Companies Acts

1963-2009

Companies Acts

1963-2009

General editors

Lyndon MacCann
BA (Mod), M Litt, SC

Dr Thomas B. Courtney
BA, LLB, LLD
Partner, Arthur Cox
Chairman of CLRG

Editors

Eleanor Daly
LLB, AITI, Solicitor
Fexco

Paul Egan
BA (Mod)
Partner, Mason, Hayes+Curran

Aidan Lambe
FCA
Director, ICAI

Gary McCarthy
LLB, BL

Ailbhe O'Neill
BL, LLB, LLM, PhD

Aillil O'Reilly
BA (Mod), BL

Bloomsbury Professional

Published by
Bloomsbury Professional
Maxwelton House
41–43 Boltro Road
Haywards Heath
West Sussex
RH16 1BJ

Bloomsbury Professional
The Fitzwilliam Business Centre
26 Upper Pembroke Street
Dublin 2

ISBN 978 1 84766 481 5

British Library Cataloguing-in-Publication Data
A catalogue record for this book is available from the British Library

Typeset by Marlex Editorial Services Ltd., Dublin, Ireland
Printed and bound in Great Britain by
CPI William Clowes, Beccles NR34 7TL

Preface

It is only sixteen months since the previous edition of this book was published. In that time there have been several important developments in company law, both in terms of legislation and case law.

At a legislative level, important amendments have been made to the Companies Acts by three statutes, namely the Companies (Amendment) Act 2009, the Companies (Miscellaneous Provisions) Act 2009 and the National Asset Management Agency Act 2009. In addition changes have been brought about by way of secondary legislation, including the European Communities (Directive 2006/46) Regulations 2009, the important Shareholders' Rights (Directive 2007/36/EC) Regulations 2009 and the European Communities (Mergers and Divisions of Companies) (Amendment) Regulations 2009.

Within the judicial sphere there has also been much activity, with decisions being handed down in areas involving, *inter alia*, the restriction and disqualification of directors, the Rule in *Foss v Harbottle*, the section 205 oppression remedy and fraudulent and reckless trading. However, if there has been one topic above all others that has attracted judicial attention in the last 16 months it has been that of examinerships. In this regard, it is of some significance that many of these decisions have been handed down by the Supreme Court, often in the context of appeals that have been heard only days after the original High Court rulings on the matter.

Insofar as possible, reference has been made to all recent Irish case law together with important decisions from the UK courts. Inevitably, however, individual decisions (particularly those that are unreported) may be overlooked and I would therefore invite readers to bring to our attention judgments that we have missed but which may merit our consideration.

As with previous editions, this latest edition has been anything but a solo effort and in this regard I would like to pay particular thanks to Tom Courtney for his invaluable input, particularly in relation to the legislative updates.

I would also like to express my thanks and gratitude to my publishers, Bloomsbury Professional, for their continued support and assistance. In particular I would like to record my appreciation for all that Sandra Mulvey has done to ensure the publication of this latest edition so soon after the enactment of the legislation referred to above. Thanks also go to Marian Sullivan who typeset the book with great skill within a particularly short timeframe.

Finally, although the work in this edition has been a collaborative effort, ultimate responsibility lies with me. I have taken every care to state the law as it is on 5 February 2010. If there are any errors or omissions I accept moral but not legal responsibility and, as with the previous editions, if there are any mistakes or shortcomings which strike the reader, I would be glad to be told of them.

5 February 2010

LYNDON MAC CANN SC
1 ARRAN SQUARE
ARRAN QUAY
DUBLIN 7

Table of Contents

Division A: Primary Legislation

Division B: Secondary Legislation

Division C: European Legislation

Division D: Rules

List of Abbreviations

Primary Legislation

CA 1963	Companies Act 1963
CA 1990	Companies Act 1990
C(AA)A 2003	Companies (Auditing and Accounting) Act 2003
C(A)(No 1)A 1999	Companies (Amendment) (No 1) Act 1999
C(A)(No 2)A 1999	Companies (Amendment) (No 2) Act 1999
C(A)A 1977	Companies (Amendment) Act 1977
C(A)A 1982	Companies (Amendment) Act 1982
C(A)A 1983	Companies (Amendment) Act 1983
C(A)A 1986	Companies (Amendment) Act 1986
C(A)A 1990	Companies (Amendment) Act 1990
C(A)A 1999	Companies (Amendment) Act 1999
C(A)A 2009	Companies (Amendment) Act 2009
C(MP)A 2009	Companies (Miscellaneous Provisions) Act 1999
CBFSAIA 2003	Central Bank and Financial Services Authority of Ireland Act 2003
CBFSAIA 2004	Central Bank and Financial Services Authority of Ireland Act 2004
CLEA 2001	Company Law Enforcement Act 2001
FA	Finance Act
IA 2005	Interpretation Act 2005
IFCMPA 2005	Investment Funds, Companies and Miscellaneous Provisions Act 2005
IFCMPA 2006	Investment Funds, Companies and Miscellaneous Provisions Act 2006
NAMA Act 2009	National Asset Management Agency Act 2009
RBNA 1963	Registration of Business Names Act 1963
SDCA 1999	Stamp Duties Consolidation Act 1999
STA 1963	Stock Transfer Act 1963

Secondary Legislation

CA 1963 (A8S) O 2009 SI 302/2009	Companies Act 1963 (Alterations of Eighth Schedule) Order 2009
CA1963(S377(1))O 1999 SI 64/1999	Companies Act 1963 (Section 377(1)) Order 1999

CA1990(A)R 1992 SI 259/1992	Companies Act 1990 (Auditors) Regulations 1992
CA1990(FCDDR)R 2002 SI 39/2002	Companies Act 1990 (Form and Content of Documents Delivered to Registrar) Regulations 2002
CA1990(PIV;PVII)R 1991 SI 209/1991	Companies Act 1990 (Parts IV And VII) Regulations 1991
CA1990(US)R 1996 SI 68/1996	Companies Act 1990 (Uncertificated Securities) Regulations 1996
CLEA2001(S56)R 2002 SI 324/2002	Company Law Enforcement Act 2001 (Section 56) Regulations 2002
EC(A)R 1993 SI 396/1993	European Communities (Accounts) Regulations 1993
EC(AMP)R 2007 SI 286/2007	European Communities (Admissions to Listings and Miscellaneous Provisions) Regulations 2007
EC(BD)R 1993 SI 395/1993	European Communities (Branch Disclosures) Regulations 1993
EC(C)(A)R 2007 SI 49/2007	European Communities (Companies) (Amendment) Regulations 2007
EC(C)R 1973 SI 163/1973	European Communities (Companies) Regulations 1973
EC(CBM)R 2008 SI 157/2008	European Communities (Cross-Border Mergers) Regulations 2008
EC(CGA)R 1992 SI 201/1992	European Communities (Companies: Group Accounts) Regulations 1992
EC(CI)(FVA)R 2004 SI 720/2004	European Communities (Credit Institutions) (Fair Value Accounting) Regulations 2004
EC(CI)R 2002 SI 333/2002	European Communities (Corporate Insolvency) Regulations 2002
EC(CIA)R 1992 SI 294/1992	European Communities (Credit Institutions: Accounts) Regulations 1992
EC(EEIG)R 1989 SI 191/1989	European Communities (European Economic Interest Groupings) Regulations 1989
EC(EPLLC)R 2007 SI 21/2007	European Communities (European Public Limited Liability Company) Regulations 2007
EC(EPLLC)(F)R 2007 SI 22/2007	European Communities (European Public Limited Liability Company) (Forms) Regulations 2007
EC(FVA)R 2004 SI 765/2004	European Communities (Fair Value Accounting) Regulations 2004
EC(IFRSMA)R 2005 SI 116/2005	European Communities (International Financial Reporting Standards and Miscellaneous Amendments) Regulations 2005
EC(IUA)R 1996 SI 23/1996	European Communities (Insurance Undertakings: Accounts) Regulations 1996
EC(MDC)(A)R 2008 SI 572/2008	European Communities (Mergers and Division of Companies) (Amendment) Regulations 2008

EC(MDC)R 1987 SI 137/1987	European Communities (Mergers and Division of Companies) Regulations 1987
EC(PLC)R 2008 SI 89/2008	European Communities (Public Limited Companies — Directive 2006/68/EC) Regulations 2008
EC(PLCS)R 1997 SI 67/1997	European Communities (Public Limited Companies Subsidiaries) Regulations 1997
EC(SE)R 1984 SI 282/1984	European Communities (Stock Exchange) Regulations 1984
EC(SMPLC)R 1994 SI 275/1994	European Communities (Single-Member Private Limited Companies) Regulations 1994
EC(TBD)R 2006 SI 255/2006	European Communities (Takeover Bids (Directive 2004/25/EC)) Regulations 2006
Market Abuse Regulations SI 342/2005	Market Abuse (Directive 2003/6/EC) Regulations 2005
Prospectus Regulations SI 324/2005	Prospectus (Directive 2003/71/EC) Regulations 2005
Transparency Regulations SI 277/2007	Transparency (Directive 2004/109/EC) Regulations 2007
Shareholders' Rights Regulations SI 316/2009	Shareholders' Rights (Directive 2007/36/EC) Regulations 2009

Other

AGM	annual general meeting
ASB	Accounting Standards Board
CLRG	Company Law Review Group
CRO	Companies Registration Office
DPP	Director of Public Prosecutions
IFRS	International Financial Reporting Standards
ODCE	Office of the Director of Corporate Enforcement
plc	public limited company
RSC	Rules of the Superior Court

Table of Cases

A

B

D

E

F

G

H

I

K

N

Q

R

W

X

Y

Z

Division A: Primary Legislation

Registration of Business Names Act 1963

No 30/1963

ARRANGEMENT OF SECTIONS

An Act to Provide for the Registration of Persons carrying on Business under Business Names and for Purposes Connected therewith. [11th December, 1963.]

Be it Enacted by the Oireachtas as Follows:

1 Commencement

This Act shall come into operation on such day as the Minister appoints by order.

Notes

RBNA 1963 was commenced on 1 April 1964: Registration of Business Names Act, 1963 (Commencement) Order 1964 (SI 46/1964).

---

2 Interpretation

(1) In this Act—

'business' includes profession;

'business name' means the name or style under which any business is carried on, and, in relation to a newspaper, includes the title of the newspaper;

'Christian name' includes any forename;

'director', in relation to a body corporate, includes a member of the managing body thereof;

'firm' means an unincorporated body of two or more individuals, or one or more individuals and one or more bodies corporate, or two or more bodies corporate, who have entered into partnership with one another with a view to publishing a newspaper or to carrying on business for profit;

'initials' includes any recognised abbreviation of a Christian name;

'the Minister' means the Minister for Industry and Commerce;

'newspaper' means any paper containing public news or observations thereon, or consisting wholly or mainly of advertisements, which is printed for sale and is published in the State either periodically or in parts or numbers at intervals not exceeding thirty-six days;

'prescribed' means prescribed by regulations made in pursuance of this Act;

'the repealed enactment' means the Registration of Business Names Act, 1916, repealed by this Act;

'surname', in the case of a person usually known by a title different from his surname, means that title.

(2) References in this Act to a former Christian name or surname do not include—

(a) in the case of a person usually known by a title different from his surname, the name by which he was known previous to the adoption of or succession to the title; or

(b) in the case of any person, a former Christian name or surname where that name or surname was changed or disused before the person bearing the name attained the age of 18 years or has been changed or disused for a period of not less than 20 years; or

(c) in the case of a married woman, the name or surname by which she was known previous to the marriage.

3 Persons to be registered

(1) Subject to the provisions of this Act—

(a) every firm having a place of business in the State and carrying on business under a business name which does not consist of the true surnames of all partners who are individuals and the corporate names of all partners which are bodies corporate without any addition other than the true Christian names of individual partners or initials of such Christian names;

(b) every individual having a place of business in the State and carrying on business under a business name which does not consist of his true surname without any addition other than his true Christian names or the initials thereof;

(c) every individual or firm having a place of business in the State, who, or a member of which, has either before or after the passing of this Act changed his name, except in the case of a woman in consequence of marriage;

(d) every body corporate having a place of business in the State and carrying on business under a business name which does not consist of its corporate name without any addition;

(e) without prejudice to the generality of the foregoing, every person having a place of business in the State and carrying on the business of publishing a newspaper,

shall be registered in the manner directed by this Act.

(2) Where the addition merely indicates that the business is carried on in succession to a former owner of the business, that addition shall not of itself render registration necessary.

(3) Where two or more individual partners have the same surname, the use of the plural form of that surname shall not of itself render registration necessary.

(4) The use by a body corporate of a recognised abbreviation for 'Company' or 'Limited' or for any analogous expression forming part of its corporate name shall not of itself render registration necessary.

(5) Where the business is carried on by an assignee or trustee in bankruptcy, a trustee of the estate of an arranging debtor, or a receiver or manager appointed by any court, registration shall not be necessary under paragraph (a), (b) or (d) of subsection (1).

(6) An individual or firm shall not require to be registered by reason only of a change of his name or of the name of a partner in the firm, if the change has taken place before the person who has changed his name has attained the age of eighteen years or if not less than twenty years have elapsed since it took place, or by reason only of the adoption by an individual of a title to which he has succeeded.

Definitions

'business': RBNA 1963, s 2(1); 'business name': RBNA 1963, s 2(1); 'Christian name': RBNA 1963, s 2(1); 'director': RBNA 1963, s 2(1); 'firm': RBNA 1963, s 2(1); 'initials': RBNA 1963, s 2(1); 'surname': RBNA 1963, s 2(1).

Notes

The obligation to register business names is cast very widely and applies to every firm of partners,[1] individual, firm or individual who has changed their name, body corporate or person publishing a newspaper who or which has a place of business in the State and who or which carry on business under a 'business name' which does not consist of their true surnames, corporate names, or surnames without addition save a true Christian name or initials as the case may be. An Irish company that carries on business under a name other than its corporate name is required by CA 1963, s 22(1) to register under the RBNA 1963; a building society which carries on business under a name other than its registered name is required by BSA 1989, s 13(3)(b)(ii) to register that name under the RBNA 1963.

1 See Twomey, *Partnership Law* (Tottel Publishing, 2000) at paras [3.56]–[3.79] for consideration of the issues that affect partnerships.

4 Manner and particulars of registration

(1) Every person required under this Act to be registered shall furnish by sending by post or delivery to the registrar a statement in writing in the prescribed form containing the following particulars:

(a) the business name, including, in the case of the proprietor of a newspaper, the title of the newspaper;

(b) the general nature of the business;

(c) the principal place of the business;

(d) where the registration to be effected is that of a firm, the present Christian name and surname, any former Christian name or surname, the nationality, if not Irish, the usual residence, and the other business occupation (if any) of each of the individuals who are partners, and the corporate name and registered or principal office in the State of every body corporate which is a partner;

(e) where the registration to be effected is that of an individual, the present Christian name and surname, any former Christian name or surname, the nationality, if not Irish, the usual residence, and the other business occupation (if any) of such individual;

(f) where the registration to be effected is that of a body corporate, its corporate name and registered or principal office in the State;

(g) the date of the adoption of the business name by that person.

(2) Where a business is carried on under two or more business names, each of those business names must be stated.

Definitions

'business': RBNA 1963, s 2(1); 'business name': RBNA 1963, s 2(1); 'Christian name': RBNA 1963, s 2(1); 'director': RBNA 1963, s 2(1); 'firm': RBNA 1963, s 2(1); 'initials': RBNA 1963, s 2(1); 'surname': RBNA 1963, s 2(1).

Notes

The prescribed forms are: an RBN1 (for an individual), an RBN1A (for a partnership) and an RBN1B (for a body corporate): originally published in the Business Names Regulations 1963 (SI 47/1964).

5 Statement to be signed by persons registering

(1) The statement required for the purpose of registration must be signed—

(a) in the case of an individual—by him, and

(b) in the case of a body corporate—by a director or secretary thereof, and

(c) in the case of a firm, either—

(i) by all the individuals who are partners, and by a director or the secretary of all bodies corporate who are partners, or

(ii) by some individual who is a partner, or a director or the secretary of some body corporate which is a partner, and in a case to which paragraph (c)(ii) applies must be verified by a statutory declaration made by the signatory.

(2) A statutory declaration stating that any person other than the declarant is a partner, or omitting to state that any person other than the declarant is a partner, shall not be evidence for or against any such other person in respect of his liability or non liability as a partner.

(3) The High Court may on application of any person alleged or claiming to be a partner direct the rectification of the register and decide any question arising under this section.

Definitions

'business': RBNA 1963, s 2(1); 'business name': RBNA 1963, s 2(1); 'Christian name': RBNA 1963, s 2(1); 'director': RBNA 1963, s 2(1); 'firm': RBNA 1963, s 2(1); 'initials': RBNA 1963, s 2(1); 'surname': RBNA 1963, s 2(1).

6 Time for registration

(1) The particulars required to be furnished under this Act by any person shall be furnished within one month after his adoption of the business name.

(2) If the person has adopted the business name before the commencement of this Act, the particulars shall, if not already furnished under the repealed enactment, be furnished within one month from the commencement of this Act.

(3) This section shall apply, where registration is required in consequence of a change of name, as if for references to the date of adoption of the business name there were substituted references to the date of such change.

Definitions

'business': RBNA 1963, s 2(1); 'business name': RBNA 1963, s 2(1); 'Christian name': RBNA 1963, s 2(1); 'director': RBNA 1963, s 2(1); 'firm': RBNA 1963, s 2(1); 'initials' : RBNA 1963, s 2(1); 'surname' : RBNA 1963, s 2(1).

7 Registration of changes

Whenever a change is made or occurs in any of the particulars registered in respect of any person, that person shall, within one month after the change or, if such change occurred before the commencement of this Act, within one month after such commencement, furnish by sending by post or delivering to the registrar a statement in writing in the prescribed form specifying the nature and date of the change signed, and where necessary verified, in like manner as the statement required on registration.

Notes

The prescribed forms for registering changes are: an RBN2 (for an individual), an RBN2A (for a partnership) and an RBN2B (for a body corporate): originally published in the Business Names Regulations 1963 (SI 47/1964).

8 Certificate of registration

(1) On receiving a statement under section 4, or a statement under section 7 specifying a change in the business name, the registrar shall send by post or deliver a certificate of the registration thereof to the person registering.

(2) A certificate of registration shall be kept exhibited in a conspicuous position at, in the case of a firm or individual, the principal place of business and, in the case of a body corporate, its registered or principal office in the State and, in every case, in every branch office or place where the business is normally carried on, and if not kept so exhibited, the person registered or, in the case of a firm, every partner in the firm shall be liable on summary conviction to a fine not exceeding [€127.90][a].

Amendments

a £100 converted to €127.90 by Council Regulations (EC) No 1103/97, No 974/98 and No 2866/98 and the Economic and Monetary Union Act 1998, s 6.

Definitions

'business name': RBNA 1963, s 2(1); 'firm': RBNA 1963, s 2(1).

9 Duty to furnish particulars

(1) The Minister may require any person to furnish to him within such time as the Minister may require a statement of such particulars as appear necessary to the Minister for the purpose of ascertaining whether or not that person or the firm of which he is partner should be registered under this Act, or an alteration made in the registered particulars.

(2) If from any information so furnished it appears to the Minister that any person ought to be registered under this Act, or an alteration ought to be made in the registered particulars, the Minister may require that person to furnish to the registrar the required particulars within such time as may be allowed by the Minister but, where any default under this Act has been discovered from the information acquired under this section, no proceedings under this Act shall be taken against any person in respect of such default prior to the expiration of the time within which that person is so required to furnish particulars to the registrar.

10 Penalty for default in furnishing statements

If any person required under this Act to furnish a statement of particulars or of any change in particulars makes default without reasonable excuse in so doing, the person so in default or, in the case of a firm, every partner in the firm shall be liable on summary conviction to a fine not exceeding [€127.90][a].

Amendments

a £100 converted to €127.90 by Council Regulations (EC) No 1103/97, No 974/98 and No 2866/98 and the Economic and Monetary Union Act 1998, s 6.

11 Penalty for false statements

If any statement furnished under this Act contains any matter which is false in any material particular to the knowledge of any person signing it, that person shall, on summary conviction, be liable to imprisonment for a term not exceeding six months or to a fine not exceeding [€127.90][a], or to both.

Amendments

a £100 converted to €127.90 by Council Regulations (EC) No 1103/97, No 974/98 and No 2866/98 and the Economic and Monetary Union Act 1998, s 6.

12 Removal of names from register

(1) If a person registered under this Act in respect of a business name ceases to carry on business under that name, it shall be the duty of that person or, in the case of an individual who dies, of his personal representative or, in the case of a firm, of every person who was a partner in the firm at the time when it ceased to carry on business under that name, and also, in the case of a body corporate, of any liquidator, within three months thereafter to send by post or deliver to the registrar a statement in the prescribed form to that effect, and if he makes default in doing so he shall be liable on summary conviction to a fine not exceeding [€127.90][a].

(2) On receipt of such statement the registrar may delete from the register the particulars relating to that business name.

(3) Where, by virtue of subsection (6) of section 3, a person registered under this Act no longer requires to be so registered—

(a) the registrar, if so requested by that person, shall remove that person from the register, and

(b) section 8 shall no longer require that person to keep exhibited the certificate of registration,

and where the particulars registered under this Act in respect of any person include a former name or surname which, by virtue of subsection (2) of section 2, no longer requires to be included among those particulars, the registrar, if so requested by that person, shall amend the particulars by deleting that name or surname.

(4) Where the registrar has reasonable cause to believe that any person registered under this Act in respect of a business name is not carrying on business under that name, he may send to that person by registered post a notice that, unless an answer is received to such notice within one month from the date thereof, the particulars relating to that business name may be deleted from the register.

(5) If the registrar either receives an answer to the effect that the person is not carrying on business under that business name or does not within one month after sending the notice receive an answer, he may delete the particulars relating to that name from the register.

Amendments

a £100 converted to €127.90 by Council Regulations (EC) No 1103/97, No 974/98 and No 2866/98 and the Economic and Monetary Union Act 1998, s 6.

13 Index of business names

The registrar shall keep an index of all business names registered under this Act.

14 Undesirable business names

(1) The Minister may refuse to permit the registration under this Act of any name which in his opinion is undesirable but an appeal shall lie to the High Court against such refusal.

(2) Where registration of a business name is refused under this section any person or, in the case of a firm, every partner in the firm, carrying on business under that name in such circumstances as to require registration under this Act, shall be liable on summary conviction to a fine not exceeding [€127.90][a].

(3) The registration of a business name under this Act shall not be construed as authorising the use of that name if apart from such registration the use thereof could be prohibited.

Amendments

a £100 converted to €127.90 by Council Regulations (EC) No 1103/97, No 974/98 and No 2866/98 and the Economic and Monetary Union Act 1998, s 6.

Notes

Sub-s (3) clarifies that where a person registers a business name, they will not become immune from civil action by an aggrieved third party where that person claims that there has been a passing off or infringement of a trademark.[1]

1 *DSG Retail Ltd v PC World Ltd* [1998] IEHC 3 (Costello J).

15 Registrar, assistant registrars and offices

(1) The registrar of companies or such other person as the Minister may determine shall be the registrar for the purposes of this Act.

(2) Such persons as the Minister may determine shall be assistant registrars for the purposes of this Act.

(3) For the purposes of the registration of persons under this Act, the Minister shall maintain and administer an office or offices in the State at such places as the Minister thinks fit.

16 Inspection, production and evidence of registered documents

(1) Any person may—

(a) inspect the documents kept by the registrar, on payment of such fee as may be prescribed;

(b) require a certificate of the registration of any person or a copy of or extract from any other document or any part of any other document, to be certified by the registrar, an assistant registrar or other officer authorised by the Minister, on payment for the certificate, certified copy or extract of such fees as may be prescribed.

(2) No process for compelling the production of any document kept by the registrar shall issue from any court except with the leave of that court, and any such process if issued shall bear thereon a statement that it is issued with the leave of the court.

(3) A certificate of registration or a copy of, or extract from, any document kept by the registrar, certified under the hand of the registrar, an assistant registrar or other officer authorised by the Minister (whose official position or authority it shall not be necessary to prove), shall in all legal proceedings be admissible in evidence.

17 Regulations

(1) The Minister may make regulations concerning any of the following matters—

(a) the fees to be paid to the registrar under this Act;

(b) the forms to be used under this Act;

(c) generally the conduct and regulation of registration under this Act, and any matters incidental thereto.

(2) All fees payable in pursuance of this Act shall be paid into or disposed of for the benefit of the Exchequer in such manner as the Minister for Finance shall direct.

(3) Regulations made under this Act shall be laid before each House of the Oireachtas as soon as may be after they are made and, if a resolution annulling the regulations is passed by either House within the next twenty-one days on which that House has sat after the regulations are laid before it, the regulations shall be annulled accordingly but without prejudice to the validity of anything previously done thereunder.

18 Publication of true names, etc

(1) A person required by this Act to be registered shall, in all business letters, circulars and catalogues on or in which the business name appears and which are sent by that person to any person, state in legible characters—

(a) in the case of an individual, his present Christian name, or the initials thereof, and present surname, any former Christian names and surnames, and his nationality, if not Irish;

(b) in the case of a firm, the present Christian names, or the initials thereof, and present surnames, any former Christian names and surnames, and the nationality, if not Irish, of all the partners in the firm or, in the case of a body corporate being a partner, the corporate name;

(c) in the case of a body corporate (not being a company to which section 196 of the Companies Act, 1963, applies), its corporate name, and the present Christian name, or the initials thereof, the present surname, any former Christian names and surnames, and the nationality, if not Irish, of every director or, in the case of a body corporate being a director, the corporate name.

(2) If default is made in compliance with this section the person or, in the case of a firm, every partner in the firm shall be liable on summary conviction for each offence to a fine not exceeding [€31.74][a].

Amendments

a £25 converted to €31.74 by Council Regulations (EC) No 1103/97, No 974/98 and No 2866/98 and the Economic and Monetary Union Act 1998, s 6.

Notes

Where a business name is used in business letters, circulars and catalogues the legal name of the person (whether a natural person or a legal entity) must also be stated; the registered business name alone is not sufficient.[1]

[1] In *Kent Adhesive Products company t/a KAPCO v Ryan* (5 November 1993, unreported) HC (Costello J) an undertaking was required by the court from a company to put its name on its letterheads and refrain from using letterheads which did not contain its name.

19 Offences by bodies corporate

Where a body corporate is guilty of an offence under this Act every director, secretary and officer of the body corporate who is knowingly a party to the default shall be guilty of a like offence and liable to a like penalty.

20 Summary proceedings

(1) Summary proceedings in relation to an offence under this Act may be brought and prosecuted by the Minister.

(2) Notwithstanding subsection (4) of section 10 of the Petty Sessions (Ireland) Act, 1851, summary proceedings for an offence under this Act may be instituted within three years from the date of the offence.

21 Repeals and consequential provisions

(1) The Registration of Business Names Act, 1916, is hereby repealed.

(2) The Defamation Act, 1961 , is hereby amended—

(a) by the deletion, in the definition of 'newspaper' in section 2, of 'except in section 27',

(b) by the repeal of section 27.

(3) The register kept under the repealed enactment shall be deemed part of the register for the purposes of this Act.

(4) All statements and particulars furnished, statutory declarations made, notices, certificates, certified copies and extracts given and things done under the repealed enactment shall have effect as if furnished, made, given or done under this Act.

22 Expenses

The expenses incurred by the Minister in the administration of this Act shall to such extent as may be sanctioned by the Minister for Finance be paid out of moneys, provided by the Oireachtas.

23 Short title

This Act may be cited as the Registration of Business Names Act, 1963.

Companies Act 1963

(Number 33 of 1963)

Arrangement of Sections

Part I
Preliminary

Part II
Incorporation of Companies and Matters incidental thereto

Memorandum of Association

Articles of Association

Form of Memorandum and Articles

Registration

Provisions relating to Names of Companies

MEETINGS AND PROCEEDINGS

ACCOUNTS AND AUDIT

Supplementary Provisions as to Winding Up

Provisions as to Dissolution

Rules of Court

Disposal of Documents filed with Registrar

PART VII
RECEIVERS

PART VIII
APPLICATION OF ACT TO COMPANIES FORMED OR REGISTERED UNDER FORMER ACTS

PART IX
COMPANIES NOT FORMED UNDER THIS ACT AUTHORISED TO REGISTER UNDER THIS ACT

PART X
WINDING UP OF UNREGISTERED COMPANIES

PART XI

COMPANIES INCORPORATED OUTSIDE THE STATE ESTABLISHING A PLACE OF BUSINESS WITHIN THE STATE

PART XII

RESTRICTIONS ON SALE OF SHARES AND OFFERS OF SHARES FOR SALE

PART XIII

GENERAL PROVISIONS AS TO REGISTRATION

PART XIV

MISCELLANEOUS PROVISIONS RELATING TO BANKING COMPANIES, PARTNERSHIPS AND UNREGISTERED COMPANIES

PROVISIONS RELATING TO BANKING COMPANIES

SCHEDULES

FIRST SCHEDULE

TABLE A, TÁBLA A, AND TABLES B, C, D, AND E

SECOND SCHEDULE

FORM OF STATEMENT IN LIEU OF PROSPECTUS TO BE DELIVERED TO REGISTRAR BY A PRIVATE COMPANY ON BECOMING [AN UNLIMITED PUBLIC COMPANY] AND REPORTS TO BE SET OUT THEREIN

THIRD SCHEDULE

MATTERS TO BE SPECIFIED IN PROSPECTUS AND REPORTS TO BE SET OUT THEREIN

FOURTH SCHEDULE

FORM OF STATEMENT IN LIEU OF PROSPECTUS TO BE DELIVERED TO REGISTRAR BY A COMPANY WHICH DOES NOT ISSUE A PROSPECTUS OR WHICH DOES NOT MAKE AN ALLOTMENT ON A PROSPECTUS ISSUED, AND REPORTS TO BE SET OUT THEREIN

FIFTH SCHEDULE

CONTENTS AND FORM OF ANNUAL RETURN OF A COMPANY HAVING A SHARE CAPITAL

SIXTH SCHEDULE

ACCOUNTS

SEVENTH SCHEDULE

MATTERS TO BE EXPRESSLY STATED IN AUDITORS' REPORT

EIGHTH SCHEDULE

FEES TO BE PAID TO THE REGISTRAR OF COMPANIES

NINTH SCHEDULE

PROVISIONS OF THIS ACT APPLIED TO UNREGISTERED COMPANIES

TENTH SCHEDULE

PROVISIONS REFERRED TO IN SECTION 380

ELEVENTH SCHEDULE

AMENDMENTS OF OTHER ACTS

TWELFTH SCHEDULE

ENACTMENTS REPEALED

THIRTEENTH SCHEDULE

ENACTMENT SAVED

Companies Act 1963

(Number 33 of 1963)

An Act to consolidate with amendments certain enactments relating to companies and for purposes connected with that matter. [23rd December, 1963]
Be It Enacted by the Oireachtas as Follows:

PART I
PRELIMINARY

1 Short title and commencement

(1) This Act may be cited as the Companies Act, 1963.

(2) This Act shall come into operation on such day as the Minister appoints by order.

Cross reference

'commencement': IA 2005, Sch, Pt 1.

Definitions

'company': CA 1963, s 2(1); 'Minister': CA 1963, s 2(1).

Notes

Operative date: The operative date for CA 1963 was 1 April 1964.[1]

[1] Companies Act 1963 (Commencement) Order 1964 (SI 41/1964).

Consolidating Act: In its title, CA 1963 is described as being a consolidating and amending Act. However, in the light of the vast amount of corporate legislation which has been enacted in the last 20 years, it is something of a misnomer to continue to refer to CA 1963 as a consolidating Act. The Acts it consolidated were the Companies (Consolidation) Act 1908 (the 1908 Act), the Companies Act 1913, the Companies (Particulars as to Directors) Act 1917 and Companies Act 1959. With regard to the amending provisions, these were in large part based upon recommendations of the Cox Committee[1] and of the Jenkins Committee[2] whose reports were published in 1958 and 1962 respectively.

[1] Report of the Company Law Reform Committee (1958) Prl 4523.

[2] Report of the Company Law Committee (1962) Cmnd 1749.

Interpretation: In so far as CA 1963 is a consolidating Act, it will be presumed that the legislature did not intend to change the law so that prima facie the same effect ought to be given to the consolidating provisions as was given to those of the Acts for which it was substituted[1].

[1] *Mitchell v Simpson* (1890) 25 QBD 183; *DPP v Schildkamp* [1971] AC 1.

---

2 General provisions as to interpretation

(1) In this Act unless the context otherwise requires:

['annual accounts' or 'accounts' means—

(a) individual accounts required by section 148, and

(b) group accounts required by section 150;

'Act of 1986' means the Companies (Amendment) Act 1986;

'Act of 1990' means the Companies Act 1990;

'Act of 2003' means the Companies (Auditing and Accounting) Act 2003;] [a]

'agent' does not include a person's counsel acting as such;

['annual return' means the return required to be made under section 125;

'annual return date' means the date in each year not later than that to which the annual return shall be made up, the calculation of which is provided for in section 127;] [b]

'articles' means the articles of association of a company, as originally framed or as altered by [a resolution of the company],[c] including, so far as they apply to the company, the regulations contained (as the case may be) in Table B in the Schedule annexed to the Joint Stock Companies Act, 1856, or in Table A in the First Schedule to the Companies Act, 1862, or in that Table as altered in pursuance of section 71 of the last mentioned Act, or in Table A in the First Schedule to the Companies (Consolidation) Act, 1908;

'bank holiday' means a day which is a bank holiday under the Public Holidays Acts, 1871 to 1924;

'the Bankruptcy Acts' means the Irish Bankrupt and Insolvent Act, 1857, the Bankruptcy (Ireland) Amendment Act, 1872, the Debtors Act (Ireland) 1872 and the Local Bankruptcy (Ireland) Act, 1888;

'book and paper' and 'book or paper' include accounts, deeds, writings and documents;

['Companies Act accounts' means Companies Act individual accounts (within the meaning of section 148) or Companies Act group accounts (within the meaning of section 150);

'Companies Act group accounts' shall be read in accordance with section 150;

'Companies Act individual accounts' shall be read in accordance with section 148;] [d]

'company' means a company formed and registered under this Act, or an existing company;

'company limited by guarantee' and 'company limited by shares' have the meanings assigned to them respectively by subsection (2) of section 5;

['company traded on a regulated market' means a company whose registered office is in the State and whose shares are admitted to trading on a regulated market situated or operating within a Member State and does not include—

(a) collective investment undertakings within the meaning of Article 1(2) of Council Directive 85/611/EEC of 20 December 1985 on the coordination of laws, regulations and administrative provisions relating to undertakings for collective investment in transferable securities (UCITS) (OJ L 375, 31.12.1985, p 3), or

(b) undertakings the sole object of which is the collective investment of capital provided by the public within the meaning of Article 1(3)(b) of Directive 2007/36/EC of the European Parliament and of the Council of 11 July 2007 on the exercise of certain rights of shareholders in listed companies (OJ L 184, 14.07.2007, p 17);][e]

'contributory' has the meaning assigned to it by section 208;

['the court' unless the context otherwise requires 'the court' used in any provision of the Companies Acts in relation to a company means:

(a) the High Court, or

(b) where another court is prescribed for the purposes of that provision, that court;][f]

['1993 Regulations' means the European Communities (Accounts) Regulations 1993 (S.I. No. 396 of 1993);

'Credit Institutions Regulations' means the European Communities (Credit Institutions: Accounts) Regulations 1992 (S.I. No. 294 of 1992);][g]

'creditors' voluntary winding up' has the meaning assigned to it by subsection (7) of section 256;

'debenture' includes debenture stock, bonds and any other securities of a company whether constituting a charge on the assets of the company or not;

'director' includes any person occupying the position of director by whatever name called;

['Directive 2004/25/EC' means Directive 2004/25/EC of the European Parliament and of the Council of 21 April 2004, on takeover bids (OJ L 142, 30.4.2004, p 1);][h]

'document' includes summons, notice, order and other legal process, and registers;

['EEA state' means a state, including the State, which is a Contracting Party to the EEA Agreement;

'EEA Agreement' means the Agreement on the European Economic Area signed at Oporto on 2 May 1992, as adjusted by the Protocol signed at Brussels on 17 March 1993;][i]

['electronic means' are means of electronic equipment for the processing (including digital compression), storage and transmission of data, employing wires, radio, optical technologies, or any other electromagnetic means;][j]

'existing company' means a company formed and registered in a register kept in the State under the Joint Stock Companies Acts, the Companies Act, 1862, or the Companies (Consolidation) Act, 1908;

'extended notice' has the meaning assigned to it by section 142;

'financial year' means, [subject to subsection (1A)][k], in relation to any body corporate, the period in respect of which any profit and loss account of the body corporate laid before it in general meeting is made up, whether that period is a year or not;

has the meaning assigned to it by subsection (1) of section 150;

['Group Accounts Regulations' means the European Communities (Companies: Group Accounts) Regulations 1992 (S.I. No. 201 of 1992);

'IAS Regulation' means Regulation (EC) No. 1606/2002 of the European Parliament and of the Council of 19 July 2002;

'income statement' means a financial statement prepared in accordance with international financial reporting standards and is equivalent to a profit and loss account;

'individual accounts' shall be read in accordance with section 148;

'IFRS accounts' means IFRS individual accounts (within the meaning of section 148) or IFRS group accounts (within the meaning of section 150);

'IFRS group accounts' shall be read in accordance with section 150;

'IFRS individual accounts' shall be read in accordance with section 148;][l]

'holding company' means a holding company as defined by section 155;

['insolvency proceedings' means insolvency proceedings opened under Article 3 of the Insolvency Regulation in a member state of the European Communities other than the State and Denmark where the proceedings relate to a body corporate;

'Insolvency Regulation' means Council Regulation (EC) No. 1346/2000 of 29 May 2000 on insolvency proceedings;][m]

['Insurance Undertakings Regulations' means the European Communities (Insurance Undertakings: Accounts) Regulations 1996 (S.I. No. 23 of 1996);

'international financial reporting standards' means the international financial reporting standards, within the meaning of the IAS Regulation, adopted from time to time by the European Commission in accordance with the IAS Regulation;][n]

'issued generally' means, in relation to a prospectus, issued to persons who are not existing members or debenture holders of the company;

'Joint Stock Companies Acts' means the Joint Stock Companies Act, 1856, the Joint Stock Companies Acts, 1856, 1857, the Joint Stock Banking Companies Act, 1857, and the Act to enable Joint Stock Banking Companies to be formed on the principle of limited liability, or any one or more of those Acts as the case may require, but does not include the Act 7 & 8 Victoria, Chapter 110;

'members' voluntary winding up' has the meaning assigned to it by subsection (7) of section 256;

'the minimum subscription' has the meaning assigned to it by subsection (2) of section 53;

'memorandum' means the memorandum of association of a company, as originally framed or as altered in pursuance of any statute (including this Act);

'Minister' means the Minister for Industry and Commerce;

'officer' in relation to a body corporate includes a director or secretary;

['parent company' or 'parent undertaking', means a company that has one or more subsidiary undertakings within the meaning of in the Group Accounts Regulations;][o]

'the operative date' means the date on which this Act comes into operation;

'prescribed' means, in relation to the provisions of this Act dealing with the winding up of companies, prescribed by rules of court, and in relation to the other provisions of this Act, prescribed by order made by the Minister;

'printed' includes reproduced in any legible and durable form approved by the registrar of companies;

'private company' has the meaning assigned to it by subsection (1) of section 33;

['profit and loss account', in relation to a company which prepares IFRS accounts, includes an income statement required to be prepared by international financial reporting standards;] [p]

['property' –

(a) in relation to proceedings opened in the State under Article 3(1) of the Insolvency Regulation, includes property situated outside the State, and

(b) in relation to proceedings so opened under Article 3(2) of the Regulation, does not include property so situated;] [q]

'prospectus' means any prospectus, notice, circular, advertisement or other invitation, offering to the public for subscription or purchase any shares or debentures of a company;

['recognised stock exchange' a recognised stock exchange for the purposes of any provision of the Companies Acts is an exchange prescribed by the Minister for the purposes of that section;] [r]

'the registrar of companies' or, when used in relation to registration of companies, 'the registrar' means the officer performing under this Act the duty of registration of companies;

['regulated market' has the same meaning as in Directive 2004/39/EC of the European Parliament and of the Council of 21 April 2004 on markets in financial instruments;] [s]

'resolution for reducing share capital' has the meaning assigned to it by subsection (3) of section 72;

'a resolution for voluntary winding up' has the meaning assigned to it by subsection (2) of section 251;

'share' means share in the share capital of a company, and includes stock except where a distinction between stock and shares is expressed or implied;

'share warrant' has the meaning assigned to it by subsection (2) of section 88;

[...], [t]

'subsidiary' means a subsidiary as defined by section 155;

'Table A' means Table A in the First Schedule;

'Tábla A' means Tábla A in the First Schedule;

'the time of the opening of the subscription lists' has the meaning assigned to it by subsection (1) of section 56;

['undertaking', means a body corporate, a partnership, or an unincorporated body of persons engaged for gain in the production, supply or distribution of goods, the provision of a service or the making or holding of investments;] [u]

['undischarged bankrupt' means a person who is declared bankrupt by a court of competent jurisdiction, within the State or elsewhere, and who has not obtained a certificate of discharge or its equivalent in the relevant jurisdiction] [v] 'unlimited company' has the meaning assigned to it by subsection (2) of section 5.

[(1A) The first financial year of a company commences on its date of incorporation and each subsequent financial year commences on the day after the end of the previous financial year.

(1B) References in this Act to annual accounts giving a 'true and fair view' are references—

(a) in the case of Companies Act individual accounts, to the requirement under section 149A that those accounts give a true and fair view,

(b) in the case of Companies Act group accounts, to the requirement under section 150A that those accounts give a true and fair view, and

(c) in the case of IFRS accounts, to the equivalent requirement under international financial reporting standards.][w]

(2) A person shall not be deemed to be, within the meaning of any provision of this Act, a person in accordance with whose directions or instructions the directors of a company are accustomed to act, by reason only that the directors of a company act on advice given by him in a professional capacity.

(3) References in this Act to a body corporate or to a corporation shall be construed as not including a corporation sole, but as including a company incorporated outside the State.

(4) Any provision of this Act overriding or interpreting a company's articles shall, except as provided by this Act, apply in relation to articles in force on the operative date as well as to articles coming into force thereafter, and shall apply also in relation to a company's memorandum as it applies in relation to its articles.

(5) References in this Act to any enactment shall, unless the context otherwise requires, be construed as references to that enactment as amended or extended by any subsequent enactment including this Act.

(6) In this Act, a reference to a Part, section or schedule is to a Part, section or schedule of this Act, unless it is indicated that reference to some other enactment is intended.

(7) In this Act, a reference to a subsection, paragraph, subparagraph or other division is to the subsection, paragraph, subparagraph or other division of the provision in which the reference occurs, unless it is indicated that reference to some other provision is intended.

Amendments

a Definition of 'annual accounts' or 'accounts' substituted for the definition of 'accounts' and definitions of C(A)A 1986, CA 1990 and C(AA)A 2003 inserted by European Communities (International Financial Reporting Standards and Miscellaneous Amendments) Regulations 2005 (SI 116/2005), Sch 1, Pt 1, Item No. 1, (a)(i) with effect from 24 February 2005.

b Definition of 'annual return' substituted and definition of 'annual return date' inserted by CLEA 2001, s 84(a) with effect from 1 March 2002.[1]

c Definition of 'articles' amended by substitution of the words 'a resolution of the company' for 'special resolution' by C(A)A 1983, Sch 1, para 1 with effect from 13 October 1983.[2]

d Definition of 'Companies Act accounts', 'Companies Act group accounts' and 'Companies Act individual accounts' inserted by European Communities (International Financial Reporting Standards and Miscellaneous Amendments) Regulations 2005 (SI 116/2005), Sch 1, Pt 1, Item No. 1, (a)(ii) with effect from 24 February 2005.

e Definition of 'company traded on a regulated market' inserted by Shareholders' Rights Regulations 2009, reg 3(a).

f Definition of 'the court' substituted by CA 1990, s 235 with effect from 27 December 1990.[3]

g Definition of '1993 Regulations' and 'Credit Institutions Regulations' inserted by European Communities (International Financial Reporting Standards and Miscellaneous Amendments) Regulations 2005 (SI 116/2005), Sch 1, Pt 1, Item No. 1, (a)(iii) with effect from 24 February 2005.

h Definition of 'Directive 2004/25/EC' inserted by Shareholders' Rights Regulations 2009, reg 3(a).

i Definition of 'EEA state' and 'EEA Agreement' inserted by European Communities (International Financial Reporting Standards and Miscellaneous Amendments) Regulations 2005 (SI 116/2005), Sch 1, Pt 1, Item No. 1, (a)(iv) with effect from 24 February 2005.

j Definition of 'electronic means' inserted by Shareholders' Rights Regulations 2009, reg 3(a).

k Definition of 'financial year' amended by inserting 'subject to sub-section (1A)' after 'means' by European Communities (International 116/2005), Sch 1, Pt 1, Item No. 1, (a)(viii) with effect from 24 February 2005.

l Definition of 'Group Accounts Regulations', 'IAS Regulation', 'income statement', 'individual accounts', 'IFRS accounts', 'IFRS group accounts' and 'IFRS individual accounts' inserted by European Communities (International Financial Reporting Standards and Miscellaneous Amendments) Regulations 2005 (SI 116/2005), Sch 1, Pt 1, Item No. 1, (a)(v) with effect from 24 February 2005.

m Definition of 'insolvency proceedings' and 'Insolvency Regulation' inserted by European Communities (Corporate Insolvency) Regulations 2002 (SI 333/2002), r 3(a) with effect from 31 May 2002.

n Definition of 'Insurance Undertakings Regulations' and 'international financial reporting standards' inserted by European Communities (International Financial Reporting Standards and Miscellaneous Amendments) Regulations 2005 (SI 116/2005), Sch 1, Pt 1, Item No. 1, (a)(vi) with effect from 24 February 2005.

o Definition of 'parent company' or 'parent undertaking' inserted by European Communities (International Financial Reporting Standards and Miscellaneous Amendments) Regulations 2005 (SI 116/2005), Sch 1, Pt 1, Item No. 1, (a)(ix) with effect from 24 February 2005.

p Definition of 'profit and loss account' inserted by European Communities (International Financial Reporting Standards and Miscellaneous Amendments) Regulations 2005 (SI 116/2005), Sch 1, Pt 1, Item No. 1, (a)(vii) with effect from 24 February 2005.

q Definition of 'property' inserted by European Communities (Corporate Insolvency) Regulations 2002 (SI 333/2002), r 3(a) with effect from 31 May 2002.

r Definition of 'recognised stock exchange' substituted by CA 1990, s 3(2) with effect from 27 December 1990.[4]

s Definition of 'regulated market' substituted by Shareholders' Rights Regulations 2009, reg 3(b).

t Definitions of 'statutory meetings' and 'statutory reports' repealed by C(A)A 1983, Sch 3, Pt I.

u Definition of 'undertaking' inserted by European Communities (International Financial Reporting Standards and Miscellaneous Amendments) Regulations 2005 (SI 116/2005), Sch 1, Pt 1, Item No. 1, (a)(xi) with effect from 24 February 2005.

v Definition of 'undischarged bankrupt' inserted by CLEA 2001, s 84(b) with effect from 1 March 2002.[5]

w CA 1963, s 2(1A) and (1B) inserted by European Communities (International Financial Reporting Standards and Miscellaneous Amendments) Regulations 2005 (SI 116/2005), Sch 1, Pt 1, Item No. 1, (b) with effect from 24 February 2005.

1 Company Law Enforcement Act, 2001 (Commencement) (No 2) Order 2001 (SI 438/2001).

2 Companies (Amendment) Act, 1983 (Commencement) Order 1983 (SI 288/1983).

3 Companies Act, 1990 (Commencement) Order 1990 (SI 336/1990).

4 Companies Act, 1990 (Commencement) Order 1990 (SI 336/1990).

5 Company Law Enforcement Act, 2001 (Commencement) (No 2) Order 2001 (SI 438/2001).

Cross reference

CA 1963, ss 148–151 (relating the preparation of individual and group accounts) were substituted by European Communities (International Financial Reporting Standards and Miscellaneous Amendments) Regulations 2005 (SI 116/2005), r 4.

See definition of 'member' at CA 1963, s 31.

Reference in the Companies Acts to the 'Minister' is to the Minister for Industry and Commerce (as amended by statutory instrument from time to time[1]) and currently refers to the Minister for Enterprise, Trade and Employment.[2]

1 Minister for Industry, Commerce and Energy, pursuant to the Industry and Commerce (Alteration of Name of Department and Title of Minister) Order 1977 (SI 306/1977); Minister for Industry, Commerce and Tourism, pursuant to the Industry, Commerce and Energy (Alteration of Name of Department and Title of Minister) Order 1980 (SI 10/1980); Minister for Trade, Commerce and Tourism, pursuant to the Industry, Commerce and Tourism (Alteration of Name of Department and Title of Minister) Order 1981 (SI 190/1981); Minister for Industry, Trade, Commerce and Tourism pursuant to the Trade, Commerce and Tourism (Alteration of Name of Department and Title of Minister) Order 1983 (SI 384/1983); Minister for Industry and Commerce pursuant to the Industry, Trade, Commerce and Tourism (Alteration of Name of Department and Title of Minister) Order 1986 (SI 41/1986); Minister for Enterprise and Employment pursuant to the Industry and Commerce (Alteration of Name of Department and Title of Minister) Order 1993 (SI 19/1993).

2 Minister for Enterprise and Employment (Alteration of Name of Department and Title of Minister) Order 1997 (SI 1997/305), with effect from 8 July 1997.

Definitions

'accounts': CA 1963, s 2(1); 'annual accounts': CA 1963, s 2(1); 'articles': CA 1963, s 2(1); 'company': CA 1963, s 2(1); 'the court': CA 1963, s 2(1); 'director': CA 1963, s 2(1); 'debenture': CA 1963, s 2(1); 'document': CA 1963, s 2(1); 'EEA Agreement': CA 1963, s 2(1); 'existing company': CA 1963, s 2(1); 'group accounts': CA 1963, s 2(1); 'Group Accounts Regulations': CA 1963, s 2(1); 'IFRS accounts': CA 1963, s 2(1); 'IFRS group accounts': CA 1963, s 2(1); 'IFRS individual accounts': CA 1963, s 2(1); 'income statement': CA 1963, s 2(1); 'individual accounts': CA 1963, s 2(1); 'international financial reporting standards': CA 1963, s 2(1); 'Minister': means CA 1963, s 2(1); 'memorandum': CA 1963, s 2(1); 'officer': CA 1963, s 2(1); 'the operative date': CA 1963, s 2(1); 'prescribed': CA 1963, s 2(1); printed': CA 1963, s 2(1); 'prospectus': CA 1963, s 2(1); 'the registrar of companies': CA 1963, s 2(1); 'rules of court': IA 2005, Sch, Part 1; CA 1963; 'share': CA 1963, s 2(1).

Notes

Bankruptcy Acts: The Irish Bankrupt and Insolvent Act 1857, the Bankruptcy (Ireland) Amendment Act 1872, the Debtors Act (Ireland) 1872, s 11, ss 12 & 14–22, and the Local Bankruptcy (Ireland) Act 1888 have all been repealed and have been replaced by the provisions of the Bankruptcy Act 1988.

With regard to the definition of 'undischarged bankrupt' the relevant provision for the discharge of bankrupts is now the Bankruptcy Act 1988, s 85.

Books and paper: The above definition is largely replicated in the definition of 'books and documents' and 'books or documents' contained in CA 1990, s 3(1). Bearing in mind therefore that the Companies Acts are to be construed as one Act[1], the definition (although clearly not exhaustive) extends to accounts, deeds, writings, summonses, notices, orders and other legal processes, registers and records made in any other manner.[2]

1 CA 1990, s 1(3).

2 See also CA 1990, ss 248 and 249 which permit the delivery of 'documents' to the Registrar of Companies (the Registrar) either in the traditional legible form or alternatively in 'non-legible form' (eg on a computer disc).

Company: The definition of 'company' extends to any company formed and registered under CA 1963 to 2006,[1] the 1908 Act, Companies Act 1862 (the 1862 Act) or the Joint Stock Companies Acts.[2] Only companies registered but not formed under any of these Acts fall to be dealt with by the provisions contained in CA 1963, s 325 and Pt IX. The winding up of 'unregistered companies' is governed by CA 1963, Pt X, whereas foreign companies establishing a place of business within the State fall to be dealt with by CA 1963, Pt XI.

1 As to the definition of the 'Companies Act', see notes to IFCMPA 2006, s 1.

2 For the application of the provisions of CA 1963 to 2005 to companies formed and registered under the Joint Stock Companies Acts, the 1862 Act or the 1908 Act, see CA 1963, s 324.

Court: To date the Minister has not prescribed any other court as being a 'court' for the purposes of the Companies Acts and accordingly almost exclusive jurisdiction rests with the High Court. Exceptions are to be found in (i) C(A)A 1990, s 3(9) which confers limited jurisdiction on the Circuit Court in relation to companies which have been placed under the protection of the court; and (ii) C(A)A 1982, s 12B(8)[1] whereby the Registrar and/or creditors of a company may apply to the Circuit Court in order to have a company which has been struck off, restored to the register. The procedure governing company law applications before the High Court is set out in RSC Ord 74, Ord 75, Ord 75A and Ord 75B.

1 As amended by C(A)(No 2)A 1999, s 46.

Debenture: It is quite clear from the definition contained in CA 1963, s 2 that a document can constitute a 'debenture' without at the same time creating a charge.[1] Rather, the essence of a debenture is that it creates or acknowledges a debt. As Chitty J stated in *Levy v Abercorris Slate and Slab Company*: [2]

> 'In my opinion, a debenture means a document which either creates a debt or acknowledges it, and any document which fulfils either of these conditions is a 'debenture'. I cannot find any precise legal definition of the term, it is not either in law or in commerce a strictly technical term, or what is called a term of art.'

This definition, whilst perhaps not exhaustive, has nonetheless been accepted in numerous other cases, including *The British India Steam Navigation Company v Commissioners of Inland Revenue*[3] and *Lemon v Austin Friars Investment Trust Ltd*[4] and represents the clearest judicial pronouncement to date. Thus, the following documents have all been held to be debentures: a legal mortgage of land;[5] an issue of income bonds by which a loan to the company was repayable only out of profits;[6] an unsecured loan note;[7] and a receipt for a deposit made with a company (which was not a bank) in circumstances where the deposit was repayable after a fixed period of time.[8] Clearly, the scope of the definition of 'debenture' is quite wide. However, Palmer points out[9] that not every document which creates or acknowledges a debt will be regarded by commercial men or by lawyers as being debentures. For example, it is suggested that bills of exchange, cheques and other negotiable instruments would fall outside the definition.

Debenture stock differs from a normal debenture in that a normal debenture is a document evidencing a debt, whereas debenture stock is an equitable interest under an instrument (typically a debenture stock trust deed) which evidences a collective debt. Unlike a debenture which is always for a fixed or ascertainable sum and which is transferable only in its entirety, debenture stock is divisible into and can be transferred as smaller units. In the absence of any provisions to the contrary, the stock may be transferred in whatever fractions the holder wishes. As a matter of practical convenience, however, the terms of issue of the debenture stock or the articles of association may instead stipulate that the stock can only be divided into and transferable as specific stock units, such as units of €1, €10 or €100. Debenture stock is therefore somewhat akin to a share, with the important exception that the holder of the debenture stock is no more than a creditor of the company, whereas the shareholder is a member and owner of the company.[10] There is, however, a hybrid type of debenture stock, known as the convertible debenture, which although initially constituting part of the company's loan capital, may, pursuant to its terms of issue, be converted into share capital at some later date or upon the happening of a specified event or contingency. Upon conversion the holder of the stock ceases to be creditor of the company and instead becomes entitled to have his name entered in the register of members.

Whilst it is permissible to issue debenture stock at a discount (ie at less than the par value of the unit of stock)[11], the same rule does not apply to the allotment of shares.[12] Thus, convertible debentures may not be used as a method of effecting a disguised allotment of shares at a discount. For example, it would be impermissible to convert a 50 cent debenture into a €1 share. Similarly, the company could not issue €1 debenture at a discount and then convert that debenture into a €1 share.[13]

A debenture need not necessarily be under seal in order to validly create or acknowledge a debt. Indeed, in so far as the debenture purports to create a charge, a failure to properly seal the document will not prevent it from creating a valid equitable security.[14] Equally well, a document does not cease to be a debenture simply because it does not provide for repayment on any fixed date but only in certain contingencies, such as the company going into liquidation.[15] Similarly, it is permissible to stipulate that the debenture is irredeemable or is only redeemable after a very long period of time.[16]

1 This point was also confirmed in *British India Steam Navigation Co v IRC* (1881) 7 QBD 165; *Speyer Bros v IRC* [1907] 1 KB 246; and *Lemon v Austin Friars Investment Trust* [1926] Ch 1.

2 *Levy v Abercorris Slate and Slab Company* (1887) 37 Ch D 260. See also the observations of the same judge in *Edmonds v Blaina Furnaces Co* [1887] 36 Ch D 215 at 219.

3 *British India Steam Navigation Company v Commissioners of Inland Revenue* [1881] 7 QBD 165.

4 *Lemon v Austin Friars Investment Trust Ltd* [1926] Ch 1.

5 *Knightsbridge Estates Trust Ltd v Byrne* [1940] AC 613.

6 *Lemon v Austin Friars Investment Trust Ltd* [1926] Ch 1.

7 *British India Steam Navigation Co v IRC* (1881) 7 QBD 165.

8 *United Dominions Trust Ltd v Kirkwood* [1966] 2 QB 431.

9 *Palmer's Company Law* (Sweet and Maxwell) para 13.017.

10 For the precise definition of 'member', see CA 1963, s 31.

11 See, for example, *Re Regent's Canal Ironworks Co* (1876) 3 Ch D 43.

12 C(A)A 1983, s 27.

13 See *Mosely v Koffyfontein Mines Ltd* [1904] AC 613; *Famatina Development Corporation v Bury* [1910] AC 439.

14 *British India Steam Co v IRC* (1881) 7 QBD 165; *Biggerstaff v Rowatt's Wharf* [1896] 2 Ch 93; *Re Fireproof Doors* [1916] 2 Ch 142.

15 See CA 1963, s 94.

16 CA 1963, s 94.

Director: By virtue of the above definition, any person occupying the position of director will be regarded as such, regardless of the title actually ascribed to him by the company. For example, the articles of association might describe the directors as trustees or as a committee or council of management. The name they are given is immaterial: if they act as directors, they will be regarded as directors.

Similarly, even where the directors are described as such in the memorandum and articles of association, certain persons may occupy the position of director even though they have not been so registered pursuant to CA 1963, s 195. For example, the company may originally have been a 'shelf company' and the new owners may have failed to register the change of shareholders and directors with the Registrar. Thus, the original incorporators will still appear in the records of the Companies Registration Office (CRO) as being the directors. Notwithstanding the lack of registration, those persons who are now responsible for the management of the company will be regarded as its directors. Equally, a person may wish to conceal his management of the company from the public by registering nominees as directors instead. If however, that person in fact manages the company, he will be regarded as one of its directors. Alternatively, if he instructs the directors as to how they should act, he may instead be regarded as a shadow director within the meaning of CA 1990, s 27(1). Notably though, both CA 1963, s 2(2) and CA 1990, s 27(1) provide that a person shall not be regarded ether as a director or a shadow director by reason only of the fact that he gives advice to the directors in a professional capacity.

Officer: Apart from the secretary and directors, the auditor may also be regarded as an officer of the company, at least in relation to the performance of his statutory functions.[1] However, the auditor of a company is not to be regarded as an officer of the company if he is appointed as an electronic filing agent[2] for the purposes of CA 1990, s 187(2)(a), which prohibits an officer of the Company from acting as the auditor of that company.

1 *R v Shacter* [1960] 1 All ER 61.

2 See IFCMPA 2005, s 57.

Prospectus: The term 'prospectus' is also defined in IFCMPA 2005[1] and in the Prospectus Regulations 2005.[2] The definition of 'prospectus' contained in CA 1963, s 2(1) applies to the use of the term in sections of CA 1963 not inserted or amended by IFCMPA 2005, Pt 5.[3] In relation to prospectuses generally, see IFCMPA 2005, Pt 5, the Prospectus Regs 2005 and notes thereto.

1 IFCMPA 2005, s 38(1): 'a document or documents in such form and containing such information as may be required by or under this Part or *EU prospectus law,* howsoever the document or documents are constituted, but does not include any advertisements in newspapers or journals derived from the foregoing'.

2 Prospectus Regs 2005, r 2(1): 'the document or documents required to be published for the purposes of a public offer or admission to trading in accordance with EU prospectus law and includes where the context admits any supplement thereto'.

3 IFCMPA 2005, s 39(1).

Recognised Stock Exchange: The Irish Stock Exchange[1] has been prescribed by the Minister as a 'recognised stock exchange' for the purposes of CA 1963, ss 44, 45, 361, 362 & Sch 6 para 28, C(A)A 1977, s 1 and CA 1990, ss 65, 66, 78, 90–96, 107, 112, 115–118, 120, 212, 229 and 230.[2]

1 See definition of 'Irish Stock Exchange', Stock Exchange Act 1995, s 3(1).

2 Companies (Stock Exchange) Regulations 1995 (SI 310/1995).

UK legislation

See CA 1985, ss 735, 741, 742, 744; IA 1985; FSA 1986, s 212(3), Sch 17, Pt I; Building Societies Act 1986, s 108, Sch 6, para 18(8) and Sch 7, Pt I; CA 1989, s 23, Sch 10, para 16 and s 212, Sch 24; Criminal Justice Act 1993, s 79(13), Sch 5, Pt I para 4; Companies (Single Member Private Limited Companies) Regulations 1992 (SI 1992/1699); Companies Act 1985 (Electronic Communications) Order 2000; and Companies Act 1985 (International Accounting Standards and Other Accounting Amendments) Regulations 2004 (SI 2004/2947).

---

3 Repeal and savings

(1) The enactments mentioned in the Twelfth Schedule are hereby repealed to the extent specified in the third column of that Schedule.

(2) Nothing in this Act shall affect any Order in Council, order, rule, regulation, appointment, conveyance, mortgage, deed or agreement made, resolution passed, direction given, proceeding taken, instrument issued or thing done under any former enactment relating to companies, but any such Order in Council, order, rule, regulation, appointment, conveyance, mortgage, deed, agreement, resolution, direction, proceeding, instrument or thing shall, if in force immediately before the operative date continue in force, and so far as it could have been made, passed, given, taken, issued or done under this Act shall have effect as if made, passed, given, taken, issued or done under this Act.

(3) Nothing in this Act shall affect the operation of sections 109 and 110 of the Companies (Consolidation) Act, 1908, as regards inspectors appointed before, or the continuance of an inspection began by inspectors appointed before, the operative date, and section 172 shall apply to a report of inspectors appointed under the said sections as it applies to a report of inspectors appointed under sections 165 and 166.

(4) Nothing in this Act shall affect:

- (a) the provisions of section 5 of the Trade Union Act, 1871 (which avoids the registration of a trade union under the enactments relating to companies);
- (b) the enactment set out in the Thirteenth Schedule, being an enactment continued in force by section 205 of the Companies Act, 1862,

or be construed as repealing any provision of the Insurance Acts, 1909 to 1961.

(5) Subject to the provisions of subsection (4), any document referring to any former enactment relating to companies shall be construed as referring to the corresponding enactment of this Act.

(6) Any person, appointed to any office under or by virtue of any former enactment relating to companies, who is in office immediately before the operative date shall be deemed to have been appointed to that office under or by virtue of this Act.

(7) Any register kept under any former enactment relating to companies shall be deemed part of the register to be kept under the corresponding provisions of this Act.

(8) All funds and accounts constituted under this Act shall be deemed to be in continuation of the corresponding funds and accounts constituted under the former enactments relating to companies.

(9) The repeal by this Act of any enactment shall not affect:

- (a) the incorporation of any company registered under any enactment hereby repealed;

(b) Table B in the Schedule annexed to the Joint Stock Companies Act, 1856, or any part thereof, so far as the same applies to any company existing on the operative date;

(c) Table A in the First Schedule annexed to the Companies Act, 1862, or any part thereof, either as originally contained in that Schedule or as altered in pursuance of section 71 of that Act, so far as the same applies to any company existing on the operative date;

(d) Table A of the First Schedule to the Companies (Consolidation) Act, 1908, or any part thereof, so far as the same applies to any company existing on the operative date.

(10) Where any offence, being an offence for the continuance of which a penalty was provided, has been committed under any former enactment relating to companies, proceedings may be taken under this Act in respect of the continuance of the offence after the operative date, in the same manner as if the offence had been committed under the corresponding provisions of this Act.

(11) In this section 'former enactment relating to companies' means any enactment repealed by this Act and any enactment repealed by the Companies (Consolidation) Act, 1908.

Cross reference

CA 1963, ss 165–173 (Inspection) were repealed by CA 1990, s 6(1) and have been replaced by CA 1990, Pt II (Investigations) (as amended by CLEA 2001, Pt 3).

Definitions

'accounts': CA 1963, s 2(1); 'company': CA 1963, s 2(1); 'document': CA 1963, s 2(1): 'the operative date': CA 1963, s 2(1); 'former enactment relating to companies': CA 1963, s 3(11).

Notes

No retrospective effect: The effect of CA 1963, s 3(2) is to prevent CA 1963 from having retrospective effect. On the constitutional presumption against retrospectivity in legislation generally, see Delaney, 'Statutory Interpretation – Can Legislation Have Retrospective Effect?' (1992) 10 ILT (ns) 133. Thus, the reckless trading provisions of CA 1963, s 297A were held not to have retrospective effect.[1] However, although a statute cannot be operated retrospectively so as to invalidate or render illegal a transaction which has already taken place, it may be invoked to at least examine or investigate such prior transactions.[2]

1 *Re Hefferon Kearns Ltd (No 1)* [1992] ILRM 51 noted by MacCann, 'Reckless Trading: No Looking Back' (Parts 1 and 2), (1992) ILT 10 31, 61.

2 *Chestvale Properties Ltd v Glackin* [1992] ILRM 221.

---

4 Construction of references in other Acts to companies registered under the Companies (Consolidation) Act, 1908

Notwithstanding subsection (1) of section 20 of the Interpretation Act, 1937, (which provides that where an Act repeals and re-enacts, with or without modification, any provisions of a former Act, references in any other Act to the provisions so repealed shall, unless the contrary intention appears, be construed as references to the provisions so re-enacted) references in any Act other than this Act to a company formed and registered, or registered, under the Companies (Consolidation) Act, 1908, shall, unless the contrary intention appears, be construed as references to a company formed and registered, or registered, under that Act or this Act.

Cross reference

See generally IA 2005. The IA 1937 was repealed in full by the IA 2005,[1] with effect from 1 January 2006.[2]

[1] IA 2005, s 3.

[2] IA 2005, s 1(2).

Definitions

'company': CA 1963, s 2(1).

Notes

Prior to the enactment of the CA 1963, the 1908 Act had been the principal piece of companies legislation in the State. For a brief history of Irish company law see Keane, *Company Law* (4th edn, Tottel Publishing, 2007) Ch 2; Courtney, *The Law of Private Companies* (2nd edn, Tottel Publishing, 2002) paras 1.045–1.073 and MacCann, *A Casebook on Company Law*, (Butterworths, 1991) paras 1.16–1.59.

PART II
INCORPORATION OF COMPANIES AND MATTERS INCIDENTAL THERETO

Memorandum of Association

5 Way of forming incorporated company

(1) Any seven or more persons or, where the company to be formed will be a private company [or an investment company (within the meaning of Part XIII of the Companies Act, 1990)],[a] any two or more persons, associated for any lawful purpose may, by subscribing their names to a memorandum of association and otherwise complying with the requirements of this Act relating to registration, form an incorporated company, with or without limited liability.

(2) Such a company may be either:

(a) a company having the liability of its members limited by the memorandum to the amount, if any, unpaid on the shares respectively held by them (in this Act termed 'a company limited by shares'); or

(b) a company having the liability of its members limited by the memorandum to such amount as the members may respectively thereby undertake to contribute to the assets of the company in the event of its being wound up (in this Act termed 'a company limited by guarantee'); or

(c) a company not having any limit on the liability of its members (in this Act termed 'an unlimited company').

Amendments

a Words inserted by CA 1990, s 260 (as substituted by C(A)(No 2)A 1999, s 54(3)).

Cross reference

'an investment company': CA 1990, s 252(1).

Definitions

'company': CA 1963, s 2(1); 'a company limited by guarantee': CA 1963, s 2(1), 5(2)(b); 'a company limited by shares': CA 1963, s 2(1), 5(2)(a); 'member': CA 1963, s 31; 'memorandum': CA 1963, s 2(1); 'private company': CA 1963, s 2(1), s 33(1); 'share': CA 1963, s 2(1); 'an unlimited company': CA 1963, s 2(1), s 5(2)(c).

Notes

No constitutional right of incorporation: There is no constitutional right of incorporation. Incorporation is instead a right conferred, and therefore capable of being removed or curtailed by, statute.[1]

1 *Private Motorists' Provident Society Ltd and Moore v Attorney General* (15 July 1981, unreported) HC (Carroll J).

Minimum number of subscribers: The minimum number of subscribers for a public company is seven. Until 1 October 1994[1] the minimum number of subscribers for a private company was two. EC(SMPLC)R 1994 (SI 275/1994) which implements the Twelfth Companies Directive[2] (and which ought to have been implemented by 1 January 1992) provides for single member companies in certain circumstances.[3] In particular EC(SMPLC)R 1994, r 3(1) provides that:

> 'Notwithstanding any enactment or rule of law to the contrary, a private company limited by shares or by guarantee may be formed by one person, and may have one member ...'

Even though it is now possible to form single-member companies in certain circumstances, such companies must still have at least two directors.[4] This requirement is somewhat anomalous and ought to be dispensed with. In this regard, it is now possible in the UK to have single-member private companies with one director only.[5]

In the case of companies which do not enjoy the benefit of EC(SMPLC)R 1994, such as plcs, there is nothing in the Companies Acts which requires the various shareholders to be independent of one another or to be unconnected. So, for example, where there are seven subscribers to the memorandum, there is nothing to prevent six of the subscribers from holding their shares as trustees or nominees for the seventh.[6]

1 The operative date of EC(SMPLC)R 1994.

2 (89/667/EEC) 32 OJ 1989, L395/40, 30 December 1989.

3 For an analysis of the Twelfth Companies Directive, see MacCann, 'Company Law Reform: One Man Companies' (1990) 8 ILT 166 and Courtney, *The Law of Private Companies* (2nd edn, Butterworths 2002) para 1.119–1.125.

4 CA 1963, s 174.

5 CA 1985, s 282(3).

6 *Salomon v Salomon and Co* [1897] AC 22; *Attorney General for Canada v Standard Trust Co of New York* [1911] AC 498; *Tunstall v Steigmann* [1962] 2 QB 593; *Lee v Lee's Air Farming Ltd* [1961] AC 12; *Macaura v Northern Assurance Co* [1925] AC 619; *Taylor v Smith* [1991] IR 142.

Corporate subscribers: The IA 2005, s 18(c) provides that a reference in a statute to a 'person' is to be construed as including a reference to a body corporate, subject, of course, to any indications to the contrary. Thus, the subscribers to the memorandum of association may be either individuals or bodies corporate.[1] However, a body corporate cannot, subject only to limited exceptions[2] be a member of a company which is its holding company.[3]

1 *Re Barned's Banking Co; ex parte Contract Corp* (1867) 3 Ch App 105; *Royal Bank of India's Case* (1868) LR 7 Eq 91.

2 See CA 1963, s 32(2)–(5) and CA 1990, s 224 and notes thereto.

3 See CA 1963, s 32 and notes thereto.

Foreign subscribers: It is permissible for all the subscribers to the memorandum to be foreigners and although at common law a company could have as its sole object the carrying on of business abroad, now, pursuant to C(A)(No2)A 1999, s 42(1), a company shall not be formed and registered unless it appears to the Registrar that the company will, when registered, carry on an activity in the State.[1] Such a company is deemed to have an Irish domicile and Irish nationality,[2] and since 6 April 1999 (subject to limited exceptions[3]) such a company is deemed to be resident in the State for tax purposes.[4] Furthermore, although having Irish nationality, the company may be regarded, in times of war, as having enemy status because of its foreign control.[5]

1 *Re General Co for Promotion of Land Credit* (1870) 5 Ch App 363; aff'd sub nom *Reuss (Princess) v Bos* (1871) LR 7 HL 176; *Attorney General v Jewish Colonization Association* [1901] 1 KB 123.

2 *Janson v Dreifontein Mines Ltd* [1902] AC 484; *Gasque v IRC* [1940] 2 KB 80.

3 TCA 1997, s 23A(3)-(4) as inserted by FA 1999, s 82(1). In the event that a company comes within such an exception, then actual residence is determined by the location of the management and control of that company; *De Beers Consolidated Mines Ltd v Howe* [1906] AC 455; *John Hood and Co Ltd v Magee* [1918] 2 IR 34; *Unit Construction Ltd v Bullock* [1960] AC 1.

4 TCA 1997, s 23A(2) as inserted by FA 1999, s 82(1).

5 *Daimler Co Ltd v Continental Tyre and Rubber Co (Great Britain) Ltd* [1916] 2 AC 307.

Minor subscribers: Minors (ie those under the age of 18) may also subscribe for shares in a company[1] unless the memorandum[2] or articles of association provides to the contrary. The capacity of a minor to take shares is subject to the general law of contract.[3] Accordingly, whilst a minor can apply for shares and become a member of the company, he is entitled, within a reasonable period of time after attaining majority, to repudiate the allotment, thereby terminating his membership[4]. Similarly, if the minor repudiates a transfer of shares, the transferor again becomes a member of the company and becomes liable for any calls on the shares.[5] Until repudiation, however, the minor remains a member of the company and cannot plead his minority as a defence to calls made upon him,[6] but if he repudiates, he cannot be sued for the calls, whether they were made before or after the date of repudiation.[7]

1 *Re Laxon and Co (No 2)* (1892) 3 Ch 555; *Hill v City of Glasgow Bank* (1880) 7 R 68.

2 *Seymour v Royal Naval School* [1910] 1 Ch 806 at 811.

3 See generally Clark, *Contract Law in Ireland* (5th edn, Roundhall Sweet & Maxwell, 2004) Ch 16.

4 *Re Blakely Ordnance Co, Lumley's Case* (1868) 4 Ch App 31; *Re Constantinople and Alexandria Hotel Co, Ebbett's Case* (1870) 5 Ch App 302; *Re Alexandra Park Co, Hart's Case* (1868) LR 6 Eq 512.

5 *Re China SS and Labaun Coal Co, Capper's Case* (1868) 3 Ch App 458.

6 *Cork and Bandon Railway Co v Cazenove* (1847) 10 QB 935.

7 *Newry and Enniskillen Railway Co v Coombe* (1849) 3 Exch 565.

Lawful purpose: The Registrar may refuse to register a company where one or more of its proposed objects necessarily involves a criminal offence.[1] If the Registrar erroneously registers a company which has an unlawful object, his decision is not readily subject to review since the certificate of incorporation is deemed to be 'conclusive evidence' of compliance with the statutory registration requirements.[2] However, the registration of the company may possibly be open to challenge by the Attorney General by way of *certiorari*.[3]

1 *R v Registrar of companies, ex parte Bowen* [1914] 3 KB 1161; *R v Registrar of Joint Stock companies ex parte More* [1931] 2 KB 197; *Bowman v Secular Society Ltd* [1917] AC 406; *McEllistrim v Ballymacelligott Co-operative and Dairy Society Ltd* [1919] AC 549.

2 C(A)A 1983, s 5(4).

3 *Bowman v Secular Society Ltd* [1917] AC 406; *R v Registrar of Joint Stock companies, ex parte More* [1931] 2 KB 197; *R v Registrar of Companies, ex parte Attorney General* [1991] BCLC 476. Cf *Byrne v Ireland* where the Supreme Court held that the State did not inherit the old Crown privilege of immunity from the provisions of its own statutes. *Quaere* whether the exemption of the certificate of incorporation from judicial review is unconstitutional: *Maher v Attorney General* [1973] IR 146; *Tormey v Attorney General* [1985] IR 289.

No incorporation without proof of intended activity in the State: Prior to the coming into force of C(A)(No 2)A 1999, s 42 on 18 April 2000[1] a company could lawfully be incorporated in the State even though its sole intended purpose was to operate as a non-resident company. Now, however, the company will not be registered and a certificate of incorporation will not be issued without proof that one of the activities mentioned in its objects clause will be carried on in the State.[2] However, the Registrar may accept as sufficient proof a statutory declaration in the prescribed form[3] that the purpose or one of the purposes for which the company is being formed is to carry on an activity in the State.[4] The statutory declaration, which may be made by one of the persons who are to be named in the statement to be filed with the Registrar under C(A)A 1982, s 3 as being the first directors of the company[5] or being the first secretary or one of the first joint secretaries of the company[6] or which may be made by a solicitor engaged in the formation of the company,[7] must give details of the activity to be carried on in the State[8] or the principal activity if two or more such activities are to be carried on,[9] including details of the place or places in the State where such activity is proposed to be carried on.[10] Furthermore, details must also be given of the place (whether in the State or abroad) where the central administration of the company will normally be carried on.[11] Although it is clearly contrary to the spirit of a European Union, it still remains to be seen whether the requirement that every newly formed company carry on an activity in the State amounts to an unlawful curtailment of the freedom of establishment provided for in Art 43 of the EC Treaty.

1 Companies (Amendment) (No 2) Act 1999 (Commencement) Order 2000 (SI 61/2000), r 3.
2 C(A)(No 2)A 1999, s 42(1).
3 Companies (Forms) No 2 Order 2004 (SI 829/2004), Form A1. In this form the declarant not only confirms compliance with the provisions of C(A)(No 2)A 1999, s 42 but also confirms compliance generally with the registration requirements of the Companies Acts, as required by C(A)A 1983, s 5(5). Making this combined declaration is expressly provided by C(A)(No 2)A 1999, s 42(5).
4 C(A)(No 2)A 1999, s 42(2).
5 C(A)(No 2)A 1999, s 42(4)(a).
6 C(A)(No 2)A 1999, s 42(4)(b).
7 C(A)(No 2)A 1999, s 42(4)(c).
8 C(A)(No 2)A 1999, s 42(2)(a) and (b).
9 C(A)(No 2)A 1999, s 42(3).
10 C(A)(No 2)A 1999, s 42(2)(c).
11 C(A)(No 2)A 1999, s 42(2)(d). With regard to the place of a company's central administration, see the notes to CA 1963, s 113.

Consequences of incorporation: See the notes to CA 1963, s 18.

Liability of members: The memorandum of association must define the liability of the members[1] and any provision in the articles which purports to modify or delimit that liability to the prejudice of the company's creditors is void.[2] On the other hand, any attempt to amend the provisions of the memorandum or articles so as to increase a member's liability *qua contributory*[3] will be void unless actually agreed upon by that particular member.[4] However, a provision in the memorandum or articles which exposes the members to a liability in some other capacity (eg to lend money to the company at interest) will be binding.[5]

1 CA 1963, s 6.
2 *Dent's Case* (1873) LR 15 Eq 407; on appeal (1873) 8 Ch App 768, 775.

3 For the definition of contributory, see CA 1963, s 208.
4 CA 1963, s 27. See also *Edwards v Haliwell* [1950] 2 All ER 1064.
5 *Peninsular Co v Fleming* (1872) 27 LT 93.

UK legislation

See CA 1985, s 1; C(SMPLC)R 1992, reg 2, Sch, para 1.

6 Requirements in relation to memorandum

[(1) The memorandum of every company must state—

(a) in the case of a public limited company, the name of the company, with 'public limited company' or 'cuideachta phoiblí theoranta' as the last words of the name;

(b) in the case of a company (other than a public limited company) which is limited by shares or by guarantee, the name of the company, with 'limited' or 'teoranta' as the last word of the name;

(c) the objects of the company.][a]

(2) The memorandum of a company limited by shares or by guarantee must also state that the liability of its members is limited.

(3) The memorandum of a company limited by guarantee must also state that each member undertakes to contribute to the assets of the company in the event of its being wound up while he is a member, or within one year after he ceases to be a member, for payment of the debts and liabilities of the company contracted before he ceases to be a member, and of the costs, charges and expenses of winding up, and for adjustment of the rights of the contributories among themselves, such amount as may be required, not exceeding a specified amount.

(4) In the case of a company having a share capital—

(a) the memorandum must also, unless the company is an unlimited company, state the amount of share capital with which the company proposes to be registered, and the division thereof into shares of a fixed amount;

(b) no subscriber of the memorandum may take less than one share;

(c) each subscriber must write opposite to his name the number of shares he takes.

Amendments

a CA 1963, s 6(1) substituted by C(A)A 1983, Sch 1, para 2.

Definitions

'company': CA 1963, s 2(1); 'a company limited by guarantee': CA 1963, s 2(1), 5(2)(b); 'a company limited by shares': CA 1963, s 2(1), 5(2)(a); 'member': CA 1963, s 31; 'memorandum': CA 1963, s 2(1); 'share': CA 1963, s 2(1); 'an unlimited company': CA 1963, s 2(1), s 5(2)(c).

Notes

Registration of standard form memoranda and articles: CLEA 2001, s 80 allows for the filing of standard form memoranda and articles of association to which reference numbers will be assigned by the Registrar. Thereafter, the promoters of a company need only file a memorandum and articles of association specifying those matters peculiar to the company itself, together with a statement identifying the reference number(s) of the standard form documents which are to be deemed also to have been incorporated therein.

Memorandum is part of company's constitution: The constitution of a company is made up of two documents, namely the memorandum and articles of association.[1] Of the two, the memorandum is the principal and dominant document,[2] acting as its charter and containing the fundamental conditions upon which the company is allowed to be incorporated.[3] As to the relationship between the memorandum and the articles, see the notes to CA 1963, s 11.

1 *TJ Wilson (Inspector of Taxes) v Dunnes Stores (Cork) Ltd* [1982] ILRM 444.
2 *Guinness v Land Corporation of Ireland* (1882) 22 Ch D 349; *Roper v Ward* [1981] ILRM 408.
3 *Guinness v Land Corporation of Ireland* (1882) 22 Ch D 349.

Name Clause and Liability Clause:

Corporate name: The memorandum of association must state the name of the company. However, undesirable names may not be registered.[1] The company is at liberty at any stage to change its name, subject to compliance with the procedure set out in CA 1963, s 23. The company may also carry on business under a name other than its corporate name provided that the trade name is first registered under the Registration of Business Names Act 1963.[2] Even so, the corporate name must still appear on the company's business letters, and other official documentation, including cheques, promissory notes and orders for money or goods. A failure to accurately state the corporate name on such documentation may result in both criminal and civil liability for the officers in default.[3]

'Public Limited Company': It is an offence for a company which is not a public limited company to carry on any trade, profession or business under a name which includes as its last part, the words 'public limited company', the Irish equivalent or their respective abbreviations.[4]

'Limited': A limited liability company other than a plc must include the word 'limited' or 'teoranta' or the appropriate abbreviation thereof at the end of its name unless it is exempted from so doing pursuant to CA 1963, s 24 as substituted by CLEA 2001, s 88.[5] Conversely, it is an offence for any person or persons who have not been so incorporated to trade or carry on business under any name or title of which 'limited' or 'teoranta' or any contraction or imitation thereof is the last word.[6]

1 CA 1963, s 21. For what constitutes an 'undesirable' see the notes to CA 1963, s 21.
2 See CA 1963, s 22(1).
3 CA 1963, s 114.
4 C(A)A 1983, s 56(1). For the permissible abbreviations, see CA 1963, s 22(2).
5 For the permissible abbreviations, see CA 1963, s 22(2).
6 CA 1963, s 381.

Objects Clause:[1]

Specific objects: The memorandum of association must state specific objects of the company.[2] It is not permissible to provide that the company can do whatever it wants 'because that is to have no object at all.[3] Nonetheless, an object of 'carrying on business ... as merchants generally' may be regarded as sufficiently specific for the purposes of the Act.[4]

Main objects rule: By virtue of a rule known as the 'main objects rule', if a main or dominant object can be ascertained from the objects clause, then all other stated objects will be treated as merely ancillary to the main object and will only be capable of being pursued while the main object is itself being pursued.[5] Therefore, and by analogy with the *ejusdem generis* rule of statutory interpretation, any broadly stated objects which follow more narrowly defined objects will typically be subordinated to those narrower objects.[6] In some exceptional cases however, the court may be prepared to construe the broad or general objects rather than more particular objects as being the main objects of the company.[7] In other cases the court may seek to determine a company's main object by reference to its name.[8]

Two principal devices have been used by draftsmen to circumvent the constraints of the 'main objects rule'. The first is known as the 'Independent Objects Clause' and the second is known as the 'Bell Houses Clause.'

Independent objects clause: The independent objects clause is generally the last paragraph of the company's objects clause and will appear after a long list of stated 'objects.' It deems every stated 'object' to be a substantive and independent activity of the company, so that no one 'object' is to be treated as being merely subsidiary or ancillary to any other. A typical independent objects clause will be in the following terms:

> 'It is hereby declared that the objects specified in the preceding sub-clauses shall be regarded as independent objects and shall be construed independently of the other sub-clauses of it, and that none of the objects mentioned in any preceding sub-clause shall be deemed to be merely subsidiary to the objects expressed in any other sub-clause.'

The House of Lords first expressed itself willing to give effect to the literal wording of such clauses in *Cotman v Brougham*.[9] In that case a company was permitted to engage in the stated object of underwriting an allotment of shares in circumstances where what would otherwise have been its 'main object' (ie developing rubber plantations) had since ceased.

1 For a general discussion of the capacity of companies and the operation of the *ultra vires* rule, see MacCann, 'The Capacity of the Company' (1992) 10 ILT 79 and 151; Courtney, *The Law of Private Companies*, (2nd edn, Tottel Publishing, 2002) p 342 *et seq*.

2 *Re Crown Bank* (1890) 44 Ch D 634.

3 Per Harman LJ *Re Introductions Ltd* [1968] 2 All ER 1221. See also *Re Crown Bank* (1890) 44 Ch D 634.

4 *Re New Finance and Mortgage Co Ltd* [1975] Ch 420. See also *Newstead v Frost* [1980] 1 WLR 135, where Viscount Dilhorne consider obiter, that a company could legitimately have an object to engage in 'all kinds ... of other operations.'

5 *Ashbury Railway Carriage and Iron Co v Riche* (1875) LR 7 HL 653. See also *Anglo-Overseas Agencies Ltd v Green* [1961] 1 QB 1, where the rule was described in the following terms:

> '... [W]here the memorandum of association expresses the object of the company in a series of paragraphs, and one paragraph or the first two or three paragraphs, appear to embody the 'main object' of the company, all other paragraphs are treated as merely ancillary to the 'main object', and as limited and controlled thereby.'

6 *Re German Date Coffee Co Ltd* (1882) 20 Ch D 169; *Re Haven Gold Mining Co* (1882) 20 Ch D 151; *Stephens v Mysore Reefs (Kangundy) Mining Co Ltd* [1902] 1 Ch 745; *Pedlar v Road Block Gold Mines of India* [1905] 2 Ch 427.

7 *Re Kitson and Co Ltd* [1946] 1 All ER 435.

8 *Re Crown Bank* (1890) 4 Ch D 634.

9 *Cotman v Brougham* [1918] AC 514. See also *Anglo-Overseas Agencies Ltd v Green* [1961] 1 QB 1.

Bell Houses Clause: The Bell Houses Clause derives its name from the case of *Bell Houses Ltd v City Wall Properties Ltd*[1] where its validity was first upheld in England.[2] Essentially, the Bell Houses Clause permits the company to extend its activities into any business which the members or directors honestly believe would be of benefit to the company's main business, even where that other business is not specifically provided for in the objects clause itself. Thus, in the *Bell Houses* case itself, a property development company was empowered to act as a money-broker or financier for another company simply because the directors came to the *bona fide* opinion that such an activity would be of profit to the company's main business.

A typical Bell Houses Clause will permit the company to do the following:

'To carry on any other business whatsoever which can, in the opinion of the company or the board of directors, be advantageously carried on in connection with or as ancillary to any of the above businesses or the general business of the company.'

As can be seen from the foregoing, the main limitation on the Bell Houses Clause is that it can only be invoked whilst the company is also carrying on one of its stated objects.[3]

1 *Bell Houses Ltd v City Wall Properties Ltd* [1966] 2 QB 656.

2 Such clauses had already been judicially recognised by the High Court of Australia in *HA Stephenson and Son Ltd v Gillanders Arbuthnot and Co* (1831) 45 CLR 476.

3 *Re Introductions Ltd* [1970] CH 199.

Express and implied powers: As noted above, the typical objects clause of a company will be divided into various sub-clauses. Many of these will contain what are undoubtedly substantive 'objects' of the company. However, others will be found to contain what are no more than mere 'powers'. The basic distinction between the two is that the 'objects' are those activities which the company was formed to achieve, whereas the 'powers' are merely ancillary or incidental to the achievement of those objects.[1] However, apart from any express powers contained in the memorandum of association, the company also has an implied power to do whatever may fairly be regarded as incidental to, or consequential upon, its stated objects.[2] The following are some of the implied powers which a company has been held to enjoy:

(i) appointing agents; [3]

(ii) engaging employees; [4]

(iii) borrowing money and giving security for such borrowings; [5]

(iv) acquiring property for the company and disposing of same; [6]

(v) entering into partnerships or joint ventures for the carrying on of any business which the company could have pursued on its own; [7]

(vi) instituting, defending and compromising legal proceedings; [8]

(vii) paying gratuities to its employees; [9]

(viii) paying pensions to former officers and employees and their dependants;[10] and

(ix) making other gratuitous dispositions which are reasonably incidental to the company's business.[11]

As a general rule, a company will not have an implied power to give guarantees for the debts of third parties, even where the third party is a major shareholder[12] or an associated company.[13] However, if the affairs of the two parties are closely linked or intertwined (eg with various inter-party loans and other transactions) then it might be reasonably incidental to the company's business to guarantee the debts of that other party, since the collapse of that other party could lead to the collapse of the company itself.[14]

Where the company's memorandum contains an independent objects clause, this may have the effect of raising some express powers to the status of substantive objects.[15] Thus, for example, an express power to make gifts[16] or to grant pensions to present or former officers and employees or their dependants,[17] is capable of being elevated to the status of a substantive object. It is to be noted though that to the extent that a transaction amounts to a gift or gratuity directly or indirectly in favour of one or more of the company's members, then even though it may be permitted by the wording of the company's objects clause, it will be unlawful except to the extent that the company has distributable profits available to it within the meaning of C(A)A 1983, s 45.[18] It is also to be noted that, some powers by their very nature can never be objects, such as, the power to borrow money,[19] or to promote the company's interests by advertising its products or services.[20]

1 *Re Horsley and Weight Ltd* [1982] 3 All ER 1045, 1050; *Rolled Steel Products (Holdings) Ltd v British Steel Corporation* [1985] 3 All ER 52, 81.

2 *Attorney General v Great Eastern Railway Co* (1880) 5 App Cas 473; *Martin v Irish Industrial Benefit Building Society* (1960) Ir Jur Rep 42; *Rolled Steel Products (Holdings) Ltd* [1985] 3 All ER 52, at 81–82; *Northern Bank Finance Corporation Ltd v Quinn and Achates Investment Company* [1979] ILRM 221.

3 *Ferguson v Wilson* (1866) 2 Ch App 77, 89.

4 *Ferguson v Wilson* (1866) 2 Ch App 77, 89.

5 *General Auction Estate and Monetary Co v Smith* [1891] 3 Ch 432.

6 *Re Kingsbury Collieries Ltd and Moore's Contract* [1907] 2 Ch 259.

7 *Newstead (Inspector of Taxes) v Frost* [1979] 2 All ER 129, 137 aff'd [1980] 1 All ER 363.

8 *Re Norwich Provident Insurance Society* (1878) 8 Ch D 334.

9 *Hampson v Price's Patents Candle Co* (1876) 45 LJ Ch 437; *Hutton v West Cork Railway Co* (1883) 23 Ch D 654. Cf *Parke v The Daily News Ltd* [1962] 2 All ER 929 where it was held to be *ultra vires* for a company to pay gratuities to its employees after it had ceased trading since the payments could no longer be regarded as 'reasonably incidental' to any business.

10 *Henderson v Bank of Australasia* (1888) 40 Ch D 170.

11 *Hutton v West Cork Railway Co* (1883) 23 Ch D 654; *Re Metro Investment Trust Ltd* (26 May 1977, unreported) HC (McWilliam J); *Re PMPA Garage (Longmile) Ltd (No 1)* [1992] ILRM 337; *Simmonds v Heffer* [1983] BCLC 298; *Rolled Steel Products (Holdings) Ltd v British Steel Corporation* [1986] Ch 246. A gratuitous disposition will not be regarded as being reasonably incidental to the business of the company in circumstances where the business is insolvent and in a state of imminent collapse, since the effect of such a disposition would be to prejudice the position of the persons having a beneficial interest in the remaining assets, namely the creditors; indeed, in such circumstances a gratuitous disposition by the company will not only be *ultra vires* but will also be illegal and therefore void: *Re Frederick Inns Ltd* [1994] 1 ILRM 387; *Re Greendale Developments Ltd* (20 February 1997, unreported) SC (Keane J); *Kinsela v Russell Kinsela Property Ltd* [1986] 4 NSWLR 722.

12 For restrictions on the giving, inter alia, of guarantees to directors ad those connected with them, see CA 1990, ss 31–40.

13 *Rolled Steel Products (Holdings) Ltd v British Steel Corporation* [1986] Ch 246; *Northern Bank Finance Corporation Ltd v Quinn and Achates Investment Co* [1979] ILRM 221.

14 *Charterbridge Corporation Ltd v Lloyds Bank Ltd* [1970] 1 Ch 62; *Re Metro Investment Trust Ltd* (26 May 1977, unreported) HC (McWilliam J); *Parkes and Sons Ltd v Hong Kong and Shanghai Banking Corporation* [1990] ILRM 341; *Re PMPA Garage (Longmile) Ltd (No 1)* [1992] ILRM 337.

15 *Re Horsley and Weight Ltd* [1982] 3 ALL ER 1045.

16 *Brady v Brady* [1989] AC 755; *Re Horsely and Weight Ltd* [1982] 3 All ER 1045; *Re Greendale Developments Ltd* [1998] 1 IR 8.

17 *Re Horsley and Weight Ltd* [1982] 3 All ER 1045.

18 *Brady v Brady* [1989] AC 755; *Aveling Barford Ltd v Perion* [1989] BCLC 626; *Barclays Bank plc v British and Commonwealth Holdings plc* [1996] 1 BCLC 1; *Plain Ltd v Kenley* [1931] 1 DLR 468.

19 *Re Introductions Ltd* [1970] Ch 199.

20 *Re Horsley and Weight Ltd* [1982] 3 All ER 1045.

Re-classification of transactions: As a preliminary step to determining whether or not a transaction is *ultra vires*, the court is entitled to ignore the labels or descriptions given to the transaction by the parties and to look instead at the true substance of the matter.[1]

1 *Re Halt Garage* (1964) Ltd [1982] 3 All ER 1016; *Aveling Barford Ltd v Perion* [1989] BCLC 626; *Barclays Bank plc v British and Commonwealth Holdings plc* [1996] 1 BCLC 1.

Enforceability of *ultra vires* transactions: Since a company is only entitled to pursue its stated objects, the traditional position, both at common law and in equity, has been that any transaction beyond those objects is wholly void and unenforceable.[1] For statutory and other exceptions to this rule, see both CA 1963, s 8 and EC(C)R 1973, reg 6 and the notes thereto.

1 *Ashbury Railway Carriage and Iron Co v Riche* (1875) LR 7 HL 653; *Pacific Coast Coal Mines v Arbuthnot* [1917] AC 607.

Alteration of objects clause: The objects of the company are freely alterable by following the procedure set out in CA 1963, s 10. However, if the alteration gives rise to a failure of substratum[1] then, apart from the remedies prescribed by CA 1963, s 10, the company could find itself faced with a petition for winding up on the just and equitable ground pursuant to CA 1963, s 213(f).[2]

1 ie a breach of the understanding between the members as to the purpose for which the company was formed.

2 *Re German Date Coffee Co* (1882) 20 Ch D 169; *Cotman v Brougham* [1918] AC 514; *Re Tivoli Freeholds Ltd* [1972] VR 338.

Capital Clause

Share capital – contents of memorandum: The memorandum of association is only required to state the amount of the authorised or nominal share capital and to detail its division into shares of a fixed amount (eg €100,000 divided into 200,000 shares of 50c each). Other matters, such as the division of the shares into different classes with different rights, need not necessarily be contained in the memorandum but may instead by regulated by the articles and by the terms of issue.[1] In the absence of an express provision to the contrary, all shares will be deemed to rank *pari passu*.[2]

The authorised or nominal share capital of the company is the maximum amount which can be allotted (subject of course to any increase in the authorised capital pursuant to CA 1963, s 68(a)) and accordingly if the company purports to issue shares in excess of its nominal capital, the allotment will be void and the subscribers will be entitled to claim a return of the money which they have paid to the company on the ground of total failure of consideration.[3]

Minimum amount of share capital: Whilst in the case of a plc there must be at least €38,092.14[4] of issued (and not just authorised) share capital,[5] the share capital of most private companies can be as large or as small as the promoters choose subject to the amount payable on application on each share being not less than 5% of the nominal amount of the share: CA 1963, s 53(3). However, if any director, secretary or promoter of a company is subject to a restriction order under CA 1990, s 150, that company will be required to have a minimum issued share capital, paid up in cash. The minimum permissible capital in such circumstances is €63,486.90[6] for a private company and €317,434.51[7] for a plc.

Denomination of share capital: In the case of private companies the amount of the share capital need not necessarily be expressed in Irish Punts but may instead be denominated in one or more foreign currencies or as a mixture of Irish and foreign currency.[8] In the case of a plc, although the 'authorised minimum'[9] (ie €38,092.14) must be expressed in Euro the remainder of the authorised capital may be denominated in whatever currency or currencies the company sees fit.[10]

Increase and reduction in authorised share capital: The amount of the company's authorised share capital may be increased or reduced, as the case may be, by following the procedures prescribed by CA 1963, ss 68(a) and 68(e) respectively. Also of relevance in relation to capital reduction is Part XI of the CA 1990 which permits a company, in certain circumstances, to buy back its own shares from its members.

Guarantee fund: The fund of money which the members of a company undertake to contribute in the event of a winding up is known as the 'guarantee fund' and cannot be mortgaged or otherwise used by the company to finance its trading.[11]

Capital contribution: Apart from subscribing for shares, members may also make 'capital contributions' which are not treated as loan capital but which are instead treated as akin to share premia.[12] In the event of a liquidation, after the discharge of the company's liabilities, any remaining portion of the capital contribution is distributable amongst the shareholders in accordance with their respective shareholdings rather than simply being paid back directly to the person or persons who made the contribution in the first place.[13]

1 See, for example, reg 2 of Table A which permits the company by ordinary resolution to divide the share capital into different classes and to determine the nature of the rights attaching to each such class of shares.
With regard to the variation of class rights, see CA 1963, s 78 and C(A)A 1983, s 38.
2 *Birch v Cropper* (1889) 14 App Cas 525.
3 *Bank of Hindustan, China and Japan Ltd v Alison* (1871) LR 6 CP 222.
4 £30,000 converted to €38,092.14 by Council Regulation (EC)No 1103/97, No 974/98 and No 2866/98 and the Economic and Monetary Union Act 1998, s 6.
5 Known as the 'authorised minimum'. See C(A)A 1983, s 19.
6 £50,000 converted to €63,486.90 by Council Regulation (EC) No 1103/97, No 974/98 and No 2866/98 and the Economic and Monetary Union Act 1998, s 6.
7 £250,000 converted to €317,434.52 by Council Regulation (EC)No 1103/97, No 974/98 and No 2866/98 and the Economic and Monetary Union Act 1998, s 6.
8 *Re Scandinavian Bank Group plc* [1987] BCLC 466.
9 See C(A)A 1983, s 19.
10 See C(A)A 1983, s 19.
11 *Re Mayfair Property Co Ltd* [1898] 2 Ch 28; *Re Irish Club* [1906] WN 127; *Re Industrial and Agricultural Fair Cork 1932* (1933) 67 ILTR 175.
12 *Kellar v Stanley Williams (Turks and Caicos Islands)* [2000] 2 BCLC 390.
13 *Kellar v Stanley Williams (Turks and Caicos Islands)* [2000] 2 BCLC 390.

Additional clauses: Apart from the clauses prescribed by CA 1963, s 6, the memorandum may also contain whatever additional clauses the subscribers and members choose. These additional clauses may be amended by following the procedure set out in CA 1963, s 28.

Subscribers: Private limited companies require at least one subscriber;[1] private unlimited companies and public companies require a minimum of two and seven subscribers respectively.[2] Any shares taken by a subscriber to the memorandum of a plc in pursuance of an undertaking of his in the memorandum and any premium on the shares shall be paid in cash.[3] Furthermore, any transaction whereby a non-cash asset is bought from or sold to a subscriber, by a plc within two years from the date of being issued with its trading certificate, for a consideration equal to or greater than 10% of the value of its issued share capital, must first be independently valued and approved by ordinary resolution of the members in general meeting.[4]

1 EC(SMPLC)R 1994, reg 3(1).
2 CA 1963, s 5(1).
3 C(A)A 1983, s 35.
4 C(A)A 1983, s 32.

UK legislation

See CA 1985, ss 2 and 25; Companies Act 1985 (Electronic Communications) Order 2000 (SI 2000/3373).

7 Printing, stamp and signature of memorandum

The memorandum must be printed [in an entire format or in a form pursuant to section 80 of the Company Law Enforcement Act, 2001][a] [...][b] and must be signed by each subscriber in the presence of at least one witness who must attest the signature.

Amendments

a The words 'in an entire format or in a form pursuant to section 80 of the Company Law Enforcement Act 2001' inserted by CLEA 2001, s 81.

b The words ', must bear the same stamp as if it were a deed,' deleted by FA 1996, s 112(1)(a).

Cross reference

See CLEA 2001, s 80.

Definitions

'memorandum': CA 1963, s 2(1); 'printed': CA 1963, s 2(1).

Notes

Signing the memorandum: The subscriber may sign the memorandum personally or may authorise an agent to sign the document on his behalf.[1]

1 *Re Whitley Partners Ltd* (1886) 32 Ch D 337.

Memorandum not a deed: The memorandum is not a deed. However, once they have been registered, the memorandum and articles bind the company and its members as if they were deeds.[1]

1 See CA 1963, s 25 and notes thereto.

Registration of standard form memoranda and articles: CLEA 2001, s 80 allows for the filing of standard form memoranda and articles of association to which reference numbers will be assigned by the Registrar. Thereafter the promoters of a company need only file a memorandum and articles of association specifying those matters peculiar to the company itself, together with a statement identifying the reference number(s) of the standard form documents which are to be deemed also to have been incorporated therein.

UK legislation

See CA 1985, s 2(6); Companies Act 1985 (Electronic Communications) Order 2000 (SI 2000/3373).

---

8 Modification of the *ultra vires* rule

(1) Any act or thing done by a company which if the company had been empowered to do the same would have been lawfully and effectively done, shall, notwithstanding that the company had no power to do such act or thing, be effective in favour of any person relying on such act or thing who is not shown to have been actually aware, at the time when he so relied thereon, that such act or thing was not within the powers of the company, but any director or officer of the company who was responsible for the doing by the company of such act or thing shall be liable to the company for any loss or damage suffered by the company in consequence thereof.

(2) The court may, on the application of any member or holder of debentures of a company, restrain such company from doing any act or thing which the company has no power to do.

Cross reference

See, generally, the Company Law Review Group, First Report, (2000–2001), Ch 10. This recommends, *inter alia*, that the doctrine of *ultra vires* be abolished for private companies limited by shares.

Definitions

'company': CA 1963, s 2(1); 'the court': CA 1963, s 2(1); 'debenture': CA 1963, s 2(1); 'director': CA 1963, s 2(1); 'member': CA 1963, s 31; 'officer': CA 1963, s 2(1).

Notes

Enforceability of *ultra vires* transactions: Since, a company is only entitled to pursue its stated objects, the traditional position, both at common law and in equity has been that any transaction beyond those objects is wholly void.[2] Being void, the *ultra vires* transaction was not only unenforceable by the company as against outsiders, but was also unenforceable as against the company by any outsider who knew of the purpose for which the company was acting, since that outsider was deemed to have constructive knowledge of the contents of the memorandum as being a document registered in the CRO (whether or not he had actually read the document) and accordingly he was presumed to know that the transaction was beyond the company's objects.[3] On the other hand, if the outsider was unaware of the purpose for which the company was exercising its powers (eg the power to borrow money), he was entitled to assume that the powers were being exercised for an *intra vires* purpose (even if that was not the case) and accordingly would be able to enforce the transaction against the company.[4]

In England it has been held that an *ultra vires* transaction cannot be ratified, even by the assent of every member of the company.[5] These cases were, however, decided at a time when the objects clause of a company was not freely alterable. In this jurisdiction, however, the objects may be varied by following the procedure set out in CA 1963, s 10. It has been held by the Supreme Court in *Bank of Ireland Finance Ltd v Rockfield Ltd*[6] that in order for effective ratification of a contract to take place, three requirements must be fulfilled:

(i) The person must have purported to act on behalf of a principal;

(ii) The principal must have been in existence at the time;[7] and

(iii) The principal must have been legally capable of doing the act himself 'at the time of ratification.'

Ussher suggests therefore[8] that if a company were to amend its objects and then ratify what would otherwise have been an *ultra vires* transaction, the ratification should be valid since the company would itself be legally capable of entering into the transaction itself 'at the time of ratification.'[9] The possibility of ratification, as put forward by *Ussher* does appear to be predicated upon the objects clause having first been expressly amended. If no such amendment has taken place, then the transaction will remain *ultra vires* notwithstanding the fact that it has received the unanimous assent, whether prospective or retrospective, of the members of the company.[10]

Subject therefore, to any possible ratification following an alteration of the objects clause, how can an *ultra vires* contract be enforced, either by the company or by an outsider who knows of the purpose of the contract (regardless of whether or not he knows that that purpose is beyond the company's objects)?

1 See generally and Courtney, *The Law of Private Companies* (2nd edn, Tottel Publishing 2002) p 342 *et seq*, and MacCann, 'The Capacity of a Company' (1992) 10 ILT 79 and 151.

2 *Ashbury Railway Carriage and Iron Co v Riche* (1875) LR 7 HL 653; *Pacific Coast Coal Mines v Arbuthnot* [1917] AC 607.

3 *Re Jon Beauforte (London) Ltd* [1953] 1 All ER 634.

4 *Re David Payne and Co Ltd* [1904] 2 Ch 608; *Re MJ Cummins Ltd* [1939] IR 61; *Charterbridge Corporation v Lloyds Bank* [1970] 1 Ch 62; *Re Metro Investments Ltd* (26 May 1977, unreported) HC (McWilliam J).

5 *Ashbury Railway Carriage and Iron Co v Riche* (1875) LR 7 HL 653; *Pacific Coast Coal Mines v Arbuthnot* [1917] AC 607; *Baroness Wenlock v River Dee Co* (1883) 36 Ch D 675n; 681n, 686n.

6 *Bank of Ireland Finance Ltd v Rockfield Ltd* [1979] IR 21, 35, citing *Firth v Staines* [1897] 2 QB 70.

7 For an exception allowing a company to ratify pre-incorporation contracts, see CA 1963, s 37.

8 Ussher, *Company Law in Ireland* (London, Sweet & Maxwell, 1986) p 131.

9 For a contrary view, see Borrie, *Commercial Law* (6th edn, Butterworths, 1988) p 37.

10 *Re Greendale Developments Ltd* [1998] 1 IR 8.

Enforcement by outsider under CA 1963, s 8: In an effort to protect innocent outsiders from the unjust effects of the *ultra vires* rule, CA 1963, s 8 was introduced by the legislature.

'Lawfully and effectively done': This section only applies to acts which, but for the lack of capacity in the objects clause, could otherwise have been 'lawfully and effectively done' by the company. The section therefore has no application to acts which are not only *ultra vires* but are also illegal.[1]

'In favour of any person': The 'person' to whom CA 1963, s 8 refers is a person dealing with the company. Thus the section only applies to the enforcement of transactions against the company and not to the enforcement of transactions by the company. The phrase 'any person' is quite wide in its scope and potentially extends not only to outsiders (ie persons having no connection with the company) but also to shareholders[2] or directors having dealings with the company.[3] In reality, however, it may be difficult for a shareholder or director to show that he was unaware of the fact that the transaction in question was *ultra vires* the company.[4]

'Relying on such act or thing': If the person is to avail of the protection of CA 1963, s 8, he must satisfy two requirements. First, he must show that he was relying on the *ultra vires* transaction. There should be no difficulty in proving reliance where the transaction is a contract and involves the agreement of the person to give good consideration in return for the performance by the company of its part of the bargain. Equally well, however, it seems that where the transaction in question involved a gift or other voluntary disposition by the company, the person could still be said to have relied on same where he has altered his position as a result (eg where the charity receives a donation from the company and then expends the sum on charitable acts).

'Who is not shown to have been actually aware': The second requirement for the person seeking to rely on CA 1963, s 8 is to show that at the time of reliance on the 'act or thing' (typically the time of the making of the contract) he was not 'actually aware' that the 'act or thing' was *ultra vires* the company. The burden of proving actual awareness rest with the company. The effect of CA 1963, s 8 is therefore to abolish the doctrine of constructive notice, at least in so far as the contents of the company's objects clause is concerned. Thus, a person who is aware of the purpose for which the company is exercising a particular power but who has not read the objects clause, will not be regarded as being 'actually aware' that the company is acting *ultra vires*. On the other hand, it has been held that a person will be deemed to be 'actually aware' that a transaction is *ultra vires* in circumstances where he has read the objects clause but failed to appreciate its meaning and effect.[5]

1 *Bank of Ireland Finance Ltd v Rockfield Ltd* [1979] IR 21; *Re Frederick inns Ltd* [1991] ILRM 582 aff'd [1994] 1 ILRM 387: *Re Greendale Developments Ltd* [1998] 1 IR 8; *Ulster Factors Ltd v Entonglen Ltd* [1997] IEHC 34 (Laffoy J).

2 *EIC Services Ltd v Phipps* [2003] 3 All ER 804.

3 *Smith v Henniker-Major and Co* [2002] 2 BCLC 655.

4 *Smith v Henniker-Major and Co* [2002] 2 BCLC 655.

5 *Northern Bank Finance Corporation Ltd v Quinn and Achates Investment Co* [1979] ILRM 221. Notably, in this case, the company was unlimited and therefore did not enjoy the protection of EC(C)R 1973, Reg 6. Keane (who happened to be the trial judge) has suggested at para 12.05 that if Reg 6 could have been invoked the result of the case might have been quite different. His lordship is of the view that if a person reads the objects clause but genuinely fails to understand therefrom that the transaction is *ultra vires*, he may still be regarded as acting in 'good faith' within the meaning of Reg 6, so as to be able to enforce the transaction against the company.

Enforcement under Reg 6: Apart from the protection afforded to persons under CA 1963, s 8, the legislature, in implementing the First EU Directive on Company Law[1] has also seen fit to afford similar protection pursuant to Reg 6, the effect of which is considered in the notes thereto.

1 (68/151/EEC) OJ Special Edition 1968(1), pp 41–45.

Persons without the protection of CA 1963, s 8 or Reg 6: As noted above, *ultra vires* transactions are void and *prima facie,* therefore are unenforceable either by or against the company. However, even if the outsider is unable to avail of the benefit of CA 1963, s 8 or Reg 6 (eg because he was at all times aware that the company was acting beyond its capacity) he may still be able to invoke common law and equitable relief to prevent the company from being unjustly enriched at his expense. In the first place, he may be entitled to avail of a remedy which is a right akin to subrogation whereby *ultra vires* borrowings of a company will be treated as valid to the extent that the moneys were used for the agreed purpose of discharging *intra vires* debts and liabilities.[1] However, the *ultra vires* creditor cannot claim subrogation to any securities or priorities of the *intra vires* creditor whose debt has been discharged, although any securities held by the *ultra vires* creditor will be validated to the extent that the loan itself is validated by subrogation.[2] Similarly, if the transaction is only impeachable on the ground that it is *ultra vires*, the outsider may be able to have it set aside in quasi-contract on terms that both parties are restored to their original positions.[3] Thus, although an insurance company could deny cover under an *ultra vires* insurance policy, it could at the same time be forced to return to the policyholder any premiums which had been paid by him.[4] Traditionally, the quasi-contractual remedy could not be invoked by the outsider if it would result in the indirect enforcement of the *ultra vires* transaction (eg where the outsider seeks repayment of moneys which had been advanced under an *ultra vires* loan).[5] However, more recent decisions, applying the doctrine of unjust enrichment, have held that no such limitation in fact exists.[6]

Another possible remedy for the outsider without the protection of CA 1963, s 8 or Reg 6 may have an action *in rem* to trace the moneys which have been paid or advanced to the company in pursuance of the *ultra vires* transaction[7] and/or to recover the moneys as held on a constructive trust.[8]

1 *Re Lough Neagh Ship Co, ex parte Workman* [1895] 1 IR 523.

2 *Re Wrexham, Mold and Connah's Quay Railway Co* [1899] 1 Ch 440.

3 *Re Irish Provident Assurance Co* [1913] 1 IR 352; *Flood v Irish Provident Assurance Co* (1912) 46 ILTR 214.

4 *Re Irish Provident Assurance Co* [1913] 1 IR 352; *Flood v Irish Provident Assurance Co* (1912) 46 ILTR 214.

5 *Sinclair v Brougham* [1914] AC 398.

6 *Re PMPA Garage (Longmile) Ltd (No 2)* [1992] ILRM 349; *Barclays Bank plc v Glasgow City Council* [1994] 4 All ER 865; *Westdeutsche Landesbank Girozentrale v Islington London Borough Council* [1994] 4 All ER 890; *Kleinwort Benson Ltd v South Tyneside Metropolitan Borough Council* [1994] 4 All ER 972; *South Tyneside Metropolitan Borough Council v Svenska International plc* [1995] 1 All ER 545; *Kleinwort Benson Ltd v Birmingham City Council* [1996] 4 All ER 733.

7 *Sinclair v Brougham* [1914] AC 398; *Re PMPA Garage (Longmile) Ltd (No 1)* [1992] ILRM 337; *Re PMPA Garage (Longmile) Ltd (No 2)* [1992] ILRM 349.

8 *Belmont Finance Corporation Ltd v Williams Furniture Ltd* [1980] 1 All ER 393; *Re Frederick Inns Ltd* [1994] 1 ILRM 387; *Ulster Factors Ltd v Entonglen Ltd* [1997] IEHC 34 (Laffoy J).

Enforcement of *ultra vires* transactions by the company: Although it cannot avail of either CA 1963, s 8 or Reg 6, the company may be able to maintain an action *in rem* for moneys paid in pursuance of an *ultra vires* transaction in order to prevent unjust enrichment of the outsider.[1] In addition the quasi-contractual remedy should be available to restore the parties to their original positions[2] even where this has the effect of indirectly enforcing the transaction (eg repayment of an *ultra vires* loan which had been made to an outsider).[3] In addition it has also been recently suggested by Murphy J in *Re PMPA Garage (Longmile) Ltd*[4] that where money paid by the company under an *ultra vires* contract is no longer recoverable in quasi-contract or by tracing (eg because it is no longer in the possession of the outsider) then the only solution in order to prevent 'manifest injustice' may be to treat those dealing with the company as being estopped from denying the validity of the transaction, so as to enable the company to directly enforce any other remedies purportedly given to it under the contract, such as a guarantee from a third party.[5]

1 *Sinclair v Brougham* [1914] AC 398; *Simmonds v Heffer* [1983] BCLC 298; *Re PMPA Garage (Longmile) Ltd (No 1)* [1992] ILRM 337; *Re PMPA Garage (Longmile) Ltd (No 2)* [1992] ILRM 349; *Barclays Bank plc v Glasgow City Council* [1994] 4 All ER 865; *Westdeutsche Landesbank Girozentrale v Islington London Borough Council* [1994] 4 All ER 890; *Kleinwort Benson Ltd v South Tyneside Metropolitan Borough Council* [1994] 4 All ER 972; *Kleinwort Benson Ltd v Birmingham City Council* [1996] 4 All ER 733.

2 *Simmonds v Heffer* [1983] BCLC 298.

3 *Brougham v Dwyer* (1913) 108 LT 504; *Re PMPA Garage (Longmile) Ltd (No 2)* [1992] ILRM 349; *Barclays Bank plc v Glasgow City Council* [1994] 4 All ER 865; *Westdeutsche Landesbanke Girozentrale v Islington London Borough Council* [1994] 4 All ER 890; *Kleinwort Benson Ltd v South Tyneside Metropolitan Borough Council* [1994] 4 All ER 972; *South Tyneside Metropolitan Borough Council v Svenska International plc* [1995] 1 All ER 545; *Kleinwort Benson Ltd v Birmingham City Council* [1996] 4 All ER 733.

4 *Re PMPA Garage (Longmile) Ltd* [1992] ILRM 349, citing *Re Coltman* (1881) 19 Ch D 6; *Re KL Tractors Ltd* (1961) 106 CLR 318 and *Breckenridge Speedway v The Queen (in the right of Alberta)* (1967) DLR 2d 488.

5 This decision, whilst undoubtedly achieving a 'just' solution, does appear to strike at the very root of the *ultra vires* rule – something which the legislature had heretofore only seen fit to do for the protection of outsiders. For a more traditional view as to the unenforceability of *ultra vires* contracts by companies, see *Cabaret Holdings Ltd v Meeanee Sports and Rodeo Club Inc* [1982] 1 NZLR 673; *Credit Suisse v Waltham Forest London Borough Council* (1996) TLR 311.

Liability of company officers for *ultra vires* acts: CA 1963, s 8(1) clearly stipulates that even if an *ultra vires* transaction is enforceable against the company, this does not absolve the officers in default from liability in damages for any loss which the company suffers as a result. This is however, no more than a restatement of the pre-existing common law position.[1]

1 *Re David Payne and Co Ltd* [1904] 2 Ch 608; *Re MJ Cummins: Barton v Bank of Ireland* [1939] IR 60; *Rolled Steel Products (Holdings) Ltd v British Steel Corporation* [1986] 1 Ch 246; *Parkes and Sons Ltd v Hong Kong and Shanghai Banking Corporation* [1990] ILRM 341; *Re Frederick Inns Ltd* [1994] 1 ILRM 387.

Injunction to restrain *ultra vires* scts: At common law, a member of a company could apply for an injunction restraining the company or its directors from engaging in *ultra vires* acts.[1] This remedy has now been extended to debenture holders by CA 1963, s 8, although presumably the entitlement to injunctive relief is still subject to the innocent outsider's rights of enforcement under CA 1963, s 8(1). If an injunction were to be refused on the ground that the innocent outsider's rights should not be prejudiced, the company could still maintain an action for damages against the officers in default for any loss sustained by it as a result of the enforcement of the transaction.

1 *Colman v Eastern Counties Ryl Co* (1846) 10 Beav 1; *Simpson v Westminster Palace Hotel Co* (1860) 8 HL Cas 712; *Maunsell v Midland Great Eastern (Ireland) Rly Co* (1863) 1 Hem and M 130; *Spokes v Grosvenor Hotel Co* [1897] 2 QB 4; *McGilligan and Bowen v O'Grady* [1999] 1 IR 346.

UK legislation

See CA 1985, s 35[1]; CA 1989, s 108(1).

1 CA 1985, s 35 is more far reaching than CA 1963, s 8.

---

9 Restriction on alteration of memorandum

A company may not alter the provisions contained in its memorandum except in the cases, in the mode and to the extent for which express provision is made in this Act.

Definitions

'company': CA 1963, s 2(1); 'memorandum': CA 1963, s 2(1).

Notes

The following are the provisions for the alteration of the clauses of the memorandum:

(i) objects: CA 1963, s 10.

(ii) name: CA 1963, s 23.

(iii) alteration to liability of members: CA 1963, s 27.

(iv) additional clauses: CA 1963, s 28.

(v) capital: CA 1963, ss 68 and 72.

(vi) variation of class rights: CA 1963, s 78 and C(A)A 1983, s 38.

(vii) imposition of personal liability on directors: CA 1963, s 198.

(viii) schemes of arrangement: CA 1963, ss 201–203.

(ix) relief of minority oppression: CA 1963, s 205(3).

(x) amendments to memorandum on re-registration of private company as a plc: C(A)A 1983, s 9(2).

(xi) amendments to memorandum on re-registration of unlimited company as plc: C(A)A 1983, s 11(2).

(xii) amendments to memorandum on re-registration of plc as private company: C(A)A 1983, s 14(2).

UK legislation

See CA 1985, s 2(7); Companies Act 1985 (Electronic Communications) Order 2000 (SI 2000/3373).

10 Way in which and extent to which objects of company may be altered

(1) Subject to subsection (2), a company may, by special resolution, alter the provisions of its memorandum by abandoning, restricting or amending any existing object or by adopting a new object and any alteration so made shall be as valid as if originally contained therein, and be subject to alteration in like manner.

(2) If an application is made to the court in accordance with this section for the alteration to be cancelled, it shall not have effect except in so far as it is confirmed by the court.

(3) Subject to subsection (4), an application under this section may be made—

(a) by the holders of not less in the aggregate than 15% in nominal value of the company's issued share capital or any class thereof or, if the company is not limited by shares, not less than 15% of the company's members; or

(b) by the holders of not less than 15% of the company's debentures, entitling the holders to object to alterations of its objects.

(4) An application shall not be made under this section by any person who has consented to or voted in favour of the alteration.

(5) An application under this section must be made within 21 days after the date on which the resolution altering the company's objects was passed, and may be made on

behalf of the persons entitled to make the application by such one or more of their number as they may appoint in writing for the purpose.

(6) On an application under this section, the court may make an order cancelling the alteration or confirming the alteration either wholly or in part and on such terms and conditions as it thinks fit, and may, if it thinks fit, adjourn the proceedings in order that an arrangement may be made to the satisfaction of the court for the purchase of the interests of dissentient members, and may give such directions and make such orders as it may think expedient for facilitating or carrying into effect any such arrangement[...].[a]

[(6A) An order under this section may, if the court thinks fit, provide for the purchase by the company of the shares of any members of the company and for the reduction accordingly of the company's capital and may make such alterations in the memorandum and articles of the company as may be required in consequence of that provision.

(6B) Where an order under this section requires the company not to make any, or any specified, alteration in its memorandum or articles, then, notwithstanding anything in the Companies Acts, 1963 to 1983 the company shall not have power without the leave of the court to make any such alteration in breach of that requirement.

(6C) Any alteration in the memorandum or articles of a company made by virtue of an order under this section, other than one made by resolution of the company, shall be of the same effect as if duly made by resolution of the company, and the provisions of the Companies Acts, 1963 to 1983, shall apply to the memorandum or articles as so altered accordingly.][b]

(7) The debentures entitling the holders to object to alterations of a company's objects shall be any debentures secured by a floating charge which were issued or first issued before the operative date or form part of the same series as any debentures so issued, and a special resolution altering a company's objects shall require the same notice to the holders of any such debentures as to members of the company, so however that not less than 10 days' notice shall be given to the holders of any such debentures.

In default of any provisions regulating the giving of notice to any such debenture holders, the provisions of the company's articles regulating the giving of notice to members shall apply.

(8) In the case of a company which is, by virtue of a licence from the Minister, exempt from the obligation to use the word 'limited' or 'teoranta' as part of its name, a resolution altering the company's objects shall also require the same notice to the [registrar of companies][c] as to holders of debentures.

(9) Where a company passes a resolution altering its objects—

- (a) if no application is made with respect thereto under this section, it shall, within 15 days from the end of the period for making such an application, deliver to the registrar of companies a printed copy of its memorandum as altered; and
- (b) if such an application is made, it shall—
  - (i) forthwith give notice of that fact to the registrar; and
  - (ii) within 15 days from the date of any order cancelling or confirming the alteration, deliver to the registrar an office copy of the order and, in the

case of an order confirming the alteration, a printed copy of the memorandum as altered.

The court may by order at any time extend the time for delivery of documents to the registrar under paragraph (b) for such period as the court may think proper.

(10) If a company makes default in giving notice or delivering any document to the registrar as required by subsection (9), the company and every officer of the company who is in default [shall be guilty of an offence and liable to a fine] [d] not exceeding [€1,904.61].[e]

(11) In relation to a resolution for altering the provisions of a company's memorandum relating to the objects of the company passed before the operative date, this section shall have effect as if, in lieu of subsections (2) to (10), there had been enacted subsections (2) to (7) of section 9 of the Companies (Consolidation) Act, 1908.

Amendments

a Words 'so, however, that no part of the capital of the company shall be expanded in any such purchase', deleted by C(A)A 1983, Sch 1, para 3(a).

b CA 1963, s 10(6A),(6C) and (6B) inserted by C(A)A 1983, Sch 1, para 3(b).

c 'registrar of companies' substituted for 'Minister' by CLEA 2001, s 85.

d CA 1963, s 10(10) words 'shall be guilty of an offence and liable to a fine' substituted for 'shall be liable to a fine' by C(A&A)A 2003, Sch 2, Item No 1.

e '£250' substituted for '£50' by C(A)A 1982, Sch 1, increased to £1,500 by CA 1990, s 240(7) as inserted by CLEA 2001, s 104(c) and converted to €1,904.61 by Council Regulations (EC) No 1103/97, No 974/98 and No 2866/98 and the Economic and Monetary Union Act 1998, s 6.

Definitions

'articles': CA 1963, s 2(1); 'company': CA 1963, s 2(1); 'the court': CA 1963, s 2(1); 'debenture': CA 1963, s 2(1); 'document': CA 1963, s 2(1): 'member': CA 1963, s 31; 'memorandum': CA 1963, s 2(1); 'Minister': CA 1963, s 2(1); 'officer': CA 1963, s 2(1); 'the operative date': CA 1963, s 2(1); 'printed': CA 1963, s 2(1); 'the registrar of companies': CA 1963, s 2 (1); 'share': CA 1963, s 2(1).

Notes

No retrospectivity to amendment: An alteration of the company's objects will not *per se* retrospectively validate a prior *ultra vires* transaction.[1] *Quaere*: whether the company having altered its objects could then validly ratify the transaction.[2]

1 *Northern Bank Finance Corporation v Quinn and Achates Investment Co* [1979] ILRM 221.

2 See the notes to CA 1963, s 8.

Application to court by dissentients: The complaint must be made by the applicants qua members or debentureholders, as the case may be, and not in some other capacity (eg as solicitors).[1] The application is brought by way of petition[2] and apart from being served on the company within three days after being filed in the Central Office[3] must also be published in such newspapers as the court directs.[4] An application under CA 1963, s 10 will only be successful if it can be shown that the alteration of the objects was unfair as between the members.[5] Shareholders or debenture holders appearing on the petition and opposing the alteration of the objects may be awarded their costs even though the petition is unsuccessful and the alteration is confirmed.[6]

1 *Re Munster and Leinster Bank* [1907] 1 IR 237; *Re Hearts of Oak Life and General Assurance Co* [1920] 1 Ch 544.
2 RSC (1986) Order 75, rule 4(a).
3 RSC (1986) Order 75, rule 20.
4 RSC (1986) Order 75, rule 13.
5 *Re Jewish Colonial Trust* [1908] 2 Ch 287.
6 *Re Patent Tyre Co* [1923] 2 Ch 222.

Failure of substratum: Apart from the risk of an application by dissentients under CA 1963, s 10, the company might possibly be faced with a petition to have the company wound up under s 213(f) on the ground that the alteration in the objects has resulted in a failure of substratum.[1] Substratum is the understanding between the members as to the type of activities which the company should pursue. It is a question of law as to whether or not a transaction is *ultra vires* but it is a matter of equity as to whether there has been a failure of substratum.[2] Unlike an application by dissentients under CA 1963, s 10, there is no minimum shareholding required to petition for a winding up order in respect of a failure of substratum.[3] Although since the advent of the ability to alter a company's objects clause, the failure of substratum as a ground to base a petition to wind up a company has become anachronistic[4] each case will be looked at on its merits.[5]

1 *Re Germn Date Coffee Co* (1882) 20 Ch D 169; *Re Tivoli Freeholds Ltd* [1972] VR 338.
2 *Cotman v Brougham* [1918] AC 514; *Ebrahimi v Westbourne Galleries Ltd* [1973] AC 360; *Re Murph's Restaurant Ltd* [1979] ILRM 141.
3 *Bryanston Finance Ltd v de Vries (No 2)* [1976] Ch 63.
4 As noted by Laffoy J in *Re Metafile Ltd* [2006] IEHC 407, citing Courtney, The Law of Private Companies (2nd edn, Tottel Publishing, 2002) para 25.087.
5 See *Re Kitson & Co Ltd* [1946] 1 All ER 435; *Re Perfectair Holdings Ltd* [1990] BCLC 423 and *Re Taldua Rubber Co Ltd* [1946] 2 All ER 763, mentioned by Laffoy J in *Re Metafile Ltd* [2006] IEHC 407.

Delivery of documents to the Registrar and publication in the Companies Registration Office Gazette: The special resolution amending the memorandum and the amended text of the memorandum must be forwarded to the Registrar within 15 days of the passing of such resolution.[1] Pursuant to EC(C) R 1973, reg 4, a company shall also cause to be published[2] in the Companies Registration Office Gazette,[3] a notice of delivery of such documents. In practice, it is in fact the Registrar who generally causes such notices to be published in the Companies Registration Office Gazette.

1 CA 1963, s 143(1).
2 Within six weeks of the relevant delivery date; EC(C)R 1973, reg 4(2).
3 Reference to *Iris Oifigiúil* was substituted by reference to the Companies Registration Office Gazette by virtue of EC(C)R 2004, reg 5.

UK legislation

See CA 1985, s 4; CA 1989, s 110(2).

See CA 1985, s 5; The Companies (Acquisition of Own Shares) (Treasury Shares) Regulations 2003 (SI 2003/1116), reg 4, Sch, para 1.

See CA 1985, s 6.

Articles of Association

11 Articles prescribing regulations for companies

[There may, in the case of a company limited by shares and in the case of a company limited by guarantee and not having a share capital, and there shall, in the case of a company limited by guarantee and having share capital or unlimited, be registered with the memorandum articles of association signed by the subscribers to the memorandum and prescribing regulations for the company.][a]

Amendments

a CA 1963, s 11, substituted by C(A)A 1982, s 2.

Definitions

'articles': CA 1963, s 2(1); 'company': CA 1963, s 2(1); 'a company limited by guarantee': CA 1963, s 2(1), 5(2)(b); 'a company limited by shares': CA 1963, s 2(1), 5(2)(a); 'memorandum': CA 1963, s 2(1); 'share': CA 1963, s 2(1).

Notes

Registration of standard form memoranda and articles: CLEA 2001, s 80 allows for the filing of standard form memoranda and articles of association to which reference numbers will be assigned by the Registrar. Thereafter the promoters of a company need only file a memorandum and articles of association specifying those matters peculiar to the company itself, together with a statement identifying the reference number(s) of the standard form documents which are to be deemed also to have been incorporated therein. The result, whilst legally valid, can give rise to uncertainty as to what a company's memorandum and articles of association are and third parties must take care to ensure they are reading the correct memorandum and articles of association.

The constitution of the company: The constitution of a company is made up of two documents, namely the memorandum and articles of association.[1] Of the two, the memorandum is the principal and dominant document,[2] acting as its charter and containing the fundamental conditions upon which alone the company is allowed to be incorporated.[3] On the other hand, the articles are the internal regulations of the company.[4]

1 *TJ Wilson (Inspector of Taxes) v Dunnes Stores (Cork) Ltd* [1982] ILRM 444.
2 *Guinness v Land Corporation of Ireland* (1882) 22 Ch D 349; *Roper v Ward* [1981] ILRM 408.
3 *Guinness v Land Corporation of Ireland* (1882) 22 Ch D 349.
4 *Guinness v Land Corporation of Ireland* (1882) 22 Ch D 349.

Relationship between memorandum and articles: Where there is a conflict between a provision in the memorandum and a provision in the articles, the former prevails.[1] As a result, the conflicting article will be void to the extent of the conflict, even though the provision in the memorandum with which it conflicts was not required by law to be there.[2] The articles may, however, be relied upon to explain or clear up any ambiguity in the memorandum[3] or to supplement the memorandum as to any matter upon which it is silent.[4] This is subject to one important proviso, in that one cannot have resort to the articles to clear up an ambiguity in the memorandum if the provision in question is one which, by law, is required to be in the memorandum, such as the objects clause.[5] In such a case the memorandum must be construed on its own.

1 *Guinness v Land Corporation of Ireland* (1882) 22 Ch D 349; *Re Southern Brazilian Rio Grande do Sul Railway Co Ltd* [1905] 2 Ch 78.
2 *Ashbury v Watson* (1885) 30 Ch D 376; *Welton v Saffrey* [1897] AC 299; *Re Peveril Gold Mines Ltd* [1898] 1 Ch 122; *Re Greene* [1949] Ch 333. See CA 1963, s 6 for the statutory requirements as to the contents of the memorandum.
3 *Roper v Ward* [1981] ILRM 408; *Re Bansha Woollen Mill Co Ltd* (1887) 21 LR Ir 181.
4 *Re Duncan Gilmour Co Ltd* [1952] 2 All ER 871; *Harrison v Mexican Railway Co* (1875) LR 19 Eq 358; *Re South Durham Brewery Co* (1885) 31 Ch D 261; *Re Edward Love and Co Pty Ltd* [1969] VR 230.

[5] *Guinness v Land Corporation of Ireland* (1882) 22 Ch D 349; *Re Southern Brazilian Rio Grande do Sul Railway Co Ltd* [1905] 2 Ch 78.

Contractual effect of memorandum and articles: As to the contractual effect of the memorandum and articles, see CA 1963, s 25 and the notes thereto.

Interpretation of memorandum and articles: Although the court may be prepared to infer a term in the articles purely by way of constructional implication[1] or to give the articles business efficacy,[2] it will not go further and imply a term from extrinsic circumstances, particularly where the suggested term is inconsistent with the express wording of the articles.[3]

[1] *Bratton Seymour Service Co Ltd v Oxborough* [1992] BCLC 693.

[2] *Rayfield v Hands* [1960] Ch 1; *Holmes v Keyes* [1959] Ch 199; *Roper v Ward* [1981] ILRM 408. Thus, in *Zytan Nominees Pty Ltd v Laverton Gold NL* (1988) 14 ACLR 524, where the company was listed on the stock exchange, the court was prepared to imply a term in the articles that the company would comply with the Stock Exchange Listing Rules.

[3] *Bratton Seymour Service Co Ltd v Oxborough* [1992] BCLC 693; *Towcester Racecourse Co Ltd v The Racecourse Association Ltd* [2003] 1 BCLC 260; *FA Tamplin Steamship Co Ltd v Anglo Mexican Petroleum Products Co Ltd* [1916] 2 AC 397. Cf *Buche v Box Pty Ltd* (1993) 31 NSWLR 368 where the articles were ambiguous as to whether certain shares carried rights on a winding up, and the court therefore looked to the reasons why the company, a family company, was established and the tax planning arrangements of which it was a part.

No rectification of memorandum or articles: Although the memorandum and articles, once registered, are deemed to have contractual effect,[1] the court has no jurisdiction to order that either document be rectified[2] other than pursuant to CA 1963, s 205(3). Instead, any errors or omissions must be rectified by following the various procedures in the Acts themselves for altering the memorandum and articles.[3]

[1] See CA 1963, s 25.

[2] *Scott v Frank F Scott (London) Ltd* [1940] CH 794; *Santos Ltd v Pettingel* (1979) 4 ACLR 110.

[3] See CA 1963, ss 10, 11 and 15 and notes thereto.

Table A: See CA 1963, ss 13 and 13A for the circumstances in which the model form articles contained in Tables A and C will apply to companies limited by shares and to companies limited by guarantee and not having a share capital respectively. In the event of a conflict between the model form articles and the company's own articles, the latter will prevail.[1]

[1] *McNeill v McNeill's Sheepfarming Co Ltd* [1955] NZLR 15.

UK legislation

See CA 1985, s 7(1); CA 1985 (Electronic Communications) Order 2000 (SI 2000/3373).

---

12 Regulations required in the case of an unlimited company or company limited by guarantee

(1) In the case of an unlimited company, the articles must state the number of members with which the company proposes to be registered and, if the company has a share capital, the amount of share capital with which the company proposes to be registered.

(2) In the case of a company limited by guarantee, the articles must state the number of members with which the company proposes to be registered.

(3) Where an unlimited company or a company limited by guarantee has increased the number of its members beyond the registered number, it shall, within 15 days after the increase was resolved on or took place, give to the registrar notice of the increase, and he shall record the increase.

If default is made in complying with this subsection, the company and every officer of the company who is in default [shall be guilty of an offence and liable to a fine] [a] not exceeding [€1,904.61].[b]

Amendments

a CA 1963, s 12(3) words 'shall be guilty of an offence and liable to a fine' substituted for 'shall be liable to a fine' by C(AA)A 2003, Sch 2, Item No 1.

b '£250' substituted for '£50' by C(A)A 1982, Sch 1, increased to £1,500 by CA 1990, s 240(7) as inserted by CLEA 2001, s 104(c), and converted to €1,904.61 by Council Regulations (EC) No 1103/97, No 974/98 and No 2866/98 and the Economic and Monetary Union Act 1998, s 6.

Definitions

'articles': CA 1963, s 2(1); 'company': s CA 1963, 2(1); 'a company limited by guarantee': CA 1963, s 2(1), s 5(2)(b); 'member': CA 1963, s 31; 'officer': CA 1963, s 2(1); 'an unlimited company': CA 1963, s 2 (1), s 5(2)(c).

Notes

Number of subscribers: Under EC(SMPLC)R 1994 (SI No 275/1994) it is possible to have just one subscriber in the case of private companies limited by shares or limited by guarantee and having a share capital.[1] In the case of a company limited by guarantee and not having a share capital, it will, by definition, be a public company and accordingly will be required to have at least seven subscribers.[2] On the same basis, an unlimited company which does not have a share capital is a public company and must, therefore, have at least seven subscribers. However, in practice most unlimited companies do in fact have a share capital. In such a case, if the unlimited company is a private company within the meaning of CA 1963, s 33, it will be required to have at least two subscribers.[3]

1 See the notes to CA 1963, s 5 and see also the notes to the EC(SMPLC)R 1994.
2 See CA 1963, ss 5(1) and 33.
3 CA 1963, s 5(1).

Table A: See CA 1963, ss 13 and 13A for the circumstances in which the model form articles contained in Tables A and C will apply to companies limited by shares and to companies limited by guarantee and not having a share capital respectively.

Registration of standard form memoranda and articles: CLEA 2001, s 80 allows for the filing of standard form memoranda and articles of association to which reference numbers will be assigned by the Registrar. Thereafter the promoters of a company need only file a memorandum and articles of association specifying those matters peculiar to the company itself, together with a statement identifying the reference number(s) of the standard form documents which are to be deemed also to have been incorporated therein.

UK legislation

See CA 1985, s 7(2); Companies Act 1985 (Electronic Communications) Order 2000 (SI 2000/ 3373)).

---

13 Adoption and application of Table A or Tábla A

(1) Articles of association may adopt all or any of the regulations contained in Table A, or of the equivalent regulations in the Irish language contained in Tábla A.

(2) In the case of a company limited by shares and registered after the operative date, if articles are not registered or, if articles are registered, in so far as the articles do not exclude or modify the regulations contained in Table A, those regulations shall, so far as applicable, be the regulations of the company in the same manner and to the same extent as if they were contained in duly registered articles.

(3) If the memorandum of the company is in the Irish language, the references in subsection (2) to Table A shall be construed as references to Tábla A.

Definitions

'articles': CA 1963, s 2(1); 'company': CA 1963, s 2(1); 'a company limited by shares': CA 1963, s 2(1), 5(a); 'memorandum': CA 1963, s 2(1); 'the operative date': CA 1963, s 2(1); 'share': CA 1963, s 2(1); 'Table A': CA 1963, s 2(1); 'Tábla A': CA 1963, s 2(1).

Notes

Table A: Table A may be seen as representing the views of the legislature as to the matters contained therein[1] and accordingly no article will be considered ultra vires if its terms are the same as or are substantially similar to an equivalent article in Table A.[2] In the case of a conflict between Table A and the express provisions of such articles as the company may actually register, the latter will prevail.[3]

1 *Re Pyle Works* (1890) 44 Ch D 534, 571; *Re Barned's Banking Co, ex parte Contract Corporation* (1867) 3 Ch App 105, 113, 114.

2 *Lock v Queensland Investment and Land Mortgage Co* [1896] 1 Ch 397, 406; aff'd [1986] AC 461, 465; *New Elkis Eerstelling Ltd v Randt Gold Mining Co* [1940] AC 165.

3 *McNeill v McNeill's Sheepfarming Co Ltd* [1955] NZLR 15.

Table A, Parts I and II: Table A is divided into two parts. Part I applies to public companies, whereas Part II applies to private companies.

Registration of standard form memoranda and articles: CLEA 2001, s 80 allows for the filing of standard form memoranda and articles of association to which reference numbers will be assigned by the Registrar. Thereafter the promoters of a company need only file a memorandum and articles of association specifying those matters peculiar to the company itself, together with a statement identifying the reference number(s) of the standard form documents which are to be deemed also to have been incorporated therein.

UK legislation

See CA 1985, s 8(1), (2).

[13A Adoption and application of Table C

(1) In the case of a company limited by guarantee and not having a share capital articles of association may adopt all or any of the regulations contained in Table C or all or any of the regulations contained in the version in the Irish language of Table C set out in the First Schedule to the Principal Act.

(2) In the case of a company limited by guarantee and not having a share capital and registered after the commencement of the Companies (Amendment) Act, 1982, if articles are not registered or, if articles are registered, in so far as the articles do not exclude or modify the regulations contained in Table C, those regulations shall, so far as

applicable, be the regulations of the company in the same manner and to the same extent as if they were contained in duly registered articles.

(3) If the memorandum of the company is in the Irish language, the references in subsection (2) to Table C shall be construed as references to the regulations contained in the version in the Irish language of Table C set out in the First Schedule to the Principal Act.][a]

Amendments

a CA 1963, s 13A inserted by C(A)A 1982, s 14.

Definitions

'articles': CA 1963, s 2(1); 'company': CA 1963, s 2(1); 'a company limited by guarantee': CA 1963, s 2(1), s 5(2)(b); 'memorandum': CA 1963, s 2(1); 'share': CA 1963, s 2(1).

Notes

Table A: Table C may be seen as representing the views of the legislature as to the matters contained therein[1] and accordingly no article will be considered *ultra vires* if its terms are the same as or are substantially similar to an equivalent article in Table C.[2] In the case of a conflict between Table C and the express provisions of such articles as the company may actually register, the latter will prevail.[3]

1 *Re Pyle Works* (1890) 44 Ch D 534, 571; *Re Barned's Banking Co, ex parte Contract Corporation* (1867) 3 Ch App 105, 113, 114.

2 *Lock v Queensland Investment and Land Mortgage Co* [1896] 1 Ch 397, 406; aff'd [1986] AC 461, 465; *New Elkis Eerstelling Ltd v Randt Gold Mining Co* [1940] AC 165.

3 *McNeill v McNeill's Sheepfarming Co Ltd* [1955] NZLR 15.

Registration of standard form memoranda and articles: CLEA 2001, s 80 allows for the filing of standard form memoranda and articles of association to which reference numbers will be assigned by the Registrar. Thereafter the promoters of a company need only file a memorandum and articles of association specifying those matters peculiar to the company itself, together with a statement identifying the reference number(s) of the standard form documents which are to be deemed also to have been incorporated therein. See note CA 1963, s 11.

UK legislation

See CA 1985, s 8(4).

---

14 Printing, stamp and signature of articles

Articles must—

(a) be printed [in an entire format or in a form pursuant to section 80 of the Company Law Enforcement Act, 2001];[a]

(b) be divided into paragraphs numbered consecutively;

(c) [...][b]

(d) be signed by each subscriber of the memorandum in the presence of at least one witness who must attest the signature.

Amendments

a The words 'in an entire format or in a form pursuant to section 80 of the Company Law Enforcement Act, 2001' inserted by CLEA 2001, s 82.[1]

b CA 1963, s 14(c) deleted by FA 1996, s 112.[2]

1 With effect from 1 October 2001; Company Law Enforcement Act 2001 (Commencement) (No 2) Order 2001 (SI 438/2001).

2 With effect from 15 May 1996.

Definitions

'articles': CA 1963, s 2(1); 'memorandum': CA 1963, s 2(1); ' printed': CA 1963, s 2(1).

Notes

Registration of standard form memoranda and articles: CLEA 2001, s 80 allows for the filing of standard form memoranda and articles of association to which reference numbers will be assigned by the Registrar. Thereafter the promoters of a company need only file a memorandum and articles of association specifying those matters peculiar to the company itself, together with a statement identifying the reference number(s) of the standard form documents which are to be deemed also to have been incorporated therein. See note to CA 1963, s 11.

Number of subscribers: Under EC(SMPLC)R 1994 it is possible to have just one subscriber in the case of private companies limited by shares or limited by guarantee and having a share capital.[1] In the case of a company limited by guarantee and not having a share capital, it will, by definition, be a public company and accordingly will be required to have at least seven subscribers.[2] On the same basis, an unlimited company which does not have a share capital is a public company and must therefore have at least seven subscribers. However, in practice most unlimited companies do in fact have a share capital. In such a case, if the unlimited company is a private company within the meaning of CA 1963, s 33, it will be required to have at least two subscribers.[3]

1 See the notes to CA 1963, s 5 and see also the notes to EC(SMPLC)R 1994.

2 See CA 1963, ss 5(1) and 33.

3 CA 1963, s 5(1).

UK legislation

See CA 1985, s 7(3); Companies 1985 (Electronic Communications) Act 2000 (SI 3373/2000).

15 Alteration of articles by special resolution

(1) Subject to the provisions of this Act and to the conditions contained in its memorandum, a company may by special resolution alter or add to its articles.

(2) Any alteration or addition so made in the articles shall, subject to the provisions of this Act, be as valid as if originally contained therein, and be subject in like manner to alteration by special resolution.

Definitions

'articles': CA 1963, s 2(1); 'company': CA 1963, s 2(1); 'memorandum': CA 1963, s 2(1).

Notes

Alteration of articles of single-member company: The articles of a single-member company may be altered by a decision of that member which is drawn up in writing and which is formally notified to the company.[1]

1 EC(SMPLC)R 1994, reg 9.

Alteration of class rights: If the proposed alteration of the article in question would involve the variation of class rights, special procedures beyond those contained in CA 1963, s 15 may have to be followed.[1]

1 See CA 1963, s 78, reg 3 of Table A and C(A)A 1983, s 38.

Informal alteration of articles: Notwithstanding the provisions of CA 1963, s 15, it would appear that the articles may also be altered by an informal decision of all the members of the company.[1]

1 *Re Express Engineering Works Ltd* [1920] 1 Ch 466; *Re Oxted Motor Co* [1921] 3 KB 32; *Re Duomatic Ltd* [1969] 2 Ch 365; *Cane v Jones* [1981] 1 All ER 533; *Re SM Barker Ltd* [1950] IR 123; *Peter Buchanan Ltd v McVey* [1954] IR 89; *Re PMPA Garage (Longmile) Ltd (No 1)* [1992] 1 ILRM 337; *Re Shannonside Holdings Ltd* (20 May 1993, unreported) HC (Costello J). Moreover, although CA 1963, s 141(8) provides that a resolution in writing signed by all the members is as valid as if passed at a properly convened general meeting, it would appear from *Re PMPA Garage (Longmile) Ltd and Re Shannonside Holdings Ltd* that an oral resolution or decision of all the members can, in certain circumstances, still suffice. On the same basis, although EC(SMPLC)R 1994, reg 9(3) requires the decision of a single-member to be recorded in writing, it seems arguable that an oral decision or resolution which is not so recorded will still be valid.

Alterations are subject to the memorandum and the Acts: CA 1963, s 15 clearly states that any alteration of the articles is subject to the provisions of the Companies Acts and the provisions of the memorandum. Thus, for example, if the memorandum states that a particular provision in the articles cannot be altered without the consent of a third party, such as a Minister, any purported alteration without that consent will be void.[1]

1 *Hennessy v National Agricultural and Industrial Development Association* [1947] IR 159.

Alteration by court order: One of the reliefs against oppression and disregard of interests of members which may be granted by the court under CA 1963, s 205(3) is to alter or add to the company's memorandum or articles. Any such alteration has the same effect as if made by special resolution of the members and, once made, cannot be cancelled or varied, except with the leave of the court.[1]

1 See *Re R Ltd* [1989] ILRM 757.

Company cannot bind itself not to alter its articles: CA 1963, s 15 confers a positive right on the members of a company to alter its articles by special resolution. Consequently, the company cannot contract with a third party not to alter the articles since to do so would deprive the members of their rights under the section.[1] Any such contract will therefore be void to that extent[2]; similarly, a stipulation in the articles that a particular provision is unalterable will be void.[3] On the other hand, if a third party has a contract with a company and the company proceeds to alter its articles in a manner which is inconsistent with the contract, then even though the third party cannot obtain an injunction restraining the alteration,[4] the company nonetheless cannot rely on the alteration to justify the breach of contract[5] and in appropriate circumstances may therefore be liable to the third party in an action for damages.[6]

1 *Walker v London Tramways Co* (1879) 12 ChD 705; *Andrews v Gas Meter Co* [1897] 1 Ch 361, 369; *Punt v Symons and Co Ltd* [1903] 2 Ch 506; *Baily v British Equitable Assurance Co* [1904]

1 Ch 374 (reversed on other grounds [1906] AC 35); *Peter's American delicacy Co Ltd Heath* (1938–39) 61 CLR 457; *Southern Foundries Ltd v Shirlaw* [1940] 2 All ER 445; *Carvill v Irish Industrial Bank* [1968] IR 325; *Cumbrian Newspapers Group Ltd v Cumberland and Westmoreland Herald Newspaper and Printing Co Ltd* [1987] Ch 1; *Russell v Northern Bank Development Corporation Ltd* [1992] 3 All ER 161. Cf *British Murac Syndicate Ltd v Alperton Rubber Co Ltd* [1915] 2 Ch 186 where an injunction was granted restraining the company from altering its articles in circumstances where the alteration would have resulted in a breach of contract with a third party. This decision was founded on the mistaken belief that *Punt v Symons and Co Ltd* had been overruled by the House of Lords in *Baily v British Equitable Assurance Co* [1906] AC 35. However, the House of Lords in that case had reversed the decision of the Court of Appeal on other grounds but had not dissented from the view that a company cannot contract not to alter its articles. Accordingly, the decision in the *British Murac* case appears to have been *per incuriam*.

2 *Allen v Gold Reefs of West Africa Ltd* [1900] 1 Ch 656; *Malleson v National Insurance and Guarantee Corporation* [1894] 1 Ch 200.

3 *Peter's American Delicacy Co Ltd v Heath* (1939) 61 CLR 457; *Russell v Northern Bank Development Corporation Ltd* [1992] 3 All ER 161.

4 *Punt v Symons and Co Ltd* [1903] 2 Ch 506; *Southern Foundries (1926) Ltd v Shirlaw* [1940] AC 701.

5 *Baily v British Equitable Assurance Co* [1904] 1 Ch 374.

6 *Baily v British Equitable Assurance Co* [1904] 1 Ch 374; *Southern Foundries (1926) Ltd v Shirlaw* [1940] AC 701.

Members may agree not to alter articles: Although the company itself cannot contract not to alter the articles, the members may individually enter into such an agreement, since it is upon them that the statutory right of alteration has been conferred.[1] Such shareholders will, however, only bind those members who are parties thereto.

1 *Re A and BC Chewing Gum Ltd* [1975] 1 All ER 1017; *Russell v Northern Bank Development Corporation Ltd* [1992] 3 All ER 161.

Alteration increasing members' liability: No member shall be bound by an alteration made in the memorandum or articles after the date on which he became a member, if and so far as the alteration requires him to take or subscribe for more shares than the number held by him at the date on which the alteration is made, or which in any way increases his liability as at that date to contribute to the share capital of, or otherwise to pay money to, the company, unless he agrees in writing either before or after the alteration is made.[1] Thus, an amendment to the articles obliging members to make payments in respect of recurring administrative and maintenance expenses of the company was invalid as against those members who did so agree to the amendment.[2]

1 CA 1963, s 27.

2 *Ding v Sylvania Waterways Ltd* [1999] NSWSC 58.

Alteration of articles must be made 'bona fide for the benefit of the company as a whole': Apart from complying with the procedure in CA 1963, s 15, in order for an alteration of the articles to be valid, it must have been made in good faith and for the benefit of the company as a whole.[1] The phrase 'the company as a whole' does not mean the company as a commercial entity, distinct from the members; it means the members as a general body, ie the interests of the 'individual hypothetical shareholder.'[2] A resolution altering the articles may therefore be impeached if the effect of the alteration is to discriminate between the majority shareholders and the minority shareholders so as to give the former an advantage of which the latter is deprived.[3]

It is for the shareholders and not for the court to say whether an alteration is for the benefit of the company, provided there are reasonable grounds upon which the alteration could be regarded as beneficial.[4] The following have all been upheld by the court as being objectively justifiable alterations for the benefit of the company as a whole: an alteration of the articles permitting the creation of a class of preference shares in circumstances where the memorandum was silent as to the division of shares into different classes;[5] the creation of a lien over fully paid shares, even though, at the time of the alteration, only one member was affected thereby;[6] the insertion of an article requiring any member who carried on a competing business to transfer his shares at fair value to a nominee of the directors;[7] the insertion of an article which permitted the removal of a permanent director;[8] the alteration of an article which conferred pre-emption rights, so as to allow the transfer of certain shares to the person named in the resolution;[9] and an alteration of voting rights attaching to certain shares which had the effect of conferring voting control on a shareholder who had arranged a private placement of shares and a substantial line of credit from the company's bank and who had personally guaranteed the company's borrowings.[10] On the other hand, the court has declared invalid a special resolution which purported to amend the articles so as to empower the majority of the members to determine that the shares of any member (other than one specified individual), whether in competition with the company or not, should be offered for sale at fair value to such persons as they should deem fit.[11] Similarily invalid was an amendment purporting to allow a specified majority to buy out the shares of the minority.[12]

An alteration of the articles may be valid even though it retrospectively affects the rights of members.[13] However, the alteration cannot retrospectively vary the terms of any contract which is based on the articles.[14]

1 *Clark v Workman* [1920] 1 IR 107; *Allen v Gold Reefs Co of West Africa* [1900] 1 Ch 656; *Sidebottom v Kershaw, Leese and Co Ltd* [1920] 1 Ch 154; *Dafen Tinplate Co v Llanelly Steel Co* (1907) Ltd [1920] 2 Ch 124; *Shuttleworth v Cox Bros and Co (Maidenhead) Ltd* [1927] 2 KB 9; *Peter's American Delicacy Co Ltd v Heath* (1939) 61 CLR 457; *Greenhalgh v Arderne Cinemas Ltd* [1951] Ch 286; *Rights and Issues Investment Trust Ltd v Stylo Shoes Ltd* [1965] Ch 250; *Citco Banking Corp NV v Pusser's Ltd* [2007] 2 BCLC 483. See also *Clemens v Clemens Bros Ltd* [1976] 2 All ER 268 where the question of alteration of the articles was examined in terms of oppression (within the meaning of CA 1963, s 205). Rather than apply the traditional test of 'bona fide for the benefit of the company as a whole' which was considered to be too general, the court held that the shareholders could not exercise their voting rights in any way they pleased, but were instead subject to 'equitable considerations' which might make it 'unjust' for them to exercise their voting rights in a particular way.

2 *Greenhalgh v Arderne Cinemas Ltd* [1951] Ch 286. See also *G and S Doherty Ltd v Doherty* (19 June 1969, unreported) HC (Henchy J).

3 *Greenhalgh v Arderne Cinemas Ltd* [1951] Ch 286. See also *G and S Doherty Ltd v Doherty* (19 June 1969, unreported) HC (Henchy J).

4 *Shuttleworth v Cox Bros and Co (Maidenhead) Ltd* [1927] 2 KB 9; *Rights and Issues Investment Trust Ltd v Stylo Shoes Ltd* [1965] Ch 250; *Citco Banking Corp NV v Pusser's Ltd* [2007] 2 BCLC 483.

5 *Andrews v Gas Meter Co* [1897] 1 Ch 361.

6 *Allen v Gold Reefs of West Africa* [1900] 1 Ch 656.

7 *Sidebottom v Kershaw, Leese and Co Ltd* [1920] 1 Ch 154. Presumably such a clause would now be subject to the provisions of the Competition Act 1991.

8 *Shuttleworth v Cox Bros and Co (Maidenhead) Ltd* [1927] 2 KB 9.

9 *Greenhalgh v Arderne Cinemas Ltd* [1951] Ch 286.

10 *Citco Banking Corp NV v Pusser's Ltd* [2007] 2 BCLC 483

11 *Dafen Tinplate Co v Llanelly Steel Co Ltd* [1920] 2 Ch 124.

12 *Gambotto v WCP Ltd* (1995) 13 ACLC 342.

13 *Allen v Gold Reefs of West Africa Ltd* [1900] 1 Ch 656.

14 *Swabey v Port Darwin Gold Mining Co* (1889) 1 Meg 385; *Re Anglo Austrian Printing and Publishing Union; Isaac's Case* [1892] 2 Ch 158.

Alteration of articles may be oppressive: Although the members are entitled to have regard to their own interests when voting on a resolution in general meeting, they are not entitled to completely disregard the interests of other members and accordingly if one group of shareholders passes a resolution which is in disregard of another group of shareholders, that resolution may conceivably be struck down pursuant to CA 1963, s 205.[1]

1 *Re Williams Group Tullamore Ltd* [1985] IR 613; *Clemens v Clemens Bros Ltd* [1976] 2 All ER 268; *Gambotto v WCP Ltd* (1995) 13 ACLC 342.

Delivery of documents to the Registrar and publication in the Companies Registration Office Gazette: The special resolution amending the articles and the amended text of the articles must be forwarded to the Registrar within 15 days of the passing of such resolution.[1] Pursuant to EC(C) R 1973, reg 4, a company shall also cause to be published[2] in the Companies Registration Office Gazette,[3] a notice of delivery of such documents. In practice, it is in fact the Registrar who generally causes such notices to be published in the Companies Registration Office Gazette.

1 CA 1963, s 143(1).

2 Within six weeks of the relevant delivery date; EC(C)R 1973, reg 4(2).

3 Reference to *Iris Oifigiúil* was substituted by reference to the Companies Registration Office Gazette by virtue of EC(C)R 2004, reg 5.

Implied terms: Terms will not be implied into the articles from the extrinsic surrounding circumstances which are inconsistent with the express terms of the articles.[1]

1 *Towcester Racecourse Co Ltd v The Racecourse Association Ltd* [2003] 1 BCLC 260; *FA Tamplin Steamship Co Ltd v Anglo Mexican Petroleum Products Co Ltd* [1916] 2 AC 397.

UK legislation

See CA 1985, s 9.

Form of Memorandum and Articles

16 Statutory forms of memorandum and articles

The form of—

(a) the memorandum of a company limited by shares;

(b) the memorandum [...][a] of a company limited by guarantee and not having a share capital;

(c) the memorandum and articles of a company limited by guarantee and having a share capital;

(d) the memorandum and articles of an unlimited company having a share capital;

shall be respectively in accordance with the forms set out in Tables B, C, D and E in the First Schedule or as near thereto as circumstances admit.

Amendments

a The words 'and articles' deleted by C(A)A 1982, s 17 with effect from 3 August 1982.[1]

1 Companies (Amendment) Act, 1982 (Commencement) Order 1982 (SI 225/1982).

Definitions

'articles': CA 1963, s 2(1); 'company': CA 1963, s 2 (1); 'a company limited by guarantee': CA 1963, s 2(1), 5(2)(b); 'a company limited by shares': CA 1963, s 2(1), 5(2)(a); 'memorandum': CA 1963, s 2(1); 'share': CA 1963, s 2(1); 'an unlimited company': CA 1963, s 2 (1), s 5(2)(c).

Notes

Form of memorandum and articles: The prescribed memoranda and articles in CA 1963, s 16 are models as to form only and not as to content.[1] For the prescribed form of memorandum for a plc, see C(A)A 1983, Sch 2.

1 *Gaiman v National Association for Mental Health* [1971] Ch 317.

Registration of standard form memoranda and articles: CLEA 2001, s 80 allows for the filing of standard form memoranda and articles of association to which reference numbers will be assigned by the Registrar. Thereafter the promoters of a company need only file a memorandum and articles of association specifying those matters peculiar to the company itself, together with a statement identifying the reference number(s) of the standard form documents which are to be deemed also to have been incorporated therein.

Signing of memorandum by subscribers: The memorandum must be signed by the subscribers.[1] Under EC(SMPLC)R 1994 it is possible to have just one subscriber in the case of private companies limited by shares or limited by guarantee and having a share capital.[2] In the case of a company limited by guarantee and not having a share capital, it will, by definition, be a public company and accordingly will be required to have at least seven subscribers.[3] On the same basis, an unlimited company which does not have a share capital is a public company and must therefore have at least seven subscribers. However, in practice most unlimited companies do in fact have a share capital. In such a case, if the unlimited company is a private company within the meaning of CA 1963, s 33, it will be required to have at least two subscribers.[4]

1 CA 1963, s 7.

2 See the notes to CA 1963, s 5 and see also the notes to the EC(SMPLC)R 1994.

3 See CA 1963, ss 5(1) and 33.

4 CA 1963, s 5(1).

UK legislation

See CA 1985, s 3; Companies (Tables A–F) Regulations 1985 (SI 1985/805).

Registration

17 Registration of memorandum and articles

The memorandum and the articles, if any, shall be delivered to the registrar of companies [in an entire format or in a form pursuant to section 80 of the Company Law Enforcement Act, 2001],[a] and he shall retain and register them.

Amendments

a The words 'in an entire format or in a form pursuant to section 80 of the Company Law Enforcement Act, 2001' inserted by CLEA 2001, s 83 with effect from 1 October 2001.[1]

1 Company Law Enforcement Act, 2001 (Commencement) (No 2) Order, 2001 (SI 438/2001).

Definitions

'articles': CA 1963, s 2(1); 'memorandum': CA 1963, s 2(1); 'the registrar of companies': CA 1963, s 2(1).

Notes

Registration of standard form memoranda and articles: CLEA 2001, s 80 allows for the filing of standard form memoranda and articles of association to which reference numbers will be assigned by the Registrar. Thereafter the promoters of a company need only file a memorandum and articles of association specifying those matters peculiar to the company itself, together with a statement identifying the reference number(s) of the standard form documents which are to be deemed also to have been incorporated therein.

Documents to be delivered to Registrar: Apart from the memorandum and articles,[1] the subscribers must also deliver to the Registrar a statement of the first directors and secretary and registered office of the company together with signed consents to act from the persons named in the statement.[2] The form must also incorporate a statutory declaration by one of the proposed directors or the proposed secretary or by a solicitor engaged in the formation of the company to the effect that the requirements of the Companies Acts have been complied with in respect of the registration of the company.[3] If the company is to be formed as a plc its memorandum must state the share capital to be not less than the authorised minimum of €38,092.14.[4]

1 CA 1963, s 17.

2 C(A)A 1982, s 3. The appropriate form is Companies (Forms) Order 2004 (SI 829/2004), Form A1. If none of the proposed directors is an Irish resident, the Form must have appended to it a bond in the form required by C(A)(No 2)A 1999, s 43.

3 C(A)A 1983, s 5(5).

4 C(A)A 1983, ss 5(2and 19 (1). £30,000 converted to €38,092.14 by Council Regulations (EC) No 1103/97, No 974/98 and No 2866/98 and the Economic and Monetary Union Act 1988, s 6.

Documents to be delivered to the Revenue Commissioners: Every company incorporated in the State or which commences to carry on a trade, profession or business in the State, must within 30 days deliver to the Revenue Commissioners a statement containing details of the name of the company, the addresses of its registered office and principal place of business, the name and address of the secretary, the date of commencement of and the nature of the trade, profession or business, the date to which its accounts will be made up, and such other information as the Revenue Commissioners may consider necessary for the purposes of the Tax Acts (as defined in TCA 1997).[1] Any material change in these particulars must be delivered within 30 days.[2] Furthermore, an inspector oftaxes may serve a notice on such a company at any time requiring the delivery of such particulars within 30 days of the date of the notice.[3] Failure to deliver the particulars in any of these circumstances may result in the default being notified to the Registrar, who may in turn rely upon that default to strike the name of the company off the register pursuant to C(A)A 1982, s 12A.[4]

1 TCA 1997, s 882(2)(i). Additional information is required under s 882(2)(ii) in respect of Irish incorporated non-resident companies and under 882(2)(iii) in respect of companies incorporated and resident abroad but carrying on a trade, profession or business in the State.

2 TCA 1997, s 882(2)(a).

3 TCA 1997, s 882(2)(b).

4 TCA 1997, s 882(3) (as amended by the FA 2000, s 78). See also C(A)A 1982, s 12A and notes thereto.

Proof of activity in Ireland: Prior to the coming into force of C(A)(No 2)A 1999, s 42 on 18 April 2000[1] a company could lawfully be incorporated in the State even though its sole intended purpose was to operate as a non-resident company. Now, however, the company will not be registered and a certificate of incorporation will not be issued without proof that one of the activities mentioned in its objects clause will be carried on in the State.[2] However, the Registrar may accept as sufficient proof a statutory declaration in the prescribed form[3] that the purpose or one of the purposes for which the company is being formed is to carry on an activity[4] in the State.[5] The statutory declaration, which may be made by one of the persons who are to be named in the statement to be filed with the Registrar under C(A)A 1982, s 3 as being the first directors of the company[6] or being the first secretary or one of the first joint secretaries of the company[7] or which may be made by a solicitor engaged in the formation of the company,[8] must give details of the activity to be carried on in the State[9] or the principal activity if two or more such activities are to be carried on,[10] including details of the place or places in the State where such activity is proposed to be carried on.[11] Furthermore, details must also be given of the place (whether in the State or abroad) where the central administration of the company will normally be carried on.[12] It remains to be seen whether the requirement that every newly formed company carry on an activity in the

State amounts to an unlawful curtailment of the freedom of establishment provided for in Art 43 of the EC Treaty.

1 Companies (Amendment) (No 2) Act 1999 (Commencement) Order 2000 (SI 61/2000).

2 C(A)(No 2)A 1999, s 42(1).

3 Companies (Forms) Order 2004 (SI 829/2004), Form A1. In this form the declarant not only confirms compliance with the provisions of CA 1963, s 42 but also confirms compliance generally with the registration requirements of the Companies Acts, as required by C(A)A 1983, s 5(5). Making this combined declaration is expressly provided by C(A)(No 2)A 1999, s 42(5).

4 The activity of the Company must be classified with reference to an appropriate NACE Code Classification ie the common basis for statistical classifications of economic activities within the European Union as set out in the Annex to Council Regulation (EEC) No 3037/90 of 9 October 1990). If such classification is not possible, a precise description of the activity must be given.

5 C(A)(No 2)A 1999, s 42(2).

6 C(A)(No 2)A 1999, s 42(4)(a).

7 C(A)(No 2)A 1999, s 42(4)(b).

8 C(A)(No 2)A 1999, s 42(4)(c).

9 C(A)(No 2)A 1999, s 42(2)(a) and (b).

10 C(A)(No 2)A 1999, s 42(3).

11 C(A)(No 2)A 1999, s 42(2)(c).

12 C(A)(No 2)A 1999, s 42(2)(d). With regard to the place of a company's central administration, see the notes to CA 1963, s 113.

Duty of Registrar: Once the prescribed documentation has been lodged, it is then the duty of the Registrar to determine whether the requirements of the Companies Acts have been fulfilled. In particular he will look to see whether the company has the correct number of subscribers under CA 1963, s 5(1) and under EC(SMPLC)R 1994 and whether the company is being formed for a lawful purpose[1] as well as ascertaining whether the proposed name of the company is undesirable within the meaning of s 21. In exercising these functions, the Registrar is acting quasi-judicially and is therefore amenable to judicial review.[2] Once these have been satisfied, the Registrar has no entitlement to refuse registration and, if necessary, may be made amenable to an order of *mandamus* to compel him to do so.[3]

1 *R v Registrar of Joint Stock Companies, ex parte More* [1931] 2 KB 197.

2 *Bowman v Secular Society* [1917] AC 406, 439.

3 *Princess Reuss v Bos* (1871) LR 5 HL 176, 192; *R v Registrar of Companies, ex parte Bowen* [1914] 3 KB 1161.

UK legislation

See CA 1985, ss 10, 12; Companies (Particulars of Usual Residential Address) (Confidentiality Orders) Regulations 2002 (SI 2002/912), r 16, Sch 2 para 1(1),(2) and (3); Companies Act (Electronic Communications) 1985 Order 2000 (SI 2000/3773), art 4.

---

18 Effect of registration

(1) On the registration of the memorandum of a company the registrar shall certify under his hand that the company is incorporated and, in the case of a limited company, that the company is limited.

(2) From the date of incorporation mentioned in the certificate of incorporation, the subscribers of the memorandum, together with such other persons as may from time to time become members of the company, shall be a body corporate with the name contained in the memorandum, capable forthwith of exercising all the functions of an incorporated company, and having perpetual succession and a common seal, but with

such liability on the part of the members to contribute to the assets of the company in the event of its being wound up as is mentioned in this Act.

Definitions

'company': CA 1963, s 2(1); 'member': CA 1963, s 31; 'memorandum': CA 1963, s 2(1).

Notes

Authority of members to act on behalf of the company: From the date of incorporation the members have authority to act on behalf of the board. Although in most instances day-to-day management will be delegated to a board of directors[1] the members have a residual authority to act where there is no board of directors[2] or where the board is deadlocked.[3] They may also ratify acts which are beyond the authority of the company's agents but within the powers of the company itself.[4] However, ratification may not take place where the act in question is beyond not only the powers of the agent but also the powers of the company.[5]

1 See Table A, reg 80.

2 *Mahoney v East Holyford Mining Co* (1875) Lr 7 HL 869.

3 *Barron v Potter* [1914] 1 Ch 895.

4 *Re Burke Clancy and Co Ltd* (23 May 1974, unreported) HC (Kenny J); *Irvine v Union Bank of Australia* (1877) 2 AC 366; *Grant v United Kingdom Switchback Railway Co* (1888) 40 Ch D 135.

5 *Ashbury Railway Carriage and Iron Co v Riche* (1875) LR 7 HL 653; *Northern Bank Finance Corporation v Quinn Achates Investment Company* [1979] ILRM 221; *Boschoek Proprietary Co Ltd v Fuke* [1906] 1 Ch 148; *Towey v Irish Livestock Exporters' and Traders' Association Ltd* (3 December 1941, unreported) HC (Gavan Duffy P).

Corporate personality: It is a fundamental principle of company law that after a company has been duly incorporated, it acquires its own legal personality, separate and distinct from the personality of its member or members.[1]

1 *Salomon v Salomon and Co* [1897] AC 22; *Kodak Ltd v Clark* [1902] 2 KB 450, aff'd [1903] 1 KB 505; *Janson v Driefontein Mines* [1902] AC 484; *Gramophone and Typewriter Ltd v Stanley* [1906] 2 KB 856, aff'd [1908] 2 KB 89; *State (Melbarien Enterprises Ltd) v Revenue Commissioners* [1985] IR 706; *Re Frederick Inns Ltd* [1991] 582, at 587, aff'd [1994] 1 ILRM 387.

Consequences of incorporation: *Blackstone*[1] has identified five principle consequences of incorporation, namely:

(i) perpetual succession;

(ii) the ability to hold property in its own name;

(iii) the ability to sue and be sued in its own name;

(iv) a common seal;

(v) the ability to make its own bye-laws and internal regulations.

(i) *Perpetual succession*: The concept of perpetual succession is expressly referred to in CA 1963, s 18. The company has 'no soul to be saved or body to be kicked' and, accordingly, even though its members may change from time to time, or become insane or even all die[2], the company itself will continue in existence until such time as it is dissolved in accordance with the provisions of the Companies Acts.[3]

(ii) *Holding property*: A corollary of perpetual succession is that the company is able to hold property in its own right. [4] Consequently, the property of the company is to be regarded as belonging to the company itself rather than belonging to its members. [5] Thus, a sale of property by a person to a company of which he is a member, is a transfer to a distinct corporate body, involving a transfer of ownership[6] and attracting stamp duty.[7]

If damage is done to the company's property, the cause of action lies with the company itself and not with the members, whether acting collectively or individually;[8] similarly, because the company owns and conducts its own business, any defamatory statement made about that business defames the company rather than its members and accordingly, only the company can sue in respect of such remarks.[9] Indeed, the company could even sue one of its own members for libel or slander.[10]

A further consequence of the company owning its own property is that the members have no insurable interest therein and cannot therefore effect a valid policy of insurance in respect thereof.[11] They may, however, be able to indirectly cover themselves against such loss by insuring their shares against any diminution in value arising by virtue of damage done to the company's assets.[12]

Since the company owns its own property, the members may be convicted of conspiring to defraud it[13] or of stealing from it[14] even though the act of appropriation has in fact been unanimously approved by them.[15] Equally well, they may be found guilty of conspiring with the company[16] or of aiding and abetting the company to commit a crime.[17] Outsiders, too, act at their own peril if they ignore the separate legal personality of the company. For example, a bank which treated the company's property as belonging to the controlling member and credited the member's account with the proceeds of cheques made payable to the company was found liable in conversion when that member subsequently misappropriated the moneys in question.[18]

(iii) *Suing and being sued*: Since the company has its own separate legal personality, it is capable of suing and being sued in its own right.[19] Thus, a shareholder cannot per se sue upon a contract which has been entered into by his company with a third party[20] nor can he per se be sued upon such a contract.[21] However, the fact that an individual is the controlling shareholder and director of the company, does not prevent him from entering into a contract with the company.[22]

The company's capacity to sue and be sued is not, however confined to contractual claims. Actions in tort may be brought in the name of the company (but not in the names of the members)[23] in respect of wrongs done to the company, even though the wrong may have be done to the company in connection with an *ultra vires* business which it was operating.[24] Because of its abstract nature, however, there are some torts which cannot be suffered by a company, such as assault, battery and false imprisonment. Just as a company may sue in tort, so too it can be sued,[25] even if the tort arises out of an activity which is *ultra vires* the company.[26]

A company may also be prosecuted for criminal offences[27] including those requiring *mens rea.*[28] There are, however, some offences such as bigamy, rape or sexual assault, which, by their very nature can only be carried out by natural persons and are therefore incapable of being committed by a body corporate.[29] Similarly, there are some punishments such as imprisonment which by their very nature can only be imposed on natural persons and to which a company cannot accordingly be subjected.[30]

In a series of cases it was suggested that corporate bodies were incapable of enjoying any of the rights afforded by the Constitution.[31] More recently, however, in *Iarnrod Éireann v Ireland*[32] it has been accepted by Keane J that a company may enjoy constitutional rights (eg property rights) provided that they are not by their nature rights which could only arise by virtue of the human characteristics of a person (eg the right to bodily integrity).

Unlike an individual, a company is an abstract legal entity, and therefore cannot represent itself in court, nor may it be represented through its controlling shareholder, managing director or other officer. Instead it must be legally represented.[33]

(iv) *Common seal*: CA 1963, s 18(2) expressly provides that the company is to have a common seal.[34]

(v) *Internal regulations*: The bye-laws and internal regulations which the company is empowered to make are to be found in the memorandum and articles of association.

1 *Commentaries on the Laws of England* (18th Edn, Blackstone, 1825) Vol 1. On the nature of corporate personality, see also *Maclaine Watson and Co Ltd v Department of Trade and Industry* [1989] 3 All ER 523; *Attorney General v Nissan* [1969] 1 All ER 629. See also Courtney, *The Law of Private Companies* (2nd edn, Tottel Publishing, 2002), Ch 4.

2 *Re Noel Tedman Holding Pty Ltd* [1967] Qd R 561.

3 For the provisions dealing with dissolution see CA 1963, ss 310–311A and C(A)A 1982, s 12.

4 *Borland's Trustee v Steel Bros and Co Ltd* [1901] 1 Ch 279; *Casey v Bentley* [1902] 1 IR 376; *Attorney General for Ireland v Jameson* [1904] 2 IR 644; *Short v Treasury Commissioners* [1948] AC 534; *Provincial Bank of Ireland Ltd v O'Connor* (10 October 1974, unreported) HC (Kenny J); *Lee and Co (Dublin) Ltd v Egan (Wholesale) Ltd* (18 October 1979, unreported) HC (Kenny J); *Keaney v Sullivan* [2007] IEHC 8.

5 *Ibid.*

6 *Farrar v Farrars Ltd* (1888) 40 Ch D 395.

7 *John Foster and Sons v IRC* [1894] 1 QB 516.

8 *Foss v Harbottle* (1843) 2 Hare 461; *Prudential Assurance Co Ltd v Newman Industries Ltd (No 2)* [1982] Ch 204; *O'Neill v Ryan* [1993] ILRM 557. For a more detailed discussion of the Rule in *Foss v Harbottle* and the exceptions thereto, see the notes to CA 1963, s 205.

9 *Metropolitan Saloon Omnibus Co Ltd v Hawkins* (1859) 4 H and N 87; *South Hetton Coal Co Ltd v North-Eastern News Association Ltd* [1894] 1 QB 133; *Irish People's Assurance Society v Dublin City Assurance Co* [1929] IR 25.

10 *Metropolitan Saloon Omnibus Co Ltd v Hawkins* (1859) 4 H and N 87.

11 *Macaura v Northern Assurance Co Ltd* [1925] AC 619; *Verdarame v Commercial Union Assurance Co plc* [1992] BCLC 793. See, however, *Constitution Insurance Co of Canada v Kosmopoulos* 34 DLR (4th) 208 where the Supreme Court of Canada held that the concept of an insurable interest was to be determined by the factual expectancy test so that the member of a single-member company did have an insurable interest in its property.

12 *Wilson v Jones* (1866) LR 1 Exch 193.

13 *Adams v R* [1995] 2 BCLC 17.

14 *R v Arthur* (1967) 111, sJ 435; *R v Pearlberg, R v O'Brien* [1982] Crim LR 829; *R v Sullivan* [1984] Crim LR 405.

15 *Attorney-General's Reference (No 2)* [1984] QB 624; *R v Philippou* (1989) 89 Cr App R 290; *DPP v Gomez* [1993] AC 442. Cf *R v Roffel* [1985] VR 511.

16 *Taylor v Smyth* [1991] IR 142. Cf *R v McDonnell* [1966] 1 QB 146. See generally MacCann, 'Companies and Conspiracy' (1990) ILT 197.

17 *McMahon v Murtagh Properties Ltd* [1982] ILRM 342.

18 *AL Underwood Ltd v Bank of Liverpool* [1924] 1 KB 775.

19 A company cannot, however, act as a common informer for the purpose of instituting criminal proceedings: *Cumann Luthchleas Gael Teo v District Justice Windle* [1994] 1 IR 533.

20 *Dunlop Pneumatic Tyre Co Ltd v Selfridge and Co Ltd* [1915] AC 847.

21 *Dunlop Pneumatic Tyre Co Ltd v Selfridge and Co Ltd* [1915] AC 847; *Maclaine Watson and Co Ltd v Department of Trade and Industry* [1990] BCLC 102; *Schouls v Canadian Meat processing Corp* (1983) 147 DLR (3d) 81. The corollary is of course that the company cannot be sued in contract or in tort for the acts and omissions of its shareholders: *Bell v Lever Bros Ltd* [1932] AC 161.

22 *Lee v Lee's Air Farming Ltd* [1961] AC 12. However, for statutory restrictions on the ability of a company and its directors to contract with one another see CA 1963, s 194 and CA 1990, Pt III.

23 *Rainham Chemical Works Ltd v Belvedere Fish Guano Co Ltd* [1921] AC 465; *British Thomson-Houston Co v Sterling Accessories Ltd* [1924] 2 Ch 33.

24 *National Telephone Co Ltd v The Constables of St Peter's Port* [1900] AC 317.

25 *Campbell v Paddington Corporation* [1911] 1 KB 869.

26 *Campbell v Paddington Corporation* [1911] 1 KB 869. Cf *Poulton v London and South Western Railway Co* (1867) LR 2 QB 534.

27 *The King (Cottingham) v The Justices of County Cork* [1906] 2 IR 415; *The King v The Chairman and Justices of Antrim* [1906] 2 IR 298; *R v British Steel plc* [1995] 1 WLR 1356.

28 *DPP v Kent and Sussex Contractors Ltd* [1944] 1 KB 146; *R v ICR Haulage Ltd* [1944] 1 KB 551; *Moore v Bresler Ltd* [1944] 2 All ER 515; *Tesco Supermarkets Ltd v Natrass* [1972] AC 153; *R v British Steel plc* [1995] 1 WLR 1356; *R v Associated Octel Co Ltd* [1996] 1 WLR 1543.

29 The offence of manslaughter is one offence which, at first sight, one might think capable only of being committed by a natural person but which can in fact be committed by a body corporate: *R v P and O European Ferries (Dover) Ltd* (1991) 93 Cr App R 72.

30 *The King (Cottingham) v The Justices of County Cork* [1906] 2 IR 415; *Pearks, Gunston and Tee Ltd v Ward* [1902] 2 KB 1; *Hawke v E Hulton and Co* [1909] 2 KB 93; *R v The Daily Mirror Newspapers Ltd* (1922) 16 Cr App R 131.

31 *Quinn's Supermarkets Ltd v Attorney General* [1972] IR 1; *Private Motorists' Provident Society v Attorney General* [1983] IR 339; *Chestvale Properties Ltd v Glackin* [1993] 3 IR 35. Cf *Bula Ltd v Tara Mines Ltd* [1987] IR 85; *Society for the Protection of Unborn Children (Ireland) Ltd v Coogan* [1989] IR 738 and *Attorney General for England and Wales v Brandon Books Publishers Ltd* [1986] IR 579 where it appears to have been implicitly accepted that a company could enjoy some constitutional rights, including a right of access to the courts and freedom of expression.

32 *Iarnrod Éireann v Ireland* [1995] 2 ILRM 161. See also *Society for the Protection of Unborn Children (Ireland) Ltd v Coogan* [1989] IR 738; *Lancefort Ltd v An Bord Pleanála* [1998] 2 IR 511; *Attorney General for England and Wales v Brandon Book Publishers Ltd* [1986] IR 579.

33 *Battle v Irish Art Promotion Centre Ltd* [1968] IR 252; *Fallon v An Bord Pleanála* [1991] ILRM 779. Similar principles apply regarding representation before a tribunal: *Tritonia Ltd v Equity and Law Life Assurance Society* [1934] AC 584. The constitutionality of the distinction between the representation of individuals and companies in court has been upheld by the Supreme Court in *Abbey Films Ltd v Attorney General* [1981] IR 158. Cf *Arbuthnot Leasing Ltd v Havelet Leasing Ltd* [1990] BCLC 802 where the court held that it has an inherent jurisdiction to allow a company to be represented by one of its members or directors. The court, however, refused to so exercise its discretion in *Re a company, ex parte F Ltd* [1991] BCLC 567. For a statutory exception to the requirement that companies be legally represented, see CA 1963, s 382.

34 As to the affixing of the common seal, see reg 115 of Table A and the notes thereto. There is no requirement for a company incorporated under CA 1985 to hold a common seal; CA 1985, s 36A (as inserted by CA 1989, s 130).

Lifting the veil of incorporation: Although the separate legal personality of the company is fundamental to company law, there are certain circumstances in which the veil of incorporation is lifted, both by the courts and by the legislature. The effect of lifting the veil of incorporation is typically to impose personal liability on the members or directors for debts, liabilities and other obligations for which the company itself would otherwise be exclusively liable.

Attribution of human characteristics: Although the company is an abstract legal entity, there are several instances where it is necessary to attribute to it certain human characteristics.

(i) *Domicile and nationality*: A company is domiciled in and is a national of the country in which it has its registered office.[1]

(ii) *Residence*: A company is deemed to reside in the country where its central management and control actually abides.[2] The location of a company's central management and control is always a matter of fact.[3] It may be found to exist in the place where the majority of directors reside[4] or in the place where general meetings are held[5] or in the place where the board of its parent company resides,[6] even though its memorandum stipulates that it is to be managed in another country. [7] Where the company's management is divided between two or more countries, it may be deemed to have more than one residence. [8]

(iii) *Enemy status*: In times of war a company, although registered in the State, may be deemed to have enemy status where all its members are nationals of an enemy state or if those persons in control of its affairs are enemies. [9]

(iv) *Criminal liability*: [10] Being an abstraction, a company cannot be guilty of a crime involving personal violence, such as murder, rape etc, [11] or which must otherwise, by necessity involve a human element, such as bigamy or driving. [12] Presumably, however, the company could be guilty of aiding or abetting a crime of personal violence, as where it pays an assassin to carry out a murder. Even if guilty, however, the company could not be punished by death, corporal punishment or imprisonment. [13] Accordingly, the only effective penalties against a company are fines or orders for sequestration.

At common law there is no vicarious liability for crimes[14] although exceptions arise for certain statutory offences and also for public nuisance. [15] Subject to these (and unless the offence is one of strict liability) [16] a company will only be personally liable for crimes by attributing to the company the acts and state of mind of the person or persons within the company who were in control of and who were entrusted with the particular situation. [17] The state of mind of such a person is the state of mind of the company and is treated by the law as such. [18] Subject to the foregoing, the following are some examples of offences of which a company may be convicted: acting with intent to deceive and making a statement which it knows to be false; [19] conspiracy to defraud;[20] criminal contempt of court;[21] breaching health and safety legislation;[22] manslaughter [23] and making false tax returns.[24] The fact that the company has also suffered loss as a result of the crime will not prevent the state of mind of the controlling officer from being attributed to the company so as to secure a conviction.[25] Apart from being identified with the company for the purpose of convicting the company, those persons who were in control of the particular situation which gave rise to the crime may also be found guilty of conspiring with the company[26] or of aiding and abetting the company to commit the crime. [27]

(v) *Victim of crime*: Certain crimes require a state of mind on the part of the victim before they can be regarded as having occurred. In the case of fraud, for example, deception of the victim is an essential prerequisite. A company will be deemed to have been defrauded if the employee or agent whose state of mind stood as that of the company, has been deceived. [28]

(vi) *Character*: Under the licensing acts, the applicant for the licence must be of good character. Where the applicant is a company, the court adopts a similar approach to that taken in criminal cases for the purpose of determining the company's character. It examines the character of the person or persons within the company who will be in control of and who are to be entrusted with the management of the licensed premises.[29] Similarly, in civil actions, where state of knowledge or the mental intent of the company is relevant (eg in actions for fraud) the company will look to the directing mind and will of the person in control of the given situation,[30] rather than simply looking at the state of mind of the person or persons having responsibility for the general management of the company. [31] Nevertheless, if the company is itself the target and primary victim of the individual's wrongdoing, then his mental intent and his acts and omissions will not be attributed to the company.[32]

1 *Janson v Dreifontein Mines Ltd* [1902] AC 484; *Gasque v IRC* [1940] 2 KB 80.

2 *De Beers Consolidated Mines Ltd v Howe* [1906] AC 455; *Unit Construction Ltd v Bullock* [1960] AC 351; *John Hood and Co Ltd v Magee* [1918] 2 IR 34; *Re Little Olympian Each Ways Ltd (No 2)* [1995] 1 BCLC 48. Cf *Adams v Cape Industries plc* [1990] Ch 433.

3 *Re Little Olympian Each Ways Ltd (No 2)* [1995] 1 BCLC 48.

4 *De Beers Consolidated Mines Ltd v Howe* [1906] AC 455; *Re Little Olympian Each Ways Ltd (No 2)* [1995] 1 BCLC 48.

5 *John Hood and Co Ltd v Magee* [1918] 2 IR 34.

6 *Unit Construction Ltd v Bullock* [1960] AC 351.

7 *Unit Construction Ltd v Bullock* [1960] AC 351. However, a provision in the company's memorandum stating that management is to take place in a particular country will be of relevance in determining residence in circumstances where there is no evidence to suggest that the provision has been breached: *Re Little Olympian Each Ways Ltd (No 2)* [1995] 1 BCLC 48.

8 *Swedish Central Railway v Thompson* [1925] AC 495; *Egyptian Delta Land and Investment Co Ltd v Todd* [1929] AC 1. See generally Corrigan, 'Place of Abode Test in Establishing Tax Residence' (1986) 6 ILT 106.

9 *Daimler v Continental Tyre and Rubber Co (Great Britain) Ltd* [1916] 2 AC 307; *Re Badische Co* [1921] 2 Ch 331; *Kuenigl v Donnersmarck* [1955] 1 All ER 46; *The Roumanian* [1915] P 26.

10 See, generally: Winn, 'The Criminal Responsibility of Corporations' (1929) 3 CLJ 398; Welsh 'The Criminal Liability of Corporations' (1946) 62 LQR 345; Wells, 'Corporations and Criminal Responsibility' (London, 1993).

11 *Manchester Corporation v Williams* [1891] 1 QB 94; *R v Murray Wright Ltd* [1970] NZLR 476.

12 *Richmond London Borough Council v Pinn and Wheeler Ltd* [1989] TRT 354.

13 *The King (Cottingham) v The Justices of County Cork* [1906] 2 IR 415, 427; *Pearks, Gunton and Tee Ltd v Ward* [1902] 2 KB 1; *Hawke v E Hulton and Co* [1909] 2 KB 93; *R v The Daily Mirror Newspapers Ltd* (1922) 16 Cr App R 131.

14 *Tesco Supermarkets Ltd v Natrass* [1972] 2 AC 153, 199.

15 *R v Great North of England Railway Co* (1846) 9 QB 315.

16 For instances where a company has been made liable for an offence of strict liability, see *R (King) v The Chairman and Justices of Antrim* [1906] 2 IR 298; *Wedick v Osmond and Son (Dublin) Ltd* [1935] IR 820; *Pearks, Gunston Tee Ltd v Ward* [1902] 2 KB 1; *Moussell Bros Ltd v London and North Western Railway Co* [1917] 2 KB 836; *Alphacell Ltd v Woodward* [1972] AC 824.

17 *Superwood Holdings plc v Sun Alliance and London Insurance plc* [1993] 3 IR 303; *Taylor v Smyth* [1991] 1 IR 142; *Attorney General's Reference (No 2 of 1999)* [2000] QB 796; *R v Associated Octel Co Ltd* [1996] 1 WLR 1543; *R v Rozeik* [1996] 1 BCLC 380; *Meridian Global Funds Management Asia Ltd v Securities Commission* [1995] 2 AC 500; *R v British Steel plc* [1995] 1 WLR 1356; *El Ajou v Dollar Land Holdings plc* [1994] 2 All ER 685; *Tesco Supermarkets Ltd v Natrass* [1972] AC 153, 171, 187, 200; *R v Andrews-Weatherfoil Ltd* [1972] 1 All ER 65; *HL Bolton (Engineering) Ltd v TJ Graham and Sons Ltd* [1957] 1 QB 159; *DPP V Kent and Sussex Contractors Ltd* [1944] KB 146; *Moore v I Bresler Ltd* [1944] 2 All ER 515; *R v Fane Robinson Ltd* [1941] 3 DLR 409; *Canadian Dredge and Dock Co Ltd v R* (1985) 19 DLR (4d) 314, 336–337; *R v P and O European Ferries (Dover) Ltd* (1991) 93 Cr App R 72; *Re Supply of Ready Mixed Concrete* [1995] 1 BCLC 613.

18 *Ibid.*

19 *DPP v Kent and Sussex Contractors Ltd* [1944] KB 146.

20 *R v ICR Haulage Ltd* [1944] KB 551.

21 *Re Hibernia National Review* [1976] IR 338, 392; *R v JG Hammond and Co Ltd* [1914] 2 KB 866; *Re Supply of Ready Mixed Concrete (No 2)* [1990] BCLC 613.

22 *R v British Steel plc* [1995] 1 WLR 1356; *R v Gateway Foodmarkets Ltd* [1997] 2 Cr App R 40.

23 *R v P and O European Ferries (Dover) Ltd* (1991) 93 Cr App R 72.

24 *Moore v I Bresler Ltd* [1944] 2 All ER 515.

25 *Moore v I Bresler Ltd* [1944] 2 All ER 515.

26 *Taylor v Smyth* [1991] IR 142. Cf *R v McDonnell* [1966] 1 QB 146. See, generally, MacCann, 'Companies and Conspiracy' (1990) ILT 197.

27 *McMahon v Murtagh Properties Ltd* [1982] ILRM 342.

28 *R v Rozeik* [1996] 1 BCLC 380.

29 *R (Cottingham) The Justices of County Cork* [1906] 2 IR 415; *The State (Hennessy and Chariot Inns Ltd) v Commons* [1976] IR 238; *McMahon v Murtagh Properties Ltd* [1982] ILRM 342. It is to be noted that not every action of a director can be said to be reflected sufficiently on a company so as to adversely affect its character for licensing purposes: *Re Whitesheet Inn Ltd* [2003] 2 IR 156.

30 *HL Bolton (Engineering) Ltd v TJ Graham and Sons Ltd* [1957] 1 QB 159; *Lennards Carrying Co Ltd v Asiatic Petroleum Co Ltd* [1915] AC 705; *The Lady Gwendolen* [1965] P 294; *El Ajou*

v Dollar Land Holdings plc [1994] 2 All ER 685; *Re Supply of Ready Mixed Concrete* [1995] 1 BCLC 613; *Meridian Global Funds Management Asia Ltd v Securities Commission* [1995] 2 BCLC 116; *Superwood Holdings plc v Sun Alliance and London Insurance plc* [1993] 3 IR 303; *Taylor v Smyth* [1991] 1 Ir 142.

31 *HL Bolton (Engineering) Ltd v TJ Graham and Sons Ltd* [1957] 1 QB 159; *Lennards Carrying Co Ltd v Asiatic Petroleum Co Ltd* [1915] AC 705; *The Lady Gwendolen* [1965] P 294; *El Ajou v Dollar Land Holdings plc* [1994] 2 All ER 686; *Re Supply of Ready Mixed Concrete* [1995] 1 BCLC 613. *Meridian Global Funds Management Asia Ltd v Securities Commission* [1995] 2 BCLC 116; *Superwood Holdings plc v Sun Alliance and London Insurance plc* [1993] 3 IR 303; *Taylor v Smyth* [1991] 1 IR 142; *Lebon v Aqua Salt Co Ltd* [2009] 1 BCLC 549.

32 *Stone & Rolls Ltd v Moore Stephens* [2009] 4 All ER 431.

Company used as a vehicle for fraud or avoiding legal existing obligations: Apart from looking behind the veil of incorporation for the purpose of attributing human characteristics to a company, the courts will also be willing to pierce the corporate veil and to impose personal liability for the liabilities of a company in circumstances where the company has been formed or is being used for a fraudulent or other wrongful purpose or to circumvent the existing legal obligations of its members.[1] Thus the corporate veil was pierced where the corporator formed a company and assigned a licence for a patent to the company, not with a view to the company working the patent but rather to enable him to avoid further royalty payments.[2] Likewise, an attempt by an employer to avoid a claim for wrongful dismissal by transferring his assets to a new company, was thwarted when the court acceded to an application to lift the veil of incorporation and to treat the new company as being liable for the debts of the employer.[3] The court was also prepared to look behind the corporate facade where the company had been set up to carry on a business which its controlling shareholder was prohibited from carrying on by virtue of a restrictive covenant in his own contract of employment,[4] similarly, an attempt to avoid an action for specific performance of a contract for the sale of land by transferring the property to a company which had been set up for the purpose, was unsuccessful.[5] Where the shareholder had used a series of companies for the purpose of concealing his criminal activities and perpetrating serious frauds on the Revenue Commissioners the court was also prepared to lift the veil of incorporation.[6] A failure on the part of the directors to effect compulsory insurance on behalf of the company will not result in the imposition of civil liability,[7] similarly, mere mismanagement or incompetence will not, however, entitle the court to look behind the corporate façade,[8] although incompetence which, amounts to recklessness may attract personal liability under CA 1963, s 297A.

1 *Cummings v Stewart* [1911] 1 IR 236; *Mastertrade (Exports) Ltd v Phelan* (4 December 2001, unreported) HC (Murphy J); *Gilford Motor Co Ltd v Horne* [1933] Ch 939; *Jones v Lipman* [1962] 1 All ER 442; *Merchandise Transport Ltd v British Transport Commission* [1962] 2 QB 173; *Re A Company* [1985] BCLC 333; *Alec Lobb (Garages) Ltd v Total Oil (Great Britain) Ltd* [1985] 1 WLR 173; *Creasey v Breachwood Motors Ltd* [1993] BCLC 480; *Ord v Belhaven Pubs Ltd* [1998] 2 BCLC 447; *Trustor AB v Smallbone* [2001] 2 BCLC 436; *Albert Locke (1940) Ltd v Winsford Urban District Council* (1973) 71 LGR 308. The veil of incorporation will not, however, be lifted where the company has been formed for the purpose of avoiding future or prospective legal liabilities: *Adams v Cape Industries plc* [1990] Ch 433. See also *Roundabout Ltd v Beirne* [1959] IR 423.

2 *Cummings v Stewart* [1911] 1 IR 236.

3 *Creasey v Breachwood Motors Ltd* [1993] BCLC 480. cf *Ord v Belhaven Pubs Ltd* [1998] 2 BCLC 447.

4 *Gilford Motor Co Ltd v Horne* [1933] Ch 939.

5 *Jones v Lipman* [1962] 1 All ER 442. Notably, in both this case and *Gilford Motor Co Ltd v Horne* [1933] Ch 939, the court made orders not only against the corporator but also against the company itself, thereby implicitly recognising the validity of the companies' incorporation.

6 *Re H* [1996] 2 All ER 391.

7 *Richardson v Pitt-Stanley* [1995] 1 All ER 460.

8 *Ellis v Nolan* (6 May 1983, unreported) HC (McWilliam J); *Dublin County Council v Elton Homes Ltd* [1984] ILRM 297; *Dublin County Council v O'Riordan* [1986] ILRM 104; *Dun Laoghaire Corporation v Parkhill Developments Ltd* [1989] IR 447.

Exercise of judicial discretion: In other instances, the courts have availed of a discretion conferred upon them by a particular statute or by the Rules of Court in order to look behind the corporate facade.[1] In one case[2] for example, the court exercised its discretion under a provision, similar to CA 1963, s 204 to grant relief against the compulsory purchase of a member's shares in a take-over where the bidder company was no more than a 'hollow sham' which had been established by the majority shareholders in the target company for the specific purpose of expropriating the minority. Similarly, where legislation prohibited public hauliers from carrying their own goods and also prohibited private hauliers from carrying the goods of others, the court upheld the exercise by the licensing authority of its statutory discretion to refuse a haulier's licence. The applicant was the subsidiary of a manufacturing company and had acquired its parents existing fleet of trucks with the clear objective of carrying its parent's goods on outward journeys and carrying the goods of others on return journeys. The court clearly viewed the actions of the subsidiary in establishing the subsidiary as a subterfuge aimed at circumvent in the restriction on private haulier's carrying third parties' goods.[3] More recently, the courts have relied on the 'polluter pays' principle, which underlies the Waste Management Act 1996 and the European Directives which it implements, to look behind the corporate façade and to fix the directors/shareholders with personal liability in circumstances where the company does not have the financial wherewithal to make the payment itself.[4]

In another instance, the court exercised its inherent jurisdiction to grant a stay of execution of a judgment against a company until the parent company's claim against the judgment creditor had been determined.[5]

A not uncommon experience in practice is for a plaintiff to obtain judgment against a company, only to find that the company is hopelessly insolvent. In England, the court has a statutory discretion to award 'wasted costs' incurred by a party as a result of the conduct of that party's legal or other representative. Relying on this statutory discretion, the court has awarded costs personally against the director of an insolvent company who improperly caused the company to defend a claim and to prosecute a bogus counterclaim.[6] It remains to be seen as to whether or not an Irish court would regard itself as having a similar inherent jurisdiction.

1 *Re Bugle Press Ltd* [1961] Ch 270; *Merchandise Transport Ltd v British Transport Commission* [1962] 2 QB 173; *Chemical Bank Ltd v Peter McCormack* [1983] ILRM 350; *Esso Standard (Inter-America) Inc v JW Enterprises Inc* (1963) 37 DLR (2d) 598; *Burnet v Francis Industries plc* [1987] 1 WLR 802. Cf *Re Tecnion Investments Ltd* [1985] BCLC 434.

2 *Re Bugle Press Ltd* [1961] Ch 270.

3 *Merchandise Transport Ltd v British Transport Commission* [1962] 2 QB 173.

4 *Wicklow Co Co v Fenton (No 2)* [2002] 4 IR 44; *Laois Co Co v Scully* [2006] 2 IR 292.

5 *Burnet v Francis Industries plc* [1987] 1 WLR 802.

6 *H Leverton Ltd v Crawford Offshore (Exploration) Services Ltd* (1996) TLR 663.

Group companies – single economic entity: Finally, there is some authority for the proposition that the court may treat two or more companies within a group as a single entity so as to render one company liable for the debts and liabilities of the other in circumstances where this conforms to the 'economic and commercial realities of the situation' and the 'justice of the case so requires.'[1] Although the entitlement of the Irish courts to lift the veil on 'just and equitable' grounds has been described in one recent case as being a 'well established' principle of law,[2] there is also a line of UK authority to the contrary.[3] Indeed, the proposition that the veil of incorporation could be lifted so as to treat two companies as one and impose general liability on one company for the debts of another simply because they are part of the same economic entity, has been recently described by both the High Court and the Supreme Court as being 'so fundamentally at variance with the principle of separate corporate legal personality laid down in *Saloman v Saloman and Co Ltd*[4] and the concept of limited liability that it is wholly unstateable'.[5] Notwithstanding these observations, the Irish legislature has seen fit to allow for the lifting of the veil of incorporation on related companies in some limited circumstances. In particular, CA 1990 allows for one company to be rendered liable for the debts of a related company in circumstances where it is 'just and equitable' to do so,[6] as well as allowing for the pooling of the assets of related companies on similar grounds where both are being wound up.[7]

In so far as judicial veil lifting is concerned, this should take place only where there is a factual identification of the affairs of the acts of one body corporate with another,[8] as where the parties themselves have treated the two companies as being one and the same[9] or where the corporators have ignored the formalities required by the Companies Acts and have in essence operated the two businesses as one.[10] However, the veil of incorporation will not be lifted simply because the two companies have a similar management team[11] or because they operate out of the same premises[12] or because one company gratuitously pays certain debts of the other in circumstances where that latter company is in financial difficulties.[13] Nor will the court be justified in piercing the corporate veil simply because a subsidiary is incorporated a subsidiary to undertake future business and to thereby reduce the parent's potential for future tortious liability.[14]

Whatever the entitlement of an outsider to have the veil of incorporation lifted as against the company, it will not normally be permissible for the company itself to seek to have its own veil of incorporation lifted.[15] As Finlay P stated in *Gresham Industries Ltd v Cannon*:[16]

> 'It seems to me ... a fundamental principle of the law that if a person decides to obtain and use the benefit of trading through limited liability companies ... he cannot subsequently be heard to ignore the existence of the legal entities consisting of different companies and to look upon the entire transaction as a personal one.'

On the other hand, the companies themselves may be entitled to have the veil of incorporation lifted on themselves where the other party to the relevant transaction has himself at all material times treated the two companies as one.[17] Moreover, even though it is effectively lifting the veil on its own group structure, a parent company may be entitled to sue for damages in respect of a loss suffered by its wholly owned subsidiary, in that every €1 loss suffered by the subsidiary will result in a €1 loss to the balance sheet or profits of that parent.[18]

Furthermore, even if the court is not prepared to lift the veil of incorporation and treat two related companies as one, the facts may be such as to point to an agency between the two companies,[19] even though such an agency does not automatically arise by virtue of two companies being connected.[20] Factors that the court will look at in determining whether or not one company is the agent of the other, include the following: whether the first company is effectively and constantly controlled by the second and whether the profits of the first company are treated as being the profits of the second, without the need for a formal declaration of dividends by the first.[21]

1 *DHN Ltd v Tower Hamlets London Borough Council* [1976] 3 All ER 462; *Power Supermarkets Ltd v Crumlin Investments Ltd* (22 June 1981, unreported) HC (Costello J); *Re Bray Travel and Bray Travel (Holdings) Ltd* (13 July 1981, ex tempore) SC noted by Keane at p 121; *State (McInerney and Co Ltd) v Dublin County Council* [1985] ILRM 513; *Albert De Bary and Co NV v TF O'Mullane* (2 June 1992, unreported) HC (Barron J).

2 *Lac Minerals Ltd v Chevron Mineral Corporation of Ireland* [1995] 1 ILRM 161, 187 (per Murphy J). Cf the comments of Laffoy J in *Allied Irish Coal Supplies Ltd v Powell Duffryn International Ltd* [1997] 1 ILRM 306.

3 *Woolfson v Strathclyde Regional Council* 1978 SC 90; *Bank of Tokyo Ltd v Karoon* [1987] AC 45; *National Dock Labour Board v Pinn and Wheeler Ltd* [1989] BCLC 647; *Adams v Cape Industries plc* [1990] Ch 433; *Re Polly Peck International plc* [1996] 2 All ER 433. Of these cases, the leading decision is that of the Court of Appeal in *Adams v Cape Industries plc* where the court, having reviewed the earlier authorities in some detail, went on to conclude that:

'... save in cases which turn on the wording of particular statutes or contracts, the court is not free to disregard the principle of *Saloman v Saloman and Co Ltd* [1897] AC 22 merely because it considers that justice so requires. Our law, for better or for worse, recognises the creation of subsidiary companies, which though in one sense the creature of their parent companies, will nevertheless under the general law fall to be treated as separate legal entities with all the rights and liabilities which would normally attach to separate legal entities'. (See [1990] Ch 433 at 536.)

4 *Saloman v Saloman and Co Ltd* [1897] AC 22.

5 *Allied Irish Coal Supplies Ltd v Powell Duffryn International Fuels Ltd* [1998] 2 IR 519.

6 CA 1990, s 140.

7 CA 1990, s 141. With regard to both s 141 and s 140 the legislature has expressly stipulated that it will not be just and equitable to lift the veil of incorporation on the company unless it has been responsible for the insolvency of the other related company.

8 *Lac Minerals Ltd v Chevron Mineral Corporation of Ireland* [1995] 1 ILRM 161.

9 *Ibid.*

10 *Power Supermarkets Ltd v Crumlin Investments Ltd* (22 June 1981, unreported) HC (Costello J).

11 *Rex Pet foods Ltd v Lamb Bros Ltd* [1985] IEHC 65 (Costello J); *National Dock Labour Board v Pinn and Wheeler Ltd* [1989] BCLC 647; *The Queen v Waverley Construction Ltd* (1973) DLR (3d) 224.

12 *Ibid.*

13 *Rex Pet Foods Ltd v Lamb Bros (Dublin) Ltd* [1985] IEHC 65 (Costello J).

14 *Adams v Cape Industries plc* [1990] Ch 433.

15 *State (Thomas McInerney and Co Ltd) v Dublin County Council* [1985] ILRM 513; *Gresham Industries Ltd (In Liquidation) v Cannon* (2 July 1980, unreported) HC (Finlay P).

16 *Gresham Industries Ltd v Cannon* (2 July 1980, unreported) HC. Cf *Munton Bros Ltd v Secretary of State* [1983] NI 369 where Gibson LJ stated, obiter that if the 'justice' of the case so requires, members of a group of companies may themselves be entitled to apply to have the veil of incorporation lifted.

17 *Lac Minerals Ltd v Chevron Mineral Corporation of Ireland* [1995] 1 ILRM 161.

18 *George Fischer (Great Britain) Ltd v Multi Construction Ltd* [1995] 1 BCLC 260.

19 *Smith, Stone and Knight Ltd v Birmingham Corporation* [1939] 4 All ER 116; *Re FG (Films) Ltd* [1953] 1 WLR 483; *Firestone Tyre and Rubber Co Ltd v Llewellin* [1957] 1 WLR 464.

20 *Ebbw Vale Urban District Council v South Wales Traffic Area Licensing Authority* [1951] 2 KB 366, 370.

21 *Smith Stone and Knight Ltd v Birmingham Corporation* [1939] 4 All ER 116.

Tortious liability of company's agents: While a director of a company is not automatically to be identified with his company for the purpose of the law of tort, however small the company may be and however powerful his control over its affairs, there may be circumstances where the imposition of personal liability in tort may be warranted.[1] For example, if he specifically procures or directs the commission of the tort he may be personally liable for the damage flowing from it.[2]

Where the tort is that of deceit the court will be much more willing to find that the culpable director is personally liable along with the company as a joint tortfeasor.[3]

In the realm of negligent misstatement it has been held[4] that in order to fix a director with personal liability, it must be shown that he assumed personal responsibility for the statements made on behalf of the company. Having regard to the importance of the status of limited liability, the director is only to be held personally liable if the plaintiffs can establish some special circumstances setting the case apart from the ordinary; and in the case of a one-man company particular vigilance is needed, lest the protection of incorporation be virtually nullified. But once such special circumstances are established, the fact of incorporation, even in the case of a one-man company, does not preclude the establishment of personal liability. In each case the decision is one of fact and degree.[5] However, in order to find the director personally liable there is no requirement for the director and the plaintiff to have had personal dealings.[6]

Finally, as has already been noted above, it is possible for a director or other agent to be found liable for the tort of conspiring with his company.[7]

1 *C Evans and Sons Ltd v Spritebrand Ltd* [1985] 1 WLR 317.

2 *Wah Tat Bank v Chan Cheung Kum* [1975] AC 507; *Performing Right Society Ltd v Ciryl Theatrical Syndicate Ltd* [1924] 1 KB 1; *Fairline Shipping Corp v Adamson* [1974] 2 All ER 967; *Shinkwin v Quin-Con Ltd* [2001] 1 IR 514; *MCA Records Inc v Charly Records Ltd* [2003] 1 BCLC 93.

3 *Trustor AB v Smallbone* [2001] 2 BCLC 436; *Standard Chartered Bank v Pakistan National Shipping Corp* [2003] 1 BCLC 244.

4 *Williams v Natural Life Health Foods Ltd* [1998] 2 All ER 577; *Henderson v Merrett Syndicates Ltd* [1995] 2 AC 145; *Trevor Ivory v Anderson* [1992] 2 NZLR 517.

5 *Ibid.*

6 *Ibid.*

7 *Taylor v Smyth* [1991] IR 142.

Imposition of personal liability under Companies Acts: Under the Companies Acts, personal liability may be imposed in various circumstances, including the following:[1] where the number of members is reduced below the statutory minimum;[2] where the company's name is incorrectly stated on bills of exchange, promissory notes, cheques or orders for money or goods;[3] where the memorandum of association provides for directors with unlimited liability;[4] where a person acts in breach of a restriction order or disqualification;[5] where a person involved in the management of a company acts on the directions of another person who is himself subject to a restriction order or disqualification order;[6] where there has been a failure to meet the capital requirements for a company whose director, secretary or promoter is subject to a restriction order;[7] where there has been a failure to keep proper books of account for the company;[8] where the company, although in a members' voluntary winding up, is in fact insolvent and the directors did not have reasonable grounds for believing that the declaration of solvency was accurate;[9] and where those involved in the management of the company have been guilty of fraudulent or reckless trading.[10] Similarly, under the Rules of the Superior Courts, where a company has been guilty of contempt of court, the court may not only sequestrate the assets of the company but may also attach and commit the directors or other officers and sequestrate their personal property.[11]

1 For a general discussion of statutory 'veil lifting' see MacCann, 'Personal liability for Corporate Debts' (1991) 9 ILT 206 and 232 and Courtney, '*The Law of Private Companies*' (2nd edn, Tottel Publishing, 2002) Ch 5.

2 CA 1963, s 36. This provision is, however, disapplied in the case of single-member companies: EC(SMPLC)R 1994, reg 7 (SI 275/1994).

3 CA 1963, s 114(4).

4 CA 1963, ss 197 and 198.

5 CA 1990, s 163.

6 CA 1990, s 165.

7 CA 1990, s 163(4).

8 CA 1990, s 204.

9 CA 1963, s 256(8).

10 CA 1963, s 297A.

11 Order 42, rule 32. *Phonographic Performance Ltd v Amusement Caterers (Peckham) Ltd* [1963] 3 All ER 493. It should be noted, however, that the remedy of attachment lies only against the directors and officers and not against persons who are only shareholders: *Northern Counties Securities Ltd v Jackson and Steeple Ltd* [1974] 2 All ER 625. See generally Courtney, *The Law of Private Companies* (2nd edn, Tottel Publishing, 2002) at para 6.088 *et seq.*

Imposition of personal liability under Companies Acts: Personal liability may be imposed on directors and/or shareholders pursuant to provisions of legislation other than the Companies Acts, for wrongs committed by the company. For example, under the 'polluter pays' principles of the

Planning Acts, personal liability may be imposed on the directors of a company for corporate pollution.[1]

1 *Wicklow County Council v Fenton (No 2)* [2002] 4 IR 44; *Laois County Council v Scully* [2006] 2 IR 292.

UK legislation

See CA 1985, s 13(1)-(4) (amended by IA 1986, s 439(1), Sch 13, Pt I.

---

19 Conclusiveness of certificate of incorporation

[...][a]

Amendments

a CA 1963, s 19 repealed by C(A)A 1983, Sch 3.

---

20 Registration of unlimited company as limited

(1) Subject to the provisions of this section, a company registered as unlimited may register under this Act as limited, or a company already registered as a limited company may re-register under this Act, but the registration of an unlimited company as a limited company shall not affect the rights or liabilities of the company in respect of any debt or obligation incurred, or any contract entered into by, to, with or on behalf of the company before the registration, and those rights or liabilities may be enforced in manner provided by Part IX of this Act in the case of a company registered in pursuance of that Part.

(2) On registration in pursuance of this section, the registrar shall close the former registration of the company, and may dispense with the delivery to him of copies of any documents with copies of which he was furnished on the occasion of the original registration of the company, but, save as aforesaid, the registration shall take place in the same manner and have effect as if it were the first registration of the company under this Act, and as if the provisions of the Acts under which the company was previously registered and regulated had been contained in different Acts from those under which the company is registered as a limited company.

Definitions

'company': CA 1963, s 2(1); 'document': CA 1963, s 2(1): 'an unlimited company': CA 1963, s 2 (1), s 5(2)(c).

Notes

Since 13 October 1983,[1] CA 1963, s 20 has ceased to have effect and unlimited companies can no longer re-register pursuant to this section.[2] Instead, re-registration must now takes place pursuant to C(A)A 1983, s 53 which provides that the re-registration of an unlimited company as a limited company must first be authorised by a special resolution of the members.[3]

1 'the appointed day': C(A) A 1983, s 2(1).; Companies (Amendment) Act 1983 (Commencement) Order 1983 (SI 288/1983).

2 C(A)A 1983, s 54.

3 On the liability of members of a formerly unlimited company in the event of liquidation, see C(A)A 1983, s 53(7).

Provisions relating to Names of Companies

21 Prohibition of registration of companies by undesirable names

No company shall be registered by a name which, in the opinion of the [registrar of companies][a], is undesirable but an appeal shall lie to the court against a refusal to register.

Amendments

a The words 'registrar of companies' substituted for 'Minister' by CLEA 2001, s 86.

1 With effect from 1 October 2001; Company Law Enforcement Act 2001 (Commencement) (No 2) Order 2001 (SI 438/2001).

Cross reference

See IFCMPA 2005, ss 59 and 60 and notes thereto.

Definitions

'company': CA 1963, s 2(1); 'the court': CA 1963, s 2(1); 'the registrar of companies': CA 1963, s 2(1).

Notes

Undesirable names: Since 1 October 2001 it is the responsibility of the Registrar to determine what is an undesirable name for a company.[1] In particular, a name will not be registered if:

(a) it is identical to a name already appearing or which has appeared on the register of companies in the previous 20 years;[2]

(b) in the opinion of the Registrar, it is offensive;

(c) it would suggest State sponsorship;

(d) the name includes 'bank' or cognate words, unless permission has been given by the Financial Regulator;

(e) the name includes the word 'insurance' or cognate words unless permission has been given by the Department of Enterprise, Trade and Employment;

(f) the name includes the words 'society', 'Co-Op' or 'Co-Operative' unless permission has been given by the Registrar of Friendly Societies; and

(g) the name includes the word 'university' unless permission has been given by the Department of Education.

Where a company has been dissolved[3] and wishes to have its name restored to the register,[4] but another company has in the meantime been registered with the same name, the court will only make the order of restoration on the undertaking of the petitioner to change the restored company's name and not to carry on any business until the change of name has been effected.[5]

1 CLEA 2001, s 86; Company Law Enforcement Act 2001 (Commencement) (No 2) Order 2001 (SI 438/2001). See also http://www.cro.ie for guidance in this regard.

2 Associated companies may, however, be registered with similar names: *Irish Permanent Building Society v Cauldwell* [1981] ILRM 240.

3 For the circumstances in which a company may be dissolved, see CA 1963, ss 249, 263, 273 and 311, and C(A)A 1982, s 12.

4 Eg pursuant to CA 1963, s 310 or C(A)A 1982, s 12.

5 *Re Repton Foundry Ltd* (1942) 86, Sol Jo 331.

Injunction to restrain use of similar names: If a company is about to register under a name which is so similar to that of an existing business as to be calculated to deceive,[1] the court may grant an injunction restraining registration even though the plaintiff's business is not operated by a registered company.[2] Likewise, even though the Registrar has already registered the new company, the court may still grant an injunction restraining the company from carrying on business under its corporate name, where it is shown that the name of the new company is calculated to deceive or cause confusion.[3] In appropriate cases, however, the court will suspend the operation of the injunction for sufficient time to enable the company to change its name to one which is not deceptive.[4]

In deciding whether a name is likely to deceive the court should consider: (1) the respective businesses of the old company and the new company; and (2) the name of the old company. Moreover, the court will not restrain the use of a word which is in ordinary use in the English or Irish language and which is descriptive only.[5]

1 A name may be calculated, though not intended, to deceive: *Manchester Brewery v North Cheshire and Manchester Brewery* [1898] 1 Ch 539; aff'd [1899] AC 83.

2 *Hendriks v Montagu* (1881) 17 Ch D 638; *Tussaud v Tussaud* (1890) 44 Ch D 678; *Ewing v Buttercup Margarine Co* [1917] Ch 1; *Waring and Gillow Ltd v Gillow and Gillow Ltd* (1916) 32 TLR 389.

3 *Merchant Banking Co of London v Merchants' Joint Stock Bank* (1878) 9 Ch D 560; *Guardian Fire and Life Assurance Co v Guardian and General Insurance Co* (1880) 50 LJ (Ch) 253; *Accident Insurance Co v Accident Disease and General Insurance Corporation* (1884) 54 LJ (Ch) 104; *Standard Bank of South Africa v Standard Bank* (1909) 25 TLR 420; *Ewing v Buttercup Margarine Co* [1917] Ch 1; *Waring and Gillow Ltd v Gillow and Gillow Ltd* (1916) 32 TLR 389; *Heels v Stafford Heels Ltd* (1927) 44 RPC 299; *Heppells Ltd v Eppels Ltd* (1928) 46 RPC 96; *Madeira House Co Ltd v Madeira House (London) Ltd* (1930) 47 RPC 481; *Sturtevant Engineering Co Ltd v Sturtevant Mill Co of USA Ltd* [1936] 3 All ER 137; *Music Corporation of America v Music Corporation (Great Britain) Ltd* (1946) 64 RPC 41; *Exxon Corporation v Exxon Insurance Consultants International Ltd* [1982] Ch 119. And the fact that the plaintiff is a foreign company without any branch or establishment in the State will not prevent the court from restraining an Irish company from operating under a name which is calculated to deceive: *S Ades Anciens Etablissments Panhard et Levassor v Levassor Motor Co* [1901] 2 Ch 513.

4 *FW Woolworth and Co Ltd v Woolworths (Australia) Ltd* (1930) 47 RPC 337; *British Legion v British Legion Club (Street) Ltd* (1931) 47 TLR 571.

5 *Aerators Ltd v Tolitt* [1902] 2 Ch 319; *British Vacuum Cleaner Co Ltd v New Vacuum Cleaner Co Ltd* [1907] 2 Ch 312.

Power of Registrar to require change of name: As to the power of the Registrar to compel a company to change its corporate name, see CA 1963, s 23(2).

UK legislation

See generally CA 1985, s 26; Companies (Audit, Investigations and Community Enterprise) Act 2004, s 33(6), Sch 6, paras 1, 2(1), (2)(a); Open-Ended Investment Companies Regulations 2001(2001/1228), reg 84, Sch 7, Pt I, para 3(1),(2); Open-Ended Investment Companies (Investment Companies with Variable Capital) Regulations 1996 (SI 1996/2827), reg 75, Sch 8, para 4(a).

---

22 Registration of business name

(1) Every company carrying on business under a name other than its corporate name shall register in the manner directed by law for the registration of business names.

[(2) The use of the abbreviation 'Ltd.' for 'Limited' or 'Teo.' for 'Teoranta' or 'p.l.c.' for 'public limited company' or 'c.p.t.' for 'cuideachta phoiblí theoranta' shall not of itself render such registration necessary.][a]

Amendments

a CA 1963, s 22(2) substituted by C(A)A 1983, Sch 1, para 4. With effect from 13 October 1983; Companies (Amendment) Act 1983 (Commencement) Order 1983 (SI 288/1983).

Definitions

'company': CA 1963, s 2(1).

Notes

Registration of business names: Registration of a business name is effected pursuant to the Registration of Business Names Act 1963.

[1] See generally Companies Registration Office, 'Business Name Registration'; September 2005, Information Leaflet No. 14.

23 Change of name

(1) A company may, by special resolution and with the approval of the [registrar of companies][a] signified in writing, change its name.

(2) If, through inadvertence or otherwise, a company on its first registration, or on its registration by a new name, is registered by a name which, in the opinion of the [registrar of companies],[a] is too like the name by which a company in existence is already registered, the firstmentioned company may change its name with the sanction of the [registrar of companies][a] and, if he so directs within 6 months of its being registered by that name, shall change it within a period of 6 weeks from the date of the direction or such longer period as the [registrar of companies][a] may think fit to allow.

If a company makes default in complying with a direction under this subsection, it shall be liable to a fine not exceeding [€1,904.61].[b]

(3) Where a company changes its name under this section, the registrar shall enter the new name in the register in place of the former name, and shall issue a certificate of incorporation altered to meet the circumstances of the case.

(4) A change of name by a company under this section shall not affect any rights or obligations of the company, or render defective any legal proceedings by or against the company, and any legal proceedings which might have been continued or commenced against it by its former name may be continued or commenced against it by its new name.

(5) A company which was registered by a name specified by statute, may, notwithstanding anything contained in that statute, change its name in accordance with subsection (1), [but if the registrar of companies is of opinion that any Minister][c] is concerned in the administration of the statute which specified the name of the company he shall not approve of the change of name save after consultation with [that Minister].[c]

(6) Where the winding up of a company commences within one year after the company has changed its name, the former name as well as the existing name of the company shall appear on all notices and advertisements in relation to the winding up.

[(7) Summary proceedings in relation to an offence under subsection (2) may be brought and prosecuted by the registrar of companies.][d]

Amendments

a In CA 1963, s 23(1) and (2) 'registrar of companies' substituted for 'Minister' wherever occurring by CLEA 2001, s 87(a).

b '£500' substituted for '£100' by C(A)A 1982, Sch 1, increased to £1,500 by CA 1990, s 240(7), as inserted by CLEA 2001, s 104(c), and converted to €1,904.61 by Council Regulations (EC) No 1103/97, No 974/98 and No 2866/98 and the Economic and Monetary Union Act 1998, s 6.

c In CA 1963, s 23(5); 'but if the registrar of companies is of opinion that any Minister' and 'that Minister' substituted for 'but if the Minister is of opinion that any other Minister' and 'that other Minister' respectively by CLEA 2001, s 87(b).

d CA 1963, s 23(7) inserted by CLEA 2001, s 87(c).

Definitions

'company': CA 1963, s 2(1); 'the registrar of companies': CA 1963, s 2(1).

Notes

Companies with similar names: Although the Registrar is empowered to require a company to change its name where it is too like that of an existing company, he will not normally impose such a requirement where the two companies are associated. Indeed, in practice where an existence company wishes to form a subsidiary with a similar name, the Registrar will accept a letter confirming the association.[1] It has been held in the United Kingdom[2] that the court does not have jurisdiction, under analogous provisions contained in CA 1985,[3] to change the name of a company where no special resolution of the company has been passed to that effect.

Notably, there is a time limit of six months from the date of registration within which the Registrar can demand a name change pursuant to CA 1963, s 23(2). Thereafter, any order requiring the name of the company to be changed will have to be obtained from the court on the application of the other company and on the ground that the name of the new company is calculated to deceive.[4]

1 *Irish Permanent Building Society v Cauldwell* [1981] ILRM 240.

2 *Halifax plc and ors v Halifax Repossessions Ltd and ors* [2004] 2 BCLC 455.

3 CA 1985, s 28(1)

4 See the notes to CA 1963, s 21.

Company cannot change to an undesirable name: Although a company may avail of the procedure laid down in CA 1963, s 23 to change its name, it will be precluded from changing to an 'undesirable' name.[1]

1 See CA 1963, s 21.

Effect of change of name: Once a company changes its name, it is issued with a new certificate of incorporation.[1] However, the company is not formed anew: it is still the same corporate body that existed before the change of name, with the same rights and liabilities as before[2], so that its date of incorporation is still deemed to be the date upon which its first certificate of incorporation was issued.[3]

In civil litigation the name of the defendant company must be amended in the title of the proceedings once the plaintiff learns of the change of name, but the amendment may be made as of right so that the leave of the court will be given as a matter of course.[4]

1 CA 1963, s 23(3).

[2] CA 1963, s 23(4).

[3] *Oshkosh B'Gosh Inc v Dan Marbel Inc Ltd* [1989] BCLC 507; *Cross v Aurora Group Ltd* (1988) 4 NZCLC 64,909.

[4] *Mitchell v Harris Engineering Co Ltd* [1967] 2 QB 703.

UK legislation

See CA 1985, s 28(1), (2) and (4).

---

24 Power to dispense with 'limited' or 'teoranta' in name of charitable and other companies

[(1) A company shall, notwithstanding its registration as a company with limited liability, be exempt from the provisions of this Act relating to the use of the word 'limited' or 'teoranta' as part of its name and the publishing of its name, but shall enjoy all the privileges and shall (subject to this section) be subject to all the obligations of limited companies, where—

(a) its objects are the promotion of commerce, art, science, education, religion, charity or any other prescribed object, and

(b) its memorandum or articles of association—

(i) require its profits (if any) or other income to be applied to the promotion of its objects,

(ii) prohibit the payment of dividends to its members, and

(iii) require all the assets which would otherwise be available to its members to be transferred on its winding up to another company whose objects comply with paragraph (a) and which meets the requirements of this paragraph, and

(c) a director or secretary of the company (or, in the case of an association about to be formed as a limited company, one of the persons who are to be the first directors or the person who is to be the first secretary of the company) has delivered to the registrar of companies a statutory declaration in the prescribed form that the company complies or, where applicable, will comply with the requirements of paragraphs (a) and (b).

(2) The registrar shall refuse to register as a limited company any association about to be formed as a limited company by a name which does not include the word 'limited' or 'teoranta' unless a declaration as provided for under subsection (1)(c) has been delivered to the registrar.

(3) An application by a company registered as a limited company for a change of name including or consisting of the omission of the word 'limited' or 'teoranta' shall be made in accordance with section 23 and the registrar shall refuse to grant the application unless a declaration as provided for under subsection (1)(c) has been delivered to the registrar.

(4) A company which is exempt under subsection (1) and whose name does not include the word 'limited' or 'teoranta' shall not alter its memorandum or articles of association so that it ceases to comply with the requirements of that subsection.

(5) If it appears to the registrar that a company which is registered under a name not including the word 'limited' or 'teoranta'—

(a) has carried on any business other than the promotion of any of the objects mentioned in subsection (1)(a),

(b) has applied any of its profits or other income otherwise than in promoting such objects, or

(c) has paid a dividend to any of its members,

the registrar may, in writing, direct the company to change its name within such period as may be specified in the direction so that its name ends with the word 'limited' or 'teoranta', and the change of name shall be made in accordance with section 23.

(6) A company which has received a direction under subsection (5) shall not thereafter be registered by a name which does not include the word 'limited' or 'teoranta' without the approval of the registrar.

(7) A person who—

(a) provides incorrect, false or misleading information in a statutory declaration under subsection (1)(c),

(b) alters its memorandum or articles of association in contravention of subsection (4), or

(c) fails to comply with a direction from the registrar under subsection (5),

shall be guilty of an offence.

(8) Summary proceedings in relation to an offence under subsection (7) may be brought and prosecuted by the registrar of companies.][a].

Amendments

a CA 1963, s 24 has been repealed and substituted by CLEA 2001, s 88 with effect from 1 March 2002.[1]

1 Company Law Enforcement Act 2001 (Commencement) (No 3) Order 2001 (SI 523/2001).

Definitions

'articles': CA 1963, s 2(1); 'company': CA 1963, s 2(1); 'director': CA 1963, s 2(1); 'document': CA 1963, s 2(1); 'member': CA 1963, s 31; 'memorandum': CA 1963, s 2(1); 'the registrar of companies': CA 1963, s 2(1).

Notes

Exemption from use of 'limited': Under the original CA 1963, s 24 a company of the type described in subsection (1) which wished to be exempted from the requirement to have 'limited' or 'teoranta' or the relevant abbreviation thereof at the end of its name had to apply for a licence to that effect from the Minister for Enterprise, Trade and Employment. Whilst existing licences remain valid,[1] exemption is now automatic for such a company where on first registration[2] or on applying for a change of name,[3] one of the directors or the secretary delivers a statutory declaration in the prescribed form[4] confirming the company's compliance with the requirements of CA 1963, s 24(1)(a) and (b).

A company benefiting from this exemption may not alter its memorandum or articles of association so that it no longer complies with CA 1963 s 24(1)(a) and (b).[5] In this regard, if it appears to the Registrar that the company is engaging in a non-qualifying activity[6] or applying its income or profits for a non-qualifying activity[7] or paying a dividend to members[8] he may direct it to include 'limited' or 'teoranta' at the end of its name.[9]

1 CLEA 2001, s 88(2).

[2] CA 1963, s 24(2). See generally Companies Registration Office, 'Exemption From Use of 'Limited'/'Teoranta' as Part of Company Name', June 2006, Information Leaflet No. 24.

[3] CA 1963, s 24(3). See generally Companies Registration Office, 'Exemption From Use of 'Limited'/'Teoranta' as Part of Company Name', June 2006, Information Leaflet No. 24.

[4] See the Companies Act 1963 (Section 24) Regulations 2001 (SI 571/2001), which prescribes Form G5, 'Statutory Declaration of Compliance' for the purposes of CA 1963, s 24.

[5] CA 1963, s 24(4).

[6] CA 1963, s 23 (5)(a).

[7] CA 1963, s 23 (5)(b).

[8] CA 1963, s 23 (5)(c).

[9] CA 1963, s 24 (6).

Letterheads: Every company which is exempt from the obligation to use the word 'limited' or teoranta' at the end of its name, must state on all its letters and order forms that it is a limited company.[1]

[1] EC(C)R 1973, (SI 163/1973) reg 9(1)(c), as amended by EC(C)(A)R 2007 (SI 49/2007).

UK legislation

See CA 1985, s 30; Companies Act 1985 (Electronic Communications) Order 2000 (SI 2000/3373), arts 2(a)–(b), 3 and 5(1); Companies (Audit, Investigations and Community Enterprise) Act 2004, s 33(6), Sch 6, paras 1 and 4.

See also CA 1985, s 31.

General provisions relating to memorandum and articles

25 Effect of memorandum and articles

(1) Subject to the provisions of this Act, the memorandum and articles shall, when registered, bind the company and the members thereof to the same extent as if they respectively had been signed and sealed by each member, and contained covenants by each member to observe all the provisions of the memorandum and of the articles.

(2) All money payable by any member to the company under the memorandum or articles shall be a debt due from him to the company.

(3) An action to recover a debt created by this section shall not be brought after the expiration of 12 years from the date on which the cause of action accrued.

Definitions

'articles': CA 1963, s 2(1); 'company': CA 1963, s 2(1); 'member': CA 1963, s 31; 'memorandum': CA 1963, s 2(1).

Notes

Statutory contract: Upon registration, the memorandum and articles take on the status of a contract under seal. The contract has been described as being 'of the most sacred character'[1] although it is not unalterable.[2] The parties to the contract are the company and the members. Accordingly, the provisions of such a 'section 25' contract may be enforced by the company against its members and likewise may be enforced by the members against the company.[3] The contract may also be enforced by one member against another.[4] The CA 1963, s 25 contract can, however, only be enforced by a member of the company in respect of rights conferred upon him in his capacity as member and not in respect of rights conferred on him in some other capacity such as director or solicitor.[5] Similarly, the section 25 contract can only be enforced against the member in respect of liabilities and obligations imposed upon him *qua* member and not in respect of liabilities and obligations imposed on him in some other capacity.[6] Nevertheless, as regards rights or obligations conferred on the member by the memorandum or articles otherwise than in his capacity as member, a separate or collateral but non-statutory contract may well be found to exist which is capable of being enforced as between the member and the company.[7] Such a contract is commonly referred to as a special contract.[8]

Section 25 does not give rise to a contract between the company and persons who are not its members[9] although a separate contract may be implied between the company and the third party based upon the terms of the articles, albeit that the terms of such a contract are subject to variation if and when the articles themselves are properly altered.[10]

1 Per Ross J, *Clark v Workman* [1920] 1 IR 107, 112. See, generally Courtney, *The Law of Private of Companies* (2nd edn, Tottel Publishing, 2002) paras 3.096–3.108.

2 The following are the provisions for the alteration of the clauses of the memorandum and articles:
- (i) objects: CA 1963, s 10.
- (ii) name: CA 1963, s 23;
- (iii) alteration to liability of members: CA 1963, s 27;
- (iv) additional clauses: CA 1963, s 28;
- (v) capital: CA 1963, ss 68 and 72;
- (vi) variation of class rights: CA 1963, s 78 and C(A)A 1983, s 38;
- (vii) imposition of personal liability on directors: CA 1963, s 198;
- (viii) schemes of arrangement: CA 1963, ss 201–203;
- (ix) relief of minority oppression: CA 1963, s 205(3);
- (x) amendments to memorandum on re-registration of private company as a plc: C(A)A 1983, s 9(2);
- (xi) amendments to memorandum on re-registration of unlimited company as plc: C(A)A 1983, s 11(2); and
- (xii) amendments to memorandum on re-registration of plc as private company: C(A)A 1983, s 14(2).

3 *Wood v Odessa Waterworks Co* (1889) 42 Ch D 636; *Hickman v Kent or Romney Marsh Sheepbreeders' Association* [1915] 1 Ch 881; *Attorney General for Ireland v Jameson* [1904] 2 IR 644; *Clark v Workman* [1920] 1 IR 107; *Beattie v Beattie* [1938] Ch 708; *Lee and Co (Dublin) Ltd v Egan (Wholesale) Ltd* (27 April 1978, unreported) HC (Kenny J); *Roper v Ward* [1981] ILRM 408, 412; *Kerry Co-Operative Creameries Ltd v An Bord Bainne Co-Operative Ltd* [1990] ILRM 664; *Kerry Co-Operative Creameries Ltd v An Bord Bainne Co-Operative Ltd* [1991] ILRM 851; *Bratton Seymour Service Co Ltd v Oxborough* [1992] BCLC 693, 698; *Bailey v New South Wales Medical Defence Union Ltd* (1996) 18 ACSR 521; *Towcester Racecourse Co Ltd v The Racecourse Association Ltd* [2003] 1 BCLC 260. See generally Courtney, '*The Law of Private Companies*', (2nd edn, Tottel Publishing, 2002) paras 3.096 to 3.108.

4 *Attorney General for Ireland v Jameson* [1904] 2 IR 644; *Rayfield v Hands* [1960] Ch 1; *Lee and Co (Dublin) Ltd v Egan (Wholesale) Ltd* (27 April 1978, unreported) HC (Kenny J). These cases all related to the enforcement of pre-emption rights in the articles. See generally Courtney, *The Law of Private Companies* (2nd edn, Tottel Publishing, 2002) paras 3.096 to 3.108.

5 *Eley v The Positive Government Security Life Assurance Co Ltd* (1876) 1 Ex D 20; *Hickman v Kent or Romney Marsh Sheepbreeders' Association* [1915] 1 Ch 881; *Beattie v Beattie* [1938] Ch 708; *London Sack and Bag Co Ltd v Dixon and Lugton Ltd* [1943] 2 All ER 763; *Bratton Seymour Service Co Ltd v Oxborough* [1992] BCLC 693, 698.

6 *Bailey v New South Wales Medical Defence Union Ltd* (1996) 18 ACSR 521.

7 *Bailey v New South Wales Medical Defence Union Ltd* (1996) 18 ACSR 521.

8 *Bailey v New South Wales Medical Defence Union Ltd* (1996) 18 ACSR 521, para 14.

9 *Browne v La Trinidad* (1887) 37 Ch D 1.

10 *Swabey v Port Darwin Gold Mining Co* (1889) 1 Meg 385; *Re Anglo Austrian and Publishing Union; Isaac's Case* [1892] 2 Ch 158; *Shuttleworth v Cox Bros and Co (Maidenhead) Ltd* [1927] 2 KB 9.

Debts due to member: Any debt due to the member *qua* member pursuant to CA 1963, s 25(2) will rank as a deferred debt in the event of a winding-up, payable after the claims of the ordinary unsecured creditors.[1]

1 CA 1963, s 207(1)(g).

UK legislation

See CA 1985, s 14.

---

26 Provisions as to memorandum and articles of company limited by guarantee

(1) In the case of a company limited by guarantee and not having a share capital, and registered on or after the 1st day of January, 1901, every provision in the memorandum or articles, or in any resolution of the company, purporting to give any person a right to participate in the divisible profits of the company, otherwise than as a member, shall be void.

(2) For the purpose of the provisions of this Act relating to the memorandum of a company limited by guarantee and of this section, every provision in the memorandum or articles, or in any resolution, of a company limited by guarantee and registered on or after the date aforesaid, purporting to divide the undertaking of the company into shares or interests, shall be treated as a provision for a share capital, notwithstanding that the nominal amount or number of the shares or interests is not specified thereby.

Definitions

'articles': CA 1963, s 2(1); 'company': CA 1963, s 2(1); 'a company limited by guarantee': CA 1963, s 2(1), 5(2)(b); 'memorandum': CA 1963, s 2(1); 'share': CA 1963, s 2(1).

Notes

Participation in divisible profits: The scope of CA 1963, s 26(1) appears to be quite far-reaching and, on a literal interpretation, would appear to prohibit the issue of debentures whose interest rates vary with the company's distributable profits.

Companies limited by guarantee and having a share capital: CA 1963, s 25(2) explicitly recognises the validity of companies limited by guarantee and having a share capital, even though such companies are not expressly mentioned in CA 1963, s 5(2). Companies limited by guarantee and having a share capital are something of a hybrid and although permitted by statute, since 13 October 1983 it has only been possible to form such companies as private companies.[1]

1 See C(A)A 1983, s 7 and notes thereto.

UK legislation

See CA 1985, s 15; CC(CP)A 1985, s 10.

---

27 Alterations in memorandum or articles increasing liability to contribute to share capital not to bind existing members without consent

(1) Subject to subsection (2), and notwithstanding anything in the memorandum or articles of a company, no member of the company shall be bound by an alteration made in the memorandum or articles after the date on which he became a member, if and so

far as the alteration requires him to take or subscribe for more shares than the number held by him at the date on which the alteration is made, or in any way increases his liability as at that date to contribute to the share capital of, or otherwise to pay money to, the company.

(2) Subsection (1) shall not apply in any case where the member agrees in writing, either before or after the alteration is made, to be bound thereby.

Definitions

'articles': CA 1963, s 2(1); 'company': CA 1963, s 2(1); 'member': CA 1963, s 31; 'memorandum': CA 1963, s 2(1); 'share': CA 1963, s 2(1).

Notes

Alteration void without written consent: Any such alteration increasing the liability of the member will be void and unenforceable as against him, unless he consents thereto in writing.[1] Thus, an amendment to the articles obliging members to make payments in respect of recurring administrative and maintenance expenses of the company was invalid as against those members who did so agree to the amendment.[2]

1 *Hole v Garnsey* [1930] AC 472; *MacDonald v Normandy Co-Operative* [1923] NZLR 122; *Shalfoon v Cheddar Valley Co-Operative* [1924] NZLR 561; *Hennessy v National Agricultural and Industrial Association* [1947] IR 159.

2 *Ding v Sylvania Waterways Ltd* [1999] NSWSC 58.

Form of written consent: CA 1963, s 26 does not require any particular form of written consent by a member to an alteration in his liability. Presumably, therefore, the consent could be in the form of a letter to the company or a resolution which has been signed by all the members. Furthermore, it does not seem necessary that the member need receive any consideration for his agreement to an increase in his liability. Moreover, rather than agreeing to a specific increase in liability, the member could agree to the company altering its constitution so as to permit it to demand contributions at future dates from its members.[1]

1 *Black, White and Grey Cabs Ltd v Reid* [1980] 1 NZLR 40.

Type of increase in liability: The types of increase in liability envisaged by CA 1963, s 27 are not confined to subscriptions for more shares. The increase could, for example, take the form of a resolution empowering the directors to demand monetary contributions to the general funds of the company from time to time.[1]

1 *Black, White and Grey Cabs Ltd v Reid* [1980] 1 NZLR 40; *Ding v Sylvania Waterways Ltd* [1999] NSWSC 58.

UK legislation

See CA 1985, s 16.

---

28 Power to alter provisions in memorandum which could have been contained in articles

(1) Subject to subsection (2) and sections 27 and 205, any provision contained in a company's memorandum which could lawfully have been contained in articles of association instead of in the memorandum may, subject to the provisions of this section, be altered by the company by special resolution.

(2) If an application is made to the court for the alteration to be cancelled, it shall not have effect except in so far as it is confirmed by the court.

(3) This section shall not apply where the memorandum itself provides for or prohibits the alteration of all or any of the said provisions, and shall not authorise any variation or abrogation of the special rights of any class of members.

(4) Subsections (3), (4), (5), (6), [(6A), (6B), (6C),][a] (9) and (10) of section 10 (except paragraph (b) of the said subsection (3)) shall apply in relation to any alteration and to any application made under this section as they apply in relation to alterations and to applications made under that section.

(5) This section shall apply to a company's memorandum whether registered before, on or after the operative date.

Amendments

a The figures '(6A), (6B), (6C)', inserted into CA 1963, s 28 (4) by C(A)A 1983, Sch 1, para 5 with effect from 13 October 1983.[1]

1 Companies (Amendment) Act 1983 (Commencement) Order 1983 (SI 288/1983).

Definitions

'articles': CA 1963, s 2(1); 'company': CA 1963, s 2(1); 'the court': CA 1963, s 2(1); 'member': CA 1963, s 31; 'memorandum': CA 1963, s 2(1); 'the operative date': CA 1963, s 2(1).

Notes

Non-compulsory clauses: CA 1963, s 28 applies to provisions which could have been contained in the articles but which the members have seen fit to include in the memorandum instead. Such provisions might, for example, deal with the appointment of directors for life, or the division of the share capital into different classes.

Alteration of class rights: The procedure for alteration of additional clauses in the memorandum is expressed by CA 1963, s 28(3) not to apply in the case of class rights. Rather, class rights can only be altered by way of a scheme of arrangement pursuant to CA 1963, s 201 or alternatively by following the procedure for the alteration of such rights laid down by CA 1963, s 78 and C(A)A 1983, s 38.

Entrenched rights: Similarly, any provisions contained in the memorandum which could lawfully have been contained in the articles, and which are expressed in the memorandum to be unalterable, cannot be varied pursuant to CA 1963, s 28[1] but can instead only be varied by way of a scheme of arrangement under CA 1963, s 201.[2]

1 See CA 1963, s 28(3).

2 *Re City Property Investment Trust Corporation Ltd, Petitioners*, 1951 SC 570, 1951 SLT 371, Ct of Sess; *re JA Nordberg Ltd* [1951] 2 Ch 439.

Alternative procedure for variation: The statutory procedure for altering non-compulsory clauses in the memorandum will likewise be disapplied if the memorandum itself contains some alternative procedure for alteration. Conceivably, such a procedure could take any form (eg an ordinary resolution, or a resolution of a particular class or classes of members, or indeed a resolution of the board of directors).

Protection of dissentients: CA 1963, s 28(4) expressly incorporates the provisions from CA 1963, s 10 dealing with the protection of dissentient minorities. The application by such a dissentient minority must therefore be brought within 21 days after the date of the passing of the resolution, by dissentients holding not less than 15% of the issued share capital or any class thereof or by dissentients holding not less than 15% of the company's debentures. The objection to the alteration must also be made by the applicants *qua* members or debenture holders, as the case may be, and not in some other capacity (eg as solicitors).[1] The application is brought by way of petition[2] and, apart from being served on the company within three days after being filed in the Central Office,[3] must also be published in such newspapers as the court directs.[4] An application under CA 1963, s 28(2) will only be successful if it can be shown that the alteration of the memorandum was unfair as between the members.[5] Shareholders or debenture holders appearing on the petition and opposing the alteration of the memorandum may be awarded their costs even though the petition is unsuccessful and the alteration is confirmed.[6]

1 *Re Munster and Leinster Bank* [1907] 1 IR 237; *Re Hearts of Oak Life and General Assurance Co* [1920] 1 Ch 544.
2 RSC (1986) Order 75, rule 4(a).
3 RSC (1986) Order 75, rule 20.
4 RSC (1986) Order 75, rule 13.
5 *Re Jewish Colonial Trust* [1908] 2 Ch 287; *Re Cyclists' Touring Club* (1907) 1 Ch 269.
6 *Re Patent Tyre Co* [1923] 2 Ch 222.

Failure of substratum or oppression: Quite apart from the risk of an application by dissentients under CA 1963, s 28(2) the company may run the risk of a winding-up petition under CA 1963, s 205 or s 213(f) if the alteration is oppressive to or in disregard of the interests of the petitioner or if it violates some understanding between the members on the basis of which the company was formed.[1]

1 *Re Murph's Restaurant Ltd* [1979] ILRM 141; *Ebrahimi v Westbourne Galleries Ltd* [1973] AC 360; and *Re Metafile Ltd* [2006] IEHC 407 (Laffoy J).

Conversion of shares into redeemable shares: If the alteration of the memorandum involves the conversion of shares into redeemable shares, the alteration will not bind dissenting shareholders who, before the date of conversion, signify to the company their unwillingness to have their shares converted.[1]

1 CA 1990, s 210.

Delivery of documents to the Registrar and publication in the Companies Registration Office Gazette: The special resolution amending the memorandum and the amended text of the memorandum must be forwarded to the Registrar within 15 days of the passing of such resolution.[1] Pursuant to EC(C) R 1973, reg 4, a company shall also cause to be published[2] in the Companies Registration Office Gazette[3] a notice of delivery of such documents. In practice, it is in fact the Registrar who generally causes such notices to be published in the Companies Registration Office Gazette.

1 CA 1963, s 143(1).
2 Within six weeks of the relevant delivery date; EC(C)R 1973, reg 4(2).
3 Reference to *Iris Oifigiúil* was substituted by reference to the Companies Registration Office Gazette by virtue of EC(C)R 2004, reg 5.

UK legislation

See CA 1985, s 17.

---

29 Copies of memorandum and articles to be given to members

(1) A company shall, on being so required by any member, send to him a copy of the memorandum and of the articles, if any, and a copy of any Act of the Oireachtas which alters the memorandum, subject to payment in the case of a copy of the memorandum and of the articles, of [76 cents][a] or such less sum as the company may prescribe, and, in the case of a copy of such Act, of such sum not exceeding the published price thereof as the company may require.

(2) If a company makes default in complying with this section, the company and every officer of the company who is in default shall be liable for each offence to a fine not exceeding [€1,904.61].[b]

Amendments

a 5s converted to 60p and converted again to 76 cents by Council Regulation (EC) No 1103/97, No 974/98 and No 2866/98 and the Economic Monetary Union Act 1998, s 6.

b '£25' substituted for '£5' by C(A)A 1982, Sch 1 increased to £1,500 by CA 1990, s 240(7) as inserted by CLEA 2001, s 104(c), and converted to €1,904.61 by Council Regulation (EC) No 1103/97, No 974/98 and No 2866/98 and the Economic Monetary Union Act 1998, s 6) with effect from 1 October 2001: Company Law Enforcement Act 2001 (Commencement) (No 2) Order 2001 (SI 438/2001).

Definitions

'articles': CA 1963, s 2(1); 'company': CA 1963, s 2(1); 'member': CA 1963, s 31; 'memorandum': CA 1963, s 2(1); 'officer': CA 1963, s 2(1).

Notes

Accuracy of copy documents furnished to members: The company owes a duty of care, only to those persons to whom the memorandum and articles are sent, to ensure that they do not contain any inaccuracies or misprints.[1] If such a person acts to his detriment on foot of an inaccuracy in the memorandum or articles (eg where a person subscribes for shares in the erroneous belief that they enjoy certain rights), the company may be liable for any loss which that person suffers as a result.[2]

1 *Securities Trust Ltd v Hugh Moore and Alexander Ltd* [1964] IR 417.

2 *Securities Trust Ltd v Hugh Moore and Alexander Ltd* [1964] IR 417.

UK legislation

See CA 1985, s 19.

30 Issued copies of memorandum to embody alterations

(1) Where an alteration is made in the memorandum of a company, every copy of the memorandum issued after the date of the alteration shall be in accordance with the alteration.

(2) If, where any such alteration has been made, the company at any time after the date of the alteration issues to any person any copy of the memorandum which is not in accordance with the alteration, it shall be liable to a fine not exceeding [€1,904.61],[a] and every officer of the company who is in default shall be liable to the like penalty.

Amendments

a '£125' substituted for '£25' by C(A)A 1982, Sch 1, increased to £1,500 by CA 1990, s 240(7) as inserted by CLEA 2001, s 104(c) and converted to €1,904.61 by Council Regulations (EC) No 1103/97, No 974/98 and No 2866/98 and the Economic and Monetary Union Act 1998, s 6 with effect from 1 October 2001: Company Law Enforcement Act 2001 (Commencement) (No 2) Order 2001 (SI 438/2001).

Definitions

'company:' CA 1963, s 2(1); 'memorandum': CA 1963, s 2(1); 'officer': CA 1963, s 2(1).

Notes

Delivery of documents to the Registrar and publication in the Companies Registration Office Gazette: The special resolution amending the memorandum and the amended text of the memorandum must be forwarded to the Registrar within 15 days of the passing of such resolution.[1] Pursuant to EC(C) R 1973, reg 4, a company shall also cause to be published[2] in the Companies Registration Office Gazette,[3] a notice of delivery of such documents. In practice, it is in fact the Registrar who generally causes such notices to be published in the Companies Registration Office Gazette.

1 CA 1963, s 143(1).

2 Within six weeks of the relevant delivery date; EC(C)R 1973, reg 4(2).

3 Reference to *Iris Oifigiúil* was substituted by reference to the Companies Registration Office Gazette by virtue of EC(C)R 2004, reg 5.

UK legislation

See CA 1985, s 20.

Membership of company

31 Definition of member

(1) The subscribers of the memorandum of a company shall be deemed to have agreed to become members of the company, and, on its registration, shall be entered as members in its register of members.

(2) Every other person who agrees to become a member of a company, and whose name is entered in its register of members, shall be a member of the company.

Definitions

'company': CA 1963, s 2(1); 'memorandum': CA 1963, s 2(1).

Notes

Membership: The members of the company are defined as being the subscribers of the company and any other person who agrees to become a member and is entered into the register of members as such.[1]

1 As to the register of members generally, see CA 1963, ss 116–124.

Subscribers:

Automatic membership: A subscriber, having signed the memorandum, automatically becomes a member upon registration of the company, even if his name is not entered in the register of members[1] and even if the company fails to allot any shares to him.[2] On the other hand, if the company issues the entire of its nominal capital to other persons, the subscriber cannot continue to be regarded as a member[3] unless, of course, the company increases its nominal capital in accordance with the procedure prescribed by CA 1963, s 68.[4]

Obligation to acquire shares: While there are shares available for the subscriber he is under a contractual and a statutory obligation to take them and pay for them[5] and this obligation will not be discharged either by lapse of time[6] or by misrepresentation made by a promoter before incorporation.[7]

If the subscriber fails to write the number of shares he is taking opposite his name on the memorandum (as is required by CA 1963, s 6(4)(c)) he will be deemed to take one share only.[8]

The subscriber must take his shares by allotment from the company[9] and accordingly his obligations will not be fulfilled by accepting shares which have been forfeited[10] or by taking a transfer of shares which have already been allotted to some one else.[11] A subscriber's obligations will of course be fulfilled if he takes an allotment from the company of more than the number of shares mentioned opposite his name in the memorandum.[12] Equally well, his obligations as a subscriber will be discharged if he takes an allotment of the same amount of shares, but of a different class (eg ordinary shares rather than preference shares).[13]

Payment for subscriber shares: Subscriber shares may be allotted for a non-cash consideration in the case of private companies;[14] however, in the case of a plc, such consideration must first be independently valued.[15]

1 *Nicol's Case* (1885) 29 Ch D 421; *Alexander v Automatic Telephone Co* [1900] 2 Ch 56.
2 *Evan's Case* (1867) 2 Ch App 427; *Re London and Provincial Consolidated Coal Co* (1877) 5 Ch D 525.
3 *Mackley's Case (*1875) 1 Ch D 247; *Kipling v Todd* (1878) 3 CPD 350.
4 *Evan's Case* (1867) 2 Ch App 427.
5 *Re Tyddn Sheffrey Quarries Co Ltd* (1868) 20 LT 105; *Re FW Jarvis and Co Ltd* [1899] 1 Ch 193.
6 *Levick's Case* (1870) 40 LJ (ch) 180; *Sidney's Case* (1871) LR Eq 228; *Tooth's Case* [1868] WN 270.
7 *Lord Lurgan's Case* [1902] 1 Ch 707.
8 *Migotti's Case; Re South Blackpool Hotel Co* (1867) LR 4 Eq 238.
9 *Dalton Time Lock Co v Dalton* (1892) 66 LT 704; *Re FW Jarvis and Co Ltd* [1899] 1 Ch 193. These cases also establish that until the allotment has been made, the subscriber, although a member of the company, cannot actually deal with the shares.
10 *Mackley's Case* (1875) 1 Ch D 247.
11 *Migotti's Case; Re South Blackpool Hotel Co* (1867) LR 4 Eq 238.
12 *Elliott's Case* (1866) 15 LT 406; *Gilman's Case* (1886) 31 Ch D 420; *Dunster's Case* [1894] 3 Ch 473; *Drummond's Case; re China SS and Labuan Coal Co* (1896) 4 Ch App 772.
13 *Duke's Case; Re New Buxton Lime Co* (1876) 1 Ch D 620.
14 *Pell's Case; Re Heyford Co* (1869) 5 Ch App 11; *Drummond's Case; Re China SS and Labuan Coal Co* (1869) 4 Ch App 772.
15 C(A)A 1983, s 30.

Members other than subscribers:

Dual requirements for membership: Apart from subscribers, the only members are those who:

(a) agree to become members, and
(b) whose names are entered in the register of members.

Both of the above requirements must be fulfilled, so that mere agreement to become a member, without entry of one's name in the register of members, will be not be sufficient to render a person a member of the company.[1] Conversely, a person whose name has been entered in the register of members without his agreement, will not be regarded as a member of the company and will be entitled to apply to the court for rectification of the register.[2] However, a person may be estopped from denying membership where his name has wrongfully been entered in the register but after becoming aware of that fact, he acts in a manner consistent with membership (eg by attending general meetings or by voting on the shares or by selling them).[3] Similarly, he may be estopped from denying membership where he fails to take any steps to rectify the register, thereby leading others to believe that he is indeed a member, and thus inducing them to alter their position (eg by extending credit to the company or subscribing for shares etc).[4]

Beneficial ownership of shares: Beneficial ownership of a share cannot necessarily be equated with membership of the company. If the share is registered in the name of a nominee or trustee, that nominee or trustee, rather than the beneficial owner, will be regarded as the member.[5]

Capacity to become member: Subject to one exception in the case of subsidiaries[6] the Companies Acts do not place any specific restriction on the entitlement or ability of persons to become members of a company.

1 *Nicol's Case* (1885) 29 Ch D 421; *Re a company* [1986] BCLC 391.

2 For rectification of the register, see CA 1963, s 122.

3 *Cunninghame v City of Glasgow Bank* (1879) 4 Ch App 607; *Linz v Electric Wire Co of Palestine* [1948] AC 371.

4 *Re Cachar Co* (1867) LR 2 Ch 412, 417; *Sewell's Case; Re New Zealand Banking Corporation* (1868) 3 Ch App 131; *Re Scottish Petroleum Co* (1883) 23 Ch D 413; *Re Railway Timetables Publishing Co* (1889) 42 Ch D 98.

5 *Re Munster Bank; Dillon's Claim* (1886–87) 17 LR Ir 341; *Casey v Bentley* [1902] 1 IR 376, 387; *Re Allied Metropole Hotel Ltd* (19 December 1988, unreported) HC (Gannon J) noted by MacCann, 'Locus Standi and Section 205 of the Companies Act 1963' (1989) 7 ILT 195; *Re Via Net Works Ireland Ltd* [2002] 2 IR 47; *Re a company* [1986] BCLC 391; *Re Quickdome Ltd* [1988] BCLC 370. Furthermore, CA 1963, s 123 provides that no notice of any trust is to be entered on the register of members.

6 See CA 1963, s 32 and CA 1990, s 224.

Minors: The capacity of a minor to take shares is subject to the general law of contract.[1] Accordingly, whilst a minor can apply for shares and become a member of the company, he is entitled, within a reasonable period of time after attaining majority, to repudiate the allotment, thereby terminating his membership.[2] Similarly, if the minor repudiates a transfer of shares, the transferor again becomes a member of the company and becomes liable for any calls on the shares.[3] Until repudiation, however, the minor remains a member of the company and cannot plead his minority as a defence to calls made upon him;[4] but if he repudiates, he cannot be sued for the calls, whether they were made before or after the date of repudiation.[5]

1 See generally Clark, *Contract Law in Ireland* (5th edn, Roundhall, Sweet & Maxwell, 2004) Ch 16.

2 *Re Blakely Ordnance Co, Lumley's Case* (1868) 4 Ch App 31; *Re Constantinople and Alexandria Hotel Co, Ebbett's Case* (1870 5 Ch App 302); *Re Alexandra Park Co, Hart's Case* (1868) LR 6 Eq 512.

3 *Re China SS and Labaun Coal Co, Capper's Case* (1868) 3 Ch App 458.

4 *Cork and Bandon Railway Co v Cazenove* (1847) 10 QB 935.

5 *Newry and Enniskillen Railway Co v Coombe* (1849) 3 Exch 565.

Foreigners: A foreigner (ie non-Irish national) may become a member of an Irish company in the same way as an Irish citizen.[1] Furthermore, even though all the members are foreigners, the company will still be an Irish national.[2] Since 6 April 1999, a company incorporated in Ireland is deemed (subject to limited expectations[3]) to be resident in the State for tax purposes.[4]

1 *Princess Reuss v Bos* (1871) LR 5 HL 176; *R v Arnaud* (1846) 9 QB 806.

2 *Gasque v IRC* [1940] 2 KB 80.

3 TCA 1997, s 23A(3)–(4) as inserted by FA 1999, s 82(1). In the event that a company comes within such an exception, then actual residence is determined by the location of the management and control of that company; *De Beers Consolidated Mines Ltd v Howe* [1906] AC 455; *John Hood and Co Ltd v Magee* [1918] 2 IR 34; *Unit Construction Ltd v Bullock* [1960] AC 1.

4 TCA 1997, s 23A (2) as inserted by FA 1999, s 82 (1).

Bankrupts: Bankruptcy shall not prohibit an individual from becoming a member of a company.[1] However, where an individual is already a member of a company and thereafter is adjudicated bankrupt, his shares automatically vest in the Official Assignee[2] and the Official Assignee in turn may apply to have his own name entered in the register of members.

1 *Morgan v Gray* [1953] CH 83; *Birch v Sullivan* [1957] 1 WLR 1247.

2 Bankruptcy Act 1988, s 44.

Bodies Corporate: One company may become a member of another company provided that it is so permitted by its objects clause.[1]

1 *Re Barned's Banking Co* (1867) LR 3 Ch 105. See, however, CA 1963, s 32 and CA 1990, s 224 as well as EC(PLCS)R 1997, reg 5 for restrictions on the entitlement of a subsidiary to become a member of its parent company.

Restrictions in memorandum: If the memorandum prohibits certain classes of persons from membership of the company, any allotment of shares to such a person will be void. Furthermore, even if such a person purports to take a transfer of existing shares, he will not be entitled to have his name entered in the register of members. In addition Table A, Pt I, reg 24 confirms the right of directors to decline to register any transfer of shares to a person 'of whom they do not approve'.[1]

1 See CA 1963, Table A, Pt I, art 23 and notes thereto.

UK legislation

See CA 1985, s 22.

---

32 Membership of holding company

(1) Subject to the provisions of this section, a body corporate cannot be a member of a company which is its holding company, and any allotment or transfer of shares in a company to its subsidiary shall be void.

(2) Nothing in this section shall apply where the subsidiary is concerned as personal representative, or where it is concerned as trustee, unless the holding company or a subsidiary thereof is beneficially interested under the trust and is not so interested only by way of security for the purposes of a transaction entered into by it in the ordinary course of a business which includes the lending of money.

(3) This section shall not prevent a subsidiary which on the 5th day of May, 1959, was a member of its holding company, from continuing to be a member.

(4) This section shall not prevent a company which at the date on which it becomes a subsidiary of another company is a member of that other company, from continuing to be a member.

(5) This section shall not prevent a subsidiary which is a member of its holding company from accepting and holding further shares in the capital of its holding company if such further shares are allotted to it in consequence of a capitalisation by such holding company and if the terms of such capitalisation are such that the subsidiary is not thereby involved in any obligation to make any payment or to give other consideration for such further shares.

(6) Subject to subsection (2), a subsidiary which is a member of its holding company shall have no right to vote at meetings of the holding company or any class of members thereof.

(7) Subject to subsection (2), this section shall apply in relation to a nominee for a body corporate which is a subsidiary, as if references therein to such a body corporate included references to a nominee for it.

(8) Where a holding company makes an offer of shares to its members it may sell, on behalf of a subsidiary, any such shares which the subsidiary could, but for this section, have taken by virtue of shares already held by it in the holding company, and pay the proceeds of sale to the subsidiary.

(9) In relation to a company limited by guarantee, or unlimited, which is a holding company, the reference in this section to shares, whether or not it has a share capital, shall be construed as including a reference to the interests of its members as such, whatever the form of that interest.

Cross reference

See CA 1990, ss 224–226 and notes thereto.

Definitions

'company': CA 1963, s 2(1); 'a company limited by guarantee': CA 1963, s 2(1), 5(2)(b); 'holding company': CA 1963, s 2(1), s 155; 'member': CA 1963, s 31; 'share': CA 1963, s 2(1); 'subsidiary': CA 1963, s 2(1), s 155.

Notes

Prohibition on acquisition of shares in holding company: The general prohibition on the acquisition by a subsidiary of shares in its holding company has been largely supplanted by the provisions of CA 1990, ss 224–226[1] which now permits most types of subsidiary to acquire such shares provided that the acquisition is approved in advance by both companies and is paid for out of distributable profits.[2] Furthermore, once the subsidiary has acquired such shares the subsidiary's distributable profits are treated as being reduced by the total cost of the shares acquired[3] and it cannot exercise any voting rights which attach to those shares.[4] No such restriction on the exercise of voting rights applies, however, if the shares have been acquired by the subsidiary in its capacity as trustee or nominee pursuant to CA 1963, s 32.[5] If the subsidiary is a member of an approved stock exchange[6] acting in the ordinary course of its business as a professional dealer in securities, the restrictions and limitations on the acquisition of shares by a subsidiary in its holding company will not apply.[7] A holding company must treat any shares held by such a subsidiary as treasury shares.[8]

1 For a more detailed discussion of the new procedure for the acquisition of shares in a holding company, see the notes to CA 1990, s 224. See also EC(PLCS)R 1997, r 5 for additional restrictions that apply in the case of the subsidiary of a plc.

2 If the subsidiary is a limited company and its holding company is a plc, it will be absolutely prohibited from either subscribing for shares in the plc or purchasing shares in the plc which are not fully paid up: EC(PLCS)R 1997, r 5(2).

3 CA 1990, s 224(2)(b)(i).

4 CA 1990, s 224(2)(b)(iii).

5 See CA 1963, s 32(6).

6 Under the Stock Exchange Act 1995, s 17(2) authorisation for membership of an approved stock exchange may be given by the Central Bank, or by a competent authority of another EU member state under the Investment Services Directive 93/22/EEC or to a European Communities credit institution under First Banking Co-ordination Directive 77/780/EEC, as amended.

7 CLEA 2001, s 111(1).

8 CA 1990, s 224 (2)(b)(ii).

Validation of invalid acquisitions of shares: If the subsidiary makes an invalid acquisition of shares in its holding company it may apply to the High Court for an order of validation.[1]

[1] CA 1963, s 89.

UK legislation

See CA 1985, s 23; CA 1989, s 129(1); Company (Membership of Holdings Company) (Dealers in Securities) Regulations 1997(SI 1997/2306), reg 2; Financial Services and Markets Act 2000 (Consequential Amendments and Repeals) Order 2001 (SI 2001/3649), art 4(1)–(4).

Private companies

33 Meaning of 'private company'

[(1) For the purposes of this Act, 'private company' means a company which has a share capital and which, by its articles—

(a) restricts the right to transfer its shares, and

(b) limits the number of its members to 99 or fewer persons, not including persons who are in the employment of the company and persons who, having been formerly in the employment of the company, were, while in that employment, and have continued after the determination of that employment to be, members of the company, and

(c) prohibits any invitation or offer to the public to subscribe for any shares, debentures or other securities of the company.

(2) A provision of a company's articles that prohibits any invitation to the public to subscribe for any shares or debentures of the company shall be construed as a prohibition on any invitation or offer being made to the public to subscribe for any shares, debentures or other securities of the company.

(3) Where two or more persons hold one or more shares in a company jointly, they shall, for the purposes of this section, be treated as a single member.

(4) Subsections (5) and (6) shall apply for the purposes of—

(a) subsection (1)(c), and

(b) unless a contrary intention appears in the company's articles, any provision of a company's articles which—

(i) corresponds in its terms to those of subsection (1)(c),

(ii) incorporates by reference the terms of subsection (1)(c), or

(iii) has the same legal effect as subsection (1)(c) even though its terms are not identical to those of sub section (1)(c) (and the cases to which this subparagraph applies include the case where subsection (2) applies to the interpretation of the provision).

(5) Each of the following offers of debentures by a company (wheresoever made) shall not be regarded as falling within subsection (1)(c) or the provision of a company's articles referred to in subsection (4)(b), namely—

(a) an offer of debentures addressed solely to qualified investors,

(b) an offer of debentures addressed to fewer than 100 persons, other than qualified investors,

(c) an offer of debentures addressed to investors where the minimum consideration payable pursuant to the offer is at least €50,000 per investor, for each separate offer,

(d) an offer of debentures whose denomination per unit amounts to at least €50,000,

(e) an offer of debentures where the offer expressly limits the amount of the total consideration for the offer to less than €100,000,

(f) an offer of those classes of instruments which are normally dealt in on the money market (such as treasury bills, certificates of deposit and commercial papers) having a maturity of less than 12 months.

(6) The following offer of shares by a company (of any amount or wheresoever made) shall not be regarded as falling within subsection (1)(c) or the provision of a company's articles referred to in subsection (4)(b), namely an offer of shares addressed to—

(a) qualified investors, or

(b) 99 or fewer persons, or

(c) both qualified investors and 99 or fewer other persons.

(7) A word or expression that is used in this section and is also used in the Prospectus (Directive 2003/71/EC) Regulations 2005 (S.I. No. 324 of 2005) shall have in this section the same meaning as it has in those Regulations.

(8) For the purposes of subsection (7), the Regulations referred to in that subsection, shall have effect as if Regulation 8 were omitted therefrom.][a]

Amendments

a This section was substituted by IFCMPA 2006, s 7 with effect from 1 July 2005.[1]

1 IFCMPA 2006, s 2(3): CA 1963, s 33, as amended by IFCMPA 2006, s 7, is deemed to come into effect on 1 July 2005. This is the date on which Directive 2003/71/EC was implemented in Ireland by virtue of the Prospectus (Directive 2003/71/EC) Regulations 2005 (SI 324/2005) and IFCMPA 2005.

Definitions[1]

'articles': CA 1963, s 2(1); 'company': Prospectus Regs, reg 2(1); 'debenture': CA 1963, s 2(1); 'member': CA 1963, s 31; 'officer': CA 1963, s 2(1); 'offer of securities to the public' or 'public offer': Prospectus Regs, reg 2(1); 'officer': CA 1963, s 2(1); 'officer in default': CA 1963, s 383; 'person': IA 2005, s 18(c); 'private company': CA 1963, s 2(1), s 33(1); 'qualified investors': Prospectus Regs, reg 2(1); 'securities': Prospectus Regs, reg 2(1); 'share': CA 1963, s 2(1).

1 Words and expressions used in CA 1963, s 33 and also used in Prospectus (Directive 2003/71/EC) Regulations 2005 (SI 324/2005) have the same meaning as is given to those words and expressions in Prospectus Regs, save that in relation to such words and expressions, Prospectus Regs is to be have effect as if Prospectus Regs, reg 8 were omitted therefrom.

Notes

Company with share capital: Since a private company must have a share capital, it follows that companies limited by guarantee and not having a share capital, as well as unlimited companies not having a share capital, are public companies,[1] single-member companies must by definition be private companies.[2]

1 Notably, companies limited by guarantee and having a share capital can only be formed as private companies after 13 October 1983: C(A)A 1983, s 7.

2 EC(SMPLC)R 1994, reg 3(1).

Restriction on transfer of shares: CA 1963, s 33 does not require any particular level of restriction on the transfer of shares in order to qualify as a private company. Therefore, although a company might elect to adopt the restrictions on transfer contained in Table A[1] it would appear that less Draconian restrictions will also suffice for the purpose of qualifying as a private company.[2]

1 See, for example, reg 24 of Part I and reg 3 of Part II of Table A.

2 See, for example, *Attorney General for Ireland v Jameson* [1904] 2 IR 644; *Tangey v Clarence Hotels Ltd* [1933] IR 51.

Maximum number of members: Private companies must, by their articles, limit the number of members to 99 or less[1] (not including any existing employees and any former employees who, while in the employment of the company were, and still are members of the company). A director is not, per se, an employee of the company[2] although an employment contract may be implied if he is an executive director.[3] Furthermore, where a share is held jointly by two or more persons, they shall be treated as a single member for the purpose of CA 1963, s 33.[4]

1 IFCMPA 2006, s 7 amended CA 1963, s 33(1)(b) by increasing the maximum number of members of a private company from 50 to 99.

2 *Hutton v West Cork Railway Co* (1883) 23 Ch D 654; *Glover v BLN Ltd* [1973] IR 388; *Re Dairy Lee Ltd* [1976] IR 314; *Normandy v Ind Coope and Co Ltd* [1908] 1 Ch 84.

3 *Re Dairy Lee Ltd* [1976] IR 314.

4 CA 1963, s 33(23).

Prohibition on offer or invitation to public to subscribe for shares or debentures: The third provision required in the articles of a private company is a prohibition on the issue of an invitation or offer to the public[1] to subscribe for shares or, debentures inor other securities[2] of the company. See CA 1963, s 34 and notes thereto in relation to the consequences of breaches of CA 1963, s 33(1).

This prohibition is further reinforced by C(A)A 1983, s 21[3] which makes it an offence for a private company and its officers to offer, allot or agree to allot to the public, shares or debentures in the company. Provided such offers or allotments do not come within those exclusions listed in C(A)A 1983, s 21(2), such offers of or invitations to subscribe for shares or debentures can therefore only be made by public companies and will be attended by various forms of investor protection, such as the requirement for a prospectus or listing particulars, as the case may be[2] in circumstances where a prospectus has been published or such offer or invitation is exempt from the requirement to publish a prospectus. While the Prospectus (Directive 2003/71/EC) Regulations 2005 (SI 324/2005), reg 9 excludes certain offers of securities made in the state, the exclusions contained in CA 1963, sub-ss 33(5) and (6) apply to such offers, 'wheresoever' made.

IFCMPA 2006, s 8 also introduces CA 1963, s 33(2) whereby any provision in the company's articles which prohibits an invitation to the public, in accordance with CA 1963, s 33(1)(c) is to be construed as also being a prohibition on any invitation or offer being made to the public to subscribe for any shares, debentures or other securities of the company. The effect of this amendment would be, for instance, in relation to the articles of association of a private company limited by shares as contained in Table A, Pt II, reg 2(c), that where they refer to 'any invitation to the public to subscribe for any shares or debentures of the company is prohibited' the articles are to be interpreted as prohibiting any invitation or offer being made to the public to subscribe for any shares, debentures or other securities of the company. Likewise any alternative form of words with the same effect as Table A, Pt II, reg 2(c) is to be construed in this way.

1 See definition of 'offer of securities to the public' or 'public offer': Prospectus Regs, reg 2(1). It is worth noting that for the purpose of this definition 'communication' shall include an invitation to treat: Prospectus Regs, reg 2(6).

2 See generally Prospectus Regs; EC(SE)R 1984, 1991 and 1994; EC(TSSE)R 1992; definition of 'securities': Prospectus Regs, reg 2(1).

3 C(A)A 1983, s 21 was substituted by IFCMPA 2006, s 7.

What offers or invitations of securities can be made by a private company?: CA 1963, sub-ss 33(5) and (6) set out those offers which are expressly exempt from the restrictions contained in CA 1963, s 33(1)(c). A private company may offer or invite subscriptions for debentures provided that the offer or invitation is—

(a) addressed exclusively to qualified investors;[1]

(b) addressed to less than 100 persons (other than qualified investors);[2]

(c) one where the minimum consideration payable per investor is at least €50,000;[3]

(d) in respect of securities having a denomination per unit of at least €50,000;[4]

(e) one where the total consideration is less then €100,000;[5]

(f) in respect of certain money market instruments with a maturity of less than 12 months.[6]

Such offers of debentures follow more closely those offers by public companies which, under the Prospectus (Directive 2003/71/EC) Regulations 2005 (SI 324/2005), reg 9, do not require a prospectus to be published. A different regime applies in the context of offers of shares of private companies. Such offers are not prohibited by CA 1963, s 33(1)(c) if—

(a) the offer is addressed to qualified investors;[7] or

(b) 99 or fewer persons;[8] or

(c) both qualified investors or 99 or fewer persons.[9]

Notwithstanding the fact that the offer can be made to an unlimited number of qualified investors the general restriction on the number of members of a private company of 99 or fewer, still applies.

1 CA 1963, s 33(5)(a). See also definition of 'qualified investors': Prospectus Regs, reg 2(1).
2 CA 1963, s 33(5)(b).
3 CA 1963, s 33(5)(c).
4 CA 1963, s 33(5)(d).
5 CA 1963, s 33(5)(e).
6 CA 1963, s 33(5)(f). See also definition of 'securities': Prospectus Regs 2005, reg 2(1) and 'money market instruments': Directive 93/22/EEC (10 May 1993 OJL 141, 11.6.1993, p 27), Art 1(5).
7 CA 1963, s 33(6)(a).
8 CA 1963, s 33(6)(b).
9 CA 1963, s 33(6)(c).

Consequences of breaches of CA 1963, s 33(1): The consequences of a breach of the restrictions in CA 1963, s 33(1) are spelt out in CA 1963, s 34. Although the company does not cease to be a private company, it loses the privileges which would otherwise be enjoyed by private companies under the following sections:

CA 1963, s 36: The provisions of CA 1963, s 36 no longer apply to private limited companies, since such companies are now permitted by EC(SMPLC)R 1994 to become single-member companies.[1] In the circumstances therefore, CA 1963, s 36, as extended by CA 1963, s 34, only remains of relevance for unlimited private companies. Where such a company breaches the restrictions in its articles which are required by CA 1963, s 33(1) it will be treated as if its minimum membership should have been seven, and accordingly, if it carries on business for more than six months while its membership is below that number, every person who is a member of the company during the time that it so carries on business after those six months and who knows that it is carrying on business with fewer than seven members, shall be severally liable for the payment of the whole of the debts of the company contracted during that time and may be severally sued therefor. The main significance of CA 1963, s 36 for the members of an unlimited private company is that they may be sued directly by the creditor concerned without the company first having to be wound up, whereas in the normal course of events their liability would have been indirect, in that they would only have been liable to contribute to the company, and even then their liability would only have arisen upon the liquidation of the company.[2]

CA 1963, s 128(4)(a): This section exempted private companies from annexing their annual accounts to their annual returns. However, it has been largely superseded by C(A)A 1986, s 7 which, subject to certain exceptions,[3] requires such documents to be annexed to the annual returns of both public and private limited companies, and by EC(A)R 1993 which imposes similar obligations unlimited companies whose members are themselves limited companies. In the circumstances therefore, CA 1963, s 128(4)(a) only remains of relevance to unlimited companies whose members are either individuals or bodies corporate with unlimited liability. This very limited category of companies will lose the benefit of CA 1963, s 128(4)(a) if they breach the provisions of CA 1963, s 33(1).

CA 1963, ss 213(d) and 215: Where a private company breaches the provisions of CA 1963, s 33(1), it may be wound up on the petition of any creditor or contributory on the ground that it has less than seven members.

1 EC(SMPLC)R 1994, regs 3, 5 and 7 and notes thereto. See also CA 1963, s 5 and notes thereto.

2 CA 1963, s 207.

3 For the exceptions, see C(A)A 1986, ss 10 and 17.

Relief from consequences of a breach of CA 1963, s 33(1): If the court is satisfied that the breach of CA 1963, s 33(1) was accidental or due to inadvertance or some other sufficient cause, or that it on other grounds it is just and equitable to grant relief, it may, on the application of the company or any interested person, and on such terms and conditions as it considers just and expedient, order that the company be relieved from the consequences of that breach.

Removal of relevant restrictions from articles: If the company, rather than simply breaching the relevant restrictions which CA 1963, s 33(1) requires to be in the articles, instead removes them altogether, it will cease to be a private company.[1] However, the alteration in the articles will not take effect unless and until the company has first been re-registered either as a plc pursuant to C(A)A 1983, s 9 or alternatively has been re-registered as an unlimited public company pursuant to C(A)A 1983, s 52.[2] Moreover, if the company is to re-register as an unlimited public company, the application to do so must be accompanied by a statement in lieu of a prospectus which meets the requirements of CA 1963, s 35.

1 CA 1963, s 35(1).

2 CA 1963, s 35(2).

UK legislation

See CA 1985, s 1(3).

34 Consequences of default in complying with conditions constituting a company a private company

(1) Subject to subsection (2), where the articles of a company include the provisions which, under section 33, are required to be included in the articles of a company in order to constitute it a private company, but default is made in complying with any of those provisions, the company shall cease to be entitled to the privileges and exemptions conferred on private companies under section 36, paragraph (a) of subsection (4) of section 128, paragraph (d) of section 213, and subparagraph (i) of paragraph (a) of section 215, and thereupon, sections 36, 128, 213 and 215, shall apply to the company as if it were not a private company.

(2) The court, on being satisfied that the failure to comply with the conditions was accidental or due to inadvertence or to some other sufficient cause, or that, on other grounds, it is just and equitable to grant relief, may, on the application of the company, or any other person interested, and on such terms and conditions as seem to the court just and expedient, order that the company be relieved from the consequences referred to in subsection (1).

Definitions

'company': CA 1963, s 2(1); 'the court': CA 1963, s 2(1); 'private company': CA 1963, s 2(1), s 33(1).

Notes

Consequences of breaches of CA 1963, s 33(1): The consequences of a breach of the restrictions in CA 1963, s 33(1) are spelt out in CA 1963, s 34. Although the company does not cease to be a private company, it loses the privileges which would otherwise be enjoyed by private companies under the following sections:

CA 1963, s 36: The provisions of CA 1963, s 36 no longer apply to private limited companies, since such companies are now permitted by EC(SMPLC)R 1994 to become single-member companies.[1] In the circumstances, therefore, CA 1963, s 36, as extended by CA 1963, s 34, only remains of relevance for unlimited private companies. Where such a company breaches the restrictions in its articles which are required by CA 1963, s 33(1) it will be treated as if its minimum membership should have been seven, and accordingly, if it carries on business for more than six months while its membership is below that number, every person who is a member of the company during the time that it so carries on business after those six months and who knows that it is carrying on business with fewer than seven members, shall be severally liable for the payment of the whole of the debts of the company contracted during that time and may be severally sued therefor. The main significance of CA 1963, s 36 for the members of an unlimited private company is that they may be sued directly by the creditor concerned without the company first having to be wound up, whereas in the normal course of events their liability would have been indirect, in that they would only have been liable to contribute to the company, and even then their liability would only have arisen upon the liquidation of the company.[2]

CA 1963, s 128(4)(a): This section exempted private companies from annexing their annual accounts to their annual returns. However, it has been largely superseded by C(A)A 1986, s 7 which, subject to certain exceptions,[3] requires such documents to be annexed to the annual returns of both public and private limited companies, and by EC(A)R 1993 which imposes similar obligations on unlimited companies whose members are themselves limited companies. In the circumstances, therefore, CA 1963, s 128(4)(a) only remains of relevance to unlimited companies whose members are either individuals or bodies corporate with unlimited liability. This very limited category of companies will lose the benefit of CA 1963, s 128(4)(a) if they breach the provisions of CA 1963, s 33(1).

CA 1963, ss 213(d) and 215: Where a private company breaches the provisions of CA 1963, s 33(1), it may be wound up on the petition of any creditor or contributory on the ground that it has less than seven members.

1 EC(SMPLC)R 1994, regs 3, 5 and 7 and notes thereto. See also CA 1963, s 5 and notes thereto.

2 CA 1963, s 207.

3 For the exceptions, see C(A)A 1986, ss 10 and 17.

Relief from consequences of a breach of CA 1963, s 33(1): If the court is satisfied that the breach of CA 1963, s 33(1) was accidental or due to inadvertance or some other sufficient cause, or that on other grounds it is just and equitable to grant relief, it may, on the application of the company or any interested person, and on such terms and conditions as it considers just and expedient, order that the company be relieved from the consequences of that breach.

---

35 [Statement in lieu of prospectus to be delivered to registrar by company on ceasing to be a private company

(1) Subject to subsection (2), if a company, being a private company, alters its articles in such a manner that they no longer include the provisions which, under section 33, are required to be included in the articles of a company in order to constitute it a private company, the company shall cease to be a private company.

(2) The alteration referred to in subsection (1) shall not take effect unless the company has been re-registered as a public limited company in accordance with section 9 of the Companies (Amendment) Act, 1983 or as an unlimited public company in accordance with section 52 of that Act.

(3) Where an application is made to re-register a private company as an unlimited public company, there shall be delivered with the application for re-registration a statement in lieu of prospectus in the form and containing the particulars set out in Part I of the Second Schedule, and, in the cases mentioned in Part II of that Schedule, setting out the reports specified therein, and the said Parts I and II shall have effect subject to the provision contained in Part III of that Schedule.

(4) A statement in lieu of prospectus need not be delivered under subsection (3) if a prospectus relating to the company which complies, or is deemed by virtue of a certificate of exemption under section 45 to comply, with the Third Schedule, is issued and is delivered to the registrar of companies as required by section 47.

(5) Every statement in lieu of prospectus delivered under subsection (3) shall, where the persons making any such report as referred to in that subsection have made therein or have, without giving the reasons, indicated therein any such adjustments as are mentioned in paragraph 5 of Part III of the Second Schedule, have endorsed thereon or attached thereto a written statement signed by those persons, setting out the adjustments and giving the reasons therefor.

(6) If default is made in complying with subsection (2), (3) or (5), the company and every officer of the company who is in default shall be guilty of an offence and shall be liable on summary conviction to a fine not exceeding [€1,904.61][b].

(7) Where a statement in lieu of prospectus, delivered to the registrar under subsection (3) includes any untrue statement, any person who authorised the delivery of the statement in lieu of prospectus for registration shall be guilty of an offence and shall be liable—

(a) on conviction on indictment, to imprisonment for a term not exceeding 2 years or a fine not exceeding [€3,174.35],[c] or both, or

(b) on summary conviction, to imprisonment for a term not exceeding 6 months or a fine not exceeding [€1,904.61][b] or both;

unless he proves either that the untrue statement was immaterial or that he had reasonable ground to believe and did, up to the time of the delivery for registration of the statement in lieu of prospectus, believe that the untrue statement was true.

(8) For the purposes of this section—

(a) a statement included in a statement in lieu of prospectus shall be deemed to be untrue if it is misleading in the form and context in which it is included, and

(b) a statement shall be deemed to be included in a statement in lieu of prospectus if it is contained therein or in any report or memorandum appearing on the face thereof, or by reference incorporated therein.][a]

Amendments

a CA 1963, s 35 substituted by C(A)A 1983, Sch 1, para 6.

b Fines increased from £500 to £1,500 by CA 1990, s 240(7) as inserted by CLEA 2001, s 104(c) and converted to €1,904.61 by Council Regulations (EC) No 1103/97, No 974/98 and No 2866/98 and the Economic and Monetary Union Act 1998, s 6.

c £2,500 converted to €3,174.35 by Council Regulations (EC) No 1103/97, No 974/98 and No 2866/98 and the Economic and Monetary Union Act 1998, s 6.

Cross reference

See Prospectus Regs 2005, IFCMPA 2005, Pt 5 and notes thereto.

CA 1963, ss 45, 47 and Sch 4 repealed by IFCMPA 2005, s 40.

Definitions

'articles': CA 1963, s 2(1); 'company': CA 1963, s 2(1); 'memorandum': CA 1963, s 2(1); 'officer': CA 1963, s 2(1); 'officer in default': CA 1963, s 383; 'person': IA 2005, s 18(c); 'private company': CA 1963, s 2(1), s 33(1); 'prospectus': CA 1963, s 2(1); 'the registrar of companies': CA 1963, s 2(1).

Notes

Requirement for statement in lieu of prospectus: If a private company removes from its articles all or some of those provisions which are required by CA 1963, s 33, it must either re-register as a plc or an unlimited public company.[1] Moreover, the alteration to the articles will not take effect until re-registration takes place.[2] Re-registration as an unlimited public company is a rare event, but where it occurs, the company will be required to deliver a statement in lieu of prospectus which complies with CA 1963, Sch 2.

Prior to the repeal of CA 1963, s 54[3] a statement in lieu of a prospectus also had to be delivered to the Registrar at least three days before the first allotment of shares by an unlimited public company which either did not issue a prospectus on or with reference to its formation, or which alternatively, had issued such a prospectus but had not proceeded to allot any of the shares which had been offered to the public for subscription.

1 CA 1963, s 35(1).

2 CA 1963, s 35(2).

3 IFCMPA 2005, s 40 repealed CA 1963, s 54 and Sch 4.

Exemption from requirement for delivery of statement in lieu of prospectus: A private company which re-registers as an unlimited public company will not be required to deliver a statement in lieu of prospectus if it instead delivers an actual prospectus or is not required to issue such a prospectus.[1]

1 See Prospectus Regs 2005, IFCMPA 2005, Pt 5 and notes thereto.

Untrue statements: Criminal liability arises for any person who authorises[1] the delivery of a statement in lieu of prospectus which contains an untrue statement, unless he proves either that the statement was immaterial[2] or that he had reasonable grounds to believe and did believe up to the time of delivery to the Registrar, that the statement was true.[3] In this regard, the person who authorised the issue of the document will not be deemed to have had reasonable grounds for believing the untrue statement if the facts contained therein were easily capable of verification.[4] Statements will be deemed to be untrue if they convey a misleading impression to persons reading the document.[5] Moreover, because under CA 1963, s 35(8)(a) one has to look at form and context in which the statement is included in the document, concealment of facts can be regarded as an untrue statement, if it renders some other statement which is actually contained in the document, untrue.[6]

1 It is a question of fact as to who authorizes the issue of the statement in lieu of prospectus. Presumably, it would normally include the directors and any expert who consents to the inclusion of his expert statement in the document.

2 Matters of a merely artistic or decorative nature or linked to the form of presentation will not normally be regarded as being material: *FNCB Waltons Corporation v CAC* [1975] 2 NSWLR 493.

3 CA 1963, s 35(7).

4 *Adams v Thrift* [1915] 1 Ch 557; on appeal [1915] 2 Ch 21.

5 *Greenwood v Leather Shod Wheel Co* [1900] 1 Ch 421, 434.

6 *Components Tube Co v Naylor* [1900] 2 IR 1, 59; *New Brunswick and Canada Pty Ltd v Muggeridge* (1860) 1 Dr and Sm 363; *R v Kylsant* [1932] 1 KB 442.

Reduction of Number of Members below Legal Minimum

36 Members severally liable for debts where business carried on with fewer than seven, or in case of private company [or an investment company (within the meaning of Part XIII of the Companies Act, 1990)][a], two members

If at any time the number of members of a company is reduced, in the case of a private company [or an investment company (within the meaning of Part XIII of the Companies Act, 1990)][a], below two, or, in the case of any other company, below seven, and it carries on business for more than 6 months while the number is so reduced, every person who is a member of the company during the time that it so carries on business after those 6 months and knows that it is carrying on business with fewer than two members, or seven members, as the case may be, shall be severally liable for the payment of the whole debts of the company contracted during that time, and may be severally sued therefor.

Amendments

a 'or an investment company (within the meaning of Part XIII of the Companies Act, 1990)' inserted by CA 1990, s 260(1) which was substituted by C(A)(No 2) 1999, s 54 with effect from 21 December 1999.[1]

1 Companies (Amendment) (No 2) Act 1999 (Commencement) Order 1999 (SI 406/1999).

Definitions

'company': CA 1963, s 2(1); 'member': CA 1963, s 31; 'private company': CA 1963, s 2(1), s 33(1).

Notes

Private limited companies: The provisions of CA 1963, s 36 no longer apply to private companies limited by shares or limited by guarantee and having a share capital, since such companies are now permitted by EC(SMPLC)R 1994 to become single-member companies.[1] In the circumstances, therefore, CA 1963, s 36 only remains of relevance for the following:

(a) public companies; and

(b) unlimited private companies.

The main significance of CA 1963, s 36 for the members of an unlimited private company is that they may be sued directly by the creditor concerned without the company first having to be wound up, whereas in the normal course of events their liability would have been indirect, in that they would only have been liable to contribute to the company, and even then their liability would only have arisen upon the liquidation of the company.[2] The CLRG has recommended the repeal of CA 1963, s 36.[3]

1 EC(SMPLC)R 1994, regs 3, 5 and 7 and notes thereto. See also CA 1963, s 5 and notes thereto.

2 CA 1963, s 207.

3 The Company Law Review Group, First Report (2001), para 4.9.3.

Extent of Personal liability[1]: If a company carries on business for more than six months while its membership is reduced below the statutory minimum, every person who is a member of the company during the period that it so carries on business after those six months and who knows that the membership is less than the statutory minimum, shall be severally liable for the payment of the whole of the debts of the company contracted during that time,[2] and may be severally sued therefor. Personal liability may not, however, be imposed for other corporate liabilities, such as claims for damages for breach of contract or for breach of statutory duty or for torts. Nor does CA 1963, s 36 extend to other liabilities of the company arising under statute, such as claims for damages for unfair or wrongful dismissal. Furthermore, even if a member does incur personal liability under CA 1963, s 36, he is entitled to an indemnity from the company since the company is still primarily liable to discharge of the debt.[3]

1 See generally MacCann, 'Personal Liability for Corporate Debts' (1991) ILT 206 and 232.

2 ie debts incurred after the expiry of the initial six month period.

3 *Brook's Wharf Ltd v Goodman Bros* [1937] 1 KB 534.

Causes of reduction in membership below statutory minimum: A reduction in the number of members below the basic minimum may be brought about, for example, by the death of a member[1], since neither his personal representative nor those entitled to his shares under the law of succession will become members of the company until such time as they are entered on the register of members.[2] Such a situation could also arise where one member sells his shares to another.[3] If the sale is to an outsider, the reduction may be only temporary provided that the name of the transferee is in turn entered in the register of members.[4] On the other hand, the reduction is potentially permanent if the sale is to another member. However, that member can bring the membership back up to the legal minimum by transferring some of his shares to nominees and by having the nominees' names entered in the register.[5]

1 *Re Bowling and Welby's Contract* [1895] 1 Ch 663.

2 See CA 1963, s 33; *Re Bowling and Welby's Contract* [1895] 1 Ch 663.

3 *Nisbet v Shepherd* [1994] 1 BCLC 300.

4 Registration of the transfer will, however, be subject to any discretion conferred on the directors by the articles. See, for example, reg 3 of Part II of Table A.

5 Such a course of action was attempted in *Shepherd v Nisbet* [1994] 1 BCLC 300.

UK legislation

See CA 1985, s 24; C(SMPLC)R 1992, reg 2 (1)(b), Sch, para 2; Companies (Acquisition of Own Shares) (Treasury Shares) Regulations 2003 (SI 2003/1116), reg 4, Sch, para 2.

Contracts, Deeds and Powers of Attorney

37 Pre-incorporation contracts

(1) Any contract or other transaction purporting to be entered into by a company prior to its formation or by any person on behalf of the company prior to its formation may be ratified by the company after its formation and thereupon the company shall become bound by it and entitled to the benefit thereof as if it had been in existence at the date of such contract or other transaction and had been a party thereto.

(2) Prior to ratification by the company the person or persons who purported to act in the name or on behalf of the company shall in the absence of express agreement to the contrary be personally bound by the contract or other transaction and entitled to the benefit thereof.

(3) This section shall not apply to a company incorporated before the operative date.

Definitions

'company': CA 1963, s 2(1); 'the operative date': CA 1963, s 2(1).

Notes

Common law position: A company cannot enter into a contract before its incorporation since it does not yet exist as a matter of law. Because of this, the traditional position at common law was that a company could not validly ratify a contract which a person had purported to enter into on its behalf pre-incorporation.[1] This was because ratification presupposes that the principal was in existence at the time when the 'agent' purported to act on his behalf.[2] As a result, persons who purported to enter into pre-incorporation contracts for companies were treated as having contracted on their own behalf and were personally liable thereunder.[3]

1 *Kelner v Baxter* (1866) LR 2 CP 174; *Scott v Lord Ebury* (1867) LR 2 CP 255; *Natal Land and Colonisation Co Ltd v Pauline Colliery and Development Syndicate* [1904] AC 120; *Re National Motor Mail-Coach Co Ltd* [1908] 2 Ch 515.

2 *Firth v Staines* [1897] 2 QB 70, 75.

3 *Kelner v Baxter* (1866) LR 2 CP 174; *Scott v Lord Ebury* (1867) LR 2 CP 255.

Ratification under s 37: The common law position has been reversed by CA 1963, s 37(1). As a result a company[1] may now ratify contracts and other transactions which are purportedly entered by it in its own name[2] or which are purportedly entered into on its behalf before incorporation.[3] In this regard, a person may purport to act on behalf of a company even though it is known by both parties at the time that the company has not yet been incorporated.[4] Once ratification takes place the company becomes bound by the contract or other transaction and is entitled to the benefit thereof as if it had been a party from the very outset. Notably, however, the company is under no obligation to actually ratify the contract or other transaction (unless perhaps required to do so by its memorandum or articles). Where ratification does take place, it need not necessarily be done by way of a formal resolution of the members or directors at a properly convened meeting.[5] Instead, ratification may in certain circumstances occur informally, as where after incorporation, the controlling shareholders or directors simply cause the company to implement the contract.[6]

Moreover, ratification may take place despite the fact that the company has since gone into liquidation and is thus unable to any longer perform its part of the bargain.[7]

1 The term 'company' is defined by CA 1963, s 2(1) as including only Irish registered companies and accordingly foreign companies fall outside the scope of CA 1963, s 37: *Rover International Ltd v Cannon Film Sales Ltd* [1987] BCLC 540. The provisions of CA 1963, s 37 are, however, applied to certain types of unregistered companies by CA 1963, s 377.

2 See, for example, *HKN Invest OY v Incotrade PVT Ltd* [1993] 3 IR 152.

3 CA 1963, s 37 has no application, however, to contracts entered into on behalf of an existing company under its proposed new name but before the new certificate of incorporation consequent upon the change of name has been issued by the Registrar pursuant to CA 1963, s 23(3): *Oshkosh B'Gosh Inc v Dan Marbel Inc Ltd* [1989] BCLC 507. The section is also *inapplicable of being* invoked by a company which has been restored to the register pursuant to CA 1963, s 310 to enable it to ratify contracts purportedly entered into by it whilst dissolved: *Cotronic (UK) Ltd v Dezonie* [1991] BCLC 721. However, if the company has been restored to the register pursuant to CA 1963, s 311A or C(A)A 1982, ss 12C or 12D no problem should arise since the restoration order operates restrospectively and the company is treated as if it had never been dissolved, thereby curing any defect that might otherwise have existed in respect of the company's position under the contract.

4 *Phonogram Ltd v Lane* [1981] 3 All ER 182. However, if the 'agent' does not purport to act for and on behalf of the as yet unincorporated company but instead contracts in his own name or the name of some other party, the contract will not be capable of ratification under CA 1963, s 37: *Badgerhill Properties Ltd v Cottrell* [1991] BCLC 805, 813.

5 *HKN Invest OY v Incotrade PVT Ltd* [1993] 3 IR 152, 160.

6 *HKN Invest OY v Incotrade PVT Ltd* [1993] 3 IR 152, 160.

7 *HKN Invest OY v Incotrade PVT Ltd* [1993] 3 IR 152.

Position of agent: Until the company ratifies the contract or other transactions, the agent shall, in the absence of any agreement to the contrary, be personally liable thereunder.[1] In this regard, describing oneself as 'agent' of the company will not amount to a sufficient exclusion of personal liability.[2]

If the agent has received any payments under the contract and the contract is subsequently ratified by the company, he will be deemed to hold the amount of the payments on trust for the company.[3]

1 CA 1963, s 37(2).

2 *Phonogram Ltd v Lane* [1981] 3 All ER 182.

3 *HKN Invest OY v Incotrade PVT Ltd* [1993] 3 IR 152.

Planning Permissions: CA 1963, s 37 cannot be used to grant planning permission to a company which has not yet been incorporated since it is an integral part of the planning code that the planning authority and the public should have an opportunity of assessing the identity of the applicant for the planning permission.[1] In such circumstances, the planning permission, if issued, will be deemed to have been granted to the applicant promoter personally, so that he will be personally liable for compliance with the conditions attaching to the permission.[2]

1 *The State (Finglas Industrial Estate Ltd) v Dublin County Council* [1983] IESC 8; *Inver Resources Ltd v Limerick Corporation* [1988] ILRM 47.

2 *Inver Resources Ltd v Limerick Corporation* [1988] ILRM 47.

UK legislation

See CA 1985, s 36C; CA 1989, s 130(4).

38 Form of contracts

(1) Contracts on behalf of a company may be made as follows:

(a) a contract which if made between private persons would be by law required to be in writing and to be under seal, may be made on behalf of the company in writing under the common seal of the company;

(b) a contract which if made between private persons would be by law required to be in writing, signed by the parties to be charged therewith, may be made on behalf of the company in writing, signed by any person acting under its authority, express or implied;

(c) a contract which if made between private persons would by law be valid although made by parol only, and not reduced into writing may be made by parol on behalf of the company by any person acting under its authority, express or implied.

(2) A contract made according to this section shall bind the company and its successors and all other parties thereto.

(3) A contract made according to this section may be varied or discharged in the same manner in which it is authorised by this section to be made.

Definitions

'company': CA 1963, s 2(1).

Notes

Contracts under seal: Every company is required by law to have a seal on which its name is engraved in legible characters.[1] Deeds may be executed by a company under its own seal.[2] Under Table A, the company's seal may only be used by the authority of the directors or of a duly authorised committee of directors and every instrument to which the seal is affixed must either be signed by two directors or alternatively by a director and the secretary or by a director and some other person appointed by the directors for the purpose.[3] A failure to comply with the sealing requirements in the articles (eg by having the document signed by one director rather than two) will render the execution of the deed ineffective.[4] Nonetheless, even if the deed has not been signed, the company may still be bound thereby if there has been part performance by the other party and the company has taken the benefits of any covenants and terms contained therein.[5] Furthermore, as an alternative to executing the deed itself, the company may instead appoint an attorney to act on its behalf.[6] In this regard, the attorney will use his own seal rather than the common seal of the company.[7] A company may have an official seal for use outside the State[8] and a company, other than a private company may have an official seal for use in connection with securities issued by that company.[9] In the case of a company in liquidation, a deed may be executed under seal on behalf of that company by affixing the seal and having the document signed by the liquidator. [10] Electronic sealing of documents is also possible.[11]

1 CA 1963, s 114(1)(b). See also CA 1963, s 18(2) which provides that upon incorporation every company shall have a common seal. See generally Courtney, *The Law of Private Companies* (2nd edn, Tottel Publishing, 2002) paras 7.014–7.032 and Kearney, 'Execution of Commercial Documents' (1994) 16 DULJ 1.

2 CA 1963, s 33(1)(a). The primary type of contract which is required by law to be made under seal is a conveyance of land: Real Property Act 1845, ss 2 and 3.

3 Art 115 of Table A. In the case of companies whose articles incorporate Table A of the Companies (Consolidation) Act 1908, the affixing of the seal must be authorised by resolution of the board and must be attested by two directors and by the secretary. See *Safeera Ltd v Wallis and O'Regan* (12 July 1994, unreported) HC (Morris J). See also CA 1963, s 177, whereby it is

confirmed that the execution under seal of a deed by a person in their capacities as director and secretary of the same company would not be effective.

4 *Safeera Ltd v Wallis and O'Regan* (12 July 1994, unreported) HC (Morris J).

5 *McDonald v John Twiname Ltd* [1953] 2 QB 304.

6 *Industrial Development Authority v Moran* [1978] IR 159; *Ferguson v Wilson* (1866) 2 Ch App 77. See also reg 81 of Table A which expressly empowers the board of directors to execute powers of attorney. It is no longer necessary that an attorney executing and/or delivering a deed under seal must be appointed under seal; see Powers of Attorney Act 1996, s 15(2).

7 *Ibid.*

8 C(A)A 1977, s 3 and notes thereto.

9 CA 1963, s 41 and notes thereto.

10 CA 1963, s 231(b) and notes thereto.

11 Electronic Commerce Act 2000, s 16.

Foreign contracts under seal: If the company's objects require or comprise the transaction of business outside the State it may, if authorised by its articles,[1] have an official seal, which is a facsimile of its common seal, for use in the execution of deeds abroad.[2] Alternatively, the company may appoint an attorney to act on its behalf abroad,[3] and that attorney will act under his own seal rather than the company's common seal.[4] Specific provision has been made in the UK for foreign companies, such as a company incorporated and registered in Ireland, to execute deeds in the way that such companies would execute deeds in the place of their incorporation.[5]

1 Table A contain no such authorisation.

2 See CA 1963, s 41 and the notes thereto.

3 CA 1963, s 40(1).

4 CA 1963, s 40(2).

5 Foreign Companies (Execution of Documents) Regulations 1994 (SI 950/1994).

Written Contracts: Contracts which are required by law to be in writing and signed by the parties[1] could of course be made under the common seal of the company. However, rather than use a seal, CA 1963, s 38(1)(b) also permits such contracts to be made in writing on behalf of the company, and to be signed on its behalf by a duly authorised agent.[2] The document will be deemed to have been adequately signed if the agent puts his own printed signature onto it or impresses the printed name of the company on it.[3] Mere initialling however, may not suffice.[4]

1 Contracts which must be in writing and signed, include the guarantees, contracts for the sale of land, and contracts which are not to be performed within the space of one year (Statute of Frauds (Ireland) 1695, s 2); hire-purchase contracts (Hire Purchase Act 1946, s 3) and certain credit agreements under the Consumer Credit Act 1995. See generally, Clark, *Contract Law in Ireland* (5th edn, Roundhall Sweet & Maxwell, 2004), Ch 4. See the Electronic Commerce Act 2000, ss 12–23 for the circumstances in which contracts can be made and signed electronically. For the classes of contracts which cannot be made electronically, see the Electronic Commerce Act 2000, s 10.

2 See *Dundalk AFC Interim Company Ltd v The FAI National League* [2001] 1 IR 434; *London County Council v Vitamins Ltd* [1955] 2 All ER 229. See also CA 1963, s 39 which allows for bills of exchange and promissory notes to be made, accepted and endorsed in the name of or by or on behalf or on account of the company by a person acting under its authority. In order to avoid the risk of personal liability on the contract, the agent should make it abundantly clear that he is acting in a representative capacity only on behalf of the company: *F Goldsmith (Sicklesmere) Ltd v Baxter* [1969] 3 All ER 733. See generally Kearney, 'Execution of Commercial Documents' (1994) 16 DULJ 1.

3 *McDonald v John Twiname Ltd* [1953] 2 QB 304.

4 *Henley Forklift (Ireland) Ltd v Lansing Bagnall and Co Ltd* [1979] ILRM 257.

Oral contracts: Contracts which may be validly made by parol by an individual, may also be validly made by parol on behalf of a company by its duly authorised agent. However, if a single-member private limited company enters into an oral contract with its sole member otherwise than in the ordinary course of business and the sole member also represents the company in the transaction, the terms of the contract must forthwith be set out in a written memorandum or alternatively must be recorded in the minutes of the next board meeting.[1] Failure to do so will not affect the validity of the contract[2] but may expose the company and every officer in default to criminal liability.[3]

1 EC(SMPLC)R 1994, reg 13(1).
2 EC(SMPLC)R 1994, reg 13(5).
3 EC(SMPLC)R 1994, reg 13(3).

Agent acting without authority: As to the position regarding the enforcement of a contract which has been entered into by an agent without authority, see the notes to EC(C)R 1973, reg 6.

***Ultra vires* contracts**: With regard to the enforcement of *ultra vires* contracts either by or against a company, see CA 1963, s 8 as well as EC(C)R 1973, reg 6 and the notes thereto.

UK legislation

See CA 1985, s 36; CA 1989, s 130(1).

See CA 1985, s 36A; CA 1989 s 130(2); The Regulatory Reform (Execution of Deeds and Documents) Order 2005 (SI 2005/1906), art 1(1)–(2).

---

39 Bills of exchange and promissory notes

A bill of exchange or promissory note shall be deemed to have been made, accepted or endorsed on behalf of a company, if made, accepted or endorsed in the name of or by or on behalf or on account of, the company by any person acting under its authority.

Cross reference

'bill of exchange': SDCA 1999, s 1(1); 'promissory note': SDCA 1999, s 1(1).

Definitions

'company': CA 1963, s 2(1).

Notes

Liability: If, on the true construction of the instrument as a whole, the bill or note was made, accepted or endorsed on behalf of the company, the company and not the agent will be entitled to sue and will be liable to be sued on it.[1] It is a question of fact and construction in each case as to whether a person is acting as agent or in a personal capacity when, in signing the instrument, he describes himself as 'director', 'receiver', 'liquidator', 'examiner' etc.[2] However, even if he is acting in a representative capacity, he may incur personal liability on a bill or note which he signs, if it fails to state the company's name either accurately or at all.[3]

1 *Okell v Charles* (1876) 34 LT 822; *Chapman v Smethurst* [1909] 1 KB 927; *Alexander v Sizer* (1869) LR 4 Exch 102.
2 *McCollin v Gilpin* (1880) 5 QBD 390, on appeal (1881) 6 QBD 516; *Elliott v Bax-Ironside* [1925] 2 KB 301; *Kettle v Dunster and Wakefield* (1927) 138 LT 158; *Rolfe, Lubell and Co v Keith* [1979] 1 All ER 860.
3 See CA 1963, s 114 and the notes thereto.

Stamp duty: Where a bill of exchange or promissory note is stamped by means of an adhesive stamp[1] rather than an impressed stamp, the person making the relevant instrument on behalf of the company must, in addition to signing that instrument, ensure that it bears the necessary adhesive stamp[2] and that the stamp is cancelled in accordance with the requirements of SDCA 1999, s 10(2).[3]

1 SDCA 1999, s 25(1).

2 SDCA 1999, Sch 1 as amended by FA 2003, s 143. Stamp duty of €0.15 applies to such instruments.

3 ie 'by writing on or across the stamp his or her name or initials, or the name or initials of his or her firm, together with the true date of his or her so writing, or otherwise effectively cancels the stamp...'

UK legislation

See CA 1985, s 37.

40 Execution of deeds outside the State

(1) A company may, by writing under its common seal, empower any person, either generally or in respect of any specified matters, as its attorney, to execute deeds on its behalf in any place outside the State.

(2) A deed signed by such attorney on behalf of the company and under his seal shall bind the company and have the same effect as if it were under its common seal.

Definitions

'company': CA 1963, s 2(1)

Notes

Foreign contracts under seal: If the company's objects require or comprise the transaction of business outside the State it may, if authorised by its articles,[1] have an official seal, which is a facsimile of its common seal, for use in the execution of deeds abroad.[2] Alternatively, the company may appoint an attorney to act on its behalf abroad,[3] and that attorney will act under his own seal rather than the company's common seal.[4]

1 Table A contain no such authorisation.

2 See CA 1963, s 41 and the notes thereto.

3 CA 1963, s 40(1).

4 CA 1963, s 40(2).

UK legislation

See CA 1985, s 38; CA 1989, s 130(7), Sch 17, para 1.

41 Power for company to have official seal for use abroad

(1) A company whose objects require or comprise the transaction of business outside the State may, if authorised by its articles, have for use in any territory, district or place not situate in the State, an official seal which shall be a facsimile of the common seal of the company with the addition on its face of the name of every territory, district or place where it is to be used.

(2) A deed or other document to which an official seal is duly affixed shall bind the company as if it had been sealed with the common seal of the company.

(3) A company having an official seal for use in any such territory, district or place, may, by writing under its common seal, authorise any person appointed for the purpose in that

territory, district or place to affix the official seal to any deed or other document to which the company is party in that territory, district or place.

(4) The authority of any such agent shall, as between the company and any person dealing with the agent, continue during the period, if any, mentioned in the instrument conferring the authority, or, if no period is there mentioned, then until the notice of revocation or determination of the agent's authority has been given to the person dealing with him.

(5) The person affixing any such official seal shall, by writing under his hand, certify on the deed or other instrument to which the seal is affixed the date on which and the place at which it is affixed.

Definitions

'agent': CA 1963, s 2(1); 'articles': CA 1963, s 2(1); 'company': CA 1963, s 2(1). 'document': CA 1963, s 2(1).

Notes

Power of company to use an official seal: The use of an official seal for the execution of documents abroad is an alternative to the appointment of an attorney to execute them.[1] Before using an official seal, the company must first be authorised to do so by its articles. Such authorisation is to be found in Table A, reg 82.

1 As to execution of documents abroad by an attorney, see CA 1963, s 40.

Authority of company's agent to use official seal: Unlike the company's common seal,[1] which under Table A[2] can only be used by having two directors or a director and secretary or a director and authorised person sign the relevant instrument, the official seal may be used by a single agent who has been duly authorised to do so by the company.[3] If the instrument conferring authority on the agent to use the official seal is stated to be for a fixed period then, in so far as any person dealing with him is concerned, that authority is treated as being irrevocable for the duration of the period in question.[4] Similarly, if the instrument conferring authority is open ended in duration, the person dealing with the agent may treat it as continuing in force until such time as he is notified to the contrary.[5]

1 As to the common seal, see CA 1963, s 38 and the notes thereto.

2 Reg 115 of Table A.

3 CA 1963, s 41(3).

4 CA 1963, s 41(4).

5 CA 1963, s 41(4).

UK legislation

See CA 1985, s 39; CA 1989, s 130(7), Sch 17, para 2.

Authentication of Documents

42 Authentication of documents

A document or proceeding requiring authentication by a company may be signed by a director, secretary or other authorised officer of the company, and need not be under its common seal.

Definitions

'company': CA 1963, s 2(1); 'director': CA 1963, s 2(1); 'document': CA 1963, s 2(1): 'officer': CA 1963, s 2(1).

UK legislation

See CA 1985, s 41; CA 1989, s 130(7), Sch 17, para 4.

PART III

SHARE CAPITAL AND DEBENTURES

Prospectus

43 Dating of prospectus

[...][a]

Amendments

a Section repealed by IFCMPA 2005, s 40(1)(a).

44 Matters to be stated and reports to be set out in prospectus

[...][a]

Amendments

a Section repealed by IFCMPA 2005, s 40(1)(a).

45 Exclusion of section 44 and relaxation of Third Schedule in case of certain prospectuses

[...][a]

Amendments

a Section repealed by IFCMPA 2005, s 40(1)(a).

46 Expert's consent to issue of prospectus containing statement by him

[...][a]

Amendments

a Section repealed by IFCMPA 2005, s 40(1)(a).

47 Registration of prospectus

[...][a]

Amendments

a Section repealed by IFCMPA 2005, s 40(1)(a).

48 Restriction on alteration of terms mentioned in prospectus or statement in lieu of prospectus

[...][a]

Amendments

a CA 1963, s 48 repealed by C(A)A 1983 Sch 3.

49 Civil liability for mis-statements in prospectus

[...][a]

Amendments

a Section repealed by IFCMPA 2005, s 40(1)(a).

50 Criminal liability for mis-statements in prospectus

[...][a]

Amendments

a Section repealed by IFCMPA 2005, s 40(1)(a).

51 Document containing offer of shares or debentures for sale deemed to be a prospectus

[...][a]

Amendments

a Section repealed by IFCMPA 2005, s 40(1)(a).

52 Interpretation of provisions relating to prospectuses

[...][a]

Amendments

a Section repealed by IFCMPA 2005, s 40(1)(a).

Allotment

53 Minimum subscription and amount payable on application

[(1) Where a prospectus states the minimum amount which, in the opinion of the directors, must be raised from an issue of shares and that no allotment shall be made of any of those shares unless that minimum amount has been subscribed and the sum payable on application for the amount so stated has been paid up, then no such allotment shall be made unless that minimum amount has been subscribed and the said sum so payable has been paid up.][a]

(2) The amount so stated in the prospectus shall be reckoned exclusively of any amount payable otherwise than in cash and is in this Act referred to as 'the minimum subscription'.

(3) [Except in the case of a public limited company the amount payable][b] on application on each share shall not be less than 5 per cent. of the nominal amount of the share.

(4) If the conditions aforesaid have not been complied with on the expiration of 40 days after the first issue of the prospectus, all money received from applicants for shares shall be forthwith repaid to them without interest, and, if any such money is not so repaid within 48 days after the issue of the prospectus, the directors of the company shall be jointly and severally liable to repay that money with interest at the rate of 5 per cent. per annum from the expiration of the forty-eighth day, so however that a director shall not be liable if he proves that the default in the repayment of the money was not due to any misconduct or negligence on his part.

(5) Any condition requiring or binding any applicant for shares to waive compliance with any requirement of this section shall be void.

(6) This section, except subsection (3) thereof, shall not apply to any allotment of shares subsequent to the first allotment of shares offered to the public for subscription.

Amendments

a Sub-s (1) substituted by IFCMPA 2005, s 53.

b Words substituted by C(A)A 1983, Sch 1, para 7.

Definitions

'company': CA 1963, s 2(1); 'director': CA 1963, s 2(1); 'the minimum subscription': CA 1963, s 2(1), s 53(2); 'prospectus': CA 1963, s 2(1); 'share': CA 1963, s 2(1).

Notes

Distinction between 'allotment' and 'issue' of shares: The term 'issue' in relation to shares means something distinct from allotment and imports some subsequent act by the company whereby the title of the allottee is completed. Shares are therefore deemed to have been issued once the subscriber has been notified of the amount of shares which have been allotted to him and his name has been entered on the register of members.[1] It is not necessary, however, that the allottee should actually be issued with a share certificate in order for the shares to be regarded as having been issued.[2]

1 *National Westminster Bank plc v Inland Revenue Commissioners* [1994] 2 BCLC 239; *Re Ambrose Lake Tin and Copper Co, Clarke's Case* (1878) 8 Ch D 635; *Oswald Tillotson Ltd v Inland Revenue Commissioners* [1933] 1 KB 134.

2 *Re Heaton's Steel and Iron Co, Clarke's Case* (1878) 8 Ch D 635; *Attorney-General v Regent's Canal and Dock Co* [1904] 1 KB 263.

Contract of allotment

Meaning of 'allotment': 'Allotment' is generally taken to mean neither more nor less than acceptance by the company of an offer to take shares.[1]

Offer and acceptance: An agreement to take shares may be made orally or in writing.[2] In so far as there is an invitation to treat, this is to be found in the listing particulars or prospectus, if any, issued by the company. The offer arises by the applicant applying to the company for a particular number of shares or debentures,[3] and the contract is concluded by the company communicating its acceptance to the offeror.[4]

Lapse and revocation of offer: An application to subscribe for shares or debentures, like any other offer, will lapse unless it is accepted within a reasonable period of time. Furthermore, the offer may be withdrawn at any time before communication of an acceptance[5] unless the application has, for valuable consideration, been made irrevocable,[6] or unless the application has been made in pursuance of a prospectus issued generally,[7] in which case, the application is irrevocable until after the expiration of nine days from the date on which the prospectus was first issued or until one of the persons potentially liable pursuant to s 49 for untrue statements in the prospectus gives a public notice under that section for the purpose of limiting or excluding liability,[8] whichever is earlier.[9] The withdrawal may be made orally[10] or by some other act which is made known to the company and which is inconsistent with the continuance of the offer.[11]

Communication of acceptance: Mere entry of the applicant's name in the register of members is not sufficient acceptance, since the applicant is not under any duty to examine the register.[12] Instead, there must be communication of an acceptance, whether in writing or orally or by conduct (eg by demanding payment for the shares).[13] Without communication of an acceptance there is no contract.[14] However, if the acceptance is communicated by post, it is effective as soon as the letter is posted,[15] despite the fact that the letter may never actually reach the applicant.[16]

Acceptance must be unconditional: The acceptance as communicated to the applicant must be unconditional in order to be effective. Thus, where an applicant applies for shares which are to be credited as fully paid, the company cannot accept by allotting him shares which are credited as being only partly paid[17] unless of course the applicant expressly or implicitly agrees to such a variation of terms.[18] Similarly, if an applicant applies for securities on condition that the company agrees to purchase goods from him, the company cannot validly accept the application unless it also agrees to acquire the goods.[19]

1 *Re Florence Land and Public Works Co, Nicol's Case* (1883) 29 Ch D 421.

2 *Re Olympic Fire and General Insurance Co* [1920] 1 Ch 582, aff'd [1920] 2 Ch 341.

3 If the securities are being issued by way of a *rights issue*, the letter of rights which details the number of shares or debentures to which the person is entitled is in itself an offer, and the contract is made by the member or debentureholder communicating his acceptance to the company: *Re New Eberhardt Co, ex parte Menzies* (1889) 43 Ch D 118, 126. Indeed, if the rights issue takes the form of a provisional letter of allotment, the contract will be completed by the person either paying an instalment of the issue price to the company or by renouncing the letter of allotment to another person. On the other hand, if the rights issue is by way of *open offer* (as to the meaning of which, see the notes to CA 1963, s 43), the offer is made by the applicant specifying the number of shares or debentures for which he wishes to subscribe, and by the company communicating its acceptance of the offer.

4 *Re Oriental Bank, Alabaster's Case* (1868) LR 7 Eq 273; *Re Peruvian Railways Co, Robinson's Case* (1869) 4 Ch App 322; *Re Florence Land and Public Works Co, Nicol's Case* (1883) 29 Ch D 421; *Re Metropolitan Fire Insurance Co, Wallace's Case* [1900] 2 Ch 671.

5 *Ramsgate Victoria Hotel Co v Montefiore* (1866) LR 1 Exch 109; *Hebb's Case* (1867) LR 4 Eq 9; *Pentelow's Case* (1869) 4 Ch App 178.

6 *Re Olympic Fire and General Reinsurance Co* [1920] 1 Ch 582; on appeal [1920] 2 Ch 341.

7 'Issued generally' means issued to persons other than existing members or debentureholders: CA 1963, s 2(1).

8 As to the types of notice that may be given and the circumstances in which same might be required, see CA 1963, s 49 and the notes thereto.

9 CA 1963, s 56(5).

10 *Re Natal Investment Co* (1869) 20 LT 962; *Truman's Case* [1894] 3 Ch 272.

11 *Dickinson v Dodds* (1876) 2 Ch D 463.

12 Registration of the allotment without express communication to the applicant may, however, be effective where the applicant is one of the directors of the company since he will be deemed to have notice, in such circumstances, of what has happened: *Bird's Case* (1864) 4 De GJ and Sm 200; *Levita's Case* (1867) 3 Ch App 36; *Fletcher's Case* (1867) 37 LJ Ch 49.

13 *Forget v Cement Products Co of Canada* [1916] WN 259.

14 *Re Richmond Hill Hotel Co, Pellat's Case* (1867) 2 Ch App 527; *Hebb's Case* (1867) LR 4 Eq 9; *Gunn's Case* (1867) 3 Ch App 40; *Sahlgreen and Carroll's Case* (1868) 3 Ch App 323; *Ward's Case* (1870) LR 10 Eq 659; *Re Land Shipping Colliery Co, Milford Haven Ltd* (1868) 18 LT 786.

15 *Adams v Lindsell* (1818) 1 B and Ald 681; *MacLagan's case* [1882] WN 98; *Harris' Case* (1872) 7 Ch App 587; *Hebb's Case* (1867) LR 4 Eq 9; *Wall's Case* (1872) LR 15 Eq 18.

16 *Household Fire and Carriage Accident Insurance Co v Grant* (1879) 4 Ex D 216. However, if the applicant wishes to withdraw his offer, mere posting will be insufficient. Rather, he will have to ensure that the communication actually reaches the company: *Byrne v Van Tienhoven* (1880) 5 CPD 344; *Henthorn v Fraser* [1892] 2 Ch 27.

17 *Re Richmond Hill Hotel Co, Pellatt's Case* (1867) 2 Ch App 527; *Re United Ports and General Insurance Co* (1873) 8 Ch App 1002; *Beck's Case* (1874) 9 Ch App 392; *Re Barangah Oil Refining Co, Arnot's Case* (1887) 36 Ch D 702.

18 *Re Richmond Hill Hotel Co, Elkington's Case* (1867) 2 Ch App 511.

19 *Re Sunken Vessels Recovery Co, Wood's Case* (1858) 3 De G and J 85.

Minimum subscription for shares of unlimited public companies: The provisions of CA 1963, s 53 have been largely superseded by C(A)A 1983, s 22. Accordingly, s 53 only continues to have any practical application in the case of unlimited public companies. Such companies are prohibited from making a first allotment[1] of shares[2] which have been offered to the public[3] for subscription[4] unless there has first been paid to and received[5] by the company, the amount stated in the prospectus as the minimum amount which, in the opinion of the directors, is necessary in order to meet the following:

(a) the purchase price of any property which has been or is to be acquired, and which is to be wholly or partly paid for out of the proceeds of the issue of shares;[6]

(b) any preliminary expenses of the company and any commission payable to underwriters;[7]

(c) the repayment of any moneys which were borrowed to pay the foregoing;[8] and

(d) the company's working capital requirements.[9]

The minimum amount payable per share on application therefor by the subscriber is 5% of the par value.[10] Moreover, in calculating whether the minimum amount as so stated in the prospectus has in fact been received, one must take into account only such sums as have been paid in cash.[11] Clearly, payment by cheque will be regarded as payment in cash.[12]

1 CA 1963, s 53(6) expressly confines the application of s 53, other than s 53(3), to the first allotment of shares to the public.

2 Notably the issue of debentures are excluded from the application of the section.

3 For the definition of an 'offer to the public' see CA 1963, s 61.

4 The reference to 'subscription' takes *offers for sale* outside the scope of the section. In any event the problem of undersubscription will not arise in the case of an *offer for sale* since the issuing

house will already have agreed to take the entire amount of the issue. Accordingly, any risk of inadequate public demand for the shares lies with the issuing house itself and not with the company.

5 A sum is deemed to have been paid to and received by the company is a cheque in that amount is received in good faith by the company and the directors have no reason for suspecting that the cheque will not be honoured: CA 1963, s 53(2).

6 CA 1963, Sch 3, para 4(a)(i).

7 CA 1963, Sch 3, para 4(a)(ii).

8 CA 1963, Sch 3, para 4(a)(iii).

9 CA 1963, Sch 3, para 4(a)(iv).

10 CA 1963, s 53(3).

11 CA 1963, s 53(2).

12 CA 1963, s 53(2). See also CA 1963, s 58 and the notes thereto as to what constitutes a cash consideration for shares.

Minimum subscription by a plc: In the case of a plc, C(A)A 1983, s 22, states that no allotment may be made of shares which have been offered for subscription unless:

(a) the capital has been subscribed for in full; or

(b) the offer states that even if the capital is not subscribed for in full, the amount actually subscribed for may be allotted in any event or in the event of the conditions specified in the offer being satisfied, and the conditions in question have in fact been satisfied.[1]

For the purposes of s 22, the word 'subscribed' is deemed to include payment for shares either in cash or alternatively by way of non-cash consideration.[2] Two types of non-cash consideration are, however, unacceptable, namely:

(a) an undertaking by a person that he or another will do work or perform services for the plc or for any other person;[3] and

(b) an undertaking which is to be performed more than five years after the date of the allotment.[4]

In addition to these limitations, the Registrar cannot issue the plc with a certificate entitling it to commence business unless, inter alia, the nominal its issued share capital is not less than the 'authorised minimum' (currently €38,092.14).[5]

1 C(A)A 1983, s 22(1).

2 C(A)A 1983, s 22(3). The non-cash consideration will, however, have to be independently valued before any allotment can take place. See C(A)A 1983, ss 28–36.

3 C(A)A 1983, s 26.

4 C(A)A 1983, s 29.

5 C(A)A 1983, ss 6 and 19.

Return of moneys, etc in the event of undersubscription: If the minimum subscription is not received, in the case of an unlimited public company, or if there has not been full subscription in the case of a plc, within 40 days after the first issue of the prospectus, the company must return to the subscribers any moneys paid by them for the shares.[1] Failure to make the repayments within 48 days after the issue of the prospectus exposes the directors to joint and several liability for the unreturned amounts together with interest thereon at 5% per annum.[2] A director may, however, avoid personal liability by showing that the failure to repay was not due to any misconduct or negligence on his part.[3]

Before suing either the company or the directors for a return of his moneys, the plaintiff must first rescind the allotment.[4]

1 CA 1963, s 53(4). In the case of a plc, where shares have been paid for by way of non-cash consideration, the company must either return the non-cash consideration itself or, if this is not reasonably practicable, the monetary equivalent thereof: C(A)A 1983, s 22(2) and (3).

2 CA 1963, s 53(4).

3 CA 1963, s 53(4).
4 *Burton v Bevan* [1908] 2 Ch 240.

Effect of irregular allotment: If an allotment of shares is made by the company without having received the minimum subscription (in the case of an unlimited public company) or the full subscription (in the case of a plc), that allotment will be voidable at the instance of the subscriber[1] within one month[2] after the date of the allotment and even though the company may have gone into liquidation in the meantime.[3]

Where the subscriber avoids the allotment within the prescribed time limit, the company must within one month thereafter deliver to the Registrar a notice to that effect.[4] Failure to deliver this notice is a criminal offence.[5]

In addition to the foregoing, any director of the company who knowingly[6] makes an allotment in contravention of CA 1963, s 53 and C(A)A 1983, s 22, shall be liable to compensate the company and the allottee respectively for any loss, damages or costs which may have been sustained or incurred thereby.[7] Proceedings against the directors must be commenced within two years from the date of the allotment or they will become statute barred.[8]

1 See *Finance and Issue Ltd v Canadian Produce Corporation* [1905] 1 Ch 37.
2 It is not necessary that legal proceedings should have been instituted within the month. Rather, it will suffice to give notice of avoidance within the month, provided that this notice is followed promptly by legal proceedings: *Re National Motor Mail-Coach Co* [1908] 2 Ch 515.
3 CA 1963, s 55(1).
4 CA 1963, s 55(2).
5 CA 1963, s 55(2), applying the provisions of CA 1963, s 58(3) and (4).
6 'Knowingly' means 'with knowledge of the facts which give rise to the contravention': *Burton v Bevan* [1908] 2 Ch 240.
7 CA 1963, s 55(3).
8 CA 1963, s 55(3).

Time limits for allotment of shares: Even if there has been a sufficient subscription for the shares, no allotment may be made in pursuance of a prospectus which has been 'issued generally'[1] until the beginning of the fourth day after the date on which the prospectus was first issued or until such later time as may be specified in the prospectus itself.[2]

1 'Issued generally' means 'issued to persons other than existing members and debentureholders': CA 1963, s 2(1).
2 CA 1963, s 56.

Investment companies: The provisions of CA 1963, s 53 do not apply to investment companies.[1]

1 CA 1990, 260(2).

UK legislation

See CA 1985, s 83.

---

54 Prohibition of allotment in certain cases unless statement in lieu of prospectus delivered to registrar

[...][a]

Amendments

a Section repealed by IFCMPA 2005, s 40(1)(a).

---

55 Effect of irregular allotment

[(1) An allotment made by a company to an applicant in contravention of sections 53 [...][b], shall be voidable at the instance of the applicant within one month after the date of the allotment, and not later, and shall be so voidable notwithstanding that the company is in the course of being wound up.][a]

(2) Where an allotment is avoided under this section the company shall within one month thereafter deliver to the registrar of companies for registration a notice to that effect, and subsections (3) and (4) of section 58, shall apply in relation to this subsection as they apply in relation to that section.

(3) If any director of a company knowingly contravenes, or permits or authorises the contravention of, any of the provisions of [section 53][b] with respect to allotment, he shall be liable to compensate the company and the allottee respectively for any loss, damages or costs which the company or allottee may have sustained or incurred thereby, so however that proceedings to recover any such loss, damages or costs shall not be commenced after the expiration of 2 years from the date of the allotment.

Amendments

a CA 1963, s 55(1) substituted by C(A)A 1983, Sch 1, para 9.

b Reference to section 54 removed by IFCMPA 2005, s 54.

Definitions

'company': CA 1963, s 2(1); 'director': CA 1963, s 2(1); ' the registrar of companies': CA 1963, s 2(1).

Notes

See the notes entitled 'effect of irregular allotment' in CA 1963, ss 53 and 54.

UK legislation

See CA 1985, s 85.

---

56 Applications for, and allotment of, shares and debentures

[...][a]

Amendments

a Section repealed by IFCMPA 2005, s 40(1)(a).

---

57 Allotment of shares and debentures to be dealt in on stock exchange

(1) Where a prospectus, whether issued generally or not, states that application has been or will be made for permission for the [securities][a] offered thereby to be dealt in on any stock exchange [or regulated market],[b] any allotment made on an application in pursuance of the prospectus shall, whenever made, be void if the permission has not been applied for before the third day after the first issue of the prospectus or if the permission has not been granted within 6 weeks from the date of the closing of the subscription lists.

(2) Where the permission has not been applied for as aforesaid or has not been granted, the company shall forthwith repay without interest all money received from applicants in pursuance of the prospectus, and, if any such money is not repaid within 8 days after the company becomes liable to repay it, the directors of the company shall be jointly and severally liable to repay that money with interest at the rate of 5 per cent. per annum from the expiration of the eighth day, so however that a director shall not be liable if he proves that the default in the repayment of the money was not due to any misconduct or negligence on his part.

(3) All money received as aforesaid shall be kept in a separate bank account so long as the company may become liable to repay it under subsection (2); and, if default is made in complying with this subsection, the company and every officer of the company who is in default shall be [guilty of an offence and liable to a fine][c] not exceeding [€1,904.61].[d]

(4) Any condition requiring or binding any applicant for [securities][a] to waive compliance with any requirement of this section shall be void.

(5) This section shall have effect—

- (a) in relation to any [securities][a] agreed to be taken by a person underwriting an offer thereof by a prospectus as if he had applied therefor in pursuance of the prospectus, and
- (b) in relation to a prospectus offering [securities][a] for sale with the following modifications,—
  - (i) references to sale shall be substituted for references to allotment,
  - (ii) the persons by whom the offer is made, and not the company, shall be liable under subsection (2) to repay money received from applicants, and references to the company's liability under that subsection shall be construed accordingly, and
  - (iii) for the reference in subsection (3) to the company and every officer of the company who is in default there shall be substituted a reference to any person by or through whom the offer is made and who knowingly and wilfully authorises or permits the default.

(6) In reckoning for the purposes of this section the third day after another day, any intervening day which is a Saturday or Sunday or which is a bank holiday shall be disregarded and if the third day (as so reckoned) is itself a Saturday or Sunday or such a bank holiday there shall for the said purposes be substituted the first day thereafter which is none of them.

[(7) The provisions of this section shall not apply in relation to an allotment of non-equity securities.][e]

Amendments

a Substitution of 'securities' for 'shares or debentures': IFCMPA 2005, s 55(a).

b Insertion of reference to 'regulated market': IFCMPA 2005, s 55(b).

c CA 1963, s 57(3) words 'shall be guilty of an offence and liable to a fine' substituted for 'shall be liable to a fine' by C(A&A)A 2003, Sch 2, Item No 1.

d '£500' substituted for '£100' by C(A)A 1982, Sch 1 and increased to £1,500 by CA 1990, s 240(7) as inserted by CLEA 2001, s 104(c) and converted to €1,904.61 by Council

Regulations (EC) No 1103/97, No 974/98 and No 2866/98 and the Economic and Monetary Union Act 1998, s 6.

e Sub-s (7) inserted by IFCMPA 2005, s 55(c).

Definitions

'bank holiday': CA 1963, s 2(1); 'company': CA 1963, s 2(1); 'debenture': CA 1963, s 2(1); 'director': CA 1963, s 2(1); 'issued generally': CA 1963, s 2(1); 'officer': CA 1963, s 2(1); 'officer in default': CA 1963, s 383; 'prospectus': CA 1963, s 2(1); 'share': CA 1963, s 2(1).

Notes

Allotment of securities for which listing is to be sought*:* If a company or issuing house issues a prospectus stating that a Stock Exchange listing is to be sought for the securities in question, any allotment or sale of such securities whether to a member of the public or to an underwriter [1] shall be void if:

(a) the application for listing has not been made before the third day after the first issue of the prospectus;[2] or

(b) the listing has not been granted within 6 weeks from the date of the closing of the subscription lists.[3]

1 See CA 1963, s 57(5)(a).

2 As to the date upon which a prospectus issued generally is deemed to have been first issued, see CA 1963, s 56(2) and (6).

3 The Companies Acts do not require the prospectus to fix any time for the closing of the subscription lists and therefore it would technically be permissible for the company to keep the lists open unless and until the issue is fully subscribed. In practice, however, it is usual for the prospectus to state that the list will be closed on or before a particular date.

Return of moneys: If the prospectus comes within the terms of CA 1963, s 57 and the company either fails to apply for a listing before the third day after the first issue of the prospectus or alternatively has its application rejected by the Stock Exchange, it must forthwith repay without interest any moneys which were received by it from persons who had applied for the securities in question. Moreover, if the money is not repaid within eight days, the directors shall become jointly and severally liable for the unreturned amounts together with interest thereon at 5% per annum.[1] A director may, however, avoid personal liability by showing that the failure to repay was not due to any misconduct or negligence on his part.[2]

Pending allotment of the securities or a return of moneys, as the case may be, the company must keep the sums in question in a separate bank account.[3] These moneys will therefore be impressed with a trust in favour of the applicants and they will be entitled to trace the amounts paid by them into the account in the event of the company going into liquidation.[4]

1 CA 1963, s 57(2).

2 CA 1963, s 57(2).

3 CA 1963, s 57(3).

4 *Re Nanwa Gold Mines Ltd, Ballantyne v Nanwa Gold Mines Ltd* [1955] 3 All ER 219.

UK legislation

See CA 1985, ss 86, 87.

---

58 Return as to allotments

(1) Whenever a company limited by shares or a company limited by guarantee and having a share capital makes any allotment of its shares, the company shall within one month thereafter deliver to the registrar of companies for registration—

(a) a return of the allotments, stating the number and nominal amount of the shares comprised in the allotment, the names, addresses [...][a] of the allottees and the amount, if any, paid or due and payable on each share; and

(b) in the case of shares allotted as fully or partly paid up otherwise than in cash, a contract in writing constituting the title of the allottee to the allotment together with any contract of sale, or for services or other consideration in respect of which that allotment was made, such contracts being duly stamped, and a return stating the number and nominal amount of shares so allotted, the extent to which they are to be treated as paid up, and the consideration for which they have been allotted,

provided that, where shares are allotted to the members of a company on a capitalisation or provisionally allotted on a rights issue, it shall not be necessary to make a return of the particular allottees, notwithstanding that in either case there may be a right of renunciation.

(2) Where such a contract as above mentioned is not reduced to writing, the company shall within one month after the allotment deliver to the registrar of companies for registration the prescribed particulars of the contract stamped with the same stamp duty as would have been payable if the contract had been reduced to writing, and those particulars shall be deemed to be an instrument within the meaning of the Stamp Act, 1891, and the registrar may, as a condition of filing the particulars, require that the duty payable thereon be adjudicated under section 12 of that Act.

(3) If default is made in complying with this section, every officer of the company who is in default [shall be guilty of an offence and liable to a fine][b] not exceeding [€1,904.61].[c]

(4) In case of default in delivering to the registrar of companies within one month after the allotment any document required to be delivered by this section, the company, or any officer liable for the default, may apply to the court for relief, and the court, if satisfied that the omission to deliver the document was accidental or due to inadvertence or that it is just and equitable to grant relief, may make an order extending the time for the delivery of the document for such period as the court may think proper.

Amendments

a Words 'and occupations' deleted by C(A)A 1963, s 19.

b CA 1963, s 58(3) words 'shall be guilty of an offence and liable to a fine' substituted for 'shall be liable to a fine' by C(A&A)A 2003, Sch 2, Item No 1.

c '£500' substituted for '£100' by C(A)A 1982, Sch 1, increased to £1,500 by CA 1990, s 240(7) as inserted by CLEA 2001, s 104(c) and converted to €1,904.61 by Council Regulations (EC) No 1103/97, No 974/98 and No 2866/98 and the Economic and Monetary Union Act 1998, s 6.

Definitions

'company': CA 1963, s 2(1); 'company limited by guarantee': CA 1963, s 2(1), 5(2); 'company limited by shares': CA 1963, s 2(1), 5(1); 'the court': CA 1963, s 2(1); 'document': CA 1963, s 2(1): 'member': CA 1963, s 31; 'officer': CA 1963, s 2(1); 'officer in default': CA 1963, s 383; 'prescribed': CA 1963, s 2(1); 'the registrar of companies': CA 1963, s 2(1); 'share': CA 1963, s 2(1).

Notes

Payment for shares

Cash and non-cash consideration: CA 1963, s 58 clearly envisages the possibility of shares being allotted otherwise than for cash. This is reinforced by C(A)A 1983, s 26 which expressly states that subject to certain exceptions, shares may be allotted for 'money or money's worth (including goodwill and expertise).'[1]

Whether shares are allotted for cash or for a non-cash consideration, they cannot be issued at a discount (ie at less than their nominal value).[2]

Plcs and non-cash consideration: Under C(A)A 1983, s 26 *et seq* restrictions are imposed on plcs in relation to the allotment of shares for a non-cash consideration. In particular, a plc may not accept by way of consideration for the allotment of shares either of the following:

(a) an undertaking from any person that he or another will do work or perform services for the company or for any other person;[3] or

(b) a non-cash consideration that includes an undertaking which is to be or may be performed more than five years after the date of allotment.[4]

If a plc proceeds to allot the shares in contravention of these restrictions the allottee becomes liable to pay to the company in cash an amount equivalent to the value attributed by the parties to the non-cash consideration, together with interest thereon,[5] even though he still remains liable to pay to the company the non-cash consideration as well.[6] The allottee may however apply to the court for relief against what could in effect be a double liability for the price of the shares.[7]

Even if the non-cash consideration is of a type which is not *per se* prohibited by the Companies Acts, the allotment of the shares must first be preceded by an independent valuation of the consideration in question.[8] Failure to obtain such a valuation will result in the allottee being required to pay both the non-cash consideration as well as the cash equivalent and interest,[9] although, in appropriate cases he may apply to the court for relief against this dual exposure.[10]

Private companies and non-cash consideration: Unlike plcs, there is no statutory mechanism for the valuation of the non-cash consideration paid to a private company for an allotment of shares. Indeed, the courts have held that they will not enquire into the adequacy of the consideration paid for the shares[11] unless:

(a) there is evidence of fraud; or

(b) the contract demonstrates on its face that the consideration is manifestly inadequate or illusory.[12]

Although the court will not normally assess the adequacy of the non-cash consideration which is paid for the shares, it may be prepared to do so where the directors have themselves failed to make any such assessment in advance of the allotment.[13] Moreover, the absence of a bona fide valuation by the directors will result in the shares being treated as wholly unpaid and the shareholder will therefore be liable to pay to the company the nominal value of the shares in cash.[14] But if the allottee is unaware of the fact, he may be able to repudiate the allotment and thus avoid liability.[15]

Past consideration: As a matter of general contract law, past consideration is no consideration.[16] Accordingly shares allotted for such consideration will be treated as unpaid and the allottee will be liable for the full cash amount.[17]

What constitutes payment in cash?: A share in a company is deemed to have been paid up in cash or allotted for cash if the consideration for the allotment or the payment up is cash[18] received by the company or is a cheque received by the company in good faith which the directors have no good reason for suspecting will not be paid.[19] Likewise, shares are allotted for cash to the extent that they are credited as paid up when being issued to a creditor in discharge of a liquidated debt owed by the company,[20] or where the cash amount payable under the contract of allotment is set off against moneys due by the company to the subscriber pursuant to a separate transaction.[21] Indeed, to the extent that the creditor agrees to the discharge of his debt by the issue to a third party of shares which are credited as fully paid, an allotment for cash will be deemed to have taken place.[22]

On the other hand, the following will not be regarded as allotments for cash:

(a) payment of, or an undertaking to pay, cash to any person other than the company;[23]

(b) the issue of shares in settlement of a liquidated claim for damages;[24]

(c) an allotment by way of accord and satisfaction;[25]

(d) the allotment of shares in discharge of liquidated sums which will become payable by the company at a future date;[26] and

(e) the assignment to the company of a debt owed to the allottee by a third party.[27]

1 See, for example, *McCoy v Greene* [1984] IEHC 70 (Costello J) where shares were allotted in consideration for the supply of services.

2 See C(A)A 1983, s 27 and the notes thereto.

3 C(A)A 1983, s 26(2).

4 C(A)A 1983, s 29(1).

5 C(A)A 1983, ss 26(3) and 29(2).

6 C(A)A 1983, s 36.

7 See C(A)A 1983, s 34.

8 C(A)A 1983, ss 30–33.

9 C(A)A 1983, s 36.

10 C(A)A 1983, s 34.

11 *Re Leinster Contract Corporation* [1902] 1 IR 349; *Re Wragg* [1897] 1 Ch 796; *Re Heyford Co, Pell's Case* (1869) 5 Ch App 11; *Hong Kong and China Glass Co v Glen* [1914] 1 Ch 527; *Re Baglan Hall Colliery Co* (1870) 5 Ch App 346; *Ooregum Gold Mining Co of India v Roper* [1892] AC 125; *Re Theatrical Trust Ltd, Chapman's Case* [1895] 1 Ch 771.

12 *Re Theatrical Trust Ltd, Chapman's Case* [1895] 1 Ch 771, 774; *Ooregum Gold Mining Co of India v Roper* [1892] AC 125, 148; *Re Wragg* [1897] 1 Ch 796, 836; *Mosley v Koffyfontein Mines Ltd* [1904] 2 Ch 108; *Park Business Interiors Ltd v Park* [1992] BCLC 1034.

13 *Tintin Exploration Syndicate Ltd v Sandys* (1947) 177 LT 412; *Hong Kong and China Gas Co Ltd v Glen* [1914] 1 Ch 527; *Re White Star Line Ltd* [1938] 1 All ER 607; *Re Alkaline Reduction Syndicate, Ames' Case* [1896] WN 79; *Park Business Interiors Ltd v Park* [1992] BCLC 1034.

14 *Re White Star Line Ltd* [1938] 1 All ER 607. The allottee, although liable to pay the nominal value of the shares in cash, should be able to sue for a *quantum valebant* or *quantum meruit* for the value of the non-cash consideration which he has furnished to the company. In a liquidation, however, such a claim cannot be the subject of a set-off as between the shareholder and the company. Instead, the shareholder must first pay the full cash price to the liquidator and the prove in the winding up for the value of his claim: *Re Overend, Gurney and Co, Grissell's Case* (1866) 1 Ch App 528.

15 *Re MacDonald Sons and Co* [1894] 1 Ch 89.

16 Clark, *Contract Law in Ireland* (3rd edn, Roundhall Sweet & Maxwell) Ch 2 at p 47 *et seq*.

17 *Re Eddystone Marine Insurance Co* [1893] 3 Ch 9; *Re Leinster Contract Corporation* [1902] 1 IR 349.

18 'Cash' includes foreign currency: C(A)A 1983, s 2(3).

19 C(A)A 1983, s 2(3)(a).

20 *Re Harmony and Montague Tin and Copper Mining Co, Spargo's Case* (1873) 8 Ch App 407.

21 *Re Gibson, Little and Co Ltd* (1880–81) 5 LR Ir 139, 155; *Spargo's Case* (1873) 8 Ch App 407 *Re Limehouse Works Co, Coates' Case* (1873) LR 17 Eq 169; *Larocque v Beauchemin* [1897] AC 358; *North Sydney Investment and Tramway Co v Higgins* [1899] AC 263; *Adamson's Case* (1874) LR 18 Eq 670; *Re Regent United Service Stores, ex parte Bentley* (1879) 12 Ch D 850; *Re Foreign and Colonial Gas Co, ex parte Wilson* [1874] WN 139. To the extent that payment is by

way of set-off, the allottee will receive credit against calls which have not yet been made: *Re Jones, Lloyd and Co* (1889) 41 Ch D 159. However, if the company is wound up before all calls have been made, the allottee cannot rely on the set-off to resist payment to the liquidator of the outstanding calls. Instead, he will have to pay the calls and prove in the liquidation for the balance: *Re Paraguassu Steam Tramway Co, Black and Co's Case* (1872) 8 Ch App 254; *Re Johannesburg Hotel Co, ex parte Zoutpansberg Prospecting Co* [1891] 1 Ch 119; *Re Overend, Gurney and Co, Grissell's Case* (1866) 1 Ch App 528; *Re General Works Co, Gill's Case* (1879) 12 Ch D 755.

22 *Re Paragassu Steam Tramway Co, Ferrao's Case* (1879) 9 Ch App 355; *Re Barrow-in-Furness and Northern Counties Land and Investment Co* (1880) 14 Ch D 400; *Re Jones, Lloyd and Co* (1889) 41 Ch D 159; *North Sydney Investment and Tramway Co v Higgins* [1899] AC 263.

23 C(A)A 1983, s 2(3)(b).

24 *Re Barangah Oil Refining Co, Arnot's Case* (1887) 36 Ch D 702.

25 *Re Johannesburg Hotel Co, ex parte Zoutpansberg Prospecting Co* [1891] 1 Ch 119.

26 *Re Richmond Hill Hotel Co, Elkington's Case* (1867) 2 Ch App 511; *Re Richmond Hill Hotel Co, Pellatt's Case* (1867) 2 Ch App 527; *Re Land Development Association, Kent's Case* (1888) 39 Ch D 259.

27 *System Control plc v Munro Corporate plc* [1990] BCLC 659.

Contents of return as to allotments: Whenever a company limited by shares or limited by guarantee and having a share capital allots shares, it must, within one month of the date of allotment, make a return to the Registrar stating the number and par value of the shares in question, as well as giving details of the names and addresses of the allottees and the amount paid or payable by them for the shares.

If all or part of the consideration for the allotment is otherwise than in cash, the return must state the nature of the consideration and the number of shares being paid for in this manner as well as explaining the extent to which the shares are to be treated as having thereby been paid for. Moreover, there must be included with the return either:

(a) a duly stamped copy[1] of the contract giving rise to the non-cash consideration; or

(b) in the event that the contract was not made in writing, a duly stamped memorandum setting out the essential terms of the agreement between the parties; and

(c) in the case of a plc, an independent person's report, valuing the non-cash consideration.[2]

Although it will be sufficient to include in the return a general rather than a particular description of the consideration[3] the requirement of the section will not be satisfied if the consideration is merely stated by reference to a document which has not been included with the return.[4] Nor will it suffice to state that the consideration is the fact that some other contract has been entered into.[5]

1 *Re Frost and Co* [1899] 2 Ch 207, 214.

2 C(A)A 1983, s 31(2).

3 *Re Frost and Co* [1898] 2 Ch 556, 560, aff'd [1899] 2 Ch 207; *Re Robert Watson and Co* [1899] 2 Ch 509, 514.

4 *Re Frost and Co* [1899] 2 Ch 207, 216; *Re Robert Watson and Co* [1899] 2 Ch 509; *Re British Columbia Electric Railway Co* [1899] WN 260.

5 *Re Frost and Co* [1899] 2 Ch 207, 216.

Publication of allotment in Companies Registration Office Gazette: All returns of allotments made by a plc must be published in Companies Registration Office Gazette.[1]

1 C(A)A 1983, s 55(1)(g), as amended by IFMCA 2005, s 72.

Investment companies: The provisions of CA 1963, s 58 do not apply to investment companies.[1]

1 CA 1990, 260(2).

UK legislation

See CA 1985, s 88.

Commissions and Discounts and Financial Assistance for Purchase of Shares

59 Power to pay certain commissions, and prohibition of payment of all other commissions and discounts

[...][a]

Amendments

a Section repealed by IFCMPA 2005, s 40(1)(a).

60 Giving of financial assistance by a company for the purchase of its shares

(1) Subject to subsections (2), (12) and (13), it shall not be lawful for a company to give, whether directly or indirectly, and whether by means of a loan, guarantee, the provision of security or otherwise, any financial assistance for the purpose of or in connection with a purchase or subscription made or to be made by any person of or for any shares in the company, or, where the company is a subsidiary company, in its holding company.

(2) Subsection (1) shall not apply to the giving of financial assistance by a company if—

(a) such financial assistance is given under the authority of a special resolution of the company passed not more than 12 months previously; and

(b) [the company has forwarded with each notice of the meeting at which the special resolution is to be considered, or, if the procedure referred to in subsection (6) is followed, the company has appended to the resolution, a copy of a statutory declaration which complies with subsections (3) and (4) and also delivers, within 21 days after the date on which the financial assistance was given, a copy of the declaration to the registrar of companies for registration.][a]

(3) The statutory declaration shall be made at a meeting of the directors held not more than 24 days before the said meeting and shall be made by the directors or, in the case of a company having more than two directors, by a majority of the directors.

(4) The statutory declaration shall state—

(a) the form which such assistance is to take;

(b) the persons to whom such assistance is to be given;

(c) the purpose for which the company intends those persons to use such assistance;

(d) that the declarants have made a full inquiry into the affairs of the company and that, having done so, they have formed the opinion that the company, having carried out the transaction whereby such assistance is to be given, will be able to pay its debts in full as they become due.

(5) Any director of a company making the statutory declaration without having reasonable grounds for the opinion that the company having carried out the transaction whereby such assistance is to be given will be able to pay its debts in full as they become due, [shall be guilty of an offence and liable to imprisonment for a period not exceeding

6 months or to a fine not exceeding €1,904.61][b] or to both; and if the company is wound up within the period of 12 months after the making of the statutory declaration and its debts are not paid or provided for in full within the period of 12 months after the commencement of the winding up, it shall be presumed until the contrary is shown that the director did not have reasonable grounds for his opinion.

(6) [The special resolution referred to in subsection (1)(a) may be passed in accordance with section 141(8).][c]

(7) Unless all of the members of the company entitled to vote at general meetings of the company vote in favour of the special resolution, the transaction whereby such assistance is to be given shall not be carried out before the expiry of 30 days after such special resolution has been passed or, if an application under subsection (8) is made, until such application has been disposed of by the court.

(8) If application is made to the court in accordance with this section for the cancellation of the special resolution, such special resolution shall not have effect except to the extent to which it is confirmed by the court.

(9) Subject to subsection (10), an application under subsection (8) may be made by the holders of not less in the aggregate than 10 per cent. in nominal value of the company's issued share capital or any class thereof.

(10) An application shall not be made under subsection (8) by any person who has consented to or voted in favour of the special resolution.

(11) An application under subsection (8) must be made within 28 days after the date on which the special resolution was passed and may be made on behalf of the persons entitled to make the application by such one or more of their number as they may appoint in writing for the purpose.

[(12) Nothing in this section shall be taken to prohibit—

(a) the payment by a company of a dividend or making by it of any distribution out of profits of the company available for distribution;

(b) the discharge by a company of a liability lawfully incurred by it;

(c) the provision of finance or delivery of security to discharge, or effect what is commonly known as refinancing of, an existing loan or other liability or security in relation to that existing loan where the incurring of the existing loan or liability or the delivery of the existing security had occurred under the authority of a special resolution of the company passed in accordance with subsection (2);

(d) subject to subsection (13), where the lending of money is part of the ordinary business of the company, the lending of money by a company in the ordinary course of its business;

(e) subject to subsection (13), the provision by a company, in accordance with any scheme for the time being in force, of money for the purchase of, or subscription for, fully paid shares in the company or its holding company, being a purchase or subscription of or for shares to be held by or for the benefit of employees or former employees of the company or of any subsidiary of the company including any person who is or was a director holding a salaried employment or office in the company or any subsidiary of the company;

(f) subject to subsection (13), the making by a company of loans to persons, other than directors, bona fide in the employment of the company or any subsidiary of the company with a view to enabling those persons to purchase or subscribe for fully paid shares in the company or its holding company to be held by themselves as beneficial owners thereof;

(g) the making or giving by a company of one or more representations, warranties or indemnities to a person who has purchased or subscribed for, or proposes to purchase or subscribe for, shares in the company or its holding company for the purpose of or in connection with that purchase or subscription;

(h) the payment by a company of fees and expenses of the advisers of any subscriber for shares in the company or its holding company that are incurred in connection with that subscription;

(i) the incurring of expenses (including professional fees and expenses) by a company either or both—

(i) in the preparation and publication of a prospectus concerning any shares in the company or its holding company,

(ii) for the purpose of facilitating the admission of any shares in the company or its holding company to, or the continuance of a facility afforded to the company or its holding company for the trading of such shares on, a regulated market;

(j) the incurring of expenses by a company for the purpose of facilitating the admission of any shares in the company or its holding company to, or the continuance of a facility afforded to the company or its holding company for the trading of such shares on, a regulated market or other securities market (including the expense of preparation and publication of any documents required for that purpose by the laws of the jurisdiction in which that market is established);

(k) the incurring of any expenses by a company in order to ensure compliance by the company or its holding company with the Irish Takeover Panel Act 1997 or an instrument thereunder or any measures for the time being adopted by the State to implement Directive 2004/25/EC of the European Parliament and of the Council of 21 April 2004 on takeover bids (OJ L142, 30.4.2004, p. 12);

(l) the reimbursement by a company which is an offeree (within the meaning of the Irish Takeover Panel Act 1997) or by a subsidiary of such an offeree of expenses of an offeror (within the meaning of that Act) pursuant to an agreement approved by, or on terms approved by, the Irish Takeover Panel;

(m) in connection with an allotment of shares by a company or its holding company, the payment by the company of commissions not exceeding 10 per cent of the money received in respect of such allotment to intermediaries, and the payment by the company of professional fees;

(n) to the extent that provision of this kind is not authorised by paragraph (e) or (f), the provision of financial assistance by a holding company or a subsidiary of it in connection with the holding company or subsidiary purchasing or subscribing for shares in the holding company on behalf of—

(i) the present or former employees of the holding company or any subsidiary of it,

(ii) an employees' share scheme within the meaning of the Companies (Amendment) Act 1983, or

(iii) an employee share ownership trust referred to in section 519 of the Taxes Consolidation Act 1997.

(13) (a) A public limited company may, in accordance with paragraph (d), (e) or (f) of subsection (12), give financial assistance to any person only if the company's net assets are not thereby reduced or, to the extent that those assets are thereby reduced, if the financial assistance is provided out of profits which are available for dividend.

(b) In this section 'net assets' means the aggregate of the company's assets less the aggregate of its liabilities; and 'liabilities' includes any provision (within the meaning of the Schedule to the Companies (Amendment) Act 1986) except to the extent that provision is taken into account in calculating the value of any asset to the company.][d]

(14) Any transaction in breach of this section shall be voidable at the instance of the company against any person (whether a party to the transaction or not) who had notice of the facts which constitute such breach.

(15) If a company acts in contravention of this section every officer of the company who is in default shall be liable;

(a) on conviction on indictment, to imprisonment for a term not exceeding [5][e] years or to a fine not exceeding [€3,174.35][f] or to both, or

(b) on summary conviction, to imprisonment for a term not exceeding 6 months or to a fine not exceeding [€1,904.61][g] or to both.

[(15A) Subsections (2) to (11) shall not apply to a public limited company originally incorporated as such or to a company registered or re-registered as a public limited company under the Companies (Amendment) Act, 1983 unless a special resolution as provided under subsection (2) was passed before the company's application for registration or re-registration.][h]

[....][i]

[....][j]

(16) Nothing in this section shall prejudice the provisions of section 72.

Amendments

a CA 1963, s 60(2)(b) substituted by CLEA 2001, s 89(a).

b Words substituted by C(AA)A 2003, s 57 and Sch 2 with effect from 8 April 2004 (SI 132/2004).

c CA 1963, s 60(6) substituted by CLEA 2001, s 89(b).

d Sub-s (12) and (13) substituted by IFCMPA 2005, s 56(1).

e '5' substituted for '2' by CA 1990, s 240(8) as inserted by CLEA 2001, s 104(c).

f '£2,500' substituted for '£500' by C(A)A 1982, Sch 1.

g £100 increased to £1,500 by CA 1990, s 240(7) as inserted by CLEA 2001, s 104(c) and converted to €1,904.61 by Council Regulations (EC) No 1103/97, No 974/98 and No 2866/98 and the Economic and Monetary Union Act 1998, s 6.

h Sub-s (15A) inserted by C(A)A 1983, s 3 and commenced 13 October 1983 (SI 288/1983).

i Sub-s (15B) which was inserted by C(A)A 1983, s 3 was repealed by IFCMPA 2005, s 40 with effect from 1 July 2005.

j Sub-s (15C) which was inserted by C(A)A 1983, s 3 with effect from 13 October 1983 (SI 288/1983) was substituted by EC(IFRSMA)R 2005 with effect from 1 January 2005 but subsequently repealed by IFCMPA 2005, s 40 with effect from 1 July 2005 (SI 393/2005).

Definitions

'articles': CA 1963, s 2(1); 'company': CA 1963, s 2(1) and NAMA Act 2009, s 228(1); 'the court': CA 1963, s 2(1); 'director': CA 1963, s 2(1); 'holding company': CA 1963, s 2(1), s 155; 'member': CA 1963, s 31; 'officer': CA 1963, s 2(1); 'officer in default: CA 1963, s 383; 'the registrar of companies': CA 1963, s 2(1); 'share': CA 1963, s 2(1); 'subsidiary': CA 1963, s 2(1), s 155.

Cross references in other enactments

NAMA Act 2009, s 218(1) provides that an acquired bank asset within the meaning of NAMA Act 2009 is 'not invalidated or rendered void or voidable as against NAMA or a NAMA group entity or their successors in title' by operation of CA 1963, s 60.

NAMA Act 2009, s 228(1) provides that a reference to a 'company' in CA 1963, s 60(1) 'shall be taken not to include a NAMA group entity' within the meaning of NAMA Act 2009.

Notes

Purpose of prohibition: The prohibition against companies giving direct or indirect financial assistance for the purchase of their own shares forms one of the many capital maintenance rules,[1] the underlying philosophy of which is to ensure that the company's capital is applied only towards the payment of the legitimate debts and liabilities of the company. Consequently, distributions should only be made to the members out of capital in circumstances where the interests of the creditors are adequately protected.

1 Other such rules are that shares should not be issued at a discount (C(A)A 1983, s 27), that a company should not normally expend its moneys in the purchase of its own shares (C(A)A 1983, s 41) and that dividends should only be paid out of distributable profits (C(A)A 1983, s 45). On capital maintenance generally Keane, *Company Law*, (4th edn, Tottel Publishing, 2007) ch 15; Courtney, *The Law of Private Companies* (2nd edn, Tottel Publishing, 2002) ch 18 and Ussher, *Company Law in Ireland* (Sweet & Maxwell, 1986) ch 10.

The basic prohibition:[1] CA 1963, s 60(1) prohibits the company from giving direct or indirect financial assistance for the acquisition of its own shares or the shares of its holding company, unless the assistance comes within one of the exceptions set out in the section itself.[2] Furthermore, such assistance is prohibited whether the acquisition of the shares is by way of subscription or purchase. However, financial assistance given by the company in connection with the acquisition of debentures is not caught by the section.

1 In relation to CA 1963, s 60 generally, see MacCann, 'Section 60 of the Companies Act 1963: Law and Procedure' (1994) 1 CLP 74; Cotter, 'Section 60 of the Companies Act 1963' (2000) 7 CLP 111.

2 See, however, CA 1990, s 224 which allows a subsidiary to acquire shares in its holding company in certain circumstances.

Meaning of 'financial assistance'

Non-exhaustive statutory definition: Although CA 1963, s 60(1) itself refers to assistance by way of loans, guarantees and the provision of security, the use of the words 'or otherwise' makes it quite clear that this list is not intended to be all-embracing and that other forms of financial assistance may also be prohibited. In *Charterhouse Investment Trust Ltd v Tempest Diesels Ltd*[1] Hoffmann J observed that the phrase 'the giving of financial assistance' has no technical meaning and must instead be construed by reference to 'the language of ordinary commerce'. He also pointed out that:

> 'One must examine the commercial realities of the transaction and decide whether it can properly be described as the giving of financial assistance by the company, bearing in mind that the section is a penal one and should not be strained to cover transactions which are not fairly within it.'

Direct and indirect financial assistance: While Hoffmann J was correct in stating that the language of s 60 should not be 'strained to cover transactions which are not fairly within it,' the section would be rendered largely inoperative if it were to be given an unduly restrictive interpretation. Indeed, the law reports abound with instances where the parties have channelled the assistance through a series of transactions involving shelf companies, trusts and other vehicles, rather than giving the assistance directly to the person who is acquiring the shares.[2] Moreover, as Murphy J observed in *Eccles Hall Ltd v Bank of Nova Scotia*[3] the phrase 'financial assistance ... in connection with a purchase or subscription' is of 'wide import' and potentially covers a large range of transactions.[4] It is important to note therefore that the prohibition in s 60 applies whether the financial assistance is given 'directly or indirectly.' In determining whether a violation of the section has taken place the approach of the court has therefore been to look at the net effect of the series of connected transactions rather than to simply look at each transaction in isolation. As Lord Denning stated in *Wallersteiner v Moir*:[5]

> 'The transactions are extremely complicated, but the end result is clear. You look to the company's money and see what has become of it. You look to the company's shares and see into whose hands they have got. You will soon see if the company's money has been used to finance the purchase.'

1 *Charterhouse Investment Trust Ltd v Tempest Diesels Ltd* [1986] BCLC 1. See also *CH (Ireland) Inc v Credit Suisse Canada* [1999] 4 IR 542; *Anglo Petroleum Ltd v TFB (Mortgages) Ltd* [2008] 1 BCLC 185.

2 See for example *Selangor Rubber Estates Ltd v Cradock (No 3)* [1968] 1 WLR 1555; *Karak Rubber Co Ltd v Burden* [1971] 1 WLR 1748; *Wallersteiner v Moir* [1974] 1 WLR 991.

3 *Eccles Hall Ltd v Bank of Nova Scotia* (3 February 1995, unreported) HC (Murphy J).

4 *Eccles Hall Ltd v Bank of Nova Scotia* (3 February 1995, unreported) HC at p 16 of the transcript.

5 *Wallersteiner v Moir* [1974] 1 WLR 991, 1014.

Types of transactions which are prohibited: The following are some specific examples of financial assistance, the giving of which is prohibited by CA 1963, s 60.

1. *Loans*: In the first place, the section expressly provides that a company may not directly or indirectly give 'a loan' to a third party 'for the purpose of or in connection with' the acquisition by that third party of shares in the company or in its holding company.[1]

2. *Guarantees and security*: The two other types of financial assistance expressly referred to in s 60(1) are the giving of guarantees and the provision of security by the company. Both types of assistance are clearly related and may therefore be conveniently considered together. For example, a third party may obtain a loan from a bank for the purpose of acquiring the shareholding in a company, and after acquiring control of the company he may arrange for it to give either a secured or an unsecured guarantee to the bank in respect of his loan. The giving of

the guarantee will itself amount to an infringement of s 60(1), as will the provision of any security in connection therewith.[2]

3. *Other types of financial assistance*: Turning to other classes of transaction which could be regarded 'in the language of ordinary commerce'[3] as amounting to the giving of financial assistance, the following have also been held to fall within s 60:

(a) a gift by the company of all or part of the purchase price of the shares;[4]

(b) the purchase by the company of an asset at an inflated price in circumstances where the vendor then uses the proceeds of sale to buy shares in the company or in its holding company;[5]

(c) a purchase of an asset at a fair price or any other sound commercial transaction negotiated at arm's length, in circumstances where the purpose thereof is to put the purchaser in funds to buy shares in the company;[6]

(d) an agreement between the seller and the buyer of shares in a private company that instead of the buyer paying the full purchase price, he would pay part only and that the balance would be paid to the sellers by way of consultancy fees from the company over a period of four years, based on a percentage of increased turnover;[7]

(e) releasing a debt owed to the company by the shareholder, thereby enabling the shareholder to sell the shares at a reduced price;[8]

(f) the company's giving of warranties as part of a share purchase agreement or share subscription agreement, at least to the extent that they have been given with the intention that the company will be called upon to pay damages and to provide funds in connection with the acquisition of shares;[9]

(g) a target company engaging and paying accountants to conduct a due diligence for the benefit of a bidder company in the context of an intended take-over bid.[10]

1 See, for example, *Steen v Law* [1964] AC 287; *Selangor United Rubber Estates Ltd v Cradock (No 3)* [1968] 1 WLR 1555; *Securities Trust Ltd v Associated Properties Ltd and Estate Developments Ltd* (1963–1993) Irish Company Law Reports 121.

2 For examples of secured and/or unsecured guarantees given by companies in respect of loans which have been used to acquire the company's shareholding, see *Victor Battery Co Ltd v Curry's Ltd* [1946] Ch 242; *Heald v O'Connor* [1971] 1 WLR 497; *Bank of Ireland Finance Ltd v Rockfield Ltd* [1979] IR 21; *Re Northside Motor Co Ltd* (24 July 1985, unreported) HC (Costello J); *Lombard and Ulster Banking Ltd v Bank of Ireland* (1963–1993) Irish Company Law Reports 223; *CH (Ireland) Inc v Credit Suisse Canada* [1999] 4 IR 542.

3 *Charterhouse Investment Trust Ltd v Tempest Diesels Ltd* [1986] BCLC 1, *per* Hoffmann J.

4 *Re Greenore Trading Ltd* [1980] ILRM 94; *Re VGM Holdings Ltd* [1942] Ch 235.

5 *Belmont Finance Corporation Ltd v Williams Furniture Ltd* [1980] 1 All ER 393; *Eccles Hall Ltd v Bank of Nova Scotia* (3 February 1995, unreported) HC (Murphy J). A violation of CA 1963, s 60 will probably also be deemed to have occurred where the asset has been acquired by the company at fair value but for the sole purpose of putting the person in funds to buy the shares. On the other hand, if the purchase of the asset by the company was *bona fide* and in the ordinary course of its business, then the subsequent use of the proceeds of sale to acquire the shares will probably be protected by s 60(12).

6 *Eccles Hall Ltd v Bank of Nova Scotia* (3 February 1995, unreported) HC (Murphy J).

7 *Independent Steels Property Ltd v Ryan* [1990] VR 247.

8 *EH Dey Property Ltd v Dey* [1966] VR 464.

9 *Barclays Bank plc v British and Commonwealth Holdings plc* [1996] 1 BCLC 1 at 41; *Burton v Palmer* [1980] 2 NSWLR 878 at 889–890.

10 *Chaston v SWP Group plc* [2003] 1 BCLC 675; cf *MT Realisations Ltd v Digital Equipment Co Ltd* [2002] 2 BCLC 688.

Assistance to purchaser or third party: Although a narrow reading of CA 1963, s 60 might lead one to conclude that it is confined to situations where the financial assistance has been given, whether directly or indirectly, to the person acquiring the shares, it has been held that the prohibition is not confined to financial assistance to the purchaser: it is directed to financial assistance to whomsoever given, provided that it be for the purpose of a purchase of shares or in connection with a purchase of shares.[1]

Thus, it was also held[2] that the section extends to financial assistance given to the vendor of shares, since the vendor would not otherwise have proceeded with the sale.

1 *EH Dey Property Ltd v Dey* [1966] VR 464, 470.

2 *Armour Hicks Northern Ltd v Armour Trust Ltd* [1980] 3 All ER 833; *Eccles Hall Ltd v Bank of Nova Scotia* (3 February 1995, unreported) HC (Murphy J).

Assistance by foreign subsidiary: Since the prohibition contained in CA 1963, s 60(1) applies only to a 'company' (ie a company formed and registered under the Companies Acts or previous Irish companies legislation),[1] financial assistance given by a foreign subsidiary for the acquisition of shares in its Irish parent will not normally be caught by s 60.[2] The foreign subsidiary will, however, be caught if it is a limited company and its parent is a plc.[3]

1 See CA 1963, s 2(1).

2 *Arab Bank plc v Merchant Holdings Ltd* [1994] 1 BCLC 330; *AMG Global Nominees (Private) Ltd v SMM Holdings Ltd* [2009] 1 BCLC 281.

3 EC(PLCS)R 1997, regs 4(2) and 5(2).

Permitted financial assistance: Although CA 1963, s 60 prohibits the giving of financial assistance for the acquisition of shares, this prohibition is not absolute and certain specific exceptions are expressly mentioned in the section.

1. *Payment of dividends*: According to sub-s (12), nothing in s 60 is to be taken as prohibiting the payment of a dividend by a company out of profits available for distribution. The key requirement here is undoubtedly that the dividend be paid in accordance with the provisions of C(A)A 1983, Part IV.

By way of example, the company may declare a dividend for a particular year in accordance with the requirements of C(A)A 1983, Part IV. A particular shareholder who would otherwise have been financially unable to do so, uses the dividend to acquire further shares in the company. Whilst undoubtedly the payment of the dividend constitutes financial assistance to the shareholder for the purchase of these additional shares, the transaction will not be regarded as having violated s 60.

A more extreme example is one where a take-over bidder takes out a short-term loan to acquire the share capital of a company which has large amounts of undistributed but distributable reserves, within the meaning of C(A)A 1983, Part IV. Once the take-over bid has been completed and the bidder has acquired control of the company, he may then declare a dividend in respect of the distributable reserves and apply same towards the discharge of the loan, without infringing CA 1963, s 60.

Such 'asset stripping' may be unobjectionable where the bidder has acquired control of the entire share capital of the company. If, however, he has acquired a mere majority of the shares, the minority may view the declaration 'asset stripping' dividends as being oppressive or in disregard of their interests as members of the company, thereby entitling them to petition for relief under CA 1963, s 205.[1]

2. *Discharge of liabilities*: A further type of financial assistance expressly provided for by sub-s (12) is 'the discharge of a liability lawfully incurred' by the company. According to *Ussher*[2] the phrase 'the discharge of a liability lawfully incurred' means 'an *intra vires* debt properly incurred in the course of its business, and not the type of bogus transaction characteristic of attempts to evade legislation of this kind.'[3]

An example of such a 'bogus transaction' is one whereby the company purchases an asset from a third party at an inflated price and that person then uses the proceeds of sale to buy shares in the company or in its holding company.[4] It is a question of degree, however, as to whether an infringement of s 60 occurs where a person sells an asset to a company at a fair or market value and then uses the proceeds of sale to acquire shares in the company or in its holding company. As Forde suggests[5] a violation of the section will probably be deemed to have occurred if the sole purpose of the acquisition of the asset by the company was to put the person in funds to buy the shares. On the other hand, if the purchase of the asset was made by the company *bona fide* and in the ordinary course of its business, then the subsequent use of the proceeds of sale to acquire the shares will probably be protected by s 60(12).

3. *Refinancings:* By an amendment introduced in IFCMPA 2005, a loan to refinance a loan which has been validated by statutory declaration and special resolution in accordance with sub-s (2) to (11) is not affected by the prohibition in sub-s (1). Similarly any security put in place to replace other security in a refinancing is intended not to be caught by the prohibition. There has been some commentary as to the significance of the mismatch between the words 'loan, guarantee, the provision of security or otherwise' in sub-s (1) and 'the provision of finance or delivery of security' in sub-s (12)(c).

4. *Loans by financial institutions*: The next type of financial assistance for the acquisition of shares which is permitted by a company is 'the lending of money by the company in the ordinary course of its business' in circumstances where 'the lending of money is part of the ordinary business of the company.'[6] In order to be regarded as having been made in the ordinary course of business the loan will presumably have to be made on terms and conditions which are neither less nor more favourable than loans of equivalent amounts which are intended to be used by the borrower for similar purposes. However, if the company is a plc, there is a further restriction in that it may only give financial assistance in accordance with sub-ss(12)(d), (e) or (f) provided that its net assets are not thereby reduced or, to the extent that they are so reduced, that the loan is made out of profits which are available for dividend.[7] In practice, however, this limitation should not be of little concern to the financial institution. As Hoffmann J observed in *Charterhouse Investment Trust Ltd v Tempest Diesels Ltd*[8] the making of a loan will leave the balance sheet undisturbed in that the cash paid out is replaced by an asset of equivalent value, namely a cause of action against the borrower.

5. *Employee shares*: Two further classes of financial assistance permitted by s 60 relate to the acquisition of shares by company employees and are to be found in sub-ss (12)(e) and (f). Again, if the company is a plc, it may only give such financial assistance provided that its net assets are not thereby reduced or, to the extent that they are so reduced, that the loan is made out of profits which are available for dividend.[9] As has been indicated above, where the financial assistance involves the giving of a loan there should be no affect on the net asset value of the company. The financial assistance will, however, have to come out of distributable profits where it involves the establishment of an employee share scheme which is paid for by the company itself.

6. *Corporate transactions*: IFCMPA 2005 introduced two useful exemptions from the financial assistance prohibition: (i) the giving by a company of representations, warranties and indemnities in connection with a share purchase or subscription; and (ii) the now express ability of a company to pay the advisory expenses of a subscriber for shares in the company.

7. *Securities markets expenses*: IFCMPA 2005 introduced exemptions clarifying that the expense of preparing disclosure documents such as prospectuses in connection with the admission to trading of the company's shares did not constitute prohibited financial assistance. This is particularly relevant since 2005 where a company may have to assist a seller of shares, which seller might be obliged to prepare a prospectus in respect of a secondary offering of shares to the public.

8. *Take-overs of public companies*: Companies to which the Irish Takeover Panel Act 1997 or the European Communities (Takeover Bids (Directive 2004/25/EC)) Regulations 2006 (SI 255/2006) apply are required to engage a 'Rule 3' adviser when the company is in an offer period. The expense of such engagement is now expressly not subject to the financial assistance prohibition. In addition, inducement fees paid by companies whereby an outbid offeror's costs will be paid by the target company when a successful third party offers more for the company are also expressly exempted from the prohibition on financial assistance.

1 *Re Greenore Trading Co* [1980] ILRM 94.

2 Ussher, *Company Law in Ireland* (Sweet & Maxwell, 1986) at p 321.

3 The comments of Ussher reflect those of Fitzgibbon LJ in *Dale v Martin* (1883–84) 11 LR Ir 371, 376 where he stated that 'payments ... in discharge of lawful obligations' do not constitute infringements of the capital maintenance rules. For an example of payments found to be in discharge of legitimate debts and thus protected by s 60(12), see *Eccles Hall Ltd v Bank of Nova Scotia* (3 February 1995, unreported) HC (Murphy J); *Anglo Petroleum Ltd v TFB (Mortgages) Ltd* [2008] 1 BCLC 185.

4 *Belmont Finance Corporation Ltd v Williams Furniture Ltd* [1980] 1 All ER 393.

5 Forde, *Company Law* (3rd edn, Roundhall Sweet & Maxwell, 1999) at p 308.

6 CA 1963, s 60(12)(d).

7 CA 1963, s 60(13)(a). For the definition of 'net assets' see s 60(13)(b). As to the profits available for dividend, see C(A)A 1983, s 45.

8 *Charterhouse Investment Trust Ltd v Tempest Diesels Ltd* [1986] BCLC 1.

9 CA 1963, s 60(15B).

Authorisation of financial assistance by private companies: In addition to the specific instances cited above where the company is permitted to give financial assistance for the acquisition of shares, CA 1963, s 60(2)–(11) also provides a procedure whereby the members of a private company may authorise the company to give financial assistance which would otherwise be prohibited by sub-s (1).[1] It should be noted, however, that this procedure may not even be availed of by a private company at a time when a person who is the subject to a restriction order under CA 1990, s 150 is appointed or acts in any way, whether directly or indirectly, as director or secretary or is concerned in or takes part in the promotion or formation of that company.[2] The procedure is also not open to a private company which is a subsidiary of a plc.[3] The procedural steps which must be followed by the company in order to validly authorise the giving of financial assistance are set out below and basically involve the directors in making a statutory declaration as to the nature of the assistance which is to be given and as to the solvency of the company. Thereafter a meeting of the members is convened for the purpose of passing a special resolution authorising the giving of the assistance. Alternatively, if so permitted by the articles,[4] the company may dispense with the need for a formal general meeting and may instead pass the resolution by having it signed by all of the members who would otherwise be entitled to attend and vote on the resolution at a general meeting.[5]

Strict compliance with procedure: The procedure as laid down by CA 1963, s 60(2)–(11) must be strictly complied with for authorisation of financial assistance to be valid.[6] Thus, the failure to make the necessary declaration of solvency within the prescribed period of time before obtaining shareholder approval will negate the authorisation.[7] Similarly, the passing of the special resolution of authorisation *after* rather than *before* the giving of the financial assistance, will render the authorisation null and void.[8]

Since such strict compliance is required by the courts it is therefore appropriate to examine in some detail the steps which must actually be taken by the company in order to validly authorise the giving of financial assistance for the acquisition of shares in itself or in its holding company.

Statutory declaration: The first step is for a meeting of the directors to make a statutory declaration as to both the nature of the assistance which is to be given and the solvency of the company. In the case of a company with only two directors it must be made by them both and in the case of a company with a larger board, it must be made by a majority of the directors.[9]

The declaration must be made not more than 24 days before the general meeting at which the resolution for the giving of financial assistance is to be considered by the members,[10] and must state the following:[11]

(a) the form which such assistance is to take;

(b) the persons to whom such assistance is to be given;

(c) the purpose for which the company intends those persons to use such assistance; and

(d) that the directors have made a full inquiry into the affairs of the company and that, having done so, they have formed the opinion that the company, having carried out the transaction whereby such assistance is to be given, will be able to pay its debts in full as they become due.

If, despite what is said in the declaration, the directors have not in fact made sufficient inquiries into the financial affairs of the company to honestly satisfy themselves as to the solvency of the company after the giving of the financial assistance, the declaration will be treated as null and void and of no effect.[12] Moreover, since the principal purpose of the statutory declaration is to ensure that despite the giving of financial assistance, the company will remain capable of paying its debts as they fall due, the directors must ensure that the declaration contains sufficient particulars to the proposed assistance to enable the reader to make an informed judgement on the matter.[13] Indeed, it has been held that the declaration will be regarded as ineffective if it is 'materially inaccurate and misleading.'[14]

Consequences for directors if declaration is inaccurate: Any director who joins in making the statutory declaration without having reasonable grounds for the opinion that the company having given the financial assistance will be able to pay its debts in full as they become due, will be guilty of an offence punishable by up to six months' imprisonment and/or by a fine of up to €1,904.61.[15] Moreover, if the company is wound up within twelve months of the date of the statutory declaration and is unable to pay its debts in full within twelve months of the commencement of the winding up, it will be presumed until the contrary is shown, that the directors did not have reasonable grounds for the opinion as to solvency expressed in the statutory declaration.[16] In the UK directors have been found to be accountable for any benefit obtained by them on foot of unlawful financial assistance.[17]

Convening of general meeting: After the statutory declaration has been made, the next step is either to convene a general meeting of creditors to pass a special resolution authorising the giving of such financial assistance[18] or alternatively to have a written resolution signed by all of the members who would be entitled to attend and vote on such a resolution at a formal general meeting.[19]

Length of notice of meeting: Not more than 24 days must elapse between the date of the making of the statutory declaration and the date of the general meeting.[20] Moreover, since the meeting is to consider a special resolution, as opposed to an ordinary resolution, it will be necessary to give the members not less than 21 days' clear notice.[21] The resolution may however, be proposed and passed on shorter notice, if not less than 90% of the members who are entitled to attend and vote so agree.[22]

Contents of notice: In sending out notice of the meeting, the company should ensure that the notice specifies either the entire text or the entire substance of the proposed resolution, otherwise the meeting will be invalid.[23] In addition, the company must forward with each notice of the meeting a copy of the statutory declaration.[24] Alternatively, if the company decides to pass the resolution using the procedure contained in CA 1963, s 141(8), a copy of the statutory declaration must be appended to the text of the resolution which circulates to the members for signing.[25]

Registration of statutory declaration: Within 21 days of the date on which the financial assistance is actually given a copy of the statutory declaration should be delivered to the registrar of companies for registration.[26]

Approval and implementation of special resolution: If a formal general meeting is held, the special resolution authorising the giving of the financial assistance will require at least three quarters of the votes actually cast at the meeting in order to be passed.[27] Alternatively the resolution can be passed by having it signed by all of the members who would be entitled to attend and vote on such a resolution at a formal general meeting.[28] Moreover, unless all of the members of the company entitled to vote at general meetings vote in favour of the special resolution, the transaction whereby the assistance is to be given may not be carried out before the expiry of 30 days after the passing of the special resolution, or if an application is made under CA 1963, s 60(8) for an order cancelling the special resolution, until such time as such application has been disposed of by the court.[29] Furthermore, just as the statute imposes time limits before which the special resolution cannot be implemented, so too, it imposes time limits beyond which it cannot be put into operation. In particular s 60(2)(a) provides that the financial assistance cannot be given if the special resolution in question was passed more than 12 months previously.

Application to cancel special resolution: Under CA 1963, s 60(8) members holding not less than 10% in nominal value of the company's issued share capital or any class thereof[30] who have neither consented to nor voted for the special resolution[31] may apply to the High Court to have it cancelled. While any such application is pending, the special resolution will have no effect and even then it will only have effect, if at all, to the extent that it is actually confirmed by the court.[32] Any such application must be made within 28 days after the date on which the special resolution was passed.[33] This time limit will be rigidly applied and is not subject to extension.

The procedure laid down by s 60(8) for challenging the special resolution would appear to relate to a situation where the resolution would otherwise be valid. If however, the proposed financial assistance would be *ultra vires* the company, then the special resolution will be void.[34] In such circumstances the dissentients will not be bound by the time limits imposed by the subsection, but will instead be entitled to challenge the validity of the resolution by way of ordinary declaratory proceedings.

Although no guidance is given by the statute as to the factors which the court will take into account in determining whether to cancel an otherwise valid special resolution pursuant to s 60(8), by analogy with the procedure in CA 1963, s 10 for the cancellation of alterations in the objects clause, it would appear that the resolution may be struck down if its operation would create some unfairness as between the members.[35]

1 The procedure laid down by CA 1963, s 60(2)–(11) used to apply to all companies, but is now excluded in the case of plcs by s 60(15A) as inserted by C(A)A 1983, Sch 1 para 10. It is also inapplicable in the case of an Irish or foreign limited company whether private or public which is itself a subsidiary of a plc and which wishes to provide financial assistance for the acquisition of shares in that plc: EC(PLCS)R 1997, regs 4(2) and 5(2).

2 CA 1990, s 155(2).

3 EC(PLCS)R 1997, reg 5(2)(c).

4 Table A, part II, reg 6 contains such an authorisation.

5 CA 1963, s 141(8) as applied by s 60(6).

6 *Re Northside Motor Co Ltd* (24 July 1985, unreported) HC (Costello J); *Lombard and Ulster Banking Ltd v Bank of Ireland* (1963–1993) Irish Company Law Reports 223; *RE SH and Co (Realisations) 1990 Ltd* [1993] BCLC 1309; *Re RW Peak (Kings Lynn) Ltd* [1998] 1 BCLC 193; cf *Re NL Electrical Ltd, Ghosh v 3i plc* [1994] 1 BCLC 22.

7 *Lombard and Ulster Banking Ltd v Bank of Ireland* (1963–1993) Irish Company Law Reports 223.

8 *Re Northside Motor Co Ltd* (24 July 1985, unreported) HC.

9 CA 1963, s 60(3).
10 CA 1963, s 60(3).
11 CA 1963, s 60(14).
12 *Re In A Flap Envelope Co Ltd* [2004] 1 BCLC 64.
13 *Re SH and Co (Realisations) 1990 Ltd* [1993] BCLC 1309.
14 *Re Northside Motor Co Ltd* (24 July 1985, unreported) HC (Costello J). However, the approval of the financial assistance will not necessarily be invalidated simply because the directors used an out-of-date statutory form on which to make their declaration of solvency: *Re NL Electrical Ltd, Ghosh v 3i plc* [1994] 1 BCLC 22.
15 CA 1963, s 60(5).
16 CA 1963, s 60(5).
17 *Re In A Flap Envelope Co Ltd* [2004] 1 BCLC 64.
18 CA 1963, s 60(2)(a).
19 CA 1963, s 60(6).
20 CA 1963, s 60(3). If the company dispenses with the holding of a formal meeting and instead opts to have a resolution signed by all members who would be entitled to attend and vote on such a resolution at a formal general meeting, the date on which the last such member signs the resolution will be taken to be the notional date of the meeting for the purposes of s 60(3). See CA 1963, s 141(8)(b).
21 CA 1963, s 141(1).
22 CA 1963, s 141(2). See also CA 1963, s 141(8) and the notes thereto, in relation to the entitlement of the members acting unanimously to pass such resolutions without the need for a formal general meeting.
23 *Re Moorgate Mercantile Holdings Ltd* [1980] 1 WLR 227.
24 CA 1963, s 60(2)(b).
25 CA 1963, s 60(2)(b).
26 CA 1963, s 60(2)(b).
27 CA 1963, s 141(1).
28 CA 1963, s 60(6).
29 CA 1963, s 60(7).
30 CA 1963, s 60(9).
31 CA 1963, s 60(10).
32 CA 1963, s 60(8).
33 CA 1963, s 60(11).
34 *Securities Trust Ltd v Associated Properties Ltd* (1963–1993) Irish Company Law Reports 121.
35 *Re Jewish Colonial Trust* [1908] 2 Ch 287.

Criminal liability for illegal financial assistance: If the company gives financial assistance in breach of CA 1963, s 60(1) every officer of the company who is in default shall be liable on conviction on indictment to imprisonment for a term of up to five years and/or to a fine of up to €3,174.35; on summary conviction they may be liable to imprisonment for a term of up to six months and/or to a fine of up to €1,904.61.[1]

1 CA 1963, s 60(15).

Civil consequences if illegal financial assistance given

Avoidance of transaction: CA 1963, s 60(14) provides that any transaction in breach of s 60 is voidable at the instance of the company against any person (whether a party to the transaction or not) who had notice of the facts which constitute the breach but is not void *ab initio*.[1] In this regard it has been held that 'notice' means 'actual notice' rather than 'constructive notice.'[2] The onus is on the company seeking to set aside the transaction to establish such notice on the balance of probabilities.[3] Furthermore, although the financial assistance may well be part of a series of circular transactions, s 60(14) does not permit the avoidance of all of those transactions, but is instead confined to the avoidance of the particular 'transaction' or 'transactions' to which the company was a party and pursuant to which the impugned financial assistance was given.[4]

Transactions which are capable of being performed either with or without contravening s 60: If the transaction is one which, on its terms, is equally capable of being performed either in a manner which is in breach of CA 1963, s 60 or alternatively in a manner which does not infringe the provisions of the section, the company will not be allowed to set it aside.[5] So, for example, where the owner of shares in one of a group of companies agreed to transfer his shares in that company to his sons in consideration of the group as a whole paying him a salary of £100,000 per annum together with a percentage of net group profits, the transaction was held to be valid and enforceable, because, at the time of the making of the agreement, the cost of making the payments did not necessarily have to come out of the company in which the shares were held but was instead capable of being met in full by the other group companies and it was open to the directors to structure the group's affairs thereafter to ensure that the cost of the payments continued to be met out of the assets of these other companies.[6] Similarly, if an executory contract envisages the giving of financial assistance within the meaning of s 60(1), specific performance will not necessarily be refused where its terms are capable of being interpreted as envisaging the use of the whitewash procedure in s 60(2) as a prerequisite to the actual giving of the financial assistance.[7]

Liability of directors and others: Apart from being entitled to avoid the transaction, the company may also sue the responsible directors and officers and others who 'assisted with knowledge' in the transaction, for any loss which it has suffered as a result.[8] Furthermore, participation in or failure to detect and prevent breaches of CA 1963, s 60 may expose the directors to the risk of disqualification under CA 1990, s 160.[9] If the company's solicitors negligently fail to identify the fact that the transaction will amount to a breach of s 60, they may be liable in damages to the company for any consequential loss suffered by it.[10] However, it would appear that the company has no cause of action against the solicitors for the counterparty arising from their failure to identify the applicability of s 60.[11]

Oppression of members: Finally, it was held in *Re Greenore Trading Co Ltd*[12] that where a company gives financial assistance in breach of CA 1963, s 60, the transaction may be not only illegal, but may also be oppressive to and in disregard of the interests of the members within the meaning of CA 1963, s 205. In such circumstances, the aggrieved members may be entitled to petition to have their shares purchased at the price at which they would have stood but for the oppressive conduct.

1 *Lombard and Ulster Banking Ltd v Bank of Ireland* (1963–1993) Irish Company Law Reports 223.

2 *Bank of Ireland Finance Ltd v Rockfield Ltd* [1979] IR 21; *Re Northside Motor Co Ltd* (24 July 1985, unreported) HC (Costello J); *Lombard and Ulster Banking Ltd v Bank of Ireland* (1963–1993) Irish Company Law Reports 223; *Eccles Hall Ltd v Bank of Nova Scotia* (3 February 1995, unreported) HC (Murphy J); *CH (Ireland) Inc v Credit Suisse Canada* [1999] 4 IR 542.

3 *Lombard and Ulster Banking Ltd v Bank of Ireland* (1963–1993) Irish Company Law Reports 223; *CH (Ireland) Inc v Credit Suisse Canada* [1999] 4 IR 542. See also *McCormick v Cameo Investments Ltd Investments Ltd* [1978] ILRM 191.

4 *CH (Ireland) Inc v Credit Suisse Canada* [1999] 4 IR 542.

5 *Parlett v Guppys (Bridport) Ltd* [1996] 2 BCLC 34; *Vision Express (UK) Ltd v Wilson* [1998] BCC 173. See also *McGill v Bogue* (11 July 2000, unreported) SC.

6 *Parlett v Guppys (Bridport) Ltd* [1996] 2 BCLC 34.

7 *McGill v Bogue* (11 July 2000, unreported) SC.

8 *Selangor Rubber Estates Ltd v Cradock (No 3)* [1968] 1 WLR 1555; *Belmont Finance Corporation Ltd v Williams Furniture Ltd* [1979] Ch 250; *Steen v Law* [1964] AC 287; *Ryan v Bank of New South Wales* [1978] VR 555; *Consul Development Property Ltd v DPC Estates Property Ltd* (1975) 132 CLR 373.

9 *Re Continental Assurance Co* [1997] 1 BCLC 48.

10 *BDG Roof-Bond Ltd v Douglas* [2000] 1 BCLC 401.

11 *BDG Roof-Bond Ltd v Douglas* [2000] 1 BCLC 401.

12 *Re Greenore Trading Co Ltd* [1980] ILRM 94.

Investment companies: The provisions of CA 1963, s 60 do not apply to investment companies.[1]

1 CA 1990, 260(2).

UK legislation

See CA 1985, ss 151, 152, 153 (amended by IA 1985, s 439(1), Sch 13, Part I) FSA 1986, s 196; CA 1989, ss 132, 144(4), Sch 18 para 33), 154, 155, 156 (amended by IA 1985, s 439(1), Sch 13 Part I), 157, 158.

Construction of References to Offering Shares or Debentures to the Public

61 Construction of references to offering shares or debentures to the public

[...][a]

Amendments

a Section repealed by IFCMPA 2005, s 40(1)(a).

Issues of Shares at Premium and Discount and Redeemable Preference Shares

62 Application of premiums received on issue of shares

(1) Where a company issues shares at a premium, whether for cash or otherwise, a sum equal to the aggregate amount or value of the premiums on those shares shall be transferred to an account, to be called 'the share premium account', and the provisions of this Act relating to the reduction of the share capital of a company shall, except as provided in this section [and section 207(2) of the Companies Act, 1990],[a] apply as if the share premium account were paid up share capital of the company.

(2) The share premium account may, notwithstanding anything in subsection (1) be applied by the company in paying up unissued shares of the company (other than redeemable [...][b] shares) [to be allotted][c] to members of the company as fully paid bonus shares, in writing off

(a) the preliminary expenses of the company, or

(b) the expenses of, or the commission paid or discount allowed on, any issue of shares or debentures of the company;

or in providing for the premium payable on redemption of any redeemable preference shares [in pursuance of section 220 of the Companies Act, 1990],[d] or of any debentures of the company.

(3) Where a company has before the operative date issued any shares at a premium, this section shall apply as if the shares had been issued after the operative date, so however that any part of the premiums which has been so applied that it does not at the operative date form an identifiable part of the company's reserves within the meaning of the Sixth Schedule shall be disregarded in determining the sum to be included in the share premium account.

Amendments

a Words inserted by CA 1990, s 231, with effect from 1 July 1991 (SI 117/1991).

b Word deleted by CA 1990, s 231, with effect from 1 July 1991 (SI 117/1991).

c Words substituted by C(A)A 1983, s 3, with effect from 13 October 1983 (SI 288/1983).

d Words inserted by CA 1990, s 231, with effect from 1 July 1991 (SI 117/1991).

Definitions

'company': CA 1963, s 2(1); 'debenture': CA 1963, s 2(1); 'member': CA 1963, s 31; 'the operative date': CA 1963, s 2(1); 'share': CA 1963, s 2(1).

Notes

Share premium: A share is regarded as having been issued at a premium, if it is allotted by the company for a price in excess of the nominal or par value. Thus, if a share has a par value of €1.00 but is issued for €1.50, the premium will be 50c. CA 1963, s 62(1) clearly envisages however, that a premium could also arise in the case of an allotment of shares for a non-cash consideration.[1] Thus, an allotment of 100 €1.00, shares in return for €500 worth of goods will give rise to a premium of €400. Similarly, a premium could arise in the case of a share for share exchange, as where company A issues shares in itself in exchange for the shares in company B, but the nominal value of those shares being issued is less than the market value of the shares being acquired.[2]

1 With regard to what constitutes a non-cash consideration, see CA 1963, s 58 and the notes thereto.

2 *Henry Head and Co Ltd v Ropner Holdings Ltd* [1952] Ch 124; *Shearer v Bercain Ltd* [1980] 3 All ER 295.

Share premium account: CA 1963, s 62(1) states that the share premium account is treated as part of the capital of the company and is therefore subject to the same provisions regarding the reduction of capital as apply to the share capital itself.[1] The share premium account may be used in a reduction of capital not only to write-off past losses[2] but also to make provision for future losses which are anticipated on the company's profit and loss account.[3] Furthermore, the court will not be precluded from confirming a reduction of the share premium account simply because the event giving rise to the premium is the same as the event giving rise to the application for the reduction of capital.[4]

Apart from any cancellation of the share premium account that may arise by virtue of a duly confirmed reduction of capital, s 62(2) identifies four additional uses to which the account may be put and which in themselves may result in the account being either cancelled or reduced:

(i) issuing fully paid bonus shares (other than redeemable shares)[5] to the members;

(ii) writing off the preliminary expenses of the company;

(iii) writing off the expenses of, or the commission paid[6] or discount allowed[7] on any issue of shares or debentures of the company; and

(iv) providing for any premium payable on redemption or purchase by a company of its own shares pursuant to CA 1990, Part XI or on redemption of any of its debentures.

1 For the reduction of capital, see CA 1963, ss 72–77 and the notes thereto. For examples of reductions of capital involving the share premium account, see *Re Barry Artist Ltd* [1985] BCLC 283; *Re Grosvenor Press plc* [1985] BCLC 286; *Re Ratners Group plc* [1988] BCLC 685; *Re European Home Products plc* [1988] BCLC 690; *Re Thorn EMI plc* [1989] BCLC 612; *Re Quayle Munro Ltd, Petitioners* [1994] 1 BCLC 410.

2 *Re Barry Artist Ltd* [1985] BCLC 283; *Re Grosvenor Press plc* [1985] BCLC 286; *Re Ratners Group plc* [1988] BCLC 685; *Re European Home Products plc* [1988] BCLC 690; *Re Thorn EMI plc* [1989] BCLC 612; *Re Quayle Munro Ltd, Petitioners* [1994] 1 BCLC 410.

3 *Re Quayle Munro Ltd, Petitioners* [1994] 1 BCLC 410.

4 *Re Ratners Group plc* [1988] BCLC 685.

5 For the provisions governing redeemable shares see CA 1990, Part XI.

6 For the circumstances in which commission may be paid in connection with an issue of shares or debentures, see CA 1963, s 59.

7 Although debentures may be issued at a discount, such discounts are prohibited in respect of allotments of shares: C(A)A 1983, s 27.

UK legislation

See CA 1985, s 130.

---

63 Power to issue shares at a discount

[...][a]

Amendments

a CA 1963, s 63 repealed by C(A)A 1983, Sch 3.

Definitions

'share': CA 1963, s 2(1).

---

64 Power to issue redeemable preference shares

[(1) Subject to the provisions of this section, a company limited by shares may, if so authorised by its articles, issue preference shares which are, or at the option of the company are to be liable, to be redeemed, so, however, that—

(a) no such shares shall be redeemed except out of profits of the company which would otherwise be available for dividend or out of the proceeds of a fresh issue of shares made for the purposes of the redemption;

(b) no such shares shall be redeemed unless they are fully paid;

[(c) the premium, if any, payable on redemption must have been provided for out of the profits of the company which would otherwise be available for dividend or out of the company's share premium account before the shares are redeemed;][b]

(d) where any such shares are redeemed otherwise than out of the proceeds of a fresh issue, there shall out of profits which would otherwise have been available for dividend be transferred to a reserve fund to be called 'the capital redemption reserve fund', a sum equal to the nominal amount of the shares redeemed and the provisions of this Act relating to the reduction of the share capital of a company shall, except as provided in this section, apply as if the capital redemption reserve fund were paid up share capital of the company.

(2) Subject to the provisions of this section, the redemption of preference shares thereunder may be effected on such terms and in such manner as may be provided by the articles of the company.

(3) The redemption of preference shares under this section by a company shall not be taken as reducing the amount of the company's authorised share capital.

(4) Subject to subsection (5), where in pursuance of this section a company has redeemed or is about to redeem any preference shares, it shall have power to issue shares up to the nominal amount of the shares redeemed or to be redeemed as if those shares had never been issued, [and, accordingly, for the purposes of section 68 of the Finance Act, 1973, shares issued by a company in place of shares redeemed under this section shall constitute a chargeable transaction if, but only if, the actual value of the shares so issued exceeds the actual value of the preference shares redeemed at the date of their redemption and, where the issue of the shares does constitute a chargeable transaction for those purposes, the amount on which stamp duty on the relevant statement relating to that transaction is chargeable under section 69 of the Finance Act, 1973, shall be the difference between—

(a) the amount on which the duty would be so chargeable if the shares had not been issued in place of shares redeemed under this section, and

(b) the value of the shares redeemed at the date of their redemption.][c]

(5) Where new shares are issued before the redemption of the old shares, the new shares shall not, so far as relates to stamp duty, be deemed to have been issued in pursuance of subsection (4) unless the old shares are redeemed within one month after issue of the new shares.

(6) The capital redemption reserve fund may, notwithstanding anything in this section, be applied by the company in paying up unissued shares of the company (other than redeemable preference shares) [to be allotted][d] to members of the company as fully paid bonus shares.][a]

Amendments

a Repealed by CA 1990, s 220 but has some application to preference shares issued prior to commencement of CA 1990, Pt XI.

b CA 1963, s 64(1)(c) substituted by C(A)A 1983, Sch 1 para 12(a).

c Words substituted by FA 1990, s 119.

d CA 1963, s 64(6) substituted by C(A)A 1983, Sch 1 para 12(b).

Definitions

'articles': CA 1963, s 2 (1); 'company': CA 1963, s 2(1); 'company limited by shares': CA 1963, s 2(1), 5(1); 'member': CA 1963, s 31; 'share': CA 1963, s 2(1).

Notes

Redeemable shares: Prior to the coming into force of CA 1990, the only type of redeemable shares capable of being issued by a company were redeemable preference shares. Such issues were governed by the provisions of CA 1963, s 64. This section has since been repealed by CA 1990, s 220 and now it is possible for a company, if so authorised by its articles,[1] to issue any class of redeemable shares. The provisions concerning the issue and redemption of such shares are to be found in CA 1990, Part XI. In so far as any redeemable preference shares were issued pursuant to s 64 prior to its repeal, redemption of the nominal or par value of the shares may be funded out of distributable profits or out of the proceeds of a fresh issue of shares[2] although any premium payable thereon may be funded either out of distributable profits or out the share premium account or out of both.[3]

1 No such authorisation is to be found in Model Form articles.

[2] CA 1990, s 207.
[3] CA 1990, s 220.

65 Power to redeem preference shares issued before 5th May, 1959

(1) Subject to the provisions of this section, a company limited by shares may, if so authorised by its articles, redeem any preference shares issued by it before the 5th day of May, 1959, so, however, that—

(a) no such shares shall be redeemed unless they are fully paid;

(b) no such shares shall be redeemed except out of profits of the company which would otherwise be available for dividend or out of the proceeds of a fresh issue of shares made for the purposes of the redemption;

(c) no such shares shall be redeemed at a sum greater than the issue price of such shares;

(d) the redemption of such shares and the terms and the manner thereof must have been authorised by a special resolution of the company;

(e) notice of the meeting at which the special resolution referred to in paragraph (d) is to be proposed and a copy of the said resolution must be published in [Companies Registration Office Gazette][a] and in at least one daily newspaper circulating in the district in which the registered office of the company is situated not less than 14 days and not more than 30 days before the date of the meeting;

(f) no holder of such shares shall be obliged to accept redemption thereof;

(g) in the case of a private company the redemption must have been sanctioned by the court.

(2) The powers conferred by this section may be availed of only by means of an offer made to all the holders of the preference shares concerned.

(3) Where any such shares are redeemed otherwise than out of the proceeds of a fresh issue, there shall out of profits which would otherwise have been available for dividend be transferred to a reserve fund to be called 'the capital redemption reserve fund' a sum equal to the nominal amount of the shares redeemed, and the provisions of this Act relating to the reduction of the share capital of a company shall, except as provided in this section, apply as if the capital redemption reserve fund were paid up share capital of the company.

(4) Subject to the provisions of this section, the redemption of preference shares under this section may be effected on such terms and in such manner as may be provided by the special resolution referred to in paragraph (d) of subsection (1).

(5) The redemption of preference shares under this section by a company shall not be taken as reducing the amount of the company's authorised share capital.

(6) Subject to subsection (7), where in pursuance of this section a company has redeemed or is about to redeem any preference shares, it shall have power to issue shares up to the nominal amount of the shares redeemed or to be redeemed as if those shares had never been issued, and accordingly the share capital of the company shall not for the purposes of any enactments relating to stamp duty be deemed to be increased by the issue of shares in pursuance of this subsection.

(7) Where new shares are issued before the redemption of the old shares, the new shares shall not, so far as relates to stamp duty, be deemed to have been issued in pursuance of subsection (6) unless the old shares are redeemed within one month after the issue of the new shares.

(8) The capital redemption reserve fund may, notwithstanding anything in this section, be applied by the company in paying up unissued shares of the company (other than redeemable preference shares) to be issued to members of the company as fully paid bonus shares.

Amendments

a Substituted for '*Iris Oifigiúil*' by IFCMPA 2005, s 72.

Definitions

'articles': CA 1963, s 2(1); 'company': CA 1963, s 2(1); 'company limited by shares': CA 1963, s 2(1), 5(2); 'the court': CA 1963, s 2(1); 'member': CA 1963, s 31; 'private company': CA 1963, s 2(1), s 33(1); 'share': CA 1963, s 2(1).

Miscellaneous Provisions as to Share Capital

66 Power of company to arrange for different amounts being paid on shares

A company, if so authorised by it articles, may do any one or more of the following things—

(a) make arrangements on the issue of shares for a difference between the shareholders in the amounts and times of payment of calls on their shares;

(b) accept from any member the whole or a part of the amount remaining unpaid on any shares held by him, although no part of that amount has been called up;

(c) pay a dividend in proportion to the amount paid up on each share where a larger amount is paid up on some shares than on others.

Definitions

'articles': CA 1963, s 2(1); 'company': CA 1963, s 2(1); 'member': CA 1963, s 31; 'share': CA 1963, s 2(1).

Notes

Equality when making calls: As a general principle, calls should be made *pari passu* as between shareholders.[1] Regardless therefore of the provisions of CA 1963, s 66(a), even if the directors are so authorised by the articles[2] they should only depart from the principle of making calls on a *pari passu* basis in exceptional circumstances.[3]

1 *Preston v Grand Collier Dock Co* (1840) 11 Sim 327, 347.

2 Authorisation to make calls otherwise than on a *pari passu* basis is contained in reg 20 of Table A.

3 *Galloway v Halle Concerts Society Ltd* [1915] 2 Ch 233; *Alexander v Automatic Telephone Co* [1900] 2 Ch 56.

Acceptance of capital in advance of calls: CA 1963, s 66(b) empowers the company, if authorised by its articles, to accept the whole or part of amounts remaining unpaid in respect of shares, before any calls have been made in respect thereof. Such authorisation is to be found in reg 21 of Table A, which further empowers the directors to pay to the member interest of up to 5% per annum on such amounts for the period from the date of payment until the date when the member would otherwise have been called upon to pay same.

Payment of dividends in proportion to amounts paid up: CA 1963, s 66(c) empowers the company, if so authorised by its articles, to pay dividends in proportion to the amount paid up on each share in circumstances where larger amounts are paid up on some shares than on others. Such authorisation is to be found in reg 120 of Table A which in fact makes it mandatory to pay dividends in proportion to the amount paid up on each share.

UK legislation

See CA 1985, s 119.

---

67 Reserve liability of limited company

A limited company may be special resolution determine that any portion of its share capital which has not been already called up shall not be capable of being called up except in the event and for the purposes of the company being wound up, and thereupon that portion of its share capital shall not be capable of being called up except in the event and for the purposes aforesaid.

Definitions

'company': CA 1963, s 2(1); 'share': CA 1963, s 2(1).

Notes

Reserve capital: Any capital which the members resolve pursuant to CA 1963, s 67 not to call up unless and until liquidation, is known as the 'reserve capital' of the company.[1] Reserve capital may arise either by creating a reserve liability on shares which have already been issued or by issuing new shares with reserve liability. Reserve capital is not subject to the control of the board of directors and therefore cannot be mortgaged, charged, pledged or otherwise disposed of by them.[2] Reserve liability can, however, be cancelled on a reduction of capital pursuant to CA 1963, s 72.[3]

1 With regard to the creation of a reserve capital by an unlimited company, when re-registering as a limited company, see CA 1963, s 71.

2 *Re Pyle Works* (1890) 44 Ch D 534, 586, 587. See also *Re Mayfair Property Co* [1898] 2 Ch 28; *Re Irish Club* [1906] WN 127; *Re Industrial and Agricultural Fair Cork 1932* (1933) 67 ILTR 175.

3 *Re Midland Railway Carriage and Wagon Co* [1907] WN 175.

UK legislation

See CA 1985, s 120.

---

68 Power of company to alter its share capital

(1) A company limited by shares or a company limited by guarantee and having a share capital, if so authorised by its articles, may in general meeting alter the conditions of its memorandum as follows, that is, it may—

(a) increase its share capital by new shares of such amount as it thinks expedient;

(b) consolidate and divide all or any of its share capital into shares of larger amount than its existing shares;

(c) convert all or any of its paid up shares into stock, and re-convert that stock into paid up shares of any denominations;

(d) subdivide its shares, or any of them, into shares of smaller amount than is fixed by the memorandum, so however, that in the subdivision the proportion between the amount paid and the amount, if any, unpaid on each reduced share shall be the same as it was in the case of the share from which the reduced share is derived;

(e) cancel shares which, at the date of the passing of the resolution in that behalf, have not been taken or agreed to be taken by any person, and diminish the amount of its share capital by the amount of the shares so cancelled.

(2) A cancellation of shares in pursuance of this section shall not be deemed to be a reduction of share capital within the meaning of this Act.

Definitions

'articles': CA 1963, s 2(1); 'company': CA 1963, s 2(1); 'company limited by guarantee': CA 1963, s 2(1), 5(2); 'company limited by shares': CA 1963, s 2(1), 5(1); 'memorandum': CA 1963, s 2(1); 'share': CA 1963, s 2(1).

Notes

Increase in authorised share capital: Authorisation for increases in the authorised share capital of a company is to be found in Model Form Articles.[1] Such an increase will be required where the company wishes to allot new shares but the entire of its existing share capital has been fully issued. Whilst the company cannot contractually bind itself not to increase its capital, the members can be so bound, as for example, by a provision to that effect in a shareholders' agreement.[2]

1 Table A, reg 44.
2 *Russell v Northern Bank Development Corp Ltd* [1992] 3 All ER 161.

Consolidation and subdivision of shares: Authorisation for the consolidation of shares into larger units, and for the subdivision of shares into smaller units, is also to be found in Model Form Articles.[1] Although 'as a matter of business' a subdivision of one class of shares may result in an increase in the voting strength of one class and a dilution of the voting strength of others, the subdivision will not be regarded as a matter of law, as constituting a variation of the rights of those other classes of shareholders.[2] The subdivision might, however, amount to oppression or disregard of the interests of those other shareholders so as to entitle them to relief under CA 1963, s 205.[3]

1 Table A, reg 45(a) and (b).
2 *Greenhalgh v Arderne Cinemas Ltd* [1946] 1 All ER 512; *White v Bristol Aeroplane Co Ltd* [1953] Ch 65. See also *Underwood v London Music Hall Ltd* [1901] 2 Ch 309.
3 *Re Williams Group Tullamore Ltd* [1985] IR 613. See also the notes to CA 1963, s 205.

Conversion of shares into stock and vice versa: Model Form articles authorise the conversion of shares into stock as well as the reconversion of stock into shares.[1] The primary difference between stock and shares is that a share is only transferable as a complete unit, whereas stock is transferable in any money fractions.[2] Furthermore, the company cannot issue its capital directly as stock. Instead, it must first issue shares and only after the shares have been paid in full, may it then convert them into stock.[3] A direct issue of stock, although irregular, will be cured by a lapse of time.[4] However, even a lapse of time will not cure a bonus issue of stock, since the allottee will not have been required to make any payment therefor.[5]

1 Table A, reg 40.
2 See *Morrice v Aylmer* (1874) 10 Ch App 148.
3 *Re Home and Foreign Investment and Agency Co* [1912] 1 Ch 72.
4 *Re Home and Foreign Investment and Agency Co* [1912] 1 Ch 72.
5 *Re Home and Foreign Investment and Agency Co* [1912] 1 Ch 72.

Cancellation of shares: Authorisation for the cancellation of unissued share capital is to be found in Model Form articles.[1] Such a cancellation does not constitute a reduction of capital and therefore does not need to be confirmed by the court.[2]

1 Table A, reg 45(c).
2 CA 1963, s 68(2). In relation to reductions of capital, see CA 1963, ss 72–77.

Publication in Companies Registration Office Gazette: Notice of any alteration of capital effected pursuant to CA 1963, s 68 must be notified to the Registrar[1] and published in the Companies Registration Office Gazette.[2]

1 CA 1963, ss 69 and 70.
2 EC(C)R 1973, reg 4.

Copy of altered memorandum: An alteration of capital pursuant to CA 1963, s 68 will result in a variation in the capital clause of the memorandum of association. A copy of the memorandum, as so altered, must be delivered to the Registrar of Companies, together with a copy of the resolution which effected the alteration.[1]

1 EC(C)R 1973, reg 5.

UK legislation

See CA 1985, s 121.

---

69 Notice to registrar of certain alterations in share capital

(1) If a company having a share capital has—

(a) consolidated and divided its share capital into shares of larger amount than its existing shares; or

(b) converted any shares into stock; or

(c) reconverted stock into shares; or

(d) subdivided its shares or any of them; or

(e) redeemed any redeemable preference shares; or

(f) redeemed any preference shares; or

(g) cancelled any shares, otherwise than in connection with a reduction of share capital under section 72:

it shall, within one month after so doing, give notice thereof to the registrar of companies, specifying, as the case may be, the shares consolidated, divided, converted, subdivided, redeemed or cancelled, or the stock reconverted.

(2) If default is made in complying with this section, the company and every officer of the company who is in default [shall be guilty of an offence and liable to a fine][a] not exceeding [€1,904.61].[b]

Amendments

a CA 1963, s 69(2) words 'shall be guilty of an offence and liable to a fine' substituted for 'shall be liable to a fine' by C(AA)A 2003, Sch 2, Item No 1.

b '£250' substituted for '£50' by C(A)A 1982, Sch 1, increased to £1,500 by CA 1990, s 240(7) as inserted by CLEA 2001, s 104(c) and converted to €1,904.61 by Council Regulations (EC) No 1103/97, No 974/98 and No 2866/98 and the Economic and Monetary Union Act 1998, s 6.

Definitions

'company': CA 1963, s 2(1); 'officer': CA 1963, s 2(1); 'officer in default': CA 1963, s 383; 'the registrar of companies': CA 1963, s 2(1); 'share': CA 1963, s 2(1).

Notes

Alterations of capital other than redemption: The various types of alteration of capital referred to in CA 1963, s 69, other than redemptions of shares, are governed by CA 1963, s 68.

Redemption of shares: Prior to the coming into force of CA 1990, Part XI, the only class of shares capable of redemption were redeemable preference shares.[1] Now, however, any class of shares may be made redeemable and may be redeemed in the manner prescribed by CA 1990, Part XI. Furthermore, any references in earlier Acts to 'redeemable preference shares' is now to be construed as a reference to 'redeemable shares.'[2]

1 See CA 1963, s 64.

2 CA 1990, s 221.

Investment companies: The provisions of CA 1963, s 69 do not apply to investment companies.[1]

1 CA 1990, s 260(1). For the definition of 'investment company' see CA 1990, s 252(1).

UK legislation

See CA 1985, s 122.

70 Notice of increase of share capital

(1) Where a company, having a share capital, whether its shares have or have not been converted into stock, has increased its share capital above the registered capital, it shall, within 15 days after the passing of the resolution increasing its share capital, give to the registrar of companies notice of the increase, and the registrar shall record the increase.

(2) The notice to be given as aforesaid shall include such particulars as may be prescribed with respect to the classes of shares affected, and the conditions subject to which the new shares have been or are to be issued.

(3) If default is made in complying with this section, the company and every officer of the company who is in default [shall be guilty of an offence and liable to a fine][a] not exceeding [€1,904.61].[b]

Amendments

a CA 1963, s 70(3) words 'shall be guilty of an offence and liable to a fine' substituted for 'shall be liable to a fine by C(AA)A 2003, Sch 2, Item No 1.

b ‘£250’ substituted for ‘£50’ by C(A)A 1982, Sch 11, increased to £1,500 by CA 1990, s 240(7) as inserted by CLEA 2001, s 104(c) and converted to €1,904.61 by Council Regulations (EC) No 1103/97, No 974/98 and No 2866/98 and the Economic and Monetary Union Act 1998, s 6.

Definitions

‘company’: CA 1963, s 2(1); ‘officer’: CA 1963, s 2(1); ‘officer in default’: CA 1963, s 383; ‘prescribed’: CA 1963, s 2(1); ‘the registrar of companies’: CA 1963, s 2(1); ‘share’: CA 1963, s 2(1).

Notes

Increase in share capital: An increase in the authorised share capital of the company may be effected pursuant to CA 1963, s 68(1).

Investment companies: The provisions of CA 1963, s 70 do not apply to investment companies.[1]

1 CA 1990, s 260(1). For the definition of ‘investment company’ see CA 1990, s 252(1).

UK legislation

See CA 1985, s 123.

---

71 Power of unlimited company to provide for reserve share capital on re-registration

An unlimited company having a share capital may, by its resolution for registration as a limited company in pursuance of this Act, do either or both of the following things:

(a) increase the nominal amount of its share capital by increasing the nominal amount of each of its shares, but subject to the condition that no part of the increased capital shall be capable of being called up, except in the event and for the purposes of the company being wound up;

(b) provide that a specified portion of its uncalled share capital shall not be capable of being called up except in the event and for the purposes of the company being wound up.

Definitions

‘company’: CA 1963, s 2(1); ‘share’: CA 1963, s 2(1); ‘unlimited company’: CA 1963, s 2(1), s 5(2).

Notes

Re-registration as limited company: The procedure for re-registering as a limited company is governed by C(A)A 1983, s 53.

Reserve capital: See the notes to CA 1963, s 67.

UK legislation

See CA 1985, s 124.

Reduction of share capital

72 Power of company to reduce its share capital

(1) Except in so far as this Act expressly permits, it shall not be lawful for a company limited by shares or a company limited by guarantee and having a share capital [...][a] to reduce its share capital in any way.

(2) Subject to confirmation by the court, a company limited by shares or a company limited by guarantee and having a share capital, may, if so authorised by its articles, by special resolution reduce its share capital in any way and, in particular, without prejudice to the generality of the foregoing power, may—

(a) extinguish or reduce the liability on any of its shares in respect of share capital not paid up; or

(b) either with or without extinguishing or reducing liability on any of its shares, cancel any paid up share capital which is lost or unrepresented by available assets; or

(c) either with or without extinguishing or reducing liability on any of its shares, pay off any paid up share capital which is in excess of the wants of the company;

and may, if and so far as is necessary, alter its memorandum by reducing the amount of its share capital and of its shares accordingly.

(3) A special resolution under this section is, in this Act, referred to as 'a resolution for reducing share capital'.

Amendments

a Words deleted by CA 1990, s 231.

Definitions

'articles': CA 1963, s 2(1); 'company': CA 1963, s 2(1) and NAMA Act 2009, s 228(1); 'company limited by guarantee': s 2(1), 5(2); 'company limited by shares': CA 1963, s 2(1), 5(2); 'the court': CA 1963, s 2(1); 'memorandum': CA 1963, s 2(1); 'resolution for reducing share capital': CA 1963, s 2(1), s 72(3); 'share': CA 1963, s 2(1).

Cross references in other enactments

NAMA Act 2009, s 228(1) provides that a reference to a 'company' in CA 1963, s 72(1) 'shall be taken not to include a NAMA group entity' within the meaning of NAMA Act 2009.

Notes

Unlimited companies: CA 1963, s 72(1) only applies to companies limited by shares or limited by guarantee and having a share capital. An unlimited company may however reduce its capital in any manner it wishes.[1] Unlimited companies are not required to have a share capital. Accordingly, if the capital was stated in the memorandum, any such reduction would be effected pursuant to CA 1963, s 28 or by such other procedure, if any, as may be specified in the memorandum itself. On the other hand, if the capital is stated in the articles, any alteration will have to be effected pursuant to CA 1963, s 15.

1 *Re Borough Commercial and Building Society* [1893] 2 Ch 242.

Guarantee companies: CA 1963, s 72(1) does not refer to companies limited by guarantee and not having a share capital. In principle, therefore, such companies ought also to be entitled to reduce their capital in whatever manner they think fit. However, the procedure for making such a reduction would appear to be even more involved than that applicable under s 72. Since a guarantee company is required to state the amount of its capital in the memorandum of association, CA 1963, s 28 cannot be invoked to effect the alteration. Section 28 can only be invoked to alter clauses which are not required by law to be contained in the memorandum. Consequently, a reduction of the capital of a company limited by guarantee and not having a share capital could only be reduced by way of a scheme of arrangement pursuant to CA 1963, ss 201–203.

Investment companies: The provisions of CA 1963, s 72 do not apply to investment companies.[1]

1 CA 1990, s 260(1). For the definition of 'investment company' see CA 1990, s 252(1).

Authorisation for reduction in articles: In order to be able to invoke CA 1963, s 72, the company must be authorised by its articles to reduce its share capital. Such authorisation is to be found in Model Form articles.[1] If the company's articles do not contain such authorisation, they must first be so amended and only then can a resolution be passed approving the reduction of capital. A single special resolution simultaneously amending the articles and approving the reduction, will not suffice.[2] It would however appear to be permissible to pass the two resolutions one after the other at the same meeting.

1 Table A, reg 46.

2 *Re West India and Pacific Steamship Co* (1868) 9 Ch App 23; *Re Patent Invert Sugar Co* (1885) 31 Ch D 166.

Notice convening the general meeting: With regard to the meeting at which the special resolution authorising the reduction of capital is to be considered, a heavy onus lies on the company to ensure that the circular or other information sent to members is accurate.[1] Any inaccuracy which could have influenced the minds of reasonable shareholders may well result in the court refusing to confirm the reduction of capital.[2]

1 *Re European Home Products plc* [1988] BCLC 690.

2 *Re European Home Products plc* [1988] BCLC 690.

Publication of resolution: A plc which passes a special resolution approving a reduction of its share capital, must publish in Companies Registration Office Gazette notice of delivery to the registrar of a copy of the resolution.[1]

1 C(A)A 1983, s 55(1)(i).

Conditional resolution: Where a resolution for the reduction of the company's share capital is expressed to be conditional, the court has jurisdiction to confirm the reduction provided that the specified condition has been fulfilled prior to confirmation.[1]

1 *Re Tip-Europe Ltd* [1988] BCLC 231.

Meaning of 'share capital': The phrase 'share capital' in CA 1963, s 72, means the issued share capital of the company, and includes any share premium account[1] and any capital redemption reserve fund,[2] as well as any capital conversion reserve fund.[3] However, a cancellation of unissued shares is regarded as a 'diminution of share capital' rather than a reduction of share capital[4] and may instead be effected pursuant to CA 1963, s 68(1).

1 CA 1963, s 62(1).

2 CA 1990, s 208.

3 Economic and Monetary Union Act 1998, s 26(4)(b).

4 CA 1963, s 68(2).

Mode of reduction of share capital: CA 1963, s 72(1) allows the company, having followed the prescribed procedure, to reduce its share capital 'in any way'. The different modes of reduction of capital referred to in s 72(2) should therefore not be regarded as exhaustive.[1]

Extinguishing or reducing liability on shares: The first type of reduction of capital expressly referred to in CA 1963, s 72(2) is where a company extinguishes or reduces the liability on any of its shares which have not been fully paid up. This may be done where the company already has more capital than it requires to finance its business.[2] The liability which is being extinguished or reduced may be in respect of called or uncalled amounts and may even be in respect of the company's 'reserve capital.'[3] So, for example, where the company has shares with a nominal value of €1 each, on which only 50c had been paid up, the liability of the members could be extinguished by reducing the nominal value of each share to 50c. Indeed, the same result could be achieved by cancelling every second share held by each shareholder and crediting the remaining shares with the amount which had been paid up on the cancelled shares.[4] However, the liability of a shareholder can neither be reduced nor extinguished by crediting him with having paid up more than has in fact been paid up.[5]

Cancellation of paid up share capital: The second type of reduction of capital referred to in CA 1963, s 72(2) involves the cancellation of any paid up share capital which is lost or unrepresented by available assets. This may be necessary to bring the company's balance sheet into line with its true financial position after it has incurred realised revenue or capital losses. Under C(A)A 1983, s 45 dividends cannot be paid by a company until its accumulated realised losses have been written off in a reduction or reorganisation of capital duly made. By writing down a sufficient amount of paid-up capital (which technically represents a liability to the shareholders), the company may be able to write off its losses and return to a position whereby it is able to declare dividends.[6] In this regard, the reduction could take the form of a cancellation of whole shares[7] or might alternatively involve a reduction in their nominal value.[8] However, whatever the method actually chosen, the court will be concerned to ensure that the effect of the reduction of capital is not to cause prejudice to the creditors of shareholders of the company.[9]

Before the court will confirm a cancellation of shares as being lost or unrepresented by available assets, there must first be evidence that the loss is permanent.[10] The mere fact that capital has been sunk into an asset which is not readily saleable, such as goodwill, does not mean that the capital has been lost or that it is unrepresented by assets.[11] This is because, in the sale of the company's business, some value would probably be attributed to the goodwill. If there is some prospect that the loss might be recovered at some future date (eg through litigation against third parties) the court, in confirming the reduction, may order (or require the company to undertake) that any amount so recovered be placed in a capital reserve fund which is to be treated as undistributable for so long as any of the liabilities of the company as of the date of the reduction of capital shall remain undischarged.[12] Indeed, subject to the imposition of such a restriction (whether by way of order or undertaking) a company may be permitted to cancel a sufficient amount of capital not only to write off existing losses but also to write off future deficits on the profit and loss account.[13]

If the company is a plc and it reduces its share capital below the authorised minimum of €38,092.14, the order of the court confirming the reduction will not take effect until the company has re-registered as some other type of company.[14]

Repayment of share capital: The third type of reduction of capital expressly referred to in CA 1963, s 72(2) involves the return of capital to its members and may involve the payment of cash or the transfer of assets *in specie*.[15] In the case of a payment *in specie* the market value of the assets being paid out need not equate with and may indeed exceed the value of the capital being reduced, provided of course that the interests of the creditors, of the shareholders and of members of the public having dealings with the company, are adequately safeguarded.[16] Furthermore, such a reduction may be made unconditionally or may be made on terms whereby the members are liable to repay the amount in question if called upon to do so.[17] For example, in the case of a fully paid €1 share, the reduction could take any one of the following forms:

(a) a return of the whole of the nominal value of the share to the shareholder, thereby turning the share into an unpaid share and thus exposing the shareholder to a potential liability to contribute €1 to the company in the event of a liquidation; or

(b) a return of part of the nominal value of the share (eg 60c), thereby turning the share into a partly paid share and exposing the shareholder to potential liability to contribute 40c to the company in the event of a liquidation; or

(c) a return of the whole of the nominal value of the share, coupled with a cancellation of the share itself, thereby extinguishing any liability on the part of the shareholder;[18] or

(d) a return of part of the nominal value of the share (eg 60c) coupled with a reduction in the nominal value of the share to 40c, thereby extinguishing any liability on the part of the shareholder.

A return of capital may take place where the company has more than sufficient funds to finance its activities and simply wishes to return part of that money to its members[19] or where the members wish to realise all or part of their investment in the company.[20] Another legitimate motive for such a reduction might be to get rid of a class of preference shareholders whose fixed dividend entitlement is in excess of prevailing interest rates, thereby making that class of share capital more costly to the company than loan capital.[21] In this regard, the court will not be precluded from confirming the reduction, simply because the return which the preference shares can expect if they re-invest their capital is less than the yield they would otherwise have obtained on their shares.[22]

In so far as the proposed reduction involves the repayment of capital to shareholders and the cancellation of their shares, the company, rather than invoking CA 1963, s 72, could instead simply purchase the shares in accordance with the procedures laid down in CA 1990, Part XI.

1 *Re Phoebe Gold Mining Co* [1900] WN 182; *Re Hoare and Co* [1910] WN 87; *Poole v National Bank of China* [1907] AC 229; *Ex parte Westburn Sugar Refineries* [1951] AC 625.

2 *Re Northern Bank Ltd* [1963] NI 90.

3 *Re Midland Railway Carriage and Wagon Co* [1907] WN 175. For the meaning of 'reserve capital' see CA 1963, s 67 and the notes thereto.

4 *Re Doloswella Rubber and Tea Estates Ltd* [1917] 1 Ch 213. Cf *Re Walker Steam Trawl Co* 1908 SC 123 where confirmation of such a scheme was refused as being a conversion of share capital rather than a reduction of share capital.

5 *Re Development Co of Central and West Africa* [1902] 1 Ch 547.

6 *Re Ratners Group plc* [1988] BCLC 685.

7 *Bannantyne v Direct Spanish Telegraph Co* (1886) 34 Ch D 287; *Re Jupiter House Investments (Cambridge) Ltd* [1985] 1 WLR 975; *Re Grosvenor Press plc* [1985] 1 WLR 980; *Re John Power and Son Ltd* [1934] IR 412.

8 *Carruth v ICI Ltd* [1937] AC 707.

9 *Re Grosvenor Press plc* [1985] 1 WLR 980; *Re Ratners Group plc* [1988] BCLC 685; *Re Quayle Munro Ltd* [1994] 1 BCLC 410.

10 *Re Jupiter House Investments (Cambridge) Ltd* [1985] 1 WLR 975; *Re Grosvenor Press plc* [1985] 1 WLR 980; *Caldwell v Caldwell and Co* [1916] WN 70; *Re Floating Dock of St Thomas Ltd* [1895] 1 Ch 691; *Re London and New York Investment Corporation* [1895] 2 Ch 860; *Re Barrow Haematite Steel Co* [1901] 2 Ch 746; *Re Welsbach Incandescent Gas Light Co Ltd* (1903) 9 E and E Dig 161.

11 *Re Abstainers and General Insurance Co* [1891] 2 Ch 124.

12 *Re Grosvenor Press plc* [1985] 1 WLR 980; *Re Ratners Group plc* [1988] BCLC 685; *Re Jupiter House Investments (Cambridge) Ltd* [1985] 1 WLR 975.

13 *Re Quayle Munro Ltd* [1994] 1 BCLC 410; *Re Thorn EMI plc* [1989] BCLC 612; *Re Ratners Group plc* [1988] BCLC 685.

14 C(A)A 1983, s 17(1) and (3).

15 *Ex parte Westburn Sugar Refineries Ltd* [1951] AC 625.

16 *Ex parte Westburn Sugar Refineries Ltd* [1951] AC 625.

17 *Re Fore Street Warehouse Co* [1888] WN 155; *Re Watson, Walker and Quickfall* [1898] WN 69; *Re Brown Sons and Co* 1931 SC 701; *Re Stevenson Anderson and Co Ltd* 1951 SC 346.

18 See, however, CA 1963, s 76 which limits somewhat the absolute extinguishing of liability of the shareholder.

19 *Cork Electricity Supply Co v Concannon* [1932] IR 314.

20 *British and American Trustee and Finance Corporation v Couper* [1894] AC 399.

21 *Re Lamson Store Service Co* [1897] 1 Ch 875n; *Re Nixon's Navigation Co* [1897] 1 Ch 872; *Re Mackenzie and Co* [1916] 2 Ch 450; *Re St James' Court Estate Ltd* [1944] Ch 6; *Re Chatterley-Whitfield Collieries Ltd* [1948] 2 All ER 593; *Re Saltdean Estate Co Ltd* [1968] 1 WLR 1844; *Re Holders Investment Trust Ltd* [1971] 1 WLR 583; *House of Fraser plc v ACGE Investments Ltd* [1987] AC 387; *Re Credit Finance Bank plc* (1963–1993) Irish Company Law Reports 170.

22 *Scottish Insurance Corporation Ltd v Wilson and Clyde Coal Co Ltd* [1949] AC 462; *Prudential Assurance Co Ltd v Chatterley-Whitfield Collieries Ltd* [1949] AC 512.

Adjustment in authorised share capital: Where the reduction in capital involves the cancellation of issued share capital, whether by way of a return of capital to shareholders or because the capital is lost or no longer represented by available assets, the proper practice is also to reduce the company's authorised or nominal share capital by a corresponding amount.[1]

1 *Re Anglo-French Exploration Co* [1902] 2 Ch 845, 852.

Reduction must be fair and equitable: A reduction of share capital will not be confirmed by the court if it is unfair or inequitable as between the shareholders generally or as between different classes of shareholders.[1]

Proper order of priorities: The reduction will, however, be regarded as fair and equitable as between different classes of shareholders if the same order of priorities is followed as would pertain in a winding up.[2] Thus, if the reduction involves a repayment of capital and the preference shareholders would have priority as to a return of capital in a winding up, they must be paid off before any ordinary shareholders.[3] Conversely, in the above example, if the reduction involved a cancellation of paid up shares as a result of losses sustained by the company, it would be the ordinary shares which would have to be cancelled first since it is the ordinary share capital which would be repaid last in the event of a liquidation.[4] However, if the different classes rank equally as to a return of capital in a winding up, or if all the shares are of the one class, the reduction of capital must be effected rateably as between all shares[5] in proportion to their respective nominal values.[6] The court will only depart from this principle of equality in the most exceptional of circumstances, as where no shareholders appear in court to oppose confirmation of the reduction[7] or where the shareholders or the class of shareholder who are adversely affected, actually consent.[8]

If the reduction of capital follows the same order of priority as would apply in a winding up, it will not amount to a variation of class rights and accordingly it will not be necessary to have the reduction approved by the different classes of shareholders.[9] However, if a class meeting is in fact required, because of the nature of the proposed reduction of capital, the shareholders, when voting at the class meetings, must have regard to the interests of the class as a whole, rather than having regard to the interests of some other class.[10]

Proper amount to be repaid: In the case of a reduction of capital which involves the repayment and cancellation of preference shares, the preference shareholders will only be entitled to receive the nominal value of their shares together with any outstanding dividends. The company is neither obliged to compensate them for the fact that they would receive a higher value if they sold their shares on the open market,[11] nor for the fact that it deprives them of the possibility of future dividends.[12] Equally well, they have no entitlement to compensation for the fact that they would have been entitled to participate in the surplus assets in a winding up[13] unless of course, such a liquidation is actually in prospect.[14]

Form of repayment of capital: If the proposed reduction involves the return of capital to shareholders, the payment will usually take the form of cash. A return of assets *in specie* may also be permitted.[15] Equally well, however, a reduction of capital may be confirmed by the court as being fair and equitable in circumstances where the shareholders, rather than receiving cash, are instead obliged to take loan stock or other securities.[16]

1 *British and American Trustee and Finance Corporation v Couper* [1894] AC 399; *Re Welsbach Incandescent Gas Light Co* [1904]1 Ch 87; *Poole v National Bank of China Ltd* [1907] AC 229; *Re Showell's Brewery Co* (1914) 30 TLR 428; *Re John Power and Son Ltd* [1934] IR 412; *Re Credit Finance Bank plc* (1963–1993) Irish Company Law Reports 170.

2 *Re MacKenzie and Co* [1916] 2 Ch 450; *Re Chatterley-Whitfield Collieries Ltd* [1948] 2 All ER 593 aff'd *sub nom Prudential Assurance Co Ltd v Chatterley-Whitfield Collieries Ltd* [1949] AC 512; *Re John Power and Son Ltd* [1934] IR 412; *House of Fraser plc v ACGE Investments Ltd* [1987] AC 387; *Re Credit Finance Bank plc* (1963–1993) Irish Company Law Reports 170.

3 *Re MacKenzie and Co* [1916] 2 Ch 450; *Re Chatterley-Whitfield Collieries* [1948] 2 All ER 593; *Scottish Insurance Corporation Ltd v Wilsons and Clyde Coal Co Ltd* [1949] AC 462; *Re Saltdean Estate Co Ltd* [1968] 1 WLR 1844; *Re Credit Finance plc* (1963–1993) Irish Company Law Reports 170.

4 *Bannantyne v Direct Spanish Telegraph Co* (1886) 34 Ch D 287; *Re Agricultural Hotel Co* [1895] 1 Ch 691; *Re Floating Dock Co of St Thomas Ltd* [1895] 1 Ch 691; *Re London and New York Investment Corporation* [1895] 2 Ch 860; *Re John Power and Son Ltd* [1934] IR 412.

5 *Bannantyne v Direct Spanish Telegraph Co* (1886) 34 Ch D 287; *Re Barrow Haematite Steel Co* (1888) 39 Ch D 582; *Re Quebrada Railway, Land and Copper Co* (1889) 40 Ch D 363; *Re Union Plate Glass Co* (1889) 42 Ch D 513; *Re MacKenzie and Co* [1916] 2 Ch 450. cf *Re Barrow Haematite Steel Co* [1900] 2 Ch 846, aff'd [1901] 2 Ch 746.

6 *Re Credit Assurance and Guarantee Corporation Ltd* [1902] 2 Ch 601.

7 *Re Robert Stephen Holdings Ltd* [1968] 1 WLR 522.

8 *Re Walsbach Incandescent Gas Light Co Ltd* [1904] 1 Ch 87; *Re Showells Brewery Co* (1914) 30 TLR 428; *Carruth v Imperial Chemical Industries* [1937] AC 707.

9 *Re MacKenzie and Co* [1916] 2 Ch 450; *Re Saltdean Estate Co Ltd* [1968] 1 WLR 1844; *House of Fraser plc v ACGE Investments Ltd* [1987] AC 387; *Re Credit Finance Bank plc* (1963–1993) Irish Company Law Reports 170.

10 *Re Holders Investment Trust Ltd* [1971] 1 WLR 583.

11 *Scottish Insurance Corporation Ltd v Wilsons and Clyde Coal Co Ltd* [1949] AC 462; *Re Saltdean Estate Co Ltd* [1968] 1 WLR 1844.

12 *Re Saltdean Estate Co Ltd* [1968] 1 WLR 1844.

13 *Scottish Insurance Corporation Ltd v Wilsons and Clyde Coal Co Ltd* [1949] AC 462.

14 *Re William Jones and Sons Ltd* [1969] 1 WLR 146.

15 *Ex parte Westburn Sugar Refineries Ltd* [1951] AC 625.

16 *Re Thomas de la Rue and Co Ltd* [1911] 2 Ch 361; *Ex parte Westburn Sugar Refineries Ltd* [1951] AC 625.

Creditor protection: Apart from ensuring that the reduction of capital is fair and equitable as between the shareholders, the court will also be concerned to see that the position of the creditors and members of the public having dealings with the company is being adequately protected.[1] With regard to the question of creditor protection see CA 1963, s 73 and the notes thereto.

1 *Ex parte Westburn Sugar Refineries Ltd* [1951] AC 625.

Motive for reduction: Provided the reduction is fair and equitable as between the members, and is not prejudicial to the creditors, the court will be prepared to confirm the scheme and will not be concerned as to the factors which motivated the company. Thus, the court was prepared in one case to confirm a reduction of capital where the motive was to avoid the effects of nationalisation[1] and in another case where the motive was tax avoidance.[2]

1 *Ex parte Westburn Sugar Refineries Ltd* [1951] AC 625.

2 *Re David Bell Ltd* 1954 SC 33.

UK legislation

See CA 1985, s 135.

73 Application to court for confirming order, objections by creditors and settlement of list of objecting creditors

(1) Where a company has passed a resolution for reducing share capital, it may apply to the court for an order confirming the reduction.

(2) Where the proposed reduction of share capital involves either diminution of liability in respect of unpaid share capital, or the payment to any shareholder of any paid up share capital, and in any other case if the court so directs, the following provisions shall have effect, subject nevertheless to subsection (3);

[(a) in the case of a public limited company—

(i) every creditor of the company who—

(I) at the date fixed by the court, is entitled to a debt or claim that, if that date were the commencement of the winding up of the company, would be admissible in proof against the company, and

(II) can credibly demonstrate that the proposed reduction in the share capital would be likely to put the satisfaction of that debt or claim at risk, and that no adequate safe-guards have been obtained from the company, is entitled to object to the reduction, and

(ii) the court shall settle a list of creditors entitled to object, and for that purpose may publish notices fixing a day or days within which creditors are to claim to be entered on the list or are to be excluded from the right of objecting to the reduction of capital;

(b) in the case of any other company—

(i) every creditor of the company who, at the date fixed by the court, is entitled to any debt or claim that, if that date were the commencement of the winding up of the company, would be admissible in proof against the company is entitled to object to the reduction;

(ii) the court shall settle a list of creditors so entitled to object, and for that purpose shall ascertain, as far as possible without requiring an application from any creditor, the names of those creditors and the nature and amount of their debts or claims, and may publish notices fixing a day or days within which creditors not entered on the list are to claim to be so entered or are to be excluded from the right of objecting to the reduction;][a]

(c) [in either case][b] where a creditor entered on the list whose debt or claim is not discharged or has not determined does not consent to the reduction, the court may, if it thinks fit, dispense with the consent of that creditor, on the company securing payment of his debt or claim by appropriating, as the court may direct, the following amount:–

(i) if the company admits the full amount of the debt or claim, or, though not admitting it, is willing to provide for it, then the full amount of the debt or claim;

(ii) if the company does not admit and is not willing to provide for the full amount of the debt or claim, or, if the amount is contingent or not ascertained, then an amount fixed by the court after the like inquiry and adjudication as if the company were being wound up by the court.

(3) Where a proposed reduction of share capital involve either the diminution of any liability in respect of unpaid share capital or the payment to any shareholder of any paid up share capital, the court may, if, having regard to any special circumstances of the case, it thinks proper so to do, direct that subsection (2) shall not apply as regards any class or any classes of creditors.

Amendments

a CA 1963, s 73(2)(a) and (b) inserted by EC(PLC)R 2008, reg 3(a)(i).

b Words 'in either case' inserted by EC(PLC)R 2008, reg 3(a)(ii).

Definitions

'company': CA 1963, s 2(1); 'the court': CA 1963, s 2(1); 'resolution for reducing share capital': CA 1963, s 2(1), s 72(3); 'share': CA 1963, s 2(1).

Notes

Application to court: The application to court for confirmation of the reduction of capital is brought by way of petition[1] and is required to be in the Form No 1 of Appendix of the Rules of the Superior Courts.[2] Having presented the petition in the Central Office, a motion is then brought before the court for directions as to the hearing of the petition.[3]

1 RSC, Ord 75, r 4(h).
2 RSC, Ord 75, r 3(3).
3 RSC, Ord 75, r 6(1).

Publication of notice of petition: At the hearing of the motion for directions the court will order that notice of the hearing of the petition be advertised in one or more newspapers.[1]

1 RSC, Ord 75, rr 6(2)(a) and 13. The advertisement must be in the Form No 10 in Appendix N with such variations as the circumstances of the case may require.

Enquiry as to debts and liabilities: If the proposed reduction of capital involves either a diminution of shareholders' liability for unpaid share capital or the repayment of paid-up share capital, the court must normally direct at the hearing of the Motion for Directions, that an enquiry be held as to the debts, claims and liabilities of the company.[1] A reduction which involves cancelling fully paid-up shares and replacing them with debentures credited as paid up to the same extent, constitutes a repayment of capital, such as to attract the requirement for an enquiry as to debts and liabilities.[2] In special circumstances, as where the company will still have sufficient cash or other readily realisable assets, after the reduction of capital so as to be able to meet its provable debts and liabilities in full as they fall due, the court may dispense with the settling of a list of creditors and may further dispense with the entitlement of creditors to object at the hearing of the petition.[3] Conversely, even if the proposed scheme involves neither a diminution in the liability of shareholders for unpaid share capital nor a return of paid-up share capital, the court may still, if it thinks fit, direct that an enquiry as to debts and liabilities be held.[4]

Where an enquiry as to debts and liabilities is ordered to be held, the court may further direct that notices be published fixing a time within which creditors not entered on the list are to claim to be so entered or are to be excluded from objecting to the reduction.[5]

1 CA 1963, s 73(2)(b) and RSC, Ord 75, r 6(2)(b). For the procedure that is involved in settling the list of creditors, see RSC, Ord 75, rr 7–12.
2 *Re Lawrie and Symington Ltd* (1969) SLT 221.
3 CA 1963, s 73(3). See *Re Unifruitco SS Co* (1930) SC 1104 (sufficient assets and evidence of debts being regularly discharged); *Re Antwerp Waterworks Co Ltd* [1931] WN 186 (sufficient assets); *Re Cadzow Coal Co Ltd* 1931 SC 272 (existing creditors either paid off or consenting); *Re Lucania Temperance Billiard Halls (London) Ltd* [1966] Ch 98 (guarantee of liabilities by third party).
4 CA 1963, s 73(2).
5 CA 1963, s 73(2)(b). See also *Re Credit Foncier of England* (1871) LR 11 Eq 356; *Re Patent Ventilating Granary Co* (1879) 12 Ch D 254.

Hearing of petition: If the reduction of capital simply involves the revaluation or cancellation of fully paid-up shares the court will normally only entertain representations from the members concerned.[1] On the other hand, if the scheme involves either a diminution in the liability of shareholders for unpaid share capital or a return of paid-up share capital, then unless the court has dispensed with the holding of an enquiry as to the company's debts and liabilities, every person appearing on the settled list of creditors shall be entitled to come in and be heard on the petition.[2] Before a creditor may be heard, he must first give two clear days' notice in writing to the company's solicitor of his intention to so appear.[3] If a creditor whose debt or claim is not discharged or has not been determined, does not consent[4] to the reduction of capital, the court may, if it thinks fit, dispense with that creditor's consent, provided that the company first secures his debt or claim, either by appropriating the full amount thereof or, in the case of a disputed or contingent or unascertained debt or claim, by appropriating such amount as the court may consider would be provable if the company were being wound up.[5] If necessary, the court may adjourn the hearing of the petition in order to allow the company time to secure the debt or claim of the creditor in question.[6]

1 *Re Meux Brewery Co Ltd* [1919] 1 Ch 28; *Re Barrow Haematite Steel Co* [1900] 2 Ch 846, aff'd [1901] 2 Ch 746.
2 CA 1963, s 73(2)(a).
3 RSC, Ord 75, r 14.
4 A creditor who takes a neutral stance and neither actively supports nor opposes the petition cannot be regarded as having 'consented' to the reduction of capital: *Re Patent Ventilating Granary Co* (1879) 12 Ch D 254.
5 CA 1963, s 73(2)(c).
6 RSC, Ord 75, r 16.

Creditors who are unaware of the hearing: If the company goes into insolvent liquidation after the confirmation of the reduction of the capital, any creditor who was ignorant of 'the proceedings for reduction, or of their nature and effect' may pursue the members for an amount equivalent to that by which their liability to contribute to the assets of the company has been so reduced.[1]

1 CA 1963, s 76.

UK legislation

See CA 1985, s 136.

---

74 Order confirming reduction and powers of court on making such order

(1) The court, if satisfied in relation to every creditor of the company who, under section 73, is entitled to object to the reduction, that either his consent to the reduction has been obtained or that his debt or claim has been discharged or has determined, or has been secured, may make an order confirming the reduction on such terms and conditions as it thinks fit.

(2) Where the court makes any such order, it may—

(a) if for any special reason it thinks proper so to do, make an order directing that the company shall, during such period, commencing on or at any time after the date of the order, as is specified in the order, add to its name as the last words thereof the words 'and reduced' or where the word 'teoranta' is part of such name, the words 'agus laghdaithe',

(b) make an order requiring the company to publish as the court directs the reasons for reduction or such other information in regard thereto as the court may think expedient, with a view to giving proper information to the public, and, if the court thinks fit, the causes which led to the reduction.

(3) Where a company is ordered to add to its name the words 'and reduced', or the words 'agus laghdaithe' those words shall, until the expiration of the period specified in the order, be deemed to be part of the name of the company.

Definitions

'company': CA 1963, s 2(1); 'the court': CA 1963, s 2(1).

Notes

Reduction subject to terms and conditions: The court has a discretion whether or not to confirm the reduction of capital. In this regard, it may confirm the reduction subject to terms and conditions,[1] eg requiring the articles to be altered so as to reduce the voting power of the shares in question.[2]

1 CA 1963, s 74(1) and RSC, Ord 75, r 17.
2 *Re Pinkney and Sons Steamship Co* [1893] 3 Ch 125. See also *Re Continental Union Gas Co* (1891) 7 TLR 476.

Re-registration of plc: Where the court makes an order confirming a reduction of the capital of a plc which has the effect of bringing the nominal value of its issued share capital below the authorised minimum, the court may authorise the plc to re-register as some other form of company without having to pass a special resolution to that effect under C(A)A 1983, s 14, and in granting such authorisation the court must specify the alterations in the memorandum and articles which are to be made in connection with the re-registration.[1]

1 C(A)A 1983, s 17(4).

Approval of minute: As part of the order confirming the reduction of capital, rather than by way of a separate order,[1] the court must also approve a minute showing, with respect to the share capital as altered, the amount of the share capital, the number of shares into which it is to be divided, and the amount of each share, and the amount, if any, deemed to be paid up on each share.[2]

1 *Re Lees Brook Spinning Co* [1906] 2 Ch 394; *Re Anglo-Italian Bank* [1906] WN 202; *Re General Industrials Development Syndicate* [1907] WN 23.
2 CA 1963, s 75(1).

Registration of minute: Upon production to him of a copy of the order of the court confirming the reduction of capital, and the delivery to him of copies of the order and minute, the Registrar of Companies must register same[1] whereupon the reduction of capital shall take effect.[2] In the case of a plc, however, if the reduction of capital brings the issued share capital below the authorised minimum, the Registrar shall not register the order unless the court otherwise directs or the plc first re-registers as some other from of company.[3]

1 CA 1963, s 75(1).

2 CA 1973, s 75(2). A copy of the memorandum and articles as altered by the reduction of capital must also be delivered to the Registrar: EC(C)R 1973, reg 5.

3 C(A)A 1983, s 17(3).

Publication of notice of order and minute: Notice of the registration of the order of the court and the minute must be published in the Companies Registration Office Gazette[1] and in such newspapers or in such other manner as the court may direct.[2]

1 EC(C)R 1973, reg 3(c) and (d).

2 CA 1963, s 75(3) and RSC, Ord 75, r 17.

UK legislation

See CA 1985, s 137.

---

75 Registration of order and minute of reduction

(1) The registrar of companies, on production to him of an order of the court confirming the reduction of the share capital of a company, and the delivery to him of a copy of the order and of a minute approved by the court showing, with respect to the share capital of the company as altered by the order, the amount of the share capital, the number of shares into which it is to be divided, and the amount of each share, and the amount, if any, at the date of the registration deemed to be paid up on each share, shall register the order and minute.

(2) On the registration of the order and minute, and not before, the resolution for reducing share capital as confirmed by the order so registered shall take effect.

(3) Notice of the registration shall be published in such manner as the court may direct.

(4) The registrar shall certify under his hand the registration of the order and minute, and his certificate shall be conclusive evidence that all the requirements of this Act relating to reduction of share capital have been complied with, and that the share capital of the company is such as is stated in the minute.

(5) The minute when registered shall be deemed to be substituted for the corresponding part of the memorandum, and shall be valid and alterable as if it had been originally contained therein.

(6) The substitution of any such minute as aforesaid for part of the memorandum of the company shall be deemed to be an alteration of the memorandum within the meaning of section 30.

Definitions

'company': CA 1963, s 2(1); 'the court': CA 1963, s 2(1); 'memorandum': CA 1963, s 2(1); 'the registrar of companies': CA 1963, s 2(1); 'resolution for reducing share capital': CA 1963, s 2(1), s 72(3); 'share': CA 1963, s 2(1).

Notes

Conclusiveness of certificate of registration: For the possible constitutional implications of the certificate of registration of the minute and order being 'conclusive evidence' as to compliance with all the requirements of the Companies Acts relating to the reduction of capital, see *Maher v Attorney General*.[1]

1 *Maher v Attorney General* [1973] IR 146. For a possible way out of such constitutional difficulties, see Courtney, *The Law of Private Companies* (2nd edn, Tottel Publishing, 2002) at paras 4.018 and 4.019.

Form of minute: Apart from providing details of the share capital consequent upon the reduction, the minute should also give details of the amount and division of shares from which it was reduced.[1]

1 *Re Barrow Haematite Steel Co* (1888) 39 Ch D 582; *Re West Cumberland Iron and Steel Co* [1888] WN 54; *Re Brittania Mills Co, Huddersfield* [1888] WN 103.

Approval, registration and publication of minute: See the notes to CA 1963, s 74.

UK legislation

See CA 1985, s 138.

---

76 Liability of members in respect of reduced shares

(1) Subject to subsection (2), in the case of a reduction of share capital, a member of the company, past or present, shall not be liable in respect of any share to any call or contribution exceeding in amount the difference, if any, between the amount of the share as fixed by the minute and the amount paid, or the reduced amount, if any, which is to be deemed to have been paid, on the share, as the case may be.

(2) If any creditor entitled in respect of any debt or claim to object to the reduction of the share capital, is, by reason of his ignorance of the proceedings for reduction, or of their nature and effect with respect to his debt or claim, not entered on the list of creditors, and, after the reduction, the company is unable within the meaning of the provisions of this Act relating to winding up by the court, to pay the amount of his debt or claim, then—

(a) every person who was a member of the company at the date of the registration of the order for reduction and minute, shall be liable to contribute for the payment of that debt or claim an amount not exceeding the amount which he would have been liable to contribute if the company had commenced to be wound up on the day before the said date, and

(b) if the company is wound up, the court, on the application of any such creditor and proof of his ignorance as aforesaid, may, if it thinks fit, settle accordingly a list of persons so liable to contribute, and make and enforce calls and orders on the contributories settled on the list, as if they were ordinary contributories in a winding up.

(3) Nothing in this section shall affect the rights of the contributories among themselves.

Definitions

'company': CA 1963, s 2(1); 'the court': CA 1963, s 2(1); 'member': CA 1963, s 31; 'share': CA 1963, s 2(1).

Notes

See the notes to CA 1963, s 73.

UK legislation

See CA 1985, s 140 (amended by IA 1985, s 439(1), Sch 13, Pt I).

77 Penalty for concealment of certain matters in proceedings for reduction

If any officer of [a company (other than a public limited company) the subject of an application under section 73][a]—

(a) wilfully conceals the name of any creditor entitled to object to the reduction; or

(b) wilfully misrepresents the nature or amount of the debt or claim of any creditor,

he shall be liable on summary conviction to a fine not exceeding [€1,904.61][b].

Amendments

a Words 'the company' substituted by 'a company (other than a public limited company) the subject of an application under section 73' by EC(PLC)R 2008, reg 3(b).

b '£500' substituted for '£100' by C(A)A 1982, Sch 1, increased to £1,500 by CA 1990, s 240(7) as inserted by CLEA 2001, s 104(c) and converted to €1,904.61 by Council Regulations (EC) No 1103/97, No 974/98 and No 2866/98 and the Economic and Monetary Union Act 1998, s 6.

Definitions

'company': CA 1963, s 2(1); 'officer': CA 1963, s 2(1).

UK legislation

See CA 1985, s 141.

Variation of Shareholders' Rights

78 Rights of holders of special classes of shares

(1) If, in the case of a company the share capital of which is divided into different classes of shares, provision is made by the memorandum or articles for authorising the variation of the rights attached to any class of shares in the company, subject to the consent of any specified proportion of the holders of the issued shares of that class or the sanction of a resolution passed at a separate meeting of the holders of those shares, and in pursuance of the said provision the rights attached to any such class of shares are at any time varied, the holders of not less in the aggregate than 10 per cent of the issued shares of that class, being persons who did not consent to or vote in favour of the resolution for the variation, may apply to the court to have the variation cancelled and, where any such application is made, the variation shall not have effect unless and until it is confirmed by the court.

(2) An application under this section must be made within 28 days (or such longer period as the court, on application made to it by any shareholder before the expiry of the said 28 days, may allow) after the date on which the consent was given or the resolution was passed, as the case may be, and may be made on behalf of the shareholders entitled to make the application by such one or more of their number as they may appoint in writing for the purpose.

(3) On any such application the court, after hearing the applicant and any other persons who apply to the court to be heard and appear to the court to be interested in the application, may, if it is satisfied having regard to all the circumstances of the case that the variation would unfairly prejudice the shareholders of the class represented by the applicant, disallow the variation and shall, if not so satisfied, confirm the variation.

(4) The decision of the court on any such application shall be final but an appeal shall lie to the Supreme Court from the determination of the court on a question of law.

(5) The company shall, within 21 days after the making of an order by the court on any such application, forward a copy of the order to the registrar of companies and, if default is made in complying with this provision, the company and every officer of the company who is in default, [shall be guilty of an offence and liable to a fine][a] not exceeding [€1,904.61].[b]

(6) In this section 'variation' includes abrogation, and 'varied' shall be construed accordingly.

Amendments

a CA 1963, s 78(5) words 'shall be guilty of an offence and liable to a fine' substituted for 'shall be liable to a fine' by C(AA)A 2003, Sch 2, Item No 1.

b '£250' substituted for '£50' by C(A)A 1982, Sch 1, increased to £1,500 by CA 1990, s 240(7) as inserted by CLEA 2001, s 104(c) and converted to €1,904.61 by Council Regulations (EC) No 1103/97, No 974/98 and No 2866/98 and the Economic and Monetary Union Act 1998, s 6.

Definitions

'articles': CA 1963, s 2(1); 'company': CA 1963, s 2(1); 'the court': CA 1963, s 2(1); 'memorandum': CA 1963, s 2(1); 'officer': CA 1963, s 2(1); 'the registrar of companies': CA 1963, s 2(1); 'share': CA 1963, s 2(1).

Notes

Different classes of shares: All shares will be presumed to rank equally *inter se*.[1] This presumption may, however, be rebutted by a provision, whether in the memorandum or articles of association or in the terms of issue or, perhaps, in a shareholders' agreement,[2] dividing the share capital into different classes.

1 *Birch v Cropper* (1889) 14 App Cas 525.

2 *Harman v BML Group Ltd* [1994] 1 WLR 893.

Authority to create different classes of shares: Model Form articles confer a power to create and issue different classes of shares.[1] However, even if the memorandum and articles are silent on the matter, such a power will normally be implied.[2] If the memorandum requires all shares to rank equally, a conflicting provision in the articles which authorises the division of shares into different classes will be void.[3] Where there are different classes of shares, these should be identified in the register of members.[4]

1 Table A, reg 2.

2 *Bushell v Faith* [1970] AC 1099.

3 *Andrews v Gas Meter Co* [1897] 1 Ch 361; *Campbell v Rofe* [1933] AC 91, 98.

4 *Re Performing Rights Society Ltd* [1978] 2 All ER 712.

Presumption of equality between classes: In the absence of an express provision to the contrary, all classes of shares will be presumed to rank equally as regards (a) the right to vote, (b) the right to dividends, (c) the right to a return of capital in a winding up, and (d) the right to participate in any surplus assets in a winding up.[1] A preference regarding one such right does not imply a preference in respect of any other rights.[2]

1 *Birch v Cropper* (1889) 14 App Cas 525.
2 *Birch v Cropper* (1889) 14 App Cas 525.

Ordinary shares: Ordinary shares (as their name suggests) are the residuary class of shares. Unless otherwise stated, all shares will be deemed to be ordinary shares and will rank equally *inter se*.[1] Even within the ordinary shares, however, it may be possible to create separate classes, so that one class might be voting ordinary shares and the other, non-voting ordinary shares.

1 *Birch v Cropper* (1889) 14 App Cas 525.

Preference shares: Preference shares are shares carrying certain preferential rights, whether as to dividend, capital or voting. As against this, their rights may, in other respects, be curtailed. Thus, for example, a preference share may carry preferential dividend entitlements, yet confer no voting rights or, perhaps, a right to vote only when dividends are in arrear.

Preferential dividend rights

1. *Fixed dividend*: Shares carrying preferential dividend rights usually entitle the shareholder to receive a fixed dividend in priority to the ordinary shareholders. Thus, '8% preference shares' would entitle the holders to a fixed dividend of 8% of the par value per annum.

2. *Declaration of dividend:* As with ordinary shares, however, the dividend on a preference share will normally only become payable once it has been declared in the manner provided by the articles.[1]

3. *Cumulative preference shares*: Unlike an ordinary share, a preference share will be presumed to carry cumulative dividend rights[2], so that once a dividend is declared for a particular year, the preference shareholder will also be entitled to receive payment of a dividend in respect of all the previous years in which no dividend had been declared.[3] Where preference shares of the same class have been issued at different times, so that different arrears on some shares are greater than on others, any dividend that is eventually paid, must be applied rateably towards satisfaction of the arrears.[4] Whether undeclared arrears of dividends on cumulative preference shares are payable in a liquidation depends very much on the terms of issue. If the dividends are expressed to be payable 'out of profits' the arrears will not be provable since the concept of 'profits' does not survive the commencement of the winding up.[5] Terminology that avoids any reference to 'profits' may, however, render the arrears of dividends capable of proof.[6] Furthermore, all dividends that have actually been declared or which are payable without having to be declared, will be provable in the liquidation, ranking for payment after the other creditors of the company.[7]

4. *Non-cumulative preference shares*: Although the presumption is that preference shares are cumulative as to dividend entitlements, this presumption may be rebutted by wording to the contrary. Thus, a preference share was held to be non-cumulative where the dividend was expressed to be payable 'out of the net profits each year.'[8] A similar conclusion was also reached in circumstances where the terms of issue stated that the dividend 'in any one year' should not exceed 9%.[9]

5. *Fixed dividend entitlement is exhaustive*: In so far as the preference shares carry a right to a fixed dividend, this will be presumed to be exhaustive of the preference shareholders' dividend entitlements.[10] This presumption may of course be rebutted by an express provision to the contrary.[11]

Preferential rights as to capital: Apart from any priority as to dividends that may be enjoyed, preference shares may also carry a right to priority of return of capital in the event of a winding up. Such a right of priority will not, however, be regarded as exhaustive of all rights of the preference shareholder in a winding up and will not, *per se*, preclude him from participating in the surplus assets.[12]

Preferential voting rights: As noted above, preference shares often carry no voting rights whatsoever or perhaps only a limited entitlement to vote. Exceptionally, however, preference shares might be given 'loaded' voting rights. For example, each €1 preference share might carry 10 votes whilst ordinary shares would carry 1 vote each. The validity of loaded voting rights has long been recognised.[13]

1 See Table A, regs 116–124. For examples of articles which were interpreted as entitling the preference shareholders to payment of a dividend every year, without the need for it to be declared, see *Re Lafayette Ltd* [1950] IR 100 and *Re Imperial Hotel (Cork) Ltd* [1950] IR 115.

2 *Henry v Great Northern Railway Co* (1857) 1 De G and J 606; *Corry v Londonderry and Enniskillen Railway Co* (1860) 29 Beav 263; *Webb v Earle* (1875) LR 20 Eq 556; *Re F de Jong and Co Ltd* [1946] Ch 211.

3 *Re Wakley, Wakley v Vachell* [1920] 2 Ch 205; *Godfrey Phillips Ltd v Investment Trust Corporation Ltd* [1953] Ch 449.

4 *First Garden City Ltd v Bonham-Carter* [1928] Ch 58.

5 *Re Lafayette Ltd* [1950] IR 100; *Re Crichton's Oil Co* [1902] 2 Ch 86; *Wilson (Inspector of Taxes) v Dunnes Stores (Cork) Ltd* [1982] ILRM 444.

6 *Re Walter Symons Ltd* [1934] Ch 308; *Re Wood, Skinner and Co Ltd* [1944] Ch 323; *Re F de Jong and Co Ltd* [1946] Ch 211; *Re E W Savory Ltd* [1951] 2 All ER 1036.

7 CA 1963, s 207(1)(g). See also *Re The Imperial Hotel (Cork) Ltd* [1950] IR 115; *Re Belfast Empire Theatre of Varieties* [1963] IR 41; *Re Severn and Wye and Severn Bridge Railway Co* [1896] 1 Ch 559; *Re Artisans' Land and Mortgage Corporation* [1904] 1 Ch 796.

8 *Staples v Eastman Photographic Materials Co* [1896] 2 Ch 303.

9 *JI. Thornycroft and Co v Thornycroft* (1927) 44 TLR 9. See also *Adair v Old Bushmills Distillery Co* [1908] WN 24.

10 *Will v United Lankat Plantations Co Ltd* [1914] AC 11.

11 See, for example, *Steel Company of Canada Ltd v Ramsay* [1931] AC 270; *Re Isle of Thanet Electricity Supply Co Ltd* [1950] Ch 161; *Re Saltdean Estate Co Ltd* [1968] 1 WLR 1844.

12 *Re Cork Electricity Supply Co Ltd* [1932] IR 314; *Birch v Cropper* (1889) 14 App Cas 525. In England, a contrary view has been taken so that a priority as to return of capital is deemed to be exhaustive of all rights in the liquidation: *Will v United Lankat Plantations Co* [1914] AC 11; *Scottish Insurance Corporation Ltd v Wilsons and Clyde Coal Co* [1949] AC 462; *Prudential Assurance Co v Chatterley-Whitfield Collieries Co Ltd* [1949] AC 462; *Re Isle of Thanet Electricity Supply Co Ltd* [1950] Ch 161.

13 *Bushell v Faith* [1970] AC 1099.

Class rights need not attach to specific shares: Where a company, by its memorandum or articles, confers special rights on one or more of its shareholders *qua* shareholder, those rights, even if not expressed to attach to any specific share or shares, will nonetheless be regarded as class rights and will only be capable of variation in accordance with the procedures laid down in the Companies Acts.[1] On the other hand, if the right as contained in the memorandum or articles is conferred on the shareholder in some other capacity, it will not be regarded as being a class right and may therefore be altered or abrogated in the ordinary way.[2]

1 *Cumbrian Newspapers Group Ltd v Cumberland and Westmoreland Herald Newspaper and Printing Co Ltd* [1986] BCLC 286.

2 *Re Blue Arrow plc* [1987] BCLC 585. With regard to the appropriate procedures for so altering such a provision, see CA 1963, ss 15 and 28.

Variation of class rights: The remedy for dissenting minorities in CA 1963, s 78 arises in circumstances where either the memorandum or articles contains a provision authorising a variation of class rights with the consent of the holders of a specified proportion of the affected class. Such authorisation is to be found in Model Form articles.[1] Section 78 has, however, been largely superseded by C(A)A 1983, s 38 which contains much more detailed provisions regarding both the circumstances in which class rights may be varied and the remedies available to opponents of the variation.

1 Table A, reg 3.

What constitutes a variation of class rights: The rights of a class of shareholders are neither varied nor 'affected' by the issue of new shares ranking *pari passu* with existing shares of that class.[1] Similarly, a dilution of the voting strength of one class of shares by an increase in voting strength of another class, although possibly affecting the rights of the first class 'as a matter of business' will not be regarded as varying their rights 'as a matter of law.'[2] Likewise, if a reduction of share capital follows the same order of priority as would apply in a winding up, it will not be regarded as a variation of class rights.[3] On the other hand, an alteration of a 'variation of class rights clause' contained in the articles, or the insertion of such a clause, is itself treated as being a variation of class rights.[4]

1 *White v Bristol Aeroplane Co* [1953] Ch 65; *Re Schweppes Ltd* [1914] 1 Ch 322; *Re John Smith's Tadcaster Brewery Co Ltd* [1953] 2 WLR 516.

2 *Greenhalgh v Arderne Cinemas Ltd* [1946] 1 All ER 512.

3 *Re MacKenzie and Co* [1916] 2 Ch 450; *Re Chatterley-Whitfield Collieries Ltd* [1948] 2 All ER 593 aff'd *sub nom Prudential Assurance Co Ltd v Chatterley-Whitfield Collieries Ltd* [1949] AC 512; *Re John Power and Son Ltd* [1934] IR 412; *House of Fraser plc v ACGE Investments Ltd* [1987] AC 387; *Re Credit Finance Bank plc* (1963–1993) Irish Company Law Reports 170.

4 C(A)A 1983, s 38(7).

Application for relief pursuant to s 78: An applicant under CA 1963, s 78 who purports to act not only on his own behalf but also on behalf of others must first show that he has in fact been so appointed in writing[1] and that the authority to so act had indeed been communicated to him.[2]

1 *Re Suburban and Provincial Stores* [1943] Ch 156.

2 *Re Sound City (Films)* [1947] Ch 169.

Unfair prejudice: To succeed in an application under CA 1963, s 78 the applicant must show that the variation was unfairly prejudicial to the affected class. This may be established by showing that the majority of the class did not vote *bona fide* in the interests of the class as a whole, but were instead motivated by some other interest (eg the benefit that they would derive as ordinary shareholders by abrogating the rights of preference shareholders).[1]

1 *Re Holders Investment Trust Ltd* [1971] 1 WLR 583; *Re Wedgewood Coal and Iron Co* [1877] 6 Ch D 627; *British American Nickel Corporation v O'Brien* [1927] AC 369; *Greenhalgh v Arderne Cinemas Ltd* [1951] Ch 286.

Oppression of minority: Apart from any relief to which the dissenting minority may be entitled, either under CA 1963, s 78 or under C(A)A 1983, s 38, they may also be entitled to seek relief under CA 1963, s 205 if they can show that the variation in class rights is oppressive or in disregard of their own interests as members.[1] Unlike the remedy contained in s 78, there is no minimum shareholding required before the member may petition for relief under s 205.

1 *Re Williams Group Tullamore Ltd* [1985] IR 613; *Clemens v Clemens Bros Ltd* [1976] 2 All ER 268.

UK legislation

See CA 1985, s 127.

Numbering and Transfer of and Evidence of Title to Shares and Debentures

79 Nature of shares

The shares or other interest of any member in a company shall be personal estate, transferable in manner provided by the articles of the company, and shall not be of the nature of real estate.

Definitions

'articles': CA 1963, s 2(1); 'company': CA 1963, s 2(1); 'member': CA 1963, s 31; 'share': CA 1963, s 2(1).

Notes

Nature of shares: Shares are items of personal property.[1] Despite earlier views to the contrary,[2] it is now well established that ownership of shares does not confer on the shareholder a right to any specific portion of the company's property.[3] Nor are the shares 'goods' within the meaning of the Sale of Goods Acts.[4] Rather, they are choses in action.[5]

A share has been defined as being:

> 'the interest of a person in the company, that interest being composed of rights and obligations which are defined by the Companies Act and by the memorandum and articles of the company.'[6]

The leading definition is that of Farwell J in *Borland's Trustee v Steel Bros and Co Ltd*[7] where he stated as follows: 'A share is the interest of a shareholder measured by a sum of money for the purpose of liability in the first case and of interest in the second, but also consisting of a series of mutual covenants[8] entered into by all the shareholders *inter se* in accordance with [the Companies Acts]. The contract contained in the articles of association is one of the original incidents of the share. A share is not a sum of money ... but is an interest measured by a sum of money and made up of various rights contained in the contract, including the right to a sum of money of a more or less amount'.

More recently, Keane J in *Re Sugar Distributors Ltd*[9] described a share in the following terms: 'A share in a company is, in effect, a bundle of proprietary rights which can be sold or exchanged for money or other valuable consideration.'

It has been held that although the share is a constitutionally protected property right,[10] the nature and extent of that right must be ascertained by reference to the terms for the time being of the company's memorandum and articles of association.[11]

1 CA 1963, s 79. See also *Lee and Co (Dublin) Ltd v Egan (Wholesale) Ltd* (18 October 1979, unreported) HC (Kenny J).

2 *Child v Hudson's Bay Co* (1723) 2 P Wms 207; *Harrison v Pryse* (1740) Barn Ch 324.

3 *Attorney General for Ireland v Jameson* [1904] 2 IR 644; *Kerry Co-Operative Creameries Ltd v An Bord Bainne Co-Operative Ltd* [1990] ILRM 664, aff'd [1991] ILRM 851; *Short v Treasury Commissioners* [1948] 1 KB 116.

4 *Lee and Co (Dublin) Ltd v Egan (Wholesale) Ltd* (18 October 1979, unreported) HC (Kenny J).

5 *Lee and Co (Dublin) Ltd v Egan (Wholesale) Ltd* (18 October 1979, unreported) HC (Kenny J); *Colonial Bank v Whiiney* (1886) 11 App Cas 426; *R v Williams* [1942] AC 541, 549; *Re VGM Holdings Ltd* [1942] Ch 235.

6 *IRC v Crossman* [1937] AC 26.

7 *Borland's Trustee v Steel Bros and Co Ltd* [1901] 1 Ch 279. Cited with approval by Fitzgibbon LJ in *Casey v Bentley* [1902] 1 IR 376. See also *Provincial Bank of Ireland Ltd v O'Connor* (10 October 1974, unreported) HC (Kenny J); *Attorney General for Ireland v Jameson* [1904] 2 IR 644; *Kerry Co-Operative Creameries Ltd v An Bord Bainne Co-Operative Ltd* [1990] ILRM 664 aff'd [1991] ILRM 851.

8 The 'mutual covenants' referred to by Farwell J are those contained in the memorandum and articles, the contractual effect of which is discussed in the notes to CA 1963, s 25.

9 *Re Sugar Distributors Ltd* [1995] 2 IR 194 at 207.

10 *Private Motorists' Provident Society and Moore v Attorney General* [1984] ILRM 988.

11 *Kerry Co-Operative Creameries Ltd v An Bord Bainne Co-Operative Ltd* [1990] ILRM 664, aff'd [1991] ILRM 851.

Denomination of shares: The share capital of the company must be divided into shares of a fixed amount.[1] In certain circumstances the shares must be individually numbered although this requirement will not apply, *inter alia*, where all the capital is fully paid up.[2]

1 CA 1963, s 6(4). In relation to the redenomination of Irish Punt share capital into Euro, see the Economic and Monetary Union Act 1998, s 24.

2 CA 1963, s 80.

Proper law: The appropriate law to decide questions of title to shares in a company is the law of the place where the shares are situated (the *lex situs*) which in the ordinary course of events is the place where the company is incorporated.[1]

1 *MacMillan Inc v Bishopsgate Investment Trust plc (No 3)* [1996] 1 All ER 585.

Transferability of shares: According to CA 1963, s 79, the share capital of the company is transferable in whatever manner is provided for by the articles of association.[1] In the absence of restrictions contained in the articles, the shares will therefore be freely transferable[2] and the directors will not be entitled to refuse to register the transfer.[3] So, where a transferee presents an instrument of transfer which under the existing articles entitles him to be registered, the company cannot, by altering the articles, defeat his right to have the transfer registered.[4]

1 With regard to the mechanics of transfer, including the registration of the transfer of shares, see CA 1963, s 81 and the notes thereto.

2 *Re Hafner* [1943] IR 426.

3 *Re Smith, Knight and Co, Weston's Case* (1868) 4 Ch App 20; *Re National Provincial Marine Insurance Co, Gilbert's Case* (1870) 5 Ch App 559; *Re Stranton Iron and Steel Co* (1873) LR 16 Eq 559; *Re Cawley and Co* (1889) 42 ChD 209; *Re Discoverers Finance Corporation Ltd, Lindlar's Case* [1910] 1 Ch 312; *Re Bede Steam Shipping Co* [1917] 1 Ch 123; *Re Smith and Fawcett* [1942] Ch 304; *Greenhalgh v Mallard* [1943] 2 All ER 234; *Re New Cedos Engineering Co Ltd* [1994] 1 BCLC 797, 806; *Stothers v William Steward (Holdings) Ltd* [1994] 2 BCLC 266.

4 *W and A M'Arthur Ltd v Gulf Line Ltd* 1909 SC 732.

Restrictions on transfer of shares: Restrictions on the transfer of shares are provided for by Model Form articles both for public and private companies.[1] Indeed, every private company must contain some such restriction in its articles,[2] albeit that the restriction need not be in the same terms as those contained in Table A.[3] However, the articles cannot be so restrictive as to prevent the member from transferring his shares at all to anybody, since such a restriction would amount to an abrogation of the *right* of transfer which is conferred on shareholders by the CA 1963, s 79.[4] Provisions in the articles restricting the transfer of shares do not offend against the rule against perpetuities since the member's shareholding is a contractual right and does not confer upon him any interest in land.[5]

1 Table A, reg 24 (for public companies) and Part II, reg 3 (for private companies). See also the notes to these articles for a discussion of the nature and extent of the restrictions thereby imposed. See generally Courtney, *The Law of Private Companies* (2nd edn, Tottel Publishing, 2002) paras 16.017–16.021.

2 CA 1963, s 33(1).

3 For an example of restrictions on the transfer of shares which satisfied the requirements of CA 1963, s 33 without being as onerous as those contained in Table A, see *Attorney-General for Ireland v Jameson* [1904] IR 644.

4 *Re Hafner* [1943] IR 426.

5 *Re Hafner* [1943] IR 426; *Casey v Bentley* [1902] 1 IR 376; *Borland's Trustee v Steel Bros and Co Ltd* [1901] 1 Ch 279.

Pre-emption rights on transfer of shares: One of the more common forms of restriction found in the articles of private companies is where the transferee is obliged to first offer his shares at fair value to the other members or directors, before offering them for sale to third parties.[1] Because shares are otherwise freely transferable, any restriction on transfer will be construed strictly by the courts.[2] Thus, any time limit for the exercise of the option to purchase the transferor's shares will be construed narrowly and rigidly.[3] On the other hand, a purported transfer of the beneficial, as opposed to the legal interest, will be regarded as a mere 'subterfuge' and will be ineffective to avoid the application of the pre-emption provisions.[4] A transaction which is in breach of the pre-emption provisions will be ineffective to create any interest (whether legal or beneficial) in the shares concerned.[5]

Pre-emption rights are regarded as forming part of the bundle of contractual entitlements conferred on shareholders by CA 1963, s 25 and will readily be enforced by the courts.[6] Accordingly, where the pre-emption clause requires a person who wishes to sell his shares to first serve a 'transfer notice' on his fellow members, that provision will automatically be brought into operation as soon as he purports to sell his shares to an outsider.[7] Moreover, a contract to sell the shares to an outsider will be unenforceable until such time, if any, as those persons entitled to exercise pre-emption rights have elected not to do so.[8] If a person puprorts to sell shares in breach of the pre-emption provisions, the purchaser will be unable to obtain a decree of specific performance against the vendor, but may be in a position to seek damages for breach of contract.[9]

1 See, for example, *Lee and Co (Dublin) Ltd v Egan (Wholesale) Ltd* (27 April 1978, unreported) HC (Kenny J); *McAuliffe v Lithographic Group Ltd* (2 November 1993, unreported) SC; *Attorney General for Ireland v Jameson* [1904] 2 IR 644; *Lyle and Scott Ltd v Scott's Trustees* [1959] AC 763; *Rayfield v Hands* [1960] Ch 1; *Jarvis Motors (Harrow) Ltd v Carabott* [1964] 3 All ER 89; *Safeguard Industrial Investments Ltd v National Westminster Bank Ltd* [1982] 1 All ER 449.

2 *Safeguard Industrial Investments Ltd v National Westminster Bank Ltd* [1982] 1 All ER 449; *Hurst v Crampton Bros (Coopers) Ltd* [2003] 1 BCLC 304.

3 *Re New Cedos Engineering Co Ltd* [1994] 1 BCLC 797.

4 *Lyle and Scott Ltd v Scott's Trustees* [1959] 2 All ER 661; *Phelan v Goodman* (11 September 2001, uneported) HC (Murphy J); cf *Safeguard Industrial Investments Ltd v National Westminster Bank Ltd* [1982] 1 All ER 449; *Theakston v London Trust plc* [1984] BCLC 390; *Hawks v McArthur* [1951] 1 All ER 22.

5 *Lee and Company (Dublin) Ltd v Egan (Wholesale) Ltd* (27 April 1978, uneported) HC (Kenny J); *Re Hafner* [1943] IR 426; *Hunter v Hunter* [1936] AC 222; cf *Hawks v McArthur* [1951] 1 All ER 22.

6 See for example *Lee and Company (Dublin) Ltd v Egan (Wholesale) Ltd* (27 April 1978, unreported) HC (Kenny J); *Attorney General for Ireland v Jameson* [1904] 2 IR 644; *Re Champion Publications Ltd* (4 June 1991, unreported) HC (Blayney J); *Rayfield v Hands* [1960] Ch 1. In determining whether the pre-emption provisions have been breached, the execution and delivery of a share transfer form will be treated as constituting a 'transfer': *Hurst v Crampton Bros (Coopers) Ltd* [2003] 1 BCLC 304.

7 *Lyle and Scott Ltd v Scott's Trustees* [1959] AC 763. An agreement for the sale of shares expressly which stipulates that the vendor is to do nothing that would contravene the pre-emption provisions, will be regarded as failing to demonstrate the necessary intent to transfer the legal title to the shares and accordingly will not be treated as activating the pre-emption clause: *Re Sedgefield Steeplechase Company (1927) Ltd* [2000] 2 BCLC 211.

8 *Lee and Company (Dublin) Ltd v Egan (Wholesale) Ltd* (27 April 1978, unreported) HC (Kenny J); *Tett v Phoenix Property and Investment Co Ltd* [1986] BCLC 149.

9 *Lee and Company (Dublin) Ltd v Egan (Wholesale) Ltd* (27 April 1978, unreported) HC (Kenny J); *O'Gorman v Kelleher* [1999] IEHC 239 (Carroll J).

Directors' discretion to refuse to register transfers: In Model Form articles the restriction on the transfer of shares consists of a discretion on the part of the board of directors to refuse to register the transfer.

Extent of directors' discretion: The extent of the discretion depends on the type of company involved. If it is a public company, the directors may refuse to register the transfer if the transferee is a person of whom they do not approve or if they are of the opinion that the transfer would imperil or prejudicially affect the status of the company in the State or would imperil any tax concession or rebate to which the members of the company are entitled or which might involve the company in the payment of any additional stamp or other duties on any conveyance of any property made or to be made by the company.[1] In the case of private companies, however, the discretion is far more wide-ranging since the directors may:

> '... in their absolute discretion, and without assigning any reason therefor, decline to register *any* transfer of any share, whether or not it is a fully paid share.'[2] (emphasis added)

In practice most litigation arises in the context of the discretion of directors of private companies. This may be due in part to the fact that public companies with a Stock Exchange listing are prohibited from imposing any restrictions on the transferability of their shares.[3]

Discretion must be exercised in a proper manner: The discretion conferred on the directors to refuse to register a transfer of shares is a form of fiduciary power and must therefore be exercised *bona fide* for a proper purpose and for the benefit of the company as a whole.[4] In the absence of any evidence to the contrary, the directors will be presumed to have acted properly[5] and in this regard it should be noted that the directors are not obliged to give any reasons for the exercise of their discretion.[6] Consequently, an aggrieved transferee may find it extremely difficult to challenge their decision. If the plaintiff can adduce *some* evidence of impropriety, although not sufficient on its own to discharge the legal burden of proof, and this allegation goes unchallenged by the directors, the court may draw an adverse inference from their silence, so as to conclude that the plaintiff has established his case.[7] Of course, if the directors volunteer reasons for their decision, the court will then consider whether those reasons are legitimate, ie whether they are *bona fide* and proper.[8] However, the directors are not confined to the reasons, if any, given by them at the time of the refusal and may rely upon justifying grounds which subsequently come to their attention.[9] Moreover, the court will not interfere with their decision simply because it might have come to a different conclusion itself.[10] The following have all been held by the court to be illegitimate reasons for refusing to register a transfer of shares: where the transferee wanted to challenge the directors' 'bloated emoluments'[11] and where the directors wanted to force the transferee to sell his shares to them at an undervalue[12] or where the directors simply have a personal dislike for the transferee.[13] On the other hand, the court has refused to interfere with a decision of the directors to refuse to register a transfer of controlling interest to an individual who was the managing director of a competitor and whose threatened control was apprehended by the directors to be detrimental to the interests of the company as a whole.[14]

Relief under section 205: If the transferee is already a member in respect of other shares or if he is either a personal representative of a deceased member or a person entitled to the deceased member's shares under a will or intestacy, he may be entitled to apply to the court for relief against the refusal to register the transfer/transmission of shares pursuant to CA 1963, s 205 on the ground that such refusal is oppressive or in disregard of his interests.

Lapse of directors' discretion: Whereas the shareholder has a *right* to transfer his shares, the directors only have a *power* to refuse to register the transfer. This power will lapse if not exercised within a reasonable period of time.[15] Typically a period of two months will be regarded as 'reasonable' for deciding whether or not to refuse to register the transfer, since that is the period specified by CA 1963, s 84 within which the company must notify the transferee if registration is being refused.[16] Despite the fact that s 84 forms the basis for determining, in most cases, what constitutes a 'reasonable time' it has been held that a decision by the directors to refuse to register a transfer of shares which has been made within the requisite two-month period will not be invalidated simply because they then fail to notify the transferee of their decision.[17]

1 Table A, Part I, reg 24.

2 Table A, Part II, reg 3.

3 See the Admissions Directive, Sch A.II(2) and Admission of Securities to listing s 1, ch 2 para 4.

4 See *Banfi Ltd v Moran et al* [2006] IEHC 257 where Laffoy J referred, with approval, to the review and analysis of the law by reference to Courtney, *The Law of Private Companies* (2nd edn, Tottel Publishing, 2002) para 16.037 et seq. See also *Clark v Workman* [1920] 1 IR 107; *Re Hafner* [1943] IR 426; *Re Dublin North City Milling Co* [1909] 1 IR 179; *Re Smith and Fawcett Ltd* [1942] 1 Ch 304; *Re Coalport China Co* [1895] 2 Ch 404.

5 *Re Gresham life Assurance Society, ex parte Penney* (1872) 8 Ch App 446, 452; *Re Hafner* [1943] IR 426.

6 See Table A, Part II, reg 3 quoted above. See also *Re Dublin North City Milling Co* [1909] 1 IR 179; *Re Hafner* [1943] IR 426; *Berry and Stewart v Tottenham Hotspur Football and Athletic Co Ltd* [1935] 1 Ch 718; *Re Smith and Fawcett Ltd* [1942] Ch 304.

7 *Re Hafner* [1943] IR 426, 439 and 440; *Clark v Workman* [1920] 1 IR 107, 118.

8 *Tett v Phoenix Property and Investment Co Ltd* [1986] BCLC 149; *Re Smith and Fawcett Ltd* [1942] Ch 304; *Re Bell Bros, ex parte Hodgson* (1891) 65 LT 245; *Re Bede Steam Shipping Co* [1917] 1 Ch 123.

9 *Village Cay Marine Ltd v Acland* [1998] 2 BCLC 327.

10 *Tett v Phoenix Property and Investment Co Ltd* [1986] BCLC 149; *Re Smith and Fawcett Ltd* [1942] Ch 304; *Re Bell Bros, ex parte Hodgson* (1891) 65 LT 245; *Re Bede Steam Shipping Co* [1917] 1 Ch 123.

11 *Re Hafner* [1943] IR 426.

12 *Re Smith and Fawcett Ltd* [1942] 1 Ch 304, 309.

13 *Popely v Planarrive Ltd* [1997] 1 BCLC 8, at 15/16.

14 *Re Dublin North City Milling Co* [1909] 1 IR 179. See also the comments of Lord Greene MR in *Re Smith and Fawcett Ltd* [1942] Ch 304, at 309 where he held that the directors could take into account 'whether by passing a particular transfer the transferee would obtain too great a weight in the affairs of the company or might even obtain control.' Clearly his lordship was envisaging a situation where the directors were apprehensive that the transferee would act to the detriment of the company if he gained control. However, if they have no such apprehension, then they may be considered as acting improperly simply because the transferee stands to obtain control of a majority interest in the company: *Tett v Phoenix Property and Investment Co Ltd* [1986] BCLC 149. The fact that the transferee is a fraudster and a liar may constitute good grounds for refusing to register the transfer of shares: *Popely v Planarrive Ltd* [1997] 1 BCLC 8, at 15/16.

15 *Re Hackney Pavilion Ltd* [1924] 1 Ch 276; *Moodie v W and J Shepherd (Bookbinders) Ltd* [1949] 2 All ER 1044; *Re Swaledale Cleaners Ltd* [1968] 1 WLR 1710; *Tett v Phoenix Property and Investment Co Ltd* [1986] BCLC 149; *Re New Cedos Engineering Co Ltd* [1994] 1 BCLC 797.

16 *Re Swaledale Cleaners Ltd* [1968] 1 WLR 1710; *Tett v Phoenix Property and Investment Co Ltd* [1986] BCLC 149; *Re New Cedos Engineering Co Ltd* [1994] 1 BCLC 797; *Re Inverdeck Ltd* [1998] 2 BCLC 242.

17 *Popely v Planarrive Ltd* [1997] 1 BCLC 8.

Transmission of shares: Transmission involves the passing of ownership automatically by operation of law on death or bankruptcy rather than by way of a voluntary *inter vivos* disposition. The restrictions on the registration of transfers of shares contained in the Model Form Articles are expressed to apply also in the case of transmission.[1]

1 Table A, reg 31.

Specific performance of transfer: Where the articles contain a provision empowering the directors to refuse to register a transfer of shares and they so refuse, the court will not order specific performance of the contract of sale unless it is also in a position to compel the directors to reverse their decision (eg where the decision was clearly made *male fides* or for an improper purpose).[1] A refusal by the directors to register the transfer of the shares will be regarded as the failure of a condition subsequent in the contract for the sale of the shares and will entitle the transferee to rescind the sale and obtain a refund of the purchase price.[2] Pending rescission, however, the contract remains in existence.[3]

1 *Bermingham v Sheridan, Re Waterloo Life Assurance Co (No 4) (*91864) 33 Beav 660; *Casey v Bentley* [1902] 1 IR 376.

2 *Casey v Bentley* [1902] 1 IR 376; cf *Stray v Russell (*91859) 1 E and E 888; *London Founder's Association v Clarke* (1888) 20 QBD 576.

3 *Skinner v City of London Marine Insurance Corporation* (1885) 14 QBD 882.

Position pending registration or after a refusal of registration: Until the transfer is registered, if at all, the legal title to the share remains in the transferor and it is he who continues to be regarded as the 'member' of the company.[1] Although still a 'member', he will have no *locus standi* to petition for relief under CA 1963, s 205, since, being contractually bound to divest himself of his shareholding, he can no longer have any legitimate interest in the affairs of the company.[2] If the transferor has been paid for the shares, he holds them as a nominee for the unregistered transferor, who must indemnify him against any liability arising under the shares (eg for calls made).[3] As a nominee, he must account for any dividends he receives and must vote in accordance with the wishes of the unregistered transferee.[4] On the other hand, if he has not been paid, the dividends belong to him and he may vote in accordance with his own wishes.[5]

1 *Casey v Bentley* [1902] 1 IR 376; *Re Munster Bank (Dillon's Claim)* (1886–87) 17 LR Ir 341; *Musselwhite v CH Musselwhite and Son Ltd* [1962] Ch 964; *Hawks v McArthur* [1951] 1 All ER 22; *Tett v Phoenix Property and Investment Co Ltd* [1986] BCLC 149.

2 *Re Via Net Works (Ireland) Ltd* [2002] 2 IR 47.

3 *Casey v Bentley* [1902] 1 IR 376; *Musselwhite v CH Musselwhite and Son Ltd* [1962] Ch 964; *Hawks v McArthur* [1951] 1 All ER 22. See also CA 1990 (US) Regs 1996, reg 18.

4 *Musselwhite v CH Musselwhite and Son Ltd* [1962] Ch 964; *Michaels v Harley House (Marleybone) Ltd* [1999] 1 All ER 356.

5 *Musselwhite v CH Musselwhite and Son Ltd* [1962] Ch 964. See, however, *O'Gorman v Kelleher* [1999] IEHC 239 (Carroll J) where an unpaid vendor was restrained from exercising the votes attaching to his shares in such a way as would damage the interests of the purchaser.

Rectification of share register: If the directors wrongfully refuse to register a transfer of shares or if their power of refusal lapses, then either the transferor or transferee may apply to the court for an order directing them to rectify the share register.[1] If the applicant is successful, the costs of such proceedings will normally be awarded against the company.[2] However, where the directors have acted in bad faith or where, although acting in good faith, they have refused to register a transfer of shares without having any entitlement to do so under the articles, they may be joined in the proceedings for the purpose of having an award of costs made against them personally.[3]

1 CA 1963, s 122.

2 *Re Keith Prowse and Co Ltd* [1918] 1 Ch 487.

3 *Morgan v Morgan Insurance Brokers Ltd* [1993] BCLC 676.

Mechanics of transfer: See CA 1963, s 81 and the notes thereto.

UK legislation

See CA 1985, s 182(1).

80 Numbering of shares

(1) Subject to subsections (2) and (3), each share in a company having a share capital shall be distinguished by its appropriate number.

(2) If at any time all the issued shares in a company, or all the issued shares therein of a particular class, are fully paid up and rank *pari passu* for all purposes, none of those shares need thereafter have a distinguishing number, so long as it remains fully paid up and ranks *pari passu* for all purposes with all shares of the same class for the time being issued and fully paid up.

(3) Where new shares are issued by a company on the terms that, within a period not exceeding 12 months, they will rank *pari passu* for all purposes with all the existing shares, or all the existing shares of a particular class, in the company, neither the new shares nor the corresponding existing shares need have distinguishing numbers so long as all of them are fully paid up and rank *pari passu* but the share certificates of the new shares shall, if not numbered, be appropriately worded or enfaced.

Definitions

'company': CA 1963, s 2(1); 'share': CA 1963, s 2(1).

UK legislation

See CA 1985, s 182(2).

81 Transfer not to be registered unless instrument of transfer delivered to the company

(1) Subject to subsection (2), and notwithstanding anything in the articles of a company, it shall not be lawful for the company to register a transfer of shares in or debentures of the company unless a proper instrument of transfer has been delivered to the company.

(2) Nothing in subsection (1) shall prejudice any power of the company to register as shareholder or debenture holder any person to whom the right to any shares in, or debentures of the company, has been transmitted by operation of law.

Definitions

'articles': CA 1963, s 2(1); 'company': CA 1963, s 2(1); 'debenture': CA 1963, s 2(1); 'share': CA 1963, s 2(1).

Notes

Mechanics of transfer:

Transfer in legible form: A contract for the sale of shares can be oral and will be effective to transfer equitable ownership of the shares.[1] Similarly, there may be an equitable assignment of shares by way of gift without the delivery of an executed share transfer form.[2] However, in order to transfer legal title, a 'proper instrument of transfer' must be delivered to the company, and must in turn be duly registered by the directors. The instrument must be duly stamped[3] and executed.[4] In this regard, the company has no obligation to register an unstamped instrument, but if it elects to do so, the absence of stamping will not render the registration of the transfer invalid.[5]

In this regard, Model Form articles require the instrument to be executed by both the transferor and the transferee.[6] Commonly, however, the articles will be modified so as to allow for execution by the transferor alone. Alternatively, if the shares are fully paid, the parties may avail of the pre-printed stock transfer form set out in the First Schedule to the Stock Transfer Act 1963. This form has to be executed by the transferor only.[7]

The executed instrument of transfer and the share certificate are then handed over by the transferor to the transferee who in turn submits them to the company for the purpose of effecting registration.[8] Unless registration is refused by the directors[9] the name of the transferee will be entered in the register of members and the transferee will be issued with a new share certificate by the company.[10]

Where the transferor is selling only some of his shares he will not want to deliver the share certificate to the transferee since the certificate will also relate to the shares which he is retaining. Instead he will lodge the instrument of transfer and share certificate directly to the company. The company may in turn 'certify' the instrument of transfer (ie endorse the instrument with a statement that there have been produced to the company such documents as on the face of them show a *prima facie* title to the shares).[11] The transferor fulfils his contractual obligations to the transferee by delivering to him a certificated instrument of transfer. Upon completion of the transaction the company then issues two new certificates of transfer – one being delivered to the transferee in respect of the shares which he has just acquired, and the other being issued to the transferor in respect of the shares which he still retains.

Transfer in non-legible form: In the case of public companies listed on the Stock Exchange, transfers of shares and debenture stock have heretofore been effected by means of a system known as TALISMAN and have involved the transfer of the securities in the first instance to a nominee company, Sepon Ltd, followed by an onward transfer from Sepon Ltd to the ultimate transferee. Only the latter transfer has attracted stamp duty. However, TALISMAN, as a system, has been largely paper based, requiring the delivery of a 'proper instrument of transfer' and the issue of a share certificate or debenture certificate, as the case may be, to the ultimate transferee. In order to speed up the settlement of bargains, the Stock Exchange had for some time been pressing for a completely electronic system for recording and transferring securities. The system is known as CREST and was introduced pursuant to the CA 1990 (US) Regs 1996.[12] Securities governed by these Regs are known as 'uncertificated units of security.'[13] Title to such securities is recorded electronically by the company and may likewise be transferred electronically rather than by way of an 'instrument of transfer.'[14] Despite the absence of an instrument of transfer, the transaction still attracts stamp duty.[15] Furthermore, because title to such shares is recorded and transferred electronically, the company is no longer allowed to issue a share certificate or debenture certificate, as the case may be, to the holder of the relevant security.[16] A document purporting to be a share certificate or debenture certificate in respect of an uncertificated unit of security, shall not be regarded as evidence of title thereto.[17] Instead, title is deemed to be evidenced by the recording of the name and address of the security holder as well as details of the number of uncertificated units of security held by him, in the register of members or the register of debentureholders, as the case may be.[18] IFCMPA 2006, s 12 amends CA 1990, s 239 by providing for the power to provide by regulations for mandatory dematerialisation: see IFCMPA 2006, s 12.

1 *Guardian Builders Ltd v Sleecon Ltd and Berville Ltd* (18 August 1988, unreported) HC (Blayney J); *Bowlby v Bell* (1846) 3 CB 284.

2 *Pennington v Waine* [2002] 2 BCLC 448.

3 CA 1963, s 86(1).

4 Any attempt by the articles to circumvent the legal requirement that the transfer be executed, at least by the transferor, will be void: *Re Greene* [1949] 1 All ER 167.

5 *Re Motor Racing Circuits Ltd* (31 January 1997, unreported) SC per Blayney J; *Nisbet v Shepherd* [1994] 1 BCLC 300; *Re Paradise Motor Co Ltd* [1968] 2 All ER 625; *Powell v London and Provincial Bank* [1893] 2 Ch 555.

6 Table A, reg 22.
7 STA 1963, s 2(1).
8 *Skinner v City of London Marine Insurance Corporation* (1885) 14 QBD 882, 887. Submission of the application for registration is, however, just as valid if made by the transferor: CA 1963, s 83.
9 For the circumstances in which the directors may typically refuse to register a transfer see the notes to CA 1963, s 79.
10 CA 1963, s 86. For the status of the share certificate as a warranty as to title, see CA 1963, s 87 and the notes thereto.
11 See CA 1963, s 85 in relation to the certification of transfers and the civil consequences where such certification is made negligently.
12 For a fuller discussion of this computer-based system see the CA 1990 (US) Regs 1996 and the notes thereto.
13 Reg 3(1).
14 Regs 4(1), 6(1) and 9(1).
15 Reg 4(2) and (3).
16 Reg 19(1).
17 Reg 19(2).
18 Regs 10 and 11.

UK legislation

See CA 1985, s 183(1), (2).

82 Transfer by personal representative

A transfer of the share or other interest of a deceased member of a company made by his personal representative shall, although the personal representative is not himself a member of the company, be as valid as if he had been such a member at the time of the execution of the instrument of transfer.

Definitions

'company': CA 1963, s 2(1); 'member': CA 1963, s 31; 'share': CA 1963, s 2(1).

Notes

The production to the company of any document which is by law sufficient evidence of the will or letters of administration, shall in turn be accepted by the company as sufficient evidence of the personal representative's title to act in relation to the transfer of shares.[1] With regard to the position of the personal representative generally, pending a disposal by him of the shares, see Table A, regs 29–32.

1 CA 1963, s 87(2).

UK legislation

See CA 1985, s 183(3).

83 Registration of transfer at request of transferor

On application of the transferor of any share or interest in a company, the company shall enter in its register of members the name of the transferee in the same manner and subject to the same conditions as if the application for the entry were made by the transferee.

Definitions

'company': CA 1963, s 2(1); 'share': CA 1963, s 2(1).

Notes

The purpose of this section is to protect the transferor where the transferee fails to fulfil his obligation to deliver the necessary documentation to the company for registration of the transfer.[1] This may be of particular relevance where the company is unlimited and the transferor wishes to avoid the risk of personal liability for the debts of the company.[2]

1 *Skinner v City of London Marine Insurance Corporation* (1885) 14 QBD 882.

2 See, for example, *Casey v Bentley* [1902] 1 IR 376.

UK legislation

See CA 1985, s 183(4).

84 Notice of refusal to register transfer

(1) If the company refuses to register a transfer of any shares or debentures, the company shall, within 2 months after the date on which the transfer was lodged with the company, send to the transferee notice of the refusal.

(2) If default is made in complying with this section, the company and every officer of the company who is in default [shall be guilty of an offence and liable to a fine][a] not exceeding [€1,904.61].[b]

Amendments

a CA 1963, s 84(2) words 'shall be guilty of an offence and liable to a fine' substituted for 'shall be liable to a fine' by C(AA)A 2003, Sch 2, Item No 1.

b '£250' substituted for '£50' by C(A)A 1982, Sch 1, increased to £1,500 by CA 1990, s 240(7) as inserted by CLEA 2001, s 104(c) and converted by €1,904.61 by Council Regulations (EC) No 1103/97, No 974/98 and No 2866/98 and the Economic and Monetary Union Act 1998, s 6.

Definitions

'company': CA 1963, s 2(1); 'debenture': CA 1963, s 2(1); 'officer': CA 1963, s 2(1); 'share': CA 1963, s 2(1); 'officer in default': CA 1963, s 383.

Notes

Discretion to refuse to register transfer: See the notes to CA 1963, s 79. Although obliged to inform the transferee if it refuses to register the transfer, the company is not under any obligation to so notify the transferor, even if the application for the transfer was lodged by the transferor.[1]

1 *Gustard's Case* (1869) LR 8 Eq 438; *Shipman's Case* (1868) LR 5 Eq 219.

Time limit for delivery of share certificate: Unless registration of the transfer is validly refused, the company must have the share certificate ready for delivery within two months after the date upon which the transfer was lodged with it.[1]

1 CA 1963, s 86(1).

Uncertificated securities:[1] In order to speed up the settlement of bargains, the Stock Exchange had for some time been pressing for a completely electronic system for recording and transferring securities. The system is known as CREST and was introduced pursuant to the CA 1990 (US) Regs 1996.[2] Securities governed by these Regs are known as 'uncertificated units of security.'[3] Title to such securities is recorded electronically by the company and may likewise be transferred electronically rather than by way of an 'instrument of transfer.'[4] Despite the absence of an instrument of transfer, the transaction still attracts stamp duty.[5] Furthermore, because title to such shares is recorded and transferred electronically, the company is no longer allowed to issue a share certificate or debenture certificate, as the case may be, to the holder of the relevant security.[6] A document purporting to be a share certificate or debenture certificate in respect of an uncertificated unit of security, shall not be regarded as evidence of title thereto.[7] Instead, title is deemed to be evidenced by the recording of the name and address of the security holder as well as details of the number of uncertificated units of security held by him, in the register of members or the register of debentureholders, as the case may be.[8]

1 For an explanation of what is meant by 'an uncertificated unit of security' see Transfers in Non-Legible Form in the notes to CA 1963, s 81.
2 For a fuller discussion of this computer-based system see the CA 1990 (US) Regs 1996 and the notes thereto.
3 Reg 3(1).
4 Regs 4(1), 6(1) and 9(1).
5 Reg 4(2) and (3).
6 Reg 19(1).
7 Reg 19(2).
8 Regs 10 and 11.

UK legislation

See CA 1985, s 183(5), (6).

85 Certification of transfers

(1) The certification by a company of any instrument of transfer of shares in or debentures of the company shall be taken as a representation by the company to any person acting on the faith of the certification that there have been produced to the company such documents as on the face of them show a *prima facie* title to the shares or debentures in the transferor named in the instrument of transfer, but not as a representation that the transferor has any title to the shares or debentures.

(2) Where any person acts on the faith of a false certification by a company made negligently, the company shall be under the same liability to him as if the certification had been made fraudulently.

(3) For the purposes of this section—

(a) an instrument of transfer shall be deemed to be certificated if it bears the words, 'certificate lodged' or words to the like effect;

(b) the certification of an instrument of transfer shall be deemed to be made by a company if—

(i) the person issuing the instrument is a person authorised to issue certificated instruments of transfer on the company's behalf, and

(ii) the certification is signed by a person authorised to certificate transfers on the company's behalf or by any officer or servant either of the company or of a body corporate so authorised;

(c) a certification shall be deemed to be signed by any person if—

(i) it purports to be authenticated by his signature or initials (whether hand written or not), and

(ii) it is not shown that the signature or initials was or were placed there neither by himself nor by any person authorised to use the signature or initials for the purpose of certificating transfers on the company's behalf.

Definitions

'company': CA 1963, s 2(1); 'debenture': CA 1963, s 2(1); 'document': CA 1963, s 2(1); 'officer': CA 1963, s 2(1); 'share': CA 1963, s 2(1).

Notes

Certification of transfers: Where the transferor is selling all of his shares he will normally deliver, not only the instrument of transfer, but also his share certificate to the transferee who in turn will submit the documentation to the company for registration. The company will then issue him with a new certificate in his own name. However, where the transferor is selling only some of his shares he will not want to deliver the share certificate to the transferee, since the certificate will also relate to shares which he is retaining. Accordingly, a practice developed, now recognised by CA 1963, s 85, whereby the transferor will instead lodge the instrument of transfer and share certificate directly with the company. The company may then in turn 'certify' the instrument of transfer (ie endorse the instrument with a statement that there have been produced to the company such documents as on the face of them show a *prima facie* title to the shares). The transferor fulfils his contractual obligations to the transferee by delivering to him a certificated instrument of transfer. Upon completion of the transaction the company then issues two new certificates of transfer – one being delivered to the transferee in respect of the shares which he has just acquired, and the other being issued to the transferor in respect of the shares which he still retains.

Certification of transfers can also arise where the transferor is selling the entire of his shareholding, but to two or more different transferees. He obviously cannot deliver the original share certificate to all of the transferees. Instead, he will arrange for certificated instruments of transfer to be delivered to them, having first lodged the share certificate with the company.

Consequences of certification of transfers: A company which gives a certification will be estopped from denying the truth of, and will be liable in respect of the representation contained therein, ie that there have been produced to the company documents which on their face show a *prima facie* title to the shares or debentures.[1] The certification of transfer is not, however, to be regarded as a representation that the transferor has any title to the shares or debentures or that the documents lodged with the company are valid.[2]

1 CA 1963, s 85(2). See also *Bishop v Balkis Consolidated Co* (1890) 25 QBD 77, aff'd 25 QBD 512.

2 CA 1963, s 84(1). See also *Longman v Bath Electric Tramways* [1905] 1 Ch 646; *Bishop v Balkis Consolidated Co* (1890) 25 QBD 77, aff'd 25 QBD 512.

Liability for acts of agents: CA 1963, s 85(3) set out the pre-conditions for liability on the part of the company for false certifications purportedly given on its behalf. There are two steps involved. The first is the signing of the certification and the second is the issuing of the certificated instrument of transfer. If the agent is an officer or servant it would seem that he need not be specifically authorised to sign the certification and/or issue the certificated instrument. If he is some other class of agent, he must be so authorised. What is not clear, however, is whether such authority has to be actual or whether ostensible authority will suffice.

Share certificate as evidence of title: With regard to the status of a share certificate as evidence of title, see CA 1963, s 87.

Uncertificated securities:[1] Provision has been made by the CA 1990 (US) Regs 1996 for computer-based systems for the holding and transferring of shares. The Regulations were made primarily to allow for the introduction by the Stock Exchange of its new electronic system, known as CREST. Shares governed by these Regulations are known as 'uncertificated units of security.' Title is recorded electronically by the company and consequently share certificates are not issued to shareholders. The whole process of the certification of transfers is therefore redundant for such securities.

1 For an explanation of what is meant by 'an uncertificated unit of security' see Transfers in Non-Legible Form in the notes to CA 1963, s 81.

UK legislation

See CA 1985, s 184.

86 Duties of company in relation to the issue of certificates

(1) Every company shall, within 2 months after the allotment of any of its shares, debentures or debenture stock, and within 2 months after the date on which a transfer of any such shares, debentures or debenture stock is lodged with the company, complete and have ready for delivery the certificates of all shares, the debentures, and the certificates of all debenture stock allotted or transferred, unless the conditions of issue of the shares, debentures or debenture stock otherwise provide.

The expression 'transfer' for the purpose of this subsection means a transfer duly stamped and otherwise valid, and does not include such a transfer as the company is, for any reason, entitled to refuse to register and does not register.

(2) If default is made in complying with this section, the company and every officer of the company who is in default [shall be guilty of an offence and liable to a fine][a] not exceeding [€1,904.61].[b]

(3) If any company on which a notice has been served requiring the company to make good any default in complying with the provisions of subsection (1) fails to make good the default within 10 days after the service of the notice, the court may, on the application of the person entitled to have the certificates or the debentures delivered to him, make an order directing the company and any officer of the company to make good the default within such time as may be specified in the order, and any such order may provide that all costs of and incidental to the application shall be borne by the company or by any officer of the company responsible for the default.

Amendments

a CA 1963, s 86(2) words 'shall be guilty of an offence and liable to a fine' substituted for 'shall be liable to a fine' by C(AA)A 2003, Sch 2, Item No 1.

b '£100' substituted for '£20' by C(A)A 1982, Sch 1, increased to £1,500 by CA 1990, s 240(7) as inserted by CLEA 2001, s 104(c) and converted to €1,904.61 by Council Regulations (EC) No 1103/97, No 974/98 and No 2866/98 and the Economic and Monetary Union Act 1998, s 6.

Definitions

'company': CA 1963, s 2(1); 'the court': CA 1963, s 2(1); 'debenture': CA 1963, s 2(1); 'officer': CA 1963, s 2(1); 'officer in default': CA 1963, s 383; 'share': CA 1963, s 2(1).

Notes

Discretion to refuse to register transfer of shares: See the notes to CA 1963, s 79.

Sepon Ltd: The obligation to issue share certificates and debenture certificates did not apply in respect of temporary transfers of listed shares or debentures to Sepon Ltd or to any other stock exchange nominee company.[1]

1 C(A)A 1977, s 2. For an explanation of Sepon Ltd, see 'Mechanics of Transfer' in the notes to CA 1963, s 81.

Uncertificated securities: See note on uncertificated securities after s 81.

1 For a fuller discussion of this computer based system see the CA 1990 (US) Regs 1996 and the notes thereto.

UK legislation

See CA 1985, s 185 (amended by the Financial services and Markets Act 2000 (Consequential Amendments and Repeals) Order 2001, Art 7).

87 Evidence of title, probate and letters of administration

[(1) A certificate under the common seal of the company or the seal kept by the company (not being a private company) by virtue of section 3 of the Companies (Amendment) Act, 1977, specifying any shares held by any member shall be *prima facie* evidence of the title of the member to the shares.][a]

(2) The production to a company of any document which is by law sufficient evidence of probate of the will or letters of administration of the estate of a deceased person having been granted to some person shall be accepted by the company, notwithstanding anything in its articles, as sufficient evidence of the grant.

Amendments

a CA 1963, s 87(1) substituted by C(A)A 1977, s 5.

Definitions

'articles': CA 1963, s 2(1); 'company': CA 1963, s 2(1); 'document': CA 1963, s 2(1); 'member': CA 1963, s 31; 'private company': CA 1963, s 2(1), s 33(1); 'share': CA 1963, s 2(1).

Notes

Certificate as representation of title: The share certificate constitutes a representation by the company that the person to whom it is granted is entitled to the particular shares and that he is entitled to sell them.[1] The company is accordingly estopped from denying the truth of the representation as against any person who relies thereon and acts to his detriment as a result.[2] Moreover, the estoppel applies regardless of the fact that the share certificate was originally obtained by fraud or mistake.[3]

1 *Re Bahia and San Fransisco Rly Co* (1868) LR 3 QB 584; *Balkis Consolidated Co v Tomkinson* [1893] AC 396; *Royal Bank of Scotland plc v Sandstone Properties Ltd* [1998] 2 BCLC 429; *Cadbury Schweppes plc v Halifax Share Dealing Ltd* [2007] 1 BCLC 497. The representation is only as to legal title. Equitable title may lie with some third party, eg pursuant to a trust or mortgage. Equitable interests are, in any event, incapable of being entered by the company in the register of members: CA 1963, s 123.

2 *Balkis Consolidated Co v Tomkinson* [1893] AC 396, 405; *Royal Bank of Scotland plc v Sandstone Properties Ltd* [1998] 2 BCLC 429; *Cadbury Schweppes plc v Halifax Share Dealing Ltd* [2007] 1 BCLC 497.

3 *Bahia and San Francisco Railway Co* (1868) LR 3 QB 584; *Cadbury Schweppes plc v Halifax Share Dealing Ltd* [2007] 1 BCLC 497.

Remedy for misrepresentation: Although the erroneous certificate raises an estoppel against the company, it does not operate so as to confer title to the shares.[1] Indeed, an estoppel as to title will not arise even where the company has erroneously treated the individual as a shareholder and has paid him a dividend.[2] The aggrieved party therefore cannot compel the company to enter or keep his name in the register of members. Rather, his remedy will lie in an action for damages.[3] The measure of damages is the value of the shares, not at the date of the purported purchase but rather at the date when the company refuses to register the transfer.[4]

1 *Re Bahia and San Francisco Railway Co* (1868) LR 3 Eq 584; *Hart v Frontino and Bolivia South American Gold Mining Co* (1870) LR 5 Exch 111.

2 *Foster v Tyne Pontoon and Dry Docks Co and Renwick* (1893) 63 LJ QB 50.

3 *Re Bahia and San Francisco Railway Co* (1868) LR 3 Eq 584; *Balkis Consolidated Co v Tomkinson* [1893] AC 396; *Dixon v Kennaway and Co* [1900] 1 Ch 833; *Sheffield Corp v Barclay* [1905] AC 392.

4 *Re Ottos Kopje Diamond Mines* [1893] 1 Ch 618.

Forged transfer: Since a forged transfer is a nullity, the true owner of the shares will be entitled to apply to have the share register rectified in the event of the company registering the purported change in ownership.[1]

A transferee who presents a transfer to the company for registration impliedly warrants that it is genuine so that if it turns out to be a forgery or to have been executed without due authorisation, the company will not be estopped from denying the transferee's title to the shares, even though the transferee was unaware of the forgery or lack of authorisation, when presenting it for registration.[2] Rather, the transferee will be liable in such circumstances to indemnify the company in respect of any loss suffered by it as a result of acting on the forged or unauthorised transfer.[3]

1 *Royal Bank of Scotland plc v Sandstone Properties Ltd* [1998] 2 BCLC 429.

2 *Simm v Anglo-American Telegraph Co* (1879) 5 QBD 188; *Balkis Consolidated Co v Tomkinson* [1893] AC 396, 406; *Dixon v Kennaway and Co* [1900] 1 Ch 833, 841; *Ruben v Great Fingall Consolidated* [1906] AC 439, 446; *A-G v Odell* [1906] 2 Ch 47.

3 *Sheffield Corporation v Barclay* [1905] AC 392; *Yeung Kei Yung v Hong Kong and Shanghai Banking Corporation* [1981] AC 787.

Forged certificate: The company is not bound by a forged share certificate.[1]

1 *Ruben v Great Fingall Consolidated* [1906] AC 439. In this case the 'forgery' involved the genuine but unauthorised use of the company's seal by a director and secretary of the company. Because the attesting of their signatures was genuine, the case did not involve forgery within the true meaning of the word. Rather, it was an instance of the company's agents acting in excess of their authority. Having regard to the doctrine of ostensible authority, the Rule in *Turquand's Case* (1869) LR 4 Ch App 376 and the provisions of Reg 6 of the EC(C)R 1973, it would seem that this case was incorrectly decided in so far as it treated genuine but unauthorised signatures as a forgery. However, the principle that a forgery does not bind the company remains good law.

Estoppel as to amount paid on shares: Where a share certificate wrongly stated that shares were fully paid up, the company could in the past have been estopped from making a call for the unpaid amount, whether as against the original allottee[1] or as against a subsequent transferee.[2] These cases have since been superseded by C(A)A 1983, s 27 which prohibits the issue of shares at a discount. The section also obliges both the allottee and any subsequent holders of the share to pay the outstanding amounts plus interest to the company. Relief is, however, afforded to persons (other than the allottee) who can prove that they purchased the shares for value and without actual notice of the fact of the discount.[3]

1 *Parbury's Case* [1896] 1 Ch 100; *Bloomenthal v Ford* [1897] AC 156.

2 *Burkinshaw v Nicolls* (1878) 3 App Cas 1004.

3 C(A)A 1983, s 27(2).

Evidence of title of personal representative: CA 1963, s 87(2) only requires the company to recognise Irish grants of probate and letters of administration. It is not required to act on foreign grants.[1]

1 *New York Breweries Co v Attorney General* [1899] AC 62.

See *Schweppes Ltd v Halifax* (23 May 2006) EWHC. Also *Sheffiled Corporation v Barclay* re implied indemnity. Also Case on prices to be paid for shares under a warrant: *Oxus v Templeton Insurance Ltd* [2007] EWHC 770.

UK legislation

CA 1985, s 186.

---

88 Issue and effect of share warrants to bearer

(1) A company limited by shares if so authorised by its articles, may, in relation to any fully paid up shares, issue under its common seal a warrant stating that the bearer of the warrant is entitled to the shares therein specified, and may provide by coupons or otherwise for the payment of the future dividends on the shares included in the warrant.

(2) Such a warrant as aforesaid is in this Act referred to as 'a share warrant'.

(3) A share warrant shall entitle the bearer thereof to the shares therein specified, and the shares may be transferred by delivery of the warrant.

Definitions

'articles': CA 1963, s 2(1); 'company limited by shares': CA 1963, s 2(1), 5(1); 'share': CA 1963, s 2(1); 'share warrant': CA 1963, s 2(1), s 88(2).

Notes

Share warrants: In practice, share warrants may only be used in public companies because the articles of private companies are required to contain provisions restricting the right to transfer shares.[1] Transfer by simple delivery of the share warrant would be in conflict with such restrictions.

1 CA 1963, s 33.

Authorisation for share warrants: CA 1963, s 88(1) provides that a company can issue share warrants, if so authorised by its articles. No such authorisation is to be found, however, in Model Form articles.

UK legislation

See CA 1985, s 188; CA 1989, s 130(7), Sch 17, para 6.

---

89 Validation of invalid issue, redemption or purchase of shares

[(1) If a company has created or issued shares in its capital, or acquired any of its shares by a redemption or purchase in purported compliance with Part XI of the Companies

Act, 1990, and if there is reason to apprehend that such shares were invalidly created, issued or acquired as aforesaid, the court may, on the application of the company, any holder or former holder of such shares or any member or former member or creditor, or the liquidator, of the company, declare that such creation, issue or acquisition shall be valid for all purposes if the court is satisfied that it would be just and equitable to do so and thereupon such shares shall from the creation, issue or acquisition thereof, as the case may be, be deemed to have been validly created, issued or acquired.

(2) Where shares have been redeemed or purchased in contravention of paragraph (d), (e) or (f) of section 207 (2) or section 207 (3) of the Companies Act, 1990, then the court shall not make a declaration under subsection (1) above in respect of those shares.

(3) The grant of relief by the court under this section shall, if the court so directs, not have the effect of relieving the company or its officers of any liability incurred under section 41 (3) of the Companies (Amendment) Act, 1983.][a]

Amendments

a CA 1963, s 89 substituted by CA 1990, s 227.

Definitions

'company': CA 1963, s 2(1); 'the court': CA 1963, s 2(1); 'member': CA 1963, s 31; 'officer': s 2(1); 'share': CA 1963, s 2(1).

Notes

Validation of irregular allotments, redemptions etc: While it is envisaged by CA 1963, s 89 that the court may make an order validating a creation, allotment, redemption or purchase of shares where it is satisfied that it is 'just and equitable' to do so, it does not follow that the discretion conferred by the section is unrestricted. Although the court has a wide discretion under the section, it is a discretion which must be exercised in a judicial manner and in accordance with appropriate criteria and having regard to the underlying policy of the section.[1] In this regard, it has been held that the policy of the section is to prevent possible hardship to persons who innocently subscribe for or pay for shares and who find that they may have spent their money for no return because of a defect in the relevant transaction of which they had no knowledge and could not be expected to have had any knowledge.[2] Even then, however, the court can still only validate the transaction if it is possible to do so in a manner which will not produce unjust or inequitable results having regard to the interests of any other persons who were or might be affected by the transaction in question.[3] Furthermore, the section cannot be invoked where the purpose of the application is to retrospectively validate seriously irregular transactions and thereby obtain for the company a tax advantage to which it would not otherwise have been legitimately entitled[4]: (1) ie where the redemption or purchase has been funded other than out of either distributable profits or a fresh issue of shares and (2) ie where a company has wrongfully acquired some of its own shares.

1 *Re Sugar Distributors Ltd* [1995] 2 IR 194.

2 *Re Sugar Distributors Ltd* [1995] 2 IR 194; *MillHeim v Barewa Oil and Mining NL* [1971] WAR 65.

3 *Re Sugar Distributors Ltd* [1995] 2 IR 194; *MillHeim v Barewa Oil and Mining NL* [1971] WAR 65.

4 *Re Sugar Distributors Ltd* [1995] 2 IR 194.

90 Penalty for personation of shareholder

If any person falsely and deceitfully personates any owner of any share or interest in any company, or of any share warrant or coupon, issued in pursuance of this Act, and thereby obtains or endeavours to obtain any such share or interest or share warrant or coupon, or receives or endeavours to receive any money due to any such owner, or votes at any meeting, as if the offender were the true and lawful owner, he shall be liable, on conviction on indictment, to imprisonment for a term not exceeding [5][a] years or to a fine not exceeding [€3,174.35][b] or to both, or, on summary conviction to imprisonment for a term not exceeding 6 months or to a fine not exceeding [€1,904.61][c] or to both.

Amendments

a '5' substituted for '2' by CA 1990, s 240(8) as inserted by CLEA 2001, s 104(c).

b '£2,500' substituted for '£500' by C(A)A 1982, Sch 1 and converted to €3,174.35 by Council Regulations (EC) No 1103/97. No 974/98 and No 2866/98 and the Economic and Monetary Union Act 1998, s 6.

c '£500' substituted for '£100' by C(A)A 1982, Sch 1, increased to £1,500 by CA 1990, s 240(7) as inserted by CLEA 2001, s 104(c) and converted to €1,904.61 by Council Regulations (EC) No 1103/97. No 974/98 and No 2866/98 and the Economic and Monetary Union Act 1998, s 6.

Definitions

'company': CA 1963, s 2(1); 'share': CA 1963, s 2(1); 'share warrant': CA 1963, s 2(1), s 88(2).

Special Provisions as to Debentures

91 Provisions as to register of debenture holders

(1) Every company shall keep a register of holders of debentures of the company and enter therein the names and addresses of the debenture holders and the amount of debentures currently held by each.

For the purposes of this subsection, debentures do not include any debenture which does not form part of a series ranking *pari passu* nor any debenture which is transferable by delivery.

(2) A company shall keep such register at the registered office of the company, any other office of the company at which the work of making it up is done, or if the company arranges with some other person for the making up of the register to be undertaken on behalf of the company by that other person, at the office of that other person at which the work is done.

(3) Subject to subsection (4), every company shall send notice to the registrar of companies of the place where the register is kept, and of any change in that place.

(4) A company shall not be bound to send notice under subsection (3) where the register has, at all times since it came into existence, or, in the case of a company which came into existence after the operative date, at all times since then, been kept at the registered office of the company.

(5) Where a company makes default in complying with subsection (1) or (2) or makes default for 14 days in complying with subsection (3), the company and every officer of

the company who is in default [shall be guilty of an offence and liable to a fine][a] not exceeding [€1,904.61].[b]

Amendments

a CA 1963, s 91(5) words 'shall be guilty of an offence and liable to a fine' substituted for 'shall be liable to a fine' by C(AA)A 2003, Sch 2, Item No 1.

b '£250' substituted for '£50' by C(A)A 1982, Sch 1, increased to £1,500 by CA 1990, s 240(7) as inserted by CLEA 2001, s 104(c) and converted to €1,904.61 by Council Regulations (EC) No 1103/97, No 974/98 and No 2866/98 and the Economic and Monetary Union Act 1998, s 6.

Definitions

'company': CA 1963, s 2(1); 'debenture': CA 1963, s 2(1); 'officer': CA 1963, s 2(1); 'officer in default': s 383; 'the operative date': CA 1963, s 2(1); 'the registrar of companies': CA 1963, s 2(1).

Notes

Register of debentureholders: The register prescribed by CA 1963, s 91(1) applies only to series of debenture stock and not to individual loan instruments.[1]

1 For an explanation of what is meant by 'debenture stock' see the notes on the definition of 'debenture' in CA 1963, s 2(1).

Place for keeping of register: The company is given a degree of choice as to where it keeps the register of debentureholders. Although it may be kept at the registered office, CA 1963, s 91(2) also allows for it to be kept at any other office of the company or at the office of any agent of the company at which the work of maintaining the register is done, such as a company secretarial service, or a firm of solicitors, accountants or stockbrokers.

Register in Non-Legible Form: The register of debentureholders may be kept in non-legible form (eg on a computer system) provided that it is capable of being reproduced in legible form.[1]

1 C(A)A 1977, s 4(2).

Uncertificated units of security:[1] Listed companies participating in the Stock Exchange's CREST system must, in addition to the general requirements of CA 1963, s 91, also enter on the register of debentureholders, details of the number of units of debenture stock held by the debentureholder in certificated and uncertificated form respectively.[2]

1 For an explanation of what is meant by 'an uncertificated unit of security' see Transfers in Non-Legible Form in the notes to CA 1963, s 81.

2 CA 1990 (US) Regs 1996, reg 10(2).

UK legislation

See CA 1985, s 190.

92 Rights of inspection of register of debenture holders and to copies of register and trust deed

(1) Every register of holders of debentures of a company shall, except when duly closed (but subject to such reasonable restrictions as the company in general meeting may impose, so that not less than 2 hours in each day shall be allowed for inspection), be open to the inspection of the registered holder of any such debentures or any holder of

shares in the company without fee, and of any other person on payment of a fee of [6 cent][a] or such less sum as may be prescribed by the company.

(2) Any such registered holder of debentures or holder of shares as aforesaid or any other person may require a copy of the register of the holders of debentures of the company or any part thereof, on payment of [8 cent][b] for every 100 words required to be copied.

(3) A copy of any trust deed for securing any issue of debentures shall be forwarded to every holder of any such debentures at his request on payment in the case of a printed trust deed of the sum of [32 cent][c] or such less sum as may be prescribed by the company, or, where the trust deed has not been printed, on payment of [8 cent][b] for every 100 words required to be copied.

(4) If inspection is refused, or a copy is refused or not forwarded, the company and every officer of the company who is in default [shall be guilty of an offence and liable to a fine][d] not exceeding [€1,904.61].[e]

(5) Where a company is in default as aforesaid, the court may by order compel an immediate inspection of the register or direct that the copies required shall be sent to the person requiring them.

(6) For the purposes of this section, a register shall be deemed to be duly closed if closed in accordance with provisions contained in the articles or in the debentures or, in the case of debenture stock, in the stock certificates, or in the trust deed or other document securing the debentures or debenture stock, during such period or periods, not exceeding in the whole 30 days in any year, as may be therein specified.

Amendments

a One shilling (5 pence) converted to 6.5 cent by Council Regulations (EC) No 1103/97, No 974/98 and No 2866/98 and the Economic and Monetary Union Act 1998, s 6.

b Sixpence converted to 8 cent by Council Regulations (EC) No 1103/97, No 974/98 and No 2866/98 and the Economic and Monetary Union Act 1998, s 6.

c Five shillings (25p) converted to 32 cent by Council Regulations (EC) No 1103/97, No 974/98 and No 2866/98 and the Economic and Monetary Union Act 1998, s 6.

d CA 1963, s 92(4) words 'shall be guilty of an offence and liable to a fine' substituted for 'shall be liable to a fine' by C(AA)A 2003, Sch 2, Item No 1.

e '£125' substituted for '£25' by C(A)A 1982, Sch 1, increased to £1,500 by CA 1990, s 240(7) as inserted by CLEA 2001, s 104(c) and converted to €1,904.61 by Council Regulations (EC) No 1103/97, No 974/98 and No 2866/98 and the Economic and Monetary Union Act 1998, s 6.

Definitions

'articles': CA 1963, s 2 (1); 'company': CA 1963, s 2(1); 'the court': CA 1963, s 2(1); 'debenture': CA 1963, s 2(1); 'document': CA 1963, s 2(1): 'officer': CA 1963, s 2(1); 'prescribed': CA 1963, s 2(1); ' printed': CA 1963, s 2(1); 'share': CA 1963, s 2(1).

Notes

Inspection of register kept in non-legible form: If the register of debentureholders is kept in non-legible form, the company will be obliged to allow inspection of, or to furnish, a reproduction of the recording of the relevant part of it in legible form.[1]

[1] C(A)A 1977, s 4(3).

UK legislation

See CA 1985, s 191 (amended by CA 1989, ss 143(4), 212, Sch 24).

93 Liability of trustees for debenture holders

(1) Subject to subsections (2) to (4), any provision contained in a trust deed for securing an issue of debentures, or in any contract with the holders of debentures secured by a trust deed, shall be void in so far as it would have the effect of exempting a trustee thereof from or indemnifying him against liability for breach of trust where he fails to show the degree of care and diligence required of him as trustee, having regard to the provisions of the trust deed conferring on him any powers, authorities or discretions.

(2) Subsection (1) shall not invalidate—

(a) any release otherwise validly given in respect of anything done or omitted to be done by a trustee before the giving of the release; or

(b) any provision enabling such a release to be given—

(i) on the agreement thereto of a majority of not less than three-fourths in value of the debenture holders present and voting in person or, where proxies are permitted, by proxy at a meeting summoned for the purpose, and

(ii) either with respect to specific acts or omissions or on the trustee dying or ceasing to act.

(3) Subsection (1) shall not operate—

(a) to invalidate any provision in force on the operative date so long as any person then entitled to the benefit of that provision or afterwards given the benefit thereof under subsection (4) remains a trustee of the deed in question; or

(b) to deprive any person of any exemption or right to be indemnified in respect of anything done or omitted to be done by him while any such provision was in force.

(4) While any trustee of a trust deed remains entitled to the benefit of a provision saved by subsection (3), the benefit of that provision may be given either—

(a) to all trustees of the deed, present and future; or

(b) to any named trustee or proposed trustees thereof;

by a resolution passed by a majority of not less than three-fourths in value of the debenture holders present in person or, where proxies are permitted, by proxy at a meeting summoned for the purpose in accordance with the provisions of the deed or, if the deed makes no provision for summoning meetings, a meeting summoned for the purpose in any manner approved by the court.

Definitions

'the court': CA 1963, s 2(1); 'debenture': CA 1963, s 2(1); 'the operative date': CA 1963, s 2(1).

Notes

With regard to the degree of care and diligence that may be required of trustees generally, see Keane, *Equity and the Law of Trusts in the Republic of Ireland* (Butterworths, 1988), Ch 10 and Delany, *Equity and the Law of Trusts in Ireland* (3rd edn, Sweet & Maxwell, 2003) Ch 12.

A release may be given to a trustee in respect of a breach of trust where all the beneficiaries under the trust deed are *sui generis* and so resolve.[1]

1 *Brice v Stokes* (1805) 11 Ves 319; *Roche v O'Brien* (1810) I Ball and B 330.

UK legislation

See CA 1985, s 192.

94 Perpetual debentures

A condition contained in any debentures or in any deed for securing any debentures, whether issued or executed before or after the operative date, shall not be invalid by reason only that the debentures are thereby made irredeemable or redeemable only on the happening of a contingency, however remote, or on the expiration of a period, however long, notwithstanding any rule of law to the contrary.

Definitions

'debenture': CA 1963, s 2(1); 'the operative date': CA 1963, s 2(1).

Notes

Clog on equity of redemption: But for CA 1963, s 94, a provision in a debenture making it irredeemable (even in the event of liquidation) or postponing the redemption to some very remote or distant date, would amount to a 'clog on the equity of redemption' thereby rendering the instrument void.[1]

1 See Snell's *Principles of Equity* (28th edn, London 1982) pp 390–394; *Knightsbridge Estates Trust Ltd v Byrne* [1940] AC 613. Cases such as *Wallace v Universal Automatic Machines Co* [1894] 2 Ch 547 which held that there could be no such thing as an 'irredeemable debenture' and that a debenture so described became immediately repayable upon liquidation, were decided prior to the enactment in the Companies Act 1907 of the precursor to the present section.

Types of debenture affected: The provisions of CA 1963, s 94 apply equally to a single debenture in favour of an individual as they do to a debenture forming part of a series of debenture stock.[1]

1 *Knightsbridge Estates Trust Ltd v Byrne* [1940] AC 613.

UK legislation

See CA 1985, s 193.

95 Power to re-issue redeemed debentures

(1) Where either before, on or after the operative date, a company has redeemed any debentures, then—

(a) unless any provision to the contrary, whether express or implied, is contained in the articles or in any contract entered into by the company; or

(b) unless the company has, by passing a resolution to that effect or by some other act, shown its intention that the debentures shall be cancelled;

the company shall have, and shall be deemed always to have had, power to re-issue the debentures, either by re-issuing the same debentures or by issuing other debentures in their place.

(2) Subject to section 96, on a re-issue of redeemed debentures, the person entitled to the debentures shall have, and shall be deemed always to have had, the same priorities as if the debentures had never been redeemed.

(3) Where a company has, either before, on or after the operative date deposited any of its debentures to secure advances from time to time on current account or otherwise, the debentures shall not be deemed to have been redeemed by reason only of the account of the company having ceased to be in debit whilst the debentures remained so deposited.

(4) Subject to subsection (5), the re-issue of a debenture or the issue of another debenture in its place under the power by this section given to, or deemed to have been possessed by, a company, whether the re-issue or issue was made before, on or after the operative date, shall be treated as the issue of a new debenture for the purposes of stamp duty, but it shall not be so treated for the purposes of any provision limiting the amount or number of debentures to be issued.

(5) Any person lending money on the security of a debenture re-issued under this section, which appears to be duly stamped, may give the debenture in evidence in any proceedings for enforcing his security without payment of the stamp duty or any penalty in respect thereof, unless he had notice or, but for his negligence, might have discovered that the debenture was not duly stamped, but in any such case the company shall be liable to pay the proper stamp duty and penalty.

Definitions

'articles': CA 1963, s 2(1); 'company': CA 1963, s 2(1); 'debenture': CA 1963, s 2(1); 'the operative date': CA 1963, s 2(1).

Notes

Re-issue of redeemed debentures: Prior to the enactment of CA 1963, s 95, any debentures forming part of a series of debentures which were redeemed, were automatically extinguished and could not be re-issued by the company.[1] Thus, any fresh issue of debentures would rank after the unredeemed remainder of the first issue.[2] The provisions of s 94 have no application, however, unless the debentures are re-issued on the same terms as applied before redemption.[3] Thus, for example, the company could not redeem the debentures and then re-issue them with a different redemption date.[4]

1 *Re George Routledge and Sons Ltd* [1904] 2 Ch 474.

2 *Re George Routledge and Sons Ltd* [1904] 2 Ch 474.

3 *Re Antofagasta (Chili) and Bolivia Rly Co Ltd's Trust Deed* [1939] Ch 732.

4 *Re Antofagasta (Chili) and Bolivia Rly Co Ltd's Trust Deed* [1939] Ch 732.

Re-issue of redeemed shares: With regard to the power of the company to re-issue shares which it has previously redeemed or purchased, see CA 1990, ss 209 and 211.

UK legislation

See CA 1985, s 194.

96 Saving of rights of certain mortgagees in case of re-issued debentures

Where any debentures which have been redeemed before the operative date are re-issued on or subsequently to that date, the re-issue of the debentures shall not prejudice and shall be deemed never to have prejudiced any right or priority which any person would have had under or by virtue of any mortgage or charge created before the operative date, if section 104 of the Companies (Consolidation) Act, 1908, had been enacted in this Act instead of section 95.

Definitions

'debenture': CA 1963, s 2(1); 'the operative date': CA 1963, s 2(1).

UK legislation

See CC(CPC)A 1985, s 13.

97 Specific performance of contracts to subscribe for debentures

A contract with a company to take up and pay for any debentures of the company may be enforced by an order for specific performance.

Definitions

'company': CA 1963, s 2(1); 'debenture': CA 1963, s 2(1).

Notes

Prior to the enactment of the precursor to this CA 1963, s 97,[1] the company could not sue for specific performance of a contract to subscribe for debentures and could only sue for damages equivalent to the amount of the loss actually suffered as a result of the breach of contract.[2] Even now, however, the company will not be entitled to an order for payment of outstanding instalments by the debentureholder in circumstances where it has forfeited the debenture and any instalments which have already been paid.[3]

1 CA 1907, s 16.

2 *South African Territories v Wallington* [1898] AC 309.

3 *Kuala Pahi Rubber Estates v Mowbray* [1914] WN 321.

UK legislation

See CA 1985, s 195.

98 Preferential payments when receiver is appointed under floating charge

(1) Where either a receiver is appointed on behalf of the holders of any debentures of a company secured by a floating charge, or possession is taken by or on behalf of those debenture holders of any property comprised in or subject to the charge, then, if the company is not at the time in course of being wound up, the debts which in every winding up are, under the provisions of Part VI relating to preferential payments to be

paid in priority to all other debts, shall be paid out of any assets coming to the hands of the receiver or other person taking possession as aforesaid in priority to any claim for principal or interest in respect of the debentures.

(2) In the application of the said provisions section 285 of this Act shall be construed as if the provision for payment of accrued holiday remuneration becoming payable on the termination of employment before or by the effect of the winding up order or resolution, were a provision for payment of such remuneration becoming payable on the termination of employment before or by the effect of the appointment of the receiver or possession being taken as aforesaid.

(3) The periods of time mentioned in the said provisions of Part VI shall be reckoned from the date of the appointment of the receiver or of possession being taken as aforesaid, as the case may be.

(4) Where the date referred to in subsection (3) occurred before the operative date, subsections (1) and (3) shall have effect with the substitution for references to the said provisions of Part VI of references to the provisions which, by virtue of subsection (12) of the said section 285 are deemed to remain in force in the case therein mentioned, and subsection (2) of this section shall not apply.

(5) Any payments made under this section shall be recouped so far as may be out of the assets of the company available for payment of general creditors.

Definitions

'company': CA 1963, s 2(1); 'debenture': CA 1963, s 2(1); 'the operative date': CA 1963, s 2(1).

Notes

Preferential debts: In relation to the categories of preferential claims that may be made in a receivership or liquidation, see CA 1963, s 285 and the notes thereto.

Receiver appointed on behalf of debentureholder: The provisions of CA 1963, s 98 only apply where the receiver is appointed by or on behalf of a debentureholder pursuant to the terms of a floating charge or where the debentureholder takes possession himself. It has no application where the receiver is appointed by order of the court.[1] However, in so far as s 98 applies, the preferential creditors would appear to be afforded priority not only over the floating charge pursuant to which the receiver was appointed or the debentureholder took possession, but also over all other charges which, as of the date of the receiver's appointment or the debentureholder's taking of possession, were floating charges.[2]

1 *Re PMPA Oil Co* (28 April 1988, unreported) HC (Costello J).

2 *Re H and K(Medway) Ltd* [1997] 1 BCLC 545; cf *Griffiths v Yorkshire Bank plc* [1994] 1 WLR 1427.

Fixed charges: The provisions of CA 1963, s 98 apply only to debentures which are still floating charges at the date of the appointment of the receiver on the date of the taking of possession by the debentureholder, as the case may be. The section has no application if the debenture has already crystallised and become a fixed charge before either the appointment of a receiver or the taking of possession by the debenture holder;[1] nor will it apply if the debenture is one which, from the very outset, was a fixed charge.[2] Of course, whether a charge is fixed or floating depends on the characteristics and substance of the security created by the debenture rather than on the description given to it by the parties.[3]

1 *Re Brightlife Ltd* [1987] 2 WLR 197; *Re Permanent Houses (Holdings) Ltd* [1988] BCLC 563; *Re Griffin Hotel Co* [1940] 4 All ER 324; *Re Christanette International Ltd* [1982] 3 All ER 225.

2 *IRC v Goldbaltt* [1972] Ch 498; *Re GL Saunders Ltd* [1986] BCLC 40; *Re United Bars Ltd* [1991] 1 IR 396; *Re Eisc Teo* [1991] ILRM 760. See TCA 1007, s 1001 in relation to the priority afforded to the claims of the Revenue Commissioners as against a creditor whose debt is secured by a fixed charge over the company's book debts.

3 *Re Armagh Shoes Ltd* [1982] NI 59; *Re Keenan Bros Ltd* [1985] IR 401; *Northern Bank Ltd v Ross* [1990] NI 53; *Re Wogans (Drogheda) Ltd* [1993] 1 IR 157; *Re Holidair Ltd* [1994] 1 IR 416; *Re GE Turnbridge Ltd* [1995] BCLC 34.

Fixed and floating charge: Where the debenture contains both a fixed charge and a floating charge, the priority given to the preferential creditors by CA 1963, s 98 will be confined to those assets which are subject to the floating charge only.[1] Accordingly, any surplus from realisations on the fixed charge element of the debenture go back to the company rather than to the preferential creditors.[2] It should be noted, however, that even if the debentureholder has been paid in full out of the fixed charge realisations, the receiver or debentureholder, as the case may be, remains under a duty to pay the preferential creditors out of the floating charge assets and, so far as is necessary, to realise those assets, rather than simply returning them directly to the company[3] or paying them to a subsequent debentureholder.[4]

1 *Re Lewis Merthyr Consolidated Collieries* [1929] 1 Ch 498.

2 *Re GL Saunders Ltd* [1986] BCLC 40; *Re United Bars Ltd* [1991] 1 IR 396; *Re Eisc Teo* [1991] ILRM 760.

3 *Re Eisc Teo* [1991] ILRM 760.

4 *Re Manning Furniture Ltd* [1996] 1 ILRM 13.

Liability of receiver to preferential creditors: A receiver and manager who carries on the company's business at a loss, and thereby reduces the funds available for the preferential creditors, will be liable to make good the deficiency.[1] Similarly, the receiver will be liable in damages if he pays away the assets to the debentureholder without having first satisfied the claims of the preferential creditors.[2]

1 *Woods v Winskill* [1913] 2 Ch 303; *Westminster Corporation v Haste* [1950] 2 All ER 65; *IRC v Goldblatt* [1972] Ch 498; *Re Tarjan Construction Co Pty Ltd* (1963) 80 WN (NSW) 1342.

2 *Woods v Winskill* [1913] 2 Ch 303; *Westminster Corporation v Haste* [1950] 2 All ER 65; *IRC v Goldblatt* [1972] Ch 498; *Re Custom Card (NSW) Pty Ltd* [1979] 1 NSWLR 241; *Steinberg v Herbert* (1988) 14 ACLR 80.

Liability of debentureholder to preferential creditors: If a receiver is unaware of a particular preferential claim or has been induced by the debentureholder to believe that the claim is unfounded, and thus proceeds to pay the debentureholder without first discharging that claim, he may be entitled to call upon the debentureholder to indemnify him if he is subsequently sued in damages by the preferential creditor.[1] Moreover, a debentureholder who has been paid out of floating charge realisations may be sued directly by an unpaid preferential creditor to the extent that he had notice of a the receiver's breach of CA 1963, s 98.[2]

1 *Westminster City Council v Treby* [1936] 2 All ER 21.

2 *IRC v Goldblatt* [1972] Ch 498.

Costs and expenses of receivership: Preferential claims are paid after allowing for the costs and expenses of the receivership.[1]

1 *Re Glyncorrwg Colliery Co* [1926] Ch 951; *Waters v Widdows* [1984] VR 503.

Dual preferential claims: The making of a preferential claim in a receivership does not preclude the creditor making a seprate preferential claim in a subsequent winding up of the company.

1 *Re H Williams (Tallaght) Ltd* [1996] 3 IR 531.

UK legislation

See CA s 1986; IA 1986, s 439(1), Sch 13 Part I.

PART IV
REGISTRATION OF CHARGES
Registration of Charges with Registrar of Companies

99 Registration of charges created by companies

(1) Subject to the provisions of this Part, every charge created after the fixed date by a company, and being a charge to which this section applies, shall, so far as any security on the company's property or undertaking is conferred thereby, be void against the liquidator and any creditor of the company, unless the prescribed particulars of the charge, verified in the prescribed manner, are delivered to or received by the registrar of companies for registration in manner required by this Act within 21 days after the date of its creation, but without prejudice to any contract or obligation for repayment of the money thereby secured, and when a charge becomes void under this section, the money secured thereby shall immediately become payable.

(2) This section applies to the following charges—

(a) a charge for the purpose of securing any issue of debentures;

(b) a charge on uncalled share capital of the company;

(c) a charge created or evidenced by an instrument which, if executed by an individual, would require registration as a bill of sale;

(d) a charge on land, wherever situate, or any interest therein, but not including a charge for any rent or other periodical sum issuing out of land;

(e) a charge on book debts of the company;

(f) a floating charge on the undertaking or property of the company;

(g) a charge on calls made but not paid;

[(h) a charge on a ship or aircraft or any share in a ship or aircraft;][a]

(i) a charge on goodwill, on a patent or a licence under a patent, on a trade mark or on a copyright or a licence under a copyright.

[(2A) The Minister may by regulations amend subsection (2) so as to add any description of charge to, or remove any description of charge from, the charges requiring registration under this section.

(2B) The power of the Minister under subsection (2A) shall include a power to amend by regulations the description of any charge referred to in subsection (2).

(2C) Every regulation made by the Minister under this section shall be laid before each House of the Oireachtas as soon as may be after it is made and, if a resolution annulling the regulation is passed by either House within the next 21 days on which that House has sat after the regulation is laid before it, the regulation shall be annulled accordingly, but without prejudice to the validity of anything previously done thereunder.][b]

(3) In the case of a charge created out of the State comprising property situate outside the State, 21 days after the date on which the prescribed particulars could, in due course of post, and if despatched with due diligence, have been received in the State shall be

substituted for 21 days after the date of the creation of the charge as the time within which the particulars are to be delivered to the registrar.

(4) Where a charge is created in the State but comprises property outside the State, the prescribed particulars may be sent for registration under this section, notwithstanding that further proceedings may be necessary to make the charge valid or effectual according to the law of the country in which the property is situate.

(5) Where a charge comprises property situate outside the State and registration in the country where the property is situate is necessary to make the charge valid or effectual according to the law of that country, a certificate in the prescribed form stating that the charge was presented for registration in the country where the property is situate on the date on which it was so presented shall be delivered to the registrar of companies for registration.

(6) Where a negotiable instrument has been given to secure the payment of any book debts of a company, the deposit of the instrument for the purpose of securing an advance to the company shall not, for the purposes of this section, be treated as a charge on those book debts.

(7) The holding of debentures entitling the holder to a charge on land shall not, for the purposes of this section, be deemed to be an interest in land.

(8) Where a series of debentures containing, or giving by reference to any other instrument, any charge to the benefit of which the debenture holders of that series are entitled *pari passu* is created by a company, it shall, for the purposes of this section, be sufficient if there are delivered to or received by the registrar, within 21 days after the execution of the deed containing the charge, or, if there is no such deed, after the execution of any debentures of the series, the following particulars—

(a) the total amount secured by the whole series; and

(b) the dates of the resolutions authorising the issue of the series, and the date of the covering deed, if any, by which the security is created or defined; and

(c) a general description of the property charged; and

(d) the names of the trustees, if any, for the debenture holders;

so, however, that where more than one issue is made of debentures in the series, there shall be sent to the registrar for entry in the register particulars of the amount and date of each issue, but an omission to do this shall not affect the validity of the debentures issued.

(9) Where any commission, allowance or discount has been paid or made either directly or indirectly by a company to any person in consideration of his subscribing or agreeing to subscribe, whether absolutely or conditionally, for any debentures of the company, or procuring or agreeing to procure subscriptions, whether absolute or conditional, for any such debentures, the particulars required to be sent for registration under this section shall include particulars as to the amount and rate per cent of the commission, discount or allowance so paid or made, but omission to do this shall not affect the validity of the debentures issued, so, however, that the deposit of any debentures as security for any debt of the company shall not, for the purposes of this subsection, be treated as the issue of the debentures at a discount.

(10) In this Part—

(a) 'charge' includes mortgage;

(b) 'the fixed date' means, in relation to the charges specified in paragraphs (a) to (f), of subsection (2), the 1st July, 1908, and in relation to the charges specified in paragraphs (g) to (i), the operative date.

Amendments

a CA 1963, s 99(h) substituted by CA 1990, s 122.

b CA 1963, s 99(2A), (2B), (2C) inserted by CA 1990, s 122.

Definitions

'company': CA 1963, s 2(1); 'debenture': CA 1963, s 2(1); 'Minister': CA 1963, s 2(1); 'the operative date': CA 1963, s 2(1); 'prescribed': CA 1963, s 2(1); 'the Registrar of Companies': CA 1963, s 2(1); 'share': CA 1963, s 2(1).

Cross references in other enactments

NAMA Act 2009, s 218(1) provides that an acquired bank asset within the meaning of NAMA Act 2009 is 'not invalidated or rendered void or voidable as against NAMA or a NAMA group entity or their successors in title' by operation of CA 1963, s 99.

Notes[1]

Foreign companies: The registration requirements of CA 1963, s 99 apply to companies formed and registered under the CA.[2] However, foreign companies which establish a place of business in the State are also required to deliver particulars of charges created or acquired by them over Irish property.[3]

1 See, generally, Gough, *Company Charges* (2nd edn, Butterworths, 1996) chs 27–32 and Courtney, *The Law of Private Companies* (2nd edn, Tottel Publishing, 2002) chs 20 and 21.

2 CA 1963, s 2(1).

3 See CA 1963, s 111 and the notes thereto.

Mortgages and charges: For the purposes of CA 1963, s 99 the term 'charge' is deemed to include mortgages: CA 1963, s 99(10). There is, however, a technical distinction between the two concepts. A mortgage involves the transfer (or conveyance or assignment) of the legal title in the mortgaged property from the debtor to the creditor by way of security, subject to an express or implied term that the property will be transferred back to the debtor when he has fulfilled his obligations (usually the repayment of the capital and interest). A charge, on the other hand, involves an agreement between the creditor and the debtor that a particular asset or assets are to be appropriated towards the satisfaction of the debt in the event of default by the debtor.[1] A charge does not, however, involve a transfer of ownership. It follows, therefore, that since the transfer of ownership in a mortgage amounts to a right of appropriation, every mortgage is a charge but not every charge is a mortgage.[2] Accordingly, only two of the four categories of consensual security (mortgage, charge, lien and pledge)[3] require registration under CA 1963, s 99(1). A contractual lien, even if coupled with a power of sale, does not amount to a charge and is not registerable, since it is a purely possessory security and is lost if possession of the asset is lost, whereas a 'charge' strictly so defined is not dependent on possession.[4] In a similar vein, it has been held that a pledge is not registerable as a charge under s 99.[5]

1 *Re Cosslett (Contractors) Ltd [1997] 4 All ER 115; Re TXU Europe Group plc* [2004] 1 BCLC 519. A payment of moneys paid into court to abide the outcome of litigation may not involve a sufficient act of appropriation such as to give rise to a charge: *Flightline Ltd v Edwards* [2003] 1 BCLC 427.

2 *Shea v Moore* [1894] IR 158 at 163, per Walker LC.

3 *Re Cosslett (Contractors) Ltd* [1997] 4 All ER 115 (Millett LJ in the Court of Appeal).

4 *Re Hamlet International plc* [1998] 2 BCLC 164; *Waitomo Wools (NZ) Ltd v Nelsons (NZ) Ltd* [1974] 1 NZLR 484.

5 *Highland Finance (Ireland) Ltd v Sacred Heart College* [1997] 2 ILRM 87.

Creation of charge: The provisions of CA 1963, s 99 only extend to charges 'created' by a company. Accordingly, security interests arising automatically and by operation of law, such as a purchaser's lien or an unpaid vendor's lien, are not registerable.[1]

1 *London and Cheshire Insurance Co Ltd v Laplagrene Pty Co Ltd* [1971] Ch 499; *Bank of Ireland Finance Ltd v DJ Daly Ltd* [1978] IR 79; *Re Barrett Apartments Ltd* [1985] IR 350; *Lovell Construction Ltd v Independent Estates plc* [1994] 1 BCLC 31.

Date of creation: For the purpose of the running of time under CA 1963, s 99, the date of creation of the charge is the date upon which the instrument is executed[1] unconditionally, or the deposit of title deeds is made,[2] and not, in the case of a charge securing future advances or an issue of debenture stock, the date of the making of the advance or the issue of the stock, as the case may be.[3] The period within which particulars of a charge can be delivered to the Registrar of Companies (ie 'within 21 days after the date of its creation') includes the day the charge is created.[4]

1 *Sun Tai Cheung Credits Ltd v Attorney General of Hong Kong* (1987) 3 BCC 357 at 360–362.

2 *Sun Tai Cheung Credits Ltd v Attorney General of Hong Kong* (1987) 3 BCC 357 at 360–362.

3 *Dublin City Distillery v Doherty* [1914] AC 823; *Esberger and Son v Capital and Counties Bank* [1913] 2 Ch 366.

4 See IA 2005, s 18(h) of which provides 'Where a period of time is expressed to begin on *or be reckonable from a particular day*, that day shall be deemed to be included in the period and, where a period of time is expressed to end on or be reckoned to a particular day, that day shall be deemed to be included in the period'. (Emphasis added).

Instrument of charge: Although most charges will be created or evidenced in writing, the delivery of particulars will be required even if there is no instrument, as where the security comprises an equitable deposit of title deeds, unaccompanied by any written memorandum.[1]

1 *Re Molton Finance Ltd* [1968] Ch 325; *Re Wallis and Simmonds (Builders) Ltd* [1974] 1 All ER 561.

Agreement or undertaking to create charge: Equity looks on that as done which ought to have been done.[1] Thus, an agreement or undertaking by or on behalf of a company to create a charge will itself be treated as conferring an equitable security on the creditor, capable of being registered under CA 1963, s 99.[2] Thus, a solicitors' undertaking to deposit their client's title deeds as security for a loan is itself an equitable charge requiring registration.[3] The intention of the parties is of paramount importance in determining whether a charge comes into being.[4]

1 See Delany, *Equity and the Law of Trusts in Ireland* (3rd edn, Thomson Round Hall, 2003) ch 2.

2 In *Re Chargecard Services Ltd* [1986] 3 All ER 288 Millett J said: 'the essence of an equitable charge is that, without any conveyance or assignment to the chargee specific property of the chargor is expressly or constructively appropriated to or made answerable for payment of a debt and the chargee is given the right to resort to the property for the purpose of having it realised and applied in or towards payment of the debt. The availability of equitable remedies has the effect of giving the chargee a proprietary interest by way of security in the property charged'. In *Murray v Wilken* (31 July 2003, unreported) HC, Finlay Geoghegan J said she had no difficulty in accepting this as an appropriate definition of an equitable charge for the purposes of Irish law and that an undertaking given by a solicitor to hold the title deeds of a client's property for the benefit of another person had long been recognised as the creation of an equitable charge. See also *Alexander Hull and Co Ltd v O'Carroll Kent and Co Ltd* (1952) 89 ILTR 70; *Re Valley Ice Cream (Ireland) Ltd* [1998] IEHC 119 (McCracken J); *Fullerton v Provincial Bank of Ireland* [1903] 1 IR 483; *Oldham and others v Kyrris and another* [2004] BCC 111.

3 *Re Farm Fresh Frozen Foods Ltd* [1980] ILRM 131.

4 *Re TXU Europe Group plc (in administration)* [2004] 1 BCLC 519.

Present and future property: A charge of the type referred to in CA 1963, s 99(2) will be registerable regardless of whether it is in respect of present or future property of the company or both.[1]

1 *Independent Automatic Sales Ltd v Knowles and Foster* [1962] 1 WLR 974.

Particulars to be registered: It is delivery of the prescribed particulars, rather than their actual registration by the Companies Registration Office, which must take place within 21 days.[1] The actual particulars to be delivered to the Registrar are as set out in CA 1963, s 99(8) and (9)[2] and CA 1963, s 103.[3] In addition, where the charge created by the company comprises property outside the State, and registration in the foreign state is necessary to make the charge valid, a certificate in the prescribed form[4], stating that the charge has been presented for registration abroad, must also be presented to the Irish Registrar[5] and although under s 99(2A) and (2B) the Minister has power to make regulations extending the classes of charges or particulars requiring registration, no such regulations have been made as of yet.

The relevant forms[6] for the registration of particulars relating to charges are Form C1 (creation of ordinary charge), Form 47A (series of debentures), Form 47B (property acquired by company already subject to a charge),[7] Form 47C (certificate the particulars of charge over foreign property has been presented for registration abroad) and Form 8E (charge created over Irish assets by foreign company with place of business in Ireland).

1 *Slavenburg's Bank NV v Intercontinental Natural Resources Ltd* [1980] 1 All ER 955.

2 For the circumstances in which commissions, allowances and discounts of the type referred to in CA 1963, s 99(9) may be paid, see CA 1963, s 59 and the notes thereto.

3 See also Form C1 of the Companies (Forms) Orders 1964–2004.

4 Form 47C.

5 CA 1963, s 99(5). *Quaere* whether failure to register this certificate renders the charge void under Irish law.

6 See the Companies (Forms) Orders 1964–2004.

7 See CA 1963, s 101.

Extension of time for registration: The 21-day period for delivery of the prescribed particulars is extended as a matter of course for charges created out of the State in respect of foreign property.[1] As regards the extension of time for registration in other cases, see CA 1963, s 106.

1 CA 1963, s 99(3).

Consequences of non-registration: CA 1963, s 99(1) provides that failure to deliver the prescribed particulars for registration within the stipulated time limit has the effect of rendering the charge void as against any liquidator or creditor of the company.[1]

1. *Secured and execution creditors*: In the context of s 99, 'creditor' means a secured creditor or execution creditor.[2] It is only as against these classes of creditor that the charge will be invalid prior to liquidation. Indeed, the unregistered charge will be invalid as against another secured creditor even though he was aware of its existence when he obtained his own security from the company.[3]

2. *The company*: The charge is not void as against the company itself prior to liquidation. Sub-section (1) provides that the moneys secured thereby become immediately payable. Unless and until the company is wound up, the charge will remain fully enforceable as against the company,[4] and will be effective for the purpose of passing good title to a purchaser.[5] It follows therefore that to the extent that the chargee has enforced his security prior to winding up, the liquidator will not be entitled to seek recovery of the proceeds from him.[6] However, once the company goes into liquidation, the charge will be prospectively set aside.[7]

3. *Unsecured creditors*: In so far as the ordinary unsecured creditors of the company are concerned, they cannot seek to invalidate an unregistered charge prior to winding up; rather, they must await the appointment of a liquidator.[8] Moreover, even in a winding up, the only person with *locus standi* to actually challenge the charge is the liquidator himself and not individual creditors,[9] although in an action brought by the holder of the unregistered charge against a third party during the course of the liquidation, the third party will be entitled to plead the invalidity of the charge by way of defence.[10]

4. *No entitlement to lien on deeds*: If a charge is void for non-registration, the chargee is not entitled, as against a liquidator or another secured or execution creditor, to seek to rely on a lien over the deeds of the property charged, since the lien which arises by operation of law will have merged with the void charge and must therefore fall with it.[11]

1 CA 1963, s 99(1). See also *Smith (Administrator of Cosslett (Contractors) Ltd)) v Bridgend County Borough Council* [2002] 1 All ER 292. However, in the case of a charge securing an issue of debentures, failure to deliver particulars of the matters set out in s 99(9) will not invalidate the security: CA 1963, s 99(9).

2 *Re Monolithic Building Co* [1915] 1 Ch 643.

3 *Re Monolithic Building Co* [1915] 1 Ch 643; *Re Ashpurton Estates Ltd* [1983] Ch 110; *Re Interview Ltd* [1975] IR 382.

4 *Re Monolithic Building Co* [1915] 1 Ch 643; *Alexander Hull and Co Ltd v O'Carroll Kent and Co Ltd* (1955) 89 ILTR 70; *Independent Automatic Sales Ltd v Knowles and Foster* [1962] 3 All ER 27; *Bank of Scotland v TA Neilson and Co* 1991 SLT 8.

5 *Re Overseas Aviation Engineering (GB) Ltd* [1963] Ch 24 at 38.

6 *Mercantile Bank of India Ltd v Chartered Bank of India and China, and Strauss and Co Ltd* [1937] 1 All ER 231; *Saunderson and Co v Clark* (1913) 29 TLR 579 at 580; *Re Row Dal Constructions Pty Ltd* [1966] VR 249; *Re J and D Contracting Pty Ltd* [1970] QWN 40; *NV Slavenburg's Bank v Intercontinental Natural Resources Ltd* [1980] 1 All ER 955 at 968; *Re Alton Corporation* [1985] BCLC 27 at 31; *Mace Builders (Glasgow) Ltd v Lunn* [1987] Ch 191.

7 *Smith (Administrator of Cosslett (Contractors) Ltd v Bridgend County Borough Council* [2002] 1 All ER 292.

8 *Re Row Dal Constructions Pty Ltd* [1966] VR 249.

9 *Re Ayala Holdings Ltd* [1993] BCLC 256 at 261. Individual creditors may, however, be entitled to apply to the court for directions under CA 1963, s 231 or s 280, requiring the liquidator to make such a challenge.

10 *Orion Finance Ltd v Crown Financial Management Ltd* [1994] 2 BCLC 607.

11 *Re Molton Finance Ltd* [1968] Ch 325.

Classes of registerable charges[1]

Charge for the purpose of securing any issue of debentures: The wording of CA 1963, s 99(2)(a) is potentially all embracing but has been interpreted as referring to a charge which secures a series of debenture stock as opposed to a single debenture.[2]

Charge on uncalled share capital: This refers to the creation of a charge on the uncalled capital of the company itself and contrasts with the position of companies limited by guarantee which are not entitled to mortgage or charge the guarantee fund.[3] A charge on uncalled capital does not affect the power of the directors under the articles to forfeit shares for non-payment of calls.[4] A serious gap in the legislation is to be found in the fact that a fixed charge on shares in the company's subsidiary is not registerable, even though the real worth of the group may lie in the subsidiary rather than in the parent company.[5]

Charges created or evidenced by an instrument which, if executed by an individual, would require registration as a bill of sale: This sub-section only extends to transactions securing the repayment of money which, if executed by an individual, would require registration under the Bills of Sale (Ireland) Acts 1879–1883.[6] A genuine sale, leasing or hire-purchase transaction is not registerable under CA 1963, s 99(2)(c).[7] However, even if the transaction is described as a sale, it will require registration under s 99(2)(c) if it is actually intended by the parties to act as a security and it is in substance a charge.[8]

A charge of the type referred to in s 99(2)(c) which is created by a company need only be registered in the Companies Registration Office, and does not need to be registered under the Bills of Sale Acts as well.[9] The charge must be in respect of 'personal chattels' which are defined in the 1878 Act as not including, *inter alia*, shares or choses in action.[10] Similarly, a charge over a 'ship or vessel' is not such as would require registration as a bill of sale, if executed by an individual;[11] for a charge on a ship created by a company, see CA 1963, s 99(2)(h).

CA 1963, s 99(2)(c) makes it clear that the registration requirement only arises where the charge is created or evidenced by an instrument. Thus, a pledge of goods completed by delivery of possession of the goods or of the documents of title[12] to the pledgee is not registerable,[13] even if the goods or documents are then returned to the company against a trust receipt.[14] On the other hand, whilst a written agreement to pledge, without delivery either of the goods themselves or of the documents of title, is registerable under the Bills of Sale Act if created by an individual, it will not be registerable under s 99(2)(c) for to be registerable under this head, it must constitute a 'charge'.[15] As with a pledge, a purely possessory lien, such as a solicitor's lien, will be exempt from registration.[16] In the case of a contractual lien coupled with a power of sale, even though it is created by an instrument, it will not require registration for the simple reason that it does not amount to a mortgage or charge.[17]

Charge on land wherever situate, or any interest therein, but not including a charge for any rent or other periodical sum issuing out of land: An agreement or undertaking to create a mortgage or charge over land is itself an equitable charge on land requiring registration under CA 1963, s 99(2)(d).[18] However, a contract between a company, a lender and a third party, whereby the third party is to buy from the company certain property (over which the lender already has a charge) in the event of default by the company on the loan, is not a charge on land within the meaning of s 99(2)(d).[19] Nor is a fixed charge over the future proceeds of sale of land deemed to be registerable whether as a charge on land or as a charge on an interest in land or as a charge on a book debt.[20] There is no inconsistency between the existence of a fixed charge and a contractual right on the part of the chargor-company to require the chargee to release property from the charge and the existence of such a contractual right does not render the charge a floating charge.[21] Apart from requiring registration under s 99, to secure priority against others, charges on land situated in Ireland will need to be registered in the Registry of Deeds or Land Registry, as the case may be.[22] Furthermore, in so far as the land is situate abroad, registration may be required under the *lex situs*.[23]

Charge on book debts of the company: This type of charge may encompass present or future book debts or both.[24] 'Book debts' mean 'all such debts accruing in the ordinary course of business as would usually be entered in well kept trade books', although to constitute a book debt it is not necessary that the debt should have been actually entered in a book.[25] A bank balance is not a book debt.[26] Nor are the following to be regarded as book debts: bank deposit investments;[27] the future proceeds of sale of a company's lands;[28] a contractual right of retention conferred on a bank in respect of credit balances maintained by a customer with that bank;[29] moneys held by an agent or other fiduciary in trust for his principal;[30] moneys held in escrow pending completion of work under a contract;[31] moneys due by way of refund of insurance premiums;[32] an absolute assignment of book debts under a 'block discounting' agreement;[33] a deposit of a negotiable instrument for the purpose of securing an advance to the company, in circumstances where the negotiable instrument was given to secure payment of any book debts of the company;[34] an agreement to hold on trust moneys received in breach of the terms of a subordination arrangement.[35] On the other hand, the following have all been held to be examples of registerable charges on book debts: a contractual lien on sub-freights created by a company under a time charter in favour of the shipowner;[36] a charge on debts due in respect of cheques, bills of exchange, promissory notes and credit card transactions arising out of sales of stock;[37] a letter of hypothetication;[38] a charge on instalment payments under leases, hire-purchase contracts etc;[39] an 'assignment' to a head lessor of rentals due under a sub-lease as security for the head rent;[40] a charge on progress payments and/or completion payments under construction contracts or contracts for work and materials;[41] a charge on the proceeds of litigation seeking damages for breach of a contract which had been entered into by the company in the ordinary course of its business.[42]

Although a charge on a book debt inevitably carries with it a charge over its proceeds, the converse, namely that a charge over proceeds inevitably arose out of a charge over a debt, does not necessarily hold good.[43]

1 See Courtney, *The Law of Private Companies* (2nd edn, Tottel Publishing, 2002) paras 21.033 to 21.056.

2 *Automatic Association (Canterbury) Inc v Australasian Secured Deposits Ltd* [1973] 1 NZLR 417.

3 *Re Mayfair Property Co Ltd* [1898] 2 Ch 28; *Re Irish Club* [1906] WN 127; *Re Industrial and Agricultural Fair Cork 1932* (1933) 67 ILTR 175.

4 *Re Agency Land and Finance Co of Australia* (1903) 20 TLR 41.

5 This gap has been noted by several commentators. See Fitzgerald, (1968) Ir Jur (ns) 258; McCormack, (1984) ILT 67; Ussher, *Company Law in Ireland* (Sweet & Maxwell, 1986) at p 457. See also *Re Arthur D Little Ltd* [2002] 2 BCLC 799.

6 *Stoneleigh Finance Ltd v Phillips* [1965] 2 QB 537; *Re Castlemahon Poultry Products Ltd* (3 May 1985, unreported) HC (Barrington J).

7 *Manchester Rly Co v North Wagon Co* (1888) 13 App Cas 554.

8 *Welsh Development Agency v Export Finance Co Ltd* [1992] BCLC 148; *Re Curtain Dream plc* [1990] BCLC 925.

9 *Re Royal Marine Hotel, Kingston Ltd* [1895] IR 368; *Re Standard Manufacturing Co* [1891] 1 Ch 627. Indeed, the Bills of Sale Act 1883, s 17 expressly states that nothing in the Act regarding registration etc is to be treated as applying to companies.

10 Bills of Sale (Ireland) Act 1879, s 4.

11 See Bills of Sale (Ireland) Act 1879, s 4 and *Barber v Burke; Re South Coast Boatyard Ltd* [1980] ILRM 186.

12 *Dublin City Distillery v Doherty* [1914] AC 823 at 843; *Wrightson v McArthur and Hutchinsons (1919) Ltd* [1921] 2 KB 807.

13 *Highland Finance (Ireland) Ltd v Sacred Heart College* [1997] 2 ILRM 87.

14 *Re David Allester Ltd* [1922] 2 Ch 211.

15 *Dublin City Distillery Ltd v Doherty* [1914] AC 823.

16 *George Barker (Transport) Ltd v Eynon* [1974] 1 All ER 900.

17 *Re Hamlet International plc* [1998] 2 BCLC 164; *Waitomo Wools (NZ) Ltd v Nelsons (NZ) Ltd* [1974] 1 NZLR 484.

18 *Re Valley Ice Cream (Ireland) Ltd* [1998] IEHC 119 (McCracken J); *Fullerton v Provincial Bank of Ireland* [1903] 1 IR 483.

19 *Nunan v Group 4 Securities (International) Ltd BV* (1963–1993) Irish Company Law Reports 216.

20 *Re Kum Tong Restaurant (Dublin) Ltd; Byrne v Allied Irish Banks Ltd* [1978] IR 446; *Anglo Irish Bank Corporation plc v Edward Kavanagh* [2003] IEHC 113.

21 *Queen's Moat Houses plc v Capita IRG Trustees Ltd* [2005] BCC 347 (Lightman J).

22 For a general overview of the registration requirement for charges on land, see Wylie, *Irish Land Law* (3rd edn, Tottel Publishing, 1997) chs 12, 13, 21 and 22. A floating charge over registered land cannot be registered as a burden but may be registered as a caution. Upon crystallization, however, the charge (which has thus become a fixed charge) may indeed be registered as a burden: *Re Mono Food Equipment Ltd* (21 May 1996, unreported) HC (Flood J).

23 See CA 1963, s 99(4) and (5) and Binchy, *Irish Conflicts of Law* (Tottel Publishing, 1988), ch 20.

24 *Independent Automatic Sales Ltd v Knowles and Foster* [1962] 3 All ER 27; *Holroyd v Marshall* (1862) 10 HLC 191; *White v Anderson* (1850) 1 Ir Ch 419; *Creed v Carey* (1857) 7 Ir Ch 295; *Galavin v Dunne* (1881–82) 7 LR Ir 144.

25 *Paul and Frank Ltd v Discount Bank (Overseas) Ltd* [1966] 2 All ER 922; *Re Kent and Sussex Sawmills Ltd* [1947] Ch 177; *Re Brian Tucker Ltd; Farrell v Equity Bank Ltd* [1990] 2 IR 549; *Jackson v Lombard and Ulster Banking Ltd* [1992] 1 IR 94.

26 *Re Brightlife Ltd* [1987] 2 WLR 197; *Re Permanent Houses (Holdings) Ltd* [1988] BCLC 563; *Re SSSL Realisations (2002) Ltd* [2005] 1 BCLC 1; *Northern Bank Ltd v Ross* [1990] NI 53, [1991] BCLC 504; and per Walsh J in *Re Keenan Bros Ltd* [1985] ILRM 641, 644; *Dempsey v Bank of Ireland* (1963–1993) Irish Company Law Reports 207; *Perrins v State Bank of Victoria* [1991] 1 VR 749 at 754.

27 *Perrins v State Bank of Victoria* [1991] 1 VR 749.

28 *Re Kum Tong Restaurant (Dublin) Ltd; Byrne v Allied Irish Banks Ltd* [1978] IR 446; *Anglo Irish Bank Corporation plc v Edward Kavanagh* [2003] IEHC 113.

29 *Re Charge Card Services Ltd* [1987] Ch 150 at 173–175. The right of retention was used in the past because Millett J expressed the view in *Re Charge Card Services Ltd* [1986] 3 All ER 288 (echoed by Murphy J in *Re Euro Travel Ltd; Dempsey v Bank of Ireland* [1963–93] Irish Company Law Reports 207) that it would be conceptually impossible for a bank to take a charge over a credit balance held in an account with that bank since the credit balance amounted to a debt due by the bank to the customer. More recently, however, in *Re BCCI (No 8)* [1997] 4 All ER 568 Lord Hoffmann has expressed the view that the creation of such a charge is in fact possible.

30 *Re Law Car and General Insurance Corporation Ltd* [1911] WN 91.

31 *Lovell Construction Ltd v Independent Estates Ltd* [1994] 1 BCLC 31.

32 *Re Brian Tucker Ltd* [1990] 2 IR 549; *Jackson v Lombard and Ulster Banking Ltd* [1992] 1 IR 94; *Perrins v State Bank of Victoria* [1991] 1 VR 749.

33 *Lloyds and Scottish Finance Ltd v Cyril Lord Carpet Sales Ltd* [1992] BCLC 609.

34 CA 1963, s 99(6).

35 *Re SSSL Realisations (2002) Ltd* [2005] 1 BCLC 1.

36 *Re Welsh Irish Ferries Ltd* [1985] BCLC 327.

37 *Northern Bank Ltd v Ross* [1990] NI 53; *Re Charge Card Services Ltd* [1987] Ch 150; *Dawson v Isle* [1906] 1 Ch 633; *Siebe Gorman and Co Ltd v Barclays Bank Ltd* [1979] 2 Lloyd's Rep 142; *Chase Manhattan Asia Ltd v Official Receiver and Liquidator of First Bangkok City Finance Ltd* [1990] BCC 514.

38 *Ladenburg and Co v Goodwin Ferreira Co Ltd and Garnett* [1912] KB 275.

39 *Re Ind Cooper and Co Ltd* [1911] 2 Ch 223; *Independent Automatic sales Ltd v Knowles and Foster* [1962] 3 All ER 27.

40 *Orion Finance Ltd v Crown Financial Management Ltd* [1996] 1 BCLC 78.

41 *Re Row Dal Constructions Pty Ltd* [1966] VR 249; *Contemporary Cottages (NZ) Ltd v Margin Traders Ltd* [1981] 2 NZLR 114.

42 *Re National Westminster Finance Australia Ltd* [1991] QdR 130; *Perrins v State Bank of Victoria* [1991] VR 749.

43 *Re SSSL Realisations (2002) Ltd* [2007] 1 BCLC 29.

Fixed charge on book debts:[1] A charge over book debts will be regarded as a fixed charge provided the terms of the charge restrict the freedom of the company to deal with such debts in the ordinary course of business.[2] Where under the terms of a charge a company is permitted to collect book debts but required to pay them into a specified bank account, the categorisation of that charge will depend upon what, if any, restrictions there are on the use the company can make of the credit to the account as reflected by each payment in.[3]

The restriction on the freedom to deal with the debts in the ordinary course of business, which must be *de jure* rather than *de facto*,[4] may involve (a) prohibiting the company from assigning or further charging the book debts without the consent of the debentureholder; and (b) requiring the proceeds of such debts be placed either in a special receivables account or in the company's ordinary trading account, and upon terms that no withdrawal of the proceeds may be made without the consent of the debentureholder.[5] Indeed, the charge will even be regarded as a fixed charge where the debentureholder is entitled to designate an account into which the proceeds of book debts are to be paid, but has not ever done so, provided that the debenture restricts the company's ability to use the moneys in the ordinary course of business in the event of a designation of such an account actually taking place.[6]

Whether a particular charge is a fixed or a floating charge is a matter or substance, not of form. [7]

An assignment to a third party of the benefit of a fixed charge over book debts does not have the effect of converting the charge into a floating charge, but simply has the effect of requiring the consent of the transferee, rather than the original debentureholder, in order for the company to be able to use the book debts in the course of its business. [8]

A fixed charge on a book debt extends not only to the debt while it is outstanding, but also, by implication, to the proceeds of the debt once collected by or on behalf of the company, [9] but a stand alone charge on the proceeds of a book debt has been held not to be a book debt. [10]

One of the primary reasons for a financial institution to take a fixed rather than a floating charge over book debts is to avoid preferential creditors gaining priority under CA 1963, s 98 or s 285 in the case of a receivership of liquidation, as the case may be. However, the advantage of a fixed charge on book debts in such circumstances has been significantly eroded by TCA 1997, s 1001, which in certain circumstances[11] allows the Revenue Commissioners to serve a notice on the debentureholder, advising of various taxes which are owing by the company and (subject to certain limitations) requiring the debentureholder to pay to the Revenue any proceeds received by it pursuant to the fixed charge.

A floating charge on the undertaking or property of the company:[12] A floating charge is a charge over a company's present or future property or both, which hovers or floats over the property which it is intended to affect until some event occurs or act is done which causes it to 'crystallise' and attach to the property, thereby becoming a fixed charge.[13] In determining whether a charge is fixed or floating, the court will look at the substance of the transaction rather than at the description given to it by the parties.[14] The essential characteristic of a floating charge is that pending crystallisation the company is free to deal with and dispose of the property the subject matter of the charge in the ordinary course of business.[15] The words 'ordinary course of business' are to be given their ordinary meaning in English and a transaction can be in the ordinary course of business even it is was exceptional or unprecedented.[16]

An entitlement to call upon the chargee to release a property from a 'fixed charge' provided that the value of the remaining property caught by the charge is not less than 175% of the value of the chargee's outstanding indebtedness to the chargor, does not have the effect of rendering the charge a floating charge.[17]

Although the charge 'floats' until crystallisation, it is nonetheless a present rather than a future security over the assets expressed to be included in it.[18] Accordingly, where shares in another company were expressed to be included in the charge, and the chargee granted an option to buy the shares which had not been exercised by the date of crystallisation, it was held that the shares remained subject to the security and were assigned in equity to the debentureholder upon crystallisation.[19]

Since it is an essential characteristic of a floating charge that the company is free to deal with and dispose of its assets in the ordinary course of business until crystallisation, it follows that a sale of all or some of those assets will result in them no longer being subject to the charge.[20] Similarly, unless the debenture provides to the contrary, the company will be free, pending crystallisation, to create other charges on the assets (eg fixed charges or mortgages) ranking in priority to the floating charge,[21] even though the floating charge is described as a first charge on the assets and undertaking.[22] In an attempt to protect his position, the debentureholder will typically include a clause in the charge, known as a 'negative pledge clause', prohibiting the company from creating any other security ranking in priority to or *pari passu* with the floating charge. Such clauses are not, per se, anti-competitive.[23] However, whilst such a clause undoubtedly binds the company, the holder of a fixed charge which has been created by the company in breach of the negative pledge clause, will only be prevented from taking priority over the floating charge if he had actual or express notice, as opposed to constructive notice, of the prohibition which had been placed upon the company, and the holder of the fixed charge will not be deemed to have actual notice of the negative pledge clause simply because such clauses are 'more or less common form in modern debentures' – such notice is constructive only. [24] 'Although creating no more than a negative contractual right, a restrictive clause can affect the quality of, and therefore bind, a subsequent proprietary interest through actual knowledge of the restriction. In equity it would be unconscionable to permit a subsequent third party to take his interest free of the restrictive right in spite of his actual knowledge that to do so would constitute a breach of a floating charge contract by the (sic) charger'. [25]

Furthermore, save in the case of a negative pledge clause contained in a floating charge in favour of the Central Bank and Financial Services Authority of Ireland (see s 103(1)(b)(iiia)) since a negative pledge clause is not one of the prescribed particulars under CA 1963, ss 99 and 103, voluntary registration of the clause will not automatically fix other parties with binding notice of its existence of contents. Rather, a third party will only be bound if he has inspected and read the particulars, which include the negative pledge clause, before he takes his own security.[26] Furthermore, the existence of a negative pledge clause will not preclude an examiner appointed under C(A)A 1990 from exercising any borrowing powers granted to him by the court, and using the floating charge assets as security for those borrowings.[27]

When the charge crystallises, the debentureholder takes subject to any pre-existing equities. Thus, for example, a solicitor's lien[28] or a registered judgment mortgage[29] will take priority over the crystallised floating charge. With regard to execution creditors, they too will take priority over a floating charge provided execution is complete before crystallisation. In the case of a garnishee application, execution is completed not by the making of the garnishee order but by payment being made by the garnishee,[30] and in the case of an order of *fieri facias*, the execution creditor will only have priority to the extent that the assets have been sold by the sheriff prior to crystallisation of the charge.[31] Similarly, the charge will be subject to any pre-existing right of set-off as between the company and a third party.[32] On the other hand, if the cross-claim against the company only arises after crystallisation, set-off cannot normally be claimed since there will have been an intervening equitable assignment of the assets to the debentureholder.[33]

With regard to the events causing crystallisation, it is well established that a floating charge will crystallise automatically (a) upon the appointment of a receiver; (b) if the debentureholder goes into possession; or (c) if the company is wound up.[34] Older authority suggests that in the absence of an express provision to the contrary, crystallisation will not occur merely because the company ceases trading.[35] However, more recent authorities take a contrary view[36] and indeed the very fact of the company selling its business may cause the charge to crystallise.[37] The parties to the floating charge are also free to stipulate whatever other events they wish as causing the charge to crystallise.[38] Until recently, it was generally considered that a floating charge, having crystallised, could not subsequently de-crystallise. It has, however, been held that where the charge crystallises upon the appointment of a receiver, and an examiner is then appointed, de-crystallisation will occur.[39] Whether de-crystallisation can occur in other circumstances, remains to be seen.

A charge on calls made but not paid: Such a charge is to be distinguished from a charge of the type of charge referred to in CA 1963, s 99(2)(b), ie a charge on uncalled capital.

A charge on a ship or aircraft or any share in a ship or aircraft: A three tonne yacht has been held to not be a 'ship' for the purposes of CA 1963, s 9.[40] A legal charge on a ship or any share in a ship may also have to be registered under s 50 of the Mercantile Marine Act 1955. In the case of aircraft, charges must be registered under the Air Navigation and Transport (Nationality and Registration of Aircraft) Orders 1963–1984.

A charge on goodwill, on a patent or a licence under a patent, on a trade mark or on a copyright or a licence under a copyright: A charge on a patent or trade mark must also be registered in the Patents Office pursuant to the Patents Acts 1992 and the Trade Marks Act 1996.[41]

1 In relation to fixed charges on book debts generally, see Pearce, 'Fixed Charges Over Book Debts' [1987] JBL 18 and McCormack, 'Fixed Charges on Future Book Debts' (1987) 8 Company Lawyer 3.

2 *Re Lakeglen Construction Ltd* [1980] IR 347; *Siebe Gorman and Co Ltd v Barclays Bank Ltd* [1979] 2 Lloyd's Rep 142; *Re Keenan Bros Ltd* [1985] IR 401; *Re AH Masser Ltd; McCann and Long v Revenue Commissioners* [1978–1987] 3 ITR 706; *Re Wogan's (Drogheda) Ltd* [1993] 1 IR 157; *Re Holidair Ltd* [1994] 1 IR 416; *Re Atlantic Computer Systems plc* [1991] BCLC 606; *Re Atlantic Medical Ltd* [1993] BCLC 386; *Chalk v Kahn* [2000] 2 BCLC 361.

3 *National Westminster Bank plc v Spectrum Plus Ltd et al* [2005] 2 BCLC 269; *Agnew v IRC* [2001] 2 AC 710; *Re Beam Tube Products Ltd* [2007] 2 BCLC 732.

4 *Re Double S Printers Ltd* [1999] BCC 303.

5 *Re Lakeglen Construction Ltd* [1980] IR 347; *Siebe Gorman and Co Ltd v Barclays Bank Ltd* [1979] 2 Lloyd's Rep 142; *Re Keenan Bros Ltd* [1985] IR 401; *Re AH Masser Ltd; McCann and Long v Revenue Commissioners* [1978–1987] 3 ITR 706; *Re Wogan's (Drogheda) Ltd* [1993] 1 IR 157; *Re Holidair Ltd* [1994] 1 IR 416. If the terms of the debenture are such that the receivables are simply to be paid into the company's ordinary trading account with no restriction on their use or application thereafter, the charge will be treated as a floating charge: *Chalk v Kahn* [2000] 2 BCLC 361.

6 *Re Wogans (Drogheda) Ltd* [1993] 1 IR 157. Cf *Re New Bullas Trading Ltd* [1994] 1 BCLC 485; *Re ASRS Establishment Ltd* [2000] 1 BCLC 727; *National Westminster Bank plc v Spectrum Plus Ltd et al* [2005] 2 BCLC 269; *Agnew v IRC* [2001] 2 AC 710; *Re Beam Tube Products Ltd* [2007] 2 BCLC 732. In *Re Holidair Ltd* [1994] 1 IR 416 the debenture empowered the chargee to nominate an account into which the proceeds of the book debts were to be lodged. No such nomination had ever taken place. Unlike the charge in *Re Wogan's (Drogheda) Ltd*, the debenture did not place any limitations on the use of the moneys in the ordinary course of the company's business in the event of the nomination of such a account taking place. Accordingly the debenture was held to create a floating rather than a fixed charge.

7 *Re Keenan Bros Ltd* [1985] IR 401. See also *National Westminster Bank plc v Spectrum Plus Ltd et al* [2005] 2 BCLC 269 where the House of Lords approved of the substance over form approach taken by McCarthy J in the *Keenan Bros Ltd* case. See Breslin and Smith, 'The House of Lords decision in *Spectrum Plus* – the Implications for Irish Banking Law', (2005) CLP 228.

8 *William Gaskell Group Ltd v Highley* [1994] 1 BCLC 197.

9 *Royal Trust Bank v National Westminster Bank plc* [1996] 2 BCLC 682; *Re Brumark Investments Ltd* [2001] 2 BCLC 188.

10 *Re SSSL Realisations (2002) Ltd* [2007] 1 BCLC 29.

11 See Courtney, *The Law of Private Companies* (2nd edn, Tottel Publishing, 2002) paras 20.054 to 20.059.

12 On the nature and characteristics of floating charges generally, see Courtney, *The Law of Private Companies* (2nd edn, Tottel Publishing, 2002) paras 20.063 to 20.096.

13 *Re Yorkshire Woolcombers' Association Ltd* [1903] 2 Ch 284 at 295; *Illingworth v Houldsworth* [1904] AC 333 at 358; *Tempany v Hynes* [1976] IR 101; *Welch v Bowmaker (Ireland) Ltd* [1980] IR 251 at 258; *Re GE Turnbridge Ltd* [1995] 1 BCLC 34; *Re Cimex Tissues Ltd* [1995] 1 BCLC 409; *Re BHT (UK) Ltd* [2004] BCC 301. A letter of indemnity is not a floating charge: *Dempsey v Bank of Ireland* (1963–1993) Irish Company Law Reports 207.

14 *Re Armagh Shoes Ltd* [1982] NI 59; *Re Lakeglen Construction Ltd; Kelly v Mahon Ltd* [1980] IR 347; *Re Keenan Bros Ltd* [1985] IR 401; *Re AH Masser Ltd* [1978–87] 3 ITR 706; *Re Wogan's (Drogheda) Ltd* [1993] 1 IR 157; *Re Holidair Ltd* [1994] 1 IR 416; *Re GE Tunbridge Ltd* [1995] 1 BCLC 34; *Re Cimex Tissues Ltd* [1995] 1 BCLC 409.

15 *Re Old Bushmills Distillery Co, ex parte Brett* [1897] 1 IR 488; *Re Lakeglen Construction Ltd; Kelly v Mahon Ltd* [1980] IR 347 at 353; *Welch v Bowmaker (Ireland) Ltd* [1980] IR 251 at 258;

Re Keenan Bros Ltd [1985] IR 401; *Re AH Masser Ltd* [1978–87] 3 ITR 706; *Re Wogan's (Drogheda) Ltd* [1993] 1 IR 157; *Re Holidair Ltd* [1994] 1 IR 416; *Re GE Tunbridge Ltd* [1995] 1 BCLC 34; *Re Cimex Tissues Ltd* [1995] 1 BCLC 409; *Smith (Administrator of Cosslett (Contractors) Ltd v Bridgend County Borough Council* [2002] 1 ALL ER 292; *Re Arthur D Little Ltd* [2002] 2 BCLC 799; *National Westminster Bank plc v Spectrum Plus Ltd et al* [2005] 2 BCLC 269; *Agnew v IRC* [2001] 2 AC 710; *Russell-Cooke Trust Co Ltd v Elliott* [2007] 2 BCLC 637; *Re Beam Tube Products Ltd* [2007] 2 BCLC 732.

16 *Ashborder BV and others v Green Gas Power Ltd and others* [2005] 1 BCLC 623.

17 *Queen's Moat Houses plc v Capita IRG Trustees Ltd* [2005] 2 BCLC 199.

18 *Evans v Rival Granite Quarries Ltd* [1910] 2 KB 979 at 999; *Re Tullow Engineering (Holdings) Ltd* [1990] 1 IR 452 at 458. Cf *Smith (Administrator of Cosslett (Contractors)) Ltd) v Bridgend County Borough Council* [2002] 1 ALL ER 292 where the House of Lords expressed the view that some types of floating charge (such as those stated to come into being on the occurrence of an uncertain future event) could operate as future rather than present charges (albeit still requiring registration upon creation). However, irrespective of whether the charge is regarded as a present or a future security, the chargee has no proprietary interest in the assets in question unless and until crystallization occurs: *Smith (Administrator of Cosslett (Contractors) Ltd) v Bridgend County Borough Council* [2002] 1 ALL ER 292.

19 *Re Tullow Engineering (Holdings) Ltd* [1990] 1 IR 452.

20 *Re Florence Land and Public Works Co, ex parte Moor* (1878) 10 Ch D 530 at 540 and 547; *Moor v Anglo-Italian Bank* (1879) 10 Ch D 681 at 687; *Re Hamilton's Windsor Ironworks Co, ex parte Pitman and Edwards* (1879) 12 Ch D 707 at 710, 712 and 714; *Biggerstaff v Rowatt's Wharf* [1896] 2 Ch 93; *Evans v Rival Granite Quarries Ltd* [1910] 2 KB 979 at 999. If a company sells an asset and is paid for it, so that it holds as a bare trustee for the purchaser, the asset will not be caught by the floating charge, even if crystallisation occurs before the purchaser's legal title has been perfected: *Sharpn v Woolwich Building Society* [1998] BCC 115.

21 *Re Hamilton's Windsor Ironworks Co, ex parte Pitman and Edwards* (1879) 12 Ch D 707; *Moor v Anglo-Italian Bank* (1879) 10 Ch D 681.

22 *Wheatley v Silkstone and Haigh Moor Coal Co* (1885) 29 Ch D 715; *Cos Moore v Peruvian Corporation* [1908] 1 Ch 604.

23 *Oakdale (Richmond) Ltd v National Westminster Bank plc* [1997] 1 BCLC 63.

24 *Welch v Bowmaker (Ireland) Ltd* [1980] IR 251 at 256.

25 *In re Salthill Properties Ltd* [2006] IESC 35 McCracken J cited this passage from Gough, *Company Charges* (2nd edn, Butterworths, 1996) at p 228 with approval.

26 *Welch v Bowmaker (Ireland) Ltd* [1980] IR 251 at 256.

27 *Re Holidair Ltd* [1994] 1 IR 416.

28 *Brunton v Electrical Engineering Corporation* [1892] 1 Ch 434.

29 *Tempany v Hynes* [1976] IR 101.

30 *Geisse v Taylor* [1905] 2 KB 658; *Norton v Yates* [1906] 1 KB 112; *Cairney v Back* [1906] 2 KB 746.

31 *Re Standard Manufacturing Co* [1891] 1 Ch 627; *Taunton v Sheriff of Warwickshire* [1895] 1 Ch 734, on appeal [1895] 2 Ch 319.

32 *Re Russell Murphy* [1976] IR 15; *Rother Iron Works Ltd v Canterbury Precision Engineers Ltd* [1974] QB 1.

33 *NW Robbie and Co Ltd v Witney Warehouse Co Ltd* [1963] 3 All ER 613; *Business Computers Ltd v Anglo-African Leasing Ltd* [1977] 2 All ER 741.

34 *Halpin v Cremin* [1954] IR 19; *Re Panama, New Zealand and Australian Royal Mail Co* (1870) 10 Ch D 530; *Nelson and Co v Faber and Co* [1903] 2 KB 367; *Evans v Rival Granite Quarries Ltd* [1910] 2 KB 979; *NW Robbie and Co v Witney Warehouse Co* [1963] 3 All ER 316.

35 *Halpin v Cremin* [1954] IR 19.

36 *Re Woodroffes (Musical Instruments) Ltd* [1986] 1 Ch 366; *Re The Real Meat Co Ltd* [1996] BCC 254.

37 *Re The Real Meat Co Ltd* [1996] BCC 254.

38 *Re Brightlife Ltd* [1987] 2 WLR 197; *Re Permanent Houses (Holdings) Ltd* [1988] BCLC 563; *Stein v Saywell* (1969) 121 529; *Re Manurewa Transport Ltd* [1971] NZLR 909. cf *R v Consolidated Churchill Copper Corporation Ltd* [1978] 5 WWR 652.

39 *Re Holidair Ltd* [1994] 1 ILRM 481. See also the notes to C(A)A 1990, s 5.

40 *Re South Coast Boatyard Ltd; Barber v Bourke* [1980] ILRM 186. See, however, CA 1963, s 13(2) of the Jurisdiction of Courts (Maritime Conventions) Act 1989, which defines a 'ship' as including 'every description of vessel used in navigation'. In the context of that Act a dredger has been held to constitute a 'ship': *Targe Towing Ltd v The Owners and all persons claiming an interest in the vessel 'Von Rocks'* [1998] 1 ILRM 481.

41 See generally Hackett, 'Taking Security Over Intellectual Property Rights in Ireland' (1994) CLP 50.

Retention of title clauses:[1] The parties to a contract of sale of goods may agree that title will not pass until all the agreed conditions have been fulfilled.[2] Such clauses are known as 'retention of title' or 'reservation of title' clauses. A question that arises in practice is whether such clauses are, in substance, charges of the type referred to in CA 1963, s 99(2)(c), so as to require registration.

1. *Simple clause*: If the clause reserves legal title to the goods in their unaltered form pending payment of the price (a 'simple clause'), it will not be regarded as a charge or bill of sale and will therefore not require registration.[3] However, if the clause merely purports to retain 'equitable and beneficial' title to the goods, it will be regarded as a charge and will require to be registered.[4]

2. *Current account clause*: Another valid and non-registerable clause is the 'current account clause' or 'all moneys clause', pursuant to which the vendor reserves legal title to the goods in their unaltered form until the purchaser has not only paid the contract price but has also fully discharged all other accrued debts which are due to the vendor.[5] Clear words, however, must be used to create an 'all-moneys' clause rather than a simple clause.[6]

3. *Aggregation clause*: A retention of title clause which purports to claim title to goods after the original identity of the goods has been lost (eg through being used in a manufacturing process) or which purports to claim title to any products into which the goods have been incorporated or with which the goods have been made ('an aggregation clause'), constitutes a bill of sale or charge requiring registration under CA 1963, s 99(2)(c).[7] Similarly, where goods have become fixtures to real property, the original title of the seller will be deemed to have passed to the buyer so that any clause purporting to 'retain' title pending payment of the price will constitute a registerable charge.[8] However, if even after intermingling, the goods are still identifiable and can be removed from the manufactured product without causing damage either to the goods themselves or to the remainder of the manufactured product, the retention of clause may be valid as such and may not require registration as a charge.[9]

Proceeds of sale clause: In some cases[10] it has been held that a clause which purports to retain the proceeds of a sub-sale of goods until the purchase price has been paid, will be not be regarded as a registerable charge provided that it satisfies all or some of the following criteria:

(a) it expressly creates a fiduciary relationship between the seller and the buyer;

(b) it stipulates that in any sub-sale the buyer is to be regarded as acting for and on behalf of the seller;[11]

(c) it imposes a duty on the buyer to keep the proceeds of any sub-sale separate from the buyer's other moneys; and

(d) it requires the buyer to account for such proceeds to the seller.

Most recent cases[12] have, however, leaned against the view that a clause in the above terms in fact constitutes a true retention of title. The point is made that in a sub-sale the price payable will in all probability be greater that the price payable on the original sale. Thus, even if the proceeds of the sub-sale were to be kept in a separate account on an alleged 'trust', the reality is that the original buyer would not be obliged to account to the vendor for the full amount of the proceeds of the sub-sale but rather would only be bound to account to the vendor for the amount of the original price.

Such a situation, in the view of the certain judges, has all the characteristics of a charge, so as to give rise to a registration obligation under CA 1963, s 99.

1 In relation to retention of title clauses generally, see Courtney, *The Law of Private Companies* (2nd edn, Tottel Publishing, 2002) paras 21.058 to 21.071; Pearce, 'Reservation of Title on the Sale of Goods in Ireland' (1985) 20 Ir Jur (ns) 264; Goode, *Proprietary Rights and Insolvency in Sales Transactions* (2nd edn, Sweet and Maxwell, 1989); McCormack, *Reservation of Title* (Sweet & Maxwell, 1990); *Debt Collection: (2) Retention of Title*, Law Reform Commission 28–1989.

2 Sale of Goods Act 1893, ss 17 and 19.

3 *Bateman v King* (1868) IR 2 CL 166; *Sugar Distributors Ltd v Monaghan Cash and Carry Ltd* [1982] ILRM 399; *Frigoscandia (Contracting) Ltd v Continental Irish Meat Ltd* [1982] ILRM 396; *Re Galway Concrete Ltd* [1983] ILRM 402; *Somers v James Allen (Ireland) Ltd* [1984] ILRM 437; *Clough Mill Ltd v Martin* [1985] BCLC 64; *Re Highway Foods International Ltd* [1995] 1 BCLC 209.

4 *Re Bond Worth Ltd* [1979] 3 All ER 919; *Frigoscandia (Contracting) Ltd v Continental Irish Meats Ltd* [1982] ILRM 396.

5 *John Snow and Co Ltd v DBG Woodcroft and Co Ltd* [1985] BCLC 54; *Clough Mill Ltd v Martin* [1985] BCLC 64; *Armour v Thyssen Edelstahlwerke AG* [1991] BCLC 28; *Re Stokes and McKiernan Ltd* [1978] ILRM 240.

6 *Re Stokes and McKiernan Ltd* [1978] ILRM 240.

7 *Borden (UK) Ltd v Scottish Timber Products Ltd* [1981] Ch 25; *Kruppstahl AG v Quitmann Products Ltd* [1982] ILRM 551; *Re Peachdart Ltd* [1983] 3 All ER 204; *Somers v Allen* [1984] ILRM 437; *Clough Mill Ltd v Martin* [1985] BCLC 64; *Pfeifer Weinkellerei v Arbuthnot Factors Ltd* [1988] 1 WLR 150; *Re Weldtech Ltd* [1991] BCLC 393; *Compaq Computers Ltd v Abercorn Group Ltd* [1991] BCC 484; *Modelboard Ltd v Outerbox Ltd* [1993] BCLC 623; *Ian Chisholm Textiles Ltd v Griffiths* [1994] BCC 96; *Chaigley Farms Ltd v Crawford, Kaye and Greyshire Ltd* [1996] BCC 957. cf *Carbery Pig Producers Co-Operative Society Ltd v Lunham Bros Ltd* (16 May 1986, unreported) HC (Carroll J) where the trial judge permitted several sellers to claim title to various types of pork product processed from pigs supplied by them. See also *Associated Alloys Pty Ltd v Metropolitan Engineering and Fabrication Ltd* [1998] NSWSC 442 where the careful creation of a trust relationship in respect of the finished products and proceeds of sale prevented the clause from being catergorised as a registerable charge.

8 *Aircool Installations v British Telecommunications* (1995) Current Law Week, 19 May 1995.

9 *Hendy Lennox Ltd v Grahame Puttick Ltd* [1984] 1 WLR 485.

10 *Re Andrabell Ltd* [1984] 3 All ER 407; *EI Pfeiffer Weinkellerei-Weinenkauf GmbH and Co v Arbuthnot Factors Ltd* [1988] 1 WLR 150; *Re WJ Hickey Ltd; Uniacke v Cassidy Electrical Supply Co Ltd* [1988] IR 126; *Associated Alloys Pty Ltd v Metropolitan Engineering and Fabrication Ltd* [1998] NSWSC 442. cf the earlier cases of *Re Stokes and McKiernan Ltd* [1978] ILRM 240, *Sugar Distributors Ltd v Monaghan Cash and Carry Ltd* [1982] ILRM 399, *SA Foundries du Lion MV v International Factors (Ireland) Ltd* [1985] ILRM 66 and *Aluminum Industrie Vaases BV v Romapla Ltd* [1976] 1 WLR 676 where the mere existence of a simple retention of title clause was regarded as sufficient to entitle the seller to claim the proceeds of sub-sales. It is thought that these earlier cases no longer represent good law.

11 If the retention of title clause purports to assign to the supplier any claims which the buyer may have against sub-buyers, the proper inference is that title had passed to the buyer at some time prior to the sub-sale and that accordingly the clause in fact creates a registerable charge over the proceeds: *Re Interview Ltd* [1975] IR 382; *EI Pfeiffer Weinkellerei-Weineinkauf GmbH and Co v Arbuthnot Factors Ltd* [1988] 1 WLR 150; *Re Weldtech Equipment Ltd* [1991] BCLC 393.

12 *Carroll Group Distributors Ltd v G and F Bourke Ltd* [1990] ILRM 285; *Tatung (UK) Ltd v Galex Telesure Ltd* (1989) 5 BCC 325; *Compaq Computer Ltd v Abercorn Group Ltd* [1993] BCLC 602; *Modelboard Ltd v Outer Box Ltd* [1993] BCLC 623; *Re Highway Foods International Ltd* [1995] 1 BCLC 209.

UK legislation

See CA 1985, ss 395, 396, 399; CA 1989, ss 93, 95.

100 Duty of company to register charges created by company

(1) It shall be the duty of a company to send to the registrar of companies for registration within the time required by section 99 the particulars of every charge created by the company, and of the issues of debentures of a series requiring registration under section 99, together with any documents required by that section, but registration of any such charge may be effected on the application of any person interested therein.

(2) Where registration is effected on the application of some person other that the company, that person shall be entitled to recover from the company the amount of any fees properly paid by him to the registrar on the registration.

(3) If any company makes default in sending to the registrar for registration the particulars of any charge created by the company or of the issues of debentures of a series requiring registration under section 99 or any documents required by that section then, unless registration has been effected on the application of some other person, the company and every officer of the company who is in default [shall be guilty of an offence and liable to a fine][a] not exceeding [€1,904.61][b].

(4) Proceedings in relation to an offence under this section may be brought and prosecuted by the registrar of companies.

Amendments

a Words substituted by C(AA)A 2003, s 57 and Sch 2, para 1.

b '£500' substituted for '£100' by C(A)A 1982, Sch 1 and increased to £1,500 by CA 1990, s 240(7) as inserted by CLEA 2001, s 104(c); £1,500 converted to €1,904.61 by Council Regulations (EC) No 1103/97, No 974/98 and No 2866/98 and the Economic and Monetary Union Act, 1988, s 6.

Definitions

'company': CA 1963, s 2(1); 'debenture': CA 1963, s 2(1); 'document': CA 1963, s 2(1); 'officer': CA 1963, s 2(1); 'the registrar of companies': CA 1963, s 2(1); 'officer in default': CA 1963, s 383.

Cross references in other enactments

NAMA Act 2009, s 218(1) provides that an acquired bank asset within the meaning of NAMA Act 2009 is 'not invalidated or rendered void or voidable as against NAMA or a NAMA group entity or their successors in title' by operation of CA 1963, s 100.

Notes

***Locus standi* to register charge**: CA 1963, s 100(1) imposes a primary obligation on the company itself to register the charge. But CA 1963, s 100(2) also confers standing on 'any person interested' to effect registration. This would undoubtedly extend to the debentureholder. Indeed, given the fact that non-registration renders the charge void, the debentureholder has a greater interest than the company in ensuring that the prescribed particulars are duly delivered to the Registrar. In practice, therefore, the delivery of particulars will normally be undertaken by the debentureholder itself. Fees incurred in effecting registration can then be recouped from the company.

UK legislation

See CA 1985, s 398; CA 1989, s 95.

101 Duty of company to register charges existing on property acquired

(1) Where a company acquires any property which is subject to a charge of any such kind as would, if it had been created after the acquisition of the property, have been required to be registered under this Part, the company shall cause the prescribed particulars of the charge, verified in the prescribed manner, to be delivered to the registrar of companies for registration in manner required by this Act within 21 days after the date on which the acquisition is completed so, however, that if the property is situated outside the State, 21 days after the date on which the prescribed particulars could, in due course of post and if despatched with due diligence, have been received in the State, shall be substituted for 21 days after the completion of the acquisition as the time within which the particulars are to be delivered to the registrar.

(2) If default is made in complying with this section, the company and every officer of the company who is in default [shall be guilty of an offence and liable to a fine][a] not exceeding [€1,904.61][b]

Amendments

a Words substituted by C(AA)A 2003, s 57 and Sch 2, para 1.

b '£500' substituted for '£100' by C(A)A 1982, Sch 1 and increased to £1,500 by CA 1990, s 240(7) as inserted by CLEA 2001, s 104(c); £1,500 converted to €1,904.61 by Council Regulations (EC) No 1103/97, No 974/98 and No 2866/98 and the Economic and Monetary Union Act, 1988, s 6.

Definitions

'company': CA 1963, s 2(1); 'officer': CA 1963, s 2(1); 'prescribed': CA 1963, s 2(1); 'the Registrar of Companies': CA 1963, s 2(1); 'officer in default': CA 1963, s 383.

Cross references in other enactments

NAMA Act 2009, s 218(1) provides that an acquired bank asset within the meaning of NAMA Act 2009 is 'not invalidated or rendered void or voidable as against NAMA or a NAMA group entity or their successors in title' by operation of CA 1963, s 101.

Notes

Pre-acquisition charge: Where the company can only complete a purchase of property by borrowing money for the security of which it is contractually bound to grant a mortgage to the lender *ex instante* with the execution of the conveyance in its favour, the company cannot in reality be ever said to acquire even for a *scintilla temporis* the unencumbered fee simple or leasehold interest in the property, but instead acquires no more than an equity of redemption.[1] To this extent therefore the company arguably 'acquires ... property which is subject to a charge.' Nonetheless, that charge is one which has been 'created' by the company and requires registration pursuant to CA 1963, s 99 rather than s 101.[2] In summary, therefore, it would seem that s 101 only applies where the property is acquired by the company subject to an existing charge which has been created by the vendor or his predecessors in title.

[1] *Abbey National Building Society v Cann* [1991] 1 AC 56, (overruling *Church of England Building Society v Piskor [1954] Ch 553*); *Security Trust Co v Royal Bank of Canada* [1976] AC 503; *Re Connolly Bros Ltd (No 2)* [1912] 2 Ch 25; *Wilson v Kelland* [1910] 2 Ch 306; *Bunbury Foods Pty Ltd v National Bank of Australia Ltd* [1985] WAR 126; *Composite Buyers Ltd v State Bank of New South Wales* (1991) 3 ACSR 196; *Sogelease Australia Pty Ltd v Boston Australia Ltd* (1991) 26 NSWLR 1.

[2] *Capital Finance Co Ltd v Stokes* [1968] 1 All ER 573, aff'd [1968] 3 All ER 625; *Security Trust Co v Royal Bank of Canada* [1976] AC 503 at 520–521.

Consequences of non-registration: Unlike a charge created by the company which is void for non-registration,[1] failure to register an existing charge on property which is acquired by the company simply results in a potential fine.

[1] CA 1963, s 99(1).

UK legislation

See CA 1985, s 398; CA 1989, s 95.

---

102 Registration of judgment mortgages

(1) When judgment is recovered against a company and such judgment is subsequently converted into a judgment mortgage affecting any property of the company, the judgment creditor shall cause 2 copies (certified by the Land Registry or the Registry of Deeds, as the case may be, to be correct copies) of the affidavit required for the purpose of registering the judgment as a mortgage to be delivered to the company within 21 days after the date of such registration, and the company shall within 3 days of receipt of such copies deliver one of such copies to the registrar of companies for registration in manner required by this Act. By way of further precaution, the Land Registry, or Registry of Deeds, shall as soon as may be deliver a copy of the said affidavit to the registrar of companies.

[(2) If a judgment creditor makes default in complying with subsection (1) he shall be guilty of an offence and liable to a fine not exceeding €1,904.61, and if a company makes default in complying with that subsection, the company and every officer who is in default shall be guilty of an offence and liable to a fine not exceeding €1,904.61.][a]

(3) This section shall not apply to any judgment mortgage created before the operative date.

Amendments

a CA 1963, s 102(2) substituted by C(AA)A 2003, s 57 and Sch 2, para 3.

Definitions

'company': CA 1963, s 2(1); 'officer': CA 1963, s 2(1); 'the operative date': CA 1963, s 2(1); 'the Registrar of Companies': CA 1963, s 2(1); 'officer in default': CA 1963, s 383.

Notes

Creation of judgment mortgages: As regards the procedure for the conversion of judgments into judgment mortgages, see Keane, *Company Law* (4th edn. Tottel Publishing, 2007), para 21.36–38 and Wylie, *Irish Land Law* (3rd edn, Tottel Publishing, 1997) at p 792 *et seq*.

Consequences of non-registration: Failure to comply with the requirements of CA 1963, s 102 does not render the judgment mortgage void. However, any judgment registered as a judgment mortgage against property of the company within three months before the commencement of the winding up will be void.[1]

1 See CA 1963, s 284(2) (which incorporates s 331 of the Irish Bankrupt and Insolvent Act 1857 into company law). See also *Re Irish Attested Sales Ltd* [1962] IR 70.

103 Register of charges to be kept by registrar of companies

(1) The registrar of companies shall keep, in relation to each company, a register in the prescribed form of all the charges requiring registration under this Part, and shall, on payment of such fee as may be prescribed, enter in the register, in relation to such charges, the following particulars:

(a) in the case of a charge to the benefit of which the holders of a series of debentures are entitled, such particulars as are specified in subsection (8) of section 99;

(b) in the case of any other charge—

(i) if the charge is a charge created by the company, the date of its creation;

(ii) if the charge was a charge existing on property acquired by the company, the date of the acquisition of the property;

(iii) if the charge was a judgment mortgage, the date of the creation of such judgment mortgage;

[(iiia) if the charge is a floating one, granted by a company to the Central Bank and Financial Services Authority of Ireland for the purposes either of providing or securing collateral, particulars of any provision of the charge that has the effect of prohibiting or restricting the company from issuing further securities that rank equally with that charge or modifying the ranking of that charge in relation to securities previously issued by the company;] [a]

(iv) the amount secured by the charge;

(v) short particulars of the property charged;

(vi) the persons entitled to the charge.

(2) The register kept in pursuance of this section shall be open to inspection by any person on payment of such fee as may be prescribed.

Amendments

a CBFSAIA 2004, s 33 and Sch 3, Pt 2 inserted sub-para (iiia) after s 103(1)(b)(iii).

Definitions

'company': CA 1963, s 2(1); 'debenture': CA 1963, s 2(1); 'prescribed': CA 1963, s 2(1); 'the Registrar of Companies': CA 1963, s 2(1).

Notes

Registration fees: The applicable fee for registration of a charge is currently €40 (since 1 December 2005).[1]

1 See the Companies (Fees) (No 3) Order 2005 (SI 517/2005).

Prescribed forms: See the Companies (Forms) Orders 1964–2004.

Prescribed particulars: Apart from the particulars referred to in CA 1963, s 103(1), particulars of commissions, allowances and discounts which have been paid or made either directly or indirectly by the company to any person in consideration of his subscribing or agreeing to subscribe, whether absolutely or conditionally, for any debentures of the company, or procuring or agreeing to procure subscriptions, whether absolute or conditional for such debentures, must also be registered.[1] Furthermore, where the charge comprises property outside the State and registration in the country where the property is situate is necessary to make the charge valid or effectual according to the law of that country, a certificate in the prescribed form stating that the charge was presented for registration in the country where the property is situate on the date on which it was so presented, are to be delivered to the Registrar for registration.[2]

The insertion of (iiia) into s 103(1)(b) was at the instigation of the Central Bank and Financial Services Authority of Ireland ('CBFSAI') and was designed to require the delivery of particulars to the Registrar of negative pledge clauses contained in floating charges granted to the CBFSAI. This would arise where Irish credit institutions grant security by way of floating charge over Tier II assets, eg a pool of mortgages, to CBFSAI to secure their short-term indebtedness to CBFSAI for Eurosystem monetary policy operations.

1 CA 1963, s 99(9).

2 CA 1963, s 99(5).

Validity of debenture: The Registrar is not required to adjudicate upon the validity of the charge before entering it on the register.[1]

1 *Re Heathstar Properties Ltd (No 2)* [1966] 1 All ER 1000; *Sun Tai Cheung Credits Ltd v Attorney General of Hong Kong* (1987) 3 BCC 357 at 360–362.

UK legislation

See CA 1985, s 397(1), (2); CA 1989, s 94.

---

104 Certificate of registration

The registrar shall give a certificate under his hand of the registration of any charge registered in pursuance of this Part, stating the amount thereby secured, and the certificate shall be conclusive evidence that the requirements of this Part as to registration have been complied with.

Definitions

'the Registrar of Companies': CA 1963, s 2(1).

Notes

Conclusiveness of certificate: Once the prescribed particulars of the charge have been registered, the Registrar issues a certificate of registration which, according to CA 1963, s 104, is 'conclusive evidence' that the statutory registration requirements have been complied with.[1] Because of the conclusiveness of the certificate it has been held that the registration of the charge cannot be challenged even where the registration requirements have not in fact been observed.[2] Despite the wording of s 104 it has been suggested that the court would be prepared to look behind the certificate in cases of fraud or where there is an error on the face of the certificate itself.[3] Furthermore, the certificate is only conclusive evidence as to compliance with the registration requirements in respect of the prescribed particulars of the charge; it affords no protection in respect of other errors that may exist in the documentation as filed with the Registrar of Companies, as where the wrong company name or number has been inserted in the Form C1.[4]

[1] See generally O'Riordan and Pearce, 'The Conclusiveness of Certificates of Registration of Company Charges' (1986) 80 Gazette 281; Prentice, 'Defectively Registered Charges' (1970) 34 Conv 410; McCormack, 'Conclusiveness in the Registration of Company Charge Procedure' (1989) 10 Company Lawyer 175; Pye, 'The s 104 certificate of Registration – An Impenetrable Shield No More' (1985) 3 ILT (ns) 212.

[2] *Lombard and Ulster Banking (Ireland) Ltd v Amurec Ltd* [1976–77] ILRM 222 (charge delivered for registration more than 21 days after date of creation); *Re Valley Ice Cream (Ireland) Ltd* [1998] IEHC 119 (McCracken J) (Form C1 referred to the wrong schedule to the debenture as identifying the charged assets); *R v Registrar of Companies, ex parte Central Bank of India* [1986] 1 QB 1114; *Re Eric Holmes (Property) Ltd* [1965] Ch 1052 (charge delivered for registration more than 21 days after date of creation); *Re CL Nye Ltd* [1971] Ch 442 (charge delivered for registration more than 21 days after date of creation); *Exeter Trust Ltd v Screenways Ltd* [1991] BCLC 888 (charge registered pursuant to order of court extending time for registration, which order was subsequently set aside); *Re Shannonside Holdings Ltd* (20 May 1993, unreported) HC (Costello J) (error in particulars as to amount secured); *Re Mechanisations (Eaglescliffe) Ltd* [1966] Ch 20 (error in particulars as to amount secured); *National Provincial and Union Bank of England v Charnley* [1924] 1 KB 431 (error in particulars as to the property charged); *Re Yolland, Husson and Birkett* [1907] 2 Ch 471, aff'd [1908] 1 Ch 152 (omission from the prescribed form of particulars of rights *inter se*, of the holders of a series of debenture stock); *Cunard SS Co v Hopwood* [1908] 2 Ch 564 (omission from the prescribed form of particulars of date of resolution creation series of debenture stock). cf *Esberger and Son Ltd v Capital and Counties Bank* [1913] 2 Ch 366 where the court was prepared to look behind the certificate of registration.

[3] *Re v Registrar of Companies, ex parte Central Bank of India* [1986] 1 QB 1114, at 1169–1170 (per Lawton LJ); *Sun Tai Cheung Credits Ltd v Attorney General of Hong Kong* (1987) 3 BCC 357 at 360; *National Provincial and Union Bank of England v Charnley* [1924] 1 KB 431 at 454.

[4] *Re Advantage Healthcare (T10) Ltd* [2000] BCC 985. The error in that case, involving the insertion of the wrong company number, was not held to be fatal since it was not an error regarding the particulars of the charge itself.

Unconstitutionality of s 104: *Quaere* whether the 'conclusive' nature of the Registrar's certificate is unconstitutional, either as an infringement of the separation of powers' provisions contained in Art 6 or as an attempt to oust the High Court's full original jurisdiction under Art 34 to hear and determine all justiciable matters.[1] In England it has been held that because legislation does not bind the Crown except where expressly so stated, an erroneously issued certificate of registration could be challenged through the *fiat* of the Attorney General.[2] It is thought, however, that a similar position would not pertain in Ireland since the Royal Prerogatives, including the non-application of statutes, have been held not to have survived the enactment of the Constitution.[3]

[1] *Murren v Brennan* [1942] IR 466; *Maher v Attorney General* [1973] IR 146; *Tormey v Ireland* [1985] IR 289.

[2] *R v Registrar of Companies, ex parte Central Bank of India* [1986] 1 QB 1114 at 1169–1170 (per Lawton LJ) and at 1171–1172 (per Slade LJ).

[3] *Byrne v Ireland* [1972] IR 241; *Webb v Ireland* [1988] IR 353; *Howard v Commissioners of Public Works* [1993] ILRM 665.

Liability of the Registrar: Even if the conclusiveness of the certificate were to be constitutionally upheld so as to preclude a challenge to the charge itself, an aggrieved third party might nevertheless have a cause of action in damages against the company for delivering or causing the delivery of wrong particulars[1] or against the Registrar of Companies for registering the wrong particulars.[2]

[1] *First City Corporation Ltd v Downsview Nominees Ltd* [1990] 3 NZLR 265; *Re Advantage Healthcare (T10) Ltd* [2000] BCC 985.

[2] *Re Advantage Healthcare (T10) Ltd* [2000] BCC 985.

Substantive invalidity: The conclusiveness of the certificate of registration is only in relation to compliance with the statutory registration requirements, and does not operate to confer validity on a charge which is invalid for other reasons.[1]

1 *R v Registrar of Companies, ex parte Central Bank of India* [1986] 1 QB 1114 at 1177; *Re Mechanisations (Eaglescliffe) Ltd* [1966] Ch 20 at 35–36; *Wilde v Australia Trade Equipment Co Pty Ltd* (1980) 145 CLR 590.

UK legislation

See CA 1985, s 347 (3)–(5); CA 1989, s 94.

105 Entries of satisfaction and release of property from charge

The registrar of companies, on evidence being given to his satisfaction with respect to any registered charge

(a) that the debt in relation to which the charge was created has been paid or satisfied in whole or in part; or

(b) that part of the property or undertaking charged has been released from the charge or has ceased to form part of the company's property or undertaking;

and after giving notice to the person to whom such charge was originally given or to the judgment creditor, as the case may be, may enter on the register a memorandum of satisfaction in whole or in part, or of the fact that part of the property or undertaking has been released from the charge or has ceased to form part of the company's property or undertaking, as the case may be, and where he enters a memorandum of satisfaction in whole he shall, if required, furnish the company with a copy thereof.

Definitions

'company': CA 1963, s 2(1); 'memorandum': CA 1963, s 2(1); 'the Registrar of Companies': CA 1963, s 2(1).

Notes

Evidence of satisfaction: Evidence of satisfaction and release of the property from the charge is presented to the Registrar on the prescribed Form C6.[1]

1 Companies (Forms) Orders 1964–2002.

Incorrect entry of satisfaction: An incorrect entry of satisfaction may be cancelled by order of the High Court.[1]

1 *Re C Light and Co* [1917] WN 77.

UK legislation

See CA 1985, s 403; CA 1989, s 98.

106 Extension of time for registration of charges

(1) The court, on being satisfied that the omission to register a charge within the time required by this Act or that the omission or mis-statement of any particular with respect to any such charge or in a memorandum of satisfaction was accidental, or due to inadvertence or to some other sufficient cause, or is not of a nature to prejudice the position of creditors or shareholders of the company, or that on other grounds it is just

and equitable to grant relief, may, on the application of the company or any person interested, and on such terms and conditions as seem to the court just and expedient, order that the time for registration shall be extended, or, as the case may be, that the omission or mis-statement shall be rectified.

(2) The grant of relief by the court under this section shall, if the court so directs, not have the effect of relieving the company or its officers of any liability already incurred under section 100.

Definitions

'company': CA 1963, s 2(1); 'the court': CA 1963, s 2(1); 'memorandum': CA 1963, s 2(1); 'officer': CA 1963, s 2(1); 'officer in default': CA 1963, s 383.

Notes

Prescribed time for delivery of particulars: For the respective periods of time within which particulars of charges must to the Registrar, see CA 1963, s 99(1) and (3), s 101 and s 102.

Dispute regarding charge: The court may extend the time for registration of a charge even though there is a dispute as to its existence, validity or registerability.[1]

1 *Re Cunard SS Co* [1908] WN 160; *Re Heathstar Properties Ltd (No 2)* [1966] 1 All ER 1000.

Jurisdiction of court: According to CA 1963, s 106(1) the court may extend the time for registration or may allow the rectification of the delivered particulars where it is satisfied:

(a) that the error was accidental, inadvertent or due to some other sufficient cause;[1] or

(b) that the error will not prejudice the position of the company's creditors[2] or shareholders; or

(c) that it is otherwise just and equitable to grant relief.[3]

The affidavit grounding the application must, however, state the reason for the error. Thus a bald assertion of 'inadvertance' will not be sufficient.[4] Ultimately, the making of an order pursuant to s 106 is a matter within the discretion of the court[5], so that where the applicant was guilty of unreasonable delay and failed to disclose that the company had been struck off the register, the court refused to allow later registration.[6]

1 For examples of accidental or inadvertent non-registration, see *Re Chantry House Developments plc* [1990] BCLC 813; *Re Resinoid and Mica Products Ltd* [1983] Ch 132; *Re RM Arnold and Co Ltd* [1984] BCLC 535. For examples of 'other sufficient cause' see *Re S Abrahams and Sons* [1902] 1 Ch 695 (non-registration through ignorance of the law); *Re Joplin Brewery Co Ltd* [1902] 1 Ch 79 (illness).

2 By 'creditors' is meant secured creditors: *Watson v Duff, Morgan and Vermont Holdings Ltd* [1974] 1 WLR 450.

3 It may be just and equitable to make an order under CA 1963, s 106 even where the omission was neither accidental nor inadvertent but where the prospect of insolvency is remote: *Re MIG Trust Ltd* [1933] Ch 542 at 560; *Re Braemar Investments Ltd* [1988] BCLC 556 at 560–561; *Re Chantry House Developments plc* [1990] BCLC 813.

4 *Re International Retail Ltd* (1963–1993) Irish Company Law Reports 199 at 202; *Re Kris Cruisers Ltd* [1949] Ch 138.

5 *Re Kris Cruisers Ltd* [1949] Ch 138.

6 *Re Telomatic Ltd* [1994] 1 BCLC 90.

Extension of time:

Position of secured creditors: An order extending the time for registration of a charge will usually be made subject to a proviso that it is to be without prejudice to the rights of any other secured creditors acquired after the expiry of the original 21-day period and before the time of actual registration.[1] Thus a subsequent debentureholder will have priority even though he had notice of the unregistered charge at the time he obtained his own charge.[2] However, if the subsequent charge is expressly subordinated to the earlier charge, that earlier charge will regain priority after late registration has been effected.[3] Moreover, the proviso regarding the protection of the rights of other secured creditors will not be included in the order of the court, if the charges created in the interim have been executed in favour of the directors of the company[4] and a director who is aware that his company did not register a prior debenture in favour of a third party cannot, in good faith, register a later debenture in his own favour.[5]

Actual or imminent liquidation: If a winding up of the company is imminent, late registration may be refused altogether.[6] Alternatively, the proviso for late registration may stipulate that the charge will be void in the event of the company being wound up before the actual date of late registration[7] or instead, that if the company is wound up within a specified time after late registration, the liquidator or any unsecured creditor company may apply to have the charge removed from the register.[8] However, if the company has already gone into liquidation, the court will not extend the time for registration of the charge.[9]

Position of Unsecured Creditors: The position of the ordinary unsecured creditors is not normally protected by the proviso attaching to the order for late registration, except insofar as the order provides for the avoidance of the charge in the event of a liquidation. The position of preferential creditors may, however, be preserved by the proviso, at least where a receiver has been appointed under some other debenture which includes a floating charge.[10] In Australia, the position of unsecured creditors may be taken into account, even if a liquidation has neither commenced nor is imminent.[11] Also, where the company is insolvent, so that the real beneficial interest in the company's assets lies with its creditors rather than its shareholders, the court may direct that late registration is to be without prejudice to the interests of all creditors, including the unsecured creditors,[12] and may even direct that notice of the making of the order for late registration should be given to the unsecured creditors so as to enable them to apply to set aside the charge if they so wish.[13]

1. *Re O'Carroll Kent and Co Ltd* (1952) 89 ILTR 72; *Re Telford Motors Ltd* (1963–1993) Irish Company Law Reports 202; *Re Joplin Brewery Co* [1902] 1 Ch 79; *Re Ehrmann Bros Ltd* [1906] 2 Ch 709; *Re Monolithic Building Co* [1915] 1 Ch 643; *Watson v Duff, Morgan and Vermont Holdings Ltd* [1974] 1 WLR 450; *Re Braemar Investments Ltd* [1988] BCLC 556.
2. *Re Monolithic Building Co* [1915] 1 Ch 643.
3. *Re Clarets Ltd; Spain v McCann* [1978] ILRM 215.
4. *Re Fablehill Ltd* [1991] BCLC 830.
5. *Confiance Ltd v Timespan Images Ltd and another* [2005] 2 BCLC 693.
6. *Re International Retail Ltd* (1963–1993) Irish Company Law Reports 199; *Re Farm Fresh Frozen Foods Ltd* [1980] ILRM 131; *Re Bootle Cold Storage Co* [1901] WN 54 *Re Resinoid and Mica Products Ltd* [1983] Ch 132; *Victoria Housing Estates Ltd v Ashpurton Estates Ltd* [1983] Ch 110.
7. *Re Telford Motors Ltd* (1963–1993) Irish Company Law Reports 202.
8. *Re International Retail Ltd* (1963–1993) Irish Company Law Reports 199; *Re LH Charles and Co Ltd* [1935] WN 15; *Re Braemar Investments Ltd* [1988] BCLC 556; *Re Chantry House Developments plc* [1990] BCLC 813; *Barclays Bank plc v Stuart Landon Ltd* [2001] 2 BCLC 316.
9. *Re International Retail Ltd* (1963–1993) Irish Company Law Reports 199; *Re Telford Motors Ltd* (1963–1993) Irish Company Law Reports 202; *Re Farm Fresh Frozen Foods Ltd* [1980] ILRM 131; *Re Spiral Globe Ltd* [1902] 1 Ch 396; *Victoria Housing Estates Ltd v Ashpurton Estates Ltd* [1983] Ch 110; *Re Resinoid and Mica Products Ltd* [1983] Ch 132. For an exceptional situation where late registration was permitted despite the presentation of a winding-up petition, see *Re RM Arnold and Co Ltd* [1984] BCLC 535. This case can, however, be

explained on the basis that the only party prejudiced by late registration was another secured creditor who was consenting to the application.

10 *Re Manning Furniture Ltd* [1996] 1 ILRM 13.
11 *Re Flinders Trading Property Co Ltd* (1978) 3 ACLR 218.
12 *Re Chantry House Developments plc* [1990] BCLC 813.
13 *Re Chantry House Developments plc* [1990] BCLC 813.

Error in particulars: An error in the particulars delivered to the Registrar will not affect the validity of the charge, once a certificate of registration has been issued pursuant to CA 1963, s 104.[1] Courtney argues therefore[2] that an application for rectification may be superfluous, particularly if the court were to impose the same conditions as are applied in the case of an order extending time. In any event, the jurisdiction conferred on the court by s 106 only allows it to correct an omission or misstatement in the delivered particulars and does not allow for the deletion of an entire entry.[3] Furthermore, the court's jurisdiction is confined to rectifying errors in the particulars which are required by law to be delivered to the registrar of companies: there is no jurisdiction to order the rectification of factual errors in particulars the delivery of which is not required by law.[4]

An error in the company's registered number in the Form C1 or other appropriate form delivered to the Registrar, will not invalidate the charge because that number is not a 'particular of the charge' in the true sense.[5]

1 *Re Shannonside Holdings Ltd* (20 May 1993, unreported) HC (Costello J); *Re Valley Ice Cream (Ireland) Ltd* [1998] IEHC 119 (McCracken J); *Re Mechanisations (Eaglescliffe) Ltd* [1964] 3 All ER 840.
2 Courtney, *The Law of Private Companies* (2nd edn, Tottel Publishing, 2002) para 21.090.
3 *Re CL Nye Ltd* [1971] CH 443 (application to delete an entry of satisfaction which had been incorrectly made).
4 *Igroup Ltd v Ocwen* [2003] 4 All ER 1063.
5 *Grove v Advantage Healthcare (T10) Ltd* [2000] 1 BCLC 661.

UK legislation

See CA 1985, s 400; CA 1989, s 95.

107 Notice to registrar of appointment of receiver, and of receiver ceasing to act

(1) If any person obtains an order for the appointment of a receiver of the property of a company or appoints such a receiver under any powers contained in any instrument, he shall, within 7 days after the date of the order or of the appointment, publish in [the Companies Registration Office Gazette][a] and in at least one daily newspaper circulating in the district where the registered office of the company is situated, and deliver to the registrar of companies, a notice in the form prescribed.

(2) When any person appointed receiver of the property of a company ceases to act as such receiver, he shall, on so ceasing, deliver to the registrar of companies a notice in the form prescribed.

(3) If any person makes default in complying with the requirements of this section, he [shall be guilty of an offence and liable to a fine][b] not exceeding [€1,904.61].[c]

Amendments

a 'the Companies Registration Office Gazette' substituted for 'Iris Oifigiúil' by IFCMPA 2005, s 72.

b Words inserted by C(AA)A 2003, s 57 and Sch 2, para 1.

c ‘£500’ substituted for ‘£100’ by C(A)A 1982, Sch 1 and increased to £1,500 by CA 1990, s 240(7) as inserted by CLEA 2001, s 104(c); £1,500 converted to €1,904.61 by Council Regulations (EC) No 1103/97, No 974/98 and No 2866/98 and the Economic and Monetary Union Act, 1988, s 6.

Definitions

‘company’: CA 1963, s 2(1); ‘prescribed’: CA 1963, s 2(1); ‘the Registrar of Companies’: CA 1963, s 2(1).

Notes

Notice of appointment: The obligation under this section to give notice of the receiver's appointment falls not upon the receiver, but upon the person who either appointed him or obtained an order of the court for his appointment.[1] However, the receiver is obliged, personally, to give notice of his appointment under other provisions of the Companies Acts.[2]

1 As to the circumstances in which the court may, in the exercise of its equitable jurisdiction, appoint a receiver of the property of a company, see Picarda, *The Law Relating to Receivers, Managers and Administrators* (2nd edn, Butterworths, 1990) ch 21.

2 See CA 1963, ss 317 and 319.

Notice of ceasing to act: The obligation under CA 1963, s 107(2) to give notice of ceasing to act falls upon the receiver himself. Moreover, if he resigns office he must give at least one month's notice to:

(a) the holders of any floating charges over all or part of the company's property;

(b) the company or its liquidator; and

(c) the holders of any fixed charge over all or any part of the company's property.[1]

And if he has been appointed by the court, he can only resign with the leave of the court.[2]

1 CA 1963, s 322C(1).

2 CA 1963, s 322C(2).

UK legislation

See CA 1985, s 409; CA 1989, s 100.

---

108 Effect of provisions of former Companies Acts as to registration of charges on land

Paragraph (d) of subsection (1) of section 10 of the Companies Act, 1907, and paragraph (d) of subsection (1) of section 93 of the Companies (Consolidation) Act, 1908 (by virtue whereof charges created on land by a company required registration under those Acts respectively), shall be deemed never to have applied to a charge for any rent or other periodical sum issuing out of the land.

Definitions

‘company’: CA 1963, s 2(1).

Provisions as to copies of Instruments creating Charges

109 Copies of instruments creating charges to be kept at registered office

Every company shall cause a copy of every instrument creating any charge requiring registration under this Part, including every affidavit a copy of which has been delivered to the company under section 102, to be kept at the registered office of the company so, however, that, in the case of a series of uniform debentures, a copy of one debenture of the series shall be sufficient.

Definitions

'company': CA 1963, s 2(1); 'debenture': CA 1963, s 2(1).

UK legislation

See CA 1985, s 411; CA 1989, s 101.

Notes

Registerable charges: For the charges requiring to be registered, see CA 1963, ss 99, 101 and 102.

Affidavit: The affidavit referred to is the one pursuant to which the judgment was registered as a judgment mortgage in the Land Registry or Registry of Deeds, as the case may be.

---

110 Right to inspect copies of instruments creating charges

(1) The copies of instruments referred to in section 109 may be inspected during business hours (but subject to such reasonable restrictions as the company in general meeting may impose, so that not less than 2 hours in each day shall be allowed for inspection) by any creditor or member of the company without fee.

(2) If inspection is refused, every officer of the company who is in default [shall be guilty of an offence and liable to a fine][a] not exceeding [€1,904.61].[b]

(3) In the event of any such refusal, the court may by order compel an immediate inspection.

Amendments

a Words substituted by C(AA)A 2003, s 57 and Sch 2, para 1.

b '£500' substituted for '£100' by C(A)A 1982, Sch 1 and increased to £1,500 by CA 1990, s 240(7) as inserted by CLEA 2001, s 104(c); £1,500 converted to €1,904.61 by Council Regulations (EC) No 1103/97, No 974/98 and No 2866/98 and the Economic and Monetary Union Act, 1988, s 6.

Definitions

'company': CA 1963, s 2(1); 'the court': CA 1963, s 2(1); 'member': CA 1963, s 31; 'officer': CA 1963, s 2(1); 'officer in default': CA 1963, s 383.

UK legislation

See CA 1985, s 412; CA 1989, s 101.

Application of this part to companies incorporated outside the State

111 Application of this Part to companies incorporated outside the State

The provisions of this Part shall extend to charges on property in the State which are created on or after the operative date, and to charges on property in the State which is acquired on or after the operative date, by a company incorporated outside the State which has an established place of business in the State, and to judgment mortgages created on or after the operative date and affecting property in the State of such a company and to receivers, appointed on or after the operative date, of property in the State of such a company, and for the purposes of those provisions, the principal place of business of such a company in the State shall be deemed to be its registered office.

Definitions

'company': CA 1963, s 2(1); 'the operative date': CA 1963, s 2(1).

Cross references in other enactments

NAMA Act 2009, s 218(1) provides that an acquired bank asset within the meaning of NAMA Act 2009 is 'not invalidated or rendered void or voidable as against NAMA or a NAMA group entity or their successors in title' by operation of CA 1963, s 111.

Notes

Registered and unregistered foreign companies: The provisions of CA 1963, s 111 apply to a foreign company which has an established place of business in the State, even though the company has failed to register on the external register of companies pursuant to CA 1963, Part XI.[1] However, because unregistered foreign companies do not have a registration number, it is not feasible for the Registrar to register the charge in the normal way. Instead, the charge is entered in what is colloquially known as the 'Slavenburg file.' Moreover, because the company is not registered pursuant to CA 1963, Part XI the Registrar will not issue the company with a certificate of registration, but instead merely writes confirming receipt of the prescribed particulars.[2]

1 *NV Slavenburg's Bank v Intercontinental Natural Resources Ltd* [1980] 1 All ER 955; *Re Oriel Ltd* [1985] BCLC 343; *Re Alton Corporation* [1985] BCLC 27.

2 See generally Courtney, *The Law of Private Companies* (2nd edn, Tottel Publishing, 2002) paras 21.076–21.087.

Established place of business: A company may have an established place of business within the State even though the business carried on in the jurisdiction is only incidental to its main business and no transactions falling within its main business are concluded within the State.[1] However, carrying on business in the State is not the same thing as having an established place of business in the State.[2] It is essential to an 'established place of business' that there should be some visible sign or physical indication that the company has a connection with a particular premises.[3] Having an established place of business therefore connotes, not only setting up a place of business at a specific location, but a degree of permanency or recognisability as being a location of the company's business; it involves some more or less permanent location, not necessarily owned or even leased by the company, but at least associated with the company and from which habitually, or with some degree of regularity, business is conducted.[4]

An 'established place of business' does not have the same meaning as a 'branch' within the meaning of the Branch Disclosures Regulations, and it is generally accepted that whilst every 'branch' will also be a place of business, not every 'place of business' will be a 'branch'.[5]

1 *South India Shipping Corp Ltd v The Export-Import Bank of Korea* [1985] BCLC 163; *Rome v Punjab National Bank (No 2)* [1989] BCLC 328.

2 *Re Oriel Ltd* [1985] BCLC 343; *Cleveland Museum of Art v Capricorn Art International SA* [1990] BCLC 546.

3 *Re Oriel Ltd* [1985] BCLC 343; cf *Donovan v North German Lloyd Steamship Co* [1933] IR 33.

4 *Re Oriel Ltd* [1985] BCLC 343; *South India Shipping Corp Ltd v The Export-Import Bank of Korea* [1985] BCLC 163; *Rome v Punjab National Bank (No 2)* [1989] BCLC 328; *Cleveland Museum of Art v Capricorn Art International SA* [1990] BCLC 546; *Derverall v Grant Advertising Inc* [1954] 3 All ER 389; *Lord Advocate v Huron and Erie Loan and Savings Co* 1911 SC 612; and *Matchnet plc v William Blair & Co LLC [2003] 2 BCLC 195.*

5 See the European Communities (Branch Disclosures) Regulations, 1993 (SI 395/1993), considered *post*.

Relevant date: The relevant date for determining whether or not the company has an established place of business is the date of creation of the charge,[1] or the date of the acquisition of the property subject to a pre-existing charge,[2] or the date of the registration of the judgment mortgage,[3] as the case may be.[4] Thus, in the case of a charge created by a foreign company, if the company has an established place of business in the State at the date of creation, CA 1963, s 111 will apply, even though the company subsequently leaves the country.[5] On the other hand, if the property is acquired by the foreign company for the first time and immediately charged, it cannot be regarded as an 'established place of business' even if the company intends for it to become such.[6]

1 CA 1963, s 99.

2 CA 1963, s 101.

3 CA 1963, s 102.

4 *Re Oriel Ltd* [1985] BCLC 343.

5 *NV Slavenburg's Bank v Intercontinental Natural Resources Ltd* [1980] 1 All ER 955.

6 *Re Oriel Ltd* [1985] BCLC 343.

Location of assets: The provisions of CA 1963, s 111 apply not only to assets of the company located in Ireland at the date of creation of the charge, or at the date of the acquisition of the property subject to a pre-existing charge, as the case may be, but also to property located outside the State at the time, which is subsequently brought into the State by the company.[1]

1 *NV Slavenburg's Bank v Intercontinental Natural Resources Ltd* [1980] 1 All ER 955.

UK legislation

See CA 1985, ss 703A–703N; CA 1989, s 105, Sch 15.

Registration of charges existing before application of this Act

112 Registration of charges existing before application of this Act

(1) It shall be the duty of a company within 6 months after the operative date to send to the registrar of companies for registration the prescribed particulars of

(a) any charge created by the company before the operative date and remaining unsatisfied at that date which would have been required to be registered under paragraphs (g), (h) and (i) of subsection (2) of section 99 or under section 111, if the charge has been created after the operative date;

(b) any charge to which any property acquired by the company before the operative date is subject and which would have been required to be registered under section 101 or under section 111 if the property had been acquired after the operative date;

(c) any charge created before the operative date to which any property of the company is subject and which would have required registration under section 102 or under section 111 if created after the operative date.

(2) The registrar on payment of the prescribed fee shall enter the said particulars on the register kept by him in pursuance of this Part.

(3) If a company fails to comply with this section, the company and every officer of the company or other person who is knowingly a party to the default shall be liable to a fine not exceeding [€1,904.61].[a]

(4) The failure of the company to send to the registrar the prescribed particulars of any charge mentioned in paragraphs (a), (b) and (c) of subsection (1) shall not prejudice any rights which any person in whose favour the charge was made may have thereunder.

(5) For the purposes of this section, 'company' includes a company incorporated outside the State which has an established place of business in the State.

(6) In relation to a company incorporated outside the State which, on or after the operative date, establishes a place of business in the State, this section shall have effect as if—

(a) for the references to the operative date there were substituted references to the date of such establishment, and

(b) for the references to charges created or property acquired before the operative date there were substituted references to charges created or property acquired before such establishment, whether before the operative date or not.

Amendments

a '£500' substituted for '£100' by C(A)A 1982, Sch 1, increased to £1,500 by CA 1990, s 240(7) as inserted by CLEA 2001, s 104(c) and converted to €1,904.61 by Council Regulations (EC) No 1103/97, No 974/98 and No 2866/98 and the Economic and Monetary Union Act, 1988, s 6.

Definitions

'company': CA 1963, s 2(1); 'officer': CA 1963, s 2(1); 'the operative date': CA 1963, s 2(1); 'prescribed': CA 1963, s 2(1); 'the Registrar of Companies': CA 1963, s 2(1); 'officer in default': CA 1963, s 383.

Notes

Unlike other provisions that provide that contravention renders a person 'liable to a fine' which were changed by C(AA)A 2003, s 57 and Sch 2, para 1 to read 'guilty of an offence and liable to a fine', s 112(3) was not so amended, presumably because s 112 is now redundant.

PART V
MANAGEMENT AND ADMINISTRATION

Registered Office and Name

113 [Registered office of company

(1) A company shall, at all times, have a registered office in the State to which all communications and notices may be addressed.

(2) Particulars of the situation of the company's registered office shall be specified in the statement delivered pursuant to section 3 of the Companies (Amendment) Act, 1982, prior to the incorporation of the company.

(3) Notice of any change in the situation of the registered office of a company shall be given within fourteen days after the date of the change to the registrar who shall record the same. The inclusion in the annual return of a company of a statement as to the address of its registered office shall not be taken to satisfy the obligation imposed by this subsection.

(4) Where the memorandum of a company has been delivered to the registrar for registration under section 17 of the Principal Act prior to the commencement of the Companies (Amendment) Act, 1982, that company shall—

(a) as from the date on which it begins to carry on business, or as from the fourteenth day after the date of its incorporation, whichever is the earlier, have a registered office in the State to which all communications and notices may be addressed, and

(b) give notice of the situation of the registered office, and of any change therein within 14 days after the date of the incorporation of the company, or of the change as the case may be, to the registrar who shall record the same.

The inclusion in the annual return of a company of a statement as to the address of its registered office shall not be taken to satisfy the obligation imposed by this subsection.

(5) If default is made in complying with this section, the company and every officer of the company who is in default [shall be guilty of an offence and liable to a fine][b] not exceeding [€1,904.61][c].

(6) Proceedings in relation to an offence under this section may be brought and prosecuted by the registrar of companies.][a]

Amendments

a CA 1963, s 113 substituted by C(A)A 1982, s 4.

b Words 'shall be guilty of an offence and liable to a fine' substituted for 'shall be liable for a fine' by C(AA)A 2003, s 57 and Sch 2, Item No. 1.

c Penalty increased to £1,500 by CA 1990, 240(7) as inserted by CLEA 2001, s 104(c) and converted to €1,904.61 by Council Regulations (EC) No 1103/97, No 974/98 and No 2866/98 and the Economic and Monetary Union Act 1998, s 6.

Definitions

'annual return': CA 1963, s 2(1); 'company': CA 1963, s 2(1); 'memorandum': CA 1963, s 2(1); 'officer': CA 1963, s 2(1); 'officer in default': CA 1963, s 383; 'the Principal Act'; C(A)A 1982, s 1; 'the registrar of companies': CA 1963, s 2(1).

Notes

First registered office: CA 1963, s 113 requires a company to have a registered office at all times. To ensure that this is the case, details of the address of the registered office must be included among the particulars which are delivered to the Registrar pursuant to C(A)A 1983, s 3 prior to the incorporation of the company.[1] Failure to do so will result in the Registrar not issuing a certificate of incorporation.

1 CA 1963, s 113(2).

Change of registered office: A resolution of the board of directors pursuant to the general delegation of the company's powers of management in Table A, Pt I, reg 80 will suffice to change the location of the registered office.[1]

1 See Pennington, *Company Law* (7th edn, LexisNexis, 1995) at p 81.

Service of documents: A document may be served on the company by leaving it at or sending it by unregistered post[1] to the registered office (as recorded by the Registrar): CA 1963, s 379.

1 *TO Supplies (London) Ltd v Jerry Creighton Ltd* [1952] 1 KB 42.

Documents to be kept at registered office: The following categories of documents are required to be kept at the company's registered office: the register of debenture holders;[1] copies of instruments creating charges over property of the company;[2] the register of members;[3] the register of directors and secretary;[4] the register of directors' and secretaries' interests in shares and debentures;[5] in the case of a plc, the register of substantial shareholdings;[6] the books of account of the company.[7]

1 CA 1963, s 91. The register may however be kept at some other location instead, proved that the Registrar is so notified s 91(3) and (4).

2 CA 1963, s 109.

3 CA 1963, s 116. Section 116(5)(a) and (b) also allow for the register to be kept at some other office of the company, if that is where the work of making up the register is actually done. Alternatively, if the register is maintained on behalf of the company by some third party such as the company secretarial division of a bank or firm of accountants, the register may be kept at the office of that third party instead. Under s 116(7) the Registrar be notified if the register is kept otherwise than at the registered office.

4 CA 1963, s 195(1).

5 CA 1990, ss 59 and 60(5)(a). Alternatively, the register may be kept at the place where the register of members is kept: s 60(5)(b). If kept otherwise than at the registered office, the Registrar must be so notified: s 60(6).

6 CA 1990, s 80.

7 CA 1990, s 202(5). the directors may however resolve to keep the books elsewhere.

Domicile and residence of company:[1] As the place of the company's registered office must at all times be within the State[2], it follows that the company is to be treated as being an Irish national[3] and Irish domiciled.[4] Since 6 April 1999 (subject to limited exceptions[5]) a company incorporated in the State is deemed to be resident here for tax purposes.[6] In the event that a company comes within such an exception, then actual residence depends on where its 'central management and control' actually abides.[7] Where the company's control is divided, it may be simultaneously resident in several jurisdictions.[8] It is a question of fact in each case as to where central management and control actually abides. The provisions of the company's constitution are persuasive but by no means binding in determining where a company resides.[9] Where the central management and control takes a shape contrary to that required by the company's constitution, the following factors can be taken into account by the court in determining where central management and control actually abide:

(a) the place where the company holds its general meetings;[10]

(b) the place where the directors reside[11] even though the articles state that all board meetings are to be held elsewhere;[12]

(c) the provisions of the objects clause;[13]

(d) the place of incorporation;[14]

(e) the place where the real trade and business of the company are carried on;[15]

(f) the place where the books of the company are kept;[16]

(g) the place where the administrative work of the company is done;[17]

(h) the place where the chief office of the company is located;[18]

(i) the place where the secretary is to be found.[19]

1 See generally, Corrigan, 'Place of Abode Test in Establishing Tax Residence' (1988) 6 ILT (ns) 106.

2 CA 1963, s 113(1).

3 *Janson v Dreifontein Mines Ltd* [1902] AC 484.

4 TCA 1997, s 23A(3)-(4) as inserted by Finance Act 1999, s 82(1).

5 TCA 1997, s 23A(2) as inserted by Finance Act 1999, s 82 (1).

6 *Gasque v IRC* [1940] 2 KB 80; *Egyptian Delta Land and Investment Co v Todd* [1929] AC 1 at 13.

7 *John Hood and Co Ltd v Magee* [1918] 2 IR 34; *De Beers Consolidated Mines Ltd v Howe* [1906] AC 455; *Unit Construction Ltd v Bullock* [1960] AC 351; *Re Little Olympian Each Ways Ltd (No 2)* [1995] 1 BCLC 48.

8 *Swedish Central Railway v Thompson* [1925] AC 495; *Egyptian Delta Land and Investment Co Ltd v Todd* [1929] AC 1. Multiple residency could have disastrous taxation consequences for the company in that, subject to any relevant double taxation treaties, it could end up being liable to corporation tax on the same profits in two or more jurisdictions.

9 *Re Little Olympian Each Ways Ltd (No 2)* [1995] 1 BCLC 48.

10 *John Hood and Co Ltd v Magee* [1918] 2 IR 34.

11 *De Beers Consolidate Mines Ltd v Howe* [1906] AC 455; *Unit Construction Ltd v Bullock* [1960] AC 351.

12 *Unit Construction Ltd v Bullock* [1960] AC 351.

13 *Re Little Olympian Each Ways Ltd (No 2)* [1995] 1 BCLC 48.

14 *Re Little Olympian Each Ways Ltd (No 2)* [1995] 1 BCLC 48.

15 *Re Little Olympian Each Ways Ltd (No 2)* [1995] 1 BCLC 48.

16 *Re Little Olympian Each Ways Ltd (No 2)* [1995] 1 BCLC 48.

17 *Re Little Olympian Each Ways Ltd (No 2)* [1995] 1 BCLC 48.

18 *Re Little Olympian Each Ways Ltd (No 2)* [1995] 1 BCLC 48.

19 *Re Little Olympian Each Ways Ltd (No 2)* [1995] 1 BCLC 48.

UK legislation

See CA 1985, s 287; CA 1989, s 136.

---

114 Publication of name by company

(1) Every company—

(a) shall paint or affix, and keep painted or affixed, its name on the outside of every office or place in which its business is carried on, in a conspicuous position, in letters easily legible;

(b) shall have its name engraven in legible characters on its seal;

(c) shall have it name mentioned in legible characters in all business letters of the company and in all notices and other official publications of the company, and in all bills of exchange, promissory notes, endorsements, cheques and orders for money or goods purporting to be signed by or on behalf of the company and in all invoices, receipts and letters of credit of the company.

(2) If a company does not paint or affix its name in manner directed by this Act, the company and every officer of the company who is in default [shall be guilty of an offence and liable to a fine][a] not exceeding [€1,904.61][b], and if a company does not keep its name painted or affixed in manner so directed, the company and every officer of

the company who is in default [shall be guilty of an offence and liable to a fine][a] not exceeding [€1,904.61][b].

(3) If a company fails to comply with paragraph (b) or paragraph (c) of subsection (1), the company [shall be guilty of an offence and liable to a fine][c] not exceeding [€1,904.61][d].

(4) If an officer of a company or any person on its behalf—

(a) uses or authorises the use of any seal purporting to be a seal of the company whereon its name is not so engraven as aforesaid, or

(b) issues or authorises the issue of any business letter of the company or any notice or other official publication of the company, or signs or authorises to be signed on behalf of the company any bill of exchange, promissory note, endorsement, cheque or order for money or goods wherein its name is not mentioned in manner aforesaid, or

(c) issues or authorises the issue of any invoice, receipt or letter of credit of the company wherein its name is not mentioned in manner aforesaid;

he [shall be guilty of an offence and liable to a fine][c] not exceeding [€1,904.61] [d], and shall further be personally liable to the holder of the bill of exchange, promissory note, cheque or order for money or goods for the amount thereof unless it is duly paid by the company.

[(5) The use of the abbreviation 'Ltd.' for 'Limited' or 'Teo.' for 'Teoranta' or 'p.l.c.' for 'public limited company' or 'c.p.t.' for 'cuideachta phoiblí theoranta' shall not be a breach of the provisions of this section.][e]

Amendments

a Words 'shall be guilty of an offence and liable to a fine' in CA 1963, s 114(2) substituted for 'shall be liable for a fine' by C(AA)A 2003, s 57 and Sch 2, Item No. 4.

b '£125' substituted for '£25' by C(A)A 1982, Sch 1, increased to £1,500 by CA 1990, s 240(7) as inserted by CLEA 2001, s 104(c) and converted to €1,904.61 by Council Regulations No 1103/97, No 974/98 and No 2866/98 and the Economic and Monetary Union Act 1998, s 6.

c Words 'shall be guilty of an offence and liable to a fine' in CA 1963, s 114(3) and (4) substituted for ' shall be liable for a fine' by C(AA)A 2003, s 57 and Sch 2, Item No. 1.

d '£250' substituted for '£50' by C(A)A 1982, Sch 1, increased to £1,500 by CA 1990, s 240(7) as inserted by CLEA 2001, s 104(c) and converted to €1,904.61 by Council Regulations No 1103/97, No 974/98 and No 2866/98 and the Economic and Monetary Union Act 1998, s 6.

e CA 1963, s 114(5) substituted by C(A)A 1983, Sch 1, para 13.

Definitions

'company': CA 1963, s 2(1); 'officer': CA 1963, s 2(1); 'officer in default': CA 1963, s 383

Notes

Name on company seal: The name which must be engraved on the company's seal is its corporate name rather than any trading name.[1]

1 *OTV Birwelco Ltd v Technical and General Guarantee Co Ltd* [2002] 2 BCLC 723.

Business letters: All business letters, notices and other official publications of the company, and all bills of exchange, promissory notes, endorsements, cheques and orders for money or goods[1] purporting to be signed by or on behalf of the company, as well as all invoices, receipts and letters of credit of the company, must clearly state the company's registered name.[2] For certain classes of documents however, the following particulars must also be stated:

Business letters

(a) the present Christian name (or the initials thereof) and present surname, as well as any former Christian names and surnames of the each director, together with details of his nationality, if not Irish.[3]

Business letters, order forms, web sites and emails

(b) the place of registration and registered number of the company;[4]

(c) the registered office;[5]

(d) in the case of a company exempt under CA 1963, s 24 from the obligation to use the word 'limited' or 'teoranta' as part of its name, the fact that it is a limited company;[6]

(e) if there is reference to the share capital of the company, the reference shall be to the paid-up share capital.[7]

Business letters, order forms and invoices

(f) in the case of a company that is being wound up,[8] (and the fact that it is so[9]) or is in receivership[10] or that is under the protection of the court.[11]

1 *Semble* orders for services do not come within the ambit of the section.

2 CA 1963, s 114(1)(c).

3 CA 1963, s 196(1). CA 1963, s 196 (2): In special circumstances, the Minister may, either conditionally or unconditionally, exempt the company from the requirement to set out details of its directors on business letters.

4 EC(C)R 1973, reg 9(1)(a).

5 EC(C)R 1973, reg 9(1)(b).

6 EC(C)R 1973, reg 9(1)(c).

7 EC(C)R 1973, reg 9(2).

8 CA 1963, s 303(1).

9 EC(C)R 1973, reg 9(1)(d).

10 CA 1963, s 317(1).

11 C(A)A 1990, s 12(4).

Personal liability for misstatement of name

Grounds for imposition of liability: If an officer of the company or any person on its behalf signs or authorises to be signed on behalf of the company any bill of exchange, promissory note, endorsement, cheque or order for money or goods[1] on which the company's registered name is not clearly stated, that person will be personally liable to the holder of the bill, note, cheque or order, as the case may be, for the amount thereof unless it is paid by the company.[2] Even if the misstatement of the company's name has been made by the holder of the document, the company's agent is nonetheless obliged to ensure that the name is accurately stated on the document before he signs it or authorises the signing of it.[3] However, in the case of a bill of exchange, if the words of acceptance are prescribed by the holder thereof and they contain a misstatement of the company's name, he may be estopped from enforcing the statutory liability against the persons who signed or authorised the signing of the bill.[4]

Document must be signed for liability to arise: Even if the company's name has been inaccurately stated on the bill of exchange, promissory note, cheque or order for money or goods, personal liability cannot arise unless the document has actually been signed on behalf of the company.[5] Moreover, where it is sought to impose personal liability – not on the actual signatory – but on the person who authorised the signing of the document, it must be shown that he not only authorised the signing of the relevant document but also that he authorised it to be signed in such a way that the name of the company would not properly appear thereon.[6] The giving of such authority may be inferred in appropriate circumstances, as where the person who authorised the signing of the document knew at the time that there was a misprint of the name in the company's stationery.[7]

What constitutes a misstatement of the company name: It has been held in the UK that the company's name will not be regarded as having been properly stated on the bill of exchange, promissory note, cheque or order for money or goods, in the following circumstances:

(a) where the company's registered name is completely omitted from the document;[8]

(b) where part of the company's registered name is omitted;[9]

(c) where extra words are added to the company's name;[10]

(d) where words in the company's registered name are abbreviated.[11] It is, however, permissible to abbreviate 'company' to 'co'[12] and to abbreviate the words 'limited', 'teoranta', 'public limited company' and 'ciudeachta phoiblí theoranta' to 'ltd', 'teo', 'plc' and 'cpt' respectively;[13]

(e) in the case of a limited company, where the appropriate statement of limited liability (or the abbreviation thereof, as the case may be) is omitted altogether from the end of the company's name.[14]

No rectification of irregular document: Rectification of the document will not be ordered after it has been signed by the company's officer or agent, where the purpose of such an order would be to avoid personal liability under CA 1963, s 114(4).[15]

Liability of officer or agent is secondary: Civil liability under s 114(4) is secondary to that of the company, so that the company's agent, if called upon to pay, will be entitled to claim an indemnity from the company itself.[16]

Who is the 'holder' of the document: The person entitled to maintain a claim under s 114 is the holder of the bill of exchange, promissory note etc. It has been held that the 'holder' is the person to whom the document is addressed and who is to benefit by it.[17]

1 *Semble* orders for services do not come within the ambit of the section.

2 CA 1963, s 114(4).

3 *Lindholst and Co A/S v Fowler* [1988] BCLC 166.

4 *Durham Fancy Goods Ltd v Michael Jackson (Fancy Goods) Ltd* [1968] 2 QB 839.

5 *Oshkosh B'Gosh Inc v Dan Marbel Inc Ltd* [1989] BCLC 507.

6 *John Wilkes Footwear Ltd v Lee International Footwear Ltd* [1985] BCLC 444.

7 *John Wilkes Footwear Ltd v Lee International Footwear Ltd* [1985] BCLC 444.

8 *Rafsanjan Pistachio Producers Co-Operative v Reiss* [1990] BCLC 352.

9 *Penrose v Merthyr* (1858) EB and E 499; *Atkins and Co v Wardle* (1889) 6 ILT 23; *Hendon v Adelman* (1973) 117 Sol Jo 631; *British Airways Board v Parish* [1979] 2 Lloyd's Rep 361; *Maxform SpA v Mariani and Goodville Ltd* [1979] 2 Lloyd's Rep 385; *Barber and Nicholls Ltd v R and G Associates (London) Ltd* (1981) 132 NLJ 1076; *Blum v OCP Repatriation SA* [1988] BCLC 170; *Lindholst and Co A/S v Fowler* [1988] BCLC 166. A trivial misspelling of the company's name, which leaves nobody in any doubt as to the identity of the company with which they are dealing, will not, however, result in personal liability being incurred: *Jenice Ltd v Dan* [1993] BCLC 1349.

10 *Nassau Steam Press v Tyler* (1894) 70 LT 376.

11 *Durham Fancy Goods Ltd v Michael Jackson (Fancy Goods) Ltd* [1968] 2 All ER 987.

12 *Banque de l'Indochine et de Suez SA v Euroseas Group Finances Co Ltd* [1981] 3 All ER 198.

13 CA 1963, s 114(5). *Stacey and Co v Wallis* (1912) 106 LT 544.

14 *Penrose v Merthyr* (1858) EB and E 499; *Lindholst and Co A/S v Fowler* [1988] BCLC 166.

[15] *Blum v OCP Repartition SA* [1988] BCLC 170; *Rafsanjan Pistachio Producers Co-Operative v Reiss* [1990] BCLC 352.

[16] *Brook's Wharf and Bull Ltd v Goodman Bros* [1937] 1 KB 534.

[17] *Civil Service Co-Operative Society Ltd v Chapman* (1914) 30 TLR 376.

UK legislation

See CA 1985, ss 348, 349, 350; CA 1989, s 130(7), Sch 17, para 7.

Restrictions on Commencement of Business

115 Restrictions on commencement of business

(1) Where a company having a share capital has issued a prospectus inviting the public to subscribe for its shares, the company shall not commence any business or exercise any borrowing powers unless—

(a) shares held subject to the payment of the whole amount thereof in cash have been allotted to an amount not less in the whole than the minimum subscription; and

(b) every director of the company has paid to the company on each of the shares taken or contracted to be taken by him and for which he is liable to pay in cash, a proportion equal to the proportion payable on application and allotment on the shares offered for public subscription; and

(c) no money is or may become liable to be repaid to applicants for any shares or debentures which have been offered for public subscription by reason of any failure to apply for or to obtain permission for the shares or debentures to be dealt in on any stock exchange; and

(d) there has been delivered to the registrar of companies for registration a statutory declaration by the secretary or one of the directors, in the prescribed form, that the aforesaid conditions have been complied with.

(2) Where a company having a share capital has not issued a prospectus inviting the public to subscribe for its shares, the company shall not commence any business or exercise any borrowing powers unless—

(a) there has been delivered to the registrar of companies for registration a statement in lieu of prospectus; and

(b) every director of the company has paid to the company, on each of the shares taken or contracted to be taken by him and for which he is liable to pay in cash, a proportion equal to the proportion payable on application and allotment on the shares payable in cash; and

(c) there has been delivered to the registrar of companies for registration a statutory declaration by the secretary or one of the directors, in the prescribed form, that paragraph (b) of this subsection has been complied with.

(3) The registrar of companies shall, on the delivery to him of the said statutory declaration, and, in the case of a company which is required by this section to deliver a statement in lieu of prospectus, of such a statement, certify that the company is entitled to commence business, and that certificate shall be conclusive evidence that the company is so entitled.

(4) Any contract made or ratified by a company before the date at which it is entitled to commence business shall be provisional only, and shall not be binding on the company until that date, and on that date it shall become binding.

(5) Nothing in this section shall prevent the simultaneous offer for subscription or allotment of any shares and debentures or the receipt of any money payable on application for debentures.

[(6)If any company commences business or exercises borrowing powers in contravention of this section, every person who is responsible for the contravention shall, without prejudice to any other liability, be guilty of an offence and liable to a fine not exceeding €1,904.61]. [a]

(7) Nothing in this section shall apply to—

(a) a private company, or

(b) a company registered before the 1st day of January, 1901, or

(c) a company registered before the 1st day of July, 1908, which has not issued a prospectus inviting the public to subscribe for its shares.

[(d) a public limited company registered as such on its original incorporation under the Companies (Amendment) Act, 1983.][b]

Amendments

a CA 1963, s 115(6) substituted by IFCMPA 2005, s 73.

b CA 1963, s 115(7)(d) inserted by C(A)A 1983, Sch 1, para 14.

Cross references

See generally Prospectus (Directive 2003/71/EC) Regulations 2005 (SI 324/2005) and notes thereto.

See also C(A)A 1983, s 6 and notes thereto.

Definitions

'company': CA 1963, s 2(1); 'debenture': CA 1963, s 2(1); 'director': CA 1963, s 2(1); 'the minimum subscription': CA 1963, s 2(1), s 53(2); 'prescribed': CA 1963, s 2(1); 'private company': CA 1963, s 2(1), s 33(1); 'prospectus': CA 1963, s 2(1); 'the registrar of companies': CA 1963, s 2(1); 'share': CA 1963, s 2(1); 'officer in default': CA 1963, s 383.

Notes

Public unlimited companies: The provisions of CA 1963, s 115 impose restrictions on certain types of company commencing business until they have been issued with a trading certificate by the Registrar. The section is expressed not to apply to private companies or to companies formed as plcs,[1] and as a result, is only of practical application to companies which are incorporated as public unlimited companies. It should be noted, however, that similar, though not identical, restrictions on the commencement of business are imposed on plcs by C(A)A 1983, s 6.

1 CA 1963, s 115(7).

Issue of prospectus: For circumstances in which a prospectus will be required, see Prospectus (Directive 2003/71/EC) Regulations 2005 (SI 324/2005)and notes thereto.

Statement in lieu of prospectus: For the circumstances in which a statement in lieu of prospectus will be required, see CA 1963, s 35.

Issue of trading certificate: Once a statutory declaration has been submitted to the Registrar confirming the requirements of CA 1963, s 115(1) or (2), as the case may be, have been complied with, the Registrar issues the company with a trading certificate, entitling it to commence business.

Consequences of commencing business without trading certificate: The absence of a trading certificate will not prevent the company from offering for subscription or allotting any shares nor will it prevent the company from receiving payment for such securities.[1] However, any other contract made or ratified by the company shall only be 'provisional', unless and until a trading certificate is issued.[2] While the contract is 'provisional', it will not be binding on the company.[3]

1 CA 1963, s 115(5).

2 CA 1963, s 115(4).

3 *Re Otto Electrical Manufacturing Co (1905) Ltd, Jenkin's Claim* [1906] 2 Ch 390; *New Druce-Portland Co v Blakiston* (1908) 24 TLR 583.

Register of Members

116 Register of members

(1) Subject to subsection (4), every company shall keep a register of its members and enter therein the following particulars—

(a) the names, addresses [...][a] of the members, and, in the case of a company having a share capital, a statement of the shares held by each member, distinguishing each share by its number so long as the share has a number, and of the amount paid or agreed to be considered as paid on the shares of each member;

(b) the date at which each person was entered in the register as a member;

(c) the date at which any person ceased to be a member.

(2) The entries required under paragraphs (a) and (b) of subsection (1) shall be made within 28 days after the conclusion of the agreement with the company to become a member or, in the case of a subscriber of the memorandum, within 28 days after the registration of the company.

(3) The entry required under paragraph (c) of the subsection (1) shall be made within 28 days after the date when the person concerned ceased to be a member, or, if he ceased to be a member otherwise than as a result of action by the company, within 28 days of production to the company of evidence satisfactory to the company of the occurrence of the event whereby he ceased to be a member.

(4) Where the company has converted any of its shares into stock and given notice of the conversion to the registrar of companies, the register shall show the amount of stock held by each member instead of the amount of shares and the particulars relating to shares specified in paragraph (a) of subsection (1).

(5) Subject to subsection (6), the register of members shall, except when it is closed under the provisions of this Act, be kept at the registered office of the company, so, however, that—

(a) if the work of making it up is done at another office of the company, it may be kept at that other office; and

(b) if the company arranges with some other person for the making up of the register to be undertaken on behalf of the company by that other person, it may be kept at the office of that other person at which the work is done.

(6) The register of members shall not be kept at a place outside the State.

(7) Subject to subsection (8), every company shall send notice to the registrar of companies of the place where its register of members is kept and of any change in that place.

(8) A company shall not be bound to send notice under subsection (7) where the register has, at all times since it came into existence or, in the case of a register in existence on the operative date, at all times since then, been kept at the registered office of the company.

(9) Where a company makes default in complying with any of the requirements of subsections (1) to (6) or makes default for 14 days in complying with subsection (7), the company and every officer of the company who is in default [shall be guilty of an offence and liable to a fine][b] not exceeding [€1,904.61].[c]

Amendments

a Words 'and occupations' deleted by C(A)A 1982, s 20.

b Words substituted by C(AA)A 2003, s 57 and Sch 2, Item No 1.

c '£500' substituted for '£100' by C(A)A 1982 Sch 1, increased to £1,500 by CA 1990, s 240(7) as inserted b CLEA 2001, s 104(c) and converted to €1,904.61 by Council Regulations (EC) No 1103/97, No 974/98 and No 2866/98 and the Economic and Monetary Union Act 1998, s 6.

Cross reference

See generally CLRG, First Report, at para 4.4, 'Register of members and other registers'.

Definitions

'company': CA 1963, s 2(1); 'member': CA 1963, s 31; 'memorandum': CA 1963, s 2(1); 'officer': CA 1963, s 2(1); 'officer in default': CA 1963, s 383; 'the operative date': CA 1963, s 2(1); 'the registrar of companies': CA 1963, s 2(1); 'share': CA 1963, s 2(1).

Notes

Classes of shares held: Where the share capital of the company is divided into different classes the register, apart from stating the total number of shares held by the member, must also specify the classes of shares he holds and the number of shares in each class.[1]

1 *Re Performing Rights Society Ltd* [1978] 2 All ER 712.

Uncertificated shares: In order to speed up the settlement of bargains, the Stock Exchange had for some time been pressing for a completely electronic system for recording and transferring securities. The system is known as CREST and was introduced pursuant to the CA 1990 (US) regs 1996.[1] Securities governed by these regulations are known as 'uncertificated units of security.[2] Title to such securities is recorded electronically by the company and may likewise be transferred electronically rather than by way of an 'instrument of transfer'.[3] Where a company participates in CREST, it must enter on its register of members, in respect of any class of shares which is a participating security, the number of shares each member holds in uncertificated form (ie electronically) and certificated form respectively.[4]

1 For a fuller discussion of this computer based system see the Companies Act 1990 (Uncertificated Securities) Regulations 1996 and the notes thereto.
2 Companies Act 1990 (Uncertificated Securities) Regulations 1996, reg 3(1).
3 Companies Act 1990 (Uncertificated Securities) Regulations 1996, regs 4(1), 6(1) and 9(1).
4 Companies Act 1990 (Uncertificated Securities) Regulations 1996, reg 10(1).

Conversion of shares into stock: If the company converts any of its shares into stock, details of the amount of stock held by each member shall be entered in the register opposite the member's name in substitution for the reference to the amount of shares held by him.[1]

1 CA 1963, s 116(4). For the distinction between stock and shares and for the procedure governing such conversions, see CA 1963, s 69 and the notes thereto.

Rectification of register:[1] Changes in the particulars contained in the register of members should be effected only under the authority of the board of directors and by the company secretary or other person charged with that administrative task.[2] CA 1963, s 116(1), (2) and (3) lay down time limits for the making of entries in the register of members regarding the acquisition or cessation of membership of the company. If the company fails to make such entries, the person aggrieved, or any other member of the company may apply to the court for an order directing that the register be rectified accordingly.[3]

1 In relation to the rectification of the register generally, see CA 1963, s 122 and the notes thereto.
2 *Wheatcroft's Case* (1873) 29 LT 324.
3 CA 1963, s 122(1). The power of the court to direct rectification is discretionary: *Trevor v Whitworth* (1887) 12 App Cas 409 at 440.

Transfer or transmission of shares: In standard form articles the registration of a transfer or transmission of shares is subject to the discretion of the directors.[1] In the case of a transfer of shares, if the company refuses to enter the transfer in the register in the register of members, it must so advise the transferee within two months.[2] A failure to make such notification may result in the directors power of veto lapsing, whereupon the shareholder will be entitled to apply, as a 'person aggrieved'[3] for an order rectifying the register accordingly.[4]

1 See CA 1963, s 79 and the notes thereto as well as Table A, Part I, reg 24 and reg 30, and Part II, reg 3.
2 CA 1963, s 84.
3 CA 1963, s 22(1).
4 *Re Hackney Pavilion Ltd* [1924] 1 Ch 276; *Moodie v W and J Shepherd (Bookbinders) Ltd* [1949] 2 All ER 1044; *Re Swaledale Cleaners Ltd* [1968] 1 WLR 1710; *Tett v Phoenix Property and Investment Co Ltd* [1986] BCLC 149; *Re New Cedos Engineering Co Ltd* [1994] 1 BCLC 797.

Register kept otherwise than in legible form: The register of members may be kept in non-legible form (eg on a computer system) provided that it is capable of being reproduced in legible form.

1 C(A)A 1977, s 4(2); see also CA 1963, s 378.

Register of substantial interests: Every plc must keep and maintain a register of beneficial interests in shares held by individuals which exceed the 'notifiable percentage' under CA 1990, Part IV ie 5%.[1] The individual must notify to the company and the company must enter in the register, details of the extent of the individual beneficial interest in 'relevant share capital'[2] of the company, as well details of any upward or downward movement in the amount of shares held by him. Moreover, if the company is listed, the individual must make the same disclosure of his interests to the Stock Exchange as he does to the company.[3]

1 CA 1990, s 80.
2 For the definition of 'relevant share capital', see CA 1990, s 67(2).
3 CA 1990, s 91.

Beneficial Interests in Shares: Beneficial interests in shares are not capable of being entered in the register of members.[1]

[1] See CA 1963, s 123 and the notes thereto.

UK legislation

See CA 1985, ss 352, 353; The Companies (Acquisition of Own Shares) (Treasury Shares) No 2 Regulations) 2003 (SI 2003/3031), reg 4, Sch, para 18.

---

117 Index of members

(1) Every company having more than fifty members shall, unless the register of members is in such a form as to constitute in itself an index, keep an index of the names of the members of the company and shall, within 14 days after the date on which any alteration is made in the register of members, make any necessary alteration in the index.

(2) The index shall in respect of each member contain a sufficient indication to enable the account of that member in the register to be readily found.

(3) The index shall be at all times kept at the same place as the register of members.

(4) If default is made in complying with this section, the company and every officer of the company who is in default [shall be guilty of an offence and liable to a fine][a] not exceeding [€1,904.61][b].

Amendments

a Words substituted by C(AA)A 2003, s 57 and Sch 2, Item No 1.

b '£250' substituted for '£50' by C(A)A 1982 Sch 1, increased to £1,500 by CA 1990, s 240(7) as inserted by CLEA 2001, s 104(c) and converted to €1,904.61 by Council Regulations (EC) No 1103/97, No 974/98 and No 2866/98 and the Economic and Monetary Union Act 1998, s 6.

Definitions

'company': CA 1963, s 2(1); 'member': CA 1963, s 31; 'officer': CA 1963, s 2(1); 'officer in default': CA 1963, s 383.

Notes

Company with more than 50 members: The requirement for a separate index of members arises only if the register of members is not itself kept in such a form as to constitute an index, and even then, only where the company has more than 50 members.

UK legislation

See CA 1985, s 354.

---

118 Provisions as to entries in register in relation to share warrants

(1) On the issue of a share warrant the company shall strike out of its register of members the name of the member then entered therein as holding the shares specified in the warrant as if he had ceased to be a member and shall enter in the register the following particulars:

(a) the fact of the issie of the warrant; and

(b) a statement of the shares included in the warrant, distinguishing each share by its number so long as the share has a number; and

(c) the date of the issue of the warrant.

(2) The bearer of a share warrant shall, subject to the articles of the company, be entitled on surrendering it for cancellation to have his name entered as a member in the register of members.

(3) The company shall be responsible for any loss incurred by any person by reason of the company entering in the register the name of a bearer of a share warrant in respect of the shares therein specified without the warrant being surrendered and cancelled.

(4) Until the warrant is surrendered, the particulars specified in subsection (1) shall be deemed to be the particulars required by this Act to be entered in the register of members, and, on surrender, the date of the surrender must be entered.

(5) Subject to the provisions of this Act, the bearer of a share warrant may, if the articles of the company so provide, be deemed to be a member of the company within the meaning of this Act, either to the full extent or for any purposes defined in the articles.

Definitions

'articles': CA 1963, s 2(1); 'company': CA 1963, s 2(1); 'member': CA 1963, s 31; 'share': CA 1963, s 2(1); 'share warrant': CA 1963, s 2(1), s 88(2).

Notes

Share warrants: Share warrants are bearer securities. Ownership of the shares may be transferred, and membership of the company may thus be altered, by simply effecting delivery of the securities from one person to another.[1] In practice, share warrants may only be used in public companies because CA 1963, s 33(1)(a) requires the articles of each private company to contain provisions restricting the right to transfer shares; a transfer of shares by simple delivery of the share warrant would be in *prima facie* conflict with such restrictions.

1 In relation to share warrants generally, see CA 1963, s 88.

Entry of name in register of members:[1] If the articles so provide, the holder of a share warrant may present it to the company for cancellation and thereafter have his name entered in the register of members.[2] No such article is to be found, however, in Table A. Nor indeed, does Table A contain any provision for the issue of share warrants or for the holders of such securities to be treated as members of the company. Instead, membership is as defined by CA 1963, s 31.

1 In relation to the register of members generally, see CA 1963, s 116.

2 CA 1963, s 118(2).

UK legislation

See CA 1985, s 355.

---

119 Inspection of register and index

(1) Except when the register of members is closed under the provisions of this Act, the register, and index of the names, of the members of a company shall during business hours (subject to such reasonable restrictions as the company in general meeting may impose, so that not less than 2 hours in each day be allowed for inspection) be open to

the inspection of any member without charge, and of any other person on payment of one shilling, or such less sum as the company may prescribe, for each inspection.

(2) Any member or other person may require a copy of the register, or of any part thereof, on payment of [8 cent][a], or such less sum as the company may prescribe, for every 100 words or fractional part thereof required to be copied.

The company shall cause any copy so required by any person to be sent to that person within a period of 10 days commencing on the day next after the day on which the requirement is received by the company.

(3) If any inspection required under this section is refused or if any copy required under this section is not sent within the proper period, the company and every officer of the company who is in default shall be liable in respect of each offence to a fine not exceeding [€1,904.61][b].

(4) In the case of any such refusal or default, the court may by order compel an immediate inspection of the register and index or direct that the copies required shall be sent to the persons requiring them.

Amendments

a 'Sixpence' converted to 8 cent by by Council Regulations (EC) No 1103/97, No 974/98 and No 2866/98 and the Economic and Monetary Union Act 1998, s 6.

b '£250' substituted for '£50' by C(A)A 1982, Sch 1, increased to £1,500 by CA 1990, s 240(7) as inserted by CLEA 2001, s 104(c) and converted to €1,904.61 by Council Regulations (EC) No 1103/97, No 974/98 and No 2866/98 and the Economic and Monetary Union Act 1998, s 6.

Cross references

CA 1990, s 105(1): the Minister may, by order alter any of the charges referred to in CA 1963, s 119(1), (2).

Definitions

'company': CA 1963, s 2(1); 'the court': CA 1963, s 2(1); 'member': CA 1963, s 31; 'officer': CA 1963, s 2(1); 'officer in default': CA 1963, s 383.

Notes

Inspection of register and index: The register of members and the index, if any,[1] must be open to public inspection for at least two hours per day, subject, however, to the entitlement of the company to close the register for a period of up to 30 days per year.[2] The person seeking to inspect the register need not specify his reasons for so doing.[3] Moreover, inspection of the register cannot be refused on the ground that the applicant is the solicitor for parties who are engaged in litigation against the company, even though the inspection is in the interests of the applicant's clients and not in the interests of the company or any individual member of the company.[4]

1 For the circumstances in which an index of members is required to be kept, see CA 1963, s 117 and the notes thereto.

2 CA 1963, ss 119(1) and 121.

3 *Holland v Dickson* (1888) 37 Ch D 669; *Davies v Gas Light and Coke Co* [1909] 1 Ch 248, aff'd [1909] 1 Ch 708.

4 *R v Wiltshire and Berkshire Canal Navigation* (1874) 29 LT 922.

Winding up: The entitlement to inspect the register of members and the index and to take copies has been held to cease when the company goes into liquidation.[1]

[1] *Re Kent Coalfields Syndicate* [1898] 1 QB 754.

Investment companies: The provisions of CA 1963, s 119 regarding the inspection of the register and index do not apply to investment companies.[1]

[1] CA 1990, s 260(1).

Lien on register and index: Solicitors, accountants and others are unable to claim a lien on the register of members or on the index, because of the fact that the Act requires these documents to be kept at and to be open for inspection at the registered office or at such other place where the work of maintaining them is carried out.[1]

[1] *Re Capital Fire Insurance Association* (1883) 24 Ch D 408; *DTC (CNC) Ltd v Gary Sargent* [1996] 2 All ER 369.

UK legislation

See CA 1985, s 356; CA 1989, ss 143(8), 212, Sch 24.

---

120 Consequences of failure to comply with requirements as to register owing to agent's default

Where, by virtue of paragraph (b) of subsection (5) of section 116, the register of members is kept at the office of some person other than the company, and by reason of any default of his the company fails to comply with subsection (7) of that section or subsection (3) of section 117 or section 119, or with any requirements of this Act as to the production of the register, that other person shall be liable to the same penalties as if he were an officer of the company who is in default, and the power of the court under subsection (4) of section 119, shall extend to the making of orders against that other person and his officers or servants.

Definitions

'agent'; CA 1963, s 2(1); 'company': CA 1963, s 2(1); 'the court': CA 1963, s 2(1); 'member': CA 1963, s 31; 'officer': CA 1963, s 2(1); 'officer in default': CA 1963, s 383.

Notes

Liability of third parties: CA 1963, s 120 applies to a situation where the register of members is kept and maintained on behalf of the company by a third party such as the company secretarial division of a bank or firm of solicitors or accountants. Criminal penalties may be imposed upon such a third party for failure to notify the Registrar that the register is being kept by him[1] or for failure to keep the register and index at the same place[2] or for failure to produce the register for inspection.[3] Notably, however, s 120 does not purport to impose any liability on the third party for complete failure to maintain the register.

[1] CA 1963, s 116(7).
[2] CA 1963, s 117(3).
[3] CA 1963, s 119.

UK legislation

See CA 1985, s 357.

---

121 Power to close register

A company may, on giving notice by advertisement in some newspaper circulating in the district in which the registered office of the company is situate, close the register of members for any time or times not exceeding in the whole 30 days in each year.

Definitions

'company': CA 1963, s 2(1); 'member': CA 1963, s 31.

Notes

Closing the register: CA 1963, s 121 permits the company to close the register for up to 30 days per year, having first advertised this fact in a newspaper. The temporary closing of the register may take place, for example, during the period between the giving of notice of a general meeting and the date of the meeting itself.

UK legislation

See CA 1985, s 358.

122 Rectification of register

(1) If—

- (a) the name of any person is, without sufficient cause, entered in the register of members or omitted therefrom in contravention of subsections (1) and (2) of section 116; or
- (b) default is made in entering on the register within the period fixed by subsection (3) of section 116 the fact of any person having ceased to be a member;

the person aggrieved, or any member of the company, or the company, may apply to the court for rectification of the register.

(2) Where an application is made under this section, the court may either refuse the application or may order rectification of the register and payment by the company of compensation for any loss sustained by any party aggrieved.

(3) On an application under this section the court may decide any question relating to the title of any person who is a party to the application to have his name entered in or omitted from the register, whether the question arises between members or alleged members, or between members or alleged members on the one hand and the company on the other hand, and generally may decide any question necessary or expedient to be decided for rectification of the register.

(4) In the case of a company required by this Act to send a list of its members to the registrar of companies, the court when making an order for rectification of the register shall by its order direct notice of the rectification to be given to the registrar.

(5) A company may, without application to the court, at any time rectify any error or omission (whether occurring before, on or after the operative date) in the register but such a rectification shall not adversely affect any person unless he agrees to the rectification made. The company shall, within 21 days, give notice of the rectification to the registrar of companies if the error or omission also occurs in any document forwarded by the company to him.

Definitions

'company': CA 1963, s 2(1); 'the court': CA 1963, s 2(1); 'document': CA 1963, s 2(1): 'member': CA 1963, s 31; 'the operative date': CA 1963, s 2(1); 'the registrar of companies': CA 1963, s 2(1).

Notes

Jurisdiction of the court: The jurisdiction of the court to order rectification of the register arises where:

(a) the name of a member is 'without sufficient cause' entered in or omitted from the register;[1] or

(b) the company fails to remove the name of a former member from the register within the relevant 28 day period prescribed by CA 1963, s 116(3). [2]

On the hearing of the application the court is empowered to determine any question relating to the title of the shares[3] and apart from ordering rectification, may also award damages against the company by way of compensation for any loss suffered by any party aggrieved.[4] If costs are to be awarded against individual directors as opposed to the company, those directors should be named as respondents to the proceedings.[5] If the rectification involves removing the name of an allottee from the register (eg where he was induced by fraud or misrepresentation on the part of the company to take the shares in the first place) damages may be measured as the amount paid for the shares together with interest thereon.[6] On the other hand, if the rectification involves the specific performance of a contract to allot shares, damages will be measured as the amount of declared dividends which the applicant would otherwise have received together with interest.[7]

The court's power under the section is discretionary[8] and, in the case of a transfer or transmission of shares, the following may be sufficient grounds for refusing to rectify the register:

(a) that the company has not been given a 'reasonable time' to register the transfer or transmission, as the case may be.[9]

(b) that the directors have, within a reasonable time, properly exercised a power conferred on them by the articles to decline to register the transfer or transmission;[10]

(c) that the applicant has been guilty of undue delay in seeking to have th register rectified.[11]

1 CA 1963, s 122(1)(a).

2 CA 1963, s 122(1)(a).

3 CA 1963, s 122(3). See *Re Hoicrest Ltd, Keane v Martin* [2000] 1 BCLC 194.

4 CA 1963, s 122(2).

5 *Morgan v Morgan Insurance Brokers Ltd* [1993] BCLC 676.

6 *Re Metropolitan Coal Consumers' Association, ex parte Wainwright* [1890] WN 3.

7 *Sri Lanka Omnibus Co Ltd v Perera* [1952] AC 76.

8 *Trevor v Whitworth* (1887) 12 App Cas 409; *Re Olde Court Holiday Hostel Ltd* [2006] IEHC 424.

9 *Kinsella v Alliance and Dublin Consumers Gas Co* [1982] IEHC 22 (Barron J).

10 For the type of discretion conferred on directors pursuant to standard form articles to refuse to register a transfer or transmission of shares, and the fiduciary constraints regarding the exercise of such powers, see CA 1963, s 79 and the notes thereto, as well as Table A, Part I, regs 24 and 30 and Part II, reg 3. As regards what constitutes a reasonable time within which to decide whether or not to refuse to register a transfer of shares CA 1963, s 84 and the notes thereto.

11 *Re Isis Factors plc* [2003] 2 BCLC 411; *Banfi Ltd v Moran & ors* [2006] IEHC 257: Laffoy J found that a delay of two years was not sufficient to prevent a successful applicaton to have the register rectified.

'Without sufficient cause': The following have all been held to circumstances warranting rectification of the register:

1. Where the company removed the name of one person from the register and entered the name of another on foot of a forged share transfer.[1]
2. Where the company has wrongfully forfeited shares.[2]
3. Where the applicant was induced to acquire the shares and to become a member as a result of an untrue statement in a prospectus or as a result of some other misrepresentation.[3] Rectification may be refused, however, if the applicant has been guilty of unreasonable delay,[4] or if the company has since gone into liquidation.[5]
4. Where the directors' power to refuse to register a transfer or transmission of shares has lapsed.[6]
5. Where shares have been allotted to members other than the applicant in breach of pre-emption provisions.[7]
6. Where the directors have, in breach of the provisions of the articles, wrongfully refused to register a transfer or transmission of shares.[8]
7. Where a purported transfer of shares had been registered by the company notwithstanding the fact that the purported transfer was unauthorised by the true owner, was unsupported by any consideration and was not effected pursuant to properly executed share transfer forms.[9]
8. Where due to an administrative oversight, a transfer of shares from one person to another was not recorded in the register of members.[10]
9. Where a company issued a share certificate to an individual in respect of a particular number of shares but then failed to record that holding in the register.[11]
10. Where a company had effected an unlawful bonus issue of shares.[12]
11. Where shares were transferred in breach of restrictive provisions containd in the articles of association.[13]

1 *Davis v Bank of England* [1824] 2 Bing 393; *Sloman v Bank of England* [1845] 14 Sim 475; *Re Bahia and San Francisco Railway* (1868) LR 3 QB 584; *Barton v London and Northwestern Railway* (1888) 38 ChD 144; *Welch v Bank of England* [1955] Ch 508.

2 *Re Ystalyfera Gas Co* [1887] WN 30. In relation to the company's power of forfeiture see CA 1963, Table A, Pt I, regs 33–39.

3 *Stewart's Case* (1886) 1 Ch App 574; *Component's Tube Co v Naylor* [1900] 2 IR 1. See also CA 1963, s 49 and the notes thereto.

4 *Sewell's Case* (1868) 3 Ch App 131; *Re Scottish Petroleum Co* (1883) 23 Ch D 413.

5 *Oakes v Turquand and Harding; Peek v Turquand and Harding* [1867] LR 2 HL 325; *Tennant v City of Glasgow Bank* (1880) 5 App Cas 317.

6 See CA 1963, ss 79 and 84 and the notes thereto. See also *Re Inverdeck Ltd* [1998] 2 BCLC 242.

7 *Re Thundercrest Ltd* [1995] 1 BCLC 117.

8 *Banfi Ltd v Moran & ors* [2006] IEHC 257; *Re New Cedos Engineering Co Ltd* [1994] 1 BCLC 797.

9 *International Credit and Investment Co (Overseas) Ltd v Adham* [1994] 1 BCLC 66.

10 *Re New Millenium Experience Co Ltd* [2004] 1 BCLC 19; *Re Fagin's Bookshop plc* [1992] BCLC 118.

11 *Alipour v UOC Corp* [2002] 2 BCLC 770.

12 *Re Cleveland Trust plc* [1991] BCLC 424.

13 *Re Picadilly Radio plc* [1989] BCLC 683.

Rectification after forfeiture: A person whose name has been improperly entered in the register of members may obtain an order for rectification even though the shares have been forfeited in the meantime and the forfeiture has been entered on the register.[1]

1 *Re Bank of Hindustan, China and Japan, ex parte Los* (1865) 34 LJ Ch 609; *Re Bank of Hindustan, China and Japan, ex parte Martin* (1865) 2 Hem and M 669.

Rectification without executed instrument of transfer: Even though a proper share transfer form has not been executed in favour of the applicant, the court, in the exercise of its jurisdiction to decide questions of title under CA 1963, s 122(3), may nonetheless order rectification of the register in favour of the applicant in circumstances where it is satisfied that the applicant has good title to the shares (ie where he can show that he is legally entitled to an order directing the registered holder to execute an instrument of transfer in his favour).[1]

1 *Re Hoicrest Ltd, Keene v Martin* [2000] 1 BCLC 194.

Notification of membership to Registrar: Every company having a share capital is required to include in its annual return details of the ownership of its shares, including details of any change in ownership which has taken place since the filing of the last annual return.[1] If the court makes an order rectifying the register of members, it may direct the company to furnish details of the rectification to the Registrar as well.[2]

1 CA 1963, s 125 and Form B1: Companies (Forms) Order 2004 (SI 2004/133).

2 CA 1963, s 122(4).

Rectification of register after liquidation: An order for rectification may be made by the court notwithstanding the fact that the company has been wound up.[1] Rectification may be ordered in such circumstances to give effect, for example, to an unregistered allotment or transfer of shares or set aside a transfer which had been procured by fraud or through a forgery.[2] Rectification in such terms is permissible because it results in the substitution of the name of one person for another in the register of members. The person whose name appears on the register after rectification will be treated as the 'contributory' for the purpose of the liquidation. However, rectification will not be allowed, where the relief sought would result in the rescission of an allotment of shares, thereby reducing the total number of contributories of the company.[3]

1 CA 1963, s 235(1). See *Re New Millenium Experience Co Ltd* [2004] 1 BCLC 19.

2 *Hill's Case* (1867) 4 Ch App 769n; *Evans v Wood* (1867) LR 5 Eq 9; *Fyfe's Case* (1869) 4 Ch App 768; *Re Hercules Insurance Co, Lowe's Case* (1870) LR 9 Eq 589; *Re Onward Building Society* [1891] 2 QB 463; *Re Sussex Brick Co* [1904] 1 Ch 598.

3 *Oakes v Turquand and Harding; Peek v Turquand and Harding* [1867] LR 2 HL 325; *Tennant v City of Glasgow Bank* (1880) 5 App Cas 317.

Challenging the rectification order: Normally the creditors of a company will not be regarded as having a sufficient standing to challenge an order for the rectification of the register of members.[1]

1 *Re New Millenium Experience Co Ltd* [2004] 1 BCLC 19.

Rectification without application to court: Where an error is recorded in the register of members, a company may rectify that error without making an application to court, provided that such rectification does not adversely affect any person unless he or she agrees to the rectification. Where in addition to making an error or omission in the register of members, the company also advised the Registrar of Companies of that matter in say an annual return (B1) or allotment of shares (B5), the company must give notice of the rectification within 21 days of the rectification.

UK legislation

See CA 1985, s 359.

123 Trusts not to be entered on register

No notice of any trust, express, implied or constructive, shall be entered on the register or be receivable by the registrar.

Definitions

'the registrar of companies': CA 1963, s 2(1).

Notes

No registration of beneficial interests: CA 1963, s 123 does not prevent the creation of beneficial interests in shares whether by way of trust or charge or otherwise, but only prevents the entry of such interests on the register of members.[1] Because only the name of the legal owner appears in the register of members, any equitable interests in the shares may be defeated by a sale to a *bona fide* purchaser for value without notice.[2]

1 *Rearden v Provincial Bank of Ireland* [1896] 1 IR 532; *Société Generale de Paris v Walker* (1885) 11 App Cas 20.

2 *Société Generale de Paris v Walker* (1885) 11 App Cas 20; *Ireland v Harte* [1902] 1 Ch 522.

Beneficial interests cannot be ignored by company: Partly reflecting the provisions of CA 1963, s 123, Table A, reg 7 states that:

> 'Except as required by law, no person shall be recognised by the company as holding any share upon any trust, and the company shall not be bound by or compelled in any way to recognise (even when having notice thereof) any equitable, contingent, future or partial interest in any share or any interest in any fractional part of a share (except only by these regulations or by law otherwise provided) and any other rights in respect of any share except an absolute right to the entirety threof in the registered holder: this shall not preclude the company from requiring the members or a transferee of shares to furnish the company with information as to beneficial ownership of any share when such information is reasonably required by the company.'[1]

Notwithstanding the provisions of reg 7, the company is not entitled to disregard trusts and other equitable interests of which it has actual knowledge.[2] Thus, a company was precluded from claiming a lien on shares for a debts owed to it by a member in circumstances where it was aware of the fact that the member held the shares on trust for a third party.[3] Moreover, even if the member holds the shares in his own right rather than on trust, the company cannot claim priority for its own lien on the shares if, before the coming into being of the lien, the company had been given notice of the creation of a security on the shares in favour of some other person.[4] Similarly, where a resolution had been carried with the votes of trustees of shares, and the company was aware that the trustees were acting in breach of trust by voting in the manner in which they did, the court held the resolution to be null and void.[5]

1 CA 1963, Table A, Pt I, reg 7.

2 *Rearden v Provincial Bank of Ireland* [1896] 1 IR 532; *MacKereth v Wigan Coal and Iron Co Ltd* [1916] 2 Ch 293; *McGrattan v McGrattan* [1985] NI 28. The law governing such equitable interests will normally be the law of the place of incorporation of the company, being the *lex situs* of the shares: *Re Harvard Securities Ltd* [1997] 2 BCLC 369.

3 *Rearden v Provincial Bank of Ireland* [1896] 1 IR 532; *MacKereth v Wigan Coal and Iron Co* [1916] 2 Ch 293.

4 *Bradford Banking Co v Briggs and Co* (1886) 12 Ch App Cas 29; *Bank of Africa v Salisbury Gold Mining Co* [1892] AC 281; *Rainford v James Keith and Blackman Co* [1905] 2 Ch 147 at 161.

5 *McGrattan v McGrattan* [1985] NI 28.

Register of directors' shareholdings: Although beneficial interests in shares will not be entered in the register of members itself, every company must keep a separate register[1] in which is recorded details of any beneficial interests held by the directors and secretary or by their spouses and minor children[2] in shares or debentures of the company or of any other body corporate being the company's subsidiary or holding company or a subsidiary of the company's holding company.[3] In order to ensure that the register is accurate and kept up to date, the directors and secretary are under a continuing obligation of disclosure to the company regarding the acquisition or disposal of any such interests.[4] Furthermore, in the case of a listed company, any details of beneficial interests disclosed to the company by its directors and secretary, must in turn be communicated by the company to the Stock Exchange which may publish the information in such manner as it may determine.[5]

1 CA 1990, s 53.
2 CA 1990, s 64.
3 CA 1990, ss 59 and 64 and notes thereto. See also CA 1990, ss 60–63 for further details regarding the maintenance of the register.
4 CA 1990, ss 53–58.
5 CA 1990, s 65.

Register of substantial shareholdings: Every plc must keep and maintain a register of beneficial interests in shares held by individuals which exceed the 'notifiable percentage' under CA 1990, Part IV, ie 5%.[1] The individual must notify to the company and the company must enter in the register, details of the extent of the individual beneficial interest in 'relevant share capital'[2] of the company, as well details of any upward or downward movement in the amount of shares held by him. Moreover, if the company is listed, the individual must make the same disclosure of his interests to the Stock Exchange as he does to the company.[3]

1 CA 1990, s 80.
2 For the definition of 'relevant share capital', see CA 1990, s 67(2).
3 CA 1990, s 91.

Investigations as to share ownership: Where necessary for the effective administration of company law, or for the effective discharge by the ODCE of its functions under the Companies Acts or in the public interest, the Director may either appoint one or more inspectors or alternatively carry out an enquiry himself, to determine the identity of the true persons who are or have been financially interested in the success or failure (real or apparent) of the company or able to control or materially influence the policy of the company.[1] This may involve, *inter alia*, ascertaining the identity of the real individuals (as opposed to bodies corporate) who are beneficially interested in the shares or debentures of the company.[2] Furthermore, in the case of plcs, the company itself may of its own motion or upon being requisitioned to do so, conduct its own investigation into the beneficial ownership of its shares;[3] and information obtained upon such an investigation must be entered on the register of substantial shareholdings, referred to above,[4] and must also be published in a report which is to be made for inspection at the registered office.[5]

1 CA 1990, ss 14 and 15. See also CA 1990, s 16 in relation to the power of the Director to impose restrictions on shares or debentures in the company where either he or the inspector, as the case may be, is facing difficulty in finding out who really owns or controls the company.
2 *Lyons v Curran* [1993] ILRM 375; *Desmond and Dedeir v Glackin (No 2)* [1993] 3 IR 67. See also the notes to CA 1990, s 14.
3 CA 1990, s 81 and 83.
4 CA 1990, s 82.
5 CA 1990, s 84.

Notice to restrain transfer of stock: Any person claiming to be interested in any shares of a company may, upon filing a notice of the nature of his beneficial interest in the Central Office, serve a 'stop notice' on the company.[1] Having been served with a copy of the affidavit and the stop notice, it shall not be lawful for the company to permit the stock to be transferred, nor, if the notice is expressed to be intended to stop the payment of dividends, to pay dividends in respect of the shares, for so long as the notice shall remain operative.[2] Any person aggrieved by the service of the notice may apply to court to have it set aside.[3] In any event, the stop notice does not operate to totally freeze the shares. The registered owner of the shares may call upon the company to permit the shares to be transferred or to pay dividends in respect of the shares, and unless the court otherwise orders, the company will not be entitled to refuse to do so for more than eight days after the date of the request.[4] During this eight day period however, it will be open to the person claiming a beneficial interest in the shares to take whatever steps he considers appropriate to protect his position.

1 RSC 1986, Ord 46, r 6.

2 RSC 1986, Ord 46, r 10.

3 RSC 1986, Ord 46, r 11.

4 RSC 1986, Ord 46, r 12.

UK legislation

See CA 1985, s 360.

---

124 Register to be evidence

The register of members shall be *prima facie* evidence of any matters by this Act directed or authorised to be inserted therein.

Definitions

'member': CA 1963, s 31.

Notes

***Prima facie* evidence**: The register is only *prima facie* evidence of the matters contained therein and may be rectified by order of the court[1] upon evidence being adduced to show that entries in the register are untrue.[2]

1 CA 1963, s 122.

2 *Re Briton Medical and General Life Assurance Association* (1888) 39 Ch D 61.

UK legislation

See CA 1985, s 361.

Annual return

125 [Annual Return

(1) Every company shall, once at least in every year, subject to section 127, make a return to the registrar of companies, being its annual return, in the prescribed form.

(2) If a company fails to comply with this section, the company and—

(a) every officer of the company who is in default, and

(b) any person in accordance with whose directions or instructions the directors of the company are accustomed to act and to whose directions or omissions the default is attributable,

shall be guilty of an offence.

(3) Proceedings in relation to an offence under this section may be brought and prosecuted by the registrar of companies.][a]

Amendments

a CA 1963, s 125 repealed and substituted by CLEA 2001, s 59.

Cross references

CA 1990, s 260 provides that the provisions of CA 1963, s 125 shall not apply to an 'investment company'.[1]

1 'investment company': CA 1990, s 252(1).

Definitions

'annual return': CA 1963, s 2(1); 'company': CA 1963, s 2(1); 'debenture': CA 1963, s 2(1); 'director': CA 1963, s 2(1); 'member': CA 1963, s 31; 'officer': CA 1963, s 2(1); 'officer in default': CA 1963, s 383; 'prescribed': CA 1963, s 2(1); 'the registrar of companies': CA 1963, s 2(1); 'share': CA 1963, s 2(1).

Notes

The annual return:[1] Prior to 1 March 2002[2] the annual return had to be completed within 60 days after the annual general meeting ('AGM') for the year. Now, however, under CA 1963, ss 125 and 127 as substituted by CLEA 2001, ss 59 and 60, new rules have been introduced regarding the making up and filing of annual returns. Every company must file an annual return in the prescribed form[3] at least once in every year.[4]

1 See generally, Rice and Walker, 'The New Annual Return Date ('ARD') Provisions under the Companies Acts' (2002) CLP 75.

2 The operative date of CLEA 2001, s 59 which replaced CA 1963, ss 125 and 126. Company Law Enforcement Act, 2001 (Commencement) (No 2) Order 2001 (SI 438/2001).

3 For the prescribed form, see Form B1 of the Companies (Forms) Order 2004 (SI 2004/133). See also the Companies (Form and Content of Documents Delivered to the Registrar) regs 2002 (SI 2002/39).

4 CA 1963, s 125(1).

Form and contents of annual return: The contents of the annual return were originally specified in CA 1963, Sch 5. That Schedule has however since been repealed.[1] Instead, the form and content of the annual return are now as prescribed by Form B1.[2] The return must state the date up to which it has been made and must identify the company's financial year. The names and addresses of the directors, secretary and members of the company must be specified, along with details of the authorised and issued share capital of the company and the number of shares held by each members. The address of the registered office must be stated along with details of political donations in excess of €5,079.[3]

1 CLEA 2001, s 63(2).

2 Companies (Forms) Order 2004 (SI 2004/133).

3 Electoral Act 1997, s 26.

Companies not required to annex accounts to the annual return: The entitlement not to annex audited accounts, even in an abridged from, to the annual return arises only for a very few types of company eg a private limited company which is not trading for gain by its members or an unlimited company which has at least one member who (in the case of a natural person) or which (in the case of a body corporate) does not have limited liability. For details of the companies required to annex accounts to the annual return see CA 1963, s 128 and notes thereto.

Returns in non-legible form: CA 1990, s 249 empowers the Minister to make regulations for the delivery to the Registrar of documents, including annual returns, in non-legible form (eg electronically). CA 1990, s 249 has not yet been commenced, however IFCMPA 2005, ss 57 and

58 introduced a system for appointing electronic filing agents for signing and delivery of documents to the Registrar.[1] At the moment it is only possible to sign and deliver annual returns[2] (and even then, where accounts are required to be annexed to the annual return, the accounts cannot be filed electronically) however, it is anticipated that it will be possible to file additional forms in due course.

1 See IFCMPA 2005, ss 57 and 58 and notes thereto. See also CLRG, First Report, para 7.7.

2 Form B1: Companies (Forms) Order 2004 (SI 133/2004).

Consequences of failure to comply with obligations: A failure to make an annual return may result in criminal liability for the company and its officers[1] and may result in disqualification proceedings being brought against those officers.[2] In addition, the Registrar may take steps to dissolve the company by having its name struck off the register of companies.[3] If the annual return is filed more than 28 days after the ARD or if the return has been made up to a date earlier than the ARD, more than 28 days after that ARD a penalty fee will be incurred.[4] The payment of late filing fees does not affect the ability of the Registrar to prosecute the Company or any of its officers under CA 1963, s 125.[5] On the spot fines may also be levied for more persistant late filing.[6]

In addition, where forms filed are not fully compliant with any requirement of the Companies Acts, the Registrar may reject the form and serve notice on the person filing such forms, indicating why the form has been rejected. If a corrected form is not refiled wihtin 14 days, the original form is deemed not to have been delivered.[7] If the company's annual return for the current year or previous year was not filed on time, the company cannot avail of the audit exmption, if applicable.[8]

1 CA 1963, s 125(2).

2 CA 1990, s 160(2)(f) and (h).

3 C(A)A 1982, s 12.

4 CLEA, s 63(3).

5 *Registrar of Companies v Judge David Andersen and another* [2004] IESC 103.

6 CLEA, s 66.

7 See CA 1990, ss 248 and 249A and notes thereto. See also Companies Act 1990 (Form and Content of Documents Delivered to the Registrar) Regulations (SI 39/2002).

8 C(A)(No 2)A 1999, s 32A (as inserted by C(AA)A 2003, s 53.

Definition of 'director' and 'officer': For the purposes of CA 1963, s 125, 'director' and 'officer' are deemed to include any person in accordance with whose directions or instructions the directors are accustomed to act[1] unless the directors are accustomed so to act by reason only of advice given by that person in a professional capacity.[2] This definition is therefore essentially the same as that of 'shadow director' contained in CA 1990, s 27.

1 CA 1963, s 125(2).

2 CA 1963, s 2(2).

Investment companies: The provisions of CA 1963, s 125 do not apply to investment companies.[1] Instead, such companies are subject to the supervisory and reporting requirements imposed upon them by the Central Bank.[2]

1 CA 1990, s 260(1). 'investment company': CA 1990 s 252(1).

2 CA 1990, s 257(4).

UK legislation

See CA 1985, ss 363, 364, 364A; CA 1989, s 139(1); Companies (Contents of Annual Return) Regulations 1999 (SI 1999/2322).

126 Annual return to be made by company not having a share capital

[...][a]

Amendments

a CA 1963, s 126 repealed by CLEA 2001, s 59.

127 [Annual return date

[(1) The annual return of a company shall be made up to a date that is not later than its annual return date, except that the first annual return of a company incorporated after the commencement of section 46 of the Companies (Auditing and Accounting) Act 2003, shall be made up to the date that is its first annual return date.][b]

(2) Subject to subsection (3), the annual return shall be delivered to the registrar of companies—

(a) in the case of the first annual return following the commencement date of a company incorporated before the commencement date — not later than 28 days after the annual return date or 3 months after the commencement date, whichever is the later, and

(b) in any other case — not later than 28 days after the annual return date, unless it is made up to an earlier date in which case it shall be delivered to the registrar not later than 28 days after that earlier date.

(3) The court, on an application made (on notice to the registrar of companies) by a company, may, if it is satisfied that it would be just to do so, make an order extending the time for the purposes of paragraph (a) or (b) of subsection (2) in which the annual return of the company in relation to a particular year may be delivered to the registrar of companies.

(4) As soon as practicable after the making of an order under subsection (3), the company to whom the order relates shall deliver an office copy of the order to the registrar of companies and, if the company fails to do so, the company and every officer of the company who is in default shall be guilty of an offence.

(5) For companies incorporated before the commencement date, the annual return date is[, subject to subsection (8),][c] each anniversary of the date to which the then most recent annual return delivered to the registrar by the company was made up, but if no annual return had been delivered by the company to the registrar, the first annual return date is[, subject to subsection (8),][c] the first day after the commencement date that is 6 months after the date on which the anniversary of incorporation of the company falls and, subject to subsection (8), subsequent annual return dates fall on each anniversary of that first annual return date.

(6) For companies incorporated on or after the commencement date, the first annual return date is the day 6 months after the date of incorporation of the company and, subject to subsection (8), subsequent annual return dates fall on each anniversary of the first annual return date.

(7) Notwithstanding anything to the contrary in the Companies Acts, companies incorporated on or after the commencement date shall not be required to annex accounts

to the first annual return delivered to the registrar after the commencement date in compliance with the Companies Acts.

[(8) Where the annual return of a company is made up to a date earlier than its annual return date, the annual return date shall thereafter be each anniversary of the date to which that annual return is made up, unless the company elects in the annual return to retain its existing annual return date or establishes a new annual return date pursuant to subsection (9).][d]

(9) A company may establish a new annual return date by—

(a) delivering an annual return to the registrar not later than 28 days after the annual return date to which, notwithstanding any provision to the contrary in the Companies Acts, it is by virtue of this subsection not required to annex accounts, and

(b) nominating to the registrar, on the prescribed form, the new annual return date, which date shall be no later than 6 months after the existing annual return date.

(10) Where a company has established a new annual return date pursuant to subsection (9), it shall not again establish a new annual return date pursuant to that subsection until at least 5 years have elapsed since the establishment of the first-mentioned new annual return date.

(11)(a) Notwithstanding subsection (5), a company incorporated before the commencement date may establish a new annual return date by—

(i) delivering an annual return to the registrar not later than 28 days after the first annual return date after the commencement date to which, notwithstanding anything to the contrary in the Companies Acts, it is by virtue of this subsection not required to annex accounts, and

(ii) nominating to the registrar, on the prescribed form, the new annual return date, which date shall be no later than 6 months after the existing annual return date.

(b) Where a company has nominated a new annual return date pursuant to paragraph (a), it may not establish a new annual return date pursuant to subsection (9) before such time as it has delivered to the registrar an annual return made up to the new annual return date nominated pursuant to paragraph (a)(ii).

(12) If a company fails to comply with this section, the company and—

(a) every officer of the company who is in default, and

(b) any person in accordance with whose directions or instructions the directors of the company are accustomed to act, and on whose directions or omissions the default is attributable,

shall be guilty of an offence.

(13) Proceedings in relation to an offence under this section may be brought and prosecuted by the registrar of companies.

(14) In this section, 'commencement date' means the date of commencement of section 60 of the Company Law Enforcement Act, 2001.][a]

Amendments

a CA 1963, s 127 substituted by CLEA 2001, s 60.

b CA 1963, s 127(1) substituted by C(AA)A 2003, s 46(a).

c Words ', subject to subsection (8),' inserted in CA 1963, s 127(5) by C(AA)A 2003, s 46(b).

d CA 1963, s 128(8) substituted by C(AA)A 2003, s 46(c).

Definitions

'annual return': CA 1963, s 2(1); 'annual return date': CA 1963, s 2(1); 'company': CA 1963, s 2(1); 'commencement': IA, Sch, Pt 1; 'director': CA 1963, s 2(1) 'officer': CA 1963, s 2(1); 'the registrar of companies': CA 1963, s 2(1); 'officer in default': CA 1963, s 383.

Notes

Completion and filing of annual return: See CA 1963, s 125 and the notes thereto.

The annual return date: The return must be made up to a date not later than its 'annual return date' except that the first annual return of a company incorporated after the commencement of C(AA)A 2003, s 46 must be made up to the date that is its first annual return date.[1] The annual return date of a company depends on whether it was incorporated before or after the coming into force of the substituted CA 1963, ss 125 and 127 on 1 March 2002.[2] In the case of companies incorporated before that date, the annual return date is the anniversary of the date to which the then most recent annual return delivered to the Registrar was made up, but if no annual return had been delivered to the Registrar, the annual return date is six months after the date on which the anniversary of incorporation occurs.[3] As regards companies incorporated on or after 1 March 2002, the first annual return date is the date six months after the date of incorporation, with each subsequent annual return date falling on the anniversary of the first annual return date.[4]

Notably, where the annual return of a company is made up to a date earlier than its annual return date, the annual return date shall thereafter be each anniversary of the date to which that annual return is made up, unless the company elects in its annual return to retain its existing annual return date or establishes a new annual return date in the manner described below.[5]

A company may alter its annual return date by delivering to the Registrar an annual return (without accounts annexed) not later than 28 days after its existing annual return date, nominating on the prescribed form[6] a new annual return date which must not be later than six months after the existing annual return date.[7] However, having made such an amendment, the company is precluded from doing so again for at least five years.[8]

1 CA 1963, s 127(1).
2 Company Law Enforcement Act, 2001 (Commencement) (No 2) Order 2001 (SI 438/2001).
3 CA 1963, s 127(5).
4 CA 1963, s 127(6).
5 CA 1963, s 127(8) as substituted by C(AA)A 2003, s 46(c).
6 Form B73: Companies (Forms) Order 2002 (SI 38/2002).
7 CA 1963, s 127(9). See also the transitional provisions of CA 1963, s 127(11) which allowed companies incorporated before 1 March 2002 to similarly amend their annual return dates.
8 CA 1963, s 127(10).

Group annual return dates: In relation to the steps that may be taken to harmonise the annual return dates of the various companies in a group, see CA 1963, s 153(2)[1] and notes thereto.

The time for filing the annual return: The annual return must be delivered to the Registrar not later than 28 days after the annual return date.[2] However, on an application made to it by the company (on notice to the Registrar) the court may extend the time for filing the annual return, provided that it considers the making of such an order to be 'just' in the circumstances.[3] If such an order is made, a copy thereof must be to the Registrar as soon as practicable.[4] Failure to do so is a criminal offence.[5]

1 CA 1963, s 153(2) was subisitituted by CLEA 2001, s 61d.
2 CA 1963, s 127(2)(b).
3 CA 1963, s 127(3).
4 CA 1963, s 127(4).
5 CA 1963, s 127(4).

UK legislation

See CA 1985, s 363; CA 1989, s 139(1).

---

128 Documents to be annexed to annual return

(1) Subject to the provisions of this Act, there shall be annexed to the annual return—

(a) a written copy certified both by a director and by the secretary of the company to be a true copy of every balance sheet laid before the annual general meeting of the company held during the period to which the return relates (including every document required by law to be annexed to the balance sheet); and

(b) a copy certified as aforesaid of the report of the auditors on, and of the report of the directors accompanying, each such balance sheet; and

(c) where any such balance sheet or document required by law to be annexed thereto is in any language other than the English or Irish language, there shall be annexed to that balance sheet a translation in English or Irish of the balance sheet or document certified in the prescribed manner to be a correct translation.

(2) If any such balance sheet as aforesaid or document required by law to be annexed thereto did not comply with the requirements of the law as in force at the date of the audit with respect to the form of balance sheets or documents aforesaid, as the case may be, there shall be made such additions to and corrections in the copy as would have been required to be made in the balance sheet or document in order to make it comply with the said requirements, and the fact that the copy has been so amended shall be stated thereon.

(3) If a company fails to comply with this section, the company and every officer of the company who is in default [shall be guilty of an offence and liable to a fine][a] not exceeding [€1,904.61].[b]

For the purposes of this subsection, 'officer' shall include any person in accordance with whose directions or instructions the directors of the company are accustomed to act.

(4) This section shall not apply to—

(a) a private company; or

(b) [...][c]

(c) a company, not having a share capital, which is formed for an object that is charitable and is under the control of a religion recognised by the State under Article 44 of the Constitution, and which exercises its functions in accordance with the laws, canons and ordinances of the religion concerned.

(5) (a) The Commissioners of Charitable Donations and Bequests for Ireland may, if they think fit, by order exempt, either altogether or for a limited period, from

the application of this section a specified company, formed for charitable purposes, not having a share capital.

(b) The Commissioners may by order revoke an order under paragraph (*a*).

(c) A sealed copy of every order of the Commissioners under this subsection shall be delivered by the company to the registrar of companies for registration within fourteen days of the making of the order.

[(6) Nothing in this section requires the balance sheet of a private company or any document or report relating to the balance sheet, other than the report prepared in accordance with subsection (6B), to be annexed to the annual return.

(6A) Nothing in subsection (4) or in section 2(1) of the Companies (Amendment) Act 1986 exempts any of the following companies from the requirement to annex to its annual return the report prepared in accordance with subsection (6B):

(a) a private company not trading for the acquisition of gain by the members;

(b) a company to which subsection (4)(c) applies;

(c) a company in respect of which an order under subsection (5) is in force.

(6B) The auditors of a company referred to in subsection (6) or (6A) shall prepare a separate report to the directors which—

(a) confirms that they audited the accounts for the relevant year, and

(b) includes within it the report made to the members of the company pursuant to section 193 [of the Act of 1990].[d]

(6C) A copy of the report prepared in accordance with subsection (6B) shall be certified by a director and by the secretary of the company to be a true copy of that report and shall be attached to the company's annual return.][e]

(7) Proceedings in relation to an offence under this section may be brought and prosecuted by the registrar of companies.

Amendments

a Words in CA 1963, s 128(3) substituted by C(AA)A 2003, s 57 and Sch 2, Item No 1.

b '£1,000' substituted for '£500' by CA 1990, s 244, increased to £1,500 by CA 1990, s 240(7) as inserted by CLEA 2001, s 104(c) and converted to €1,904.61 by Council Regulations (EC) No 1103/97, No 974/98 and No 2866/98 and the Economic and Monetary Union Act 1998, s 6.

c CA 1963, s 128(4)(b) repealed by EC(IUA)R 1996, reg 20(1).

d Words inserted by IFCMPA 2005, s 61.

e CA 1963, s 128(6) substituted and CA 1963, s 128(6A)–(6C) inserted by C(AA)A 2003, s 47.

Definitions

'annual return': CA 1963, s 2(1); 'company': CA 1963, s 2(1); 'director': CA 1963, s 2(1); 'document': CA 1963, s 2(1): 'officer': CA 1963, s 2(1); 'prescribed': CA 1963, s 2(1); 'private company': CA 1963, s 2(1), s 33(1): 'the registrar of companies': CA 1963, s 2(1); 'share': CA 1963, s 2(1); 'officer in default': CA 1963, s 383.

For the purposes of CA 1963, s 128, the term 'officer' is to be interpreted in accordance with CA 1963, s 128(3).

Notes

Documents to be annexed to the annual return: Most companies are now required to annex copies of their annual accounts and as well copies of their auditors' reports and directors' reports to their annual returns. It should be noted though, that no accounts, etc need be annexed to a company's first annual return.[1] Furthermore, in the case of a private limited company which has validly availed of an audit exemption under C(A)(No 2)A 1999, Part III, there will be no requirement to annex an auditors' report to the annual return.

In the case of a holding company[2] or parent undertaking,[3] copies of the group accounts and of the group auditors' report and directors' report must also be annexed to the annual return. Originally the obligation to annex the accounts etc to the annual return only applied to public companies.[4] However, over the last three decades, the disclosure requirements for companies have been expanded upon in the manner set out below.

1 CA 1963, s 127(7).
2 For the definition of 'holding company' see CA 1963, ss 2(1) and 155.
3 For the definition of 'parent undertaking' see CA 1963, s 2(1) (as inserted by EC(IFRSMA)R 2005), Sch I, Pt I, Item No. 1.
4 CA 1963, s 128. This section provides an exemption however, to certain classes of religious and general charitable companies. See CA 1963, s 128(4) and (5).

C(A)A 1986: This Act applies to most classes of Irish registered private and public limited companies. Those companies not governed directly by its disclosure provisions are as follows:

(a) companies not trading for the acquisition of gain by its members;[1]

(b) religious charitable companies limited by guarantee;[2]

(c) any charitable company limited by guarantee in respect of which the Commissioners of Charitable Donations and Bequests for Ireland have made an order exempting it from the obligation to annex its accounts to the annual return;[3]

(d) licensed life and non-life insurance companies as well as reinsurance companies.[4]

The documents to be annexed to the annual return of a limited company comprise the balance sheet, profit and loss acocunt, directors' report and auditor's report.[5] Certain modifications apply however for 'small and medium sized' private companies.[6]

1 C(A)A 1986, s 2(1)(a).
2 C(A)A 1986, s 2(1)(b).
3 C(A)A 1986, s 2(1)(c).
4 C(A)A 1986, s 2(3).
5 C(A)A 1986, s 7.
6 These companies are defined by reference to balance sheet value, annual turnover and the size of the workforce. See C(A)A 1986, s 8. The exemptions from disclosure do not apply, however, to banks, finance companies and other credit institutions: C(A)A 1986, s 2(2).

Dispensation for small and medium sized companies: In the case of a small company, it will suffice to annex to the return an abridged balance sheet[1] together with a special report from the auditors certifying that the company is entitled to the small company exemptions and that the accounts have been properly prepared.[2] The dispensations for a medium sized company are slightly less extensive in that the return for such a company must at least have annexed to it an abridged balance sheet, an abridged profit and loss account and a copy of the directors' report,[3] as well as a special report from the auditors certifying that the company is entitled to the medium company exemptions and that the accounts have been properly prepared.[4]

1 C(A)A 1986, ss 10 and 12.
2 C(A)A 1986, s 18(3)–(5).
3 C(A)A 1986, s 11 and 12.

4 C(A)A 1986, s 18(3)–(5).

Dispensation for subsidiary undertakings: A subsidiary of a parent undertaking established under the laws of a member state of the European Union may, in certain circumstances, be exempted from annexing its accounts to its annual return.[1] This lack of disclosure may, however, be compensated for by the fact that any company which owns a subsidiary or which holds a 'qualifying capital interest'[2] of 20% or more in an undertaking (defined as 'an undertaking of substantial interest'), may be required to include certain financial and other information regarding the subsidiary or undertaking of substantial interest, in the documentation annexed to its own annual return, either by way of note to the accounts or by way of separate statement signed by a director and the secretary.[3]

1 See C(A)A 1986, s 17 and the notes thereto.

2 For the definition of 'qualifying capital interest' see EC(CGA)R 1992, reg 35(2).

3 C(A)A 1986, s 16.

EC(CGA)R 1992: These regulations implement Council Directive 83/349/EEC[1] and apply to public and private limited holding companies[2] which are engaged for gain in the production, supply or distribution of goods, the provision of a service or the making or holding of investments.[3] The regulations do not apply, however, to the following:

(a) licensed banks;[4]

(b) certified trustee savings banks;[5]

(c) other companies engaged in the business of accepting deposits or other repayable funds or granting credit for its own account;[6]

(d) companies engaged solely in the making of hire-purchase agreements and credit-sale agreements;[7]

(e) authorised life and non-life insurance companies;[8]

(f) companies which meet at least two of the three following criteria –

  (i) the group balance sheet does not exceed €7,618,428.47,

  (ii) the group turnover does not exceed €15,236,856.94 per annum,

  (iii) the group workforce does not exceed 250,[9] and in respect of which neither the parent company not any of its subsidiaries is listed on a stock exchange established in a member state;[10]

(g) certain parent companies which are themselves subsidiaries of other EC companies.[11]

Apart from annexing copies of its own accounts, directors' report and auditors' report to its annual return, a parent company governed by EC(CGA)R 1992 must annex thereto a copy of its group accounts as well as copies of the group directors' report and the group auditors' report.[12] If the parent undertaking is itself a subsidiary of another company, it may be exempted from the requirement to prepare and file group accounts provided, *inter alia*, that it annexes copies of the second parent's group accounts to its own annual return.[13]

1 OJ No L 193, 18.7,1983, pp 1–17.

2 EC(CGA)R 1992, reg 5(1) and (2).

3 EC(CGA)R 1992, reg 3(1).

4 EC(CGA)R 1992, reg 6(2)(a).

5 EC(CGA)R 1992, reg 6(2)(b).

6 EC(CGA)R 1992, reg 6(2)(d).

7 EC(CGA)R 1992, reg 6(2)(c).

8 EC(CGA)R 1992, reg 6(2)(g).

9 EC(CGA)R 1992, reg 7(1).

10 EC(CGA)R 1992, reg 7(8).

11 EC(CGA)R, 1992 regs 8 and 9.
12 EC(CGA)R 1992, reg 39.
13 EC(CGA)R 1992, regs 8 and 9.

EC(CI:A)R 1992: These regulations give effect to Council Directives 86/635/EEC[1] and 89/117/EEC[2] and apply to banks and other financial institutions. Such entities were already obliged to annex their annual accounts, directors' reports and auditors' reports to their annual returns.[3] Now, however, under these regulations, if the company is a parent undertaking it must also annex copies of its group accounts and group auditors' report to the return.[4] Nonetheless, if the parent undertaking is itself a subsidiary of another company, it may be exempted from the requirement to prepare and file group accounts provided, *inter alia*, that it annexes copies of the second parent's group accounts to its own annual return.[5]

1 OJ No L 372, 31.12.1986.
2 OJ No L 44, 16.02.1989.
3 C(A)A 1986, s 2(2) and s 7. The exemptions for small and medium sized companies contained in C(A)A 1986 do not apply to financial institutions.
4 EC(CI:A)R 1992, reg 5(3) and (4).
5 EC(CI:A)R 1992, reg 8.

EC(A)AR 1993: Unlimited public companies have always been obliged to annex a copy balance sheet and auditors' report to the annual return.[1] The disclosure requirements have however been expanded by EC(A)R 1993, the provisions of which apply to the following:

'1. unlimited companies and partnerships where all the members thereof who do not have a limit on their liability are:

(a) companies limited by shares or by guarantee, or

(b) bodies not governed by the law of the State but equivalent to those in paragraph (a) or

(c) any combination of the types of bodies referred to in sub-paragraphs (a) and (b) and

2. unlimited companies and partnerships where all the members thereof who do not have a limit on their liability are:

(a) (i) unlimited companies or partnerships of the type referred to in paragraph (1) that are governed by the laws of a member state, or

(ii) bodies governed by the laws of a member state that are of a legal form comparable to those referred to in paragraph (i) or

(b) any combination of the types of bodies referred to in sub-paragraph (a) and sub-paragraphs (a) and (b) of paragraph 1.'[2]

The provisions of C(A)A 1986 and EC(CGA)R 1992 regarding the format and content of annual accounts and the annexing of accounts to the annual return, as well as the exemptions for small and medium sized companies, apply to these unlimited companies as they apply to limited companies.[3]

1 CA 1963, s 128.
2 EC(A)R 1993, reg 6.
3 EC(A)R 1993, regs 7,9 and 13.

EC(BD)R 1993: A foreign limited company which establishes a branch in the State is obliged each year to file with the Registrar copy annual accounts as drawn up, audited and where so required, disclosed in accordance with the law of the State of incorporation.[1] Moreoever, if the foreign company is incorporated under the laws of another EU member state, the accounts must comply with the provisions of the Fourth, Seventh and Eighth Company Law Directives.[2] In the case of a non-EU company, if there is no requirement under the laws of the State of incorporation to draw up annual accounts, the accounts as delivered to the Registrar must comply with the provisions of the Fourth and Seventh Company Law Directives[3] and indeed, even where the law of the non-EU State requires the drawing up of accounts, the foreign company rather than delivering to the Irish Registrar copies of the accounts as drawn up under the law of the state of incorporation, may instead deliver accounts which are drawn up in accordance with the provisions of the aforementioned Directives.[4] The accounts must be filed within 11 months of the end of the company's financial year or at the time of publication under the law of the state of incorporation, whichever is earlier,[5] although, if there is no obligation to draw up accounts under the law of the state of incorporation, filing must simply take place within 11 months of the financial year end.[6] The accounts as filed shall include a directors' report and an auditor's report and, if applicable, consolidated group accounts[7] together with translations into English or Irish, if not already in either one of these languages.[8]

1 EC(BD)R 1993, reg 11(1).
2 Council Directives 78/660/EEC, 83/349/EEC and 84/253/EEC. See EC(BD)R 1993, reg 11(1).
3 EC(BD)R 1993, reg 11(2).
4 EC(BD)R 1993, reg 11(3).
5 EC(BD)R 1993, reg 11(4).
6 EC(BD)R 1993, reg 11(5).
7 EC(BD)R 1993, reg 12.
8 EC(BD)R 1993, reg 13.

EC(IUA)R 1996: Insurance companies had heretofore been largely exempted from the disclosure requirements of the Companies Acts.[1] The format and content of the accounts of insurance companies and reinsurance companies are now governed by EC(IUA)R 1996. Where the companies form part of a group, the parent undertaking must deliver a return to the Registrar each year with copies of the group accounts, directors' report and auditors' report annexed thereto.[2] Nonetheless, if the parent undertaking is itself a subsidiary of another company, it may be exempted from the requirement to prepare and file group accounts provided, *inter alia*, that it annexes copies of the second parent's group accounts to its own annual return.[3]

1 CA 1963, s 128(4)(b); C(A)A 1986, s 2(3).
2 EC(IUA)R 1996, reg 17.
3 EC(IUA)R 1996, reg 12.

Definition of 'director' and 'officer': For the purposes of CA 1963, s 128, 'director' and 'officer' are deemed to include any person in accordance with whose directions or instructions the directors are accustomed to act[1] unless the directors are accustomed so to act by reason only of advice given by that person in a professional capacity.[2] This definition is therefore essentially the same as that of 'shadow director' contained in CA 1990, s 27.

1 CA 1963, s 128(3).
2 CA 1963, s 2(2).

UK legislation

See CA 1985, s 242; CA 1989, s 11; The Directors' Remuneration Report Regulations 2002 (SI 2002/1986), reg 1(2); Companies Act 1985 (Operating and Financial Review and Directors Report etc) Regulations 2005 (2005/1011), reg 19, sch, paras 1, 5(a); Companies Act 1985 (Operating and Financial Review)(Repeal) Regulations 2005 (SI 2005/3442), reg 1(2).

---

129 Certificates to be sent by private company with annual return

A private company shall send with the annual return required by section 125 a certificate signed both by a director and by the secretary of the company that the company has not, since the date of the last return or, in the case of a first return, since the date of the incorporation of the company, issued any invitation to the public to subscribe for any shares or debentures of the company, and, where the annual return discloses the fact that the number of members of the company exceeds fifty, also a certificate so signed that the excess consists wholly of persons who, under paragraph (b) of subsection (1) of section 33 are not to be included in reckoning the number of fifty.

Definitions

'annual return': CA 1963, s 2 (1); 'company': CA 1963, s 2 (1); 'director': CA 1963, s 2 (1); 'debenture': CA 1963, s 2 (1); 'member': CA 1963, s 31 (1): 'private company': CA 1963, ss 2 (1) 33 (1).

Cross references

See CA 1963, ss 125, 127 and notes thereto.

See also Form B1: Companies (Forms) Order 2004 (SI 133/2004).

See generally Prospectus Regs 2005, in relation to invitation to public to subscribe for shares.

Notes

The continued reference to the number of members exceeding 'fifty' is an anomaly, most likely occassioned by an oversight, since the amendment of CA 1963, s 33 to provide that a private company may have 99 members, effected by IFCMPA 2006, s 7.

Meetings and Proceedings

130 Statutory meeting and statutory report

[...][a]

Amendments

a CA 1963, s 130 repealed by C(A)A 1983, Sch 3, Pt 1.

131 Annual general meeting

(1) Subject to subsection (2), every company shall in each year hold a general meeting as its annual general meeting in addition to any other meetings in that year and shall specify the meeting as such in the notices calling it and not more than 15 months shall elapse between the date of one annual general meeting of a company and that of the next.

(2) So long as a company holds its first annual general meeting within 18 months of its incorporation, it need not hold it in the year of its incorporation or in the following year.

(3) If default is made in holding a meeting of the company in accordance with subsection (1), the [Director][a] may, on the application of any member of the company, call or direct the calling of a general meeting of the company and give such ancillary or consequential directions as the [Director][a] thinks expedient, including directions modifying or supplementing in relation to the calling, holding and conducting of the meeting, the operation of the company's articles, and it is hereby declared that the directions which may be given under this subsection include a direction that one

member of the company present in person or by proxy shall be deemed to constitute a meeting.

(4) A general meeting held in pursuance of subsection (3) shall, subject to any directions of the [Director][a], be deemed to be an annual general meeting of the company but, where a meeting so held is not held in the year in which the default in holding the company's annual general meeting occurred, the meeting so held shall not be treated as the annual general meeting for the year in which it is held unless at that meeting the company resolves that it shall be so treated.

(5) Where a company resolves that a meeting shall be so treated, a copy of the resolution shall, within 15 days after the passing thereof, be forwarded to the registrar of companies and recorded by him.

(6) If default is made in holding a meeting of the company in accordance with subsection (1), or in complying with any direction of the [Director] [a] under subsection (3), the company and every officer of the company who is in default [shall be guilty of an offence and liable to a fine][b] not exceeding [€1,904.61][c], and if default is made in complying with subsection (5), the company and every officer of the company who is in default [shall be guilty of an offence and liable to a fine][b] not exceeding [€1,904.61][d].

Amendments

a 'Director' substituted for 'Minister' by CLEA 2001, s 14.

b Words 'shall be guilty of an offence and liable to a fine' substituted for 'shall be liable for a fine' in CA 1963, s 131(6) substituted by C(AA)A 2003, s 57 and Sch 2, Item No 4.

c '£500' substituted for '£100' by C(A)A 1982, Sch 1, increased to £1,500 by CA 1990, s 240(7) as inserted by CLEA 2001, s 104(c) and converted to €1,904.61 by Council Regulations (EC) No 1103/97, No 974/98 and No 2866/98 and the Economic and Monetary Union Act 1998, s 6.

d '£100' substituted for '£20' by C(A)A 1982, Sch 1, increased to £1,500 by CA 1990, s 240(7) as inserted by CLEA 2001, s 104(c) and converted to €1,904.61 by Council Regulations (EC) No 1103/97, No 974/98 and No 2866/98 and the Economic and Monetary Union Act 1998, s 6.

Definitions

'articles': CA 1963, s 2(1); 'company': CA 1963, s 2(1); 'Director': CLEA 2001, s 3(1); 'member': CA 1963, s 31; 'Minister': CA 1963, s 2(1); 'officer': CA 1963, s 2(1); 'officer in default': CA 1963, s 383; 'the registrar of companies': CA 1963, s 2 (1).

Notes

General meetings and class meetings: Meetings of members of the company may be divided into two broad categories, namely general meetings and class meetings.

General meetings: General meetings pass resolutions which affect the company as a whole.[1] Subject to any restrictions contained either in the memorandum and articles or in the terms of issue of a particular class or classes of shares, all members will be entitled to attend and vote at such meetings. There are two types of general meeting, both of which are considered below, namely AGMs and extraordinary general meetings ('EGMs').

1 On company meetings, see, generally, Courtney, *The Law of Private Companies* (2nd edn, Tottel Publishing, 2002), ch 9.

Class meetings: Class meetings are more limited in nature, being convened to pass resolutions which affect a particular class of members rather than the company as a whole. Only members of the particular class can attend and vote at such meetings.[1] Except where otherwise stated, the provisions of the Companies Acts and the company's memorandum and articles which govern the convening and holding of general meetings apply equally to class meetings.

1 *Carruth v ICI Ltd* [1937] AC 707.

Ordinary and special resolutions: The two types of resolution capable of being passed at general meetings and class meetings are ordinary resolutions and special resolutions. An ordinary resolution is not defined by the Companies Acts. It is a resolution of which the normal notice for an AGM or EGM, as the case may be, has been given and which has been passed by a simple majority of those who were present in person or by proxy at the meeting and who were entitled to vote.[1] On the other hand, a special resolution is one which has been passed by a majority of not less than 75% of those who were present in person or by proxy at the meeting and who were entitled to vote, at a meeting of which not less than 21 days' notice, specifying the intention to propose the resolution as a special resolution, was duly given.[2] Regardless of whether an ordinary resolution or a special resolution is involved, persons abstaining are to be ignored in determining whether or not the necessary majority has been achieved.[3]

1 *Bushell v Faith* [1970] AC 1099.

2 CA 1963, s 141(1).

3 *Re William Dixon Ltd* (1948) SLT 423.

Time within which to hold AGM: CA 1963, s 131(1) requires every company to hold an AGM once in each year, but so that no more than 15 months elapse between the holding of one AGM and the next. In this context 'year' means a calendar year (ie 1 January to 31 December).[1] This requirement to hold an AGM in every calendar year constitutes an overriding obligation for the company, so that although the company might otherwise be allowed to let fifteen months lapse between the holding of one AGM and the next, it cannot do so in circumstances where this would result in no AGM whatsoever being held for a particular calendar year.

Example 1

Company X holds an AGM on 30 April 2006. It can allow fifteen months to elapse before the next AGM, since to do so would still result in the Company holding its AGM within the 2007 calendar year.

Example 2

Company Y holds its AGM on 30 November 2006. It cannot allow fifteen months to elapse before the holding of the next AGM since to do so would result in the AGM being held in 2008 rather than 2007. Accordingly, the maximum period that can elapse before the holding of the next AGM is thirteen months since that would allow the AGM to be held just within the 2007 calendar year (ie on 31 December 2007).

In the case of newly-formed companies, CA 1963, s 131(2) modifies the strict requirement for the holding of an AGM in every calendar year, where the company has only just been incorporated. Such companies need not hold an AGM's either in the calendar year of incorporation or in the following year, provided that one such meeting is held not more than 18 months after the date of incorporation. So, for example, if a company is incorporated in December 2006 it may hold its first AGM in April 2007, and that meeting will be deemed to be the AGM for 2006, 2007 and 2008.

1 *Gibson v Barton* (1875) LR 10 QB 329.

Convening of AGM

Directors: Under Table A the power and duty to convene the AGM rests with the board of directors.[1] In this regard the AGM may be called by directors whose term of office has expired but who have still continued to act as the *de facto* directors of the company,[2] or may be called by the directors at a board meeting of which proper notice has not been given to all of their number.[3] However, if the directors deliberately exclude some of their number from the board meeting, they cannot validly transact any business, including the convening of a general meeting.[4] Where there are insufficient directors in the State to form a quorum, Table A authorises any one director to convene an EGM.[5] A similar power is not however conferred on the director regarding the convening of an AGM. Presumably therefore, such a meeting would have to be convened either by the Director of Corporate Enforcement ('Director') (see CA 1963, s 131(3) and note below) or by the court (see CA 1963, s 135 and notes thereto). Unless expressly empowered to do so, the company secretary cannot validly convene a general meeting, nor can any meeting purportedly convened by him be held, unless the board later ratifies his acts.[6]

Members: Table A confers no authority whatsoever on members of the company to convene AGMs although, where there are insufficient directors in the State to form a quorum, any two members of the company may convene an EGM.[7] However, in the case of single-member company, all the powers exercisable by the company in general meeting are exercisable by the sole member without the need for a formal general meeting.[8]

ODCE: If a company fails to hold its AGM for any year, the Director may, on the application of any member, call or direct the calling of a general meeting himself and may give whatever consequential or ancillary directions he thinks expedient for the calling, holding and conducting of the meeting, including directions modifying or supplementing the operation of the company's articles.[9] Such directions might, for example, provide for the temporary modification of the articles so as to allow the member who applied to the Director, rather than the board, to send out notice of the meeting. The section also allows the Director to direct that one person present in person or by proxy shall be deemed to constitute a meeting.[10] The power to declare that one member present in person or by proxy shall constitute a meeting is necessary because of the fact that in companies other than single member companies, a general meeting must by definition have at least two members in attendance.[11]

Court: See CA 1963, s 135 and the notes thereto.

1 CA 1963, Table A, Pt I, regs 48(2) and 80. The notice provisions applicable to the convening of the AGM are as set out in CA 1963, ss 133 and 141.

2 *Gibson v Barton* (1875) LR 10 QB 329; *Boschoel Proprietary Co Ltd v Fuke* [1906] 1 Ch 148.

3 *Browne v La Trinidad* (1887) 37 Ch D 1; *Re State of Wyoming Syndicate* [1901] 2 Ch 431 at 437.

4 *Harben v Phillips* (1883) 23 Ch D 14 at 34.

5 CA 1963, Table A, Pt I, reg 50.

6 *Re Haycraft Gold Reduction and Mining Co* [1900] 2 Ch 230; *Re State of Wyoming Syndicate* [1901] 2 Ch 431 at 437.

7 CA 1963, Table A, Pt I, reg 50. See also CA 1963, s 132 regarding the entitlement of members to convene an EGM themselves where they have requisitioned such a meeting but the the directors have failed to act.

8 EC(SMPLC)R 1994, reg 9.

9 CA 1963, s 131(3).

10 CA 1963, s 133(4). See also CA 1963, s 135 for similar powers which are conferred on the court in relation to the convening of meetings, including giving directions that one person constitute a quorum.

11 *Sharp v Dawes* (1876) 2 QBD 26; *Re London Flats Ltd* [1969] 2 All ER 744; *Re El Sombrero Ltd* [1958] Ch 900. In the case of single-member companies, the sole member present in person or by

proxy, is deemed to be a quorum, even though this results in the rather artificial concept of him meeting with himself: EC(SMPLC)R 1994, reg 10.

Holding of AGM in the State: Subject to anything to the contrary in the articles, CA 1963, s 140 allows for the first AGM of the company may be held abroad.[1] However, all other AGMs must be held in the State unless:

(a) either all the members entitled to attend and votes at the meeting consent in writing to its being held elsewhere or a resolution providing that it be held elsewhere has been passed at the preceding AGM; and

(b) the articles do not provide that the AGM is to be held in the State.[2]

In fact, Table A stipulates that all general meetings of the company, and not just the AGM, are to be held in the State.[3] Any business transacted at an AGM outside the State, in breach of the above provisions, will be void.[4]

1 CA 1963, s 140(2).
2 CA 1963, s 140(1).
3 CA 1963, Table A, Pt I, reg 47.
4 CA 1963, s 140(1). In the case of an EGM, however, where there is no statutory provision requiring the meeting to be held in the State, the unanimous consent of the members (whether express or implied), to the holding of a particular meeting abroad will be regarded as overruling Table A, Pt I, reg 47, so as to render any business transacted at the meeting valid: *Re Shannonside Holdings Ltd* (20 May 1993, unreported) HC (Costello J).

Business of AGM: A distinction is made in company law between the ordinary business and the special business of a general meeting. The notice convening the meeting will be invalid unless it at least sets out the general nature of the special business which is to be transacted.[1] Table A provides that all business transacted at the AGM shall be deemed special business, with the exception of declaring a dividend, the consideration of the accounts, balance sheets and the reports of the directors and auditors, the election of directors in the place of those retiring, the re-appointment of retiring auditors and the fixing of the remuneration of the auditors.[2] In practice, the articles will often be amended so as to include the fixing of the remuneration of the directors among the items of ordinary business. However, the only items of business which *must* be transacted at the meeting are the presentation of the annual accounts[3] and the appointment of auditors.[4]

1 *Roper v Ward* [1981] ILRM 408.
2 CA 1963, Table A, Pt I, reg 53.
3 CA 1963, s 148.
4 CA 1963, s 160.

Conduct of the meeting: See CA 1963, s 134 and Table A, Pt I, regs 53–74, as well as the notes thereto.

Retirement of directors by rotation: Where Table A applies in their unmodified form, a proportion of the board of directors must retire at each AGM.[1] If no AGM is held, the appropriate number of directors will still be deemed to have automatically vacated office at the end of the last day on which the meeting could lawfully have been held.[2]

1 CA 1963, Table A, Pt I, regs 92–100.
2 *Re Consolidated Nickel Mines Ltd* [1914] 1 CH 883; *Morris v Kanssen* [1946] AC 459; *Re Zinotty Properties Ltd* [1984] 3 All ER 754. Cf *Phoenix Shannon plc v Purkey* [1998] 4 IR 597 where Costello J purported to follow this line of authority yet came to a wholly contradictory conclusion. It is thought that the decision of Costello J does not represent good law.

Dispensing with AGM for single-member companies: The sole member of a single-member private limited company may, at any time, dispense with the holding of AGMs.[1] He is meant to do so by drawing up a decision to that effect in writing and by forwarding a copy of the decision to the company,[2] whereupon the company is meant to record that decision and any other decisions made by him, in a separate book or by some other suitable means maintained for that purpose.[3] Notwithstanding these procedural requirements, there is considerable authority to support the proposition that an unwritten decision of the sole member to dispense with the holding of AGMs should be just as valid as a written decision to that effect.[4] Indeed, it is notable that under the EC(SMPLC)R 1994 it is expressly stated that neither a failure to give written notice of the decision to the company nor a failure by the company to record the decision, will affect the validity of the decision itself.[5]

A decision to dispense with the holding of AGMs shall have effect for the year in which it is made and subsequent years, but will not affect any liability already incurred for failing to comply with CA 1963, s 131 in the past.[6] Moreover, even if the sole member decides to dispense with AGMs, either he or the company's auditor can, in any given year, still require such a meeting being held, by serving notice to that effect on the company itself at least three months before the end of the year in question.[7]

If the AGM is dispensed with, annual accounts must still be prepared. However, rather than presenting a balance sheet, profit and loss account, auditor's report and directors' report and, if appropriate, group accounts, to the company in AGM, copies of these documents will simply be sent directly are simply sent to the sole member.[8] The time limits for sending copies of the accounts to the member vary depending on the particular circumstances of the case. If the company was formed as or converted into a single-member company, and the decision to dispense with AGMs was made before the due date for the first such meeting, the accounts will have to be sent to the member within 21 days of the end of the month in which the anniversary of incorporation falls.[9] In all other cases, the accounts must be sent to the member within 21 days of the end of the month in which the anniversary of the last AGM falls.[10] The accounts themselves must be made up to a date not more than nine months prior to the date upon which they have to be furnished to the member.[11]

Finally, in relation to the filing of annual returns, this obligation continues to apply regardless of the fact that the company now has single-member status and has dispensed with the holding of AGMs.[12]

1 EC(SMPLC)R 1994, reg 8(1).

2 EC(SMPLC)R 1994, reg 9(3) and (4).

3 EC(SMPLC)R 1994, reg 9(4).

4 *Re Express Engineering Works Ltd* [1920] 1 Ch 466; *Re Oxted Motor Co* [1921] 3 KB 32; *Re Duomatic Ltd* [1969] 2 Ch 365; *Cane v Jones* [1981] 1 All ER 533; *Re SM Barker Ltd* [1950] IR 123; *Peter Buchanan Ltd v McVey* [1954] IR 89; *Re PMPA Garage (Longmile) Ltd (No 1)* [1992] 1 ILRM 337; *Re Shannonside Holdings Ltd* (20 May 1993, unreported) HC (Costello J).

5 EC(SMPLC)R 1994, reg 9(8).

6 EC(SMPLC)R 1994, reg 8(2).

7 EC(SMPLC)R 1994, reg 8(3).

8 EC(SMPLC)R 1994, reg 8(5) and (6).

9 EC(SMPLC)R 1994, reg 8(9)(a) and (b).

10 EC(SMPLC)R 1994, reg 8(9)(c).

11 CA 1963, s 148, as amended by EC(SMPLC)R 1994, reg 8(8)(b).

12 CA 1963, s 127 as amended by EC(SMPLC)R 1994, reg 8(8)(a) and reg 8(9).

Power of court to direct holding of meetings: See CA 1963, s 135 and the notes thereto.

UK legislation

See CA 1985, ss 366, 367.

132 Convening of extraordinary general meeting on requisition

(1) The directors of a company, notwithstanding anything in its articles, shall, on the requisition of members of the company holding at the date of the deposit of the requisition not less than one-tenth of such of the paid up capital of the company as at the date of the deposit carries the right of voting at general meetings of the company, or, in the case of a company not having a share capital, members of the company representing not less than one-tenth of the total voting rights of all the members having at the said date a right to vote at general meetings of the company, forthwith proceed duly to convene an extraordinary general meeting of the company.

[(1A) Notwithstanding subsection (1) or anything in its articles, the directors of a company traded on a regulated market, shall, on the requisition of members of the company holding at the date of the deposit of the requisition not less than 5 per cent of such of the paid up capital of the company as at the date of the deposit carries the right of voting at general meetings of the company, forthwith proceed duly to convene an extraordinary general meeting of the company.][a]

(2) The requisition must state the objects of the meeting and must be signed by the requisitionists and deposited at the registered office of the company and may consist of several documents in like form each signed by one or more requisitionists.

(3) If the directors do not within 21 days from the date of the deposit of the requisition proceed duly to convene a meeting to be held within 2 months from the said date, the requisitionists, or any of them representing more than one half of the total voting rights of all of them, may themselves convene a meeting, but any meeting so convened shall not be held after the expiration of 3 months from the said date.

(4) A meeting convened under this section by the requisitionists shall be convened in the same manner as nearly as possible as that in which meetings are to be convened by directors.

(5) Any reasonable expenses incurred by the requisitionists by reason of the failure of the directors duly to convene a meeting shall be repaid to the requisitionists by the company and any sum so repaid shall be retained by the company out of any sums due or to become due from the company by way of fees or other remuneration in respect of their services to such of the directors as were in default.

(6) For the purposes of this section, the directors shall, in the case of a meeting at which a resolution is to be proposed as a special resolution, be deemed not to have duly convened the meeting if they do not give such notice thereof as is required by section 141.

Amendments

a CA 1963, s 132(1A) inserted by Shareholders' Rights Regulations 2009, reg 4.

Cross references

See C(A)A 1983, s 40 and notes thereto in relation to convening an EGM in the event of a serious capital loss.

Definitions

'articles': CA 1963, s 2(1); 'company': CA 1963, s 2(1); 'company traded on a regulated market': CA 1963, s 2(1); 'director': CA 1963, s 2(1); 'document': CA 1963, s 2(1); 'regulated market': CA 1963, s 2(1); 'share': CA 1963, s 2(1).

Notes

Extraordinary general meetings: Every general meeting of the company other than the AGM is deemed to be an EGM.[1]

1 CA 1963, Table A, Pt I, reg 49.

Convening of EGM: Under Table A the power to convene EGMs rests primarily with the board of directors[1] although under CA 1963, s 132(3) persons who have requisitioned an EGM may convene the meeting themselves if the directors fail to do so. Furthermore, Table A provides that if at any time there are not sufficient directors in the State capable of acting to form a quorum, any one director or any two members of the company may convene an EGM in the same manner as nearly as possible as that in which meetings may be convened by the board.[2]

1 CA 1963, Table A, Pt I, reg 50. See also the notes to CA 1963, s 131 in relation to the power of the directors to convene general meetings.

2 CA 1963, Table A, Pt I, reg 50.

Holding of EGM in the State: Under Table A every general meeting of the company must be held in the State.[1] Nonetheless, the unanimous consent of the members (whether express or implied) to the holding of a particular meeting abroad will be regarded as overruling this requirement so as to render any business transacted at the meeting, valid.[2]

1 CA 1963, Table A, Pt I, reg 47.

2 *Re Shannonside Holdings Ltd* (20 May 1993, unreported) HC (Costello J).

Business of EGM: A distinction is made in company law between the ordinary business and the special business of a general meeting. The notice convening the meeting will be invalid unless it at least sets out the general nature of the special business which is to be transacted.[1] Table A provides that all business transacted at the EGM shall be deemed special business.[2] Where the net asset value of the company fall to half or less of the called-up share capital, the directors are obliged to convene an EGM in order to enable the members to consider the position, albeit that there is no specific statutory obligation imposed upon the members to then take any remedial action.[3]

1 *Roper v Ward* [1981] ILRM 408.

2 CA 1963, Table A, Pt I, reg 53.

3 C(A)A 1983, s 40.

Conduct of the meeting: See CA 1963, s 134 and Table A, Pt I, regs 53–74, as well as the notes thereto.

Requisitioning of EGM of companies not traded on a regulated market

Number of requisitionists: CA 1963, s 132(1) refers to the EGM being requisitioned by 'members' holding not less than one-tenth of the paid up capital of the company carrying voting rights or in the case of a company not having a share capital[1] by 'members' holding not less than one-tenth of the voting rights in general meeting. Despite the reference to 'members,' it is clear that the meeting may also be requisitioned by a single member holding not less than the prescribed minimum amount of paid up share capital or voting rights, as the case may be.[2]

Form of requisition: The requisition may consist of a single document or a series of documents.[3] In the latter case, it is not necessary that all of the documents be identical in form, provided that their general purport is the same.[4] The requisition must state the objects of the meeting and must be signed by each of the requisitionists.[5] A requisition by the joint holders of a share must be signed by each of them.[6] The requisition will be valid despite the fact that it records the wrongly held opinion of the requisitionist that the directors are opposed to the items of business proposed to be transacted at the meeting.[7]

Depositing the requisition: Service of the requisition on the company may be effected by hand delivery, by post or by fax.[8]

Objects of meeting: The only items of business which the requisitionists are entitled to have dealt with at the meeting are those specified in the requisition[9] although the directors may add their own items of business to the agenda if they so wish.[10] If one of several objects stated in the requisition cannot legally be implemented by the company, the directors will be justified in excluding that object from the notice which they send out, convening the meeting.[11] However, if the entire of the objects of the meeting as stated in the requisition are incapable of being legally be carried into effect in any manner by the company, the directors will be entitled to refuse to requisition the meeting altogether.[12]

Failure to convene the EGM: If the directors do not proceed within 21 days from the date of deposit of the requisition to convene an EGM to be held within two months from that date, they may expose themselves to an action for oppression and/or disregard of interests under CA 1963, s 205.[13] Moreover, the requisitionists or not less than half in value of them, may proceed to convene the meeting themselves, provided that the meeting must be held not later than three months from the date on which the requisition was originally deposited by them.[14] Any reasonable expenses incurred by the requisitionists in convening the meeting themselves is to be repaid by the company which can then recoup the expenses from the directors in default by retaining the amount in question out of any fees or other remuneration which would otherwise have been payable to them.[15]

Requisitioning of EGM by resigning auditor: An auditor of a company who resigns may also require the directors to convene an EGM to consider an explanation by him of his reasons for resigning.[16] Notably, if the directors refuse to convene the meeting, the auditor has no entitlement to convene it himself, albeit that he has a right to attend at the next AGM of the company and to give his explanation there instead.[17]

1 Eg a guarantee company or an unlimited company not having a share capital.
2 *Re El Sombrero Ltd* [1958] Ch 900.
3 *Fruit and Vegetable Growers' Association v Kekewick* [1912] 2 Ch 52.
4 *Fruit and Vegetable Growers' Association v Kekewick* [1912] 2 Ch 52.
5 CA 1963, s 132(2).
6 *Patent Wood Keg Syndicate v Pearse* [1906] WN 164.
7 *Rose v McGivern* [1998] 2 BCLC 593.
8 *PNC Telecom plc v Thomas* [2004] 1 BCLC 88.
9 *Patent Wood Keg Syndicate Ltd v Pearse* [1906] WN 164; *Ball v Metal Industries Ltd* 1957 SC 315; *Rose v McGivern* [1998] 2 BCLC 593.
10 *Ball v Metal Industries Ltd* 1957 SC 315; *Rose v McGivern* [1998] 2 BCLC 593.
11 *Turner v Berner* [1978] 1 NSWLR 66; *Rose v McGivern* [1998] 2 BCLC 593.
12 *Isle of Wight Rly Co v Tahourdin* (1883) 25 Ch D 320, 334; *National Roads and Motorists' Association v Parker* (1986) 6 NSWLR 517; *Rose v McGivern* [1998] 2 BCLC 593.
13 *McGuinnes v Bremner plc* [1988] BCLC 673.
14 CA 1963, s 132(3).
15 CA 1963, s 132(5).
16 See CA 1990, s 186 and the notes thereto.
17 CA 1990, s 186(5). See *Jarvis plc v PricewaterhouseCoopers* [2001] BCC 670.

Requisitioning of EGM of companies traded on a regulated market

The Shareholders' Rights Regulations 2009 introduced a new regime for companies traded on a regulated market, ie companies whose registered office is in the State and whose shares are admitted to trading on a regulated market situated or operating within an EU Member State (excluding collective investment undertakings and undertakings with the sole object of the collective investment of capital provided by the public: see CA 1963, s 2(1)). In the case of such companies, the threshold entitling shareholders to convene an EGM is reduced from having to hold not less than 10% of such of the paid up capital carrying the right of voting at general meetings to having to hold only not less than 5% of such paid up capital. This enhanced right for shareholders of companies traded on a regulated market applies notwithstanding anything in the articles of association. It may be that a complete ban on 'contracting out' was not achieved because of the absence of any reference to anything to the contrary in any agreement between the shareholders and the company. Where elsewhere the Companies Acts seek an outright ban on 'contracting out' they have used language such as 'notwithstanding anything in its articles or in any agreement', eg CA 1963, s 182(1).

Power of court to direct holding of meetings: See CA 1963, s 135 and the notes thereto.

UK legislation

See CA 1985, s 368; CA 1989, s 145, Sch 19 para 9; The Companies (Acquisition of Own Shares)(Treasury Shares) Regulations 2003. reg 4, Sch, para 19.

[132A Equal treatment of members

A company traded on a regulated market shall ensure equal treatment for all members who are in the same position with regard to the exercise of voting rights and participation in a general meeting.][a]

Amendments

a CA 1963, s 132A inserted by Shareholders' Rights Regulations 2009, reg 5.

Notes

Equal treatment of members

The Shareholders' Rights Regulations 2009 require the equal treatment of shareholders in companies traded on a regulated market. The requirement is to ensure equal treatment of all members 'who are in the same position' so members who have different rights in accordance with the class of shares they hold can continue to be treated differently. Moreover, the requirement is only in regard to 'the exercise of voting rights and participation in a general meeting'.

---

133 Length of notice for calling meetings

(1) Any provision of a company's articles shall be void in so far as it provides for the calling of a meeting of the company (other than an adjourned meeting) by a shorter notice than—

(a) in the case of the annual general meeting, 21 days' notice in writing; and

(b) in the case of a meeting (other than an annual general meeting or a meeting for the passing of a special resolution) 14 days' notice in writing where the company is neither a private company nor an unlimited company and 7 days' notice in writing where it is a private company [or an unlimited company, and][a] [(c) in the case of a company traded on a regulated market, without prejudice to Articles 9(4) and 11(4) of Directive 2004/25/EC—

(i) in the case of an annual general meeting, 21 days' notice in writing, and

(ii) in the case of a general meeting (other than an annual general meeting or a meeting for the passing of a special resolution) 14 days' notice in writing where—

(I) the company offers the facility for members to vote by electronic means accessible to all members who hold shares that carry rights to vote at general meetings, and

(II) a special resolution reducing the period of notice to 14 days has been passed at the immediately preceding annual general meeting, or at a general meeting held since that meeting.][b]

(2) Save in so far as the articles of a company make other provision in that behalf (not being a provision avoided by sub-section (1)) a meeting of the company (other than an adjourned meeting) may be called—

(a) in the case of the annual general meeting by 21 days' notice in writing; and

(b) in the case of a meeting (other than an annual general meeting or a meeting for the passing of a special resolution), by 14 days' notice in writing where the company is neither a private company nor an unlimited company and by 7 days' notice in writing where it is a private company [or an unlimited company, and][c]

[(c) in the case of a company traded on a regulated market, without prejudice to Articles 9(4) and 11(4) of Directive 2004/25/EC—

(i) in the case of an annual general meeting, 21 days' notice in writing, and

(ii) in the case of a general meeting (other than an annual general meeting or a meeting for the passing of a special resolution) 14 days' notice in writing where—

(I) the company offers the facility for members to vote by electronic means accessible to all members who hold shares that carry rights to vote at general meetings, and

(II) a special resolution reducing the period of notice to 14 days has been passed at the immediately preceding annual general meeting, or at a general meeting held since that meeting.][d]

(3) A meeting of a company[, other than a company traded on a regulated market,][e] shall, notwithstanding that it is called by shorter notice than that specified in subsection (2) or in the company's articles, as the case may be, be deemed to have been duly called if it is so agreed by the auditors of the company and by all the members entitled to attend and vote thereat.

Amendments

a Words 'or an unlimited company, and' substituted for 'or an unlimited company.' by Shareholders' Rights Regulations 2009, reg 6(a).

b CA 1963, s 133(1)(c) inserted by Shareholders' Rights Regulations 2009, reg 6(b).

c Words 'or an unlimited company, and' substituted for 'or an unlimited company.' by inserted by Shareholders' Rights Regulations 2009, reg 6(c).

d CA 1963, s 133(2)(c) inserted by Shareholders' Rights Regulations 2009, reg 6(d).

e Words ', other than a company traded on a regulated market,' inserted by Shareholders' Rights Regulations 2009, reg 6(e).

Definitions

'articles': CA 1963, s 2(1); 'company': CA 1963, s 2(1). 'private company': CA 1963, s 2(1), s 33(1); 'unlimited company': CA 1963, s 2 (1), s 5(2)(c).

Cross references

See generally CLRG, First Report, para 4.5.10.

Notes

Notice of general meetings for companies other than those traded on a regulated market: CA 1963, s 133, stipulates different notice periods depending on the nature of the general meeting and also depending on whether the company is a private company or a public company. At least 21 days' notice in writing must be given for an AGM, regardless of the type of company.[1] In the case of an EGM at least 14-days' notice in writing must be given by a plc or a guarantee company and at least seven days' notice in writing must be given by all other companies.[2] In this context 'notice' means 'clear notice' (ie exclusive both of the day on which the notice is served and of the day of the meeting).[3] Although s 133(2) clearly envisages the possibility of the articles stipulating longer notice periods, any provision in the articles for shorter notice will be void.[4]

1 CA 1963, s 133(1)(a) and (2).

2 CA 1963, s 133(1)(b) and (2).

3 CA 1963, Table A, Pt I, reg 51. See also *Re Hector Whaling Ltd* [1936] Ch 208; *Re Railway Sleepers Supply Co* (1885) 29 Ch D 204 at 208. cf *Re Neil McLeod and Sons Ltd* 1967 SLT 46.

4 CA 1963, s 133(1). The notice periods provided for in CA 1963, s 133 are replicated in Table A. See Table A, Pt I, reg 51 for plc's and Table A, Pt II, reg 4 for private companies limited by shares. For companies limited by guarantee and not having a share capital see Table C, reg 8.

Notice of general meetings for companies traded on a regulated market: The Shareholders' Rights Regulations 2009 amend s 133 by restricting the circumstances in which companies traded on a regulated market can rely on a 14-day notice period for general meetings (other than AGMs or general meetings for the passing of a special resolution). Such companies may only have a 14-day notice period where the company offers the facility to vote by electronic means accessible to all members who hold shares that carry voting rights and a special resolution reducing the period to 14 days has been passed at the immediately preceding AGM or at an EGM held since the AGM.

The *Guidance Notes* issued by the Department of Enterprise Trade and Employment express the view that the effect of this change to s 133 is that if a company decides not to retain the 14 days' notice period then all general meetings will be held at 21 days' notice. It is not clear that this is the effect of the amendment, however, and it is thought that a company traded on a regulated market would not contravene s 133(1) if its articles specified that the notice for calling an EGM to pass an ordinary resolution is 15 days.

Period of notice for special resolutions: If the company wishes to pass a special resolution, the members must be given not less than 21 days' clear notice.[1] So, for example, if a private company wishes to pass a special resolution at an EGM, the normal 7-day notice period provided for in CA 1963, s 133 will be replaced by a 21-day notice period.

1 CA 1963, s 141(1).

Extended notice: 'Extended notice' refers to the period of notice which must be given to the company, rather than by the company, of notice of intention to move certain types of resolution.[1] The resolutions requiring 'extended notice' are as follows:

1. a resolution at an agm of a company appointing as auditor a person other than a retiring auditor or providing expressly that a retiring auditor shall not be re-appointed;[2]
2. a resolution at a general meeting of a company removing an auditor before the expiration of his term of office;[3]
3. a resolution at a general meeting of a company filling a casual vacancy in the office of auditor;[4]
4. a resolution at a general meeting of a company to remove a director or to appoint somebody else instead of a director so removed at the meeting at which he is removed.[5]

Such a resolution will not be effective (except where the directors of the company have resolved to submit it) unless notice of the intention to move it has been given to the company not less than 28 days before the meeting at which it is moved.[6] Having received such notice the company must then give its members notice of the proposed resolution at the same time and in the same manner as it gives notice of the meeting[7] or, if that is not practicable, it must give them notice thereof, either by advertisement in a daily newspaper circulating in the district in which the registered office of the company is situate or in any other mode allowed by the articles, not less than 21 days before the meeting.[8] Notably, if after receiving notice of the intention to move the resolution, the company then calls the general meeting for a date 28 days or less after the date of receipt of the notice, the notice, though not strictly given within the prescribed time, will nonetheless be deemed to have been properly given.[9]

The provisions of CA 1963, s 142 are, however, purely procedural and confer no substantive rights on individual members, so that although an individual member might submit a resolution to the company of the type outlined above (eg for the dismissal of a director) he has no right to force a meeting to be called to consider the resolution unless he can muster sufficient support to requisition an EGM pursuant to CA 1963, s 132.[10]

1 CA 1963, s 142.

2 CA 1963, s 161(1)(a).

3 CA 1963, s 161(1)(b).

4 CA 1963, s 161(1)(c).

5 CA 1963, s 182(2).

6 CA 1963, s 142(1).

7 Thus, for example, in the case of a private company where someone other than the board of directors proposes to move a resolution for the dismissal of a director at a forthcoming EGM, the proposer of the resolution must give notice of the proposed resolution to the company at least 28 days before the meeting, but the company will only be obliged to give the normal period of notice to the members, namely seven days.

8 CA 1963, s 142(1).

9 CA 1963, s 142(2). Presumably this is to prevent the company from frustrating the member's intention to move the resolution by deliberately calling the meeting for a date which would result in the company technically not having received 'extended notice.'

10 *Pedley v Inland Waterwats Association Ltd* [1977] 1 All ER 209.

Abridging the period of notice to members: CA 1963, s 133(3) permits the holding of a general meeting on shorter notice than that specified above, if it is so agreed by the company's auditors and by all the members who are entitled to attend and vote at the particular meeting. It would appear that this agreement does not need to be in writing in order to be effective. A company traded in a regulated market may not call a meeting on shorter notice than that set out in s 133(2) or its articles of association even if this is agreed to by its auditors and all of the members entitled to attend and vote thereat. In reality this amendment probably added nothing to the law since it would be virtually impossible to secure the agreement of all of the members of a company traded on a regulated market.

In so far as the company wishes to abridge the notice period for the passing of a special resolution, it may do so with a majority of not less than 90% in value of the members having the right to attend and vote at the meeting.[1] However, the members' purported consent to short notice will not be valid and effective unless they appreciate that what they are consenting to is in fact short notice rather than the normal statutory notice period.[2]

1 CA 1963, s 141(2).

2 *Re Pearce Duff and Co Ltd* [1960] 1 WLR 1014.

Persons entitled to receive notice: The articles of association determine who is entitled to receive notice of, and to attend, speak and vote at general meetings of the company. If the articles are silent, all members are to receive notice,[1] even though certain of them have no right to vote at the meeting.[2] Table A provides that notice is to be given to every member and to every person upon whom the ownership of a share devolves by reason of his being a personal representative or the Official Assignee in bankruptcy of a member, where the member but for his death or bankruptcy would be entitled to receive notice of the meeting.[3] In addition, however, the auditors are entitled not only to receive all notices of, and other communications relating to any general meeting of the company, but also to attend at the meeting and to be heard on any part of the business which concerns them as auditors.[4] Similarly, an auditor who resigns before the end of his term of office, is entitled to receive notice of, and to attend and speak at the next AGM after his resignation.[5]

1 CA 1963, s 134(a). See also *Carruth v ICI Ltd* [1937] AC 707.

2 *Re Mackenzie and Co Ltd* [1916] 2 Ch 450.

3 CA 1963, Table A, Pt I, reg 136(a) and (b). Personal representatives and the Official Assignee are not, however, entitled to vote at general meetings and will not be counted in the quorum: *Arulchelvan v Wright* (7 February 1996, unreported) HC (Carroll J).

4 CA 1990, s 193(5). See also CA 1963, Table A, Pt I, reg 136(c).

5 CA 1990, s 186(5).

Method of giving notice: Table A provides that notice may be given to any member either personally or by sending it by post to him to his registered address (ie the address given for him in the register of members).[1] However, if the articles permit notices of meetings to be sent to a member at alternative addresses, the obligation to give notice will be satisfied by posting the notice to any one of the alternative addresses which the company chooses.[2] In the case of a share held in joint names, the notice may be sent out to the first of the persons whose name appears in the register in respect of the share rather than to all of the holders.[3] Moreover, where a member has died or been adjudged bankrupt, notice may be given to his personal representatives or to the Official Assignee, as the case may be, by posting it to such address as may have been furnished by him or them, and if no such address has been furnished, by posting it to the registered address of the deceased or bankrupt member.[4]

Where a notice is sent by post, service is deemed to have been effected 24 hours after the posting of a properly addressed, pre-paid letter containing the notice.[5] The company will not however be entitled to rely on this deemed service if it is aware of facts which would lead to the conclusion that service could not have taken place, as where a nationwide postal strike is in place at the time of posting.[6]

If the articles permit service by way of advertisement, service will be deemed to have been effected at the time of publication of the advertisement.[7]

1 CA 1963, Table A, Pt I, reg 133.

2 *Parkstone Ltd v Gulf Guarantee Bank plc* [1990] BCLC 850.

3 CA 1963, Table A, Pt I, reg 134.

4 CA 1963, Table A, Pt I, reg 135.

5 CA 1963, Table A, Pt I, reg 133. However, if the member is resident in another country where the notice will not reach him as speedily by post as members resident in the State, the company may dispense altogether with notifying him: *Re Warden and Hotchkiss Ltd* [1945] Ch 270.

6 *Bradman v Trinity Estates plc* [1989] BCLC 757.

7 *Mercantile Investment and General Trust Co v International Co of Mexico* (1891) [1893] 1 Ch 484n.

Contents of notice

Special business: The business of a general meeting may be divided into ordinary and special business.[1] The distinction between ordinary and special business is important since resolutions passed at the meeting will be invalid if the notice convening the meeting fails to give adequate notice of the general nature of the special business.[2] In this regard it suffices that the notice calling the meeting gives sufficient details as to the nature of the business to be transacted to enable members to decide whether or not they should attend.[3] Under Table A, all business at an EGM is deemed to be special, as is all business at the AGM with the exception of the declaration of a dividend, the consideration of the accounts, balance sheets, the reports of the directors and auditors, the election of directors in place of those retiring, the re-appointment of the retiring auditors and the fixing of the auditors' remuneration.[4] In practice, the Table A is commonly amended so as to include the fixing of the directors' remuneration within the ordinary business of the AGM.

Special resolutions: Either ordinary or special resolutions may be passed at the general meeting.[5] In the case of a special resolution, the notice convening the meeting will be invalid if it fails to specify either the entire text or the entire substance of the proposed resolution.[6] Mere typographical or otherwise inconsequential discrepancies between the contents of the notice and the special resolution, as passed, will be overlooked by the court.[7]

Interests of directors: If the directors have any interest in a proposed resolution, details of that interest must be fully disclosed in the notice calling the meeting and a failure to make such disclosure may render the resolution, if passed, invalid.[8] In this regard, the disclosure in the notice should relate not only of the nature but also of the extent of the directors' interest in the outcome of the resolution.[9]

Circulars: The directors are entitled, at the company's expense, to issue circulars to the members prior to the meeting in support of the board's position on the proposed resolutions, provided that, in so acting, they intend to benefit the company as a whole.[10] Conversely, the directors are under no duty to send out to the members a circular which has been prepared by a group of members who are opposed to the board's policy or who wish to encourage the members generally to vote in a particular way on a specified resolution or resolutions.[11]

Misleading notices and circulars: The company may be restrained from holding a general meeting (whether for the purpose of passing ordinary resolutions or special resolutions) where the notice convening it, or any accompanying circular is inaccurate or misleading.[12] Indeed, the court may refuse to uphold the validity of resolutions passed at a meeting convened on foot of a misleading notice or circular.[13] However, the validity of the resolutions may be confirmed by the court if it can be shown that although the notice or circular contained inaccurate information the shareholders were not in fact misled.[14]

1 CA 1963, Table A, Pt I, reg 53.

2 *Roper v Ward* [1981] ILRM 408; *Jackson v Munster Bank* (1884–85) 13 LR Ir 118.

3 *Choppington Collieries Ltd v Johnson* [1944] 1 All ER 762; *Re Trench Tubeless Tyre Co* [1900] 1 Ch 408; *MacConnell v E Prill and Co Ltd* [1916] 2 Ch 57; *Young v South African and Australian Exploration and Development Syndicate* [1896] 2 Ch 268; *Normandy v Ind Coope and Co Ltd* [1908] 1 Ch 84.

4 CA 1963, Table A, Pt I, reg 53.

5 For the definition of 'ordinary resolution' and 'special resolution' see the notes to CA 1963, s 131 and CA 1963, s 141.

6 *Re Moorgate Mercantile Holdings Ltd* [1980] 1 WLR 227; *MacConnell v E Prill and Co Ltd* [1916] 2 Ch 57.

7 *Re Willaire Systems plc* [1987] BCLC 67.

8 *Kaye v Croydon Tramways Co* [1898] 1 Ch 358; *Tiessen v Henderson* [1899] 1 Ch 861; *Baillie v Oriental Telephone and Electric Co Ltd* [1915] 1 Ch 503.

9 *Tiessen v Henderson* [1899] 1 Ch 861; *Baillie v Oriental Telephone and Electric Co Ltd* [1915] 1 Ch 503.

10 *Peel v London and North Western Rly Co* [1907] 1 Ch 5; *Campbell v Australian Mutual Provident Society* (1908) 77 LJPC 117.

11 *Campbell v Australian Mutual Provident Society* (1908) 77 LJPC 117.

12 *Jackson v Munster Bank* (1884–85) 13 LR Ir 118.

13 *Re Teele and Bishop* (1901) 70 LJ 409; *Re European Home Products plc* (1988) 4 BCC 779.

14 *Re European Home Products plc* (1988) 4 BCC 779. See also *Re Trench Tubeless Tyre Co* [1900] 1 Ch 408.

Failure to give notice: A deliberate failure to give notice to a person who is entitled to receive such notice renders the meeting and any business transacted thereat, invalid.[1] However, under Table A the accidental omission to give notice of a meeting to, or the non-receipt of notice of a meeting by, any person entitled to receive a notice shall not invalidate the proceedings at the meeting.[2] It has been held that the phrase 'accidental omission' covers the accidental failure through oversight, to put a notice to a member in the post[3] but does not cover a deliberate omission to send out notices to certain members in consequence of a misinterpretation of the articles of association.[4] Sending notice by post to members during a postal strike may also be regarded as a deliberate rather than an accidental failure to give notice, such as would invalidate any business purportedly transacted at the meeting and which may therefore justify the court in granting an injunction restraining the company from allowing the meeting to proceed.[5]

1 *Smyth v Darley* (1849) 2 HL Cas 789; *Musselwhite v CH Musselwhite and Son Ltd* [1962] Ch 964; *Colthurst v La Touche Colthurst* [2000] IEHC 14 (McCracken J).

2 CA 1963, Table A, Pt I, reg 52.

3 *Re West Canadian Collieries Ltd* [1962] 1 All ER 26.

4 *Royal Mutual Benefit Building Society v Sharman* [1963] 2 All ER 242.

5 *Bradman v Trinity Estates plc* [1989] BCLC 757.

Informal acts of the members: Notwithstanding the notice requirements of the Companies Acts, an informal decision made by all of the members who have voting rights, will be as valid and effective as if it had been passed as a formal resolution at a properly convened general meeting of the company.[1]

1 *Re Oxted Motor Co* [1921] 3 KB 32; *Re Duomatic Ltd* [1969] 2 Ch 365; *Cane v Jones* [1981] 1 All ER 533; *Re SM Barker Ltd* [1950] IR 123; *Peter Buchanan Ltd v McVey* [1954] IR 89; *Re PMPA Garage (Longmile) Ltd (No 1)* [1992] 1 ILRM 337; *Re Shannonside Holdings Ltd* (20 May 1993, unreported) HC (Costello J); *Euro Brokers Holdings Ltd v Monecor (London) Ltd* [2003] 1 BCLC 506. Moreover, although CA 1963, s 141(8) provides that a resolution in writing signed by all the members is as valid as if passed at a properly convened general meeting, it would appear from *Re PMPA Garage (Longmile) Ltd and Re Shannonside Holdings Ltd* that an oral resolution or decision of all the members will still suffice. On the same basis, although EC(SMPLC)R 1994, reg 9(3) requires the decision of a single-member to be recorded in writing, it seems that an oral decision or resolution which is not so recorded will still be valid. In relation to the Duomatic Principle generally, see the notes to CA 1963, s 141.

UK legislation

See CA 1985, s 369; CA 1989, s 115(3); Companies Act 1985 (Electronic Communications) Order 2000 (SI 2000/3373), art 18; The Companies (Acquisition of Own Shares)(Treasury Shares) Regulations 2003 (SI 2003/1116), art 1(1), 4, sch, para 20).

[133A Further provisions on notice

(1) Notwithstanding section 13 or anything contained in its articles, this section applies to a company traded on a regulated market.

(2) Notice of a general meeting shall be issued, free of charge, in a manner ensuring fast access to the notice on a non-discriminatory basis, using such media as may reasonably be relied upon for the effective dissemination of information to the public throughout Member States.

(3) Notice of a general meeting under subsections (1)(c) and (2)(c) of section 133 shall set out:

(a) when and where the meeting is to take place and the proposed agenda for the meeting;

(b) a clear and precise statement of any procedures a member must comply with in order to participate and vote in the meeting, including—

(i) the right of a member to put items on the agenda of a general meeting and to table draft resolutions pursuant to section 133B and to ask questions relating to items on the agenda pursuant to section 134C, and the time limits applicable to the exercise of any of those rights,

(ii) the right of a member entitled to attend, speak, ask questions and vote, to appoint a proxy pursuant to section 136 (including a proxy who is not a member) by electronic means or otherwise or, where allowed, one or more proxies, to attend, speak, ask questions and vote instead of the member,

(iii) the procedure for voting by proxy pursuant to section 136, including the forms to be used and the means by which the company is prepared to accept electronic notification of the appointment of a proxy, and

(iv) the procedure (where applicable) to be followed pursuant to sections 134B and 138 for voting electronically or by correspondence respectively;

(c) the record date for eligibility for voting as defined in section 134A and state that only members registered on the record date shall have the right to participate and vote in the general meeting;

(d) where and how the full, unabridged text of the documents and draft resolutions referred to in subsection 4(c) and (d) may be obtained, and

(e) the internet site at which the information contained in subsection (4) shall be made available.

(4) A company shall make available to its members on its internet site, for a continuous period beginning not later than 21 days before a general meeting (inclusive of the day of the meeting), the following—

(a) a notice under section 133A(2),

(b) the total number of shares and voting rights at the date of the giving of the notice (including separate totals for each class of shares where the company's capital is divided into 2 or more classes of shares),

(c) the documents to be submitted to the meeting,

(d) a copy of any draft resolution or, where no such resolution is proposed to be adopted, a comment from the board of directors on each item of the proposed agenda of the meeting,

(e) a copy of forms to be used to vote by proxy and to vote by correspondence unless these forms are sent directly to each member.

(5) The company shall make available, on its internet site as soon as possible following their receipt, draft resolutions tabled by members.

(6) Where the forms referred to in subsection (4)(e) cannot be made available on the company's internet site for technical reasons, the company shall indicate on its internet site how the forms may be obtained in hard copy form and the company shall send the forms by post, free of charge, to every member who requests them.

(7) Where notice of a general meeting is issued later than on the twenty first day before the meeting pursuant to section 133(1)(c)(ii) or 133(2)(c)(ii) or Articles 9(4) or 11(4) of Directive 2004/25/EC, the period specified in subsection (4) shall be reduced accordingly.][a]

Amendments

a CA 1963, s 133A inserted by Shareholders' Rights Regulations 2009, reg 7.

Notes

Additional provisions on notice for companies traded on a regulated market: Section 133A applies only to companies traded on a regulated market and was inserted by the Shareholders' Rights Regulations 2009. This provision requires such companies to provide additional information to shareholders in their notices of general meetings and also to make available specified information on their Internet sites.

[133B Right to put items on the agenda of the general meeting and to table draft resolutions

(1) A member of a company traded on a regulated market, shall have the right, by electronic or postal means, at an address specified by the company, to—

(a) put an item on the agenda of an annual general meeting, provided that each such item is accompanied by stated grounds justifying its inclusion or a draft resolution to be adopted at the general meeting, and

(b) table a draft resolution for an item on the agenda of a general meeting,

subject to the member or members concerned holding 3 per cent of the issued share capital, representing at least 3 per cent of the total voting rights of all the members who have a right to vote at the meeting to which the request for inclusion of the item relates.

(2) A request by a member to put an item on the agenda or to table a draft resolution under subsection (1)(a) shall be received by the company in hardcopy form or in electronic form at least 42 days before the meeting to which it relates.

(3) Where the exercise of the right conferred by subsection (1)(a) involves a modification of the agenda for the annual general meeting, in situations where the agenda has already been communicated to the members, and only in such situations, the company shall make available a revised agenda in the same manner as the previous agenda in advance of the applicable record date (as defined in section 134A) of share-ownership for purposes of entitlement to vote, or, if no such record date applies, sufficiently in advance of the date of the annual general meeting so as to enable other members to appoint a proxy or, where applicable, to vote by correspondence.

(4) In order to facilitate a member to avail of subsection (1)(a), the company shall ensure that the date of the next annual general meeting is placed on its internet site by—

(a) the end of the previous financial year, or

(b) not later than 70 days prior to the annual general meeting,

whichever is the earlier.][a]

Amendments

a CA 1963, s 133B inserted by Shareholders' Rights Regulations 2009, reg 7.

Definitions

'company traded on a regulated market': CA 1963, s 2(1); 'record date': CA 1963, s 134A.

Notes

Right to put items on the agenda of general meetings of companies traded on a regulated market: For companies traded on a regulated market, a significant new right is afforded to shareholders by the Shareholders' Rights Regulations 2009. Members of such companies holding 3% of the issued share capital and representing at least 3% of the total voting rights of all members who have a right to vote at such meetings, now have a statutory rights to (a) put an item on the agenda of the AGM or a draft resolution to be adopted and to (b) table a draft resolution for an item on the agenda of an EGM. To facilitate members exercising the right in s 133(1)(a), such companies must ensure that the date of the next AGM is placed on its Internet site by either the end of the previous financial year or not later than 70 days prior to the AGM, whichever is the earlier. Where the exercise of the right in s 133(1)(a) involves a modification of the agenda for the AGM in circumstances where the AGM has already been communicated to members, the company must make available a revised agenda in the same manner as the previous agenda in advance of the applicable record date of share-ownership for purposes of entitlement to vote or, if no such record date applies, sufficiently in advance of the date of the AGM to enable the other members to appoint a proxy or vote by correspondence.

There are a number of important conditions which must be met by shareholders exercising such rights.

In the first place, the rights may be exercised by electronic or postal means, but in either case to an address specified by the company; therefore, it is essential that a shareholder wishing to exercise these rights sends their notice to the address specified by the company for such purposes and a notice sent to any other address will be ineffective.

Secondly, in the case of a request to put an item on the agenda of an AGM, the request must be accompanied by either stated grounds justifying the inclusion of the item or a draft resolution to be adopted at the general meeting.

Thirdly, a request to put an item on the agenda or to table a draft resolution at an AGM must be sent in sufficient time to ensure that it is received by the company in hard copy form or in electronic form at least 42 days before the meeting to which it relates.

134 General Provisions as to meetings and votes

The following provisions shall have effects in so far as the articles of the company do not make other provision in that behalf—

(a) notice of the meeting of a company shall be served on every member of the company in the manner in which notices are required to be served by Table A and for the purpose of this paragraph 'Table A' means that Table as for the time being in force;

(b) two or more members holding not less than one-tenth of the issued share capital or, if the company has not a share capital, not less than 5 per cent in number of all the members of the company may call a meeting;

(c) in the case of a private company two members, and in the case of any other company three members, personally present shall be a quorum;

(d) any member elected by the members present at a meeting may be chairman thereof;

(e) in the case of a company originally having a share capital, every member shall have one vote in respect of each share or each [€12.69][a] of stock held by him, and in any other case, every member shall have one vote.

Amendments

[a] £10 converted to €12.69 by Council Regulations (EC) No 1103/97, No 974/98 and No 2866/98 and the Economic and Monetary Union Act 1998, s 6.

Definitions

'articles': CA 1963, s 2(1); 'company': CA 1963, s 2(1); 'member': CA 1963, s 31; 'private company': s 2(1), s 33(1) 'share': CA 1963, s 2(1); 'Table A': CA 1963, s 2(1); 'Tábla A': CA 1963, s 2(1).

Notes

Notice: See CA 1963, s 133 and notes thereto in relation to persons entitled to receive notice and in relation to the mode of giving notice. See Table A, Pt I, reg 51 (as modified by Table A, Pt I, regs 48(2) and 50) as regards the contents of a notice.

See CA 1963, s 133.

Quorum

Table A: CA 1963, s 134(c) provides that unless the articles otherwise provide, the quorum for a general meeting shall, in the case of public company be three members and in the case of a private company, two members, *personally present*. In Table A, however, a meeting of a private company is deemed to be quorate if there are at least two members present in person or by proxy.[1] In this regard it has been held that one person holding proxies from several members cannot constitute a quorum on his own.[2] On the other hand, it has been held that one person can constitute a quorum for a class meeting when he is the only member of that class.[3]

Shareholders' agreement: The provisions of CA 1963, s 134, as to what constitutes a quorum may also be superseded by the terms of a shareholders' agreement (eg where the agreement provides that a quorum will not be present unless at least one member of a particular class attends).[4]

Single member companies: In the case of single member companies, the provisions of CA 1963, s 134(c) are superseded by EC(SMPLC)R 1994 which state that a quorum is deemed to be the sole member present either in person or by proxy.[5]

Only those entitled to vote: In ascertaining whether or not a quorum exists, regard can only be had to members who are entitled to vote at the meeting.[6] In this regard, neither the personal representatives of a deceased member nor the Official Assignee of a bankrupt member who have not themselves been entered on the register in respect of the deceased's shares can be counted in the quorum since they do not rank as members.[7]

Absence of quorum: Table A states that if within half an hour from the time appointed for the meeting a quorum is not present, the meeting, if convened upon the requisition of members,[8] shall be dissolved and in any other case shall stand adjourned to the same day in the next week, at the same time and place or to such other day and at such other time and place as the directors may determine.[9] If at the adjourned meeting a quorum is not present within half an hour from the time appointed for the meeting, the members present shall be a quorum[10] provided of course that that there are at least two of them.[11]

Departure of quorum: Because of the particular wording of Table A, provided a quorum is present at the beginning of a meeting, the subsequent departure of one or more members will not affect the validity of business transacted after their departure, notwithstanding the fact that the meeting is no longer quorate.[12] This is subject to the proviso, however, that if only one person remains, there can no longer be a meeting.[13] Unless otherwise ordered by the Director of Corporate Enforcement[14] or by the court,[15] only single member companies can have a meeting of one person.[16]

Use of technology: The CLRG recommends that CA 1963, s 134 be amended to provide that a company should be able to hold a meeting at two or more venues using any technology which gives the members as a whole a reasonable opportunity to participate.[17]

1 CA 1963, Table A, Part II, reg 5.

2 *Re Sanitary Carbon Co* [1877] WN 223; *Arulchelvan v Wright* (7 February 1996, unreported) HC (Carroll J).

3 *East v Bennett Bros Ltd* [1911] 1 Ch 163.

4 *Harman v BML Group Ltd* [1994] 1 WLR 893.

5 EC(SMPLC)R 1994, reg 10.

6 *Hennessy v National Agricultural and Industrial Development Association* [1947] IR 159 at 198; *Arulchelvan v Wright* (7 February 1996, unreported) HC (Carroll J); *Young v South African and Australian Exploration and Development Syndicate* [1896] 2 Ch 268 at 277.

7 *Arulchelvan v Wright* (7 February 1996, unreported) HC (Carroll J). See also Table A, Pt I, reg 32.

8 See CA 1963, s 132 regarding the requisitioning of meetings.

9 CA 1963, Table A, Pt I, reg 55.

10 CA 1963, Table A, Pt I, reg 55.

11 *Re London Flats Ltd* [1969] 1 WLR 711; *Re El Sombrero Ltd* [1958] Ch 900; *Sharp v Dawes* (1876) 2 QBD 26.

12 *Re Hartley Baird Ltd* [1955] Ch 143.

13 *Arulchelvan v Wright* (7 February 1996, unreported) HC (Carroll J); *Re London Flats Ltd* [1969] 1 WLR 711; *Re El Sombrero Ltd* [1958] Ch 900; *Sharp v Dawes* (1876) 2 QBD 26.

14 See CA 1963, s 131(3).

15 CA 1963, s 135(1).

16 EC(SMPLC)R 1994, reg 10.

17 CLRG, First Report, para 6.5.6.

Chairman: Subject to anything to the contrary in the articles, CA 1963, s 134(d) entitles any member of the company to be appointed chairman of a general meeting. The acts of a person who assumes the role of chairman of a general meeting or class meeting without being elected or designated to that post, are null and void.[1] Under Table A the appointment of an ordinary member of the company as chairman is very much a measure of last resort. The chairman of the board of directors should normally act as chairman of a general meeting.[2] However, if the board has no chairman or he is either not present within 15 minutes after the time appointed for the holding of the meeting or is unwilling to act, the directors are to elect a member of the board to be chairman.[3] Ultimately, if no director is willing to act as chairman or if no director is present within 15 minutes after the time appointed for the holding of the meeting, the members present may then proceed to choose one of their own number to chair the meeting.[4] In the case of an equality of votes, the chairman has a casting vote.[5]

1 *Re Bradford Investments plc* [1991] BCLC 224.

2 CA 1963, Table A, Pt I, reg 56.

3 CA 1963, Table A, reg 56.

4 CA 1963, Table A, Pt I, reg 57.

5 CA 1963, Table A, Pt I, reg 61. With regard to the other powers, functions and duties of the chairman, see Table A, Pt 1, regs 58–62 and the notes thereto.

Adjournment of meetings

Power to adjourn: There is no power to adjourn a validly convened general meeting of a company unless expressly provided for in the articles.[1] However, under Table A the chairman may, with the consent of any meeting at which a quorum is present, and must if so directed, adjourn the meeting.[2] Although entitled to briefly suspend proceedings so as to restore order,[3] the chairman is not, however, entitled to adjourn the meeting at his own will and pleasure and if he attempts to do so, the meeting can go on without him and the members may appoint someone else to replace him in the chair.[4] An adjournment will also be permitted for purely logistical reasons, as where the room is too small to accommodate all those who are present or where there is a failure of the public address system or audio-visual equipment with which it was anticipated to communicate with those in attendance.[5]

Attendance at adjourned meeting: A member may attend at an adjourned meeting even though he did not attend at the original one.[6]

Business of adjourned meeting: No business is to be transacted at an adjourned meeting other than business left unfinished from the previous occasion.[7]

Notice of adjourned meeting: At common law it is not necessary to give notice of the business to be transacted at an adjourned meeting.[8] However, under Table A, where the meeting is adjourned for 30 days or more, notice of the adjourned meeting must be given as in the case of a original meeting.[9] Failure to give this notice will render any business transacted at the adjourned meeting invalid.[10]

Deemed date of resolutions: A resolution passed at an adjourned meeting is treated as having been passed on the date on which it was in fact passed and is not to be deemed to have been passed on any earlier date (such as the original date of the meeting).[11] In the case of a resolution on which a poll is taken the date on which the resolution is deemed to have been passed is that date on which the result of the poll is known.[12]

1 *Smith v Paringa Mines Ltd* [1906] 2 Ch 193.

2 CA 1963, Table A, Pt I, reg 58. If Table A does not apply, the chairman will not be obliged, at common law, to adjourn the meeting, even if a majority of those present wish him to do so: *Salisbury Gold Mining Co v Hathorn* [1897] AC 268.

3 *John v Rees* [1970] Ch 345.

4 *Salisbury Gold Mining Co v Hathorn* [1897] AC 268; *National Dwellings Society v Sykes* [1894] 3 Ch 159; *Catesby v Burnett* [1916] 2 Ch 325.

5 *Byng v London Life Association Ltd* [1990] Ch 170.

6 *R v D'Oyly* (1840) 12 Ad and El 139.

7 Table A, Pt I, reg 58. See also *Robert Batcheller and Sons Ltd v Batcheller* [1945] Ch 169.

8 *Wills v Murray* (1850) 4 Exch 843.

9 Table A, Pt I, reg 58. See CA 1963, s 133 and the notes thereto for details of the notice provisions applicable to general meetings.

10 *Robert Batcheller and Sons Ltd v Batcheller* [1945] Ch 169 at 171.

11 CA 1963, s 144 and notes thereto.

12 *Holmes v Keyes* [1959] 1 Ch 199.

Moving of resolutions: If a resolution is one which need not be set out verbatim or substantially verbatim in the notice, the fact that it has been set out verbatim does not prevent the passing of a different resolution at the meeting itself so long as the substance of the business transacted is the same.[1] Thus, a resolution to appoint a named person as director[2] or as liquidator[3] may amended so as to appoint someone else instead. However a resolution to sell the undertaking of the company cannot be amended to one for the winding up of the company since that would be to change in a fundamental way the nature of the business of the meeting.[4]

Although amendments to a special resolution may be permitted, this is so only provided that the substance of the resolution is not altered, however slightly.[5] A refusal by the chairman to put a permissible amendment to the meeting will result in the resolution, if carried, being void.[6]

The meeting may resolve to close discussion on a proposed resolution and to take a vote, but only after the members have had a reasonable opportunity to discuss the substance of the matters in issue, and any closure of business which is intended to simply stifle discussion will render the substantive decision on the resolution void.[7]

1 *Betts and Co Ltd v Macnaghten* [1910] 1 Ch 430; *Catesby v Burnett* [1916] 2 Ch 325; *Choppington Collieries Ltd v Johnson* [1944] 1 All ER 762.

2 *Betts and Co Ltd v Macnaghten* [1910] 1 Ch 430; *Catesby v Burnett* [1916] 2 Ch 325; *Choppington Collieries Ltd v Johnson* [1944] 1 All ER 762.

3 *Re Trench Tubeless Tyre Co* [1900] 1 Ch 408.

4 *Re Teede and Bishop Ltd* [1901] 70 LJ Ch 409.

5 *Re Moorgate Mercantile Holdings Ltd* [1980] 1 All ER 40.

6 *Henderson v Bank of Australasia* (1890) 45 Ch D 330.

7 *Wall v London and Northern Assets Corporation* [1898] 2 Ch 469.

Voting

Only registered members may vote: Only those persons whose names are entered on the register of members, or their duly appointed proxies, may vote at the general meeting.[1] If the memorandum or articles of association lay down a procedure for the admission of a person to membership (eg approval by the board of directors) that procedure must be fully observed before the person can acquire any voting rights.[2] The chairman is under no obligation to adjourn the meeting to allow unregistered transfers to be entered on the register of members,[3] nor will the court restrain the holding of a general meeting simply on the ground that the outcome would be different if unregistered transfers were in fact registered.[4] Nevertheless the directors must act *bona fide* in determining the date of the general meeting and if they choose a date in bad faith and for the dominant purpose of frustrating the exercise of voting rights attaching to particular shares, the affected shareholder or shareholders may be entitled to an injunction restaining the company from holding the meetng on that date.[5]

Voting entitlements of registered members: The voting rights of members are governed principally by the articles of association or by the terms of issue of the shares.[6] In so far as the articles or terms of issue are silent, CA 1963, s 134(e) stipulates that every member shall have one vote per share or per €12.69 of stock held by him and that in the case of a company not having a share capital, voting shall simply be on the basis of one vote per member. Where the company is governed by Table A, then subject to any rights or restrictions for the time being attaching to any class or classes of shares, voting shall be as follows:

(a) on a show of hands every member present in person and every proxy shall have one vote, so, however, that no individual shall have more than one vote; and

(b) on a poll, every member shall have one vote for every share held by him.[7]

In practice it is not uncommon to find companies with different classes of shares with varying voting rights. For example, on class may have no rights whatsoever, whereas a second class may have a right to vote only in limited circumstances (eg where their dividends are in arrears) and a third class may have a right to vote in all circumstances. Furthermore, rather than provide for just one vote per member or per share, as the case may be, the company may provide in its articles or in the terms of issue, that the holders of certain classes of shares are to enjoy 'loaded' voting rights (eg 10 votes per share or 100 votes per share, or a majority of votes, etc) on all resolutions or in respect of certain types of resolutions (eg for the removal of directors). The validity of loaded voting rights has long been recognised.[8]

Regardless of whether the vote is on a show of hands or on a poll, Table A provides that no member shall be entitled to vote unless all calls or other sums immediately payable by him in respect of his shares have been paid.[9] Thus, if sums are owing in respect of some only of his shares, he will be precluded from voting in respect of any of them, even those that are fully paid up.[10]

Joint holders of share: Where there are joint holders of a share, and the company is governed by Table A, the vote of the person whose name appears first in the register of members in respect of the share, whether given in person or by proxy, shall be accepted to the exclusion of the votes of all other joint holders of the share.[11] However, in so far as the shareholding comprises more than one share, the joint holders are entitled as against the company to have the shareholding split into several holdings with their names in different orders so as to enable each joint holder to attend and vote.[12]

Members of unsound mind: In the case of a company governed by Table A, a member of unsound mind against whom an order has been made by the court under the Lunacy Regulation (Ireland) Act 1871, may vote, whether on a show of hands or on a poll, by his committee, receiver, guardian or other person appointed by the court.[13]

Proxies: See CA 1963, s 136 as well as Table A, Pt 1, regs 68–73 and the notes thereto.

Representation of corporate shareholders: See CA 1963, s 139 as well as Table A, Pt I, reg 74 and the notes thereto.

Voting on a show of hands first: At common law, votes should first be taken on a show of hands.[14] This is reflected in Table A.[15] Nonetheless, a resolution passed on a poll first without having had a show of hands, will still be valid.[16]

Chairman's declaration on a show of hands: Table A provide that unless a poll is demanded, a declaration by the chairman that a resolution has, on a show of hands, been carried or carried unanimously, or by a particular majority, or lost, an entry to that effect in the minute book is to be 'conclusive evidence' of that fact without proof of the number or proportion of the votes recorded in favour of or against the particular resolution.[17] Nonetheless, the declaration is susceptible to challenge in the case of fraud[18] or where there is plainly an error on the face of it.[19] Nor will the declaration be treated as conclusive evidence where the resolution though proposed and seconded, was never actually put to a vote.[20]

Voting on a poll: See CA 1963, ss 137 and 138 as well as Table A, Pt I, regs 59–62 in relation to the right to demand and to vote on a poll.

Objection to qualification of voter: Under Table A no objection can be raised to the qualification of a voter except at the meeting or adjourned meeting at which the vote is given or tendered, and every vote not disallowed at the meeting will be treated as valid for all purposes.[21] In this regard the decision of the chairman as to the qualification of the voter is deemed to be final and conclusive,[22] in the absence of fraud or *mala fides*.[23]

Personal interest of member in the resolution: As a general rule, a member may vote in whatever way he thinks fit on a resolution in general meeting, and will not be disqualified from voting on the ground that he has a personal interest in the outcome.[24] Moreover, in so voting, he may put his own personal interests ahead of those of the company,[25] and may even bind himself by contract with a third party to vote in a particular way.[26] This general principle is, however, subject to certain exceptions:

1. any amendment to the memorandum or articles must be made *bona fide* for the benefit of the company as a whole;[27]
2. a member may be restrained from exercising his voting rights in an illegal or *ultra vires* manner;[28]
3. a member will not be allowed to exercise his voting rights in such a way as to perpetrate a fraud on the minority;[29]
4. in the case of a company which is insolvent or threatened with insolvency the members cannot exercise their voting rights in such a manner as to perpetrate a fraud on the general body of creditors;[30]
5. in extreme cases, a member may be prevented from voting in a particular way on his shares, if to do so would result in the collapse of the company;[31]
6. a member may be restrained from voting in a manner which would be oppressive to or in disregard of the interests of other members of the company.[32]

[1] *Arulchelvan v Wright* (7 February 1996, unreported) HC (Carroll J); *Kinsella v Alliance and Dublin Consumers Gas Co* (1963–1993) Irish Company Law Reports 129; *Powell v London and Provincial Bank* [1893] 2 Ch 555.

[2] *POW Services Ltd v Clare* [1995] 2 BCLC 435.

[3] *Kinsella v Alliance and Dublin Consumers Gas Co* (1963–1993) Irish Company Law Reports 129.

[4] *Kinsella v Alliance and Dublin Consumers Gas Co* (1963–1993) Irish Company Law Reports 129.

[5] *Cannon v Trask* (1875) 20 Eq 669.

[6] See CA 1963, Table A, Pt I, regs 3 and 4 for the entitlement of the company to issue classes of shares with different class rights whether as to voting or otherwise.

[7] CA 1963, Table A, Pt I, reg 63.

[8] See for example, *Bushell v Faith* [1970] AC 1099.

[9] CA 1963, Table A, Pt I, reg 66.

[10] *Re Bradford Investments plc* [1991] BCLC 224.

[11] CA 1963, Table A, Pt I, reg 64.

[12] *Burns v Siemens Bros Dynamo Works* [1919] 1 Ch 225.

[13] CA 1963, Table A, Pt I, reg 65

[14] *Re Horbury Bridge, Coal Iron and Waggon Co* (1879) 11 Ch D 109; *Duggan v Bank of Ireland* [1998] IEHC 124 (McCracken J).

[15] CA 1963, Table A, Pt I, reg 59.

[16] *Re Credit Finance plc* (1963–1993) Irish Company Law Reports 170; *Holmes v Keyes* [1959] 1 Ch 199.

17 CA 1963, Table A, Pt I, reg 59. See also *Re Graham's Morocco Co* (1932) SC 269; *Re Hadleigh Castle Gold Mines Ltd* [1900] 2 Ch 419. *Quaere*: whether the 'conclusive' nature of the chairman's decision is unconstitutional, either as an infringement of the separation of powers provisions contained in Art 6 of the Constitution or as an attempt to oust the High Court's full original jurisdiction under Art 34 of the Constitution to hear and determine all justiciable matters: *Murren v Brennan* [1942] IR 466; *Maher v AG* [1973] IR 146; *Tormey v Ireland* [1985] IR 289.

18 *Re Hadleigh Castle Gold Mines Ltd* [1900] 2 Ch 419; *Arnot v United African Lands* [1901] 1 Ch 618.

19 *Re Hadleigh Castle Gold Mines Ltd* [1900] 2 Ch 419; *Re Caratal (New) Mines Ltd* [1902] 2 Ch 498.

20 *Re The Citizens Theatre Ltd* 1948 SC 14.

21 CA 1963, Table A, Pt I, reg 67.

22 CA 1963, Table A, Pt I, reg 67. See also *Re Hadleigh Castle Gold Mines Ltd* [1900] 2 Ch 419; *Arnot v United African Lands Ltd* [1901] 1 Ch 618. *Quaere*: whether the 'conclusive' nature of the registrar's certificate is unconstitutional, either as an infringement of the separation of powers provisions contained in Art 6 of the Constitution or as an attempt to oust the High Court's full original jurisdiction under Art 34 of the Constitution to hear and determine all justiciable matters: *Murren v Brennan* [1942] IR 466; *Maher v AG* [1973] IR 146; *Tormey v Ireland* [1985] IR 289.

23 *Wall v London and Northern Assets Corporation Ltd* [1899] 1 Ch 550; *Wall v Exchange Investment Corporation Ltd* [1926] Ch 143.

24 *Pender v Lushington* (1877) 6 Ch D 70; *North-West Transportation Co v Beatty* (1887) 12 App Cas 589; *Burland v Earle* [1902] AC 83.

25 *Pender v Lushington* (1877) 6 Ch D 70; *North-West Transportation Co v Beatty* (1887) 12 App Cas 589; *Burland v Earle* [1902] AC 83.

26 *Greenwell v Porter* [1902] 1 Ch 530; *Puddephatt v Leith* [1916] 1 Ch 200.

27 *Clark v Workman* [1920] 1 IR 107; *Allen v Gold Reefs Co of West Africa* [1900] 1 Ch 656; *Sidebottom v Kershaw, Leese and Co Ltd* [1920] 1 Ch 154; *Dafen Tinplate Co v Llanelly Steel Co* (1907) *Ltd* [1920] 2 Ch 124; *Shuttleworth v Cox Bros and Co (Maidenhead) Ltd* [1927] 2 KB 9; *Peter's American Delicacy Co Ltd v Heath* (1939) 61 CLR 457; *Greenhalgh v Arderne Cinemas Ltd* [1951] Ch 286; *Rights and Issues Investment Trust Ltd v Stylo Shoes Ltd* [1965] Ch 250; *Clemens v Clemens Bros Ltd* [1976] 2 All ER 268.

28 *ultra vires* acts: See CA 1963, s 8(3) and *Colman v Eastern Counties Ryl Co* (1846) 10 Beav 1; *Simpson v Westminster Palace Hotel Co* (1860) 8 HL Cas 712; *Maunsell v Midland Great Eastern (Ireland) Rly Co* (1863) 1 Hem and M 130; *Spokes v Grosvenor Hotel Co* [1897] 2 QB 4.

Illegal acts: See *Buchanan Ltd v McVey* [1954] IR 89; *Hennessy v National Agricultural and Industrial Development Association* [1947] IR 159; *Cockburn v Newbridge Sanitary Steam Laundry Co* [1915] 1 IR 237.

29 *Menier v Hooper's Telegraph Works Ltd* (1874) 9 Ch App 350; *North-West Transportation Co v Beatty* (1887) 12 app Cas 589; *Cook v Deeks* [1916] 1 AC 554; *Pavlides v Jensen* [1956] 2 All ER 518; *Daniels v Daniels* [1978] Ch 406; *Estmanco (Kilner House) Ltd v Greater London Council* [1982] 1 All ER 437; *Smith v Croft (No 3)* [1987] BCLC 355. See generally the commentary entitled 'Exceptions to the Rule in *Foss v Harbottle*' in the notes to CA 1963, s 205.

30 *Byrne v Shelbourne FC Ltd* [1984] IEHC 46; *Re John C Parkes and Sons Ltd* [1990] ILRM 341; *Re Frederick Inns Ltd* [1994] 1 ILRM 387; *Winkworth v Edward Baron Development Ltd* [1987] 1 All ER 114; *West Mercia Safetywear Ltd v Dodd* [1988] BCLC 250; *Kuwait Asia Bank EC v National Mutual Life Nominees Ltd* [1990] 3 All ER 404. *Walker v Wimborne* (1976) 50 ALJR 446; *Nicholson v Permakraft (NZ) Ltd* (1986) 4 ACLC 213; *Grove v Flavel* (1986) 4 ACLC 654; *David Neil and Co Ltd v Neil Tekapo Motor Inn Ltd* (1987) 3 NZCLC 100.

31 *Standard Chartered Bank v Walker* [1992] BCLC 603.

32 *Re Williams Group Tullamore Ltd* [1985] IR 613. See generally CA 1963, s 205 and the notes thereto.

UK legislation

See CA 1985, s 370; The Companies (Acquisition of Own Shares)(Treasury Shares) Regulations 2003 (SI 2003/1116), reg 4, sch, para 21.

[134A Requirements for participation and voting in general meeting

(1) This section applies to a company traded on a regulated market.

(2) In this section—

'record date' means a date not more than 48 hours before the general meeting to which it relates;

'register of securities' has the same meaning as it has in Regulation 3 of the Companies Act 1990 (Uncertificated Securities) Regulations 1996 (S.I. No. 68 of 1996).

(3) A person shall be entered on the relevant register of securities by the record date in order to exercise the right of a member to participate and vote at a general meeting and any change to an entry on the relevant register of securities after the record date shall be disregarded in determining the right of any person to attend and vote at the meeting.

(4) The right of a member to participate in a general meeting and to vote in respect of his shares shall not be subject to any requirement that the shares be deposited with, or transferred to, or registered in the name of another person before the general meeting.

(5) A member is free to sell or otherwise transfer shares in a company at any time between the record date and the general meeting to which it applies if the right to sell would not otherwise be subject to such a restriction.

(6) Proof of qualification as a member may be made subject only to such requirements as are necessary to ensure the identification of the member and only to the extent that such requirements are proportionate to the achievement of that objective.][a]

Amendments

a CA 1963, s 134A inserted by Shareholders' Rights Regulations 2009, reg 8.

Definitions

'company traded on a regulated market': CA 1963, s 2(1); 'record date': CA 1963, s 134A; 'register of securities': CA1990(US)R 1996, reg 3.

Notes

This is a new provision inserted by the Shareholders' Rights Regulations 2009 which provides new requirements for participation and voting in general meetings of companies traded on a regulated market. Subsection (3) provides that in order to be entitled to exercise the right to participate and vote at a general meeting, a person must be entered in the relevant register of securities by the 'record date'. 'Record date' is defined as meaning a date not more than 48 hours before the general meeting to which it relates. This section also expressly provides that a member's right to participate and vote at a general meeting may not be subject to any requirement that the member's shares be deposited with or transferred to or registered in the name of another person before the general meeting.

Section 134A also seeks to stop the practice of 'share-blocking', a phenomenon relatively common in some EU Member States (but not in Ireland) the effect of which is to prevent the sale of shares after a record date but before the general meeting to which it relates. Accordingly, sub-s (5) expressly provides that a member is free to sell his shares in a company at any time between the record date and the general meeting unless the right to sell is otherwise restricted in some way.

Proof that a person is a member may be subject only to such requirements as are necessary to ensure the identification of the member and only to the extent that they are proportionate to the achievement of that objective.

[134B Participation in general meeting by electronic means

(1) A company traded on a regulated market may provide for participation in a general meeting by electronic means including—

(a) a mechanism for casting votes, whether before or during the meeting, and the mechanism adopted shall not require the member to be physically present at the meeting or require the member to appoint a proxy who is physically present at the meeting,

(b) real time transmission of the meeting,

(c) real time two way communication enabling members to address the meeting from a remote location.

(2) (a) The use of electronic means pursuant to subsection (1) may be made subject only to such requirements and restrictions as are necessary to ensure the identification of those taking part and the security of the electronic communication, to the extent that such requirements and restrictions are proportionate to the achievement of those objectives.

(b) Members shall be informed of any requirements or restrictions which a company puts in place pursuant to paragraph (a).

(c) A company that provides electronic means for participation at a general meeting by a member shall ensure, as far as practicable, such means—

(i) guarantee the security of any electronic communication by the member,

(ii) minimise the risk of data corruption and unauthorised access,

(iii) provide certainty as to the source of the electronic communication, and

(iv) are remedied as soon as practicable, in the case of any failure or disruption.][a]

Amendments

a CA 1963, s 134B inserted by Shareholders' Rights Regulations 2009, reg 8.

Definitions

'company traded on a regulated market': CA 1963, s 2(1).

Notes

The Shareholders' Rights Regulations 2009 facilitate participation in a general meeting of a company traded on a regulated market by electronic means. This is an enabling provision which allows such companies to provide for the electronic casting of votes, transmission of the meeting and real-time, two-way, communication between members and the meeting.

Although facilitative, where such companies elect to provide for such participation, they become subject to certain requirements. In the first place, the use of electronic means may be made subject only to proportionate requirements and restrictions necessary to ensure the identification of participants and the security of the electronic communications. Members must also be informed of any requirements or restrictions and companies that provide such facilities are secure.

[134C Right to ask questions

(1) A member of a company traded on a regulated market has the right to ask questions related to items on the agenda of a general meeting and to have such questions answered by the company subject to any reasonable measures the company may take to ensure the identification of the member.

(2) An answer to a question asked pursuant to subsection (1) is not required where—

(a) to give an answer would interfere unduly with the preparation for the meeting or the confidentiality and business interests of the company,

(b) the answer has already been given on the company's internet site in a question and answer forum, or

(c) it appears to the Chairman of the meeting that it is undesirable in the interests of good order of the meeting that the question be answered.][a]

Amendments

a CA 1963, s 134C inserted by Shareholders' Rights Regulations 2009, reg 8.

Definitions

'company traded on a regulated market': CA 1963, s 2(1).

Notes

The right to ask questions: It may come as a surprise to members of listed companies, but prior to this amendment to the CA 1963 effected by the Shareholders' Rights Regulations 2009, there was no statutory right to ask questions at general meetings. This has now been changed and members of a company traded on a regulated market have the right to ask questions related to items on the agenda of a general meeting and to have such questions answered by the company. It is recognised, however, that questions can relate to confidential matters, be repetitious or otherwise objectionable and so the right to receive answers is not unconditional.

---

135 Power of court to order a meeting

(1) If for any reason it is impracticable to call a meeting of a company in any manner in which meetings of that company may be called, or to conduct the meeting of the company in manner prescribed by the articles or this Act, the court may, either of its own motion or on the application of any director of the company or of any member of the company who would be entitled to vote at the meeting, order a meeting of the company to be called, held and conducted in such manner as the court thinks fit, and where any such order is made may give such ancillary or consequential directions as it thinks expedient; and it is hereby declared that the directions that may be given under this subsection include a direction that one member of the company present in person or by proxy shall be deemed to constitute a meeting.

(2) Any meeting called, held and conducted in accordance with an order under subsection (1) shall for all purposes be deemed to be a meeting of the company duly called, held and conducted.

Definitions

'articles': CA 1963, s 2(1); 'company': CA 1963, s 2(1); 'the court': CA 1963, s 2(1); 'director': CA 1963, s 2(1); 'member': CA 1963, s 31; 'prescribed': CA 1963, s 2(1).

Notes

Jurisdiction of the court[1]: The power of the court to order a meeting to be called in circumstances where it would otherwise be 'impracticable' to do so. Accordingly, the court will not make an order pursuant to CA 1963, s 135 where the meeting could, without difficulty, be convened and held in accordance with the procedures prescribed by the articles[2] or where the applicant has as yet to exhaust all other procedures under the articles which might enable the meeting to be called.[3] Whilst the existence of a petition in respect of the company under CA 1963, s 205 will not operate an an automatic bar to the making of an order under CA 1963, s 135, it will result in the court approaching the application with a greater degree of caution.[4] The following are examples of situations where the court has ordered the calling of a meeting on the grounds that it would otherwise be impracticable to do so: where the names and addresses of some of the members were not known as a result of the destruction of the register of members and it was therefore necessary to give notice of the meeting to them by way of advertisement rather than by post;[5] where a postal strike prevented the company from sending out notice of a meeting in the ordinary way, so that it was necessary to give notice by way of advertisement instead;[6] where certain members refused to attend, thereby rendering any potential meeting inquorate, so that an order was needed, deeming one person present in person or by proxy to be a quorum.[7] The court will not however direct that a meeting be convened and that one person or a specific number of persons be deemed to be a quorum, where to do so would result in a breach of the class rights of some other class (eg where the articles or a shareholders' agreement provides that the meeting shall be inquorate without the attendance of a particular person or representatives from a particular class of shareholders).[8] Furthermore, the court has held that CA 1963, s 135 is not an appropriate vehicle for resolving deadlock between two equal shareholders since the section does not empower the court to break a deadlock at either a board or general meeting of a company.[9] The section is procedural only and is not designed to affect substantive voting rights or to shift the balance of power between shareholders by permitting a 50% shareholder to override the wishes of the other 50% shareholder where they had agreed that power would be shared equally and where a potential deadlock was a matter which must be taken to have been agreed on with the consent and for the protection of each of them.[10]

In one exceptional case, in order to prevent a breach of the peace at the general meeting the court went so far as to direct that only the directors could attend in person and that all other members of the company were required to exercise their votes by way of postal ballot.[11]

1 See generally Milman, 'The Courts and Company Meetings' (1997) Palmer's In Company, Issue 8/97, 18 September 1997.

2 *Angelis v Algemene Bank Nederland (Ireland) Ltd* (1963–1993) Irish Company Law Reports 539.

3 *Arulchelvan v Wright* (7 February 1996, unreported) HC (Carroll J).

4 *Re Whitechurch Consultants Ltd* [1993] BCLC 1359; *Re Sticky Fingers Restaurant Ltd* [1992] BLCL 84.

5 *Payne v Coe* [1947] 1 All ER 841.

6 *Re Waterford Foods plc*, reported in *Irish Times* 12 May 1992 and noted by Courtney. *The Law of Private Companies* (2nd edn, Tottel Publishing, 2002), ch 9.

[7] *Re El Sombrero Ltd* [1958] Ch 900; *Re HR Paul and Son Ltd* (1974) 118 Sol J 166; *Re Opera Photographic Ltd* [1989] BCLC 763; *Re Sticky Fingers Restaurant Ltd* [1992] BLCL 84; *Re Whitechurch Consultants Ltd* [1993] BCLC 1359; *Re Woven Rugs Ltd* [2002] 1 BCLC 324; *Union Music Ltd v Watson* [2003] 1 BCLC 453.

[8] *Harman v BML Group Ltd* [1994] 1 WLR 893; *Re Woven Rugs Ltd* [2002] 1 BCLC 324; *Union Music Ltd v Watson* [2003] 1 BCLC 453.

[9] *Ross v Telford* [1998] 1 BCLC 82.

[10] *Ross v Telford* [1998] 1 BCLC 82.

[11] *Re British Union for the Abolition of Vivisection* [1995] 2 BCLC 1.

UK legislation

See CA 1985, s 371.[1]

[1] CA 1985, s 371 applies to both general and directors' meetings.

---

136 Proxies

(1) Subject to subsection (2), any member of a company entitled to attend and vote at a meeting of the company shall be entitled to appoint another person (whether a member or not) as his proxy to attend and vote instead of him, and a proxy so appointed shall have the same right as the member to speak at the meeting and to vote on a show of hands and on a poll.

[(1A)(a) This subsection applies to a company traded on a regulated market.

(b) A proxy appointed may be any natural or legal person (whether a member or not) and shall act in accordance with any instructions given by the member by whom the proxy is appointed.

(c) A proxy shall be appointed by written notification to a company or by electronic means.

(d) A member shall be entitled to—

(i) appoint a proxy by electronic means, to an address specified by the company,

(ii) have the electronic notification of such appointment accepted by the company, and

(iii) have at least one effective method of notification of a proxy by electronic means offered to it by a company.

(e) The appointment and notification of appointment of a proxy to a company and the issuing of voting instructions to a proxy may be subject only to such formal requirements as are necessary to ensure identification of a member, or the proxy, or the possibility of verifying the content of voting instructions, if any, and only to the extent that those requirements are proportionate to achieving those objectives.

(1B) Subsection (1A) shall apply mutatis mutandis to the revocation of the appointment of a proxy.][a]

(2) Unless the articles otherwise provide—

(a) subsection (1) shall not apply in the case of a company not having a share capital; and

(b) a member of a company shall not be entitled to appoint more than one proxy to attend on the same occasion.

[(2A) Notwithstanding subsection (2) or anything in its articles, in the case of a company traded on a regulated market—

(a) no limitation may be placed on the right of a member to appoint more than one proxy to attend and vote at a general meeting in respect of shares held in different securities accounts, and

(b) subject to paragraph (a), a member shall not be entitled to appoint more than one proxy to attend and vote on the same occasion, provided however that a member (being a natural or legal person) acting as an intermediary on behalf of a client, shall not be prohibited from granting a proxy to each of his clients or to any third party designated by a client. Such intermediary shall be permitted to cast votes attaching to some of the shares differently from others.][b]

(3) In every notice calling a meeting of a company having a share capital there shall appear with reasonable prominence a statement that a member entitled to attend and vote is entitled to appoint a proxy or, where that is allowed, one or more proxies, to attend, speak and vote instead of him, and that a proxy need not be a member; and if default is made in complying with this subsection in relation to any meeting, every officer of the company who is in default [shall be guilty of an offence and liable to a fine][c] not exceeding [€1,904.61][d].

(4) Any provision contained in a company's articles shall be void in so far as it would have the effect of requiring the instrument appointing a proxy, or any other document necessary to show the validity of or otherwise relating to the appointment of a proxy, to be received by the company or any other person more than 48 hours before a meeting or adjourned meeting in order that the appointment may be effective thereat.

[(4A) Any provision contained in the articles of a company traded on a regulated market (other than a requirement that a person appointed as a proxy shall possess legal capacity) shall be void in so far as it would have the effect of restricting the eligibility of a person to be appointed as a proxy.][e]

(5) Subject to subsection (6), if for the purpose of any meeting of a company invitations to appoint as proxy a person or one of a number of persons specified in the invitations are issued at the company's expense to some only of the members entitled to be sent a notice of the meeting and to vote thereat by proxy, every officer of the company who knowingly and wilfully authorises or permits their issue as aforesaid [shall be guilty of an offence and liable to a fine][f] not exceeding [€1,904.61][g].

(6) An officer shall not be liable under subsection (5) by reason only of the issue to a member at his request in writing of a form of appointment naming the proxy or of a list of persons willing to act as proxy if the form or list is available on request in writing to every member entitled to vote at the meeting by proxy.

(7) This section shall apply to meetings of any class of members of a company as it applies to general meetings of the company.

Amendments

a CA 1963, s 136(1A) and (1B) inserted by Shareholders' Rights Regulations 2009, reg 9(a).

b CA 1963, s 136(2A) inserted by Shareholders' Rights Regulations 2009, reg 9(b).

c Words 'shall be guilty of an offence and liable to a fine' substituted for 'shall be liable to a fine' in CA 1963, s 136(3) by C(AA)A 2003, s 57 and Sch 2, Item No 1.

d '£250' substituted for '£50' by C(A)A 1982, Sch 1, increased to £1,500 by CA 1990, s 240(7) as inserted by CLEA 2001, s 104(c) and converted to €1,904.61 by Council Regulations (EC) No 1103/97, No 974/98 and No 2866/98 and the Economic and Monetary Union Act 1998, s 6.

e CA 1963, s 136(4A) inserted by Shareholders' Rights Regulations 2009, reg 9(c).

f Words 'shall be guilty of an offence and liable to a fine' substituted for 'shall be liable to a fine' in CA 1963, s 136(5) by C(AA)A 2003, s 57 and Sch 2, Item No 1.

g '£500' substituted for '£100' by C(A)A 1982, Sch 1, increased to £1,500 by CA 1990, s 240(7) as inserted by CLEA 2001, s 104(c) and converted to €1,904.61 by Council Regulations (EC) No 1103/97, No 974/98 and No 2866/98 and the Economic and Monetary Union Act 1998, s 6.

Definitions

'articles': CA 1963, s 2(1); 'company': CA 1963, s 2(1); 'company traded on a regulated market': CA 1963, s 2(1); 'document': CA 1963, s 2(1): 'member': CA 1963, s 31; 'officer': CA 1963, s 2(1); 'share': CA 1963, s 2(1); 'officer in default': CA 1963, s 383.

Notes

Right to vote by proxy: At common law there was no right to vote by proxy.[1] This position is, however, reversed by CA 1963, s 136 and by Table A, Pt I, reg 2 which allow for voting by proxy both on a show of hands and on a poll. In the case of a vote on a show of hands the proxy can only exercise one vote, even though he has been appointed by several members.[3]

1 *Harben v Phillips* (1883) 23 Ch D 14.

2 CA 1963, Table A, Pt I, reg 68 and Table C, reg 25.

3 *Ernest v Loma Gold Mines Ltd* [1897] 1 Ch 1. See also Table A, Pt I, reg 63.

Notice of right to appoint proxy: In the case of a company having a share capital, every notice convening a general meeting or class meeting must state with reasonable prominence that any member who is entitled to attend and vote at the meeting is also entitled to appoint a proxy in his stead and that the proxy need not be a member.[1]

1 CA 1963, s 136(3).

Appointment of proxy: Unless the articles otherwise provide,[1] a member cannot appoint more than one proxy.[2] The proxy need not, however, be a member of the company.[3] The appointment of the proxy is deemed to confer authority on him not only to vote in whatever way is stipulated or allowed by the instrument itself, but also to demand or join in demanding a poll.[4]

1 Table A is silent on the matter.

2 CA 1963, s 136(2)(b). *Quaere*, whether this subsection is intended to prohibit the appointment of different proxies in respect of different shares or to simply prohibit the appointment of alternate individuals as proxies in respect of the same share.

3 Table A, Pt I, reg 69 and Table C, reg 20.

4 CA 1963, s 137(2). See also Table A, Pt I, reg 72 and Table C, reg 20.

Form of instrument of proxy: Table A prescribes a form of instrument for the appointment of a proxy. It must, in the case of an individual member, be in writing, signed by the member or by the member's attorney duly authorised in writing, and in the case of a corporate member must either be under seal or under the hand of a duly authorised officer or attorney.[1] However, insofar as the articles allow for an instrument as near as the circumstances permit to the form actually prescribed by the articles, it appears that any instrument which would otherwise be valid as a matter of general law, will be effective for the purpose of appointing a proxy.[2]

1 Table A, Pt I, reg 69 and Table C, reg 26. For the actual form of instrument prescribed by Table A for the appointment of a proxy, see Table A, Pt I, reg 71 and Table C, reg 28.

2 *Isaacs v Chapman* [1915] 32 TLR 183.

Revocation of appointment of proxy: Unless the appointment of the proxy was made for valuable consideration and expressed to be irrevocable, there is nothing to prevent the member from revoking the appointment[1] or, even if the proxy remains unrevoked, from attending and voting in person instead.[2]

A vote in accordance with the terms of an instrument of proxy will be treated as valid despite the previous death or insanity of the principal or revocation of the proxy or authority under which the proxy was executed or the transfer of the share in respect of which the proxy is given, provided that no intimation in writing of such death, insanity, revocation or transfer, as the case may be, has been received by the company at its office before the start of the meeting or adjourned meeting at which the proxy is used.[3] Presumably however, if the chairman is actually aware of the death, insanity, revocation or transfer, as the case may be, he should not accept the proxy's vote, even if written notice of the fact in question has not yet been received at the company's office.

1 *Spiller v Mayo (Rhodesia) Co* [1926] WN 78.

2 *Cousins v International Brick Co* [1931] 2 Ch 90.

3 Table A, Pt I, reg 73 and Table C, reg 27.

Time for deposit of instrument appointing proxy: CA 1963, s 136(4) renders void any provision in a company's articles to the extent that it stipulates that the appointment of a proxy will not be effective unless the instrument appointing the proxy, and any other documents necessary to show the validity of or otherwise relating to the appointment, have to be received by the company more than 48 hours before the meeting or adjourned meeting, as the case may be. The relevant provision in Table A falls just short of being invalid, since it stipulates that the said documentation must be received by the company 'not less than 48 hours' beforehand.[1]

1 See Table A, Pt I, reg 70 and Table C, reg 27.

Partial distribution of proxy forms: If invitations are issued at the company's expense, inviting the appointment of a named person or one of a number of named persons as proxy, they must be sent to all and not just some of those who would be entitled to attend and vote at the meeting.[1] The purpose of this is to prevent the directors from soliciting only those members who are unlikely to oppose the views of the board.

1 CA 1963, s 136(5).

Two-way proxy forms: Although Table A provides for two-way proxies,[1] it is nonetheless permissible for the directors of an unlisted company to issue 'one way' proxy forms at company's expense, provided they are issued to all members who are entitled to attend and vote at the meeting.[2] In the case of publicly quoted companies, however, only 'two-way' proxy forms are permitted.[3]

1 Table A, Pt I, reg 71 and Table C, reg 28.

2 *Peel v London and North Western Rly Co* [1907] 1 Ch 5; *Campbell v Australian Mutual Provident Society* (1908) 77 LJPC 117.

3 The Stock Exchange 'Listing Rules', Ch 9, para 9.26 and Ch 13, para 28 and 29.

Regulation of proxies in companies traded on a regulated market: Irish company law has always been facilitative of proxy voting. The mischief which the Shareholders' Rights Directive (2007/36/EC) is intended to curb is largely to be found in non-common law EU Member States. Nevertheless, the Shareholders' Rights Regulations 2009 seek to give effect to the Directive to copper-fasten the position in Ireland. Section 136(1A) – which applies only to companies traded on a regulated market – makes explicit that which had always been understood, namely, that a proxy may be a natural or legal person. In the case of such companies, it is also provided that proxies do not need to be members of the company and, somewhat unnecessarily, it is expressly provided that proxies must act in accordance with the appointing member's instructions. Proxies must be appointed in writing or electronically. In the case of electronic appointments, the appointment must be sent to an address specified by the company and members also have a right to appoint a proxy electronically, rather than this being left to the company to decide. Moreover, it is provided that the revocation of the appointment of a proxy shall also be covered, *mutatis mutandis*, by the foregoing provisions. The amendments to s 136 also provide that in the case of such companies, notwithstanding anything in a company's articles, no limitation may be placed on the right to appoint more than one proxy to attend and vote at general meetings in respect of shares held in different securities accounts provided that a member shall not be entitled to appoint more than one proxy to attend and vote on the same occasion unless the member is an intermediary acting on behalf of clients. Members who are intermediaries cannot be prohibited from granting a proxy to each of their clients or their clients' nominees and also cannot be prevented from casting some votes differently to others. The only restriction on the appointment of a proxy which such companies can legitimately impose is that the proxy possesses the legal capacity to act as such.

UK legislation

See CA 1985, s 372; Companies Act 1985 (Electronic Communications) Order 2000 (SI 2000/3373), art 19(1), (2) and (5).

---

137 Right to demand a poll

(1) Any provision contained in a company's articles shall be void in so far as it would have the effect either—

(a) of excluding the right to demand a poll at a general meeting on any question other than the election of the chairman of the meeting or the adjournment of the meeting, or

(b) of making ineffective a demand for a poll on any such question which is made—

(i) by not less than five members having the right to vote at the meeting, or

(ii) by a member or members representing not less than one-tenth of the total voting rights of all the members having the right to vote at the meeting, or

(iii) by a member or members holding shares in the company conferring a right to vote at the meeting, being shares on which an aggregate sum has been paid up equal to not less than one-tenth of the total sum paid up on all the shares conferring that right.

(2) The instrument appointing a proxy to vote at a meeting of a company shall be deemed also to confer authority to demand or join in demanding a poll, and for the purposes of subsection (1), a demand by a person as proxy for a member shall be the same as a demand by the member.

Cross reference

See CA 1990, s 213(4) and notes thereto. See also Table A, Pt I, reg 59 and notes thereto.

Definitions

'articles': CA 1963, s 2(1); 'company': CA 1963, s 2(1); 'member': CA 1963, s 31; 'share': CA 1963, s 2(1).

Notes

Vote to be on a show of hands first: At common law, votes should first be taken on a show of hands.[1] This is reflected in Table A.[2] Nonetheless, a resolution passed on a poll without first having had a show of hands, will still be valid.[3]

1 *Re Horbury Bridge, Coal Iron and Waggon Co* (1879) 11 Ch D 109; *Duggan v Bank of Ireland* [1998] IEHC 124 (McCracken J). In relation to voting, generally, see CA 1963, s 134 and the notes thereto.

2 Table A, Pt I, reg 59.

3 *Re Credit Finance plc* (1963–1993) Irish Company Law Reports 170; *Holmes v Keyes* [1959] 1 Ch 199.

Chairman's declaration on a show of hands: Table A provides that unless a poll is demanded, a declaration by the chairman that a resolution has, on a show of hands, been carried or carried unanimously, or by a particular majority, or lost, an entry to that effect in the minute book is to be 'conclusive evidence' of that fact without proof of the number or proportion of the votes recorded in favour of or against the particular resolution.[1] Nonetheless, the declaration is susceptible to challenge in the case of fraud[2] or where there is plainly an error on the face of it.[3] Nor will the declaration be treated as conclusive evidence where the resolution though proposed and seconded, was never actually put to a vote.[4]

1 Table A, Pt I, reg 59. *Quaere*: whether the 'conclusive' nature of the chairman's decision is unconstitutional, either as an infringement of the separation of powers provisions contained in reg 6 or as an attempt to oust the High Court's full original jurisdiction under reg 34 to hear and determine all justiciable matters: *Murren v Brennan* [1942] IR 466; *Maher v AG* [1973] IR 146; *Tormey v Ireland* [1985] IR 289.

2 *Arnot v United African Lands* [1901] 1 Ch 618.

3 *Re Caratal (New) Mines Ltd* [1902] 2 Ch 498.

4 *Citizens Theatre Ltd, Petitioners* 1946 SC 14.

Right to demand a poll: At common law any person who was entitled to attend and vote at a meeting was also entitled to demand a poll unless the constitution of the association provided otherwise.[1] The common law rule has, however, been strengthened somewhat by CA 1963, s 137, in that articles precluding a right to demand a poll will be void to the extent specified in sub-section (1).

Under Table A the right to demand a poll is more generous than that provided for in CA 1963, s 137. The poll may be demanded in respect of any resolution including one for the appointment of a chairman.[2] Moreover, the persons have standing to make such a demand are the following:[3]

(a) the chairman; or

(b) at least three members present in person or by proxy;[4] or

(c) any member or members present in person or by proxy and representing not less than one-tenth of the total voting rights of all the members having the right to vote at the meeting; or

(d) by a member or members holding shares in the company conferring the right to vote at the meeting being shares on which an aggregate sum has been paid up equal to not less than one-tenth of the total sum paid up on all the shares conferring that right.

It is to be noted though that notwithstanding any limitations contained in CA 1963, s 137 and/or in the articles, any member of the company may demand a poll on a resolution to authorise an off-market purchase by a company of its own shares.[5]

1 *Marx v Estates and General Investments Ltd* [1975] 3 All ER 1064; *R v Wimbledon Local Board* (1882) 8 QBD 459.

2 CA 1963, Table A, Pt I, reg 59.

3 CA 1963, Table A, Pt I, reg 59.

4 It would appear that although these members would have to be entitled to attend the meeting, they would not necessarily have to be entitled to vote, in order to demand a poll.

5 CA 1990, s 213(4).

Duty of chairman to demand a poll: The right of a chairman under the articles to demand a poll[1] is not a personal right to be exercised according to his own personal wishes and desires but is instead to be exercised where he considers it necessary to ascertain the feeling of the meeting.[2] Indeed, he must exercise that power where he has reason to believe that the result of the poll would be different from the result of the vote taken on a show of hands.[3] On the other hand, if the articles confer no right on the chairman to demand a poll, he is under no obligation to invite members to demand a poll despite the fact that he believes that the outcome of a poll would be different from the vote on the show of hands.[4]

1 See Table A, Pt I, reg 59.

2 *Second Consolidated Trust Ltd v Ceylon Amalgamated Tea and Rubber Estates Ltd* [1943] 2 All ER 567.

3 *Second Consolidated Trust Ltd v Ceylon Amalgamated Tea and Rubber Estates Ltd* [1943] 2 All ER 567.

4 *Re Hockerill Athletic Club Ltd* [1990] BCLC 921.

Conduct of poll: The manner of conducting the poll is a matter for the discretion of the chairman.[1] Table A provides, logically, that if the poll relates to the election of a chairman or a question of an adjournment, it must be taken forthwith.[2] Otherwise the poll is to be taken at such time as the chairman directs, and any other business of the meeting may be proceeded with pending the taking of the poll.[3] In this regard the chairman may decide to defer the holding of the poll until a later day, or alternatively may resolve to hold it then and there.[4]

Where resolutions have been put separately to the meeting and polls are demanded, there must be a separate poll for each resolution,[5] although the chairman may put them *en bloc* if no member objects.[6]

Normally when a poll has been validly demanded the chairman should invite votes from those wishing to vote either way n the resolution. However, if to save time, he only calls for those wishing to vote against the resolution to cast their votes, this decision will not necessarily invalidate the poll provided he already knows from the amount of proxies submitted in favour of the resolution that no matter how many votes are cast against the resolution on the poll, the resolution will still be carried.[7]

1 Table A, Pt I, reg 60.

2 Table A, Pt I, reg 62.

3 Table A, Pt I, reg 62.

4 *R v D'Oyly* (1840) 12 Ad and El 139; *Re Chillington Iron Co* (1885) 29 Ch D 159. *cf Re Horbury Bridge Coal, Iron and Waggon Co* (1879) 11 Ch D 109 where it was held that the chairman should defer the holding of the poll to a later day so as to afford an opportunity to the members who are not present at the meeting to vote as well.

5 *Blair Open Hearth Furnace Co v Reigart* (1913) 108 LT 665.

6 *Re Jones Ltd* (1933) 50 TLR 31.

7 *Duggan v Bank of Ireland* [1998] IEHC 124 (McCracken J).

Withdrawal of demand for a poll: Table A permits a demand for a poll to be withdrawn,[1] although they do not specify the time up to which the withdrawal may be made. *Quaere*: whether the demand may be withdrawn after the close of the meeting.[2]

1 Table A, Pt I, reg 59.

2 *R v Mayor of Dover* [1903] 1 KB 668.

Voting on a poll

Generally: See generally CA 1963, s 134 and the notes thereto in relation to voting on resolutions

Voting by proxies: Where proxies have been submitted there is no absolute requirement that the proxy holders cast their votes in writing, so that where a chairman orally announces how the proxies held by him have been voted, this was held to suffice for the purpose of the poll.[1]

Member with more than one vote: Where a member, present in person or by proxy, is entitled to exercise more than one vote on a poll, he need not cast all his votes in the same way.[2]

Casting vote of chairman: At common law the chairman has no casting vote whether on a show of hands or on a poll.[3] However, this position is reversed by Table A.[4] A resolution which has been carried by the casting vote of an invalidly appointed chairman will itself be invalid.[5]

Members who did not attend the meeting: A member who was neither present in person nor by proxy at the meeting, will still be entitled to vote on the poll if the chairman resolves that it be deferred to a later day.[6]

1 *Duggan v Bank of Ireland* [1998] IEHC 124 (McCracken J).

2 CA 1963, s 138. This provision is presumably in aid of trustees and nominees who hold shares on behalf of various beneficiaries, not all of whom wish to have votes cast in the same way: *Northern Counties Securities Ltd v Jackson and Steeple Ltd* [1974] 1 WLR 1133 at 1147.

3 *Nell v Longbottom* [1894] 1 QB 767.

4 Table A, Pt I, reg 61.

5 *Clark v Workman* [1920] 1 IR 107.

6 *R v D'Oyly* (1840) 12 Ad and El 139.

Date of resolution carried on a poll: A resolution which has been carried on a poll is deemed to have been passed on the date on which the result of the poll is declared and not the date on which the meeting was originally held.[1]

1 *Holmes v Keyes* [1959] 1 Ch 199.

Disclosure of how people voted: The way in which shareholders or their proxies cast their votes is not confidential information such as could only be disclosed with the consent of the individual concerned. Accordingly, the chairman or scrutineers may reveal to the company and its members who voted and in which way they voted.[1]

1 *Haarhaus and Co GmbH v Law Debenture Trust Corporation plc* [1988] BCLC 640.

Wrongful refusal to hold a poll: Where a poll has been lawfully demanded by a member or his proxy but has been refused, the member may obtain an injunction restraining the implementation of resolutions passed at the meeting, even though his votes on the poll would not have effected the outcome.[1]

1 *Pender v Lushington* (1877) 6 Ch D 70.

UK legislation

See CA 1985, s 373; Companies Act 1985 (Electronic Communications) Order 2000 (SI 2000/3373), art 20; The Companies (Acquisition of Own Shares)Regulations 2003 (SI 2003/3031), reg 4, sch, para 22(a)(b).

[138 Voting on a poll

(1) On a poll taken at a meeting of a company or a meeting of any class of members of a company, a member, whether present in person or by proxy, entitled to more than one vote need not, if he votes, use all his votes or cast all the votes he uses in the same way.

(2) A company traded on a regulated market, may provide for a vote exercised under subsection (1) to include a vote cast in advance by correspondence, subject only to such requirements and restrictions as are necessary to ensure the identification of the person voting, and as are proportionate to the achievement of that objective.

(3) A company traded on a regulated market shall only be required to count votes cast in advance by correspondence pursuant to subsection (2), where such votes are received before the date and time specified by the company, provided the date and time is no more than 24 hours before the time at which the vote is to be concluded.][a]

Amendments

a CA 1963, s 138 substituted by Shareholders' Rights Regulations 2009, reg 10.

Cross reference

See CA 1963, s 137 and notes thereto.

Definitions

'company': CA 1963, s 2(1); 'member': CA 1963, s 31.

Notes

Subsections (2) and (3) apply only to companies traded on a regulated market and were introduced by the Shareholders' Rights Regulations 2009. The effect is to facilitate the taking of a poll by correspondence entered into prior to a meeting; however, companies wishing to avail of this option would be required to make provision for such in their articles of association since most articles of association would only provide for voting at the general meeting. This option is not mandatory and companies may elect to permit or not permit voting by correspondence. Where companies elect to permit voting by correspondence, companies may only insist on proportionate requirements and restrictions necessary to ensure identification of the member and are only obliged to count votes cast by correspondence where they are received before the date and time specified by the company provided such is no more than 24 hours before the time at which the vote is to be concluded.

Voting by correspondence is not the same as proxy voting; in the case of voting by correspondence, the member casts their own vote in advance of the general meeting. In the case of proxy voting, the member appoints another person to cast the member's vote as directed by the member at a future time, usually at the general meeting.

UK legislation

See CA 1985, s 374.

---

139 Representation of bodies corporate at meetings of companies and of creditors

(1) A body corporate may—

(a) if it is a member of a company, by resolution of its directors or other governing body authorise such person as it thinks fit to act as its representative at any meeting of the company or at any meeting of any class of members of the company [....][a]

(b) if it is a creditor (including a holder of debentures) of a company, by resolution of its directors or other governing body authorise such person as it thinks fit to act as its representative at any meeting of any creditors of the company held in pursuance of this Act or of any rules made thereunder or in pursuance of the provisions contained in any debenture or trust deed, as the case [may be, and][b].

[(c) if it has been appointed as the proxy to attend and vote at a general meeting of a company traded on a regulated market on behalf of a member of the company, by resolution of its directors or other governing body authorise such person as it thinks fit to act as its representative at any meeting of the company or at any meeting of any class of members of the company for the purpose of such appointment.][c]

(2) A person authorised as aforesaid shall be entitled to exercise the same powers on behalf of the body corporate which he represents as that body corporate could exercise if it were an individual member, creditor or holder of debentures of the company.

Amendments

a Word 'and' deleted by Shareholders' Rights Regulations 2009, reg 11(a).

b Words 'may be, and' substituted for 'may be.' by Shareholders' Rights Regulations 2009, reg 11(b).

c CA 1963, s 139(1)(c) inserted by Shareholders' Rights Regulations 2009, reg 11(c).

Cross references

See Table A, Pt I, reg 74.

Definitions

'company': CA 1963, s 2(1); 'company traded on a regulated market': CA 1963, s 2(1); 'debenture': CA 1963, s 2(1); 'director': CA 1963, s 2(1); 'member': CA 1963, s 31.

Notes

Representation of corporate members and creditors: A body corporate, being an artificial legal entity, cannot attend meetings in person.[1] However, where such a body corporate is a member of a company it may attend and vote at meetings in either of two ways. It may appoint a proxy,[2] or alternatively its board of directors 'or other governing body' may appoint someone pursuant to CA 1963, s 139 to act as its duly authorised representative at the meeting.[3] The representative is deemed to be the body corporate for the purposes of the meeting and enjoys all of its powers with regard to speaking, voting, demanding polls etc.[4] He is not a proxy and accordingly there is no need to notify his appointment to the company before the meeting.[5] Nor do any of the restrictions in the articles which relate to proxies apply to him.

Where the body corporate is in liquidation or receivership, the power of appointment under CA 1963, s 136 is exercisable by the liquidator or receiver, as the case may be, rather than by the directors.[6]

In the case of creditors' meetings the body corporate is similarly entitled to appoint a duly authorised representative to attend and vote on its behalf.[7] Furthermore, if the meeting is one in the context of a winding up, there is also a power to appoint a proxy if the body corporate so wishes.[8]

Quaere, whether the company can demand evidence that the representative has been duly appointed by the body corporate.[9]

1 *Mauri Development Corporation Ltd v Power Beat International Ltd* [1995] 2 NZLR 568.

2 See CA 1963, s 136 and the notes thereto in relation to the appointment of proxies.

3 The provisions of CA 1963, s 139 are replicated in Table A, Pt I, reg 74 in so far as they apply to general meetings and class meetings.

4 CA 1963, s 139(2). See also *Hillman v Crystal Bowl Amusements Ltd* [1973] 1 All ER 379; *Re Kelantan Coconut Estates Ltd* [1920] WN 274.

5 See CA 1963, s 136(4) and Table A, Pt I, reg 70 in relation to the notification of proxies to the company prior to the meeting.

6 *Hillman v Crystal Bowl Amusements Ltd* [1973] 1 All ER 379.

7 CA 1963, s 139(1)(b).

8 See RSC 1986, Ord 74, rr 74–83.

9 *Colonial Gold Reef v Free State Rand* [1914] 1 Ch 382.

Appointment of bodies corporate as proxy: In the case of a body corporate that is appointed as the proxy of a member to attend and vote on that member's behalf at a general meeting of a company traded on a regulated market, it may by resolution of its directors authorise a person to act as its representative at any meeting of the company. It is unfortunate that this creates a distinction between companies traded on a regulated market and other companies since it casts a doubt as to whether a body corporate appointed proxy for a member in another company can appoint a representative when the entitlement to do this has never been disputed.

UK legislation

See CA 1985, s 375.

---

140 Annual general meeting to be held in the State

(1) Subject to subsection (2), the annual general meeting of a company shall be held in the State and any business transacted at a meeting held in breach of this requirement shall be void unless—

(a) either all the members entitled to attend and vote at such meeting consent in writing to its being held elsewhere or a resolution providing that it be held elsewhere has been passed at the preceding annual general meeting, and

(b) the articles do not provide that the annual general meeting shall be held in the State.

(2) Subsection (1) shall not apply to the first annual general meeting of a company held on or after the operative date.

Cross reference

Table A, Pt I, reg 47: requires all general meetings and not just the AGM to be held in the State.

Definitions

'articles': CA 1963, s 2(1); 'company': CA 1963, s 2(1); 'member': CA 1963, s 31; 'the operative date': CA 1963, s 2(1).

Notes

Holding of AGM in the State: Subject to anything to the contrary in the articles, CA 1963, s 140 allows for the first AGM of the company may be held abroad.[1] However, all other AGMs must be held in the State unless:

(a) either all the members entitled to attend and votes at the meeting consent in writing to its being held elsewhere or a resolution providing that it be held elsewhere has been passed at the preceding AGM; and

(b) the articles do not provide that the AGM is to be held in the State.[2]

In fact, Table A stipulates that all general meetings of the company, and not just the AGM, are to be held in the State.[3] Any business transacted at an AGM outside the State, in breach of the above provisions, will be void.[4]

1 CA 1963, s 140(2).

2 CA 1963, s 140(1).

3 CA 1963, Table A, Pt I, reg 47.

4 CA 1963, s 140(1). In the case of an EGM, however, where there is no statutory provision requiring the meeting to be held in the State, the unanimous consent of the members (whether express or implied), to the holding of a particular meeting abroad will be regarded as overruling Table A, Pt I, reg 47, so as to render any business transacted at the meeting valid: *Re Shannonside Holdings Ltd* (20 May 1993, unreported) HC (Costello J).

141 Resolutions

(1) A resolution shall be a special resolution when it has been passed by not less than three-fourths of the votes cast by such members as, being entitled so to do, vote in person or, where proxies are allowed, by proxy at a general meeting of which not less than 21 days' notice, specifying the intention to propose the resolution as a special resolution, has been duly given.

(2) A resolution may be proposed and passed as a special resolution at a meeting of which less than 21 days' notice has been given if it is so agreed by a majority in number of the members having the right to attend and vote at any such meeting, being a majority together holding not less than ninety per cent. in nominal value of the shares giving that right or, in the case of a company not having a share capital, together representing not less than ninety per cent. of the total voting rights at that meeting of all the members.

(3) At any meeting at which a special resolution is submitted to be passed, a declaration of the chairman that the resolution is carried shall, unless a poll is demanded, be conclusive evidence of the fact without proof of the number or proportion of the votes recorded in favour of or against the resolution.

(4) For the purposes of this section, notice of a meeting shall be deemed to be duly given and the meeting to be duly held when the notice is given and the meeting held in manner provided by this Act or the articles.

(5) The terms of any resolution (whether special or otherwise) before a general meeting may be amended by ordinary resolution moved at the meeting provided that the terms of the resolution as amended will still be such that adequate notice of the intention to pass the same can be deemed to have been given.

(6) Any reference to an extraordinary resolution contained in any statute which was passed or document which existed before the operative date shall, in relation to a resolution passed or to be passed on or after the operative date, be deemed to be a reference to a special resolution.

(7) Where before the operative date a meeting has been convened for the purpose of passing an extraordinary resolution as defined in the Companies Acts, 1908 to 1959, and at that meeting that resolution has after the operative date been passed in the manner required by those Acts for the passing of an extraordinary resolution and such resolution

would under the Companies Acts, 1908 to 1959, have been effective for its purpose, such resolution shall be as effective as if it had been a special resolution.

(8) (a) Notwithstanding anything to the contrary in this Act, in any case in which a company is so authorised by its articles, a resolution in writing signed by all the members for the time being entitled to attend and vote on such resolution at a general meeting (or being bodies corporate by their duly appointed representatives) shall be as valid and effective for all purposes as if the resolution had been passed at a general meeting of the company duly convened and held, and if described as a special resolution shall be deemed to be a special resolution within the meaning of this Act.

(b) Any such resolution shall be deemed to have been passed at a meeting held on the date on which it was signed by the last member to sign, and where the resolution states a date as being the date of his signature thereof by any member the statement shall be *prima facie* evidence that it was signed by him on that date.

(c) This section does not apply to a resolution for any of the purposes of section 160 or 182.

Cross reference

See CA 1963, ss 160 and 182 and notes thereto.

Definitions

'articles': CA 1963, s 2(1); 'company': CA 1963, s 2(1). 'document': CA 1963, s 2(1): 'member': CA 1963, s 31; 'the operative date': CA 1963, s 2(1); 'share': CA 1963, s 2(1).

Notes

Ordinary and special resolutions: The two types of resolution capable of being passed at general meetings and class meetings are ordinary resolutions and special resolutions. An ordinary resolution is not defined by the Companies Acts. It is a resolution of which the normal notice for an AGM or EGM, as the case may be, has been given and which has been passed by a simple majority of those who were present in person or by proxy at the meeting and who were entitled to vote.[1] On the other hand, a special resolution is one which has been passed by a majority of not less than 75% of those who were present in person or by proxy and entitled to vote, at a meeting of which not less than 21 days' notice, specifying the intention to propose the resolution as a special resolution, was duly given.[2]

1 *Bushell v Faith* [1970] AC 1099.

2 CA 1963, s 141(1). For the notice periods that are otherwise applicable to AGMs and EGMs at which special resolutions are not being proposed, see CA 163, s 133 and the notes thereto. See Table A, Pt I, reg 53: all business at an EGM is deemed to be special business.

Contents of notice for special resolution: In the case of a special resolution, the notice convening the meeting will be invalid if it fails to specify either the entire text or the entire substance of the proposed resolution.[1] Mere typographical or otherwise inconsequential discrepancies between the contents of the notice and the special resolution, as passed, will be overlooked by the court.[2]

1 *Re Moorgate Mercantile Holdings Ltd* [1980] 1 WLR 227; *MacConnell v E Prill and Co Ltd* [1916] 2 Ch 57.

2 *Re Willaire Systems plc* [1987] BCLC 67.

Abridgement of notice period: In so far as the company wishes to abridge the notice period for the passing of a special resolution, it may do so with a majority of not less than 90% in value of the members having the right to attend and vote at the meeting.[1] However, the members' purported consent to short notice will not be valid and effective unless they appreciate that what they are consenting to is in fact short notice rather than the normal statutory notice period.[2] See also CA 1963, s 133(3) and notes thereto in relation to the ability to shorten the notice period for general meetings.

1 CA 1963, s 141(2).

2 *Re Pearce Duff and Co Ltd* [1960] 1 WLR 1014.

Chairman's declaration on a show of hands: CA 1963, s 141(3) provides that unless a poll is demanded, a declaration by the chairman that a special resolution has been carried shall be 'conclusive evidence' without proof of the number or proportion of the votes recorded in favour of or against the particular resolution. Nonetheless, the declaration is susceptible to challenge in the case of fraud[1] or where there is plainly an error on the face of it.[2] The declaration will not be treated as conclusive evidence where the resolution, though proposed and seconded, was never actually put to a vote.[3]

1 *Arnot v United African Lands* [1901] 1 Ch 618.

2 *Re Caratal (New) Mines Ltd* [1902] 2 Ch 498.

3 *Citizens Theatre Ltd, Petitioners* 1946 SC 14.

Informal resolutions of the members: At common law an *intra vires* decision made unanimously, albeit informally, by those members having an entitlement to vote is as valid and effective as if it had been passed as a formal resolution at a properly convened meeting.[1] As stated by Kingsmill Moore J in the Supreme Court in one leading case:[2]

> 'It is now settled law that neither meeting nor resolution is necessary. If all the corporators agree to a certain course then, however informal the manner of their agreement, it is an act of the company and binds the company, subject only to two pre-requisites ...The two necessary pre-requisites are (1) that the transaction to which the corporators agree should be intra vires the company; (2) that the transaction should be honest.'

The requirement that the transaction be otherwise lawful and honest is of course of fundamental importance. Accordingly, it has been held that the unanimous approval of the shareholders will be ineffective where it is shown that the transaction itself was not bona fide or honest or was likely to jeopardise the company's solvency or cause loss to its creditors.[3] Similarly, the unanimous approval of the members will not operate to validate the payment of a dividend which would have been unlawful even if it had been declared at a formal general meeting.[4]

If a decision of the members is, on its face, *ultra vires*, the fact that it has been unanimously adopted, will not operate so as to implicitly alter the objects clause and thereby render it *intra vires* the company.[5] Instead, an express alteration of the objects will first be required before the decision can be validly made.

Subject to the foregoing, the informal consent of the members does not have to be given at the same time and in the same place, but can be given individually and at different times.[6] However, in order for the informal consent to be valid and effective it must be given by all, and not just a majority, of the members entitled to attend and vote on the transaction.[7] Similarly, the principle cannot be invoked by a surviving shareholder to validate transactions effected by him following the death of his fellow shareholder.[8] However, where the only persons entitled to vote on the transaction are shareholders of a particular class, the transaction will be validated where it can be shown that all of the members of that class have given their consent, albeit informally.[9]

Where the legal and beneficial ownership of a share is split, with one person holding as bare nominee or bare trustee for another, the consent of the beneficial owner of the share is the relevant consent in determining whether the particular transaction or course of action has the unanimous approval of the shareholders.[10]

The unanimous consent of the members has been relied upon in the following circumstances to cure what would otherwise be irregularities:

1. Debts which the members owed to the company were cancelled by the unanimous, albeit informal agreement.[11]
2. The execution of a guarantee without the approval of the board was deemed to be ratified in circumstances where the annual accounts (which reflected the giving of the guarantee) were approved by all the members.[12]
3. A prohibition in the articles against the holding of general meetings outside the State was held to have been implicitly overridden by the attendance of all members at an EGM in the USA.[13]
4. A breach by the directors, of provisions in the articles prohibiting them from voting on contracts in which they were interested was cured by the fact that the directors were also the only members of the company.[14]
5. A failure to give sufficient notice of a general meeting of the company was cured by the attendance of all the members.[15]
6. Acts performed by improperly appointed directors were validated by reason of the fact that they had been informally approved by all the members.[16]
7. The payment of remuneration to the directors without the prior approval of the company in general meeting was cured in one year by reason of the fact that the annual accounts (which reflected the payments) were signed by two directors who happened to be the only two shareholders; in another year where accounts were not drawn up, the consent of the members (who now numbered more than two) was expressed informally but not at a general meeting.[17] On the other hand, it has been held that members' approval of annual accounts which happened to record unauthorised drawings by a director, did not amount to a validation of those drawings in circumstances where the members were unaware that the drawings were in fact being improperly made.[18]
8. A provision in the articles conferring a casting vote on the chairman was deemed to have been implicitly repealed by a shareholders' agreement to the contrary.[19]
9. Acts done by a minority of the board and without the authority of a board resolution were cured by reason of the fact that the minority directors were also the only shareholders.[20]
10. The retainer of a firm of solicitors to act in relation to the hearing of a winding-up petition against the company was deemed to have been validated by the unanimous informal agreement of the members.[21]
11. A capital call approved by all the members was held to be valid and effective notwithstanding the fact that t had been made in a way which did not comply with certain procedural requirements laid down by a shareholders' agreement to which those members were parties.[22]
12. A buy-back by a company by some of its own shares would have been validated by the court (but for the absence of distributable profits) in circumstances where it had been endorsed by all of the members but, where contrary to the requirements of CA 1990, s 213(5)(a) the purchase contract had not been available for inspection by members for at least 21 days prior to the members' decision to approve the transaction.[23]
13. The validity of a contract giving a director security of tenure for at least seven years was upheld in circumstances where, although contrary to the requirements of CA 1990, s 28(4) it had not been available for inspection at the registered office by members of the company prior to being voted on, it had in fact been informally approved by all of the members of the company.[24]

14. The creation of debentures in favour of third party which required the prior approval of a particular class of shareholders, was validated by the informal unanimous consent of the members of that class.[25]
15. A substantial property transaction between a company and some of its directors was validated in circumstances where, even though there was no formal shareholders' resolution under the UK equivalent of CA 1990, s 29, the transaction had been unanimously approved in advance by a resolution of the directors, three of whom also held the entire issued share capital in the company.[26]
16. A transfer of shares which has been approved by all the shareholders will be valid even though the Articles confer on the directors a discretion to refuse to register such a transfer.[27]

In all of the above examples, it was possible to override the various procedural requirements whether statutory or contractual, because they existed for the protection of members only.[28] However, if the procedural requirement is one whch exists for the protection of creditors then it cannot be overridden by the unanimous consentof the members.[29]

1 *Re SM Barker Ltd* [1950] IR 123; *Peter Buchanan Ltd v McVey* [1954] IR 89; *Re PMPA Garage (Longmile) Ltd (No 1)* [1992] ILRM 337; *Re Shannonside Holdings Ltd* (20 May 1993, unreported) HC (Costello J); *Re Greendale Developments Ltd* (20 February 1997, unreported) SC (Keane J); *Re Express Engineering Works Ltd* [1920] 1 Ch 466; *Re Oxted Motor Co* [1921] 3 KB 32; *Parker and Cooper Ltd v Reading* [1926] Ch 975; *Re Duomatic Ltd* [1969] 2 Ch 365; *Cane v Jones* [1981] 1 All ER 533; *Re Horsley and Weight Ltd* [1982] 3 All ER 1045; *Re Fletcher Hunt (Bristol) Ltd* [1989] BCLC 109. The absence of unanimity will render the informal acts null and void: *EBM Co Ltd v Dominion Bank* [1937] 3 All ER 555.

2 *Peter Buchanan Ltd v McVey* [1954] IR 89.

3 *Bowthorpe Holdings Ltd v Hills* [2003] 1 BCLC 226; *Official Receiver v Stern* [2002] 1 BCLC 119 at 129; *Precision Dippings Ltd v Precision Dippings Marketing Ltd* [1985] BCLC 385; *Multinational Gas v Multinational Services* [1983] BCLC 461 at 468; *West Mercia Safetywear v Dodd* [1988] BCLC 250; *Re Express Engineering Works* [1920] 1 Ch 466 at 471; *A-G for Canada v Standard Trust* [1911] AC 498 at 505; *Nicholson v Permakraft (NZ) Ltd* [1985] 1 NZLR 242 at 250; *Kinsela v Russell Kinsela Property Ltd (in liq)* (1986) 4 NSWLR 722 at 732; *Re Frederick Inns Ltd* [1994] 1 ILRM 387.

4 *Inn Spirit Ltd v Burns* [2002] 2 BCLC 780; *Bairstow v Queens Moat Houses plc* [2001] 2 BCLC 531.

5 *Re Greendale Developments Ltd* (20 February 1997, unreported) SC (Keane J).

6 *Parker and Cooper Ltd v Reading* [1926] Ch 975.

7 *Extrasure Travel Insurances Ltd v Scattergood* [2003] 1 BCLC 598.

8 *Re New Cedos Engineering Ltd* [1994] 1 BCLC 797.

9 *Re Torvale Ltd* [1999] [1999] 2 BCLC 605. See also *Re Bradford Investments Ltd* [1991] BCLC 224.

10 *Deakin v Faulding* [2001] EWHC Ch 7.

11 *Re SM Barker Ltd* [1950] IR 123.

12 *Re PMPA Garage (Longmile) Ltd (No 1)* [1992] ILRM 337. See also *Re Gee and Co (Woolwich) Ltd* [1975] Ch 52.

13 *Re Shannonside Holdings Ltd* (20 May 1993, unreported) HC (Costello J).

14 *Re Express Engineering Works Ltd* [1920] 1 Ch 466.

15 *Re Oxted Motor Co* [1921] 3 KB 32.

16 *Parker and Cooper Ltd v Reading* [1926] Ch 975.

17 *Re Duomatic Ltd* [1969] 2 Ch 365. See also *Re Gee and Co (Woolwich) Ltd* [1975] Ch 52.

18 *Clark v Cutland* [2003] 2 BCLC 393 at 395/396.

19 *Cane v Jones* [1981] 1 WLR 1451.

20 *Re Horsley and Weight Ltd* [1982] 3 All ER 1045.

21 *Re Fletcher Hunt (Bristol) Ltd* [1989] BCLC 109. See also *Re Bailey, Hay and Co Ltd* [1971] 3 All ER 693.

22 *Euro Brokers Holdings Ltd v Monecor (London) Ltd* [2003] 1 BCLC 506.

23 *BDG Roof-Bond Ltd v Douglas* [2000] 1 BCLC 401. See *Kinlan v Crimmin* [2007] 2 BCLC 67 where a unanimously approved share buy-back was held to be valid despite the fact that the contract had not been available for inspection for the prescribed period prior to the passing of the special resolution. Cf *Re RW Peak (Kings Lynnn) Ltd* [1998] 1 BCLC 193.

24 *Wright v Atlas Wright (Europe) Ltd* [1999] 2 BCLC 301.

25 *Re Torvale Group Ltd* [1999] 2 BCLC 605.

26 *Re Conegrade Ltd* [2003] BPIR 358. cf *Demite Ltd v Protec Health Ltd* [1998] BCC 638.

27 *Re Zinotty Properties Ltd* [1984] BCLC 375.

28 See for example the comments of the court in *Re Torvale Group Ltd* [1999] 2 BCLC 605, *BDG Roof-Bond Ltd v Douglas* [2000] 1 BCLC 401 and *Kinlan v Crimmin* [2007] 2 BCLC 67.

29 *Precision Dippings Ltd v Precision Dippings Marketing Ltd* [1985] BCLC 385; *Kinlan v Crimmin* [2007] 2 BCLC 67.

Effect of subsection (8) on informal resolutions: Under CA 1963, s 141(8), if a company is so authorised by its articles,[1] a resolution in writing signed by all the members entitled to attend and vote on such a resolution at a general meeting, is deemed to be as valid and effective as if it had been passed at a properly convened meeting, unless it is a resolution relating to the appointment or removal of an auditor[2] or the dismissal of a director.[3]

A question that arises is whether the common law position regarding the validity of informal acts of all the members has in any way been modified by the provisions of CA 1963 and in particular ss 133(3) and 141(8). For example, can general meetings only be called on shorter notice pursuant to s 133(3) (ie. with the consent of all members entitled to vote and the auditors)? Furthermore, if a resolution is to be passed without a formal general meeting, must it comply with s 141(8) (ie must it (a) be in writing, (b) be signed by all the members entitled to vote and (c) be described as a special or ordinary resolution, as the case may be)? Ussher expresses the view[4] that the common law position has been so modified. In the first relevant Irish case decided after the coming into force of CA 1963[5] Keane J avoided any reference to s 141(8) but held that where the members had unanimously and informally approved a resolution they would then be estopped from challenging it subsequently. The weakness of such an estoppel, however, is that it only binds the parties thereto and would have no effect on a third party such as a person who subsequently becomes a member or a person who is subsequently appointed as a receiver, liquidator or examiner of the company. However, in two more recent cases,[6] the High Court, without actually referring to s 141(8), has nonetheless adopted the traditional common law principles regarding the validity of informal unanimous acts of those members having voting rights, so that presumably such acts do not in fact have to be in writing or be signed or be described as resolutions in order to have the same effect and validity as resolutions passed at properly convened meetings.

1 Such authorisation is to be found, in the case of private companies, in CA 1963, Table A, Part II, reg 6. It is to be noted that the provisions of reg 6 do not automatically apply to companies incorporated under C(C)A 1908: *Safeera Ltd v Wallis and O'Regan* (12 July 1994, unreported) HC (Morris J).

2 CA 1963, s 160.

3 CA 1963, s 182.

4 Ussher, *Company Law in Ireland* (Sweet & Maxwell, 1986) at pp 76–77.

5 *Re Greenore Trading Co Ltd* [1980] ILRM 94.

6 *Re PMPA Garage (Longmile) Ltd (No 1)* [1992] ILRM 337; *Re Shannonside Holdings Ltd* (20 May 1993, unreported) HC (Costello J).

Informal acts in single-member companies: In the case of a single-member company, all the powers capable of being exercised by a company in general meeting, other than those relating to the removal of an auditor from office, are exercisable by the sole member without the need to hold a general meeting for that purpose.[1] The member is required to draw up his decision in writing and forward a copy to the company which is in turn to record that decision in a book or by some other suitable means maintained for that purpose.[2] Although a failure to comply with these procedures may constitute an offence[3] the inherent validity of the decision itself would not appear to be affected.[4]

1 EC(SMPLC)R 1994, reg 9(1) and (2).

2 EC(SMPLC)R 1994, reg 9(3)-(5).

3 EC(SMPLC)R 1994, reg 9(7).

4 EC(SMPLC)R 1994, reg 9(8). See also the notes above on the validity at common law of informal acts of the members which are not necessarily recorded in writing.

UK legislation

See CA 1985, ss 378, 381A; CA 1989, ss 113(2), 115; The Companies (Acquisition of Own Shares) (Treasury Shares) Regulations 2003 (SI 2003/1116), reg 4, sch, para 24; Deregulation (Resolutions of Private Companies) Order 1996 (SI 1996/1471), art 3(2)(a), (3).

---

142 Extended notice

(1) Subject to subsection (2), where by any provision hereafter contained in this Act extended notice is required of a resolution, the resolution shall not be effective unless (except when the directors of the company have resolved to submit it) notice of the intention to move it has been given to the company not less than 28 days before the meeting at which it is moved, and the company shall give its members notice of any such resolution at the same time and in the same manner as it gives notice of the meeting or, if that is not practicable, shall give them notice thereof, either by advertisement in a daily newspaper circulating in the district in which the registered office of the company is situate or in any other mode allowed by the articles, not less than 21 days before the meeting.

(2) If, after notice of the intention to move such a resolution has been given to the company, a meeting is called for a date 28 days or less after the notice has been given, the notice though not given within the time required by subsection (1) shall be deemed to have been properly given for the purposes of that subsection.

Cross references

See CA 1963, s 161: resolution at an AGM to appoint a person other than a retiring auditor.

See also CA 1963, s 182: resolution to remove a director.

Definitions

'articles': CA 1963, s 2(1); 'company': CA 1963, s 2(1); 'director': CA 1963, s 2(1); 'extended notice': CA 1963, s 2(1), s 142; 'member': CA 1963, s 31.

Notes

Extended notice: 'Extended notice' refers to the period of notice which must be given to the company, rather than by the company, of notice of intention to move certain types of resolution.[1] The resolutions requiring 'extended notice' are as follows:

1. a resolution at an agm of a company appointing as auditor a person other than a retiring auditor or providing expressly that a retiring auditor shall not be re-appointed;[2]
2. a resolution at a general meeting of a company removing an auditor before the expiration of his term of office;[3]

3. a resolution at a general meeting of a company filling a casual vacancy in the office of auditor;[4]
4. a resolution at a general meeting of a company to remove a director or to appoint somebody else instead of a director so removed at the meeting at which he is removed.[5]

Such a resolution will not be effective (except where the directors of the company have resolved to submit it) unless notice of intention to move it has been given to the company not less than 28 days before the meeting at which it is moved.[6] Having received such notice the company must then give its members notice of the proposed resolution at the same time and in the same manner as it gives notice of the meeting[7] or, if that is not practicable, must give them notice thereof, either by advertisement in a daily newspaper circulating in the district in which the registered office of the company is situate or in any other mode allowed by the articles, not less than 21 days before the meeting.[8] Notably, if after receiving notice of intention to move the resolution, the company then calls the general meeting for a date 28 days or less after the date of receipt of the notice, the notice, though not strictly given within the prescribed time, will nonetheless be deemed to have been properly given.[9]

The provisions of CA 1963, s 142 are, however, purely procedural and confer no substantive rights on individual members, so that although an individual member might submit a resolution to the company of the type outlined above (eg for the dismissal of a director) he has no right to force a meeting to be called to consider the resolution unless he can muster sufficient support to requisition an EGM pursuant to CA 1963, s 132.[10]

1 CA 1963, s 142.

2 CA 1963, s 161(1)(a).

3 CA 1963, s 161(1)(b).

4 CA 1963, s 161(1)(c).

5 CA 1963, s 182(2).

6 CA 1963, s 142(1).

7 Thus, for example, in the case of a private company where someone other than the board of directors proposes to move a resolution for the dismissal of a director at a forthcoming EGM, the proposer of the resolution must give notice of the proposed resolution to the company at least 28 days before the meeting, but the company will only be obliged to give the normal period of notice to the members, namely seven days.

8 CA 1963, s 142(1).

9 CA 1963, s 142(2). Presumably this is to prevent the company from frustrating the member's intention to move the resolution by deliberately calling the meeting for a date which would result in the company technically not having received 'extended notice.'

10 *Pedley v Inland Waterwats Association Ltd* [1977] 1 All ER 209.

UK legislation

See CA 1985, s 379.

---

143 Registration of, and obligation of company to supply copies of certain resolutions and agreements

(1) A printed copy of every resolution or agreement to which this section applies shall, within 15 days after the passing or making thereof, be forwarded to the registrar of companies and recorded by him.

(2) Where articles have been registered, a copy of every such resolution or agreement for the time being in force shall be embodied in or annexed to every copy of the articles issued after the passing of the resolution or the making of the agreement.

(3) A copy of every such resolution or agreement shall be forwarded to any member at his request on payment of one shilling or such less sum as the company may direct.

(4) This section shall apply to:

(a) special resolutions;

(b) resolutions which have been agreed to by all the members of a company, but which, if not so agreed to, would not have been effective for their purpose unless they had been passed as special resolutions;

(c) resolutions or agreements which have been agreed to by all the members of some class of shareholders but which, if not so agreed to, would not have been effective for their purpose unless they had been passed by some particular majority or otherwise in some particular manner, and all resolutions or agreements which effectively bind all the members of any class of shareholders though not agreed to by all those members;

(d) resolutions increasing the share capital of a company;

(e) resolutions that a company be wound up voluntarily passed under paragraph (*a*) or paragraph (c) of subsection (1) of section 251.

[(f) resolutions attaching rights or restrictions to any share;

(g) resolutions varying any such rights or restrictions;

(h) resolutions classifying any unclassified share;

(i) resolutions converting shares of one class into shares of another class;][a]

[(j) resolutions of the directors of a company passed by virtue of sections 12(3)(a) and 43(3) of the Companies (Amendment) Act, 1983.][b]

(5) If a company fails to comply with subsection (1), the company and every officer of the company who is in default [shall be guilty of an offence and liable to a fine][c] not exceeding [€1,904.61].[d]

(6) If a company fails to comply with subsection (2) or subsection (3), the company and every officer of the company who is in default [shall be guilty of an offence and liable to a fine][e] not exceeding [€1,904.61][f] for each copy in respect of which default is made.

(7) For the purposes of subsections (5) and (6), a liquidator of a company shall be deemed to be an officer of the company.

Amendments

a CA 1963, s 143(4)(f)–(i) inserted by C(A)A 1982, s 5.

b CA 1963, s 143(4)(j) inserted by C(A)A 1983, Sch1, para 15.

c Words 'shall be guilty of an offence and liable to a fine' substituted for 'shall be liable to a fine' in CA 1963, s 143(5) by C(AA)A 2003, s 57 and Sch 2, Item No 1.

d '£250' substituted for '£50' by C(A)A 1982, Sch 1, increased to £1,500 by CA 1990, s 240(7) as inserted by CLEA 2001, s 104(c) and converted to €1,904.61 by Council Regulations (EC) No 1103/97, No 974/98 and No 2866/98 and the Economic and Monetary Union Act 1998, s 6.

e Words 'shall be guilty of an offence and liable to a fine' substituted for 'shall be liable to a fine' in CA 1963, s 143(6) by C(AA)A 2003, s 57 and Sch 2, Item No 1.

f 	'£5' substituted for '£1' by C(A)A 1982, Sch 1, increased to £1,500 by CA 1990, s 240(7) as inserted by CLEA 2001, s 104(c) and converted to €1,904.61 by Council Regulations (EC) No 1103/97, No 974/98 and No 2866/98 and the Economic and Monetary Union Act 1998, s 6.

Definitions

'articles': CA 1963, s 2(1); 'company': CA 1963, s 2(1); 'director': CA 1963, s 2(1); 'member': CA 1963, s 31; 'officer': CA 1963, s 2(1); ' printed': CA 1963, s 2(1); 'the registrar of companies': CA 1963, s 2(1); 'share': CA 1963, s 2(1); 'officer in default': CA 1963, s 383.

Notes

Doctrine of constructive notice: At common law persons dealing with a company were deemed to have notice of all documents which were required by law to be registered in the CRO (including the memorandum and articles and resolutions of the type referred to in CA 1963, s 143).[1] So, for example, if the articles provided that the directors could only borrow beyond a specific sum if so authorised special resolution of the members, a person dealing with the company would be deemed to have constructive notice not only of the fact that such a resolution was required but also of the fact that the resolution had or had not been passed, as the case may be, because both the articles and the special resolution require to be registered in the Companies Registration Office.[2] Similarly a person dealing with the company was deemed to have constructive notice of the company's objects clause and to know whether or not a particular transaction was therefore *ultra vires*.[3] Although one recent case has suggested that a person dealing with a company will not be bound by provisions in the articles unless he has express notice thereof[4] this decision is against the weight of previous authority and probably does not of itself displace the common law position in relation to constructive notice. Nonetheless, it should be noted that very considerable statutory inroads have been made into the doctrine of constructive notice both by CA 1963, s 8 (ie *ultra vires* contracts) and by EC(C)R 1973, reg 6 (ie *ultra vires* contracts as well as *intra vires* transactions which have been entered into by the company's agents without authority). For a fuller account of the impact of these two provisions see the notes thereto.

1 	*Ernest v Nicholls* (1857) 6 HL Cas 401 at 419; *Mahony v East Holyford Mining Co* (1875) 7 HL 869 at 893; *Re Jon Beauforte (London) Ltd* [1953] 1 All ER 634.

2 	*Irvine v Union Bank of Australia* (1877) 2 App Cas 366.

3 	*Re Jon Beauforte (London) Ltd* [1953] 1 All ER 634.

4 	*Re Shannonside Holdings Ltd* (20 May 1993, unreported) HC (Costello J).

Documents required to be registered: Under CA 1963, s 143(4) all special resolutions must be registered[1] as well as any informal resolutions which, if passed at formal meetings, would have been passed as special resolutions.[2] Resolutions affecting class rights must also be registered.[3] Although ordinary resolutions do not generally require registration, there are some exceptions, namely resolutions increasing the share capital[4] or authorising market purchases of the company's own shares[5] as well as certain resolutions to wind up a company voluntarily[6] and resolutions which by giving, varying, revoking or renewing a board of directors' authority to allot shares, thereby amend the Articles.[7] Similarly, most board resolutions will not have to be registered, although a notable exception is in relation to any resolution of the directors of a plc to cancel shares which have been forfeited or surrendered or which have been acquired by the company otherwise than for valuable consideration.[8]

Resolutions of the type described in s 143(4) which are passed informally by the sole member of a single member company must also be registered.[9]

1 	CA 1963, s 413(4)(a). See CA 1963, s 141(1) for the definition of a special resolution.

2 	CA 1963, s 143(4)(b). See CA 1963, s 141(8) and the notes thereto in relation to the effectiveness of informal resolutions.

3 CA 1963, s 143(4)(c),(f),(g) and (i). In relation to the variation of class rights generally, see CA 1963, s 78 and C(A)A 1983, s 38.

4 CA 1963, s 143(4)(d). The authority for such resolutions is to be found in CA 1963, s 68.

5 CA 1990, s 215(2).

6 CA 1963, s 143(4)(e).

7 C(A)A 1983, s 20(6).

8 CA 1963, s 143(4)(j). See also C(A)A 1983, ss 41 and 43.

9 EC(SMPLC)R 1994, reg 9(6).

Publication in the Companies Registration Office Gazette: Apart from requiring to be registered in the CRO, many of the above resolutions will also require to be published in the Companies Registration Office Gazette.[1]

1 EC(C)R 1973, reg 4. Reference to the Companies Registration Office Gazette is substituted for '*Iris Ofigiúil*' by European Communities (Companies) Regulations, 2004 (SI 839/2004).

UK legislation

See CA 1985, s 380; IA 1985, s 439(1), Sch 13 Part I; CA 1989, s 116(3); Uncertified Securities Regulations 1995 (SI 1995/3272), reg 40(3), Uncertified Securities Regulations 2001(SI 2001/3755), reg 52, reg 51 and Sch 7, Pt 1, para 10; The Companies (Acquisition of Own Shares)(Treasury Shares) Regulations 2003 (SI 2003/1116), reg 4, sch, para 25).

144 Resolutions passed at adjourned meetings

Where a resolution is passed at an adjourned meeting of—

(a) a company;

(b) the holders of any class of shares in a company;

(c) the directors of a company;

the resolution shall for all purposes be treated as having been passed on the date on which it was in fact passed and shall not be deemed to have been passed on any earlier date.

Cross references

See CA 1963, s 134 and notes thereto.

See also Table A, Pt I, reg 58 in relation to the adjournment of meetings.

Definitions

'company': CA 1963, s 2(1); 'director': CA 1963, s 2(1); 'share': CA 1963, s 2(1).

Notes

Deemed date of resolutions: A resolution passed at an adjourned meeting is treated as having been passed on the date on which it was in fact passed and is not to be deemed to have been passed on any earlier date (such as the original date of the meeting).[1] In the case of a resolution on which a poll is taken the date on which the resolution is deemed to have been passed is that date on which the result of the poll is known.[2]

1 CA 1963, s 144, and notes thereto.

2 *Holmes v Keyes* [1959] 1 Ch 199.

UK legislation

See 1985, s 381.

145 Minutes of proceedings of meetings of company and directors

(1) Every company shall as soon as may be cause minutes of all proceedings of general meetings and all proceedings at meetings of its directors or committees of directors to be entered in books kept for that purpose.

(2) Any such minute if purporting to be signed by the chairman of the meeting at which the proceedings were had, or by the chairman of the next succeeding meeting, shall be evidence of the proceedings.

(3) Where minutes have been made in accordance with this section of the proceedings at any general meeting of the company or meeting of directors or committee of directors, then, until the contrary is proved, the meeting shall be deemed to have been duly held and convened, and all proceedings had thereat to have been duly had, and all appointments of directors or liquidators shall be deemed to be valid.

[(3A) A company shall, if required by the Director, produce to the Director for inspection the book or books kept in accordance with subsection (1) and shall give to the Director such facilities for inspecting and taking copies of the contents of the book or books as the Director may require.][a]

(4) If a company fails to comply with subsection (1) [or 3A][b], the company and every officer of the company who is in default [shall be guilty of an offence and liable to a fine][c] not exceeding [€1,904.61][d].

Amendments

a CA 1963, s 145(3A) inserted by CLEA 2001, s 19(a).

b The words 'or (3A)' in CA 1963, s 145(4) inserted by CLEA 2001, s 19(b)

c The words 'shall be guilty of an offence and liable to a fine' in CA 1963, s 145(4) substitute by C(AA)A 2003, s 57 and Sch 2, Item No. 1.

d '£500' substituted for '£100' by C(A)A 1982, Sch 1, increased to £1,500 by CA 1990, s 240(7) as inserted by CLEA 2001, s 104(c) and converted to €1,904.61 by Council Regulations (EC) No 1103/97, No 974/98 and No 2866/98 and the Economic and Monetary Union Act 1998, s 6.

Cross references

See Table A, Pt I, reg 89 and notes thereto.

See also CA 1963, ss 146, 378 and notes thereto.

See also CA 1963, s 194 and CA 1990, s 27 and notes thereto.

See also C(A)A 1977, s 4 and notes thereto.

Definitions

'company': CA 1963, s 2(1); 'director': CA 1963, s 2(1); 'Director'; CLEA 2001, s 3 (1) 'officer': CA 1963, s 2(1); 'officer in default': CA 1963, s 383.

Notes

Form of minute book: The minute books of a company may be kept either 'by making entries in bound books or by recording the matters in question in any other manner';[1] provided that where a bound book is not used, 'adequate precautions' are taken to guard against falsification and to facilitate their discovery.[2] Although C(A)A 1977, s 4, permits a company to keep most classes of records and registers on computer, minute books are expressly excluded from this dispensation and must continue to be maintained in a legible form. In *Hearts of Oak Assurance Co v Flower and Son*[3] it was held that a loose-leaf minute book was not a proper minute book for the purposes of the section.

1 CA 1963, s 378(1).
2 CA 1963, s 378(2).
3 *Hearts of Oak Assurance Co v Flower and Son* [1936] 1 Ch 76.

Evidential status of minutes: Although, under CA 1963, s 145(2) and (3) the signed minutes are evidence of the proceedings, they are not, however, conclusive evidence and may be rebutted by proof to the contrary.[1] Moreover, if the minutes are to be valid and to have the status of *prima facie* evidence of the proceedings, they must be made and signed within a reasonable time after the conclusion of the meeting.[2] If a particular matter has not been recorded in the minutes, it may be proved by some other method (eg oral evidence of a person who was present).[3] Once signed, the minutes may constitute a sufficient note or memorandum for the purposes of the Statute of Frauds.[4]

1 *Tothill's Case* (1865) 1 Ch App 85.
2 *Toms v Cinema Trust* [1915] WN 29.
3 *Knight's Case* [1867] 2 Ch App 321; *Re Fireproof Doors Ltd* [1916] 1 Ch 142; *HL Bolton (Engineering) Co Ltd v TJ Graham and Sons Ltd* [1957] 1 QB 159.
4 *Jones v Victoria Graving Dock Co* (1877) 2 QBD 314; *Re Strathblaine Estates Ltd* [1948] Ch 228.

Inspection of minute books: As a result of the amendments effected by CLEA 2001, s 19 the Director is given an express right of access to the minute books of every company. A similar right of inspection is enjoyed by the members themselves under CA 1963, s 146.

UK legislation

See CA 1985, s 382.

[145A Voting Results

(1) This section applies to a company traded on a regulated market.

(2) Where a member requests a full account of a vote before or on the declaration of the result of a vote at a general meeting, then with respect to each resolution proposed at a general meeting the company shall establish—

(a) the number of shares for which votes have been validly cast,

(b) the proportion of the company's issued share capital at close of business on the day before the meeting represented by those votes,

(c) the total number of votes validly cast, and

(d) the number of votes cast in favour of and against each resolution and, if counted, the number of abstentions.

(3) Where no member requests a full account of the voting before or on the declaration of the result of a vote at a general meeting, it shall be sufficient for the company to

establish the voting results only to the extent necessary to ensure that the required majority is reached for each resolution.

(4) A company shall ensure that a voting result established in accordance with this section is published on its internet site not later than the end of the fifteenth day after the date of the meeting at which the voting result was obtained.][a]

Amendments

a CA 1963, s 145A inserted by Shareholders' Rights Regulations 2009, reg 12.

Definitions

'company traded on a regulated market': CA 1963, s 2(1).

Notes

This provision, inserted by the Shareholders' Rights Regulations 2009, applies only to companies traded on a regulated market. This provides that any member of such a company has a right to request a full account of a vote before or on the declaration of the result of a vote at a general meeting. In the absence of any such demand, companies can proceed by way of a show of hands. Given that this applies to listed companies, the likelihood is that there will always be someone who will want to exercise the right so companies would be well advised to always proceed on the basis that it will be exercised.

146 Inspection of minute books

(1) The books containing the minutes of proceedings of any general meeting of a company held after the operative date shall be kept at the registered office of the company, and shall during business hours (subject to such reasonable restrictions as the company may by its articles or in general meeting impose, so that not less than 2 hours in each day be allowed for inspection) be open to the inspection of any member without charge.

(2) Any member shall be entitled to be furnished within 7 days after he has made a request in that behalf to the company with a copy of any such minutes as aforesaid at a charge not exceeding one shilling for every 100 words.

(3) If any inspection required under this section is refused or if any copy required under this section is not sent within the proper time, the company and every officer of the company who is in default shall be liable in respect of each offence to a fine not exceeding [€1,904.61][a].

(4) In the case of any such refusal or default, the court may by order compel an inspection of the books in respect of all proceedings of general meetings or direct that the copies required shall be sent to the persons requiring them.

Amendments

a '£125' substituted for '£25' by C(A)A 1982, Sch 1, increased to £1,500 by CA 1990, s 240(7) as inserted by CLEA 2001, s 104(c) and converted to €1,904.61 by Council Regulations (EC) No 1103/97, No 974/98 and No 2866/98 and the Economic and Monetary Union Act 1998, s 6.

Cross reference

See CA 1990, s 105(1)(b): The Minister may by order alter any of the charges referred to in CA 1963, s 146(2).

Definitions

'articles': CA 1963, s 2(1); 'company': CA 1963, s 2(1); 'the court': CA 1963, s 2(1); 'member': CA 1963, s 31; 'officer': CA 1963, s 2(1); 'officer in default': CA 1963, s 383; 'the operative date': CA 1963, s 2(1) 'person': IA 2005, s 18(c).

Notes

Inspection of minute books: CA 1963, s 146 applies to minutes of general meetings only and there is no statutory entitlement for members to see minutes of proceedings of the board of directors. Unless there is a specific provision in the articles of association or a subscription or shareholders' agreement, no such right exists.[1] The auditors of the company have a right of access at all reasonable times to the books of the company.[2] The Director may also require sight of such minutes.[3]

1 See *R v Mariquita Mining Co* (1859) 1 E & E 289.

2 CA 1990, s 193(3).

3 CA 1963, s 145 (3A) as inserted by CLEA 2001, s 19(b).

UK legislation

See CA 1985, ss 383 and 389A; CA 1989, ss 143(9), 212, Sch 24; Companies (Inspection and Copying of Registers Indexes and Documents) Regulations 1991 (SI 1991/1998).

Accounts and Audit

147 Keeping of books of account

[...][a]

Amendments

a CA 1963, s 147 repealed by CA 1990, s 6.

[148 Duty to prepare individual accounts

(1) The directors of every company shall on a date not later than 18 months after the incorporation of the company and subsequently once at least in every calendar year prepare accounts for the company for each financial year (to be known and in this Act referred to as 'individual accounts').

(2) Subject to subsections (3) to (11), a company's individual accounts shall be prepared—

(a) in accordance with section 149 (to be known and in this Act referred to as 'Companies Act individual accounts'), or

(b) in accordance with international financial reporting standards and section 149A (to be known and in this Act referred to as 'IFRS individual accounts').

(3) Companies Act individual accounts shall be prepared by a company—

(a) not trading for the acquisition of gain by the members, or

(b) to which section 128(4)(c) applies, or

(c) in respect of which an order under section 128(5) is in force.

(4) After the first financial year in which the directors of a company prepare IFRS individual accounts (in this section referred to as 'the first IFRS year'), all subsequent individual accounts of the company shall be prepared in accordance with international financial reporting standards unless there is a relevant change of circumstances as referred to in subsection (5).

(5) There is a relevant change of circumstances where at any time during or after the first IFRS year—

(a) the company becomes a subsidiary undertaking of another undertaking that does not prepare IFRS individual accounts,

(b) the company ceases to be a company with securities admitted to trading on a regulated market, or

(c) a parent undertaking of the company ceases to be an undertaking with securities admitted to trading on a regulated market.

(6) Where, following a relevant change of circumstances, Companies Act individual accounts are prepared, the directors may subsequently prepare IFRS individual accounts for the company and subsections (4) and (5) apply as if that financial year for which such IFRS individual accounts are subsequently prepared was the first IFRS year.

(7) The directors of the company shall lay the individual accounts before the annual general meeting of the company within 9 months of the balance sheet date.

(8) Subsection (7) shall not apply to the profit and loss account or income statement of a company where—

(a) the company is a parent company,

(b) the company prepares group accounts in accordance with section 150, and

(c) the notes to the company's individual balance sheet show the company's profit or loss for the financial year determined in accordance with section 149 or 149A, as appropriate.

(9) Where, in the case of a company, advantage is taken of subsection (8), that fact shall be disclosed—

(a) in the notes on the company's individual accounts, and

(b) in the notes on the group accounts referred to in subsection (8)(b).

(10) For the purposes of this Act unless the contrary intention appears—

(a) a reference to a balance sheet or profit and loss account or income statement shall include any notes thereon or document annexed thereto giving information required by this Act and allowed by this Act to be so given, and

(b) a reference to a profit and loss account shall be read, in the case of a company not trading for profit, as referring to its income and expenditure account, and references to profit or to loss and, if the company has subsidiaries, references to a consolidated profit and loss account shall be read accordingly.

(11) Where any person being a director of a company fails to take all reasonable steps to comply with this section, the person is, in respect of each offence, liable on summary conviction to imprisonment for a term not exceeding 6 months or to a fine not exceeding €635 or to both, so, however that—

(a) in any proceedings against a person in respect of an offence under this section, it shall be a defence to prove that the person had reasonable ground to believe and did believe that a competent and reliable person was charged with the duty of seeing that this section was complied with and was in a position to discharge that duty, and

(b) a person shall not be sentenced to imprisonment for such an offence unless, in the opinion of the court dealing with the case, the offence was committed wilfully.][a]

Amendments

a CA 1963, s 148 was repealed and replaced by reg 4 of EC(IFRSMA)R 2005.

Definitions

'accounts' CA 1963, s 2(1); 'annual accounts': CA 1963, s 2(1);. 'company': CA 1963, s 2(1); 'Companies Act accounts': CA 1963, s 2(1); 'Companies Act individual accounts': CA 1963, s 2(1); 'the court': CA 1963, s 2(1); 'director': CA 1963, s 2(1); 'Financial year': CA 1963, s 22(1); 'IFRS accounts': CA 1963, s 2(1); 'IFRS individual accounts': CA 1963, s 2(1); 'Income statement': CA 1963, s 2(1); 'Individual accounts' CA 1963, s 2(1); 'International financial reporting standards': CA 1963, s 2(1); 'Parent company': CA 1963, s 2(1); 'Parent undertaking': CA 1963, s 2(1); 'Profit and loss account': CA 1963, s 2(1); 'Regulated market': CA 1963, s 2(1); 'Undertaking': CA 1963, s 2(1); 'First financial year': CA 1963, s 2(1A).

Notes

Requirement for annual accounts: CA 1963, s 148 imposes a general requirement for every company to prepare and lay before the AGM a set of accounts (to be known as 'individual accounts'). EC(IFRSMA)R 2005 was a direct consequence of Regulation (EC) No 1606/2002 of the European Parliament and of the Council. This regulation applied directly to the group accounts of listed entities throughout the European Union by requiring these to be prepared in accordance with International Financial Reporting Standards ('IFRS').

The main purpose of the IFRS regs was to avail of a number of EU member state options contained in Regulation EC 1606/2002 of the European Parliament of the the Council ('the EU IAS Regulation'). The EU IAS regs requires all listed entities required to prepare consolidated (or group) accounts to do so in accordance with International Financial Reporting Standards ('IFRS') as adopted for use in the European Union. IFRS (previously known as International Accounting Standards or 'IAS') are issued by the International Accounting Standards Board ('IASB'). Each IFRS requires formal adoption by the European Union, after which, when published in the Official Journal, they have full legal recognition.

The EU IAS regs also allows member states to 'permit or require' the use of IFRS for the preparation of individual company accounts, regardless of whether such companies are listed or not. In implementing the IFRS regs, Ireland has opted for a permissive regime and the following choices have been reflected in CA 1963:

- debt-only listed parent companies may avail of an option not to prepare group accounts in accordance with IFRS until accounting periods beginning on or after 1 January 2007; and
- all other companies have the option to use IFRS in preparing their group or individual accounts.

Therefore as a result of the IFRS regs, all companies and groups (that are not directly impacted by the EU IAS regs) have a choice as to the financial reporting framework they apply in preparing their individual and group accounts.

The choice is not available to the following types of company;

- a company not trading for the acquisition of gain by members;
- a company not having a share capital formed for charitable purposes (see s 128(4) (c) of CA 1963);
- a company in respect of which an order under s 128(5) is in force.

Such companies must continue to prepare Companies Act accounts. Companies Act accounts are prepared in accordance with the format requirements of the Companies Acts and accounting standards. The applicable standards are the Financial Reporting Standards ('FRS') issued by the Accounting Standards Board ('ASB') and promulgated in the Republic of Ireland by the Institute of Chartered Accountants in Ireland.

Generally, if a company opts to move from preparing Companies Act accounts to IFRS accounts, it is a one-way street. Such a company may not subsequently revert to preparing Companies Act accounts except where there has been a 'relevant change of circumstances'. Subsection (5) sets out the situations when such a change may arise.

The IFRS regs apply to accounting periods beginning on or after 1 January 2005.

Two reports must also be annexed or attached to the balance sheet. The first is an auditors' report[1] as to accuracy of the accounts[2] and the second is a directors' report which summarises the state of affairs of the company for the last financial year.[3]

The balance sheet, profit and loss account, directors' report and auditors' report must be sent to every member of the company (whether he is or is not entitled to receive notice of general meetings), to every debentureholder and to any other persons legally entitled to receive same,[4] not less than 21 days before the date of the annual general meeting.[5]

1 CA 1963, s 157.

2 See CA 1990, s 193 for the precise contents of the auditors' report.

3 CA 1963, s 158.

4 eg bankers under the terms of a loan agreement.

5 CA 1963, s 159(1). If the company does not have a share capital, copies of the accounts and reports need not be sent to any members or debentureholders who are not entitled to receive notice of general meetings: CA 1963, s 159(2).

Group accounts: If the company is a holding company it is obliged not only to prepare and present annual accounts dealing with its own financial affairs but also to prepare and present group accounts dealing with the affairs of the group as a whole.[1]

1 CA 1963, s 150; EC(CGA)R 1992, reg 5; EC(A)R 1993, reg 9; EC(IUA)R 1996, reg 10.

Form and content of annual accounts: The form and content of a company's annual accounts were originally governed by CA 1963, s 149 and Sch 6, with group accounts being governed by CA 1963, ss 151 and 152. These provisions have been largely rendered redundant over the last three decades as a result of the enactment of C(A)A 1986, EC(CGA)R 1992, EC(A)R 1993 and EC(IUA)R 1996. With the enactment of the IFRS regs, the form and content of Companies Act accounts continues to be governed by C(A)A 1986. However, for those preparing IFRS accounts, the form and content will be in accordance with IFRS plus certain mandatory disclosures as set out in CA 1963 s 149A (1) (b). The overriding requirement of all of these statutory provisions is that the accounts should present a 'true and fair view' (or, in the language of IFRS, 'give a fair presentation') of the state of affairs of the company or of the group, as the case may be.[1]

1 See also CA 1963, s 191 and CA 1990, ss 41–45 for the disclosure of directors' interests in the annual accounts.

Day-to-day books of account: Apart from the duty to prepare annual accounts, the directors of a company are also obliged to keep proper books of account recording the company's transactions on a day-to-day basis.[1]

1 CA 1990, s 202.

Balance sheet as an acknowledgement of debt: Every balance sheet and profit and loss account must be signed on behalf of the company by two of its directors.[1] Once signed, the balance sheet is capable of operating as an acknowledgement of debt for the purposes of the Statute of Limitations 1957, s 56.[2] However, if the debt is one due to the directors or to one of them, they cannot acknowledge the debt[3] unless authorised to do so by the company in general meeting.[4]

1 CA 1963, s 156(1). Note, in the case of a bankruptcy company, three directors and the secretary: CA 1963, s 156(2).

2 *Re Atlantic and Pacific Fibre Importing and Manufacturing Co* [1928] Ch 836; *Jones v Bellgrove Properties Ltd* [1949] 2 KB 700; *Re Gee and Co (Woolwich) Ltd* [1975] Ch 152; *Re Compania de Electricidad de la Provincia de Buenos Aires Ltd* [1978] 3 All ER 668; *The Stage Club Ltd v Millers Hotel Pty Ltd* (1982) 56 ALJR 113; *Re Overmark Smith Warden Ltd* [1982] 1 WLR 1195.

3 *Re Coliseum (Barrow) Ltd* [1930] 2 Ch 44; *Re Transplanters (Holding Co) Ltd* [1958] 1 WLR 822.

4 *Re Gee and Co (Woolwich) Ltd* [1975] Ch 52.

Exemption from audit requirement: Normally, every company should have its annual accounts audited.[1] However, in the case of a private limited company,[2] being one to which the provisions of C(A)A 1986 apply,[3] the requirement to appoint an auditor and to have the annual accounts audited may be disapplied provided that certain conditions are met. In essence, the directors must form the opinion that both in respect of the financial year in question and also in respect of the immediately preceding financial year[4] the company meets the criteria set out in CA 1963, s 148(3), namely that:

(a) its does not exceed any of the specified thresholds as to turnover, balance sheet value or number of employees;[5]

(b) it must neither be a parent undertaking nor a subsidiary undertaking within the meaning of EC(CGA)R 1992;[6]

(c) it must not be a licensed bank,[7] an insurance company[8] or a financial services company of the type referred to in Sch 2;[9] and

(d) the filing of its annual returns must be fully up-to-date.[10]

Once they have concluded that these criteria are being satisfied the directors may determine to disapply the audit provisions of the Companies Acts insofar as they pertain to the company. That determination must be recorded in the board minutes.[11] Any person who records in the minutes a decision to avail of the audit exemption knowing that the company does not in fact qualify for the exemption, is guilty of an offence.[12]

1 See in particular CA 1990, s 193.

2 See C(A)(No 2)A 1999, s 31 and s 32(1)(a).

3 See C(A)(No 2)A 1999, s 32(3)(a)(i). As to the categories of company covered by C(A)A 1986, see ss 1 and 2 thereof and the notes thereto.

4 C(A)(No 2)A 1999, s 32(1). Of course, if the company is in its first financial year, the relevant criteria need only be met in respect of that year: s 32(1)(b).

5 C(A)(No 2)A 1999, s 32(3)(a)(ii)–(iv).

6 C(A)(No 2)A 1999, s 32(3)(a)(v)(I).

7 C(A)(No 2)A 1999, s 32(3)(a)(v)(II).

8 C(A)(No 2)A 1999, s 32(3)(a)(v)(III).

9 C(A)(No 2)A 1999, s 32(3)(a)(v)(IV).

10 C(A)(No 2)A 1999, s 32(3)(b).

11 C(A)(No 2)A 1999, s 32(1)(a[illegible]

12 C(A)(No 2)A 1999, s 37.

Entitlement of members to insist on a[illegible] Even if the directors wish to avail of the audit exemption, they may be prevented from [illegible] by the members. In this regard, members holding shares carrying not less than 10% o[illegible] rights may serve a notice insisting on the relevant audit provisions continuing to apply to [illegible] reactivated in respect of the company for a given financial year.[2] The notice must be served [illegible] company not less than one month before the end of the financial year which precedes that [illegible]h the exemption might otherwise be availed of.[3]

1 In determining whether or not the 10% has been achie[illegible] regard is not had to voting rights which are only exercisable in special circumstances: C(A)([illegible] A 1999, s 33(7).

2 C(A)(No 2)A 1999, s 33(1).

3 C(A)(No 2)A 1999, s 33(2).

Statement in the accounts: Even if a company validly avails of the audit exemption, it must still prepare and present to its members accounts which are prepared in accordance with the Companies Acts and which present a true and fair view of the company's financial position.[1] Moreover, a statement to that effect must be contained in the balance sheet as signed by the directors.[2] The statement must also clearly state that the audit exemption is being availed of[3] and must confirm that no notice of the type referred to above, has been served on the company reactivating the audit provisions.[4] If the statement is false in any material respect, any director who participated in the making of the statement knowing it to be false, will be guilty of an offence.[5]

1 C(A)(No 2)A 1999, s 33(4)(d).

2 C(A)(No 2)A 1999, s 33(4)(d) and (5).

3 C(A)(No 2)A 1999, s 33(4)(a) and (b).

4 C(A)(No 2)A 1999, s 33(4)(c).

5 C(A)(No 2)A 1999, s 37.

UK legislation

See CA 1985, ss 226 to 227; CA 1989, s 11. See also SI 2004/2947.

[149 Companies Act individual accounts

(1) Companies Act individual accounts shall comprise—

(a) a balance sheet as at the last day of the financial year, and

(b) a profit and loss account.

(2) The balance sheet shall give a true and fair view of the state of affairs of the company as at the end of the financial year and the profit and loss account shall give a true and fair view of the profit or loss of the company for the financial year.

(3) Companies Act individual accounts shall—

(a) in the case of an undertaking to which the Act of 1986 applies, comply with that Act,

(b) in the case of an undertaking to which the 1993 Regulations apply, comply with those Regulations and the Act of 1986,

(c) in the case of an undertaking to which the Credit Institutions Regulations apply, comply with those Regulations,

(d) in the case of an undertaking to w... Insurance Undertakings Regulations apply, comply with those Regula...

(e) in all other cases comply with ...visions of the Sixth Schedule in so far as that Schedule applies to Co... Act individual accounts.

(4) Save as expressly provided in ...ions (5) and (6) or in Part III of the Sixth Schedule, the requirements of s... ...ion (3)(e) and of the Sixth Schedule shall be without prejudice either to the ... ...al requirements of subsection (2) or to any other requirements of this Act.

(5) The profits or losses attri... ...ble to any shares in a subsidiary for the time being held by a holding company or ... other of its subsidiaries shall not, for any purpose, be treated in the holding co... ...ny's accounts as revenue profits or losses so far as they are profits or losses for th... ...eriod before the date on or as from which the shares were acquired by the comp... or any of its subsidiaries, and for the purpose of determining whether any profits o... ...osses are to be treated as profits or losses for the said period the profit or loss for a... financial year of the subsidiary may, if it is not practicable to apportion it with r...asonable accuracy by reference to the facts, be treated as accruing from day to day during that year and be apportioned accordingly. Provided however that where the directors and the auditors are satisfied and so certify that it would be fair and reasonable and would not prejudice the rights and interests of any person, the profits or losses attributable to any shares in a subsidiary may be treated in a manner otherwise than in accordance with this subsection.

(6) Where, in relation to any accounts laid before the annual general meeting of a company, any person being a director of a company fails to take all reasonable steps to secure compliance with this section and with the other requirements of this Act as to the matters to be stated in accounts, the person is, in respect of each offence, liable on summary conviction to imprisonment for a term not exceeding 6 months or to a fine not exceeding €635 or to both, so, however, that—

(a) in any proceedings against a person in respect of an offence under this section, it shall be a defence to prove that the person had reasonable ground to believe and did believe that a competent and reliable person was charged with the duty of seeing that this section or those other requirements, as the case may be, were complied with and was in a position to discharge that duty, and

(b) a person shall not be sentenced to imprisonment for any such offence unless, in the opinion of the court dealing with the case, the offence was committed wilfully.][a]

Amendments

a CA 1963, s 149 was repealed and replaced by reg 4 of EC(IFRSMA)R 2005.

Definitions

'Act of 1986': CA 1963, s 2(1); 'company': CA 1963, s 2(1); 'the court': CA 1963, s 2(1); 'accounts': CA 1963, s 2(1); 'Companies Act accounts': CA 1963, s 2(1); 'Companies Act individual accounts': CA 1963, s 2(1); 'director': CA 1963, s 2(1); 'Credit Institutions Regulations': CA 1963, s 2(1); 'Financial year': CA 1963, s 22(1); 'Holding company': CA 1963, s 2(1); 'Individual accounts' CA 1963, s 2(1); 'Insurance Undertakings Regulations': CA 1963, s 2(1); 'Profit and loss account': CA 1963, s 2(1); 'Undertaking': CA 1963, s 2(1); 'First financial year': CA 1963, s 2(1A); '1993 Regulations': CA 1963, s 2(1).

Notes

Undertakings opting to prepare Companies Act individual accounts must do so in accordance with section 149. Compliance with the disclosure requirements of the Companies Acts and accounting standards are normally necessary in order for accounts to give a true and fair view.[1] The relevant accounting standards for companies preparing Companies Act individual accounts are the Financial Reporting Standards (FRSs) issued by the Accounting Standards Board and promulgated in the Republic of Ireland by the Institute of Chartered Accountants in Ireland.

The format and content of Companies Act individual accounts is governed by the particular legislation applicable to a particular undertaking. Therefore, undertakings to which the CA(A) 1986 applies, comply with formats and accounting requirements of that Act when preparing Companies Act individual accounts. Similarly, undertakings to which the 1993 Regulations,[a] the Credit Institutions Regulations,[b] the Insurance Undertakings Regulations,[c] or the Sixth Schedule of CA 1963 apply comply with the requirements of those enactments.

1 *Dolan v AB Ltd* [1969] IR 282; *Lloyd Cheyham and Co Ltd v Littlejohn and Co* [1987] BCLC 303; *IRC v Duple Motor Bodies Ltd* [1961] 1 WLR 739.

C(A)A 1986: This Act gives legal effect to Council Directive 78/660/EEC. It governs the format and contents of the annual accounts of all private and public limited companies[1] other than:

(a) companies not trading for the acquisition of gain by its members;[2]

(b) religious charitable companies limited by guarantee;[3]

(c) any charitable company limited by guarantee in respect of which the Commissioners of Charitable Donations and Bequests for Ireland have made an order exempting it from the obligation to annex its accounts to the annual return;[4]

(d) licensed banks;[5]

(e) certified trustee savings banks;[6]

(f) other companies engaged in the business of accepting deposits or other repayable funds or granting credit for its own account;[7]

(g) companies engaged solely in the making of hire-purchase agreements and credit-sale agreements;[8]

(h) authorised life and non-life insurance companies.[9]

The provisions of s 149(5) continue to apply to any company whose accounts are governed by C(A)A 1986.[10]

1 C(A)A 1986, s 1(1).
2 C(A)A 1986, s 2(1)(a).
3 C(A)A 1986, s 2(1)(b).
4 C(A)A 1986, s 2(1)(c).
5 C(A)A 1986, s 2(2)(a).
6 C(A)A 1986, s 2(2)(b).
7 C(A)A 1986, s 2(2)(d).
8 C(A)A 1986, s 2(2)(c).
9 C(A)A 1986, s 2(3).
10 C(A)A 1986, s 3(1).

[a] *EC(A)R 1993*: These Regulations give legal effect, *inter alia*, to Council Directive 90/605/EEC and govern the format and content of the annual accounts for unlimited companies in circumstances where, broadly speaking, the members of the company are themselves either Irish or foreign limited companies.[1]

[b] *EC(CIA)R 1992*: These regs, which give effect to Council Directive 86/635/EEC, govern the form and content of annual accounts for banks and other financial institutions.

[c] *EC(IUA)R 1996*: These Regulations implement Council Directive 91/674/EEC and govern the form and content of annual accounts for insurance companies to which the European Communities (Non-Life Insurance) regs 1976 or the European Communities (Life Assurance) regs 1984 apply, as well as reinsurance companies.

[1] EC(A)R 1993, reg 6. The Regulations also apply to certain 'partnerships'.

UK legislation

See CA 1985, ss 226 to 227; CA 1989, s 11. See also SI 2004/2947.

[149A IFRS individual accounts

(1) Where the directors of a company prepare IFRS individual accounts—

- (a) they shall state in the notes to those accounts that the accounts have been prepared in accordance with international financial reporting standards, and
- (b) shall ensure that those notes contain the information required by—
  - (i) section 191 and paragraph 39(6) of the Schedule to the Act of 1986 (details of directors' remuneration),
  - (ii) sections 41 to 45 of the Act of 1990 to be disclosed in individual accounts (transactions with directors),
  - (iii) section 63 of the Act of 1990 unless it is disclosed in the directors' report (interests in shares and debentures),
  - (iv) sections 16 and 16A (inserted by Regulation 23 of the 1993 Regulations) of the Act of 1986 (details on group undertakings),
  - (v) paragraphs 26 to 28 of the Schedule to the Act of 1986 (details of share capital and debentures),
  - (vi) paragraph 32A (inserted by section 233 of the Act of 1990) of the Schedule to the Act of 1986 (restriction on distributability of profits),
  - (vii) paragraph 36 of the Schedule to the Act of 1986 (guarantees and other financial commitments),
  - (viii) paragraph 37(2) of the Schedule to the Act of 1986 (financial assistance for the purchase of own shares),
  - (ix) paragraph 42 of the Schedule to the Act of 1986 (details of staff numbers and remuneration),
  - (x) paragraph 46 of the Schedule to the Act of 1986 (shares and debentures held by subsidiary undertakings), [...][b]
  - (xi) paragraph 39(5) of the Schedule to the Act of 1986 and section 205D (inserted by section 44 of the Act of 2003) of the Act of 1990 [(remuneration of auditors), and][c]][a]
  - [(xii) where appropriate, paragraph 36A of the Schedule to the Act of 1986.][d]

Amendments

a Section 149A was inserted by reg 4 of EC(IFRSMA)R 2005.

b Word 'and' deleted by European Communities (Directive 2006/46/EC) Regulations 2009, reg 11(a).

c Section 149A(1)(b)(xi) amended by European Communities (Directive 2006/46/EC) Regulations 2009, reg 11(b).

d Subparagraph (xii) inserted by European Communities (Directive 2006/46/EC) Regulations 2009, reg 11(c).

Definitions

'Act of 1986': CA 1963, s 2(1); 'Act of 1990': CA 1963, s 2(1); 'accounts' CA 1963, s 2(1): 'company': CA 1963, s 2(1); 'the court': CA 1963, s 2(1); 'debenture': CA 1963, s 2(1) 'director': CA 1963, s 2(1); 'Financial year': CA 1963, 22(1); 'IFRS accounts': CA 1963, s 2(1); 'IFRS individual accounts': CA 1963, s 2(1); 'Income statement': CA 1963, s 2(1); 'Individual accounts' CA 1963, s 2(1); 'International financial reporting standards': CA 1963, s 2(1); 'share': CA 1963, s 2(1); '1993 Regulations': CA 1963, s 2(1).

Notes

Companies opting to prepare IFRS accounts comply with the format and disclosure requirements of IFRS rather than the formats and disclosures required by the Companies Acts. Section 149A applies to IFRS accounts, those Companies Act disclosure requirements not addressed by IFRS but with which all companies should comply. At the time of writing, s 205D of CA 1990, referred to in s 149A(1)(b)(xi), had not been commenced.

UK legislation

See CA 1985, ss 226 to 227; CA 1989, s 11. See also SI 2004/2947.

[150 Duty to prepare group accounts

(1) Where at the end of its financial year a company is a parent company, the directors, as well as preparing individual accounts for the year, shall prepare consolidated accounts (to be known and in this Act referred to as 'group accounts') for the group for that year.

(2) (a) Subject to paragraph (b), companies are obliged for financial years commencing on or after 1 January 2005 to prepare their group accounts in accordance with international financial reporting standards (to be known and in this Act referred to as 'IFRS group accounts') if, at their balance sheet date their securities are admitted to trading on a regulated market of any EEA State.

(b) The requirements referred to in paragraph (a) shall only apply for each financial year starting on or after 1 January 2007 to those companies whose debt securities only have been admitted to trading on a regulated market of any EEA State.

(3) Subject to subsections (4) to (11), other companies which are required to prepare group accounts shall prepare—

(a) group accounts in accordance with section 150A (to be known and in this Act referred to as 'Companies Act group accounts'), or

(b) IFRS group accounts.

(4) Companies Act group accounts shall be prepared by a parent company—

(a) not trading for the acquisition of gain by the members, or

(b) to which section 128(4)(c) applies, or

(c) in respect of which an order under section 128(5) is in force.

(5) After the first financial year in which the directors of a parent company prepare IFRS group accounts (in this section referred to as 'the first IFRS year'), all subsequent group accounts of the company shall be prepared in accordance with international financial reporting standards unless there is a relevant change of circumstances as referred to in subsection (6).

(6) There is a relevant change of circumstances where at any time during or after the first IFRS year—

(a) the company becomes a subsidiary undertaking of another undertaking that does not prepare IFRS group accounts,

(b) the company ceases to be a company with securities admitted to trading on a regulated market, or

(c) a parent undertaking of the company ceases to be an undertaking with securities admitted to trading on a regulated market.

(7) Where, following a relevant change of circumstances, Companies Act group accounts are prepared, the directors may subsequently prepare IFRS group accounts for the company and subsections (5) and (6) apply as if that financial year for which such IFRS group accounts are subsequently prepared was the first IFRS year.

(8) In the case of a company to which the Group Accounts Regulations, the Credit Institutions Regulations or the Insurance Undertakings Regulations apply, this section is subject to the exemptions from the preparation of group accounts provided by those Regulations as applicable to the company concerned and set out in—

(a) Regulations 7, 8, 8A and 9 of the Group Accounts Regulations,

(b) Regulations 7, 8, 8A and 9 of the Credit Institutions Regulations, and

(c) Regulations 10, 12 and 12A of the Insurance Undertakings Regulations.

(9) The directors of the company shall lay any group accounts prepared in accordance with subsection (1) before the annual general meeting of the company when the individual accounts are so laid.

(10)(a) Where the group accounts do not deal with a subsidiary of the company, any member of the company shall be entitled to be furnished without charge within 14 days after the member has made a request in that behalf to the company with a copy of the latest balance sheet of that subsidiary which has been sent to the members of the subsidiary together with a copy of every document required by law to be annexed thereto and a copy of the directors' and auditors' reports.

(b) Where any copy required under paragraph (a) is not sent within the period specified in that paragraph, the company and every officer of the company who is in default is liable, in respect of each offence, to a fine not exceeding €635 unless it is proved that the member has already made a demand for and been furnished with a copy and in the case of any default under this subsection the court may direct that the copies required shall be sent to the member requiring them.

(11) Where, in relation to a company, any person being a director of a company fails to take all reasonable steps to secure compliance with this section the person is, in respect

of each offence, liable on summary conviction to imprisonment for a term not exceeding 6 months or to a fine not exceeding €635 or to both, so, however, that—

(a) in any proceedings against a person in respect of an offence under this section, it shall be a defence to prove that the person had reasonable ground to believe and did believe that a competent and reliable person was charged with the duty of seeing that the requirements of this section were complied with and was in a position to discharge that duty, and

(b) a person shall not be sentenced to imprisonment for an offence under this section unless, in the opinion of the court dealing with the case, the offence was committed wilfully.][a]

Amendments

a CA 1963, s 150 was repealed and replaced by reg 4 of EC(IFRSMA)R 2005.

Definitions

'accounts': CA 1963, s 2(1); 'annual accounts': CA 1963, s 2(1); 'company': CA 1963, s 2(1); 'Companies Act accounts': CA 1963, s 2(1); 'Companies Act group accounts': CA 1963, s 2(1); 'the court': CA 1963, s 2(1); 'Credit Institutions Regulations': CA 1963, s 2(1); 'director': CA 1963, s 2(1); 'EEA State': CA 1963, s 2(1); 'Financial year': CA 1963, s 22(1); 'Group Accounts': CA 1963, s 2(1). 'Group Accounts Regulations': CA 1963, s 2(1); 'IFRS accounts': CA 1963, s 2(1); 'IFRS group accounts': CA 1963, s 2(1); 'Individual accounts' CA 1963, s 2(1); 'Insurance Undertakings Regulations': CA 1963, s 2(1); 'International financial reporting standards': CA 1963, s 2(1); 'Parent company': CA 1963, s 2(1); 'Parent undertaking': CA 1963, s 2(1); 'Profit and loss account': CA 1963, s 2(1); 'Regulated market': CA 1963, s 2(1); 'subsidiary': CA 1963, s 2(1); 'Undertaking': CA 1963, s 2(1); 'First financial year': CA 1963, s 2(1A).

Notes

Requirement for group accounts: CA 1963, s 150 imposes a general requirement for the directors of every company that is a parent company, as well as preparing individual accounts, also to prepare consolidated accounts (known as 'group accounts'). The International Financial Reporting Standards regs were a direct consequence of Regulation (EC) No. 1606/2002 of the European Parliament and of the Council. This Regulation applied directly to the group accounts of listed entities throughout the European Union by requiring these to be prepared in accordance with the IFRS.

The main purpose of the IFRS regs was to avail of a number of EU member state options contained in Regulation (EC) 1606/2002 of the European Parliament of the the Council ('the EU IAS Regulation'). The EU IAS Regulation requires all listed entities required to prepare consolidated (or group) accounts to do so in accordance with the IFRS as adopted for use in the European Union. IFRS (previously known as International Accounting Standards or 'IAS') are issued by the International Accounting Standards Board ('IASB'). Each IFRS requires formal adoption by the European Union, after which, when published in the Official Journal, it has full legal recognition.

The EU IAS Regulation also allows member states to 'permit or require' the use of IFRS for the preparation of individual company accounts, regardless of whether such companies are listed or not. In implementing the IFRS regs, Ireland has opted for a permissive regime and the following choices have been reflected in CA 1963;

- debt-only listed parent companies may avail of an option not to prepare group accounts in accordance with IFRS until accounting periods beginning on or after 1 January 2007; and
- all other companies have the option to use IFRS in preparing their group or individual accounts.

Therefore as a result of the IFRS Regulations, all companies and groups (that are not directly impacted by the EU IAS Regulation) have a choice as to the financial reporting framework they apply in preparing their individual and group accounts.

The choice is not available to the following types of company that prepare group accounts;

- a company not trading for the acquisition of gain by members;
- a company not having a share capital formed for charitable purposes (see section 128(4)(c) of CA 1963);
- a company in respect of which an order under s 128(5) is in force.

Such companies must continue to prepare Companies Act group accounts. Companies Act accounts are prepared in accordance with the format requirements of the Companies Acts and accounting standards. The applicable standards are the Financial Reporting Standards ('FRS') issued by the Accounting Standards Board ('ASB') and promulgated in the Republic of Ireland by the Institute of Chartered Accountants in Ireland.

Generally, if a company opts to move from preparing Companies Act group accounts to IFRS accounts, it is a one-way street. Such a company may not subsequently revert to preparing Companies Act group accounts except where there has been a 'relevant change of circumstances'. Subsection (6) sets out the situations when such a change may arise.

The IFRS regs apply to accounting periods beginning on or after 1 January 2005.

CA 1963, s 150A addresses the content and format of Companies Act group accounts. This is determined by whether an undertaking is subject to the Group Accounts regs,[1] the 1993 regs,[2] the Credit Institutions regs,[3] or the Insurance Undertakings regs.[4] However, certain exemptions from the requirement to prepare group accounts are available and are set out in subsection 150(8) (a), (b) and (c).

For a company to which the Group Accounts regs apply, the exemptions are set out in regs 7, 8, 8A, and 9 of the Group Accounts regs.

The exemption in reg 7 relate to the size of the group, in terms of aggregate balance sheet total, turnover, and employees numbers of the parent and its subsidiaries.

The exemptions in regs 8 and 9 relate to circumstances where the parent company in question is fully or 90 percent owned by other EC undertakings (excluding parent undertakings that have securities admitted to trading on a regulated market of any EEA State. An incorrect reference (8A) appears to be have been transposed by the IFRS regs. However, a further exemption was inserted by SI 116, 9A, which applies to parent undertakings included in non-EEA group accounts, provided certain conditions are complied with.

See Regulations 7 to 9A of the Group Accounts regs.

For a company to which the Credit Institutions regs apply, the exemptions are set out regs 7, 8, 8A, and 9 of the Credit Institutions regs. Again, there appears to be a referencing error in subsection 150(8)(b) as the exemptions are contained in Regulations 8 and 9 of the Credit Institutions Regulations and relate to parent companies that are wholly owned subsidiaries of undertakings established in an EEA State or are included in the group accounts of a non-EEA parent undertaking. See regs 8 and 8A of the Credit Institutions regs.

For a company to which the Insurance Undertakings regs apply, similar exemptions are also available by virtue of regs 12 and 12A of those regs. Reference to reg 10 in subsection 150(8)(c) appears to be an error.

1 European Communities (Companies: Group Accounts) regs 1992 (SI 201/1992).

2 European Communities (Accounts) regs 1993.

3 European Communities (Credit Institutions: Accounts) regs 1992.

4 European Communities (Insurance Undertakings: Accounts) regs 1996.

UK legislation

See CA 1985, s 227 and SI 2004/2947.

[150A Companies Act group accounts

(1) Without prejudice to section 151, Companies Act group accounts shall comprise—

(a) a consolidated balance sheet dealing with the state of affairs of the parent company and its subsidiary undertakings (including those in liquidation), and

(b) a consolidated profit and loss account dealing with the profit or loss of the parent company and its subsidiary undertakings (including those in liquidation).

(2) The Companies Act group accounts shall give a true and fair view of the state of affairs as at the end of the financial year, and the profit or loss for the financial year, of the undertakings included in the consolidation as a whole, so far as concerns members of the company.

(3) Companies Act group accounts shall—

(a) in the case of an undertaking to which the Group Accounts Regulations apply, comply with those Regulations,

(b) in the case of an undertaking to which the 1993 Regulations apply, comply with those Regulations and the Group Accounts Regulations,

(c) in the case of an undertaking to which the Credit Institutions Regulations apply, comply with those Regulations,

(d) in the case of an undertaking to which the Insurance Undertakings Regulations apply, comply with those Regulations, and

(e) in all other cases comply with this section and sections 151 to 155.][a]

Amendments

a CA 1963, s 150A was inserted by reg 4 of EC(IFRSMA)R 2005.

Definitions

'Companies Act group accounts': CA 1963, s 2(1); 'company': CA 1963, s 2(1); 'Credit Institutions Regulations': CA 1963, s 2(1); 'Financial year': CA 1963, s 22(1); 'Group Accounts': CA 1963, s 2(1); 'Group Accounts Regulations': CA 1963, s 2(1); 'Insurance Undertakings Regulations': CA 1963, s 2(1); 'Profit and loss account': CA 1963, s 2(1); 'subsidiary': CA 1963, s 2(1); 'Undertaking': CA 1963, s 2(1); 'financial year': CA 1963, s 2(1); '1993 Regulations': CA 1963, s 2(1).

Notes

Companies Act group accounts: Undertakings preparing Companies Act individual accounts must do so in accordance with section 150A. Compliance with the disclosure requirements of the Companies Acts and accounting standards are normally necessary in order for accounts to give a true and fair view.[1] The relevant accounting standards for companies preparing Companies Act group accounts are the Financial Reporting Standards (FRSs) issued by the Accounting Standards Board and promulgated in Ireland by the Institute of Chartered Accountants in Ireland.

1 *Dolan v AB Ltd* [1969] IR 282; *Lloyd Cheyham and Co Ltd v Littlejohn and Co* [1987] BCLC 303; *IRC v Duple Motor Bodies Ltd* [1961] 1 WLR 739.

The format and content of Companies Act group accounts is governed by the particular legislation applicable to a particular undertaking. Therefore, undertakings to whom the Group Accounts Regulations apply comply with formats and accounting requirements of those regs and C(A)A, 1986 when preparing Companies Act group. Similarly, undertakings to whom the 1993 Regulations, the Credit Institutions regs, the Insurance Undertakings regs, or the Sixth Schedule of CA 1963 apply comply with the requirements of those enactments.

UK legislation

See CA 1985, s 227A and SI 2004/2947.

[150B IFRS group accounts

(1) Where the directors of a parent company prepare IFRS group accounts, they shall state in the notes to those accounts that the accounts have been prepared in accordance with international financial reporting standards.

(2) Where the directors of a parent company prepare IFRS group accounts in compliance with section 150(2)(a) or under section 150(3)(b), they shall ensure that the notes to those group accounts include the information required by—

(a) section 191 and paragraph 16 of the Schedule to the Group Accounts Regulations (details of directors' remuneration),

(b) sections 41 to 45 of the Act of 1990 to be disclosed in group accounts by virtue of paragraph 17 of the Schedule to the Group Accounts Regulations (transactions with directors),

(c) section 63 of the Act of 1990 unless it is disclosed in the directors' report (interests in shares and debentures),

(d) subject to Regulation 36 of the Group Accounts Regulations, paragraphs 18 to 22 of the Schedule to those Regulations (details of group undertakings),

(e) paragraph 15 of the Schedule to the Group Accounts Regulations (details of staff numbers and remuneration),

(f) paragraphs 26 to 28 of the Schedule to the Act of 1986 (details of share capital and debentures),

(g) paragraph 32A of the Schedule to the Act of 1986 (restriction on distributability of profits),

(h) paragraph 36 of the Schedule to the Act of 1986 (guarantees and other financial commitments),

(i) paragraph 37(2) of the Schedule to the Act of 1986 (financial assistance for the purchase of own shares),

(j) paragraph 46 of the Schedule to the Act of 1986 (shares and debentures held by subsidiary undertakings), [...][b]

(k) paragraph 39(5) of the Schedule to the Act of 1986 and section 205D of the Act of 1990 [(remuneration of auditors), and][c][a] [(*l*) where appropriate, Regulation 7(1)(a) of the European Communities (Directive 2006/46/EC) Regulations 2009.][d]

Amendments

a CA 1063, s 150B was inserted by reg 4 of EC(IFRSMA)R 2005.

b Word 'and' deleted by European Communities (Directive 2006/46/EC) Regulations 2009, reg 12(a).

c Words '(remuneration of auditors).' substituted by '(remuneration of auditors), and' by European Communities (Directive 2006/46/EC) Regulations 2009, reg 12(b).

d Subparagraph (l) inserted by European Communities (Directive 2006/46/EC) Regulations 2009, reg 12(c).

Definitions

'accounts': CA 1963, s 2(1); 'Act of 1986': CA 1963, s 2(1); 'Act of 1990': CA 1963, s 2(1); 'annual accounts': CA 1963, s 2(1); 'company': CA 1963, s 2(1); 'director': CA 1963, s 2(1); 'group accounts': CA 1963, s 2(1); 'Group Accounts Regulations': CA 1963, s 2(1); 'IFRS group accounts': CA 1963, s 2(1); 'International financial reporting standards': CA 1963, s 2(1); 'Parent company': CA 1963, s 2(1); 'Profit and loss account': CA 1963, s 2(1); 'subsidiary': CA 1963, s 2(1); 'Undertaking': CA 1963, s 2(1).

Notes

Directors of parent companies opting to prepare IFRS accounts comply with the format and disclosure requirements of IFRS rather than the formats and disclosures required by the Companies Acts. Section 149A applies to IFRS accounts those Companies Act disclosure requirements not addressed by IFRS but with which all companies should comply. At the time of writing, section 205D of CA 1990, referred to in s 149A(1)(b)(xi) had not been commenced.

UK legislation

See CA 1985, s 227B and SI 2004/2947.

[150C Consistency of accounts

(1) The directors of a parent company shall ensure that the individual accounts of—

(a) the parent company, and

(b) each of the subsidiary undertakings of the parent company,

are all prepared using the same financial reporting framework, except to the extent that in their opinion there are good reasons for not doing so, and those reasons are disclosed in the individual accounts of the parent company.

(2) Subsection (1) only applies to accounts of subsidiary undertakings that are required to be prepared under this Act.

(3) Subsection (1) does not apply:

(a) where the directors do not prepare group accounts for the parent company;

(b) to the accounts of undertakings to which section 148(3) applies.

(4) Subsection (1)(a) does not apply where the directors of a parent company prepare IFRS group accounts and IFRS individual accounts for the parent.][a]

Amendments

a CA 1963, s 150C was inserted by reg 4 of EC(IFRSMA)R 2005.

Definitions

'accounts': CA 1963, s 2(1); 'director': CA 1963, s 2(1); 'Group Accounts': CA 1963, s 2(1); 'IFRS accounts': CA 1963, s 2(1); 'IFRS group accounts': CA 1963, s 2(1); 'IFRS individual accounts': CA 1963, s 2(1); 'Individual accounts' CA 1963, s 2(1); 'Parent company': CA 1963, s 2(1); 'subsidiary': CA 1963, s 2(1); 'Undertaking': CA 1963, s 2(1).

Notes

The IFRS regs impose 'consistency' requirements on the directors of a parent company that prepares group accounts. The requirement is that directors should ensure that the same financial reporting framework (ie Companies Act or IFRS accounts) is used in the individual accounts of the parent entity and in the individual accounts of all subsidiaries. A reason for this is to avoid 'accounting arbitrage' being used by different companies within the same group. There are a few limitations to this consistency requirement. Firstly, it applies only to parent companies that prepare group accounts; secondly, it applies only to Irish subsidiaries; and thirdly, it applies unless there are 'good reasons' (which need to be disclosed) for doing otherwise. A further exemption from this 'consistency requirement' is that the individual parent entity can follow the framework used for the consolidated accounts where the consolidated accounts are prepared using IFRS.

It should be noted that those parts of company law that do not deal with the preparation of accounts still continue to apply to all Irish companies regardless of which financial reporting framework they apply to their accounts. Therefore the rules regarding the filing and signing of accounts, the rules regarding purchase and redemption of own shares or financial assistance for purchase of own shares and the rules regarding distributions still continue to apply to companies act and IFRS accounts.

UK legislation

Section 227C CA 1985 and SI 2004/2947.

[151 Form of group accounts

(1) Subject to subsections (2) and (3), Companies Act group accounts prepared in accordance with sections 151 to 155 shall be group accounts comprising—

(a) a consolidated balance sheet dealing with the state of affairs of the parent company and all the subsidiaries to be dealt with in group accounts, and

(b) a consolidated profit and loss account dealing with the profit or loss of the parent company and those subsidiaries.

(2) Notwithstanding anything in section 150 or 150A, Companies Act group accounts prepared in accordance with this section—

(a) shall not be required where the company is, at the end of its financial year, the wholly owned subsidiary of another body corporate incorporated in the State, and

(b) need not deal with a subsidiary of the company where the company's directors are of the opinion that—

(i) it is impracticable, or would be of no real value to members of the company, in view of the insignificant amounts involved, or would involve expenses or delay out of proportion to the value to members of the company, or

(ii) the result would be misleading,

and if the directors are of such an opinion about each of the company's subsidiaries, group accounts shall not be required.

(3) If the company's directors are of the opinion that it is better for the purpose—

(a) of presenting the same or equivalent information about the state of affairs and profit or loss of the company and those subsidiaries, and

(b) and of so presenting that information that it may be readily appreciated by the company's members, the group accounts may be prepared in a form other than that required by subsection (1) and, in particular, may consist of—

(i) more than one set of consolidated accounts dealing respectively with the company and one group of subsidiaries and with other groups of subsidiaries, or

(ii) individual accounts dealing with each of the subsidiaries, or

(iii) statements expanding the information about the subsidiaries in the company's own accounts, or

(iv) any combination of those forms.

(4) The group accounts may be wholly or partly incorporated in the company's own balance sheet and profit and loss account.

(5) For the purposes of this section, a body corporate shall be deemed to be the wholly owned subsidiary of another if it has no members except that other and that other's wholly owned subsidiaries and its or their nominees.][a]

Amendments

a CA 1963, s 151 was repealed and replaced by reg 4 of the EC(IFRSMA)R 2005.

Definitions

'accounts': CA 1963, s 2(1); 'annual accounts': CA 1963, s 2(1); 'company': CA 1963, s 2(1); 'Companies Act group accounts': CA 1963, s 2(1); 'director': CA 1963, s 2(1); 'Financial year': CA 1963, s 22(1); 'Group Accounts': CA 1963, s 2(1); 'Parent company': CA 1963, s 2(1); 'Profit and loss account': CA 1963, s 2(1); 'subsidiary': CA 1963, s 2(1); 'financial year': CA 1963, s 2(1A).

Notes

Applicability of ss 151, 152 and 154: The requirement to prepare group accounts and the format and content of those accounts were originally governed by CA 1963, ss 150, 151, 152 and 154. Over the last three decades, however, the relevance and applicability of these provisions has been largely eroded by the following enactments:

EC(CGA)R 1992: These regs implement Council Directive 83/349/EEC and deal with the format and content of group accounts of public and private limited holding companies[1] which are engaged for gain in the production, supply or distribution of goods, the provision of a service or the making or holding of investments.[2] The regs do not apply, however, to the following:

(a) licensed banks;[3]

(b) certified trustee savings banks;[4]

(c) other companies engaged in the business of accepting deposits or other repayable funds or granting credit for its own account;[5]

(d) companies engaged solely in the making of hire-purchase agreements and credit-sale agreements;[6]

(e) authorised life and non-life insurance companies;[7]

(f) companies which meet at least two of the three following criteria:

(i) the group balance sheet does not exceed €7,618,428.47,

(ii) the group turnover does not exceed €15,236,856.94 per annum,

(iii) the group workforce does not exceed 250; [8] and in respect of which neither the parent company not any of its subsidiaries is listed on a stock exchange established in a member state;[9]

(g) certain parent companies which are themselves subsidiaries of other EC companies.[10]

1 EC(CGA)R 1992, reg 5.
2 EC(CGA)R 1992, reg 3(1).
3 EC(CGA)R 1992, reg 6(2)(a).
4 EC(CGA)R 1992, reg 6(2)(b).
5 EC(CGA)R 1992, reg 6(2)(d).
6 EC(CGA)R 1992, reg 6(2)(c).
7 EC(CGA)R 1992, reg 6(2)(g).
8 EC(CGA)R 1992, reg 7(1).
9 EC(CGA)R 1992, reg 7(8).
10 EC(CGA)R, regs 8 and 9.

EC(CIA)R 1992: These regs, which give effect to Council Directive 86/635/EEC, govern the format and content of annual accounts and group accounts for banks and other financial institutions.

EC(A)R 1993: These regs give legal effect, *inter alia*, to Council Directive 90/605/EEC and govern the format and content of the annual accounts for unlimited companies in circumstances where, broadly speaking, the members of the company are themselves either Irish or foreign limited companies.[1] The group accounts of such companies are, with some modifications, to be drawn up in accordance with the provisions of EC(CGA)R 1992.[2]

1 EC(A)R 1993, reg 6. The Regulations also apply to partnerships.
2 EC(A)R 1993, reg 9.

EC(IUA)R 1996: These regs implement Council Directive 91/674/EEC and govern the form and content of annual accounts and group accounts for insurance companies to which the European Communities (Non-Life Insurance) Regulations 1976 or the European Communities (Life Assurance) Regulations 1984 apply, as well as reinsurance companies.

As a result of the various enactments cited above, the provisions of CA 1963, ss, 151, 152 and 154 now apply to only a very few types of holding company, eg a limited company which is not trading for gain by its members,[1] or a limited company whose group profit, turnover and workforce do not exceed €7,618,428.47, €15,236,856.94 and 250 respectively,[2] or an unlimited company which has at least one human being as a member.[3]

1 Such a company is governed wholly by the provisions of CA 1963.
2 Such a company is governed by CA 1963, ss 151–154, but because it is trading for gain, the format and content of its group accounts are governed by C(A)A 1986 and references CA 1963, s 152(3) to CA 1963, Sch 6 are instead to be construed as references to the Schedule to C(A)A 1986.
3 Such companies are governed solely by C(A)A 1986.

Dispensing in whole or in part with group accounts: If the holding company is one to which CA 1963, s 151 might otherwise apply, it may still be relieved in whole or in part from its obligation to prepare group accounts. If it is a private company, it may elect to dispense altogether with group accounts,[1] although its members will be entitled to receive copies of each subsidiary's accounts not only for the current year but also for each year since the coming into force of CA 1963.[2] Furthermore, under s 150(2)(a), group accounts will not be required if the company is in turn a wholly-owned subsidiary of another Irish company[3], since that other company will itself be obliged to prepare group accounts. Furthermore, if the directors are of the opinion that it would be impracticable, of no real value, disproportionately expensive or misleading to either prepare accounts or alternatively to include a particular subsidiary or subsidiaries in the group accounts, then they may dispense with such accounts altogether or exclude the particular subsidiary or subsidiaries therefrom, as the case may be.[4]

1 CA 1963, s 154(1).

2 CA 1963, s 154(2) and (3).

3 See CA 1963, s 151(5) for the definition of 'wholly-owned subsidiary'.

4 CA 1963, s 151(2)(b).

Harmonising group year ends: In relation to the steps that may be taken to harmonise the financial year ends of the various companies within a group see CA 1963, s 153(2).

---

152 Contents of group accounts

(1) [Companies Act group accounts prepared in accordance with sections 151 to 155 of this Act][a] laid before the annual general meeting of a company shall give a true and fair view of the state of affairs and profit or loss of the company and the subsidiaries dealt with thereby as a whole, so far as concerns members of the company.

(2) Where the financial year of a subsidiary does not coincide with that of the holding company, [the group accounts referred to in subsection (1)][b] shall deal with the subsidiary's state of affairs as at the end of its financial year ending with or last before that of the holding company and with the subsidiary's profit or loss for the financial year.

(3) Without prejudice to subsection (1), [the group accounts referred to in subsection (1)][b], if prepared as consolidated accounts, shall comply with the requirements of the Sixth Schedule so far as applicable thereto, and if not so prepared shall give the same or equivalent information.

Amendments

a Words substituted by EC(IFRSMA)R 2005, reg 9, Sch 1, Pt 1, Item No 3(a).

b Words substituted by EC(IFRSMA)R 2005, reg 9, Sch 1, Pt 1, Item No 3(b).

Definitions

'accounts': CA 1963, s 2(1); 'company': CA 1963, s 2(1); 'Companies Act group accounts': CA 1963, s 2(1); 'financial year': CA 1963, s 2(1); 'group accounts'; CA 1963, s 2(1), s 150(1); 'holding company': CA 1963, s 2(1), s 155; 'member': CA 1963, s 31; 'subsidiary': CA 1963, s 2(1), s 155.

Notes

Applicability of s 152: See notes to CA 1963, s 151.

True and fair view: The basic requirement for group accounts, as with any other annual accounts, is that they should give a 'true and fair view' of the financial state of affairs of the company, or of the group, as the case may be, for the year in question. To a large extent, CA 1963, Sch 6 is determinative as to what constitutes a properly-prepared set of accounts.[1] However, to the extent that the legislation is silent on any particular matter, compliance with the recognised practices and standards of the accountancy profession in preparing the company's accounts will be strong, but not conclusive evidence that the accounts give a 'true and fair view' of the company's financial position.[2]

1 See also CA 1963, s 191 and CA 1990, ss 41–45 for the disclosure of directors' interests in the annual accounts.

2 *Dolan v AB Ltd* [1969] IR 282; *Lloyd Cheyham and Co Ltd v Littlejohn and Co* [1987] BCLC 303; *IRC v Duple Motor Bodies Ltd* [1961] 1 WLR 739. The recognised practices of the accountancy profession may be found in its Statements of Standard Accounting Practice (SSAPs) and in its Auditing Guidelines.

Financial year of holding company and subsidiaries to coincide: Except where there are good reasons to the contrary, the financial year of each of the subsidiaries should coincide with that of the holding company.[1]

1 CA 1963, s 153.

UK legislation

See CA 1985, s 228; CA 1989, s 5(1).

---

153 Financial year and annual return date of holding company and subsidiary

(1) A holding company's directors shall secure that except where there are good reasons against it, the financial year of each of its subsidiaries shall coincide with the company's own financial year.

(2) [Where it appears to the Minister desirable for a holding company or a holding company's subsidiary to extend its financial year so that the subsidiary's financial year may end with that of the holding company, and for that purpose to postpone the submission of the relevant accounts to an annual general meeting from one calendar year to the next, or for a holding company or a holding company's subsidiary to extend its annual return date so that the subsidiary's annual return date may correspond with that of the holding company, the Minister may—

(a) on the application or with the consent of the directors of the company whose financial year is to be extended, direct that in the case of that company, the submission of accounts to an annual general meeting or the holding of an annual general meeting shall not be required in the earlier of the calendar years, or

(b) on the application or with the consent of the directors of the company whose annual return date is to be extended, direct that an extension is to be permitted in the case of that company.][a]

(3) If any person being a director of a company fails to take all reasonable steps to secure compliance by the company with the provisions of this section, he shall in respect of each offence be liable on summary conviction to a fine not exceeding [€1,904.61].[b]

(4) No proceedings shall be instituted under this section except by, or with the consent of, the Minister.

(5) This section shall not apply to a private company which is a holding company and which takes advantage of subsection (1) of section 154.

Amendments

a CA 1963, s 153(2) substituted by CLEA 2001, s 61.

b '£250' substituted for '£50' by C(A)A 1982 Sch 1, increased to £1,500 by CA 1990, s 240(7) as inserted by CLEA 2001, s 104(c) and converted to €1,904.61 by Council Regulations (EC) No 1103/97, No 974/98 and No 2866/98, and the Economic and Monetary Union Act 1998, s 6.

Definitions

'accounts': CA 1963, s 2(1); 'annual return': CA 1963, s 2(1); 'company': CA 1963, s 2(1); 'director': CA 1963, s 2(1); 'financial year': CA 1963, s 2(1); 'holding company': CA 1963, s 2(1), s 155; 'Minister': CA 1963, s 2(1); 'private company': CA 1963, s 2(1), s 33(1); 'subsidiary': CA 1963, s 2(1), s 155.

UK legislation

See CA 1985, s 223(5); CA 1989, s 3.

---

154 Right of member of private company to get balance sheet of subsidiary

(1) Notwithstanding section 150, a private company which is a holding company need not prepare group accounts but if it does not do so the subsequent provisions of this section shall apply.

(2) Any member of the company shall be entitled to be furnished without charge within 14 days after he has made a request in that behalf to the company with a copy of the latest balance sheet of each of its subsidiaries which has been sent to the members of that subsidiary together with a copy of every document required by law to be annexed thereto and a copy of the directors' and auditors' reports.

(3) Without prejudice to subsection (2), any member of the company shall be entitled to be furnished within 14 days after he has made a request in that behalf to the company with a copy of any balance sheet (including every document required by law to be annexed thereto and a copy of the directors' and auditors' reports) of any subsidiary of the company laid before any annual general meeting of such subsidiary held since the operative date, at a charge not exceeding [13 cent][a] for each balance sheet so furnished so, however, that a member shall not be entitled to be furnished with a copy of any balance sheet laid before an annual general meeting held more than 10 years before the date on which such request is made.

(4) Copies of balance sheets need not be sent to any member of a private company if, on the application either of the company or of any person who claims to be aggrieved, the court is satisfied that the rights conferred by this section are being abused, and the court may order the company's costs on an application under this subsection to be paid in whole or in part by the member who has made the request for such copies.

(5) Subject to subsection (4), if any copy required under this section is not sent within the proper time, the company and every officer of the company who is in default shall be liable, in respect of each offence, to a fine not exceeding [€1,904.61][b] unless it is proved that the member has already made a demand for and been furnished with a copy.

(6) In the case of any default under this section, the court may direct that the copies required shall be sent to the member requiring them.

Amendments

a ‘2 shillings’ converted to 13 cent by Council Regulations (EC) No 1103/97, No 974/98 and No 2866/98 and the Economic and Monetary Union Act 1998, s 6.

b ‘£500’ substituted for ‘£100’ by C(A)A 1982, Sch 1, increased to £1,500 by CA 1990, s 240(7) as inserted by CLEA 2001, s 104(c) and converted to €1,904.61 by Council Regulations (EC) No 1103/97, No 974/98 and No 2866/98 and the Economic and Monetary Union Act 1998, s 6.

Definitions

‘accounts’: CA 1963, s 2(1); company: CA 1963, s 2 (1); ‘the court’: CA 1963, s 2(1); ‘director’: CA 1963, s 2(1); ‘document’: CA 1963, s 2(1): ‘group accounts’; CA 1963, s 2(1), s 150(1); ‘holding company’: CA 1963, s 2(1), s 155; ‘member’: CA 1963, s 31; ‘officer’: CA 1963, s 2(1); ‘officer in default: CA 1963, s 383; ‘the operative date’: CA 1963, s 2(1); ‘private company’: CA 1963, s 2(1), s 33(1); ‘subsidiary’: CA 1963, s 2(1), s 155.

Notes

The provisions of CA 1963, s 154 do not apply to companies governed by EC(CGA)R 1992,[1] EC(CIA)R 1992,[2] EC(A)R 1993,[3] or by EC(IUA)R 1996.[4]

1 EC(CGA)R 1992, reg 5(5).
2 EC(CIA)R 1992, reg 7(2).
3 EC(A)AR 1993, reg 9.
4 EC(IUA)R 1996, reg 10(2).

155 Meaning of ‘holding company’ and ‘subsidiary’

(1) For the purposes of this Act, a company shall, subject to subsection (3), be deemed to be a subsidiary of another if, but only if—

(a) that other—

(i) is a member of it and controls the composition of its board of directors, or

(ii) holds more than half in nominal value of its equity share capital, or

(iii) holds more than half in nominal value of its shares carrying voting rights (other than voting rights which arise only in specified circumstances); or

(b) the first-mentioned company is a subsidiary of any company which is that other’s subsidiary.

(2) For the purposes of subsection (1), the composition of a company’s board of directors shall be deemed to be controlled by another company if, but only if, that other company by the exercise of some power exercisable by it without the consent or concurrence of any other person can appoint or remove the holders of all or a majority of the directorships; but for the purposes of this provision that other company shall be deemed to have power to appoint to a directorship in relation to which any of the following conditions is satisfied—

(a) that a person cannot be appointed thereto without the exercise in his favour by that other company of such a power as aforesaid; or

(b) that a person's appointment thereto follows necessarily from his appointment as director of that other company.

(3) In determining whether one company is a subsidiary of another—

(a) any shares held or power exercisable by that other in a fiduciary capacity shall be treated as not held or exercisable by it;

(b) subject to paragraphs (c) and (d), any shares held or power exercisable—

(i) by any person as a nominee for that other (except where that other is concerned only in a fiduciary capacity); or

(ii) by, or by a nominee for, a subsidiary of that other, not being a subsidiary which is concerned only in a fiduciary capacity;

shall be treated as held or exercisable by that other;

(c) any shares held or power exercisable by any person by virtue of the provisions of any debentures of the first-mentioned company or of a trust deed for securing any issue of such debentures shall be disregarded;

(d) any shares held or power exercisable by, or by a nominee for, that other or its subsidiary (not being held or exercisable as mentioned in paragraph (*c*)) shall be treated as not held or exercisable by that other if the ordinary business of that other or its subsidiary, as the case may be, includes the lending of money and the shares are held or power is exercisable as aforesaid by way of security only for the purposes of a transaction entered into in the ordinary course of that business.

(4) For the purposes of this Act, a company shall be deemed to be another's holding company if, but only if, that other is its subsidiary.

(5) In this section 'company' includes any body corporate and 'equity share capital' means, in relation to a company, its issued share capital excluding any part thereof which, neither as respects dividends nor as respects capital, carries any right to participate beyond a specified amount in a distribution.

Definitions

'company': CA 1963, s 2(1); 'debenture': CA 1963, s 2(1); 'director': CA 1963, s 2(1); 'Equity Share Capital': CA 1963, s 155 (5); 'holding company': CA 1963, s 2(1), s 155; 'member': CA 1963, s 31; 'share': CA 1963, s 2(1); 'subsidiary': CA 1963, s 2(1), s 155.

Notes

Exhaustive definition: CA 1963, s 155(1) and (4) make it quite clear that the definition of 'holding company' and 'subsidiary' contained in s 155 is exhaustive. The four ways in which the relationship can arise are as follows:

(a) *Control of composition of board*:[1] This involves an entitlement on the part of Company A without the consent or concurrence of any other person to appoint or remove a majority of the board of Company B or to exercise a right of veto in respect of the appointment of a majority of the board.[2] A person may be able to control the composition of the board of directors by reason, *inter alia*, of (i) having a majority of the votes in general meeting; (ii) a shareholders' agreement giving such control; (iii) a provision in the memorandum or articles of association conferring a power appoint and dismiss the board or a majority of the board. Ultimately however, whatever form the control takes, it must be *de jure* control rather than mere *de facto* control in order for one company to be treated as the subsidiary of another.[3]

(b) *More than half in nominal value of the equity share capital*:[4] The phrase 'equity share capital' is defined in CA 1963, s 155(5) and excludes any shares which are limited to a specified amount in a distribution *both* as respects dividends and as respects capital.

(c) *More than half in value of shares carrying voting rights*: Notably, what is required here is not necessarily the holding of more than half of the voting rights in general meeting, but rather, more than half in value of the shares carrying voting rights. It is well established that a company may create shares with loaded voting rights.[5] So, for example, Company A might hold a class of shares in Company B which, although representing only a small number of the shares carrying voting rights, nonetheless represents a voting block of more than 50% in general meeting. If these loaded voting rights are created in such a way as to give Company A control of every aspect of Company B's affairs other than the election and removal of the directors, Company B will not be deemed to be a subsidiary of Company A.

(d) *Subsidiary of a subsidiary*: If Company B is a subsidiary of Company A, but in turn has its own subsidiary, Company C, then Company C will also be deemed to be a subsidiary of Company A.

1 CA 1963, s 155(1)(a)(i). See, generally, Courtney, *The Law of Private Companies* (2nd edn, Tottel Publishing, 2002) Ch 17.

2 CA 1963, s 155(2).

3 *Mount Edon Gold Mines (Australia) Ltd v Burmine Ltd* (1994) 12 ACLC 185; *Bluebird Investments Pty Ltd v Graf* (1994) 12 ACLC 724.

4 CA 1963, s 155(1)(a)(ii).

5 *Bushell v Faith* [1970] AC 1099.

Shares and powers held in a fiduciary capacity: Where shares are held or powers are exercisable by a company in a fiduciary capacity, they are to be ignored in determining whether that company is the holding company of another entity.[1] Conversely, if shares are held or powers are exercisable by a third party as its bare nominee, those shares or powers may be taken into consideration in determining whether or not a holding company/subsidiary relationship exists.[2] If shares have been registered in the name of an entity as mortgagee, those shares are to be taken into account in determining whether the mortgagee has thereby become the company's holding company.[3]

1 CA 1963, s 155(3)(a). See *Michaels v Harley House (Marleybone) Ltd* [1999] 1 BCLC 670.

2 CA 1963, s 155(3)(b). See the exception in s 155(3)(d) for shares taken as security by a financial institution in the ordinary course of its business.

3 *Enviroco Ltd v Farstad Supply A/S* [2009] 2 BCLC 225.

Subsidiary of a plc for purposes of CA 1990, Part XI: For the purpose of CA 1990, Part XI and for no other purposes, a limited company[1] will also be deemed to be a subsidiary of a plc if, but only if, the plc is itself a shareholder or member of that limited company and controls alone, pusuant to an agreement with other shareholders or members, a majority of the shareholders' or members' voting rights in the company in question.[2]

1 'Limited company' includes not only an Irish limited company but also an equivalent foreign company: EC(PLCS)R 1997, reg 4(2).

2 EC(PLCS)R 1997, reg 4(1).

Foreign companies: Because under CA 1963, s 155(5) the phrase 'company' is to be construed as referring to any body corporate, the holding company/subsidiary relationship can be deemed to arise not only where both companies are registered under the Companies Acts, but also where one of them is registered abroad.

Control through debentures: If Company A controls Company B through voting rights or other powers which are conferred by a series of debentures rather than by shares, etc, this does not constitute relevant control for the purposes of s 155[1] even though it may be just as effective as the other forms of control which are recognised by the section.

1 CA 1963, s 155(3)(c).

Parent and subsidiary undertakings: One of the original purposes behind defining 'holding company' and 'subsidiary' was to identify the companies in respect of which group accounts were to be prepared. However, for companies governed by EC(CGA)R 1992, EC(CIA)R 1992 or EC(A)R 1993, the requirement for group accounts is now dependent on whether the relationship of 'parent undertaking' and 'subsidiary undertaking' exists.[1]

1 The definition of these phrases is to be found in EC(CGA)R 1992, reg 3(1) and reg 4.

Single economic unit: As regards the entitlement to lift the veil of incorporation on a group of companies which forms one single economic entity, see CA 1963, s 18 and the notes thereto.

UK legislation

See CA 1985, s 736; CA 1989, s 144.

---

156 Signing of balance sheet and profit and loss account

[(1) (a) Where the directors of a company prepare Companies Act individual accounts, every balance sheet and profit and loss account of the company shall be signed on behalf of the directors by 2 of the directors of the company.

(b) Where the directors of a company prepare IFRS individual accounts, every balance sheet and income statement of a company shall be signed on behalf of the directors by 2 of the directors of the company.

(2) In the case of a banking company registered after 15 August 1879, the balance sheet and profit and loss account, or, where the directors of a company prepare IFRS accounts, the income statement, must be signed by the secretary and where there are more than 3 directors of the company by at least 3 of those directors, and where there are not more than 3 directors by all the directors.][a]

(3) If any copy of a balance sheet or profit and loss account which has not been signed as required by this section is issued, circulated or published, the company and every officer of the company who is in default [shall be guilty of an offence and liable to a fine][b] not exceeding [€1,904.61].[c]

(4) Subsection (3) shall not prohibit the issue, circulation or publication of—

(a) a fair and accurate summary of any profit and loss account and balance sheet and the auditors' report thereon after such profit and loss account and balance sheet shall have been signed on behalf of the directors;

(b) a fair and accurate summary of the profit or loss figures for part of the company's financial year.

Amendments

a CA 1963, s 156(1) and (2) substituted by EC(IFRSMA)R 2005, Sch 1, Pt 1, Item No 4.

b Words in CA 1963, s 156(3) substituted by C(AA)A 2003, s 57 and Sch 2, para 1.

c '£500' substituted for '£100' by C(A)A 1982, Sch 1, increased to £1,500 by CA 1990, s 240(7) as inserted by CLEA 2001, s 104(c) and converted to €1,904.61 by Council Regulations (EC) No 1103/97, No 974/98 and No 2866/98 and the Economic and Monetary Union Act 1998, s 6.

Definitions

'company': CA 1963, s 2(1); 'Companies Act individual accounts': CA 1963, s 2(1); 'director': CA 1963, s 2(1); 'financial year': CA 1963, s 2(1); 'income statement': CA 1963, s 2(1); 'IFRS accounts': CA 1963, s 2(1); 'IFRS individual accounts': CA 1963, s 2(1); 'officer': CA 1963, s 2(1); 'officer in default'; CA 1963, s 383.

Notes

Signed balance sheet as an acknowledgement of debt: See CA 1963, s 148 and the notes thereto.

UK legislation

See CA 1985, s 233; CA 1989, s 7.

---

157 Documents to be attached and annexed to balance sheet

(1) The profit and loss account and, so far as not incorporated in the balance sheet or profit and loss account, any group accounts laid before the annual general meeting of a company shall be annexed to the balance sheet and the auditors report shall be attached thereto and any accounts so annexed shall be approved by the board of directors before the balance sheet and profit and loss account are signed on their behalf.

(2) If any copy of a balance sheet is issued, circulated or published without compliance with subsection (1), the company and every officer of the company who is in default [shall be guilty of an offence and liable to a fine][a] not exceeding [€1,904.61][b].

Amendments

a Words in CA 1963, s 157(2) substituted by C(AA)A 2003, s 57 and Sch 2, para 1.

b '£500' substituted for '£100' by C(A)A 1982, Sch 1, increased to £1,500 by CA 1990, s 240(7) as inserted by CLEA 2001, s 104(c) and converted to €1,904.61 by Council Regulations (EC) No 1103/97, No 974/98 and No 2866/98 and the Economic and Monetary Union Act 1998, s 6.

Definitions

'accounts': CA 1963, s 2(1); 'company': CA 1963, s 2(1); 'director': CA 1963, s 2(1); 'document': CA 1963, s 2(1): 'group accounts'; CA 1963, s 2(1), s 150(1); 'officer': CA 1963, s 2(1); 'officer in default'; CA 1963, s 383.

Notes

Auditors' Report: The requirement for the auditors to prepare a report and the contents of that report are governed primarily by CA 1990, s 193. In addition, however, see CA 1963, s 191(8) and C(A)A 1986, s 15, EC(CGA)R 1992, reg 38, EC(CAI)R 1992, reg 13 and EC(IUA)R 1996, reg 16.

UK legislation

See CA 1985, s 241.

158 Directors' report to be attached to balance sheet and contents of such report

(1) There shall be attached to every balance sheet laid before the annual general meeting of a company a report by the directors on the state of the company's affairs and, if the company is a holding company, on the state of affairs of the company and its subsidiaries as a group, the amount, if any, which they recommend should be paid by way of dividend and the amount, if any, which they propose to carry to reserves within the meaning of the Sixth Schedule.

(2) The said report shall be signed on behalf of the directors by two of the directors of the company.

(3) The said report shall deal, so far as is material for the appreciation of the state of the company's affairs, with any change during the financial year in the nature of the business of the company or of the company's subsidiaries, or in the classes of business in which the company has an interest whether as a member of another company or otherwise.

(4) The said report shall contain a list of bodies corporate in relation to which either of the following conditions is fulfilled at the end of the company's financial year—

(a) the body corporate is a subsidiary of the company;

(b) although the body corporate is not a subsidiary of the company, the company is beneficially entitled to more than 20 per cent in nominal value of its shares carrying voting rights (other than voting rights which arise only in specified circumstances).

(5) The list referred to in subsection (4) shall distinguish between bodies corporate falling within paragraph (a) and paragraph (b) thereof and shall state in relation to each such body corporate—

(a) its name;

(b) where it is incorporated; and

(c) the nature of the business carried on by it.

(6) Subsections (4) and (5) shall not apply to a company which is principally engaged in the acquisition and underwriting of shares or other securities of companies carrying on a trade or industry in the State and which holds a certificate of exemption issued by the Minister from the requirements of those subsections.

[(6A) The report referred to in subsection (1) shall contain a statement of the measures taken by the directors to secure compliance with the requirements of section 202 of the Companies Act, 1990, with regard to the keeping of proper books of account and the exact location of those books.][a]

[(6B) The report referred to in subsection (1) shall contain a copy of any Disclosure Issue Notice issued under section 33AK (inserted by the Central Bank and Financial Services Authority of Ireland Act 2003) during the financial year ending with the relevant balance sheet date.][b]

[(6C) Subject to subsection (6E), a company whose securities are admitted to trading on a regulated market shall include a corporate governance statement in respect of the financial year in the report by the directors referred to in subsection (1).

(6D) The corporate governance statement referred to in subsection (6C) shall be included as a specific section of the report of the directors referred to in subsection (1), and shall include, at least, all of the following information:

(a) a reference to—

(i) the corporate governance code—

(I) to which the company is subject and where the relevant text is publicly available, or

(II) which the company has voluntarily decided to apply and where the relevant text is publicly available, and

(ii) all relevant information concerning corporate governance practices applied in respect of the company which are additional to any statutory requirement, and where the information on such corporate governance practices is available for inspection by the public;

(b) where the company departs, in accordance with any statutory provision, from a corporate governance code referred to in clause (I) or (II) of paragraph (a)(i)—

(i) an explanation by the company as to which parts of the corporate governance code it departs from in accordance with the statutory provision and the extent to which it departs from such code and

(ii) the reasons for such departure,

and where the company has decided not to apply any provisions of a corporate governance code referred to in clause (I) or (II) of paragraph (a)(i), the company shall explain its reasons for doing so;

(c) a description of the main features of the internal control and risk management systems of the company in relation to the financial reporting process;

(d) the information required under subparagraphs (c), (d), (f), (h) and (i) of paragraph (2) of Regulation 21 of the European Communities (Takeover Bids (Directive 2004/25/EC)) Regulations 2006 (S.I. 255 of 2006), where the company is subject to those Regulations;

(e) a description of the operation of the shareholder meeting, the key powers of the shareholder meeting, shareholders' rights and the exercise of such rights;

(f) the composition and operation of the board of directors and the committees of the board of directors with administrative, management and supervisory functions.

(6E) The information required under subsection (6D) may be set out in a separate report published in conjunction with the annual report in accordance with subsections (6F) or (6G), or provided by a reference in the annual report to where the separate report is publicly available on the website of the company, and where a separate report is provided, the corporate governance statement may contain a reference to the annual report where the information referred to in subsection (6D)(d) is provided.

(6F) Where a company produces a corporate governance statement in the form of a separate report, such report shall be attached to every balance sheet, referred to in subsection (1), laid before the annual general meeting of the company and shall be signed on behalf of the directors by 2 of the directors of the company.

(6G) Where a company produces a corporate governance statement in the form of a separate report—

(a) a copy of such report shall be published on the website of the company, and a statement that a copy of the report has been so published together with the address of the website of the company, shall be included in the report of the directors of the company, or

(b) be annexed to the annual return, under section 7 of the Act of 1986, of the company and shall be certified both by a director and the secretary of the company to be a true copy of such corporate governance statement laid or to be laid before the annual general meeting of the company.

(6H) Where a company produces a corporate governance statement the auditors of the company, when preparing the report required by section 193 of the Act of 1990, in respect of the company, shall—

(a) establish that the company has produced a corporate governance statement and whether such statement contains the information required by paragraphs (a), (b), (e) and (f) of subsection (6D),

(b) provide an opinion concerning the consistency or otherwise of the information given in the corporate governance statement under subsection (6D)(c) relating to the financial year concerned is consistent with the outcome of their evaluation and testing of the relevant systems for the purposes of preparing that report and the auditors shall state in the report under section 193 of the 1990 Act whether, in their opinion, such information is so consistent, and

(c) provide an opinion as to whether the information given in the corporate governance statement under subsection (6D)(d) relating to the financial year concerned is consistent.

(6I) Paragraphs (a), (b), (e) and (f) of subsection (6D) shall not apply to companies which have only issued securities other than shares admitted to trading on a regulated market, unless such companies have issued shares which are traded in a multilateral trading facility.

(6J) In subsection (6I), 'multilateral trading facility' has the meaning assigned to it by Article 4(1), point (15) of Directive 2004/39/EC6.][c]

(7) If any person, being a director of a company, fails to take all reasonable steps to comply with the requirements of this section he shall in respect of each offence be liable on summary conviction to imprisonment for a term not exceeding 6 months or to a fine not exceeding [€1,904.61][d] or to both so, however, that—

(a) in any proceedings against a person in respect of an offence under this section it shall be a defence to prove that he had reasonable ground to believe and did believe that a competent and reliable person was charged with the duty of seeing that the provisions of this section were complied with and was in a position to discharge that duty; and

(b) a person shall not be liable to be sentenced to imprisonment for such an offence unless, in the opinion of the court dealing with the case, the offence was committed wilfully.

Amendments

a CA 1963, s 158(6A) inserted by CLEA 2001, s 90.

b Subsection (6B) inserted by CBFSAIA 2003, s 35(1) and Sch 1, Pt 4.

c Subsections (6C)–(6J) inserted by European Communities (Directive 2006/46/EC) Regulations 2009, reg 13.

d '£500' substituted for '£100' by C(A)A 1982, Sch 1, increased to £1,500 by CA 1990, s 240(7) as inserted by CLEA 2001, s 104(c) and converted to €1,904.61 by Council Regulations (EC) No 1103/97, No 974/98 and No 2866/98 and the Economic and Monetary Union Act 1998, s 6.

Definitions

'company': CA 1963, s 2(1); 'the court': CA 1963, s 2(1); 'director': CA 1963, s 2(1); 'financial year': CA 1963, s 2(1); 'holding company': CA 1963, s 2(1), s 155; 'member': CA 1963, s 31; 'Minister': CA 1963, s 2(1); 'share': CA 1963, s 2(1); 'subsidiary': CA 1963, s 2(1), s 155.

Notes

Directors' report: The requirements of CA 1963, s 158 are as to the prescribed contents of the directors' report. They have been expanded upon, however, by subsequent legislation.

C(A)A 1986: In the case of companies governed by C(A)A 1986, the provisions of sub-ss (4) and (5) do not apply,[1] with the information being contained instead in the notes to the accounts.[2] Also, the reference to CA 1963, Sch 6 is instead to be construed as a reference to the provisions of C(A)A 1986.[3] Furthermore, the report must contain the following additional information:

(a) a fair review of the development of the business of the company and of its subsidiaries, if any, during the financial year;[4]

(b) particulars of any important events affecting the company or any of its subsidiaries during the year;[5]

(c) an indication of likely future development in the business of the company and of its subsidiaries, if any;[6]

(d) an indication of the activities, if any, of the company and its subsidiaries, if any, in the field of research and development;[7]

(e) an indication of the existence of any branches of the company outside the State and the country in which each such branch is located;[8]

(f) details of the amount, value, etc of any of its own shares which have been acquired by the company by forfeiture or surrender in lieu of forfeiture;[9]

(g) details of the amount, value, etc of any of its own shares which the company has otherwise acquired or disposed of; and the consideration, if any, paid to or received by the company, se the case may be, in respect thereof;[10]

(h) in the case of a plc, details of the amount, value, etc of any of its won shares which have been acquired by a subsidiary;[11]

(i) details of the amount, value, etc of any of its own shares over which the company has acquired a lien or charge, and the reasons for taking the lien or charge.[12]

1 C(A)A 1986, s 16(5).

2 C(A)A 1986, s 16(1)–(3).

3 C(A)A 1986, s 3(1)(e)(ii).

4 C(A)A 1986, s 13.

5 C(A)A 1986, s 13.

6 C(A)A 1986, s 13.

7 C(A)A 1986, s 13.

8 C(A)A 1986, s 13(e).

9 C(A)A 1986, s 14.

10 C(A)A 1986, s 14.

11 C(A)A 1986, s 14 as extended by EC(PLCS)R 1997, reg 6.

12 C(A)A 1986, s 14.

CA 1990 (as amended by C(AA)A 2003): In the case of a plc, the directors' report must include a report from the audit committee on the committee's activities during the financial year including its work in monitoring the performance and quality of the auditors' work and the auditors' independence from the company.[1] Furthermore, the directors' report of each 'large private company' and each 'relevant undertaking'[2] must state:

(a) whether the company or undertaking, as the case may be, has established an audit committee or decided not to do so,

(b) if it has established such a committee, whether it has all or some only of the responsibilities provided for in CA 1990, s 205B(2), and

(c) if it has decided not to establish such a committee, the reasons for that decision.[3]

1 CA 1990, s 205B(2)(n).

2 For the definitions of 'large private company' and 'relevant undertaking' see CA 1990, s 205B(1).

3 CA 1990, s 205B(4).

EC(CGA)R 1992: The additional information to be included in the directors' report accompanying group accounts governed by these regs in similar to that contained in paragraphs (a)–(d) above for companies governed by C(A)A 1986.[1] In addition, there must be contained, either in the notes to the accounts or in the directors' report details of the number and nominal value of shares in the parent undertaking held by that undertaking itself, by its subsidiary undertakings or by a person acting in his own name but on behalf of those undertakings.[2]

1 EC(CGA)R 1992, reg 37.

2 EC(CGA)R 1992, reg 37.

EC(CIA)R 1992: The additional information to be contained in the directors' report of a parent company governed by these regs is similar to that prescribed by C(A)A 1986 and EC(CGA)R 1992.[1]

1 EC(CIA)R 1992, reg 11.

EC(IUA)R 1996: The additional information to be contained in the directors' report of a parent company governed by these regs is similar to that prescribed by C(A)A 1986 and EC(CGA)R 1992.[1]

1 EC(UI:A)R 1996, reg 14.

UK legislation

See CA 1985, ss 234, 234A, Sch 7 (amended by CA 1989, s 8(2), Sch 5, s 137(2)): CA 1989, s 8.

159 Obligation of company to send copies of balance sheets and directors' and auditors' reports

(1) Subject to subsections (2) and (3), a copy of every balance sheet including every document required by law to be annexed thereto, which is to be laid before the annual general meeting of a company together with a copy of the directors' and auditors' reports shall, not less than 21 days before the date of the meeting, be sent to every member of the company (whether he is or is not entitled to receive notices of general meetings of the company), every holder of debentures of the company (whether he is or is not so entitled) and all persons other than members or holders of debentures of the company who are so entitled.

(2) In the case of a company not having a share capital, subsection (1) shall not require a copy of the documents referred to in that subsection to be sent to a member of the company who is not entitled to receive notices of general meetings of the company or to a holder of debentures of the company who is not so entitled.

(3) If the copies of the documents referred to in subsection (1) are sent less than 21 days before the date of the meeting, they shall, notwithstanding that fact, be deemed to have been duly sent if it is so agreed by all the members entitled to attend and vote at the meeting.

(4) Any member of a company, whether he is or is not entitled to have sent to him copies of the company's balance sheets, and any holder of debentures of the company, whether he is or is not so entitled, shall be entitled to be furnished on demand without charge with a copy of the last balance sheet of the company, including every document required by law to be annexed thereto, together with copies of the directors' and auditors' reports.

(5) If default is made in complying with subsection (1), the company and every officer of the company who is in default [shall be guilty of an offence and liable to a fine][a] not exceeding [€1,904.61][b], and if, when any person makes a demand for any document with which he is by virtue of subsection (4) entitled to be furnished, default is made in complying with the demand within 7 days after the making thereof, the company and every officer of the company who is in default [shall be guilty of an offence and liable to a fine][a] not exceeding [€1,904.61][b] unless it is proved that that person has already made a demand for and been furnished with a copy of the document.

(6) Subsection (4) shall not apply to a balance sheet of a private company laid before it before the operative date and the right of any person to be furnished with a copy of any such balance sheet and the liability of the company in respect of a failure to satisfy that obligation shall be the same as they would have been if this Act had not been passed.

Amendments

a Words in CA 1963, s 156(3) substituted by C(AA)A 2003, s 57 and Sch 2 and 4.

b '£250' substituted for '£50' by C(A)A 1982, Sch 1, increased to £1,500 by CA 1990, s 240(7) as inserted by CLEA 2001, s 104(c) and converted to €1,904.61 by Council Regulations (EC) No 1103/97, No 974/98 and No 2866/98 and the Economic and Monetary Union Act 1998, s 6.

Definitions

'company': CA 1963, s 2(1); 'debenture': CA 1963, s 2(1); 'director': CA 1963, s 2(1); 'document': CA 1963, s 2(1): 'member': CA 1963, s 31; 'officer': CA 1963, s 2(1); 'officer in default'; CA 1963, s 383; 'the operative date': CA 1963, s 2(1); 'private company': CA 1963, s 2(1), s 33(1); 'share': CA 1963, s 2(1).

Notes

As to the meaning of 'not less than 21 days' see CA 1963, s 133 and the notes thereto.

UK legislation

See CA 1985, ss 238, 239; CA 1989, s 10.

---

160 Appointment and remuneration of auditors

(1) Subject to subsection (2), every company shall at each annual general meeting appoint an auditor or auditors to hold office from the conclusion of that until the conclusion of the next annual general meeting.

(2) Subject to subsection (3), at any annual general meeting a retiring auditor, however appointed, shall be re-appointed without any resolution being passed unless—

(a) he is not qualified for re-appointment; or

(b) a resolution has been passed at that meeting appointing somebody instead of him or providing expressly that he shall not be re-appointed; or

(c) he has given the company notice in writing of his unwillingness to be re-appointed.

(3) Where notice is given of an intended resolution to appoint some other person or persons in place of a retiring auditor, and by reason of the death, incapacity or disqualification of that person or of all those persons, as the case may be, the resolution cannot be proceeded with, the retiring auditor shall not be automatically re-appointed by virtue of subsection (2).

(4) Where, at an annual general meeting, no auditors are appointed or re-appointed, the Minister may appoint a person to fill the vacancy.

[(5) Without prejudice to any rights of the auditor in relation to his removal under this subsection, a company may, by ordinary resolution at a general meeting, remove an auditor other than an auditor who is the first auditor or one of the first auditors of the company and appoint in his place any other person who has been nominated for appointment by any member of the company, who is qualified under the Companies Acts to be an auditor of a company and of whose nomination notice has been given to its members.

[(5A)(a) A company shall—

(i) within one week of the Minister's power under subsection (4) becoming exercisable, give the Minister notice of that fact, and

(ii) where a resolution removing an auditor is passed, give notice of that fact in the prescribed form to the registrar of companies within 14 days of the meeting at which the resolution removing the auditor was passed.

(b) If a company fails to give notice as required by paragraph (a) of this subsection, the company and every officer of the company who is in default shall be guilty of an offence and liable, on summary conviction, to a fine not exceeding [€1,904.61][b].][a]

(6) Subject as hereinafter provided, the first auditors of a company may be appointed by the directors at any time before the first annual general meeting, and auditors so appointed shall hold office until the conclusion of that meeting, so, however, that—

(a) the company may at a general meeting remove any such auditors and appoint in their place any other persons who have been nominated for appointment by any member of the company, and of whose nomination notice has been given to the members of the company not less than 14 days before the date of the meeting; and

(b) if the directors fail to exercise their powers under this subsection, the company in general meeting may appoint the first auditors, and thereupon the said powers of the directors shall cease.

[(7) The directors of a company or the company in general meeting may fill any casual vacancy in the office of auditor, but while any such vacancy continues, the surviving or continuing auditor or auditors, if any, may act.][c]

(8) The remuneration of the auditors of a company—

(a) in the case of an auditor appointed by the directors or by the Minister, may be fixed by the directors or by the Minister, as the case may be;

(b) Subject to paragraph (a), shall be fixed by the company at the annual general meeting or in such manner as the company at the annual general meeting may determine.

For the purposes of this subsection, any sums paid by the company in respect of the auditors' expenses shall be deemed to be included in the term 'remuneration'.

(9) The appointment of a firm by its firm name to be the auditors of a company shall be deemed to be an appointment of those persons who shall from time to time during the currency of the appointment be the partners in that firm as from time to time constituted and who are qualified to be auditors of that company.

Amendments

a CA 1963, s 160(5) substituted and subs (5A) inserted by CA 1990, s 183.

b '£1,000' increased to '£1,500' by CA 1990, s 240(7) as inserted by CLEA 2001, s 104(c) and converted to €1,904.61 by Council Regulations (EC) No 1103/97, No 974/98 and No 2866/98 and the Economic and Monetary Union Act 1998, s 6.

c CA 1963, s 160(7) substituted by CA 1990, s 183.

Definitions

'company': CA 1963, s 2(1); 'director': CA 1963, s 2(1); 'member': CA 1963, s 31; 'Minister': CA 1963, s 2(1); 'officer': CA 1963, s 2(1); 'office in default': CA 1963, s 383; 'prescribed': CA 1963, s 2(1); 'registrar of companies': CA 1963, s 2(1).

Notes

Appointment of first auditor: Every company must have an auditor or auditors.[1] The first appointment may be made by the directors at any time before the first AGM[2] although if the board fails to act, the members in general meeting may appoint the first auditors themselves.[3]

If the directors make the first appointment, the company in general meeting may appoint a replacement nominated by any member of the company and whose nomination has been notified to the members at least 14 days before the date of the meeting.[4]

1 CA 1963, s 160(1).
2 CA 1963, s 160(6). As to the holding of the first AGM, see CA 1963, s 131(2).
3 CA 1963, s 150(6).
4 CA 1963, s 160(6).

Subsequent appointments: Once appointed, an auditor normally holds office until the conclusion of the next AGM of the company.[1] Moreover, at the next AGM he will be deemed to have been automatically re-appointed without the need for any formal resolution to that effect unless:

(a) he is not qualified for re-appointment;[2]

(b) a resolution has been passed at the AGM appointing someone else instead of him or providing expressly that he should not be re-appointed;[3] or

(c) he has given written notice of his unwillingness to be re-appointed.[4]

1 CA 1963, s 160(1).
2 CA 1963, s 160(2)(a).
3 CA 1963, s 160(2)(b).
4 CA 1963, s 160(2)(c).

Appointment by Minister: If, at the AGM of the company, no auditors are appointed or re-appointed, the Minister may appoint a person to fill the vacancy.[1] In order to enable the Minister to exercise this power, the company must notify him of the vacancy within one week of the occurrence of same.[2] The Minister's power of appointment would seem to be without prejudice to the right of the members to fill the vacancy themselves at an EGM convened for that purpose.

1 CA 1963, s 160(4).
2 CA 1963, s 160(5A)(a)(i).

Casual vacancy: Casual vacancies in the office of auditor[1] may be filled by the directors or by the company in general meeting,[2] although in the latter case extended notice[3] of the proposed resolution will be required.[4] In either case, while the vacancy continues, the surviving or continuing auditor or auditors, if any, will still be entitled to act.[5]

1 eg where an auditor resigns or dies.
2 CA 1963, s 160(7).
3 For the definition of 'extended notice' see CA 1963, s 142.
4 CA 1963, s 161(1)(c).
5 CA 1963, s 160(7).

Appointment of a firm: A resolution appointing a firm to be the auditors of the company, is to be deemed to be an appointment of all those persons who, from time to time, are partners in that firm and are qualified to so act.[1]

1 CA 1963, s 160(9).

Qualification to act as auditor: With regard to the qualification of an individual to act an the auditor of a company, see CA 1990, ss 187–192, 198 and 199 as amended by C(AA)A 2003, Part 3 and the notes thereto.

Resolution not to re-appoint or to appoint someone else: Extended notice[1] is required for a resolution at the AGM appointing someone else as auditor or expressly providing that the retiring auditor should not be re-appointed.[2]

If the resolution is one for the appointment of someone else and it cannot be proceeded with because the other nominee dies or is incapable of or is disqualified from acting, the retiring auditor will not be deemed to have been automatically re-appointed.[3] However, if the resolution is simply defeated on a vote, the retiring auditor will be automatically re-appointed.[4]

1 For the definition of 'extended notice' see CA 1963, s 142.
2 CA 1963, s 161(a).
3 CA 1963, s 160(3).
4 CA 1963, s 160(1).

Removal of auditor during term of office: Although an auditor's appointment will normally continue until the next AGM, he may be removed before the expiration of his term of office by an ordinary resolution of the members passed in general meeting, and may be replaced by someone else qualified to so act who has been nominated by any member of the company and of whose nomination due notice has been given to all the members.[1] Extended notice is required for the resolution to remove the auditor.[2]

Apart from being entitled to be heard at the general meeting at which he is to be removed, the auditor is also entitled to receive notice of, to attend at and be heard at the next AGM of the company and at the general meeting at which it is proposed to appoint someone to fill the vacancy created by his removal.[3] His right of audience only extends, however, to that part of the business of the meeting which concerns him as former auditor of the company.[4]

Where an auditor has been removed from office, the company must give notice of this fact to the registrar of companies within 14 days of the meeting at which the resolution removing him was passed.[5]

1 CA 1963, s 160(5).
2 CA 1963, s 161(1)(b). For the definition of 'extended notice' see CA 1963, s 142.
3 CA 1963, s 161(2A).
4 CA 1963, s 161(2A).
5 CA 1963, s 160(5A)(ii).

Procedure for removal etc: In the case of:

(a) a resolution to replace the directors' appointee as auditor with a members' nominee;[1]

(b) a resolution at an AGM to appoint someone other than the retiring auditor or to expressly not re-appoint the retiring auditor;[2]

(c) a resolution to remove an auditor other than the first auditor during his term of office;[3] or

(d) a resolution of the company in general meeting to fill a casual vacancy,[4]

the following procedure must be observed by the company in addition to any additional requirements imposed by the memorandum or articles of association.

Upon receipt of notice of the intended resolution, the company must send a copy of the intended resolution to the auditor[5] who may in turn make written representations to the company not exceeding a reasonable length and request their notification to the members.[6] Having received such a request from the auditor, the company must, unless it is already too late to do so, mention in the notice convening the meeting that such representations have been made and it must also send a copy of the representations to each such member, either along with the notice itself or separately.[7] If the representations are not sent out to the members, whether because of the company's own default or because they were simply received too late, the auditor (without prejudice to his right to be heard orally) may insist on the representations being read out at the meeting.[8]

If the auditor is abusing his right to make representations in order to secure needless publicity for defamatory matter, the court on the application of the company or any other aggrieved person, may direct that the representations are not to be circulated and/or read at the general meeting.[9]

1 CA 1963, s 161(5).
2 CA 1963, s 161(1)(a).
3 CA 1990, s 184(2).
4 CA 1963, s 161(1)(c).

5. CA 1963, s 161(2). Of course, in the case of a casual vacancy, there may not be a former auditor to whom notice can be sent, eg because he has died.
6. CA 1963, s 161(3).
7. CA 1963, s 161(3).
8. CA 1963, s 161(3).
9. CA 1963, s 161(4).

Resignation of auditor or unwillingness to be re-appointed: An auditor who wishes to resign or who is unwilling to be re-appointed at the next AGM must serve written notice to this effect on the company[1] and must within 14 days thereafter send a copy thereof to the registrar of companies.[2] In the case of a resignation, this takes effect on the date of the service of the notice on the company or on such later date as may be specified therein.[3]

The notice as served on the company must contain either:

(a) a statement that there are no circumstances connected with the resignation or unwillingness to be re-appointed that the auditor considers should be brought to the notice of the members or creditors of the company; or

(b) a statement of any such circumstances.[4]

Circumstances which the auditor might wish to bring to the attention of the members might include the non co-operation of the directors in relation to the conduct of the audit, or attempts by the directors to force the auditor not to qualify the accounts. If such circumstances are specified in the notice, the company must, not later than 14 days after the date of service thereof by the auditor, send a copy to every person who is entitled to receive copies of the annual accounts.[5] However, if the auditor is abusing his position in order to secure needless publicity for defamatory matter, the court on the application of the company or any other aggrieved person, may direct that the notice need not be circulated to the members.[6] The application to court must be made by the company within 14 days of service of the notice.[7] This is a strict time limit which cannot and will not be extended by the court.[8] If the company is unsuccessful in preventing dissemination of the auditors' statement, it may be required to pay the auditors' legal costs on an indemnity basis.[9]

In giving notice to the company which indicated that there are circumstances which should be brought to the attention of the members or creditors, the auditor may also requisition a general meeting of the company for the purpose of receiving and considering an account and explanation from him of the circumstances connected with his resignation or unwillingness to be re-appointed.[10] Upon being so requisitioned, the directors must within 14 days proceed to convene a general meeting for a date not more than 28 days from the date upon which the auditor originally served the notice.[11] The auditor has an entitlement to make written representations to the members which is similar to that described above in connection with removal from office, etc[12] and also has a similar right to attend the next AGM of the company and to attend any general meeting at which it is proposed to fill the vacancy caused by his resignation or unwillingness to be re-appointed.[13]

1. CA 1990, s 185(1) and (5).
2. CA 1990, s 185(3)(a).
3. CA 1990, s 185(1).
4. CA 1990, s 185(2).
5. CA 1990, s 185(3)(b).
6. CA 1990, s 185(4).
7. CA 1990, s 185(3)(b).
8. *P and P Design plc v PricewaterhouseCoopers* [2002] 2 BCLC 648.
9. *Jarvis plc v PricewaterhouseCoopers* [2000] 2 BCLC 368.
10. CA 1990, s 186(1).
11. CA 1990, s 186(2).
12. CA 1990, s 186(3) and (4).
13. CA 1990, s 186(5).

Removal of auditor through use of audit exemption: In the case of a private limited company[1] being one to which the provisions of C(A)A 1986 apply[2] the requirement to appoint an auditor and to have the annual accounts audited, may be disapplied provided that certain conditions are met. In essence, the directors must form the opinion that both in respect of the financial year in question and also in respect of the immediately preceding financial year[3] the company meets the criteria set out in CA 1963, s 160(3), namely that:

(a) its does not exceed any of the specified thresholds as to turnover, balance sheet value or number of employees;[4]

(b) it must neither be a parent undertaking nor a subsidiary undertaking within the meaning of EC(CGA)R 1992;[5]

(c) it must not be a licensed bank,[6] an insurance company[7] or a financial services company of the type referred to in Sch 2;[8] and

(d) the filing of its annual returns must be fully up-to-date.[9]

Once they have concluded that these criteria are being satisfied the directors may determine to disapply the audit provisions of the Companies Acts insofar as they pertain to the company. That determination must be recorded in the board minutes.[10] Any person who records in the minutes a decision to avail of the audit exemption knowing that the company does not in fact qualify for the exemption, is guilty of an offence.[11]

Where the directors validly resolve that the company shall avail of the audit exemption, this does not automatically result in the removal of the auditor from office, albeit that his functions and powers are suspended.[12] Rather, a separate decision must be taken to terminate the appointment of the auditor for the whole or part of the year in respect of which the exemption is be availed.[13] Normally, removal of an auditor would require a resolution of the members in general meeting[14] with all of the attendant rights on the part of the auditor to attend and be heard at the meeting and to have his written representations, if any, circulated to the members in advance of the meeting.[15] However, where the removal is consequent solely upon the company availing of the audit exemption, it would seem to be implicit that those procedures are disapplied by CA 1963, s 32(2)(a) as being provisions which 'require anything to be done ... as respects an auditor.' Instead, the procedures prescribed by s 34 itself are deemed to apply. It seems therefore that a decision to remove the auditor before the expiration of his term of office may be taken by the board of directors.[16] However, it does not become effective[17] unless and until the auditor serves a notice on the company stating either that there are no circumstances connected with the decision to avail of the audit exemption which ought to be brought to the attention of the members or creditors, or alternatively stating what those circumstances are.[18] The auditor must serve this notice on the company within 21 days of being notified of the decision to terminate his appointment[19] and within a further 14 days thereafter he must copy same to the registrar of companies.[20] Significantly, if the notice does indeed state that there are circumstances connected with the decision to avail of the audit exemption which ought to be brought to the attention of the members or creditors, the company must within the same 14 day period send a copy of the notice to every person who would be entitled to copies of the annual accounts under CA 1963, s 159(1).[21] However, if the notice contains defamatory matter application may be made to the court by the company itself or by any other aggrieved person for an order preventing its circulation.[22] Furthermore, if the auditor's statement is false in any material particular and he made it knowing it to be false, he will be guilty of an offence.[23]

Normally, where an auditor has been removed from office, he will be entitled to attend the next AGM at which, but for his prior removal, his term of office would otherwise have expired and to attend any other general meeting (such as an EGM in advance of the next AGM) at which it is proposed to fill the vacancy occasioned by his removal.[24] However, this right of attendance is not enjoyed by an auditor removed under s 34.[25]

1 See C(A)(No 2)A 1999, s 31 and s 32(1)(a).

2 See C(A)(No 2)A 1999, s 32(3)(a)(i). As to the categories of company covered by C(A)A 1986, see ss 1 and 2 thereof and the notes thereto.

3 C(A)(No 2)A 1999, s 32(1). Of course, if the company is in its first financial year, the relevant criteria need only be met in respect of that year: s 32(1)(b).

4 C(A)(No 2)A 1999, s 32(3)(a)(ii)–(iv).

5 C(A)(No 2)A 1999, s 32(3)(a)(v)(I).

6 C(A)(No 2)A 1999, s 32(3)(a)(v)(II).

7 C(A)(No 2)A 1999, s 32(3)(a)(v)(III).

8 C(A)(No 2)A 1999, s 32(3)(a)(v)(IV).

9 C(A)(No 2)A 1999, s 32(3)(b).

10 C(A)(No 2)A 1999, s 32(1)(a).

11 C(A)(No 2)A 1999, s 37.

12 C(A)(No 2)A 1999, s 32(2) and Sch 1.

13 C(A)(No 2)A 1999, s 34(1).

14 CA 1963, s 161.

15 CA 1963, s 161.

16 Presumably the provisions of and procedures contained in C(A)(No 2)A 1999, s 34 will also apply where the auditor is not removed from office during the course of the financial year but where his appointment lapses instead at the following AGM in accordance with CA 1963, s 160(1) as a result of no resolution being proposed and passed for his re-election.

17 C(A)(No 2)A 1999, s 34(1)(ii). Presumably the delay in the vacation of office becoming effective also applies in the case of an auditor whose appointment lapses under s 160(1) at the following AGM in accordance with CA 1963, s 160(1) as a result of no resolution being proposed and passed for his re-election.

18 C(A)(No 2)A 1999, s 34(2).

19 C(A)(No 2)A 1999, s 34(1)(i).

20 C(A)(No 2)A 1999, s 34(3)(a).

21 C(A)(No 2)A 1999, s 34(3)(b). Under CA 1963, s 159(1) the persons entitled to receive the copies of the annual accounts are the members (whether or not entitled to receive notice of general meetings) and every holder of debentures (whether or not entitled to receive notice of general meetings) and every other person who would be entitled to receive notice of general meetings (eg where such entitlement is conferred by the articles of association).

22 C(A)(No 2)A 1999, s 34(4).

23 C(A)(No 2)A 1999, s 37.

24 CA 1963, s 161(2A).

25 C(A)(No 2)A 1999, s 34(5).

Reappointment after loss of audit exemption: Where a company ceases to be entitled to avail of the audit exemption, the directors must take steps 'as soon as may be' to appoint a new auditor,[1] assuming of course that the previous appointee has indeed ceased to hold office.[2] If the directors fail to make the appointment, the members in general meeting may do so instead.[3] In either event, the newly appointed auditor holds office until the next general meeting at which annual accounts are to be presented.[4]

1 C(A)(No 2)A 1999, s 35(1).

2 The previous auditor may have been removed before the expiration of his term of office under CA 1963, s 34 or alternatively his appointment may have lapsed under CA 1963, s 160(1) in circumstances where, at the AGM following the decision to avail of the audit exemption, the members resolved not to re-elect him.

3 C(A)(No 2)A 1999, s 35(3). If neither the directors nor the members appoint an auditor, then the Minister may do so (at least where there has since been an AGM) pursuant to CA 1963, s 160(4).

4 C(A)(No 2)A 1999, s 35(2). With regard to the laying of accounts before a general meeting of the members, see CA 1963, s 148.

Status of auditor: Auditors are officers of the company once appointed under CA 1963, s 160.[1] They are therefore subject to the various provisions of the Companies Acts, both civil and criminal, which are expressed to apply to such 'officers'[2] as well as being entitled to rely on CA 1963, s 391 which allows for the grant of relief to 'officers' in respect of negligence, breach of duty, etc.[3] Equally well, they are entitled to avail of any provisions in the articles of association which provide for the indemnification of the company's officers.[4]

Despite being an officer, however, an auditor is not an agent of the company[5] and does not, *per se*, have any authority to manage the company's affairs and therefore does not have any ostensible authority to make representations on behalf of, or to bind the company.[6] Similarly, the company is not to be automatically fixed with any knowledge which has been acquired by him in the course of the audit.[7]

1 *Mutual Reinsurance Co Ltd v Peat Marwick Mitchell and Co* [1997] 1 BCLC 1; *R v Shacter* [1960] 2 QB 252; *Re Western Counties Steam Bakeries and Milling* [1897] 1 Ch 617; *Re London and General Bank* [1895] 2 Ch 673.

2 *R v Shacter* [1960] 2 QB 252.

3 *Commissioners of Customs and Excise v Hedon Alpha Ltd* [1981] QB 818.

4 *Mutual Reinsurance Co Ltd v Peat Marwick Mitchell and Co* [1997] 1 BCLC 1.

5 *Re London and General Bank* [1895] 2 Ch 673; *Re Transplanters Ltd* [1958] 1 WLR 822.

6 *Re Transplanters Ltd* [1958] 1 WLR 822.

7 *Re London and General Bank* [1895] 2 Ch 673; *Markham v SA Finance and Industrial Co Ltd* 1962 (2) SA 5 (W).

Rights, duties and liabilities of auditors: See CA 1990, ss 193–197 and the notes thereto.

Remuneration and expenses: The remuneration of the auditors is to be fixed at the AGM or in such manner as the AGM by the AGM may determine,[1] which may include delegating the matter to the board of directors. If the appointment has been made by the directors or by the Minister, then the remuneration is determined by the board or by the Minister, as the case may be.[2] In this regard, any sums paid to the auditors in respect of expenses are to be regarded as remuneration.[3]

Whilst the auditor may, in appropriate circumstances, exercise a lien over property, books and records of the company for unpaid fees, he is not entitled to exercise such a lien in respect of books, records, registers, etc which either under the Companies Acts or under the memorandum or articles of association, are required to be kept at the registered office of the company or which are required, under the Companies Acts, to be available for a particular purpose such as inspection.[4] Moreover, even if he has a valid lien, it may be subject to the rights of any liquidator, provisional liquidator or examiner who is appointed to the company.[5]

1 CA 1963, s 160(8).

2 CA 1963, s 160(8).

3 CA 1963, s 160(8).

4 *Re Capital Fire Insurance Association* (1883) 24 ChD 408; *Re JJ Hopkins and Co* (1959) 93 ILTR 32; *Re Darion Fashions Ltd* [1981] 2 NZLR 47; *Re Firedart Ltd* [1994] 2 BCLC 340; *DTC (CNC) Ltd v Gary Sargent and Co* [1996] 2 All ER 369. As to the classes of documents which must be kept at the registered office, see the notes to CA 1963, s 113.

5 CA 1963, s 244A.

UK legislation

See CA 1985, ss 384, 385, 387, 388, 390A; CA 1989, ss 26, 119(1), 121.

---

161 Provisions as to resolutions relating to appointment and removal of auditors

[(1) Extended notice within the meaning of section 142 shall be required for—

(a) a resolution at an annual general meeting of a company appointing as auditor a person other than a retiring auditor or providing expressly that a retiring auditor shall not be re-appointed,

(b) a resolution at a general meeting of a company removing an auditor before the expiration of his term of office, and

(c) a resolution at a general meeting of a company filling a casual vacancy in the office of auditor.

(2) On receipt of notice of such an intended resolution as is mentioned in subsection (1), the company shall forthwith—

(a) if the resolution is a resolution mentioned in paragraph (a) of the said subsection (1), send a copy thereof to the retiring auditor (if any),

(b) if the resolution is a resolution mentioned in paragraph (b) of the said subsection (1), send a copy thereof to the auditor proposed to be removed, and

(c) if the resolution is a resolution mentioned in paragraph (*c*) of the said subsection (1), send a copy thereof to the person (if any) whose ceasing to hold the office of auditor of the company occasioned the casual vacancy.

(2A) An auditor of a company who has been removed shall be entitled to attend—

(a) the annual general meeting of the company at which, but for his removal, his term of office as auditor of the company would have expired, and

(b) the general meeting of the company at which it is proposed to fill the vacancy occasioned by his removal, and

to receive all notices of, and other communications relating to, any such meeting which a member of the company is entitled to receive and to be heard at any general meeting that such a member attends on any part of the business of the meeting which concerns him as former auditor of the company.][a]

(3) Subject to subsection (4), where notice is given of such an intended resolution as aforesaid, and the retiring auditor makes in relation to the intended resolution representations in writing to the company (not exceeding a reasonable length) and requests their notification to members of the company, the company shall, unless the representations are received by it too late for it to do so—

(a) in any notice of the resolution given to members of the company, state the fact of the representations having been made; and

(b) send a copy of the representations to every member of the company to who notice of the meeting is sent (whether before or after receipt of the representations by the company);

and if a copy of the representations is not sent as aforesaid because received too late or because of the company's default, the auditor may (without prejudice to his right to be heard orally) require that the representations shall be read out at the meeting.

(4) Copies of the representations need not be sent out as aforesaid and the representations need not be read out at the meeting as aforesaid if, on the application either of the company or of any other person who claims to be aggrieved, the court is satisfied that the rights conferred by this section are being abused to secure needless publicity for defamatory matter and the court may order the company's costs on an

application under this section to be paid in whole or in part by the auditor, notwithstanding that he is not a party to the application.

(5) Subsections (3) and (4) shall apply to a resolution to remove the first auditors by virtue of subsection (6) of section 160 as they apply in relation to a resolution that a retiring auditor shall not be re-appointed.

Amendments

a CA 1963, s 161(1), (2) substituted and (2A) inserted by CA 1990, s 184.

Definitions

'company': CA 1963, s 2(1); 'the court': CA 1963, s 2(1); 'extended notice': CA 1963, s 2(1), s 142; 'member': CA 1963, s 31.

Notes

See the notes to CA 1963, s 160. Also note what CA 1990 s 184(2) says about how CA 1963 s 161(5) is to be construed.

UK legislation

See CA 1985, ss 391, 391A; CA 1989, s 122(1).

---

162 Qualifications for appointment as auditor

[...][a]

Amendments

a CA 1963, s 162 repealed by CA 1990, s 6.

Notes

CA 1963, s 162 replaced by CA 1990, ss 187–192.

---

163 Auditors' report and right of access to books and to attend and be heard at general meetings

[...][a]

Amendments

a CA 1963, s 163 repealed by CA 1990, s 6.

Notes

CA 1963, s 163 replaced by CA 1990, s 193.

---

164 Construction of references to documents annexed to accounts

(1) Subject to subsection (2), references in this Act to a document annexed or required to be annexed to a company's accounts or any of them shall not include the directors' report or the auditors' report.

(2) Any information which is required by this Act to be given in accounts, and is thereby allowed to be given in a statement annexed, may be given in the directors' report instead of in the accounts and, if any such information is so given, the report shall be annexed to the accounts, and this Act shall apply in relation thereto accordingly, except that the auditors shall report thereon only so far as it gives the said information.

Definitions

'accounts': CA 1963, s 2(1); 'company': CA 1963, s 2(1); 'director': CA 1963, s 2(1); 'document': CA 1963, s 2(1).

Notes

The applicability of this section has been largely curtailed as a result of the narrowing of the scope of CA 1963, s 149 and Sch 6. As to the companies to which these provisions continue to apply, see the notes to s 149, above.

UK legislation

See CA 1985, s 261; CA 1989, s 22.

---

165 Investigation of company's affairs on application of members

[...][a]

Amendments

a CA 1963, s 165 repealed by CA 1990, s 6.

Notes

CA 1963, ss 165–173 provided for inspectors to be appointed primarily by the Minister. Such appointments were, however, rarely made. The provisions in question have all been repealed and have been replaced by CA 1990, Part II which has expanded upon the circumstances in which an inspector may be appointed and has also transferred to the High Court the primary jurisdiction to appoint inspectors. The Minister is, however, given a power to appoint inspectors to investigate the ownership of companies, as well as being empowered to conduct less formal examinations himself or through an 'authorised officer.'

---

166 Investigation of company's affairs in other cases

[...][a]

Amendments

a CA 1963, s 166 repealed by CA 1990, s 6.

---

167 Power of inspectors to extend investigation into affairs of related companies

[...][a]

Amendments

a CA 1963, s 167 repealed by CA 1990, s 6.

168 Production of documents, and evidence, on investigation

[...][a]

Amendments

a CA 1963, s 168 repealed by CA 1990, s 6.

169 Inspectors' report

[...][a]

Amendments

a CA 1963, s 169 repealed by CA 1990, s 6.

170 Proceedings on inspectors' report

[...][a]

Amendments

a CA 1963, s 170 repealed by CA 1990, s 6.

171 Expenses of investigation of company's affairs

[...][a]

Amendments

a CA 1963, s 171 repealed by CA 1990, s 6.

172 Inspectors' report to be evidence

[...][a]

Amendments

a CA 1963, s 172 repealed by CA 1990, s 6.

173 Saving for solicitors and bankers

[...][a]

Amendments

a CA 1963, s 173 repealed by CA 1990, s 6.

Directors and Other Officers

174 Directors

Every company shall have at least two directors.

Definitions

'company': CA 1963, s 2(1); 'director': CA 1963, s 2(1).

Notes

Status of a director: The director is an office holder and not an employee.[1] Apart from his status as office holder, however, he may also have a service contract with the company, pursuant to which he may become an employee. The contract may be express or, particularly in the case of a full-time executive director, implied.[2]

1 *Hutton v West Cork Rly Co* (1883) 23 Ch D 654; *Glover v BLN Ltd* [1973] IR 388; *Re Dairy Lee Ltd* [1976] IR 314.

2 *Carvill v Irish Industrial Bank Ltd* [1968] IR 325; *Re Dairy Lee Ltd* [1976] IR 314; *Re Beeton and Co Ltd* [1913] 1 Ch 84; *Anderson v James Sutherland (Peterhead) Ltd* [1932] 2 Ch 46.

Sole directors not permitted: The Twelfth Companies Directive,[1] which was implemented in Ireland with effect from 1 October 1994,[2] provides for one man private companies limited by shares or by guarantee. It is permissible for companies to be managed by sole directors in England and Wales: CA 1985, s 282, however CA 1963, s 174 stipulates that two directors are required.

1 (89/667/EEC) 32 OJ 1989, L395/40, 30 December 1989.

2 EC(SMPLC)R 1994. See generally MacCann, 'Company Law Reform: One Man Companies' (1991) 8 ILT 166.

UK legislation

See CA 1985, s 282.

175 Secretary

(1) Every company shall have a secretary, who may be one of the directors.

(2) Anything required or authorised to be done by or to the secretary may, if the office is vacant or there is for any other reason no secretary capable of acting, be done by or to any assistant or deputy secretary or, if there is no assistant or deputy secretary capable of acting, by or to any officer of the company authorised generally or specially in that behalf by the directors.

Cross reference

See C(A)A 1982, s 3(3), the name of the first secretary must be notified to the Registrar when an application is made to incorporate a company and the first secretary must consent to act as such.

See also CA 1990, s 236, there are certain qualification requirements for any secretary of a plc.

See also CA 1963, s 176, bodies corporate are not restricted from acting as company secretaries, unlike the restriction on bodies corporate acting as directors.

Definitions

'company': CA 1963, s 2(1); 'director': CA 1963, s 2(1) 'officer': CA 1963, s 2(1).

UK legislation

See CA 1985, s 283(1)–(3).[1]

[1] In England and Wales, the sole director of a company may not act as that company's secretary.

---

176 Prohibition of body corporate being director

(1) A company shall not, after the expiration of 3 months from the operative date, have as director of the company a body corporate.

(2) A body corporate which, on the operative date is a director of a company shall within a period of 3 months from that date vacate its office as director of the company, and all acts or things purporting to be made or done after the expiration of that period, by a body corporate as director of any company shall be null and void.

Definitions

'company': CA 1963, s 2(1); 'director': CA 1963, s 2(1); 'the operative date': CA 1963, s 2(1).

Notes

Corporate directors: In England and Wales there is no prohibition against bodies corporate acting as directors,[1] including companies incorporated under the Irish Companies Acts. It had been held in other jurisdictions that a body corporate can be a shadow director of a company.[2] More recently in *Fyffes v DCC*[3] and *Re Worldport Ltd*[4] the courts have confirmed that it is possible for a body corporate to be a 'shadow director' within the meaning of CA 1990, s 27.

[1] *Re Bulawayo Market and Offices Co Ltd* [1907] 2 Ch 458.

[2] *Ex p Copp* [1989] BCLC 12; *Standard Chartered Bank of Australia Ltd v Antico* (1995) 13 ACLC 1381.

[3] *Fyffes Plc v DCC Plc & Ors* [2005] IEHC 477.

[4] *Re Worldport Ltd* [2009] 1 IR 398.

UK legislation

See CA 1985, s 283(4).

---

177 Avoidance of acts done by person in dual capacity as director and secretary

A provision requiring or authorising a thing to be done by or to a director and the secretary shall not be satisfied by its being done by or to the same person acting both as director and as, or in place of, the secretary.

Definitions

'director': CA 1963, s 2(1); 'person': IA 2005, s 18(c).

Notes

Acts which require to be done by a director and the secretary include the signing of the annual return in the prescribed form[1] and certification of certain documents to be annexed to the annual return.[2] See also the sealing requirements in Table A, Pt 1, reg 115.

1 CA 1963, s 125: for the prescribed form, see Form B1 contained in Companies (Forms) Order 2004 (SI 133/2004).

2 CA 1963, s 128(1): balance sheet and auditors' report.

UK legislation

See CA 1985, s 284.

---

178 Validity of acts of directors

The acts of a director shall be valid notwithstanding any defect which may afterwards be discovered in his appointment or qualification.

Cross reference

See CA 1963, s 181(3), whereby the prohibition on a single resolution to appoint two or more directors is not to be taken as excluding the operation of CA 1963, s 178.

See also CA 1963, s 180, in relation to share qualifications of directors.

See also CA 1963, s 377 and Sch 9 (as amended by CA 1990, s 250) which applies CA 1963, s 178 to unregistered companies.

Definitions

'director': CA 1963, s 2(1).

Notes

This is effectively a statutory application of the Rule in *Turquand*.[1] This section only applies in the case of a procedural error in the appointment and affords no protection if the error concerns the substantive provisions relating to the appointment, nor is it of any avail if there never has been any appointment at all.[2] Similarly, the section has no application in a situation where the director, although originally validly appointed, subsequently vacates office (eg because of bankruptcy or a disqualification order) but nonetheless continues to act as if he were a director.[3] There are no requirements, under statute or common law, as to the professional qualifications of a director.[4]

1 *Royal British Bank v Turquand* (1856) 6 E & B 327.

2 *Morris v Kanssen* [1946] AC 459.

3 *Morris v Kanssen* [1946] AC 459.

4 *Re Brazilian Rubber Plantations & Estates Ltd* [1911] 1 Ch 425.

UK legislation

See CA 1985, s 285.

---

179 Restrictions on appointment or advertisement of director

(1) A person shall not be capable of being appointed a director of a company by the articles, and shall not be named as a director or proposed director of a company in a prospectus issued by or on behalf of the company, or as proposed director of an intended company in a prospectus issued in relation to that intended company, or in a statement in

lieu of prospectus delivered to the registrar by or on behalf of a company unless, before the registration of the articles or the publication of the prospectus or the delivery of the statement in lieu of prospectus, as the case may be, he has by himself or by his agent authorised in writing—

(a) signed and delivered to the registrar of companiesfor registration a consent in writing to act as such director; and

(b) either—

(i) signed the memorandum for a number of shares not less than his qualification, if any; or

(ii) taken from the company and paid or agreed to pay for his qualification shares, if any; or

(iii) signed and delivered to the registrar for registration an undertaking in writing to take from the company and pay for his qualification shares, if any; or

(iv) made and delivered to the registrar for registration a statutory declaration to the effect that a number of shares, not less than his qualification, if any, are registered in his name.

(2) Where a person has signed and delivered as aforesaid an undertaking to take and pay for his qualification shares, he shall, as regards those shares, be in the same position as if he had signed the memorandum for that number of shares.

(3) References in this section to a share qualification of a director or proposed director shall be construed as including only a share qualification required on appointment or within a period determined by reference to the time of appointment, and references therein to qualification shares shall be construed accordingly.

(4) On the application for registration of the memorandum and articles of a company, the applicant shall deliver to the registrar a list of the persons who have consented to be directors of the company and, if this list contains the name of any person who has not so consented, the applicant [shall be guilty of an offence and liable to a fine][a] not exceeding [€1,904.61][b].

(5) This section shall not apply to—

(a) a company not having a share capital; or

(b) a private company; or

(c) a company which was a private company before becoming a public company; or

(d) a prospectus issued by or on behalf of a company after the expiration of one year from the date on which the company was entitled to commence business.

Amendments

a Words 'shall be guilty of an offence and liable to a fine' substituted for 'shall be liable to a fine' in CA 1963, s 179(4) by C(AA)A 2003, Sch 2, Item No 1.

b '£250' substituted for '£50' by C(A)A 1982, Sch 1, increased to £1,500 by CA 1990, s 240(7) as inserted by CLEA 2001, s 104(c) and converted to €1,904.61 by Council Regulations (EC) No 1103/97, No 974/98 and No 2866/98 and the Economic and Monetary Union Act 1998, s 6.

Cross reference

See CA 1963, s 180 and Table A, Pt 1, reg 77.

See C(A)A 1983, s 9, for the procedure to convert a private company into a public company.

See also CA 1963, s 115, C(A)A 1983, s 6, for the restrictions on a company and public limited company, respectively, commencing business.

Definitions

'agent': CA 1963, s 2(1); 'articles': CA 1963, s 2(1); 'company': CA 1963, s 2(1); 'director': CA 1963, s 2(1); 'memorandum': CA 1963, s 2(1); 'person': IA 2005, s 18(c); 'private company': CA 1963, s 2(1), s 33(1); 'prospectus': CA 1963, s 2(1); 'the registrar of companies': CA 1963, s 2(1); 'share': CA 1963, s 2(1).

Notes

Qualification shares in public companies: The provisions of CA 1963, s 179 apply to public companies only.[1] Table A, Pt 1, reg 77 provides that if a shareholding qualification is not fixed by the company in general meeting, then none such shall apply.[2] Therefore, if there is no share qualification imposed by the company, the director will not have to comply with any of the requirements of CA 1963, s 179(1)(b). In the case of the first directors of all companies, and not just those companies to which CA 1963, s 179 applies, there must be delivered to the Registrar a statement containing the names and other prescribed particulars of the directors, together with their signed consents to act.[3] Where a director has signed and delivered to the Registrar an undertaking to take and pay for qualification shares, he shall be deemed to have agreed to become a member of the company in the same way as if he had been a subscriber to the memorandum.[4] If the requirements of CA 1963, s 179 are not fulfilled, the person applying to the Registrar to incorporate the company shall be liable to a fine.[5] In the event that, following a period of two months after his appointment (or such shorter time as is required by the articles), the director has not acquired the necessary shares, the director's office will be vacated until such time as the shares are acquired.[6]

1 CA 1963, s 179(5): this includes public companies limited by shares or guarantee (not having a share capital) and public companies which have been converted from a private company.

2 The CLRG, First Report, para 4.8.4: recommends that Table A, Pt 1, reg 77 be repealed on grounds of obsolescence.

3 C(A)A 1982, s 3; Companies (Forms) (No 2) Order 2004 (SI /2004/829), Form A1.

4 CA 1963, s 179(2). See CA 1963, s 31(1) and notes thereto.

5 CA 1963, s 179(4): a fine, not exceeding €1,904.61, shall apply.

6 CA 1963, s 180(3) and notes thereto.

---

180 Share qualifications of directors

(1) Without prejudice to the restrictions imposed by section 179, it shall be the duty of every director who is by the articles of the company required to hold a specified share qualification, and who is not already qualified, to obtain his qualification within 2 months after his appointment, or such shorter time as may be fixed by the articles.

(2) For the purpose of any provision in the articles requiring a director to hold a specified share qualification, the bearer of a share warrant shall not be deemed to be the holder of the shares specified in the warrant.

(3) The office of director of a company shall be vacated if the director does not within 2 months from the date of his appointment or within such shorter time as may be fixed by

the articles, obtain his qualification, or if after the expiration of the said period or shorter time, he ceases at any time to hold his qualification.

(4) A person vacating office under this section shall be incapable of being re-appointed director of the company until he has obtained his qualification.

(5) If after the expiration of the said period or shorter time any unqualified person acts as a director of the company, he [shall be guilty of an offence and liable to a fine][a] not exceeding [€1,904.61][b].

Amendments

a Words 'shall be guilty of an offence and liable to a fine' substituted for 'shall be liable to a fine' in CA 1963, s 180(5) by C(AA)A 2003, Sch 2.

b '£500' substituted for '£100' by C(A)A 1982, Sch 1, and increased to £1,500 by CA 1990, s 240(7) as inserted by CLEA 2001, s 104(c) and converted to €1,904.61 by Council Regulations (EC) No 1103/97, No 974/98 and No 2866/98 and the Economic and Monetary Union Act 1998, s 6.

Cross reference

See also CA 1963, s 179 and Table A, Pt 1, regs 77 and 91(a).

Definitions

'articles': CA 1963, s 2(1); 'company': CA 1963, s 2(1); 'director': CA 1963, s 2(1); 'person': IA Act 2005, s 18(c); 'share': CA 1963, s 2(1); 'share warrant': CA 1963, s 2(1), s 88(2).

Notes

Subject to any provision to the contrary in the articles, a director does not fail to satisfy the share qualification simply because he is not the beneficial owner of the shares.[1] Conversely, even if a director is the beneficial owner of the requisite number of shares, he will not be deemed to have satisfied the share qualification, unless he is registered in respect of them.[2] If an unqualified person continues to act as a director, after the two-month grace period (or such shorter time as the articles might require), such person is guilty of an offence and liable to a fine of up to €1,904.61.[3] For an example of a case where this provision operated, see *Duggan v Bourke* (30 May 1983, unreported) HC (Costello J).

1 *Pulbrook v Richmond Consolidated Mining Co* (1878) 9 Ch D 610; *Bainbridge v Smith* (1889) 41 Ch D 462.

2 *Spencer v Kennedy* [1926] Ch 125.

3 CA 1963, s 180(5).

UK legislation

See CA 1985, s 291.

181 Appointment of directors to be voted on individually

(1) At a general meeting of a company, a motion for the appointment of two or more persons as directors of the company by a single resolution shall not be made, unless a resolution that it shall be so made has first been agreed to by the meeting without any vote being given against it.

(2) Subject to subsections (3) and (4), a resolution moved in contravention of this section shall be void, whether or not its being so moved was objected to at the time.

(3) Subsection (2) shall not be taken as excluding the operation of section 178.

(4) Where a resolution moved in contravention of this section is passed, no provision for the automatic re-appointment of retiring directors in default of another appointment shall apply.

(5) For the purposes of this section, a motion for approving a person's appointment or for nominating a person for appointment shall be treated as a motion for his appointment.

(6) Nothing in this section shall apply to a resolution altering the company's articles.

Cross reference

See CA 1963, s 178 and Table A, Pt 1, reg 95.

Definitions

'articles': CA 1963, s 2(1); 'company': CA 1963, s 2(1); 'director': CA 1963, s 2(1) 'person': IA 2005, s 18(c).

Notes

Individual appointment of directors: This provision is included to ensure that one candidate about whom the members might otherwise object, is not elected on the strength of another candidate. Effectively, each candidate must be elected on his own merit. For an example of a case, where this provision operated, see *Moylan v Irish Whiting Manufacturers Ltd* (14 April 1980, unreported) HC (Hamilton J). It would appear from CA 1963, s 181(6) that it would be permissible to pass one special resolution inserting into the articles a provision for the collective appointment of a number of persons to the board. However, if such a provision were to be inserted into the memorandum instead, it would presumably have to comply with the requirements of CA 1963, s 181(1).

UK legislation

See CA 1985, ss 285, 292.

---

182 Removal of directors

(1) A company may by ordinary resolution remove a director before the expiration of his period of office notwithstanding anything in its articles or in any agreement between it and him so, however, that this subsection shall not, in the case of a private company, authorise the removal of a director holding office for life.

(2) Extended notice within the meaning of section 142 shall be required of any resolution to remove a director under this section or to appoint somebody instead of the director so removed at the meeting at which he is removed, and on receipt of notice of an intended resolution to remove a director under this section, the company shall forthwith send a copy thereof to the director concerned, and the director (whether or not he is a member of the company) shall be entitled to be heard on the resolution at the meeting.

(3) Subject to subsection (4), where notice is given of an intended resolution to remove a director under this section and the director concerned makes in relation thereto representations in writing to the company (not exceeding a reasonable length) and requests their notification to the members of the company, the company shall, unless the representations are received by it too late for it to do so—

(a) in any notice of the resolution given to members of the company, state the fact of the representations having been made; and

(b) send a copy of the representations to every member of the company to whom notice of the meeting is sent (whether before or after receipt of the representations by the company);

and if a copy of the representations is not sent as aforesaid because received too late or because of the company's default, the director may (without prejudice to his right to be heard orally) require that the representations shall be read out at the meeting.

(4) Copies of the representations need not be sent out as aforesaid, and the representations need not be read out at the meeting as aforesaid if, on the application either of the company or of any other person who claims to be aggrieved, the court is satisfied that the rights conferred by this section are being abused to secure needless publicity for defamatory matter, and the court may order the company's costs on an application under this section to be paid in whole or in part by the director concerned, notwithstanding that he is not a party to the application.

(5) A vacancy created by the removal of a director under this section may be filled at the meeting at which he is removed and, if not so filled, may be filled as a casual vacancy.

(6) A person appointed director in place of a person removed under this section shall be treated, for the purpose of determining the time at which he or any other director is to retire, as if he had become director on the day on which the person in whose place he is appointed was last appointed director.

(7) Nothing in this section shall be taken as depriving a person removed thereunder of compensation or damages payable to him in respect of the determination of his appointment as director or compensation or damages payable to him in respect of the determination of any appointment terminating with that as director or as derogating from any power to remove a director which may exist apart from this section.

Cross reference

See CA 1963, s 142.

See also Table A, Pt I, regs 98–100: casual vacancies may be filled either by the board itself or by the company in general meeting.

See also Table A, Pt 1, regs 92–100: as regards retirement by rotation.

CA 1963, s 182 is disapplied in relation to the Investor Compensation Company Limited under the Investor Compensation Act 1989, s 16 and in relation to the Irish Takeover Panel under the Irish Takeover Panel Act 1997, s 6.

Definitions

'articles': CA 1963, s 2(1); 'company': CA 1963, s 2(1); 'the court': CA 1963, s 2(1); 'director': CA 1963, s 2(1); 'extended notice': CA 1963, s 2(1), s 142; 'member': CA 1963, s 31; 'private company': CA 1963, s 2(1), s 33(1) 'person': IA 2005, s 18(c).

Notes

Power to remove a director[1]: Even a life director may ultimately be subject to CA 1963, s 182, if the members can muster a sufficient majority to remove the provision in the memorandum or articles which confers the life directorship.[2] In dismissing a director, the company must observe not only the requirements of CA 1963, s 182, but also the requirements of natural justice.[3] It has been held in other jurisdictions that a company cannot agree under contract not to exercise the power to remove a director,[4] however it has also been held that shareholders may contract, as between themselves, that they will not remove a director by way of a resolution brought under provisions analogous CA 1963, s 182.[5] The dismissal of one of the directors by resolution of the board will be valid if expressly authorised by the articles and if the power to dismiss has been exercised bona fide and in the best interests of the company.[6]

1 See generally Dunleavy, 'The Power of Shareholders to Remove Directors under s 182 of the Companies Act 1963 (1999) Bar Law Review 265.

2 *Shuttleworth v Cox Brothers and Co Ltd* [1927] 1 KB 9.

3 *Glover v BLN* [1973] IR 388.

4 *Russell v Northern Bank Development Corpn Ltd* [1992] 1 WLR 588.

5 *Stewart v Schwab* 1956 (4) SA 791, PD (Transvaal).

6 *Lee v Chou Wen Hsien* [1985] BCLC 45.

Director's options: If the director has a service contract with the company he may be able to avail of the remedies provided by the Unfair Dismissals Act 1977–2005. With the exception of a claim for damages for breach of the rules of natural justice, a claim for compensation or damages will only arise if the director had an express or implied service contract, the terms of which were inconsistent with peremptory dismissal.[1] Damages may be claimed, for example, where the director has a fixed term contract and is dismissed before the expiry of that term.[2] Apart from the question of damages for breach of contract, it is possible that a director may be entitled, if he is also a member of the company, to petition in appropriate circumstances for relief under CA 1963, ss 205, 213(f).[3]

1 *Nelson v James Nelson and Sons Ltd* [1914] 2 KB 770. See also CA 1963, s 183(7), which confirms that removal under CA 1963, s 182 does not deprive a director from receiving compensation or damages as a result of the termination of his appointment.

2 *Southern Foundries (1926) Ltd v Shirlaw* [1940] AC 701; *Shindler v Northern Raincoat Co Ltd* [1960] 1 WLR 1038.

3 *Ebrahimi v Westbourne Galleries* [1973] AC 360. *Re Murph's Restaurant Ltd* [1979] ILRM 141. See also *Avoca Capital Holdings v Companies Acts* [2005] IEHC 302, *Feighery v Feighery* [1999] 1 IR 321 (Laffoy J) and *McGilligan & Bowen v O'Grady* [1999] 1 IR 346 in the context of an injunction to prevent the removal of a director under CA 1963, s 182, pending the hearing of a petition under CA 1963, s 205. Keane CJ, in *McGilligan & Bowen v O'Grady*, in the Supreme Court, took a different view from that of Laffoy J in *Feighery v Feighery*, and acknowledged that the court has jurisdiction to award such interlocutory relief, where it would preserve the plaintiffs rights pending the hearing of the proceedings under CA 1963, s 205.

Notice of termination: If the director is to be employed for a period in excess of five years, the contract may have to be approved beforehand by the company in general meeting, and failure to obtain such approval (where required) will render the contract liable to termination on 'reasonable notice'.[1] Where the contract is not for a fixed term, the court may be prepared (at least in the case of a senior executive director) to imply a notice period of up to one year.[2] In some cases, however, the actual terms of the contract will be so spartan as to allow for peremptory dismissal.[3]

1 See CA 1990, s 28.

2 *Carvill v Irish Industrial Bank Ltd* [1968] IR 325.

3 *Read v Astoria Garage (Streatham) Ltd* [1952] Ch 637.

UK legislation

See CA 1985, ss 303, 304; CC(CP)A 1985, s 14 (in relation to removal of life directors).

183 [Prohibition of undischarged bankrupts acting as directors and other officers of companies

(1) Subject to subsection (2), if any person being an undischarged bankrupt acts as officer, auditor, liquidator or examiner of, or directly or indirectly takes part or is concerned in the promotion, formation or management of, any company except with the leave of the court, he shall be guilty of an offence.

(2) Where a person is convicted of an offence under subsection (1) he shall be deemed to be subject to a disqualification order from the date of such conviction if he was not, or was not deemed to be, subject to such an order on that date.

(3) In this section 'company' includes a company incorporated outside the State which has an established place of business within the State.][a]

Amendments

a CA 1963, s 183 substituted by CA 1990, s 169.

Cross reference

See CA 1990, Pt VII and notes thereto: concerning the power of the court to either restrict or disqualify directors and other officers of the company.See also CA 1963, Sch 1, Table A, Pt I, reg 91(b), (f): requiring the office of director to be vacated if a director is adjudged bankrupt or convicted of an indictable offence.

See also CA 1963, s 352 and notes thereto: a foreign company which has an established place of business in the State is required to register as an external company.[1]

See also CA 1963, s 183A and notes thereto: improvement of enforcement regime surrounding CA 1963, s 183.

[1] See generally CA 1963, Pt XI and Gill, 'Foreign Companies and Establishing 'A Place of Business'' (1989) ILT 264.

Definitions

'company': CA 1963, s 2(1); 'the court': CA 1963, s 2(1); 'director': CA 1963, s 2(1); 'examiner': C(A)A 1990, s 1, s 2; 'disqualification order': CA 1990, s 159;[1] 'officer': CA 1963, s 2(1); 'undischarged bankrupt': CA 1963, s 2(1).[2]

[1] The definitions contained in CA 1990, s 159 (including the definition of the term 'disqualification order') are said to apply to CA 1990, Pt VII, Ch 2 and Ch 3. Presumably this definition of 'disqualification order' is also intended to apply to that term, as used in CA 1963, s 183 (as inserted by CA 1990, s 169).

[2] 'undischarged bankrupt' inserted in CA 1963, s 2(1) by CLEA 2001, s 84(b).

UK legislation

See Company Directors Disqualification Act 1986, s 11; Enterprise Act 2002, s 257(3), Sch 21, para 5.

[183A Examination as to solvency status

Where the Director has reason to believe that a director of a company is an undischarged bankrupt, the Director may require the director of the company to produce by a specified date a sworn statement of all relevant facts pertaining to the company director's financial position, both within the State and elsewhere, and, in particular, to any matter pertaining to bankruptcy as at a particular date.

The court may, on the application of the Director, require a director of a company who has made a statement under subsection (1) to appear before it and answer on oath any question pertaining to the content of the statement.

The court may, on the application of the Director, make a disqualification order (as defined in section 159 of the Companies Act, 1990) against a director of a company on the grounds that he is an undischarged bankrupt.

A director of a company who fails to comply with a requirement under subsection (1) shall be guilty of an offence.][a]

Amendments

a CA 1963, s 183A inserted by CLEA 2001, s 40.

Cross reference

See CA 1963, s 183 and notes thereto.

Definitions

'company': CA 1963, s 2(1); 'the court': CA 1963, s 2(1); 'director': CA 1963, s 2(1); 'Director': CLEA 2001, s 3(1); 'disqualification order': CA 1990, s 159;[1] 'oath': IA 2005, Sch, Pt 1; 'undischarged bankrupt': CA 1963, s 2(1).[2]

1 The definition 'disqualification order', as used in CA 1963, s 183A, is specifically acknowledged as being that definition contained in CA 1990, s 159.

2 'undischarged bankrupt' inserted in CA 1963, s 2(1) by CLEA 2001, s 84(b).

Notes

Improved enforcement measures: It is intended that CA 1963, s 183A will facilitate enforcement of the prohibition of undischarged bankrupts acting as directors. Where the Director suspects that a director of a company is an undischarged bankrupt,[1] a mechanism now exists whereby the Director can require the director concerned to furnish a sworn statement of his or her financial position (in particular dealing with any matter relating to bankruptcy at a particular date).[2] In addition, the Director may have such a director examined before the court and may apply to the court to have a disqualification order made against the person.[3] The Director may apply to the court for a disqualification order against the director on the grounds that the director is an undischarged bankrupt.[4] The application is made on the basis of information before the court arising from the examination under CA 1963, s 183(A)(2). This allows the Director to take immediate action to disqualify a director who is an undischarged bankrupt rather than go making prosecution under CA 1963, s 183, which can be a time consuming process, particularly where evidence of the director's bankruptcy is in a foreign jurisdiction. In an application for a disqualification order under CA 1963, s 183A, evidence may be presented by affidavit, thus facilitating the presentation of testimony from persons outside the State.

1 CA 1963, s 183: it is an offence for a director, who is an undischarged bankrupt, to so act.

2 CA 1963, s 183A(1).

3 CA 1963, s 183A(2).

4 CA 1963, s 183A(3).

---

184 Power of court to restrain certain persons from acting as directors of or managing companies

[...][a]

Amendments

a CA 1963, s 184 repealed by CA 1990, s 6.

Cross reference

CA 1963, s 184 replaced by CA 1990, Pt VII.

CA 1990, s 159: definition of 'disqualification order' makes specific reference to CA 1963, s 184.

Definitions

'company': CA 1963, s 2(1); 'the court': CA 1963, s 2(1); 'director': CA 1963, s 2(1).

185 Prohibition of tax-free payments to directors

(1) It shall not be lawful for a company to pay a director remuneration (whether as director or otherwise) free of income tax or of income tax and sur-tax or of sur-tax, or otherwise calculated by reference to or varying with the amount of his income tax or his income tax and sur-tax or his sur-tax, or to or with the rate of income tax or sur-tax except under a contract which was in force on the 31st day of March, 1962, and provides expressly, and not by reference to the articles, for payment of remuneration as aforesaid.

(2) Any provision contained in a company's articles or in any contract other than such a contract as aforesaid, or in any resolution of a company or a company's directors, for payment to a director of remuneration as aforesaid shall have effect as if it provided for payment, as a gross sum subject to income tax and sur-tax, of the net sum for which it actually provides.

(3) This section shall not apply to remuneration due before the operative date or in respect of a period before the operative date.

Definitions

'articles': CA 1963, s 2(1); 'company': CA 1963, s 2(1); 'director': CA 1963, s 2(1); 'the operative date': CA 1963, s 2(1).

Notes

Income tax liability: Presumably, if a payment to a director is not liable to income tax in the first instance,[1] CA 1963, s 185 shall have no application. It would appear that, under similar legislation in the United Kingdom,[2] if a company fails to deduct the required income tax from a director's pay, the Inland Revenue may claim the unpaid tax from the director if he was aware that the company had wilfully failed to make the necessary deductions.[3]

1 For instance, a statutory redundancy payment made under the Redundancy Payment Acts 1967–2003 is not liable to income tax.

2 CA 1985, s 311(2).

3 *R v Inland Revenue Commissioners ex parte Sims* [1987] STC 211.

UK legislation

See CA 1985, s 311; CC(CP)A 1985, s 15.

---

186 Approval of company necessary for payment by it to director for loss of office

It shall not be lawful for a company to make to any director of the company any payment by way of compensation for loss of office, or as consideration for or in connection with his retirement from office, without particulars relating to the proposed payment (including the amount thereof) being disclosed to the members of the company and the proposal being approved by the company in general meeting.

Cross reference

See CA 1963, s 189: supplemental provisions relating to CA 1963, ss 186–188.

Definitions

'company': CA 1963, s 2(1); 'director'[1]: CA 1963, s 2(1); 'member': CA 1963, s 31.

1 CA 1963, s 189(5): reference to 'director' in CA 1963, s 186 includes reference to a past director.

Notes

Approval by the members: In the context of this section, disclosure must be made to all members of the company, and not just to those with voting rights.[1] Particulars of the proposed payment must be disclosed not only at the meeting itself, but also in the notice convening the meeting.[2] No approval is required, however, for any bona fide payment by way of damages for breach of contract or by way of pension for past services.[3] In this regard, 'pension' includes any superannuation allowance, superannuation gratuity or similar payment.[4] Disclosure of such payments in the company's accounts, after the fact, is not sufficient to satisfy the 'approval' required.[5]

1 *Re Duomatic Ltd* [1969] 1 All ER 161.

2 *Kaye v Croydon Tramways Co* [1898] 1 Ch 358.

3 CA 1963, s 189(3). See also *Taupo Totara Timber Co Ltd v Rowe* [1978] AC 537; followed in *Lander v Premier Pict Petroleum Ltd* [1998] BCC 248.

4 CA 1963, s 189(3).

5 *Mercer v Heart of Midlothian plc* (2001) SLT 945.

Payment held in trust: There is no reference in CA 1963, s 186 to such a payment being held in trust for the company or otherwise. Compare this position with payments caught by CA 1963, ss 187[1] and 188.[2]

1 Payment is held in trust for the company, as a separate legal entity.

2 Payment is held in trust for the individual members.

UK legislation

See CA 1985, s 312.

---

187 Approval of company necessary for payment to director of compensation in connection with transfer of property

(1) It is hereby declared that it is not lawful in connection with the transfer of the whole or any part of the undertaking or property of a company for any payment to be made to any director of the company by way of compensation for loss of office or as consideration for or in connection with his retirement from office, unless particulars relating to the proposed payment (including the amount thereof) have been disclosed to the members of the company and the proposal approved by the company in general meeting.

(2) Where a payment which is hereby declared to be illegal is made to a director of the company, the amount received shall be deemed to have been received by him in trust for the company.

Cross reference

See CA 1963, s 189: supplemental provisions relating to CA 1963, ss 186–188.

Definition

'company': CA 1963, s 2(1); 'director'[1]: CA 1963, s 2(1); 'member': CA 1963, s 31; 'undertaking': CA 1963, s 2(1).

1 CA 1963, s 189(5): reference to 'director' in CA 1963, s 186 includes reference to a past director.

Notes

Approval by the members: In the context of this section, disclosure must be made to all members of the company, and not just to those with voting rights.[1] Particulars of the proposed payment must be disclosed not only at the meeting itself, but also in the notice convening the meeting.[2] No approval is required, however, for any bona fide payment by way of damages for breach of contract or by way of pension for past services.[3] In this regard, 'pension' includes any superannuation allowance, superannuation gratuity or similar payment.[4] Disclosure of such payments in the Company's accounts, after the fact, is not sufficient to satisfy the 'approval' required.[5]

1 *Re Duomatic Ltd* [1969] 1 All ER 161.

2 *Kaye v Croydon Tramways Co* [1898] 1 Ch 358.

3 CA 1963, s 189(3). See also *Taupo Totara Timber Co Ltd v Rowe* [1978] AC 537; followed in *Lander v Premier Pict Petroleum Ltd* [1998] BCC 248.

4 CA 1963, s 189(3).

5 *Mercer v Heart of Midlothian plc* (2001) SLT 945.

Payment held in trust: The payment is held in trust for the company as a separate legal entity. Compare this position with payments caught by CA 1963, ss 186[1] and 188.[2]

1 The payment is not required to be held in trust for either the company or the individual shareholders.

2 The payment is held in trust for the individual shareholders.

UK legislation

See CA 1985, s 313.

188 Duty of director to disclose to company payments to be made to him in connection with transfer of shares in a company

(1) Where, in connection with the transfer to any persons of all or any of the shares in a company being a transfer resulting from—

(a) an offer made to the general body of shareholders; or

(b) an offer made by or on behalf of some other body corporate, with a view to the company becoming its subsidiary or a subsidiary of its holding company; or

(c) an offer made by or on behalf of an individual with a view to his obtaining the right to exercise or control the exercise of not less than one-third of the voting power at any general meeting of the company; or

(d) any other offer which is conditional on acceptance to a given extent;

a payment is to be made to a director of the company by way of compensation for loss of office, or as a consideration for or in connection with his retirement from office, it shall be the duty of that director to take all reasonable steps to secure that particulars of the proposed payment (including the amount thereof) shall be included in or sent with any notice of the offer made for their shares which is given to any shareholders.

(2) If—

(a) any such director fails to take reasonable steps as aforesaid; or

(b) any person who has been properly required by any such director to include the said particulars in or send them with any such notice as aforesaid fails so to do,

he [shall be guilty of an offence and liable to a fine][a] not exceeding [€1,904.61][b].

(3) Unless—

(a) the requirements of subsection (1) are complied with in relation to any such payment as is therein mentioned; and

(b) the making of the proposed payment is, before the transfer of any shares in pursuance of the offer, approved by a meeting summoned for the purpose of the holders of the shares to which the offer relates and of other holders of shares of the same class as any of the said shares,

any sum received by the director on account of the payment shall be deemed to have been received by him in trust for any persons who have sold their shares as a result of the offer made, and the expenses incurred by him in distributing that sum amongst those persons shall be borne by him and not retained out of that sum.

(4) Where the shareholders referred to in paragraph (*b*) of subsection (3) are not all the members of the company and no provision is made by the articles for summoning or regulating such a meeting as is mentioned in that paragraph, the provisions of this Act and of the company's articles relating to general meetings of the company shall, for that purpose, apply to the meeting either without modification or with such modifications as the Minister on the application of any person concerned may direct for the purpose of adapting them to the circumstances of the meeting.

(5) If at a meeting summoned for the purpose of approving any payment as required by paragraph (*b*) of subsection (3), a quorum is not present and, after the meeting has been adjourned to a later date, a quorum is again not present, the payment shall be deemed, for the purposes of that subsection, to have been approved.

Amendments

a Words 'shall be guilty of an offence and liable to a fine' substituted for 'shall be liable to a fine' in CA 1963, s 188(2) by C(AA)A 2003, Sch 2, Item No. 1.

b '£125' substituted for '£25' by C(A)A 1982, Sch 1, increased to £1,500 by CA 1990, s 240(7) as inserted by CLEA 2001, s 104(c) and converted to €1,904.61 by Council Regulations (EC) No 1103/97, No 974/98 and No 2866/98 and the Economic and Monetary Union Act 1998, s 6.

Cross reference

See CA 1963, s 189: supplemental provisions relating to CA 1963, ss 186–188.

Definitions

'articles': CA 1963, s 2(1); 'company': CA 1963, s 2(1); 'director'[1]: CA 1963, s 2(1); 'holding company': CA 1963, s 2(1), s 155; 'member': CA 1963, s 31; 'Minister': CA 1963, s 2(1); 'share': CA 1963, s 2(1); 'subsidiary': CA 1963, s 2(1), s 155.

1 CA 1963, s 189(5): reference to 'director' in CA 1963, s 186 includes reference to a past director.

Notes

Approval by shareholders: It should be noted that unlike CA 1963, ss 186 and 187, reference is made not to approval by 'members' but instead to approval by 'shareholders'. For the circumstances in which a shareholder might not be a member of the company, see CA 1963, s 31 and notes thereto. The term 'shareholder' could include a person who has acquired shares but has not yet had his name entered in the register of members.[1] In the context of this section, particulars of the proposed payment must be sent to all shareholders whose shares are the subject of the offer, and not just to those shareholders with voting rights.[2] No approval is required, however, for any bona fide payment by way of damages for breach of contract or by way of pension for past services.[3] In this regard, 'pension' includes any superannuation allowance, superannuation gratuity or similar payment.[4]

1 See *Kaye v Croydon Tramways Co* [1898] 1 Ch 358.

2 *Re Duomatic Ltd* [1969] 1 All ER 161.

3 CA 1963, s 189(3). See also *Taupo Totara Timber Co Ltd v Rowe* [1978] AC 537; followed in *Lander v Premier Pict Petroleum Ltd* [1998] BCC 248.

4 CA 1963, s 189(3).

Payment held in trust: The sum is held in trust for those persons who have sold their shares as a result of the offer made[1] rather than for the company as a separate legal entity.[2] It is suggested in *Pennington's Company Law*[3] that the sum held in trust by the director is distributable between the shareholders in question in proportion to the nominal value of their shares, and that if the offer relates to two or more classes of shares, the amount is distributable only between the shareholders of classes which have not approved the making of the payment to the director.

1 CA 1963, s 188(3).

2 Compare this position with payments caught by CA 1963, s 186.

3 Pennington, *Pennington's Company Law* (6th edn, Butterworths, 1990).

UK legislation

See CA 1985, ss 314, 315.

189 Provisions supplementary to sections 186, 187 and 188

(1) Where in proceedings for the recovery of any payment as having, by virtue of subsections (1) and (2) of section 187 or subsections (1) and (3) of section 188, been received by any person in trust, it is shown that—

(a) the payment was made in pursuance of any arrangement entered into as part of the agreement for the transfer in question, or within one year before or 2 years after that agreement or the offer leading thereto; and

(b) the company or any person to whom the transfer was made was privy to that arrangement;

the payment shall be deemed, except in so far as the contrary is shown, to be one to which the subsections apply.

(2) If in connection with any such transfer as is mentioned in section 187 or section 188—

(a) the price to be paid to a director of the company for any shares in the company held by him is in excess of the price which could at the time have been obtained by other holders of the like shares; or

(b) any valuable consideration is given to any such director,

the excess or the money value of the consideration, as the case may be, shall, for the purposes of that section, be deemed to have been a payment made to him by way of compensation for loss of office or as consideration for or in connection with his retirement from office.

(3) It is hereby declared that references in sections 186, 187 and 188 to payments to any director of a company by way of compensation for loss of office, or as consideration for or in connection with his retirement from office, include payments to him by way of compensation for loss of office as director of the company or for the loss, while director of the company, or on or in connection with his ceasing to be a director of the company, of any other office in connection with the management of the company's affairs or of any office as director or otherwise in connection with the management of the affairs of any subsidiary company but do not include any *bona fide* payment by way of damages for breach of contract or by way of pension in respect of past services, and for the purposes of this subsection 'pension' includes any superannuation allowance, superannuation gratuity or similar payment.

(4) Nothing in sections 187 and 188 shall be taken to prejudice the operation of any rule of law requiring disclosure to be made with respect to any such payments as are therein mentioned or with respect to any other like payments made or to be made to the directors of a company or to prejudice the operation of any rule of law in relation to the accountability (if any) of any director for any such payment received by him.

(5) References in sections 186, 187, 188 and this section to a director include references to a past-director.

Cross reference

See CA 1963, ss 186, 187, 188 and notes thereto.For further disclosure requirements that may arise with regard to payments, see CA 1963, s 194. See also CA 1990, ss 29 and 31 and notes thereto.

Definitions

'company': CA 1963, s 2(1); 'director'[1]: CA 1963, s 2(1); 'person': IA 2005, Sch, Pt 1; 'share': CA 1963, s 2(1); 'subsidiary': CA 1963, s 2(1), s 155.

1 CA 1963, s 189(5): reference to 'director' in CA 1963, s 186 includes reference to a past director.

Notes

Directors' remuneration:[1] The purpose of the restrictions imposed by CA 1963, ss 187 and 188 is to prevent an abuse by directors of their position in a take-over either of the company's business or the shareholding in the company. The directors will be aware that once the take-over has been implemented, they may be forced to vacate office. In particular, if the undertaking has been sold, there will be no business left to manage; and if instead the shareholding has been acquired, the new controller will be in a position to use his control of the general meeting to dismiss the existing board and replace it with his own nominees. The purchaser may therefore promise the existing board direct or disguised payments to them for their loss of office in return for their co-operation and assistance in ensuring that the take-over is approved. The purpose of CA 1963, s 189(1), (2) is to prevent the making of disguised payment to the directors in an attempt to circumvent CA 1963, ss 187 and 188.

1 In relation to CA 1963, ss 186–189 generally, see MacCann, 'Directors' Remuneration and Loans Part I' (1991) 9 ILT 250.

UK legislation

See CA 1985, s 316.

190 Register of directors' shareholdings

(1) Every company shall keep a register showing, in relation to each director and secretary of the company, the number, description and amount of any shares in or debentures of the company or any other body corporate, being the company's subsidiary or holding company, or a subsidiary of the company's holding company, which are held by, or in trust for, him or his spouse or any child of his or of which he or they have any right to become the holder (whether on payment or not), so however, that the register need not include shares in any body corporate which is the wholly-owned subsidiary of another body corporate, and for this purpose a body corporate shall be deemed to be the wholly-owned subsidiary of another if it has no members but that other and that other's wholly-owned subsidiaries and its or their nominees.

(2) Subject to subsection (3), where any shares or debentures have to be, or cease to be, recorded in the said register in relation to any director or secretary by reason of a transaction entered into after the operative date and while he is a director or secretary the register shall also show the date of, and price or other consideration for, the transaction.

(3) Where there is an interval between the agreement for any such transaction as aforesaid and the completion thereof, the date shall be that of the agreement.

(4) The nature and extent of the interest or right in or over any shares or debentures recorded in relation to a director or secretary in the said register shall, if he so requires, be indicated in the register.

(5) The company shall not, by virtue of anything done for the purposes of this section, be affected with notice of, or put upon inquiry as to, the rights of any person in relation to any shares or debentures.

(6) Subject to subsection (7), the said register shall be kept at the same office as the register of members is kept, and shall be open to inspection during business hours (subject to such reasonable restrictions as the company may by its articles or in general meeting impose, so that not less than 2 hours in each day be allowed for inspection) by any member or holder of debentures of the company.

(7) The said register shall also be produced at the commencement of the company's annual general meeting and shall remain open and accessible during the continuance of the meeting to any person attending the meeting.

(8) Any member or holder of debentures of the company may require a copy of the register, or of any part thereof, on payment of one shilling, or such less sum as the company may prescribe, for every 100 words or fractional part thereof required to be copied.

The company shall cause any copy so required by any person to be sent to that person within a period of 10 days commencing on the day next after the day on which the requirement is received by the company.

(9) If default is made in complying with subsection (7), the company and every officer of the company who is in default [shall be guilty of an offence and liable to a fine][a] not exceeding [€1,904.61][b]; and if default is made in complying with subsection (1) or subsection (2), or if any inspection required under this section is refused or if any copy required under this section if not sent within the proper period, the company and every officer of the company who is in default [shall be guilty of an offence and liable to a fine][a] not exceeding [€1,904.61][c].

(10) To ensure compliance with the provisions of this section the court may by order compel an inspection of the register or direct that the copies required shall be sent to the persons requiring them.

(11) For the purposes of this section—

(a) any person in accordance with whose directions or instructions the directors of a company are accustomed to act shall be deemed to be a director of the company; and

(b) a person shall be deemed to hold, or to have an interest in or right over, any shares or debentures in which he has an interest jointly or in common with any other person or a limited, reversionary or contingent interest or an interest as the object of a discretionary trust; and

(c) a person shall be deemed to hold, or to have an interest or right in or over any shares or debentures if a body corporate other than the company holds them or has that interest or right in or over them, and either—

   (i) that body corporate or its directors are accustomed to act in accordance with his directions or instructions; or

   (ii) he is entitled to exercise or control the exercise of one-third or more of the voting power at any general meeting of that body corporate.

(12) This section shall not apply to a private company if and so long as all the members of such private company are directors thereof.

Amendments

a Words 'shall be guilty of an offence and liable to a fine' substituted for 'shall be liable to a fine' in both instances where it occurs in CA 1963, s 190(9) by C(AA)A 2003, Sch 2, Item No 4. Notwithstanding the fact that CA 1963, s 190 ceased to have effect on 1 August 1991 (the operative date of CA 1990, s 53), it was amended by C(AA)A 2003.

b '£250' substituted for '£50' by C(A)A 1982, Sch 1, increased to £1,500 by CA 1990, s 240(7) as inserted by CLEA 2001, s 104(c) and converted to €1,904.61 by Council Regulations (EC) No 1103/97, No 974/98 and No 2866/98 and the Economic and Monetary Union Act 1998, s 6.

c '£500' substituted for '£100' by C(A)A 1982, Sch 1, increased to £1,500 by CA 1990, s 240(7) as inserted by CLEA 2001, s 104(c) and converted to €1,904.61 by Council Regulations (EC) No 1103/97, No 974/98 and No 2866/98 and the Economic and Monetary Union Act 1998, s 6.

Cross reference

CA 1990, s 53(11): CA 1963, s 190 has ceased to have effect and is replaced by CA 1990, s 59. In this regard, see generally CA 1990, Pt IV, Ch 1.

Definitions

'articles': CA 1963, s 2(1); 'company': CA 1963, s 2(1); 'the court': CA 1963, s 2(1); 'debenture': CA 1963, s 2(1); 'director': CA 1963, s 2(1) and note that as CA 1963, s 190(11)(a): reference to a director in CA 1963, s 190 includes any person in accordance with whose directions or instructions the directors of a company are accustomed to act; 'holding company': CA 1963, s 2(1), s 155; 'member': CA 1963, s 31; 'officer': CA 1963, s 2(1); 'officer in default': CA 1963, s 383; 'the operative date': CA 1963, s 2(1); 'private company': CA 1963, s 2(1), s 33(1); 'share': CA 1963, s 2(1); 'subsidiary': CA 1963, s 2(1), s 155.

191 Particulars of directors' salaries and payments to be given in accounts

(1) In any accounts of a company laid before the annual general meeting or in a statement annexed thereto, there shall, subject to and in accordance with the provisions of this section, be shown so far as the information is contained in the company's books and papers or the company has the right to obtain it from the persons concerned—

(a) the aggregate amount of the directors' emoluments;

(b) the aggregate amount of directors' or past-directors' pensions; and

(c) the aggregate amount of any compensation to directors or past-directors in respect of loss of office.

(2) The amount to be shown under paragraph (a) of subsection (1)—

(a) shall include any emoluments paid to or receivable by any person in respect of his services as director of the company or in respect of his services, while director of the company, as director of any subsidiary thereof or otherwise in connection with the management of the affairs of the company or any subsidiary thereof; and

(b) shall distinguish between emoluments in respect of services as director, whether of the company or of its subsidiary, and other emoluments;

and, for the purposes of this section, 'emoluments' in relation to a director, includes fees and percentages, any sums paid by way of expenses allowance in so far as those sums are charged to income tax, any contribution paid in respect of him under any pension scheme, and the estimated money value of any other benefits received by him otherwise than in cash in so far as the same are charged to income tax.

(3) The amount to be shown under paragraph (b) of subsection (1) —

(a) shall not include any pension paid or receivable under a pension scheme if the scheme is such that the contributions thereunder are substantially adequate for the maintenance of the scheme, but save as aforesaid, shall include any pension paid or receivable in respect of any such services of a director or past-director of the company as are mentioned in subsection (2), whether to or by him or, on his nomination or by virtue of dependence on or other connection with him, to or by any other person; and

(b) shall distinguish between pensions in respect of services as director, whether of the company or its subsidiary, and other pensions;

and, for the purposes of this section, 'pension' includes any superannuation allowance, superannuation gratuity or similar payment, and 'pension scheme' means a scheme for the provision of pensions in respect of services as director or otherwise which is maintained in whole or in part by means of contributions, and 'contribution' in relation to a pension scheme means any payment (including an insurance premium) paid for the purposes of the scheme by or in respect of persons rendering services in respect of which pensions will or may become payable under the scheme, except that it does not include any payment in respect of two or more persons if the amount paid in respect of each of them is not ascertainable.

(4) The amount to be shown under paragraph (*c*) of subsection (1) —

(a) shall include any sums paid to or receivable by a director or past-director by way of compensation for loss of office as director of the company or for the loss, while director of the company, or on or in connection with his ceasing to be a director of the company, of any other office in connection with the management of the company's affairs or of any office as director or otherwise in connection with the management of the affairs of any subsidiary thereof; and

(b) shall distinguish between compensation in respect of the office of director, whether of the company or of its subsidiary, and compensation in respect of other offices;

and, for the purposes of this section, references to compensation for loss of office shall include sums paid as consideration for or in connection with a person's retirement from office.

(5) The amounts to be shown under each paragraph of subsection (1)—

(a) shall include all relevant sums paid by or receivable from—

(i) the company; and

(ii) the company's subsidiaries; and

(iii) any other person;

except sums to be accounted for to the company or any of its subsidiaries or, by virtue of section 188, to past or present members of the company or any of its subsidiaries or any class of those members; and

(b) shall distinguish, in the case of the amount to be shown under paragraph (*c*) of subsection (1), between the sums respectively paid by or receivable from the company, the company's subsidiaries and persons other than the company and its subsidiaries.

(6) The amounts to be shown under this section for any financial year shall be the sums receivable in respect of that year, whenever paid, or, in the case of sums not receivable in respect of a period, the sums paid during that year, so, however, that where—

(a) any sums are not shown in the accounts for the relevant financial year on the ground that the person receiving them is liable to account therefor as mentioned in paragraph (a) of subsection (5), but the liability is thereafter wholly or partly released or is not enforced within a period of 2 years; or

(b) any sums paid by way of expenses allowances are charged to income tax after the end of the relevant financial year;

those sums shall, to the extent to which the liability is released or not enforced or they are charged as aforesaid, as the case may be, be shown in the first accounts in which it is practicable to show them, or in a statement annexed thereto, and shall be distinguished from the amounts to be shown therein apart from this provision.

(7) Where it is necessary so to do for the purpose of making any distinction required by this section in any amount to be shown thereunder, the directors may apportion any payments between the matters in respect of which they have been paid or are receivable in such manner as they think appropriate.

(8) If in the case of any accounts the requirements of this section are not complied with, it shall be the duty of the auditors of the company by whom the accounts are examined to include in the report thereon, so far as they are reasonably able to do so, a statement giving the required particulars.

(9) In this section, any reference to a company's subsidiary—

(a) in relation to a person who is or was, while a director of the company, a director also, by virtue of the company's nomination, direct or indirect, of any other body corporate, shall, subject to the following paragraph, include that body corporate, whether or not it is or was in fact the company's subsidiary; and

(b) shall, for the purposes of subsections (2) and (3), be taken as referring to a subsidiary at the time the services were rendered, and, for the purposes of subsection (4), be taken as referring to a subsidiary immediately before the loss of office as director of the company.

Cross reference

CA 1963, s 191 does not apply to group accounts prepared in accordance with EC(CGA)R 1992, Sch, Pt 2, para 16(a).

CA 1963, s 191 does not apply to a company to which EC(CI:A) R 1992, reg 7 or EC(IUA)R 1996, reg 10 applies.

CA 1963, s 191 applies to a 'society' (as that term is defined in the Building Society Act 1989) as if the society were a company.

See also C(A)A 1986, Sch paras 36(4), (5), 39(6).

See also CA 1963, s 148: in relation to the accounts which must be laid before the AGM.

See also CA 1990, ss 41–45: with regard to the obligation to disclose particulars of loans and quasi-loans to and credit transactions with directors of the company or of a holding company or with persons connected with such a director.

See also CA 1963, ss 186–189: for other disclosure requirements that arise concerning the payment of compensation for loss of office.

Definitions

'accounts': CA 1963, s 2(1); 'books and paper': CA 1963, s 2(1); 'company': CA 1963, s 2(1); 'director': CA 1963, s 2(1); 'financial year': CA 1963, s 2(1); 'member': CA 1963, s 31; 'subsidiary': CA 1963, s 2(1), s 155.

In CA 1963, s 191 generally, reference to 'emoluments' will be interpreted in accordance with CA 1963, s 191(2); reference to 'pension', 'pension scheme' and 'contributions' will be interpreted in accordance with CA 1963, s 191(3); and reference to 'subsidiary' will be in accordance with CA 1963, s 191(9).

Notes

There is no express obligation to disclose whether the emoluments paid represent the true value of the services rendered by the director.

UK legislation

See CA 1985, s 232; CA 1989, s 6, Sch 6 Pt I; Directors' Remuneration Report Regulations 2002 (SI 2002/1986), reg 2.

---

192 Particulars of loans to directors to be given in accounts

(1) The accounts which, in pursuance of this Act, are to be laid before the annual general meeting of every company shall, subject to the provisions of this section, contain particulars showing—

(a) the amount of any loans made during the company's financial year to—

(i) any director of the company;

(ii) any person who, after the making of the loan, became during that year a director of the company; and

(iii) any body corporate in which the directors of the company (or any of them) are beneficially entitled to more than 20 per cent in nominal value of the shares of such body corporate which carry voting rights other than voting rights which arise only in specified circumstances;

by the company or a subsidiary thereof or by any other person under a guarantee from or on a security provided by the company or a subsidiary thereof (including any such loans which were repaid during that year); and

(b) the amount of any loans made in manner aforesaid to any such director, person or body corporate as aforesaid at any time before the company's financial year and outstanding at the expiration thereof.

(2) Subsection (1) shall not require the inclusion in accounts of particulars of—

(a) a loan made in the ordinary course of its business by the company or a subsidiary thereof, where the ordinary business of the company, or, as the case may be, the subsidiary, includes the lending of money; or

(b) a loan made by the company or a subsidiary thereof to an employee of the company or subsidiary, as the case may be, if the loan does not exceed [€2,539.48][a] and is certified by the directors of the company or subsidiary, as the case may be, to have been made in accordance with any practice adopted or about to be adopted by the company or subsidiary relating to loans to its employees;

not being, in either case, a loan made by the company under a guarantee from or on a security provided by a subsidiary thereof or a loan made by a subsidiary of the company under a guarantee from or on a security provided by the company or any other subsidiary thereof.

(3) If in the case of any such accounts as aforesaid, the requirements of this section are not complied with, it shall be the duty of the auditors of the company by whom the accounts are examined to include in their report on the balance sheet of the company, so far as they are reasonably able to do so, a statement giving the required particulars.

(4) References in this section to a subsidiary shall be taken as referring to a subsidiary at the end of the company's financial year (whether or not a subsidiary at the date of the loan).

Amendments

a £2,000 converted to €2,539.48 by Council Regulations (EC) No 1103/97, No 974/98 and No 2866/98 and the Economic and Monetary Union Act 1998, s 6.

Cross reference

See generally CA 1990, ss 28–40 and notes thereto.

Definitions

'accounts': CA 1963, s 2(1); 'company': CA 1963, s 2(1); 'director': CA 1963, s 2(1); 'financial year': CA 1963, s 2(1); 'share': CA 1963, s 2(1); 'subsidiary': CA 1963, s 2(1), s 155.

Notes

CA 1963, s 192 ceased to have effect by virtue of CA 1990, s 49, except in relation to any accounts and directors' reports for: (i) financial years ending before the commencement of CA 1990, s 49; and (ii) the first financial year after the commencement of CA 1990, s 49, but only in relation to loans and contracts entered into before the commencement of that section.[1]

[1] 1 February 1991: Companies Act 1990 (Commencement) Order 1991 (SI 10/1991).

UK legislation

See also CA 1985, Sch 9, Pt II.

193 General duty to make disclosure for the purposes of sections 190, 191 and 192

(1) It shall be the duty of every director and secretary of a company to give notice in writing to the company as soon as may be of such matters relating to himself and to his spouse and children as may be necessary for the purposes of section 190.

(2) It shall be the duty of every director of a company to give notice in writing to the company of such matters relating to himself as may be necessary for the purposes of sections 191 and 192 except in so far as the latter section relates to loans made by the company or by any other person under a guarantee from or on a security provided by the company to a director thereof.

(3) If any such notice is not given at a meeting of directors, the director or secretary, as the case may be, giving it shall take reasonable steps to secure that it is brought up and read at the next meeting of the directors after it is given.

(4) Any person who fails to comply with this section [shall be guilty of an offence and liable to a fine][a] not exceeding [€1,904.61][b].

Amendments

a Words 'shall be guilty of an offence and liable to a fine' substituted for 'shall be liable to a fine' in CA 1963, s 193(4) by C(AA)A 2003, Sch 2, Item No. 1.

b '£500' substituted for '£100' by C(A)A 1982, Sch 1, increased to £1,500 by CA 1990, s 240(7) as inserted by CLEA 2001, s 104(c) and converted to €1,904.61 by Council Regulations (EC) No 1103/97, No 974/98 and No 2866/98 and the Economic and Monetary Union Act 1998, s 6.

Cross reference

CA 1990, s 53(11): CA 1963, s 193, as much as it relates to CA 1963, s 190 has ceased to have effect and is replaced by CA 1990, s 53. See generally CA 1990, Pt IV, Ch 1.

See also CA 1963, ss 191, 192 and notes thereto.

Definitions

'company': CA 1963, s 2(1); 'director': CA 1963, s 2(1).

UK legislation

See CA 1985, s 232(2); CA 1989, s 6(3); Directors' Remuneration Report Regulations 2002 (SI 2002/1986), reg 2.

---

194 Duty of director to disclose his interest in contracts made by the company

(1) It shall be the duty of a director of a company who is in any way, whether directly or indirectly, interested in a contract or proposed contract with the company to declare the nature of his interest at a meeting of the directors of the company.

(2) In the case of a proposed contract the declaration required by this section to be made by a director shall be made at the meeting of the directors at which the question of entering into the contract is first taken into consideration, or if the director was not at the date of that meeting interested in the proposed contract, at the next meeting of the directors held after he became so interested, and in a case where the director becomes

interested in a contract after it is made, the said declaration shall be made at the first meeting of the directors held after the director becomes so interested.

[(3) Subject to subsection (4), for the purposes of this section, a general notice given to the directors of a company by a director to the effect that—

(a) he is a member of a specified company or firm and is to be regarded as interested in any contract which may, after the date of the notice, be made with that company or firm; or

(b) he is to be regarded as interested in any contract which may after the date of the notice be made with a specified person who is connected with him (within the meaning of section 26 of the Companies Act, 1990),

shall be deemed to be a sufficient declaration of interest in relation to any such contract.] [a]

(4) No such notice as aforesaid shall be of effect unless either it is given at a meeting of the directors or the director takes reasonable steps to secure that it is brought up and read at the next meeting of the directors after it is given.

(5) (a) A copy of every declaration made and notice given in pursuance of this section shall, within 3 days after the making or giving thereof, be entered in a book kept for this purpose. Such book shall be open for inspection without charge by any director, secretary, auditor or member of the company at the registered office of the company and shall be produced at every general meeting of the company, and at any meeting of the directors if any director so requests in sufficient time to enable the book to be available at the meeting.

(b) If a company [fails to comply with this subsection or subsection (5A)][b] the company and every officer of the company who is in default [shall be guilty of an offence and liable to a fine][c] not exceeding [€1,904.61][d] and if any inspection or production required thereunder is refused, the court may by order compel an immediate inspection or production.

[(5A) A company shall, if required by the Director, produce to the Director for inspection the book kept by it in accordance with subsection (5)(a) and shall give the Director such facilities for inspecting and taking copies of the contents of the book as the Director may require.][e]

(6) Any director who fails to comply with this section [shall be guilty of an offence and liable to a fine][f] not exceeding [€1,904.61][d].

(7) Nothing in this section shall be taken to prejudice the operation of any rule of law restricting directors of a company from having any interest in contracts with the company.

Amendments

a CA 1963, s 194(3) substituted by CA 1990, s 47(3).

b Words 'fails to comply with this subsection or subsection (5A)' substituted for 'fails to comply with this subsection' in CA 1963, s 194(5)(b) by C(A)A 2009, s 2(a).

c Words 'shall be guilty of an offence and liable to a fine' substituted for 'shall be liable to a fine' in CA 1963, s 194(5)(b) and (6) by C(AA)A 2003, Sch 2, Item No. 1.

d ‘£500’ substituted for ‘£100’ by C(A)A 1982, Sch 1, increased to £1,500 by CA 1990, s 240(7) as inserted by CLEA 2001, s 104(c) and converted to €1,904.61 by Council Regulations (EC) No 1103/97, No 974/98 and No 2866/98 and the Economic and Monetary Union Act 1998, s 6.

e CA 1963, s 194(5A) inserted by C(A)A 2009, s 2(b).

f Words ‘shall be guilty of an offence and liable to a fine’ substituted for ‘shall be liable to a fine’ in CA 1963, s 194(6) and (6) by C(AA)A 2003, Sch 2, Item No. 1.

Cross references

See CA 1990, ss 26, 27 and 47 and notes thereto.

In the case of certain designated bodies, such as Bord na Móna, Coras Iompair Éireann, the provisions of CA 1963, s 194 do not apply but are instead replaced by the provisions of s 20 of the Worker Participation (State Enterprises) Acts 1977 and 1988.

Definitions

‘company’: CA 1963, s 2(1); ‘connected person’: CA 1990, s 26; ‘the court’: CA 1963, s 2(1); ‘director’: CA 1963, s 2(1); ‘member’: CA 1963, s 31; ‘officer’: CA 1963, s 2(1); ‘officer in default’: CA 1963, s 383.

Notes

What requires to be disclosed?: Any direct or indirect interest of a director in any contract or proposed contract with the company must be disclosed. It is important to note that there is no *de minimis* and on its fact the provision appears to apply to every contract. In practice, this provision has been interpreted as only applying to contracts or proposed contracts that are such as to be considered by a company’s board of directors and not to apply to contracts entered into by companies in the ordinary course of business at arms’ length. The primary obligation is contained in sub-s (1) and this only applies to contracts in which *directors* are directly or indirectly interested. Curiously, sub-s (3), inserted by the CA 1990, facilitates the giving of a general notice by a director to the effect that (a) he is a member of a specified company or firm and so is to be regarded as interested in any contract made with that company or firm and (b) he is to be regarded as interested in any contract made with a person who is connected to him within the meaning of CA 1990, s 26. Given that there is no obligation to notify interests in contracts between a director’s company and persons connected with a director, this provision can only apply to where a director is beneficially interested in a contract made between his company and such people.

What constitutes effective disclosure?: Disclosure, to be effective under CA 1963, s 194, must be to the full board duly convened and not merely to a sub-committee of the board.[1] Moreover, disclosure must be to an independent board of directors and not to directors who are equally interested in the contract.[2]

1 *Guinness plc v Saunders* [1988] 2 All ER 940.

2 *Hopkins v Shannon Transport Ltd* (10 July 1972, unreported) HC (Pringle J).

Consequences of disclosure: Subject to certain statutory restrictions[1] and subject to the disclosure requirements laid down by CA 1963, s 194, Table A, Pt I, reg 85 permits directors to be interested in contracts with the company. However, if a director fails to disclose his interest in a contract pursuant to CA 1963, s 194, then he loses the protection of Table A, Pt I, reg 85, and in addition to being liable to a fine[2] the contract generally becomes voidable at the instance of the company[3] and he becomes accountable for any profits which he has made.[4] Under Table A, Pt II, reg 7, a director of a private company may be counted towards a quorum and vote in favour of a contract in which he is interested and has disclosed such interest.

1 See CA 1990, ss 28–40 and notes thereto for statutory restrictions on contracts between directors and the company.

2 CA 1963, s 194(6).

3 *Craven Textile Engineers Ltd v Batley Football Club Ltd* [2001] BCC 697: in the particular circumstances of that case, the parties could not be restored to their original position, therefore it was held that the company could not avoid the contract, notwithstanding the fact that the director had failed to disclose his interest. See also *Aberdeen Railway Co v Blaikie Bros* (1854) 1 Macq 461; *Bristol & West Building Society v Mothew* [1996] 4 All ER 698; *Gwembe Valley Development Co Ltd v Koshy* [2004] 1 BCLC 131; *Newgate Stud Co v Penfold* [2008] 1 BCLC 46.

4 *Guinness plc v Saunders* [1988] 2 All ER 940; *Hely-Hutchinson v Brayhead Ltd* [1967] 3 All ER 98; *Hopkins v Shannon Transport Ltd* (10 July 1972, unreported) HC (Pringle J); *Aberdeen Railway Co v Blaikie Bros* (1854) 1 Macq 461; *Bristol & West Building Society v Mothew* [1996] 4 All ER 698; *Gwembe Valley Development Co Ltd v Koshy* [2004] 1 BCLC 131; *Newgate Stud Co v Penfold* [2008] 1 BCLC 46.

Shadow directors: The disclosure requirements contained in CA 1963, s 1990 also extend to shadow directors.[1] In the case of a shadow director, disclosure, rather than being made at a board meeting, is made by notice in writing to the directors.[2] It seems implicit from subsection (3)(b) that he is to be deemed to be interested in any contract in which a person connected with him is interested. However, at common law a fiduciary was not to be regarded as under an automatic duty of disclosure in respect of a transaction between the company and his spouse or domestic partner, at least unless that spouse or partner was acting as his nominee: *Newgate Stud Co v Penfold* [2008] 1 BCLC 46.

1 CA 1990, s 27(3).

2 CA 1990, s 27(3).

Deemed interest: A director or shadow director is deemed to be interested in transactions and arrangements of the kind described in CA 1990, s 31 (ie loans, quasi-loans, credit transactions etc.).[1] It seems implicit from subsection (3)(b) that he is to be deemed to be interested in any contract in which a person connected with him is interested. However, at common law a fiduciary was not to be regarded as under an automatic duty of disclosure in respect of a transaction between the company and his spouse or domestic partner, at least unless that spouse or partner was acting as his nominee.[2]

1 CA 1990, s 47(2).

2 *Newgate Stud Co v Penfold* [2008] 1 BCLC 46.

Right to inspect book in which declarations are kept: The ODCE has the right to require companies to produce for inspection the book in which declarations are kept and to provide facilities for inspecting and taking copies of its contents.

UK legislation

See also CA 1985, s 317.

[195 Register of directors and secretaries

(1) Every company shall keep at its registered office a register of its directors and secretaries.

(2) Subject to subsection (3), the said register shall contain the following particulars relating to each director—

(a) his present forename and surname and any former fore-name and surname; and

(b) his date of birth; and

(c) his usual residential address; and

(d) his nationality; and

(e) his business occupation, if any; and

(f) particulars of any other directorships of bodies corporate, whether incorporated in the State or elsewhere, held by him or which have been held by him.

(3) It shall not be necessary for the said register to contain on any day particulars of any directorship—

(a) which has not been held by a director at any time during the ten years preceding that day;

(b) which is held or was held by a director in bodies corporate of which the company is or was the wholly owned subsidiary or which are or were the wholly owned subsidiaries either of the company or of another body corporate of which the company is or was the wholly owned subsidiary;

and for the purposes of this subsection a body corporate shall be deemed to be the wholly owned subsidiary of another if it has no members except that other and that other's wholly owned subsidiaries and its or their nominees.

(4) Subject to subsection (5), the said register shall contain the following particulars relating to the secretary or, where there are joint secretaries, in relation to each of them—

(a) in the case of an individual, his present forename and surname, any former forename and surname and his usual residential address; and

(b) in the case of a body corporate, the corporate name and registered office.

(5) Where all partners in a firm are joint secretaries of a company, the name and principal office of the firm may be stated instead of the said particulars.

(6) The company shall, within the period of 14 days from the happening of—

(a) any change among its directors or in its secretary, or

(b) any change in any of the particulars contained in the register,

send to the registrar of companies a notification in the prescribed form of the change and of the date on which it occurred.[b]

(6A) In the case of a person who is a director of more than one company (the 'relevant companies') the following provisions apply—

(a) the person may send a notification in the prescribed form to the registrar of companies of a change in his or her usual residential address or of a change in his or her name and (in each case) of the date on which the change occurred,

(b) if such a notification is sent to the registrar and the relevant companies are listed in the notification as being companies of which the person is a director—

(i) each of the relevant companies shall be relieved, as respects, and only as respects, that particular change or, as the case may be, those particular changes, of the obligation under subsection (6) to send a notification of it or them to the registrar,

and

(ii) the registrar may proceed to record the relevant change or changes concerning the person in relation to each of the relevant companies.

(7) A notification sent to the registrar of companies pursuant to subsection (6) of the appointment of a person as a director, secretary or joint secretary of a company shall be accompanied by a consent signed by that person to act as director, secretary or joint secretary, as the case may be.

[(8) Without prejudice to subsection (7), if the notification to be sent to the registrar of companies pursuant to subsection (6) is a notification of the appointment of a person as a director of a company and that person is a person who is disqualified under the law of another state (whether pursuant to an order of a judge or a tribunal or otherwise) from being appointed or acting as a director or secretary of a body corporate or an undertaking, that person shall ensure that the notification is accompanied by (but as a separate document from the notification) a statement in the prescribed form signed by him specifying—

(a) the jurisdiction in which he is so disqualified,

(b) the date on which he became so disqualified, and

(c) the period for which he is so disqualified.][c]

(9) Subsection (6) shall not apply to any change in the particulars contained in a company's register of directors and secretaries made solely by reason of the coming into force of section 51 of the Companies Act, 1990 but if after any such change has occurred and before the company makes its next annual return, any other change in those particulars occurs, the company shall send to the registrar of companies a notification in the prescribed form of any such earlier changes and the date on which they occurred at the same time as it notifies the registrar of the later changes in accordance with this section.

(10) The register to be kept under this section shall, during business hours (subject to such reasonable restrictions as the company may by its articles or in general meeting impose, so that not less than 2 hours in each day be allowed for inspection) be open to the inspection of any member of the company without charge, and of any other person, on payment of one pound or such less sum as the company may prescribe, for each inspection.

[(10A) Any member of a company or other person may require the company to supply to him a copy of the register required to be kept under this section, or any part of the register, on payment of [19c][d], or such less sum as the company may prescribe, for every hundred words or fractional part thereof required to be copied. The company shall cause a copy so required by a person to be sent to the person within 10 days of the receipt by the company of the request, and if it fails to do so it shall be guilty of an offence.][e]

(11) It shall be the duty of each director and secretary of a company to give information in writing to the company as soon as may be of such matters as may be necessary to enable the company to comply with this section.

[(11A) If a company fails to send, in accordance with subsection (6), a notification, in the prescribed form, to the registrar of companies of the fact of a person's having ceased, for whatever reason, to be a director or secretary of the company and of the date on which that event occurred that person may serve on the company a notice—

(a) requesting it to send forthwith the notification of that matter, in the prescribed form, to the registrar, and

(b) stating that if the company fails to comply with that request within 21 days of the service of the notice on it, he will forward to the registrar of companies and to every person who, to his knowledge, is an officer of the company a copy of any notice of resignation by him as a director or secretary of the company or any other documentary proof of his having ceased to be such a director or secretary together with—

(i) in the case of the registrar of companies, such additional information as may be prescribed (which may include a statutory declaration made by the person stating the names of the persons who, to his knowledge, are officers of the company), and

(ii) in the case of every other person as aforesaid, a written request of the person that he take such steps as will ensure that the failure of the company to comply with the notice continues no further.

(11B) If a company fails to comply with a request made of it under a notice referred to in subsection (11A) the person who served the notice may forward to the registrar of companies and to every person who, to his knowledge, is an officer of the company a copy of the notice of resignation or other documentary proof referred to in subsection (11A) if, but only if, there is forwarded together with that notice or proof, in the case of the registrar, the additional information referred to in that subsection and, in the case of every other person as aforesaid, the written request referred to in that subsection.

(11C) No notice of resignation or other documentary proof of a person's having ceased to be a director or secretary of a company which is forwarded to the registrar of companies by that person (other than such a notice or other proof which is forwarded by him under and in accordance with subsections (11A) and (11B), or section 43(9) of the Companies (Amendment) (No. 2) Act, 1999) shall be considered by the registrar.

(11D) No additional information referred to in subsection (11A)(b)(i) that is included in a notice of resignation or other documentary proof referred to in this section which is forwarded, under and in accordance with the foregoing provisions, to the registrar of companies shall, of itself, be regarded as constituting defamatory matter.

(11E) Any person may give notice (accompanied by such proof of the matter concerned as may be prescribed) to the registrar of companies of the fact that a person holding the office of director or secretary of a particular company has died.][f]

(12) If an inspection required under this section is refused or if default is made in complying with subsections (1), (2), (4), (6) or (7), the company and every officer of the company who is in default [shall be guilty of an offence and liable to a fine][g] not exceeding [€1,904.61][h] and, for continued contravention, to a daily default fine not exceeding [€63.49][i].

(13) In the case of any such refusal, the court may by order compel an immediate inspection of the register.

(14) A person who fails to comply with subsection (11) shall be guilty of an offence and liable to a fine.

(15) For the purposes of this section—

(a) in the case of a person usually known by a title different from his surname, the expression 'surname' means that title;

(b) references to a 'former forename' or 'surname' do not include—

(i) in the case of a person usually known by a title different from his surname, the name by which he was known previous to the adoption of or succession to the title; or

(ii) in the case of any person, a former forename or surname where that name or surname was changed or disused before the person bearing the name attained the age of 18 years or has been changed or disused for a period of not less than 20 years; or

(iii) in the case of a married woman, the name or surname by which she was known previous to the marriage.][a]

Amendments

a CA 1963, s 195 substituted by CA 1990, s 51.

b CA 1963, s 195(6A) inserted by IFCMPA 2005, s 62. This provision has not yet been commenced.

c CA 1963, s 195(8) substituted by C(A)A 1982, s 8; deleted by C(A)(No 2)A 1999 s 47; inserted by CLEA 2001, s 91. CA 1963, s 195(8) is not yet operative.

d 15p converted to 19c by Council Regulations (EC) No 1103/97, No 974/98 and No 2866/98 and the Economic and Monetary Union Act 1998, s 6.

e CA 1963, s 10A inserted by CLEA 2001, s 91.

f CA 1963, ss (11A) – (11E) inserted by CLEA C(A)(No 2)A 1999, s 47.

g Words 'shall be guilty of an offence and liable to a fine' substituted for 'shall be liable to a fine' in CA 1963, s 195(12) by C(AA)A 2003, Sch 2.

h £1,000 increased to £1,500 by CA 1990, s 240(7) as inserted by CLEA 2001, s 104(c) and converted to €1,904.61 by Council Regulations (EC) No 1103/97, No 974/98 and No 2866/98 and the Economic and Monetary Union Act 1998, s 6.

i £50 converted to €63.49 by Council Regulations (EC) No 1103/97, No 974/98 and No 2866/98 and the Economic and Monetary Union Act 1998, s 6.

Cross reference

The phrase 'directors' is deemed to include 'shadow directors': CA 1990, s 27(1).

See also CA 1990, s 51.

Definitions

'annual return': CA 1963, s 2(1); 'articles': CA 1963, s 2(1); 'company': CA 1963, s 2(1); 'the court': CA 1963, s 2(1); 'director': CA 1963, s 2(1); 'member': CA 1963, s 31; 'officer': CA 1963, s 2(1); 'officer in default': CA 1963, s 383; 'person': IA 2005, s 18(c); 'Registrar of Companies': CA 1963, s 2(1); 'subsidiary': CA 1963, s 2(1), s 155.

Notes

Register of directors and secretaries: Companies registered under the Companies Acts and certain unregistered companies[1] must keep a register of directors and secretaries.[2] The register must show for each director: name; any former name (other than where a woman has changed her name on marriage); usual residential address; nationality; occupation; other directorships; and date of birth.[3] 'Other directorships' includes directorships in all bodies corporate, irrespective of where registered, and director ships held in the previous ten years.[4] It is not necessary to list companies which are wholly owned within the same group of companies.[5] The register must show for secretaries: name, former name; and usual residential address.[6] If the secretary is a body corporate, its corporate name and the address of its registered or principal office must be shown.[7] Where all the partners of a firm are joint secretaries, the name and principal office of the firm may be stated instead.[8] The Company must inform the Registrar or any change on the register within 14 days.[9] CA 1963, s 195(6A) gives effect to the recommendation of the CLRG[10] that a director should, by way of a single prescribed form, be able to file a change of personal details with the Registrar in respect of more than one company. However, CA 1963, s 195(6A) has yet to be commenced. It is the duty if each director and secretary to give information in writing to the company as soon as may be necessary to enable the company to comply with CA 1963, s 195[11] and failure to provide this information is an offence and liable to a fine.[12]

1 CA 1963, s 377 and Sch 9.
2 CA 1963, s 195(1).
3 CA 1963, s 195(2).
4 CA 1963, s 195(3)(a).
5 CA 1963, s 195(3)(b).
6 CA 1963, s 195(4)(a).
7 CA 1963, s 195(4)(b).
8 CA 1963, s 195(5).
9 CA 1963, s 195(6)(b).
10 The Company Law Review Group, First Report, para 7.8.3.
11 CA 1963, s 195(11).
12 CA 1963, s 195(14). CA 1990, s 240(2)(a): as the amount of the fine is not specified it will be an amount not exceeding €1,904.61.

Consent and ability of directors and secretaries to act: Prior to the enactment of C(A)A 1982, s 3, although every company was required to notify the Registrar of any change in its directors or secretary,[1] there was no requirement to notify him of the first such officers. This lacuna was filled by imposing an obligation on the company's subscribers to deliver to the Registrar, prior to incorporation, not only a copy of the memorandum and articles of association,[2] but also a statement in the prescribed form[3] containing particulars of the first directors and secretary as well as their signed consents to so act.[4] On appointment, any director or secretary, must also confirm their consent to act.[5]

If any person notified to the Registrar as a director is disqualified under the law of another state from being appointed or acting as a director of a body corporate or undertaking, that person must ensure that the statement delivered to the Registrar is accompanied by a separate document in the prescribed form, signed by him specifying the jurisdiction in which he is disqualified, the date of his disqualification and the period of his disqualification.[6] If he fails to do so, or if he signs such a statement knowing it to be false or misleading in any material respect, he will automatically be disqualified in this jurisdiction for a period equivalent to the unexpired term of the foreign disqualification order or orders.[7]

1 CA 1963, s 195(6) and (7) (before amendment by C(A)A 1982, s 8).
2 CA 1963, s 17 (as amended by CLEA 2001, s 80).
3 Companies (Forms) (No 2) Order 2004 (SI 829/2004), Form A1.
4 C(A)A 1982, s 3(1) and (2).
5 CA 1963, s 195(7) (as amended by C(A)A 1982, s 8).
6 CA 1963, s 195(6A). See Companies (Forms) (No 2) Order 2002 (SI 2002/54), Form B74. In relation to the disqualification of directors and secretaries, see CA 1990, Pt VII, Ch 2. See also CA 1963, s 176 (prohibition of body corporate being a director).
7 CA 1990, s 160(1A) and (1B) as amended by CLEA 2001, ss 14 and 42.

Notification to the registrar of cessation to act as a director or secretary: It was possible for any person who had ceased to be a director or secretary of a company to send to the Registrar a notification of their ceasing to so act as at a particular date.[1] However, it became apparent that such a provision would cause serious administrative difficulties as it could result in companies remaining on the register, notwithstanding the fact that such companies had no registered directors or secretary. This would arise in circumstances where the company did not notify the Registrar, of officers who would replace those ceasing to act. Therefore, it was decided not to commence this particular subsection of CA 1990, s 51. However, it was recognised that provision should be made for officers to be able to notify the Registrar in circumstances where they had ceased to act and the company had not made the appropriate notification to the Registrar and therefore C(A)(No 2)A 1999, s 47 introduced CA 1963, s 195(11A)–(11E).

CA 1963, s 195(11A)–(11E) allow a director or secretary of a company, in circumstances where the company has not made the necessary notification to the Registrar, to notify the Registrar of their ceasing to act subject to certain conditions. Firstly, the director or secretary must request the that the company notify the Registrar, stating that if the company fails to so notify the Registrar within 21 days, that the director or secretary will sent to the Registrar and all other officers of the company a copy of his resignation.[2] Such a director or secretary must make a statutory declaration stating the names of the persons to are 'to his knowledge' officers of the company.[3] If the company fails to notify the Registrar as requested, the director or secretary may then proceed to notify the Registrar of his cessation to act.[4] No representation made pursuant to this section to the Registrar will be regard as constituting defamatory matter.[5] Any person may give notice to the Registrar (accompanied by the prescribed proof)[6] of the death of any director or secretary.[7]

1 See CA 1963, s 195(8)(as inserted by CA 1990, s 51, but not commenced), prior to its deletion by C(A)(No 2)A 1999, s 47 and replacement by CLEA 2001, s 91.

2 CA 1963, s 195(11A).

3 CA 1963, s 195(11A)(b); Companies (Forms) Order 2000 (SI 62/2000): Form B69.

4 CA 1963, s 195(11B).

5 CA 1963, s 195(11D).

6 Companies (Forms) Order 2000 (SI 62/2000): Form B70, accompanied with official copy death certificate.

7 CA 1963, s 195(11E).

Inspection of registers: The register of directors and secretaries must be kept at the registered office of the company. Subject to such reasonable restrictions as the articles or the company in general meeting may impose, the register must be available for inspection by members and non-members during business hours. Notwithstanding any such restrictions, the register must be available for inspection for not less than two hours each business day. There is no charge to members for inspecting the register, however, non-members may be required to pay a fee of €1.27.[1] In addition, members and non-members may require the company to supply copies of the register (or part thereof) on payment of a maximum of 19c[2] for every 100 words to be copied; such copies to be supplied within ten days of receipt of the request by the company.[3]

1 CA 1963, s 195(10).

2 '15p' converted to 19c by Council Regulations (EC) No 1103/97, No 974/98 and No 2866/98 and the Economic and Monetary Union Act 1998, s 6.

3 CA 1963, s 195(10A).

UK legislation

See CA 1985, s 288, 289 and 290; CA 1989, ss 23, Sch 10 para 9; 143(6); 145, Sch 19, para 2, 3; 212, Sch 24; The Companies (Particulars of Usual Residential Address)(Confidentiality Orders) Regulations 2002, r 16, Sch 2; Criminal Justice and Police Act 2001, s 45(1), (3); The Companies Act (Audit Exemption)(Amendment) Regulations 2000, r 8(7).

196 Particulars relating to directors to be shown on all business letters of the company

(1) Subject to subsection (2), every company to which this section applies shall, in all business letters on or in which the company's name appears and which are sent by the company to any person, state in legible characters in relation to every director the following particulars:

(a) his present Christian name, or the initials thereof, and present surname; and

(b) any former Christian names and surnames; and

(c) his nationality, if not Irish.

(2) If special circumstances exist which render it in the opinion of the Minister expedient that such an exemption should be granted, the Minister may, subject to such conditions as he may think fit, grant exemption from the obligations imposed by this section.

(3) This section shall apply to—

(a) every company registered under this Act or under the Companies (Consolidation) Act, 1908, unless it was registered before the 23rd day of November, 1916, and

(b) every company incorporated outside the State which has an established place of business within the State, unless it had established such a place of business before the said date; and

(c) every company licensed under the Moneylenders Act, 1933, whenever it was registered or whenever it established a place of business.

(4) Subject to subsection (5), if a company makes default in complying with this section, every officer of the company who is in default shall be liable on summary conviction for each offence to a fine not exceeding [€1,904.61],[a] and, for the purpose of this subsection, where a body corporate is an officer of the company, any officer of the body corporate shall be deemed to be an officer of the company.

(5) No proceedings shall be instituted under this section except by, or with the consent of, the Minister.

(6) For the purposes of this section—

(a) 'director' includes any person in accordance with whose directions or instructions the directors of the company are accustomed to act, and 'officer' shall be construed accordingly; and

(b) 'initials' includes a recognised abbreviation of a Christian name; and paragraphs (b), (c) and (d) of subsection (12) of section 195 shall apply as they apply for the purposes of that section.

Amendments

a '£125' substituted for '£25' by C(A)A 1982, Sch 1, increased to £1,500 by CA 1990, s 240(7) as inserted by CLEA 2001, s 104(c) and converted to €1,904.61 by Council Regulations (EC) No 1103/97, No 974/98 and No 2866/98 and the Economic and Monetary Union Act 1998, s 6.

Cross reference

See CA 1990, s 27(1): the definition of 'director' in CA 1963, s 196 is remarkably similar to that definition of 'shadow director'.

See also CA 1963, s 195(15): in relation to use of names.[1]

See also CA 1963, s 114 and notes thereto: further disclosure requirements on companies.

See also CA 1963, s 352 and notes thereto: a foreign company which has an established place of business in the State is required to register as an external company.[2]

1 Presumably reference in CA 1963, s 196(6) to CA 1963, s 195(12)(b),(c) and (d) should be to CA 1963, s 195(15).

2 See generally CA 1963, Pt XI and Gill, 'Foreign Companies and Establishing 'A Place of Business'' (1989) ILT 264

Definitions

'company': CA 1963, s 2(1); 'director': CA 1963, s 2(1), s 196(6); 'Minister': CA 1963, s 2(1); 'officer': CA 1963, s 2(1); 'officer in default': CA 1963, s 383.

In CA 1963, s 196 generally, reference to 'director' will be interpreted in accordance with CA 1963, s 196(6)(b).

Notes

Company letterhead disclosure requirements: The requirements of CA 1963, s 196 apply to companies registered under the Companies Acts and under the Companies (Consolidation) Act 1908,[1] foreign companies with an established place of business in the State[2] and all companies registered under the Moneylenders Act 1933.[3] The Minister for Enterprise Trade and Employment may grant a exemption from these requirements (subject to such conditions as he may require).[4] The Minister for Enterprise Trade and Employment, in deciding whether such an exemption should be granted, will consider whether a company has a history of frequent changes of director and whether its annual returns are up to date.[5] It is the Minister who may institute or give consent to the institution of proceedings under this section.[6]

1 CA 1963, s 196(3)(a).

2 CA 1963, s 196(3)(b).

3 CA 1963, s 196(3)(c). The Moneylenders Act 1933 was repealed and replaced by the Consumer Credit Act 1995. See IA 2005, s 26(2).

4 CA 1963, s 196(2).

5 See the website of the Department of Enterprise, Trade and Employment: http://www.entemp.ie. A subsidiary,whose parent company has been granted the exemption, may also be granted the exemption if the parent company's annual returns are up to date.

6 CA 1963, s 196(5).

UK legislation

See CA 1985, s 305; CA 1989, s 145, Sch 19, para 4.

---

197 Limited company may have directors with unlimited liability

(1) In a limited company the liability of the directors, or of the managing director, may, if so provided by the memorandum, be unlimited.

(2) In a limited company in which the liability of a director is unlimited, the directors of the company and the member who proposes a person for election or appointment to the office of director, shall add to that proposal a statement that the liability of the person

holding that office will be unlimited, and before the person accepts the office or acts therein, notice in writing that his liability will be unlimited shall be given to him by the following or one of the following persons, namely, the promoters of the company, the directors of the company, and the secretary of the company.

(3) If any director or proposer makes default in adding such a statement, or if any promoter or director or secretary makes default in giving such a notice, he [shall be guilty of an offence and liable to a fine][a] not exceeding [€1,904.61][b] and shall also be liable for any damage which the person so elected or appointed may sustain from the default, but the liability of the person elected or appointed shall not be affected by the default.

Amendments

a Words 'shall be guilty of an offence and liable to a fine' substituted for 'shall be liable to a fine' in CA 1963, s 197(3) by C(AA)A 2003, Sch 2, Item No. 1.

b '£500' substituted for '£100' by C(A)A 1982, Sch 1, increased to £1,500 by CA 1990, s 240(7) as inserted by CLEA 2001, s 104(c) and converted to €1,904.61 by Council Regulations (EC) No 1103/97, No 974/98 and No 2866/98 and the Economic and Monetary Union Act 1998, s 6.

Cross reference

See CA 1963, s 207(2): includes directors with unlimited liability as being a class of contributory, bound to contribute to the assets of a company in the event of its being wound up.

See CA 1963, s 5(2)(a), (b): reference to 'company limited by shares' and 'company limited by guarantee'.

Definitions

'company': CA 1963, s 2(1); 'director': CA 1963, s 2(1) 'member': CA 1963, s 31; 'memorandum': CA 1963, s 2(1).

Notes

Consequences of failure to notify: The directors or members proposing a person for election as a director of a company which provides in its memorandum of association that the liability of such a director is unlimited are obliged to make this fact known to the proposed director (i) in a statement contained in the proposal of that director and (ii) by notice in writing prior to the proposed director being appointed or acting as such.[1] In the event that any proposer, director or secretary fails to include such a statement or give such a notice, then they will be guilty of an offence and liable to a fine of up to €1,904.61. In addition, notwithstanding the fact that the director so appointed continues to have unlimited liability, the promotor, director or secretary in default is also liable for any damage which that person suffers as a result of their default.[2]

1 CA 1963, s 197(2).

2 See MacCann, 'Personal Liability for Corporate Debts' (1991) 9 ILT 206.

UK legislation

See CA 1985, s 306.

---

198 Power of limited company to make liability of directors unlimited

(1) A limited company, if so authorised by its articles, may, by special resolution, alter its memorandum so as to render unlimited the liability of its directors or of any managing director.

(2) Upon the passing of any such special resolution, the provisions thereof shall be as valid as if they had been originally contained in the memorandum.

Cross reference

See CA 1963, s 207(2): includes directors with unlimited liability as being a class of contributory, bound to contribute to the assets of a company in the event of its being wound up.

See CA 1963, s 5(2)(a), (b): reference to 'company limited by shares' and 'company limited by guarantee'.

Definitions

'articles': CA 1963, s 2(1); 'company': CA 1963, s 2(1); 'director': CA 1963, s 2(1); 'memorandum': CA 1963, s 2(1).

Notes

CLRG: The CLRG has recommended that CA 1963, s 198 be repealed on the grounds of obsolescence.[1]

Prospective effect only:[2] Presumably any such amendment could only operate prospectively. Any attempt to make the amendment retrospective by imposing personal liability on the director for debts of the company which had already accrued could amount to an unjust attack and unconstitutional attack on his property rights.[3] The effect of CA 1963, s 198(2) is that the company is relieved from the necessity of having the memorandum in its altered form signed again by the subscribers, attested by witnesses and then reprinted.[4]

1 The Company Law Review Group, First Report (2001), para 6.11.1.

2 See MacCann, Personal Liability for Corporate Debts (1991) 9 ILT 206.

3 *Re Hefferon Kearns Ltd* [1992] ILRM 51; *Hamilton v Hamilton* [1982] IR 466; *O'H v O'H* [1991] ILRM 108. See also *Delaney* (1992) ILT (ns) 133.

4 *Northern Bank Finance Corp Ltd v Quinn* [1979] ILRM 221.

UK legislation

See CA 1985, s 307.

199 Provisions as to assignment of office by directors

If in the case of any company provision is made by the articles or by any agreement entered into between any person and the company for empowering a director of the company to assign his office as such to another person, any assignment of office made in pursuance of the said provision shall, notwithstanding anything to the contrary contained in the said provision, be of no effect unless and until it is approved by a special resolution of the company.

Cross reference

See also Table A, Pt II, reg 9: appointment of alternate directors.

Definitions

'articles': CA 1963, s 2(1); 'company': CA 1963, s 2(1); 'director': CA 1963, s 2(1).

Notes

Assignment of office: Table A does not provide for the assignment of the office of director; the articles of association of a company will have to provide specifically for such a power of assignment. A distinction can be made between the appointment of an alternate director (which is provided for in Table A[1] in respect of private companies), in that an assigning director ceases to act as a director, however a director appointing an alternate continues in office. In addition, the appointment of an alternate director must be approved by a majority of the directors rather than by special resolution of the members. CA 1963, s 199 does not apply to a power to appoint a successor upon death.[2]

1 CA 1963, Sch I, Table A, Pt II, reg 9.

2 *Fitzpatrick v Fitzpatricks Footwear Ltd* (18 November 1970, unreported) HC (Kenny J).

UK legislation

See CA 1985, s 308.

Avoidance of Provisions in Articles or Contracts relieving Officers from Liability

200 Avoidance of provisions exempting officers and auditors of company from liability

[(1)][a] Subject as hereinafter provided, any provision whether contained in the articles of a company or in any contract with a company or otherwise for exempting any officer of the company or any person employed by the company as auditor from, or indemnifying him against, any liability which by virtue of any rule of law would otherwise attach to him in respect of any negligence, default, breach of duty or breach of trust of which he may be guilty in relation to the company shall be void, so, however, that—

(a) nothing in this section shall operate to deprive any person of any exemption or right to be indemnified in respect of anything done or omitted to be done by him while any such provision was in force; and

(b) notwithstanding anything in this section, a company may, in pursuance of any such provision as aforesaid, indemnify any such officer or auditor against any liability incurred by him in defending proceedings, whether civil or criminal, in which judgment is given in his favour or in which he is acquitted, or in connection with any application under section 391 [or section 42 of the Companies (Amendment) Act, 1983][b] in which relief is granted to him by the court.

[(2) Notwithstanding subsection (1), a company may purchase and maintain for any of its officers or auditors insurance in respect of any liability referred to in that subsection.

(3) Notwithstanding any provision contained in an enactment, the articles of a company or otherwise, a director may be counted in the quorum and may vote on any resolution to purchase or maintain any insurance under which the director might benefit.

(4) Any directors' and officers' insurance purchased or maintained by a company before the date on which the amendments made to this section by the Companies (Auditing and Accounting) Act 2003 came into operation is as valid and effective as it would have

been if those amendments had been in operation when that insurance was purchased or maintained.

(5) In this section a reference to an officer or auditor includes any former or current officer or auditor of the company, as the case may be.][c]

Amendments

a CA 1963, s 200 renumbered as s 200(1) by C(AA)A 2003, s 56.[1]

b Words 'or section 42 of the Companies (Amendment) Act, 1983' inserted by C(A)A 1983, Sch 1, para 16.

c CA 1963, s 200(2)–(5) inserted by C(AA)A 2003, s 56.

1 Amendments to CA 1963, s 200 were introduced to the Companies (Auditing and Accounting) Bill 2003 by way of amendment at the Select Committee on Enterprise and Small Business, 4 December 2003.

Cross reference

See also CA 1963, s 391 and notes thereto; C(A)A 1983, s 42 and notes thereto.

Definitions

'articles': CA 1963, s 2(1); 'company': CA 1963, s 2(1); 'the court': CA 1963, s 2(1); 'officer': CA 1963, s 2(1).

Notes

Directors' and officers' insurance: Prior to 6 April 2004,[1] there was significant doubt as to the effectiveness of directors' and officers' insurance policies. Notwithstanding this doubt, such policies were freely available and availed of by companies to which CA 1963, s 200 applied. The CLRG recommended that CA 1963, s 200 should be amended to specifically permit companies to take out and fund directors' and officers' insurance.[2] It is now clear that a company may purchase and maintain insurance in respect of any liability in respect of any negligence, default, breach of duty or breach of trust on the part of an officer or auditor.[3] At any meeting of the board of directors where the purchase of such a policy of insurance is approved, a director, who may benefit from such insurance, may count towards a quorum and vote on any such resolution.[4] Policies of insurance purchased prior to the 6 April 2004 are to be treated as valid, notwithstanding the fact that CA 1963, s 200(2) had not yet come into effect.[5]

1 Companies (Auditing and Accounting) Act, 2003 (Commencement) Order, 2004 (SI 132/2004).

2 The Company Law Review Group, First Report, para 11.6.4.

3 CA 1963, s 200(2).

4 CA 1963, s 200(3).

5 CA 1963, s 200(4).

Release from liability by agreement: Although a provision in an agreement with a director waiving or exempting liability will be void, it is permissible for the company to draft its articles in such a way that, by modifying the directors' duties, the possibility of liability for breach of duty will not arise in the first place.[1] Notwithstanding the provisions of CA 1963, s 200, the company in general meeting may by resolution forgive or ratify a breach of duty by a director.[2]

1 *Movitex Ltd v Bulfield* [1988] BCLC 104, 120. See also Birds, 'The Permissible Scope of Articles Excluding the Duties of Company Directors' (1976) 39 MLR 394 and Gregory 'The Scope of the Companies Act 1948, Section 205' (1982) 98 LQR 413.

2 *Multinational Gas and Petrochemical Co v Multinational Gas and Petrochemical Services Ltd* [1983] Ch 258.

UK legislation

See CA 1985, ss309A, 309B, 309C,[1] 310;[2] CA 1989, s 137(1); Companies (Audit, Investigations and Community Enterprise) Act 2004, ss 19, 64 and Sch 8).

1 CA 1985, ss 309A, 309B and 309C relates to directors only.

2 CA 1985, s 310 relates to auditors only.

Arrangements and Reconstructions

201 Compromise between company and its member or creditors

(1) Where a compromise or arrangement is proposed between a company and its creditors or any class of them or between the company and its members or any class of them, the court may, on the application of the company or of any creditor or member of the company, or, in the case of a company being wound up, of the liquidator, order a meeting of the creditors or class of creditors, or of the members of the company or class of members, as the case may be, to be summoned in such manner as the court directs.

(2) Whenever such an application as is mentioned in subsection (1) is made, the court may on such terms as seem just, stay all proceedings or restrain further proceedings against the company for such period as to the court seems fit.

(3) If a majority in number representing three-fourths in value of the creditors or class of creditors or members or class of members, as the case may be, present and voting either in person or by proxy at the meeting, vote in favour of a resolution agreeing to any compromise or arrangement, the compromise or arrangement shall, if sanctioned by the court, be binding on all the creditors or the class of creditors, or on the members or class of members, as the case may be, and also on the company or, in the case of a company in the course of being wound up, on the liquidator and contributories of the company.

(4) Section 144 shall apply to any such resolution as is mentioned in subsection (3) which is passed at any adjourned meeting held under this section.

(5) An order made under subsection (3) shall have no effect until an office copy of the order has been delivered to the registrar of companies for registration, and a copy of every such order shall be annexed to every copy of the memorandum of the company issued after the order has been made, or, in the case of a company not having a memorandum, of every copy so issued of the instrument constituting or defining the constitution of the company.

(6) If a company fails to comply with subsection (5), the company and every officer of the company who is in default [shall be guilty of an offence and liable to a fine][a] not exceeding [€1,904.61][b].

[(6A) For the avoidance of doubt, nothing in this section or sections 202 to 204 prejudices the jurisdiction of the Irish Takeover Panel under the Irish Takeover Panel Act, 1997, with respect to a compromise or scheme of arrangement that is proposed between a relevant company (within the meaning of that Act) and its members or any class of them and which constitutes a takeover within the meaning of that Act and, accordingly, the said Panel has, and shall be deemed always to have had, power to make rules under section 8 of the said Act in relation to a takeover of the kind aforesaid, to the same extent and subject to the like conditions, as it has power to make rules under that section in relation to any other kind of takeover.

(6B) The Irish Takeover Panel, in exercising its powers under the Irish Takeover Panel Act, 1997, and the High Court, in exercising its powers under this section and sections 203 and 204, shall each have due regard to the other's exercise of powers under the said Act or those sections, as the case may be.][c]

(7) In this section and in section 202, 'company' means any company liable to be wound up under this Act, and 'arrangement' includes a reorganisation of the share capital of the company by the consolidation of shares of different classes or by the division of shares into shares of different classes or by both those methods.

Amendments

a Words 'shall be guilty of an offence and liable to a fine' substituted for 'shall be liable to a fine' in CA 1963, s 201(6) by C(AA)A 2003, Sch 2, Item No. 1.

b '£100' substituted for '£20' by C(A)A 1982, Sch 1, increased to £1,500 by CA 1990, s 240(7) as inserted by CLEA 2001, s 104(c) and converted to €1,904.61 by Council Regulations (EC) No 1103/97, No 974/98 and No 2866/98 and the Economic and Monetary Union Act 1998, s 6.

c CA 1963, s 201(6A) and (6B) inserted by CLEA 2001, s 92.

Cross reference

See CA 1963, ss 202 and 203 and notes thereto.

See also CA 1963, ss 144 and notes thereto.

See also C(A)A 1983, s 38(10); and European Communities (Mergers and Divisions of Companies) Regulations 1987 (SI 137/1987), regs 5 and 25.

Definitions

'company': CA 1963, s 201(7); 'the court': CA 1963, s 2(1); 'member': CA 1963, s 31; 'memorandum': CA 1963, s 2(1); 'officer': CA 1963, s 2(1); 'officer in default': CA 1963, s 383; 'person': IA 2005, s 18(c); 'Registrar of Companies': CA 1963, s 2 (1); 'relevant company': Takeover Panel Act 1997, s 2; 'share': CA 1963, s 2(1); 'takeover': Takeover Panel Act 1997, s 1(1).

In CA 1963, s 201 generally, reference to 'company' and 'arrangement' will be interpreted in accordance with CA 1963, s 201(7).

Notes

Scheme 'between' the company and its members: In order for a proposed scheme to come within CA 1963, s 201, it must be 'between' the company and its creditors or members. Thus, some consideration must be provided not only by the members and/or creditors, as the case may be, but also by the company itself.[1] If the proposals merely require members or creditors to surrender all their rights and entitlements against the company, then there is no consideration being provided by the company and thus the proposed scheme will not fall within CA 1963, s 201.[2] Nevertheless, it is not a necessary element of a scheme for the purposes of the section that it should alter the rights existing between the company and the creditors or members with whom it is made, provided that the context and content of the scheme are such as to properly constitute an arrangement between them.[3]

CA 1963, s 72 will apply in circumstances where the scheme of arrangement would result in the reduction of the company's capital.[4]

1 *Singer Manufacturing Co v Robinow* (1971) SC 11; *Re NFU Development Trust Ltd* [1973] 1 All ER 135; *Re Savoy Hotel Ltd* [1981] 3 WLR 441.

2 *Re NFU Development Trust Ltd* [1973] 1 All ER 135.

3 *Re T & N Ltd (No 3)* [2007] 1 BCLC 563; *Re Savoy Hotel Ltd* [1981] 3 WLR 441.

4 *Re Cooper, Cooper & Johnson Ltd* [1902] WN 119.

Class meetings: Where the court orders meetings of creditors and/or members to be summoned to consider the proposals, the company must take great care to ensure that the affected parties are segregated into the correct classes. Each class must be confined to 'those persons whose rights are not so dissimilar as to make it impossible for them to consult together with a view to their common interest'.[1] In this regard, the emphasis in segregating persons into classes is on legal rights and not commercial or other interests, and on the similarity or dissimilarity of rights, not whether those rights are identical. Moreover, the court should not require persons to be divided into separate classes unless it is absolutely necessary to do so to give effect to these principles, lest by ordering separate meetings the court inappropriately gives an effective veto to some minority group.[3] A member or creditor who falls into two classes should properly be treated by the company as a member of each class.[4]

The court will not rule in advance regarding the proper class to which a particular creditor or member belongs.[5] If a particular creditor or member is placed in an incorrect class, the mistake may be deemed fatal and the scheme may not be sanctioned by the court.[6]

The company may enter into agreements with some members of a class whereby those members bind themselves to vote in favour of the scheme. Such an agreement is not open to objection if the member in question would not reasonably have voted differently in the absence of such an agreement, as, for example, where he can withdraw from the agreement in the event that reasonable grounds exist for a change of mind.[7] Moreover, the existence of such an agreement does not make the persons who enter into it a separate class for voting purposes save where in consideration of entering into the agreement they obtain benefits not available to other members of the class.[8] Nevertheless, the existence of such an agreement is relevant to the exercise of the court's discretion whether or not to sanction the scheme.[9]

At each meeting of creditors or members, as the case may be, the majority must vote *bona fide* in the interest of the class as a whole.[10] Moreover, unless the class is comprised of one person only, a class meeting attended in person or by proxy by just one member of that class will be inquorate and the court will therefore have no jurisdiction to sanction the scheme.[11]

1 *Sovereign Life Assurance Co v Dodd* (1892) 2 QB 573; *Re BTR plc* [1999] 2 BCLC 675; *Re Anglo American Insurance Ltd* [2001] 1 BCLC 755; *Re Hawk Insurance Co Ltd* [2001] 2 BCLC 480; *Re Equitable Life Assurance Society* [2002] 2 BCLC 510; *Re Telewest Communications plc (No 1)* [2005] 1 BCLC 752; *Re British Aviation Insurance Co Ltd* [2006] 1 BCLC 665; *Re Sovereign Marine and General Insurance Co Ltd* [2007] 1 BCLC 228; *Re Cape plc* [2007] 2 BCLC 546.

2 *Re Hawk Insurance Co Ltd* [2001] 2 BCLC 480; *Re British Aviation Insurance Co Ltd* [2006] 1 BCLC 665; *Re Cape plc* [2007] 2 BCLC 546.

3 *Re Hawk Insurance Co Ltd* [2001] 2 BCLC 480; *Re Cape plc* [2007] 2 BCLC 546.

4 *Re Alabama, New Orleans, Texas and Pacific Junction Rly Co* [1891] 1 Ch 213; *Re Cape plc* [2007] 2 BCLC 546.

5 *Re Pye (Ireland) Ltd* [1985] IEHC 62 (Costello J).

6 *Re Pye (Ireland) Ltd* (11 March 1985, unreported) HC (Costello J). See also *Re Hellenic Trust Ltd* [1975] 3 All ER 382; *Re T & N Ltd (No 3)* [2007] 1 BCLC 563. Note that in the United Kingdom, Practice Statement [2002] 1 WLR 1345 has been issued to enable issues surrounding the composition of classes of creditor and the summoning of meetings to be identified and, where appropriate, resolved early in proceedings.

7 *Re Depfa Bank plc* [2007] IEHC 463.

8 *Re Depfa Bank plc* [2007] IEHC 463.

9 *Re Depfa Bank plc* [2007] IEHC 463.

10 *Re John Power and Sons Ltd* [1934] IR 412; *Re Alabama, New Orleans, Texas and Pacific Railway Co* [1891] 1 Ch 213; *Re Dorman Long and Co Ltd* [1934] Ch 65; *Carruth v Imperial Chemical Industries Ltd* [1937] 2 All ER 422; *British America Nickel Corporation Ltd v MJ O'Brien Ltd* [1927] AC 369; *Re Wedgewood Coal and Iron Co* (1877) 6 Ch D 627.

11 *Re Altitude Scaffolding Ltd* [2007] 1 BCLC 199.

Court sanction: The court will not sanction a scheme which is *ultra vires* the company.[1] Nor will the scheme be sanctioned unless it has been approved by the company whether through the board, liquidator, receiver or if appropriate, by means of a simple majority of the members in general meeting.[2] The court will only confirm a scheme if it is satisfied that: (i) sufficient steps have been taken to identify and notify all interested parties; (ii) the statutory provisions and procedures and all directions of the court have been complied with; (iii) the classes were properly constituted; (iv) the prescribed majorities at each meeting acted *bona fide* and no issue of coercion arises; and (v) the compromise or arrangement is 'fair and equitable' such that an intelligent and honest man, a member of the class concerned, acting in respect of his interest might reasonably approve.[3] The court may however sanction a scheme of arrangement despite the dissent of a class of members or creditors if it is satisfied that the value of the company's assets is such that the class in question can have no interest in them.[4] While the function of the court is not merely to act as a rubber stamp, nevertheless it will be slow to differ with those who voted at the class meeting(s) and will not refuse to sanction a scheme merely because as a matter of business judgment, it might have reached a contrary conclusion regarding the proposals.[5]

In sanctioning a scheme, the court may impose such conditions or modifications as it thinks fit in order to ensure that the arrangement or compromise is fair and equitable.[6] Once a scheme has been sanctioned and the order has been duly registered, it becomes binding and can normally only be altered by order of the court.[7] Nevertheless, in exceptional cases the court may approve a scheme which contains internal machinery for making future amendments to the scheme itself.[8]

Previously the English courts had suggested that where the scheme of arrangement involved a reconstruction which could have been effected under CA 1963, s 260, it would only be sanctioned by the court if the dissenting shareholders were given the same protection as they would have enjoyed under CA 1963, s 260.[9] Similarly, it had been indicated that the court would not sanction a scheme of arrangement which provides for a compulsory purchase of the shares of dissenting members in circumstances where they could not be compulsorily purchased under CA 1963, s 204.[10] That line of case law would however no longer appear to represent good law and instead it would seem that there is no reason why affected parties should not simply be confined to relying on the checks and balances contained in s 201 itself.[11]

The arrangement may, for example, involve creditors converting loan capital into share capital;[12] or it may involve deferring the enforcement by creditors of all or part of their claims either to ease the company's cash flow position or to facilitate a more advantageous realisation of assets than would be achieved in a liquidation.[13]

1 *Re Guardian Assurance Co* [1917] 1 Ch 431; *Re Savoy Hotel Co* [1981] 3 WLR 441.

2 *Re Savoy Hotel Co* [1981] 3 WLR 441; *Re International Contract Co* (1872) 26 LT 358; *Re Oceanic Steam Navigation Co Ltd* [1938] 3 All ER 740.

3 *Re Colonia Insurance (Ireland) Ltd* [2005] 1 IR 497; *Re Depfa Bank plc* [2007] IEHC 463; *Re John Power and Sons Ltd* [1934] IR 412; *Re Dorman Long and Co Ltd* [1934] Ch 635; *Carruth v Imperial Chemical Industries Ltd* [1937] 2 All ER 422; *Re TDG plc* [2009] 1 BCLC 445.

4 *Re Tea Corporation Ltd* [1904] 1 Ch 12.

5 *Re Colonia Insurance (Ireland) Ltd* [2005] 1 IR 497; *Re Depfa Bank plc* [2007] IEHC 463; *Re London Chartered Bank of Australia* [1893] 3 Ch 540.

6 *Re Canning Jarrah Timber Co (Western Australia) Ltd* [1900] 1 Ch 708.

7 *Srimata Premila Devi v Peoples Bank of Northern India Ltd* [1938] 4 All ER 337; *Re Equitable Life Assurance Society* [2002] 2 BCLC 510.

8 *Re Cape plc* [2007] 2 BCLC 546.

9 *Re Anglo-Continental Supply Co Ltd* [1922] 2 Ch 723.

10 *Re Hellenic and General Trust Ltd* [1975] 3 All ER 382.

11 *Re TDG plc* [2009] 1 BCLC 445. See also *Re National Bank Ltd* [1966] 1 WLR 819.

12 *Re Empire Mining Co Ltd* (1890) 44 Ch D 402.

13 *Re Pye (Ireland) Ltd* [1985] IEHC 62 (Costello J); *UDL Argos Engineering v Li Lo Lin* [2001] HKCFA 53. See also *Re Dorman Long and Co Ltd* [1934] Ch 635 where the scheme involved paying some trade creditors and securing the claims of others; or *Shaw v Royce Ltd* [1911] 1 Ch 138 where the scheme was used to release a guarantee.

Irish Takeover Panel: The Irish Takeover Panel supervises certain transactions, particularly takeovers, concerning Irish registered companies listed on the Irish Stock Exchange. As an increasing number of schemes of arrangement involved companies supervised by the Takeover Panel, it was necessary to clarify the respective roles and responsibilities of the court and the Takeover Panel in transactions where both the Takeover Panel Act 1997 and CA 1963, s 201 applied. Accordingly, CA 1963, s 201(6A) and (6B) were introduced. Firstly, it is confirmed that nothing contained in CA 1963, s 201 prejudices the jurisdiction of the Irish Takeover Panel where a proposed scheme of arrangement also falls to be supervised by the Irish Takeover Panel.[1] Secondly, both the court and the Takeover Panel must have due regard to the exercise by the other of their respective powers in relation to such a transaction.[2] It should also be noted that since 5 December 2005, RSC, ord 75 has been amended[3] to facilitate the requirements of CA 1963, s 201(6A) and (6B). In particular, the court may invite the Takeover Panel to provide any report or other information which appears relevant to the exercise of the Courts jurisdiction in relation to the scheme.[4] In addition the applicant or other moving party must promptly provide the Takeover Panel with copies of any motion or petition in relation to any takeover scheme proceedings and details of the terms of any court order.[5] The Takeover Panel is at liberty to be heard in any such takeover scheme proceedings.[6]

1 CA 1963, s 201(6A).

2 CA 1963, s 201(6B).

3 Rules of the Superior Courts (Takeover Schemes) 2005 (SI 688/2005).

4 RSC, ord 74, r 24(5).

5 RSC, ord 74, r 24(3).

6 RSC, ord 74, r 24(4).

Other consents: There are certain circumstances where an order may not be made by the court under CA 1963, s 201 until regulatory consents have been obtained, such as:

Central Bank Act 1989, s 88;
Stock Exchange Act 1995, s 49;
Investment Intermediaries Act 1995, s 48; and
Competition Act 2002, s 16(1)(a).[1]

1 See McCarthy and Power, *Irish Competition Law: The Competition Act 2002* (Tottel Publishing, 2003) at para [9.18]. Specific reference was made in the Mergers, Take-Overs and Monopolies (Control) Act 1978, s 14 to CA 1963, s 201. However the Mergers, Take-Overs and Monopolies (Control) Act 1978 was repealed by the Competition Act 2002.

Foreign and other companies: By virtue of s 201(7) the provisions of ss 201 and 202 are applied to any company that may be wound up under the Companies Acts, including certain categories of foreign companies and certain types of companies formed by charter or under other legislation. They are more particularly identified in CA 1963, Part X and in the Insolvency Regulation.[1]

1 See the notes to CA 1963, Part X and the Insolvency Regulation for the categories of companies that may be wound up under these provisions. See also *Re Sovereign Marine and General Insurance Co Ltd* [2007] 1 BCLC 228.

UK legislation

See CA 1985, s 425; IA 1985, s 109(1), Sch 6 para 11; Enterprise Act 2002, s 248(3), Sch 17, paras 3, 5).

---

202 Information as to compromises with members and creditors

(1) Where a meeting of creditors or any class of creditors or members or any class of members is summoned under section 201 there shall—

(a) with every notice summoning the meeting which is sent to a creditor or member, be sent also a statement explaining the effect of the compromise or arrangement and in particular stating any material interests of the directors of the company, whether as directors or as members or as creditors of the company or otherwise, and the effect thereon of the compromise or arrangement, in so far as it is different from the effect on the like interests of other persons; and

(b) in every notice summoning the meeting which is given by advertisement, be included either such a statement as aforesaid or a notification of the place at which and the manner in which creditors or members entitled to attend the meeting may obtain copies of such a statement as aforesaid.

(2) Where the compromise or arrangement affects the rights of debenture holders of a company, the said statement shall give the like explanation in relation to the trustees of any deed for securing the issue of the debentures as it is required to give in relation to the company's directors.

(3) Where a notice given by advertisement includes a notification that copies of a statement explaining the effect of a compromise or arrangement proposed can be obtained by creditors or members entitled to attend the meeting, every such creditor or member shall, on making application in the manner indicated by the notice, be furnished by the company free of charge with a copy of the statement.

(4) Subject to subsection (5), where a company fails to comply with any requirement of this section, the company and every officer of the company who is in default [shall be guilty of an offence and liable to a fine][a] not exceeding [€1,904.61][b], and for the purpose of this subsection any liquidator of the company and any trustee of a deed for securing the issue of debentures of the company shall be deemed to be an officer of the company.

(5) A person shall not be liable under subsection (4) if that person shows that the default was due to the refusal of any other person, being a director or trustee for debenture holders, to supply the necessary particulars as to his interests.

(6) It shall be the duty of any director of the company and of any trustee for debenture holders of the company to give notice to the company of such matters relating to himself as may be necessary for the purposes of this section, and any person who makes default in complying with this subsection [shall be guilty of an offence and liable to a fine][a] not exceeding [€1,904.61][c].

Amendments

a Words 'shall be guilty of an offence and liable to a fine' substituted for 'shall be liable to a fine' in CA 1963, s 202(4) and (6) by C(AA)A 2003, Sch 2, Item 1.

b '£500' substituted for '£100' by C(A)A 1982, Sch 1, increased to £1,500 by CA 1990, s 240(7) as inserted by CLEA 2001, s 104(c) and converted to €1,904.61 by Council Regulations (EC) No 1103/97, No 974/98 and No 2866/98 and the Economic and Monetary Union Act 1998, s 6.

c '£250' substituted for '£50' by C(A)A 1982, Sch 1, increased to £1,500 by CA 1990, s 240(7) as inserted by CLEA 2001, s 104(c) and converted to €1,904.61 by Council Regulations (EC) No 1103/97, No 974/98 and No 2866/98 and the Economic and Monetary Union Act 1998, s 6.

Cross reference

See also CA 1963, ss 201, 203 and notes thereto.

Definitions

'company': CA 1963, s 201(7); 'debenture': CA 1963, s 2(1); 'director': CA 1963, s 2(1); 'member': CA 1963, s 31; 'officer': CA 1963, s 2(1); 'officer in default': CA 1963, s 383; 'person': IA 2005, s 18(c).

In CA 1963, s 202, reference to 'company' and 'arrangement' will be interpreted in accordance with CA 1963, s 201(7).

Notes

Statement of effect and interests: When notices of meetings being held in connection with a scheme of arrangement under CA 1963, s 201, are circulated, the company is required to give certain specified information regarding the effect of the scheme and the interests of directors[1] and debenture stock trustees.[2] Where the notices of meetings are given by way of advertisement, such a statement must be included in the advertisement or copies of the statement made available for creditors or members to obtain.[3] Failure to provide such a statement makes the company and every defaulting officer guilty of an offence and liable to a fine.[4] Similarly, failure by any director of the company or trustee for debenture holders to give the company notice of such matters for the purposes of CA 1963, s 202 will make them guilty of an offence and liable to a fine.[5] The company will not be guilty of an offence or liable to a fine if a director or trustee had failed to provide it with the necessary information.[6] If, after notices have been issued, there is a subsequent change in the directors' material interests, it would be prudent to disclose such facts before or at the relevant meeting.[7] The court may decline to sanction the scheme if the notice convening the meeting was misleading or confusing.[8]

1 CA 1963, s 202(1)(a).

2 CA 1963, s 202(2).

3 CA 1963, s 202(1)(b).

4 CA 1963, s 202(4): Liquidators and any trustees under a debenture trust deed are deemed to be officers for the purposes of this subsection.

5 CA 1963, s 202(6).

6 CA 1963, s 202(5).

7 *Re Minister Assets plc* [1985] BCLC 200; *Re MB Group plc* [1989] 6 BCLC 672.

8 *Re John Power and Sons Ltd* [1934] IR 412; *Re National Bank Ltd* [1966] 1 WLR 819; *Jackson v Munster Bank Ltd* (1884–85) 13 LR Ir 118; *Re TDG plc* [2009] 1 BCLC 445.

UK legislation

See CA 1985, s 426; IA 1985, s 109(1) Sch 6, para 12.

203 Provisions to facilitate reconstruction and amalgamation of companies

(1) Where an application is made to the court under section 201 for the sanctioning of a compromise or arrangement proposed between a company and any such persons as are mentioned in that section, and it is shown to the court that the compromise or arrangement has been proposed for the purposes of or in connection with a scheme for the reconstruction of any company or companies or the amalgamation of any two or more companies, and that under the scheme the whole or any part of the undertaking or the property of any company concerned in the scheme (in this section referred to as 'a transferor company') is to be transferred to another company (in this section referred to as 'the transferee company'), the court may, either by the order sanctioning the compromise or arrangement or by any subsequent order make provision for all or any of the following matters—

(a) the transfer to the transferee company of the whole or any part of the undertaking and of the property or liabilities of any transferor company;

(b) the allotting or appropriation by the transferee company of any shares, debentures, policies or other like interests in that company which under the compromise or arrangement are to be allotted or appropriated by that company to or for any person;

(c) the continuation by or against the transferee company of any legal proceedings pending by or against any transferor company;

(d) the dissolution, without winding up, of any transferor company;

(e) the provision to be made for any persons who, within such time and in such manner as the court directs, dissent from the compromise or arrangement;

(f) such incidental, consequential and supplemental matters as are necessary to secure that the reconstruction or amalgamation shall be fully and effectively carried out.

(2) Where an order under this section provides for the transfer of property or liabilities, that property shall, by virtue of the order, be transferred to and vest in, and those liabilities shall, by virtue of the order, be transferred to and become the liabilities of the transferee company, and in the case of any property, if the order so directs, freed from any charge which is, by virtue of the compromise or arrangement, to cease to have effect.

(3) Where an order is made under this section, every company in relation to which the order is made shall cause an office copy thereof to be delivered to the registrar of companies for registration within 21 days after the making of the order, and if default is made in complying with this subsection, the company and every officer of the company who is in default [shall be guilty of an offence and liable to a fine][a] not exceeding [€1,904.61][b].

(4) In this section, 'property' includes property, rights and powers of every description, and 'liabilities' includes duties.

(5) Notwithstanding subsection (7) of section 201, 'company' in this section does not include any company other than a company within the meaning of this Act.

Amendments

a '£125' substituted for '£25' by C(A)A 1982, Sch 1, increased to £1,500 by CA 1990, s 240(7) as inserted by CLEA 2001, s 104(c) and converted to €1,904.61 by Council Regulations (EC) No 1103/97, No 974/98 and No 2866/98 and the Economic and Monetary Union Act 1998, s 6.

b Words 'shall be guilty of an offence and liable to a fine' substituted for 'shall be liable to a fine' in CA 1963, s 203(3) by C(AA)A 2003, Sch 2, Item No.1.

Cross reference

See the European Communities (Mergers and Divisions of Companies) Regulations 1987: in relation to the amalgamation or merger of companies. See also RSC, ord 75, r 24 as inserted by the Rules of the Superior Courts (Takeover Schemes) 2005 (SI 688/2005).

See also CA 1963, ss 201 and 202 and notes thereto.

Definitions

'company': CA 1963, s 2(1); 'the court': CA 1963, s 2(1); 'debenture': CA 1963, s 2(1); 'officer': CA 1963, s 2(1); 'officer in default': CA 1963, s 383; 'person': IA 2005, s 18(c); 'Registrar of Companies': CA 1963, s 2(1); 'share': CA 1963, s 2(1); 'undertaking': CA 1963, s 2(1).

In CA 1963, s 203, the term 'company' is refers only to companies registered under the Companies Acts and not to companies liable to wound up under the Companies Acts, as is the case under CA 1963, s 201(7);[1] and the terms 'property' and 'liabilities' will be interpreted in accordance with CA 1963, s 203(4).

1 CA 1963, s 201(5).

Notes

Court powers: In order for a proposed scheme of arrangement or compromise to be binding on the relevant parties, the court must first sanction the scheme.[1] Where a proposed scheme of arrangement or compromise is which is shown to the court to be for the purpose of or in connection with a scheme of reconstruction[2] or amalgamation and that as part of that scheme the whole or part of the undertaking or property of any company is to be transferred to another, then the court may, either with the order sanctioning the scheme[3] or by way of a subsequent order facilitate the implementation of the proposed scheme by a wide variety of means.[4] Every company in relation to which such an order is made is obliged to forward a copy to the Registrar within 21 days and in default shall be guilty of an offence and liable to a fine.[5]

1 CA 1963, s 201(3).

2 See *Re MyTravel Group plc* [2005] 2 BCLC 123 in relation to whether a scheme constituted a reconstruction for the purposes of CA 1985, s 427.

3 As envisaged by CA 1963, s 201(3).

4 CA 1963, ss 203(1)(a)–(f) and (2).

5 CA 1963, s 203(3).

UK legislation

See CA 1985, ss 427, 427A; CA 1989 s 114(2); Enterprise Act 2002, s 248(3), Sch 17, paras 3, 6; The Companies (Mergers and Divisions) Regulations 1987(SI 1987/1991).

204 Power to acquire shares of shareholders dissenting from scheme or contract which has been approved by majority

(1) Subject to subsection (2), where a scheme, contract or offer involving the acquisition by one company, whether a company within the meaning of this Act or not (in this section referred to as 'the transferee company') of the beneficial ownership of all the shares (other than shares already in the beneficial ownership of the transferee company) in the capital of another company, being a company within the meaning of this Act (in this section referred to as 'the transferor company') has become binding or been approved or accepted in respect of not less than four-fifths in value of the shares affected not later than the date 4 months after publication generally to the holders of the shares affected of the terms of such scheme, contract or offer, the transferee company may at any time before the expiration of the period of 6 months next following such publication give notice in the prescribed manner to any dissenting shareholder that it desires to acquire the beneficial ownership of his shares, and when such notice is given the transferee company shall, unless on an application made by the dissenting shareholder within one month from the date on which the notice was given, the court thinks fit to order otherwise, be entitled and bound to acquire the beneficial ownership of those shares on the terms on which under the scheme, contract or offer, the beneficial ownership of the shares in respect of which the scheme, contract or offer has become binding or been approved or accepted is to be acquired by the transferee company.

(2) Where shares in the transferor company are, at the date of such publication, already in the beneficial ownership of the transferee company to a value greater than one-fifth of the aggregate value of those shares and the shares affected, subsection (1) shall not apply unless the assenting shareholders besides holding not less than four-fifths in value of the shares affected are not less than three-fourths in number of the holders of those shares.

(3) For the purpose of this section, shares in the transferor company in the beneficial ownership of a subsidiary of the transferee company shall be deemed to be in the beneficial ownership of the transferee company, the acquisition of the beneficial ownership of shares in the transferor company by a subsidiary of the transferee company shall be deemed to be the acquisition of such beneficial ownership by the transferee company and shares shall not be treated as not being in the beneficial ownership of the transferee company merely by reason of the fact that those shares are or may become subject to a charge in favour of another person.

(4) Where, in consequence of any such scheme, contract or offer, the beneficial interest in shares in the transferor company is acquired by the transferee company and as a result of such acquisition the transferee company has become the beneficial owner of four-fifths in value of all the shares in the transferor company then—

(a) the transferee company shall, within one month of the date of such acquisition, give notice of that fact in the prescribed manner to all holders of shares in the transferor company not in the beneficial ownership of the transferee company; and

(b) any such holder may, within 3 months from the giving of the notice to him, require the transferee company to acquire his shares;

and, where a shareholder gives notice under paragraph (*b*) in relation to any shares, the transferee company shall be entitled and bound to acquire the beneficial ownership of those shares on the terms on which under the scheme, contract or offer the beneficial ownership of the shares of the assenting shareholders was acquired by it, or on such other terms as may be agreed or as the court on the application either of the transferee company or of a shareholder thinks fit to order, and subsections (5), (6) and (7) shall be applicable *mutatis mutandis* as if any reference therein to a notice given under subsection (1) were a reference to a notice given under paragraph (*b*).

(5) Where a notice has been given by the transferee company under subsection (1) and the court has not, on application made by the dissenting shareholder, ordered to the contrary, the transferee company shall, on the expiration of one month from the date on which the notice was given, or, if an application to the court by the dissenting shareholder is then pending, after that application has been disposed of, transmit to the transferor company a copy of the notice together with an instrument of transfer of the shares of the dissenting shareholder executed on behalf of the dissenting shareholder as transferor by any person appointed by the transferee company and by the transferee (being either the transferee company or a subsidiary of the transferee company or a nominee of the transferee company or of such a subsidiary) and pay to or vest in the transferor company the amount or other consideration representing the price payable by the transferee company for the shares the beneficial ownership of which by virtue of this section the transferee company is entitled to acquire, and the transferor company shall thereupon register as the holder of those shares the person who executed such instrument as the transferee, so however, that an instrument of transfer shall not be so required for any share for which a share warrant is for the time being outstanding.

(6) Any sums received by the transferor company under this section shall be paid into a separate bank account and any such sums and any other consideration so received shall be held by that company on trust for the several persons entitled to the shares in respect of which the said sums or other consideration were respectively received.

(7) The transferor company or a nominee of the transferor company shall not be entitled to exercise any right of voting conferred by any shares in the transferee company issued to it or to its nominee as aforesaid except by and in accordance with instructions given by the shareholder in respect of whom those shares were so issued or his successor in title.

(8) In this section, 'the shares affected' means the shares the acquisition of the beneficial ownership of which by the transferee company is involved in the scheme, contract or offer, 'assenting shareholder' means a holder of any of the shares affected in respect of which the scheme, contract or offer has become binding or been approved or accepted and 'dissenting shareholder' means a holder of any of the shares affected in respect of which the scheme, contract or offer has not become binding or been approved or accepted or who has failed or refused to transfer his shares in accordance with the scheme, contract or offer.

(9) Where the scheme, contract or offer becomes binding on or is approved or accepted by a person in respect of a part only of the shares held by him, he shall be treated as an assenting shareholder as regards that part of his holding and as a dissenting shareholder as regards the remainder of his holding.

(10) Where the scheme, contract or offer provides that an assenting shareholder may elect between 2 or more sets of terms for the acquisition by the transferee company of the beneficial ownership of the shares affected, the notice given by the transferee company under subsection (1) shall be accompanied by or embody a notice stating the alternative sets of terms between which assenting shareholders are entitled to elect and specifying which of those sets of terms shall be applicable to the dissenting shareholder if he does not before the expiration of 14 days from the date of the giving of the notice notify to the transferee company in writing his election as between such alternative sets of terms, and the terms upon which the transferee company shall under this section be entitled and bound to acquire the beneficial ownership of the shares of the dissenting shareholder shall be the set of terms which the dissenting shareholder shall so notify or, in default of such notification, the set of terms so specified as applicable.

(11) In the application of this section to a transferor company the share capital of which consists of two or more classes of shares, references to the shares in the capital of the transferor company shall be construed as references to the shares in its capital of a particular class.

(12) Subject to subsection (13), this section shall not apply to a scheme, contract or offer the terms of which were published generally to the holders of the shares affected before the operative date and section 8 of the Companies Act, 1959, shall continue to apply to any such scheme, contract or offer and for the purposes of any such scheme, contract or offer, the said section shall be deemed to remain in full force.

(13) Where any such scheme, contract or offer as is mentioned in subsection (1) was approved or accepted in the manner described in that subsection at any time before the passing of the Companies Act, 1959, the court may by order on an application made to it by the transferee company within 6 months after the operative date authorise notice to be given under this section within such time after the making of the order as the court shall direct, and this section shall apply accordingly, except that the terms on which the shares of the dissenting shareholder are to be acquired shall be such terms as the court may by the order direct, instead of the terms provided by the scheme, contract or offer.

Cross reference

See European Communities (Takeover Bids (Directive 2004/25/EC)) Regulations 2006 (SI 225/2005), Pt 5.

See European Communities (Mergers and Divisions of Companies) Regulations 1987 (SI 137/1987), regs 5 and 25.

See also RSC, ord 75, r 24(b).[1]

1 As inserted by the Rules of the Superior Courts (Takeover Schemes) 2005 (SI 688/2005).

Definition

'company': CA 1963, s 2(1); 'the court': CA 1963, s 2(1); 'the operative date': CA 1963, s 2(1); 'prescribed': CA 1963, s 2(1); 'share': CA 1963, s 2(1); 'share warrant': CA 1963, s 2(1), s 88(2); 'subsidiary': CA 1963, s 2(1), s 155.

In CA 1963, s 204, reference to 'the shares affected', 'assenting shareholder' and 'dissenting shareholder' will be interpreted in accordance with CA 1963, s 204(8).

Notes

Power to acquire remaining shares: Since 20 May 2006,[1] CA 1963, s 204 no longer applies to takeover bids which the Irish Takeover Panel has jurisdiction to supervise.[2] CA 1963, s 204 applies so as to permit shares in a company registered under the Companies Acts (the 'transferor company')[3] to be compulsorily acquired by a company[4] (whether registered under the Companies Acts or not)(the 'transferee company') in circumstances where the transferee company has already acquired or is bound to acquire 80% of the value of the shares in the transferor company. The power to buy out the shares in this manner is designed to facilitate the acquisition of the entire transferor company.[5]

A scheme, contract or offer to acquire all (and not some only) of the shares in the transferor company must be made by the transferee company. The scheme, contract or offer must have become binding or been approved or accepted by at least 80% of the value of the shares in the transferor company at least four months after the date of the publication of the terms of the proposed transaction. In order to acquire the remaining shares, the transferee company must notify[6] those shareholders who have not accepted or approved or in respect of whom, the scheme, contract or offer, has not become binding (the dissenting shareholders[7]) of its intention to acquire the beneficial ownership in their shares. If no dissenting shareholder makes an application to court for relief within one month of the date of the notice from the transferee company, then the transferee company becomes entitled and bound[8] to acquire the shares of the dissenting shareholders on the same terms[9] as have been offered to the assenting shareholders.[10]

If, on the date of publication of the scheme, arrangement or offer, the transferee company is the beneficial owner of more than 20% of the aggregate value of all of the shares in the transferor company, then the transferee company cannot apply under CA 1963, s 204(1), unless the assenting shareholders, in addition to representing 80% in value of the shares, are also the holders[11] of not less than 75% of those shares.[12]

1 The operative date of European Communities (Takeover Bids (Directive 2004/25/EC)) Regulations 2006 (SI 225/2006), see also notes thereto.

2 See European Communities (Takeover Bids (Directive 2004/25/EC)) Regulations 2006 (SI 225/2006), reg 6 in relation to the jurisdiction of the Irish Takeover Panel.

3 Other than a company to which the European Communities (Takeover Bids (Directive 2004/25/EC)) Regulations 2006 (SI 225/2006).

4 Not an individual.

5 See generally Clarke, *Takeovers and Mergers Law in Ireland* (Round Hall Sweet & Maxwell, 1999).

6 In the prescribed form: Companies Forms Order 1964 (SI 45/1964), Sch, Form 18.

7 CA 1963, s 204(8): 'dissenting shareholders'.

8 CA 1963, s 204(4). Companies Forms Order 1964 (SI 45/1964), Sch, Form 19.

9 CA 1963, s 204(10).

10 CA 1963, s 204(8): 'assenting shareholders'.

11 See *Re Simo Securities Trust Ltd* [1971] 3 All ER 999 (in relation to the Companies Act 1948, s 209) where the English High Court considered the point in time at which 'holders' are to be identified.

12 CA 1963, s 204(2).

Dissenting shareholders:[1] The onus is on the dissenting shareholder who applies to court for relief to show that the terms of the take-over are not fair.[2] In this regard, the court will pay great attention to the views of the majority who accepted the bid, although acceptance by shareholders in the transferor company who are associated directly or indirectly with the transferee company will not carry the same weight or influence as acceptance by truly independent shareholders.[3] Provided the offer is for the market value, it will not be regarded as unfair simply because some of the details of the scheme are open to valid criticism or because it could be improved upon, and this is so even though it results in a loss to the dissenting shareholder.[4] On the other hand, if the section is being used in an artifical way by the existing majority shareholders of a company as a means of compulsorily acquiring the shares of the minority at an unfair price, then relief may be granted by the court.[5]

The dissenting shareholders, whose shares are to be compulsorily acquired are entitled to be furnished with reasonably full particulars of the take-over. If such details are not provided by the transferee company they must then be furnished by the directors of the transferor company.[6] Curiously CA 1963, s 204(4) does not extend to a situation where the transferee company is a subsidiary of another company which has shares in the transferor company.[7] Nonetheless, in such a situation, the court may in its discretion grant the dissenting minority relief from compulsory purchase.[8]

1 A shareholder may be both a dissenting shareholder as regards part of his shareholding and an assenting shareholder as regards the remainder of his shareholding.

2 *Walls v PJ Walls Holdings Ltd* [2008] 1 IR 732; *Re Fitzwilton plc* [2000] 2 IRLM 263; *Re Hoare and Co* (1934) 150 LT 374; *McCormick v Cameo Investments Ltd* [1978] ILRM 191.

3 *Re Hoare and Co* (1934) 150 LT 374; *Securities Trust Ltd v Associated Properties Ltd* (19 November 1980, unreported) HC (McWilliam J); *Re Fitzwilton plc* [2000] 2 IRLM 263; *Walls v PJ Walls Holdings Ltd* [2008] 1 IR 732.

4 *McCormick v Cameo Investments Ltd* [1978] ILRM 191; *Re Grierson, Oldham and Adams Ltd* [1968] Ch 17; *Walls v PJ Walls Holdings Ltd* [2008] 1 IR 732.

5 *Re Bugle Press Ltd* [1960] 3 All ER 791.

6 *Securities Trust Ltd v Associated Properties Ltd* (19 November 1980, unreported) HC (McWilliam J). Cf *Evertite Locknuts* [1945] Ch 220.

7 See *Re Fitzwilton plc* [2000] 2 IRLM 263 at 274.

8 *Esso Standard (Inter America) IC v JW Enterprises* (1963) 37 DLR (2d) 598.

Funds held on trust: Any cash consideration must be paid into a separate bank account and any such cash and any other form of consideration must be held on trust by the transferor company for the persons whose shares have been compulsorily acquired.[1] The transferor company, as trustee, is subject to various statutory and common law duties in respect of such funds.[2] The CLRG have recommended that any such unclaimed consideration should be held on trust for no longer than 7 years and thereafter, should be paid into the Exchequer.[3]

1 CA 1963, s 204(6).

2 See generally Trustee Act 1931 and Trustee (Authorised Investments) Act 1958 (as amended).

3 The Company Law Review Group, First Report, para 6.9.5.

UK legislation

See CA 1985, ss 429, 430, 430A–430C; FSA 1986, s 172(1), Sch 12; The Companies (Acquisition of Own Shares)(Treasury Shares) Regulations 2003 (SI 2003/1116), r 4, Sch, para 26(a), (b); r 6(a),(b)), para 27(a),(b); r 7(1)(a), (b), 7(2) and (3).

Minorities

205 Remedy in cases of oppression

(1) Any member of a company who complains that the affairs of the company are being conducted or that the powers of the directors of the company are being exercised in a manner oppressive to him or any of the members (including himself), or in disregard of his or their interests as members, may apply to the court for an order under this section.

(2) In a case falling within subsection (3) of section 170, the Minister may apply for an order under this section.

(3) If, on any application under subsection (1) or subsection (2) the court is of opinion that the company's affairs are being conducted or the directors' powers are being

exercised as aforesaid, the court may, with a view to bringing to an end the matters complained of, make such order as it thinks fit, whether directing or prohibiting any act or cancelling or varying any transaction or for regulating the conduct of the company's affairs in future, or for the purchase of the shares of any members of the company by other members of the company or by the company and in the case of a purchase by the company, for the reduction accordingly of the company's capital, or otherwise.

(4) Where an order under this section makes any alteration in or addition to any company's memorandum or articles, then, notwithstanding anything in any other provision of this Act but subject to the provisions of the order, the company concerned shall not have power without the leave of the court to make any further alteration in or addition to the memorandum or articles inconsistent with the provisions of the order; but, subject to the foregoing provisions of this subsection, the alterations or additions made by the order shall be of the same effect as if duly made by resolution of the company, and the provisions of this Act shall apply to the memorandum or articles as so altered or added to accordingly.

(5) An office copy of any order under this section altering or adding to or giving leave to alter or add to a company's memorandum or articles shall, within 21 days after the making thereof, be delivered by the company to the registrar of companies for registration; and if a company fails to comply with this subsection, the company and every officer of the company who is in default [shall be guilty of an offence and liable to a fine][a] not exceeding [€1,904.61].[b]

(6) The personal representative of a person who, at the date of his death was a member of a company, or any trustee of, or person beneficially interested in, the shares of a company by virtue of the will or intestacy of any such person, may apply to the court under subsection (1) for an order under this section and, accordingly, any reference in that subsection to a member of a company shall be construed as including a reference to any such personal representative, trustee or person beneficially interested as aforesaid or to all of them.

(7) If, in the opinion of the court, the hearing of proceedings under this section would involve the disclosure of information the publication of which would be seriously prejudicial to the legitimate interests of the company, the court may order that the hearing of the proceedings or any part thereof shall be *in camera*.

Amendments

a Words 'shall be guilty of an offence and liable to a fine' substituted for 'shall be liable to a fine' in CA 1963, s 203(3) by C(AA)A 2003, Sch 2, Item No. 1.

b '£125' substituted for '£25' by C(A)A 1982, Sch 1, increased to £1,500 by CA 1990, s 240(7) as inserted by CLEA 2001, s 104(c) and converted to €1,904.61 by Council Regulations (EC) No 1103/97, No 974/98 and No 2866/98 and the Economic and Monetary Union Act 1998, s 6.

Cross reference

CA 1963, s 170 was repealed by CA 1990, s 6 and replaced by CA 1990, s 12.

[1] See IA 2005, s 26(2).

Definitions

'articles': CA 1963, s 2(1); 'company': CA 1963, s 2(1); 'the court': CA 1963, s 2(1); 'director': CA 1963, s 2(1); 'member': CA 1963, s 31; 'memorandum': CA 1963, s 2(1); 'Minister': CA 1963, s 2(1); 'officer': CA 1963, s 2(1); 'officer in default': CA 1963, s 383; 'the registrar of companies': CA 1963, s 2 (1); 'share': CA 1963, s 2(1).

Notes

Application for relief: Subject to CA 1963, s 205(6),[1] relief under CA 1963, s 205 is only available to 'members' of the company.[2] However, a registered member who no longer holds a beneficial interest in shares, but whose name remains registered in the register of members, may not seek relief.[3] Conversely, a person will not be precluded from petitioning in respect of oppressive conduct which commenced whilst he was a mere beneficial owner of shares provided that he has since become the registered holder of those shares and provided also that the oppression is still ongoing.[4] Although the heading to s 205 is entitled 'Minorities', the section does not require that the petitioner should in fact be a minority shareholder and in this regard a member may be oppressed in circumstances where the minority in fact have control of the company (eg through loaded voting rights).[5] Although only a member may petition for relief under CA 1963, s 205, where his complaint is of oppression, he need not have suffered qua member but may instead have suffered in some other capacity, as for example qua director or creditor.[6] Relief may be claimed under CA 1963, s 205 even if some other form of remedy would also be available to the petitioner, such as a derivative action.[7] In this regard, the courts will not take a 'narrow legalistic view' in defining 'oppression' and 'disregard of interest', but will have regard instead to the particular facts of each case.[8] Where the members of the company are parties to a shareholders' agreement which regulates the conduct of the company's affairs and which provides for disputes to be referred to arbitration, proceedings under s 205 may be stayed by the court in favour of arbitration.[9]

1 CA 1963, s 205(6): Personal representatives of deceased members, trustees and persons beneficially interested in shares by virtue of a will or intestacy may petition the court for relief under CA 1963, 205.

2 As defined in CA 1963, s 31, ie the subscribers to the memorandum and such other persons whose names have, with their agreement, been entered on the register of members. See *Re Allied Metropole Hotel Ltd* (19 December 1988, unreported) HC (Gannon J), noted by MacCann, 'Locus Standi and Section 205 of the Companies Act 1963' (1989) 7 ILT 195; *Re McCarthy Surfacing Ltd* [2009] 1 BCLC 622; *Re Emerald Group Holdings Ltd* [2009] IEHC 440.

3 *Re Via Net Works Ireland Ltd* [2002] 2 IR 47.

4 *Re Emerald Group Holdings Ltd* [2009] IEHC 440.

5 *Re HR Harmer Ltd* [1959] 1 WLR 62; *Re Westwinds Holding Co Ltd* (21 May 1974, unreported) HC (Kenny J).

6 *Re Murph's Restaurant Ltd* [1979] ILRM 141; *Re a company* [1983] 1 WLR 927; *Re a company* [1986] BCLC 376; *Gamlestaden Fastigheter AB v Baltic Partners Ltd* [2008] 1 BCLC 468. Cf *Re Emerald Group Holdings Ltd* [2009] IEHC 440 where it appears to have been agreed by the parties that the oppression had to be suffered *qua* member. Whatever the position regarding oppression, it is clear that disregard of interests, must indeed be suffered *qua* member.

7 *Re Westwinds Holding Co Ltd* (21 May 1974, unreported) HC (Kenny J); *Re Greenore Trading Co Ltd* [1980] ILRM 94.

8 *Scottish Wholesale C-Operative v Meyer* [1959] AC 324.

9 *Re Via Net Works (Ireland) Ltd* [2002] 2 IR 47.

Oppression: The conduct or exercise of powers complained of in a petition under CA 1963, s 205 must relate to the internal management of the affairs of the company (including but not necessarily limited to the exercise of the powers of the directors).[1] Dealings in respect of the company's issued share capital do not constitute the 'affairs of the company', but rather involve the affairs of the shareholders personally and thus fall outside the ambit of s 205.[2] A single act of oppression or disregard of interests may suffice for the purpose of bring proceedings under CA 1963, s 205.[3] The wording of the section envisages that the oppression or disregard of interests is operative and ongoing at the time the petition is presented. However, if the acts complained of have not been redressed prior to the presentation of the petition, then the oppression or disregard of interests, as the case may be, will be duly regarded as operative and ongoing.[4]

However, it may at least be said that 'oppression' connotes conduct which is 'burdensome, harsh and wrongful'.[5] Acts may be oppressive, even if done honestly and in good faith.[6] Oppression may involve illegal acts,[7] however, not every illegal act relating to the internal affairs of a company will constitute oppression and conversely, in appropriate circumstances, relief may be claimed under CA 1963, s 205 in respect of conduct (such as a failure to consult members) which although oppressive or in disregard of interests, is not strictly illegal.[8]

Examples of oppression have included the diversion or misappropriation of corporate assets,[9] the imposition of an unfair financial burden on a petitioner,[10] exclusion of the petitioner from management of the affairs of a quasi-partnership company,[11] a board's continued failure to declare dividends where the company had distributable profits[12] and a failure to consult members in respect of important transactions affecting the company.[13] On the other hand, the waiver of a genuinely irrecoverable debt (including a debt owed by a related or associated company) will not, of itself, amount to oppression.[14] Mismanagement will not constitute oppression *per se*.[15] In more recent English cases and in one recent Irish case it has been held that only in extreme cases would the court be prepared to grant relief under the equivalent of CA 1963, s 205 in respect of mismanagement.[16]

1 *Re Irish Visiting Motorists' Bureau Ltd* (27 January 1972, unreported) HC (Kenny J); *Re Emerald Group Holdings Ltd* [2009] IEHC 440; *Re Saul D Harrison & Sons plc* [1995] 1 BCLC 14; *Oak Investment Partners XII v Boughtwood* [2009] 1 BCLC 453.

2 *Re New Ad Advertising Co Ltd* [2007] IEHC 436; *Re Leeds United Holdings plc* [1996] 2 BCLC 545; *Re Legal Costs Negotiators Ltd* [1999] BCLC 171.

3 *Re Williams Group Tullamore Ltd* [1985] IR 613; *Re Westwinds Holding Co Ltd* (21 May 1974, unreported) HC (Kenny J).

4 *Re Greenore Trading Co Ltd* [1980] ILRM 94; *Re Emerald Group Holdings Ltd* [2009] IEHC 440.

5 *Re Greenore Trading Co Ltd* [1980] ILRM 94; *Scottish Wholesale Co-Operative Society Ltd v Meyer* [1959] AC 324; *Re Jermyn Street Turkish Baths Ltd* [1971] 1 WLR 1042; *Re New Ad Advertising Co Ltd* [2007] IEHC 436; *Re Emerald Group Holdings Ltd* [2009] IEHC 440.

6 *Re Irish Visiting Motorists Bureau Ltd* (27 January 1972, unreported) HC (Kenny J); *Re Emerald Group Holdings Ltd* [2009] IEHC 440.

7 eg *Re Westwinds Holding Co Ltd* (21 May 1974, unreported) HC (Kenny J).

8 *Re Clubman Shirts Ltd* [1983] ILRM 323; *Re Neath Rugby Ltd* [2008] 1 BCLC 527.

9 *Scottish Co-Operative Wholesale Society Ltd v Meyer* [1959] AC 324; *Re Westwinds Holding Co Ltd* (21 May 1974, unreported) HC (Kenny J); *Re Emerald Group Holdings Ltd* [2009] IEHC 440; *Re McCarthy Surfacing Ltd* [2009] 1 BCLC 622.

10 *Re Irish Visiting Motorists Bureau Ltd* (27 January 1972, unreported) HC (Kenny J).

11 *Re HR Harmer Ltd* [1959] 1 WLR 62; *Re a company* [1986] BCLC 376; *Re Murphs Restaurants Ltd* [1979] ILRM 141.

12 *Re McCarthy Surfacing Ltd* [2009] 1 BCLC 622.

13 *Re Clubman Shirts Ltd* [1983] ILRM 323. It may not be oppressive though to withhold from a member information which would be used by him to compete with the company: *PMPA Insurance Co Ltd v New Ireland Assurance Co Ltd* (22 October 1975) HC (Kenny J) reported in The Irish Times 23 October 1975.

14 *Re New Ad Advertising Co Ltd* [2007] IEHC 436.

15 *Re Five Minute Car Wash Service Ltd* [1966] 1 WLR 745. However, both Keane, *Company Law* (2nd edn, Tottel Publishing, 1991) at para 28.17 and Ussher, *Company Law in Ireland* (Sweet & Maxwell, 1986) at p 263, take the view that in such circumstances a claim might be successfully mounted on the ground that there had been a disregard of members' interests.

16 In this regard, see *Re Sam Weller and Sons Ltd* [1990] BCLC 80 and *Re Elgindata Ltd* [1991] BCLC 959 and *Re New Ad Advertising Co Ltd* [2007] IEHC 436.

Disregard of interests: The word 'interests' in CA 1963, s 205 is wider than the term 'rights' and its presence in s 205, suggests that the Oireachtas recognised that members may have different interests, even if their rights as members are the same.[1] The alteration of the rights of one class of shareholders, although technically valid, may nonetheless be objectionable as being in disregard of the interests of another class of shareholders.[2]

1 *Re Sam Weller and Sons Ltd* [1990] BCLC 80.

2 *Re Williams Group Tullamore Ltd* [1985] IR 613.

Estoppel: Where a member fails to object at the time to conduct which he considers to be oppressive or in disregard of his interests, he may be estopped from subsequently seeking relief in respect of those transactions under s 205.[1]

1 *Re New Ad Advertising Co Ltd* [2007] IEHC 436; *Re Greenore Trading Co Ltd* [1980] ILRM 94.

Remedies: Most commonly, the remedy granted by the court is an order that the oppressive majority, or the company itself, buy out the petitioner's shares at a price which reflects the value they would have had, but for the oppressive conduct.[1] Exceptionally, the court may instead order the oppressive majority to sell their shareholding in the company to the petitioner.[2] Indeed, sub-s (3) makes it quite clear that the order to purchase shares may also be made as against the company itself. The conduct of the parties will be relevant in determining whether their respective shareholdings are to be valued *pro rata* or whether a discount should be applied in respect of the petitioner's minority interest.[3]

The buy out of one party by the other is not, however, the only remedy at the court's disposal. It may for example, cancel an oppressive resolution or restrain the company from implementing it.[4] It would even be possible for the court to direct that the oppressor, rather than buying out the petitioner or being bought out himself, simply be prevented from taking any active role in the company's affairs.[5] Where it is proposed that a director who is also a member be removed from office,[6] the court may grant interlocutory relief preventing the removal of such a director pending the hearing of a petition under CA 1963, s 205.[7] Nevertheless, the court will be extraordinarily cautious before imposing a director on a company (at least in an active management role) by way of interlocutory remedy.[8] One remedy that is not, however, open to the court under s 205 is to award damages to the petitioner.[9]

It should be noted, though, that whatever the nature of the relief involved, it may only be ordered as against a person who has been named as a party to the proceedings.[10] Every company in relation to which such an order is made is obliged to forward a copy to the Registrar within 21 days and in default shall be guilty of an offence and liable to a fine.[11]

1 *Re Greenore Trading Co Ltd* [1980] ILRM 94; *Re Clubman Shirts Ltd* [1983] ILRM 323 and [1991] ILRM 43; *Re Westwinds Holding Co Ltd* (21 May 1974, unreported) HC (Kenny J); *Scottish Wholesale Co-Operative Society Ltd v Meyer* [1959] AC 324; *Re OC (Transport) Services Ltd* [1984] BCLC 251; *Re Emerald Group Holdings Ltd* [2009] IEHC 440. The rejection by the petitioner of a pre-litigation offer to buy out his shareholding will not necessarily render his proceedings under s 205 an abuse of process: *Re Murray Consultants Ltd* [1997] 3 IR 23. Nevertheless, the court is entitled to have regard to any such offers in determining whether he should ultimately be entitled to any relief: *Re New Ad Advertising Co Ltd* [2007] IEHC 436.

2 *Re a Company (No 00789 of 1987) ex parte Shooter (No 2)* [1991] BCLC 267.

3 *Re Bird Precision Bellows Ltd* [1986] Ch 658; *Re London School of Electronics Ltd* [1985] BCLC 273.

4 *Re Irish Visiting Motorists Bureau Ltd* (27 January 1972, unreported) HC (Kenny J); *Re Williams Group Tullamore Ltd* [1985] IR 613.

5 *Re HR Harmer Ltd* [1959] 1 WLR 62. In an *ex tempore* judgment, *Re Christy Kenneally Communications Ltd* Costello J disqualified the respondents from acting as directors and replaced them with two court appointed directors (both of whom were chartered accountants and whose role was de facto very much similar to that of a court appointed receiver).

6 See CA 1963, s 182 (right of members to remove a director by ordinary resolution) and notes thereto.

7 *Avoca Holdings v Companies Acts* [2005] IEHC 302; *McGilligan and Bowen v O'Grady* [1999] ILRM 303.

8 *Pringle v Callard* [2008] 2 BCLC 505.

9 *Irish Press plc v Ingersoll Publications Ltd* [1995] 2 IR 175.

10 *Re New-Ad Advertising Co Ltd* (26 March 1998, unreported) SC.

11 CA 1963, s 203(3).

Proceedings in camera: Proceedings will only be heard in camera[1] if a public hearing (a) would involve the disclosure of information which would be seriously prejudicial to the legitimate interests of the company and (b) would fall short of doing justice.[2]

1 CA 1963, s 205(7).

2 *Irish Press plc v Ingersoll Irish Publications Ltd* [1993] ILRM 747; *Re R Ltd* [1989] ILRM 757.

The Rule in *Foss v Harbottle*[1] and the Derivative Action: Prior to the enactment of CA 1963, s 205, the main remedy for a minority shareholder complaining of wrongdoing in relation to the internal management of a company was to seek to proceed by way of a derivative action. In this regard, the Rule in *Foss v Harbottle*[2] states that where a wrong is done to a company the proper plaintiff is normally the company itself rather than an individual shareholder. Moreover, where the transaction is one which might be made binding on the company and all its members by a simple majority of its members, no individual member of the company is allowed to maintain an action in respect of the matter for the simple reason that, if a mere majority of the members of the company is in favour of what has been done, then *cadit quaestio*, no wrong has actually been done to the company and there is nothing in respect of which anyone can sue.[3] By way of a corollary to this rule, it follows that where the only loss suffered by an individual shareholder is a reflective loss, ie a diminution in the valuation of his shareholding as a result of damage done to the company itself, the proper plaintiff remains the company and the individual shareholder has no *locus standi* to sue.[4] On the other hand, if the wrong in question is one done to the shareholder personally (eg an interference with his right to vote), then he may bring a personal action against the wrongdoer.[5] By way of exception to the Rule in *Foss v Harbottle* an individual shareholder may be entitled to proceed by way of what is known as a 'derivative action' in respect of a wrong done to the company itself in certain limited circumstances. In such circumstances, although the individual shareholder is the plaintiff, he sues for the benefit of the company and thus the company is joined as a co-defendant to the proceedings so that if the claim against the true defendant is successful, the award against that defendant may be made in the company's favour.[6] The circumstances in which a derivative action may be brought by an individual shareholder are where:

(a) the act is illegal or *ultra vires* the company;[7]

(b) the act is one which requires more than a simple majority to be ratified;[8]

(c) the act infringes the personal rights of the shareholder;[9] or

(d) the act constitutes a fraud on the minority and the wrongdoers are themselves in control of the company.[10]

There has also been some suggestion that a derivative action may be brought where the justice of the case requires it, although the position in this regard still remains far from clear.[11]

Even though the shareholder may be able to bring himself within one of the above exceptions, nevertheless he may not be entitled to proceed by way of derivative action where the majority of the independent shareholders (ie shareholders other than the proposed defendants) are opposed to the action.[12] Before an individual shareholder institutes a derivative action he may first seek the leave of the court to proceed and if he obtains such leave he will have a high likelihood of being indemnified as to costs out of the assets of the company, irrespective of the outcome of the proceedings.[13] Where such an application for leave is brought the court will first determine whether the plaintiff has the necessary *locus standi* to sue and he must also show, on the basis of affidavit evidence, supported by counsel's opinion, that he has a realistic prospect of success.[14] Moreover, even if he satisfies these tests the court still has a discretion whether to grant leave and may take into account factors such as delay on the plaintiff's part, whether he has an ulterior motive for proceeding, whether the proceedings might of themselves damage the company and whether there is some alternative remedy available.[15]

A shareholder of a parent company who can bring himself within one of the exceptions identified above may be allowed to proceed by way of derivative action not only in respect of a wrong done to the parent company but also in respect of a wrong done to one or more of its subsidiaries.[16]

1 *Foss v Harbottle* (1843) 2 Hare 461.

2 *Ibid.*

3 *Edwards v Halliwell* [1950] 2 All ER 1064; *Prudential Assurance Co Ltd v Newman Industries Ltd (No 2)* [1982] 1 Ch 204; *Balkanbank v Taher* (19 January 1995, unreported) SC.

4 *Prudential Assurance Co Ltd v Newman Industries Ltd (No 2)* [1982] 1 Ch 204; *O'Neill v Ryan* [1993] ILRM 557; *Johnson v Gore Wood & Co* [2001] 1 BCLC 313.

5 *MacDougall v Gardiner* (1875) 1 ChD 13; *Pender v Lushington* (1877) 6 ChD 70; *Edwards v Halliwell* [1950] 2 All ER 1064; *Choudhury v Bhattar* [2009] 2 BCLC 108.

6 *Spokes v Grosvenor Hotel Co Ltd* [1897] 2 QB 124; *Wallersteiner v Moir (No 2)* [1975] 1 QB 373; *Barrett v Duckett* [1995] 1 BCLC 243.

7 *Simpson v Westminster Palace Hotel* (1860) 8 HL Cas 712; *Hoole v Great Western Railway Co* (1867) LR 3 Ch App 262; *Russell v Wakefield Waterworks Co* (1875) LR 20 Eq 474; *Smith v Croft (No3)* [1987] BCLC 355; *Cockburn v Newbridge Sanitary Steam Laundry Co* [1915] 1 IR 237; *Hennessy v National Agricultural and Industrial Development Association* [1947] IR 159; *Fanning v Murtagh* [2009] 1 IR 551.

8 *Edwards v Halliwell* [1950] 2 All ER 1064; *Fanning v Murtagh* [2009] 1 IR 551. The question of whether or not the wrong is capable of ratification may not arise in circumstances where the dispute is as to the composition of the general body of shareholders: *Choudhury v Bhattar* [2009] 2 BCLC 108.

9 *MacDougall v Gardiner* (1875) 1 ChD 13; *Pender v Lushington* (1877) 6 ChD 70; *Edwards v Halliwell* [1950] 2 All ER 1064; *Choudhury v Bhattar* [2009] 2 BCLC 108; *Fanning v Murtagh* [2009] 1 IR 551. *Quaere* whether this is a true exception to the Rule in *Foss v Harbottle* at all.

10 *Menier v Hooper's Telegraph Works Ltd* (1874) 9 Ch App 350, where it was held that the 'fraud' need simply be that 'the majority have put something in their pockets at the expense of the minority'. See also *Burland v Earle* [1902] AC 83; *Cook v Deeks* [1916] 1 AC 554; *Crindle Investments v Wymes* [1999] 4 IR 578; *Glynn v Owen* [2007] IEHC 328; *Fanning v Murtagh* [2009] 1 IR 551.

11 See *Moylan v Irish Whiting Manufacturers Ltd* (14 April 1980), HC (Hamilton J); *O'Neill v Ryan* [1993] ILRM 557; *Crindle Investments v Wymes* [1999] 4 IR 578; *Glynn v Owen* [2007] IEHC 328; *Fanning v Murtagh* [2009] 1 IR 551.

12 *Smith v Croft (No3)* [1987] BCLC 355; *Glynn v Owen* [2007] IEHC 328; *Fanning v Murtagh* [2009] 1 IR 551.

13 *Fanning v Murtagh* [2009] 1 IR 551.

14 *Ibid.*

15 *Ibid.*

16 *Waddington Ltd v Thomas* [2009] 2 BCLC 82.

UK legislation

See CA 1985, ss 459, 460 and, 461; IA 1985, s 109, Sch 6, para 24; IA 1986, s 439(1), Sch, 13 Pt I; CA 1989, ss 145, Sch 19, para 11; and 212, Sch 24.

PART VI
WINDING UP
(I) PRELIMINARY
Modes of Winding Up

[205A Restriction of this Part

This Part is subject to Chapters I (general provisions) and III (secondary insolvency proceedings) of the Insolvency Regulation.][a]

Amendments

a CA 1963, s 205A inserted by EC(CI)R 2002, reg 3(b).

Notes

Overview of the Insolvency Regulation: Council Regulation (EC) No. 1346/2000 of the 22nd of May 2000 came into effect in all EU member states other than Denmark on the 31 May 2002.[1] The function of the Insolvency Regulation is to govern, between member states of the European Union, matters of jurisdiction in relation to opening cross-border insolvency proceedings, judgments on the basis of insolvency proceedings and the recognition and enforcement of such judgments.[2] It also harmonises, to the extent that it applies, the law applicable to insolvency proceedings in member states[3] and in that regard replaces the national rules of private international law. It does not however provide uniform rules on which Insolvency Proceedings may be opened in the individual member states; nor does it seek to harmonise or affect national insolvency rules and procedures which continue to apply. The Insolvency Regulation has priority over domestic winding-up provisions in so far as they conflict and this is reflected in the provisions of CA 1963, s 205A.[4]

1 In relation to the Insolvency Regulations generally see Moss, Fletcher & Isaacs *EC Regulation and Insolvency Proceedings* (OUP, 2000). See also O'Neill, 'Cross-Border Insolvency Regulation in the Supreme Court – some (EURO) food for thought' CLP May 2005 119; Greer, 'Eurofoods IFSC Limited – An End to Forum Shopping' CLP June 2006; Givens & O'Riordan, 'Eurofoods IFSC Limited Judicial Clarification of Insolvency Regulation 1346/2000' *Bar Review* July 2006 p 111. Insolvency proceedings commenced before 31 May 2002 do not fall to be governed by the Insolvency Regulations, even if they were still ongoing as of that date: art 43. See also *Oakley v Vehicle Design Ltd* [2005] EWHC 872 (Ch); *Re Ultra Motorhomes International Ltd* [2006] BCC 57.

2 Recital 6.

3 Recital 23.

4 *Re Cedarlease Ltd* [2005] 1 IR 470 where the court held that, in relation to the jurisdiction to wind up a company based on a foreign revenue debt, the old common law rule that a foreign revenue judgment could not be enforced in another member state, had been rendered inapplicable by Council Regulation 1346/2000.

Scope of the regulation: Under Article 1(1) of the Insolvency Regulation applies to collective Insolvency Proceedings which entail the partial or total divestment of a debtor and the appointment of a liquidator. Insolvency proceedings are defined in 2(a) as the collective proceedings referred to in art 1(1) listed at Appendix A to the Insolvency Regulation[1].

1 In Ireland this includes a compulsory winding up of the court, bankruptcy, administration and bankruptcy of the estate of persons dying insolvent, winding up in bankruptcy of partnerships, creditors voluntary winding up (with confirmation of a court), arrangements under the control of the court which involve the vesting of all or part of the property of the debtor in the official assignee for realisation and distribution and company examinership. In relation to a creditors' voluntary winding up CA 1963, s 267A (as implemented by SI 333/2002) provides that where a liquidator is appointed in a creditors' voluntary winding up of a company in pursuance of s 267 and the centre of the company's main interests (COMI) is situate in the state, the Master of the High Court may, on application by the liquidator, confirm the creditors' voluntary winding up for the purposes of the Insolvency Regulation and shall so certify.

Applicable law: In general the national law of the member state where proceedings have been commenced (whether main, or secondary) is the applicable law.[1] But Articles 5 to 15 of the Insolvency Regulation contain a number of conflict provisions. In brief, the following categories are expressly excluded from the provisions of the EU Regulations so that they are covered solely by the law of the State where the issues arise (and not the law of the member state where main insolvency proceedings have been commenced). These excluded categories are third party rights in rem,[2] set off,[3] retention of title,[4] contract relating to a moveable property,[5] payment systems and financial markets,[6] contracts of employment,[7] effects on rights subject to registration,[8] EU patents and trademarks,[9] detrimental acts,[10] protection of third party purchases[11] and effects of insolvency proceedings and pending lawsuits/actions.[12]

1 *Re Flightlease Ireland Ltd (in voluntary liquidation)* [2005] IEHC 274 where the court held that, as regards a claim by a foreign corporation, art 4 of the Regulation requires the claim to be determined by the Irish court in accordance with Irish law governing the lodging, verification and admission of claims in insolvency proceedings.

2 Article 5.

3 Article 6.

4 Article 7.

5 Article 8.

6 Article 9.

7 Article 10.

8 Article 11.

9 Article 12.

10 Article 13.

11 Article 14.

12 Article 15. See *Re Flightlease Ireland Ltd (in voluntary liquidation)* [2005] IEHC 274 where the court held that the proceedings did not, on the facts of that case, have to be determined in accordance with French law.

Centre of main interests ('COMI'): The insolvency proceedings only apply where the company's COMI is located in a member state. There is a rebuttable presumption that the COMI of a company is the place of its registered offices[1]. The main insolvency proceedings can only be commenced in that member state. The term COMI is not defined in the European Regulation itself. The only assistance provided is recital 13 which defines the COMI as the place where a company conducts the administration of its interests on a regular basis and therefore ascertainable by third parties. The location of COMI is important for a number of reasons. The first reason is that only the courts of the member state in which a company's COMI is situate have exclusive jurisdiction to open main insolvency proceedings under the regulation[2]. The second reason is that the applicable law in relation to the insolvency shall be the law of the member state where the main proceedings were opened.[3]

The issue of a company's COMI was recently considered in the ECJ decision in *Eurofoods IFSC Ltd*[4] which held that the COMI should correspond to the place where the company conducts the administration of its interests on a regular basis and therefore is ascertainable by third parties. The court noted that COMI must be identified by reference to criteria that are both objective and ascertainable by third parties. It also confirmed that in the case of a 'letterbox company' which is not carrying out any business in the territory of the member state in which its registered office is situate, the court will look elsewhere to determine the company's COMI. However, where a company carries on its business in the territory of the member state where its registered office is situate, the mere fact that its economic choices are or can be controlled by a parent company in another member state is not enough to rebut the presumption as to COMI laid down by the regulation.

In a number of decisions of the United Kingdom, the court has held that COMI was not the place of the registered offices.[7]

1 Article 3(1). See *Re Ci4net.com Inc* [2005] BCC 277; *Re AIM Underwriting Agencies (Ireland) ltd* [2004] EWHC 2114; *Re Collins & Aikman Corporation Group* [2005] EWHC 1754.

2 Article 3(1)

3 Article 4(1) provides that the law of the member state opening the proceedings shall determine the conditions for the opening of the proceedings, their conduct and their closure. Article 4(2) particularises on a non-exclusive basis what this entails. Article 16(1) provides that a judgement opened in a member state shall be recognised in other member states, subject to the public policy exception contained in Article 16(2).

4 *Re Eurofood IFSC Ltd* [2006] 3 WLR 309.

6 In the case of *Re Daisytek* [2003] BCC 562, the court ruled that three German and one French subsidiaries of an English company had their COMI in the United Kingdom as most of the subsidiaries' trade creditors were aware that many of the subsidiaries important functions are carried out at the parent company's registered office within the jurisdiction. In the case of *Re Brac Rent-A-Car International Inc* [2003] 1 WLR 1421 it was held that the company's place of incorporation was of little import. This case related to an American company whose registered offices were situate in Delaware. The court held that as the company's COMI was within England and Wales, the EU Regulation applied and the company could petition for its administration within the UK jurisdiction. In *Geveran Trading v Skjevesland* [2003] BPIR it was emphasised that, in relation to a bankruptcy petition the important test was where a debtor conducted the administration of his interests on a regular basis (and where it is ascertainable by third parties). Registrar Jaques also felt that the important criteria were where third parties, ie creditors, perceived a debtor's COMI to be. In *Re Dollarland (Manhattan) Ltd* [2005] All ER (D) 35 (Nov) the court had to consider whether or not a company's centre of main interests was in England and Wales. In that case the court had to consider where the presumption in art 3(1) as to the centre of main interests had been rebutted. The court held that pursuant to recital 13 of the Regulation it was of great importance that the debtor's centre of main interests were ascertainable by third parties. On the evidence it was found that it was not ascertainable by third parties that the company's centre of main interests was outside England and Wales and accordingly that the company had failed to displace the presumption in art 3.1. However, the Court found that it had jurisdiction to hear the application. In *Re 3T Telecom Ltd* [2005] All ER (D) 91 (Jan) Ch D, the company was involved in the telecommunications market. It has been incorporated in Northern Ireland and its registered office was located there. However the court found that on the facts of the case the administrative functions took place in England and that the company's customers and suppliers were based there. The court concluded that the COMI was in England and that the company had only limited connection with Northern Ireland.

Secondary proceedings: Secondary proceedings may be opened in a member state other than the member state that has the company's centre of main interests. However, in order to commence secondary proceedings a company must have an 'establishment' within the member state.[1] Secondary Proceedings are limited to the realisation of assets within the jurisdiction where those proceedings have been commenced.

1 Defined in art 2(h) as any place of operations where the debtor carries out a non-transitory economic activity with human means and goods.

Public policy exception – art 16 of EU Regulation: In *Eurofoods IFSC Ltd*[1] the ECJ held that on the proper interpretation of art 26 of the Insolvency Regulation a member state may refuse to recognise insolvency proceedings opened in another member state where the decision to open the proceedings was taken in flagrant breach of the fundamental right to be heard, which a person concerned by such proceedings enjoys.

Practical effect of EU Insolvency Regulation: It is suggested that all petitions for winding up of companies should now contain a standard wording confirming the whereabouts of the company's COMI and a statement as to whether or not the EU Insolvency Regulation applies. In the UK there is a practice direction which states that it is a necessary requirement for the hearing of a petition to include the standard wording to reflect the above.[2]

In relation to creditors' voluntary liquidations, as is set out above, pursuant to SI 333/2002 in order for a creditors' voluntary liquidation to be subject to the EU Insolvency Regulation they must seek court confirmation pursuant to CA 1963, s 267A. Confirmation is obtained by using the prescribed form before the Master of the High Court.[3] It is suggested that in any creditor's voluntary liquidation where there are foreign operations, foreign assets or foreign creditors, the liquidator should seek confirmation of court. In the event that he fails to do so, he runs the risk that main insolvency proceedings might be opened in another member state that will also prevent the local realisation of assets held abroad.

1 (Case C–341/04) [2006] 3 WLR 309.

2 Insolvency Proceedings – Practice Note 1 of 2002.

3 For an English example of a creditors' voluntary winding up confirmed by the court and governed by the Regulation, see *Re TXU Europe German Finance BV* [2005] BPIR 209.

---

206 Modes of winding up

(1) The winding up of a company may be—

(a) by the court; or

(b) voluntary.

(2) The provisions of this Act relating to winding up apply, unless the contrary appears, to the winding up of a company in either of those modes.

Definitions

'company': CA 1963, s 2(1); 'the court': CA 1963, s 2(1).

Notes

General: Subject to Council Regulation (EC) No 1346/2000 and CA 1963, s 205A, the High Court has exclusive jurisdiction regarding the winding up of companies.[1] CA 1963, s 213 sets out the circumstances in which a company may be wound up by the court, whereas CA 1963, s 251 sets out the circumstances in which a company may be wound up voluntarily. Winding up by the Court is also known as a compulsory winding up.

1 CA 1963, s 212.

Company: A company is defined as a company formed and registered under the Act, or an existing company[1]. An existing company means a company formed and registered in a register kept in the State under the Joint Stock Companies Acts, the Companies Act 1862, or the Companies (Consolidation) Act 1908.[2] The court also has the jurisdiction to wind up 'unregistered companies' including foreign companies which have a place of business or assets in the State or which otherwise have a sufficiently close connection with the State to warrant the Irish court exercising its jurisdiction over them.[3]

1 CA 1963, s 2.

2 CA 1963, s 2.

3 See CA 1963, s 345 and the notes thereto and CA 1963, s 205A.

Commencement of a winding up: In the case of a compulsory winding up, once the winding-up order has been made by the court, the commencement of the liquidation is backdated to the date of the presentation of the petition in the Central Office.[1] In the case of a voluntary winding up CA 1963, s 253 provides that the winding up commences at the time of the passing of the resolution to wind up the company.

1 CA 1963, s 220 and notes. See also *Emo Oil Ltd v Sun Alliance Ltd and London Insurance plc* [2005] IEHC 474 and the judgment of Kelly J in *Re Eurofood IFSC Ltd* [2004] 4 IR 370.

UK legislation

See IA 1986, s 73.

Contributories

207 Liability as contributories of past and present members

(1) In the event of a company being wound up, every present and past member shall be liable to contribute to the assets of the company to an amount sufficient for payment of its debts and liabilities, and the costs, charges and expenses of the winding up, and for the adjustment of the rights of the contributories among themselves, subject to subsection (2) and the following qualifications—

(a) a past member shall not be liable to contribute if he has ceased to be a member for one year or more before the commencement of the winding up;

(b) a past member shall not be liable to contribute in respect of any debt or liability of the company contracted after he ceased to be a member;

(c) a past member shall not be liable to contribute unless it appears to the court that the existing members are unable to satisfy the contributions required to be made by them in pursuance of this Act;

(d) in the case of a company limited by shares, no contribution shall be required from any member exceeding the amount, if any, unpaid on the shares in respect of which he is liable as a present or past member;

(e) in the case of a company limited by guarantee, no contribution shall, subject to subsection (3), be required from any member exceeding the amount undertaken to be contributed by him to the assets of the company in the event of its being wound up;

(f) nothing in this Act shall invalidate any provision contained in any policy of insurance or other contract whereby the liability of individual members on the policy or contract is restricted, or whereby the funds of the company are alone made liable in respect of the policy or contract;

(g) a sum due to any member of the company, in his character of a member, by way of dividends, profits or otherwise, shall not be deemed to be a debt of the company, payable to that member in a case of competition between himself and any other creditor not a member of the company, but any such sum may be taken into account for the purpose of the final adjustment of the rights of the contributories among themselves.

(2) In the winding up of a limited company, any director, whether past or present, whose liability is, under this Act, unlimited, shall, in addition to his liability (if any) to

contribute as an ordinary member, be liable to made a further contribution as if he were at the commencement of the winding up a member of an unlimited company, so, however, that—

(a) a past director shall not be liable to make such further contribution if he has ceased to hold office for a year or more before the commencement of the winding up;

(b) a past director shall not be liable to make such further contribution in respect of any debt or liability of the company contracted after he ceased to hold office;

(c) subject to the articles of the company, a director shall not be liable to make such further contribution unless the court deems it necessary to require that contribution in order to satisfy the debts and liabilities of the company and the costs, charges and expenses of the winding up.

(3) In the winding up of a company limited by guarantee which has a share capital, every member of the company shall be liable, in addition to the amount undertaken to be contributed by him to the assets of the company in the event of its being wound up, to contribute to the extent of any sums unpaid on any shares held by him.

Definitions

'articles': CA 1963, s 2(1); 'company': CA 1963, s 2(1); 'company limited by guarantee': CA 1963, s 2(1), 5(2); 'company limited by shares': CA 1963, s 2(1), 5(2); 'contributory': CA 1963, s 2(1), s 208; 'the court': CA 1963, s 2(1); 'director': CA 1963, s 2(1); 'member': CA 1963, s 31; 'share': CA 1963, s 2(1); 'unlimited company': CA 1963, s 2(1), s 5(2).

Notes

Liability of existing members: CA 1963, s 5(2) sets out the liability of a member prior to liquidation. In the case of an unlimited company, as its name suggests, the liability of the members is for the full amount of whatever deficit is ultimately found to exist. In the case of a company limited by guarantee, the liability of the member is confined to whatever amount that member has agreed to contribute to the 'guarantee fund'.[1] In the case of a company limited by shares the liability of a member is the amount, if any, which remains unpaid on his shares. This liability is enforced by making a call on the shares. The articles of association usually contain a procedure for this. In Table A, articles 15–21 provide that the directors may at their discretion make calls from time to time. However when a company goes into liquidation, CA 1963, s 207 imposes a new liability that is not discretionary. The contributions due form part of the assets of the company available for distribution by the liquidator.[2] Irrespective of the limits on liability prescribed by s 207, if the articles provide for the imposition of a greater liability on members, that greater liability can be enforced against them by the liquidator as a contractual indebtedness.[3]

1 As regards the 'guarantee fund' see CA 1963, s 5 and the notes thereto.

2 See generally *Hansraj Gupta v Asthana* [1932] 60 Ind App 1.

3 *Maxwell's Case* (1875) LR 20 Eq 585; *McKewan's Case* (1877) 6 Ch D 447; *Lion Assurance Association v Tucker* (1883) 12 QBD 176.

Liability of past members:[1] A past member[2] is not liable to contribute in respect of debts due at the winding up that were contracted after his ceasing to be a member.[3] Before a past member of a company is liable it must appear to the court that the existing members are unable to satisfy the contributions required to be made by them.[4] Where a share has been transferred from one member to another, the former holder is entitled to be indemnified by the transferee and by any subsequent holder in respect of any liability to which he may be exposed under CA 1963, s 207.[5]

1 In relation to the liability of a past member of an unlimited company which re-registered as a limited company before being wound up, see C(A)A 1983, s 53(7).

2 A person whose shares are forfeited, ranks as a past member for the purposes of s 207: *Needham's Case* (1867) LR 4 Eq 135; *Creyke's Case* (1869) 5 Ch App 63; *Marshall v Glamorgan Iron and Coal Co* (1868) LT 7 Eq 129; *Bridger's Case and Neill's Case* (1869) 4 Ch App 266; *Ladies' Dress Association v Pulbrook* [1900] 2 QB 376. Even in respect of calls which were due at the time of forfeiture, the person is still treated as a 'past member' rather than as a 'present member': *Knight's Case* (1867) 2 Ch App 321; *Bath's Case* (1878) 8 ChD 334. Thus, he is only liable to contribute if the present members' contributions are insufficient to meet the deficit in the winding up.

3 CA 1963, s 207(1)(b). The past member is however potentially liable for debts before he became a member: *Helbert's Case* (1868) LR 6 Eq 509, aff'd (1871) LR 5 HL 28.

4 CA 1963, s 207(1)(c). Although a past member is liable only in respect of debts incurred before he ceased being a member, his contribution, once made, forms part of the general assets in the winding up and is available for the benefit of all creditors of the company: *Webb v Whiffin* (1872) LR 5 HL 711.

5 *Kellock v Enthoven* (1873) LR 8 QB 458, aff'd (1874) LR 9 QB 241; *Morton v Bigham* [1873] WN 226.

Liability of directors: Apart from past and present members, directors with unlimited liability also rank as contributories,[1] albeit that they can only be called on to contribute by order of the court, and then only where it appears that even with contributions from past and present members, there will still be a deficit in the winding up.[2] Such a director ceases to have any liability if he has ceased to hold office for a year or more before the commencement of the winding up.[3] Moreover, even if the company is wound up less than a year after he ceases to hold office, he will have no liability for debts or liabilities incurred since his departure.[4]

1 CA 1963, s 207(2). See CA 1963, s 197 as to the circumstances in which a director may have unlimited liability. In practice, such directorships are unheard of.

2 CA 1963, s 207(2)(c).

3 CA 1963, s 207(2)(a).

4 CA 1963, s 207(2)(b).

Procedure for calls on contributories: To enforce the liability of the contributories the liquidator makes out a list of persons whom he claims to treat as contributories [1]. The list is made out in two parts: Part A consists of the present members and Part B of the past members.[2] 'A' members are primarily liable,[3] whereas 'B' members are only called upon to contribute if the present members' contributions are exhausted.[4] In the case of a compulsory winding up the list is settled by the Examiner of the High Court. If there is a dispute regarding settlement of the list or the contributories fail to meet their liabilities, application can be made to court for directions or for an order for payment as the case may be.[5] The application is grounded on an affidavit of the liquidator and must be served six clear days at least before the hearing of the application on every contributory proposed to be included in the call. The court can direct that notice is to be given by taking out a newspaper advertisement.[6] In reality most liquidators will realise little by way of moneys from contributories of insolvent companies for the simple reason that the vast majorities of companies are companies limited by shares with only a small issued share capital, all or most of which will already be fully paid up.

1 RSC 1986, O 74, r 92–94, sets out the full procedure. The court can however dispense with the settling of such a list under CA 1963, s 235.

2 This is so whether the company is limited or unlimited: *Re Premier Underwriting Association (No 1)* [1913] 2 Ch 29.

3 The contributions of the A contributories are applied pro rata in respect of all creditors, irrespective of when their debts were incurred: *Morris' Case* (1872) 7 Ch App 200 and (1873) 8 Ch App 800; *Webb v Whiffin* (1872) LR 5 HL 711.

4 *Wright's Case* (1868) LR 12 Eq 335; *McEwen's Case* (1871) 6 Ch App 582; *Needham's Case* (1867) LR 4 Eq 135.

5 See also notes to CA 1963, s 235.

6 See generally Keane, *Company Law* (4th edn, Tottel Publishing, 2007).

Entitlement to a dividend where a company is being wound up: A shareholder's entitlement to further dividends ceases once a winding up commences. Moreover, his right to sue in respect of accrued dividends is deferred until the debts owed to the company's ordinary creditors have been satisfied.[1] This does not mean, however, that the shareholder loses his entitlement to the dividend altogether. It may be taken into account in calculating the extent of the shareholder's right, as against other shareholders, to participate in the distribution of any remaining assets in the winding up.[2] It will rank in priority to any claim by shareholders to a return of capital.

1 This subordination of claims also applies to former shareholders in respect of any dividends still due to them: *Re Consolidated Goldfields of New Zealand Ltd* [1953] Ch 689.

2 *Re Imperial Hotel (Cork) Ltd* [1950] IR 115 as referred to as *Re Lafayette* [1950] IR 100. See also *Wilson (Inspector Taxes) v Dunnes Stores (Cork) Ltd* (22 January 1976, unreported). See also notes to CA 1963, s 78.

UK legislation

See IA 1986, ss 74, 75.

208 Definition of 'contributory'

The term 'contributory' means every person liable to contribute to the assets of a company in the event of its being wound up, and for the purposes of all proceedings for determining, and all proceedings prior to the final determination of, the persons who are to be deemed contributories, includes any person alleged to be a contributory.

Definitions

'company': CA 1963, s 2(1); 'contributory': CA 1963, s 2(1), s 208.

Notes

Definition: The definition is not limited to persons who are actually liable to contribute to the assets of the company in the event of it being wound up. The holders of fully paid shares are included in the definition even though they will have no actual liability. In essence any person who has a potential liability to contribute to the assets of the Company falls within the definition.[1]

1 *Re Anglesea Colliery Co* [1866] 1 Ch App 555; *Re Phoenix Oil and Transport Co Ltd* [1958] Ch 560, [1957] 2 All ER 218.

A contributory can petition to wind up the company: CA 1963, s 215(a) provides that a contributory can present a petition to wind up the company in limited circumstances. There is UK authority to suggest that the court will be reluctant to allow an individual holder of fully paid shares to petition to wind up a company unless it can be shown the company is solvent and that a substantial surplus of assets will be available to the members, since otherwise the member will not have a tangible interest in the winding up.[1] However, it is thought that in this jurisdiction, if the company is insolvent and ought to be wound up, but the directors have failed to take steps either to convene the necessary meetings for a creditors' voluntary winding up or alternatively to have the company authorise the presentation of a petition in the company's own name, the court would accede to a petition presented by an individual contributory who, although no longer having any tangible interest in the company because of the net asset deficiency, nonetheless wishes to ensure that there is an orderly realisation of assets for the benefit of the general body of creditors.[2]

1 *Re Instrumentation Electrical Services Ltd* [1988] BCLC 550. See also the notes to CA 1963, s 215(a).

2 In the case of *Re Irish Tourist Promotion Board Ltd* (22 April 1974, unreported) HC (Kenny J) a contributory succeeded in winding up a company on the just and equitable ground despite the fact that it was insolvent and that the majority of the creditors of the company were against the winding up. Kenny J noted the insolvency of the company and the fact that in that case the petitioner accepted that he could not hope to get anything out of a liquidation. In coming to that conclusion no authority was cited but the decision is consistent with CA 1963, s 216(1).

UK legislation

See IA 1986, s 79.

---

209 Liability of contributory

(1) The liability of a contributory shall create a debt accruing due from him at the time when his liability commenced, but payable at the times when calls are made for enforcing the liability.

(2) An action to recover a debt created by this section shall not be brought after the expiration of 12 years from the date on which the cause of action accrued.

Definitions

'contributory': CA 1963, s 2(1), s 208.

Notes

Liability to contribute: The obligation to contribute constitutes a debt by specialty[1] with liability commencing on the date on which the person becomes a member of the company.[2] However, until a call is made, the debt does not accrue due and accordingly until then time does not begin to run for the purposes of CA 1963, s 209(2).[3] Applying the same reasoning, a member who is also a creditor of the company cannot exercise a right of set off in respect of calls which had not been made prior to the commencement of the winding up.[4]

1 *Buck v Robson* (1870) LR 10 Eq 629.

2 *Re Vaughan, ex parte Canwell* (1864) De GJ and Sm 539; *Williams v Harding* (1866) LR 1 HL 9; *Re West of England Bank, ex parte Hatcher* (1879) 12 Ch D 284.

3 *Re Vaughan, ex parte Canwell* (1864) De GJ and Sm 539; *Williams v Harding* (1866) LR 1 HL 9; *Re West of England Bank, ex parte Hatcher* (1879) 12 Ch D 284.

4 *Grissell's Case* (1866) 1 Ch App 528.

UK legislation

See IA 1986, s 80.

---

210 Contributories in case of death of member

(1) If a contributory dies, either before or after he has been placed on the list of contributories, his personal representatives shall be liable in due course of administration to contribute to the assets of the company in discharge of his liability and shall be contributories accordingly.

(2) If the personal representatives make default in paying any money ordered to be paid by them, proceedings may be taken for the administration of the estate of the deceased contributory or otherwise for compelling payment thereout of the money due.

Definitions

'company': CA 1963, s 2(1); 'contributory': CA 1963, s 2(1), s 208; 'member': CA 1963, s 31.

Notes

Liability of personal representatives: The liability of the personal representatives of a deceased contributory under CA 1963, s 210(1) is representative rather than personal unless they have personally accepted the shares[1] or have made themselves liable for a *devastavit*.[2]

1 *Buchan's Case* (1879) 4 App Cas 549.

2 *Taylor v Taylor* (1870) LR 10 Eq 477.

Joint holders of shares: If shares are registered in the names of joint holders, they are treated as joint tenants insofar as the legal interest in the shares is concerned. Accordingly, in the absence of anything to the contrary in the articles, they will be treated as jointly rather than jointly and severally liable to pay calls and thus, in the death of one holder, the survivor becomes solely liable.[1] In practice, though, Model Form Articles expressly provide for the joint and several liability of joint holders.[2]

1 *Hill's Case* (1875) LR 20 Eq 585.

2 See CA 1963, Table A, part I, reg 17.

Civil Liability Act 1961, s 9(2): Notwithstanding the provisions of CA 1963, s 209(2), it would appear that by virtue of the Civil Liability Act 1961, s 9(2) no proceedings shall be maintainable against the estate of a deceased contributory unless they were instituted within the relevant limitation period and were pending at the date of death or alternatively were commenced within two years after the death, or whichever period expires first.

UK legislation

See IA 1986, s 81.

211 Contributories in case of bankruptcy of member

If a contributory becomes bankrupt, either before or after he has been placed on the list of contributories—

(a) the Official Assignee shall represent him for all the purposes of the winding up, and shall be a contributory accordingly, and may be called on to admit to proof against the estate of the bankrupt or otherwise to allow to be paid out of his assets in due course of law any money due from the bankrupt in respect of his liability to contribute to the assets of the company; and

(b) there may be proved against the estate of the bankrupt the estimated value of his liability to future calls as well as calls already made.

Definitions

'contributory': CA 1963, s 2(1), s 208; 'member': CA 1963, s 31.

Notes

Bankrupt contributory: The provisions of CA 1963, s 211 apply whether the bankrupt held the shares in his own right or as trustee for another.[1] Although the Official Assignee may be liable to admit the call to proof in the bankruptcy, he does not have the corresponding entitlement of a contributory to present a petition for the winding up of the company.[2]

1 *Re Wolverhampton Steel and Iron Co Ltd* [1977] 3 All ER 467.

2 *Re HL Bolton Engineering Co Ltd* [1956] Ch 577 at 583/4.

UK legislation

See IA 1986, s 82.

(II) WINDING UP BY THE COURT

Jurisdiction

212 Jurisdiction to wind up companies

The High Court shall have jurisdiction to wind up any company.

Definitions

'company': CA 1963, s 2(1).

Notes

Procedure: By virtue of this section the High Court is the only court in the State with original jurisdiction to make an order for the winding up of a company.[1] A company may be wound up by the court on presentation of a petition under Part VI of the CA 1963.[2] The petition for the winding up of the company must be verified by affidavit[3] and must be presented at the Central Office[4]. Every petition must be advertised seven clear days before the hearing, once in *Iris Oifigiúil* and once at least in two Dublin daily morning newspapers or in such other newspapers as the Registrar when appointing the time and place in which the petition is to be heard shall direct[5].

1 Of course the Supreme Court has jurisdiction to make such an order on appeal from a decision of the High Court pursuant to RSC 1986, Ord 58.

2 RSC 1986, Ord 74, r 7.

3 RSC 1986, Ord 74, r 12.

4 RSC 1986, Ord 74, r 8.

5 RSC 1986, Ord 74, r 10.

Cases in which Company may be wound up by the Court

213 Circumstances in which company may be wound up by the court

A company may be wound up by the court if—

(a) the company has by special resolution resolved that the company be wound up by the court;

(b) [...];[a]

(c) the company does not commence its business within a year from its incorporation or suspends its business for a whole year;

(d) the number of members is reduced, in the case of a private company, [or an investment company (within the meaning of Part XIII of the Companies Act, 1990],[b] below two, or, in the case of any other company, below seven;

(e) the company is unable to pay its debts;

[(ea) the company is an SE, within the meaning of the European Communities (European Public Limited – Liability Company) Regulations 2007, that no longer complies with the requirements specified in Article 7 of Council Regulation (EC) No 2157/2001 on the Statute for a European company;][c]

(f) the court is of opinion that it is just and equitable that the company [other than an investment company within the meaning of Part XIII of the Companies Act, 1990, or the European Communities (Undertakings for Collective Investment in Transferable Securities) Regulations, 1989 (SI No 78 of 1989,][d] should be wound up;

[(fa) the court is of opinion that it is just and equitable that the company, being an investment company within the meaning aforesaid, should be wound up and the following conditions are complied with—

(i) in the case of an investment company within the meaning of Part XIII of the Companies Act, 1990—

(I) the petition for such winding-up has been presented by the trustee of the company, that is to say, the person nominated by the Central Bank of Ireland under section 257(4)(c) of the Companies Act, 1990, in respect of that company;

(II) the said trustee has notified the investment company of its intention to resign as such trustee and six or more months have elapsed since the giving of that notification without a trustee having been appointed to replace it;

(III) the court, in considering the said petition, has regard to—

(A) any conditions imposed under section 257 of the Companies Act, 1990, in relation to the resignation from office of such a trustee and the replacement of it by another trustee; and

(B) whether a winding-up would best serve the interests of shareholders in the company; and

(IV) the petition for such winding-up has been served on the company (if any) discharging, in relation to the first-mentioned company, functions of a company referred to in conditions imposed under section 257 of the Companies Act, 1990, as a 'management company'; and

(ii) in the case of an investment company within the meaning of the European Communities (Undertakings for Collective Investment in Transferable Securities) Regulations, 1989, such conditions as the Minister may prescribe by regulations.][e]

(g) the court is satisfied that the company's affairs are being conducted, or the powers of the directors are being exercised, in a manner oppressive to any member or in disregard of his interests as a member and that, despite the existence of an alternative remedy, winding up would be justified in the general circumstances of the case so, however, that the court may dismiss a petition to wind up under this paragraph if it is of opinion that proceedings under section 205 would, in all the circumstances, be more appropriate.

[(h) after the end of the general transitional period, within the meaning the of the Companies (Amendment) Act, 1983, the company is an old public limited company within the meaning of that Act;

(i) after the end of the transitional period for share capital, within the meaning of the Companies (Amendment) Act, 1983, the company has not complied with the conditions specified in section 12 (9) of that Act.][f]

Amendments

a CA 1963, s 213(b) repealed by C(A)A 1983, Sch 3.

b CA 1963, s 213(d) amended by CA 1990, s 260(1) as substituted by C(A)(No 2)A 1999, s 54(3).

c CA 1963, s 213(ea) inserted by EC(EPLLC)R 2007, reg 25(4).

d CA 1963, s 213(f) amended by CLEA 2001, s 93(a) by the insertion after 'company' of ', other than an investment company within the meaning of Part XIII of the Companies Act, 1990, or the European Communities (Undertakings for Collective Investment in Transferable Securities) Regulations 1989 (SI 78 of 1989),'.

e CA 1963, s 213(fa) inserted by CLEA 2001, s 93(b). The provisions of para (fa)(ii) have yet to be brought into force.

f CA 1963, s 213(h) and (i) inserted by C(A)A 1983, Sch 1 para 17.

Definitions

'company': CA 1963, s 2(1); 'the court': CA 1963, s 2(1); 'director': CA 1963, s 2(1); 'member': CA 1963, s 31; 'old public limited company': C(A)A 1983, s 12(1); 'private company': CA 1963, s 2(1), s 33(1); 'share': CA 1963, s 2(1); 'special resolution': CA 1963, s 141.

Notes

Circumstances in which a company may be wound up:

The members have resolved by special resolution to wind up the company: It is unusual for the members of a company to pass a special resolution to petition the court to place the company in compulsory winding up. Instead, if the members wish to have the company wound up it is more usual for them to proceed by way of voluntary liquidation pursuant to the provisions of CA 1963, Part VI (iii). From the point of view of both members and creditors, voluntary winding up is often preferable to a compulsory winding up, as representing the less costly option, with the consequent possibility of a higher dividend being paid.

The company does not commence its business within a year from its incorporation or suspends its business for a whole year: It is rare for an application to be made under this ground. The court's power under this section is discretionary and the fact that a petitioner establishes that the company has not commenced business does not give him an automatic right to an order.[1] The order will only be granted where there is a fair indication that there is no intention of carrying on the business. The order may be made despite the opposition of the majority of shareholders.[2] The non-commencement of business refers to business activities and not to the allotment of shares.[3] If a company suspends only part of its business an order will not be made.[4] The court will not make an order on the grounds of suspension of business if the majority of shareholders oppose the application and there is a genuine intention to proceed with the business.[5]

1 *Re Metropolitan Railway Warehousing Co* (1867) 36 LJ (Ch) 827.

2 *Re Tumacacori Mining Co* (1874) LR 17 Eq 534.

3 *Re South Luipaards Vlei Gold Mines* (1897) 13 TLR 504.

4 *Re Norwegian Titanic Iron Co Ltd* [1965] 35 Beav 223.

5 *Re Middlesborough Assembly Rooms Co* [1880] 14 Ch 827.

The number of members is reduced in the case of a private company below two or in the case of any other company below seven: In the case of private limited companies this is no longer a ground to petition the court to have such a company wound up.[1] It is also of no application to investment companies as a result of amendments to CA 1963, s 213(d) effected by C(A)(No2)A 1999, s 54(3).

1 Regulation 11 of the EC(SMPLC)R 1994 provides that this section no longer applies to a private company limited by shares or limited by guarantee and having a share capital. This ground, however, continues to apply in full force and effect in the case of public companies and unlimited private companies.

The company is unable to pay its debts: Inability to pay debts is defined in CA 1963, s 214. In relation to winding up a company for inability to pay its debts see generally the notes to CA 1963, s 214.

The court is of the opinion that it is just and equitable that the company (not being an investment company) should be wound up: The circumstances in which a company other than an investment company may be wound up are wide-ranging and are by no means limited by reference to the other grounds for winding up recited in s 213.[1]

1 *Ebrahimi v Westbourne Galleries Ltd* [1973] AC 360 at 374; *Re Murph's Restaurants Ltd* [1979] ILRM 141 at 153.

Illegality: Where a company has been formed for an illegal purpose[1] or actively participates in, condones or supports corrupt or criminal conduct, it may be just and equitable to have the company wound up.[2] Similarly if the company is being used as an instrument of fraud, the company can be wound up on the just and equitable ground [3]. However, it is not a pre-condition to the exercise of the court's jurisdiction under CA 1963, s 213(f) that those opposing the petition should have been guilty of a 'lack of probity' in their dealings with the petitioner,[4] and in this regard the court has acknowledged that its jurisdiction is analogous to that found in the provisions of the Partnership Act 1890, s 35(f).[5]

Failure of substratum: Where there has been a failure of substratum, the court has been prepared to make a winding-up order on the just and equitable ground. There is a failure of substratum where the purpose for which the company was formed is no longer pursued, or where the company pursues a different venture to that originally envisaged.[6] However, a company will not be wound up under the just and equitable ground on the basis that a particular prominent purpose, even the most important and most prominent purpose, identified for the company in its memorandum is no longer capable of being achieved if it is the case that other commercial purposes authorised by the memorandum remained capable of being achieved.[7] Nor will the company be wound up for failure of substratum in circumstances where its principal object is conducted by the members for a period of time through the medium of an associated company and where, after the associated company has gone into liquidation, the principal object is capable of being resumed by the company itself.[8]

Breakdown of mutual trust and confidence: In the case of a company which is a quasi-partnership, it may be just and equitable to make a winding-up order where the relationship of mutual trust and confidence which previously existed between the members no longer exists.[9] In practice a petition for relief under s 213(f) in respect of a quasi-partnership may also seek relief under CA 1963, ss 205 and 213(g) on grounds of alleged oppression and/or disregard of interests. The following have all been held to constitute situations justifying the making of a winding-up order on the just and equitable ground following the breakdown of such a relationship of trust and confidence:

(i) where it was understood that all shareholders would be entitled to participate in the management of the business, but the majority subsequently sought to exclude a minority shareholder;[10]

(ii) where an individual subscribed for shares on the understanding that he would be elected to the board of directors of the company but was never in fact so elected; and[11]

(iii) where a breakdown in relations between equal shareholders resulted in deadlock both at board level and in general meetings.[12]

Whilst the court may refuse to make a winding-up order where the breakdown in the relationship between the parties has been entirely due to the fault of the petitioner,[13] relief will not be refused where the petitioner has merely contributed to that breakdown.[14]

It is to be noted though that even if the petitioner establishes that there has been a breakdown in the relationship between the parties which has not been caused solely by him, he may still be refused relief if the respondents can show that the company is solvent and that they have made a fair offer to buy his shares which he has unreasonably refused to accept.[15] Furthermore, if the affairs of the company are governed by a shareholders' agreement which contains a sufficiently widely drafted arbitration clause, the court may possibly be prepared to stay any petition under CA 1963, s 213(f) thereby requiring the parties to arbitrate their differences instead.[16]

Public interest: It may be just and equitable to wind up a company in the public interest. So, for example, where a company had been formed specifically to carry out the policies and directions of a public body, but refused to comply with those policies and directions, the court was prepared to place it in liquidation.[17] The court may also wind up a company on the public interest grounds that the business of the company was founded and continued on the basis of a fraud or deception.[18] In a similar vein, the ODCE may petition to have a body corporate wound up where it appears from an inspector's report made under CA 1990, s 11 or from information obtained as part of an inquiry under CA 1990, Part II that the making of such an order would be just and equitable.[19] The court will make such an order where the ODCE has established that it is in the public interest to do so.[20] Weighty and substantial reasons will, however, have to be established by the ODCE in order to convince the court that the making of a winding-up order is indeed in the public interest and in this context, mere proof of some unlawful acts may not of itself be sufficient to warrant placing the company in liquidation,[21] particularly if the company has since taken or is taking steps to address the issues not merely by word but also by deed.[22] The court will also have regard to any adverse consequences for members of the public, including customers and creditors, in the event of a winding-up order being made.[23] However, the fact that the company refuses to co-operate with an investigation or inquiry being conducted under CA 1990, Part II may of itself render it just and equitable to wind up the company.[24] If the body corporate is a foreign company, a winding-up order will not, however, be made on public interest grounds unless that company has a real and sufficient connection with the jurisdiction of the Irish court.[25]

1 *R v Registrar of Joint Stock Companies* [1931] 2 KB 197; *Bowman v Secular Society Ltd* [1917] AC 406; *McEllistrim v Ballymacelligott Co-Operative and Dairy Society Ltd* [1919] AC 549.

2 *Re Shrinkpak Ltd* (20 December 1989, unreported) HC (Barron J) referred to by Courtney in *Law of Private Companies* (2nd edn Tottel Publishing, 2002) para 25.090.

3 *Re Newbridge Sanitary Steam Laundry Ltd* [1917] 1 IR 67; *Re Shrinkpak Ltd* (20 December 1989, unreported) HC (Barron J); *Re Senator Hanseatische Verwaltunggesellschaft GmbH* [1996] 2 BCLC 562; *Re Delfin International (SA) Ltd* [2000] 1 BCLC 71; *Re a company* [2000] 1 BCLC 427; *Re North West Holdings plc* [2001] 1 BCLC 468; *Re ForceSun Ltd* [2002] 2 BCLC 302; *Re Alpha Club (UK) Ltd* [2002] 2 BCLC 612.

4 *Symington v Symington's Quarries Ltd* (1905) 8 F 121 at 130; *Re Yenidje Tobacco Ltd* [1916] 2 Ch 426 at 431–432; *Ebrahimi v Westbourne Galleries Ltd* [1973] AC 360 at 383; *Re Murph's Restaurants Ltd* [1979] ILRM 141 at 153.

5 *Symington v Symington's Quarries Ltd* (1905) 8 F 121 at 130; *Re Yenidje Tobacco Ltd* [1916] 2 Ch 426 at 431–432; *Ebrahimi v Westbourne Galleries Ltd* [1973] AC 360 at 383; *Re Murph's Restaurants Ltd* [1979] ILRM 141 at 153.

6 *Cotman v Brougham* [1918] AC 514; *Re German Date Coffee Co* (1882) 20 ChD 169; *Re Haven Gold Mining Co* (1882) 20 ChD 151; *Re Crown Bank* (1890) 44 ChD 634; *Re Anglo Continental Produce Ltd* [1939] 1 All ER 99; *Re Kitson and Co Ltd* [1946] 1 All ER 435; *Re Perfectair Holdings Ltd* [1990] BCLC 423. For the meaning of 'substratum' see the notes to CA 1963, s 10.

7 *Re Kitson & Co Ltd* [1946] 1 All ER 435. *Re Taldua Rubber Co Ltd* [1946] 2 All ER 763 as approved by Scott J in *Re Perfectair Holdings Ltd* [1990] BCLC 423.

8 *Re Metafile Ltd* [2007] 2 IR 613. In that case Laffoy J expressed the view that winding up for failure of substratum had become anachronistic as a result of the ability to alter a company's objects clause pursuant to CA 1963, s 10.

9 *Ebrahimi v Westbourne Galleries Ltd* [1973] AC 360; *Re Murph's Restaurants Ltd* [1979] ILRM 141; *Re Irish Tourist Promotions Ltd* (1963–1993) Irish Company Law Reports 382; *Re Vehicle Buildings and Insulations Ltd* [1986] ILRM 239; *Re Tradalco Ltd, Bluzwed Metals Ltd v Transworld Metals SA* (9 May 2001, unreported) HC (Lavan J); *Re Yenidje Tobacco Co Ltd* [1916] 2 Ch 426; *Re Lundie Bros Ltd* [1965] 2 All ER 692.

10 *Re Lundie Bros Ltd* [1965] 2 All ER 692; *Ebrahimi v Westbourne Galleries Ltd* [1973] AC 360; *Tay Bok Choon v Tahansan Sdn Bhd* [1987] BCLC 472; *CVC/Opportunity Equity Partners Ltd v Demarco Almeida* [2002] 2 BCLC 108; *Re Murph's Restaurants Ltd* [1979] ILRM 141; *Re Wondoflex Textiles Pty Ltd* [1951] VR 458.

11 *Re Zinotty Properties Ltd* [1984] 3 All ER 754.

12 *Re Yenidje Tobacco Co Ltd* [1916] 2 Ch 426; *Re Davis Investments (East Ham) Ltd* [1961] 3 All ER 926; *Re A and BC Chewing Gum Ltd* [1975] 1 All ER 1017; *Re Irish Tourist Promotions Ltd* (1963–1993) Irish Company Law Reports 382; *Re Vehicle Buildings and Insulations Ltd* [1986] ILRM 239; *Re Tradalco Ltd, Bluzwed Metals Ltd v Transworld Metals SA* (9 May 2001, unreported) HC (Lavan J).

13 *Ebrahimi v Westbourne Galleries Ltd* [1973] AC 360 at 387.

14 *Re Vehicle Buildings and Insulations Ltd* [1986] ILRM 239; *Re Tradalco Ltd, Bluzwed Metals Ltd v Transworld Metals SA* (9 May 2001, unreported) HC (Lavan J).

15 *CVC/Opportunity Equity Partners Ltd v Demarco Almeida* [2002] 2 BCLC 108; *Fuller v Cyracuse Ltd* [2001] 1 BCLC 187; *Re a company* (1988) 4 BCC 80; *Re a company* [1987] BCLC 562; *Thomas v HW Thomas Ltd* [1985] LRC (Comm) 802; *Re a company* [1983] BCLC 151. These cases, which admittedly concern the more drastic remedy of liquidation may be contrasted with *Horgan v Murray* [1997] 3 IR 23 where a reasonable offer to buy out the petitioner's shares may not justify the dismissal of a petition under CA 1963, s 205.

16 *Re Via Net Works (Ireland) Ltd* [2002] 2 IR 47. cf *Re Peveril Gold Mines Co Ltd* [1898] 1 Ch 122.

17 *Re Dublin and Eastern Regional Tourism Organisation Ltd* [1990] 1 IR 579.

18 *Re Supporting Link* [2004] 2 BCLC 486; *Re Millennium Advanced Technology Ltd* [2004] 2 BCLC 77; *Re Drivertime Recruitment Ltd* [2005] 1 BCLC 411; *Re UK-Euro Group plc* [2007] 1 BCLC 812.

19 CA 1990, s 12(2).

20 *Re Walter L Jacob and Co Ltd* [1989] BCLC 345; *Re Senator Hanseatische Verwaltunggesellschaft GmbH* [1996] 2 BCLC 562; *Re Titan International Inc* [1998] 1 BCLC 102; *Re Market Wizard Systems (UK) Ltd* [1998] 2 BCLC 282; *Re Delfin International (SA) Ltd* [2000] 1 BCLC 71; *Re a company* [2000] 1 BCLC 427; *Secretary of State for Trade and Industry v Leyton Housing Trustees Ltd* [2000] 2 BCLC 808; *Re North West Holdings plc* [2001] 1 BCLC 468; *Re ForceSun Ltd* [2002] 2 BCLC 302; *Re Alpha Club (UK) Ltd* [2002] 2 BCLC 612.

21 *Re Portfolios of Distinction Ltd* [2006] 2 BCLC 261.

22 *Re National Irish Bank Ltd (No 3)* [2004] 4 IR 186; *Secretary of State for Trade and Industry v Bell Davies Trading Ltd* [2005] 1 BCLC 516.

23 *Re National Irish Bank Ltd (No 3)* [2004] 4 IR 186.

24 *Re Equity and Provident Ltd* [2002] 2 BCLC 78; *Secretary of State for Business Enterprise and Regulatory Reform v Art It plc* [2009] 1 BCLC 262.

25 *Re Real Estate Development Co Ltd* [1991] BCLC 210; *Re Titan International Inc* [1998] 1 BCLC 102.

The court is of the opinion that it is just and equitable that the company (being an investment company) should be wound up: In the case of an investment company, a winding-up petition on the just and equitable ground will have to observe the procedural requirements contained in CA 1963, s 213(fa). However, to date only subparagraph (i) of s 213(fa) has been brought into force. The only person entitled to present a petition under s 213(fa)(i) is the trustee appointed by IFSRA under CA 1990, s 257(4)(c).

Company's affairs being conducted or powers of directors being exercised in a manner oppressive to a member or in disregard of his interests: For a fuller discussion on oppression and disregard of interests, see notes to CA 1963, s 205.

Failure of old public companies to re-register within the transitional period: Every old public company had to re-register as some other form of company or go into voluntary liquidation before the end of the transitional period, namely 13 October 1986. Failure to do so entitled the Registrar of Companies to petition to have that company wound up compulsorily.

Winding up of insurance undertakings: See the European Communities (Reorganisation and Winding-up of Insurance Undertakings) Regs 2003.

***Locus standi* to present a winding-up petition**: See CA 1963, s 215 and the notes thereto.

UK legislation

See IA 1986, s 122.

214 Circumstances in which company deemed to be unable to pay its debts

A company shall be deemed to be unable to pay its debts—

(a) if a creditor, by assignment or otherwise, to whom the company is indebted in a sum exceeding [€1,269.74][a] then due, has served on the company, by leaving it at the registered office of the company, a demand in writing requiring the company to pay the sum so due, and the company has for 3 weeks thereafter neglected to pay the sum or to secure or compound for it to the reasonable satisfaction of the creditor; or

(b) if execution or other process issued on a judgment, decree or order of any court in favour of a creditor of the company is returned unsatisfied in whole or in part; or

(c) if it is proved to the satisfaction of the court that the company is unable to pay its debts, and in determining whether a company is unable to pay it debts, the court shall take into account the contingent and prospective liabilities of the company.

Amendments

a '£1,000' substituted for '£50' by CA 1990, s 213. £1,000 converted to €1,269.74 by Council Regulation (EC) 1103/97, No 974/98 and No 2866/98 and the Economic and Monetary Union Act, s 6.

Definitions

'**company**': CA 1963, s 2(1); '**the court**': CA 1963, s 2(1).

Notes

Winding up where the company is unable to pay its debts: A petition for winding up may be presented under CA 1963, s 213(e) where a company is unable to pay its debts. The petition may be presented by the company itself (in which case it must have been authorised by resolution of the members in general meeting)[1] or it may be presented by a creditor or contributory.[2] Inability to pay debts may be established by the service of a statutory demand for not less than €1,2369.74 which goes unsatisfied for at least three weeks[3] or by the return unsatisfied in whole or in part of any execution or other process on a judgment, decree or order of any court.[4] In addition, however, inability to pay debts (by which is meant inability to pay debts as they fall due)[5] may be established by any other available evidence (eg the company's own accounts, cheques being dishonoured, the company admitting insolvency etc).[6] This may allow for the quicker presentation of the petition since there is no need to allow three weeks to elapse before it can be presented.[7]

1 *Re Galway and Salthill Tramways Co* [1918] 1 IR 62.

2 CA 1963, s 215. For the restrictions on the presentation of a petition by a contributory, see s 215(a).

3 CA 1963, s 213(a).

4 CA 1963, s 213(b).

5 *JSF Finance and Currency Exchange Co Ltd v Akma Solutions Inc* [2001] 2 BCLC 307.

6 CA 1963, s 214(c). See the dicta of Barron J in *H Albert d Barry NV v O'Mullane* (2 June 1992), pp 54–55. See also Forde, *The Law of Company Insolvency* (Round Hall, 1993) pp 151–152.

7 *Taylors Industrial Flooring Ltd v MandH Plant Hire (Manchester) Ltd* [1990] BCLC 216; See also Courtney, *Law of Private Companies* (2nd edn, Tottel Publishing, 2002) at paras 25.063–25.064.

Statutory demand: There is no requirement that the letter takes any particular form. All the section requires is that the demand is made in writing. However, in order to be effective, the demand should be unequivocal, of a peremptory character and unconditional.[1] If the debt is contingent only, it may not be relied upon to form the basis of a statutory demand unless and until the contingency has occurred.[2] The demand should be left at the registered office of the Company by hand. A demand by way of fax or telex is not good service, as it was not 'left' at the company's office.[3] Once the demand has been duly served, 21 clear days must elapse before the presentation of the petition. The general rule in the computation of periods of time is that unless there is a sufficient indication to the contrary, fractions of the day should be ignored.[4]

1 *Re a company* [1985] BCLC 37; *Re WMG Toughening Ltd* [2001] 3 IR 113 (reversed on other grounds at [2003] 1 IR 389).

2 *JSF Finance and Currency Exchange Co Ltd v Akma Solutions Inc* [2001] 2 BCLC 307.

3 *Re a company* [1985] BCLC 37; *Re WMG Toughening Ltd* [2001] 3 IR 113 (reversed on other grounds at [2003] 1 IR 389).

4 *Re Lympne Investments Ltd* [1972] 2 All ER 385; *Re Catholic Publishing and Book Selling Co Ltd* (1864) 2 De Gj and Sm 116.

Demand in respect of an assigned debt: CA 1963, s 214(a) allows for the statutory demand to be served in respect of a debt originally due to the creditor or alternatively acquired by assignment. Although assignment includes an equitable assignment[1] it does not include a part assignment of the debt.[2] Thus, the assignee of part only of a debt cannot serve an effective demand under s 214(a). Either the demand must be made by the assignor in whom the legal title to the debt is still vested[3] or alternatively the assignee may seek to establish the company's insolvency by some means other than the service of a statutory demand.[4]

1 *Re Montgomery Moore Ship Collision Doors Syndicate* [1903] WN 121; *Re Steel Wing Co* [1921] 1 Ch 349.

2 *Re Steel Wing Co* [1921] 1 Ch 349.

3 *Re Steel Wing Co* [1921] 1 Ch 349; *Parmalat Capital Finance Ltd v Food Holdings Ltd* [2009] 1 BCLC 274.

4 *Re Steel Wing Co* [1921] 1 Ch 349.

Disputed debt: A petitioning creditor who has proved that the company is unable to pay its debt is normally entitled to a winding-up order *ex debito justitiae*.[1] On the other hand, if the debt is bona fide disputed on substantial grounds the petition will be dismissed.[2] The appropriate course is to litigate the debt instead.[3] Indeed, the very presentation of a petition on foot of a genuinely disputed debt may amount to an abuse of the process of the court,[4] in which event the company may be entitled to its costs on an indemnity basis.[5] A debt will also be regarded as being disputed where the company has a valid cross-claim which equals or exceeds the amount of the petition debt.[6] In relation to a cross-claim the test to be applied is whether the cross-claim is made in good faith and on substantial grounds. The issue should not be whether the claim will succeed but is whether or not it is a claim made in good faith and on substantial grounds [7] However, if the cross-claim is less than the amount of the creditor's claim, so that at least €1,269.74 of the petition debt remains undisputed, the petition will be normally allowed to proceed and a winding-up order will be made in respect of the company.[8] Similarly, if the entire of the debt is disputed, but the grounds of defence are shown to have no substance, the court will accede to the petition and wind up the company.[9]

1 *Re P and J Macrae* [1961] 1 All ER 302.

2 *Mann and Another v Goldstein and another* [1968] 2 All ER 769; *Stonegate Securities v Gregory* [1980] Ch 576; *Re Pageboy Couriers Ltd* [1983] ILRM 510; *Re Bula Ltd* [1990] 1 IR 440; *Re a company ex parte Rousell* [1992] BCLC 562; *Re Wallace Smith and Co Ltd* [1992] BCLC 970; *Clandown Ltd v Davis* [1994] 2 ILRM 536; *Truck and Machinery Sales Ltd v Marubeni Komatsu Ltd* [1996] 1 IR 12; *Re Ringinfo Ltd* [2002] 1 BCLC 210; *Re UK (Aid) Ltd* [2003] 2 BCLC 351; *Re WMG (Toughening)Ltd* [2003] 1 IR 389; *Coalport Building Co Ltd v Castle Contracts (Ireland) Ltd* (19 January 2004, unreported) HC (Laffoy J); *Re ICT International Cotton and Textile Trading Co Ltd* [2004] IEHC 55; *Re Mares Associates Ltd* [2006] IEHC 73; *Re VP Developments Ltd* [2005] 2 BCLC 607; *Re 3H Europe Ltd* [2006] All ER (D) 25; *Bolsover District Council v Dennis Rye Ltd* [2009] 4 All ER 1140.

3 *Re Claybridge Shipping Co SA (1981)* [1997] 1 BCLC 572; *Re Bayoil SA* [1999] 1 All ER 374; *Montgomery v Wanda Modes Ltd* [2002] 1 BCLC 289; *Re UK (Aid) Ltd* [2003] 2 BCLC 351. *Re ICT International Cotton and Textile Trading Company Ltd* [2004] IEHC 55.

4 *Mann and Another v Goldstein and another* [1968] 2 All ER 769; *Stonegate Securities v Gregory* [1980] Ch 576; *Re Pageboy Couriers Ltd* [1983] ILRM 510; *Re Bula Ltd* [1990] 1 IR 440; *Re a company* [1992] BCLC 865; *Re Dubned Exports Ltd* [1986] IEHC 31 (Costello J); *Re a company* [1998] 2 BCLC 111; *Truck and Machinery Sales Ltd v Marubeni Komatsu Ltd* [1996] 1 IR 12; *Re Ringinfo Ltd* [2002] 1 BCLC 210; *Re WMG (Toughening)Ltd* [2003] 1 IR 389.

5 *Re a company* [2003] 2 BCLC 346; *Re a company* [1992] BCLC 865.

6 *Re Bayoil SA* [1999] 1 All ER 374; *Montgomery v Wanda Modes Ltd* [2002] 1 BCLC 289; *Re WMG (Toughening)Ltd* [2003] 1 IR 389. See also *Chan v Appasamy* [2008] 1 BCLC 314.

7 See *Re Pageboy Securities Ltd* [1983] ILRM 510 as approved by Clarke J in *Re Emerald Portable Building Systems* [2005] IEHC 301.

8 *Re Tweeds Garages Ltd* [1962] Ch 406; *Mann v Goldstein* [1968] 2 All ER 769; *Bryanston Finance Ltd v De Vries (No 2)* [1976] 1 Ch 63; *Stonegate Securities v Gregory* [1980] Ch 576; *Taylor's Industrial v M and H Plant Hire* [1990] BCLC 216; *Patrick Butterly and Sons Ltd v Top Securities Ltd* (27 September 1995, unreported) HC (Keane J); *Truck and Machinery Sales Ltd v Marubeni Komatsu Ltd* 1 IR [1996] 12.

9 *In the matter of Millhouse Taverns Ltd* [2000] IEHC 55 (Finnegan J); *Re a company* [1997] 1 BCLC 639; *Greenacre Publishing Group v The Manson Group* [2000] BCC 11; *Orion Media Marketing Ltd v Media Brook Ltd* [2002] 1 BCLC 184; *Re Cooling Equipment Wholesale Ltd* [2002] 2 BCLC 745; *Parmalat Capital Finance Ltd v Food Holdings Ltd* [2009] 1 BCLC 274.

Restraining the presentation or advertising of a petition: As noted above, the presentation of a petition in respect of a debt which is disputed in good faith and on substantial grounds, constitutes an abuse of process. The commercial implications of the commencement of winding-up proceedings for a company may be extreme. Accordingly, whilst it will only exercise such a jurisdiction with great caution, where a *prima facie* case of abuse of process has been made out, the court will normally be prepared to grant an injunction restraining the presentation and/or advertisement of such a petition.[1]

1 *Re Tweeds Garages Ltd* [1962] Ch 406; *Mann v Goldstein* [1968] 2 All ER 769; *Bryanston Finance Ltd v De Vries (No 2)* [1976] 1 Ch 63; *Stonegate Securities v Gregory* [1980] Ch 576; *Coulson Sanderson and Ward v Ward* [1986] BCLC 99; *Taylor's Industrial v M and H Plant Hire* [1990] BCLC 216; *Re a company* [1992] BCLC 633; *Re a company* [1992] BCLC 865; *Patrick Butterly and Sons Ltd v Top Securities Ltd* (27 September 1995, unreported) HC (Keane J); *Re a company* [1998] 2 BCLC 54; *Re Ringinfo Ltd* [2002] 1 BCLC 210. Although Morris J was prepared to restrain the presentation of a petition where only part of the debt was disputed in the case of *Clandown Ltd v Davis* [1994] 2 ILRM 536, that decision was questioned by Keane J in the case of *Truck and Machinery Sales Ltd v Marubeni Komatsu Ltd* 1 IR [1996] 12. Thus an injunction will only be granted where the entire of the debt is disputed in good faith on substantial grounds, or where the undisputed portion of the debt is less than €1,269.74. See also *Meridian Communications Ltd v Eircell Ltd* [2001] IESC 42 (McGuinness J). See also *Coalport Building Company Ltd v Castle Contracts (Ireland) Ltd* [2004] IEHC 6, *Celtech International Ltd v Dalkia Utility Services plc* [2004] EWHC 193 (ch) [2004] All ER (d) 197; *Re A Company (no 4298 of 2006)* [2006] All ER (D) 277; *Re 3H Europe Ltd* [2006] All ER (D) 25.

The tort of malicious presentation of petition: In addition to constituting an abuse of process, the presentation of a winding-up petition in respect of a debt which is genuinely disputed on substantial grounds may also constitute an actionable tort, provided it can be shown that there was an absence of reasonable or probable cause for presenting the petition in the first place and provided it can also be shown that there was malice or improper motive on the part of the petitioner in presenting the petition.[1]

1 *Radivojevic v LR Industries Ltd* (22 November 1984, unreported) CA (Eng); *Business Computers International Ltd v Registrar of Companies* [1987] 3 All ER 465; *Partizan Ltd v OJ Kilkenny and Co Ltd* [1998] 1 BCLC 451.

Court's overriding discretion: As noted above, where a petitioning creditor establishes that a company is unable to pay its debts, he will normally be entitled to a winding-up order *ex debito justitiae*.[1] Nevertheless, the court still retains an overriding and unfettered discretion to refuse to order to wind up the company, albeit that it will only exercise this discretion sparingly and where good cause is shown.[2] If there is opposition to the making of a winding-up order from other creditors or from shareholders the court may, in accordance with CA 1963, s 309, have regard to their wishes[3] and may in its discretion decline to make the order,[4] as where it is established that the petition has been presented for an ulterior purpose,[5] or where it is established that the making of the winding-up order would operate to the detriment rather than to the benefit of creditors generally.[6] In a recent case where the petition was presented by the persons who represented a majority of the board and there was evidence that moneys owed by them to the company would, if repaid, be sufficient to render the company solvent again, the court exercised its discretion to stay the petition pending quantification in separate proceedings of the precise amount due by the petitioners to the company.[7]

1 *Re P and J Macrae* [1961] 1 All ER 302.

2 *Re Bula Ltd* [1990] 1 IR 440; *Re Genport Ltd* [1996] IEHC 34 (McCracken J); *Re Genport Ltd (No 2)* [2001] IEHC 156 (McCracken J); *Re Demaglass Holdings Ltd* [2001] 2 BCLC 633; *Re RW Sharman Ltd* [1957] 1 All ER 737; *Re P and J Macrae* [1961] 1 All ER 302; *Re Southard & Co Ltd* [1979] 1 WLR 1198; *Re Minrealm Ltd* [2008] 2 BCLC 141.

3 *Re Minrealm Ltd* [2008] 2 BCLC 141. Less weight may be attached to the views of connected creditors than to the views of independent creditors: *Re Lummus Agricultural Services Ltd* [1999] BCC 953.

4 *Re Bula Ltd* [1990] 1 IR 440; *Re Genport Ltd* ([1996] IEHC 34 (McCracken J); *Re Genport Ltd (No 2)* [2001] IEHC 156 (McCracken J); *Re Demaglass Holdings Ltd* [2001] 2 BCLC 633.

5 *Re Bula Ltd* [1990] 1 IR 440; *Re Genport Ltd* [1996] IEHC 34 (McCracken J); *Re Genport Ltd (No 2)* [2001] IEHC 156 (McCracken J).

6 *Re Genport Ltd* [1996] IEHC 34 (McCracken J); *Re Genport Ltd (No 2)* [2001] IEHC 156 (McCracken J); *Re Demaglass Holdings Ltd* [2001] 2 BCLC 633.

7 *Re Minrealm Ltd* [2008] 2 BCLC 141.

UK legislation

See IA 1986, s 123.

Petition for Winding Up and Effects thereof

215 Provisions as to applications for winding up

An application to the court for the winding up of a company shall be by petition presented, subject to the provisions of this section, either by the company or by any creditor or creditors (including any contingent or prospective creditor or creditors), contributory or contributories, or by all or any of those parties, together or separately, so, however, that—

(a) a contributory shall not be entitled to present a winding up petition unless—

(i) either the number of members is reduced, in the case of a private company [or an investment company (within the meaning of Part XIII of the Companies Act, 1990][a], below two, or in the case of any other company, below seven; or

(ii) the shares in respect of which he is a contributory, or some of them, either were originally allotted to him or have been held by him, and registered in his name, for at least 6 months during the 18 months before the commencement of the winding up, or have devolved on him through the death of a former holder; and

(b) [...],[b]

(c) the court shall not give a hearing to a winding-up petition presented by a contingent or prospective creditor until such security for costs has been given as the court thinks reasonable, and until a prima facie case for winding up has been established to the satisfaction of the court; and

(d) in a case falling within subsection (3) of section 170 a winding-up petition may be presented by the Minister; and

(e) a petition for winding up on the grounds mentioned in paragraph (g) of section 213 may be presented by any person entitled to bring proceedings for an order under section 205.

[(f) a petition for winding up on the grounds mentioned in section 213 (h) or (i), may be presented by the registrar of companies;][c] [...][d]

[(g) a petition presented for winding-up on the grounds mentioned in paragraph (fa) of section 213 shall be presented by the person referred to in subparagraph (i) of that paragraph or, as the case may be, the person specified in that behalf by regulations under subparagraph (ii) of that [paragraph; and[e]][f] [(h) a petition for winding-up on the grounds mentioned in paragraph (ea) of section 213 may be presented by the Director.][g]

Amendments

a Words inserted by CA 1990, s 260 which was substituted by C(A)(No 2)A 1999, s 54.

b CA 1963, s 215(b) repealed by C(A)A 1983, Sch 3.

c CA 1963, s 215(f) inserted by C(A)A 1983, Sch 1 para 18 and amended by CLEA 2001, s 94.

d 'and' deleted by EC(EPLLC)R 2007, reg 25(5)(a).

e 'paragraph; and' substituted for 'paragraph' by EC(EPLLC)R 2007, reg 25(5)(b).

f CA 1963, s 215(g) inserted by CLEA 2001, s 94.

g CA 1963, s 215(h) inserted by EC(EPLLC)R 2007, reg 25(5)(c).

Definitions

'company': CA 1963, s 2(1); 'contributory': CA 1963, s 2(1), s 208; 'the court': CA 1963, s 2(1); 'member': CA 1963, s 31; 'Minister': CA 1963, s 2(1); 'private company': CA 1963, s 2(1), s 33(1); 'the Registrar of Companies': CA 1963, s 2(1); 'share': CA 1963, s 2(1).

Notes

Procedure and form of petition: For procedure and the form of the petition, see notes to CA 1963, s 212.

Petition by the company: It is rare for companies to petition to wind up as they can resolve to be wound up voluntarily instead. In any event, a petition may not be presented by the directors in the company's own name unless they have been authorised to do so by resolution of the members in general meeting.[1]

1 *Re Galway and Salthill Tramways Co* [1918] 1 IR 62; *Re Cannock Ltd* (8 September 1984, unreported) HC (Murphy J); *Re Emmadart Ltd* [1979] 1 All ER 599.

Petition by a creditor: See notes to CA 1963, s 214. The definition of creditor includes a secured creditor even if he has obtained the appointment of a receiver in an action.[1] In this regard a secured creditor does not lose his security by presenting a winding-up petition.[2] The phrase 'creditor' also includes not only a person who has obtained judgment in a claim for unliquidated damages [3] but also a local authority in respect of unpaid rates.[4] A person having a claim that is statute barred at the date of presentation of the petition is not a creditor within the meaning of the section.[5] In the case of a contingent or prospective creditor,[6] there is a heavier onus to discharge. The creditor needs to establish a *prima facie* case for a winding-up order and may have to provide security for costs.[7] In relation to the existence or otherwise of a prima facie case, this should be determined by way of a preliminary hearing.[8]

1 *Re Borough of Portsmouth Tramways Co* [1892] 2 Ch 362.

2 *Moor v Anglo-Italian Bank* (1879) 10 ChD 681; *Re Great Western (Forest of Dean) Coal Consumers Co* (1882) 21 ChD 679.

3 *Re Pen-y-van Colliery Co* [1877] 6 Ch D 477.

4 *Re North Bucks Furniture Depositories Ltd* [1939] 2 All ER 126 *Re Karnos Property Co Ltd* [1989] BCLC 340.

5 *Re a Debtor* (No 50A SD of 1995) [1997] 1 BCLC 280. This case concerned bankruptcy but Judge Paul Baker QC held there was no material difference in this context between bankruptcy proceedings and winding-up proceedings.

6 A person with an unliquidated but undisputed claim for damages is a prospective creditor: *Re Dollar Land Holdings plc* [1994] 1 BCLC 404.

7 CA 1963, s 215 (c). See also *Truck and Machinery Sales Ltd v Marubeni Komatsu Ltd* [1996] 1 IR 12 at 27; *Holt Southey v Catnic Components Ltd* [1978] 1 WLR 630.

8 *Re Fitness Centre (South East) Ltd* [1986] BCLC 518; *Truck and Machinery Sales Ltd v Marubeni Komatsu Ltd* [1996] 1 IR 12 at 27; *Holt Southey v Catnic Components Ltd* [1978] 1 WLR 630.

Petition by a contributory: A contributory is a person who is liable to contribute to the assets of the company in the event of it being wound up, and for the purposes of all proceedings for determining, and all proceedings prior to final determination of, the term 'contributories' includes any person alleged to be a contributory,[1] as well as the personal representative of a deceased contributory.[2] Where a company has issued a share certificate to a person in respect of shares which have been allotted to him but has failed to enter his name in the register of members, the company will be estopped from denying his status as a contributory and from challenging his *locus standi* to present a winding-up petition.[3] In the event of a dispute as to whether the shares of a petitioning contributory are properly registered in his name, the court may adjourn the petition until the matter has been resolved or have the matter determined as a preliminary issue.[4] A contributory is restricted in his right to bring a petition by virtue of CA 1963, s 215(a), in that he cannot petition unless he has either held his shares for the period of time prescribed by s 215(a)(ii) or, in the case of a public company or an unlimited private company, the number of members is reduced below the statutory minimum.[5] These restrictions are present to prevent past or present disgruntled members from petitioning unless they have substantial reason to do so.[6] Whilst the English courts have been reluctant to allow the holder of a fully paid share to petition to wind up a company unless it can be shown that the member will have a tangible interest in the liquidation, as where there will be a substantial surplus of assets available for members,[7] the Irish courts have been prepared to make a winding-up order on a creditor's petition even where there is no prospect of a dividend in the liquidation.[8] The fact that a shareholder is in arrears of a call that has been made is not a bar to his petition so long as he pays all the arrears into Court.[9] Furthermore, because the right to present a petition is a statutory right, it cannot be varied or abrogated by the memorandum or articles of association.[10]

1 See CA 1963, s 208 and the notes thereto.

2 CA 1963, s 210.

3 *Alipour v UOC Corp* [2002] 2 BCLC 770.

4 *Re JN2 Ltd* [1978] 1 WLR 183; *Re Garage Door Associates Ltd* [1984] 1 All ER 434; *Re a company, Alipour v Ary* [1997] 1 BCLC 557.

5 Regulation 11 of European Communities (Single Member Private Limited Companies) Regulations 1994 disapplies CA 1963, s 215(a)(i) in the case of private limited companies.

6 See Palmer, Schmitthoff (ed) op cit, 88–15.

7 *Re Instrumentation Electrical Services Ltd* [1988] BCLC 550; *Re WR Willcocks Ltd* [1973] 3 WLR 669; *Re Expanded Plugs Ltd* [1966] 1 WLR 514.

8 *Re Irish Tourist Promotions Ltd* (1963–1993) Irish Company Law Reports 382.

9 *Re Diamond Fuel Co* [1879] 13 Ch D 400.

10 *Re Peveril Gold Mines Co Ltd* [1898] 1 Ch 122. Cf *Re Via Net Works Ltd* [2002] 2 IR 47.

Voluntary liquidation already in progress: If the company is already in voluntary winding up, this will operate as a *prima facie* bar but not an absolute bar to the making of a winding-up order on a contributory's petition[1] and the court may make a winding-up order if it is satisfied that the voluntary winding up would prejudice the rights of the contributory.[2] Where the petition is presented by a creditor, the court may have regard to the wishes of the other creditors in determining whether to make a winding up order.[3] Ultimately though, the court will be reluctant to dislodge a voluntary liquidator and, in approaching the matter, will have due regard to the costs involved in a winding up by the court, the delays which will be incurred, the overall value of the assets to be administered, the complexity or simplicity of the task facing the liquidator, and any other relevant factors which may give the creditors a legitimate sense of grievance such as *mala fides* on the part of persons involved in the company.[4]

1 *Re Bank of Gibraltar* [1865] I Ch App 69.

2 *Re National Company for Distribution of Electricity* [1902] 2 Ch 34. See also CA 1963, s 282.

3 *Re Wicklow Textiles Ltd* (1953) 87 ILTR 72; *Re Lowerstoft Traffic Services Ltd* [1986] BCLC 81; *Re Palmer Marine Surveys Ltd* [1986] BCLC 106; *Re HJ Tomkins and Son Ltd* [1990] BCLC 76. See also CA 1963, s 309.

4 *Re Gilt Construction Ltd* [1994] 2 ILRM 456; *Re NAIAD Ltd t/a Metal Products Fasteners* (13 February 1995, unreported) HC (McCracken J): *Re Eurochick (Ireland) Ltd* [1998] IEHC 51 (McCracken J), *Re Hayes Homes Ltd* [2004] IEHC 124; *Re Permanent Formwork Systems Ltd* [2007] IEHC 268; *Re Balbradagh Developments Ltd* [2009] 1 IR 597.

Petition by the Registrar of Companies: The Registrar of Companies can only petition the court to have a company wound up on the grounds set out in CA 1963, s 213(h) and (i). Since the transitional period has long since elapsed, this ground for winding up is now effectively redundant.

The Director of Corporate Enforcement: The Director of Corporate Enforcement can petition for the winding up of the company on the grounds set out in CA 1990, s 12. For a fuller discussion, see the note in relation to 'public interest' petitions in the notes to CA 1963, s 213(f).

The trustees of investment companies: An investment company can be wound up by the trustee of an investment company (the person nominated by the Central Bank under CA 1990, s 257(4)(c))[1].

1 CA 1963, s 215(g) provides that the trustee of an investment company is the only person with *locus standi* to petition for the winding up of an investment on the just and equitable ground under CA 1963, s 213(fa).

UK legislation

See IA 1986, s 124 (amended by CA 1989, s 60(2)).

---

216 Powers of court on hearing petition

(1) On hearing a winding-up petition, the court may dismiss it, or adjourn the hearing conditionally or unconditionally, or make any interim order, or any other order that it thinks fit, but the court shall not refuse to make a winding-up order on the ground only that the assets of the company have been mortgaged to an amount equal to or in excess of those assets, or that the company has no assets.

[(2) The court shall not make an order for the winding up of a company unless—

(a) the court is satisfied that the company has no obligations in relation to a bank asset that has been transferred to the National Asset Management Agency or a NAMA group entity, or

(b) if the company has any such obligation—

(i) a copy of the petition has been served on that Agency, and

(ii) the court has heard that Agency in relation to the making of the order.

(3) In subsection (2) 'bank asset' and 'NAMA group entity' have the same respective meanings as in the National Asset Management Agency Act 2009.][a]

Amendments

a CA 1963, s 216(2) repealed by C(A)A 1983, Sch 3. New subsections (2) and (3) inserted by NAMA Act 2009, s 233.

Definitions

'company': CA 1963, s 2(1); 'the court': CA 1963, s 2(1).

Notes

Procedure: The winding-up petition must be in the prescribed form.[1] It must be presented in the Central office of the High Court[2] and must be advertised at least seven days before the hearing once in *Iris Oifigiúil* and once at least in two Dublin daily morning newspapers or in such other newspapers as the Registrar may direct.[3] It must also be served on the company.[4] Every person who intends to appear at the hearing of the petition shall serve a notice of intention to appear on the petitioner not later than 5 o'clock on the day prior to the day appointed for the hearing of the petition. Affidavits in opposition to a petition must be filed within seven days of the publication of the last advertisement of the petition.[5] The petitioner must prepare a list of the names and addresses of the persons who have given their notice of intention to appear at the hearing of the petition, and on the day of the hearing a copy of the list shall be handed to the Registrar prior to the hearing of the petition.[6]

1 RSC 1986, Ord 74, r 7 and Appendix M, Forms 2–4.
2 RSC 1986, Ord 74, r 8.
3 RSC 1986, Ord 74, r 10.
4 RSC 1986, Ord 74, r 11.
5 RSC 1986 Ord 74, r 15.
6 The list is in the form set out at Appendix M Form 9 of the Rules of the Superior Court.

Substitution of petitioner: When a petitioner either consents to withdraw his petition, allows it to be dismissed, fails to appear in support of a petition when it is called in court or when appearing does not apply for an order in the terms of the prayer of his petition, the court may upon such terms as it shall deem just, substitute as petitioner any person who would have a right to present a petition and who desires to prosecute the petition.[1] It is desirable that for the sake of convenience and for saving costs, a company should be the subject-matter of one petition only and not the subject of two or more petitions. However if the substituting petitioner is a creditor rather than a contributory, the court may order the petition to be re-advertised.[2]

1 RSC 1986, Ord 74, r 18.
2 *Re Creative Handbooks Ltd* [1985] BCLC 1.

Discretion of the court: The court has a complete and unfettered judicial discretion as to whether to make the order or not but will exercise its discretion in accordance with certain guiding principles.[1] The court may take into consideration the position of creditors or contributories and may direct the meeting of contributories to be called.[2] If the company is insolvent, the court will attach little weight to the wishes of contributories in comparison to the wishes of an unpaid creditor.[3] If the company is solvent, however, the court will attach more weight to the wishes of contributories.[4] A creditor is *prima facie* entitled to an order winding up the company if it complies with CA 1963, s 214(a) subject to the discretion referred to above. The bare fact that a majority of creditors oppose the petition is not sufficient of itself to entitle them to have the order refused. There must be some good reason for refusing to make the order,[5] as where it is established that the petition has been presented for an ulterior purpose,[6] or where it is established that the making of the winding-up order would operate to the detriment, rather than to the benefit, of creditors generally.[7] Where the creditors do oppose the petition for good reason their opposition should prevail in the absence of proof by the petitioner of special circumstances which would justify the making up of the winding-up order.[8] In this regard, the Court has jurisdiction to make a winding-up order even though the company has no assets and the only purpose of the order is to enable an investigation into the company's affairs to take place.[9]

1 *Re P and J Macrae Ltd* [1961] 1 All ER 302; *Re Demaglass Holdings Ltd* [2001] 2 BCLC 633.

2 CA 1963, s 309; RSC 1986 O 74, r 54; *Belfast Tailor's Co Partnership Ltd, Re* [1909] 1 IR 49. See generally Courtney *The Law of Private Companies* (2nd edn, Tottel Publishing, 2002) paras 25.052–25.053.

3 *Re Camburn Petroleum Products Ltd* [1979] 3 All ER 298.

4 Keane, *Company Law* (4th edn, Tottel Publishing, 2007) para 36.58.

5 *Re Bula Ltd* [1990] 1 IR 440; *Re Genport Ltd* [1996] IEHC 34 (McCracken J); *Re Genport Ltd (No 2)* [2001] IEHC 156 (McCracken J); *Re Demaglass Holdings Ltd* [2001] 2 BCLC 633.

6 *Re Bula Ltd* [1990] 1 IR 440; *Re Genport Ltd* [1996] IEHC 34 (McCracken J); *Re Genport Ltd (No 2)* [2001] IEHC 156 (McCracken J).

7 *Re Genport Ltd* [1996] IEHC 34 (McCracken J); *Re Genport Ltd (No 2)* [2001] IEHC 156 (McCracken J); *Re Demaglass Holdings Ltd* [2001] 2 BCLC 633.

8 *Re P and J Macrae Ltd* [1961] 1 All ER 302; *Re Bula Ltd* [1990] 1 IR 440; *Re Genport Ltd* [1996] IEHC 34 (McCracken J); *Re Genport Ltd (No 2)* [2001] IEHC 156 (McCracken J).

9 CA 1963, s 216. See also *Re Bell Group Finance [BTY] Ltd (in liquidation) v Bell Group (UK) Holdings Ltd* [1996] 1 BCLC 304 where Chadwick J approved the following dictum of Buckley in *Re Crigglestone Coal Co Ltd* [1906] 2 CH 327: 'The Company will often put forward, as if it were a matter of defence; that there are no assets to wind up. It is not a matter of defence at all. The court has often refused an order upon that ground, but not because it lies in the debtor's mouth to say that he is not amenable to the jurisdiction because he has no property but because the Court does not make an order where no benefit can result. If the order will be useful (not necessarily fruitful) there is jurisdiction to make it. This view is illustrated by the fact that in many cases, and in particularly since the Act of 1890 the Court will make an order, not because there are assets, but in order to provide the machinery for ascertaining whether there cannot be shewn to be assets'.

Adjournment of petitions: The Court is reluctant to grant lengthy adjournments of a winding up petitions.[1] Adjournments are often undesirable because the winding-up order (if made) dates back to the presentation of the petition.[2] Furthermore if the matter is not dealt with quickly the books of the company tend to be out of date or lost (quite apart from any question of dishonest behaviour on the part of Officers). Officers and employees who could provide valuable information sometimes leave and cannot be traced. Dispositions made between the presentation of the petition and the making up of the winding up are void and any delay increases the number of these transactions and makes their examination more difficult.[3] In certain circumstances the Court has granted an adjournment pending litigation between parties.[4] Similarly, in exceptional circumstances an adjournment may be granted for a substantial period of time for some creditable reason such as to facilitate the realisation of a substantial asset for the benefit of the creditors.[5]

1 *Re Demaglass Holdings Ltd* [2001] 2 BCLC 633; *Re Coolfadda Developers Ltd* (14 July 2009, unreported) SC (Denham J).

2 CA 1963, s 218.

3 CA 1963, s 218. *Practice Direction Chancery Division (Companies Court)* [1977] 3 All ER 64.

4 *Re Genport Ltd* [1996] IEHC 34 (McCracken J). See also *Bluzwed Metals Ltd v Transworld Metals SA* (9 May 2001, unreported) HC (Lavan J) where the Court refused to grant a lengthy adjournment of a petition to allow the determination of Swiss proceedings including the parties to the petition.

5 *Northern Development (Holdings) Ltd v UDT Securities Ltd* [1977] 1 All ER 747; *MHMH Ltd v Carwood Barker Holdings Ltd* [2006] 1 BCLC 279; *Re Coolfadda Developers Ltd* (14 July 2009, unreported) SC (Denham J).

Costs: Although the Court has a general discretion as to costs, the general practice is that if the petition succeeds the costs will be awarded to the petitioner against the company in liquidation.

These costs are paid in priority to any other costs in the liquidation.[1] Creditors who appear at the hearing of a petition are not entitled to costs as of right. They must show a reasonable ground for appearing.[2] Where a petition is brought on the basis of a disputed debt against a solvent company, the court may order costs of the company to be paid by the petitioner on an indemnity basis and as the petition is an abuse of process.[3] On the other hand, if the debt is undisputed and is paid after the presentation of the petition, the petitioner should normally be entitled to his costs against the company.[4]

1 CA 1963, s 285 and RSC 1986, Ord 74, r 128.

2 *Re Hull and County Bank* Ch D 130.

3 *Re a company* [2003] 2 BCLC 346; *Re a company (No. 0012209 of 1991)* [1992] BCLC 865.

4 *Re Ryan Developments Ltd* [2002] 2 BCLC 792; *Re Nowmost Co Ltd* [1996] 2 BCLC 64; *Re Pendigo Ltd* [1996] 2 BCLC 64.

UK legislation

See IA 1986, s 125.

217 Power to stay or restrain proceedings against company

At any time after the presentation of a winding-up petition, and before a winding-up order has been made, the company or any creditor or contributory may—

(a) where any action or proceeding against the company is pending in the High Court or on appeal in the Supreme Court apply to the court in which the action or proceeding is pending for a stay of proceedings therein; and

(b) where any other action or proceeding is pending against the company, apply to the High Court to restrain further proceedings in the action or proceeding;

and the court to which application is so made may, as the case may be, stay or restrain the proceedings accordingly on such terms and for such period as it thinks fit.

Definitions

'company': CA 1963, s 2(1); 'contributory': CA 1963, s 2(1), s 208; 'the court': CA 1963, s 2(1).

Notes

General: CA 1963, s 217 applies to the period between the presentation of the winding up petition and the making of a winding up order. Once a winding-up order has been made, the leave of the court must be obtained before commencing any action or proceeding.[1]

1 See notes to CA 1963, s 222.

Court's discretion: The jurisdiction to stay is discretionary and in its exercise regard must be had to the primary object of the winding up, namely the collection and distribution of the assets *parri passu* among unsecured creditors after payment of preferential debts.[1]

1 *Smith Fleming and Co's case, Gledstanes and Co's case* [1866] 1 Ch App 538 Act 545; *Herbert Berry Associates Ltd v IRC* [1978] 1 All ER 161.

Action or proceeding: The courts have given a wide interpretation to 'action' or 'proceeding' for the purpose of CA 1963, s 217. The expression 'proceeding' includes not only any process of execution of a judgment or order[1] but also includes any method of enforcing a claim against the company's assets which does not involve litigation. Accordingly the court may restrain landlords and other persons from levying a distress on the company's chattels after a winding up petition has been presented.[2] In the absence of special circumstances the court will restrain the action or proceedings if the assets of the company would otherwise be diminished.[3]

1 *Re Exhall Coal Mining Co* (1864) 4 De GJ and Sm 377; *Re Lancashire Cotton Spinning Co, ex parte Carnelley* (1887) 35 Ch D 656; *Re Higginshaw Mills and Spinning Co* [1896] 2 Ch 544; *Croshaw v Lyndhurst Ship Co* [1897] 2 Ch 154; *Re Traders' North Staffordshire Carrying Co ex parte North Staffordshire Railway Co* (1874) LR 19 Eq 60; *Re Universal Disinfector Co* (1875) LR 20 Eq 162; *Re Artistic Colour Printing Co* (1880) 14 Ch D 502; *Re Twentieth Century Equitable Friendly Society* [1910] WN 236. See also CA 1963, s 219 pursuant to which any attachment, sequestration, distress or execution put in force against the assets of the company after the commencement of the winding up is rendered void. Further under CA 1863, s 291 any execution or attachment against assets of the company which has been begun but not completed before the commencement of the winding up, is invalidated.

2 *Venners Electrical Cooking and Heating Appliances Ltd v Thorpe* [1915] 2 Ch 404; *Re Bellaglade Ltd* [1977] 1 All ER 319. See also *Re Roundwood Colliery Co, Lee v Roundwood Clliery Co* [1897] 1 Ch 373.

3 *Bowkett v Fuller's United Electric Works* [1923] 1 KB 160; *Hudson's Concrete Products Ltd v DB Evans (Bilston) Ltd* (1861) 105 Sol Jo 281; *D Wilson (Birmingham) Ltd v Metropolitan Property Developments Ltd* [1975] 2 All ER 814; *Rainbow v Moorgate Properties Ltd* [1975] 2 All ER 821.

Practice: The application may be made *ex parte*.[1] The applicant must give an undertaking as to damages as is required in interlocutory injunctions.[2] A plaintiff in an action stayed under this section is entitled to be paid by the applicant the costs of appearing in the motion to stay.[3]

1 *Re London and Suburban Bank* [1871] 25 LT 23.

2 *Re London and Suburban Bank* [1871] 25 LT 23.

3 *Pierce v Wexford Picture House Co* [1915] 2 IR 310.

UK legislation

See IA 1986, s 126.

---

218 Avoidance of dispositions of property and transfer of shares after commencement of winding up

In a winding up by the court, any disposition of the property of the company, including things in action, and any transfer of shares or alteration in the status of the members of the company, made after the commencement of the winding up, shall, unless the court otherwise orders, be void.

Definitions

'company': CA 1963, s 2(1); 'the court': CA 1963, s 2(1); 'member': CA 1963, s 31; 'share': CA 1963, s 2(1).

Notes

General: It is a basic concept of the law governing the liquidation of insolvent companies that the unencumbered assets of the company as at the date of commencement of the liquidation should be available for realisation and distribution amongst the creditors in accordance with the proper order of priorities.[1] The courts have constantly held[2] that it would be improper to prefer one unsecured creditor over another and that each should be placed on an equal footing. Unsurprisingly, therefore, CA 1963, s 218 provides that all dispositions of the company's assets are void after the commencement of the winding up.

Retrospection of winding up: In the event of a winding-up order being made, the commencement of the winding up relates back to the time at which the petition was presented in the Central Office of the High Court.[3] Thus, for example, where an insurance policy provided cover against customers going into liquidation, it was held that the insured was entitled to cover where the petition in respect of the customer was presented before but the winding up order was made after the policy had lapsed.[4]

1 *Re Gray's Inns Construction Ltd* [1980] 1 WLR 711; *Re Pat Ruth Ltd* [1981] ILRM 51; *Re Ashmark Ltd (No 2)* [1990] ILRM 455; *Dennehy v John Hudson and Co Ltd* [1992] BCLC 901.

2 See for example, *Re Gray's Inns Construction Ltd* [1980] 1 WLR 711 at 717.

3 CA 1963, s 220. See also *Re Eurofoods IFSC Ltd* [2004] 4 IR 370; *UPM Kymmene Corp v BMG Ltd* (11 June 1999, unreported) HC (Laffoy J); *Emo Oil Ltd v Sun Alliance and London Insurance plc* [2005] IEHC 474; *Kanwell Developments Ltd v Salthill Properties Ltd* [2008] IEHC 3.

4 *Emo Oil Ltd v Sun Alliance and London Insurance plc* [2005] IEHC 474.

Voidance of Dispositions: CA 1963, s 218 covers all dispositions of a company's property made between the presentation of the petition and the making of the winding up order. The concept of a 'disposition' has been widely construed as meaning 'any conveyance, transfer, assignment, settlement, delivery, payment or any other alienation of property'[1]. Any payment out of a bank account, whether the account is overdrawn or in credit, is clearly a disposition in favour of the payee within the meaning of the section.[2] In addition, it is also regarded as a disposition in favour of the bank.[3] This is because of the well established debtor/creditor relationship that exists between the bank and its customer. Money held in a bank account is not owned, as such, by the customer. Rather, the bank owes the sum standing to the credit of the account to the customer. Similarly, if a customer deposits money into a bank account they are in fact lending money to the bank. This has an impact on the interpretation of s 218 because with every transaction on the account the bank is either lending to or borrowing money from the customer. In either case, there is a disposition.[4] Similarly, lodgements into a company's overdrawn account constitute dispositions in favour of the bank, since the lodgement results in a pro tanto reduction in the company's indebtedness to the bank.[5] The position is, however, less obvious in the case of a lodgement into a company account which is in credit. In the UK the courts have taken the view that such a transaction does not constitute a disposition in favour of the bank,[6] whereas a contrary view has been adopted in Ireland.[7]

As regards the time when the disposition occurs, it has been held that drawing of a cheque on the account does not of itself operate as the 'disposition' of funds: rather the disposition occurs when the cheque is paid.[8] The debiting of interest from the account does not, however, amount to a disposition within the meaning of the section.[9] Where, before the presentation of a winding up petition, a company has entered into an unconditional contract for the sale of property which was specifically enforceable, the completion of the contract after the petition has been presented does not constitute a disposition within the meaning of the section.[10] Similarly, there is no 'disposition' where a receiver is appointed on foot of a debenture executed prior to the presentation of the petition.[11]

1 *McGain v Commissioner for Taxation* [1965] 112 CLR (3) at 528 as approved by Kearns J in *Re Industrial Services Company (Dublin) Ltd* [2001] 2 IR 118.

2 *Re Gray's Inn Construction Co Ltd* [1980] 1 WLR 711; *Re Pat Ruth Ltd* [1981] ILRM 51; *Re Tain Construction Ltd, Rose v AIB Group (UK) plc* [2003] 2 BCLC 374.

3 *Re Industrial Services Company (Dublin) Ltd* [2001] 2 IR 118; *Re Worldport Ireland Ltd* [2005] IEHC 189.

4 The courts in the UK have analysed the position differently. In *Hollicourt (Contracts) Ltd v Bank of Ireland* [2001] 1 BCLC 233 the Court of Appeal held that the bank, in paying a cheque to a third party, is acting as agent of the customer and accordingly that there is no disposition as between the bank and the customer. The Court of Appeal also held that a bank in honouring the

company's cheques is merely acting on the instructions of its principal to pay out the principal's money. The court took the view that the beneficial ownership of the property represented by the cheque was never transferred to the bank and as such there was no alienation of the company's property and accordingly there was no disposition within the meaning of s 218. The reasoning in the *Hollicourt* case was rejected by Kearns J in *Re Industrial Services Company (Dublin) Ltd* [20001] 2 IR 118. His decision was subsequently followed by Clarke J in *Re Worldport Ireland Ltd [In Liquidation]* [2005] IEHC 189.

5 *Re Gray's Inn Construction Co Ltd* [1980] 1 WLR 711; *Re Pat Ruth Ltd* [1981] ILRM 51; *Re Tain Construction Ltd, Rose v AIB Group (UK) plc* [2003] 2 BCLC 374.

6 *Re Barn Crown Ltd* [1994] 2 BCLC 186.

7 *Re Industrial Services Company (Dublin) Ltd* [2001] 2 IR 118; *Re Worldport Ireland Ltd* [2005] IEHC 189.

8 *Re Ashmark Ltd (No 2)* [1990] ILRM 455.

9 *Re Ashmark Ltd, Ashmark Ltd v Allied Irish Banks plc* [1994] 1 ILRM 223.

10 *Re French's (Wine Bar) Ltd* [1987] BCLC 499.

11 *Re Motor Racing Circuits Ltd* (31 January 1997, unreported, nem diss) SC (Blayney J).

Effect on garnishee proceedings: Because of the retrospective effect of a winding up under s 218, the court will generally lean against making an order of garnishee against a company when it has a winding up petition pending against it.[1] Conversely, the court will lean against winding up a company solely on the basis of a debt owed to a petitioner where that debt has, prior to the presentation of the petition, been the subject of an order nisi of garnishee.[2]

1 *Kanwell Developments Ltd v Salthill Properties Ltd* [2008] IEHC 3.

2 *Kanwell Developments Ltd v Salthill Properties Ltd* [2008] IEHC 3.

Property recovered under s 218: Since post-petitions are rendered void by CA 1963, s 218 it follows that if the property disposed of was subject to a charge, it remains subject to that charge and is available for the debentureholder rather than the general body of creditors if and when recovered from the disponeee by the liquidator.[1]

1 *Mond v Hammond Suddards* [1996] 2 BCLC 470.

Validation of dispositions: CA 1963, s 218 confers on the court a jurisdiction to validate post-petition dispositions. Whilst the absence of notice of the presentation of the petition on the part of the disponee and a change of position by the donee are factors the court may take into account in the exercise of its jurisdiction to validate,[1] the entire burden of the authorities is to the effect that the disposition will not be validated unless it can be shown to be for the benefit of the company or at least desirable in the interests of the unsecured creditors as a body.[2] Accordingly, whilst a transaction at full market value post-petition involves no dissipation of company assets and will therefore be validated,[3] the court will not sanction a disposition at an undervalue[4] and will not, except in exceptional circumstances, validate a transaction which results in one or more pre-petition creditors being paid in full where other such creditors will only receive a dividend.[5] Nevertheless, where it is shown to be in the interests of creditors generally that the company should continue to trade until the making of any winding up order, payments by the company in the ordinary course of business may be validated,[6] at least where the payees are unconnected third parties.[7] Similarly, where a company's lease would have been forfeit upon the making of a winding up order, an assignment of that lease after the date of the presentation of the petition and before the making of the winding-up order was found to be for the benefit of creditors and was thus validated.[8]

1 *Re Leslie Engineers Co Ltd* [1976] 2 All ER 85; *Re Gray's Inns Construction Ltd* [1980] 1 WLR 711; *Re Pat Ruth Ltd* [1981] ILRM 51; *Re Ashmark Ltd (No.1)* [1990] ILRM 330; *Dennehy v John Hudson and Co Ltd* [1992] BCLC 901; *Re Tain Construction Ltd, Rose v AIB Group (UK) plc* [2003] 2 BCLC 374.

[2] *Re McBirney and Co Ltd* (2 July 1992, unreported) HC (Murphy J); *Re Lynch, Monaghan and O'Brien Ltd* (9 June 1989, unreported) HC (Costello J); *Re Pat Ruth Ltd* [1981] ILRM 51; *Re Ashmark Ltd (No 1)* [1990] ILRM 330; *Re Gray's Inns Construction Ltd* [1980] 1 WLR 711; *Re AI Levy (Holdings) Ltd* [1963] 2 All ER 556; *Re Fairway Graphics Ltd* [1991] BCLC 468; *Dennehy v John Hudson and Co Ltd* [1992] BCLC 901; *Re Tain Construction Ltd, Rose v AIB Group (UK) plc* [2003] 2 BCLC 374; *Re Industrial Services Company (Dublin) Ltd (in liquidation)* [2002] 4 IR 394; *Re Wellingford Construction Ltd* [2005] IEHC 392.

[3] *Dennehy v John Hudson and Co Ltd* [1992] BCLC 901; *Re Lynch, Monaghan and O'Brien Ltd* (9 June 1989, unreported) HC (Costello J); *Re Wellingford Construction Ltd* [2005] IEHC 392.

[4] *Re Rescupine Ltd* [2003] 1 BCLC 661.

[5] *Dennehy v John Hudson and Co Ltd* [1992] BCLC 901; *Re Ashmark Ltd (No 1)* [1990] ILRM 330; *Re Ashmark Ltd (No 2)* [1990] ILRM 455; *Re Gray's Inns Construction Ltd* [1980] 1 WLR 711; *Re Fairway Graphics Ltd* [1991] BCLC 468; *Re Tain Construction Ltd, Rose v AIB Group (UK) plc* [2003] 2 BCLC 374.

[6] *Re Pat Ruth Ltd* [1981] ILRM 51; *Re McBirney and Co Ltd* (2 July 1992, unreported) HC (Murphy J); *Re Industrial Services Company (Dublin) Ltd (No 2)* [2002] 4 IR 394; *Denney v John Hudson and Company* [1992] BCLC 901; *Countrywide Banking Corporation Ltd v Dean* [1998] 2 WLR 441. See also *Re Wiltshire Iron Co* (1868) 3 Ch App 443 at 446–447.

[7] *Re McBirney and Co Ltd* (2 July 1992, unreported) HC (Murphy J); *Re McBirney and Co Ltd (No 2)* (15 June 1993, unreported) HC (Murphy J); *Re Industrial Services Company (Dublin) Ltd (No 2)* [2002] 4 IR 394; *Denney v John Hudson and Company* [1992] BCLC 901.

[8] *Re AI Levy (Holdings) Ltd* [1963] 2 All ER 556.

Transfer of shares: Any transfer of shares in the company made after the commencement of the winding up is void under CA 1963, s 218 unless the court otherwise orders. Transfers made and completed in ignorance of the petition may be validated,[1] although an uncompleted agreement for the purchase of shares will not be enforced.[2] As between the transferor and transferee, an uncompleted agreement for the sale of shares will not be rendered void, but rather the consequence is that the court will not, except in exceptional circumstances, allow for the transfer to be registered.[3]

[1] *Emmerson's Case* (1866) LR 2 Eq 231, on appeal (1866) 1 Ch App 433; *Walker's Case* (1866) LR 2 Eq 554; *Paine v Hutchinson* (1868) 3 Ch App 388.

[2] *Emmerson's Case* (1866) LR 2 Eq 231, on appeal (1866) 1 Ch App 433; *Walker's Case* (1866) LR 2 Eq 554; *Paine v Hutchinson* (1868) 3 Ch App 388.

[3] *Re Onward Building Society* [1891] 2 QB 463 at 483.

Alteration of member's status: Any alteration in the status of members made after the commencement of the winding up, other than occasioned by a transfer sanctioned by the court, is also void unless the Court otherwise orders.

UK legislation

See IA 1986, s 127.

---

219 Avoidance of executions against property of company

Where any company is being wound up by the court, any attachment, sequestration, distress or execution put in force against the property or effects of the company after the commencement of the winding up shall be void to all intents.

Definitions

'company': CA 1963, s 2(1); 'the court': CA 1963, s 2(1).

Notes

Execution etc put in force against the company: In the period after the presentation of the petition and before the making of any winding-up order, application may be made to court to stay any attachment, sequestration, distress or execution which is being effected against the assets of the company.[1] If a winding-up order is ultimately made, any such process which has been 'put in force' against the assets of the company after the date of the presentation of the petition will be invalidated under CA 1963, s 219. Such a process is only 'put in force' if it is commenced after the presentation of the petition.[2] If the process is commenced but not completed before the presentation of the petition, it will, upon the making of the winding up order, be invalidated to the extent that it has not been completed, not by s 219 but rather by CA 1963, s 291. On the other hand, to the extent that the process was completed prior to the presentation of the petition, the creditor will be entitled to retain the proceeds for his own benefit.[3]

1 CA 1963, s 217.

2 *Re Great Ship Co, Parry's Case* (1863) 4 De GJ and Sm 63.

3 *Re Andrews, ex parte Official Receiver* [1937] Ch 122. See generally CA 1963, s 291 and the notes thereto.

UK legislation

See IA 1986, s 128.

Commencement of Winding Up

220 Commencement of winding up by the court

(1) Where, before the presentation of a petition for the winding up of a company by the court, a resolution has been passed by the company for voluntary winding up, the winding up of the company shall be deemed to have commenced at the time of the passing of the resolution, and unless the court, on proof of fraud or mistake, thinks fit to direct otherwise, all proceedings taken in the voluntary winding up shall be deemed to have been validly taken.

(2) In any other case, the winding up of a company by the court shall be deemed to commence at the time of the presentation of the petition for the winding up.

Definitions

'company': CA 1963, s 2(1); 'the court': CA 1963, s 2(1).

Notes

Date of commencement of winding up: By virtue of CA 1963, s 220(2) the date of commencement of a winding up normally relates back to the date of the presentation of the petition, with consequent avoidance of transactions that occurred post-petition and pre-order.[1] If the company was previously in voluntary winding up, the date of the commencement of the winding up is the date of the winding up resolution,[2] even where the resolution was passed after the presentation of the petition and before the date of the making of the winding up order.[3]

1 See CA 1963, ss 218 and 219. See *Re Eurofood IFSC Ltd* [2004] 4 IR 370; *Re Eurofood IFSC Ltd* [2006] 3 WLR 309; *Emo Oil Ltd v Sun Alliance and London Insurance plc* [2005] IEHC 474.

2 CA 1963, ss 220(1) and 253.

3 *Weston's Case* (1868) 4 Ch App 20.

UK legislation

See IA 1986, s 129.

221 Copy of order for winding up to be forwarded to registrar

(1) On the making of a winding-up order, an office copy of the order must forthwith be delivered by the company, or by such person as the court may direct, to the registrar of companies for registration.

(2) If a company makes default in complying with subsection (1), the company and every officer of the company who is in default [shall be guilty of an offence and liable to a fine][a] not exceeding [€1,904.61][b] and if any other person makes default in complying with subsection (1) such person [shall be guilty of an offence and liable to a fine][a] not exceeding [€1,904.61].[b]

Amendments

a Words in CA 1963, s 221(2) substituted by C(AA)A 2003, s 57 and Sch 2, para 4.

b '£125' increased to '£1,500' by CA 1990, s 240(7) as inserted by CLEA 2001, s 104(c) and converted to €1,904.61 by Council Regulation (EC) 1103/97, No 974/98 and No 2866/98 and the Economic and Monetary Union Act 1998, s 6.

Definitions

'company': CA 1963, s 2(1); 'the court': CA 1963, s 2(1); 'officer': CA 1963, s 2(1); 'the Registrar of Companies': CA 1963, s 2(1).

Notes

Practice: In addition to the filing obligation contained in CA 1963, s 221(1) there is an obligation to file notice of the filing of the order in *Iris Oifigiúil* within a period of six weeks.[1] Furthermore, unless the court otherwise directs, the order itself must be advertised in Iris Oifigiuil and in each of the newspapers in which the petition was advertised within twelve days of the date of the order or within such other period as the court may allow.[2] A copy of the order for winding up of a company certified by the petitioner or his solicitor shall be left at the examiners office within ten days after same has been perfected.[3] A copy of every order for winding up of a company certified by the petitioner shall be served on the company by pre-paid letter addressed to its registered office.[4] This does not apply where the company is the petitioner.[5]

1 European Communities (Companies) Regulations 1973, reg 4(1)(i) and (2).

2 RSC 1986, Ord 74, r 20.

3 RSC 1986, Ord 74, r 21.

4 RSC 1986, Ord 74, r 22.

5 RSC 1986, Ord 74, r 22.

UK legislation

IA 1986, s 130(1).

222 Actions against company stayed on winding-up order

When a winding-up order has been made or a provisional liquidator has been appointed, no action or proceeding shall be proceeded with or commenced against the company except by leave of the court and subject to such terms as the court may impose.

Definitions

'company': CA 1963, s 2(1); 'the court': CA 1963, s 2(1).

Notes

General: The function of this section is to ensure that individual creditors should not be allowed to proceed with a multiplicity of separate actions against the company.[1] This section is not intended for the purposes of harassing, impeding or injuring third parties but for the purposes of preserving the limited assets of the company in the best way for distribution among all the persons who have claims upon them.[2] Thus actions and proceedings against the company are completely stopped unless leave is obtained from the court.[3] The stay under CA 1963, s 222 does not, however, apply to proceedings against the company before the Employment Appeals Tribunal[4] nor does it apply to proceedings against the directors [5] or to proceedings against the company in a foreign jurisdiction.[6] On the other hand, if the proceedings are within the State but relate to assets outside the State, the stay will apply.[7]

1 Keane, *Company Law* (4th edn, Tottel Publishing, 2007) p 507.
2 *Re David Lloyd and Company v David Lloyd and Co* [1877] 6 Ch D 339.
3 *Re Waterloo Life Insurance Co (No2)* (1862) 31 Beav 586.
4 C(A)A 1986, s 23.
5 *Re New Zealand Banking Corporation, ex parte Hankey* [1869] WN 226.
6 *Re Oriental Inland Steam Co, ex parte Scinde Railway co* (1874) 9 Ch App 557; *Re Vocalion (Foreign)* [1932] 2 Ch 196.
7 *Re South Eastern Portugal Railway Co* (1869) 17 WR 982; *Re Wanzer Ltd* [1891] 1 Ch 305.

Court's discretion: The court has a very wide discretion regarding whether or not to grant leave under CA 1963, s 222. In exercise of the discretion the court has a free hand to do what is right and fair in the circumstances.[1] If the proposed action for which leave is sought raises issues, which can be conveniently decided in the course of the winding up, then in the absence of special circumstances, permission to bring the action should be refused.[2] There is a positive benefit in having the issue decided in the liquidation proceedings, as this should be less expensive and quicker than an independent cause of action.[3] Also, as the liquidator is obliged to act even handily as between each class of claimant, the settlement of claims through the winding-up procedure will normally not cause prejudice to any particular class of claimant.[4] When deciding on individual cases, the court will enquire as to what is most convenient. If the debt is undisputed, leave to proceed will usually not be granted, but if the debt is disputed, it may be considered most convenient to allow the action to proceed.[5] Even if leave to proceed is granted, the applicant will be required to undertake not to enforce any judgment he may obtain against the company without the leave of the court.[6] The court will usually allow an action for specific performance to proceed in respect of a right *in rem*.[7] Contempt proceedings in respect of a breach of an order to deliver up the applicant's property will also be permitted.[8] The appointment of a receiver on foot of a debenture does not fall within the definition of an 'action or proceeding'[9] and accordingly does not require the leave of the court. However, if a secured creditor wishes to commence proceedings to enforce his security against the company (eg by seeking an order for possession and sale of charged property), leave will be given as a matter of course.[10]

1 *Re Grosvenor Metal Co Ltd* [1949] 2 All ER 948; *Re Aro Co Ltd* [1980] 1All ER 1067; *Canon (Scotland) Business Machines Ltd v GA Business Systems Ltd* [1993] BCLC 1194.
2 *Re Exchange Securities and Commodities Ltd* [1983] BCLC 186; *Wilson v Natal Investment Co* [1867] WN 68.
3 *Re Exchange Securities and Commodities Ltd* [1983] BCLC 186.
4 *Re Exchange Securities and Commodities Ltd* [1983] BCLC 186.
5 *Cook v X Chair Patents Co Ltd* [1959] 3 All ER 906.

6 *Mc Ewen v London, Bombay and Mediterranean Bank* [1866] WN 407; *Hagell v Currie, Re Breech-Loading Armoury Co* [1867] WN 75.

7 *Re Coregrange Ltd* [1984] BCLC 453 where the court held that 'if a proposing plaintiff has unimpugnable claim for specific performance of an agreement to sell property belonging to a company which is being wound up, then it would, it seems to me, be wholly wrong for the Court to deprive him of that proprietary right and remit him to a claim for damages. If he has such an unimpugnable right to specific performance he is to be treated in equity as the owner of the property to which that right extends, and it would be unjust for the court to deprive him of the property and put him back into the pool for the benefit of the unsecured creditors generally'. See also *Canon (Scotland) Business Machines Ltd v GA Business Systems Ltd* [1993] BCLC 1194; *Thames Plate Glass Co v Land and Sea Telegraph Co* (1870) LR 7 Eq 129, on appeal (1871) 6 Ch App 643; *Marshall v Glamorgan Iron and Coal Co* (1868) LR 7 Eq 129; *Blakely v Dent, Re Blakely Ordnance Co* (1867) 15 WR 663.

8 *Canon (Scotland) Business Machines Ltd v GA Business Systems Ltd* [1993] BCLC 1194.

9 *Re MotorRacing Circuits Ltd* (31 January 1997, unreported) SC.

10 *David Lloyd and Co v David Lloyd and Company* [1877] 6 Ch 339 where the court held that a secured creditor is in a position where he can justly claim that he is independent of the liquidation since he is enforcing a right, not against the company, but to his own property.

Proceedings commenced without leave: If proceedings are commenced against the company without leave they are a nullity and cannot be retrospectively validated under CA 1963, s 222.[1]

1 *Re National Employers Mutual General Insurance Association Ltd* [1995] 1 BCLC 232.

UK legislation

See IA 1986, s 130(2).

---

223 Effect of winding-up order

An order for winding up a company shall operate in favour of all the creditors and of all the contributories of the company, as if made on the joint petition of a creditor and of a contributory.

Definitions

'company': CA 1963, s 2(1); 'contributory': CA 1963, s 2(1), s 208.

UK legislation

See IA 1986, s 130(4).

---

224 Statement of company's affairs to be filed in court

(1) Where the court has made a winding-up order or appointed a provisional liquidator, there shall, unless the court thinks fit to order otherwise and so orders, be made out and filed in the court a statement as to the affairs of the company in the prescribed form, verified by affidavit, and showing the particulars of its assets, debts and liabilities, the names, residences and occupations of its creditors, the securities held by them respectively, the dates when the securities were respectively given, and such further or other information as may be prescribed or as the court may require.

(2) The statement shall be filed and verified by one or more of the persons who are at the relevant date the directors and by the person who is at that date the secretary of the

company or by such of the persons hereinafter mentioned in this subsection as the court may require to file and verify the statement, that is, persons—

(a) who are or have been officers of the company;

(b) who have taken part in the formation of the company at any time within one year before the relevant date;

(c) who are in the employment of the company, or have been in the employment of the company within the said year, and are in the opinion of the court, capable of giving the information required;

(d) who are or have been within the said year officers of or in the employment of a company which is, or within the said year was, an officer of the company to which the statement relates.

(3) The statement shall be filed within 21 days from the relevant date or within such extended time as the court may for special reasons appoint.

(4) Any person making or concurring in making the statement and affidavit required by this section shall be allowed, and shall be paid out of the assets of the company, such costs and expenses incurred in and about the preparation and making of the statement and affidavit as the court may allow.

(5) If any person, without reasonable excuse, makes default in complying with the requirements of this section, he [shall be guilty of an offence and liable to a fine][a] not exceeding [€1,904.61].[b]

(6) Any person who states in writing that he is a creditor or contributory of the company shall be entitled by himself or by his agent at all reasonable times, on payment of the prescribed fee, to inspect the statement filed in pursuance of this section, and to a copy thereof or extract therefrom.

(7) Any person untruthfully so stating himself to be a creditor or contributory shall be guilty of a contempt of court and shall, on the application of the liquidator, be punishable accordingly.

(8) In this section, 'the relevant date' means, in a case where a provisional liquidator is appointed, the date of his appointment, and, in a case where no such appointment is made, the date of the winding-up order.

Amendments

a Words in CA 1963, s 224(5) substituted by C(AA)A 2003, s 57 and Sch 2, para 1.

b '£500' increased to £1,500 by CA 1990, s 240(7) as inserted by CLEA 2001, s 104(c). £1,500 converted to €1,904.61 by Council Regulation (EC) 1103/97, No 974/98 and No 2866/98 and the Economic and Monetary Union Act 1998, s 6.

Definitions

'agent': CA 1963, s 2(1); 'company': CA 1963, s 2(1); 'contributory': CA 1963, s 2(1), s 208; 'the court': CA 1963, s 2(1); 'director': CA 1963, s 2(1); 'officer': CA 1963, s 2(1); 'prescribed': CA 1963, s 2(1); 'relevant date': CA 1963, s 224(8).

Notes

Practice: The statement of affairs must be in the prescribed form[1] and must be verified by affidavit.[2] It must be filed in the Central Office[3]. Normally the statement of affairs should be filed within 21 days of the date of the making of the winding-up order although the Court may, for special reasons, make an order extending the time for so doing.[4] It is the person who requires the extension of time who should normally make the application.[5] Any person required to make or concur in making the statement of affairs may apply to the liquidator or to the court to sanction payment out of the assets of the company in respect of costs or expenses which it is intended to incur in performing that task.[6] Whilst the court may make an order under CA 1963, s 224(1) dispensing with the requirement to make out and file a statement of affairs, any application for such a dispensation should be supported by a report of the official liquidator showing the special circumstances which, in his opinion, render such a course desirable.[7] Unless the court otherwise orders, the liquidator must, as soon as practicable, send to each creditor mentioned in the statement of affairs and to each contributory a summary of the statement of affairs including the causes of the company's failure and any observations thereon which the liquidator may think fit to make.[8] The purpose of CA 1963, s 224 is to ensure that information relating to the affairs of a company is made available to an outsider, liquidator or receiver.[9]

1 RSC 1986, Ord 74, r 27 and Appendix M Form 13.

2 RSC 1986, Ord 74, r 24.

3 RSC 1986, Ord 74, r 24.

4 CA 1963, s 224(3).

5 RSC 1986, Ord 74, r 24(3).

6 RSC 1986, Ord 74, r 25.

7 RSC 1986, Ord 74, r 26.

8 RSC 1986, Ord 74, r 28.

9 *Somers v Kennedy* [1998] 1 IR 1.

CA 1990, s 150: The failure to fulfil the statutory obligation to file a statement of affairs under CA 1963, s 224 is sufficient reason to make a restriction order against directors or former directors under CA 1990, s 150.[1]

1 *Re Dunleckney* [2001] 1 IR 103 (Carroll J).

Information contained in the statement of affairs: Information contained in the statement of affairs can be used in evidence against any person making or concurring in making it.[1]

1 CA 1990, s 18.

Examination as to the company's affairs: The court can require all or any of the persons who could be required by CA 1963, s 224 to file a statement of affairs to attend before a court for the purposes of them giving such information in relation to the company as the court may think fit.[1]

1 RSC 1986, Ord 74, r 24(2); see also CA 1963, ss 245 and 282B and the notes thereto.

UK legislation

See IA 1986, s 131.

Liquidators

225 Appointment of liquidator

For the purpose of conducting the proceedings in winding up a company and performing such duties in reference thereto as the court may impose, the court may appoint a liquidator or liquidators.

Definitions

'company': CA 1963, s 2(1); 'the court': CA 1963, s 2(1).

Cross references in other enactments

NAMA Act 2009, s 150(2) provides:

> 'The appointment of a liquidator to a company whose assets or any part of them are under the control of a statutory receiver does not displace the statutory receiver and does not affect his or her powers, authority and agency.'

Notes

Status of liquidator: The liquidator is an agent of the company with fiduciary obligations arising from his office and statutory obligations imposed on him by legislation.[1] The liquidator is not in a strict sense a trustee, and is not a trustee for each creditor or contributory of the company.[2] The official liquidator is an executive officer appointed by the court.[3] The liquidator is in a different position to that of the official assignee in bankruptcy in that the assets of the company are not automatically vested in him.[4] A vesting order can be made, though, pursuant to CA 1963, s 230.

1 *Re Belfast Empire Theatre of Varieties Ltd* [1963] IR 41; *Re Tailteann Freight Services Ltd* [1975] IR 376; *Re Gertzenstein Ltd* [1937] Ch 115; *Stewart v Engel* [2000] BCC 741.

2 *Knowles v Scott* [1891] 1 Ch 717 where Rowe J held that 'in my view a ... Liquidator is more rightly described as the agent of the company – an agent who has, no doubt, cast upon him by statute and otherwise special duties, amongst which may be mentioned the duty of applying the company's assets in paying creditors and distributing the surplus amongst the shareholders'.

3 *Re Whiterock Quarries Ltd* (1933) IR 363.

4 Bankruptcy Act 1988, s 44 (1).

Liquidator's duties: Every liquidator is subject to a myriad of statutory duties laid down by the CA.[1] He may be sued for a breach of these statutory duties[2]. As a fiduciary he is under a duty to avoid a conflict of interests[3] and is also required not to make any secret profit from his office.[4] If he is in breach of his fiduciary duties or is guilty of negligence he may be sued for misfeasance[5] and may also in appropriate circumstances be disqualified under CA 1990, s 160.[6] Since the liquidator's duties are owed primarily to the company itself,[7] the misfeasance summons under CA 1963, s 298 will normally represent the most appropriate method for seeking financial recompense since any award of damages, etc will go to the company itself.[8] However, in special circumstances the liquidator may owe duties to individual creditors which may therefore be actionable by those individual creditors by way of normal plenary proceedings.[9]

1 For a brief summary of those duties, see Courtney, *The Law of Private Companies* (2nd edn, Tottel Publishing, 2002) paras 26.020–26.023.

2 *A & J Fabrications Ltd v Grant Thornton* [1998] 2 BCLC 227; *Pulsford v Devenish* [1903] 2 Ch 625; *James Smith and Sons (Norwood) Ltd v Goodman* [1936] Ch 216.

3 *Re Corbenstoke Ltd* (2) [1990] BCLC 60.

4 *Re Gertzenstein Ltd* [1936] 3 All ER 341. See also RSC 1986, Ord 74, r 40 which precludes the liquidator from making any profit arising out of the purchase of goods for the carrying on of the business of the company during the liquidation.

5 *Kyrris v Oldham* [2004] 1 BCLC 305; *A &J Fabrications Ltd v Grant Thornton* [1998] 2 BCLC 227.

6 See *Re CB Readymix Ltd, Cahill v Grimes* [2002] 1 IR 372 where Smyth J made an order disqualifying a person from acting as a liquidator for a period of seven years.

7 *Knowles v Scott* [1891] 1 Ch 717.

8 *Kyrris v Oldham* [2004] 1 BCLC 305; *A & J Fabrications Ltd v Grant Thornton* [1998] 2 BCLC 227; *Pulsford v Devenish* [1903] 2 Ch 625; *James Smith and Sons (Norwood) Ltd v Goodman* [1936] Ch 216. See also *Re Esal (Commodities) Ltd* [1997] 1 BCLC 705.

9 *Kyrris v Oldham* [2004] 1 BCLC 305; *A & J Fabrications Ltd v Grant Thornton* [1998] 2 BCLC 227; *Pulsford v Devenish* [1903] 2 Ch 625; *James Smith and Sons (Norwood) Ltd v Goodman* [1936] Ch 216.

Liquidator's personal liability: As an agent of the company, the liquidator will not, as a general rule, have any personal liability, whether in contract or in tort, in respect of his dealings with third parties.[1] However, as is the case with any agent, he may positively elect to contract on terms which show that he is undertaking a personal liability.[2] Ultimately, though, it is a question of fact in each case as to whether he has so elected.[3]

1 *Stewart v Engel* [2000] 2 BCLC 528.

2 *Re Anglo-Moravian Hungarian Railway Co ex p Watkin* (1875) 1 Ch D 130; *Stead Hazel and Co v Cooper* [1933] 1 KB 840.

3 *Re Anglo-Moravian Hungarian Railway Co ex p Watkin* [1875] 1 Ch D 130; *Stead Hazel and Co v Cooper* [1933] 1 KB 840.

Effect of appointment of liquidator on directors' powers: Upon the appointment of an official liquidator the board of directors become *functus officio* and its powers are assumed by the liquidator.[1]

1 *Union Accident Insurance Co Ltd* [1972] 1 All ER 1105; *Re Mawcon Ltd* [1969] 1 All ER 188; *Re Farrow's Bank Ltd* [1921] 2 Ch 164; *Re Ebsworth and Tidy's Contract* (1889) 42 ChD 23.

Effect of appointment of liquidator on employees: The making of the winding-up order and the appointment of the liquidator operate as an automatic dismissal of the company's workforce.[1] In contrast, the appointment of a provisional liquidator does not automatically result in the dismissal of the employees.[2] The official liquidator may waive the effect of the winding-up order as an automatic discharge of employees, either generally or in relation to specific employees only.[3]

1 *Donnelly v Gleeson* (11 July 1978, unreported) HC (Hamilton J).

2 *In re Le Gourmet Restaurants Ltd* (1984) Irish Times, 4 August (Egan J).

3 *Evan Henry Ltd* (15 May 1996, unreported) HC (Murphy J).

Practice: The identity of the person to be appointed as liquidator is a matter for the discretion of the court.[1] In practice the same person is often appointed as liquidator of several related companies even though there may be a potential conflict between the interest of one company and another. The appropriate method of resolving any such conflicts, as and when they arise, is for the liquidator to apply to the court for directions.[2] Following the making of a winding-up order the court adjourns the matter to the examiner's list for further consideration. The court requires the liquidator to prepare a preliminary report which deals with the value of the assets and liabilities of the company, the cause of the failure of the company and whether further enquiry is desirable regarding the formation or failure of the company or the conduct of the business. The report should also deal with whether, in the liquidator's opinion, any fraud has been committed in relation to the company since its formation, the estimation of time required to complete and any other matter that is relevant.[3] The report, (unless otherwise requested by the court) should be limited to a simple statement of facts and the liquidator should be wary of incurring extensive costs in the preparation of the report and should follow the court's guidelines in the matter.[4] The liquidator is also required at this stage to enter into a bond, the amount of which will be dictated by the estimated realisable value of the company's assets.[5]

1 *Parmalat Capital Finance Ltd v Food Holdings Ltd* [2009] 1 BCLC 274.

2 *Ibid.*

3 *Re Custom Line Ltd* (27 February 1984, unreported) HC (Murphy J).

4 *Re Merchant Banking Ltd* [1997] ILRM 260.

5 RSC 1986, Ord 74, rr 31–33. See also CA 1963, s 228(a).

226 Appointment and powers of provisional liquidator

(1) Subject to subsection (2), the court may appoint a liquidator provisionally at any time after the presentation of a winding-up petition and before the first appointment of liquidators.

(2) Where a liquidator is provisionally appointed by the court, the court may limit and restrict his powers by the order appointing him.

Definitions

'the court': CA 1963, s 2(1).

Cross references in other enactments

NAMA Act 2009, s 150(2) provides:

> 'The appointment of a liquidator to a company whose assets or any part of them are under the control of a statutory receiver does not displace the statutory receiver and does not affect his or her powers, authority and agency.'

Notes

Grounds for appointment of a provisional liquidator: An application to appoint a provisional liquidator may be made at any time after the presentation of a winding-up petition. The primary reason for the appointment of a provisional liquidator is to preserve the status quo pending the hearing of the petition and to prevent any one creditor from getting priority over another.[1] Nevertheless, whilst such an appointment is normally made in circumstances where there is a danger of the assets being dissipated before the hearing of the petition,[2] this is not the only ground for making such an order.[3] So, for example, the court has appointed a provisional liquidator in cases where the company was obviously insolvent and a winding up was inevitable[4] or where it was in the public interest to have the company's business under the stewardship of an insolvency practitioner during the period between the date of the presentation of the petition and the date on which the petition was scheduled to be heard[5] or where an immediate investigation into the affairs of the company was warranted.[6] In the case of a solvent company, where the shareholders are in dispute with one another and have caused deadlock in the administration of the company's affairs, the court may appoint a provisional liquidator to take over management of the company pending the hearing of a petition under CA 1963, s 205 and/or s 213(f).[7] In a recent case a provisional liquidator was appointed to prevent the controllers of a company from attempting to thwart the jurisdiction of the Court to make a winding-up order under Council Regulation (EC) No 1346/ 2000 of 29 May 2000 by changing its centre of main interests.[8] In a rather exceptional case the court was even prepared to appoint a provisional liquidator and to defer the hearing of the petition for a lengthy period so as to prevent the company from losing an income stream that was specified to terminate in the event of the making of a winding up order.[9] Normally, however, a provisional liquidator will not be left in place by the court for any lengthy period of time.[10]

1 *Re Dry Docks Corporation of London* (1888) 39 Ch D 306; *Re a company* [1991] BCLC 539; *Re Forrester and Lamego* Ltd [1997] 2 BCLC 155;Re *Namco UK Ltd* [2003] 2 BCLC 78.

2 *Re Dry Docks Corporation of London* (1888) 39 Ch D 306; *Levy v Napier* (1962) SLT 261; *International Westminster Bank plc v Okeanos Maritime Corp* [1987] BCLC 450; *Re a company* [1991] BCLC 539; *Re Forrester and Lamego* Ltd [1997] 2 BCLC 155;Re *Namco UK Ltd* [2003] 2 BCLC 78.

3 *Re Union Accident Insurance Co Ltd* [1972] 1 All ER 1105.

4 *Re Railway Finance Co Ltd* (1886) 35 Beav 473,14 LT 507.

5 *Re Union Accident Insurance Co Ltd* [1972] 1 All ER 1105; *Re Highfield Commodities Ltd* [1984] BCLC 623; *Re Goodwill Merchant Financial Services Ltd* [2001] 1 BCLC 259.

6 *Re a company* [1997] 2 BCLC 139; *Re Pinstripe Farming Co Ltd* [1996] 2 BCLC 295.

7 *Re Tradalco Ltd* [2001] IEHC 89.

8 *Re Eurofood IFSC Ltd, ex tempore*, (27 January 2004, unreported) HC (Lavan J) referred to in *Re Eurofood IFSC Ltd* [2004] 4 IR 370; See also R*e Eurofood IFSC Ltd* [2006] 3 WLR 309.

9 *MHMH Ltd & Ors v Carwood Baker Holdings Ltd* [2006] 1 BCLC 279.

10 *Re Coolfadda Developers Ltd* (14 July 2009, unreported) SC (Denham J).

Effect of appointment of provisional liquidator: The appointment of a provisional liquidator amounts to the opening of insolvency proceedings for the purposes of Council Regulation (EC) No 1346/2000 of 29 May 2000.[1] It also operates to suspend the powers of the directors[2] albeit that they retain a residual authority to act on behalf of the company in opposing the making of any winding up order.[3] Nevertheless, if the directors unreasonably oppose the making of the winding up order, they may face a personal liability in costs.[4] The provisional liquidator's appointment may also operate to suspend or terminate the authority of agents who have previously been appointed by the board to act on behalf of the company.[5] The appointment of the provisional liquidator does not, however, operate to automatically determine the contracts of employment of the company's workforce, at least where he has been given liberty to carry on the business of the company pending the hearing of the petition.[6]

1 *Re Eurofood IFSC Ltd [2004] 4 IR 370; Re Eurofood IFSC Ltd* [2006] 3 WLR 309.

2 *Re Mawcon Ltd* [1969] 1 WLR 78.

3 *Re Union Accident Insurance Co Ltd* [1972] 1 All ER 1105.

4 *Re Brackland Magazines Ltd* [1994] 1 BCLC 190.

5 *Pacific and General Insurance Co Ltd v Hazell* [1997] BCC 400.

6 *Donnelly v Gleeson* (11 July 1978, unreported) HC (Hamilton J).

Functions and duties of provisional liquidator: The provisional liquidator does not represent any one creditor or class of creditors but instead acts, albeit under the direction of the court, for the benefit of the creditors generally.[1] The primary function of the provisional liquidator will be to ensure the preservation of the company's assets thereby enabling the official liquidator, once appointed, to effect an orderly realisation and distribution of those assets.[2] The provisional liquidator is therefore required to take into his custody and under his control all of the property and choses in action to which the company is or appears to be entitled.[3]

1 *Bank of Credit and Commerce SA (No 2)* [1992] BCLC 579.

2 *Bank of Credit and Commerce International SA (No 2)* [1992] BCLC 579.

3 CA 1963, s 229 (1). See also *Levy v Napier* (1962) S L T 261.

Powers of the provisional liquidator: The powers of the provisional liquidator must be set out in the order made appointing him. These are usually limited to preserving the status quo pending the hearing of the petition.[1] He may therefore be empowered to appoint solicitors to act on his behalf, to open a bank account, to take possession of the company's assets,[2] to hire security personnel and, if necessary, to dismiss employees.[3] In certain circumstances the court may confer further powers on the provisional liquidator, such as the power to carry on the company's business.[4] He may also apply to the court for an order directing that any relevant persons be examined concerning the promotion, formation, trade, dealing, affairs or property of the company.[5] The court may also invoke the power to order the arrest of an absconding contributory, director, shadow director or other officer on proof of probable cause for believing that the contributory is about to quit the State or otherwise to abscond or to remove or conceal any of the property.[6] If there is any doubt about the powers of a provisional liquidator, he should apply to the court for directions or approval of any course of action.[7]

1 In practice the order usually limits the powers to 'taking possession of, collecting and protecting the assets … but such assets are not to be distributed or parted with until further order'.

2 See, for example, *Re Marseilles Extension Railway and Land Co* [1867] WN 64.

3 *Re Union Accident Insurance Co Ltd* [1972] 1 All ER 1105; *Re Joseph Phillips Ltd* [1964] 1 all ER 441.

4 *Re Dry Docks Corporation of London* (1888) 39 ChD 306; *Donnelly v Gleeson* (11 July 1978, unreported) HC (Hamilton J); *Re Gourmet Restaurants Ltd* (3 August 1984) The Irish Times, 4 August (Egan J). See also Ussher, *Company Law in Ireland* (Sweet & Maxwell), pp 487 and 488.

5 CA 1963, s 245.

6 CA 1963, s 247 (as amended by CLEA 2001).

7 CA 1963, s 280.

Practice and procedure: The application is made *ex parte* by a creditor, contributory or the company grounded on an affidavit setting out the grounds for the appointment.[1] The order appointing the provisional liquidator must state the nature and a short description of the property of which he is to take possession and the duties to be performed by him.[2] The appointment of the provisional liquidator triggers the obligation to make out and file a statement of affairs, subject of course to any order of the court to the contrary.[3] On the appointment of a provisional liquidator no action may be commenced or proceeded with against the company except with the leave of the court.[4] A provisional liquidator is displaced by the appointment of an official liquidator. Where the court refuses the petition to wind up the company the provisional liquidator is discharged and any order made against any third party based upon the existence of a provisional liquidator is discharged.[5] If no order for the winding up of the company is made, the court may nevertheless order that his costs, charges and expenses be paid out of the property of the company.[6]

1 RSC 1986, Ord 74, r 14(1).

2 RSC 1986, Ord 74, r 14(2).

3 CA 1963, s 224.

4 See CA 1963, s 222 and the notes thereto.

5 *Re Kingscroft Insurance Co Ltd* [1994] 2 BCLC 80.

6 RSC 1986, Ord 74, r 14(3). See *Re UOC Corp* [1997] 2 BCLC 569; *Re a company* [1988] BCLC 182.

227 Publication by liquidator of his appointment

(1) In a winding up by the court, the liquidator shall within 21 days after his appointment, publish in [the Companies Registration Office Gazette][a] a notice of his appointment and deliver to the registrar of companies an office copy of the court order appointing him.

(2) If the liquidator fails to comply with subsection (1), he [shall be guilty of an offence and liable to a fine][b] not exceeding [€1,904.61].[c]

Amendments

a The Companies Registration Office Gazette substituted for *Iris Oifigiúil* by IFCMPA 2005, s 72.

b Words in CA 1963, s 227(2) substituted by C(AA)A 2003, s 57 and Sch 2 para 1.

c '£250' increased to '£1,500' by CA 1990, s 240(7) as inserted by CLEA 2001, s 104(c). £1,500 converted to €1,904.61 by Council Regulation (EC) 1103/97, No 974/98 and No 2866/98 and the Economic and Monetary Union Act 1998, s 6.

Definitions

'the court': CA 1963, s 2(1); 'the Registrar of Companies': CA 1963, s 2(1).

Notes

Publication of liquidator's appointment: This section deals with the publication of the appointment of a liquidator by order of the Irish High Court. In relation to the publication pursuant to the Insolvency Regulation of notice of the appointment of liquidators in other EU member States, see CA 1963, ss 227A and 227B.

UK legislation

See IA 1986, s 109.

[227A Registration of Judgements given in insolvency proceedings

(1) Without prejudice to Article 16(1) of the Insolvency Regulation, a liquidator appointed in insolvency proceedings who intends—

(a) to request under Article 21 of the Regulation that notice of the judgment opening the proceedings and, where appropriate, the decision appointing him or her be published in the State, or

(b) to take any other action in the State under the Regulation,

shall deliver to the Registrar of Companies for registration a duly certified copy of the judgment and, where appropriate, of the decision appointing the liquidator.

(2) Registration under subsection (1) may also be effected by the Registrar of Companies on application by a liquidator who does not intend to take any action in the State under the Insolvency Regulation.

(3) The certified copy or copies mentioned in subsection (1) shall be accompanied by—

(a) if the judgment or decision is not expressed in Irish or English, a translation, certified to be correct by a person competent to do so, into either of those languages,

(b) the prescribed form, and

(c) the fee payable under the Eighth Schedule, as altered by order of the Minister under section 395(2).

(4) The Registrar shall issue a certificate of the registration to the liquidator.

(5) In any proceedings a document purporting to be—

(a) a duly certified copy of a judgment opening insolvency proceedings or a decision appointing a liquidator in such proceedings, or

(b) a translation of such a document which is certified as correct by a person competent to do so,

shall, without further proof, be admissible as evidence of the judgment, the liquidator's appointment or the translation, unless the contrary is shown.][a]

Amendments

a Section inserted by EC(CI)R 2002, reg 31.

Notes

Registration and publication of foreign appointments: This section was inserted by EC (CI)R 2002 for the purpose of giving effect to Council Regulation (EC) No 1346/2000(1) of 29 May

2000 on insolvency proceedings. It stipulates that a liquidator appointed in another member state who wishes to have his appointment published in the State must deliver to the Registrar of Companies a certified copy of the judgment or order pursuant to which he was appointed. The judgment or order may also be delivered for registration even if the liquidator is not seeking to have his appointment so published.[1]

Publication of the appointment in the State is optional unless the company has an establishment here.[2] If the company does have an establishment in the State the foreign liquidator must ensure that publication of his appointment takes place as soon as practicable after the opening of the foreign insolvency proceedings.[3] The publication must be effected in the Companies Registration Office Gazette and in at least two daily morning newspapers circulating in the state[4] and should comprise the following—[5]

(a) notice of the judgment opening the insolvency proceedings;

(b) where appropriate, the decision appointing the liquidator in those proceedings (as where a voluntary liquidator is appointed by resolution of the members);

(c) the name and business address of the liquidator; and

(d) an indication as to whether the liquidator's appointment is as part of main insolvency proceedings under art 3.1 of the Insolvency Regulation or as part of secondary insolvency proceedings under art 3.2.[6]

See also the notes to the Insolvency Regulation, arts 19–21.

1 CA 1963, s 227A(2).
2 See Insolvency Reg, art 21 and CA 1963, s 227B.
3 CA 1963, s 227B(3).
4 CA 1963, s 227B(1).
5 CA 1963, s 227B(1).
6 For an explanation of the distinction between main insolvency proceedings and secondary proceedings see the notes to CA 1963, s 205A as well as the notes to the Insolvency Reg, art 3.

[227B Publication in relation to insolvency proceedings

(1) In this section 'publication' means publication of—

(a) notice of the judgment opening the insolvency proceedings concerned,

(b) where appropriate, the decision appointing the liquidator in those proceedings,

(c) the name and business address of the liquidator, and

(d) the provision (either paragraph 1 or paragraph 2) of Article 3 of the Insolvency Regulation giving jurisdiction to open the proceedings,

in [the Companies Registration Office Gazette][b] and once at least in two daily morning newspapers circulating in the State.

(2) Without prejudice to section 227A(1), publication shall be effected by the liquidator concerned.

(3) Where the debtor company has an establishment (within the meaning of Article 2(h) of the Insolvency Regulation) in the State, the liquidator or any authority mentioned in Article 21(2) of the Regulation shall ensure that publication takes place as soon as practicable after the opening of the insolvency proceedings.][a]

Amendments

a Section inserted by EC(CI)R 2002, reg 3.

b Words inserted by reg 9 of the European Communities (Companies) Regulations 2004 (SI 839/2004).

Notes

General: CA 1963, s 227B was inserted by the Insolvency Regulations for the purpose of giving effect to Council Regulation (EC) No 1346/2000(1) of 29 May 2000 on insolvency proceedings. See generally the notes to CA 1963, s 227B as well as the notes to the Insolvency Regulation, arts 19–21.

228 General provisions as to liquidators

The following provisions relating to liquidators shall have effect on a winding-up order being made—

(a) the court may determine whether any and what security is to be given by a liquidator on his appointment;

(b) a liquidator shall be described by the style of 'the official liquidator' of the particular company in respect of which he is appointed and not by his individual name;

(c) a liquidator appointed by the court may resign or, on cause shown, be removed by the court;

(d) a person appointed liquidator shall receive such salary or remuneration by way of percentage or otherwise as the court may direct, and if more such persons than on are appointed liquidators, their remuneration shall be distributed among them in such proportions as the court directs;

(e) a vacancy in the office of a liquidator appointed by the court shall be filled by the court;

(f) if more than one liquidator is appointed by the court, the court shall declare whether any act by this Act required or authorised to be done by the liquidator is to be done by all or any one or more of the persons appointed;

(g) subject to section 300, the acts of a liquidator shall be valid notwithstanding any defects that may afterwards be discovered in his appointment or qualification.

Definitions

'company': CA 1963, s 2(1); 'the court': CA 1963, s 2(1).

Notes

The official liquidator as fiduciary: see the notes to CA 1963, s 225.

The powers of the official liquidator: See CA 1963, ss 229–231, 236, 244A–245A, 247, 286–290, 277A and 298 and CA 1990, ss 139–141.

The liquidator's bond: A bond is taken out to protect the creditors of the company from misappropriation of the assets in an official liquidation. After an order for winding up has been made, the court will adjourn the matter to the examiner's list for further consideration. At this stage the court will make an order directing that the official liquidator obtain an indemnity in the form of a bond.[1] The bond must be in the same format as Form No 22 of Appendix G of the Rules of the Superior Courts. The court usually accepts an insurance company as sole surety[2]. In exceptional circumstances the court may authorise the official liquidator to act without entering into a bond.[3] The bond must be filed in the Central Office.[4]

1 RSC 1986, Ord 74, r 31.

2 In the majority of cases the court will direct that the insurance bond be in the form of a fidelity bond provided by an insurance company.

3 RSC 1986, Ord 74, r 31. This dispensation may arise where there are no assets in the liquidation.

4 RSC 1986, Ord 74, r 33.

Disqualification for appointment as liquidator: A body corporate may not act as a liquidator and will be guilty of a criminal offence if it attempts to do so.[1] In addition, certain individuals are not qualified for appointment as liquidators, namely:[2]

(a) a person who is, or has within 12 months of the commencement of the winding up been, an officer or servant of the company;

(b) except with the leave of the court, a parent, spouse, brother, sister or child of an officer of the company;

(c) a person who is a partner or in the employment of an officer or servant of the company; and

(d) A person who is not qualified for appointment as liquidator of any other body corporate which is that company's subsidiary or holding company or a subsidiary of that company's holding company, or would be so disqualified if the body corporate were an Irish registered company.

For the purposes of the foregoing, references to an 'officer or servant of the company' are taken to include an auditor of the company.[3]

A liquidator who becomes disqualified from so acting must thereupon vacate office, giving fourteen days' notice in writing of that fact to the court.[4] If he fails to do so, he is guilty of an offence.[5]

1 CA 1963, s 300.

2 CA 1963, s 300A. This section only applies to liquidations commenced after the 1 August 1991.

3 CA 1963, s 300A(1).

4 CA 1963, s 300A(3). In the case of a members' voluntary winding up the notice must be given to the company, whereas in the case of a creditors' voluntary winding up the notice must be given to the company and to the creditors.

5 CA 1963, s 300A(4).

Resignation of liquidator: Under CA 1963, s 228(c) a liquidator appointed by the court may resign but there is nothing in this section or in the Rules of the Superior Courts that requires that the resignation should be accepted or approved by the court. however, it is deemed advisable in a compulsory winding up to obtain an order from the court either accepting or approving the resignation.[1] The resignation of a liquidator is not fully effective until he has been released by the court and has had his bond vacated.[2] The resigning liquidator shall deliver all books kept by him and all other books, documents' papers and accounts in his possession relating to his office to his replacement[3]. However, orders have been made in this jurisdiction discharging an official liquidator and vacating his bond without appointing another in his place.[4] The Rules of the Superior Court do not appear to contemplate the release of an official liquidator until he has been replaced.[5] In this regard the Rules of the Superior Courts stipulate that upon the resignation of an official liquidator a new liquidator is to be appointed in the same manner as the first liquidator and the application to court to effect that appointment may be brought by such party as the court authorises.[6]

1 Per Hamilton J in *Re Palgrave Murphy Ltd* 112 ILTR 81.

2 See *Re Northern Waterproofs Ltd* [1967] NI 17 where it was held that before granting the release to the liquidator the Court had to be satisfied that an acceptable successor had been found and that a report had been prepared concerning the conduct of the retiring liquidator.

3 RSC 1986, Ord 74, r 43.

4 In *Re Harold's Cross Public Utility Society* (1956, unreported) Dixon J and in *Re Mersey Meat Packaging Company* (1962, unreported) Budd J as referred to by Lowry J In *Re Northern Waterproofs Ltd*.

5 RSC 1986, Ord 74, r 43.

6 RSC 1986, Ord 74, r 36.

Removal of liquidator: The official liquidator may be removed for 'cause shown' under CA 1963, s 228(c). In this regard, the application may only properly be made by a person having a legitimate interest in the outcome of the liquidation.[1] So, whilst a creditor of the company might have *locus standi* to bring the application, a contributory who was not also a creditor would have no such standing unless he could show that there was a likelihood of a surplus being available for the members.[2] Similarly, a debtor or alleged debtor of a company in liquidation would have no entitlement to apply for the removal of the liquidator.[3] In the case where joint liquidators have been appointed, one joint liquidator will be regarded as having *locus standi* to seek the removal of the other.[4]

The burden of showing cause is on the applicant. Earlier authorities had suggested that in order to show cause the applicant had to show some personal unfitness, impropriety or breach of duty on the part of the liquidator.[5] However, it is now accepted that it would be wrong for the court to seek to limit or define the grounds warranting removal and accordingly it may be appropriate to remove a liquidator even though nothing can be said against him, either personally or in his conduct of the particular liquidation.[6] The touchstone for an appraisal of whether good cause has been shown for the removal of a liquidator is the real, substantial and honest interests of the liquidation and the purpose for which the liquidator was appointed.[7] Essentially, in order to show cause, the applicant must satisfy the court that it is for the general advantage of those interested in the assets of the company that the liquidator be removed.[8] Instances that have been found to warrant the removal of the liquidator include the following: where the liquidator failed to display sufficient vigour in carrying out his duties;[9] where he preferred the interests of members over creditors; [10] where there was a deficiency of assets and he insisted on prosecuting an action contrary to the wishes of the majority of creditors;[11] where he was guilty of a conflict of interest;[12] where as a joint liquidator it was no longer practicable for him and the other joint liquidator to work together.[13] The application to remove a liquidator may be brought by a motion on notice to the liquidator. The principal creditors should also be put on notice of the application as the parties with the greatest material interest in the outcome of the liquidation. Upon the removal of the official liquidator a new liquidator is to be appointed in the same manner as the first liquidator and, if he not appointed within the same application that resulted in the first liquidator being removed, the application to court to effect the new appointment may be brought by such party as the court authorises.[14]

1 *Re Buildhead Ltd (No 2)* [2005] BCC 138; *Deloitte and Touche AG v Johnson* [2000] 1 BCLC 485. See also *Corbenstoke Ltd (No 2)* [1990] BCLC 60; *Re A and C Supplies Ltd* [1998] 1 BCLC 603; *City and Suburban Pty Ltd v Smith* [1998] 822 FCA (9 July 1998). *Clements and Or v Udal* [2002] 2 BCLC 606; *AMP Music Box Enterprises Ltd v Hoffman & Anor* [2002] BCLC 996.

2 *Re Corbenstoke Ltd (No 2)* [1990] BCLC 60; *Deloitte and Touche AG v Johnson* [2000] 1 BCLC 485; *Re Doherty Advertising Ltd* [2006] IEHC 198.

3 *Re Doherty Advertising Ltd* [2006] IEHC 198; *Deloitte and Touche AG v Johnson* [2000] 1 BCLC 485; *Walker Morris (a firm) v Khalastchi* [2001] 1 BCLC 1.

4 *Re A & C Supplies Ltd* [1998] 1 BCLC 603.

5 *Per* Jessel MR in the case of *Sir John Moore Gold Mining Company* (1879) 12 Ch D 325.

6 *Re Keypak Homecare Ltd* [1987] BCLC 409. See also *Re Marseilles Extension Rly and Land Co* (1867) LR Eq 692; *City and Suburban Pty Ltd v Smith* 1998] 822 FCA (9 July 1998).

7 *Re Buildlead Ltd (no 2)* [2006] 1 BCLC 9.

8 *Re A & C Supplies Ltd* [1998] 1 BCLC 603. See also *Re Adam Eyton Ltd, ex parte Charlesworth* (1887) 36 Ch D 299; *Re The Mutual Life Stock Financial and Agency Company Ltd* (1886) 12 VLR 777; *Dallinger v Halcha Holdings Pty Ltd* (1995) 134 ALR 178; *City and Suburban Pty Ltd v Smith* 1998] 822 FCA (9 July 1998).

9 *Re Keypak Homecare Ltd* [1987] BCLC 409.

10 *Re Rubber and Produce Investment Trust* [1915] 1 Ch 382.

11 *Re Tavistock Ironworks Co* (1871) 24 LT 605; *Re Rubber and Produce Investment Trust* [1915] 1 Ch 382.

12 *Re P Turner (Wilsden) Ltd* [1987] BCLC 149; *Re Corbenstoke Ltd (No 2)* [1990] BCLC 60.

13 *Re A and C Supplies Ltd* [1998] 1 BCLC 603.

14 RSC 1986, Ord 74, r 36.

Defects in appointment or qualification of a liquidator: The language of CA 1963, s 228(g) is similar to that used in CA 1963, s 178 which deals with defects in the appointment or qualification of directors. It has been held that s 178 only applies in the case of a procedural error in the appointment and affords no protection if the error concerns substantive provisions relating to the appointment, nor is it of any avail if there has never been any appointment at all.[1] In this regard, it is to be noted that s 228(g) is expressly subordinated to CA 1963, s 300 (and presumably, by inference, s 300A) dealing with the disqualification of persons for appointment as liquidator. Thus, if the liquidator was disqualified from acting from the outset or becomes disqualified, acts purportedly done by him during a period of disqualification will not be saved under s 228(g).

1 *Morris v Kanssen* [1946] AC 459. See generally the notes to CA 1963, s 178.

Remuneration of liquidator: The remuneration of the official liquidator ranks as a cost of the liquidation[1] and may be fixed either at the time of his appointment or at any time thereafter.[2] In practice remuneration is allowed on an interim basis on foot of applications made from time to time by the liquidator during the course of the winding up, with the final measuring of remuneration taking place as part of the official liquidator's application for final orders.[3] There is no scale of fees fixed for the liquidator's remuneration; instead, the court will allow such remuneration as is fair in the particular circumstances of the case.[4] The liquidator's remuneration will normally be determined by reference to the number of hours worked by the liquidator and his staff.[5] In this regard, the court is in no sense bound by the scales of fees fixed for accountancy work by professional institutions, although it may take such scales into account in determining what is fair remuneration in the circumstances.[6] In practice, the court seeks to ensure that there is reasonable uniformity as between the remuneration fixed for the liquidator *qua* liquidator, and the remuneration payable for other accountancy work of a similar type.[7] In order to achieve this result a practice has developed of appointing a creditor – usually the Revenue – to represent the general body of creditors at the hearing to determine the liquidator's remuneration.[8]

Where there have been two or more liquidators of the company, one in succession to the other, and there is an insufficiency of assets to pay them both in full, their remuneration should abate rateably.[9]

1 See RSC 1986, Ord 74, r 128.

2 See generally RSC 1986, Ord 74, r 46.

3 In relation to the final orders application, see RSC 1986, Ord 74, r 137.

4 *Re Amalgamated Syndicates Ltd* [1901] 2 Ch 181; *Re Merchant Banking Ltd* [1987] ILRM 163.

5 *Re Car Replacements Ltd* (15 December 1999, unreported) HC (Murphy J); *Re Independent Insurance Co Ltd (No 2)* [2003] 21 BCLC 640.

6 *Re Merchant Banking Ltd* [1987] ILRM 163.

7 *Re Merchant Banking Ltd* [1987] ILRM 163; *Re Independent Insurance Co Ltd (No 2)* [2003] 21 BCLC 640.

[8] *Re Merchant Banking Ltd* [1987] ILRM 163.
[9] *Re Salters Hall School Ltd* [1998] 1 BCLC 401.

UK legislation

See IA 1986, ss 231, 232.

---

229 Custody of company's property

(1) Where a winding-up order has been made or where a provisional liquidator has been appointed, the liquidator or the provisional liquidator, as the case may be, shall take into his custody or under his control all the property and things in action to which the company is or appears to be entitled.

(2) If and so long as there is no liquidator, all the property of the company shall be deemed to be in the custody of the court.

Definitions

'company': CA 1963, s 2(1); 'the court': CA 1963, s 2(1).

Notes

Taking custody of property: This section empowers the court not only to order the delivery up of property to which the company 'is entitled' but also property to which it 'appears to be entitled', thereby conferring on it jurisdiction to order the delivery up of property even though there is a dispute as to its ownership.[1] The dispute as to title can then be resolved either within the liquidation process itself or by way of separate proceedings.[2] If the property comprises documents (eg documents of title), the assertion of a lien will not operate so as to prevent delivery up to the liquidator or provisional liquidator.[3]

[1] *Re London Iron and Steel Co Ltd* [1990] BCLC 372. See also RSC 1986, Ord 74, r 91 which allows the liquidator to serve notice on any person being a contributory, trustee, receiver, banker, agent or officer of the company to deliver up any money, property, books or papers in that person's hands to which the company is *prima facie* entitled. If the notice is not complied with the liquidator may seek an order under CA 1963, s 236 for the delivery up of the items in question. Notably though, whilst the words 'appear to be entitled' in s 229 are wide enough to encompass assets whose ownership is disputed, the words '*prima facie* entitled' in Ord 74, r 91 and s 236 do not appear to be wide enough to encompass assets whose ownership is in dispute: *Re London Iron and Steel Co Ltd* [1990] BCLC 372.
[2] *Re London Iron and Steel Co Ltd* [1990] BCLC 372.
[3] See CA 1963, s 244A and the notes thereto.

UK legislation

See IA 1986, s 144.

---

230 Vesting of property of company in liquidator

Where a company is being wound up by the court, the court may, on the application of the liquidator, by order direct that all or any part of the property of whatsoever description belonging to the company or held by trustees on its behalf shall vest in the liquidator by his official name, and thereupon the property to which the order relates shall vest accordingly, and the liquidator may, after giving such indemnity, if any, as the court may direct, bring or defend in his official name any action or other legal proceeding which relates to that property or which it is necessary to bring or defend for the purpose of effectually winding up the company and recovering its property.

Definitions

'company': CA 1963, s 2(1); 'the court': CA 1963, s 2(1).

Notes

General: Upon the making of a winding-up order all property of the company remains vested in the company and not the liquidator. The court may, on the liquidator's *ex parte* application,[1] make an order vesting all or any part of the assets in him in his official name. This will enable the liquidator to institute or defend proceedings in his official name relating to that property. Otherwise, such proceedings should be brought by him in the name of the company.[2] If a vesting order is made in respect of property the liquidator does not become personally liable in respect of obligations attaching to the property[3]. The position in a liquidation can be compared to the position in bankruptcy where the assets of the bankrupt automatically vest in the Official Assignee once the bankruptcy order has been made.[4] Even if a vesting order is not made (and such orders are only very rarely made) the proper person to give a receipt for assets realised in the liquidation is the liquidator himself.[5]

1 *Re Albert Life Assurance Co* (1869) 18 WR 91.

2 See CA 1963, s 231 regarding the requirement to obtain the leave of the court or the committee of inspection in order to bring or defend legal proceedings in the name of the company.

3 *Graham v Edge* (1888) 20 QBD 538, aff'd (1888) 20 OBD 683; *Re Ebsworth and Tidy's Contract* (1889) 42 Ch D 23.

4 Bankruptcy Act 1988, s 44(1).

5 *Re Private Motorists' Provident Society Ltd, Horgan v Minister for Justice* (23 June 1995, unreported) HC (Murphy J).

UK legislation

See IA 1986, s 145.

---

231 Powers of liquidator

(1) The liquidator in a winding up by the court shall have power, with the sanction of the court or of the committee of inspection—

(a) to bring or defend any action or other legal proceeding in the name and on behalf of the company;

(b) to carry on the business of the company so far as may be necessary for the beneficial winding up thereof;

(c) to appoint a solicitor to assist him in the performance of his duties;

(d) to pay any classes of creditors in full;

(e) to make any compromise or arrangement with creditors or persons claiming to be creditors, or having or alleging themselves to have any claim present or future, certain or contingent, ascertained or sounding only in damages against the company, or whereby the company may be rendered liable;

(f) to compromise all calls and liabilities to calls, debts and liabilities capable of resulting in debts, and all claims, present or future, certain or contingent, ascertained or sounding only in damages, subsisting or supposed to subsist between the company and a contributory or alleged contributory or other debtor or person apprehending liability to the company, and all questions in any way relating to or affecting the assets or winding up of the company, on such terms as may be agreed, and take any security for the discharge of any such call, debt, liability or claim, and give a complete discharge in respect thereof.

[(1A)(a) The liquidator of a company shall not sell by private contract a non-cash asset of the requisite value to a person who is, or who, within three years prior to the date of commencement of the winding-up, has been, an officer of the company unless the liquidator has given at least 14 days notice of his intention to do so to all creditors of the company who are known to him or who have been intimated to him.

(b) In this subsection—

(i) 'non-cash asset' and 'requisite value' have the meanings assigned to them by section 29 of the Companies Act, 1990, and

(ii) 'officer' includes a person connected, within the meaning of section 26 of the Companies Act, 1990, with a director, and a shadow director.][a]

(2) The liquidator in a winding up by the court shall have power—

(a) to sell the real and personal property and things in action of the company by public auction or private contract, with power to transfer the whole thereof to any person or company or to sell the same in lots and for the purpose of selling the company's land or any part thereof to carry out such sales by fee farm grant, sub fee farm grant, lease, sub-lease or otherwise, and to sell any rent reserved on any such grant or any reversion expectant upon the determination of any such lease;

(b) to do all acts and to execute, in the name and on behalf of the company, all deeds, receipts and other documents, and for that purpose to use, when necessary, the company's seal;

(c) where any contributory has been adjudged bankrupt or has presented a petition for arrangement with his creditors in pursuance of the Bankruptcy Acts, to prove, rank and claim in the bankruptcy or arrangement for any balance against his estate, and to receive dividends in the bankruptcy or arrangement in respect of that balance, as a separate debt due from the bankrupt or arranging debtor, and rateably with the other separate creditors;

(d) to draw, accept, make and endorse any bill of exchange or promissory note in the name and on behalf of the company, with the same effect with respect to the liability of the company as if the bill or note had been drawn, accepted, made or endorsed by or on behalf of the company in the course of its business;

(e) to raise on the security of the assets of the company any money requisite;

(f) to take out in his official name letters of administration to any deceased contributory and to do in his official name any other act necessary for obtaining payment of any money due from a contributory or his estate which cannot be conveniently done in the name of the company, and in all such cases the money due shall, for the purpose of enabling the liquidator to take out the letters of administration or recover the money, be deemed to be due to the liquidator himself;

(g) to give security for costs in any proceedings commenced by the company or by him in the name of the company;

(h) to appoint an agent to do any business which the liquidator is unable to do himself;

(i) to do all such other things as may be necessary for winding up the affairs of the company and distributing its assets.

(3) The exercise by the liquidator in a winding up by the court of the powers conferred by this section shall be subject to the control of the court, and any creditor or contributory may apply to the court in relation to any exercise or proposed exercise of any of those powers.

(4) The court may provide by any order that the liquidator may, where there is no committee of inspection, exercise any of the powers mentioned in paragraph (a) or paragraph (b) of subsection (1) without the sanction or intervention of the court.

Amendments

a CA 1963, s 231(1A) inserted by CA 1990, s 124.

Definitions

'agent': CA 1963, s 2(1); 'company': CA 1963, s 2(1), s 2(1); 'the Bankruptcy Acts': CA 1963, s 2(1); 'contributory': CA 1963, s 2(1), s 208; 'the court': CA 1963, s 2(1); 'director': CA 1963, s 2(1); 'document': CA 1963, s 2(1): 'officer': CA 1963, s 2(1).

Notes

1. Powers exercisable with the sanction of the court or the committee of inspection.

Test to be applied by the court or committee of inspection in granting leave to exercise powers: In determining whether or not to grant leave to exercise all or any of the powers listed in CA 1963, s 231(1), the court or committee of inspection, as the case may be, must have regard to whether the exercise of that power is in the best interests of those creditors or contributories of the company who have a real interest in the assets of the company.[1] Nevertheless, whilst the court or committee may have regard to the wishes of the creditors generally, there is a residual discretion to depart from their views in exceptional circumstances.[2] If leave is being sought from the court rather than from the committee, the application, although normally made *ex parte*, must nevertheless be heard in public.[3]

1 *Re Greendale Developments Ltd* [1997] 3 IR 540; *Re Bank of Credit and commerce International SA (No 3)* [1993] BCLC 106, aff'd [1993] BCLC 1490; *Re Bank of Credit and Commerce International SA (No 10)* [1995] 1 BCLC 362; *Re Edennote Ltd (No 2)* [1997] 2 BCLC 89; *Re Greenhaven Motors Ltd* [1999] 1 BCLC 635; *Re Barings plc (No 7)* [2002] 1 BCLC 401.

2 *Re Bank of Credit and Commerce International SA (No 3)* [1993] BCLC 106, aff'd [1993] BCLC 1490.

3 *Re Greendale Developments Ltd* [1997] 3 IR 540.

Legal proceedings: Leave of the court or of the committee of inspection (if one has been appointed)[1] must be obtained to bring or defend any action or any other legal proceeding in the name and on behalf of the company.[2] Such leave should be sought even if the proceedings were commenced before the company went into liquidation.[3] Moreover, if judgment is obtained against the company the only party with standing to bring an appeal on behalf of and in the name of the company is the liquidator himself.[4]

If the leave of the court is sought to bring, continue or defend proceedings (and in practice it is normal for the liquidator to seek leave from the court rather than the committee), the application will be made *ex parte* grounded on an affidavit of the official liquidator, exhibiting an opinion of counsel as to the likelihood of success in the proceedings. Moreover, whilst the application, if made to the court, is heard in public,[5] it may be legitimate to exclude the adverse party to the litigation or proposed litigation, in determining whether or not to grant leave to the liquidator.[6]

The defendant to proceedings brought by a liquidator in the name of the company cannot object to those proceedings on the ground that the sanction of the court has not been obtained.[7] In this regard, it should also be noted that the court has jurisdiction to retrospectively sanction the proceedings, albeit that the liquidator may be at risk as to costs incurred by him prior to that sanction being obtained.[8]

Where the proceedings are being taken or defended by the liquidator in the name of the company rather than in his own name, he has no personal liability for any award of costs that may be made in favour of the other party to the litigation,[9] at least provided there has been no personal impropriety on his part.[10] The costs will, however, rank as a cost or expense of the winding up and will rank ahead of the liquidator's own remuneration.[11] Nevertheless there are certain statutory causes of action that must be taken by the liquidator in his own name, such as fraudulent or reckless trading proceedings under CA 1963, s 297A, misfeasance proceedings under CA 1963, s 298 and proceedings under CA 1990, s 204 to impose personal liability for failure to keep proper books of account, which must be taken by the liquidator in his own name.[12] As regards such proceedings, the adverse litigant is entitled to look to the liquidator personally to meet any award of costs, albeit that the liquidator has a right to be indemnified out of the assets in the winding up.[13]

1 See CA 1963, ss 232 and 233 in relation to committees of inspection, their appointment and functions.

2 CA 1963, s 231(1)(a).

3 *Re Greendale Developments Ltd* [1997] 3 IR 540.

4 *Cork County Council v CB Readymix Ltd* (12 December 1997, unreported) SC, noted in (1999) 17 ILT (ns) 2.

5 *Re Greendale Developments Ltd* [1997] 3 IR 540.

6 *Re Hinckley Island Hotel Ltd* [1998] 2 BCLC 526.

7 *Dublin City Distillery Ltd v Doherty* [1914] AC 823.

8 *Gresham International Ltd v Moonie* [2009] 2 BCLC 256; *Re London Metallurgical Co* [1897] 2 Ch 262.

9 *Fraser v Province of Bescia Steam Tramways Co* (1887) 56 LT 771.

10 *Metalloy Supplies Ltd v MA (UK) Ltd* [1997] 1 BCLC 165.

11 *Comhlucht Páipéar Riomhaireachta Teo v Udarás na Gaeltachta* [1990] 1 IR 320. See also RSC 1986, Ord 74, r 128. If the dispute is as between the liquidator and a debentureholder and involves an unsuccessful attempt by the liquidator to retain assets as against the debentureholder or a receiver appointed pursuant to the debenture, the costs of that litigation will have to be borne personally by the liquidator and he will not be entitled to any indemnity out of the assets of the company at least to the extent that any such claim would rank in priority to the claim of the debentureholder: *Re MC Bacon Ltd* [1990] BCLC 607; *Re R S and M Engineering Co Ltd* [1999] 2 BCLC 485.

12 *Southern Mineral Oil Ltd v Cooney* [1997] 3 IR 549; *Southern Mineral Oil Ltd v Cooney (No 2)* [1999] 1 IR 237.

13 *Re Hounslow Brewery Co* [1896] WN 45; *Re W Powell and Sons* [1896] 1 Ch 681; *Sichell's Case* (1867) 3 Ch App 119; *Re Wilson Lovatt and Sons Ltd* [1977] 1 All ER 274. Recent UK cases have cast doubt upon the liquidator's entitlement to be indemnified out of the assets of the company: *Re MC Bacon Ltd (No 2)* [1990] BCLC 607; *Re Floor Fourteen Ltd* [2001] 2 BCLC 392; *Re Demaglass Ltd* [2003] 1 BCLC 412; *Re MT Realisations Ltd* [2004] 1 BCLC 119. These cases have all been predicated on the assumption that such causes of action may instituted by the liquidator without the leave of the court. However, in this jurisdiction the invariable practice is

that the leave of the court is required by the liquidator to bring proceedings whether they are in the company's name or in his own name. It is questionable therefore whether these more recent authorities would represent good law in this jurisdiction.

Carrying on the business of the company: The power to carry on the business can only be exercised to the extent 'necessary' for the beneficial winding up of the company[1] and is not exercisable for some other purpose such as a reconstruction of the company, even if such a course of action is supported by a majority of the creditors.[2] Whether or not it is necessary for the beneficial winding up of the company is something that must be determined by the Court having regard to all the circumstances of the case and include what may be called a mercantile necessity.[3] There is no question of the liquidator being allowed to carry on the business for a long period with a view to making a profit.[4] However, even if the carrying on of the business over a shorter period ultimately proves to have been the wrong decision, the liquidator will not face any personal exposure provided, at the time of seeking leave to trade, he reasonably and *bona fide* believed that such a course of action was indeed necessary for the beneficial winding up of the company.[5]

Where the official liquidator carries on the business of the company, he may not, without the express sanction of the court, purchase goods for the carrying on of that business from any person whose connection with him is of such a nature as would result in his obtaining any portion of the profit, if any, arising out of the transaction.[6]

All debts and liabilities incurred in the course of the carrying on of the business are classified as an expense of the liquidation and rank in priority to the debts and liabilities of the company, as well as being in priority to the liquidator's own remuneration.[7]

1 CA 1963, s 231(1)(b).
2 *Re Wreck Recovery and Salvage Co* (1880) 15 Ch D 353.
3 *Re Wreck Recovery and Salvage Co* (1880) 15 Ch D 353; *Willis v Association of Universities of the British Commonwealth* [1965] 1 QB 140; *Re The 19th Ltd* [1989] ILRM 652.
4 *Re Great Eastern Electric Co Ltd* (1941) All ER 409; *Re. Davis (SI) and Co* [1945] Ch 402; *Re Batey, ex parte Emmanuel* (1881) 17 Ch D 35.
5 *Re Great Eastern Electric Co Ltd* (1941) All ER 409.
6 RSC 1986, Ord 74, r 40. Se also the notes to CA 1963, s 225 regarding the duty of liquidators to avoid any conflict of interests.
7 *Re Davis (SI) and Co* [1945] Ch 402.

Appointment of solicitor: There is no general rule that the liquidator may not retain the petitioning creditor's solicitors. In fact such a course may offer advantages to all the creditors in so far as the petitioner's solicitors may already have some familiarity with the company, its assets and affairs.[1] If the petitioning creditor is the largest creditor and no difficulties are expected in quantifying the provable debts, the risk of a conflict of interest may only be a distant possibility.[2] If however a conflict of interest can be identified but there is no real risk of confidential information miscarrying or being misused, a balancing exercise might be appropriate to determine whether the conflict was something which the court might countenance.[3] In order to deal with any possible conflict a separate firm of solicitors could be appointed to deal with the conflicted area.[4]

Whilst the liquidator is not personally liable for the costs of his solicitor,[5] the solicitor's costs will rank as a cost or expense of the liquidation in priority ahead of the liquidator's remuneration.[6] A solicitor is not entitled to any lien over the company's money and documents that he acquired during the course of the winding up.[7]

1 *Re Schuppan (a bankrupt)* [1997] 1 BCLC 211; *Re Recover Ltd (in liquidation)* [2003] 2 BCLC 186; *Re Maxwell Communications Corporation plc* [1992] 1 BCLC 465; *Re Baron Investment (Holdings) Ltd (in Liquidation), Halstuk v Venvil* [2000] 1 BCLC 272.
2 *Re Schuppan (a bankrupt)* [1997] 1 BCLC 211; *Re Maxwell Communications Corporation plc* [1992] 1 BCLC 465; *Re Baron Investment (Holdings) Ltd (in Liquidation), Halstuk v Venvil* [2000] 1 BCLC 272.
3 *Re Schuppan (a bankrupt)* [1997] 1 BCLC 211.

[4] *Re Schuppan (a bankrupt)* [1997] 1 BCLC 211; *Re Maxwell Communications Corporation plc* [1992] 1 BCLC 465; *Re Baron Investment (Holdings) Ltd (in Liquidation), Halstuk v Venvil* [2000] 1 BCLC 272.

[5] *Re Anglo-Moravian Hungarian Junction Railway Co, ex parte Watkin* (1875) 1 Ch D 130.

[6] CA 1963, s 281; RSC 1986, Ord 74, r 128.

[7] *Re Motor Cabs Ltd* [1911] 2 Ch 557.

Compromise of claims by or against the company: The court or committee of inspection, as the case may be, must have sufficient information put before it by the liquidator to allow it to exercise its discretion in a fully informed manner when deciding whether or not to compromise a claim under CA 1963, s 231(1)(e) or (f).[1] In this regard the court has jurisdiction to rescind a compromise made with its sanction if it has been obtained by misrepresentation or by the suppression of material facts.[2] It is usual for an application to be made *ex parte* to the court grounded on an affidavit of the liquidator which exhibits counsel's opinion. The court will refuse to sanction a compromise of proceedings if it precludes the liquidator from pursuing any other actions against the defendants without good cause.[3] If the proposed compromise is with a class of creditors, the appropriate way for the liquidator to effect same may be by way of a scheme of arrangement under CA 1963, s 201,[4] unless of course, the convening of meetings of those creditors is impracticable in the circumstances.[5]

[1] *Re South Eastern of Portugal Railway Co* (1869) 20 LT 800; *Re Northumberland and Durham District Banking Co, ex parte Totty* (1860) 1 Drew and Sm 273.

[2] *Re Leeds Banking Co, ex parte Clarke* (1866) 14 LT 789; *Re Central Darjeeling Tea Co* [1866] WN 361; *Re Home Counties Life Assurance Co, ex parte Garstin* (1862) 6 LT 374.

[3] *Irish Commercial Society Ltd* (10 September 1996, unreported) HC (O'Hanlon J) where the Court refused to sanction the compromise of an action against six defendants in circumstances where the terms of the compromise would have precluded the liquidator from pursuing not only the existing action but also any other action against all or any of the defendants. According to O'Hanlon J there was *prima facie* evidence to support a second action against the first-named defendant on separate grounds. The compromise was therefore refused as not having being made on the best possible terms.

[4] *Re Trix Ltd* [1970] 3 All ER 397.

[5] *Re Bank of Credit and Commerce International SA* [1993] BCLC 106, aff'd [1993] BCLC 1490.

2. Powers Exercisable without leave but subject to restriction

Sales of assets to ex-officers of the company: CA 1963, s 231(1A) was inserted to curb the ability of liquidators to sell the company's assets at below market prices to former officers of the company.[1] It is aimed at curbing the 'Phoenix syndrome' whereby the directors arise out of the ashes of their latest liquidation and resume the same business with a new company. It should therefore be read in conjunction with the restrictions on directors imposed by CA 1990, Part VII.

CA 1963, s 231(1A) does not apply to every sale of assets to a former officer. Firstly, it applies only to sales by private contract and not to sales by public auction. Secondly, it applies only if the asset is a 'non-cash asset'[2] of the 'requisite value'.[3] Thirdly, it only applies if the purchaser or one or more of the purchasers (a) has been an officer within the three years prior to the commencement of the winding up, or (b) is connected with such an officer within the meaning of CA 1990, s 26.

Notably, although the creditors must be given at least 14 days' notice of the proposed sale of such non-cash assets, no remedy is expressly prescribed for an aggrieved creditor. Presumably, however, an application could be made to the court by an aggrieved creditor for a relief under CA 1963, s 231(3).

[1] Dáil Special Committee Debates, Cols 482/483, 6 February 1990.

[2] A 'non-cash asset' comprises any property or interest in property other than cash (including foreign currency): CA 1990, s 29(9)(a). Furthermore, any reference to the acquisition of a non-cash asset is deemed to include a reference to the creation or extinction of an estate or interest in,

or a right over any property and also a reference to the discharge of any person's liability other than a liability for a liquidated sum: CA 1990, s 29(9)(b).

3 The non-cash asset is of the 'requisite value' if its value is not less than €1,269.74, but subject to that, exceeds €63,486.90 or 10% of the amount of the company's 'relevant assets'. The amount of a company's 'relevant assets' is its net asset value as per its last annual accounts or, if it has no such accounts, the amount of its called-up share capital: CA 1990, s 29(2).

3. Powers exercisable without leave or restriction

Most of the powers recited in CA 1963, s 231(2) are self-explanatory. They are all exercisable without sanction either from the court or from the committee of inspection and require little comment.

Sale of the company's property other than to former officers and persons connected with them: By virtue of CA 1963, s 231(2)(a) the liquidator is mandated to sell all or the real and personal property of the company, including any choses of action owned by the company.[1] In this regard, the liquidator may validly dispose of a right to litigate enjoyed by the company even though such a disposal might, but for the intervening liquidation, have amounted to the tort of maintenance or champerty.[2] The sale may however be impugned as champertous and thus as tortious where the liquidator is selling a beneficial interest in the fruits of the recoveries rather than the cause of action itself.[3] Furthermore, causes of action enjoyed by the liquidator rather than by the company itself, such as the entitlement to bring fraudulent or reckless trading proceedings under CA 1963, s 297A, or misfeasance proceedings under CA 1963, s 298 or proceedings under CA 1990, s 204 to impose personal liability for failure to keep proper books of account, cannot validly be assigned.[4]

It is the duty of the official liquidator to secure the best price reasonably obtainable for the company's assets.[5] In this regard, if the property is to be sold at a price below the best possible available an injunction may be obtained by a creditor or contributory restraining the sale.[6] Where the terms of the contract made by the official liquidator include the proviso 'subject to and conditional upon the consent of the High Court hereto', the time for deciding whether the best price was being obtained by that contract is when that question is before the High Court and not the date upon which the contract was made.[7] If however the official liquidator applies to the High court and obtains leave to sell property at a particular price and subsequently a further offer is received the court will not repudiate this contract for the sake of a better one.[8] The conditions or contract of sale in respect of the sale of property must be settled and approved by the court unless the court otherwise directs and the court may, on any sale by public auction, fix a reserve.[9] The conditions and contracts of sale must provide for the payment of any deposit into a joint deposit account bearing interest in the names of the official liquidator and the examiner and the purchase moneys must be paid by the purchaser into the bank of the official liquidator.[10]

In order to prevent the possibility of a conflict of interests, the Rules of the Superior Courts stipulate that the official liquidator may not directly or indirectly purchase any part of the company's assets except by leave of the court and any such purchase made without leave is capable of being set aside on the application of any creditor or contributory of the company.[11]

1 A milk quota is an asset of the company capable of being sold by the liquidator: *Swift v Dairywise Farms Ltd* [2001] 1 BCLC 672.

2 *Seear v Lawson* (1880) 15 Ch D 426; *Re Park Gate Wagon Works Co* (1881) 17 Ch D 234; *Grovewood Holdings plc v James Capel and Co Ltd* [1994] 2 BCLC 782; *Re Oakleague Ltd* [1995] 2 BCLC 624; *Norglen Ltd v Reeds Rains Prudential Ltd* [1996] 1 BCLC 690, aff'd [1998] 1 BCLC 176; *Circuit Systems Ltd v Zuken-Redac (UK) Ltd* [1996] 2 BCLC 349, aff'd [1998] 1 BCLC 176; *Re Oasis Merchandising Services Ltd* [1997] 1 BCLC 689; *Abraham v Thompson* [1997] 4 All ER 362; *Re Edennote Ltd (No 2)* [1997] 2 BCLC 89; *Stocznia Gdanska SA v Latreefers Inc (No 2)* [2001] 2 BCLC 116; *Farmer v Moseley (Holdings) Ltd* [2001] 2 BCLC 572. See also *O'Keefe v Scales* [1998] 2 ILRM 393.

3 *Grovewood Holdings plc v James Capel and Co Ltd* [1994] 2 BCLC 782.

4 *Re Oasis Merchandising Services Ltd* [1997] 1 BCLC 689. See also *Re MC Bacon Ltd (No 2)* [1990] BCLC 607; *Re Floor Fourteen Ltd* [2001] 2 BCLC 392; *Re Demaglass Ltd* [2003] 1 BCLC 412; *Re MT Realisations Ltd* [2004] 1 BCLC 119.

5 *Van Hool McArdle Ltd v Rohan Industrial Estates Ltd* [1980] IR 237.

6 *Re Brook Cottage* [1976] NI 78.

7 *Van Hool McArdle Ltd v Rohan Industrial Estates Ltd* [1980] IR 237. The official liquidator in that case obtained agreement to sell the property for the sum of £730,000 'subject to and conditional upon the consent of the High Court' being obtained. Four days later the liquidator received a second offer to buy the property for the sum of £850,000. When the liquidator applied to the court for approval of the contract he informed the court of the second offer. The Supreme Court held that the second offer must be accepted, as the primary duty of the court and of the liquidator in a court winding up is to get the maximum price for its assets.

8 *Hibernian Transport Companies Ltd* [1972] IR 190.

9 RSC 1986, Ord 74, r 124.

10 RSC 1986, Ord 74, r 124.

11 RSC 1986, Ord 74, r 39.

Appointing an agent: Although the liquidator may appoint agents to act on his behalf under CA 1963, s 231(2)(h), he is not entitled to delegate his discretion on matters that require the exercise of professional judgement.[1] Furthermore, the official liquidator cannot receive payment in respect of tasks delegated that should have been performed by him.[2]

1 *Rendall v Conroy* (1897) 8 QLJ 89; *Re Timberlands Ltd* (1979) 4 ACLR 259.

2 RSC 1986, Ord 74, r 47.

Applications to court by creditors or contributories: Any creditor or contributory of the company may apply to the court in relation to any exercise or proposed exercise by a liquidator of all or any of the powers contained in CA 1963, s 231[1] provided he can show that he is directly affected by what has been done or is proposed to be done by the liquidator.[2] Any such application must be heard in public.[3]

1 CA 1963, s 231(3).

2 *Mahomed v Morris* [200] 2 BCLC 536.

3 *Re Greendale Developments Ltd* [1997] 3 IR 540.

UK legislation

See IA 1986, s 167, Sch 4.

Committees of Inspection

232 Meetings of creditors and contributories to determine whether committee of inspection should be appointed

(1) When a winding-up order has been made by the court, the liquidator shall if the court by order so directs summon a meeting of the creditors of the company or separate meetings of the creditors and contributories of the company for the purpose of determining whether or not an application is to be made to the court for the appointment of a committee of inspection to act with the liquidator and who are to be the members of the committee if appointed.

(2) The court may make any appointment and order required to give effect to any such determination, and if there is a difference between the determinations of the meetings of the creditors and contributories in respect of the matters aforesaid, the court shall decide the difference and make such order thereon as the court may think fit.

Definitions

'company': CA 1963, s 2(1); 'contributory': CA 1963, s 2(1), s 208; 'the court': CA 1963, s 2(1); 'member': CA 1963, s 31.

Notes

Meetings to consider appointing committee: The court may direct that a committee of inspection be appointed by the creditors. Where it directs a meeting of the creditors or separate meetings of the creditors and contributories to be summoned, the liquidator must give notice in writing (or if the court so directs, by advertisement) seven clear days before the day appointed for the meeting or meetings to every creditor or, as the case may be, to every creditor and contributory, of the time and place appointed for the meeting or meetings, indicating that the purpose thereof is to determine whether an application should be made to the court for the appointment of a committee of inspection and, if so, to further determine who should be members of that committee.[1] The liquidator, or if he is unable to act, someone nominated by him, must act as chairman and that individual must report the result of the meeting or meetings to the court.[2] If there is a difference between the determinations at the respective meetings of creditors and contributories, the court must, on the application of the liquidator, fix a time and place (of which at least seven days' notice must be given by advertisement) for considering the resolutions and determinations of the meetings, deciding differences and making such order as may be necessary.[3] After that second hearing has taken place (or if there has been no difference between the meetings, upon the hearing to consider the report of the chairman of the meetings) and after hearing the liquidator and any creditor or contributory of the company, the court may make such appointments as may be necessary to give effect to the resolutions or determinations of the meetings.[4] The appointments must then be advertised by the liquidator in whatever manner the court directs, unless of course the court dispenses altogether with the need to place any such advertisements.[5]

1 RSC 1986, Ord 74, r 50.
2 RSC 1986, Ord 74, r 50.
3 RSC 1986, Ord 74, rr 50 and 51.
4 RSC 1986, Ord 74, rr 50–52.
5 RSC 1986, Ord 74, r 53.

Functions of the committee: The functions of the committee are to supervise the liquidator's activities and to give him practical assistance and advice.[1] A further important function of the committee is to consider and rule on applications by the liquidator for leave to exercise all or any of the powers listed in CA 1963, s 231(1), at least in so far as the liquidator does not look to the court for leave instead.

1 See generally Forde, *The Law of Company Insolvency* (Round Hall Press, 1993), p 193. See also *City and Suburban Pty Ltd v Smith* [1998] 822 FCA (9 July 1998).

Status of members of committee of inspection: The members of a committee are in a fiduciary position towards the company and the members may not purchase the assets of the company without the sanction of the court.[1]

1 *Dowling v Lord Advocate* [1965] SLT 146; 1963 SC 272. See also RSC 1986, Ord 74, r 39.

Constitution and proceedings of the committee: See CA 1963, s 233.

UK legislation

See IA 1986, ss 141, 142.

233 Constitution and proceedings of committee of inspection

(1) A committee of inspection appointed in pursuance of this Act shall consist of creditors and contributories of the company or persons holding general powers of attorney from creditors or contributories in such proportions as may be agreed on by the meetings of creditors and contributories or as, in case of difference, may be determined by the court.

(2) The committee shall meet at such times as they from time to time appoint, and the liquidator or any member of the committee may also call a meeting of the committee as and when he thinks necessary.

(3) The committee may act by a majority of their members present at a meeting but shall not act unless a majority of the committee are present.

(4) A member of the committee may resign by notice in writing signed by him and delivered to the liquidator.

(5) If a member of the committee becomes bankrupt or compounds or arranges with his creditors or is absent from 5 consecutive meetings of the committee without the leave of those members who, together with himself, represent the creditors or contributories, as the case may be, his office shall thereupon become vacant.

(6) A member of the committee may be removed by an ordinary resolution at a meeting of creditors, if he represents creditors, or of contributories, if he represents contributories, of which 7 days' notice has been given, stating the object of the meeting.

(7) Subject to subsection (8), on a vacancy occurring in the committee the liquidator shall forthwith summon a meeting of creditors or of contributories, as the case may require, to fill the vacancy, and the meeting may, by resolution, reappoint the same or appoint another person, qualified under subsection (1) to be a member of the committee, to fill the vacancy.

(8) If the liquidator, having regard to the position in the winding up, is of opinion that it is unnecessary for a vacancy occurring in the committee to be filled, he may apply to the court and the court may make an order that the vacancy shall not be filled or shall not filled except in such circumstances as may be specified in the order.

(9) The continuing members of the committee, if not less than two, may act notwithstanding any vacancy in the committee.

Definitions

'contributory': CA 1963, s 2(1), s 208; 'the court': CA 1963, s 2(1); 'member': CA 1963, s 31.

Notes

Committee of inspection: See CA 1963, s 232 and the notes thereto.

UK legislation

See IA 1986, ss 141, 142.

General Powers of Court in case of Winding Up by the Court

234 Power to annul order for winding up or to stay winding up

(1) The court may at any time after an order for winding up, on the application of the liquidator or any creditor or contributory and on proof to the satisfaction of the court that the order for winding up ought to be annulled, make an order annulling the order for winding up on such terms and conditions as the court thinks fit.

(2) The court may at any time after an order for winding up, on the application of the liquidator or any creditor or contributory, and on proof to the satisfaction of the court that all proceedings in relation to the winding up ought to be stayed, make an order staying the proceedings, either altogether or for a limited time, on such terms and conditions as the court thinks fit.

(3) On any application under this section the court may, before making an order, require the liquidator to furnish to the court a report relating to any facts or matters which are in his opinion relevant to the application.

(4) An office copy of every order made under this section shall forthwith be forwarded by the company, or by such person as the court may direct, to the registrar of companies for registration.

(5) If a company makes default in complying with subsection (4), the company and every officer of the company who is in default [shall be guilty of an offence and liable to a fine][a] not exceeding [€1,904.61][b] and if any other person makes default in complying with subsection (4) such person [shall be guilty of an offence and liable to a fine][a] not exceeding [€1,904.61].[b]

Amendments

a Words in CA 1963, s 234(5) substituted by C(AA)A 2003, s 57 and Sch 2 para 4.

b '£125' substituted for '£25' by C(A)A 1982, Sch 1 and increased to '£1,500' by CA 1990, s 240(7) as inserted by CLEA 2001, s 104(c). £1,500 converted to €1,904.61 by Council Regulation (EC) 1103/97, No 974/98 and No 2866/98 and the Economic and Monetary Union Act 1998, s 6.

Definitions

'company': CA 1963, s 2(1); 'contributory': CA 1963, s 2(1), s 208; 'the court': CA 1963, s 2(1); 'officer': CA 1963, s 2(1); 'the Registrar of Companies': CA 1963, s 2 (1).

Notes

General: Applications to annul or stay a winding-up order are rarely made. If the validity of the winding up is disputed, the application should be to annul rather than to stay the winding-up order.[1] Any such application ought to be made promptly.[2]

On those rare occasions where the liquidator finds himself with sufficient assets, not only to pay the creditors in full but also to hand back the business of the company to its shareholders, a stay may be sought, if so desired by the members.[3] Similarly, an application for a stay may be appropriate for the purpose of giving effect to a reconstruction or scheme of arrangement whereby a compromise is put in place with creditors, new capital is injected and the company resumes trading.[4] In exercising its discretion, the court will consider the interests of commercial morality and not merely the wishes of creditors, and will refuse a stay if there is evidence of misfeasance, or of irregularities that demand investigation.[5] Unless there is a firm and acceptable proposal for satisfying all creditors, the court will be reluctant to make an order staying the liquidation.[6]

1 *Re Empire Builders Ltd* [1919] WN 178.

2 *Re Oakwood Storage Services Ltd* [2004] 2 BCLC 404.

3 *Re James McMenamin Ltd (In Vol Liquidation)* [2005] IEHC 339; *Re Calgary and Edmonton Land Co Ltd* [1975] 1 All ER 1046.

4 *Re Stephen Walters and Sons* [1926] WN 236.

5 *Re Telescriptor Syndicate* [1903] 2 Ch 174; *Re Calgary and Edmonton Land Co* [1975] 1 All ER 1046.

6 *Re Lowston* [1991] BCLC 570 where the court held that it had to be satisfied that it was right to stay the winding up proceedings and if there were matters on which the Court had doubts it should not grant the stay; *Re Piccadilly Property Management Ltd* [1999] 2 BCLC 145.

Voluntary winding up: In a voluntary winding up the Court has power pursuant to CA 1963, s 280 to invoke the powers contained in s 234 to annul or stay the winding-up resolution.[1] So, for example, the Court has annulled a winding-up resolution in respect of a member's voluntary winding up where the necessary statutory declaration of solvency was not made or the independent person's report was not attached thereto, as required by CA 1963, s 256, made before the resolution was passed.[2] The court has, however, required an undertaking that steps be taking immediately upon the resolution being annulled, to properly and effectively place the company in members' voluntary winding up.[3]

1 *Re James McMenamin Ltd (In Vol Liquidation)* [2005] IEHC 339; *Re Oakthorpe Holdings Ltd* [1988] ILRM 62; *Re Favon Investments Ltd* [1993] IR 87 (Costello J); *Re Titian Steamship Co* [1888] WN 17; *Re Schanschieff Electric Battery Syndicate* [1888] WN 166; *Re Stephen Walters and Sons* [1926] WN 236; *Re Calgary and Edmonton Land Co Ltd* [1975] 1 All ER 1046.

2 *Re Oakthorpe Holdings Ltd* [1988] ILRM 62; *Re Favon Investments Ltd* [1993] IR 87 (Costello J).

3 *Re Oakthorpe Holdings Ltd* [1988] ILRM 62; *Re Favon Investments Ltd* (13 July 1992, unreported) HC (Costello J).

Prosecution by the Registrar: Criminal proceedings under CA 1963, s 234(4) may be prosecuted by the Registrar of Companies.[1]

1 C(A)A 1982, s 16.

UK legislation

See IA 1986, s 147.

---

235 Settlement of list of contributories and application of assets

(1) Subject to subsection (2), as soon as may be after making a winding-up order, the court shall settle a list of contributories, with power to rectify the register of members in all cases where rectification is required in pursuance of this Act, and shall cause the assets of the company to collected and applied in discharge of its liabilities.

(2) Where it appears to the court that it will not be necessary to make calls on or adjust the rights of contributories, the court may dispense with the settlement of a list of contributories.

(3) In settling the list of contributories, the court shall distinguish between persons who are contributories in their own right and persons who are contributories as being representatives of or liable for the debts of others.

Definitions

'company': CA 1963, s 2(1); 'contributory': CA 1963, s 2(1), s 208; 'the court': CA 1963, s 2(1); 'member': CA 1963, s 31.

Notes

Rectification of the register of members: One of the powers conferred on the court by CA 1963, s 235(1) is to rectify the register of members of the company. The official liquidator is not entitled to effect such a rectification himself without the leave of the court.[1] Moreover, any application on behalf of the company to have the court rectify the register should be made in the name of the company itself rather than in the name of the liquidator.[2] As between a vendor and purchasers of shares under a contract made after the commencement of the winding up, the court will be slow to order rectification of the register, save in the most exceptional circumstances.[3]

In addition to making any necessary rectifications to the register, the court is also required to adjust the rights of contributories among themselves and to distribute the surplus, if any, among the persons entitled thereto.[4]

1 *Trevor v Whitworth* (1887) 12 App Cas 409. In relation to the rectification of the register generally, see the notes to CA 1963, s 122.

2 *Re Bank of Hindustan, China and Japan, ex parte Kintrea* (1869) 5 Ch App 95.

3 *Re Onward Building Society* [1891] 2 QB 463. See CA 1963, s 218 which provides, *inter alia*, that any transfer of shares after the commencement of the winding up is void unless the court otherwise orders.

4 See CA 1963, s 242 and the notes thereto.

Practice concerning list of contributories: Unless the court grants an order of dispensation under CA 1963, s 235(5), the official liquidator must, at such time as the court directs, make out and leave at the examiner's office a list of the contributories of the company, which must be verified by affidavit in form No 25 of Appendix M to the Rules of the Superior Courts.[1] So far as practicable, the list must state the address of and the number of shares or the extent of interest to be attributed to each contributory and the amount called up and the amount paid in respect of such shares or interest and must distinguish the several classes of contributories,[2] as well as distinguishing between persons who are contributories in their own right and persons who are contributories as being representatives of or liable for the debts of others.[3] When the list has been left at the examiner's office, the official liquidator must obtain an appointment from the examiner to settle the list, whereupon he is required to give notice in writing of the meeting in Form No 27 of Appendix M to the Rules of the Superior Courts to every person included in such list, stating in what character and for what number of shares, or extent of interest, such person is included in the list and that any application for the removal of the person's name from the list or for the variation of the list should be made to the examiner at the time appointed for the settlement of the list.[4] In this regard, a person may wish to apply to have his name removed from the list of contributories (and to have the register of members rectified) in circumstances where he has previously transferred his shares but his name has erroneously been left on the register of members.[5] The result of the settlement of the list must be stated in a certificate by the examiner.[6] The list may be varied from time to time but any such variation must go through the same process of settlement as described above.[7] Resettling of the list may be required, for example, following an order of the court for the rectification of the register of members.[8]

1 RSC 1986, Ord 74, r 86.

2 RSC 1986, Ord 74, r 86.

3 CA 1963, s 235(3) and RSC 1986, O 74, r 86.

4 RSC 1986 Ord 74, r 87.

5 *Fyfe's Case* (1869) 4 Ch App 768; *Minshall's Case* (1873) LT 29; *Joshua Murgatroyd's Case* (1873) 18 Sol Jo 28; *Thomas Brown's Case* (1873) 17 Sol Jo 310.

6 *Fyfe's Case* (1869) 4 Ch App 768; *Minshall's Case* (1873) LT 29; *Joshua Murgatroyd's Case* (1873) 18 Sol Jo 28; *Thomas Brown's Case* (1873) 17 Sol Jo 310.

7 RSC 1986, Ord 74, r 89.

8 *Re Onward Building Society* [1891] 2 QB 463; *Re Sussex Brick Co* [1904] 1 Ch 598; *Re Anglo-Indian and Colonial, Industrial and Commercial Institution, Grey's Case* [1888] WN 137, on appeal [1888] WN 211; *Re Scottish Universal Finance Bank, Breckenridge's Case* (1865) 2 Hem and M 642.

Practice regarding collection and distribution of the company's assets: For the purpose of acquiring and retaining possession of the company's assets, the official liquidator is in the same position as if he were the receiver of the property appointed by the court and the court may on his application enforce such acquisition or retention accordingly.[1] In this regard, he may serve notice on any person being a contributory, trustee, receiver, banker, agent or officer of the company to deliver up any money, property, books or papers in that person's hands to which the company is *prima facie* entitled.[2] Delivery up may, if necessary, be enforced by order of the court, under CA 1963, s 236. In relation to the collection of the assets of the company from other persons, the liquidator may be obliged to sue in the name of the company if those assets are not voluntarily handed over.[3] The leave of the court will, however, be required to institute such proceedings.[4] In relation to the setting aside of antecedent and other transactions so as to swell the assets available for distribution to the creditors in the winding up, see CA 1963, ss 218, 286–290, 297A and 298 and CA 1990, ss 139–141 and 204.

In relation to the order of priorities in the distribution of the proceeds of sale of the company's assets (excluding assets subject to fixed charges or mortgages) is as follows:

(i) the super-preferential debts;[5]

(ii) the costs and expenses of the winding up;[6]

(iii) the preferential debts;[7]

(iv) the debts secured by floating charges;[8]

(v) the ordinary unsecured debts; and[9]

(vi) debts due to members *qua* members.[10]

1 RSC 1986, Ord 74, r 90.

2 RSC 1986, Ord 74, r 91. If there is a dispute as to the ownership of the assets, the company cannot be said to be '*prima facie*' entitled to them, but in such circumstances an order for delivery up may instead by sought by the liquidator pursuant to CA 1963, s 229: *Re London Iron and Steel Co Ltd* [1990] BCLC 372.

3 *Re Private Motorists Provident Society Ltd, Horgan v Minister for Justice* (23 June 1995, unreported) HC (Murphy J).

4 See CA 1963, s 231(1)(a).

5 Social Welfare (Consolidation) Act 1993, s 16(2).

6 CA 1963, ss 244 and 285(8) and RSC 1986, Ord 74, r 128.

7 CA 1963, s 285.

8 CA 1963, s 285(7)(b).

9 CA 1963, ss 284 and 285(2).

10 CA 1963, s 207(1)(g). See *Soden v British and Commonwealth Holdings plc* [1997] 2 BCLC 501.

UK legislation

See IA 1986, s 148.

236 Delivery of property of company to liquidator

The court may, at any time after making a winding-up order, require any contributory for the time being on the list of contributories and any trustee, receiver, banker, agent or officer of the company to pay, deliver, convey, surrender or transfer forthwith, or within such time as the court directs, to the liquidator any money, property or books and papers in his hands to which the company is prima facie entitled.

Definitions

'agent': CA 1963, s 2(1); 'books and paper': CA 1963, s 2(1); 'company': CA 1963, s 2(1); 'contributory': CA 1963, s 2(1), s 208; 'the court': CA 1963, s 2(1); 'officer': CA 1963, s 2(1).

Notes

Delivery up of property to which the company is *prima facie* entitled: The provisions of CA 1963, s 236 may only be used against those particular classes of persons recited therein. In this regard, the 'officers' of the company will be regarded as including the company's solicitors,[1] but not an accountant (as distinct from the auditor) to whom the books have been handed for the purpose of preparing a balance sheet.[2] Furthermore, a person is not a 'banker' of the company unless he holds as banker for and not adversely to the company.[3]

The procedure to be followed by the liquidator is that he first serve notice on the contributory, trustee, receiver, banker, agent or officer, as the case may be, requiring that person to deliver up any money, property, books or papers in that person's hands to which the company is *prima facie* entitled.[4] If the notice is complied with, the liquidator may apply to the court by motion on notice to the other person, for an order directing the delivery up of the items in question.[5]

The provisions of s 236 cannot be availed of by the liquidator in circumstances where the ownership of the property in question is disputed.[6] Instead, whilst the liquidator might be in a position to obtain physical custody of the items under CA 1963, s 229 pending a determination of the dispute as to ownership,[7] the actual question of ownership will have to be determined by ordinary plenary proceedings brought by the liquidator in the name of the company, having first obtained the leave of the court to do so under CA 1963, s 231(1)(a).

1 *Re Palace Restaurants Ltd* [1914] 1 Ch 492.

2 *Findlay v Waddell* [191] SC 670.

3 *Re Imperial Land Co of Marseilles, Re National Bank* (1870) LR 10 Eq 298.

4 RSC 1986, Ord 74, r 91.

5 RSC 1986, Ord 74, r 136. See also *Re Commercial Union Wine Co* (1865) 35 Beav 35.

6 *Re Vimbos Ltd* [1900] 1 Ch 470; *Re Palace Restaurants Ltd* [1914] 1 Ch 492; *Re London Iron and Steel Co Ltd* [1990] BCLC 372.

7 *Re London Iron and Steel Co Ltd* [1990] BCLC 372. See also CA 1963, s 229 and the notes thereto.

UK legislation

See IA 1986, s 234(2).

237 Payment of debts due by contributory to the company and extent to which set-off allowed

(1) The court may, at any time after making a winding up order, make an order on any contributory for the time being on the list of contributories, to pay in manner directed by the order, any money due from him or from the estate of the person whom he represents

to the company, exclusive of any money payable by him or the estate by virtue of any call in pursuance of this Act.

(2) The court in making such an order may—

(a) in the case of an unlimited company, allow to the contributory by way of set-off any money due to him or to the estate which he represents from the company on any independent dealing or contract with the company, but not any money due to him as a member of the company in respect of any dividend or profit; and

(b) in the case of a limited company, make to any director whose liability is unlimited or to his estate a like allowance.

(3) In the case of any company, whether limited or unlimited, when all the creditors are paid in full, any money due on any account whatever to a contributory from the company may be allowed to him by way of set-off against any subsequent call.

Definitions

'company': CA 1963, s 2(1); 'contributory': CA 1963, s 2(1), s 208; 'the court': CA 1963, s 2(1); 'director': CA 1963, s 2(1); 'member': CA 1963, s 31; 'unlimited company': CA 1963, s 2(1), s 5(2).

Notes

General: Under CA 1963, s 237(1) the court may call on those persons whose names are on the list of contributories[1] to pay into the liquidation such sum or sums as may be payable by them *qua* contributories.[2] The section goes on to provide for the circumstances in which the contributory may set off moneys due to him by the company against the amount he is called upon to contribute to the winding up. In this regard, at common law the amount of the contribution was not regarded as being a debt due to the company but rather as being an amount recoverable by the liquidator.[3] Thus, even if the company owed other moneys to the contributory there was no mutuality and thus no set-off could be allowed against the amount of the contribution.[4] Now, however, by virtue of s 237(2), in the case of an unlimited company or in the very rare case of a director of a limited company with unlimited liability,[5] set-off of calls will be allowed against amounts due by the company to the contributory *qua* member, such as the amount of any arrears of dividends declared but not paid.[6] Furthermore[7], under s 237(3) once all of the creditors have been paid in full, set-off will be allowed without restriction regardless of the type of company involved.

1 In relation to the settling of the list of contributories, see CA 1963, s 235 and the notes thereto.

2 See CA 1963, s 207 and the notes thereto in relation to the extent of the liability of contributories in a winding up.

3 *Re Whitehouse and Co* (1878) 9 Ch D 595; *Re West of England and South Wales District Bank, ex parte Branwhite* [1879] WN 86.

4 *Re Whitehouse and Co* (1878) 9 Ch D 595; *Re West of England and South Wales District Bank, ex parte Branwhite* [1879] WN 86.

5 In relation to the concept of a director with unlimited liability, see CA 1963, s 197.

6 With regard to the deferred status of unpaid dividends in a liquidation, see CA 1963, s 207(1)(g). See also *Re Imperial Hotel (Cork) Ltd* [1950] IR 115; *Re Lafayette Ltd* [1950] IR 100; *Re Belfast Empire Theatre of Varieties* [1963] IR 41.

7 So, for example, amounts due by the company in respect of arrears of dividend might be set-off against calls made on the member in respect of the costs and expenses of the winding up.

UK legislation

See IA 1986, s 149.

238 Power of court to make calls

(1) The court may, at any time after making a winding up order, and either before or after it has ascertained the sufficiency of the assets of the company, make calls on all or any of the contributories for the time being on the list of contributories to the extent of their liability, for payment of any money which the court considers necessary to satisfy the debts and liabilities of the company, and the costs, charges and expenses of winding up, and for the adjustment of the rights of the contributories among themselves, and make an order for payment of any calls so made.

(2) In making a call, the court may take into consideration that some of the contributories may partly or wholly fail to pay the call.

Definitions

'company': CA 1963, s 2(1); 'contributory': CA 1963, s 2(1), s 208; 'the court': CA 1963, s 2(1).

Notes

General: Although CA 1963, s 238 empowers the court to make calls on the contributories in respect of the debts and liabilities of the company together with the costs, charges and expenses of winding up, the reality is somewhat different.[1] In the vast majority of private companies liquidators will not realise much, if anything, from the contributories of insolvent companies because the vast majority of companies are limited companies with a small issued share capital, all of which tends to have been paid up in full.

[1] See notes to CA 1963, s 207.

UK legislation

See IA 1986, ss 150, 161.

239 Payment into bank of moneys due to company

(1) The court may order any contributory, purchaser or other person from whom money is due to the company to pay the amount due into such bank as the court may appoint to the account of the liquidator instead of to the liquidator, and any such order may be enforced in like manner as if it had directed payment to the liquidator.

(2) All moneys and securities paid or delivered into any such bank as aforesaid in the event of a winding up by the court shall be subject in all respects to the orders of the court.

Definitions

'company': CA 1963, s 2(1); 'contributory': CA 1963, s 2(1), s 208; 'the court': CA 1963, s 2(1).

Notes

Bank account: CA 1963, s 239 allows for the court to order that calls on contributories be paid directly into the liquidator's account. In this regard, the Rules of the Superior Courts stipulate that the liquidator must open a liquidation account in the Bank of Ireland into which all moneys received by him in the course of the winding up must be lodged.[1] If he fails to pay any such collections into the account within seven days from the receipt he can be charged interest and have all or part of his remuneration disallowed.[2] All cheques must be signed by the liquidator and countersigned by the examiner[3].

1 RSc 1986, Ord 74, r 32.

2 RSC 1986, Ord 74, r 117.

3 RSC 1986, Ord 74, r 121.

UK legislation

See IA 1986, s 151.

---

240 Order on contributory to be conclusive evidence

(1) An order made by the court on a contributory shall, subject to any right of appeal, be conclusive evidence that the money, if any, thereby appearing to be due or ordered to be paid is due.

(2) All other relevant matters stated in the order shall be taken to be truly stated as against all persons and in all proceedings.

Definitions

'contributory': CA 1963, s 2(1), s 208; 'the court': CA 1963, s 2(1).

UK legislation

See IA 1986, s 152.

---

241 Power to exclude creditors not proving in time

The court may fix a time or times within which creditors are to prove their debts or claims or to be excluded from the benefit of any distribution made before those debts are proved.

Definitions

'the court': CA 1963, s 2(1).

Notes

Ascertainment of the company's liabilities: For the purpose of ascertaining the debts and claims due from the company and for the purpose of requiring the creditors to come in and prove their debts or claims, an advertisement must be published in the terms of Form No 35 of Appendix M to the Rules of the Superior Courts.[1] The advertisement must fix a time for the creditors to send their names and addresses and the particulars of their debts and claims, and the names and registered places of business of their solicitors (if any) to the official liquidator and must further appoint a day for adjudicating on those debts and claims.[2] The creditors need not attend upon the adjudication nor prove their debts or claims unless they are required to do so by notice from the official liquidator.[3] The liquidator is required to investigate the debts and claims sent in to him, and ascertain in so far as he is able which of those debts and claims are legally due from the company, and he must make out and leave at the examiner's office a list, verified by affidavit, of all the debts and claims sent in to him distinguishing which of the debts and claims, or parts thereof, are in his opinion legally due and proper to be admitted without further evidence, and which of them in his opinion ought to be proved by the creditor.[4] In so far as possible, debts and claims should be valued as of the date of the winding-up order.[5] At the time appointed for adjudicating upon the debts and claims, or at an adjournment thereof, the examiner may either allow the debts and claims on the basis of the contents of the liquidator's affidavit or may require all or some of those debts and claims to be formally proved by the creditors in question.[6] The examiner must give notice to those creditors whose debts or claims have been admitted, informing them of the fact that their debts or claims have been so admitted.[7] Equally, any creditors who are required to come and formally prove their debts of claims (or part thereof) must be given not less than seven days' notice of the requirement to do so and they must further be notified that if they fail to do so, their debts or claims (or the relevant parts thereof) will be disallowed.[8] Creditors who attend and prove their debts or claims, having been called upon to do so by the examiner, are entitled to their costs as costs of the winding up.[9]

Under CA 1963, s 241 the court is empowered to fix a time or times within which creditors are to prove their debts or claims, in default of which they will be excluded from the benefit of any distribution made before those debts are proved. The fixing of such a time limit is aimed at ensuring that the liquidator can make distributions to those creditors who have submitted their proofs in a timely manner. Nevertheless, a creditor may come in and prove at any time before the company is dissolved; the only penalty for late proof being that the creditor is excluded from the benefit of any distribution made before proof.[10] Even if a claim is proved within the time prescribed by the official liquidator, he is obliged to exclude the debt if it is statute barred.[11] A liquidator, when adjudicating on a proof of debt, can only inquire into the consideration for a judgment debt if there was evidence of fraud, collusion, or some other miscarriage of justice – otherwise the judgment is conclusive.[12]

1 RSC 1986, Ord 74, r 95.

2 RSC 1986, Ord 74, r 95.

3 RSC 1986, Ord 74, r 96.

4 RSC 1986, Ord 74, r 97. In relation to the debts and claims which are provable in a winding up, see CA 1963, s 284 and the notes thereto as well as RSC 1986, Ord 74, rr 102–111.

5 RSC 1986, Ord 74, r 99.

6 RSC 1986, Ord 74, r 98.

7 RSC 1986, Ord 74, r 98.

8 RSC 1986, Ord 74, r 98.

9 RSC 1986, Ord 74, r 100.

10 *Re Kit Hill Tunnel, ex parte Williams* 16 Ch D 590; *Re Metcalfe, Hicks v May* (1879) 13 Ch D 236; *Butler v Broadhead* [1975] Ch 97.

11 *Re Lafayette Ltd* [1950] IR 100: *Re Imperial Hotel (Cork) Ltd* [1950] IR 115; *Re Belfast Empire Theatre of Varieties* [1963] IR 41; *Re Joshua Shaw and Sons Ltd* [1989] BCLC 362; *Re Maxwell Fleet and Facilities Management Ltd* [1999] 2 BCLC 721.

12 *Re Shruth* [2006] 1 BCLC 293.

UK legislation

See IA 1986, s 153.

---

242 Adjustment of rights of contributories

The court shall adjust the rights of the contributories among themselves and distribute any surplus among the persons entitled thereto.

Definitions

'contributory': CA 1963, s 2(1), s 208; 'the court': CA 1963, s 2(1).

Notes

Adjustment of rights of contributories by court: CA 1963, s 242, the application of which is mandatory,[1] only applies to a compulsory winding up. In the case of a members' or a creditors' voluntary winding up, it is the duty of the liquidator to adjust the rights of the contributories amongst themselves.[2]

1 *Re Phoenix Oil and Transport Co Ltd (No 2)* [1958] Ch 565; *Re Paragon Holdings Ltd* [1961] Ch 346.

2 CA 1963, s 276(2).

Return of capital to contributories: The return of capital to members and the distribution of any surplus only occurs after the other debts and liabilities of the company have been paid in full.[1] For a detailed analysis of the rights of different classes of shareholders and their rights to a return of capital see the notes to CA 1963, s 78. All shares will be presumed to rank equally unless the contrary is provided for in the memorandum or articles of association of the company.[2] The equality relates to the right to vote, the right to a dividend and, most importantly in respect of this section, the right to a return of capital and the right to participate in the event of their being a surplus of assets in a winding up. Shares carrying preferred rights as to the return of capital are presumed to be entitled to participate equally in the distribution of any surplus of assets in the winding up along with any other shareholders.[3] The position is different in the UK where the courts have held that a statement of a preference shareholder's right to participate in capital is an exhaustive definition of their rights.[4]

1 See CA 1963, s 235 and the notes thereto regarding as well as CA 1963, s 207(1)(g) regarding the order of priority of the debts and liabilities in the winding up.

2 *Birch v Cropper* (1889) 14 App Cas 525.

3 *Cork Electric Supply Co Ltd v Concannon* [1932] IR 314; *Re William Metcalf and Son Ltd* [1933] Ch 142.

4 *Will v The United Lanket Plantations Co* [1914] AC 11; *Re National Telephone Co* [1914] I Ch 755; *Scottish Insurance Corporation v Wilsons and Clyde Coal Co* [1949] AC 462; *Prudential Assurance Co v Chatterley-Whitfield Collieries Co Ltd* [1949] AC 512.

UK legislation

See IA 1986, s 154.

243 Inspection of books by creditors, contributories and director

(1) The court may, at any time after making a winding up order, make such order for inspection of the books and papers of the company by creditors and contributories as the court thinks just, and any books and papers in the possession of the company may be inspected by creditors or contributories accordingly, but not further or otherwise.

[(1A) The court may, on the application of the Director, make an order for the inspection by the Director of any books and papers in the possession of a company the subject of a winding-up order and the company, every officer of the company and the liquidator shall give to the Director such access to and facilities as are necessary for inspecting and taking copies of those books and papers as the Director may require.][a]

(2) Nothing in this section shall be taken as excluding or restricting any statutory rights of a Minister of the Government or a person acting under the authority of a Minister of the Government.

Amendments

a CA 1963, s 243(1A) inserted by CLEA 2001, s 43.

Definitions

'books and paper': CA 1963, s 2(1); 'company': CA 1963, s 2(1); 'contributory': CA 1963, s 2(1), s 208; 'the court': CA 1963, s 2(1); 'Minister': CA 1963, s 2(1).

Notes

Books and papers in the possession of the company: CA 1963, s 243 only applies to books and papers in the actual possession of the company.[1] This section cannot be used to compel a liquidator of a company to demand the return of books and records of the company that had been seized by the police.[2]

1 *Re North Brazilian Sugar Factories* (1887) 37 Ch D 83.

2 *Re DPR Futures Ltd* [1989] BCLC 634.

Inspection must be for the purposes of the winding up: An order under this section will only be made for the benefit of the winding up,[1] such as to allow the liquidator to bring civil proceedings or the ODCE to bring criminal or disqualification proceedings against directors or other.[2] The greater the indebtedness, the more willing the court will be to accede to the application.[3] In exceptional circumstances, the section may be used where the winding-up petition is pending, so as to enable the petitioner to respond to an affidavit sworn in opposition by an officer of the company.[4] However, the section cannot be used to help a director prepare his defence to criminal charges which are outside the remit of the winding up of the company.[5]

1 If the company is not being wound up and the reason or principal reason why this is so is the insufficiency of its assets, the provisions of the section may be invoked by individual members or creditors or by the ODCE upon application to the court pursuant to CA 1990, s 251.

2 *Re DPR Futures Ltd* [1989] BCLC 634; In *Re North Brazilian Sugar Factories* (1887) 37 Ch D 83.

3 *Re Joint Stock Discount Co, ex parte Buchan* (1866) 36 LJ (Ch) 150; *Re Imperial Land Co of Marseilles* [1882] WN 134.

4 *Re Emma Silver Mining co* (1875) 10 Ch App 194; *Re Lisbon Steam Tramways Co* [1875] WN 54.

5 *Re DPR Futures Ltd* [1989] BCLC 634; In *Re North Brazilian Sugar Factories* (1887) 37 Ch D 83.

UK legislation

See IA 1986, s 155.

---

244 Power to order costs of winding up to be paid out of assets

The court may, in the event of the assets being insufficient to satisfy the liabilities, make an order as to the payment out of the assets of the costs, charges and expenses incurred in the winding up in such order of priority as the court thinks just.

Definitions

'the court': CA 1963, s 2(1).

Notes

Costs of successful litigant in post-liquidation proceedings: Where an action is brought by a company after liquidation, an award of costs in favour of a successful defendant will rank in priority to all of the costs and expenses of the winding up.[1] The same priority will also attach to an award of costs in favour of a successful plaintiff in proceedings brought against the company, with the leave of the court, after the commencement of the winding up.[2] However, damages payable by the company on foot of an undertaking as to damages given by the liquidator in injunction proceedings, rather than ranking ahead of the costs and expenses of the winding up, would instead appear to rank as part of those costs and expenses.[3]

1 *Comhlucht Páipéar Riomhaireachta Teo v Udarás na Gaeltachta* [1990] 1 IR 320; *Re CHA Ltd* [1999] 1 IR 437; *Re Home Investment Society* (1880) 14 ChD 167; *Re National Building and Land Investment Co, ex parte Clitheroe* (1885) 15 LR Ir 47; *Re London Metallurgical Co* (1895) 1 Ch 758; *Re Pacific Coast Syndicate Ltd* [1913] 2 Ch 26.

2 *Re CHA Ltd* [1999] 1 IR 437.

3 *Irish Commercial Society Ltd v Plunkett* (6 June 1984, unreported) HC (Carroll J).

Priority of costs and expenses: RSC 1986, Ord 74, r 128, sets out the order of priority of the costs and expenses of a compulsory winding up.[1] Ranking ahead of everything else are the fees and expenses properly incurred in preserving, realising or getting in the assets, including where a company has previously commenced to be wound up voluntarily such remuneration, costs and expenses as the court may allow to the voluntary liquidator. Thereafter, the costs and expenses rank as follows—

(i) the costs of the petition, including the costs of any person appearing on the petition whose costs are allowed by the court;

(ii) the costs and expenses of any person who makes or concurs in the company's statement of affairs;

(iii) the necessary disbursements of the official liquidator other than expenses properly incurred in preserving, realising or getting in the assets;

(iv) the costs payable to the solicitor for the official liquidator;

(v) the remuneration of the official liquidator; and

(vi) the out-of-pocket expenses necessarily incurred by the committee of inspection (if any).

It is to be noted though, that by virtue of CA 1963, s 244 it is open to the court, in its discretion to impose such other order of priority as it thinks fit in the circumstances.[2] Furthermore, within any particular ranking of costs and expenses, unless the court orders otherwise, the claimants will abate rateably in the event of a deficiency of funds.[3]

The costs and expenses of the winding up are not payable out of assets secured by a fixed charge or by a floating charge which has crystallised prior to the commencement of the winding up, until the debt due to the debentureholder has been paid in full and (in the case of a crystallised floating charge) until the preferential debts payable under CA 1963, s 98 have been paid in full.[4]

1 See, however, C(A)A 1990, s 29 which provides for the costs and expenses of any examinership which may have preceded the liquidation to rank ahead of the costs and expenses of the winding up.

2 *Re CHA Ltd* [1999] 1 IR 437. See also *Re Beni-Felkai Mining Co* [1934] Ch 406.

3 *Re Audley Hall Cotton Spinning Co* (1868) LR 6 Eq 245.

4 *Re Leyland Daf Ltd* [2004] 1 BCLC 281.

Fees and expenses properly incurred in preserving, realising or getting in the assets: Examples of fees and expenses incurred in the liquidation in preserving, realising or getting in the assets of the company would include the necessary costs of maintaining the company's buildings as well as wages for caretaking.[1] Costs and expenses properly incurred by the liquidator in realising assets subject to charges or mortgages are payable in priority to the claims of the incumbrancers.[2] Legal costs of the liquidator in suing for the recovery of company assets would also fall within this heading,[3] as would any damages payable by the company on foot of an undertaking as to damages given by the liquidator in injunction proceedings.[4] However, the liquidator's costs of an unsuccessful challenge to the validity of a charge over the company's assets will not be allowed as a cost or expense of the winding up, at least in so far as the effect of doing so would be to confer on those costs priority over the claim of the debentureholder.[5] Corporation tax referable to a capital gain made by a company on the disposal of an asset in the winding up does not rank as an expense incurred in the realisation of that asset within the meaning of Ord 74, r 128.[6] It does however rank as a 'necessary disbursement' of the liquidator and has priority accordingly.[7] Corporation tax on income earned by the company after the commencement of the winding up ranks neither as a properly incurred expense nor as a necessary disbursement[8] of the liquidator and accordingly is not provable at all in the winding up.[9]

1 *Re Van Hool McArdle Ltd; Revenue Commissioners v Donnelly* [1983] ILRM 329, per O'Higgins CJ.

2 *Re Marine Mansions Co* (1867) LR 4 Eq 601; *Re Oriental Hotels Co, Perry v Oriental Hotels Co* (1871) LR 12 Eq 126; *Re Regent's Canal Ironworks Co, ex parte Grissell* (1875) 3 Ch D 411; *Lathom v Greenwich Ferry Co* [1895] WN 77; *Re Northern Milling Co* [1908] 1 IR 473.

3 *Re Floor Fourteen Ltd; Lewis v IRC* [2001] 2 BCLC 392.

4 *Irish Commercial Society Ltd v Plunkett* [1984] IEHC 51 (Carroll J).

5 *Re MC Bacon Ltd (No 2)* [1990] BCLC 607; *Re R S and M Engineering Co Ltd* [1999] 2 BCLC 485.

6 *Re Van Hool McArdle Ltd* [1982] ILRM 340, aff'd sub nom *Revenue Commissioners v Donnelly* [1983] ILRM 329. See also *Re Mesco Properties Ltd* [1980] 1 WLR 96.

7 TCA 1997, s 571, reversing *Re Van Hool McArdle Ltd* [1982] ILRM 340, aff'd sub nom *Revenue Commissioners v Donnelly* [1983] ILRM 329.

8 *Hibernian Transport Companies Ltd* [1984] ILRM 583. cf *Re Toshoku Finance UK plc* [2000] 1 BCLC 683.

9 See *Re National Building and Land Co* (1885–86) 15 LR Ir 47 where Chatterton V-C stated that there is a distinction between 'debts and liabilities of the company at the commencement of the winding up which must be approved for and paid for *pari passu,* and must abate rateably in case the assets of the company prove insufficient, and debts and liabilities which arise only in the course of a liquidation, and as incidental to it, which must be paid before a distribution of the assets'.

Petition costs: Where a company has been formed or operated for a dishonest purpose and the directors cause the company to unsuccessfully resist the winding-up petition, the court in the exercise of its discretion under Ord 99, r 1 may order that the costs of the proceedings be borne by the directors and may further direct that none of the company's costs should be paid directly or indirectly out of the company's own assets until after the unsecured creditors have been paid in full.[1]

1 *Re Aurum Marketing Ltd* [2000] 2 BCLC 645.

Necessary disbursements of the official liquidator: Whilst it has been held that corporation tax referable to a capital gain made by a company on the disposal of an asset in the winding up did not rank as a 'necessary disbursement' of the liquidator,[1] that position has been reversed by TCA 1997, s 571. However, in the case of corporation tax on income earned by the company after the commencement of the compulsory winding up it remains the case that same ranks neither as a properly incurred expense nor as a necessary disbursement of the liquidator [2] and accordingly is not provable at all in the winding up.[3] This contrasts with the position in a voluntary winding up where corporation tax on income arising during the course of the liquidation does indeed rank as a cost, charge or expense of the winding up.[4] In relation to VAT payable on the sale of property which completes after the commencement of the winding up, this ranks as an expense of the liquidation even though the contract was enetered into prior to the winding up.[5]

1 *Re Van Hool McArdle Ltd* [1982] ILRM 340, aff'd sub nom *Revenue Commissioners v Donnelly* [1983] ILRM 329.

2 *Hibernian Transport Companies Ltd* [1984] ILRM 583. Cf *Re Toshoku Finance UK plc* [2000] 1 BCLC 683.

3 See *Re National Building and Land Co* (1885–86) 15 LR Ir 47.

4 See CA 1963, s 281 and *Re A Noyek and Sons Ltd* [1989] ILRM 155; *Spa Estates Ltd v O'Hargain* (30 June 1975, unreported) HC (Kenny J); *City of Dublin Steam Packet Co v Revenue Commissioners (No 2)* [1930] IR 217.

5 *Re Fitz-Pack Cartons Ltd* [2008] 4 IR 19.

Legal cost accountant: The costs of a legal cost accountant employed to tax the costs of the liquidator's solicitors are not costs properly incurred by the liquidator in a winding up.[1]

1 *Re Castle Brand Ltd* [1990] ILRM 97 where Carroll J held that it was long-established law that the costs of a legal cost accountant must be borne by the solicitor. Because the cost was incurred for his benefit and not for the benefit of the liquidation, it could not be allowed as part of the costs of the winding up.

Leasehold property held by a liquidator. Where the liquidator retains a company's leasehold property for the benefit of the winding up, any rent accruing constitutes an expense of the liquidation and is payable accordingly.[1]

1 *Re CHA Ltd* [1999] 1 IR 437; *Re GWI Ltd* [1987] IEHC 21 (Murphy J); *Tempany v Royal Liver Trustees Ltd* [1984] ILRM 273; *Grant v Aston* (1969) 1031 ILTR 39; *Re Lundy Granite Co* (1871) 6 Ch App 462; *Re Oak Pits Colliery Co* (1882) 21 Ch D 322; *Re ABC Coupler and Engineering Ltd* [1970] 1 WLR 702; *Re Downer Enterprises Ltd* [1974] 1WLR 146.

Voluntary liquidation: CA 1963, s 281 provides that in the case of a voluntary winding up 'all costs, charges and expenses properly incurred in the winding up including the remuneration of the liquidator shall be payable out of the assets of the company in priority to all other claims'.[1] The order of priority of costs and expenses in a compulsory winding up will, subject to appropriate modifications, be used as a guide to the priority of the costs, charges and expenses in a voluntary winding up.[2]

1 CA 1963, s 281. Ord 74, r 128 does not apply in respect of voluntary liquidations.

2 *Re Redbreast Preserving Co (Ireland) Ltd* [1958] IR 234.

UK legislation

See IA 1986, s 156.

[244A No lien over company's books, records, etc

Where the court has appointed a provisional liquidator or a company is being wound up by the court or by means of a creditors' voluntary winding up, no person shall be entitled as against the liquidator or provisional liquidator to withhold possession of any deed, instrument, or other document belonging to the company, or the books of account, receipts, bills, invoices, or other papers of a like nature relating to the accounts or trade, dealings or business of the company, or to claim any lien thereon provided that—

(a) where a mortgage, charge or pledge has been created by the deposit of any such document or paper with a person, the production of the document or paper to the liquidator or provisional liquidator by the person shall be without prejudice to the person's rights under the mortgage, charge or pledge (other than any right to possession of the document or paper),

(b) where by virtue of this section a liquidator or provisional liquidator has possession of any document or papers of a receiver or that receiver is entitled to examine, the liquidator or provisional liquidator shall, unless the court otherwise orders, make the document or papers available for inspection by the receiver at all reasonable times.][a]

Amendments

a CA 1963, s 244A inserted by CA 1990, s 125.

Notes

No lien on documents: CA 1963, s 244A, which may be availed of not only by a liquidator or provisional liquidator, but also by the examiner of a company under the protection of the court,[1] was inserted by CA 1990, s 125 to ensure that advisors and other third parties could not withhold possession of files or documents belonging to the company by exercising a lien over them as security for unpaid fees.[2] The section does not have retrospective effect and accordingly if the work was done by the advisor and if the lien was created prior to the enactment of CA 1990, the advisor will still be entitled to assert the lien so as to withhold possession of the documents.[3]

1 CA 1990, s 180(2).

2 See *Re Macks Bakeries Ltd* [2003] 2 IR 396.

3 *Kelly v Scales* [1994] 1 IR 42.

UK legislation

See IA 1986, s 246.

245 Power of court to summon persons for examination

[(1) The court may, [of its own motion or on the application of the Director,][b] at any time after the appointment of a provisional liquidator or the making of a winding-up order, summon before it any officer of the company or person known or suspected to have in his possession any property of the company or supposed to be indebted to the company, or any person whom the court deems capable of giving information relating to the promotion, formation, trade, dealings, affairs or property of the company.

(2) The court may examine such person on oath concerning the matters aforesaid, either by word of mouth or on written interrogatories, and may reduce his answers to writing and require him to sign them.

(3) The court may require such person to produce any accounting records, deed, instrument, or other document or paper relating to the company that are in his custody or power.

(4) The court may, before the examination takes place, require such person to place before it a statement, in such form as the court may direct, of any transactions between him and the company of a type or class which the court may specify.

(5) If, in the opinion of the court, it is just and equitable to do so, it may direct that the costs of the examination be paid by the person examined.

[(6) A person who is examined under this section shall not be entitled to refuse to answer any question put to him on the ground that his answer might incriminate him and any answer by him to such a question may be used in evidence against him in any proceedings whatsoever (save proceedings for an offence (other than perjury in respect of such an answer)).][c]

(7) If a person without reasonable excuse fails at any time to attend his examination under this section, he shall be guilty of contempt of court and liable to be punished accordingly.

(8) In a case where a person without reasonable excuse fails at any time to attend his examination under this section or there are reasonable grounds for believing that a person has absconded, or is about to abscond, with a view to avoiding or delaying his examination under this section, the court may cause that person to be arrested and his books and documents and moveable personal property to be seized and him and them to be detained until such time as the court may order.][a]

Amendments

a CA 1963, s 245, substituted by CA 1990, s 126.

b The words 'of its own motion or on the application of the Director' inserted in CA 1963, s 245(1) by CLEA 2001, s 44(a).

c Subsection (6) substituted by CLEA 2001, s 44(b).

Definitions

'company': CA 1963, s 2(1); 'the court': CA 1963, s 2(1); 'document': CA 1963, s 2(1): 'officer': CA 1963, s 2(1).

Notes

Persons who may apply for examination: Although the ODCE is the only party expressly given *locus standi* to apply under CA 1963, s 245, it is well-established practice that the application for examination may also be made by the official liquidator or provisional liquidator. Indeed, a contributory or creditor of the company may also make the application although the court will be reluctant to order the examination in such circumstances unless it can be shown that some benefit will probably accrue to the applicant as a result.[1] In reaching its decision on the application the court will ordinarily attach considerable weight to the views of the liquidator whereas the views of an applicant creditor or contributory will not attract the same weight.[2]

1 *Re Comet Food Machinery Company Ltd* [1999] 1 IR 485; *Re Embassy Art Products* [1988] BCLC 1.

2 *Re Comet Food Machinery Company Ltd* [1999] 1 IR 485; *Re Embassy Art Products* [1988] BCLC 1.

Voluntary winding up: In the case of a voluntary winding up, the application for examination is made pursuant to CA 1963, s 282B rather than pursuant to s 245.

Other insolvent companies: If the company is not being wound up and the reason or principal reason for this is the insufficiency of the company's assets, individual creditors or shareholders may seek to invoke the provisions of ss 245 and 245A by following the procedures laid down in CA 1990, s 251.

Discretion of the Court to make an order for examination: The court has an inherent discretion to grant or refuse an order for examination.[1] The primary function of the section is to enable the Liquidator or the ODCE, as the case may be, to complete his functions as effectively as possible and with as little expense and as much expedition as possible.[2] An application under this section is subject to the overriding requirement that the examination must be necessary in the interests of the winding up or the performance of the ODCE's functions, as the case may be, and must not be oppressive, unfair or unjust to the respondent.[3] If the object of the liquidator is to simply obtain information, which will enable him to assist to decide whether or not the company has a valid claim against the third party, the court will normally grant the application.[4] However, if the evidence shows that the purpose of the liquidator or the ODCE in seeking the examination is to achieve an advantage beyond the ordinary litigant in proceedings which he has already commenced or which he has definitely decided to commence, the pre-disposition of the court will normally be to refuse the application as being tantamount to an abuse of process, unless of course the applicant can show special grounds to the contrary[5] (as where the proposed line of questioning goes not to the merits of the case, but simply to understand the affairs of the company or to identify the whereabouts of assets owned by the company).[6] The case for making an order against an officer or former officer of the company would usually be stronger than against a third party who has no duty to co-operate with the liquidator [7] and that oral examination is likely to be more oppressive than an order for the production of documents.[8] The order will be made even though its stated purpose is to gather information to be used against a director in restriction or disqualification proceedings.[9] Nevertheless, an order for the production of documents may be oppressive where the person against whom the order is directed is being required to produce documents which do not belong to him but which belong to some other party, such as his employer.[10]

If the application is brought by a creditor by first invoking the provisions of CA 1990, s 251, there is an onus on a creditor to demonstrate that the examination would probably result in a benefit to him.[11] That onus is more rigorous than the onus borne by a contributory or a creditor in a compulsory or a voluntary winding up.[12] Thus, the application for examination will be dismissed if the court forms the view that the creditor is merely on a 'fishing expedition'.[13]

The application is usually made on an *ex parte* basis and if a person is aggrieved by the making of the order he can apply to have the order set aside. The courts will set aside the order, *inter alia*, if, for example, there was no purpose to be served by the examination or where the examinee would be liable to some sanction in a foreign jurisdiction if questions were answered which would make it unduly oppressive to require him to answer any questions put to him.[14] If, however, the only purpose of the application to set aside the order was to assert that there would be some questions which could not be answered, then the convenient course was likely to be to allow the cross examination to proceed but provide in the order that objection could be raised at the cross-examination to those questions.[15]

1 *Re Comet Food Machinery Company Ltd* [1999] 1 IR 485.

2 *Re Rolls Razor Ltd* [1968] 3 All ER 698; *Re British and Commonwealth Holdings plc (Nos 1 and 2)* [1992] BCLC 641, aff'd sub nom *British and Commonwealth Holdings plc v Spicer and Oppenheim* [1993] BCLC 168.

3 *Re Embassy Art Products Ltd* [1988] BCLC 1; *Re Adlards Motor Group Holding Ltd* [1990] BCLC 68; *Cloverbay Ltd v Bank of Credit and Commerce International SA* [1991] BCLC 135; *Re British and Commonwealth Holdings plc (Nos 1 and 2)* [1992] BCLC 641, aff'd sub nom *British and Commonwealth Holdings plc v Spicer and Oppenheim* [1993] BCLC 168; *Re Arrows (No 2)* [1994] 1 BCLC 355; *Re Bank of Credit and Commerce International SA (No 7)* [1994] 1 BCLC 455; *Re Bank of Credit and Commerce International SA (No 12)* [1997] 1 BCLC 526; *Bellmex International Ltd v British American Tobacco Ltd* [2001] 1 BCLC 91; *Re Westmead Consultants Ltd* [2002] 1 BCLC 384.

4 *Re British and Commonwealth Holdings plc (Nos 1 and 2)* [1992] BCLC 641, aff'd sub nom *British and Commonwealth Holdings plc v Spicer and Oppenheim* [1993] BCLC 168; *Re Bank of Credit and Commerce International SA (No 12)* [1997] 1 BCLC 526; *Re Sasea Finance Ltd* [1998] 1 BCLC 559.

5 *Re Castle New Homes Ltd* [1979] 1 WLR 1075; *Clover Bay Ltd v Bank of Credit and Commerce International Ltd* [1991] BCLC 135; *Re British and Commonwealth Holdings plc (Nos 1 and 2)* [1992] BCLC 641 aff'd sub nom *British and Commonwealth Holdings plc v Spicer and Oppenheim* [1993] BCLC 168; *Re Bishopsgate Investment Management Ltd (No 2)* [1994] BCC

732; *Re PFTZM Ltd* [1995] 2 BCLC 354; *Re Sasea Finance Ltd* [1998] 1 BCLC 559; *Daltel Europe Ltd v Makki* [2005] 1 BCLC 594.

6 *Re Richbell Strategic Holdings Ltd* [2000] 2 BCLC 794. See also *Re Brook Martin and Co (Nominees) Ltd* [1993] BCLC 328; *Re RBJ Resources Ltd, Sierson v Rastogi* [2002] All ER (D) 124.

7 *Re British and Commonwealth Holdings plc (Nos 1 and 2)* [1992] BCLC 641; *Re Westmead Consultants Ltd* [2002] 1 BCLC 384.

8 *Clover Bay Ltd v Bank of Credit and Commerce International Ltd* [1991] BCLC 135.

9 *Re Pantmaenog Timber Co Ltd* [2003] 2 BCLC 257.

10 *Re Westmead Consultants Ltd* [2002] 1 BCLC 384.

11 *Re Powertech Logistics Ltd* [2007] IEHC 43.

12 *Re Powertech Logistics Ltd* [2007] IEHC 43.

13 *Re Powertech Logistics Ltd* [2007] IEHC 43.

14 *Re Casterbridge Properties Ltd (in liquidation)* [2004] 1 BCLC 96.

15 *Re Casterbridge Properties Ltd (in liquidation)* [2004] 1 BCLC 96.

Persons who may be examined or ordered to produce documents: The court may for the purpose of an examination summon before it an officer of the company, a person known or suspected to have in its possession any property of the company or a person who is supposed to be indebted to the company or any person who the court deems capable of giving information relating to the promotion, formation, trade dealings, affairs or property of the company.[1] The order may be directed against such a person even if resident abroad.[2] Examples of persons summonsed for examination have included the following: the directors;[3] shareholders who have traded with the company and who are conversant with its affairs;[4] a person indebted to a contributory such as a former partner;[5] the managing clerk of a bank where a contributory had an account;[6] a broker who has made a transfer of shares to an infant;[7] a stockbroker asserted to have acted improperly;[8] a creditor of the company who claimed for commission for services and work carried out as an agent for the company;[9] a director and general manager of another company which had important dealings with the company immediately prior to the resolution to wind up;[10] a surveyor of taxes to obtain information on the company's income tax returns;[11] the secretary of the bank with regard to tracing payments of money and calls for shares;[12] shareholders of a debtor company;[13] the auditors of the company;[14] However, the section cannot be used simply to examine a creditor on his proof of debt.[15]

1 CA 1963, s 245(1).

2 *Re Seagull Manufacturing Co Ltd* [1992] BCLC 1.

3 *Re Comet Food Machinery Company Ltd* [1999] 1 IR 485; *Re Brook Martin and Co (Nominees) Ltd* [1993] BCLC 328; *Re Richbell Strategic Holdings Ltd* [2000] 2 BCLC 794.

4 *Re Bank of Credit and Commerce International SA (No 12)* [1997] 1 BCLC 526.

5 *Trower and Lawsons Case* [1872] LR 14 Eq 8.

6 *Re Financial Insurance Company* [1867] 36 LJ (Ch) 687.

7 *Re Clement Case* [1868] LR 13 Eq 179n.

8 *Re Contract Corporation Ex parte Carter* [1870] 40 LJ Ch 15.

9 *Re English Joint Stock Bank* [1866] LR 3 Eq 203.

10 *Re Rolls Razor Ltd (No. 2)* [1970] Ch 576.

11 *Re Joseph Hargreaves Ltd* [1900] 1 Ch 347.

12 *Re Smith Knight and Company* [1869] 4 Ch App 421.

13 *Contract Corpn* (1871) 6 Ch App.

14 *British and Commonwealth Holdings plc v Spicer and Oppenheim* [1993] BCLC 168.

15 *Bellmex International Ltd v British American Tobacco Ltd* [2001] 1 BCLC 91; *Re Bank of Credit and Commerce International (No 7)* [1994] 1 BCLC 455 at 460; *Re Accidental and Marine Insurance Corporation* [1867] LR 5 Eq 22.

Order to produce documents: The court may order the person to be examined to produce any accounting records, deed, instrument, or other document or paper relating to the company that are in his custody or power[1] including documents located abroad.[2] Any such documents are only required to relate to the affairs of the company and need not necessarily be the property of the company[3]. In relation to the company's books, the company secretary is ordinarily regarded as having them[4]. A witness who is a banker is not required to disclose anything that may affect the account of a person not directly connected with the investigation.[5] The existence of a lien over documents will not prevent an order for their production even though the production may deprive the lien of much of its practical value.[6] Reports held by an insurance company claims officer in relation to fire damage were held to be privileged and therefore an examination did not extend to them[7]. It is open to the liquidators of a parent company to make documents obtained under examination available to the directors or liquidators of subsidiaries to assist them in gathering in assets or defending assets for the ultimate benefit not merely of the subsidiary but also of the parent itself.[8]

1 CA 1963, s 245(3).

2 *Re Mid East Trading Ltd* [1998] 1 BCLC 240.

3 *Re British Commonwealth Holdings Plc* [No 2] [1992] BCLC 314.

4 *Gladstone v McCullen* 23 R(c) SESS 783.

5 *Re Druitts case* [1872] LR 14 Eq 6.

6 *Re South Essex Estuary and Reclamation Company* [1869] 4 Ch App 215.

7 *Re High Grade Traders Ltd* [1984] BCLC 151.

8 In *Re Esal (Commodities) Ltd* [1990] BCC 708.

Arrest of witness: Prior to the amendments to CA 1963, s 245 effected by CA 1990, s 126 there was no statutory power to arrest a witness until after the examination order had been made and he had failed, without reasonable excuse, to attend at the time and place stipulated in the court order.[1] The position has now changed and an order can also be made for the arrest of such a person if there are grounds for believing that the person is about to abscond with a view to avoiding or delaying his examination.[2] These arrest provisions should be read in conjunction with CA 1963, s 247 which empowers the court to order the arrest of absconding contributories and officers of the company.

1 *Re J Ellis Pharmaceuticals* (1988) The Irish Times, 13 August; *Re Oriental Credit Ltd* [1988] 2 WLR 172. In these cases the court instead exercised its inherent equitable jurisdiction to grant injunctions restraining the respondents from leaving the country. See also *Re A Company* (No 003318 of 1987)(1987) 3 BCC 564; *O'Neill v O'Keefe* (19 February 2002, unreported) HC (Kearns J).

2 CA 1963, s 245(8).

Committal for failure to co-operate: A person who is summonsed for examination and without reasonable excuse fails to attend at any time shall be guilty of contempt of Court and liable to be punished accordingly.[1] Witnesses who refuse to attend may be made to pay the costs of compelling their attendance.[2] A person who is summonsed for examination or to produce documents must attend even though he does not possess such documents.[3]

1 CA 1963, s 245(7).

2 *Trower and Lawson's Case* (1872) LR 14 Eq 8; *Re Lisbon Steam Tramways Company* (1876) 2 Ch D 575.

3 *Re LeitnerElectric Company* [1916] 32 TLR 474.

Privilege: CA 1963, s 245(6) abrogates the common law privilege against self-incrimination by prohibiting a person being examined from refusing to answer a question on the grounds of self-incrimination. The evidence cannot be used in any other criminal proceedings, save that of perjury in respect of such an answer. However, such evidence may be used in civil proceedings.[1] There is no prohibition on the use of evidence in proceedings against a third party.[2] A witness who is being examined must answer all questions referred to above including those referring to hearsay evidence.[3] The only basis upon which a witness may refuse to answer would be on grounds of privilege.[4]

1 *Re Aluminium Fabricators Ltd* [1984] ILRM 399.

2 *Irish Commercial Society Ltd v Plunkett* [1986] ILRM 624; *Re Jeffrey S. Levitt Ltd* [1992] 2 All ER 509.

3 *Re Ottoman Company* [1867] 15 WR 1069.

4 If, for example, a lawyer refuses to answer a question based on breach of confidence the remedy is to ask the question of the client directly.

Costs: In the normal course of events costs of conducting the examination form part of the costs of the liquidation, although the court may direct that the person examined pay all or part of the costs.[1] Such an order may be made where the person's conduct had contributed materially to the uncertainty concerning the affairs of the company.[2]

1 CA 1963, S 245(5).

2 *Re David Ireland and Co Ltd* [1905] IR 133.

Delivery of money or property by witness: If in the course of an examination under CA 1963, s 245 it appears to the court that the person being examined is indebted to the company or has in his possession or control any money, property or documents belonging to the company, the court may make an order for the repayment of all or part of the debt or for the delivery up of all or part of the money, property or documents, as the case may be.[1] In order to give effect to such an order the court may make a further order on the application of the liquidator or the ODCE authorising the entry into and search of premises and for the seizure of any money, property or documents of the company found on the premises.[2] The outcome of any such entry, search and seizure must be reported to the court which may then make consequential orders concerning the disposition of anything so seized.[3]

1 CA 1963, s 245A(1).

2 CA 1963, s 245A(2).

3 CA 1963, s 245A(3) and (4).

Practice and procedure: The application to have a person cross-examined is initially made *ex-parte*[1] grounded on an affidavit in which the applicant sets out the basis upon which the application is made. It is open to the respondent to apply subsequently to have the order for examination set aside. While the witness is entitled to reasonable notice of an examination,[2] there is no requirement that he be provided with the list of questions to be asked prior to the examination.[3] The examination is conducted in public[4] and is normally held before the Master of the High Court and usually the cross-examination is conducted by a solicitor or counsel. The witness is entitled to be attended by his own solicitors and counsel[5] and may be re-examined by them for the purpose of explaining answers given by him.[6]. Evidence is usually recorded and the witness may be required to sign a transcript;[7] they may correct any errors and sign subject to corrections.[8]

1 A contrary practice has been adopted in the UK. See *Re PFTZM Ltd* [1995] 2 BCLC 354.

2 *Re North Wheal Exmouth Mining Company* (1862) 31 Beav 628.

3 *Re Rolls Razor (No 2)* [1971] 1 Ch 576.

4 See *Re R Ltd* [1988] ILRM 126, reversing *Re Redbreast Preserving Co (Ireland) Ltd* 91 ILTR 12.

5 *Re Breech-Loading Armoury Co, Re Merchant's Co* (1867) LR 4 Eq 453.

6 *Re Cambrian Mining Company* (1881) 20 Ch D 376.

7 CA 1963, s 245(2)

8 *Re Milton Hindle Ltd* [1963] 3 All ER 161.

UK legislation

See IA 1986, ss 133, 134, 236.

[245A Order for payment or delivery of property against person examined under section 245 of Principal Act

[(1) If in the course of an examination][b] under section 245 it appears to the court that any person being examined—

(a) is indebted to the company, or

(b) has in his possession or control any money, property or books and papers of the company,

[the court may, of its own motion or on the application of the Director, order such person][c]—

(i) to pay to the liquidator the amount of the debt or any part thereof, or

(ii) to pay, deliver, convey, surrender or transfer to the liquidator such money, property or books and papers or any part thereof, as the case may be, at such time and in such manner and on such terms as the court may direct.

[(2) Where the court has made an order under subsection (1), it may, on the application of the Director or the liquidator, make a further order permitting the applicant, accompanied by such persons as the applicant thinks appropriate, to enter at any time or times within one month from the date of issue of the order, any premises (including a dwelling) owned or occupied by the person the subject of the order under subsection (1) (using such force as is reasonably necessary for the purpose), to search the premises and to seize any money, property or books and papers of the company found on the premises.

(3) Where the court has made an order under subsection (2), the applicant shall report to it as soon as may be on the outcome of any action on foot of the court's order and the court shall direct the applicant as to the disposition of anything seized on foot of the order.

(4) A direction under subsection (3) shall not be made in favour of the Director except in respect of the Director's costs and reasonable expenses.

(5) A person who obstructs the exercise of a right of entry, search and seizure conferred by virtue of an order made under subsection (2) or who obstructs the exercise of a right so conferred to take possession of anything referred to in that subsection, shall be guilty of an offence.

(6) Proceedings on foot of an offence under subsection (5) shall not prejudice the power of the court to issue proceedings for contempt of court for failure by a person to comply with an order under this section.][d]][a]

Amendments

a CA 1963, s 245A inserted by CA 1990, s 127.

b '(1) If in the course of an examination' substituted for 'If in the course of an examination' by CLEA 2001, s 45(a).

c 'the court may, of its own motion or on the application of the Director, order such person' substituted for 'the court may order such person' by CLEA 2001, s 45(b).

d CA 1963, s 245A(2)–(6) inserted by CLEA 2001, s 45(c).

Definitions

'books and paper': CA 1963, s 2(1); 'company': CA 1963, s 2(1); 'the court': CA 1963, s 2(1).

Notes

See the notes to CA 1963, s 245.

UK legislation

See IA 1986, ss 212, 236(2), 237.

246 Attendance of officers of company at meetings

In the case of a winding up by the court, the court shall have power to require the attendance of any officer of the company at any meeting of creditors or of contributories or of a committee of inspection for the purpose of giving information as to the trade, dealings, affairs or property of the company.

Definitions

'company': CA 1963, s 2(1); 'the court': CA 1963, s 2(1); 'officer': CA 1963, s 2(1).

Notes

General. Unlike an examination under CA 1963, s 245, the privilege against self-incrimination is not expressed to be abrogated when an officer of the company attends a meeting of creditors or of contributories or of the committee of inspection.

247 Power to arrest absconding contributory or officer of company

[The court, at any time either before or after making a winding-up order, on proof of probable cause for believing that a contributory, director, shadow director, secretary or other officer is about to quit the State or otherwise to abscond or to remove or conceal any of his property for the purpose of evading payment of calls or of avoiding examination about the affairs of the company, may, of its own motion or on the application of the Director, a creditor of the company or any other interested person, cause the contributory, director, shadow director, secretary or other officer to be arrested, and his books and papers and movable personal property to be seized and him and them to be detained until such time as the court may order.][a]

Amendments

a CA 1963, s 247, substituted by CLEA 2001, s 46.

Definitions

'books and paper': 'company': CA 1963, s 2(1); s 2(1); 'contributory': CA 1963, s 2(1), s 208; 'the court': CA 1963, s 2(1).

Notes

Absconding contributories and officers: Before the amendments effected by CLEA 2001, s 46, this section was only available for use against absconding contributories who wished to avoid payment of calls or who wished to avoid being examined. Since, typically, the issued share capital of a company is fully paid up, there will not normally be any question of contributories absconding to avoid paying calls. Moreover, the section could not be used against an officer who intended to abscond to avoid being examined unless it could be shown that he was also a contributory. Thus, the section was little used in practice.[1] The amendment of the section to apply to officers irrespective of whether they are also contributories may result in greater use of this statutory power of arrest in future.

1 For examples of the use of the section, see *Re Central Trust Investment Society* (1982) *The Irish Times,* 31 August; *Re O'Shea's (Dublin) Ltd* (1984) The Irish Times, 6 July and 5 May 1987. See also *Re J Ellis Pharmaceuticals Ltd* (1988) The Irish Times, 13 August; *Re Mark Synnott (Life and Pensions) Brokers Ltd* (1991) The Irish Times, 3 July; *Re Tipperary Self-Drive Ltd* (1992) The Irish Times, 4 February.

Probable cause must be shown: A heavy onus is placed on the applicant to show that there is probable cause for believing not only that the contributory or officer is about to abscond but also that he intends to do so for the purpose of avoiding payment of calls or being examined, as the case may be.[1]

1 *Felton v Callis* [1968] 3 All ER 673; *Re Underwood* (1903) 51 WR 335; *Re The Ulster Land, Building and Investment Co Ltd* (1887) 17 LR Ir 591; *Re Imperial Mercantile Credit company* (1867) LR 5 Eq 264; *Sichel v Raphael* (1861) 4 LT 114. See also *Bayer AG v Winter* [1986] 1 All ER 733; *O'Neill v O'Keefe* (19 February 2002, unreported) HC (Kearns J). Most of these cases involved either the exercise of the court's equitable jurisdiction to grant injunctions or alternatively, the use of the writ of *ne exeat regno*.

Voluntary winding up: In the case of a voluntary winding up, the application for arrest is made pursuant to CA 1963, s 282D rather than pursuant to s 247.

Other insolvent companies: If the company is not being wound up and the reason or principal reason for this is the insufficiency of the company's assets, individual creditors or shareholders may seek to invoke the provisions of s 247 by following the procedures laid down in CA 1990, s 251.

Freezing order against directors and officers: In addition to these powers of arrest, the court may, on the application of a company, director, member, liquidator, receiver, creditor or the ODCE, grant *Mareva*-type injunctive relief against a director or other officer of a company, directing him not to remove his assets from the State and/or not to reduce his assets within the State below a specified amount.[1] In order to obtain such relief the applicant must show that he has a substantive civil cause of action against the director or officer (including a right to seek an order imposing personal liability for all or some of the debts and liabilities of the company) and he must further show that there are grounds for believing that unless otherwise restrained, the director or officer will attempt to remove or dispose of his assets or the company's assets with a view to evading his or the company's obligations and frustrating an order of the court.[2]

1 CLEA 2001, s 55.

2 CLEA 2001, s 55.

UK legislation

See IA 1986, s 158.

248 Powers of court cumulative

Any powers by this Act conferred on the court shall be in addition to and not in restriction of any existing powers of instituting proceedings against any contributory or debtor of the company or the estate of any contributory or debtor, for the recovery of any call or other sums.

Definitions

'company': CA 1963, s 2(1); 'contributory': CA 1963, s 2(1), s 208; 'the court': CA 1963, s 2(1).

UK legislation

See IA 1986, s 159.

249 Dissolution of company

(1) When the affairs of a company have been completely wound up, the court, if the liquidator makes an application in that behalf, shall make an order that the company be dissolved from the date of the order, and the company shall be dissolved accordingly.

(2) An office copy of the order shall within 21 days from the date thereof be forwarded by the liquidator to the registrar of companies for registration.

(3) If the liquidator makes default in complying with the requirements of this section, he [shall be guilty of an offence and liable to a fine][a] not exceeding [€1,904.61].[b]

Amendments

a Words in CA 1963, s 249(3) substituted by C(AA)A 2003, s 57 and Sch 2, para 1.

b '£250' substituted for '£50' by C(A)A 1982, Sch 1, increased to '£1,500' by CA 1990, s 240(7) as inserted by CLEA 2001, s 104(c) and converted to €1,904.61 by Council Regulation (EC) 1103/97, No 974/98 and No 2866/98 and the Economic and Monetary Union Act 1998, s 6.

Definitions

'company': CA 1963, s 2(1); 'the court': CA 1963, s 2(1); 'the Registrar of Companies': CA 1963, s 2(1).

Notes

Dissolution following final orders application: In the case of a compulsory winding up, once the official liquidator's final account has been passed he applies to the court for final orders (as to payment of final dividends, remuneration, costs and expenses etc) including an order for the dissolution of the company.[1] The court will direct that the company be dissolved once the examiner of the High Court has issued a certificate to the effect that any remaining balance of funds in the liquidation has been disposed of and that the affairs of the company have been completely wound up.[2] The liquidation is deemed to have been concluded on the date on which the order dissolving the company has been delivered to the Registrar of Companies by the official liquidator.[3] Notice of delivery of the order to the Registrar of Companies must be published in *Iris Oifigiúil*.[4]

1 RSC 1986, Ord 74, r 137.

2 RSC 1986, Ord 74, r 137.

3 RSC 1986, Ord 74, r 129(a).

4 EC(C)R 1973, reg 4(1)(j).

Members' voluntary winding up: CA 1963, s 263(4) provides that in the case of a member's winding up, the company is dissolved on the expiration of three months from the registration of the liquidator's final return with the Companies Registration Office.

Creditors' voluntary winding up: CA 1963, s 273(4) provides that in the case of a creditor's voluntary winding up, the company is dissolved on the expiration of three months from the registration of the liquidator's final return.

Reinstatement of company: CA 1963, s 310 allows a liquidator or any interested person to apply within two years to have the dissolution declared void. Alternatively, under CA 1963, s 311(8) an application to restore the company may be made by the company itself or by any member or creditor within a period of twenty years from the date of dissolution.[1]

1 For a fuller discussion, see the notes to CA 1963, ss 310 and 311.

UK legislation

See IA 1986, s 205.

Enforcement of Orders made in Winding Up by Courts outside the State

250 Enforcement of orders made in winding up by courts outside the State

(1) Any order made by a court of any country recognised for the purposes of this section and made for or in the course of winding up a company may be enforced by the High Court in the same manner in all respects as if the order had been made by the High Court.

(2) When an application is made to the High Court under this section, an office copy of any order sought to be enforced shall be sufficient evidence of the order.

(3) In this section, 'company' means a body corporate incorporated outside the State, and 'recognised' means recognised by order made by the Minister.

[(4) This section does not apply in relation to an order made by a court of a member state of the European Communities other than the State and Denmark.][a]

Amendments

a CA 1963, s 250(4) inserted by EC(CI)R 2002, reg 3.

Definitions

'company': CA 1963, s 2(1); 'Minister': CA 1963, s 2(1).

Notes

Enforcement of orders in foreign insolvency proceedings: Only Great Britain and Northern Ireland were 'recognised' by Ministerial Order.[1] However, the provisions of CA 1963, s 250 have now been superseded in respect of insolvency orders made in EU member states other than Denmark, by Council Regulation (EC) No 1346/2000 of 29 May 2000 which came into effect on 31 May 2002.[2] Under the terms of the Regulation there is provision for the recognition and enforcement in the courts of one member state of the insolvency proceedings of another member state.[3] The assistance to be given to the foreign insolvency procedure under this section may extend to directing an Irish liquidator to pay over to foreign liquidators sums collected and/or moneys realised in Ireland.[4]

1 Companies (Recognition of Countries) Order 1964.

2 In relation to the Insolvency Reg generally, see Moss, Fletcher and Isaacs, *EC Regulation on Insolvency Proceedings* (Oxford, 2002).

3 See Chapter II of the Insolvency Regulation. See also CA 1963, ss 227A and 227B and the notes thereto.

4 *Re HIH Casualty and General Insurance Ltd* [2008] 3 All ER 869.

UK legislation

See IA 1986, s 426.

(III) Voluntary Winding Up

Resolutions for and Commencement of Voluntary Winding Up

251 Circumstances in which company may be wound up voluntarily

(1) A company may be wound up voluntarily—

(a) when the period, if any, fixed for the duration of the company by the articles expires, or the event, if any, occurs, on the occurrence of which the articles provide that the company is to be dissolved, and the company in general meeting has passed a resolution that the company be wound up voluntarily;

(b) if the company resolves by special resolution that the company be wound up voluntarily;

(c) if the company in general meeting resolves that it cannot by reason of its liabilities continue its business, and that it be wound up voluntarily.

(2) In this Act, 'a resolution for voluntary winding up' means a resolution passed under any paragraph of subsection (1).

Notes

Different types of voluntary winding up: A company can be wound up voluntarily in three different ways:

(i) *Dissolution after a fixed period of time.* Where a company provides in its articles of association that it is dissolved after a fixed period of time.[1]

(ii) *Members' voluntary winding up.* Where the members at a general meeting resolve to wind up a solvent company on the basis that it is able to pay its debts within twelve months of the passing of the resolution.[2] The resolution is a special resolution. It will be valid if consented to by all the members having voting rights, even though there may be some procedural defect in the manner in which it was passed.[3]

(iii) *Creditors' voluntary winding up.* Where the company is insolvent, a company can resolve at an EGM to wind up the company. The members must pass an ordinary resolution at which it is declared that the company is unable to pay its debts as they fall due.[4]

1 CA 1963, s 251(1)(a).

2 CA 1963, s 251(1)(b).

3 *Re Bailey, Hay & Co Ltd* [1971] 3 All ER 693.

4 CA 1963, s 251(1)(c).

252 Publication of resolution to wind up voluntarily

(1) When a company has passed a resolution for voluntary winding up, it shall, within 14 days after the passing of the resolution, give notice of the resolution by advertisement in [the Companies Registration Office Gazette].[a]

(2) If default is made in complying with this section, the company and every officer of the company who is in default [shall be guilty of an offence and liable to a fine][b] not exceeding [€1,904.61][c] and for the purposes of this subsection, the liquidator of the company shall be deemed to be an officer of the company.

Amendments

a Words substituted by IFCMPA 2005, s 72.

b Words substituted by C(AA)A 2003, s 57 and Sch 2.

c '£125' substituted for '£25' by C(A)A 1982 Sch 1, increased to £1,500 by CA 1990, s 240(7) as inserted by CLEA 2001, s104 and converted to €1,904.61 by Council Regulations (EC) No 1103/97, No 974/98 and No 2866/98 and the Economic and Monetary Union Act 1998, s 6.

Cross reference

In addition the company must within 15 days deliver a copy of the resolution to the Registrar of Companies for registration pursuant to CA 1963, s 143.

The Registrar of Companies may bring and prosecute proceedings for a breach of the section: C(A)A 1982, s 16.

Definitions

'company': CA 1963, s 2(1); 'officer': CA 1963, s 2(1); 'a resolution for voluntary winding up': CA 1963, s 2(1), s 251(2).

Notes

Publication: In addition to the requirements set out in CA 1963, s 252 the company must also within fifteen days deliver a copy of the resolution to wind up the company to the Registrar of Companies.[1] If the company fails to do so the Registrar of Companies may prosecute the company.[2]

1 CA 1963, s 143.

2 C(A)(A) 1982, s 16.

UK legislation

See IA 1986, s 85.

---

253 Commencement of voluntary winding up

A voluntary winding up shall be deemed to commence at the time of the passing of the resolution for voluntary winding up.

Cross reference

For the date of the commencement of a compulsory winding up, see CA 1963, s 220.

Definitions

'a resolution for voluntary winding up': CA 1963, s 2(1), s 251(2).

UK legislation

See IA 1986, s 86.

Consequences of Voluntary Winding up

254 Effect of voluntary winding up on business and status of company

In case of a voluntary winding up, the company shall, from the commencement of the winding up, cease to carry on its business, except so far as may be required for the beneficial winding up thereof, so, however, that the corporate state and corporate powers of the company shall, notwithstanding anything to the contrary in its articles, continue until it is dissolved.

Cross reference

For other consequences of the commencement of the winding up, see CA 1963, ss 255, 258, 269.

Definitions

'articles': CA 1963, s 2(1); 'company': CA 1963, s 2(1).

Notes

Directors: The passing of a winding-up resolution does not cause the directors to cease to hold office.[1] It is the appointment of the liquidator rather than the passing of a resolution that takes a director's power away. Upon the appointment of a liquidator all directors' powers cease except in so far as they are sanctioned by the company in general meeting (in the case of a members' voluntary winding up[2]) or with the sanction of the committee of inspection (in a creditors' voluntary winding up[3]).

1 *Madrid Bank Ltd v Bayley* (1866) LR 2 QB 37.
2 CA 1963, s 258.
3 CA 1963, s 269.

Carrying on the business of the company: The company must cease to carry on its business except in so far as may be required for its beneficial winding up.[1] If carrying on the business post-liquidation is genuinely considered to be beneficial to the winding up, post-liquidation liabilities may be paid in priority to pre-liquidation creditors as an expense of the winding up. However, if the carrying on of the business of the company is later found not to have been for the beneficial winding up of the company, then the post liquidation creditors will not get such priority.[2]

1 See notes to CA 1963, s 231.
2 *Re Great Eastern Electric Company Ltd* [1941] Ch 241; 1 All ER 409.

Authority of agents: Any authority given to a person to act on behalf of the company in the ordinary course of his business ceases upon the passing of the winding-up resolution.[1] After the commencement of the winding up, the liquidator becomes the company's authorised agent.[2]

1 *Freaney v Bank of Ireland* [1975] IR 376 in which the court held that the company's bankers are entitled to pay cheques drawn on the company before the winding-up resolution and presented for payment after that date.
2 *Freaney v Bank of Ireland* [1975] IR 376.

Position of employees: Unlike a compulsory winding up the passing of the resolution does not automatically operate to dismiss the company's employees.[1] Whether or not the passing of a resolution constitutes a notice of determination of an employee's contract depends on factors such as the terms of contract and the intention of the liquidator concerning the business of the company. The test is whether, in all the circumstances, the employee is justified in regarding the winding up as indicating an intention by the company to repudiate its obligations under the contract of employment.[2]

1 See notes to CA 1963, s 225; *Midland Counties District Bank v Attwood* [1905] 1 Ch 357.

2 *Reigate v Union Mfg Co* [1918] I KB 592. See generally, Graham, 'The Effect of Liquidation on a Contract of Service' 15 MLR 48 (1952).

UK legislation

See IA 1986, s 87.

255 Avoidance of transfers of shares after commencement of voluntary winding up

Any transfer of shares, not being a transfer made to or with the sanction of the liquidator, and any alteration in the status of the members of the company, made after the commencement of a voluntary winding up, shall be void.

Definitions

'company': CA 1963, s 2(1); 'member': CA 1963, s 31; 'share': CA 1963, s 2(1).

Notes

Post-liquidation transfer of shares: This section prohibits post-liquidation transfers of shares, except where sanctioned by the liquidator. The section also applies to a transfer of shares which has been executed but not registered prior to the commencement of the winding up, and the transferee in such circumstances cannot insist on being registered.[1] Similarly, rescission of a contract to take shares will not be permitted after the commencement of the winding up, even if the contract was induced by misrepresentation.[2] It is to be noted, though, that the section applies only to transfers of shares and does not prevent or release the company from any duty it may be under to register a transfer of debentures.[3] Nor may the section be used by the liquidator to cancel a valid forfeiture of shares made by the directors prior to the passing of the winding-up resolution.[4]

1 *Re Violet Consolidated Gold-Mining Co* (1889) 68 LJ (Ch) 535.

2 *Oakes v Turquand and Harding*; *Peek v Turquand and Harding* (1867) LR 2 HL 325; *Re Addlestone Linoleum Co* (1887) 36 Ch D 191.

3 *Re Goy & Co* [1900] 2 Ch 149.

4 *Dawes' Case* (1868) LR 6 Eq 232.

UK legislation

See IA 1986, s 88.

Declaration of Solvency

256 [Statutory declaration of solvency in case of proposal to wind up voluntarily

(1) Where it is proposed to wind up a company voluntarily, the directors of the company or, in the case of a company having more than two directors, the majority of the directors may, at a meeting of the directors, make a statutory declaration to the effect that they have made a full inquiry into the affairs of the company, and that having done so, they have formed the opinion that the company will be able to pay its debts in full within such

Notes

General: Where a statutory declaration has not been made and delivered in accordance with CA 1963, s 256, the result is that the winding up becomes a creditors' voluntary winding up by operation of law.[1] The failure to hold a meeting of creditors pursuant to CA 1963, s 266 on the day of or on the day after the passing of the winding-up resolution results in the appointment of a liquidator becoming null and void. The court has no jurisdiction under CA 1963, s 280 to extend the time for the making and filing of the report of the independent expert so the winding up becomes a creditors' voluntary winding up. Where the company is out of time for holding a creditors' meeting in accordance with CA 1963, s 266 the court may annul the resolution that the company be wound up.[2]

1 CA 1963, s 256(2).

2 See notes to CA 1963, s 234, 280. *Re James McMenamin Ltd (in Vol Liquidation)* [2005] IEHC 339, In *Re Favon Investment Co Ltd (in liquidation)* [1993] IR 87; *Re Oakthorpe Holdings Ltd; Walsh v Registrar of Company* [1988] ILRM 62. In the latter case Carroll J felt that the appropriate course of action would be for a creditor or contributory of the company either to petition to have the company wound up by the court or alternatively to apply pursuant to CA 1963, s 234 and s 280 to have the winding-up resolution annulled.

UK legislation

See IA 1986, ss 89, 90.

Provisions applicable to a Members' Voluntary Winding Up

257 Provisions applicable to a members' voluntary winding up

Sections 258 to 264 shall, subject to the last-mentioned section, apply to a members' voluntary winding up.

Cross reference

See also CA 1963, ss 258–264.

Definitions

'member': CA 1963, s 31; 'members' voluntary winding up': CA 1963, s 2(1), s 256(7).

---

258 Power of company to appoint and fix remuneration of liquidators

(1) The company in general meeting shall appoint one or more liquidators for the purpose of winding up the affairs and distributing the assets of the company, and may fix the remuneration to be paid to him or them.

(2) On the appointment of a liquidator all the powers of the directors shall cease, except so far as the company in general meeting or the liquidator sanctions the continuance thereof.

Definitions

'company': CA 1963, s 2(1); 'director': CA 1963, s 2(1).

Cross references in other enactments

NAMA Act 2009, s 150(2) provides:

'The appointment of a liquidator to a company whose assets or any part of them are under the control of a statutory receiver does not displace the statutory receiver and does not affect his or her powers, authority and agency.'

Notes

Liquidator's remuneration: If the company in general meeting does not fix the liquidator's remuneration, it may be fixed by the Court.[1]

1 *Re Amalgamated Syndicates Ltd* [1901] 2 Ch 181.

Powers of directors after liquidator's appointment: As regards the powers of the directors in a creditors' voluntary winding up, see CA 1963, s 269. By way of contrast with sub-s (2), in the case of a compulsory liquidation the appointment of a liquidator renders the directors *functus officio*.[1]

1 *Re Union Accident Insurance Co Ltd* [1972] 1 All ER 1105; *Re Mawcon* [1969] 1 All ER 118.

Director's powers prior to liquidator's appointment.[1] In the time period between the passing of the resolution to wind up the company and the appointment of the liquidator, the directors still retain the power to act on behalf of the company, but it is thought that their power must be limited by restrictions contained in CA 1963, s 254, 255 and 218.[2]

1 See notes to CA 1963, s 225.

2 *In re a Company (No 006341 of 1992), ex parte B Ltd* [1994] 1 BCLC 225.

UK legislation

See IA 1986, s 91.

---

259 Power to fill vacancy in office of liquidator

(1) If a vacancy occurs by death, resignation or otherwise in the office of liquidator appointed by the company, the company in general meeting may fill the vacancy.

(2) For that purpose a general meeting may be convened by any contributory or, if there are more liquidators than one, by the continuing liquidators.

(3) The meeting shall be held in manner provided by this Act or by the articles or in such manner as may, on application by any contributory or by the continuing liquidators, be determined by the court.

Cross reference

As regards the provisions concerning meetings, see CA 1963, ss 131–146 and Table A, regs 4–30.

Definitions

'articles': CA 1963, s 2(1); 'company': CA 1963, s 2(1); 'contributory': CA 1963, s 2(1), s 208; 'the court': CA 1963, s 2(1).

UK legislation

See IA 1986, s 92.

---

260 Power of liquidator to accept shares as consideration for sale of property of company

(1) Where a company is proposed to be, or is in course of being, wound up voluntarily, and the whole or part of its business or property is proposed to be transferred or sold to another company, whether a company within the meaning of this Act or not (in this section referred to as 'the transferee company'), the liquidator of the first-mentioned company (in this section referred to as 'the transferor company') may, with the sanction of a special resolution of that company, conferring either a general authority on the liquidator or an authority in respect of any particular arrangement, receive in compensation or part compensation for the transfer or sale, shares, policies or other like interests in the transferee company for distribution among the members of the transferor company, or may enter into any other arrangement whereby the members of the transferor company may, in lieu of receiving cash, shares, policies or other like interests, or in addition thereto, participate in the profits of or receive any other benefit from the transferee company.

(2) Any sale or arrangement in pursuance of this section shall be binding on the members of the transferor company.

(3) If the voting rights conferred by any shares in the company were not cast in favour of the special resolution and the holder of those shares expresses his dissent from the special resolution in writing addressed to the liquidator and left at the registered office of the company within 7 days after the passing of the special resolution, he may require the liquidator either to abstain from carrying the resolution into effect or to purchase that part of his interest which those shares represent at a price to be determined by agreement or by arbitration in manner provided by this section.

(4) If the liquidator elects to purchase the member's interest, the purchase money must be paid before the company is dissolved and, unless otherwise provided for, shall be deemed to be and shall be paid as part of the costs, charges and expenses of the winding up.

(5) A special resolution shall not be invalid for the purposes of this section by reason that it is passed before or concurrently with a resolution for voluntary winding up or for appointing liquidators, but, if an order is made within a year for winding up the company by the court, the special resolution shall not be valid unless sanctioned by the court.

(6) For the purposes of an arbitration under this section, the provisions of the Companies Clauses Consolidation Act, 1845, relating to the settlement of disputes by arbitration, shall be incorporated with this Act, and in the construction of those provisions this Act shall be deemed to be the special Act, and 'the company' shall mean the transferor company, and any appointment by the said incorporated provisions directed to be made under the hand of the secretary or any two of the directors may be made under the hand of the liquidator, or, if there is more than one liquidator, then of any two or more of the liquidators.

Cross reference

In relation to the merger of plcs, see also the EC(MDC)R 1987. As regards the application of s 260 in a creditors' voluntary winding up, see CA 1963, s 271.

Definitions

'company': CA 1963, s 2(1); 'the court': CA 1963, s 2(1); 'director': CA 1963, s 2(1); 'member': CA 1963, s 31; 'a resolution for voluntary winding up': CA 1963, s 2(1), s 251(2): 'share': CA 1963, s 2(1).

Notes

General: The reconstruction procedure provided for in this section allows a liquidator of a company to transfer the assets of the company to a new company where members in the old company are given shares in the new company. CA 1963, s 260 only applies where the company is solvent and is being wound up as a members' voluntary winding up. A similar scheme can apply where the company is insolvent, and is being wound up by way of a creditors' voluntary winding up, but subject to the modification that the powers of the liquidator shall not be exercised except with the sanction of the court or the committee of inspection.[1] There is no definition of the types of schemes that fall within this section but its use has many advantages over CA 1963, s 201 in that it only requires a special resolution of the company to initiate the scheme and there is no requirement for court approval.[2] If the company is wound up within a year the sanction of the court is required.[3]

1 CA 1963, s 271.

2 Unlike CA 1963, s 201.

3 CA 1963, s 260(5) requires the court's sanction if the company is compulsorily wound up within twelve months of the passing of the special resolution. The court will not sanction the scheme if the position of creditors are not protected by the disappearance of the company's assets in exchange for the mere paper of the transferee company.

Position of creditors: The reconstruction does not, however, bind the creditors and accordingly the liquidator must either retain sufficient funds to meet the creditors' claim or alternatively obtain an adequate indemnity from the transferee company. Failure to so will render him personally liable to any creditor whose claim is not paid in full.[1]

1 *Pulsford v Devenish* [1903] 1 Ch 331.

Dissentient members: Unlike CA 1963, s 201, dissentient shareholders are not bound by the reconstruction and they can serve a notice of dissent at the registered offices of the company.[1] The notice served on the liquidator must give him an option to either abstain from the reconstruction or to purchase the dissenting shareholder's shares.[2] If a dissenting shareholder does not agree to the reconstruction, the liquidator will in practice be obliged to purchase shares from the dissenting shareholder. If a price cannot be agreed it will be determined by arbitration under the procedure laid down in the Companies Clause Consolidation Act 1845. [3] In establishing the value of the dissenting shareholder's shares, the shareholders are not entitled to question the company's officers and in the absence of fraud or proven inaccuracy, are not entitled to discovery of the books and records of the company.[4] Even if a shareholder does not dissent as provided for by CA 1963, s 260(3) it does not prevent them from refusing to accept the new shares.[5] The shareholders of the transferee company cannot be compelled to pay further sums as part of the reconstruction (for example by accepting shares in the transferee company as being partly paid up) unless they expressly consent.[6] The court will not sanction a scheme under CA1963, s 201 (thus allowing the rights of dissenting shareholders to be circumvented) if the scheme could have been carried out under CA 1963, s 260, unless the dissentient shareholders are given the same rights as they enjoy under CA 1963, s 260(3).[7] Any provision in the memorandum of association or articles of association which attempts to deprive dissenting shareholders of their rights under CA 1963, s 260(3) is null and void.[8]

1 CA 1963, s 260(3).

2 *Re Demerara Rubber Company Ltd* [1923] 1 Ch 331.

[3] CA 1963, s 260(6).
[4] *Re British Building Stone Co Ltd* [1908] 2 Ch 450; *Re Glamorganshire Banking Co; Morgan's case* (1885) 28 Ch D 620.
[5] *Higgs' case* [1865] 2 H&N 657 at 655.
[6] *Re Imperial Mercantile Credit Association* (1871) LR 12 Eq 504.
[7] *Re Anglo – Continental Supply Co Ltd* [1922] 2 Ch 723.
[8] *Bisgood v Henderson's Transvaal Estates Ltd* [1908] 1 Ch 331; *Payne v Cork Co Ltd* [1900] 1 Ch 308.

UK legislation

See IA 1986, ss 110, 111.

261 [Duty of liquidator to call creditors' meeting if he is of opinion that company unable to pay its debts

(1) If the liquidator is at any time of the opinion that the company will not be able to pay its debts in full within the period stated in the declaration under section 256 he shall—

(a) summon a meeting of creditors for a day not later than the fourteenth day after the day on which he formed that opinion;

(b) send notices of the creditors' meeting to the creditors by post not less than seven days before the day on which that meeting is to be held;

(c) cause notice of the creditors' meeting to be advertised, at least ten days before the date of the meeting, once in [the Companies Registration Office Gazette][b] and once at least in two daily newspapers circulating in the locality in which the company's principal place of business in the State was situated during the relevant period; and

(d) during the period before the day on which the creditors' meeting is to be held, furnish creditors free of charge with such information concerning the affairs of the company as they may reasonably require;

and the notice of the creditors' meeting shall state the duty imposed by paragraph (d).

(2) The liquidator shall also—

(a) make out a statement in the prescribed form as to the affairs of the company, including a statement of the company's assets and liabilities, a list of the outstanding creditors and the estimated amount of their claims;

(b) lay that statement before the creditors' meeting; and

(c) attend and preside at that meeting.

(3) As from the day on which the creditors' meeting is held under this section, the Companies Acts shall have effect as if—

(a) without prejudice to the powers of the court under section 256, the directors' declaration under that section had not been made; and

(b) the creditors' meeting and the company meetings at which it was resolved that the company be wound up voluntarily were the meetings mentioned in section 266;

and, accordingly, the winding up shall become a creditors' voluntary winding up and any appointment made or committee established by the creditors' meeting shall be deemed to have been made or established by the creditors' meeting so mentioned.

(4) The appointment of a liquidator at a meeting called under this section shall not, subject to subsection (5), affect the validity of any action previously taken by the liquidator appointed by the members of the company.

(5) Where the creditors appoint a liquidator at a meeting called under this section and there is a dispute as to any or all of the costs, charges or expenses incurred by, including the remuneration of, the liquidator appointed by the members of the company, the liquidator appointed by the creditors, or any creditor, may apply to the court to determine the dispute and the court may, on such application, make such order as it deems fit.

(6) Nothing in this section shall be deemed to take away any right in this Act of any person to present a petition to the court for the winding up of a company.

(7) If the liquidator fails to comply with subsection (1) he [shall be guilty of an offence and liable to a fine].[c]][a]

Amendments

a CA 1963, s 261 substituted by CA 1990, s 129.

b 'the Companies Registration Office Gazette' substituted for '*Iris Oifigiúil*' by IFCMPA 2005, s 72.

c Words substituted by C(AA)A 2003, s 57 and Sch 2.

Cross-reference

See also CA 1963, s 256.

See also CA 1963, s 266.

Proceedings for a breach of the section may be brought and prosecuted by the Registrar of Companies: C(A)A 1982, s 16. As regards the level of the fine, see CA 1990, s 240.

Definitions

'company': CA 1963, s 2(1); 'the court': CA 1963, s 2(1); 'creditors' voluntary winding up': CA 1963, s 2(1), s 256(7); 'director': CA 1963, s 2(1); 'member': CA 1963, s 31; 'prescribed': CA 1963, s 2(1).

Notes

General: There is a similar requirement to hold a general meeting of the company where the winding up continues for more than one year in the case of a creditors' winding up.[1]

1 CA1963, s 272.

UK legislation

See IA 1986, s 95.

---

262 Duty of liquidator to call general meeting at end of each year

(1) Subject to section 264, in the event of the winding up continuing for more than one year, the liquidator shall summon a general meeting of the company at the end of the first year from the commencement of the winding up, and of each succeeding year, or at the first convenient date within 3 months from the end of the year and shall lay before the meeting an account of his acts and dealings and of the conduct of the winding up

during the preceding year and shall within 7 days after such meeting send a copy of that account to the registrar.

(2) If the liquidator fails to comply with this section, he [shall be guilty of an offence and liable to a fine][a] not exceeding [€1,904.61].[b]

Amendments

a Words substituted by C(AA)A 2003, s 57 and Sch 2.

b '£250' substituted for '£50' by C(A)A 1982, Sch 1. '£250' increased to '£1,000' by CA 1990, s 145 and further increased to £1,500 by CA 1990, s 240(7) as inserted by CLEA 2001, s104. £1,500 converted to €1,904.61 by Council Regulations (EC) No 1103/97, No 974/98 and No 2866/98 and the Economic and Monetary Union Act 1998, s 6. See also CA 1990, s 145(2).

Cross references

See also CA 1963, s 264.

Proceedings for a breach of the section may be brought and prosecuted by the Registrar of Companies: C(A)A 1982, s 16.

Definitions

'company': CA 1963, s 2(1).

UK legislation

See IA 1986, s 93.

263 Final meeting and dissolution

(1) Subject to section 264, as soon as the affairs of the company are fully wound up, the liquidator shall make up an account of the winding up showing how the winding up has been conducted and the property of the company has been disposed of, and thereupon shall call a general meeting of the company for the purpose of laying before it the account and giving any explanation thereof.

(2) The meeting shall be called by advertisement in 2 daily newspapers circulating in the district where the registered office of the company is situate, specifying the time, place and object thereof, and published 28 days at least before the meeting.

(3) Within one week after the meeting, the liquidator shall send to the registrar of companies a copy of the account, and shall make a return to him of the holding of the meeting and of its date, and if the copy is not sent or the return is not made in accordance with this subsection, the liquidator [shall be guilty of an offence and liable to a fine][a] not exceeding [€1,904.61],[b] so, however, that if a quorum is not present at the meeting, the liquidator shall, in lieu of the return hereinbefore mentioned, make a return that the meeting was duly summoned and that no quorum was present thereat, and upon such a return being made, the provisions of this subsection as to the making of the return shall be deemed to have been complied with.

(4) Subject to subsection (5), the registrar on receiving the account and either of the returns hereinbefore mentioned shall forthwith register them, and on the expiration of 3 months from the registration of the return the company shall be deemed to be dissolved.

(5) The court may, on the application of the liquidator or of any other person who appears to the court to be interested, make an order deferring the date at which the dissolution of the company is to take effect for such time as the court thinks fit.

(6) It shall be the duty of the person on whose application an order of the court under this section is made, within 14 days after the making of the order, to deliver to the registrar an office copy of the order for registration, and if that person fails so to do he [shall be guilty of an offence and liable to a fine][a] not exceeding [€1,904.61].[c]

(7) If the liquidator fails to call a general meeting of the company as required by this section, he [shall be guilty of an offence and liable to a fine][a] not exceeding [€1,904.61].[d]

Amendments

a Words substituted by C(AA)A 2003, s 57 and Sch 2.

b '£500' substituted for '£100' by C(A)A 1982, Sch 1 and increased to £1,500 by CA 1990, s 240(7) as inserted by CLEA 2001, s 104. £1,500 converted to €1,904.61 by Council Regulations (EC) No 1103/97, No 974/98 and No 2866/98 and the Economic and Monetary Union Act 1998, s 6.

c '£25' substituted for '£5' by C(A)A 1982, Sch 1 and increased to £1,500 by CA 1990, s 240(7) as inserted by CLEA 2001, s 104. £1,500 converted to €1,904.61 by Council Regulations (EC) No 1103/97, No 974/98 and No 2866/98 and the Economic and Monetary Union Act 1998, s 6.

d '£250' substituted for '£25' by C(A)A 1982, Sch 1 and increased to £1,500 by CA 1990, s 240(7) as inserted by CLEA 2001, s 104. £1,500 converted to €1,904.61 by Council Regulations (EC) No 1103/97, No 974/98 and No 2866/98 and the Economic and Monetary Union Act 1998, s 6.

Cross reference

See also CA 1963, s 264.

As regards the power of the court to declare the dissolution void and restore the name of the company to the register, see CA 1963, s 310.

Proceedings for a breach of the section may be brought and prosecuted by the Registrar of Companies: C(A)A 1982, s 16. In addition, a breach of CA 1963, s 263(3) may also constitute an offence under CA 1990, s 145.

Definitions

'company': CA 1963, s 2(1); 'the court': CA 1963, s 2(1); 'the registrar of companies': CA 1963, s 2(1).

Notes

Setting aside dissolution: Any dissolution of a company pursuant to CA 1963, s 263 can be declared to be void within two years upon the application of a liquidator or any interested person. If a dissolution is set aside it is as if the company was never dissolved.[1] See notes to CA 1963, s 310.

1 CA 1963, s 310.

UK legislation

See IA 1986, ss 94, 201.

264 Alternative provisions as to annual and final meetings if liquidator is of opinion that company unable to pay its debts

(1) Subject to subsection (2), where section 261 has effect, sections 272 and 273 shall apply to the winding up to the exclusion of sections 262 and 263, as if the winding up were a creditors' voluntary winding up and not a members' voluntary winding up.

(2) The liquidator shall not be required to summon a meeting of creditors under section 272 at the end of the first year from the commencement of the winding up, unless the meeting held under section 261 is held more than 3 months before the end of that year.

Cross reference

See also CA 1963, ss 261, 262, 263, 272, 273.

See also CA 1963, ss 261, 272.

Definitions

'company': CA 1963, s 2(1); 'creditors' voluntary winding up': CA 1963, s 2(1), s 256(7); 'member': CA 1963, s 31; 'members' voluntary winding up': CA 1963, s 2(1), s 256(7).

UK legislation

See IA 1986, s 96.

Provisions applicable to a Creditors' Voluntary Winding Up

265 Provisions applicable to a creditors' voluntary winding up

Sections 266 to 273, shall apply in relation to a creditors' voluntary winding up.

Cross reference

See also CA 1963, ss 266, 273.

Definitions

'creditors' voluntary winding up': CA 1963, s 2(1), s 256(7).

UK legislation

See IA 1986, s 97.

266 Meeting of creditors

(1) The company shall cause a meeting of the creditors of the company to be summoned for the day, or the day next following the day, on which there is to be held the meeting at which the resolution for voluntary winding up is to be proposed, and shall cause the notices of the said meeting of creditors to be sent by post to the creditors at least 10 days before the date of the said meeting of the company.

(2) The company shall cause notice of the meeting of the creditors to be advertised [, at least ten days before the date of the meeting,][a] once at least in 2 daily newspapers circulating in the district where the registered office or principal place of business of the company is situate.

(3) The directors of the company shall—

(a) cause a full statement of the position of the company's affairs, together with a list of the creditors of the company and the estimated amount of their claims to be laid before the meeting of the creditors to be held as aforesaid; and

(b) appoint one of their number to preside at the said meeting.

(4) It shall be the duty of the director appointed to preside at the meeting of creditors to attend the meeting and preside thereat.

(5) If the meeting of the company at which the resolution for voluntary winding up is to be proposed is adjourned and the resolution is passed at an adjourned meeting, any resolution passed at the meeting of the creditors held in pursuance of subsection (1) shall have effect as if it had been passed immediately after the passing of the resolution for winding up the company.

[(6) If default is made—

(a) by the company in complying with subsections (1) and (2);

(b) by the directors of the company in complying with subsection (3);

(c) by any director of the company in complying with subsection (4);

the company, directors or director, as the case may be, shall be guilty of an offence and liable to a fine not exceeding €1,904.61, and in case of default by the company, every officer of the company who is in default shall be guilty of an offence and liable to a fine not exceeding €1,904.61.][b]

Amendments

a Words inserted by CA 1990, s 130.

b Subsection (6) substituted by C(AA)A 2003, s 57 and Sch 2.

Cross-reference

See also CA 1990, s 131 which limits the power of a liquidator nominated by the members to act in relation to the affairs of the company pending the holding of the creditors' meeting.

Definitions

'company': CA 1963, s 2(1); 'director': CA 1963, s 2(1); 'officer': CA 1963, s 2(1); 'a resolution for voluntary winding up': CA 1963, s 2(1), s 251(2).

Notes

Publication: As is set out in CA 1963, s 266(1) a creditors' meeting must be held on the same day or the day next following the members' general meeting. Notices of the creditors' meeting must be sent by post to the creditors at least ten days before the date of the meeting[1] together with two proxy forms[2] giving the creditors the right to appoint the Chairman of the meeting or someone else by proxy.[3] An advertisement should be placed at least ten days before the creditors' meeting, once at least, in two daily newspapers circulating in the district where the company has its registered office or principal place of business.[4]

1 CA 1963, s 266 (1).

2 RSC 1986, Ord 74, r 76.

3 RSC 1986, Ord 74, r 77.

4 CA 1963, s 266(2).

Procedures to be adopted: The procedures to be adopted are determined by the Rules of the Superior Court 1986. Order 74, r 66 provides that the quorum must be three creditors provided that if there are less than three creditors present those present must represent all of the company's creditors. Unless a quorum is present a meeting may not act for any purpose apart from the election of the chairman and the adjournment of the meeting.

Votes of unsecured creditors: In order to be entitled to vote a creditor must have an ascertained debt and a creditor shall not be entitled to vote in respect of any unliquidated or contingent debt, the value of which is not ascertained.[1]

1 RSC 1986, Ord 74, r 68.

Votes of secured creditors: A secured creditor is only allowed to vote at a meeting of creditors in respect of the amount of the debt (if any) which is not secured. If a vote is taken over a secured part of his debt this has the effect of surrendering the security unless the court is satisfied that the omission was due to inadvertence.[1] It is not usual for a secured creditor to vote at a meeting and they will generally not become involved in the liquidation and seek to rely upon their security.

1 RSC 1986, Ord 74, r 69.

Admission or rejection of proof of debts: The Chairman of the meeting is given the power to admit or reject a proof for the purpose of voting, subject to an appeal to the High Court.[1] A creditor is entitled to have his claim admitted to proof, and to be permitted to vote accordingly, if the debt claimed by him is not one excluded by RSC 1986, Ord 74, r 68. If the claim was clearly excluded by r 68, then the chairman is entitled to reject it, subject to appeal to the High Court. However, in the event of doubt, the chairman ought to allow the creditor to vote subject to that vote being declared invalid in the event of the objection being sustained.[2]

1 RSC 1986, Ord 74, r 71.

2 RSC 1986, Ord 74, r 71 expressly provides that a decision of the chairman to reject a claim is subject to an appeal. However, neither r 71 itself, nor any other provision of Ord 74, gives any real guidance as to the nature and extent of such appeal, though some assistance can be obtained from the decision of the High Court in *In Re Titan Transport Logistics Ltd* (In voluntary liquidation) (19 February 2003, unreported) HC (Kelly J). In that case the court refused the challenge to the vote. Kelly J expressed the view that the application should have been made within a two-week period despite the fact that the rules did not lay down a time limit. Clearly, in the event of a contest the application should be made immediately. In principle, it would seem that, if the court determines that a claim has been wrongly rejected, it ought to make whatever consequential orders as are necessary to give full effect to that determination.

Failure to comply with s 266: If default is made in complying with CA 1963, s 266(1) or CA 1963, s 266(2) by a company or by directors, an application can be made to court for directions.[1] Pending the holding of the creditors' meeting, the liquidator's powers are circumscribed in the manner laid down in CA 1990, s 131.

1 CA 1990, s 131.

UK legislation

See IA 1986, ss 98, 99.

267 Appointment of liquidator

(1) Subject to subsection (2), the creditors and the company at their respective meetings mentioned in section 266 may nominate a person to be liquidator for the purpose of winding up the affairs and distributing the assets of the company, and if the creditors and the company nominate different persons, the person nominated by the creditors shall be liquidator, and if no person is nominated by the creditors, the person, if any, nominated by the company shall be liquidator.

(2) Where different persons are nominated as liquidator, any director, member or creditor of the company may, within 14 days after the date on which the nomination was made by the creditors, apply to the court for an order either directing that the person nominated as liquidator by the company shall be liquidator instead of or jointly with the person nominated by the creditors, or appointing some other person to be liquidator instead of the person appointed by the creditors.

[(3) If at a meeting of creditors mentioned in section 266(1) a resolution as to the creditors' nominee as liquidator is proposed, it shall be deemed to be passed when a majority, in value only, of the creditors present personally or by proxy and voting on the resolution have voted in favour of the resolution.][a]

Amendments

a Subsection (3) inserted by CLEA 2001, s 47.

Cross references in other enactments

See also CA 1963, s 266.

NAMA Act 2009, s 150(2) provides:

> 'The appointment of a liquidator to a company whose assets or any part of them are under the control of a statutory receiver does not displace the statutory receiver and does not affect his or her powers, authority and agency.'

Definitions

'company': CA 1963, s 2(1); 'the court': CA 1963, s 2(1); 'director': CA 1963, s 2(1); 'member': CA 1963, s 31.

Notes

Resolution for the appointment of a liquidator: In the case of a resolution to appoint the creditors' nominee as liquidator, the resolution is deemed to be passed when a majority in value only of the creditors present personally or by proxy and voting on the resolution have voted in favour of the resolution.[1] For all other resolutions the resolution is deemed passed when a majority in number and value of those present personally or by proxy vote in favour.[2] There will be no basis for disregarding the votes of directors of the company who are also connected creditors in the absence of sufficient evidence to merit a finding that the asserted debts were significantly exaggerated if not largely fictitious and included in the statement of affairs to defeat an anticipated motion for a creditor's nominee to be appointed instead.[3]

1 CA 1963, s 267(3). This subsection was inserted by CLEA 2001, s 47 so as to overcome a problem that often arose in practice whereby the directors of a company might procure proxies from a large number of creditors with small claims and use those proxies to vote in favour of the members' nominee. This could lead to a most unsatisfactory position whereby the vast majority in value of the creditors might want to appoint someone other than the members' nominee but

would be prevented from doing so because they did not also represent the majority in number of the creditors' votes being cast.

2 RSC 1986, Ord 74, r 62.

3 *Re Balbradagh Developments Ltd* [2009] 1 IR 597.

Displacing the liquidator appointed at a meeting of creditors.[1] If a party wishes to displace a liquidator who has been appointed at the creditors' meeting, he has a number of options. Either an application can be made under CA 1963, s 267(2) or alternatively under CA 1963, s 282 asking the court to allow the winding up proceed as a compulsory winding up. The court, when considering whether or not to proceed with a voluntary liquidation or a compulsory liquidation, will have due regard to the costs involved in the winding up by the court and the delays which will be incurred compared to the overall value of the assets to be administered and the complexity or simplicity of the task facing the liquidator.[2] The court should be disposed to replacing a voluntary liquidator if the evidence suggests that the goodwill of the business has gone to an associated company without payment and the liquidation is in the hands of a nominee of the person who had control over both the company and the connected or associated companies and where the nominee of the majority creditors who stand to lose substantial moneys has been rejected.[3] An order may be made directing the liquidation to proceed as a compulsory liquidation where there is found to be some wrongdoing by the company which needs to be investigated or where it can be shown that the directors of the company are removing assets from the company before the winding up.[4] Dissatisfaction as to the conduct of the creditor's meeting is not usually sufficient to persuade the court to allow the liquidation proceed as a compulsory liquidation.[5] In exercising its discretion the court is not obliged to give equal weight to all debts of an equal amount and may have due regard to the interests of non-connected creditors.[6]

1 See generally O'Donnell, 'Opposing A Creditor's Voluntary Liquidation – Learning to Swallow a Bitter Pill' 1995 CLP 79.

2 O'Hanlon J in *In the Matter of Gilt Construction Ltd* (1994) 2 ILRM 456 as approved by McCracken J in *In the Matter of Naiad Ltd* (13 February 1995, unreported) and *In the Matter of Eurochick Ireland Ltd* [1998] IEHC 51 (McCracken J).

3 *In the matter of Hayes Homes Ltd* [2004] IEHC 124; see also *Parma Surveys Ltd* [1986] BCLC 106; *Falcon RJ Developments Ltd* [1987] BCLC 437.

4 *In the matter of Eurochick Ireland Ltd* [1998] IEHC 51 (McCracken J).

5 *In Re Naiad* (13 February 1995, unreported) HC (McCracken J).

6 *Re Falcon RJ Developments Ltd* [1987] BCLC 437: as accepted by Costello J in an ex-tempore judgment of *Metro Express Ireland Ltd (In Liquidation)*. See also *Re George Downs & Co Ltd* [1943] IR 420; *Re Wicklow Textiles Ltd* (1953) 87 ILTR 72; *Swain (JD) Ltd* [1965] 2 All ER 761; *Re Medisco Equipment Ltd* [1983] BCLC 305; *Re Lowerstoft Traffic Services Ltd* [1986] BCLC 81; *Re Falcon RJ Developments Ltd* [1987] BCLC 437; *Re HJ Thomkins & Son Ltd* [1990] BCLC 76.

Appointment of liquidator. Certain persons are disqualified from acting or being appointed as a liquidator.[1] A creditor who has a connection with the proposed liquidator must make known the connection to the chairman who must in turn disclose the fact to the meeting before any resolution is put to the creditors for the appointment of the proposed liquidator.[2] The appointment of a liquidator shall be of no effect unless he has, prior to his appointment, signified his consent in writing to the appointment.[3]

1 CA 1963, ss 300, 300(A) and 301.

2 CA 1963, s 301(A).

3 CA 1963, s 276(A).

UK legislation

See IA 1986, s 100.

[267A Confirmation of creditors' voluntary winding up

(1) Where—

(a) a liquidator is appointed in a creditors' voluntary winding up of a company in pursuance of section 267, and

(b) the centre of the company's main interests is situated in the State,

the Master of the High Court may, on application by the liquidator in the prescribed form and payment of the prescribed fee, confirm the creditors' voluntary winding up for the purposes of the Insolvency Regulation and shall so certify.][a]

Amendments

a Inserted by EC(CI)R 2002, reg 3.

Notes

Confirmation of winding up: This section enables the liquidator to have the winding up confirmed by the court, so as to allow for the recognition and enforcement of the liquidation in the other members states of the EU governed by the EC(CI)R 2002. In this regard, se generally the notes to EC(CI)R 2002, infra.

---

268 Appointment of committee of inspection

(1) Subject to subsection (2), the creditors at the meeting to be held in pursuance of section 266 or at any subsequent meeting may, if they think fit, appoint a committee of inspection consisting of not more than five persons, and, if such committee is appointed the company may, either at the meeting at which the resolution for voluntary winding up is passed or at any time subsequently in general meeting, appoint three persons to act as members of the committee, provided that the number of members of the committee shall not at any time exceed eight.

(2) The creditors may, if they think fit, resolve that all or any of the persons so appointed by the company ought not to be members of the committee of inspection, and if the creditors so resolve, the persons mentioned in the resolution shall not, unless the court otherwise directs, be qualified to act as members of the committee, and on any application to the court under this subsection the court may, if it thinks fit, appoint other persons to act as such members in place of the persons mentioned in the resolution.

(3) Subject to subsections (1) and (2), and to rules of court, section 233 (except subsection (1)) shall apply to a committee of inspection appointed under this section as it applies to a committee of inspection appointed in a winding up by the court.

Cross-reference

See also CA 1963, s 266.

See also CA 1963, s 233.

For the applicable rules of court, see RSC 1986, Ord 74, rr 50–53.

Definitions

'company': CA 1963, s 2(1); 'the court': CA 1963, s 2(1); 'member': CA 1963, s 31; 'a resolution for voluntary winding up': CA 1963, s 2(1), s 251(2).

Notes

General: The power to appoint a committee of inspection is given to the creditors.[1] It will consist of no more than five nominees of the creditor and three of the company.[2] The members of the committee of inspection may not purchase the assets of the company nor may they make a profit from the winding up, except with the leave of the court or the sanction of a general meeting of the creditors.[3]

1 CA 1963, s 268(2).
2 CA 1963, s 268(1).
3 *Dowling v Lord Advocate* (1963) SLT 146.

Procedure: The constitution of and proceedings relating to the committee of inspection is set out in CA 1963, s 233 and also in Ord 74, rr 50–53. The proceedings are similar for both a creditors' voluntary winding up and a compulsory winding up.[1] The members of the committee of inspection are not entitled to be paid but are entitled to recoup their expenses.[2]

1 For status of committee of inspection see notes to s 232. For procedure see notes to CA 1963, s 233.
2 RSC 1986, Ord 74, r 129.

UK legislation

See IA 1986, s 101.

269 Fixing of liquidators' remuneration and cesser of directors' powers

(1) The committee of inspection, or if there is no such committee, the creditors, may fix the remuneration to be paid to the liquidator or liquidators.

(2) Within 28 days after the remuneration to be paid to the liquidator or liquidators has been fixed by the committee of inspection or by the creditors, any creditor or contributory who alleges that such remuneration is excessive may apply to the court to fix the remuneration to be paid to the liquidator or liquidators.

(3) On the appointment of a liquidator, all the powers of the directors shall cease, except so far as the committee of inspection or, if there is no such committee, the creditors, sanction the continuance thereof.

Cross reference

As regards the effect of a members' voluntary winding up on the powers of the directors, see CA 1963, s 258.

Definitions

'contributory': CA 1963, s 2(1), s 208; 'the court': CA 1963, s 2(1); 'director': CA 1963, s 2(1).

Notes

Liquidator's remuneration: If the liquidator's remuneration is not fixed by the committee of inspection or the creditors it may be fixed instead by the court.[1] See notes to CA 1963, s 228 as to quantum of liquidator's remuneration.

Cessation of powers of directors: In the case of a compulsory liquidation the powers of the director automatically cease and they become *functus officio* upon the making of the winding-up order.[2] In a voluntary liquidation all powers of the directors shall cease (in the absence of a sanction from the committee of inspection or the creditors where there is no committee). Normally, the powers of directors will not be continued under this section.[3]

1 *Re Amalgamated Syndicates Ltd* [1901] 2 Ch 181.

2 *Re Union Accident Insurance Co Ltd* [1972] 1 All ER 1105; *Re Mawcon Ltd* [1969] 1 All ER 118: *Re Farrow's Bank Ltd* [1921] 2 Ch 164: *Re Ebsworth & Tidy's Contract* (1889) 42 Ch D 23. See also notes to CA 1963, s 228.

3 See generally Lynch, Marshall and O'Ferrall, *Corporate Insolvency and Rescue* (Tottel Publishing, 1996) at para 3.49.

UK legislation

See IA 1986, s 103.

270 Power to fill vacancy in office of liquidator

If a vacancy occurs by death, resignation or otherwise in the office of a liquidator, other than a liquidator appointed by, or by the direction of, the court, the creditors may fill the vacancy.

Cross reference

In relation to the qualifications and independence of the liquidator, see CA 1963, ss 300, 300A, 301.

Definitions

'the court': CA 1963, s 2(1).

Notes

General: If a liquidator appointed in a members' voluntary winding up dies or resigns, the company in general meeting may fill the vacancy.[1] The court has the power to remove a liquidator and appoint another liquidator on cause shown.[2] Any creditor who has a connection with the proposed liquidator must make known the connection to the chairman who must in turn disclose the fact to the meeting before any resolution is put to the creditors for the appointment of the proposed liquidator.[3]

1 CA1963, s 259.

2 CA 1963, s 277.

3 CA 1963, s 301A.

UK legislation

See IA 1986, s 104.

271 Application of section 260 to a creditors' voluntary winding up

Section 260 shall apply in the case of a creditors' voluntary winding up as in the case of a members' voluntary winding up, with the modification that the powers of the liquidator under that section shall not be exercised except with the sanction either of the court or of the committee of inspection.

Cross reference

See also CA 1963, s 260.

Definitions

'the court': CA 1963, s 2(1); 'creditors' voluntary winding up': CA 1963, s 2(1), s 256(7); 'member': CA 1963, s 31; 'members' voluntary winding up': CA 1963, s 2(1), s 256(7).

UK legislation

See IA 1986, ss 110, 111.

272 Duty of liquidator to call meetings of company and of creditors at end of each year

(1) In the event of the winding up continuing for more than one year, the liquidator shall summon a general meeting of the company and a meeting of the creditors at the end of the first year from the commencement of the winding up, and of each succeeding year, or at the first convenient date within 3 months from the end of the year, and shall lay before the meetings an account of his acts and dealings and of the conduct of the winding up during the preceding year and shall within 7 days after the later of such meetings send a copy of that account to the registrar.

(2) If the liquidator fails to comply with this section, he [shall be guilty of an offence and liable to a fine][a] not exceeding [€1,904.61].[b]

Amendments

a Words substituted by C(AA)A 2003, s 57 and Sch 2.

b '£1000' substitued for '£250' by CA 1990, s 145 and increased to £1,500 by CA 1990, s 240(7) as inserted by CLEA 2001, s 104. £1,500 converted to €1,904.61 by Council Regulations (EC) No 1103/97, No 974/98 and No 2866/98 and the Economic and Monetary Union Act 1998, s 6. See also CA 1990, s 145(2).

Cross reference

Apart from meetings under CA 1963, s 272, the liquidator may himself from time to time summon, hold and conduct meetings of creditors for the purpose of ascertaining their wishes in all matters relating to the winding up: CA 1963, s 309 and RSC 1986, Ord 74, r 54(2).

Proceedings for a breach of CA 1963, s 272 may be brought and prosecuted by the Registrar of Companies: C(A)A 1982, s 16. For the applicable penalties, see CA 1990, s 145(2).

Definitions

'company': CA 1963, s 2(1).

Notes

General: Apart from meetings under this section, the liquidator may himself from time to time, summon, hold and conduct meetings of creditors for the purposes of ascertaining their wishes in any matters relating to the winding up.[1]

1 CA 1963, s 309 and RSC 1986, Ord 74, r 54(2).

Prosecution of offences: The Registrar of Companies is responsible for prosecuting a failure on the part of the liquidator to call meetings with the company and/or creditors within the meaning of this section.[1]

1 C(A) 1982, s 16. For the applicable penalties, see CA 1990, s 145(2).

UK legislation

See IA 1986, s 105.

---

273 Final meeting and dissolution

(1) As soon as the affairs of the company are fully wound up, the liquidator shall make up an account of the winding up, showing how the winding up has been conducted and the property of the company has been disposed of, and thereupon shall call a general meeting of the company and a meeting of the creditors for the purpose of laying the account before the meetings and giving any explanation thereof.

(2) Each such meeting shall be called by advertisement in 2 daily newspapers circulating in the district where the registered office of the company is situate, specifying the time, place and object thereof, and published 28 days at least before the meeting.

(3) Within one week after the date of the meetings, or if the meetings are not held on the same date, after the date of the later meeting, the liquidator shall send to the registrar of companies a copy of the account, and shall make a return to him of the holding of the meetings and of their dates, and if the copy is not sent or the return is not made in accordance with this subsection, the liquidator [shall be guilty of an offence and liable to a fine][a] not exceeding [€1,904.61],[b] so, however, that if a quorum is not present at either such meeting, the liquidator shall, in lieu of the return hereinbefore mentioned, make a return that the meeting was duly summoned and that no quorum was present thereat, and upon such a return being made, the provisions of this subsection as to the making of the return shall, in respect of that meeting, be deemed to have been complied with.

(4) Subject to subsection (5), the registrar on receiving the account and, in respect of each such meeting, either of the returns hereinbefore mentioned, shall forthwith register them, and on the expiration of 3 months from the registration thereof the company shall be deemed to be dissolved.

(5) The court may, on the application of the liquidator or of any other person who appears to the court to be interested, make an order deferring the date at which the dissolution of the company is to take effect for such time as the court thinks fit.

(6) It shall be the duty of the person on whose application an order of the court under this section is made, within 14 days after the making of the order, to deliver to the registrar an office copy of the order for registration, and if that person fails so to do, he [shall be guilty of an offence and liable to a fine][a] not exceeding [€1,904.61].[b]

(7) If the liquidator fails to call a general meeting of the company or a meeting of the creditors as required by this section, he [shall be guilty of an offence and liable for a fine][a] not exceeding [€1,904.61].[b]

Amendments

a Words substituted by C(AA)A 2003, s 57 and Sch 2.

b '£250' substituted for '£50' by C(A)A 1982, Sch 1, increased to £1,500 by CA 1990, s 240(7) as inserted by CLEA 2001, s104 and converted to €1,904.61 by Council Regulations (EC) No 1103/97, No 974/98 and No 2866/98 and the Economic and Monetary Union Act 1998, s 6. See also CA 1990, s 145(2).

Cross reference

Proceedings for a breach of CA 1963, s 272 may be brought and prosecuted by the Registrar of Companies: C(A)A 1982, s 16. A breach of s 273(3) is also an offence under CA 1990, s 145 .

Definitions

'company': CA 1963, s 2(1); 'the court': CA 1963, s 2(1); 'the registrar of companies': CA 1963, s 2(1).

Notes

Affairs of the company fully wound up: The company is dissolved three months following the liquidator filing a return with the Registrar of Companies. It is not necessary that the affairs of the company have been fully wound up before the liquidator can validly make his return, only that they should have been fully wound up so far as the liquidator is aware. If the liquidator had discharged all the liabilities of which he was aware when he made his final account and the registration was affected under the provisions of this section, the company is deemed to be dissolved three months after the date of such registration.[1]

1 *In Re Cornish Manures Ltd* [1967] 1 WLR 807. In this case the liquidator made arrangements for a final meeting and received a demand for tax a day after the final meeting. A creditor of the company issued a motion outside the two-year time provided for under the equivalent section of CA1963, s 310 seeking a declaration that their dissolution was void. On the question of whether or not the court had jurisdiction to re-open the liquidation on the grounds that the company was not fully wound up, the court held that the affairs had been fully wound within the meaning of this section. As more than two years had elapsed of dissolution, the application was refused.

Prosecution of offences: The Registrar of Companies is responsible for prosecuting a failure on the part of the liquidator under CA 1963, s 273(3).[1] A breach of CA 1963, s 273(3) is also an offence under CA 1990, s 145.

1 C (A) 1982, s 16.

Setting aside dissolution. Any dissolution of a company under CA 1963, s 273 can be declared to be void within two years upon the application of a liquidator or any interested person. If dissolution is set aside and the company is placed back on the Company Register, the company is treated as if it had never been dissolved.[1]

1 CA 1963, s 310.

UK legislation

See IA 1986, ss 106, 201.

Provisions applicable to every Voluntary Winding Up

274 Provisions applicable to every voluntary winding up

Sections 275 to 282 shall apply to every voluntary winding up whether a members' or a creditors' winding up.

Cross reference

See also CA 1963, ss 275–282.

Definitions

'member': CA 1963, s 31.

275 [Distribution of property of company

(1) Subject to the provisions of this Act as to preferential payments, the property of a company on its winding up—

(a) shall, subject to subsection (2), be applied in satisfaction of its liabilities *pari passu*, and

(b) shall, subject to such application, and unless the articles otherwise provide, be distributed among the members according to their rights and interests in the company.

(2) Nothing in paragraph (a) of subsection (1) shall in any way affect any rights or obligations of the company or any other person arising as a result of any agreement entered into (whether before or after the commencement of section 132 of the Companies Act, 1990) by any person under which any particular liability of the company to any general creditor is postponed in favour of or subordinated to the rights or claims of any other person to whom the company may be in any way liable.

(3) In subsection (2)—

'liability' includes a contingent liability; and
'person' includes a class of persons.][a]

Amendments

CA 1963, s 275 substituted by CA 1990, s 132.

Cross references

See also CA 1990, s 132.

As regards preferential debts, see CA 1963, s 285.

Definitions

'articles': CA 1963, s 2(1); 'company': CA 1963, s 2(1); 'member': CA 1963, s 31.

Notes

***Parri passu* principle of distribution**: The general rule enshrined in insolvency law is that creditors of an insolvent company are to be paid *parri passu* so that if the assets are insufficient to pay all creditors fully, they are paid in equal proportion to their debts. The courts defend the principle of *parri passu* and where the effect of a contract is that an asset which is owned by a company at the commencement of its liquidation would be dealt with otherwise than to that extent, the contract as a matter of public policy is voided, whether or not the contract was entered into for consideration and for bona fide commercial reasons and whether or not the contractual provision affecting those assets is expressed to take effect only on insolvency.[1] The *parri passu* principle set out in CA 1963, s 275(1) is not to be interpreted as meaning that every contract is void by which a party to it obtains rights over a company's assets superior to those given to ordinary creditors under this section. Such an interpretation would mean, for example, that retention of title clauses in contracts for the sale of goods, and clauses in building contracts conferring rights and builder owners over retention moneys would be void, which is obviously not the case.[2] The section only impugns a transaction if a contract is one for the disposal of an asset belonging to the company.[3] However, as insolvency law has evolved, there have been many exceptions to this rule such as CA 1963, s 285 which deals with preferential debts.[4] Furthermore secured creditors prove their debt outside the liquidation and therefore are not subject to the *parri passu* rule.

1 A summary of the case of *British Eagle International Airlines Ltd v Air France* [1975] 1 WLR 758 by Peter Gibson J in *Carreras Rothmans Ltd v Freeman Matthews Treasure Ltd* [1985] Ch 207. See also *Perpetual Trustee Co Ltd v BNY Corporate Trustee Services Ltd* [2009] 2 BCLC 400.

2 As per Costello J in *Glow Heating Ltd v The Eastern Health Board* [1988] IR 110.

3 *Glow Heating v The Eastern Health Board, Patrick Rooney and others* [1998] IR 110.

4 See notes to CA1963, s 285 below.

Subordination agreements: CA 1963, s 275(2) provides for another exception to the *parri passu* principle for agreements commonly known as subordination agreements. A subordination agreement is an agreement under which an unsecured creditor agrees with another unsecured creditor to be paid off at a different time.

Compulsory liquidations: Although the principle of *parri passu* distribution is only expressly referred to in the Companies Acts in the context of voluntary liquidations, nevertheless, it also applies to compulsory liquidations.[1] It is of note that there is no provision for the subordination of claims in a compulsory winding up.

1 CA 1963, s 284 states that in the winding up of an insolvent company 'the same rules shall prevail and be observed relating to the respective rights of secured and unsecured creditors and to debts provable and to the valuation of annuities and future and contingent liabilities as in force for the time being under the laws of bankruptcy relating to the estates of persons adjudged bankrupt.' This has been interpreted by Lynch, Marshall and O'Ferrall, in *Corporate Insolvency and Rescue* (Tottel Publishing, 1996) as implying that the principle of *parri passu* applies to compulsory liquidations. See also *Attorney General v McMillen & Loughwood Ltd* [1991] 1ZLR 53; Oditah, 'Treatment of Claims and Insolvency' 108 LQR [1992] 459 at 463–468.

Returns to members in case of solvency:[1] Where a surplus arises in liquidation it is presumed that all classes of shareholders rank equally as regards a return of capital and as regards participation of any surplus assets.[2] In the absence of some other express provision to the contrary, a provision conferring priority as to a return of capital in a winding up on one class of shareholders will not be deemed to exhaust the rights of that class to participate rateably in any surplus of assets.[3] It is presumed, in the absence of an express provision to the contrary, that cumulative preference shareholders are not entitled to arrears of undeclared dividends in a winding up. However, this presumption may be readily rebutted.[4] Members who are owed dividends by the company when it goes into liquidation do not lose their claims although they do not rate as creditors. They are only paid after all other creditors have been paid.[5]

1 See generally notes to CA 1963, s 78.

2 *Birch v Cropper* (1889) 14 App Cas 525.

3 *Re Cork Electric Supply Co Ltd* [1932] IR 314: *Re William Metcalf & Son Ltd* [1933] Ch 142.

4 *F De Jong & Co Ltd* [1946] Ch 211: *Re E Gap W Savory* [1951] 2 All ER 1036.

5 See *Wilson (Inspector of Taxes) v Dunnes Stores (Cork) Ltd* (22 January 1976, unreported) HC, per Kenny J.

UK legislation

See IA 1986, s 107.

276 Powers and duties of liquidator in voluntary winding up

(1) The liquidator may—

(a) in the case of a members' voluntary winding up, with the sanction of a special resolution of the company, and, in the case of a creditors' voluntary winding up, with the sanction of the court or the committee of inspection or (if there is no such committee) a meeting of the creditors, exercise any of the powers given by paragraphs (d), (e) and (f) of subsection (1) of section 231 to a liquidator in a winding up by the court;

(b) without sanction, exercise any of the other powers by this Act given to the liquidator in a winding up by the court;

(c) exercise the power of the court under this Act of settling a list of contributories, and the list of contributories shall be *prima facie* evidence of the liability of persons named therein to be contributories;

(d) exercise the power of the court of making calls;

(e) summon general meetings of the company for the purpose of obtaining the sanction of the company by resolution or for any other purpose he may think fit.

(2) The liquidator shall pay the debts of the company and shall adjust the rights of the contributories among themselves.

(3) When several liquidators are appointed, any power given by this Act may be exercised by such one or more of them as may be determined at the time of their appointment, or, in default of such determination, by any number not less than two.

Definitions

'company': CA 1963, s 2(1); 'contributory': CA 1963, s 2(1), s 208; 'the court': CA 1963, s 2(1).

Notes

Limitation of the liquidator's powers pending the meeting of creditors: A liquidator who has been appointed by the members cannot exercise most of the powers granted to him by CA 1963, s 276 before the creditors' meeting is held. The limitation does not apply to the liquidator's power to (a) take into his custody and under his control all the property to which the company is or appears to be entitled; (b) dispose of perishable goods and other goods the value of which is likely to diminish if they are not immediately disposed of; and (c) do all such things as may be necessary for the protection of the company's assets.[1]

1 CA 1990, s 131(3). This section was inserted to end the practice which became known as 'Centre-Binding' after the case of *Re Centre Bind Ltd*. In that case the members of an insolvent company put the company into voluntary liquidation and appointed a liquidator. Prior to the creditors' meeting the liquidator prevented the UK Inland Revenue from proceeding against the company's assets. Although it was later held to have been a valid exercise of his powers it was believed that less scrupulous companies might have caused a members' meeting to be held for the sole purpose of appointing a liquidator with whom they could collude so as to have the assets of the company acquired by another company controlled by them.

UK legislation

See IA 1986, ss 165, 166, Sch 4.

[276A Consent to appointment as liquidator and notification of appointment

(1) The appointment of a liquidator shall be of no effect unless the person nominated has, prior to his appointment, signified his written consent to the appointment.

(2) The chairman of any meeting at which a liquidator is appointed shall, within 7 days of the meeting, notify the liquidator in writing of his appointment, unless the liquidator or his duly authorised representative is present at the meeting where the appointment is made.

(3) A person who fails to comply with subsection (2) [shall be guilty of an offence and liable to a fine][b] not exceeding [€1,904.61][c].][a]

Amendments

a CA 1963, s 276A substituted by CA 1990, s 133.

b Words substituted by C(AA)A 2003, s 57 and Sch 2.

c £1,000 to increased to £1,500 by CA 1990, s 240(7) as inserted by CLEA 2001, s 104. £1,500 converted to €1,904.61 by Council Regulations (EC) No 1103/97, No 974/98 and No 2866/98 and the Economic and Monetary Union Act 1998, s 6.

Notes

General: Prior to the enactment of this section the appointment of a liquidator could be foisted upon an unwilling nominee. It is now essential that the liquidator's consent is obtained. If there is a failure to obtain his consent, the appointment of the liquidator is not valid.

277 Power of court to appoint and remove liquidator in a voluntary winding up

(1) If from any cause whatever there is no liquidator acting, the court may appoint a liquidator.

(2) The court may, on cause shown, remove a liquidator and appoint another liquidator.

Definitions

'the court': CA 1963, s 2(1).

Notes

General: For removing the liquidator on cause shown, see notes to CA 1963, s 228. In relation to the power of the court to fill vacancies in the office of liquidator in members' and creditors' voluntary winding up, respectively, see CA 1963, ss 259(1), 270. In appropriate circumstances there might be good cause to remove a liquidator notwithstanding the failure of the applicant to prove misfeasance as such and even though no reasonable criticism could be made of his conduct. It might, for example, be appropriate to have a proper investigation of matters relating to intercompany transfers with certain creditors.[1]

1 *Re Buildlead Ltd, Quikson (South and West) Ltd v Katz* [2004] All ER (D) 138 (Aug) where Etherton J allowed an application for the removal of a joint voluntary liquidator. The company in that case entered into a creditors' voluntary liquidation in 1997. Later information was obtained

which raised questions about the relationship between the company and a particular group of creditors and an application was successfully made to have the liquidators removed.

UK legislation

See IA 1986, s 108.

278 Notice by liquidator of his appointment

(1) The liquidator shall, within 14 days after his appointment, deliver to the registrar of companies for registration a notice of his appointment [and the registrar shall forward a copy to the Director][a].

(2) If the liquidator fails to comply with the requirements of this section, he [shall be guilty of an offence and liable to a fine][b] not exceeding [€1,904.61].[c]

Amendments

a Words inserted by CLEA 2001, s 48.

b Words substituted by C(AA)A 2003, s 57 and Sch 2.

c '£250' substituted for '£50' by C(A)A 1982, Sch 1, increased to £1,500 by CA 1990, s 240(7) as inserted by CLEA 2001, s 104 and converted to €1,904.61 by Council Regulations (EC) No 1103/97, No 974/98 and No 2866/98 and the Economic and Monetary Union Act 1998, s 6.

Cross reference

Proceedings for a breach of the section may be brought and prosecuted by the Registrar of Companies: C(A)A 1982, s 16.

Definitions

'the registrar of companies': CA 1963, s 2(1).

UK legislation

See IA 1986, s 109.

279 Provisions as to arrangement binding creditors

(1) Any arrangement entered into between a company about to be, or in the course of being, wound up and its creditors shall, subject to the right of appeal under this section, be binding on the company if sanctioned by a special resolution and on the creditors if acceded to by three-fourths in number and value of the creditors.

(2) Any creditor or contributory may, within 3 weeks from the completion of the arrangement, appeal to the court against it, and the court may thereupon, as it thinks just, amend, vary or confirm the arrangement.

Cross reference

On the power of the liquidator to enter into such arrangements, see CA 1963, s 231(1)(e).

Rather than using CA 1963, s 279 for the arrangement, the liquidator could instead avail of the procedure contained in CA 1963, ss 201–203.

Definitions

'company': CA 1963, s 2(1); 'contributory': CA 1963, s 2(1), s 208; 'the court': CA 1963, s 2(1).

Notes

General: The procedures set out in this section are similar to the powers of the liquidator to avail of a scheme of arrangement under CA 1963, ss 201–203 and may be used as an alternative. Although both sections may be similar, there are differences in that (a) there is no need for permission of the court in this section (as is in the case of CA 1963, ss 201–203); (b) it only applies where the company is about to be or is in the course of being wound up (whereas CA 1963, ss 201–203 applies to both solvent and insolvent companies); and (c) using the procedure under this section there is no form of protection given to a company (unlike the position with companies availing of arrangement under CA 1963, ss 201–203). The requisite majority of creditors is three-fourths in numbers and in value of *all creditors* and not just three-fourths in number and value of those creditors who are attending in person and by proxy and voting at the meeting.

UK legislation

See IA 1986, ss 5, 6.

---

280 Power to apply to court to have questions determined or powers exercised

(1) The liquidator or any contributory or creditor may apply to the court to determine any question arising in the winding up of a company, or to exercise in relation to the enforcing of calls or any other matter, all or any of the powers which the court might exercise if the company were being wound up by the court.

(2) The court, if satisfied that the determination of the question or the required exercise of power will be just and beneficial, may accede wholly or partially to the application on such terms and conditions as it thinks fit or may make such other order on the application as it thinks just.

(3) An office copy of an order made by virtue of this section annulling the resolution to wind up or staying the proceedings in the winding up shall forthwith be forwarded by the company to the registrar of companies for registration.

(4) If a company fails to comply with subsection (3), the company and every officer of the company who is in default [shall be guilty of an offence and liable to a fine][a] not exceeding [€1,904.61].[b]

Amendments

a Words substituted by C(AA)A 2003, s 57 and Sch 2.

b '£125' substituted for '£25' by C(A)A 1982, Sch 1, increased to £1,500 by CA 1990, s 240(7) as inserted by CLEA 2001, s 104 and converted to €1,904.61 by Council Regulations (EC) No 1103/97, No 974/98 and No 2866/98 and the Economic and Monetary Union Act 1998, s 6.

Cross reference

The powers of the court which may be invoked pursuant to CA 1963, s 280 are to be found in CA 1963, ss 234–248.

Applications pursuant to CA 1963, s 280 are brought by way of an Originating Notice of Motion: RSC 1986, Ord 74, r 138 as amended by RSC (No 4) 1991, r 2(4).

Proceedings for a breach of CA 1963, s 280(4) may be brought and prosecuted by the Registrar of Companies: C(A)A 1982, s 16.

Definitions

'company': CA 1963, s 2(1); 'contributory': CA 1963, s 2(1), s 208; 'the court': CA 1963, s 2(1); 'officer': CA 1963, s 2(1); 'the registrar of companies': CA 1963, s 2(1).

Notes

General: The object of allowing liquidations to proceed voluntarily is to allow the company, its contributories and creditors to proceed with the winding up of the company without interference from the court, but at the same time providing them with a means of access to the court if any questions need to be determined.[1] The powers of the court which may invoked pursuant to CA 1963, s 280 are to be found in CA 1963, ss 234–248.

1 *Gilt Construction Ltd (In Voluntary Liquidation)* [1994] 2 ILRM 456 in which O'Hanlon J stated when refusing to allow the winding up proceed as a compulsory winding up, that if any unexpected problems should arise where the guidance of the court is needed by the voluntary liquidator or any contributor or creditor, access to the court has to be provided by CA 1963, s 280.

Practice and procedure: Applications to CA 1963, s 280 are brought by way of originating notice of motion.[1] Where the application under s 280 is by a voluntary liquidator seeking directions, the court should be presented with some overview of the winding up, with the type of report which is furnished to the court in compulsory winding up matters being the appropriate template.[2] The detail required in any case will depend on the case, on the stage which the winding up had reached and the issues which the court has to address on the application for directions.[3]

1 RSC 1986, Ord 74, r 138 as amended by RSC (No 4) 1991, r 4.

2 *Re Olde Court Holiday Hostel Ltd* [2006] IEHC 424.

3 *Re Olde Court Holiday Hostel Ltd* [2006] IEHC 424.

Annulling a resolution to wind up the company: The court is empowered by CA 1963, s 280 in the appropriate case to annul the resolution to wind up a company voluntarily.[1]

1 *In re Oakthorphe Holdings (In Voluntary Liquidation) v the Registrar of Companies* [1987] IR 632 where Carroll J stated that 'by analogy with the power of the Court under CA 1963, s 234 to annul a winding in a Court order by reference at CA 1963, s 280(3) to an order … annulling the resolution to windup the Court was empowered by CA 1963, s 280 to annul the resolution to wind up a company voluntarily. She stated there is no express power conferred on the Court in a voluntary winding up to annul a resolution to wind up. But sub-section 3 of s 280 must be given a meaning. Therefore the reference in sub-section 3 to an order annulling the resolution to wind up must mean that by analogy with the power of the Court in a Court winding up to annul a winding up order the Court in a voluntary winding up annul the resolution to windup in an appropriate case, just as it can stay proceedings'.

UK legislation

See IA 1986, s 112.

281 Costs of voluntary winding up

All costs, charges and expenses properly incurred in the winding up, including the remuneration of the liquidator, shall be payable out of the assets of the company in priority to all other claims.

Cross-reference

See CA 1963, s 244; RSC 1986, Ord 74, r 128 in relation to the order of priority of costs and expenses from a compulsory winding up.

Definitions

'company': CA 1963, s 2(1).

Notes

General: See notes to CA 1963, s 244. The order of priority of costs and expenses in a compulsory liquidation is governed by RSC 1986, Ord 74, r 128.[1] Although RSC 1986, Ord 74, r 128 does not apply to a voluntary liquidation, the order of priority of costs and expenses for a compulsory liquidation will, subject to appropriate modifications, be used as a guide as to the priority of costs and expenses in a voluntary winding up.[2] There is a difference between a voluntary winding up and a compulsory winding up. For a voluntary winding up, CA 1963, s 281 states that 'all costs, charges and expenses' properly incurred are to be paid out of the assets of the company in priority to all other claims. Such costs will include the remuneration of the liquidator. However in a compulsory liquidation, RSC 1986, Ord 74, r 128 distinguishes between the costs associated with the collection and realisation of assets and other costs of the liquidation.[3]

1 See notes to CA 1963, s 244.
2 *Re Redbreast Preserving Co (Ireland) Ltd* [1958] IR 234.
3 RSC 1986, Ord 74, r 128 provides that first the assets in a winding up will be subject to the 'payment of fees and expenses properly incurred in preserving, realising or getting in the assets'. See notes to CA 1963, s 244.

Pre-liquidation legal expenses: Fees and expenses due to a firm of solicitors for pre-liquidation services and advice as to the procedures to be followed to place a company into creditors' voluntary liquidation are not 'expenses properly incurred in the winding up of the company' within the meaning of the section.[1]

1 *In the matter of Compustore Ltd* [2007] 3 IR 556.

Post winding-up corporation tax and VAT: Corporation tax on income arising to the company after the commencement of a voluntary winding up is a cost, charge or expenses properly incurred in the liquidation.[1] The position is different in a compulsory winding up as was seen in *Re Van Hool McCardle Ltd*.[2] In relation to VAT payable on the sale of property which completes after the commencement of the winding up, this ranks as an expense of the liquidation even though the contract was entered into prior to the winding up.[3]

1 *Re Noyek & Sons Ltd* [1989] ILRM 155; *City of Dublin Steam Packet Co v Revenue Commissioners (No. 2)* [1930] IR 217; *Spa Estates Ltd v O'Hargain* (30 June 1975, unreported) HC (Kenny J).
2 *Re Van Hool McCardle Ltd* [1982] ILRM 340. In this case it was held that corporation tax payable after the commencement of a winding up was not an 'expense' or a necessary disbursement within the meaning of CA 1963, s 244. This was subsequently amended by FA 1983, s 56. The basis for the distinction between voluntary and compulsory liquidations was the reference to 'charges' in CA 1963, s 281 and the absence of such in RSC 1986, Ord 74, r 129(1).
3 *Re Fitz-Pack Cartons Ltd* [2008] 4 IR 19.

Leasehold property held by a liquidator: Where a liquidator retains a company's leasehold property for the benefit of the winding up, any rent accruing constitutes an expense of the liquidation and is payable accordingly.[1]

1 *Re CHA Ltd (In Liquidation)* [1999] 1 IR 437; *Re GWI Ltd* [1987] IEHC 21 (Murphy J); *Re Lundy Granite Co* (1871) 6 Ch App 462; *Re Oak Pits Colliery Co* (1882) 21 Ch D 322; *Re ABC*

Coupler & Engineering Ltd [1970] 1 WLR 702; *Re Downer Enterprises Ltd* [1974] 1 WLR 146; *Re M Power & Sons Ltd; Grant v Aston* (1969) 103 ILTR 39; *Tempany v Royal Liver Trustees Ltd* [1984] ILRM 273.

Proceedings during liquidation: Where an action is brought after a winding-up order has been made, the costs of the successful litigant against the company rank in priority to all other claims.[1] Similarly the damages payable on foot of an undertaking given in interlocutory proceedings rank as an expense of the liquidation.[2]

1 *Comhlucht Paipear Riomhaireachta Teoranta v Udaras na Gaeltachta* [1990] ILRM 266.

2 *Irish Commercial Society Ltd v Plunkett* [1984] IEHC 51 (Carroll J).

Costs of realising charged assets: The costs of the liquidator have no priority over the claims of a secured creditor except in so far as incurred in realising or preserving the security for the benefit of that creditor.[1]

1 *Re Regent's Canal Ironworks Co, ex parte Grissell* (1875) 3 ChD 411.

UK legislation

See IA 1986, s 115.

282 Savings for rights of creditors and contributories

The winding up of a company shall not bar the right of any creditor or contributory to have it wound up by the court, but in the case of an application by a contributory the court must be satisfied that the rights of the contributories will be prejudiced by a voluntary winding up.

Definitions

'company': CA 1963, s 2(1); 'contributory': CA 1963, s 2(1), s 208; 'the court': CA 1963, s 2(1).

Notes

General: See notes to CA 1963, s 267. This section is used to terminate a voluntary liquidation and have it replaced by a compulsory liquidation. The court, in exercising its discretion, will have due regard to the costs involved in the winding up and the delays which have been incurred compared to the overall value of the assets to be administered and also to the complexity or simplicity of the task facing the liquidator.[1] Generally speaking in order for it to be successful it must be shown that there is some wrongdoing by the company which needs to be investigated or if it is suspected or shown that the directors of the company have removed assets from the company before the winding up.[2] The court's normal practice is to allow the views of the majority of creditors to prevail where their views are rationally based and not tainted by interests other than their interests as creditors.[3] The court will also make an order directing that the company be compulsorily wound up where the rights of a contributory petitioner will be prejudiced if the voluntary winding up were to continue.[4] Where there is no reasonable case for suspicion, the court will not order a compulsory liquidation bearing in mind that a voluntary liquidation is cheaper thus increasing the eventual dividend for all creditors.[5]

1 *In the matter of Gilt Construction Ltd* [1994] 2 ILRM 456.

2 *In the matter of Eurochick Ireland Ltd* [1998] IEHC 51 (McCracken J).

3 *Re Hewitt Brannan (Tools) Co Ltd* [1991] BCLC 80. In this case the liquidator did not convene the meeting with the committee of inspection or a meeting with creditors. In addition he did not pay cash balances in his possession into the appropriate bank account with the Bank of England. He also failed to account for corporation tax and failed to comply with the statutory duty to make

returns. The court made an order directing that the voluntary liquidation be replaced by a compulsory liquidation so that the affairs of the company could be investigated. The court believed that it was in the public interest to do so.

4 *Re Zinotty Properties Ltd* [1984] 3 All ER 754.

5 *Re Belfast Tailor's Co Partnership Ltd* [1909] 1 IR 49 where the court refused to grant an order for compulsory liquidation as there was a relatively small amount of assets involved and the integrity and independence of a liquidator had not been impugned and there had been no allegations at all of lack of bona fides in the conduct of the company's affairs.

UK legislation

See IA 1986, s 116.

[282A Inspection of books in voluntary winding-up

(1) The court may, on the application of the Director, make an order for the inspection by the Director of any books and papers in the possession of a company which is in voluntary liquidation and the company, every officer of the company and the liquidator shall give to the Director such access and facilities as are necessary for inspecting and taking copies of those books and papers as the Director may require.

(2) Nothing in this section shall be taken as excluding or restricting any statutory rights of a Minister of the Government or a person acting under the authority of a Minister of the Government.][a]

Amendments

a Section inserted by CLEA 2001, s 49.

[282B Power of court to summon persons for examination in voluntary winding up

(1) The court may, of its own motion or on the application of the Director, at any time where a company is in voluntary liquidation, summon before it any officer of the company or person known or suspected to have in his possession any property of the company or supposed to be indebted to the company, or any person whom the court deems capable of giving information relating to the promotion, formation, trade, dealings, affairs or property of the company.

(2) The court may examine such person on oath concerning the matters aforesaid, either by word of mouth or on written interrogatories, and may reduce his answers to writing and require him to sign them.

(3) The court may require such person to produce any accounting records, deed, instrument, or other document or paper relating to the company that are in his custody or power.

(4) The court may, before the examination takes place, require such person to place before it a statement, in such form as the court may direct, of any transactions between him and the company of a type or class which the court may specify.

(5) If, in the opinion of the court, it is just and equitable so to do, it may direct that the costs of the examination be paid by the person examined.

(6) A person who is examined under this section is not entitled to refuse to answer any question put to him on the ground that his answer might incriminate him and any answer

by him to such a question may be used in evidence against him in any proceedings whatsoever (save proceedings for an offence (other than perjury in respect of such an answer)).

(7) If a person without reasonable excuse fails at any time to attend his examination under this section, he shall be guilty of contempt of court and liable to be punished accordingly.

(8) In a case where a person without reasonable excuse fails at any time to attend his examination under this section or there are reasonable grounds for believing that a person has absconded, or is about to abscond, with a view to avoiding or delaying his examination under this section, the court may cause the person to be arrested and his books and documents and moveable personal property to be seized and him and them to be detained until such time as the court may order.][a]

Amendments

a Section inserted by CLEA 2001, s 49.

Notes

This section confers a power to summons persons for examination in a voluntary winding up which is virtually identical to that arising in a compulsory winding up. In this regard, see the notes to CA 1963, s 245.

[282C Order for payment or delivery of property against person examined under section 282B

(1) If in the course of an examination under section 282B it appears to the court that any person being examined—

(a) is indebted to the company, or

(b) has in his possession or control any money, property or books and papers of the company,

the court may, of its own motion or on the application of the Director, order the person—

(i) to pay to the liquidator the amount of the debt or any part thereof, or

(ii) to pay, deliver, convey, surrender or transfer to the liquidator such money, property or books and papers or any part thereof,

as the case may be, at such time and in such manner and on such terms as the court may direct.

(2) Where the court has made an order under subsection (1), it may, on the application of the Director or the liquidator, make a further order permitting the applicant, accompanied by such persons as the applicant thinks appropriate, to enter at any time or times within one month from the date of issue of the order any premises (including a dwelling) owned or occupied by the person the subject of the order under subsection (1) (using such force as is reasonably necessary for the purpose), to search the premises and to seize any money, property or books and papers of the company found on the premises.

(3) Where the court has made an order under subsection (2), the applicant shall report to it as soon as may be on the outcome of any action on foot of the court's order and the

court shall direct the applicant as to the disposition of anything seized on foot of the order.

(4) A direction under subsection (3) shall not be made in favour of the Director except in respect of the Director's costs and reasonable expenses.

(5) A person who obstructs the exercise of a right of entry, search and seizure conferred by virtue of an order made under subsection (2) or who obstructs the exercise of a right so conferred to take possession of anything referred to in that subsection, shall be guilty of an offence.

(6) Proceedings on foot of an offence under subsection (5) shall not prejudice the power of the court to issue proceedings for contempt of court for failure by a person to comply with an order under this section.][a]

Amendments

a Section inserted by CLEA 2001, s 49.

Notes

See the notes to CA 1963, s 245A.

[282D Power to arrest absconding contributory or officer of company in voluntary winding-up

The court, at any time in respect of a voluntary winding-up, on proof of probable cause for believing that a contributory, director, shadow director, secretary or other officer is about to quit the State or otherwise to abscond or to remove or conceal any of his property for the purpose of evading payment of calls or of avoiding examination about the affairs of the company, may, of its own motion or on the application of the Director, a creditor of the company or any other interested person, cause the contributory, director, shadow director, secretary or other officer to be arrested, and his books and papers and movable personal property to be seized and him and them to be detained until such time as the court may order.][a]

Amendments

a Section inserted by CLEA 2001, s 49.

Notes

See the notes to CA 1963, s 247.

(IV) Provisions Applicable to Every Mode of Winding Up

Proof and Ranking of Claims

283 Debts which may be proved

(1) Subject to subsection (2), in every winding up (subject, in the case of insolvent companies, to the application in accordance with the provisions of this Act of the law of bankruptcy) all debts payable on a contingency, and all claims against the company, present or future, certain or contingent, ascertained or sounding only in damages, shall

be admissible to proof against the company, a just estimate being made, so far as possible, of the value of such debts or claims which may be subject to any contingency or which sound only in damages, or for some other reason do not bear a certain value.

(2) Where a company is being wound up, dividends declared by the company more than 6 years preceding the commencement of the winding up which have not been claimed within the said 6 years shall not be a claim admissible to proof against the company for the purposes of the winding up, unless the articles of the company or the conditions of issue provide otherwise.

Cross reference

As regards the proof of debts pursuant to the law of bankruptcy, see the Bankruptcy Act 1988, Sch 1.

Thus damages for breach of contract and tort are provable. See also Civil Liability Act 1961, s 61.

In relation to the proof of debts generally, see RSC 1986, Ord 74, rr 102–111.

See CA 1963, s 241 in relation to the power of the court to limit the time within which creditors may prove their claims.

Definitions

'articles': CA 1963, s 2(1); 'company': CA 1963, s 2(1).

Notes

Practice and procedure: The first schedule to the Bankruptcy Act 1988 and RSC 1986, Ords 102–111 set out the procedure for proving a debt. The liquidator places an advertisement advising the creditors where and when they should send their claims. The liquidator fixes a time within which the creditors are to prove their debts.[1] Creditors are asked to give their names and addresses, particulars of the debts and claims and the names and addresses of their solicitors.[2] Creditors will not be obliged to attend before the liquidator to prove their debts unless the liquidator so requires.[3] The liquidator investigates claims that have been notified to him and identifies claims which he believes are valid and those which require to be proved further.[4] At the adjudication the examiner decides which debts should be allowed upon the liquidator's affidavit and which creditors should come in and prove their debts.[5] The liquidator then gives notice to the latter category of creditors of the time in which they are to attend before the examiner and prove their claims.[6] After the adjudication by the examiner he issues a certificate in respect of each of the creditors.

1 CA 1963, s 241.
2 RSC 1986, Ord 74, r 95.
3 RSC 1986, Ord 74, r 96.
4 RSC 1986, Ord 74, r 97.
5 RSC 1986, Ord 74, r 95.
6 RSC 1986, Ord 74, r 95.

Liquidator's liability: When deciding whether to admit a claim to proof the liquidator is described as acting in a quasi-judicial capacity and his standards are as exacting as those of a court or judge.[1] He must take care that any legally enforceable claims are admitted to proof. His failure to take proper steps to investigate a claim can amount to misfeasance or breach of duty, rendering him personally liable for a claim which is improperly paid.[2]

1 *Tanning Research Laboratories Inc v O'Brien* 64 ALJLR 21 (1990).
2 *Re Home and Colonial Insurance Co* [1930] 1 Ch 102.

Future debts: All debts, be they present or future, are admissible to proof by CA 1963, s 283. A creditor may prove for a debt not payable at the date of the winding-up order or resolution as if it were payable presently and may receive dividends equally with other creditors. However the liquidator can deduct a rate of interest at 6% per annum computed from the declaration of the dividend at the time of the debt that would have become payable according to the terms on which it was contracted.[1]

1 RSC 1986, Ord 74, r 108.

Unliquidated claims: An unliquidated debt or claim is a present existing liability where the actual amount cannot yet be ascertained. Examples include most claims in tort and some claims for breach of contract and for breach of fiduciary duty. Prior to s 61 of the Civil Liability Act 1961[1] tort creditors were prevented from proving in a liquidation. The inclusion of unliquidated tort claims was recognised in s 75(1) of the Bankruptcy Act 1988.[2]

1 'Notwithstanding any other enactment or any rule of law, a claim for damages or contribution in respect of a wrong shall be provable in bankruptcy where the wrong out of which the liability to damages or the right of contribution arose was committed before the time of bankruptcy.'

2 'claims in the nature of un-liquidated damages which the bankrupt ... is liable ... by reason of a wrong within the meaning of the Civil Liability Act 1961 can be proved'.

Contingent claims: A contingent claim is one in respect of a liability that might very well occur but nevertheless may never occur. An example of a contingent liability is a claim on foot of a guarantee. It is contingent because it will only arise if the principle debtor defaults. Section 75(1) of the Bankruptcy Act 1998 allows for contingent claims to be proved.[1] In the event of there being difficulties in placing a value on a contingent claim, the court can make an estimate of its value to be proved.[2]

1 Section 75(1) of the Bankruptcy Act 1988 which provides that 'debts and liabilities present or future, certain or contingent', can be proved.

2 Section 75(4) of the Bankruptcy Act 1988.

Periodic payments: Where a company which is liable to make any periodic payment (for example rent) is wound up on a day other than the day in which such payment becomes due, the person entitled to the payment may prove for a proportionate part of the payment for the period from the date when the last payment became to the date of the commencement of the winding up, as if the payment accrued from day to day.[1]

1 Bankruptcy Act 1988, Sch 1 para 16; RSC 1986, Ord 74, r 106.

Interest: In the case of the liquidation of an insolvent company, interest on unsecured claims is generally payable up to the commencement of the liquidation whether it is a voluntary or compulsory liquidation. In a compulsory liquidation, where interest has not been agreed, and the debt is overdue at the time of the commencement of the liquidation, the creditor may prove for interest at the rate of not more than 6% per annum from the date the sum was payable to the date of the commencement of the liquidation.[1] No further interest is payable after the date of the commencement of the winding up.[2] Where a secured creditor is entitled to interest his right does not end on the commencement of the liquidation. A secured creditor is entitled to interest up to the date of realisation of the security.[3]

1 RSC 1986, Ord 74, r 107.

2 *Daly v Allied Irish Banks* (27 January 1997, unreported) HC. See also Re *Car Replacement and the Companies Acts* [1995] 1 ILRM 221.

3 *Re McCairns (PMPA) plc* [1991] 2 IR 465.

Debts in foreign currencies. Foreign currency claims must be valued at the exchange rate applicable on the date of the commencement of the winding up.[1]

1 *Re Lines Bros Ltd* [1983] 1 Ch 1.

284 Application of bankruptcy rules in winding up of insolvent companies

(1) In the winding up of an insolvent company the same rules shall prevail and be observed relating to the respective rights of secured and unsecured creditors and to debts provable and to the valuation of annuities and future and contingent liabilities as are in force for the time being under the law of bankruptcy relating to the estates of persons adjudged bankrupt, and all persons who in any such case would be entitled to prove for and receive dividends out of the assets of the company may come in under the winding up and make such claims against the company as they respectively are entitled to by virtue of this section.

(2) [Section 51 of the Bankruptcy Act, 1988,][a] shall apply in the winding up of an insolvent company and accordingly the reference in that section to the filing of the petition shall be read as a reference to the presentation of a petition for the winding up of the company by the court or the passing of a resolution for voluntary winding up, as the case may be, and where, before the presentation of a petition for the winding up of the company by the court, a resolution has been passed by the company for voluntary winding up, shall be read as a reference to the passing of the resolution.

(3) Subsection (2) shall not apply to a judgment mortgage created before the operative date.

Amendments

a CA 1963, s 284 amended by the Bankruptcy Act 1988, s 51(2).

Cross reference

In relation to the priority of rent as a cost or expense of the winding up, see CA 1963, ss 244, 281.

Definitions

'company': CA 1963, s 2(1); 'the operative date': CA 1963, s 2(1); 'a resolution for voluntary winding up': CA 1963, s 2(1), s 251(2).

Notes

General: Although the bankruptcy rules apply in relation to the winding up of insolvent companies it is only in respect of: (a) the respective rights of secured and unsecured creditors; (b) debts provable; and (c) the valuation of annuities and future and contingent liabilities.[1] The Companies Acts does not import all of the rules of bankruptcy into the law relating to the winding up of the company.[2]

1 CA 1963, s 284.

2 *In the Matter of Irish Attested Sales Ltd (In voluntary liquidation)* [1962] IR 70. In this case Kenny J held that a judgment mortgage registered by a creditor of the company within a period of three months of the winding up of the company is valid and enures for the benefit of the judgment mortgagee as against the simple contract creditors.

Secured creditors: If a secured creditor realises his security, he may prove for the balance due to him after deducting the net amount realised and receive dividends thereon but not so as to disturb any dividend then already declared. If he surrenders his security for the general benefit of the creditors, he may prove the whole of his debt.[1] He may at any time amend the valuation on proof upon showing that the valuation and proof were made bona fide on a mistaken estimate, but every such amendment shall be made at the cost of the creditor and upon such terms as the court shall order, unless the Official Assignee allows the amendment without application to the court. If the valuation has reduced the value of the security and a dividend has already been declared, the secured creditor shall (subject to the availability of funds) be paid the balance of the dividend which he would have received but for the inaccuracy of the original valuation.[2] If a secured creditor, having valued his security, subsequently realises it, the net amount realised shall be treated as an amended valuation thereof with any necessary adjustments regarding the payment or repayment of dividends being made accordingly.[3] Failure on the part of the secured creditor in his proof to state that he is a secured creditor shall debar him from sharing in any dividend, unless the court's permits him to amend his proof accordingly.[4] Providing the secured creditor does not bring the property the subject of the charge into the winding up and does not seek to prove it in the winding up, he may claim interest at the rate provided for up to the date of redemption.[5] As seen from notes to CA 1963, s 283 unsecured creditors may only claim interest up to the date of commencement of the winding up.[6]

1 Bankruptcy Act 1988, Sch 1 para 24(a) and (b).

2 Bankruptcy Act 1988, Sch 1 para 24(5)(6).

3 Bankruptcy Act 1988, Sch 1 para 24(7).

4 Bankruptcy Act 1988, Sch 1 para 24(8),(9).

5 *Re McCairns (PMPA) Plc* [1992] ILRM 19.

6 *Re Humber Ironworks and Shipbuilding Co* (1869) LR 4 Ch App 643.

Set off: Where there are mutual credits or debts as between a company and any person claiming as a creditor, one debt or demand may be set off against the other and only the balance found owing shall be recoverable on one side or the other.[1] Moreover, an unsecured debt may be set off against a secured debt.[2] However, a right of set off can only apply to moneys actually owing to and by the company at the date of the liquidation. Moneys paid into the company's account by mistake are akin to lost property and in the absence of a defence of equitable estoppel, may be traced by the payer and may not be subjected to a set off by the company's bankers.[3]

1 Bankruptcy Act 1988, Sch 1 para 17(1). See also *Re Newman, ex parte Brock* (1876) 3 Ch D 494; *Freaney v Bank of Ireland* [1975] IR 376; *Re McCairns (PMPA) plc* [1992] ILRM 19.

2 *McKinnon v Armstrong* (1877) 2 App Cas 531.

3 *Re Irish Shipping Ltd* [1986] ILRM 518.

Solicitor's lien. A solicitor who has a lien on a company document for his costs is deemed to be a secured creditor.[1]

1 *Re Safety Explosives Ltd* [1904] 1 Ch 226.

Landlord. A landlord will not be regarded as a secured creditor merely because of his power of distress.[1]

1 *Re Coal Consumers Association* (1876) 4 Ch D 625.

---

285 Preferential payments in a winding up

(1) In this section 'the relevant date' means—

(i) where the company is ordered to be wound up compulsorily, the date of the appointment (or first appointment) of a provisional liquidator or, if no such appointment was made, the date of the winding-up order, unless in either case the company had commenced to be wound up voluntarily before that date; and

(ii) where subparagraph (i) does not apply, the date of the passing of the resolution for the winding up of the company.

(2) In a winding up there shall be paid in priority to all other debts—

(a) the following rates and taxes,—

(i) all local rates due from the company at the relevant date and having become due and payable within 12 months next before that date;

(ii) all assessed taxes, including income tax and corporation profits tax, assessed on the company up to the 5th day of April next before the relevant date and not exceeding in the whole one year's assessment;

(iii) any amount due at the relevant date in respect of sums which an employer is liable under the Finance (No. 2) Act, 1959, and any regulations thereunder to deduct from emoluments to which Part II of that Act applies paid by him during the period of 12 months next before the relevant date reduced by any amount which he was under that Act and any regulation thereunder liable to repay during the said period, with the addition of interest payable under section 8 of that Act;

(b) all wages or salary (whether or not earned wholly or in part by way of commission) of any clerk or servant in respect of services rendered to the company during the 4 months next before the relevant date;

(c) all wages (whether payable for time or for piece work) of any workman or labourer in respect of services rendered to the company during the 4 months next before the relevant date;

(d) all accrued holiday remuneration becoming payable to any clerk, servant, workman or labourer (or in the case of his death to any other person in his right) on the termination of his employment before or by the effect of the winding-up order or resolution;

[(e) unless the company is being wound up voluntarily merely for the purposes of reconstruction or of amalgamation with another company—

(i) all amounts due in respect of contributions which are payable during the 12 months next before the relevant date by the company as the employer of any persons under the Social Welfare Acts,and

(ii) all amounts due in respect of contributions which would have been payable under the provisions of section 10(1)(b) of the Social Welfare (Consolidation) Act, 1981, by the company as the employer of any persons in respect of any remuneration in respect of any period of employment during the 12 months next before the relevant date even if such remuneration is paid after the relevant date;][a]

(f) unless the company is being wound up voluntarily merely for the purposes of reconstruction or of amalgamation with another company, all amounts (including costs) due in respect of compensation or liability for compensation under the Workmen's Compensation Acts, 1934 to 1955 (being amounts which have accrued before the relevant date), to the extent that the company is not effectively indemnified by insurers against liability for such compensation;

(g) unless the company is being wound up voluntarily merely for the purposes of reconstruction or of amalgamation with another company, all amounts due from the company in respect of damages and costs or liability for damages and costs, payable to a person employed by it in connection with an accident occurring before the relevant date and in the course of his employment with the company, to the extent that the company is not effectively indemnified by insurers against such damages and costs;

[(h) all sums due to any employee pursuant to any scheme or arrangement for the provision of payments to the employee while he is absent from employment due to ill health;

(i) any payments due by the company pursuant to any scheme or arrangement for the provision of superannuation benefits to or in respect of employees of the company whether such payments are due in respect of the company's contribution to that scheme or under that arrangement or in respect of such contributions payable by the employees to the company under any such scheme or arrangement which have been deducted from the wages or salaries of employees.][b]

(3) Subject to subsection (4), and notwithstanding anything in paragraphs (b) and (c) of subsection (2) the sum to which priority is to be given under those paragraphs respectively shall not, in the case of any one claimant, exceed [€3,174.35].[c]

(4) Where a claimant under paragraph (c) of subsection (2) is a farm labourer who has entered into a contract for payment of a portion of his wages in a lump sum at the end of the year of hiring, he shall have priority in respect of the whole of such sum, or such part thereof as the court may decide to be due under the contract, proportionate to the time of service up to the relevant date.

(5) Where any compensation under the Workmen's Compensation Acts, 1934 and 1955 is a weekly payment, the amount due in respect thereof shall, for the purposes of paragraph (f) of subsection (2) be taken to be the amount of the lump sum for which the weekly payment could be redeemed if the employer made an application for that purpose under the said Acts.

(6) Where any payment has been made—

(a) to any clerk, servant, workman or labourer in the employment of a company, on account of wages or salary; or

(b) to any such clerk, servant, workman or labourer or, in the case of his death, to any other person in his right, on account of accrued holiday remuneration;

[or

(c) to any such clerk, servant, workman or labourer while he is absent from employment due to ill health or pursuant to any scheme or arrangement for the provision of superannuation benefit to or in respect of him;][d]

out of money advanced by some person for that purpose, the person by whom the money was advanced shall, in a winding up, have a right of priority in respect of the money so advanced and paid up to the amount by which the sum, in respect of which the clerk, servant, workman or labourer or other person in his right, would have been entitled to priority in the winding up has been diminished by reason of the payment having been made.

(7) The foregoing debts shall—

(a) rank equally among themselves and be paid in full, unless the assets are insufficient to meet them, in which case they shall abate in equal proportions; and

(b) so far as the assets of the company available for payment of general creditors are insufficient to meet them, have priority over the claims of holders of debentures under any floating charge created by the company, and be paid accordingly out of any property comprised in or subject to that charge.

(8) Subject to the retention of such sums as may be necessary for the costs and expenses of the winding up, the foregoing debts shall be discharged forthwith so far as the assets are sufficient to meet them, and in the case of debts to which priority is given by paragraph (e) of subsection (2), formal proof thereof shall not be required except in so far as is otherwise provided by rules of court.

(9) Subject to subsection (10), in the event of a landlord or other person distraining or having distrained on any goods or effects of the company within 3 months next before the relevant date, the debts to which priority is given by this section shall be a first charge on the goods or effects so distrained on, or the proceeds of the sale thereof.

(10) In respect of any money paid under any such charge as is referred to in subsection (9), the landlord or other person shall have the same rights or priority as the person to whom the payment is made.

(11) Any remuneration in respect of a period of holiday [or absence from work through][e] good cause shall be deemed to be wages in respect of services rendered to the company during that period.

(12) This section shall not apply in the case of a winding up where the relevant date occurred before the operative date, and in such a case, the provisions relating to preferential payments which would have applied if this Act had not been passed shall be deemed to remain in full force.

[(13) The Minister may by order made under this subsection vary the sum of money specified in subsection (3) of this section.][f]

[(14) The priority conferred by subsection (2) shall apply only to those debts which, within the period of six months after advertisement by the liquidator for claims in at least two daily newspapers circulating in the district where the registered office of the company is situated, either—

(a) have been notified to him; or

(b) have become known to him.][g]

Amendments

a Subsection (e) substituted by the Social Welfare Act 1991, s 37.

b CA 1963, s 285(2)(h)–(i) inserted by C(A)A 1982, s 10.

c '£2,500' substituted for '£300' by C(A)A 1982, s 10 and converted to €3,174.35 by Council Regulations (EC) No 1103/97, No 974/98 and No 2866/98 and the Economic and Monetary Union Act 1998, s 6.

d CA 1963, s 285(6)(c) inserted by C(A)A 1982, s 10.

e Words substituted by C(A)A 1982, s 10.

f CA 1963, s 285(13) inserted by C(A)A 1982, s 10.

g CA 1963, s 285(14) inserted by CA 1990, s 134.

Cross references

See also CA 1963, s 98(2), (4) regarding preferential payments when receiver is appointed under floating charge.

With regard to the application of CA 1963, s 285 in a receivership, see CA 1963, s 98.

Value added tax together with interest thereon is also a preferential debt to the extent of the tax due in the twelve months next before the relevant date: FA 1976, s 62.

Definitions

'company': CA 1963, s 2(1); 'debenture': CA 1963, s 2(1); 'Minister': CA 1963, s 2(1); 'the operative date': CA 1963, s 2(1).

Notes

General: As an exception to the principle of *parri passu* the legislature has intervened and granted preferential status to a number of creditors. The principle benefactors of this section are the Revenue Commissioners and employees.[1] Where there are not sufficient sums to pay the preferential creditors in full, they are to rank equally amongst themselves.

1 For a discussion on the justification for attaching preferential status under this section, see Lynch, Marshall and O'Ferrall, *Corporate Insolvency and Rescue* (Tottel Publishing, 1986) p 100.

Super preferential debts: The Social Welfare (Consolidation) Act 1993, s 16 provides that the assets of a company in the winding up shall not include any sums deducted by an employer from the employee's remuneration in respect of PRSI. This section appears to impress a form of trust on the fund deducted by the employer and they rank before all other preferential debts. It also appears that they rank before the liquidator's remuneration and expenses.[1] It is a condition precedent to the super preferential status that it be a sum deducted by the employer in respect of the employment contribution of the employee which remains due and owing by the employer. Super preferential status is not afforded to sums which ought to have been deducted in respect of the employment contributions of an employee but were not.[2] If moneys ought to have been deducted but were not deducted they still obtained priority by virtue of CA 1963, s 285(2)(a)(ii). In a receivership such claims rank as ordinary unsecured creditors.[3]

1 See Forde, 'The Law of Company Insolvency' p 361.

2 *Re Coombe Importers Ltd* [1999] I IR 492.

3 CA 1963, s 285(2)(e).

Preferential Revenue claims: Preferential status is given to local rates and all assessed taxes not exceeding one year.[1] The Revenue Commissioners can choose whatever year they wish for the different kinds of assessed taxes due and will of course select the largest outstanding year each tax.[2]

1 This includes income tax, corporation tax, valued added tax and capital gains tax.

2 *Re Pratt* [1951]1 Ch 229.

Wages and salaries: Priority is given to unpaid wages and salaries owing for services rendered to the employer up to a maximum of €3,174.35 for every claimant.[1] The priority only applies to the persons employed under a contract of service and not the individuals working under a contract for service.[2] As to the amounts capable of being claimed under sub-s 92(a)(iii), see the TCA 1997, ss 995 and 1000. The right to claim will not necessarily be lost simply because the contract of employment was tainted by illegality due to the making of 'under the counter payments' by the employer.[3]

1 Limited to sums due during the four months prior to the liquidation.

2 *The Sunday Tribune (In Liquidation)* [1994] IR 505; *Re Dairy Lee* [1976] IR 314.

3 *Re Red Sail Frozen Foods Ltd* [2007] 2 IR 361.

Sick and holiday pay and pension contributions: Accrued holiday remuneration, sums due under an arrangement for sick pay and outstanding pension contributions are preferred with no financial ceiling. The outstanding pension contributions are preferred whether they are employer's contributions or those deducted from the employees remuneration. The right to claim will not necessarily be lost simply because the contract of employment was tainted by illegality due to the making of 'under the counter payments' by the employer.[1]

1 *Re Red Sail Frozen Foods Ltd* [2007] 2 IR 361.

Compensation for dismissal and damages for accident at work: Any sums paid to an employee under the Unfair Dismissals Act 1977, The Minimum Notice and Terms of Employment Act 1973 and/or The Redundancy Payments Act 1979 are given priority under this section. In the event that the employer is unable to pay the compensation the employee can claim such sums from the Redundancy and Employers' Insolvency Fund.[1] Where such sums are paid by the Redundancy and Employers' Insolvency Fund, the Department of Enterprise is entitled to claim these payments in liquidation as a preferential claim.[2] Where an employer in insured, the injured party may claim directly against the insurance company.[3] The term 'accident' in CA 1963, s 285 (2)(g) does not include hearing loss incurred as a result of ongoing exposure during the course of employment.[4] The right to claim will not necessarily be lost simply because the contract of employment was tainted by illegality due to the making of 'under the counter payments' by the employer.[5]

1 Payable under the Protection of Employees (Insolvency) Act 1984.

2 C(A)A 1982, s 10.

3 Civil Liability Act 1961 s 62; *Dunne v White Construction Co Ltd* [1989] IRLM 803.

4 *Irish Ispat Ltd (in Voluntary Liquidation)* [2004] IEHC 604.

5 *Re Red Sail Frozen Foods Ltd* [2007] 2 IR 361.

Subrogated claims: Where money is advanced to the company for the purpose of paying employees' wages or salary, holiday remuneration or pension benefits, the lender is preferred to the extent that those employees would have been preferred if they had been paid what is owing to them.[1] Although it may not be easy for a bank or other financial institution to establish that an account was opened expressly with a view to funding the payment of salaries or wages, it has been held that a benevolent rather than a narrow construction should be given to this section.[2] A further right of statutory subrogation is given to the Minister for Enterprise and Employment under the Protection of Employees (Insolvency) Act 1984.[3] The Minister is given by s 10 the same priority as an employee would have enjoyed in respect of any of the debts. However, it is to be noted that if, during the course of the winding up, someone other than the Minister pays the employee's outstanding wages, that person will not enjoy any entitlement to be subrogated to the employee's preferential claim in the liquidation up but will instead rank only as an ordinary unsecured creditor.[4]

1 CA 1963, s 285(6).

2 Plowman J In *Re Rampgill Mill Ltd* [1967] Ch 1138 as approved by Carroll J in *Re Station Motors Ltd* (22 November 1994, unreported).

3 Section 10 Protection of Employees (Employer's Insolvency) Act 1984.

4 *Re Bell Lines Ltd* [2006] IEHC 188.

Scheme of arrangement under CA 1963, ss 201–203: The parties to a scheme of arrangement under CA 1963, ss 201–203 may be bound by a term which confers on an ordinary unsecured creditor preferential status in a winding up.[1]

1 *Re MFN Construction Co Ltd* (12 May 1988, unreported) SC.

Time limit: The order of priority provided for in CA 1963, s 285(2) only applies to those debts which are notified or have become known to the liquidator within six months of his advertisement for claims in at least two daily newspapers.[1] The six-month time limit cannot be extended and notice has been interpreted as either actual notification or actual knowledge.[2]

1 CA 1963, s 285(14).

2 In *Re H William (Tallaght) Ltd* [1996] 3 IR 531.

UK legislation

See IA 1986, ss 386, 387, Sch 6 (amended by ICTA 1988, s 844, Sch 29 para 32; SI 1987/2093 reg 2(1),(3)).

Effect of Winding Up on Antecedent and other Transactions

286 [Fraudulent preference

(1) Subject to the provisions of this section, any conveyance, mortgage, delivery of goods, payment, execution or other act relating to property made or done by or against a company which is unable to pay its debts as they become due in favour of any creditor, or of any person on trust for any creditor, with a view to giving such creditor, or any surety or guarantor for the debt due to such creditor, a preference over the other creditors, shall, if a winding-up of the company commences within 6 months of the making or doing the same and the company is at the time of the commencement of the winding-up unable to pay its debts (taking into account the contingent and prospective liabilities), be deemed a fraudulent preference of its creditors and be invalid accordingly.

(2) Any conveyance or assignment by a company of all its property to trustees for the benefit of all its creditors shall be void to all intents.

(3) A transaction to which subsection (1) applies in favour of a connected person which was made within two years within two years before the commencement of the winding up of the company shall, unless the contrary is shown, be deemed in the event of the company being wound up—

- (a) to have been made with a view to giving such person a preference over the other creditors, and
- (b) to be a fraudulent preference,

and be invalid accordingly.

(4) Subsections (1) and (3) shall not affect the rights of any person making title in good faith and for valuable consideration through or under a creditor of the company.

(5) In this section, 'a connected person' means a person who, at the time the transaction was made, was—

- (a) a director of the company;
- (b) a shadow director of the company;
- (c) a person connected, within the meaning of section 26 (1)(a) of the Companies Act, 1990, with a director;
- (d) a related company, within the meaning of section 140 of the said Act, or
- (e) any trustee of, or surety or guarantor for the debt due to, any person described in paragraph (a), (b), (c) or (d).][a]

Amendments

a CA 1963, s 286 substituted by CA 1990, s 135.

Definitions

'company': CA 1963, s 2(1); 'director': CA 1963, s 2(1).

Cross references in other enactments

NAMA Act 2009, s 218(1) provides that an acquired bank asset within the meaning of NAMA Act 2009 is 'not invalidated or rendered void or voidable as against NAMA or a NAMA group entity or their successors in title' by operation of CA 1963, s 286.

NAMA Act 2009, s 228(2) provides that NAMA Act 2009, s 286 'shall not be taken to invalidate or render void a payment made to NAMA or to another person at NAMA's direction'.

Notes

General:[1] It is a basic concept of the law governing the liquidation of an insolvent company that the assets of the insolvent company at the commencement of the liquidation are to be distributed rateable amongst the company's unsecured creditors as of the date of the commencement of the liquidation.[2] CA 1963, s 286 restricts the powers of the controllers of the company to dispose of its assets on the verge of it being wound up. If a transaction is a fraudulent preference within the meaning of CA 1963, s 286 and is made within six months of the winding up of the company, it is invalid. If the preferential transaction is made in favour of a connected person,[3] it is invalid where it is made within two years of the commencement of the winding up.[4] The making of a fraudulent preference payment does not amount to fraudulent trading for the purposes of CA 1963, s 297A.[5]

1 See generally, Keirse, 'Object and effect: the vexed question of intent in fraudulent preference cases', [2005] CLP 182.

2 *In Re Grays Inns Constructions Ltd* [1980] 1 WLR 711. See also notes to CA1963, s 218.

3 As defined in CA 1963, s 286(5) as a director or shadow director of the company, a director's spouse, parent, sibling or child, a related company within the meaning of CA 1990, s 140(5) or a trustee of, or surety or guarantor for the debt due to any person.

4 CA 1963, s 286(3).

5 *Re Sarflax Ltd* [1979] Ch 592.

Inability to pay debts: The company must be unable to pay its debts as they fall due at the time of the disposition and at the time of the commencement of the winding up.[1] A bona fide belief that the company will be able to pay its debts in full at some future date does not negate an intention to prefer in circumstances where, at the time of the payment, the company was well aware of its own insolvency.[2]

1 CA 1963, s 286(1).

2 *Re FP & CH Matthews Ltd* [1982] 2 WLR 495.

Onus of proof: The onus of proof is on the liquidator to establish a dominant intention to prefer one creditor over another.[1] Where a preferential transaction is made in favour of a connected person,[2] it is presumed to have been made with a view to giving such a person a preference over other creditors unless the contrary is shown.[3] At times it can be difficult for the liquidator to discharge the onus of proof as he must prove the state of mind of the controller of the company who made the disposition. The liquidator has to look at the circumstances as a whole and draw the appropriate inferences from the evidence such as it is. Because the liquidator was not a participant in the relevant events, he is faced with this difficulty and he knows only what appears from the books and papers of the company and what he is told by the participants in those events.[4] In the absence of direct evidence of an intention to prefer, the court may be prepared to infer such an intention from the surrounding circumstances.[5] Such an intention may be inferred where a debt has been paid shortly before the commencement of the winding up, having been outstanding for a long time previously.

1 *Re Welding Plant Ltd* (27 June 1984, unreported) HC (McWilliam J); *Corran Construction Co Ltd v Bank of Ireland Finance Ltd* [1976/7] ILRM 175; *Re Northside Motors Ltd* (24 July 1978, unreported) HC (Costello J); *Station Motors Ltd v Allied Irish Banks Ltd* [1985] IR 756; *Le Chatelaine Thudichum Ltd v Conway* [2008] IEHC 349.

2 As defined in CA1963, s 286(5).

3 For an example of a case where the respondent was unable to rebut the presumed intention to prefer, see *Clements v Henry Hadaway Organisation Ltd* [2008] 1 BCLC 223. In that instance, the respondent director had levied 'management charges' which were found to be excessive and which had been calculated without the company receiving any independent advice.

4 *Re Clasper Group Services Ltd* [1989] BCLC 143.

5 *Station Motors Ltd v Allied Irish Banks Ltd* [1985] IR 756; *Re Northside Motors Ltd* (24 July 1978, unreported) HC (Costello J); *Re Industrial Design and Manufacturing Ltd* (25 June 1984, unreported) High Court of Northern Ireland (Carswell J); *Peat v Gresham Trust Ltd* [1934] AC 252; *Re M Kushler Ltd* [1943] 2 All ER 22; *Le Chatelaine Thudichum Ltd v Conway* [2008] IEHC 349.

Intention to prefer: In order to prove that a transaction is a preference, it is not sufficient to show that the effect of the transaction was to give a preference[1]; rather the phrase 'with a view to giving ...' has been interpreted as meaning that the transaction must have been entered into with a dominant intention to prefer.[2] It is not enough to prove that there was actual preferment from which an intention to prefer can, with hindsight, be inferred. The liquidator must prove an intention to prefer at the time the payment is made.[3] Where there is no direct evidence of intention, the court can draw an inference of an intention to prefer in a case where some other possible explanation is open.[4] The method of ascertaining the state of mind of the payer is the ordinary method of evidence and inference, to be dealt with on the same principles which are commonly employed in drawing inferences of fact.[5]

1 Although a transaction will not amount to a preference unless it has the effect of preferring the creditor, surety or guarantor: *Re Welding Plant Hire Ltd* (27 June 1984, unreported) HC (McWilliam J).

2 *Corran Construction Co. Ltd v Bank of Ireland Finance* [1976/7] ILRM 175; *Station Motors Ltd v Allied Irish Banks Ltd* [1985] IR 756; *Kelleher v Continental Irish Meats Ltd* (9 May 1978, unreported) HC (Costello J); *Re Northside Motor Co Ltd* (24 July 1978, unreported) HC (Costello J).

3 *Re M Kushler Ltd* (1943) 2 All ER 22 as approved by Carroll J in *Station Motors v AIB Ltd* [1995] IR 761.

4 *Re M Kushler Ltd* [1943] 2 All ER 22.

5 *Per* Lloyd Green MR in the case of *M Kushler Ltd* [1943] 2 All ER 22 where he states that 'the inference to be drawn in a case of fraudulent preference is an inference of something which has about it, at the very least, the taint of dishonesty, and, in extreme cases, very much more than a mere taint of dishonesty, and that being so, the Court, on ordinary principals, is not in the habit of drawing inferences which involve dishonesty or something approaching dishonesty, unless there are solid grounds for drawing them'.

Examples of intention to prefer: The following are instances where an intention to prefer has been found and where the transaction has accordingly been set aside as a fraudulent preference: where a company's directors and shareholders gave joint and several guarantees for the company's overdraft for the bank and sought to use the company's assets to pay off the liability of the bank;[1] the repayment of a loan to the auditor of a company;[2] the payment of the sum of Stg£2,000 to the son of the beneficial owner and managing director of a company one month before the company went into liquidation; [3] the company giving a charge to a previously unsecured creditor, although not contractually obliged to do so;[4] For an analysis of the evidence that a court will draw inference from, see the judgment of Lord Greene MR *in Re M Kushler*.[5]

1 *Re Station Motors Ltd* [1985] IR 756.

2 *Re John Daly & Co Ltd* (1886) 19 LRIr 83.

3 *Re Clasper Group Services Ltd* [1989] BCLC 143.

4 *Re Eric Holmes (Property) Ltd* [1965] 1Ch 1052.

5 *Re M Kushler* [1943] 2 All ER 22 where he stated as follows: 'the weight of evidence of conduct in these cases may vary much according to the particular type of case with which the Court is concerned. In the case of a creditor who is an entire stranger to the debtor (or the person who is acting for the debtor) circumstances may be insufficient to justify an inference of an intention to prefer, when there can be no benefit at all to the debtor who is making the payment. That is one type of case. At the other end of the scale comes the type of case which is extremely familiar nowadays, where the person (such as a director) who makes the payment on behalf of the debtor is himself going to obtain by means of it a direct and immediate personal benefit. These cases of guarantees of overdrafts and securities deposited to cover overdrafts are very common indeed and where, for example, you have directors who have given guarantees, the circumstances of that strong element of private advantage may justify the Court in attaching to the other facts much greater weight then would have been attached to precisely similar facts in a case where that element did not exist'.

Examples of absence of intention to prefer: The following are all instances where the transaction has been held not to be a fraudulent preference because of the absence of an intention to prefer: where the creditor, surety or guarantor as the case may be, has put sufficient pressure on the company to pay the debt so as to overbear the will of the company's controllers the transaction;[1] a payment made in fear of losing a client;[2] the giving of a fresh mortgage by a company; where the member/director's will had been overborne by pressure applied by the bank;[3] The result of these cases is perversely that the more weak willed the company's controller is, and the more oppressive the creditor, the less likely that the payment will be regarded as a fraudulent preference. This has been said to be 'overtly at odds with the aim of achieving an equitable distribution of the assets of an insolvent company'.[4]

1 *Corran Construction Co Ltd v Bank of Ireland Finance Ltd* [1976/7] ILRM 175; *Re Boyd* (1885) 15 LR Ir 521; *Taylor Assignees of v Thompson* (1869/70) IRCL129; *Re Daly & Co Ltd* (1887–88) 19 LR 1r 83 where Porter MR said that 'where pressure exists so as to overbear the volition of the debtor a payment is not made with a view to prefer to the creditor exerting it, but because the debtor cannot help it. The view to prefer is absent; or at least is not the real view, or motive or reason actuating the debtor ...'

2 *Assignees of Taylor v Thompson* (1969/90) IRCL 129.

3 *Corran Construction Co Ltd v Bank of Ireland Finance Ltd* [1976/7] ILRM 175.

4 See Ussher, *Company Law in Ireland* (Sweet & Maxwell, 1986) p 508.

Fraudulent preference compared to fraudulent dispositions: A transaction will not constitute a fraudulent preference if it only amounts to a fraudulent preference compared to fraudulent dispositions. A transaction will not constitute a fraudulent preference unless the person preferred is a creditor, a surety or guarantor of the company.[1] If the person preferred is merely the creditor, a surety or guarantor of some other company (albeit an associated company), then CA 1963, s 286 can have no application.[2] A fraudulent disposition of corporate property is liable to be subject to a court order that the property so disposed be returned to the company. Pursuant to CA 1990, s 139 different considerations apply to determining whether or not there has been a fraudulent preference or a fraudulent disposition. The categories of fraudulent preference and fraudulent disposition are not necessarily mutually exclusive.[3] It has been held that it is immaterial that the disposition by way of a fraudulent preference is far in excess of the amount owed provided that it was made in favour of a creditor.[4] The repayment of a debt due by an insolvent company to a director or connected person, apart from being a fraudulent preference, may also amount to a breach by the directors of their fiduciary duty to act in the best interest of the creditors generally.[5]

1 *Re Welding Plant Ltd* (27 June 1984, unreported) HC (McWilliam J).

2 *Re John C Parkes & Sons Ltd v Hong Kong and Shanghai Banking Corporation* [1990] 1 ILM 341 noted by MacCann (1990) 8ILT (ns 111).

3 *Re Clasper Group Services Ltd* [1989] BCLC 143.

4 *Re Clasper Group Services Ltd* [1989] BCLC 143 although this decision has been described as not persuasive by Courtney in *The Law of Private Companies* (2nd edn, Tottel Publishing, 2002). See also, CA 1990, s 139(2).

5 *West Mercia Safetywear Ltd v Dodd* [1988] BCLC 250.

UK legislation

See IA 1986, ss 239, 240, 241, 243.

---

287 Liabilities and rights of certain persons who have been fraudulently preferred

(1) Where—

(a) a company is being wound up; and

(b) anything made or done on or after the operative date is void under section 286 as a fraudulent preference of a person interested in property mortgaged or charged to secure the company's debt;

then (without prejudice to any rights or liabilities arising apart from this section) the person preferred shall be subject to the same liabilities and shall have the same rights as if he had undertaken to be personally liable as surety for the debt to the extent of the charge on the property or the value of his interest, whichever is the less.

(2) The value of the said person's interest shall be determined as at the date of the transaction constituting the fraudulent preference, and shall be determined as if the interest were free of all encumbrances other than those to which the charge for the company's debt was then subject.

(3) On any application made to the court in relation to any payment on the ground that the payment was a fraudulent preference of a surety or guarantor, the court shall have jurisdiction to determine any questions relating to the payment arising between the person to whom the payment was made and the surety or guarantor, and to grant relief in respect thereof notwithstanding that it is not necessary so to do for the purposes of the winding up, and for that purpose may give leave to bring in the surety or guarantor as a third party as in the case of an action for the recovery of the sum paid.

(4) Subsection (3) shall apply, with the necessary modifications, in relation to transactions other than the payment of money as it applies to payments.

Definitions

'company': CA 1963, s 2(1); 'the operative date': CA 1963, s 2(1).

UK legislation

See IA 1986, ss 241, 243.

---

288 [Circumstances in which floating charge is invalid

(1) Where a company is being wound up, a floating charge on the undertaking or property of the company created within 12 months before the commencement of the winding up shall, unless it is proved that the company immediately after the creation of the charge was solvent, be invalid, except as to money actually advanced or paid, or the actual price or value of goods or services sold or supplied, to the company at the time of or subsequently to the creation of, and in consideration for, the charge, together with interest on that amount at the rate of 5 per cent per annum.

(2) For the purposes of subsection (1) the value of any goods or services sold or supplied by way of consideration for a floating charge is the amount in money which at the time they were sold or supplied could reasonably have been expected to be obtained for the goods or services in the ordinary course of business and on the same terms (apart from the consideration) as those on which they were sold or supplied to the company.

(3) Where a floating charge on the undertaking or property of a company is created in favour of a connected person, subsection (1) shall apply to such a charge as if the period of 12 months mentioned in that subsection were a period of 2 years.

(4) In this section 'a connected person' means a person who, at the time the transaction was made, was—

(a) a director of the company;

(b) a shadow director of the company;

(c) a person connected, within the meaning of section 26 (1) (a) of the Companies Act, 1990, with a director;

(d) a related company, within the meaning of section 140 of the said Act; or

(e) any trustee of, or any surety or guarantor for the debt due to, any person described in paragraph (a), (b), (c) or (d).][a]

Amendments

a CA 1963, s 288 substituted by CA 1990, s 136.

Definitions

'company': CA 1963, s 2(1); 'director': CA 1963, s 2(1).

Cross references in other enactments

NAMA Act 2009, s 218(1) provides that an acquired bank asset within the meaning of NAMA Act 2009 is 'not invalidated or rendered void or voidable as against NAMA or a NAMA group entity or their successors in title' by operation of CA 1963, s 288.

Notes

General: The purpose of CA 1963, s 288 is to prevent a company on its last legs from creating floating charges to secure past debts or for moneys which do not go to swell their assets and become available for creditors.[1] The parties to the charge will not be able to circumvent s 288 merely by describing it as a fixed charge; rather the court will look to the substance of the transaction to see whether in fact the instrument created was instead a floating charge.[2]

1 *Re Orleans Motor Co Ltd* [1911] 2 Ch 41.

2 *Re Keenan Bros Ltd* [1985] IR 401.

The test of solvency: There is a presumption that a floating charge that is created within the operative time limits (ie 12 months or 2 years for a connected person[1]) is invalid, and the onus is on the holder of the floating charge to prove that the company was solvent immediately after the creation of the charge.[2] The test to be applied in determining whether or not the company is solvent is whether immediately after the creation of the charge the company was able to pay its debts as they became due. The question is not whether its assets exceed the estimated value of its liabilities or whether or not a businessman would have regarded it as solvent.[3]

1 As defined in CA 1963, s 288(4).

2 See Keane, *Company Law* (4th edn, Tottel Publishing, 2007). The date that the floating charge is created rather than the date of its registration is the relevant date.

3 *Re Creation Printing Ltd* [1981] IR 353 where Kenny J rejected the proposition that solvency equals assets exceeding liabilities. He preferred the cash flow test and decided that the question of whether a company was solvent on a specified date is one of fact and involves very many difficult inferences. He stated that 'if there is or there is likely to be, a large deficiency of assets when the liquidation starts, the temptation is to hold that the company was not solvent or strong. But the deficiency may have been caused by some change in economic or market conditions happening after the charge was given. So an examination of the financial history of the company, both before and after the charges were given is necessary'. The court held that it was wrong to include the value of the company's fixed assets in considering the company's solvency because such assets were required for the purpose of generating income, and would not, in the normal course of things, be sold by a company which intended to stay in business.

Securities realised prior to winding up: CA 1963, s 288 does not apply where a floating charge holder enforces his security before the company goes into liquidation.[1]

1 *Mace Builders (Glasgow) Ltd v Lunn* [1987] BCLC 55.

The charge is valid to the extent of money actually advanced or paid: CA 1963, s 288 does not apply if the floating charge is given in consideration for 'money actually advanced or paid' to the company either when the charge was created or later. The payment does not have to be made unconditionally and can have been on terms that it is used to extinguish an existing liability of the company.[1] In deciding whether or not the chargee paid money to the company in consideration of the charge, the court is concerned as to the substance of any transaction that took place and not simply its form.[2] It also looks to see if the company received a benefit. It is only where no benefit at all accrues to the company that the cash paid should be disregarded.[3] There are several reported instances of payments to companies which have been held to be mere devices for obtaining a security for an existing debt. In the case of *Re Orleans Motor Co*[4] the directors obtained a floating charge for advancing money to the company, but that money was used for re-paying its overdraft which the directors had guaranteed. The court had no hesitation in invalidating the charge. In *Re Port Supermarket Ltd*[5] the court held that the charge (which concerned a series of transactions within a group of companies) was simply a device to transfer a debt from one subsidiary to its parent under the cover of receiving new cash. In *Faraway Magazines Ltd*[6] the moneys had been lodged by the debentureholder directly into the company's overdrawn account. The court did not validate the payment since the effect of the transaction would merely have been to substitute one debt for another.[7] Where the charge has been created to secure the company's existing indebtedness as well as future advances, the rule in *Clayton's case* provides that any lodgement after the creation of the charge to the company's overdrawn account will be appropriated towards discharging the company's unsecured indebtedness to the Bank first.[8] 'Money paid' includes cheques met by the bank on behalf of the company.[9] Forbearance to sue does not constitute 'cash paid'.[10]

1 *Re Matthew Ellis Ltd* [1933] Ch 58 which appeared to overrule the Court of Appeal decision in *Revere Trust Ltd v Wellington Handkerchief Works Co Ltd* [1931] NI 55. See also Keane,

Company Law (4th edn, Tottel Publishing, 2002) at 20.81 where it is stated that the entire advance is still treated as cash paid even if the money is used to extinguish an existing liability.

2 *Revere Trust Ltd v Wellington Handkerchief Works Co Ltd* [1931] NI 55.

3 Keane, *Company Law* (4th edn, Tottel Publishing, 2007); See also *Re Destone Fabrics Ltd* [1941] 1 Ch 319 where the court held that the test of whether the company indeed received funds in exchange for security is whether the transaction benefited the transaction or those behind it. *Re G T White & Co Ltd* [1983] BCLC 311 where the court held that the creation of a floating charge was in a substance no more than the substitution for an unsecured debt, or of a better for an existing security.

4 *Re Orleans Motor Co* [1911] 2 CH 41.

5 *Re Port Supermarket Ltd* [1978] 1 NZ LR 330.

6 *Fairway Magazines Ltd* [1993] BCLC 643.

7 *Clayton's Case* (1816) 1 MER 572.

8 *Re Daniel Murphy Ltd* [1964] IR 1; *Re Yeogil Glove Co Ltd* [1962] 3 All ER 400.

9 *Re Yeogil Glove Co. Ltd* [1962] 3 All ER 400; *Re Thomas Mortimer Ltd* [1965] Ch 186.

10 *Lake Glen Construction Ltd* [1980] IR 347.

Timing of the payment: Although CA 1963, s 288 provides that money should be paid at the time of or subsequent to the creation and in consideration for the charge, a delay between the agreement to make the charge and the actual creation is not automatically fatal. The delay between the agreement to give the floating charge and the creating of the floating charge must not have been with a view to deceive creditors.[1] There is no one firm test to be applied in determining how long time may elapse between the first payment and the execution of the charge for the proviso of CA 1963, s 288(1) to be excluded.[2]

1 *Daniel Murphy Ltd* [1964] IR 1 where the court held that a delay of 55 days was not held to have been unreasonable because the solicitors acting for both parties acted as fast as they would have done in any other transaction. See also *Re Faraway Magazines Ltd* [1993] BCLC 643; *Re Shoe Lace Ltd* [1992] BCLC 636.

2 *Smurfit Paribas Bank Ltd v AAB Export Finance Ltd (No 2)* [1991] 2 IR 19 where Baron J held that two years and three months was too much of a delay. He stated: 'in order to treat payment made to the company before the execution of the charge as payments made at the time of the charge, the necessary elements to be established are: An honest transaction; advances made before the execution of the charge and reasonable expedition in and about the preparation and execution of the charge'.

UK legislation

See IA 1986, s 245.

289 Other circumstances in which floating charge is invalid

(1) Subject to subsection (2), where—

(a) a company is being wound up; and

(b) the company was within 12 months before the commencement of the winding up indebted to any officer of the company; and

(c) such indebtedness was discharged whether wholly or partly by the company or by any other person; and

(d) the company created a floating charge on any of its assets or property within 12 months before the commencement of the winding up in favour of the officer to whom such company was indebted;

then (without prejudice to any rights or liabilities arising apart from this section) such charge shall be invalid to the extent of the repayment referred to in paragraph (c) unless it is proved that the company immediately after the creation of the charge was solvent.

(2) Subsection (1) shall not apply if the charge referred to in paragraph (d) was created before the operative date.

(3) In this section, 'officer' includes the spouse, child or nominee of an officer.

Definitions

'company': CA 1963, s 2(1); 'officer': CA 1963, s 2(1); 'the operative date': CA 1963, s 2(1).

Notes

General: Unlike CA 1963, s 288 there is no saver for the charge to the extent of money paid, goods sold or services supplied at the time of or subsequent to the creation of, and in consideration for the charge.

UK legislation

See IA 1986, s 245; CC(CP)A 1985, s 18.

290 Disclaimer of onerous property in case of company being wound up

(1) Subject to subsections (2) and (5), where any part of the property of a company which is being wound up consists of land of any tenure burdened with onerous covenants, of shares or stock in companies, of unprofitable contracts, or of any other property which is unsaleable or not readily saleable by reason of its binding the possessor thereof to the performance of any onerous act or to the payment of any sum of money, the liquidator of the company, notwithstanding that he has endeavoured to sell or has taken possession of the property or exercised any act of ownership in relation thereto, may, with the leave of the court and subject to the provisions of this section, by writing signed by him, at any time within 12 months after the commencement of the winding up or such extended period as may be allowed by the court, disclaim the property.

(2) Where any such property as aforesaid has not come to the knowledge of the liquidator within one month after the commencement of the winding up, the power under this section of disclaiming the property may be exercised at any time within 12 months after he has become aware thereof or such extended period as may be allowed by the court.

(3) The disclaimer shall operate to determine, as from the date of disclaimer, the rights, interests and liabilities of the company, and the property of the company, in or in respect of the property disclaimed, but shall not, except so far as is necessary for the purpose of releasing the company and the property of the company from liability, affect the rights or liabilities of any other person.

(4) The court, before or on granting leave to disclaim, may require such notices to be given to persons interested and impose such terms as a condition of granting leave, and make such other order in the matter as the court thinks just.

(5) The liquidator shall not be entitled to disclaim any property under this section in any case where an application in writing has been made to him by any persons interested in the property requiring him to decide whether he will or will not disclaim, and the liquidator has not, within a period of 28 days after the receipt of the application or such further period as may be allowed by the court, given notice to the applicant that he intends to apply to the court for leave to disclaim.

(6) The court may, on the application of any person who is, as against the liquidator, entitled to the benefit or subject to the burden of a contract made with the company, make an order rescinding the contract on such terms as to payment by or to either party of damages for the non-performance of the contract, or otherwise as the court thinks just, and any damages payable under the order to any such person shall be deemed to be a debt proved and admitted in the winding up.

(7) Subject to subsection (8), the court may, on an application by any person who either claims any interest in any disclaimed property or is under any liability not discharged by this Act in respect of any disclaimed property and on hearing any such persons as it thinks fit, make an order for the vesting of the property in or the delivery of the property to any person entitled thereto, or to whom it may seem just that the property should be delivered by way of compensation for such liability as aforesaid, or a trustee for him, and on such terms as the court may think just, and on any such vesting order being made, the property comprised therein shall vest accordingly in the person therein named in that behalf without any conveyance or assignment for the purpose.

(8) Where the property disclaimed is of a leasehold nature, the court shall not make a vesting order in favour of any person claiming under the company, whether as under-lessee or as mortgagee by demise, except upon the terms of making that person—

(a) subject to the same liabilities and obligations as those to which the company was subject under the lease in respect of the property at the commencement of the winding up; or

(b) if the court thinks fit, subject only to the same liabilities and obligations as if the lease had been assigned to that person at that date;

and in either event (if the case so requires), as if the lease had comprised only the property comprised in the vesting order, and any mortgagee or under-lessee declining to accept a vesting order upon such terms shall be excluded from all interest in and security upon the property, and, if there is no person claiming under the company who is willing to accept an order upon such terms, the court shall have power to vest the estate and interest of the company in the property in any person liable either personally or in a representative character, and either alone or jointly with the company, to perform the lessee's covenants in the lease, freed and discharged from all estates, encumbrances and interests created therein by the company.

(9) Any person damaged by the operation of a disclaimer under this section shall be deemed to be a creditor of the company to the amount of the damages, and may accordingly prove the amount as a debt in the winding up.

Definitions

'company': CA 1963, s 2(1); 'the court': CA 1963, s 2(1); 'share': CA 1963, s 2(1).

Notes

General: CA 1963, s 290 applies the bankruptcy rules about disclaiming onerous obligations.[1] The power to disclaim onerous property and certain contracts is given to the liquidator to enable him to realise and dispose of the company's assets without needlessly protracting the winding up. The exclusive concern of the court in an application to disclaim must be the interests of all persons interested in the liquidation.[2]

1 Bankruptcy Act 1988, s 56(1).
2 *Tempany v Royal Liver Trustees Ltd* [1984] ILRM 273.

Practice and procedure: The liquidator must apply to court within twelve months of his appointment seeking its leave to disclaim.[1] Where a property or contract does not come to his notice until more than a month has elapsed from the date of the liquidation, the twelve-month period runs from when he became aware of them and that period may be extended by the court in appropriate circumstances.[2] The application for leave to disclaim is usually made ex-parte by the liquidator.[3] Other persons interested in the property or contract can compel the liquidator to make up his mind to disclaim and if he elects not to disclaim he is thenceforth prevented from doing so.[4] For this purpose an application in writing must be made to him and he has 28 days or such further period as the court may allow to decide on the matter. If before that time he has not disclaimed a contract he has deemed to have adopted it. A party to a contract with the company or a person 'entitled to the benefit of subject to the burden' of such contract can apply to the court for an order to have it rescinded.[5] Before giving leave to disclaim, the court will usually require that persons interested are duly notified so that they can appear in the proceedings. Although there is no express provision for attaching conditions to the disclaimer, the court has a general discretion pursuant to his inherent jurisdiction to impose conditions.[6]

1 CA 1963, s 290(1).
2 CA 1963, s 290(2).
3 RSC 1986, Ord 75, r 84.
4 CA 1963, s 290(5).
5 CA 1963, s 290(6).
6 *Tempany v Royal Liver Trustees Ltd* [1984] ILRM 273.

Property and interests capable of being disclaimed: CA 1963, s 290(1) sets out the property and interests that are capable of being disclaimed. In this regard, a contract is not an 'unprofitable contract' merely because it is financially disadvantageous or merely because the company could have made a better bargain.[1] In the context of a disclaimer, it is a necessary feature of an 'unprofitable contract' that it imposes future obligations the performance of which might be detrimental to the company's creditors by prejudicing the liquidator's obligation to realise the company's property and pay a dividend to the creditors within a reasonable time.[2] Moreover, for the purposes of disclaimer, property is not 'unsaleable or not readily saleable by reason of binding the possessor thereof to the performance of any onerous act or to the payment of any sum of money' in circumstances where it is simply valueless but is in no other way harmful.[3] So, for example, a liquidator has been held not to be able to disclaim a chattel such as chlorinated waste oil which exposes him to no liability and which is simply valueless[4] nor could he disclaim a contract for the sale of land merely because he found a purchaser who would pay a higher price.[5] Examples of matters which can be disclaimed would include leases,[6] shares that are not fully paid up,[7] a contract to continue works in a mine that does not appear to have any immediate benefit,[8] the benefit of an Environmental Protection Agency license.[9] The liquidator cannot, however, use s 290 to disclaim a legally enforceable contract for the sale of land, even if the property has since increased in value.[10] The entire of the property or contract must be disclaimed and a liquidator will not be allowed to disclaim part only and keep the remainder.[11]

1 *Re SSSL Realisations (2002) Ltd* [2007] 1 BCLC 29; *Re Park Air Services plc* [1999] 1 BCLC 155.

2 *Re SSSL Realisations (2002) Ltd* [2007] 1 BCLC 29.
3 *Re Potters Oil Ltd (In Liquidation)* [1985] BCLC 203.
4 *Re Potters Oil Ltd (In Liquidation)* [1985] BCLC 203. See also *Environment Agency v Hillridge Ltd* [2004] 2 BCLC 358.
5 *Abbeyford Estates Ltd* (29 October 1993, unreported) HC (Flood J).
6 *Re Grant v Aston Ltd* 103 ILTR 39 (1969).
7 *Re Hallett* (1894) 1 mans 380.
8 *Re Grundy* (1829) Mont & M 231.
9 *In the matter of ISPAT (in voluntary liquidation)* [2004] IEHC 143.
10 *Re Bastable* [1901] 2 KB 518; *Re Abbeyford Estates Ltd* [1993] IEHC 232. cf *Capital Prime Properties plc v Worthgate Ltd* [2000] 1 BCLC 647.
11 *Re Fussell* (1882) 20 Ch D 321.

The effect of a disclaimer: CA 1963, s 290(3) sets out the effect of a legal disclaimer. In *Tempany v Royal Liver Trustees Ltd*[1] Keane J held that the exclusive concern of the court in an application for leave to disclaim must be the interest of all persons interested in the liquidation. The rights and liabilities of persons other than the company, including any guarantor of the tenant company's obligations, will remain intact and that the courts will seek to construe the section in such a way as to remove the company's onerous obligations while seeking to interfere with other party's rights as little as possible.[2] Thus, the court will also refuse to release an original lessee who previously assigned the lease to the company.[3] The date upon which the Liquidator gives notice of the intention to disclaim is treated as the date of disclaimer.[4]

1 *Tempany v Royal Liver Trustees Ltd* [1984] ILRM 273. In this case a liquidator sought to disclaim a lease held by a company. The lease represented a liability of £1.5 million because the rent paid by the company was greatly in excess of the market value. A schedule of dilapidations had been served by the landlord and there was no prospect of assigning the interest for value. The defendant in the proceedings was the guarantor of the company's obligation under the lease and opposed the application for disclaimer by the liquidator.
2 *Tempany v Royal Liver Trustees Ltd* [1984] ILRM 273; *Capital Prime Properties Plc v Worthgate Ltd* [2000] 1 BCLC 647; *Shaw v Doleman* [2009] 2 BCLC 123.
3 *Tempany v Royal Liver Trustees Ltd* [1984] ILRM 273.
4 *Tempany v Royal Liver Trustees Ltd* [1984] ILRM 273. See also *RHH Realisations Ltd* (1975) 31 P at CR49; *Grant v Aston* (1969) 103 ILTR 30.

Vesting Orders: CA 1963 s 290 (8) allows the court to make vesting orders in favour of persons claiming an interest in the disclaimed property or who are under a liability in respect of that property which is not discharged by the disclaimer. Until such time, if any, as the court makes a vesting order, the disclaimed property remains in the form of a legal limbo, continuing to exist, but vested in nobody.[1]

1 *Tempany v Royal Liver Trustees Ltd* [1984] ILRM 273; *Re Town Investments Ltd Underlease* [1954] Ch 301; *Re Thompsons and Cottrells Contract* [1943] Ch 97; *East and West India Co v Hill* (1882) 22 Ch D 14.

Power to rescind contacts and award damages: Pursuant to the provisions of CA 1963, s 290(6) the court has the power to make an order rescinding the contract on such terms as to payment of damages as it thinks fit. If the onerous property is a lease, the measure of damages will be the difference between the rent which would have been paid by the company under the lease and the rent which the lessor is likely to obtain under the unexpired residue of the term.[1] Any rent accruing in respect of the period prior to this disclaimer and during which the liquidator has retained the property for the benefit of the creditors, ranks in priority as a cost or expense of the winding up.[2] In *GWI Ltd*[3] the High Court refused to allow arrears of rent in priority from the commencement of the winding up to the date of disclaimer as the court found that there had been no affirmation of the company's interest in the property.

1 *Re Ranks (Ireland) Ltd* [1988] ILRM 751.

2 *Re Ranks (Ireland) Ltd* [1988] ILRM 751; *Re Oak Pits Colliery Co* (1882) 21 Ch D 322; *Re HH Realisations Ltd* (1975) 31 P & CR 249; *Tempany v Royal Liver Trustees Ltd* [1984] ILRM 273.

3 *GWI Ltd* [1987] IEHC 21 (Murphy J).

UK legislation

See IA 1986, ss 178–182, 186.

---

291 Restriction of rights of creditor as to execution or attachment in case of company being wound up

(1) Subject to subsections (2) to (4), where a creditor has issued execution against the goods or lands of a company or has attached any debt due to the company, and the company is subsequently wound up, he shall not be entitled to retain the benefit of the execution or attachment against the liquidator in the winding up of the company unless he has completed the execution or attachment before the commencement of the winding up.

(2) Where any creditor has had notice of a meeting having been called at which a resolution for voluntary winding up is to be proposed, the date on which the creditor so had notice shall, for the purposes of subsection (1), be substituted for the date of the commencement of the winding up.

(3) A person who purchases in good faith under a sale by the sheriff any goods of a company on which an execution has been levied shall in all cases acquire a good title to them against the liquidator.

(4) The rights conferred by subsection (1) on the liquidator may be set aside by the court in favour of the creditor to such extent and subject to such terms as the court thinks fit.

(5) For the purposes of this section, an execution against goods shall be taken to be completed by seizure and sale, and an attachment of a debt shall be deemed to be completed by receipt of the debt, and an execution against land shall be deemed to be completed by seizure and, in the case of an equitable interest, by the appointment of a receiver.

(6) Nothing in this section shall give any validity to any payment constituting a fraudulent preference.

(7) In this section, 'goods' includes all chattels personal and 'sheriff' includes any officer charged with the execution of a writ or other process.

Cross references

See CA 1963, s 284(2) as regards the effect of the commencement of a winding up on judgment mortgages registered against the property of the company.

See CA 1963, s 292(1) as regards the power of the liquidator to demand the delivery up by the sheriff of goods and money taken in uncompleted executions.

Definitions

'company': CA 1963, s 2(1); 'the court': CA 1963, s 2(1); 'officer': CA 1963, s 2(1); 'a resolution for voluntary winding up': CA 1963, s 2(1), s 251(2).

Notes

General: The principle behind this section is to ensure that unsecured creditors of the company are to be treated equally in the case of a winding up. It is in those circumstances that if execution is not complete[1] before the commencement of the winding up the creditor cannot rely upon a security. Where a creditor has had notice of a meeting at which it is proposed to resolve to wind up a company, the date of the notice is substituted for the date of the commencement of the winding up.[2] Judgment mortgages registered against the company's property within three months of the commencement of the winding up are invalid.[3]

1 As further provided for by CA 1963, s 291(5). In *Caribbean Producers (Yam Importers) Ltd* [1966] CH 331 where Russell LJ stated that attachment was only complete where the execution creditor is in actual receipt of the money. In this case execution was not completed when the creditor learned of the intention to wind up the company but was completed when the actual winding up commenced.

2 CA 1963, s 291(4) provides for the setting aside of the rights conferred on a liquidator by reason of the operation of this section. The courts will be reluctant to exercise its validating jurisdiction under this subsection by reason of the purpose of the section as referred to above. See also *Caribbean Producers (Yam Importers) Ltd* [1966] CH 331 where Harmon J observed that it is in accordance with 'the policy of law both in bankruptcy and in the liquidation of the companies, that all unsecured creditors shall be treated alike from the date when there comes to their notice that an act ... which in the case of a limited company amounts to 'notice of intention to liquidate'. From that critical time the creditor 'loses his right to enforce a security. If he improperly obtains payment by wrongfully enforcing the security this is a wrong against the liquidator'.

3 Bankruptcy Act 1988, s 51 as incorporated in the Companies Acts by virtue of CA 1963, s 284(2); *Re Shannon Side Holdings Ltd* (20 May 1993, unreported) (Costello J).

UK legislation

See IA 1986, s 183.

---

292 Duties of sheriff as to goods taken in execution

(1) Subject to subsection (3), where any goods of a company are taken in execution, and, before the sale thereof or the completion of the execution by the receipt or recovery of the full amount of the levy, notice is served on the sheriff that a provisional liquidator has been appointed or that a winding-up order has been made or that a resolution for voluntary winding up has been passed, the sheriff shall, on being so required, deliver the goods and any money seized or received in part satisfaction of the execution to the liquidator, but the costs of the execution shall be a first charge on the goods or the money so delivered, and the liquidator may sell the goods or a sufficient part thereof for the purpose of satisfying that charge.

(2) Subject to subsection (3), where under an execution in respect of a judgment for a sum exceeding [€25.39][a] the goods of a company are sold or money is paid in order to avoid sale, the sheriff shall deduct the costs of the execution from the proceeds of the sale or the money paid and retain the balance for 14 days, and if within that time notice is served on him of a petition for the winding up of the company having been presented or of a meeting having been called at which there is to be proposed a resolution for the voluntary winding up of the company and an order is made or a resolution is passed, as the case may be, for the winding up of the company, the sheriff shall pay the balance to the liquidator who shall be entitled to retain it as against the execution creditor.

(3) The rights conferred by this section on the liquidator may be set aside by the court in favour of the creditor to such extent and subject to such terms as the court thinks fit.

(4) In this section, 'goods' includes all chattels personal and 'sheriff' includes any officer charged with the execution of a writ or other process.

Amendments

a £20 converted to €25.39 by Council Regulations (EC) No 1103/97, No 974/98 and No 2866/98 and the Economic and Monetary Union Act 1998, s 6.

Definitions

'company': CA 1963, s 2(1); 'the court': CA 1963, s 2(1); 'officer': CA 1963, s 2(1); 'a resolution for voluntary winding up': CA 1963, s 2(1), s 251(2).

Notes

General: Where goods are taken but not yet sold or the proceeds of a sale not handed over to the execution creditor, and the Sheriff is notified that a winding-up order has commenced, the Sheriff must deliver up to the liquidator those goods or proceeds. The rights conferred on the liquidator may be set aside by the court in favour of the creditor to such an extent as the court thinks fit.[1]

1 CA 1963, s 292(3).

UK legislation

See IA 1986, s 184 (amended by SI 1986/1996, art 2, Sch, Pt I).

Offences antecedent to or in the course of Winding Up

293 Offences by officers of companies in liquidation

(1) Subject to subsection (2), if any person, being a past or present officer of a company which at the time of the commission of the alleged offence is being wound up, whether by the court or voluntarily, or is subsequently ordered to be wound up by the court or subsequently passes a resolution for voluntary winding up—

(a) does not to the best of his knowledge and belief fully and truly disclose to the liquidator when he requests such disclosure all the property, real and personal, of the company and how and to whom and for what consideration and when the company disposed of any part thereof, except such part as has been disposed of in the ordinary way of the business of the company; or

(b) does not deliver up to the liquidator, or as he directs, all such part of the real and personal property of the company as is in his custody or under his control, and which he is required by law to deliver up; or

(c) does not deliver up to the liquidator, or as he directs, all books and papers in his custody or under his control belonging to the company and which he is required by law to deliver up; or

(d) within 12 months next before the commencement of the winding up or at any time thereafter conceals any part of the property of the company to the value of [€12.70][a] or upwards, or conceals any debt due to or from the company; or

(e) within 12 months next before the commencement of the winding up or at any time thereafter fraudulently removes any part of the property of the company to the value of [€12.70][a] or upwards; or

(f) makes any material omission in any statement relating to the affairs of the company; or

(g) knowing or believing that a false debt has been proved by any person under the winding up, fails for the period of a month to inform the liquidator thereof; or

(h) after the commencement of the winding up prevents the production of any book or paper affecting or relating to the property or affairs of the company; or

(i) within 12 months next before the commencement of the winding up or at any time thereafter conceals, destroys, mutilates or falsifies or is privy to the concealment, destruction, mutilation or falsification of any book or paper affecting or relating to the property or affairs of the company; or

(j) within 12 months next before the commencement of the winding up or at any time thereafter makes or is privy to the making of any false entry in any book or paper affecting or relating to the property or affairs of the company; or

(k) within 12 months next before the commencement of the winding up or at any time thereafter fraudulently parts with, alters or makes any omission in, or is privy to the fraudulent parting with, altering or making any omission in, any document affecting or relating to the property or affairs of the company; or

(l) after the commencement of the winding up or at any meeting of the creditors of the company within 12 months next before the commencement of the winding up attempts to account for any part of the property of the company by fictitious losses or expenses; or

(m) has within 12 months next before the commencement of the winding up or at any time thereafter, by any false representation or other fraud, obtained any property for or on behalf of the company on credit which the company does not subsequently pay for; or

(n) within 12 months next before the commencement of the winding up or at any time thereafter, under the false pretence that the company is carrying on its business, obtains on credit for or on behalf of the company, any property which the company does not subsequently pay for; or

(o) within 12 months next before the commencement of the winding up or at any time thereafter pawns, pledges or disposes of any property of the company which has been obtained on credit and has not been paid for, unless such pawning, pledging or disposing is in the ordinary way of business of the company; or

(p) is guilty of any false representation or other fraud for the purpose of obtaining the consent of the creditors of the company or any of them to an agreement with reference to the affairs of the company or to the winding up;

he shall in the case of an offence mentioned in paragraph (m), (n) or (o), be liable, on conviction on indictment, to penal servitude for a term not exceeding 5 years or to imprisonment for a term not exceeding [5][b] years or to a fine not exceeding [€6,348.69][d] or to both such penal servitude or imprisonment and such fine and, in the case of an offence mentioned in any other paragraph, be liable, on conviction on indictment, to imprisonment for a term not exceeding [5][b] years or to a fine not exceeding [€3,174.35][c] or to both, or, in the case of any offence under this subsection, be liable, on summary conviction, to imprisonment for a term not exceeding 6 months or to a fine not exceeding [€634.87][e] or to both.

(2) It shall be a good defence to a charge under any of paragraphs (a), (b), (c), (d), (f), (n) and (o) of subsection (1), if the accused proves that he had no intent to defraud and to a charge under any of paragraphs (h), (i) and (j) of subsection (1), if he proves that he had no intent to conceal the state of affairs of the company or to defeat the law.

(3) Where any person pawns, pledges or disposes of any property in circumstances which amount to an offence under paragraph (o) of subsection (1), every person who takes in pawn or pledge or otherwise receives the property knowing it to be pawned, pledged or disposed of in such circumstances as aforesaid shall be guilty of an offence and shall be liable to be punished in the same way as if he had been guilty of an offence under the said paragraph (o).

(4) For the purposes of this section, 'officer' shall include any person in accordance with whose directions or instructions the directors of a company have been accustomed to act.

Amendments

a £10 converted to €12.70 by Council Regulations (EC) No 1103/97, No 974/98 and No 2866/98 and the Economic and Monetary Union Act 1998, s 6.

b '2 years' increased to '5 years' by CA 1990, s 240(8) as inserted by CLEA 2001, s 104.

c '£5,000' substituted for '£1,000' by C(A)A 1982, Sch 1 and converted to €6,348.69 by Council Regulations (EC) No 1103/97, No 974/98 and No 2866/98 and the Economic and Monetary Union Act 1998, s 6.

d £2,500 converted to €3,174.35 by Council Regulations (EC) No 1103/97, No 974/98 and No 2866/98 and the Economic and Monetary Union Act 1998, s 6.

e '£500' substituted for '£100' by C(A)A 1982, Sch 1 and converted to €634.87 by Council Regulations (EC) No 1103/97, No 974/98 and No 2866/98 and the Economic and Monetary Union Act 1998, s 6.

Definitions

'books and paper': CA 1963, s 2(1); 'book or paper': CA 1963, s 2(1); 'company': CA 1963, s 2(1); 'director': CA 1963, s 2(1); 'document': CA 1963, s 2(1): 'officer': CA 1963, s 2(1); 'a resolution for voluntary winding up': CA 1963, s 2(1), s 251(2).

Notes

Officer: The offences in s 293 apply to past and present officers of the company. The definition of 'officer' in sub-s (4) extends to shadow directors. As regards the other classes of persons who may constitute 'officers' of a company, see *R v Shacter*[1] (auditors) and *Director of Corporate Enforcement v D'Arcy*[2] (senior management).

1 *R v Shacter* [1960] 2 QB 252.

2 *Director of Corporate Enforcement v D'Arcy* [2006] 2 IR 163.

Defence of absence of fraudulent intent: Subsection (2) provides a defence to certain of the offences enumerated in subsection (1) where the accused had no intent to defraud. For certain of the other offences an absence of intent to conceal the state of affairs of the company is a good defence. In each instance, the onus is on the accused to prove that he did not have such intent.[1]

[1] *R v Richmond Magistrates' Court* [2008] 1 BCLC 681.

UK legislation

See IA 1986, ss 206, 208, 210, 211.

294 Alteration or falsification of books

[...][a]

Amendments

a Repealed by CA 1990, s 6. See instead CA 1990, s 243.

295 Frauds by officers of companies which have gone into liquidation

If any person, being at the time of the commission of the alleged offence an officer of a company which is subsequently ordered to be wound up by the court or subsequently passes a resolution for voluntary winding up—

(a) has by false pretences or by means of any other fraud induced any person to give credit to the company;

(b) with intent to defraud creditors of the company, has made or caused to be made any gift or transfer of or charge on, or has caused or connived at the levying of any execution against, the property of the company;

(c) with intent to defraud creditors of the company, has concealed or removed any part of the property of the company since or within 2 months before the date of any unsatisfied judgment or order for payment of money obtained against the company;

he shall be liable, on conviction on indictment, to imprisonment for a term not exceeding [5][a] years or to a fine not exceeding [€3,174.35][b] or to both or, on summary conviction, to imprisonment for a term not exceeding 6 months or to a fine not exceeding [€1,904.61][c] or to both.

Amendments

a '2 years' increased to '5 years' by CA 1990, s 240(8) as inserted by CLEA 2001, s 104.

b '£2,500' substituted for '£500' by C(A)A 1982, Sch 1 and converted to €3,174.35 by Council Regulations (EC) No 1103/97, No 974/98 and No 2866/98 and the Economic and Monetary Union Act 1998, s 6.

c '£500' substituted for '£100' by C(A)A 1982, Sch 1 and increased to £1,500 by CA 1990, s 240(7) as inserted by CLEA 2001, s 104 and converted to €1,904.61 by Council Regulations (EC) No 1103/97, No 974/98 and No 2866/98 and the Economic and Monetary Union Act 1998, s 6.

Cross-references

See also CA 1963, s 293(m), (n).

Such conduct may also constitute fraudulent trading within the meaning of CA 1963, ss 297 and 297A .

See also CA 1963, s 293(d), (e).

Definitions

'company': CA 1963, s 2(1); 'the court': CA 1963, s 2(1); 'officer': CA 1963, s 2(1); 'a resolution for voluntary winding up': CA 1963, s 2(1), s 251(2).

UK legislation

See IA 1986, s 207.

296 Liability where proper books of account not kept

[…][a]

Amendments

a CA 1963, s 296 repealed by CA 1990, s 6.

297 [Criminal liability of persons concerned for fraudulent trading of company

(1) If any person is knowingly a party to the carrying on of the business of a company with intent to defraud creditors of the company or creditors of any other person or for any fraudulent purpose, that person shall be guilty of an offence.

(2) Any person who is convicted of an offence under this section shall be liable–

(a) on summary conviction to imprisonment for a term not exceeding 12 months or to a fine not exceeding [€1,904.61][b] or to both, or

(b) on conviction on indictment, to imprisonment for a term not exceeding 7 years or to a fine not exceeding [€63,486.90][c] or to both.][a]

Amendments

a CA 1963, s 297 substituted by CA 1990, s 137.

b £1,000 increased to £1,500 by CA 1990, s 240(7) as inserted by CLEA 2001, s 104 and increased to €1,904.61 by Council Regulations (EC) No 1103/97, No 974/98 and No 2866/98 and the Economic and Monetary Union Act 1998, s 6.

c £50,000 converted to €63,486.90 by Council Regulations (EC) No 1103/97, No 974/98 and No 2866/98 and the Economic and Monetary Union Act 1998, s 6.

Definitions

'company': CA 1963, s 2(1).

UK legislation

See CA 1985, s 458.

[297A Civil liability of persons concerned for fraudulent or reckless trading of company

(1) If in the course of winding up of a company or in the course of proceedings under the Companies (Amendment) Act, 1990, it appears that—

(a) any person was, while an officer of the company, knowingly a party to the carrying on of any business of the company in a reckless manner; or

(b) any person was knowingly a party to the carrying on of any business of the company with intent to defraud creditors of the company, or creditors of any other person or for any fraudulent purpose;

the court, on the application of the receiver, examiner, liquidator or any creditor or contributory of the company, may, if it thinks it proper to do so, declare that such person shall be personally responsible, without any limitation of liability, for all or any part of the debts or other liabilities of the company as the court may direct.

(2) Without prejudice to the generality of subsection (1) (a), an officer of a company shall be deemed to have been knowingly a party to the carrying on of any business of the company in a reckless manner if—

(a) he was a party to the carrying on of such business and, having regard to the general knowledge, skill and experience that may reasonably be expected of a person in his position, he ought to have known that his actions or those of the company would cause loss to the creditors of the company, or any of them, or

(b) he was a party to the contracting of a debt by the company and did not honestly believe on reasonable grounds that the company would be able to pay the debt when it fell due for payment as well as all its other debts (taking into account the contingent and prospective liabilities).

(3) Notwithstanding anything contained in subsection (1) the court may grant a declaration on the grounds set out in paragraph (a) of that subsection only if—

(a) paragraph (a), (b) or (c) of section 214 applies to the company concerned, and

(b) an applicant for such a declaration, being a creditor or contributory of the company, or any person on whose behalf such application is made, suffered loss or damage as a consequence of any behaviour mentioned in subsection (1).

(4) In deciding whether it is proper to make an order on the ground set out in subsection (2) (b), the court shall have regard to whether the creditor in question was, at the time the debt was incurred, aware of the company's financial state of affairs and, notwithstanding such awareness, nevertheless assented to the incurring of the debt.

(5) On the hearing of an application under this section, the applicant may himself give evidence or call witnesses.

(6) Where it appears to the court that any person in respect of whom a declaration has been sought under subsection (1) (a), has acted honestly and responsibly in relation to the conduct of the affairs of the company or any matter or matters on the ground of which such declaration is sought to be made, the court may, having regard to all the circumstances of the case, relieve him either wholly or in part, from personal liability on such terms as it may think fit.

(7) Where the court makes any such declaration, it may—

(a) give such further directions as it thinks proper for the purpose of giving effect to that declaration and in particular may make provision for making the liability of any such person under the declaration a charge on any debt or obligation due from the company to him, or on any mortgage or charge or any interest in any mortgage or charge on any assets of the company held by or vested in him or any company or person on his behalf, or any person claiming as assignee from or through the person liable or any company or person acting on his behalf, and may from time to time make such further order as may be necessary for the purpose of enforcing any charge imposed under this subsection;

(b) provide that sums recovered under this section shall be paid to such person or classes of persons, for such purposes, in such amounts or proportions at such time or times and in such respective priorities among themselves as such declaration may specify.

(8) Subsection (1) (a) shall not apply in relation to the carrying on of the business of a company during a period when the company is under the protection of the court.

(9) This section shall have effect notwithstanding that—

(a) the person in respect of whom the declaration has been sought under subsection (1) may be criminally liable in respect of the matters on the ground of which such declaration is to be made; or

(b) any matter or matters on the ground of which the declaration under subsection (1) is to be made have occurred outside the State.

(10) For the purposes of this section—

'assignee' includes any person to whom or in whose favour, by the directions of the person liable, the debt, obligation, mortgage or charge was created, issued or transferred or the interest created, but does not include an assignee for valuable consideration (not including consideration by way of marriage) given in good faith and without notice of any of the matters on the ground of which the declaration is made;

'company' includes any body which may be wound up under the Companies Acts; and

'officer' includes any auditor, liquidator, receiver, or shadow director.][a]

Amendments

a CA 1963, s 297A inserted by CA 1990, s 138.

Cross reference

See also CA 1963, s 214(a), (b), (c).

Definitions

'company': CA 1963, s 2(1); 'contributory': CA 1963, s 2(1), s 208; 'the court': CA 1963, s 2(1); 'director': CA 1963, s 2(1); 'officer': s 2(1).

Notes

Reckless and fraudulent trading: Section 297A provides for the imposition of personal liability for reckless or fraudulent trading. Fraudulent trading also attracts potential criminal liability under

CA 1963, s 297. Each of the two concepts is considered separately below. Thereafter, consideration is given to aspects of s 297A common to both remedies.

1 Reckless trading

Definition of recklessness: CA 1963, s 297A(1)(a) introduces the concept of reckless trading. The leading Irish decision is *Re Hefferon Kearns Ltd.*[1] In that case Lynch J approved the definition of reckless in *Donovan v Landys Ltd*[2] and *Shawinigan v Vokins.*[3] Prior to the decision there had been debate as to whether the court would prefer a subjective or objective test when interpreting recklessness.[4] Lynch J opted for an objective test. However, in interpreting the section he placed particular emphasis on the inclusion of the word 'knowingly' and concluded that although the test for recklessness is objective it was tempered by subjectivity.[5] Other jurisdictions have favoured the objective test, such as the New Zealand case of *Thomas Thompson v Innes*[6] and the South African case of *SV Goertz* where it has been held that the term 'recklessness' was to be assessed objectively.[7] In assessing the conduct of the respondent officers, the court will be concerned not to judge them with the benefit of hindsight and will be conscious of the fact that directors of a company which gets into financial difficulty will be faced with a real and unenviable dilemma of deciding whether to close down and go into liquidation or to trade on and try to turn the company around.[8] If a decision is made to trade on and that decision is arrived at in a responsible and conscientious manner (eg by taking independent professional advice), the court will not regard their actions as reckless and will therefore decline to impose personal liability.[9] On the other hand, a decision to continue trading through the use of moneys which the officers know to have been deducted in respect of PAYE, PRSI, VAT, RCT etc and which ought properly to have been paid to the Revenue Commissioners, has been held to constitute reckless trading.[10]

1 *Dublin Heating Company v Hefferon Kearns Ltd* [1993] 3 IR 191, Lynch J; *Re PSK Construction Ltd* (7 December 2009, unreported) HC (Finlay Geoghegan J). See also *Re Produce Marketing Consortium Ltd (No 2)* [1989] BCLC 520; *Re DKG Construction Ltd* [1990] BCC 905.

2 *Donovan v Landys Ltd* [1993] 3 IR 19.

3 *Shawinigan v Vokins* [1961] 1 WLR 1206.

4 See generally Courtney, *Law of Private Companies* (2nd edn, Tottel Publishing, 2002) paras 10.083–10.085.

5 Judge Lynch stated as follows ' the inclusion of the word 'knowingly' in sub-section (1)(a) of s 33 now Section 297A(1)(a) must have been intended by the Oireachtas to have some effect on the nature of the reckless conduct required to come within the subsection. I think that its inclusion requires that the director is party to carrying on the business in a manner which the director knows very well involves an obvious and serious risk of loss or damage to others yet ignores the risk because he does not care whether such others suffer loss or damage or because of his selfish desire to keep his own company alive overrides any concern which he ought to have for others'. See also *Re PSK Construction Ltd* (7 December 2009, unreported) HC (Finlay Geoghegan J).

6 *Thomas Thompson v Innes* [1985] 2 NZ CLC 99.

7 *SV Goertz* 1980 (1) SA 269 where Fagan J held that it was not necessary to prove an actual awareness of the risk and a conscious decision to ignore it. He stated 'the plain meaning of the word 'recklessly' does not limit it to dolus eventualis (an actual awareness of the risk and a decision to ignore it). I can, furthermore, find no indication in S 424(E) that the legislation intended to place such a restricted meaning upon the word. I can also find nothing disturbing in legislation aiming at punishing those who carry on business of a company recklessly in the sense is grossly negligently ... It is thus not incumbent upon the State to establish that the appellant foresaw a detriment to a company. What was required was proof that the appellant acted recklessly judged by the standards of reasonable businessmen. The test is an objective one, not a subjective one. Proof of gross negligence is sufficient to obtain a conviction.'

8 *Re Hefferon Kearns Ltd (*No 2) [1993] 3 IR 191; *Re PSK Construction Ltd* (7 December 2009, unreported) HC (Finlay Geoghegan J); *Re Continental Assurance Co of London plc (No 4)* [2007] 2 BCLC 287.

9 *Re Continental Assurance Co of London plc (No 4)* [2007] 2 BCLC 287.

10 *Re PSK Construction Ltd* (7 December 2009, unreported) HC (Finlay Geoghegan J).

Deemed reckless trading: CA 1963, s 297A(2) provides a recital of types of conduct that will be deemed to constitute reckless trading, even in the absence of knowledge on the part of the respondent that his conduct is wrongful. In this regard, it has been held that sub-s (2) does not affect or extend the meaning of 'reckless' but does extend its application.[1] The first limb for the test for deemed recklessness effectively introduces an objective standard which must be observed by the officers of the company and may properly be classified as a liability for gross negligence. It does not matter that the officer did not actually foresee the loss to creditors. For a liability to be imposed it suffices that he ought to have foreseen that his actions are those that would cause loss to the creditors of the company or any of them.[2] The second limb of the test for deemed recklessness applies where a person did not honestly believe on reasonable grounds that the company would be able to pay its debts if they fell due. Lynch J held that this was also an objective test.[3]

1 Per Lynch J in *Re Hefferon Kearns Ltd* [1993] 3 IR 191 where the judge says subsection (2) does not affect or extend the meaning of subsection (1)(a) but extends the application of subsection 1(a). The case is mentioned in paragraphs (a) and (b) of subsection (2) even though the director was not guilty of reckless trading within the meaning of subsection(1)(a) itself. Subsection (2) deems a director be guilty of reckless trading in the circumstances set out in paragraph (A) and (B) and presupposes that otherwise he would not be so guilty. See also *Re PSK Construction Ltd* (7 December 2009, unreported) HC (Finlay Geoghegan J).

2 In the case of *Re Hefferon Kearns Ltd (No 2)* [1993] 3 IR 191 Lynch found no evidence within CA 1963, s 197A(2)(a) by which to deem the directors guilty of reckless trading. He said that it was required that there be found 'knowledge or imputed knowledge that the ... Defendant's actions or those of the company would cause loss to the creditors. It is not sufficient that there might be some worry or uncertainty as to the ability to pay all creditors. The requirement is that the ... Defendant knew or ought to have known that his actions or those of the company would cause loss to the creditors.' See also *Re PSK Construction Ltd* (7 December 2009, unreported) HC (Finlay Geoghegan J).

3 He stated that the directors in the case were for a period of time deemed to have traded recklessly within the meaning of CA 1963, s 297A(2)(a) in that 'the director was in fact a party to the contracting of debts, by the company at a time when he knew that those debts, together with the other debts of the company,(including contingent and prospective liabilities), could not be paid by the company as they fell due'. Lynch J went on to absolve the director by invoking his discretionary jurisdiction provided for in CA 1963, s 297A(6). See below.

Parties against whom order may be sought: Subsection (1)(a) only allows for the imposition of liability on 'officers' of the company who have been guilty of reckless trading. A non-exhaustive definition of 'officer' is contained in sub-s (1). As regards the other classes of persons who may constitute 'officers' of a company, see *R v Shacter*[1] (auditors) and *Director of Corporate Enforcement v D'Arcy*[2] (senior management).

1 *R v Shacter* [1960] 2 QB 252.

2 *Director of Corporate Enforcement v D'Arcy* [2006] 2 IR 163.

Knowingly a party: An officer will not be deemed to be knowingly a party to reckless trading simply because he is aware of reckless conduct on the part of other officers. Instead, only active participation will attract liability.[1] There is no collective responsibility for reckless trading but rather the conduct of each individual officer must be looked at on his own.[2] Each person must be a party to the carrying on of a business and must take some positive or active part in the actual conduct of the business operations of the company. The positive and active part may take various forms and would include the giving of advice.[3] In the case of *Re Hunting Lodges Ltd* [4] Carroll J accepted the meaning of 'to be a party to' as indicating no more than participating in, taking part in, or concurring in, that it remains to be determined whether or not inert disinterest will constitute knowingly being a party where a director who is also a large shareholder in the company never became actively involved in the business of the company. It was held that she had wrongly refrained from exercising proper control of the company and that that her inertia had facilitated the mismanagement by her co-director.[5]

1 *Re Maidstown Building Provisions Ltd* [1971] 3 All ER 363; *Re Kellys Carpetdrome Ltd* (No 2) [1984] IEHC 87 (O'Hanlon J); *Re PSK Construction Ltd* (7 December 2009, unreported) HC (Finlay Geoghegan J).

2 *Re Petherick Exclusive Fashions Ltd* (1987) 3 NZCLC 99; *Re PSK Construction Ltd* (7 December 2009, unreported) HC (Finlay Geoghegan J).

3 *Thomas Thompson v Innes* [1985] 2 NZ CLC 99.

4 *Re Hunting Lodges Ltd* [1985] ILRM 75.

5 Courtney in *The Law of Private Companies* (2nd edn, Tottel Publishing, 2002) at 10.091. He refers to the case of *Cronjeno v Stone* (1985) (3) SA 597 T. *Morris v Bank of India* [2005] All ER (d) 242 (Jun).

Relief from liability for reckless trading: In one case[1] Lynch J expressed the view that that the terms of CA 1963 s 297A(2)(b) appear to be very wide ranging and draconian. He noted that the sub-section could apply to every company which had become insolvent and had to cease trading. For that reason he held that it would not be in the interests of the community that whenever there might appear to be any significant danger that the company was going to become insolvent, that the directors should immediately cease trading and close down its business. He noted that many businesses which might have survived by continuing to trade coupled with remedial measures would be lost to the community. It is for this reason that he believed, that the exceptions contained in CA 1963 s 297A(6) was included and he concluded that the director had acted honestly and responsibly in relation to the conduct and affairs of the company and was accordingly relieved him from liability.[2] As reckless trading has been found to be referable to an objective standard it is difficult to see how a person can have been said to have acted both recklessly and responsibly at the same time.[3]

1 *Re Hefferon Kearns Ltd (No 2)* [1993] 3 IR 191.

2 *Re Hefferon Kearns Ltd* (No 2) [1993] 3 IR 191 at 225. See also *Re Continental Assurance Co of London plc (No 4)* [2007] 2 BCLC 287.

3 See generally MacCann, 'Reckless Trading, No Looking Back Part 1' (1993) ILT 31.

2 Fraudulent trading

Parties against whom an order can be made. Liability for reckless trading may only be imposed on officers of the company. However, liability for fraudulent trading may be imposed on any person who was a party to the impugned conduct,[1] including a creditor of the company,[2] its bankers,[3] a purchaser of the company's property,[4] or a person to whom the company's property has been transferred for the purpose of putting those assets beyond the reach of creditors.[5]

1 *Re Augustus Barnett Ltd* (1986) BCC 98, 904.

2 *Re Gerald Cooper Chemicals Ltd* [1978] 2 WLR 867.

3 *Morris v Bank of India* [2005] 2 BCLC 328. In that case the key issue on liability was whether those at the defendant bank responsible for entering into the transaction knew that they were thereby assisting the company to perpetrate a fraud on its creditors and whether their knowledge should be attributed to the bank. The court found in favour of the liquidator and held that the chief manager of the defendant bank had knowledge that the transactions were entered into for a fraudulent purpose and that his knowledge was to be attributed to the cefendant bank even though the chief manager was not on the board of directors.

4 *Re Hunting Lodges Ltd* [1985] ILRM 75.

5 *Re Kelly's Carpetdrome Ltd (No 1)* (1 July 1983, unreported) HC (Costello J).

Knowingly a party to the fraud: A person will not be deemed to be knowingly a party to fraudulent trading simply because he is aware of fraudulent trading by others.[1] There is no collective responsibility for fraudulent trading but rather the conduct of each individual officer must be looked at on his own.[2] Each person must be a party to the carrying on of a business and must take some positive or active part in the actual conduct of the business operations of the company. The positive and active part may take various forms and would include the giving of advice.[3] In the case of *Re Hunting Lodges Ltd* [4] Carroll J accepted the meaning of 'to be a party to' as indicating no more than participating in, taking part in, or concurs in, that it remains to be determined where or not inert disinterest will constitute knowingly being a party where a director who is also a large shareholder in the company never became actively involved in the business of the company. It was held that she had recklessly refrained from exercising proper control of the company and that that her inertia had facilitated the mismanagement by her co-director.[5]

1 *Re Maidstown Building Provisions Ltd* [1971] 3 All ER 363; *Re Kellys Carpetdrome Ltd* (No 2) [1984] IEHC 87 (O'Hanlon J).

2 *Re Petherick Exclusive Fashions Ltd* (1987) 3 NZCLC 99.

3 *Thomas Thompson v Innes* [1985] 2 NZ CLC 99.

4 *Re Hunting Lodges Ltd* [1985] ILRM 75.

5 Courtney in *The Law of Private Companies* (2nd edn, Tottel Publishing, 2002) at 10.091. He refers to the case of *Cronjeno v Stone* (1985) (3) SA 597 T. *Morris v Bank of India* [2005] All ER (d) 242 (Jun).

Intention to defraud: It is difficult to prove an intention to defraud due to the subjective nature of the test. It will certainly be established where an individual causes the company to incur debts and liabilities in the actual knowledge that there is no reasonable prospect of the creditors ever receiving payment of their debts.[1] The applicant must prove a subjective intention to defraud.[2] The words 'intent to defraud' and 'fraudulent purpose' are words which denote actual dishonesty involving, according to current notions, a fair trading among commercial men, real moral blame.[3] It has been said that fraudulent trading involves conduct which goes 'well beyond the bounds of what ordinary people engaged in business would regard as honest'.[4] If a company continues to carry on a business and to incur debts at a time when there is, to the knowledge of the directors, no prospect of the creditors ever receiving payment of those debts, it is, in general, a proper inference that the company is carrying on business with intent to defraud.[5] A person may also be guilty of fraudulent trading if he incurs credit on behalf of the company knowing that there is no good reason to think that funds will be available to pay the debt when it becomes due or shortly thereafter.[6] Tax evasion will amount to fraudulent trading, as will attempts to conceal the company's assets from its creditors.[7]

1 *Re William C Leitch Bros Ltd* [1932] All ER 892; *Re White and Osmond (Parkinstone) Ltd* (30 June 1960, unreported) English High Court per Buckley J.

2 *Hardy v Hanson* (1960) 105 CLR 451 (Australia) where Dixon CJ stressed the need for 'the intent to defraud creditors must be express or actual and real, nothing constructed, imputed or implied will do.'

3 *Re Patrick and Lyon Ltd* [1933] Ch 786; *R v Cox; Rv Hodges* [1983] BCLC 169, *Hardy v Hanson* (1960) 105 CLR 451; *Re Peake and Hall Ltd* (1985) PCC 87; *Re EB Tractors Ltd* (21 March 1986, unreported) High Court of Justice in Northern Ireland (Murray J); *Re Augustus Barnett and Son Ltd* (1986) BCC 98 904; *Aktieselskabet Dansk Skibfinansiering v Brothers* [2001] 2 BCLC 324.

4 *Re EB Tractors Ltd* (21 March 1986, unreported) High Court of Justice in Northern Ireland (Murray J).

5 *Re William C Leitch Bros Ltd* [1932] All ER 892.

6 *Re Grantham* [1984] 3 All ER 166; *Re PSK Construction Ltd* (7 December 2009, unreported) HC (Finlay Geoghegan J).

7 *Re Kelly's Carpetdrome* (No 1) (1 July 1983, unreported) HC (Costello J); *Aluminium Fabricators Ltd, Re* [1984] ILRM 399 (O'Hanlon J); *Re Hunting Lodges Ltd* [1985] ILRM 75.

Constitutionality of s 297A:[1] In *O'Keefe v Ferris*[2] the constitutionality of s 297A was upheld notwithstanding the fact that personal liability may be imposed on the respondent on a punitive basis rather than just in propertion to his own wrongdoing.

1 See generally Duffy, 'Fraudulent Trading and the decision of *O'Keefe v Ferris*' CLP (1994) 255.

2 *O'Keefe v Ferris* [1997] 3 IR 463; *Southern Mineral Oil Ltd* [1997] 3 IR 550. See also *Re PSK Construction Ltd* (7 December 2009, unreported) HC (Finlay Geoghegan J).

Illustrations of circumstances where the court have held that there has been fraudulent trading: In each of the cases where the courts have held that there has been fraudulent trading, the facts unequivocally showed fraudulent conduct motivated mainly by a desire to defraud the Revenue Commissioners. In *Re Kelly's Carpetdrome Ltd*[1] proper books of account were not kept, financial records were deliberately destroyed, assets were siphoned off to a friendly holder and, when the Revenue was closing in, the company's remaining stock was transferred to an associated company which the company paid the creditors rather than the Revenue Commissioners. In *Re Aluminium Fabricators Ltd*[2] the fraud involved the keeping of two separate books of account, the false set being for the auditors and the Revenue Commissioners and the true set being for the controllers of the company. In *Re Hunting Lodges Ltd*[3] the fraud involved paying party of the price for the company's assets 'under the table' so as to reduce the stamp duty payable on the transaction. In *Re Contract Packaging Ltd*[4] the fraud involved false invoicing and the diverting company moneys into bank accounts which were not recorded in the company's records. In *Re PSK Construction Ltd*[5] the underdeclaration of taxes and the use of those tax moneys to fund continued insolvent trading was found to amount to fraud.

1 *Re Kelly's Carpetdrome Ltd* (1 July 1983, unreported) HC, Per Costello J.

2 *Re Aluminium Fabricators Ltd* [1984] ILRM 399.

3 *Re Hunting Lodges Ltd* [1995] ILRM 75.

4 *Re Contract Packaging Ltd* (1992) *The Irish Times* 16 January.

5 *Re PSK Construction Ltd* (7 December 2009, unreported) HC (Finlay Geoghegan J).

Provisions common to reckless and fraudulent trading

Carrying on any business of the company: An isolated transaction may properly be regarded as the carrying on of any business of the company.[1] In this regard, liability may be imposed whether the fraud is being perpetrated on the company's creditors or on customers.[2]

1 In *Re Hunting Lodges* [1985] ILRM 75; *Re PSK Construction Ltd* (7 December 2009, unreported) HC (Finlay Geoghegan J); *Re Gerald Cooper Chemicals Ltd* [1978] 2 WLR 867; *Re Nimbus Trawling Co Ltd* (1986) 3 NZCLC 99–646. cf *Morphites vBernasconi* [2003] 2 BCLC 53.

2 *R v Kemp* [1988] BCLC 217.

Requirements that the company is insolvent: The company must be unable to pay its debts within the meaning of CA 1963, s 214.[1] This requirement should not be too difficult to satisfy in most cases. The majority of liquidations relate to insolvent companies, and a company can only be placed under the protection of the court if it is or is likely to be unable to pay its debts.[2]

1 Section 297A(3)(a).

2 Section 2(1)(a) of C(A)A 1990.

Potential applicants: The application may be made by the receiver, examiner, liquidator or any creditor or contributory of the company but only if the company is at the time in the course of being wound up or under the protection of the court.[1] If the proceedings are being taken for the benefit of the company, rather than by an individual creditor or contributory, the liquidator should be named as the applicant rather than the company itself.[2]

1 Section 297A(1); *In Re Hefferon Kearns Ltd* No (2) [1993] 3 IR 191.

2 *Southern Mineral Oils Ltd v Cooney (No 2)* [1999] 3 IR 549.

(b) to contribute such sum to the assets of the company by way of compensation in respect of the misapplication, retainer, misfeasance or other breach of duty as the court thinks just.

(3) This section has effect notwithstanding that the offence is one for which the offender may be criminally liable.][a]

Amendments

a CA 1963, s 298 substituted by CA 1990, s 142.

Definitions

'company': CA 1963, s 2(1); 'contributory': CA 1963, s 2(1), s 208; 'the court': CA 1963, s 2(1); 'director': CA 1963, s 2(1); 'officer': CA 1963, s 2(1).

Notes

General: This section provides for a summary procedure whereby redress may be obtained in respect of breaches of duty perpetrated by the directors and others. It is not necessary to launch an entire action and the summary procedure provides for the examination of the conduct of a promoter, liquidator, director or officer and following the examination the court has jurisdiction to compel the directors to repay or restore the money or property to the company or to contribute to the assets by way of compensation.[1] This section is procedural in nature and does not create any new cause of action and the acts covered by the section are acts which are wrongful according to the established rules of law and equity.[2] The procedure is only available where the company is in liquidation or where CA 1990, s 251 is applicable.[3] If the proceedings are being taken for the benefit of the company rather than by an individual creditor or contributory, the liquidator should be named as the applicant rather than the company itself.[4]

1 CA 1963, s 298(2). See for example, *Re Greendale Developments Ltd (No 2)* [1998] 1 IR 8.

2 *In Re B Johnson & Co (Builders) Ltd* [1955] Ch 634.

3 CA 1990, s 251 facilitates the invocation of various statutory remedies where a company is insolvent even though it is not being would up. In the case of a company that is not being wound up and where execution has not been possible and it is proved to the satisfaction of the court that the company is unable to pay its debts and the principle reason for it not being would up is insufficiency of assets, an application can be made to court in order to apply various statutory remedies (including misfeasance proceedings pursuant to CA 1963, s 298). See notes to CA 1990, s 251.

4 *Southern Mineral Oil Ltd v Cooney (No 2)* [1999] 3 IR 549.

The scope of misfeasance proceedings: The operation of this section is not applicable to every case in which a company has a right of action against an officer, but is limited to cases where there has been a breach of duty by an officer of the company that has caused a pecuniary loss to the company.[1] A claim based exclusively on common law negligence and/or an ordinary claim for damages for negligence would not be covered by this section.[2] Neither every error of judgment nor every act of negligence amounts to misfeasance. Rather, it requires something more than carelessness, such as gross negligence in failing to carry out a duty owed by a director to his company.[3]

1 In *Re Etic Ltd* [1928] Ch 861; *Cavendish-Bentinck v Finn* (1887) 12 App Cas 652; *Re George Newman & Co* [1895] 1 Ch 674; *Re SM Barker Ltd* [1950] IR 123; *Re Irish Provident Assurance Co* [1913] 1 IR 352; *Re Greendale Developments Ltd (No 2)* [1998] 1 IR 8. See also *Re Continental Assurance Co of London plc (No 4)* [2007] 2 BCLC 287 where it was observed by Park J that the 'loss' suffered by the company should be based on the increase in the net deficiency of the company between the date of the wrongdoing and the date of the liquidation.

2 *Re B Johnson & Co. (Builders)* [1955] Ch 634.

3 *Re Mont Clare Hotel Ltd (In Liquidation) Ray Jackson v Pauline Mortell & others* (2 December 1986, unreported) HC (Costello J) in which Costello J held 'it is not every error of judgement that amounts to misfeasance in law and it is not every act of negligence that amounts to misfeasance in law. It seems to me that something more than mere carelessness is required, some act, that perhaps, may amount to gross negligence in failing to carry out a duty owed by a director to his company'.

Potential respondents to an action: The terms of CA 1963, s 298 provide that any person who has taken part in the formation or promotion of the company or any past or present officer, liquidator, receiver or examiner of the company can be the subject of an action under this section. This section has been held not to apply to a solicitor who was instructed to do exclusively legal work.[1] The term 'officer' has, however, been construed sufficiently broadly to include a company's auditors.[2] It will also include a shadow director.[3] Where the company being wound up is a subsidiary, proceedings may also be commenced against any director of the holding company who has been guilty of misfeasance in relation to the subsidiary.[4] A liquidator can also be made liable for misfeasance.[5] Furthermore, it is to be noted that a director may be guilty of misfeasance committed even after he has retired from office.[6]

1 *Re Great Wheal Polgooth Co* (1883) 53 LJ Ch 42.

2 *Re R v Shacter* [1960] 2 QB 252.

3 CA 1963, s 27.

4 CA 1990, s 148.

5 *Re Home and Colonial Insurance Company Ltd* [1930] 1 Ch 102.

6 *Brosnan v Sommerville* [2007] 4 IR 135; *Curtis's Furnishing Stores Ltd v Freedman* [1966] 1 WLR 1219.

Limitation period: In the absence of any extension of time under the Statute of Limitations 1957, as amended (eg because of fraudulent concealment of the cause of action) the limitation period for a claim under s 298 is six years from the date of the misfeasance and not six years from the date of the commencement of the winding up.[1] Thus, depending on when the misfeasance occurred, the cause of action could be statute barred before the liquidation even commences.

1 *Re Eurocruit Europe Ltd* [2007] 2 BCLC 598. See also *Southern Mineral Oils Ltd v Cooney* [1997] 1 IR 237; *Southern Mineral Oils Ltd v Cooney (No 2)* [1999] 3 IR 549.

UK legislation

See IA 1986, s 212.

---

299 Prosecution of criminal offences committed by officers and members of company

[(1) If it appears to the court in the course of a winding-up by the court that any past or present officer, or any member, of the company has been guilty of an offence in relation to the company for which he is criminally liable, the court may either on the application of any person interested in the winding-up or of its own motion direct the liquidator to refer the matter to the Director of Public Prosecutions and in such a case the liquidator shall furnish to the Director of Public Prosecutions such information and give to him such access to and facilities for inspecting and taking any copies of any documents, being information or documents in the possession or under the control of the liquidator and relating to the matter in question, as the Director of Public Prosecutions may require.][a]

[(1A) Where the court directs a liquidator, in accordance with subsection (1), to refer a matter to the Director of Public Prosecutions, it shall also direct the liquidator to refer the matter to the Director and, in such a case, the liquidator shall furnish to the Director such information, and give to the Director such access to and facilities for inspecting and taking copies of any documents, being information or documents in the possession or under the control of the liquidator and relating to the matter in question, as the Director may require.][b]

(2) If it appears to the liquidator in the course of a voluntary winding up that any past or present officer, or any member, of the company has been guilty of any offence in relation to the company for which he is criminally liable, he shall forthwith report the matter to the [Director of Public Prosecutions][b] and shall furnish to the [Director of Public Prosecutions][b] such information and give to him such access to and facilities for inspecting and taking copies of any documents, being information or documents in the possession or under the control of the liquidator and relating to the matter in question, as the [Director of Public Prosecutions][b] may require.

[(2A) Where a liquidator, in accordance with subsection (2), reports a matter to the Director of Public Prosecutions, the liquidator shall also refer the matter to the Director and, in such a case, the liquidator shall furnish to the Director such information and give to the Director such access to and facilities for inspecting and taking copies of any documents, being information or documents in the possession or under the control of the liquidator and relating to the matter in question, as the Director may require.][b]

(3) If it appears to the court in the course of a voluntary winding up that any past or present officer, or any member, of the company has been guilty as aforesaid, and that no report relating to the matter has been made by the liquidator to [the Director of Public Prosecutions under subsection (2), or to the Director under subsection (2A)][b], the court may, on the application of any person interested in the winding up or of its own motion, direct the liquidator to make such a report, and on a report being made accordingly, this section shall have effect as though the report had been made [in pursuance of subsection (2) or subsection (2A), as the case may be][b].

(4) If, where any matter is reported or referred to the [Director of Public Prosecutions and the Director under this section, either the Director of Public Prosecutions or the Director considers][b] that the case is one in which a prosecution ought to be instituted and institutes proceedings accordingly, it shall be the duty of the liquidator and of every officer and agent of the company past and present (other than the defendant in the proceedings) to give all assistance in connection with the prosecution which he is reasonably able to give.

For the purposes of this subsection, 'agent' in relation to a company shall be deemed to include any banker or solicitor of the company and any person employed by the company as auditor, whether that person is or is not an officer of the company.

(5) If any person fails or neglects to give assistance in the manner required by subsection (4), the court may, on the application [of the Director of Public Prosecutions or of the Director][b], direct that person to comply with the requirements of that subsection, and where any such application is made in relation to a liquidator the court may, unless it appears that the failure or neglect to comply was due to the liquidator not having in his hands sufficient assets of the company to enable him so to do, direct that the costs of the application shall be borne by the liquidator personally.

Amendments

a CA 1963, s 299(1) substituted by CA 1990, s 143.

b Sub-ss (1A) and (2A) inserted and words substituted by CLEA 2001, s 51.

Cross reference

In relation to the extension of the provisions of this sub-s to receivers, see CA 1990, s 179.

Definitions

'agent': CA 1963, s 2(1); 'company': CA 1963, s 2(1); 'the court': CA 1963, s 2(1); 'document': CA 1963, s 2(1): 'member': CA 1963, s 31; 'officer': CA 1963, s 2(1).

UK legislation

See IA 1986, ss 218 (amended by CA 1989, s 78), 219.

Supplementary Provisions as to Winding Up

300 Disqualification for appointment as liquidator

A body corporate shall not be qualified for appointment as liquidator of a company whether in a winding up by the court or in a voluntary winding up and—

(a) any appointment made in contravention of this provision shall be void; and

(b) any body corporate which acts as liquidator of a company [shall be guilty of an offence and liable to a fine][a] not exceeding [€1,904.61][b].

Amendments

a Words in CA 1963, s 300(b) substituted by C(AA)A 2003, s 57 and Sch 2, para 1.

b '£500' substituted for '£100' by C(A)A 1982, Sch 1, increased to '£1,500' by CA 1990, s 240(7) as inserted by CLEA 2001, s 104(c) and £1,500 converted to €1,904.61 by Council Regulations (EC) No 1103/97, No 974/98 and No 2866/98 and the Economic and Monetary Union Act 1998, s 6.

Definitions

'company': CA 1963, s 2(1); 'the court': CA 1963, s 2(1).

Notes

See the notes to CA 1963, s 228 entitled 'Disqualification for appointment as liquidator'.

UK legislation

See IA 1986, ss 389, 390(1).

[300A Disqualification for appointment as liquidator

(1) None of the following persons shall be qualified for appointment as liquidator of a company—

(a) a person who is, or who has within 12 months of the commencement of the winding up been, an officer or servant of the company;

(b) except with the leave of the court, a parent, spouse, brother, sister or child of an officer of the company;

(c) a person who is a partner or in the employment of an officer or servant of the company;

(d) a person who is not qualified by virtue of this subsection for appointment as liquidator of any other body corporate which is that company's subsidiary or holding company or a subsidiary of that company's holding company, or would be so disqualified if the body corporate were a company.

References in this subsection to an officer or servant of the company include references to an auditor.

(2) An application for leave under subsection (1)(b) shall be supported by such evidence as the court may require.

(3) If a liquidator becomes disqualified by virtue of this section he shall thereupon vacate his office and give notice in writing within 14 days to—

(a) the court in a court winding up,

(b) the company in a members' voluntary winding up,

(c) the company and the creditors in a creditors' voluntary winding up,

that he has vacated it by reason of such disqualification.

(4) Any person who acts as a liquidator when disqualified by this section from so doing or who fails to comply with subsection (3), if that subsection applies to him, shall be guilty of an offence and shall be liable—

(a) on summary conviction, to a fine not exceeding [€1,904.61][b] and, for continued contravention, a daily default fine not exceeding [€63.49][c];

(b) on conviction on indictment, to a fine of [€12,697.38][d] and, for continued contravention, a daily default fine not exceeding [€317.43][e].

(5) This section shall not apply to a winding-up commenced before the commencement of section 146 of the Companies Act, 1990].[a]

Amendments

a CA 1963, s 300A inserted by CA 1990, s 146.

b '£1,000' increased to '£1,500' by CA 1990, s 240(7) as inserted by CLEA 2001, s 104(c) and converted to €1,904.61 by Council Regulations (EC) No 1103/97, No 974/98 and No 2866/98 and the Economic and Monetary Union Act 1998, s 6.

c £50 converted to €63.49 by Council Regulations (EC) No 1103/97, No 974/98 and No 2866/98 and the Economic and Monetary Union Act 1998, s 6.

d £10,000 converted to €12,697.38 by Council Regulations (EC) No 1103/97, No 974/98 and No 2866/98 and the Economic and Monetary Union Act 1998, s 6.

e £250 converted to €317.43 by Council Regulations (EC) No 1103/97, No 974/98 and No 2866/98 and the Economic and Monetary Union Act 1998, s 6.

Definitions

'company': CA 1963, s 2(1); 'the court': CA 1963, s 2(1); 'creditors' voluntary winding up': CA 1963, s 2(1), s 256(7); 'holding company': CA 1963, s 2(1), s 155; 'member': CA 1963, s 31; 'members' voluntary winding up': CA 1963, s 2(1), s 256(7); 'officer': CA 1963, s 2(1); 'subsidiary': CA 1963, s 2(1), s 155.

Notes

See the notes to CA 1963, s 228 entitled 'Disqualification for appointment as liquidator'.

UK legislation

See IA 1986, ss 389, 390.

---

301 Corrupt inducement affecting appointment as liquidator

Any person who gives or agrees or offers to give to any member or creditor of a company any valuable consideration with a view to securing his own appointment or nomination or to securing or preventing the appointment or nomination of some person other than himself as the company's liquidator [shall be guilty of an offence and liable to a fine][a] not exceeding [€1,904.61].[b]

Amendments

a Words substituted by C(AA)A 2003, s 57 and Sch 2.

b '£500' substituted for '£100' by C(A)A 1982, Sch 1, increased to '£1,500' by CA 1990, s 240(7) as inserted by CLEA 2001, s 104(c) and converted to €1,904.61 by Council Regulations (EC) No 1103/97, No 974/98 and No 2866/98 and the Economic and Monetary Union Act 1998, s 6.

Definitions

'company': CA 1963, s 2(1); 'member': CA 1963, s 31.

Notes

Bribe to secure appointment of liquidator: Whilst it is an offence for a person to pay a bribe to a member or creditor of a company either to secure his own or someone else's appointment or nomination as liquidator, the payment of the bribe does not appear to invalidate the appointment or nomination itself. Nevertheless, if the liquidator has been party to such corrupt conduct, grounds would appear to exist justifying his disqualification under CA 1990, s 160.

UK legislation

See IA 1986, s 164.

[301A Disclosure of interest by creditors, etc. at creditors' meeting

(1) Where, at a meeting of creditors, a resolution is proposed for the appointment of a liquidator, any creditor who has a connection with the proposed liquidator shall, before the resolution is put, make such connection known to the chairman of the meeting who shall disclose that fact to the meeting, together with details thereof.

(2) Subsection (1) shall also apply to any person at the meeting, being a representative of a creditor and entitled to vote on the resolution on his behalf.

(3) Where the chairman of a meeting of creditors has any such connection as is mentioned in subsection (1), he shall disclose that fact to the meeting, together with details thereof.

(4) For the purposes of this section, a person has a connection with a proposed liquidator if he is—

(a) a parent, spouse, brother, sister or child of, or

(b) employed by, or a partner of,

the proposed liquidator.

(5) A person who fails to comply with this section [shall be guilty of an offence and liable to a fine][b] not exceeding [€1,904.61].[c]

(6) In exercising its jurisdiction under sections 267 (2) or 272 (2) (which relate to the appointment or removal of a liquidator) the court may have regard to any failure to comply with this section.][a]

Amendments

a CA 1963, s 301A inserted by CA 1990, s 147.

b Words in CA 1963, s 301A(5) substituted by C(AA)A 2003, s 57 and Sch 2, para 1.

c '£1,000' increased to '£1,500' by CA 1990, s 240(7) as inserted by CLEA 2001, s 104(c). £1,500 converted to €1,904.61 by Council Regulations (EC) No 1103/97, No 974/98 and No 2866/98 and the Economic and Monetary Union Act 1998, s 6.

Definitions

'the court': CA 1963, s 2(1).

Notes

See the notes to CA 1963, s 267. Curiously, the employer of a proposed liquidator is not deemed to be connected with him and seemingly therefore does not have to make disclosure under this section. Nevertheless, the relationship is one which the court would undoubtedly take into account if a subsequent challenge were to be made to the appointment under CA 1963, s 267 or s 277.

---

302 Enforcement of duty of liquidator to make returns

(1) If any liquidator who has made any default in filing, delivering or making any return, account or other document, or in giving any notice which he is by law required to file, deliver, make or give, fails to make good the default within 14 days after the service on him of a notice requiring him to do so, [or such greater period as may be specified in the notice],[a] the court may, on an application made to the court by any contributory or creditor of the company or by the registrar of companies, make an order directing the liquidator to make good the default within such time as may be specified in the order.

(2) Any such order may provide that all costs of and incidental to the application shall be borne by the liquidator.

(3) Nothing in this section shall be taken to prejudice the operation of any enactment imposing penalties on a liquidator in respect of any such default as aforesaid.

Amendments

a Words inserted by IFCMPA 2005, s 63.

Definitions

'company': CA 1963, s 2(1); 'contributory': CA 1963, s 2(1), s 208; 'the court': CA 1963, s 2(1); 'document': CA 1963, s 2(1): 'the registrar of companies': CA 1963, s 2(1).

Notes

Enforcement of duty to make returns: CA 1963, s 302 empowers the Registrar of Companies and any creditor or contributory of a company to serve on the liquidator notice requiring him to make good any default on his part in filing, delivering or making any return, account or other document and, if he fails to make good that default within 14 days or such longer period as may have been specified in the notice, to apply to the court for a mandatory order directing him to remedy the position. The following are examples of cases where the liquidator's default might form the subject of an application under s 302:

(i) a failure on the part of an official liquidator to deliver to the Registrar of Companies an office copy of the order appointing him;[1]

(ii) a failure on the part of a voluntary liquidator to deliver to the Registrar of Companies notice of his appointment;[2]

(iii) a failure to file with the Registrar of Companies a certified copy of a resolution of a meeting of creditors or contributories;[3]

(iv) a failure on the part of an official liquidator to leave his accounts of receipts and payments at the Examiner's Office of the High Court;[4]

(v) a failure on the part of a voluntary liquidator to file a copy of his annual account with the Registrar of Companies;[5]

(vi) a failure on the part of a liquidator to file with the Registrar of Companies yearly (or in the case of a voluntary liquidation, half yearly) statements as to the progress of the winding up, in so far as not completed within two years;[6]

(vii) a failure to send notice to any creditor of a declared interim or final dividend;[7]

(viii) a failure on the part of a voluntary liquidator to file his final account and return as to the holding of final meetings with the Registrar of Companies;[8] and

(ix) a failure on the part of an official liquidator to file with the Registrar of Companies an office copy of the final order in the winding up pursuant to which the company is dissolved.[9]

Apart from the remedies available under s 302, the Registrar of Companies and any creditor or contributory as well as the ODCE may apply to the court under CA 1963, s 371 for an order requiring any officer (including a liquidator) to make good any default under the Companies Acts (and not just a default regarding the delivery/filing of documents). The provisions of s 371 which had been invoked on a few occasions by the Registrar of Companies are now being more regularly invoked as a result of the ODCE being included in the category of persons entitled to seek orders thereunder. In this regard see generally the notes to CA 1963, s 371.

For the possible criminal consequences of a breach of s 302, see CA 1990, s 145.

1 CA 1963, s 227(1).
2 CA 1963, s 278(1).
3 RSC 1986, Ord 74, r 63.
4 RSC 1986, Ord 74, rr 32 and 42.
5 CA 1963, ss 262(1) and 272(1).
6 CA 1963, s 306 and RSC 1986, Ord 74, r 130.
7 RSC 1986, Ord 74, r 113.
8 CA 1963, ss 263(3) and 273(3).
9 CA 1963, s 249(2).

UK legislation

See IA 1986, s 170.

303 Notification that a company is in liquidation

(1) Where a company is being wound up, whether by the court or voluntarily, every invoice, order for goods or business letter issued by or on behalf of the company or a liquidator of the company, or a receiver of the property of the company, being a document on or in which the name of the company appears, shall contain a statement that the company is being wound up.

(2) If default is made in complying with this section, the company and any of the following persons who knowingly and wilfully authorises or permits the default, namely, any officer of the company, any liquidator of the company and any receiver, [shall be guilty of an offence and liable to a fine][a] not exceeding [€1,904.61].[b]

Amendments

a Words in CA 1963, s 303(2) substituted by C(AA)A 2003, s 57 and Sch 2, para 1.

b '£250' substituted for '£50' by C(A)A 1982, Sch 1, increased to '£1,500' by CA 1990, s 240(7) as inserted by CLEA 2001, s 104(c) and converted to €1,904.61 by Council Regulations (EC) No 1103/97, No 974/98 and No 2866/98 and the Economic and Monetary Union Act 1998, s 6.

Definitions

'company': CA 1963, s 2(1); 'the court': CA 1963, s 2(1); 'document': CA 1963, s 2(1); 'officer': CA 1963, s 2(1).

Notes

Only those documents specified in CA 1963, s 303 must state that the company is in liquidation. No such statement is required on other company documents such as cheques.

UK legislation

See IA 1986, s 188.

304 Books of company to be evidence

When a company is being wound up, all books and papers of the company and of the liquidators shall, as between the contributories of the company, be *prima facie* evidence of the truth of all matters purporting to be recorded therein.

Definitions

'books and paper': CA 1963, s 2(1); 'company': CA 1963, s 2(1); 'contributory': CA 1963, s 2(1), s 208.

Notes

Books of the company as evidence: By virtue of CA 1963, s 304 the books and records of the company are *prima facie* evidence as between the company and the contributories and as between the contributories *inter se*. Being only *prima facie* evidence, their contents may be rebutted by other evidence to the contrary. Furthermore, this *prima facie* evidence does not apply to proceedings between the company and third parties such as creditors or debtors of the company.

UK legislation

See IA 1986, s 191.

305 Disposal of books and papers of company in winding up

(1) When a company has been wound up and is about to be dissolved, the books and papers of the company and of the liquidator may be disposed of as follows—

(a) in the case of a winding up by the court, in such way as the court directs;

(b) in the case of a members' voluntary winding up, in such way as the company by special resolution directs, and in the case of a creditors' voluntary winding up, in such way as the committee of inspection or, if there is no such committee, as the creditors of the company, may direct, so, however, that such books and papers shall be retained by the liquidator for a period of 3 years from the date of the dissolution of the company and, in the absence of any direction as to their disposal, he may then dispose of them as he thinks fit.

(2) If a liquidator fails to comply with the requirements of this section he [shall be guilty of an offence and liable to a fine][a] not exceeding [€1,904.61].[b]

Amendments

a Words in CA 1963, s 305(2) substituted by C(AA)A 2003, s 57 and Sch 2, para 1.

b '£500' substituted for '£100' by C(A)A 1982, Sch 1, increased to '£1,500' by CA 1990, s 240(7) as inserted by CLEA 2001, s 104(c) and converted to €1,904.61 by Council Regulations (EC) No 1103/97, No 974/98 and No 2866/98 and the Economic and Monetary Union Act 1998, s 6.

Definitions

'books and paper': CA 1963, s 2(1); 'company': CA 1963, s 2(1); 'the court': CA 1963, s 2(1); 'creditors' voluntary winding up': CA 1963, s 2(1), s 256(7); 'member': CA 1963, s 31; 'members' voluntary winding up': CA 1963, s 2(1), s 256(7).

Notes

Disposal of books and records by the liquidator: In the case of a voluntary winding up the liquidator is required to maintain the books and records for at least three years from the date of dissolution. In practice the court will impose a similar requirement on official liquidators. It is to be noted though that under CLEA 2001, s 57 the ODCE is empowered to inspect the liquidator's books (as distinct from the company's books) for up to six years after the completion of the winding up. It is a criminal offence for a liquidator to fail to co-operate or fail to deliver up his books when requested to do so by the ODCE.[1] The effectiveness of such an investigation by the ODCE could well be frustrated if the company's books no longer existed and if the ODCE only had the liquidator's own books available for inspection. In this regard the liquidator's books might only be capable of meaningful analysis by reference to the underlying records of the company itself. Accordingly, liquidators may be well advised to retain their records for longer than the minimum period prescribed by the court or by CA 1963, s 305, as the case may be, so as to avoid frustrating any such investigation as might be undertaken by the ODCE.

1 CLEA 2001, s 57(4).

306 Information about progress of liquidation

(1) If, where a company is being wound up, the winding up is not concluded within 2 years after its commencement, the liquidator shall, at such intervals as may be prescribed, until the winding up is concluded, send to the registrar of companies a statement in the prescribed form and containing the prescribed particulars about the proceedings in and position of the liquidation.

(2) If a liquidator fails to comply with this section, he [shall be guilty of an offence and liable to a fine][a] not exceeding [€1,904.61].[b]

(3) An offence under this section may be prosecuted by the registrar of companies.

Amendments

a Words in CA 1963, s 306(2) substituted by C(AA)A 2003, s 57 and Sch 2, para 1.

b '£1,000' substituted for '£500' by CA 1990, s 145 and increased to '£1,500' by CA 1990, s 240(7) as inserted by CLEA 2001, s 104(c). £1,500 converted to €1,904.61 by Council Regulations (EC) No 1103/97, No 974/98 and No 2866/98 and the Economic and Monetary Union Act 1998, s 6.

Definitions

'company': CA 1963, s 2(1); 'concluded' winding up': RSC 1986, Ord 74, r 129; 'the registrar of companies': CA 1963, s 2(1).

Notes

Statement as to progress of older liquidations: The statement as to the progress of any liquidation which has not been concluded within a period of two years must be in the form prescribed by Form No 44 of the Rules of the Superior Courts and must be verified by affidavit in the form prescribed by Form No 45.[1] In the case of a compulsory winding up the statement must be sent to the Registrar of Companies annually, whereas in the case of a voluntary winding up it must be sent on a half yearly basis.[2] Moreover, regardless of the form of the liquidation, once the assets of the company have been fully realised and distributed, a final statement must be delivered to the Registrar of Companies forthwith.[3]

1 RSC 1986, Ord 74, r 130(b).

2 RSC 1986, Ord 74, r 130(a).

3 RSC 1986, Ord 74, r 130(a).

Conclusion of winding up: In the case of a compulsory winding up, once the official liquidator's final account has been passed he applies to the court for final orders (as to payment of final dividends, remuneration, costs and expenses etc) including an order for the dissolution of the company.[1] The court will direct that the company be dissolved once the Examiner of the High Court has issued a certificate to the effect that any remaining balance of funds in the liquidation has been disposed of and that the affairs of the company have been completely wound up.[2] The liquidation is deemed to have been concluded on the date on which the order dissolving the company has been delivered to the Registrar of Companies by the official liquidator.[3]

In the case of a voluntary liquidation, the winding up is deemed to be concluded on the date of the dissolution of the company by the Registrar pursuant to CA 1963, s 263 or s 273, as the case may be.[4] However, if on the date of dissolution any funds or assets of the company remain undistributed, the winding up shall not be deemed to be concluded until such funds or assets have either been distributed or paid into The Companies Liquidation Account.[5]

1 RSC 1986, Ord 74, r 137.

2 RSC 1986, Ord 74, r 137.

3 RSC 1986, Ord 74, r 129(a).

4 RSC 1986, Ord 74, r 129(b).

5 RSC 1986, Ord 74, r 129(b). In relation to The Companies Liquidation Account, see CA 1963, s 307.

UK legislation

See IA 1986, s 192.

307 Unclaimed dividends and balances to be paid into Companies Liquidation Account

(1) Where a company has been wound up voluntarily and is about to be dissolved, the liquidator shall lodge to an account to be known as The Companies Liquidation Account in the Bank of Ireland in such manner as may be prescribed by rules of court the whole unclaimed dividends admissible to proof and unapplied or undistributable balances.

(2) The Companies Liquidation Account shall be under the control of the court.

(3) Any application by a person claiming to be entitled to any dividend or payment out of a lodgment made in pursuance of subsection (1), and any payment out of such lodgment in satisfaction of such claim, shall be made in manner prescribed by rules of court.

(4) At the expiration of 7 years from the date of any lodgment made in pursuance of subsection (1), the amount of the lodgment remaining unclaimed shall be paid into the Exchequer, but where the court is satisfied that any person claiming is entitled to any dividend or payment out of the moneys paid into the Exchequer, it may order payment of the same and the Minister for Finance shall issue such sum as may be necessary to provide for that payment.

Definitions

'company': CA 1963, s 2(1); 'the court': CA 1963, s 2(1); 'prescribed': CA 1963, s 2(1).

Notes

The Companies Liquidation Account: The Companies Liquidation Account, which is maintained in the Bank of Ireland, is the account into which the liquidator must lodge unclaimed or undistributed balances in a liquidation. Although CA 1963, s 307 refers to the account as being applicable in the case of voluntary liquidations, it is also the practice in the case of compulsory liquidations for the court in making its final orders to direct that any such unclaimed or undistributed amounts be paid into that account. Amounts may be unclaimed or undistributed, for example, where creditors have failed to cash their dividend cheques or where particular creditors cannot be located or, in the case of corporate creditors, where they have since been dissolved or where, in the case of a deceased creditor, his estate has since been administered and there is no longer a personal representative acting on its behalf.

For the procedural aspects of payments into and out of The Companies Liquidation Account, see RSC 1986, Ord 74, r 131.

308 Resolutions passed at adjourned meetings of creditors and contributories

Where a resolution is passed at an adjourned meeting of any creditors or contributories of a company, the resolution shall, for all purposes, be treated as having been passed on the date on which it was in fact passed and shall not be deemed to have been passed on any earlier date.

Definitions

'company': CA 1963, s 2(1); 'contributory': CA 1963, s 2(1), s 208.

UK legislation

See IA 1986, s 194.

---

309 Meetings to ascertain wishes of creditors and contributories

(1) The court may, as to all matters relating to the winding up of a company, have regard to the wishes of the creditors or contributories of the company, as proved to it by any sufficient evidence, and may, if it thinks fit, for the purpose of ascertaining those wishes, direct meetings of the creditors or contributories to be called, held and conducted in such manner as the court directs, and may appoint a person to act as chairman of any such meeting and report the result thereof to the court.

(2) In the case of creditors, regard shall be had to the value of each creditor's debt.

(3) In the case of contributories, regard shall be had to the number of votes conferred on each contributory by this Act or the articles.

Definitions

'articles': CA 1963, s 2(1); 'company': CA 1963, s 2(1); 'contributory': CA 1963, s 2(1), s 208; 'the court': CA 1963, s 2(1).

Notes

Ascertaining the wishes of creditors and contributories: To date, the provisions of CA 1963, s 309 have not been given much consideration. However, an area where the court has had regard to the wishes of creditors and, to a lesser extent, contributories, has been in relation to the hearing of an opposed winding-up petition, particularly one which is alleged to have been presented in respect of a disputed debt or for an ulterior purpose.[1]

1 See the notes to CA 1963, s 214 and, in particular, the observations of McCracken J in *Re Genport Ltd* [1996] IEHC 34.

UK legislation

See IA 1986, s 195.

Provisions as to Dissolution

310 Power of court to declare dissolution of company void

(1) Where a company has been dissolved, the court may at any time within 2 years of the date of the dissolution, on an application being made for the purpose by the liquidator of the company or by any other person who appears to the court to be interested, make an order, upon such terms as the court thinks fit, declaring the dissolution to have been

void, and thereupon such proceedings may be taken as might have been taken if the company had not been dissolved.

(2) It shall be the duty of the person on whose application the order was made, within 14 days after the making of the order, or such further time as the court may allow, to deliver to the registrar of companies for registration an office copy of the order, and if that person fails to do so, he [shall be guilty of an offence and liable to a fine][a] not exceeding [€1,904.61].[b]

Amendments

a 'shall be guilty of an offence and liable to a fine' substituted for 'shall be liable to a fine' by CA(A)A 2003, s 57 and Sch 2.

b '£25' substituted for '£5' by C(A)A 1982, Sch 1, increased to £1,500 by CA 1990, s 240(7) as inserted by CLEA 2001, s 104 (c) and converted to €1,904.61 by Council Regulations (EC) No 1103\97, No 974\98 and No 2866\98 and the Economic and Monetary Union Act 1998, s 6.

Definitions

'company': CA 1963, s 2(1); 'the court': CA 1963, s 2(1); 'the Registrar of Companies': CA 1963, s 2(1).

Notes

Dissolution of companies: For the circumstances in which a company may be dissolved, see CA 1963, ss 249, 263, 273 and 311 and C(A)A 1982, ss 12 and 12A and C(A)(No2)A 1999, ss 43(15) and 48.

Restoration to the register[1]: Whilst the provisions of CA 1963, s 310 will normally only be availed of for the purpose of resurrecting a company that has been dissolved following a winding up (eg to facilitate the distribution of an overlooked asset or to facilitate a claim by a creditor),[2] it may be availed of in other circumstances[3] as where the company has been struck off by the register as being defunct[4] or for failure to have any registered directors[5] or at least one Irish director a bond in lieu thereof[6] or for failure to file annual returns[7] or tax returns.[8] Unlike restoration under C(A)A 1982, s 12B this application can only be made before the High Court.[9]

1 See generally, Courtney, *Law of Private Companies* (2nd edn, Tottel Publishing, 2002) paras 12.152–12.174, O'Higgins, 'How to Restore a Struck-Off Company to the Register' (2001) Gazette 40 and Leonard, 'Restoring companies to the register' (2000) 6(3) Bar Review 182.

2 *Stanhope Pension Trust Ltd v Registrar of Companies* [1994] 1 BCLC 628 at 635; *Re Oakleague Ltd* [1995] 2 BCLC 624.

3 *Re Belmont and Co Ltd* [1951] 2 All ER 898; *Re Test Holdings (Clifton) Ltd* [1970] Ch 285; *Re Wood and Martin Ltd* [1971] 1 WLR 293; *Re Thompson and Riches Ltd* [1981] 1 WLR 682.

4 See CA 1963, s 311.

5 C(A)(No2)A 1999, s 48.

6 See C(A)(No2)A 1999, s 43(15).

7 See C(A)A 1982, s 12.

8 See C(A)A 1982, s 12A.

9 The phrase 'the court' is defined by CA 1963, s 2(1) as meaning the High Court. See C(A)A 1982, s 12B and notes thereto.

Who may petition: The application to have the company restored may be made by the liquidator or by an interested person.[1] A person purportedly appointed as voluntary liquidator of a company at a time when, unbeknownst to the parties, the company was already dissolved, is not strictly speaking a 'liquidator' and accordingly does not have *locus standi* in that capacity to apply to have the dissolution declared void.[2] He will, however, be entitled to so apply as a 'person interested'.[3] A member or creditor would also appear to be a 'person interested'.[4] In this regard, the creditors so entitled to apply would include contingent or prospective creditors of the company.[5] However, in the case of a contingent or prospective creditor, he may be required to establish that his claim is neither frivolous nor vexatious and is being bona fide maintained, in order to be allowed by the court to proceed with his petition.[6] The Revenue Commissioners will only be regarded as creditors of the company if, and to the extent that, they have raised assessments on the company prior to the date upon which its name was dissolved.[7] A person who after the date of dissolution acquires shares in the company, or takes an assignment of one of its debts, will not be regarded as a 'member or creditor'[8] but clearly would be a 'person interested'.

1 CA 1963, s 310(1).

2 *Re Wood and Martin Ltd* [1971] 1 WLR 293.

3 *Re Wood and Martin Ltd* [1971] 1 WLR 293.

4 *Re Thompson and Riches Ltd* [1981] 1 WLR 682.

5 *Re Deauville Communications Worldwide Ltd* [2002] 2 IR 32; *Re Industrial Glazing Systems Ltd* (6 November 2000, unreported) HC (Barr J); *City of Westminster Assurance Co Ltd v Registrar of Companies* (1997) BCC 960; *Re Harvest Lane Motor Bodies Ltd* [1969] 1 Ch 457; *Re Mixhurst Ltd* [1994] 2 BCLC 19; *Re Jayham Ltd* [1995] 2 BCLC 455.

6 *Re Deauville Communications Worldwide Ltd* [2002] 2 IR 32.

7 *Re Nelson Car Hire Ltd* (1973) 107 ILTR 97; *Re Supatone (Eire) Ltd* (1973) 107 ILTR 105.

8 *Re Test Holdings (Clifton) Ltd* [1970] Ch 285; *Re New Timbiqui Gold Mines Ltd* [1961] Ch 319.

Notice parties: Any application to declare the dissolution void should be on notice to the relevant State authorities,[1] such as the Chief State Solicitor and the Registrar. There are no statutory requirements as to notice parties under CA 1963, s 311, unlike C(A)A 1982, s 12B(3).[2]

1 *Re Belmont and Co* [1951] 2 All ER 898.

2 C(A)A 1982, s 12B(3) requires that notice be given to the Registrar, the Revenue Commissioners and the Minister for Finance.

Consequences of restoration: Upon the dissolution being declared void, the company's corporate existence is restored and any property which had previously vested in the State under the State Property Act 1954, s 28 reverts to the company without the need for any formal vesting order.[1] Proceedings may be taken by or against the company as if it had not been dissolved.[2] However, the order of the court does not have the effect of retrospectively validating transactions purportedly entered into by or with the company during the period of dissolution.[3] Accordingly, proceedings which had been commenced by or against the company either prior to or during the period of dissolution, will not be retrospectively validated.[4] While the avoidance of the dissolution of the company is not retrospective, the period of actual dissolution will nonetheless be taken into account in determining whether a claim by or against the company is statute barred.[5]

1 *Re CW Dixon Ltd* [1947] Ch 251.

2 CA 1963, s 310(1).

3 *Morris v Harris* [1927] AC 252; *Re Mixhurst Ltd* [1994] 2 BCLC 19; *Re Townreach Ltd* [1995] Ch 28; *Re Philip Powis Ltd* [1998] 1 BCLC 440; *Re Amantiss Enterprises Ltd; Framus plc v CRH plc* [2000] 2 ILRM 177.

4 *Morris v Harris* [1927] AC 252; *Re Mixhurst Ltd* [1994] 2 BCLC 19; *Re Townreach Ltd* [1995] Ch 28; *Re Philip Powis Ltd* [1998] 1 BCLC 440; *Re Amantiss Enterprises Ltd; Framus plc v CRH plc* [2000] 2 ILRM 177. This contrasts with the position where a company is restored to the register under CA 1963, s 311(8) or under C(A)A 1982, s 12B. In those circumstances the validation is indeed retrospective: *Re Amantiss Enterprises Ltd; Framus plc v CRH plc* [2000] 2 ILRM 177; *Re Deauville Communications Worldwide Ltd* [2002] 2 IR 32; *Top Creative Ltd v St Albans DC* [2000] 2 BCLC 379; *Tyman's Ltd v Craven* [1952] 1 All ER 613; *Re Dunleckney Ltd* [2001] 1 IR 103.

5 *Re Philip Powis Ltd* [1998] 1 BCLC 440; *Smith v White Knight Laundry Ltd* [2001] 2 BCLC 206. In this respect the position differs from a restoration under C(A)A 1982, s 12B, where the court may order that the period of dissolution be ignored for the purpose of calculating the relevant limitation period: *Re Donald Kenyon Ltd* [1956] 3 All ER 596. Notably, in the UK where the dissolution is declared void under the equivalent of CA 1963, s 310, the court has express jurisdiction in respect of personal injuries and fatal injuries claims to declare that the period of dissolution be ignored for the purpose of the limitation period.

UK legislation

See CA 1985, s 651; CA 1989, ss 141(2), (3), 212, Sch 24.

311 Power of registrar to strike defunct company off register

[(1) Where the registrar of companies has reasonable cause to believe that a company is not carrying on business, he may send to the company by post a registered letter inquiring whether the company is carrying on business and stating that, if an answer is not received within one month from the date of that letter, a notice will be published in [the Companies Registration Office Gazette][a] with a view to striking the name of the company off the register.

(2) If the registrar either receives an answer to the effect that the company is not carrying on business or does not within one month after sending the letter receive any answer, he may publish in [the Companies Registration Office Gazette][a] and send to the company by registered post a notice that at the expiration of one month from the date of that notice, the name of the company mentioned therein will, unless cause is shown to the contrary, be struck off the register, and the company will be dissolved.

(3) If in any case where a company is being wound up the registrar has reasonable cause to believe either that no liquidator is acting, or that the affairs of the company are fully wound up, and the returns required to be made by the liquidator have not been made for a period of 6 consecutive months, the registrar shall publish in [the Companies Registration Office Gazette][a] and send to the company or the liquidator, if any, a like notice as is provided in subsection (2).

(4) ...][b]

(5) Subject to subsections (6) and (7), at the expiration of the time mentioned in the notice, the registrar may, unless cause to the contrary is previously shown by the company, strike its name off the register, and shall publish notice thereof in [the Companies Registration Office Gazette][a] and on the publication in [the Companies Registration Office Gazette][a] of this notice, the company shall be dissolved.

(6) The liability, if any, of every director, officer and member of the company shall continue and may be enforced as if the company had not been dissolved.

(7) Nothing in subsection (5) or (6) shall affect the power of the court to wind up a company the name of which has been struck off the register.

(8) If a company or any member or creditor thereof feels aggrieved by the company having been struck off the register, the court, on an application made (on notice to the registrar) by the company or member or creditor before the expiration of 20 years from the publication in [the Companies Registration Office Gazette][a] of the notice aforesaid, may, if satisfied that the company was at the time of the striking off carrying on business or otherwise that it is just that the company be restored to the register, order that the

name of the company be restored to the register, and upon an office copy of the order being delivered to the registrar for registration, the company shall be deemed to have continued in existence as if its name had not been struck off; and the court may by the order give such directions and make such provisions as seem just for placing the company and all other persons in the same position as nearly as may be [as if the name of the company had not been struck off or make such other order as seems just (and such other order is referred to in subsection (8A) as an 'alternative order').][c]

[(8A) An alternative order may, if the court considers it appropriate that it should do so, include a provision that, as respects a debt or liability incurred by, or on behalf of, the company during the period when it stood struck of the register, the officers of the company or such one or more of them as is or are specified in the order shall be liable for the whole or part (as the court thinks just) of the debt or liability.][d]

(9) A notice to be sent under this section to a liquidator may be addressed to the liquidator at his last known place of business, and a letter or notice to be sent under this section to a company may be addressed to the company at its registered office, or, if no office has been registered, to the care of some officer of the company, or, if there is no officer of the company whose name and address are known to the registrar of companies, may be sent to each of the persons who subscribed the memorandum, addressed to him at the address mentioned in the memorandum.

Amendments

a 'the Companies Registration Office Gazette' substituted for '*Iris Oifigiúil*' by IFCMPA 2005, s 72.

b CA 1963, s 311(1), (2), (3) substituted and sub-s (4) deleted by C(A)A 1982, s 11.

c The words 'as if the name of the company had not been struck off or make such other order as seems just (and such other order is referred to in subsection (8A) as an 'alternative order')' substituted for 'as if the name of the company had not been struck off' in CA 1963, s 311(8) by C(A)(No 2)A 1999, s 49, para (a).

d CA 1963, s 311(8A) inserted by C(A)(No 2)A 1999, s 49, para (b).

Definitions

'company': CA 1963, s 2(1); 'the court': CA 1963, s 2(1); 'director': CA 1963, s 2(1); 'member': CA 1963, s 31; 'memorandum': CA 1963, s 2(1); 'officer': CA 1963, s 2(1); 'the Registrar of Companies': CA 1963, s 2(1).

Notes

Striking off for failure to carry on business:[1] CA 1963, s 311 empowers the Registrar to dissolve a company where he has reasonable cause to believe that it is not carrying on business.[2] He will be deemed to have good grounds for such a belief where the company does not have the names and prescribed details of any continuing directors registered in the CRO.[3] The section may also be invoked against the company which is not exempt from C(A)(No2)A 1999, s 43 and which does not have at least one Irish resident director or a bond in lieu thereof.[4]

Having sent a warning letter under CA 1963, s 311(1), if within one month he either receives no answer or alternatively receives an answer to the effect that the company is no longer carrying on business, he may send to the company and publish a notice in the Companies Registration Office Gazette that unless the company shows cause to the contrary within one further month, its name will be struck of the register.[5] A similar notice may be sent and published in the case of any company which the Registrar believes to be in liquidation and in respect of which liquidators' returns[6] have not been made for six consecutive months.[7] Dissolution takes place upon the publication of notice of the striking off in the Companies Registration Office Gazette.[8]

1 In relation to the operation of this section generally, see MacCann, 'Striking off the Register and Section 12 of the Companies (Amendment) Act 1982' (1990) 84 Gazette 125; Mooney, 'Restoring companies to the register' 1997 (2) Bar Review 226.
2 CA 1963, s 311(1).
3 C(A)(No 2)A 1999, s 48.
4 C(A)(No 2)A 1999, s 43(15).
5 CA 1963, s 311(2).
6 See CA 1963, ss 263 (3) and 273 (3) and notes thereto.
7 CA 1963, s 311(3).
8 CA 1963, s 311(5).

Other grounds for dissolution: The power of the Registrar to dissolve companies under this section is in addition to his power to strike off companies which fail to file their annual returns[1] or which fail to deliver certain statements to the Revenue Commissioners.[2]

1 C(A)A 1982, s 12.
2 C(A)A 1982, s 12A.

Consequences of dissolution: Upon dissolution, all real and personal property of the company vests in the State.[1] The liability, if any, of its directors, officers and members, will however continue and may be enforced as if dissolution had not occurred.[2] Liability, in this context, might include criminal liability for breaches of provisions of the Companies Acts or civil liability under specific provisions of the Acts, such as for fraudulent or reckless trading[3] or for failure to keep proper books of account[4] or for issuing an order for goods on which the company's name is not legibly stated.[5] The director, officer or member will not, however, be personally liable for corporate debts unless he was also so liable before the date of the dissolution. In the UK the courts have held that where a company which holds a lease is dissolved and the Crown subsequently disclaims any interest in the lease, the liability of any sureties under the lease is extinguished.[6] However, these cases rely on the decision in *Stacey v Hill*[7] which held that the disclaimer of a lease by a liquidator or trustee in bankruptcy had the effect of relieving the sureties of any liability thereunder. The decision in *Stacey v Hill* was expressly disapproved of by Keane J in *Tempany v Royal Liver Trustees Ltd*[8] and accordingly these English cases on the effect of dissolution of the company and subsequent Crown disclaimer must be viewed with some caution.

1 State Property Act 1954, s 28. Property held by the company in trust does not, however, vest in the State: *Re Kavanagh and Cantwell* [1984] IEHC 55 (Costello J); *Re Heidelstone Co Ltd* [2007] 4 IR 175.
2 CA 1963, s 311(6).
3 CA 1963, s 297A.
4 CA 1990, s 204.
5 CA 1963, s 114(4).
6 *Re Yarmarine (IW) Ltd* [1992] BCLC 276; *Allied Dunbar Assurance plc v Fowle* [1994] 2 BCLC 197.
7 *Stacey v Hill* [1901] 1 QB 660.
8 *Tempany v Royal Liver Trustees Ltd* [1984] ILRM 273.

Winding up of dissolved company: A company may be wound up by order of the court notwithstanding the fact that it has already been dissolved.[1] Voluntary winding up is not, however, an option. The proper practice in this regard is for the petition to ask first for the restoration of the company's name to the register and then for it to be wound up.[2]

1 CA 1963, s 311(7).
2 *Re Cambridge Coffee Room Association Ltd* [1952] 1 All ER 112.

Restoration to the register:[1] Where the name of a company has been struck off the register under CA 1963, s 311 application may be made to the court by any one of several applicants[2] for an order restoring the company to the register.[2] Rather curiously, given the fact that it no longer exists, the company itself may apply, as may any member or creditor, including a contingent or prospective creditor.[3] However, in the case of a contingent or prospective creditor, he may be required to establish that his claim is neither frivolous nor vexatious and is being bona fide maintained, in order to be allowed by the court to proceed with his petition.[4] The Revenue Commissioners will only be regarded as creditors of the company for the purposes of an application under CA 1963, s 311(8) if, and to the extent that, they have raised assessments on the company prior to the date upon which its name was struck off the register.[5] A person who after the date of dissolution acquires shares in the company, or takes an assignment of one of its debts, will not be regarded as a 'member or creditor' of that company within CA 1963, s 311(8) and accordingly will not have standing to present a petition for the restoration of the name of the company to the register.[6]

1 See generally, O'Higgins, 'How to Restore a Struck-Off Company to the Register' (2001) Gazette 40 and Leonard, 'Restoring companies to the register' (2000) 6 (3) Bar Review 1982.

2 CA 1963, s 311(8).

3 *Re Deauville Communications Worldwide Ltd* [2002] 2 IR 32; *Re Industrial Glazing Systems Ltd* (6 November 2000, unreported) HC (Barr J); *City of Westminster Assurance Co Ltd v Registrar of Companies* (1997) BCC 960; *Re Harvest Lane Motor Bodies Ltd* [1969] 1 Ch 457; *Re Mixhurst Ltd* [1994] 2 BCLC 19; *Re Jayham Ltd* [1995] 2 BCLC 455.

4 *Re Deauville Communications Worldwide Ltd* [2002] 2 IR 32.

5 *Re Nelson Car Hire Ltd* (1973) 107 ILTR 97; *Re Supatone (Eire) Ltd* (1973) 107 ILTR 105.

6 *Re Test Holdings (Clifton) Ltd* [1970] Ch 285; *Re New Timbiqui Gold Mines Ltd* [1961] Ch 319.

Grounds for restoration: CA 1963, s 311(8) enables the court to restore the name of the company to the register if it is satisfied that the company was carrying on business at the time of dissolution or otherwise that it is 'just' to do so.[1] If the company is already being wound up[2] or is otherwise carrying on operations[3] this will constitute a good ground for restoration to the register. Moreover, in the case of a petition by a creditor, it may be 'just' to restore the name of the company to the register in order to enable the creditor pursue some legal claim against the company or its officers[4] provided that the claim is not already patently statute barred.[5] Similarly, it may be 'just' to restore a company to the register to enable it to prove as a creditor in the liquidation of another body corporate[6] or to enable a member to bring proceedings under CA 1963, s 205.[7] In this regard, as a statement of general principle, it has been held that the exercise by the court of its discretion to refuse to restore the company to the register should be the exception rather than the rule.[8]

1 See C(A)A 1982, s 12B(3), under which the only ground for restoring a company to the register is that it is 'just' to do so.

2 *Re Outlay Assurance Society* (1887) 34 Ch D 479; *Re Johannesburg Mining and General Syndicate* [1901] WN 46.

3 *Re Portrafram Ltd* [1986] BCLC 533.

4 *Re Haltone (Cork) Ltd* [1996] 1 IR 32; *Re Workvale Ltd* [1991] BCLC 528; *City of Westminster Assurance Co v Registrar of Companies* (1997) BCC 960.

5 *Re Workvale Ltd (No 2)* [1991] BCLC 531, aff'd [1992] BCLC 544.

6 *Re Eden Quay Investments Ltd* (11 April 1994, unreported) HC (Keane J) reported in *The Irish Times*, 12 April 1994. See also *Stanhope Pension Trust Ltd v Registrar of Companies* [1994] 1 BCLC 628.

7 *Re New Ad Advertising Company Ltd* [2006] IEHC 19 (Laffoy J).

8 *Re Priceland Ltd* [1997] 1 BCLC 467; *Re Blenheim Leisure (Restaurants) Ltd (No 2)* [2000] BCC 821.

Notice parties: The application for restoration of the name of the company to the register is brought by way of petition and verifying affidavit pursuant to RSC 1986, Ord 75. By analogy with the requirements of C(A)A 1982, s 12, it should be on notice to the Registrar of Companies, the Revenue Commissioners and the Minister for Finance.[1] The costs of these three notice parties must normally be paid by the petitioner.[2]

As a matter of general principle, the application for restoration is a matter exclusively between the petitioner, the company and the regulatory authorities and accordingly third parties should not normally be allowed to intervene.[3] Nonetheless, the court has jurisdiction to join as a party to the application any person whose rights would be affected by the restoration of the company to the register.[4] In this regard, the test to be applied in determining whether the third party should be joined to a petition by a creditor is whether the third party merely wishes to argue that the petitioning creditor has no claim against the company or that the proceedings which the revived company proposed to bring against him have no prospect of success, in which case he would not be entitled to intervene in the application, or whether the order for restoration would directly affect the rights of the third party irrespective of whether the petitioning creditor had any claim against the company or the company had any claim against the third-party, in which case the joinder would be allowed.[5] The third party prejudice must therefore arise out of the restoration itself and not simply out of some contractual arrangement which is revived by the restoration.[6] An example of third-party prejudice arising from the restoration itself is where the bringing of the company back into existence would have resulted in residuary legatees under a will being divested of their bequests.[7] If a third party has been dealing with the officers of a dissolved company under the mistaken belief that the company is still in existence, he will not be prejudiced by the restoration of the company to the register, even though such an order would have the effect of precluding any action by him against the company's officers personally for breach of contract or breach of warranty of authority.[8] It is to be noted, though, that even if a third party has been validly joined as a notice party to the application for restoration to the register, costs should only be awarded in favour of that notice party in exceptional circumstances.[9]

1 CA 1963, s 12B(3). The reason for putting the State on notice is that the company's property will have vested in the Minister for Finance upon dissolution pursuant to the State Property Act 1954, s 28. The State's consent is therefore required in order for the property to re-vest in the company. In practice, such consent is normally communicated by the Chief State Solicitor acting on behalf of the Registrar and the two Ministers.

2 *Re Conrad Hall and Co* [1916] WN 275; *Re Haltone (Cork) Ltd* [1996] 1 IR 32.

3 *Re Bloomberg Developments Ltd* [2002] 2 IR 613.

4 *Re Servers of the Blind League* [1960] 2 All ER 298; *Re H Clarkson (Overseas) Ltd* (1987) 3 BCC 606; *Stanhope Pension Trust Ltd v Registrar of Companies* [1994] 1 BCLC 628; *Re Jayham Ltd* [1995] 2 BCLC 455. If the purpose of restoring the company to the register is to enable a creditor to pursue a personal injuries claim in respect of which the company is insured, it may be proper but is by no means necessary to join the insurance company as a notice party to the application: *Re Workvale Ltd* [1991] BCLC 528. Restoration of the company to the register is a necessary prerequisite to the enforcement of the company's insurance policy since it has been held by the House of Lords in *Bradley v Eagle Star Insurance Co Ltd* [1989] 1 All ER 961 that there could be no indemnity under a policy of insurance in respect of a company which no longer existed and whose liability could therefore not be determined. See also *Re Workvale Ltd (No 2)* [1991] BCLC 531, aff'd [1992] BCLC 544.

5 *Re Jayham Ltd* [1995] 2 BCLC 455.

6 *Re Priceland Ltd* [1997] 1 BCLC 467; cf *Smith v White Knight Laundry Ltd* [2001] 2 BCLC 206.

7 *Re Servers of the Blind League* [1960] 2 All ER 298.

8 *Re Rortrafram Ltd* [1986] BCLC 533.

9 *Re Bloomberg Developments Ltd* [2002] 2 IR 613; *Re Brown Bayley's Steel Works* (1905) 21 TLR 374; *Re Langlaatge Proprietary Co Ltd* (1912) 28 TLR 529.

Consequences of restoration: If the court makes an order for the restoration of the company to the register it will typically direct that the order, to be valid, must be delivered to the Registrar within a period of three months.[1] As soon as an office copy of the order restoring the name of the company to the register has been delivered to the Registrar for registration, the company and all other persons are placed in the same position as if the company had continued in existence and never been dissolved.[2] Thus, any property which had previously vested in the State under the State Property Act 1954, s 28 reverts to the company without the need for any formal vesting order.[3] Similarly proceedings which had been commenced by or against the company either prior to or during the period of dissolution, are retrospectively validated.[4] Where particulars of a charge over the company's property were delivered to the Registrar within 21 days of creation of the charge, but at a time when unbeknownst to the parties the company had been dissolved the court may direct that the delivery of particulars of the charge will be regarded as having been duly and properly made for the purposes of CA 1963, s 99.[5]

1 Failure to file the order in time will result in it lapsing: *Re Barrowland Ltd* [2003] IEHC 54.

2 CA 1963, s 311(8). See also *Tyman's Ltd v Craven* [1952] 1 All ER 613.

3 *Re CW Dixon Ltd* [1947] Ch 251.

4 *Re Amantiss Enterprises Ltd; Framus plc v CRH plc* [2000] 2 ILRM 177; *Re Deauville Communications Worldwide Ltd* [2002] 2 IR 32; *Top Creative Ltd v St Albans DC* [2000] 2 BCLC 379; *Tyman's Ltd v Craven* [1952] 1 All ER 613. Proceedings in the name of the liquidator of the company, such as proceedings under CA 1990, s 150 for a restriction order against the directors, will similarly be validated: *Re Dunleckney Ltd* [2001] 1 IR 103.

5 In *Re Boxco Ltd* [1970] Ch 442, the court directed that delivery of particulars of a charge under the equivalent of CA 1963, s 99 should be regarded as having been properly made, thus avoiding the necessity of making a separate application under the equivalent of CA 1963, s 106.

Special directions for restoration: Apart from ordering the restoration of the company, the court may also give such directions and make such provisions as it considers just for placing the company and third parties in the same position as if dissolution had never occurred.[1] It is also open to the court to direct that even though upon restoration the company is deemed never to have been dissolved, nonetheless all or some of the company's officers should be fixed with personal liability in respect of all or certain of the debts and liabilities incurred by the company during the period when it was actually dissolved.[2]

1 See also CA 1963, s 311(A) cf *Re Lindsay Bowman Ltd* [1969] 3 All ER 601.

2 *Richmond Building Products Ltd v Sound Gables Ltd* [2005] 1 ILRM 497. In that case the defendant had for sometime been struck off the register of companies but was subsequently restored to it. The plaintiff had obtained judgment against the company in respect of payment for goods sold and delivered to the company during the period when it was being struck off and then sought relief against the directors of the company. Finnegan P refused to make the directors personally liable because the order restoring the company had the effect of releasing directors from a personal liability which they had incurred while the company was struck off. He rationalised his decision by placing reliance on the principles set out in *East End Dwellings Co Limited v Finsbury Council* [1951] 2 ALL ER 587.

New company with same name: Currently it is the practice of the CRO not to incorporate a new company with the same name as a company which has been struck off the register for a period of twenty years from the date of strike off. However, if though inadvertantly, since the date of dissolution of the company, a company has been incorporated with, or changed its name to the same or similar name to that of the company which has been struck off, the court may make it a condition of restoration to the register that the first company change its name and the court may further preclude the company from carrying on business until this change of name has been effected.[1] It would appear that no objection can be lodged with the Registrar of Companies, on behalf of a company which has been struck off, under CA 1963, s 23.[2]

1 *Re Rapton Foundry Ltd* Sol Jo 331.

2 Under CA 1963, s 23 (as amended by CLEA 2001, s 87) the Registrar has the power to direct, within six months of a second company being registered with the same or similar name to a name by which a company in existence is already registered, that the second company alters its name.

Other provisions for restoration to the register by order of the court: The court is also empowered to restore dissolved companies to the register pursuant to CA 1963, ss 310 and C(A)A 1982, s 12B. For a discussion of these sections see the notes thereto.

Restoration to register by Registrar: On the power of the Registrar to restore the company to the register within 12 months of dissolution, see also C(A)A 1982, s 12C and CA 1963, s 311A.

UK legislation

See CA 1985, ss 652, 653.

[311A Restoration to register of company struck off

[(1) Without prejudice to the provisions of section 311 (8) of this Act or subsection or (7) of section 12B or subsection 1 of section 12C of the Companies (Amendment) Act, 1982][b], if a company feels aggrieved by having been struck off the register, the registrar of companies, on an application made in the prescribed form by the company before the expiration of twelve months after the publication in [the Companies Registration Office Gazette][c] of the notice striking the company name from the register, and provided he has received all annual returns outstanding, if any, from the company, may restore the name of the company to the register.

(2) Upon the registration of an application under subsection (1) and on payment of such fees as may be prescribed, the company shall be deemed to have continued in existence as if its name had not been struck off.

(3) Subject to any order made by the court in the matter, the restoration of the name of a company to the register under this section shall not affect the rights or liabilities of the company in respect of any debt or obligation incurred, or any contract entered into by, to, with or on behalf of, the company between the date of its dissolution and the date of such restoration.][a]

Amendments

a CA 1963, s 311A inserted by CA 1990, s 246.

b The words 'Without prejudice to the provisions of section 311(8) of this Act or subsection (3) or (7) of section 12B, or subsection (1) of section 12C, of the Companies (Amendment) Act 1982,' substituted for 'Without prejudice to the provisions of section 311(8) of this Act and section 12(6) of the Companies (Amendment) Act, 1982,' in CA 1963, s 311A by C(A)(No 2)A 1999, s 50.

c 'the Companies Registration Office Gazette' substituted for '*Iris Oifigiúil*' by IFCMPA 2005, s 72.

Definitions

'annual return': CA 1963, s 2(1); 'company': CA 1963, s 2(1); 'the court': CA 1963, s 2(1); 'prescribed': CA 1963, s 2(1); 'the Registrar of Companies': CA 1963, s 2(1).

Notes

Restoration to register by filing outstanding annual returns: In C(A)A 1982, s 12B provision is made for the court to restore a company to the register which has been struck off for failure to file its annual returns and/or to deliver any statement required by TCA 1997, s 882. In the case of striking-off for failure to file annual returns, restoration may be effected by the Registrar upon application by the company itself (despite the fact that it technically no longer exists!), provided that the application is made to him in the prescribed form,[1] within 12 months of the notice of striking off appearing in the Companies Registration Office Gazette and provided he receives all outstanding annual returns that have since been filed.[2]

1 Form H1: Companies (Forms) Order 1991 (SI 161/1991).

2 CA 1963, s 311A(1). A similar power of restoration is vested in the Registrar under C(A)A 1982, s 12C where the company has been struck off for failure to file its tax returns.

Consequences of restoration: Once the application has been registered and the prescribed fees have been paid, the company is deemed to have always been in existence and is deemed never to have been dissolved.[1] Thus, any property which had previously vested in the State under the State Property Act 1954, s 28 reverts to the company without the need for any formal vesting order.[2] Similarly proceedings which had been commenced by or against the company, either prior to or during the period of dissolution, are retrospectively validated.[3]

Where particulars of a charge over the company's property were delivered to the Registrar within 21 days of creation of the charge, but at a time when unbeknownst to the parties the company had been dissolved, the court may direct that the delivery of particulars of the charge will be regarded as having been duly and properly made for the purposes of CA 1963, s 99.[4]

1 CA 1963, s 311A(2). See also *Tyman's Ltd v Craven* [1952] 1 ALL ER 613.

2 *Re CW Dixon Ltd* [1947] Ch 251.

3 *Re Amantiss Enterprises Ltd; Framus plc v CRH plc* [2000] 2 ILRM 177; *Re Deauville Communications Worldwide Ltd* [2002] 2 IR 32; *Top Creative Ltd v St Albans DC* [2000] 2 BCLC 379; *Tyman's Ltd v Craven* [1952] 1 All ER 613. Proceedings in the name of the liquidator of the company, such as proceedings under CA 1990, s 150 for a restriction order against the directors, will similarly be validated: *Re Dunleckney Ltd* [2001] 1 IR 103.

4 In *Re Boxco Ltd* [1970] Ch 442 the court directed that delivery of particulars of a charge under the equivalent of CA 1963, s 99 should be regarded as having been properly made thus avoiding the necessity of making a separate application under the equivalent of CA 1963, s 106.

Rules of Court

312 Rules of Court for winding up

Section 68 of the Courts of Justice Act, 1936 (which confers power on a rule-making authority to make rules regulating the practice and procedure of the court in certain cases) shall extend to the making of rules in respect of the winding up of companies 3 whether by the court or voluntarily.

Definitions

'company': CA 1963, s 2(1); 'the court': CA 1963, s 2(1).

Notes

Rules of court for liquidations: Section 68 of the Courts of Justice Act 1936 conferred power on the Superior Courts Rules Committee to make rules for the practice and procedure of the court to be applied in relation compulsory liquidations. That rule making power was extended to voluntary liquidations by CA 1963, s 312. The relevant rules for both types of liquidation are to be found in RSC, Ord 74 as amended by RSC (No 4) 1991.

UK legislation

See IA 1986, s 411.

Disposal of Documents filed with Registrar

313 Disposal of documents filed with registrar

The registrar of companies, shall, after the expiration of 20 years from the dissolution of a company, send all the documents filed in connection with such company to the Public Record Office.

Definitions

'company': CA 1963, s 2(1); 'document': CA 1963, s 2(1): 'the registrar of companies': CA 1963, s 2(1).

UK legislation

See CA 1985, s 707A(2), (3); CA 1989, s 126(1).

[313A Provision of certain documents to liquidator or examiner

On—

(a) the making of—

(i) a winding up order, or

(ii) an order under section 2 of the Companies (Amendment) Act 1990 appointing an examiner to a company, or

(b) the issue of a certificate by the Master of the High Court under section 267A (inserted by the European Communities (Corporate Insolvency) Regulations 2002 (S.I. No 333 of 2002)) of this Act in relation to the confirmation by the Master of a creditors' voluntary winding up,

the proper officer of the Central Office of the High Court shall, on request and payment of the prescribed fee and subject to any conditions that may be specified in rules of court, give to the liquidator or examiner concerned—

(i) a copy of the order or certificate, certified by the officer to be a true copy, and

(ii) any other prescribed particulars.][a]

Amendments

a CA 1963, s 313A inserted by EC(CI)R 2002, reg 3(f).

PART VII
RECEIVERS

314 Disqualification of body corporate for appointment as receiver

A body corporate shall not be qualified for appointment as receiver of the property of a company, and any body corporate which acts as such a receiver [shall be guilty of an offence and liable to a fine][a] not exceeding [€1,904.61][b].

Amendments

a Section 314 amended an offence created by C(AA)A 2003, s 57 and Sch 2 with effect from 6 April 2004.

b '£500' substituted for '£100' by C(A)A 1982, Sch 1, increased to £1,500 by CA 1990, s 240(7) as inserted by CLEA 2001, s 104 and converted to €1,904.61 by Council Regulations (EC) No 1103/97, No 974/98 and No 2866/98 and the Economic and Monetary Union Act 1998, s 6.

Definitions

'company': CA 1963, s 2(1); 'month' is a calendar month: IA 2005, s 21, Sch 1, Pt 2.

Notes

Qualification to act as receiver: There are no formal qualifications necessary for appointment as a receiver in Ireland. However, there are certain grounds upon which a person may be disqualified from acting as a receiver.[1] A receiver of the property of a gas undertaking has all powers in relation to that property as if had he been appointed as a receiver of the property of a company, whether by reason of the relevant debenture or other instrument or otherwise: Gas Regulation Act 1982 (No. 16 of 1982), s 7.

For a general discussion of the law relating to receivers, see Courtney, *The Law of Private Companies* (2nd edn, Tottel Publishing, 2002), ch 22.

1 See CA 1963, s 314 and CA 1963, s 315. In addition, any person who is subject to a disqualification order pursuant to CA 1990, Pt VII is disqualified from acting as a receiver.

UK legislation

See IA 1986, s 30.

315 [Disqualification for appointment as receiver

(1) None of the following persons shall be qualified for appointment as receiver of the property of a company—

(a) an undischarged bankrupt;

(b) a person who is, or who has within 12 months of the commencement of the receivership been, an officer or servant of the company;

(c) a parent, spouse, brother, sister or child of an officer of the company;

(d) a person who is a partner of or in the employment of an officer or servant of the company;

(e) a person who is not qualified by virtue of this subsection for appointment as receiver of the property of any other body corporate which is that company's subsidiary or holding company or a subsidiary of that company's holding company, or would be so disqualified if the body corporate were a company.

References in this subsection to an officer or servant of the company include references to an auditor.

(2) If a receiver of the property of a company becomes disqualified by virtue of this section, he shall thereupon vacate his office and give notice in writing within 14 days to—

(a) the company;

(b) the registrar of companies;

(c) (i) the debenture-holder, if the receiver was appointed by a debenture-holder, or

(ii) the court, if the receiver was appointed by the court,

that he has vacated it by reason of such disqualification.

(3) Subsection (2) is without prejudice to sections 107, 319 (2) and 321.

(4) Nothing in this section shall require a receiver appointed before the commencement of section 170 of the Companies Act, 1990, to vacate the office to which he was so appointed.

(5) Any person who acts as a receiver when disqualified by this section from so doing or who fails to comply with subsection (2), if that subsection applies to him, shall be guilty of an offence and shall be liable—

(a) on summary conviction, to a fine not exceeding [€1,904.61][b] and, for continued contravention, to a daily default fine not exceeding [€63.49][b];

(b) on conviction on indictment, to a fine not exceeding [€6,348.69][b] and, for continued contravention, to a daily default fine not exceeding [€317.43][b].][a]

Amendments

a CA 1963, s 315 substituted by CA 1990, s 170.

b '£1,000' in sub-s (5)(a) increased to £1,500 by CA 1990, s 240(7) as inserted by CLEA 2001, s 104 and converted to €1,904.61; £50 converted to €63.49; £5,000 converted to €6,348.69 and £250 converted to €317.43 by Council Regulations (EC) No 1103/97, No 974/98 and No 2866/98 and the Economic and Monetary Union Act 1998, s 6.

Definitions

'company': CA 1963, s 2(1); 'the court': CA 1963, s 2(1); 'debenture': CA 1963, s 2(1); 'holding company': CA 1963, s 2(1), s 155; 'officer': CA 1963, s 2(1); 'the registrar of companies': CA 1963, s 2(1); 'subsidiary': CA 1963, s 2(1), s 155; 'undischarged bankrupt': CA 1963, s 2(1).

Notes

Disqualification as receiver: CA 1963, s 315(1) further disqualifies the following categories of persons from being appointed as a receiver of the property of a company:

(a) an undischarged bankrupt;

(b) a person who is, or who has within 12 months of the commencement of the receivership been, an officer[1] or servant of the company;[2]

(c) a parent, spouse, brother, sister or child of an officer of the company;

(d) a person who is a partner of or in the employment of an officer or servant of the company; and

(e) a person disqualified from acting as a receiver of the company's holding company or subsidiaries or of a subsidiary of its holding company.

Restriction, pursuant to CA 1990, s 150, of a person who was a director of an insolvent company does not, in and of itself, act as a bar to the appointment of a person as a receiver. However, the facts giving rise to the restriction may have a bearing on the suitability of the person to act as receiver.

See CA 1990, s 237 wherein the Minister may make regulations adding to the list of persons who are disqualified from acting as a receiver. To date no such regulations have been made.

[1] References in CA 1963, s 315(1) include references to an officer or servant of the company and include references to an auditor. See also *R v Shacter* [1960] 2 QB 252. Presumably, a shadow director would also fall within the definition of an 'officer'. For a fuller discussion of what constitutes an 'officer' see *Director of Corporate Enforcement v D'Arcy* [2006] 2 IR 163.

[2] In *Wise Finance Company Ltd v O'Regan* (26 June 1996, unreported) HC Laffoy J held that under s 315(1)(d) the secretary of company could not validly be appointed as receiver.

Section 315(2) provides that when a receiver of the property of a company becomes disqualified by virtue of this section, he shall thereupon vacate his office and give notice of such disqualification in writing within 14 days to:

(a) the company;

(b) the Registrar of Companies;

(c) the debentureholder, if the receiver was appointed by a debentureholder, or the court, if the receiver was appointed by the court.

Where a person disqualified from acting as receiver nevertheless does so act, he is guilty of an offence.

UK legislation

See IA 1986, s 31.

---

316 Power of receiver to apply to the court for directions and his liability on contracts

[(1) Where a receiver of the property of a company is appointed under the powers contained in any instrument, any of the following persons may apply to the court for directions in relation to any matter in connection with the performances or otherwise by the receiver of his functions, that is to say—

(a) (i) the receiver;

(ii) an officer of the company;

(iii) a member of the company;

(iv) employees of the company comprising at least half in number of the persons employed in a full-time capacity by the company;

(v) a creditor of the company; and

(b) (i) a liquidator;

(ii) a contributory;

and on any such application, the court may give such directions, or make such order declaring the rights of persons before the court or otherwise, as the court thinks just.

(1A) An application to the court under subsection (1), except an application under paragraph (a) (i) of that subsection, shall be supported by such evidence that the applicant is being unfairly prejudiced by any actual or proposed action or omission of the receiver as the court may require.

(1B) For the purposes of subsection (1), 'creditor' means one or more creditors to whom the company the company is indebted by more, in aggregate, than [€12,697.38][b].][a]

(2) A receiver of the property of a company shall be personally liable on any contract entered into by him in the performance of his functions (whether such contract is entered into by him in the name of such company or in his own name as receiver or otherwise) unless the contract provides that he is not to be personally liable on such contract, and he shall be entitled in respect of that liability to indemnity out of the assets; but nothing in this subsection shall be taken as limiting any right to indemnity which he would have apart from this subsection, or as limiting his liability on contracts entered into without authority or as conferring any right to indemnity in respect of that liability.

(3) Where a receiver of the property of a company has been appointed or purported to be appointed and it is subsequently discovered that the charge or purported charge in respect of which he was so appointed or purported to be appointed was not effective as a charge on such property or on some part of such property, the court may, if it thinks fit, on the application of such receiver, order that he be relieved wholly or to such extent as the court shall think fit from personal liability in respect of anything done or omitted by him in relation to any property purporting to be comprised in the charge by virtue of which he was appointed or purported to be appointed which if such property had been effectively included in such charge or purported charge would have been properly done or omitted by him and he shall be relieved from personal liability accordingly, but in that event the person by whom such receiver was appointed or purported to be appointed shall be personally liable for everything for which, but for such order, such receiver would have been liable.

(4) This section shall apply whether the receiver was appointed before, on, or after the operative date, but subsection (2) shall not apply to contracts entered into before the operative date.

Amendments

a CA 1963, s 316(1) substituted and CA 1963, s 316(1A) and (1B) inserted by CA 1990, s 171.

b £10,000 converted to €12,697.38 by Council Regulations (EC) No 1103/97, No 974/98 and No 2866/98 and the Economic and Monetary Union Act 1998, s 6.

Definitions

'company': CA 1963, s 2(1); 'contributory': CA 1963, s 2(1), s 208; 'the court': CA 1963, s 2(1); 'member': CA 1963, s 31; 'officer': CA 1963, s 2(1); 'the operative date': CA 1963, s 2(1).

Notes

See notes at CA 1963, s 314 on Gas Regulation Act 1982, s 7.

Power of receiver to apply for directions: CA 1963, s 316(1) provides that a receiver appointed under a debenture[1] may apply to the High Court for directions in relation to any matter arising in connection with the performance of his functions.[2] CA 1990, s 171, amended s 316(1) by extending the entitlement to seek directions to any officer, member, liquidator or contributory of the company, as well as any creditor(s) owed at least €12,697.38, and any employees constituting at least 50% of the full-time workforce. However, with the exception of the receiver, unfair prejudice must be established in order to be able to seek the directions of the court.[3]

The application is made by Originating Notice of Motion and the court may make such order declaring the rights of the persons before the court as it thinks just.[4] The court should be presented with some overview of the receivership and, in this regard, the type of report which is furnished to the court in compulsory winding up matters will be regarded as an appropriate template.[5] The detail required in any case will depend on the case, on the stage which the receivership up had reached and the issues which the court has to address on the application for directions.[6]

Most applications for directions are likely to concern the nature of the receiver's role as agent, the duties of the receivers and his responsibilities to the company, guarantors or creditors and his role in a company in liquidation. The court has jurisdiction on an application under this section to determine any matter including the priority of charges, the repudiation of liability under a contract of insurance between an insurer and the company, and liability for non-domestic rates.[7]

1 CA 1963, s 316 has no application where the receiver has been appointed by the court.

2 In relation to the status, powers and functions of receivers generally, see Keane, *Company Law* (4th edn, Tottel Publishing, 2007) ch 22, Picarda, *The Law Relating to Receivers, Managers and Administrators* (3rd edn, Tottel Publishing, 2006), Courtney, *The Law of Private Companies* (2nd edn, Tottel Publishing, 2002) ch 22 and Lightman and Moss, *The Law of Receivers and Administrators of Companies* (3rd edn, Sweet and Maxwell, 2000).

3 For an example of a case where a contributory failed in his application for directions because of an inability to show unfair prejudice, see *Kinsella v Somers* [1999] IEHC 44 (Budd J).

4 RSC 1986, Ord 75, r 5(aa).

5 *Re Olde Court Holiday Hostel Ltd* [2006] IEHC 424.

6 *Re Olde Court Holiday Hostel Ltd* [2006] IEHC 424

7 *Bula Ltd v Crowley* (No 4) [2003] 2 IR 430; *In re Salthill Properties Ltd* [2006] IESC 35, *Becks Foods Ltd, Re, Rees v Boston Borough Council* [2001] 2 BCLC 663.

Other examples of Irish cases where directions were sought by the receiver from the court include the following: *Re Manning Furniture Ltd*[1] which concerned the receiver's obligations to discharge preferential creditors from the surplus on realised assets of the company, where there was late registration of the charge; *Re Edenfell Holdings Ltd*[2] which concerned the completion of a contract for sale of company assets; *Irish Oil and Cake Mills Ltd v Donnelly*[3] which concerned the extent of the duty of a receiver to keep the company appraised of how the business of the company is going or to account to the company whose affairs he is managing; *McGowan v Gannon*[4] which concerned the extent to which the receiver owes a duty of care to the guarantor of the company; and *Bula Ltd v Crowley (No 4)*[5] which concerned whether the best price had been obtained by a receiver for a charged asset.

1 *Re Manning Furniture Ltd* [1996] 1 ILRM 13.

2 *Re Edenfell Holdings Ltd* [1999] 1 IR 458.

3 *Irish Oil and Cake Mills Ltd v Donnelly* [1983] IEHC 57. See also *Smiths Ltd v Midleton* [1979] 3 All ER 842.

4 *McGowan v Gannon* [1983] ILRM 516 at 518.

5 *Bula Ltd v Crowley (No 4)* [2003] 2 IR 430.

Agency of receiver: In the absence of a provision to the contrary in a debenture, the receiver will be regarded as the agent of the debentureholder.[1] A receiver receives the assets of the mortgagor for the benefit of the mortgagee. In practice standard form debentures deem the receiver to be the company's agent. In this way the debentureholder avoids any liability for the acts or omissions of the receiver. This procedure was considered by Barr J in *Bula Ltd v Crowley*[2] in which he pointed to two distinct relationships involved in a receivership:

> 'First, between the appointing mortgagee and the Receiver which relates to the fundamental objective of the receivership, being entry into possession of the company's assets for the purpose of sale in the interest of the mortgagee …
>
> The Second relationship is that between the Receiver and third parties arising out of the receivership. Debentures normally provide, as in the instant case, that such dealings are conducted by the Receiver as agent of the company in receivership. The mortgagees have no right to interfere in the receivership in that regard.' Adding that
>
> 'In my view there is no inconsistency between the foregoing relationships which represent long established commercial good sense.'

If the receiver is deemed to be the company's agent under the terms of the debenture appointing him, that agency terminates upon the company going into liquidation.[3] However, even though his agency terminates upon the company going into liquidation, he remains entitled to deal with and realise the charged assets,[4] subject to any application that may be made to the court by the liquidator under CA 1963, s 322B to determine or limit the receivership. In exercising his powers during the course of the winding up, the receiver is deemed to act as principal, although if the debentureholder directs his conduct, he may by implication become the debentureholder's agent.[5]

Although a receiver is normally deemed to be an agent of the company by virtue of the terms of the debenture, his duty of care is owed primarily to the debentureholder[6] and he may not be dismissed by the company even though it is, strictly speaking, his principal.[7]

The receiver owes a fiduciary duty to a debentureholder, who has a right, as against the receiver, to be put in possession of all the information concerning the receivership available to the receiver[8].

1 See *Kerr on Receivers* (16th edn, Sweet and Maxwell) 304 and Courtney, *The Law of Private Companies* (2nd ed, Tottel Publishing, 2002) ch 22; *Robinson Printing Co Ltd v Chic Ltd* [1905] 2 Ch 123.

2 *Bula Ltd v Crowley* [2003] 1 ILRM 55.

3 *Gosling v Gaskell* [1897] AC 575; *Sowman v David Samuel Trust Ltd* [1976] 1 WLR 22.

4 *Sowman v David Samuel Trust Ltd* [1976] 1 WLR 22; *Goughs Garages Ltd v Puglsey* [1930] 1 KB 615.

5 *Re Della Rocell's Estate* (1892) 29 LR Ir 464; *Standard Chartered Bank Ltd v Walker* [1982] 3 All ER 938.

6 *Bula v Crowley (No 3)* [2003] 1 IR 396; *Re B Johnson and Co (Builders) Ltd* [1955] Ch 634; *Ardmore Studios (Ir) Ltd v Lynch and Others* [1965] IR 1; *Lynch v Ardmore Studios (Ireland) Ltd* [1966] IR 133; *Rottenberg v Monjack* [1993] BCLC 374; *Gomba Holdings Ltd v Minories Finance Ltd* [1988] 1 WLR 1231; *In re B Johnson & Co (Builders)* [1955] 1 Ch 634.

7 See *Kerr on Receivers* (16th edn, Sweet and Maxwell) 304; *Bula Ltd v Crowley* [2003] 1 ILRM 55.

8 *Bula v Crowley (No 3)* [2003] 1 IR 396; *Gomba Holdings Ltd v Minories Finance Ltd* [1988] 1 WLR 1231; *In re Magadi Soda Co Ltd* (1925) 41 TLR 297. In relation to the receiver's duty to equitably account to persons other than the debentureholder, see the notes to CA 1963, s 319.

Receiver and manager: Where the charge extends over the entire assets of a company the debentureholder may appoint a receiver and manager[1]. Under standard form debentures the receiver will be given wide powers to manage the company, to act in its name, to carry on the company's business and to realise the assets.

1 *Irish Oil and Cake Mills Ltd v Donnelly* [1983] IEHC 57.

Positon of directors during receivership: While the appointment of a receiver and manager may suspend most of the powers of the directors[1], at least in respect of the charged assets, the powers vested by law in the directors of the company are not wholly terminated. They may not exercise their powers in such a manner as to inhibit the receiver in dealing with and disposing of the charged assets, nor may they act so as to adversely affect the position of the debentureholders by threatening or imperilling the assets which are subject to the charge.[2] However, they still retain the power to institute proceedings in the name of the company, provided the action is in the company's interest and does not impinge prejudicially on the conduct of the receivership or imperil the charged assets.[3] If the receiver is expressly empowered to sue to enforce claims of the company, the directors rather than instituting debt collection proceedings in the name of the company should instead apply to the court for a direction that the receiver should initiate the action himself.[4]

The directors also retain power to institute proceedings in the name of the company challenging the validity of the security under which the receiver has been appointed and/or challenging the validity of the appointment itself.[5] A company may maintain proceedings against a debentureholder, notwithstanding the subsequent appointment of a receiver,[6] because, if the debenture under which a receiver is appointed is found to be invalid so too will be the receiver's appointment.[7] However, where the directors initially cooperate with the receiver, they may be estopped from subsequently challenging the validity of the appointment.[8]

A debentureholder who is contractually entitled to appoint a receiver is free to do so to protect his own interests and is under no duty to refrain from exercising his rights on the grounds that this might cause loss to the company or its creditors, or because the appointment of a receiver is allegedly unnecessary in that it would merely duplicate the efforts of the liquidator.[9] But there must first have been an event of default, provided for in the debenture, which permits the appointment of a receiver. A receiver may be appointed at any time after such default.[10]

Where there is no debenture or, where the debenture document does not give sufficient power to any single creditor to appoint a receiver, an application may be made to the High Court which may appoint a receiver under its inherent equitable jurisdiction[11] or, pursuant to the Supreme Court of Judicature (Ireland) Act 1877, s 28(8).[12]

1 *Village Cay Marine Ltd v Acland et al* [1998] BCC 417.

2 *Lascomme Ltd v UDT Bank* [1993] 3 IR 412 at 416; *Bula Ltd and others v Crowley and others* [2003] 1 ILRM 55.

3 *Wymes v Crowley* (27 February 1987, unreported) HC (Murphy J); *Newhart Developments Ltd v Cooperative Commercial Bank Ltd* [1978] QB 814; [1978] 2 All ER 896; cf *Tudor Grange Holdings Ltd v Citibank NA* [1991] 4 All ER 1; *GE Capital Commercial Finance Ltd v Sutton and others Anglo Petroleum Ltd v GE Capital Commercial Finance Ltd* [2004] All ER (D) 387 (Mar).

4 *Tudor Grange Holdings Ltd v Citibank NA* [1992] Ch 53; [1991] 4 All ER 1.

5 *Hawkesbury Development Co Ltd v Landmark Finance Pty Ltd* [1969] 2 NSWLR 782, 790 per Street J 'A valid receivership and management will ordinarily supersede, but not destroy, the company's own organs through which it conducts its affairs'; *Brooklands Motor Co Ltd v Bridge Wholesale Acceptance Corporation (Australia) Ltd* [1994] MCLR 193. *In Re Reprographic Exports* (1978) 122 Sol J 400 directors were permitted to oppose the equivalent of a winding-up petition brought by a receiver appointed to the company.

6 *Lascomme Ltd v UDT Bank* [1993] 3IR 412, [1994] 1 ILRM 227; See also *Tudor Grange Holdings Ltd v Citibank NA* [1992] CH 53.

7 *Madden v Anglo Irish Bank plc* [1998] IESC 6.

8 *Bank of Baroda v Panessar* [1986] 3 All ER 751.

9 *Re Potters Oils Ltd (No 2)* [1986] 1 WLR 201, [1986] BCLC 98; *Shamji v Johnson Matthey Bankers Ltd* [1986] BCLC 278; *South Australian Asset Management Corp v Sheahan and Health and Life Care Ltd* (1995) 65 SASR 59; [1995] SASC 5182. The Australian courts accept that if the creditor in fact exercises the power to appoint a receiver in the circumstances, and for the purposes, stipulated in the contract then the debtor will find it exceptionally hard to claim that it was unreasonable for the creditor to exercise that contractual right: *Canberra Advance Bank Ltd*

v Benny (1992) 88 FCR 427, at 433–434; *White & Carter (Councils) Ltd v McGregor* [1962] AC 413, at 429–430. See, however, CA 1963, s 322B.

10 *Brighty v Norton* [1862] 122 ER 116: *Bank of Baroda v Panessar* [1986] 3 All ER 75; *Sheppard and Cooper Ltd v TSB Bank plc* [1996] 2 All ER 654.

11 See *Angelis v Algemene Bank Nederland (Ireland) Ltd* (4 June 1974, unreported) HC at 2 per Kenny J.

12 See also RSC 1986, Ord 50, r 6(1).

Contractual liability of the receiver

Section 316(2) provides that a receiver is personally liable on any contract entered into by him, in his own name or that of the company, in the performance of his functions, unless the contract provides otherwise. He is entitled, however, to be indemnified by the company in respect of his personal liability.

(i) Contracts in existence prior to the appointment of the receiver: The receiver does not have any personal liability as regards pre-appointment contracts entered into by the company, unless there is novation[1] (ie where a contract is varied and the receiver takes on the rights and obligations of the company)[2]. Mere continuance of a pre-appointment contract does not amount to a novation and thus where a receiver allows employees to continue in employment, the company, rather than the receiver, is liable for their wages.[3] Furthermore, if the receiver causes the company to break a pre-appointment contract he will not be guilty of the tort of inducing a breach of contract[4].

The appointment of a receiver does not terminate the company's pre-existing contracts which remain binding on the company.[5] Except for specific employees whose continued employment would be inconsistent with the role and functions of the receiver and manager, the company's employment contracts will also remain binding where the receiver is appointed pursuant to a debenture.[6] By contrast, the appointment of a receiver and manager by the court operates to dismiss all the company's employees.[7]

The receiver is not obliged to fulfil all existing contracts as this would mean that unsecured creditors would be in a position to require fulfilment of their contracts before the receiver could realise the security[8].

However, if a contract entered into by a company before the appointment of the receiver is for the sale of land or the granting of a lease or if it is otherwise capable of enforcement by an order for specific performance in the form of a mandatory injunction, specific performance may, indeed, be ordered by the court, notwithstanding the commencement of the receivership[9].

A receiver may apply to the court, pursuant to s 139 of CA 1990, to set aside antecedent transactions disposing of the company's property where such disposal has been to perpetrate a fraud on the company, its creditors or members.[10]

1 *Ardmore Studios (Ireland) Ltd v Lynch* [1965] IR 1; *Re B Johnson and Co (Builders) Ltd* [1955] 1 Ch 634; *Re Newdigate Colliery Co Ltd* [1912] 1 Ch 68; *Parsons v Sovereign Bank of Canada* [1913] AC 160; *Airline Airspaces Ltd v Handley Page Ltd* [1970] Ch 193; *Nicoll v Cutts* [1986] BCLC 99.

2 *Parsons v Sovereign Bank of Canada* [1913] AC 160.

3 *Nicoll v Cutts* [1985] BCLC 322.

4 *Said v Butt* [1920] 3 KB 497; *G Scammel and Nephew Ltd v Jurley* [1929] 1 KB 419; *DC Thompson and Co Ltd v Deakin* [1952] Ch 646, see also *Lathia v Dronsfield Bros Ltd* 1987 BCLC 321.

5 *Triffit Nurseries v Salads Etcetera Ltd* [2000] BCC 98.

6 *Griffiths v Secretary of State for Social Services* [1974] QB 468; *Nicoll v Cutts* [1985] BCLC 322.

7 *Reid v Explosives Co Ltd* (1887)19 QB 264.

8 See generally Davies, *Gower and Davies: Principles of Modern Company Law* (6th edn, Sweet and Maxwell) ch 15.

[9] *Freevale Ltd v Metrostore (Holdings) Ltd* [1984] Ch 199; *AMEC Properties Ltd v Planning Research and Systems plc* [1992] BCLC 1149; *Telemetrix plc v Modern Engineers of Bristol (Holdings) plc* [1985] BCLC 213; *Land Rover Group Ltd v UPF (UK) Ltd* [2003] 2 BCLC 222.

[10] CA 1990, s 139 as extended by CA 1990, s 178

(ii) Contracts entered into post appointment of the receiver: A receiver is personally liable on all new contracts entered into by him on behalf of the company unless he expressly excludes such liability at the time.[1] A receiver will not be deemed to have excluded personal liability on a post-appointment contract simply by describing himself as 'agent' of the company[2]. If, however, he does succeed in excluding personal liability on such a contract, the claim of the other party will rank as an expense of the receivership having priority over the claims of the debentureholder[3].

Nevertheless, it is legitimate for a creditor to demand payment of all arrears and to require an undertaking of personal liability from the receiver as a pre-condition for the continuance of supplies during the course of a receivership.[4] A receiver is entitled to make a 'salvage payment' in this situation in order, in effect, to preserved the mortgaged property. This extends to the payment of unsecured creditors (such as utilities that are, on the facts, vital to the charged property).[5]

[1] CA 1963, s 316(2).

[2] *Phonogram Ltd v Lane* [1981] 3 WLR 736.

[3] *Re British Power Traction and Lighting Co* [1906] 1 Ch 497; *Healy v Oliver* [1918] 1 IR 366; *Moore v Donnelly* [1985] IEHC 52 (Carroll J).

[4] *W and L Crowe Ltd v ESB* [1984] IEHC 22 (Costello J); *Husey v London Electric Supply Corporation* [1902] 1 Ch 411; *Paterson v Gas Light and Coke Company* [1896] 2 Ch 476.

[5] See Fisher and Lightwood, *The Law of Mortgage* (10th edn, LexisNexis) ch 16; *Wildy v Mid-Hants Rly Co* (1868) 16 WR 409; *Re Casrhalton Park Estate Ltd, Graham v Carshalton Park Estate Ltd* [1908] 2 Ch 62; *Higginstown v German Athenaeum Ltd* (1916) 32 TLR 277.

CA 1963, s 316(3) provides that where a receiver has been appointed under a charge which subsequently transpires to be ineffective[1], the receiver may make an application to the High Court to be relieved from personal liability as the court thinks fit. Where the court makes such an order, the person who appointed the receiver becomes personally liable.[2]

[1] The charge could, for example, be ineffective as a result of a failure to register pursuant to CA 1963, s 99, or in the case of a floating charge, it might be invalid under CA 1963, s 288.

[2] See *Re Goldburg (No 2)* [1912] 1 KB 606 where it was held that where a charge under which a receiver has been appointed is invalid, so too is his appointment, and he is a trespasser in respect of all assets of which he takes possession.

UK legislation

See IA 1986, ss 35, 37.

[316A Duty of receiver selling property to get best possible price reasonably obtainable

(1) A receiver, in selling property of a company, shall exercise all reasonable care to obtain the best price reasonably obtainable for the property as at the time of sale.

(2) Notwithstanding the provisions of any instrument—

(a) it shall not be a defence to any action or proceeding brought against a receiver in respect of a breach of his duty under subsection (1) that the receiver was acting as the agent of the company or under a power of attorney given by the company; and

(b) notwithstanding anything in section 316(2), a receiver shall not be entitled to be compensated or indemnified by the company for any liability he may incur as a result of a breach of his duty under this section.

(3) (a) A receiver shall not sell by private contract a non-cash asset of the requisite value to a person who is, or who, within three years prior to the date of appointment of the receiver, has been, an officer of the company unless he has given at least 14 days' notice of his intention to do so to all creditors of the company who are known to him or who have been intimated to him.

(b) In this subsection—

(i) 'non-cash asset' and 'requisite value' have the meanings assigned to them by section 29 of the Companies Act, 1990, and

(ii) 'officer' includes a person connected, within the meaning of section 26 of the Companies Act, 1990, with a director, and a shadow director.][a]

Amendments

a CA 1963, s 316A inserted by CA 1990, s 172.

Definitions

'agent': CA 1963, s 2(1); 'company': CA 1963, s 2(1); 'director': CA 1963, s 2(1); 'officer': CA 1963, s 2(1).

Notes

Restatement of common law duty of care: CA 1963, s 316(A)(1) provides that a receiver in selling the property of a company shall exercise all reasonable care to obtain the best price reasonably obtainable for the property as at the time of the sale. In *Re Edenfell Holdings* Ltd,[1] Laffoy J commented that this duty is 'merely a statutory restatement of the common law duty of care owed by a receiver in relation to the sale of property charged by a debenture under which he is appointed'[2]. This was confirmed by Denham J in the decision on the various appeals heard and adjudged on together in *Bula Ltd v Crowley (No 4)*.[3]

1 *Re Edenfell Holdings Ltd* [1999] 1 IR 443. See also *Ruby Property Company Ltd v Kilty* [1999] IEHC 50 where McCracken J similarly acknowledged that s 316A(1) is merely a restatement of the position at common law.

2 In relation to the position at common law, see *Holohan v Friends Provident and Century Life Office* [1966] IR 1; *Cuckmere Brick Co Ltd v Mutual Finance Ltd* [1971] Ch 949; *Casey v Irish Intercontinental Bank Ltd* [1979] IR 364; *Latchford v Beirne* [1981] 2 All ER 705; *Standard Chartered Bank Ltd v Walker* [1982] 3 All ER 938; *Lambert Jones Estates Ltd v Donnelly* [1982] IEHC 25 (O'Hanlon J); *McGowan v Gannon* [1983] ILRM 516; *Irish Oil and Cake Mills v Donnelly* [1983] IEHC 57 (Costello J); *American Express International Banking Corporation v Hurley* [1985] 3 All ER 564; *Tse Kwong Lam v Wong Chit Sen* [1983] 3 All ER 54; *Knight v Lawrence* [1993] BCLC 215; *Downsview Nominees Ltd v First City Corp Ltd* [1994] 1 BCLC 49; *Medforth v Blake* [1999] 3 All ER 97; *Yorkshire Bank plc v Hall* [1999] 1 WLR 1713; *Silven Properties Ltd v Royal Bank of Scotland plc* [2004] 1 BCLC 359; *Bell v Long* [2008] 2 BCLC 706.

3 *Bula Ltd v Crowley* (No. 4) [2003] 2 IR 430.

Timing and manner of sale: It has been consistently held by the courts that the receiver's statutory duty is only a duty to obtain the best price reasonably obtainable 'at the time of the sale' and is not obliged to postpone a sale in the hope of an upswing in the market.[1] Furthermore, it may be reasonable for him to impose a deadline within which bids are to be submitted and to elect not to treat with persons who fail to adhere to that deadline.[2] In this regard, it has been emphasised by the court that to adopt any other position would be to run the risk of trying to judge the receiver with the benefit of hindsight.[3]

In deciding to put the property up for sale the receiver is under no duty to take steps such as the carrying out of repairs or the obtaining of planning permission in order to enhance its value.[4]

The receiver should, however, exercise reasonable care as to the manner in which the property is to be marketed and sold and, where appropriate, should act on professional advice.[5] If there is evidence that the receiver is acting negligently, the court may restrain the disposal of a property at an undervalue[6] and in this regard a decision by the receiver to sell the property at auction does not necessarily amount to a sufficient discharge by him of his duty of care, particularly if the only bidder is a party connected with the company in receivership.[7]

One particularly problematic area for a receiver and manager, in exercising his duty of care under s 316A, is determining whether he should cause the company to continue trading with a view to trying to sell the business as a going concern. Some cases had suggested that a receiver and manager might well be under a duty to continue the business and preserve the goodwill, at least in circumstances where a failure to do so would adversely affect the price obtainable for the charged assets[8] However, the better view would now seem to be that no such duty arises.[9] Nevertheless, if he does decide to trade, he must exercise reasonable care to try to do so profitably.[10]

In *Medforth v Blake*[11] Sir Richard Scott VC set out the duties of a receiver/manager in deciding whether or not to trade, as follows:

'(1) A Receiver managing mortgaged property owes duties to the mortgagor and any one else with an interest in the equity of redemption,

(2) The duties include, but are not necessarily confined to, a duty of good faith,

(3) The extent and scope of any duty additional to that of good faith will depend on the facts and circumstances of a particular case,

(4) In exercising his powers of management the primary duty of the Receiver is to try and bring about a situation in which the interest on the security can be paid and the debt itself repaid,

(5) Subject to the primary duty, the Receiver owes a duty to manage the property with due diligence,

(6) Due diligence does not oblige the Receiver to continue to carry on a business on the alleged premises previously carried out by the mortgagor,

(7) If the Receiver does carry on a business on the mortgaged premises, due diligence requires reasonable steps to be taken in order to do so profitably.'

In *Moorview Developments Ltd v First Active plc*[12] Clarke J has left open the question of whether *Medforth v Blake* represents good law in this jurisdiction, at least in so far as that case suggests that the receiver might owe a duty of care to the company regarding the management of the company's assets and undertakings. Be that as it may, if the receiver does decide to trade and does so at a loss, thereby reducing the amount that would otherwise have been payable to the preferential creditors out of the floating charge realisations, he may be personally liable to the preferential creditors to make up the consequential shortfall.[13]

1 *Casey v Irish Intercontinental Bank* [1979] IR 364; *Bank of Cyprus (London) Ltd v Gill* [1980] 2 Lloyd's Rep 51; *Standard Chartered Bank Ltd v Walker* [1982] 3 All ER 938; *McGowan v Gannon* [1983] ILRM 516; *Bank of Cyprus (London) Ltd v Gill* [1980] 2 Lloyds' Reports 51; *Routestone Ltd v Minories Finance Ltd* [1997] BCC 180; *Re Edenfell Holdings Ltd* [1999] 1 IR 458; *Re Bula Ltd* [2002] 2 ILRM 513; *Bula Ltd v Crowley (No 4)* [2003] 2 IR 430; *Ruby Property Co Ltd v Kilty* (31 January 2003, unreported) HC (McKechnie J); *Silven Properties Ltd v Royal Bank of Scotland plc* [2004] 1 BCLC 359; *Bell v Long* [2008] 2 BCLC 706.

2 *Grace v ACC Bank plc* [2006] IEHC 315;

3 *Re Edenfell Holdings Ltd* [1999] 1 IR 458; *Grace v ACC Bank plc* [2006] IEHC 315.

4 *Silven Properties Ltd v Royal Bank of Scotland plc* [2004] 1 BCLC 359; *Meftah v Lloyds TSB Bank plc* [2001] 2 All ER (Comm) 741; *Garland v Ralph Pay & Ranson (a firm)* [1984] EGLR 147; *Den Norske Bank v Acemex Management Co* [2004] 1 Lloyd's Rep 1.

5 *Cuckmere Brick Co Ltd v Mutual Finance Ltd* [1971] Ch 949; *American Express International Banking Corporation v Hurley* [1985] 3 All ER 564; *Lambert Jones Estates Ltd v Donnelly* [1982] IEHC 25 (O'Hanlon J); *Re Edenfell Holdings Ltd* [1999] 1 IR 458; *Re Bula plc* [2002] 2 ILRM 513; *Ruby Property Co Ltd v Kilty* (31 January 2003, unreported) HC (McKechnie J); *Bula Ltd v Crowley (No 4)* [2003] 2 IR 430.

6 *Holohan v Friends Provident and Century Life Office* [1966] IR 1.

7 *Tse Kwong Lam v Won, Chit Sen* [1983] 1 WLR 1349.

8 *R v Board of Trade, ex parte St Martins Preserving Co Ltd* [1965] 1 QB 603; *Airline Airspaces Ltd v Handley Page Ltd* [1970] 1 Ch 193.

9 *Medforth v Blake* [2000] Ch 86. See also *Re B Johnson & Co Builders) Ltd* [1955] Ch 634.

10 *Medforth v Blake* [2000] Ch 86.

11 [2000] Ch 86.

12 *Moorview Developments Ltd v First Active plc* [2009] IEHC 214.

13 *Westminster City Corporation v Haste* [1950] Ch 442.

To whom is the duty of care owed: The receiver's duty of care is owed primarily to the debentureholder who appointed him.[1] He also owes a secondary duty of care to third parties who have guaranteed the debt due to the debentureholder,[2] at least in so far as they have any interest as guarantors in the equity of redemption.[3] Moreover, whilst he may have a limited duty of care to the company itself to the extent that it has any interest in the equity of redemption,[4] he owes no duty of care to individual creditors of the company.[5] Nor does he owe any duty of care to individual directors, shareholders or employees of the company.[6]

1 *Re B Johnson & Co (Builders) Ltd* [1955] 1 Ch 634; *Rottenberg v Monjack* [1993] BCLC 374; *Bula Ltd v Crowley (No 3)* [2003] 1 IR 396.

2 *Standard Chartered Bank Ltd v Walker* [1982] 3 All ER 938; *American Express International Banking Corporation v Hurley* [1985] 3 All ER 564; *McGowan v Gannon* [1983] ILRM 516; *Irish Oil and Cake Mills Ltd v Donnelly* [1983] IEHC 57 (Costello J); *Ruby Property Co Ltd v Kilty* (31 January 2003, unreported) HC (McKechnie J).

3 *Burgess v Auger* [1998] 2 BCLC 478; *Downsview Nominees Ltd v First City Corp* [1994] 1 BCLC 49.

4 *McGowan v Gannon* [1983] ILRM 516; *Re Bula Ltd* [2002] 2 ILRM 513; *Ruby Property Co Ltd v Kilty* (31 January 2003, unreported) HC (McKechnie J).

5 *Lathia v Dronsfield Bros Ltd* [1987] BCLC 321; *Ruby Property Co Ltd v Kilty* (31 January 2003, unreported) HC (McKechnie J). cf The comments of O'Hanlon J in *Lambert Jones Estates Ltd v Donnelly* [1982] IEHC 25 (O'Hanlon J).

6 *Burgess v Auger* [1998] 2 BCLC 478.

CA 1963, s 316A(2) provides that a receiver may not avoid his statutory duty to obtain the best price reasonably obtainable for the property at the time of sale by claiming that he is acting as agent or attorney for the company. Furthermore, a receiver may not be compensated or indemnified by the company for any liability he may incur as a result of breach of his duty under this section.

CA 1963, s 316A(3) prohibits the receiver from selling by private contract a non-cash asset of requisite value[1] to any person who is or was an officer[2] of the company within three years of the receiver's appointment, unless he has given at least 14 days notice to all creditors known to him. The purpose of this provision is to restrict the ability of the past and present officers of the company to buy the assets of the company at a knock down price.

In *Demite v Protec Health Ltd*[3] which concerned the English equivalent to CA 1990, s 29[4] regulating transactions involving directors, Park J held that this section applied to the sale of company assets by receivers. Courtney has convincingly argued that it would be highly unlikely that this decision would be followed in Ireland on the grounds that s 316A(3) implicitly displaces the operation of s 29 of the 1990 Act.[5]

1 'non-cash asset' and 'requisite value' have the meanings assigned to these terms by a 29 of CA 1990.

2 'office' includes a person connected, within the meaning of s 26 of CA1990, with a director, and a shadow director.

3 *Demite Ltd v Protec Health Ltd* [1998] BCC 638.

4 UK Companies Act 1985, s 320.

5 Courtney, 'Receiverships in Ireland in the Wake of *Demite Ltd v Protec Health Ltd*' Commercial Law Practitioner, November 1998. See also Courtney, *The Law of Private Companies* (2nd edn, Tottel Publishing, 2002) at para 22.049.

317 Notification that receiver appointed

(1) Where a receiver of the property of a company has been appointed, every invoice, order for goods or business letter issued by or on behalf of the company or the receiver or the liquidator of the company, being a document on or in which the name of the company appears, shall contain a statement that a receiver has been appointed.

(2) If default is made in complying with the requirements of this section, the company and any of the following persons who knowingly and wilfully authorises or permits the default, namely, any officer of the company, any liquidator of the company and any receiver, [shall be guilty of an offence and liable to a fine][a] of [€1,904.61][b].

Amendments

a Offence created by C(AA)A 2003, s 57 and Sch 2 with effect from 6 April 2004.

b '£100' substituted for '£20' by C(A)A 1982, Sch 1. £100 increased to £1,500 by CA 1990, s 240(7) as inserted by CLEA 2001, s 104, and converted to €1,904.61 by Council Regulations (EC) No 1103/97, No 974/98 and No 2866/98 and the Economic and Monetary Union Act 1998, s 6.

Definitions

'company': CA 1963, s 2(1); 'document': CA 1963, s 2(1): 'officer': CA 1963, s 2(1).

UK legislation

See IA 1986, s 39.

318 Power of court to fix remuneration of receiver

(1) The Court may, on an application made to it by the liquidator of a company or by any creditor or member of the company, by order fix the amount to be paid by way of remuneration to any person who, under the powers contained in any instrument, has been appointed as receiver of the property of the company notwithstanding that the remuneration of such receiver has been fixed by or under that instrument.

(2) Subject to subsection (3), the power of the court under subsection (1) shall, where no previous order has been made in relation thereto under that subsection—

(a) extend to fixing the remuneration for any period before the making of the order or the application therefor; and

(b) be exercisable notwithstanding that the receiver has died or ceased to act before the making of the order or the application therefor; and

(c) where the receiver has been paid or has retained for his remuneration for any period before the making of the order any amount in excess of that fixed by the court for that period, extend to requiring him or his personal representatives to account for the excess or such part thereof as may be specified in the order.

(3) The power conferred by paragraph (c) of subsection (2) shall not be exercised in relation to any period before the making of the application for the order unless in the opinion of the court there are special circumstances making it proper for the power to be so exercised.

(4) The court may from time to time on an application made by the liquidator or by any creditor or member of the company or by the receiver, vary or amend an order made under subsection (1).

(5) This section shall apply whether the receiver was appointed before, on, or after the operative date and to periods before, as well as to periods after, the operative date.

Definitions

'company': CA 1963, s 2(1); 'the court': CA 1963, s 2(1); 'member': CA 1963, s 31; 'the operative date': CA 1963, s 2(1).

Notes

CA 1963, s 318(1) provides that the court may fix the remuneration of a receiver appointed under a debenture on the application of a liquidator, creditor or member of the company.

CA 1963, s 318(2) provides that the court can determine the remuneration for a period prior to the making of an order or application, and can do so even in the case where a receiver dies or ceases to act and may require a receiver to account for any fees already fees paid or retained by him in excess of the remuneration fixed ordered by the court.

CA 1963, s 318(3) provides that CA 1963, s 318(2)(c) shall not be exercised in relation to any period before the making of the application for the order unless in the opinion of the court there are special circumstances making it proper for the power to be so exercised.

The scope of s 318 is confined to the receiver's remuneration, and confers no jurisdiction to interfere with the receiver's right to be indemnified pursuant to CA 1963, s 316(2) for disbursements which have been properly incurred.[1] Interference by the court should be confined to cases in which the receiver's remuneration can clearly be seen as excessive.[2]

Where a receiver is appointed on foot of a debenture his remuneration will generally be agreed by the debentureholder. Where appointed by the court his remuneration will be fixed by the court.[3] Such remuneration will be determined by the court by reference to such scales or rates of professional charges as it thinks fit.[4] The receiver must justify the reasonableness and prudence of incurring disbursements for which he seeks allowance and reimbursement.[5]

In *Re City Car Sales Ltd*[6], Geoghegan J gave CA 1963, s 318 a purposive or teleological interpretation and indicated that it did not prohibit the approval of a higher amount in respect of remuneration than 5 per cent of the value of realisations that would otherwise be allowed by s 24 of the Conveyancing Act 1881. Section 318 is designed to prevent excessive payment to a receiver and therefore the court will only interfere with contractual rights where the remuneration is clearly excessive. A rate in excess of 5 per cent of the value of the realisations will be permitted where the fee has been charged by the receiver in a proper and bona fide manner and where the level of that fee represents the remuneration that would be claimed as a matter of normal accountancy practice for work of that type.[7]

See notes at CA 1963, s 314 on Gas Regulation Act 1982, s 7.

1 *Re Potters Oils Ltd (No 2)* [1986] BCLC 98; [1986] 1 WLR 201.
2 *Re Potters Oils Ltd (No 2)* [1986] BCLC 98; [1986] 1 WLR 201.
3 RSC 1986, Ord 50, r 16(1).
4 Lightman and Moss, *The Law of Receivers and Administrators of Companies* (3rd edn, Sweet and Maxwell, 2000) ch 22, p 424.
5 *Mirror Group Newspapers plc v Maxwell* [1998] 1 BCLC 638.
6 *Re City Car Sales Ltd* [1995] 1 ILRM 221.
7 *Re City Car Sales Ltd* [1995] 1 ILRM 221; *Re Red Sail Frozen Foods Ltd* [2007] 2 IR 361.

UK legislation

See IA 1986, s 36.

---

319 Information to be given when receiver is appointed

(1) Where a receiver of the whole or substantially the whole of the property of a company (hereinafter in this section and in section 320 referred to as 'the receiver') is appointed on behalf of the holders of any debentures of the company secured by a floating charge, then subject to the provisions of this section and section 320—

(a) the receiver shall forthwith send notice to the company of his appointment; and

(b) there shall, within 14 days after receipt of the notice, or such longer period as may be allowed by the court or by the receiver, be made out and submitted to the receiver in accordance with section 320 a statement in the prescribed form as to the affairs of the company; and

(c) the receiver shall within 2 months after receipt of the said statement send to the registrar of companies, to the court, to the company, to any trustees for the debenture holders on whose behalf he was appointed and, so far as he is aware of their addresses, to all such debenture holders, a copy of the statement and of any comments he sees fit to make thereon.

(2) The receiver shall within one month after the expiration of the period of 6 months from the date of his appointment and of every subsequent period of 6 months, and within one month after he ceases to act as receiver of the property of the company, send to the registrar of companies an abstract in the prescribed form showing the assets of the company of which he has taken possession since his appointment, their estimated value, the proceeds of sale of any such assets since his appointment, his receipts and payments during that period of 6 months or, where he ceases to act as aforesaid, during the period from the end of the period to which the last preceding abstract related up to the date of his so ceasing, and the aggregate amounts of his receipts and of his payments during all preceding periods since his appointment.

[(2A) Where a receiver ceases to act as receiver of the property of the company, the abstract under subsection (2) shall be accompanied by a statement from the receiver of his opinion as to whether or not the company is solvent and the registrar shall, on receiving the statement, forward a copy of it to the Director.][a]

(3) Where a receiver is appointed under the powers contained in any instrument, this section shall have effect with the omission of the references to the court in subsection

(1), and in any other case, references to the court shall be taken as referring to the court by which the receiver was appointed.

(4) Subsection (1) shall not apply in relation to the appointment of a receiver to act with an existing receiver or in place of a receiver dying or ceasing to act, except that, where that subsection applies to a receiver who dies or ceases to act before it has been fully complied with, the references in paragraphs (b) and (c) thereof to the receiver shall (subject to subsection (5)) include references to his successor and to any continuing receiver.

Nothing in this subsection shall be taken as limiting the meaning of 'the receiver' where used in or in relation to subsection (2).

(5) This section and section 320, where the company is being wound up, shall apply notwithstanding that the receiver and the liquidator are the same person, but with any necessary modifications arising from that fact.

(6) Nothing in subsection (2) shall be taken to prejudice the duty of the receiver to render proper accounts of his receipts and payments to the persons to whom, and at the times at which, he may be required to do so apart from that subsection.

[(7) Where the registrar of companies becomes aware of the appointment of a receiver under this section, he shall forthwith inform the Director of the appointment.

(8) If the receiver makes default in complying with this section, he shall be guilty of an offence.][a]

Amendments

a CA 1963, s 319(2A), (7) and (8) were inserted by CLEA 2001, s 52.

Definitions

'accounts': CA 1963, s 2(1); 'company': CA 1963, s 2(1); 'the court': CA 1963, s 2(1); 'debenture': CA 1963, s 2(1); 'prescribed': CA 1963, s 2(1); 'the registrar of companies': CA 1963, s 2(1) 'Director': CLEA 2001, s 3(1).

Notes

Information to be provided to the receiver: Section 319(1) provides that where a receiver is appointed under a debenture of a company secured by a floating charge, he must immediately notify the company of his appointment. Within 14 days of the receipt of that notice a statement of affairs of the company must be provided to the receiver in accordance with CA 1963, s 320.[1] Within a further two months the receiver must provide a copy of the statement along with his comments to the Registrar of Companies, debentureholders or their trustees and to the court where he is appointed by the court.[2] If the statement of affairs is not submitted to the receiver or if it is submitted otherwise than in the prescribed form, he or any creditor may apply to the court under CA 1963, s 320A for an order compelling compliance with ss 319 and 320.

1 The prescribed form of the statement of affairs is Form 17 Companies (Forms) Order (SI 1964/45).

2 See CA 1963, s 319(3).

Filing of accounts: CA 1963, s 319(2) provides that a receiver must provide to the Registrar of Companies an abstract detailing the assets of the company of which he has taken possession, of the disposals of any such assets and of his receipts and payments for each six-month period following his appointment. He must provide this information abstract in a proscribed form[1] within one month following each six-month period. Where he ceases to act, he must provide details of the aggregate amounts of his receipts and payments from the date of the last abstract up to the date he ceased to act, within one month of ceasing to act.

See also the duty to provide accounts under CA 1963, s 321.

1 Companies Forms Order 1964 (SI 45/1964) Form 57.

CA 1963, s 319(2A)[1] provides that where a receiver ceases to act he should provide to the Director of Corporate Enforcement, in addition to the abstract under s 319(2), a statement setting out his opinion as to whether the company is solvent.

Where the receiver fails to comply with s 319, he is guilty of an offence[2] the penalties for which are set out at CA 1990, s 145.

Equitable duty to account: Apart from the accounting obligations imposed on a receiver pursuant to s 316(2) he also has an equitable duty to account to the debentureholder and the company.[3] The extent and nature of the equitable duty of the receiver to account will depend upon the facts of each individual case.[4]

Although the same equitable duty to account is owed both to the debentureholder and to the company at the end of the receivership, different considerations apply during the course of the receivership. The duty to supply reasonable information during the course of the receivership is certainly owed to the debentureholder for whose benefit the receiver is acting, but the right of the company to such information depends upon proof that it is needed to enable the directors to exercise their residual powers or to perform their duties. Any right which the company has to obtain information from the receiver must be qualified by the receiver's primary responsibility to the debentureholder, so that the receiver is entitled to withhold information from the company where he has formed the opinion that to disclose it would be contrary to the interests of the debentureholder in realising the security[5].

In *Gomba Holdings v Minories Finance*[6] Fox LJ in the Court of Appeal held, in relation to documents held by receiver following a receivership, that the ownership of the documents depends on whether they were created or received in discharge of the receiver's duties to the company or the debentureholder or neither. Only documents generated or received by the receivers pursuant to their duty to manage the businesses of the companies or dispose of their assets belong to the company.

The receiver is not under any equitable duty to account to guarantors of the company's debts.[7]

1 As substituted by CLEA 2001, s 52.

2 CA 1963, s 319(7) as substituted by CLEA 2001, s 52.

3 *McGowan v Gannon* [1983] ILRM 516; *Irish Oil and Cake Mills Ltd v Donnelly* [1983] IEHC 57 (Costello J); *Smith Ltd v Middleton* [1979] 3 All ER 843; *Gomba Holdings (UK) Ltd v Homan* [1986] BCLC 331.

4 *McGowan v Gannon* [1983] ILRM 516; *Irish Oil and Cake Mills Ltd v Donnelly* [1983] IEHC 57; *Smith Ltd v Middleton* [1979] 3 All ER 843; *Gomba Holdings (UK) Ltd v Homan* [1986] BCLC 331; *Kinsella v Somers* [1999] IEHC 44 (Budd J).

5 *Gomba Holdings (UK) Ltd v Homan* [1986] BCLC 331; *Irish Oil and Cake Mills Ltd v Donnelly* [1983] IEHC 57 (Costello J).

6 *Gomba Holdings v Minories Finance* [1989] BCLC 115.

7 *McGowan v Gannon* [1983] ILRM 516; *Re Bula Ltd* [2002] 2 ILRM 513.

UK legislation

See IA 1986, ss 36, 46, 47.

320 Contents of statement to be submitted to receiver

(1) The statement as to the affairs of a company required by section 319 to be submitted to the receiver (or his successor) shall show as at the date of the receiver's appointment particulars of the company's assets, debts and liabilities, the names and residences of its creditors, the securities held by them respectively, the dates when the securities were respectively given and such further or other information as may be prescribed.

(2) The said statement shall be submitted by, and be verified by affidavit of, one or more of the persons who are, at the date of the receiver's appointment, the directors and by the person who is at that date the secretary of the company, or by such of the persons hereafter in this subsection mentioned as the receiver (or his successor), may require to submit and verify the statement, that is, persons—

(a) who are or have been officers of the company;

(b) who have taken part in the formation of the company at any time within one year before the date of the receiver's appointment;

(c) who are in the employment of the company or have been in the employment of the company within the said year, and are in the opinion of the receiver capable of giving the information required;

(d) who are or have been within the said year officers of or in the employment of a company which is, or within the said year was, an officer of the company to which the statement relates.

(3) Any person making the statement and affidavit shall be allowed, and shall be paid by the receiver (or his successor) out of his receipts, such costs and expenses incurred in and about the preparation and making of the statement and affidavit as the receiver (or his successor) may consider reasonable, subject to an appeal to the court.

(4) Where the receiver is appointed under the powers contained in any instrument, this section shall have effect with the substitution for references to an affidavit of references to a statutory declaration; and in any other case references to the court shall be taken to refer to the court by which the receiver was appointed.

[(5) If any person to whom subsection (2) applies makes default in complying with the requirements of this section, he shall, unless he can prove to the satisfaction of the court that it was not possible for him to comply with the requirements of the section, be liable—

(a) on summary conviction, to imprisonment for a term not exceeding six months or to a fine not exceeding [€1,904.61][a] or to both; or

(b) on conviction on indictment, to imprisonment for a term not exceeding three years or to a fine not exceeding [€6,348.69][b] or to both.][c]

(6) References in this section to the receiver's successor shall include a continuing receiver.

Amendments

a £1,000 increased to £1,500 by CA 1990, s 240(7) and converted to €1,904.61 by Council Regulations (EC) No 1103/97, No 974/98 and No 2866/98 and the Economic and Monetary Union Act 1998, s 6.

b £5,000 converted to €6,348.69 by Council Regulations (EC) No 1103/97, No 974/98 and No 2866/98 and the Economic and Monetary Union Act 1998, s 6.

c CA 1963, s 320(5) substituted by CA 1990, s 173.

Definitions

'company': CA 1963, s 2(1); 'the court': CA 1963, s 2(1); 'director': CA 1963, s 2(1); 'officer': CA 1963, s 2(1); 'prescribed': CA 1963, s 2(1).

Notes

Section 320(1) provides that the statement of affairs[1] to be provided by the directors to the receiver pursuant to CA 1963, s 319 must include the following details:

(i) particulars of the company's assets;

(ii) particulars of the company's debts and liabilities;

(iii) the names and residence of all creditors;

(iv) the security held by creditor;

(v) the dates when the securities were respectively given; and

(vi) any further information as may be prescribed.

The Registrar of Companies may prosecute offences under this section. See C(A)A 1982, s 16.

1 For the prescribed form of statement of affairs, see Companies (Forms) Order (SI 45/1964), Form 17.

CA 1963, s 320(2) provides that the statement of affairs submitted to the receiver must be verified on affidavit by either (i) a director, (ii) the company secretary, (iii) one who is or has been an officer of the company, (iv) a person involved in the formation of the company, (v) a present or former employee capable of giving the information required, or (vi) an officer or employee of a company to which the statement relates.

CA 1963, s 320(3) provides that the person making this statement and affidavit shall be paid by the receiver for any costs and expenses incurred in doing so, as considered reasonable by the receiver, and subject to appeal to the court. The persons making out the statement of affairs are not bound to use outside experts, because they are only obliged to provide such information as is within their own knowledge, and in any event, the receiver will himself typically be an expert himself and will have access to any additional outside expertise that may be necessary to construe the construe and analyse the statement of affairs.[1]

CA 1963, s 320(5)[2] provides that failure by any of the above persons to verify the statement of affairs is a criminal offence. It is a defence, where one can prove to the satisfaction of the court, that it was not possible for the person in default to comply with the requirements of this section.[3] Verification of the statement of affairs on affidavit permits the relevant officers to be cross-examined as to its contents. If the statement of affairs is not submitted to the receiver or if it is submitted otherwise than in the prescribed form, he or any creditor may apply to the court under CA 1963, s 320A for an order compelling compliance with ss 319 and 320.

1 *Somers v Kennedy* [1998] 1 IR 1.

2 CA 1963, s 320(5) substituted by CA 1990, s 173.

3 Proceedings for a breach of this section may be brought and prosecuted by the registrar of companies: C(A)A 1982, s 16.

UK legislation

See IA 1986, s 47.

[320A Consequences of contravention of section 319 or 320

Where, in contravention of section 319 (1) (b) and section 320, a statement of affairs is not submitted to the receiver as required by those provisions, the court may, on the application of the receiver or any creditor of the company, and notwithstanding the provisions of section 320 (5) (inserted by section 173 of the Companies Act, 1990), makes whatever order it thinks fit, including an order compelling compliance with section 319 and section 320.][a]

Amendments

a CA 1963, s 320A inserted by CA 1990, s 174.

Definitions

'company': CA 1963, s 2(1); 'the court': CA 1963, s 2(1).

Notes

Where there is failure to submit a statement of affairs to the receiver, as required by CA 1963, ss 319(1) and 320, the court may on application from the receiver or any creditor, make an order compelling compliance with these sections.

This provision may be of particular importance to creditors who wish to obtain financial information about the company in order to determine whether or not to pursue the officers of the company for misfeasance, fraudulent or reckless trading, etc.[1] There is no statutory time limit for invoking the provisions of s 320A.

1 Pursuant to CA 1990, s 251.

321 Delivery to registrar of accounts of receivers

(1) Except where subsection (2) of section 319 applies, every receiver of the property of a company shall, within one month after the expiration of the period of 6 months from the date of his appointment and of every subsequent period of 6 months, and within one month after he ceases to act as receiver, deliver to the registrar of companies for registration an abstract in the prescribed form showing the assets of the company of which he has taken possession since his appointment, their estimated value, the proceeds of sale of any such assets since his appointment, his receipts and his payments during that period of 6 months or, where he ceases to act as aforesaid, during the period from the end of the period to which the last preceding abstract related up to the date of his so ceasing, and the aggregate amounts of his receipts and of his payments during all the preceding periods since his appointment.

(2) Every receiver who makes default in complying with this section [shall be guilty of an offence and liable to a fine][a] not exceeding [€1,904.61].[b]

Amendments

a Words substituted by C(AA)A 2003, s 57 and Sch 2.

b '£1000' substituted for '£500' by CA 1990, s 145, increased to £1,500 by CA 1990, 240(7) as inserted by CLEA 2001, s 104 and converted to €1,904.61 by Council Regulations (EC) No 1103/97, No 974/98 and No 2866/98 and the Economic and Monetary Union Act 1998, s 6.

Definitions

'accounts': CA 1963, s 2(1); 'company': CA 1963, s 2(1); 'prescribed': CA 1963, s 2(1); 'the registrar of companies': CA 1963, s 2(1).

Notes

This section applies if the receiver has been appointed over some only of the company's assets. If he has been appointed over the whole or substantially the whole of the property of the company, the provisions of CA 1963, s 319 apply instead. For a fuller discussion of the receiver's statutory and equitable accounting obligations, see the notes to s 319.

UK legislation

See IA 1986, s 38.

---

322 Enforcement of duty of receiver to make returns

(1) If any receiver of the property of a company—

(a) having made default in filing, delivering or making any return, account or other document, or in giving any notice, which a receiver is by law required to file, deliver, make or give, fails to make good the default within 14 days after the service on him of a notice requiring him to do so; or

(b) having been appointed under the powers contained in any instrument, has, after being required at any time by the liquidator of the company to do so, failed to render proper accounts of his receipts and payments and to vouch the same and to pay over to the liquidator the amount properly payable to him;

the court may, on an application made for the purpose, make an order directing the receiver to make good the default within such time as may be specified in the order.

(2) In the case of any such default as is mentioned in paragraph (a) of subsection (1), an application for the purposes of this section may be made by any member or creditor of the company or by the registrar of companies, and in the case of any such default as is mentioned in paragraph (b) of that subsection, the application shall be made by the liquidator, and in either case the order may provide that all costs of and incidental to the application shall be borne by the receiver.

(3) Nothing in this section shall be taken to prejudice the operation of any enactments imposing penalties on receivers in respect of any such default as is mentioned in subsection (1).

Definitions

'accounts': CA 1963, s 2(1); 'company': CA 1963, s 2(1); 'the court': CA 1963, s 2(1); 'document': CA 1963, s 2(1): 'member': CA 1963, s 31; 'the registrar of companies': CA 1963, s 2(1).

Notes

CA 1963, s 322(1) provides that if a receiver (a) fails to files returns, accounts or other documents which by law he is required to do and fails to rectify this default within 14 days of receipt of notice of such default, or (b) fails to provide proper accounts of his receipts and payments duly vouched and to pay over to the liquidator amounts properly payable to him, the court may, 'on an application made for the purpose, make an order directing the receiver to make good the default within such time as may be specified in the order'.

CA 1963, s 322(2) provides that an application under s 322(1)(a) may be made by any member or creditor of the company or the Registrar of Companies, and under sub-s (1)(b) by the liquidator, and in either case the court may order that the costs of the application be paid by the receiver.

CA 1963, s 322(3) provides that this section does not affect any other penalties which may be imposed on a receiver for similar statutory breaches to that set out in sub-s (1).

Criminal penalties for failure by a receiver to make proper returns are set out at CA 1963, ss 319 and 321 and at s 145 of CA 1990.

Under CA 1963, s 322(1)(b) the liquidator may only require proper accounts of receipts and payments made by the receiver personally and not of his predecessor who has retired, died or otherwise vacated office.[1] For the purposes of CA 1963, s 322(1)(b) 'proper accounts' constitute more than a mere abstract of receipts and payments.[2]

The receiver is entitled to make reasonable charges for necessary work done in preparing proper accounts for a liquidator under CA 1963, s 322(1)(b), at least in so far as they are more detailed than the statutory accounts which he must file under CA 1963, ss 319 or 321.[3]

1 *Stewart v Campbell* (13 June 1986, unreported) HC (Carroll J).
2 *Stewart v Campbell* (13 June 1986, unreported) HC (Carroll J).
3 *Stewart v Campbell* (13 June 1986, unreported) HC (Carroll J).

UK legislation

See IA 1986, s 41.

[322A Removal of receiver

(1) The court may, on cause shown, remove a receiver and appoint another receiver.

(2) Notice of such proceedings shall be served on the receiver and on the person who appointed him not less than 7 days before the hearing of such proceedings and, in any such proceedings, the receiver and the person who appointed him may appear and be heard.][a]

Amendments

a CA 1963, s 322A inserted by CA 1990, s 175.

Definitions

'the court': CA 1963, s 2(1).

Notes

CA 1963, s 322A provides that the court may 'on cause shown' remove a receiver and appoint another person as receiver. The phrase 'on cause shown' is used in CA 1963, s 228(c) in respect of liquidators. See the notes at CA 1963, s 228(c).

The onus is on the applicant to show cause why the receiver should be removed.[1] To show cause it is not necessary to prove misconduct, impropriety or unfitness on the part of the receiver.[2] Whilst a receiver will undoubtedly be removed for breach of duty[3] he may also be removed where he has merely failed to display sufficient vigour in carrying out his duties and the interests of the general creditors are best served by his removal.[4] Similarly, it may be appropriate to remove the receiver where, although he is not in breach of CA 1963, s 315, his independence is nonetheless compromised.

Notice of an application to remove a receiver must be served on the receiver and the person who appointed him not less than seven days before the proceedings are heard and both may appear and be heard.

A receiver appointed pursuant to the terms of a debenture cannot be removed by the company even though he is the company's agent.[5] The company would, however, be entitled to apply pursuant to CA 1963, s 322A to have him removed by the court.

Standard form debentures confer a power on the debentureholder to remove the receiver, which obviates the need to apply for an order pursuant to CA 1963, s 322A.

On the presentation of a petition seeking the appointment of an examiner, the court may order *inter alia* that the receiver shall cease to act.[6]

1 *Re Keypak Homecare Ltd* [1990] BCLC 440. The test for due cause remains that set out in *Re Adam Eyton Ltd ex parte Charlesworth* (1887) 36 Ch D 229 per Bowen LJ at 306: 'The due cause is to be measured by reference to the real, substantial, honest interests of the liquidation, and to the purpose for which the liquidator is appointed.' This test has recently been adopted by Etherton J in *Re Buildlead Ltd* (No 2) [2005] BCC 138.

2 *Re Adam Eyton Ltd* (1887) 36 ChD 299. See also *Re Marseilles Extension Railway and Land Company* (1867) LR 4 Eq 692; *Re Keypak Homecare Ltd* [1987] BCLC 409.

3 *Re St George's Estate* (1887) 19 LR Ir 556.

4 Per Neuberger J in *AMP Enterprises (t/a Total Home Entertainment) v Hoffman* [2003] 1 BCLC 319. See also *Quickson (South and West) Ltd v Katz* [2006] 1 BCLC 9; *Chua Boon Chin v McCormack* [1979] 2 MLJ 156, 158; *Procam (Pte) Ltd v Nangle* [1990] 3 MLJ 269.

5 *Gosling v Gaskell* [1896] 1 QB 669, 692 approved and upheld at [1897] AC 575.

6 C(A)A 1990, s 6(1), as amended by C(A)(No 2)A 1999, s 16; see also C(A)A 1990, s 3(6).

[322B Court may determine or limit receivership on application of liquidator

(1) On the application of the liquidator of a company that is being wound up (other than by means of a members' voluntary winding up) and in respect of which a receiver has been appointed (whether before or after the commencement of the winding up), the court may—

(a) order that the receiver shall cease to act as such from a date specified by the court, and prohibit the appointment of any other receiver; or

(b) order that the receiver shall, from a date specified by the court, act as such only in respect of certain assets specified by the court.

An order under this subsection may be made on such terms and conditions as the court thinks fit.

(2) The court may from time to time, on an application made either by the liquidator or by the receiver, rescind or amend an order made under subsection (1).

(3) A copy of an application made under this section shall be served on the receiver and on the person who appointed him not less than 7 days before the hearing of the application, and the receiver and any such party may appear before and be heard by the court in respect of the application.

(4) Except as provided in subsection (1), no order make under this section shall affect any security or charge over the undertaking or property of the company.][a]

Amendments

a CA 1963, s 322B inserted by CA 1990, s 176.

Definitions

'company': CA 1963, s 2(1); 'the court': CA 1963, s 2(1); 'member': CA 1963, s 31; 'members' voluntary winding up': CA 1963, s 2(1), s 256(7).

Notes

Section 322B (1) provides that where a liquidator has been appointed he may make an application to the court seeking to determine or limit the role of the receiver in the liquidation process. A court has the power to make such order on such terms and conditions as the court sees fit. Keane has commented that 'problems have been caused for everyone concerned by the existence side by side of a receivership and a winding up and (CA 1963, s 322B) seeks to deal with these difficulties.'[1] Courtney has commented that CA 1963, 322B is a radical change in the law, while emphasising the saver contained at s 322B(4). A court determining that a receiver should cease to act in respect of a charged asset must give sufficient weight to the effect of depriving a debentureholder of his agent (and control of his property) and will have to decide what influence the debentureholder will subsequently exert over the liquidator in respect of his charge (and his property).

This section reverses the decision in *Re Joshua Stubbs Ltd*[2] where it was held that the court will not displace a receiver, appointed pursuant to the terms of a debenture, following the appointment of a liquidator. The effect of this amendment may be to avoid two sets of costs and expenses being incurred in respect of the same insolvent company, thus increasing the prospects of a dividend for ordinary unsecured creditors.

It is well established at common law that the commencement of a winding up does not preclude the appointment of a receiver[3] nor does the appointment of a liquidator automatically terminate the receivership. However, a receiver requires the leave of the court to take possession of charged assets which are already in the possession of the liquidator but would normally be entitled to that leave as of right.[4]

A copy of an application made under this section shall be served on the receiver and on the person who appointed him not less than 7 days before the hearing of the application, and the receiver and any such party may appear before and be heard by the court in respect of the application.

CA 1963, s 322B(2) permits the court on application by a receiver or liquidator to amend or rescind an order made under CA 1963, 322B(1). No time limit is placed on this application.

CA 1963, s 322B(4) provides that no order under this section will affect any security or charge over the company or its assets. Accordingly the section is concerned with the manner, and cost effectiveness of, and the person responsible for, realising some or all of the charged assets of the company, rather than the assets themselves.

1 Keane, *Company Law* (4th edn, Tottel Publishing, 2007) para 22.41.

2 [1891] 1 Ch 475.

3 *Re Henry Pound, Son and Hutchins* (1889) 42 Ch D 402.

4 *Re Henry Pound, Son and Hutchins* (1889) 42 Ch D 402.

[322C Resignation of receiver

(1) A receiver of the property of a company appointed under the powers contained in any instrument may resign, provided he has given one month's notice thereof to—

(a) the holders of floating charges over all or any part of the property of the company;

(b) the company or its liquidator; and

(c) the holders of any fixed charge over all or any part of the property of the company.

(2) A receiver appointed by the court may resign only with the authority of the court and on such terms and conditions, if any, as may be laid down by the court.

(3) If any person makes default in complying with the requirements of this section, he [shall be guilty of an offence and liable to a fine][b] not exceeding [€1,269.74][c]][a].

Amendments

a CA 1963, s 322C inserted by CA 1990, s 177.

b Words substituted by C(AA)A 2003, s 57 and Sch 2 with effect from 6 April 2004.

c £1,000 increased to £1,500 by CA 1990, s 240(7) as inserted by CLEA 2001, s 104 and converted to €1,904.61 by Council Regulations (EC) No 1103/97, No 974/98 and No 2866/98 and the Economic and Monetary Union Act 1998, s 6.

Definitions

'company': CA 1963, s 2(1); 'the court': CA 1963, s 2(1).

Notes

CA 1963, s 322C(1) provides that where a receiver is appointed by a debentureholder he must give one month's notice of his resignation to the holders of floating charges, the company and liquidator and the holder of any fixed charge over all or part of the property of the company. Prior to the enactment of this section, a receiver appointed pursuant to a debenture would be liable for breach of contract if he resigned without the consent the debentureholder[1]. The effect of the section is to make the resignation of a receiver appointed on foot of a debenture largely a matter of contract. The section does not imply any additional term into the contractual relationship between a receiver and a debentureholder.

CA 1963, s 322C(2) provides that a receiver appointed by the court may resign only with the consent of and on such terms and conditions as may be fixed by the court.

1 *Chinnock v Sainsbury* (1860) 3 LT 258; *Morris v Delobbel-Flipo* [1892] 2 Ch 352.

323 Construction of references to receiver

It is hereby declared that, unless the contrary intention appears—

(a) any reference in this Act to a receiver of the property of a company includes a reference to a receiver and manager of the property of a company and to a manager of the property of a company and includes a reference to a receiver or to a receiver and manager or to a manager, of part only of that property, and to a receiver only of the income arising from that property or from part thereof; and

(b) any reference in this Act to the appointment of a receiver under powers contained in any instrument includes a reference to an appointment made under powers which, by virtue of any enactment, are implied in and have effect as if contained in an instrument.

Definitions

'company': CA 1963, s 2(1).

Notes

CA 1963, s 323 provides that any reference in the Act to a receiver of a company includes a reference to a receiver and manager of the property of a company. Further, any reference to an instrument under which a receiver is appointed includes statutory powers implied in such an instrument.

See notes at CA 1963, s 314 on Gas Regulation Act 1982, s 7.

See Article 2 of the Gas Regulation Act, 1982 (Section 7) Order, 1986 (SI 110/1986).

UK legislation

See IA 1986, s 29.

[323A Director may request production of receiver's books

(1) The Director may, where he considers it necessary or appropriate, request (specifying the reason why the request is being made) the production of a receiver's books for examination, either in regard to a particular receivership or to all receiverships undertaken by the receiver.

(2) Where the Director has requested the production of a receiver's books for examination under subsection (1), the receiver to whom the request is made shall furnish the books to the Director and answer any questions concerning the content of the books and the conduct of a particular receivership or receiverships, and give to the Director all assistance in the matter as the receiver is reasonably able to give.

(3) A request under subsection (1) may not be made in respect of books relating to a receivership that has concluded more than 6 years prior to the request.

(4) If the receiver makes default in complying with this section, he shall be guilty of an offence.][a]

Amendments

a CA 1963, s 323A inserted by CLEA 2001, s 53.

Definitions

'company': CA 1963, s 2(1); 'Director': CLEA 2001, s 3(1).

Notes

CA 1963, s 323A provides that the Director of Corporate Enforcement may request the production of the receiver's books for examination, either to a particular receivership or to all receiverships undertaken by that receiver.[1] The director must specify the reason for such request. A receiver is obliged to furnish the books requested to the Director and answer any questions concerning the content of the books and the conduct of a particular receivership or receiverships, and give to the Director all assistance in the matter as the receiver is reasonably able to give.[2] A request may not be made in respect to a receivership that has concluded more than 6 years prior to the request.[3] It is an offence to fail to comply with a request from the Director of Corporate Enforcement.[4]

Relevant in this context is CLEA 2001, s 58 concerning the obligation on a disciplinary committee or tribunal of a professional body to report to the Director of misconduct by liquidators or receivers. Such obligation arises where such committee or tribunal finds that a member conducting a liquidation or receivership has not maintained appropriate records, or it has reasonable grounds for believing that a member has committed an indictable offence under the Companies Acts during the course of a liquidation or receivership[5].

[1] As inserted by CLEA 2001, s 53(1).

[2] As inserted by CLEA 2001, s 53(2).

[3] As inserted by CLEA 2001, s 53(3).

[4] As inserted by CLEA 2001, s 53(3).

[5] See Courtney, *The Law of Private Companies* (2nd edn, Tottel Publishing, 2002) ch 12.

UK legislation

See IA 1986, s 29.

PART VIII
APPLICATION OF ACT TO COMPANIES FORMED OR REGISTERED UNDER FORMER ACTS

324 Application of Act to companies formed and registered under former Companies Acts

(1) Subject to subsection (2), in the application of this Act to existing companies, it shall apply in the same manner—

(a) in the case of a limited company other than a company limited by guarantee, as if the company had been formed and registered under this Act as a company limited by shares;

(b) in the case of a company limited by guarantee, as if the company had been formed and registered under this Act as a company limited by guarantee; and

(c) in the case of a company other than a limited company, as if the company had been formed and registered under this Act as an unlimited company.

(2) Reference, express or implied, to the date of registration shall be construed as a reference to the date at which the company was registered under the Joint Stock Companies Acts, the Companies Act, 1862, or the Companies (Consolidation) Act, 1908, as the case may be.

Definitions

'company': s 2(1); 'company limited by guarantee': s 2(1), 5(2); 'company limited by shares': s 2(1), 5(2); 'Joint Stock Companies Acts': s 2(1); 'unlimited company': s 2 (1), s 5(2).

Notes

The purpose of this section is to apply the Companies Acts to companies incorporated that were both formed and registered under former Companies Acts (ie before the coming into force of CA 1963 on 1 April 1964). For a general history of Irish Company Law, see Keane, ch 2, MacCann, ch 1 and Courtney, ch 1.

UK legislation

See CA 1985, s 675.

---

325 Application of Act to companies registered but not formed under former Companies Acts

(1) Subject to subsection (2), this Act shall apply to every company registered (in a register kept in the State) but not formed under the Joint Stock Companies Acts, the

Companies Act, 1862, or the Companies (Consolidation) Act, 1908, in the same manner as it is in Part IX declared to apply to companies registered but not formed under this Act.

(2) Reference, express or implied, to the date of registration shall be construed as a reference to the date at which the company was registered under the Joint Stock Companies Acts, the Companies Act, 1862, or the Companies (Consolidation) Act, 1908, as the case may be.

Definitions

'company': s 2(1); 'Joint Stock Companies Acts': s 2(1).

Notes

The purpose of this section is to apply the Companies Acts to companies formed before 1 April 1964 which, although registered under the former Companies Acts, were formed in some other manner (eg by special Act of Parliament or by Charter). In this regard see CA 1963, Part IX.

UK legislation

See CA 1985, s 676.

---

326 Application of Act to unlimited companies re-registered as limited companies under former Companies Acts

(1) Subject to subsection (2), this Act shall apply to every unlimited company registered (in a register kept in the State) as a limited company in pursuance of the Companies Act, 1879, or section 57 of the Companies (Consolidation) Act, 1908, in the same manner as it applies to an unlimited company registered in pursuance of this Act as a limited company.

(2) Reference, express or implied, to the date of registration shall be construed as a reference to the date at which the company was registered as a limited company under the said Act of 1879 or the said section 57, as the case may be.

Definitions

'unlimited company': s 2 (1), s 5(2).

Notes

With regard to the provisions applicable to an unlimited company which re-registers as a limited company, see CA 1963, s 20; C(A)A 1983, s 53.

UK legislation

See CA 1985, s 677.

---

327 Provisions as to companies registered under Joint Stock Companies Acts

(1) A company registered under the Joint Stock Companies Acts may cause its shares to be transferred in manner hitherto in use, or in such other manner as the company may direct.

(2) The power of altering articles under section 15 shall, in the case of an unlimited company formed and registered under the Joint Stock Companies Acts, extend to altering any regulations relating to the amount of capital or to its distribution into shares, notwithstanding that those regulations are contained in the memorandum.

Cross reference

See also CA 1963, s 15.

Definitions

'articles': s 2(1); 'company': s 2(1); 'memorandum': s 2(1); 'Joint Stock Companies Acts': s 2(1); 'share': s 2(1); 'unlimited company': s 2 (1), s 5(2).

UK legislation

See CA 1985, s 678.

PART IX

COMPANIES NOT FORMED UNDER THIS ACT AUTHORISED TO REGISTER UNDER THIS ACT

328 Companies capable of being registered

(1) With the exceptions and subject to the provisions contained in this section—

(a) any company consisting of seven or more members, which was in existence on the 2nd day of November, 1862, including any company registered under the Joint Stock Companies Acts; and

(b) any company formed after the date aforesaid, whether before or after the operative date, in pursuance of any statute other than this Act, or of letters patent, or being otherwise duly constituted according to law, and consisting of seven or more members;

may at any time register under this Act as an unlimited company, or as a company limited by shares, or as a company limited by guarantee; and the registration shall not be invalid by reason that it has taken place with a view to the company's being wound up.

(2) This section shall not apply to a company registered under the Companies Act, 1862, or the Companies (Consolidation) Act, 1908, or to a company which has not its registered office or principal place of business in the State.

(3) A company having the liability of its members limited by statute or letters patent, and not being a joint stock company as hereinafter defined, shall not register in pursuance of this section.

(4) A company, having the liability of its members limited by statute or letters patent, shall not register in pursuance of this section as an unlimited company or as a company limited by guarantee.

(5) A company that is not a joint stock company as hereinafter defined shall not register in pursuance of this section as a company limited by shares.

(6) A company shall not register in pursuance of this section without the assent of a majority of such of its members as are present in person or by proxy at a general meeting summoned for the purpose.

(7) Where a company, not having the liability of its members limited by statute or letters patent, is about to register as a limited company, the majority required to assent as aforesaid shall consist of not less than three-fourths of the members present in person or by proxy at the meeting.

(8) Where a company is about to register as a company limited by guarantee, the assent to its being so registered shall be accompanied by a resolution declaring that each member undertakes to contribute to the assets of the company, in the event of its being wound up while he is a member, or within one year after he ceases to be a member, for payment of the debts and liabilities of the company contracted before he ceased to be a member, and of the costs and expenses of winding up and for the adjustment of the rights of the contributories among themselves, such amount as may be required, not exceeding a specified amount.

(9) In computing any majority under this section when a poll is demanded, regard shall be had to the number of votes to which each member is entitled according to the regulations of the company.

Definitions

'company': CA 1963, s 2(1); 'company limited by guarantee': CA 1963, s 2(1), 5(2); 'company limited by shares': CA 1963, s 2(1), 5(2); 'contributory': CA 1963, s 2(1), s 208; 'member': CA 1963, s 31; 'Joint Stock Companies Acts': CA 1963, s 2(1); 'joint stock company': CA 1963, s 329; 'the operative date': CA 1963, s 2(1); 'unlimited company': CA 1963, s 2 (1), s 5(2).

Notes

This section is primarily of relevance for companies formed otherwise than in pursuance of the former Companies Acts[1] and which wish to re-register under CA 1963–1990. They would include industrial and provident societies[2] as well as companies formed under some other Act of Parliament or under letters patent or a Charter from the Crown.[3] For the background to such companies see Keane, *Company Law* (4th edn, Tottel Publishing, 2007) ch 2 and MacCann, ch 1.

As sub-s (2) makes clear, registration under Pt IX cannot take place in the case of a company which does not its registered office or principal place of business in the State.[4]

Corporations sole also appear to be excluded from the application of this section. Members of companies referred to sub-s (7) may have their liability limited otherwise than by statute or letters patent, eg contract or equitable principles.

Voting in sub-s (7) is in accordance with number represented at the meeting, not value, unless the regulations of the company expressly permit voting according to value.

1 For the application of CA 1963–1990 to companies formed under the old Companies Acts, see CA 1963, Pt VIII. In relation to companies incorporated outside the State with an established place of business within the State, see CA 1963, Pt XI. See also CA 1963, Pt X, in relation to the winding up of unregistered companies.

2 *Re Sheffield and Hallamshire Society, Fountain's Case* (1865) 4 De GJ & Sm 699.

3 *R v Joint Stock Co's Registrar, ex parte Johnston* [1891] 2 QB 598; *Re Cussons Ltd* (1904) 73 LJ Ch 296.

4 *Bulkeley v Schutz* (1871) LR 3 PC 764; *Bateman v Service* (1881) 6 App Cas 386.

UK legislation

See CA 1985, ss 680, 681.

329 Definition of joint stock company

For the purposes of this Part, as far as relates to registration of companies as companies limited by shares, a joint stock company means a company having a permanent paid up or nominal share capital of fixed amount divided into shares, also of fixed amount, or held and transferable as stock, or divided and held partly in one way and partly in the other, and formed on the principle of having for its members the holders of those shares or that stock, and no other persons, and such a company when registered with limited liability under this Act shall be deemed to be a company limited by shares.

Definitions

'company': CA 1963, s 2(1); 'company limited by shares': CA 1963, s 2(1), s 5(2); 'member': CA 1963, s 31; 'share': CA 1963, s 2(1).

Notes

The obligation of a member to contribute to the assets of a company, in one way or another, the nominal amount of the shares, is part or the statutory constitution of every joint stock company.

UK legislation

See CA 1985, s 683.

330 Requirements for registration of joint stock companies

Before the registration in pursuance of this Part of a joint stock company, there shall be delivered to the registrar the following documents—

(a) a list showing the names, addresses and occupations of all persons who, on a day named in the list, not being more than 6 clear days before the day of registration, were members of the company, with the addition of the shares or stock held by them respectively, distinguishing, in cases where the shares are numbered, each share by its number;

(b) a copy of any statute, charter, letters patent, deed of settlement, contract of co-partnery or other instrument constituting or regulating the company; and

(c) if the company is intended to be registered as a limited company, a statement specifying the following particulars—

(i) the nominal share capital of the company and the number of shares into which it is divided, or the amount of stock of which it consists;

(ii) the number of shares taken and the amount paid on each share;

[(iii) the name of the company with the addition of the word 'limited' or 'teoranta' as the last word thereof or, in the case of a public limited company, with the addition of the words 'public limited company' or 'cuideachta phoiblí theoranta' as the last words thereof; and][a]

(iv) in the case of a company intended to be registered as a company limited by guarantee, the resolution declaring the amount of the guarantee.

Amendments

a Subparagraph (c)(iii) substituted by C(A)A 1963, Sch 1, para 19.

Definitions

'company': CA 1963, s 2(1); 'company limited by guarantee': CA 1963, s 2(1), s 5(2) 'document': CA 1963, s 2(1); 'joint stock company': CA 1963, s 329; 'member': CA 1963, s 31; 'share': CA 1963, s 2(1).

UK legislation

See CA 1985, ss 684 (amended by CA 1989, s 145, Sch 19 para 12), 687.

---

331 Requirements for registration of company not being a joint stock company

Before the registration in pursuance of this Part of any company not being a joint stock company, there shall be delivered to the registrar—

(a) a list showing the names, addresses and occupations of the directors of the company; and

(b) a copy of any statute, letters patent, deed of settlement, contract of co-partnery or other instrument constituting or regulating the company; and

(c) in the case of a company intended to be registered as a company limited by guarantee, a copy of the resolution declaring the amount of the guarantee.

Definitions

'company': CA 1963, s 2(1); 'company limited by guarantee': CA 1963, s 2(1), s 5(2); 'director': CA 1963, s 2(1); 'joint stock company': CA 1963, s 329.

Notes

Companies that are not joint stock companies may only register as companies limited by guarantee or an unlimited companies: CA 1963, s 328(1), (5). 'A contract of co-partnery' was a contract of partnership in Scotland.

UK legislation

See CA 1985, s 686(1) (amended by CA 1989, s 145, Sch 19 para 5).

---

332 Verification of lists of members and directors of company for purposes of registration

The lists of members and directors and any other particulars relating to the company required to be delivered to the registrar shall be verified by a statutory declaration of any two or more directors or other principal officers of the company.

Definitions

'company': CA 1963, s 2(1); 'director': CA 1963, s 2(1); 'member': CA 1963, s 31; 'officer': CA 1963, s 2(1).

UK legislation

See CA 1985, s 686(2).

---

333 Registrar may require evidence as to nature of company

The registrar may require such evidence as he thinks necessary for the purpose of satisfying himself whether any company proposing to be registered is or is not a joint stock company as hereinbefore defined.

Definitions

'company': CA 1963, s 2(1); 'joint stock company': CA 1963, s 329.

UK legislation

See CA 1985, s 686(3).

334 Change of name for purposes of registration

(1) Subject to subsection (2), where the name of a company seeking registration under this Part is one by which it may not be so registered by reason of the name being, in the opinion of the [registrar of companies][a], undesirable, it may, with the approval of the [registrar of companies][a] signified in writing, change its name with effect from its registration as aforesaid.

(2) The like assent of the members of the company shall be required to the change of name as is by section 328 required to the registration under this Act.

Amendments

a Words substituted by CLEA 2001, s 95, with effect from 1 October 2001.

Notes

For the prohibition on the registration of a company with an 'undesirable' name, see CA 1963, s 21 and the notes thereto. Regarding s 334(2), see CA 1963, s 328(7)–(9).

Definitions

'company': CA 1963, s 2(1); 'member': CA 1963, s 31; 'Minister': CA 1963, s 2(1).

UK legislation

See CA 1985, s 682.

335 Addition of 'limited' or 'teoranta' to name

[(1) Subject to subsection (2), when a company registers in pursuance of this Part with limited liability, the word 'limited' or 'teoranta' or in the case of a public limited company the words 'public limited company' or 'cuideachta phoiblí theoranta' shall form and be part of its name.][a]

(2) Subsection (1) shall not be taken as excluding the operation of section 24.

Amendments

a Substituted by C(A)A 1983, Sch 1 para 20.

Definitions

'company': CA 1963, s 2(1).

Notes

In relation to the names of companies generally and the use of the word 'limited' or 'teoranta', etc, see CA 1963, s s 22–24 & C(A)A 1983, ss 4 and 56.

UK legislation

See CA 1985, s 687.

---

336 Certificate of registration of existing companies

[(1)][a] On compliance with the requirements of this Part relating to registration, and on payment of such fees, if any, as are payable under the following provisions of this Act, the registrar shall certify under his hand that the company applying for registration is incorporated as a company under this Act, and in the case of a limited company that it is limited and thereupon the company shall be so incorporated.

[(2) A certificate given under this section in respect of a company shall be conclusive evidence that the requirements of this Part in respect of registration and of matters precedent and incidental thereto have been complied with.][b]

Amendments

a Renumbered by C(A)A 1983, Sch 1 para 21.

b Inserted by C(A)A 1983, Sch 1 para 21.

Definitions

'company': CA 1963, s 2(1).

Notes

Is the according of 'conclusive' status to the certificate of incorporation an unconstitutional interference with the exercise of judicial power by the courts as well as being an attempt to oust the full original jurisdiction of the High Court to determine all matters and questions? See *Maher v Attorney General*;[1] *Tormey v Attorney General*.[2] See also C(A)A 1983, s 5 and the notes thereto.

Even if the certificate of incorporation has 'conclusive' status, it may still be challenged by the Attorney General: *Bowman v Secular Society Ltd*.[3]

In the case of a company registered other than in accordance with the provisions of this Part, in respect of which a certificate of incorporation is issued, the High Court would be required to adjudicate on the validity or otherwise of the actions of the Registrar of Companies. It would not be open to the Registrar of Companies to set aside or revoke the certificate granted by him on grounds of irregularities (of the company applying for registration) associated with its grant. The best that might be said of the certificate from the point of view of the newly incorporated company is that its certificate was voidable only at the instance of the High Court on judicial review. In this regard, it should be borne in mind that ceriorari is a discretionary remedy and delay may constitute a bar to relief. See *de Róiste v Minister for Defence*.[4] In relation to whether the registrar of companies might owe a duty care in the operation of his statutory duty see *Glencar Explorations plc v Mayo County Council*.[5]

1 *Maher v Attorney General* [1973] IR 146.

2 *Tormey v Attorney General* [1985] ILRM 375.

3 *Bowman v Secular Society Ltd* [1917] AC 406.

4 *de Róiste v Minister for Defence* [2001] 1 IR 190 at 216 and 221 *per* Fennelly J (SC).

5 *Glencar Explorations plc v Mayo County Council* [2001] 1 IR 84.

UK legislation

See CA 1985, s 688(1)–(3).

337 Vesting of property on registration

(1) All property, real and personal (including things in action) belonging to or vested in a company at the date of its registration in pursuance of this Part, shall on registration pass to and vest in the company as incorporated under this Act for all the estate and interest of the company therein.

[(2) ...][a]

Amendments

a Deleted by FA 1998, Sch 8 with effect from 27 March 1998.

Cross reference

See also FA 1895, s 12.

Definitions

'company': CA 1963, s 2(1); 'document': CA 1963, s 2(1).

UK legislation

See CA 1985, s 689, Sch 21 (amended by CA 1989, s 108(2)).

338 Saving for existing liabilities

Registration of a company in pursuance of this Part shall not affect the rights or liabilities of the company in respect of any debt or obligation incurred, or any contract entered into by, to, with or on behalf of, the company before registration.

Definitions

'company': CA 1963, s 2(1).

Notes

The provisions of s 339 have no application to the case of a pure contributory[1] so that if a previously unlimited company is registered under Pt IX with limited liability, he member will have no liability beyond the price paid or payable for his shares.[1] Conversely, where the policies of an association limited liability to the assets of the association, and the association subsequently re-registered as an unlimited company, it was held that policyholders were bound by the terms of their contracts and could not look to the members personally in a liquidation for payment.[2]

1 *Re Sheffield and Hallamshire Society, Fountain's Case* (1865) De GJ & Sm 699.

2 *Lethbridge v Adams, ex parte International Life Assurance Society* (1872) LR 13 Eq 547.

UK legislation

See CA 1985, s 689, Sch 21 (amended by CA 1989, s 108(2)).

339 Continuation of existing actions

(1) Subject to subsection (2), all actions and other legal proceedings which at the time of the registration of a company in pursuance of this Part are pending by or against the company, or the public officer or any member thereof, may be continued in the same manner as if the registration had not taken place.

(2) Execution shall not issue against the effects of any individual member of the company on any judgment, decree or order obtained in any such action or proceeding, but, in the event of the property and effects of the company being insufficient to satisfy the judgment, decree or order, an order may be obtained for winding up the company.

Definitions

'company': CA 1963, s 2(1); 'member': CA 1963, s 31; 'officer': CA 1963, s 2(1).

UK legislation

See CA 1985, s 689, Sch 21 (amended by CA 1989, s 108(2)).

340 Effect of registration under this Part

(1) When a company is registered in pursuance of this Part, subsections (2) to (7) shall have effect.

(2) All provisions contained in any statute or instrument constituting or regulating the company, including, in the case of a company registered as a company limited by guarantee, the resolution declaring the amount of the guarantee [and including any statement under section 330 (c)][a], shall be deemed to be conditions and regulations of the company, in the same manner and with the same incidents as if so much thereof as would, if the company had been formed under this Act, have been required to be inserted in the memorandum, were contained in a registered memorandum, and the residue thereof were contained in registered articles.

(3) All the provisions of this Act shall apply to the company and the members, contributories and creditors thereof, in the same manner in all respects as if it had been formed under this Act, subject as follows—

- (a) Table A or Tábla A shall not apply unless adopted by special resolution;
- (b) the provisions of this Act relating to the numbering of shares shall not apply to any joint stock company whose shares are not numbered;
- (c) subject to the provisions of this section, the company shall not have power to alter any provision contained in any statute relating to the company;
- (d) subject to the provisions of this section, the company shall not have power without the sanction of the Minister, to alter any provision contained in any letters patent relating to the company;
- (e) the company shall not have power to alter any provision contained in a charter or letters patent relating to the objects of the company;

(f) in the event of the company being wound up, every person shall be a contributory, in respect of the debts and liabilities of the company contracted before registration, who is liable to pay or contribute to the payment of any debt or liability of the company contracted before registration or to pay or contribute to the payment of any sum for the adjustment of the rights of the members among themselves in respect of any such debt or liability, or to pay or contribute to the payment of the costs and expenses of winding up the company, so far as relates to such debts or liabilities as aforesaid;

(g) in the event of the company being wound up, every contributory shall be liable to contribute to the assets of the company, in the course of the winding up, all sums due from him in respect of any such liability as aforesaid, and, in the event of the death or bankruptcy of any contributory, the provisions of this Act relating to the personal representatives of deceased contributories and to the assignees of bankrupt contributories shall apply.

(4) The provisions of this Act relating to—

(a) the registration of an unlimited company as limited;

(b) the powers of an unlimited company on registration as a limited company to increase the nominal amount of its share capital and to provide that a portion of its share capital shall not be capable of being called up except in the event of winding up;

(c) the power of a limited company to determine that a portion of its share capital shall not be capable of being called up except in the event of winding up;

shall apply notwithstanding any provisions contained in any statute, charter or other instrument constituting or regulating the company.

(5) Nothing in this section shall authorise the company to alter any such provisions contained in any instrument constituting or regulating the company, as would, if the company had originally been formed under this Act, have been required to be contained in the memorandum and are not authorised to be altered by this Act.

(6) None of the provisions of this Act (apart from those of subsection (4) of section 205) shall derogate from any power of altering its constitution or regulations which may, by virtue of any statute or other instrument constituting or regulating the company, be vested in the company.

(7) In this section, 'instrument' includes deed of settlement, contract of co-partnery and letters patent.

Amendments

a Words inserted by C(A)A 1983, Sch 1 para 22.

Definitions

'articles': CA 1963, s 2(1); 'company': CA 1963, s 2(1); 'company limited by guarantee': CA 1963, s 2(1), s 5(2); 'contributory': CA 1963, s 2(1), s 208; 'joint stock company': CA 1963, s 329; 'member': CA 1963, s 31; 'memorandum': CA 1963, s 2(1); 'Minister': CA 1963, s 2(1); 'share': CA 1963, s 2(1); 'Table A': CA 1963, s 2(1); 'unlimited company': CA 1963, s 2 (1), s 5(2).

Notes

See notes after s 338 in relation to the continuation of rights or liabilities after registration. 'A contract of co-partnery' was a contract of partnership in Scotland.

UK legislation

See CA 1985, s 689, Sch 21 (amended by CA 1989, s 108(2)).

341 Power to substitute memorandum and articles for deed of settlement

(1) Subject to subsections (2) to (4), a company registered in pursuance of this Part may by special resolution alter the form of its constitution by substituting a memorandum and articles for a deed of settlement.

(2) The provisions of section 10 relating to applications to the court for cancellation of alterations of the objects of a company and matters consequential on the passing of resolutions for such alterations shall, so far as applicable, apply to an alteration under this section with the following modifications—

(a) there shall be substituted for the printed copy of the altered memorandum required to be delivered to the registrar of companies a printed copy of the substituted memorandum and articles; and

(b) on the delivery to the registrar of a printed copy of the substituted memorandum and articles or on the date when the alteration is no longer liable to be cancelled by order of the court, whichever last occurs, the substituted memorandum and articles shall apply to the company in the same manner as if it were a company registered under this Act with that memorandum and those articles, and the company's deed of settlement shall cease to apply to the company.

(3) An alteration under this section may be made either with or without any alteration of the objects of the company under this Act.

(4) In this section, 'deed of settlement' includes any contract of co-partnery or other instrument constituting or regulating the company, not being a statute, charter or letter patent.

Definitions

'articles': CA 1963, s 2(1); 'company': CA 1963, s 2(1); 'the court': CA 1963, s 2(1); 'memorandum': CA 1963, s 2(1); 'printed': CA 1963, s 2(1); 'the registrar of companies': CA 1963, s 2(1).

Notes

'A contract of co-partnery' was a contract of partnership in Scotland.

UK legislation

See CA 1985, s 690.

342 Power of court to stay or restrain proceedings

The provisions of this Act relating to staying and restraining actions and proceedings against a company at any time after the presentation of a petition for winding up and before the making of a winding-up order shall, in the case of a company registered in pursuance of this Part, where the application to stay or restrain is by a creditor, extend to actions and proceedings against any contributory of the company.

Definitions

'company': CA 1963, s 2(1); 'contributory': CA 1963, s 2(1), s 208.

Notes

For the power to stay or restrain proceedings pending the hearing of a winding up petition, see CA 1963, s 217 and the notes thereto.

UK legislation

See IA 1986, s 126(2).

343 Actions stayed on winding-up order

Where an order has been made for winding up a company registered in pursuance of this Part, no action or proceeding shall be commenced or proceeded with against the company or any contributory of the company in respect of any debt of the company, except by leave of the court, and subject to such terms as the court may impose.

Definitions

'company': CA 1963, s 2(1); 'contributory': CA 1963, s 2(1), s 208; 'the court': CA 1963, s 2(1).

Notes

See also CA 1963, s 222 and the notes thereto.

UK legislation

See IA 1986, s 130(3).

PART X

WINDING UP OF UNREGISTERED COMPANIES

[343A Restriction of this Part

This Part is subject to Chapters I (general provisions) and III (secondary insolvency proceedings) of the Insolvency Regulation.][a]

Amendments

a Inserted by EC(CI)R 2002, reg 3, with effect from 1 July 2002.

Definitions

'Insolvency Regulation': CA 1963, s 2(1); Council Regulation (EC) No. 1346/2000 of 29 May 2000 on insolvency proceedings.

UK legislation

See IA 1986, s 225(2).

344 Meaning of unregistered company

For the purposes of this Part, 'unregistered company' shall include any trustee savings bank certified under the Trustee Savings Banks Acts, 1863 to 1958, any partnership, whether limited or not, any association and any company with the following exceptions—

(a) a company as defined by section 2;

(b) a partnership, association or company which consists of less than eight members and is not formed outside the State.

Definitions

'company': CA 1963, s 2(1); 'member': CA 1963, s 31.

Notes

Unregistered company: The following are examples of unregistered companies:

(a) a foreign company[1] incorporated and having its 'centre of main interests' in a country which is not subject to the provisions of the Insolvency Regulation;[2]

(b) companies formed by special Act of Parliament or of the Oireachtas;[3]

(c) companies incorporated by charter;[4]

(d) friendly societies;[5]

(e) companies registered but not formed under one or other of the Joint Stock Companies Acts, the Companies Act 1862 or the Companies (Consolidation) Act 1908; and[6]

(f) European Economic Interest Groupings.[7]

A club or non-trading society is not an 'unregistered company' for the purposes of Pt X[8] although other unicorpororated trading associations do come within the scope of the definition.[9]

1 *Re Mercantile Bank of Australia* [1892] 2 Ch 204; *Russian Commercial and Industrial Bank v Le Comptoir D'Escompte de Mulhouse* [1925] AC 112.

2 *Re Sovereign Marine and General Insurance Co Ltd* [2007] 1 BCLC 228. For the definition of 'centre of main interests' and for a discussion of the Insolvency Regulations generally, see the notes to the Insolvency Regulations, below.

3 *Re St Neots Water Co* (1906) 22 TLR 478; *Re Barton-upon-Humber Water Co* (1889) 42 Ch D 585; *Re Brentford and Isleworth Tramways Co* (1884) 26 Ch D 527; *Re Basingstoke Canal (Proprietors)* (1866) 14 WR 956.

5 *Re Commercial Buildings* [1938] IR 477; *Re Independent Protestant Loan Society* [1895] 1 IR 1; *Re Irish Mercantile Loan Society* [1907] 1 IR 98; *Re Twentieth Century Equitable Friendly Society* [1910] WN 236; *Re Victoria Society, Knottingley* [1913] 1 Ch 167.

6 *Bowes v Hope Mutual Life Assurance Company* (HL) [1861–73] All ER Rep Ext 1443.

7 See reg 22 of the European Communities (European Economic Interest Groupings) Regulations 1989 (SI 191/1989).

8 *Re Bristol Athenoeum* (1889) 43 Ch D 236.

9 *Re Family Endowment Society* (1870) LR 4 Eq 695.

UK legislation

See IA 1986, s 220.

345 Winding up of unregistered companies

(1) Subject to the provisions of this Part, any unregistered company may be wound up under this Act, and all the provisions of this Act relating to winding up shall apply to an unregistered company, with the exceptions and additions mentioned in this section.

(2) The principal place of business in the State of an unregistered company shall, for all the purposes of the winding up, be deemed to be the registered office of the company.

(3) No unregistered company shall be wound up under this Act voluntarily.

(4) The circumstances in which an unregistered company may be wound up are as follows—

(a) if the company is dissolved, or has ceased to carry on business, or is carrying on business only for the purpose of winding up its affairs;

(b) if the company is unable to pay its debts;

(c) if the court is of opinion that it is just and equitable that the company should be wound up.

(5) An unregistered company shall, for the purposes of this Act, be deemed to be unable to pay its debts—

(a) if a creditor, by assignment or otherwise, to whom the company is indebted in a sum exceeding [€1,269.74][a] then due, has served on the company, by leaving at its principal place of business in the State, or by delivering to the secretary or some director or principal officer of the company, or by serving otherwise in such manner as the court may approve or direct, a demand in writing requiring the company to pay the sum so due, and the company has, for 3 weeks after the service of the demand, neglected to pay the sum or to secure or compound for it to the satisfaction of the creditor;

(b) if any action or other proceeding has been instituted against any member for any debt or demand due or claimed to be due, from the company, or from him in his character of member, and notice in writing of the institution of the action or proceeding having been served on the company by leaving the same at its principal place of business in the State, or by delivering it to the secretary, or some director or principal officer of the company, or by otherwise serving the same in such manner as the court may approve or direct, the company has not within 10 days after service of the notice paid, secured or compounded for the debt or demand, or procured the action or proceeding to be stayed, or indemnified the defendant to his reasonable satisfaction against the action or proceeding, and against all costs, damages and expenses to be incurred by him by reason of the same;

(c) if in the State or in any country recognised by the Minister for the purposes of section 250, execution or other process issued on a judgment, decree or order obtained in any court in favour of a creditor against the company, or any member thereof as such, or any person authorised to be sued as nominal defendant on behalf of the company, is returned unsatisfied;

(d) if it is otherwise proved to the satisfaction of the court that the company is unable to pay its debts.

(6) A petition for winding up a trustee savings bank may be presented by the Minister for Finance as well as by any person authorised under the other provisions of this Act to present a petition for winding up a company.

(7) Where a company incorporated outside the State which has been carrying on business in the State ceases to carry on business in the State, it may be wound up as an unregistered company under this Part, notwithstanding that it has been dissolved or otherwise ceased to exist as a company under or by virtue of the laws of the country under which it was incorporated.

(8) [...][b]

Amendments

a ‘£1,000’ substituted for ‘£50’ by CA 1990, s 213 and increased to £1,500 by CA 1990, s 240(7) as inserted by CLEA 2001, s 104. £1,500 converted to €1,904.61 by Council Regulations (EC) No 1103/97, No 974/98 and No 2866/98 and the Economic and Monetary Union Act 1998, s 6.

b Subsection (8) was repealed by the Bankruptcy Act 1988, Sch 2.

Definitions

‘the Bankruptcy Acts: CA 1963, s 2(1); ‘company’: CA 1963, s 2(1); ‘the court’: CA 1963, s 2(1); ‘director’: CA 1963, s 2(1); ‘member’: CA 1963, s 31; ‘officer’: CA 1963, s 2(1).

Notes

Winding up foreign companies: A foreign company incorporated and having its ‘centre of main interests’ in a country which is not subject to the provisions of the Insolvency Regulation,[1] may be wound up by the Irish courts even if it has not done business within the State and has no assets in the jurisdiction, provided that: (i) a sufficiently close connection can be established between the company’s business and this country; (ii) there is a reasonable possibility that a winding up order will benefit those applying for it; and (iii) the court can exercise jurisdiction over one or more persons interested in the distribution of the company’s assets.[2] In order to establish a sufficient connection between the company and Ireland, it is not necessary to show that the foreign company carried on business in the jurisdiction,[3] although clearly if there is neither a business nor assets in the jurisdiction, it is always going to be somewhat difficult to convince the courts of the existence of a sufficient connection with Ireland such as to warrant the making of a winding-up order in the first place.[4] Factors that were held by the court to give rise to a sufficient connection with Ireland such as to warrant the making of a winding-up order included the drawing down of loans in the jurisdiction[5] or the possibility of a liquidator being in a position to bring proceedings against directors for the imposition of personal liability in respect of fraudulent and/or reckless trading.[6] By virtue of sub-s (7) the foreign company may be wound up even though it has been dissolved under the law of its incorporation. The predecessor to sub-s (7) was enacted to remove doubts which had arisen concerning the jurisdiction of the English courts to wind up companies which had been formed under Imperial Russian company law and which had been dissolved shortly after the 1917 Revolution.[7]

1 For the definition of ‘centre of main interests’ and for a discussion of the Insolvency Reg generally, see the notes to the Insolvency Reg, infra.

2 *International Westminster Bank v Okeanos* [1987] BCLC 450; *Banque des Marchands de Moscou v Kindersley* [1951] 1 Ch 112; *Re Azoff-Don Commercial Bank* [1954] 1 Ch 315; *Inland*

Revenue v Highland Engineering Ltd (1975) SLT 203; *Re Compania Merabello San Nicholas SA* [1973] 1 Ch 75; *Re Allebrogia Steamship Corp* [1978] 3 All ER 423; *Re Eloc Electro-Optieck and Communicatie BV* [1981] 2 All ER 1111; *Re Real Estate Development Company* [1991] BCLC 210; *Re Paramount Airways Ltd* [1993] Ch 223; *Banco Nacional De Cuba v Cosmos Trading Corporation* [2000] 1 BCLC 116; *Stocznia Gdanska SA v Latreefers Inc (No 2)* [2001] BCLC 11; *Re OJSC Ank Yugraneft* [2009] 1 BCLC 298.

3 *Banque des Marchandes de Moscou v Kindersley* [1951] Ch 112; *Re Azoff-Don Commercial Bank* [1954] Ch 315; *Re Compania Merabello San Nicholas SA* [1973] Ch 75; *International Westminster Bank v Okeanos* [1997] BCLC 450.

4 See, for example *Re Real Estate Development Company* [1991] BCLC 210; *Re Titan International Inc* [1998] 1 BCLC 102.

5 *Re A Company* (No 00359 of 1987) [1988] Ch 210; *Re A Company* (No 003102 of 1991) *Ex parte Nyckelyn Finance Company Ltd* [1991] BCLC 539.

6 *Re A Company (No 00359 of 1987)* [1988] Ch 210.

7 *Re Russian and English Bank* [1932] 1 Ch 663; *Russian and Florence Montefiore Guedalla v Baring Bros & Co Ltd* [1936] AC 405; *Banque des Marchandes de Moscou v Kindersley* [1951] 1 Ch 112; *Re Azoff-Don Commercial Bank* [1954] 1 Ch 315; *Inland Revenue v Highland Engineering Ltd* 1975 SLT 203; *Re Compania Merabello San Nicholas SA* [1973] 1 Ch 75; *Re Allobrogia Steamship Corp* [1978] 3 All ER 423; *Re Eloc Electro-Optieck and Communicatie BV* [1981] 2 All ER 1111; *Stocznia Gdanska SA v Latreefers Inc and other appeals* [2001] 2 BCLC 116, [2000] All ER (D) 148; *Re HIH Casualty and General Insurance Ltd* [2006] All ER (D).

Illegal associations: An association which, under CA 1963, s 372, ought to have been but has not been registered as a company under the Companies Acts, may not be wound up as an unregistered company.[1]

1 *Re Padstow Total Loss and Collision Assurance Association* (1882) 20 ChD 137.

Inability to pay debts: CA 1963, see CA 1963, ss 213 and 214 and the notes thereto.

UK legislation

See IA 1986, ss 221–225.

346 Contributories in winding up of unregistered company

(1) In the event of an unregistered company being wound up, every person shall be deemed to be a contributory who is liable to pay or contribute to the payment of any debt or liability of the company, or to pay or contribute to the payment of any sum for the adjustment of the rights of the members among themselves, or to pay or contribute to the payment of the costs and expenses of winding up the company, and every contributory shall be liable to contribute to the assets of the company all sums due from him in respect of any such liability as aforesaid.

(2) In the event of the death or bankruptcy of any contributory, the provisions of this Act relating to the personal representatives of deceased contributories and to the assignees of bankrupt contributories respectively shall apply.

Definitions

'company': CA 1963, s 2(1); 'contributory': CA 1963, s 2(1), s 208; 'member': CA 1963, s 31.

Notes

Contributories: In relation to the position of contributories, see CA 1963, ss 207 to 211 and the notes thereto. A contributory of an unregistered company has *locus standi* to petition to wind up that company. It is sufficient if a contributor is an allottee of shares who has a right to be included on the register.[1]

1 *Re JN (2) Ltd* [1977] 3 All ER 1104, [1978] 1 WLR 183 at 187; *Alipour v UOC Corp* [2002] EWHC 937 (Ch).

UK legislation

See IA 1986, s 226.

---

347 Power of court to stay or restrain proceedings

The provisions of this Act relating to staying and restraining actions and proceedings against a company at any time after the presentation of a petition for winding up and before the making of a winding-up order shall, in the case of an unregistered company, where the application to stay or restrain is by a creditor, extend to actions and proceedings against any contributory of the company.

Definitions

'company': CA 1963, s 2(1); 'contributory': CA 1963, s 2(1), s 208.

Notes

Staying or restraining proceedings: CA 1963, see CA 1963, s 217 and the notes thereto.

UK legislation

See IA 1986, s 227.

---

348 Actions stayed on winding-up order

Where an order has been made for winding up an unregistered company, no action or proceeding shall be proceeded with or commenced against any contributory of the company in respect of any debt of the company, except by leave of the court, and subject to such terms as the court may impose.

Cross references

In this regard, see CA 1963, s 222.

Definitions

'company': CA 1963, s 2(1); 'contributory': CA 1963, s 2(1), s 208; 'the court': CA 1963, s 2(1).

Notes

See CA 1963, s 222 and the notes thereto.

UK legislation

See IA 1986, s 228.

---

349 Provisions of this Part to be cumulative

The provisions of this Part relating to unregistered companies shall be in addition to and not in restriction of any provisions hereinbefore contained in this Act relating to winding up companies by the court, and the court or liquidator may exercise any powers or do any act in the case of unregistered companies which might be exercised or done by it or him in winding up companies formed and registered under this Act.

Definitions

'company': CA 1963, s 2(1); 'the court': CA 1963, s 2(1).

UK legislation

See IA 1989, s 229.

---

350 Saving for enactments providing for winding up under former Companies Acts

Nothing in this Part shall affect the operation of any enactment which provides for any partnership, association or company being wound up, or being wound up as a company or as an unregistered company under the Companies (Consolidation) Act, 1908 or any enactment repealed by that Act.

Definitions

'company': CA 1963, s 2(1).

UK legislation

See CC(CP)A 1985, s 31(8)(c).

PART XI
COMPANIES INCORPORATED OUTSIDE THE STATE ESTABLISHING A PLACE OF BUSINESS WITHIN THE STATE

351 Application of this Part

This Part shall apply to all companies incorporated outside the State which, after the operative date, establish a place of business within the State, and to companies incorporated outside the State which have, before the operative date, established a place of business within the State and continue to have an established place of business within the State on the operative date.

Definitions

'company': CA 1963, s 2(1); 'the operative date': CA 1963, s 2(1); 'place of business': CA 1963, s 360.

Notes

Non-application of Part XI: Part XI does apply to a Societas Europeae.[1] Nor does it apply to a foreign company with a branch in Ireland which is subject to the disclosure requirements of the EC(BD)R 1993 (SI 395/1993).[2]

The EC(BD)R 1993 gave effect to Council Directive No 89/666/EEC of 21 December 1989 (OJ No. L395, 30.12.89, pp 36–39) which concerns disclosure requirements in respect of branches opened in a member state by foreign limited liability companies. Prior to the introduction of these regs, CA 1963, Pt XI applied to branches opened in Ireland by such companies.

Place of business or branch?: It is probably the case that most places of business established in the State by limited liability companies are also fact branches for the purposes of the Branch Disclosure Regs and, accordingly, the Regs will apply instead of Pt XI for those companies. Where a place of business (as per CA 1963, Pt XI), which is not a branch, has been established, then CA 1963 applies. A company incorporated outside Ireland does not 'establish a place of business' in the State where it merely acts through an agent in the state, even though that agent may himself have his own place of business in the state.[3] The CRO considers that places of business that perform operations ancillary or incidental to the company's business are (in general terms) not branches within the meaning of the Branch Disclosure Directive.[4]

1 See Council Regulation (EC) No 2157/2001of 8 October 2001 on the Statute for a European company (SE).

2 EC(BD)R 1993, reg 14(1).

3 *Lord Advocate v Huron and Erie Loan and Savings Co* [1911] SC 612; *Re Tovarishestvo Manufactur Liudvig-Rabenek* [1944] Ch 404; *Rakusens Ltd v Baser Ambalaj Plastik Sanayi Ticaret AS* [2002] 1 BCLC 104; *Donovan v North German Lloyd Steamship Co* [1933] IR 33.

4 With regard to what constitutes a `branch' see the notes to reg 3 of the EC(BD)R 1993.

UK legislation

See CA 1985, s 744.

---

352 Documents to be delivered to registrar by certain companies incorporated outside the State

(1) Companies incorporated outside the State, which, after the operative date, establish a place of business within the State, shall, within one month of the establishment of the place of business, deliver to the registrar of companies for registration—

(a) a certified copy of the charter, statutes or memorandum and articles of the company, or other instrument constituting or defining the constitution of the company, and, if the instrument is not written in the English or Irish language, a certified translation thereof;

(b) a list of the directors and secretary of the company containing the particulars mentioned in subsection (2);

(c) the names and addresses of some one or more persons resident in the State authorised to accept on behalf of the company service of process and any notices required to be served on the company and also the address of the company's principal place of business in the State.

(2) Subject to subsection (3), the list referred to in paragraph (b) of subsection (1) shall contain the following particulars—

(a) in relation to each director—

(i) in the case of an individual, his present Christian name and surname, and any former Christian name or surname, his usual residential address, his nationality (if not Irish) and his business occupation (if any), and particulars of any other directorships of bodies corporate incorporated in the State held by him; and

(ii) in the case of a body corporate, its corporate name and registered or principal office:

(b) in relation to the secretary or, where there are joint secretaries, in relation to each of them—

(i) in the case of an individual, his present Christian name and surname, any former Christian name and surname and his usual residential address; and

(ii) in the case of a body corporate, its corporate name and registered or principal office.

Paragraphs (b), (c) and (d) of subsection (12) of section 195 shall apply for the purpose of the construction of references in this subsection to present and former Christian names and surnames as they apply for the purpose of the construction of such references in that section.

(3) Where all the partners in a firm are joint secretaries of the company, the name and principal office of the firm may be stated instead of the particulars mentioned in paragraph (b) of subsection (2).

(4) Companies to which this Part applies, other than those mentioned in subsection (1), shall, if on the operative date they have not delivered to the registrar the documents and particulars specified in subsection (1) of section 274 of the Companies (Consolidation) Act, 1908, deliver the documents and particulars mentioned in subsection (1) of this section within 2 months after the operative date.

Definitions

'articles': CA 1963, s 2(1); 'company': CA 1963, s 2(1); 'director': CA 1963, s 2(1), s 360; 'document': CA 1963, s 2(1): 'memorandum': CA 1963, s 2(1); 'the operative date': CA 1963, s 2(1); 'the registrar of companies': CA 1963, s 2(1); 'place of business': CA 1963, s 360; 'secretary': CA 1963, s 360; 'month' is a calendar month: IA 2005, s 21, Sch 1, pt 2.

Notes

Time limit for filing documents: The word 'of' in sub-s (1) carries the meaning 'after' with the effect that the date of registration is excluded in the calculation of the time limit, in contra-distinction to IA 2005, s 18(h).

Documents previously filed under the Branch Disclosure Regs: The disclosure requirements in sub-s (1)(a) & (b) and in sub-s (2) may be deemed to have been satisfied where the company has previously filed equivalent material under the EC(BD)R 1993.[1]

Submission to jurisdiction: The registration of a company under Pt XI amounts to a submission to the jurisdiction of the Irish courts.[2] In this regard, whilst the names and addresses of persons authorised to accept service of proceedings may be changed from time to time under s 353, the company cannot withdraw one name without substituting another unless it is ceasing altogether to have a place of business in the state.[3]

Consequence of failure to register under Pt XI: A failure to comply with the registration obligation of Pt XI will not *per se* render unenforceable a contract entered into by the foreign company.[4]

1 Reg 16 of the EC(BD)R 1993.

2 *Employers' Liability Assurance Corporation v Sedgwick, Collins & Co* [1927] AC 95.

3 *Employers' Liability Assurance Corporation v Sedgwick, Collins & Co* [1927] AC 95.

[4] *Curragh Investments Ltd v Cook* [1974] 1 WLR 1559.

UK legislation

See CA 1985, s 691 (amended by CA 1989, s 145, Sch 19 para 6).

353 Return to be delivered to registrar where documents altered

If, in the case of any company to which this Part applies, any alteration is made in—

(a) the charter, statutes or memorandum and articles of the company, or other instrument constituting or defining the constitution of the company; or

(b) the directors or secretary of the company or the particulars contained in the list of the directors and secretaries; or

(c) the names or addresses of the persons authorised to accept service on behalf of the company or the address of its principal place of business in the State;

the company shall, within the prescribed time, deliver to the registrar of companies for registration a return containing the prescribed particulars of the alteration.

Definitions

'articles': CA 1963, s 2(1); 'company': CA 1963, s 2(1); 'director': CA 1963, s 2(1), s 360; 'document': CA 1963, s 2(1): 'memorandum': CA 1963, s 2(1); 'the registrar of companies': CA 1963, s 2(1); 'place of business': CA 1963, s 360; 'secretary': CA 1963, s 360; 'month' is a calendar month: IA 2005, s 21, Sch 1, pt 2.

Notes

Change in particulars of persons for service: Whilst the names and addresses of persons authorised to accept service of proceedings may be changed from time to time under s 353, the company cannot withdraw one name without substituting another unless it is ceasing altogether to have a place of business in the state.[1]

[1] *Employers' Liability Assurance Corporation v Sedgwick, Collins & Co* [1927] AC 95.

UK legislation

See CA 1985, s 692.

354 Accounts of company to which this Part applies to be delivered to registrar

(1) Every company to which this Part applies shall, in every calendar year, make out a balance sheet and profit and loss account and, if the company is a holding company, group accounts, in such form and containing such particulars and including such documents, as under the provisions of this Act it would, if it had been a company within the meaning of this Act, have been required to make out and lay before the company in general meeting, and deliver copies of those documents to the registrar of companies.

(2) If any such document as is mentioned in subsection (1) is not written in the English or Irish language, there shall be annexed to it a certified translation thereof.

(3) The Minister may grant to any company or to any class of companies exemption from the obligation imposed by subsection (1) subject to such conditions as he may think fit.

(4) Subsection (1) shall not apply to any company having provisions in its constitution that would entitle it to rank as a private company if it had been registered in the State.

Definitions

'accounts': CA 1963, s 2(1); 'certified': CA 1963, s 360; 'company': CA 1963, s 2(1); 'document': CA 1963, s 2(1): 'group accounts'; s 2(1), s 150(1); 'holding company': CA 1963, s 2(1), s 155; 'Minister': CA 1963, s 2(1); 'private company': CA 1963, s 33; ' the registrar of companies': CA 1963, s 2(1).

Notes

See art 5 of the EC(CGA)R 1992 which provides that the reference to 'group accounts' in sub-s (1) is to be construed as a reference to group accounts prepared in accordance with the provisions of those regs.

UK legislation

See CA 1985, ss 700, 702; CA 1989 s 23, Sch 10 para 13.

355 Obligation to state name of company to which this Part applies, whether limited and country where incorporated

Every company to which this Part applies shall—

(a) in every prospectus inviting subscriptions for its shares or debentures in the State state the country in which the company is incorporated; and

(b) exhibit conspicuously on every place where it carries on business in the State the name of the company and the country in which the company is incorporated; and

(c) cause the name of the company and of the country in which the company is incorporated to be stated in legible characters on all billheads and letter-paper, and in all notices and other official publications of the company; and

(d) if the liability of the members of the company is limited, cause notice of that fact to be stated in legible characters in every such prospectus as aforesaid and in all billheads, letter-paper, notices and other official publications of the company in the State, and to be affixed on every place where it carries on its business.

Definitions

'company': CA 1963, s 2(1); 'debenture': CA 1963, s 2(1); 'member': CA 1963, s 31; 'share': CA 1963, s 2(1); 'prospectus': CA 1963, s 360.

UK legislation

See CA 1985, s 693 (amended by FSA 1986).

356 Service of documents on company to which this Part applies

(1) Subject to subsection (2), any process or notice required to be served on a company to which this Part applies shall be sufficiently served if addressed to any person whose name has been delivered to the registrar of companies under the foregoing provisions of this Part and left at or sent by post to the address which has been so delivered.

(2) A document may be served on any such company by leaving it at or sending it by post to any place of business established by the company in the State—

(a) where the company makes default in delivering to the registrar the name and address of a person resident in the State who is authorised to accept on behalf of the company service of process or notices; or

(b) if at any time all the persons whose names and addresses have been so delivered are dead or have ceased so to reside, or refuse to accept service on behalf of the company, or for any reason cannot be served.

(3) This section shall cease to apply to a company on the expiration of two years after it has given the notice referred to in section 357.

Definitions

'company': CA 1963, s 2(1); 'document': CA 1963, s 2(1): 'the registrar of companies': CA 1963, s 2 (1); 'place of business': CA 1963, s 360.

Notes

Service on nominated person: CA 1963, service on a person whose name and address have not been filed with the registrar under s 352(1)(c) will not be good service for the purposes of s 356.[1] Moreover, because s 356 constitutes a statutory code for service, it follows that the court cannot retrospectively deem some other form of service to be good service under RSC 1986, Ord 9, r 15.[2] It may, however, be able to prospectively allow for substituted service in some other form under Ord 10. Service effected on a person that the company has notified to the CRO for the purposes of s 352(1)(c) will be good service even though the company may have ceased to have an established place of business in the State and may have notified that fact to the CRO.[3] In the case of an insurance company having an establishe dplace of business in the State, service may not only be effected in the manner prescribed by s 356 but it may also be effected by leaving the document with, or by sending it by pre-paid ordinary post, to the person notified to the Minister under the Insurance Acts as the authorised agent in the state of the company.[4]

Service at place of business: Where service is to effected under s 356(2) rather than being effected on the nominated person, under sub-s (1), the service must be on an existing place of business rather than a former place of business, unless the company has held itself out as still carrying on business at the old location.[5]

1 *Rakusens Ltd v Baser Ambalaj Plastik Sanayi Ticaret AS* [2002] 1 BCLC 104.

2 *Boocock v Hilton International Co* [1993] 4 All ER 19.

3 *Rome and another v Punjab National Bank (No 2)* [1990] 1 All ER 58.

4 Insurance Act 1989, s 4.

5 *Deverall v Grant Advertising Inc* [1955] Ch 111.

UK legislation

See CA 1985, s 695.

357 Notice to be given when company to which this Part applies ceases to carry on business in the State

If any company to which this Part applies ceases to have a place of business in the State, it shall forthwith give notice of the fact to the registrar of companies, and as from the date on which notice is so given, the obligation of the company to deliver any document to the registrar shall cease.

Definitions

'company': CA 1963, s 2(1); 'document': CA 1963, s 2(1): 'the registrar of companies': CA 1963, s 2(1); 'place of business': CA 1963, s 360.

UK legislation

See CA 1985, s 696(3); CA 1989, s 145, Sch 19 para 13.

358 Penalties for non-compliance with this Part

If any company to which this Part applies fails to comply with any of the foregoing provisions of this Part, the company and every officer or agent of the company who knowingly and wilfully authorises or permits the default [shall be guilty of an offence and liable to a fine][a] not exceeding [€1,904.61].[b]

Amendments

a Words substituted by C(AA)A 2003, s 57 and Sch 2 with effect from 6 April 2004.

b '£500' substituted for '£100' by C(A)A 1982, Sch 1 and increased to £1,500 by CA 1990, s 240(7) as inserted by CLEA 2001, s 104. £1,500 converted to €1,904.61 by Council Regulations (EC) No 1103/97, No 974/98 and No 2866/98 and the Economic and Monetary Union Act 1998, s 6.

Definitions

'agent': CA 1963, s 2(1); 'company': CA 1963, s 2(1); 'officer': CA 1963, s 2(1).

UK legislation

See CA 1985, ss 697, 703; CA 1989 s 23, Sch 10 para 13.

359 Construction of section 275 of Companies (Consolidation) Act, 1908

In its application to the State, section 275 of the Companies (Consolidation) Act, 1908, shall be deemed to have always applied as if—

(a) the words 'in Northern Ireland or in Great Britain or in a British possession' were substituted for the words 'in a British possession', and

(b) the words 'the State' were substituted for the words 'the United Kingdom'.

360 Interpretation of this Part

For the purposes of this Part—

'certified' means certified in the prescribed manner to be a true copy or a correct translation;

'director' in relation to a company includes any person in accordance with whose directions and instructions the directors of the company are accustomed to act;

'place of business' includes a share transfer or share registration office;

'prospectus' has the same meaning as when used in relation to a company incorporated under this Act;

'secretary' includes any person occupying the position of secretary by whatever name called.

Definitions

'company': CA 1963, s 2(1); 'director': CA 1963, s 2(1), s 360; 'prescribed': CA 1963, s 2(1); 'share': CA 1963, s 2(1); 'shadow director': CA 1990 s 27.

UK legislation

See CA 1985, s 698.

PART XII
RESTRICTIONS ON SALE OF SHARES AND OFFERS OF SHARES FOR SALE

361 Prospectuses relating to companies incorporated outside the State

[…][a]

Amendments

a Section 361 repealed by IFCMPA 2005, s 40(1)(a).

---

362 Exclusion of section 361 and relaxation of Third Schedule in case of certain prospectuses

[…][a]

Amendments

a Section 362 repealed by IFCMPA 2005, s 40(1)(a).

---

363 Provisions as to expert's consent and allotment

[…][a]

Amendments

a Section 363 repealed by IFCMPA 2005, s 40(1)(a).

---

364 Registration of prospectus

[…][a]

Amendments

a Section 364 repealed by IFCMPA 2005, s 40(1)(a).

365 Penalty for contravention of section 361 to 364

[…][a]

Amendments

a Section 365 repealed by IFCMPA 2005, s 40(1)(a).

366 Civil liability for mis-statements in prospectus

[…][a]

Amendments

a Section 366 repealed by IFCMPA 2005, s 40(1)(a).

367 Interpretation of provisions as to prospectuses

[…][a]

Amendments

a Section 367 repealed by IFCMPA 2005, s 40(1)(a).

PART XIII
GENERAL PROVISIONS AS TO REGISTRATION

368 Registration office

(1) For the purposes of the registration of companies under this Act, the Minister shall maintain and administer an office or offices in the State at such places as the Minister thinks fit.

(2) The Minister may appoint such registrars and assistant registrars as he thinks necessary for the registration of companies under this Act, and may make regulations with respect to their duties and may remove any persons so appointed.

(3) The Minister may direct a seal or seals to be prepared for the authentication of documents required for or connected with the registration of companies.

(4) Whenever any act is by this Act or by any statute directed to be done to or by the registrar of companies, it shall, until the Minister otherwise directs, be done to or by the existing registrar of joint stock companies or, in his absence, to or by such person as the Minister may for the time being authorise.

Definitions

'company': CA 1963, s 2(1); 'document': CA 1963, s 2(1): 'Minister': CA 1963, s 2(1); ' person': IA 2005, s 18(c); 'the Registrar of Companies': CA 1963, s 2(1).

Cross reference

See C(A)(No 2)A 1999, s 52.

Notes

Delegation to assistant registrars and other officials: CA 1963, s 368(2) allows for the appointment of assistant registrars of companies. Under that section, however, such assistant registrars were not automatically authorised to exercise the functions of the actual Registrar of Companies. Delegation of authority was dependent on the making of appropriate regulations by the Minister for Enterprise, Trade and Employment. Doubt was therefore cast on the validity of acts performed on behalf of the Registrar of Companies by officials in the Companies Registration Office. To remove these doubts C(A)(No 2)A 1999, s 52(1) retrospectively ratifies any acts performed on behalf of the registrar whether by an assistant registrar or by some other official employed in the CRO. Furthermore, C(A)(No 2)A 1999, s 52(2) prospectively provides for the delegation of the Registrar's functions to assistant registrars and other officials, not only for the purposes of the Companies Acts but also for the purposes of the Registration of Business Names Act 1963 and the Limited Partnership Act 1907. CA 1963, s 368 (4), which dealt with such delegation previously, ceases to have effect as of 21 December 1999.[1]

1 Companies (Amendment) (No 2) Act 1999 (Commencement) Order 1999 (SI 406/1999).

UK legislation

See CA 1985, s 704 and CA 2006, s 1060.[1]

1 With effect from 6 April 2007: The Companies Act 2006 (Commencement No 1, Transitional Provisions and Savings) Order 2006 (SI 2006/3428), art 4(3)(a).

369 Fees

(1) Subject to subsection (2), in respect of the several matters mentioned in the first column of the table set out in Part I of the Eight Schedule, there shall, subject to the limitations imposed by Part II of that Schedule, be paid to the registrar the several fees specified in the second column of that table.

(2) No fees shall be charged in respect of the registration in pursuance of Part IX of a company if it is not registered as a limited company, or if before its registration as a limited company, the liability of the shareholders was limited by statute or letters patent.

(3) All fees paid to the registrar in pursuance of this Act shall be paid into or disposed of for the benefit of the Exchequer in such manner as the Minister for Finance may direct.

Definitions

'company': CA 1963, s 2(1); ' Minister for Finance': Ministers and Secretaries Act 1924, s 1(ii); 'the Registrar of Companies': CA 1963, s 2(1).

Cross reference

In relation to the fees currently applicable see CA 1963, Sch 8 as amended by Companies (Fees) (No 3) Order, 2005 (SI 517/2005), with effect from 1 December 2005.

UK legislation

See CA 1985, s 708 (amended by CA 1989, ss 127(2), 212, Sch 24) and CA 2006, s 1063.[1]

[1] With effect from 6 April 2007: The Companies Act 2006 (Commencement No 1, Transitional Provisions and Savings) Order 2006 (SI 2006/3428), art 4(1)(a).

---

370 Inspection, production and evidence of documents kept by registrar

(1) Any person may—

(a) inspect the documents kept by the registrar of companies, on payment of such fee as may be fixed by the Minister;

(b) require a certificate of the incorporation of any company, or a copy or extract of any other document or any part of any other document, to be certified by the registrar, on payment for the certificate, certified copy or extract of such fees as the Minister may fix.

(2) No process for compelling the production of any document kept by the registrar shall issue from any court except with the leave of that court, and any such process if issued shall bear thereon a statement that it is issued with the leave of the court.

(3) A copy of, or extract from, any document kept and registered at the office for the registration of companies, certified to be a true copy under the hand of the registrar, assistant registrar or other officer authorised by the Minister (whose official position it shall not be necessary to prove), shall in all legal proceedings by admissible in evidence as of equal validity with the original document.

[(4) A certificate in writing made by the registrar of companies as to-

(a) the contents of a register kept by the registrar,

(b) the date on which a document was filed or registered with or delivered to the registrar,

(c) the date on which a document was received by the registrar, or

(d) the most recent date (if any) on which a requirement under the Companies Acts was complied with by or in relation to a company,

shall in all legal proceedings be admissible without further proof, until the contrary is shown, as evidence of the facts stated in the certificate.][a]

Amendments

a CA 1963, s 370(4) inserted by CLEA 2001, s 62 with effect from 1 October 2001: Company Law Enforcement Act 2001 (Commencement) (No 2) Order 2001 (SI 438/2001).

Definitions

'company': CA 1963, s 2(1); 'Companies Acts': CLEA 2001, s 3(1); 'the court': CA 1963, s 2(1); 'document': CA 1963, s 2(1); 'Minister': CA 1963, s 2(1); 'officer': CA 1963, s 2(1); 'the Registrar of Companies': CA 1963, s 2 (1).

Notes

Evidence from the Registrar: CA 1963, s 370 governs the inspection, production and evidence of documents kept by the Registrar. In addition to the provisions as to the admissibility of copies of or extracts from certain documents contained in CA 1963, s 370(3), CA 1963, s 370(4) now provides that a certificate in writing from the Registrar as to the contents of a register;[1] the date on which a document was filed, registered with or delivered[2] to or received[3] by the Registrar; or the date on which a requirement under the Companies Acts was complied with[4] shall be admissible in all legal proceedings as prima facie evidence, provided that evidence to the contrary is not adduced. In circumstances where the facts given in a certificate of the Registrar are disputed, those facts will not be admitted in evidence without further proof. This amendment is intended to avoid the necessity of the attendance in court of an officer representing the Registrar at every case in which facts relating to CRO registers, or their contents, are presented in evidence. Nevertheless, it is to be noted that the provision for certification is limited to allowing for the introduction of copy documents rather than originals and cannot be utilised to render otherwise inadmissible documents admissible.[5]

1 CA 1963, s 370(4)(a).

2 CA 1963, s 370(4)(b).

3 CA 1963, s 370(4)(c).

4 CA 1963, s 370(4)(d).

5 *Re Bovale Developments Ltd, Director of Corporate Enforcement v Bailey* [2008] 2 ILRM 13.

UK legislation

See CA 2006, ss 1085–1092.[1]

1 With effect from 1 January 2007: The Companies Act 2006 (Commencement No 1, Transitional Provisions and Savings) Order 2006 (SI 2006/3428), art 2(1)(f).

---

371 Enforcement of duty of comply with Act

(1) If a company or any officer of a company having made default in complying with any provision of this Act fails to make good the default within 14 days after the service of a notice on the company or officer requiring it or him to do so, [or such greater period as may be specified in the notice],[a] the court may, on an application made to the court by any member or creditor of the company [, by the Director][b] or by the registrar of companies, make an order directing the company and any officer thereof to make good the default within such time as may be specified in the order.

(2) Any such order may provide that all cost of and incidental to the application shall be borne by the company or by any officers of the company responsible for the default.

(3) Nothing in this section shall be taken to prejudice the operation of any enactment imposing penalties [(including restriction under section 150, or disqualification under section 160, of the Companies Act, 1990)][c] on a company or its officers in respect of any such default as aforesaid.

[(4) In this section, 'officer of a company' and cognate words include a director, a shadow director, an officer, a promoter, a receiver, a liquidator or an auditor of a company.][d]

Amendments

a Words 'or such greater period as may be specified in the notice' inserted in CA 1963, s 371(1) by IFCMPA 2005, s 64 with effect from 30 June 2005.[1]

b Words ', by the Director' inserted in CA 1963, s 371(1) by CLEA 2001, s 96 with effect from 28 November 2001.[2]

c Words '(including restriction under section 150, or disqualification under section 160, of the Companies Act, 1990)' inserted in CA 1963, s 371(3) by CLEA 2001, s 96 with effect from 28 November 2001.[3]

d CA 1963, s 371(4) inserted by CLEA 2001, s 96 with effect from 28 November 2001.[4]

1 Investment Funds, Companies and Miscellaneous Provisions Act 2005 (Commencement) Order 2005 (SI 323/2005).

2 Company Law Enforcement Act 2001 (Commencement) (No 3) Order, 2001 (SI 523/2001).

3 Company Law Enforcement Act 2001 (Commencement) (No 3) Order, 2001 (SI 523/2001).

4 Company Law Enforcement Act 2001 (Commencement) (No 3) Order, 2001 (SI 523/2001).

Definitions

'company': CA 1963, s 2(1); 'the court': CA 1963, s 2(1); 'director': CA 1963, s 2(1); 'Director': CLEA 2001, s 3(1); 'member': CA 1963, s 31; 'officer': CA 1963, s 2(1); ' the Registrar of Companies': CA 1963, s 2(1); 'shadow director': CA 1990, s 27(1).

Notes

Company law enforcement: The Registrar, the Director,[1] and any member or creditor of a company has the right to apply to the High Court for an order requiring a company or officer of a company to make good a default in complying with a provision of the Companies Acts.[2] Such an order may be made where the company or officer concerned has failed to make good the default in question within 14 days of the service of a notice requiring them to do so, or such longer time as may be specified in the notice.[3] Where the court makes an order under CA 1963, s 371, such an order will not prejudice the making of an application for restriction[4] or disqualification[5] of a person based on the same default to which the order relates.[6] CA 1963, s 371(4)[7] provides a definition of the term 'officer of a company' for the purposes of determining those persons against whom orders under CA 1963, s 371 may be made. Where a person has by resignation ceased to be an 'officer', an order may still be made against them in certain circumstances. Where the request to comply with a provision of the Companies Acts was initiated while he or she was an officer.[8]

1 CA 1963, s 371(1) as amended by CLEA 2001, s 96(a).

2 CA 1963, s 371(1). The section may, for example, be used by a director to enforce the duty of the company and of his fellow directors to make the company's books of account available for inspection by him pursuant to CA 1990, s 202: *Brosnan v Sommerville* [2007] 4 IR 135. The section may also be sued to force the filing of outstanding annual returns: *Re Powertech Logistics Ltd* [2007] IEHC 43.

3 IFCMPA 2005, s 63 extended the time within which such a company or officer could comply with such a notice from the CRO, in order to encourage more widespread use of this enforcement mechanism.

4 CA 1990, s 150.

5 CA 1990, s 160.

6 CA 1963, s 371(3).

7 As inserted by CLEA 2001, s 96(c).

8 *Brosnan et al v Sommerville* [2007] 4 IR 134.

UK legislation

See CA 1985, s 713 (amended by CA 1989, s 127(4).

[371A Power to compel compliance with requirement made under section 19(3)(b) of Act of 1990

(1) If a person having made default in complying with a requirement made of him under [section 19(3)(c)][b] of the Companies Act, 1990, fails to make good the default within 14 days after the service of a notice on him requiring him to do so, the court may, on an application made to the court by the Director, make an order directing the person to make good the default within such time as may be specified in the order.

(2) Any such order may provide that all costs of and incidental to the application shall be borne by the person who has made the default concerned.

(3) Nothing in this section shall be taken to prejudice the operation of section 19(6) of the Companies Act, 1990.][a]

Amendments

a CA 1963, s 371A inserted by CLEA 2001, s 97 with effect from 28 November 2001.[1]

1 Company Law Enforcement Act 2001 (Commencement) (No 3) Order 2001 (SI 523/2001).

b Words 'section 19(3)(c)' substituted for 'section 19(3)(b)' by C(A)A 2009, s 3.

Definitions

'company': CA 1963, s 2(1); 'the court': CA 1963, s 2(1); 'Director': CLEA 2001, s 3(1); 'person': IA 2005, s 18(c).

Notes

Enforcement of compliance under CA 1990, s 19(3)(c): CA 1990, s 19(3)(c)[1] gives the Director the power to require that any person[2] shall provide the Director with such books and documents that the Director believes to be related to the books and documents of a company whose books are being examined under the provisions of CA 1990, s 19. It was anticipated that the Director would need to require persons who were not officers of a company to produce books and documents under CA 1990, s 19(3)(c) and therefore it was necessary to insert CA 1963, s 371A, as the existing provisions under CA 1963, s 371 only dealt with orders to require the company or officers of the company to comply.

1 As amended by CLEA 2001, s 29.

2 Not just the company or any officer of the company.

UK legislation

See CA 1985, s 713 (amended by CA 1989, s 127(4)).

PART XIV
MISCELLANEOUS PROVISIONS RELATING TO BANKING COMPANIES, PARTNERSHIPS AND UNREGISTERED COMPANIES

Provisions relating to Banking Companies

372 Prohibition of banking partnerships with more than ten members

No company, association or partnership consisting of more than ten persons shall be formed for the purpose of carrying on the business of banking, unless it is registered as a company under this Act, or is formed in pursuance of some other statute.

Definitions

'company': CA 1963, s 2(1); 'member': CA 1963, s 31; 'person': IA 2005, s 18(c).

Cross reference

See generally CBA 1971 in relation to the meaning of 'banking business'.[1]

[1] See also Keane, *Company Law* (4th edn, Tottel Publishing, 2007), paras 1.37–1.39 and Johnston et al, *Arthur Cox Banking Law Handbook* (Tottel Publishing, 2007), pp 181–182.

UK legislation

See generally The Regulatory Reform (Removal of 20 Member Limit in Partnerships etc.) Order 2002 (SI 2002/3203).

---

373 Notice to be given to customers on registration of banking company with limited liability

(1) Where a banking company which was in existence on the 7th day of August, 1862, proposes to register as a limited company under this Act, it shall, at least 30 days before so registering, give notice of its intention so to register to every person who has a banking account with the company, either by delivery of the notice to him, or by posting it to him at, or by delivering it at, his last known address.

(2) If the company omits to give the notice required by this section then, as between the company and the person for the time being interested in the account in respect of which the notice ought to have been given, and so far as respects the account down to the time at which notice is given, but not further or otherwise, the certificate of registration with limited liability shall have no operation.

Definitions

'company': CA 1963, s 2(1); 'person': CA 1963, s 2(1).

---

374 Liability of bank of issue unlimited in respect of notes

[...][a]

Amendments

a CA 1963, s 374 was repealed by the CBA 1989, s 4 and Sch with effect from 12 July 1989.[1]

[1] Central Bank Act 1989 (Commencement) Order 1989 (SI 176/1989).

375 Privileges of banks making annual return

(1) Where a company carrying on the business of bankers has duly forwarded to the registrar of companies the annual return required by section 125 and has added thereto a statement of the names of the several places where it carries on business, the company shall not be required to furnish any returns under the Bankers (Ireland) Act, 1825, or section 22 of the Bankers (Ireland) Act, 1845.

(2) The fact of the said annual return and statement having been duly forwarded may be proved in any legal proceedings by the certificate of the registrar.

Definitions

'annual return': CA 1963, s 2(1); 'company': CA 1963, s 2(1); ' the Registrar of Companies': CA 1963, s 2(1).

Cross reference

Bankers (Ireland) Act 1825 and Bankers (Ireland) Act 1845, s 22 were repealed by CBA 1971, s 5 and Sch.

See generally CBA 1971, s 18 (as amended) 'Holders of licences and others to provide Bank with required information and returns'.

Prohibition of Partnerships with more than twenty Members

376 Prohibition of partnerships with more than twenty members

No company, association or partnership consisting of more than twenty persons shall be formed for the purpose of carrying on any business (other than the business of banking), that has for its object the acquisition of gain by the company, association or partnership, or by the individual members thereof, unless it is registered as a company under this Act or is formed in pursuance of some other statute.

Definitions

'company': CA 1963, s 2(1); 'member':.CA 1963, s 31; 'person': IA 2005, s 18(c).

Cross reference

Investment Limited Partnerships Act 1994, s 4 states that CA 1963, s 376 does not apply to investment limited partnerships.

Notes

Partnerships with more than 20 members: CA 1963, s 376 prohibits partnerships with more than 20 members. However, C(A)A 1982, s 13 provides an exemption for:

(a) firms of accountants where all of the partners are qualified to act as auditors;[1]

(b) firms of solicitors;[2] and

(c) such other types of partnership as the Minister may from time to time prescribe.[3]

To date the only such partnerships to have been so prescribed are those established for the purposes of carrying on or promoting the business of thoroughbred horse breeding[4] and those whose main business consists of the provision of investment and loan finance and ancillary facilities and services to persons engaged in industrial or commercial activities.[5]

1 C(A)A 1982, s 13(1)(a).
2 C(A)A 1982, s 13(1)(b).
3 C(A)A 1982, s 13(2).
4 SI 54/1988.
5 SI 506/2004.

UK legislation

See generally The Regulatory Reform (Removal of 20 Member Limit in Partnerships etc.) Order 2002 (SI 2002/3203).

Application of certain Provisions of this Act to Unregistered Companies

377 Application of certain provisions of this Act to unregistered companies

[(1) The provisions specified in the Ninth Schedule shall apply to all bodies corporate incorporated in and having a principal place of business in the State, other than those mentioned in subsection (2), as if they were companies registered under this Act and subject to such adaptations and modifications (if any) as may be prescribed.][a]

(2) The said provisions shall not apply by virtue of this section to any of the following bodies—

(a) any body corporate incorporated by or registered under any public general statue; and

(b) any body corporate not formed for the purpose of carrying on a business which has for its object the acquisition of gain by the body or by the individual members thereof; and

(c) any body corporate which is prohibited by statute or otherwise from making any distribution of its income or property among its members while it is a going concern or when it is in liquidation; and

(d) any body corporate for the time being exempted by direction of the Minister.

(3) The said provisions shall apply also in like manner in relation to any unincorporated body of persons entitled by virtue of letters patent to any of the privileges conferred by the Chartered Companies Act, 1837, and not registered under any other public general statute, but subject to the like exceptions as are provided for in the case of bodies corporate by paragraphs (b), (c) and (d) of subsection (2).

(4) This section shall not repeal or revoke in whole or in part any enactment, charter or other instrument constituting or regulating any body in relation to which the said provisions are applied by virtue of this section, or restrict the power of the Government to grant a charter in lieu of or supplementary to any such charter as aforesaid; but in relation to any such body, the operation of any such enactment, charter or instrument shall be suspended in so far as it is inconsistent with any of the said provisions as they apply for the time being to that body.

(5) Every body to which this section applies and which was in existence before the operative date shall within six months after the operative date deliver to the registrar of companies for registration a certified copy of the charter, statutes, memorandum and articles, or other instrument constituting or defining the constitution of the body.

(6) Every body to which this section applies and which comes into existence on or after the operative date shall within three months after coming into existence deliver to the registrar of companies for registration a certified copy of the charter, statutes, memorandum and articles or other instrument constituting or defining the constitution of the body.

(7) If default is made in complying with subsection (5) or (6), the body and every officer of the body who is in default [shall be guilty of an offence and liable to a fine][b] not exceeding [€1,904.61][c].

Amendments

a CA 1963, s 377(1) substituted by CA 1990, s 250(1)(a) with effect from 1 August 1991.[1]

b Words 'shall be guilty of an offence and liable to a fine' substituted for 'shall be liable to a fine' in CA 1963, s 180(5) by C(AA)A 2003, Sch 2 with effect from 6 April 2004.[2]

c '£500' substituted for '£100' by C(A)A 1982, Sch 1, increased to £1,500 by CA 1990, s 240(7) as inserted by CLEA 2001, s 104(c) and converted to €1,904.61 by Council Regulations (EC) No 1103/97, No 974/98 and No 2866/98 and the Economic and Monetary Union Act 1998, s 6.

1 Companies Act, 1990 (Commencement) (No 2) Order, 1991(SI 117/1991).

2 Companies (Auditing and Accounting) Act, 2003 (Commencement) Order, 2004 (SI 132/2004).

Definitions

'articles': CA 1963, s 2(1); 'body corporate': CA 1963, s 2(3); 'company': CA 1963, s 2(1); 'Government': IA 2005, Sch, Pt 1; member': CA 1963, s 31; 'memorandum': CA 1963, s 2(1); 'Minister': CA 1963, s 2(1); 'officer': CA 1963, s 2(1); 'prescribed': CA 1963, s 2(1); ' the Registrar of Companies': CA 1963, s 2(1).

Notes

Application of the Companies Acts to unregistered companies: This section applies to companies formed by private Act of Parliament, by charter or by letters patent and which have not registered pursuant to CA, Part IX. It is understood that there is now only one unregistered company trading, namely The Governor and Company of the Bank of Ireland. A limited company which is not a joint stock company within the meaning of CA 1963, s 329, is precluded from registering pursuant to CA 1963, Pt IX.[1] The various provisions of the Companies Acts listed in CA 1963, Sch 9 (as amended) are applicable to unregistered companies, other than those unregistered companies excluded by virtue of CA 1963, s 377(2).[2]

It is questionable as to whether the Royal Prerogative to grant charters survived the creation of the Free State and the subsequent enactment of the Constitution, so that the creation of replacement or supplementary charters under CA 1963, s 377(4) may be unconstitutional.[3]

1 CA 1963, s 328(3).

2 CA 1963, s 377(1).

3 See *Webb v Ireland* [1988] IR 353.

UK legislation

See CA 1985, s 718 (amended by SIs 1996/2827 and 2001/1228 and Statute Law (Repeals) Act 2004). Subordinate legislation: SIs 1985/680, 1990/438, 1990/1394, 1990/2571, 2001/86).

PART XV
GENERAL

Form of Registers

378 Form of registers, minute books and books of account

(1) Any register, index, minute book or book of account required by this Act to be kept by a company or by the registrar of companies may be kept either by making entries in bound books or by recording the matters in question in any other manner.

(2) Where any register, index, minute book or book of account to be kept by a company is not kept by making entries in a bound book but by some other means, adequate precautions shall be taken for guarding against falsification and facilitating its discovery, and where default is made in complying with this subsection, the company and every officer of the company with this subsection, the company and every officer of the company who is in default [shall be guilty of an offence and liable to a fine][a] not exceeding [€1,904.61]. [b]

Amendments

a Words 'shall be guilty of an offence and liable to a fine' substituted for 'shall be liable to a fine' by C(AA)A 2003, Sch 2.

b '£250' substituted for '£50' by C(A)A 1982, Sch 1, increased to £1,500 by CA 1990, s 240(7) as inserted by CLEA 2001, s 104(c) and converted to €1,904.61 by Council Regulations (EC) No 1103/97, No 974/98 and No 2866/98 and the Economic and Monetary Union Act 1998, s 6.

Cross reference

See C(A)A 1977, s 4 and notes thereto.

See also CA 1990, s 249 and notes thereto in relation to delivery of documents in non-legible form to the CRO.

See also CA 1963, s 377 and Sch 9 (as amended by CA 1990, s 250) which applies CA 1963, s 378 to unregistered companies.

Definitions

'company': CA 1963, s 2(1); 'officer': CA 1963, s 2(1); 'officer in default': CA 1963, s 383; 'Registrar of Companies': CA 1963, s 2(1).

Notes

Registers kept on computer: The combined effect of the provisions of CA 1963, s 378(2) and C(A)A 1977, s 4 permits registers, books etc to be maintained on computer provided that 'adequate' precautions[1] are taken to safeguard the falsification of such records and their discovery.[2]

1 CA 1963, s 378 (2).

2 See consideration given to the meaning of 'adequate' precautions: Courtney, *The Law of Private Companies* (2nd edn, Tottel Publishing, 2002) para 15.017. 'Where the register is kept on computer disk, a backup copy, made at regular intervals, should be password protected and kept on another disk to be placed in a secure and safe place.'

UK legislation

See CA 1985, ss 722; Uncertificated Securities Regulations 2001 (SI 2001/3755), Sch 4.

See generally CA 1985, s 723; Companies (Registers and other Records) Regulations 1985 (SI 1985/724).

Service of Documents

379 Service of documents on a company

(1) A document may be served on a company by leaving it at or sending it by post to the registered office of the company or, if the company has not given notice to the registrar of companies of the situation of its registered office, by registering it at the office for the registration of companies.

(2) For the purposes of this section, any document left at or sent by post to the place for the time being recorded by the registrar of companies as the situation of the registered office of a company shall be deemed to have been left at or sent by post to the registered office of the company notwithstanding that the situation of its registered office may have been changed.

Cross reference

In relation to the service of legal proceedings, see also RSC 1986, ords 9, 10.

In relation to the service of documents on a company for the purposes of tax legislation, see TCA 1997, s 869.

See also CA 1963, s 377 and Sch 9 (as amended by CA 1990, s 250) which applies CA 1963, s 379 to unregistered companies.

Definitions

'company': CA 1963, s 2(1); 'document': CA 1963, s 2(1): 'Registrar of Companies': CA 1963, s 2(1).

Notes

Reference to a company which has not given notice to the Registar of the situation of its registered office would only apply to companies incorporated prior to the coming into force of C(A)A 1982, s 3.[1] Since that date,[2] it has not been possible for a company to be incorporated without having notified the CRO of details of the registered office.[3]

1 3 August 1982.

2 The operative date of C(A)A 1982, s 3; Companies (Amendment) Act 1982 (Commencement) Order 1982 (SI 255/1982).

3 See generally, Courtney, *The Law of Private Companies* (2nd edn, Tottel Publishing, 2002) para 6.011–6.013.

UK legislation

See CA 1985, s 725.

Offences

380 Penalty for false statements

[...][a]

Amendments

a Repealed by CA 1990, s 6 and replaced by CA 1990, s 242.

UK legislation

See CA 1985, s 451 (substituted by the Companies (Audit, Investigations and Community Enterprise) Act 2004 (SI 2004/3322), s 25(1), Sch 2, Pt 3, paras 16, 19).

381 Improper use of 'limited' or 'teoranta'

[(1) If any person or persons trade or carry on business under a name or title of which 'limited' or 'teoranta', or any contraction or imitation of either word, is the last word, that person or those persons shall be, unless duly incorporated with limited liability, guilty of an offence.

(2) If any person or persons, having committed an offence under subsection (1), fails within 14 days after the service of a notice on him or them to do so, to cease to so trade or carry on business, in breach of that subsection, the court may, on the application of the registrar of companies or the Director, make an order directing the person or persons to so cease within such time as may be specified in the order and the person or persons shall comply with the order.

(3) An order under subsection (2) may provide that all costs of and incidental to the application shall be borne by the person or persons against whom it is made.][a]

Amendments

a CA 1963, s 381 repealed and substituted by CLEA 2001, s 98.

Definitions

'the court': CA 1963, s 2(1); 'Director': CLEA 2001, s 3(1); 'Registrar of Companies': CA 1963, s 2(1).

Notes

Improved enforcement: In an attempt to improve company law compliance by means of an enhanced enforcement regime,[1] CLEA 2001, s 98 amended the existing offence contained under CA 1963, s 381 in a number of ways. Firstly, the set fine of €634.87 was replaced. Where a provision of the Companies Acts does not specify the penalty applicable in respect of a particular offence, the general provisions of CA 1990, s 240 will apply so that the relevant penalty is a fine of €1,904.61 and/or imprisonment for up to 12 months.[2] Secondly, both the Director and the Registrar have the ability to make an application to court for an order prohibiting persons from continuing to trade using the word 'limited', if such persons have already failed to observe a notice formally requiring them to cease trading in this manner.[3] Thirdly, express provision is made for the possibility of award of costs against any person in respect of whom an application is made under CA 1963, s 381(2).[4] Clearly this is designed as an added deterrent against offending.

1 See The Report of the Working Group on Company Law Compliance and Enforcement (1998), para 3.31.

2 CA 1963, s 381(1).

3 CA 1963, s 381(2).

4 CA 1963, s 381(3).

UK legislation

See CA 1985, s 34.

---

382 Prosecution of companies on indictment

(1) Where a company is charged either alone or jointly with some other person with an indictable offence the subsequent provisions of this section shall have effect.

(2) The company may appear at all stages of the proceedings by a representative and the answer to any question to be put to a person charged with an indictable offence may be made on behalf of the company by that representative but if the company does not so appear it shall not be necessary to put the questions and the District Court may, notwithstanding its absence, take depositions and send forward the company for trial.

(3) Any right of objection or election conferred upon the accused person by any enactment may be exercised on behalf of the company by its representative.

(4) Any plea which may be entered or signed by an accused person, whether before the District Court or before the trial judge, may be entered in writing on behalf of the company by its representative, and, if the company does not appear by its representative or, though it does so appear, fails to enter any such plea, the trial shall proceed as though the company had duly entered a plea of not guilty.

(5) In this section, 'representative' in relation to a company means a person duly appointed by the company to represent it for the purpose of doing any act or thing which the representative of a company is by this section authorised to do, but a person so appointed shall not, by virtue only of being so appointed, be qualified to act on behalf of the company before any court for any other purpose.

(6) A representative for the purpose of this section need not be appointed under the seal of the company and a statement in writing purporting to be signed by a managing director of the company or by some other person (by whatever name called) having, or being one of the persons having, the management of the affairs of the company, to the effect that the person named in the statement has been appointed as the representative of the company for the purposes of this section shall be admissible without further proof as evidence that that person has been so appointed.

(7) In this section, 'company' includes a company incorporated outside the State which has an established place of business in the State.

Definitions

'company': CA 1963, s 2(1), s 382(7); 'District Court': IA 2005, Sch, Pt 1; 'representative': CA 1963, s 382(5).

Notes

One of the consequences of incorporation[1] is the fact that a company may be sued in its own name, independent of the persons who have incorporated that company. It is a manifestation of this independence from its incorporators that in civil proceedings, a company cannot appear by one of its agents, but must instead be represented by a solicitor or barrister.[2] Prior to the enactment of CA 1963, s 382, it appeared that a company could not be returned for trial on indictment, as a company could not appear in person.[3] However, since its enactment it has been possible for a duly appointed representative[4] of a company to answer questions,[5] exercise any right of objection or election,[6] and enter any plea[7] on behalf of the company. There are a number of circumstances where statutes have applied the provisions of CA 1963, s 382 to proceedings involving unincorporated bodies[8] and bodies corporate not governed by the Companies Acts.[9]

1 See CA 1963, s 18 and notes thereto.

2 *Battle v Irish Art Promotion Centre Ltd* [1968] IR 252.

3 *The State (Batchelor & Co Ireland Ltd) v O'Leannain* [1957] IR 1.

4 CA 1963, s 382(5).

5 CA 1963, s 382(2).

6 CA 1963, s 382(3).

7 CA 1963, s 382(4).

8 Livestock Marts Act 1967, s 9.

9 Package Holidays and Travel Trade Act 1995, s 7; Air Navigation and Transport (Amendment) Act 1998, s 8; Public Health (Tobacco) Act 2002, s 6.

383 Meaning of 'officer in default'

[(1) For the purpose of any provision of the Companies Acts which provides that an officer of a company who is in default shall be liable to a fine or penalty, an officer who is in default is any officer who authorises or who, in breach of his duty as such officer, permits, the default mentioned in the provision.

(2) For the purposes of this section, an officer shall be presumed to have permitted a default by the company unless the officer can establish that he took all reasonable steps to prevent it or that, by reason of circumstances beyond his control, was unable to do so.

(3) It is the duty of each director and secretary of a company to ensure that the requirements of the Companies Acts are complied with by the company.

(4) In this section 'default' includes a refusal or contravention.][a]

Amendments

a CA 1963, s 383 repealed and substituted by CLEA 2001, s 100.

Cross reference

See CA 1963, s 377 and Sch 9 (as amended by CA 1990, s 250) which applies CA 1963, s 383 to unregistered companies.

Definitions

'Companies Acts': CLEA 2001, s 3(1), IA 2005, Sch, Pt 2; 'company': CA 1963, s 2(1); 'director': CA 1963, s 2(1); 'officer': CA 1963, s 2(1); 'officer in default': CA 1963, s 383.

In CA 1963, s 383 reference to 'default' includes a refusal or contravention.

Notes

'officer who is in default': CA 1963, s 383 (as amended) provides a definition of the term 'officer who is in default', wherever that term is used in the Companies Acts. Previously, this term referred to any officer of the company who 'knowingly and wilfully' authorised or permitted the relevant default, refusal or contravention. Now, an officer is guilty of an offence if he authorises or, in breach of his duty as an officer, permits the default in question.[1] This removes the necessity under the previous CA 1963, s 383 of establishing that the officer acted 'knowingly and wilfully' in authorising or permitting the default in question. In addition, there is now a presumption that the relevant officer had permitted the default, unless the officer may establish that he took reasonable steps to prevent the default or that he was unable to prevent it because of reasons outside of his or her control.[2] This places the onus on the officer to disprove to the court, any fault on his part.

1 CA 1963, s 383(1).

2 CA 1963, s 383(2).

Duty to comply with Companies Acts: CA 1963, s 383(3) places a statutory responsibility on directors and secretaries of companies to ensure that the requirements of the Companies Acts are complied with by the company. It is also clarified that reference to 'default' includes any refusal of an officer to comply with or contravention of a particular requirement of the Companies Acts.[1] Given the fact that most company secretaries will only have those powers as have been delegated to them by the directors, it is somewhat anomalous to impose upon secretaries a blanket duty 'to ensure that the requirements of the Companies Acts are complied with by the company.' It is thought that the words 'being requirements that are within the secretary's control' must be implied into subsection (3).

1 CA 1963, s 383(4).

UK legislation

See CA 1985, s 730(5); CA 1989, s 145, Sch 19, para 17.

---

384 Production and inspection of books when offence suspected

(1) If on an application to a Judge of the High Court by the Attorney General, the [Director][a] or a Superintendent of the Garda Síochána, there is shown to be reasonable cause to believe that any person has, while an officer of a company, committed an offence in connection with the management of the company's affairs and that evidence of the commission of the offence is to be found in any books or papers of or under the control of the company, an order may be made—

(a) authorising any person named therein to inspect the said books or papers or any of them for the purpose of investigating and obtaining evidence of the offence; or

(b) requiring the secretary of the company or such other officer thereof as may be named in the order to produce the said books or any of them to a person named in the order at a place so named.

(2) Subsection (1) shall apply also in relation to any books or papers of a person carrying on the business of banking so far as they relate to the company's affairs, as it applies to any books or papers of or under the control of the company, except that no such order as is referred to in paragraph (b) thereof shall be made by virtue of this subsection.

(3) The decision of a Judge of the High Court on an application under this section shall be final subject to an appeal to the Supreme Court on a question of law.

(4) In this section, 'company' includes a company incorporated outside the State which has an established place of business in the State.

Amendments

a CA 1963, s 384 word 'Director' substituted for 'Minister' by CLEA 2001, s 14.

Cross reference

See CA 1963, s 377 and Sch 9 (as amended by CA 1990, s 250) which applies CA 1963, s 384 to unregistered companies.

Definitions

'company': CA 1963, s 2(1); 'High Court': IA 2005, Sch, Pt 2; 'Minister': CA 1963, s 2(1); 'officer': CA 1963, s 2(1); 'Supreme Court': IA 2005, Sch, Pt 2.

UK legislation

See CA 1985, s 721.

---

385 Summary proceedings

[...][a]

Amendments

a Repealed by CA 1990, s 6.

Cross reference

See CA 1990, s 240 (as amended) and notes thereto.

---

386 Minimum fine for second or subsequent offences

Where a person is convicted of an offence under this Act and is subsequently convicted of another offence under this Act, the fine to be imposed by the court in respect of such second or subsequent offence shall not be less than [€1,904.61][a] unless the court, having regard to all the circumstances of the case, otherwise decides.

Amendments

a '£250' substituted for '£50' by C(A)A 1982 Sch 1, increased to £1,500 by CA 1990, s 240(7) as inserted by CLEA 2001, s 104(c) and converted to €1,904.61 by Council Regulations (EC) No 1103/97, No 974/98 and No 2866/98 and the Economic and Monetary Union Act 1998, s 6.

Cross reference

See CA 1963, s 377 and Sch 9 (as amended by CA 1990, s 250) which applies CA 1963, s 386 to unregistered companies.

Definitions

'the court': CA 1963, s 2(1).

387 Saving for privileged communications

Where proceedings are instituted under this Act against any person, nothing in sections 170 or 299 shall be taken to require any person who has acted as solicitor for the company to disclose any privileged communication made to him otherwise than as such solicitor.

Cross reference

CA 1963, s 170 was repealed by CA 1990, s 6.

See also CA 1963, s 377 and Sch 9 (as amended by CA 1990, s 250) which applies CA 1963, s 387 to unregistered companies.

Definitions

'company': CA 1963, s 2(1).

Notes

In relation to legal professional privilege generally, see Fennell, *The Law of Evidence in Ireland* (2nd edn, Tottel Publishing, 2003), paras 8.05–8.48. See see CA 1990, s 10 in relation to the obligation to produce documents and evidence on investigation and also CA 1990, s 23 which protects the claim of legal professional privilege in respect of inspections and investigations (as well as proceedings on foot thereof) pursuant to CA 1990, Part II.

UK legislation

See CA 1985, s 732(3); Companies (Audit, Investigations and Community Enterprise) Act 2004 (SI 2004/3322), s 25(1), Sch 2, Pt 3, paras 16, 22(c).

388 Proof of incorporation of companies incorporated outside the State

A copy of any Act by which a corporation is incorporated, purporting to be published by the Government publishers of any country prescribed by the Minister for the purposes of this section, shall without further proof be *prima facie* evidence of the incorporation of that corporation.

Cross reference

Northern Ireland and Great Britain are recognised for the purposes of CA 1963, s 388 by Companies (Recognition of Countries) Order 1964 (SI 1964/42), reg 2.

[1] Companies (Recognition of Countries) Order 1964 (SI 42/1964) has been revoked to the extent that it is for the purposes of CA 1963, s 367, pursuant to IFCMPA 2005, s 40(2).

Definitions

'Minister': CA 1963, s 2(1); 'prescribed': CA 1963, s 2(1).

389 Proof of certificates as to incorporation

A certificate signed by any person purporting to hold the office of registrar of companies or assistant registrar of companies or any office similar thereto in any country prescribed by the Minister for the purposes of this section, certifying that a company named in such certificate has been incorporated in that country, shall be *prima facie* evidence of such incorporation without proof of the signature of the person signing such certificate and without proof that the person signing such certificate holds that office.

Cross reference

Northern Ireland and Great Britain are recognised for the purposes of CA 1963, s 389 by Companies (Recognition of Countries) Order 1964 (SI 42/1964), reg 2.[1]

[1] Companies (Recognition of Countries) Order 1964 (SI 1964/42) has been revoked to the extent that it is for the purposes of CA 1963, s 367, pursuant to IFCMPA 2005, s 40(2).

Definitions

'company': CA 1963, s 2(1); 'Minister': CA 1963, s 2(1); 'prescribed': CA 1963, s 2(1).

Legal Proceedings

390 Security for costs by company

Where a limited company is plaintiff in any action or other legal proceeding, any judge having jurisdiction in the matter, may, if it appears by credible testimony that there is reason to believe that the company will be unable to pay the costs of the defendant if successful in his defence, require sufficient security to be given for those costs and may stay all proceedings until the security is given.

Cross reference

See RSC, ord 29.

Definitions

'company': CA 1963, s 2(1).

Notes

Security for costs against corporate plaintiffs:[1] A defendant[2] in any action or any other legal proceeding may seek an order under CA 1963, s 390, where the plaintiff is a limited company. An order may also be sought under s 390 by a plaintiff against whom an insolvent company is bringing a counterclaim.[3] Reference to a 'limited company' has been held to include companies limited by guarantee.[4] The phrase 'other legal proceedings' refers to any matter in which the jurisdiction of the court is invoked by an originating process rather than by a summons; a summons properly speaking commences an action. Thus the word 'plaintiff' indicates not only a company which would be described as a plaintiff but also covers a company which has involved the jurisdiction of the court by any other originating process including a petition or an originating notice of motion.[5] There is no requirement for costs to have been first sought from and refused by the company before an application may be made.[6] Security can only be ordered in respect of costs incurred after the demand for security for costs has first been made by the defendant.[7]

1 See generally Barr, 'Security for costs under s 390 ofthe Companies Act 1963 – an overview' 14 (3) 2009 BR 61.

2 A notice party may also apply for security for costs under CA 1963, s 390: *Broadnet Ireland Ltd v Office of the Director of Telecommunications Regulation and Eircom plc* [2000] 3 IR 281.

3 *Boyle v McGilloway* [2006] IEHC 37; *Hart Investments Ltd v Larchpark Ltd* [2008] 1 BCLC 589.

4 *West Donegal Land League Ltd v Údarás na Gaelt*achta [2007] 1 ILRM 1. The fact that a company might have charitable status would not prevent the application of CA 1963, s 390: *West Donegal Land League Ltd v Údarás na Gaeltachta* [2003] IEHC 125.

5 *Village Residents Association Ltd v An Bord Pleanála* [2000] 4 IR 321; *Usk District Residents Association Ltd v The Environmental Protection Agency* [2006] IESC 1; *Boyle v McGilloway* [2006] IEHC 37; *Re Unisoft Group Ltd (No 1)* [1993] BCLC 528. A review of a decision of the Taxing Master under RSC, ord 99, r 38 comes within the meaning of 'other legal proceeding': *Superwood Holdings plc & Ors v Sun Alliance and London Insurance Plc & Ors* [2006] IEHC 123.

6 *Lancefort Ltd v An Bord Pleanála* [1998] 2 IR 511 (Morris J).

7 *SEE Co Ltd v Public Lighting Services Ltd* [1987] ILRM 255.

Matters to be proven by the applicant and the burden of proof: Firstly, there is an onus on the applicant to establish by credible evidence an inability, on the part of the respondent company, to discharge the costs of the applicant.[1] Secondly, there is an onus on the applicant to satisfy the court that he has a prima facie defence.[2] Once the court is satisfied of these two matters, the burden of proof is then placed on the respondent company, who must satisfy the court that 'special circumstances' exist, such that the court should exercise its discretion not to order security for costs.[3] The court can take into account the strength of the plaintiff's case in determining whether to order security for costs.[4] However, the strength of the plaintiff's case will not, on its own, be a ground for refusing an order for security for costs, unless the strength is such as to show that the defendant has no real defence.[5]

1 *SEE Co Ltd v Public Lighting Services Ltd* [1987] ILRM 255; *Bula Ltd v Tara Mines Ltd (No 3)* [1987] IR 494; *Irish Press plc v EM Warburg Pincus & Co International Ltd* [1997] 2 ILRM 263, 271; *Interfinance Group Ltd v KPMG Peat Marwick* [1998] IEHC 217 (Morris P); *Usk District Residents Association Ltd v The Environmental Protection Agency* [2006] IESC 1; *Boyle v McGilloway* [2006] IEHC 37; *PDC (Moate) Ltd v Allied Irish Banks plc* (25 July 2008, unreported) HC (Finlay Geoghegan J).

2 *Bula Ltd v Tara Mines Ltd* [1987] IR 494; *Comhlucht Páipéar Ríomhaireachta Teo v Údarás na Gaeltachta* [1990] ILRM 266; *Interfinance Group Ltd v KPMG Peat Marwick* (29 June 1998, unreported) HC (Morris P); *Lismore Homes Ltd v Bank of Ireland Finance Ltd* [1999] 1 IR 501, 529; *Usk District Residents Association Ltd v The Environmental Protection Agency* [2006] IESC 1; *Boyle v McGilloway* [2006] IEHC 37; *PDC (Moate) Ltd v Allied Irish Banks plc* (25 July 2008, unreported) HC (Finlay Geoghegan J).

3 *Jack O'Toole Ltd v MacEoin Kelly Associates* [1987] ILRM 269; *Bula Ltd v Tara Mines Ltd (No 3)* [1987] IR 494; *Irish Commercial Society Ltd v Plunkett* [1988] IR 1; *Interfinance Group Ltd v KPMG Peat Marwick* [1998] IEHC 217 (Morris P); *Usk District Residents Association Ltd v The Environmental Protection Agency* [2006] IESC 1; *Boyle v McGilloway* [2006] IEHC 37; *West Donegal Land League Ltd v Údarás na Gaeltachta* [2007] 1 ILRM 1; *Dublin International Arena Ltd v Campus & Stadium Ireland Development Ltd* [2008] 1 ILRM 496.

4 *Irish Commercial Society Ltd v Plunkett* [1988] IR 1; *Bula Ltd v Tara Mines Ltd* (*op cit*); *Interfinance Group Ltd v KPMG Peat Marwick* [1998] IEHC 217 (Morris P); *Usk District Residents Association Ltd v The Environmental Protection Agency* [2006] IESC 1; *Boyle v McGilloway* [2006] IEHC 37.

5 *Comhlucht Páipéar Ríomhaireachta Teo v Údarás na Gaeltachta* [1990] ILRM 266; *Interfinance Group Ltd v KPMG Peat Marwick* [1998] IEHC 217 (Morris P); *Usk District*

Residents Association Ltd v The Environmental Protection Agency [2006] IESC 1; *Boyle v McGilloway* [2006] IEHC 37.

Court will only exercise its discretion in 'special circumstances': In each case the court must determine whether the necessary 'special circumstances' exist for it to exercise its discretion to make an order for costs.[1] Such 'special circumstances' are considered below.

Lack of bona fides by the applicant: The conduct of the defendant or (in the case of a company) the persons actually controlling its affairs, may also be taken into account by the court in considering how to exercise its discretion under CA 1963, s 390.[2]

The company's insolvency having been caused by the applicant: The court may refuse the application for security for costs where the respondent company adduces prima facie evidence that its insolvency has been caused by the wrongful act of the defendant which is the subject-matter of the proceedings. To discharge the onus of proof, however, it is not sufficient for the respondent company to make a mere bald statement of fact that its insolvency has been caused by the defendant.[3] If the respondent company is seeking to invoke remedies against the defendant which can only be exercised in a liquidation (eg to set aside a transaction as a fraudulent preference under CA 1963, s 298), the liquidator cannot plead that the wrongful act the subject matter of the proceedings has caused the insolvency, by way of answer to a claim for security for costs.[4]

The company seeking to vindicate the public interest: While it would appear that, to date, no case has arisen where it was successfully argued that such 'special circumstances' existed, it has been acknowledged that this is one of the grounds on which the discretion under CA 1963, s 390 may be exercised.[5]

The existence of a natural co-plaintiff: A natural person runs the risk of bankruptcy in the event that an award of costs is made against him, unlike the members of a limited company. Consideration has been given as to whether the natural co-plaintiff would be able to meet any such order for costs[6] and the bona fides of the presence of the natural co-plaintiff in the proceedings.[7]

The applicant's delay in applying for an order for security for costs: Delay on the part of the defendant in bringing the application under CA 1963, s 390 may result in the court ordering security for costs in a lesser amount, or in exceptional cases, refusing the application altogether.[8]

1 *West Donegal Land League Ltd v Údarás na Gaeltachta* [2007] 1 ILRM 1; *Hidden Ireland Heritage Holidays Ltd v Indigo Services Ltd* [2005] 2 IR 115. See also Courtney, *The Law of Private Companies* (2nd edn, Tottel Publishing, 2002) para 6.042 *et seq* and Delany and McGrath, *Civil Procedure in the Superior Courts,* (2nd edn, Thomson, Round Hall, 2005) para 12.42 *et seq*.

2 *Irish Commercial Society Ltd v Plunkett* [1988] IR 1.

3 *Jack O'Toole Ltd v MacEoin Kelly Associates* [1987] ILRM 269; *SEE Co Ltd v Public Lighting Services Ltd* [1987] ILRM 255; *Peppard & Co Ltd v Bogoff* [1962] IR 180; *Irish Commercial Society Ltd v Plunkett* [1987] ILRM 504; *Bula Ltd v Tara Mines Ltd* [1987] IR 494.

4 *Comhlucht Páipear Ríomhaireachta Teo v Údarás na Gaeltachta* [1990] ILRM 266.

5 *Broadnet Ireland Ltd v Office of the Director of Telecommunications Regulation and Eircom plc* [2000] 3 IR 281; *Village Residents Association Ltd v An Bord Pleanála and McDonald's Restaurants of Ireland Ltd* [2000] 4 IR 321.

6 *Bula Ltd v Tara Mines* Ltd [1987] IR 494.

7 *In Bonis Mooney* [1938] IR 354.

8 *Thalle v Soares* [1957] IR 182; *SEE Co Ltd v Public Lighting Services Ltd* [1987] ILRM 255.

'Sufficient security': CA 1963, s 390 (unlike in the case of an order for costs under RSC, ord 29) stipulates that the amount should represent 'sufficient security'. Its meaning has been given consideration recently in the Supreme Court,[1] where Murphy J concluded that the phrase required the court to 'make a reasonable estimate or assessment of the actual costs which it is anticipated that the defendant will have to meet'. This is at variance with the interpretation of this phrase in the UK.[2] This approach should also be contrasted against the quantum of security for costs awarded pursuant to RSC, ord 29.[3]

1 *Lismore Homes v Bank of Ireland* [2002] 1 ILRM 541.

2 *Re Unisoft Group Ltd (No 2)* [1993] BCLC 532.

3 See Delaney and McGrath, *Civil Procedure in the Superior Courts* (2nd edn, Thomson, Round Hall, 2005), paras 12.26–12.32.

UK legislation

See CA 1985, s 726.

391 Power of court to grant relief to officers of company

(1) If in any proceeding for negligence, default, breach of duty or breach of trust against an officer of a company or a person employed by a company as auditor, it appears to the court hearing the case that that officer or person is or may be liable in respect of the negligence, default, breach of duty or breach of trust, but that he has acted honestly and reasonably, and that, having regard to all the circumstances of the case, including those connected with his appointment, he ought fairly to be excused for the negligence, default, breach of duty or breach of trust, that court may relieve him, either wholly or partly from his liability on such terms as the court may think fit.

(2) Where any such officer or person as aforesaid has reason to apprehend that any claim will or might be made against him in respect of any negligence, default, breach of duty or breach of trust, he may apply to the court for relief, and the court on any such application shall have the same power to relieve him as under this section it would have had if it had been a court before which proceedings against that person for negligence, default, breach of duty or breach of trust had been brought.

(3) Where any case to which subsection (1) applies is being tried by a judge with a jury, the judge, after hearing the evidence, may, if he is satisfied that the defendant ought in pursuance of that subsection to be relieved, either in whole or in part, from the liability sought to be enforced against him, withdraw the case in whole on in part from the jury, and direct judgment to be entered for the defendant on such terms as to costs or otherwise as the judge may think proper.

Definitions

'company': CA 1963, s 2(1); 'the court': CA 1963, s 2(1); 'officer': CA 1963, s 2(1).

Cross reference

See CA 1963, s 377 and Sch 9 (as amended by CA 1990, s 250) which applies CA 1963, s 391 to unregistered companies.

Notes

Availability of relief under CA 1963, s 391: Relief may not be granted under CA 1963, s 391 against any of the criminal penalties imposed by the Companies Acts; however, it may be granted in respect of a liability arising by reason of a breach of duty, negligence, default or trust by the officer in any action brought by the company.[1] Relief cannot be granted, even where the liability of the officer is to the company and not to a third party, unless he has acted honestly and reasonably.[2] CA 1963, s 391 only allows the court to grant relief to the officer or auditor in respect of liability to the company itself. Thus, the section is inapplicable to any claims brought by third parties (eg fraudulent or reckless trading claims or claims in respect of breach of a duty owed directly by the officer to a member or creditor of the company).[3] Relief may be granted under CA 1963, s 391 in respect of *ultra vires* acts.[4] Furthermore, relief may be granted, even if the application under CA 196, s 391 is opposed by the members.[5] Relief will be refused, however, if the officer, although not guilty of dishonest conduct, has wrongfully received and still retains company property.[6] In deciding whether to make an officer of a company liable, CA 1963, s 391 gives the court a discretion to take all the circumstances of the case into account.[7]

1 *Commissioners of Customs & Excise v Hedon Alpha Ltd* [1981] QB 818. cf *Re Barry and Staines Linoleum Ltd* [1934] Ch 227.

2 *Re Duomatic Ltd* [1969] 1 All ER 161; *Bairstow v Queens Moat Houses plc* [2001] 2 BCLC 531; *Queensway Systems Ltd v Walker* [2007] 2 BCLC 577; *PNC Telecom plc v Thomas (No 2)* [2008] 2 BCLC 95.

3 *Commissioners of Customs & Excise v Hedon Alpha Ltd* [1981] QB 818; *Re Produce Marketing Consortium Ltd* [1989] 3 All ER 1.

4 *Re Claridge's Patent Asphalte Co Ltd* [1921] 1 Ch 543.

5 *Re Gilt Edge Safety Glass Ltd* [1940] 2 All ER 237.

6 *Guinness plc v Saunders* [1990] 1 All ER 652.

7 *Coleman Taymar Ltd v Oakes* [2001] BCLC 749.

UK legislation

See CA 1985, s 727.

General Provisions as to the Minister

392 Annual report by the Minister

The Minister shall cause a general annual report of matters within this Act to be prepared and laid before both Houses of the Oireachtas [not later than 7 months after the end of the calendar year to which the report relates][a].

Amendments

a Words 'not later than 7 months after the end of the calendar year to which the report relates' inserted after 'Houses of the Oireachtas' in CA 1963, s 392 by CLEA 2001, s 99.

Definitions

'Minister': CA 1963, s 2(1); 'Oireachtas': IA 2005, Sch, Pt 2.

Notes

The annual Companies Report is available to download from the CRO's website, http://www.cro.ie and the Department of Enterprise Trade and Employment's website, http://www.entemp.ie.

UK legislation

See CA 1985, s 729.

393 Expenses

The expenses incurred by the Minister in the administration of this Act shall to such extent as may be sanctioned by the Minister for Finance be paid out of moneys provided by the Oireachtas.

Definitions

'Minister': CA 1963, s 2(1); 'Minister for Finance': Ministers and Secretaries Act 1924, s 1(ii); 'Oireachtas': IA 2005, Sch, Pt 2.

394 Authentication of documents issued by the Minister

Any approval, sanction, direction or licence or revocation of licence which under this Act may be given or made by the Minister may be under the hand of any person authorised in that behalf by the Minister.

Definitions

'document': CA 1963, s 2(1): 'Minister': CA 1963, s 2(1).

395 Power to alter Tables and Forms

(1) The Minister shall have power by order to alter or add to the requirements of this Act as to the matters to be stated in a company's balance sheet, profit and loss account and group accounts, and in particular of those of the Sixth Schedule; and any reference in this Act to the Sixth Schedule shall be construed as a reference to that Schedule with any alterations of additions made by orders for the time being in force under this subsection.

[(2) The Minister may by order—

(a) alter Table A, Tábla A and the Third, Seventh and Eighth Schedules;

(b) alter or add to Tables B, C, D and E in the First Schedule[...][a]; and

(c) alter the forms set out in the Second Schedule to the Companies (Amendment) Act, 1983;

but no alteration made by the Minister in Table A or in Tábla A shall affect any company registered before the alteration, or repeal in relation to that company any portion of Table A or Tábla A.][b]

[(3) To avoid doubt, an alteration to the Eighth Schedule under subsection (2)(a) may provide for different fees to be charged for the registration of documents depending on whether they are delivered to the registrar of companies within a specified time or at various times after a specified time.] [c]

Amendments

a Words 'and the form in Part II of the Fifth Schedule' deleted from CA 1963, s 395(2)(b) by CLEA 2001, s 63(1)(a).[1]

b CA 1963, s 385(2) substituted by C(A)A 1983, Sch 1, para 23.

c CA 1963, s 395(3) inserted by CLEA 2001, s 63(1)(b).[2]

1 With effect from 1 March 2002; the Company Law Enforcement Act 2001 (Commencement) (No 2) Order 2001 (SI 438/2001), reg 5.

2 With effect from 26 October 2001; the Company Law Enforcement Act 2001 (Commencement) (No 2) Order 2001 (SI 438/2001), reg 4.

Cross reference

See CA 1963, s 377 and Sch 9 (as amended by CA 1990, s 250) which applies CA 1963, s 395(1) to unregistered companies.

Definitions

'accounts': CA 1963, s 2(1); 'company': CA 1963, s 2(1); 'document': CA 1963, s (1); 'group accounts'; CA 1963, s 2(1), s 150(1); 'Minister': CA 1963, s 2(1); 'Registrar of Companies': CA 1963, s 2(1); 'Table A'; CA 1963, s 2(1); 'Tábla A'; CA 1963, s 2(1).

Notes

Late filing fees: The purpose of the addition of CA 1963, s 395(3) by CLEA 2001, s 63(b) is to confirm the statutory basis for the levying of progressively increasing late filing penalties in respect of returns to be made to the Registrar. It is intended that such increasing fees will serve to provide an ongoing incentive to make the required filing, even in circumstances where the initial filing deadline has passed. The payment of any such late filing penalty will not prevent a prosecution under CA 1963, s 125 in respect of the same return.[1]

1 *Registrar of Companies v Judge David Anderson & Ors* [2004] IESC 103.

UK legislation

See CA 1985, ss 3, 6, 257, 365; CA 1989, ss 20, 139(1).

---

396 Laying of orders before Houses of Oireachtas and power to revoke or amend orders and to prescribe forms

(1) Every order made under this Act shall be laid before each House of the Oireachtas as soon as may be after it is made and if a resolution annulling the order is passed by either House within the next 21 days on which that House has sat after the order is laid before it, the order shall be annulled accordingly but without prejudice to the validity of anything previously done thereunder.

(2) The Minister may by order revoke or amend an order (other than an order made under subsection (2) of section 1) made under this Act.

(3) The Minister may by order prescribe forms to be used in connection with any of the provisions of this Act other than those relating to the winding up of companies.

Definitions

'company': CA 1963, s 2(1); 'Minister': CA 1963, s 2(1); 'prescribed' CA 1963, s 2(1); 'Oireachtas': IA 2005, Sch, Pt 2.

Supplemental

397 Restriction of section 58 of Solicitors Act, 1954

Notwithstanding section 58 of the Solicitors Act, 1954, a person to whom paragraph (a) or (b) of subsection (1) of section 162 applies may draw or prepare any document for the purpose of this Act other than a deed or a memorandum or articles of association.

Cross reference

CA 1963, s 162, '*Qualifications for appointment as auditor*' was repealed by CA 1990, s 6 and replaced by CA 1990, s 187.

Definitions

'articles': CA 1963, s 2(1); 'document': CA 1963, s 2(1): 'memorandum': CA 1963, s 2(1).

398 Provisions as to winding-up proceedings commenced before the operative date

(1) The provisions of this Act relating to winding up (other than subsections (2) and (3)) shall not apply to any company of which the winding up commenced before the operative date but every such company shall be wound up in the same manner and with the same incidents as if this Act (apart from the enactments aforesaid) had not been passed, and for the purposes of the winding up, the Act or Acts under which the winding up commenced shall be deemed to remain in full force.

(2) An office copy of every order staying the proceedings in a winding up commenced as aforesaid shall forthwith be forwarded by the company or by such person as the court may direct, to the registrar of companies for registration.

(3) If a company fails to comply with subsection (2), the company and every officer of the company who is in default [shall be guilty of an offence and liable to a fine] [a] not exceeding [€1,904.61],[b] and if any other person fails to comply with subsection (2) such person [shall be guilty of an offence and liable to a fine][a] not exceeding [€1,904.61].[b]

Amendments

a Words 'shall be guilty of an offence and liable to a fine' substituted for 'shall be liable to a fine' in both instances where they occur in CA 1963, s 398 by C(AA)A 2003, Sch 2, para 4.

b '£125' substituted for '£25' by C(A)A 1982, Sch 1, increased to £1,500 by CA 1990, s 240(7) as inserted by CLEA 2001, s 104(c) and converted to €1,904.61 by Council Regulations (EC) No 1103/97, No 974/98 and No 2866/98 and the Economic and Monetary Union Act 1998, s 6.

Definitions

'company': CA 1963, s 2(1); 'the court': CA 1963, s 2(1); 'officer': CA 1963, s 2(1); 'officer in default': CA 1963, s 383; 'the operative date': CA 1963, s 2(1); 'Registrar of Companies': CA 1963, s 2(1).

UK legislation

See CC(CP)A 1985, s 22.

399 Amendments of other Acts

The enactments set out in the Eleventh Schedule shall have effect subject to the amendments specified in that Schedule.

SCHEDULES

FIRST SCHEDULE

TABLE A [...][a] AND TABLES B, C, D AND E

TABLE A

PART I

REGULATIONS FOR MANAGEMENT OF A COMPANY LIMITED BY SHARES NOT BEING A PRIVATE COMPANY

Interpretation

1. In these regulations:

'the Act' means the Companies Act, 1963 (No. 33 of 1963);

'the directors' means the directors for the time being of the company or the directors present at a meeting of the board of directors and includes any person occupying the position of director by whatever name called;

'the register' means the register of members to be kept as required by section 116 of the Act;

'secretary' means any person appointed to perform the duties of the secretary of the company;

'the office' means the registered office for the time being of the company;

'the seal' means the common seal of the company.

Expressions referring to writing shall, unless the contrary intention appears, be construed as including references to printing, lithography, photography, and any other modes of representing or reproducing words in a visible form.

Unless the contrary intention appears, words or expressions contained in these regulations shall bear the same meaning as in the Act or in any statutory modification thereof in force at the date at which these regulations become binding on the company.

Amendments

a The Irish language version of Table A is omitted from this book.

Notes

It is virtually unknown for an Irish public company to adopt, without amendment, Table A, Part I articles of association. [1] Most public companies limited by shares will adopt bespoke articles of association and completely eschew Table A, Part I. Ironically, those companies that most frequently adopt most (although not all) of Table A, Part I are private companies limited by shares which do so by the express adoption of Part II which in reg 1, states that the regulations contained in Part I of Table A (with the exception of regs 8, 24, 51, 54, 84 and 86) shall apply to the private company limited by shares.

> 'Unless the contrary intention appears, words or expressions contained in these regulations shall bear the same meaning as in the Act or in any statutory modification thereof in force at the date at which these regulations become binding on the company'

The effect of this provision is that unless the contrary is provided for, words and phrases defined in a company's articles of association are defined by reference to their statutory meanings in the Companies Acts, being those Companies Acts in force as at the time of their adoption.

In the UK it has been decided that the Interpretation Act applies to the interpretation of both Table A regulations and bespoke articles adopted by a company where these together comprise a company's articles of association as otherwise there could be two different principles of interpretation.[2] Where a company adopts articles of association that entirely eschew Table A, in the absence of a provision to the contrary, it would seem that IA 2005 cannot apply since they could, in no circumstance, be considered to be an enactment.[3]

1 For a comprehensive review of the contents of the UK's comparable Table A, see Nicholson, *Table A Articles of Association*, (Sweet & Maxwell, 1977).

2 See *Fell v Derby Leather Company Ltd* [1931] 2 Ch 252 at 254 *per* Bennett J and see also *Jarvis Motors (Harrow) Ltd and another v Carabott and another* [1964] 1 WLR 1101.

3 'Enactment' as defined as 'an Act or a statutory instrument or any portion of an Act or statutory instrument' by IA 2005, s 2(1).

Share Capital and Variation of Rights

2. Without prejudice to any special rights previously conferred on the holders of any existing shares or class of shares, any share in the company may be issued with such preferred, deferred or other special rights or such restrictions, whether in regard to dividend, voting, return of capital or otherwise, as the company may from time to time by ordinary resolution determine.

Definitions

'company': CA 1963, s 2(1); 'share': CA 1963, s 2(1).

Notes

If the terms of issue do not differentiate between the different classes of shareholders regarding the right (a) to dividend, (b) to a return of capital, (c) to participate in surplus assets in a winding up, or (d) to vote, the presumption is that they all rank equally in all regards.[1] Furthermore, a preference regarding any one of these rights does not imply a preference in respect of another right.[2] It has been recognised, however, that enhanced rights can also be conferred upon certain shares which entitled the holders to weighted voting rights in general or particular cases.[3]

If the terms of the issue give the preference shareholders a right of priority to a fixed dividend, this is deemed to be exhaustive of their dividend entitlements, in the absence of an express provision to the contrary.[4] However, if the terms of issue give the preference shareholders priority as to a return of capital, this is not presumed to be exhaustive of their rights in a winding up, in the absence of an express provision to the contrary.[5]

1 *Birch v Cropper* (1889) 14 App Cas 525; *British & American Trustee & Finance Corporation v Couper* [1894] AC 399.

2 *Birch v Cropper* (1889) 14 App Cas 525.

3 *Bushell v Faith* [1970] AC 1099.

4 *Will v United Lankat Plantations Co Ltd* [1914] AC 11.

5 *Re Cork Electric Supply Co Ltd* [1932] IR 314.

[**3**. If at any time the share capital is divided into different classes of shares, the rights attached to any class may, whether or not the company is being wound up, be varied or abrogated with the consent in writing of the holders of three-fourths of the issued shares of that class, or with the sanction of a special resolution passed at a separate general meeting of the holders of the shares of the class.][a]

Amendments

a Substituted by C(A)A 1983, Sch 1 para 24.

Definitions

'share': CA 1963, s 2(1).

4. The rights conferred upon the holders of the shares of any class issued with preferred or other rights shall not, unless otherwise expressly provided by the terms of issue of the shares of that class, be deemed to be varied by the creation or issue of further shares ranking *pari passu* therewith.

Definitions

'share': CA 1963, s 2(1).

Notes

This provision states the common law position.[1] The issue of extra shares ranking *pari passu*, although strictly permissible, could be in disregard of the interests of the existing shareholders within the meaning of CA 1963, s 205.[2]

1 *White v Bristol Aeroplane Co* [1953] Ch 65. See also *Re Schweppes Ltd* [1914] 1 Ch 322; *Re John Smith's Tadcaster Brewery Co Ltd* [1953] 2 WLR 516; *Greenhalgh v Arderne Cinemas Ltd* [1946] 1 All ER 512.

2 See *Re Williams Group Tullamore Ltd* [1985] IR 613.

[**5**. Subject to the provisions of these regulations relating to new shares, the shares shall be at the disposal of the directors, and they may (subject to the provisions of the Companies Acts, 1963 to 1983) allot, grant options over or otherwise dispose of them to such persons, on such terms and conditions and at such times as they may consider to be in the best interests of the company and its shareholders, but so that no share shall be issued at a discount and so that, in the case of shares offered to the public for subscription by a public limited company, the amount payable on application on each share shall not be less than one-quarter of the nominal amount of the share and the whole of any premium thereon.] [a]

Amendments

a Substituted by C(A)A 1983, Sch 1 para 24.

Notes

This regulation is necessitated by the provisions of C(A)A 1983, s 20. The actual power of allotment conferred by this article is subject to the pre-emption provisions contained in C(A)A 1983, s 23. However, under s 24 of that Act it is possible to confer a power of allotment which excludes the pre-emption provisions.

The directors must exercise the power of allotment *bona fide* for the benefit of the company as a whole and for its proper purpose.[1] Where the power of allotment has been used for two or more purposes, the court will be concerned with whether the main or dominant purpose was proper.[2] It is improper for the directors to use the power of allotment to give themselves control of the company.[3] Furthermore, an allotment of shares for the purpose of reducing a member's stake in the company may be oppressive within the meaning of CA 1963, s 205.[4] It may also be improper to use the power of allotment to fend off a take-over bid.[5]

1 *Nash v Lancegaye Safety Glass (Ireland) Ltd* (1958) 92 ILTR 11; *Bamford v Bamford* [1969] 2 WLR 1107.

2 *Howard Smith Ltd v Ampol Petroleum Ltd* [1974] AC 821; *Mills v Mills* (1938) 60 CLR 150; *Harlowe's Nominees Pty Ltd v Woodside (Lakes Entrance) Oil Co NL* [1968] 121 CLR 483; *Teck Corporation v Millar* (1972) 33 DLR (3d) 288.

3 *Nash v Lancegaye Safety Glass (Ireland) Ltd* (1958) 92 ILTR 11; *Hogg v Cramphorn Ltd* [1967] Ch 254.

4 *Clemens v Clemens Bros Ltd* [1976] 2 All ER 268.

5 *Hogg v Cramphorn Ltd* [1967] Ch 254; *Howard Smith Ltd v Ampol Petroleum Ltd* [1974] AC 821. cf *Teck Corporations Ltd v Millar* (1972) 33 DLR (3d) 288.

---

6. The company may exercise the powers of paying commissions conferred by section 59 of the Act, provided that the rate per cent. and the amount of the commission paid or agreed to be paid shall be disclosed in the manner required by that section, and the rate of the commission shall not exceed the rate of 10 per cent. of the price at which the shares in respect whereof the same is paid are issued or an amount equal to 10 per cent. of such price (as the case may be). Such commission may be satisfied by the payment of cash or the allotment of fully or partly paid shares or partly in one way and partly in the other. The company may also, on any issue of shares, pay such brokerage as may be lawful.

Definitions

'the Act': CA 1963, Sch 1 para 1; 'company': CA 1963, s 2(1); 'share': CA 1963, s 2(1).

---

7. Except as required by law, no person shall be recognised by the company as holding any share upon any trust, and the company shall not be bound by or be compelled in any way to recognise (even when having notice thereof) any equitable, contingent, future or partial interest in any share or any interest in any fractional part of a share or (except only as by these regulations or by law otherwise provided) any other rights in respect of any share except an absolute right to the entirety thereof in the registered holder: this shall not preclude the company from requiring the members or a transferee of shares to furnish the company with information as to the beneficial ownership of any share when such information is reasonably required by the company.

Definitions

'company': CA 1963, s 2(1); 'share': CA 1963, s 2(1).

Notes

Regulation 7 reflects the statutory provisions of CA 1963, s 123, which prohibits the notice of any trust being entered on the register of members or receivable by the Registrar of Companies. Where notice of a trust is sent to a company it has been held that the company is under no obligation to record it anywhere,[1] although it has been held in Ireland that reg 7 does not entitle the company to ignore beneficial interests of which it has notice.[2]

[1] *Societe Generale de Paris v Tramways Union Co Ltd* (1884) 14 QBD 424 and (1885) 11 App Cas 20 HL.

[2] *Rearden v Provincial Bank of Ireland* [1896] 1 IR 532.

[**8**. Every person whose name is entered as a member in the register shall be entitled without payment to receive within 2 months after allotment or lodgement of a transfer (or within such other period as the conditions of issue shall provide) one certificate for all his shares or several certificates each for one or more of his shares upon payment of [16 cent][b] for every certificate after the first or such less sum as the directors shall from time to time determine, so, however, that in respect of a share or shares held jointly by several persons the company shall not be bound to issue more than one certificate, and delivery of a certificate for a share to one of several joint holders shall be sufficient delivery to all such holders. Every certificate shall be under the seal or under the official seal kept by the company by virtue of section 3 of the Companies (Amendment) Act, 1977, and shall specify the shares to which it relates and the amount paid up thereon.][a]

Amendments

a Reg 8 substituted by C(A)A 1977, s 5.

b '12½ new pence' converted to 16 cent by Council Regulations (EC) No 1103/97, No 974/98 and No 2866/98 and the Economic and Monetary Union Act 1998, s 6.

Definitions

'company': CA 1963, s 2(1); 'director': CA 1963, s 2(1), Sch 1, reg 1; 'member': CA 1963, s 31; 'register': CA 1963, Sch 1 para 1; 'share': CA 1963, s 2(1).

Notes

Regulation 8 applies only in the case of public companies, not private companies.

9. If a share certificate be defaced, lost or destroyed, it may be renewed on payment of [27 cent][a] or such less sum and on such terms (if any) as to evidence and indemnity and the payment of out-of-pocket expenses of the company of investigating evidence as the directors think fit.

Amendment

a '2s. 6d.' converted to 27 cent by Council Regulations (EC) No 1103/97, No 974/98 and No 2866/98 and the Economic and Monetary Union Act 1998, s 6.

Definitions

'company': CA 1963, s 2(1); 'director': CA 1963, s 2(1), Sch 1, reg 1; 'share': CA 1963, s 2(1).

10. The company shall not give, whether directly or indirectly, and whether by means of a loan, guarantee, the provision of security or otherwise, any financial assistance for the purpose of or in connection with a purchase or subscription made or to be made by any person of or for any shares in the company or in its holding company, but this regulation shall not prohibit any transaction permitted by section 60 of the Act.

Definitions

'Act': 1963, Sch 1, reg 1; 'company': CA 1963, s 2(1); 'share': CA 1963, s 2(1).

Lien

11. The company shall have a first and paramount lien on every share (not being a fully paid share) called or payable at a fixed time in respect of that share [...][a] but the directors may at any time declare any share to be wholly or in part exempt from the provisions of this regulation. The company's lien on a share shall extend to all dividends payable thereon.

Amendments

a Words deleted by C(A)A 1963, Sch 3.

Definitions

'company': CA 1963, s 2(1); 'director': CA 1963, s 2(1), Sch 1, reg 1; 'share': CA 1963, s 2(1).

Notes

Regulation 11 only gives a company a lien in respect of partly paid shares and only extends to moneys owed in respect of those shares, not to moneys owed generally by the shareholder to the company.[1]

1 *Re Dunlop* (1882) 21 Ch D 583.

12. The company may sell, in such manner as the directors think fit, any shares on which the company has a lien, but no sale shall be made unless a sum in respect of which the lien exists is immediately payable, nor until the expiration of 14 days after a notice in writing, stating and demanding payment of such part of the amount in respect of which the lien exists as is immediately payable, has been given to the registered holder for the time being of the share, or the person entitled thereto by reason of his death or bankruptcy.

Definitions

'company': CA 1963, s 2(1); 'director': CA 1963, s 2(1), Sch 1, reg 1; 'share': CA 1963, s 2(1).

13. To give effect to any such sale, the directors may authorise some person to transfer the shares sold to the purchaser thereof. The purchaser shall be registered as the holder of the shares comprised in any such transfer, and he shall not be bound to see to the application of the purchase money, nor shall his title to the shares be affected by any irregularity or invalidity in the proceedings in reference to the sale.

Definitions

'director': CA 1963, s 2(1), Sch 1, reg 1; 'share': CA 1963, s 2(1).

14. The proceeds of the sale shall be received by the company and applied in payment of such part of the amount in respect of which the lien exists as is immediately payable, and the residue, if any, shall (subject to a like lien for sums not immediately payable as existed upon the shares before the sale) be paid to the person entitled to the shares at the date of the sale.

Definitions

'company': CA 1963, s 2(1); 'share': CA 1963, s 2(1).

Calls on Shares

15. The directors may from time to time make calls upon the members in respect of any moneys unpaid on their shares (whether on account of the nominal value of the shares or by way of premium) and not by the conditions of allotment thereof made payable at fixed times, provided that no call shall exceed one-fourth of the nominal value of the share or be payable at less than one month from the date fixed for the payment of the last preceding call, and each member shall (subject to receiving at least 14 days' notice specifying the time or times and place of payment) pay to the company at the time or times and place so specified the amount called on his shares. A call may be revoked or postponed as the directors may determine.

Definitions

'director': CA 1963, s 2(1), Sch 1, reg 1; 'member': CA 1963, s 31; 'share': CA 1963, s 2(1).

Notes

Regulation 12 gives the directors power to make calls on members in respect of moneys unpaid on their shares. As with all directors' powers, this power must be exercised *bona fide* and in the interests of the company.[1] In the absence of evidence of bad faith in exercising this power, the courts will generally not investigate the circumstances giving rise to the making of a call.[2] In order for a call to be valid, the precise requirements of the regulation must be complied with.[3]

1 *Nash v Lancegaye Safety Glass (Ireland) Ltd* (1958) 92 ILTR 11; *Bamford v Bamford* [1969] 2 WLR 1107.

2 *Odessa Tramways Co v Mendel* (1878) 8 Ch D 235.

3 *Re Cawley & Co* (1889) 42 Ch D 209.

16. A call shall be deemed to have been made at the time when the resolution of the directors authorising the call was passed and may be required to be paid by instalments.

Definitions

'director': CA 1963, s 2(1), Sch 1, reg 1.

17. The joint holders of a share shall be jointly and severally liable to pay all calls in respect thereof.

Definitions

'share': CA 1963, s 2(1).

18. If a sum called in respect of a share is not paid before or on the day appointed for payment thereof, the person from whom the sum is due shall pay interest on the sum from the day appointed for payment thereof to the time of actual payment at such rate, not exceeding 5 per cent. per annum, as the directors may determine, but the directors shall be at liberty to waive payment of such interest wholly or in part.

Definitions

'director': CA 1963, s 2(1), Sch 1, reg 1; 'share': CA 1963, s 2(1).

Notes

Interest cannot be claimed from the date of the call, only from the date that payment falls due.[1]

1 *Johnson v Lyttle's Iron Agency* (1877) 5 Ch D 687.

19. Any sum which by the terms of issue of a share becomes payable on allotment or at any fixed date, whether on account of the nominal value of the share or by way of premium, shall, for the purposes of these regulations, be deemed to be a call duly made and payable on the date on which, by the terms of issue, the same becomes payable, and in case of non-payment all the relevant provisions of these regulations as to payment of interest and expenses, forfeiture or otherwise, shall apply as if such sum had become payable by virtue of a call duly made and notified.

Definitions

'share': CA 1963, s 2(1).

20. The directors may, on the issue of shares, differentiate between the holders as to the amount of calls to be paid and the time of payment.

Definitions

'share': CA 1963, s 2(1).

Notes

Despite the provisions of reg 20, calls should normally be made *pari passu* on all shareholders, so that special grounds will be required to justify a departure from this principle.[1]

1 *Galloway v Halle Concerts Society Ltd* [1915] 2 Ch 233; *Alexander v Automatic Telephone Co* [1900] 2 Ch 56.

21. The directors may, if they think fit, receive from any member willing to advance the same, all or any part of the moneys uncalled and unpaid upon any shares held by him, and upon all or any of the moneys so advanced may (until the same would, but for such advance, become payable) pay interest at such rate not exceeding (unless the company in general meeting otherwise directs) 5 per cent. per annum, as may be agreed upon between the directors and the member paying such sum in advance.

Definitions

'company': CA 1963, s 2(1); 'director': CA 1963, s 2(1), Sch 1 para 1; 'member': CA 1963, s 31; 'share': CA 1963, s 2(1).

Notes

This power must be exercised by the directors bona fide for the benefit of the company as a whole and for its proper purpose. For example, in the case of an insolvent company, the directors should not seek payment of uncalled capital in advance for the purpose of paying their own fees.[1]

1 *Syke's Case* (1872) LR 13 Eq 255.

Transfer of Shares

22. The instrument of transfer of any share shall be executed by or on behalf of the transferor and transferee, and the transferor shall be deemed to remain the holder of the share until the name of the transferee is entered in the register in respect thereof.

Definitions

'share': CA 1963, s 2(1); 'register': CA 1963, Sch 1, reg 1.

Notes

Pending registration of the transfer, the transferor holds the shares as nominee or trustee for the transferee and is entitled to be indemnified by the transferee against any liability in respect of the shares.[1] Regulation 22 envisages the execution of the instrument of transfer by or on behalf of both the transferor and transferee. However, under the STA 1963, an instrument of transfer is provided for, which is signed by the transferor alone. The provisions of the STA 1963 apply, however, only to fully paid shares.

1 *Casey v Bentley* [1902] 1 IR 376; *Musselwhite v CH Musselwhite & Son Ltd* [1962] Ch 964; *Tett v Phoenix Property Co* [1984] BCLC 599; *Hawks v McArthur* [1951] 1 All ER 22.

23. Subject to such of the restrictions of these regulations as may be applicable, any member may transfer all or any of his shares by instrument in writing in any usual or common form or any other form which the directors may approve.

Definitions

'director': CA 1963, s 2(1), Sch 1, reg 1; 'member': CA 1963, s 31; 'share': CA 1963, s 2(1).

Notes

In the case of fully paid shares, the instrument of transfer may be in the form prescribed by the STA 1963. Note that CA 1963, s 81 requires the transfer to be by instrument. However, CA 1990, s 239 empowers the Minister to make provision by regulations for enabling title to securities to be evidenced and transferred without a written instrument.

24. The directors may decline to register the transfer of a share (not being a fully paid share) to a person of whom they do not approve, and they may also decline to register the transfer of a share on which the company has a lien. The directors may also decline to register any transfer of a share which, in their opinion, may imperil or prejudicially affect the status of the company in the State or which may imperil any tax concession or rebate to which the members of the company are entitled or which may involve the company in the payment of any additional stamp or other duties on any conveyance of any property made or to be made to the company.

Definitions

'company': CA 1963, s 2(1); 'director': CA 1963, s 2(1), Sch 1, reg 1; 'member': CA 1963, s 31; 'share': CA 1963, s 2(1).

Notes

Regulation 24 applies only in the case of public companies not private companies.[1] The power of the directors to decline to register the transfer of a share must be exercised *bona fide* in the interests of the company as a whole and for the proper purposes.[2] Since registration may only be declined on specific grounds, the court can enquire as to whether the directors did in fact decline on one of the grounds prescribed.[3]

1 CA 1963, Sch 1, Pt II, reg 1.

2 *Re Dublin North City Milling Co* [1909] 1 IR 179; *Re Smith & Fawcett Ltd* [1942] Ch 304; *Re Hafner* [1943] IR 426.

3 *Re Bede Shipping Co Ltd* [1917] 1 Ch 123.

25. The directors may also decline to recognise any instrument of transfer unless—

(a) a fee of 2s. 6d. or such lesser sum as the directors may from time to time require, is paid to the company in respect thereof; and

(b) the instrument of transfer is accompanied by the certificate of the shares to which it relates, and such other evidence as the directors may reasonably require to show the right of the transferor to make the transfer; and

(c) the instrument of transfer is in respect of one class of share only.

Definitions

'company': CA 1963, s 2(1); 'director': CA 1963, s 2(1), Sch 1, reg 1; 'share': CA 1963, s 2(1).

26. If the directors refuse to register a transfer they shall, within 2 months after the date on which the transfer was lodged with the company, send to the transferee notice of the refusal.

Definitions

'company': CA 1963, s 2(1); 'director': CA 1963, s 2(1), Sch 1, reg 1.

Notes

The power to decline to register the transfer of a share will lapse if not exercised within the two-month period.[1]

1 *Re Hackney Pavilion Ltd* [1924] 1 Ch 276; *Moodie v W & J Shepherd (Bookbinders) Ltd* [1949] 2 All ER 1044; *Re Swaledale Cleaners Ltd* [1968] 1 WLR 1710; *Tett v Phoenix Property Co* [1984] BCLC 599.

---

27. The registration of transfers may be suspended at such times and for such periods, not exceeding in the whole 30 days in each year, as the directors may from time to time determine.

Definitions

'director': CA 1963, s 2(1), Sch 1, reg 1.

Notes

Typically, the register of members will be closed for the notice period prior to and for the date of the company's annual general meeting.

---

28. The company shall be entitled to charge a fee not exceeding [27 cent][a] on the registration of every probate, letters of administration, certificate of death or marriage, power of attorney, notice as to stock or other instrument.

Amendment

a '2s. 6d.' converted to 27 cent by Council Regulations (EC) No 1103/97, No 974/98 and No 2866/98 and the Economic and Monetary Union Act 1998, s 6.

Definitions

'company': CA 1963, s 2(1).

Transmission of Shares

29. In the case of the death of a member, the survivor or survivors where the deceased was a joint holder, and the personal representatives of the deceased where he was a sole holder, shall be the only persons recognised by the company as having any title to his interest in the shares; but nothing herein contained shall release the estate of a deceased joint holder from any liability in respect of any share which had been jointly held by him with other persons.

Definitions

'company': CA 1963, s 2(1); 'member': CA 1963, s 31; 'share': CA 1963, s 2(1).

Notes

Although a deceased member's personal representatives are the only persons entitled to be recognised by the company as having any title to a deceased member's interest in shares, unless a personal representative is registered as a member, he or she will not become personally liable on the deceased member's shares or personally entitled to any benefit accruing[1] such as the right to vote.[2] A deceased member's estate will remain entitled to the member's rights and subject to any obligations on the member until such time as the new member is registered.[3] Pending registration, a personal representative will have rights indicative of his fiduciary position.[4]

1 *Buchan's Case* (1879) App Cas 549.
2 *Arulchelvan v Wright* (7 February 1996, unreported) HC (Carroll J).
3 *James v Buena Ventura Nitrate Grounds Syndicate* [1896] 1 Ch 456.
4 *Gabbett v Lawder* (1883) 11 LR Ir 295.

30. Any person becoming entitled to a share in consequence of the death or bankruptcy of a member may, upon such evidence being produced as may from time to time properly be required by the directors and subject as hereinafter provided, elect either to be registered himself as holder of the share or to have some person nominated by him registered as the transferee thereof, but the directors shall, in either case, have the same right to decline or suspend registration as they would have had in the case of a transfer of the share by that member before his death or bankruptcy, as the case may be.

Definitions

'director': CA 1963, s 2(1), Sch 1, reg 1; 'member': CA 1963, s 31; 'share': CA 1963, s 2(1).

Notes

For the power to decline to register the transmission of the share, see reg 24 or, in the case of a private company that adopts Part II, reg 3 of Part II. In the absence of such a provision, however, the person taking by transmission has an unrestricted right to be registered in respect of the share.[1] A personal representative is not in a more privileged position than an ordinary transferor.[2]

1 *Safeguard Industrial Investments Ltd v National Westminster Bank Ltd* [1982] 1 All ER 449; *Re Ray-Ger Ltd* (28 April 1983, unreported) HC (Costello J).
2 *Village Cay Marine Ltd v Acland (Barclays Bank plc third party)* [1998] 2 BCLC 327.

31. If the person so becoming entitled elects to be registered himself, he shall deliver or send to the company a notice in writing signed by him stating that he so elects. If he elects to have another person registered, he shall testify his election by executing to that person a transfer of the share. All the limitations, restrictions and provisions of these regulations relating to the right to transfer and the registration of transfers of shares shall be applicable to any such notice or transfer as aforesaid as if the death or bankruptcy of the member had not occurred and the notice or transfer were a transfer signed by that member.

Definitions

'company': CA 1963, s 2(1); 'member': CA 1963, s 31; 'share': CA 1963, s 2(1).

32. A person becoming entitled to a share by reason of the death or bankruptcy of the holder shall be entitled to the same dividends and other advantages to which he would be entitled if he were the registered holder of the share, except that he shall not, before being registered as a member in respect of the share, be entitled in respect of it to exercise any right conferred by membership in relation to meetings of the company, so, however, that the directors may at any time give notice requiring any such person to elect either to be registered himself or to transfer the share, and if the notice is not complied with within 90 days, the directors may thereupon withhold payment of all dividends, bonuses or other moneys payable in respect of the share until the requirements of the notice have been complied with.

Definitions

'company': CA 1963, s 2(1); 'director': CA 1963, s 2(1), Sch 1, reg 1; 'member': CA 1963, s 31; 'share': CA 1963, s 2(1).

Forfeiture of Shares

33. If a member fails to pay and call or instalment of a call on the day appointed for payment thereof, the directors may, at any time thereafter during such time as any part of the call or instalment remains unpaid, serve a notice on him requiring payment of so much of the call or instalment as is unpaid together with any interest which may have accrued.

Definitions

'company': CA 1963, s 2(1); 'director': CA 1963, s 2(1), Sch 1, reg 1.

34. The notice shall name a further day (not earlier than the expiration of 14 days from the date of service of the notice) on or before which the payment required by the notice is to be made, and shall state that in the event of non-payment at or before the time appointed the shares in respect of which the call was made will be liable to be forfeited.

Definitions

'share': CA 1963, s 2(1).

35. If the requirements of any such notice as aforesaid are not complied with, any share in respect of which the notice has been given may at any time thereafter, before the payment required by the notice has been made, be forfeited by a resolution of the directors to that effect.

Definitions

'director': CA 1963, s 2(1), Sch 1, reg 1; 'share': CA 1963, s 2(1).

36. A forfeited share may be sold or otherwise disposed of on such terms and in such manner as the directors think fit, and at any time before a sale or disposition the forfeiture may be cancelled on such terms as the directors think fit.

Definitions

'director': CA 1963, s 2(1), Sch 1, reg 1; 'share': CA 1963, s 2(1).

Notes

In the case of a plc, if the forfeited shares have not been disposed of by the company within three years from the date of forfeiture, they must be cancelled and the share capital of the company must be reduced accordingly: C(A)A 1983, s 43. Furthermore, if the cancellation of the shares brings the issued share capital of the plc below the 'authorised minimum', it must re-register as some other form of company: C(A)A 1983, s 43.

37. A person whose shares have been forfeited shall cease to be a member in respect of the forfeited shares, but shall, notwithstanding, remain liable to pay to the company all moneys which, at the date of forfeiture, were payable by him to the company in respect of the shares, but his liability shall cease if and when the company shall have received payment in full of all such moneys in respect of the shares.

Definitions

'company': CA 1963, s 2(1); 'share': CA 1963, s 2(1).

38. A statutory declaration that the declarant is a director or the secretary of the company, and that a share in the company has been duly forfeited on a date stated in the declaration, shall be conclusive evidence of the facts therein stated as against all persons claiming to be entitled to the share. The company may receive the consideration, if any, given for the share on any sale or disposition thereof and may execute a transfer of the share in favour of the person to whom the share is sold of disposed of and he shall thereupon be registered as the holder of the share, and shall not be bound to see to the application of the purchase money, if any, nor shall his title to the share be affected by any irregularity or invalidity in the proceedings in reference to the forfeiture, sale or disposal of the shares.

Definitions

'company': CA 1963, s 2(1); 'director': CA 1963, s 2(1), Sch 1, reg 1; ' secretary': CA 1963, s 2(1), Sch 1, reg 1; 'share': CA 1963, s 2(1).

39. The provisions of these regulations as to forfeiture shall apply in the case of non-payment of any sum which, by the terms of issue of a share, becomes payable at a fixed time, whether on account of the nominal value of the share or by way of premium, as if the same had been payable by virtue of a call duly made and notified.

Definitions

'share': CA 1963, s 2(1).

Conversion of Shares into Stock

40. The company may by ordinary resolution convert any paid up shares into stock, and reconvert any stock into paid up shares of any denomination.

Definitions

'company': CA 1963, s 2(1); 'share': CA 1963, s 2(1).

41. The holders of stock may transfer the same, or any part thereof, in the same manner, and subject to the same regulations, as and subject to which the shares from which the stock arose might previously to conversion have been transferred, or as near thereto as circumstances admit; and the directors may from time to time fix the minimum amount of stock transferable but so that such minimum shall not exceed the nominal amount of each share from which the stock arose.

Definitions

'share': CA 1963, s 2(1).

42. The holders of stock shall, according to the amount of stock held by them, have the same rights, privileges and advantages in relation to dividends, voting at meetings of the company and other matters as if they held the shares from which the stock arose, but no such right, privilege or advantage (except participation in the dividends and profits of the company and in the assets on winding up) shall be conferred by an amount of stock which would not, if existing in shares, have conferred that right, privilege or advantage.

Definitions

'company': CA 1963, s 2(1).

43. Such of the regulations of the company as are applicable to paid up shares shall apply to stock, and the words 'share' and 'shareholder' therein shall include 'stock' and 'stockholder'.

Definitions

'share': CA 1963, s 2(1).

Alteration of Capital

44. The company may from time to time by ordinary resolution increase the share capital by such sum, to be divided into shares of such amount, as the resolution shall prescribe.

Definitions

'company': CA 1963, s 2(1); 'share': CA 1963, s 2(1).

45. The company may by ordinary resolution—

(a) consolidate and divide all or any of its share capital into shares of larger amount than its existing shares;

(b) subdivide its existing shares, or any of them, into shares of smaller amount than is fixed by the memorandum of association subject, nevertheless, to section 68(1)(d) of the Act;

(c) cancel any shares which, at the date of the passing of the resolution, have not been taken or agreed to be taken by any person.

Definitions

'Act': CA 1963, Sch 1, reg 1; 'company': CA 1963, s 2(1); 'memorandum': CA 1963, s 2(1); 'share': CA 1963, s 2(1).

46. The company may by special resolution reduce its share capital, any capital redemption reserve fund or any share premium account in any manner and with and subject to any incident authorised, and consent required, by law.

Definitions

'company': CA 1963, s 2(1); 'share': CA 1963, s 2(1).

General Meetings

47. All general meetings of the company shall be held in the State.

Definitions

'company': CA 1963, s 2(1).

48. (1) Subject to paragraph (2) of this regulation, the company shall in each year hold a general meeting as its annual general meeting in addition to any other meeting in that year, and shall specify the meeting as such in the notices calling it; and not more than 15 months shall elapse between the date of one annual general meeting of the company and that of the next.

(2) So long as the company holds its first annual general meeting within 18 months of its incorporation, it need not hold it in the year of its incorporation or in the year following. Subject to regulation 47, the annual general meeting shall be held at such time and place as the directors shall appoint.

Definitions

'company': CA 1963, s 2(1).

49. All general meetings other than annual general meetings shall be called extraordinary general meetings.

50. The directors may, whenever they think fit, convene an extraordinary general meeting, and extraordinary general meetings shall also be convened on such requisition, or in default, may be convened by such requisitionists, as provided by section 132 of the Act. If at any time there are not within the State sufficient directors capable of acting to form a quorum, any director or any 2 members of the company may convene an extraordinary general meeting in the same manner as nearly as possible as that in which meetings may be convened by the directors.

Definitions

'Act': CA 1963, Sch 1, reg 1; 'company': CA 1963, s 2(1); 'director': CA 1963, s 2(1), Sch 1, reg 1; 'member': CA 1963, s 31.

Notes

Where there are no remaining directors and only one remaining member, it may be necessary to apply to the court pursuant to CA 1963, s 135 for an order convening the EGM and directing that the sole surviving member shall constitute the meeting on his own.

Notice of General Meetings

51. Subject to sections 133 and 141 of the Act, an annual general meeting and a meeting called for the passing of a special resolution shall be called by 21 days' notice in writing at the least, and a meeting of the company (other than an annual general meeting or a meeting for the passing of a special resolution) shall be called by 14 days' notice in writing at the least. The notice shall be exclusive of the day on which it is served or deemed to be served and of the day for which it is given, and shall specify the place, the day and the hour of the meeting, and in the case of special business, the general nature of that business, and shall be given, in manner hereinafter mentioned, to such persons as are, under the regulations of the company, entitled to receive such notices from the company.

Definitions

'Act': CA 1963, Sch 1, reg 1; 'company': CA 1963, s 2(1).

Notes

Regulation 51 applies only to public companies, not private companies. The notice of the meeting will be void, if it or any accompanying circular is misleading. Where it is proposed to pass a special resolution at the meeting, the notice will be invalid if it fails to specify either the entire text or the entire substance of the proposed resolution.[2]

1 *Jackson v Munster Bank Ltd* (1884–85) 13 LR Ir 118.

2 *Re Moorgate Mercantile Holdings Ltd* [1980] 1 WLR 227.

52. The accidental omission to give notice of a meeting to, or the non-receipt of notice of a meeting by, any person entitled to receive notice shall not invalidate the proceedings at the meeting.

Notes

Deliberate omission to give notice of a meeting to a person entitled to receive such notice, renders the meeting invalid.[1]

1 *Musselwhite v CH Musselwhite & Son Ltd* [1962] Ch 964.

Proceedings at General Meetings

53. All business shall be deemed special that is transacted at an extraordinary general meeting, and also all that is transacted at an annual general meeting, with the exception of declaring a dividend, the consideration of the accounts, balance sheets and the reports of the directors and auditors, the election of directors in the place of those retiring, the re-appointment of the retiring auditors and the fixing of the remuneration of the auditors.

Definitions

'director': CA 1963, s 2(1), Sch 1, reg 1.

Notes

The notice convening a meeting will be invalid if it fails to set out at least the general nature of the special business which is to be transacted thereat.[1]

1 *Roper v Ward* [1981] ILRM 408.

54. No business shall be transacted at any general meeting unless a quorum of members is present at the time when the meeting proceeds to business; save as herein otherwise provided, three members present in person shall be a quorum.

Definitions

'member': CA 1963, s 31.

Notes

Regulation 54 applies only to public companies, not private companies.

If a quorum is present at the beginning of a meeting, the subsequent departure of a member reducing the meeting below the number required for the quorum will not invalidate proceedings of the meeting after his departure.[1] However, if the number of members present falls to one, then there will no longer be a meeting.[2]

Where it is impracticable to obtain a quorum, it may be necessary to apply to the court pursuant to CA 1963, s 135 for an order convening the meeting and directing that one member present in person or by proxy shall constitute a meeting.

1 *Re Hartley Baird Ltd* [1955] Ch 143.

[2] *Re London Flats Ltd* [1969] 1 WLR 711; *Sharp v Dawes* (1876) 2 QBD 26; *Re El Sombrero Ltd* [1958] Ch 900.

55. If within half an hour from the time appointed for the meeting a quorum is not present, the meeting, if convened upon the requisition of members, shall be dissolved; in any other case it shall stand adjourned to the same day in the next week, at the same time and place or to such other day and at such other time and place as the directors may determine, and if at the adjourned meeting a quorum is not present within half an hour from the time appointed for the meeting, the members present shall be a quorum.

Definitions

'director': CA 1963, s 2(1), Sch 1, reg 1; 'member': CA 1963, s 31.

Notes

However, if there is only one member present, a meeting cannot exist.[1]

[1] *Re London Flats Ltd* [1969] 1 WLR 711; *Sharp v Dawes* (1876) 2 QBD 26; *Re El Sombrero Ltd* [1958] Ch 900.

56. The chairman, if any, of the board of directors shall preside as chairman at every general meeting of the company, or if there is no such chairman, or if he is not present within 15 minutes after the time appointed for the holding of the meeting or is unwilling to act, the directors present shall elect one of their number to be chairman of the meeting.

Definitions

'company': CA 1963, s 2(1); 'director': CA 1963, s 2(1), Sch 1, reg 1.

57. If at any meeting no director is willing to act as chairman or if no director is present within 15 minutes after the time appointed for holding the meeting, the members present shall choose one of their number to be chairman of the meeting.

Definitions

'director': CA 1963, s 2(1), Sch 1, reg 1; 'member': CA 1963, s 31.

58. The chairman may, with the consent of any meeting at which a quorum is present, and shall if so directed by the meeting, adjourn the meeting from time to time and from place to place, but no business shall be transacted at any adjourned meeting other than the business left unfinished at the meeting from which the adjournment took place. When a meeting is adjourned for 30 days or more, notice of the adjourned meeting shall be given as in the case of an original meeting. Save as aforesaid it shall not be necessary to give any notice of an adjournment or of the business to be transacted at an adjourned meeting.

59. At any general meeting a resolution put to the vote of the meeting shall be decided on a show of hands unless a poll is (before or on the declaration of the result of the show of hands) demanded—

(a) by the chairman; or

(b) by at least three members present in person or by proxy; or

(c) by any member or members present in person or by proxy and representing not less than one-tenth of the total voting rights of all the members having the right to vote at the meetings; or

(d) by a member or members holding shares in the company conferring the right to vote at the meeting being shares on which an aggregate sum has been paid up equal to not less than one-tenth of the total sum paid up on all the shares conferring that right.

Unless a poll is so demanded, a declaration by the chairman that a resolution has, on a show of hands, been carried or carried unanimously, or by a particular majority, or lost, and an entry to that effect in the book containing the minutes of the proceedings of the company shall be conclusive evidence of the fact without proof of the number or proportion of the votes recorded in favour of or against such resolution.

The demand for a poll may be withdrawn.

Definitions

'company': CA 1963, s 2(1); 'member': CA 1963, s 31; 'share': CA 1963, s 2(1).

60. Except as provided in regulation 62, if a poll is duly demanded it shall be taken in such manner as the chairman directs, and the result of the poll shall be deemed to be the resolution of the meeting at which the poll was demanded.

61. Where there is an equality of votes, whether on a show of hands or on a poll, the chairman of the meeting at which the show of hands takes place or at which the poll is demanded, shall be entitled to a second or casting vote.

Notes

Any resolution carried on the casting vote of an invalidly appointed chairman is itself invalid.[1]

1 *Clark v Workman* [1920] 1 IR 107.

62. A poll demanded on the election of a chairman or on a question of adjournment shall be taken forthwith. A poll demanded on any other question shall be taken at such time as the chairman of the meeting directs, and any business other than that on which a poll is demanded may be proceeded with pending the taking of the poll.

Votes of Members

63. Subject to any rights or restrictions for the time being attached to any class or classes of shares, on a show of hands every member present in person and every proxy shall have one vote, so, however, that no individual shall have more than one vote, and on a poll every member shall have one vote for each share of which he is the holder.

Definitions

'director': CA 1963, s 2(1), Sch 1, reg 1; 'member': CA 1963, s 31.

64. Where there are joint holders, the vote of the senior who tenders a vote, whether in person or by proxy, shall be accepted to the exclusion of the votes of the other joint holders; and for this purpose, seniority shall be determined by the order in which the names stand in the register.

65. A member of unsound mind, or in respect of whom an order has been made by any court having jurisdiction in lunacy, may vote, whether on a show of hands or on a poll, by his committee, receiver, guardian or other person appointed by that court, and any such committee, receiver, guardian or other person may vote by proxy on a show of hands or on a poll.

Definitions

'court': CA 1963, s 2(1); 'member': CA 1963, s 31.

66. No member shall be entitled to vote at any general meeting unless all calls or other sums immediately payable by him in respect of shares in the company have been paid.

Definitions

'company': CA 1963, s 2(1); 'member': CA 1963, s 31.

67. No objection shall be raised to the qualification of any voter except at the meeting or adjourned meeting at which the vote objected to is given or tendered, and every vote not disallowed at such meeting shall be valid for all purposes. Any such objection made in due time shall be referred to the chairman of the meeting, whose decision shall be final and conclusive.

68. Votes may be given either personally or by proxy.

Cross reference

In relation to proxies generally, see CA 1963, s 136.

69. The instrument appointing a proxy shall be in writing under the hand of the appointer or of his attorney duly authorised in writing, or, if the appointer is a body corporate, either under seal or under the hand of an officer or attorney duly authorised. A proxy need not be a member of the company.

Definitions

'seal': CA 1963, Sch 1, reg 1.

70. The instrument appointing a proxy and the power of attorney or other authority, if any, under which it is signed, or a notarially certified copy of that power or authority shall be deposited at the office or at such other place within the State as is specified for that purpose in the notice convening the meeting, not less than 48 hours before the time for holding the meeting or adjourned meeting at which the person named in the instrument proposes to vote, or, in the case of a poll, not less than 48 hours before the time appointed for the taking of the poll, and, in default, the instrument of proxy shall not be treated as valid.

71. An instrument appointing a proxy shall be in the following form or a form as near thereto as circumstances permit—

'Limited.

I/We of ....

in the Country of.., being a

member/members of the above-named company hereby appoint ....

....

....

of..

or failing him, ...

of..

as my/our proxy to vote for me/us on my/our behalf at the (annual or extraordinary, as the case may be) general meeting of the company to be held on the .... day of ...., 19.............. and at any adjournment thereof.

Signed this.................day of............................, 19.......

This form is to be used *in favour/against the resolution.

Unless otherwise instructed the proxy will vote as he thinks fit.

*Strike out whichever is not desired.'

72. The instrument appointing a proxy shall be deemed to confer authority to demand or join in demanding a poll.

73. A vote given in accordance with the terms of an instrument of proxy shall be valid notwithstanding the previous death or insanity of the principal or revocation of the proxy or of the authority under which the proxy was executed or the transfer of the share in respect of which the proxy is given, if not intimation in writing of such death, insanity, revocation or transfer as aforesaid is received by the company at the office before the commencement of the meeting or adjourned meeting at which the proxy is used.

Definitions

'company': CA 1963, s 2(1); 'share': CA 1963, s 2(1).

Bodies Corporate acting by Representatives at Meetings

74. Any body corporate which is a member of the company may, by resolution of its directors or other governing body, authorise such person as it thinks fit to act as its representative at any meeting of the company or of any class of members of the company, and the person so authorised shall be entitled to exercise the same powers on behalf of the body corporate which he represents as that body corporate could exercise if it were an individual member of the company.

Definitions

'company': CA 1963, s 2(1); 'director': CA 1963, s 2(1), Sch 1, reg 1; 'member': CA 1963, s 31.

Directors

75. The number of the directors and the names of the first directors shall be determined in writing by the subscribers of the memorandum of association or a majority of them.

Definitions

'director': CA 1963, s 2(1), Sch 1, reg 1; 'memorandum': CA 1963, s 2(1).

76. The remuneration of the directors shall from time to time be determined by the company in general meeting. Such remuneration shall be deemed to accrue from day to day. The directors may also be paid all travelling, hotel and other expenses properly incurred by them in attending and returning from meetings of the directors or any committee of the directors or general meetings of the company or in connection with the business of the company.

Definitions

'company': CA 1963, s 2(1); 'director': CA 1963, s 2(1), Sch 1, reg 1.

Notes

If the company in general meeting fails or refuses to determine the remuneration of the directors, they do not have any implied right to be paid for the performance of their function and have no claim to payment on a *quantum meruit*. [1] Accordingly, they may be compelled to return any sums they have paid to themselves without the necessary authority, even if they acted *bona fide* in the belief that the payments were permissible. [2] The company in general meeting cannot retrospectively alter the directors' right to payment of accrued remuneration. [3] Where the company in general meeting has determined the remuneration of the board, but the appointment of one of the directors is defective, he may nonetheless be entitled to payment on a *quantum meruit* for services performed. [4] If the company is insolvent and determines the remuneration of the directors at a level which is excessive in the circumstances, the court may be entitled to reclassify the payment as an unlawful gift out of capital. [5] It should be noted that any remuneration paid to the directors under reg 76 is distinct from any payable to them as employees pursuant to any service contracts they may have with the company.

1. *Hutton v West Cork Rly Co* (1883) 23 Ch D 654; *Dunston v The Imperial Gas, Light & Coke Co* (1832) 3 B & Ad 125; *Woolf v East Niger Gold Mining Co Ltd* [1905] 21 TLR 660; *Guinness plc v Saunders* [1990] 2 WLR 324.
2. *Brown and Green Ltd v Harp* (1920) 36 TLR 330; *Guinness plc v Saunders* [1990] 2 WLR 324.
3. *Swabey v Port Darwin Gold Mining Co* (1889) 1 Meg 385.

[4] *Craven-Ellis v Canons Ltd* [1936] 2 KB 403.

[5] *Re Halt Garage (1964) Ltd* [1982] 3 All ER 1016.

77. The shareholding qualification for directors may be fixed by the company in general meeting and unless and until so fixed, no qualification shall be required.

Definitions

'director': CA 1963, s 2(1), Sch 1, reg 1.

78. A director of the company may be or become a director or other officer of, or otherwise interested in, any company promoted by the company or in which the company may be interested as shareholder or otherwise, and no such director shall be accountable to the company for any remuneration or other benefits received by him as a director or officer of, or from his interest in, such other company unless the company otherwise directs.

Definitions

'company': CA 1963, s 2(1); 'director': CA 1963, s 2(1), Sch 1, reg 1; 'officer': CA 1963, s 2(1).

Notes

This provision appears to reverse the decision in *Regal (Hastings) Ltd v Gulliver* [1942] 1 All ER 378.

Borrowing Powers

79. The directors may exercise all powers of the company to borrow money, and to mortgage or charge its undertaking, property and uncalled capital, or any part thereof, and [subject to section 20 of the Companies (Amendment) Act, 1983][a] to issue debentures, debenture stock and other securities, whether outright or as security for any debt, liability or obligation of the company or of any third party, so, however, that the amount for the time being remaining undischarged of moneys borrowed or secured by the directors as aforesaid (apart from temporary loans obtained from the company's bankers in the ordinary course of business) shall not at any time, without the previous sanction of the company in general meeting, exceed the nominal amount of the share capital of the company for the time being issued, but nevertheless no lender or other person dealing with the company shall be concerned to see or inquire whether this limit is observed. No debt incurred or security given in excess of such limit shall be invalid or ineffectual except in the case of express notice to the lender or the recipient of the security at the time when the debt was incurred or security given that the limit hereby imposed had been or was thereby exceeded.

Amendments

a Inserted by C(A)A 1983, Sch 1 para 24.

Definitions

'company': CA 1963, s 2(1); 'debenture': CA 1963, s 2(1); 'director': CA 1963, s 2(1), Sch 1, reg 1.

Powers and Duties of Directors

80. The business of the company shall be managed by the directors, who may pay all expenses incurred in promoting and registering the company and may exercise all such powers of the company as are not, by [the Companies Acts, 1963 to 1983][a] or by these regulations, required to be exercised by the company in general meeting, subject, nevertheless, to any of these regulations, to the provisions of the Act and to such directions, being not inconsistent with the aforesaid regulations or provisions, as may be given by the company in general meeting; but no direction given by the company in general meeting shall invalidate any prior act of the directors which would have been valid if that direction had not been given.

Amendments

a Substituted by C(A)A 1983, Sch 1 para 24.

Definitions

'Act': CA 1963, Sch 1, reg 1; 'company': CA 1963, s 2(1); 'director': CA 1963, s 2(1), Sch 1, reg 1.

Notes

Under the precursor to reg 80 (ie reg 71 of the Companies (Consolidation) Act 1908) and under the former English equivalent (ie reg 70 of Table A of the Companies Act 1948) it had been held that the members, having delegated the powers of management of the company to the board of directors, could only interfere by way of special resolution.[1] This position has now been expressly entrenched in England by the updated version of reg 80 (ie reg 70 of Table A of the Companies (Tables A to F) Regulations 1985 (SI 1985/805). The wording of reg 80 is, however, slightly different to the equivalent provisions in the 1908 and 1948 Acts. Whereas reg 80 refers to 'directions' of the general meeting, the other provisions referred to 'regulations'. The 'directions' must be taken to mean 'ordinary resolutions' of the company in general meeting.[2] Thus, in most aspects of the management of the business of the company, the members may interfere by way of ordinary resolution. In the case of a specific power conferred on the directors by some other article (eg the power to elect the chairman under reg 104), the members may only interfere by way of special resolution.[3] Furthermore, if a specific power has been conferred on the directors by statute, the members cannot interfere (whether by ordinary or special resolution) since they have no authority to circumvent legislative provisions.[4]

1 *John Shaw & Sons (Salford) Ltd v Shaw* [1935] 2 KB 113; *Automatic Self-Cleansing Filter Syndicate Co v Cunninghame* [1906] 2 Ch 34; *Salmon v Quinn & Axtens Ltd* [1909] 1 Ch 311; *Breckland Group Holdings Ltd v London & Suffolk Property Ltd* [1989] BCLC 100; *Nash v Lancegaye Safety Glass (Ireland) Ltd* (1958) 92 ILTR 11; *Clark v Workman* [1920] 1 IR 107.

2 See *J Temple Lang* (1973) Gazette 241, and Ussher, *Company Law In Ireland* (Butterworths, 1986), p 87.

3 *Clark v Workman* [1920] 1 IR 107; *Kehoe v Waterford and Limerick Railways* (1888–89) 21 LR Ir 221.

4 See, generally, Courtney, *The Law of Private Companies* (2nd edn, Tottel Publishing, 2002), para 8.004 et seq.

81. The directors may from time to time and at any time by power of attorney appoint any company, firm or person or body of persons, whether nominated directly or indirectly by the directors, to be the attorney or attorneys of the company for such purposes and with such powers, authorities and discretions (not exceeding those vested in or exercisable by the directors under these regulations) and for such period and subject to such conditions as they may think fit, and any such power of attorney may contain such provisions for the protection of persons dealing with any such attorney as the directors may think fit, and may also authorise any such attorney to delegate all or any of the powers, authorities and discretions vested in him.

Definitions

'company': CA 1963, s 2(1); 'director': CA 1963, s 2(1), Sch 1, reg 1.

Notes

It is usual practice for debentures secured by a fixed and/or floating charge over the company's property to contain a provision giving any receiver appointed by the debenture holder a power of attorney to act in the name of and on behalf of the company.[1]

1 See *Industrial development Authority v Moran* [1978] IR 159.

82. The company may exercise the powers conferred by section 41 of the Act with regard to having an official seal for use abroad, and such powers shall be vested in the directors.

Definitions

'Act': CA 1963, Sch 1, reg 1; 'company': CA 1963, s 2(1); 'seal': CA 1963, Sch 1, reg 1.

83. A director who is in any way, whether directly or indirectly, interested in a contract or proposed contract with the company shall declare the nature of his interest at a meeting of the directors in accordance with section 194 of the Act.

Definitions

'Act': CA 1963, Sch 1, reg 1; 'company': CA 1963, s 2(1); 'director': CA 1963, s 2(1), Sch 1, reg 1.

Notes

Failure to make the necessary disclosure to the board under s 194 will result in the director losing the benefit of reg 85.[1]

1 *Hely-Hutchinson v Brayhead Ltd* [1967] 3 All ER 98; *Movitex Ltd v Bulfield* [1988] BCLC 104; *Guinness plc v Saunders* [1988] 2 All ER 940 aff'd [1990] 1 All ER 652; *Hopkins v Shannon Transport Ltd* (10 July 1972) HC (Pringle J).

84. A director shall not vote in respect of any contract or arrangement in which he is so interested, and if he shall so vote, his vote shall not be counted, nor shall he be counted in the quorum present at the meeting but neither of these prohibitions shall apply to—

(a) any arrangement for giving any director any security or indemnity in respect of money lent by him to or obligations undertaken by him for the benefit of the company; or

(b) any arrangement for the giving by the company of any security to a third party in respect of a debt or obligation of the company for which the director himself has assumed responsibility in whole or in part under a guarantee or indemnity or by the deposit of security; or

(c) any contract by a director to subscribe for or underwrite shares or debenture of the company; or

(d) any contract or arrangement with any other company in which he is interested only as an officer of such other company or as a holder of shares or other securities in such other company;

and these prohibitions may at any time be suspended or relaxed to any extent and either generally or in respect of any particular contract, arrangement or transaction by the company in general meeting.

Definitions

'company': CA 1963, s 2(1); 'director': CA 1963, s 2(1), Sch 1, reg 1; 'officer': CA 1963, s 2(1); 'share': CA 1963, s 2(1).

Notes

Regulation 84 applies only in the case of public companies, not private companies. This provision reverses the decision in *Cox v Dublin City Distillery Ltd (No 2)* [1915] 1 IR 345. The quorum must be looked at separately for each item of business transacted in which any director has an interest, and one transaction in which two or more directors are interested cannot be artificially split into several transactions, so as to create the necessary quorum.[1]

1 *North Eastern Insurance Co Ltd* [1919] 1 Ch 198.

85. A director may hold any other office or place of profit under the company (other than the office of auditor) in conjunction with his office of director for such period and on such terms as to remuneration and otherwise as the directors may determine, and no director or intending director shall be disqualified by his office from contracting with the company either with regard to his tenure of any such other office or place of profit or as vendor, purchaser or otherwise, nor shall any such contract or any contract or arrangement entered into by or on behalf of the company in which any director is in any way interested, be liable to be avoided, nor shall any director so contracting or being so interested be liable to account to the company for any profit realised by any such contract or arrangement by reason of such director holding that office or of the fiduciary relation thereby established.

Notes

In so far as reg 85 applies, it reverses the decision in *Aberdeen Railway Co v Blaikie Bros* (1854) 1 Macq 461. The benefit of this article is dependent, however, on disclosure under CA 1963, s 194.[1] If the benefit of reg 85 has been lost through failure to make disclosure to the board under s 194, the contract becomes voidable at the instance of the company, and the director will be liable to account for any profit made as well as being liable in damages for breach of fiduciary duty.[2] Where the contract is voidable, it may nonetheless be ratified and the breach of duty may be forgiven by the company in general meeting.[3] Furthermore, the director may, in his capacity as member, vote in favour of ratification, unless to do so would amount to a fraud on the minority.[4]

1 *Hely-Hutchinson v Brayhead Ltd* [1967] 3 All ER 98; *Movitex Ltd v Bulfield* [1988] BCLC 104; *Guinness plc v Saunders* [1988] 2 All ER 940 aff'd [1990] 1 All ER 652; *Hopkins v Shannon Transport Ltd* (10 July 1972, unreported) HC (Pringle J).

2 *Aberdeen Railway Co v Blaikie Bros* (1854) 1 Macq 461.

3 *Northwest Transportation Co Ltd v Beatty* (1887) 12 App Cas 589.

4 *Northwest Transportation Co Ltd v Beatty* (1887) 12 App Cas 589.

86. A director, notwithstanding his interest, may be counted in the quorum present at any meeting whereat he or any other director is appointed to hold any such office or place of profit under the company or whereat the terms of any such appointment are arranged, and he may vote on any such appointment or arrangement other than his own appointment or the arrangement of the terms thereof.

Definitions

'company': CA 1963, s 2(1); 'director': CA 1963, s 2(1), Sch 1, reg 1.

Notes

Regulation 86 applies only in the case of public companies not private companies.

87. Any director may act by himself or his firm in a professional capacity for the company, and he or his firm shall be entitled to remuneration for professional services as if he were not a director; but nothing herein contained shall authorise a director or his firm to act as auditor to the company.

Definitions

'company': CA 1963, s 2(1); 'director': CA 1963, s 2(1), Sch 1, reg 1.

Notes

In so far as reg 86 applies, it reverses the decision in *Aberdeen Railway Co v Blaikie Bros* (1854) 1 Macq 461. The benefit of this article is dependent, however, on disclosure under CA 1963, s 194.[1] If the benefit of reg 86 has been lost through failure to make disclosure to the board under s 194, the contract becomes voidable at the instance of the company, and the director will be liable to account for any profit made as well as being liable in damages for breach of fiduciary duty.[2] Where the contract is voidable, it may nonetheless be ratified and the breach of duty may be forgiven by the company in general meeting.[3] Furthermore, the director may, in his capacity as member, vote in favour of ratification, unless to do so would amount to a fraud on the minority.[4]

1 *Hely-Hutchinson v Brayhead Ltd* [1967] 3 All ER 98 *Movitex Ltd v Bulfield* [1988] BCLC 104; *Guinness plc v Saunders* [1988] 2 All ER 940 aff'd [1990] 1 All ER 652; *Hopkins v Shannon Transport Ltd* (10 July 1972, unreported) HC (Pringle J).

2 *Aberdeen Railway Co v Blaikie Bros* (1854) 1 Macq 461.

3 *Northwest Transportation Co Ltd v Beatty* (1887) 12 App Cas 589.

4 *Northwest Transportation Co Ltd v Beatty* (1887) 12 App Cas 589.

88. All cheques, promissory notes, drafts, bills of exchange and other negotiable instruments and all receipts for moneys paid to the company shall be signed, drawn, accepted, endorsed or otherwise executed, as the case may be, by such person or persons and in such manner as the directors shall from time to time by resolution determine.

Definitions

'company': CA 1963, s 2(1); 'director': CA 1963, s 2(1), Sch 1, reg 1.

89. The directors shall cause minutes to be made in books provided for the purpose—

(a) of all appointment of officers made by the directors;

(b) of the names of the directors present at each meeting of the directors and of any committee of the directors;

(c) of all resolutions and proceedings at all meetings of the company and of the directors and of committees of directors.

Definitions

'director': CA 1963, s 2(1), Sch 1, reg 1; 'officer': CA 1963, s 2(1).

90. The directors on behalf of the company may pay a gratuity or pension or allowance on retirement to any director who has held any other salaried office or place of profit with the company or to his widow or dependants, and may make contributions to any fund any pay premiums for the purchase or provision of any such gratuity, pension or allowance.

Definitions

'company': CA 1963, s 2(1); 'director': CA 1963, s 2(1), Sch 1, reg 1.

Notes

This power must be exercised bona fide for the benefit of the company as a whole and for its proper purpose.[1] If the company's objects clause contains an express power to grant pensions and also has an independent and substantive object of the company. [2] If, however, the company is insolvent, the granting of a pension, whether permitted by the memorandum or articles, may nonetheless be unlawful if it has the effect of perpetrating a fraud on the company's creditors. [3]

1 *Re W & M Roith Ltd* [1967] 1 All ER 427.

2 *Re Horsley & White Ltd* [1982] 3 All ER 1045.

3 *Re Frederick Inns Ltd* [1991] ILRM 582 and see also CA 1990, s 139.

Disqualification of Directors

91. The office of director shall be vacated if the director—

(a) ceases to be a director by virtue of section 180 of the Act; or

(b) is adjudged bankrupt in the State or in Northern Ireland or Great Britain or makes any arrangement or composition with his creditors generally; of

(c) becomes prohibited from being a director by reason of any order made under section 184 of the Act; or

(d) becomes of unsound mind; or

(e) resigns his office by notice in writing to the company; or

(f) is convicted of an indictable offence unless the directors otherwise determine; or

(g) is for more than 6 months absent without permission of the directors from meetings of the directors held during that period.

Definitions

'Act': CA 1963, Sch 1, reg 1; 'director': CA 1963, s 2(1), Sch 1, reg 1.

Rotation of Directors

92. At the first annual general meeting of the company all the directors shall retire from office, and at the annual general meeting in every subsequent year, one-third of the directors for the time being, or, if their number is not three or a multiple of three, then the number nearest one-third shall retire from office.

Definitions

'director': CA 1963, s 2(1), Sch 1, reg 1.

Notes

Where the company fails to hold its AGM, those directors who ought to have retired by rotation in that year are deemed to automatically vacate office at the end of the last day upon which the meeting could lawfully have been held.[1]

1 *Re Zinotty Properties Ltd* [1984] 3 All ER 754; *Morris v Kanssen* [1946] AC 459; *Re Consolidated Nickel Mines Ltd* [1914] 1 Ch 883.

---

93. The directors to retire in every year shall be those who have been longest in office since their last election but as between persons who became directors on the same day, those to retire shall (unless they otherwise agree among themselves) be determined by lot.

Definitions

'director': CA 1963, s 2(1), Sch 1, reg 1.

---

94. A retiring director shall be eligible for re-election.

Definitions

'director': CA 1963, s 2(1), Sch 1, reg 1.

95. The company, at the meeting at which a director retires in manner aforesaid, may fill the vacated office by electing a person thereto, and in default the retiring director shall, if offering himself for re-election, be deemed to have been re-elected, unless at such meeting it is expressly resolved not to fill such vacated office, or unless a resolution for the re-election of such director has been put to the meeting and lost.

Definitions

'company': CA 1963, s 2(1); 'director': CA 1963, s 2(1), Sch 1, reg 1.

96. No person other than a director retiring at the meeting shall, unless recommended by the directors, be eligible for election to the office of director at any general meeting unless not less than 3 nor more than 21 days before the day appointed for the meeting there shall have been left at the office notice in writing signed by a member duly qualified to attend and vote at the meeting for which such notice is given, of his intention to propose such person for election and also notice in writing signed by that person of his willingness to be elected.

Definitions

'director': CA 1963, s 2(1), Sch 1, reg 1.

97. The company may from time to time by ordinary resolution increase or reduce the number of directors and may also determine in what rotation the increased or reduced number is to go out of office.

Definitions

'company': CA 1963, s 2(1); 'director': CA 1963, s 2(1), Sch 1, reg 1.

98. The directors shall have power at any time and from time to time to appoint any person to be a director, either to fill a casual vacancy or as an addition to the existing directors, but so that the total number of directors shall not at any time exceed the number fixed in accordance with these regulations. Any director so appointed shall hold office only until the next following annual general meeting, and shall then be eligible for re-election but shall not be taken into account in determining the directors who are to retire by rotation at such meeting.

Definitions

'director': CA 1963, s 2(1), Sch 1, reg 1.

99. The company may, by ordinary resolution, of which extended notice has been given in accordance with section 142 of the Act, remove any director before the expiration of his period of office notwithstanding anything in these regulations or in any agreement between the company and such director. Such removal shall be without prejudice to any claim such director may have for damages for breach of any contract of service between him and the company.

Definitions

'Act': CA 1963, Sch 1, reg 1; 'company': CA 1963, s 2(1); 'director': CA 1963, s 2(1), Sch 1, reg 1.

100. The company may, by ordinary resolution, appoint another person in place of a director removed from office under regulation 99 and without prejudice to the powers of the directors under regulation 98 the company in general meeting may appoint any person to be a director either to fill a casual vacancy or as an additional director. A person appointed in place of a director so removed or to fill such a vacancy shall be subject to retirement at the same time as if he had become a director on the day on which the director in whose place he is appointed was last elected a director.

Definitions

'company': CA 1963, s 2(1); 'director': CA 1963, s 2(1), Sch 1, reg 1.

Notes

Even if reg 100 is excluded, the members will still have an implied power to fill any casual vacancies.[1]

1 *Worcester Corsetry Ltd v Whiting* [1936] Ch 640.

Proceedings of Directors

101. The directors may meet together for the despatch of business, adjourn and otherwise regulate their meetings as they think fit. Questions arising at any meeting shall be decided by a majority of votes. Where there is an equality of votes, the chairman shall have a second or casting vote. A director may, and the secretary on the requisition of a director shall, at any time summon a meeting of the directors. If the directors so resolve, it shall not be necessary to give notice of a meeting of directors to any director who, being resident in the State, is for the time being absent from the State.

Definitions

'director': CA 1963, s 2(1), Sch 1, reg 1.

Notes

Reasonable notice must be given of any meeting of directors.[1] Whether or not notice is reasonable depends on the circumstances. For example, five minutes' notice was held to be sufficient where all directors were physically present and were not otherwise engaged.[2] However, where the directors were all in the same city, but some had prior engagements, three hours' notice was held to be insufficient.[3] Failure to provide reasonable notice of the directors' meeting renders any resolutions passed at it void.[4] It has been held that there is no requirement to provide an agenda for directors' meetings.[5] Any resolution carried on the casting vote of an invalidly appointed chairman is itself invalid.[6]

1 *Barron v Potter* [1914] 1 Ch 895; *Holland v McGill* (16 March 1990, unreported) HC (Murphy J).

2 *Browne v La Trinidad* (1887) 37 Ch D 1.

3 *Re Homer District Consolidated Gold Mines Ltd, ex parte Smith* (1888) 39 Ch D 546.

4 *Re Homer District Consolidated Gold Mines Ltd, ex parte Smith* (1888) 39 Ch D 546; *Re East Norfolk Tramways Co* (1877) 5 Ch D 963. cf. *Browne v La Trinidad* (1887) 37 Ch D 1.

5 *Holland v McGill* (16 March 1990, unreported) HC (Murphy J).

6 *Clark v Workman* [1920] 1 IR 107.

---

102. The quorum necessary for the transaction of the business of the directors may be fixed by the directors, and unless so fixed shall be two.

Definitions

'director': CA 1963, s 2(1), Sch 1, reg 1.

Notes

Under reg 54 it appears at a general meeting of the members a quorum need only be present when the meeting proceeds to business.[1] However, the wording of reg 102 seems to require a quorum throughout the meeting. In any event, if there is only one director present, he cannot constitute a meeting on his own.[2]

1 *Re Hartley Baird Ltd* [1955] Ch 143; *Re London Flats Ltd* [1969] 1 WLR 711.

2 *Re London Flats Ltd* [1969] 1 WLR 711.

---

103. The continuing directors may act notwithstanding any vacancy in their number but, if and so long as their number is reduced below the number fixed by or pursuant to the regulations of the company as the necessary quorum of directors, the continuing directors or director may act for the purpose of increasing the number of directors to that number or of summoning a general meeting of the company but for no other purpose.

Definitions

'company': CA 1963, s 2(1); 'director': CA 1963, s 2(1), Sch 1, reg 1.

---

104. The directors may elect a chairman of their meeting and determine the period for which he is to hold office, but if no such chairman is elected, or, if at any meeting the chairman is not present within 5 minutes after the time appointed for holding the same, the directors present may choose one of their number to be chairman of the meeting.

Definitions

'director': CA 1963, s 2(1), Sch 1, reg 1.

Notes

The members in general meeting can only interfere with the directors' power of appointment of a chairman by way of special resolution.[1]

1 *Clark v Workman* [1920] 1 IR 107.

105. The directors may delegate any of their powers to committees consisting of such member or members of the board as think fit; any committee so formed shall, in the exercise of the powers so delegated, conform to any regulations that may be imposed on it by the directors.

Definitions

'director': CA 1963, s 2(1), Sch 1, reg 1; 'member': CA 1963, s 31.

Notes

The power to delegate to a committee must not be used for the purpose of excluding a particular director from participating in the management of the company's affairs.[1]

1 *Kyushu v Alturas Gold Ltd* (1888) 4 TLR 331.

106. A committee may elect a chairman of its meetings; if no such chairman is elected, or if at any meeting the chairman is not present within 5 minutes after the time appointed for holding the same, the members present may choose one of their number to be chairman of the meeting.

Definitions

'member': CA 1963, s 31.

107. A committee may meet and adjourn as it thinks proper. Questions arising at any meeting shall be determined by a majority of votes of the members present, and where there is an equality of votes, the chairman shall have a second or casting vote.

Definitions

'member': CA 1963, s 31.

Notes

Any resolution carried on the casting vote of an invalidly appointed chairman is itself invalid.[1]

1 *Clark v Workman* [1920] 1 IR 107.

108. All acts done by any meeting of the directors or of a committee of directors or by any person acting as a director shall, notwithstanding that it be afterwards discovered that there was same defect in the appointment of any such director or person acting as aforesaid, or that they or any of them were disqualified, be as valid as if every such person had been duly appointed and was qualified to be a director.

Definitions

'director': CA 1963, s 2(1), Sch 1, reg 1.

109. A resolution in writing signed by all the directors for the time being entitled to receive notice of a meeting of the directors shall be as valid as if it had been passed at a meeting of the directors duly convened and held.

Definitions

'director': CA 1963, s 2(1), Sch 1, reg 1.

Managing Director

110. The directors may from time to time appoint one or more of themselves to the office of managing director for such period and on such terms as to remuneration and otherwise as they think fit, subject to the terms of any agreement entered into in any particular case, may revoke such appointment. A director so appointed shall not, whilst holding that office, be subject to retirement by rotation or be taken into account in determining the rotation of retirement of directors but (without prejudice to any claim he may have for damages for breach of any contract of service between him and the company), his appointment shall be automatically determined if he ceases from any cause to be a director.

Definitions

'director': CA 1963, s 2(1), Sch 1, reg 1.

Notes

The managing director is both an officer and an employee of the company.[1] In relation to claims for damages for breach of his service contract resulting from his dismissal as managing director, see the notes to CA 1963, s 182.

1 *Carvill v Irish Industrial Banks Ltd* [1968] IR 325; *Re Dairy Lee Ltd* [1976] IR 314; *Anderson v James Sutherland (Peterhead) Ltd* [1941] SC 203.

111. A managing director shall receive such remuneration whether by way of salary, commission or participation in the profits, or partly in one way and partly in another, as the directors may determine.

Definitions

'director': CA 1963, s 2(1), Sch 1, reg 1.

112. The directors may entrust to and confer upon a managing director any of the powers exercisable by them upon such terms and conditions and with such restrictions as they may think fit, and either collaterally with or to the exclusion of their own powers, and may from time to time revoke, withdraw, alter or vary all or any of such powers.

Definitions

'director': CA 1963, s 2(1), Sch 1, reg 1.

Notes

As appears from reg 112, the powers of a managing director are not fixed by law, but instead depend upon the terms of appointment as fixed from time to time by the board of directors.[1]

1 *Harold Holdsworth & Co (Wakefield) Ltd v Cadies* [1955] 1 WLR 352.

Secretary

113. [Subject to section 3 of the Companies (Amendment) Act, 1982,][a] the secretary shall be appointed by the directors for such term, at such remuneration and upon such conditions as they may think fit; and any secretary so appointed may be removed by them.

Amendments

a Words inserted by C(A)A 1982, s 21.

Definitions

'director': CA 1963, s 2(1), Sch 1, reg 1; ' secretary': CA 1963, Sch 1, reg 1.

114. A provision of the Act or these regulations requiring or authorising a thing to be done by or to a director and the secretary shall not be satisfied by its being done by or to the same person acting both as director and as, or in place of, the secretary.

Definitions

'Act': CA 1963, Sch 1, reg 1; 'director': CA 1963, s 2(1), Sch 1, reg 1; ' secretary': CA 1963, Sch 1, reg 1.

The Seal

115. The seal shall be used only by the authority of the directors or of a committee of directors authorised by the directors in that behalf, and every instrument to which the seal shall be affixed shall be signed by a director and shall be countersigned by the secretary or by a second director or by some other person appointed by the directors for the purpose.

Definitions

'director': CA 1963, s 2(1), Sch 1, reg 1; 'seal': CA 1963, Sch 1, reg 1; 'secretary': CA 1963, Sch 1, reg 1.

Notes

Regulation 76 of Table A of the Companies (Consolidation) Act 1908 contained a similar provision but required two directors and the secretary, or such other person as the directors might appoint, to sign every instrument to which the seal was affixed ie three signatures. It has been held that where reg 76 applied to a company, an indenture to which the seal is affixed but which has been signed by only two such persons was not effective to convey the company's interest in property.[1]

A power of attorney conferred on a receiver pursuant to the terms of a debenture, although allowing him to use his own seal to execute deeds on behalf of the company, does not entitle him to use the company's seal.[2]

1 *Safeera Ltd v Wallis and O'Regan* (12 July 1994, unreported) HC (Morris J).

2 *Industrial Development Authority v Moran* [1978] IR 159.

Dividends and Reserve

116. The company in general meeting may declare dividends, but no dividend shall exceed the amount recommended by the directors.

Definitions

'company': CA 1963, s 2(1); 'director': CA 1963, s 2(1), Sch 1, reg 1.

Notes

There is no legal obligation on the company to declare a dividend, even where there are sufficient distributable profits available.[1] See also reg 119. It is, however, possible that a refusal to declare a dividend could amount to oppression or disregard of interests within the meaning of CA 1963, s 205.

1 *Burland v Earle* [1902] AC 83.

---

117. The directors may from time to time pay to the members such interim dividends as appear to the directors to be justified by the profits of the company.

Definitions

'company': CA 1963, s 2(1); 'director': CA 1963, s 2(1), Sch 1, reg 1; 'member': CA 1963, s 31.

[**118**. No dividend or interim dividend shall be paid otherwise than in accordance with the provisions of Part IV of the Companies (Amendment) Act, 1983 which apply to the company.][a]

Amendments

a Substituted by C(A)A 1983, Sch 1 para 24.

Notes

Directors who knowingly or negligently cause the company to pay an unlawful dividend are personally liable to compensate the company for the amount so paid.[1]

1 *Re Exchange Banking Co; Flitcroft's Case* (1882) 21 Ch D 519; *Re City Equitable Fire Assurance Co* [1905] Ch 207; *Dovey v Cory* [1901] AC 477.

---

119. The directors may, before recommending any dividend, set aside out of the profits of the company such sums as they thinks proper as a reserve or reserves which shall, at the discretion of the directors, be applicable for any purpose to which the profits of the company may be properly applied, and pending such application may, at the like discretion, either be employed in the business of the company or be invested in such investments as the directors may lawfully determine. The directors may also, without placing the same to reserve, carry forward any profits which they may think it prudent not to divide.

Definitions

'company': CA 1963, s 2(1); 'director': CA 1963, s 2(1), Sch 1, reg 1.

---

120. Subject to the rights of persons, if any, entitled to shares with special rights as to dividend, all dividends shall be declared and paid according to the amounts paid or credited as paid on the shares in respect whereof the dividend is paid, but no amount paid or credited as paid on a share in advance of calls shall be treated for the purposes of this regulation as paid on the share. All dividends shall be apportioned and paid proportionately to the amounts paid or credited as paid on the shares during any portion or portions of the period in respect of which the dividend is paid; but if any share is issued on terms providing that it shall rank for dividend as from a particular date, such share shall rank for dividend accordingly.

Definitions

'share': CA 1963, s 2(1).

---

121. The directors may deduct from any dividend payable to any member all sums of money (if any) immediately payable by him to the company on account of calls or otherwise in relation to the shares of the company.

Definitions

'company': CA 1963, s 2(1); 'director': CA 1963, s 2(1), Sch 1, reg 1; 'member': CA 1963, s 31; 'share': CA 1963, s 2(1).

---

122. Any general meeting declaring a dividend or bonus may direct payment of such dividend or bonus wholly or partly by the distribution of specific assets and in particular of paid up shares, debentures or debenture stock of any other company or in any one or more of such ways, and the directors shall give effect to such resolution, and where any difficulty arises in regard to such distribution, the directors may settle the same as they think expedient, and in particular may issue fractional certificates and fix the value for distribution of such specific assets or any part thereof and may determine that cash payment shall be made to any members upon the footing of the value so fixed, in order to adjust the rights of all the parties, and may vest any such specific assets in trustees as may seem expedient to the directors.

Definitions

'company': CA 1963, s 2(1); 'debenture': CA 1963, s 2(1); 'director': CA 1963, s 2(1), Sch 1, reg 1; 'share': CA 1963, s 2(1).

123. Any dividend, interest or other moneys payable in cash in respect of any shares may be paid by cheque or warrant sent through the post directed to the registered address of the holder, or, where there are joint holders, to the registered address of that one of the joint holders who is first named on the register or to such person and to such address as the holder or joint holders may in writing direct. Every such cheque or warrant shall be made payable to the order of the person to whom it is sent. Any one of two or more joint holders may give effectual receipts for any dividends, bonuses or other moneys payable in respect of the shares held by them as joint holders.

Definitions

'share': CA 1963, s 2(1).

124. No dividend shall bear interest against the company.

Definitions

'company': CA 1963, s 2(1).

Accounts

125. The directors shall cause proper books of account to be kept relating to—

(a) all sums of money received and expended by the company and the matters in respect of which the receipt and expenditure takes place; and

(b) all sales and purchases of goods by the company; and

(c) the assets and liabilities of the company.

Proper books shall not be deemed to be kept if there are not kept such books of account as are necessary to give a true and fair view of the state of the company's affairs and to explain its transactions.

Definitions

'company': CA 1963, s 2(1); 'director': CA 1963, s 2(1), Sch 1, reg 1.

126. The books of account shall be kept at the office or, subject to section 147 of the Act, at such other place as the directors think fit, and shall at all reasonable times be open to the inspiration of the directors.

Definitions

'Act': CA 1963, Sch 1, reg 1; 'director': CA 1963, s 2(1), Sch 1, reg 1.

127. The directors shall time to time determine whether and to what extent and at what times and places and under what conditions or regulations the accounts and books of the company or any of them shall be open to the inspection of members, not being directors, and no member (not being a director) shall have any right of inspection any account or book or document of the company except as conferred by statute or authorised by the directors or by the company in general meeting.

Definitions

'company': CA 1963, s 2(1); 'director': CA 1963, s 2(1), Sch 1, reg 1; 'member': CA 1963, s 31.

128. The directors shall from time to time, in accordance with sections 148, 150, 157 and 158 of the Act cause to be prepared and to be laid before the annual general meeting of the company such profit and loss accounts, balance sheets, group accounts and reports as are required by those sections to be prepared and laid before the annual general meeting of the company.

Definitions

'Act': CA 1963, Sch 1, reg 1; 'company': CA 1963, s 2(1); 'director': CA 1963, s 2(1), Sch 1, reg 1.

129. A copy of every balance sheet (including every document required by law to be annexed thereto) which is to be laid before the annual general meeting of the company together with a copy of the directors' report and auditors' report shall, not less than 21 days before the date of the annual general meeting be sent to every person entitled under the provisions of the Act to receive them.

Definitions

'Act': CA 1963, Sch 1, reg 1; 'company': CA 1963, s 2(1); 'director': CA 1963, s 2(1), Sch 1, reg 1.

Capitalisation of Profits

130. The company in general meeting may upon the recommendation of the directors resolve that any sum for the time being standing to the credit of any of the company's reserves (including any capital redemption reserve fund or share premium account) or to the credit of profit and loss account be capitalised and applied on behalf of the members who would have been entitled to receive the same if the same had been distributed by way of dividend and in the same proportions either in or towards paying up amounts for the time being unpaid on any shares held by them respectively or in paying up in full unissued shares or debentures of the company of a nominal amount equal to the sum capitalised (such shares or debentures to be allotted and distributed credited as fully paid up to and amongst such holders in the proportions aforesaid) or partly in one way and partly in another, so however, that the only purpose for which sums standing to the credit of the capital redemption reserve fund or the share premium account shall be applied shall be those permitted by sections 62 and 64 of the Act.

Definitions

'Act': CA 1963, Sch 1, reg 1; 'company': CA 1963, s 2(1); 'debenture': CA 1963, s 2(1); 'director': CA 1963, s 2(1), Sch 1, reg 1; 'share': CA 1963, s 2(1).

[130A. The company in general meeting may on the recommendation of the directors resolve that it is desirable to capitalise any part of the amount for the time being standing to the credit of any of the company's reserve accounts or to the credit of the profit and loss account which is not available for distribution by applying such sum in paying up in full unissued shares to be allotted as fully paid bonus shares to those members of the company who would have been entitled to that sum if it were distributed by way of dividend (and in the same proportions), and the directors shall give effect to such resolution.][a]

Amendments

a Inserted by C(A)A 1983, Sch 1 para 24.

Definitions

'company': CA 1963, s 2(1); 'director': CA 1963, s 2(1), Sch 1, reg 1; 'member': CA 1963, s 31; 'share': CA 1963, s 2(1).

131. [Whenever a resolution is passed in pursuance of regulation 130 or 130A] [a], the directors shall make all appropriations and applications of the undivided profits resolved to be capitalised thereby and all allotments and issues of fully paid shares or debentures, if any, and generally shall do all acts and things required to give effect thereto with full power to the directors to make such provision as they shall think fit for the case of shares or debentures becoming distributable in fractions (and, in particular, without prejudice to the generality of the foregoing, to sell the shares or debentures represented by such fractions and distribute the net proceeds of such sale amongst the members otherwise entitled to such fractions in due proportions) and also to authorise any person to enter on behalf of all the members concerned into an agreement with the company providing for the allotment to them respectively credited as fully paid up of any further shares or debentures to which they may become entitled on such capitalisation or, as the case may require, for the payment up by the application thereto of their respective proportions of the profits resolved to be capitalised of the amounts remaining unpaid on their existing shares and any agreement made under such authority shall be effective and binding on all such members.

Amendments

a Words substituted by C(A)A 1983, Sch 1 para 24.

Definitions

'company': CA 1963, s 2(1); 'debenture': CA 1963, s 2(1); 'director': CA 1963, s 2(1), Sch 1, reg 1; 'member': CA 1963, s 31; 'share': CA 1963, s 2(1).

Audit

132. Auditors shall be appointed and their duties regulated in accordance with sections 160 to 163 of the Act.

Definitions

'Act': CA 1963, Sch 1, reg 1.

Notices

133. A notice may be given by the company to any member either personally or by sending it by post to him to his registered address. Where a notice is sent by post, service of the notice shall be deemed to be effected by properly addressing, prepaying and posting a letter containing the notice, and to have been effected in the case of the notice of a meeting at the expiration of 24 hours after the letter containing the same is posted, and in any other case at the time at which the letter would be delivered in the ordinary course of post.

Definitions

'company': CA 1963, s 2(1); 'member': CA 1963, s 31.

134. A notice may be given by the company to the joint holders of a share by giving the notice to the joint holder first named in the register in respect of the share.

Definitions

'company': CA 1963, s 2(1); 'share': CA 1963, s 2(1).

135. A notice may be given by the company to the persons entitled to a share in consequence of the death or bankruptcy of a member by sending it through the post in a prepaid letter addressed to them by name or by the title of representatives of the deceased of Official Assignee in bankruptcy or by any like description at the address supplied for the purpose by the persons claiming to be so entitled, or (until such an address has been so supplied) by giving the notice in any manner in which the same might have been given if the death or bankruptcy had not occurred.

Definitions

'company': CA 1963, s 2(1); 'member': CA 1963, s 31; 'share': CA 1963, s 2(1).

136. Notice of every general meeting shall be given in any manner hereinbefore authorised to—

(a) every member; and

(b) every person upon whom the ownership of a share devolves by reason of his being a personal representative or the Official Assignee in bankruptcy of a member, where the member but for his death or bankruptcy would be entitled to receive notice of the meeting; and

(c) the auditor for the time being of the company.

No other person shall be entitled to receive notices of general meetings.

Definitions

'company': CA 1963, s 2(1); 'member': CA 1963, s 31; 'share': CA 1963, s 2(1).

Winding Up

137. If the company is wound up, the liquidator may, with the sanction of a special resolution of the company and any other sanction required by the Act, divide among the members in specie or kind the whole or any part of the assets of the company (whether they shall consist of property of the same kind or not) and may, for such purpose, set such value as he deems fair upon any property to divided as aforesaid any may determine how such division shall be carried out as between the members or different classes of members. The liquidator may, with the like sanction, vest the whole or any part of such assets in trustees upon such trusts for the benefit of the contributories as the liquidator, with the like sanction, shall think fit, but so that no member shall be compelled to accept any shares or other securities whereon there is any liability.

Definitions

'Act': CA 1963, Sch 1, reg 1; 'company': CA 1963, s 2(1); 'member': CA 1963, s 31.

Indemnity

138. Every director, managing director, agent, auditor, secretary and other officer for the time being of the company shall be indemnified out of the assets of the company against any liability incurred by him in defending any proceedings, whether civil or criminal, in relation to his acts while acting in such office, in which judgment is given in his favour or in which he is acquitted or in connection with any application under section 391 of the Act in which relief is granted to him by the court.

Definitions

'Act': CA 1963, Sch 1, reg 1; 'company': CA 1963, s 2(1); 'court': CA 1963, s 2(1); 'director': CA 1963, s 2(1), Sch 1, reg 1; 'officer': CA 1963, s 2(1); ' secretary': CA 1963, Sch 1, reg 1.

PART II
REGULATIONS FOR THE MANAGEMENT OF A PRIVATE COMPANY LIMITED BY SHARES

1. The regulations contained in Part I of Table A [(with the exception of regulations 8, 24, 51, 54, 84 and 86)][a] shall apply.

Amendments

a Words substituted by C(A)A 1977, s 5.

Definitions

'Table A': CA 1963, s 2(1).

2. The company is a private company and accordingly—

(a) the right to transfer shares is restricted in the manner hereinafter prescribed;

(b) the number of members of the company (exclusive of persons who are in the employment of the company and of persons who, having been formerly in the employment of the company, were while in such employment, and have continued after the determination of such employment to be, members of the company) is limited to fifty, so, however, that where two or more persons hold one or more shares in the company jointly, they shall, for the purpose of this regulation, be treated as a single member;

(c) any invitation to the public to subscribe for any shares or debentures of the company is prohibited;

(d) the company shall not have power to issue share warrants to bearer.

Definitions

'company': CA 1963, s 2(1); 'member': CA 1963, s 31; 'prescribed': CA 1963, s 2(1); 'private company': CA 1963, s 2(1), s 33(1).

3. The directors may, in their absolute discretion, and without assigning any reason therefor, decline to register any transfer of any share, whether or not it is a fully paid share.

Definitions

'director': CA 1963, s 2(1), Sch 1, reg 1; 'share': CA 1963, s 2(1).

Notes

The power of the directors to decline to register the transfer of a share must be exercised *bona fide* in the interests of the company as a whole and for the proper purposes.[1] As appears from the express words of reg 3, the directors cannot be compelled to give reasons as to why they have declined to refuse to register the transfer.[2] If, however, the directors volunteer reasons for their decision, the court may consider whether the reasons given justify the decision reached. [3] Furthermore, if the applicant can produce some evidence that the directors reached their decision *mala fides* or for an improper purpose, and they fail to refute the allegation made, the court may then draw an adverse inference from their silence.[4] Even if bad faith or an improper purpose cannot be proved against the directors, the applicant may (if already registered in respect of other shares or if entitled to the shares by virtue of the death of an existing member) be entitled to petition for relief under CA 1963, s 205. The power to decline to register a transfer of shares may lapse if not exercised within two months from the date on which the transfer was lodged. See CA 1963, s 84, reg 26.

1 *Re Dublin North City Milling Co* [1909] 1 IR 179; *Re Smith & Fawcett Ltd* [1942] Ch 304; *Re Hafner* [1943] IR 426; *Mactra Properties Ltd v Morshead Mansions Ltd* [2009] 1 BCLC 179.

2 *Re Dublin North City Milling Co* [1909] 1 IR 179; *Re Hafner* [1943] IR 426; *Tett v Phoenix Property Co* [1984] BCLC 104.

3 *Tett v Phoenix Property Co* [1984] BCLC 104; *Mactra Properties Ltd v Morshead Mansions Ltd* [2009] 1 BCLC 179.

4 *Re Hafner* [1943] IR 426; *Clark v Workman* [1920] 1 IR 107.

---

4. Subject to section 133 and 141 of the Act, an annual general meeting and a meeting called for the passing of a special resolution shall be called by 21 days' notice in writing at the least and a meeting of the company (other than an annual general meeting or a meeting for the passing of a special resolution) shall be called by 7 days' notice in writing at the least. The notice shall be exclusive of the day on which it is served or deemed to be served and of the day for which it is given and shall specify the day, the place and the hour of the meeting and, in the case of special business, the general nature of that business and shall be given in manner authorised by these regulations to such persons as are under the regulations of the company entitled to receive such notices from the company.

Definitions

'Act': CA 1963, Sch 1, reg 1; 'company': CA 1963, s 2(1).

Notes

The notice of the meeting will be void if it or any accompanying circular is misleading.[1] Where it is proposed to pass a special resolution at the meeting, the notice will be invalid if it fails to specify either the entire text or the entire substance of the proposed resolution.[2]

1 *Jackson v Munster Bank Ltd* (1884–85) 13 LR Ir 118.

2 *Re Moorgate Mercantile Holdings Ltd* [1980] 1 WLR 227.

---

5. No business shall be transacted at any general meeting unless a quorum of members is present at the time when the meeting proceeds to business; save as herein otherwise provided, two member present in person or by proxy shall be a quorum.

Definitions

'member': CA 1963, s 31.

Notes

The wording of reg 5 appears to envisage that a quorum need only be present at the beginning of the meeting so that the subsequent departure of a member reducing the meeting below the number required for the quorum would not invalidate proceedings of the meeting after his departure.[1] However, if the number of members present falls to one, then there will no longer be a meeting.[2]

Where it is impracticable to obtain a quorum, it may be necessary to apply to the court pursuant to CA 1963, s 135 for an order convening the meeting and directing that one member present in person or by proxy shall constitute a meeting.

1 *Re Hartley Baird Ltd* [1955] Ch 143.

2 *Re London Flats Ltd* [1969] 1 WLR 711; *Sharp v Dawes* (1876) 2 QBD 26; *Re El Sombrero Ltd* [1958] Ch 900.

---

6. Subject to section 141 of the Act, a resolution in writing signed by all the members for the time being entitled to attend and vote on such resolution at a general meeting (or being bodies corporate by their duly authorised representatives) shall be as valid and effective for all purposes as if the resolution had been passed at a general meeting of the company duly convened and held, and if described as a special resolution shall be deemed to be a special resolution within the meaning of the Act.

Definitions

'Act': CA 1963, Sch 1, reg 1; 'company': CA 1963, s 2(1); 'member': CA 1963, s 31.

---

7. A director may vote in respect of any contract, appointment or arrangement in which he is interested, and he shall be counted in the quorum present at the meeting.

Definitions

'director': CA 1963, s 2(1), Sch 1, reg 1.

Notes

This provision effectively reverses *Cox v Dublin City Distillery (No 2)* [1915] 1 IR 345. Note that it is considerably wider than reg 84 which applies to public companies.

---

8. The directors may exercise the voting powers conferred by the shares of any other company held or owned by the company in such manner in all respects as they think fit and in particular they may exercise the voting powers in favour of any resolution appointing the directors or any of them as directors or officers of such other company or providing for the payment of remuneration or pensions to the directors or officers of such other company. Any director of the company may vote in favour of the exercise of such voting rights, notwithstanding that he may be or may be about to become a director or officer of such other company, and as such or in any other manner is or may be interested in the exercise of such voting rights in manner aforesaid.

Definitions

'company': CA 1963, s 2(1); 'director': CA 1963, s 2(1), Sch 1, reg 1; 'officer': CA 1963, s 2(1); 'share': CA 1963, s 2(1).

---

9. Any director may from time to time appoint any person who is approved by the majority of the directors to be an alternate or substitute director. The appointee, while he holds office as an alternate director, shall be entitled to notice of meetings of the directors and to attend and vote thereat as a director and shall not be entitled to be remunerated otherwise than out of the remuneration of the director appointing him. Any appointment under this regulation shall be effected by notice in writing given by the appointer to the secretary. Any appointment so made may be revoked at any time by the appointer or by a majority of the other directors or by the company in general meeting. Revocation by an appointer shall be effected by notice in writing given by the appointer to the secretary.

Definitions

'company': CA 1963, s 2(1); 'director': CA 1963, s 2(1), Sch 1, reg 1; ' secretary': CA 1963, Sch 1, reg 1.

[**10**. Every person whose name is entered as a member in the register shall be entitled without payment to receive within 2 months after allotment or lodgment of a transfer (or within such other period as the conditions of issue shall provide) one certificate for all his shares or several certificates each for one or more of his shares upon payment of 12½ new pence for every certificate after the first or such less sum as the directors shall from time to time determine, so, however, that in respect of a share or shares held jointly by several persons the company shall not be bound to issue more than one certificate, and delivery of a certificate for a share to one of several joint holders shall be sufficient delivery to all such holders. Every certificate shall be under the seal and shall specify the shares to which it relates and the amount paid up thereon.] [a]

Amendments

a Reg 10 inserted by C(A)A 1977, s 5.

Definitions

'company': CA 1963, s 2(1); 'director': CA 1963, s 2(1), Sch 1, reg 1; 'register': CA 1963, Sch 1, reg 1; 'share': CA 1963, s 2(1).

[Note: Regulations 3, 4, 5 and 10 of this Part are alternative to regulations 24, 51, 54 and 8 respectively of Part 1. Regulations 7 and 8 of this Part are alternative to regulations 84 and 86 of Part I.] [a]

Amendments

a Note substituted by C(A)A 1977, s 5.

TABLE B

FORM OF MEMORANDUM OF ASSOCIATION OF A COMPANY LIMITED BY SHARES

1. The name of the company is 'The Western Mining Company, Limited'.

2. The objects for which the company is established are the mining of minerals of all kinds and the doing of all such other things as are incidental or conducive to the attainment of the above object.

3. The liability of the members is limited.

4. The share capital of the company is £200,000, divided into 200,000 shares of £1 each.

We, the several persons whose names and addresses are subscribed, wish to be formed into a company in pursuance of this memorandum of association, and we agree to take the number of shares in the capital of the company set opposite our respective names.

Names, Addresses and Descriptions of Subscribers	Number of Shares taken by Each Subscriber
1. James Walsh of.................................... in the County of...................................... Solicitor.	50
2. John Murphy of .... in the County of...................................... Engineer.	2,700
3. Patrick Ryan of.................................... in the County of...................................... Geologist.	1,250
4. Thomas O'Connell of.......................... in the County of...................................... Engineer.	500
5. Daniel Clarke of.................................... in the County of...................................... Geologist.	50
6. Patrick Byrne of.................................... in the County of...................................... Accountant.	300
7. John Collins of.................................... in the County of...................................... Solicitor.	150
Total Shares taken	5,000

Dated the.............................day of......................................, 19.....................

Witness to the above Signatures: ....

Name:...

Address: ....

TABLE C

FORM OF MEMORANDUM AND ARTICLES OF ASSOCIATION OF A COMPANY LIMITED BY GUARANTEE AND NOT HAVING A SHARE CAPITAL

Memorandum of Association

1. The name of the company is 'The Scientific Research Association, Limited.'

2. The objects for which the company is established are the promotion of research into matters of a scientific nature and the doing of all such other things as are incidental or conducive to the attainment of the above object.

3. The liability of the members is limited.

4. Every member of the company undertakes to contribute to the assets of the company in the event of its being wound up while he is a member, or within one year afterwards, for payment of the debts and liabilities of the company contracted before he ceases to be a member, and the costs, charges and expenses of winding up, and for the adjustment of the rights of the contributories among themselves, such amount as may be required not exceeding £1.

We, the several persons whose names and addresses are subscribed, wish to be formed into a company in pursuance of this memorandum of association.

Names, Addresses and Descriptions of Subscribers

1. Charles O'Brien of...........in the County of..........University Professor.
2. Francis Power of..............in the County of..........Research Chemist.
3. James O'Connor of..........in the County of...........Biologist.
4. Thomas Daly of...............in the County of...........Science Teacher.
5. Richard O'Donnell of........in the County of...........Librarian.
6. Joseph Murray of............in the County of.................Physicist.
7. Michael Nolan of............in the County of..................Statistician.

Dated the.............................day of.................................., 19......................

Witness to the above signatures:..

Name: ....

Address:...

ARTICLES OF ASSOCIATION TO ACCOMPANY PRECEDING MEMORANDUM OF ASSOCIATION

Interpretation

1. In these articles—

'the Act' means the Companies Act, 1963 (No. 33 of 1963);

'the directors' means the directors for the time being of the company or the directors present at a meeting of the board of directors and includes any person occupying the position of director by whatever name called;

'secretary' means any person appointed to perform the duties of the secretary of the company;

'the seal' means the common seal of the company;

'the office' means the registered office for the time being of the company.

Expressions referring to writing shall, unless the contrary intention appears, be construed as including references to printing, lithography, photography and any other modes of representing or reproducing words in a visible form.

Unless the contrary intention appears, words or expressions contained in these articles shall bear the same meaning as in the Act or any statutory modification thereof in force at the date at which these articles become binding on the company.

Members

2. The number of members with which the company proposes to be registered is 500, but the directors may from time to time register an increase of members.

Definitions

'company': CA 1963, s 2(1); 'director': CA 1963, s 2(1), Sch 1, reg 1; 'member': CA 1963, s 31.

---

3. The subscribers to the memorandum of association and such other persons as the directors shall admit to membership shall be members of the company.

Definitions

'company': CA 1963, s 2(1); 'director': CA 1963, s 2(1), Sch 1, reg 1; 'member': CA 1963, s 31; 'memorandum': CA 1963, s 2(1).

General Meetings

4. All general meetings of the company shall be held in the State.

Definitions

'company': CA 1963, s 2(1).

---

5. (1) Subject to paragraph (2), the company shall in each year hold a general meeting as its annual general meeting in addition to any other meetings in that year and shall specify the meeting as such in the notices calling it; and not more than 15 months shall elapse between the date of one annual general meeting of the company and that of the next.

(2) So long as the company holds its first annual general meeting within 18 months of its incorporation, it need not hold it in the year of its incorporation or in the following year. Subject to article 4, the annual general meeting shall be held at such time and at such place in the State as the directors shall appoint.

Definitions

'company': CA 1963, s 2(1); 'director': CA 1963, s 2(1), Sch 1, reg 1.

---

6. All general meetings other than annual general meetings shall be called extraordinary general meetings.

7. The directors may, whenever they think fit, convene an extraordinary general meeting and extraordinary general meetings shall also be convened on such requisition, or, in default, may be convened by such requisitionists, as provided by section 132 of the Act. If at any time there are not within the State sufficient directors capable of acting to form a quorum, any director or any two members of the company may convene an extraordinary general meeting in the same manner as nearly as possible as that in which meeting may be convened by the directors.

Definitions

'Act': CA 1963, Sch 1, reg 1; 'company': CA 1963, s 2(1); 'director': CA 1963, s 2(1), Sch 1, reg 1; 'member': CA 1963, s 31.

Notes

Where there are no remaining directors and only one remaining member, it may be necessary to apply to the court pursuant to CA 1963, s 135 for an order convening the EGM and directing that the sole surviving member shall constitute the meeting on his own.

Notice of General Meetings.

8. Subject to sections 133 and 141 of the Act, an annual general meeting and a meeting called for the passing of a special resolution shall be called by 21 days' notice in writing at the least, and a meeting of the company (other than an annual general meeting or a meeting for the passing of a special resolution) shall be called by 14 days' notice in writing at the least. The notice shall be exclusive of the day on which it is served or deemed to be served and of the day for which it is given and shall specify the place, the day and the hour of meeting and, in the case of special business, the general nature of that business and shall be given, in manner hereinafter mentioned, to such persons as are, under the articles of the company, entitled to receive such notices from the company.

Definitions

'Act': CA 1963, Sch 1, reg 1; 'company': CA 1963, s 2(1); 'articles': CA 1963, s 2 (1); 'company': CA 1963, s 2(1).

Notes

The notice of the meeting will be void if it or any accompanying circular is misleading.[1] Where it is proposed to pass a special resolution at the meeting, the notice will be invalid if it fails to specify either the entire text or the entire substance of the proposed resolution.[2]

1 *Jackson v Munster Bank Ltd* (1884–85) 13 LR Ir 118.

2 *Re Moorgate Mercantile Holdings Ltd* [1980] 1 WLR 227.

---

9. The accidental omission to give notice of a meeting to, or the non-receipt of notice of a meeting by, any person entitled to receive notice shall not invalidate the proceedings at that meeting.

Notes

Deliberate omission to give notice of a meeting to a person entitled to receive such notice renders the meeting invalid. [1]

[1] *Musselwhite v CH Musselwhite & Son Ltd* [1962] Ch 964.

Proceedings at General Meetings

10. All business shall be deemed special that is transacted at an extraordinary general meeting, and also all that is transacted at an annual general meeting with the exception of declaring a dividend, the consideration of the accounts, balance sheets and the reports of the directors and auditors, the election of directors in the place of those retiring, the re-appointment of the retiring auditors, and the fixing of the remuneration of the auditors.

Definitions

'accounts': CA 1963, s 2(1); 'director': CA 1963, s 2(1), Sch 1, reg 1.

Notes

The notice convening a meeting will be invalid if it fails to set out at least the general nature of the special business which is to be transacted thereat.[1]

[1] *Roper v Ward* [1981] ILRM 408.

11. No business shall be transacted at any general meeting unless a quorum of members is present at the time when the meeting proceeds to business; save as herein otherwise provided, three members present in person shall be a quorum.

Definitions

'member': CA 1963, s 31.

Notes

If a quorum is present at the beginning of a meeting, the subsequent departure of a member reducing the meeting below the number required for the quorum will not invalidate proceedings of the meeting after his departure.[1] If, however, the number of members present falls to one, then there will no longer be a meeting. [2] Where it is impracticable to obtain a quorum, it may be necessary to apply to the court pursuant to CA 1963 s 135 for an order convening the meeting and directing that one member present in person or by proxy shall constitute a meeting.

[1] *Re Hartley Baird Ltd* [1955] Ch 143.

[2] *Re London Flats Ltd* [1969] 1 WLR 711; *Sharp v Dawes* (1876) 2 QBD 26; *Re El Sombrero Ltd* [1958] Ch 900.

12. If within half an hour from the time appointed for the meeting a quorum is not present, the meeting, if convened upon the requisition of members, shall be dissolved; in any other case it shall stand adjourned to the same day in the next week at the same time and place, or to such other day and at such other time and place as the directors may determine, and if at the adjourned meeting a quorum is not present within half an hour from the time appointed for the meeting, the members present shall be a quorum.

Definitions

'director': CA 1963, s 2(1), Sch 1, reg 1; 'member': CA 1963, s 31.

Notes

However, if there is only one member present, a meeting cannot exist.[1]

1 *Re London Flats Ltd* [1969] 1 WLR 711; *Sharp v Dawes* (1876) 2 QBD 26; *Re El Sombrero Ltd* [1958] Ch 900.

13. The chairman, if any, of the board of directors shall preside as chairman at every general meeting of the company, or if there is no such chairman, or if he is not present within 15 minutes after the time appointed for the holding of the meeting or is unwilling to act, the directors present shall elect one of their number to be chairman of the meeting.

Definitions

'company': CA 1963, s 2(1); 'director': CA 1963, s 2(1), Sch 1, reg 1.

14. If at any meeting no director is willing to act as chairman or if no director is present within 15 minutes after the time appointed for holding the meeting, the members present shall choose one of their number to be chairman of the meeting.

Definitions

'director': CA 1963, s 2(1), Sch 1, reg 1; 'member': CA 1963, s 31.

15. The chairman may with the consent of any meeting at which a quorum is present (and shall, if so directed by the meeting), adjourn the meeting from time to time and from place to place, but no business shall be transacted at any adjourned meeting other than the business left unfinished at the meeting from which the adjournment took place. When a meeting is adjourned for 30 days or more, notice of the adjourned meeting shall be given as in the case of an original meeting. Save as aforesaid, it shall not be necessary to give any notice of an adjournment or of the business to be transacted at an adjourned meeting.

16. At any general meeting a resolution put to the vote of the meeting shall be decided on a show of hands unless a poll is (before or on the declaration of the result of the show of hands) demanded—

(a) by the chairman; or

(b) by at least three members present in person or by proxy; or

(c) by any member or members present in person or by proxy and representing not less than one-tenth of the total voting rights of all the members having the right to vote at the meeting.

Unless a poll is so demanded, a declaration by the chairman that a resolution has, on a show of hands, been carried or carried unanimously or by a particular majority or lost, and an entry to that effect in the book containing the minutes of proceedings of the company shall be conclusive evidence of the fact without proof of the number or proportion of the votes recorded in favour of or against such resolution.

Definitions

'member': CA 1963, s 31.

The demand for a poll may be withdrawn.

17. Except as provided in article 19, if a poll is duly demanded it shall be taken in such manner as the chairman directs and the result of the poll shall be deemed to be the resolution of the meeting at which the poll was demanded.

18. Where there is an equality of votes, whether on a show of hands or on a poll, the chairman of the meeting at which the show of hands takes place or at which the poll is demanded, shall be entitled to a second or casting vote.

Notes

Any resolution carried on the casting vote of an invalidly appointed chairman is itself invalid.[1]

[1] *Clark v Workman* [1920] 1 IR 107.

---

19. A poll demanded on the election of a chairman, or on a question of adjournment shall be taken forthwith. A poll demanded on any other question shall be taken at such time as the chairman of the meeting directs, and any business other than that upon which a poll has been demanded may be proceeded with pending the taking of the poll.

20. Subject to section 141 of the Act, a resolution in writing signed by all the members for the time being entitled to attend and vote on such resolution at a general meeting (or being bodies corporate by their duly authorised representatives) shall be as valid and effective for all purposes as if the resolution had been passed at a general meeting of the company duly convened and held, and if described as a special resolution shall be deemed to be a special resolution within the meaning of the Act.

Definitions

'Act': CA 1963, Sch 1, reg 1; 'company': CA 1963, s 2(1); 'member': CA 1963, s 31.

Votes of Members

21. Every member shall have one vote.

Definitions

'member': CA 1963, s 31.

---

22. A member of unsound mind, or in respect of whom an order has been made by any court having jurisdiction in lunacy, may vote, whether on a show of hands or on a poll, by his committee, receiver, guardian, or other person appointed by that court, and any such committee, receiver, guardian, or other person may vote by proxy on a show of hands or on a poll.

Definitions

'member': CA 1963, s 31.

---

23. No member shall be entitled to vote at any general meeting unless all moneys immediately payable by him to the company have been paid.

Definitions

'company': CA 1963, s 2(1); 'member': CA 1963, s 31.

---

24. No objection shall be raised to the qualification of any voter except at the meeting or adjourned meeting at which the vote objected to is given or tendered, and every vote not disallowed at such meeting shall be valid for all purposes. Any such objection made in due time shall be referred to the chairman of the meeting whose decision shall be final and conclusive.

25. Votes may be given either personally or by proxy.

26. The instrument appointing a proxy shall be in writing under the hand of the appointer or of his attorney duly authorised in writing, or, if the appointer is a body corporate, either under seal or under the hand of an officer or attorney duly authorised. A proxy need not be a member of the company.

Definitions

'company': CA 1963, s 2(1); 'member': CA 1963, s 31; 'officer': CA 1963, s 2(1).

---

27. The instrument appointing a proxy and the power of attorney or other authority, if any, under which it is signed or a notarially certified copy of that power or authority shall be deposited at the office or at such other place within the State as is specified for that purpose in the notice convening the meeting not less than 48 hours before the time for holding the meeting or adjourned meeting at which the person named in the instrument purposes to vote, or, in the case of a poll, not less than 48 hours before the time appointed for the taking of the poll, and in default the instrument of proxy shall not be treated as valid.

28. An instrument appointing a proxy shall be in the following form or a form as near thereto as circumstances permit—

' Limited.

I/We,..

of...

in the County of.., being a member/members of the

above-named company, hereby appoint...

of...

or failing him, ...

of...

as may/our proxy to vote for me/us on my/our behalf at the (annual or extra-ordinary, as the case may be) general meeting of the company to be held on the .... day of ...., 19............ and at any adjournment thereof.

Signed this..............................day of......................................., 19..................

This form is to be used *in favour of/against the resolution. Unless otherwise instructed, the proxy will vote as he thinks fit.'

*Strike out whichever is not desired.

29. The instrument appointing a proxy shall be deemed to confer authority to demand or join in demanding a poll.

30. A vote given in accordance with the terms of an instrument of proxy shall be valid notwithstanding the previous death or insanity of the principal or revocation of the proxy or of the authority under which the proxy was executed, if no intimation in writing of such death, insanity or revocation as aforesaid is received by the company at the office before the commencement of the meeting or adjourned meeting at which the proxy is used.

Definitions

'company': CA 1963, s 2(1).

Bodies Corporate acting by Representatives at Meetings

31. Any body corporate which is a member of the company may by resolution of its directors or other governing body authorise such person as it thinks fit to act as its representative at any meeting of the company, and the person so authorised shall be entitled to exercise the same powers on behalf of the body corporate which he represents as that body corporate could exercise if it were an individual member of the company.

Definitions

'company': CA 1963, s 2(1); 'director': CA 1963, s 2(1), Sch 1, reg 1; 'member': CA 1963, s 31.

Directors

32. The number of the directors and the names of the first directors shall be determined in writing by the subscribers of the memorandum of association or a majority of them.

Definitions

'director': CA 1963, s 2(1), Sch 1, reg 1; 'memorandum': CA 1963, s 2(1).

33. The remuneration of the directors shall from time to time be determined by the company in general meeting. Such remuneration shall be deemed to accrue from day to day. The directors may also be paid all travelling, hotel and other expenses properly incurred by them in attending and returning from meetings of the directors or any committee of the directors or general meetings of the company or in connection with the business of the company.

Definitions

'company': CA 1963, s 2(1); 'director': CA 1963, s 2(1), Sch 1, reg 1.

Notes

If the company in general meeting fails or refuses to determine the remuneration of the directors, they do not have any implied right to be paid for the performance of their function and have no claim to payment on a *quantum meruit*.[1] Accordingly, they may be compelled to return any sums they have paid to themselves without the necessary authority, even if they acted *bona fide* in the belief that the payments were permissible.[2] The company in general meeting cannot retrospectively alter the directors' right to payment of accrued remuneration.[3] Where the company in general meeting has determined the remuneration of the board, but the appointment of one of the directors is defective, he may nonetheless be entitled to payment on a *quantum meruit* for services performed.[4] It should be noted that any remuneration paid to the directors under reg 33 is distinct from any payable to them as employees pursuant to any service contracts they may have with the company.

1 *Hutton v West Cork Rly Co* (1883) 23 Ch D 654; *Dunston v The Imperial Gas, Light & Coke Co* (1832) 3 B & Ad 125; *Woolf v East Niger Gold Mining Co Ltd* [1905] 21 TLR 660; *Guinness plc v Saunders* [1990] 2 WLR 324.

2 *Brown and Green Ltd v Harp* (1920) 36 TLR 330; *Guinness plc v Saunders* [1990] 2 WLR 324.

3 *Swabey v Port Darwin Gold Mining Co* (1889) 1 Meg 385.

4 *Craven-Ellis v Canons Ltd* [1936] 2 KB 403.

Borrowing Powers

34. The directors may exercise all the powers of the company to borrow money and to mortgage or charge its undertaking and property or any part thereof, and to issue debentures, debenture stock and other securities, whether outright or as security for any debt, liability or obligation of the company or of any third part.

Definitions

'company': CA 1963, s 2(1); 'debenture': CA 1963, s 2(1); 'director': CA 1963, s 2(1), Sch 1, reg 1.

Powers and Duties of Directors

35. The business of the company shall be managed by the directors, who may pay all expenses incurred in promoting and registering the company, and may exercise all such powers of the company as are not by the Act or by these articles required to be exercised by the company in general meeting, subject nevertheless to the provisions of the Act and of these articles and to such directions, being not inconsistent with the aforesaid provisions, as may be given by the company in general meeting: but no direction given by the company in general meeting shall invalidate any prior act of the directors which would have been valid if that direction had not been given.

Definitions

'Act': CA 1963, Sch 1, reg 1; 'company': CA 1963, s 2(1); 'director': CA 1963, s 2(1), Sch 1, reg 1.

Notes

Under the precursor to reg 35 in the Companies (Consolidation) Act 1908 and under the former English equivalent in the Companies Act 1948 it had been held that the members, having delegated the powers of management of the company to the board of directors, could only interfere by way of special resolution.[1] This position has now been expressly entrenched in England by the updated version of reg 35 (in the Companies (Tables A to F) Regulations 1985 (SI 1985/805)). The wording of reg 35 is, however, slightly different to the equivalent provisions in the 1908 and 1948 Acts. Whereas reg 35 refers to 'directions' of the general meeting, the other provisions referred to 'regulations'. The 'directions' must be taken to mean 'ordinary resolutions' of the company in general meeting.[2] Thus, in most aspects of the management of the business of the company, the members may interfere by way of ordinary resolution. In the case of a specific power conferred on the directors by some other article (eg the power to elect the chairman under reg 53), the members may only interfere by way of special resolution.[3] Furthermore, if a specific power has been conferred on the directors by statute, the members cannot interfere (whether by ordinary or special resolution) since they have no authority to circumvent legislative provisions.

1 *John Shaw & Sons (Salford) Ltd v Shaw* [1935] 2 KB 113; *Automatic Self-Cleansing Filter Syndicate Co v Cunninghame* [1906] 2 Ch 34; *Salmon v Quin & Axtens Ltd* [1909] 1 Ch 311; *Breckland Group Holdings Ltd v London & Suffolk Property Ltd* [1989] BCLC 100; *Nash v Lancegaye Safety Glass (Ireland) Ltd* (1958) 92 ILTR 11; *Clark v Workman* [1920] 1 IR 107.

2 See *J Temple Lang* (1973) Gazette 241, and Ussher, *Company Law In Ireland* (Butterworths, 1986), p 87.

3 *Clark v Workman* [1920] 1 IR 107; *Kehoe v Waterford and Limerick Railways* (1888–89) 21 LR Ir 221.

---

36. The directors may from time to time and at any time by power of attorney appoint any company, firm or person or body of persons, whether nominated directly or indirectly by the directors, to be the attorney or attorneys of the company for such purposes and with such powers, authorities and discretions (not exceeding those vested in or exercisable by the directors under these articles) and for such period and subject to such conditions as they may think fit, and any such powers of attorney may contain such provisions for the protection and convenience of persons dealing with any such attorney as the directors may think fit, and may also authorise any such attorney to delegate all or any of the powers, authorities and discretions vested in him.

Definitions

'company': CA 1963, s 2(1); 'director': CA 1963, s 2(1), Sch 1, reg 1.

Notes

It is usual practice for debentures secured by a fixed and/or floating charge over the company's property to contain a provision giving any receiver appointed by the debentureholder a power of attorney to act in the name of and on behalf of the company. [1]

[1] See *Industrial Development Authority v Moran* [1978] IR 159.

---

37. All cheques, promissory notes, drafts, bills of exchange and other negotiable instruments, and all receipts for moneys paid to the company, shall be signed, drawn, accepted, endorsed or otherwise executed, as the case may be, by such person or persons and in such manner as the directors shall from time to time by resolution determine.

Definitions

'director': CA 1963, s 2(1), Sch 1, reg 1.

---

38. The directors shall cause minutes to be made in books provided for the purpose-

(a) of all appointment of officers made by the directors;

(b) of the names of the directors present at each meeting of the directors and of any committee of the directors;

(c) of all resolutions and proceedings at all meetings of the company, and of the directors and of committees of directors.

Definitions

'company': CA 1963, s 2(1); 'director': CA 1963, s 2(1), Sch 1, reg 1; 'officer': CA 1963, s 2(1).

Disqualification of Directors

39. The office of director shall be vacated if the director—

(a) without the consent of the company in general meeting holds any other office or place of profit under the company; or

(b) is adjudged bankrupt in the State or in Northern Ireland or Great Britain or makes any arrangement or composition with his creditors generally; or

(c) becomes prohibited from being a director by reason of any order made under section 184 of the Act; or

(d) becomes of unsound mind; or

(e) resigns his office by notice in writing to the company; or

(f) is convicted of an indictable offence unless the directors otherwise determine; or

(g) is directly or indirectly interested in any contract with the company and fails to declare the nature of his interest in manner required by section 194 of the Act.

Definitions

'Act': CA 1963, Sch 1, reg 1; 'company': CA 1963, s 2(1); 'director': CA 1963, s 2(1), Sch 1, reg 1.

Voting on Contracts

40. A director may vote in respect of any contract in which he is interested or any matter arising thereout.

Definitions

'director': CA 1963, s 2(1), Sch 1, reg 1.

Notes

This provision effectively reverses *Cox v Dublin City Distillery (No 2)* [1915] 1 IR 345. Note that it is considerably wider than reg 84 which applies to public limited companies: CA 1963, see Part I of Table A.

Rotation of Directors

41. At the first annual general meeting of the company, all the directors shall retire from office and at the annual general meeting in every subsequent year one-third of the directors for the time being, or, if their number is not three or a multiple of three, then the number nearest one-third, shall retire from office.

Definitions

'company': CA 1963, s 2(1); 'director': CA 1963, s 2(1), Sch 1, reg 1.

Notes

Where the company fails to hold its AGM, those directors who ought to have retired by rotation in that year are deemed to automatically vacate office at the end of the last day upon which the meeting could lawfully have been held.[1]

1 *Re Zinotty Properties Ltd* [1984] 3 All ER 754; *Morris v Kassen* [1946] AC 459; *Re Consolidated Nickel Mines Ltd* [1914] 1 Ch 883.

42. The directors to retire in every year shall be those who have been longest in office since the last election, but as between persons who became directors on the same day, those to retire shall (unless they otherwise agree amongst themselves) be determined by lot.

Definitions

'director': CA 1963, s 2(1), Sch 1, reg 1.

43. A retiring director shall be eligible for re-election.

Definitions

'director': CA 1963, s 2(1), Sch 1, reg 1.

44. The company, at the meeting at which a director retires in manner aforesaid, may fill the vacated office electing a person thereto, and in default the retiring director shall, if offering himself for re-election, be deemed to have been re-elected, unless at such meeting it is expressly resolved not to fill such vacated office or unless a resolution for the re-election of such director has been put to the meeting and lost.

Definitions

'company': CA 1963, s 2(1); 'director': CA 1963, s 2(1), Sch 1, reg 1.

45. No person other than a director retiring at the meeting shall, unless recommended by the directors, be eligible for election to the office of director at any general meeting unless, not less than 3 nor more than 21 days before the date appointed for the meeting, there has been left at the office notice in writing, signed by a member duly qualified to attend and vote at the meeting for which such notice is given, of his intention to propose such a person for election, and also notice in writing signed by that person of his willingness to be elected.

Definitions

'director': CA 1963, s 2(1), Sch 1, reg 1; 'member': CA 1963, s 31.

46. The company may from time to time by ordinary resolution increase or reduce the number of directors, and may also determine in what rotation the increased or reduced number is to go out of office.

Definitions

'company': CA 1963, s 2(1); 'director': CA 1963, s 2(1), Sch 1, reg 1.

47. The directors shall have power at any time, and from time to time, to appoint any person to be a director, either to fill a casual vacancy or as an addition to the existing directors, but so that the total number of directors shall not at any time exceed the number fixed in accordance with these articles. Any director so appointed shall hold office only until the next annual general meeting, and shall then be eligible for re-election, but shall not be taken into account in determining the directors who are to retire by rotation at such meeting.

Definitions

'articles': CA 1963, s 2 (1); 'director': CA 1963, s 2(1), Sch 1, reg 1.

48. The company may by ordinary resolution of which extended notice has been given in accordance with section 142 of the Act remove any director before the expiration of his period of office, notwithstanding anything in these articles or in any agreement between the company and such director. Such removal shall be without prejudice to any claim such director may have for damages for breach of any contract of service between him and the company.

Definitions

'Act': CA 1963, Sch 1, reg 1; 'articles': CA 1963, s 2 (1)'company': CA 1963, s 2(1); 'director': CA 1963, s 2(1), Sch 1, reg 1.

49. The company may by ordinary resolution appoint another person in place of a director removed from office under article 48. Without prejudice to the powers of the directors under article 47, the company in general meeting may appoint any person to be a director, either to fill a casual vacancy or as an additional director. A person appointed in place of a director so removed or to fill such a vacancy shall be subject to retirement at the same time as if he had become a director on the day on which the director in whose place he is appointed was last elected a director.

Definitions

'company': CA 1963, s 2(1); 'director': CA 1963, s 2(1), Sch 1, reg 1.

Notes

Even if reg 49 is excluded, the members will still have an implied power to fill any casual vacancies.[1]

1 *Worcester Corsetry Ltd v Whiting* [1936] Ch 640.

Proceedings of Directors

50. The directors may meet together for the despatch of business, adjourn and otherwise regulate their meetings as the think fit. Questions arising at any meeting shall be decided by a majority of votes. Where there is an equality of votes, the chairman shall have a second or casting vote. A director may, and the secretary on the requisition of a director shall, at any time summon a meeting of the directors. If the directors so resolve it shall not be necessary to give notice of a meeting of directors to any director who being resident in the State is for the time being absent from the State.

Definitions

'director': CA 1963, s 2(1), Sch 1, reg 1; 'secretary': CA 1963, Sch 1, reg 1.

Notes

Reasonable notice must be given of any meeting of directors.[1] Whether or not notice is reasonable depends on the circumstances. For example, five minutes' notice was held to be sufficient where all directors were physically present and were not otherwise engaged. [2] However, where the directors were all in the same city, but some had prior engagements, three hours' notice was held to be insufficient.[3] Failure to provide reasonable notice of the directors' meeting renders any resolutions passed at it void.[4] It has been held that there is no requirement to provide an agenda for directors' meetings.[5] Any resolution carried on the casting vote of an invalidly appointed chairman is itself invalid.[6]

1 *Barron v Potter* [1914] 1 Ch 895; *Holland v McGill* (16 March 1990, unreported) HC (Murphy J).
2 *Browne v La Trinidad* (1887) 37 Ch D 1.
3 *Re Homer District Consolidated Gold Mines Ltd, ex parte Smith* (1888) 39 Ch D 546.
4 *Re Homer District Consolidated Mines Ltd ex parte Smith* (1888) 39 Ch D 546; *Re East Norfolk Tramways Co* (1877) 5 Ch D 963. cf. *Browne v La Trinidad* (1887) 37 Ch D 1.
5 *Holland v McGill* (16 March 1990, unreported) HC (Murphy J).
6 *Clark v Workman* [1920] 1 IR 107.

51. The quorum necessary for the transaction of the business of the directors may be fixed by the directors, and unless so fixed shall be two.

Definitions

'director': CA 1963, s 2(1), Sch 1, reg 1.

Notes

The wording of reg 51 seems to require a quorum throughout the meeting. In any event, if there is only one director present, he cannot constitute a meeting on his own.[1]

1 *Re London Flats Ltd* [1969] 1 WLR 711.

52. The continuing directors may act notwithstanding any vacancy in their number but, if and so long as their number is reduced below the number fixed by or pursuant to the articles of the company as the necessary quorum of directors, the continuing directors or director may act for the purpose of increasing the number of directors to that number or of summoning a general meeting of the company, but for no other purpose.

Definitions

'articles': CA 1963, s 2 (1)'company': CA 1963, s 2(1); 'director': CA 1963, s 2(1), Sch 1, reg 1.

53. The directors may elect a chairman of their meetings and determine the period for which he is to hold office; but, if no such chairman is elected, or if at any meeting the chairman is not present within 5 minutes after the time appointed for holding the same, the directors present may choose one of their number to be chairman of the meeting.

Definitions

'director': CA 1963, s 2(1), Sch 1, reg 1.

Notes

The members in general meeting can only interfere with the directors' power of appointment of a chairman, by way of special resolution.[1]

1 *Clark v Workman* [1920] 1 IR 107.

54. The directors may delegate any of their powers to committees consisting of such member or members of the board as they think fit; any committee so formed shall, in the exercise of the powers so delegated, conform to any regulations that may be imposed on it by the directors.

Definitions

'director': CA 1963, s 2(1), Sch 1, reg 1; 'member': CA 1963, s 31.

Notes

The power to delegate to a committee must not be used for the purpose of excluding a particular director from participating in the management of the company's affairs.[1]

1 *Kyushu v Alturas Gold Ltd* (1888) 4 TLR 331.

55. A committee may elect a chairman of its meetings; if no such chairman is elected, or if at any meeting the chairman is not present within 5 minutes after the time appointed for holding the same, the members present may choose one of their number to be chairman of the meeting.

Definitions

'member': CA 1963, s 31.

56. A committee may meet and adjourn as it thinks proper. Questions arising at any meeting shall be determined by a majority of votes of the members present, and when there is an equality of votes, the chairman shall have a second or casting vote.

Definitions

'member': CA 1963, s 31.

Notes

Any resolution carried on the casting vote of an invalidly appointed chairman is itself invalid.[1]

1 *Clark v Workman* [1920] 1 IR 107.

57. All acts done by any meeting of the directors or of a committee of directors or by an person acting as a director shall, notwithstanding that it is afterwards discovered that there was some defect in the appointment of any such director or person acting as aforesaid, or that they or any of them were disqualified, be as valid as if every such person had been duly appointed and was qualified to be a director.

Definitions

'director': CA 1963, s 2(1), Sch 1, reg 1.

58. A resolution in writing, signed by all the directors for the time being entitled to receive notice of a meeting of the directors, shall be as valid as if it had been passed at a meeting of the directors duly convened and held.

Definitions

'director': CA 1963, s 2(1), Sch 1, reg 1.

Secretary

59. [Subject to section 3 of the Companies (Amendment) Act, 1982,] [a] the secretary shall be appointed by the directors for such term and at such remuneration and upon such conditions as they may think fit; and any secretary so appointed may be removed by them.

Amendments

a Words inserted by C(A)A 1982, s 21.

Definitions

'director': CA 1963, s 2(1), Sch 1, reg 1; 'secretary': CA 1963, Sch 1, reg 1.

60. A provision of the Act or these articles requiring or authorising a thing to be done by or to a director and the secretary shall not be satisfied by its being done by or to the same person acting both as director and as, or in place of, the secretary.

Definitions

'Act': CA 1963, Sch 1, reg 1; 'articles': CA 1963, s 2 (1); 'director': CA 1963, s 2(1), Sch 1, reg 1; ' secretary': CA 1963, Sch 1, reg 1.

The Seal

61. The seal shall be used only by the authority of the directors or of a committee of directors authorised by the directors in that behalf, and every instrument to which the seal shall be affixed shall be signed by a director and shall be countersigned by the secretary or by a second director or by some other person appointed by the directors for the purpose.

Definitions

'director': CA 1963, s 2(1), Sch 1, reg 1; 'seal': CA 1963, Sch 1, reg 1; 'secretary': CA 1963, Sch 1, reg 1.

Notes

Regulation 76 of Table A of the Companies (Consolidation) Act 1908 contained a similar provision but required two directors and the secretary or such other person as the directors might appoint to sign every instrument to which the seal was affixed ie three signatures. It has been held that where reg 76 applied to a company, an indenture to which the seal is affixed but which has been signed by only two such persons was not effective to convey the company's interest in property.[1]

A power of attorney conferred on a receiver pursuant to the terms of a debenture, although allowing him to use his own seal to execute deeds on behalf of the company, does not entitle him to use the company's seal.[2]

1 *Safeera Ltd v Wallis and O'Regan* (12 July 1994, unreported), HC (Morris J).

2 *Industrial Development Authority v Moran* [1978] IR 159.

Accounts

62. The directors shall cause proper books of account to be kept relation to—

(a) all sums of money received and expended by the company and the matters in respect of which the receipt and expenditure takes place.

(b) all sales and purchases of goods by the company; and

(c) the assets and liabilities of the company.

Proper books shall not be deemed to be kept if there are not kept such books of account as are necessary to give a true and fair view of the state of the company's affairs and to explain its transactions.

Definitions

'company': CA 1963, s 2(1); 'director': CA 1963, s 2(1), Sch 1, reg 1.

---

63. The books of account shall be kept at the office or, subject to section 147 of the Act, at such other place as the directors think fit, and shall at all reasonable times be open to the inspection of the directors.

Definitions

'Act': CA 1963, Sch 1, reg 1; 'director': CA 1963, s 2(1), Sch 1, reg 1; 'office': CA 1963, Sch 1, reg 1.

---

64. The directors shall from time to time determine whether and to what extent and at what times and places and under what conditions or regulations the accounts and books of the company or any of them shall be open to the inspection of members not being directors, and no member (not being a director) shall have any right of inspecting any account or book or document of the company except as conferred by statute or authorised by the director or by the company in general meeting.

Definitions

'accounts': CA 1963, s 2(1); 'company': CA 1963, s 2(1); 'director': CA 1963, s 2(1), Sch 1, reg 1; 'document': CA 1963, s 2(1): 'member': CA 1963, s 31.

---

65. The directors shall from time to time in accordance with sections 148,150, 157 and 158 of the Act cause to be prepared and to be laid before the annual general meeting of the company such profit and loss accounts, balance sheets, group accounts and reports as are required by those sections to be prepared and laid before the annual general meeting of the company.

Definitions

'Act': CA 1963, Sch 1, reg 1; 'accounts': CA 1963, s 2(1); 'company': CA 1963, s 2(1); 'director': CA 1963, s 2(1), Sch 1, reg 1; 'group accounts'; s 2(1), s 150(1).

66. A copy of every balance sheet (including every document required by law to be annexed thereto) which is to be laid before the annual general meeting of the company together with a copy of the directors' report and auditors' report shall, not less than 21 days before the date of the annual general meeting, be sent to every person entitled under the provisions of the Act to receive them.

Definitions

'Act': CA 1963, Sch 1, reg 1; 'company': CA 1963, s 2(1); 'director': CA 1963, s 2(1), Sch 1, reg 1; 'document': CA 1963, s 2(1).

Audit

67. Auditors shall be appointed an their duties regulated in accordance with sections 160 to 163 of the Act.

Definitions

'Act': CA 1963, Sch 1, reg 1.

Notices

68. A notice may be given by the company to any member either personally or by sending it by post to him to his registered address. Where a notice is sent by post, service of the notice shall be deemed to be effected by properly addressing, prepaying and posting a letter containing the notice, and to have been effected in the case of a notice of a meeting at the expiration of 24 hours after the letter containing the same is posted and in any other case at the time at which the letter would be delivered in the ordinary course of post.

Definitions

'company': CA 1963, s 2(1); 'member': CA 1963, s 31.

69. Notice of every general meeting shall be given in any manner hereinbefore authorised to—

(a) every member;

(b) every person being a personal representative or the Official Assignee in bankruptcy or a member where the member but for his death or bankruptcy would be entitled to receive notice of the meeting; and

(c) the auditor for the time being of the company.

No other person shall be entitled to receive notices of general meetings.

Names, Addresses and Descriptions of Subscribers

1. Charles O'Brien of..................in the County of..................University Professor.
2. Francis Power of..................in the County of..................Research Chemist.
3. James O'Connor of...............in the County of..................Biologist.
4. Thomas Daly of....................in the County of..................Science Teacher.
5. Richard O'Donnell of............in the County of..................Librarian.
6. Joseph Murray of..................in the County of..................Physicist.
7. Michael Nolan of..................in the County of..................Statistician.

Dated the......................... day of......................................., 19...........................

Witness to the above signatures:...

Name:...

Address: ....

Definitions

'company': CA 1963, s 2(1); 'member': CA 1963, s 31.

TABLE D

PART I

FORM OF MEMORANDUM AND ARTICLES OF ASSOCIATION OF A COMPANY LIMITED BY GUARANTEE AND HAVING A SHARE CAPITAL

Memorandum of Association

1. The name of the company is 'The Western Counties Tourist Development Company, Limited.'

Definitions

'company': CA 1963, s 2(1).

2. Objects for which the company is established are the promotion of tourism in the western counties of Ireland by providing facilities for tourists, and the doing of all such other things as are incidental or conducive to the attainment of the above object.

Definitions

'company': CA 1963, s 2(1).

3. The liability of the members is limited.

Definitions

'member': CA 1963, s 31.

4. Every member of the company undertakes to contribute to the assets of the company in the event of its being wound up while he is a member, or within one year afterwards, for payment of the debts and liabilities of the company contracted before he ceases to be a member, and the costs, charges and expenses of winding up, and for the adjustment of the rights of the contributories among themselves, such amount as may be required, not exceeding £5.

Definitions

'company': CA 1963, s 2(1); 'member': CA 1963, s 31.

5. The share capital of the company is £100,000 divided into 10,000 shares of £1 each. We, the several persons whose names and addresses are subscribed, wish to be formed into a company in pursuance of this memorandum of association, and we agree to take the number of shares in the capital of the company set opposite our respective names.

Names, Addresses and Descriptions of Subscribers	*Number of shares taken by each subscriber*
1. Patrick Walsh of.................in the County of.................Solicitor	100
2. Thomas Murphy of................in the County of................Hotel Proprietor	500
3. James Ryan of...............in the County of...............Engineer	45
4. Francis O'Brien of...............in the County of..............Travel Agent	100
5. Thomas Duffy of..............in the County of..............Farmer	100
6. Joseph Moran of..............in the County of..............Architect	150
7. Martin O'Reilly of..............in the County of..............Clerk	5

Total shares taken..............1,000

Dated the......................day of.., 19....................

Witness to the above signatures:...

Name:...

Address:...

Definitions

'company': CA 1963, s 2(1); 'memorandum': CA 1963, s 2(1); 'share': CA 1963, s 2(1).

PART II

ARTICLES OF ASSOCIATION TO ACCOMPANY PRECEDING MEMORANDUM OF ASSOCIATION WHERE THE COMPANY IS NOT A PRIVATE COMPANY

[...][a]

Amendments

a Repealed by C(A)A 1983, Sch 3.

PART III

ARTICLES OF ASSOCIATION TO ACCOMPANY PRECEDING MEMORANDUM OF ASSOCIATION WHERE THE COMPANY IS A PRIVATE COMPANY

1. The number of members with which the company proposes to be registered is 40 but the directors may from time to time, subject to Article 2, register an increase of members.

Definitions

'company': CA 1963, s 2(1); 'director': CA 1963, s 2(1), Sch 1, reg 1; 'member': CA 1963, s 31; 'private company': CA 1963, s 2(1), s 33(1).

---

2. The regulations of Table A, Part II, set out in the First Schedule to the Companies Act, 1963, shall be deemed to be incorporated with these articles and shall apply to the company.

Names, Addresses and Descriptions of Subscribers

1. Patrick Walsh of.........................in the County of................Solicitor.
2. Thomas Murphy of.....................in the County of................Hotel Proprietor.
3. James Ryan of............................in the County of.................Engineer.
4. Francis O'Brien of.....................in the County of.................Travel Agent.
5. Thomas Duffy of.......................in the County of.................Farmer.
6. Joseph Moran of.......................in the County of.................Architect.
7. Martin O'Reilly of.....................in the County of..................Clerk.

Dated the..............................day of.., 19.....................

Witness to the above signatures:...

Name...

Address:..

TABLE E

PART I

FORM OF MEMORANDUM AND ARTICLES OF ASSOCIATION OF AN UNLIMITED COMPANY HAVING A SHARE CAPITAL

Memorandum of Association

1. The name of the company is 'The Turf Harvester Company'.

Definitions

'company': CA 1963, s 2(1); 'unlimited company': CA 1963, s 2(1), s 5(2).

2. The object for which the company is established are the development of improved methods of cutting and harvesting turf and the doing of all such things as are incidental or conducive to the attainment of the above object.

We, the several persons whose names and addresses are subscribed, wish to be formed into a company in pursuance of this memorandum of association, and we agree to take the number of shares in the capital of the company set opposite our respective names.

Names, Addresses and Descriptions of Subscribers			*Number of shares taken by each subscriber*
1. Patrick O'Connor of	in the County of	Merchant	100
2. Joseph O'Brien of	in the County of	, Solicitor	500
3. Thomas Ryan of	in the County of	, Engineer	50
4. James Murphy of	in the County of	, Engineer	500
5. Patrick Nolan of	in the County of	, Farmer	350
6. James Byrne of	in the County of	, Metal Worker	50
7. James Duffy of	in the County of	, Farmer	50
Total shares taken			1,600

Dated the..................................day of................................., 19.................

Witness to the above signatures: ....

Name: ....

Address: ....

PART II

ARTICLES OF ASSOCIATION TO ACCOMPANY PRECEDING MEMORANDUM OF ASSOCIATION WHERE THE COMPANY IS NOT A PRIVATE COMPANY

1. The number of members with which the company proposes to be registered is 100 but the directors may from time to time register an increase of members.

Definitions

'articles': CA 1963, s 2(1); 'company': CA 1963, s 2(1); 'director': CA 1963, s 2(1), Sch 1, reg 1; 'member': CA 1963, s 31; 'memorandum': CA 1963, s 2(1); 'private company': CA 1963, s 2(1), s 33(1).

2. The share capital of the company is £10,000 divided into 10,000 shares of £1 each.

Definitions

'company': CA 1963, s 2(1); 'share': CA 1963, s 2(1).

3. The company may by special resolution—

(a) increase the share capital by such to be divided into shares of such amount as the resolution may prescribe;

(b) consolidate its shares into shares of a larger amount than its existing shares;

(c) subdivide its shares into shares of a smaller amount than its existing shares;

(d) cancel any shares which at the date of the passing of the resolution have not been taken or agreed to be taken by an person;

(e) reduce its share capital in any way.

Definitions

'company': CA 1963, s 2(1); 'share': CA 1963, s 2(1).

---

4. Subject to sections 133 and 141 of the Act, an annual general meeting and a meeting called for the passing of a special resolution shall be called by 21 days' notice in writing at the least, and a meeting of the company other than—

(a) an annual general meeting, or

(b) a meeting for the passing of a special resolution;

shall be called by 7 days' notice in writing at the least. The notice shall be exclusive of the day on which it is served or deemed to be served and of the day for which it is given, and shall specify the place, the day and the hour of the meeting, and, in the case of special business, the general nature of that business, and shall be given in manner authorised by these articles to such persons as are, under the articles of the company, entitled to receive such notices from the company.

Definitions

'Act': CA 1963, Sch 1, reg 1; 'articles': CA 1963, s 2 (1); 'company': CA 1963, s 2(1).

---

5. The regulations of Table A, Part I, set out in the First Schedule to the Companies Act, 1963 (other than regulations 40 to 46 (inclusive) and 51) shall be deemed to be incorporated with these articles and shall apply to the company.

Names, Addresses and Descriptions of Subscribers

1. Patrick O'Connor of....................in the County of...................., Merchant.
2. Joseph O'Brien of......................in the County of...................., Solicitor.
3. Thomas Ryan of.........................in the County of...................., Engineer.
4. James Murphy of........................in the County of...................., Engineer.
5. Patrick Nolan of.........................in the County of...................., Farmer.
6. James Byrne of..........................in the County of...................., Metal Worker.
7. James Duffy of...........................in the County of...................., Farmer.

Dated the..................................day of.................................., 19................

Witness to the above signatures:..

Name: ....

Address:...

PART III

ARTICLES OF ASSOCIATION TO ACCOMPANY PRECEDING MEMORANDUM OF ASSOCIATION WHERE THE COMPANY IS A PRIVATE COMPANY

1. The number of members with which the company proposes to be registered is 40 but the directors may from time to time, subject to Article 4, register an increase of members.

Definitions

'articles': CA 1963, s 2(1); 'company': CA 1963, s 2(1); 'director': CA 1963, s 2(1), Sch 1, reg 1; 'member': CA 1963, s 31; 'memorandum': CA 1963, s 2(1); 'private company': CA 1963, s 2(1), s 33(1).

2. The share capital of the company is £10,000 divided into 10,000 shares of £1 each.

Definitions

'company': CA 1963, s 2(1); 'share': CA 1963, s 2(1).

3. The company may by special resolution—

(a) increase the share capital by such sum to be divided into shares of such amount as the resolution may prescribe;

(b) consolidate its shares into shares of a larger amount than its existing shares;

(c) subdivide its shares into shares of a smaller amount than its existing shares;

(d) cancel any shares which at the date of the passing of the resolution have not been taken or agreed to be taken by any person;

(e) reduce its share capital in any way.

Definitions

'company': CA 1963, s 2(1); 'share': CA 1963, s 2(1).

4. The regulations of Table A, Part II set out in the First Schedule to the Companies Act, 1963, (with the exception of regulations 40 to 46 (inclusive) of Part I of that Table), shall be deemed to be incorporated with these articles and shall apply to the company.

Names, Addresses and Descriptions of Subscribers

1. Patrick O'Connor of....................in the County of...................., Merchant.

2. Joseph O'Brien of.......................in the County of....................., Solicitor.

3. Thomas Ryan of..........................in the County of...................., Engineer.

4. James Murphy of..........................in the County of...................., Engineer.

5. Patrick Nolan of..........................in the County of...................., Farmer.

6. James Byrne of..........................in the County of...................., Metal Worker.

7. James Duffy of..........................in the County of...................., Farmer.

Dated the..................................day of.................................., 19.................

Witness to the above signatures:...

Name:...

Address: ....

SECOND SCHEDULE

FORM OF STATEMENT IN LIEU OF PROSPECTUS TO BE DELIVERED TO REGISTRAR BY A PRIVATE COMPANY ON BECOMING [AN UNLIMITED PUBLIC COMPANY][a] AND REPORTS TO BE SET OUT THEREIN

Amendments

a Words substituted by C(A)A 1983, Sch 1 para 26.

Definitions

'private company': CA 1963, s 2(1), s 33(1); 'prospectus': CA 1963, s 2(1); 'registrar of companies': CA 1963, s 2(1).

Part I

Form of Statement and Particulars to be contained therein

The Companies Act, 1963

Statement in lieu of prospectus delivered for registration by

(Insert the name of the company)

Pursuant to section 35 of the Companies Act, 1963

Delivered for registration by

1.	The nominal share capital of the company	1.	£
2.	Divided into	2.	Shares of £ each Shares of £ each
3	Amount, if any, of above capital which consists of redeemable preference shares.	3.	Shares of £ each
4.	The earliest date on which the company has power to redeem these shares.	4.	
5.	Names, descriptions and addresses of directors or proposed directors.	5.	

6.	Number of shares issued and amounts paid up thereon.	6.	Shares of £ each on which £ paid up shares of £ paid up on which £ paid up
7.	Amount of commissions paid or payable in connection with the issue of any shares or debentures.	7.	£
8	Amount of discount, if any, allowed on the issue of any shares, or so much thereof as has not been written off at the date of the statement.	8.	£
9.	Unless more than 2 years have elapsed since the date on which the company was entitled to commence business:—	9.	
	(a) Amount of preliminary expenses.	(a)	£
	(b) By whom these expenses have been paid or are payable.	(b)	
	(c) Amount paid to any promoter.	(c)	Name of promotor
	(d) Consideration for the payment.	(d)	Consideration
	(e) Any other benefit given to any promoter.	(e)	Name of promoter: Nature and value of benefit
	(f) Consideration for giving of benefit.	(f)	Consideration
10.	If the share capital of the company is divided into different classes of shares, the right of voting at meetings of the company conferred by and the rights in respect of capital and dividends attached to the several classes of shares respectively.	10.	
11.	Number and amount of shares and debentures issued within the 2 years preceding the date of this statement as fully or partly paid up otherwise than for cash or agreed to be so issued at the date of this statement.	11.	(a) shares of £ fully paid (b) shares upon which £ per share credited as paid (c) debentures £
	Consideration for the issue of those shares or debentures.		(d) Consideration
12.(a)	Number, description and amount of any shares or debentures which any person has or is entitled to be given an option to subscribe for, or to acquire from a person to whom they have been allotted or agreed to be allotted with a view to his offering them for sale.	12.	(a) shares of £ and debentures of £

(b) Period during which option is exercisable.	(b) Until
(c) Price to be paid for shares or debentures subscribed for or acquired under option.	(c)
(d) Consideration for option or right to option.	(d) Consideration:
(e) Persons to whom option or right to option was given or, if given to existing shareholders or debenture holders as such, the relevant shares or debentures.	(e) Names and addresses
13.(a) Names and addresses of vendors of property (1) purchased or acquired by the company within the 2 years preceding the date of this statement or (2) agreed or proposed to be purchased or acquired by the company, except where the contract for its purchase or acquisition was entered into in the ordinary course of business and there is no connection between the contract and the company ceasing to be a private company or where the amount of the purchase money is not material.	13. (a)
(b) Amount (in cash, shares or debentures) paid or payable to each separate vendor.	(b)
(c) Amount paid or payable in cash, shares or debentures for any such property, specifying the amount paid or payable for goodwill.	(c) Total purchase £ Cash £ Shares £ Debentures £ Goodwill £
14. Short particulars of any transaction relating to any such property which was completed within the 2 preceing years and in which any vendor to the company or any person who is, or was at the time thereof, a promoter, director or proposed director of the company, had any interest direct or indirect.	14.

15. Dates of parties to, and general nature of every material (other than contracts entered into in the ordinary course of business carried on by the company or entered into more than 2 years before the delivery of this statement.	15.
16. Time and place at which the contracts or copies thereof may be inspected or (1) in the case of a contract not reduced into writing, a memorandum giving full particulars thereof, and (2) in the case of a contract wholly or partly in a language other than English or Irish, a copy of a translation thereof in English or Irish or embodying a translation in English or Irish of the parts not in English or Irish, as the case may be, being a translation certified in the prescribed manner to be a correct translation.	16.
17. Names and addresses of the auditors of the company.	17.
18. Full particulars of the nature and extent of the interest of every director in any property purchased or acquired by the company within the 2 years preceding the date of this statement or proposed to be purchased or acquired by the company or, where the interest of such a director consists in being a partner in a firm, the nature and extent of the interest of the firm, with a statement of all sums paid or agreed to be paid to him or to the firm in cash or shares or otherwise by any person either to induce him to become, or to qualify him as, a director, or otherwise for services rendered or to be rendered to the company by him or by the firm.	18.

19. Rates of the dividends, if any, paid by the company in respect of each class of shares in the company in each of the 5 financial years immediately preceding the date of this statement or since the incorporation of the company whichever period is the shorter.	19.
20. Particulars of the cases in which no dividends have been paid in respect of any class of shares in any of these years.	20.

(Signatures of the persons above-named as directors or proposed director or of their agents authorised in writing).

Date ....

....

PART II
REPORTS TO BE SET OUT

1. If unissued shares or debentures of the company are to be applied in the purchase of a business, a report made by accountants (who shall be named in the statement) upon—

(a) the profits or losses of the business in respect of each of the 5 financial years immediately preceding the delivery of the statement to the registrar; and

(b) the assets and liabilities of the business at the last date to which the accounts of the business were made up.

Definitions

'accounts': CA 1963, s 2(1); 'company': CA 1963, s 2(1); 'debenture': CA 1963, s 2(1); 'financial year': CA 1963, s 2(1); 'registrar of companies': CA 1963, s 2(1); 'share': CA 1963, s 2(1).

---

2. (1) If unissued shares or debentures of the company are to be applied directly or indirectly in any manner resulting in the acquisition of shares in a body corporate which by reason of the acquisition or anything to be done in consequence thereof or in connection therewith will become a subsidiary of the company, a report made by accountants (who shall be named in the statement) upon the profits and losses and assets and liabilities of the other body corporate in accordance with subparagraph (2) or (3), as the case requires, indicating how the profits or losses of the other body corporate dealt with by the report would, in respect of the shares to be acquired, have concerned members of the company, and what allowance would have had to be made, in relation to assets and liabilities so dealt with, for holders of other shares, if the company had at all material times held the shares to be acquired.

(2) If the other body corporate has no subsidiaries, the report referred to in subparagraph (1) shall—

(a) so far as regards profits and losses, deal with the profits or losses of the body corporate in respect of each of the 5 financial years immediately preceding the delivery of the statement to the registrar; and

(b) so far as regards assets and liabilities, deal with the assets and liabilities of the body corporate at the last date to which the accounts of the body corporate were made up.

(3) If the other body corporate has subsidiaries, the report referred to in subparagraph (1) shall—

(a) so far as regards profits and losses, deal separately with the other body corporate's profits or losses as provided by subparagraph (2), and in addition deal either—

(i) as a whole with the combined profits or losses of its subsidiaries, so far as they concern members of the other body corporate; or

(ii) separately with the profits or losses of each subsidiary, so far as they concern members of the other body corporate;

or, instead of dealing separately with the other body corporate's profits or losses, deal as a whole with the profits or losses of the other body corporate and, so far as they concern members of the other body corporate, with the combined profits or losses of its subsidiaries; and

(b) so far as regards assets and liabilities, deal separately with the other body corporate's assets and liabilities as provided by subparagraph (2) and in addition, deal either—

(i) as a whole with the combined assets and liabilities of its subsidiaries, with or without the other body corporate's assets and liabilities; or

(ii) separately with the assets and liabilities of each subsidiary;

and shall indicate in relation to the assets and liabilities of the subsidiaries, the allowance to be made for persons other than members of the company.

Definitions

'accounts': CA 1963, s 2(1); 'company': CA 1963, s 2(1); 'debenture': CA 1963, s 2(1); 'financial year': CA 1963, s 2(1); 'member': CA 1963, s 31; 'registrar of companies': CA 1963, s 2(1); 'share': CA 1963, s 2(1); 'subsidiary': CA 1963, s 2(1), s 155.

Part III

Provisions applying to Parts I and II

3. In this Schedule, 'vendor' includes a vendor as defined in Part III of the Third Schedule and 'financial year' has the meaning assigned to it in that Part of that Schedule.

Definitions

'financial year': CA 1963, s 2(1).

---

4. If in the case of a business which has been carried on, or of a body corporate which has been carrying on business, for less than 5 years, the accounts of the business or body corporate have been made up only in respect of 4 years, 3 years, 2 years or one year, Part II shall have effect as if references to 4 years, 3 years, 2 years or one year, as the case may be, were substituted for references to 5 years.

Definitions

'accounts': CA 1963, s 2(1).

5. Any report required by Part II shall either indicated by way of note any adjustments relating to the figures of any profits or losses or assets and liabilities dealt with by the report which appear to the persons making the report necessary or shall make those adjustments and indicate that adjustments have been made.

6. Any report by accountants required by Part II shall be made by accountants qualified under this Act for appointment as auditors of the company.

Definitions

'Act': CA 1963, Sch 1, reg 1; 'company': CA 1963, s 2(1).

THIRD SCHEDULE

MATTERS TO BE SPECIFIED IN PROSPECTUS AND REPORTS TO BE SENT OUT THEREIN

[...][a]

Amendments

a Repealed by IFCMPA 2005, s 40.

FOURTH SCHEDULE

FORM OF STATEMENT IN LIEU OF PROSPECTUS TO BE DELIVERED TO REGISTRAR BY A COMPANY WHICH DOES NOT ISSUE A PROSPECTUS OR WHICH DOES NOT MAKE AN ALLOTMENT ON A PROSPECTUS ISSUED, AND REPORTS TO BE SET OUT THEREIN

[...][a]

Amendments

a Repealed by IFCMPA 2005, s 40.

FIFTH SCHEDULE

SECTIONS 125, 395

CONTENTS AND FORM OF ANNUAL RETURN OF A COMPANY HAVING A SHARE

CAPITAL

[...][a]

Amendments

a Repealed by CLEA 2001, s 63(2) with effect from 1 March 2002.[1]

[1] Company Law Enforcement Act 2001 (Commencement) (No. 2) Order 2001 (SI 438/2001).

Cross reference

See CA 1963, ss 125 and 127 and notes thereto.

See also Companies (Forms) Order 2004 (SI 133/2004): Form B1.

Definitions

'annual return': CA 1963, s 2(1); 'company': CA 1963, s 2(1); 'share': CA 1963, s 2(1).

SIXTH SCHEDULE

Notes

This schedule still applies to limited companies of the type referred to in C(A)A 1986, s 2(1).

ACCOUNTS

Preliminary

1. Paragraphs 2 to 11 apply to the balance sheet and 12 to 14 to the profit and loss account and are subject to the exceptions and modifications provided for by Parts II and III of this Schedule; and this Schedule has effect in addition to sections 191 and 192.

PART I

GENERAL PROVISIONS AS TO BALANCE SHEET AND PROFIT AND LOSS *Account*

BALANCE SHEET

2. The authorised share capital, issued share capital, liabilities and assets shall be summarised, with such particulars as are necessary to disclose the general nature of the assets and liabilities, and there shall be specified—

(a) any part of the issued capital that consists of redeemable preference shares, the amount of the premium (if any) payable on redemption, the earliest and latest dates on which the company has power to redeem those shares and whether redemption is at the option of the company or obligatory;

(b) any part of the issued capital that consists of preference shares which are redeemable in accordance with a resolution passed under section 65, the amount of the premium (if any) payable on redemption, the earliest and latest dates on which the company has power to redeem those shares and whether redemption is at the option of the company or obligatory;

(c) the amount of the share premium account;

(d) particulars of any redeemed debentures which the company has power to re-issue.

Definitions

'company': CA 1963, s 2(1); 'debenture': CA 1963, s 2(1); 'share': CA 1963, s 2(1).

3. There shall be stated under separate headings, so far as they are not written off—

(a) the preliminary expenses;

(b) any expenses incurred in connection with any issue of share capital or debentures;

(c) any sums paid by way of commission in respect of any shares or debentures;

(d) any sums allowed by way of discount in respect of any debentures; and

(e) the amount of the discount allowed on any issue of shares at a discount.

Definitions

'debenture': CA 1963, s 2(1); 'share': CA 1963, s 2(1).

4. (1) Subject to subparagraphs (2) and (3), the reserves, provisions, liabilities and fixed and current assets shall be classified under headings appropriate to the company's business. Amounts set aside to meet future tax liabilities or for tax equalisation purposes shall be treated as provisions but separately indicated.

(2) Where the amount of any class is not material, it may be included under the same heading as some other class.

(3) Where any assets of one class are not separable from assets of another class, those assets may be included under the same heading.

(4) Fixed assets shall also be distinguished from current assets.

(5) The method or methods used to arrive at the amount of the fixed assets under each heading shall be stated.

Definitions

'company': CA 1963, s 2(1).

5. (1) The method of arriving at the amount of any fixed asset shall, subject to subparagraph (2), be to take the difference between—

(a) its cost or, if it stands in the company's books at a valuation, the amount of the valuation; and

(b) the aggregate amount provided or written off since the date of acquisition or valuation, as the case may be, for depreciation or diminution in value;

and for the purposes of this paragraph the net amount at which any assets stand in the company's books on the operative date (after deduction of the amounts previously provided or written off for depreciation or diminution in value) shall, if the figures relating to the period before the operative date cannot be obtained without unreasonable expense or delay, be treated as if it were the amount of a valuation of those assets made on the operative date and, where any of those assets are sold, the said net amount less the amount of the sales shall be treated as if it were the amount of the valuation so made of the remaining assets.

(2) Subparagraph (1) shall not apply—

(a) to assets for which the figures relating to the period beginning with the operative date cannot be obtained without unreasonable expense or delay; or

(b) to assets the replacement of which is provided for wholly or partly—

(i) by making provision for renewals and charging the cost of replacement against the provision so made; or

(ii) by charging the cost of replacement direct to revenue; or

(c) to any investments of which the market value (or, in the case of investments not having a market value, their value as estimated by the directors) is shown either as the amount of the investments or by way of note; or

(d) to goodwill, patents or trademarks.

(3) For the assets under each heading whose amount is arrived in accordance with subparagraph (1), there shall be shown—

(a) the aggregate of the amounts referred to in head (a) of that subparagraph; and

(b) the aggregate of the amounts referred to in head (b) thereof.

(4) As respects the assets under each heading whose amount is not arrived at in accordance with subparagraph (1) because their placement is provided for as mentioned in subparagraph (2)(b), there shall be stated—

(a) the means by which their replacement is provided for; and

(b) the aggregate amount of the provision (if any) made for renewals and not used.

Definitions

'company': CA 1963, s 2(1); 'director': CA 1963, s 2(1), Sch 1 reg 1; 'the operative date': CA 1963, s 2(1).

6.(1) Subject to subparagraph (2), the aggregate amounts respectively of capital reserves, revenue reserves and provisions (other than provisions for depreciation, renewals or diminution in value of assets) shall be stated under separate headings.

(2) Subparagraph (1) shall not require a separate statement of any of the 3 amounts referred to in that subparagraph which is not material.

7. (1) There shall also be shown (unless it is shown in the profit and loss account or a statement or report annexed thereto or the amount involved is not material)—

(a) where the amount of the capital reserves, of the revenue reserves or of the provisions (other than provisions for depreciation, renewals or diminution in value of assets) shows an increase as compared with the amount at the end of the immediately preceding financial year, the source from which the amount of the increase has been derived; and

(b) where—

(i) the amount of the capital reserves or of the revenue reserves shows a decrease as compared with the amount at the end of the immediately preceding financial year; or

(ii) the amount at the end of the immediately preceding financial year of the provisions (other than provisions for depreciation, renewals or diminution in value of assets) exceeded the aggregate of the sums since applied and amounts still retained for the purposes thereof;

the application of the amounts derived from the difference.

(2) Where the heading showing any of the reserves or provisions aforesaid is divided into subheadings, this paragraph shall apply to each of the separate amounts shown in the subheadings instead of applying to the aggregate amount thereof.

Definitions

'financial year': CA 1963, s 2(1).

---

8. There shall be shown under separate headings—

(a) the aggregate amounts respectively of the company's quoted investments and unquoted investments;

(b) the amount of the goodwill so far as ascertainable from the books of the company or from any contracts or documents relating to the purchase or sale of property and so far as not written off;

(c) the amount of the patents and trademarks so far as ascertainable and so far as not written off;

(d) the aggregate amount of any outstanding loans permitted by section 60 (other than loans to which paragraph (a) of subsection (13) refers) indicating separately loans permitted by paragraphs (b) and (c) of subsection (13);

(e) the aggregate amount of bank loans and overdrafts;

(f) the net aggregate amount (after deduction of income tax) which is recommended for distribution by way of dividend.

Definitions

'company': CA 1963, s 2(1); 'document': CA 1963, s 2(1).

---

9. Where any liability of the company is secured otherwise than by operation of law on any assets of the company, the fact that that liability is so secured shall be stated but it shall not be necessary to specify the assets on which the liability is secured.

Definitions

'company': CA 1963, s 2(1).

---

10. Where any of the company's debentures are held by a nominee of or a trustee for the company, the nominal amount of the debentures and the amount paid for such debentures by the company shall be stated.

Definitions

'company': CA 1963, s 2(1); 'debenture': CA 1963, s 2(1).

11. (1) The matters referred to in subparagraphs (2) to (10) shall be stated by way of note, or in statement or report annexed, if not otherwise shown.

(2) The amount of any arrears of fixed cumulative dividends on the company's shares and the period for which the dividends or, if there is more than one class, each class of them are in arrear the amount to be stated before deduction of income tax, except that, in the case of tax free dividends, the amount shall be shown free of tax and the fact that it is so shown shall also be stated.

[(2A) Where shares in a public limited company, other than an old public limited company within the meaning of the Companies (Amendment) Act, 1983 are acquired by the company by forfeiture or surrender in lieu of forfeiture, or in pursuance of section 41 of that Act, or are acquired by another person in circumstances where paragraph (c) or (d) of section 43 (1) of that Act applies or are made subject to a lien or charge taken (whether expressly or otherwise) by the company and permitted by section 44 (2) (a), (c) or (d) of that Act—

(a) the number and nominal value of the shares so acquired by the company, acquired by another person in such circumstances and so charged respectively during the financial year;

(b) the maximum number and nominal value of shares which, having been so acquired by the company, acquired by another person in such circumstances or so charged (whether or not during the financial year) are held at any time by the company or that other person during that year;

(c) the number and nominal value of the shares so acquired by the company, acquired by another person in such circumstances or so charged (whether or not during that year) which are disposed of by the company or that other person or cancelled by the company during that year;

(d) where the number and nominal value of the shares of any particular description are stated in pursuance of any of the preceding paragraphs, the percentage of the called-up share capital which shares of that description represent;

(e) where any of the shares have been so charged, the amount of the charge in each case; and

(f) where any of the shares have been disposed of by the company or the person who acquired them in such circumstances for money or money's worth, the amount or value of the consideration in each case.

(2B) Any distribution by an investment company within the meaning of Part IV of the Companies (Amendment) Act, 1983, which reduces the amount of its net assets to less than the aggregate of its called-up share capital and undistributable reserves. In this subparagraph 'net assets' and 'called up share capital' have the same meanings as in section 2 of the Companies (Amendment) Act, 1983 and 'undistributable reserves' has the same meaning as in section 46(2) of that Act.][a]

(3) Particulars of any charge on the assets of the company to secure the liabilities of any other person, including, where practicable, the amount secured.

(4) The general nature of any other contingent liabilities not provided for and, where practicable, the aggregate amount or estimated amount of those liabilities, if it is material.

(5) The aggregate amount or estimated amount, if it is material, of contracts for capital expenditure, so far as not provided for.

(6) If in the opinion of the directors any of the current assets have not a value, on realisation in the ordinary course of the company's business, at least equal to the amount at which they are stated, the fact that the directors are of that opinion.

(7) The aggregate market value of the company's quoted investments where it differs from the amount of the investments as stated, and the stock exchange value of any investments of which the market value is shown (whether separately or not) and is taken as being higher than their stock exchange value.

(8) The basis on which foreign currencies have been converted into Irish currency where the amount of the assets or liabilities affected is material.

(9) The basis on which the amount, if any, set aside for taxation on profits is computed.

(10) Except in the case of the first balance sheet laid before the company after the operative date, the corresponding amounts at the end of the immediately preceding financial year for all items shown in the balance sheet.

Amendments

a Sub-paragraphs (2A) and (2B) inserted by C(A)A 1983, Sch 1, para 27.

Definitions

'company': CA 1963, s 2(1); 'director': CA 1963, s 2(1), Sch 1 reg 1; 'financial year': CA 1963, s 2(1); 'share': CA 1963, s 2(1).

Profit and Loss Account

12. There shall be shown—

(a) the amount charged to revenue by way of provision for depreciation, renewals or diminution in value of fixed assets;

(b) the amount of the interest on the company's debentures and other fixed loans;

(c) the amount of the charge for income tax and other taxation on profits including income tax and other taxation payable outside the State on profits and distinguishing where practicable between income tax and other taxation;

[(d) the amounts respectively provided for purchase of the company's share capital, for redemption of share capital and for redemption of loans;][a]

(e) the amount set aside or proposed to be set aside to, or withdrawn from reserves, excluding amounts which would not, in accordance with good accountancy practice, normally pass through the profit and loss account;

(f) the amount set aside to provisions other than provisions for depreciation, renewals or diminution in value of assets or, as the case may be, the amount, if material, withdrawn from such provisions and not applied for the purposes thereof, excluding amounts which would not, in accordance with good accountancy practice, normally pass through the profit and loss account;

(g) the amount of income from investments;

(h) the aggregate amount of the dividends paid;

(i) the aggregate amount of the dividends proposed.

Amendments

a Sub–paragraph (d) substituted by CA 1990, s 231.

Definitions

'company': CA 1963, s 2(1); 'debenture': CA 1963, s 2(1).

---

13. The amount of remuneration of the auditors shall be shown under a separate heading, and for the purposes of this paragraph, any sums paid by the company for the auditors' expenses shall be deemed to be included in the expression 'remuneration'.

Definitions

'company': CA 1963, s 2(1).

---

14. (1) The matters referred to in subparagraphs (2) to (7) shall be stated by way of note, if not otherwise shown.

(2) If depreciation or replacement of fixed assets is provided for by some method other than a depreciation charge or provision for renewals, or is not provided for, the method by which it is provided for or the fact that it is not provided for, as the case may be, but this subparagraph shall not apply to freehold land.

(3) The basis on which the charge for income tax and other taxation on profits (whether payable in or outside the State) is computed.

(4) Whether or not the amount stated for dividends paid is for dividends subject to deduction of income tax.

(5) Whether or not the amount stated for dividends proposed is for dividends subject to deduction of income tax.

(6) Except in the case of the first profit and loss account laid before the company after the operative date, the corresponding amounts for the immediately preceding financial year for all items shown in the profit and loss account.

(7) Any material respects in which any items shown in the profit and loss account are affected—

(a) by transactions of a sort not usually undertaken by the company or otherwise by circumstances of an exceptional or non-recurrent nature; or

(b) by any change in the basis of accounting.

Definitions

'company': CA 1963, s 2(1); 'financial year': CA 1963, s 2(1); 'the operative date': CA 1963, s 2(1).

PART II
SPECIAL PROVISIONS WHERE THE COMPANY IS A HOLDING COMPANY OR A SUBSIDIARY COMPANY

Modifications of and Additions to Requirements as to Company's own Accounts

15. (1) This paragraph shall apply where the company is a holding company, whether or not it is itself a subsidiary of another body corporate but subparagraphs (4), (5) and (6) shall not apply to a private company taking advantage of subsection (1) of section 154 nor to a company which is at the end of its financial year the wholly owned subsidiary of another body corporate incorporated in the State.

(2) The aggregate amount of assets consisting of shares in, or amounts owing (whether on account of a loan or otherwise) from, the company's subsidiaries, distinguishing shares from indebtedness, shall be set out in the balance sheet separately from all the other assets of the company, and the aggregate amount of its indebtedness (whether on account of a loan or otherwise) to the company's subsidiaries shall be so set out separately from all its other liabilities, and—

(a) the references in Part I to the company's investments shall not include investments in its subsidiaries required by this paragraph to be separately set out; and

(b) paragraph 5, subparagraph (a) of paragraph 12, and subparagraph (2) of paragraph 14 shall not apply in relation to fixed assets consisting of interests in the company's subsidiaries.

(3) There shall be shown by way of note on the balance sheet or in a statement or report annexed thereto the number, description and amount of the shares in and debentures of the company held by its subsidiaries or their nominees, but excluding any of those shares or debentures in the case of which the subsidiary is concerned as personal representative or in the case of which it is concerned as trustee and neither the company nor any subsidiary thereof is beneficially interested under the trust, otherwise than by way of security only for the purposes of a transaction entered into by it in the ordinary course of a business which includes the lending of money.

(4) Where group accounts are not submitted, there shall, subject to subparagraph (5), be annexed to the balance sheet a statement showing—

(a) the reasons why subsidiaries are not dealt with in group accounts;

(b) the net aggregate amount (so far as it concerns members of the holding company) of the subsidiaries' profits after deducting the subsidiaries' losses, or vice versa, for the respective financial years of the subsidiaries ending with or during the financial year of the company—

(i) so far as dealt with in the company's accounts for that year; and

(ii) so far as not so dealt with;

(c) the net aggregate amount, so far as concerns members of the holding company, of the subsidiaries' profits after deducting the subsidiaries' losses, or vice versa, for their previous financial years since they respectively became subsidiaries of the holding company—

(i) so far as dealt with in the company's accounts for the year referred to in head (b)(i); and

(ii) so far as not dealt with in the company's accounts for that or previous years;

(d) any qualifications contained in the report of the auditors of the subsidiaries on their accounts for their respective financial years ending as aforesaid, and any note or saving contained in those accounts to call attention to a matter which, apart from the note or saving, would properly have been referred to in such a qualification, in so far as the matter which is the subject of the qualification or note is not covered by the company's own accounts and is material from the point of view of its members;

or, in so far as the information required by this subparagraph is not obtainable, a statement that it is not obtainable.

(5) Heads (b) and (c) of subparagraph (4) shall apply only to profits and losses of a subsidiary which may properly be treated in the holding company's accounts as revenue profits or losses.

(6) Where group accounts are not submitted, there shall be annexed to the balance sheet a statement showing, in relation to the subsidiaries, if any, whose financial years did not end with that of the company—

(a) the reasons why the company's directors consider the subsidiaries' financial years should not end with that of the company; and

(b) the dates on which the subsidiaries' financial years ending last before that of the company respectively ended or the earliest and latest of those dates.

Definitions

'accounts': CA 1963, s 2(1); 'company': CA 1963, s 2(1); 'debenture': CA 1963, s 2(1); 'director': CA 1963, s 2(1), Sch 1, reg 1; 'financial year': CA 1963, s 2(1); 'group accounts'; CA 1963, s 2 (1), s 150(1); 'holding company': CA 1963, s 2(1), s 155; 'member': CA 1963, s 2(1); 'private company': CA 1963, s 2(1), s 33(1); 'share': CA 1963, s 2 (1); 'subsidiary': CA 1963, s 2(1), s 155.

16. (1) The balance sheet of a company which is a subsidiary of another body corporate, whether or not it is itself a holding company, shall show the aggregate amount of its indebtedness to all bodies corporate of which it is a subsidiary or a fellow subsidiary and the aggregate amount of the indebtedness of all such bodies corporate to it, distinguishing in each case between indebtedness in respect of debentures and otherwise.

(2) For the purposes of this paragraph a company shall be deemed to be a fellow subsidiary of another body corporate if both are subsidiaries of the same body corporate but neither is the other's.

Definitions

'company': CA 1963, s 2(1); 'holding company': CA 1963, s 2(1), s 155; 'subsidiary': CA 1963, s 2(1), s 155.

Consolidated Accounts of Holding Company and Subsidiaries

17. Subject to paragraphs 18 to 22, the consolidated balance sheet and profit and loss account shall combine the information contained in the separate balance sheets and profit and loss accounts of the holding company and of the subsidiaries dealt with by the consolidated accounts, but with such adjustments, if any, as the directors of the holding company think necessary.

Definitions

'accounts': CA 1963, s 2(1); 'company': CA 1963, s 2(1); 'director': CA 1963, s 2(1), Sch 1, reg 1 1; 'holding company': CA 1963, s 2(1), s 155; 'subsidiary': CA 1963, s 2(1), s 155.

18. Subject as aforesaid and to Part III, the consolidated accounts shall, in giving the said information, comply, so far as practicable, with the requirements of this Act as if they were the accounts of an actual company.

Definitions

'accounts': CA 1963, s 2(1); 'Act': Sch 1, reg 1; 'company': CA 1963, s 2(1).

19. Sections 191 and 192 shall not, by virtue of paragraphs 17 and 18 apply for the purpose of the consolidated accounts.

Definitions

'accounts': CA 1963, s 2(1).

20. Paragraph 7 shall not apply for the purpose of any consolidated accounts laid before a company with the first balance sheet so laid after the operative date.

Definitions

'accounts': CA 1963, s 2(1); 'company': CA 1963, s 2(1); 'the operative date': CA 1963, s 2(1).

21. In relation to any subsidiaries of the holding company not dealt with by the consolidated accounts—

(a) subparagraphs (2) and (3) of paragraph 15 shall apply for the purpose of those accounts as if those accounts were the accounts of an actual company of which they were subsidiaries; and

(b) there shall be annexed the like statement as is required by subparagraph (4) of that paragraph where there are no group accounts, but as if references therein to the holding company's accounts were references to the consolidated accounts.

Definitions

'accounts': CA 1963, s 2(1); 'company': CA 1963, s 2(1); 'group accounts'; CA 1963, s 2(1), s 150(1); 'holding company': CA 1963, s 2(1), s 155; 'subsidiary': CA 1963, s 2(1), s 155.

---

22. In relation to any subsidiaries (whether or not dealt with by the consolidated accounts), whose financial years did not end with that of the company, there shall be annexed the like statement as is required by subparagraph (6) of paragraph 15 where there are no group accounts.

Definitions

'accounts': CA 1963, s 2(1); 'company': CA 1963, s 2(1); 'financial year': CA 1963, s 2(1); 'group accounts'; CA 1963, s 2(1), s 150(1).

PART III
EXCEPTIONS FOR SPECIAL CLASSES OF COMPANY

23. (1) A banking or discount company shall not be subject to the requirements of Part I other than—

(a) in relation to its balance sheet, those of paragraphs 2 and 3, paragraph 4 (so far as it relates to fixed and current assets), paragraph 8 (except subparagraph (e)), paragraphs 9 and 10 and paragraph 11 (except subparagraph (7)); and

(b) in relation to its profit and loss account, those of subparagraphs (h) and (i) of paragraph 12, paragraph 13 and subparagraphs (1), (4), (5) and (6) of paragraph 14;

but where in its balance sheet capital reserves, revenue reserves or provisions (other than provisions for depreciation, renewals or diminution in value of assets) are not stated separately, and heading stating an amount arrived at after taking into account such a reserve or provision shall be so framed or marked as to indicate that fact, and its profit and loss account shall indicate by appropriate words the manner in which the amount stated for the company's profit or loss has been arrived at.

(2) The accounts of a banking or discount company shall not be deemed, by reason only of the fact that they do not comply with any requirements of Part I from which the company is exempt by virtue of this paragraph, not to give the true and fair view required by this Act.

(3) In this paragraph, 'banking or discount company' means any company which satisfies the Minister that it ought to be treated for the purposes of this Schedule as a banking company or as a discount company.

Definitions

'accounts': CA 1963, s 2(1); 'Act': Sch 1, reg 1; 'company': CA 1963, s 2(1); 'Minister': CA 1963, s 2(1).

24. In relation to an assurance company within the meaning of the Insurance Acts, 1909 to 1961, which is subject to and complies with the requirements of those Acts relating to the preparation and deposit with the Minister of a balance sheet and profit and loss account, paragraph 23 shall apply as it applies in relation to a banking or a discount company, and such an assurance company shall also not be subject to the requirements of subparagraph (a) of paragraph 8 and subparagraph (3), (4), (6) and (9) of paragraph 11.

Definitions

'Minister': CA 1963, s 2(1).

25. (1) A company to which this paragraph applies shall not be subject to the following requirements of this Schedule:

- (a) in relation to its balance sheet, those of paragraph 4 (except so far as that paragraph relates to fixed and current assets) and paragraphs 5, 6 and 7; and
- (b) in relation to its profit and loss account, those of subparagraph (a), (e) and (f) of paragraph 12;

but a company taking advantage of this paragraph shall be subject, instead of the said requirements, to any prescribed conditions in relation to matters to be stated in its accounts or by way of note thereto and in relation to information to be furnished to the Minister or a person authorised by the Minister to require it.

(2) The accounts of a company shall not be deemed, by reason only of the fact that they do not comply with any of the requirements of Part I from which the company is exempt by virtue of this paragraph, not to give the true and fair view required by this Act.

(3) Subject to subparagraph (4), this paragraph applies to companies of any class prescribed for the purposes thereof, and a class of companies may be so prescribed if it appears to the Minister desirable in the public interest.

(4) If the Minister is of opinion that any of the conditions prescribed for the purposes of this paragraph have not been complied with in the case of any company, the Minister may direct that so long as the direction continues in force this paragraph shall not apply to the company.

Definitions

'Act': CA 1963, Sch 1, reg 1; 'company': CA 1963, 2(1); 'Minister': CA 1963, s 2(1); 'prescribed': CA 1963, s 2(1);

26. Where a company entitled to the benefit of any provision contained in this Part is a holding company, the references in Part II to consolidated accounts complying with the requirements of this Act shall, in relation to consolidated accounts of that company, be construed as referring to those requirements in so far only as they apply to the separate accounts of that company.

Definitions

'Act'; CA 1963, Sch 1, reg 1; 'accounts': CA 1963, s 2(1); 'company': CA 1963, s 2(1); 'holding company': CA 1963, s 2(1), s 155;

PART IV
INTERPRETATION OF SCHEDULE

27. (1) For the purposes of this Schedule—

(a) 'provision' shall, subject to subparagraph (2), mean any amount written off or retained by way of providing for depreciation, renewals or diminution in value of assets or retained by way of providing for any known liability of which the amount cannot be determined with substantial accuracy;

(b) 'reserve' shall not, subject as aforesaid, include any amount written off or retained by way of providing for depreciation, renewals or diminution in value of assets or retained by way of providing for any known liability;

(c) 'capital reserve' shall not include any amount regarded as free for distribution through the profit and loss account, and 'revenue reserve' shall mean any reserve other than a capital reserve;

and in this paragraph 'liability' shall include all liabilities in respect of expenditure contracted for and all disputed or contingent liabilities.

(2) Where—

(a) any amount written off or retained by way of providing for depreciation, renewals or diminution in value of assets, not being an amount written off in relation to fixed assets before the operative date; or

(b) any amount retained by way of providing for any known liability;

is in excess of that which in the opinion of the directors is reasonably necessary for the purpose, the excess shall be treated for the purposes of this Schedule as a reserve and not as a provision.

Definitions

'director': CA 1963, s 2(1), Sch 1, reg 1; 'the operative date': CA 1963, s 2(1).

---

28. For the purposes aforesaid 'quoted investment' means an investment for which there has been granted a quotation or permission to deal on a recognised stock exchange within the State or on any stock exchange of repute outside the State, and 'unquoted investment' shall be construed accordingly.

Definitions

'recognised stock exchange': CA 1963, s 2(1), CA 1990, s 3(2).

SEVENTH SCHEDULE

MATTERS TO BE EXPRESSLY STATED IN AUDITORS' REPORT

[...][a]

Amendments

a Repealed by CA 1990, s 6 and replaced by CA 1990, s 193.

EIGHTH SCHEDULE

FEES TO BE PAID TO THE REGISTRAR OF COMPANIES

[PART I

'electronic form' means in relation to the doing of any act specified in the first column to the table set out in this Part the doing of that act by means of—

(a) the electronic form filing system in use by the registrar of companies, or

(b) the Companies Registration Office disk electronic filing system where the act is also effected in paper form;

'paper form' means, in relation a matter specified in the first column to the table set out in this Part—

(a) the filing of documents or an application in paper form, or

(b) the inspection of documents or an application submitted in paper form, or

(c) the submission of documents in paper form;

'Societas Europaea' or European Public Limited Liability Company shall be construed in accordance with the European Communities (European Public Limited Liability Company) Regulations 2007 (S.I. No. 21 of 2007).

TABLE OF FEES

Matter in respect of which Fee is payable	*Amount of Fee*
Provision of an electronic certified copy certificate of incorporation for public sector use pursuant to section 370(1)(b)	Paper form — not applicable Electronic form — nil
Provision of a certified copy of any matter entered in the register kept by the registrar of companies for the registration of companies (including the register referred to in section 103) pursuant to section 370(1)(b)	Paper form — €12 Electronic form — not applicable
Each inspection of any register kept in the office for the registration of companies (including the register referred to in section 103) pursuant to section 370(1)(a)	Paper form — €3.50 Electronic form — €3.50

Matter in respect of which Fee is payable	*Amount of Fee*
Provision of an uncertified copy of any matter entered in the register aforesaid pursuant to section 370(1)(b)	Paper form — €2.50 Electronic form — €2.50
Registration of any company (other than a Societas Europaea) under the Companies Acts	Paper form — €100 Electronic form — €50
Registration of a company to which section 328(1) applies	Paper form — €100 Electronic form — €50
Application for a certificate pursuant to section 6 of the Companies (Amendment) Act 1983 (No. 13 of 1983)	Paper form — €300 Electronic form — not applicable
Delivery, pursuant to section 352, for registration of documents referred to in that section by a company incorporated outside the State	Paper form — €60 Electronic form — not applicable
Registration of a company to which Part II or III of the European Communities (Branch Disclosures) Regulations 1993 (S.I. No. 395 of 1993) applies	Paper form — €60 Electronic form — not applicable
Re-registration of a company in any of the ways provided for under the Companies Acts	Paper form — €60 Electronic form — not applicable
Registration of an annual return made up to a date prior to 1 March 2002	Paper form — €1,240 Electronic form — €1,220
Delivery of annual return within the period referred to in section 127(2) (amended by section 60 of the Company Law Enforcement Act 2001 (No. 28 of 2001))	Paper form — €40 Electronic form — €20
Delivery of an annual return later than the period referred to in section 127(2) (amended by section 60 of the Company Law Enforcement Act 2001 (No. 28 of 2001))	Paper form — €140 plus €3.00 in respect of each day on which the failure to file the return continues after the statutory filing period, subject to a maximum fee of €1,240 for each return Electronic form — €120 plus €3.00 in respect of each day on which the failure to file the return continues after the statutory filing period, subject to a maximum fee of €1,220 for each return
Entry of new name in the register in place of the former name pursuant to section 23(3)	Paper form — €100 Electronic form — €50
Registration of particulars of a series of debentures required to be registered pursuant to section 99(8)	Paper form — €40 Electronic form — not applicable

Matter in respect of which Fee is payable	*Amount of Fee*
Giving of notice of a change in the situation of the registered office of the company pursuant to subsection (3) of section 113 (inserted by section 4 of the Companies (Amendment) Act 1982 (No. 10 of 1982))	Paper form — €15 Electronic form — nil
Sending of notification of a change of director or secretary, or of any particulars contained in the register, pursuant to subsection (6) of section 195 (inserted by section 51 of the Companies Act 1990 (No. 33 of 1990))	Paper form — €15 Electronic form — nil
Sending of a notice of the place where the register of members of a company is kept or of any change in that place, pursuant to section 116(7)	Paper form — €15 Electronic form — nil
Sending of a notice of the place where the register of debenture holders of a company is kept or of a change in that place, pursuant to section 91(3)	Paper form — €15 Electronic form — nil
Sending of a notice of the place where copies and memoranda required by section 50(1) of the Companies Act 1990 (No. 33 of 1990) are kept or of any change in that place, pursuant to section 50(4) of that Act	Paper form — €15 Electronic form — nil
Delivery of a notice referred to in Regulation 4(3)(c), 7(3)(c), 4(3)(d) or 7(3)(d), of the European Communities (Branch Disclosures) Regulations 1993 (S.I. No. 395 of1993)	Paper form — €15 Electronic form — nil
Delivery pursuant to section 353 of a return containing prescribed particulars of an alteration made in respect of persons referred to in paragraph (c) of that section	Paper form — €15 Electronic form — nil
Forwarding of an ordinary resolution or agreement, or a special resolution or agreement (other than a special resolution or agreement relating to a change of name of a company pursuant to section 23) pursuant to section 143 (amended by section 5 of the Companies (Amendment) Act 1982 (No. 6 of 1982) and paragraph 15 of the First Schedule to the Companies (Amendment) Act 1983 (No. 13 of 1983)) and any document lodged in connection with such resolution	Paper form — €15 Electronic form — nil

Matter in respect of which Fee is payable	*Amount of Fee*
Notification of a company becoming a single-member company and identity of its sole member pursuant to Regulation 5 of the European Communities (Single-Member Private Limited Companies) Regulations 1994 (S.I. No. 275 of 1994)	Paper form — €15 Electronic form — nil
Notification that a company has ceased to be a single- member company, pursuant to Regulation 6 of the European Communities (Single-Member Private Limited Companies) Regulations 1994 (S.I. No. 275 of 1994)	Paper form — €15 Electronic form — nil
Sending, pursuant to section 34(3)(a) of the Companies (Amendment) (No.2) Act 1999 (No. 30 of 1999), of a copy of a notice under subsection (1)(i) of that section)	Paper form — nil Electronic form — not applicable
Filing a document to which section 80(1) of the Company Law Enforcement Act 2001 (No. 28 of 2001) applies, for the purposes of registration	Paper form — €100 Electronic form — not applicable
Application for a grant of a certificate pursuant to section 44(2) of the Companies (Amendment) (No. 2) Act 1999 (No. 30 of 1999)	Paper form — €40 Electronic form — not applicable
Delivering a notice and statutory declaration, pursuant to subsections (3)(b)(i) and (5) respectively, of section 45 of the Companies (Amendment) (No. 2) Act 1999 (No. 30 of1999)	Paper form — €40 Electronic form — not applicable
Delivery of nomination of a new annual return date, pursuant to subsection (9) of section 127 (inserted by section 60 of the Company Law Enforcement Act 2001 (No. 28 of 2001))	Paper form — €15 Electronic form — nil
Application for the formation by merger of a Societas Europaea pursuant to Regulation 4(1)(a) of the European Communities (European Public Limited Liability Company) Regulations 2007 (S.I. No. 21 of 2007)	Paper form — €100 Electronic form — not applicable
Application for the formation of a holding Societas Europaea pursuant to Regulation 4(1)(b) of the European Communities (European Public Limited Liability Company) Regulations 2007 (S.I. No. 21 of 2007)	Paper form — €100 Electronic form — not applicable

Matter in respect of which Fee is payable	*Amount of Fee*
Application for the formation of a subsidiary Societas Europaea pursuant to Regulation 4(1)(c) of the European Communities (European Public Liability Company) Regulations 2007 (S.I. No. 21 of 2007)	Paper form — €100 Electronic form — not applicable
Application for the conversion of a public limited company to a Societas Europaea pursuant to Regulation 4(1)(d) of the European Communities (European Public Limited Liability) Regulations 2007 (S.I. No. 21 of 2007)	Paper form — €100 Electronic form — not applicable
Application for the formation of a subsidiary Societas Europaea of a Societas Europaea pursuant to Regulation 4(1)(e) of the European Communities (European Public Limited Liability) Regulations 2007 (S.I. No. 21 of 2007)	Paper form — €60 Electronic form — not applicable
Application to transfer a Societas Europaea's registered office to the State pursuant to Regulation 5 of the European Communities (European Communities (European Public Limited Liability Company) Regulations 2007 (S.I. No. 21 of 2007)	Paper form — €100 Electronic form — not applicable
Application to register the transfer of an Societas Europaea's registered office from the State pursuant to Regulation 7 of the European Communities (European Public Limited Liability Company) Regulations 2007 (S.I. No. 21 of 2007)	Paper form — €100 Electronic form — not applicable
Registration of any notice and accompanying copy common draft terms of merger delivered to the registrar of companies by an Irish merging company pursuant to Regulation 8(1) of the European Communities (Cross-Border Merger) Regulations 2008 (S.I. No. 157 of 2008)	Paper form — €100 Electronic form — not applicable
Delivery to the registrar of companies of draft terms of conversion of a Societas Europaea into a public limited company for publication by the registrar of companies pursuant to Article 66(4) of Council Regulation No. 2157/2001/EC of 8 October 2001 (O.J. L.294 of 10.11.2001)	Paper form — €100 Electronic form — not applicable

Matter in respect of which Fee is payable	*Amount of Fee*
Re-registration of a Societas Europaea as a public limited company following approval by the general meeting of the Societas Europaea of the draft terms of conversion pursuant to Article 66(6) of Council Regulation No. 2157/2001/EC of 8 October 2001	Paper form — €100 Electronic form — not applicable
Delivery for registration, pursuant to Regulation 11(1)(a) of the European Communities (Mergers and Division of Companies) Regulations 1987 (S.I. No. 137 of 1987), to the registrar of companies of a copy of the draft terms of merger, signed and dated, required by Regulation 6 of those Regulations and delivery to the registrar of companies, pursuant to Regulation 4(1) of the European Communities (European Public Limited-Liability Company) Regulations 2007 (S.I. No. 21 of 2007), of particulars for publication set out in Article 21 of Council Regulation No. 2157/2001 of 8 October 2001, in respect of the formation of an Societas Europaea by means of a merger where the Societas Europaea will be registered outside the state.	Paper form — €100 Electronic form — not applicable
Subject to this Schedule, registration or application for registration of, or delivery or giving of, any document to the registrar of companies, pursuant to the Companies Acts.	Paper form — €15 Electronic form (where applicable) — nil

][a]

Amendments

a CA 1963, Sch 8 substituted by Companies Act 1963 (Alteration of Eighth Schedule) Order 2009 (SI 302/2009).

Cross reference

See CA 1963, s 369 and notes thereto.

Definitions

'annual return': CA 1963, s 2(1); 'annual return date': CA 1963, s 2(1); 'articles': CA 1963, s 2(1); 'company': CA 1963, s 2(1); 'debenture': CA 1963, s 2(1); 'director': CA 1963, s 2(1); 'member': CA 1963, s 31; 'memorandum': CA 1963, s 2(1); 'person': IA, 2005, s 18(c); 'officer': CA 1963, s 2(1); 'the registrar of companies': CA 1963, s 2(1).

[PART II
LIMITATIONS ON OPERATION OF PART I

Where the registrar directs, pursuant to section 23(2), that a company shall change its name, any fee that would, but for this Part, be required to be paid under Part I of this Schedule in respect of the registration of that change shall not be charged, levied or paid.][a]

Amendments

a CA 1963, Sch 8, Pt II substituted by Companies (Fees)(No 3) Order 2005 (SI 2005/517) Sch, Pt I.

Definitions

'company': CA 1963, s 2(1); 'the registrar of companies': CA 1963, s 2(1).

Notes

Change of name on direction of the Registrar: The Registrar can demand a name change pursuant to CA 1963, s 23(2), within in a period of six months following incorporation or change of name, if the name which has been registered is too similar to the name of a company already in existence. There is no fee charged on change of name if such circumstances exist.[1]

1 CA 1963, Sch 8, Pt 2.

NINTH SCHEDULE

[PROVISIONS APPLIED TO UNREGISTERED COMPANIES

Principal Act

Subject matter	*Provisions applied*
Acts done by company (ultra vires rule).	Section 8.
Pre-incorporation contracts.	Section 37(1) and (2).
Prospectus and allotments.	Sections 43 to 52, 56, 57, 61 and the Third Schedule.
[Validation of invalid issue, redemption or purchase of shares.	Section 89.][a]
Registered office.	Section 113 (inserted by the Companies (Amendment) Act, 1982).
Annual Return	Sections 125 to 129 and the Fifth Schedule
Accounts and Audit	Sections 148 to 153, 155 to 161, 191 and the Sixth Schedule (except subparagraphs (a) to (d) of paragraph 2, subparagraphs (c) to (e) of paragraph 3 and subparagraph (d) of paragraph 8), as amended by the Companies (Amendment) Act, 1986.
Validity of acts of directors.	Section 178.
Register of directors and secretaries. Particulars relating to directors to be shown on all business letters of the company	Sections 195 (inserted by the Companies Act, 1990) and 196.

Subject matter	*Provisions applied*
Registration of documents, enforcement and other supplemental matters.	Sections 2, 193, 369 to 371, 378, 379, 383, 384, 386, 387, 395(1) and the Eighth Schedule.
Liability of officers and others for negligence etc.	Sections 200 and 391.

Companies (Amendment) Act, 1977

Subject matter	*Provisions applied*
Share certificates	Sections 2 and 3.
Company records	Section 4.

Companies (Amendment) Act, 1983

Subject matter	*Provisions applied*
Maintenance of capital. Restrictions on distribution of profits and assets.	Sections 40 to 42, 45, 45A (inserted by the Companies (Amendment) Act, 1986, and 49 to 51. Sections 43, [43A,][b] 44, 46 and 47, with the modification that those sections shall apply to all bodies corporate to which section 377(1) of the Principal Act applies other than those which, if they were registered, would be private companies.

European Communities (Stock Exchange) Regulations, 1984 (SI No 282 of 1984)

Provisions applied

All of the Regulations

Companies (Amendment) Act, 1986

Subject matter	*Provisions applied*
Power to alter form of accounts.	Section 24.

European Communities (Mergers And Divisions of Companies) Regulations, 1987 (SI No. 137 of 1987)

Provisions applied

All of the Regulations

COMPANIES (AMENDMENT) ACT, 1990

Provisions applied

The whole Act.

COMPANIES ACT, 1990

Provisions applied

Parts I to III.

Part IV, with the modification that Chapter 2 of that Part shall apply to all bodies corporate to which section 377 (1) of the Principal Act applies other than those which, if they were registered, would be private companies and Chapter 3 of that Part shall apply to all such bodies corporate which, if they were registered, would be private companies.

Part V.

Part VI, except sections 122, 128 to 131 and 133.

Parts VII,IX,X,[XI,][c] and XII.][d]

[European Communities (Public Limited Companies Subsidiaries) Regulations, 1997 (SI No 67 of 1997)

Provisions applied

All of the Regulations][e]

Amendments

a Words 'Validation of invalid issue, redemption or purchase of shares' and 'Section 89' inserted in the first and second column respectively, under the title 'Principal Act', by Companies Act 1963 (Ninth Schedule) Regulations 1999 (SI 63/1999), reg 3(a) with effect from 1 April 1999.

b Words '43A,' inserted in the second column, under the title 'Companies (Amendment) Act, 1983' by Companies Act 1963 (Ninth Schedule) Regulations 1999 (SI 63/1999), reg 3(b) with effect from 1 April 1999.

c Words ',XI' inserted in the second column, under the title 'Companies Act, 1990' by Companies Act 1963 (Ninth Schedule) Regulations 1999 (SI 63/1999), reg 3(c) with effect from 1 April 1999.

d CA 1963, Sch 9 substituted by CA 1990, s 250 and Sch.

e Additional table inserted by Companies Act 1963 (Ninth Schedule) Regulations 1999 (SI 63/1999), reg 3(d) with effect from 1 April 1999.

Definitions

'accounts': CA 1963, s 2(1); 'annual return': CA 1963, s 2(1); 'company': CA 1963, s 2(1); 'director': CA 1963, s 2(1); 'prospectus': CA 1963, s 2(1); 'shares': CA 1963, s 2(1).

TENTH SCHEDULE

PROVISIONS REFERRED TO IN SECTION 380

[...][a]

Amendments

a CA 1963, Sch 10 repealed by CA 1990, s 6 with effect from 1 July 1991.[1]

1 Companies Act 1990 (Commencement) (No 2) Order 1991 (SI 117/1991).

Cross reference

CA 1963, s 380 and Sch 10 have been replaced by CA 1990, s 242 (as amended by CLEA 2001, s 106 and IFCMPA 2005, s 71). See CA 1990, s 242 and notes thereto.

ELEVENTH SCHEDULE

AMENDMENTS OF OTHER ACTS

THE BANKRUPTCY ACTS

1.(1) The Bankruptcy Acts shall have effect as if for section 53 of the Bankruptcy (Ireland) Amendment Act, 1872 (which relates to the avoidance of fraudulent preferences) there were substituted the following section:

> '53. Every conveyance or transfer of property or charge thereon made, every obligation incurred and every judicial proceeding taken or suffered by any person unable to pay his debts as they become due from his own moneys, in favour of any creditor or of any person in trust for any creditor, with a view to giving such creditor, or any surety or guarantor for the debt due to such creditor, a preference over the other creditors, shall, if the person making, taking, paying or suffering the same is adjudged bankrupt on a bankruptcy petition or a petition for arrangement, presented within 6 months after the date of making, taking, paying or suffering the same, be deemed fraudulent and void against the assignees or trustees of such bankrupt; but this section shall not affect the rights of any person making title in good faith and for valuable consideration through or under a creditor of the bankrupt.'

(2) Subparagraph (1) shall not apply in relation to things made or done before the operative date and section 53 of the Bankruptcy (Ireland) Amendment Act, 1872, as originally enacted shall continue to apply to things made or done before the operative date as if this Act had not been passed.

Definitions

'the Bankruptcy Acts': CA 1963, s 2(1); 'company': CA 1963, s 2(1); 'the operative date': CA 1963, s 2(1);

Cross reference

The Bankruptcy (Ireland) Amendment Act, 1872, s 53 (as amended) was repealed by the Bankruptcy Act 1988, s 6 and Sch 2. See generally the Bankruptcy Act 1988, s 57(1).

---

2. Section 287 shall apply also in relation to the said Act of 1872 (with the necessary modification of any reference to a company and to winding up) as if a reference to section 53 of the said Act of 1872 were substituted in section 287 for the reference to section 286.

Definitions

'company': CA 1963, s 2(1).

Cross reference

The Bankruptcy (Ireland) Amendment Act, 1872, s 53 (as amended) was repealed by the Bankruptcy Act 1988, s 6 and Sch 2. See generally Bankruptcy Act 1988, s 57(2).

The Insurance Acts, 1909 to 1961

3. The Insurance Acts, 1909 to 1961, shall have effect as if for subsection (5) of section 46 of the Insurance Act, 1936, there were substituted the following subsection:

> '(5) Sections 167 and 168 of the Companies Act, 1963, shall apply in relation to an inspector appointed under this section in like manner as they apply to an inspector appointed under section 165 of that Act, and any such refusal as under subsection (3) of the said section 168 is, or might be, made the ground of the punishment of an officer or agent of the company or other body corporate whose affairs are investigated by virtue of the said section 167, shall also be a ground on which the Minister may present a petition for the winding up of such company and upon which the High Court may, on the hearing of any such petition, make an order for the winding up of such company under and in accordance with the Companies Act, 1963.'

Notes

Effect of repeal and replacement of CA 1963, ss 167–168: The investigation provisions of CA 1963 were repealed and replaced by CA 1990, Pt II (as amended by CLEA 2001, Pt 3), however the Insurance Act 1936, s 46(5) (as substituted above) remains in force. It would appear from the IA 2005, s 26(2)(f) that in circumstances such as this, where an enactment is repealed and re-enacted with modifications by another enactment, then any reference in the Insurance Act 1936 to CA 1963, ss 167–168 should be read as a reference to CA 1990, ss 9–10.

TWELFTH SCHEDULE

ENACTMENTS REPEALED

Session and Chapter or Number & Year	*Short title*	*Extent of Repeal*
3 & 4 Will. 4 c. 31.	The Sunday Observance Act, 1833	The whole Act
45 & 46 Vict., c 72	The Revenue Friendly Societies and National Debt Act, 1882	Subsection (1) of Section 11 and in the First Schedule the words '6 Geo. 4, c. 42, 8 & 9 Vic., c. 37, s.22
8 Edw 7, c.69	The Companies (Consolidation) Act, 1908	The whole Act.
3 & 4 Geo.5, c. 25	The Companies Act, 1913	The whole Act.
7 & 8 Geo. 5 c. 28	The Companies (Particulars as to Directors) Act, 1917.	The whole Act.
No 9 of 1934	The Workmen's Compensation Act, 1934.	Subsections (3) and (4) of section 20.
No. 7 of 1942	The Insurance (Intermittent Unemployment) Act, 1942.	Subsections (1) and (2) of section 27.

Session and Chapter or Number & Year	*Short title*	*Extent of Repeal*
No. 11 of 1952	The Social Welfare Act, 1952.	Subsections (1) and (2) of section 58.
No. 7 of 1959	The Companies Act, 1959.	The whole Act.
No. 42 of 1959	The Finance (No. 2) Act, 1959.	Subsections (2) and (3) of section 12.

THIRTEENTH SCHEDULE

ENACTMENT SAVED

THE JOINT STOCK BANKING COMPANIES ACT, 1857, PART OF SECTION 12

Notwithstanding anything contained in any Act passed in the session holden in the seventh and eighth years of Queen Victoria, chapter one hundred and thirteen, and intituled 'An Act to regulate Joint Stock Banks in England', or in any other Act, it shall be lawful for any number of persons, not exceeding ten, to carry on in partnership the business of banking, in the same manner and upon the same conditions in all respects as any company of not more than six persons could before the passing of the Joint Stock Banking Companies Act, 1857, have carried on such business.

Definitions

'company': CA 1963, s 2(1); 'person': IA 2005, s 18(c).

Cross reference

See also CA 1963, s 372 and notes thereto.

Stock Transfer Act 1963

Number 34 of 1963

ARRANGEMENT OF SECTIONS

An Act to amend the Law with Respect to the Transfer of Securities. [24th December, 1963.]

Be It Enacted by the Oireachtas as follows:—

1 Interpretation

(1) In this Act—

'the Minister' means the Minister for Finance;

'registered securities' means securities the holders of which are entered in a register;

'securities' includes shares, stock, debentures, debenture stock, loan stock and bonds;

'stock exchange transaction' means a sale and purchase of securities in which each of the parties is a member of a stock exchange acting in the ordinary course of his business as such or is acting through the agency of such a member;

'stock exchange' means the Cork Stock Exchange, the Dublin Stock Exchange and any other stock exchange which is declared by the Minister by regulations to be a recognised stock exchange for the purposes of this Act.

[(2) References in this Act to 'a stock transfer' shall, in addition to applying to an instrument under hand in a form set out in the First Schedule to this Act, be construed, where the context so allows, as including a transfer to which section 139 of the Central Bank Act, 1989, applies as if it were a transfer in a form so set out and in respect of which no brokers transfer is necessary.] [a]

Amendments

a Central Bank Act 1989, s 139(3) inserted STA 1963, s 1(2) with effect from 12 July 1989.[1]

[1] Central Bank Act 1989 (Commencement) Order 1989 (SI 176/1989).

Cross reference

'debenture': CA 1963, s 2(1); 'instrument': SDCA 1999, s 1(1); 'Minister for Finance': Ministers and Secretaries Act 1924, s 1(ii); 'stock': SDCA 1999, s 1(1); 'recognised stock exchange': CA 1963, s 2(1); 'stock exchange': Stock Exchange Act 1995, s 3(1).

Definitions

'securities': STA 1963, s 1(1); 'stock exchange': STA 1963, s 1(1).

Notes

Operative date: STA 1963 was brought in to force on 13 January 1964[1].

1 Stock Transfer Act 1963 (Commencement) Order 1964 (SI 4/1964).

Transfer of securities by electronic means: Reference to a stock transfer in this Act includes reference to an electronic transfer made in accordance with Central Bank Act 1989, s 139 (1)[1].

1 As amended by the Central Bank Act 1997, s 63.

UK legislation

See STA 1963, s 4 (as amended by Financial Services Act 1986, s 212(2), Sch 16, para 4; Local Government Finance (Repeals, Savings and Consequential Amendments) Order 1990 (SI 776/1990), art 8, Sch 3, para 8; Local Government Finance Act 1992, s 117(1), Sch 13, para 12; Financial Services and Markets Act 2000 (Consequential Amendments and Repeals) Order (SI 3649/2001), art 271; and Fire and Rescue Services Act 2004, s 53(1), Sch 1, para 18(1), (2) and (3).

---

2 Simplified transfer of securities

(1) Registered securities to which this section applies may be transferred by means of an instrument under hand in [the form][a] set out in the First Schedule to this Act (in this Act referred to as a stock transfer), executed by the transferor only and specifying (in addition to the particulars of the consideration, of the description and number or amount of the securities, and of the person by whom the transfer is made) the full name and address of the transferee.

[Provided that—

(a) in the case of an instrument in the form set out in Part I of the Schedule to the Stock Transfer (Forms) Regulations 1980, and inserted in the said First Schedule, by Regulation 4 of those Regulations, the instrument need not specify—

(i) particulars of the consideration, or

(ii) the address of the transferee, and

(b) in the case of an instrument in the form set out in Part II of the Schedule to the said Regulations and inserted in the said First Schedule by the said Regulation 4, if the transferor is a body corporate, the instrument need not be executed under hand but shall be sufficiently executed by or on behalf of such transferor if it bears a facsimile of the corporate seal of the transferor, authenticated by the signature (whether actual or facsimile) of a director or the secretary of the transferor.][b]

[(c) in the case of an instrument in the forms set out in Parts I and II of the Schedule to the Stock Transfer (Forms) Regulations 1987, and inserted in the First Schedule, or, as the case may be, the Second Schedule, to this Act, by Regulation 4 of those Regulations, the instrument shall not specify particulars of the consideration.] [c]

[(d) designated stock may be transferred by means of—

(i) [an instrument in a form set out in the First Schedule to this Act, or an instrument in the form set out in Part II of the Second Schedule of this Act, that—][d]

(I) is produced by fax in the [Central Bank of Ireland Securities Settlements Office][e] by, or by a person acting on behalf of, a person authorised to transfer designated stock (referred to subsequently in this subsection as 'a member of the [Central Bank of Ireland Securities Settlements Office]'.

(II) bears a representation purporting to be of—

(A) the signature of the member of the [Central Bank of Ireland Securities Settlements][e] entitled to transfer the stock concerned, or

(B) the signature or signatures of a person or persons authorised to sign, on behalf of the member aforesaid, the document of which the instrument is a facsimile,

and

(III) specifies (in addition to the particulars of the consideration and of the description and the number or amount of the securities) the full name of the transferee or, if abbreviation thereof has been specified by the [Central Bank of Ireland Securities Settlements Office][e], the abbreviation.

or

(ii) an instrument of which the instrument specified in subparagraph (i) of this paragraph is a facsimile and which is received in the [Central Bank of Ireland Securities Settlements Office][e], from a member of that Office,

(e) designated stock may be transferred by means of an instrument in the form set out in Part III of the said Second Schedule that—

(i) is produced by telex in the [Central Bank of Ireland Securities Settlements Office][e] by a member of that Office,

(ii) bears the name of the member of the [Central Bank of Ireland Securities Settlements Office][e] entitled to transfer the stock concerned together with the tested code number allocated to the member for the purpose, pursuant to an agreement between the Bank and the member of the [Central Bank of Ireland Securities Settlements Office] [e], and

(iii) specifies (in addition to the particulars of the consideration and of the description and number or amount of the securities) the full name of the transferee or, if an abbreviation thereof has been specified by the [Central Bank of Ireland Securities Settlements Office][e], the abbreviation.] [f]

[(f) Exchequer Notes held by any company or other body corporate (whether incorporated in Ireland or elsewhere) may be transferred by means of an instrument in writing in the form set out in Part IV of the Second Schedule to this Act and signed by a person duly authorised in that behalf by such company or such other body corporate.] [g]

[(g) designated stock held by any company or other body corporate (whether incorporated in the State or elsewhere) may be transferred by means of an instrument in the form set out in the First Schedule to this Act, which—

(i) is or has been produced by fax in the Bank by or on behalf of such company or body corporate, and

(ii) bears a representation purporting to be the signature of a person authorised by such company or body corporate to sign, on its behalf the instrument.] [h]

(2) The execution of a stock transfer need not be attested; and where such a transfer has been executed for the purpose of a stock exchange transaction, the particulars of the consideration and of the transferee may either be inserted in that transfer or, as the case may require, be supplied by means of separate instruments in the form set out in the Second Schedule to this Act (in this Act referred to as brokers transfers), identifying the stock transfer and specifying the securities to which each such instrument relates and the consideration paid for those securities.

(3) Nothing in this section shall be construed as affecting the validity of any instrument which would be effective to transfer securities apart from this section; and any instrument purporting to be made in any form which was common or usual before the commencement of this Act, or in any other form authorised or required for that purpose apart from this section, shall be sufficient, whether or not it is completed in accordance with the form, if it complies with the requirements as to execution and contents which apply to a stock transfer.

(4) This section applies to fully paid up transferable registered securities of any description, except securities of a company limited by guarantee or an unlimited company.

[(5) In this section and in the Second Schedule to this Act

'the Bank' means the Central Bank of Ireland;

['company' means—

(a) a company within the meaning of the Companies Acts 1963 to 1999, or

(b) a body established under the laws of a state other than the State and corresponding to a body referred to in paragraph (a) of this definition;] [i]

'designated stock' means—

(a) such registered securities created by the Minister as for the time being stand specified by the Bank in relation to the [Central Bank of Ireland Securities Settlements Office] [e] [or for the purpose of paragraph (g) of the proviso to subsection (1) of this section] [j], and

(b) such other registered securities (if any) as for the time stand specified by the Minister in relation to the [Central Bank of Ireland Securities Settlements Office] [e] and as respect which the specification has been communicated in writing to the Bank;

'fax' means the system whereby a facsimile of a document is produced at a place other than that at which the document is located;

'[Central Bank of Ireland Securities Settlements Office]' [e] means the office managed by the Bank that provides a settlement service in designated stock for its members].[k]

[(6) In this section and in the Second Schedule to this Act,

Exchequer Notes means:

(a) such securities as may be issued from time to time by Ireland acting through the National Treasury Management Agency under Ireland's Exchequer Notes Programme.][l]

Amendments

a Stock Transfer (Forms) Regulations 1980 (SI 139/1980), r 4(a) substituted 'a form' for 'the form' with effect from 16 May 1980.

b Stock Transfer (Forms) Regulations 1980 (SI 139/1980), r 4(b) inserted STA 1963, sub-ss 2(1)(a) and 2(1)(b) with effect from 16 May 1980.

c Stock Transfer (Forms) Regulations 1987 (SI 117/1987), r 3 inserted STA 1963, sub-s 2(1)(c) with effect from 30 April 1987.

d Stock Transfer (Forms) Regulations 1998 (SI 546/1998), r 3 substituted the words 'an instrument in a form set out in the First Schedule to this Act, or an instrument in the form set out in Part II of the Second Schedule of this Act, that—' for 'an instrument in the form set out in Part II of the Second Schedule to this Act that—', with effect from 1 January 1998.

e Central Bank Act 1997, s 83 substituted 'Central Bank of Ireland Securities Settlements Office' for 'Gilts Settlement Office' with effect from 9 April 1997[1].

f Stock Transfer (Forms) Regulations 1991 (SI 77/1991), r 4(a) inserted STA 1963, sub-ss 2(1)(d) and 2(1)(e) with effect from 31 March 1991.

g Stock Transfer (Forms) Regulations 1994 (SI 173/1994), r 4(a) inserted sub-s 2(1)(f), with effect from 30 June 1994.

h Stock Transfer (Forms) Regulations 2000 (SI 206/2000), r 2(a) inserted sub-s 2(1)(g), with effect from 29 June 2000.

i Stock Transfer (Forms) Regulations 2000 (SI 206/2000), r 2(b)(i) inserted the definition of 'company' in STA 1963, sub-s 2(5), with effect from 29 June 2000.

j Stock Transfer (Forms) Regulations 2000 (SI 206/2000), r 2(b)(ii) inserted in STA 1963, sub-s 2(5) 'or for the purpose of the proviso to subsection (1) of this section' in para (a) of the definition of 'designated stock', with effect from 29 June 2000.

k Stock Transfer (Forms) Regulations 1991 (SI 77/1991), r 4(b) inserted STA 1963, sub-s 2(5) with effect from 31 March 1991.

l Stock Transfer (Forms) Regulations 1994 (SI 173/1994), r 4(a) inserted STA 1963, sub-s 2(6), with effect from 30 June 1994.

1 Central Bank Act 1997 Commencement Order 1997 (SI 150/1997).

Cross references

'company limited by guarantee': CA 1963, s 2(1); 'instrument': SDCA 1999, s 1(1); 'national treasury management agency': National Treasury Management Agency Act 1990, s 3(1); 'stock': SDCA 1999, s 1(1); 'stock exchange': Stock Exchange Act 1995, s 3(1); 'unlimited company': CA 1963, s 2(1); 'writing': IA 2005, Sch, Pt 1.

Definitions

'the Bank': STA 1963, s 2(5); 'Central Bank of Ireland Securities Settlements Office': STA 1963, s 2(5); 'company': STA 1963, s 2(5); 'designated stock': STA 1963, s 2(5); 'Exchequer Notes': STA 1963, s 2(6); 'fax': STA 1963, s 2(5); 'Minister'; STA 1963, s 1(1); 'registered securities': STA 1963, s 1(1); 'securities': STA 1963, s 1(1); 'stock exchange transaction': STA 1963, s 1(1); 'a stock transfer': STA 1963, s 1(2).

Notes

What constitutes a valid transfer?: The STA 1963 introduced a simplified form of transfer for fully paid shares[1]; the forms contained in STA 1963, Sch 1 are now generally accepted for the transfer of any shares (including shares in companies limited by guarantee and unlimited companies[2]). STA 1963 does not prohibit the use of any particular form; however, it does require that certain basic information is provided including the full name and address of the transferee, particulars of the consideration and of the number, type and amount of securities transferred, and details of the transferor.[3] The stock transfer forms provided in STA 1963 are alternatives to, rather than a substitute for, the provisions regarding transfer contained in a company's articles of association. Nothing contained in STA 1963, s 2 will affect the validity of an instrument which, were it not for the provisions of STA 1963, s 2 would be capable of transferring securities.[4]

CA 1963, s 81(1)[5] requires that a 'proper instrument of transfer' must be delivered to the company in order for the company to register such a transfer (irrespective of provisions of the articles of association of a company or the application of STA 1963, CA 1963). While it is thought that it is not strictly necessary to present a stamped share transfer form in order to have the transfer registered[6], CA 1963, s 86(1) relieves a company of any obligation to issue a certificate of title in respect of any transfer which has not been duly stamped. In addition SDCA 1999, s 129(1) imposes a penalty of €634.87 on any person who enrols, enters or registers an instrument which is chargeable with stamp duty if the instrument is not properly stamped[7].

Registered securities[8] may be validly transferred other than in accordance with STA 1963, including by way of a stock transfer form which is in a form which was common or usual before the commencement of STA 1963[9] or by way of forms which are 'substantially similar' to those set out in STA 1963, Schs 1 and 2.[10] It is common to see, on the reverse side of a stock transfer form, in addition to the information contained in the forms set out in STA 1963, Sch 1, a list of possible revenue certificates to be given where relief from *ad valorem* stamp duty is being claimed.[11]

1 Parliamentary Debates, Dáil Eireann, Vol 206, col 886 (10 December 1963). This legislation was introduced to Ireland in line with similar legislation enacted in the same year in the United Kingdom, implementing the principal recommendations of a committee representing the London Stock Exchange, the Bank of England and various other institutions in the City of London. See also UK legislation.

2 Notwithstanding STA 1963, s 2(4).

3 STA 1963, s 2(1).

4 STA 1963, s 2(3).

5 Which applies to all companies registered under the Companies Acts, including companies limited by guarantee and unlimited companies.

6 *Nisbet v Shepard* [1994] 1 BCLC 300.

7 Under SDCA, s 71(e), this penalty does not apply to transfers of dematerialised shares or securities effected through CREST.

8 See definition of 'registered securities', STA 1963, s 1(1).

9 STA 1963, s 2(3).

10 STA 1963, s 5(1).

11 The revenue certificates now commonly found originated from a written instruction from the Commissioners of the Inland Revenue. See Revenue Commissioners, *Stamp Duty Work Manual and Practices*, November 2001, p 43.

Execution of stock transfer forms: Section 2(1) specifically provides that stock transfer forms may be executed under hand. The forms set out in STA 1963, Sch 1 make reference[1] to the affixing of the company seal in circumstances where the transferor is a company.

Where the articles of association of the company do not require it, there would appear to be no statutory obligation for the transfer to be under seal.[2] It is interesting to note that a form of stock transfer form for Exchequer Notes[3] was introduced[4] to 'remove the need'[5] for such documents to be executed under seal. Although STA 1963, s 2 does not require a stock transfer form to be executed under seal, this does not relieve a company of the obligations regarding execution of documents and, in particular, transfers contained in that company's articles of association or under any power of attorney or otherwise.[6] Where the articles of association do require a transfer to be under seal, the directors of the company cannot waive such a requirement.[7]

Table A[8] provides that an instrument of transfer should be executed by both the transferee and the transferor, but this provision is commonly amended to bring the articles of the company into line with the requirements of STA 1963, s 2(1) which provides that the relevant instrument be 'executed by the transferor only'. It is not necessary that the execution of a stock transfer form should be attested.[9]

1 The stock transfer forms contained in STA 1963, Sch 1 do not require a company seal to be affixed, but note that 'a body corporate should execute this transfer under its common seal or otherwise in accordance with applicable statutory requirements.'

2 STA 1963, s 3(1) confirms that STA 1963, s 2 has effect 'notwithstanding anything to the contrary in any enactment ... or instrument relating to the transfer of those securities'.

3 STA 1963, Sch 2, Pt IV.

4 Stock Transfer Forms Regulations 1994 (SI 173/1994), brought into force on 30 June 1994.

5 Stock Transfer Forms Regulations 1994 (SI 173/1994), Explanatory Memorandum.

6 STA 1963, s 3(1)(b).

7 *Murray v Bush* (1873) LR 6 HL 37.

8 CA 1963, Table A, Pt 1, reg 22.

9 STA 1963, s 2(2). See also Practice Note, Law Society of Ireland, Professional Purposes Committee, 1 January 1994, in relation to witnessing transfers of Government securities.

Transfer of dematerialised securities: The Companies Act 1990, s 239 gave the Minister for Enterprise Trade and Employment power to introduce, by way of regulation[1], a system whereby dematerialised securities could be transferred without need of a written instrument of transfer. Since the introduction of the 1996 Regulations, notwithstanding the provisions of CA 1963, ss 79[2] or 81[3] or STA 1963, s 2(1),[4] transfers of dematerialised securities may be done other than by way of written instrument[5]. It is thought that the shares in a private company may not be transferred without a written instrument of transfer pursuant to the 1996 Regulations[6].

1 Companies Act 1990 (Uncertified Securities) Regulations 1996 (SI 65/1996) as amended by Companies Act 1990 (Uncertified Securities) (Amendment) Regulations 2005 (SI 693/2005) (the 1996 Regulations).

2 CA 1963, s 79 confirms that shares are choses in action (rather than real property) transferable in accordance with the articles of association of the company.

3 CA 1963, s 81 requires a proper instrument of transfer to be delivered in order for the company to register a transfer.

4 1996 Regulations, r 4(1).

5 1996 Regulations, r 5 disapplies the Statute of Frauds Act (Ireland) 1695, s 6 and the Supreme Court of Judicature (Ireland) Act 1877, s 28 (6) and any other rule of law requiring the execution under hand or seal of a document in writing for the transfer of property shall not apply to any transfer of title of uncertificated units of a security through a relevant system.

6 Courtney, *The Law of Private Companies* (2nd edn, Tottel Publishing, 2002) p 950.

Brokers transfers: Where a transfer is done to give effect to the transfer of shares listed on the Irish Stock Exchange[1], details of the consideration paid and of the transferee may be inserted either in the stock transfer form or supplied by means of a separate instrument as set out in STA 1963, Sch 2 and referred to as 'brokers transfers'.[2] Brokers transfers appropriate for use in certain circumstances in relation to Government securities[3] have also been included in STA 1963, Sch 2.

1 See definition of 'stock exchange transaction', STA 1963, s 1(1).

2 STA 1963, s 2(2).

3 See the second form contained in STA 1963, Sch 2, inserted by Stock Transfer (Forms) Regulations 1987 (SI 117/1987).

Central Bank of Ireland Securities Settlements Office[1]: Euroclear plc assumed responsibility for the settlement function for designated stock[2] and for all other Irish Government Bonds on 4 December 2000. The Central Bank of Ireland Securities Settlements Office maintains the register of bonds issued in the Irish market by the National Treasury Management Agency, the Housing Finance Agency, the European Investment Bank and Ulysses Securitisation plc.

1 Formerly the Gilts Settlement Office, Central Bank Act 1989, s 83.

2 STA 1963, s 2(5), 'designated Stock'.

UK legislation

See STA 1963, s 1 (as amended by Companies Consolidation (Consequential Provisions) Act 1985, s 30, Sch 2); Building Societies Act 1986, s 120, Sch 18, Pt I, para 5; Post Office Act 1969, s 108(1)(f); Finance Act 1964, ss 24, 26(7), Sch 8, para 10, Sch 9; Financial Services Act 1986, s 212(2), Sch 16, para 4 and Financial Services and Markets Act 2000 (Consequential Amendments and Repeals) Order (SI 3649/2001), art 271.

---

3 Supplementary provisions as to simplified transfer

(1) Section 2 of this Act shall have effect in relation to the transfer of any securities to which that section applies notwithstanding anything to the contrary in any enactment (including the Companies Act, 1963) or instrument relating to the transfer of those securities; but nothing in that section affects—

(a) any right to refuse to register a person as the holder of any securities on any ground other than the form in which those securities purport to be transferred to him; or

(b) any enactment or rule of law regulating the execution of documents by companies or other bodies corporate, or any articles of association or other instrument regulating the execution of documents by any particular company or body corporate.

(2) Subject to the provisions of this section, any enactment or instrument relating to the transfer of securities to which section 2 of this Act applies shall, with any necessary modifications, apply in relation to an instrument of transfer authorised by that section as it applies in relation to an instrument of transfer to which it applies apart from this subsection.

(3) In relation to the transfer of securities by means of a stock transfer and a brokers transfer—

(a) any reference in any enactment or instrument to the delivery or lodging of an instrument (or proper instrument) of transfer shall be construed as a reference to the delivery or lodging of the stock transfer and the brokers transfer;

(b) any such reference to the date on which an instrument of transfer is delivered or lodged shall be construed as a reference to the date by which the later of those transfers to be delivered or lodged has been delivered or lodged; and

(c) subject to paragraphs (a) and (b) of this subsection, the brokers transfer (and not the stock transfer) shall be deemed to be the conveyance or transfer for the purposes of the enactments relating to stamp duty.

Cross reference

See also SDCA 1999, Sch 1, Conveyance or Transfer on sale of any stocks or marketable securities.

Definitions

'articles': CA 1963, s 2(1); 'brokers transfer': STA, s 2(2); 'company': STA 1963, s 2(5); 'document'; CA 1963, s 2(1); 'instrument': SDCA 1999, s 1(1); 'securities': STA 1963, s 1(1); 'a stock transfer': STA 1963, s 1(2).

Notes

Application of STA 1963, s 2: A transfer done in accordance with STA 1963, s 2 does not affect the right of directors to refuse registration of a transferee of shares[1] or other securities in any way[2]. Similarly, nothing in STA 1963, s 2 has the effect of excluding any applicable rules[3] relating to execution of documents by companies and bodies corporate[4].

Any Act of the Oireachtas, statutory instrument or other document relating to the transfer of securities shall apply, *mutatis mutandis,* to a transfer of securities to which STA 1963, s 2 does not apply as it does to a transfer of securities to which STA 1963, s 2 does apply.[5]

1 See CA 1963, Table A, Pt 1, r 24 and CA 1963, s 84 and notes thereto.

2 STA 1963, s 3(1)(a).

3 Such as rules imposed by articles of association of a company, by any Act of the Oireachtas, statutory instrument or otherwise.

4 STA 1963, s 3(1)(b).

5 STA 1963, s 3(2).

Use of brokers transfers: In circumstances where a stock transfer is used with a brokers transfer, any reference to the delivery or lodging of an instrument (which included reference to a proper instrument[1]) is deemed to be reference to both the stock transfer and the brokers transfer[2]. Where a stock transfer is lodged or delivered on a different date to the lodgement or delivery of the brokers transfer, the latest date of lodgement or delivery of both forms is the date on which the transfer is to be treated as having been lodged[3]. For the purposes of the SDCA 1999 (as amended), the brokers transfer, rather than the stock transfer, is to be treated as the conveyance or transfer[4].

See also notes to STA 1963, s 2.

1 See CA 1963, s 81.

2 STA 1963, s 3(3)(a).

3 STA 1963, s 3(3)(b).

4 STA 1963, s 3(3)(c), see also SDCA 1999, Sch 1, Conveyance or Transfer on sale of any stocks or marketable securities.

UK legislation

See STA 1963, s 2 (as amended by Companies Consolidation (Consequential Provisions) Act 1985, s 30, Sch 2); FA 1999, s 139, Sch 20, Pt V(5); FA 1990, s 132, Sch 19, pt VI and Requirements of Writing (Scotland) Act 1995, s 14(2), Sch 5.

4 Prohibition of circulation of blank transfers

(1) Where a transfer in blank relating to registered securities has been delivered, pursuant to a sale of those securities, to or to the order of the purchaser or any person acting on his behalf, any person who in the State parts with possession of that transfer, or who removes it or causes or permits it to be removed from the State, before it has been duly completed shall, as well as being liable for the stamp duty chargeable in respect of that transfer, be liable to [a penalty of €634.87][a], and the penalty shall be recoverable in the same manner as if it were part of the duty.

(2) For the purposes of this section 'transfer in blank' means a transfer in which the name of the transferee has not been inserted, and a transfer shall be treated as duly completed if, and only if, the name of the transferee is inserted therein, being the name of—

(a) the purchaser of the securities under the sale;

(b) a person entitled to a charge upon the securities for money lent to that purchaser;

(c) a nominee holding as a bare trustee for that purchaser or for any such person as is mentioned in paragraph (b) of this subsection; or

(d) a person acting as the agent of that purchaser for the purposes of the sale.

(3) The foregoing provisions of this section shall apply in relation to a transfer delivered by way of or pursuant to a voluntary disposition *inter vivos*, being a transfer to which [section 30 of the Stamp Duties (Consolidation) Act, 1999][b], applies, as they apply in relation to a transfer delivered pursuant to a sale, and as if for any reference to the purchaser there were substituted a reference to the person (in this section referred to as the donee) to whom the disposition is made.

(4) References in this section to the purchaser or donee of any registered securities include references to any person to whom the rights of the purchaser or donee are transmitted by operation of law; and in relation to a transfer chargeable with duty in accordance with [subsection (1) or (2) of section 46 of the Stamp Duties (Consolidation) Act, 1999][c], references in this section to the purchaser and a sale shall be construed as references to the sub-purchaser and a sub-sale.

Amendments

a FA 1991, s 107, substituted the words and figures 'a penalty of €634.87'[1] in STA 1963, s 4 for 'a penalty of one hundred pounds' with effect from 29 May 1991.

b SDCA 1999, Sch 4 substituted the words and figures 'section 30 of the Stamp Duties (Consolidation) Act 1999' for 'section 74 of the Finance (1909–10) Act 1910' in STA 1963, s 4(3) with effect from 15 December 1999 (the date on which SDCA 1999 came in to force).

c SDCA 1999, Sch 4 substituted the words and figures 'subsection (1) or (2) of section 46 of the Stamp Duties (Consolidation) Act 1999' for 'subsection (4) or subsection (5) of section 58 of the Stamp Act, 1891' in STA 1963, s 4(4) with effect from 15 December 1999 (the date on which SDCA 1999 came in to force).

1 £500 converted to €634.87 by Council Regulations (EC) No 1103/97, No 974/98 and No 2866/98 and the Economic and Monetary Union Act 1998, s 6.

Cross reference

See SDCA 1999, s 46, 'Directions as to sub-sales'.

Definitions

'registered securities': STA 1963, s 1; 'securities': STA 1963, s 1.

Notes

Use of blank transfers: Transfers where details of the transferee have been omitted are authorised where the transfer is for the purposes of a stock exchange transaction[1] under STA 1963, s 2(2). In addition, blank transfers may be delivered with share certificates, in the context of the giving of security.[2]

1 See definition of 'stock exchange transaction', STA 1963, s 1(1).

2 See Johnston, *Banking and Security Law in Ireland* (Tottel Publishing, 1998), Ch 16.

Avoidance of stamp duty: The rationale for the inclusion of STA 1963, s 4 was to prevent avoidance of stamp duty, whereby the name of transferee was not inserted on the occasion of a transfer shares and stamp duty would be recovered only once (rather than twice) where a subsequent transferee's name was inserted into the stock transfer form and the form then presented to the Revenue Commissioners for stamping.[1] Any person found to have circulated such a transfer or to have taken it (or caused it to be taken) out of the State, prior to the transfer having been duly completed[2] will be liable to pay the stamp duty chargeable and a fine of €634.87.[3] As the fine of €634.87 is recoverable in the same manner as if it were part of the stamp duty payable, then interest will accrue on the fine in the same way as on the stamp duty payable.[4]

The provisions of STA 1963, s 4 apply in circumstances where the transfer has been by way of gift in the same way as if there had been a sale.[5] Where there is a sub-sale of property it is possible to avail of relief from stamp duty whereby stamp duty is only applied on the last conveyance or transfer.[6] In order to avail of such relief it is necessary to seek adjudication of the conveyance or transfer by the Revenue Commissioners.[7] STA 1963, s 4, does not prevent sub-sale relief from stamp duty being available for transfers of securities. In fact, STA 1963, s 4 makes specific reference to the application of that section[8] to sub-purchasers.[9]

1 Parliamentary Debates, Dáil Eireann, Vol 206, col 887 (10 December 1963).

2 For meaning of 'duly completed' see STA 1963, s 4(2)(a)–(d).

3 Amount was increased from £100 to £500 by FA 1991, s 107. £500 converted to €634.87 by Council Regulations (EC) No 1103/97, No 974/98 and No 2866/98 and the Economic and Monetary Union Act 1988, s 6.

4 At a rate of 0.0273% per day, SDCA 1999, s 14 (as amended by FA 2005, s 145).

5 STA 1963, s 3. See SDCA 1999, s 30, which provides that transfers by way of gift are liable to stamp duty in the same way as transfers on sale.

6 SDCA 1999, s 46.

7 See Warrant for Adjudication, under SDCA 1999, s 20.

8 STA 1963, s 4(4).

9 SDCA 1999, sub-ss 46(1) and (2).

UK legislation

FA 1963, s 67. This section was prospectively repealed by the FA 1990, Sch 19, Pt VI from a day to be appointed by the Treasury in accordance with FA 1990, ss 107–111. The Treasury order specifying the appointed day was to coincide with the start of paperless trading under the unsuccessful TAURUS system.

5 Additional provisions as to transfer forms

(1) References in this Act to the forms set out in the First and Second Schedules to this Act include references to forms substantially corresponding to those forms respectively.

(2) The Minister may by regulations amend the said Schedules either by altering the forms set out therein or by substituting different forms for those forms or by the addition of forms for use as alternatives to those forms; and references in this Act to the forms set out in those Schedules (including references in this section) shall be construed accordingly.

(3) Any regulations under subsection (2) of this section which substitute a different form for a form set out in the First Schedule to this Act may direct that subsection (3) of section 2 of this Act shall apply with any necessary modifications, in relation to the form for which that form is substituted as it applies to any form which was common or usual before the commencement of this Act.

[(4) Any regulations under subsection (2) of this section may—

(a) provide for forms on which some of the particulars mentioned in subsection (1) of section 2 of this Act are not required to be specified;

(b) provide for that section to have effect, in relation to such forms as are mentioned in paragraph (a) of this subsection or other forms specified in the regulations, subject to such amendments as are so specified (which may include an amendment of the reference in subsection (1) of section 2 of this Act to an instrument under hand);

(c) provide for all or any of the provisions of the regulations to have effect in such cases only as are specified in the regulations.] [a]

[(5) The Minister, having consulted with the Bank, may by regulation provide for the substitution for the references in that section of that name, or references to another name.] [b]

Amendments

a C(A)A 1977, s 8 inserted STA 1963, s 5(4) with effect from 1 April 1978.[1]

b Central Bank Act 1997, s 83 inserted STA 1963, s 5(5) with effect from 9 April 1997.[2]

1 Companies (Amendment) Act 1977 Commencement Order 1978 (SI 95/1978).

2 Central Bank Act 1997 Commencement Order 1997 (SI 150/1997).

Definitions

'the Minister': STA 1963, s 1; 'the Bank': STA 1963, s 2(5).

Notes

Ministerial powers under the Act: The Minister for Finance is given (and has exercised) specific powers to amend the scheduled forms by alteration[1] and substitution[2] and to introduce alternative[3] forms. It has been further clarified that the Minister's powers extend to introducing forms which omit particulars required by STA 1963, s 2(1),[4] and to amend the effect of STA 1963, s 2(1) in relation to such forms[5]. The Minister may also, having consulted with the Central Bank, make consequential changes necessitated by a change of name[6].

1 Eg Stock Transfer Act 1963 (Amendment of Forms) Regulations 1975 (SI 92/1975) amended the first forms set out in STA 1963, Schs 1 and 2.

2 Eg Stock Transfer (Forms) Regulations 1996 (SI 263/1996) substituted the first form set out in STA 1963, Sch 1.

3 Eg Stock Transfer (Forms) Regulations 1998 (SI 546/1998) introduced an alternative stock transfer form for use when transferring Government securities.

4 STA 1964, s 5(4)(a).

5 STA 1963, s 5(4)(b).

6 STA 1963, s 5(5).

UK legislation

See STA 1963, s 3 (as amended by Stock Exchange (Completion of Bargains) Act 1976, s 6.

6 Laying of regulations before Houses of Oireachtas

Every regulation made under this Act shall be laid before each House of the Oireachtas as soon as may be after it is made and, if a resolution annulling the regulations is passed by either such House within the next twenty-one days upon which that House has sat after the regulation is laid before it, the regulation shall be annulled accordingly, but without prejudice to the validity of anything previously done thereunder.

Cross reference

'Oireachtas': IA 2005, Sch, Pt 1.

UK legislation

See STA 1963, s 3(4).

7 Short title and commencement

(1) This Act may be cited as the Stock Transfer Act, 1963.

(2) This Act shall come into operation on such day as the Minister appoints by order.

Definitions

'the Minister': STA 1963, s 1.

Cross reference

'commencement': IA 2005, Sch, Pt 1.

UK legislation

See STA 1963, s 6.

First Schedule

Form (Stock Transfer)

(Above this line for Registrars only)

Stock Transfer Form[a]

Consideration Money €......[b]	Certificate lodged with the Registrar (For completion by the Registrar/ Stock Exchange)	
Full Name of Undertaking		
Full Description of Security		
Number or amount of Shares, Stock or other security and, in figures column only, number and denomination of units, if any.	Words	Figures (units of)
Name(s) of registered holder(s) should be given in full; the address should be given where there is only one holder. If the transfer is not made by the registered holder(s) insert also the name(s) and capacity (e.g., Executor (s)) of the person(s) making the transfer.	In the name(s) of	
I/We hereby transfer the above security out of the name(s) aforesaid to the person(s) named below *or to the several persons named in Parts 2 of Brokers Transfer Forms relating to the above security*: Delete words in italics except for stock exchange transactions. Signature(s) of transferor(s) 1................................. 2................................. 3................................. 4................................. A body corporate should execute this transfer under its common seal or otherwise in accordance with applicable statutory requirements.	Stamp of Selling Broker(s) or, for transactions which are not stock exchange transactions, of Agent(s), if any acting for the Transferor(s). Date………………………………	
Full name(s) and full postal address(es) (including County or, if applicable, Postal District number) of the person(s) to whom the security is transferred.		
Please state title, if any, or whether Mr., Mrs. or Miss. Please complete in type or in Block Capitals.		
I/ We request that such entries be made in the register as are necessary to give effect to this transfer.		

Stamp of Buying Broker(s) (if any)	Stamp or name and address of person lodging this form (if other than the Buying Broker(s))
Reference to the Registrar in this form means the registrar or registration agent of the undertaking, not the Registrar of Companies.	
(Endorsement for use only in stock exchange transactions) The security represented by the transfer overleaf has been sold as follows:—	
..........Shares/Stock ....Shares/Stock ....Shares/Stock ....Shares/Stock ....Shares/Stock ....Shares/Stock ....Shares/Stock ....Shares/Stock ....Shares/Stock ....Shares/Stock	..........Shares/Stock ....Shares/Stock ....Shares/Stock ....Shares/Stock ....Shares/Stock ....Shares/Stock ....Shares/Stock ....Shares/Stock ....Shares/Stock ....Shares/Stock
	....
Balance (if any) due to Selling Broker(s)	
Amount of Certificate(s)	
	Brokers Transfer Forms for above amounts certified
Stamp of certifying Stock Exchange	Stamp of Selling Broker(s)

Amendments

a Stock Transfer (Forms) Regulations 1996 (SI 263/1996), r 3(1) substituted the first form set out in STA 1963, Sch 1 with effect from 9 September 1996.

b '£' may be converted to '€' pursuant to the Economic and Monetary Union Act 1998, s 21.

Notes

See generally notes to STA 1963, s 2.

UK legislation

See STA 1963, Sch I (as inserted by the Stock Transfer (Addition and Substitution of Forms) Order 1996 (SI 1571/1996)).

[TALISMAN SOLD TRANSFER][a]

Amendments

a Stock Transfer (Forms) Regulations 1980 (SI 139/1980), r 5(a) inserted the Talisman Sold Transfer in 1963, Sch 1 with effect from 16 May 1980.

Notes

Because the Talisman Sold Transfer Form is no longer in use, it is not reproduced here.

UK legislation

See STA 1963, Sch I (as inserted by the Stock Transfer (Addition and Substitution of Forms) Order 1979 (SI 277/1979)).

[TALISMAN BOUGHT TRANSFER][a]

Amendments

a Stock Transfer (Forms) Regulations 1980 (SI 139/1980), r 5(b) inserted the Talisman Bought Transfer in 1963, Sch 1 with effect from 16 May 1980.

Notes

Because the Talisman Bought Transfer Form is no longer in use, it is not reproduced here.

UK legislation

See STA 1963, Sch I (as inserted by the Stock Transfer (Addition of Forms) Order 1979 (SI 277/1979) and the Stock Transfer (Substitution of Forms) Order 1990 (SI 18/1990)).

(Above this line for Registrar's use)

TRANSFER[a]	Counter Location Stamp	Barcode or reference *RN*
	Above this line for completion by the depositing system-user only.	
	Consideration Money €......[b]	Certificate(s) lodged with Registrar (To be completed by Registrar)
Name of Undertaking Description of Security		
Please complete in type or in block capitals.	Amount of shares or other security in words	Figures
Name(s) of registered holder(s) should be given in full; the address should be given where there is only one holder.	In the name(s) of	Designation (if any)
If the transfer is not made by the registered holder(s) insert also the name(s) and capacity (e.g. executor(s)) of the person(s) making the transfer.		Balance certificate(s) required

	I/We hereby transfer the above security out of the name(s) aforesaid into the name(s) of the system-member set out below and request that the necessary entries be made in the undertaking's own register of members.	Stamp of depositing system-user
Please Sign Here	1	
	2	
	3	
	4	
	A body corporate should execute this transfer under its common seal or otherwise in accordance with applicable statutory requirements.	Date
Full name(s) of the person(s) to whom the security is transferred.		Participant ID
Such person(s) must be a system-member.		Member Account ID
References to the Registrar in this form means the registrar or registration agent of the undertaking, *not* the Registrar of Companies.	is delivering this transfer at the direction and on behalf of the depositing system-user whose stamp appears herein and does not in any manner or to any extent warrant or represent the validity, genuineness or correctness of the transfer instructions contained herein or the genuineness of the signature(s) of the transferor(s). The depositing system-user by delivering this transfer to authorises to deliver this transfer for registration and agrees to be deemed for all purposes to be the person(s) actually so delivering this transfer for registration.	

Amendments

a Stock Transfer (Forms) Regulations 1996 (SI 263/1996), r 4(1) inserted the second form in STA 1963, Sch 1 with effect from 9 September 1996.[1]

b '£' may be converted to '€' pursuant to the Economic and Monetary Union Act 1998, s 21.

[1] Stock Transfer (Forms) Regulations 1996 (SI 263/1996).

Cross reference

See CA 1990, s 239, whereby the Minister made provision, by regulation for enabling title to securities to be evidenced and transferred without a written instrument.

Definitions

'the registrar of companies': CA 1963, s 2(1); 'system-member': SI 263/1996, s 3(1); 'securities': STA 1963, s 1(1); 'system-user': SI 263/1996, s 3(1).

Notes

Transfer of uncertificated securities: This stock transfer form was introduced in connection with the introduction of the equity settlement system known as CREST for the purpose of providing for the transfer of securities which are held in uncertificated form[1]. CREST was preceded by the Talisman system[2].

1 See generally McHugh, 'CREST in Ireland, The Uncertificated Securities Regulations, 1996' (1996) 3 CLP 219.

2 See Abrans, 'Talisman: A Legal Analysis' (1980) Co Law 17; and Ussher, *Company Law in Ireland* (Sweet & Maxwell 1986), p 198–199.

UK legislation

See STA 1963, Sch I (as inserted by the Stock Transfer (Addition and Substitution of Forms) Order 1996 (SI 1571/1996)).

[STOCK TRANSFER FORM][a]

(Above this line for Registrars only)

Certificate lodged with the Registrar		
(For completion by the Registrar/Stock Exchange)		
Full name of Undertaking		
Full description of Security		
Amount of security and, in figures column only, number and denomination of units, if any.	Words	Figures (units of)
Name(s) of registered holder(s) should be given in full; the address should be given where there is only one holder. If the transfer is not made by the registered holder(s) insert also the name(s) and capacity (e.g., Executor(s)) of the person(s) making the transfer.	In the name(s) of	

I/We hereby transfer the above security out of the name(s) aforesaid to the person(s) named below *or to the several persons named in Parts 2 of Brokers Transfer Forms relating to the above security:* Delete words in italics except for stock exchange transactions. Signature(s) of transferor(s) 1... 2... 3... 4... Bodies corporate should execute under their common seal	Stamp of Selling Broker(s) for transactions which are stock exchange transactions Agent(s), if any, acting for the transferor(s). Date..................................

Full name(s) and full postal address(es) (including County or, if a applicable, Postal District number) of the person(s) to whom the security is transferred. Please state title, if any, or whether Mr., Mrs. or Miss. Please complete in type-writing or in Block Capitals.	

I/ We request that such entries be made in the register as are necessary to give effect to this transfer.

Stamp of Buying Broker(s) (if any)	Stamp or name and address of person lodging this form (if other than the Buying Broker(s))

The security represented by the transfer overleaf has been sold as follows:-

....Stock	....Stock
....Stock	....Stock
....Stock	....Stock
....Stock	....Stock
....Stock	....Stock
....Stock	....Stock
....Stock	....Stock
....Stock	....Stock
....Stock	....Stock
....Stock	....Stock

Balance (if any) due to Selling Broker(s)

Amount of Certificate(s)

Brokers Transfer Forms for above amounts certified Stamp of certifying Stock Exchange	Stamp of Selling Broker(s)

Amendments

a Stock Transfer (Forms) Regulations 1987 (SI 117/1987), r 4(1) inserted STA 1963, Sch 1, Stock Transfer Form, with effect from 30 April 1987.

Cross reference

See STA 1963, ss 2 and 5(4).

Definitions

'securities': STA 1963, s 1(1); 'stock exchange transaction': STA 1963, s 1(1); 'a stock transfer': STA 1963, s 1(2).

Notes

This stock transfer form was introduced as an alternative to the first stock transfer form contained in STA 1963, Sch I, for the transfer of Government securities where details of the consideration are not included on the stock transfer form.

UK legislation

See generally Stock Transfer Act 1982 in relation to the transfer of Government securities in the United Kingdom.

[STOCK TRANSFER FORM II][a]

(Above this line for Registrars only)

Certificate lodged with the Registrar (For completion by the Registrar/Stock Exchange)			
Full name of Undertaking	GOVERNMENT SECURITIES (IRELAND)		
Full description of Security			
Amount of security and, in figures column only, number and denomination of units, if any.	Words		Figures (units of)
Name(s) of registered holder(s) should be given in full: the address should be given where there is only one holder.			
If the transfer is not made by the registered holder(s) insert also the name(s) and capacity (e.g., Executor (s)) of the person(s) making the transfer.			
I/We hereby transfer the above security out of the name(s) aforesaid to he person(s) named below *or to the several persons named in Parts 2 of Brokers Transfer Forms relating to the above security*: Delete words in italics except for stock exchange transactions. Signature(s) of transferor(s)			Stamp of Selling Broker(s) or, for transactions which are not stock exchange transactions of Agent(s), if any, acting for the Transferor(s):

<table>
<tr><td colspan="2">1..
2..
3..
4..
Bodies corporate should execute under their common seal</td><td>Date
..............................</td></tr>
<tr><td colspan="3">Full name(s) and full postal address(es) (including County or, if applicable, Postal District number of the person(s) to whom the security is transferred.
Please state title, if any, or whether Mr., Mrs. or Miss.
Please complete in typewriting or in Block Capitals.</td></tr>
<tr><td colspan="3">I/We request that such entries be made in the register as are necessary to give effect to this transfer.</td></tr>
<tr><td>Stamp of Buying Broker(s) (if any)</td><td colspan="2">Stamp or name and address of person lodging this form (if other than the Buying Broker(s))</td></tr>
<tr><td colspan="3">SCHEDULE
The security represented by the transfer overleaf has been sold as follows:-</td></tr>
<tr><td>..Stock
....Stock
....Stock
....Stock
....Stock
....Stock
....Stock
....Stock
....Stock
....Stock</td><td colspan="2">..Stock
....Stock
....Stock
....Stock
....Stock
....Stock
....Stock
....Stock
....Stock
....Stock</td></tr>
<tr><td>Balance (if any) due to Selling Broker(s)
Amount of Certificate(s)
Brokers Transfer Forms for above amounts certified
Stamp of certifying Stock Exchange</td><td colspan="2">..

Stamp of Selling Broker(s)</td></tr>
</table>

Amendments

a Stock Transfer (Forms) Regulations 1998 (SI 546/1998), r 4 inserted STA 1963, Sch 1, Stock Transfer Form II, with effect from 1 January 1999.

Cross reference

See STA 1963, s 5(4).

Definitions

'securities': STA 1963, s 1(1); 'stock exchange transaction': STA 1963, s 1(1); 'a stock transfer': STA 1963, s 1(2).

Notes

This stock transfer form was introduced as an alternative stock transfer form which would be effective to transfer title to Government securities when transmitted by fax. However, the Central Bank of Ireland Securities Settlement Office (as registrars of designated stocks[1]) no longer accept copies of stock transfer forms sent by fax as evidence of transfer of those Government securities.

[1] STA 1963, s 2(5).

UK legislation

See generally STA 1982 in relation to the transfer of Government securities in the UK.

SECOND SCHEDULE

FORM (BROKER'S TRANSFER)

BROKERS TRANSFER FORM

(Above this line for Registrars only)

<table>
<tr><td>Consideration Money € ...[a]</td><td colspan="2">Certificate lodged with the Registrar

(For completion by the Registrar/ Stock Exchange)</td></tr>
<tr><td>PART 1
[Name of Undertaking] [b]</td><td colspan="2"></td></tr>
<tr><td>[Description of Security] [b]</td><td colspan="2"></td></tr>
<tr><td>Number or amount of Shares, Stock or other security and, in figures column only, number and denomination of units, if any.</td><td>Words</td><td>Figures
(units of)</td></tr>
<tr><td>Name(s) of registered holder(s) should be given in full; the address should be given where there is only one holder.
If the transfer is not made by the registered holder(s) insert also the name(s) and capacity (e.g., Executor(s)) of the person(s) making the transfer.</td><td>In the name(s) of</td><td></td></tr>
<tr><td colspan="3">I/We confirm that the Stock Transfer Form relating to the security set out above has been lodged with the Registrar, and that the said security has been sold by me/us by a stock exchange transaction within the meaning of the Stock Transfer Act 1963.

Date and Stamp of Selling Brokers(s)</td></tr>
<tr><td>Part 2
Full name(s) and full postal address(es) (including County or, if applicable, Postal District number) of the person(s) to whom the security is transferred.
Please state title, if any, or whether Mr, Mrs. or Miss. Please complete in typewriting or in Block Capitals.</td><td colspan="2"></td></tr>
</table>

I/We confirm that the security set out in Part I above has been purchased by a stock exchange transaction within the meaning of the Stock Transfer Act, 1963 and I/we request that such entries be made in the register as are necessary to give effect to this transfer.	
Stamp of Buying Broker(s)	Stamp of Lodging Agent (if other than the Buying Broker(s)

Amendments

a £' may be converted to '€' pursuant to the Economic and Monetary Union Act 1998, s 21.

b Stock Transfer Act, 1963 (Amendment of Forms) Regulations 1975 (SI 117/1987), r 4 substituted the words 'Full name of Undertaking' and 'Full description of Security' with 'Name of Undertaking' and 'Description of Security'.

Cross reference

See notes to STA 1963, ss 2 and 5(4).

Definitions

'securities': STA 1963, s 1(1); 'stock exchange transaction': STA 1963, s 1(1); 'a stock transfer': STA 1963, s 1(2).

UK legislation

See STA 1963, Sch II (as amended by the Stock Transfer (Amendment of Forms) Order 1974).

[STOCK TRANSFER FORM][a]

(Above this line for Registrars only)

Certificate lodged with the Registrar		
(For completion by the Registrar/Stock Exchange)		
PART 1 Name of Undertaking		
Full description of Security		
Amount of security and, in figures column only, number and denomination of units, if any.	Words	Figures (units of)
Name(s) of registered holder(s) should be given in full; the address should be given where there is only one holder. If the transfer is not made by the registered holder(s) insert also the name(s) and capacity (e.g., Executor(s)) of the person(s) making the transfer.	In the name(s) of	
I/We confirm that the Stock Transfer Form relating to the security set out above has been lodged with the Registrar, and that the said security has been sold by me/us by a stock exchange transaction within the meaning of the Stock Transfer Act, 1963 . Date and Stamp of Selling Brokers(s)		

<table>
<tr><td colspan="2">PART 2
Full name(s) and full postal address(es) (including County or, if applicable, Postal District number) of the person(s) to whom the security is transferred.
Please state title, if any, or whether Mr., Mrs. or Miss. Please complete in typewriting or in Block Capitals.</td></tr>
<tr><td colspan="2">I/We confirm that the security set out in Part I above has been purchased by a stock exchange transaction within the meaning of the Stock Transfer Act, 1963, and I/we request that such entries be made in the register as are necessary to give effect to this transfer.</td></tr>
<tr><td>Stamp of Buying Broker(s)</td><td>Stamp of Lodging Agent (if other than the Buying Broker(s))</td></tr>
</table>

Amendments

a Stock Transfer (Forms) Regulations 1987 (SI 117/1987), r 4(2) inserted STA 1963, Sch 2, Form (Brokers Transfer), with effect from 30 April 1987.

Cross reference

See notes to STA 1963, ss 2 and 5(4).

Definitions

'securities': STA 1963, s 1(1); 'stock exchange transaction': STA 1963, s 1(1); 'a stock transfer': STA 1963, s 1(2).

Notes

This brokers transfer form was introduced for the purpose of providing for the transfer of certain Government securities without including details of the consideration on the brokers transfer form.

UK legislation

See generally STA 1982 in relation to the transfer of Government securities in the UK.

[PART II

FORM FOR DESIGNATED STOCK TRANSFER (FAX)][a]

Amendments

a Stock Transfer (Forms) Regulations 1991(SI 77/1991), r 5 inserted STA 1963, Sch 2, Pt II, with effect from 31 March 1991.

Cross reference

STA 1963, s 5(4).

Notes

This form was introduced for use by members of the Central Bank Securities Settlements Office[1] only, so that, instead of several individual stock transfer forms being completed, a schedule of transfers of stock could be used. The transmission by fax[2] of this form was a valid mechanism to transfer title to designated stock[3] and the use in this form of an abbreviation of the transferee's name was permitted[4]. The Central Bank of Ireland Securities Settlement Office is no longer responsible for settlement of designated stocks. Because this form is no longer in use, it is not reproduced here.

1 Formerly the Gilts Settlements Office (see Central Bank Act 1997, s 83).
2 STA 1963, s 2(1)(d).
3 STA 1963, s 2 (5), 'designated stock'.
4 STA 1963, s 2(d)(ii)(III).

[PART III

FORM FOR DESIGNATED STOCK TRANSFER (TELEX)

(FOR USE ONLY BY MEMBERS OF GILTS SETTLEMENT OFFICE)][a]

Amendments

a Stock Transfer (Forms) Regulations 1991 (SI 77/1991), r 5 inserted STA 1963, Sch 2, Pt III, with effect from 31 March 1991.

Cross reference

STA 1963, s 5(4).

Notes

This form was introduced for use by members of the Central Bank Securities Settlements Office[1] only, so that, instead of several individual stock transfer forms being completed, a schedule of transfers of stock could be used. The transmission by telex[2] of this form, was a valid mechanism to transfer title to designated stock[3] and the use in this form of an abbreviation of the transferee name was permitted[4]. The Central Bank of Ireland Securities Settlement Office is no longer responsible for settlement of designated stocks. Because this form is no longer in use, it is not reproduced here.

1 Formerly the Gilts Settlements Office (see Central Bank Act 1997, s 83).
2 STA 1963, s 2(1)(e).
3 STA 1963, s 2 (5), 'designated stock'.
4 STA 1963, s 2(e)(iii).

[PART IV

FORM OF TRANSFER FOR EXCHEQUER NOTES

NATIONAL TREASURY MANAGEMENT AGENCY][a]

A	For Completion by the National Treasury Management Agency		
	Full Name of Undertaking	Government Securities (Ireland)	
	Full Description of Security	Exchequer Note: (Number)	
	Amount of Security and, in figures column only, number and denomination of units, if any.	Words	Figures (units of)
	Name(s) of registered holder(s) should be given in full; the address should be given where there is only one holder. If the transfer is not made by the registered holder(s) insert also the name(s) and capacity (e.g. Executor(s)) of the person(s) making the transfer).	In the name(s) of	

<table>
<tr><td>B</td><td>I/We, being an authorised signatory or signatories, hereby transfer the above security out of the name(s) aforesaid to the person(s) named in Section C below:

1.____________
2.____________
3.____________
4.____________</td><td>Stamp of Selling Broker(s) or, for transactions which are not stock exchange transactions of Agent(s) if any acting for the Transferor(s).

Date: ____________</td></tr>
<tr><td>C</td><td colspan="2">Full name(s) and full postal address(es), including Country or, if applicable, Postal District number, of the person(s) to whom the security is transferred.

Bank account, name, address for payment on maturity.

Please complete in typewriting or in Block Capitals.</td></tr>
<tr><td colspan="3">I/We request that such entries be made in the register as are necessary to give effect to this transfer.</td></tr>
<tr><td colspan="2">Stamp of Buying Broker(s) (if any)</td><td>Stamp or name and address of person lodging this form (if other than the Buying Broker(s))</td></tr>
</table>

Amendments

a Stock Transfer (Forms) Regulations 1994 (SI 173/1994), r 5 inserted STA 1963, Sch 2, Pt IV, with effect from 30 June 1994.

Cross reference

'National Treasury Management Agency': National Treasury Management Agency Act 1990, s 3(1).

See also STA 1963, s 5(4).

Definitions

'securities': STA 1963, s 1(1); 'stock exchange transaction': STA 1963, s 1(1); 'a stock transfer': STA 1963, s 1(2).

Notes

This stock transfer form, which relates to transfer of Exchequer Notes[1] only, removes reference to the transfer being executed company under seal by a company or body corporate.

[1] STA 1963, s 2(6).

Companies (Amendment) Act 1977

(Number 31 of 1977)

ARRANGEMENT OF SECTIONS

SECTION

An Act to Provide for the Simplification of Certain Activities connected with the Periodic Completion of Bargains made on the Stock Exchange, for that Purpose to amend and extend the Companies Act, 1963, and to provide for other Connected Matters. [12th December, 1977]

Be it Enacted by the Oireachtas as follows:

1 Interpretation

(1) In this Act—

'the Act of 1963' means the Companies Act, 1963;

'the Minister' means the Minister for Industry, Commerce and Energy;

'stock exchange nominee' means a person designated, by regulations made by the Minister, as a nominee of a recognised stock exchange for the purposes of this Act.

(2) In this Act any word or expression to which a meaning is assigned by the Act of 1963 has that meaning except where the context requires otherwise.

Notes

Recognised stock exchange: The Irish Stock Exchange is prescribed as a recognised stock exchange for the purposes of CA 1977, s 1.[1]

[1] Companies (Stock Exchange) Regulations 1995 (SI 30/1995), reg 3(b)). The definition of 'the Irish Stock Exchange' is to be found in the Stock Exchange Act 1995, s 3(1)).

Minister: The relevant Minister is now the Minister for Enterprise, Trade and Employment.

---

2 Modification of obligation to prepare share certificates etc

A company of which shares or debentures are allotted or debenture stock is allotted to a stock exchange nominee, or with which a transfer is lodged for transferring any shares, debentures or debenture stock of the company to a stock exchange nominee, shall not be required in consequence of the allotment or the lodging of the transfer to complete and have ready for delivery in pursuance of section 86(1) of the Act of 1963 the certificates of the shares or the debentures or the certificates of the debenture stock, as the case may be.

Definitions

'debenture': CA 1963, s 2(1); 'company': CA 1963, s 2(1); 'share': CA 1963, s 2(1); 'stock exchange nominee': CA 1977, s 1(1); 'the Act of 1963': CA 1977, s 1.

Notes

Talisman settlement system and CREST: Until a few years ago a special system known as the Talisman Settlement System operated in relation to the transfer of listed securities. The objective of the Talisman system was to centralise all dealings through a central pooling system known as SEPON (Stock Exchange Pool Nominees). For the purpose of this system the designated stock exchange nominee was a company known as Sepon Ltd.[1] Shares or debentures sold on the stock exchange would be transferred on a form called the Talisman Sold Transfer to Sepon Ltd.[2] The securities would then be transferred by Sepon Ltd to the ultimate purchaser on a Talisman Bought Transfer Form.[3] By virtue of CA 1963, s 2 the company in which the shares are held did not have to issue a share certificate or debenture certificate in respect of the temporary transfer of the securities into Sepon Ltd. Instead, the company was obliged only to issue a certificate to the ultimate purchaser.

In order to speed up the settlement of bargains, the stock exchange had for some time been pressing for a completely electronic system for recording and transferring securities. This system, which replaces Talisman, is known as CREST and was introduced pursuant to Companies Act 1990 (Uncertificated Securities) Regulations 1996 (SI 68/1996).[4] Securities governed by these Regulations are known as 'uncertificated units of security'.[5] Title to such securities is recorded electronically by the company and may likewise be transferred electronically rather than by way of an 'instrument of transfer'.[6] Despite the absence of an instrument of transfer, the transaction still attracts stamp duty.[7] Furthermore, because title to such shares is recorded and transferred electronically, the company is no longer allowed to issue a share certificate or debenture certificate, as the case may be, to the holder of the relevant security.[8] A document purporting to be a share certificate or debenture certificate in respect of an uncertificated unit of security, shall not be regarded as evidence of title thereto.[9] Instead, title is deemed to be evidenced by the recording of the name and address of the security holder as well as details of the number of uncertificated units of security held by him, in the register of members or the register of debenture holders, as the case may be.[10]

1 Companies (Amendment) Act 1977 (Designation of Stock Exchange Nominee) Regulations 1979 (SI 122/1979).

2 This form was added to Part II of the Schedule to STA 1963, by the Stock Transfer (Forms) Regulations 1980 (SI 139/1980).

3 This form was added to Part II of the Schedule to STA 1963, by the Stock Transfer (Forms) Regulations 1980 (SI 139/1980).

4 For a fuller discussion of this computer-based system see the Companies Act 1990 (Uncertificated Securities) Regulations 1996 (SI 68/1996) and the notes thereto.

5 Reg 3(1).

6 Regs 4(1), 6(1) and 9(1).

7 Reg 4(2) and (3).

8 Reg 19(1).

9 Reg 19(2).

10 Regs 10 and 11.

3 Official seals for sealing share certificates etc

(1) A company other than a private company may have, for use for sealing securities issued by the company and for sealing documents creating or evidencing securities so issued, an official seal which is a facsimile of the common seal of the company with the addition on its face of the word 'Securities' or the word 'Urrúis'.

(2) A company which was incorporated before the commencement of this Act and which has such an official seal as is mentioned in subsection (1) of this section may use the seal for sealing such securities and documents as are mentioned in that subsection notwithstanding anything in any instrument constituting or regulating the company or in any instrument made before such commencement which relates to any securities issued by the company, and any provision of such an instrument which requires any such securities or documents to be signed shall not apply to the securities or documents if they are sealed with that seal.

Definitions

'company': CA 1963, s 2(1); 'document': CA 1963, s 2(1); 'private company': CA 1963, s 2(1), s 33(1); 'share': CA 1963, s 2(1).

Notes

Sealing of securities: In relation to the sealing of share certificates by companies and the status of such certificates as evidence of title, see CA 1963, s 87 and the notes thereto.

---

4 Use of computers etc for certain company records

(1) It is hereby declared that the power conferred on a company by section 378(1) of the Act of 1963 to keep a register or other record by recording the matters in question otherwise than by making entries in bound books includes power to keep the register or other record other than minute books kept pursuant to section 145 of the Act of 1963 by recording the matters in question otherwise than in a legible form so long as the recording is capable of being reproduced in a legible form.

(2) Any provision of an instrument made by a company before the commencement of this Act which requires a register of holders of debentures of the company to be kept in a legible form shall be construed as requiring the register to be kept in a legible or non-legible form, provided, however, that a register kept in non-legible form shall be capable of being reproduced in legible form.

(3) If any such register or other record of a company as is mentioned in section 378(1) of the Act of 1963 is kept by the company by recording the matters in question otherwise than in a legible form, any duty imposed on the company by virtue of that Act to allow inspection of, or to furnish a copy of, the register or other record or any part of it shall be treated as a duty to allow inspection of, or to furnish, a reproduction of the recording or of the relevant part of it in a legible form.

(4) The Minister may by regulations make such provision in addition to subsection (3) of this section as he considers appropriate in connection with such registers or other records as are mentioned in that subsection and are kept as there mentioned, and the

regulations may make modifications of provisions of the Act of 1963 relating to such registers or other records as are mentioned in that subsection.

Definitions

'company': CA 1963 s 2(1); 'debenture': CA 1963 s 2(1); 'the Minister': CA 1977, s 1(1); 'the Act of 1963': CA 1977, s 1(1).

Notes

Keeping of records on computer: CA 1977, s 4 permits a company to keep its statutory records, other than the minute book, on computer rather than in traditional 'hard copy' form. The records which may be so kept include the register of members,[1] the index of members, if any,[2] the register of directors and secretaries,[3] the register of directors' interests in shares and debentures,[4] in the case of a plc, the register of beneficial interests in shares and debentures,[5] and the books of account.[6]

CA 1990, s 239 as amended by IFCMPA 2006, s 12 enables the Minister, by regulation, to require electronic means 'for evidencing and transferring title to [certain classes of] securities shall constitute the sole and exclusive means for doing so (and, accordingly, that any purported transfer of such securities otherwise than by those means shall be void)'. This can be done only for:

(a) securities of companies admitted to trading on a regulated market;

(b) securities of companies admitted to trading on a market other than a regulated market; or

(c) securities of public limited companies of a specified class.

Returns in non-legible form: CA 1990, s 249 permits companies to make returns to the registrar of companies in non-legible form. However, the section has yet to be brought into force.

1 CA 1963, s 116.
2 CA 1963, s 117.
3 CA 1963, s 195.
4 CA 1990, s 59.
5 CA 1990, s 80.
6 CA 1990, s 202.

---

5 Consequential amendments of Act of 1963

(1) […][a]

(2) […][b]

(3) […][c]

(4) […][d]

(5) […][e]

(6) […][f]

(7) […][g]

(8) […][h]

(9) […][i]

Amendments

a CA 1977, s 5(1) substituted CA 1963, s 87(1).

b CA 1977, s 5(2) substituted CA 1963, Sch 1, Table A, Part 1, reg 8.

c CA 1977, s 5(3) substituted CA 1963, Sch 1, Table A, Part 1, reg 8.

d CA 1977, s 5(4) substituted 'with the exception of regulations 8, 24, 51, 54, 84 and 86' in CA 1963, Sch 1, Table A, Part II, reg 1 and deleted 'with the exception of regulations 24, 51, 54, 84, 86'.

e CA 1977, s 5(5) inserted CA 1963, Sch 1, Table A, Part II, reg 10.

f CA 1977, s 5(6) substituted CA 1963, Sch 1, Table A, Part II, Note.

g CA 1977, s 5(7) substituted the Irish translation of substitution by sub-s (4).

h CA 1977, s 5(8) substituted the Irish translation of the substitution by sub-s (5).

i CA 1977, s 5(9) substituted the Irish translation of substitution by sub-s (6).

6 Application of *sections 2 to 4* to unregistered companies

[...][a]

Amendments

a CA 1977, s 6 repealed by CA 1990, s 6(2).

Definitions

'company': CA 1963, s 2(1).

7 Acquisition and disposal of securities by trustees and personal representatives

A trustee or personal representative shall not be chargeable with breach of trust or, as the case may be, with default in administering the estate by reason only of the fact that—

(a) he has, for the purpose of acquiring securities which he has power to acquire in connection with the trust or estate, paid for the securities under arrangements which provide for them to be transferred to him from a stock exchange nominee but not to be so transferred until after payment of the price; or

(b) he has, for the purpose of disposing of securities which he has power to dispose of in connection with the trust or estate, transferred the securities to a stock exchange nominee under arrangements which provide that the price is not to be paid to him until after the transfer is made.

Definitions

'stock exchange nominee': CA 1977, s 1(1).

Notes

See the notes to C(A)A 1977, s 2. As to the power of trustees to buy and sell shares, see Keane, *Equity and the Law of Trusts in the Republic of Ireland*, (Butterworths, 1988), ch 10.

---

8 Forms for transfer of securities

[...][a]

Amendments

a CA 1977, s 8 inserted sub-s (4) of the STA 1963.

---

9 Laying of regulations before Houses of Oireachtas

Every regulation under this Act shall be laid before each House of the Oireachtas as soon as may be after it is made and, if a resolution annulling the regulation is passed by either House within the next 21 days on which that House has sat after the regulation is laid before it, the regulation shall be annulled accordingly, but without prejudice to the validity of anything previously done thereunder.

10 Expenses

The expenses incurred in the administration of this Act shall, to such extent as may be sanctioned by the Minister for Finance, be paid out of moneys provided by the Oireachtas.

11 Short title, collective citation and commencement

(1) This Act may be cited as the Companies (Amendment) Act, 1977.

(2) This Act and the Act of 1963 may be cited together as the Companies Acts, 1963 to 1977.

(3) This Act shall come into operation on such date as the Minister may appoint by order.

Definitions

'the Minister': CA 1977, s 1; 'the Act of 1963': CA 1977, s 1.

Notes

The commencement date for C(A)A 1977 was 3 April 1978.

Companies (Amendment) Act 1982

(Number 10 of 1982)

ARRANGEMENT OF SECTIONS

Companies (Amendment) Act 1982

(Number 10 of 1982)

An Act To Amend And Extend The Companies Act, 1963, and to Provide for Other Connected Matters. [15th June, 1982]

Be It Enacted by the Oireachtas as Follows:

1 Interpretation

In this Act 'the Principal Act' means the Companies Act, 1963.

Notes

Operative Date: C(A)A 1982 came into force on 3 August 1982.[1]

[1] Companies (Amendment) Act 1982 (Commencement) Order 1982 (SI 255/1982).

2 Articles prescribing regulations for companies

[...][a]

Amendments

a C(A)A 1982, s 2 substituted CA 1963, s 11.

Cross reference

See CA 1963, s 11 (as amended).

Definitions

'articles': CA 1963, s 2(1).

3 Particulars to be delivered with memorandum

(1) There shall be delivered to the registrar together with every memorandum of a company delivered to him pursuant to section 17 of the Principal Act a statement in the prescribed form containing the name and the particulars specified in subsection (2) of this section in relation to—

(a) the persons who are to be the first directors of the company,

(b) the person who is, or the persons who are, to be the first secretary or joint secretaries of the company, and

(c) the situation of the company's registered office.

(2) The particulars referred to in subsection (1) of this section are—

(a) in relation to a person named as director of the company concerned all particulars which are, in relation to a director, required pursuant to section 195(2) of the Principal Act to be contained in the register kept under that section,

(b) in relation to a person named as secretary, or as one of the joint secretaries, all particulars which are, in relation to the secretary or to each joint secretary, required pursuant to section 195(4) of the Principal Act to be contained in the register kept under that section, and

(c) in relation to the registered office of the company, the particulars which are required to be given to the registrar pursuant to section 113 of the Principal Act.

(3) The statement required to be delivered pursuant to this section shall be signed by or on behalf of the subscribers and shall be accompanied by a consent signed by each of the persons named in it as a director, secretary or joint secretary to act in that capacity.

(4) Where the memorandum is delivered to the registrar pursuant to section 17 of the Principal Act by a person as agent for the subscribers to the memorandum the statement required to be delivered to the registrar pursuant to this section shall so specify and shall specify the name and address of the person by whom the memorandum is delivered.

(5) The persons who are specified in the statement required to be delivered to the registrar pursuant to this section as the directors, secretary or joint secretaries of the company to which the statement refers shall, on the incorporation of the company, be deemed to have been appointed as the first directors, secretary or joint secretaries, as the case may be, of the company, and any indication in any articles delivered to the registrar with the memorandum specifying a person as a director or secretary of a company shall be void unless such person is specified as a director or as secretary in the said statement.

(6) [...][a]

Amendments

a C(A)A 1982, s 3(6) repealed by C(A)A 1983, Sch 3, Pt II.

Definitions

'agent': CA 1963, s 2(1); 'articles': CA 1963, s 2(1); 'company': CA 1963, s 2(1); 'director': CA 1963, s 2(1); 'memorandum': CA 1963, s 2(1); 'prescribed': CA 1963, s 2(1); 'the Principal Act': C(A)A 1982, s 1; 'the registrar of companies': CA 1963, s 2(1).

Notes

Particulars of first directors and secretary: Prior to the enactment of C(A)A 1982, s 3, although every company was required to notify the Registrar of Companies (the 'Registrar') of any change in its directors or secretary[1] there was no requirement to notify him of the first such officers. This lacuna has now been filled by imposing an obligation on the company's subscribers to deliver to the Registrar, prior to incorporation, not only a copy of the memorandum and articles of association,[2] but also a statement in the prescribed form[3] containing particulars of the first directors and secretary[4] as well as their signed consents to so act.[5] If any persons named in the statement as the first directors are disqualified under the law of another state from being appointed or acting as a director of a body corporate or undertaking, those persons must ensure that the statement delivered to the Registrar is accompanied by a separate document in the prescribed form signed by them specifying the jurisdiction in which they are disqualified, the date of their disqualification and the period of their disqualification.[6] If they fail to do so, or if they sign such a statement knowing it to be false or misleading in any material respect, they will automatically be disqualified in this jurisdiction for a period equivalent to the unexpired term of the foreign disqualification order or orders.[7]

If none of the proposed directors is Irish resident, a copy of the bond prescribed in such circumstances by C(A)(No 2)A 1999, s 43 must be appended to the statement made pursuant to C(A)A 1982, s 3.[8]

1 CA 1963, s 195(6) and (7).

2 CA 1963, s 17 (as amended by CLEA 2001, s 80).

3 Companies (Forms) (No 2) Order 2004 (SI 829/2004), Form A1.

4 C(A)A 1983, s 3(1) and (2).

5 C(A)A 1982, s 3(3).

6 C(A)A 1982, s 3A(1). See Companies (Forms) (No 2) Order 2002 (SI 54/2002), Form B74. In relation to the disqualification of directors and secretaries, see CA 1990, Pt VII, Ch 2. See also CA 1963, s 176 (prohibition of body corporate being a director).

7 CA 1990, s 160(1A) and (1B) as amended by CLEA 2001 ss 14 and 42.

8 C(A)(No 2)A 1999, s 43(8)(a).

Automatic appointment of officers: Once the company has been incorporated, the persons named in the statement are deemed to have been automatically appointed as its first directors and secretary.[1] Presumably, however, their appointment will only be effective provided that they are not already disqualified from holding office.[2]

1 C(A)A 1982, s 3(5).

2 In relation to the disqualification of directors and secretaries, see CA 1990, Pt VII, Ch 2. See also CA 1963, s 176 (prohibition of body corporate being a director) and CA 1990, s 236 (qualification for appointment as secretary of a plc).

Priority of statement over memorandum and articles: Although rare, it is not unheard of, particularly in the case of smaller private companies, for the articles to name the first directors and secretary. However, insofar as those persons are not named in the statement which is required to be delivered under C(A)A 1982, s 3, such appointment shall be void.[1]

1 C(A)A 1982, s 3(5).

Proof of activity in Ireland: Prior to the coming into force of C(A)(No 2)A 1999, s 42 on 18 April 2000[1] a company could lawfully be incorporated in the State even though its sole intended purpose was to operate as a non-resident company. Now, however, the company will not be registered and a certificate of incorporation will not be issued without proof that one of the activities mentioned in its objects clause will be carried on in the State.[2] Thus, the statement (which also incorporates the statutory declaration prescribed by C(A)A 1983, s 5(5)) must also state that the purpose or one of the purposes for which the company is being formed is to carry on an activity[3] in the State.[4] It must give details of the activity to be carried on in the State[5] or the principal activity if two or more such activities are to be carried on,[6] including details of the place or places in the State where such activity is proposed to be carried on.[7] Furthermore, details must also be given of the place (whether in the State or abroad) where the central administration of the company will normally be carried on.[8] It remains to be seen whether the requirement that every newly formed company carry on an activity in the State amounts to an unlawful curtailment of the freedom of establishment provided for in Art 43 of the EC Treaty.

1 Companies (Amendment)(No 2) Act 1999 (Commencement) Order 2000 (SI 61/2000).

2 C(A)(No 2)A 1999, s 42(1).

3 The activity of the company must be classified with reference to an appropriate NACE code classification (ie the common basis for statistical classifications of economic activities within the European Community as set out in the Annex to Council Regulation (EEC) No 3037/90 of 9 October 1990). If such classification is not possible, a precise description of the activity must be given.

4 C(A)(No 2)A 1999, s 42(2).

5 C(A)(No 2)A 1999, s 42(2)(a) and (b).

6 C(A)(No 2)A 1999, s 42(3).

7 C(A)(No 2)A 1999, s 42(2)(c).

8 C(A)(No 2)A 1999, s 42(2)(d). With regard to the place of a company's central administration, see the notes to CA 1963, s 113.

Documents to be delivered to the Revenue Commissioners: Every company incorporated in the State or which commences to carry on a trade, profession or business in the State, must within 30 days deliver to the Revenue Commissioners a statement containing details of the name of the company, the addresses of its registered office and principal place of business, the name and address of the secretary, the date of commencement of and the nature of the trade, profession or business, the date to which its accounts will be made up, and such other information as the Revenue Commissioners may consider necessary for the purposes of the Tax Acts (as defined in TCA 1997).[1] Any material change in these particulars must be delivered within 30 days.[2]

Furthermore, an inspector of taxes may serve a notice on such a company at any time requiring the delivery of such particulars within 30 days of the date of the notice.[3] Failure to deliver the particulars in any of these circumstances may result in the default being notified to the Registrar who may in turn rely upon that default to strike the name of the company off the register pursuant to C(A)A 1982, s 12A.[4]

1 TCA 1997, s 882(2)(i). Additional information is required under s 882(2)(ii) in respect of Irish incorporated non-resident companies and under s 882(2)(iii) companies incorporated and resident abroad but carrying on a trade, profession or business in the State.

2 TCA 1997, s 882(2)(a).

3 TCA 1997, s 882(2)(b).

4 TCA 1997, s 882(3)(as amended by the Finance Act 2000, s 78. See also notes to C(A)A 1982, s 12A.

UK legislation

See CA 1985, s 10(2)-(6).

[3A Additional statement to be delivered to the registrar

(1) If any of the persons named in the statement to be delivered pursuant to section 3 of this Act as directors of the company concerned is a person who is disqualified under the law of another state (whether pursuant to an order of a judge or a tribunal or otherwise) from being appointed or acting as a director or secretary of a body corporate or an undertaking, that person shall ensure that that statement is accompanied by (but as a separate document from that statement) a statement in the prescribed form signed by him specifying—

(a) the jurisdiction in which he is so disqualified,

(b) the date on which he became so disqualified, and

(c) the period for which he is so disqualified.

(2) This section is without prejudice to section 3(3) of this Act or the requirements of any other enactment with regard to the registration of companies.][a]

Amendments

a C(A)A 1982, s 3A was inserted by CLEA 2001, s 101.

Notes

Operative Date: C(A)A 1982, s 3A came into force on 1 March 2002.[1]

1 Company Law Enforcement Act 2001 (Commencement) (No 5) Order 2002 (SI 53/2002).

Details of disqualified persons: See the notes to C(A)A 1982, s 3.

---

4 Registered office of company

[...][a]

Amendments

a C(A)A 1982, s 4 substituted CA 1963, s 113.

Cross reference

See CA 1963, s 113 (as amended).

Definitions

'company': CA 1963, s 2(1).

5 Amendment of section 143 of Principal Act

(1) [...][a]

(2) Every company shall, within three months after the commencement of this section, forward to the registrar of companies a return containing particulars not previously forwarded to him or any right or restriction attaching to shares in the share capital of the company existing upon such commencement and the particulars shall be recorded by him.

Amendments

a C(A)A 1982, s 5(1) inserted CA 1963, s 143(4)(f)–(i).

Cross reference

See CA 1963, s 143(4) (as amended).

Definitions

'company': CA 1963, s 2(1); 'the Principal Act': C(A)A 1982, s 1; 'the registrar of companies': CA 1963, s 2(1); 'share': CA 1963, s 2(1).

6 Qualification for appointment as auditor

[...][a]

Amendments

a C(A)A 1982, s 6 substituted CA 1963, s 162.[1]

[1] CA 1963, s 162 repealed by CA 1990, s 6 with effect from 21 September 1992.

Cross reference

See CA 1963, s 162 (as amended).

7 Amendment of section 168 of Principal Act

[...][a]

Amendments

a C(A)A 1982, s 7 substituted CA 1963, s 168(3).[1]

[1] CA 1963, s 168 repealed by CA 1990, s 6 with effect from 1 July 1991.

Cross reference

See CA 1963, s 168 (as amended).

Definitions

'Principal Act': C(A)A 1982, s 1.

8 Register of directors and secretaries

[...][a]

Amendments

a C(A)A 1982, s 8(1) substituted CA 1963, s 195, sub-ss (6), (7) and (8); C(A)A 1982, s 8(2) substituted '(6), (7) or (8)' for 'or (6)'; and €634.87'[1] for '€126.97'[2] in CA 1963, s 195(1).

[1] £500 converted to €634.87 by Council Regulations (EC) No 1103/97, No 974/98 and No 2866/98 and the Economic and Monetary Union Act 1998, s 6.

[2] £100 converted to €126.97 by Council Regulations (EC) No 1103/97, No 974/98 and No 2866/98 and the Economic and Monetary Union Act 1998, s 6.

Cross reference

See CA 1963, s 195 (as amended).

Definitions

'director': CA 1963, s 2(1).

9 Amendment of section 256 of Principal Act

[...][a]

Amendments

a C(A)A 1982, s 9 substituted CA 1963, s 256(2).[1]

[1] CA 1990, s 128 substituted CA 1963, s 256. C(AA)A 2003, s 57 amended CA 1963, s 256 (7) by substitution of 'shall be guilty of an offence and liable to a fine' for 'shall be liable to a fine'.

Cross reference

See CA 1963, s 256 (as amended).

Definitions

'the Principal Act': C(A)A 1982, s 1.

10 Preferential payments in a winding up

[...][a]

Amendments

a C(A)A 1982, s 10(a) inserted CA 1963, s 285(2)(h)-(i); C(A)A 1982, s 10(b) substituted '€3,174.35[1]' for '€380.922'[2] in CA 1963, s 285(3); C(A)A 1982, s 10(c) inserted CA 1963, s 285(6)(c); C(A)A 1982, s 10(d) substituted 'or absence from work through' for ', absence from work through sickness or other' in CA 1963, s 285(11); C(A)A 1982, s 10(e) inserted CA 1963, s 285(13).

1 £2,500 converted to €3,174.35 by Council Regulations (EC) No 1103/97, No 974/98 and No 2866/98 and the Economic and Monetary Union Act 1998, s 6.

2 £300 converted to €380.92 by Council Regulations (EC) No 1103/97, No 974/98 and No 2866/98 and the Economic and Monetary Union Act 1998, s 6.

Cross reference

See CA 1963, s 285 (as amended).

11 Power of registrar to strike defunct company off register

[...][a]

Amendments

a C(A)A 1982, s 11 substituted CA 1963, s 311(1)–(3) and deleted s 311(4).

Cross reference

See CA 1963, s 311 (as amended).

Definitions

'company': CA 1963, s 2(1); 'the registrar of companies': CA 1963, s 2(1).

12 Power of registrar to strike off register companies who fail to make returns[a]

[(1) Without prejudice to the generality of section 311 of the Principal Act, where a company does not, for one or more years, make an annual return required by section 125 or 126 of the Principal Act, the registrar of companies may send to the company by post a registered letter stating that, unless all annual returns which are outstanding are delivered to him within 1 month of the date of the letter, a notice will be published in [the Companies Registration Office Gazette][b] with a view to striking the name of the company off the register.

(2) If the registrar of companies either receives an answer to the effect that the company is not carrying on business, or does not within 1 month after sending the letter receive all annual returns which are outstanding, he may publish in [the Companies Registration Office Gazette][b] a notice stating that, at the expiration of 1 month from the date of that notice, the name of the company mentioned therein will, unless all outstanding returns are delivered to the registrar, be struck off the register, and the company will be dissolved.

(3) Subject to subsections (1) and (2) of section 12B of this Act, at the expiration of the time mentioned in the notice, the registrar of companies may, unless cause to the contrary is previously shown by the company, strike its name off the register, and shall publish notice thereof in [the Companies Registration Office Gazette][b] and on the publication in [the Companies Registration Office Gazette][b] of this notice, the company shall be dissolved.][a]

Amendments

a C(A)A 1982, s 12 substituted by C(A)(No 2)A 1999, s 46.

b 'the Companies Registration Office Gazette' substituted for '*Iris Oifigiúil*' by IFCMPA 2005, s 72.

Definitions

'annual return': CA 1963, s 2(1); 'company': CA 1963, s 2(1); 'the court': CA 1963, s 2(1); 'director': CA 1963, s 2(1); 'member': CA 1963, s 31; 'memorandum': CA 1963, s 2(1); 'officer': CA 1963, s 2(1); 'the Principal Act': C(A)A 1982, s 1; 'the registrar of companies': CA 1963, s 2(1).

Notes

Striking off for failure to make annual returns:[1] C(A)A 1982, s 12 empowers the Registrar to dissolve a company which fails to make annual returns for at least one year.[2] Having sent a warning letter under s 12(1) or having published a notice to the same effect in the Companies Registration Office Gazette (where appropriate)[3] if the Registrar either receives an answer to the effect that the company is no longer carrying on business or within one month does not receive any answer or all outstanding returns, he may send notice to the company and publish same in the Companies Registration Office Gazette[4] that unless the company either shows cause or files all outstanding returns within one further month, its name will be struck off the register.[5] Dissolution takes place upon the publication of notice of the striking off in the Companies Registration Office Gazette.[6]

1 In relation to the operation of this section generally, see MacCann 'Striking off the Register and Section 12 of the Companies (Amendment) Act 1982 (1990) 84 Gazette 125; Mooney, 'Restoring companies to the register' 1997 (2) Bar Review 226 and Courtney, *The Law of Private Companies* (2nd edn, Tottel Publishing, 2002) para 12.136 et seq.

2 Prior to the coming into force of C(A)(No 2)A 1999, s 46, the company had to be in default for at least two consecutive years before the strike-off procedure could be invoked.

3 See C(A)A 1982, s 12B(8A).

4 'the Companies Registration Office Gazette' substituted for '*Iris Oifigiúil*' by IFCMPA 2005, s 72.

5 C(A)A 1982, s 12(2).

6 C(A)A 1982, s 12(3).

Other grounds for dissolution: The power of the Registrar to dissolve companies under this section is in addition to his power to strike off companies under CA 1963, s 311 where he has reasonable cause to believe that the company is not carrying on business[1].The Registrar may also strike off companies which fail either to have at least one Irish resident director or a bond in lieu thereof[2], and which fail to deliver certain statements to the Revenue Commissioners.[3]

1 Under C(A)(No 2) A 1999, s 48 the fact that there are no persons recorded as being directors constitutes good grounds for believing that the company is not carrying on business.

2 C(A)(No 2)A 1999, s 43(15).

3 C(A)A 1982, s 12A.

Consequences of dissolution: Upon dissolution, all real and personal property of the company vests in the State.[1] The liability, if any, of its directors, officers and members, will however continue and may be enforced as if dissolution had not occurred.[2] Liability, in this context, might include criminal liability for breaches of provisions of the Companies Acts or civil liability under specific provisions of the Acts, such as for fraudulent or reckless trading[3] or for failure to keep proper books of account[4] or for issuing an order for goods on which the company's name is not legibly stated.[5] The director, officer or member will not however, be personally liable for corporate debts unless he was also so liable before the date of the dissolution. In the UK the courts have held that where a company which holds a lease is dissolved and the Crown subsequently disclaims any interest in the lease, the liability of any sureties under the lease is extinguished.[6]

However, these cases rely on the decision in *Stacey v Hill*[7] which held that the disclaimer of a lease by a liquidator or trustee in bankruptcy had the effect of relieving the sureties of any liability thereunder. The decision in *Stacey v Hill* was expressly disapproved of by Keane J in *Tempany v Royal Liver Trustees Ltd*[8] and accordingly these English cases on the effect of dissolution of the company and subsequent Crown disclaimer must be viewed with some caution.

1 State Property Act 1954, s 28. Property held by the company in trust does not, however, vest in the State and accordingly those beneficially entitled to the property may apply for a vesting order in their favour pursuant to the Trustee Act 1893, s 26: *Re Kavanagh and Cantwell* [1984] IEHC 55 (Costello J); *Re Heidelstone Co Ltd* [2006] IEHC 408. See generally Courtney, *The Law of Private Companies* (2nd edn, Tottel Publishing, 2002) para [12.145].

2 C(A)A 1982, s 12B(1).

3 CA 1963, s 297A.

4 CA 1990, s 204.

5 CA 1963, s 114(4).

6 *Re Yarmarine (IW) Ltd* [1992] BCLC 276; *Allied Dunbar Assurance plc v Fowle* [1994] 2 BCLC 197.

7 *Stacey v Hill* [1901] 1 QB 660.

8 *Tempany v Royal Liver Trustees Ltd* [1984] ILRM 273.

Winding up of dissolved company: A company may be wound up by order of the court notwithstanding the fact that it has already been dissolved.[1] Voluntary winding up is not, however, an option. The proper practice in this regard is for the petition to ask first for the restoration of the company's name to the register and then for it to be wound up.[2]

1 C(A)A 1982, s 12B(1).

2 *Re Cambridge Coffee Room Association Ltd* [1952] 1 All ER 112.

Restoration to the register: See C(A)A 1982, ss 12B and 12C and the notes thereto.

Disqualification of directors: Where the court is satisfied in any proceedings or as a result of an application brought before it by the Director of Corporate Enforcement under CA 1990 s 160[1], that a person was a director of a company at the time of the sending of a warning letter by the Registrar under C(A)A 1982, s 12(1) which ultimately led to the name of the company being struck off the register[2], the court, either of its own motion or as a result of the application, may make a disqualification order in respect of that person for such period as it sees fit. So, for example, on an application for restoration to the register, the court could of its own motion disqualify all or some of the directors if it concluded that the circumstances which led to the company being struck off in the first place demonstrated sufficient neglect or default on the part of those directors.[3]

1 CA 1990, s 160(2)(h) (as inserted by CLEA 2001, s 42).

2 C(A)A 1983, s 12(3).

3 *Re Clawhammer Ltd* [2005] IEHC 85.

UK legislation

See CA 1985, ss 652 and 653 (as amended by DCOA 1994, s 13(1), Sch 5, para 3).

[12A

(1) Where the Revenue Commissioners give a notice in writing under subsection (3) of section 882 (inserted by the Finance Act, 1999) of the Taxes Consolidation Act, 1997, to the registrar of companies stating that a company has failed to deliver a statement which it is required to deliver under that section, then, without prejudice to section 311 of the Principal Act or section 12 of this Act, the registrar may send to the company by

post a registered letter stating that, unless the company delivers to the Revenue Commissioners the said statement within 1 month of the date of the letter, a notice will be published in [the Companies Registration Office Gazette][b] with a view to striking the name of the company off the register.

(2) If the statement referred to in subsection (1) of this section is not delivered by the company concerned to the Revenue Commissioners within 1 month after the sending of the letter referred to in that subsection, the registrar of companies may publish in [the Companies Registration Office Gazette][b] a notice stating that, at the expiration of 1 month from the date of that notice, the name of the company mentioned therein will, unless the said statement is delivered to the Revenue Commissioners, be struck off the register, and the company will be dissolved.

(3) Subject to subsections (1) and (2) of section 12B of this Act, at the expiration of the time mentioned in the notice, the registrar of companies may, unless cause to the contrary is previously shown by the company, strike its name off the register, and shall publish notice thereof in [the Companies Registration Office Gazette][b] and on the publication in [the Companies Registration Office Gazette][b] of this notice, the company shall be dissolved.][a]

Amendments

a C(A)A 1982, s 12A inserted by C(A)(No 2)A 1999, s 46.

b 'the Companies Registration Office Gazette' substituted for '*Iris Oifigiúil*' by IFCMPA 2005, s 72.

Definitions

'company': CA 1963, s 2(1); 'the Principal Act': C(A)A 1982, s 2(1); 'the registrar of companies': CA 1963, s 2(1).

Notes

Striking off for failure to deliver certain tax statements: C(A)A 1982, s 12A introduces an entirely new basis for the dissolution of a company, namely that it has failed to deliver certain statements[1] to the Revenue Commissioners. The Revenue Commissioners may serve on the Registrar a notice advising him of the fact that the company has failed to deliver such a statement. The Registrar may then serve a warning letter on the company.[2] If the outstanding statement is not filed with the Revenue Commissioners within one month of the warning letter, the Registrar may then publish notice in the Companies Registration Office Gazette that unless the company files the outstanding statement within one further month, its name will be struck of the register.[3] Dissolution takes place upon the publication of notice of the striking off in the Companies Registration Office Gazette.[4]

1 TCA 1997, s 882, Form 11F CRO, 'Statement of Particulars'.

2 C(A)A 1982, s 12A(1).

3 C(A)A 1982, s 12A(2).

4 C(A)A 1982, s 12A(3). The Registrar will not publish such a notice if cause is shown to the contrary.

Other grounds for dissolution: See CA 1963, s 311 and C(A)A 1982, s 12 and the notes thereto.

Consequence of dissolution: See CA 1963, s 311 and C(A)A 1982, s 12 and the notes thereto.

Winding up of dissolved company: A company may be wound up by order of the court notwithstanding the fact that it has already been dissolved.[1] Voluntary winding up is not, however, an option. The proper practice in this regard is for the petition to ask first for the restoration of the company's name to the register and then for it to be wound up.[2]

1 C(A)A 1982, s 12B(2).
2 *Re Cambridge Coffee Room Association Ltd* [1952] 1 All ER 112.

Restoration to the register: See CA 1963, s 311A, C(A)A 1982, ss 12B and 12C and the notes thereto.

Disqualification of Directors: Under CA 1990 160(2)(h) the court may, of its own motion in any proceedings or as a result of an application of the Director of Corporate Enforcement, make a disqualification order against a person who was a director of a company which has received a warning letter under C(A)A 1982, s 12(1) and the name of which company has been struck off the register [1]. There is no analogous provision allowing the court to make a disqualification order in circumstances where the name of a company is struck off the register under C(A)A 1982 s 12A.

1 See notes to C(A)A 1982, s 12(1).

[12B

(1) The liability, if any, of every director, officer and member of a company the name of which has been struck off the register under section 12(3) or 12A(3) of this Act shall continue and may be enforced as if the company had not been dissolved.

(2) Nothing in subsection (1) of this section or section 12(3) or 12A(3) of this Act shall affect the power of the court to wind up a company the name of which has been struck off the register.

(3) If any member, officer or creditor of a company is aggrieved by the fact of the company's having been struck off the register under section 12(3) or 12A(3) of this Act, the court, on an application made (on notice to the registrar of companies, the Revenue Commissioners and the Minister for Finance) by the member, officer or creditor, before the expiration of 20 years from the publication in [the Companies Registration Office Gazette] [b] of the notice referred to in section 12(3) or, as the case may be, 12A(3) of this Act, may, if satisfied that it is just that the company be restored to the register, order that the name of the company be restored to the register, and, subject to subsection (4) of this section, upon an office copy of the order being delivered to the registrar for registration, the company shall be deemed to have continued in existence as if its name had not been struck off; and the court may by the order give such directions and make such provisions as seem just for placing the company and all other persons in the same position as nearly as may be as if the name of the company had not been struck off or make such other order as seems just (and such other order is referred to in subsection (4) of this section as an 'alternative order').

(4) An alternative order may, if the court considers it appropriate that it should do so, include a provision that, as respects a debt or liability incurred by, or on behalf of, the company during the period when it stood struck off the register, the officers of the company or such one or more of them as is or are specified in the order shall be liable for the whole or a part (as the court thinks just) of the debt or liability.

(5) The court shall, unless cause is shown to the contrary, include in an order under subsection (3) of this section, being an order made on the application of a member or

officer of the company, a provision that the order shall not have effect unless, within 1 month from the date of the court's order—

(a) if the order relates to a company that has been struck off the register under section 12(3) of this Act, all outstanding annual returns required by section 125 or 126 of the Principal Act are delivered to the registrar of companies,

(b) if the order relates to a company that has been struck off the register under section 12A(3) of this Act, all outstanding statements required by section 882 of the Taxes Consolidation Act, 1997, are delivered to the Revenue Commissioners.

(6) The court shall, in making an order under subsection (3) of this section, being an order that is made on the application of a creditor of the company, direct that one or more specified members or officers of the company shall, within a specified period—

(a) if the order relates to a company that has been struck off the register under section 12(3) of this Act, deliver all outstanding annual returns required by section 125 or 126 of the Principal Act to the registrar of companies,

(b) if the order relates to a company that has been struck off the register under section 12A(3) of this Act, deliver all outstanding statements required by section 882 of the Taxes Consolidation Act, 1997, to the Revenue Commissioners.

(7) The court, on an application made by the registrar of companies (on notice to each person who, to his knowledge, is an officer of the company) before the expiration of 20 years from the publication in [the Companies Registration Office Gazette][b] of the notice referred to in section 12(3) or, as the case may be, 12A(3) of this Act, may, if satisfied that it is just that the company be restored to the register, order that the name of a company which has been struck off the register under the said section 12(3) or 12A(3) be restored to the register and, upon the making of the order by the court, the company shall be deemed to have continued in existence as if its name had not been struck off; and the court may by the order give such directions and make such provisions as seem just for placing the company and all other persons in the same position as nearly as may be as if the name of the company had not been struck off or make such other order as seems just (and such other order may, if the court considers it appropriate that it should do so, include a provision of the kind referred to in subsection (4) of this section).

(8) A letter or notice to be sent under this section to a company may be addressed to the company at its registered office, or, if no office has been registered, to the care of some officer of the company, or, if there is no officer of the company whose name and address are known to the registrar of companies, may be sent to each of the persons who subscribed to the memorandum, addressed to him at the address mentioned in the memorandum.

[(8A) For the purposes of subsection (1) of section 12 of this Act where—

(a) a company does not, for 20 or more consecutive years, make an annual return required by section 125 of the Principal Act, and

(b) no notice of the situation of the registered office of the company has been given to the registrar of companies as required by section 113 of the Principal Act,

the registrar of companies may, instead of sending, in accordance with the said subsection (1), a registered letter to the company stating that he proposes to take the course of action mentioned in that subsection in relation to the company, publish a notice in the Companies Registration Office Gazette stating that he proposes to take that course of action in relation to the company, and where the registrar publishes such a notice the reference in subsection (2) of section 12 of this Act to the sending of a letter of the foregoing kind shall be construed as a reference to the publishing of that notice.][c]

(9) Without prejudice to section 2(1) of the Principal Act where such an application is made by any other person, in the case of an application under this section that is made by a creditor of the company or the registrar of companies, 'the court', for the purposes of this section, means the Circuit Court.

(10) An application under this Act to the Circuit Court by a creditor of the company concerned shall be made to the judge of the Circuit Court for the circuit in which the registered office of the company was, immediately before it was struck off the register, situated or, if no office was registered at that time, for the circuit in which the creditor resides or, in case the creditor resides outside the State, for the Dublin Circuit.

(11) An application under this section to the Circuit Court by the registrar of companies shall be made to the judge of the Circuit Court for the Dublin Circuit.][a]

Amendments

a C(A)A 1982, s 12B inserted by C(A)(No 2)A 1999, s 46.

b 'the Companies Registration Office Gazette' substituted for '*Iris Oifigiúil*' by IFCMPA 2005, s 72.

c C(A)A 1982, s 12B(8A) inserted by IFCMPA 2005, s 65 with effect from 30 June 2005.[1]

1 Investment Funds, Companies and Miscellaneous Provisions Act 2005 (Commencement) Order 2005 (SI 323/2005).

Definitions

'annual return': CA 1963, s 2(1); 'company': CA 1963, s 2(1); 'the court': CA 1963, s 2(1) and s 12B(9); 'director': CA 1963, s 2(1); 'member': CA 1963, s 31; 'officer': CA 1963, s 2(1); 'the Principal Act': C(A)A 1982, s 2(1); 'the registrar of companies': CA 1963, s 2(1).

Notes

Restoration to the register:[1] Where the name of a company has been struck off the register either for failure to file annual returns[2] or for failure to deliver certain statements to the Revenue Commissioners'[3] application may be made to the court by any one of several applicants[4] for an order restoring the company to the register.[5] In most cases the application must be made to the High Court.[6] However, in the case of an application by the Registrar or by a creditor of the company, application may be made to the Circuit Court.[7] It should be noted however, that in such instances the Circuit Court's jurisdiction is not exclusive and it remains open to the Registrar or creditor to apply to the High Court instead.[8]

1 See generally, O'Higgins, 'How to Restore a Struck-Off Company to the Register' (2001) Gazette 40; Leonard, 'Restoring companies to the register' 2000 6 (3) Bar Review 182 and Courtney, *The Law of Private Companies* (2nd edn, Tottel Publishing, 2002) para 12.145 et seq.

2 See C(A)A 1982, s 12.

3 See C(A)A 1982, s 12A.

Any member, officer, or creditor of the company who is aggrieved by the company's having been struck off the register.

5 C(A)A 1982, s 12B(3).

6 The phrase 'the court' is defined by CA 1963, s 2(1) as meaning the High Court.
7 C(A)A 1982, s 12B(9).
8 *Re Deauville Communications Worldwide Ltd* [2002] 2 IR 32; *Re NAFTA Product Operations Ltd* (31 July 2000, unreported) HC (O'Donovan J).

Who may petition: Prior to the amendments effected by C(A)(No 2)A 1999, s 46, application could be made to the court by the company or any member or creditor to have the company restored.[1] Conferring such standing on the company itself seemed somewhat odd, because technically, the company no longer existed.[2] Now, however, the entitlement to petition to have the name of the company restored to the register may be presented[3] by (a) the Registrar;[4] (b) a member of the company;[5] (c) an officer of the company;[6] or (d) a creditor of the company,[7] including a contingent or prospective creditor.[8] However, in the case of a contingent or prospective creditor, he may be required to establish that his claim is neither frivolous nor vexatious and is being bona fide maintained, in order to be allowed by the court to proceed with his petition.[9] The Revenue Commissioners will only be regarded as creditors of the company for the purposes of an application under C(A)A 1982, s 12B(3) if, and to the extent that, they have raised assessments on the company prior to the date upon which its name was struck off the register.[10] A person who, after the date of dissolution acquires shares in the company or takes an assignment of one of its debts, will not be regarded as a 'member or creditor' of that company within s 12B(3) and accordingly will not have standing to present a petition for the restoration of the name of the company to the register.[11]

1 CA 1963, s 311(8).
2 *Re Conrad Hall and Co* [1916] WN 275; *Tymans Ltd v Craven* [1952] 1 All ER 613; *Re New Timbiqui Gold Mines Ltd* [1961] Ch 319; *Re Test Holdings (Clifton) Ltd* [1970] Ch 285.
3 In the case of a petition by a member, officer, or creditor, he must be 'aggrieved' by the dissolution. A director who has actively ensured the dissolution of the company may not be so 'aggrieved': *Re Contiv Uebersee Bank AG* (12 October 1998) Times Scots Law Report. Otherwise, a person will be sufficiently 'aggrieved' for the purposes of the section if his interests are, or are likely to be, prejudiced by the dissolution of the company: *Re Waldcourt Investment Co Pty Ltd* (1986) 11 ACLR 12.
4 C(A)A 1982, s 12B(7).
5 C(A)A 1982, s 12B(3). *Locus standi* would also seem to be enjoyed by the personal representative of a deceased member: *Re Bayswater Trading Co Ltd* [1970] 1 All ER 608. The conferral of locus standi on personal representatives of deceased members represents a stretching of the literal wording of the legislation since such persons do not themselves constitute 'members' of the company for the purposes of CA 1963, s 31.
6 C(A)A 1982, s 12B(3). A director who is disqualified after the date of dissolution would not appear to be an 'officer' of the company for the purpose of applying to have the company restored to the register: *Witherdale v Registrar of Companies* [2008] 1 BCLC 174.
7 C(A)A 1982, s 12B(3).
8 *Re Deauville Communications Worldwide Ltd* [2002] 2 IR 32; *Re Industrial Glazing Systems Ltd* (6 November 2000, unreported) HC (Barr J); *City of Westminster Assurance Co Ltd v Registrar of Companies* (1997) BCC 960; *Re Harvest Lane Motor Bodies Ltd* [1969] 1 Ch 457; *Re Mixhurst Ltd* [1994] 2 BCLC 19; *Re Jayham Ltd* [1995] 2 BCLC 455.
9 *Re Deauville Communications Worldwide Ltd* [2002] 2 IR 32.
10 *Re Nelson Car Hire Ltd* (1973) 107 ILTR 97; *Re Supatone (Eire) Ltd* (1973) 107 ILTR 105.
11 *Re Test Holdings (Clifton) Ltd* [1970] Ch 285; *Re New Timbiqui Gold Mines Ltd* [1961] Ch 319.

Grounds for restoration: C(A)A 1982, s 12B(3) enables the court to restore the name of the company to the register if it is satisfied that it is 'just' to do so.[1] If the company is already being wound up[2] or is otherwise carrying on operations,[3] this will constitute a good ground for restoration to the register. Moreover, in the case of a petition by a creditor, it may be 'just' to restore the name of the company to the register in order to enable the creditor pursue some legal claim against the company or its officers[4] provided that the claim is not already patently statute-barred.[5] Similarly, it may be 'just' to restore a company to the register to enable it to prove as a creditor in the liquidation of another body corporate[6] or to enable a member to bring proceedings under CA 1963, s 205.[7] In this regard, as a statement of general principle, it has been held that the exercise by the court of its discretion to refuse to restore the company to the register should be the exception rather than the rule.[8] Where a company has been struck off the register and at the time of its dissolution held property in trust for a third party, an application to have the legal title to the trust property vested in a new trustee under the Trustee Act 1893, s 26 in lieu of applying to have the company restored to the register can be a more cost effective and clear cut solution.[9]

1 In the version of C(A)A 1982, s 12 which operated prior to the amendments effected by C(A)(No 2)A 1999, the primary ground for restoring a company to the register was that the company was carrying on business at the time of dissolution. Restoration on the ground that it was 'just' to do so, constituted a secondary basis for relief only.

2 *Re Outlay Assurance Society* (1887) 34 ChD 479; *Re Johannesburg Mining and General Syndicate* [1901] WN 46.

3 *Re Portrafram Ltd* [1986] BCLC 533.

4 *Re Haltone (Cork) Ltd* [1996] 1 IR 32; *Re Workvale Ltd* [1991] BCLC 528; *City of Westminster Assurance Co v Registrar of Companies* (1997) BCC 960.

5 *Re Workvale Ltd (No 2)* [1991] BCLC 531 affirmed in [1992] BCLC 544.

6 *Re Eden Quay Investments Ltd* (11 April 1994, unreported) HC (Keane J) reported in *The Irish Times*, 12 April 1994. See also *Stanhope Pension Trust Ltd v Registrar of Companies* [1994] 1 BCLC 628.

7 *Re New Ad Advertising Company Ltd* [2006] IEHC 19 (Laffoy J).

8 *Re Priceland Ltd* [1997] 1 BCLC 467; *Re Blenheim Leisure (Restaurants) Ltd (No 2)* [2000] BCC 821.

9 *Re Heidlestone Co Ltd and others* [2006] IEHC 408, (24 November 2006) HC (Laffoy J).

Notice parties: The application for restoration of the name of the company to the register is brought by way of petition and verifying affidavit pursuant to RSC 1986, Ord 75. In the case of a petition by an officer, member or creditor, the notice parties must include the Registrar, the Revenue Commissioners and the Minister for Finance.[1] The costs of these three notice parties must normally be paid for by the petitioner.[2] It may also be appropriate to name the directors of the company as notice parties so as to facilitate the making of consequential orders against them under C(A)A 1982, s 12B(5) or (6) for the delivery of all outstanding annual returns or statements to the Revenue Commissioners, as the case may be.[3] Moreover, by naming them as notice parties, the petitioner may be in a position to obtain an order directing them to indemnify the petitioner in respect of the costs of the application.

If the petition is being presented by the Registrar, the notice parties must include every person who, to the knowledge of the Registrar, is an officer of the company.[4]

As a matter of general principle, the application for restoration is a matter exclusively between the petitioner, the company and the regulatory authorities and accordingly third parties should not normally be allowed to intervene.[5] Nonetheless, the court has jurisdiction to join as a party to the application any person whose rights would be affected by the restoration of the company to the register.[6] In this regard, the test to be applied in determining whether the third party should be joined to a petition by a creditor is whether the third party merely wishes to argue that the petitioning creditor has no claim against the company or that the proceedings which the revived company proposed to bring against him have no prospect of success, in which case he would not be entitled to intervene in the application, or whether the order for restoration would directly affect the rights of the third party irrespective of whether the petitioning creditor had any claim against the company or the company had any claim against the third party, in which case the joinder would be allowed.[7] The third party prejudice must therefore arise out of the restoration itself and not simply out of some contractual arrangement which is revived by the restoration.[8] An example of third party prejudice arising from the restoration itself is where the bringing of the company back into existence would have resulted in residuary legatees under a will being divested of their bequests.[9] If a third party has been dealing with the officers of a dissolved company under the mistaken belief that the company is still in existence, he will not be prejudiced by the restoration of the company to the register, even though such an order would have the effect of precluding any action by him against the company's officers personally for breach of contract or breach of warranty of authority.[10] It is to be noted though, that even if a third party has been validly joined as a notice party to the application for restoration to the register, costs should only be awarded in favour of that notice party in exceptional circumstances.[11]

1 C(A)A 1982, s 12B(3). The reason for putting the State on notice is that the company's property will have vested in the Minister for Finance upon dissolution pursuant to the State Property Act 1954, s 28. The State's consent is therefore required in order for the property to re-vest in the company. In practice, such consent is normally communicated by the Chief State Solicitor acting on behalf of the Registrar and the two Ministers.

2 *Re Conrad Hall and Co* [1916] WN 275; *Re Haltone (Cork) Ltd* [1996] 1 IR 32.

3 *Re Haltone (Cork) Ltd* [1996] 1 IR 32. In *Re Workvale Ltd* [1991] BCLC 528 it was held that the company itself could not be made a notice party to a creditor's petition since the company no longer existed.

4 C(A)A 1982, s 12(7).

5 *Re Bloomberg Developments Ltd* [2002] 2 IR 613.

6 *Re Servers of the Blind League* [1960] 2 All ER 298; *Re H Clarkson (Overseas) Ltd* (1987) 3 BCC 606; *Stanhope Pension Trust Ltd v Registrar of Companies* [1994] 1 BCLC 628; *Re Jayham Ltd* [1995] 2 BCLC 455. If the purpose for restoring the company to the register is to enable a creditor to pursue a personal injuries claim in respect of which the company is insured, it may be proper but is by no means necessary to join the insurance company as a notice party to the application: *Re Workvale Ltd* [1991] BCLC 528. Restoration of the company to the register is a necessary prerequisite to the enforcement of the company's insurance policy since it has been held by the House of Lords in *Bradley v Eagle Star Insurance Co Ltd* [1989] 1 All ER 961 that there could be no indemnity under a policy of insurance in respect of a company which no longer existed and whose liability could therefore not be determined. See also *Re Workvale Ltd (No 2)* [1991] BCLC 531, affirmed in [1992] BCLC 544.

7 *Re Jayham Ltd* [1995] 2 BCLC 455.

8 *Re Priceland Ltd* [1997] 1 BCLC 467; cf *Smith v White Knight Laundry Ltd* [2001] 2 BCLC 206.

9 *Re Servers of the Blind League* [1960] 2 All ER 298.

10 *Re Rortrafram Ltd* [1986] BCLC 533.

11 *Re Bloomberg Developments Ltd* [2002] 2 IR 613; *Re Brown Bayley's Steel Works* (1905) 21 TLR 374; *Re Langlaatge Proprietary Co Ltd* (1912) 28 TLR 529.

Consequences of restoration: If it is satisfied that it is 'just' to do so, the court may make an order for the restoration of the company to the register.[1] The court will typically direct that the order, to be valid, must be delivered to the Registrar within a period of three months.[2] As soon as an office copy of the order restoring the name of the company to the register has been delivered to the company for registration, the company and all other persons are placed in the same position as if the company had continued in existence and never been dissolved.[3] Thus, any property which had previously vested in the State under the State Property Act 1954, s 28 reverts to the company without the need for any formal vesting order.[4] Similarly proceedings commenced by or against the company either prior to or during the period of dissolution, are retrospectively validated.[5] Furthermore unless the court makes an alternative order under subsection (4) the directors will be absolved of personal liability for debts incurred by them while the company was dissolved and any proceedings against them for recovery of those debts will fail.[6] Where particulars of a charge over the company's property were delivered to the Registrar within 21 days of creation of the charge, but at a time when unbeknownst to the parties the company had been dissolved, court may direct that the delivery of particulars of the charge will be regarded as having been duly and properly made for the purposes of CA 1963, s 99.[7]

1 C(A)A 1982, s 12B(3).
2 Failure to file the order in time will result in it lapsing: *Re Barrowland Ltd* [2003] IEHC 54.
3 C(A)A 1982, s 12B(3). See also *Tyman's Ltd v Craven* [1952] 1 All ER 613.
4 *Re CW Dixon Ltd* [1947] Ch 251.
5 *Re Amantiss Enterprises Ltd; Framus plc v CRH plc* [2000] 2 ILRM 177; *Re Deauville Communications Worldwide Ltd* [2002] 2 IR 32; *Top Creative Ltd v St Albans DC* [2000] 2 BCLC 379; *Tyman's Ltd v Craven* [1952] 1 All ER 613. Proceedings in the name of the liquidator of the company, such as proceedings under CA 1990, s 150 for a restriction order against the directors, will similarly be validated: *Re Dunleckney Ltd* [2001] 1 IR 103.
6 *Richmond Building Products Ltd v Soundgables Ltd* [2005] 1 ILRM 497.
7 In *Re Boxco Ltd* [1970] Ch 442, the court directed that delivery of particulars of a charge under the equivalent of CA 1963, s 99 should be regarded as having been properly made, thus avoiding the necessity of making a separate application under the equivalent of CA 1963, s 106.

Orders to file outstanding returns: If the petition has been presented by a creditor, the court, in restoring the company to the register, must direct that one or more specified members or officers deliver all outstanding annual returns (in the case of a company dissolved under C(A)A 1982, s 12(3) or all outstanding statements to the Revenue Commissioners[1] (in the case of a company dissolved under s 12A(3)) within such period of time as the court may specify.

In the case of a petition presented by a member or officer, the court should normally make it a pre-condition to restoration to the register that all outstanding annual returns or statements to the Revenue Commissioners,[2] as the case may be, should be filed within a period of one month.[3] The court does, however, have a discretion to dispense with this requirement where cause is shown to the contrary.[4] Such a dispensation may be granted, for example, where the company has ceased trading.[5]

1 While C(A)A 1982, s 12B(6) only refers to 'all outstanding statements required by' TCA 1997, s 882, it is the practice of the Revenue Commissioners not to issue a letter of no objection to the application for restoration to the register unless all outstanding tax returns are filed for periods up to dissolution and while the company is dissolved together with relevant accounts and tax computations. In addition the Revenue Commissioners require that the petitioner provide an undertaking on his own behalf and on behalf of the company to pay all outstanding taxes of the company. See also O'Reilly, 'Undertaking Required by the Revenue Commissioners when Petitioning to Restore a Company to the Register of Companies' (2002) 9 CLP, 197.
2 A similar approach taken by the Revenue Commissioners under C(A)A 1982, s 12B(5) as is taken under C(A)A 1982, s 12B(6).
3 C(A)A 1982, s 12B(5). Thus, if the outstanding returns or statements are not filed, the restoration of the company will not take effect. In practice, regardless of whether the company has been struck off for the non-delivery of annual returns or statements to the Revenue Commissioners, the court will require evidence that the company is up-to-date in the delivery of both annual returns and tax returns before acceding to an application by a member or officer for restoration of the company to the register. See Grier, 'Companies arising from the dead' (2006) 13 CLP, 129.
4 C(A)A 1982, s 12B(5). In *Re New Ad Advertising Company Ltd* [2006] IEHC 19 (Laffoy J), Laffoy J expressed the view that the court is given a very limited discretion to dispense with the requirements of C(A)A 1982, subs 12B(5)(a) or (b).
5 *Re Haltone (Cork) Ltd* [1996] 1 IR 32.

Special directions for restoration: Apart from ordering the restoration of the company, the court may also give such directions and make such provisions as it considers just for placing the company and third parties in the same position as if dissolution had never occurred.[1] The court may therefore restore the name of the company to the register on terms that, in the case of creditors whose claims were not statute-barred at the date of dissolution, the period between the date of dissolution and the date of restoration to the register should be ignored for the purposes of the Statute of Limitations.[2] Such a direction will not be given, however, if it is not shown to be necessary,[3] as where the company was already being wound up.[4] It is also open to the court to direct that even though, upon restoration, the company is deemed never to have been dissolved, nonetheless all or some of the company's officers should be fixed with personal liability in respect of all or certain of the debts and liabilities incurred by the company during the period when it was actually dissolved.[5]

1 CA 1963 ss 310 and 311 (8) and C(A)A 1982, subs 12B(3) and (7)

2 *Re Donald Kenyon Ltd* [1956] 3 All ER 596; *Smith v White Knight Laundry Ltd* [2001] 2 BCLC 206.

3 *Re Huntington Poultry Ltd* [1969] 1 All ER 328.

4 *Re Vickers and Bott Ltd* [1968] 2 All ER 264.

5 C(A)A 1982, s 12B(4). See also Grier, 'Companies arising from the dead' (2006) 13 CLP, 129 at 132. Cf *Re Lindsay Bowman Ltd* [1969] 3 All ER 601.

New company with same name: Currently, it is the practice of the Registrar not to incorporate a new company with the same name as a company which has been struck off the register for a period of twenty years from the date of strike off. However, if through inadvertence, since the date of dissolution of the company, a company has been incorporated with, or changed its name to, the same or similar name to the company which has been struck off, the court may make it a condition of restoration to the register that the first company change its name and the court may further preclude the company from carrying on business until this change of name has been effected.[1] It would appear that no objection can be lodged with the Registrar, on behalf of a company which has been struck off under CA 1963, s 23.[2]

1 *Re Rapton Foundry Ltd* Sol Jo 331.

2 Under CA 1963, s 23 (as amended by CLEA 2001, s 87) the Registrar has the power to direct, within six months of a second company being registered with the same or similar name to a name by which a company in existence is already registered, that the second company alters its name.

Notice of intention to strike off a company: IFCMPA 2005, s 65 introduced an amendment to C(A)A 1982, s 12B whereby the Registrar, in the event that he wishes to strike off a company for failure to make an annual return under C(A)A 1982, s 12(1), may advertise his intention to do so in the Companies Registration Office Gazette. In circumstances where the Registrar does not have a record of the registered office of the company, the Registrar may advertise his intention to strike off the company rather than sending a letter, to the same effect, to the registered office of that company under C(A)A 1982, s 12(1). This would only apply to companies incorporated prior to the coming into force of C(A)A 1982, s 3[1], as after that date details of the registered office of a company had to be supplied when applying to the Registrar to incorporate a company.

1 3 August 1982; Companies (Amendment) Act 1982 (Commencement) Order 1982 (SI 255/1982).

Other provisions for restoration to the register by order of the court: The court is also empowered to restore dissolved companies to the register pursuant to CA 1963, ss 310 and 311(8). For a discussion of these sections see the notes thereto.

Restoration to register by Registrar: Regarding the power of the Registrar to restore the company to the register within 12 months of dissolution, see also C(A)A 1982, s 12C and CA 1963, s 311A.

Winding up of dissolved company: A company may be wound up by order of the court notwithstanding the fact that it has already been dissolved.[1] Voluntary winding up is not, however, an option. The proper practice in this regard is for the petition to ask first for the restoration of the company's name to the register and then for it to be wound up.[2]

1 C(A)A 1982, s 12B(1).

2 *Re Cambridge Coffee Room Association Ltd* [1952] All ER 112.

[12C

(1) Without prejudice to the provisions of section 311(8) or 311A(1) of the Principal Act or subsection (3) or (7) of section 12B of this Act, if a member or officer of a company is aggrieved by the fact of the company's having been struck off the register under section 12A(3) of this Act, the registrar of companies, on an application made in the prescribed form by the member or officer before the expiration of 12 months from the publication in [the Companies Registration Office Gazette][b] of the notice striking the company name from the register, and provided he has received confirmation from the Revenue Commissioners that all outstanding, if any, statements required by section 882 of the Taxes Consolidation Act, 1997, have been delivered to the Revenue Commissioners, may restore the name of the company to the register.

(2) Upon the registration of an application under subsection (1) of this section and on payment of such fees as may be prescribed, the company shall be deemed to have continued in existence as if its name had not been struck off.

(3) Subject to any order made by the court in the matter, the restoration of the name of a company to the register under this section shall not affect the rights or liabilities of the company in respect of any debt or obligation incurred, or any contract entered into by, to, with or on behalf of, the company between the date of its dissolution and the date of such restoration.][a]

Amendments

a C(A)A 1982, s 12C inserted by C(A)(No 2)A 1999, s 46.

b 'the Companies Registration Office Gazette' substituted for '*Iris Oifigiúil*' by IFCMPA 2005, s 72.

Definitions

'company': CA 1963, s 2(1); 'member': CA 1963, s 2(1); 'prescribed': CA 1963, s 2(1); 'the Principal Act': C(A)A 1982, s 2(1); 'the registrar of companies': CA 1963, s 2(1).

Notes

Restoration to register by filing tax statement: In C(A)A 1982, s 12B provision is made for the court to restore a company to the register which has been struck off for failure to file its annual returns and/or to deliver any statement required by TCA 1997, s 882. In the case of striking-off for failure to file any statement required by TCA 1997, s 882, restoration may be effected by the Registrar upon application by a member or officer, provided that the application is made to him in the prescribed form[1] within 12 months of the notice of striking off appearing in the Companies Registration Office Gazette and provided he receives confirmation from the Revenue Commissioners that all outstanding statements required by TCA 1997, s 882[2] have since been filed.[3]

1 Companies (Forms) Order (2000), Form H1R.

2 TCA, 1997, s 882, Form 11FCRO, Statement of Particulars.

3 C(A)A 1982, s 12C(1). A similar power of restoration is vested in the Registrar under CA 1963, s 311A in the event that the company makes an application to be restored to the register.

Consequences of restoration: Once the application has been registered and the prescribed fees have been paid, the company is deemed to have always been in existence and is deemed never to have been dissolved.[1] Thus, any property which had previously vested in the State under the State Property Act 1954, s 28 reverts to the Company without the need for any formal vesting order.[2]

Similarly, proceedings commenced by or against the company either prior to or during the period of dissolution are retrospectively validated.[3] Furthermore unless the court makes an alternative order under subsection (4) the directors will be absolved of personal liability for debts incurred by them while the company was dissolved and any proceedings against them for recovery of those debts will fail.[4] Where particulars of a charge over the company's property were delivered to the Registrar within 21 days of creation of the charge, but at a time when unbeknownst to the parties the company had been dissolved, the court may direct that the delivery of particulars of the charge will be regarded as having been duly and properly made for the purposes of CA 1963, s 99.[5]

1 See notes to C(A)A 1982, s 12B(3). See also *Tyman's Ltd v Craven* [1952] 1 All ER 613.

2 *Re CW Dixon Ltd* [1947] Ch 251.

3 *Re Amantiss Enterprises Ltd; Framus plc v CRH plc* [2000] 2 ILRM 177; *Re Deauville Communications Worldwide Ltd* [2002] 2 IR 32; *Top Creative Ltd v St Albans DC* [2000] 2 BCLC 379; *Tyman's Ltd v Craven* [1952] 1 All ER 613. Proceedings in the name of the liquidator of the company, such as proceedings under CA 1990, s 150 for a restriction order against the directors, will similarly be validated: *Re Dunleckney Ltd* [2001] 1 IR 103.

4 *Richmond Building Products Ltd v Soundgables Ltd* [2005] 1 ILRM 497.

5 In *Re Boxco Ltd* [1970] Ch 442 the Court directed that delivery of particulars of a charge under the equivalent of CA 1963 s 99 should be regarded as having been properly made, thus avoiding the necessity of making a separate application under the equivalent of CA 1963, s 106.

[12D

If the question of whether a statement which a company has failed to deliver to the Revenue Commissioners in accordance with section 882(3) of the Taxes Consolidation Act, 1997, has or has not been subsequently delivered to them falls to be determined for the purpose of the exercise by the registrar of companies of any of the powers under sections 12A to 12C of this Act, the Revenue Commissioners may, notwithstanding any obligations as to secrecy or other restriction upon disclosure of information imposed by or under statute or otherwise, disclose to the registrar any information in their possession required by him for the purpose of that determination.][a]

Amendments

a C(A)A 1982, s 12D inserted by C(A)(No 2)A 1999, s 46.

Definitions

'company': CA 1963, s 2(1); 'the registrar of companies': CA 1963, s 2(1).

Notes

Disclosure of information by Revenue Commissioners: The effect of C(A)A 1982, s 12D is that the Revenue Commissioners will not be regarded as acting in breach of their duty of confidentiality to a taxpayer by disclosing to the Registrar for the purposes of C(A)A 1982, ss 12A to 12C the fact that a taxpayer has or has not filed a statement required by TCA 1997, s 882.[1]

1 TCA 1997, s 882 (3) (as amended by the Finance Act 2000, s 78) provides similarly.

13 Non-application of section 376 of Principal Act to certain partnerships

(1) The provisions of section 376 of the Principal Act shall not apply to the formation of a partnership—

(a) for the purpose of carrying on practice as accountants in a case where each partner is a person who is qualified under section 162(1)(a) or (b) of the Principal Act, as amended by this Act, or

(b) for the purpose of carrying on practice as solicitors in a case where each partner is a solicitor.

[(2) The Minister may by an order made under this section declare that the provisions of section 376 of the Principal Act shall not apply to a partnership that is of a description, and that has been or is formed for a purpose, specified in the order.][a]

(3) Every order made under subsection (2) of this section shall be laid before each House of the Oireachtas as soon as may be after it is made and, if a resolution annulling the order is passed by either House within the next 21 days on which that House has sat after the order is laid before it, the order shall be annulled accordingly, but without prejudice to the validity of anything previously done thereunder.

(4) The Minister may revoke or amend an order made under this section, including this subsection.

(5) The provisions of section 4(2) of the Limited Partnerships Act, 1907 shall not apply to a partnership specified in subsection (1) of this section nor to a partnership specified in an order made pursuant to subsection (2) of this section.

Amendments

a C(AA)A 2003, s 55 substitutes C(A)A 1982, s 13(2).

Definitions

'Minister': CA 1963, s 2(1); 'the Principal Act': C(A)A 1982, s 1.

Notes

Partnerships with more than 20 members: CA 1963, s 376 prohibits partnerships with more than 20 members. However, C(A)A 1982, s 13 provides an exemption for:

(a) firms of accountants where all of the partners are qualified to act as auditors[1];

(b) firms of solicitors[2]; and

(c) such other types of partnership as the Minister may from time to time prescribe.[3] To date the only such partnerships to have been so prescribed are those established for the purposes of carrying on or promoting the business of thoroughbred horse breeding[4] and those whose main business consists of the provision of investment and loan finance and ancillary facilities and services to persons engaged in industrial or commercial activities.[5]

1 C(A)A 1982, s 13(1)(a).

2 C(A)A 1982, s 13(1)(b).

3 C(A)A 1982, s 13(2).

4 SI 54/1988.

5 SI 506/2004.

UK legislation

See CA 1985, s 716 (amended FSA 1986, s 212(2), Sch 16, para 22; CA 1989, s 145 Sch 19, para 15 and s 212, Sch 24).

14 Adoption and application of Table C

[...][a]

Amendments

a C(A)A 1982, s 14 inserted CA 1963, s 13A.

Cross reference

See CA 1963, s 13A and Sch 1, Table C.

15 Increase of penalties

A person convicted of an offence for which a penalty is provided in any section of the Principal Act specified in column (2) of the First Schedule at any reference number shall, in lieu of the penalty provided in any such section and specified in column (3) of that Schedule, be liable to the penalty specified in column (4) of that Schedule at that reference number, and that section shall be construed and have effect accordingly.

Definitions

'the Principal Act': C(A)A 1982, s 1.

Notes

Penalties relating to annual returns: The penalties imposed by this section for offences under CA 1963, ss 125(2),[1] 126(4),[2] 127(2)[3] and 128(3)[4] were further increased to €1,269.74 by CA 1990, s 244.

1 CA 1963, s 125 repealed and substituted by CLEA 2001, s 59.

2 CA 1963, s 126 repealed by CLEA 2001, s 59.

3 CA 1963, s 127 repealed and substituted by CLEA 2001, s 60 and amended by C(A&A)A 2003, s 46.

4 CA 1963, s 128 (3) amended by IFCMPA 2005, s 71(1)(b) substituting 'shall be guilty of an offence and liable to a fine' for 'shall be liable to a fine'.

16 Prosecution of certain offences

Proceedings in relation to offences under sections 227, 234, 249, 252, 262, 263, 272, 273, 278, 280, 319, 320 and 321 of the Principal Act may be brought and prosecuted by the registrar of companies.

Cross reference

C(A&A)A 2003, s 57 and Sch 2, Item No 1, amended CA 1963, ss 227, 249, 252, 262, 272, 273, 278, 280 and 321 by substitution of 'shall be guilty of an offence and liable to a fine' for 'shall be liable to a fine'; and C(A&A)A 2003, s 57 and Sch 2, Item No 4 amended CA 1963, s 234 by substitution of 'shall be guilty of an offence and liable to a fine' for 'shall be liable to a fine'.

Definitions

'the Principal Act': C(A)A 1982, s 1; 'the registrar of companies': CA 1963, s 2(1).

17 Amendment of section 16 of Principal Act

[...][a]

Amendments

a C(A)A 1982, s 17 deleted 'and articles' from CA 1963, s 16(a).

Cross reference

See CA 1963, s 16 (as amended).

Definitions

'the Principal Act': C(A)A 1982, s 1.

18 Amendment of section 19 of Principal Act

[...][a]

Amendments

a C(A)A 1982, s 18 substituted 'a person named as director or secretary of the company in the statement delivered pursuant to section 3 of the Companies (Amendment) Act, 1982' for 'a person named in the articles as a director or secretary of the company' in CA 1963, s 19(2).

Cross reference

See CA 1963, s 19 (as amended).

Definitions

'the Principal Act': C(A)A 1982, s 1.

19 Amendment of section 58 of Principal Act

[...][a]

Amendments

a C(A)A 1982, s 19 deleted 'and occupations' from CA 1963, s 58(1)(b).

Cross reference

See CA 1963, s 58 (as amended).

Definitions

'the Principal Act': C(A)A 1982, s 1.

20 Amendment of section 116 of Principal Act

[...][a]

Amendments

a C(A)A 1982, s 20 deleted 'and occupations' from CA 1963, s 116(1)(a).

Cross reference

See CA 1963, s 116 (as amended).

Definitions

'the Principal Act': C(A)A 1982, s 1.

21 Amendment of First Schedule to Principal Act

[...][a]

Amendments

a C(A)A 1982, s 21(a) inserted 'Subject to section 3 of the Companies (Amendment) Act, 1982,' before 'The secretary' in CA 1963, Sch 1, Table A, Pt I, Reg 113; C(A)A 1982, s 21(c) inserted 'Subject to section 3 of the Companies (Amendment) Act, 1982,' before 'The secretary' in CA 1963, Sch 1, Table C, Reg 59.

Cross reference

See CA 1963, Sch 1, Table A, Pt I, Reg 113 and CA 1963, Sch 1, Table C, Reg 59.

Definitions

'the Principal Act': C(A)A 1982, s 1.

22 Amendment of Fifth Schedule to Principal Act

[...][a]

Amendments

a C(A)A 1982, s 22(a) deleted 'and occupations' in CA 1963, Sch 5, Pt I, para 5(a); C(A)A 1982, s 22(b) deleted 'and occupations' in CA 1963, Sch 5, Pt II, para 5, Col 2.

Cross reference

CA 1963, Sch 5 was repealed by CLEA 2001, s 63(2) with effect from 1 March 2002.

[1] Company Law Enforcement Act 2001 (Commencement) (No 2) Order 2001 (SI 438/2001).

Definitions

'the Principal Act': C(A)A 1982, s 1.

23 Repeals

Sections 29 and 30 of the Industrial Research and Standards Act, 1961, are hereby repealed.

24 Short title, collective citation, construction and commencement

(1) This Act may be cited as the Companies (Amendment) Act, 1982.

(2) This Act and the Companies Acts, 1963 to 1977, shall be construed together as one Act and may be cited together as the Companies Acts, 1963 to 1982.

(3) This Act shall come into operation on such day or days as may be fixed therefor by order or orders of the Minister, either generally or with reference to a particular purpose

or provision, and different days may be so fixed for different purposes and different provisions of this Act.

Notes

Operative Date: C(A)A 1982 came into force on 3 August 1982.[1]

1 Companies (Amendment) Act 1982 (Commencement) Order 1982 (SI 255/1982).

FIRST SCHEDULE[a]

INCREASE OF PENALTIES

Amendments

a This Schedule increased the penalties in CA 1963 as follows: '€6,348.69[1]' substituted for '£1,000' in s 293(1); '€3,174.35'[2] substituted for '£500' in ss 35(5)(a), 50(1)(a), 54(5)(a), 60(15)(a), 90, 183(1), 184(5), 293(1), 294, 295, 296(1), 297(3), 365(a), 380(a); '€634.87'[3] substituted for '£100' in ss 23(2), 24(8), 35(4), 35(5)(b), 44(8), 46(2), 47(4), 50(1)(b), 54(4), 54(5)(b), 56(3), 57(3), 58(3), 59(5), 60(5), 60(15)(b), 63(5), 77, 90, 100(3), 101(2), 102(2), 107(3), 110(2), 112(3), 115(6), 116(9), 125(2); 126(4), 127(2), 128(3), 130(10), 131(6), 136(5), 145(4), 147(6), 148(3), 149(7), 150(3), 150(4), 154(5), 156(3), 157(2), 158(7), 180(5); 183(1), 184(5), 190(9), 193(4), 194(5)(b), 194(6), 197(3), 202(4), 224(5), 256(6), 263(3), 266(6), 293(1), 294, 295, 296(1), 297(3), 300, 301, 305(2), 306(2), 314, 315(1), 319(7), 320(5), 321(2), 358, 365(b), 377(7), 380(b), 381, 385; '€317.43'[4] substituted for '£50' in ss 10(10), 12(3), 69(2), 70(3), 78(5), 84(2), 91(5), 114(3), 114(4), 117(4), 119(3), 136(3), 143(5), 153(3), 159(5), 160(5), 165(2), 179(4), 190(9), 202(6), 227(2), 249(3), 261(2), 262(2), 263(7), 272(3), 273(5), 273(6), 273(7); 278(2); 303(2), 378(2), 386; '€158.72'[5] substituted for '£25' in ss 30(2), 92(4), 114(2), 146(3), 188(2), 196(4), 203(3), 205(5), 221(2), 234(5), 252(2), 256(5), 280(4), 398(3); '€126.97'[6] substituted for '£20' in 86(2), 131(6), 201(6); 317(2); '€31.74'[7] substituted for '£5' in ss 29(2), 263(6), 310(2); '€6.35'[8] substituted for '£1' in s 143(6).

1 £5,000 converted to €6,348.69 by Council Regulations (EC) No 1103/97, No 974/98 and No 2866/98 and the Economic and Monetary Union Act 1998, s 6.

2 £2,500 converted to €3,174.35 by Council Regulations (EC) No 1103/97, No 974/98 and No 2866/98 and the Economic and Monetary Union Act 1998, s 6.

3 £500 converted to €634.87 by Council Regulations (EC) No 1103/97, No 974/98 and No 2866/98 and the Economic and Monetary Union Act 1998, s 6.

4 £250 converted to €317.43 by Council Regulations (EC) No 1103/97, No 974/98 and No 2866/98 and the Economic and Monetary Union Act 1998, s 6.

5 £125 converted to €158.72 by Council Regulations (EC) No 1103/97, No 974/98 and No 2866/98 and the Economic and Monetary Union Act 1998, s 6.

6 £100 converted to €126.97 by Council Regulations (EC) No 1103/97, No 974/98 and No 2866/98 and the Economic and Monetary Union Act 1998, s 6.

7 £25 converted to €31.74 by Council Regulations (EC) No 1103/97, No 974/98 and No 2866/98 and the Economic and Monetary Union Act 1998, s 6.

8 £5 converted to €6.35 by Council Regulations (EC) No 1103/97, No 974/98 and No 2866/98 and the Economic and Monetary Union Act 1998, s 6.

Companies (Amendment) Act 1983

(Number 13 of 1983)

ARRANGEMENT OF SECTIONS

PART 1
PRELIMINARY

An Act to amend the Law Relating to Companies. [5th June, 1983]

Be It Enacted By The Oireachtas as Follows:

Notes

This Act implemented the Second EU Directive on Company Law,[1] under which a new type of entity was created, namely the 'public limited company' or 'plc'. Various requirements were imposed in relation to the capitalisation of such entities, the principal one being that there be an issued share capital of not less than €38,092.14,[2] of which the entire of any premium and at least 25% of the par value must actually be paid up.[3] The Act also introduced important provisions applicable to all companies, whether public or private and whether limited or unlimited, regarding the circumstances in which they may pay dividends or make other distributions to their members.[4]

1 Directive 77/91/EEC.

2 C(A)A 1983, ss 5, 6, 10 and 19. For the capital requirements in respect of a plc wishing to obtain a stock exchange listing, see the Admissions Directive (79/279/EEC) as implemented by EC(SE)R 1984 as amended by EC(SE)(A)R 1991, EC(SE)(A)R 1994 and EC(SE)(A)R 1995.

3 C(A)A 1983, s 28(1). This payment requirement does not apply to shares forming part of an employee share scheme: C(A)A 1983, s 28(2). However, if share forming part of such a scheme have not been aid up a least to that extent, they cannot be taken into account in determining whether the company's allotted share capital meet the minimum capital requirements of the Act: C(A)A 1983, s 6(4).

4 See C(A)A 1983, Pt IV.

PART 1
PRELIMINARY

1 Short title, collective citation and commencement

(1) This Act may be cited as the Companies (Amendment) Act, 1983.

(2) The collective citation 'the Companies Acts, 1963 to 1983' shall include this Act.

(3) This Act shall come into operation on such day as the Minister may appoint by order.

Definitions

'the appointed day': C(A)A 1983, s 1(3), s 2(1); 'the Minister': C(A)A 1983, s 2(1).

Notes

Commencement date: C(A)A 1983 came into force on 13 October 1983.[1]

1 Companies (Amendment) Act 1983 (Commencement) Order 1983 (SI 288/1983).

2 Interpretation

(1) In this Act unless the context otherwise requires—

'the appointed day' means the day appointed by the Minister under section 1(3) for the coming into operation of this Act;

'the appropriate rate', in relation to interest, means five per cent. per annum or such other rate as may be specified by order made by the Minister under subsection (7);

'the authorised minimum' has the meaning assigned to it by section 19;

'balance sheet date', in relation to a balance sheet, means the date as at which the balance sheet was prepared;

'called-up share capital', in relation to a company, means so much of its share capital as equals the aggregate amount of the calls made on its shares, whether or not those calls have been paid, together with any share capital paid up without being called and any share capital to be paid on a specified future date under the articles, the terms of allotment of the relevant shares or any other arrangements for payment of those shares, and 'uncalled share capital' shall be construed accordingly;

'the Companies Acts' means the Acts which by virtue of subsection (5) shall be construed as one Act;

'employees' share scheme' means any scheme for the time being in force, in accordance with which a company encourages or facilitates the holding of shares or debentures in the company or its holding company by or for the benefit of employees or former employees of the company or of any subsidiary of the company including any person who is or was a director holding a salaried employment or office in the company or any subsidiary of the company;

'equity security' has the meaning assigned to it by section 23(13);

'the general transitional period' means the period of 18 months commencing on the appointed day;

'hire-purchase agreement' has the same meaning as in the Hire-Purchase Act, 1946;

'the Minister' means the Minister for Trade, Commerce and Tourism;

'non-cash asset' means any property or interest in property other than cash (including foreign currency);

'old public limited company' has the meaning assigned to it by section 12 (1);

'the Principal Act' means the Companies Act, 1963;

'public company' means a company which is not a private company;

'public limited company' means a public company limited by shares or a public company limited by guarantee and having a share capital, being a company—

(a) the memorandum of which states that the company is to be a public limited company; and

(b) in relation to which the provisions of the Companies Acts as to the registration or re-registration of a company as a public limited company have been complied with on or after the appointed day;

'the re-registration period' has the meaning assigned to it by section 13(1);

'the transitional period for share capital' means the period of 3 years commencing on the appointed day.

(2) In relation to an allotment of shares in a company,the shares shall be taken for the purposes of the Companies Acts to be allotted when a person acquires the unconditional right to be included in the company's register of members in respect of those shares.

(3) For the purposes of the Companies Acts—

(a) a share in a company shall be taken to have been paid up (as to its nominal value or any premium on it) in cash or allotted for cash if the consideration for the allotment or the payment up is cash received by the company or is a cheque received by the company in good faith which the directors have no reason for suspecting will not be paid or is the release of a liability of the company for a liquidated sum or is an undertaking to pay cash to the company at a future date; and

(b) in relation to the allotment or payment up of any shares in a company, references in the Companies Acts, except in section 23, to consideration other than cash and to the payment up of shares and premiums on shares otherwise than in cash include references to the payment of, or an undertaking to pay, cash to any person other than the company;

and for the purposes of determining whether a share is or is to be allotted for cash or paid up in cash, 'cash' includes foreign currency.

(4) For the purposes of this Act—

(a) any reference to a balance sheet or to a profit and loss account shall include a reference to any notes thereon or document annexed thereto giving information which is required by the Companies Acts [or by international financial reporting standards][a] and is thereby allowed to be so given;

(b) any reference to the transfer or acquisition of a non-cash asset includes a reference to the creation or extinction of an estate or interest in, or a right over, any property and also a reference to the discharge of any person's liability, other than a liability for a liquidated sum; and

[(c) the net assets of a company are the aggregate of its assets less the aggregate of its liabilities;

and in paragraph (c) 'liabilities' includes—

(i) any provision (within the meaning of the Sixth Schedule to the Principal Act) that is made in Companies Act individual accounts except to the extent that that provision is taken into account in calculating the value of any asset to the company,

(ii) any provision for liabilities within the meaning of paragraph 70 of the Schedule to the Companies (Amendment) Act 1986 that is made in Companies Act individual accounts, and

(iii) any provision that is made in IFRS individual accounts.][b]

(5) The Companies Act, 1963, the Companies (Amendment) Act, 1977, the Companies (Amendment) Act, 1982, and this Act shall be construed together as one Act.

(6) In this Act—

(a) a reference to a Part, section or Schedule is to a Part, section or Schedule of this Act unless it is indicated that a reference to some other enactment is intended;

(b) a reference to a subsection, paragraph or subparagraph is to the subsection, paragraph or subparagraph of the provision in which the reference occurs, unless it is indicated that reference to some other provision is intended; and

(c) a reference to any other enactment shall, unless the context otherwise requires, be construed as a reference to that enactment as amended by or under any other enactment, including this Act.

(7) The Minister may by order specify that the appropriate rate of interest for the purposes of this Act shall be a rate other than five per cent. per annum.

Amendments

a Words inserted by EC(IFRSMA)R 2005 (SI 116/2005), reg 9, Part 2 of Schedule, Item No 1.

b Paragraph (c) substituted by EC(IFRSMA)R 2005 (SI 116/2005), reg 9, Part 2 of Schedule, Item No 1.

Definitions

'company': CA 1963, s 2(1); 'debenture': CA 1963, s 2(1); 'document': CA 1963, s 2(1); 'director': CA 1963, s 2(1); 'holding company': CA 1963, s 2(1), s 155; 'private company': CA 1963, s 2(1), s 33(1); 'share': CA 1963, s 2(1); 'subsidiary': CA 1963, s 2(1), s 155.

Notes

The appointed day: The appointed day for the coming into operation of the Act was 13 October 1983.[1] Thus, 'the general transitional period' comprised the period from 13 October 1983 to 12 April 1985 and 'the transitional period for share capital' comprised the period from 13 October 1983 to 12 October 1986.

[1] Companies (Amendment) Act 1983 (Commencement) Order 1983 (SI 288/1983).

The Minister: The current title of the Minister is that 'the Minister for Enterprise, Trade and Employment'. This is reflected in the definition of 'the Minister in CLEA 2001, s 3(1).

Allotment of shares: C(A)A 1983, s 2(2) stipulates that a share shall be taken as having been allotted in a company when a person acquires an unconditional right to be included n the register of members in respect of that share. It is only by being an original subscriber to the memorandum or by having his name entered in the register that a person actually becomes a member of the company.[1] In relation to the allotment of shares generally, see CA 1963, ss 53–58 and C(A)A 1983, Pt III.

1 CA 1963, s 31. See also CA 1963, s 122 in relation to the entitlement to apply to the High Court to have the register rectified by the inclusion or deletion of a person's name, as appropriate

Payment for shares in cash:[1] C(A)A 1983, s 2(3) gives statutory effect to the decisions in *Re Gibson, Little and Co Ltd*,[2] *Re Harmony and Montague Tin and Copper Mining Co Spargo's Case*[3] and *Larocque v Beauchemin*[4] as to the circumstances in which shares are to be taken as having been paid for in cash. In this regard 'cash' includes not only actual money, but also (a) a cheque (providing the directors have no reason for suspecting that it will not be paid); (b) the release of a liquidated debt owed by the company;[5] or (c) an undertaking to pay 'cash' (as so defined) at a future date. It should be noted though, that an allotment by way of accord and satisfaction will not be regarded as having been paid for in cash.[6] Similarly, the assignment of a debt to the company in return for an allotment of shares, will not be treated as a cash consideration.[7]

1 See also the notes to C(A)A 1983, s 26.

2 *Re Gibson, Little and Co Ltd* (1880–81) 5 LR Ir 139.

3 *Re Harmony and Montague Tin and Copper Mining Co Spargo's Case* (1873) 8 Ch App 407.

4 *Larocque v Beauchemin* [1897] AC 358.

5 A sale of a business for a specified price which is satisfied by the allotment of shares in the acquiring company does not constitute 'the release of a liability of the company for a liquidated sum'; rather it simply constitutes the allotment of shares for a non-cash consideration: *Re Bradford Investments plc (No 2)* [1991] BCLC 688.

6 *Re Johannesburg Hotel Co, ex parte Zoutpansberg Prospecting Co* [1891] 1 Ch 119. See also C(A)A 1983, s 2(4)(b).

7 *System Control plc v Munro Corporate plc* [1990] BCLC 659.

UK legislation

See CA 1985, ss 737–739, 743.

---

3 Amendments, repeals and savings

(1) The provisions of the Principal Act specified in the First Schedule are hereby amended to the extent specified in that Schedule.

(2) The provisions of the Principal Act and the Companies (Amendment) Act, 1982, specified in the first column of the Third Schedule are hereby repealed to the extent specified in the second column of that Schedule.

(3) Paragraphs 24 and 25 of the First Schedule (which amend Table A and Tábla A respectively in the First Schedule to the Principal Act) and any repeal specified in the Third Schedule of anything contained in the said Table A and the said Tábla A shall not affect any company registered before the appointed day.

(4) In the Principal Act, a reference to a company registered under any specified enactment shall continue to have effect as a reference to a company registered under that enactment, notwithstanding that it has subsequently been re-registered under this Act.

Definitions

'the appointed day': C(A)A 1983, s 1(3), s 2(1); 'company': CA 1963, s 2(1); 'the Principal Act': C(A)A 1983, s 2(1); 'Table A': CA 1963, s 2(1).

PART II
NAME OF PUBLIC LIMITED COMPANY, REGISTRATION AND RE-REGISTRATION OF COMPANIES

4 Name of a public limited company

(1) The name of a public limited company must end with the words 'public limited company' or 'cuideachta phoiblí theoranta' which may be abbreviated to 'p.l.c.' or 'c.p.t.' respectively and those words or abbreviations may not be preceded by the word 'limited' or its abbreviation 'ltd.' or 'teoranta' or its abbreviation 'teo.'.

(2) Subject to subsection (1), a resolution in accordance with section 12 that a company be re-registered as a public limited company may change the name of the company by deleting—

(a) the word 'company' or the words 'and company'; or

(b) the word 'cuideachta' or the words 'agus cuideachta',

including any abbreviation of them, and no fee shall be payable in respect of any change of name mentioned in this subsection.

(3) The memorandum of a public limited company which is limited by shares shall be in the form set out in Part I of the Second Schedule or, if it is a company limited by guarantee and having a share capital, in the form set out in Part II of that Schedule or, in either case, as near thereto as circumstances admit; and those forms supersede in the case of a public limited company the forms of memorandum set out respectively in Tables B and D in the First Schedule to the Principal Act.

Definitions

'company': CA 1963, s 2(1); 'company limited by guarantee': CA 1963, s 2(1); 'the Principal Act': C(A)A 1983, s 2(1); 'public limited company': C(A)A 1983, s 2(1); 'share': CA 1963, s 2(1).

Notes

Name of pubic limited company: Just as a limited company must include the word 'limited' or 'teoranta' or the appropriate abbreviation thereof at the end of its name[1], so too public limited company must include the words 'public limited company' or the abbreviation 'p.l.c.' or the Irish equivalents thereof at the end of their names.[2] Failure to do so may constitute a criminal offence.[3] Furthermore, a failure to correctly state the corporate name of the plc on a bill of exchange, promissory note, endorsement, cheque or order for money or goods may render any officer who signs such a document on behalf of the plc, jointly and severally liable with the plc itself for the debt thereby incurred.[4]

1 CA 1963, ss 6(1)(b) and 22(2). See however CA 1963, s 24 in relation to the circumstances in which charitable and other companies will be exempted from the requirement to include 'limited' etc in its name.

2 C(A)A 1983, s 4(1) and CA 1963, s 6(1)(a).

3 C(A)A 1983, s 56(2) and CA 1963, s 114(2), (3) and (4).

4 See CA 1963, s 114(4) and the notes thereto.

Registration of business name: If the plc has a business name other than its corporate name, it must be registered pursuant to the Registration of Business Names Act 1963.

Form of memorandum of association: The prescribed memoranda of association in Sch 2 are models as to form only and not as to content.[1] As to the matters which must be included in a company's memorandum of association, see CA 1963, ss 6 and 7.

[1] *Gaiman v National Association for Mental Health* [1971] Ch 317.

UK legislation

See CA 1985, ss 3, 25.

5 Registration of companies

(1) Where any memorandum is delivered for registration under section 17 of the Principal Act, the registrar shall not register the memorandum unless he is satisfied that all the requirements of the Companies Acts in respect of registration and of matters precedent and incidental thereto have been complied with.

(2) Where a memorandum which is so delivered states that the association to be registered is to be a public limited company, the amount of the share capital stated in the memorandum to be that with which the company proposes to be registered must not be less than the authorised minimum.

(3) Where the registrar registers an association's memorandum which states that the association is to be a public limited company, the certificate of incorporation given in respect of that association under section 18 of the Principal Act shall contain a statement that the company is a public limited company.

(4) A certificate of incorporation given under that section in respect of any association shall be conclusive evidence—

- (a) that the requirements mentioned in subsection (1) have been complied with, and that the association is a company authorised to be registered and is duly registered under the Principal Act; and
- (b) if the certificate contains a statement that the company is a public limited company, that the company is such a company.

(5) A statutory declaration in the prescribed form by a solicitor engaged in the formation of a company, or by a person named as a director or secretary of the company in the statement delivered under section 3 of the Companies (Amendment) Act, 1982 that the requirements mentioned in subsection (1) have been complied with shall be delivered to the registrar, and the registrar may accept such a declaration as sufficient evidence of compliance.

Definitions

'authorised minimum': C(A)A 1983, s 19; 'company': CA 1963, s 2(1); 'the Companies Acts': C(A)A 1983, s 2(1), (5); 'director': CA 1963, s 2(1); 'memorandum': CA 1963, s 2(1); 'prescribed': CA 1963, s 2(1); 'the Principal Act': C(A)A 1983, s 2(1); 'public limited company': C(A)A 1983, s 2(1); 'Registrar of Companies': CA 1963, s 2(1); 'share': CA 1963, s 2(1).

Notes

Documents to be delivered to Registrar: Apart from the memorandum and articles,[1] the subscribers must also deliver to the registrar a statement of the first directors and secretary and registered office of the company together with signed consents to act from the persons named in the statement.[2] The form must also incorporate a statutory declaration by one of the proposed directors or the proposed secretary or by a solicitor engaged in the formation of the company to the effect that the requirements of the Companies Acts have been complied with in respect of the registration of the company.[3] If the company is to be formed as a plc its memorandum must state the share capital to be not less than the authorised minimum of €38,092.14.[4]

1 CA 1963, s 17.
2 C(A)A 1982, s 3. The appropriate form is Companies (Forms) Order 2000 (SI 62/2000), Form A1. If none of the proposed directors is an Irish resident, the Form A1 must have appended to it a bond in the form required by C(A)(No 2)A 1999, s 43.
3 C(A)A 1983, s 5(5).
4 C(A)A 1983, s 5(2).

No incorporation without proof of intended activity in the state: Prior to the coming into force of C(A)(No 2)A 1999, s 42 on 18 April 2000;[1] a company could lawfully be incorporated in the State even though its sole intended purpose was to operate as a non-resident company. Now, however, the company will not be registered and a certificate of incorporation will not be issued without proof that one of the activities mentioned in its objects clause will be carried on in the State.[2] However, the Registrar of companies may accept as sufficient proof a statutory declaration in the prescribed form[3] that the purpose or one of the purposes for which the company is being formed is to carry on an activity in the state.[4] The statutory declaration, which may be made by one of the persons who are to be named in the statement to be filed with the registrar of companies under C(A)A 1982, s 3 as being the first directors of the company[5] or being the first secretary or one of the first joint secretaries of the company[6] or which may be made by a solicitor engaged in the formation of the company,[7] must give details of the activity to be carried on in the state[8] or the principal activity if two or more such activities are to be carried on,[9] including details of the place or places in the State where such activity is proposed to be carried on.[10] Furthermore, details must also be given of the place (whether in the State or abroad) where the central administration of the company will normally be carried on.[11] It remains to be seen whether the requirement that every newly formed company carry on an activity in the State amounts to an unlawful curtailment of the freedom of establishment provided for in Art 43 of the EC Treaty.

1 Companies (Amendment)(No 2) Act, 1999 (Commencement) Order 2000 (SI 61/2000).
2 C(A)(No 2)A 1999, s 42(1).
3 Companies (Forms) Order 2000 (SI 62/2000), Form A1. In this form the declarant not only confirms compliance with the provisions of C(A)A 1983, s 42 but also confirms compliance generally with the registration requirements of the Companies Acts, as required by C(A)A 1983, s 5(5). Making this combined declaration is expressly provided by C(A)(No 2)A 1999, s 42(5).
4 C(A)(No 2)A 1999, s 42(2).
5 C(A)(No 2)A 1999, s 42(4)(a).
6 C(A)(No 2)A 1999, s 42(4)(b).
7 C(A)(No 2)A 1999, s 42(4)(c).
8 C(A)(No 2)A 1999, s 42(2)(a) and (b).
9 C(A)(No 2)A 1999, s 42(3).
10 C(A)(No 2)A 1999, s 42(2)(c).
11 C(A)(No 2)A 1999, s 42(2)(d). With regard to the place of a company's central administration, see the notes to CA 1963, s 113.

Documents to be delivered to the Revenue Commissioners: Every company incorporated in the state, or which commences to carry on a trade, profession or business in the state, must within 30 days deliver to the Revenue Commissioners: a statement containing details of the name of the company; the addresses of its registered office and principal place of business; the name and address of the secretary; the date of commencement of and the nature of the trade; profession or business, the date to which its accounts will be made up; and such other information as the Revenue Commissioners may consider necessary for the purposes of the Tax Acts.[1] Any material change in these particulars must be delivered within 30 days.[2] Furthermore, an inspector taxes may serve a notice on such a company at any time requiring the delivery of such particulars within 30 days of the date of the notice.[3] Failure to deliver the particulars in any of these circumstances may result in the default being notified to the Registrar of Companies who may in turn rely upon that default to strike the name of the company off the register pursuant to C(A)A 1982, s 12A.[4]

1 TCA 1997, s 882(2)(i). Additional information is required under s 882(2)(ii) in respect of Irish-registered non-resident companies and companies incorporated and resident abroad but carrying on a trade, profession or business in the State.

2 TCA 1997, s 882(2).

3 TCA 1997, s 882(2).

4 TCA 1997, s 882(3).

Conclusive status of certificate of incorporation: A certificate of incorporation, once issued by the Registrar of Companies, is stated to be 'conclusive evidence' that the registration requirements of the Companies Acts have been complied with and that the company has been validly incorporated[1] and, as appropriate, that the company is a plc.[2] The conclusiveness of a registrar's certificate has previously been upheld in the context of the certification of the registration of a charge under CA 1963, s 99.[3] It has also been upheld in the context of a certificate of incorporation, so as to preclude the court from looking behind the date stated on the certificate as being the date of incorporation.[4] In the UK, it has been suggested that despite its stated conclusiveness, the courts would be prepared to look behind a Registrar's certificate in cases of fraud or where there is an error on the face of the certificate itself.[5] It has also been held by the UK courts that because legislation does not bind the Crown except where expressly so stated, an erroneously-issued certificate could be challenged through the *fiat* of the Attorney General.[6] It is thought, however, that a similar position would not pertain in Ireland since the Royal Prerogatives, including the non-application of statutes, have been held not to have survived the enactment of the Constitution.[7] Whilst the certainty afforded to members and creditors alike by the conclusiveness of the certificate of incorporation has been judicially acknowledged,[8] it remains to be seen, however whether that 'conclusiveness' is unconstitutional either as an infringement of the separation of powers contained in Art 6 of the Constitution or as an attempt to oust the High Court's full original jurisdiction under Art 34 of the Constitution to hear and determine all justiciable matters.[9]

1 C(A)A 1983, s 5(4)(a).

2 C(A)A 1983, s 5(4)(b).

3 See CA 1963, s 104 and the notes thereto.

4 *Jubilee Cotton Mills v Lewis* [1924] AC 958.

5 *R v Registrar of Companies, ex parte Central Bank of India* [1986] 1 QB 1114 at 1169–1170 (per Lawton LJ); *Sun Tai Cheung Credits Ltd v Attorney General of Hong Kong* (1987) 3 BCC 357 at 360; *National Provincial and Union Bank of England v Charnley* [1924] 1 KB 431 at 454.

6 *R v Registrar of Companies, ex parte Central Bank of India* [1986] 1 QB 1114 at 1169–1170 (per Lawton LJ) and at 1171–1172 (per Slade LJ).

7 *Byrne v Ireland* [1972] IR 241; *Webb v Ireland* [1988] IR 353; *Howard v Commissioners of Pubic Works* [1993] ILRM 665.

8 *Peel's Case, Re Barned's Banking Co* (1867) LR 2 Ch App 674.

9 *Murren v Brennan* [1942] IR 466; *Maher v Attorney General* [1973] IR 146; *Tormey v Ireland* [1985] IR 289.

Investment companies: The provisions of this C(A)A 1983, s 5(2) do not apply to investment companies.[1]

1 CA 1990, 260(3).

UK legislation

See CA 1985, ss 11, 12, 13(6), (7).

---

6 Restriction on commencement of business by a public limited company

(1) A company registered as a public limited company on its original incorporation shall not do business or exercise any borrowing powers unless the registrar of companies has issued it with a certificate under this section or the company is re-registered as another form of company.

(2) The registrar shall issue a public limited company with a certificate under this section if, on an application made to him in the prescribed form by the company, he is satisfied that the nominal value of the company's allotted share capital is not less than the authorised minimum, and there is delivered to him a statutory declaration complying with subsection (3).

(3) The statutory declaration shall be in the prescribed form and signed by a director or secretary of the company and shall state—

(a) that the nominal value of the company's allotted share capital is not less than the authorised minimum;

(b) the amount paid up, at the time of the application, on the allotted share capital of the company;

(c) the amount, or estimated amount, of the preliminary expenses of the company and the persons by whom any of those expenses have been paid or are payable; and

(d) any amount or benefit paid or given or intended to be paid or given to any promoter of the company, and the consideration for the payment or benefit.

(4) For the purposes of subsection (2), a share allotted in pursuance of an employees' share scheme may not be taken into account in determining the nominal value of the company's allotted share capital unless it is paid up at least as to one-quarter of the nominal value of the share and the whole of any premium on the share.

(5) The registrar may accept a statutory declaration delivered to him under subsection (2) as sufficient evidence of the matters stated therein.

(6) A certificate under this section in respect of any public limited company be conclusive evidence that the company is entitled to do business and exercise any borrowing powers.

(7) If a public limited company does business or exercises borrowing powers in contravention of this section, the company and any officer of the company who is in default shall be guilty of an offence and shall be liable on summary conviction to a fine not exceeding [€1,904.61][a].

(8) The provisions of this section are without prejudice to the validity of any transaction entered into by a public limited company; but if a public limited company enters into a transaction in contravention of those provisions and fails to comply with its obligations in connection therewith within 21 days from being called upon to do so, the directors of the company shall be jointly and severally liable to indemnify the other party to the

transaction in respect of any loss or damage suffered by him by reason of the failure of the company to comply with those obligations.

Amendments

a '£500' substituted for '£100' by C(A)A 1982, Sch 1, increased to £1,500 by CA 1990, s 240(7) as inserted by CLEA 2001, s 104(c), and converted to €1,904.61 by Council Regulations (EC) No 1103/97, No 974/98 and No 2866/98 and the Economic and Monetary Union Act 1998, s 6.

Definitions

'authorised minimum': C(A)A 1983, s 19; 'company': CA 1963, s 2(1); 'director': CA 1963, s 2(1); 'employees' share scheme': C(A)A 1983, s 2(1); 'prescribed': CA 1963, s 2(1); 'public limited company': C(A)A 1983, s 2(1); 'officer in default': CA 1963, s 383; 'the registrar of companies': CA 1963, s 2(1); 'share': CA 1963, s 2(1).

Notes

Restriction on plc commencing business:[1] Even though duly incorporated, a plc cannot commence business or exercise any of its borrowing powers until either it has been issued with a certificate from the Registrar of Companies under this section or it has re-registered as some other form of company.[2] However, the Registrar may not issue such a certificate unless he is satisfied that the plc has an allotted share capital of not less than the 'authorised minimum' of €38,092.14,[3] in respect of which the whole of any premium and not less than 25% of the par value must be paid up.[4] In this regard, a share shall be taken as having been allotted in a company only when a person acquires an unconditional right to be included in the register of members in respect of that share.[5] In determining the amount of the allotted share capital for this purpose, shares forming part of an employee share scheme are ignored unless they are paid up as to not less than 25% of the par value and the whole of any premium.[6]

The registrar may accept as sufficient proof of compliance with the requirements of This section a statutory declaration in the prescribed form[7], signed by the secretary or one of the directors stating:

(a) that the nominal value of the allotted share capital is not less than the authorised minimum;

(b) the amount paid up in respect of the allotted share capital;

(c) the amount or estimated amount of the preliminary expenses and the persons by whom any of those expenses have been paid or are payable; and

(d) any amounts or benefit paid or given or intended to be paid or given to any promoter and the consideration therefor.[8]

Notice of the delivery of the statutory declaration to the registrar of companies must be published in the Companies Registration Office Gazette.[9]

1 In relation to the restrictions on the commencement of business by a public unlimited company which has issued a prospectus, see CA 1963, s 115.

2 C(A)A 1983, s 6(1).

3 C(A)A 1983, s 6(2).

4 C(A)A 1983, s 28(1). If less than the whole of the premium and at least 25% of the par value has been paid up in respect of a share the allottee and any subsequent holder other than a purchaser for value without notice of the discount (or a person deriving title through him) will be liable to pay interest on the amount of the underpayment: s 28(2) and (4). Application may however be made to the court in appropriate circumstances for relief in whole or in part against this liability to pay interest: s 34.

5 C(A)A 1983, s 2(2).
6 C(A)A 1983, s 6(4). See also s 28(4).
7 Form 70, Companies (Forms) Order 1983, (SI 289/1983).
8 C(A)A 1983, s 6(2) and (5).
9 C(A)A 1983, s 55(1)(a).

Conclusive status of section 6 certificate: A section 6 certificate, once issued by the registrar of companies, is stated to be 'conclusive evidence' that the plc is entitled to business and exercise its borrowing powers.[1] The conclusiveness of a registrar's certificate has previously been upheld in the context of the certification of the registration of a charge under CA 1963, s 99.[2] It has also been upheld in the context of a certificate of incorporation, so as to preclude the court from looking behind the date stated on the certificate as being the date of incorporation.[3] In the UK it has been suggested that despite its stated conclusiveness, the courts would be prepared to look behind a registrar's certificate in cases of fraud or where there is an error on the face of the certificate itself.[4] It has also been held by the UK Courts that because legislation does not bind the Crown except where expressly so stated, an erroneously issued certificate could be challenged through the *fiat* of the Attorney General.[5] It is thought, however, that a similar position would not pertain in Ireland since the Royal Prerogatives, including the non-application of statutes, have been held not to have survived the enactment of the Constitution.[6] Whilst the certainty afforded to members and creditors alike by the conclusiveness of such certificates has been judicially acknowledged,[7] it remains to be seen, however whether that 'conclusiveness' is unconstitutional either as an infringement of the separation of powers contained in Article 6 of the Constitution or as an attempt to oust the High Court's full original jurisdiction under Article 34 of the Constitution to hear and determine all justiciable matters.[8]

1 C(A)A 1983, s 6(6).
2 See CA 1963, s 104 and the notes thereto.
3 *Jubilee Cotton Mills v Lewis* [1924] AC 958.
4 *R v Registrar of Companies, ex parte Central Bank of India* [1986] 1 QB 1114 at 1169–1170 (per Lawton LJ); *Sun Tai Cheung Credits Ltd v Attorney General of Hong Kong* (1987) 3 BCC 357 at 360; *National Provincial and Union Bank of England v Charnley* [1924] 1 KB 431 at 454.
5 *R v Registrar of Companies, ex parte Central Bank of India* [1986] 1 QB 1114 at 1169–1170 (per Lawton LJ) and at 1171–1172 (per Slade LJ).
6 *Byrne v Ireland* [1972] IR 241; *Webb v Ireland* [1988] IR 353; *Howard v Commissioners of Pubic Works* [1993] ILRM 665.
7 *Peel's Case, Re Barned's Banking Co* (1867) LR 2 Ch App 674.
8 *Murren v Brennan* [1942] IR 466; *Maher v Attorney General* [1973] IR 146; *Tormey v Ireland* [1985] IR 289.

Consequences of trading without s 6 certificate: If a plc carries on business or exercises any of its borrowing powers before receiving a s 6 certificate, both the plc itself and every office in default will be guilty of a criminal offence.[1] The validity of the underlying transaction will not be affected.[2] However, if the plc fails to comply with its obligations thereunder within 21 days of being called upon to do so, the directors will be rendered jointly and severally liable to indemnify the other party to the transaction in respect of any consequential loss.[3] To the extent that the directors have to make payment to the other party, they are in turn entitled to be indemnified by the plc itself.[4]

1 C(A)A 1983, s 6(7).
2 C(A)A 1983, s 6(8).
3 C(A)A 1983, s 6(8).
4 *Brook's Wharf and Bull Ltd v Goodman Bros* [1937] 1 KB 534.

Dissolution for failure to obtain a s 6 certificate: If a company is originally incorporated as a plc and fails to obtain a s 6 certificate within one year of incorporation, the registrar of companies may send a warning letter stating that a notice will be published in the Companies Registration Office Gazette with a view to having its name struck off the register of companies unless it obtains the certificate within a period of one month.[1] If the certificate has not been obtained within the prescribed one-month period the registrar may proceed to publish a further warning notice in the Companies Registration Office Gazette.[2] Thereafter unless cause is shown to the contrary within a period of one month, he may proceed to dissolve the company and publish notice of that fact in the Companies Registration Office Gazette.[3]

1 C(A)A 1983, s 8(1).

2 C(A)A 1983, s 8(2).

3 C(A)A 1983, s 8(2). As regards the procedure for restoration, see C(A)A 1983, s 8 and CA 1963, s 311 and the notes thereto.

UK legislation

See CA 1985, s 117.

---

7 Prohibition on formation of public company limited by guarantee and having a share capital

On or after the appointed day, no company shall be formed as, or become, a public company limited by guarantee and having a share capital.

Definitions

'the appointed day': C(A)A 1983, s 1(3), s 2(1); 'company': CA 1963, s 2(1); 'company limited by guarantee': CA 1963, s 2(1); 'public company': C(A)A 1983, s 2(1); 'share': CA 1963, s 2(1).

Notes

Companies limited by guarantee and having a share capital: The effect of C(A)A 1983, s 7 is to prohibit the formation of public companies[1] limited by guarantee and having share capital as and from 18 October 1983.[2] Pubic companies of that type already in existence on that date either had to re-register as plcs or as some other form of company.[3]

1 The section does not, however, prohibit the creation of private companies limited by guarantee and having a share capital. For the definition of a 'private company', see CA 1963, s 33. Neither does it prohibit the creation of public companies limited by guarantee without a share capital.

2 Companies (Amendment) Act 1983 (Commencement) Order 1983 (SI 288/1983).

3 C(A)A 1983, ss 12, 13 and 16.

UK legislation

See CA 1985, s 1(4).

---

8 Power of registrar to strike public limited company off register

(1) Where a public limited company registered as such on its original incorporation has not been issued with a certificate under section 6 within one year from the date on which it was registered, the registrar may send to the company, by registered post, a letter stating that a notice will be published in [the Companies Registration Office Gazette][a] with a view to striking the name of that public limited company off the register unless such a certificate has been issued to the company within on month from the date of that letter.

(2) Where a certificate referred to in section 6 has not been issued within one month from the date of the letter referred to in subsection (1), the registrar may publish such notice and may proceed to strike the name of the public limited company off the register in accordance with section 311 (5) of the Principal Act.

(3) Section 311 (6), [(7), (8) and (8A)][b] of the Principal Act shall apply to a public limited company the name of which has been struck off the register in accordance with subsection (2) as those subsections apply for the purposes of the said section 311.

Amendments

a *Iris Oifigiúil* replaced with 'the Companies Registration Gazette' by IFCMPA 2005, s 72.

b '(7), (8) and (8A)' substituted for '(7) and (8)' by C(A)(No 2)A 1999, s 51.

Definitions

'company': CA 1963, s 2(1); 'the Principal Act': s 2(1); 'public limited company': C(A)A 1983, s 2(1); 'registrar of companies': CA 1963, s 2(1).

Notes

Dissolution for failure to obtain s 6 certificate: See C(A)A 1983, s 6 and the notes thereto.

Consequence of dissolution: See CA 1963, s 311 and the notes thereto.

Restoration to the register: See CA 1963, s 311 and the notes thereto.

UK legislation

See CA 1985, ss 652, 653.

---

9 Re-registration of private company as public limited company

(1) Subject to section 11, a private company may be re-registered as a public limited company if—

(a) a special resolution, complying with subsection (2) that it should be so re-registered is passed; and

(b) an application for the purpose, in the prescribed form and signed by a director or secretary of the company, is delivered to the registrar together with the documents mentioned in subsection (3); and

(c) the conditions specified in subsection (5)(a) and (b) (where applicable) and section 10(1)(a) to (d) are satisfied in relation to the company.

(2) The special resolution must—

(a) alter the company's memorandum so that it states that the company is to be a public limited company;

(b) make such other alterations in the memorandum as are necessary to bring it in substance and in form into conformity with the requirements of this Act with respect to the memorandum of a public limited company; and

(c) make such alterations in the company's articles as are requisite in the circumstances.

(3) The documents referred to in subsection (1) are—

(a) a printed copy of the memorandum and articles as altered in pursuance of the resolution;

(b) a copy of a written statement by the auditors of the company that in their opinion the relevant balance sheet shows that at the balance sheet date the amount of the company's net assets was not less than the aggregate of its called-up share capital and undistributable reserves;

(c) a copy of the relevant balance sheet, together with a copy of an unqualified report by the company's auditors in relation to that balance sheet;

(d) a copy of any report prepared under subsection (5)(b); and

(e) a statutory declaration in the prescribed form by a director or secretary of the company—

(i) that the special resolution mentioned in subsection (1)(a) has been passed and that the conditions specified in subsection (1)(c) have been satisfied; and

(ii) that, between the balance sheet date and the application of the company for re-registration, there has been no change in the financial position of the company that has resulted in the amount of the company's net assets becoming less than the aggregate of its called-up share capital and undistributable reserves.

(4) The registrar may accept a statutory declaration under subsection (3)(e) as sufficient evidence that the special resolution has been passed and the said conditions have been satisfied.

(5) Where shares are allotted by the company between the balance sheet date and the passing of the special resolution as fully or partly paid up as to their nominal value or any premium on them otherwise than in cash, the company shall not make an application for re-registration under this section unless before the making of the application—

(a) the consideration for that allotment has been valued in accordance with the provisions of section 30 applied by this subsection and section 31; and

(b) a report with respect to its value has been made to the company in accordance with those provisions during the six months immediately preceding the allotment of the shares;

and subsections (2) to (8) and (12) to (14) of section 30 shall apply for the purposes of this subsection as they apply for the purposes of that section and as if the references to subsection (1) of section 30 were references to this subsection.

(6) If the registrar is satisfied on an application made under subsection (1) that a company may be re-registered under this section as a public limited company, he shall—

(a) retain the application and other documents delivered to him under that subsection; and

(b) issue the company with a certificate of incorporation stating that the company is a public limited company.

(7) The registrar shall not issue a certificate of incorporation under subsection (6) if it appears to him that the court has made an order confirming a reduction of the

company's capital which has the effect of bringing the nominal value of the company's allotted share capital below the authorised minimum.

(8) Upon the issue to a company of a certificate of incorporation under subsection (6)—

(a) the company shall by virtue of the issue of that certificate become a public limited company; and

(b) any alterations in the memorandum and articles set out in the resolution shall take effect accordingly.

(9) A certificate of incorporation issued to a company under sub-section (6) shall be conclusive evidence—

(a) that the requirements of this Act in respect of re-registration and of matters precedent and incidental thereto have been complied with; and

(b) that the company is a public limited company.

(10) The re-registration of a private company as a public limited company pursuant to this Act shall not affect any rights or obligations of the company or render defective any legal proceedings by or against the company, and any legal proceedings which might have been continued or commenced against it in its former status may be continued or commenced against it in its new status.

(11) A qualification shall be treated for the purposes of the definition of an unqualified report in subsection (13) as being not material in relation to any balance sheet if, but only if, the person making the report states in writing that the thing giving rise to the qualification is not material for the purposes of determining, by reference to that balance sheet, whether at the balance sheet date the amount of the company's net assets was not less than the aggregate of its called-up share capital and undistributable reserves.

(12) For the purposes of the making, in relation to the balance sheet of a company, of a report falling within the definition in subsection (13) of an unqualified report, section 149 of the Sixth Schedule to the Principal Act shall be deemed to have effect in relation to that balance sheet with such modifications as are necessary by reason of the fact that that balance sheet is prepared otherwise than in respect of a financial year.

(13) In this section—

'undistributable reserves' has the same meaning as in section 46(2);

'relevant balance sheet' means, in relation to a company, a balance sheet prepared as at a date not more than seven months before the company's application for re-registration under this section; and

'unqualified report' means, in relation to the balance sheet of a company, a report stating without material qualification—

[(a) that in the opinion of the person making the report, the balance sheet complies with the requirements of section 148 and either section 149 or 149A of the Principal Act, where applicable and with section 156 of the Principal Act;][a]

(b) without prejudice to paragraph (a) that, except where the company is entitled to avail itself, and has availed itself, of the benefit of any of the provisions of Part III of the Sixth Schedule to the Principal Act, in the opinion of that person, the balance sheet gives a true and fair view of the state of the company's affairs as at the balance sheet date.

Amendments

a Paragraph 13(a) substituted by EC(IFRSMA)R 2005 (SI 116/2005), reg 9, Part 2 of Schedule, Item No 2.

Definitions

'articles': CA 1963, s 2 (1); 'authorised minimum': C(A)A 1983, s 19; 'balance sheet date': C(A)A 1983, s 2(1); 'called-up share capital': C(A)A 1983, s 2(1); 'company': CA 1963, s 2(1); 'the court': CA 1963, s 2(1); 'director': CA 1963, s 2(1); 'document': CA 1963, s 2(1); 'financial year': CA 1963, s 2(1); 'memorandum': CA 1963, s 2(1); 'net assets': C(A)A 1983, s 2 (4)(c); 'prescribed': CA 1963, s 2(1); 'the Principal Act': C(A)A 1983, s 2(1); 'printed': CA 1963, s 2(1); 'private company': CA 1963, s 2(1), s 33(1); 'public company': C(A)A 1983, s 2(1); 'public limited company': C(A)A 1983, s 2(1); 'registrar of companies': CA 1963, s 2(1); 'relevant balance sheet': C(A)A 1983, s 9(13); 'share': CA 1963, s 2(1); 'undistributable reserves': s 9(13), s 46(2); 'unqualified report': C(A)A 1983, s 9(11), (13).

Notes

Re-registration of private company as a plc: Apart from special purpose plcs used in capital markets transactions, very few companies start life as plc's. Rather, it is more common to have begun as a private company, converting to public status as the business grows. C(A)A 1983, s 9 and s 10 lay down the requirements for re-registration to take place.

Special resolution: In order to effect such a conversion, the first requirement is that a special resolution to that effect be passed by the members in general meeting.[1] This resolution must not only approve the company's conversion but must also make all necessary consequential amendments to the memorandum and articles of association so as to ensure that it will comply with the statutory requirements of a plc.[2] These would include, inter alia, replacing the word 'limited' or the abbreviation thereof at the end of the company's name with 'public limited company' or 'plc'[3] and making any necessary changes to the capital clause so as to ensure that its *nominal* share capital is not less than the authorised minimum.[4]

Allotted capital requirements: The company must also ensure that its allotted share capital[5] is not less than the authorised minimum,[6] with at least 25% of the nominal value and the whole of any premium in respect of each such share being paid up.[7] Where any share or any premium payable on it has been fully- or partly-paid by an undertaking given by a person to do work or perform services for the company or for another party, that undertaking must have been performed or otherwise discharged before such shares can be taken into account in ascertaining whether or not the company's allotted share capital is not less than the authorised minimum.[8] This is because once a company is a plc, it cannot accept such an undertaking as good consideration for the allotment of shares.[9] So too, where shares have been allotted as fully- or partly-paid up as to their par value or a premium otherwise than in cash and the consideration for the allotment consists of or includes some other form of undertaking, they cannot be taken into account in determining whether or not the company's allotted share capital is not less than the authorised minimum unless either that undertaking has been performed or otherwise discharged, or alternatively a contract has been put in place between the company and the third party whereby the undertaking is to be performed within five years.[10] Again, the logic behind this requirement derives from the fact that once a company is a plc it cannot accept as full or part consideration for an allotment of shares an undertaking which is to be or may be performed more than five year from the date of allotment.[11]

If, after the date to which the last balance sheet has been made up[12] but before the date of application for re-registration, shares have been allotted wholly or partly for a non-cash consideration, the company must have had that consideration independently valued in accordance with the provisions of C(A)A 1983, ss 30 and 31, as if it were already a plc.[13]

Documents to be delivered: An application in the prescribed form[14] must be delivered to the Registrar of Companies together with the following documents:[15] (a) a printed copy of the memorandum and articles of association as amended by the special resolution; (b) a written statement by the auditors that in their opinion the relevant balance sheet (being a balance sheet made up to a date not more than seven months before the date of the application for re-registration) shows the value of the net assets to be not less than the aggregate of its called up share capital and undistributable reserves; (c) a copy of that balance sheet and an unqualified auditor's report;[16] (d) a valuation report in respect of any non-cash consideration for shares allotted between the balance sheet date and the date of the special resolution; and (e) a statutory declaration in the prescribed form[17] made by a director or the company secretary confirming that the special resolution was duly passed and that the necessary amendments were made to the memorandum and articles of association[18] and further confirming that between the balance sheet date and the date of the application for re-registration there has been no change in the company's financial position such as to reduce the value of the net assets below the aggregate of the called up share capital and undistributable reserves.

Certificate of incorporation: If the Registrar is satisfied that the requirements for re-registration have been complied with and if he is satisfied that since the date of the application for re-registration there has been no court sanctioned reduction of capital bringing the company's allotted share capital below the authorised minimum, he must issue the company with a certificate of incorporation as a plc.[19] This certificate operates as 'conclusive' evidence that the re-registration requirements have been complied with and that the company is indeed a plc.[20] The conclusiveness of a registrar's certificate has previously been upheld in the context of the certification of the registration of a charge under CA 1963, s 99.[21] It has also been upheld in the context of a certificate of incorporation, so as to preclude the court from looking behind the date stated on the certificate as being the date of incorporation.[22] In the UK it has been suggested that despite its stated conclusiveness, the courts would be prepared to look behind a Registrar's certificate in cases of fraud or where there is an error on the face of the certificate itself.[23] It has also been held by the UK courts that because legislation does not bind the Crown except where expressly so stated, an erroneously-issued certificate could be challenged through the *fiat* of the Attorney General.[24] It is thought, however, that a similar position would not pertain in Ireland since the Royal Prerogatives, including the non-application of statutes, have been held not to have survived the enactment of the Constitution.[25] Whilst the certainty afforded to members and creditors alike by the conclusiveness of such certificates has been judicially acknowledged,[26] it remains to be seen, however, whether that 'conclusiveness' is unconstitutional either as an infringement of the separation of powers contained in Article 6 of the Constitution or as an attempt to oust the High Court's full original jurisdiction under Article 34 of the Constitution to hear and determine all justiciable matters.[27]

1 C(A)A 1983, s 9(1)(a). A dissenting minority may be able to rely on applicable veto provisions in a shareholders' agreement to prevent the majority shareholders from passing or implementing from passing a special resolution to convert the company into a plc: *Growth Management Ltd v Mutafchiev* [2007] 1 BCLC 645.

2 C(A)A 1983, s 9(2).

3 C(A)A 1983, s 4(1).

4 C(A)A 1983, s 5(2).

5 A share shall be taken as having been allotted in a company only when a person acquires an unconditional right to be included in the register of members in respect of that share: C(A)A 1983, s 2(2).

6 C(A)A 1983, s 10(1)(a).

7 C(A)A 1983, s 10(1)(b). An exemption from this payment requirement applies in respect of shares forming part of an employee share scheme: C(A)A 1983, s 10(2)(b). In addition, the payment requirement is modified in respect of shares which were allotted before 12 October 1986: C(A)A 1983, s 10(2)(a) and (3).

8 C(A)A 1983, s 10(1)(c).

9 C(A)A 1983, s 26(2).

10 C(A)A 1983, s 10(1)(d).

11 C(A)A 1983, s 29(1).

12 ie a date not more than seven months before the date of the application for re-registration: C(A)A 1983, s 9(13).

13 C(A)A 1983, s 10(5).

14 Form 71, Companies (Forms) Order 1983 (SI 289/1993).

15 C(A)A 1983, s 9(1)(b) and (3).

16 As to what constitutes an 'unqualified' auditors' report, see C(A)A 1983, ss 9(11), (12) and (13).

17 Form 72, Companies (Forms Order 1983 (SI 289/1993).

18 For the Model Form Memorandum of Association of a plc see Sch 2, Pt I.

19 C(A)A 1983, s 9(6)–(8)

20 C(A)A 1983, s 9(9).

21 See CA 1963, s 104 and the notes thereto.

22 *Jubilee Cotton Mills v Lewis* [1924] AC 958.

23 *R v Registrar of Companies, ex parte Central Bank of India* [1986] 1 QB 1114 at 1169–1170 (per Lawton LJ); *Sun Tai Cheung Credits Ltd v Attorney General of Hong Kong* (1987) 3 BCC 357 at 360; *National Provincial and Union Bank of England v Charnley* [1924] 1 KB 431 at 454.

24 *R v Registrar of Companies, ex parte Central Bank of India* [1986] 1 QB 1114 at 1169–1170 (per Lawton LJ) and at 1171–1172 (per Slade LJ).

25 *Byrne v Ireland* [1972] IR 241; *Webb v Ireland* [1988] IR 353; *Howard v Commissioners of Pubic Works* [1993] ILRM 665.

26 *Peel's Case, Re Barned's Banking Co* (1867) LR 2 Ch App 674.

27 *Murren v Brennan* [1942] IR 466; *Maher v Attorney General* [1973] IR 146; *Tormey v Ireland* [1985] IR 289.

Effect of re-registration: Although re-registration converts the company into a plc, it retains the same corporate persona and thus all pre-existing rights and obligations of the company remain unaffected (including any legal proceedings commenced by or against it).[1]

1 C(A)A 1983, s 9(10).

UK legislation

See CA 1985, ss 43, 44 (amended by IA 1986, s 439(1) Sch 13, Pt I), 46 (amended by CA 1989, s 23 Sch 10 para 1), 47.

---

10 Requirements as to share capital of private company applying to re-register as public limited company

(1) Subject to subsection (2), a private company shall not be re-registered under section 9 as a public limited company unless, at the time the special resolution referred to in that section is passed—

(a) the nominal value of the company's allotted share capital is not less than the authorised minimum;

(b) each of its allotted shares is paid up at least as to one-quarter of the nominal value of that share and the whole of any premium on it;

(c) where any share in the company or any premium payable on it has been fully or partly paid up by an undertaking given by any person that he or another should do work or perform services for the company or another, the undertaking has been performed or otherwise discharged; and

(d) where shares have been allotted as fully or partly paid up as to their nominal value or any premium payable on them otherwise than in cash and the consideration for the allotment consists of or includes an undertaking (other than one to which paragraph (c) applies) to the company, either—

(i) that undertaking has been performed or otherwise discharged; or

(ii) there is a contract between the company and any person pursuant to which that undertaking must be performed within five years from that time.

(2) Subject to subsection (3), any share allotted by the company—

(a) which was allotted before the end of the general transitional period; or

(b) which was allotted in pursuance of an employees' share scheme and by reason of which the company would, but for this subsection, be precluded under subsection (1)(b), but not otherwise, from being re-registered as a public limited company,

may be disregarded for the purpose of determining whether subsection (1)(b) to (d) is complied with in relation to the company, and a share so disregarded shall be treated for the purposes of subsection (1)(a) as if it were not part of the allotted share capital of the company.

(3) A share shall not be disregarded by virtue of subsection (2)(a) if the aggregate in nominal value of that share and the other shares which it is proposed so to disregard is more than one-tenth of the nominal value of the company's allotted share capital (not including any share disregarded by virtue of subsection (2)(b)).

Definitions

'authorised minimum': C(A)A 1983, s 19; 'company': CA 1963, s 2(1); 'employees' share scheme': C(A)A 1983, s 2(1); 'the general transitional period': C(A)A 1983, s 2(1); 'private company': CA 1963, s 33(1), C(A)A 1983, s 2(1); 'public limited company': C(A)A 1983, s 2(1); 'share': CA 1963, s 2(1).

Notes

Re-registration of private company as a plc: See the notes to C(A)A 1983, s 9.

UK legislation

See CA 1985, s 45.

---

11 Re-registration of unlimited company as public limited company

(1) An unlimited company may be re-registered as a public limited company and for the purposes of such a re-registration sections 9 and 53(6) and (7) shall have effect subject to the modifications contained in this section.

(2) The special resolution required by section 9(1) must, in addition to the matters mentioned in section 9(2)—

(a) state that the liability of the members is to be limited by shares and what the share capital of the company is to be; and

(b) make such alterations in the company's memorandum as are necessary to bring it in substance and in form into conformity with the requirements of the Companies Acts with respect to the memorandum of a company limited by shares.

(3) The certificate of incorporation issued under section 9(6) shall, in addition to containing the statement required by paragraph (b) of that subsection, state that the company has been incorporated as a company limited by shares and—

(a) the company shall by virtue of the issue of that certificate become a public limited company so limited; and

(b) the certificate shall be conclusive evidence of the fact that it is such limited company.

(4) Section 53(6) and (7) shall have effect as if any reference to the re-registration of a company in pursuance of that section included a reference to the re-registration of an unlimited company as a public limited company in accordance with subsection (1), but except as aforesaid the said section 53 shall not apply in relation to the re-registration of an unlimited company as a public limited company.

Definitions

'company': CA 1963, s 2(1); 'the Companies Acts': C(A)A 1983, s 2(1), (5); 'member': CA 1963, s 31; 'public limited company': C(A)A 1983, s 2(1); 'share': CA 1963, s 2(1); 'unlimited company': CA 1963, s 2 (1), s 5(2).

Notes

Re-registration of unlimited company as a plc:[1] The procedure for re-registering an unlimited company as a plc is essentially the same as for the re-registration of a private company as a plc, as to which see C(A)A 1983, ss 9 and 10 and the notes thereto.

1 In relation to the re-registration of an unlimited company as a company limited by guarantee or as a private company limited by shares, see C(A)A 1983, s 53.

Creditor protection: In passing the necessary special resolution for re-registration the members may also if they so desire: (a) increase the nominal value of the share capital by increasing the nominal amount of each of its shares, but subject to the condition that on part of the increased capital is to be called up except in the event and for the purposes of the company being wound up; and/or (b) provide that a specified portion of its uncalled capital shall not be capable of being called up except in the event and for the purposes of the company being wound up.[1] Whilst either course of action affords the creditors less protection than if the liability of the members were to remain unlimited on an indefinite basis, it does at least ensure that some proportion of the capital is 'ring-fenced' for creditors and is kept immune from the risk of being lost in the ordinary course of the company's trading life.

It is also to be noted that if the company goes into liquidation within three years of the date of re-registration as a plc, any person who was a member at the date of re-registration will have unlimited liability for debts and liabilities incurred before the company became a plc.[2] In this regard, however, past members will only be called upon to so contribute if: (a) no persons who were members of the company at the time of re-registration are existing members at the time of the winding up; or (b) those persons who were members of the company at the time of re-

registration and are existing members at the time of the winding up are unable between them to make good the deficiency in the liquidation.[3]

[1] CA 1963, s 71 as applied by s 11(1) and (4) and s 53(6).
[2] C(A)A 1983, s 53(7) as applied by s 11(1) and (4).
[3] C(A)A 1983, s 53(7) and CA 1963, s 207(1)(c).

UK legislation

See CA 1985, s 48.

12 Old public limited companies

(1) In this Act 'old public limited company' means a public company limited by shares or a public company limited by guarantee and having a share capital in respect of which the following conditions are satisfied, that is to say—

(a) the company either existed on the appointed day or was incorporated after that day pursuant to an application made before that day; and

(b) the company has not since the appointed day or the day of the company's incorporation, as the case may be, either been re-registered as a public limited company or become another form of company.

(2) The references in the Principal Act to a company other than a private company and, after the end of the general transitional period, in this Act other than this Part to a public limited company shall, unless the context otherwise requires, include references to an old public limited company.

(3) An old public limited company may (either before or after the end of the general transitional period) be re-registered as a public limited company if—

(a) the directors pass a resolution, complying with subsection (4), that it should be so re-registered; and

(b) an application for the purpose in the prescribed form and signed by a director or secretary of the company is delivered to the registrar, together with the documents mentioned in subsection (5); and

(c) at the time of the resolution, the conditions specified in subsection (9) are satisfied.

(4) The resolution referred to in subsection (3) must alter the company's memorandum so that it states that the company is to be a public limited company and make such other alterations in it as are necessary to bring it in substance and in form into conformity with the requirements of this Act with respect to the memorandum of a public limited company.

(5) The documents referred to in subsection (3) are—

(a) a printed copy of the memorandum as altered in pursuance of the resolution; and

(b) a statutory declaration in the prescribed form by a director or secretary of the company that the resolution mentioned in subsection (3)(a) has been passed and that the conditions specified in subsection (9) were satisfied at the time of the resolution.

(6) The registrar may accept a declaration under subsection (5)(b) as sufficient evidence that the said resolution has been passed and that the said conditions were so satisfied.

(7) Subsections (6) to (9) of section 9, shall apply on an application for re-registration under this section as they apply on an application for re-registration under that section and as if the reference to subsection (1) of that section were a reference to subsection (3) of this section.

(8) If an old public limited company applies for re-registration as a public limited company in accordance with subsection (3) and at the time of making that application delivers to the registrar a statutory declaration in the prescribed form by a director or secretary of the company that the company does not at the time of the declaration satisfy the conditions specified in subsection (9), the registrar shall re-register the company as a public limited company but shall notify it that if, within the transitional period for share capital, it has not satisfied the aforesaid conditions it must re-register as another form of company or wind up voluntarily under section 251 of the Principal Act. Failure so to re-register or wind up shall constitute grounds for a winding-up by the court under section 213(i) of the Principal Act.

(9) The conditions referred to in subsections (3)(c) and (8) are that, at the time of the resolution, the nominal value of the company's allotted share capital is not less than the authorised minimum and that in the case of all the shares of the company or all those of its shares which are comprised in a portion of that capital which satisfies that condition—

(a) each share is paid up at least as to one-quarter of the nominal value of that share and the whole of any premium on it;

(b) where any of the shares in question or any premium payable on them has been fully or partly paid up by an undertaking given by any person that he or another should do work or perform services for the company or another, the undertaking has been performed or otherwise discharged; and

(c) where any of the shares in question has been allotted as fully or partly paid up as to its nominal value or any premium payable on it otherwise than in cash and the consideration for the allotment consists of or includes an undertaking (other than one to which paragraph (b) applies) to the company, either—

  (i) that undertaking has been performed or otherwise discharged; or

  (ii) there is a contract between the company and any person pursuant to which that undertaking must be performed within five years from the time of the resolution.

(10) The re-registration of an old public limited company as a public limited company pursuant to this Act shall not affect any rights or obligations of the company or render defective any legal proceedings by or against the company, and any legal proceedings which might have been continued or commenced against it in its former status may be continued or commenced against it in its new status.

Definitions

'the appointed day': C(A)A 1983, s 1(3),s 2(1); 'authorised minimum': C(A)A 1983, s 19; 'company': CA 1963, s 2(1); 'company limited by guarantee': CA 1963, s 2(1); 'the court': CA

1963, s 2(1); 'director': CA 1963, s 2(1); 'document': CA 1963, s 2(1): 'the general transitional period': C(A)A 1983, s 2(1); 'memorandum': CA 1963, s 2(1); 'old public limited company': C(A)A 1983, s 2(1), s 12(1); 'prescribed': CA 1963, s 2(1); 'the Principal Act': C(A)A 1983, s 2(1); ' printed': CA 1963, s 2(1); 'private company': CA 1963, s 2(1), s 33(1); 'public company': C(A)A 1983, s 2(1); 'public limited company': C(A)A 1983, s 2(1); 'registrar of companies': CA 1963, s 2(1); 'share': CA 1963, s 2(1); 'the transitional period for share capital': C(A)A 1983, s 2(1).

Notes

Re-registration of old public limited companies: C(A)A 1983, s 12 required public companies with limited liability which were in existence as on 13 October 1983 or which were incorporated on foot of an application lodged with the registrar before that date, to re-register as plcs or as some other form of company or wind up voluntarily. This had to be effected before 12 January 1985. Failure to do so gave rise to various criminal offences under s 13 or s 16, as the case may be and also constituted grounds for the registrar petitioning to have the company wound up compulsorily.

UK legislation

See CC(CP)A 1985, ss 1–3.

---

13 Failure by an old public limited company to re-register as public limited company

(1) If, at any time after the end of the period of fifteen months from the appointed day (in this Act referred to as 'the re-registration period'), a company which is an old public limited company has not re-registered as a public limited company under section 12, the company and any officer of the company who is in default shall be guilty of an offence unless at that time the company—

(a) has applied to be re-registered under section 12 and the application has not been refused or withdrawn;

(b) has applied to be re-registered as another form of company.

(2) A person guilty of an offence under subsection (1) shall be liable on summary conviction to a fine not exceeding [€1,904.61][a] together with, in the case of a continuing offence, a fine not exceeding [€31.74][b] for every day on which the offence continues, but not exceeding [€1,904.61][c] in total.

Amendments

a '£250' substituted for '£50' by C(A)A 1982, Sch 1, increased to £1,500 by CA 1990, s 240(7) as inserted by CLEA 2001, s 104(c), and converted to €1,904.61 by Council Regulations (EC) No 1103/97, No 974/98 and No 2866/98 and the Economic and Monetary Union Act 1998, s 6.

b £25 converted to €31.74 by Council Regulations (EC) No 1103/97, No 974/98 and No 2866/98 and the Economic and Monetary Union Act 1998, s 6.

c £500 increased to £1,500 by CA 1990, s 240(7) as inserted by CLEA 2001, s 104(c) and converted to €1,904.61 by Council Regulations (EC) No 1103/97, No 974/98 and No 2866/98 and the Economic and Monetary Union Act 1998, s 6. Note the effect of CA 1990, s 240(7) is to render the daily fine meaningless as the upper cap imposed on the fine and daily fine is now the same as the daily fine.

Definitions

'the appointed day': C(A)A 1983, s 1(3),s 2(1); 'company': CA 1963, s 2(1); 'old public limited company': C(A)A 1983, s 2(1), s 12(1); 'officer': CA 1963, s 2(1); 'officer in default': CA 1963, s 383; 'public limited company': C(A)A 1983, s 2(1); 'the re-registration period': C(A)A 1983, s 2(1), 13(1).

Notes

Re-registration of old public limited companies: See the notes to C(A)A 1983, s 12.

UK legislation

See CC(CP)A 1985, s 5.

---

14 Re-registration of public limited company as private company

(1) A public limited company may be re-registered as a private company if—

(a) a special resolution complying with subsection (2) that it should be so re-registered is passed and has not been cancelled by the court under section 15(6);

(b) an application for the purpose in the prescribed form and signed by a director or secretary of the company is delivered to the registrar, together with a printed copy of the memorandum and articles of the company as altered by the resolution; and

(c) the period during which an application for the cancellation of the resolution under section 15 (2) may be made has expired without any such application having been made; or

(d) where such an application has been made, the application has been withdrawn or an order has been made under section 15 (6) confirming the resolution and a copy of that order has been delivered to the registrar.

(2) The resolution must—

(a) alter the company's memorandum so that it no longer states that the company is to be a public limited company and must make such other alterations in the company's memorandum as are requisite in the circumstances; and

(b) make such alterations in the company's articles as are requisite in the circumstances and in such a manner that they include the provisions which, under section 33 of the Principal Act, are required to be included in the articles of a company in order to constitute it a private company.

(3) If the registrar is satisfied that a public limited company may be re-registered under subsection (1), he shall—

(a) retain the application and other documents delivered to him under that subsection; and

(b) issue the company with a certificate of incorporation appropriate to a private company.

(4) Upon the issue of a certificate of incorporation under subsection (3)—

(a) the company shall by virtue of the issue of that certificate become a private company; and

(b) the alterations in the memorandum and articles set out in the resolution shall take effect accordingly.

(5) A certificate of incorporation issued to a company under subsection (3) shall be conclusive evidence—

(a) that the requirements of this section in respect of re-registration and of matters precedent and incidental thereto have been complied with; and

(b) that the company is a private company.

(6) The re-registration of a public limited company as a private company pursuant to this Act shall not affect any rights or obligations of the company or render defective any legal proceedings by or against the company, and any legal proceedings which might have been continued or commenced against it in its former status may be continued or commenced against it in its new status.

Definitions

'articles': CA 1963, s 2 (1); 'company': CA 1963, s 2(1); 'the court': CA 1963, s 2(1); 'director': CA 1963, s 2(1); 'document': CA 1963, s 2(1): 'memorandum': CA 1963, s 2(1); 'prescribed': CA 1963, s 2(1); 'the Principal Act': C(A)A 1983, s 2(1); ' printed': CA 1963, s 2(1); 'private company': CA 1963, s 2(1), s 33(1); 'public limited company': C(A)A 1983, s 2(1); 'registrar of companies' CA 1963, s 2(1).

Notes

Re-registration of a plc as a private company: C(A)A 1983, s 14 and s 15 lay down the procedure for the re-registration of a plc as a private company.

Special resolution: In order to effect such a conversion, the first requirement is that a special resolution to that effect be passed by the members in general meeting.[1] This resolution must not only approve the plcs conversion into private company but must also make all necessary consequential amendments to the memorandum and articles of association so as to ensure that it will comply with the statutory requirements of a private company.[2] These would include provisions in the articles: (a) restricting the transfer of shares; (b) placing an upper limit of 99 on the number of members (including present employees and persons who have continued to be members after ceasing employment with the company); and (c) prohibiting any invitation or offer to the public to subscribe for shares, debentures or other securities of the company.[3]

Application to cancel the special resolution: Where a special resolution has been passed for the re-registration of a plc as a private company, any dissenting member or members representing not less than 5% of the issued share capital or any class thereof or not less than 50 members (regardless of the number of shares held by them) may apply to the High Court within 28 days for an order cancelling the special resolution.[4] The application is brought by way of petition.[5] Having been served with the proceedings, the company must in turn serve notice on the Registrar of Companies (presumably so as to ensure that the registrar does not erroneously re-register the company whilst the proceedings are ongoing).[6] A Motion for Directions will be brought regarding the advertising and manner of hearing of the petition (eg on affidavit or by way of plenary hearing).[7] The petition must be advertised in such newspapers the court directs.[8] At the hearing not only the members but any creditors who have given not less than two days' notice of intention to appear[9] may be heard by the court. The Act does not specify the factors to be taken into account by the court in determining whether or not to accede to the dissentients' application. Presumably by analogy with the court's jurisdiction under CA 1963, s 10, the dissentients would have to establish that there was something unfair or inequitable in the proposed re-registration before the court would grant them any relief.[10] Nonetheless, in hearing the application the court is seemingly given a wide discretion and may either cancel or confirm the resolution on such terms as it thinks fit,[11] including terms altering the memorandum and/or articles of association[12] and/or terms to the effect that the company may not make any or any specified alterations to its memorandum and/or articles of association except with the leave of the court.[13] It may adjourn the proceedings to enable a satisfactory arrangement to be put in place to buy out the dissentients and may make any necessary consequential orders and give any consequential directions as may be expedient for the implementation of such an arrangement.[14] Furthermore, even if such an arrangement cannot be arrived at by agreement, the court make an order of its own accord for the company itself to buy out any of the members, reducing the capital accordingly and making any other consequential amendments to the memorandum and articles of association.[15] Whilst in most cases the appropriate order would be for the company to buy out the dissentients, the legislation appears to be drafted in wide enough terms to even allow for the buy out of the majority, thereby leaving the dissentients with control of the company. Doubtless an order of this latter type would only be made in the most extreme of cases.

Documents to be delivered: An application in the prescribed form[16] must be delivered to the Registrar of Companies together with a printed copy of the memorandum and articles of association as amended by the special resolution.[17]

Certificate of incorporation: Assuming either that no petition is brought to cancel the special resolution or alternatively, that the petition is satisfactorily disposed of,[18] and provided he is satisfied that the requirements for re-registration have been complied with, the registrar must issue the plc with a certificate of incorporation as a private company.[19] This certificate operates as 'conclusive' evidence that the re-registration requirements have been complied with and that the company is indeed a private company.[20] The conclusiveness of a registrar's certificate has previously been upheld in the context of the certification of the registration of a charge under CA 1963, s 99.[21] It has also been upheld in the context of a certificate of incorporation, so as to preclude the court from looking behind the date stated on the certificate as being the date of incorporation.[22] In the UK it has been suggested that despite its stated conclusiveness, the courts would be prepared to look behind a registrar's certificate in cases of fraud or where there is an error on the face of the certificate itself.[23] It has also been held by the UK courts that because legislation does not bind the Crown except where expressly so stated, an erroneously issued certificate could be challenged through the *fiat* of the Attorney General.[24] It is thought, however, that a similar position would not pertain in Ireland since the Royal Prerogatives, including the non-application of statutes, have been held not to have survived the enactment of the Constitution.[25] Whilst the certainty afforded to members and creditors alike by the conclusiveness of such certificates has been judicially acknowledged,[26] it remains to be seen, however whether that 'conclusiveness' is unconstitutional either as an infringement of the separation of powers contained in Article 6 of the Constitution or as an attempt to oust the High Court's full original jurisdiction under Article 34 of the Constitution to hear and determine all justiciable matters.[27]

1 C(A)A 1983, s 14(1)(a). Such a special resolution will not be required where the plc has effected a reduction of capital which has brought its allotted share capital below the authorised minimum and the court in confirming the reduction of capital has made an order under s 17(4) directing that it may be registered without the need for such a special resolution.

2 C(A)A 1983, s 14(2). See CA 1963, s 33 for the matters which must be provided for in the articles of association in order to qualify as a private company. Moreover, as CA 1963, s 33 makes quite clear, only a company with a share capital can be a private company. Thus, by definition, a company limited by guarantee alone must be a public company (albeit not a plc).

3 CA 1963, s 33.

4 C(A)A 1983, s 15(2) and (3). This procedure will not be available to dissentients where the plc has effected a reduction of capital which has brought its allotted share capital below the

authorised minimum and the court in confirming the reduction of capital has made an order under s 17(4) directing that it may be registered without the need for such a special resolution. The protection for dissentients in such circumstances is that they will have had an opportunity to oppose the reduction of capital at the hearing of the petition under CA 1963, s 72.

5 RSC, Ord 75, r 4(4).
6 C(A)A 1983, s 15(5)(a).
7 RSC, Ord 75, r 6.
8 RSC, Ord 75, r 13.
9 RSC, Ord 75, r 14.
10 *Re Jewish Colonial Trust* [1908] 2 Ch 287.
11 C(A)A 1983, s 15(6)(a).
12 C(A)A 1983, s 15(9).
13 C(A)A 1983, s 15(8).
14 C(A)A 1983, s 15(8).
15 C(A)A 1983, s 15(7).
16 Form 76, Companies (Forms) Order 1983 (SI 289/1993).
17 C(A)A 1983, s 14(1)(b).
18 C(A)A 1983, s 14(1)(c) and (d)
19 C(A)A 1983, s 14(3) and (4).
20 C(A)A 1983, s 14(5).
21 See CA 1963, s 104 and the notes thereto.
22 *Jubilee Cotton Mills v Lewis* [1924] AC 958.
23 *R v Registrar of Companies, ex parte Central Bank of India* [1986] 1 QB 1114 at 1169–1170 (per Lawton LJ); *Sun Tai Cheung Credits Ltd v Attorney General of Hong Kong* (1987) 3 BCC 357 at 360; *National Provincial and Union Bank of England v Charnley* [1924] 1 KB 431 at 454.
24 *R v Registrar of Companies, ex parte Central Bank of India* [1986] 1 QB 1114 at 1169–1170 (per Lawton LJ) and at 1171–1172 (per Slade LJ).
25 *Byrne v Ireland* [1972] IR 241; *Webb v Ireland* [1988] IR 353; *Howard v Commissioners of Pubic Works* [1993] ILRM 665.
26 *Peel's Case, Re Barned's Banking Co* (1867) LR 2 Ch App 674.
27 *Murren v Brennan* [1942] IR 466; *Maher v Attorney General* [1973] IR 146; *Tormey v Ireland* [1985] IR 289.

Effect of re-registration: Although re-registration converts the company into a private company, it retains the same corporate persona and thus all pre-existing rights and obligations of the company remain unaffected (including any legal proceedings commenced by or against it).[1]

1 C(A)A 1983, s 14(6).

UK legislation

See CA 1985, ss 53, 55.

---

15 Provisions supplementary to section 14

(1) This section applies to a special resolution by a public limited company to be re-registered under section 14 as a private company.

(2) Where a special resolution to which this section applies has been passed, an application may be made to the court for the cancellation of that resolution.

(3) An application under subsection (2) may be made—

(a) by the holders of not less in the aggregate than five per cent. in nominal value of the company's issued share capital or any class thereof;

(b) if the company is not limited by shares, by not less than five per cent. of the company's members; or

(c) by not less than 50 of the company's members;

but any such application shall not be made by any person who has consented to or voted in favour of the resolution.

(4) Any such application must be made within 28 days after the passing of the resolution and may be made on behalf of the persons entitled to make the application by such one or more of their number as they may appoint in writing for the purpose.

(5) If an application is made under subsection (2), the company—

(a) shall forthwith give notice of that fact to the registrar; and

(b) where on the hearing of that application an order cancelling or confirming the resolution is made under subsection (6), shall, within 15 days from the making of that order, or within such longer period as the court may at any time by order direct, deliver an office copy of the order to the registrar.

(6) On the hearing of an application under subsection (2) the court shall make an order either cancelling or confirming the resolution and—

(a) may make that order on such terms and conditions as it thinks fit, and may, if it thinks fit, adjourn the proceedings in order that an arrangement may be made to the satisfaction of the court for the purchase of the interests of dissentient members; and

(b) may give such directions and make such orders as it thinks expedient for facilitating or carrying into effect any such arrangement.

(7) An order under this section may, if the court thinks fit, provide for the purchase by the company of the shares of any members of the company and for the reduction accordingly of the company's capital and may make such alterations in the memorandum and articles of the company as may be required in consequence of that provision.

(8) Where an order under this section requires the company not to make any, or any specified, alteration in its memorandum or articles, then, notwithstanding anything in the Companies Acts, the company shall not have power without the leave of the court to make any such alteration in breach of that requirement.

(9) Any alteration in the memorandum or articles of the company made by virtue of an order under this section, other than one made by resolution of the company, shall be of the same effect as if duly made by resolution of the company, and the provisions of the Companies Acts shall apply to the memorandum or articles as so altered accordingly.

(10) A company which fails to comply with subsection (5) and any officer of the company who is in default shall be guilty of an offence and shall be liable on summary conviction to a fine not exceeding [€1,904.61][a] together with, in the case of a continuing offence, a fine not exceeding [€31.74][b] for every day on which the offence continues, but not exceeding [€634.50][c] in total.

Amendments

a '£250' substituted for '£50' by C(A)A 1982, Sch 1, increased to £1,500 by CA 1990, s 240(7) as inserted by CLEA 2001, s 104(c), and converted to €1,904.61 by Council Regulations (EC) No 1103/97, No 974/98 and No 2866/98 and the Economic and Monetary Union Act 1998, s 6.

b £25 converted to €31.74 by Council Regulations (EC) No 1103/97, No 974/98 and No 2866/98 and the Economic and Monetary Union Act 1998, s 6.

c £500 converted to €634.50 by Council Regulations (EC) No 1103/97, No 974/98 and No 2866/98 and the Economic and Monetary Union Act 1998, s 6. Note the effect of CA 1990, s 240(7) is to render the daily fine meaningless as the upper cap imposed on the fine and daily fine is now the same as the daily fine.

Definitions

'articles': CA 1963, s 2(1); 'company': CA 1963, s 2(1); 'the Companies Acts': C(A)A 1983, s 2(1), (5); 'the court': CA 1963, s 2(1); 'member': CA 1963, s 31; 'memorandum': CA 1963, s 2(1); 'private company': CA 1963, s 2(1), s 33(1); 'public limited company': C(A)A 1983, s 2(1); 'officer in default': CA 1963, s 383 'registrar of companies': CA 1963, s 2(1); 'share': CA 1963, s 2(1).

Notes

Re-registration of a plc as a private company: See C(A)A 1983, s 14 and the notes thereto.

UK legislation

See CA 1985, s 54.

---

16 Failure by old public limited company to re-register as another form of company

(1) Where an old public limited company has within the re-registration period applied for re-registration as a form of company other than a public limited company, and the registrar has notified the company that it has failed to fulfil the requirements for such re-registration, the company and any officer of the company who is in default shall be guilty of an offence unless within a period of 12 months from the end of the re-registration period—

(a) those requirements have been fulfilled and the re-registration has taken place; or

(b) the company has been re-registered in a form other than that for which application was made; or

(c) the company has been wound up voluntarily under section 251 of the Principal Act.

(2) A person guilty of an offence under subsection (1) shall be liable on summary conviction to a fine not exceeding £250 together with, in the case of a continuing offence, a fine not exceeding £25 for every day on which the offence continues, but not exceeding £500 in total.

Definitions

'company': CA 1963, s 2(1); 'old public limited company': C(A)A 1983, s 2(1), s 12(1); 'the Principal Act': C(A)A 1983, s 2(1); 'public limited company': C(A)A 1983, s 2(1); 'the re-registration period': C(A)A 1983, s 2(1), 13(1); 'officer in default': CA 1963, s 383; 'registrar of companies': CA 1963, s 2(1).

Notes

Re-registration of old public limited companies: See the notes to C(A)A 1983, s 12.

UK legislation

See CC(CP)A 1985, s 5.

---

17 Limitation on reduction by a public limited company of its allotted share capital

(1) Subject to subsections (2) and (3), a public limited company may not reduce its allotted share capital below the authorised minimum and section 72(1) of the Principal Act shall be construed accordingly.

(2) Subsection (1) shall not apply to an old public limited company which has been re-registered as a public limited company until expiry of the transitional period for share capital.

(3) Where the court makes an order confirming a reduction of the capital of a public limited company which has the effect of bringing the nominal value of the company's allotted share capital below the authorised minimum, the registrar shall not register the order under section 75(1) of the Principal Act unless the court otherwise directs or the company is first re-registered as another form of company.

(4) A court making any such order in respect of a public limited company may authorise the company to be re-registered as another form of company without its having passed a special resolution and, where the court so authorises a public limited company, the court shall specify in the order the alterations in the company's memorandum and articles to be made in connection with that re-registration.

(5) In its application to a public limited company that applies to be re-registered as a private company in pursuance of an authority given under subsection (4), section 14, shall have effect with the following modifications—

(a) references to the special resolution of the company shall have effect as references to the order of the court under the said subsection (4);

(b) section 14 (1)(a), (c) and (d) and (2) shall not apply; and

(c) section 14 (3) shall be read as if the words— 'If the registrar is satisfied that a public limited company may be re-registered under subsection (1) he shall' were deleted and the following words substituted therefor 'On receipt of an application for re-registration under this section made in pursuance of an order of the court under section 17, the registrar shall'.

Definitions

'articles': CA 1963, s 2 (1); 'authorised minimum': C(A)A 1983, s 19; 'company': CA 1963, s 2(1); 'the court': CA 1963, s 2(1); 'memorandum': CA 1963, s 2(1); 'old public limited company': C(A)A 1983, s 2(1), s 12(1); 'the Principal Act': C(A)A 1983, s 2(1); 'private company': CA 1963, s 2(1), s 33(1); 'public limited company': C(A)A 1983, s 2(1); 'Registrar of Companies': CA 1963, s 2(1); 'share': CA 1963, s 2(1); 'the transitional period for share capital'; C(A)A 1983, s 2(1).

Notes

Reduction of capital by a plc below the authorised minimum: The procedures for implementing a reduction of capital, and the circumstances in which same may be effected, are governed by CA 1963, ss 72–77. In the case of a private company, it may, circumstances allowing, reduce its capital by any appropriate amount. However, in the case of a plc, there are restrictions on its ability to effect a reduction of capital which brings the amount of its allotted share capital below the authorised minimum of €38,092.14.[1] The Registrar is precluded from registering any order made for such a reduction of capital (thereby preventing the order from taking effect[2]) unless the court otherwise directs or the plc first re-registers as some other form of company.[3] In practice, the court has made orders directing the registrar to register such an order in circumstances where the reduction of capital forms part of a restructuring of the company's capital and the company gives an undertaking to allot a sufficient number of new shares (perhaps of a new class) immediately after the reduction of capital has been implemented, so as to bring the company's allotted share capital back above the authorised minimum of €38,092.14. On the other hand, if the company does not propose to bring its capital back above the authorised minimum, but instead indicates to the court that it proposes to re-register as a some other form of company, the court in confirming the reduction of capital may also make an order authorising it to so re-register without having to first pass a special resolution to that effect.[4] In doing so, it may also direct the changes that are to be made to the company's memorandum and articles so as to fully give effect to the process of re-registration.[5] If the court makes an order for re-registration as a private company dissentients will not be able to apply under C(A)A 1983, s 15 to seek to have the re-registration cancelled.[6] The protection for dissentients in such circumstances is that they will have had an opportunity to oppose the reduction of capital at the hearing of the petition under CA 1963, s 72.

1 C(A)A 1983, s 17(1).

2 See CA 1963, s 75(2) which stipulates that an order for the reduction of capital shall not take effect until it has been registered together with the minute prescribed by s 75(1).

3 C(A)A 1983, s 17(3). See ss 14 and 17 for the applicable procedures to re-register as a private company or as an unlimited company, respectively.

4 C(A)A 1983, s 17(4).

5 C(A)A 1983, s 17(4).

6 C(A)A 1983, s 17(5).

UK legislation

See CA 1985, s 139.

---

18 Registration of joint stock companies

(1) A joint stock company (within the meaning of section 329 of the Principal Act) applying to be registered in pursuance of Part IX of that Act as a company limited by shares may, subject to satisfying the conditions specified in section 9(5)(a) and (b) (where applicable) and section 10(1)(a) to (d), as applied by this section, and to complying with the requirements of subsection (4), apply to be so registered as a public limited company.

(2) The said sections 9(5) and 10 shall apply to a joint stock company applying to register under the said Part IX as they apply to a private company applying to be re-registered under section 9, but as if any reference to the special resolution referred to in section 9 were a reference to the resolution referred to in subsection (4)(a).

(3) In the following provisions of this section an application by a company made in pursuance of the said Part IX to register as a public company limited by shares is referred to as a relevant application.

(4) A relevant application shall be made in the prescribed form and shall be delivered to the registrar together with the following documents (as well as with the documents referred to in section 330 of the Principal Act), namely—

(a) a copy of the resolution that the company be a public limited company;

(b) a copy of a written statement by a person, who would be qualified under section 162 of the Principal Act for appointment as auditor of the company if it were a company registered under that Act, that in his opinion a relevant balance sheet shows that at the balance sheet date the amount of the company's net assets was not less than the aggregate of the called-up share capital of the company and its undistributable reserves;

(c) a copy of the relevant balance sheet together with a copy of an unqualified report by such a person in relation to that balance sheet;

(d) a copy of any report prepared under section 9(5)(b) as applied by this section; and

(e) a statutory declaration in the prescribed form by a director or secretary of the company—

(i) that the conditions specified in section 9(5)(a) and (b) (where applicable) and section 10(1)(a) to (d) have been satisfied; and

(ii) that, between the balance sheet date referred to in paragraph (b) and the date of the relevant application, there has been no change in the financial position of the company that has resulted in the amount of the company's net assets becoming less than the aggregate of its called-up share capital and undistributable reserves.

(5) The registrar may accept a declaration under subsection (4)(e) as sufficient evidence that the conditions referred to in subparagraph (i) of that paragraph have been satisfied.

(6) Where on a relevant application the registrar is satisfied that the company may be registered as a public company limited by shares, the certificate of incorporation given by him under section 336 of the Principal Act shall state that the company is a public limited company; and such a statement shall be conclusive evidence that the requirements of this section have been complied with and that the company is a public company so limited.

(7) The registration of a joint stock company as a public limited company shall not affect any rights or obligations of the company or render defective any legal proceedings by or against the company, and any legal proceedings which might have been continued or commenced against it in its former status may be continued or commenced against it in its new status.

(8) In this section—

'relevant balance sheet' means, in relation to a company, a balance sheet prepared as at a date not more than seven months before the relevant application;

'undistributable reserves' has the same meaning as in section 46(2); and

'unqualified report' has the same meaning as in section 9(13);

and section 9(11) applies to the making in pursuance of this section of an unqualified report such as is mentioned in that subsection as it applies to the making of such a report in pursuance of the said section 9.

Definitions

'balance sheet date': C(A)A 1983, s 2(1); 'called-up share capital': C(A)A 1983, s 2(1); 'company': CA 1963, s 2(1); 'company limited by shares': CA 1963, s 2(1), s 5(2); 'director': CA 1963, s 2(1); 'document': CA 1963, s 2(1): 'prescribed': CA 1963, s 2(1); 'the Principal Act': C(A)A 1983, s 2(1); 'private company': CA 1963, s 2(1), s 33(1); 'public company': C(A)A 1983, s 2(1); 'public limited company': C(A)A 1983, s 2(1); 'Registrar of Companies': CA 1963, s 2(1) 'share': CA 1963, s 2(1).

Notes

Re-registration of joint stock companies as plcs: A joint stock company is a limited liability company incorporated under the Joint Stock Companies Acts or under some other enactment (apart from the Companies Act 1862 or the Companies (Consolidation) Act 1908)[1] having a permanent paid up or nominal capital of fixed amount divided into stock and/or shares, also of fixed amount and transferable as such.[2] If such a company has not less than seven members[3] it may apply to be re-registered as a plc in the same manner as if it were a private company incorporated under the Companies Acts. In this regard see the notes to ss 9 and 10. The relevant application form is Form 78[4] whereas the statutory declaration of compliance with the re-registration procedures is Form 79.[5]

1 See CA 1963, s 328(2).

2 CA 1963, s 329.

3 CA 1963, s 328(1).

4 Companies (Forms) order 1983 (SI 289/1983).

5 Companies (Forms) order 1983 (SI 289/1983).

UK legislation

See CA 1985, s 685.

PART III

THE CAPITAL OF A COMPANY

Authorised share capital and the issue of share capital

19 Meaning of 'authorised minimum'

(1) In this Act 'the authorised minimum' means [€38,092.41][a] or such greater sum as may be specified by order made by the Minister under sub-section (2).

(2) The Minister may by order specify that the authorised minimum for the purposes of this Act shall be an amount other than [€38,092.41][a] and such and order may—

(a) require any public limited company having an allotted share capital of which the nominal value is less than the amount specified in the order as the authorised minimum to increase that value to not less than that amount or make an application to be re-registered as another form of company;

(b) make, in connection with any such requirement, provision for any of the matters for which provision is made by any enactment in the Companies Acts relating to a company's registration, re-registration or change of name, to payment for any share comprised in a company's capital and to offers of shares in or debentures of a company to the public, including provision as to the consequences (whether in criminal law or otherwise) of a failure to comply with any requirement of the order; and

(c) contain such supplemental and transitional provision as the Minister thinks appropriate, make different provision for different cases and, in particular, provide for any provision of the order to come into operation on different days for different purposes.

Amendments

a £30,000 converted to €38,092.14 by Council Regulations (EC) No 1103/97, No 974/98 and No 2866/98 and the Economic and Monetary Union Act 1998, s 6.

Definitions

'the authorised minimum': C(A)A 1983, s 2(1), s 19; 'company': CA 1963, s 2(1); 'the Companies Acts': C(A)A 1983, s 2(1); 'debenture': CA 1963, s 2(1); 'the Minister': C(A)A 1983, s 2(1); 'public limited company': C(A)A 1983, s 2(1); 'share': CA 1963, s 2(1).

Notes

Authorised minimum capital: The sum of €38,092.14 represents the minimum nominal share capital with which a plc may be incorporated[1] and the minimum allotted share capital which it needs to obtain a certificate allowing it to commence business and exercise its borrowing powers.[2] It also represents the minimum amount of allotted share capital which a private company must have in order to re-register as a plc.[3] Whilst the Minister may make orders varying the amount of the authorised minimum together with appropriate consequential orders of the type specified in C(A)A 1983, s 19(2), no such orders have been made to date.

1 C(A)A 1983, s 5(2).

2 C(A)A 1983, s 6(2).

3 C(A)A 1983, s 10(1)(a).

Investment company: The provisions of C(A)A 1983, s 19 do not apply to investment companies. See CA 1990, s 260.

20 Authority of company required for allotment of certain securities by directors

(1) The directors of a company shall not exercise any power of the company to allot relevant securities, unless the directors are, in accordance with this section, authorised to do so by—

(a) the company in general meeting; or

(b) the articles of the company.

(2) Authority for the purposes of this section may be given for a particular exercise of that power or for the exercise of that power generally, and may be unconditional or subject to conditions.

(3) Any such authority shall state the maximum amount of relevant securities that may be allotted thereunder and the date on which the authority will expire, which shall be not more than five years from whichever is relevant of the following dates—

(a) in the case of an authority contained at the time of the original incorporation of the company in the articles of the company, the date of that incorporation; and

(b) in any other case, the date on which the resolution is passed by virtue of which that authority is given;

but any such authority (including an authority contained in the articles of the company) may be previously revoked or varied by the company in general meeting.

(4) Any such authority (whether or not it has been previously renewed under this subsection) may be renewed by the company in general meeting for a further period not exceeding five years; but the resolution must state (or restate) the amount of relevant securities which may be allotted under the authority or, as the case may be, the amount remaining to be allotted thereunder, and must specify the date on which the renewed authority will expire.

(5) The directors may allot relevant securities, notwithstanding that any authority for the purposes of this section has expired, if the relevant securities are allotted in pursuance of an offer or agreement made by the company before the authority expired and the authority allowed it to make an offer or agreement which would or might require relevant securities to be allotted after the authority expired.

(6) A resolution of a company to give, vary, revoke or renew such an authority may, notwithstanding that it alters the articles of the company, be an ordinary resolution but section 143 of the Principal Act shall apply to it.

(7) Any director who knowingly and wilfully contravenes, or permits or authorises a contravention of, this section shall be guilty of an offence.

(8) Nothing in this section shall affect the validity of any allotment of relevant securities.

(9) This section does not apply to any allotment of relevant securities by a company, other than a public limited company registered as such on its original incorporation, if it is made in pursuance of an offer or agreement made before the date on which the earlier of the following events occurs, that is to say, the holding of the first general meeting of the company after its re-registration or registration as a public limited company and the end of the general transitional period; but any resolution to give, vary or revoke an authority for the purposes of this section shall have effect for those purposes if it is passed at any time after the passing of this Act.

(10) In this section 'relevant securities' means, in relation to a company,—

(a) shares in the company other than shares shown in the memorandum to have been taken by the subscribers thereto or shares allotted in pursuance of an employees' share scheme; and

(b) any right to subscribe for, or to convert any security into, shares in the company other than shares so allotted; and any reference to the allotment of relevant securities shall include a reference to the grant of such a right but shall not include any reference to the allotment of shares pursuant to such a right.

Definitions

'articles': CA 1963, s 2(1); 'company': CA 1963, s 2(1); 'director': CA 1963, s 2(1); 'employees' share scheme': C(A)A 1983, s 2(1); 'the general transitional period': C(A)A 1983, s 2(1); 'the Principal Act': C(A)A 1983, s 2(1); 'relevant securities': C(A)A 1983, s 20(10); 'share': CA 1963, s 2(1).

Notes

Duty not to misuse power of allotment: The directors of a company must exercise their powers, including the power to allot shares, in good faith for the benefit of the company as a whole and for proper purposes.[1] If the directors have mixed motives for exercising their power of allotment, regard must be had to the dominant motive in determining whether or not there has been a breach of duty.[2] So, for example, it has been held to amount to a breach of duty for directors to allot shares to themselves or their associates for the purpose of giving themselves control of the company.[3] Indeed, to so act may also amount to oppression and/or disregard of interest of the other members of the company, entitling them to relief under CA 1963, s 205.[4] It may also amount to a breach of duty for the directors to allot shares for the dominant purpose of fending off a takeover bid.[5]

1 *Nash v Lancegaye Safety Glass (Ireland) Ltd* 1958) 92 ILTR 1; *G and S Doherty Ltd v Doherty* (19 June 1969, unreported) HC (Henchy J); *Mills v Mills* (1938) 60 CLR 150; *Harlowe's Nominees Pty Ltd v Woodside (Lakes Entrance) Oil Co NL* (1968) 121 CLR 483; *Teck Corporation Ltd v Millar* (1972) 3 DLR (3d) 288; *Punt v Symons and Co Ltd* [1903] 2 Ch 506; *Piercy v S Mills and Co Ltd* [1920] 1 Ch 77; *Hogg v Cramphorn* [1967] Ch 254; *Bamford v Bamford* [1969] 2 WLR 1107; *Howard Smith Ltd v Ampol Petroleum Ltd* [1974] AC 821; *Clemens v Clemens Bros Ltd* [1976] 2 All ER 268; *Whitehouse v Carlton Party Ltd* [1976] 2 All ER 268.

2 *Nash v Lancegaye Safety Glass (Ireland) Ltd* 1958) 92 ILTR 1; *Afric Sive Ltd v Gas and Exploration Ltd* [1989] IEHC 35; *Mills v Mills* (1938) 60 CLR 150; *Harlowe's Nominees Pty Ltd v Woodside (Lakes Entrance) Oil Co NL* (1968) 121 CLR 483; *Teck Corporation Ltd v Millar* (1972) 3 DLR (3d) 288; *Hogg v Cramphorn* [1967] Ch 254; *Howard Smith Ltd v Ampol Petroleum Ltd* [1974] AC 821; *Re Jermyn Street Turkish Baths Ltd* [1971] 1 WLR 1042; *Whitehouse v Carlton Party Ltd* [1976] 2 All ER 268; *Mutual Life Insurance Co of New York v The Rank Organisation Ltd* [1985] BCLC 11; *CAS (Nominees) Ltd v Nottingham Forest plc* [2002] 1 BCLC 613.

3 *Nash v Lancegaye Safety Glass (Ireland) Ltd* 1958) 92 ILTR 1; *G and S Doherty Ltd v Doherty* (19 June 1969, unreported) HC (Henchy J); *Punt v Symons and Co Ltd* [1903] 2 Ch 506; *Piercy v S Mills and Co Ltd* [1920] 1 Ch 77; *Whitehouse v Carlton Party Ltd* [1976] 2 All ER 268.

4 *Clemens v Clemens Bros Ltd* [1976] 2 All ER 268. *Re a company* (*Case No 005136 of 1986*) [1987] BCLC 82; *Re Chez Nico (Restaurants) Ltd* [1992] BCLC 192. On the other hand, it may not be oppressive to allot shares to a director or to some other third party which confer majority control where the allotment is part of a rescue package aimed at saving the company: *Re Jermyn Street Turkish Baths Ltd* [1971] 1 WLR 1042; *CAS (Nominees) Ltd v Nottingham Forest plc* [2002] 1 BCLC 613.

5 *Hogg v Cramphorn* [1967] Ch 254; *Howard Smith Ltd v Ampol Petroleum Ltd* [1974] AC 821. However, in *Teck Corporation Ltd v Millar* (1972) 3 DLR (3d) 288 it was suggested that such an allotment might be proper where the directors honestly and reasonably believed that the interests of the company would be substantially damaged in the event of the takeover bid being successful. It must be doubtful whether such reasoning would find favour with the courts in this jurisdiction. In any event, the ability to use the power of allotment to fend of such a takeover bid is now greatly curtailed by the pre-emption provisions contained in C(A)A 1983, s 23.

Authorisation to allot shares: C(A)A 1983, Table A, Part 1, reg 5 confers on the directors a general power to allot shares which is accordingly open to potential abuse of the type described above. However that power of allotment is expressly stated to be 'subject to the provisions of the Companies Acts'. In this regard, the provisions of C(A)A 1983, s 20, whilst of course not eliminating the risk of abuse, nonetheless greatly curtail the ability of the directors to misuse their powers, by conferring on the shareholders an important role in authorising the exercise of allotment. The section stipulates that the directors may not exercise their power of allotment in respect of 'relevant securities'[1] unless authorised to do so by the company in general meeting or by the articles of association.[2] The authorisation may be given generally or for the purpose of a particular allotment and may also be given conditionally or unconditionally.[3] In either case though, the authorisation must state the maximum amount of relevant securities that may be allotted by the directors and must also stipulate a date on which the authorisation will lapse.[4] The maximum period of authorisation is five years,[5] although such authorisation may be revoked at any time by resolution of the members in general meeting.[6] It may also be renewed from time to time, again for further periods of up to five years each.[7] For the purpose of giving, varying, revoking or renewing an authorisation to allot relevant securities, an ordinary resolution will suffice, even though it may have the effect of altering the articles of association (eg where the articles provide for a five-year authorisation, but the members resolve to prematurely terminate that authorisation).[8] The resolution must however be filed in the Companies Registration Office in the same way as if it were a special resolution[9] and notice of its delivery must be published in the Companies Registration Office Gazette.[10]

1 'Relevant securities' include not only all shares (other than subscribers' shares and shares forming part of an employee share scheme) but also rights to subscribe for shares, or to convert any security such a debenture stock, into shares: C(A)A 1983, s 20(10).

2 C(A)A 1983, s 20(1).

3 C(A)A 1983, s 20(2).

4 C(A)A 1983, s 20(3).

5 C(A)A 1983, s 20(3).

6 C(A)A 1983, s 20(3).

7 C(A)A 1983, s 20(4).

8 C(A)A 1983, s 20(6). Normally, under CA 1963, s 15 a special resolution would be required to amend the articles of association.

9 C(A)A 1983, s 20(6).

10 C(A)A 1983, s 55(1)(b).

Allotments after expiry of authorisation: A share is to be taken as having been allotted in a company when a person acquires an unconditional right to be included in the register of members in respect of that share.[1] Even though the directors' power of allotment may have expired they may still allot relevant securities in pursuance of an offer or agreement validly made by the company before the authorisation actually expired and provided also that the authorisation permitted the directors to make offers or enter into agreements which would or might require the actual allotment to take place after the authorisation itself had actually expired.[2]

1 C(A)A 1983, s 2(2).

2 C(A)A 1983, s 20(5).

Allotment of relevant securities without authorisation: Any director who knowingly allots or permits or authorised an allotment of relevant securities without due authorisation, either under the articles or from the members in general meeting, is guilty of an offence.[1] The allotment itself will not be rendered validly simply because of a breach of C(A)A 1983, s 20[2] but it may be rendered invalid if capable of being impugned on some other basis, as where it is established that the allotment was effected by the directors in bad faith or for an improper purpose or otherwise than for the benefit of the company as a whole.[3] In such circumstances, the court may nonetheless validate the allotment if satisfied that it is just and equitable to do so (eg where bona fide allottees for value without notice of the breach of directors' duties would otherwise be adversely affected).[4]

Pre-emption rights on allotment of securities: See C(A)A 1983, ss 23–25 and the notes thereto.

1 C(A)A 1983, s 20(7).

2 C(A)A 1983, s 20(8).

3 *Nash v Lancegaye Safety Glass (Ireland) Ltd* 1958) 92 ILTR 1; *G and S Doherty Ltd v Doherty* (19 June 1969, unreported) HC (Henchy J); *Punt v Symons and Co Ltd* [1903] 2 Ch 506; *Piercy v S Mills and Co Ltd* [1920] 1 Ch 77; *Hogg v Cramphorn* [1967] Ch 254; *Bamford v Bamford* [1969] 2 WLR 1107; *Howard Smith Ltd v Ampol Petroleum Ltd* [1974] AC 821; *Clemens v Clemens Bros Ltd* [1976] 2 All ER 268; *Whitehouse v Carlton Party Ltd* [1976] 2 All ER 268.

4 CA 1963, s 89. See also *Re Sugar Distributors Ltd* [1995] 2 IR 194.

Investment companies: The provisions of C(A)A 1983, s 20(3) and (4) do not apply to investment companies.

1 CA 1990, 260(3).

UK legislation

See CA 1985, s 80 (amended by CA 1989, s 115(1)).

---

21 Shares and debentures of private company not to be offered to public

[(1) A private company and any officer of the company who is in default shall be guilty of an offence if the company—

(a) offers to the public (whether for cash or otherwise) any shares in or debentures of the company, or

(b) allots, or agrees to allot, (whether for cash or otherwise) any shares in or debentures of the company with a view to all or any of those shares or debentures being offered for sale to the public.

(2) Subsection (1) does not apply to the following offers or allotments (wheresoever made):

(a) an offer of debentures addressed or allotment made solely to qualified investors,

(b) an offer of debentures addressed to fewer than 100 persons, other than qualified investors,

(c) an offer of debentures addressed to investors where the minimum consideration payable pursuant to the offer is at least €50,000 per investor, for each separate offer,

(d) an offer of debentures whose denomination per unit amounts to at least €50,000,

(e) an offer of debentures where the offer expressly limits the amount of the total consideration for the offer to less than €100,000, or

(f) an offer of those classes of instruments which are normally dealt in on the money market (such as treasury bills, certificates of deposit and commercial papers) having a maturity of less than 12 months,

(g) an offer of shares addressed to—

(i) qualified investors, or

(ii) 99 or fewer persons, or

(iii) both qualified investors and 99 or fewer other persons,

(h) an allotment of shares or debentures, an agreement to make such an allotment, with a view to those shares or debentures being the subject of any one or more of the offers referred to in paragraphs (a) to (g).

(3) A word or expression that is used in this section and is also used in the Prospectus (Directive 2003/71/EC) Regulations 2005 (S.I. No.324 of 2005) shall have in this section the same meaning as it has in those Regulations.

(4) Nothing in this section shall affect the validity of any allotment or sale of shares or debentures or of any agreement to allot or sell shares or debentures.

(5) A person guilty of an offence under subsection (1) shall be liable on summary conviction to a fine not exceeding €1,904.61.][a]

Amendments

a This section was substituted by IFCMPA 2006, s 8 with effect from 1 July 2005.[1]

1 IFCMPA 2006, s 2(3): C(A)A 1983, s 21, as amended by IFCMPA 2006, s 8, is deemed to come into effect on 1 July 2005. This is the date on which Directive 2003/71/EC was implemented in Ireland by virtue of the Prospectus (Directive 2003/71/EC) Regulations 2005 (SI 324/2005) and IFCMPA 2005.

Definitions

'company': CA 1963, s 2(1), Prospectus Regs, reg 2(1); 'debenture': CA 1963, s 2(1); 'officer': CA 1963, s 2(1); 'offer (of securities) to the public': Prospectus Regs, reg 2(1). 'officer in default': CA 1963, s 383; 'qualified investors': Prospectus Regs, reg 2(1). 'the Principal Act': C(A)A 1983, s 2(1); 'person': IA 2005, s 18(c); 'private company': CA 1963, s 2(1), s 33(1); 'qualified investors': Prospectus Regs, reg 2(1); 'shares': CA 1963, s 2(1).

Notes

Offer to the public of shares in or debentures of a private company: It is an essential characteristic of a private company[1] that its articles should prohibit any invitation to the public[2] to subscribe for any of its shares or debentures. This section adds teeth to that prohibition by imposing criminal sanctions on the company itself and on any officer in default where the company makes such an offer or allots or agrees to allot shares or debentures with a view to all or any of those shares or debentures being offered for sale to the public.[3]

While Prospectus (Directive 2003/71/EC) Regulations 2005 (SI 324/2005), reg 9 excludes certain offers of securities made in the State, the exclusions from criminal sanctions contained in C(A)A 1983, s 21(2) apply to those offers, 'wheresoever' made.

Notably though, an allotment or sale or agreement to allot or sell shares or debentures made in breach of this section will not be invalidated.[4] It is also worth noting that C(A)A 1983, s 21(1)(as amended by IFCMPA 2006, s 8) does not state that it imposes criminal sanctions on the company or any officer in default where there is an offer to the public of securities (other than shares or debentures) by a private company.

1 CA 1963, s 33(1).

2 As to what constitutes an invitation to the 'public' this is now construed in accordance with the definition in the Prospectus (Directive 2003/71/EC) Regulations 2005 (SI 324/2005) which transposed the Prospectus Directive 2003/71/EC.

3 C(A)A 1983, s 21(1).

4 C(A)A 1983, s 21(4). For the consequences of failing to comply with the statutory conditions constituting a company a private company see CA 1963, s 34.

---

22 Document containing offer to state whether shares will be allotted where issue not fully subscribed

(1) Without prejudice to section 53 of the Principal Act no allotment shall be made of any share capital of a public limited company offered for subscription unless—

(a) that capital is subscribed for in full; or

(b) the offer states that, even if the capital is not subscribed for in full, the amount of that capital subscribed for may be allotted in any event or in the event of the conditions specified in the offer being satisfied.

and, where conditions are so specified, no allotment of the capital shall be made by virtue of paragraph (b) unless those conditions are satisfied.

(2) Section 53 (4) and section 55 of the Principal Act shall apply where shares are prohibited from being allotted by subsection (1) as they apply where the conditions mentioned in subsection (1) of the said section 53 are not complied with; and subsection (5) of the said section 53 shall apply to this section as it applies to that section.

(3) The provisions of this section shall apply in the case of shares offered as wholly or partly payable otherwise than in cash as they apply in the case of shares offered for subscription and—

(a) in subsection (1), the word 'subscribed' shall be construed accordingly; and

(b) in the said section 53 (4), as it applies by virtue of subsection (2) to the former case, references to the repayment of money received from applicants for shares shall include references to the return of any other consideration so received (including, if the case so requires, the release of the applicant from any undertaking) or, if it is not reasonably practicable to return the consideration, the payment of money equal to the value of the consideration at the time it was so received, and references to interest shall have effect accordingly.

Definitions

'the Principal Act': C(A)A 1983, s 2(1); 'public limited company': C(A)A 1983, s 2(1); 'shares': CA 1963, s 2(1).

Notes

Minimum subscription for a plc's shares: See CA 1963 and the notes thereto.

UK legislation

See CA 1985, s 84 (amended by FSA 1986).

Pre-emption rights

23 Pre-emption rights

(1) Subject to the following provisions of this section and sections 24 and 25, a company proposing to allot any equity securities—

(a) shall not allot any of those securities on any terms to any person unless it has made an offer to each person who holds relevant shares or relevant employee shares to allot to him on the same or more favourable terms a proportion of those securities which is as nearly as practicable equal to the proportion in nominal value held by him of the aggregate of relevant shares and relevant employee shares;

and

(b) shall not allot any of those securities to any person unless the period during which any such offer may be accepted has expired or the company has received notice of the acceptance or refusal of every offer so made.

(2) Subsection (3) applies to any provision of the memorandum or articles of a company which requires the company, when proposing to allot equity securities consisting of relevant shares of any particular class, not to allot those securities on any terms unless it has complied with the condition that it makes such an offer as is described in subsection (1) to each person who holds relevant shares or relevant employee shares of that class.

(3) If, in accordance with a provision to which this subsection applies—

(a) a company makes an offer to allot any securities to such a holder; and

(b) he or anyone in whose favour he has renounced his right to their allotment accepts the offer.

subsection (1) shall not apply to the allotment of those securities and the company may allot them accordingly; but this subsection is without prejudice to the application of subsection (1) in any other case.

(4) Subsection (1) shall not apply in relation to a particular allotment of equity securities if the securities are, or are to be, wholly or partly paid up otherwise than in cash.

(5) Securities which a company has offered to allot to a holder of relevant shares or relevant employee shares may be allotted to him or anyone in whose favour he has renounced his right to their allotment without contravening subsection (1)(b).

(6) Subsection (1) shall not apply in relation to the allotment or any securities which would apart from a renunciation or assignment of the right to their allotment be held under an employees' share scheme.

(7) An offer which is required by subsection (1) or by any provision to which subsection (3) applies to be made to any person shall be made by serving it on him in the manner in which notices are authorised to be given by regulations 133, 134 and 135 of Table A; but where he is the holder of a share warrant the offer may instead be made by causing the offer, or a notice specifying where a copy of the offer can be obtained or inspected, to be published in [the Companies Registration Office Gazette][a].

(8) Any such offer as is mentioned in subsection (7) must state a period of not less than 21 days during which the offer may be accepted; and the offer shall not be withdrawn before the end of that period.

(9) Subsections (7) and (8) shall not invalidate a provision to which subsection (3) applies by reason that that provision requires or authorises an offer thereunder to be made in contravention of one or both of those subsections, but, to the extent that the provision requires or authorises such an offer to be so made, it shall be of no effect.

(10) Subsection (1), (7) or (8) may, in its application in relation to allotments by a private company of equity securities or to such allotments of a particular description, be excluded by a provision contained in the memorandum or articles of that company; and a requirement or authority contained in the memorandum or articles of a private company shall, if it is inconsistent with any of those subsections, have effect as a

provision excluding that subsection, but a provision to which subsection (3) applies shall not be treated as being inconsistent with subsection (1).

(11) Where there is a contravention of subsections (1), (7) or (8) or of a provision to which subsection (3) applies, the company, and every officer of the company who knowingly authorised or permitted the contravention, shall be jointly and severally liable to compensate any person to whom an offer should have been made under the subsection or provision contravened for any loss, damage, costs or expenses which that person has sustained or incurred by reason of the contravention; but no proceedings to recover any such loss, damage, costs or expenses shall be commenced after the expiration of two years from the delivery to the registrar of companies of the return of allotments in question or, where equity securities other than shares are granted, from the date of the grant.

(12) In relation to any offer to allot any securities required by subsection (1) or by any provision to which subsection (3) applies, references in this section (however expressed) to the holder of shares of any descriptions shall be read as including references to any person who held shares of that description on any day within the period of twenty-eight days ending with the day immediately preceding the date of the offer.

(13) In this section and sections 24 and 25—

'equity security', in relation to a company, means a relevant share in the company(other than a share shown in the memorandum to have been taken by a subscriber thereto or a bonus share) or a right to subscribe for, or to convert any securities into, relevant shares in the company, and references to the allotment of equity securities or of equity securities consisting of relevant shares of a particular class shall include references to the grant of a right to subscribe for, or to convert any securities into, relevant shares in the company or, as the case may be, relevant shares of a particular class, but shall not include references to the allotment of any relevant shares pursuant to such a right;

'relevant employee shares', in relation to a company, means shares of the company which would be relevant shares in the company but for the fact that they are held by a person who acquired them in pursuance of an employees' share scheme; and

'relevant shares' in relation to a company, means shares in the company other than—

(a) shares which as respects dividends and capital carry a right to participate only up to a specified amount in a distribution; and

(b) shares which are held by a person who acquired them in pursuance of an employees' share scheme, or, in the case of shares which have not been allotted, are to be allotted in pursuance of such a scheme;

and any reference to a class of shares shall be construed as a reference to shares to which the same rights are attached as to voting and as to participation, both as respects dividends and as respects capital, in a distribution.

Amendments

a Words substituted by IFCMPA 2005, s 72.

Definitions

'articles': CA 1963, s 2(1); 'company': CA 1963, s 2(1); 'employees' share scheme': C(A)A 1983, s 2(1); 'equity securities': C(A)A 1983, s 23(13); 'memorandum': CA 1963, s 2(1); 'private company': CA 1963, s 2(1), s 33(1); 'officer': CA 1963, s 2(1); 'Registrar of Companies': CA 1963, s 2(1); 'relevant shares': C(A)A 1983, s 23(13); 'relevant employee shares': C(A)A 1983, s 23(13); 'shares': CA 1963, s 2(1).

Notes

Forms of pre-emption rights: There are two broad types of pre-emption rights that may be enjoyed by the members of a company. The first is a right of pre-emption in respect of the transfer of shares already in issue, whereas the second is a right of pre-emption in respect of the allotment of new securities. Prior to the coming into force of C(A)A 1983 on 13 October 1983,[1] there was no statutory scheme for the conferral of either type of pre-emption right on the existing members of a company. Instead, such rights would often be provided for either by way of express provisions in the memorandum or articles of association[2] or by way of a separate shareholders' agreement.[3] Whilst C(A)A 1983, s 23 now provides statutory pre-emption rights in respect of the allotment of certain types of securities, it affords no such rights in respect of the transfer of shares which still fall to be governed by whatever contractual provisions, if any, the members themselves may have chosen to adopt. Moreover, even the statutory pre-emption rights may be disapplied in the circumstances set out in s 24.

1 Companies (Amendment) Act 1983 (Commencement) Order 1983 (SI 288/1983).

2 There are no pre-emption provisions in the Model Form Articles contained in C(A)A 1983, Table A.

3 In relation to the ability of a shareholders' agreement to override the provisions of the memorandum and articles of association see by way of example *TGM v Al Babtain Trading* [1982] ILRM 349; *Telenor Invest AS v IIU Nominees Ltd and Esat Telecom Holdings Ltd* [1999] IEHC 188 (O'Sullivan J); *Cane v Jones* [1981] 1 All ER 533; *Harman v BML Group Ltd* [1994] 1 WLR 893.

Securities covered by statutory pre-emption rights: Not every type of security issued by a company will be caught by the pre-emption provisions of C(A)A 1983, s 23. In the first place, the section applies only to the allotment of 'equity securities'[1] which are defined[2] as meaning 'relevant shares' and rights to subscribe for, or to convert other securities into 'relevant shares'. A share is not a 'relevant share' if: (a) as respects dividends and capital, it carries a right to participate only up to a specified amount in a distribution;[3] or (b) it is allotted as part of an employee share scheme or if the person holding it acquired it in pursuance of such a scheme.[4] Also excluded from the scope of the statutory pre-emption provisions are allotments of bonus shares[5] and allotments of shares which are, or are to be, wholly- or partly-paid up by way of a non-cash consideration.[6]

1 C(A)A 1983, s 23(1).

2 C(A)A 1983, s 23(13).

3 C(A)A 1983, s 23(13). It would seem therefore that a share may be a 'relevant share' if the restriction on participation beyond a specified amount in a distribution applies only as to dividends or capital, but not as to both.

4 C(A)A 1983, s 23(13). See also s 23(6).

5 C(A)A 1983, s 23(13). Bonus shares fall outside the definition of equity securities.

6 C(A)A 1983, s 23(4).

Nature of statutory pre-emption rights: According to C(A)A 1983, s 23(1) a company may not allot any equity securities' to a third party without first offering them *pro rata* on the same or more favourable terms to the existing holders of the company's 'relevant shares' and 'relevant employee shares'[1] and to all persons who held such shares in the period of 28 days immediately preceding the date of the offer.[2] Such an offer is to be served on the existing members in the same manner as is prescribed by C(A)A 1983, Table A, regs 13–135 for the service of notices on members and must afford members not less than 21 days within which to accept.[4] During that period of time, the offer cannot be withdrawn[5] and the securities cannot be allotted to anyone else.[6] Curiously, the section does not state what is to happen if only some of the securities are taken up in pursuance of this offer. Should the company keep offering the balance of the securities to willing members until they have all been taken up or should it instead proceed to start offering the balance to interested third parties? The adoption of either course would appear to be in conformity with the legislation. To avoid any uncertainty as to how the directors should proceed, the manner of dealing with any securities not taken up by existing members in pursuance of the statutory offer should be dealt with in the memorandum or articles of association or alternatively in the actual terms of offer.

1 'Relevant employee shares' are shares which would be 'relevant shares but for the fact that they have been acquired in pursuance of an employee share scheme. The effect of this definition is, therefore, that where what would otherwise be 'relevant shares' are being allotted as part of an employee share scheme, the pre-emption provisions do not apply and the shares do not have to first be offered to the other members of the company. However, once they have been allotted they enjoy the same pre-emption rights as 'relevant shares' and accordingly if any new equity securities' they enjoy the same pre-emption rights as 'relevant shares'.

2 C(A)A 1983, s 23(12).

3 C(A)A 1983, s 23(7). Such service may be effected personally or by post to the member's registered address. In the case of joint holders of a share, service may be effected on the person fist named in the register of members in respect of the share. In the case of the death or bankruptcy of a member, service may be effected on the personal representatives or on the official assignee, as the case may be, provided that their respective addresses have been notified to the company.

4 C(A)A 1983, s 23(8). Rather than taking the shares himself, an existing member may renounce his right of allotment in favour of a third party. An allotment of shares to the person in whose favour the renouncement has been made, will not be regarded as being a breach of the statutory pre-emption provisions: C(A)A 1983, s 23(2) and (3).

5 C(A)A 1983, s 23(8).

6 C(A)A 1983, s 23(1)(b).

Effect of a breach of the statutory pre-emption provisions: Notably, an allotment of shares will not be invalidated merely for being in breach of the statutory pre-emption provisions. It may, however, be rendered invalid if capable of being impugned on some other basis, as where it is established that the allotment was effected by the directors in bad faith or for an improper purpose or otherwise than for the benefit of the company as a whole.[1] However, if and insofar as there has been a breach of C(A)A 1983, s 24 the company and every officer who knowingly authorised or permitted the breach will be jointly and severally liable to compensate any person to whom an offer of share should have been made and who has suffered loss, damage, costs or expenses as a result.[2] Any such proceedings must be commenced within two years of the delivery of the return of allotments to the Registrar[3] or within two years of the date of the grant of the options to subscribe for or convert securities into shares, as the case may be.[4]

1 *Nash v Lancegaye Safety Glass (Ireland) Ltd* 1958) 92 ILTR 1; *G and S Doherty Ltd v Doherty* (19 June 1969, unreported) HC (Henchy J); *Punt v Symons and Co Ltd* [1903] 2 Ch 506; *Piercy v S Mills and Co Ltd* [1920] 1 Ch 77; *Hogg v Cramphorn* [1967] Ch 254; *Bamford v Bamford* [1969] 2 WLR 1107; *Howard Smith Ltd v Ampol Petroleum Ltd* [1974] AC 821; *Clemens v Clemens Bros Ltd* [1976] 2 All ER 268; *Whitehouse v Carlton Party Ltd* [1976] 2 All ER 268.

2 C(A)A 1983, s 23(11).

3 See CA 1963, s 58 in relation to the filing of returns of allotments.

4 C(A)A 1983, s 23(11). A share is to be taken as having been allotted in a company when a person acquires an unconditional right to be included in the register of members in respect of that share: C(A)A 1983, s 2(2).

Disapplication of statutory pre-emption provisions: The statutory pre-emption provisions may be disapplied in several situations. Firstly, they may be disapplied by a provision to that effect in the company's memorandum or articles of association.[1] Secondly, where the directors have been generally authorised to allot shares under C(A)A 1983, s 20, they may be given power by the articles or by a special resolution to allot equity securities as if s 23 did not apply or applied only in some modified form.[2] Thirdly, where the directors have been authorised (whether generally or otherwise) by s 20 to allot shares, they may be authorised by special resolution in relation to a particular allotment to effect that allotment as if s 23 did not apply or applied only in some modified form.[3] In these second and third instances, the authorisation to disapply or modify s 23 will lapse with the s 20 authorisation itself.[4] However, just as the s 20 authorisation may be renewed, so too the disapplication or modification of s 23 may be renewed, albeit by special resolution.[5] Furthermore, even though the power or resolution authorising the directors to allot equity securities without regard for s 23 may have expired, they may still allot equity securities in pursuance of an offer or agreement validly made by the company before that power or resolution actually expired and provided also that the power or resolution, as the case may be, permitted the directors to make offers or agreement which would or might require the actual allotment to take place after the power or resolution had actually expired.[6] Finally, it is to be noted that the statutory pre-emption provisions do not apply to investment companies.[7]

1 C(A)A 1983, s 23(10). According to this subsection, any inconsistent provision in the memorandum or articles of a private company will have the effect of disapplying C(A)A 1983, s 23. Accordingly, the very fact of a private company devising its own pre-emption rules would seemingly result in s 23 being disapplied. On the other hand, in the case of a public company, the disapplication would seemingly have to be express.

2 C(A)A 1983, s 24(1). In the case of a special resolution disapplying the statutory pre-emption provisions notice of its delivery to the Registrar of Companies must be published in the Companies Registration Office Gazette: C(A)A 1983, s 55(1)(c).

3 C(A)A 1983, s 24(2). Notice of the delivery of the special resolution to the Registrar of Companies must be published in the Companies Registration Office Gazette: C(A)A 1983, s 55(1)(c). Such a resolution cannot be proposed nor can any resolution be proposed for its renewal unless it has been recommended by the directors and there has been circulated, with the notice of the meeting at which the resolution is to be proposed a written statement by the directors setting out their reasons for making the recommendation and the amount to be paid to the company in respect of the securities to be allotted: C(A)A 1983, s 24(5).

4 C(A)A 1983, s 24(3).

5 C(A)A 1983, s 24(3). Notice of the delivery of the special resolution to the Registrar of Companies must be published in the Companies Registration Office Gazette: C(A)A 1983, s 55(1)(c).

6 C(A)A 1983, s 24(4).

7 CA 1990, s 260(2).

Pre-emption rights on transfer of shares: As observed above, such rights arise as a matter of contract only and not pursuant to statute. In this regard, see CA 1963, s 79 and the notes thereto.

Investment company: The provisions of C(A)A 1983, ss 23–25 do not apply to investment companies. See CA 1990, s 260.

UK legislation

See CA 1985, ss 89–92, 94.

24 Further provisions relating to pre-emption rights

(1) Where the directors of a company are generally authorised for the purposes of section 20, they may be given power by the articles or by a special resolution of the company to allot equity securities pursuant to that authority as if—

(a) section 23(1) did not apply to the allotment;

or

(b) that subsection applied to the allotment with such modifications as the directors may determine;

and where the directors make an allotment under this subsection, the said section 23, shall have effect accordingly.

(2) Where the directors of a company are authorised for the purposes of section 20 (whether generally or otherwise), the company may by special resolution resolve either—

(a) that section 23(1) shall not apply to a specified allotment of equity securities to be made pursuant to that authority; or

(b) that that subsection shall apply to the allotment with such modifications as may be specified in the resolution;

and where such a resolution is passed the said section 23 shall have effect accordingly.

(3) A power conferred by virtue of subsection (1) or a special resolution under subsection (2) shall cease to have effect when the authority to which it relates is revoked or would, if not renewed, expire, but if that authority is renewed, the power or, as the case may be, the resolution may also be renewed, for a period not longer than that for which the authority is renewed, by a special resolution of the company.

(4) Notwithstanding that any such power or resolution has expired, the directors may allot equity securities in pursuance of an offer or agreement previously made by the company, if the power or resolution enabled the company to make an offer or agreement which would or might require equity securities to be allotted after it expired.

(5) A special resolution under subsection (2), or a special resolution to renew such a resolution, shall not be proposed unless it is recommended by the directors and there has been circulated, with the notice of the meeting at which the resolution is proposed, to the members entitled to have that notice a written statement by the directors setting out—

(a) their reasons for making the recommendation;

(b) the amount to be paid to the company in respect of the equity securities to be allotted; and

(c) the directors' justification of that amount.

(6) A person who knowingly or recklessly authorises or permits the inclusion in a statement circulated under subsection (5) of any matter which is misleading, false or deceptive in a material particular shall be guilty of an offence.

Definitions

'company': CA 1963, s 2(1); 'director': CA 1963, s 2(1); 'equity securities': C(A)A 1983, s 2(1), s 23(13).

Notes

Disapplication of statutory pre-emption provisions: See C(A)A 1983, s 23 and the notes thereto.

Investment companies: The provisions of C(A)A 1983, ss 23–25 do not apply to investment companies.[1]

1 CA 1990, s 260(2).

UK legislation

See CA 1985, s 95.

---

25 Transitional provisions relating to pre-emption rights

(1) Sections 23 and 24, shall not apply—

(a) to any allotment of equity securities made by a company, other than a public limited company registered as such on its original incorporation, before the date on which the earlier of the following events occurs, that is to say, the holding of the first general meeting of the company after its re-registration or registration as a public limited company and the end of the general transitional period; or

(b) where subsection (2) applies, to an allotment of the equity securities which are subject to the requirement mentioned in that subsection.

(2) This subsection applies where any company which is re-registered or registered as a public limited company is or, but for the provisions of this Act, would be subject at the time of re-registration or, as the case may be, registration to a requirement imposed (whether by the company's memorandum or articles or otherwise) before the relevant time by virtue of which it must, when making an allotment of equity securities, make an offer to allot those securities or some of them in a manner which (otherwise than by virtue of its involving a contravention of section 23(7) or (8)) is inconsistent with section 23.

(3) Any requirement which—

(a) is imposed on a private company before the relevant time otherwise than by the company's memorandum or articles;

and

(b) if contained in the memorandum or articles of the company, would have effect by virtue of section 23(10) to the exclusion of any provision of that section,

shall have effect, so long as the company remains a private company, as if it were contained in the memorandum or articles of the company.

(4) If at the relevant time a company, other than a public limited company registered as such on its original incorporation, is subject to a requirement such as is mentioned in section 23(2) and which was imposed otherwise than by the company's memorandum or articles, the requirement shall be treated for the purposes of that section as if it were contained in the company's memorandum or articles.

(5) In this section 'the relevant time' means—

(a) except in a case falling within paragraph (b), the end of the general transitional period;

and

(b) in the case of a company which is re-registered or registered as a public limited company in pursuance of an application made before the end of that period, the time at which the application is made.

Definitions

'articles': CA 1963, s 2(1); 'company': CA 1963, s 2(1); 'equity securities' C(A)A 1983, s 2(1), s 23(13); 'the general transitional period': C(A)A 1983, s 2(1); 'memorandum': CA 1963, s 2(1); 'private company': CA 1963, s 2(1), s 33(1); 'public limited company': C(A)A 1983, s 2(1).

Notes

Transitional pre-emption provisions: C(A)A 1983, s 25 contained transitional pre-emption provisions covering the period to 12 April 1985.

Investment companies: The provisions of C(A)A 1983, ss 23–25 do not apply to investment companies.[1]

[1] CA 1990, s 260(2).

UK legislation

See CA 1985, s 96.

Payment for share capital

26 Subscription of share capital

(1) Subject to the following provisions of this Part, shares allotted by a company and any premium payable on them may be paid up in money or money's worth (including goodwill and expertise).

(2) A public limited company shall not accept at any time in payment up of its shares or any premium on them, an undertaking given by any person that he or another should do work or perform services for the company or any other person.

(3) Where a public limited company accepts such an undertaking as payment up of its shares or any premium payable on them, the holder of the shares when they or the premium are treated as paid up, in whole or in part, by the undertaking—

(a) shall be liable to pay the company in respect of those shares an amount equal to their nominal value, together with the whole of any premium or, if the case so requires, such proportion of that amount as is treated as paid up by the undertaking; and

(b) shall be liable to pay interest at the appropriate rate on the amount payable under paragraph (a).

(4) Where any person becomes a holder of any shares in respect of which—

(a) there has been a contravention of this section; and

(b) by virtue of that contravention, another is liable to pay any amount under this section, that person also shall be liable to pay that amount (jointly and severally with any other person so liable) unless either he is a purchaser for value and, at the time of the purchase, he did not have actual notice of the contravention or he derived title to the shares (directly or indirectly) from a person who became a holder of them after the contravention and was not so liable.

(5) Subsection (1) shall not prevent a company from allotting bonus shares in the company to its members or from paying up, with sums available for the purpose, any amounts for the time being unpaid on any of its shares (whether on account of the nominal value of the shares or by way of premium).

(6) References in this section to a holder, in relation to any shares in a company, include references to any person who has an unconditional right to be included in the company's register of members in respect of those shares or to have an instrument of transfer of the shares executed in his favour.

Definitions

'the appropriate rate': C(A)A 1983, s 2(1), (7); 'company': CA 1963, s 2(1); 'member': CA 1963, s 31; 'public limited company': C(A)A 1983, s 2(1); 'share': CA 1963, s 2(1).

Notes

Payment for shares

Cash and non-cash consideration: C(A)A 1983, s 26(1) recognises a well-established principle at common law, namely that a company may allot shares not only for cash but also for a non-cash consideration.[1] So, for example, shares have been allotted in consideration of the following: the transfer of a business of a company;[2] the transfer of patents;[3] the provision of services.[4] However, since as a matter of general contract law past consideration is no consideration,[5] it follows that shares allotted for such consideration will be treated as unpaid and the allottee will be liable to pay the full cash amount to the company.[6]

Prohibited non-cash consideration for a plc: Restrictions are imposed on the ability of a plc (or a private company or an unlimited company which has duly resolved to re-register as a plc)[7] to accept non-cash consideration for the allotment of shares. Subscriber shares must be paid for in cash.[8] Also, such a company may not accept either of the following in payment for shares:

(a) an undertaking from any person that he or another will do work or perform services for the company or for any other person;[9] or

(b) a non-cash consideration that is or includes an undertaking which is to be or may be performed more than five years after the date of allotment.[10]

If the company proceeds to allot shares in contravention of these restrictions or allots shares for a non-cash consideration, which consists of or includes an undertaking which was to be performed within five years of the date of allotment but which remains either wholly or partly unperformed at the end of that five-year period, the allottee becomes liable to pay to the company in cash an amount equivalent to the value attributed to the undertaking in question,[11] together with interest,[12] even though he still remains liable to the company to perform the undertaking as well.[13] Moreover, any subsequent holder of the shares (other than a purchaser for value without notice of the contravention or a person deriving his title from an innocent purchaser) will also be jointly and severally liable to pay the aforementioned cash amount plus interest, even though he may already have duly paid his predecessor in title.[14] The allottee or subsequent holder may, however, apply to court for relief from what would otherwise be a double liability to pay all or part of the price of the shares.[15]

Valuation of non-cash consideration payable to a plc: Even if the non-cash consideration payable to the plc (or payable to a private company or an unlimited company which has duly resolved to re-register as a plc)[16] is of a type which is not per se prohibited by the Companies Acts, the allotment must be preceded by an independent valuation of the consideration in question.[17] Failure to obtain such a valuation will result in the allottee being required to pay not only the non-cash consideration but also the cash equivalent and interest,[18] though in appropriate cases though, he may apply to court for relief against this double exposure.[19]

Valuation of non-cash consideration payable to other companies: In the case of other companies, there is no statutory mechanism for the valuation of the non-cash consideration payable in respect of an allotment of shares. Indeed, the courts have consistently held[20] that they will not inquire into the adequacy of the consideration paid for such shares unless:–

(a) there is evidence of fraud; or

(b) the contract demonstrates on its face that the consideration is manifestly inadequate or illusory.[21]

Although the court will not normally assess the adequacy of the non-cash consideration which has been paid for shares, it may be prepared to do so where the directors have themselves failed to make any such assessment in advance of the allotment.[22] Moreover, the absence of a bona fide valuation by the directors will result in the shares being treated as wholly unpaid and the shareholder will therefore be liable to pay to the company the nominal value of the shares in cash.[23] But if the allottee is unaware of the fact that there has been no bona fide valuation, he may be able to repudiate the allotment and thus avoid any liability.[24]

What constitutes payment in cash?: A share in a company is deemed to have been paid up in cash or to have been allotted for cash if the consideration for the allotment or the payment up is actual cash (whether domestic or foreign currency) received by the company or is an undertaking to pay cash to the company at a future date or is a cheque received by the company in good faith which the directors have no good reason for suspecting will not be paid.[25] In addition, shares are regarded as having been paid up in cash or allotted for cash to the extent that the consideration comprises the release of a liability of the company for a liquidated sum,[26] or where the cash amount payable under the contract of allotment is set off against moneys due by the company to the allottee pursuant to a separate transaction.[27] Indeed, to the extent that the creditor agrees to the discharge of his debt by the issue to a third party of shares which are credited as fully paid up, an allotment for cash will be regarded as having taken place.[28] On the other hand, the following will not be regarded as allotments for cash:

(a) payment of, or an undertaking to pay, cash to any person other than he company;[29]

(b) the allotment of shares in settlement of a liquidated claim for damages;[30]

(c) an allotment by way of accord and satisfaction;[31]

(d) an allotment of shares in discharge of liquidated sums which will be come payable by the company at a future date;[32] and

(e) the assignment to the company of a debt owed to the allottee by a third party.[33]

Return as to allotments: Every company having a share capital must make a return to the Registrar of Companies as to allotments of shares made by it.[34] Such returns must include, inter alia, details of any non-cash consideration paid or payable in respect of the shares. In this regard see CA 1963, s 58 and the notes thereto. In the case of a plc or a private company or unlimited which has duly resolved to re-register as a plc, any independent person's report on the value of non-cash consideration paid or payable to the company must be delivered to the Registrar of Companies at the same time as the return of allotments.[35] All returns of allotments made by a plc must be published in the Companies Registration Office Gazette.[36]

1 *Re Heyford Co, Pell's Case* (1869) 5 Ch App 11; *Re Wragg Ltd* [1897] 1 Ch 796; *Re Leinster Contract Corporation* [1902] 1 IR 349; *Mc Coy v Greene* [1984] IEHC 70 (Costello J).

2 *Re Wragg Ltd* [1897] 1 Ch 796.

3 *Re Leinster Contract Corporation* [1902] 1 IR 349.

4 *Mc Coy v Greene* [1984] IEHC 70 (Costello J).

5 Clark, *Contract Law in Ireland* (edn), ch 2.

6 *Re Eddystone Marine Insurance Co* [1893] 3 Ch 9; *Re Leinster Contract Corporation* [1902] 1 IR 349.

7 See C(A)A 1983, s 37(1).

8 C(A)A 1983, s 35.

9 C(A)A 1983, s 26(2).

10 C(A)A 1983, s 29(1). Any variation of a contract by a plc (including a contract made by it before it was registered or re-registered as a plc) will be unlawful if the effect of the variation is that shares are being or have been allotted wholly or partly in consideration of an undertaking which is to be or may be performed more than five years after the date of allotment: C(A)A 1983, s 29(3) and (4).

11 In the case of an undertaking which was to have been performed within five years of the date of allotment but which remains partly unperformed, the liability to make payment in cash relates only to the value attributable to that unperformed part: C(A)A 1983, s 29(5).

12 C(A)A 1983, s 26(3) and s 29(2) and (5).

13 C(A)A 1983, s 36.

14 C(A)A 1983, s 26(4) and s 29(6).

15 C(A)A 1983, s 34.

16 See C(A)A 1983, s 37(1).

17 C(A)A 1983, ss 30–33.

18 C(A)A 1983, s 36.

19 C(A)A 1983, s 34.

20 *Re Heyford Co, Pell's Case* (1869) 5 Ch App 11; *Re Baglan Hall Colliery Co* (1870) 5 Ch App 346; *Ooregum Gold Mining Co of India v Roper* [1892] AC 125; *Re Theatrical Trust Ltd, Chapman's Case* [1895] 1 Ch 771; *Re Wragg Ltd* [1897] 1 Ch 796; *Re Leinster Contract Corporation* [1902] 1 IR 349; *Hong Kong and China Glass Co v Glen* [1914] 1 Ch 527; *Pilmer v Duke Group Ltd* [2001] 2 BCLC 773.

21 *Ooregum Gold Mining Co of India v Roper* [1892] AC 125; *Re Theatrical Trust Ltd, Chapman's Case* [1895] 1 Ch 771; *Re Wragg Ltd* [1897] 1 Ch 796; *Mosley v Koffyfontein Mines Ltd* [1904] 2 Ch 108; *Park Business Interiors Ltd v Park* [1992] BCLC 1034.

22 *Tintin Exploration Syndicate Ltd v Sandys* (1947) 177 LT 412; *Hong Kong and China Gas Co Ltd v Glen* [1914] 1 Ch 527; *Re White Star Line Ltd* [1938] 1 All ER 607; *Re Alkaline Reduction Syndicate, Ames' Case* [1896] WN 79; *Park Business Interiors Ltd v Park* [1992] BCLC 1034.

23 *Re White Star Line Ltd* [1938] 1 All ER 607. The allottee, although liable to pay the nominal value of the shares in cash, should be able to sue for a quantum valebant or quantum meruit for the value of the non-cash consideration which he has furnished to the company. In a liquidation, however, such a claim cannot be the subject of set-off as between the shareholder and the company. Instead, the shareholder must first pay the full cash price to the liquidator and then prove in the winding up for the value of his claim: *Re Overend, Gurney and Co, Grissell's Case* (1866) 1 Ch App 528.

24 *Re MacDonald Sons and Co* [1894] 1 Ch 89.

25 C(A)A 1983, s 2(3).

26 C(A)A 1983, s 2(3). See also *Re Harmony and Montague Tin and Copper Mining Co, Spargo's Case* (1873) 8 Ch App 407; *Larocque v Beauchemin* [1897] AC 358. A sale of a business for a specified price which is satisfied by the allotment of shares in the acquiring company does not constitute 'the release of a liability of the company for a liquidated sum'; rather it simply constitutes the allotment of shares for a non-cash consideration: *Re Bradford Investments plc (No 2)* [1991] BCLC 688.

27 *Re Gibson, Little and Co Ltd* (1880–81) 5 LR Ir 139; *Re Limehouse Works Co Coates' Case* (1873) LR 17 Eq 169; *Re Harmony and Montague Tin and Copper Mining Co, Spargo's Case* (1873) 8 Ch App 407; *Larocque v Beauchemin* [1897] AC 358; *North Sydney Investment and Tramway Co v Higgins* [1899] AC 263; *Adamson's Case* (1874) LR 18 Eq 670; *Re Regent United Service Stores, ex parte Bentley* (1879) 12 ChD 850; *Re Foreign ad Colonial Gas Co, ex parte Wilson* [1874] WN 139. To the extent that payment is by way of set–off, the allottee will receive credit against calls which have not yet been made: *Re Jones, Lloyd and Co* (1889) 41 ChD 159. However, if the company is wound up before all calls have been made, the allottee cannot rely on the set–of to resist payment to the liquidator of the outstanding calls. Instead he will have to pay the calls and then prove in the liquidation for the balance: *Re Johannesburg Hotel Co, ex parte Zoutpansberg Prospecting Co* [1891] 1 Ch 119; *Re Overend, Gurney Co, Grissell's Case* (1866) 1 Ch App 528; *Re General Works Co, Gill's Case* (1879) 12 ChD 755.

28 *Re Paragassu Steam Tramway Co, Ferrao's Case* (1879) 9 Ch App 355; *Re Barrow-in-Furness and Northern Counties Land and Investment Co* (1880) 14 ChD 400; *Re Jones, Lloyd and Co* (1889) 41 ChD 159; *North Sydney Investment and Tramway Co v Higgins* [1899] AC 263.

29 C(A)A 1983, s 2(3)(b).

30 *Re Barangah Oil Refining Co, Arnot's Case* (1887) 36 ChD 702.

31 *Re Johannesburg Hotel Co, ex parte Zoutpansberg Prospecting Co* [1891] 1 Ch 119.

32 *Re Richmond Hill Hotel Co, Elkington's Case* (1867) 2 Ch App 511; *Re Richmond Hill Hotel Co Pellatt's Case* (1867) 2 Ch App 527; *Re Land Development Association, Kents Case* (1888) 39 ChD 259.

33 *System Control plc v Munro Corporate plc* [1990] BCLC 659.

34 CA 1963, s 58.

35 C(A)A 1983, s 31(2).

36 C(A)A 1983, s 55(1)(g).

UK legislation

See CA 1985, s 99.

---

27 Prohibition on allotment of shares at a discount

(1) Subject to subsection (4) the shares of a company shall not be allotted at a discount.

(2) Where shares are allotted in contravention of subsection (1), the allottee shall be liable to pay the company an amount equal to the amount of the discount and shall be liable to pay interest thereon at the appropriate rate.

(3) Section 26(4) shall apply for the purposes of this section as it applies for the purposes of that section.

(4) The repeal of section 63 of the Principal Act effected by section 3(2) shall not affect an application for an order sanctioning the issue of shares at a discount which has been made to the court under that section and which has not been withdrawn or disposed of before the appointed day, or an order made on or after that day in pursuance of any such application, and—

(a) any such application may be proceeded with and any such order, if not made before the appointed day, may be made as if that section had not been repealed; and

(b) shares may be allotted at a discount in accordance with any such order (whether made, before, on or after the appointed day) accordingly.

Definitions

'the appointed day': C(A)A 1983, s 1(3), s 2(1); 'the appropriate rate': C(A)A 1983, s 2(1), (7); 'company': CA 1963, s 2(1); 'the court': CA 1963, s 2(1); 'the Principal Act': C(A)A 1983, s 2(1); 'share' CA 1963, s 2(1).

Notes

Prohibition on allotment of shares at a discount: C(A)A 1983, s 27 places on a statutory footing a well established common law principle, namely that a company may not issue shares at a discount (ie below par value).[1] Payment of at least the par value is the price for shareholders of achieving limited liability.[2] So, for example, a company may not issue €1 debentures which are convertible into shares with a par value of less than €1 since to do so would be to indirectly issue shares at a discount.[3] One way of effecting a discount allotment of shares at a discount would be to allot the shares for a non-cash consideration the value of which was artificially inflated.[4] As a guard against such potential abuses it is stipulated that in the case of a plc (or a private company or an unlimited company which has duly resolved to re-register as a plc)[5] the allotment must be preceded by an independent valuation of the consideration in question.[6] However, in the case of other companies, there is no statutory mechanism for the valuation of the non-cash consideration payable in respect of an allotment of shares. Indeed, the courts have consistently held[7] that they will not inquire into the adequacy of the consideration paid for such shares unless:

(a) there is evidence of fraud; or
(b) the contract demonstrates on its face that the consideration is manifestly inadequate or illusory.[8]

Although the court will not normally assess the adequacy of the non-cash consideration which has been paid for shares, it may be prepared to do so where the directors have themselves failed to make any such assessment in advance of the allotment.[9]

1 See *Ooregum Gold Mining Co of India v Roper* [1892] AC 125; *Re Theatrical Trust Ltd, Chapman's Case* [1895] 1 Ch 771, *Re Wragg* [1897] 1 Ch 796, *Mosely v Koffyfontein Mines Ltd* [1904] 2 Ch 108.

2 *Ibid.*

3 *Mosley v Koffyfontein Mines Ltd* [1904] 2 Ch 108.

4 Shares may be issued either for cash or for a non-cash consideration: C(A)A 1983, s 26. See, however, both C(A)A 1983, ss 26, 29 and 37 for the restrictions on the types of non-cash consideration which may be accepted by a plc or by a private company or unlimited company which has resolved to re-register as a plc.

5 See C(A)A 1983, s 37(1).

6 C(A)A 1983, ss 30–33.

7 *Re Heyford Co, Pell's Case* (1869) 5 Ch App 11; *Re Baglan Hall Colliery Co* (1870) 5 Ch App 346; *Ooregum Gold Mining Co of India v Roper* [1892] AC 125; *Re Theatrical Trust Ltd, Chapman's Case* [1895] 1 Ch 771; *Re Wragg Ltd* [1897] 1 Ch 796; *Re Leinster Contract Corporation* [1902] 1 IR 349; *Hong Kong and China Glass Co v Glen* [1914] 1 Ch 527; *Pilmer v Duke Group Ltd* [2001] 2 BCLC 773.

8 *Ooregum Gold Mining Co of India v Roper* [1892] AC 125; *Re Theatrical Trust Ltd, Chapman's Case* [1895] 1 Ch 771; *Re Wragg Ltd* [1897] 1 Ch 796; *Mosley v Koffyfontein Mines Ltd* [1904] 2 Ch 108; *Park Business Interiors Ltd v Park* [1992] BCLC 1034.

9 *Tintin Exploration Syndicate Ltd v Sandys* (1947) 177 LT 412; *Hong Kong and China Gas Co Ltd v Glen* [1914] 1 Ch 527; *Re White Star Line Ltd* [1938] 1 All ER 607; *Re Alkaline Reduction Syndicate, Ames' Case* [1896] WN 79; *Park Business Interiors Ltd v Park* [1992] BCLC 1034.

Consequence of allotting shares at a discount: If shares are issued at a discount, the allottee becomes liable to pay to the company in cash a sum equivalent to the amount of the discount together with interest.[1] Moreover, any subsequent holder of the shares (other than a purchaser for value without notice of the contravention or a person deriving his title from an innocent purchaser) will also be jointly and severally liable to pay to the company the amount of the discount plus interest, even though he may already have paid duly paid his predecessor in title full value for the shares.[2] The liability of the allottee or subsequent holder to pay the amount of this discount plus interest arises regardless of whether he holds the shares in his own right or as agent, trustee or nominee or by way of security.[3] Moreover, where the company goes into liquidation, this liability to pay up the discount plus interest arises even if there are sufficient assets to pay the creditors in full.[4] Furthermore, if the company is unable to recover the amount of the discount from the allottee or from subsequent holders of the shares, it will be entitled to recoup the sum in question from the directors who were responsible for the discount, even though they had acted in good faith and in what they considered to be the company's best interests in effecting the allotment at a discount.[5]

1 C(A)A 1983, s 27(2).
2 C(A)A 1983, s 27(3).
3 *Re Munster Bank (Dillon's Claim)* (1886–87) 17 LR Ir 341.
4 *Re Newtownards Gas Co* (1885–86) 15 LR Ir 51; *Welton v Saffrey* [1897] AC 299.
5 *Hirsche v Sims* [1894] AC 654.

UK legislation

See CA 1985, s 100.

---

28 Payment for allotted shares

(1) Subject to subsection (4), a public limited company shall not allot a share except as paid up at least as to one-quarter of the nominal value of the share and the whole of any premium on it.

(2) Where a public limited company allots a share in contravention of subsection (1), the share shall be treated as if one-quarter of its nominal value together with the whole of any premium had been received, but the allottee shall be liable to pay the company the minimum amount which should have been received in respect of the share under that subsection less the value of any consideration actually applied in payment up (to any extent) of the share and any premium on it, and interest at the appropriate rate on the amount payable under this subsection.

(3) Subsection (2) shall not apply in relation to the allotment of a bonus share in contravention of subsection (1) unless the allottee knew or ought to have known the share was so allotted.

(4) Subsections (1) to (3) shall not apply to shares allotted in pursuance of an employees' share scheme.

(5) Section 26 (4) shall apply for the purposes of this section as it applies for the purposes of that section.

Definitions

'the appropriate rate': C(A)A 1983, s 2(1), (7); 'company': CA 1963, s 2(1); 'employees' share scheme': C(A)A 1983, s 2(1); 'public limited company': C(A)A 1983, s 2(1); 'share': CA 1963, s 2(1).

Notes

Payment for shares in a plc: Apart from having an authorised share capital of not less than authorised minimum' of €38,092.14,[1] it must also have an allotted share capital of not less than that amount before the Registrar can issue it with a s 6 certificate entitling it to carry on business and exercise its borrowing powers. As regards each issued share, the whole of any premium, and not less than 25% of the par value must be paid up.[2] A share shall be taken as having been allotted in a company only when a person acquires an unconditional right to be included in the register of members in respect of that share.[3] In determining the amount of the allotted share capital for this purpose, shares forming part of an employee share scheme are ignored unless they are paid up as to not less than 25% of the par value and the whole of any premium.[4]

1 C(A)A 1983, s 5(2).
2 C(A)A 1983, s 28(1). If less than the whole of the premium and at least 25% of the par value has been paid up in respect of a share, the allottee and any subsequent holder other than a purchaser for value without notice of the discount (or a person deriving title through him) will be liable to pay interest on the amount of the underpayment: C(A)A 1983, s 28(2) and (4). Application may however be made to the court in appropriate circumstances for relief in whole or in part against this liability to pay interest: C(A)A 1983, s 34.
3 C(A)A 1983, s 2(2).
4 C(A)A 1983, s 6(4). See also s 28(4).

UK legislation

See CA 1985, s 101.

---

29 Payment of non-cash consideration

(1) A public limited company shall not allot shares as fully or partly paid up (as to their nominal value or any premium payable on them) otherwise than in cash if the consideration for the allotment is or includes an undertaking which is to be or may be performed more than five years after the date of the allotment.

(2) Where a public limited company allots shares in contravention of subsection (1), the allottee of the shares shall be liable to pay the company an amount equal to their nominal value, together with the whole of any premium, or, if the case so requires, such proportion of that amount as is treated as paid up by the undertaking and shall be liable to pay interest at the appropriate rate on the amount payable under this subsection.

(3) Where a contract for the allotment of shares does not contravene subsection (1), any variation of the contract which has the effect that the contract would have contravened that subsection if the terms of the contract as varied had been its original terms shall be void.

(4) Subsection (3) shall apply to the variation by a public limited company of the terms of a contract entered into before the company was registered or re-registered as a public limited company.

(5) Where a public limited company allots shares for a consideration which consists of or includes (in accordance with subsection (1)) an undertaking which is to be performed within five years of the allotment but that undertaking is not performed within the period allowed by the contract for the allotment of the shares, the allottee of the shares in question shall be liable to pay the company at the end of that period an amount equal to the nominal value of the shares, together with the whole of any premium, or, if the case so requires, such proportion of that amount as is treated as paid up by the

undertaking, together with interest at the appropriate rate on the amount payable under this subsection.

(6) Section 26 (4) shall apply in relation to a contravention of this section and to a failure to carry out a term of a contract as mentioned in subsection (5) as it applies in relation to a contravention of that section.

(7) Any reference in this section to a contract for the allotment of shares includes a reference to an ancillary contract relating to payment in respect of those shares.

Definitions

'the appropriate rate': C(A)A 1983, s 2(1), (7); 'company': CA 1963, s 2(1); 'payment in cash': C(A)A 1983, s 2(3); 'public limited company': C(A)A 1983, s 2(1); 'share': CA 1963, s 2(1).

Notes

Payment of shares by way of long-term undertaking: See C(A)A 1983, s 26 and the note entitled 'Prohibited non-cash consideration for a plc'.

UK legislation

See CA 1985, s 102.

---

30 Experts' reports on non-cash consideration before allotment of shares

(1) Subject to subsection (2), a public limited company shall not allot shares as fully or partly paid up (as to their nominal value or any premium payable on them) otherwise than in cash unless—

(a) the consideration for the allotment has been valued in accordance with the following provisions of this section;

(b) a report with respect to its value has been made to the company by a person appointed by the company in accordance with those provisions during the six months immediately preceding the allotments of the shares; and

(c) a copy of the report has been sent to the proposed allottee of the shares.

(2) Subject to subsection (3), subsection (1) shall not apply to the allotment of shares by a company in connection with—

(a) an arrangement providing for the allotment of shares in that company on terms that the whole or part of the consideration for the shares allotted is to be provided by the transfer to that company or the cancellation of all or some of the shares, or of all or some of the shares of a particular class, in another company (with or without the issue to that company of shares, or of shares of any particular class, in that other company); or

(b) a proposed merger of that company with another company.

(3) Subsection (2)(a) does not exclude the application of subsection (1) to the allotment of shares by a company in connection with any such arrangement as is there mentioned unless it is open to all the holders of the shares in the other company in question or, where the arrangement applies only to shares of a particular class, to all the holders of shares in that other company of that class, to take part in the arrangement. In determining whether that is the case, shares held by or by a nominee of the company

proposing to allot the shares in connection with the arrangement, or by or by a nominee of a company which is that company's holding company or subsidiary or a company which is a subsidiary of its holding company, shall be disregarded.

(4) For the purposes of subsection (2)(b) there is a proposed merger of two companies when one of them proposes to acquire all the assets and liabilities of the other in exchange for the issue of shares or other securities in that one to shareholders of the other, with or without any cash payment to those shareholders.

(5) The valuation and report required by subsection (1) shall be made by an independent person, that is to say, a person qualified at the time of the report to be appointed or to continue to be auditor of the company, except that where it appears to him to be reasonable for the valuation of the consideration, or a valuation of part of the consideration, to be made, or to accept such a valuation made, by any person who—

(a) appears to him to have the requisite knowledge and experience to value the consideration or that part of the consideration; and

(b) is not an officer or servant of the company or any other body corporate which is that company's subsidiary or holding company or a subsidiary of that company's holding company or a partner or employee of such an officer or servant,

that independent person may arrange for or accept such a valuation, together with a report which will enable him to make his own report under that subsection and provide a note in accordance with subsection (8).

(6) The independent person's report under subsection (1) shall state—

(a) the nominal value of the shares to be wholly or partly paid for by the consideration in question;

(b) the amount of any premium payable on those shares;

(c) the description of the consideration and, as respects so much of the consideration as he himself has valued, a description of that part of the consideration, the method used to value it and the date of the valuation; and

(d) the extent to which the nominal value of the shares and any premium are to be treated as paid up—

(i) by the consideration;

(ii) in cash.

(7) Where any consideration is valued under this section by a person other than the independent person, the latter's report under subsection (1) shall state that fact and shall also—

(a) state the former's name and what knowledge and experience he has to carry out the valuation; and

(b) describe so much of the consideration as was valued by that other person, the method used to value it and state the date of valuation.

(8) The report of the independent person made under subsection (1) shall contain or be accompanied by a note by him—

(a) in the case of a valuation made by another person, that it appeared to the independent person reasonable to arrange for it to be so made, or to accept a valuation so made;

(b) whoever made the valuation, that the method of valuation was reasonable in all the circumstances;

(c) that it appears to the independent person that there has been no material change in the value of the consideration in question since the valuation; and

(d) that on the basis of the valuation the value of the consideration, together with any cash by which the nominal value of the shares or any premium payable on them is to be paid up, is not less than so much of the aggregate of the nominal value and the whole of any such premium as is treated as paid up by the consideration and any such cash.

(9) Subsection (10) applies where a public limited company allots any share in contravention of subsection (1) and either—

(a) the allottee has not received a report under this section; or

(b) there has been some other contravention of this section and the allottee knew or ought to have known that it amounted to a contravention.

(10) Where this subsection applies, the allottee shall be liable to pay the company an amount equal to the nominal value of the shares, together with the whole of any premium or, if the case so requires, such proportion of that amount as is treated as paid up by the consideration, and shall be liable to pay interest at the appropriate rate on the amount payable under this subsection.

(11) Section 26(4) shall apply for the purposes of this section as it applies for the purposes of that section.

(12) Where the consideration is accepted partly in payment up of the nominal value of the shares and any premium and partly for some other consideration given by the company, the provisions of this section shall apply as if references to the consideration accepted by the company included references to the proportion of that consideration which is properly attributable to the payment up of that value and any premium; and

(a) the independent person shall carry out or arrange for such other valuations as will enable him to determine that proportion; and

(b) his report under subsection (1) shall state what valuations have been made by virtue of this subsection and also the reason for and method and date of any such valuations and any other matters which may be relevant to that determination.

(13) It is hereby declared for the avoidance of doubt that subsection (1) does not apply by reference to the application of an amount for the time being standing to the credit of any of the company's reserve accounts or to the credit of its profit and loss account in paying up (to any extent) any shares allotted to members of the company or any premiums on any shares so allotted; and in relation to any such allotment references in this section to the consideration for the allotment do not include any such amount so applied.

(14) In this section—

(a) 'arrangement' means any agreement, scheme or arrangement (including an arrangement sanctioned in accordance with section 201 or 260 of the Principal Act);

(b) any reference to a company, except where it is or is to be construed as a reference to a public limited company, includes a reference to any body corporate and any body to which letters patent have been issued under the Chartered Companies Act, 1837; and

(c) any reference to an officer or servant shall not include a reference to an auditor.

Definitions

'the appropriate rate': C(A)A 1983, s 2(1), (7); 'company': CA 1963, s 2(1); 'holding company': CA 1963, s 2(1), s 155; 'officer': CA 1963, s 2(1); 'payment in cash': C(A)A 1983, s 2(3); 'the Principal Act': C(A)A 1983, s 2(1); 'public limited company': C(A)A 1983, s 2(1); 'shares': CA 1963, s 2(1); 'subsidiary': CA 1963, s 2(1), s 155.

Notes

Valuation of non-cash consideration for plcs: As noted above,[1] in the case of most companies, there is no statutory mechanism for the valuation of the non-cash consideration payable in respect of an allotment of shares. Indeed, the courts have consistently held[2] that they will not inquire into the adequacy of the consideration paid for such shares unless:

(a) there is evidence of fraud; or

(b) the contract demonstrates on its face that the consideration is manifestly inadequate or illusory.[3]

However, in the case of a plc (or a private or unlimited company which has duly resolved to re-register as a plc)[4] any permitted non-cash consideration[5] for the allotment of shares by such companies must be independently valued within the period of six months preceding the allotment by a person qualified to act as auditor of the company[6] and a copy of the independent person' report must also have been sent to the proposed allottee.[7] In preparing his report, the independent person may engage the assistance of such other independent experts as it may be reasonable for him to retain to assist him in valuing the particular type of non-cash consideration.[8] So, for example, if he is valuing lands to be transferred to the company in return for the allotment of shares, it may be reasonable for him to engage the services of an estate agent/auctioneer to assist him in the valuation of those lands. Both the independent person and any expert engaged by him are entitled to such information and explanations from the company's officers as the may reasonably require for the purpose of carrying out their respective tasks.[9] If an expert has been retained to value the whole or part of the non-cash consideration, details thereof (including details of the expert's knowledge and experience) must be recited in the independent person's report[10] together with confirmation that the expert's valuation has been accepted.[11] Regardless of who actually carried out the valuation the report must also state the following:

(a) the nominal value of the shares being allotted;[12]

(b) the amount of the premium payable on those shares;[13]

(c) a description of the consideration payable,[14] the method of valuation used by him[15] and/or by such expert or experts as may have been engaged by him[16] and confirmation that whoever conducted the valuation, the method of valuation was reasonable in the circumstances;[17]

(d) the extent of the nominal value and premium to be treated as paid up by way of cash and non-cash consideration respectively;[18]

(e) confirmation that there has been in material change in the value of the non-cash consideration between the actual date of valuation and the date of the report;[19] and

(f) confirmation that the aggregate value of the non-cash consideration and any cash payable is not less than the aggregate of the nominal value and premium payable in respect of the shares in question.[20]

1 See C(A)A 1983, s 26 and the notes thereto.

2 *Re Heyford Co, Pell's Case* (1869) 5 Ch App 11; *Re Baglan Hall Colliery Co* (1870) 5 Ch App 346; *Ooregum Gold Mining Co of India v Roper* [1892] AC 125; *Re Theatrical Trust Ltd, Chapman's Case* [1895] 1 Ch 771; *Re Wragg Ltd* [1897] 1 Ch 796; *Re Leinster Contract Corporation* [1902] 1 IR 349; *Hong Kong and China Glass Co v Glen* [1914] 1 Ch 527; *Pilmer v Duke Group Ltd* [2001] 2 BCLC 773.

3 *Ooregum Gold Mining Co of India v Roper* [1892] AC 125; *Re Theatrical Trust Ltd, Chapman's Case* [1895] 1 Ch 771; *Re Wragg Ltd* [1897] 1 Ch 796; *Mosley v Koffyfontein Mines Ltd* [1904] 2 Ch 108; *Park Business Interiors Ltd v Park* [1992] BCLC 1034.

4 C(A)A 1983, s 37.

5 As regards prohibited forms of non-cash consideration for the allotment of shares by such companies, see C(A)A 1983, s 26(2) and s 29.

6 C(A)A 1983, s 30(1) and (5). As regards the qualifications for appointment as an auditor, see CA 1990, ss 187–192.

7 C(A)A 1983, s 30(1)(c).

8 C(A)A 1983, s 30(3).

9 C(A)A 1983, s 31(1). It is an offence to knowingly or recklessly make a false statement to the expert or independent person.

10 C(A)A 1983, s 30(7) and (8)(a).

11 C(A)A 1983, s 30(8)(a).

12 C(A)A 1983, s 30(6)(a).

13 C(A)A 1983, s 30(6)(b).

14 C(A)A 1983, s 30(6)(c).

15 C(A)A 1983, s 30(6)(c).

16 C(A)A 1983, s 30(7)(b).

17 C(A)A 1983, s 30(8)(b).

18 C(A)A 1983, s 30(6)(d).

19 C(A)A 1983, s 30(8)(c).

20 C(A)A 1983, s 30(8)(d). If the report concludes that the shares are being issued a less than par value the provisions of C(A)A 1983, s 27 will apply.

Consequences of breach of s 30: The apparent purpose of these valuation provisions is to ensure that a plc does not issue shares either at a discount or at less than fair value. In this regard, if there has been a failure altogether to provide the allottee with a copy of an independent person's report or of there is some other breach of C(A)A 1983, s 30 regarding the valuation of the shares of which the allottee knew or ought to have known, then he and any subsequent holder (other than a purchaser for value without notice of the contravention or a person deriving title through him) will be liable to pay to the company so much of the nominal value of the shares and so much of the premium as was to have been treated as paid up by way of the non-cash consideration together with interest,[1] regardless of the fact that the non-cash consideration may still be payable or indeed may also have been paid over. In appropriate cases though, such a person may apply to court for relief against this double exposure.[2]

1 C(A)A 1983, s 30(9) and (10).

2 C(A)A 1983, s 34.

Filing an independent person's report: The independent person's report on the value of non-cash consideration paid or payable to the company must be delivered to the Registrar of

Companies at the same time as the return of allotments.[1] Notice of the delivery of the report to the Registrar must be published in the Companies Registration Office Gazette.[2]

1 C(A)A 1983, s 31(2). In relation to the delivery of returns of allotments, see CA 1963, s 58 and the notes thereto.

2 C(A)A 1983, s 55(1)(d).

Allotments exempted from valuation: A bonus issue or capitalisation of profits by way of allotment of shares to existing members will be exempted from the valuation provisions of s 30,[1] as will be:

(a) an allotment of shares in consideration for the transfer or cancellation of all or some of the shares in another company (eg as part of a take-over or restructuring);[2]

(b) an allotment of shares as part of a merger involving the acquisition by one company of the assets and liabilities of another in return for the allotment of shares (either with or without an additional cash payment) to the members of the target company;[3]

(c) an allotment of shares by any company formed for the purposes of a merger by formation of a new company pursuant to EC(MDC)R 1987.[4]

1 C(A)A 1983, s 30(13).

2 C(A)A 1983, s 30(2)(a). The offer of shares must be open to all members of the other company or all members of the relevant class, as the case may be (ignoring shares held by the allotting company or by its nominee or holding company or subsidiary or by a fellow subsidiary of a common holding company): C(A)A 1983, s 30(3).

3 C(A)A 1983, s 30(2)(b) and (4).

4 EC(MDC)R 1987, reg 10.

Investment company: The provisions of C(A)A 1983, s 30 do not apply to investment companies. See CA 1990, s 260.

Mergers: The provsions of C(A)A 1983, s 30 do not apply to the issue of shares by a new company formed for the purposes of a merger. See reg 10 of the EC(MDC) Regs 1987.

UK legislation

See CA 1985, s 103 (amended by IA 1986, s 439(1), Sch 13, Pt I), 108, 112(1).

---

31 Experts' reports: supplementary

(1) Any person carrying out a valuation or making a report under section 30 with respect to any consideration proposed to be accepted or given by a company shall be entitled to require from the officers of the company such information and explanation as he thinks necessary to enable him to carry out the valuation or to make the report and provide a note, under that section.

(2) A company to which such a report is made as to the value of any consideration for which, or partly for which, it proposes to allot shares shall deliver a copy of the report to the registrar of companies for registration at the same time that it files the return of the allotments of those shares under section 58 of the Principal Act, and subsections (3) and (4) of that section shall apply to a default in complying with this subsection as they apply to a default in complying with that section.

(3) Any person who knowingly or recklessly makes a statement which—

(a) is misleading, false or deceptive in a material particular, and

(b) is a statement to which this subsection applies,

shall be guilty of an offence.

(4) Subsection (3) applies to any statement made (whether orally or in writing) to any person carrying out a valuation or making a report under section 30, being a statement which conveys or purports to convey any information or explanation which that person requires, or is entitled to require, under subsection (1).

Definitions

'company': CA 1963, s 2(1); 'officer': CA 1963, s 2(1); 'the Principal Act': C(A)A 1983, s 2(1); 'Registrar of Companies': CA 1963, s 2(1); 'share': CA 1963, s 2(1).

Notes

False statements to independent person or expert: See C(A)A 1983, s 30 and the notes thereto.

Filing of independent person's report: See C(A)A 1983, s 30 and the notes thereto.

Investment company: The provisions of C(A)A 1983, s 31 do not apply to investment companies. See CA 1990, s 260.

Mergers: The provsions of C(A)A 1983, s 31 do not apply to the issue of shares by a new company formed for the purposes of a merger. See reg 10 of the EC(MDC) Regs 1987.

UK legislation

See CA 1985, s 110.

---

32 Experts' reports on non-cash assets acquired from subscribers, etc.

(1) A public limited company, other than a company re-registered under section 12, shall not, unless the conditions mentioned in subsection (3) have been complied with, enter into an agreement with a relevant person for the transfer by him during the initial period of one or more non-cash assets to the company or another for a consideration to be given by the company equal in value at the time of the agreement to at least one-tenth of the nominal value of the company's share capital issued at that time.

(2) In this section—

(a) in relation to a company formed as a public limited company, 'relevant person' means any subscriber to the memorandum of the company and 'initial period' means the period of two years beginning with the date on which the company is issued with a certificate under section 6 that it is entitled to do business;

(b) in relation to a company re-registered, or registered in accordance with section 18, as a public limited company, 'relevant person' means any person who was a member of the company on the date of the re-registration or registration and 'initial period' means the period of two years beginning with that date.

(3) The conditions referred to in subsection (1) are that—

(a) the consideration to be received by the company (that is to say, the asset to be transferred to the company or the advantage to the company of its transfer to another person) and any consideration other than cash to be given by the company have been valued under the following provisions of this section (without prejudice to any requirement to value any consideration under section 30);

(b) a report with respect to the consideration to be so received and given has been made to the company in accordance with those provisions during the six months immediately preceding the date of the agreement;

(c) the terms of the agreement have been approved by an ordinary resolution of the company; and

(d) not later than the giving of the notice of the meeting at which the resolution is proposed, copies of the resolution and report have been circulated to the members of the company entitled to receive that notice and, if the relevant person is not then such a member, to that person.

(4) Subsection (1) shall not apply to the following agreements for the transfer of an asset for a consideration to be given by the company, that is to say—

(a) where it is part of the ordinary business of the company to acquire or arrange for other persons to acquire assets of a particular description, an agreement entered into by the company in the ordinary course of its business for the transfer of an asset of that description to it or such a person, as the case may be; or

(b) an agreement entered into by the company under the supervision of the court or an officer authorised by the court for the purpose, for the transfer of an asset to the company or to another.

(5) Section 30 (5) and (7) shall apply to a valuation and report of any consideration under this section as those subsections apply to a valuation of and report on any consideration under subsection (1) of that section.

(6) The report of the independent person under this section shall—

(a) state the consideration to be received by the company, describing the asset in question, specifying the amount to be received in cash, and the consideration to be given by the company, specifying the amount to be given in cash;

(b) state the method and date of valuation;

(c) contain or be accompanied by a note as to the matters mentioned in section 30 (8)(a) to (c); and

(d) contain or be accompanied by a note that on the basis of the valuation the value of the consideration to be received by the company is not less than the value of the consideration to be given by it.

(7) If a public limited company enters into an agreement with any relevant person in contravention of subsection (1) and either he has not received a report under this section or there has been some other contravention of this section or section 30 (5) or (7) which he knew or ought to have known amounted to a contravention, then, subject to subsection (8)—

(a) the company shall be entitled to recover from the relevant person any consideration given by the company under the agreement or an amount equivalent to its value at the time of the agreement; and

(b) the agreement, so far as not carried out, shall be void.

(8) Where a company enters into an agreement in contravention of subsection (1) and that agreement is or includes an agreement for the allotment of shares in that company, then, whether or not the agreement also contravenes section 30—

(a) subsection (7) shall not apply to the agreement insofar as it is an agreement for the allotment of shares; and

(b) section 26 (4) and section 30 (10) shall apply in relation to the shares as if they had been allotted in contravention of section 30.

Definitions

'company': CA 1963, s 2(1); 'court': CA 1963, s 2(1); 'memorandum': CA 1963, s 2(1); 'member': CA 1963, s 31; 'non-cash asset': C(A)A 1983, s 2(1); 'officer': CA 1963, s 2(1); 'payment in cash': C(A)A 1983, s 2(3); 'public limited company'; C(A)A 1983, s 2(1); 'share': CA 1963, s 2(1).

Notes

Valuation of non-cash assets acquired from the subscribers and others:[1] This section requires a plc, *inter alia,* to obtain an independent valuation of any agreement which it proposes to enter into within the period of two years from the date of obtaining its s 6 certificate for the transfer to it or to any other person of any non-cash assets from any of its subscribers in circumstances where the value of consideration payable by the plc equals or exceeds 10% of the nominal value of the issued share capital.[2] In the case of a company which re-registers as a plc, the valuation requirement is triggered where the company proposes within two years of its re-registration to enter into an agreement for the transfer of any non-cash assets to it or another person from any of the persons who were members at the date of re-registration and where the value of consideration payable by the plc equals or exceeds 10% of the nominal value of the issued share capital.[3] For the purpose of effecting the valuation, the relevant provisions of C(A)A 1983, s 30 are deemed to apply.[4] Moreover, the contents of the independent person's report largely mirror those of a s 30 report.[5] In order for the company to lawfully enter into the agreement to acquire the non-cash asset the following must first occur:

(a) the valuation must be duly carried out and the independent person must preset his report which must be made up to a date not more than six month prior to the date of the proposed agreement;[6]

(b) the report must be circulated to all members entitled to receive notice of general meetings together with a draft resolution to approve the proposed agreement;[7]

(c) the proposed agreement must be duly approved by ordinary resolution of the members.[8]

1 See also CA 1990, s 29 in relation to the restrictions on the transfer of non-cash assets of the stipulated value between by a company (whether or not a plc) on the one hand and any of its directors or any directors of its holding company or any persons connected with any such directors on the other hand.

2 C(A)A 1983, s 32(1) and (2)(a).

3 C(A)A 1983, s 32(1) and (2)(b).

4 C(A)A 1983, s 32(5). See C(A)A 1983, s 30 and the notes thereto for a discussion of the valuation provisions. The independent person, and any expert engaged by him, have the same

entitlement to information and explanations from the company's officer as if the report were one being commissioned under s 30. See C(A)A 1983, s 33(1).

5 See C(A)A 1983, s 32(6).

6 C(A)A 1983, s 32(3)(a) and (b).

7 C(A)A 1983, s 32(3)(d). If the other party to the proposed agreement is not a member entitled to reeve notice of general meetings as where he has since ceased to be a member or holds shares which do not entitle him to such notice), a copy of the report and draft resolution must also be circulated to him.

8 C(A)A 1983, s 32(3)(c).

Consequence of breach of s 32: If the plc proceeds to enter into an agreement of the type described above without first providing the contracting party with a copy of the independent person's report, or if the agreement is otherwise entered into in circumstances here there has been some breach of C(A)A 1983, s 32 of which the other contracting party knew or ought to have known, the agreement will be void in so far as not already carried out.[1] Moreover, to the extent that the agreement has already been performed, the company will be entitled to recover any consideration which has actually been paid by it[2] notwithstanding the fact that the non-cash asset may already have been transferred by the other party. In appropriate circumstances though, relief against this potential liability may be obtained upon application to the court.[3] It should also be noted that if and to the extent that the consideration payable by the company would have involved the allotment of shares, the civil consequences are those stipulated by s 30.[4]

1 C(A)A 1983, s 32(7)(b).

2 C(A)A 1983, s 32(7)(a).

3 C(A)A 1983, s 34(6).

4 C(A)A 1983, s 32(8). See the notes to C(A)A 1983, s 30 for the relevant civil consequences.

Filing of resolution and report: A copy of the resolution approving the acquisition together with a copy of the independent person's report must be delivered to the Registrar of Companies within 15 days of the actual passing of the resolution. Failure to do so is a criminal offence.[1] Notice of the delivery of the report must also be published in the Companies Registration Office Gazette.[2]

1 C(A)A 1983, s 33(2)(b).

2 C(A)A 1983, s 55(1)(e).

Transactions exempted from s 32: Even though an asset is being acquired from a person to subscriber etc within the relevant two-year period and for a consideration equivalent to not less than 10% of the issued share capital, the provisions of C(A)A 1983, s 32 will not apply where: (a) the ordinary business of the company involves either acquiring such assets or (whether the asset is to be transferred to someone else) arranging for the acquisition of such assets by other persons;[1] or (b) the agreement is entered into under the supervision of the court or under the supervision of an officer appointed by the court for that purpose.[2]

1 C(A)A 1983, s 32(4)(a). So, for example, a property development company could acquire development land for itself and a company carrying on business as estate agents and auctioneers could enter into an agreement for the transfer of lands to a third party without either having to go through the procedures laid down by s 32.

2 C(A)A 1983, s 32(4)(b). A transfer supervised by the court or by an officer of the court appointed for that purpose might occur in the context of a scheme of arrangement under CA 1963, ss 201–203 or as part of relief granted under CA 1963, s 205 or in the context of a scheme of arrangement proposed by an examiner under C(A)A 1990.

Investment company: The provisions of C(A)A 1983, s 32 do not apply to investment companies. See CA 1990, s 260.

UK legislation

See CA 1985, s 104, 105, 109.

33 Provisions supplementary to section 32

(1) Any person carrying out a valuation or making a report under section 32, shall be entitled to require from the officers of the company such information and explanation as he thinks necessary to enable him to carry out the valuation or make the report and provide the note required by that section; and section 31(3) shall apply in relation to any such valuation and report as it applies in relation to a valuation and report under section 30(1) with the substitution of a reference to this subsection for the reference in section 31(4) to section 31(1).

(2) A company which has passed a resolution under section 32 with respect to the transfer of an asset shall, within 15 days of the passing of the resolution, deliver to the registrar of companies a copy of the resolution together with the report required by that section and, if it fails to do so, the company and every officer of the company who is in default shall be liable on summary conviction to a fine not exceeding [€1,904.61][a] together with, in the case of a continuing offence, a fine not exceeding [€31.74][b] for every day on which the offence continues, but not exceeding [€1,904.61][c] in total.

(3) Any reference in section 32 or this section to consideration given for the transfer of an asset includes a reference to consideration given partly for its transfer but—

(a) the value of any consideration partly so given shall be taken to be the proportion of that consideration properly attributable to its transfer;

(b) the independent person shall carry out or arrange for such valuations of anything else as will enable him to determine that proportion; and

(c) his report under that section shall state what valuation has been made by virtue of this paragraph and also the reason for and method and date of any such valuation and any other matters which may be relevant to that determination.

Amendments

a '£250' substituted for '£50' by C(A)A 1982, Sch 1, increased to £1,500 by CA 1990, s 240(7) as inserted by CLEA 2001, s 104(c), and converted to €1,904.61 by Council Regulations (EC) No 1103/97, No 974/98 and No 2866/98 and the Economic and Monetary Union Act 1998, s 6.

b £25 converted to €31.74 by Council Regulations (EC) No 1103/97, No 974/98 and No 2866/98 and the Economic and Monetary Union Act 1998, s 6.

c £500 increased to £1,500 by CA 1990, s 240(7) as inserted by ClEA 2001, s 104(c) and converted to €1,904.61 by Council Regulations (EC) No 1103/97, No 974/98 and No 2866/98 and the Economic and Monetary Union Act 1998, s 6.

Definitions

'company'; CA 1963, s 2(1); 'officer': CA 1963, s 2(1); 'officer in default'; CA 1963, s 383; 'Registrar of Companies'; CA 1963, s 2(1).

Notes

False statements to independent person or expert: See C(A)A 1983, s 32 and the notes thereto.

Filing of independent person's report: See C(A)A 1983, s 32 and the notes thereto.

Investment company: The provisions of C(A)A 1983, s 33 do not apply to investment companies. See CA 1990, s 260.

UK legislation

See CA 1985, ss 109(3), 110(1), 111.

34 Relief

(1) Where any person is liable to a company under section 26, 29, 30 or 32 in relation to payment in respect of any shares in the company or is liable by virtue of any undertaking given to the company in, or in connection with, payment for any such shares, the person so liable may make an application to the court under this subsection to be exempted in whole or in part from that liability.

(2) Where the liability mentioned in subsection (1) arises under any of those sections in relation to payment in respect of any shares, the court may, on an application under that subsection, exempt the applicant from that liability only—

(a) if and to the extent that it appears to the court just and equitable to do so having regard to the following, namely—

(i) whether the applicant has paid, or is liable to pay, any amount in respect of any other liability arising in relation to those shares under any of those sections or of any liability arising by virtue of any undertaking given in or in connection with payment for those shares;

(ii) whether any person other than the applicant has paid or is likely to pay (whether in pursuance of an order of the court or otherwise) any such amount; and

(iii) whether the applicant or any other person has performed, in whole or in part, or is likely so to perform any such undertaking or has done or is likely to do any other thing in payment or part payment in respect of those shares;

(b) if and to the extent that it appears to the court just and equitable to do so in respect of any interest which he is liable to pay to the company under any of those sections.

(3) Where the liability mentioned in subsection (1) arises by virtue of an undertaking given to the company in, or in connection with, payment for any shares in the company, the court may, on an application under that subsection, exempt the applicant from that liability only if and to the extent that it appears to the court just and equitable to do so having regard to the following, namely—

(a) whether the applicant has paid or is liable to pay any amount in respect of any liability arising in relation to those shares under sections 26, 29, 30 or 32; and

(b) whether any person other than the applicant has paid or is likely to pay (whether in pursuance of an order of the court or otherwise) any such amount.

(4) In determining in pursuance of an application under subsection (1) whether it should exempt the applicant in whole or in part from any liability, the court shall have regard to the following overriding principles, namely—

(a) that a company which has allotted shares should receive money or money's worth at least equal in value to the aggregate of the nominal value of those shares and the whole of any premium or, if the case so requires, so much of that aggregate as is treated as paid up; and

(b) subject to paragraph (a), that where such a company would, if the court did not grant that exemption, have more than one remedy against a particular person, it should be for the company to decide which remedy it should remain entitled to pursue.

(5) Where a person brings any proceedings against another ('the contributor') for a contribution in respect of any liability to a company arising under any of sections 26 to 30 and 32 and it appears to the court that the contributor is liable to make such a contribution, the court may, if and to the extent that it appears to the court, having regard to the respective culpability in respect of the liability to the company of the contributor and the person bringing the proceedings, that it is just and equitable to do so—

(a) exempt the contributor in whole or in part from his liability to make such a contribution; or

(b) order the contributor to make a larger contribution than, but for this subsection, he would be liable to make.

(6) Where a person is liable to a company by virtue of section 32(7)(a), the court may, on an application under this subsection, exempt that person in whole or in part from that liability if and to the extent that it appears to the court just and equitable to do so having regard to any benefit accruing to the company by virtue of anything done by that person towards the carrying out of the agreement mentioned in that subsection.

Definitions

'company': CA 1963, s 2(1); 'court'; CA 1963, s 2(1); 'share': CA 1963, s 2(1).

Notes

Circumstances in respect of which relief may be required: A plc is prohibited from accepting certain types of undertaking as payment or part-payment for the allotment of shares.[1] In addition, if shares are being issued wholly or partly for a non-cash consideration, that non-cash consideration must first be independently valued.[2] There is a similar requirement to independently value non-cash assets of a certain value being acquired within a specified period of time by a plc's subscribers or persons who, in the case of a company which re-registers as a plc, were members at the time of re-registration.[3]

If a plc proceeds to allot shares for a consideration which comprises or includes a prohibited undertaking the allottee becomes liable to pay to the company in cash an amount equivalent to the value attributed to the undertaking in question,[4] together with interest,[5] even though he still remains liable to the company to perform the undertaking as well.[6] Moreover, any subsequent holder of the shares (other than a purchaser for value without notice of the contravention or a person deriving his title from an innocent purchaser) will also be jointly and severally liable to pay the aforementioned cash amount plus interest, even though he may already have paid duly paid his predecessor in title.[7] Similarly, if there been failure altogether to provide the allottee with a copy of an independent person's valuation report or of there is some other breach of C(A)A 1983, s 30 regarding the valuation of the shares of which the allottee knew or ought to have known, then he and any subsequent holder (other than a purchaser for value without notice of the contravention or a person deriving title through him) will be liable to pay to the company so much of the nominal value of the shares and so much of the premium as was to have been treated as paid up by way of the non-cash consideration together with interest[8] even though the non-cash consideration may still be payable or, indeed, may already have been paid.

In addition, if a plc proceeds to enter into an agreement caught by C(A)A 1983, s 32 without first providing the contracting party with a copy of the independent person's report or if the agreement is otherwise entered into in circumstances here there has been some breach of s 32 of which the other contracting party knew or ought to have known, the agreement will be void in so far as not already carried out.[9] Moreover, to the extent that the agreement has already been performed, the company will be entitled to recover any consideration which has actually been paid by it[10] notwithstanding the fact that the non-cash asset may already have been transferred by the other party.

1 See C(A)A 1983, ss 26 and 29 for the types of undertaking which are prohibited.
2 See C(A)A 1983, s 30 and the notes thereto.
3 See C(A)A 1983, s 32 and the notes thereto.
4 In the case of an undertaking which was to have been performed within five years of the date of allotment but which remains partly unperformed, the liability to make payment in cash relates only to the value attributable to that unperformed part: C(A)A 1983, s 29(5).
5 C(A)A 1983, s 26(3) and s 29(2) and (5).
6 C(A)A 1983, s 36.
7 C(A)A 1983, s 26(4) and s 29(6).
8 C(A)A 1983, s 30(9) and (10).
9 C(A)A 1983, s 32(7)(b).
10 C(A)A 1983, s 32(7)(a).

Application for relief: Where any of the above–mentioned situations involves an allotment of shares the allottee or subsequent holder of the shares may apply[1] to the court for relief, in whole or in part, from the statutory liability that has been imposed on them.[2] The court may grant relief where it considers it just and equitable to do so[3] and in this regard it would appear that the overriding consideration for the court is to ensure that the company has received money or money's worth at least equal the aggregate of the nominal value of the shares and the whole premium payable in respect thereof.[4] The court may thus take into account the value of any other non-cash consideration paid or payable in respect of the shares by the allottee or any subsequent holder[5] and may also have regard to any other cash payments paid or payable in respect of the shares by the allottee or any subsequent holder.[6] So, for example, if 1,000,000 shares of €1 each are allotted in return for a non-cash consideration which has not been valued under C(A)A 1983, s 30, but which is subsequently shown by the allottee or subsequent holder to be worth €750,000, relief from liability might well be granted except to the extent of €250,000 which would remain payable in cash together with interest.

Where the transaction does not involve the allotment of shares but merely involves the acquisition by the company of a non-cash asset in breach of s 32, the contracting party may similarly apply[7] to the court for relief against his liability to reimburse any moneys paid by the company,[8] as where he can show that he has already transferred the asset or assets to the company under the impugned agreement. So, for example, if the company has paid him €750,000 and he could establish that the value of the assets transferred by him was €600,000, he might well obtain relief except to the extent of €150,000 plus interest.

1 Such applications are brought by way of petition: RSC 1986, Ord 75, r 4(q).
2 C(A)A 1983, s 34(1). In an action for a contribution as between several persons with liability under the relevant section to make a cash payment to the company in respect of the shares, the court may determine the extent of the respective obligations to contribute so as to take account of

the respective degrees of culpability and may even exempt particular individuals in appropriate circumstances from liability to make any contribution whatsoever: C(A)A 1983, s 34(5).

3 C(A)A 1983, s 34(2).

4 C(A)A 1983, s 34(4)(a).

5 C(A)A 1983, s 34(2).

6 C(A)A 1983, s 34(3).

7 Such applications are brought by way of petition: RSC 1986, Ord 75, r 4(q).

8 C(A)A 1983, s 34(6).

UK legislation

See CA 1985, s 113.

---

35 Special provisions as to issue of shares to subscribers

Any shares taken by a subscriber to the memorandum of a public limited company in pursuance of an undertaking of his in the memorandum and any premium on the shares shall be paid up in cash.

Definitions

'cash': C(A)A 1983, s 2(3); 'memorandum'; CA 1963, s 2(1); 'public limited company': C(A)A 1983, s 2(1); 'share': CA 1963, s 2(1).

Notes

Payment for subscriber shares in a plc: See C(A)A 1983, s 26 and the note thereto entitled 'Prohibited non-cash consideration for a plc'. See also CA 1963, s 6 in relation to the undertaking of a subscriber to take shares in the company.

UK legislation

See CA 1985, s 106.

---

36 Contravention of sections 26 to 35

(1) Where a company contravenes any of the provisions of sections 26 to 30, 32 and 35, the company and any officer of the company who is in default shall be guilty of an offence.

(2) Subject to section 34, an undertaking given by any person in or in connection with payment for shares in a company to do work or perform services or to do any other thing shall, if it is enforceable by the company apart from this Act, be so enforceable notwithstanding that there has been a contravention in relation thereto of sections 26, 29 or 30 and where such an undertaking is given in contravention of section 32 in respect of the allotment of any shares it shall be so enforceable notwithstanding that contravention.

Definitions

'company'; CA 1963, s 2(1); 'officer': CA 1963, s 2(1); 'officer in default': CA 1963, s 383; 'share': CA 1963, s 2(1).

Notes

Double liability to pay for shares: See C(A)A 1983, s 26 and the note thereto entitled 'Prohibited non-cash consideration for a plc'. See also C(A)A 1983, s 30 and the notes thereto.

UK legislation

See CA 1985, ss 114, 115.

---

37 Application of sections 26 to 36 in special cases

(1) Subject to subsection (2), sections 26, 28 to 31 and 34 to 36, shall apply—

(a) to a company which has passed and not revoked a special resolution to be re-registered under section 9 or section 11;

(b) to a company whose directors have passed and not revoked a resolution to be re-registered under section 12; and

(c) to a joint stock company (within the meaning of section 329 of the Principal Act) which has passed and not revoked a resolution that the company be a public limited company;

as those sections apply to a public limited company.

(2) Section 26 and sections 28 to 31, shall not apply to the allotment of shares by a company, other than a public limited company registered as such on its original incorporation, where the contract for their allotment was entered into—

(a) except in a case falling within paragraph (b), before the end of the general transitional period;

(b) in the case of a company re-registered or registered as a public limited company in pursuance of a resolution of any description mentioned in subsection (1) that is passed before the end of that period, before the date on which that resolution is passed.

Definitions

'company'; CA 1963, s 2(1); 'director': CA 1963, s 2(1); 'the general transitional period': C(A)A 1983, s 2(1); 'the Principal Act': C(A)A 1983, s 2(1); 'public limited company': C(A)A 1983, s 2(1); 'share': CA 1963, s 2(1).

Notes

Payment for shares in a company re-registering as a plc: The effect of C(A)A 1983, s 37 is to extend to a private company or an unlimited company which has duly resolved to re-register as a plc, the restrictions that apply to plcs regarding the payment of non-cash consideration for the allotment of shares (including the provisions for the independent valuation of such shares). In this regard, see C(A)A 1983, ss 26 and 30 and the notes thereto.

UK legislation

See CA 1985, s 116 (amended by CA 1989, s 131(2)).

Class rights

38 Variation of rights attached to special classes of shares

(1) This section shall have effect with respect to the variation of the rights attached to any class of shares in a company whose share capital is divided into shares of different classes.

(2) Where the rights are attached to a class of shares in the company otherwise than by the memorandum, and the articles of the company do not contain provisions with respect to the variation of the rights, those rights may be varied if, but only if—

(a) the holders of three-quarters in nominal value of the issued shares of that class consent in writing to the variation; or

(b) a special resolution passed at a separate general meeting of the holders of that class sanctions the variation;

and any requirement (howsoever imposed) in relation to the variation of those rights is complied with to the extent that it is not comprised in paragraphs (a) and (b).

(3) Where—

(a) the rights are attached to a class of shares in the company by the memorandum or otherwise;

(b) the memorandum or articles contain provision for the variation of those rights; and

(c) the variation of those rights is connected with the giving, variation, revocation or renewal of an authority for the purposes of section 20 or with a reduction of the company's share capital under section 72 of the Principal Act,

those rights shall not be varied unless—

(i) the condition mentioned in subsection (2)(a) or (b) is satisfied; and

(ii) any requirement of the memorandum or articles in relation to the variation of rights of that class is complied with to the extent that it is not comprised in the condition in subparagraph (i).

(4) Where the rights are attached to a class of shares in the company by the memorandum or otherwise and—

(a) where they are so attached by the memorandum, the articles contain provision with respect to their variation which had been included in the articles at the time of the company's original incorporation; or

(b) where they are so attached otherwise, the articles contain such provision (whenever first so included);

and in either case the variation is not connected as mentioned in subsection (3)(c), those rights may only be varied in accordance with that provision of the articles.

(5) Where the rights are attached to a class of shares in the company by the memorandum and the memorandum and articles do not contain provision with respect to the variation of the rights, those rights may be varied if all the members of the company agree to the variation.

(6) The provision of sections 133 and 134 of the Principal Act and the provisions of the articles relating to general meetings shall, so far as applicable, apply in relation to any meeting of shareholders required by this section or otherwise to take place in connection

with the variation of the rights attached to a class of shares, and shall so apply with the necessary modifications and subject to the following provisions, namely—

(a) the necessary quorum at any such meeting other than an adjourned meeting shall be two persons holding or representing by proxy at least one-third in nominal value of the issued shares of the class in question and at an adjourned meeting one person holding shares of the class in question or his proxy;

(b) any holder of shares of the class in question present in person or by proxy may demand a poll.

(7) Any alteration of a provision contained in the articles of a company for the variation of the rights attached to a class of shares or the insertion of any such provision into the company's articles shall itself be treated as a variation of those rights.

(8) Section 78 of the Principal Act shall apply in relation to subsection (2) as it applies in relation to a provision of the memorandum or articles of a company to the like effect.

(9) In this section and, except where the context otherwise requires, in any provision for the variation of the rights attached to a class of shares contained in the company's memorandum or articles references to the variation of those rights shall include references to their abrogation.

(10) Nothing in subsections (2) to (5) shall be construed as derogating from the powers of the court under section 15 or any of the following sections of the Principal Act, that is to say, sections 10, 201, 203 and 205.

(11) This section shall not apply in relation to any variation made by a company, other than a public limited company registered as such on its original incorporation, before the date on which the earlier of the following events occurs, that is to say, the re-registration or registration of the company as a public limited company and the end of the general transitional period.

Definitions

'articles': CA 1963, s 2(1); 'company'; CA 1963, s 2(1); 'the general transitional period': C(A)A 1983, s 2(1); 'memorandum': CA 1963, s 2(1); 'the Principal Act': C(A)A 1983, s 2(1); 'public limited company': C(A)A 1983, s 2(1); 'share': CA 1963, s 2(1).

Notes

Different classes of shares: All shares will be presumed to rank equally *inter se*.[1] This presumption may, however, be rebutted by a provision, whether in the memorandum or articles of association or in the terms of issue or, perhaps, in a shareholders' agreement,[2] dividing the share capital into different classes.

1 *Birch v Cropper* (1889) 14 App Cas 525.

2 *Harman v BML Group Ltd* [1994] 1 WLR 893.

Authority to create different classes of shares: Model Form Articles confer a power to create and issue different classes of shares.[1] However, even if the memorandum and articles are silent on the matter, such a power will normally be implied.[2] If the memorandum requires all shares to rank equally, a conflicting provision in the articles which authorises the division of shares into different classes will be void.[3] Where there are different classes of shares, these should be identified in the register of members.[4]

1 C(A)A 1983, Table A, reg 2.

2 *Bushell v Faith* [1970] AC 1099. *cf Campbell v Rofe* [1933] AC 91 at 98.

[3] *Andrews v Gas Meter Co* [1897] 1 Ch 361; *Campbell v Rofe* [1933] AC 91.
[4] *Re Performing Rights Society Ltd* [1978] 2 All ER 712.

Presumption of equality between classes: In the absence of an express provision to the contrary, all classes of shares will be presumed to rank equally as regards: (a) the right to vote; (b) the right to dividends; (c) the right to a return of capital in a winding up; and (d) the right to participate in any surplus assets in a winding up.[1] A preference regarding one such right does not imply a preference in respect of any other rights.[2]

[1] *Birch v Cropper* (1889) 14 App Cas 525.
[2] *Birch Cropper* (1889) 14 App Cas 525.

Ordinary shares: Ordinary shares (as their name suggests) are the residuary class of shares. Unless otherwise stated, all shares will be deemed to be ordinary shares and will rank equally *inter se*.[1] Even within the ordinary shares, however, it may be possible to create separate classes, so that one class might be voting ordinary shares and the other, non-voting ordinary shares.[2]

[1] *Birch Cropper* (1889) 14 App Cas 525.
[2] *Re Hellenic and General Trust Ltd* [1975] 3 All ER 382.

Preference shares: Preference shares are shares carrying certain preferential rights, whether as to dividends, capital or voting or a combination of all or some of the foregoing. As against this, however, their rights may in other respects, be curtailed. Thus, for example a preference share may carry preferential dividend entitlements, yet carry no voting rights or perhaps, a right to vote only when dividends are in arrear.

Preferential dividend rights

1. *Fixed dividend*: Shares carrying preferential dividend rights usually entitle the shareholder to receive a fixed dividend in priority to the ordinary shareholders. Thus, '8% preference shares' would entitle the holders to a fixed dividend of 8% of the par value per annum in priority to the payment of any dividend to the ordinary shareholders.[1]
2. *Declaration of dividend*: As with ordinary shares, however, the dividend on a preference share will normally only become payable once it has been declared in the manner provided by the articles.[2]
3. *Cumulative preference shares*: Unlike an ordinary share, a preference share will be presumed to carry cumulative dividend rights[3], so that once a dividend is declared for a particular year, the preference shareholder will also be entitled to receive payment of a dividend in respect of all the previous years in which no dividend has been declared.[4] Where preference shares of the same class have been issued at different times, so that different arrears are greater on some shares than on others, any dividend that is eventually paid must be applied rateably towards the satisfaction of those arrears.[5] Whether undeclared arrears of dividends on cumulative preference shares are payable in a liquidation depends very much n the terms of issue. If the dividends are expressed to be payable 'out of profits' the arrears will not be provable since the concept of 'profits' does not survive the commencement of the winding up.[6] Terminology that avoids any reference to 'profits' may, however, render the arrears of dividend capable of proof.[7]
4. *Non-cumulative preference shares*: Although the presumption is that preference shares are cumulative as to dividend entitlements, this presumption may be rebutted by wording to the contrary. Thus preference shares were held to be non-cumulative where the dividend was expressed to be payable 'out of the net profits each year'.[8] A similar conclusion was also reached in circumstances where the terms of issue stated that the dividend in any one year' should not exceed 9%.[9]
5. *Fixed dividend entitlement is exhaustive*: In so far as the preference shares carry a right to a fixed dividend, this will be presumed to be exhaustive of the preference shareholder's

dividend entitlements.[10] This presumption may of course be rebutted by an express provision to the contrary.[11]

6. *Preferential rights as to capital*: Apart from any priority as to dividends that may be enjoyed, preference shares may also or alternatively carry a priority to a return of capital in the event of a winding up. Such a right of priority will not, however, be regarded as exhaustive of all rights of the preference shareholder in a winding up and will not, per se, prelude him from participating in the surplus assets.[12]

7, *Preferential voting rights*: As noted above, preference shares often carry no voting rights whatsoever or perhaps only a limited entitlement to vote. Exceptionally, however, preference shares may be given 'loaded' voting rights. For example, each €1 preference share might carry 10 votes whilst ordinary shares would carry only one vote each. The validity of such loaded voting rights has long been recognised.[13]

1 *Re Lafayette Ltd* [1950] IR 100; *Webb v Earle* (1875) LR 20 Eq 556; *Re F de Jong and Company Ltd* 1946] Ch 211.

2 See C(A)A 1983, Table A, regs 116–124. For an example of articles which were interpreted as entitling the preference shareholders to payment of a dividend every year without the need for it to be declared, see *Re Lafayette Ltd* [1950] IR 100 and *Re Imperial Hotel (Cork) Ltd* [1950] IR 115. See also *RE WJ Hall and Co Ltd* [1909] 1 Ch 521; *Re Spanish Prospecting Co Ltd* [1911] 1 Ch 92.

3 *Henry v Great Northern Railway Co* (1857) 1 De G and J 606; *Corry v Londonderry and Enniskillen Railway Co* (1860) 29 Beav 263; *Webb v Earle* (1875) LR 20 Eq 556; *Re F de Jong and Company Ltd* 1946] Ch 211.

4 *Re Wakley, Wakley v Vachell* [1920] 2 Ch 205; *Godfrey Phillips Ltd v Investment Trust Corporation Ltd* [1953] Ch 449. As regards the profits available for distribution by way of dividend, see C(A)A 1983, s 45 and the notes thereto.

5 *First Garden City Ltd v Bonham-Carter* [1928] Ch 58.

6 *Re Lafayette Ltd* [1950] IR 100; *Re Crichton's Oil Co* [1902] 2 Ch 86; *Wilson (Inspector of Taxes) v Dunnes Stores (Cork) Ltd* [1982] ILRM 444.

7 *Re Walter Symons Ltd* [1934] Ch 308; *Re Wood, Skinner and Co Ltd* [1944] Ch 323; *Re de Jong and Co Ltd* [1946] Ch 211; *Re EW Savory Ltd* [1951] 2 All ER 1036.

8 *Staples v Eastman Photographic Materials Co* [1896] 2 Ch 303.

9 *JI Thornycroft and Co v Thornycroft* (1927) 44 TLR 9. See also *Adair v Old Bushmills Distillery Co* [1908] WN 24.

10 *Will v United Plankat Plantations Co Ltd* [1914] AC 11.

11 See for example, *Steel Company of Canada Ltd v Ramsay* [1931] AC 270; *Re Isle of Thanet Electricity Supply Co Ltd* [1950] Ch 161; *Re Saltdean Estate Co Ltd* [1968] 1 WLR 1844.

12 *Re Cork Electricity Supply Co Ltd* [1932] IR 314; *Birch v Cropper* (1889) 14 App Cas 525. In England, a contrary view has been taken so that priority as to return of capital is presumed to be exhaustive of all rights in the liquidation: *Will v United Lankat Plantations Co* [1914] AC 11; *Scottish Insurance Corporation Ltd v Wilson and Clyde Coal Co* [1949] AC 462; *Prudential Assurance Co v Chatterley-Whitfield Collieries Co Ltd* [1949] AC 462; *Re Isle of Thanet Electricity Supply Co Ltd* [1950] Ch 161.

13 *Bushell v Faith* [1970] AC 1099.

Class rights need not attach to specific shares: Where a company, by its memorandum or articles, confers special rights on one or more of its shareholders *qua* shareholder, those rights, even if not expressed to attach to any specific share or shares, will nonetheless be regarded as class rights and will only be capable of variation in accordance with the procedures laid down in the Companies Acts.[1] On the other hand, if the right as contained in the memorandum or articles, is conferred in the shareholder in some other capacity, it will not be regarded as being a class right and may therefore be altered or abrogated in the ordinary way.[2]

1 *Cumbrian Newspaper Group Ltd v Cumberland and Westmoreland Herald Newspaper and Printing Co Ltd* [1986] BCLC 286.

2 *Re Blue Arrow plc* [1987] BCLC 585. With regard to the appropriate procedures for so altering such a provision, see CA 1963, ss 15 and 28.

Registration of class rights: Where class rights are contained in the memorandum or articles or in a resolution which has been registered pursuant to CA 1963 (such as a special resolution or a resolution under C(A)A 1983, s 20 authorising the directors to allot shares), they will be readily capable of being ascertained by an examination of the Companies Registration Office file. If the class rights arose otherwise (eg pursuant to shareholders' agreement) they would not necessarily be known to persons dealing with or proposing to invest in the company. Accordingly, where a company allots shares with rights which are not specified in the memorandum or articles or in a resolution requiring registration under CA 1963, s 143, then unless the shares being allotted are in all respects uniform with shares previously allotted, the company must, within one month of the allotment, deliver to the Registrar a statement in the prescribed form[1] containing particulars of those rights.[2] Similar registration requirements arise where the rights attaching to existing shares are varied otherwise than by an amendment to the memorandum or articles or pursuant to a resolution requiring registration under CA 1963, s 143.[3] In addition, if a company assigns a name or other designation, or a new name or other designation, to any class of shares, otherwise than by an amendment to the memorandum or articles or pursuant to a resolution requiring registration under CA 1963, s 143, then a statement in the prescribed form[4] containing full particulars thereof must be delivered to the Registrar of companies within a period of one month.[5] Failure to observe these registration requirements constitutes a criminal offence.[6]

1 Form 80, Companies (Forms) Order 1983 (SI 289/1983).

2 C(A)A 1983, s 39(1). Shares will not be regarded as being different merely because they have different dividend entitlements from existing shares for a period of to 12 months from the date of allotment: s 38(2).

3 C(A)A 1983, s 38(3). The prescribed form in such circumstances is Form 81 of the Companies (Forms Order 1983 (SI 283/1983).

4 Form 82, Companies (Forms) Order 1983 (SI 289/1983).

5 C(A)A 1983, s 38(4).

6 C(A)A 1983, s 38(5).

What constitutes a variation of class rights?: The rights of a class of shareholders are neither varied nor 'affected' by the issue of new shares ranking *pari passu* with existing shares of that class.[1] Similarly, a dilution of the voting strength of one class of shares by an increase in the voting strength of another class, although possibly affecting the rights of the first class 'as a matter of business' will not be regarded as varying their rights 'as a matter of law'.[2] Likewise, if a reduction of share capital follows the same order of priority as would apply in a winding up, it will not be regarded as a variation of class rights.[3] On the other hand, the insertion or alteration of a clause in the articles laying down procedures for the variation of class rights is itself to be regarded as a variation of class rights.[4]

1 *White v Bristol Aeroplane Co* [1953] Ch 65; *Re John Smith's Tadcaster Brewery Co Ltd* [1953] 2 WLR 516; *Re Schweppes Ltd* [1914] 1 Ch 322.

2 *Greenhalgh v Arderne Cinemas Ltd* [1946] 1 All ER 512. It is possible, however that the dilution in voting strength could amount to oppression or disregard of interests within the meaning of CA 1963, s 205: *Re Williams Group Tullamore Ltd* [1985] IR 613.

3 *Re MacKenzie and Co* [1916] 2 Ch 450; *Re Chatterley-Whitfield Collieries Ltd* [1948] 2 All ER 593, aff'd sub nom *Prudential Assurance Co Ltd Chatterley-Whitfield Collieries Ltd* [1949] AC 512; *Re John Power and Son Ltd* [1934] IR 412; *House of Fraser plc v ACGE Investments Ltd* [1987] AC 387; *Re Credit Finance Bank plc* (1963–1993) Irish Company Law Reports 170.

4 C(A)A 1983, s 38(7). Curiously the insertion or alteration of such a clause in the memorandum of association does not appear to attract the same statutory protection.

Procedure for variation of class rights:[1] The procedure for the variation of class rights depends on where those rights are to be founds and on whether the memorandum or articles contain an express procedure for effecting such a variation. The scenarios are as follows:

1. If the class rights are to be found otherwise than in the memorandum or articles (as where they are to be found in the terms of issue) and if there is no procedure for variation either in the memorandum or articles, the variation may only be effected by a special resolution of that class or by the written consent of not less than 75% in nominal value of the shares of that class.[2]
2. Regardless of where the class rights are to be found, if the proposed variation relates to the giving, revocation or renewal of an authorisation to the directors under C(A)A 1983, s 20 to allot shares or if it relates to a reduction of capital under CA 1963, s 72, then in addition to any procedures that may be prescribed by the memorandum or articles, the company must also obtain either a special resolution of that class or the written consent of not less than 75% in nominal value of the shares of that class.[3]
3. Subject to C(A)A 1983, s 38(2), if the class rights are to be found in the memorandum and the articles have from the original incorporation of the company contained a procedure for the variation of class rights, that procedure will be applicable.[4]
4. Subject to C(A)A 1983, s 38(2), if the class rights are to be found otherwise than in the memorandum and the articles contain a procedure for variation (even if that procedure has not been in place from the company's original incorporation), the procedure as so prescribed will be applicable.[5]
5. If the class rights are to be found in the memorandum, and neither the memorandum nor the articles contain a procedure for the variation of such rights, no variation will in fact be effective unless consented to by all the members of the company (and not just all the members of that class).[6]

With regard to the foregoing, it is to be noted that the insertion or alteration of a clause in the articles laying down procedures for the variation of class rights is itself to be regarded as a variation of class rights which can only be effected in the manner described above.[7]

1 Unless the context otherwise requires, a 'variation' of class rights includes a complete abrogation of those rights: C(A)A 1983, s 38(9).

2 C(A)A 1983, s 38(2). As it happens, Table A, Pt I, reg 3 contains a procedure for variation of class rights which requires similar class consent.

3 C(A)A 1983, s 38(3).

4 C(A)A 1983, s 38(4)(a). Such a procedure is in fact to be found in Table A, Pt I, reg 3. However, if or whatever reason, reg 3 was disapplied on the incorporation of the company, the variation of class rights contained in the memorandum will only be effective if either the company has a procedure for variation in the memorandum itself or alternatively the consent of all members is obtained under s 38(5).

5 C(A)A 1983, s 38(4)(b).

6 C(A)A 1983, s 38(5).

7 C(A)A 1983, s 38(7). Curiously, the insertion or alteration of such a clause in the memorandum of association does not appear to attract the same statutory protection. Such a provision, where found in the memorandum of association, may be amended by special resolution of the company in general meeting (as opposed to a special resolution of the affected class) pursuant to CA 163, s 28.

Objection to court by dissentients: Where the procedure for varying class rights is contained in the memorandum or articles and provides for the separate consent of the affected class,[1] or where the provisions of C(A)A 1983, s 38 require the separate consent of that class, any dissenting member or members of that class holding between them not less than 10% of the nominal value of the shares of that class may apply to the court within 28 days of the date on which the variation was approved to have the variation cancelled.[2] Where such an application is ending the variation of class rights is suspended unless and until confirmed by the court.[3] An applicant who purports to act not only on his own behalf but also on behalf of others must first show that he has in fact been so appointed in writing[4] and that the authority to so act has indeed been communicated to him.[5] To succeed in such an application the dissentient must show that the variation is unfairly prejudicial to the affected class. This may be established by showing that the majority of the class did not vote *bona fide* in the interests of the class as a whole, but were instead motivated by some other interest (eg the benefit that they would derive as ordinary shareholders by varying or abrogating the rights of preference shareholders).[6]

1 As is the case in C(A)A 1983, Table A, Pt I, reg 3.

2 CA 1963, s 78(1) and (2) as applied by s 38(8).

3 CA 1963, s 78(1) as applied by s 38(8).

4 CA 1963, s 78(2). See also *Re Suburban and Provincial Stores* [1943] Ch 156.

5 *Re Sound City (Films) Ltd* [1947] Ch 169.

6 *Re Holders Investment Trust Ltd* [1971] 1 WLR 583; *Re Wedgewood Coal and Iron Co* [1877] 6 ChD 627; *British American Nickel Corporation v O'Brien* [1927] AC 369; *Greenhalgh v Arderne Cinemas Ltd (No 2)* [1945] 2 All ER 719; *Greenhalgh v Arderne Cinemas Ltd* [1951] Ch 286.

Oppression of minority: Apart from any relief to which the dissenting minority might be entitled under CA 1963, s 78 as applied by s 38(8), they may also be entitled to seek relief under CA 1963, s 205 if they can show that the variation in class rights is oppressive or in disregard of their own interests as members.[1] Unlike the remedy contained in CA 1963, s 78, there is no minimum shareholding required before a member can petition for relief under s 205.

1 *Re Williams Group Tullamore Ltd* [1985] IR 613; *Clemens v Clemens Bros Ltd* [1976] 2 All ER 268.

UK legislation

See CA 1985, ss 125, 126.

---

39 Registration of particulars of special rights

(1) Where a company allots shares with rights which are not stated in its memorandum or articles or in any resolution or agreement to which section 143 of the Principal Act applies, the company shall, unless the shares are in all respects uniform with shares previously allotted, deliver to the registrar of companies within one month from allotting the shares a statement in the prescribed form containing particulars of those rights.

(2) Shares allotted with such rights shall not be treated for the purposes of subsection (1) as different from shares previously allotted by reason only of the fact that the former do not carry the same rights to dividends as the latter during the twelve months immediately following the former's allotment.

(3) Where the rights attached to any shares of a company are varied otherwise than by an amendment of the company's memorandum or articles or by resolution or agreement to which the said section 143 applies, the company shall within one month from the date on which the variation is made deliver to the registrar of companies a statement in the prescribed form containing particulars of the variation.

(4) Where a company (otherwise than by any such amendment, resolution or agreement as is mentioned in subsection (3)) assigns a name or other designation, or a new name or

other designation, to any class of its shares it shall within one month from doing so deliver to the registrar of companies a notice in the prescribed form giving particulars thereof.

(5) If a company fails to comply with this section, the company and every officer of the company who is in default shall be guilty of an offence and shall be liable on summary conviction to a fine not exceeding [€1,904.61][a] together with, in the case of a continuing offence, a fine not exceeding [€31.74][b] for every day on which the offence continues but not exceeding [€1,904.61][c] in total.

Amendments

a '£250' substituted for '£50' by C(A)A 1982, Sch 1, increased to £1,500 by CA 1990, s 240(7) as inserted by CLEA 2001, s 104(c), and converted to €1,904.61 by Council Regulations (EC) No 1103/97, No 974/98 and No 2866/98 and the Economic and Monetary Union Act 1998, s 6.

b £25 converted to €31.74 by Council Regulations (EC) No 1103/97, No 974/98 and No 2866/98 and the Economic and Monetary Union Act 1998, s 6.

c £500 increased to £1,500 by CA 1990, s 240(7) as inserted by CLEA 2001, s 104(c) and converted to €1,904.61 by Council Regulations (EC) No 1103/97, No 974/98 and No 2866/98 and the Economic and Monetary Union Act 1998, s 6.

Definitions

'articles': CA 1963, s 2(1); 'company': CA 1963, s 2(1); 'memorandum': CA 1963, s 2(1); 'officer'; CA 1963, s 2(1); 'officer in default': CA 1963, s 383; 'Prescribed': CA 1963, s 2(1); 'the Principal Act': C(A)A 1983, s 2(1); 'Registrar of Companies': CA 1963, s 2(1); 'share'; CA 1963, s 2(1).

Notes

Registration of class rights: See C(A)A 1983, s 38 and the notes thereto.

Investment company: The provisions of C(A)A 1983, s 40 do not apply to investment companies. See CA 1990, s 260.

UK legislation

See CA 1985, s 128.

Maintenance of capital

40 Obligation to convene extraordinary general meeting in event of serious loss of capital

(1) Subject to subsection (4), where the net assets of a company are half or less of the amount of the company's called-up share capital, the directors of the company shall, not later than 28 days from the earliest day on which that fact is known to a director of the company, duly convene an extraordinary general meeting of the company for a date not later than 56 days from that day for the purpose of considering whether any, and if so what, measures should be taken to deal with the situation.

(2) If there is a failure to convene an extraordinary general meeting of a company as required by subsection (1), each of the directors of the company who—

(a) knowingly and wilfully authorises or permits that failure; or

(b) after the expiry of the period during which that meeting should have been convened, knowingly and wilfully authorises or permits that failure to continue,

shall be guilty of an offence.

(3) Nothing in this section shall be taken as authorising the consideration, at a meeting convened in pursuance of subsection (1), of any matter which could not have been considered at that meeting apart from this section.

(4) This section shall not apply where the day mentioned in subsection (1) is before the appointed day.

Definitions

'the appointed day': C(A)A 1983, s 1(3), s 2(1); 'called-up share capital': C(A)A 1983, s 2(1); 'company': CA 1963, s 2(1); 'director': CA 1963, s 2(1).

Notes

EGM to consider serious loss of capital: Where a company, other than an investment company[1], suffers a serious loss of capital (eg as a result of adverse trading conditions) such that the value of its net assets is 50% or less of the called up share capital, the directors are obliged by this section to convene an EGM to consider what measures, if any, should be taken to deal the situation.[2] The convening of the meeting does not, however, operate so as to allow the consideration of other items of business,[3] unless the general nature of those other items has been specifically included in the notice convening the meeting as items of special business.[4] Furthermore, whilst the meeting must be convened and held within the time limits prescribed by C(A)A 1983, s 40(2), there is apparently no obligation on the members, to attend the meeting let alone, having considered the situation, to actually take any steps to redress the loss of capital. Nonetheless, if they cause or permit the company to trade whilst insolvent, they may ultimately face exposure under CA 1963, s 297A.

1 CA 1990, s 260(2).

2 C(A)A 1983, s 40(1).

3 C(A)A 1983, s 40(3).

4 See C(A)A 1983, Table A, reg 53 and *Roper v Ward* [1981] ILRM 408. See also CA 1963, s 141(8) and the notes thereto in relation to the ability of the members acting unanimously to dispense with any formal requirements regarding the convening and holding of meetings and the passing of resolutions.

UK legislation

See CA 1985, s 142.

---

41 Restriction on company acquiring its own shares

(1) Subject to the following provisions of this section, no company limited by shares or limited by guarantee and having a share capital shall acquire its own shares (whether by purchase, subscription or otherwise).

(2) A company limited by shares may acquire any of its own fully paid shares otherwise than for valuable consideration.

(3) If a company purports to act in contravention of this section the company and every officer of the company who is in default shall be guilty of an offence and the purported acquisition shall be void.

(4) Subsection (1) shall not apply in relation to—

[(a) the redemption of preference shares in pursuance of section 65 of the Principal Act or the redemption or purchase of shares in pursuance of Part XI of the Companies Act, 1990];[a]

(b) the acquisition of any shares in a reduction of capital duly made;

(c) the purchase of any shares in pursuance of an order of the court under section 15 or under section 10 or section 205 of the Principal Act; or

(d) the forfeiture of any shares, or the acceptance of any shares surrendered in lieu, in pursuance of the articles for failure to pay any sum payable in respect of those shares.

Amendments

a C(A)A 1983, s 41(a) substituted by CA 1990, s 232.

Definitions

'company': CA 1963, s 2(1) and NAMA Act 2009, s 229; 'company limited by guarantee': CA 1963, s 2(1), s 5(2); 'company limited by shares'; CA 1963, s 2(1); s 5(2); 'the Principal Act': C(A)A 1983, s 2(1); 'share': CA 1963, s 2(1).

Cross references in other enactments

NAMA Act 2009, s 229 provides that a reference to a 'company' in C(A)A 1983, s 41(1) 'shall be taken not to include a NAMA group entity' within the meaning of NAMA Act 2009.

Notes

Acquisition by company of its own shares: This general prohibition on a company acquiring its own shares was not only already well established at common law[1] but was also to be found in the opening words of CA 1963, s 72(1). The rule exists for the protection of creditors, the rationale being that no part of the company's capital should be paid out except in the legitimate course of the company's business.[2] Nor can a company circumvent this restriction by having its own shares issued to or purchased by a nominee (or in the case of a plc, to or by a nominee of its subsidiary). Instead: if such shares are issued to or purchased by a nominee purportedly in his own right,[3] they will be treated for all purposes as being owned by the nominee on his own account and the company will not be regarded as having any beneficial interest in them.[4] Moreover, in the case of shares held by such a nominee, if the nominee fails to pay any part of the par value or any part of any premium within 21 days of being called upon to do so, the directors (or the other subscribers, if the shares held by the nominee are subscriber shares) shall be jointly and severally liable along with the nominee to pay up the amount in question.[5] The imposition of this joint and several liability reflects the culpability of the directors or subscribers as the case may be, in seeking to circumvent the restriction on a company acquiring its own shares, by having those shares acquired through a nominee instead. In this regard, however, in any proceedings against a director or subscriber for the unpaid amount,[6] if the person can show that he has acted honestly and reasonably and that having regard to all the circumstances of the case he ought fairly to be excused from liability (as here he can show that the other directors or subscribers concealed from him the fact that the person acquiring the shares was in fact a nominee of the company), the court may, if it thinks fit, excuse him in whole or in part from the liability to pay the said sum.[7]

1 *Trevor v Whitworth* (1887) 12 App Cas 409; *Re Irish Provident Assurance Co Ltd* [1913] 1 IR 352; *Barclays Bank plc v British and Commonwealth Holdings plc* [1996] 1 BCLC 1; *Re RW Peak (Kings Lynn) Ltd* [1998] 1 BCLC 193.

2 *Trevor v Whitworth* (1887) 12 App Cas 409.

3 Needless to say, there can be no ground for objecting to the company's nominee being issued with or otherwise acquiring shares as agent, personal representative or trustee for some other person and in circumstances where the company itself is going to have no beneficial interest in those shares, since in such a case there is no question of the company either directly or indirectly breaching the prohibition on the acquisition of its own shares: C(A)A 1983, s 42(6). Nor is the position affected by the fact that as trustee, personal representative, etc the nominee is entitled to recover his expenses or be remunerated out of the property in question (ie the shares): s 42(6).

4 C(A)A 1983, s 42(1) as extended by EC(PLCS)R 1997, reg 5(4). If, however, the shares are acquired by a nominee of a plc otherwise than by subscription and with direct or indirect financial assistance from the plc itself, the beneficial interest of the plc will be recognised, irrespective of any breach of CA 1963, s 60, but the shares must either be disposed of or cancelled with one year of their acquisition: C(A)A 1983, s 42(5) and s 43.

5 C(A)A 1983, s 42(2).

6 As an alternative to waiting to be sued, the director or subscriber may apply to the court for relief in advance of the actual commencement of any proceedings against him: C(A)A 1983, s 42(4).

7 C(A)A 1983, s 42(3).

Permitted share acquisitions: Where the company acquires its own shares otherwise than for valuable consideration (eg a gift or bequest), the acquisition will be lawful because it involves no dissipation of the company's assets.[1] Forfeiture of shares or surrender in lieu of forfeiture, in accordance with the articles of association[2] (ie on terms whereby the shareholder remains liable for any amounts accrued in respect of his shares) will similarly be permitted[3] whereas a surrender of shares which involves the release of a shareholder from liability in respect of accrued amounts is equivalent to a purchase of shares and is therefore void.[4] In relation to the other forms of share acquisition permitted by C(A)A 1983, s 41(4), a redemption of purchase of shares under CA 1990, Part XI may only be effected out of distributable profits or out of the proceeds of a fresh issue of shares whereas the other forms of acquisition can only occur pursuant to court order. A court will be most unlikely to allow a company's moneys to be used in buying back its own shares unless it is satisfied that the company will still have sufficient funds to meet its liabilities to its creditors as they fall due. In this regard see C(A)A 1983, s 15 and CA 1963, ss 10, 72 and 205 and the notes thereto.

1 C(A)A 1983, s 41(2). If the shares are beneficially so acquired by a plc they must either be disposed of within three years or be cancelled: s 43.

2 See C(A)A 1983, Table A, regs 33–39 in relation to the forfeiture of shares.

3 C(A)A 1983, s 41(4)(d). If the shares are beneficially so acquired by a plc they must either be disposed of within three years or be cancelled: s 43.

4 *Bellerby v Rowland and Marwood's Steamship Co Ltd* [1902] Ch 14.

Acquisition of shares in shareholder companies: Whilst a company may well be precluded from acquiring its own shares, there is no prohibition on a company acquiring shares in another company which is in turn one of its own shareholders,[1] unless that other company is its holding company in which event the restrictions prescribed by CA 1990, ss 224 and 225 as extended by EC(PLCS)R 1997, reg 5(2) and (5) will apply.

1 *Acatos and Hutcheson plc v Watson* [1995] 1 BCLC 218. In that case, Lightman J held that the court will nonetheless carefully scrutinise the directors' motives for having the company effect the acquisition, lest they should have caused the company to purchase the shares not for the benefit of the company but to enable them to exercise indirect control over a greater number of shares for the protection of their own position. See also *Dyason v JC Hutton Pty Ltd* (1935) Argus LR 419; *August Investments Pty Ltd v Poseidon Ltd and Samin Ltd* [1971] 2 SASR 71; *Trade Practices Commission v Australian Iron and Steel Pty Ltd* (1990) 92 ALR 395.

Liens and other charges on shares: Model Form Articles provide that a company has a lien on its own shares and any dividends payable in respect thereof.[1] Typically, these Model Form Articles are varied so as to provide that the lien will extend not only to sums payable in respect of the shares themselves but also to any other sums payable by the shareholder to the company. In such circumstances, a lien could be exercised on a share notwithstanding the fact that t was fully paid up. However, C(A)A 1983, s 44 curtails the ability of a plc to take a lien or charge on its own shares. Such security will be taken on unpaid shares and in respect of moneys payable in the shares themselves.[2] In the case of a plc which carries on business as a bank, moneylender or finance house, it may take a charge in its own shares (whether or not fully paid) provided it does so in the ordinary course of business.[3] If a private or unlimited company re-registers as a plc, these restrictions on the taking of liens and other charges will only apply to such securities to the extent that they are taken after the date of the application for re-registration.[4]

1 See C(A)A 1983, regs 11–14.

2 C(A)A 1983, s 43(2)(a).

3 C(A)A 1983, s 43(2)(b).

4 C(A)A 1983, s 43(2)(c).

Unlimited companies and investment companies: The prohibition on a company acquiring its own shares which is contained in s 41 does not apply to unlimited companies nor does it apply to investment companies.[2]

1 See C(A)A 1983, s 41(1).

2 CA 1990, s 260(2)

UK legislation

See CA 1985, s 143.

---

42 Acquisition of shares in a company by company's nominee

(1) Subject to subsections (5) and (6), where shares are issued to a nominee of a company referred to in section 41(1) or are acquired by a nominee of such a company from a third party as partly paid up, then, for all purposes the shares shall be treated as held by the nominee on his own account and the company shall be regarded as having no beneficial interest in them.

(2) Subject to subsection (6), if a person is called on to pay any amount for the purpose of paying up, or paying any premium on, any shares in any such company which were issued to him, or which he otherwise acquired, as the nominee of the company and he fails to pay that amount within 21 days from being called on to do so, then—

(a) if the shares were issued to him as a subscriber to the memorandum by virtue of an undertaking of his in the memorandum, the other subscribers to the memorandum; or

(b) if the shares were otherwise issued to or acquired by him, the directors of the company at the time of the issue or acquisition,

shall be jointly and severally liable with him to pay that amount.

(3) If in proceedings for the recovery of any such amount from any such subscriber or director under this section it appears to the court that he is or may be liable to pay that amount, but that he has acted honestly and reasonably and that, having regard to all the circumstances of the case, he ought fairly to be excused from liability, the court may

relieve him, either wholly or partly, from his liability on such terms as the court thinks fit.

(4) Where any such subscriber or director has reason to apprehend that a claim will or might be made for the recovery of any such amount from him, he may apply to the court for relief and on the application the court shall have the same power to relieve him as it would have had in proceedings for the recovery of that amount.

(5) Subsection (1) shall not apply to shares acquired otherwise than by subscription by a nominee of a public limited company in a case falling within section 43(1)(d).

(6) Subsections (1) and (2) shall not apply—

(a) to shares acquired by a nominee of a company where the company has no beneficial interest in those shares (disregarding any right which the company itself may have as trustee, whether as personal representative or otherwise, to recover its expenses or be remunerated out of the trust property); or

(b) to shares issued in consequence of an application made before the appointed day or transferred in pursuance of an agreement to acquire them made before that day.

Definitions

'the appointed day': C(A)A 1983, s 1(3), s 2(1); 'company': CA 1963, s 2(1); 'director': CA 1963, s 2(1); 'memorandum': CA 1963, s 2(1) 'public limited company': C(A)A 1983, s 2(1); 'shares'; CA 1963, s 2(1).

Notes

Acquisition of own shares through a nominee: See C(A)A 1983, s 41 and the notes thereto.

UK legislation

See CA 1985, ss 144–145.

---

43 Treatment of shares held by or on behalf of a public limited company

(1) Subject to subsections (12) and (15), this section applies to a public limited company—

(a) where shares in the company are forfeited, or are surrendered to the company in lieu, in pursuance of the articles for failure to pay any sum payable in respect of those shares;

(b) where shares in the company are acquired by the company otherwise that by any of the methods mentioned in section 41(4) and the company has a beneficial interest in those shares;

(c) where the nominee of the company acquires shares in the company from a third person without financial assistance being given directly or indirectly by the company and the company has a beneficial interest in those shares; or

(d) where any person acquires shares in the company with financial assistance given to him directly or indirectly by the company for the purpose of or in connection with the acquisition and the company has a beneficial interest in those shares.

(2) In determining for the purposes of subsection (1)(b) and (c) whether a company has a beneficial interest in any shares, there shall be disregarded, in any case where the company is a trustee (whether as personal representative or otherwise), any right of the company (as trustee) to recover its expenses or be remunerated out of the trust property.

(3) Unless the shares or any interest of the company in them are previously disposed of, the company must not later than the end of the relevant period from their forfeiture or surrender or, in a case to which subsection (1)(b), (c) or (d) applies, their acquisition—

(a) cancel them and reduce the amount of the share capital by the nominal value of the shares; and

(b) where the effect of cancelling the shares will be that the nominal value of the company's allotted share capital is brought below the authorised minimum, apply for re-registration as another form of company, stating the effect of the cancellation,

and the directors may take such steps as are requisite to enable the company to carry out its obligations under this subsection without complying with sections 72 and 73 of the Principal Act, including passing a resolution in accordance with subsection (5).

(4) The company and, in a case falling within subsection (1)(c) or (d), the company's nominee or, as the case may be, the other shareholder must not exercise any voting rights in respect of the shares and any purported exercise of those rights shall be void.

(5) The resolution authorised by subsection (3) may alter the company's memorandum so that it no longer states that the company is to be a public limited company and may make such other alterations in the memorandum and articles as are requisite in the circumstances.

(6) The application for re-registration required by subsection (3)(b) must be in the prescribed form and signed by a director or secretary of the company and must be delivered to the registrar together with a printed copy of the memorandum and articles of the company as altered by the resolution.

(7) If a public limited company required to apply to be re-registered as another form of company under this section fails to do so before the end of the relevant period, section 21 shall apply to it as if it were a private company such as is mentioned in that section, but, except as aforesaid, the company shall continue to be treated for the purposes of the Companies Acts as a public limited company until it is re-registered as another form of company.

(8) If a company when required to do so by subsection (3) fails to cancel any shares in accordance with paragraph (a) of that subsection or to make an application for re-registration in accordance with paragraph (b) of that subsection, the company and every officer of the company who is in default shall be guilty of an offence and shall be liable on summary conviction to a fine not exceeding [€1,904.61][a] together with, in the case of a continuing offence, a fine not exceeding [€31.74][b] for every day on which the offence continues, but not exceeding [€1,904.61][c] in total.

(9) If the registrar is satisfied that a company may be re-registered in accordance with this section he shall—

(a) retain the application and other documents delivered to him under subsection (6); and

(b) issue the company with an appropriate certificate of incorporation.

(10) Upon the issue of a certificate of incorporation under subsection (9)—

(a) the company shall by virtue of the issue of that certificate become the form of company stated in the certificate; and

(b) the alterations in the memorandum and articles set out in the resolution shall take effect accordingly.

(11) A certificate of incorporation issued to a company under subsection (9) shall be conclusive evidence—

(a) that the requirements of this section in respect of re-registration and of matters precedent and incidental thereto have been complied with; and

(b) that the company is the form of company stated in the certificate.

(12) Where, after shares in a company—

(a) are forfeited in pursuance of the articles of the company or are surrendered to the company in lieu of forfeiture or are otherwise acquired by the company;

(b) are acquired by a nominee of the company in the circumstances mentioned in subsection (1)(c); or

(c) are acquired by any person in the circumstances mentioned in subsection (1)(d),

the company is re-registered as a public limited company, the foregoing provisions of this section shall apply to the company as if it had been a public limited company at the time of the forfeiture, surrender or acquisition and as if for any reference to the relevant period from the forfeiture, surrender or acquisition there were substituted a reference to the relevant period from the re-registration of the company as a public limited company.

(13) [...][d]

(14) In this section 'relevant period', in relation to any shares, means—

(a) in the case of shares forfeited or surrendered to the company in lieu of forfeiture or acquired as mentioned in subsection (1)(b) or (c), three years;

(b) in the case of shares acquired as mentioned in subsection (1)(d), one year.

(15) Notwithstanding anything in section 12(2), a reference in this section to a public limited company does not include a reference to an old public limited company.

Amendments

a '£250' substituted for '£50' by C(A)A 1982, Sch 1, increased to £1,500 by CA 1990, s 240(7) as inserted by CLEA 2001, s 104(c), and converted to €1,904.61 by Council Regulations (EC) No 1103/97, No 974/98 and No 2866/98 and the Economic and Monetary Union Act 1998, s 6.

b £25 converted to €31.74 by Council Regulations (EC) No 1103/97, No 974/98 and No 2866/98 and the Economic and Monetary Union Act 1998, s 6.

c £500 converted to €1,904.61 by Council Regulations (EC) No 1103/97, No 974/98 and No 2866/98 and the Economic and Monetary Union Act 1998, s 6.

d C(A)A 1983, s 43(13) repealed by CA 1990, s 232.

Definitions

'articles': CA 1963, s 2(1); 'the authorised minimum': C(A)A 1983, s 2(1), s 19; 'the Companies Acts': C(A)A 1983, s 2(1); 'company': CA 1963, s 2(1); 'director': CA 1963, s 2(1); 'document': CA 1963, s 2(1): 'memorandum': CA 1963, s 2(1); 'officer': CA 1963, s 2(1); 'officer in default': CA 1963, s 383; 'old public limited company': C(A)A 1983, s 2(1), s 12(1); 'prescribed': CA 1963, s 2(1); 'the Principal Act': C(A)A 1983, s 2(1); 'printed': CA 1963, s 2(1); 'private company': CA 1963, s 2(1), s 33(1); 'public limited company': C(A)A 1983, s 2(1); 'Registrar of Companies'; CA 1963, s 2(1); 'share': CA 1963, s 2(1).

Notes

Acquisition of shares by a plc: A plc may validly acquire shares otherwise than for valuable consideration[1] (eg by way of gift or bequest) or by any of the other methods described in C(A)A 1983, s 41(4).[2] However, if the plc, or a company which re-registers as a plc has acquired any such shares beneficially and other than pursuant to one or other of the methods described in C(A)A 1983, s 41(4)(1)(a)–(c), it must either dispose of or cancel those shares within three years of the acquisition or re-registration, as the case may be, or within one year where the acquisition was by way of forfeiture or surrender in lieu of forfeiture.[3] If the company opts to cancel rather than dispose of the shares, the company's capital must be reduced accordingly, albeit that this may be done by the directors without having to obtain either the approval of the shareholders or the confirmation of the court under CA 1963, ss 72 and 73.[4] Nonetheless, if the effect of the reduction of capital is to bring the plc's allotted share capital below the authorised minimum of €38,092.14, it must take the necessary steps to re-register as some other form of company.[5] If the plc fails to so re-register within the relevant period of time, it will be treated as a private company to the extent that it will be precluded from offering its shares or debentures to the public[6] but will otherwise be regarded as a plc unless and until formal re-registration is actually effected.[7] Furthermore, the company itself and every officer in default will be guilty of a criminal offence where re-registration ought to have been but has not been effected.[8]

1. C(A)A 1983, s 41(2).
2. However, if: (a) the shares are acquired by a nominee of the plc from a third party without direct or indirect financial interest from the plc but in circumstances where the plc obtains a beneficial interest in those shares; or (b) the shares are acquired by any person with direct or indirect financial assistance from the plc and the plc acquires a beneficial interest in those shares, no voting rights shall be exercisable in respect of those shares: C(A)A 1983, s 43(4).
3. C(A)A 1983, s 43(1), (3), (12) and (14). This obligation to dispose of or cancel the shares arises even if the shares have been acquired by way of gift, bequest, etc.
4. C(A)A 1983, s 43(3).
5. C(A)A 1983, s 43(3) and (5). See C(A)A 1983, ss 14, 15 and 52 for the procedures applicable in the case of re-registration as private company or an unlimited company.
6. C(A)A 1983, s 43(7).
7. C(A)A 1983, s 43(7).
8. C(A)A 1983, s 43(8).

Plc subsidiaries: Where a plcs subsidiary purchases, subscribes for or holds shares in its plc and: (a) the shares were not fully paid when they were purchased; or (b) the authorisation required by CA 1990, s 224(3) has not been obtained; or (c) the shares are held as treasury shares in excess of the limited referred to in CA 1990, s 209(2) or (d) the purchase or subscription was effected with financial assistance in purported reliance on the whitewash procedure contained in CA 1963, s 60(2)–(11), then the provisions of s 43(3) shares will apply with the modification that the shares in question must be disposed of or cancelled within a period of 12 months.[1]

1. EC(PLCS)R 1997, reg 5(5). See, however, reg 5(6) for the circumstances in which a plc's subsidiary may lawfully acquire and hold shares in the plc.

UK legislation

See CA 1985, ss 146, 147, 148(1), (2), 149.

[43A Accounting for own shares

Where a company or a nominee of a company holds shares in the company or an interest in such shares, such shares shall not be shown in the balance sheet of the company as an asset, but—

(a) the deduction of the cost of the acquired shares from the profits available for distribution, and

(b) the nominal value of such shares,

shall be disclosed in the notes to the accounts and the profits available for distribution shall accordingly be restricted by the amount of such deduction.][a]

Amendments

a C(A)A 1983, s 43A inserted by CA 1990, s 232.

Definitions

'accounts': CA 1963, s 2(1); 'company': CA 1963, s 2(1); 'share': CA 1963, s 2(1).

Notes

Accounting treatment for own shares acquired by a company: If a company acquires any of its own shares,[1] it cannot treat that acquisition as an asset for accounting purposes. Rather, C(A)A 1983, s 43A stipulates that whilst the nominal value of the shares so acquired must be shown in the notes to the accounts, the amount of the profits available for distribution[2] must be reduced by an amount equivalent to the cost of the acquisition.

1 See C(A)A 1983, s 41 and the notes thereto for the circumstances in which a company may lawfully acquire its own shares.

2 See C(A)A 1983, s 45 and the notes thereto for the determination of what constitutes distributable profits.

UK legislation

See CA 1985, s 148(4).

44 Charges taken by public limited companies on own shares

(1) A lien or other charge of a public limited company on its own shares (whether taken expressly or otherwise), except a charge permitted by subsection (2), is void.

(2) The following are permitted charges, that is to say—

(a) in the case of every description of company, a charge on its own shares (not being fully paid) for any amount payable in respect of the shares;

(b) in the case of a public limited company whose ordinary business includes the lending of money or consists of the provision of credit or the bailment or hiring of goods under a hire-purchase agreement, or both, a charge of the company on its own shares (whether fully paid or not) which arises in connection with a transaction entered into by the company in the ordinary course of its business;

(c) in the case of a company (other than a company in relation to which paragraph (d) applies) which is re-registered or is registered under section 18 as a public limited company, a charge on its own shares which was in existence immediately before its application for re-registration or, as the case may be, registration;

(d) in the case of any company which after the end of the re-registration period remains or remained an old public limited company and did not before the end of that period apply to be re-registered under section 12 as a public limited company, any charge on its own shares which was in existence immediately before the end of that period.

Definitions

'company': CA 1963, s 2(1); 'hire-purchase agreement': C(A)A 1983, s 2(1); 'old public limited company': C(A)A 1983, s 2(1), s 12(1); 'public limited company': C(A)A 1983, s 2(1); 'the re-registration period': C(A)A 1983, s 2(1), 13(1); 'share': CA 1963, s 2(1).

Notes

Restrictions on liens and charges taken by a plc on its own shares: See C(A)A 1983, s 41 and the notes thereto.

PART IV

RESTRICTIONS ON DISTRIBUTION OF PROFITS AND ASSETS

45 Profits available for distribution

(1) A company shall not make a distribution (as defined by section 51) except out of profits available for the purpose.

(2) For the purposes of this Part, but subject to section 47(1), a company's profits available for distribution are its accumulated, realised profits, so far as not previously utilised by distribution or capitalisation, less its accumulated, realised losses, so far as not previously written off in a reduction or reorganisation of capital duly made.

(3) A company shall not apply an unrealised profit in paying up debentures or any amounts unpaid on any of its issued shares.

[(4)For the purposes of subsections (2) and (3)—

(a) where the company prepares Companies Act individual accounts, any provision (within the meaning of the Sixth Schedule to the Principal Act or paragraph 70 of the Schedule to the Companies (Amendment) Act 1986), other than one in respect of any diminution in value of a fixed asset appearing on a revaluation of all the fixed assets or of all the fixed assets other than goodwill of the company, shall be treated as a realised loss, and

(b) where the company prepares IFRS individual accounts, a provision of any kind shall be treated as a realized loss.][a]

(5) Subject to section 49(8), any consideration by the directors of a company of the value at any particular time of any fixed asset of the company shall be treated as a revaluation of that asset for the purposes of determining whether any such revaluation of the company's fixed assets as is required for the purposes of the exception from

subsection (4) has taken place at that time; but where any such assets which have not actually been revalued are treated as revalued for those purposes by virtue of this subsection that exception shall only apply if the directors are satisfied that their aggregate value at the time in question is not less than the aggregate amount at which they are for the time being stated in the company's accounts.

(6) If, on the revaluation of a fixed asset, an unrealised profit is shown to have been made and, on or after the revaluation, a sum is written off or retained for depreciation of that asset over a period, then, an amount equal to the amount by which that sum exceeds the sum which would have been so written off or retained for depreciation of that asset over that period, if that profit had not been made, shall be treated for the purposes of subsections (2) and (3) as a realised profit made over that period.

(7) Where there is no record of the original cost of an asset of a company (whether acquired before, on or after the appointed day) or any such record cannot be obtained without unreasonable expense or delay, then, for the purposes of determining whether the company has made a profit or loss in respect of that asset, the cost of the asset shall be taken to be the value ascribed to it in the earliest available record of its value made on or after its acquisition by the company.

(8) Where the directors of a company are, after making all reasonable enquiries, unable to determine whether a particular profit made before the appointed day is realised or unrealised they may treat the profit as realised, and where after making such enquiries they are unable to determine whether a particular loss so made is realised or unrealised, they may treat the loss as unrealised.

(9) In this section 'fixed asset' includes any other asset which is not a current asset.

Amendments

a Sub-s (4) substituted by by EC(IFRSMA)R 2005, reg 9, Part 2 of Schedule, Item No 3.

Definitions

'accounts': CA 1963, s 2(1); 'the appointed day': C(A)A 1983, s 1(3), s 2(1); 'company': CA 1963, s 2(1) and NAMA Act 2009, s 229; 'debenture': CA 1963, s 2(1); 'director': CA 1963, s 2(1); 'distribution': C(A)A 1983, s 51; 'the Principal Act': C(A)A 1983, s 2(1); 'share': CA 1963, s 2(1).

Cross references in other enactments

NAMA Act 2009, s 229 provides that a reference to a 'company' in C(A)A 1983, s 45(1) and s 45(3) 'shall be taken not to include a NAMA group entity' within the meaning of NAMA Act 2009.

Notes

Profits available for distribution: Prior to the coming into force of this section, a company could declare a dividend out of profits earned during the particular year without having to first make provision for losses sustained in previous financial years.[1] Now, however, in an effort to give greater effect to the common law rule that there should be no distributions out of capital (since to do so amounts to a disguised reduction of capital in breach of CA 1963, s 72),[2] provision must first be made for past losses, since a company's distributable profits are defined as being 'its accumulated realised profits, so far as not previously utilised by distribution or capitalisation, less its accumulated, realised losses, so far as not previously written off in a reduction or reorganisation of capital duly made.'[3] In this regard, unless the context otherwise requires, a realised profit or loss may be a realised revenue or capital profit or loss.[4] In determining whether there has been a realised profit or loss, as the case may be, reference is to be had to the company's latest properly prepared and audited annual accounts,[5] although where the proposed distribution would infringe s 45 if judged solely by the last annual accounts, reference may also be had to properly prepared interim or 'management' accounts which have been delivered to the Registrar of Companies, insofar as same are necessary to make a reasonable judgment as to the amount if any of the profits available for distribution.[6] Furthermore, whether reference is being had to audited annual accounts or interim accounts they will only be regarded as having been 'properly prepared' if they are in compliance with the accounting provisions of the Companies Acts and present a true and fair view of the company's financial position[8] and if they are also in accord with accepted accounting practice.[9]

An increase in the value of a fixed asset[10] in the financial statements consequent upon a revaluation, constitutes an unrealised profit[11] and is accordingly not available for distribution.[12] On the other hand, a provision made in the accounts must be treated as a realised loss[13] unless the provision is in respect of a diminution in value of a fixed asset appearing on a revaluation of all fixed assets or of all fixed assets other than goodwill (and where of course the general revaluation may have yielded unrealised profits as well as losses) that provision need not be treated as a realised loss.[14]

It is to be noted that where development costs are shown as an asset in a company's accounts, they are to be treated as a realised loss in determining the amount of profits available for distribution[15] unless there are special circumstances justifying the directors in treating them otherwise,[16] in which event this different treatment and the circumstances relied upon as justifying same must be fully explained by way of a note to the accounts.[17]

1 See *Ammonia Soda Company Ltd v Chamberlain* [1981] 1 Ch 266; *Kehoe v Waterford and Limerick Railway Co* (1888–89) LR Ir 221.

2 See *Re Exchange Banking Co; Flitcroft's Case* (1882) 21 ChD 519; *Kehoe v Waterford and Limerick Railway Co* (1888–89) LR Ir 221.

3 It is to be noted that this limitation applies whether the company is limited or unlimited. This compares with the reduction of capital provisions contained in CA 1963, s 72 et seq which apply only to limited companies.

4 C(A)A 1983, s 51(4).

5 C(A)A 1983, s 49(1), (2)(a) and (3). If the auditors' report is qualified, the accounts cannot be relied upon for the purpose of making a distribution unless the auditors have also made a statement which has been laid before the company in general meeting, to the effect that the qualification is not material for the purpose of determining whether the a distribution would be unlawful: C(A)A 1983, s 49(3)(c) and (d) and s 49(4). Of course, in the case of a company which is audit exempt there will be no need for any report or statement from any auditors in order for reference to be had to the accounts in determining the level of profits, if any, available for distribution: C(A)(No 2)A 1999, Sch 2 para 3.

6 C(A)A 1983, s 49(2)(b) and (5). Interim accounts may also be relied upon where a company is in its first financial year and has therefore not yet produced audited annual accounts: C(A)A 1983, s 49(2)(c) and (6).

7 For the relevant provisions of the Companies Acts governing the format and content of a company's accounts, see in particular CA 1963, ss 149, 151–153, 156–158, C(A)A 1986, EC(CGA)R 1992, EC(CIA)R 1992, EC(A)R 1993, EC(IUA)R 1996 and C(A)(No 2)A 1999, Pt III.

8 C(A)A 1983, ss 49(9) and (10).

9 *Dolan v AB Co Ltd* [1969] IR 247; *Lloyd Cheyham Ltd v Littlejohn and Company* [1987] BCLC 303; *IRC v Duple Motor Bodies Ltd* [1961] 1 WLR 739; *Dovey v Cory* [1901] AC 477.

10 A 'fixed asset' is rather unhelpfully defined in C(A)A 1983, s 45(9) as being an asset which is not a current asset. Further guidance is, however, to be found in C(A)A 1986, Sch, para 60 which defines 'fixed assets' as those which are 'intended for use on a continuing basis in the company's

activities'. Any assets not intended for such use (eg raw materials and stock-in-trade) are deemed to be current assets. Whether an asset is current or fixed depends on the nature of the company's business rather than on the nature of the asset. For example motors cars will be fixed assets in the hands of a car-hire firm but will be current assets in the hands of a car manufacturer.

11 C(A)A 1983, s 45(6).

12 An unrealised profit may however be used for a capitalisation or bonus issue since neither comes within the definition of a 'distribution': C(A)A 1983, s 51(2)(a).

13 C(A)A 1983, s 45(4). It is compulsory to make provision for depreciation in respect of fixed assets whose value has been permanently reduced: C(A)A 1986, Sch para 7(2).

14 C(A)A 1983, s 45(4).

15 C(A)A 1983, s 45A(1). This treatment does not have to be applied to any part of the development costs which are properly shown in the accounts as an unrealised profit (and thus as an asset) consequent upon a revaluation of those costs: C(A)A 1983, s 45A(2).

16 C(A)A 1983, s 45A(3)(a).

17 C(A)A 1983, s 45A(3)(b).

Additional restrictions on distributions by a plc: In the case of a plc there is a further restriction on its ability to make a distribution, namely that it may only do so if at that time, the amount of its net assets is not less that the aggregate of its called-up share capital and undistributable reserves and if and to the extent that the distribution does not reduce the amount of those to less than that aggregate.[1] The 'undistributable reserves' of a plc comprise[2] of the share premium account;[3] the capital redemption reserve fund;[4] the amount by which the plc's accumulated unrealised profits, so far as not previously utilised by any capitalisation, exceed its accumulated unrealised losses so far as not previously written off in a reduction or reorganisation of capital duly made; and any other reserve which the plc is prohibited from distributing, whether by a statute or by it memorandum or articles of association.[5] A plc is also prohibited from treating any part of its uncalled capital as an asset in determining the level of profits, if any, available for distribution.[6]

1 C(A)A 1983, s 46(1).

2 C(A)A 1983, s 46(2).

3 In relation to a company's share premium account, see CA 1963, s 62.

4 In relation to a company's capital redemption reserve fund, see CA 1963, s 64 and CA 1990, ss 208 and 211.

5 Such a fund might include a capital conversion reserve fund arising upon a renominalisation of the par value of the shares pursuant to the Economic and Monetary Union Act 1998 in which the par value has been decreased by the plc following the introduction of the euro.

6 C(A)A 1983, s 46(4).

Restrictions imposed by the memorandum or articles of association: Quite apart from the statutory restrictions on the making of distributions, it is also open to the company to impose additional restrictions in its memorandum or articles of association on the sums that may be paid out to its members.[1] In this regard, for example, the memorandum or articles may provide that some classes of shares are to be more limited than others, as to the dividends and other distributions payable in respect thereof.

1 C(A)A 1983, s 51(5).

Definition of a distribution: In common parlance a distribution is a dealing out or bestowing in proportions or shares amongst many, allotting or apportioning to each his own share.[1] As a matter of company law it has its own technical meaning[2] which will be presumed to apply where it is used in the context of an agreement governing the regulation of all or some of the internal affairs of a company.[3] In this regard, the phrase encompasses every description of a company's assets to members of the company, whether in cash or otherwise, exception distributions made by way of: (a) an issue of shares as fully or partly paid bonus shares; (b) a redemption or purchase of shares pursuant to CA 1990, Pt XI out of the proceeds of a fresh issue of shares made for that purpose (including the payment of any premium out of the share premium account); a reduction of capital pursuant to CA 1963, s 72 by extinguishing or reducing the liability of any of the members on any of its shares in respect of share capital not paid up or by paying off paid up share capital; and (d) a distribution of assets to members of the company on its winding up.[4] In order to constitute a 'distribution' to a member the payment may be either direct or indirect.[5] So, for example, if a company makes a gratuitous disposition to one of its members or to a company controlled by him, the transaction will be regarded as being a distribution.[6] Similarly, to the extent that the company directly or indirectly transfers an asset to a member at an undervalue, the transfer will amount to a distribution. It is however essential that the payment be made to the member in his capacity as member and not in some other capacity such as deferred remuneration *qua* employee, in order to constitute a distribution.[7]

1 *Igote Ltd Badsey Ltd* [2001] 4 IR 511.

2 See C(A)A 1983, s 51(2).

3 *Igote Ltd Badsey Ltd* [2001] 4 IR 511.

4 C(A)A 1983, s 51(1) and (2).

5 *Barclays Bank plc v British and Commonwealth Holdings plc* [1996] 1 BCLC 1; *Aveling Barford Ltd v Perion Ltd* [1989] BCLC 626; *Brady v Brady* [1988] BCLC 20. See also *Shaker v Al-Bedrawi* [2003] 1 BCLC 157 at 197.

6 *Barclays Bank plc v British and Commonwealth Holdings plc* [1996] 1 BCLC 1; *Aveling Barford Ltd v Perion Ltd* [1989] BCLC 626; *Brady v Brady* [1989] AC 755; *Re Greendale Developments Ltd* [1998] 1 IR 8; *Plain Ltd v Kenley* [1931] 1 DLR 468 at 479. See also *Shaker v Al-Bedrawi* [2003] 1 BCLC 157 at 197.

7 *MacPherson v European Strategic Bureau Ltd* [2000] 2 BCLC 683.

Investment companies and life assurance companies: Special rules apply to plcs carrying on business as investment companies and to life assurance companies respectively in determining the level of profits available for distribution. In this regard see C(A)A 1983, ss 47 and 48.

Consequences of an unlawful distribution: If a company makes a distribution in breach of Part IV, that distribution (or so much of it as is unlawful) will be recoverable against any recipient member who knows or has reasonable grounds for believing that there has been a breach of Part IV.[1] However, if the distribution has been made otherwise in cash, the member will instead be liable to repay a sum equivalent to the value of the distribution or such art thereof as is unlawful.[2] In addition, any director who knowingly or negligently causes or permits the company to make an unlawful distribution will be personally liable to compensate the company in damages for the amount of such distribution.[3] In this regard, the director's liability will be for the full amount of the distribution and not just that portion which was unlawful.[4] Furthermore, the company's auditors may also be liable in damages if, through their negligence, the company was caused to make a distribution out of false or non-existent profits.[5]

1 C(A)A 1983, s 50(1). The member is deemed to hold the distribution as a constructive trustee for the company: *Precision Dippings Ltd v Precision Dippings Marketing Ltd* [1985] BCLC 385.

2 C(A)A 1983, s 50(1).

3 *Re Exchange Banking Co; Flitcroft's Case* (1882) 21 ChD 519; *Dovey v Cory* [1901] AC 477; *Re City Equitable Fire Assurance Co* [1905] Ch 207; *Bairstow v Queens Moat Houses plc* [2001] 2 BCLC 531; *MacPherson v European Strategic Bureau Ltd* [2000] 2 BCLC 683. This liability in negligence could arise, for example, where the directors ought reasonably to have caused the company to make provision for a particular liability in the company's accounts but failed to do so, with the consequence that dividends were paid out of false profits: *Re Paycheck Services 3 Ltd* [2008] 2 BCLC 613.

4 *Bairstow v Queens Moat Houses plc* [2001] 2 BCLC 531; *Re Paycheck Services 3 Ltd* [2008] 2 BCLC 613.

5 *Re Thomas Gerrard and Son Ltd* [1968] Ch 455.

UK legislation

See CA 1985, ss 263(1), (3), (4), (5), 275(1)–(5).

[45A Development costs shown as an asset of a company to be set off against company's distributable profits

(1) Subject to the following provisions of this section, where development costs are shown as an asset in a company's accounts, any amount shown in respect of those costs shall be treated—

(a) for the purposes of section 45, as a realised loss and

(b) for the purposes of section 47, as a realised revenue loss.

(2) Subsection (1) shall not apply to any part of the amount aforesaid representing an unrealised profit made on revaluation of those costs.

(3) Subsection (1) shall not apply if—

(a) there are special circumstances justifying the directors of the company concerned in deciding that the amount mentioned in respect thereof in the company's accounts shall not be treated as required by that subsection, and

[(b) it is stated—

(i) where the company prepares Companies Act individual accounts, in the note to the accounts required by paragraph 8(2) of the Schedule to the Companies (Amendment) Act 1986, or

(ii) where the company prepares IFRS individual accounts, in any note to the accounts, that that amount is not to be so treated, and the note explains the circumstances relied upon to justify the decision of the directors to that effect']^b.]^a

---

Amendments

a Section 45A inserted by C(A)A 1986, s 20.

b Sub-s (3)(b) substituted by EC(IFRSMA)R 2005, reg 9, Part 2 of Schedule, Item No 4.

Definitions

'accounts': C(A)A 1983, s 2(1); 'company': C(A)A 1983, s 2(1); 'director': C(A)A 1983, s 2(1).

Notes

Deduction of development costs from profits available for distribution: See C(A)A 1983, s 45 and the notes thereto.

UK legislation

See CA 1985, s 269 (amended by the Companies Act 1985 (Accounts of Small and Medium Sized Companies and Minor Accounting Amendments) Regs 1997, regs 1(4) and 7(7)).

---

46 Restriction on distribution of assets

(1) Subject to section 47, a public limited company may only make a distribution at any time—

(a) if at that time the amount of its net assets is not less than the aggregate of the company's called-up share capital and its undistributable reserves; and

(b) if, and to the extent that, the distribution does not reduce the amount of those assets to less than that aggregate.

(2) For the purposes of this section the undistributable reserves of a public limited company are—

(a) the share premium account;

(b) the capital redemption reserve fund;

(c) the amount by which the company's accumulated, unrealised profits, so far as not previously utilised by any capitalisation, exceed its accumulated, unrealised losses, so far as not previously written off in a reduction or reorganisation of capital duly made; and

(d) any other reserve which the company is prohibited from distributing by any enactment, other than one contained in this Part, or by its memorandum or articles.

(3) Subsections (4) to (8) of section 45, shall apply for the purposes of this section as they apply for the purposes of that section.

(4) A public limited company shall not include any uncalled share capital as an asset in any account relevant for the purposes of this section.

Definitions

'articles': CA 1963, s 2(1); 'called-up share capital': C(A)A 1983, s 2(1); 'company': CA 1963, s 2(1); 'distribution': C(A)A 1983, s 51(2); 'memorandum': CA 1963, s 2(1); 'net assets': C(A)A 1983, s 2(4); 'public limited company': C(A)A 1983, s 2(1); 'share': CA 1963, s 2(1).

Notes

Additional restrictions on distributions by a plc: See C(A)A 1983, s 45 and the notes thereto.

UK legislation

See CA 1963, s 264.

---

47 Other distributions of investment companies

(1) Subject to the following provisions of this section, an investment company may also make a distribution at any time out of its accumulated, realised revenue profits, so far as not previously utilised by distribution or capitalisation, less its accumulated revenue losses (whether realised or unrealised), so far as not previously written off in a reduction or reorganisation of capital duly made—

(a) if at that time the amount of its assets is at least equal to one and a half times the aggregate of its liabilities [to creditors][a]; and

(b) if, and to the extent that, the distribution does not reduce that amount to less than one and a half times that aggregate.

[(2) In subsection (1) ['liabilities to creditors'][b] includes—

(a) any provision [for liabilities to creditors][c] (within the meaning of the Sixth Schedule to the Principal Act) that is made in Companies Act individual accounts except to the extent that that provision is taken into account in calculating the value of any asset to the company,

(b) any provision [for liabilities to creditors][c] within the meaning of paragraph 70 of the Schedule to the Companies (Amendment) Act 1986 that is made in Companies Act individual accounts, and

(c) any provision [for liabilities to creditors][c] that is made in IFRS individual accounts, and subsection (4) of section 46 shall apply for those purposes as it applies for the purposes of that section.][d]

(3) In this Part 'investment company' means a public limited company which has given notice in writing (which has not been revoked) to the registrar of its intention to carry on business as an investment company (the 'requisite notice') and has since the date of that notice complied with the requirements set out in subsection (4).

(4) The requirements referred to in subsection (3) are—

(a) that the business of the company consists of investing its funds mainly in securities, with the aim of spreading investment risk and giving members of the company the benefit of the results of the management of its funds;

(b) that none of the company's holdings in companies other than companies which are for the time being investment companies represents more than 15 per cent. by value of the investing company's investment;

(c) that distribution of the company's capital profits is prohibited by its memorandum or articles of association;

(d) that the company has not retained, otherwise than in compliance with this Part in respect of any financial year more than 15 per cent. of the income it derives from securities.

(5) An investment company may not make a distribution by virtue of subsection (1) unless its shares are listed on a recognised stock exchange and, during the period beginning with the first day of the financial year immediately preceding the financial year in which the proposed distribution is to be made or, where the distribution is proposed to be made during the company's first financial year, the first day of that financial year and ending with the date of the distribution (whether or not any part of those financial years falls before the appointed day), it has not—

(a) distributed any of its capital profits; or

(b) applied any unrealised profits or any capital profits (realised or unrealised) in paying up debentures or any amounts unpaid on any of its issued shares.

(6) An investment company may not make a distribution by virtue of subsection (1) unless the company gave the requisite notice—

(a) before the beginning of the appropriate period referred to in subsection (5); or

(b) where that period began before the appointed day, as soon as may be reasonably practicable after the appointed day;

or

(c) where the company was incorporated on or after the appointed day, as soon as may be reasonably practicable after the date of its incorporation.

(7) A notice by a company to the registrar under subsection (3) may be revoked at any time by the company on giving notice to the registrar that it no longer wishes to be an

investment company within the meaning of this section and, on giving such notice, the company shall cease to be such an investment company.

(8) In determining capital and revenue profits and losses for the purposes of this section an asset which is not a fixed asset or a current asset shall be treated as a fixed asset.

(9) An investment company shall include the expression 'investment company' on its letters and order forms.

(10) Where a company fails to comply with subsection (9), the company and every officer of the company who is in default shall be guilty of an offence and shall be liable on summary conviction to a fine not exceeding [€1,904.61].[e]

(11) Proceedings in relation to an offence under this section may be brought and prosecuted by the registrar of companies.

(12) For the purposes of paragraph (b) of subsection (4)—

(a) 'holding' means the shares or securities (whether of one class or more than one class) held in any one company;

(b) holdings in companies which are members of a group (whether or not including the investing company) and are not excluded from the said paragraph (b) shall be treated as holdings in a single company;

(c) where the investing company is a member of a group, money owed to it by another member of the group shall be treated as a security of the latter held by the investing company and accordingly as, or as part of, the holding of the investing company in the company owing the money,

and for the purposes of this subsection 'group' means a company and all companies which are its subsidiaries within the meaning of section 155 of the Principal Act.

Amendments

a Words inserted by SI 840/2005, reg 8(a).

b Words substituted by SI 840/2005, reg 8(b)(i).

c Words inserted by SI 840/2005, reg 8(b)(ii).

d Sub-s (2) was substituted by EC(IFRSMA)R 2005, reg 9, Part 2 of Schedule, Item No 5.

e '£250' increased to £1,500 by CA 1990, s 240(7) as inserted by CLEA 2001, s 104(c), and converted to €1,904.61 by Council Regulations (EC) No 1103/97, No 974/98 and No 2866/98 and the Economic and Monetary Union Act 1998, s 6.

Definitions

'the appointed day': C(A)A 1983, s 1(3), s 2(1); 'articles': CA 1963, s 2(1); 'company': CA 1963, s 2(1); 'debenture': CA 1963, s 2(1); 'distribution': C(A)A 1983, s 51(2); 'financial year': CA 1963, s 2(1); 'member': CA 1963, s 31; 'memorandum': CA 1963, s 2(1); 'officer': CA 1963, s 2(1); 'the Principal Act': C(A)A 1983, s 2(1); 'public limited company': C(A)A 1983, s 2(1); 'recognised stock exchange': CA 1963, s 2(1), CA 1990, s 3(2); 'the Registrar of Companies': CA 1963, s 2(1); 'share': CA 1963, s 2(1).

Notes

Distributions by an investment company: In the case of a plc which is listed on a recognised stock exchange and which not only carries on business as an investment company but which has also given notice of that fact to the Registrar, a more liberal regime applies regarding the making of distributions. In determining the amount of its distributable profits such a company need only have regard to its revenue profits and losses. Subject to the provisions of subsection (5), capital profits and losses may be ignored. The purpose behind this provision is to avoid a situation whereby an investment company might otherwise be prevented from declaring dividends under C(A)A 1983, s 46 because of temporary fluctuations in the value of its investments (ie its capital assets).[1] In the case of an investment company which was not a plc, s 46 would not apply and temporary fluctuations in the value of its assets could be ignored, since provision for depreciation need only be made if there has been a permanent reduction in the value of the asset.[2]

1 See also Art 15(4) of the Second EEC Companies Directive (77/91/EEC).

2 See C(A)A 1986, Sch, para 7(2).

UK legislation

See CA 1985, s 265 (amended by FSA 1986, s 212(2) and Sch, para 19, by the Companies (Investment Companies) (Distribution of Profits) Regs 1999, regs 2 and 4 and by the Financial Services and Markets Act 2000 (Consequential Amendments and Repeals) Order 2001, Arts 17(1), (2) and (3)) and s 266 (amended by FSA 1986, s 117(3) and by the Companies (Investment Companies) (Distribution of Profits) Regs 1999, reg 3(a) and (b)).

---

48 Realised profits of assurance companies

(1) In the case of an assurance company carrying on life assurance business, or industrial assurance business or both, any amount properly transferred to the profit and loss account of the company from a surplus in the fund or funds maintained by it in respect of that business and any deficit in that fund or those funds shall be respectively treated for the purposes of this Part as a realised profit and a realised loss, and, subject to the foregoing, any profit or loss arising on the fund or funds maintained by it in respect of that business shall be left out of account for those purposes.

(2) In subsection (1)—

(a) the reference to a surplus in any fund or funds of an assurance company is a reference to an excess of the assets representing that fund or those funds over the liabilities of the company attributable to its life assurance or industrial assurance business, as shown by an actuarial investigation; and

(b) the reference to a deficit in any such fund or funds is a reference to the excess of those liabilities over those assets, as so shown.

(3) In this section—

'actuarial investigation' means an investigation to which section 5 of the Assurance Companies Act, 1909 applies;

'life assurance business' and 'industrial assurance business' have the same meanings as in section 3 of the Insurance Act, 1936.

Definitions

'company': CA 1963, s 2(1).

Notes

Profits available for distribution: See C(A)A 1983, s 45 and the notes thereto.

UK legislation

See CA 1985, s 268 (amended by the Companies Act 1985 (Miscellaneous Accounting Amendments) Regs 1996, regs 13(1), (2) and (3) and 16(6) and by the Financial Services and Markets Act 2000 (Consequential Amendments and Repeals) Order 2001, art 18)).

---

49 The relevant accounts

(1) Subject to the following provisions of this section, the question whether a distribution may be made by a company without contravening section 45, 46 or 47 (the relevant section) and the amount of any distribution which may be so made shall be determined by reference to the relevant items as stated in the relevant accounts, and the relevant section shall be treated as contravened in the case of a distribution unless the requirements of this section about those accounts are complied with in the case of that distribution.

(2) The relevant accounts for any company in the case of any particular distribution are—

(a) except in a case falling within paragraph (b) or (c), the last annual accounts that is to say, the accounts prepared in accordance with the requirements of the Principal Act [(and, where applicable, in accordance with the requirements of Article 4 of the IAS Regulation)][a] which were laid in respect of the last preceding financial year in respect of which accounts so prepared were laid;

(b) if that distribution would be found to contravene the relevant section if reference were made only to the last annual accounts, such accounts (interim accounts) as are necessary to enable a reasonable judgment to be made as to the amounts of any of the relevant items;

(c) if that distribution is proposed to be declared during the company's first financial year or before any accounts are laid in respect of that financial year, such accounts (initial accounts) as are necessary as aforesaid.

(3) The following requirements apply where the last annual accounts of a company constitute the only relevant accounts in the case of any distribution, that is to say—

(a) those accounts must have been properly prepared or have been so prepared subject only to matters which are not material for the purpose of determining, by reference to the relevant items as stated in those accounts, whether that distribution would be in contravention of the relevant section;

(b) the auditors of the company must have made a report under section 163 of the Principal Act in respect of those accounts;

(c) if, by virtue of anything referred to in that report, the report is not an unqualified report, the auditors must also have stated in writing (either at the time the report was made or subsequently) whether, in their opinion, that thing is material for the purpose of determining, by reference to the relevant items as stated in those accounts, whether that distribution would be in contravention of the relevant section; and

(d) a copy of any such statement must have been laid before the company in general meeting.

(4) A statement under subsection (3)(c) suffices for the purposes of a particular distribution not only if it relates to a distribution which has been proposed but also if it relates to distributions of any description which include that particular distribution, notwithstanding that at the time of the statement it has not been proposed.

(5) The following requirements apply to interim accounts prepared for a proposed distribution by a public limited company, that is to say—

- (a) the accounts must have been properly prepared or have been so prepared subject only to matters which are not material for the purpose of determining, by reference to the relevant items as stated in those accounts, whether that distribution would be in contravention of the relevant section;
- (b) a copy of those accounts must have been delivered to the registrar of companies;
- (c) if the accounts are in a language other than the English or Irish language, a translation into English or Irish of the accounts which has been certified in the prescribed manner to be a correct translation must also have been delivered to the registrar.

(6) The following requirements apply to initial accounts prepared for a proposed distribution by a public limited company, that is to say—

- (a) those accounts must have been properly prepared or have been so prepared subject only to matters which are not material for the purpose of determining, by reference to the relevant items as stated in those accounts, whether that distribution would be in contravention of the relevant section;
- (b) the auditors of the company must have made a report stating whether in their opinion the accounts have been properly prepared;
- (c) if, by virtue of anything referred to in that report, the report is not an unqualified report, the auditors must also have stated writing whether, in their opinion, that thing is material for the purpose of determining, by reference to the relevant items as stated in those accounts, whether that distribution would be in contravention of the relevant section;
- (d) a copy of those accounts, of the report made under paragraph (b) and of any such statement must have been delivered to the registrar of companies; and
- (e) if the accounts are, or that report or statement is, in a language other than the English or Irish language, a translation into English or Irish of the accounts, the report or statement, as the case may be, which has been certified in the prescribed manner to be a correct translation, must also have been delivered to the registrar.

(7) For the purpose of determining by reference to particular accounts whether a proposed distribution may be made by a company, this section shall have effect, in any case where one or more distributions have already been made in pursuance of determinations made by reference to those same accounts, as if the amount of the proposed distribution was increased by the amount of the distributions so made.

(8) Where subsection (3)(a), (5)(a) or (6)(a) applies to the relevant accounts, section 45(5) shall not apply for the purposes of determining whether any revaluation of the company's fixed assets affecting the amount of the relevant items as stated in those accounts has taken place, unless it is stated in a note to those accounts—

(a) that the directors have considered the value at any time of any fixed assets of the company without actually revaluing those assets;

(b) that there are satisfied that the aggregate value of those assets at the time in question is or was not less than the aggregate amount at which they are or were for the time being stated in the company's accounts; and

(c) that the relevant items affected are accordingly stated in the relevant accounts on the basis that a revaluation of the company's fixed assets which by virtue of section 45(5) included the assets in question took place at that time.

(9) In this section—

'properly prepared' means, in relation to any accounts of a company, that the following conditions are satisfied in relation to those accounts, that is to say—

[(a) in the case of annual individual accounts, that they have been properly prepared in accordance with the Principal Act,

(b) in the case of interim or initial accounts that they comply with the requirements of section 148 and either section 149 or 149A (inserted by the European Communities (International Financial Reporting Standards and Miscellaneous Amendments) Regulations 2005) of the Principal Act, where applicable, and any balance sheet comprised in those accounts has been signed in accordance with section 156 of the Principal Act; and][b]

(c) in either case, without prejudice to the foregoing, that, except where the company is entitled to avail itself, and has availed itself, of any of the provisions of Part III of the Sixth Schedule to the Principal Act—

(i) so much of the accounts as consists of a balance sheet gives a true and fair view of the state of the company's affairs as at the balance sheet date; and

(ii) so much of those accounts as consists of a profit and loss account gives a true and fair view of the company's profit or loss for the period in respect of which the accounts were prepared;

['relevant item' means the following amounts as dealt with in the company's relevant accounts—

(a) profits, losses, assets and liabilities,

(b) where the company prepares Companies Act individual accounts, any provisions mentioned in the Companies (Amendment) Act 1986 or any provisions mentioned in the Sixth Schedule to the Principal Act (depreciation, diminution in value of assets, retention to meet liabilities, etc,),

(c) where the company prepares IFRS individual accounts, provisions of any kind, and

(d) share capital and reserves;][c]

'reserves' includes undistributable reserves within the meaning of section 46(2);

'unqualified report' in relation to any accounts of a company, means a report, without qualification, to the effect that in the opinion of the person making the report the accounts have been properly prepared; and for the purposes of this section, accounts are laid if section 148 of the Principal Act has been complied with in relation to those accounts.

(10) For the purpose of paragraph (b) of the definition of 'properly prepared' in subsection (9), [section 148 and either section 149 or 149A of the Principal Act, where applicable, of,][d] and the Sixth Schedule to the Principal Act shall be deemed to have effect in relation to interim and initial accounts with such modifications as are necessary by reason of the fact that the accounts are prepared otherwise than in respect of a financial year.

Amendments

a Words inserted by EC(IFRSMA)R 2005 (SI 116/2005), reg 9, Part 2 of Schedule, Item No 5.

b Sub-s (9)(a) and (b) in definition of 'properly prepared', substituted by EC(IFRSMA)R 2005 (SI 116/2005), reg 9, Part 2 of Schedule, Item No 5.

c Definition of 'relevant item' substituted by EC(IFRSMA)R 2005 (SI 116/2005), reg 9, Part 2 of Schedule, Item No 5.

d Words inserted by EC(IFRSMA)R 2005 (SI 116/2005), reg 9, Part 2 of Schedule, Item No 5.

Definitions

'accounts': CA 1963, s 2(1); 'balance sheet date': C(A)A 1983, s 2(1); 'company': CA 1963, s 2(1); 'director': CA 1963, s 2(1); 'financial year': CA 1963, s 2(1); 'prescribed': CA 1963, s 2(1); 'the Principal Act': C(A)A 1983, s 2(1); 'public limited company': C(A)A 1983, s 2(1); 'the Registrar of Companies': CA 1963, s 2(1); 'share': CA 1963, s 2(1).

Notes

Properly prepared accounts for making a distribution: See C(A)A 1983, s 45 and the note thereto entitled 'Profits available for distribution'.

UK legislation

See CA 1985, ss 270, 171 (amended by CA 1989, s 23 Sch 10 para 4), 272 (amended by CA 1989, s 23 Sch 10 paras 5, 6), 273 (amended by CA 1989, s 23 Sch 10 para 6), 274(1), 275(6).

50 Consequences of making unlawful distribution

(1) Where a distribution, or part of one, made by a company to one of its members is made in contravention of the provisions of this Part and, at the time of the distribution, he knows or has reasonable grounds for believing that it is so made, he shall be liable to repay it or that part, as the case may be, to the company or (in the case of a distribution made otherwise than in cash) to pay the company a sum equal to the value of the distribution or part at that time.

(2) The provisions of this section are without prejudice to any obligation imposed apart from this section on a member of a company to repay a distribution unlawfully made to him.

Definitions

'company': CA 1963, s 2(1); 'member': CA 1963, s 31.

Notes

Consequences of in unlawful distribution: See C(A)A 1983, s 45 and the notes thereto.

UK legislation

See CA 1985, s 277(1), (2).

---

51 Ancillary provisions

(1) Where immediately before the appointed day a company is authorised by any provision of its articles to apply its unrealised profits in paying up in full or in part unissued shares to be allotted to members of the company as fully or partly paid bonus shares, that provision shall, subject to any subsequent alteration of the articles, continue to be construed as authorising those profits to be so applied after the appointed day.

(2) In this Part 'distribution' means every description of distribution of a company's assets to members of the company, whether in cash or otherwise, except distributions made by way of—

(a) an issue of shares as fully or partly paid bonus shares;

[(b) the redemption of preference shares pursuant to section 65 of the Principal Act out of the proceeds of a fresh issue of shares made for the purposes of redemption;][a]

[(bb) the redemption of or purchase of shares pursuant to Part XI of the Companies Act, 1990 out of the proceeds of a fresh issue of shares made for the purposes of the redemption or purchase and the payment of any premium out of the company's share premium account on a redemption pursuant to section 220 in the said Part;][b]

(c) the reduction of share capital by extinguishing or reducing the liability of any of the members on any of its shares in respect of share capital not paid up or by paying off paid up share capital; and

(d) a distribution of assets to members of the company on its winding up.

(3) In this Part 'capitalisation', in relation to any profits of a company, means any of the following operations, whether carried out before, on or after the appointed day, that is to say, applying the profits in wholly or partly paying up unissued shares in the company to be allotted to members of the company as fully or partly paid bonus shares or transferring the profits to the capital redemption reserve fund.

(4) In this Part reference to profits and losses of any description are references respectively to profits and losses of that description made at any time, whether before, on, or after the appointed day and, except where the context otherwise requires, are references respectively to revenue and capital profits and revenue and capital losses.

(5) The provisions of this Part are without prejudice to any enactment or rule of law or any provision of a company's memorandum or articles restricting the sums out of which, or the cases in which, a distribution may be made.

(6) The provision of this Part shall not apply to any distribution made by a company, other than a public limited company registered as such on its original incorporation, before the date on which the earlier of the following events occurs, that is to say, the re-

registration or registration of the company as a public limited company and the end of the general transitional period.

Amendments

a Section 51(2)(b) substituted by CA 1990, s 232(d).

b Section 51(2)(bb) substituted by CA 1990, s 232(e).

Definitions

'the appointed day': C(A)A 1983, s 1(3), s 2(1); 'articles': CA 1963, s 2(1); 'company': CA 1963, s 2(1); 'the general transitional period': C(A)A 1983, s 2(1); 'member': CA 1963, s 31; 'memorandum': CA 1963, s 2(1); 'the Principal Act': C(A)A 1983, s 2(1); 'public limited company': C(A)A 1983, s 2(1); 'share': CA 1963, s 2(1).

Notes

Definition of a 'distribution': See C(A)A 1983, s 45 and the notes thereto.

Paying off paid-up share capital: The expression 'paid-up share capital' is not defined in the Companies Acts but recognition of the share premium account as part of paid-up share capital is found in two provisions of the Companies Acts.

Section 2(3) of the Companies (Amendment) Act 1983, states 'For the purposes of the Companies Acts, a share is taken to have been paid up (as to its nominal value and any premium on it) " … according to circumstances stated in that section ie 'paid-up' includes both par value and premium. Section 62 of the Companies Act, 1963, states that the provisions of the Companies Acts relating to the reduction of the share capital of a company 'shall apply as if the share premium account were paid-up share capital of the company'.

A company may pay off paid-up share capital with the consent of the court in the case of a limited company and without the consent of the court in the case of an unlimited company. For the purposes of the provisions of the Companies Acts concerning reduction of capital, "paid-up share capital" includes share premium.

UK legislation

See CA 1985, ss 263(2), 278, 280, 281.

PART V
CHANGE OF STATUS OF CERTAIN COMPANIES

52 Re-registration of limited company as unlimited

(1) A company which, on the appointed day, is registered as limited or thereafter is so registered (otherwise than in pursuance of section 53) may be re-registered under the Principal Act as unlimited in pursuance of an application in that behalf complying with the requirements of subsection (2), made in the prescribed form and signed by a director or by the secretary of the company and delivered to the registrar together with the documents mentioned in subsection (3).

(2) The requirements referred to in subsection (1) are that the application must—

(a) set out alterations in the company's memorandum as—

(i) if it is to have a share capital, are requisite to bring it, both in substance and in form into conformity with the requirements imposed by the

Principal Act with respect to the memorandum of a company to be formed under that Act as an unlimited company having a share capital; or

(ii) if it is not to have a share capital, are requisite in the circumstances; and

(b) if articles have been registered, set out such alterations therein and additions thereto as—

(i) if it is to have a share capital, are requisite to bring them, both in substance and in form, into conformity with the requirements imposed by the Principal Act with respect to the articles of a company to be formed under that Act as an unlimited company having a share capital; or

(ii) if it is not to have a share capital, are requisite in the circumstances; and

(c) if articles have not been registered—

(i) have annexed thereto, and request the registration of, printed articles, bearing the same stamp as if they were contained in a deed, being, if the company is to have a share capital, articles complying with the said requirements; or

(ii) if it is not to have a share capital, articles appropriate to the circumstances.

(3) The documents referred to in subsection (1) are—

(a) the prescribed form of assent to the company's being registered as unlimited subscribed by or on behalf of all members of the company.

(b) a statutory declaration made by the directors of the company that the persons by whom or on whose behalf the form of assent is subscribed constitute the whole membership of the company, and, if any of the members have not subscribed that form themselves, that the directors have taken all reasonable steps to satisfy themselves that each person who subscribed it on behalf of a member was lawfully empowered so to do;

(c) a printed copy of the memorandum incorporating the alterations therein set out in the application; and

(d) if articles have been registered, a printed copy thereof incorporating the alterations therein and additions thereto set out in the application.

(4) The registrar shall retain the application and other documents delivered to him under subsection (1), shall, if articles are annexed to the application, register them and shall issue to the company a certificate of incorporation appropriate to the status to be assumed by the company by virtue of this section, and upon the issue of the certificate—

(a) the status of the company shall, by virtue of the issue, be changed from limited to unlimited; and

(b) the alterations in the memorandum set out in the application and (if articles have been previously registered) any alterations and additions to the articles so set out shall, notwithstanding anything in the Principal Act, take effect as if duly made by resolution of the company and the provisions of the Principal Act shall apply to the memorandum and articles as altered or added to by virtue of this section accordingly.

(5) A certificate of incorporation issued by virtue of this section shall be conclusive evidence that the requirements of this section with respect to re-registration and of

matters precedent and incidental thereto have been complied with, and that the company was authorised to be re-registered under the Principal Act in pursuance of this section and was duly so re-registered.

(6) Where a company is re-registered in pursuance of this section a person who, at the time when the application for it to be re-registered was delivered to the registrar, was a past member of the company and did not thereafter again become a member thereof shall not, in the event of the company's being wound up, be liable to contribute to the assets of the company more than he would have been liable to contribute thereto had it not been so re-registered.

(7) The re-registration of a limited company as an unlimited company pursuant to this Act shall not affect any rights or obligations of the company, or render defective any legal proceedings by or against the company, and any legal proceedings which might have been continued or commenced against it in its former status may be continued or commenced against it in its new status.

(8) For the purposes of this section—

- (a) subscription to a form of assent by the legal personal representative of a deceased member of a company shall be deemed to be subscription by him;
- (b) a trustee in bankruptcy of a person who is a member of a company shall, to the exclusion of that person, be deemed to be a member of the company.

Definitions

'the appointed day': C(A)A 1983, s 1(3), s 2(1); 'articles': CA 1963, s 2(1); 'company': CA 1963, s 2(1); 'director': CA 1963, s 2(1); 'document': CA 1963, s 2(1): 'member': CA 1963, s 31; 'memorandum': CA 1963, s 2(1); 'prescribed': CA 1963, s 2(1); 'the Principal Act': C(A)A 1983, s 2(1); 'printed': CA 1963, s 2(1); 'Registrar of Companies': CA 1963, s 2(1): 'share': CA 1963, s 2(1); 'unlimited company': CA 1963, s 2(1), s 5(2).

Notes

Re-registration of limited company as unlimited: Prior to the appointed day of 13 October 1983,[1] there had been no procedure for the conversion of a limited company into an unlimited company. Now, however, such re-registration may be effected in accordance with the procedures laid down by this section provided that the company is not one which has previously converted from unlimited to limited liability pursuant to C(A)A 1983, s 53.[2] In this regard the re-registration may be as an unlimited company either with or without share capital, although in either case, the necessary amendments will have to be made to the company's memorandum and articles of association.[3]

Documents to be delivered to Registrar: The amended constitutional documents must be appended to the application for re-registration,[4] which must itself be in the prescribed form[5] and must be signed by the secretary or by one of the directors. In addition, because the memorandum and articles cannot be altered so as to increase a member's liability without his consent,[6] the application form must have appended to it a written consent to re-registration from each and every member (or his duly authorised representative)[7] together with a statutory declaration from the directors that all members have so consented and that where such consent has been given on behalf of a member rather than by the member personally, that they have taken all reasonable steps to satisfy themselves as to the authority of that person to so consent n behalf of the member in question.[8]

Certificate of incorporation: Provided he is satisfied that the requirements for re-registration have been complied with, the Registrar must issue the company with a certificate of incorporation as an unlimited company.[9] This certificate operates as 'conclusive' evidence that the re-registration requirements have been complied with and that the company is indeed an unlimited company.[10] The conclusiveness of a Registrar's certificate has previously been upheld in the context of the certification of the registration of a charge under CA 1963, s 99.[11] It has also been upheld in the context of a certificate of incorporation, so as to preclude the court from looking behind the date stated on the certificate as being the date of incorporation.[12] In the UK it has been suggested that despite its stated conclusiveness, the courts would be prepared to look behind a Registrar's certificate in cases of fraud or where there is an error on the face of the certificate itself.[13] It has also been held by the UK courts that because legislation does not bind the Crown except where expressly so stated, an erroneously issued certificate could be challenged through the fiat of the Attorney General.[14] It is thought, however, that a similar position would not pertain in Ireland since the Royal Prerogatives, including the non-application of statutes, have been held not to have survived the enactment of the Constitution.[15] Whilst the certainty afforded to members and creditors alike by the conclusiveness of such certificates has been judicially acknowledged,[16] it remains to be seen, however whether that 'conclusiveness' is unconstitutional either as an infringement of the separation of powers contained in Article 6 of the Constitution or as an attempt to oust the High Court's full original jurisdiction under Article 34 of the Constitution to hear and determine all justiciable matters.[17]

1 Companies (Amendment) Act 1983 (Commencement) Order 1983 (SI 288/1983).

2 C(A)A 1983, s 52(1).

3 C(A)A 1983, s 52(2).

4 C(A)A 1983, s 52(3)(c) and (d).

5 Form D6, Companies (Forms) Order 1987 (SI 147/1987).

6 CA 1963, s 27.

7 C(A)A 1983, s 52(3)(a). A consent from the personal representative of a deceased member or from the Official Assignee in the case of a bankrupt member shall be deemed to be the consent of the member himself, rather than merely the consent of his agent: C(A)A 1983, s 52(8).

8 C(A)A 1983, s 52(3)(b).

9 C(A)A 1983, s 52(4).

10 C(A)A 1983, s 52(5).

11 See CA 1963, s 104 and the notes thereto.

12 *Jubilee Cotton Mills v Lewis* [1924] AC 958.

13 *R v Registrar of Companies, ex parte Central Bank of India* [1986] 1 QB 1114 at 1169–1170 (per Lawton LJ); *Sun Tai Cheung Credits Ltd v Attorney General of Hong Kong* (1987) 3 BCC 357 at 360; *National Provincial and Union Bank of England v Charnley* [1924] 1 KB 431 at 454.

14 *R v Registrar of Companies, ex parte Central Bank of India* [1986] 1 QB 1114 at 1169–1170 (per Lawton LJ) and at 1171–1172 (per Slade LJ).

15 *Byrne v Ireland* [1972] IR 241; *Webb v Ireland* [1988] IR 353; *Howard v Commissioners of Pubic Works* [1993] ILRM 665.

16 *Peel's Case, Re Barned's Banking Co* (1867) LR 2 Ch App 674.

17 *Murren v Brennan* [1942] IR 466; *Maher v Attorney General* [1973] IR 146; *Tormey v Ireland* [1985] IR 289.

Effect of re-registration: Although re-registration converts the company into an unlimited company, it retains the same corporate persona and thus all pre-existing rights and obligations of the company remain unaffected (including any legal proceedings commenced by or against it).[1] In the case of persons who had ceased to be members of the company before its re-registration with unlimited liability, they will have no greater liability to contribute in a winding up than if the company had continued to be a limited company.[2]

1 C(A)A 1983, s 52(7).

[2] C(A)A 1983, s 52(6). By virtue of CA 1963, s 207 a person who has ceased to be a member for more than one year prior to the commencement of the winding up. Moreover, even if he has only ceased to be member in the 12 months preceding the liquidation, he will only be liable to contribute such amount as may be unpaid on his former shares and even then, only if the existing members are unable to make the contributions required from them.

UK legislation

See CA 1985, ss 49, 50; IA 1986, s 78.

---

53 Re-registration of unlimited company as limited

(1) A company which, on the appointed day, is registered as unlimited or thereafter is so registered (otherwise than by virtue of section 52) may be re-registered under the Principal Act as limited if a special resolution that it should be so re-registered (complying with the requirements of subsection (2)) is passed and an application in that behalf, made in the prescribed form and signed by a director or by the secretary of the company, is delivered to the registrar, together with the documents mentioned in subsection (3) not earlier than the day on which the copy of the resolution forwarded to him in pursuance of section 143 of the Principal Act is received by him.

(2) The said requirements are that the resolution must state whether the company is to be limited by shares or by guarantee and—

(a) if it is to be limited by shares, must state what the share capital is to be and provide for the making of such alterations in the memorandum as are necessary to bring it, both in substance and in form, into conformity with the requirements of the Companies Acts with respect to the memorandum of a company so limited, and such alterations in the articles as are requisite in the circumstances;

(b) if it is to be limited by guarantee, must provide for the making of such alterations in its memorandum and articles as are necessary to bring them, both in substance and in form, into conformity with the requirements of the Principal Act with respect to the memorandum and articles of a company so limited.

(3) The documents referred to in subsection (1) are a printed copy of the memorandum as altered in pursuance of the resolution and a printed copy of the articles as so altered.

(4) The registrar shall retain the application and other documents delivered to him under subsection (1) and shall issue to the company a certificate of incorporation appropriate to the status to be assumed by the company by virtue of this section; and upon the issue of the certificate—

(a) the status of the company shall, by virtue of the issue, be changed from unlimited to limited; and

(b) the alterations in the memorandum specified in the resolution and the alterations in, and additions to, the articles so specified shall, notwithstanding anything in the Principal Act, take effect.

(5) A certificate of incorporation issued by virtue of this section shall be conclusive evidence that the requirements of this section with respect to re-registration and of matters precedent and incidental thereto have been complied with, and that the company

was authorised to be re-registered under the Principal Act in pursuance of this section and was duly so re-registered.

(6) Section 71 of the Principal Act shall have effect as if, for the reference to its resolution for registration as a limited company in pursuance of that Act, there were substituted a reference to its resolution for registration as a limited company in pursuance of that Act or re-registration as a limited company in pursuance of this section.

(7) In the event of the winding-up of a company re-registered in pursuance of this section, the following provisions shall have effect—

(a) notwithstanding paragraph (a) of subsection (1) of section 207 of the Principal Act, a past member of the company who was a member thereof at the time of re-registration shall, if the winding-up commences within the period of three years beginning with the day on which the company is re-registered, be liable to contribute to the assets of the company in respect of its debts and liabilities contracted before that time;

(b) where no persons who were members of the company at that time are existing members of the company, a person who, at that time, was a present or past member thereof shall, subject to paragraph (a) of the said subsection (1) and to paragraph (a) of this subsection, but notwithstanding paragraph (c) of the said subsection (1), be liable to contribute as aforesaid notwithstanding that the existing members have satisfied the contributions required to be made by them in pursuance of the Principal Act;

(c) notwithstanding paragraphs (d) and (e) of the said subsection (1), there shall be no limit on the amount which a person who, at that time, was a past or present member of the company is liable to contribute as aforesaid.

(8) The re-registration of an unlimited company as a limited company pursuant to this Act shall not affect any rights or obligations of the company, or render defective any legal proceedings by or against the company, and any legal proceedings which might have been continued or commenced against it in its former status may be continued or commenced against it in its new status.

Definitions

'the appointed day': C(A)A 1983, s 1(3), s 2(1); 'articles': CA 1963, s 2(1); 'the Companies Acts': C(A)A 1983, s 2(1); 'company': CA 1963, s 2(1); 'company limited by guarantee': CA 1963, s 2(1), s 5(2); 'company limited by shares': CA 1963, s 2(1), s 5(2); 'director': CA 1963, s 2(1); 'document': CA 1963, s 2(1); 'member': CA 1963, s 31; 'memorandum': CA 1963, s 2(1); 'prescribed': CA 1963, s 2(1); 'the Principal Act': C(A)A 1983, s 2(1); 'printed': CA 1963, s 2(1); 'Registrar of Companies': CA 1963, s 2(1): 'share': CA 1963, s 2(1); 'unlimited company': CA 1963, s 2 (1), s 5(2).

Notes

Re-registration of unlimited company as a limited company: Prior to the appointed day of 13 October 1983,[1] an unlimited company wishing to re-register as a limited company would do so in accordance with the procedures laid down by CA 1963, s 20. Now, however, re-registration must be effected in accordance with the procedures laid down by this section,[2] unless the re-registration is to be as a plc, in which case the procedure to be followed is as laid down in C(A)A 1983, s 11.

The application for re-registration must be authorised by special resolution of the members[3] which must stipulate whether the company is to be limited by shares and/or by guarantee[4] and it must also effect any necessary changes to the memorandum and articles of association to reflect this proposed change in status.[5]

Documents to be delivered to the Registrar: An application for re-registration in the prescribed form[6], signed by one of the directors or by the company secretary must be delivered to the Registrar of Companies together with printed copies of the amended memorandum and articles that are to apply upon re-registration.[7]

Certificate of incorporation: Provided he is satisfied that the requirements for re-registration have been complied with, the Registrar must issue the company with a certificate of incorporation as a limited company of the appropriate type.[8] This certificate operates as 'conclusive' evidence that the re-registration requirements have been complied with and that the company is such a limited company.[9] The conclusiveness of a Registrar's certificate has previously been upheld in the context of the certification of the registration of a charge under CA 1963, s 99.[10] It has also been upheld in the context of a certificate of incorporation, so as to preclude the court from looking behind the date stated on the certificate as being the date of incorporation.[11] In the UK it has been suggested that despite its stated conclusiveness, the courts would be prepared to look behind a Registrar's certificate in cases of fraud or where there is an error on the face of the certificate itself.[12] It has also been held by the UK courts that because legislation does not bind the Crown except where expressly so stated, an erroneously issued certificate could be challenged through the *fiat* of the Attorney General.[13] It is thought, however, that a similar position would not pertain in Ireland since the Royal Prerogatives, including the non-application of statutes, have been held not to have survived the enactment of the Constitution.[14] Whilst the certainty afforded to members and creditors alike by the conclusiveness of such certificates has been judicially acknowledged,[15] it remains to be seen, however whether that 'conclusiveness' is unconstitutional either as an infringement of the separation of powers contained in Article 6 of the Constitution or as an attempt to oust the High Court's full original jurisdiction under Article 34 of the Constitution to hear and determine all justiciable matters.[16]

1 Companies (Amendment) Act 1983 (Commencement) Order 1983 (SI 288/1983).

2 See C(A)A 1983, s 54.

3 C(A)A 1983, s 53(1).

4 C(A)A 1983, s 53(2). Note, however, that if the company is to be a public company it cannot be a company limited by guarantee and having a share capital: s 7.

5 C(A)A 1983, s 53(2). See CA 1963, ss 11, 12, 13, 13A, 14 and 16 and Tables A, B, C and D for the Model Form memoranda and articles of association of limited companies.

6 Form 86, Companies (Forms) order 1983 (SI 289/1983).

7 C(A)A 1983, s 53(1) and (3).

8 C(A)A 1983, s 53(4).

9 C(A)A 1983, s 53(5).

10 See CA 1963, s 104 and the notes thereto.

11 *Jubilee Cotton Mills v Lewis* [1924] AC 958.

12 *R v Registrar of Companies, ex parte Central Bank of India* [1986] 1 QB 1114 at 1169–1170 (per Lawton LJ); *Sun Tai Cheung Credits Ltd v Attorney General of Hong Kong* (1987) 3 BCC 357 at 360; *National Provincial and Union Bank of England v Charnley* [1924] 1 KB 431 at 454.

13 *R v Registrar of Companies, ex parte Central Bank of India* [1986] 1 QB 1114 at 1169–1170 (per Lawton LJ) and at 1171–1172 (per Slade LJ).

14 *Byrne v Ireland* [1972] IR 241; *Webb v Ireland* [1988] IR 353; *Howard v Commissioners of Pubic Works* [1993] ILRM 665.

15 *Peel's Case, Re Barned's Banking Co* (1867) LR 2 Ch App 674.

16 *Murren v Brennan* [1942] IR 466; *Maher v Attorney General* [1973] IR 146; *Tormey v Ireland* [1985] IR 289.

Effect of re-registration: Although re-registration converts the company into a limited company, it retains the same corporate persona and thus all pre-existing rights and obligations of the company remain unaffected (including any legal proceedings commenced by or against it).[1]

1 C(A)A 1983, s 53(8).

Creditor protection: In passing the necessary special resolution for re-registration, the members may also if they so desire: (a) increase the nominal value of the share capital by increasing the nominal amount of each of its shares, but subject to the condition that no part of the increased capital is to be called up except in the event and for the purposes of the company being wound up; and/or (b) provide that a specified portion of its uncalled capital shall not be capable of being called up except in the event and for the purposes of the company being wound up.[1] Whilst either course of action affords the creditors less protection than if the liability of the members were to remain unlimited on an indefinite basis, it does at least ensure that some proportion of the capital is 'ring-fenced' for creditors and is kept immune from the risk of being lost in the ordinary curse of the company's trading life.

It is also to be noted that if the company goes into liquidation within thee years of the date of re-registration as a plc, any person who was a member at the date of re-registration will have unlimited liability for debts and liabilities incurred before the company became a plc.[2] In this regard, however, past members will only be called upon to so contribute if: (a) no persons who were members of the company at the time of re-registration are existing members at the time of the winding up; or (b) those persons who were members of the company at the time of re-registration and are existing members at the time of the winding up are unable between them the make good the deficiency in the liquidation.[3]

1 CA 1963, s 71 as applied by s 53(6).
2 C(A)A 1983, s 53(7).
3 C(A)A 1983, s 53(7) and CA 1963, s 207(1)(c).

UK legislation

See CA 1985, ss 51, 52; IA 1986, s 77.

---

54 Cesser of section 20 of Principal Act

No company shall register or re-register in pursuance of section 20 (1) of the Principal Act after the appointed day except upon an application in that behalf made before that day.

Definitions

'the appointed day': C(A)A 1983, s 1(3), s 2(1); 'company': CA 1963, s 2(1); 'the Principal Act': C(A)A 1983, s 2(1).

Notes

Re-registration of an unlimited company as a limited company: Prior to the appointed day of 13 October 1983,[1] an unlimited company wishing to re-register as a limited company would do so in accordance with the procedures laid down by CA 1963, s 20. Now, however, re-registration must be effected in accordance with the procedures laid down by C(A)A 1983, s 53, unless the re-registration is to be as a plc, in which case the procedure to be followed is as laid down in s 11.

1 Companies (Amendment) Act 1983 (Commencement) Order 1983 (SI 288/1983).

PART VI
MISCELLANEOUS

55 Public limited company to publish certain matters in [the Companies Registration Office Gazette][a]

(1) A public limited company shall publish in [the Companies Registration Office Gazette][a] notice of the delivery to the registrar of companies of the following documents—

(a) a statutory declaration under section 6(2);

(b) a copy of a resolution which gives, varies, revokes or renews an authority for the purposes of section 20;

(c) a copy of a special resolution under section 24(1), (2) or (3);

(d) any expert's valuation report on a non-cash consideration under section 31(2);

(e) any expert's valuation report on a non-cash asset acquired from a subscriber under section 33(2);

(f) any statement or notice under section 39(1), (3) or (4);

(g) any return of allotments under section 58(1) of the Principal Act;

(h) any notification of the redemption of preference shares under section 69(1) of the Principal Act;

(i) a copy of a special resolution to reduce its share capital under section 72(2) of the Principal Act;

(j) a copy of any resolution or agreement to which section 143 of the Principal Act applies and which—

(i) states the rights attached to any shares in the company, other than shares which are, in all respects, uniform (for the purposes of section 39(1)) with shares previously allotted;

(ii) varies rights attached to any shares in the company; or

(iii) assigns a name or other designation, or a new name or other designation, to any class of shares in the company.

(2) The notice mentioned in subsection (1) shall be published within six weeks of the relevant delivery.

(3) Where a company fails to comply with this section, the company and every officer of the company who is in default shall be guilty of an offence and shall be liable on summary conviction to a fine not exceeding [€1,904.61].[b]

(4) Proceedings in relation to an offence under this section may be brought and prosecuted by the registrar of companies.

Amendments

a Words substituted by IFCMPA 2005, s 72.

b '£250' increased to £1,500 by CA 1990, s 240(7) as inserted by CLEA 2001, s 104(c), and converted to €1,904.61 by Council Regulations (EC) No 1103/97, No 974/98 and No 2866/98 and the Economic and Monetary Union Act 1998, s 6.

Definitions

'company': CA 1963, s 2(1); 'document': CA 1963, s 2(1); 'non-cash asset': C(A)A 1983, s 2(1); 'officer': CA 1963, s 2(1); 'officer in default': CA 1963, s 383; 'the Principal Act': C(A)A 1983, s 2(1); 'public limited company': C(A)A 1983, s 2(1); 'the Registrar of Companies': CA 1963, s 2(1); 'share': CA 1963, s 2(1).

Notes

Publication of notice in the Companies Registration Office Gazette: This section adds to the list of documents already prescribed by EC(C)R 1973, reg 4, in respect of which notice of delivery to the Registrar of Companies, must be published in the Companies Registration Office Gazette. It may be noted that, in practice, the Registrar of Companies causes the notice of the delivery to be published.

Redeemable preference shares: The reference to redeemable preference shares in C(A)A 1983, s 55(1)(h) is deemed to be a reference to 'redeemable shares'.[1]

[1] CA 1990, s 221.

UK legislation

See CA 1986, s 711 (amended by IA 1986, s 439(1) Sch 13, Pt 1; CA 1989, s 23 Sch 10 para 14).

---

56 Trading under misleading name

(1) A person who is not a public limited company or (after the end of the general transitional period) is an old public limited company shall be guilty of an offence if he carries on any trade, profession or business under a name which includes, as its last part, the words 'public limited company', or 'cuideachta phoiblí theoranta' or abbreviations of those words.

(2) A public limited company other than an old public limited company shall be guilty of an offence if, in circumstances in which the fact that it is a public limited company is likely to be material to any person, it uses a name which may reasonably be expected to give the impression that it is a company other than a public limited company.

(3) Where, within the re-registration period, an old public limited company applies to be re-registered under section 12 as a public limited company, then—

- (a) during the twelve months following the re-registration, any provision of section 114(1)(b) or (c) of the Principal Act; and
- (b) during the three years following the re-registration, section 114(1)(a) of the Principal Act or any provision of any other Act or statutory instrument requiring or authorising the name of the company to be shown on any document or other object.

shall apply as if any reference in that provision to the name of the company were a reference to a name which either is its name or was its name before re-registration.

(4) Subsection (1) shall not apply to any company—

- (a) to which Part XI of the Principal Act applies; and
- (b) which has provisions in its constitution that would entitle it to rank as a public limited company if its had been registered in the State.

(5) A person guilty of an offence under subsection (1) or (2) and, if that person is a company, any officer of the company who is in default shall be liable on summary

conviction to a fine not exceeding [€1,904.61][a] together with, in the case of a continuing offence, a fine not exceeding [€31.74][b] for every day on which the offence continues, but not exceeding [€1,904.61][c] in total.

Amendments

a '£500' substituted for '£50' by C(A)A 1982, Sch 1, increased to £1,500 by CA 1990, s 240(7) as inserted by CLEA 2001, s 104(c), and converted to €1,904.61 by Council Regulations (EC) No 1103/97, No 974/98 and No 2866/98 and the Economic and Monetary Union Act 1998, s 6.

b £50 converted to €31.74 by Council Regulations (EC) No 1103/97, No 974/98 and No 2866/98 and the Economic and Monetary Union Act 1998, s 6.

c £1,000 increased to £1,500 by CA 1990, s 240(7) as inserted by CLEA 2001, s 104(c) and converted to €1,904.61 by Council Regulations (EC) No 1103/97, No 974/98 and No 2866/98 and the Economic and Monetary Union Act 1998, s 6.

Definitions

'company': CA 1963, s 2(1); 'document': CA 1963, s 2(1); 'officer': CA 1963, s 2(1); 'officer in default': CA 1963, s 383; 'old public limited company': C(A)A 1983, s 2(1), s 12(1); 'the Principal Act': C(A)A 1983, s 2(1); 'public limited company': C(A)A 1983, s 2(1); 'the re-registration period': C(A)A 1983, s 2(1), 13(1).

Notes

Trading under misleading name: Just as it is an offence for any person or company other than a limited liability company to carry on business under a name or title which includes the word 'limited' or 'teoranta' or any abbreviation or imitation thereof,[1], so too it is an offence to carry on business under a name or title which includes the words 'public limited company' or 'cuideachta phoiblí theoranta' or the relevant abbreviation thereof unless the entity in question actually is a plc[2] or is the foreign equivalent of a plc[3] or is a foreign company having an established place of business in the State (even if not actually the foreign equivalent of a plc).[4] Furthermore, just as it is an offence to pretend to be a plc, so too it is an offence for a plc to use a name which could reasonably be expected to give the impression that it is some other type of entity in circumstances where the fact of it being a plc is likely to be material to the person dealing with it.[5]

1 CA 1963, s 381.
2 C(A)A 1983, s 56(1).
3 C(A)A 1983, s 56(4)(b).
4 C(A)A 1983, s 56(4)(a).
5 C(A)A 1983, s 56(2).

Exemption for use of 'limited' in the name of plc: In its original form, CA 1963, s 24 empowered the Minister to licence certain charitable and other companies (whether pubic or private) to dispense with the use of the word 'limited' in their names. That power of dispensation was removed for plcs by C(A)A 1983, s 58. However, the provisions of CA 1963, s 24 have since been repealed and substituted by CLEA 2001, s 88 and now the Minister no longer grants a licence dispensing with the use of the word 'limited'. Instead, the company automatically obtains such a dispensation upon incorporation provided its constitution meet the requirements prescribed by the section and provided a statutory declaration is filed on behalf of the company confirming compliance with the section's requirements. On its face, the new s 24 would appear to extend the dispensation regarding the use of the word 'limited' to any company with limited liability, including a plc. It is not clear whether this is intentional or an oversight. In this regard C(A)A 1983, s 58 was neither amended nor repealed by CLEA 2001. Accordingly, it may be that the reference in s 58 to no 'licence' being granted to a plc under CA 1963, s 24, should now be read as meaning that no plc will be entitled to avail of the exemption provided by CA 1963, s 24 as substituted by CLEA 2001, s 88.

UK legislation

See CA 1985, s 33.

57 Penalties

(1) A company or other person guilty of an offence under section 20 or 36, shall be liable, on conviction on indictment, to a fine not exceeding [€3,174.35].[a]

(2) A company or other person guilty of an offence under section 24, 40 or 41 shall be liable, on conviction on indictment—

- (a) in the case of a company, to a fine not exceeding [€3,174.35];[a]
- (b) in the case of a person other than a company, to a fine not exceeding [€3,174.35][a] or, at the discretion of the court, to imprisonment for a term not exceeding [5][b] years or to both the fine and the imprisonment.

(3) Any person guilty of an offence under section 31, shall be liable on conviction on indictment to a fine not exceeding [€6,348.69][c] or, at the discretion of the court, to imprisonment for a term not exceeding [5][d] years or to both the fine and the imprisonment.

(4) A Justice of the District Court shall have jurisdiction to try summarily an offence under sections 20, 24, 31, 36, 40 and 41 if—

- (a) the Justice is of the opinion that the facts proved or alleged against the defendant charged with any such offence constitute a minor offence fit to be tried summarily;
- (b) the Director of Public Prosecutions consents; and
- (c) the defendant (on being informed by the Justice of his right to be tried by a jury) does not object to being tried summarily,

and, upon conviction under this subsection the said defendant shall be liable—

- (i) in the case where the defendant is guilty of an offence under section 20 or 36, to a fine not exceeding [€1,904.61];[e]
- (ii) in the case where the defendant is guilty of an offence under section 24, 31, 40 or 41—
  - (I) in the case of a company, to a fine not exceeding [€1,904.61];[e]
  - (II) in the case of a person other than a company, to a fine not exceeding [€1,904.61][e] or, at the discretion of the Court, to imprisonment for a term not exceeding 6 months or to both the fine and the imprisonment.

(5) Section 13 of the Criminal Procedure Act, 1967, shall apply in relation to an offence under the said section 20, 24, 31, 36, 40 and 41 as if, in lieu of the penalties specified in subsection (3) of the said section 13, there were specified therein the penalty provided for by subsection (4) of this section, and the reference in subsection 2 (a) of the said section 13 to the penalties provided for in subsection (3) of the said section 13, shall be construed and have effect accordingly.

Amendments

a £2,500 converted to €3,174.35 by Council Regulations (EC) No 1103/97, No 974/98 and No 2866/98 and the Economic and Monetary Union Act 1998, s 6.

b 2 years increased to 5 years by CA 1990, s 240(8).

c £2,500 converted to €6,348.69 by Council Regulations (EC) No 1103/97, No 974/98 and No 2866/98 and the Economic and Monetary Union Act 1998, s 6.

d 3 years increased to 5 years by CA 1990, s 240(8).

e £500 increased to €1,500 by CA 1990, s 240(7) and converted to €1,904.61 by Council Regulations (EC) No 1103/97, No 974/98 and No 2866/98 and the Economic and Monetary Union Act 1998, s 6.

Definitions

'company': CA 1963, s 2(1); 'the court': CA 1963, s 2(1).

58 Revocation of power under section 24 of Principal Act to dispense with 'limited' in name of public limited companies

(1) No licence under section 24 of the Principal Act shall be granted in respect of a public limited company or an association about to be formed into a public limited company or have effect in respect of such a company.

(2) Any such licence already granted to a company shall cease to have effect if, after the appointed day, the company is registered or re-registered as a public limited company.

Definitions

'the appointed day': C(A)A 1983, s 1(3), s 2(1); 'company': CA 1963, s 2(1); 'the Principal Act': C(A)A 1983, s 2(1); 'public limited company': C(A)A 1983, s 2(1).

Notes

Exemption for use of 'limited' in the name of plc: In its original form, CA 1963, s 24 empowered the Minister to licence certain charitable and other companies (whether pubic or private) to dispense with the use of the word 'limited in their names. That power of dispensation was removed for plc's by C(A)A 1983, s 58. However, the provisions of CA 1963, s 24 have since been repealed and substituted by CLEA 2001, s 88 and now the Minister no longer grants a licence dispensing with the use of the word 'limited. Instead, the company automatically obtains such a dispensation upon incorporation provided its constitution meet the requirements prescribed by the section and provided a statutory declaration is filed on behalf of the company confirming compliance with the section's requirements. On its face, the new s 24 would appear to extend the dispensation regarding the use of the word 'limited' to any company with limited liability, including a plc. It is not clear whether this is intentional or an oversight. In this regard C(A)A 1983, s 58 was neither amended nor repealed by CLEA 2001. Accordingly, it may be that the reference in s 58 to no 'licence' being granted to a plc under CA 1963, s 24, should now be read as meaning that no plc will be entitled to avail of the exemption provided by CA 1963, s 24 as substituted by CLEA 2001, s 88.

59 Power by order to prescribe forms and to revoke and amend orders

(1) The Minister may by order prescribe forms to be used in connection with any of the provisions of this Act.

(2) The Minister may by order revoke or amend an order (other than an order made under section 1(3)) made under this Act.

Definitions

'the Minister': C(A)A 1983, s 2(1).

Notes

Prescribed forms: The forms prescribed for the purposes of C(A)A 1983 are those contained in the Companies (Forms) Order 1983 (SI 289/1983).

60 Laying of orders before Houses of Oireachtas

Every order made under this Act shall be laid before each House of the Oireachtas as soon as may be after it is made and if a resolution annulling the order is passed by either House within the next 21 days on which that House has sat after the order is laid before it, the order shall be annulled accordingly but without prejudice to the validity of anything previously done thereunder.

61 Expenses

The expenses incurred in the administration of this Act shall, to such extent as may be sanctioned by the Minister for Finance, be paid out of moneys provided by the Oireachtas.

FIRST SCHEDULE

MINOR AND CONSEQUENTIAL AMENDMENTS TO THE COMPANIES ACT, 1963

Section 3

1. [...][a]

Amendments

This para substituted 'a resolution of the company' for 'special resolution' in the definition of 'articles' in CA 1963, s 2(1).

2. [...][a]

Amendments

C(A)A 1983, Sch 1, para 2, substituted CA 1963, s 6(1).

3. [...][a]

Amendments

This para deleted 'so, however, that no part of the capital of the company shall be expended in any such purchase' in CA 1963, s 10(6); para (b) inserted CA 1963, s 10(6A),(6B),(6C).

4. [...][a]

Amendments

CA 1963, s 22(2) substituted by this para.

5. [...][a]

Amendments

This para substituted '(6A), (6B), (6C),' in CA 1963, s 28(4).

6. [...][a]

Amendments

a C(A)A 1983, Sch 1, para 6, substituted CA 1963, s 35.

7. [...][a]

Amendments

a C(A)A 1983, Sch 1, para 7, substituted 'Except in the case of a public limited company the amount payable' for 'The amount payable' in CA 1963, s 53.

8. [...][a]

Amendments

a C(A)A 1983, Sch 1, para 8, substituted CA 1963, s 54(3).

9. [...][a]

Amendments

a C(A)A 1983, Sch 1, para 9, substituted CA 1963, s 55(1).

10. [...][a]

Amendments

a C(A)A 1983, Sch 1, para 10 inserted CA 1963, s 60(15A), (15B).

11. [...][a]

Amendments

a C(A)A 1983, Sch 1, para 11, substituted 'to be allotted' for 'to be issued' in CA 1963, s 62(2).

12. [...][a]

Amendments

a C(A)A 1983,, Sch 1, para 12, substituted CA 1963, s 64(1)(c).

13. [...][a]

Amendments

a C(A)A 1983, Sch 1, para 12, substituted CA 1963, s 114(5).

14. [...][a]

Amendments

a C(A)A 1983, Sch 1, para 14 inserted CA 1963, s 115(7)(d).

15. [...][a]

Amendments

a C(A)A 1983, Sch 1, para 15 inserted CA 1963, s 143(4)(j).

16. [...][a]

Amendments

a C(A)A 1983, Sch 1, para 16 inserted 'or section 42 of the Companies (Amendment) Act, 1983' after 'section 391' in CA 1963, s 200(b).

17. [...][a]

Amendments

a C(A)A 1983, Sch 1, para 17 inserted CA 1963, s 213(h)–(i).

18. [...][a]

Amendments

a C(A)A 1983, Sch 1, para 18 inserted CA 1963, s 215(f).

19. [...][a]

Amendments

a C(A)A 1983, Sch 1, para 19, substituted CA 1963, s 330(c)(iii).

20. [...][a]

Amendments

a C(A)A 1983, Sch 1, para 20 substituted CA 1963, s 335(1).

21. [...][a]

Amendments

a C(A)A 1983, Sch 1, para 21 renumbered CA 1963, s 336 and inserted sub-s (2).

22. [...][a]

Amendments

a C(A)A 1983, Sch 1, para 22 inserted 'and including any statement under section 330 (c)' after 'the amount of the guarantee' in CA 1963, s 340.

23. [...][a]

Amendments

a C(A)A 1983, Sch 1, para 23, substituted CA 1963, s 395(2).

24. [...][a]

Amendments

a C(A)A 1983, Sch 1, para 24(a) substituted CA 1963, Sch 1, Table A, Pt I, reg 3; C(A)A 1983, Sch 1, para 24(b) substituted CA 1963, Sch I, Table A, Pt I, reg 5; C(A)A 1983, Sch 1, para 24(c) inserted ' the following ', subject to section 20 of the Companies (Amendment) Act, 1983' after 'or any part thereof,' in CA 1963, Sch 1, Table A, Pt I, reg 79; C(A)A 1983, Sch 1, para 24(d) substituted the 'Companies Acts, 1963 to 1983' for 'the Act' in CA 1963, Sch 1, Table A, Pt I, reg 80; C(A)A 1983, Sch 1, para 24(e) substituted CA 1963, Sch 1, Table A, Pt I, reg 118; C(A)A 1983, Sch 1, para 24(f) inserted CA 1963, Sch 1, Table A, Pt I, reg 130A; C(A)A 1983, Sch 1, para 24(g) substituted 'Whenever a resolution is passed in pursuance of regulation 130 or 130A' for 'Whenever such a resolution as aforesaid shall have been passed' in CA 1963, Sch 1, Table A, Pt I, reg 131.

25. [...][a]

Amendments

a C(A)A 1983, Sch 1, para 25, substituted CA 1963, Sch 1, Table A, Pt 1; regs 3, 5, 79, 80, 118, 130, 131.

26. [...][a]

Amendments

a C(A)A 1983, Sch 1, para 26, substituted 'AN UNLIMITED PUBLIC COMPANY' for 'A PUBLIC COMPANY' in the heading of CA 1963, Sch 2.

27. [...][a]

Amendments

a C(A)A 1983, Sch 1, para 27 inserted CA 1963, Sch 6 para 11(2A) and (2B).

28. [...][a]

Amendments

a C(A)A 1983, Sch 1, para 28 inserted CA 1963, Sch 7 para 5.

29. [...][a]

Amendments

a C(A)A 1983, Sch 1, para 29 inserted 'Particulars relating to directors to be shown on all business letters of the company' after 'Register of directors and secretaries' in CA 1963 Sch 9.

30. [...][a]

Amendments

a C(A)A 1983, Sch 1, para 30 deleted '130 Statutory meeting and statutory report' from CA 1963, Sch 10.

SECOND SCHEDULE

FORM OF MEMORANDUM OF ASSOCIATION OF A PUBLIC LIMITED COMPANY

Section 4

PART 1

A PUBLIC COMPANY LIMITED BY SHARES

1. The name of the company is 'The Northern Mining, public limited company'.

2. The company is to be a public limited company.

3. The objects for which the company is established are the mining of minerals of all kinds and the doing of all such other things as are incidental or conducive to the attainment of the above object.

4. The liability of the member is limited.

5. The share capital of the company is £30,000, divided into 30,000 shares of £1 each.

We, the several persons whose names and addresses are subscribed, wish to be formed into a company in pursuance of this memorandum of association, and we agree to take the number of shares in the capital of the company set opposite our respective names.

Names, Addresses and Descriptions of Subscribers	*Number of Shares taken by each Subscriber*
1. James Maher of .... in the County of .... Solicitor	5
2. John O'Brien of .... in the County of .... Engineer	375
3. Michael Nolan of .... in the County of .... Solicitor	225

Names, Addresses and Descriptions of Subscribers	*Number of Shares taken by each Subscriber*
4. Patrick Hayes of .... in the County of .... Geologist	55
5. Paul McCarthy of .... in the County of .... Geologist	10
6. Thomas Kennedy of .... in the County of .... Accountant	30
7. Joseph O'Meara of .... in the County of .... Solicitor	15
Total shares taken	715

Dated the .... day of ...., 19..........

Witness to the above signatures:

Name:

Address:

Definitions

'company': CA 1963, s 2(1); 'member': CA 1963, s 31; 'memorandum': CA 1963, s 2(1); 'share': CA 1963, s 2(1); 'public limited company': C(A)A 1983, s 2(1).

PART II

A PUBLIC COMPANY LIMITED BY GUARANTEE AND HAVING A SHARE CAPITAL

1. The name of the company is 'The Southern Counties Tourist Development,

2. The company is to be a public limited company.

3. The objects for which the company is established are the promotion of tourism in the southern counties of Ireland by providing facilities for tourists, and the doing of all such other things as are incidental or conducive to the attainment of the above object.

4. The liability of the member is limited.

5. Every member of the company undertakes to contribute to the assets of the company in the event of its being wound up while he is a member, or within one year afterwards, for payment of the debts and liabilities of the company contracted before he ceases to be a member, and the costs, charges and expenses of winding up, and for the adjustment of the rights of the contributories among themselves, such amount as may be required, not exceeding £25.

6. The share capital of the company shall consist of £30,000 divided into 30,000 shares of £1 each.

We, the several persons whose names and addresses are subscribed, wish to be formed into a company in pursuance of this memorandum of association, and we agree to take the number of shares in the capital of the company set opposite our respective names.

Names, Addresses and Descriptions of Subscribers	*Number of Shares taken by each Subscriber*
1. John Boland of .... in the County of .... Solicitor	5
2. Martin Cullen of .... in the County of .... Hotel Proprietor	375
3. Sean Keogh of .... in the County of .... Engineer	225
4. James Mangan of .... in the County of .... Travel Agent	55
5. Paul Roche of .... in the County of .... Farmer	10
6. Kevin O'Sullivan of .... in the County of .... Architect	30
7. Teresa O'Connell of .... in the County of .... Housewife	15
Total shares taken	715

Dated the .... day of ...., 19..........

Witness to the above signatures:

Name:

Address:

Definitions

'company': CA 1963, s 2(1); 'public limited company': C(A)A 1983, s 2(1); 'member': CA 1963, s 31; 'memorandum': CA 1963, s 2(1); 'share': CA 1963, s 2(1).

THIRD SCHEDULE
REPEALS

Notes

a Part I repealed. It also repealed definitions of 'statutory meeting' and 'statutory report' in s (2)(1), (6), s 19, s 48, s 63, s 130, s 149, s 213(b), s 215(b), s 216(2), words ',and the company shall also have a first and paramount lien on all shares (other than fully paid shares) standing registered in the name of a single person for all moneys immediately payable by him or his estate to the company' in Sch 1, Table A, Pt I. Pt II repealed C(A)A 1982, s 3(6).

Companies (Amendment) Act 1986

(Number 25 of 1986)

Section

PART V

[SPECIAL PROVISIONS WHERE A COMPANY IS A PARENT UNDERTAKING OR SUBSIDIARY UNDERTAKING]

PART VI

SPECIAL PROVISIONS WHERE A COMPANY IS AN INVESTMENT COMPANY

PART VII

INTERPRETATION OF SCHEDULE

An Act to amend the Law Relating To Companies. [12th July, 1986]

Be it Enacted by the Oireachtas as Follows:

1 Interpretation

(1) In this Act, except where the context otherwise requires—

'the Act of 1983' means the Companies (Amendment) Act, 1983;

['abridged accounts' has the meaning given to it by section 19 of the Principal Act;][a]

'company' does not include an unlimited company;

'private company' does not include an unlimited company;

'public company' means a company other than a private company;

'the Principal Act' means the Companies Act, 1963.

(2) In this Act, except where the context otherwise requires, a reference to a balance sheet or profit and loss account shall include a reference to any notes to or documents annexed to the accounts in question giving information which is required by any provision of the Companies Acts, 1963 to 1986, and required or allowed by any such provision to be given in a note to or a document annexed to a company's accounts.

[(3) In this Act, except where the context otherwise requires, a reference to a subsidiary is to a subsidiary undertaking as defined in Regulation 4 of the European Communities (Companies: Group Accounts) Regulations, 1992, and a reference to a holding company shall be construed accordingly.][b]

Amendments

a Definition inserted by the Schedule to EC(IFRSMA)R 2005. However, the reference to the 'Principal Act' appears to be an error. The correct reference should be to s 19 of C(A)A 1986.

b C(A)A 1986, s 1(3) inserted by EC(CGA)R 1992, reg 42.

Definitions

'accounts': CA 1963, s 2(1); 'company': CA 1963, s 2(1); 'document': CA 1963, s 2(1); 'private company': CA 1963, s 33; CA 1963, s 2(1), 'subsidiary': CA 1963, s 155.

Notes

Scope of C(A)A 1986: C(A)A 1986 gives legal effect to Council Directive 78/660/EEC. It deals, in broad terms, with two main issues. The first relates to the format and contents of the annual accounts for most types of private and public limited companies, and the second relates to the nature and extent of the disclosure of accounts which must be made by such companies when filing their annual returns.

However, with the advent of the EC(IFRSMA)R 2005 ('IFRS Regulations'), the requirements for companies to produce accounts changed significantly.

The IFRS Regulations was a direct consequence of Regulation (EC) No 1606/2002 of the European Parliament and of the Council. This Regulation applied directly to the group accounts of listed entities throughout the European Union by requiring these to be prepared in accordance with International Financial Reporting Standards ('IFRS').

The main purpose of the IFRS Regulations was to avail of a number of EU member state options contained in Regulation EC 1606/2002 of the European Parliament of the the Council ('the EU IAS Regulation'). The EU IAS Regulation requires all listed entities that are required to prepare consolidated (or group) accounts to do so in accordance with International Financial Reporting Standards ('IFRS') as adopted for use in the European Union. IFRS (previously known as International Accounting Standards or 'IAS') are issued by the International Accounting Standards Board ('IASB'). Each IFRS requires formal adoption by the European Union, after which, when published in the Official Journal, it has full legal recognition.

The EU IAS Regulation also allows member states to 'permit or require' the use of IFRS for the preparation of individual company accounts, regardless of whether such companies are listed or not. In implementing the IFRS Regulation, Ireland has opted for a permissive regime and the following choices have been reflected in CA 1963:

- debt-only listed parent companies may avail of an option not to prepare group accounts in accordance with IFRS until accounting periods beginning on or after 1 January 2007; and
- all other companies have the option to use IFRS in preparing their group or individual accounts.

Therefore, as a result of the IFRS Regulation, all companies and groups (that are not directly impacted by the EU IAS Regulation) have a choice as to the financial reporting framework they apply in preparing their individual and group accounts, known as Companies Act individual and group accounts or IFRS individual and group accounts.

The choice is not available to the following types of company:

- a company not trading for the acquisition of gain by members;
- a company not having a share capital formed for charitable purposes (see CA 1963, s 128(4)(c)); or
- a company in respect of which an order under CA 1963, s 128(5) is in force.

Such companies must continue to prepare Companies Act accounts. Companies Act accounts are prepared in accordance with the formats accounting requirements of the Companies Acts and accounting standards. The applicable standards are the Financial Reporting Standards ('FRS') issued by the Accounting Standards Board ('ASB') and promulgated in the Republic of Ireland by the Institute of Chartered Accountants in Ireland.

Generally, if a company opts to move from preparing Companies Act accounts to IFRS accounts, it is a one-way street. Such a company may not subsequently revert to preparing Companies Act accounts except where there has been a 'relevant change of circumstances'. Subsection 5 sets out the situations when such a change may arise.

The IFRS Regulation applies to accounting periods beginning on or after 1 January 2005.

See also notes on C(A)A 1986, s 3 below.

Insofar as the annual accounts of companies do not fall within the ambit of CA 1963 or C(A)A 1986, they fall to be dealt with by the EC(CGA)R 1992: these Regulations implement Council Directive 83/349/EEC and deal with the format and content of group accounts of public and private limited holding companies[2] which are engaged for gain in the production, supply or distribution of goods, the provision of a service or the making or holding of investments.[3] The Regulations do not apply, however, to the following:

(a) licensed banks[4];

(b) certified trustee savings banks[5];

(c) other companies engaged in the business of accepting deposits or other repayable funds or granting credit for its own account[6];
(d) companies engaged solely in the making of hire-purchase agreements and credit-sale agreements[7];
(e) authorised life and non-life insurance companies[8];
(f) companies which meet at least two of the three following criteria:
    (i) the group balance sheet does not exceed €7,618,428.47,
    (ii) the group turnover does not exceed e15,236,856.94 per annum,
    (iii) the group workforce does not exceed 250,[9] and in respect of which neither the parent company nor any of its subsidiaries is listed on a stock exchange established in a member state[10];
(g) certain parent companies which are themselves subsidiaries of other EC companies.[11]

1 See CA 1963, s 149 and the notes thereto as to the types of company still governed by that section and by CA 1963, Sch 6.

2 EC(CGA)R 1992, reg 5.

3 EC(CGA)R 1992, reg 3(1).

4 EC(CGA)R 1992, reg 6(2)(a).

5 EC(CGA)R 1992, reg 6(2)(b).

6 EC(CGA)R 1992, reg 6(2)(d).

7 EC(CGA)R 1992, reg 6(2)(c).

8 EC(CGA)R 1992, reg 6(2)(g).

9 EC(CGA)R 1992, reg 7(1).

10 EC(CGA)R 1992, reg 7(8).

11 EC(CGA)R, regs 8 and 9.

EC(CIA)R 1992: These Regulations, which give effect to Council Directive 86/635/EEC, govern the form and content of annual accounts for banks and other financial institutions.

EC(A)R 1993: These Regulations give legal effect, *inter alia*, to Council Directive 90/605/EEC and govern the format and content of the annual accounts for unlimited companies in circumstances where, broadly speaking, the members of the company are themselves either Irish or foreign limited companies.[1]

1 EC(A)R 1993, reg 6. The Regulations also apply to partnerships.

EC(IUA)R 1996: These Regulations implement Council Directive 91/674/EEC and govern the form and content of annual accounts for insurance companies to which the European Communities (Non-Life Insurance) Regs 1976 or the European Communities (Life Assurance) Regs 1984 apply, as well as reinsurance companies.

Subsidiary: Note that for the purposes of this Act the definition of 'subsidiary' contained in CA 1963, s 155 is replaced by the definition of 'subsidiary undertaking' contained in EC(CGA)R 1992.

---

2 Scope of Act

(1) This Act does not apply to—

(a) a company not trading for the acquisition of gain by the members,

(b) a company to which subsection (4)(c) of section 128 of the Principal Act applies,

(c) a company in respect of which there is in force an order under subsection (5) of that section.

(2) Sections 3 to 6, 8 to 12, 17 to 19, and 24 of this Act do not apply in relation to—

(a) a company that is the holder of a licence under the Central Bank Act, 1971,

(b) a company that is a trustee savings bank certified under the Trustee Savings Banks Acts, 1863 to 1965,

(c) a company engaged solely in the making of hire-purchase agreements (within the meaning of the Hire-Purchase Act, 1946) and credit-sale agreements (within the meaning of that Act), in respect of goods owned by the company,

(d) a company engaged in the business of accepting deposits or other repayable funds or granting credit for its own account,

(e) [...],[a]

(f) Fóir Teoranta, or

(g) [...].[b]

[(3) Sections 3 to 6, 8, 12, 17, 18 and 24 of this Act do not apply in relation to undertakings to which the European Communities (Insurance Undertakings: Accounts) Regulations 1996 (No 23 of 1991) apply by virtue of regulation 3 of those Regulations).][c]

Amendments

a C(A)A 1986, s 2(2)(e) repealed by ACC Bank Act 2001, s 12(1).

b C(A)A 1986, s 2(2)(g) repealed by ICC Bank Act 2000, s 7(1).

c C(A)A 1986, s 2(3) substituted by EC(IUA)R 1996, reg 20(2)(a).

Definitions

'company': C(A)A 1986, s 1(1), CA 1963, s 2(1); 'member': CA 1963, s 31; 'the Principal Act': C(A)A 1986, s 1(1).

Notes

Scope of C(A)A 1986: See notes to C(A)A 1986, s 1.

UK legislation

See CA 1985, s 226.

3 General provisions in relation to accounts

[(1)Companies Act individual accounts, including a balance sheet and profit and loss account, prepared in accordance with section 149 of the Principal Act shall comply with the following requirements]:[a]

(a) every such balance sheet and profit and loss account shall comply with the provisions of sections 4 and 5 of, and the Schedule to, this Act,

(b) every such balance sheet of a company shall give a true and fair view of the state of affairs of the company as at the end of its financial year and every such profit and loss account of a company shall give a true and fair view of the profit or loss of the company for the financial year,

(c) where a balance sheet or profit and loss account drawn up in accordance with paragraph (a) of this subsection would not provide sufficient information to comply with paragraph (b) of this subsection, any necessary additional information shall be provided in that balance sheet or profit and loss account or in a note to the accounts,

(d) where, owing to special circumstances, the preparation of accounts of a company in compliance with the said paragraph (a) would prevent those accounts from complying with paragraph (b) (even if additional information were provided under paragraph (c) of this subsection), the directors of the company shall depart from the requirements of the Schedule to this Act in preparing those accounts insofar as is necessary in order to comply with that paragraph,

(e) where the directors of a company depart from the requirements of this section, they shall attach a note to the accounts of the company giving details of the particular departures made, the reasons therefor and the effect of those departures on the accounts, and, accordingly, in the Companies Acts, 1963 to 1982, and the Companies (Amendment) Act, 1983, in relation to a company to which this Act applies—

(i) references to the said section 149, shall be construed as references to subsection (5) and, insofar as it relates to the said subsection (5), subsection (7) of the said section 149 and to the provisions of this Act corresponding to the other provisions of the said section 149, and

(ii) references to the Sixth Schedule shall be construed as references to the corresponding provisions of this Act.

(2) [...][b]

(3) [...][b]

(4) Subsection (1)(b) of this section overrides the requirements of sections 4 and 5 of, and the Schedule to, this Act and all other requirements of the Companies Acts, 1963 to 1986, as to the matters to be included in the accounts of a company or in notes to those accounts; and, accordingly, where a balance sheet or profit and loss account of a company drawn up in accordance with those requirements would not provide sufficient information to comply with the said subsection (1)(b), any necessary additional information shall be provided in that balance sheet or profit and loss account or in a note to the accounts.

Amendments

a Amended by EC(IFRSMA)R 2005, reg 5(a)(i).

b C(A)A 1986, s 3(2) and (3) deleted by EC(IFRSMA)R 2005, reg 5(a)(ii).

Definitions

'accounts': CA 1963, s 2(1); 'companies act individual accounts' CA 1963, s 2(1); 'company'; C(A)A 1986, s 1(1), CA 1963, s 2(1); 'director': CA 1963, s 2(1); 'group accounts': CA 1963, s 2(1), s 150(1), EC(CGA) 1992, reg 3(1), reg 13; 'financial year' CA 1963, s 2(1); 'parent undertaking': EC(CGA) 1992, reg 3(1); 'the Principal Act': C(A)A 1986, s 1(1).

Notes

Disapplication of CA 1963, s 149 and Sch 6: See notes to C(A)A 1986, s 1.

As a result of the amendments introduced by the IFRS Regulation, the primary obligation to prepare accounts, previously contained in C(A)A 1986, s 3 (individual company accounts) and Regulation 5 of the EC(CGAR), 1992 has 'moved' to CA 1963, s 148 for individual accounts, and CA 1963, s 150 for group accounts. The format and content of Companies Act individual accounts is governed by the particular legislation applicable to a particular undertaking. Therefore, undertakings to which the CA(A) 1986 apply, comply with formats and accounting requirements of that Act when preparing Companies Act individual accounts. Similarly, undertakings to which the 1993 Regulations[1], the Credit Institutions Regulations[2], the Insurance Undertakings Regulations[3], or the Sixth Schedule of CA 1963 apply comply with the requirements of those enactments.

1 *EC(A)R 1993*: These Regulations give legal effect, *inter alia*, to Council Directive 90/605/EEC and govern the format and content of the annual accounts for unlimited companies in circumstances where, broadly speaking, the members of the company are themselves either Irish or foreign limited companies.

2 *EC(CIA)R 1992*: These Regulationss, which give effect to Council Directive 86/635/EEC, govern the form and content of annual accounts for banks and other financial institutions.

3 *EC(IUA)R 1996*: These Regulations implement Council Directive 91/674/EEC and govern the form and content of annual accounts for insurance companies to which the European Communities (Non-Life Insurance) Regs 1976 or the European Communities (Life Assurance) Regs 1984 apply, as well as reinsurance companies.

True and fair view: The basic requirement for a company's annual accounts is that they should give a 'true and fair view' (or in the language of IFRS, give a 'fair presentation') of the financial state of affairs of the company, or of the group, as the case may be, for the year in question. To a large extent, compliance with a relevant accounting framework and the provisions of the accounting and disclosure requirements of the Companies Acts themselves are determinative as to what constitutes a properly prepared set of accounts. However, to the extent that the legislation is silent on any particular matter, compliance with 'generally accepted accounting practice' ('GAAP') in preparing the company's accounts will be strong but not conclusive evidence that the accounts give a 'true and fair view' of the company's financial position.[1]

1 *Dolan v AB Ltd* [1969] IR 282; *Lloyd Cheyham and Co Ltd v Littlejohn and Co* [1987] BCLC 303; *IRC v Duple Motor Bodies Ltd* [1961] 1 WLR 739. The recognised practices of the accountancy profession may be found in its Statements of Standard Accounting Practice (SSAPs) and in its Auditing Guidelines.

Small and medium-sized companies: The requirement for complete compliance with the provisions of CA 1963, s 3 and the Schedule is modified by C(A)A 1986 which allows for the preparation of abridged accounts in the case of small and medium-sized companies. Prior to the IFRS Regulations, the requirement for these abridged accounts to give a 'true and fair view' still pertained. This has always been somewhat anomalous as a set of accounts either gives a true and fair view or it does not. There are not 'degrees of true and fair'. However, the IFRS Regulations have addressed this anomaly by their substitution of C(A)A, 1986, ss 10 and 11 which has effectively removed the previous cross referecences to C(A)A 1986, s 3(1)(b) and the 'reference' 'true and fair' for abridged accounts.

Information about subsidiaries and 'undertakings of substantial interest': If the company is governed by C(A)A 1986 and it has a subsidiary or holds a 'qualifying capital interest'[1] of 20 per cent or more in another company, (referred to as an 'undertaking of substantial interest'), it must include certain information about that subsidiary or undertaking of substantial interest in the notes to its accounts,[2] unless—

(a) it already prepares group accounts in accordance with EC(CGA)R 1992 which contain equivalent information[3];

(b) the subsidiary or undertaking of substantial interest is not required to publish its accounts,[4] and the 'qualifying capital interest' of the company in that entity is less than 50 per cent[5]; or

(c) the information is not material.[6]

The information includes the name and address of the entity in question, the amount and proportion of its share capital which is held by the company, as well as details of its capital and reserves and profit or loss for the last financial year.[7]

However, if the directors are of the opinion that to include such information in the notes to the accounts would result in the notes being of excessive length, then unless the financial state of the subsidiary or undertaking of substantial interest has a substantial effect on the financial position of the company itself, the directors may instead set out the information in a separate statement which must be signed by one director and the secretary and which must be annexed to the annual return.[8]

1 For the definition of 'qualifying capital interest' see EC(CGA)R 1992, reg 35(2).

2 C(A)A 1986, s 16(1).

3 C(A)A 1986, s 16(2)(a) and (b).

4 As to the types of company which do not need to publish their accounts, see CA 1963, ss 125 and C(A)A 1986, s 7 as well as the notes thereto. Such companies include private limited companies not trading for gain by their members and unlimited companies in which there is at least one individual (ie non-corporate) member.

5 C(A)A 1986, s 16(2)(c).

6 C(A)A 1986, s 16(2)(d).

7 C(A)A 1986, s 16(1).

8 C(A)A 1986, s 16(3)). By including the information concerning subsidiaries or undertakings of substantial interest in a statement annexed to the annual return, rather than in the notes to the accounts, the directors would seem to be able to avoid presenting such information to the members at the annual general meeting.

UK legislation

See CA 1985, s 230.

---

4 Format of accounts

(1) [Where the directors of a company prepare Companies Act individual accounts and subject to this section,][a] every balance sheet of a company shall show the items listed in either of the balance sheets formats set out in the Schedule to this Act and every profit and loss account of a company shall show the items listed in any one of the profit and loss accounts formats so set out in either case in the order and under the headings and sub-headings given in the format adopted.

(2) Subsection (1) of this section shall not be construed as requiring the heading or sub-heading for any item in the balance sheet, or profit and loss account, of a company to be distinguished by any letter or number assigned to that item in the formats set out in the Schedule to this Act.

(3) Where the balance sheet, or profit and loss account, of a company has been prepared by reference to one of the formats set out in the Schedule to this Act, the directors of the

company shall adopt the same format in preparing the accounts for subsequent financial years unless, in their opinion, there are special reasons for a change.

(4) Where any change is made in accordance with subsection (3) of this section in the format adopted in preparing a balance sheet, or profit and loss account, of a company, the reasons for the change, together with full particulars of the change, shall be given in a note to the accounts in which the new format is first adopted.

(5) Any item required in accordance with the Schedule to this Act to be shown in the balance sheet, or profit and loss account, of a company, may be shown in greater detail than that required by the format adopted.

(6) Any items to which an Arabic number is assigned in any of the formats set out in the Schedule to this Act may be combined in the accounts of a company—

(a) in any case where the individual amounts of such items are not material to assessing the state of affairs or profit or loss of the company for the financial year concerned, or

(b) in any case where the combination of such items facilitates that assessment.

(7) Where items are combined in a company's accounts pursuant to subsection (6)(b) of this section, the individual amounts of any items so combined shall be disclosed in a note to the accounts.

[(8) In respect of every item shown in the balance sheet, or profit and loss account, of a company, the corresponding amount for the financial year immediately preceding that to which the balance sheet or profit and loss account refers shall also be shown. Where that corresponding amount is not comparable with the amount to be shown for the item in question in respect of the financial year to which the balance sheet or profit and loss account relates, the former amount may be adjusted, and, if the former amount is adjusted, particulars as regards the respect or respects in which the foregoing amounts are not comparable and of the adjustment shall be given in a note to the accounts.][b]

(9) Subject to subsection (10) of this section, a heading or sub-heading corresponding to an item listed in the format adopted in preparing the balance sheet, or profit and loss account, of a company, shall not be included in the balance sheet or profit and loss account, as the case may be, if there is no amount to be shown for that item in respect of the financial year to which the balance sheet or profit and loss account relates.

(10) Subsection (9) of this section shall not apply in any case where an amount can be shown for the item in question in respect of the financial year immediately preceding that to which the balance sheet or profit and loss account relates, and that amount shall be shown under the heading or sub-heading required by the format adopted as aforesaid.

(11) Amounts in respect of items representing assets or income may not be set off in the accounts of a company against amounts in respect of items representing liabilities or expenditure, as the case may be, or vice versa.

(12) The balance sheet, or profit and loss account, of a company may include an item representing or covering the amount of any asset or liability or income or expenditure not otherwise covered by any of the items listed in the format adopted but the following shall not be treated as assets in the balance sheet of a company—

(a) preliminary expenses,

(b) expenses of, and commission on, any issue of shares or debentures, and

(c) costs of research.

(13) In preparing the balance sheet, or profit and loss account, of a company, the directors of the company shall adapt the arrangement and headings and sub-headings otherwise required by subsection (1) of this section in respect of items to which an arabic number is assigned in the format adopted, in any case where the special nature of the company's business requires such adaptation.

(14) Every profit and loss account of a company shall show the amount of the profit or loss of the company on ordinary activities before taxation.

[(15) The notes to the profit and loss account of a company shall show—

(a) dividends paid (other than dividends for which a liability existed at the immediately preceding balance sheet date) or which the company is liable to pay,

(b) separately, any transfers between the profit and loss account and other reserves,

(c) any increase or reduction in the balance on the profit and loss account since the immediately preceding financial year,

(d) the profit or loss brought forward at the beginning of the financial year, and

(e) the profit or loss carried forward at the end of the financial year.

(16) There shall be shown in the notes to the accounts the aggregate amount of any dividends proposed before the date of approval of the accounts which have not been shown in the notes to the profit and loss account in accordance with subsection (15) of this section.][c]

Amendments

a Amended by EC(IFRSMA)R 2005, reg 5(b)(i).

b Substituted by SI 840/2005, reg 4.

c Amended by EC(IFRSMA)R 2005, reg 5(b)(ii).

Definitions

'accounts': CA 1963, s 2(1); 'companies act individual accounts' CA 1963, s 2(1); 'company': C(A)A 1986, s 1(1), CA 1963, s 2(1); 'debenture': CA 1963, s 2(1); 'director': CA 1963, s 2(1); 'financial year': CA 1963, s 2(1); 'share': CA 1963, s 2(1).

Notes

Small and medium-sized companies: As to the format of the balance sheet and profit and loss account for small and medium-sized companies, see C(A)A 1986, ss 10–12.

SI 840/2005: Companies that opt to prepare accounts in accordance with International Accounting Standards ('IAS'), now known as International Financial Reporting Standards ('IFRS'), no longer have to comply with the detailed accounting requirements of the Companies Acts, save for certain disclosures as detailed in section 149A(1)(b) of CA 1963. Companies continuing to prepare 'companies act accounts' continue to comply with the companies act requirements.

IFRS 1 'First-time adoption of International Financial Reporting Standards': provides exemption from the requirement to restate comparative information relating primarily to financial instruments, now required to be accounted for at 'fair value'. SI 840/2005 (along with FRS 28) provides a similar exemption for companies preparing 'companies act accounts'. Henceforth, it will fall to accounting standards to specify when corresponding amounts should be restated.

Accounting for dividends: The IFRS Regulations have also changed the timing of the recognition of proposed dividends. A proposed dividend is not considered a liability until companies have completed the necessary approval processes. Consequently, dividends proposed to the shareholders for approval at the Annual General Meeting will not be a liability in the accounts of the company at the end of the financial year. Instead, they will be disclosed separately in the notes to those accounts for information. This brings the law into line with current accounting standard requirements.

Directive 2003/51/EC 'The Modernisation Directive': The amendments to section 4(15) and (16) are a consequence of the Modernisation Directive. This Directive amends Directives 78/660/EEC, 83/349/EEC, 86/635/EEC and 91/674/EEC on the annual and consolidated accounts of certain types of companies, banks and other financial institutions and insurance undertakings. These are the four EU Directives that form the basis of European accounting requirements:

- The Fourth and Seventh Directives on the annual and consolidated accounts of companies;
- The Bank Accounts Directive on the annual and consolidated accounts of banks; and
- The Insurance Accounts Directive on the annual and consolidated accounts of insurance companies.

The Modernisation Directive was designed to:

- Remove conflicts between the accounting directives and International Accounting Standard ('IAS') (now referred to as International Financial Reporting Standards ('IFRS')) in existence at the time the Directive was drafted; and
- Ensure that those optional accounting treatments available under IAS/IFRS in existence when the Directive was finalised are available were available to EU companies which would not be preparing accounts under IAS/IFRS.

In general, the Modernisation Directive amendments relating to accounting requirements were 'technical' in nature.

UK legislation

See CA 1985, Sch 4, paras 1–5.

5 Accounting principles

Subject to section 6 of this Act, the amount to be included in the accounts of a company in respect of the items shown shall be determined in accordance with the following principles:

(a) the company shall be presumed to be carrying on business as a going concern,

(b) accounting policies shall be applied consistently from one financial year to the next,

(c) the amount of any item in the accounts shall be determined on a prudent basis and in particular—

(i) only profits realised at the balance sheet date shall be included in the profit and loss account, and

(ii) [all liabilities which have arisen][a] in respect of the financial year to which the accounts relate, or a previous financial year, shall be taken into account, including those liabilities and losses which only become apparent between the balance sheet date and the date on which the accounts are signed in pursuance of section 156 of the Principal Act,

(d) all income and charges relating to the financial year to which the accounts relate shall be taken into account without regard to the date of receipt or [payment][b]

(e) in determining the aggregate amount of any item the amount of each individual asset or liability that fails to be taken into account shall be determined [separately, and][c]

[(f) in determining how amounts are presented within items in the profit and loss account and balance sheet, the directors of a company shall have regard to the substance of the reported transaction or arrangement, in accordance with generally accepted accounting principles or practice.][d]

Amendments

a Amended by EC(IFRSMA)R 2005, reg 5(c)(i).

b Amended by EC(IFRSMA)R 2005, reg 5(c)(ii).

c Amended by EC(IFRSMA)R 2005, reg 5(c)(iii).

d Amended by EC(IFRSMA)R 2005, reg 5(c)(iv).

Definitions

'accounts': CA 1963, s 2(1); 'company': C(A)A 1986, s 1(1), CA 1963, s 2(1); 'financial year': CA 1963, s 2(1); 'the Principal Act': C(A)A 1986, s 1(1).

Notes

True and fair view: The basic requirement for a company's annual accounts is that they should give a 'true and fair view' (or in the language of IFRS, give a 'fair presentation') of the financial state of affairs of the company, or of the group, as the case may be, for the year in question.[1] To a large extent, compliance with a relevant accounting framework and the provisions of the accounting and disclosure requirements of the Companies Acts themselves are determinative as to what constitutes a properly prepared set of accounts. However, to the extent that the legislation is silent on any particular matter, compliance with 'generally accepted accounting practice' ('GAAP') in preparing the company's accounts will be strong but not conclusive evidence that the accounts give a 'true and fair view' of the company's financial position[1].

1 C(A)A 1986, s 3(1).

2 *Dolan v AB Ltd* [1969] IR 282; *Lloyd Cheyham and Co Ltd v Littlejohn and Co* [1987] BCLC 303; *IRC v Duple Motor Bodies Ltd* [1961] 1 WLR 739). The recognised practices of the accountancy profession may be found in its Statements of Standard Accounting Practice (SSAPs) and in its Auditing Guidelines.

Insertion of ss 5(f): This amendment has introduced a 'new' accounting principle into Irish company law. This requires that in accounting for a transaction, its substance and not just its legal form should be considered. This was a member state option in the Modernisation Directive which was availed of by the Irish Government. This reflects a long standing principle that has already been embodied in accounting standards.

UK legislation

See CA 1985, Sch 1, paras 5A, 9, 10, 11.

6 Departure from the accounting principles

If it appears to the directors of a company that there are special reasons for departing from any of the principles specified in section 5 of this Act, they may so depart, but particulars of the departure, the reasons for it and its effect on the balance sheet and profit and loss account of the company shall be stated in a note to the accounts, for the financial year concerned, of the company.

Definitions

'accounts': CA 1963, s 2(1); 'company': C(A)A 1986, s 1(1); CA 1963, s 2(1); 'director': CA 1963, s 2(1).

Notes

Although the directors may, under C(A)A 1986, s 6, depart in special circumstances from the accounting principles set out in CA 1963, s 5, they remain under an overriding obligation to ensure that the accounts present a true and fair view of the company's financial position.[1]

1 See C(A)A 1986, s 3(1) and the notes thereto.

UK legislation

See CA 1985, Sch 4, para 15.

7 Documents to be annexed to annual return

(1) Subject to the provisions of this Act, there shall be annexed to the annual return—

(a) [(i) in the case of a company other than a company to which section 2(2) or (3) of this Act applies, a copy of the company's individual accounts which shall be either IFRS individual accounts or Companies Act individual accounts prepared in accordance with sections 3, 4 and 5 of, and the Schedule to, this Act,

(ii) in the case of a company to which section 2(2) of this Act applies, a copy of the company's individual accounts which shall be either IFRS individual accounts or Companies Act individual accounts prepared in accordance with the Credit Institutions Regulations,

(iii) in the case of an undertaking to which section 2(3) of this Act applies, a copy of the undertaking's individual accounts which shall be either IFRS individual accounts or Companies Act individual accounts prepared in accordance with the Insurance Undertakings Regulations,

and a copy of the report of the auditors on, and the report of the directors accompanying, each such individual accounts, and each such copy shall be certified both by a director, and the secretary of the company, to be a true copy of such individual accounts, or report, as the case may be, laid or to be laid before the annual general meeting of the company for that year, and][a]

(b) where a document, being a balance sheet, profit and loss account, report, or statement, annexed to the annual return, is in a language other than the English language or the Irish language, there shall be annexed to each such document a translation in the English language or the Irish language certified in the prescribed manner to be a correct translation.

[(1A) Subsection (1) of this section shall not apply to the profit and loss account or income statement of a company where—

(a) the company is a parent undertaking,

(b) the company prepares group accounts in accordance with section 150 of the Principal Act, and

(c) the notes to the company's individual balance sheet show the company's profit or loss for the financial year determined in accordance with this Act or section 149A of the Principal Act, as appropriate.

(1B) Where, in the case of a company, advantage is taken of subsection (1A) of this section, that fact shall be disclosed—

(a) in the notes on the company's individual accounts, and

(b) in the notes on the group accounts referred to in subsection (1A)(b) of this section.] [b]

[[(1C)] Every document, being a balance sheet, profit and loss account, report or statement, annexed to the annual return in accordance with paragraph (a) of subsection (1) shall cover the period—

(a) in the case of the first annual return to which such documents are annexed – since the incorporation of the company, and

(b) in any other case – since the end of the period covered by the balance sheet, profit and loss account, report or statement, as the case may be, annexed to the preceding annual return,

made up to a date not earlier by more than 9 months than the date to which the annual return is made up.] [c]

(2) If a document required by this section to be annexed to the annual return referred to in subsection (1) of this section does not comply with the provisions of the law in force at the date of the relevant audit with respect to the form and the contents of the document, there shall be made by the company concerned such amendment sin the copy as are necessary in order to bring it into compliance with those provisions, and the fact that the copy has been so amended shall be stated therein.

(3) Section 128 of the Principal Act shall not apply to a company to which this section applies.

Amendments

a C(A)A 1986, s 7(a)(i)–(iii) amended by EC(IFRSMA)R 2005, reg 5(d)(i).

b C(A)A 1986, s 7(1A) and (1B) inserted by EC(IFRSMA)R 2005, reg 5(d)(ii)

c C(A)A 1986, s 7(1A) inserted by CLEA 2001, s 64(b) and renumbered as s 7(1C) by EC(IFRSMA)R 2005, reg 5(d)(ii).

Definitions

'annual return': CA 1963, s 2 (1); 'companies act individual accounts': CA 1963, s 2(1); 'company': C(A)A 1986, s 1(1), CA 1963, s 2(1); 'director': CA 1963, s 2(1); 'document': CA 1963, s 2(1): 'financial year': CA 1963, s 2(1); 'IFRS individual accounts': CA 1963, s 2(1); 'parent undertaking'; EC(CGA) 1992, reg 3(1); 'prescribed': CA 1963, s 2(1); 'the Principal Act': C(A)A 1986, s 1(1).

Notes

Documents to be annexed; position pre C(A)A 1986: Most companies are required to annex copies of their annual accounts, including the auditor's report and directors' report to the annual return. Originally this obligation only applied to public companies.[1] However, over the last three decades, the disclosure requirements for companies have been expanded upon by the following legislation.

1 CA 1963, s 128. This section provided an exemption, however, to certain classes of religious and general charitable companies. See sub-ss (4) and (5).

C(A)A 1986: Section 7 requires the annexing of accounts to the annual returns of all private and public limited companies[1] other than:

(a) companies not trading for the acquisition of gain by its members[2];

(b) religious charitable companies limited by guarantee[3];

(c) any charitable company limited by guarantee in respect of which the Commissioners of Charitable Donations and Bequests for Ireland have made an order exempting it from the obligation to annex its accounts to the annual return[4];

(d) certified trustee savings banks[5];

(i) authorised life and non-life insurance companies.[6]

1 C(A)A 1986, ss 7–12 and 16–18. The reason why C(A)A 1986 does not apply to unlimited companies is because 'company' is defined in s 1(1) of that Act as meaning only limited companies.

2 C(A)A 1986, s 2(1)(a).

3 C(A)A 1986, s 2(1)(b).

4 C(A)A 1986, s 2(1)(c).

5 C(A)A 1986, s 7(1)(a)(ii).

6 C(A)A 1986, s 2(3).

Documents to be annexed; position post C(A)A 1986: The documents to be annexed to the annual return of a limited company governed by C(A)A 1986 comprise the balance sheet, profit and loss account, directors' report and auditors' report.[1] Section 7(1)(A) grants an exemption from annexing to the annual return (and therefore an exemption from filing with the Companies Registration Office) the individual profit and loss account or income statement of a parent undertaking where that undertaking prepares group accounts in accordance with section 150 of CA 1963. The notes to the individual balance sheet of the company, however, must show the company's profit or loss for the financial year and both the notes to the company's individual accounts and group accounts must disclose that advantage has been taken of this exemption.

Certain modifications apply for 'small and medium sized' private companies and for private companies which meet the audit exemption requirements set out in C(A)(No 2)A 1999, Part III.

1 C(A)A 1986, s 7.

2 These companies are defined by reference to balance sheet value, annual turnover and the size of the workforce. See C(A)A 1986, s 8.

Period covered by annexed documents: All documents which have to be annexed to the annual return must cover the period from the date of incorporation (in the case of a first annual return) or (in any other case) the period since that covered by the relevant documents annexed to the last annual return and must in any event be made up to a date not more than nine months before the date to which the annual return itself is made up.[1]

1 C(A)A 1986, s 7(1A).

Dispensation for small companies: In the case of a small company, it will suffice to annex to the return an abridged balance sheet[1] together with a special report from the auditors containing:

(a) their ordinary auditors' report under CA 1990, s 193; and

(b) a report certifying that they are satisfied that the company is entitled to the small company exemptions and that the accounts have been properly prepared.[2]

1 C(A)A 1986, ss 10 and 12.

2 C(A)A 1986, s 18(3)–(5).

Dispensation for medium-sized companies: The dispensations for a medium-sized company are slightly less extensive in that the return for such a company must at least have annexed to it an abridged balance sheet, an abridged profit and loss account and a copy of the directors' report,[1] as well as a special report from the auditors containing:

(a) their ordinary auditors' report under CA 1990, s 193; and

(b) a report certifying that they are satisfied that the company is entitled to the medium company exemptions and that the accounts have been properly prepared.[2]

1 C(A)A 1986, ss 11 and 12.

2 C(A)A 1986, s 18(3)-(5).

Dispensation for audit exempt companies: The requirement to have the accounts audited may, however, be dispensed with in the case of a private limited company which meets the requirements set out in C(A)(No 2)A 1990, Part III. Such a company accordingly does not have to have an auditors' report annexed to its annual return.[1]

1 C(A)(No 2)A 1999, Sch 1. The exemption in respect of the auditors' reporting obligations in such circumstances also extends to the matters specified in C(A)A 1986, s 18(3), (4) and (5).

Dispensation for subsidiary undertakings: A subsidiary of a parent undertaking[1] established under the laws of a member state of the European Union may, in certain circumstances, be exempted from annexing its accounts to its annual return[2]. This lack of disclosure may, however, be compensated for by the fact that any company which owns a subsidiary or which holds a 'qualifying capital interest'[3] of 20 per cent or more in an undertaking (defined as 'an undertaking of substantial interest'), may be required to include certain financial and other information regarding the subsidiary or undertaking of substantial interest, in the documentation annexed to its own annual return, either by way of note to the accounts or by way of separate statement signed by a director and the secretary.[4]

1 For the definition of 'parent undertaking' and 'subsidiary undertaking' see EC(CGA)R 1992, regs 3(1) and 4.

2 See C(A)A 1986, s 17 and the notes thereto.

3 For the definition of 'qualifying capital interest' see EC(CGA)R 1992, reg 35(2).

4 C(A)A 1986.

EC(A)R 1992: Unlimited public companies have always been obliged to annex a copy balance sheet and auditors' report to the annual return.[1] The disclosure requirements have, however, been expanded by EC(A)R 1993, the provisions of which apply to the following:

1. Unlimited companies and partnerships where all the members thereof who do not have a limit on their liability are:

   (a) companies limited by shares or by guarantee, or

   (b) bodies not governed by the law of the State but equivalent to those in (a) or

   (c) any combination of the types of bodies referred to in subparas (a) and (b).

2. Unlimited companies where all the members thereof who do not have a limit on their liability are:

   (a) (i) unlimited companies or partnerships of the type referred to in para (1) that are governed by the laws of a member state, or

   (ii) bodies governed by the laws of a member state that are of a legal form comparable to those referred to in para (i) or

   (b) any combination of the types of bodies referred to in subpara (a) and subparas (a) and (b) of para 1[2].

The provisions of C(A)A 1986 and EC(CGA)R 1992 regarding the format and content of annual accounts and the annexing of accounts to the annual return, as well as the exemptions for small and medium-sized companies, apply to these unlimited companies as they apply to limited companies.[3]

1 CA 1963, s 128.
2 EC(A)R 1993, reg 6.
3 EC(A)R 1993, regs 7, 9 and 13.

EC(BD)R 1993: A foreign limited company which establishes a branch in the State is obliged each year to file with the registrar copy annual accounts as drawn up, audited and where so required, disclosed in accordance with the law of the State of incorporation.[1] Moreover, if the foreign company is incorporated under the laws of another EU member state, the accounts must comply with the provisions of the Fourth, Seventh and Eighth Company Law Directives.[2] In the case of a non-EU company, if there is no requirement under the laws of the State of incorporation to draw up annual accounts, the accounts as delivered to the Irish Registrar of Companies must comply with the provisions of the Fourth and Seventh Company Law Directives[3] and indeed, even where the law of the non-EU state requires the drawing up of accounts, the foreign company rather than delivering to the Irish registrar copies of the accounts as drawn up under the law of the state of incorporation, may instead deliver accounts which are drawn up in accordance with the provisions of the aforementioned Directives.[4] The accounts must be filed within 11 months of the end of the company's financial year or at the time of publication under the law of the state of incorporation, whichever is earlier,[5] although, if there is no obligation to draw up accounts under the law of the state of incorporation, filing must simply take place within 11 months of the financial year end.[6] The accounts as filed shall include a directors' report and an auditor's report and, if applicable, consolidated group accounts[7] together with translations into English or Irish, if they are not already in either one of these languages.[8]

1 EC(BD)R 1993, reg 11(1).
2 Council Directives 78/660/EEC, 83/349/EEC and 84/253/EEC. See EC(BD)R 1993, reg 11(1).
3 EC(BD)R 1993, reg 11(2).
4 EC(BD)R 1993, reg 11(3).
5 EC(BD)R 1993, reg 11(4).
6 EC(BD)R 1993, reg 11(5).
7 EC(BD)R 1993, reg 12.
8 EC(BD)R 1993, reg 13.

EC(IUA)R 1996: Insurance companies had heretofore been largely exempted from the disclosure requirements of the Companies Acts.[1] The format and content of the accounts of insurance companies and reinsurance companies are now governed by EC(IUA)R 1996. Where the companies form part of a group, the parent undertaking must deliver a return to the registrar each year with copies of the group accounts, directors' report and auditors' report annexed thereto.[2]

1 CA 1963, s 128(4)(b); C(A)A 1986, s 2(3).
2 EC(IUA)R 1986, reg 17.

Unit of currency for annual return: The documents annexed to the annual return may have the money amount referred to therein expressed in European currency units ('ECU'), in addition to their expression in the currency in which the documents concerned were drawn up.[1] However, where the company avails of this option, the exchange rate to be used is that prevailing on the date of the balance sheet.[2] Moreover, the exchange rate must also be disclosed in a note to the accounts.[3]

1 EC(A)R 1993, reg 5(1).
2 EC(A)R 1993, reg 5(2).
3 EC(A)R 1993, reg 5(2).

UK legislation

See CA 1985, s 242.

---

8 Small companies and medium-sized companies

(1) Subject to section 9 of this Act—

(a) a private company[, subject to subsection (1A)][a] shall qualify to be treated as a small company for the purposes of this Act in respect of any financial year of the company if, in respect of that year and the financial year of the company immediately preceding that year, the company satisfies at least two of the conditions specified in subsection (2) of this section, and

(b) a private company[, subject to subsection (1B)][b] shall qualify to be treated as a medium-sized company for the purposes of this Act in respect of any financial year of the company if, in respect of that year and the financial year of the company immediately preceding that year, the company satisfies at least two of the conditions specified in subsection (3) of this section.

[(1A) Subsection (1)(a) shall not apply to a private company whose securities are admitted to trading on a regulated market.

(1B) Subsection (1)(b) shall not apply to a private company whose securities are admitted to trading on a regulated market.][c]

(2) The qualifying conditions for a company to be treated as a small company in respect of any financial year are as follows:

(a) its balance sheet total for that year shall not exceed [€1,904,607],[d]

(b) the amount of its turnover for that year shall not exceed [€3,809,214],[e] and

(c) the average number of persons employed by the company in that year shall not exceed 50.

(3) The qualifying conditions for a company to be treated as a medium-sized company in respect of any financial year are as follows:

(a) its balance sheet total for that year shall not exceed [€7,618,428],[f]

(b) the amount of its turnover for that year shall not exceed [€15,236,857],[g] and

(c) the average number of persons employed by the company in that year shall not exceed 250.

(4) In this section 'balance sheet total', in relation to any financial year of a company, means—

(a) where Format 1 of the balance sheet formats set out in the Schedule to this Act is adopted by the company, the aggregate of the amounts shown in the company's balance sheet for that year under headings corresponding to items A and B in that Format, [...][h]

(b) where Format 2 of those formats is adopted by the company, the aggregate of the amounts so shown [under 'Assets', and][i]

[(c) where the company prepares IFRS individual accounts, the aggregate of the amounts shown as assets in the balance sheet.][j]

(5) In this section 'amount of turnover', in relation to any financial year of a company, means the amounts of the turnover shown in the profit and loss account of the company under headings corresponding to the relevant items in any of the Formats of profit and loss accounts set out in the Schedule to this Act.

(6) In the application of this section to any period which is a financial year of a company, but is not in fact a year, the amounts specified in subsections (2)(b) and (3)(b) of this section shall be proportionately adjusted.

(7) A private company which is incorporated on or after the commencement of this section shall qualify to be treated as a small company or, as the case may be, as a medium-sized company, in respect of its first financial year if it satisfies at least two of the relevant qualifying conditions specified in subsection (2) or (3), as may be appropriate, of this section in respect of that financial year.

(8) A private company which was incorporated before such commencement shall qualify to be treated under subsection (1) of this section as a small company or, as the case may be, as a medium-sized company, in respect of the first financial year of the company in which accounts of the company are required to be prepared in accordance with section 3 of this Act if it satisfies at least two of the relevant qualifying conditions specified in subsection (2) or (3), as may be appropriate, of this section in respect of either that first financial year or the financial year immediately preceding that year.

(9) For the purposes of subsection (2)(c) and (3)(c) of this section, the average number of persons employed by a company shall be determined by applying the method of calculation prescribed by paragraph 42(4) of the Schedule to this Act for determining the number required by subparagraph (1) of that paragraph to be stated in a note to the accounts of a company.

(10) In determining for the purposes of subsection (8) of this section whether a company satisfies at least two of the relevant conditions specified in subsection (2) or (3), as may be appropriate, of this section in respect of a financial year in a case where the accounts of the company in respect of that year prepared under the Companies Acts, 1963 to 1983 are not prepared in accordance with this Act, subsection (4) of this section shall be construed as referring to the aggregate of any amounts included in the balance sheet of the company for that year which correspond to the amounts mentioned in paragraph (a) or (b), as may be appropriate, of that subsection.

(11) The Minister may by order substitute different amounts, totals and numbers, respectively, for the amounts, totals and number specified for the time being in subsections (2) and (3) of this section and those subsections shall have effect in accordance with any order for the time being in force under this section.

(12) An order under this section shall be laid before each House of the Oireachtas as soon as may be after it is made and, if a resolution annulling the order is passed by either such House within the next twenty-one days on which that House has sat after the order is laid before it, the order shall be annulled accordingly but without prejudice to the validity of anything previously done thereunder.

[(13) In subsections (1A) and (1B), 'regulated market' has the meaning assigned to it by Article 4(1), point (14) of Directive 2004/39/EC (OJ L 145, 30.4.2004, p 1).][k]

Amendments

a Words inserted by European Communities (Directive 2006/46/EC) Regulations 2009, reg 4(a).

b Words inserted by European Communities (Directive 2006/46/EC) Regulations 2009, reg 4(b).

c Subsections (1A) and (1B) inserted by European Communities (Directive 2006/46/EC) Regulations 2009, reg 4(c).

d '£1,500,000' substituted for '£1,250,000' by EC(A)R 1992, reg 4 and converted to €1,904,607 by Council Regulation (EC) No 1103/97, No 974/98, No 2866/98 and the European and Monetary Act 1998, s 6.

e '£3,000,000' substituted for '£2,500,000' by EC(A)R 1992, reg 4 and converted to €3,809,214 by Council Regulation (EC) No 1103/97, No 974/98, No 2866/98 and the European and Monetary Act 1998, s 6.

f '£6,000,000' substituted for '£5,000,000' by EC(A)R 1992, reg 4 and converted to €7,618,428 by Council Regulation (EC) No 1103/97, No 974/98, No 2866/98 and the European and Monetary Act 1998, s 6.

g '£12,000,000' substituted for '£10,000,000' by EC(A)R 1992, reg 4 and converted to €15,236,957 by Council Regulation (EC) No 1103/97, No 974/98, No 2866/98 and the European and Monetary Act 1998, s 6.

h Amended by EC(IFRSMA)R 2005, reg 5(e)(i).

i Amended by EC(IFRSMA)R 2005, reg 5(e)(ii).

j Amended by EC(IFRSMA)R 2005, reg 5(e)(iii).

k Subsection (13) inserted by European Communities (Directive 2006/46/EC) Regulations 2009, reg 4(d).

Definitions

'accounts': CA 1963, s 2(1); 'company': C(A)A 1986, s 1(1), CA 1963, s 2(1); 'financial year': CA 1963, s 2(1); 'Minister': CA 1963, s 2(1); 'private company': C(A)A 1986, s 1(1), CA 1963, s 2(1), s 33(1).

Notes

Small and medium-sized companies: Qualification as a small company or as a medium-sized company is dependent upon compliance for at least two successive financial years with the conditions set out in C(A)A 1986, s 8(2) or (3), as the case may be.[1] In the case of a newly incorporated company, however, qualification for such status will be judged by reference to the company's results for the first financial year alone.[2]

Having qualified as a small or medium-sized company, such status will be lost if the company fails to comply with at least two of the conditions set out in C(A)A 1986, s 8(2) or (3), as the case may be, for two consecutive financial years.[3]

1 C(A)A 1986, s 8(1).

2 C(A)A 1986, s 8(7).
3 C(A)A 1986, s 9.

Benefit of small or medium-sized company status: The benefit of qualifying as a small or medium-sized company is that the company will be allowed to prepare abridged accounts[1] and will be given certain exemptions as to the documents which they must annex to their annual returns.[2]

1 See C(A)A 1986, s 10, 11 and 12 for the abridgments permissible in respect of such companies.
2 See C(A)A 1986, ss 7 and 17, and the notes thereto.

UK legislation

See CA 1985, ss 246, 246A, 247, and 247A, Sch 8.

9 Reclassification of small companies and medium-sized companies

(1) Where a private company has qualified to be treated as a small company under subsection (1) of section 8 of this Act, it shall continue to be so qualified, unless, in the latest financial year of the company and the financial year of the company immediately preceding that year, it does not satisfy at least two of the conditions set out in subsection (2) of the said section 8 and if, during each of those two years, it does not satisfy at least two of those conditions, it shall, in respect of its latest financial year, cease to be so qualified.

(2) Where a private company has qualified to be treated as a medium-sized company under subsection (1) of section 8 of this Act, it shall continue to be so qualified unless, in the latest financial year of the company and the financial year of the company immediately preceding that year, it does not satisfy at least two of the conditions set out in subsection (3) of the said section 8 for treatment as a medium-sized company and, if during each of those two years, it does not satisfy at least two of those conditions, it shall, in respect of its latest financial year, cease to be so qualified.

(3) A company which qualified to be treated as a medium-sized company under subsection (2) of this section in the financial year immediately preceding its latest financial year shall qualify to be treated as a small company for the purposes of this Act in respect of its latest financial year if, in those two years, it satisfies at least two of the conditions set out in section 8(2) of this Act.

(4) Where a private company ceases to be qualified as specified in subsection (1) or (2) of this section, section 8 of this Act shall apply in respect of the company as if it had never previously qualified to be treated as a small company or a medium-sized company under that section.

Definitions

'company': C(A)A 1986, s 1(1), CA 1963, s 2(1); 'financial year': CA 1963, s 2(1); 'private company': C(A)A 1986, s 1(1), CA 1963, s 2(1) and s 33(1).

Notes

See the notes to C(A)A 1986, s 8.

UK legislation

See CA 1985, s 247.

10 Exemption for small companies from certain provision of sections 3 and 7

[(1) A company treated as a small company pursuant to section 8(1) of this Act may, in lieu of complying with the requirements in that behalf in section 7 of this Act, annex to the annual return in relation to the company referred to in the said section 7 a copy of the abridged balance sheet of the company drawn up in accordance with subsection (2) of this section in respect of the period to which the return refers and, notwithstanding section 7 of this Act, the company shall not be required to annex to the return a copy of the profit and loss account of the company or the report of the directors accompanying the balance sheet of the company.

(2) (a) Where the directors of a company prepare IFRS individual accounts and the company is to be treated as a small company pursuant to section (8)(1) of this Act, the abridged balance sheet referred to in subsection (1) of this section shall comprise the full balance sheet included in the IFRS individual accounts.

(b) Where the directors of a company prepare Companies Act individual accounts and the company is to be treated as a small company pursuant to section (8)(1) of this Act, the directors may extract from the balance sheet of the company prepared in accordance with section 3(1) of this Act an abridged balance sheet showing only those items preceded by letters or roman numerals in Formats 1 and 2 of the balance sheet formats set out in the Schedule to this Act but the total amounts falling due within one year and after one year shall be shown separately for item B. II in Format 1 and items B. II under 'Assets' and C under 'Liabilities' in Format 2 of the balance sheet formats in relation to debtors and creditors.][a]

Amendments

a C(A)A 1986, s 10 substituted by EC(IFRSMA)R 2005, reg 5(f).

Definitions

'annual return': CA 1963, s 2 (1); 'companies act individual accounts'; CA 1963, s 2(1) 'company': C(A)A 1986, s 1(1); CA 1963, s 2(1); 'director': CA 1963, s 2(1); 'IFRS individual accounts': CA 1963, s 2(1).

Notes

Abridged balance sheet: A small company is permitted to prepare an abridged balance sheet to lay before the members at the AGM.[1] In addition, it is afforded certain exemptions as to the information to be given in the notes to the accounts.[2] The exemptions are similar regardless of whether the company prepares companies acts individual accounts of IFRS individual accounts.

1 As to the obligation to lay the balance sheet and profit and loss account before the AGM, see CA 1963, s 148. Notably, under s 8 it is not permissible to prepare an abridged profit and loss account. However, that document, although presented to the members in general meeting, need not be annexed to the annual return, thereby preserving some degree of confidentiality for the company.

2 C(A)A 1986, s 12.

Documents to be annexed to annual return: A small company will not be obliged to annex its profit and loss account or income statement or directors' report to the annual return. Instead, only the abridged balance sheet and a special auditors' report need be so annexed[1].

[1] C(A)A 1986, ss 10(2) and 18.

UK legislation

See CA 1985, Sch 8.

---

11 Exemption for medium-sized companies from certain provisions of sections 3 and 7

[(1) A company treated as a medium-sized company pursuant to section 8(1) of this Act may, in lieu of complying with the requirements in that behalf in section 7 of this Act, annex to the annual return in relation to the company referred to in the said section 7 a copy of the abridged balance sheet of the company drawn up in accordance with subsection (2) of this section and an abridged profit and loss account or abridged income statement of the company drawn up in accordance with subsection (3) of this section in respect of the period to which the return refers.

(2) (a) Where the directors of a company prepare IFRS individual accounts and the company is to be treated as a medium-sized company pursuant to section 8(1) of this Act, the abridged balance sheet referred to in subsection (1) of this section shall comprise the full balance sheet included in the IFRS individual accounts.

(b) (i) Subject to subparagraph (ii) of this paragraph, where the directors of a company prepare Companies Act individual accounts and the company is to be treated as a medium-sized company pursuant to section 8(1) of this Act, the directors may extract from the balance sheet of the company prepared in accordance with section 3(1) of this Act an abridged balance sheet showing only those items preceded by letters or roman numerals in Formats 1 and 2 of the balance sheet formats set out in the Schedule to this Act but the amounts in respect of the following items shall be disclosed separately either in the balance sheet of the company or in the notes to the accounts of the company-

(I) in Format 1 of the balance sheet formats, items A. I. 3, A. II. 1, 2, 3 and 4, A. III. 1, 2, 3, 4 and 7, B. II. 2, 3 and 6, B. III. 1 and 2, C. 1, 2, 6, 7, 8 and 9 and F. 1, 2, 6, 7, 8 and 9, and

(II) in Format 2 of the balance sheet formats, under 'Assets', items A. I. 3, A. II. 1, 2, 3 and 4, A. III. 1, 2, 3, 4 and 7, B. II. 2, 3 and 6 and B. III. 1 and 2 and under 'Liabilities', items C. 1, 2, 6, 7, 8 and 9.

(ii) The balance sheet of the company shall show separately—

(I) the amounts falling due within one year and after one year in respect of items B. II in the said Format 1 in total and in respect, individually, of items B. II. 2 and 3 in the said Format 1, and

(II) the amounts falling due in a similar manner in respect of the total of the amounts in respect of the following items, that is to say, in the said Format 2 under 'Assets' item B. II and under 'Liabilities' item C and in respect, individually, of the following items, that is to say, in the said Format 2 under 'Assets' items B. II. 2 and 3 and under 'Liabilities' items C. 1, 2, 6 and 7.

(3) (a) Where the directors of a company prepare IFRS individual accounts and the company is to be treated as a medium-sized company pursuant to section 8(1) of this Act, the directors may extract from the income statement, prepared in accordance with international financial reporting standards and section 149A (inserted by the European Communities (International Financial Reporting Standards and Miscellaneous Amendments) Regulations 2005) of the Principal Act, an abridged income statement which combines as one item the company's revenue and certain expenses for the period.

(b) The expenses that may be combined as one item with the revenue of the company are—

(i) where expenses are classified by function, only those expenses classified as 'cost of sales' may be so combined, and

(ii) where expenses are classified by nature, only changes in finished goods and work-in-progress and raw materials and consumables used may be so combined.

(c) Where the directors of a company prepare Companies Act individual accounts and the company is to be treated as a medium-sized company pursuant to section 8(1) of this Act, the directors may extract from the profit and loss account of the company prepared in accordance with section 3(1) of this Act an abridged profit and loss account which combines as one item under the heading 'gross profit or loss' the following items:

(i) items 1, 2, 3 and 6 in Format 1 of the profit and loss account formats set out in the Schedule to this Act;

(ii) items 1 to 5 in Format 2 of the said profit and loss account formats;

(iii) items A.1, B.1 and B.2 in Format 3 of the said profit and loss account formats;

(iv) items A.1, A.2 and B.1 to B.4 in Format 4 of the said profit and loss account formats.][a]

Amendments

a C(A)A 1986, s 11 was replaced by EC(IFRSMA)R 2005, reg 5(f).

Definitions

'accounts': CA 1963, s 2(1); 'annual return': CA 1963, s 2 (1); 'companies act individual accounts': CA 1963, s 2(1); 'company': C(A)A 1986, s 1(1); CA 1963, s 2(1); 'director': CA 1963, s 2(1); 'IFRS individual accounts': CA 1963, s 2(1).

Notes

Abridged balance sheet and profit and loss account: A medium-sized company is permitted to prepare both an abridged balance sheet and an abridged profit and loss account or income statement to lay before the members at the AGM.[1] The abridgements to the balance sheet are not as extensive as those permitted for small companies.[2] In addition to the foregoing, the medium-sized company is afforded certain exemptions as to the information to be given in the notes to the accounts.[3]

[1] As to the obligation to lay the balance sheet and profit and loss account before the AGM, see CA 1963, s 148.

[2] See C(A)A 1986, s 10 for the abridgments permissible for small companies.

[3] C(A)A 1986, s 12.

Documents to be annexed to annual return: Unlike small companies, there is no exemption for medium-sized companies in respect of the obligation to annex a copy of the directors' report to the annual return. Instead, the documents to be annexed to the return are the abridged balance sheet,[1] the abridged profit and loss account or income statement,[2] and a special auditors' report.[3]

[1] C(A)A 1986, s 11(2).

[2] C(A)A 1986, s 11(3).

[3] C(A)A 1986, s 18.

UK legislation

See CA 1985, Sch 8.

12 Exemptions in relation to notes to accounts for small companies and medium-sized companies

[(1) (a) Where the directors of a company prepare IFRS individual accounts and the company is to be treated as a small company in accordance with section 8(1) of this Act, the following notes shall be extracted from those accounts and included with the abridged balance sheet annexed to the annual return pursuant to section 10(1) of this Act:

(i) accounting policies applied in the preparation of the accounts;

(ii) information in relation to the maturity of non-current liabilities and any security given in respect of those liabilities;

(iii) disclosures made in accordance with section 149A(2)(a) to (k) of the Principal Act.

(b) Where the directors of a company prepare Companies Act individual accounts and the company is to be treated as a small company in accordance with section 8(1) of this Act, any notes resulting from the provisions of the Schedule to this Act (other than paragraphs 24, 26, 27, 31B, 31C, 33, 34 and 44) may be excluded from the abridged balance sheet annexed to the annual return pursuant to section 11(1) of this Act;

(2) (a) Where the directors of a company prepare IFRS individual accounts and the company is to be treated as a medium-sized company in accordance with section 8(1) of this Act, all notes forming part of those accounts shall be included with the abridged balance sheet and abridged income statement annexed to the annual return pursuant to section 11(1) of this Act, except that items that are combined on the face of the income statement need not be separately identified in the notes.

(b) Where the directors of a company prepare Companies Act individual accounts and the company is to be treated as a medium-sized company in accordance with section 8(1) of this Act, all notes forming part of those accounts shall be included with the abridged balance sheet and abridged profit and loss account annexed to the annual return pursuant to section 11(1) of this Act, except that the information required by paragraph 41 of the Schedule to this Act need not be given.][a]

Amendments

a C(A)A, 1986, s 12 replaced by EC(IFRSMA)R 2005, reg 5(f).

Definitions

'accounts': CA 1963, s 2(1); 'annual return': CA 1963, s 2 (1); 'company': C(A)A 1986, s 1(1), CA 1963, s 2(1).

UK legislation

See CA 1985, Sch 8.

13 Information to be included in directors' report

[(1)][a] The report of the directors of a company under section 158 of the Principal Act shall contain, in addition to the information specified in that section, the following information:

[(a) a fair review of the development and performance of the company's business and of its position and, in relation to its subsidiary undertakings, if any, of the development and performance of their business and of their position, during the financial year ending with the relevant balance sheet date together with a description of the principal risks and uncertainties that they face, which review—

(i) shall be a balanced and comprehensive analysis of the development and performance of the company's business and of its position and, in relation to its subsidiary undertakings, if any, of the development and performance of their business and of their position, consistent with the size and complexity of the business, and

(ii) to the extent necessary for an understanding of the company's development, performance or position, and that of its subsidiary undertakings, if any, shall include an analysis of financial, and, where appropriate, non-financial key performance indicators relevant to the particular business, including information relevant to environmental and employee matters,

and, where appropriate, the report shall include additional explanations of amounts included in the annual accounts;][b]

(b) particulars of any important events affecting the company or any of its subsidiaries, if any, which have occurred since the end of that year;

[(c) an indication of likely future developments in the business of the company and of its subsidiaries, if any;

(d) an indication of the activities, if any, of the company and its subsidiaries, if any, in the field of research and development;

(e) an indication of the existence of branches (within the meaning of Council Directive 89/666/EEC[1]) of the company outside the State and the country in which each such branch is located, and] [c] [(f) in relation to the use by the company and its subsidiaries, if any, of financial instruments and where material for the assessment of the assets, liabilities, financial position and profit or loss of the company and, as the case may be, the group—

(i) the financial risk management objectives and policies of the company and the group, including the policy for hedging each major type of forecasted transaction for which hedge accounting is used, and

(ii) the exposure of the company and the group to price risk, credit risk, liquidity risk and cash flow risk.][d]

[(2) Where a company is to be treated as a small or medium sized company pursuant to section 8(1) of this Act, the directors shall be exempt from the requirement to include in the report of the directors the information required by subsection (1)(a)(ii) and (f) of this section.][e]

Amendments

a C(A)A 1986, s 13 renumbered by EC(IFRSMA)R 2005, reg 5(g)(ii).

b C(A) A 1986 s 13 (1)(a) substituted by EC(IFRSMA)R 2005, reg 5(g)(i).

c C(A)A 1986, s 13(1)(c), (d) and (e) inserted by EC(FVA)R 2004, reg 3.

d C(A)A 1986, s 13(1) (f) inserted by EC(FVA)R 2004, reg 5.

e C(A)A 1986, s 13(2) inserted by EC(IFRSMA)R 2005, reg 5(g)(ii).

Definitions

'company': C(A)A 1986, s 1(1); CA 1963, s 2(1); 'director': CA 1963, s 2(1); 'financial year': CA 1963, s 2(1); 'subsidiary': CA 1963, s 2(1) and s 155; 'the Principal Act': C(A)A 1986, s 1(1).

Notes

Contents of directors' report: See CA 1963, s 158 and the notes thereto, as well as C(A)A 1986, s 14, and CA 1990, s 205D and s 205E as inserted by C(AA)A 2003.

Amendments to s 13 of C(A)A 1986 arise from the Modernisation Directive. The aim of the amendment is to promote greater consistency in the quality of the required 'reviews' by directors and to encourage company directors to move away from the use of 'boiler plate' language'.

Subsection 1(f) was inserted by EC(FVA)R 2004. These Regulations implemented Directive 2001/65/EC ('the Fair Value Directive') which amended Directives 78/660/EEC, 83/349/EEC and 86/635/EEC as regards the valuation rules for the annual and consolidated accounts of certain types of companies as well as banks and other financial institutions. The Fair Value Directive permits certain financial instruments to be recorded at fair value (essentially current market value), in line with international accounting practice.

Subsidiary: Note that for the purposes of this Act the definition of 'subsidiary' contained in CA 1963, s 155 is replaced by the definition of 'subsidiary undertaking' contained in EC(CGA)R 1992.

UK legislation

See CA 1985, s 234, 234ZZB, Sch 7 (amended by CA 1989, s 8, Sch 5).

---

14 Information to be included in directors' report regarding acquisition by company of own shares

Where, in any financial year of a company, shares in the company—

(a) are acquired by the company by forfeiture or surrender in lieu of forfeiture, or

(b) are acquired by the company in pursuance of section 41 of the Act of 1983, or

(c) are required by another person in the circumstances specified in paragraph (c) or (d) of section 43(1) of that Act, or

(d) are made subject to a lien or other charge that is taken (whether expressly or otherwise) by the company and is permitted by paragraph (a), (c) or (d) of section 44(2) of that Act,

the directors' report with respect to that financial year of the company shall state—

(i) the number and nominal value of any shares of the company acquired as aforesaid by the company, the number and nominal value of any shares of the company acquired as aforesaid by another person, and the number and nominal value of any shares charged as aforesaid, respectively,

(ii) the maximum number and nominal value of any shares which, having been acquired as aforesaid (whether or not during that year) by the company or by another person or charged as aforesaid (whether or not during that year) are held at any time by the company or that other person during that year,

(iii) the number and nominal value of any shares acquired as aforesaid (whether or not during that year) by the company or another person or charged as aforesaid (whether or not during that year) which are disposed of by the company or that other person or cancelled by the company during that year,

(iv) where the number and nominal value of the shares of any particular description are stated in pursuance of any of the preceding paragraphs, the percentage of the called-up share capital of the company which shares of that description represent.

(v) in the case of a charge as aforesaid, the amount of the charge in each case, and

(vi) in the case of an [acquisition or disposal][a] as aforesaid for money or money's worth, the amount or value of the consideration in each case.

[(vii) the reasons for the acquisition, lien or charge, as the case may be].[b]

Amendments

a Words substituted by CA 1990, s 233.

b C(A)A 1986, s 14(vii) inserted by CA 1990, s 233.

Definitions

'the Act of 1983': C(A)A 1986, s 1(1); 'company': C(A)A 1986, s 1(1); CA 1963, s 2(1); 'director': CA 1963, s 2(1); 'financial year': CA 1963, s 2(1); 'share': CA 1963, s 2(1).

Notes

Own-share acquisitions: CA 1963, s 158 and C(A)A 1986, s 13 deal in general terms with the prescribed contents of a directors' report. This section is more specific and requires the directors to include in their report details of:

(a) acquisitions of its own shares made by the company during the course of the financial year;

(b) any charges or liens which it has taken on its own shares.[1]

In so far as acquisitions of shares are concerned, these may have occurred in various ways, all of which are identified in C(A)A 1983, s 41. They include the following—

(a) a transaction such as a gift or testamentary disposition which does not involve the giving of valuable consideration by the company;[2]

(b) a redemption or purchase in pursuance of CA 1990, Part XI;[3]

(c) a purchase of the shares pursuant to an order of the court under CA 1963, s 10 in circumstances where a dissenting minority has objected to an alteration in the objects clause;[4]

(d) a purchase of shares pursuant to an order of the court under CA 1963, s 205 on grounds of oppression or disregard of interests;[5]

(e) a purchase of shares pursuant to an order of the court under C(A)A 1983, s 15 in circumstances where a dissenting minority has objected to the re-registration of a plc as a private company;[6]

(f) a forfeiture or surrender in lieu of forfeiture.[7]

1 In relation to liens and charges on shares, see C(A)A 1983, s 44 and Table A, regs 11–14, as well as the notes thereto.

2 C(A)A 1983, s 41(2). Included under this heading are transactions whereby shares in a plc are acquired on its behalf by a nominee or other third party, and whether with or without valuable consideration flowing from the company itself.

3 C(A)A 1983, s 41(4)(a).

4 C(A)A 1983, s 41(4)(c).

5 C(A)A 1983, s 41(4)(c).

6 C(A)A 1983, s 41(4)(c).

7 C(A)A 1983, s 41(4)(d).

Acquisition of shares of subsidiary: If the company is a plc and in any financial year an acquisition of its shares is made by a subsidiary, details of that acquisition must also be included in the directors' report[1].

1 EC(PLCS)R 1997, reg 6.

UK legislation

See CA 1985, s 234, 234 ZZB, Sch 7.

---

15 Consideration by auditors of consistency of directors' report with company's accounts

It shall be the duty of the auditors of a company, in preparing the report in relation to the company required by [section 193 of the Companies Act 1990],[a] to consider whether the information given in the report of the directors of the company relating to the financial year concerned is consistent with the accounts prepared by the company for that year and they shall state in the report whether, in their opinion, such information is consistent with those accounts.

Amendments

a C(A)A 1986, s 15 amended by EC(IFRSMA)R 2005, reg 5(h).

Definitions

'accounts': CA 1963, s 2(1); 'company': C(A)A 1986, s 1(1); CA 1963, s 2(1); 'director': CA 1963, s 2(1); 'financial year': CA 1963, s 2(1); 'the Principal Act': C(A)A 1986, s 1(1).

Notes

Contents of auditors' report: The reference to CA 1963, s 163, should instead be to CA 1990, s 193 which is now the primary provision governing both the obligation to prepare an auditors' report and the contents thereof. In addition, however, see CA 1963, s 191(8), EC(CGA)R 1992, reg 38, EC(CAI)R 1992, reg 13 and EC(IUA)R 1996, reg 16.

Dispensation for audit exempt companies: The requirement to have the accounts audited may be dispensed with in the case of a private limited company which meets the requirements set out in C(A)(No 2)A 1990, Part III. In such circumstances an auditors' report will not be required and accordingly the provisions of this section shall not apply.[1]

1 C(A)(No 2)A 1999, Sch 1.

UK legislation

See CA 1985, s 253(3).

16 Publication of information regarding subsidiary and associated companies

(1) Subject to the provisions of this section, where at the end of the financial year of a company, the company—

(a) has a subsidiary, or

[(b) holds a qualifying capital interest equal to 20 per cent or more of all such interests in an undertaking that is not its subsidiary undertaking (in this section referred to as 'an undertaking of substantial interest');][a]

[(c) for the purposes of subparagraph (b), interests held by persons acting in their own name but on behalf of the company shall be deemed to be held by the company,

(d) in this section, 'qualifying capital interest' shall have the meaning assigned to it in Regulation 35(2) of the European Communities (Companies: Group Accounts) Regulations, 1992,

(e) paragraph (4) of Regulation 35 of the European Communities (Companies: Group Accounts) Regulations, 1992, shall apply in determining the percentage of qualifying capital interests held by a company in an undertaking with share capital, for the purposes of this section];[b]

a note shall be included in the accounts of the company for that year annexed to the annual return distinguishing between the subsidiaries and the [undertaking of substantial interest][c] and giving the following information in relation to them—

(i) the name and registered office of each subsidiary or [undertaking of substantial interest][c] and the nature of the business carried on by it,

(ii) the identity of each class of shares held by the company in each subsidiary or [undertaking of substantial interest][c] and the proportion of the nominal value of the allotted shares in the subsidiary or [undertaking of substantial interest][c] of each such class represented by the shares of that class held by the company,

(iii) the aggregate amount of the capital and reserves of each subsidiary or [undertaking of substantial interest][c] as at the end of the financial year of the subsidiary or [undertaking of substantial interest][c] ending with or last before the end of the financial year of the company to which the accounts relate, and

(iv) the profit or loss of the subsidiary or [undertaking of substantial interest][c] for the financial year thereof mentioned in paragraph (iii) of this subsection.

[(2) Paragraphs (iii) and (iv) of subsection (l) of this section shall not apply—

[(a) in respect of a subsidiary undertaking of a company, if the company prepares Companies Acts group accounts in accordance with section 150 of the Principal Act, and either—

(i) the subsidiary undertaking is dealt with in the group accounts prepared by the company or where the company avails of the exemption in Regulation 8, 9 or 9A of the Group Accounts Regulations, the group accounts referred to in Regulation 8(3)(a) or 9A(2)(a) of those Regulations, or

(ii) the qualifying capital interest of the company in the subsidiary undertaking is included in or in a note to the company's accounts by way of the equity method of valuation,

or

(aa) in respect of a subsidiary undertaking of a company, where the company prepares IFRS group accounts in accordance with section 150 of the Principal Act, and either—

(i) the subsidiary undertaking is dealt with in the IFRS group accounts prepared by the company, or

(ii) where the company is exempt from preparing IFRS group accounts, the subsidiary undertaking is dealt with in IFRS group accounts prepared by a parent undertaking of the company,] [d]

(b) in respect of an undertaking of substantial interest of a company if the qualifying capital interest in the undertaking of substantial interest is included in or in a note to the company's accounts by way of the equity method of valuation,

or

(c) if—

(i) the subsidiary undertaking or the undertaking of substantial interest is not required to publish its accounts, and

(ii) the qualifying capital interest held in the subsidiary undertaking or the undertaking of substantial interest do not amount to at least 50 per cent of all such interests,

(d) if the information specified in subsection (l) of this section is not material.];[e]

(3) (a) Subject to paragraph (b) of this subsection, the information specified in subsection (1) of this section may, in lieu of being stated in a note to the accounts of the company concerned for any particular financial year of the company, be given in a statement in writing signed by a director, and the secretary, of the company and annexed to the first annual return made by the company next after its accounts for that year are laid before the annual general meeting of the company if, in the opinion of the directors of the company, compliance with subsection (1) of this section would require a note to the accounts of the company of excessive length.

(b) Paragraph (a) of this subsection shall not apply in relation to information concerning a subsidiary or associated company of a company (referred to subsequently in this paragraph as the 'second-mentioned company') if the financial state of the subsidiary or associated company, as disclosed by its accounts, has, in the opinion of the directors of the second-mentioned company, a substantial effect on the profit or loss, or the amount of the assets, of the second-mentioned company and its subsidiaries.

(c) A copy of a statement annexed, pursuant to paragraph (a) of this subsection, to the annual return referred to in that subsection made by a company shall be certified both by a director, and the secretary, of the company to be a true copy of such statement.

(4) [...][f]

(5) Subsection (4) and (5) of section 158 of the Principal Act shall not apply to a company to which this section applies.

(6) [...][f]

Amendments

a C(A)A 1986, s 16(1)(b) substituted by EC(CGA)R 1992, reg 44(a).

b C(A)A 1986, s 16(1)(c)–(e) inserted by EC(CGA)R 1992, reg 44(b).

c 'undertaking of substantial interest' substituted for 'associated company' by EC(CGA)R 1992, reg 44(c).

d C(A)A 1986, s 16(2)(a)–(aa) substituted by EC(IFRSMA)R 2005, reg 5(i).

e C(A)A 1986, s 16(2) substituted by EC(CGA)R 1992, reg 44(d).

f C(A)A 1986, s 16(4) and (6) deleted by EC(CGA)R 1992, reg 44(e).

Definitions

'accounts': CA 1963, s 2(1); 'annual return': CA 1963, s 2 (1); 'companies act group accounts': CA 1963, s 2(1)'company': C(A)A 1986, s 1(1); CA 1963, s 2(1); 'director': CA 1963, s 2(1); 'financial year': CA 1963, s 2(1); 'group accounts'; CA 1963, s 2(1) and s 150(1), EC(CGA)R 1992, reg 3(1), reg 13; 'IFRS group accounts': CA 1963, s 2(1); 'share': CA 1963, s 2(1); 'subsidiary': CA 1963, s 2(1) and s 155 as modified by C(A)A 1986, s 1(3); 'the Principal Act': C(A)A 1986, s 1(1); 'undertaking': EC(CGA)R 1992, reg 3(1); 'subsidiary undertaking': EC(CGA)R 1992, reg 4.

Notes

Information about subsidiaries and undertakings of substantial interest: If the company is one governed by section 150 of CA 1963, preparing companies act group accounts or IFRS group accounts and it has a subsidiary or holds a 'qualifying capital interest'[1] of 20 per cent of more in another company, (referred to as an 'undertaking of substantial interest') it must include certain information about that subsidiary or undertaking of substantial interest in the notes to its accounts,[2] unless:

(a) it already prepares group accounts in accordance with EC(CGA)R 1992 which contain equivalent information;[3]

(b) the subsidiary or undertaking of substantial interest is not required to publish its accounts 4, and the 'qualifying capital interest' of the company in that entity is less than 50 per cent;[5] or

(c) the information is not material.[6]

The information includes the name and address of the entity in question, the amount and proportion of its share capital which is held by the company, as well as details of its capital and reserves and profit or loss for the last financial year.[7]

However, if the directors are of the opinion that to include such information in the notes to the accounts would result in the notes being of excessive length, then unless the financial state of the subsidiary or undertaking of substantial interest has a substantial effect on the financial position of the company itself, the directors may instead set out the information in a separate statement which must be signed by one director and the secretary and which must be annexed to the annual return.[8]

1 For the definition of 'qualifying capital interest' see EC(CGA)R 1992, reg 35(2).
2 C(A)A 1986, s 16(1).
3 C(A)A 1986, s 16(2)(a) and (b).
4 As to the types of company which do not need to publish their accounts, see CA 1963, ss 125–128 and C(A)A 1986, s 7 as well as the notes thereto. Such companies include private limited companies not trading for gain by their members and unlimited companies in which there is at least one individual (ie non-corporate) member.
5 C(A)A 1986, s 16(2)(c).
6 C(A)A 1986, s 16(2)(d).
7 C(A)A 1986, s 16(1).
8 C(A)A 1986, s 16(3). By including the information about subsidiaries or undertakings of substantial interest in a statement annexed to the annual return, rather than in the notes to the accounts, the directors would seem to be able to avoid presenting such information to the members at the annual general meeting.

Qualifying capital interest: The phrase 'qualifying capital interest' is defined by EC(CGA)R 1992, reg 35(2) as meaning:

(a) in relation to an undertaking with share capital, an interest in the allotted share capital of that undertaking;[1]

(b) in relation to an undertaking with capital but no shares[2], an interest conferring rights to participate in the capital of that undertaking;

(c) in relation to an undertaking with no capital[3], an interest conferring rights to participate in the profits or a liability to contribute to the losses of that undertaking or to giving rise to an obligation to contribute to the debts and expenses in the event of a winding up;

(d) an interest which is convertible into a qualifying capital interest (eg debenture stock which is convertible into shares); or

(e) an option to acquire any such qualifying capital interest.

Disapplication of CA 1963, s 158(4) and (5): CA 1963, s 158(4) and (5) required information regarding subsidiaries to be included in the directors' report. These provisions no longer apply, however, to companies governed by C(A)A 1986 because such information must in any event be included by way of note in the accounts under C(A)A 1986, s 16.

1 EC(CGA)R 1992, reg 35(4) provides that the percentage of qualifying capital interest held in an undertaking with share capital shall be the percentage that the nominal value of the shares held represents of the nominal value of the allotted share capital of that undertaking,

2 For example, a company limited by guarantee.

3 For example, an unlimited company with no share capital.

[16A

(1) A note shall be included in the accounts of the company annexed to the annual return stating the name, the head or registered office and the legal form of each of the undertakings of which the company is a member having unlimited liability, unless such information is of negligible importance only for the purpose of section 3(1)(b).

(2) Subsection 3 of section 16, shall apply to the information referred to in subsection (1) of this section.][a]

Amendments

a C(A)A 1986, s 16A inserted by EC(A)R 1993, reg 23.

Notes

Unlimited liability undertakings: Each company must include a note in the accounts which it annexes to the annual return stating the name, head office or registered office and the legal form of every undertaking of which it is a member unless such information is of negligible importance in the context of ensuring that the accounts give a true and fair view of the affairs of the company.[1] For the purpose of this section it should be noted that the term 'undertaking' includes not only companies, but also partnerships and other unincorporated bodies.[2]

However, if the directors are of the opinion that to include such information in the notes to the accounts would result in the notes being of excessive length, then unless the financial state of the subsidiary or undertaking of substantial interest has a substantial effect on the financial position of the company itself, the directors may instead set out the information in a separate statement which must be signed by one director and the secretary and which must be annexed to the annual return.[3]

1 C(A)A 1986, s 16A(1).

2 EC(CGA)R 1992, reg 3(1).

3 C(A)A, s 16(3) as applied by s 16A(2). By including the information about subsidiaries or undertakings of substantial interest in a statement annexed to the annual return, rather than in the notes to the accounts, the directors would seem to be able to avoid presenting such information to the members at the annual general meeting.

17 Exemption for subsidiaries from section 7

[(1) Where a private company is a subsidiary undertaking of a parent undertaking established under the laws of a member state, the company shall, as respects any particular financial year of the company, stand exempted from the provisions of section 7 (other than subsection (1)(b)) of this Act if, but only if, the following conditions are fulfilled:

(a) every person who is a shareholder of the company on the date of the holding of the next annual general meeting of the company after the end of that financial year [or on the next annual return date of the company after the end of that financial year, which ever is the earlier],[b] shall declare his consent to the exemption,

[(b) there is in force in respect of the whole of that financial year an irrevocable guarantee by the parent undertaking of—

(i) the liabilities of the company referred to in section 5(c) of this Act in respect of that financial year, in a case where the company prepares Companies Act individual accounts, or

(ii) all liabilities in respect of that financial year, in a case where the company prepares IFRS individual accounts,

and the company has notified in writing every person referred to in paragraph (a) of this subsection of the guarantee,],[c]

(c) the annual accounts of the company for that financial year are consolidated in the group accounts prepared by the parent undertaking and the exemption of the company under this section is disclosed in a note to the group accounts,

(d) a notice stating that the company has availed of the exemption under this section in respect of that financial year and a copy of the guarantee and notification referred to in paragraph (b) of this subsection, together with a declaration by the company in writing that paragraph (a) of this subsection has been complied with in relation to the exemption, is annexed to the annual return for the financial year made by the company under the Principal Act to the registrar of companies,

[(e) the group accounts of the parent undertaking are drawn up in accordance with the requirements of the Seventh Council Directive 83/349/EEC of 13 June 1983 or in accordance with international financial reporting standards, and][d]

(f) the group accounts of the parent undertaking are annexed to the annual return aforesaid and are audited in accordance with Article 37 of the said Seventh Council Directive.

(2) The Minister may make such orders (if any) as may be necessary for the purpose of enabling this section to have full effect.][a]

Amendments

a C(A)A 1986, s 17, substituted by EC(CGA)R 1992, reg 45.

b Words inserted by CLEA 2001, s 65.

c C(A)A 1986, s 17(1)(b) substituted by EC(IFRSMA)R 2005, reg 5(j)(i).

d C(A)A 1986, s 17(1)(e) substituted by EC(IFRSMA)R 2005, reg 5(j)(ii).

Definitions

'accounts': CA 1963, s 2(1); 'annual return': CA 1963, s 2 (1); 'companies act group accounts': CA 1963, s 2(1); 'company'; C(A)A 1986, s 1(1); CA 1963, s 2(1); 'financial year': CA 1963, s 2(1); 'group accounts'; CA 1963, s 2(1), s 150(1), EC(CGA)R 1992, reg 3(1), reg 13; 'IFRS group accounts': CA 1963, s 2(1); 'member state': EC(CGA)R 1992, reg 3(1); 'Minister': CA 1963, s 2(1), EC(CGA)R 1992, reg 3(1); 'parent undertaking': EC(CGA)R 1992, reg 3(1); 'private company': C(A)A 1986, s 1(1); CA 1963, s 2(1), s 33(1); 'the registrar of companies': CA 1963, s 2 (1); 'share': CA 1963, s 2(1); 'subsidiary': CA 1963, s 2(1), s 155; 'the Principal Act': C(A)A 1986, s 1(1); 'subsidiary': CA 1963, s 2(1) and s 155 as modified by C(A)A 1986, s 1(3); 'undertaking': EC(CGA)R 1992, reg 3(1); 'subsidiary undertaking': EC(CGA)R 1992, reg 4.

Notes

Exemption from disclosure for subsidiaries: C(A)A 1986, s 17 exempts a subsidiary undertaking from the obligation to annex its accounts to the annual return provided:

1. every shareholder of the parent undertaking so consents;
2. there is in force an irrevocable undertaking from the parent undertaking in respect of the subsidiary's liabilities for the particular financial year, and the members of the parent undertaking have been given written notice of this guarantee;
3. the subsidiaries' accounts are consolidated into group accounts of the parent undertaking which must comply as to format and contents with the requirements of the Seventh Companies Directive as implemented by EC(CGA)R 1992;
4. details of the exemption from disclosure must be contained in a note to the group accounts;
5. the annual return of the subsidiary undertaking must have the following documents annexed to it:
   (a) a notice stating that the exemption from disclosure has been availed of;
   (b) a copy of the guarantee from the parent undertaking together with a copy of the notification of the guarantee to the members;
   (c) a declaration that all the members consent to the company availing of the exemption from disclosure;
   (d) a copy of the group accounts.

Consent of members: With regard to the requirement for the consent of the members to non-disclosure of the accounts of the subsidiary, Ussher,[1] queries the purpose of same, since the members will, in any event, be entitled to copies of the accounts under CA 1963, s 159. The members will not suffer from the non-disclosure and therefore their consent seems superfluous. In reality, if there is any group which could potentially benefit from disclosure of the accounts, it would be the subsidiary's creditors, yet they have no say at all in relation to whether or not the accounts should be disclosed.

1 *Company Law in Ireland* (Sweet & Maxwell, 1986), p 362.

Guarantee from parent undertaking: Ussher,[1] also questions why the members of the subsidiary need to be informed of the guarantee, particularly since the guarantee is designed primarily for the protection of the creditors. Furthermore, if the subsidiary is wholly owned by the parent undertaking, then the parent undertaking effectively ends up informing itself of its own guarantee.

A further question arises in relation to the enforceability of the guarantee. Is it enforceable only by the subsidiary undertaking or can it be enforced by individual creditors of the subsidiary? To date there has been no judicial guidance on the matter.

1 *Company Law in Ireland* (Sweet & Maxwell, 1986), at p 362.

18 Provisions in relation to documents delivered to registrar of companies

[(1) Abridged accounts (within the meaning of section 19 of this Act) annexed to the annual return required by the Principal Act to be made by the company to the registrar of companies shall be signed as required by section 156 of the Principal Act and the abridged balance sheet so annexed shall contain the statement required by subsection (2) of this section in a position immediately above the signatures appended pursuant to the said section 156 and shall be accompanied by a copy of the report of the auditors of the company in relation to the abridged accounts of the company under subsection (3) of this section.][a]

(2) [An abridged balance sheet][b] of a company prepared pursuant to any of the provisions of sections 10 to 12 of this Act and annexed to the said annual return shall contain a statement by the directors that—

(a) they have relied on specified exemptions contained in the said sections 10 to 12, and

(b) they have done so on the ground that the company is entitled to the benefit of those exemptions as a small company or (as the case may be) as a medium-sized company.

[(3) Abridged accounts delivered to the registrar of companies need not be accompanied by the report of the auditors under section 193 of the Companies Act 1990 on the company's individual accounts, but shall be accompanied by a special report of the auditors containing—

(a) a copy of the report made by the auditors of the company under subsection (4) of this section on those abridged accounts, and

(b) a copy of the report of the auditors under section 193 of the Companies Act 1990 on the company's individual accounts.][c]

(4) Where the directors of a company propose to annex to the annual return [abridged accounts][d] for any accounting period prepared pursuant to any of the provisions of sections 10 to 12 of this Act and the auditors of the company are satisfied that the directors of the company are entitled, for that purpose, to rely on exemptions specified in sections 10 to 12 of this Act and that the [abridged accounts][d] have been properly prepared pursuant to those provisions, it shall be the duty of the auditors of the company to provide the directors of the company with a report in writing stating that, in the opinion of the auditors of the company, the directors of the company are entitled to annex those [abridged accounts][d] to the annual return and that the [abridged accounts][d] so annexed are properly prepared as aforesaid.

(5) A copy of the report of the auditors of a company under subsection (3) of this section furnished to the registrar of companies pursuant to this section shall be certified both by a director, and the secretary, of the company to be a true copy of such report.

Amendments

a C(A)A 1986, s 18(1) substituted by EC(IFRSMA)R 2005, reg 5(k)(i).

b C(A)A 1986, s 18(2) amended by EC(IFRSMA)R 2005, reg 5(k)(ii).

c C(A)A 1986, s 18(3) substituted by EC(IFRSMA)R 2005, reg 5(k)(iii).

d C(A)A 1986, s 18(4) amended by EC(IFRSMA)R 2005, reg 5(k)(iv).

Definitions

'accounts': CA 1963, s 2(1); 'annual return': CA 1963, s 2(1); 'company': C(A)A 1986, s 1(1); CA 1963, s 2(1); 'director': CA 1963, s 2(1); 'document': CA 1963, s 2(1): 'the registrar of companies': CA 1963, s 2(1); 'the Principal Act': C(A)A 1986, s 1(1).

Notes

See the notes to C(A)A 1986, s 7.

UK legislation

See CA 1985, Sch 8.

19 Publication of full or abbreviated accounts

[(1) Where a company publishes its full individual accounts, it shall also publish with those accounts any report of the auditors made in accordance with section 193 of the Companies Act 1990.

(1A) Where a company publishes its abridged accounts, it shall also publish with those accounts any report in relation to those accounts specified in subsection (3) of section 18 of this Act and, if the auditors of the company have refused to provide the directors of the company with a report under subsection (4) of that section, an indication of the refusal.][a]

(2) Where a company publishes abbreviated accounts relating to any financial year, it shall also publish a statement indicating—

- (a) that the accounts are not the accounts copies of which are required by this Act to be annexed to the annual return,
- (b) whether the copies of the accounts so required to be so annexed have in fact been so annexed,
- (c) whether the auditors of the company have made a report under section 163 of the Principal Act in respect of the accounts of the company which relate to any financial year with which the abbreviated accounts purport to deal,
- [(d) whether any matters referred to in the auditors' report were qualified or unqualified, or whether the auditors' report included a reference to any matters to which the auditors drew attention by way of emphasis without qualifying the report.][b]

(3) Where a company published abbreviated accounts, it shall not publish with those accounts any such report of the auditors as is mentioned in subsection (2)(c) of this section.

[(3A) Where a company publishes its full individual accounts for a financial year it shall indicate if group accounts have been prepared and, if so, where those group accounts can be obtained.][c]

(4) In this section—

'abbreviated accounts', in relation to a company, means any balance sheet or profit and loss account, or summary or abstract of a balance sheet or profit and loss account, relating to a financial year of the company which is published by the company otherwise than as part of the full accounts of the company for that financial year and, in relation to a holding company, includes an account in any form purporting to be a balance sheet or profit and loss account, or a summary or abstract of a balance sheet or profit and loss account, of the group consisting of the holding company and its subsidiaries;

['abridged accounts', in relation to a company, means accounts of the company prepared in accordance with sections 10 to 12 of this Act and, except in the case of a company which is exempt by virtue of section 10 of this Act from annexing a copy of such a report to the annual return, the report of the directors of the company specified in section 158(1) of the Principal Act;][d]

['full individual accounts', in relation to a company, means the accounts of the company prepared in accordance with section 148 of the Principal Act;][e]

'publish', in relation to a document, includes issue, circulate or otherwise make it available for public inspection in a manner calculated to invite the public generally, or any class of members of the public, to read the document, and cognate words shall be construed accordingly.

Amendments

a C(A)A 1986, s 19(1) and (1A) substituted by EC(IFRSMA)R 2005, reg 5(l)(i).

b C(A)A 1986, s 19(2)(d) substituted by EC(IFRSMA)R 2005, reg 5(l)(ii).

c C(A)A 1986, s 19(3A) inserted by EC(CGA)R 1992, reg 46.

d Definition of 'abridged accounts' in C(A)A 1986, s 19(4) inserted by EC(IFRSMA)R 2005, reg 5(l)(iii)(I).

e Definition of 'full individual accounts' in C(A)A 1986, s 19(4) amended by EC(IFRSMA)R 2005, reg 5(l)(iii)(II).

Definitions

'accounts': CA 1963, s 2(1); 'annual return': CA 1963, s 2 (1); 'company'; C(A)A 1986, s 1(1); CA 1963, s 2(1); 'director': CA 1963, s 2(1); 'document': CA 1963, s 2(1): 'financial year': CA 1963, s 2(1); 'group accounts'; CA 1963, s 2(1) and s 150(1), EC(CGA)R 1992, reg 3(1), reg 13; 'holding company': CA 1963, s 2(1), s 155; 'the Principal Act': C(A)A 1986, s 1(1); 'subsidiary': CA 1963, s 2(1), s 155.

Notes

Publication of accounts: The reference to 'publication' in C(A)A 1986, s 19 is to situations such as the publishing of the full or abbreviated accounts of the company in a national newspaper, rather than to the filing of accounts with the annual return.

Similar obligations are imposed with regard to the publication of group accounts.[1]

1 EC(CGA)R 1992, reg 40.

Dispensation for audit exempt companies: The requirement to have the accounts audited may be dispensed with in the case of a private limited company which meets the requirements set out in C(A)(No 2)A 1990, Part III. In such circumstances the provisions of this section shall not apply insofar as they relate to an auditors' report.[1]

1 C(A)(No 2)A 1999, Sch 1.

UK legislation

See CA 1985, s 240.

---

20 Amendment of Act of 1983

[...][a]

Amendments

a C(A)A 1986, s 20 inserted CA 1963, s 45A.

Definitions

'Act of 1983': C(A)A 1986, s 1(1).

21 Power to apply Act to unregistered companies

[...][a]

Amendments

a C(A)A 1986, s 21 repealed by CA 1990, s 6(2)(c).

22 Offences and penalties

(1) (a) If a company fails to comply with a provision of section 5, 6, 7, 10, 11, 16, 18 or 19 of this Act, the company and every officer of the company who is in default [shall be guilty of an offence][a].

(b) [Summary proceedings][b] for an offence under this subsection, in relation to sections 7, 10, 11, 16 or 18 of this Act, may be brought and prosecuted by the registrar of companies.

(2) If any person, being a director of a company, fails to take all reasonable steps to secure compliance with the requirements of section 3 or section 4 (other than subsections (3) and (13)) of this Act or to comply with the provisions of subsections (3) or (13) of section 4 or section 13 or 14 of this Act, he shall – [in respect of each such failure be guilty of an offence, but—][c]

(a) in any proceedings against a person in respect of an offence under this subsection, it shall be a defence to prove that he had reasonable grounds to believe and did believe that a competent and reliable person was charged with he duty of ensuring that the provisions of the said section 3 or section 4 (other than subsections (3) and (13)), as may be appropriate, were complied with and that the latter person was in a position to discharge that duty, and

(b) a person shall not be liable to be sentenced to imprisonment for such an offence unless, in the opinion of the court, the offence was committed wilfully.

(3) If any person in any return, report, certificate, balance sheet or other documents required by or for the purposes of any of the provisions of this Act wilfully makes a statement false in any material particular, knowing it to be false, he shall be liable –

(a) on conviction on indictment, to imprisonment for a term not exceeding three years or a fine not exceeding [€3,174.35][d] or both, or

(b) on summary conviction, to imprisonment for a term not exceeding six months or a fine not exceeding [€1,904.61][e] or both.

(4) Section 385 of the Principal Act shall have effect as if for the sum mentioned in subsection (1) there were substituted [€1,269.74][f].

(5) In this section 'director' and 'officer' includes any person in accordance with whose directions or instructions the directors of the company are accustomed to act.

Amendments

a C(A)A 1986, s 22(1)(a) amended by IFCMPA 2005, s 66.

b C(A)A 1986, s 22(1)(b) amended by IFCMPA 2005, s 66.

c C(A)A 1986, s 22(2) amended by IFCMPA 2005, s 66.

d '£2,500' converted to €3,174.35 by Council Regulation (EC) No 1103/97, No 974/98, No 2866/98 and the European and Monetary Act 1998, s 6.

e '£1,000' increased to £1,500 by CA 1990, s 240(7) as inserted by CLEA 2001, s 104(c), and converted to €1,904.61 by Council Regulations (EC) No 1103/97, No 974/98 and No 2866/98 and the Economic and Monetary Union Act 1998, s 6.

f '£1,000' converted to €1,269.74 by Council Regulation (EC) No 1103/97, No 974/98, No 2866/98 and the European and Monetary Act 1998, s 6.

Definitions

'company': C(A)A 1986, s 1(1), CA 1963, s 2(1); 'the court': CA 1963, s 2(1); 'director': CA 1963, s 2(1); 'document': CA 1963, s 2(1): 'officer': CA 1963, s 2(1); 'officer in default': CA 1963, s 385; ' the registrar of companies': CA 1963, s 2 (1); 'the Principal Act': C(A)A 1986, s 1(1).

Notes

Meaning of 'officer' and 'director': The definition of 'officer' and 'director' for the purposes of C(A)A 1986, s 22 is deemed to include any person in accordance with whose directions or instructions the directors of the company are accustomed to act. This definition is similar to that of 'shadow director' contained in CA 1990, s 27. Notably, however, unlike in CA 1990, s 27, there is no saving provision for circumstances where the directors are accustomed to so act by reason only that they do so on advice given by the person in a professional capacity. It is at least arguable therefore that if the directors are accustomed to act on the professional advice of an accountant regarding, for example, the filing of the annual return, that accountant could be regarded as being a 'director' or 'officer' for the purposes of s 22.

UK legislation

See CA 1985, s 730 (amended by CA 1989, s 145, Sch 9 para 17), Sch 24.

---

23 Restriction of section 222 of Principal Act

Section 222 of the Principal Act shall not apply to proceedings before the Employment Appeals Tribunal.

Definitions

'the Principal Act': C(A)A 1986, s 1(1).

Notes

Proceedings before Employment Appeals Tribunal: The effect of C(A)A 1986, s 23 is to dispense with the requirement for the leave of the High Court before commencing or continuing proceedings before the Employment Appeals Tribunal against a company which is being compulsorily wound up.

---

24 Power of Minister to modify Act in certain respects

(1) The Minister may by order alter or add to the provisions of this Act, in so far as it relates to the balance sheet and profit and loss account of a company and the notes to and documents to be attached to such a balance sheet or profit and loss account, either generally or in relation to a specified class or classes of company.

(2) An order under this section shall be laid before each House of the Oireachtas as soon as may be after it is made and, if a resolution annulling the order is passed by either such House within the next 21 days on which that House has sat after the order is laid before it, the order shall be annulled accordingly but without prejudice to the validity of anything previously done thereunder.

Definitions

'company': C(A)A 1986, s 1(1); CA 1963, s 2(1); 'document': CA 1963, s 2(1): 'Minister': CA 1963, s 2(1).

Notes

Power to make amendments: The only amendments made to date by Order of the Minister are those contained in EC(CGA)R 1992.

UK legislation

See CA 1985, s 257.

---

25 Short title, collective citation, construction and commencement

(1) This Act may be cited as the Companies (Amendment) Act, 1986.

(2) The Companies Acts, 1963 to 1982, the Companies (Amendment) Act, 1983, section 6 of the Designated Investment Funds Act, 1985, and this Act may be cited together as the Companies Acts, 1963 to 1986.

(3) The Companies Acts, 1963 to 1982, the Companies (Amendment) Act, 1983, section 6 of the Designated Investment Funds Act, 1985, and this Act shall be construed together as one.

(4) Save as is otherwise specifically provided thereby, this Act shall come into operation on such day or days as, by order or orders made by the Minister under this section, may be fixed therefor either generally or with reference to any particular purpose or provision and different days may be so fixed for different purposes and different provisions.

(5) (a) Subject to paragraph (b) of this subsection, each provision of this Act shall apply as respects the accounts of a company, and the report by the directors of a company specified in section 158 of the Principal Act, for each financial year of the company beginning or ending, as may be specified by the Minister by order, after such date after the commencement of the provision as may be specified by the Minister by order.

(b) Paragraph (a) of this subsection does not apply in relation to subsection (7) or (8) of section 8 of this Act.

Definitions

'accounts': CA 1963, s 2(1); 'company': C(A)A 1986, s 1(1); CA 1963, s 2(1); 'director': CA 1963, s 2(1); 'financial year': CA 1963, s 2(1); 'Minister': CA 1963, s 2(1); 'the Principal Act': C(A)A 1986, s 1(1).

Notes

All sections of C(A)A 1986, other than s 7(1)(a)(ii) (which was inserted by EC(CGA)R 1992), came into operation on 1 August 1986.

SCHEDULE

FORM AND CONTENTS OF ACCOUNTS

PART I

THE REQUIRED FORMATS FOR ACCOUNTS

Preliminary

1. References in this Part of this Schedule to the items listed in any of the formats set out in this Part are references to those items read together with any notes following the formats which apply to any of those items.

2. A number in brackets following any item in, or any heading to, any of the formats set out in this Part is a reference to the note of that number in the notes following the formats.

3. In the notes following the formats—

(a) the heading of each note gives the required heading or subheading for the item to which it applies and a reference to any letters and numbers assigned to that item in the formats set out in this Part; and

(b) references to a numbered format are references to the balance sheet format or (as the case may require) to the profit and loss account format of that number set out in this Part.

BALANCE SHEET FORMATS

Format 1

A. Fixed Assets

I. Intangible assets

1. Development costs
2. Concessions, patents, licences, trade marks and similar rights and assets (1)
3. Goodwill (2)
4. Payments on account

II. Tangible assets

1. Land and buildings
2. Plant and machinery

3. Fixtures, fittings, tools and equipment
4. Payments on account and assets in course of construction

III. Financial assets

1. Shares in [group undertakings][a]
2. Loans to [group undertakings][a]
3. [Participating interests][b]
4. Loans to [undertakings in which a participating interest is held][c]
5. Other investments other than loans
6. Other loans
7. [...][d]

B. Current Assets

I. Stocks

1. Raw materials and consumables
2. Work in progress
3. Finished goods and goods for resale
4. Payments on account

II. Debtors (4)

1. Trade debtors
2. Amounts owed by [group undertakings][a]
3. Amounts owed by [undertakings in which a participating interest is held][c]
4. Other debtors
5. Called up share capital not paid
6. Prepayments and accrued income

III. Investments

1. Shares in [group undertakings][a]
2. [...][d]
3. Other investments

IV. Cash at bank and in hand

C. Creditors: amounts falling due within one year

1. Debenture loans (5)
2. Bank loans and overdrafts
3. Payments received on account (6)
4. Trade creditors
5. Bills of exchange payable
6. Amounts owed to [group undertakings][a]
7. Amounts owed to [undertakings in which a participating interest is held][c]
8. Other creditors including tax and social welfare (7)
9. Accruals and deferred income (8)

D. Net current assets (liabilities)

E. Total assets less current liabilities

F. Creditors: Amounts falling due after more than one year

1. Debenture loans (5)
2. Bank loans and overdrafts
3. Payments received on account (6)
4. Trade creditors
5. Bills of exchange payable
6. Amounts owed to [group undertakings][a]
7. Amounts owed to [undertakings in which a participating interest is held][c]
8. Other creditors including tax and social welfare (7)
9. Accruals and deferred income (8)

G. [Provisions for liabilities][e]

1. Pensions and similar obligations
2. Taxation, including deferred taxation
3. Other provisions

H. Capital and reserves

I. Called up share capital (9)

II. Share premium account

III. Revaluation reserve

IV. Other reserves

1. The capital redemption reserve fund
2. [...][d]
3. Reserves provided for by the articles of association
4. Other reserves

V. Profit and loss account

[Minority Interest][f]

Amendments

a 'group undertakings' substituted for 'group companies' by EC(CGA)R 1992, Sch, Pt I para 1.

b 'participating interests' substituted for 'shares in related companies' by EC(CGA)R 1992, Sch, Pt 1 para 2.

c 'undertakings in which a participating interest is held' substituted for 'related companies' by EC(CGA)R 1992, Sch, Pt 1 para 3.

d Item deleted by CA 1990, s 233(2)(a).

e 'Provisions for liabilities' substituted for 'Provisions for liabilities and charges' by EC(IFRSMA)R 2005, reg 5(m)(i)(I).

f Inserted by EC(CGA)R 1992, Sch, Pt 1 para 8(1)(a).

Cross reference

In the case of group accounts 'Participating interests' is substituted with 'Interests in associated undertakings' and 'Other participating interests'. See EC(CGA)R 1992, Sch, Pt 1 para 10.

BALANCE SHEET FORMATS

Format 2

ASSETS

A. Fixed Assets

I. Intangible assets

1. Development costs
2. Concessions, patents, licences, trade marks and similar rights and assets (1)
3. Goodwill (2)
4. Payments on account

II. Tangible assets

1. Land and buildings
2. Plant and machinery
3. Fixtures, fittings, tools and equipment
4. Payments on account and assets in course of construction

III. Financial assets

1. Shares in [group undertakings][a]
2. Loans to [group undertakings][a]
3. [Partcipating interests][b]
4. Loans to [undertakings in which a participating interest is held][c]
5. Other investments other than loans
6. Other loans
7. [...][d]

B. Current Assets

I. Stocks

1. Raw materials and consumables
2. Work in progress
3. Finished goods and goods for resale
4. Payments on account

II. Debtors (4)

1. Trade debtors
2. Amounts owed by [group undertakings][a]
3. Amounts owed by [undertakings in which a participating interest is held][c]
4. Other debtors
5. Called up share capital not paid
6. Prepayments and accrued income

III. Investments

1. Shares in [group undertakings][a]
2. [...][d]
3. Other investments

IV. Cash at bank and in hand

LIABILITIES

A. Capital and reserves

I. Called up share capital (9)

II. Share premium account

III. Revaluation reserve

IV. Other reserves

1. The capital redemption reserve fund

[...][d]

3. Reserves provided for by the articles of association

4. Other reserves

V. Profit and loss account

[Minority Interest][e]

B. [Provisions for liabilities][f]

1. Pensions and similar obligations
2. Taxation, including deferred taxation
3. Other provisions

C. Creditors (10)

1. Debenture loans (5)
2. Bank loans and overdrafts
3. Payments received on account (6)
4. Trade creditors
5. Bills of exchange payable
6. Amounts owed to [group undertakings][a]
7. Amounts owed to [undertakings in which a participating interest is held][c]
8. Other creditors including tax and social welfare (7)
9. Accruals and deferred income (8)

Amendments

a 'group undertakings' substituted for 'group companies' by EC(CGA)R 1992, Sch, Pt 1 para 1.

b 'participating interests' substituted for 'shares in related companies' by EC(CGA)R 1992, Sch, Pt 1 para 2.

c 'undertakings in which a participating interest is held' substituted for 'related companies' by EC(CGA)R 1992, Sch, Pt 1 para 3.

d Item deleted by CA 1990, s 233(2)(b).

e Inserted by EC(CGA)R 1992, Sch, Pt 1 para 8(b).

f 'Provisions for liabilities' substituted for 'Provisions for liabilities and charges' by EC(IFRSMA)R 2005, reg 5(m)(i)(II).

Cross reference

In the case of group accounts 'Participating interests' is substituted with 'Interests in associated undertakings' and 'Other participating interests'. See EC(CGA)R 1992, Sch, Pt 1 para 10.

NOTES ON THE BALANCE SHEET FORMATS

(1) *Concessions, patents, licences, trade marks and similar rights and assets*

(Formats 1 and 2, items A. I. 2)

Amounts in respect of assets shall only be included in a company's balance sheet under this item if either—

(a) the assets were acquired for valuable consideration and are not required to be shown under goodwill, or

(b) the assets in question were created by the company itself.

(2) *Goodwill*

(Formats 1 and 2, items A. I. 3)

Amounts representing goodwill shall only be included to the extent that the goodwill was acquired for valuable consideration.

(3) [...][a]

(4) *Debtors*

(Formats 1 and 2, items B. II. 1 to 6)

The amount failing due after more than one year shall be shown separately for each item included under debtors.

(5) *Debenture loans*

(Format 1, item C.1 and F.1 and Format 2, item C.1)

The amount of any convertible loans shall be shown separately.

(6) *Payments received on account*

(Format 1, items C.3 and F.3 and Format 2, item C.3)

Payments received on account of orders shall be shown for each of these items insofar as they are not shown as deductions from stocks.

(7) *Other creditors including tax and social welfare*

(Format 1, items C.8 and F.8 and Format 2, item C.8)

The amount for creditors in respect of taxation and social welfare shall be shown separately from the amount for other creditors and in respect of taxation there shall be stated separately the amounts included in respect of income tax payable on emoluments to which Chapter IV of Part V of the Income Tax Act, 1967, applies, any other income tax, corporation tax, capital gains tax, value-added tax and any other tax.

(8) *Accruals and deferred income*

(Format 1, items C. 9 and F. 9 and Format 2, item C. 9)

The amount in respect of Government grants, that is to say, grants made by or on behalf of the Government, included in this item shall be shown separately in a note to the accounts unless it is shown separately in the balance sheet.

(9) *Called up share capital*

(Format 1, item H. I and Format 2, item A. I)

The amount of allotted share capital and the amount of called up share capital which has been paid up shall be shown separately.

(10) *Creditors*

(Format 2, items C.1 to 9)

Amounts falling due within one year and after one year shall be shown separately for each of these items and their aggregate shall be shown separately for all of these items.

Amendments

a Deleted by CA 1990, s 233(c).

PROFIT AND LOSS ACCOUNT FORMATS

Format 1 (14)

1. Turnover
2. Cost of Sales (11)
3. Gross Profit or Loss
4. Distribution costs (11)
5. Administrative expenses (11)
6. Other operating income
7. Income from shares in [group undertakings][a]
8. Income from [participating interests][b]
9. Income from other financial assets (12)
10. Other interest receivable and similar income (12)
11. Amounts written off financial assets and investments held as current assets
12. Interest payable and similar charges (13)
13. Tax on profit or loss on ordinary activities
14. Profit or loss on ordinary activities after taxation
    [Minority Interest][c]
15. Extraordinary income
16. Extraordinary charges
17. Extraordinary profit or loss
18. Tax on extraordinary profit or loss
    [Minority Interest][d]
19. Other taxes not shown under the above items
20. Profit or loss for the financial year

Amendments

a 'group undertakings' substituted for 'group companies' by EC(CGA)R 1992, Sch, Pt I para 1.

b 'participating interests' substituted for 'shares in related companies' by EC(CGA)R 1992, Sch, Pt 1 para 2.

c Inserted by EC(CGA)R 1992, Sch, Pt 1 para 9(1)(a).

d Inserted by EC(CGA)R 1992, Sch, Pt 1 para 9(3)(a).

Cross reference

In the case of group accounts 'Participating interests' is substituted with 'Interests in associated undertakings' and 'Other participating interests'. See EC(CGA)R 1992, Sch, Pt 1 para 10.

PROFIT AND LOSS ACCOUNT FORMATS

Format 2

1. Turnover
2. Variation in stocks of finished goods and in work in progress
3. Own work capitalised
4. Other operating income
5. (a) Raw materials and consumables
   (b) Other external charges
6. Staff costs:
   (a) Wages and salaries
   (b) Social welfare costs
   (c) Other pension costs
7. (a) Depreciation and other amounts written off tangible and intangible fixed assets
   (b) Exceptional amounts written off current assets
8. Other operating charges
9. Income from shares in [group undertakings][a]
10. Income from [participating interests][b]
11. Income from other financial assets (12)
12. Other interest receivable and similar income (12)
13. Amounts written off financial assets and investments held as current assets
14. Interest payable and similar charges (13)
15. Tax on profit or loss on ordinary activities
16. Profit or loss on ordinary activities after taxation
    [Minority Interest][c]
17. Extraordinary income
18. Extraordinary charges
19. Extraordinary profit or loss
20. Tax on extraordinary profit or loss
    [Minority Interest][d]
21. Other taxes not shown under the above items
22. Profit or loss for the financial year

Amendments

a 'group undertakings' substituted for 'group companies' by EC(CGA)R 1992, Sch, Pt I para 1.

b 'participating interests' substituted for 'shares in related companies' by EC(CGA)R 1992, Sch, Pt 1 para 2.

c Inserted by EC(CGA)R 1992, Sch, Pt 1 para 9(1)(b).

d Inserted by EC(CGA)R 1992, Sch, Pt 1 para 9(3)(b).

Cross reference

In the case of group accounts 'Participating interests' is substituted with 'Interests in associated undertakings' and 'Other participating interests'. See EC(CGA)R 1992, Sch, Pt 1 para 10.

PROFIT AND LOSS ACCOUNT FORMATS

Format 3 (14)

A. Charges

1. Cost of sales (11)
2. Distribution costs (11)
3. Administrative expenses (11)
4. Amounts written off financial assets and investments held as current assets
5. Interest payable and similar charges (13)
6. Tax on profit or loss on ordinary activities
7. Profit or loss on ordinary activities after taxation
   [Minority Interest][a]
8. Extraordinary charges
9. Tax on extraordinary profit or loss
   [Minority Interest][b]
10. Other taxes not shown under the above items
11. Profit or loss for the financial year

B. Income

1. Turnover
2. Other operating income
3. Income from shares in [group undertakings][c]
4. Income from [participating interests][d]
5. Income from other financial assets (12)
6. Other interest receivable and similar income (12)
7. Profit or loss on ordinary activities after taxation
   [Minority Interest][a]
8. Extraordinary income
   [Minority Interest][b]
9. Profit or loss for the financial year

Amendments

a Inserted by EC(CGA)R 1992, Sch, Pt 1 para 9(1)(c).

b Inserted by EC(CGA)R 1992, Sch, Pt 1 para 9(3)(c).

c 'group undertakings' substituted for 'group companies' by EC(CGA)R 1992, Sch, Pt I para 1.

d 'participating interests' substituted for 'shares in related companies' by EC(CGA)R 1992, Sch, Pt 1 para 2.

Cross reference

In the case of group accounts 'Participating interests' is substituted with 'Interests in associated undertakings' and 'Other participating interests'. See EC(CGA)R 1992, Sch, Pt 1 para 10.

PROFIT AND LOSS ACCOUNT FORMATS

Format 4

A. Charges

1. Reduction in stocks of finished goods and in work in progress
2. (a) Raw materials and consumables
   (b) Other external charges
3. Staff costs:
   (a) Wages and salaries
   (b) Social welfare costs
   (c) Other pension costs
4. (a) Depreciation and other amounts written off tangible and intangible fixed assets
   (b) Exceptional amounts written off current assets
5. Other operating charges
6. Amounts written off financial assets and investments held as current assets
7. Interest payable and similar charges (13)
8. Tax on profit or loss on ordinary activities
9. Profit or loss on ordinary activities after taxation
   [Minority Interest][a]
10. Extraordinary charges
11. Tax on extraordinary profit or loss
    [Minority Interest][b]
12. Other taxes not shown under the above items
13. Profit or loss for the financial year

B. Income

1. Turnover
2. Increase in stocks of finished goods and in work in progress
3. Own work capitalised
4. Other operating income
5. Income from shares in [group undertakings][c]

6. Income from [participating interests][d]
7. Income from other financial assets (12)
8. Other interest receivable and similar income (12)
9. Profit or loss on ordinary activities after taxation

   [Minority Interest][a]
10. Extraordinary income

    [Minority Interest][b]
11. Profit or loss for the financial year

Amendments

a Inserted by EC(CGA)R 1992, Sch, Pt 1 para 9(1)(d).

b Inserted by EC(CGA)R 1992, Sch, Pt 1 para 9(3)(d).

c 'group undertakings' substituted for 'group companies' by EC(CGA)R 1992, Sch, Pt I para 1.

d 'participating interests' substituted for 'shares in related companies' by EC(CGA)R 1992, Sch, Pt 1 para 2.

Cross reference

In the case of group accounts 'Participating interests' is substituted with 'Interests in associated undertakings' and 'other participating interests'. See EC(CGA)R 1992, Sch, Pt 1 para 10.

NOTES ON THE PROFIT AND LOSS ACCOUNT FORMATS

(11) *Cost of sales: Distribution costs: Administrative expenses*

(Format 1, items 2, 4 and 5 and Format 3, items A. 1, 2 and 3)

These items shall be stated after taking into account any necessary provisions for depreciation or diminution in value of assets.

(12) *Income from other financial assets: other interest receivable and similar income*

(Format 1, items 9 and 10; Format 2, items 11 and 12; Format 3, items B. 5 and 6; Format 4, items B. 7 and 8)

Income and interest derived from [group undertakings][a] shall be shown separately from income and interest derived from other sources.

(13) *Interest payable and similar charges*

(Format 1, item 12; Format 2, item 14; Format 3, item A. 5; Format 4, item A. 7)

The amount payable to [group undertakings][a] shall be shown separately.

(14) *Formats 1 and 3*

The amounts of any provisions for depreciation and diminution in value of tangible and intangible fixed assets falling to be shown under items 7 (a) and A. 4 (a), respectively, in Formats 2 and 4 shall be disclosed in a note to the accounts in any case where the profit and loss account is prepared by reference to Format 1 or Format 3.

Amendments

a 'group undertakings' substituted for 'group companies' by EC(CGA)R 1992, Sch, Pt I para 1.

PART II

HISTORICAL COST RULES IN RELATION TO THE DRAWING UP OF ACCOUNTS

Preliminary

4. Subject to [Parts III and IIIA][a] of this Schedule, the amounts to be included in respect of all items shown in a company's accounts shall be determined in accordance with the rules set out in the following paragraphs of this Part.

Amendments

a 'Parts III and IIIA' substituted for 'Part III' by EC(FVA)R 2004, reg 3(c)(i).

FIXED ASSETS

General rules

5. Subject to any provision for depreciation or diminution in value made in accordance with paragraph 6 or 7 of this Schedule the amount to be included in respect of any fixed asset shall be its purchase price or production cost.

6. In the case of any fixed asset which has a limited useful economic life, the amount of—

(a) its purchase price or production cost, or

(b) where it is estimated that any such asset will have a residual value at the end of the period of its useful economic life, its purchase price or production cost less that estimated residual value,

shall be reduced by provisions for depreciation calculated to write off that amount systematically over the period of the asset's useful economic life.

7. (1) Where a financial asset of a description falling to be included under item A. III of either of the balance sheet formats set out in Part I of this Schedule has diminished in value, provisions for diminution in value may be made in respect of it and the amount to be included in respect of it may be reduced accordingly; and any such provisions which are not shown separately in the profit and loss account shall be disclosed (either separately or in aggregate) in a note to the accounts.

(2) Provisions for diminution in value shall be made in respect of any fixed asset which has diminished in value if the reduction in its value is expected to be permanent (whether its useful economic life is limited or not) and the amount to be included in respect of it shall be reduced accordingly; and any such provisions which are not shown separately in the profit and loss account shall be disclosed (either separately or in aggregate) in a note to the accounts.

(3) Where the reasons for which any provision was made in accordance with subparagraph (1) or (2) of this paragraph have ceased to apply to any extent, that

provision shall be written back to the extent that it is no longer necessary; and any amounts written back in accordance with this subparagraph which are not shown in the profit and loss account shall be disclosed (either separately or in aggregate) in a note to the accounts.

Rules for determining particular fixed asset items

8. (1) Notwithstanding that an item in respect of 'development costs' is included under 'fixed assets' in the balance sheet formats set out in Part I of this Schedule, an amount may only be included in a company's balance sheet in respect of that item in special circumstances.

(2) If an amount is included in a company's balance sheet in respect of development costs, the following information shall be given in a note to the accounts—

(a) the period over which the amount of those costs originally capitalised is being or is to be written off, and

(b) the reasons for capitalising the costs in question.

9. (1) The application of paragraphs 5 to 7 of this Schedule in relation to goodwill (in any case where goodwill is treated as an asset) is subject to the following provisions of this paragraph.

(2) Subject to subparagraph (3) of this paragraph, the amount of the consideration for any goodwill acquired by a company shall be reduced by provisions for depreciation calculated to write off that amount systematically over a period chosen by the directors of the company.

(3) The period chosen shall not exceed the useful economic life of the goodwill in question.

(4) In any case where any goodwill acquired by a company is shown or included as an asset in the company's balance sheet, the period chosen for writing off the consideration for that goodwill and the reasons for choosing that period shall be disclosed in a note to the accounts.

CURRENT ASSETS

10. Subject to paragraph 11 of this Schedule the amount to be included in respect of any current asset shall be its purchase price or production cost.

11. (1) If the net realisable value of any current asset is lower than its purchase price or production cost, the amount to be included in respect of that asset shall be the net realisable value.

(2) Where the reasons for which any provision for diminution in value was made under subparagraph (1) of this paragraph have ceased to apply to any extent, that provision shall be written back to the extent that it is no longer necessary.

MISCELLANEOUS

Excess of money owed over value received as an asset item

12. (1) Where the amount repayable on any debt owed by a company is greater than the value of the consideration received in the transaction giving rise to the debt, the amount of the difference may be treated as an asset.

(2) Where any such amount exists—

(a) it shall be written off by reasonable amounts each year and shall be completely written off before repayment of the debt; and

(b) if the amount not written off is not shown as a separate item in the company's balance sheet, it shall be disclosed in a note to the accounts.

ASSETS INCLUDED AT A FIXED AMOUNT

13. (1) Subject to subparagraph (2) of this paragraph, assets which fall to be included—

(a) amongst the fixed assets of a company under the item 'tangible assets', or

(b) amongst the current assets of a company under the item 'raw materials and consumables',

may be included at a fixed quantity and value.

(2) Subparagraph (1) of this paragraph applies to assets of a kind which are constantly being replaced, where—

(a) their overall value is not material to assessing the company's state of affairs, and

(b) their quantity, value and composition are not subject to material variation.

DETERMINATION OF PURCHASE PRICE OR PRODUCTION COST

14. (1) The purchase price of an asset shall be determined by adding to the actual price paid any expenses incidental to its acquisition.

(2) The production cost of an asset shall be determined by adding to the purchase price of the raw materials and consumables used the amount of the costs incurred by the company which are directly attributable to the production of that asset.

(3) In addition there may be included in the production cost of an asset—

(a) a reasonable proportion of the costs incurred by the company which are only indirectly attributable to the production of that asset, but only to the extent that they relate to the period of production, and

(b) interest on capital borrowed to finance the production of that asset, to the extent that it accrues in respect of the period of production:

Provided, however, in a case within clause (b) of this subparagraph that the inclusion of the interest in determining the cost of that asset is disclosed in a note to the accounts.

(4) In the case of current assets, distribution costs may not be included in production costs.

15. (1) Subject to the qualification mentioned in this subparagraph, the purchase price or production cost of—

(a) any assets which fall to be included under any item shown in a company's balance sheet under the general item 'stocks', and

(b) any assets which are fungible assets (including investments),

may be determined by the application of any of the methods mentioned in subparagraph (2) of this paragraph in relation to any such assets of the same class.

The method chosen must be one which appears to the directors to be appropriate in the circumstances of the company.

(2) Those methods are:

(a) the method known as 'first in, first out' (FIFO),

(b) a weighted average price, and

(c) any other method similar to any of the methods mentioned above.

(3) Where, in the case of any company—

(a) the purchase price or production cost of assets falling to be included under any item shown in the company's balance sheet has been determined by the application of any method permitted by this paragraph, and

(b) the amount shown in respect of that item differs materially from the relevant alternative amount given below in this paragraph,

the amount of that difference shall be disclosed in a note to the accounts.

(4) Subject to subparagraph (5) of this paragraph, for the purposes of subparagraph (3) (b) of this paragraph, the relevant alternative amount, in relation to any item shown in a company's balance sheet, is the amount which would have been shown in respect of that item if assets of any class included under that item at an amount determined by any method permitted by this paragraph had instead been included at their replacement cost as at the balance sheet date.

(5) The relevant alternative amount may be determined by reference to the most recent actual purchase price or production cost before the balance sheet date of assets of any class included under the item in question instead of by reference to their replacement cost as at that date, but only if the former appears to the directors of the company to constitute the more appropriate approach in the case of assets of that class.

(6) For the purpose of this paragraph, assets of any description shall be regarded as fungible if assets of that description are substantially indistinguishable one from another.

SUBSTITUTION OF ORIGINAL STATED AMOUNT WHERE PRICE OR COST UNKNOWN

16. Where there is no record of the purchase price or production cost of any asset of a company or of any price, expense or costs relevant for determining its purchase price or production cost in accordance with paragraph 14 of this Schedule or any such record cannot be obtained without unreasonable expense or delay, its purchase price or production cost shall be taken for the purposes of paragraphs 5 to 11 of this Schedule to be the value ascribed to it in the earliest available record of its value made on or after its acquisition or production by the company.

PART III

ALTERNATIVE RULES IN RELATION TO THE DRAWING UP OF ACCOUNTS

Preliminary

17. (1) The rules set out in Part II of this Schedule are referred to subsequently in this Schedule as the historical cost accounting rules.

(2) Those rules, with the omission of paragraphs 4, 9 and 13 to 16, are referred to subsequently in this Part of this Schedule as the depreciation rules; and references subsequently in this Schedule to the historical cost accounting rules do not include the depreciation rules as they apply by virtue of paragraph 20 of this Schedule.

18. Subject to paragraphs 20 to 22 of this Schedule, the amounts to be included in respect of assets of any description mentioned in paragraph 19 of this Schedule may be determined on any basis so mentioned.

Alternative accounting rules

19.(1) Intangible fixed assets, other than goodwill, may be included at their current cost.

(2) Tangible fixed assets may be included at a market value determined as at the date of their last valuation or at their current cost.

(3) Financial fixed assets may be included either—

(a) at a market value determined as at the date of their last valuation; or

(b) at a value determined on any basis which appears to the directors to be appropriate in the circumstances of the company,

but in the latter case particulars of the method of valuation adopted and of the reasons for adopting it shall be disclosed in a note to the accounts.

(4) Investments of any description falling to be included under item B. III of either of the balance sheet formats set out in Part I of this Schedule may be included at their current cost.

(5) Stocks may be included at their current cost.

Application of the depreciation rules

20. (1) Where the value of any asset of a company is determined on any basis mentioned in paragraph 19 of this Schedule, that value shall be, or (as the case may require) be the starting point for determining, the amount to be included in respect of that asset in the company's accounts, instead of its purchase price or production cost or any value previously so determined for that asset; and the depreciation rules shall apply accordingly in relation to any such asset with the substitution for any reference to its purchase price or production cost of a reference to the value most recently determined for that asset on any basis mentioned in the said paragraph 19.

(2) The amount of any provision for depreciation required in the case of any fixed asset by paragraph 6 or 7 of this Schedule as it applies by virtue of subparagraph (1) of this paragraph is referred to below in this paragraph as the adjusted amount; and the amount of any provision which would be required by that paragraph in the case of that asset according to the historical cost accounting rules is referred to as the historical cost amount.

(3) Where subparagraph (1) of this paragraph applies in the case of any fixed asset. the amount of any provision for depreciation in respect of that asset—

(a) included in any item shown in the profit and loss account in respect of amounts written off assets of the description in question; or

(b) taken into account in stating any item so shown which is required by note (11) of the notes on the profit and loss account formats set out in Part I of this Schedule to be stated after taking into account any necessary provisions for depreciation or diminution in value of assets included under it,

may be the historical cost amount instead of the adjusted amount:

Provided that, if the amount of the provision for depreciation is the historical cost amount, the amount of any difference between the two shall be shown separately in the profit and loss account or in a note to the accounts.

Additional information in case of departure from historical cost rules

21. (1) This paragraph applies where the amounts to be included in respect of assets covered by any items shown in a company's accounts have been determined on any basis mentioned in paragraph 19 of this Schedule.

(2) The items affected and the basis of valuation adopted in determining the amounts of the assets in question in the case of each such item shall be disclosed in a note to the accounts.

(3) In the case of each balance sheet item affected (except stocks) either—

(a) the comparable amounts determined according to the historical cost accounting rules, or

(b) the differences between those amounts and the corresponding amounts actually shown in the balance sheet in respect of that item,

shall be shown separately in the balance sheet or in a note to the accounts.

(4) In subparagraph (3) of this paragraph, references in relation to any item to the comparable amounts determined as there mentioned are references to—

(a) the aggregate amount which would be required to be shown in respect of that item if the amounts to be included in respect of all the assets covered by that item were determined according to the historical cost accounting rules, and

(b) the aggregate amount of the cumulative provisions for depreciation or diminution in value which would be permitted or required in determining those amounts according to those rules.

Revaluation reserve

22. (1) With respect to any determination of the value of an asset of a company on any basis mentioned in paragraph 19 of this Schedule, the amount of any profit or loss arising from that determination (after allowing, where appropriate, for any provisions for depreciation or diminution in value made otherwise than by reference to the value so determined and any adjustments of any such provisions made in the light of that determination) shall be credited or (as the case may be) debited to a separate reserve (referred to in this paragraph as 'the revaluation reserve').

(2) Subparagraph (1) of this paragraph applies in relation to any determination of the value of an asset of a company which takes place before the commencement of this paragraph as it applies to any such determination taking place on or after such commencement.

(3) The amount of the revaluation reserve shall be shown in the company's balance sheet under a separate sub-heading in the position given for the item 'revaluation reserve' in Format 1 or 2 of the balance sheet formats set out in Part I of this Schedule.

(4) The revaluation reserve shall be reduced to the extent that the amounts standing to the credit of the reserve are, in the opinion of the directors of the company, no longer necessary for the purpose of the accounting policies adopted by the company; but an amount may only be transferred from the reserve to the profit and loss account if either—

(a) the amount in question was previously charged to that account, or

(b) it represents realised profit.

(5) The treatment for taxation purposes of amounts credited or debited to the revaluation reserve shall be disclosed in a note to the accounts.

[PART IIIA VALUATION AT FAIR VALUE

Inclusion of financial instruments at fair value

22A. (1) Subject to subparagraphs (2) to (4) of this paragraph [and paragraph 22AA][b], financial instruments, including derivative financial instruments, may be accounted for by companies at fair value.

(2) Subparagraph (1) of this paragraph does not apply to financial instruments which constitute liabilities unless—

(a) they are held as part of a trading portfolio, or

(b) they are derivative financial instruments.

(3) Subparagraph (1) of this paragraph does not apply to—

(a) non-derivative financial instruments held to maturity,

(b) loans and receivables originated by the company and not held for trading purposes,

(c) interests in subsidiary undertakings, associated undertakings and joint ventures,

(d) equity instruments issued by the company,

(e) contracts for contingent consideration in a business combination, and

(f) other financial instruments with such special characteristics that the instruments, according to what is generally accepted, should be accounted for differently from other financial instruments.

(4) In this paragraph—

'Regulations of 1992' means the European Communities (Companies: Group Accounts) Regulations 1992 (S.I. No. 201 of 1992);

'associated undertaking' has the same meaning as in Regulation 34 of the Regulations of 1992;

'joint venture' has the same meaning as in Regulation 32 of the Regulations of 1992;

'subsidiary undertaking' has the same meaning as in Regulation 4 of the Regulations of 1992.][a]

Amendments

a Paragraph 22A inserted by EC(FVA)R 2004, reg 3(c)(ii).

b Inserted by the European Communities (Directive 2006/46/EC) Regulations 2009, reg 3(a).

[22AA. (1) Financial instruments which constitute liabilities other than such instruments referred to in subparagraphs (2)(a) and (2)(b) of paragraph 22A may be accounted for by companies at fair value if—

(a) they are accounted for in accordance with international accounting standards as adopted by the Commission Regulation on or before 5 September 2006, and

(b) the associated disclosure requirements, provided for in international financial reporting standards adopted in accordance with the IAS Regulation, are made.

(2) Financial instruments referred to in subparagraph (3) of paragraph 22A may be accounted for by companies at fair value if—

(a) they are accounted for in accordance with international accounting standards as adopted by the Commission Regulation, on or before 5 September 2006, and

(b) the associated disclosure requirements, provided for in international financial reporting standards adopted in accordance with the IAS Regulation, are made.

(3) In this paragraph—

'Commission Regulation' means Commission Regulation (EC) No. 1725/2003 (OJ L 261, 13.10.2003, p.1) of 29 September 2003;

'IAS Regulation' has the meaning assigned to by the Principal Act;

'international financial reporting standards' has the meaning assigned to it by section 2 of the Principal Act.][a]

Amendments

a Paragraph 22AA inserted by European Communities (Directive 2006/46/EC) Regulations 2009, reg 3(b).

[Methods for determining fair value

22B. (1) The fair value of a financial instrument is its value determined in accordance with this paragraph.

(2) Where a reliable market can readily be identified for a financial instrument its fair value is to be determined by reference to its market value.

(3) Where a reliable market value cannot readily be identified for a financial instrument but can be identified for its components or for a similar instrument, its fair value is to be determined by reference to the market value of its components or of the similar instrument.

(4) Where neither subparagraph (2) nor (3) of this paragraph apply, the fair value of the financial instrument is to be a value resulting from generally accepted valuation models and techniques.

(5) Valuation models and techniques used for the purposes of subparagraph (4) of this paragraph shall ensure a reasonable approximation of the market value.

(6) Financial instruments that cannot be measured reliably by any of the methods described in paragraphs (1) to (5) of this paragraph shall be measured in accordance with Part II or III of this Schedule.][a]

Amendments

a Paragraph 22B inserted by EC(FVA)R 2004, reg 3(c)(ii).

[Hedged items

22C. A company may, in respect of any assets and liabilities which qualify as hedged items under a fair value hedge accounting system, or identified portions of those assets and liabilities, value those assets and liabilities at the amount required under that system.][a]

Amendments

a Paragraph 22C inserted by EC(FVA)R 2004, reg 3(c)(ii).

[Other assets that may be included at fair value

22CA. (1) This paragraph applies to—

(a) investment property, and

(b) living animals and plants,

that, under relevant international financial reporting standards, may be included in accounts at fair value.

(2) Investment property and living animals and plants may be included at fair value, provided that all such investment property or, as the case may be, all such living animals and plants are so included where their fair value can reliably be determined.

(3) In this paragraph, 'fair value' means fair value determined in accordance with relevant international financial reporting standards.][a]

Amendments

a Paragraph 22CA inserted by EC(IFRSMA)R 2005, reg 5(m)(ii).

[Accounting for changes in fair value of financial instruments

22D.(1) This paragraph applies where the fair value at which a financial instrument is included in accordance with paragraph 22A or 22C of this Schedule [or where the fair value at which an asset is included in accordance with paragraph 22CA of this Schedule][b] is different from the value at which it was last included in accordance with that paragraph.

(2) Notwithstanding section 5(c) of this Act, and subject to subparagraphs (3) and (4) of this paragraph, the amount of the difference in value [of the financial instrument or of the investment property or living animals or plants][c] shall be included in the profit and loss account.

(3) Where—

(a) the financial instrument accounted for is a hedging instrument under a system of hedge accounting that allows some or all of the difference in value not to be shown in the profit and loss account, or

(b) the difference in value relates to an exchange difference arising on a monetary item that forms part of a company's net investment in a foreign entity,

the difference in value shall be credited to (or debited from as the case may be) a separate reserve to be known as the 'fair value reserve'.

(4) Where the instrument accounted for—

(a) is an available for sale financial asset, and

(b) is not a derivative financial instrument,

the difference in value may be credited to (or debited from as the case may be) the fair value reserve.][a]

Amendments

a Paragraph 22D inserted by EC(FVA)R 2004, reg 3(c)(ii).

b Words inserted by EC(IFRSMA)R 2005, reg 5(m)(ii)(I).

c Words inserted by EC(IFRSMA)R 2005, reg 5(m)(ii)(II).

[The fair value reserve

22E. (1) An amount may be transferred—

(a) from the fair value reserve to the profit and loss account if the amount represents realised profit, or

(b) to or from the fair value reserve any amount credited or debited to the reserve.

(2) The fair value reserve shall be adjusted when amounts therein are no longer necessary for the purposes of paragraph 22D (3) or (4) of this Schedule.

(3) The fair value reserve shall not be reduced except as provided for in this paragraph.

(4) The treatment for taxation purposes of amounts credited or debited to the fair value reserve shall be disclosed in a note to the accounts.][a]

Amendments

a Paragraph 22E inserted by EC(FVA)R 2004, reg 3(c)(ii).

PART IV

INFORMATION REQUIRED BY WAY OF NOTES TO ACCOUNTS

Preliminary

23. (1) Any information required in the case of any company by the following provisions of this Part shall (if not given in the company's accounts) be given by way of a note to those accounts.

(2) Notes to a company's accounts may be contained in the accounts or in a separate document annexed to the accounts.

24. The accounting policies adopted by the company in determining the amounts to be included in respect of items shown in the balance sheet and in determining the profit or loss of the company shall be stated (including such policies with respect to the depreciation and diminution in value of assets).

Information supplementing the balance sheet

25. Paragraphs 26 to 37 of this Schedule require information which either supplements the information given with respect to any particular items shown in the balance sheet or

is otherwise relevant to assessing the company's state of affairs in the light of the information so given.

Share capital and debentures

26. (1) The following information shall be given with respect to the company's share capital—

(a) the authorised share capital, and

(b) where shares of more than one class have been allotted, the number and aggregate nominal value of shares of each class allotted.

(2) In the case of any part of the allotted share capital that consists of redeemable shares, the following information shall be given—

(a) the earliest and latest dates on which the company has power to redeem those shares,

(b) whether those shares must be redeemed in any event or are liable to be redeemed at the option of the company, and

(c) whether any (and, if so, what) premium is payable on redemption.

27. If the company has allotted any shares during the financial year to which the accounts relate, the following information shall be given—

(a) the reason for making the allotment,

(b) the classes of shares allotted, and

(c) in respect of each class of shares, the number allotted, their aggregate nominal value and the consideration received by the company for the allotment.

28. (1) If the company has issued any debentures during the financial year to which the accounts relate, the following information shall be given—

(a) the reason for making the issue,

(b) the classes of debentures issued, and

(c) in respect of each class of debentures, the amount issued and the consideration received by the company for the issue.

(2) Particulars of any redeemed debentures which the company has power to re-issue shall also be given.

(3) Where any of the company's debentures are held by a nominee of or trustee for the company, the nominal amount of the debentures and the amount at which they are stated in the accounting records kept by the company in accordance with section 147 of the Principal Act shall be stated.

FIXED ASSETS

29. (1) In respect of each item which is or would, but for section 4 (6) (b) of this Act, be shown under the general item 'fixed assets' in the company's balance sheet, the following information shall be given—

(a) the appropriate amounts in respect of that item as at the date of the beginning of the financial year and as at the balance sheet date respectively,

(b) the effect on any amount shown in the balance sheet in respect of that item of—

(i) any revision of the amount in respect of any assets included under that item made during that year on any basis mentioned in paragraph 19 of this Schedule,

(ii) acquisitions during that year of any assets,

(iii) disposals during that year of any assets, and

(iv) any transfers of assets of the company to and from that item during that year.

(2) The reference in subparagraph (1) (a) of this paragraph to the appropriate amounts in respect of any item as at any date there mentioned is a reference to amounts representing the aggregate amounts determined, as at that date, in respect of assets falling to be included under that item either—

(a) on the basis of purchase price or production cost (determined in accordance with paragraphs 14 and 15 of this Schedule,) or

(b) on any basis mentioned in paragraph 19 of this Schedule

(leaving out of account in either case any provisions for depreciation or diminution in value).

(3) In respect of each item within subparagraph (1) of this paragraph—

(a) the cumulative amount of provisions for depreciation or diminution in value of assets included under that item as at each date mentioned in subparagraph (1) (a) of this paragraph,

(b) the amount of any such provisions made in respect of the financial year concerned,

(c) the amount of any adjustments made in respect of any such provisions during that year in consequence of the disposal of any assets, and

(d) the amount of any other adjustments made in respect of any such provisions during that year,

shall be also stated.

30. Where any fixed assets of the company (other than listed investments) are included under any item shown in the company's balance sheet at an amount determined on any basis mentioned in paragraph 19 of this Schedule, the following information shall be given—

(a) the years (so far as they are known to the directors) in which the assets were severally valued and the several values, and

(b) in the case of assets that have been valued during the financial year, the names of the persons who valued them or particulars of their qualifications for doing so and (in either case) the bases of valuation used.

Financial assets and investments held as current assets

31. (1) In respect of the amount of each item which is or would, but for section 4 (6) (b) of this Act, be shown in the company's balance sheet under the general items 'financial assets' or 'investments held as current assets' there shall be stated—

(a) how much of that amount is ascribable to listed investments, and

(b) how much of any amount so ascribable is ascribable to investments as respects which there has been granted a listing on a recognised stock exchange and how much to other listed investments.

(2) Where the amount of any listed investments is stated for any item in accordance with subparagraph (1) (a) of this paragraph, the following amounts shall also be stated—

(a) the aggregate market value of those investments where it differs from the amount so stated, and

(b) both the market value and stock exchange value of any investments of which the former value is, for the purposes of the accounts, taken as being higher than the latter.

[Information about fair valuation of assets and liabilities

31A. (1) This paragraph applies where financial instruments have been included at fair value pursuant to paragraph 22A or 22C of this Schedule.

(2) There shall be disclosed—

(a) the significant assumptions underlying the valuation models and techniques where fair values have been determined in accordance with paragraph 22B(4) of this Schedule,

(b) for each category of financial instrument, the fair value of the financial instruments in that category and the amounts—

(i) included in the profit and loss account, and

(ii) credited to or debited from the fair value reserve, in respect of instruments in that category,

(c) for each class of derivative financial instrument, the extent and nature of the instruments including significant terms and conditions that may affect the amount, timing and certainty of future cash flows, and

(d) a table showing movements in the fair value reserve during the financial year.][a]

Amendments

a Paragraph 31A inserted by EC(FVA)R 2004, reg 3(c)(iii).

[31B. Where valuation of financial instruments at fair value has not been applied, for each class of derivative financial instrument there shall be stated—

(a) the fair value of the instruments in that class, if such a value can be determined in accordance with paragraph 22B of this Schedule,

and

(b) the extent and nature of the instruments.][a]

Amendments

a Paragraph 31B inserted by EC(FVA)R 2004, reg 3(c)(iii).

[31C. (1) Subparagraph (2) of this paragraph applies where—

(a) the company has financial fixed assets that could be included at fair value by virtue of paragraph 22A of this Schedule,

(b) the amount at which those assets are included under any item in the company's accounts is in excess of their fair value, and

(c) the company has not made provision for the diminution in value of those assets in accordance with paragraph 7(1) of this Schedule.

(2) There shall be stated—

(a) the amount at which either the individual assets or appropriate groupings of those assets is stated in the company's accounts,

(b) the fair value of those assets or groupings, and

(c) the reasons for not making a provision for diminution in value of those assets, including the nature of the evidence that provides the basis for the belief that the book value will be recovered.][a]

Amendments

a Paragraph 31C inserted by EC(FVA)R 2004, reg 3(c)(iii) but substituted by EC(IFRSMA)R 2005, reg 5(m)(iv).

[Information where investment property and living animals and plants included at fair value

31D. (1) This paragraph applies where the amounts to be included in a company's accounts in respect of investment property or living animals and plants have been determined in accordance with paragraph 22CA of this Schedule.

(2) The balance sheet items affected and the basis of valuation adopted in determining the amounts of the assets concerned in the case of each such item shall be disclosed in a note to the accounts.

(3) In the case of investment property, for each balance sheet item affected there shall be shown, either separately in the balance sheet or in a note to the accounts—

(a) the comparable amounts determined according to the historical cost accounting rules, or

(b) the differences between those amounts and the corresponding amounts actually shown in the balance sheet in respect of that item.

(4) In subparagraph (3) of this paragraph, references in relation to any item to the comparable amounts determined in accordance with that subparagraph are references to—

(a) the aggregate amount which would be required to be shown in respect of that item if the amounts to be included in respect of all the assets covered by that item were determined according to the historical cost accounting rules, and

(b) the aggregate amount of the cumulative provisions for depreciation or diminution in value which would be permitted or required in determining those amounts according to those rules][a].

Amendments

a Paragraph 31D inserted by EC(IFRSMA)R 2005, reg 5(m)(v).

Reserves and provisions

32. (1) Where any amount is transferred—

(a) to or from any reserves, or

(b) to any provisions for [provisions for liabilities][a], or

(c) from any [provisions for liabilities][b] otherwise than for the purpose for which the provision was established,

and the reserves or provisions are or would, but for section 4 (6) (b) of this Act, be shown as separate items in the company's balance sheet, the information mentioned in subparagraph (2) of this paragraph shall be given in respect of the aggregate of reserves or provisions included in the same item.

(2) That information is—

(a) the amount of the reserves or provisions as at the date of the beginning of the financial year and as at the balance sheet date respectively,

(b) any amount transferred to or from the reserves or provisions during that year, and

(c) the source and application respectively of any amounts so transferred.

(3) Particulars shall be given of each provision included in the item 'other provisions' in the company's balance sheet in any case where the amount of that provision is material.

Amendments

a Words inserted by EC(IFRSMA)R 2005, reg 5(m)(vi)(I).

b Words inserted by EC(IFRSMA)R 2005, reg 5(m)(vi)(II).

[32A. Particulars of any restriction on profits available for distribution by virtue of section 224(2)(b)(i) of the Companies Act, 1990, must also be stated.][a]

Amendments

a Paragraph 32A inserted by CA 1990, s 233(3)(a).

Provision for taxation

33. The amount of any provision for taxation other than deferred taxation shall be stated.

Details of indebtedness

34. (1) In respect of each item shown under 'creditors' in the company's balance sheet there shall be stated—

(a) the aggregate amount of any debts included under that item which are payable or repayable otherwise than by instalments and fall due for payment or repayment after the end of the period of five years beginning with the day next following the end of the financial year,

(b) the aggregate amount of any debts so included which are payable or repayable by instalments any of which fall due for payment after the end of that period,

(c) the aggregate amount of any debts included under that item in respect of which any security has been given, and

(d) an indication of the nature of the securities so given,

and, in the case of debts within clause (b) of this subparagraph, the aggregate amount of instalments falling due after the end of that period shall also be disclosed for each such item.

(2) References in subparagraph (1) of this paragraph to an item shown under 'creditors' in the company's balance sheet include references, where amounts failing due to creditors within one year and after more than one year are distinguished in the balance sheet—

(a) in a case within subparagraph (1) (a) of this paragraph, to an item shown under the latter of those categories, and

(b) in a case within subparagraph (1) (d) of this paragraph, to an item shown under either of those categories,

and references to items shown under 'creditors' include references to items which would, but for section 4(6)(b) of this Act, be shown under that heading.

35. If any fixed cumulative dividends on the company's shares are in arrears, there shall be stated—

(a) the amount of the arrears, and

(b) the period for which the dividends or, if there is more than one class, each class of them are in arrears.

Guarantees and other financial commitments

36. (1) Particulars shall be given of any charge on the assets of the company to secure the liabilities of any other person, including, where practicable, the amount secured.

(2) The following information shall be given with respect to any other contingent liability not provided for—

(a) the amount or estimated amount of that liability,

(b) its legal nature, and

(c) whether any valuable security has been provided by the company in connection with that liability and, if so, what.

(3) There shall be stated, where practicable—

(a) the aggregate amount or estimated amount of contracts for capital expenditure, so far as not provided for, and

(b) the aggregate amount or estimated amount of capital expenditure authorised by the directors which has not been contracted for.

(4) Particulars shall be given of:

(a) any pension commitments included under any provision shown in the company's balance sheet, and

(b) any such commitments for which no provision has been made, and, where any such commitment relates wholly or partly to pensions payable to past directors of the company, separate particulars shall be given of that commitment so far as it relates to such pensions.

(5) The following information shall also be given:

(a) the nature of every pension scheme operated by or on behalf of the company including information as to whether or not each scheme is a defined benefit scheme or a defined contribution scheme,

(b) whether each such scheme is externally funded or internally financed,

(c) whether any pension costs and liabilities are assessed in accordance with the advice of a professionally qualified actuary and, if so, the date of the most recent relevant actuarial valuation,

(d) whether and, if so, where any such actuarial valuation is available for public inspection.

(6) Particulars shall also be given of any other financial commitments which—

(a) have not been provided for, and

(b) are relevant to assessing the company's state of affairs.

(7) [...][a]

Amendments

a Paragraph 36(7) deleted by EC(CGA)R 1992, Sch, Pt 1 para 4(6)(a).

[Information on arrangements not included in balance sheet

36A. The nature and business purpose of the arrangements of the company that are not included in its balance sheet and the financial impact on the company of those arrangements shall be provided in the notes to the accounts of the company if the risks or benefits arising from such arrangements are material and in so far as the disclosure of such risks or benefits is necessary for assessing the financial position of the company.][a]

Amendments

a Paragraph 36A inserted by European Communities (Directive 2006/46/EC) Regulations 2009, reg 6.

[Related party transactions

36. (1) Particulars shall be given in the notes to the accounts of the company of transactions which have been entered into with related parties by the company if such transactions are material and have not been concluded under normal market conditions and the particulars shall include the amount of such transactions, the nature of the related party relationship and other information about the transactions which is necessary for an understanding of the financial position of the company.

(2) Subject to subparagraph (4), the provision of particulars and other information about individual transactions may be aggregated according to their nature, except where

separate information is necessary for an understanding of the effects of related party transactions on the financial position of the company.

(3) Subparagraph (1) shall not apply to transactions which are entered into between 2 or more members of a group if any subsidiary undertaking which is party to the transaction is wholly owned by such a member.

(4) Subparagraph (2) shall not apply to a company whose securities are admitted to trading on a regulated market within the meaning of Article 4(1), point (14) of Directive 2004/39/EC6.

(5) A word or expression used in subparagraphs (1) to (3) has the same meaning as it has in Directive 2006/46/EC.][a]

Amendments

a Paragraph 36 inserted by European Communities (Directive 2006/46/EC) Regulations 2009, reg 6.

Notes

There are now two paragraphs 36 and it is thought that this is a typographical error in the Regulations and that the second paragraph 36 was intended to be 36B.

Miscellaneous matters

37. (1) Particulars shall be given of any case where the purchase price or production cost of any asset is for the first time determined under paragraph 16 of this Schedule.

(2) The aggregate amount of any outstanding loans permitted by section 60 of the Principal Act, as amended by the Act of 1983 (other than loans to which subsection (13)(a) of that section refers), shall be shown, indicating separately loans permitted by paragraphs (b) and (c) of the said subsection (13).

(3) The aggregate amount which is recommended for distribution by way of dividend shall be stated.

Information supplementing the profit and loss account

38. Paragraphs 39 to 43 of this Part require information which either supplements the information given with respect to any particular items shown in the profit and loss account or otherwise provides particulars of income or expenditure of the company or of circumstances affecting the items shown in the profit and loss account.

Separate statement of certain items of income and expenditure

39. (1) Subject to the following provisions of this paragraph, each of the amounts mentioned in subparagraphs (2) to (6) of this paragraph shall be stated.

(2) The amount of interest on or any similar charges in respect of—

(a) bank loans and overdrafts, and loans made to the company (other than bank loans and overdrafts) which—

(i) are repayable otherwise than by instalments and fall due for repayment before the end of the period of five years beginning with the day next following the end of the financial year of the company, or

(ii) are repayable by instalments the last of which falls due for payment before the end of that period, and

(b) loans of any other kind made to the company.

This subparagraph does not apply to interest or charges on loans to the company from [group undertakings][a], but, with that exception, it applies to interest or charges on all loans, whether made on the security of debentures or not.

[(3) The amounts respectively provided for the purchase of the company's share capital, for redemption of share capital and for redemption of loans.][b]

(4) The amount of income from listed and unlisted investments.

(5) The amount of the remuneration of the auditors (including any sums paid by the company in respect of the auditors' expenses).

(6) The aggregate amounts of the emoluments of, and compensation in respect of loss of office to, directors and compensation in respect of loss of office to past-directors.

Amendments

a 'group undertakings' substituted for 'group companies' by EC(CGA)R 1992, Sch, Pt I para 1.

b Para 39(3) substituted by CA 1990, s 233(3)(b).

Particulars of tax

40. (1) The basis on which the charge for corporation tax, income tax and other taxation on profits (whether payable in or outside the State) is computed shall be stated.

(2) Particulars shall be given of any special circumstances which affect liability in respect of taxation on profits, income or capital gains for the financial year concerned or liability in respect of taxation of profits, income or capital gains for succeeding financial years.

(3) The amount of the charge for corporation tax, income tax and other taxation on profits or capital gains, so far as charged to revenue, including taxation payable outside the State on profits (distinguishing where practicable between corporation tax and other taxation) shall be stated.

These amounts shall be stated separately in respect of each of the amounts which is or would, but for section 4 (6) (b) of this Act, be shown under the following items in the profit and loss account, that is to say, 'tax on profit or loss on ordinary activities' and 'tax on extraordinary profit or loss'.

Particulars of turnover

41. (1) If in the course of the financial year, the company has carried on business of two or more classes which, in the opinion of the directors, differ substantially from each other, there shall be stated in respect of each class (describing it) the amount of the turnover attributable to that class.

(2) If, in the course of the financial year, the company has supplied markets which, in the opinion of the directors, differ substantially from each other, the amount of the turnover attributable to each such market shall also be stated.

In this subparagraph 'market' means a market delimited in a geographical manner.

(3) In analysing for the purposes of this paragraph the source (in terms of business or in terms of market) of turnover, the directors of the company shall have regard to the manner in which the company's activities are organised.

(4) For the purpose of this paragraph—

(a) classes of business which, in the opinion of the directors, do not differ substantially from each other shall be treated as one class, and

(b) markets which, in the opinion of the directors, do not differ substantially from each other shall be treated as one market,

and any amounts properly attributable to one class of business or (as the case may be) to one market which are not material may be included in the amount stated in respect of another.

(5) Where in the opinion of the directors the disclosure of any information required by this paragraph would be seriously prejudicial to the interests of the company, that information need not be disclosed, but the fact that any such information has not been disclosed must be stated.

Particulars of staff

42. (1) The following information shall be given with respect to the employees of the company—

(a) the average number of persons employed by the company in the financial year, and

(b) the average number of persons employed within each category of persons employed by the company.

(2) In respect of all persons employed by the company during the financial year who are taken into account in determining the relevant annual number for the purposes of subparagraph (1) (a) of this paragraph, there shall also be stated the aggregate amounts respectively of—

(a) wages and salaries paid or payable in respect of that year to those persons,

(b) social welfare costs incurred by the company on their behalf, and

(c) other pension costs so incurred,

save insofar as these amounts or any of them are stated in the profit and loss account.

(3) The categories of persons employed by the company by reference to which the number required to be disclosed by subparagraph (1) (b) of this paragraph is to be determined shall be such as the directors may select, having regard to the manner in which the company's activities are organised.

(4) (a) For the purposes of clauses (a) and (b) of subparagraph (1) of this paragraph, the average number of persons employed by a company shall be determined by dividing the relevant annual number by the number of weeks in the financial year of the company.

(b) For the purposes of this subparagraph, the relevant annual number shall be determined by ascertaining for each week in the financial year of the company concerned—

(i) in the case of the said clause (a), the number of persons employed under contracts of service by the company in that week (whether throughout the week or not), and

(ii) in the case of the said clause (b), the number of persons in the category in question of persons so employed,

and, in either case, adding together all the weekly numbers.

Miscellaneous matters

43. (1) Where any amount relating to any preceding financial year is included in any item in the profit and loss account, the effect shall be stated.

(2) Particulars shall be given of any extraordinary income or charges arising in the financial year.

(3) The effect shall be stated of any transactions that are exceptional by virtue of size or incidence notwithstanding the fact that they fall within the ordinary activities of the company.

(4) Any amount expended on research and development in the financial year, and any amount committed in respect of research and development in subsequent years, shall be stated.

(5) Where, in the opinion of the directors, the disclosure of any information required by subparagraph (4) of this paragraph would be prejudicial to the interests of the company, that information need not be disclosed, but the fact that any such information has not been disclosed shall be stated.

General

44. (1) Where sums originally denominated in foreign currencies have been brought into account under any items shown in the balance sheet or profit and loss account, the basis on which those sums have been translated into Irish currency shall be stated.

[(2) In respect of every balance sheet or profit and loss account item which would, but for its inclusion in a note to the accounts, be shown in the balance sheet, or profit and loss account format set out in Part I of this Schedule and chosen pursuant to section 4 of this Act, there shall also be shown in a note to the accounts the corresponding amount for the financial year immediately preceding that to which the accounts relate. Where that corresponding amount is not comparable with the amount to be shown for the item in question in respect of the financial year to which the accounts relate, the former amount may be adjusted, and, if the former amount is adjusted, particulars as regards the respect or respects in which the foregoing amounts are not comparable and of the adjustment shall be given in a note to the accounts.][a]

(3) Subparagraph (2) of this paragraph does not apply in relation to any amount stated by virtue of paragraphs 29 and 32 of this Schedule.

Amendments

a Subparagraph 44(2) substituted by EC(ANAADCIC)R 2005, reg 5.

PART V
[SPECIAL PROVISIONS WHERE A COMPANY IS A PARENT UNDERTAKING OR SUBSIDIARY UNDERTAKING][A]

Amendments

a Heading of Part V substituted by EC(CGA)R 1992, Sch, Pt I para 4(1).

Company's own accounts

[45. (1) This Part applies where the company is a parent undertaking, whether or not it is itself a subsidiary undertaking.

(2) Where a company is a parent undertaking or a subsidiary undertaking and any item required by Part I of this Schedule to be shown in the company's balance sheet, in relation to group undertakings, includes—

(a) amounts attributable to dealings with or interests in any parent undertaking or fellow subsidiary undertaking, or

(b) amounts attributable to dealings with or interests in any subsidiary undertaking of the company,

the aggregate amounts within paragraph (a) and (b) respectively shall be shown as separate items, either by way of subdivision of the relevant item in the balance sheet or in a note to the company's accounts.][a]

Amendments

a Paragraph 45 substituted by EC(CGA)R 1992, Sch, Pt 1 para 4(2).

Guarantees and other financial commitments in favour of group undertakings

[45A. Commitments within any of subparagraphs (1) to (6) of paragraph 36 (guarantees and other financial commitments) which are undertaken on behalf of or for the benefit of—

(a) any parent undertaking or fellow subsidiary undertaking, or

(b) any subsidiary undertaking of the company,

shall be stated separately from the other commitments within that subparagraph, and commitments within paragraph (a) shall also be stated separately from those within paragraph (b).][a]

Amendments

a Paragraph 45A inserted by EC(CGA)R 1992, Sch, Pt 1 para 4(3).

[46. (1) Subject to subparagraph (2) of this paragraph, where the company is a parent undertaking, the number, description and amount of the shares in, and debentures of the company held by its subsidiary undertakings or their nominees shall be disclosed in a note to the company's accounts.

(2) Subparagraph (1) of this paragraph does not apply in relation to any shares or debentures—

(a) in the case of which the subsidiary undertaking is concerned as personal representative, or

(b) in the case of which it is concerned as trustee:

Provided that in the latter case neither the company nor a subsidiary undertaking of the company is beneficially interested under the trust, otherwise than by way of security only for the purposes of a transaction entered into by it in the ordinary course of a business which includes the lending of money.][a]

Amendments

a Paragraph 46 substituted by EC(CGA)R 1992, Sch, Pt 1 para 4(4).

[46A. (1) Where a company is a subsidiary undertaking, the following information shall be stated with respect to the parent undertaking of—

(a) the largest group of undertakings for which group accounts are drawn up and of which the company is a member, and

(b) the smallest such group of undertakings.

(2) The name of the parent undertaking shall be stated.

(3) There shall be stated—

(a) if the undertaking is incorporated, the country in which it is incorporated;

(b) if it is unincorporated, the address of its principal place of business.

(4) If copies of the group accounts referred to in subparagraph (1) are available to the public, there shall also be stated the addresses from which copies of the accounts can be obtained.][a]

Amendments

a Paragraph 46A inserted by EC(CGA)R 1992, Sch, Pt 1 para 4(5).

Consolidated accounts of holding company and subsidiaries

47. […][a]

Amendments

a Paragraph 47 deleted by EC(CGA)R 1992, Sch, Pt 1 para 4(6)(b).

48. […][a]

Amendments

a Paragraph 48 deleted by EC(CGA)R 1992, Sch, Pt 1 para 4(6)(b).

49. […][a]

Amendments

a Paragraph 49 deleted by EC(CGA)R 1992, Sch, Pt 1 para 4(6)(b).

50. […][a]

Amendments

a Paragraph 50 deleted by EC(CGA)R 1992, Sch, Pt 1 para 4(6)(b).

51. […][a]

Amendments

a Paragraph 51 deleted by EC(CGA)R 1992, Sch, Pt 1 para 4(6)(b).

52. […][a]

Amendments

a Paragraph 52 deleted by EC(CGA)R 1992, Sch, Pt 1 para 4(6)(b).

Group accounts not prepared as consolidated accounts

53. […][a]

Amendments

a Paragraph 53 deleted by EC(CGA)R 1992, Sch, Pt 1 para 4(6)(b).

Provisions of general application

54. (1) This paragraph applies where a company is a holding company and either—

(a) does not prepare group accounts, or

(b) prepares group accounts which do not deal with one or more of its subsidiaries,

and references in this paragraph to subsidiaries shall be read in a case within clause (b) of this subparagraph as references to such of the subsidiaries of the company concerned as are excluded from the group accounts.

(2) Subject to the following provisions of this paragraph—

(a) the reasons why subsidiaries are not dealt with in group accounts, and

(b) a statement showing any qualifications contained in the reports of the auditors of the subsidiaries on their accounts for their respective financial years ending with or during the financial year of the company, and any note or saving contained in those accounts to call attention to a matter which, apart from the note or saving, would properly have been referred to in such a qualification, insofar as the matter which is the subject of the qualification or note is not covered by the company's own accounts and is material from the point of view of its members, shall be given in a note to the company's accounts.

(3) Subject to the following provisions of this paragraph, the aggregate amount of the total investment of the holding company in the shares of the subsidiaries shall be stated in a note to the company's accounts by way of the equity method of valuation.

(4) Insofar as information required by any of the preceding provisions of this paragraph to be stated in a note to the company's accounts is not obtainable, a statement to that effect shall be given instead in a note to those accounts.

(5) Where in any case within subparagraph (1)(b) of this paragraph the group accounts are consolidated accounts, references in the preceding subparagraphs of this paragraph to the company's accounts shall be read as references to the consolidated accounts.

55. Where a company has subsidiaries whose financial years did not end with that of the company, the following information shall be given in relation to each such subsidiary (whether or not dealt with in any group accounts prepared by the company) by way of a note to the company's accounts or (where group accounts are prepared) to the group accounts, that is to say—

(a) the reasons why the company's directors consider that the subsidiaries' financial years should not end with that of the company, and

(b) the dates on which the subsidiaries' financial years ending last before that of the company respectively ended or the earliest and latest of those dates.

PART VI

SPECIAL PROVISIONS WHERE A COMPANY IS AN INVESTMENT COMPANY

56. (1) Paragraph 22 of this Schedule shall not apply to the amount of any profit or loss arising from a determination of the value of any investments of an investment company on any basis mentioned in paragraph 19 (3) of this Schedule.

(2) Any provisions made by virtue of subparagraph (1) or (2) of paragraph 7 of this Schedule in the case of an investment company in respect of any fixed asset investments need not be charged to the company's profit and loss account if they are either—

(a) charged against any reserve account to which any amount excluded by subparagraph (1) of this paragraph from the requirements of the said paragraph 22 has been credited, or

(b) shown as a separate item in the company's balance sheet under the sub-heading 'other reserves'.

(3) For the purposes of this paragraph as it applies in relation to any company, 'fixed asset investment' means any asset falling to be included under any item shown in the company's balance sheet under the subdivision 'financial assets' under the general item 'fixed assets'.

57. [(1)][a] Any distribution made by an investment company which reduces the amount of its net assets to less than the aggregate of its called-up share capital and undistributable reserves shall be disclosed in a note to the company's accounts.

[(2) In this paragraph 'net assets' means the aggregate of the company's assets less the aggregate of its liabilities, and 'liabilities' includes—

(a) any provision for liabilities within the meaning of paragraph 70 of this Schedule that is made in Companies Act individual accounts, and

(b) any provision that is made in IFRS individual accounts.][b]

Amendments

a Renumbered by EC(IFRSMA)R 2005, reg 5(m)(vii).

b Subparagraph (2) inserted by EC(IFRSMA)R 2005, reg 5(m)(vii).

58. A company shall be treated as an investment company for the purposes of this Part in relation to any financial year of the company if—

(a) during the whole of that year, it was an investment company within the meaning of Part IV of the Act of 1983,

(b) it was not at any time during that year prohibited by section 47 of that Act from making a distribution.

59. […][a]

Amendments

a Paragraph 59 deleted by EC(CGA)R 1992, Sch, Pt 1 para 4(6)(b).

PART VII
INTERPRETATION OF SCHEDULE

Assets: fixed or current

60. For the purposes of this Schedule, assets of a company shall be taken to be fixed assets if they are intended for use on a continuing basis in the company's activities, and any assets not intended for such use shall be taken to be current assets.

Balance sheet date

61. For the purposes of this Schedule, 'balance sheet date', in relation to a balance sheet, means the date as at which the balance sheet was prepared.

Capitalisation

62. References in this Schedule to capitalising any work or costs are references to treating that work or those costs as a fixed asset.

Fellow subsidiary

[63. References in this Schedule to 'fellow subsidiary undertakings' are to undertakings which are subsidiary undertakings of the same parent undertaking but are not parent undertakings or subsidiary undertakings of each other.][a]

Amendments

a Paragraph 63 substituted by EC(CGA)R 1992, Sch, Pt 1 para 5.

[Group undertakings

64. (1) For the purposes of this Schedule, 'group undertaking' in relation to any undertaking, means any undertaking which is—

(a) a parent undertaking or subsidiary undertaking of that undertaking, or

(b) a subsidiary undertaking of any parent undertaking of that undertaking.

(2) For the purposes of this paragraph, 'undertaking' shall have the meaning assigned to it by Regulation 3 of the European Communities (Companies: Group Accounts) Regulations, 1992.][b]

Amendments

a Paragraph 64 substituted by EC(CGA)R 1992, Sch, Pt 1 para 6.

Historical cost accounting rules

65. References in this Schedule to the historical cost accounting rules shall be read in accordance with paragraph 17 of this Schedule.

[Investment property

65A. In this Schedule 'investment property' means land or buildings (or both) held to earn rentals or for capital appreciation (or both).][a]

Amendments

a Paragraph 65A inserted by EC(IFRSMA)R 2005, reg 5(m)(viii).

Listed investments

66. In this Schedule, 'listed investments' means an investment as respects which there has been granted a listing on a recognised stock exchange within the State or on any stock exchange of repute outside the State.

Loans

67. For the purposes of this Schedule, a loan shall be treated as falling due for payment, and an instalment of a loan shall be treated as falling due for payment, on the earliest date on which the lender could require repayment or (as the case may be) payment, if he exercised all options and rights available to him.

Materiality

68. Amounts which in the particular context of any provision of this Schedule are not material may be disregarded for the purposes of that provision.

Provisions

69. (1) References in this Schedule to provisions for depreciation or diminution in value of assets are references to any amount written off by way of providing for depreciation or diminution in value of assets.

(2) Any reference in the profit and loss account formats set out in Part I of this Schedule to the depreciation of, or amounts written off, assets of any description is a reference to any provision for depreciation or diminution in value of assets of that description.

70. References in this Schedule to provisions for liabilities [...][a] are references to any amount retained as reasonably necessary for the purpose of providing for any [liability the nature of which is clearly defined and][b] which is either likely to be incurred, or certain to be incurred but uncertain as to amount or as to the date on which it will arise.

Amendments

a 'or changes' deleted by EC(IFRSMA)R 2005, reg 5(m)(ix)(I).

b Words substituted by EC(IFRSMA)R 2005, reg 5(m)(ix)(II).

Purchase price

71. References in this Schedule (however expressed) to the purchase price of an asset of a company or of any raw materials or consumables used in the production of any such asset shall be read as including references to any consideration (whether in cash or otherwise) given by the company in respect of that asset or in respect of those materials or consumables (as the case may require).

Realised profits

72. Without prejudice to—

(a) the construction of any other expression by reference (where appropriate) to accepted accounting principles or practice, or

(b) any specific provision for the treatment of profits of any description as realised,

it is hereby declared for the avoidance of doubt that references in this Schedule to realised profits, in relation to a company's accounts, are references to such profits of the company as fall to be treated as realised profits for the purposes of those accounts in accordance with principles generally accepted with respect to the determination for accounting purposes of realised profits at the time when those accounts are prepared.

Related companies

[73. For the purposes of this Schedule, 'participating interest' shall have the meaning assigned to it in Regulation 35 of the European Communities (Companies: Group Accounts) Regulations, 1992.][a]

Amendments

a Paragraph 73 substituted by EC(CGA)R 1992, Sch, Pt 1 para 7.

Staff costs

74. In this Schedule—

'social welfare costs' means any contribution by a company to any state social welfare, social security or pension scheme, fund or arrangement, being a fund or arrangement connected with such a scheme, and 'social welfare' means any such scheme fund or arrangement;

'pension costs' include any other contributions by a company for the purposes of any pension scheme established for the purpose of providing pensions for persons employed by the company, any sums set aside for that purpose and any amounts paid by the company in respect of pensions without first being so set aside;

and any amount stated in respect of either of the above items or in respect of the item 'wages and salaries' in a company's profit and loss account shall be determined by reference to payments made or costs incurred in respect of all persons employed by the company during the financial year concerned who are taken into account in determining the relevant annual number for the purposes of paragraph 42(1)(a) of this Schedule.

Turnover

75. For the purposes of this Schedule, 'turnover', in relation to any company, means the amounts derived from the provision of goods and services falling within the company's ordinary activities, after deduction of—

(a) trade discounts,

(b) value-added tax, and

(c) any other taxes based on the amounts so derived.

Wholly-owned Subsidiaries

76. A body corporate shall be deemed for the purposes of this Schedule to be a wholly-owned subsidiary of another if it would be so deemed for the purposes of section 150 of the Principal Act.

[Financial instruments

77. References to 'derivative financial instruments' are deemed to include commodity-based contracts that give either contracting party the right to settle in cash or some other financial instrument except where those contracts—

(a) were entered into and continue to meet the company's expected purchase, sale or usage requirements,

(b) were designed for that purpose at their inception, and

(c) are expected to be settled by delivery of the commodity.][a]

Amendments

a Paragraph 77 inserted by EC(FVA)R 2004, reg 3(iv).

[78. The words and expressions set out in the Table to this paragraph have the same meaning in this Schedule as they have in Council Directive 78/660/EEC of 25 July 1978 (OJ L222, 14/08/1978 p 11), as amended by Council Directive 2001/65/EEC of the European Parliament and of the Council of 27 September 2001 (OJ No. L283, 27.10.01, p 28).][a]

TABLE

available for sale financial asset

business combination

commodity-based contracts

equity instrument

exchange difference

fair value hedge accounting system

financial fixed asset
financial instrument
foreign entity
hedge accounting
hedge accounting system
hedged items
hedging instrument
held to maturity
held for trading purposes
monetary item
receivables
reliable market
trading portfolio

Amendments

a Paragraph 78 inserted by EC(FVA)R 2004, reg 3(iv).

UK legislation

See CA 1985, Sch 4, paras 6–8.

Companies (Amendment) Act 1990

Number 27 of 1990

ARRANGEMENT OF SECTIONS

An Act to Amend the Law Relating to Companies and to Provide for Related Matters. [29th August, 1990]

Be It Enacted By The Oireachtas As Follows:

Notes

The purpose of this Act is to provide a mechanism for the rescue of ailing companies, known colloquially as 'examinership'. It is modelled to a large extent on Chapter XI of the US Bankruptcy Code,[1] with some elements of the English system of administration as found in the Insolvency Act 1986, also being incorporated.[2] Several important changes were made to the examinership procedure by C(A)(No 2)A 1999, Part I. These include raising the standard of proof required for the appointment of an examiner and shortening the period of the examinership itself.

Briefly, a petition is presented to the High Court for the appointment of an officer known as an examiner. The petition will normally be accompanied by a report from an independent accountant expressing an opinion that, subject to the implementation of a scheme of arrangement, the company and the whole or part of its undertaking is capable of survival as a going concern. If the court is satisfied that there is a reasonable prospect of the company being rescued, it will appoint the examiner.

In England an administrator has powers analogous to those of a receiver and manager appointed under a debenture, in that his appointment ousts the directors and he takes over the management of the company. In the case of the examiner, however, his position is analogous to the trustee under Chapter XI of the US Bankruptcy Code, whose primary function is to formulate a rescue package, whilst leaving the directors in control of the management of the company. In Ireland, in appropriate circumstances, the court may direct the transfer to the examiner of all or some of the directors' powers of management for the duration of the protection period. This is unheard of in practice.

The examiner instead concentrates on trying to formulate a scheme of arrangement. In order to do this, he will typically have to find investors to inject new capital and the fund the rescue package or address a cashflow difficulty. Assuming that such a package can be put together, the examiner then convenes meetings of the members and creditors to consider and vote on his proposals. Whilst allowed to vote, the members cannot veto the scheme. This of course reflects the fact that in an insolvency situation the persons with the real beneficial interest in the company are its creditors. After the meetings have been held, the examiner reports the outcome to the court and if the requisite approval has been obtained the court may then approve the scheme with or without modifications. Presuming that the scheme is duly confirmed, it then binds the members and creditors, including those who dissented.

The promulgation of the Act invoked a procedure under Article 25.2 of the Constitution whereby, at the request of the Government and with the prior conent of Seanad Éireann the President may sign a Bill on a date which is earlier than the fifth day after the date on which the Bill shall have been presented to him.[3] The Bill was introduced into and then passed by the Dáil on 28 August 1990, then passed by the Seanad and signed by the President into law on 29 August 1990. The first application for the appointment of an examiner under the Act was acceded to at a special sitting of the High Court on 29 August 1990. The appointment was made to Goodman International and 25 related companies. The content of the Act appears largely to mirror Part IX of the Companies (No. 2) Bill 1987.[4]

1 For a useful summary of the US Bankruptcy Code, including Chapter XI, see Albergotti, *Understanding Bankruptcy in the US* (Harvard University Press, 1992).

2 A helpful analysis of the administration procedure is to be found in Picarda, *The Law Relating to Receivers, Managers and Administrators* (2nd edn, 1990).

3 126 Seanad Debates Column 1128.

4 See Gerard McCormack, Annotated Companies (Amendment) Act 1990.

---

1 Definitions

In this Act, unless the context otherwise required—

['Central Bank' means the Central Bank and Financial Services Authority of Ireland;][a]

'the Companies Acts' means the Principal Act, and every enactment (including this Act) which is to be construed as one with that Act;

'examiner' means an examiner appointed under section 2;

'interested party', in relation to a company to which section 2(1) relates, means—

(a) a creditor of the company,

(b) a member of the company;

'the Minister' means the Minister for Industry and Commerce;

'the Principal Act' means the Companies Act, 1963.

Amendments

a C(A)A 1990, s 1 inserted by the Central Bank and Financial Services Authority Act 2003, Sch 1, part 12, with effect from 1 May 2003.

Definitions

'company': CA 1963, s 2(1); 'member': CA 1963, s 31; interested party: the phrase 'interested party' is stated to include 'creditor'. In other circumstances, 'creditor' includes a contingent or prospective creditor.[1] However, C(A)A 1990, s 3(1)(c) seems to make a distinction between a creditor on the one hand and a contingent or prospective creditor on the other. If this distinction is intended to operate thought the entire of the Act, then a contingent or prospective creditor would not come within the definition of 'interested party'. This in turn would impact upon the entitlement of parties under C(A)A 1990, s 17 to be heard on the application to have the scheme of arrangement sanctioned by the Court; 'examiner': the phrase 'examiner' includes any interim examiner so appointed by the Court[2]; 'the Minister': The reference to the Minister for Industry and Commerce should now be construed as a reference to the Minister for Enterprise, Trade and Employment.

1 CA 1963, ss 215 and 311(8); C(A)A 1990, s 12B(3); *Re Industrial Glazing Systems Ltd* (6 November 2000, unreported) HC, *ex tempore* (Barr J), following *Re Harvest Lane Motor Bodies Ltd* [1969] 1 Ch 457; *Re Deauville Communications Worldwide Ltd* [2002] 2 IR 32.

2 RSC 1986, Ord 75A, r 1(4).

[1A Restriction of this Act

This Act is subject to Chapters I (general provisions) and III (secondary insolvency proceedings) of Council Regulation (EC) No 1346/2000 of 29 May 2000 (OJ L160 of 30.6.2000.) on insolvency proceedings.][a]

Amendments

a C(A)A 1990, s 1A inserted by European Communities (Corporate Insolvency) Regulations 2002 (SI 333/2002) reg 4.

Cross reference

For the view of the Office of the Director of Corporate Enforcement on the duties of Examiners see Decision Notice DN/2002/1, book 7, paragraph 4 *et seq.*

Notes

The Insolvency Regulation: The jurisdiction to open main insolvency proceedings and secondary insolvency proceedings in an EU member state other than Denmark is no longer governed solely by domestic law but is instead regulated by the provisions of Council Regulation (EC) No 1346/2000 of 29 May 2000 on insolvency proceedings ('the EC Insolvency Regulation'). Under Art 3(1) of the EC Insolvency Regulation, main insolvency proceedings (which, in Ireland, include examinership) may only be opened in the member state where the company has its centre of main interests.[1] Under Art 3(2), if the company has an establishment in another member state, secondary insolvency proceedings may be opened there as well, but those secondary proceedings must take the form of a liquidation, rather than an examinership or similar process.

1 See Case C–341/04 *Eurofood IFSC Ltd* [2006] 3 WLR 309.

2 Power of court to appoint examiner

(1) [Subject to subsection (2), where it appears to the court that][a]—

(a) a company is or is likely to be unable to pay its debts, and

[(b) no resolution subsists for the winding-up of the company, and][b]

(c) no order has been made for the winding-up of the company,

it may, on application by petition presented, appoint an examiner to the company for the purpose of examining the state of the company's affairs and performing such duties in relation to the company as may be imposed by or under this Act.

[(2) The court shall not make an order under this section unless it is satisfied that there is a reasonable prospect of the survival of the company and the whole or any part of its undertaking as a going concern.][c]

(3) For the purposes of this section, a company is unable to pay its debts if—

(a) it is unable to pay its debts as they fall due,

(b) the value of its assets is less than the amount of its liabilities, taking into account its contingent and prospective liabilities, or

(c) section 214 (a) or (b) of the Principal Act applies to the company.

(4) In deciding whether to make an order under this section the court may also have regard to whether the company has sought from its creditors significant extensions of time for the payment of its debts, from which it could reasonably be inferred that the company was likely to be unable to pay its debts.

[(5) The court shall not make an order under this section unless –

(a) the court is satisfied that the company has no obligations in relation to a bank asset that has been transferred to the National Asset Management Agency or a NAMA group entity, or

(b) if the company has any such obligation –

(i) if a copy of the petition has been served on that Agency, and

(ii) the court has heard that Agency in relation to the making of the order.

(6) In subsection (5) 'bank asset' and 'NAMA group entity' have the same respective meanings as in the National Asset Management Agency Act 2009.][d]

Amendments

a C(A)A 1990, s 2(1) amended by C(A) (No 2) 1999, s 5(a).

b C(A)A 1990, s 2(1)(b) substituted by CA 1990, s 181.

c C(A)A 1990, s 2(2) substituted by C(A) (No 2) 1999, s 5(b).

d C(A)A 1990, s 2(5) and s 2(6) inserted by NAMA Act 2009, s 234.

Definitions

'company': CA 1963, s 2(1); 'the court': CA 1963, s 2(1); 'examiner': C(A)A 1990, s 1: the phrase 'examiner' includes any interim examiner so appointed by the Court[1]; 'Principal Act': C(A)A 1990, s 1.

1 Rules of the Superior Courts 1986, Ord 75A, r 1(4).

Notes

Procedure for presentation of petition: See notes to C(A)A 1990, s 3.

Presenting a second petition: See the notes to C(A)A 1990, s 3.

Purpose for which an examiner may be appointed: Whilst C(A)A 1990, s 2(1) refers in rather general terms to the court appointing an examiner 'to examine the state of the company's affairs and to perform such duties as may be imposed by or under this Act', the real purpose of the appointment can be discerned in s 2(2), which indicates that the whole purpose of the examinership is to facilitate the survival of the company and the whole or part of its undertaking as a going concern.[1] In this regard, it has been held that the examinership process is not designed to immunise the principals or shareholders of a company from the consequences of the company getting into financial difficulties, but is instead designed to enable, in an appropriate case, an enterprise to continue in existence for the benefit of the economy as a whole and to enable as many as possible of the jobs which may be at stake to be maintained for the benefit of the community.[2] Survival must be measured over a reasonable timeframe such as there would be some point from the perspective of society as a whole in facilitating that survival even at the cost of some creditors having to forgo their strict legal entitlements.[3]

Significantly, it has been held that, unlike the administration procedure in the UK, examinership cannot be used for the purpose of a more orderly realisation of the company's assets than might be achieved in a liquidation or receivership.[4] It has also been held that a company which does no more than hold shares in other companies does not itself constitute a 'going concern' and accordingly does not qualify for the appointment of an examiner.[5]

1 *Re Gallium Ltd* [2009] 2 ILRM 11; *Re Vantive Holdings (No 1)* (11 August 2009, unreported) SC (Murray J); *Re Vantive Holdings (No 2)* [2009] IEHC 409. In *Re Atlantic Magnetics Ltd* [1993] 2 IR 570, Finlay CJ seemed to suggest (*obiter dicta*) that the appointment of an examiner might be possible for other purposes. These observations were made in the context of the wording of C(A)A 1990, s 2(2) prior to the amendments effected by C(A)(No 2)A 1999 and would no longer appear to have any application.

2 *Re Traffic Group Ltd* [2008] 1 IR 253; *Re Gallium Ltd* [2009] 2 ILRM 11; *Re Vantive Holdings (No 1)* (11 August 2009, unreported) SC (Murray J); *Re Missford Ltd* (20 January 2010, unreported) HC (Kelly J). As against this, in some circumstances jobs may still be saved in a receivership or liquidation and this is something that the court can legitimately take into account: *Re Laragan Developments Ltd* (31 July 2009, unreported) HC (Clarke J).

3 *Re Vantive Holdings (No 2)* [2009] IEHC 409.

4 *Re Vantive Holdings (No 1)* (11 August 2009, unreported) SC (Murray J).

5 *Re Tuskar Resources plc* [2001] 1 IR 668.

Standard of proof required: In its original form C(A)A 1990, s 2(2) allowed for the appointment of an examiner where the court 'considered' that such an order might facilitate the survival of the company and the whole or part of its undertaking as a going concern. This was interpreted by the courts as imposing a very low standard of proof, namely that the petitioner establish 'some prospect of survival' or some 'identifiable possibility of survival.'[1] However, the newly-worded subsection as substituted by C(A)(No 2)A 1999 has introduced significant changes which involve the imposition of a more exacting evidential standard[2]. It is negatively worded and this has been held to take away much of the court's discretion in the matter.[3] It imposes a jurisdictional threshold which must be overcome before the court can have any entitlement to even consider appointing an examiner, since it stipulates that the court 'shall not' appoint an examiner unless it is 'satisfied' that there is a 'reasonable prospect' of survival.[4] It should be noted though, that in order to establish a reasonable prospect of survival, the petitioner does not have to establish a probability of survival.[5]

The court must be 'satisfied' as to the existence of a reasonable prospect of survival based on the evidence before it, which is in the first instance the evidence of the petitioner[6] In this regard, a critical piece of evidence is the Report of the Independent Accountant under s 3 which must accompany the petition.[7] If the Report of the Independent Accountant is to be of any real assistance it should do more than just recite in a formulaic manner the accountant's conclusions in relation to each of the items listed in C(A)A 1990, s 3(3B) and should, in particular, explain in a reasoned manner why the Independent Accountant is of the view that the company and the whole or part of its undertaking has a reasonable prospect of survival as a going concern.[8] In this regard it is also to be noted that the mere fact that the company has not been actively trading in the recent past because of financial constraints, does not mean that with an appropriately structured scheme of arrangement, it cannot survive as a going concern.[9]

In determining whether or not that evidential burden has been met the court may take into consideration the wishes of the creditors. In particular, if there is no likelihood of at least one class of 'impaired' creditors voting in favour of a scheme of arrangement, the court should dismiss the petition.[10] This is because the court cannot confirm the scheme of arrangement unless it is supported by at least one class of 'impaired' creditors.[11]

Even if the court is satisfied that the petitioner has established a reasonable prospect of survival, the court still has a discretion whether or not to appoint an examiner,[12] and may, for example, exercise its discretion against making such an appointment where it is suspected that there have been serious irregularities in relation to the management of the company and those suspected irregularities could not be satisfactorily and fully investigated within the protection period.[13]

1 *Re Atlantic Magnetics Ltd* [1993] 2 IR 561; *Re Holidair Ltd* [1994] 1 IR 416; *Re Butlers Engineering Ltd* (1 March 1996, unreported) HC (Keane J); *Re Cavan Crystal Glass Ltd* [1998] 3 IR 570.

2 As McCracken J noted in *Re Circle Network (Europe) Ltd* (15 February 2001, unreported) HC and in *Re Tuskar Resources plc* [2001] 1 IR 668 and as the Supreme Court has noted in *Re Gallium Ltd* [2009] 2 ILRM 11 and *Re Vantive Holdings (No 1)* (11 August 2009, unreported) SC (Murray J), this is the standard of proof that had been articulated by Lardner J in the High Court but which had been rejected by the Supreme Court in *Re Atlantic Magnetics Ltd* [1993] 2 IR 561. See also *Re Fergus Haynes (Developments) Ltd* [2008] IEHC 327; *Re Vantive Holdings (No 2)* [2009] IEHC 409.

3 *Re Circle Network (Europe) Ltd* (15 February 2001, unreported) HC (McCracken J) at p 13; *Re Tuskar Resources plc* [2001] 1 IR 668; *Re Gallium Ltd* [2009] 2 ILRM 11; *Re Vantive Holdings (No 1)* (unreported, 11 August 2009) SC (Murray J); *Re Vantive Holdings (No 2)* [2009] IEHC 409.

4 *Re Tuskar Resources plc* [2001] 1 IR 668; *Re Fergus Haynes (Developments) Ltd* [2008] IEHC 327; *Re Gallium Ltd* [2009] 2 ILRM 11; *Re Vantive Holdings (No 1)* (unreported, 11 August 2009) SC (Murray J).

5 *Re Gallium Ltd* [2009] 2 ILRM 11; *Re Vantive Holdings (No 1)* (unreported, 11 August 2009) SC (Murray J). For guidance as to the degree of probability involved, see *Re Harris Simons Construction Ltd* [1989] BCLC 202.

6 *Re Tuskar Resources plc* [2001] 1 IR 668; *Re Gallium Ltd* [2009] 2 ILRM 11; *Re Vantive Holdings (No 1)* (unreported, 11 August 2009) SC (Murray J); *Re Vantive Holdings (No 2)* [2009] IEHC 409.

7 *Re Fergus Haynes (Developments) Ltd* [2008] IEHC 327; *Re Gallium Ltd* [2009] 2 ILRM 11; *Re Vantive Holdings (No 1)* (unreported, 11 August 2009) SC (Murray J); *Re Vantive Holdings (No 2)* [2009] IEHC 409.

8 *Re Vantive Holdings (No 1)* (unreported, 11 August 2009) SC (Murray J). These views were also expressed by members of the Supreme Court during legal argument in *Re Gallium Ltd* [2009] 2 ILRM 11.

9 *Re Fergus Haynes (Developments) Ltd* [2008] IEHC 327.

10 *Re Land and Property Trust Co plc* [1991] BCLC 849; *Re Arrows plc (No 3)* [1992] BCLC 555.

11 C(A)A 1990, s 24(4)(a). As regards the definition of 'impairment' see C(A)A 1990, s 22(5) and (6).

12 *Re Gallium Ltd* [2009] 2 ILRM 11; *Re Vantive Holdings (No 1)* (unreported, 11 August 2009) SC (Murray J); *Re Missford Ltd* (20 January 2010, unreported) HC (Kelly J).

13 *Re Missford Ltd* (20 January 2010, unreported) HC (Kelly J).

Absence of winding up: Although a petition cannot be presented for the appointment of an examiner after the company has actually gone into liquidation, C(A)A 1990, s 2(1) makes it quite clear that the petition may be presented in circumstances where there is an outstanding winding up petition against the company. Indeed, even the appointment of a provisional liquidator will not operate as a bar to the making of an order under C(A)A 1990, s 2.[1]

1 See C(A)A 1990, s 6 which spells out the effect of the appointment of an examiner on any existing provisional liquidator or receiver.

UK legislation

See IA 1986, s 8, now contained in Schedule B1 of IA 1986, para 11.

---

3 Petition for protection of the court

(1) Subject to subsection (2), a petition under section 2 may be presented by—

(a) the company, or

(b) the directors of the company, or

(c) a creditor, or contingent or prospective creditor (including an employee), of the company, or

(d) members of the company holding at the date of the presentation of a petition under that section not less than one-tenth of such of the paid-up capital of the company as carries at that date the right of voting at general meetings of the company,

or by all or any of those parties, together or separately.

(2) (a) Where the company referred to in section 2 is an insurer, a petition under that section may be presented only by the Minister, and subsection (1) of this section shall not apply to the company.

[(b) Where the company referred to in section 2 is—

(i) the holder of a licence under section 9 of the Central Bank Act, 1971,

(ii) a company which a building society has converted itself into under Part XI of the Building Societies Act, 1989,

(iii) a company which one or more trustee savings banks have been reorganised into pursuant to an order under section 57 of the Trustee Savings Banks Act, 1989,

a petition under section 2 may be presented only by the Central Bank, and subsection (1) of this section shall not apply to the company.][a]

[(c) Where the company referred to in section 2 is a company referred to in the Second Schedule to the Companies (Amendment) (No. 2) Act, 1999, (not being a company referred to in paragraph 18, 19 or 20 of that Schedule or to which paragraph (b) applies) the following provisions shall apply—

(i) a petition under section 2 may be presented by—

(I) any of the persons referred to in paragraph (a), (b), (c) or (d) of subsection (1) of this section (including by one or more of such persons acting together),

(II) the Central Bank, or

(III) one or more of such persons and the Central Bank acting together,

(ii) if the Central Bank does not present such a petition—

(I) the petitioner shall, before he presents the petition at the office of the court, cause to be received by the Central Bank a notice in writing of his intention to present the petition, and shall serve a copy of the petition on the Central Bank as soon as may be after the presentation of it at the said office,

(II) the Central Bank shall be entitled to appear and be heard at any hearing relating to the petition.][a]

(3) A petition presented under section 2 shall—

(a) nominate a person to be appointed as examiner, and

[...][b]

[(3A) In addition to the matters specified in subsection (4), a petition presented under section 2 shall be accompanied by a report in relation to the company prepared by a person (in this Act referred to as 'the independent accountant') who is either the auditor of the company or a person who is qualified to be appointed as an examiner of the company.

(3B) The report of the independent accountant shall comprise the following:

(a) the names and permanent addresses of the officers of the company and, in so far as the independent accountant can establish, any person in accordance with whose directions or instructions the directors of the company are accustomed to act,

(b) the names of any other bodies corporate of which the directors of the company are also directors,

(c) a statement as to the affairs of the company, showing in so far as it is reasonably possible to do so, particulars of the company's assets and liabilities (including contingent and prospective liabilities) as at the latest practicable date, the names and addresses of its creditors, the securities held by them respectively and the dates when the securities were respectively given,

(d) whether in the opinion of the independent accountant any deficiency between the assets and liabilities of the company has been satisfactorily accounted for or, if not, whether there is evidence of a substantial disappearance of property that is not adequately accounted for,

(e) his opinion as to whether the company, and the whole or any part of its undertaking, would have a reasonable prospect of survival as a going concern and a statement of the conditions which he considers are essential to ensure such survival, whether as regards the internal management and controls of the company or otherwise,

(f) his opinion as to whether the formulation, acceptance and confirmation of proposals for a compromise or scheme of arrangement would offer a reasonable prospect of the survival of the company, and the whole or any part of its undertaking, as a going concern,

(g) his opinion as to whether an attempt to continue the whole or any part of the undertaking would be likely to be more advantageous to the members as a whole and the creditors as a whole than a winding-up of the company,

(h) recommendations as to the course he thinks should be taken in relation to the company including, if warranted, draft proposals for a compromise or scheme of arrangement,

(i) his opinion as to whether the facts disclosed would warrant further inquiries with a view to proceedings under section 297 or 297A of the Principal Act,

(j) details of the extent of the funding required to enable the company to continue trading during the period of protection and the sources of that funding,

(k) his recommendations as to which liabilities incurred before the presentation of the petition should be paid,

(l) his opinion as to whether the work of the examiner would be assisted by a direction of the court in relation to the role or membership of any creditor's committee referred to in section 21, and

(m) such other matters as he thinks relevant.][c]

(4) A petition presented under section 2, shall be accompanied—

(a) by a consent signed by the person nominated to be examiner, and

(b) if proposals for a compromise or scheme of arrangement in relation to the company's affairs have been prepared for submission to interested parties for their approval, by a copy of the proposals.

(5) The court shall not give a hearing to a petition under section 2 presented by a contingent or prospective creditor until such security for costs has been given as the court thinks reasonable [...][d]

(6) The court shall not give a hearing to a petition under section 2 if a receiver stands appointed to the company the subject of the petition and such receiver has stood so appointed for a continuous period of at least [3 days][e] prior the presentation of the petition.

(7) On hearing a petition under this section, the court may dismiss it, or adjourn the hearing conditionally or unconditionally, or make any interim order, or any other order it thinks fit.

(8) Without prejudice to the generality of subsection (7), an interim order under that subsection may restrict the exercise of any powers of the directors or of the company (whether by reference to the consent of the court or otherwise).

(9) (a) Where it appears to the court that the total liabilities of the company (taking into account its contingent and prospective liabilities) do not exceed [€317,434.52][f] the court may, after making such interim or other orders as it thinks fit, order that the matter be remitted to the judge of the Circuit Court in whose circuit the company has its registered office or principal place of business.

(b) Where an order is made by the court under this subsection the Circuit Court shall have full jurisdiction to exercise all the powers of the court conferred by this Act in relation to the company and every reference to the court in this Act shall be construed accordingly.

(c) Where, in any proceedings under this Act which have been remitted to the Circuit Court by virtue of this subsection, it appears to the Circuit Court that the total liabilities of the company exceed [€317,434.52][f], it shall make, after making such interim orders as it thinks fit, an order transferring the matter to the court.

Amendments

a C(A)A 1990, s 3(2)(b) and (c) substituted by C(A)(No 2)A 1999, s 6. Subsection 2(b) was further substituted with effect from 28 February 2002 by ACC Bank Act 2001, s 11.

b C(A)A 1990, s 3(3)(b) and (c) repealed by C(A)(No 2)A 1999, s 30.

c C(A)A 1990, s 3(3A) and (3B) inserted by C(A)(No 2)A 1999, s 7.

d C(A)A 1990, s 3(5) amended by C(A)(No 2)A 1999, s 8.

e Words '3 days' substituted for '14 days' by CA 1990, s 180.

f £250,000 converted to €317,434.52 by Council Regulations (EC) No 1103/97, No 974/98 and No 2866/98 and the Economic and Monetary Union Act 1998, s 6.

Definitions

'Central Bank'[1] C(A)A 1990, s 1; 'company': CA 1963, s 2(1); 'court': CA 1963, s 2(1); 'director': CA 1963, s 2(1); 'examiner': C(A)A 1990, s 1; the phrase 'examiner' includes any interim examiner so appointed by the Court[2]; 'Minister': C(A)A 1990, s 1.

1 See Central Bank and Financial Services Authority of Ireland Act 2003, s 33C(1) and (2) whereby the Financial Regulator is entitled to perform the functions of the Central Bank under C(A)A 1990, ss 3, 3C, 18, 23, 24 and 27.

2 RSC, Ord 75A, r 1(4).

Notes

***Locus standi* to petition**: A petition for the appointment of an examiner may be presented by different categories of person.

The company: A petition may be presented by the company itself (ie pursuant to a decision of the members taken in general meeting).[1] Since the section is silent on the matter, an ordinary resolution would seem to suffice. Evidence of the passing of the resolution will be required before the court makes its order eg by exhibiting a copy of the resolution or the minutes of the relevant meeting to the verifying affidavit.[2]

1 C(A)A 1990, s 3(1)(a).

2 *Re Don Bluth (Entertainment) Ltd (No 1)* (27 August 1992, unreported) HC (Murphy J); *Re Aston Colour Print Ltd* [2005] 3 IR 609.

Members: Individual members of the company, holding between them not less than 10% of the paid up capital of the company carrying voting rights, are also given standing to present the petition in their own names.[1] This may be particularly useful in circumstances where, for ulterior motives, a majority of the members do not want to see the company saved or where certain members cannot be contacted at short notice for the purpose of holding a formal general meeting of the company.

1 C(A)A 1990, s 3(1)(d).

The directors: The plain meaning of subsection (1)(b) is that the directors must act collectively in order to possess *locus standi*. Whilst individual directors cannot unilaterally petition to have an examiner appointed,[1] the board of directors, acting by a majority, is authorised to present such a petition.[2] In this regard the petition is treated as having been presented by all the directors if presented by one or more of their number on foot of a properly passed board resolution.[3] The fact that some of the directors were absent from the meeting will not affect the validity of the petition provided that the board meeting was itself validly convened.[4] Evidence of the passing of the resolution should be contained in the affidavit verifying the petition.[5]

1 *Re Instrumentation Electrical Services Ltd* [1988] BCLC 550, (1988) 4 BCC 301.

2 C(A)A 1990, s 3(1)(b).

3 *Re Don Bluth Entertainment Ltd (No 1)* (27 August 1992, unreported) HC (Murphy J); *Re Don Bluth Entertainment Ltd (No 2)* [1994] 3 IR 141.

4 *Re Equiticorp International plc* [1989] BCLC 597.

5 *Re Don Bluth Entertainment Ltd (No 1)* (27 August 1992, unreported) HC (Murphy J); *Re Aston Colour Print Ltd* [2005] 3 IR 609.

Creditors: Whilst creditors of the company are entitled to petition for the appointment of an examiner,[1] the court will not hear the petition where the petitioner is a contingent or prospective creditor until such security for costs has been given as the court thinks reasonable.[2] In practice, petitions by creditors are very rare since the creditors will not normally have sufficient knowledge of the company's financial affairs to ascertain whether or not there is some prospect of its survival, unless the debts were to sister companies of a group of companies. The persons best placed to make this assessment are those in control of the company, and for this reason most petitions are in fact in presented either in the name of the board or in the name of the company itself.

1 C(A)A 1990, s 3(1)(c).

2 C(A)A 1990, s 3(5).

The Minister: In the case of insurance companies, the petition may be presented only by the Minister and not by the company or its directors or by any of the members or creditors.[1]

1 C(A)A 1990, s 3(2)(a).

The Central Bank: The only person entitled to petition in respect of a bank or building society is the Central Bank and Financial Services Authority of Ireland ('the Central Bank').[1] However, in the case of a stock exchange company, member firms of the stock exchange and their associated or related undertakings, investment business firms, investment companies, UCITS, investment limited partnerships and certain other entities regulated by the Irish Financial Services Regulatory Authority (known as the Financial Regulator) and listed in C(A)(No 2)A 1999, Sch 2, the petition may be presented not only by the Central Bank or the Irish Financial Services Regulatory Authority (known as the Financial Regulator)[2] but also by the company itself or by its directors, but also by creditors and members holding not less than 10% of the paid up capital with voting rights.[3] However, if the petitioner is someone other than the Central Bank, notice of intention to present the petition must be served on the Central Bank, followed by service of the petition itself, once presented.[4] Furthermore the Central Bank has a right of audience at the hearing of the petition.[5] It is submitted that the courts should not invalidate the presentation of a petition merely because the Central Bank has not been notified beforehand. However, if the Central Bank has not been served with the petition, the hearing should, at the very least, be adjourned so as to allow service to be effected.[6]

1 C(A)A 1990, s 3(2)(b).

2 See Central Bank and Financial Services Authority of Ireland Act 2003, s 33C(1) and (2) whereby the Financial Regulator is entitled to perform the functions of the Central Bank under C(A)A 1990, ss 3, 3C, 18, 23, 24 and 27. C(A)(No2)A 1999, Sch 2, para 7 refers to any company 'that is engaged in the business of accepting deposits or other repayable funds or granting credits for its own account'. While the Oireachtas obviously intended that para 7 would tie in with the definitions of banking business contained in the Central Bank Acts, this is not the effect. The essence of banking business is the acceptance of repayable funds *from the public* and (not as stated in para 7, which uses 'or') the granting of credits on its own account. The failure to mention the public nature of the enterprise together with the use of 'or' instead of 'and' means that on a literal interpretation, most businesses would fall under para 7. This clearly cannot have been the intention of the Oireachtas.

3 C(A)A 1990, s 3(2)(c)(i).

4 C(A)A 1990, s 3(2)(c)(ii)(I).

5 C(A)A 1990, s 3(2)(c)(ii)(II).

6 C(A)A 1990, s 3(2)(c).

Amending status of petitioner: If a person has presented a petition in one capacity which gives rise to a flaw (eg he is only one of a number of directors and has not obtained the authority of a formal board resolution) but he would have been entitled to present the petition in some other capacity (eg as creditor) the court may allow him to amend the petition to alter the capacity in which he is petitioning.[1]

1 *Re Cavan Crystal Glass Ltd* [1998] 3 IR 570.

The petition: The application for the appointment of an examiner is made by way of petition.[1] The petition must be verified by an affidavit of the applicant and the application itself will be heard solely on affidavit unless the court otherwise orders.[2] The person proposed to be appointed as examiner must be named in the petition,[3] and must be accompanied by a consent from that person to so act.[4] In the unlikely event that a scheme of arrangement has already been drafted, this too should be appended to the petition.[5] Furthermore, there is a significant obligation on the petitioner to ensure that the financial state of the company is presented to the court in as accurate a way as is practically possible in all the circumstances.[6] Nevertheless, where the statement of the company's financial position in the petition is relatively accurate, any falling off from absolute correctness will not be fatal to the application.[7]

1. C(A)A 1990, s 2(1).
2. RSC, Ord 75A, r 3 and r 4.
3. C(A)A 1990, s 3(3)(a).
4. C(A)A 1990, s 3(4)(a).
5. C(A)A 1990, s 3(4)(b).
6. *Re Traffic Group Ltd* [2008] 2 ILRM 1.
7. *Re Traffic Group Ltd* [2008] 2 ILRM 1.

Independent accountant's report: A new feature introduced by C(A)(No 2)A 1999, by way of the addition to the pre-existing obligation to present the court with an accurate picture of the company's financial position, is the requirement that the petition be accompanied by a report from an independent accountant who is either the company's auditor or someone qualified to be appointed as an examiner of the company.[1] The court has rejected any suggestion that the person who has prepared the independent accountant's report is then precluded from accepting appointment as the examiner.[2] In practice, however, the person nominated as examiner tends to be someone other than the independent accountant.[3] The report is designed to assist the court in determining whether or not the company has a reasonable prospect of survival. It must deal with various matters including the following:[4] it should identify the creditors and should detail any security held by them; it should contain a statement of affairs and should explain how the company's trading is to be funded during the protection period; it should indicate whether there is any evidence of fraudulent or reckless trading[5] and should express a view as to whether the company and the whole or part of its undertaking are capable of survival as a going concern and, if so, whether this would be facilitated by the implementation of a scheme of arrangement. In this regard, the independent accountant is only required to express his opinion as to the prospects of the company being rescued and the conditions which he considers essential for that to happen; he does not have to set out in detail the evidence which led him to that opinion.[6]

Importantly, the report should also identify any pre-petition liabilities that ought to be paid. Apart from these, the only other pre-petition liabilities that can be discharged during the protection period are those sanctioned by the court on the application of the examiner or an interested as being necessary for the continued survival of the company.[7]

In exceptional circumstances outside the control of the petitioner, the court may entertain a petition on a preliminary basis and grant interim protection for up to 10 days pending the preparation of an independent accountant's report.[8] The fact that the company has gone into receivership will not of itself constitute an 'exceptional circumstance'.[9] If the petitioner is a creditor or member, the directors must co-operate in the preparation of the independent accountant's report and may be compelled to do so by order of the court.[10] A failure on the part of the petitioner to submit the independent accountant's report within the period of up to 10 days allowed by the court will result in the protection of the court being lifted albeit without prejudice to any entitlement to re-petition.[11] Furthermore, no liabilities incurred during the period between the granting of protection and the submission of the independent accountant's report can be certified as examinership expenses.[12]

The independent accountant is obliged to furnish a copy of his report to the company and, on written application, to any interested party.[13] However, application may be made to the court for an order directing that portions of the report be withheld from the interested person(s), especially if disclosure might prejudice the survival of the company.[14] The Central Bank must also be provided with a copy where the company is one to which C(A)A 1990, s 3(2)(c) relates and the petitioner is someone other than the Central Bank itself.[15]

1 C(A)A 1990, s 3(3A).
2 *Re Tuskar Resources plc* [2001] 1 IR 668.
3 See the comments of Costello J in *Re Wogans (Drogheda) Ltd* (9 February 1993, unreported) HC, as to the need for impartiality on the part of the examiner. As against this, in *Re Tuskar Resources plc* [2001] 1 IR 668 McCracken J acknowledged the possible duplication of work and expense by appointing as examiner someone other than the independent accountant who, after all, will have already carried out a preliminary examination of the company's affairs.
4 These matters are identified in C(A)A 1990, s 3(3B).
5 If the Report discloses irregularities, the court must hold a hearing to consider the evidence: C(A)A 1990, s 13A.
6 *Re Tuskar Resources plc* [2001] 1 IR 668.
7 C(A)A 1990, s 5A.
8 C(A)A 1990, s 3A(1) and (2). If the tenth day expires on a Saturday, Sunday or public holiday, the protection will be deemed to continue until the next working day.
9 C(A)A 1990, s 3A(3).
10 C(A)A 1990, s 3A(4) and (5).
11 C(A)A 1990, s 3A(7).
12 C(A)A 1990, s 3A(8). In relation to the certification of liabilities during the examinership period and the priority attaching to examinership expenses generally see C(A)A 1990, ss 10 and 29 and the notes thereto.
13 C(A)A 1990, s 3C(1).
14 C(A)A 1990, s 3C(2) and (3).
15 C(A)A 1990, s 3C(4).

Duty of candour: When presenting a petition for the appointment of an examiner the petitioner and all those associated with the petition (including the independent accountant and proposed examiner) must disclose all material information and must exercise utmost good faith.[1] Any failure to do so may result in the petition being dismissed as an abuse of the process of the court.[2] Furthermore, if the proposed examiner has previously been employed by the company, that fact should be divulged to the court since an examiner must be impartial between the company's shareholders and its creditors and the court will therefore be very slow to appoint as examiner anyone previously associated with the company.[3]

1 C(A)A 1990, s 4A.
2 C(A)A 1990, s 4A. This section puts on a statutory footing earlier decisions of the court in cases such as *Re Selukwe Ltd* (20 December 1991, unreported) HC (Costello J); *Re Wogans (Drogheda) Ltd (No 2)* (7 May 1992, unreported) HC (Costello J); *Re Wogans (Drogheda) Ltd (No 3)* (9 February 1993, unreported) HC (Costello J); *Re Tuskar Resources plc* [2001] 1 IR 668. See also *Re Traffic Group Ltd* [2008] 1 IR 253; *Cornhill Insurance plc v Cornhill Financial Services Ltd* [1993] BCLC 914.
3 *Re Wogans (Drogheda) Ltd (No 3)* (9 February 1993, unreported) HC (Costello J).

Effect of pre-existing receivership: Once a receiver has been in place for at least three days prior to the presentation of the petition, the court will be precluded from giving a hearing to the petition.[1]

1 C(A)A 1990, s 3(6). As to the effect of the appointment of an examiner on a receiver who has been appointed for less than 3 days pre-petition, see C(A)A 1990, s 6.

***Ex parte* application to court**: The petition is presented in the Central Office of the High Court and is allocated to one of the judges assigned for the hearing of such matters.[1] On the day that the petition is presented, application must be made *ex parte* to the High Court for directions as to the proceedings to be taken in relation thereto, and in particular in relation to matters such as service and advertisement of the petition and the fixing of the date for the hearing of the application.[2] In practice, the court will normally direct that the petition be served on the Revenue Commissioners and on the four or five creditors with the largest claims and that it be advertised in *Iris Oifigiúil* as well as in at least two national daily newspapers. The importance of this *ex parte* application for directions as to advertisement and service, etc is now underscored by the statutory requirement that no order be made appointing an examiner or dismissing a petition without first affording the creditors of the company an opportunity to be heard.[3] If a provisional liquidator already stands appointed, the court may make such order as it thinks fit including an order that the provisional liquidator be appointed as interim examiner or directing that the provisional liquidator cease to act.[4] It may also direct the provisional liquidator to deliver up to any interim examiner all books and records in his possession relating to the property or undertaking of the company and to furnish a full account of his dealings as provisional liquidator.[5]

1 RSC, Ord 75A, r 2. If one of the assigned judges is unavailable, it may be dealt with by some other High Court judge.

2 RSC, Ord 75A, rr 4 and 5.

3 C(A)A 1990, s 3B as inserted by C(A)(No 2)A 1999, s 10.

4 C(A)A 1990, s 6(2)(a), (b) and (c).

5 C(A)A 1990, s 6(2)(d) and (e).

Appointment of interim examiner: At the hearing of the *ex parte* application, the court may make such interim order as it thinks fit including an order appointing an interim examiner.[1] If an interim examiner is appointed, he is deemed to have the same powers and duties in relation to the company and in relation to any related company to which he may also be appointed, as if he were an examiner appointed at the hearing of the petition itself.[2] Previously, an interim examiner would typically be appointed in cases of urgency, as where the company needs to raise finance to purchase essential supplies or to pay wages, and the bank is only willing to lend monies on foot of a certificate pursuant to C(A)A 1990, s 10. In practice, however, with the shortening of the initial protection period to 70 days, the appointment of an interim examiner is being made in almost every case so as to facilitate his examination of the company's affairs and his search for investors as quickly as possible.

The power to make an interim order, including restricting the directors' powers is predicated on the petition being heard, albeit on an interim *ex parte* basis. The power to place the company under the protection of the court is triggered by the presentation of the petition to the court. The creditors must be heard before a final pronouncement on the petition is made but the court has authority to make interim orders notwithstanding the absence of the creditors.

1 C(A)A 1990, s 3(7) and Ord 75A, 55(2).

2 RSC, O rd75A, r 5(2). As regards the appointment of an examiner to a related company, see C(A)A 1990, s 4.

Hearing of petition: On the hearing of the petition, at which the creditors must have an opportunity to be heard,[1] the court may appoint an examiner if it is satisfied that the petitioner has discharged the evidential burden placed on him for the making of such an order.[2] It may also make such further or other orders as it thinks fit,[3] including an order transferring the case to the Circuit Court if the liabilities of the company are less than €317,434.52.[4] Furthermore, if a provisional liquidator already stands appointed, the court may make such order as it thinks fit including an order that the provisional liquidator or someone else be appointed as examiner or directing that the provisional liquidator cease to act.[5] It may also direct the provisional liquidator to deliver up to the examiner any books and records in his possession relating to the property or undertaking of the company and to furnish a full account of his dealings as provisional liquidator.[6]

If an interim examiner has been appointed and upon the final hearing of the petition, no examiner is appointed to the company, the interim examiner must prepare a written report on the

Company to the Court in which he must also give an account of all liabilities certified by him under C(A)A 1990, s 10.[7]

1 C(A)A 1990, s 3B.
2 C(A)A 1990, s 3(7) and Ord 75A, r 5(4). As regards the standard of proof required, see the notes to C(A)A 1990, s 2.
3 C(A)A 1990, s 3(7) and Ord 75A, r 5(4). As regards the standard of proof required, see the notes to C(A)A 1990, s 2.
4 C(A)A 1990, s 3(9). Given the low monetary threshold involved, the transfer of cases to the Circuit Court does not happen in practice.
5 C(A)A 1990, s 6(2)(a), (b) and (c).
6 C(A)A 1990, s 6(2)(d) and (e).
7 RSC, Ord 75A, r 7.

Presenting a second petition: The provisions of C(A)A 1990 do not preclude the presentation of a second petition for the appointment of an examiner. However, a second petition may only be presented in exceptional or special circumstances and will be dismissed as an abuse of the process of the court if the 'new' material being relied on by the petitioner is material which was available or which could reasonably have been obtained for the first petition.[1]

1 *Re Vantive Holdings (No 2)* (14 October 2009, unreported) SC (Murray CJ & Denham J).

UK legislation

See IA 1986, s 9, now contained in Schedule B1 of IA 1986, paras 9 and 12.

[3A Interim protection pending report

(1) If a petition presented under section 2 shows, and the court is satisfied—

(a) that, by reason of exceptional circumstances outside the control of the petitioner, the report of the independent accountant is not available in time to accompany the petition, and

(b) that the petitioner could not reasonably have anticipated the circumstances referred to in paragraph (a), and, accordingly, the court is unable to consider the making of an order under that section, the court may make an order under this section placing the company concerned under the protection of the court for such period as the court thinks appropriate in order to allow for the submission of the independent accountant's report.

(2) That period shall be a period that expires not later than the 10th day after the date of making of the order concerned or, if the 10th day after that date would fall on a Saturday, Sunday or public holiday, the first following day that is not a Saturday, Sunday or public holiday.

(3) For the avoidance of doubt, the fact that a receiver stands appointed to the whole or any part of the property or undertaking of the company at the time of the presentation of a petition under section 2 in relation to the company shall not, in itself, constitute, for the purposes of subsection (1), exceptional circumstances outside the control of the petitioner.

(4) If the petition concerned has been presented by any of the persons referred to in paragraph (c) or (d) of section 3(1) and an order under subsection (1) is made in relation to the company concerned, the directors of the company shall cooperate in the preparation of the report of the independent accountant, particularly in relation to the matters specified in paragraphs (a), (b) and (c) of section 3(3B).

(5) If the directors of the company concerned fail to comply with subsection (4), the person who has presented the petition concerned or the independent accountant may apply to the court for an order requiring the directors to do specified things by way of compliance with subsection (4) and the court may, as it thinks fit, grant such an order accordingly.

(6) If the report of the independent accountant is submitted to the court before the expiry of the period of protection specified in an order under subsection (1), the court shall proceed to consider the petition together with the report as if they were presented in accordance with section 2.

(7) If the report of the independent accountant is not submitted to the court before the expiry of the period of protection specified in an order under subsection (1), then, at the expiry of that period, the company concerned shall cease to be under the protection of the court, but without prejudice to the presentation of a further petition under section 2.

(8) Any liabilities incurred by the company concerned during the period of protection specified in an order under subsection (1) may not be the subject of a certificate under section 10(2).][a]

Amendments

a C(A)A 1990, s 3A was inserted by C(A)(No 2)A 1999, s 9.

Definitions

'company': CA 1963, s 2(1); 'court': CA 1963, s 2(1). See also C(A)A 1990, s 3(9); 'director': CA 1963, s 2(1); 'the independent accountant': C(A)A 1990, s 3(3A).

Notes

See the notes to C(A)A 1990, s 3, under the heading 'Independent Accountant's Report'.

[3B Creditors to be heard

(1) The court shall not make an order dismissing a petition presented under section 2 or an order appointing an examiner to a company without having afforded each creditor of the company who has indicated to the court his desire to be heard in the matter an opportunity to be so heard.

(2) Nothing in this section shall affect the power of the court under section 3(7) to make an interim order in the matter.][a]

Amendments

a C(A)A 1990, s 3B was inserted by C(A)(No 2)A 1999, s 10.

Definitions

'company': CA 1963, s 2(1); 'court': CA 1963, s 2(1). See also C(A)A 1990, s 3(9); 'examiner': C(A)A 1990, s 1; The phrase 'examiner' includes any interim examiner so appointed by the Court.[1]

1 RSC, Ord 75A, r 1(4).

Notes

See the notes to C(A)A 1990, s 3 under the heading 'ex parte application' and 'hearing of petition'.

[3C Availability of independent accountant's report

(1) The independent accountant shall supply a copy of the report prepared by him under section 3(3A) to the company concerned or any interested party on written application being made to him in that behalf.

(2) If the court, on application to it in that behalf, directs that that supply may be the subject of such omission, there may be omitted from any copy of the report supplied to the company or an interested party such parts of it as are specified in the direction of the court.

(3) The court may, in particular, on such an application, direct that there may be omitted from such a supply of a copy of the report any information the inclusion of which in such a copy would be likely to prejudice the survival of the company or the whole or any part of its undertaking as a going concern.

(4) If the company concerned is a company referred to in section 3(2)(c) and the Central Bank does not propose to present, or has not presented, (whether alone or acting together with other persons) a petition under section 2 in relation to the company, the independent accountant shall, as soon as may be after it is prepared, supply a copy of the report prepared by him under section 3(3A) to the Central Bank and subsections (2) and (3) shall not apply to such a copy.][a]

Amendments

a C(A)A 1990, s 3C was inserted by C(A)(No 2)A 1999, s 11.

Definitions

'central bank'[1]: C(A)A 1990, s 1; 'company': CA 1963, s 2(1); 'court': CA 1963, s 2(1). See also C(A)A 1990, s 3(9); 'the independent accountant': C(A)A 1990, s 3(3A); 'interested party': C(A)A 1990, s 1.

1 See Central Bank and Financial Services Authority of Ireland Act 2003, s 33C(1) and (2) whereby the Financial Regulator is entitled to perform the functions of the Central Bank under C(A)A 1990, ss 3, 3C, 18, 23, 24 and 27.

Notes

See the notes to C(A)A 1990, s 3 under the heading 'Independent Accountant's Report'.

4 Related companies

(1) [Subject to subsection (2), where the court appoints an examiner to a company][a], it may, at the same or any time thereafter, make an order—

(a) appointing the examiner to be examiner for the purposes of this Act to a related company, or

(b) conferring on the examiner, in relation to such company, all or any of the powers or duties conferred on him in relation to the first-mentioned company.

(2) In deciding whether to make an order under subsection (1), the court shall have regard to whether the making of the order would be likely to facilitate the survival of the company, or of the related company, or both, and the whole or any part of its or their undertaking, as a going concern [and shall not, in any case, make such an order unless it is satisfied that there is a reasonable prospect of the survival of the related company, and the whole or any part of its undertaking, as a going concern'.][b]

(3) A related company to which an examiner is appointed shall be deemed to be under the protection of the court for the period beginning on the date of the making of an order under this section and continuing for the period during which the company to which it is related is under such protection.

(4) Where an examiner stands appointed to two or more related companies, he shall have the same powers and duties in relation to each company, taken separately, unless the court otherwise directs.

(5) For the purposes of this Act, a company is related to another company if—

(a) that other company is its holding company or subsidiary; or

(b) more than half in nominal value of its equity share capital (as defined in section 155(5) of the Principal Act) is held by the other company and companies related to that other company (whether directly or indirectly, but other than in a fiduciary capacity); or

(c) more than half in nominal value of the equity share capital (as defined in section 155(5) of the Principal Act) of each of them is held by members of the other (whether directly or indirectly, but other than in a fiduciary capacity); or

(d) that other company or a company or companies related to that other company or that other company together with a company or companies related to it are entitled to exercise or control the exercise of more than one half of the voting power at any general meeting of the company; or

(e) the businesses of the companies have been so carried on that the separate business of each company, or a substantial part thereof, is not readily identifiable; or

(f) there is another [body corporate][c] to which both companies are related;

and 'related company' has a corresponding meaning.

(6) For the purposes of this section 'company' includes any body which is liable to be wound up under the Companies Acts.

[(7) The court shall not make an order under this section unless—

(a) the court is satisfied that the related company has no obligations in relation to a bank asset that has been transferred to the National Asset Management Agency or a NAMA group entity, or

(b) if the related company has any such obligation—

(i) a copy of the petition has been served on that Agency, and

(ii) the court has heard that Agency in relation to the making of the order.

(8) In subsection (7) 'bank asset' and 'NAMA group entity' have the same respective meanings as in the National Asset Management Agency Act 2009.][d]

Amendments

a C(A)A 1990, s 4(1) amended by C(A)(No 2)A 1999, s 12(a).

b C(A)A 1990, s 4(2) amended by C(A)(No 2)A 1999, s 12(b).

c Words 'body corporate' substituted for 'company' by CA 1990, s 181.

d C(A)A 1990, s 4(7) and (8) inserted by NAMA Act 2009, s 234.

Definitions

'company': CA 1963, s 2(1); 'Companies Acts': C(A)A 1990, s 1; 'court': CA 1963, s 2(1); 'examiner': C(A)A 1990, s 1: the phrase 'examiner' includes any interim examiner so appointed by the Court[1]; 'holding company': CA 1963, s 155; 'subsidiary' CA 1963, s 155; 'Principal Act': C(A)A 1990, s 1.

1 RSC, Ord 75A, r 1(4).

Notes

Appointment of examiner to related companies: Two possible orders appear to be envisaged by C(A)A 1990, s 4(1). The first is an order under paragraph (a) appointing the examiner to the related company as well. In such circumstances, the related company also comes under the protection of the court. The second type of order is one under paragraph (b), where the examiner is not actually appointed to be examiner of the related company as well, but is nonetheless directed to examine the affairs of the related company and, if possible, to prepare rescue proposals. The provisions of subsection (3) seems to indicate that because the examiner is not 'appointed' to the related company in the case of an order made under paragraph (b), the related company will not technically be in examinership and will not have the protection of the court afforded by C(A)A 1990, s 5. Accordingly, the circumstances warranting an order under paragraph (b) rather than paragraph (a) must be very limited indeed.[1]

1 For an example of a case where an examiner had been appointed to a related company, see *Re Edenpark Construction Ltd* [1994] 3 IR 126.

Ground for appointment: Unlike a petition under C(A)A 1990, s 2 where the basis for the appointment of the examiner must be the survival of the company itself, a petition under C(A)A 1990, s 4 may be presented for the purpose of saving the company and/or the related company.

The application for appointment: If the person seeking the appointment of an examiner to a related company is the petitioner or the examiner himself, application is made *ex parte* to the Court which may then give directions in relation to matters such as service and advertisement and the fixing of a date for the hearing of the application itself.[1] Pending the hearing of the application, the court may also appoint the examiner as interim examiner of the related company.[2]

If the person seeking the appointment of the examiner to the related company is someone other than the petitioner or the examiner, it must apply by notice of motion served on the petitioner and the examiner.[3]

1 RSC, Ord 75A, r 6(1).

2 RSC, Ord 75A, r 6(1).

3 RSC, Ord 75A, r 6(3). As to the *locus standi* to make such an application, see C(A)A 1990, s 3 and the notes thereto.

Standard of proof required: See the notes to C(A)A 1990, s 2.

Hearing of the application: See C(A)A 1990, s 3 and the notes thereto.

Foreign related companies: A related entity which is incorporated under the laws of another jurisdiction will not normally rank as a 'related company' for the purposes of C(A)A 1990, s 4(5) because the definition of 'company' in CA 1963, s 2(1) refers to Irish-registered companies.[1] However, if the foreign entity is one which is capable of being wound up under the Companies Acts, eg where it has assets or a place of business in the State, then it will come within the definition of a 'related company'.[2]

1 *Re Tuskar Resources plc* [2001] 1 IR 668.

2 C(A)A 1990, s 4(6). See CA 1963, s 345 and the notes thereto, concerning the circumstances in which a foreign company may be wound up in the State.

[4A Duty to act in good faith

The court may decline to hear a petition presented under section 2 or, as the case may be, may decline to continue hearing such a petition if it appears to the court that, in the preparation or presentation of the petition or in the preparation of the report of the independent accountant, the petitioner or independent accountant—

(a) has failed to disclose any information available to him which is material to the exercise by the court of its powers under this Act, or

(b) has in any other way failed to exercise utmost good faith.][a]

Amendments

a C(A)A 1990, s 4A inserted by C(A)(No 2)A 1999, s 13.

Definitions

'court': CA 1963, s 2(1). See also C(A)A 1990, s 3(9); 'the independent accountant': C(A)A 1990, s 3(3A).

Notes

Duty to act in good faith: See C(A)A 1990, s 3 and the notes under the heading 'Duty of Candour'.

---

5 Effect of petition to appoint examiner on creditors and others

[(1) Subject to section 3A, during the period beginning with the date of the presentation of a petition under section 2 and (subject to subsections (3) and (4) of section 18) ending on the expiry of 70 days from that date or on the withdrawal or refusal of the petition, whichever first happens, the company shall be deemed to be under the protection of the court.][a]

(2) For so long as a company is under the protection of the court in a case under this Act, the following provisions shall have effect—

(a) no proceedings for the winding-up of the company may be commenced or resolution for winding-up passed in relation to that company and any resolution so passed shall be of no effect;

(b) no receiver over any part of the property or undertaking of the company shall be appointed, or, if so appointed before the presentation of a petition under section 2, shall, subject to section 6, be able to act;

(c) no attachment, sequestration, distress or execution shall be put into force against the property or effects of the company, except with the consent of the examiner;

[(d) where any claim against the company is secured by a mortgage, charge, lien or other encumbrance or a pledge of, on or affecting the whole or any part of the property, effects or income of the company, no action may be taken to realize the whole or any part of that security, except with the consent of the examiner;][b]

(e) no steps may be taken to repossess goods in the company's possession under any hire-purchase agreement (within the meaning of section 11(8)), except with the consent of the examiner;

(f) where, under any enactment, rule of law or otherwise, any person other than the company is liable to pay all or any part of the debts of the company—

(i) no attachment, sequestration, distress or execution shall be put into force against the property or effects of such person in respect of the debts of the company, and

(ii) no proceedings of any sort may be commenced against such person in respect of the debts of the company;

[(g) no order for relief shall be made under section 205 of the Principal Act against the company in respect of complaints as to the conduct of the affairs of the company or the exercise of the powers of the directors prior to the presentation of the petition];[c]

[(h) ...][d]

(3) Subject to subsection (2), no other proceedings in relation to the company may be commenced except by leave of the court and subject to such terms as the court may impose and the court may on the application of the examiner make such order as it thinks proper in relation to any existing proceedings including an order to stay such proceedings.

(4) Complaints concerning the conduct of the affairs of the company while it is under the protection of the court shall not constitute a basis for the making of an order for relief under section 205 of the Principal Act.

Amendments

a C(A)A 1990, s 5(1) substituted by C(A)(No 2)A 1999, s 14(a).

b C(A)A 1990, s 2(2)(d) substituted by C(A)(No 2)A 1999, s 14(b)(i).

c C(A)A 1990, s 5(g) inserted by CA 1990, s 180.

d C(A)A 1990, s 5(h) inserted by CA 1990, s 181 and subsequently deleted by C(A)(No 2)A 1999, s 14(b)(ii).

Definitions

'company': CA 1963, s 2(1); 'court': CA 1963, s 2(1); 'director': CA 1963, s 2(1); 'examiner': C(A)A 1990, s 1; The phrase 'examiner' includes any interim examiner so appointed by the Court;[1] 'Principal Act': C(A)A 1990, s 1.

1 RSC, Ord 75A, r 1(4).

Notes

Period of moratorium: By virtue of C(A)A 1990, s 5(1) the company enjoys a moratorium on proceedings, execution and enforcement of secured and other rights against it for an initial period of 70 days from the date of the presentation of the petition. However, the examiner may apply for further extensions of not more than 30 days to finalise his proposals, present them to the creditors and members and report back to court.[1] Moreover, once the examiner has actually presented his report, the court may grant such additional extensions of time as it considers necessary in order to enable it to make its decision on the report.[2]

1 C(A)A 1990, s 18(3).

2 C(A)A 1990, s 18(4).

The nature of the moratorium: The moratorium imposed by C(A)A 1990, s 5 applies to various forms of process by third parties against the company.

Winding up: During the protection period no winding up resolution can be passed in respect of the company, nor may any new winding up petition be presented.[1] Where a winding up petition has been presented in advance of the presentation of the petition for the appointment of an examiner, the two petitions will be listed for hearing on the same date so that if the application for the appointment of an examiner fails, the court may then proceed to hear the winding up petition and appoint a liquidator to the company.[2] Furthermore, if a provisional liquidator already stands appointed, the court may make such order as it thinks fit including an order that the provisional liquidator or someone else be appointed as examiner or directing that the provisional liquidator cease to act.[3] It may also direct the provisional liquidator to deliver up to the examiner any books and records in his possession relating to the property or undertaking of the company and to furnish a full account of his dealings as provisional liquidator.[4]

1 C(A)A 1990, s 5(2)(a).

2 C(A)A 1990, s 6(5). For an example, see *Re Tuskar Resources plc* [2001] 1 IR 668.

3 C(A)A 1990, s 6(2)(a), (b) and (c).

4 C(A)A 1990, s 6(2)(d) and (e).

Receivers: If a receiver has been in place for at least three days prior to the presentation of the petition, the court will be precluded from giving a hearing to the application for the appointment of an examiner.[1] Whilst no new receivership may be commenced after the presentation of the petition, if a receiver is already in place, he may be directed by the court to cease acting or to cease acting except in respect of specified assets and he may be directed to deliver up to the examiner any books and records in his possession relating to the property or undertaking of the company and to furnish a full account of his dealings as receiver.[2] Furthermore, if the court is satisfied that the making of such an order would be likely to facilitate the survival of the company, it may, on application made to it, relieve the director of any liability to pay the preferential claims which would otherwise have been payable in the receivership.[3] No such order will, however, be made without affording the creditors an opportunity to be heard.[4] The case for making such a relieving order is compelling in circumstances where the receiver has been forced to cease acting because of the examinership.

1 C(A)A 1990, s 3(6).

2 C(A)A 1990, s 5(2)(b) and s 6(1).

3 C(A)A 1990, s 6A(1). Although C(A)A 1990, s 6A does not identify the parties with standing to make such an application, they would presumably include the receiver, the examiner, the petitioner and the company.

4 C(A)A 1990, s 6A(2).

Secured claims: No mortgage, charge, lien, pledge or other encumbrance affecting any property of the company may be realised during the protection period to realise that security except with the consent of the examiner.[1] This restriction on the enforcement of security applies regardless of whether the party attempting to effect the realisation is the secured creditor or a receiver previously appointed by him.[2] In circumstances where a charge on the company's book debts entitles the secured creditor to designate an account into which the proceeds of book debts should be lodged and out of which no withdrawals should be made except with the creditor's consent, the purported designation of such an account by the secured creditor for the first time after the presentation of the petition and without the consent of the examiner, will amount to an attempt to realise the security and will be void accordingly.[3] Similarly void will be any attempt, without the examiner's consent, to exercise a power of sale in respect of the secured property.[4] Because the examiner is an officer of the court, attempts at realisation without his consent may amount to a contempt of court.[5] The examiner should not consent to the realisation of a security where the creditor is fully secured and will not be prejudiced by any delay which results from the placing of the company under the protection of the court.[6]

Apart from any impact on the position of the secured creditor simply through the moratorium, adverse consequences may arise in other ways. For example, the examiner may be able to invoke the provisions of C(A)A 1990, s 7(5B) and (5C) to override any negative pledge clause contained in the debenture.[7] Moreover, in the case of a floating charge, even if it has previously crystallised as a result of some other event such as the appointment of a receiver, it will immediately decrystallise on the appointment of an examiner.[8] In this regard, the examiner may certify fresh borrowings during the protection period pursuant to s 10[9] and these and any other certified liabilities will rank ahead of any claim secured by the floating charge.[10] The other costs and expenses of the examinership, including the examiner's own remuneration, will rank ahead of all secured claims, whether secured by a fixed or a floating charge.[11]

1 C(A)A 1990, s 5(2)(d).
2 *Re Holidair Ltd* [1994] 1 IR 416.
3 *Re Holidair Ltd* [1994] 1 IR 416.
4 *Bristol Airport plc v Powdrill* [1990] BCLC 585.
5 *Re Exchange Travel (Holdings) Ltd* [1991] BCLC 728.
6 *Royal Trust Bank v Buchler* [1989] BCLC 130.
7 *Re Holidair Ltd* [1994] 1 IR 416.
8 *Re Holidair Ltd* [1994] 1 IR 416.
9 See for example, *Re Holidair Ltd* [1994] 1 IR 416.
10 C(A)A 1990, s 29(3A).
11 C(A)A 1990, s 29(3).

Hire-purchase, leasing and retention of title: If goods have been supplied to the company pursuant to a hire-purchase agreement[1] or a lease agreement or have been supplied subject to a retention of title clause, no steps may be taken to repossess the goods except with the consent of the examiner.[2] If the examiner refuses to give his consent, he may, in the case of a lease or hire-purchase contract, be obliged to treat any ongoing rental liabilities as a cost or expense of the examinership and to certify them under C(A)A 1990, s 10.[3] Because the examiner is an officer of the court, attempts at repossession without his consent may amount to a contempt of court.[4]

1 The phrase 'hire-purchase agreement' is defined in C(A)A 1990, s 11(8) as including a conditional sale agreement, a retention of title agreement and an agreement for the bailment off goods which is capable of subsisting for more than 3 months.
2 C(A)A 1990, s 5(2)(e).
3 *Re Atlantic Computer Systems plc* [1991] BCLC 606.
4 *Re Exchange Travel (Holdings) Ltd* [1991] BCLC 728.

Execution and guarantee claims: During the period of protection, no attachment, distress or execution may be effected against the property of the company except with the examiner's consent.[1] A similar moratorium applies in respect of enforcement against the assets of anyone else such as a surety or guarantor, who would otherwise be liable to pay the company's debt.[2] Indeed, during the protection period no proceedings[3] of any sort can even be commenced against that third party.[4] Because the examiner is an officer of the court, attempts at enforcement without his consent may amount to a contempt of court.[5]

1 C(A)A 1990, s 5(2)(c).

2 C(A)A 1990, s 5(2)(f)(i).

3 'Proceedings' are legal proceedings or quasi-legal proceedings such as arbitration: *Bristol Airport plc v Powdrill* [1990] BCLC 585.

4 C(A)A 1990, s 5(2)(f)(ii).

5 *Re Exchange Travel (Holdings) Ltd* [1991] BCLC 728.

CA(A) 1990, s 205 proceedings: Despite the fact that the existing management remains in control of the company during the protection period[1] no complaint of oppression or disregard of interests may be made in respect of the conduct of the affairs of the company during the protection period.[2] Furthermore, even if the alleged oppression or disregard of interests relates to the period prior to the presentation of the petition for the appointment of an examiner, no order for relief may be made under s 205 during the protection period.[3]

1 Subject only to any order to the contrary pursuant to C(A)A 1990, s 9.

2 C(A)A 1990, s 5(4).

3 C(A)A 1990, s 5(2)(g).

Other proceedings: During the protection period no other proceedings may be commenced except by leave of the court, and even then only on such terms as the court may impose.[1] The application for leave must be brought by way of motion on notice to the examiner and the company[2] and should establish that the applicant has a seriously arguable case.[3]

In the case of existing proceedings, the examiner may apply to the court for a stay or for such other order as the court thinks proper.[4] The application by the examiner must be brought by motion on notice to all parties to such proceedings, including the company itself.[5] If the examiner fails to make such an application, then technically, the plaintiff can continue with his action up to and including judgment. However, he will be precluded from levying execution during the protection period except with the consent of the examiner.[6]

The phrase 'proceedings' is deemed to cover court proceedings and analogous proceedings such as arbitration and proceedings before the employment appeals tribunal.[7] Proceedings before an administrative tribunal for the revocation of a licence held by the company will not however, be caught by the provisions of C(A)A 1990, s 5.[8] It is similarly unnecessary to obtain the leave of the court to commence reckless or fraudulent trading proceedings against the officers of the company pursuant to CA 1963, s 297A.[9] Nor will the leave of the court be required before serving a notice on the company making time of the essence in a contract[10]

1 C(A)A 1990, s 5(3).

2 RSC, Ord 75A, r 8(2).

3 *Scottish Exhibition Centre Ltd v Mirestop Ltd* [1993] BCLC 1459.

4 *Scottish Exhibition Centre Ltd v Mirestop Ltd* [1993] BCLC 1459.

5 RSC, Ord 75A, r 8(1).

6 C(A)A 1990, s 5(2)(c).

7 *Bristol Airport plc v Powdrill* [1990] BCLC 585; *Air Ecosse Ltd v Civil Aviation Authority* 1987 SLT 751; *Carr v British International Helicopters Ltd* [1994] 2 BCLC 474.

8 *Air Ecosse Ltd v Civil Aviation Authority* 1987 SLT 751.

9 *Re Hefferon Kearns Ltd* [1992] ILRM 51.

10 *Re Olympia and York Canary Wharf Ltd* [1993] BCLC 453.

[5A Restriction on payment of pre-petition debts

(1) Subject to subsection (2), no payment may be made by a company, during the period it is under the protection of the court, by way of satisfaction or discharge of the whole or a part of a liability incurred by the company before the date of the presentation under section 2 of the petition in relation to it unless the report of the independent accountant contains a recommendation that the whole or, as the case may be, the part of that liability should be discharged or satisfied.

(2) Notwithstanding subsection (1), the court may, on application being made to it in that behalf by the examiner or any interested party, authorise the discharge or satisfaction, in whole or in part, by the company concerned of a liability referred to in subsection (1) if it is satisfied that a failure to discharge or satisfy, in whole or in part, that liability would considerably reduce the prospects of the company or the whole or any part of its undertaking surviving as a going concern.][a]

Amendments

a C(A)A 1990, s 5A was inserted by C(A)(No 2)A 1999, s 15.

Definitions

'company': CA 1963, s 2(1); 'court': CA 1963, s 2(1). See also C(A)A 1990, s 3(9); 'examiner': C(A)A 1990, s 1: The phrase 'examiner' includes any interim examiner so appointed by the Court[1]; 'independent accountant': C(A)A 1990, s 3(3A); 'interested party': C(A)A 1990, s 1.

1 RSC, Ord 75A, r 1(4).

Notes

Payment of pre-petition liabilities: Prior to the insertion of C(A)A 1990, s 5A by C(A)(No 2) 1999, there was no legal impediment to the company paying pre-petition liabilities during the protection period, subject of course to the availability of funds. Utilities and other essential creditors could insist on the payment of pre-petition debts as a pre-condition to continuity of supply.[1] Now, however, such liabilities can only be discharged if payment has been recommended in the independent accountant's report[2] or if the court so directs upon an application by the examiner or by an interested party. The leave of the court will only be given if failure to make the payment would considerably reduce the prospects of survival for the company.

An important aspect of this section to note in practice is its application to wages payable to the workforce. The employees will typically be paid weekly or monthly. If the petition is paid in the middle of a week or month as the case may be, work will already have been done for which payment has not yet been made. The company will not be entitled to pay the wages for pre-petition work done by them unless such payment is either recommended in the report or sanctioned by the court.

1 For an example of such a case, albeit in the context of a receivership, see *W and L Crowe Ltd v ESB* [1984] IEHC 22 (Costello J).

2 In relation to the report, see C(A)A 1990, s 3(3A) and (3B).

6 Effect on receiver or provisional liquidator of order appointing examiner

(1) [Where, at the date of the presentation of a petition under section 2 in relation to a company,][a] a receiver stands appointed to the whole or any part of the property or undertaking of that company the court may make such order as it thinks fit including an order as to any or all of the following matters—

(a) that the receiver shall cease to act as such from a date specified by the court,

(b) that the receiver shall, from a date specified by the court, act as such only in respect of certain assets specified by the court,

(c) directing the receiver to deliver all books, papers and other records, which relate to the property or undertaking of the company (or any part thereof) and are in his possession or control, to the examiner within a period to be specified by the court,

(d) directing the receiver to give the examiner full particulars of all his dealings with the property or undertaking of the company.

(2) [Where, at the date of the presentation of a petition under section 2 in relation to a company,][b] a provisional liquidator stands appointed to that company, the court may make such order as it thinks fit including an order as to any or all of the following matters—

(a) that the provisional liquidator be appointed as examiner of the company,

(b) appointing some other person as examiner of the company,

(c) that the provisional liquidator shall cease to act as such from the date specified by the court,

(d) directing the provisional liquidator to deliver all books, papers and other records, which relate to the property or undertaking of the company or any part thereof and are in his possession or control, to the examiner within a period to be specified by the court,

(e) directing the provisional liquidator to give the examiner full particulars of all his dealings with the property or undertaking of the company.

[(3) The court shall not make an order under paragraph (a) or (b) of subsection (1) or paragraph (c) of subsection (2) unless the court is satisfied that there is a reasonable prospect of the survival of the company, and the whole or any part of its undertaking, as a going concern.][c]

(4) Where the court makes an order under subsection (1) or (2), it may, for the purpose of giving full effect to the order, include such conditions in the order and make such ancillary or other orders as it deems fit.

(5) Where a petition is presented under section 2 in respect of a company at a date subsequent to the presentation of a petition for the winding-up of that company, but before a provisional liquidator has been appointed or an order made for its winding-up, both petitions shall be heard together.

Amendments

a C(A)A 1990, s 6(1) amended by C(A)(No 2) 1999, s 16(a).

b C(A)A 1990, s 6(2) amended by C(A)(No 2) 1999, s 16(b).

c C(A)A 1990, s 6(3) amended by C(A)(No 2) 1999, s 16(c).

Cross reference

See C(A)A 1990, s 2.

Definitions

'company': CA 1963, s 2(1); 'court': CA 1963, s 2(1); 'examiner': C(A)A 1990, s 1: The phrase 'examiner' includes any interim examiner so appointed by the Court[1]; 'independent accountant': C(A)A 1990, s 3(3A).

[1] RSC, Ord 75A, r 1(4).

Cross references in other enactments

NAMA Act 2009, s 150 provides:

'(1) Notwithstanding any provision of the Companies (Amendment) Act 1990, the appointment of an examiner to a company whose assets or any part of them are under the control of a statutory receiver does not—

(a) displace the statutory receiver or affect his or her powers, authority or agency,

(b) prevent the statutory receiver from enforcing any security held by NAMA or a NAMA group entity, or

(c) cause the de-crystallisation of any charge created as a floating charge over assets that are under the control of the statutory receiver.

(2) The appointment of a liquidator to a company whose assets or any part of them are under the control of a statutory receiver does not displace the statutory receiver and does not affect his or her powers, authority and agency.'

Notes

Effect on receivership: See the notes to C(A)A 1990, s 5 under the heading 'Receivers'.

Effect on provisional liquidator: See the notes to C(A)A 1990, s 5 under the heading 'Winding Up'.

UK legislation

See IA 1986, s 11.

[6A Disapplication of section 98 of Principal Act to receivers in certain circumstances

(1) Without prejudice to the generality of section 6(1), the court, on application being made in that behalf, may, in relation to a receiver who stands appointed to the whole or any part of the property or undertaking of a company, make an order providing that section 98 of the Principal Act shall not apply as respects payments made by the receiver out of assets coming into his hands as such receiver if—

(a) (i) an examiner has been appointed to the company, or

(ii) an examiner has not been appointed to the company but, in the opinion of the court, such an appointment may yet be made, and

(b) the making of the order would, in the opinion of the court, be likely to facilitate the survival of the company, and the whole or any part of its undertaking, as a going concern.

(2) An order under subsection (1) shall not be made without each creditor of the company of the following class being afforded an opportunity to be heard, namely a creditor any of the debts owed to whom by the company are debts which in a winding-up are, by virtue of the provisions of Part VI of the Principal Act relating to preferential payments, required to be paid in priority to all other debts.][a]

Amendments

a C(A)A 1990, s 6A inserted by C(A)(No 2)A 1999, s 17.

Definitions

'company': CA 1963, s 2(1); 'court': CA 1963, s 2(1). See also C(A)A 1990, s 3(9); 'examiner': C(A)A 1990, s 1: The phrase 'examiner' includes any interim examiner so appointed by the Court.[1]

[1] RSC, O 75A, r 1(4).

Notes

Payment of preferential claims by receiver: See the notes to C(A)A 1990, s 5 under the heading 'Receivers'.

7 Powers of an examiner

(1) Any provision of the Companies Acts relating to the rights and powers of an auditor of a company and the supplying of information to and co-operation with such auditor shall, with the necessary modifications, apply to an examiner.

(2) Notwithstanding any provision of the Companies Acts relating to notice of general meetings, and examiner shall have power to convene, set the agenda for, and preside at meetings of the board of directors and general meetings of the company to which he is appointed and to propose motions or resolutions and to give reports to such meetings.

(3) An examiner shall be entitled to reasonable notice of, to attend and be heard at, all meetings of the board of directors of a company and all general meetings of the company to which he is appointed.

(4) For the purpose of subsection (3) 'reasonable notice' shall be deemed to include a description of the business to be transacted at any such meeting.

(5) Where an examiner becomes aware of any actual or proposed act, omission, course of conduct, decision or contract, by or on behalf of the company to which he has been appointed, its officers, employees, members or creditors or by any other person in relation to the income, assets or liabilities of that company which, in his opinion, is or is likely to be to the detriment of that company, or any interested party, he shall, subject to the rights of parties acquiring an interest in good faith and for value in such income, assets or liabilities, have full power to take whatever steps are necessary to halt, prevent or rectify the effects of such act, omission, course of conduct, decision or contract.

[(5A) Without prejudice to subsection (5B), nothing in this section shall enable an examiner to repudiate a contract that has been entered into by the company prior to the period during which the company is under the protection of the court.

(5B) A provision referred to in subsection (5C) shall not be binding on the company at any time after the service of the notice under this subsection and before the expiration of the period during which the company concerned is under the protection of the court if the examiner is of the opinion that the provision, were it to be enforced, would be likely to prejudice the survival of the company or the whole or any part of its undertaking as a going concern and he serves a notice on the other party or parties to the agreement in which the provision is contained informing him or them of that opinion.

(5C) The provision referred to in subsection (5B) is a provision of an agreement entered into by the company concerned and any other person or persons at any time (including a time that is prior to the period during which the company is under the protection of the court) that provides that the company shall not, or shall not otherwise than in specified circumstances—

(a) borrow moneys or otherwise obtain credit from any person other than the said person or persons, or

(b) create or permit to subsist any mortgage, charge, lien or other encumbrance or any pledge over the whole or any part of the property or undertaking of the company.][a]

(6) The examiner may apply to the court to determine any question arising in the course of his office, or for the exercise in relation to the company of all or any of the powers which the court may exercise under this Act, upon the application to it of any member, contributory, creditor or director of a company.

(7) The examiner shall, if so directed by the court, have power to ascertain and agree claims against the company to which he has been appointed.

Amendments

a C(A)A 1990, s 7(5A), (5B) and (5C) inserted by C(A)(No 2)A 1999, s 18.

Cross reference

For further powers of the examiner see CA 1990, s 180(2).

For the notice requirements in respect of general meetings, see CA 1963, s 133 and Arts 51, 53. Notice of board meetings is dealt with by Art 101.

Definitions

'company': CA 1963, s 2(1); 'Companies Acts': C(A)A 1990, s 1; 'court': CA 1963, s 2(1); 'director': CA 1963, s 2(1); 'examiner': C(A)A 1990, s 1: The phrase 'examiner' includes any interim examiner so appointed by the Court[1]; 'interested party': C(A)A 1990, s 1, s 2(1); 'officer': CA 1963, s 2(1).

1 RSC, Ord 75A, r 1(4).

Notes

Conferral of rights and powers of auditors: In order to assist the examiner in the performance of his functions, he is automatically conferred with the rights and powers of an auditor. These include a right of access to the books and records of the company and a right to all necessary information and explanations from the company's officers[1] and from the officers and auditors of any Irish subsidiary.[2] This right of access to information is of particular importance if he is to determine whether or not it is feasible to put together proposals for the rescue of the company and all or part of its undertaking. The making of false statements to the examiner may constitute criminal offences.[3] The conferral on the examiner of the rights and powers of an auditor are, however, without prejudice to the powers conferred on him by C(A)A 1990, s 8 regarding the production of documents and evidence. He may also have wider powers of management conferred on him by the court pursuant to C(A)A 1990, s 9(1) and may indeed be vested with the powers of a liquidator.[4]

1 CA 1990, s 193(3).

2 CA 1990, s 196(1).

3 CA 1990, ss 197 and 242.

4 C(A)A 1990, s 9(4).

Board meetings and general meetings: Whilst C(A)A 1990, s 7(2) and (3) confer on the examiner a right to convene and set the agenda for, receive notice of[1] and preside and speak at general meetings and board meetings, one power not given to him is the right to vote.

1 For the notice periods in respect of general meetings and board meetings, see CA 1963, s 133 and C(A)A 1990, Table A, regs 51 and 53 respectively.

Halting prejudicial conduct: By virtue of C(A)A 1990, s 7(5) the examiner has full power to take whatever steps are necessary to halt, prevent or rectify the effects of any actual or proposed act, omission, course of conduct, decision or contract by the company or by any other party which he believes to be actually or potentially detrimental to the company or any interested party. It had previously been held that he could invoke this power to repudiate or override the detrimental provisions of pre-petition contracts.[1] However, this is no longer the case[2] and accordingly his power would seem to be limited to challenging post-petition activities and contracts.[3]

1 *Re Holidair Ltd* [1994] 1 IR 416. See also *Astor Chemicals Ltd v Synthetic Technology Ltd* [1990] BCLC 1.

2 C(A)A 1990, s 7(5A).

3 If the pre-petition contract amounted to onerous property within the meaning of CA 1963, s 290, the examiner could apply to the court under C(A)A 1990, s 9(4) to have a liquidator's power of disclaimer conferred on him.

Overriding negative pledge clauses: The company's existing loan facilities may contain a negative pledge clause pursuant to which it is not allowed to borrow from any third party or to create any fresh security except with the consent of its existing lenders. Whilst such a clause would otherwise be enforceable,[1] it will not be binding on the company during the protection period if the examiner is of the opinion that its enforcement would be prejudicial to the survival of the company.[2] The examiner must, however, serve notice on the affected party advising of the intention to disapply the negative pledge clause.[3]

1 *Re Old Bushmills Distillery ex parte Brydon* [1896] 1 IR 301; *English and Scottish Mercantile Investment Co v Brunton* [1892] 2 QB 700.

2 See *Re Atlantic Magnetics Ltd* [1993] 2 IR 561.

3 C(A)A 1990, s 7(5B) and (5C).

Power to seek directions: C(A)A 1990, s 7(6) contains a somewhat confusingly-worded power to apply to the court for directions. An application may be made at any stage for directions regarding any question arising in the examinership. If the application is by the examiner, it is made *ex parte*, although the court can direct that other parties be put on notice.[1] However, if the application is made by a member, contributory, creditor or director of the company, it must be by motion on notice to the examiner and the company.[2]

1 RSC, Ord 75A, r 9(1).

2 RSC, Ord 75A, r 9(2).

Power to ascertain and agree claims: This potentially useful power may be conferred on the examiner by the court pursuant to C(A)A 1990, s 7(7). It could be of assistance to him in ascertaining the extent of the company's indebtedness and thus in deciding whether or not it is possible to formulate rescue proposals for the company. In addition, it would enable him to ascertain the claims which would be admissible for voting purposes at any meetings held to consider his proposals. In practice, however, the power is rarely sought or conferred. Instead, unagreed claims are left to be determined after the scheme of arrangement has been voted on and in accordance with a mechanism set out in the scheme itself.

UK legislation

See IA 1986, ss 14,17(1), Sch 1.

8 Production of documents and evidence

(1) It shall be the duty of all officers and agents of the company or a related company to produce to the examiner all books and documents of or relating to any such company which are in their custody or power, to attend before him when required so to do and otherwise to give to him all assistance in connection with his functions which they are reasonably able to give.

(2) If the examiner considers that a person other than an officer or agent of any such company is or may be in possession of any information concerning its affairs, he may require that person to produce to him any books or documents in his custody or power relating to the company, to attend before him and otherwise to give him all assistance in connection with his functions which he is reasonably able to give; and it shall be the duty of that person to comply with the requirement.

(3) If the examiner has reasonable grounds for believing that a director [...][a] of any such company maintains or has maintained a bank account of any description, whether alone or jointly with another person and whether in the State or elsewhere, into or out of which there has been paid—

(a) any money which has resulted from or been used in the financing of any transaction, arrangement or agreement particulars of which have not been disclosed in the accounts of any company for any financial year as required by law; or

(b) any money which has been in any way connected with any act or omission, or series of acts or omissions, which on the part of that director constituted misconduct (whether fraudulent or not) towards that company or its members;

the examiner may require the director to produce to him all documents in the director's possession, or under his control, relating to that bank account; and in this subsection 'bank account' includes an account with any person exempt by virtue of section 7(4) of the Central Bank Act, 1971, from the requirement of holding a licence under section 9 of that Act [and 'director' includes any present or past director or any person connected, within the meaning of section 26 of the Companies Act, 1990, with such director, and any present or past shadow director][b].

(4) An examiner may examine on oath, either by word of mouth or on written interrogatories, the officers and agents of such company or other person as is mentioned in subsection (1) or (2) in relation to its affairs and may—

(a) administer an oath accordingly,

(b) reduce the answers of such person to writing and require him to sign them.

[(5) If any officer or agent of such company or other person—

(a) refuses to produce to the examiner any book or document which it is his duty under this section to produce, or

(b) refuses to attend before the examiner when requested to do so, or

(c) refuses to answer any question which is put to him by the examiner with respect to the affairs of the company, the examiner may certify the refusal under his hand to the court, and the court may thereupon enquire into the case and, after hearing any witnesses who may be produced against or on behalf of the said officer, agent or other person or any statement which may be offered in defence, make any order or direction it thinks fit.][c]

(5A) Without prejudice to the generality of subsection (5), the court may, after a hearing under that subsection, make a direction—

(a) to the person concerned to attend or re-attend before the examiner or produce particular books or documents or answer particular questions put to him by the examiner, or

(b) that the person concerned need not produce a particular book or document or answer a particular question put to him by the examiner.][d]

[(5B) Section 23(1) of the Companies Act, 1990, shall apply for the purposes of this section.][e]

(6) In this section, any reference to officers or to agents shall include past, as well as present, officers or agents, as the case may be, and 'agents', in relation to a company, shall include the bankers and solicitors of the company and any persons employed by the company as auditors, whether those persons are or are not officers of the company.

Amendments

a Words deleted by CA 1990, s 180.

b Words inserted by CA 1990, s 180.

c C(A)A 1990, s 8(5) substituted by C(A)(No 2)A 1999, s 19.

d C(A)A 1990, s 8(5A), inserted by CA 1990, s 180 and substituted by C(A)(No2)A 1999, s 19.

e C(A)A 1990, s 8(5B) inserted by CA 1990, s 180.

Definitions

'agent': CA 1963, s 2(1); 'company': CA 1963, s 2(1); 'court': CA 1963, s 2(1); 'director': CA 1963, s 2(1); 'document': CA 1963, s 2(1); 'examiner': C(A)A 1990, s 1: The phrase 'examiner' includes any interim examiner so appointed by the Court[1]; 'financial year': CA 1963, s 2(1); 'officer': CA 1963, s 2(1); 'related company': C(A)A 1990, s 4: 'shadow director': CA 1990, s 27.

1 RSC, Ord 75A, r 1(4).

Notes

Production of documents to and assisting the examiner: C(A)A 1990, s 8 confers on the examiner powers in relation to the production of documents and the eliciting of information which are broadly equivalent to the powers conferred on an inspector appointed by the High Court pursuant to CA 1990, Part II. In this regard see the notes to CA 1990, s 10. The power to compel the production of documents and information is, however, subject to any claim of legal professional privilege which the affected party may be entitled to assert.[1]

In practice, the company is unlikely to have much prospect of survival if the examiner is forced to use these coercive powers to obtain documentation, information and assistance. Accordingly, if the company's officers, servants and agents are not co-operating fully on a voluntary basis, the examiner would have to seriously whether there is any merit to keeping the company under the protection of the court.

1 CA 1990, s 23(1) as applied by C(A)A 1990, s 8(5B).

Examination of directors' accounts: C(A)A 1990, s 8(3) empowers the examiner the investigate accounts maintained by any past or present director or shadow director either on his own or jointly with some third party, which the examiner believes may have been used in connection with the misappropriation of moneys from the company. The examiner's entitlement to call for production of records relating to the account arises irrespective of whether the account is located in the State or abroad. The phrase 'bank account' is given a wide definition and includes any account maintained with an institution which is exempt under s 7(4) of the Central Bank Act 1971 from the requirement to hold a banking licence, namely central banks of European Community member states, the Agricultural Credit Corporation, the Industrial Credit Corporation, the Post Office Savings Bank, certified trustee savings banks, building societies, industrial and provident societies, friendly societies, credit unions and unit trusts.

UK legislation

See IA 1986, s 235.

9 Further powers of court

(1) Where it appears to the court, on the application of the examiner, that, having regard to the matters referred to in subsection (2), it is just and equitable to do so, it may make an order that all or any of the functions or powers which are vested in or exercisable by the directors (whether by virtue of the memorandum or articles of association of the company or by law or otherwise) shall be performable or exercisable only by the examiner.

(2) The matters to which the court is to have regard for the purpose of subsection (1) are—

(a) that the affairs of the company are being conducted, or are likely to be conducted, in a manner which is calculated or likely to prejudice the interests of the company or of its employees or of its creditors as a whole, or

(b) that it is expedient, for the purpose of preserving the assets of the company or of safeguarding the interests of the company or of its employees or of its creditors as a whole, that the carrying on of the business of the company by, or the exercise of the powers of, its directors or management should be curtailed or regulated in any particular respect, or

(c) that the company, or its directors, have resolved that such an order should be sought, or

(d) any other matter in relation to the company the court thinks relevant.

(3) Where the court makes an order under subsection (1), it may, for the purpose of giving full effect to the order, include such conditions in the order and make such ancillary or other orders as it sees fit.

(4) Without prejudice to the generality of subsections (1) and (3), an order under this section may provide that the examiner shall have all or any of the powers that he would have if he were a liquidator appointed by the court in respect of the company and, where such order so provides, the court shall have all the powers that it would have if it had

made a winding-up order and appointed a liquidator in respect of the company concerned.

Definitions

'articles': CA 1963, s 2(1); 'company': CA 1963, s 2(1); 'court': CA 1963, s 2(1); 'director': CA 1963, s 2(1); 'examiner': C(A)A 1990, s 1: The phrase 'examiner' includes any interim examiner so appointed by the court[1]; 'memorandum': CA 1963, s 2(1).

1 RSC, Ord 75A, r 1(4).

Notes

Transfer of directors' functions and powers: C(A)A 1990, s 9(1) confers a 'very wide discretion'[1] on the court to transfer all or some of the functions and powers of the board of directors to the examiner. This may include the conferral on the examiner of a power to borrow money to finance the continued trading of the company.[2] In granting such a power the court may declare that the monies so borrowed are to be treated as an expenses properly incurred by the examiner pursuant to s 29(1) with the consequent priority that derives from that section.[3]

In the absence of an order under subsection (1), the examiner does not usurp the functions of the board and it is the board who will continue to manage the affairs of the company during the protection period.[4] In practice, of course, the examinership process will have little prospect of success unless the directors, in exercising their power of management, liaise closely with and take on board the views of the examiner. Subsection (2) identifies the grounds upon which the court may transfer executive powers to the examiner. Such an order may be made, inter alia, where it has been sought by the company or by the directors themselves or to prevent actual or threatened prejudice to the company, its employees or creditors generally. Any such application by the examiner must be made by motion on notice to the directors, grounded on an affidavit specifying precisely which powers he is seeking to have vested in him.[5] The court may give such directions in relation to the hearing of the application as it thinks fit.[6]

In making an order under subsection (1), the court cannot authorise the examiner to do anything which would be *ultra vires* the company[7] nor may it grant to the examiner powers which would not have been exercisable by the directors themselves.[8] The conferral of greater powers on the examiner may, however, be ordered under subsection (4).[9]

1 *Re Holidair Ltd* [1994] 1 IR 416, per Finlay CJ at p440.

2 *Re Atlantic Magnetics Ltd* [1993] 2 IR 561; *Re Holidair Ltd* [1994] 1 IR 416. If the borrowing is necessary for the survival of the company, the examiner may be entitled to ignore existing negative pledge clauses: C(A)A 1990, s 7(5B) and (5C).

3 *Re Atlantic Magnetics Ltd* [1993] 2 IR 561.

4 *Re Edenpark Construction Ltd* [1994] 3 IR 126.

5 RSC, Ord 75A, r 11.

6 RSC, Ord 75A, r 11.

7 *Re Home Treat Ltd* [1991] BCLC 705.

8 *Re Holidair Ltd* [1994] 1 IR 416 at 440.

9 *Re Holidair Ltd* [1994] 1 IR 416 at 440.

Conferral of powers of a liquidator: Despite the confusion and inconsistency of the opening words of C(A)A 1990, s 9(4) which refer back to sub-s (1), it was thought that sub-s (4) vested an additional authority in the court to confer on the examiner all or any of the powers of an official liquidator and not just those powers which, pre-liquidation, would have been exercisable by the directors instead.[1] However, it now appears that the conferral of the powers of a liquidator on the examiner may only occur as part of an application pursuant to sub-s (1) whereby all or some of the directors' powers are also being conferred on him.[2] One of the liquidator's power that the examiner could, for example, seek to have conferred on him might be the power of disclaimer in respect of onerous property.[3]

1 *Re Holidair Ltd* [1994] 1 IR 416 at 441.

2 *Re Fate Park Ltd* [2009] IEHC 375.

3 CA 1963, s 290. In *Re Linen Supply of Ireland Ltd* (4 December 2009, unreported) HC, McGovern J held that the power of disclaimer could not be conferred on an examiner. However, the reasons given by him for this conclusion were rejected by the Supreme Court on appeal, albeit in the context of C(A)A 1990, s 20: (10 December 2009, unreported) SC (Murray CJ). It is thought that the reasoning of the Supreme Court therefore means that the power of disclaimer is indeed one that an examiner can seek under s 9(4).

UK legislation

See IA 1986, s 14, Sch 1.

10 Incurring of certain liabilities by examiner

(1) [Any][a] liabilities incurred by the company during the protection period which are referred to in subsection (2) shall be treated as expenses properly incurred, for the purpose of section 29, by the examiner.

(2) The liabilities referred to in subsection (1) are those certified by the examiner at the time they are incurred, in circumstances where, in the opinion of the examiner, the survival of the company as a going concern during the protection period would otherwise be seriously prejudiced.

(3) In this section, 'protection period' means the period, beginning with the appointment of an examiner, during which the company is under the protection of the court.

Amendments

a Substituted by CA 1990, s 180.

Definitions

'company': CA 1963, s 2(1); 'court': CA 1963, s 2(1); 'examiner': C(A)A 1990, s 1: The phrase 'examiner' includes any interim examiner so appointed by the Court.[1]

1 RSC, Ord 75A, r 1(4).

Notes

Certified liabilities[1]: Any post-petition liabilities which are certified by the examiner will be treated as expenses of the examinership and will therefore enjoy the priority afforded by C(A)A 1990, s 29. In this regard, whilst the remuneration and other expenses of the examinership will rank ahead of all other claims, secured or unsecured,[2] the priority afforded to liabilities certified under C(A)A 1990, s 10 is less generous. Although ranking ahead of unsecured claims and claims secured by a floating charge, they nonetheless rank behind any claim secured by a fixed charge.[3]

Pre-petition liabilities (such as the cost of presenting the petition itself) cannot be certified under C(A)A 1990, s 10.[4] In this regard, the examiner may only certify post-petition liabilities where in the opinion of the examiner, the survival of the company would otherwise be seriously prejudiced.[5] In this regard the prejudice must be foreseen as occurring during the protection period itself.[6] The decision of the examiner to certify a liability is not conclusive and may be reviewed by the court.[7] Furthermore, in appointing the examiner, the court is entitled, in appropriate circumstances, to curtail his power of certification, limiting him, for example, to certifying certain types or categories of liabilities.[8]

Great care and professional expertise must be exercised by the examiner in issuing certificates under C(A)A 1990, s 10.[9] The directors should normally submit to the examiner their proposals in relation to particular liabilities which they propose to incur and should satisfy him as to how the services or goods to be obtained will benefit the company and contribute to its survival during the protection period.[10] Furthermore, the examiner must certify the liabilities as and when they are incurred, rather than either retrospectively certifying them or certifying them *en bloc* before they have even been incurred.[11] Although the legislation does not expressly stipulate that the certificate should be in writing, the court regards documented certification as being 'an obvious and administrative necessity.'[12]

1 See generally, O'Donnell, 'Nursing the Corporate Patient – Examinership and Certification Under the Companies (Amendment) Act 1990' (1994) CLP 83.

2 C(A)A 1990, s 29(3).

3 C(A)A 1990, s 29(3A).

4 *Re Don Bluth Entertainment Ltd* [1994] 3 IR 141. In *Re Edenpark Construction Ltd* [1994] 3 IR 126 it was indicated that the costs incurred by a company in presenting a petition in respect of a related company would not be capable of certification under C(A)A 1990, s 10. This rationale is hard to understand, at least in circumstances where the placing of the related company in examinership may be necessary for the survival of the first company.

5 C(A)A 1990, s 10(2). See also *Re Edenpark Construction Ltd* [1994] 3 IR 126.

6 *Re Edenpark Construction Ltd* [1994] 3 IR 126.

7 *Re Don Bluth Entertainment Ltd* [1994] 3 IR 141; *Re Clare Textiles Ltd* [1993] 2 IR 213.

8 *Re Don Bluth Entertainment Ltd* [1994] 3 IR 141.

9 *Re Don Bluth Entertainment Ltd* [1994] 3 IR 141.

10 *Re Don Bluth Entertainment Ltd* [1994] 3 IR 141.

11 *Re Edenpark Construction Ltd* [1994] 3 IR 126; *Re Don Bluth Entertainment Ltd* [1994] 3 IR 141.

12 *Re Edenpark Construction Ltd* [1994] 3 IR 126.

UK legislation

See IA 1986, s 19(5).

---

11 Power to deal with charged property, etc

(1) Where, on an application by the examiner, the court is satisfied that the disposal (with or without other assets) of any property of the company which is subject to a security which, as created, was a floating charge or the exercise by the examiner of his powers in relation to such property would be likely to facilitate the survival of the whole or any part of the company as a going concern, the court may by order authorise the examiner to dispose of the property, or exercise his powers in relation to it, as the case may be, as if it were not subject to the security.

(2) Where, on an application by the examiner, the court is satisfied that the disposal (with or without other assets) of—

(a) any property of the company subject to a security other than a security to which subsection (1) applies, or

(b) any goods in the possession of the company under a hire-purchase agreement,

would be likely to facilitate the survival of the whole or any part of the company as a going concern, the court may by order authorise the examiner to dispose of the property as if it were not subject to the security or to dispose of the goods as if all rights of the owner under the hire-purchase agreement were vested in the company.

(3) Where property is disposed of under subsection (1), the holder of the security shall have the same priority in respect of any property of the company directly or indirectly representing the property disposed of as he would have had in respect of the property subject to the security.

(4) It shall be a condition of an order under subsection (2) that—

(a) the net proceeds of the disposal, and

(b) where those proceeds are less than such amount as may be determined by the court to be the net amount which would be realised on a sale of the property or goods in the open market by a willing vendor, such sums as may be required to make good the deficiency,

shall be applied towards discharging the sums secured by the security or payable under the hire-purchase agreement.

(5) Where a condition imposed in pursuance of subsection (4) relates to two or more securities, that condition requires the net proceeds of the disposal and, where paragraph (b) of that subsection applies, the sums mentioned in that paragraph to be applied towards [discharging][a] the sums secured by those securities in the order of their priorities.

(6) An office copy of an order under subsection (1) or (2) in relation to a security shall, within 7 days after the making of the order, be delivered by the examiner to the registrar of companies.

(7) If the examiner without reasonable excuse fails to comply with subsection (6), he [shall be guilty of an offence and liable to a fine][b] not exceeding [€1,904.61][c].

(8) References in this section to a hire-purchase agreement include a conditional sale agreement, a retention of title agreement and an agreement for the bailment of goods which is capable of subsisting for more than 3 months.

Amendments

a Word inserted by CA 1990, s 181.

b Words inserted by C(AA)A 2003, Sch 2.

c £1,000 increased to £1,500 by CA 1990, s 140(7) as inserted by CLEA 2001, s 104. £1,500 converted to €1,904.61 by Council Regulations (EC) No 1103/97, No 974/98 and No 2866/98 and the Economic and Monetary Union Act, 1998, s 6.

Definitions

'company': CA 1963, s 2(1); 'court': CA 1963, s 2(1); 'examiner': C(A)A 1990, s 1: The phrase 'examiner' includes any interim examiner so appointed by the Court[1]; 'hire purchase agreement': C(A)A 1990, s 11(8); 'registrar of companies': CA 1963, s 2(1).

1 RSC, Ord 75A, r 1(4).

Notes

Disposal of charged assets: C(A)A 1990, s 11 enables the examiner to dispose of assets which are subject to fixed or floating charges or retention of title, hire-purchase or lease-finance agreements. Such a disposal will only be permitted where it is 'likely to facilitate the survival of the whole or any part of the company as a going concern'.[1] The leave of the court will be required unless the affected creditor already consents to the disposal.[2] The application by the examiner must be by notice of motion grounded upon affidavit of the examiner and served upon the holder of the security or the creditor under the 'hire-purchase agreement', as the case may be, or upon any other person who appears to have an interest in the property.[3] On hearing the application the court may give such directions as it thinks just and proper concerning the proceeds of the disposal.[4]

If the assets are subject to a charge 'which, as created, was a floating charge'[5] the secured creditor will be deemed to have a corresponding security over the proceeds of the disposal.[6] However, if the assets are subject to a fixed charge or a 'hire-purchase agreement', it will be a condition of any disposal order that the net proceeds or the net amount which would be achieved on an open market sale by a willing vendor (whichever is the greater) be applied towards discharging the sums secured by the charge or payable under the agreement, as the case may be.[7] In the case of a fixed charge, the amount payable will include not only all principal and interest, but also any costs to which the debentureholder is entitled either under the general law or under the terms of the security.[8] *Prima facie*, these payments must be made notwithstanding the fact that the company is still in under the protection of the court and no scheme of arrangement has yet been voted on by the creditors. Accordingly, it will only be in 'quite exceptional circumstances' that the court will authorise such a disposal before the examiner has even formulated his proposals for the survival of the company and all or part of its undertaking as a going concern.[9]

1 See C(A)A 1990, s 11(1) and (2).

2 *Re Newman Shopfitters (Cleveland) Ltd* [1991] BCLC 407.

3 RSC, Ord 75A, r 12.

4 RSC, Ord 75A, r 12. In the case of a disposal of assets which are subject to a fixed charge or a 'hire-purchase agreement' any such directions of the court regarding the proceeds of sale must, of course, comply with the requirements of C(A)A 1990, s 11(4).

5 See *Re Holidair Ltd* [1994] 1 IR 416 in relation to the decrystallisation of previously crystallised floating charges which occurs upon the appointment of an examiner. See also *Re Brightlife Ltd* [1986] BCLC 418 at 425.

6 See C(A)A 1990, s 11(3).

7 See C(A)A 1990, s 11(4).

8 *Re ARV Aviation Ltd* [1989] BCLC 664.

9 *Re Consumer and Industrial Press Ltd (No 2)* (1988) 4 BCC 72.

UK legislation

See IA 1986, s 15.

---

12 Notification of appointment of examiner

(1) Where a petition is presented under section 2, notice of the petition in the prescribed form shall, within 3 days after its presentation, be delivered by the petitioner to the registrar of companies.

(2) [(a) An examiner shall, within the time limits specified in paragraph (b), cause to be published in [The Companies Registration Office Gazette][a] and in at least two daily newspapers circulating in the district in which the registered office or principal place of business of the company is situate a notice of his appointment and the date thereof.][b]

(b) The time limits referred to in paragraph (a) are—

(i) twenty-one days after his appointment in the case of [the Companies Registration Office Gazette],[a] and

(ii) three days after his appointment in the other case referred to in that paragraph.

(3) An examiner shall, within three days after his appointment, deliver to the registrar of companies a copy of the order appointing him.

[(4) Where a company is, by virtue of section 5, deemed to be under the protection of the court, every invoice, order for goods or business letter issued by or on behalf of the company, being a document on or in which the name of the company appears, shall immediately after the mention of that name, include the words 'in examination (under the Companies (Amendment) Act, 1990).][c]

(5) A person who fails to comply with the provisions of this section shall be guilty of an offence and shall be liable, on summary conviction, to a fine not exceeding [€1,904.61][d] and, on conviction on indictment, to a fine not exceeding [€12,697.38].[d]

Amendments

a 'The Companies Registration Office Gazette' substituted for '*Iris Oifigiúil*' by IFCMPA 2005, s 72.

b C(A)A 1990, s 12(2)(a) substituted by C(A)(No 2)A 1999, s 20(1).

c C(A)A 1990, s 12(4) substituted by C(A)(No 2)A 1999, s 20(2).

d £1,000 increased to £1500 by CA 1990, s 240(7) as inserted by CLEA 2001, s 104. £1,500 and £10,000 converted to €1,904.61 and €12,697.38 respectively by Council Regulations (EC) No 1103/97, No 974/98 and No 2866/98 and the Economic and Monetary Union Act, 1998, s 6.

Definitions

'company': CA 1963, s 2(1); 'court': CA 1963, s 2(1); 'document': CA 1963, s 2(1); 'examiner': C(A)A 1990, s 1: The phrase 'examiner' includes any interim examiner so appointed by the Court[1]; 'registrar of companies': CA 1963, s 2(1).

1 RSC, Ord 75A, r 1(4).

Notes

Notification of petition and appointment of examiner: In addition to the notice requirements contained in this section, see also C(A)A 1990, s 3 and the notes thereto entitled 'Ex parte application to court'. See also C(A)A 1990, s 3B.

UK legislation

See IA 1986, ss 12, 21, 430, Sch 10.

13 General provisions as to examiners

(1) An examiner may resign or, on cause shown, be removed by the court.

(2) If for any reason a vacancy occurs in the office of examiner, the court may by order fill the vacancy.

(3) An application for an order under subsection (2) may be made by—

(a) any committee of creditors established under section 21, or

(b) the company or any interested party.

(4) An examiner shall be described by the style of 'the examiner' of the particular company in respect of which he is appointed and not by his individual name.

(5) The acts of an examiner shall be valid notwithstanding any defects that may afterwards be discovered in his appointment or qualification.

(6) An examiner shall be personally liable on any contract entered into by him in the performance of his functions (whether such contract is entered into by him in the name of the company or in his own name as examiner or otherwise) unless the contract provides that he is not to be personally liable on such contract, and he shall be entitled in respect of that liability to indemnity out of the assets; but nothing in this subsection shall be taken as limiting any right to indemnity which he would have apart from this subsection, or as limiting his liability on contracts entered into without authority or as conferring any right to indemnity in respect of that liability.

(7) A company to which an examiner has been appointed or an interested party may apply to the court for the determination of any question arising out of the performance or otherwise by the examiner of his functions.

Cross reference

For the power of the examiner to apply to court for directions, see C(A)A 1990, s 7(6).

Definitions

'company': CA 1963, s 2(1); 'court': CA 1963, s 2(1);'examiner': C(A)A 1990, s 1: The phrase 'examiner' includes any interim examiner so appointed by the Court[1]; 'interested party': C(A)A 1990, s 1, s 2(1).

[1] RSC, Ord 75A, r 1(4).

Notes

Resignation of examiner: An examiner wishing to resign must do so by application *ex parte* to the court. On the hearing of the application the court may, if it thinks fit, direct that notice of the application be served on the petitioner, the company, the directors or any interested party. The application must be grounded upon an affidavit sworn by the examiner and must specify the reasons for his proposed resignation, and the date of the proposed resignation. On hearing the application the court may make such order as it thinks just and proper in the circumstances.[1]

[1] RSC, O 75A, r 13(1).

Removal of an examiner: An application to the court to remove an examiner must be made by motion on notice to the examiner, to the petitioner, to the company, to the directors and to such other parties as the court may direct.[1]. It must be grounded upon an affidavit specifying the cause alleged to justify the removal of the examiner.[2] On hearing the application the court may make such orders as appear to be just and, if it is satisfied that cause has been shown, it may order that the examiner be removed either forthwith or on such date as it may specify.[3] Furthermore, either before or after ruling on the application for removal of the examiner the court may order the production of any document or documents, or order the preparation of such report or reports as it thinks fit.[4] This could include requiring the examiner to present a report of all work done by him up to the date of the application.

[1] RSC, Ord 75A, r 13(2).

[2] RSC, Ord 75A, r 13(2).

[3] RSC, Ord 75A, r 13(2).

[4] RSC, Ord 75A, r 13(2).

Casual vacancies: An application by the company or any creditors' committee or interested party to fill a vacancy in the office of examiner must be made *ex parte* to the court. However, the court may adjourn the application and make such directions as it deems proper, including directions for service of notice of the application upon such party as it thinks proper.[1]

1 RSC, Ord 75A, r 13(3).

Contractual liability of examiner: The provisions of C(A)A 1990, s 13(6) are based on CA 1963, s 316(2) which deal with the liability of a receiver on contracts entered into by him in the performance of his functions. He is entitled to be indemnified out of the assets of the company provided that, in entering into the contract in the first place, he was acting with authority.[1] In relation to the priority which the examiner enjoys in respect of any liability so incurred by him, see C(A)A 1990, s 29.

Although the basic rule is that the examiner is personally liable on any contract entered into by him in the performance of his functions, C(A)A 1990, s 13(6) does permit him to exclude that liability. In this regard, the exclusion of liability must be expressly made and simply describing the examiner in the contract as an 'agent' of the company will not suffice.[2]. If, the examiner does succeed in excluding personal liability on such a contract, the claim of the other party should rank as an expense of the examinership under s 29.[3]

In relation to pre-appointment contracts entered into by a company, the position of the examiner would appear to be the same as that of a receiver, namely that he has no personal liability in the absence of a novation.[4] Mere continuance of a pre-appointment contract does not amount to a novation.[5]

In one important respect the contractual position of an examiner differs from that of a receiver. In this regard, a receiver is primarily appointed to realise the company's assets for the benefit of a secured creditor whereas an examiner is appointed for the benefit of the creditors generally. Accordingly, whilst a receiver is free to break pre-appointment contracts in order to protect the position of the secured creditor,[6] an examiner has no automatic right to break such contracts[7] and indeed, in appropriate circumstances he may be restrained attempting to do so.[8] However, if he can establish that the contract is 'onerous' within the meaning of CA 1963, s 290, he may apply to the court under C(A)A 1990, s 9(4) to have conferred on him a liquidator's powers of disclaimer.

1 See C(A)A 1990, s 9 and the notes thereto regarding the circumstances in which the power to enter into contracts on behalf of and/or in the name of the company, can be transferred from the directors to the examiner.

2 *Phonogram Ltd v Lane* [1981] 3 WLR 736.

3 *Re British Power Traction and Lighting Co* [1906] 1 Ch 497; *Healy v Oliver* [1918] 1 IR 366.

4 *Ardmore Studios (Ireland) Ltd v Lynch* [1965] IR 1; *Re B Johnson and Co (Builders) Ltd* [1955] 1 Ch 634; *Re Newdigate Colliery Co Ltd* [1912] 1 Ch 68; *Airline Airspaces Ltd v Handley Page Ltd* [1970] Ch 193; *Nicoll v Cutts* [1986] BCLC 99.

5 *Nicoll v Cutts* [1986] BCLC 99.

6 *Ardmore Studios (Ireland) Ltd v Lynch* [1965] IR 1.

7 C(A)A 1990, s 7(5B) and (5C). Repudiation may, however, be permitted by the court in circumstances where a scheme of arrangement is being formulated: see 20.

8 *Astor Chemicals Ltd v Synthetic Technology Ltd* [1990] BCLC 1.

Application for directions: C(A)A 1990, s 13(7) confers on the company and any interested party a right to apply to the court to determine any question arising out of the performance or non-performance by the examiner of his functions. Any such application must be made by motion on notice to the examiner and any other interested party or the company, as the case may be.[1] The examiner himself may also apply for directions under C(A)A 1990, s 7(6).

1 RSC, Ord 75A, r 9(3).

UK legislation

See IA 1986, ss 13, 19, 27.

[13A Hearing regarding irregularities

(1) Where, arising out of the presentation to it of the report of the independent accountant or otherwise, it appears to the court that there is evidence of a substantial disappearance of property of the company concerned that is not adequately accounted for, or of other serious irregularities in relation to the company's affairs having occurred, the court shall, as soon as it is practicable, hold a hearing to consider that evidence.

(2) If, before the hearing referred to in subsection (1) is held, the court directs the examiner to do so, the examiner shall prepare a report setting out any matters which he considers will assist the court in considering the evidence concerned on that hearing.

(3) The examiner shall supply a copy of a report prepared by him under subsection (2) to the company concerned on the same day as he causes the report to be delivered to the office of the court.

(4) The examiner shall also supply a copy of a report prepared by him under subsection (2) to each person who is mentioned in the report and any interested party on written application being made to him in that behalf.

(5) If the court, on application to it in that behalf, directs that that supply may be the subject of such omission, there may be omitted from any copy of the report supplied to a person referred to in subsection (4) or an interested party such parts of it as are specified in the direction of the court.

(6) The court may, in particular, on such an application, direct that there may be omitted from such a supply of a copy of the report any information the inclusion of which in such a copy would be likely to prejudice the survival of the company or the whole or any part of its undertaking as a going concern.

(7) The examiner shall, as soon as may be after it is prepared, supply a copy of the report prepared by him under subsection (2) to—

(a) if the company concerned is a company referred to in paragraph (a) of section 3(2), the Minister, or

(b) if the company concerned is a company referred to in paragraph (b) or (c) of section 3(2), the Central Bank, and subsections (5) and (6) shall not apply to such a copy.

(8) The following persons shall be entitled to appear and be heard at a hearing under this section—

(a) the examiner,

(b) if the court decided to hold a hearing under this section because of matters contained in the report of the independent accountant, the independent accountant,

(c) the company concerned,

(d) any interested party,

(e) any person who is referred to in the report of the independent accountant or the report prepared under subsection (2),

(f) if the company concerned is a company referred to in paragraph (a) of section 3 (2), the Minister,

(g) if the company concerned is a company referred to in paragraph (b)or (c) of section 3(2), the Central Bank.

(9) The court may, on a hearing under this section, make such order or orders as it deems fit (including, where appropriate, an order for the trial of any issue relating to the matter concerned).

(10) The court may, if it considers it appropriate to do so, direct that an office copy of an order under subsection (9) shall be delivered to the registrar of companies by the examiner or such other person as it may specify.][a]

Amendments

a C(A)A 1990, s 13A was inserted by C(A)(No 2)A 1999, s 21.

Definitions

'company': CA 1963, s 2(1); 'court': CA 1963, s 2(1). See also C(A)A 1990, s 3(9); 'examiner': C(A)A 1990, s 1: The phrase 'examiner' includes any interim examiner so appointed by the Court[1]; 'the independent accountant': C(A)A 1990, s 3(3A); 'interested party': C(A)A 1990, s 1; 'the Minister': C(A)A 1990, s 1.

1 RSC, Ord 75A, r 1(4).

Notes

Hearing into irregularities: If the contents of the independent accountant's report[1] disclose financial or other irregularities in relation to the company's affairs or if at any other stage during the examinership process such irregularities come to the attention of the court,[2] a hearing must be held as soon as practicable to consider the evidence.[3] The court may direct the examiner or interim examiner to prepare a report in advance of the hearing setting out any matters of relevance.[4] The report will automatically be furnished to the court and to the company by the examiner.[5] Any person named in the report and any other interested party may apply to him for a copy[6] although the court can direct that all of part of the contents of the report should not be so disclosed[7] particularly if disclosure would adversely affect the prospects for the survival of the company.[8] If the company is one in respect of which the Minister or the Central Bank were the petitioner or would have been entitled to present a petition, a copy of the report in its unredacted form must be furnished to that party as well.[9]

The examiner, the company, all interested parties and any persons named in the independent person's report or the examiner's report, as the case may be, are entitled to be heard. The Minister and the Central Bank respectively may also appear and be heard in respect of companies where petitioned or could have petitioned for the appointment of the examiner.[10] At the end of the hearing the court may make whatever order or orders it thinks fit, including an order for the trial of issues.[11] Because of the limited timescale within which an examinership must be concluded,[12] a full trial of issues may simply not be practicable.[13]. Accordingly, if the allegations of wrongdoing have sufficient weight, the more appropriate course may be to lift the protection of the court and order that the company be wound up, leaving it to the liquidator to then investigate the matter fully.

1 In relation to the independent accountant's report generally, see C(A)A 1990, s 3(3A) and (3B) and the notes thereto. It is unlikely that a company would actually present a petition for the appointment of an examiner, in circumstances where the report contains damaging allegations of irregularities. The provisions of C(A)A 1990, s 13A may therefore be of more relevance in the limited instances where the petitioner is a creditor, the Minister or the Central Bank.

2 In relation to the duty of good faith and full disclosure to the court, see C(A)A 1990, s 4A and the notes thereto.

3 C(A)A 1990, s 13A(1).

4 C(A)A 1990, s 13A(2).

5 C(A)A 1990, s 13A(3).

6 C(A)A 1990, s 13A(4).

7 C(A)A 1990, s 13A(5). In relation to persons commented upon critically in the report, the requirements of natural justice would seem to dictate that no portion of the report should be excised if to do so would result in the individual not knowing the nature of the allegations being made against him and thereby being unable to properly defend himself: *Re Haughey* [1971] IR 217; *Killiney and Ballybrack v Minister for Local Government (No 1)* (1978) 112 ILTR 9; *Kiely v Minister for Social Welfare (No 2)* [1977] IR 267.

8 C(A)A 1990, s 13A(6).

9 C(A)A 1990, s 13A(7).

10 C(A)A 1990, s 13A(8).

11 C(A)A 1990, s 13A(9).

12 See C(A)A 1990, s 5(1).

13 *Re Hefferon Kearns Ltd* [1992] ILRM 51.

14 Information to be given when examiner appointed

[...][a]

Amendments

a C(A)A 1990, s 14 was repealed by C(A)(No 2)A 1999, s 30.

15 Examination of affairs of company

[...][a]

Amendments

a C(A)A 1990, s 15 was repealed by C(A)(No 2)A 1999, s 30.

16 Examiner's report

[...][a]

Amendments

a C(A)A 1990, s 16 was repealed by C(A)(No 2)A 1999, s 30.

17 Hearing of matters arising from examiner's report

[...][a]

Amendments

a C(A)A 1990, s 17 was repealed by C(A)(No 2)A 1999, s 30.

18 Further report by examiner

[(1) An examiner shall—

(a) as soon as practicable after he is appointed, formulate proposals for a compromise or scheme of arrangement in relation to the company concerned,

(b) without prejudice to any other provision of this Act, carry out such other duties as the court may direct him to carry out.][a]

(2) Notwithstanding any provision of the Companies Acts relating to notice of general meetings, (but subject to notice of not less than three days in any case) the examiner shall convene and preside at such meetings of members and creditors as he thinks proper, [for the purpose of section 23 and shall report on those proposals to the court, within 35 days of his appointment or such longer period as the court may allow, in accordance with section 19.][b].

(3) Where, on the application of the examiner, the court is satisfied that the examiner would be unable to report to the court within the period of [70 days][c] referred to in section 5(1) but that he would be able to make a report if that period were extended, the court may by order extend that period by not more than 30 days to enable him to do so.

(4) Where the examiner has submitted a report under this section to the court and, but for this subsection, the period mentioned in section 5(1) (and any extended period allowed under subsection (3) of this section) would expire, the court may, of its own motion or on the application of the examiner, extend the period concerned by such period as the court considers necessary to enable it to take a decision under section 24.

[(5) The examiner shall supply a copy of his report under this section—

(a) to the company concerned on the same day as he causes the report to be delivered to the office of the court, and

(b) to any interested party on written application being made to him in that behalf.

(6) The examiner shall, as soon as may be after it is prepared, supply a copy of his report under this section to—

(a) if the company concerned is a company referred to in paragraph (a) of section 3(2), the Minister, or

(b) if the company concerned is a company referred to in paragraph (b) or (c) of section 3(2), the Central Bank.

(7) If the court, on application to it in that behalf, directs that that supply may be the subject of such omission, there may be omitted from any copy of the report supplied under subsection (5)(b) to an interested party such parts of it as are specified in the direction of the court.

(8) The court may, in particular, on such an application, direct that there may be omitted from such a supply of a copy of the report any information the inclusion of which in such a copy would be likely to prejudice the survival of the company or the whole or any part of its undertaking as a going concern.

(9) If the examiner is not able to enter into an agreement with the interested parties and any other persons concerned in the matter or formulate proposals for a compromise or scheme of arrangement in relation to the company concerned, he may apply to the court for the grant of directions in the matter and the court may, on such application, give such directions or make such order as it deems fit, including, if it considers it just and equitable to do so, an order for the winding-up of the company.][d]

Amendments

a C(A)A 1990, s 18(1) substituted by C(A)(No 2)A 1999, s 22(a).

b C(A)A 1990, s 18(2) amended by C(A)(No 2)A 1999, s 22(b).

c C(A)A 1990, s 18(3) amended by C(A)(No 2)A 1999, s 22(c).

d C(A)A 1990, s 18(5) and (6) substituted and subsections (7) to (9) inserted by C(A)(No 2)A 1999, s 22(d).

Definitions

'central bank'[1]: C(A)A 1990, s 1; 'company': CA 1963, s 2(1); 'Companies Acts': C(A)A 1990, s 1; 'court': CA 1963, s 2(1); 'examiner': C(A)A 1990, s 1: The phrase 'examiner' includes any interim examiner so appointed by the Court,[2] 'interested party': C(A)A 1990, s 1, s 2(1); 'member': CA 1963, s 31.

1 See Central Bank and Financial Services Authority of Ireland Act 2003, s 33C(1) and (2) whereby the Financial Regulator is entitled to perform the functions of the Central Bank under C(A)A 1990, ss 3, 3C, 18, 23, 24 and 27.

2 RSC, Ord 75A, r 1(4).

Notes

Contents of proposals: See C(A)A 1990, s 22 and the notes thereto.

Notice of meetings: The meetings of members and creditors may be held on not less than three days' notice, which is a significantly shorter notice period than would normally pertain for general meetings.[1] It reflects the fact that the examiner must operate within a relatively condensed time frame in formulating and seeking approval for any rescue package.

1 With regard to the normal notice requirements for general meetings, see CA 1963, ss 133 and 141.

Consideration of proposals by members and creditors: See C(A)A 1990, s 23 and the notes thereto.

Report to court: C(A)A 1990, s 18(2) envisages the examiner formulating his proposals, having them considered by the creditors and members, and reporting back to court all within 35 days of his appointment. In practice, this timetable is often difficult to follow and accordingly, subsection (3) allows for the granting of extensions of up to 30 additional days. The application for the extension of time is made *ex parte* by the examiner.[1] However, any party affected by the extension may apply to the court by motion on notice to the examiner to set the aside the order extending the time, and must specify in his affidavit the grounds upon which he is mounting any such challenge.[2]

Once the examiner has held the requisite meetings of creditors and members, he then presents his report to the court by way of *ex parte* application.[3] At this stage the court will fix a date for the hearing to consider the report under C(A)A 1990, s 24 and may direct that the hearing be advertised or may direct that relevant affected parties be put on notice. On the same day a copy of the report must be delivered to the company[4] and, on written application, to any interested party.[5] If the company is one in respect of which the Minister or the Central Bank could have been petitioner, then a copy of the report must be delivered to that party as well.[6]

1 RSC, Ord 75A, r 16.
2 RSC, Ord 75A, r 16.
3 RSC, Ord 75A, r 17(1).
4 C(A)A 1990, s 18(5)(a).
5 C(A)A 1990, s 18(5)(b). The court may direct that parts of the report be omitted from the copy furnished to interested parties where disclosure of the information contained therein could adversely affect the survival of the company: C(A)A 1990, s 18(7) and (8).
6 C(A)A 1990, s 18(6).

Contents of the report: The report must contain a full account of each meeting convened by the examiner and of the proposals put before each such meeting and must contain as an appendix a copy of the proposals.[1] Any modifications to the proposals adopted at the meetings must also be detailed along with the recommendations of the creditors' committee, if any.[2] The report must include a statement of the assets and liabilities of the company together with a list of creditors.[3] For each creditor there should be details of the amount owed, the security, if any held, and the preferential status, if any, enjoyed.[4] The report should identify the officers of the company and should set out any recommendations of the examiner as well as detailing any other matters which the examiner deems relevant or the court directs.[5] The examiner must also specify in his application whether, and if so what, portions of the report should be omitted from delivery to interested parties and he must draw to the attention of the court any particular aspects of the report which are or may be relevant to the exercise by the court of any of its other functions under the Act.[6]

1 RSC, Ord 75A, r 17(2)(a). See also C(A)A 1990, s 19.
2 C(A)A 1990, s 19(b) and (d).
3 C(A)A 1990, s 19(f).
4 C(A)A 1990, s 19(f).
5 C(A)A 1990, s 19(g), (h) and (i). Any misstatement of assets and liabilities in the petition or any other financial irregularity, if not already reported to the court under C(A)A 1990, s 13B, should be detailed in the C(A)A 1990, s 18 report, since evidence of such wrongdoing is a factor for the court to take into account in determining whether or not to confirm the examiner's proposals: *Re Wogans (Drogheda) Ltd (No 2)* (7 May 1992, unreported) HC (Costello J); *Re Wogans (Drogheda) Ltd (No 3)* (9 February 1993, unreported) HC (Costello J): *Re Selukwe Ltd* (20 December 1991, unreported) HC (Costello J); *Re Traffic Group Ltd* [2008] 1 IR 253.
6 RSC, O 75A, r 17(2)(b).

Extension of protection period: If the date for the C(A)A 1990, s 24 hearing is more than 70 days beyond the date on which the petition was originally presented, the court may, of its own motion or on application by the examiner, grant an extension of the protection period for such period of time as may be necessary.[1] If it is the examiner who applies for the extension of time, he must initially do so *ex parte* although the court may then direct service of notice of the application on such party or parties as it thinks fit and may adjourn the application to enable service to take place. However, if the court does direct that parties be put on notice of the application, it may nonetheless extend the protection *pro tem.*[2]

1 C(A)A 1990, s 18(4).
2 RSC, Ord 75A, r 17(3).

Inability to formulate proposals: If the examiner is unable to formulate proposals for the survival of the company and the whole or part of its undertaking as a going concern, he should apply to the court for directions in the matter.[1] Before making any order, the court may direct that notice of the application be given to all or some of the creditors and members of the company. On hearing the application, the court may make whatever order it thinks fit including an order discharging the examiner, lifting the protection of the court[2] and directing that the company be wound up.[3]

1 C(A)A 1990, s 18(9).
2 See C(A)A 1990, s 26.
3 C(A)A 1990, s 18(9).

UK legislation

See IA 1986, s 23.

19 Examiner's report under section 18

An Examiner's report under section 18 shall include—

(a) the proposals placed before the required meetings,

(b) any modification of those proposals adopted at any of those meetings,

(c) the outcome of each of the required meetings,

(d) the recommendation of the committee of creditors, if any,

(e) a statement of the assets and liabilities (including contingent and prospective liabilities) of the company as at the date of his report,

(f) a list of the creditors of the company, the amount owing to each such creditor, the nature and value of any security held by any such creditor, and the priority status of any such creditor under section 285 of the Principal Act or any other statutory provision or rule of law,

(g) a list of the officers of the company,

(h) his recommendations,

(i) such other matters as the examiner deems appropriate or the court directs.

Definitions

'company': CA 1963, s 2(1); 'court': CA 1963, s 2(1); 'examiner': C(A)A 1990, s 1: The phrase 'examiner' includes any interim examiner so appointed by the Court[1]; 'officer': CA 1963, s 2(1); 'Principal Act': C(A)A 1990, s 1.

1 RSC, Ord 75A, r 1(4).

Notes

Contents of report: See notes to C(A)A 1990, s 18.

20 Repudiation of certain contracts

(1) Where proposals for a compromise or scheme of arrangement are to be formulated in relation to a company, the company may, subject to the approval of the court, affirm or repudiate any contract under which some element of performance other than payment remains to be rendered both by the company and the other contracting party or parties.

(2) Any person who suffers loss or damage as a result of such repudiation shall stand as an unsecured creditor for the amount of such loss or damage.

(3) In order to facilitate the formulation, consideration or confirmation of a compromise or scheme of arrangement, the court may hold a hearing and make an order determining the amount of any such loss or damage and the amount so determined shall be due by the company to the creditor as a judgement debt.

(4) Where the examiner is not a party to an application to the court for the purposes of subsection (1), the company shall serve notice of such application on the examiner and the examiner may appear and be heard on the hearing of any such application.

(5) Where the court approves the affirmation or repudiation of a contract under this section, it may in giving such approval make such orders as it thinks fit for the purposes of giving full effect to its approval including orders as to notice to, or declaring the rights of, any party affected by such affirmation or repudiation.

Definitions

'company': CA 1963, s 2(1); 'court': CA 1963, s 2(1); 'examiner': C(A)A 1990, s 1: The phrase 'examiner' includes any interim examiner so appointed by the Court[1].

1 RSC, Ord 75A, r 1(4).

Notes

Repudiation of contracts: During the protection period the power of the examiner to repudiate pre-appointment contracts is extremely curtailed.[1] However, under C(A)A 1990, s 20, if the examiner is formulate a scheme of arrangement for the survival of the company and the whole or part of its undertaking as a going concern, the company (and not the examiner) may apply to the court for permission to repudiate existing contracts.[2] The application will not be permitted if the only unperformed element involves the payment of money.[3] Some other element, such as the carrying out of works or the performances of services must be outstanding in order for the court to entertain the application. In this regard, it has recently been held by the Supreme Court that one of the types of contract that may be repudiated under s 20 is a lease of land.[4]

The section gives little guidance as to the types of contract that may be repudiated nor does it indicate what factors the court must take into account in determining whether or not to grant leave to repudiate. C(A)A 1990, s 20(3) would seem to suggest that the company must establish that the contract is onerous and that its continued performance would jeopardise the survival of the company.

1 See C(A)A 1990, s 7(5A) to (5C).

2 The examiner could, however, apply to have a liquidator's power of disclaimer conferred on him pursuant to C(A)A 1990, s 9(4).

3 See C(A)A 1990, s 20(1).

4 *Re Linen Supply of Ireland Ltd* (10 December 2009, unreported) SC (Murray CJ). The decision of the Supreme Court effectively reverses the decision of Ryan J in *O'Brien's Irish Sandwich Bars Ltd* (16 October 2009, unreported) HC (Ryan J), at least in so far as the judge was questioning the jurisdiction to repudiate a lease at all.

The application to court: The application by the company for leave to repudiate must be on notice, not only to the examiner, but also on notice to the other parties to the contract as well as any person who suffers loss or damage as a result of the repudiation.[1]

1 RSC, Ord 75A, r 19.

Hearing to quantify loss: Where the court grants leave to repudiate a contract, it may also conduct a hearing to determine the loss of any affected parties. Any application by the company arising out of the repudiation, to determine the amount of the creditor's loss or damage, must be on notice to the examiner, the creditor and any other parties to the contract.[1] The damages payable to the affected creditor are essentially in respect of moneys for which, as of the date of the presentation of the petition, he was a prospective creditor, and thus they are capable of being written down in the examiner's proposals for a scheme of arrangement.[2]

1 RSC, Ord 75A, r 19.

2 *Re Linen Supply of Ireland Ltd* (3 February 2010, unreported) HC (McGovern J).

21 Appointment of creditors' committee

(1) An examiner may, and if so directed by the court shall, appoint a committee of creditors to assist him in the performance of his functions.

(2) Save as otherwise directed by the court, a committee appointed under subsection (1) shall consist of not more than five members and shall include the holders of the three largest unsecured claims who are willing to serve.

(3) The examiner shall provide the committee with a copy of any proposals for a compromise or scheme of arrangement and the committee may express an opinion on the proposals on its own behalf or on behalf of the creditors or classes of creditors represented thereon.

(4) As soon as practicable after the appointment of a committee under subsection (1) the examiner shall meet with the committee to transact such business as may be necessary.

Definitions

'court': CA 1963, s 2(1); 'examiner': C(A)A 1990, s 1: The phrase 'examiner' includes any interim examiner so appointed by the Court[1]; 'member': CA 1963, s 31.

1 RSC, Ord 75A, r 1(4).

Notes

Creditors' committee: Creditors' committees are rare in practice, unlike their counterparts in liquidations,[1] Apart from being entitled to express an opinion on the examiner's proposals, the committee is given no specific functions by the Act other than 'to assist' the examiner.

1 For the powers of a committee of inspection in a winding up, see CA 1963, ss 231 to 233 and the notes thereto.

UK legislation

See IA 1986, s 26.

---

22 Contents of proposals

(1) Proposals for a compromise or scheme of arrangement shall—

(a) specify each class of members and creditors of the company,

(b) specify any class of members and creditors whose interests or claims will not be impaired by the proposals,

(c) specify any class of members and creditors whose interests or claims will be impaired by the proposals,

(d) provide equal treatment for each claim or interest of a particular class unless the holder of a particular claim or interest agrees to less favourable treatment,

(e) provide for the implementation of the proposals,

(f) if the examiner considers it necessary or desirable to do so to facilitate the survival of the company, and the whole or any part of its undertaking, as a going concern, specify whatever changes should be made in relation to the management or direction of the company,

(g) if the examiner considers it necessary or desirable as aforesaid, specify any changes he considers should be made in the memorandum or articles of the company, whether as regards the management or direction of the company or otherwise,

(h) include such other matters as the examiner deems appropriate.

(2) A statement of the assets and liabilities (including contingent and prospective liabilities) of the company as at the date of the proposals shall be attached to each copy of the proposals to be submitted to meetings of members and creditors under section 23.

(3) There shall also be attached to each such copy of the proposals a description of the estimated financial outcome of a winding-up of the company for each class of members and creditors.

(4) The court may direct that the proposals include whatever other provisions it deems fit.

(5) For the purpose of this section and sections 24 and 25, a creditor's claim against a company is impaired if he receives less in payment of his claim than the full amount due in respect of the claim at the date of presentation of the petition for the appointment of the examiner.

(6) For the purposes of this section and sections 24 and 25, the interest of a member of a company in a company is impaired if—

(a) the nominal value of his shareholding in the company is reduced,

(b) where he is entitled to a fixed dividend in respect of his shareholding in the company, the amount of that dividend is reduced,

(c) he is deprived of all or any part of the rights accruing to him by virtue of his shareholding in the company,

(d) his percentage interest in the total issued share capital of the company is reduced, or

(e) he is deprived of his shareholding in the company.

Cross reference

With regard to the circumstances in which the interests of creditors and members will be deemed to be impaired, see C(A)A 1990, s 22(5), (6).

Definitions

'articles': CA 1963, s 2(1); 'company': CA 1963, s 2(1); 'court': CA 1963, s 2(1); 'examiner': C(A)A 1990, s 1: The phrase 'examiner' includes any interim examiner so appointed by the Court[1]; 'member': CA 1963, s 31; 'memorandum': CA 1963, s 2(1); 'share': CA 1963, s 2(1).

1 RSC, Ord 75A, r 1(4).

Notes

Contents of the proposals: It is not sufficient for the examiner to prepare proposals which would result in the survival of all or part of the business. Rather, his proposals must envisage the survival of the company as a legal entity, along with all or part of its business as a going concern.[1] Where the examiner has been appointed to a group of companies, his proposals may, where appropriate, be formulated by reference to the group as a whole, rather than preparing separate proposals for each company within the group.[2]

1 *Re Clare Textiles Ltd* [1993] 2 IR 213.

2 *Re Goodman International and related companies* (28 January 1991, unreported) HC (Hamilton P). Proposals were also prepared on a group basis in *Re Antigen Holdings Ltd* [2001] 4 IR 600.

Class meetings: In formulating its proposals for a scheme of compromise or arrangement, the company must take great care to ensure that the affected parties are segregated into their correct classes. Each class must be confined to 'those persons whose rights are not so dissimilar as to make it impossible for them to consult together with a view to their common interest'.[1] If a particular creditor or member is placed in an incorrect class, the mistake may be fatal and the scheme may not be sanctioned by the court.[2]

1 *Sovereign Life Assurance Co v Dodd* (1892) 2 QB 573; *Re Pye (Ireland) Ltd* [1985] IEHC 62 (Costello J); *Re Heron International NV* [1994] 1 BCLC 667; *Re Osiris Insurance Ltd* [1999]1 BCLC 182; *Re BTR plc* [2000] 1 BCLC 740; *Re Hawk Insurance Co Ltd* [2001] 2 BCLC 480; *Re Anglo American Insurance Co Ltd* [2001] 1 BCLC 755; *Re Equitable Life Assurance Society* [2002] 2 BCLC 510; *Re Waste Recycling Group plc* [2004] 1 BCLC 352; *Re Telewest Communications plc (No 1)* [2005] 1 BCLC 752; *Re My Travel Group plc* [2005] 2 BCLC 123; *Re British Aviation Insurance Co Ltd* [2006] 1 BCLC 665; *Re Linen Supply of Ireland Ltd* (3 February 2010, unreported) HC (McGovern J). In these cases the judge looked for a 'community of interest' between all of the creditors who had been placed in one class by the company. See also *Re Colonia Insurance (Ireland) Ltd* [2005] 1 IR 497.

2 *Re United Provident Assurance Co Ltd* [1910] 2 Ch 477; *Re Hellenic and General Trust Ltd* [1975] 3 All ER 382; *Re Pye (Ireland) Ltd* [1985] IEHC 62 (Costello J).

Impairment: The claim of a creditor will be deemed to be impaired not only where he obtains less than the full amount of his debt,[1] but also where it is to paid by instalments beyond the contractual date for payment and is either to receive no interest or is to receive less interest than that to which he would otherwise be contractually entitled.[2] In relation to the members, they may be impaired by having their shares expropriated or by having the rights attaching to those shares varied.[3] However, if the company's liabilities exceed its assets, the shares may be worthless anyway and accordingly the impairment may, in commercial terms, be more apparent than real.

1 C(A)A 1990, s 22(5).

2 *Re Jetmara Teo* [1992] 1 IR 147; *Re Antigen Holdings Ltd* [2001] 4 IR 600.

3 C(A)A 1990, s 22(6).

---

23 Consideration by members and creditors of proposals

(1) This section applies to a meeting of members or creditors or any class of members or creditors summoned to consider proposals for a [compromise or scheme of arrangement; save where expressly provided otherwise in this section, this section shall not authorise, at such a meeting, anything to be done in relation to such proposals by any member or creditor.][a]

(2) At a meeting to which this section applies a modification of the proposals may be put to the meeting but may only be accepted with the consent of the examiner.

(3) [...][b].

(4) Proposals shall be deemed to have been accepted by a meeting of creditors or of a class of creditors when a majority in number representing a majority in value of the claims represented at that meeting have voted, either in person or by proxy, in favour of the resolution for the proposals.

[(4A) Nothing in subsection (4) shall, in the case of a creditor who abstains from voting, or otherwise fails to cast a vote, in respect of the proposals, be construed as permitting such an abstention or failure to be regarded as a casting by that person of a vote against the proposals.][c]

(5) (a) Where a State authority is a creditor of the company, such authority shall be entitled to accept proposals under this section notwithstanding—

(i) that any claim of such authority as a creditor would be impaired under the proposals, or

(ii) any other enactment.

(b) In this subsection, 'State authority' means the State, a Minister of the Government[, a local authority][d] or the Revenue Commissioners.

(6) Section 144 of the Principal Act shall apply to any resolution to which subsection [...][e] (4) relates which is passed at any adjourned meeting.

(7) Section 202, subsections (2) to (6), of the Principal Act shall, with the necessary modifications, apply to meetings held under this section.

(8) With every notice summoning a meeting to which this section applies which is sent to a creditor or member, there shall be sent also a statement explaining the effect of the compromise or scheme of arrangement and in particular stating any material interests of the directors of the company, whether as directors or as members or as creditors of the company or otherwise and the effect thereon of the compromise or arrangement, insofar as it is different from the effect on the like interest of other persons.

[(9) Without prejudice to subsections (1) to (8), in the case of a company referred to in paragraph (b) or (c) of section 3(2), the examiner shall also afford the Central Bank an opportunity to consider the proposals for a compromise or scheme of arrangement and for this purpose shall furnish to the Central Bank a statement containing the like information to that referred to in subsection (8).][f]

Amendments

a C(A)A 1990, s 23(1) amended by C(A)(No 2)A 1999, s 23(a).

b C(A)A 1990, s 23(3) deleted by C(A)(No 2)A 1999, s 23(b).

c C(A)A 1990, s 23(4A) inserted by C(A)(No 2)A 1999, s 23(c).

d Words inserted by CA 1990, s 180.

e C(A)A 1990, s 23(6) amended by C(A)(No 2)A 1999, s 23(d).

f C(A)A 1990, s 23(9) inserted by C(A)(No 2)A 1999, s 23(e).

Definitions

'central bank':[1] C(A)A 1990, s 1; 'company': CA 1963, s 2(1); 'director': CA 1963, s 2(1); 'examiner': C(A)A 1990, s 1: The phrase 'examiner' includes any interim examiner so appointed by the Court[b]; 'member': CA 1963, s 31; 'Principal Act': C(A)A 1990, s 1.

1 See Central Bank and Financial Services Authority of Ireland Act 2003, s 33C(1) and (2) whereby the Financial Regulator is entitled to perform the functions of the Central Bank under C(A)A 1990, ss 3, 3C, 18, 23, 24 and 27.

2 RSC, Ord 75A, r 1(4).

Notes

Notice of meetings: The examiner must summon all meetings of creditors and members by sending by post, not less than three days before the day appointed for the meeting, to every person appearing in the company's books to be a creditor or a member of the company, notice of the meeting of creditors or members as the case may be.[1] The notice to each creditor or member must be sent to such address as may be known to the Examiner.[2] The notice should be accompanied not only by a copy of the proposals, but also by a statement in the form prescribed by C(A)A 1990, s 23(8) explaining the effect of the proposed compromise or arrangement and identifying any material interests of the directors and the effect of the proposals thereon (insofar as different from the treatment of other members or creditors). This statement should give a full and proper explanation of the proposals and should identify how it will affect the interests of each member and creditor.[3]

An affidavit by the Examiner or solicitor or by some other officer or clerk of the company or its solicitor that the notice of any meeting has been duly posted shall be sufficient evidence of such notice having been duly sent to the person to whom the same was addressed.[4] In this regard, the proceedings and resolutions of the meetings shall unless the Court otherwise orders be valid, notwithstanding that some creditors or members, as the may be, have received the notice sent to them.[5] The court may however, decline to confirm the proposals if the notices convening the meetings were misleading or confusing.[6]

1 RSC, Ord 75A, r 18(1).

2 RSC, Ord 75A, r 18(2).

3 *Re English Scottish and Australian Chartered Bank* [1893] 3 Ch 385; *Re Dorman Long and Co* [1934] Ch 635; *Re Ratners Group plc* [1988] BCLC 685; *Re Heron International NV* [1994] 1 BCLC 667; *Re Minster Assets plc* [1985] BCLC 2000; *Re MB Group plc* [1989] BCLC 672.

4 RSC, Ord 75A, r 18(3).

5 RSC, Ord 75A, r 18(5).

6 *Re John Power and Sons Ltd* [1934] IR 412; *Re National Bank Ltd* [1966] 1 WLR 819; *Jackson v Munster Bank Ltd* (1884–85) 13 LR Ir 118.

Location and time of meetings: The examiner may fix a meeting of meetings to be held at such place as in his opinion is most convenient for the majority of creditors or members, or both and different times and/or places may be named for the meetings of creditors and members.[1]

1 RSC, Ord 75A, r 18(3).

Quorum: A meeting may not act for any purpose except the adjournment of the meeting unless there are present or represented thereat in the case of a creditors meeting, at least three creditors ruled by the examiner to be entitled to vote or in the case of a meeting of members, at least two members. If within 15 minutes from the time appointed for the meeting, a quorum of creditors or members as the case may be is not present or represented, the meeting must be adjourned for the same day in the following week at the same time and place or to such other day or time or place as the examiner may appoint but so that the day appointed shall not be less than three, nor more than 21 days from the date from which the meeting was adjourned.[1]

1 RSC, Ord 75A, r 18(7).

Examiner as chairman: The examiner must preside at and be chairman of any meeting which he has convened and must conduct the business of the meeting in an orderly manner so as to ensure the proper discussion of all proposals placed by him before the said meeting.[1] The examiner may with the consent of the meeting adjourn from time to time and from place to place but the adjourned meeting shall be held at the same place as the original meeting unless in a resolution for adjournment another place is specified or unless the court otherwise orders.[2] The examiner, when acting as chairman of the meetings of members and creditors, has a duty to exercise an independent professional judgment and if he falls significantly below the standards required of a reasonably competent insolvency practitioner, the court can require him to pay all or part of the costs of legal proceedings arising out of his inadequate discharge of his duties as chairman of the meetings, including the costs of any appeal from decisions made by him in relation to the entitlement or otherwise of members or creditors to vote at such meetings.[3]

1 RSC, Ord 75A, r 18(4).
2 RSC, Ord 75A, r 18(6).
3 *Re a debtor (No 222 of 1990) ex parte Bank of Ireland (No 2)* [1993] BCLC 233.

Minutes: The examiner must cause minutes of the proceedings of the meeting to be drawn up and entered in a book kept for that purpose and the minutes must be signed by him.[1] He must also cause a list of creditors present at every meeting to be kept and every such list must be signed by him.[2]

1 RSC, Ord 75A, r 18(8)(a).
2 RSC, Ord 75A, r 18(8)(b).

Proxies: Every creditor or member may appear either in person or by proxy.[1] A general and a special form of proxy must be sent to each of the creditors or members with a notice summoning the meeting and neither the name nor the description of the examiner or any other person must be printed or inserted in the body of any instrument of proxy before it is sent.[2] A creditor or a member may appoint any person a special proxy to vote at any specified meeting or adjournment thereof on all questions relating to any matter arising at the meeting or an adjournment thereof.[3] Any creditor or member may appoint the examiner to act as his general or special proxy.[4] However, no person who is an infant may be appointed either a general or a special proxy.[5] Every instrument of proxy must be lodged with the examiner no later than 16:00 of the day before the meeting or adjourned meeting at which it is to be used and the same must be kept by the examiner.[6]

1 RSC, Ord 75A, r 18(9). For the applicable from of proxy, see RSC, Appendix M, Forms 21 and 22.
2 RSC, Ord 75A, r 18(10).
3 RSC, Ord 75A, r 18(11).
4 RSC, Ord 75A, r 18(12).
5 RSC, Ord 75, r 18(14)(b).
6 RSC, Ord 75A, r 18(14(a).

Representation of corporations: Where a person is authorised in the manner provided by CA 1963, s 139 to represent a corporation at any meeting of creditors or members, such person must produce to the examiner a copy of the resolution so authorising him. Such copies must be under the seal of the corporation or be certified to be a true copy by the secretary or director of the corporation.[1] Alternatively, any person who is duly authorised under the seal of the corporation to act, generally on behalf its behalf at meetings of creditors and members, may fill in and sign the instrument of proxy on behalf of the corporation and appoint himself to be such company's proxy and the instrument of proxy so filled in and signed by such person shall be received and dealt with as a proxy of such company.[2]

1 RSC, Ord 75A, r 18(9).
2 RSC, Ord 75A, r 18(13).

Rejection of votes: The examiner has power to allow or disallow the vote of a person claiming to be a creditor or member, if he thinks fit, but his decision may be subject to appeal to the court. If he is in doubt whether a vote should be allowed or disallowed, he must allow it and record the vote as such subject to the vote being declared invalid in the event of an objection being taken and sustained by the court.[1] The meeting is not the place to go into a lengthy debate as to the exact status of a claim by a purported member or creditor of an entitlement to vote. Accordingly, the examiner, as chairman, must look at each claim and if it is plain or obvious that it is good, he must admit it; similarly, if it is plain or obvious that it is bad, he must reject it; but if there is a question or doubt, he must admit it subject to the right of interested parties to appeal his decision.[2] If the examiner rejects a creditor's vote, that particular creditor will not be bound by the examiner's proposals, even if duly confirmed by the court.[3]

1 RSC, Ord 75A, r 18(15).
2 *Re a debtor (No 222 of 1990), ex parte Bank of Ireland* [1992] BCLC 137.
3 *Re a debtor (No 222 of 1990), ex parte Bank of Ireland* [1992] BCLC 137.

Voting at meetings: Whilst the members may vote on the proposals, by virtue of the deletion of C(A)A 1990, s 23(3), their votes no longer count in determining whether the requisite approval has been obtained. At creditor meetings, the proposals will be deemed to have been approved if a majority in number representing also a majority in value of those voting in person or by proxy, vote in favour.[1] At each such class meeting, those present must vote *bona fide* in the interest of the class as a whole and failure to do so may result in the resolution being impugned.[2] A resolution passed at an adjourned meeting is to be treated as having been passed on the date on which it was in fact passed and not on any earlier date (such as the original date of the meeting).[3]

1 See C(A)A 1990, s 23(4). Abstentions are not to be counted as votes against the proposals: C(A)A 1990, s 23(4A).
2 *Re John Power and Sons Ltd* [1934] IR 412; *Re BTR plc* [2000] 1 BCLC 740; *Re Hawk Insurance Co Ltd* [2001] 2 BCLC 480; *Re Anglo Asmerican Insurance Co Ltd* [2001] 1 BCLC 755; *Re Alabama, New Orleans, Texas and Pacific Railway Co* [1891] 1 Ch 213; *Re Dorman Long and Co Ltd* [1934] Ch 635; *Carruth v Imperial Chemical Industries Ltd* [1937] 2 All ER 422; *British America Nickel Corporation Ltd v MJ O'Brien Ltd* [1927] AC 369; *Re Wedgewood Coal and Iron Co* (1877) 6 ChD 627.
3 CA 1963, s 144, as applied by C(A)A 1990, s 23(6).

UK legislation

See IA 1986, ss 4, 24.

---

24 Confirmation of proposals

(1) The report of the examiner under section 18 shall be set down for consideration by the court as soon as may be after receipt of the report by the court.

(2) The following persons may appear and be heard at a hearing under subsection (1)—

(a) the company,

(b) the examiner,

(c) any creditor or member whose claim or interest would be impaired if the proposals were implemented,

[(d) in case the company is a company referred to in paragraph (b) or (c) of section 3(2), the Central Bank.][a]

(3) At a hearing under subsection (1) the court may, as it thinks proper, subject to the provisions of this section and section 25, confirm, confirm subject to modifications, or refuse to confirm the proposals.

(4) The court shall not confirm any proposals—

[(a) unless at least one class of creditors whose interests or claims would be impaired by implementation of the proposals has accepted the proposals, or][b]

(b) if the sole or primary purpose of the proposals is the avoidance of payment of tax due, or

(c) unless the court is satisfied that—

(i) the proposals are fair and equitable in relation to any class of members or creditors that has not accepted the proposals and whose interests or claims would be impaired by implementation, and

(ii) the proposals are not unfairly prejudicial to the interests of any interested party.

[(4A) Without prejudice to subsection (4), the court shall not confirm any proposals in respect of a company to which an examiner has been appointed under section 4 if the proposals would have the effect of impairing the interests of the creditors of the company in such a manner as to favour the interests of the creditors or members of any company to which it is related, being a company to which that examiner has been appointed examiner under section 2 or, as the case may be, 4.][c]

(5) Where the court confirms proposals (with or without modification), the proposals shall be binding on all the members or class or classes of members, as the case may be, affected by the proposal and also on the company.

(6) Where the court confirms proposals (with or without modification), the proposals shall, notwithstanding any other enactment, be binding on all the creditors or the class or classes of creditors, as the case may be, affected by the proposals in respect of any claim or claims against the company and any person other than the company who, under any statute, enactment, rule of law or otherwise, is liable for all or any part of the debts of the company.

(7) Any alterations in, additions to or deletions from the memorandum and articles of the company which are specified in the proposals shall, after confirmation of the proposals by the court and notwithstanding any other provisions of the Companies Acts, take effect from a date fixed by the court.

(8) Where the court confirms proposals under this section it may make such orders for the implementation of its decision as it deems fit.

(9) A compromise or scheme of arrangement, proposals for which have been confirmed under this section shall come into effect from a date fixed by the court, which date shall be not later than 21 days from the date of their confirmation.

(10) On the confirmation of proposals a copy of any order made by the court under this section shall be delivered by the examiner, or by such person as the court may direct, to the registrar of companies for registration.

(11) Where—

(a) the court refuses to confirm proposals under this section, or

(b) the report of an examiner under section 18 concludes that, following the required meetings of [...][d] creditors of a company under this Act, it has not been possible to reach agreement on a compromise or scheme of arrangement,

the court may, if it considers it just and equitable to do so, make an order for the winding-up of the company, or any other order as it deems fit.

[(12) Notwithstanding subsection (4), or any other provision of this Act, nothing in this Act shall prevent the examiner from including in a report under section 18 proposals which will not involve the impairment of the interests of members or creditors of the company, nor the court from confirming any such proposals',][e]

Amendments

a C(A)A 1990, s 24(2)(d) inserted by C(A)(No 2)A 1999, s 24(a).

b C(A)A 1990, s 24(4)(a) substituted by C(A)(No 2)A 1999, s 24(b).

c C(A)A 1990, s 24(4A) inserted by C(A)(No 2)A 1999, s 24(c).

d C(A)A 1990, s 24(11) amended by C(A)(No 2)A 1999, s 24(d).

e C(A)A 1990, s 24(12) inserted by CA 1990, s 180 and substituted by C(A)(No 2)A 1999, s 24(e).

Cross reference

With regard to the circumstances in which the interests of a creditor or member will be deemed to be impaired, see C(A)A 1990, s 22(5), (6).

Definitions

'central bank'[1]: C(A)A 1990, s 1; 'articles': CA 1963, s 2(1); 'company': CA 1963, s 2(1); 'Companies Acts': C(A)A 1990, s 1; 'court': CA 1963, s 2(1); 'examiner': C(A)A 1990, s 1: The phrase 'examiner' includes any interim examiner so appointed by the Court[2]; 'impaired': C(A)A 1990, s 23(5); 'interested party': C(A)A 1990, s 1, s 2(1); 'member': CA 1963, s 31; 'memorandum': CA 1963, s 2(1); 'registrar of companies': CA 1963, s 2(1).

1 See Central Bank and Financial Services Authority of Ireland Act 2003, s 33C(1) and (2) whereby the Financial Regulator is entitled to perform the functions of the Central Bank under C(A)A 1990, ss 3, 3C, 18, 23, 24 and 27.

2 RSC, Ord 75A, r 1(4).

Notes

Delivery of report to court: See C(A)A 1990, s 18 and the notes thereto.

Confirmation of proposals: The preservation of the employment of the company's workforce is a factor for the court to consider when determining whether or not to confirm proposals.[1] However, the essential requirements for the confirmation of the proposals by the court are that they should have been approved by at least one class of impaired creditors,[2] they should not have tax avoidance as their sole or primary motive, they should be fair and equitable and should not unfairly prejudice any interested part.[3] The court will not, however, refuse to approve the scheme merely because as a matter of business judgment, it might have reached a contrary conclusion regarding the proposals.[4] Moreover, proposals will not necessarily be deemed to unfair, inequitable or unfairly prejudicial, merely because they impair the interests of one or more classes of creditors (including secured creditors).[5] In practice, the court will be slow to find that proposals are unfair or inequitable or unfairly prejudicial in circumstances where the affected class will receive a higher dividend that in a liquidation.[6] Indeed, there may be circumstances where the court will be prepared to approve a scheme even though a creditor is likely to do worse than in a winding up.[7] However, if there is an extreme or disproportionate disparity between the position of a creditor on a winding up and under the proposed scheme, compared with the position of other creditors under both alternatives, this may be a factor to be properly taken into account in ruling against the confirmation of the scheme.[8] Moreover, a good explanation will be required for treating members of the same class differently. In this regard, for example, it may be fair in the case of unsecured creditors who are going to continue trading with the company, to pay them somewhat ahead of those unsecured creditors whose relationship with the company will not be continuing into the future.[9] Whilst it might be unfair to pay the members ahead of creditors out of the assets of the company,[10] there can be no objection to payments to the members in return for warranties being given by them to the investor since the giving of such warranties is an obligation which could not be imposed on them by the court pursuant to the Act.[11]

The court will not confirm proposals which are *ultra vires* the company,[12] nor does it have jurisdiction to confirm proposals which involve a reduction of the company's capital, unless that reduction has already been approved by special resolution under CA 1963, s 72.[13] Furthermore, the court will not confirm proposals, even if approved by the members and creditors, where they fail to provide for the survival of the company but provide instead for a more advantageous sale of the business than in a liquidation.[14] The proposals must be finalised and complete before the confirmation of the court is sought and in this regard the court will refuse to confirm a scheme of arrangement which is to be funded by an investor unless the investor has been found and has entered into a legally binding commitment (which apart from court sanction of the scheme is otherwise unconditional) to provide the funds[15] and (where appropriate) to continue funding the company.[16] Confirmation may also be refused for a scheme which fails to make provision for particular claims against the company.[17] The court will not, however, refuse to confirm proposals simply because they operate retrospectively to affect contracts entered into prior to the coming into operation of the Act.[18]

If the directors knowingly overstated the value of the company's assets or understated the extent of the liabilities when petitioning for the appointment of an examiner or were otherwise guilty of impropriety or lack of good faith, the court may take this into account in determining whether or not to confirm the examiner's proposals.[19] There may be cases where the wrongful actions of those involved in promoting the examinership may be so serious that the court is left with no option but, on that ground alone, to decline a scheme which is otherwise in order, although the court should also consider the extent to which it may be possible to neutralise the effects of any wrongdoing either by virtue of the provisions of the scheme as presented or by modifications suggested by the court.[20] In this regard, the court should attach significant weight to the extent to which measures can be put in place to ensure that those who may have been guilty of a lack of candour or other wrongful action do not benefit thereby.[21]

1 *Re Holidair Ltd* [1994] 1 IR 416; *Re Antigen Holdings Ltd* [2001] 4 IR 600; *Re Selukwe Ltd* (20 December 1991, unreported) HC (Costello J); *Re Traffic Group Ltd* [2008] 2 ILRM 1. In *Re Wogans (Dorgheda) Ltd (No 2)* (7 May 1992, unreported) HC (Costello J) the court refused to sanction a scheme, inter alia, because the proposals allowed the investor to revise the wages of the company's existing workforce and to dismiss them if they refused to accept the new wage rates.

2 For the definition of 'impairment' see C(A)A 1990, s 23(5).

3 See C(A)A 1990, s 24(4); *Re Laragan Developments Ltd* (31 July 2009, unreported) HC (Clarke J).

4 *Re Selukwe Ltd* (20 December 1991, unreported) HC (Costello J); *Re London Chartered Bank of Australia* [1893] 3 Ch 540.

5 *Re Jetmara Teo* [1992] 1 IR 147; *Re Atlantic Magnetics Ltd* [1993] 2 IR 561; *Re Antigen Holdings Ltd* [2001] 4 IR 600.

6 See *Re Antigen Holdings Ltd* [2001] 4 IR 600 where it as held that a comparison with the outcome in a liquidation was an important consideration, although not the only one to be taken into account. See also by way of analogy *Re Tea Corporation Ltd* [1904] 1 Ch 12, which concerned objections to a scheme of arrangement under the English equivalent of CA 1963, s 201.

7 *Re Traffic Group Ltd* [2008] 1 IR 253; *Re Linen Supply of Ireland Ltd* (3 February 2010, unreported) HC (McGovern J).

8 *Re Traffic Group Ltd* [2008] 1 IR 253; *Re Laragan Developments Ltd* (31 July 2009, unreported) HC (Clarke J); *Re Linen Supply of Ireland Ltd* (3 February 2010, unreported) HC (McGovern J). See also *Prudential Assurance Co Ltd v PRG Powerhouse Ltd* [2008] 1 BCLC 289.

9 *Re Antigen Holdings Ltd* [2001] 4 IR 600.

10 *Re Antigen Holdings Ltd* [2001] 4 IR 600.

11 *Re Antigen Holdings Ltd* [2001] 4 IR 600.

12 *Re Guardian Assurance Co* [1917] 1 Ch 431; *Re Savoy Hotel Co* [1981] 3 WLR 441.

13 *Re McEnaney Construction Ltd* [2008] 3 IR 744. See also O'Neill, 'Captial Reduction under Examinership: A Case Note on *Re McEnaney Construction Ltd* (2008) 3(1) IBL.

14 *Re Clare Textiles Ltd* [1993] 2 IR 213.

15 *Re Cisti Gugan Barra Teo* [2009] 1 ILRM 182; *Re Coombe Importers Ltd* (5 December 1990, unreported) HC (Hamilton P); *Re Wogans (Drogheda) Ltd (No 2)* (7 May 1992, unreported) HC (Costello J).

16 *Re Linen Supply of Ireland Ltd* (3 February 2010, unreported) HC (McGovern J).

17 *Re Wogans (Drogheda) Ltd (No 2)* (7 May 1992, unreported) HC (Costello J).

18 *Re Selukwe Ltd* (20 December 1991, unreported) HC (Costello J).

19 *Re Coombe Importers Ltd* (5 December 1990, unreported) HC (Hamilton P); *Re Selukwe Ltd* (20 December 1991, unreported) HC (Costello J); *Re Wogans (Drogheda) Ltd (No 2)* (7 May 1992, unreported) HC (Costello J); *Re Laragan Developments Ltd* (31 July 2009, unreported) HC (Clarke J). Cf *Re Jetmara Teo* [1992] 1 IR 147. In relation to the duty of good faith generally, see C(A)A 1990, s 4A. See also C(A)A 1990, s 13A in relation to the hearing which should take place when irregularities have been discovered.

20 *Re Traffic Group Ltd* [2008] 1 IR 253; *Re Laragan Developments Ltd* (31 July 2009, unreported) HC (Clarke J).

21 *Re Traffic Group Ltd* [2008] 2 IR 253.

Modification of proposals: The court may confirm the proposals subject to such conditions or modifications as it thinks fit in order to ensure that the arrangement or compromise is fair and equitable and is not unfairly prejudicial to the interests of any interested party.[1] The court will be slow to modify the proposals in a fundamental manner without first having the suggested modifications considered at meetings of the members and creditors.[2]

1 See C(A)A 1990, s 24(3) and (5). See also *Re Canning Jarrah Timber Co (Western Australia) Ltd* [1900] 1 Ch 708; *Re Goodman International and related companies* (28 January 1991, unreported) HC, Hamilton P; *Re Selukwe Ltd* (20 December 1991, unreported) HC (Costello J); *Re Antigen Holdings Ltd* [2001] 4 IR 600.

2 *Re Goodman International and Related Companies* (28 January 1991, unreported) HC (Hamilton P); *Re Selukwe Ltd* (20 December 1991, unreported) HC (Costello J); *Re Antigen Holdings Ltd* [2001] 4 IR 600.

Effect of confirmation: If the proposals are confirmed by the court, they become binding on all members and creditors affected thereby,[1] with effect from such date as the court may determine, which date cannot be more than 21 days from the date of the order itself.[2] In this regard, the court has no jurisdiction to extend the protection of the court beyond the effective date.[3] For the effect of the proposals on guarantees and leases, see C(A)A 1990, ss 25A and 25B.

1 C(A)A 1990, s 24(5) and (6).

2 C(A)A 1990, s 24(9).

3 *Re Cisti Gugan Barra Teo* [2009] 1 ILRM 182.

Winding-up: If the court refuses to confirm the proposals or concludes that the requisite approval of cannot be obtained for proposals, it may make whatever order it thinks fit, including an order for the winding up of the company.[1] Rather than make an immediate winding up order, the court may, if it thinks fit, direct that the examiner or some other person bring a separate application for a winding up order.[2]

1 C(A)A 1990, s 24(11).

2 RSC, Ord 75A, r 20.

UK legislation

See IA 1986, ss 5(3)(b), 24(5).

25 Objection to confirmation by court of proposals

(1) At a hearing under section 24 in relation to proposals a member or creditor whose interest or claim would be impaired by the proposals may object in particular to their confirmation by the court on any of the following grounds—

(a) that there was some material irregularity at or in relation to a meeting to which section 23 applies,

(b) that acceptance of the proposals by the meeting was obtained by improper means,

(c) that the proposals were put forward for an improper purpose,

(d) that the proposals unfairly prejudice the interests of the objector.

(2) Any person who voted to accept the proposals may not object to their confirmation by the court except on the grounds—

(a) that such acceptance was obtained by improper means, or

(b) that after voting to accept the proposals he became aware that the proposals were put forward for an improper purpose.

(3) Where the court upholds an objection under this section, the court may make such order as it deems fit, including an order that the decision of any meeting be set aside and an order that any meeting be reconvened.

Cross reference

With regard to the circumstances in which the interests of a creditor or member will be deemed to be impaired, see C(A)A 1990, s 22(5), (6).

For the procedural requirements applicable in relation to such meetings, see O 75A, r 18, discussed above in the notes to C(A)A 1990, s 23(1).

Definitions

'court': CA 1963, s 2(1); 'member': CA 1963, s 31.

Notes

Objection by impaired creditor or member: Only creditors or members whose interests or claims would be impaired under the proposals may object. As to what constitutes impairment, see C(A)A 1990, s 22 and the notes thereto.

Objection in respect of guaranteed debts: In the case of guaranteed debts, if the creditor proposes to enforce the guarantee he will have been required to serve a written notice on the guarantor within the prescribed time limits offering to transfer to the guarantor the right to vote on the proposals.[1] If the guarantor has taken up this offer, the creditor is still entitled to object to the confirmation of the proposals, regardless of how the guarantor has actually cast the transferred vote.[2]

1 C(A)A 1990, s 25A(1)(c)(i).

2 C(A)A 1990, s 25A(1)(c)(ii).

Material irregularity: One of the potential grounds of objection is if there has been a material irregularity at or in relation to any of the meetings which were convened to consider and vote on the examiner's proposals. With regard to the procedural requirements which should have been observed in relation to such meetings, see C(A)A 1990, ss 22 & 23 and the notes thereto.

Improperly procured acceptance: If the financial information furnished to the creditors contained a deliberate overstatement of the value of the company's assets or a deliberate understatement of the liabilities or if there has been some other impropriety which has induced the acceptance of the examiner's proposals, this too may operate as a basis for objection to the confirmation of the examiner's proposals.[1]

[1] See Central Bank and Financial Services Authority of Ireland Act 2003, s 33C(1) and (2) whereby the Financial Regulator is entitled to perform the functions of the Central Bank under C(A)A 1990, ss 3, 3C, 18, 23, 24 and 27. *Re Coombe Importers Ltd* (5 December 1990) HC (Hamilton P); *Re Selukwe Ltd* (20 December 1991) HC (Costello J); *Re Wogans (Drogheda) Ltd (No2)* (7 May 1992) HC (Costello J). Cf *Re Jetmara Teo* [1992] 1 IR 147. In relation to the duty of good faith generally, see s 4A. See also s 13A in relation to the hearing which should take place when irregularities have been discovered.

Improper purpose and unfair prejudice: For a consideration of the other two grounds of objection, namely that the proposals were put forward for an improper purpose, or are unfairly prejudicial, see C(A)A 1990, s 24 and the notes entitled 'confirmation of proposals'.

UK legislation

See IA 1986, s 6.

[25A Provisions with respect to guarantees

(1) The following provisions shall have effect in relation to the liability of any person ('the third person') whether under a guarantee or otherwise, in respect of a debt ('the debt') of a company to which an examiner has been appointed:

(a) subject to paragraph (b) and save where the contrary is provided in an agreement entered into by the third person and the person to whom he is liable in respect of the debt ('the creditor'), the liability shall, notwithstanding section 24(6), not be affected by the fact that the debt is the subject of a compromise or scheme of arrangement that has taken effect under section 24(9),

(b) neither paragraph (a) nor any of the subsequent provisions of this subsection shall apply if the third person is a company to which an examiner has been appointed,

(c) if the creditor proposes to enforce by legal proceedings or otherwise the obligation of the third person in respect of the liability, then—

(i) he shall—

(I) if 14 days' or more notice is given of such meeting, at least 14 days before the day on which the meeting concerned under section 23 to consider the proposals is held, or

(II) if less than 14 days' notice is given of such meeting, not more than 48 hours after he has received notice of such meeting,

serve a notice on the third person containing an offer in writing by the creditor to transfer to the third person (which the creditor is hereby empowered to do) any rights, so far as they relate to the debt, he may have under section 23 to vote in respect of proposals for a compromise or scheme of arrangement in relation to the company,

(ii) if the said offer is accepted by the third person, that offer shall, if the third person furnishes to the examiner at the meeting concerned a copy of the offer and informs the examiner of his having accepted it, operate, without the necessity for any assignment or the execution of any other instrument, to entitle the third person to exercise the said rights, but neither the said transfer nor any vote cast by the third person on foot of the transfer shall operate to prejudice the right of the creditor to object to the proposals under section 25,

(iii) if the creditor fails to make the said offer in accordance with subparagraph (ii), then, subject to subparagraph (iv), the creditor may not enforce by legal proceedings or otherwise the obligation of the third person in respect of the liability,

(iv) subparagraph (iii) shall not apply if a compromise or scheme of arrangement in relation to the company is not entered into or does not take effect under section 24(9) and the creditor has obtained the leave of the court to enforce the obligation of the third person in respect of the liability,

(d) if the third person makes a payment to the creditor in respect of the liability after the period of protection has expired, then any amount that would, but for that payment, be payable to the creditor in respect of the debt under a compromise or scheme of arrangement that has taken effect under section 24(9) in relation to the company shall become and be payable to the third person upon and subject to the same terms and conditions as the compromise or scheme of arrangement provided that it was to be payable to the creditor.

(2) Nothing in subsection (1) shall affect the operation of—

(a) section 5(2)(f), or

(b) any rule of law whereby any act done by the creditor referred to in that subsection results in the third person referred to therein being released from his obligation in respect of the liability concerned.][a]

Amendments

a Inserted by C(A)A (No2) 1999, s 25.

Definitions

'company': CA 1963, s 2(1); 'court': CA 1963, s 2(1); 'examiner': s 1; The phrase `examiner' includes any interim examiner so appointed by the Court;[1] 'impaired': s 23(5).

1 RSC, Ord 75A, r 1(4).

Notes

No release of guarantors and sureties: During the protection period guarantees and indemnities, etc in respect of company debts are unenforceable.[1] However, unless the contractual arrangement between the creditor and the guarantor otherwise provides, it will be impermissible for the proposals to affect the liability of the guarantor (other than the liability of a corporate guarantor which is also under examinership), notwithstanding the fact that the primary liability of the company itself is being compromised by the proposals.[2]

1 C(A)A 1990, s 5(2)(f).

2 C(A)A 1990, s 25A. See also *Re Selukwe Ltd* (20 December 1991) HC (Costello J); *Re Presswell Ltd* (4 November 1991, unreported) HC (Murphy J). See also *Prudential Assurance Co Ltd v PRG Powerhouse Ltd* [2008] 1 BCLC 289.

Transfer of voting rights to the guarantor: If the creditor proposes to enforce the guarantee he must serve a written notice on the guarantor within the prescribed time limits offering to transfer to the guarantor the right to vote on the proposals.[1] Failure on the part of the creditor to make this offer will preclude him from thereafter seeking to enforce the guarantee[2] unless; (a) the scheme of arrangement fails to take effect; and (b) the creditor obtains the leave of the court to proceed against the guarantor.[3] On the other hand, if the guarantor takes up this offer, the creditor does not lose his right to object to the confirmation of the proposals, regardless of how the guarantor actually casts the transferred vote.[4]

1 C(A)A 1990, s 25A(1)(c)(i).
2 C(A)A 1990, s 25A(1)(c)(iii).
3 C(A)A 1990, s 25A(1)(c)(iv).
4 C(A)A 1990, s 25A(1)(c)(ii).

Subrogation of guarantor: If the guarantor makes any payment to the creditor after the end of the protection period and after the scheme of arrangement has taken effect, he will be automatically subrogated to any amount that, but for the payment, would otherwise be payable to the creditor under that scheme.[1]

1 C(A)A 1990, s 25A(1)(d).

[25B Provisions with respect to leases

(1) Subject to subsection (3), proposals for a compromise or scheme of arrangement shall not contain, nor shall any modification by the court under section 24 of such proposals result in their containing, a provision providing for either or both—

(a) a reduction in the amount of any rent or other periodical payment reserved under a lease of land that falls to be paid after the compromise or scheme of arrangement would take effect under section 24(9) or the complete extinguishment of the right of the lessor to any such payments,

(b) as respects a failure—

(i) to pay an amount of rent or make any periodical payment reserved under a lease of land, or

(ii) to comply with any other covenant or obligation of such a lease,

that falls to be paid or complied with after the date referred to in paragraph (a), a requirement that the lessor under such a lease shall not exercise, or shall only exercise in specified circumstances, any right, whether under the lease or otherwise, to recover possession of the land concerned, effect a forfeiture of the lease or otherwise enter on the land or to recover the amount of such rent or other payment or to claim damages or other relief in respect of the failure to comply with such a covenant or obligation.

(2) Subject to subsection (3), proposals for a compromise or scheme of arrangement in relation to a company shall not be held by the court to satisfy the condition specified in paragraph (c)(ii) of section 24(4) if the proposals contain a provision relating to a lease of, or any hiring agreement in relation to, property other than land and, in the opinion of the court—

(a) the value of that property is substantial, and

(b) the said provision is of like effect to a provision referred to in paragraph (a) or (b) o f subsection (1).

(3) Subsection (1) or (2) shall not apply if the lessor or owner of the property concerned has consented in writing to the inclusion of the provision referred to in subsection (1) or (2) in the proposals for the compromise or scheme of arrangement.

(4) In deciding, for the purposes of subsection (2), whether the value of the property concerned is substantial the matters to which the court shall have regard shall include the length of the unexpired form of the lease or hiring agreement concerned.][a]

Amendments

a Inserted by C(A)(No2)A 1999, s 26.

Definitions

'company': CA 1963, s 2(1); 'court': CA 1963, s 2(1).

Notes

Lease obligations: In the case of a lease of land, the proposals as put forward by the examiner for approval by the creditors and for confirmation by the court may provide for the compromise of liabilities falling due under the lease on a date prior to the scheme of arrangement coming into effect. However, unless the landlord otherwise consents in writing,[1] the proposals cannot reduce the quantum of any rental or other payments falling due for payment under the lease after that date nor can the proposals provide for the cancellation of the landlord's right to receive such payments.[2] Furthermore, it is impermissible to contain in the proposals any provision which would curtail or extinguish all or any of the landlord's rights and remedies in respect of breaches of the lease occurring after the coming into effect of the scheme of arrangement.[3]

In the case of a lease or hire agreement concerning property other than land, the entitlement to modify payment obligations arising after the coming into effect of the scheme of arrangement and the entitlement to curtail or extinguish the rights and remedies of the lessor or hirer in respect of breaches arising after that date are similarly curtailed if but only if the court is of the opinion that value of the property the subject-matter of the agreement is `substantial'.[4] However, in determining whether or not the value of the property is `substantial' the court can have regard, inter alia, the length of the unexpired term of the agreement and thus may take into account the aggregate value of the payments yet to be made by the company thereunder.[5]

1 C(A)A 1990, s 25B(3).
2 C(A)A 1990, s 25B(1)(a).
3 C(A)A 1990, s 25B(1)(b).
4 C(A)A 1990, s 25B(2).
5 C(A)A 1990, s 25B(4).

26 Cessation of protection of company and termination of appointment of examiner

(1) Subject to section 5, the protection deemed to be granted to a company under that section shall cease—

(a) on the coming into effect of a compromise or scheme of arrangement under this Act, or

(b) on such earlier date as the court may direct.

(2) Where a company ceases to be under the protection of the court, the appointment of the examiner shall terminate on the date of such cessation.

Cross reference

a See C(A)A 1990, s 5.

Definitions

'company': CA 1963, s 2(1); 'court': CA 1963, s 2(1); 'examiner': C(A)A 1990, s 1, s 2.

Notes

Duration of protection period: The protection period lasts for 70 days from the date of the presentation of the petition.[1] If necessary in order to enable him to present his proposals and report to the court, the examiner may apply to the court for an extension of the protection of up to 30 extra days.[2] Once his report has been presented, the court may continue the protection for such additional period as may be necessary in order to enable the court to determine whether or not to confirm the proposals under s 24.[3]

1 C(A)A 1990, s 5(1).

2 C(A)A 1990, s 18(3a).

3 C(A)A 1990, s 18(4).

UK legislation

See IA 1986, s 19.

---

27 Revocation

[(1)][a] The company or any interested party may, within 180 days after the confirmation of the proposals by the court, apply to the court for revocation of that confirmation on the grounds that it was procured by fraud and the court, if satisfied that such was the case, may revoke that confirmation on such terms and conditions, particularly with regard to the protection of the rights of parties acquiring interests or property in good faith and for value in reliance on that confirmation, as it deems fit.

[(2) As soon as practicable after the revocation under this section of such a confirmation, a copy of the order made by the court shall be delivered to—

(a) the registrar of companies,

(b) in case the company to which the order relates is a company referred to in paragraph (a) o f section 3 (2), the Minister, and

(c) in case the company to which the order relates is a company referred to in paragraph (b) or (c) of section 3(2), the Central Bank,

by such person as the court may direct.][a]

Amendments

a '(1)' and subsection (2) inserted by C(A)(No2)A 1999, s 27.

Definitions

'company': CA 1963, s 2(1); 'court': CA 1963, s 2(1); 'interested party': C(A)A 1990, s 1, s 2(1).

Cross reference

See Central Bank and Financial Services Authority of Ireland Act 2003, s 33C(1) and (2) whereby the Financial Regulator is entitled to perform the functions of the Central Bank under C(A)A 1990, ss 3, 3C, 18, 23, 24 and 27.

Notes

Revocation of scheme of arrangement: An application to the court for the revocation of confirmation of the proposals must be made ex parte for directions as to the proceedings to be taken. The application must be grounded upon an affidavit which must specify the fraud alleged and must supply full particulars thereof together with the names and addresses of all parties who have or may have acquired interests or property in good faith and for value and in reliance on the confirmation of the proposals by the court.[1] Upon such application the court may make such order and give such directions for the hearing of the application including directions for service of notice of the application upon all such parties as appear proper in the circumstances and may give such further directions as to the application, including particularly, whether and if so, how the application should be advertised and if it seems fit, direct the filing of any pleadings in the matter.[2]

1 RSC, Ord 75A, r 21(1)

2 RSC, Ord 75A, r 21(2).

UK legislation

See IA 1986, s 6.

28 Disqualification of examiners

(1) A person shall not be qualified to be appointed or act as an examiner of a company if he would not be qualified to act as its liquidator.

(2) A person who acts as examiner of a company while disqualified under this section shall be guilty of an offence, and shall be liable, on summary conviction, to a fine not exceeding [€1,904.61][a] and, on conviction on indictment, to a fine not exceeding [€12,697.38].[b]

Amendments

a £1,000 increased to £1,500 by CA 1990, s 240(7) as inserted by CLEA 2001, s 104. £1,500 converted to €1,904.61 by Council Regulations (EC) No 1103/97, No 974/98 and No 2866/98 and the Economic and Monetary Union Act, 1998, s 6.

b '£10,000' converted to €12,697.38 by Council Regulations (EC) No 1103/97, No 974/98 and No 2866/98 and the Economic and Monetary Union Act, 1998, s 6.

Cross reference

In relation to the disqualification of liquidators see CA 1963, s 300A; CA 1990 Part VII, Chapter 2.

Definitions

'company': CA 1963, s 2(1); 'examiner': C(A)A 1990, s 1, s 2.

Notes

Disqualification of examiners: A person will be disqualified from acting as liquidator of a company is he would be disqualified from acting as its liquidator. As to the circumstances in which disqualification as liquidator would arise, see CA 1963, s 300A and CA 1990, Part VII, Chapter 2.

UK legislation

See IA 1986, ss 389, 390.

29 Costs and remuneration of examiners

(1) The court may from time to time make such orders as it thinks proper for payment of the remuneration and costs of, and reasonable expenses properly incurred by, an examiner.

(2) Unless the court otherwise orders, the remuneration, costs and expenses of an examiner shall be paid and the examiner shall be entitled to be indemnified in respect thereof out of the revenue of the business of the company to which he has been appointed, or the proceeds of realisation of the assets (including investments).

[(3) The remuneration, costs and expenses of an examiner which have been sanctioned by order of the court (other than the expenses referred to in subsection (3A)) shall be paid in full and shall be paid before any other claim, secured or unsecured, under any compromise or scheme of arrangement or in any receivership or winding-up of the company to which he has been appointed.

(3A) Liabilities incurred by the company to which an examiner has been appointed that, by virtue of section 10(1), are treated as expenses properly incurred by the examiner shall be paid in full and shall be paid before any other claim (including a claim secured by a floating charge), but after any claim secured by a mortgage, charge, lien or other encumbrance of a fixed nature or a pledge, under any compromise or scheme of arrangement or in any receivership or winding-up of the company to which he has been appointed.

(3B) In subsections (3) and (3A) references to a claim shall be deemed to include references to any payment in a winding-up of the company in respect of costs, charges and expenses of that winding-up (including the remuneration of any liquidator).][a]

(4) The functions of an examiner may be performed by him with the assistance of persons appointed or employed by him for that purpose provided that an examiner shall, insofar as is reasonably possible, make use of the services of the staff and facilities of the company to which he has been appointed to assist him in the performance of his functions.

(5) In considering any matter relating to the costs, expenses and remuneration of an examiner the court shall have particular regard to the proviso to subsection (4).

Amendments

a Sub-s (3) substituted and sub-ss (3A) & (3B) inserted by C(A)(No2)A 1999, s 28.

Definitions

'company': CA 1963, s 2(1); 'court': CA 1963, s 2(1); 'examiner': C(A)A 1990, s 1, s 2.

Notes

Procedure for payment application: An application by the examiner for payment to him of remuneration and costs and reasonable expenses properly incurred by him must be made by application *ex parte* to the court and upon an affidavit of the examiner in which he must set forth a full account of the work carried out by him to the date of the application and a full account of the costs and expenses incurred by him.[1] He must vouch the costs and expenses and must also give a full account of the basis for the proposed remuneration which he is seeking to be paid.[2] In addition, the affidavit must specify what use, if any, he has made of the services of the staff and/or of the facilities of the company, as required by sub-section (4).[3] The court may, where it thinks fit, order that notice of the application be given to all such persons as it may direct, and may give directions as to the service of the notice and fix a date for the hearing of the application.[4]

1 RSC, Ord 75A, r 22.
2 RSC, Ord 75A, r 22.
3 RSC, Ord 75A, r 22.
4 RSC, Ord 75A, r 22.

Examiner's remuneration, costs and expenses: The expenses 'properly incurred' by the examiner include such liabilities as are certified by him under s 10 as having been incurred in circumstances where, in his opinion, the survival of the company as a going concern during the protection period would otherwise be seriously prejudiced. With regard to the entitlement to certify liabilities, see the notes to s 10.

The court will not sanction the payment of costs, remuneration or expenses to an examiner who has acted in an unofficial capacity in the period between the presentation of the petition and the date of his actual appointment as examiner.[1] Furthermore, payment may be disallowed, either wholly or in part where the examiner has acted negligently or in breach of duty.[2] Where the examiner is aware at the time of his appointment, or subsequently discovers, that the liabilities of the company have been understated in the petition, but fails to inform the court of the true financial position, he will be deemed to have been guilty of an abuse of the process of the court, and his remuneration, costs and expenses may accordingly be disallowed.[3] Similarly, if the examiner has had a prior association with the company, such that if it had been disclosed he would probably not have been appointed in the first place, the court may well decline to sanction payment to him.[4] Likewise, where the examiner's proposals are seriously defective (for example, in failing to make provision for all known liabilities of the company), the court may, apart from refusing to confirm the proposals, also refuse to sanction the payment of his remuneration, costs or expenses.[5]

Even where the examiner has acted entirely properly, the court may disallow any element of his remuneration which is found to be excessive.[6] Moreover, if the court determines that the examinership ought to have been concluded earlier (as where it was apparent for some time that there was no longer any reasonable prospect of putting forward meaningful proposals for a scheme of arrangement), the court may only sanction payment to the examiner in respect of costs, remuneration and expenses incurred by him up to the time when he ought first have applied to be discharged.[7]

Where the examiner has been appointed to a group of companies, his remuneration, costs and expenses should be appropriately apportioned amongst those companies rather than simply attributing the entire amount to such of the companies as have assets to meet the amounts in question.[8] In so far as the court refuses to sanction the costs or expenses of the examiner, and thereby prohibits him from claiming an indemnity out of the company's assets, he will (in the absence of an express disclaimer) be personally liable under s 13(6) on any contracts made by him in the performance of his functions.

1 *Re Wogans (Drogheda) Ltd (No 3)* [1993] 1 IR 157.
2 *Re Wogans (Drogheda) Ltd (No 3)* [1993] 1 IR 157; *Re Clare Textiles Ltd* [1993] 2 IR 213; *Re Edenpark Construction Ltd* [1994] 3 IR 126.
3 *Re Wogans (Drogheda) Ltd (No 3)* [1993] 1 IR 157.
4 *Re Wogans (Drogheda) Ltd (No 3)* [1993] 1 IR 157.
5 *Re Wogans (Drogheda) Ltd (No 3)* [1993] 1 IR 157.
6 *Re Coombe Importers Ltd* (22 June 1995, unreported) SC per Hamilton CJ; *Re Don Bluth Entertainment Ltd* [1994] 3 IR 141.
7 *Re Clare Textiles Ltd* [1993] 2 IR 213; *Re Edenpark Construction Ltd* [1994] 3 IR 126.
8 *Re Sharmane Ltd* (30 July 2009, unreported) HC (Finlay Geoghegan J).

Priority of costs, remuneration and expenses: All remuneration, costs and expenses of the examiner sanctioned by the court (with the exception of liabilities certified under s 10) will rank in priority not only to claims secured by floating charges, but also in priority to claims secured by fixed charges.[1] Originally, the same priority was also afforded to liabilities which had the benefit of a s 10 certificate.[2] Now, however, the s 10 certificate will not afford any priority over claims secured by a fixed charge, lien or pledge.[3]

In the event of the company going into liquidation following examinership (as where the examiner has been unable to formulate proposals) his sanctioned costs, remuneration and expenses (including liabilities certified under s 10) will rank in priority to the costs, charges and expenses of the winding up (including the remuneration of the liquidator).[4] If, instead, the company goes into receivership after a failed examinership, the examiner's claim for payment will rank ahead of the costs and expenses of the receivership (including the receiver's remuneration) and, by virtue of sub-s (2) he wil be entitled to be paid not only out of the proceeds of the realisation of assets in the receivership, but also out of any revenue (and not just profits) generated by the receiver through continued trading of the company during the receivership.[5]

1 C(A)A 1990, s 29(3).
2 *Re Atlantic Magnetics Ltd* [1993] 2 IR 561.
3 C(A)A 1990, s 29(3A).
4 C(A)A 1990, s 29(3B), which gives effect to *Re Springline Ltd* [1999] 1 IR 478.
5 *Re Sharmane Ltd* (30 July 2009, unreported) HC (Finlay Geoghegan J).

---

30 Publicity

(1) An examiner or, where appropriate, such other person as the court may direct, shall, within 14 days after the delivery to the registrar of companies of every order made under [section 13A, 24 or 27][a], cause to be published in [the Companies Registration Office Gazette][b] notice of such delivery.

(2) Where a person fails to comply with this section, that person, and where that person is a company, the company and every officer of the company who is in default, shall be guilty of an offence and shall be liable to a fine not exceeding [€1,904.61].[c]

(3) [...][d]

Amendments

a Words amended by C(A)(No2)A 1999, s 30.

b IFCMPA 2005, s 72 substituted the 'Companies Registration Office Gazette' for *Iris Oifigiúil.*

c £1,000 increased to £1,500 by CA 1990, s 240(7) as inserted by CLEA 2001, s 104. £1,500 converted to €1,904.61 by Council Regulations (EC) No 1103/97, No 974/98 and No 2866/98 and the Economic and Monetary Union Act, 1998, s 6.

d C(A)A 1990, s 30(3) repealed by CA 1990, s 181.

Definitions

'company': CA 1963, s 2(1); 'court': CA 1963, s 2(1); 'examiner': C(A)A 1990, s 1, s 2; 'officer': CA 1963, s 2(1); 'officer in default': CA 1963, s 383; 'registrar of companies': CA 1963, s 2(1).

31 Hearing of proceedings otherwise than in public

The whole or part of any proceedings under this Act may be heard otherwise than in public if the court, in the interests of justice, considers that the interests of the company concerned or of its creditors as a whole so require.

Definitions

'company': CA 1963, s 2(1); 'court': CA 1963, s 2(1).

Notes

Proceedings *in camera*: It is a precondition to the exercise by the court of its discretion under s 31 that the hearing of the proceedings or some particular part thereof would involve the disclosure of information the publication of which would be seriously prejudicial to the legitimate interests of the company. However, even if the court is satisfied that such a situation exists, it must still balance that potential prejudice against the fundamental constitutional right vested in the public of having justice administered in public.[1]

1 *Irish Press plc v Ingersoll Irish Publications Ltd* [1993] ILRM 747; *Re R Ltd* [1989] IR 169. See also *Re Chancery plc* [1991] BCLC 712.

32 No lien over company's books, records etc

[...][a]

Amendments

a C(A)A 1990, s 32 repealed by CA 1990, s 180.

Replaced by CA 1963, s 244A (as inserted by CA 1990, s 125) and applied to companies under the protection of the court, by CA 1990, s 180(2).

33 Civil liability of persons concerned for fraudulent trading of company

[...][a]

Amendments

a C(A)A 1990, s 33 repealed by CA 1990, s 180.

34 Criminal liability of persons concerned for fraudulent trading of company

[...][a]

Amendments

a C(A)A 1990, s 34 repealed by CA 1990, s 180.

35 Power of court to order the return of assets which have been improperly transferred

[...][a]

Amendments

a C(A)A 1990, s 35 repealed by CA 1990, s 180.

C(A)A 1990, s 35 replaced by CA 1990, s 139 as applied to companies under the protection of the court by CA 1990, s 180(2).

36 Enforcement of reconstruction orders made by courts outside the State

(1) Any order made by a court of any country recognised for the purposes of this section and made for or in the course of the reorganisation or reconstruction of a company may be enforced by the High Court in all respects as if the order had been made by the High Court.

(2) When an application is made to the High Court under this section, an office copy of any order sought to be enforced shall be sufficient evidence of the order.

(3) In this section, 'company' means a body corporate incorporated outside the State, and 'recognised' means recognised by order made by the Minister.

Definitions

'company': CA 1963, s 2(1); 'Minister': s 1.

Notes

Enforcement of foreign orders: To date the Minister has not made an Order recognising any country for the purposes of s 36. Orders of foreign courts may however be enforced in this jurisdiction pursuant to Council Regulation (EC) No 1346/2000 on Insolvency Proceedings.

UK legislation

See IA 1986, s 426.

[36A Proceedings by registrar

Proceedings in relation to an offence under section 11(6), 12 or 30 may be brought and prosecuted by the registrar of companies.][a]

Amendments

a C(A)A 1990, s 36A inserted by CA 1990, s 181.

37 Short title, collective citation and construction

(1) This Act may be cited as the Companies (Amendment) Act, 1990.

(2) This Act and the Companies Acts, 1963 to 1986, may be cited together as the Companies Acts, 1963 to 1990.

(3) The Companies Acts, 1963 to 1986, and this Act shall be construed together as one Act.

Companies Act 1990

Number 33 of 1990

ARRANGEMENT OF SECTIONS

PART I
PRELIMINARY

PART II
INVESTIGATIONS

PART III
TRANSACTIONS INVOLVING DIRECTORS

PRELIMINARY

CHAPTER 2

INDIVIDUAL AND GROUP ACQUISITIONS

CHAPTER 3

DISCLOSURE ORDERS: COMPANIES OTHER THAN PUBLIC LIMITED COMPANIES

CHAPTER 4

GENERAL PROVISIONS ABOUT SHARE REGISTERS ETC

PART V

INSIDER DEALING

PART VI

WINDING UP AND RELATED MATTERS

REGISTRATION OF CHARGES

WINDING UP BY THE COURT

DECLARATION OF SOLVENCY

PROVISIONS APPLICABLE TO A MEMBERS' VOLUNTARY WINDING UP

CHAPTER 3
ENFORCEMENT

PART VIII
RECEIVERS

PART IX
COMPANIES UNDER COURT PROTECTION

PART X
ACCOUNTS AND AUDIT

PART XI
ACQUISITION OF OWN SHARES AND SHARES IN HOLDING COMPANY

PART XII
GENERAL

PART XIII
INVESTMENT COMPANIES

An Act to Amend the Law Relating to Companies and to Provide for Related Matters. [22nd December, 1990]

Be it Enacted by the Oireachtas as Follows:

PART I
PRELIMINARY

1 Short title, collective citation and construction

(1) This Act may be cited as the Companies Act, 1990.

(2) This Act and the Companies Acts, 1963 to 1986, may be cited together as the Companies Acts, 1963 to 1990.

(3) The Companies Acts, 1963 to 1986, and this Act shall be construed together as one Act.

2 Commencement

This Act shall come into operation on such day or days as may be fixed therefor by order or orders of the Minister, either generally or with reference to a particular purpose or provision, and different days may be so fixed for different purposes and different provisions of this Act.

Notes

With the exception of part of s 249 and part of s 51, all of CA 1990 has come into operation. The SIs which brought the Act into force are SI 336/1990, SI 10/1991, SI 117/1991, SI 258/1992 and SI 57/2002.

[3 Interpretation

(1) In this Act, unless the context otherwise requires—

'books and documents' and 'books or documents' include accounts, deeds, writings and records made in any other manner;

'child' includes a step-child and an adopted child and 'son', 'daughter' and 'parent' shall be construed accordingly;

['Central Bank' means the Central Bank and Financial Services Authority of Ireland;][a]

'the Companies Acts' means the Companies Act, 1963, and every enactment (including this Act) which is to be construed as one with that Act;

'connected person' has the meaning assigned to it by section 26;

'contravention' includes failure to comply;

'daily default fine' has the meaning assigned to it by section 240(6);

'the Minister' means the Minister for Industry and Commerce;

'prescribe' means prescribe by regulations;

'the Principal Act' means the Companies Act, 1963;

'recognised stock exchange' has the meaning assigned to it by subsection (2);

'related company' has the meaning assigned to it by section 140;

'shadow director' has the meaning assigned to it by section 27.

(2) (a) [A recognised stock exchange for the purposes of any provision of the Companies Acts is an exchange or a market, whether within or outside the State, prescribed by the Minister for the purposes of that provision.][b]

(b) The definition of 'recognised stock exchange' in paragraph (a) is in substitution for the definition in section 2(1) of the Principal Act.

(3) The Minister may make regulations in relation to any matter referred to in this Act as prescribed or to be prescribed.

(4) In this Act—

(a) a reference to a Part or section is to a Part or section of this Act unless it is indicated that a reference to some other enactment is intended;

(b) a reference to a subsection, paragraph or subparagraph is to the subsection, paragraph or subparagraph of the provision in which the reference occurs, unless it is indicated that reference to some other provision is intended; and

(c) a reference to any other enactment shall, unless the context otherwise requires, be construed as a reference to that enactment as amended by or under any other enactment, including this Act.][a]

Amendments

a CA 1990, s 3 inserted by CBFSAIA 2003, Sch 1.

b CA 1990, s 3(2)(a) substituted by C(MP)A 2009, s 3(a).

---

4 Periods of time

(1) Where the time limited by any provision of this Act for the doing of anything expires on a Saturday, Sunday or public holiday, the time so limited shall extend to and the thing may be done on the first following day that is not a Saturday, Sunday or public holiday.

(2) Where in this Act anything is required or allowed to be done within a number of days not exceeding six a day that is a Saturday, Sunday or public holiday shall not be reckoned in computing that number.

Notes

These provisions as to time reflect the decisions in *McGuinness v Armstrong Patents Ltd*[1] and *Prittam Kaur v S Russell & Sons Ltd*.[2]

1 *McGuinness v Armstrong Patents Ltd* [1980] IR 289.
2 *Prittam Kaur v S Russell & Sons Ltd* [1973] QB 336.

5 Orders

The Minister may by order revoke or amend an order made by him under any provision of this Act, other than section 2.

Definitions

'Minister': CA 1990, s 3(1).

6 Repeals

(1) The following provisions of the Principal Act are hereby repealed – sections 147, 162 (inserted by section 6 of the Companies (Amendment) Act, 1982), 163, 165 to 173, 184, 294, 296, 380 and 385, and the Seventh and Tenth Schedules.

(2) The following provisions are also hereby repealed—

(a) Regulation 8 of the European Communities (Companies) Regulations, 1973,

(b) section 6 of the Companies (Amendment) Act, 1977, and

(c) section 21 of the Companies (Amendment) Act, 1986.

Definitions

'Principal Act': CA 1990, s 3(1).

PART II
INVESTIGATIONS

7 Investigation of company's affairs

(1) The court may appoint one or more competent inspectors to investigate the affairs of a company in order to enquire into matters specified by the court and to report thereon in such manner as the court directs—

(a) in the case of a company having a share capital, on the application either of not less than 100 members or of a member or members holding not less than one-tenth of the paid up share capital of the company;

(b) in the case of a company not having a share capital, on the application of not less than one-fifth in number of the persons on the company's register of members;

(c) in any case, on the application of the company;

(d) in any case, on the application of a director of the company;

(e) in any case, on the application of a creditor of the company.

(2) The application shall be supported by such evidence as the court may require, including such evidence as may be prescribed.

(3) Where an application is made under this section, the court may require the applicant or applicants to give security [...][a] for payment of the costs of the investigation.

(4) Where the court appoints an inspector under this section or section 8, it may, from time to time, give such directions as it thinks fit, whether to the inspector or otherwise, with a view to ensuring that the investigation is carried out as quickly and as inexpensively as possible.

Amendments

a Words deleted by C(MP)A 2009, s 3(b).

Definitions

'company': CA 1963, s 2(1); 'court': CA 1963, s 2(1); 'director': CA 1963, s 2(1); 'member': CA 1963, s 31; 'prescribe': s 3(1); 'share': CA 1963, s 2(1).

Notes

Appointment of Inspectors by High Court: Prior to the coming into force of CA 1990, Pt II, the provisions governing the appointment of inspectors were to be found in CA 1963, ss 165–173. The main change effected by CA 1990, Pt II has been to transfer from the Minister to the High Court the jurisdiction to appoint inspectors. The provisions of Pt II are retrospective in that inspectors appointed by the High Court may investigate matters that occurred prior to the coming into force of Pt II on 1 July 1991.[1] Notably, under s 7 the High Court is not empowered to appoint an inspector of its own motion. It may however appoint an inspector notwithstanding the fact that the company in question is already in the process of being wound up.[2]

Purpose of investigation: Section 8 identified specific circumstances in which the ODCE may apply to the High Court for the appointment of an inspector to investigate the affairs of a company. These include cases where there are circumstances suggesting that there has been fraudulent or prejudicial activity or misfeasance/misconduct towards members or that the members have not been given all information that they might reasonably expect relating to the affairs of the company. It should be noted, though, that s 8 merely specifies the circumstances in which the ODCE can apply for the appointment of an inspector. The court still retains a discretion whether or not to order the appointment and will be disinclined to put an inspector in place unless the purpose of the appointment has a reasonable prospect of being achieved.[3]

The jurisdiction conferred on the court by s 7 is altogether wider and, in essence, the court is at large to exercise its own discretion in determining whether there are circumstances which warrant further investigation.[4] In this regard, whether it is exercising its discretion under s 7 or s 8, it is entitled to have consideration for the public interest in deciding whether or not to appoint inspectors and is also entitled to consider whether the appointment of inspectors would be disproportionate having regard to the information put before it.[5]

The Supreme Court has commented that the purpose of CA 1990, Pt II is 'to ensure that companies incorporated under the Acts do not abuse the privileges which incorporation confers on them to the detriment of their members, creditors or indeed the public in general.'[6] In this regard, the essential function of the inspectors is to conduct an investigation to discover whether there are facts not already known which may result in others taking action;[7] accordingly an appointment will not be warranted where the facts are already known and where the sole purpose is to provide the applicant with a procedural or evidential advantage in other proceedings.[8]

Affairs of the company: The rather wide jurisdiction conferred on the court by s 7(1) is to appoint an inspector to investigate 'the affairs of the company'. This phrase has a wide meaning and includes matters such as the conduct of a receiver appointed pursuant to the terms of a debenture as well as including the company's 'goodwill, its profits or losses, its contracts and assets, including its shareholding in and ability to control the affairs of a subsidiary and perhaps in the latter regard a sub-subsidiary.'[9]

Procedure to apply to court: RSC, Ord 75B, r 3a provides that an application under s 7 must be made by originating notice of motion. When the application is brought by a director, the papers must be served on the other directors and on the company itself. When it is brought by the company, the papers must be served on all the directors. In all other cases, the applicant must serve the papers on the company and on all of the directors.

Standard of proof: Sub-s (2) empowers the Minister to prescribe the evidence that shall support an application for the appointment of an inspector. No such regulations have been made to date. However, it would appear that in order to obtain an order appointing an inspector, the applicant should be in a position to establish at least a *prima facie* case of irregularity in relation to the company's affairs.[10] In other words, the applicant should have reasonable grounds for suspecting the irregularity which grounds his application.[11]

1 *Chestvale Proprties Ltd and Hoddle Investments Ltd v Glackin* [1993] 3 IR 35.

2 CA 1990, s 8(2)(a).

3 *Director of Corporate Enforcement v DCC plc* [2009] 1 IR 464.

4 This proposition of law has recently been endorsed by Kelly J in *Director of Corporate Enforcement v DCC plc* [2009] 1 IR 464.

5 *Director of Corporate Enforcement v DCC plc* [2009] 1 IR 464; *Dunnes Stores Ireland Company v Ryan* [2002] 2 IR 60.

6 *Dunnes Stores Ireland Company v Ryan* [2002] 2 IR 60. See also *Sage Holdings Ltd v The Unisec Group Ltd* (1982) (1) SA 337 (W) where Goldstone J held that the court may make an order for the appointment of an inspector whenever it considers that an investigation of the company's affairs is right or advisable. The court should, however, only order an investigation if it is satisfied that some object may be achieved as a result, as where the investigation might lead to the winding up of the company or the disqualification of directors or the institution of proceedings for the recovery of damages or property of the company. The court should not, however, act merely to satisfy disgruntled shareholders who have no legitimate cause for complaint.

7 *Director of Corporate Enforcement v DCC plc* [2009] 1 IR 464; *Dunnes Stores Ireland Company v Ryan* [2002] 2 IR 60; *Re Pergamon Press Ltd* [1970] 3 All ER 535 at 540; *Saunders v Eco Temp International Inc* [2007] ABB 136; *Re First Investors* [1988] AJ No 244.

8 *Director of Corporate Enforcement v DCC plc* [2009] 1 IR 464.

9 *R v Board of Trade, ex parte St Martins Preserving Co Ltd* [1965] 1 QB 603. For the jurisdiction to extend an investigation into the affairs of a related company, see CA 1990, s 9.

10 *Re Miles Aircraft Ltd (No 2)* [1948] WN 178.

11 *Dunnes Stores Ireland Company v Ryan* [2002] 2 IR 60; *Sage Holdings Ltd v The Unisec Group Ltd* (1982) (1) SA 337 (W).

Conduct of the investigation: The inspector sits in private and is not entitled to admit the public to the proceedings.[1] He does not act as a court of law and his proceedings are not judicial proceedings.[2] His functions are not judicial in nature, but are rather administrative or occasionally quasi-judicial in nature.[3] Nevertheless, he is obliged, in conducting his investigation, to observe the rules of natural justice, since findings of fact made by him may be very damaging to those named in the report and may lead to civil or criminal proceedings being brought.[4] The procedure adopted by the inspectors in the investigations into the affairs of National Irish Bank Ltd has twice been judicially endorsed,[5] as being one that complies with the rules of natural justice. The procedure was in two stages: the first stage being an information-gathering exercise by way of informal interviews; the second, which would only arise when the first stage indicated a possibility that adverse conclusions could be drawn in relation to certain individuals, consisting of a hearing at which such individuals could have legal representation,[6] could cross-examine witnesses[7] and could give evidence themselves.[8] If necessary, the individual should be afforded an adjournment of any hearing in order to allow him to properly prepare his cross-examination and to prepare his defence.[9]

Persons called upon by the inspector pursuant to s 10 to answer questions, may not decline to do so in reliance on the privilege against self-incrimination, although any answers given by them under compulsion will not, in general, be admissible against them in subsequent criminal proceedings.[10]

The inspector does not have to put his conclusions verbatim to an affected individual before making his report; rather it suffices that, during the course of the investigations, he has put to the individual, all matters of substance which would appear to call for an explanation or answer.[11]

1 *Hearts of Oak Assurance Co Ltd v AG* [1932] AC 392; *Re Pergamon Press Ltd* [1970] 3 All ER 589; *Maxwell v Department of Trade and Industry* [1974] QB 523; *Re Redbreast Preserving Co (Ireland) Ltd* 91 ILTR 12.

2 *Re Grosvenor and West End Railway Terminus Hotel Co Ltd* (1897) 76 LT 337; *Re Pergamon Press Ltd* [1970] 3 All ER 589.

3 *Chestvale Properties Ltd and Hoddle Investments Ltd v Glackin* [1993] 3 IR 35. See *Re Pergamon Press Ltd* [1970] 3 All ER 589 where the inspector's functions were described as purely administrative in nature.

4 *Re Pergamon Press Ltd* [1970] 3 All ER 589; *Maxwell v Department of Trade and Industry* [1974] QB 523; *Norwest Holst Ltd v Secretary of State for Trade* [1978] 3 All ER 28; *R v Secretary of State for Trade, ex parte Perestrello* [1980] 3 All ER 28; *Chestvale Properties Ltd and Hoddle Investments Ltd v Glackin* [1993] 3 IR 35; *Re National Irish Bank Ltd (No 1)* [1999] 3 IR 145; *Re National Irish Bank Ltd (No 2)* [1999] 3 IR 190; *Byrne v O'Leary* [2006] IEHC 412.

5 *Re National Irish Bank Ltd* (No 1) [1999] 3 IR 145; *Re National Irish Bank Ltd (No 2)* [1999] 3 IR 190.

6 See also *Re Haughey* [1971] IR 217 as regards the right to legal representation, at least where serious accusations are being made against the person.

7 In relation to the entitlement to cross-examine witnesses, see also *Re Pergamon Press Ltd* [1970] 3 All ER 589; *Re Haughey* [1971] IR 217.

8 As regards the right to introduce rebutting evidence and to address the inspector, see also *Re Haughey* [1971] IR 217.

9 *Kiely v Minister for Social Welfare* [1977] IR 267.

10 *Re National Irish Bank Ltd (No 1)* [1999] 3 IR 145. See also *Saunders v United Kingdom* [1997] BCC 872. Under s 18 such answers are admissible in civil proceedings, but are stated to be inadmissible in proceedings in criminal proceedings other than proceedings for perjury. However, it would seem that s 18 protects individuals only and not companies.

11 *Re Pergamon Press Ltd* [1970] 3 All ER 589; *Maxwell v Department of Trade and Industry* [1974] QB 523; *Byrne v O'Leary* (7 December 2006, unreported) HC (Gilligan J).

8 Investigation of company's affairs on application of [Director]

(1) Without prejudice to its powers under section 7, the court may [on the application of the Director appoint one or more competent inspectors (who may be or include an officer of officers of the Director][a] to investigate the affairs of a company and to report thereon in such manner as the court shall direct, if the court is satisfied that there are circumstances suggesting—

(a) that its affairs are being or have been conducted with intent to defraud its creditors or the creditors of any other person or otherwise for a fraudulent or unlawful purpose or in an unlawful manner or in a manner which is unfairly prejudicial to some part of its members, or that any actual or proposed act or omission of the company (including an act or omission on its behalf) is or would be so prejudicial, or that it was formed for any fraudulent or unlawful purpose; or

(b) that persons connected with its formation or the management of its affairs have in connection therewith been guilty of fraud, misfeasance or other misconduct towards it or towards its members; or

(c) that its members have not been given all the information relating to its affairs which they might reasonably expect.

(2) (a) The power conferred by section 7 or this section shall be exercisable with respect to a body corporate not withstanding that it is in course of being wound up.

(b) The reference in subsection (1)(a) to the members of a company shall have effect as if it included a reference to any person who is not a member but to whom shares in the company have been transferred or transmitted by operation of law.

Amendments

a Subsection (1) amended by the substitution for 'on the application of the Minister appoint one or more competent inspectors' of 'on the application of the Director appoint one or more competent inspectors (who may be or include an officer or officers of the Director)' by CLEA 2001, s 21.

Notes

Appointment on application by ODCE: Prior to the amendments effected by CLEA 2001, s 21 the power to apply for the appointment of an inspector under s 8 was vested in the Minister. The grounds for appointment under s 8(1) appear to be exhaustive, unlike s 7 where the discretion of the court to appoint inspectors is framed in wide and non-exhaustive terms.

Purpose of Investigation: See the notes to CA 1990, s 7.

Procedure to apply to court: RSC, Ord 75B, r 3b provides that an application under s 8 must be made by originating notice of motion and must be served on the company and all of its directors.

Standard of proof: See notes to CA 1990, s 7.

Investigation of foreign companies: Section 8(1), as well as applying to all companies formed and registered under the Companies Acts also applies, by virtue of s 17, to all bodies corporate incorporated outside the State which are carrying on, or have carried on, business in the State.[1]

Unfair prejudice: One of the grounds on which an inspector may be appointed under s 8 is where there are circumstances suggesting that the affairs of the company are being or have been conducted in a manner which is 'unfairly prejudicial' to members. The use of the term 'unfairly prejudicial' in s 8(1)(a) appears to have been imported from the UK which introduced the concept of prejudice in ss 459–461 of the UK Companies Act 1985 to replace the old concepts of oppression and disregard of interests. See CA 1963, s 205. In *Horgan v Murray*,[2] Murray J appears to have taken the view that there is little distinction of substance between the Irish and UK terminology.

Past and present irregularity: The wording of s 8(1) is such as to justify the appointment of an inspector not only where misconduct of the type specified therein is ongoing, but also where it has occurred in the past. As was noted by Keane J in *Dunnes Stores Ireland Company v Ryan*[3] (albeit in the context of an inquiry under s 19):

> 'the Minister, in the exercise of her supervisory jurisdiction over companies, may be concerned to establish how such a misuse of the privilege of incorporation took place with a view to ensuring, so far as possible, that similar abuses do not take place in this, or indeed any other companies regulated by the Acts, in the future.'

1 See also *Desmond and Dedeir v Glackin (No 2)* [1993] 3 IR 67; *Probets and Freezone Investments Ltd v Glackin* [1993] 3 IR 134; *Chestvale Properties Ltd and Hoddle Investments Ltd v Glackin* [1993] 3 IR 35; *Lyons v Curran* [1993] ILRM 375; *Minister for Justice v Siúcre Éireann* [1992] 2 IR 215.

2 *Horgan v Murray* [1997] 3 IR 23. In that case, Murray J referred to two UK decisions on the meaning of 'unfairly prejudicial': *Re a Company* [1986] BCLC 362, [1987] BCLC 94 and *Re a company, ex p Kremer* [1989] BCLC 365.

3 *Dunnes Stores Ireland Company v Ryan* [2002] 2 IR 60.

UK legislation

CA 1985, s 432 (as amended by CA 1989, s 55).

---

9 Power of inspectors to extend investigation into affairs of related companies

[(1) If an inspector][a] appointed under section 7 or 8 to investigate the affairs of a company thinks it necessary for the purposes of his investigation to investigate also the affairs of any other body corporate which is related to such company, he shall, with the approval of the court, have power so to do, and shall report on the affairs of the other body corporate so far as he thinks the results of his investigation thereof are relevant to the investigation of the affairs of the first-mentioned company.

[(2) For the purposes of this section, a body corporate which is related to a company includes a body corporate with which the company has a commercial relationship, and a commercial relationship exists where goods or services are sold or given by one party to another.][b]

Amendments

a '(1) If an inspector' substituted for 'If an inspector' by CLEA 2001, s 22(a).

b Subsection (2) inserted by CLEA 2001, s 22(b).

Notes

Investigation of related companies: The provisions of s 9 empower an inspector, whether appointed under s 7 or s 8 to investigate the affairs of a related company, without the need for a further court order, where he considers it necessary for the purposes of his own investigation. The definition of a 'related company' in sub-s (2) is extremely wide and includes not only companies related to one another in the strict legal sense as defined in CA 1990, s 140(5) but also companies that have a 'commercial relationship' simply through supplying goods and services to one another. Nevertheless, s 9 applies only to related companies and bodies corporate which are formed and registered within the State or which have been incorporated outside the State and are carrying on or have carried on business within the State.[1]

It has been held that where an inspector knows that an investigation into the affairs of a related company is necessary to perform his function he may proceed with such an investigation without the need to obtain the approval of the court. Where he merely thinks but does not know that such an investigation is necessary he must seek the approval of the court. See *Lyons, Keleghan and Murphy v Curran*.[2] See discussion of this in Courtney, *The Law of Private Companies* (2nd edn, Tottel Publishing, 2002) at 858–861.

1 See CA 1990, s 17. See also *Desmond and Dedeir v Glackin (No 2)* [1993] 3 IR 67; *Probets and Freezone Investments Ltd v Glackin* [1993] 3 IR 134; *Chestvale Proprties Ltd and Hoddle Investments Ltd v Glackin* [1993] 3 IR 35; *Lyons v Curran* [1993] ILRM 375; *Minister for Justice v Siúcre Éireann* [1992] 2 IR 215.

2 *Lyons, Keleghan and Murphy v Curran* [1993] ILRM 375.

10 Production of documents and evidence on investigation

(1) It shall be the duty of all officers and agents of the company and of all officers and agents of any other body corporate whose affairs are investigated by virtue of section 9 to produce to the inspectors all books and documents of or relating to the company, or, as the case may be, the other body corporate which are in their custody or power, to attend before the inspectors when required so to do and otherwise to give to the inspectors all assistance in connection with the investigation which they are reasonably able to give [; but where any such person claims a lien on books or documents produced by the person, the production shall be without prejudice to the lien.][a]

(2) If the inspectors consider that a person other than an officer or agent of the company or other body corporate is or may be in possession of any information concerning its affairs, they may require that person to produce to them any books or documents in his custody or power relating to the company or other body corporate, to attend before them and otherwise to give them all assistance in connection with the investigation which he is reasonably able to give; and it shall be the duty of that person to comply with the requirement [; but where any such person claims a lien on books or documents produced by the person, the production shall be without prejudice to the lien.][b]

(3) If an inspector has reasonable grounds for believing that a director of the company or other body corporate whose affairs the inspector is investigating maintains or has maintained a bank account of any description, whether alone or jointly with another person and whether in the State or elsewhere, into or out of which there has been paid—

- (a) any money which has resulted from or been used in the financing of any transaction, arrangement or agreement—
  - (i) particulars of which have not been disclosed in a note to the accounts of any company for any financial year as required by section 41; or
  - (ii) in respect of which any amount outstanding was not included in the aggregate amounts outstanding in respect of certain transactions, arrangements or agreements as required by section 43 to be disclosed in a note to the accounts of any company for any financial year; or
  - (iii) particulars of which were not included in any register of certain transactions, arrangements and agreements as required by section 44; or

(b) any money which has been in any way connected with any act or omission, or series of acts or omissions, which on the part of that director constituted misconduct (whether fraudulent or not) towards that company or body corporate or its members;

the inspector may require the director to produce to him all documents in the director's possession, or under his control, relating to that bank account; and in this subsection 'bank account' includes an account with any person exempt by virtue of section 7 (4) of the Central Bank Act, 1971, from the requirement of holding a licence under section 9 of that Act, and 'director' includes any present or past director or any person connected, within the meaning of section 26, with such director, and any present or past shadow director.

(4) An inspector may examine on oath, either by word of mouth or on written interrogatories, the officers and agents of the company or other body corporate and such person as is mentioned in subsection (2) in relation to its affairs and may—

(a) administer an oath accordingly,

(b) reduce the answers of such person to writing and require him to sign them.

[(5) If an officer or agent of the company or other body corporate, or any such person as is mentioned in subsection (2), refuses or fails within a reasonable time to—

(a) produce to the inspectors any book or document which it is his duty under this section so to produce,

(b) attend before the inspectors when required so to do, or

(c) answer a question put to him by the inspectors with respect to the affairs of the company or other body corporate as the case may be,

the inspectors may certify the refusal or failure under their hand to the court, and the court may thereupon enquire into the case and, after hearing any witnesses who may be produced against or on behalf of the person alleged to have so refused or failed and any statement which may be offered in defence, make any order or direction it thinks fit.

(6) Without prejudice to the generality of subsection (5), the court may, after a hearing under that subsection, direct—

(a) the person concerned to attend or Re-attend before the inspectors or produce particular books or documents or answer particular questions put to him by the inspectors, or

(b) that the person concerned need not produce a particular book or document or answer a particular question put to him by the inspectors.][c]

(7) In this section, any reference to officers or to agents shall include past, as well as present, officers or agents, as the case may be, and 'agents', in relation to a company or other body corporate, shall include the bankers and solicitors of the company or other body corporate and any persons employed by the company or other body corporate as auditors, [accountants, book-keepers or taxation advisers,][d] whether those persons are or are not officers of the company or other body corporate.

Amendments

a Words in sub-s (1) inserted by CLEA 2001, s 23(a).

b Words in sub-s (2) inserted by CLEA 2001, s 23(b).

c Subsections (5) and (6) inserted by CLEA 2001, s 23(c).

d Words in sub-s (7) inserted by CLEA 2001, s 23(d).

Notes

Production of books and records: Under sub-s (1) the inspector may demand production of books and records belonging to or 'relating to' the company under investigation or any related company being investigated under s 9 from any past or present officers[1] or agents[2] of those entities. Under sub-s (2) the production of books and records 'concerning' the entities under investigation may also be demanded of third parties whom the inspectors consider to be in possession of such material. The phrases 'relating to' and 'concerning' are wide enough to entitle the inspectors to demand sight not only of books and records owned by the entities under investigation but also books and records owned by third parties.[3] Under sub-s (3) he may also require the production of documents relating to bank accounts into which or out of which have been paid the proceeds of loans, quasi-loans and credit transactions made in favour of directors of the entities or directors of any holding company or made in favour of persons connected with such directors and particulars of which ought to have been but were not included in the annual accounts or which ought to have been but were not recorded in the register provided for by CA 1990, s 44.

Confidentiality and privilege: Any duty of confidentiality which a banker owes to a company as its customer is overridden by the duty to co-operate with the inspector.[4] Nor may a journalist refuse to disclose his sources to the inspector on grounds of confidentiality.[5] Moreover, amendments made to sub-ss (1) and (2) by CLEA 2001, s 23 make it clear that although an individual may not refuse to produce books and records merely because he is claiming a lien such as a solicitor's lien over them, nevertheless the actual production of the documents to the inspector will not result in the lien being lost.

Notwithstanding the provisions of s 10, a person is not required to produce books and records or to answer questions where to do so would result in the disclosure of information protected by legal professional privilege.[6] However, persons called upon by the inspector pursuant to s 10(4) to answer questions, may not decline to do so in reliance on the privilege against self-incrimination, although any answers given by them under compulsion will not, in general, be admissible against them in subsequent criminal proceedings.[7]

Conduct of Investigation: See the notes to CA 1990, s 7.

Refusal to co-operate: Under the original text of sub-s (5), refusal to co-operate was punishable as a contempt of court. That subsection was, however, found to be unconstitutional.[8] Costello J held, however, that this did not prevent the court from directing the witness to co-operate under sub-s (6).[9] The constitutional infirmities of sub-s (5) appear to have been successfully overcome by the new sub-ss (5) and (6) as inserted by CLEA 2001, s 23. These provisions enable the inspector to certify the witness's non-cooperation and to apply to the court for an order compelling him to do so. Failure to obey an order of the court made under sub-s (6) would be punishable as a contempt of court.

1 For an analysis of what is meant by the term 'officer', see *Director of Corporate Enforcement v D'Arcy* [2006] 2 IR 163.

2 By virtue of sub-s (7), the term 'agent' means bankers, solicitors, auditors, accountants, book-keepers and tax advisers.

3 *Chestvale Properties Ltd v Glackin (No 2)* [1993] 23 IR 35.

4 *Glackin v Trustee Savings Bank* [1993] 3 IR 55.

5 *Re an Inquiry under the Company Securities (Insider Dealing) Act 1985* [1988] AC 660.

6 CA 1990, s 23(1).

7 *Re National Irish Bank Ltd (No 1)* [1999] 3 IR 145. See also *Saunders v United Kingdom* [1997] BCC 872. Under s 18 such answers are admissible in civil proceedings, but are stated to be

inadmissible in proceedings in criminal proceedings other than proceedings for perjury. However, it would seem that s 18 protects individuals only and not companies.

8 *Desmond v Glackin (No 2)* [1993] 3 IR 67.

9 *Glackin v Trustee Savings Bank* [1993] 3 IR 55.

11 Inspectors' reports

(1) Inspectors appointed under section 7 or 8 may, and if so directed by the court shall, make interim reports to the court and on the conclusion of the investigation, shall make a final report to the court.

(2) Notwithstanding anything contained in subsection (1), an inspector appointed under section 7 or 8 may at any time in the course of his investigation, without the necessity of making an interim report, inform the court of matters coming to his knowledge as a result of the investigation tending to show that an offence has been committed.

(3) Where inspectors were appointed under section 7 or 8, the court shall furnish a copy of every report of theirs to the [Director][a] and the court may, if it thinks fit—

(a) forward a copy of any report made by the inspectors to the company's registered office,

(b) furnish a copy on request and payment of the prescribed fee to—

(i) any member of the company or other body corporate which is the subject of the report;

(ii) any person whose conduct is referred to in the report;

(iii) the auditors of that company or body corporate;

(iv) the applicants for the investigation;

(v) any other person (including an employee) whose financial interests appear to the court to be affected by the matters dealt with in the report whether as a creditor of the company or body corporate or otherwise;

(vi) the Central Bank, in any case in which the report of the inspectors relates, wholly or partly, to the affairs of the holder of a licence under section 9 of the Central Bank Act, 1971;[...][b]

[(ba) furnish a copy to—

(i) an appropriate authority in relation to any of the matters referred to in section 21(1)(a) to (fb); or

(ii) a competent authority as defined in section 21(3)(a) to (i); and][c]

(c) cause any such report to be printed and published.

(4) Where the court so thinks proper it may direct that a particular part of a report made by virtue of this section be omitted from a copy forwarded or furnished under [subsection (3)(a), (b) or (ba)][d] or from the report as printed and published under subsection (3)(c).

Amendments

a 'Director' substituted for 'Minister' by CLEA 2001, s 14.

b CLEA 2001, s 24(1)(a) amends CA 1990, s 11(3)(b)(vi) by the deletion of 'and' from the end thereof.

c CLEA 2001, s 24(1) inserts CA 1990, s 11(3)(ba).

d CLEA 2001, s 24(2) amends CA 1990, s 11(4) by the substitution for 'subsection (3)(a) or (b)' of 'subsection (3)(a), (b) or (ba)'.

Notes

Duty to report: If the inspector does determine facts relevant to the investigation, he has a power and a duty to include that information in his report; equally, if he is unable to make a positive determination as to relevant facts, but is able to form an opinion in relation thereto, he has a duty to include that opinion in his report.[1]

Furnishing copies of the report: The court is obliged, under sub-s (3) to furnish a copy of the inspector's report to the ODCE, irrespective of whether the inspector was appointed under s 7 or s 8. Whilst it is given a discretion whether to furnish copies to all or any of the other persons listed in paras (a), (b) and (ba), the requirements of natural justice would seem to dictate that copies should at least be furnished upon request to those persons criticised in the report.[2] However, if the decision is taken to publish the report, those persons criticised therein are not necessarily entitled to copies of the report in its final form in advance of publication.[3]

Publication of the report: The power to decide whether or not to publish the report is discretionary, and in this regard the court will be inclined to exercise its discretion in favour of ordering publication in circumstances where this is favoured by the inspectors, the company and any relevant regulatory authority.[4]

An application to have one's name omitted from a report prior to its publication cannot be heard *in camera*.[5]

The publication of the report is privileged under CA 1990, s 23(3).

Proceedings on foot of the report: See CA 1990, s 12 and the notes thereto.

Evidential status of inspector's report: See CA 1990, s 22 and the notes thereto.

1 *Lyons v Curran* [1993] ILRM 375.

2 *Re Pergamon Press Ltd* [1970] 3 All ER 589; *Maxwell v Department of Trade and Industry* [1974] QB 523; *Norwest Holst Ltd v Secretary of State for trade* [1978] 3 All ER 28; *R v Secretary of State for Trade, ex parte Perestrello* [1980] 3 All ER 28; *Chestvale Properties Ltd and Hoddle Investments Ltd v Glackin* [1993] 3 IR 35; *Re National Irish Bank Ltd (No3)* [2004] 4 IR 186.

3 *Re National Irish Bank Ltd (No3)* [2004] 4 IR 186.

4 *Re National Irish Bank Ltd (No3)* [2004] 4 IR 186.

5 *Re Ansbacher (Cayman) Ltd* [2002] 2 IR 517.

12 Proceedings on inspectors' report

(1) Having considered a report made under section 11, the court may make such order as it deems fit in relation to matters arising from that report including—

(a) an order of its own motion for the winding up of a body corporate, or

(b) an order for the purpose of remedying any disability suffered by any person whose interests were adversely affected by the conduct of the affairs of the company, provided that, in making any such order, the court shall have regard to the interests of any other person who may be adversely affected by the order.

(2) If, in the case of any body corporate liable to be wound up under the Companies Acts, it appears to the [Director][a] from—

(a) any report made under section 11 as a result of an application by the [Director][a] under section 8, or

(b) any report made by inspectors appointed by the [Director][a] under this Act, or

(c) any information or document obtained by the [Director][a] under this Part,

that a petition should be presented for the winding up of the body, the [Director][a] may, unless the body is already being wound up by the court, present a petition for it to be so wound up if the court thinks it just and equitable for it to be so wound up.

Amendments

a 'Director' substituted for 'Minister' by CLEA 2001, s 14.

Notes

Proceedings on inspector's report: The court is given a broad jurisdiction as to the orders it may make having considered the contents of the inspector's report[1]. Of its own motion, or on foot of a petition presented by the ODCE,[2] it may order that the company or other body corporate[3] be wound up. The court will only make a winding-up order of its own motion where it is satisfied that the public interest requires it.[4] Similarly, the ODCE should only present a winding-up petition in the public interest[5] and, in this regard, his decision to do so may be subject to judicial review, if he has misdirected himself on questions of law or has taken into account irrelevant matters or ignored relevant matters, or if there has been some other serious and substantial defect in the procedure which led to his decision.[6]

With regard to the foregoing, it may not be in the public interest to make such an order, despite findings of past misconduct, in circumstances where the company has since taken steps to address the issues and the consequence of placing the company in liquidation would be to adversely affect third parties dealing with the company, such as creditors and customers.[7]

Apart from being empowered to make a winding-up order, the court may also make any other order under s 12(1)(b) as it deems fit to remedy any disability suffered by any person whose interests were adversely affected by the way in which the affairs of the company were conducted. Presumably, this could include an order for the payment of restitution and/or to set aside improper transactions. In *Re Ansbacher (Cayman) Ltd*[8] Finnegan P used the section to order that certain classes of documents that had come into the possession of the inspectors during the course of the investigation be disclosed to the Revenue Commissioners so as to facilitate the recovery of taxes. The 'disability' that the Revenue Commissioners were under in that case was that they had not been paid taxes that were lawfully due. Notably, Finnegan P held that disclosure should be ordered even though the material may have been furnished to the inspectors in circumstances of confidentiality.

Section 12(1)(b) may not, however, be used as a means of third party discovery or discovery against the inspectors, where this would undermine the finality of the report.[9]

Costs of investigation: See CA 1990, s 13 and the notes thereto.

1 *Re Ansbacher (Cayman) Ltd* [2004] 3 IR 193; *Re National Irish Bank Ltd (No 3)* [2004] 4 IR 186.

2 Subsections (2)(a) and (b) empower the ODCE to petition for a winding-up order on foot of the report of an inspector appointed under s 8 or s 19 which deals with the investigation of share ownership. However, sub-s (2)(c) also allows him to present such a petition on foot of other information or documentation obtained by him under CA 1990, Pt II. Prima facie, this would include a report of an inspector appointed under s 7, since such a report must be furnished to him under s 11(3). It would also include information and documents produced to him during an inquiry under s 19.

3 It is not clear whether the references to a 'body corporate' in s 12(1) and (2) are intended just to be references to related companies investigated under s 9 or whether the references are intended to be more expansive so as to encompass any body corporate mentioned in the report.

4 *Re National Irish Bank Ltd (No 3)* [2004] 4 IR 186.
5 *Re Lubin, Rosen & Associates Ltd* [1975] 1 WLR 122.
6 *Re Walter L Jacob & Co Ltd* [1989] BCLC 345.
7 *Re National Irish Bank Ltd (No 3)* [2004] 4 IR 186.
8 *Re Ansbacher (Cayman) Ltd* [2004] 3 IR 193.
9 *Re National Irish Bank Ltd* [2006] 2 ILRM 263. See also *Re National Irish Bank Ltd (No 4)* [2005] 3 IR 90 where Kelly J refused to use s 12 to order the inspectors to disclose to the ODCE information and material which the ODCE had already obtained from the company itself.

UK legislation

CA 1985, s 441.

13 Expenses of investigation of company's affairs

(1) The expenses of and incidental to an investigation by an inspector appointed by the court under the foregoing provisions of this Act shall be defrayed in the first instance by the [relevant Minister][a] but the court may direct that any person being—

(a) a body corporate dealt with in the report, or

(b) the applicant or applicants for the investigation,

shall be liable, to such extent as the court may direct, to repay the [relevant Minister.][b]

(2) Without prejudice to subsection (1), any person who is—

(a) convicted on indictment of an offence on a prosecution instituted as a result of an investigation,

(b) ordered to pay damages or restore any property in proceedings brought as a result of an investigation, or

(c) awarded damages or to whom property is restored in proceedings brought as a result of an investigation,

may, in the same proceedings, be ordered to repay all or part of the expenses referred to in subsection (1) to the [relevant Minister][a] or to any person on whom liability has been imposed by the court under that subsection, provided that, in the case of a person to whom paragraph (c) relates, the court shall not order payment in excess of one-tenth of the amount of the damages awarded or of the value of the property restored, as the case may be, and any such order shall not be executed until the person concerned has received his damages or the property has been restored, as the case may be.

(3) The report of an inspector may, if he thinks fit, and shall, if the court so directs, include a recommendation as to the directions (if any) which he thinks appropriate, in the light of his investigation, to be given under subsection (1).

[(3A) In this section 'relevant Minister' means—

(a) in case the inspector or inspectors concerned was or were appointed under section 7, the Minister for Justice, Equality and Law Reform, and

(b) in case the inspector or inspectors concerned was or were appointed under section 8, the Minister.][c]

Amendments

a 'relevant Minister' substituted for 'Minister for Justice' by CLEA 2001, s 25.

b Words substituted by C(MP)A 2009, s 3(c).

c Subsection (3A) inserted by CLEA 2001, s 25.

Notes

Costs of investigation: This section provides for the costs to be borne in the first instance by the Minister for Justice, Equality and Law Reform in a s 7 investigation, and by the Minister for Enterprise, Trade and Employment in a s 8 investigation. However, the court may direct the applicant for the investigation to reimburse to the relevant Minister up to €317,435.51 of those costs. In addition, the court may fix all or part of the costs on any body corporate dealt with in the report. The phrase 'dealt with in the report' has been interpreted as referring only to those bodies corporate that were both under investigation and dealt with in the report.[1] Thus, costs cannot be awarded against some other company simply because it has been mentioned in the report.[2]

Where successful civil or criminal proceedings are brought against a wrongdoer as a result of the investigation, the court hearing those proceedings may direct the wrongdoer to reimburse all or part of the costs of the investigation under sub-s (2). Indeed, this is clearly the most desirable outcome and should be achieved where possible.[3] Subsection (2) also allows the court in civil proceedings brought as a result of the investigation to direct that anyone whose has recovered damages or property in consequence should pay up to 10% of the costs of the investigation.

1 *Minister for Justice v Siúcre Éireann* [1992] 2 IR 215.

2 *Minister for Justice v Siúcre Éireann* [1992] 2 IR 215.

3 *Minister for Justice v Siúcre Éireann* [1992] 2 IR 215.

14 Appointment and powers of inspectors to investigate ownership of company

(1) The [Director][a] may, subject to subsection (2), appoint one or more competent inspectors to investigate and report on the membership of any company and otherwise with respect to the company for the purpose of determining the true persons who are or have been financially interested in the success or failure (real or apparent) of the company or able to control or materially to influence the policy of the company.

(2) An appointment may be made by the [Director][a] if he is of the opinion that there are circumstances suggesting that it is necessary—

(a) for the effective administration of the law relating to companies;

(b) for the effective discharge by the [Director][a] of his functions under any enactment; or

(c) in the public interest.

(3) The appointment of an inspector under this section may define the scope of his investigation, whether as respects the matters or the period to which it is to extend or otherwise, and in particular may limit the investigation to matters connected with particular shares or debentures.

(4) Subject to the terms of an inspector's appointment his powers shall extend to the investigation of any circumstances suggesting the existence of an arrangement or understanding which, though not legally binding, is or was observed or likely to be observed in practice and which is relevant to the purposes of his investigation.

(5) For the purposes of any investigation under this section, sections 9 to 11, except section 10 (3), shall apply with the necessary modifications of references to the affairs of the company or to those of any other body corporate, so, however, that—

(a) the said sections shall apply in relation to all persons who are or have been, or whom the inspector has reasonable cause to believe to be or have been, financially interested in the success or failure or the apparent success or failure of the company or any other body corporate whose membership is investigated with that of the company, or able to control or materially to influence the policy thereof, including persons concerned only on behalf of others and to any other person whom the inspector has reasonable cause to believe possesses information relevant to the investigation, as they apply in relation to officers and agents of the company or of the other body corporate, as the case may be;

(b) if the [Director][a] is of opinion that there is good reason for not divulging any part of a report made by virtue of this section he may disclose the report with the omission of that part; and may cause to be kept by the registrar of companies a copy of the report with that part omitted or, in the case of any other such report, a copy of the whole report; and

(c) for references to the court (except in section 10(5) and (6)), there shall be substituted references to the [Director].[a]

[(6) The court may, on the application of the Director, direct that a company the subject of an investigation under this section shall be liable, to such extent as the court may direct, to repay the Director the expenses of and incidental to the investigation.

(7) Without prejudice to subsection (6) but subject to subsection (8), a person—

(a) convicted on indictment of an offence on a prosecution instituted,

(b) ordered to pay damages or restore any property in proceedings brought, or

(c) awarded damages or to whom property is restored in proceedings brought,

as a result of an investigation under this section may, in the same proceedings, be ordered to repay the Director all or part of the expenses referred to in subsection (6).

(8) The court shall not order a person to whom subsection (7)(c) relates to make payment in excess of one-tenth of the amount of the damages awarded or of the value of the property restored, as the case may be, and any such order shall not be executed until the person concerned has received his damages or the property has been restored.][b]

Amendments

a 'Director' substituted for 'Minister' by CLEA 2001, s 14.

b Subsections (6) to (8) inserted by CLEA 2001, s 26.

Notes

Appointment of inspector to investigate ownership: This section empowers the ODCE to appoint an inspector to investigate the ownership of a company. There is no requirement that the ODCE state in the warrant the reasons for the appointment of the inspectors.[1] There is, however, a requirement that the appointment be *bona fide*.[2] Moreover, whilst there is no obligation for the ODCE to notify the company in advance of his decision to appoint the inspector, he may, on request, be obliged to furnish reasons for the appointment.[3] The circumstances in which an inspector may be appointed are as set out in sub-s (2) and, in this regard, the ODCE should have reasonable grounds for his opinion that one or other of those circumstances has arisen.[4] If the ODCE has acted unreasonably or misdirected itself in deciding to appoint the inspector, that decision may be amenable to judicial review.[5]

Identity of true owners: Subsection (1) requires the inspector to determine the identity of the 'true persons' who are or have been financially interested in the success or failure (real or apparent) of the company under investigation or who have been able to control or materially influence the company's policy. In this regard, the phrase the 'true persons' means the individuals who are ultimately behind the company.[6] Thus, the inspector is not confined to ascertaining the identity of the registered members of the company; instead, where shares are held by trustees or by corporate shareholders, he must look behind those trusts and bodies corporate to ascertain the identity of the ultimate beneficial owners.[7]

Investigation of related companies: See CA 1990, s 9.

Conduct of investigation: See notes to CA 1990, s 7.

Powers of inspector: See notes to CA 1990, s 10.

Inspector's report: See notes to CA 1990, s 11.

1 *Desmond v Glackin (No 2)* [1993] 3 IR 67.

2 *Desmond v Glackin (No. 2)* [1993] 3 IR 67.

3 *Dunnes Stores Ireland Company v Maloney* [1999] 3 IR 542; *Dunnes Stores Ireland Company v Ryan* [2002] 2 IR 60.

4 *Dunnes Stores Ireland Company v Maloney* [1999] 3 IR 542; *Dunnes Stores Ireland Company v Ryan* [2002] 2 IR 60.

5 *Dunnes Stores Ireland Company v Maloney* [1999] 3 IR 542; *Dunnes Stores Ireland Company v Ryan* [2002] 2 IR 60.

6 *Lyons v Curran* [1993] ILRM 375. See also *Desmond v Glackin (No 2)* [1993] 3 IR 67; *Probets and Freezone Investments Ltd v Glackin* [1993] 3 IR 134; *Glackin v Trustee Savings Bank* [1993] 3 IR 55; *Chestvale Properties Ltd v Glackin* [1993] 3 IR 35.

7 *Lyons v Curran* [1993] ILRM 375. See also *Desmond v Glackin (No 2)* [1993] 3 IR 67; *Probets and Freezone Investments Ltd v Glackin* [1993] 3 IR 134; *Glackin v Trustee Savings Bank* [1993] 3 IR 55; *Chestvale Properties Ltd v Glackin* [1993] 3 IR 35.

15 Power to require information as to persons interested in shares or debentures

(1) Where it appears to the [Director][a] that it is necessary—

(a) for the effective administration of the law relating to companies;

(b) for the effective discharge by the [Director][a] of his functions under any enactment; or

(c) in the public interest;

to investigate the ownership of any shares in or debentures of a company and that it is unnecessary to appoint an inspector for the purpose, he may require any person whom he has reasonable cause to believe to have or to be able to obtain any information as to the present and past interests in those shares or debentures and the names and addresses of the persons interested and of any persons who act or have acted on their behalf in relation to the shares or debentures to give any such information to the [Director][a].

(2) For the purposes of this section a person shall be deemed to have an interest in a share or debenture if he has any right to acquire or dispose of the share or debenture or any interest therein or to vote in respect thereof or if his consent is necessary for the exercise of any of the rights of other persons interested therein or if the other persons interested therein can be required or are accustomed to exercise their rights in accordance with his instructions.

(3) Any person who fails to give any information required of him under this section or who in giving any such information makes any statement which he knows to be false in a material particular, or recklessly makes any statement which is false in a material particular, shall be guilty of an offence.

Amendments

a 'Director' substituted for 'Minister' by CLEA 2001, s 14.

Notes

Inquiry into share ownership: Section 15 empowers the ODCE to conduct his own inquiry into share ownership in circumstances where he considers that a formal investigation under s 14 may be unnecessary. The circumstances entitling him to conduct such an inquiry are the same as for the appointment of an inspector under s 14. In this regard, the inquiry should be *bona fide*,[1] and whilst there is no obligation on the ODCE to notify the person in advance of the decision to conduct the inquiry, he may, on request, be obliged to furnish reasons for so acting.[2] Furthermore, the ODCE should have reasonable grounds for his opinion that one or other of those circumstances specified in sub-s (1)(a) to (c) has arisen.[3] If the ODCE has acted unreasonably or misdirected itself in deciding to conduct the inquiry, that decision may be amenable to judicial review.[4]

Confidentiality and privilege: See notes to CA 1990, s 10.

1 *Desmond v Glackin (No 2)* [1993] 3 IR 67.

2 *Dunnes Stores Ireland Company v Maloney* [1999] 3 IR 542; *Dunnes Stores Ireland Company v Ryan* [2002] 2 IR 60.

3 *Dunnes Stores Ireland Company v Maloney* [1999] 3 IR 542; *Dunnes Stores Ireland Company v Ryan* [2002] 2 IR 60.

4 *Dunnes Stores Ireland Company v Maloney* [1999] 3 IR 542; *Dunnes Stores Ireland Company v Ryan* [2002] 2 IR 60.

16 Power to impose restrictions on shares or debentures

(1) Where in connection with an investigation or enquiry under section 14 or 15 it appears to the [Director][a] that there is difficulty in finding out the relevant facts about any shares (whether issued or to be issued), the [Director][a] may by notice in writing direct that the shares shall until further notice be subject to the restrictions imposed by this section.

(2) So long as a direction under subsection (1) in respect of any shares is in force—

(a) any transfer of those shares, or in the case of unissued shares any transfer of the right to be issued therewith and any issue thereof, shall be void;

(b) no voting rights shall be exercisable in respect of those shares;

(c) no further shares shall be issued in right of those shares or in pursuance of any offer made to the holder thereof; and

(d) […][b] no payment shall be made of any sums due from the company on those shares, whether in respect of capital or otherwise.

(3) Where shares are subject to the restrictions imposed by subsection (2)(a) any agreement to transfer the shares or in the case of unissued shares the right to be issued with the shares shall be void except an agreement to sell the shares pursuant to subsection (6)(b).

(4) Where shares are subject to the restrictions imposed by subsection (2)(c) or (2)(d) any agreement to transfer any right to be issued with other shares in right of those shares or to receive any payment on those shares […][c] shall be void except an agreement to transfer any such right on the sale of the shares pursuant to subsection (6)(b).

(5) Where the [Director][a] directs that shares shall be subject to the said restrictions, or refuses to direct that shares shall cease to be subject thereto, any person aggrieved thereby may apply to the court for an order that the shares shall cease to be subject thereto.

(6) Subject to subsections (7) and (13), an order of the court or a direction of the Minister that shares shall cease to be subject to the restrictions imposed by this section may be made only if—

[(a) in the case of an order by the court, the court is satisfied that the relevant facts about the shares have been disclosed to the company or, as the case requires, to the Director, or that it is otherwise equitable to lift the restrictions;

(b) in the case of a direction of the Director, the Director is satisfied that the relevant facts about the shares have been disclosed to him; or

(c) the shares are to be sold and the court or the Director approves the sale.][d]

(7) Where any shares in a company are subject to the restrictions imposed by this section, the court may on the application of the [Director][a] or the company [, having given notice to the Director][e] order the shares to be sold, subject to the approval of the court as to the sale, and may also direct that the shares shall cease to be subject to those restrictions.

(8) Where an order has been made under subsection (7) then, on application of the [Director],[a] the company, the person appointed by or in pursuance of the order to effect the sale or any person interested in the shares, the court may make such further order relating to the sale or to the transfer of the shares as it thinks fit.

(9) Where any shares are sold in pursuance of an order made under subsection (7), the proceeds of sale, less the costs of the sale, shall be paid into court for the benefit of the persons who are beneficially interested in the shares; and any such person may apply to the court for the whole or part of those proceeds to be paid to him.

(10) On an application under subsection (9) the court shall, subject to subsection (11), order the payment to the applicant of the whole of the proceeds of sale together with any interest thereon or, if any other person had a beneficial interest in the shares at the time of their sale, such proportion of those proceeds and interest as is equal to the proportion which the value of the applicant's interest in the shares bears to the total value of the shares.

(11) On granting an application for an order under subsection (7) or (8), the court may order that the costs of the applicant shall be paid out of the proceeds of sale; and, where an order under this subsection is made, the applicant shall be entitled to payment of his costs out of the proceeds of sale before any person interested in the shares in question receives any part of those proceeds.

(12) Any order or direction that shares shall cease to be subject to the said restrictions which is expressed to be made or given with a view to permitting a transfer of those shares or which is made under subsection (7) may continue the restrictions mentioned in

subsection (2)(c) and (2)(d) in whole or in part, so far as they relate to any right acquired or offer made before the transfer.

(13) Subsection (6) shall not apply in relation to any order of the court or of the [Director][a] directing that shares shall cease to be subject to any restrictions which have been continued in force in relation to those shares by virtue of subsection (12).

(14) Any person who—

(a) exercises or purports to exercise any right to dispose of any shares which, to his knowledge, are for the time being subject to the said restrictions or of any right to be issued with any such shares; or

(b) votes in respect of any such shares, whether as holder or proxy, or appoints a proxy to vote in respect thereof; or

(c) being the holder of any such shares, fails to notify of their being subject to the said restrictions any person whom he does not know to be aware of that fact but does know to be entitled, apart from the said restrictions, to vote in respect of those shares whether as holder or proxy; or

(d) being the holder of any such shares, or being entitled to any such right as is mentioned in subsection (4) enters into an agreement which is void by virtue of subsection (3) or (4);

shall be guilty of an offence.

(15) Where shares in any company are issued in contravention of the said restrictions, the company and every officer of the company who is in default shall be guilty of an offence.

(16) Summary proceedings shall not be instituted under this section except by or with the consent of the [Director].[a]

(17) This section shall apply in relation to debentures as it applies in relation to shares.

(18) The [Director][a] shall cause notice of any direction given by him under this section—

(a) to be sent to the company concerned at its registered office, and

(b) to be delivered to the registrar of companies,

(c) to be published in [the Companies Registration Office Gazette][f] and in at least two daily newspapers,

as soon as may be after the direction is given.

Amendments

a 'Director' substituted for 'Minister' by CLEA 2001, s 14.

b 'except in a liquidation' deleted from sub-s (2)(d) by CLEA 2001, s 27(a).

c '(otherwise than in a liquidation)' deleted from sub-s (4) by CLEA 2001, s 27(b).

d Paras (a) to (c) substituted by CLEA 2001, s 27(c).

e ', having given notice to the Director,' inserted by CLEA 2001, s 27(d).

f 'the Companies Registration Office Gazette' substituted for '*Iris Oifigiúil*' by IFCMPA 2005, s 72.

Notes

Freezing order in respect of shares: This section confers on the ODCE the power, by written notice, to effectively freeze all rights in respect of shares and debentures in connection with an investigation or inquiry under ss 14 or 15. The freezing order may be lifted by the court or the ODCE if the relevant information as to the ownership of the shares or debentures has been disclosed or if the shares or debentures 'are to be sold' and the court or the ODCE approves the sale. Under the equivalent UK provision, it has been held that the words 'to be sold' in sub-s (6)(c) refer to a transfer for money consideration,[1] which therefore suggests that a share-for-share transfer might not be capable of being approved by the court or the Director.[2] In any event, the court will be disinclined to approve a sale unless and until the identity of the true owner of the shares or debentures has been disclosed.[3]

Under sub-ss (7) *et seq* the ODCE or the company may also apply to court to have the shares or debentures in question sold and to have the proceeds of sale placed in court until such time as the true beneficial owner comes forward and applies to have the moneys paid out.

1 *Re Westminster Property Group plc* [1985] 1 WLR 676.

2 See discussion in Courtney, *The Law of Private Companies* (2nd edn, Tottel Publishing, 2002) at 889.

3 *Re Greers Gross plc* [1985] 1 WLR 676.

17 Extension of powers of investigation to certain bodies incorporated outside the State

Sections 8 to 11, 13, 18 and 22 shall apply to all bodies corporate incorporated outside the State which are carrying on business in the State or have at any time carried on business therein as if they were companies registered under the Principal Act, subject to any necessary modifications.

Notes

The words 'carry on a business' require a continuum of activity and one or two isolated transactions will not suffice.[1]

1 *Minister for Justice v Siúcre Éireann* [1992] 2 IR 215.

18 Admissibility in evidence of certain matters

[(1) An answer given by an individual][a] to a question put to him in exercise of powers conferred by—

(a) section 10;

(b) section 10 as applied by sections 14 and 17; or

(c) rules made in respect of the winding-up of companies whether by the court or voluntarily under section 68 of the Courts of Justice Act, 1936, as extended by section 312 of the Principal Act;

may be used in evidence against him [in any proceedings whatsoever (save proceedings for an offence (other than perjury in respect of such an answer)).][b]

[(2) A statement required by section 224 of the Principal Act may, in any proceedings whatsoever (save proceedings for an offence (other than perjury in respect of any matter contained in the statement)), be used in evidence against any individual making or concurring in making it.][c]

Amendments

a Words substituted by CLEA 2001, s 28(a).

b Words substituted by CLEA 2001, s 28(b).

c Subsection (2) inserted by CLEA 2001, s 28(c).

Notes

Privilege against self-incrimination: Persons called upon by the inspector pursuant to s 10(4) to answer questions may not decline to do so in reliance on the privilege against self-incrimination, although any answers given by them under compulsion will not, in general, be admissible against them in subsequent criminal proceedings,[1] other than proceedings for perjury.

The replacement of the word 'person' with the word 'individual' as a result of the amendments made by CLEA 2001, s 28 appears to exclude companies from the protection of sub-s (1).[2]

1 *Re National Irish Bank Ltd (No 1)* [1999] 3 IR 145. See also *Saunders v United Kingdom* [1997] BCC 872.

2 See *Re National Irish Bank* [1999] 3 IR 145, [1999] 1 ILRM 312 discussed in O'Neill, 'The Right to Silence and the Company' (2005) Ir Jur 111.

19 [Power of Director to require production of documents

(1) The Director may, subject to subsection (2), give directions to any body being—

(a) a company formed and registered under the Companies Acts;

(b) an existing company within the meaning of those Acts;

(c) a company to which the Principal Act applies by virtue of section 325 thereof or which is registered under that Act by virtue of Part IX thereof;

(d) a body corporate incorporated in, and having a principal place of business in, the State, being a body to which any of the provisions of the said Act with respect to prospectuses and allotments apply by virtue of section 377 of that Act;

(e) a body corporate incorporated outside the State which is carrying on business in the State or has at any time carried on business therein;

(f) any other body, whether incorporated or not, which is, or appears to the Director to be, an insurance undertaking to which the Insurance Acts, 1909 to 2000, or regulations on insurance made under the European Communities Act, 1972, would apply, requiring the body, at such time and place as may be specified in the directions, to produce such books or documents as may be so specified.

(2) Directions may be given by the Director if he is of the opinion that there are circumstances suggesting that—

(a) it is necessary to examine the books and documents of the body with a view to determining whether an inspector should be appointed to conduct an investigation of the body under the Companies Acts;

(b) the affairs of the body are being or have been conducted with intent to defraud—

(i) its creditors,

(ii) the creditors of any other person, or

(iii) its members;

(c) the affairs of the body are being or have been conducted for a fraudulent purpose other than described in paragraph (b);

(d) the affairs of the body are being or have been conducted in a manner which is unfairly prejudicial to some part of its members;

[(da) the affairs of the body are being or have been conducted in a manner which is unfairly prejudicial to some or all of its creditors;][b]

(e) any actual or proposed act or omission or series of acts or omissions of the body or on behalf of the body [have been, are or would][c] be unfairly prejudicial to some part of its members;

(f) any actual or proposed act or omission or series of acts or omissions of the body or on behalf of the body or by an officer of the body acting in his capacity as such officer [have been, or are likely][d] to be unlawful;

(g) the body was formed for any fraudulent purpose;

(h) the body was formed for any unlawful purpose; or

(i) the body may be in possession of books or documents containing information relating to the books or documents of a body which comes within the terms of one or more of paragraphs (a) to (h).

[(3) Where by virtue of subsection (1) the Director has power to require the production of any books or documents from any body, the Director shall have power to require the production of—

(a) those books or documents from any person who appears to the Director to be in possession of them,

(b) copies of any books or documents of the body from any person who appears to the Director to be in possession of them, and

(c) subject to subsection (4), other books or documents (whether the originals of them or otherwise) which may relate to any books or documents of the body from any person who appears to the Director to be in possession of such other books or documents,

but where any such person claims a lien on books or documents produced by him, the production shall be without prejudice to the lien.][e]

[(3A) Any requirement under subsection (3) shall be made by the giving by the Director of a direction to the person of whom the requirement is being made that specifies—

(a) the books or documents to be produced by the person, and

(b) the time and place at which they are to be produced.][f]

(4) The power under [subsection (3)(c)][g] shall not be exercised unless—

(a) in the opinion of the Director, there are reasonable grounds for believing the first and second-mentioned books or documents in [subsection (3)(c)][g] are related to one another (and those grounds may include grounds related to the relationship between the body and the person of whom the requirement under [subsection (3)(c)][g] is proposed to be made, a common origin of some or all of the information contained in the said books or documents or similar considerations), and

(b) save where the Director is of opinion that compliance with this paragraph could result in the concealment, falsification, destruction or the disposal otherwise of the books or documents concerned, the Director notifies the person of whom the requirement under [subsection (3)(c)][g] is proposed to be made ('the third party') that the Director proposes to make that requirement and states in that notification the grounds for his opinion under paragraph (a) and that the third party may (if such is his contention) make submissions to the Director, within 21 days from the date of the making of the notification, as to why he believes the said opinion of the Director to be erroneous (and the Director shall have regard to any such submissions so made before finally deciding whether to make the said requirement or not),

but in no case shall the third party be obliged to comply with such a requirement in relation to a particular book or document concerned if he would be entitled, by virtue of any rule of law or enactment, to refuse to produce, in any proceedings, the book or document on the ground of any privilege (whether the privilege to which section 23 applies or not).

(5) Any power conferred by or by virtue of this section to require a body or other person to produce books or documents shall include power—

(a) if the books or documents are produced—

(i) to take copies of them or extracts from them, and

(ii) to require that person, or any other person who is a present or past officer of, or is or was at any time employed (including in a professional, consultancy or similar capacity) by, the body in question, to provide, insofar as the person may be reasonably able so to do, an explanation of any of them, including an explanation of any apparent omissions from them or any omission of any book or document, and

(b) if the books or documents are not produced, to require the person who was required to produce them to state, to the best of his knowledge and belief, where they are,

and in either event to give all assistance to the Director as the body or person is reasonably able to give in connection with an examination or proposed examination of books or documents under this section.

(6) If a requirement to produce books or documents or provide an explanation or make a statement which is imposed by virtue of this section is not complied with, the body or other person on whom the requirement was so imposed shall be guilty of an offence; but where a person is charged with an offence under this subsection in respect of a requirement to produce any books or documents, it shall be a defence to prove that they were not in his possession or under his control and that it was not reasonably practicable for him to comply with the requirement.

(7) A statement made or an explanation provided by an individual in compliance with a requirement imposed by virtue of this section may be used in evidence against him in any proceedings whatsoever (save proceedings for an offence (other than an offence under subsection (6) or (8))).

(8) A person who provides an explanation or makes a statement required under this section which is false or misleading in a material respect, knowing it to be so false or misleading, shall be guilty of an offence.

(9) Notwithstanding section 202(9), it shall be an offence for a person or body with notice of [a direction under subsection (1) or (3A)][h] (whether given or coming to the notice of the person or body before or after the commencement of section 29 of the Company Law Enforcement Act, 2001) to destroy, mutilate, falsify or conceal any book or document the subject of a direction.

(10) The court may, on the application of the Director, direct that a body the subject of a direction under subsection (1) shall be liable, to such extent as the court may direct, to repay the Director the expenses of and incidental to the examination.

(11) Without prejudice to subsection (10) but subject to subsection (12), a person—

(a) convicted on indictment of an offence on a prosecution instituted,

(b) ordered to pay damages or restore any property in proceedings brought, or

(c) awarded damages or to whom property is restored in proceedings brought,

as a result of a direction under subsection (1) may, in the same proceedings, be ordered to repay the Director all or part of the expenses referred to in subsection (10).

(12) The court shall not order a person to whom subsection (11)(c) relates to make payment in excess of one-tenth of the amount of the damages awarded or of the value of the property restored, as the case may be, and any such order shall not be executed until the person concerned has received his damages or the property has been restored.][a]

Amendments

a Section 19 substituted by CLEA 2001, s 29.

b Subsection (2)(da) inserted by IFCMPA 2005, s 67(a).

c Words substituted by IFCMPA 2005, s 67(b).

d Words substituted by IFCMPA 2005, s 67(c).

e CA 1990, s 19(3) substituted by C(A)A 2009, s 4(1)(a).

f CA 1990, s 19(3A) inserted by C(A)A 2009, s 4(1)(a).

g Words 'subsection 3(c)' substituted for 'subsection 3(b)' by C(A)A 2009, s 4(1)(b).

h Words 'a direction under subsection (1) or (3A)' substituted for 'a direction under subsection (1)' by C(A)A 2009, s 4(1)(c).

Notes

Inquiry by ODCE: Either as a possible prelude to, or instead of, the appointment of an inspector under s 8, the ODCE may conduct an enquiry under s 19.[1] Any inquiry must be conducted *bona fide*.[2] Whilst there is no obligation for the ODCE to notify the company in advance of his decision to conduct the inquiry, he may, on request, be obliged to furnish reasons for the appointment.[3] The circumstances in which an inquiry may be appointed are as set out in sub-s (2) and, in this regard, the ODCE should have reasonable grounds for his opinion that one or other of those circumstances has arisen.[4] If the ODCE has acted unreasonably or misdirected itself in deciding to appoint the inspector, that decision may be amenable to judicial review.[5]

Persons to whom requirements may be addressed: The ODCE's primary focus of inquiry is the company itself. However, under sub-s (3)(a) he may also require copies of company records to be produced by any other person in possession of same. As regards books and records which do not belong to the company but which relate to the company's records, these may be demanded of third parties under sub-s (3)(b). Under sub-s (4) the ODCE should first give at least 21days' notice to the third party unless he is of the opinion that the records might otherwise be concealed, falsified, destroyed or disposed of. By virtue of sub-s (3), an individual may not refuse to produce books and records merely because he is claiming a lien such as a solicitor's lien over them, nevertheless the actual production of the documents to the inspector will not result in the lien being lost.

The past and present officers and employees of the company (including its professional advisers and consultants) and any other person of whom documents are demanded, may be required under sub-s (6) to provide the ODCE with all reasonable assistance and to provide all reasonable explanations in relation to the records produced.

Non-cooperation may give rise to any one of a series of offences under sub-ss (6), (8) and (9), and s 19A.

Costs of inquiry: The provisions of sub-ss (10) to (12) broadly mirror the provisions of CA 1990.

Confidentiality and privilege: Any duty of confidentiality which an individual owes to a company as its customer is overridden by the duty to co-operate with the ODCE.[6] Notwithstanding the provisions of s 10, a person is not required to produce books and records or to answer questions where to do so would result in the disclosure of information protected by legal professional privilege.[7] However, persons called upon by the ODCE pursuant to s 19(5) to answer questions may not decline to do so in reliance on the privilege against self-incrimination, although any answers given by them under compulsion will not, in general, be admissible against them in subsequent criminal proceedings.[8]

Non-disclosure of information provided to the ODCE: See CA 1990, s 21 which limited the entitlement of the ODCE to disclose information obtained under ss 19 and 20, otherwise than to the bodies and organisations specified therein.

1 See generally, Courtney, *The Law of Private Companies* (2nd edn, Tottel Publishing, 2002) at paras 14.068 et seq.

2 *Desmond v Glackin (No. 2)* [1993] 3 IR 67.

3 *Dunnes Stores Ireland Company v Maloney* [1999] 3 IR 542; *Dunnes Stores Ireland Company v Ryan* [2002] 2 IR 60.

4 *Dunnes Stores Ireland Company v Maloney* [1999] 3 IR 542; *Dunnes Stores Ireland Company v Ryan* [2002] 2 IR 60.

5 *Dunnes Stores Ireland Company v Maloney* [1999] 3 IR 542; *Dunnes Stores Ireland Company v Ryan* [2002] 2 IR 60.

6 *Glackin v Trustee Savings Bank* [1993] 3 IR 55.

7 CA 1990, s 23(1).

8 *Re National Irish Bank Ltd (No 1)* [1999] 3 IR 145. See also *Saunders v United Kingdom* [1997] BCC 872. See also sub-s (7) which, it would seem, protects individuals only and not companies.

[19A Concealing facts disclosed by documents

(1) A person who—

(a) knows or suspects that an investigation by the Director into an offence under the Companies Acts is being or is likely to be carried out, and

(b) falsifies, conceals, destroys or otherwise disposes of a document or record which he knows or suspects is or would be relevant to the investigation or causes or permits its falsification, concealment, destruction or disposal,

shall be guilty of an offence.

(2) Where a person—

(a) falsifies, conceals, destroys or otherwise disposes of a document or record, or

(b) causes or permits its falsification, concealment, destruction or disposal,

in such circumstances that it is reasonable to conclude that the person knew or suspected—

(i) that an investigation by the Director into an offence under the Companies Acts was being or was likely to be carried out, and

(ii) that the document or record was or would be relevant to the investigation,

the person shall be taken for the purposes of this section to have so known or suspected, unless the court or the jury, as the case may be, is satisfied having regard to all the evidence that there is reasonable doubt as to whether the person so knew or suspected.][a]

Amendments

a Section was inserted by CLEA 2001, s 29.

20 Entry and search of premises

[(1) If a judge of the District Court is satisfied by information on oath laid by a designated officer that there are reasonable grounds for suspecting that any material information is to be found on any premises (including a dwelling), the judge may issue a search warrant under this section.

(2) A search warrant issued under this section shall be expressed and operate to authorise a named designated officer ('the officer'), accompanied by such other persons as the officer thinks necessary, [at any time or times within the period of validity of the warrant][b], on production if so requested of the warrant, to—

(a) enter the premises named in the warrant, if necessary by force,

(b) search the premises,

(c) require any person found on the premises—

(i) to give to the officer his name, home address and occupation, and

(ii) to produce to the officer any material information which is in the custody or possession of that person,

(d) seize and retain any material information found on the premises or in the custody or possession of any person found on the premises, and

(e) take any other steps which appear to the officer to be necessary for preserving or preventing interference with material information.

[(2A) Without prejudice to subsection (2B), where—

(a) the officer finds anything at, or in the custody or possession of any person found on, the premises named in the warrant that the officer has reasonable grounds for believing may be or may contain material information, and

(b) it is not reasonably practicable for a determination to be made on the premises—

(i) whether what he has found is something that he is entitled to seize under the war-rant (whether as mentioned in subsection (2)(d) or subsection (2B)), or

(ii) the extent to which what he has found contains something that he is entitled to seize under the warrant in either of those cases,

the officer's powers of seizure under the warrant shall include power to seize so much of what he has found as it is necessary to remove from the premises to enable that to be determined (in subsections (2D) to (2G) referred to as an 'extended power of seizure').

(2B) Where—

(a) the officer finds anything at, or in the custody or possession of any person found on, the premises named in the warrant being a book, document or other thing constituting material information ('seizable information') which he would be entitled to seize but for its being comprised in something else that he has (apart from this subsection) no power to seize, and

(b) it is not reasonably practicable for the seizable information to be separated, on those premises, from that in which it is comprised,

the officer's powers of seizure shall include power to seize both the seizable information and that from which it is not reasonably practicable to separate it (in subsections (2D) to (2G) also referred to as an 'extended power of seizure').

(2C) Where, for the purposes of subsection (2A) or (2B), an issue arises as to either of the following matters, namely—

(a) whether or not it is reasonably practicable on particular premises for something to be determined, or

(b) whether or not it is reasonably practicable on particular premises for something to be separated from something else,

the issue shall be decided by reference solely to the following matters:

(i) how long it would take to carry out the determination or separation on those premises;

(ii) the number of persons that would be required to carry out that determination or separation on those premises within a reasonable period;

(iii) whether the determination or separation would (or would if carried out on those premises) involve damage to property;

(iv) the apparatus or equipment that it would be necessary or appropriate to use for the carrying out of the determination or separation;

(v) the costs of carrying out the determination or separation on those premises as against the costs of carrying out the determination or separation in another place (being a place in which the Director can show it would be appropriate to do the thing concerned and in which the Director intends to arrange, or does arrange, for the thing to be done), and

(vi) in the case of separation, whether the separation—

(I) would be likely, or

(II) if carried out by the only means that are reasonably practicable on those premises, would be likely,

to prejudice the use of some or all of the separated seizable information for a purpose for which something seized under the warrant is capable of being used.

(2D) Save where the officer is of opinion that compliance with this subsection could result in the concealment, falsification, destruction or the disposal otherwise of material information, an extended power of seizure shall not be exercised unless the officer has first made the following arrangements in relation to the thing or things, the subject of the proposed exercise of that power, namely reasonable arrangements—

(a) providing for the appropriate storage of that thing or those things,

(b) allowing reasonable access, from time to time, to that thing or those things by the owner, lawful custodian or possessor thereof (including, in the case of documents or information in non-legible form, by the making of copies or the transmission of matter by electronic means), and

(c) providing for confidentiality to be maintained as regards any confidential matter comprised in that thing or those things,

being arrangements to apply pending the making of the foregoing determination or the carrying out of the foregoing separation and the consequent return of anything to the owner, lawful custodian or possessor that is not material information; in deciding what the terms of those arrangements shall be, the officer shall have regard to any representations reasonably made on the matter by the owner, lawful custodian or possessor of the thing or things and endeavour, where practicable, to secure the agreement of that person to those terms.

(2E) Where—

(a) by reason of the officer being of the opinion referred to in subsection (2D), the arrangements referred to in paragraphs (a) to (c) of that subsection are not made in relation to the thing or things the subject of the proposed exercise of the extended power of seizure, or

(b) circumstances arise subsequent to the exercise of the extended power of seizure that make it appropriate to vary the arrangements made under that subsection,

the officer shall, as the case may be—

(i) make, as soon as practicable after the exercise of that power of seizure, the arrangements referred to in subsection (2D)(a) to (c) in relation to the thing or things concerned, or

(ii) vary the arrangements made under that subsection in a manner he considers appropriate,

and, in deciding what shall be the terms of those arrangements or that variation, the officer shall have regard to any representations on the matter reasonably made by the owner, lawful custodian or possessor of the thing or things concerned and endeavour, where practicable, to secure the agreement of that person to those terms.

(2F) Where an extended power of seizure is exercised, it shall be the duty of the officer—

(a) to carry out the determination or separation concerned as soon as practicable, and, in any event, subject to subsection (2G), within the prescribed period, after its exercise, and

(b) as respects anything seized in exercise of the power found not to be material information or, as the case may be, anything separated from another thing in the exercise of the power that is not material information, to return, as soon as practicable, and, in any event, subject to subsection (2G), within the prescribed period, after that finding or separation, the thing to its owner or the person appearing to the officer to be lawfully entitled to the custody or possession of it.

(2G) On application to the court by the Director or any person affected by the exercise of an extended power of seizure, the court may, if it thinks fit and having had regard, in particular, to any submissions made on behalf of the Director with regard to the progress of any investigation being carried on by the Director for the purpose of which the powers under this section had been exercised, give one or more of the following:

(a) a direction that the doing of an act referred to in subsection (2F)(a) or (b) shall be done within such lesser or greater period of time than that specified in that provision as the court determines,

(b) a direction with respect to the making, variation or operation of arrangements referred to in subsection (2D)(a) to (c) in relation to a thing concerned or a direction that such arrangements as the court provides for in the direction shall have effect in place of any such arrangements that have been or were proposed to be made,

(c) a direction of any other kind that the court considers it just to give for the purpose of further securing the rights of any person affected by the exercise of an extended power of seizure, including, if the exceptional circumstances of the case warrant doing so, a direction that a thing seized be returned to its owner or the person appearing to the court to be lawfully entitled to the custody or possession of it, not-withstanding that the determination or separation concerned has not occurred,

and any such direction may—

(i) relate to some or all of the things the subject of the exercise of the extended power of seizure,

(ii) be expressed to operate subject to such terms and conditions as the court specifies, including,

in the case of a direction under paragraph (c), a condition that an officer of the Director be permitted, during a specified subsequent period, to re-take and retain possession of the thing returned for the purpose of carrying out the determination or separation concerned (and, retain after the expiry of that period, that which is found to be material information or is material information).

(2H) An application under subsection (2G) shall be by motion and may, if the court directs, be heard otherwise than in public.

(2I) In subsection (2F) 'prescribed period' means—

(a) in the case of paragraph (a) of it—

(i) unless subparagraph (ii) applies, 3 months, or

(ii) such other period as the Minister prescribes in consequence of a review that may, from time to time, be carried out by or on behalf of the Minister of the operation and implementation of the amendments effected by section 5 of the Companies (Amendment) Act 2009,

(b) in the case of paragraph (b) of it—

(i) unless subparagraph (ii) applies, 7 days, or

(ii) such other period as the Minister prescribes in consequence of such a review that may, from time to time, be carried out by or on behalf of the Minister,

but no regulations made to prescribe such a period shall be read as operating to affect any direction given by the court under subsection (2G)(a) in force on the commencement of those regulations.

(2J) The Minister may make regulations providing for such supplementary, consequential and incidental matters to or in respect of subsections (2A) to (2F) as he considers necessary or expedient.][c]

(3) [...][d]

(4) The officer may—

(a) operate any computer at the place which is being searched or cause any such computer to be operated by a person accompanying the officer, and

(b) require any person at that place who appears to the officer to be in a position to facilitate access to the information held in any such computer or which can be accessed by the use of that computer—

(i) to give to the officer any password necessary to operate it,

(ii) otherwise to enable the officer to examine the information accessible by the computer in a form in which the information is visible and legible, or

(iii) to produce the information in a form in which it can be removed and in which it is, or can be made, visible and legible.

(5) The power to issue a warrant under this section is in addition to and not in substitution for any other power to issue a warrant for the search of any place or person.

(6) A person who—

(a) obstructs the exercise of a right of entry or search conferred by virtue of a search warrant issued under this section,

(b) obstructs the exercise of a right so conferred to seize and retain material information,

(c) fails to comply with a requirement under subsection (2)(c) or gives a name, address or occupation which is false or misleading, or

(d) fails to comply with a requirement under subsection (4)(b),

shall be guilty of an offence.

(7) In this section—

'computer' includes a personal organiser or any other electronic means of information storage or retrieval;

'computer at the place which is being searched' includes any other computer, whether at that place or at any other place, which is lawfully accessible by means of that computer;

'designated officer' means the Director or an officer of the Director authorised in that behalf by the Director; and

'material information' means—

(a) any books or documents of which production has been required under or by virtue of section 14, 15 or 19 and which have not been produced in compliance with that requirement, or

(b) any books or documents or other things (including a computer) which the officer has reasonable grounds for believing may provide evidence of or relating to the commission of an offence under the Companies Acts.][a]

[(8) The period of validity of a warrant shall be 1 month from its date of issue but that period of validity may be extended in accordance with subsections (9) and (10).

(9) The officer may, during the period of validity of a warrant (including such period as previously extended under subsection (10)), apply to a judge of the District Court for an order extending the period of validity of the warrant and such an application shall be grounded upon information on oath laid by the officer stating, by reference to the purpose or purposes for which the warrant was issued, the reasons why he considers the extension to be necessary.

(10) If the judge of the District Court is satisfied that there are reasonable grounds for believing, having regard to that information so laid, that further time is needed so that the purpose or purposes for which the warrant was issued can be fulfilled, the judge may make an order extending the period of validity of the warrant by such period as, in the opinion of the judge, is appropriate and just; where such an order is made, the judge shall cause the warrant to be suitably endorsed to indicate its extended period of validity.

(11) Nothing in the preceding subsections prevents a judge of the District Court from issuing, on foot of a fresh application made under subsection (1), a further search warrant under this section in relation to the same premises.][e]

Amendments

a Section substituted by CLEA 2001, s 30.

b Words 'at any time or times within the period of validity of the warrant' substituted for 'at any time or times within 1 month from the date of issue of the warrant' by C(A)A 2009, s 5(a).

c CA 1990, s 20(2A)–(2J) inserted by C(A)A 2009, s 5(b).

d Subsection (3) repealed by IFCMPA, s 68(2).

e CA 1990, s 20(8)–(11) inserted by C(A)A 2009, s 5(c).

21 Provision for security of information

[(1) No information, book or document relating to a body which has been obtained under section 19 or 20, shall, without the previous consent in writing of that body, be published or disclosed, except to a competent authority, unless the publication or disclosure is, in the opinion of the [Director][b], required—

(a) with a view to the investigation or prosecution of any offence, being an offence—

(i) under

(I) the Companies Acts;

(II) the Central Bank Acts, 1942 to 1998;

(III) the Exchange Control Acts, 1954 to 1986;

(IV) the Insurance Acts, 1909 to 1990;

[(V) the Taxes Consolidation Act, 1997, or an offence under an enactment referred to in section 1078(1) of that Act;][c]

(VI) regulations relating to insurance made under the European Communities Act, 1972;

or

(ii) entailing misconduct in connection with the management of the body's affairs or misapplication or wrongful retainer of its property;

(b) for the purpose of assessing the liability of a person in respect of a tax or duty or other payment owed or payable to the State, a local authority (within the meaning of the Local Government Act, 1941) or a health board or for the purpose of collecting an amount due in respect of such a tax or duty or other payment;

(c) for the purpose of the performance by a tribunal (to which the Tribunals of Inquiry (Evidence) Acts, 1921 to 1998, apply) of any of its functions;

(d) for the purpose of assisting or facilitating the performance by any Minister of the Government of any of his functions;

(e) for the purpose of assisting or facilitating any accountancy or other professional organisation in the performance of its disciplinary functions with respect to any of its members;

(f) for the purpose of the performance by the Irish Takeover Panel or any stock exchange established in the State of any of its functions in relation to the body or any other person who, in its opinion, is connected with the body;

[(fa) for the purpose of the performance by the Competition Authority of any of its functions;

(fb) for the purpose of the performance by a committee (being a committee within the meaning of the Committees of the Houses of the Oireachtas (Compellability, Privileges and Immunities of Witnesses) Act, 1997, to which sections 3 to 14 and 16 of that Act apply) of any of its functions;][d]

(g) for the purposes of complying with the requirements of procedural fairness, to be made to—

(i) any company in relation to which an inspector has been appointed under section 14 or any person required by the [Director][b] to give any information under section 15, or

[(ii) any body to which the Director has given a direction under section 19 or any person named in a report relating to an examination under that section;][e]

(h) for the purpose of complying with any requirement, or exercising any power, imposed or conferred by this Part with respect to reports made by inspectors appointed thereunder by the court or the [Director][b];

(i) with a view to the institution by the [Director][b] of proceedings for the winding-up under the Principal Act of the body or otherwise for the purposes of proceedings instituted by him for that purpose;

(j) for the purposes of proceedings under section 20 or 160].[a]

(2) A person who publishes or discloses any information, book or document in contravention of this section shall be guilty of an offence.

(3) For the purposes of this section 'competent authority' includes—

(a) the Minister,

(b) a person authorised by the Minister,

(c) an inspector appointed under this Act,

(d) the Minister for Finance,

(e) an officer authorised by the Minister for Finance,

[(ea) the Irish Auditing and Accounting Supervisory Authority,][f]

(f) any court of competent jurisdiction,

(g) a supervisory authority within the meaning of regulations relating to insurance made under the European Communities Act, 1972, [...][g]

[(h) the Central Bank, and

(i) any authority established outside the State in which there are vested—

(i) functions of investigating or prosecuting an offence similar to an offence referred to in paragraph (a) of subsection (1),

(ii) functions of assessing the liability of a person in respect of a tax or duty or other payment owed or payable to the state in which it is established or any other authority established in that state or of collecting an amount due in respect of such a tax or duty or other payment, or

(iii) functions which are similar to the functions referred to in paragraph (c), (d), (e) or (f) of subsection (1).][h]

Amendments

a C(A)(No 2)A 1999, s 53(2) substitutes CA 1990, s 21(1).

b CLEA 2001, s 31(a) amends CA 1990, s 21(1) by the substitution for 'Minister' where ever occurring, except in para (d) of 'Director'.

c CLEA 2001, s 31(b) substitutes CA 1990, s 21(1)(a)(i)(V).

d CLEA 2001, s 31(c) inserts CA 1990, s 21(1)(fa) and (fb).

e CLEA 2001, s 31(d) substitutes CA 1990, s 21(1)(g)(ii).

f Subsection (3)(ea) inserted by IFCMPA 2005, s 69.

g C(A)(No 2)A 1999, s 53(3)(a) amends CA 1990, s 21(3)(g) by the deletion of 'and'.

h C(A)(No 2)A 1999, s 53 (3)(b) substitutes CA 1990, s 21(3)(h) and inserts CA 1990, s 21(3)(i).

22 Inspectors' reports to be evidence

A document purporting to be a copy of a report of an inspector appointed under the provisions of this Part shall be admissible in any civil proceedings as evidence—

(a) of the facts set out therein without further proof unless the contrary is shown, and

(b) of the opinion of the inspector in relation to any matter contained in the report.

Notes

Admissibility of report: In *Countyglen plc v Carway*[1] Laffoy J held that the effect of s 22 was to render a report admissible:

> 'to give all findings of primary fact clearly expressed as such therein the status of proven fact unless disproved. Section 22 does not prescribe that facts thereby given the status of proven facts have any special probative value or that any particular weight should be attached thereto. Accordingly, the ordinary rules apply in determining whether an application for a direction should be acceded to at the end of the plaintiff's case and in determining the issue of fact when all the evidence is in.'

Inspectors' reports have been relied upon in the context of disqualification proceedings against directors under s 160 of CA 1990.[2] It has also been relied upon to ground an application for an interlocutory Mareva injuction.[3] It is not clear whether the section shifts a legal or evidential burden onto the respondent to s 160 proceedings – see O'Neill, 'Section 12 of the Companies Act 1990 as a Weapon of Mass Destruction' (2006) 13 CLP 81.

1 *Countyglen plc v Carway* [1998] 2 IR 540 at 551..

2 *Director of Corporate Enforcement v D'Arcy* [2006] 2 IR 163; *Director of Corporate Enforcement v D'Arcy* (20 March 2007, unreported) HC (Murphy J).

3 *Countyglen plc v Carway* [1995] 1 IR 208.

23 Saving for privileged information

[(1) In this section—

'computer' has the same meaning as it has in section 20;

'information' means information contained in a document, a computer or otherwise;

'privileged legal material' means information which, in the opinion of the court, a person is entitled to refuse to produce on the grounds of legal professional privilege.

(1A) Subject to subsection (1B), nothing in this Part shall compel the disclosure by any person of privileged legal material or authorise the taking of privileged legal material.

(1B) The disclosure of information may be compelled, or possession of it taken, pursuant to the powers in this Part, not-withstanding that it is apprehended that the information is privileged legal material provided the compelling of its disclosure or the taking of its possession is done by means whereby the confidentiality of the information can be maintained (as against the person compelling such disclosure or taking such possession) pending the determination by the court of the issue as to whether the information is privileged legal material.

(1C) Without prejudice to subsection (1D), where, in the circumstances referred to in subsection (1B), information has been disclosed or taken possession of pursuant to the powers in this Part, the person—

(a) to whom such information has been so disclosed, or

(b) who has taken possession of it,

shall (unless the person has, within the period subsequently mentioned in this subsection, been served with notice of an application under subsection (1D) in relation to the matter concerned) apply to the court for a determination as to whether the information is privileged legal material and an application under this subsection shall be made within 7 days after the disclosure or the taking of possession.

(1D) A person who, in the circumstances referred to in sub-section (1B), is compelled to disclose information, or from whose possession information is taken, pursuant to the powers in this Part, may apply to the court for a determination as to whether the information is privileged legal material.

(1E) Pending the making of a final determination of an application under subsection (1C) or (1D), the court may give such interim or interlocutory directions as the court considers appropriate including, without prejudice to the generality of the fore-going, directions as to—

(a) the preservation of the information, in whole or in part, in a safe and secure place in any manner specified by the court,

(b) the appointment of a person with suitable legal qualifications possessing the level of experience, and the independence from any interest falling to be determined between the parties concerned, that the court considers to be appropriate for the purpose of—

(i) examining the information, and

(ii) preparing a report for the court with a view to assisting or facilitating the court in the making by the court of its determination as to whether the information is privileged legal material.

(1F) An application under subsection (1C), (1D) or (1E) shall be by motion and may, if the court directs, be heard other-wise than in public.][a]

[(2) The Director shall not, under section 19, require the production by a person carrying on the business of banking of a document relating to the affairs of a customer, or relating to the affairs of any other person, unless either it appears to the Director that it is necessary to do so for the purposes of investigating the affairs of the person carrying on the business of banking, or the customer or other person is a person on whom a requirement has been imposed by virtue of that section.][b]

(3) The publication, in pursuance of any provision of this Part, of any report, information, book or document shall be privileged.

[(4) In this section, 'customer', in relation to a person carrying on the business of banking, includes a person who has in the past availed of one or more services of the person, as defined in section 149(12) of the Consumer Credit Act, 1995.][c]

Amendments

a C(A)A 2009, s 6 substitutes CA 1990, s 23(1) and inserts CA 1990, s 23(1A)–(1F).

b CLEA 2001, s 32(a) substitutes CA 1990, s 23(2).

c CLEA 2001, s 32(b) inserts CA 1990, s 23(4).

23A Assistance to overseas company law authorities

[(1) The powers conferred on the Director by this Part are also exercisable by the Director on foot of a request from a company law authority for assistance in connection with inquiries being carried out by it or on its behalf where the Director is satisfied that such assistance is for the purpose of the discharge by the authority of its supervisory or regulatory functions.

(2) The Director may decline to accede to a request referred to in subsection (1) if, in the opinion of the Director, it is not appropriate to so accede or where the company law authority making the request does not undertake to make such contribution to the costs attendant on the request as the Director considers appropriate.

(3) In this section, 'company law authority' means an authority outside the State which performs functions of a supervisory or regulatory nature in relation to bodies corporate or undertakings or their officers, or a person acting on behalf of such an authority.][a]

Amendments

a CLEA 2001, s 33 inserts CA 1990, s 23A.

Notes

This section empowers the ODCE to exercise its powers of inquiry under CA 1990, ss 8, 14, 15, 16 and 19 to assist an investigation by a foreign company law authority.

---

24 Power to make supplementary regulations

(1) If, in any respect, any difficulty arises in bringing any provision of this Part into operation or in relation to the operation of any such provision, the Minister may by regulations do anything which appears to him to be necessary or expedient for removing that difficulty, for bringing the provision into operation, or for securing or facilitating its operation, and any such regulations may modify any provision of this Part so far as may be necessary or expedient for carrying such provision into effect for the purposes aforesaid.

(2) Every regulation made by the Minister under this section shall be laid before each House of the Oireachtas as soon as may be after it is made and, if a resolution annulling the regulation is passed by either House within the next 21 days on which that House has sat after the regulation is laid before it, the regulation shall be annulled accordingly, but without prejudice to the validity of anything previously done thereunder.

PART III

TRANSACTIONS INVOLVING DIRECTORS

Preliminary

Notes

General: For detailed commentary on Part III, see Courtney, *The Law of Private Companies*, (2nd edn, Tottel Publishing, 2002) ch 11; Courtney and Johnston, 'Structuring Company Lending after the Company Law Enforcement Act 2001', (2001, Butterworths); and MacCann, 'Directors' Remuneration and Loans' (1991) ILT 276.

Commencement: Part III, with the exceptions of ss 28, 50 and 51 came into operation on 1 February 1991. Sections 28, 50 and 51 came into operation on 1 July 1991. The changes made to

Part III (to CA 1990, s 25(3A), s 26(1), (3) and (6), s 33(3), s 34 and s 35) by CLEA 2001, Part 9 were all commenced on 1 October 2001.

25 Interpretation of Part III

(1) In this Part, unless the context otherwise requires—

'credit transactions' has the meaning assigned to it by *subsection (3)*;

'guarantee' includes indemnity;

'quasi-loan' has the meaning assigned to it by *subsection (2)*;

'licensed bank' means the holder of a licence under section 9 of the Central Bank Act, 1971.

(2) For the purposes of this Part—

(a) a quasi-loan is a transaction under which one party ('the creditor') agrees to pay, or pays otherwise than in pursuance of an agreement, a sum for another ('the borrower') or agrees to reimburse, or reimburses otherwise than in pursuance of an agreement, expenditure incurred by another party for another ('the borrower')—

(i) on terms that the borrower (or a person on his behalf) will reimburse the creditor; or

(ii) in circumstances giving rise to a liability on the borrower to reimburse the creditor;

(b) any reference to the person to whom a quasi-loan is made is a reference to the borrower; and

(c) the liabilities of a borrower under a quasi-loan include the liabilities of any person who has agreed to reimburse the creditor on behalf of the borrower.

(3) For the purposes of this Part a credit transaction is a transaction under which one party ('the creditor')—

(a) supplies any goods or sells any land under a hire-purchase agreement or conditional sale agreement;

(b) leases or licenses the use of land or hires goods in return for periodical payments;

(c) otherwise disposes of land or supplies goods or services on the understanding that payment (whether in a lump-sum or instalments or by way of periodical payments or otherwise) is to be deferred.

[(3A) For the purposes of this Part, a lease of land which reserves a nominal annual rent of not more than [€12.70] [b] is not a credit transaction where a company grants the lease in return for a premium or capital payment which represents the open market value of the land thereby disposed of by the company.] [a]

(4) For the purposes of this Part the value of a transaction or arrangement is—

(a) in the case of a loan, the principal of the loan;

(b) in the case of a quasi-loan, the amount, or maximum amount, which the person to whom the quasi-loan is made is liable to reimburse the creditor;

(c) in the case of a transaction or arrangement, other than a loan or quasi-loan or a transaction or arrangement within paragraph (d) or (e), the price which it is reasonable to expect could be obtained for the goods, land or services to which the transaction or arrangement relates if they had been supplied at the time the transaction or arrangement is entered into in the ordinary course of business and on the same terms (apart from price) as they have been supplied or are to be supplied under the transaction or arrangement in question;

(d) in the case of a guarantee or security, the amount guaranteed or secured;

(e) in the case of an arrangement to which section 31(2) or 31(3) applies the value of the transaction to which the arrangement relates less any amount by which the liabilities under the arrangement or transaction of the person for whom the transaction was made have been reduced.

(5) For the purposes of subsection (4), the value of a transaction or arrangement which is not capable of being expressed as a specific sum of money (because the amount of any liability arising under the transaction is unascertainable, or for any other reason) shall, whether or not any liability under the transaction has been reduced, be deemed to exceed [€63,486.90].[c]

(6) For the purposes of this Part, a transaction or arrangement is made for a person if—

(a) in the case of a loan or quasi-loan, it is made to him;

(b) in the case of a credit transaction, he is the person to whom goods or services are supplied, or land is sold or otherwise disposed of, under the transaction;

(c) in the case of a guarantee or security, it is entered into or provided in connection with a loan or quasi-loan made to him or a credit transaction made for him;

(d) in the case of an arrangement to which section 31(2) or 31(3) applies, the transaction to which the arrangement relates was made for him; and

(e) in the case of any other transaction or arrangement for the supply or transfer of goods, land or services (or any interest therein), he is the person to whom the goods, land or services (or the interest) are supplied or transferred.

(7) This Part, except sections 41, 43 and 44, does not apply to arrangements or transactions entered into before the commencement of this section but, for the purposes of determining whether an arrangement is one to which section 31(2) or 31(3) applies the transaction to which the arrangement relates shall, if it was entered into before the said commencement, be deemed to have been entered into thereafter.

(8) This Part shall have effect in relation to an arrangement or transaction whether governed by the law of the State or of another country.

Amendments

a CLEA 2001, s 75 inserts CA 1990, s 25(3A).

b £10 converted to €12.70 by Council Regulations (EC) No 1103/97, No 974/98 and No 2866/98 and the Economic and Monetary Union Act 1998, s 6.

c £50,000 converted to €63,486.90 by Council Regulations (EC) No 1103/97, No 974/98 and No 2866/98 and the Economic and Monetary Union Act 1988, s 6.

UK legislation

See CA 1985, ss 331 (as amended by the Banking Act 1987, s 108(2), Sch 7, Pt I, as from 1 October 1987), 340 (as amended by the Companies (Fair Dealing by Directors) (Increase in Financial Limits) Order 1990, SI 1990/1393, as from 31 July 1990) and 347.

---

26 Connected persons

[(1) For the purposes of this Part, a person is connected with a director of a company if, but only if, the person (not being himself a director of the company) is—

(a) that director's spouse, parent, brother, sister or child;

(b) a person acting in his capacity as the trustee of any trust, the principal beneficiaries of which are the director, his spouse or any of his children or any body corporate which he controls; or

(c) in partnership, within the meaning of section 1(1) of the Partnership Act, 1890, with that director.][a]

(2) A body corporate shall also be deemed to be connected with a director of a company if it is controlled by that director.

[(3) For the purposes of this section, a director of a company shall be deemed to control a body corporate if, but only if, he is, alone or together with any other director or directors of the company, or any person connected with the director or such other director or directors, interested in one-half or more of the equity share capital of that body or entitled to exercise or control the exercise of one-half or more of the voting power at any general meeting of that body.][b]

(4) In subsection (3) —

(a) 'equity share capital' has the same meaning as in section 155 of the Principal Act; and

(b) references to voting power exercised by a director shall include references to voting power exercised by another body corporate which that director controls.

(5) The provisions of section 54, shall have effect for the purposes of subsection (3) with the substitution of the words 'more than half' for the words 'one-third or more' in subsections (5) and (6) of that section.

[(6) It shall be presumed for the purposes of this Part, until the contrary is shown, that the sole member of a single-member private limited company within the meaning of the European Communities (Single-Member Private Limited Companies) Regulations, 1994 (S.I. No. 275 of 1994) is a person connected with a director of that company.][c]

Amendments

a CLEA 2001, s 76(a) substitutes CA 1990, s 26(1).

b CLEA 2001, s 76(b) substitutes CA 1990, s 26(3).

c CLEA 2001, s 76(c) inserts CA 1990, s 26(6). Regulation 12 of the European Communities (Single-Member Private Limited Companies) Regulations, 1994 (SI No 275 of 1994) was deleted following the commencement on 1 October 2001 of s 26(6) (which was inserted by CLEA 2001, s 76(c)): see the European Communities (Single-Member Private Limited Companies) Regulations, 1994 (Amendment) Regulations, 2001 (SI No 437 of 2001).

Definitions

'child': CA 1990, s 3(1); 'connected person': CA 1990 s 3(1); 'director': CA 1963, s 2(1); 'Principal Act': CA 1990, s 3(1); 'equity share capital': CA 1963 s 155; 'body corporate' includes a company that is incorporated outside the State: s 2(3) of CA 1963; and 'interested in' shares, as used in s 26(3) is defined by CA 1990, s 54.

Notes

Commencement: CLEA 2001, s 76 was commenced on 1 October 2001: Company Law Enforcement Act, 2001 (Commencement) (No 2) Order, 2001 (SI 438/2001).

Connected persons: The definition of a person connected with a director of a company is very extensive and extends to natural persons and legal persons. So, a body corporate will be deemed to be connected with a director of a company if it is controlled by that director. As a general rule, whether a person is entitled to exercise voting rights (and thus, the question of whether he controls the company) is to be determined by looking at the register of shareholders and the company's articles, and normally it will not be permissible to look outside those documents to inquire whether there are contractual or fiduciary restraints, as between the registered shareholder and others which inhibit him in exercising those rights: nevertheless the court is entitled to look at the economic reality of the situation and thus if shares are held by a bare trustee for the director, he will be treated as being entitled to exercise the voting rights attaching to those shares.[1]

The reference in s 26(5) to 'more than half, as opposed to 'one-half or more' as used in s 26(3) is thought to be an oversight, occasioned when the section was amended by the CLEA 2001.

1 *Unidare plc v Cohen* [2006] 2 BCLC 140.

UK legislation

See CA 1985 s 346 (as amended by the Civil Partnership Act 2004, s 261(1), Sch 27, para 102, as from 5 December 2005; and the Companies (Acquisition of Own Shares) (Treasury Shares) Regulations 2003, SI 2003/1116, reg 4, Schedule, para 17, as from 1 December 2003).

---

27 Shadow directors

(1) Subject to subsection (2), a person in accordance with whose directions or instructions the directors of a company are accustomed to act (in this Act referred to as 'a shadow director') shall be treated for the purposes of this Part as a director of the company unless the directors are accustomed so to act by reason only that they do so on advice given by him in a professional capacity.

(2) A shadow director shall not be guilty of an offence under section 44(8) by virtue only of subsection (1).

(3) Section 194 of the Principal Act shall apply in relation to a shadow director of a company as it applies in relation to a director of a company, except that the shadow director shall declare his interest, not at a meeting of the directors, but by a notice in writing to the directors which is either—

(a) a specific notice given before the date of the meeting at which, if he had been a director, the declaration would be required by subsection (2) of that section to be made; or

(b) a notice which under subsection (3) of that section falls to be treated as a sufficient declaration of that interest or would fall to be so treated apart from the proviso;

and section 145 of that Act shall have effect as if the declaration had been made at the meeting in question and had accordingly formed part of the proceedings at that meeting.

Definitions

'director': CA 1963, s 2(1); 'Principal Act': CA 1990, s 3(1); 'shadow director': CA 1990, s 27.

Notes

Shadow directors

The proofs required for a finding that a person is a shadow director are: '(1) who are the directors of the company, whether de facto or de jure; (2) that the defendant directed those directors how to act in relation to the company or that he was one of those persons who did so; (3) that those directors acted in accordance with such directions; and (4) that they were accustomed so to act. What is needed is, first, a board of directors claiming and purporting to act as such; and secondly a pattern of behaviour in which the board did not exercise any discretion or judgment of its own, but acted in accordance with the directions of others'.[1]

On the meaning of 'directed or instructed', a person has been found to be a shadow director where he was 'in effect, the puppet master controlling the actions of the board'.[2] The words 'directed or instructed' are both words with a mandatory effect and when coupled with the word 'accustomed', they 'contemplate a situation where the board has cast itself in a subservient role to the 'shadow'…'.[3] The use of the words 'directed or instructed' indicated that for a person to be found to be a shadow director, the board should be subservient to the shadow director.[4] The directions or instructions emanating from the alleged shadow director must have an imperative quality; the consideration by the board of directors interposed between the direction, instruction or imperative advice does not mean that the act of the board is not to be taken into account in applying CA 1990, s 27 if the board acts in accordance with the direction, instruction or imperative advice; and CA 1990, s 27 does not require that the board should always act on the directions and instructions for a shadow directorship to exist, nor does it necessarily require that the directions and instructions should extend over the whole range of the company's activities.[5] So, for example, a bank may be a shadow director of a company in circumstances where the company has been managed in accordance with the bank's 'recommendations' or instructions as a condition of the bank not appointing a receiver.[6] Nevertheless, a shadow directorship will not necessarily be established merely because the board acts on the instructions of the person in respect of one isolated transaction.[7] Nor will a person be regarded as having automatically become a shadow director merely because he has exercised a contractual or other power, including a power under the articles of association, to appoint nominees to the board of directors.[8]

'The directors of a company' means the board or a majority of the directors.[9] A body corporate (including a company incorporated outside of the State) can be a shadow director because interpreting the word 'person' in CA 1990, s 27 is not in any way inconsistent with CA 1963, s 176, the provision which prohibits a company from having a body corporate as a director, albeit that it cannot be made the subject of a restriction order pursuant to CA 1990, s 150.[10] A person will not, however, be a shadow director where the directors are accustomed to act in accordance with his or her directions or instructions by reason only that they do so on advice given by him or her in a professional capacity.[11]

1 Millett J in *Re Hydrodam (Corby) Ltd* [1994] 2 BCLC 180.

2 *Re Unisoft Group Ltd* [1994] BCC 766.

3 *Secretary of State for Trade and Industry v Deverell* [2000] BCC 1057.

4 *Australian Securities Commission v AS Nominees Ltd* (1995) 133 ALR 1; this was, however, questioned by the English Court of Appeal in *Secretary of State for Trade and Industry v Deverell* [2000] BCC 1057.

5 *Fyffes PLC v DCC PLC et al* (21 December 2005, unreported) HC (Laffoy J); *Re Mea Corporation Ltd* [2007] 1 BCLC 618; *Gemma Ltd v Davies* [2008] 2 BCLC 281.

6 *Re a company (No 00509 of 1987)* (1988) 4 BCC 424.

7 *Unidare plc v Cohen* [2006] 2 BCLC 140.

8 *Kuwait Asia Bank EC v National Mutual Life Nominees Ltd* [1990] BCLC 868.

9 *Fyffes PLC v DCC PLC et al* (21 December 2005, unreported) HC (Laffoy J).

10 *Re Worldport Ireland Ltd* [2009] 1 IR 398; see also *Fyffes PLC v DCC PLC et al* (21 December 2005, unreported) HC (Laffoy J) and *Re a company (No 00509 of 1987); ex p Copp* [1989] BCLC 12.

11 The 'professional advice exception' was considered in *Re Vehicle Imports Ltd (in liquidation)* [2000] IEHC 90 (Murphy J); see also *Secretary of State for Trade and Industry v Deverell* [2000] BCC 1057.

UK legislation

See CA 1985 ss 317(8) and 741 (as amended by the Companies (Single Member Private Limited Companies) Regulations 1992, SI 1992/1699, reg 2, Schedule, para 3(2), as from 15 July 1992.

Particular transactions involving conflict of interest

28 Contracts of employment of directors

(1) Subject to subsection (6), a company shall not incorporate in any agreement a term to which this section applies unless the term is first approved by a resolution of the company in general meeting and, in the case of a director of a holding company, by a resolution of that company in general meeting.

(2) This section applies to any term by which a director's employment with the company of which he is the director or, where he is the director of a holding company, his employment within the group is to continue, or may be continued, otherwise than at the instance of the company (whether under the original agreement or under a new agreement entered into in pursuance of the original agreement), for a period exceeding five years during which the employment—

(a) cannot be terminated by the company by notice; or

(b) can be so terminated only in specified circumstances.

(3) In any case where—

(a) a person is or is to be employed with a company under an agreement which cannot be terminated by the company by notice or can be so terminated only in specified circumstances; and

(b) more than six months before the expiration of the period for which he is or is to be so employed, the company enters into a further agreement (otherwise than in pursuance of a right conferred by or by virtue of the original agreement on the other party thereto) under which he is to be employed with the company or, where he is a director of a holding company, within the group,

subsection (2) shall apply as if to the period for which he is to be employed under that further agreement there were added a further period equal to the unexpired period of the original agreement.

(4) A resolution of a company approving a term to which this section applies shall not be passed at a general meeting of the company unless a written memorandum setting out

the proposed agreement incorporating the term is available for inspection by members of the company both—

(a) at the registered office of the company for not less than the period of 15 days ending with the date of the meeting; and

(b) at the meeting itself.

(5) A term incorporated in an agreement in contravention of this section shall to the extent that it contravenes this section be void; and that agreement and, in a case where subsection (3) applies, the original agreement shall be deemed to contain a term entitling the company to terminate it at any time by the giving of reasonable notice.

(6) No approval is required to be given under this section by any body corporate unless it is a company within the meaning of the Principal Act or registered under Part IX of that Act, or if it is, for the purposes of section 150 of that Act, a wholly owned subsidiary of any body corporate, wherever incorporated.

(7) In this section—

(a) 'employment' includes employment under a contract for services; and

(b) 'group', in relation to a director of a holding company, means the group which consists of that company and its subsidiaries.

Definitions

'contravention': CA 1990, s 3(1); 'director': CA 1963, s 2(1) (but note that for the purposes of Part III of CA 1990 a shadow director shall be treated as a director: CA 1990, s 27(1)); 'holding company': CA 1963, s 155; 'member': CA 1963, s 31; 'subsidiary': CA 1963, s 155.

Notes

It seems clear from s 28(1) that the validating resolution must be passed before, and not after, the incorporation of the terms into the contract of employment. Even if the director has a valid fixed term contract with the company, he may still be dismissed by ordinary resolution of a company's members pursuant to CA 1963, s 182 before the expiry of the terms of the contract, subject to the director's right to apply for an interlocutory injunction to preserve the status quo.[1] It may be noted that such a dismissal is without prejudice to any claim a director may have for damages for breach of contract. The effects of s 28(3) are easily overcome. For example, if a director has a fixed term contract for five years exactly and precisely six months before it is due to expire he negotiates another fixed term contract for five years exactly, then shareholder approval will not be required because neither contract exceeds five years and since the second contract was not concluded 'more than six months' before the end of the first contract, the unexpired term of the first contract cannot be added to the term of the second contract. An ordinary resolution is sufficient for the purpose of approving the term of the contract in s 28(4).

The validity of a contract giving a director security of tenure for at least seven years was upheld in circumstances where, although contrary to the requirements of CA 1990, s 28(4) it had not been available for inspection at the registered office by members of the company prior to being voted on, it had in fact been informally approved by all of the members of the company.[2]

If the person is an executive director and his salary is fixed on an annual basis, a court may be prepared to infer that he is entitled to at least one year's notice.[3] As an employee, a director may also have remedies under unfair dismissals legislation.

1 *McGilligan & Bowen v O'Grady* [1999] 1 IR 346; [1999] 1 ILRM 303. *cf Feighery v Feighery* [1999] 1 IR 321.

2 *Wright v Atlas Wright (Europe) Ltd* [1999] 2 BCLC 301.

[3] *Carvill v Irish Industrial Bank Ltd* [1968] IR 325.

UK legislation

See CA 1985 319.

29 Substantial property transactions involving directors, etc.

(1) Subject to subsections (6), (7) and (8), a company shall not enter into an arrangement—

(a) whereby a director of the company or its holding company or a person connected with such a director acquires or is to acquire one or more non-cash assets of the requisite value from the company; or

(b) whereby the company acquires or is to acquire one or more non-cash assets of the requisite value from such a director or a person so connected;

unless the arrangement is first approved by a resolution of the company in general meeting and, if the director or connected person is a director of its holding company or a person connected with such a director, by a resolution in general meeting of the holding company.

(2) For the purposes of this section a non-cash asset is of the requisite value if at the time the arrangement in question is entered into its value is not less than [€1,269.74] [a] but, subject to that, exceeds [€63,486.90] [b] or ten per cent of the amount of the company's relevant assets, and for those purposes the amount of a company's relevant assets is—

(a) except in a case falling within paragraph (b), the value of its net assets determined by reference to the accounts prepared and laid in accordance with the requirements of section 148 of the Principal Act in respect of the last preceding financial year in respect of which such accounts were so laid;

(b) where no accounts have been prepared and laid under that section before that time, the amount of its called-up share capital.

(3) An arrangement entered into by a company in contravention of this section and any transaction entered into in pursuance of the arrangement (whether by the company or any other person) shall be voidable at the instance of the company unless—

(a) restitution of any money or any other asset which is the subject-matter of the arrangement or transaction is no longer possible or the company has been indemnified in pursuance of subsection (4)(b) by any other person for the loss or damage suffered by it; or

(b) any rights acquired bona fide for value and without actual notice of the contravention by any person who is not a party to the arrangement or transaction would be affected by its avoidance; or

(c) the arrangement is, within a reasonable period, affirmed by the company in general meeting and, if it is an arrangement for the transfer of an asset to or by a director of its holding company or a person who is connected with such a director, is so affirmed with the approval of the holding company given by a resolution in general meeting.

(4) Without prejudice to any liability imposed otherwise than by this subsection, but subject to subsection (5), where an arrangement is entered into with a company by a

director of the company or its holding company or a person connected with him in contravention of this section, that director and the person so connected, and any other director of the company who authorised the arrangement or any transaction entered into in pursuance of such an arrangement, shall (whether or not it has been avoided in pursuance of subsection (3)) be liable—

(a) to account to the company for any gain which he had made directly or indirectly by the arrangement or transaction; and

(b) (jointly and severally with any other person liable under this subsection) to indemnify the company for any loss or damage resulting from the arrangement or transaction.

(5) Where an arrangement is entered into by a company and a person connected with a director of the company or its holding company in contravention of this section, that director shall not be liable under subsection (4) if he shows that he took all reasonable steps to secure the company's compliance with this section and, in any case, a person so connected and any such other director as is mentioned in that subsection shall not be so liable if he shows that, at the time the arrangement was entered into, he did not know the relevant circumstances constituting the contravention.

(6) No approval is required to be given under this section by any body corporate unless it is a company within the meaning of the Principal Act or registered under Part IX of that Act or, if it is, for the purposes of section 150 of that Act, a wholly owned subsidiary of any body corporate, wherever incorporated.

(7) Subsection (1) shall not apply in relation to any arrangement for the acquisition of a non-cash asset—

(a) if the non-cash asset in question is or is to be acquired by a holding company from any of its wholly owned subsidiaries or from a holding company by any of its wholly owned subsidiaries or by one wholly owned subsidiary of a holding company from another wholly owned subsidiary of that same holding company; or

(b) if the arrangement is entered into by a company which is being wound up unless the winding up is a members' voluntary winding up.

(8) Subsection (1)(a) shall not apply in relation to any arrangement whereby a person acquires or is to acquire an asset from a company of which he is a member if the arrangement is made with that person in his character as such member.

(9) In this section—

(a) 'non-cash asset' means any property or interest in property other than cash, and for this purpose 'cash' includes foreign currency;

(b) any reference to the acquisition of a non-cash asset includes a reference to the creation or extinction of an estate or interest in, or a right over, any property and also a reference to the discharge of any person's liability other than a liability for a liquidated sum; and

[(c) 'net assets', in relation to a company, means the aggregate of the company's assets less the aggregate of its liabilities, and for this purpose 'liabilities' includes—

(i) any provision (within the meaning of the Sixth Schedule to the Principal Act) that is made in Companies Act individual accounts except to the extent that that provision is taken into account in calculating the value of any asset to the company,

(ii) any provision for liabilities within the meaning of paragraph 70 of the Schedule to the Companies (Amendment) Act 1986 that is made in Companies Act individual accounts, and

(iii) any provision that is made in IFRS individual accounts.] [c]

Amendments

a £1,000 converted to €1,269.74 by Council Regulations (EC) No 1103/97, No 974/98 and No 2866/98 and the Economic and Monetary Union Act 1988, s 6.

b £50,000 converted to €63,486.90 by Council Regulations (EC) No 1103/97, No 974/98 and No 2866/98 and the Economic and Monetary Union Act 1988, s 6.

c EC(IFRSMA)R 2005, reg 9, Sch 1, Pt 4, item 1 substitutes s 29(9)(c).

Cross references in other enactments

NAMA Act 2009, s 218(1) provides that an acquired bank asset within the meaning of NAMA Act 2009 is 'not invalidated or rendered void or voidable as against NAMA or a NAMA group entity or their successors in title' by operation of CA 1990, s 29.

Notes

The rationale of Section 29 – CA 1990, s 29 is designed to regulate self-dealing by directors. The rationale for this type of provision is that if directors (on behalf of their company) enter into substantial property transactions with one of their number, there is a danger that their judgment may be distorted by conflicts of interest and loyalties (even if there is no actual dishonesty). This type of provision provides a check against such distortions by requiring the members to approve the transaction.[1] Arrangements within s 29 must be first approved by a resolution of the company in general meeting *and* if the director or connected person is a director of the company's holding company, by a resolution of the company's holding company; an ordinary resolution will suffice.[2]

Although the section provides for the transaction to be approved by an ordinary resolution in general meeting, nevertheless such a transaction may be validated in circumstances where, despite the absence of a formal shareholders' resolution, the transaction has been unanimously approved in advance by a resolution of the directors, some of whom also hoeld the entire of the shares in the company.[3]

Although there is no Irish case law on CA 1990, s 29, there are several English cases on their very similar provision, Companies Act 1985, s 320.[4]

The scope of the provision – An 'arrangement' does not need to be contractually binding and includes agreements and understandings.[5] CA 1990, s 29(1) (a) and (b) applies to arrangements entered into between a company and a potentially large circle of people, namely directors of that company, directors of that company's holding company, shadow directors of either company as well as a 'person connected with such a director' (as defined by CA 1990, s 26). This latter category extends the scope of the provision to any such directors' spouse, parent, brother, sister, child, a person acting in his capacity as the trustee of any trust where the principal beneficiaries are the director, his spouse or any of his children or any body corporate he controls, a person in partnership within the meaning of PA 1890, s 1(1) with such a director and a body corporate controlled by such director. There is a rebuttable presumption that a sole member of a single member private company is a person connected with such a director. Section 29(1) has a two-way application: it regulates substantial property transactions in which a director acquires assets from his company *and* transactions in which a company acquires assets from its director.

The subject matter of a substantial property transaction – A reference to the acquisition of a non-cash asset is deemed, by s 29(9)(b) to include a reference to the creation or extinction of an estate or interest in, or a right over, any property and also a reference to the discharge of any person's liability other than a liability for a liquidated sum. A novation of a contract was considered to be arguably an acquisition of an asset within the meaning of similar English legislation.[6] The meaning of 'non-cash asset' is elaborated upon by s 29(9)(a) where it is defined to mean any property or interest in property other than cash where cash includes foreign currency). This has been recognised as being a comprehensive definition[7] but has been held not to include property or an interest in property that is brought into existence only by the 'acquisition' itself.[8]

The requisite value of the property – 'Requisite value' is defined by s 29(2). The onus of establishing that a non-cash asset is of the requisite value is on the person who invokes the provision.[9] It may be noted that further guidance as to the meaning of the 'value' of an arrangement is provided by CA 1990, s 25(4)(c) and that in this respect Irish law may differ from the similar provisions of the English Companies Act 1985, s 320.[10]

The consequences of breaching CA 1990, s 29(1) – An arrangement that contravenes CA 1990, s 29(1) is not void or illegal ab initio, but is voidable at the instance of the company.[11] The primary remedy in the case of an unlawful arrangement is 'the avoidance of the arrangement and of any transaction entered into pursuant to it with consequential repayment of the money paid and retransfer of the asset'.[12] A company's entitlement to avoid a contravening arrangement will only be barred if one of the three 'savers' identified in s 29(3) is found to apply. The third saver[13] allows a company's members to retrospectively validate an otherwise voidable arrangement by so resolving 'within a reasonable period'.[14]

The liability of directors and others for breaching CA 1990, s 29(1) – Where an arrangement is entered into in breach of this provision, the company's remedies are an account for the profit, where a director or other relevant person makes a gain from the arrangement and an indemnity, where a loss is made by the company.[15] The indemnity may extend to 'any loss or damage resulting from the arrangement or transaction', including a loss incurred on the realisation of an asset or a loss resulting from a fall in value of an acquired asset.[16] It may also extend, in the case of an acquired asset, to costs incurred by the company which have contributed to the value of the asset such as the costs of planning applications, as well as rates, insurance premia and other moneys expended in preserving the asset.[17] Where an arrangement is entered into in breach of s 29(1), it is a defence to the civil remedy against a person to show that he took all reasonable steps to secure compliance but this cannot be invoked by a director of the company, only by a person connected with a director.[18]

The exceptions – There are three exceptions which operate to exempt certain arrangements. The first exemption is provided for in s 29(7)(a) which exempts certain inter-group arrangements, namely, a non-cash asset acquired by a holding company from any of its wholly-owned subsidiaries, by a wholly-owned subsidiary from its holding company or by one wholly-owned subsidiary from another wholly-owned subsidiary. The second exemption is contained in s 29(7)(b) which exempts arrangements for the acquisition of a non-cash asset where entered into by a company which is being wound up unless the winding-up is a members' voluntary winding up. Whilst disposals of assets by an official liquidator or a liquidator in a creditors' voluntary liquidation to directors and other relevant persons are outside s 29, disposals by a liquidator in a members' voluntary winding up and by a receiver must comply with s 29(1).[19] The third exception is provided for in s 29(8) and applies to acquisitions by members acting 'qua member'; this exemption only extends, however, to s 29(1)(a).

1 *British Racing Drivers' Club Ltd v Hextall Erskine & Co (a firm)* [1996] 3 All ER 667.

2 See the Law Society's Conveyancing Committee's Practice Note on substantial property transactions: see Practice Notes (1991) Gazette ILSI 419.

3 *Re Conegrade Ltd* [2003] BPIR 358. cf *Demite Ltd v Protec Health Ltd* [1998] BCC 638

4 See generally, Courtney, *The Law of Private Companies* (2nd edn, Tottel Publishing, 2002) paras 11.023 to 11.050.

5 *Duckwari plc v Offerventure (No 2)* [1999] BCC 11.

6 *Re a Company (No 0032314 of 1992); Duckwari plc v Offerventure Ltd* [1995] BCC 89.

7 See *Lander v Premium Pict Petroleum and another* [1998] BCC 248.

8 *Micro Leisure Ltd v Country Properties & Developments Ltd (No 1)* (1999) (19 January 1999, unreported) Scottish Court of Sessions.

9 *Joint Receivers and Managers of Niltan Carson v Hawthorne* [1988] BCLC 298.

10 Cf *Micro Leisure Ltd v Country Properties & Developments Ltd (No 1)* (1999) (19 January 1999, unreported) Scottish Court of Sessions where a subjective definition of value, as in the value to a particular director, was preferred to the objective approach seen in CA 1990, s 25(4)(c).

11 *Joint Receivers and Managers of Niltan Carson v Hawthorne* [1988] BCLC 298 at 322b per Hodgson J.

12 *Re Duckwari plc* [1997] 2 WLR 48 at 53 *per* Judge Paul Baker QC.

13 As to the first two savers, these are very similar to those contained in CA 1990, s 38(1)(a) and (b) and are examined in the notes thereto.

14 As to the meaning of 'a reasonable period' see *Re Duckwari plc* [1997] 2 WLR 48 and *Demite Ltd v Protec Health Ltd* [1998] 638 at 650.

15 CA 1990, s 29(4)(a) and (b).

16 *Duckwari plc v Offerventure (No 2)* [1999] BCC 11 at 19.

17 *Duckwari plc v Offerventure (No 3)* [1999] 1 BCLC 168.

18 *Duckwari plc v Offerventure (No 2)* [1999] BCC 11.

19 *Demite Ltd v Protec Health Ltd* [1998] BCC 638.

UK legislation

See CA 1985, s 320 (as amended by Companies (Fair Dealing by Directors) (Increase in Financial Limits) Order 1990, SI 1990/1393 as from 31 July 1990) and s 321 (amended by CA 1989, s 134 Sch 19, para 8 and Financial Services and Markets Act 2000 (Consequential Amendments and Repeals) Order 2001, SI 2001/3649, art 19, as from 1 December 2001) and s 322.

30 Penalisation of dealing by director of a company in options to buy or sell certain shares in, or debentures of, the company or associated companies

(1) A director of a company who buys—

(a) a right to call for delivery at a specified price and within a specified time of a specified number of relevant shares or a specified amount of relevant debentures; or

(b) a right to make delivery at a specified price and within a specified time of a specified number of relevant shares or a specified amount of relevant debentures; or

(c) a right (as he may elect) to call for delivery at a specified price and within a specified time or to make delivery at a specified price and within a specified time of a specified number of relevant shares or a specified amount of relevant debentures;

shall be guilty of an offence.

(2) In subsection (1)—

(a) 'relevant shares', in relation to a director of a company, means shares in the company or in any other body corporate, being the company's subsidiary or holding company or a subsidiary of the company's holding company, being shares for which dealing facilities are provided by a stock exchange (whether within the State or elsewhere); and

(b) 'relevant debentures', in relation to a director of a company, means debentures of the company or of any other body corporate, being the company's subsidiary or holding company or a subsidiary of the company's holding company, being debentures as respects which there has been granted such dealing facilities as aforesaid.

(3) Nothing in this section shall be taken to penalise a person who buys a right to subscribe for shares in, or debentures of, a body corporate or buys debentures of a body corporate that confer upon the holder thereof a right to subscribe for, or to convert the debentures (in whole or in part) into, shares of the body.

[(3A) Nothing in this section shall prevent a person from acquiring a right to shares in a company pursuant to a scheme approved by the Revenue Commissioners for the purposes of the Tax Acts and the Capital Gains Tax Acts, and in respect of which approval has not been withdrawn at the time the right is obtained.][a]

(4) For the purposes of this section any reference, however expressed, to any price paid, given or received in respect of any interest in shares or debentures shall be construed as including a reference to any consideration other than money given or received in respect of any such interest, and any reference to a specified price includes a reference to a specified price range.

(5) This section shall also apply to any person (not being a director of the company) who—

(a) buys a right referred to in subsection (1), and

(b) does so on behalf or at the instigation of a director of the company.

Amendments

a CLEA 2001, s 102 inserts CA 1990, s 30(3A).

Definitions

'debenture': CA 1963 s 2(1); 'director': CA 1963 s 2(1); 'share': CA 1963 s 2(1).

Notes

See also the notes regarding insider dealing in CA 1990, Part V and the Market Abuse (Directive 2003/6/EC) Regs 2005.

UK legislation

See CA 1985, s 323 (as amended by the Companies (Acquisition of Own Shares) (Treasury Shares) No 2 Regulations 2003, 2003/3031, reg 4, as from 18 December 2003).

31 Prohibition of loans, etc. to directors and connected persons

(1) Except as provided by sections 32 to 37, a company shall not—

(a) make a loan or a quasi-loan to a director of the company or of its holding company or to a person connected with such a director;

(b) enter into a credit transaction as creditor for such a director or a person so connected;

(c) enter into a guarantee or provide any security in connection with a loan, quasi-loan or credit transaction made by any other person for such a director or a person so connected.

(2) A company shall not arrange for the assignment to it or the assumption by it of any rights, obligations or liabilities under a transaction which, if it had been entered into by the company, would have contravened *subsection (1)*; but for the purposes of this Part the transaction shall be treated as having been entered into on the date of the arrangement.

(3) A company shall not take part in any arrangement whereby—

(a) another person enters into a transaction which, if it had been entered into by the company, would have contravened subsection (1) or (2); and

(b) that other person, in pursuance of the arrangement, has obtained or is to obtain any benefit from the company or its holding company or a subsidiary of the company or its holding company.

Definitions

'company': CA 1963 s 2(1); 'director' includes 'shadow director': CA 1990 s 27; 'holding company' and 'subsidiary': CA 1963 s 155; 'quasi-loan': CA 1990 s 25(2); 'credit transaction': CA 1990 s 25(3) and s 25(3A); 'guarantee': CA 1990 s 25(1).

Cross references in other enactments

NAMA Act 2009, s 218(1) provides that an acquired bank asset within the meaning of NAMA Act 2009 is 'not invalidated or rendered void or voidable as against NAMA or a NAMA group entity or their successors in title' by operation of CA 1990, s 31.

Notes

Overview of Section 31 Prohibition – Section 31(1) – The enactment of CA 1990, s 31 was designed to curb the perceived abuse by directors of causing their companies to make loans and quasi loans, to enter into credit transactions and to enter into guarantees and provide security in connection with loans, quasi loans and credit transactions in favour of themselves, directors of the companies' holding companies or persons connected with such directors.[1] It was generally recognised in the 1990s that s 31 had been cast too widely and a number of amendments were effected to the definitions and exceptions applicable to s 31, by CLEA 2001, Part 9. Unlike CA 1990, s 29 (substantial property transactions) s 31 operates on a one-way basis only in that it prevents a company from directly or indirectly[2] making or entering into any one of the five prohibited transactions or arrangements to or for[3] a director or other relevant person unless any of the five exceptions apply. It does not, however, prevent directors and connected persons from making loans, etc to/for the benefit of the company or holding company.

The five prohibited transactions or arrangements – Section 31(1) prohibits companies from making loans and quasi loans, entering into credit transactions and entering into guarantees and providing security in connection with loans, quasi loans and credit transactions in favour of certain persons.

Loans are perhaps the most straightforward of prohibited transactions and arrangements. Loans made in contravention of s 31 are illegal and immediately recoverable by the company, irrespective of the terms and conditions upon which they may have been made.[4]

Quasi-loans are defined by CA 1990, s 25(2)(a), (b) and (c).

Credit transactions are defined by CA 1990, s 25(3) and (3A). Subsection (3A), inserted by CLEA 2001, s 75, makes clear that a lease of land that reserves a nominal annual rent of not more than €12.60 per annum is not a credit transaction where the lease is granted by a company in return for a premium or capital payment that is the open market value of the land.

Guarantees in connection with loans, quasi-loans and credit transactions is a wide category of prohibited transactions or arrangements. Guarantee is defined by CA 1990 s 25(1) to include 'indemnity'.

Security in connection with loans, quasi-loans and credit transactions is the fifth category of prohibited transaction or arrangement and would operate to prohibit the granting of, say, a surety mortgage by a company to secure the repayment of, say, a loan made by a third party to a director of the company.

The application of CA 1990, s 31 to directors and other relevant people – Subject to the five exceptions contained in ss 32 to 37, companies are prohibited from entering into any of the five types of transaction or arrangement in favour of a wide number of people. Those persons who are relevant to s 31(1) are: directors of the company, shadow directors of the company, directors of the company's holding company, shadow directors of the company's holding company and in the case of any such director, his or her spouse, parent, brother sister, child or partner, trustees of trusts where the principal beneficiaries are the director, his spouse, children or a body corporate which he controls, bodies corporate controlled by such directors, bodies corporate controlled by bodies corporate that are controlled by such directors and there is a presumption that the sole member of a single member private limited company is a person connected with a director. This represents the application of CA 1990, s 26 which defines connected persons to CA 1990 s 31(1).

1 See generally Courtney, *The Law of Private Companies* (2nd edn, Tottel Publishing, 2002) para 11.051 *et seq*; Courtney and Johnston, 'Structuring Company Lending after the Company Law Enforcement Act 2001', (2001, Butterworths); Courtney, 'The Latest Hazard to Guarantees: The Effects of s 31 of the Companies Act 1990 on Inter Company Guarantees', (1991) Gazette ILSI 261 and Courtney, 'Credit Transactions and Section 31 of the Companies Act 1990', (1994) CLP 17.

2 As to the prohibition on indirect action by a company, see CA 1990, s 25(7). Note also the effects of s 31(2) and s 31(3) in regulating transactions and arrangements that might otherwise not fall directly within the s 31(1) prohibition.

3 As to the meaning of 'for', see CA 1990, s 25(6).

4 *Tait Consibee (Oxford) Ltd v Tait* [1997] 2 BCLC 349; see also *Currencies Direct Ltd v Ellis* [2002] 1 BCLC 195, both of which considered the similar UK provision, CA 1985 s 330.

UK legislation

See CA 1985, s 330.

---

32 Arrangements of certain value

(1) Section 31, shall not prohibit a company from entering into an arrangement with a director or a person connected with a director if—

(a) the value of the arrangement, and

(b) the total amount outstanding under any other arrangements entered into by the company with any director of the company, or any person connected with a director,

together, is less than ten per cent of the company's relevant assets.

(2) For the purposes of this section—

(a) a company enters an arrangement with a person if it makes a loan or quasi-loan to, or enters into a credit transaction as creditor for, that person, and

(b) the amount of a company's relevant assets shall be determined in accordance with section 29(2).

Definitions

'company': CA 1963, s 2(1); 'director' includes 'shadow director': CA 1990, s 27; 'person connected with a director': CA 1990, s 26; 'arrangement': CA 1990, s 32(2)(a); 'quasi-loan': CA 1990, s 25(2); 'credit transaction': CA 1990, s 25(3) and s 25(3A).

Notes

The *de minimis* exception: The first exception to the prohibition contained in s 31 is the so-called *de minimis* or less-than-10% exception. This can apply where the value of an arrangement is less than 10% of a company's relevant assets. The *value* of an arrangement is defined by CA 1990 s 25(4) and depends upon whether the arrangement in question is a loan, a quasi-loan or a credit transaction.

The meaning of relevant assets: For the purpose of CA 1990, s 32 a company's *relevant assets* has the meaning assigned to it by CA 1990, s 29(2).

The scope of the *de minimis* exception: Not all five prohibited transactions and arrangements are exempted by CA 1990, s 32 which applies only to 'arrangements', which are defined in s 32(2)(a) to mean a loan, a quasi-loan or a credit transaction. Accordingly, guarantees and the provision of security in connection with loans, quasi-loans and credit transactions fall outside the *de minimis* exemption. Moreover, on a strict technical interpretation, it would seem that an arrangement, so defined, entered into by a company in favour of a director of its holding company cannot come within the *de minimis* exception because it merely states that s 31 shall not prohibit a company from entering into an arrangement 'with a director or a person so connected with a director'.

UK legislation

See CA 1985, s 334 (amended by CA 1989, s 138(b), as from 31 July 1990, subject to transitional arrangements) and s 335 (as amended by Companies (Fair Dealing by Directors) (Increase in Financial Limits) Order 1990. SI 1990/1393 as from 31 July 1990).

---

33 Reduction in amount of company's relevant assets

(1) This section applies to a company in respect of which the total amount outstanding under any arrangements referred to in section 32 comes to exceed 10 per cent of the company's relevant assets for any reason, but in particular because the value of those assets has fallen.

(2) Where the directors of a company become aware, or ought reasonably to become aware, that there exists a situation referred to in subsection (1), it shall be the duty of the

company, its directors and any persons for whom the arrangements referred to in that subsection were made, to amend, within two months, the terms of the arrangements concerned so that the total amount outstanding under the arrangements again falls within the percentage limit referred to in that subsection.

[(3) Where the terms of the arrangements referred to in subsection (2) are not amended within the period specified in that subsection, the arrangements shall be voidable at the instance of the company unless section 38(1)(a) or (b) applies.][a]

Amendments

a CLEA 2001, s 77 inserts CA 1990, s 33(3).

Definitions

'company': CA 1963, s 2(1); 'arrangement': CA 1990, s 32(2)(a); 'quasi-loan': CA 1990; 'month': IA 2005, s 21(1) and Part 1 of Schedule.

34 [Exceptions to section 31 in certain circumstances

(1) Section 31 does not prohibit a company from entering into a guarantee or providing any security in connection with a loan, quasi-loan or credit transaction made by any other person for a director of the company or of its holding company, or for a person connected with such a director, if—

- (a) the entering into the guarantee is, or the provision of the security is given, under the authority of a special resolution of the company passed not more than 12 months previously; and
- (b) the company has forwarded with each notice of the meeting at which the special resolution is to be considered or, if the procedure detailed in subsection (6) is followed, the company has appended to the resolution, a copy of a statutory declaration which complies with subsections (2) and (3) and also delivers, within 21 days after the date on which the guarantee was entered into or the date on which the security was provided, as the case may be, a copy of the declaration to the registrar of companies for registration.

(2) The statutory declaration shall be made at a meeting of the directors held not earlier than 24 days before the meeting referred to in subsection (1)(b) or, if the special resolution is passed in accordance with subsection (6), not earlier than 24 days before the signing of the special resolution, and shall be made by the directors or, in the case of a company having more than 2 directors, by a majority of the directors.

(3) The statutory declaration shall state—

- (a) the circumstances in which the guarantee is to be entered into or the security is to be provided;
- (b) the nature of the guarantee or security;
- (c) the person or persons to or for whom the loan, quasi-loan or credit transaction (in connection with which the guarantee is to be entered into or the security is to be provided) is to be made;
- (d) the purpose for which the company is entering into the guarantee or is providing the security;

(e) the benefit which will accrue to the company directly or indirectly from entering into the guarantee or providing the security; and

(f) that the declarants have made a full inquiry into the affairs of the company and that, having done so, they have formed the opinion that the company, having entered into the guarantee or provided the security, will be able to pay its debts in full as they become due.

(4) A statutory declaration under subsection (3) has no effect for the purposes of this Act unless it is accompanied by a report—

(a) drawn up in the prescribed form, by an independent person who is qualified at the time of the report to be appointed, or to continue to be, the auditor of the company; and

(b) which shall state whether, in the opinion of the independent person, the statutory declaration is reasonable.

(5) Where a director of a company makes the statutory declaration without having reasonable grounds for the opinion that the company having entered into the guarantee or provided the security will be able to pay its debts in full as they become due—

(a) the court, on the application of a liquidator, creditor, member or contributory of the company, may declare that the director shall be personally responsible, without any limitation of liability, for all or any of the debts or other liabilities of the company; and

(b) if the company is wound up within 12 months after the making of the statutory declaration and its debts are not paid or provided for in full within 12 months after the commencement of the winding-up, it shall be presumed, until the contrary is shown, that the director did not have reasonable grounds for his opinion.

(6) The special resolution referred to in subsection (1)(a) may be passed in accordance with section 141(8) of the Principal Act.

(7) Unless all of the members of the company entitled to vote at general meetings of the company vote in favour of the special resolution, the company shall not enter into the guarantee or provide the security before the expiry of 30 days after the special resolution has been passed or, if an application referred to in subsection (8) is made, until the application has been disposed of by the court.

(8) If application is made to the court in accordance with this section for the cancellation of the special resolution, the special resolution shall not have effect except to the extent to which it is confirmed by the court.

(9) Subject to subsection (10), an application referred to in subsection (8) may be made by the holders of not less in the aggregate than 10 per cent in nominal value of the company's issued share capital or any class thereof.

(10) An application shall not be made under subsection (8) by a person who has consented to, signed or voted in favour of the special resolution.

(11) An application referred to in subsection (8) must be made within 28 days after the date on which the special resolution was passed and may be made on behalf of the persons entitled to make the application by such one or more of their number as they may appoint in writing for the purpose.][a]

Amendments

a CLEA 2001, s 78 substitutes CA 1990, s 34.

Definitions

'company': CA 1963, s 2(1); 'director' includes 'shadow director': CA 1990, s 27; 'person connected with a director': CA 1990, s 26; 'arrangement': CA 1990, s 32(2)(a); 'quasi-loan': CA 1990, s 25(2); 'credit transaction': CA 1990, s 25(3) and s 25(3A); 'guarantee': CA 1990, s 25(1).

Notes

The 'new' CA 1990, s 34[1] (as substituted by CLEA 2001, s 78) introduced a validation procedure where companies wish to enter into guarantees and provide security in connection with loans, quasi-loans or credit transactions made for a director of the company or of its holding company or a person connected with such a director. Modelled on CA 1963, s 60 (the validation procedure for allowing financial assistance be given in connection with the purchase of a company's own shares), CA 1990, s 34(1) provides that s 31 shall not prevent the entering into of such a guarantee or the provision of such security where there is the authority of a special resolution to do so and the company's directors have sworn a statutory declaration of solvency. The statutory declaration must contain the matters detailed in s 34(3). CA 1990, s 34(4) requires the directors' statutory declaration to be accompanied by a report drawn up in the prescribed form[2] by an independent person, being a person qualified to be the company's auditor.

1 The 'old' CA 1990, s 34 had provided: 'Where a company is a member of a group of companies, consisting of a holding company and its subsidiaries, s 31 shall not prohibit that company from – (a) making a loan or quasi loan to another member of that group; or (b) entering into a guarantee or providing any security in connection with a loan or a quasi loan made by any person to another member of the group; by reason only that a director or one member of the group is connected with another'.

2 As prescribed by the Companies Act 1990 (Section 34) Regulations 2001 (SI 439/2001).

35 Transactions with holding company

Section 31, shall not prohibit a company from—

(a) making a loan or quasi-loan to [any company which is its holding company, subsidiary or a subsidiary of its holding company][a] or entering into a guarantee or providing any security in connection with a loan or quasi-loan made by any person to [any company which is its holding company, subsidiary or a subsidiary of its holding company][a];

(b) entering into a credit transaction as creditor for [any company which is its holding company, subsidiary or a subsidiary of its holding company][a] or entering into a guarantee or providing any security in connection with any credit transaction made by any other person for [any company which is its holding company, subsidiary or a subsidiary of its holding company][a], subsidiary or a subsidiary of its holding company][a].

Amendments

a CLEA 2001, s 79 amends CA 1990, s 35 by the substitution for 'its holding company' wherever occurring, of 'any company which is its holding company, subsidiary or a subsidiary of its holding company'.

Definitions

'company': CA 1963, s 2(1); 'holding company' and 'subsidiary': CA 1963, s 155; 'quasi-loan': CA 1990, s 25(2); 'credit transaction': CA 1990, s 25(3) and s 25(3A); 'guarantee': CA 1990, s 25(1).

Notes

As originally drafted, CA 1990, s 35 only operated to exempt from the provisions of s 31 transactions or arrangements made by a subsidiary company in favour of its holding company. The amendment effected by CLEA 2001, s 79 seems to have been intended to broaden the exemption by extending it to transactions or arrangements made by a holding company in favour of its subsidiary or one subsidiary in favour of a sister-subsidiary ie a company that is the subsidiary of its holding company. While it is thought to have been unintended, the use of the words 'for any *company*' in the first lines of s 35(a) and (b), instead of the broader term, 'body corporate' may operate on a strict technical construction of the words used to confine the exception to cases where the beneficiary group-member is a 'company' within the meaning of CA 1963, s 2 (ie an Irish formed and registered company) and not, say, a subsidiary that is, say, English registered. This interpretation is open unless a court were to find that the proximity of the words 'for any *company*' to the term 'which is its holding company' is sufficient to indicate that it was intended that the phrase 'for any *company*' was used in the sense of a company as defined in CA 1963, s 155 which defines 'company' for the purposes of the meaning of 'holding company' and 'subsidiary' as including 'any body corporate': CA 1965, s 155(5).

UK legislation

See CA 1985, ss 333 and 336.

---

36 Directors' expenses

(1) Section 31 shall not prohibit a company from doing anything to provide any of its directors with funds to meet vouched expenditure properly incurred or to be incurred by him for the purposes of the company or the purpose of enabling him properly to perform his duties as an officer of the company or doing anything to enable any of its directors to avoid incurring such expenditure.

(2) Where a company enters into any transaction pursuant to subsection (1), any liability falling on any person arising from any such transaction shall be discharged by him within six months from the date on which it was incurred.

(3) A person who contravenes subsection (2) shall be guilty of an offence.

Definitions

'company': CA 1963, s 2(1); 'director' includes 'shadow director': CA 1990, s 27.

UK legislation

See CA 1985, s 337 (as amended by Companies (Fair Dealing by Directors) (Increase in Financial Limits) Order 1990, SI 1990/1393 as from 31 July 1990).

---

37 Business transactions

Section 31, shall not prohibit a company from making any loan or quasi-loan or entering into any credit transaction as creditor for any person if—

(a) the company enters into the transaction concerned in the ordinary course of its business; and

(b) the value of the transaction is not greater, and the terms on which it is entered into are no more favourable, in respect of the person for whom the transaction is made, than that or those which—

(i) the company ordinarily offers, or

(ii) it is reasonable to expect the company to have offered,

to or in respect of a person of the same financial standing as that person but unconnected with the company.

Definitions

'Company': CA 1963 s 2(1); 'Quasi-loan': CA 1990 s 25(2); 'Credit transaction': CA 1990 s 25(3) and s 25(3A).

Notes

This exception is confined to transactions and arrangements being loans, quasi-loans and credit transactions and does not extend to transactions that are guarantees or the provision of security in connection with loans, quasi-loans and credit transactions. It would cover, for example, arm's length loans made by a bank or other financial institution as well as the arm's length supply of goods by a finance house pursuant to a lease or hire-purchase agreement. The exception would also appear to cover an arm's length lease of land or buildings by a company which ordinarily carries on the business of landlord. A transaction will not be found to be in the 'ordinary course of business' where a company has ceased trading.[1]

[1] *Re Ashmark Ltd (No 2)* [1990] ILRM 455.

UK legislation

See CA 1985, s 335(2) (as amended by Companies (Fair Dealing by Directors) (Increase in Financial Limits) Order 1990, SI 1990/1393 as from 31 July 1990) and s 338 (as amended by CA 1989, s 23 Sch 10, para 10 as from 1 April 1990 and CA 1989, s 138(c) as from 31 July 1990).

38 Civil remedies for breach of section 31

(1) Where a company enters into a transaction or arrangement in contravention of section 31 the transaction or arrangement shall be voidable at the instance of the company unless—

(a) restitution of any money or any other asset which is the subject matter of the arrangement or transaction is no longer possible, or the company has been indemnified in pursuance of subsection (2)(b) for the loss or damage suffered by it; or

(b) any rights acquired *bona fide* for value and without actual notice of the contravention by any person other than the person for whom the transaction or arrangement was made would be affected by its avoidance.

(2) Without prejudice to any liability imposed otherwise than by this subsection but subject to subsection (3), where an arrangement or transaction is made by a company for a director of the company or its holding company or person connected with such a director in contravention of section 31, that director and the person so connected and

any other director of the company who authorised the transaction or arrangement shall (whether or not it has been avoided in pursuance of subsection (1)) be liable—

(a) to account to the company for any gain which he has made directly or indirectly by the arrangement or transaction; and

(b) (jointly and severally with any other person liable under this subsection) to indemnify the company for any loss or damage resulting from the arrangement or transaction.

(3) Where an arrangement or transaction is entered into by a company and a person connected with a director of the company or its holding company in contravention of section 31 that director shall not be liable under subsection (2) if he shows that he took all reasonable steps to secure the company's compliance with that section and, in any case, a person so connected and any such other director as is mentioned in the said subsection (2) shall not be so liable if he shows that, at the time the arrangement or transaction was entered into, he did not know the relevant circumstances constituting the contravention.

Definitions

'company': CA 1963, s 2(1); 'director': CA 1963, s 2(1); director includes 'shadow director': CA 1990, s 27; 'person connected with a director': CA 1990, s 26.

Notes

Contravening transactions or arrangements are voidable at the instance of the company: A transaction or arrangement entered into by a company in contravention of CA 1990, s 31 is voidable at the instance of the company. Being 'voidable' the transaction or arrangement is valid unless the company exercises its right to avoid it. Avoidance can be initiated by the board of directors, the members of the company in general meeting or by any liquidator appointed to the company. The company's right to avoid a transaction or arrangement that contravened CA 1990, s 31 is expressly stated to be subject to the existence of either of the three 'savers' in s 38(1)(a) and (b).

Restitution impossible and indemnification: A transaction or arrangement in contravention of CA 1990, s 31 will not be voidable if restitution of any money or other assets, the subject of the transaction or arrangement, is no longer possible or if the company has been indemnified in pursuance of s 38(2)(b) for the loss and damage suffered by it.[1]

Rights acquired bona fide, for value, without actual notice of the contravention: A company may not avoid a transaction or arrangement in contravention of s 31 where to do so would affect any rights acquired bona fide, for value and without actual notice of the contravention, other than someone for whom the transaction or arrangement was made.[2] Where a receiver (who had been appointed under a debenture that it was claimed had been provide by a company as security for a loan to one or its directors) disposed of property in favour of a bona fide purchaser for value without actual notice of any contravention of s 31, it was held that any challenge to the sale by the receiver of the property must fail because the purchaser was for value, bona fide and without actual notice of any contravention.[3] To successfully invoke this 'saver' a person must have acted bona fide[4] and must not have had 'actual notice' of the contravention of CA 1990, s 31. It has been held recently by the English courts that that the distinction between 'actual' and imputed' knowledge is so well known that there should be a strong presumption that such expressions are used in their ordinary legal meanings and that 'actual knowledge' has its primary meaning, which does not include 'imputed notice'; and that the knowledge of an agent (an accountant) was not attributed to his principal.[5] An alternative approach is, however that 'there may be something about a transaction by which the principal is 'put on enquiry'. If the principal employs an agent to discharge such a duty, the knowledge of the agent will be imputed'. [6] This latter would appear to be the preferred approach in Ireland as the Supreme Court has held that actual notice includes cases where the agent gets actual notice of the equity. [7] A person cannot claim not to have actual notice where his conduct is so reckless or so intensely negligent, that the court is absolutely unable to account for it in any other way than by concluding that the person abstained from inquiry because he was satisfied as to the fact of the existence of a breach.[8]

Directors' and others' liability to account and indemnify the company: Where a transaction or arrangement is entered into by a company in contravention of s 31 the person for whom it was made and any directors who authorised it are liable to indemnity the company for any loss it suffers and to account to the company for any gain made.[9] A loan to a director in contravention of s 31 does not automatically make the director a constructive trustee of assets acquired with the proceeds of the loan: the validity of the loan unless and until avoided by the company is inimical either to the existence of a constructive trusteeship or to any other form of tracing claim in the absence of special circumstances.[10] Where a director is aware that his company has operated a loan account in favour of a fellow director in breach of s 31, he is jointly and severally liable to repay the loan to the company, even though he is not aware of the details of the individual loans that have been made to his fellow director: he is regarded in such circumstances as being in breach of his duty to take steps to have the loans repaid. [11]

1 CA 1990, s 38(1)(a).

2 CA 1990, s 38(1)(b).

3 *Ruby Property Company Ltd at al v Kilty and Superquinn* [1999] IEHC 50, McCracken J).

4 On the meaning of 'good faith' see *International Sales and Agencies Ltd v Marcuse* [1986] 1 All ER 587.

5 *Infiniteland Ltd and another v Artisan Contracting Ltd and another* [2006] 1 BCLC 632.

6 *El Ajou v Dollar Land Holdings plc* [1994] 1 BCLC 464 at 480.

7 *Bank of Ireland Finance Ltd v Rockfield Ltd* [1979] IR 21 at 37.

8 *Agra Bank Ltd v Barry* (1874) LR 7 HL 135 at 149.

9 For an example of a case where directors were liable to indemnify the company in respect of transactions which they authorised and/or to which they were counterparties, see *Queensway Systems Ltd v Walker* [2007] 2 BCLC 577.

10 *Re Ciro Citterio Menswear plc* [2002] 2 All ER 717.

11 *Neville v Krikorian et al* [2006] EWCA Civ 943. See also *Queensway Systems Ltd v Walker* [2007] 2 BCLC 577.

UK legislation

See CA 1985, s 341.

---

39 Personal liability for company debts in certain cases

(1) If a company is being wound up and is unable to pay its debts, and the court considers that any arrangement of a kind described in section 32 has contributed materially to the company's inability to pay its debts or has substantially impeded the orderly winding up thereof, the court, on the application of the liquidator or any creditor or contributory of the company, may, if it thinks it proper to do so, declare that any person for whose benefit the arrangement was made shall be personally liable, without any limitation of liability, for all, or such part as may be specified by the court, of the debts and other liabilities of the company.

(2) In deciding whether to make a declaration under subsection (1), the court shall have particular regard to whether, and to what extent, any outstanding liabilities arising under any arrangement referred to in that subsection were discharged before the commencement of the winding up.

(3) In deciding the extent of any personal liability under this section, the court shall have particular regard to the extent to which the arrangement in question contributed materially to the company's inability to pay its debts or substantially impeded the orderly winding up of the company.

Definitions

'company': CA 1963, s 2(1); 'arrangement of a kind described in s 32': CA 1990, s 32(2)(a).

40 Criminal penalties for breach of section 31

[If a company enters into a transaction or arrangement that contravenes section 31, every officer of the company who is in default shall be guilty of an offence.][a]

Amendments

a C(A)A 2009, s 7 substitutes CA 1990, s 40.

Definitions

'company': CA 1963, s 2(1); 'officer': CA 1963, s 2(1); 'officer who is in default': CA 1963, s 383.

Cross reference

For the penalties for contravention of CA 1990, s 31, see CA 1990, s 240.

Notes

Prior to the C(A)A 2009 the offence of contravening CA 1990, s 31 was directed at 'an officer of a company who authorises or permits the company to enter into a transaction or arrangement knowing or having reasonable cause to believe that the company was thereby contravening section 31'. The offence and the proofs required to establish its commission have been simplified somewhat now and the offence is now directed at 'every officer of the company [of a company entering a transaction or arrangement that contravenes section 31] who is in default'. For the meaning of 'officer who is in default' see the commentary on CA 1963, s 383.

UK legislation

See CA 1985, s 342.

Disclosure of transactions involving directors and others

41 Substantial contracts, etc., with directors and others to be disclosed in accounts

(1) Subject to subsections (5) and (6) and to section 45, group accounts prepared by a holding company in accordance with the requirements of section 150 of the Principal Act in respect of the relevant period shall contain the particulars specified in section 42 of—

(a) any transaction or arrangement of a kind described in section 31 entered into by the company or by a subsidiary of the company for a person who at any time during the relevant period was a director of the company or its holding company or was connected with such a director;

(b) any agreement by the company or by a subsidiary of the company to enter into any such transaction or arrangement for a person who at any time during the relevant period was a director of the company or its holding company or was connected with such a director;

(c) any other transaction or arrangement with the company or with a subsidiary of the company in which a person who at any time during the relevant period was a director of the company or its holding company had, directly or indirectly, a material interest.

(2) Subject as aforesaid, accounts prepared by any company other than a holding company in respect of the relevant period shall contain the particulars specified in section 42 of—

(a) any transaction or arrangement of a kind described in section 31 entered into by the company for a person who at any time during the relevant period was a director of the company or of its holding company or was connected with such a director;

(b) any agreement by the company to enter into any such transaction or arrangement for a person who at any time during the relevant period was a director of the company or of its holding company or was connected with such a director;

(c) any other transaction or arrangement with the company in which a person who at any time during the relevant period was a director of the company or of its holding company had, directly or indirectly, a material interest.

(3) Particulars which are required by subsection (1) or (2) to be contained in any accounts shall be given by way of notes to those accounts.

(4) Where by virtue of [sections 151(2) and 154] [a] of the Principal Act a company does not produce group accounts in relation to any financial year, subsection (1) shall have effect in relation to the company and that financial year as if the word 'group' were omitted.

(5) For the purposes of subsections (1)(c) and (2)(c)—

(a) a transaction or arrangement between a company and a director of the company or of its holding company or a person connected with such a director shall (if it would not otherwise be so treated) be treated as a transaction, arrangement or agreement in which that director is interested; and

(b) an interest in such a transaction or arrangement is not material if in the opinion of the majority of the directors (other than that director) of the company which is preparing the accounts in question it is not material (but without prejudice to the question whether or not such an interest is material in any case where those directors have not considered the matter).

[(6) Subsections (1) and (2) do not apply for the purposes of any accounts prepared by any company which is a licensed bank, or the holding company of a licensed bank, in relation to—

(a) a transaction or arrangement of a kind described in section 31 entered into for a person who at any time during the relevant period was connected with a director of that company or that holding company; or

(b) an agreement to enter into such a transaction or arrangement for a person so connected, to which the licensed bank is a party.][b]

(7) Subsections (1) and (2) do not apply in relation to the following transactions, arrangements and agreements—

(a) a transaction, arrangement or agreement between one company and another in which a director of the first company or of its subsidiary or holding company is interested only by virtue of his being a director of the other;

(b) a contract of service between a company and one of its directors or a director of its holding company or between a director of a company and any of that company's subsidiaries;

(c) a transaction, arrangement or agreement which was not entered into during the relevant period for the accounts in question and which did not subsist at any time during that period; and

(d) a transaction, arrangement or agreement which was made before the commencement of this section and which does not subsist thereafter.

(8) Subsections (1) and (2) apply whether or not—

(a) the transaction or arrangement was prohibited by section 31;

(b) the person for whom it was made was a director of the company or was connected with a director of the company at the time it was made;

(c) in the case of a transaction or arrangement made by a company which at any time during a relevant period is a subsidiary of another company, it was a subsidiary of that other company at the time the transaction or arrangement was made.

(9) In this section and in sections 43 and 45, 'relevant period', in relation to a company, means a financial year of the company ending not earlier than 6 months after the commencement of the section concerned.

[(10) Nothing in this section or sections 42 to 45 prejudices the operation of any—

(a) rule or other instrument; or

(b) direction or requirement,

made, issued, granted or otherwise created under the Central Bank Acts 1942 to 1998, the Central Bank and Financial Services Authority of Ireland Acts 2003 and 2004 or any other enactment requiring a licensed bank, or a holding company of a licensed bank, to disclose particulars, whether in accounts prepared by it or otherwise, of transactions, arrangements or agreements (whether of the kind described in section 31 or not) entered into by the licensed bank.

(11) Where a company makes default in complying with this section, the company and every person who at the time of that default is a director of the company shall be guilty of an offence.

(12) It shall be a defence in proceedings for an offence under subsection (11) for the defendant to prove that he took all reasonable steps for securing compliance with the requirements of this section.][c]

Amendments

a EC(IFRSMA)R 2005, reg 9 and Sch 1, Pt 4, Item 2 substitutes 'sections 151(2) and 154' for 'sections 150(2) and 154' in s 41(4).

b C(A)A 2009, s 8(1)(a) substitutes CA 1990, s 41(6).

c C(A)A 2009, s 8(1)(b) inserts CA 1990, s 41(10)–(12).

Definitions

'company': CA 1963, s 2(1); 'director': CA 1963, s 2(1); director includes 'shadow director': CA 1990, s 27; 'person connected with a director': CA 1990, s 26; 'holding company' and 'subsidiary company': CA 1963, s 155.

Notes

CA 1990, s 41 specifies certain transactions and arrangements between directors and others with their companies and their companies' subsidiaries which must be disclosed in a company's financial statements.

Transactions and arrangements requiring disclosure: Although the marginal note to CA 1990, s 41 refers to 'substantial contracts etc' with directors and others to be disclosed in accounts, the primary obligation refers not to 'substantial contracts' but instead to (a) transactions or arrangements of a kind described in CA 1990, s 31, (b) agreements to enter into such transactions or arrangements, and (c) any other transaction or arrangement in which a director had, directly or indirectly, a material interest. The matters referred to in (a) and (b) which must be disclosed are in the nature of loans, quasi-loans, credit transactions and guarantees and security in connection with such loans, quasi-loans and credit transactions and agreements to enter into such. What is included in (c) is somewhat less clear. If transaction and arrangement are given their ordinary meaning in English, outside of the context of the Companies Acts, they are very broad and would extend to practically any dealing between a company and a director. It is not certain, however, that they should be given their ordinary meaning given that both words are used elsewhere in Part III of CA 1990 in a very particular way. There is some support for saying that not every 'contract' will be a transaction or arrangement. This is because although CA 1990, s 47(1) provides that any reference in CA 1963, s 194 to a 'contract' shall be construed as including a reference to any transaction or arrangement, the converse is not provided, ie it is not said that every reference to a 'transaction or arrangement' as used in CA 1990, s 41 shall be construed as including a reference to a contract.

Certain transactions, arrangements and agreements are excluded. Those between one company and another in which a director of the first company or of its subsidiary or holding company is interested only by virtue of his being a director of the other, those not entered into during the relevant period for the accounts in question and which did not subsist at any time during that period and those made before the commencement of s 41 and which do not subsist thereafter are excluded as are service contracts between companies and its directors or directors of its holding company or between a director of a company and any of its subsidiaries.

Relevant persons with whom transactions and arrangements must be disclosed: In respect of the transactions and arrangements and agreements to enter into such described in CA 1990, s 41(1)(a) and (b) and (2)(a) and (b) the relevant persons are those who at any time during the relevant period are directors of the company, directors of the company's holding company or persons connected with such directors within the meaning of CA 1990, s 26. In the case of transactions or arrangements within the meaning of CA 1990, s 41(1)(c) and (2)(c) the only persons who are relevant are directors of the company and its holding company but not persons connected with such directors.

Exemptions for licensed banks: Companies that are licensed banks or which are the holding companies of licensed banks are not required under the Companies Acts to disclose in their accounts the transactions and arrangements described in CA 1990, s 41(1)(a) and (b) or (2)(a) and (b) in relation to those which are entered into for persons connected with directors of the company or of its holding company. This represents a change in the law. Prior to the C(A)A 2009, which was commenced on enactment on 12 July 2009, this exemption applied to directors of such companies and their holding companies as well as to connected persons.

Subsection (10), inserted by the C(A)A 2009, makes clear that nothing in ss 41 to 45 prejudices the operation of any rule or other instrument or direction or other requirement made by the Financial Regulator in relation to any company that is a licensed bank.

Contravention: The contravention of CA 1990, s 41 is an indictable offence which will be committed by the company and every person who at the time of the default is a director: sub-s (11). It is, however, a defence for a defendant to prove that he took all reasonable steps for securing compliance with the requirements of the section.

UK legislation

See CA 1985, s 232, Sch 6 (amended by CA 1989, s 6(4) Sch 4); CA 1989, s 6(3); Directors' Remuneration Report Regulations 2002, SI 2002/1986, reg 2, as from 1 August 2002).

---

42 Particulars required to be included in accounts by section 41

The particulars of a transaction, arrangement or agreement which are required by section 41 to be included in the annual accounts prepared by a company are particulars of the principal terms of the transaction, arrangement or agreement and (without prejudice to the generality of the foregoing provision)—

(a) a statement of the fact either that the transaction, arrangement or agreement was made or subsisted, as the case may be, during the financial year in respect of which those accounts are made up;

(b) the name of the person for whom it was made, and, where that person is or was connected with a director of the company or of its holding company, the name of that director;

(c) in any case where subsection (1)(c) or (2)(c) of section 41 applies, the name of the director with the material interest and the nature of that interest;

(d) in the case of a loan or an agreement for a loan or an arrangement within section 31(2) or 31(3) relating to a loan—

(i) the amount of the liability of the person to whom the loan was or was agreed to be made, in respect of principal and interest, at the beginning and at the end of that period;

(ii) the maximum amount of that liability during that period;

(iii) the amount of any interest which, having fallen due, has not been paid; and

(iv) the amount of any provision (within the meaning of the Sixth Schedule to the Principal Act or the Companies (Amendment) Act, 1986) made in respect of any failure or anticipated failure by the borrower to repay the whole or part of the loan or to pay the whole or part of any interest thereon;

(e) in the case of a guarantee or security or an arrangement within *section 31 (2)* relating to a guarantee or security—

(i) the amount for which the company (or its subsidiary) was liable under the guarantee or in respect of the security both at the beginning and at the end of the financial year in question;

(ii) the maximum amount for which the company (or its subsidiary) may become so liable; and

(iii) any amount paid and any liability incurred by the company (or its subsidiary) for the purpose of fulfilling the guarantee or discharging the security (including any loss incurred by reason of the enforcement of the guarantee or security); and

(f) in the case of any transaction, arrangement or agreement, other than those mentioned in paragraphs (d) and (e) the value of the transaction or arrangement or, as the case may be, the value of the transaction or arrangement to which the agreement relates; and

(g) in the case of arrangements to which section 32 relates, the aggregate value of such arrangements at the end of the financial year concerned, in relation to any persons specified in that section, expressed as a percentage of the company's relevant assets at that time; and

(h) any amendment of the terms of any such arrangement in accordance with section 33.

Definitions

'company': CA 1963, s 2(1); 'director': CA 1963, s 2(1); 'financial year': CA 1963, s 2(1).

UK legislation

See CA 1985, s 232, Sch 6 (amended by CA 1989, s 6(4) Sch 4); CA 1989, s 6(3); Directors' Remuneration Report Regulations 2002, SI 2002/1986, reg 2, as from 1 August 2002).

43 Particulars of amounts outstanding to be included in accounts

(1) This section applies in relation to the following classes of transactions, arrangements and agreements—

(a) loans, guarantees and securities relating to loans, arrangements of a kind described in section 31(2) or 31(3) relating to loans, and agreements to enter into any of the foregoing transactions and arrangements;

(b) quasi-loans, guarantees and securities relating to quasi-loans, arrangements of a kind described in those subsections relating to quasi-loans and agreements to enter into any of the foregoing transactions and arrangements;

(c) credit transactions, guarantees and securities relating to credit transactions and arrangements of a kind described in those subsections relating to credit transactions and agreements to enter into any of the foregoing transactions and arrangements.

(2) The group accounts of a holding company prepared in accordance with the requirements of section 150 of the Principal Act and the accounts of any other company

prepared in accordance with the requirements of section 148 of the Principal Act in respect of the relevant period shall contain a statement in relation to transactions, arrangements and agreements made by the company and, in the case of a holding company, by a subsidiary of the company for persons who at any time during the relevant period were officers of the company (but not directors) of the aggregate amounts outstanding at the end of the relevant period under transactions, arrangements and agreements within any paragraph of subsection (1) and the number of officers for whom the transactions, arrangements and agreements falling within each of those paragraphs were made.

(3) Subsection (2) shall not apply, in relation to the accounts prepared by any company in respect of any relevant period, to transactions, arrangements and agreements made by the company or any of its subsidiaries for any officer of the company if the aggregate amount outstanding at the end of that period under the transactions, arrangements and agreements so made for that officer does not exceed [€3,174.35]. [a]

(4) Subsection (2) shall not apply in relation to any transaction, arrangement or agreement made by a licensed bank for any of its officers or for any of the officers of its holding company.

[(5) The following, namely—

(a) the group accounts of a company which is, or is the holding company of, a licensed bank prepared in accordance with the requirements of section 150 of the Principal Act; and

(b) the accounts of any other company which is a licensed bank prepared in accordance with the requirements of section 148 of the Principal Act,

in respect of the relevant period shall contain a statement in relation to transactions, arrangements and agreements made by—

(i) the company preparing the accounts, if it is a licensed bank; and

(ii) in the case of a holding company, by any of its subsidiaries which is a licensed bank,

for persons who at any time during the relevant period were connected with a director of the company of—

(I) the aggregate amounts outstanding at the end of the relevant period under transactions, arrangements and agreements coming within any paragraph of sub-section (1) (which transactions, arrangements and agreements, coming within any particular such paragraph, are referred to subsequently in this section as 'relevant transactions, arrangements and agreements');

(II) the aggregate maximum amounts outstanding during the relevant period under relevant transactions, arrangements and agreements made for persons so connected;

(III) the number of persons so connected for whom relevant transactions, arrangements and agreements that subsisted at the end of the relevant period were made; and

(IV) the maximum number of persons so connected for whom relevant transactions, arrangements and agreements that subsisted at any time during the relevant period were made.

(6) A transaction, arrangement or agreement to which sub-section (5) applies need not be included in the statement referred to in that subsection if—

(a) it is entered into by the company concerned in the ordinary course of its business, and

(b) its value is not greater, and its terms no more favour-able, in respect of the person for whom it is made, than that or those which—

(i) the company ordinarily offers, or

(ii) it is reasonable to expect the company to have offered,

to or in respect of a person of the same financial standing but unconnected with the company.

(6A) In reckoning the aggregate maximum amounts or the maximum number of persons referred to in subsection (5)(II) or (IV), as appropriate, there shall not be counted, as the case may be—

(a) relevant transactions, arrangements and agreements made by the company, or a subsidiary of it, referred to in subsection (5) and which is a licensed bank for any person connected as mentioned in that subsection if the aggregate maximum amount outstanding during the relevant period under relevant transactions, arrangements and agreements made for that person does not exceed €3,174.35; or

(b) a person so connected for whom the aggregate maximum amount outstanding as mentioned in paragraph (a) does not exceed the amount there mentioned.][b]

(7) Particulars which are required by [subsection (2) or (5)][c] to be contained in any accounts shall be given by way of notes to those accounts.

(8) Where by virtue of [sections 151(2) and 154][d] of the Principal Act, a company does not produce group accounts in relation to any financial year, [subsections (2) and (5)][e] shall have effect in relation to the company and that financial year as if the word 'group' were omitted.

[...][f]

(10) For the purposes of this section, 'amount outstanding' means the amount of the outstanding liabilities of the person for whom the transaction, arrangement or agreement in question was made, or, in the case of a guarantee or security, the amount guaranteed or secured.

[(11) Where a company makes default in complying with this section, the company and every person who at the time of that default is a director of the company shall be guilty of an offence.

(12) It shall be a defence in proceedings for an offence under subsection (11) for the defendant to prove that he took all reasonable steps for securing compliance with the requirements of this section.][g]

Amendments

a £2,500 converted to €3,174.35 by Council Regulations (EC) No 1103/97, No 974/98 and No 2866/98 and the Economic and Monetary Union Act 1988, s 6.

b C(A)A 2009, s 8(2) substituted CA 1990, s 43(5) and (6) and inserted s 43(6A).

c Words 'subsection (2) or (5)' substituted for 'subsection (2), (5) or (6)' by C(A)A 2009, s 8(3)(a).

d EC(IFRSMA)R 2005, reg 9 and Sch 1, Pt 4, Item 3 substitutes 'sections 151(2) and 154' for 'sections 150(2) and 154' in s 43(8).

e Words 'subsection (2) and (5)' substituted for 'subsection (2), (5) or (6)' by C(A)A 2009, s 8(3)(c).

f C(A)A 2009, s 8(d) deletes CA 1990, s 43(9).

g C(A)A 2009, s 8(3)(d) inserts CA 1990, s 43(11) and (12).

Definitions

'company': CA 1963, s 2(1); 'director': CA 1963, s 2(1); 'financial year': CA 1963, s 2(1).

UK legislation

See CA 1985, s 232, Sch 6 (amended by CA 1989, s 6(4) Sch 4); CA 1989, s 6(3); Directors' Remuneration Report Regulations 2002 (SI 2002/1986), reg 2, as from 1 August 2002).

44 Further provisions relating to licensed banks

(1) Subject to section 45, a company which is, or is the holding company of, a licensed bank, shall maintain a register containing a copy of every transaction, arrangement or agreement of which particulars [are required by subsection (1) or (2) of section 41 or would, but for section 41(6), be required by subsection (1) or (2) of that section][a] to be disclosed in the company's accounts or group accounts for the current financial year and for each of the preceding ten financial years (but excluding any financial year ending prior to the passing of this Act) or, if such a transaction, arrangement or agreement is not in writing, a written memorandum setting out its terms.

(2) Subsection (1) shall not require a company to keep in its register a copy of any transaction, arrangement or agreement made for a connected person if—

(a) it is entered into in the ordinary course of the company's business, and

(b) its value is not greater, and its terms no more favourable, in respect of the person for whom it is made, than that or those which—

(i) the company ordinarily offers, or

(ii) it is reasonable to expect the company to have offered,

to or in respect of a person of the same financial standing but unconnected with the company.

(3) Subject to section 45, a company which is, or is the holding company of, a licensed bank shall before its annual general meeting make available, at the registered office of the company for not less than the period of 15 days ending with the date of the meeting, for inspection by members of the company a statement containing the particulars of transactions, arrangements and agreements which the company would, but for section 41 (6), be required by subsection (1) or (2) of that section to disclose in its accounts or group accounts for the last complete financial year preceding that meeting and such a statement shall also be made available for inspection by the members at the annual general meeting.

(4) Subsection (3) shall not require the inclusion in the statement of particulars of any transaction, arrangement or agreement if—

(a) it is entered into in the ordinary course of the company's business, and

(b) its value is not greater, and its terms no more favourable, in respect of the person for whom it is made, than that or those which—

(i) the company ordinarily offers, or

(ii) it is reasonable to expect the company to have offered,

to or in respect of a person of the same financial standing but unconnected with the company.

[(4A) Subsection (3) shall not require the inclusion in the statement of particulars of any transaction, arrangement or agreement if, by reason of—

(a) the company's not taking advantage of section 41(6); or

(b) the company's being required by a rule, instrument, direction or requirement referred to in section 41(10) to disclose such information in the following manner,

the company has included in the group accounts or accounts referred to in section 41(1) or (2), as the case may be, for the last complete financial year mentioned in subsection (3) particulars of the transaction, arrangement or agreement which, but for either of those reasons, it would not have disclosed in those accounts by virtue of section 41(6).

(4B) Where subsection (1) falls to be applied to a company which is the holding company of a licensed bank, each of the references in subsection (2) to the company, other than the first such reference, shall be deemed to be a reference to the licensed bank.

(4C) A company shall, if required by the Director, produce to the Director for inspection the register kept by it in accordance with subsection (1) and shall give the Director such facilities for inspecting and taking copies of the contents of the register as the Director may require.][b]

(5) It shall be the duty of the auditors of the company to examine any such statement before it is made available to the members of the company in accordance with subsection (3) and to make a report to the members on that statement; and the report shall be annexed to the statement before it is made so available.

(6) A report under subsection (5) shall state whether in the opinion of the auditors the statement contains the particulars required by subsection (3) and, where their opinion is that it does not, they shall include in the report, so far as they are reasonably able to do so, a statement giving the required particulars.

(7) Subsection (3) shall not apply in relation to a licensed bank which is for the purposes of section 150 of the Principal Act the wholly owned subsidiary of a company incorporated in the State.

(8) Where a company fails to comply with [subsection (1), (3) or (4C)][c], the company and every person who at the time of that failure is a director of the company shall be guilty of an offence and liable to a fine.

[(9) It shall be a defence in proceedings for an offence under subsection (8) (being an offence consisting of a failure to comply with subsection (1) or (3)) for the defendant to prove that he took all reasonable steps for securing compliance with subsection (1) or (3), as the case may be.][d]

Amendments

a Words 'are required by subsection (1) or (2) of section 41 or would, but for section 41(6), be required by subsection (1) or (2) of that section' substituted for 'would, but for section 41 (6), be required by subsection (1) or (2) of that section' by C(A)A 2009, s 9(a).

b C(A)A 2009, s 9(b) inserts CA 1990, s 44(4A)–(4C).

c Words 'subsection (1), (3) or (4C)' substituted for 'subsection (1) or (3)' by C(A)A 2009, s 9(c).

d C(A)A 2009, s 9(d) substitutes CA 1990, s 44(9).

Definitions

'company': CA 1963, s 2(1); 'connected person': CA 1990, ss 3(1) and 26; 'director': CA 1963, s 2(1); 'financial year': CA 1963, s 2(1); 'holding company' and 'subsidiary company': CA 1963, s 155.

Notes

The section 44 register: Licensed banks and companies that are the holding companies of licensed banks are required to maintain a register of directors' dealings. The contents of a 'section 44 register' are copies of every transaction, arrangement or agreement of which particulars are required by CA 1990, s 41 to be disclosed in the company's accounts or group accounts (even where a company is exempt from disclosing them in its accounts by reason of CA 1990, s 41(6)) for the current financial year and for each of the ten preceding financial years. Where a relevant transaction etc is not in writing, then a memorandum of its terms should be placed on the file. These requirements are subject to CA 1990, s 45 and its *de minimis* exemptions.

Copies of transactions etc relating to connected persons are not required to be entered in the register where they are entered into in the ordinary course of business on arm's length terms: CA 1990, s 44(2).

Companies required to keep a section 44 register are also required to produce it to the ODCE on request and facilitate the making of copies: CA 1990, s 44(4C).

The failure to comply with the requirement to maintain a section 44 register or with a direction given by the ODCE is an indictable offence.

The section 44 statement: Licensed banks and companies that are the holding companies of licensed banks are required to make available a statement for inspection by their members, at their registered offices for a period of 15 days before their AGMs and at their AGMs. The 'section 44 statement' must contain particulars of transactions etc which the companies would, but for CA 1990, s 41(6), be required to disclose in its accounts for the last complete financial year preceding that AGM. Exempted from this requirement are licensed banks which are wholly-owned subsidiaries of companies incorporated in the State.

Particulars of transactions etc entered into in favour of directors and others are not required to be included in the statement where they are entered into in the ordinary course of business on arm's length terms: CA 1990, s 44(4). Where companies do not take advantage of the exemption from disclosure contained in CA 1990, s 41(6) or where banks are required by the regulator to make disclosure in their accounts, and particulars of the transactions were given in the accounts, such transactions etc are not required to be included in the section 44 statement: CA 1990, s 44(4A).

It is the duty of such companies' auditors to examine the section 44 statement before it is made available to the members and to report to the members on the statement, which report must be annexed to the statement: CA 1990, s 44(5). The auditors' report must state whether in their opinion the statement contains the particulars required to be stated and where in their opinion it does not, the auditors must include in the report so far as they can a statement giving the required particulars.

The failure to comply with the requirement to make available a section 44 statement or with a direction given by the ODCE is an indictable offence.

UK legislation

See CA 1985, s 343 (amended by CA 1989, s 23 Sch 10 paras 10, 11; and Companies Act 1989 (Bank Accounts Regulations 1994, SI 1994/233, reg 6(1), (2) as and from 28 February 1994).

---

45 Arrangements excluded from sections 41 and 44

(1) Section 41(1) and (2) and section 44 do not apply to arrangements of the kind mentioned in section 32(2) entered into by a company or by a subsidiary of the company for a person who at any time during the relevant period was a director of the company or of its holding company or was connected with such a director, if the aggregate of the values of each arrangement so made for that director or any person connected with him, less the amount (if any) by which the liabilities of the person for whom the arrangement was made has been reduced, did not at any time during the relevant period exceed [€3,174.35].[a]

(2) Subsections (1)(c) and (2)(c) of section 41 do not apply, in relation to any accounts prepared by a company in respect of any relevant period, to any transaction or arrangement with a company or any of its subsidiaries in which a director of the company or of its holding company had, directly or indirectly, a material interest if—

(a) the value of each transaction or arrangement within subsection (1)(c) or (2)(c), as the case may be, in which that director had, directly or indirectly, a material interest and which was made after the commencement of that relevant period with the company or any of its subsidiaries; and

(b) the value of each such transaction or arrangement which was made before the commencement of that period less the amount (if any) by which the liabilities of the person for whom the transaction or arrangement was made have been reduced;

did not at any time during the relevant period exceed in the aggregate [€1,269.74][b] or, if more, did not exceed [€6,348.69][c] or one per cent of the value of the net assets of the company preparing the accounts in question as at the end of the relevant period for those accounts, whichever is the less and for this purpose, 'net assets' has the same meaning as in section 29 (9).

Amendments

a £2,500 converted to €3,174.35 by Council Regulations (EC) No 1103/97, No 974/98 and No 2866/98 and the Economic and Monetary Union Act 1988, s 6.

b £1,000 converted to €1,269.74 by Council Regulations (EC) No 1103/97, No 974/98 and No 2866/98 and the Economic and Monetary Union Act 1988, s 6.

c £5,000 converted to €6,348.69 by Council Regulations (EC) No 1103/97, No 974/98 and No 2866/98 and the Economic and Monetary Union Act 1988, s 6.

Definitions

'director': CA 1963, s 2(1); 'arrangements of the kind described in section 32(2)': CA 1990, s 32(2)(a).

UK legislation

See CA 1985, s 344 (amended by CA 1989, s 23 Sch 10 para 10; and Companies (Fair Dealing by Directors) (Increase in Financial Limits) Order 1990, SI 1990/1393 as from 31 July 1990).

46 Duty of auditors of company in breach of section 41 or 43

If in the case of any group or other accounts of a company the requirements of section 41 or 43 are not complied with, it shall be the duty of the auditors of the company by whom the accounts are examined to include in their report on the balance sheet of the company, so far as they are reasonably able to do so, a statement giving the required particulars.

Definitions

'accounts': CA 1963, s 2(1); 'company': CA 1963, s 2(1); 'director': CA 1963, s 2(1).

UK legislation

See CA 1985, s 237(4) (substituted by Directors' Remuneration Report Regulations 2002 SI 2002/1989, reg 6 as from 1 August 2002).

47 Disclosure by directors of interests in contracts, etc.

(1) Any reference in section 194 of the Principal Act to a contract shall be construed as including a reference to any transaction or arrangement (whether or not constituting a contract) made or entered into on or after the commencement of this section.

(2) For the purposes of the said section 194, a transaction or arrangement of a kind described in section 31 made by a company for a director of the company or a person connected with such a director shall, if it would not otherwise be so treated (and whether or not prohibited by that section), be treated as a transaction or arrangement in which that director is interested.

(3) […][a]

Amendments

a Subsection (3) substituted CA 1963, s 194(3).

Definitions

'company': CA 1963, s 2(1); 'director': CA 1963, s 2(1); 'the Principal Act': CA 1990, s 3(1).

Notes

See the notes to CA 1963, s 194.

UK legislation

See CA 1985, s 317.

Supplemental

48 Power to alter financial limits under Part III

(1) The Minister may, by order, alter any of the financial limits specified in this Part.

(2) Every order made under this section shall be laid before each House of the Oireachtas as soon as may be after it is made and if a resolution annulling the order is passed by either House within the next 21 days on which that House has sat after the order is laid before it, the order shall be annulled accordingly but without prejudice to the validity of anything previously done thereunder.

Definitions

'Minister': CA 1990, s 3(1).

UK legislation

See CA 1985, s 345 (amended by Companies (Fair Dealing by Directors) (Increase in Financial Limits) Order 1990, SI 1990/1393).

---

49 Cessation of section 192 of Principal Act

Section 192 of the Principal Act shall cease to have effect except—

(a) in relation to accounts and directors' reports prepared in respect of any financial year ending before the commencement of this section; and

(b) in relation to accounts and directors' reports prepared in respect of the first financial year ending after the commencement of this section but only in relation to loans and contracts entered into before the commencement of this section which do not subsist on or after that day.

Definitions

'accounts': CA 1963, s 2(1); 'director': CA 1963, s 2(1); 'financial year': CA 1963, s 2(1).

Notes

CA 1963, s 192 required the disclosure of loans to directors to be made in companies' annual accounts.

---

50 Inspection of director's service contracts

(1) Subject to the provisions of this section every company shall keep at an appropriate place—

(a) in the case of each director whose contract of service with the company is in writing, a copy of that contract;

(b) in the case of each director whose contract of service with the company is not in writing, a written memorandum setting out the terms of that contract;

(c) in the case of each director who is employed under a contract of service with a subsidiary of the company, a copy of that contract or, if it is not in writing, a written memorandum setting out the terms of that contract;

(d) a copy or written memorandum, as the case may be, of any variation of any contract of service referred to in paragraph (a), (b) or (c);

and all copies and memoranda kept by a company in pursuance of this subsection shall be kept at the same place.

(2) Where a contract of service is only partially in writing, paragraphs (a), (b), (c) and (d), as appropriate, of subsection (1), and subsections (4) and (5), shall also apply to such a contract.

(3) The following shall, as regards a company, be appropriate places for the purposes of subsection (1), namely—

(a) its registered office;

(b) the place where its register of members is kept if other than its registered office;

(c) its principal place of business.

(4) Every company shall send notice in the prescribed form to the registrar of companies of the place where copies and memoranda required by subsection (1) to be kept by it are kept and of any change in that place, save in a case in which they have at all times been kept at its registered office.

(5) Subsection (1) shall not apply in relation to a director's contract of service with the company or with a subsidiary of the company if that contract required him to work wholly or mainly outside the State, but the company shall keep a memorandum—

(a) in the case of a contract of service with the company, setting out the name of the director and the provisions of the contract relating to its duration;

(b) in the case of a contract of service with a subsidiary of the company setting out the name of the director, the name and place of incorporation of the subsidiary and the provisions of the contract relating to its duration,

at the same place as copies and the memoranda are kept by the company in pursuance of subsection (1).

(6) Every copy and memorandum required to be kept by subsections (1) and (5) shall, during business hours (subject to such reasonable restrictions as the company may in general meeting impose, so that not less than two hours in each day be allowed for inspection), be open to the inspection of any member of the company without charge.

[(7) If default is made in complying with subsection (1) or (5) or if an inspection required under subsection (6) is refused, the company and every officer of the company who is in default shall be guilty of an offence and liable on summary conviction to a fine not exceeding €1,904.61 and, for continued contravention, to a daily default fine not exceeding €63.49 and, if default is made for 14 days in complying with subsection (4), the company and every officer of the company who is in default shall be guilty of an offence and liable to a fine not exceeding €1,904.61 and, for continued contravention, to a daily default fine not exceeding €63.49.][a]

(8) In the case of a refusal of an inspection required under subsection (6) of a copy or memorandum the court may by order compel an immediate inspection thereof.

(9) This section shall not require to be kept a copy of, or memorandum setting out the terms of, a contract or a copy of, or memorandum setting out the terms of a variation of, a contract at a time at which the unexpired portion of the term for which the contract is

to be in force is less than three years or at a time at which the contract can, within the next ensuing three years, be terminated by the company without payment of compensation.

Amendments

a. C(AA)A 2003, s 57 and Sch 2 substitutes CA 1990, s 50(7).

Definitions

'contravention': CA 1990, s 3(1); 'court': CA 1990, s 235; 'daily default fine': CA 1990, s 3(1) and s 249(6); 'director': CA 1963, s 2(1); 'officer': CA 1963, s 2(1); 'officer in default': CA 1963, s 383; 'member': CA 1963, s 31; 'subsidiary': CA 1963, s 155.

UK legislation

CA 1985, s 318 (as amended by CA 1989, ss 143, 212, Sch 24).

51 Register of directors and secretaries

[...][a]

Amendments

a This section substituted CA 1963, s 195.

52 Directors to have regard to interests of employees

(1) The matters to which the directors of a company are to have regard in the performance of their functions shall include the interests of the company's employees in general, as well as the interests of its members.

(2) Accordingly, the duty imposed by this section on the directors shall be owed by them to the company (and the company alone) and shall be enforceable in the same way as any other fiduciary duty owed to a company by its directors.

Definitions

'director': CA 1963, s 2(1) and includes 'shadow director': CA 1990, s 26; 'member': CA 1963, s 31.

Notes

The subject of directors' duties: the general rule: CA 1990, s 52(1) introduced a statutory duty for company directors, in the performance of their functions, to have regard to the interests of the company's employees in general as well as the interests of its members.[1] The common law position, that directors' duties are only owed to their company[2] (and encapsulated in the motto, 'directors have but one master, the company')[3] is preserved by CA 1990, s 52(2) which makes clear that the duty to have regard to the interests of employees is owed by directors to the company (and the company alone) and is enforceable in the same way as any other fiduciary duty owed by a company by its directors. Although the novelty of this provision was the extension of directors' duties to employees, s 52(1) assumes that directors already owed a duty to have regard to the interests of members, which they do although only in the sense of being obliged to act for the benefit of the company as a whole and not in the interests of individual members.[4]

The duty of nominee directors: A person who has been nominated by another to be a director of a company still owes his fiduciary duties primarily to the company rather than to his nominator and is thus obliged to act in the best interests of the company, albeit that he is entitled to have regard to the interests and requirements of his nominator to the extent that those interests and requirements are not incompatible with his duty to act in the best interests of the company.[5]

The expansion of directors' duties to member-shareholders: Although the general rule is that directors' duties are not owed to member-shareholders, it has been recognised that in particular circumstances a company director may assume or otherwise find himself in a position where he owes a fiduciary duty to members which duty is enforceable by the members against the directors.[6] The clearest example of where this will arise is where directors expressly undertake certain obligations to member-shareholders.[7]

The expansion of directors' duties to creditors: It is now well established that where a company is insolvent, directors will owe duties to creditors,[8] who become 'prospectively entitled, through the mechanism of liquidation, to displace the power of the shareholders and the directors to deal with the company's assets'.[9]

1 See Courtney, *The Law of Private Companies* (2nd edn, Tottel Publishing, 2002) para 10.016 and MacCann, 'Directors' Duties: To Whom Are they Owed?' (1991) ILT 3 and 30.

2 For the common law position that directors' duties are only owed to their company, see: *Pervical v Wright* [1902] 2 Ch 421 and *Smith v Cork & Bandon Rly Co* (1870) 5 IR Eq 65.

3 Per Lord Cullen in *Dawson International plc v Coats Paton plc* [1989] BCLC 233 at 243.

4 *Crindle Investments v Wymes* [1998] 2 ILRM 275 at 288 (Keane J).

5 *Re Neath Rugby Ltd* [2008] 1 BCLC 527; *Kuwait Asia Bank EC v National Mutual Life Nominees Ltd* [1990] BCLC 868.

6 *Crindle Investments v Wymes* [1998] 2 ILRM 275; *Coleman v Myers* [1977] 2 NZLR 225; *Re Chez Nico (Restaurants) Ltd* [1992] BCLC 192; *Platt v Platt* [1999] 2 BCLC 745; *Peskin and another v Anderson* [2000] 2 BCLC 1; *Brunninghausen v Glavanics* (1999) 32 ACSR 294; *Securities Trust Ltd v Associated Properties Ltd* (19 November 1980, unreported) HC (McWilliams J).

7 As in the case of *Allen v Hyatt* (1941) 30 TLR 444.

8 *Re Frederick Inns Ltd* [1994] 1 ILRM 387; *Jones v Gunn* [1997] 2 ILRM 245; *Parkes v Hong Kong & Shanghai Bank Corp* [1990] ILRM 341; *West Mercia Safetywear Ltd v Dodd* [1988] BCLC 250; *Yukong Line Ltd of Korea v Rendsburg Investments Corporation of Liberia (No 2)* [1998] 1 WLR 294; *Cullen Gwyer & Associates Ltd v London Wharf (Limehouse) Ltd* [2003] 2 BCLC 153; *Re Pantone 485 Ltd* [2002] 1 BCLC 266; *Re Mytravel Group Plc* [2005] 1 WLR 2365; *Walker v Wimborne* (1976) 50 ALJR 446; *Kinsela v Russell Kinsela Pty Ltd* (1986) 4 ACLC 213; *Grove v Flavel* (1986) 4 ACLC 654; *Nicholson v Permakraft (NZ) Ltd* [1985] 1 NZLR 242.

9 *Per* Street CJ in *Kinsella v Russell Kinsella Property Ltd* [1986] 4 NSWLR 722, cited with approval by Blayney J in the Supreme Court in *Re Frederick Inns Ltd* [1994] 1 ILRM 387.

UK legislation

CA 1985, s 309.

PART IV
DISCLOSURE OF INTERESTS IN SHARES

Chapter 1
Share dealings by directors, secretaries and their families

53 Obligation of director or secretary to notify interests in shares or debentures of company

(1) Subject to the provisions of this section a person who, at the commencement of this section is a director or secretary of a company and is then interested in shares in, or debentures of, the company or any other body corporate, being the company's subsidiary or holding company or a subsidiary of the company's holding company or thereafter becomes a director or secretary of a company and, at the time when he becomes a director or secretary of a company, is so interested, shall notify the company in writing—

(a) of the subsistence of his interests at that time, and

(b) of the number of shares of each class in, and the amount of debentures of each class of, the company or any such other body corporate as aforesaid in which each interest of his subsists at that time.

(2) A director or secretary of a company shall notify the company in writing of the occurrence, while he is a director or secretary, of any of the following events and the date on which it occurred—

(a) any event in consequence of whose occurrence he becomes, or ceases to be, interested in shares in, or debentures of, the company or any other body corporate, being the company's subsidiary or holding company or a subsidiary of the company's holding company;

(b) the entering into by him of a contract to sell any such shares or debentures;

(c) the assignment by him of a right granted to him by the company to subscribe for shares in, or debentures of, the company; and

(d) the grant to him by another body corporate, being the company's subsidiary or holding company or a subsidiary of the company's holding company, of a right to subscribe for shares in, or debentures of, that other body corporate, the exercise of such a right granted to him and the assignment by him of such a right so granted;

stating the number or amount, and class, of shares or debentures involved.

(3) The provisions of section 54 shall have effect for the interpretation of, and otherwise in relation to, subsections (1) and (2).

(4) Section 56 shall have effect with respect to the periods within which obligations imposed by subsections (1) and (2) on persons must be fulfilled by them.

(5) Section 57 shall have effect with respect to certain circumstances in which obligations imposed by subsections (1) and (2) are to be treated as not discharged.

(6) In the case of a person who is a director or secretary of a company at the time when this section comes into operation subsection (2) shall not require the notification by him of the occurrence of an event before that time; and that subsection shall not require the

notification by a person of the occurrence of an event whose occurrence comes to his knowledge after he has ceased to be a director or secretary.

(7) A person who fails to fulfil, within the proper period, an obligation to which he is subject by virtue of subsection (1) or (2) shall be guilty of an offence.

(8) An obligation imposed by this section shall be treated as not being fulfilled unless the notice by means of which it purports to be fulfilled is expressed to be given in fulfilment of that obligation.

(9) This section applies to shadow directors as to directors, but the making of a notification by a person under this section shall not, in itself, be proof that the person making the notification is a shadow director.

(10) Nothing in this section shall operate so as to impose an obligation with respect to shares in a body corporate which is the wholly owned subsidiary of another body corporate; and for this purpose a body corporate shall be deemed to be the wholly owned subsidiary of another if it has no members but that other and that other's wholly owned subsidiaries and its or their nominees.

(11) This section and sections 54, 56, 57 and 59 shall have effect in place of section 190 of the Principal Act and of so much of section 193 of that Act as relates to section 190, and that section and so much of section 193 as relates thereto shall, accordingly, cease to have effect.

Cross reference

For the proper period within which, see CA 1990, ss 4(2) and 56.

For the civil consequences of a failure to make disclosure within the 'proper period' see CA 1990, s 58(3)–(5).

See also CA 1990, s 66 for the power of the Minister to appoint an inspector to investigate suspected breaches of ss 53 and 64.

Definitions

'debenture': CA 1963, s 2(1); 'director': CA 1963, s 2(1); 'holding company': CA 1963, s 155; 'member': CA 1963, s 31; 'Principal Act': CA 1990, s 3(1); 'shadow director': CA 1990, s 3(1) s 27; 'share': CA 1963, s 2(1); 'subsidiary': CA 1963, s 155.

Notes

The duty on the part of a director or secretary to make a notification under this section is in addition to:

(a) the duty of 'persons discharging managerial responsibilities' to disclose their personal, family and corporate interests in shares of a company whose shares are admitted to trading on a regulated market, under the Market Abuse Regulations, reg 12;

(b) the duty of major shareholders in an Irish-incorporated public limited company whose shares are not admitted to trading on a regulated market, to make disclosure of interests in the 'relevant share capital' of the public limited company, under CA 1990, ss 67 *et seq,* and the related requirement to make disclosure of agreements to acquire shares in a public limited company;

(c) the duty of major shareholders in issuers whose shares are admitted to trading on a regulated market in Ireland to disclose voting rights held, under the Transparency Regulations, Pt 5 and related Financial Regulator Transparency Rules; and

(d) the duty of shareholders in a company subject to the Irish Takeover Rules or the Substantial Acquisition Rules to notify certain dealings in shares in such a company.

Paragraph 11.10.5 of the First Report of the CLRG noted a number of anomalies:

(a) 'A director's salary will be disclosed, in the aggregate, some months following the financial year's end. On the other hand, share options or the acquisition or disposal of shares go (or at least are meant to go) on the public record immediately.

(b) The delivery of a stock transfer form is considered insufficient notification of an interest – the notification must state that it is being made for the purposes of s 53 of the 1990 Act. Therefore a director and a company may honestly disclose the identity of the directors and their shareholdings in the register of directors and register of members respectively, but because of failure to make an otiose notification under this law, the rights attaching to the shares are unenforceable.

(c) A notification cannot be made on the day of acquisition – it must be on the day after or during the four business days after that date.

(d) An honest failure to notify an interest in shares is remediable only by applying to the High Court to restore enforceability of rights attaching to shares.'

Unsurprisingly, the Report recommended substantial amendments to these provisions in respect of which certain submissions to the Review Group suggested a 'slight' level of compliance.

The reference in CA 1990, s 53(i) to 'body corporate', means that the company's holding company, subsidiary or fellow subsidiaries may be incorporated outside the State or may be an Industrial and Provident Society or other body corporate: CA 1963, s 2(3).

Whilst this part of the 1990 Act has various curious and anomalous effects, this first section provides us with a taste of what is to follow. For example, Company A is the wholly owned subsidiary of Company B. The director has no interest in the shares of Company B, but pursuant to an agreement with that company, is entitled to control the exercise of all voting rights on shares in Company A. In such circumstances the director is interested in the shares of Company A, but because it is a wholly owned subsidiary of Company B, no disclosure obligation arises.

UK legislation

See CA 1985, s 324.

---

54 Nature of an interest within section 53

(1) The provisions of this section shall apply in determining for the purposes of section 53 whether a person has an interest in shares or debentures.

(2) Any reference to an interest in shares or debentures shall be read as including a reference to any interest of any kind whatsoever in shares or debentures; and accordingly there shall be disregarded any restraints or restrictions to which the exercise of any right attached to the interest is or may be subject.

(3) Where any property is held on trust and any interest in shares or debentures is comprised in that property, any beneficiary of that trust who, apart from this subsection, does not have an interest in the shares or debentures shall be taken to have such an interest; but this subsection is without prejudice to the following provisions of this section.

(4) A person shall be taken to have an interest in shares or debentures if—

(a) he enters into a contract for their purchase by him (whether for cash or other consideration); or

(b) not being the registered holder, he is entitled to exercise any right conferred by the holding of those shares or debentures or is entitled to control the exercise of any such right.

(5) A person shall be taken to be interested in shares or debentures if a body corporate is interested in them and—

(a) that body corporate or its directors are accustomed to act in accordance with his directions or instructions; or

(b) he is entitled to exercise or control the exercise of one-third or more of the voting power at general meetings of that body corporate.

(6) Where a person is entitled to exercise or control the exercise of one-third or more of the voting power at general meetings of a body corporate and that body corporate is entitled to exercise or control the exercise of any of the voting power at general meetings of another body corporate (the 'relevant voting power'), then, for the purposes of subsection (5)(b), the relevant voting power shall be taken to be exercisable by that person.

(7) A person shall be taken to have an interest in shares or debentures if, otherwise than by virtue of having an interest under a trust—

(a) he has a right to call for delivery of the shares or debentures to himself or to his order; or

(b) he has a right to acquire an interest in shares or debentures or is under an obligation to take an interest in shares or debentures;

whether in any case the right or obligation is conditional or absolute.

(8) For the purposes of subsection (4)(b) a person shall be taken to be entitled to exercise or control the exercise of any right conferred by the holding of shares or debentures if he has a right (whether subject to conditions or not) the exercise of which would make him so entitled or is under an obligation (whether so subject or not) the fulfilment of which would make him so entitled.

(9) A person shall not by virtue of subsection (4)(b) be taken to be interested in any shares or debentures by reason only that he has been appointed a proxy to vote at a specified meeting of a company or of any class of its members and at any adjournment of that meeting or has been appointed by a body corporate to act as its representative at any meeting of a company or of any class of its members.

(10) Without prejudice to subsection (2), rights or obligations to subscribe for any shares or debentures shall not be taken for the purposes of subsection (7) to be rights to acquire, or obligations to take, any interest in shares or debentures.

(11) Where persons have a joint interest each of them shall be deemed to have that interest.

(12) It is immaterial that shares or debentures in which a person has an interest are unidentifiable.

(13) Delivery to a person's order of shares or debentures in fulfilment of a contract for the purchase thereof by him or in satisfaction of a right of his to call for delivery thereof, or failure to deliver shares or debentures in accordance with the terms of such a contract or on which such a right falls to be satisfied, shall be deemed to constitute an event in consequence of the occurrence of which he ceases to be interested in them, and so shall the lapse of a person's right to call for delivery of shares or debentures.

Cross reference

The reference to a 'body corporate' indicates that the company need not have been incorporated in the State or may be another kind of body corporate such as an Industrial and Provident Society.

Definitions

'debenture': CA 1963, s 2(1); 'director': CA 1963, s 2(1); 'member': CA 1963, s 31; 'share': CA 1963, s 2(1).

Notes

For example, subject to CA 1990, s 55(1)(d), a mortgagee or chargee of shares would be regarded as having an interest in the shares. See also CA 1990, s 64 which deems a director or secretary to be interested in shares or debentures in which his spouse or minor children have an interest. See CA 1990, s 54(2).

Where shares are held in the name of a nominee, the person on whose behalf the nominee acts will be treated as having an interest in the shares. See CA 1990, s 54(3).

A person could, for example, be regarded as having an interest in shares where although not the registered shareholder, he is entitled to control the exercise of the votes attaching to the shares or is entitled to receive any dividends declared or other distributions made in respect of the shares. Furthermore, subject to CA 1990, s 55(1)(d), a mortgage or chargee of shares would be regarded as having an interest in the shares. See CA 1990, s 54(4)(b).

Thus a shadow director would be regarded as having an interest in any shares held by the body corporate. See CA 1990, s 54(5)(a).

UK legislation

See CA 1985, Sch 13, Pt 1 (amended by FSA 1986, s 212, Sch 16).

---

55 Interests to be disregarded

(1) The following interests shall be disregarded for the purposes of section 54 and sections 56 to 58—

(a) where property is held on trust and an interest in shares or debentures is comprised in that property, an interest in reversion or remainder or of a bare trustee and any discretionary interest;

(b) an interest of a person subsisting by virtue of—

(i) his holding units in—

(I) a registered unit trust scheme within the meaning of section 3 of the Unit Trusts Act, 1972;

(II) a unit trust to which section 31 of the Capital Gains Tax Act, 1975, as amended by section 34 of the Finance Act, 1977 relates;

(III) an undertaking for collective investment in transferable securities, within the meaning of the European Communities (Undertakings for Collective Investment in Transferable Securities) Regulations, 1989 (S.I. No 78 of 1989);

(ii) a scheme made under section 46 of the Charities Act, 1961;

(c) an interest for the life of himself or another of a person under a settlement in the case of which the property comprised in the settlement consists of or includes shares or debentures, and the conditions mentioned in subsection (3) are satisfied;

(d) an interest in shares or debentures held by a member of a recognised stock exchange carrying on business as a stock broker which is held by way of security only for the purposes of a transaction entered into by the person or body concerned in the ordinary course of business of such person or body;

(e) such interests, or interests of such a class, as may be prescribed for the purposes of this paragraph by regulations made by the Minister.

(2) A person shall not by virtue of section 54(4)(b) be taken to be interested in shares or debentures by reason only that he has been appointed a proxy to vote at a specified meeting of a company or of any class of its members and at any adjournment of that meeting, or has been appointed by a body corporate to act as its representative at any meeting of a company or of any class of its members.

(3) The conditions referred to in subsection (1)(c) are, in relation to a settlement—

(a) that it is irrevocable, and

(b) that the settlor (within the meaning of section 96 of the Income Tax Act, 1967) has no interest in any income arising under, or property comprised in, the settlement.

Cross reference

Registered unit trusts, as referred to in the Unit Trusts Act 1972 are now superseded by authorised unit trusts, under the Unit Trusts Act 1990.

Definitions

'debenture': CA 1963, s 2(1); 'member': CA 1963, s 31; 'Minister': CA 1990, s 3(1); 'prescribe': CA 1990, s 3(1); 'recognised stock exchange': CA 1990, s 3(1); 'share': CA 1963, s 2(1).

Notes

Interests in a discretionary trust may be taken into account, where as a matter of practice and expectation, the trustees exercise their discretion in favour of the director or secretary.

No regulations have been made regarding s 55(1)(e).

Section 55(2) is an unnecessary repetition of s 54(9).

---

56 Periods within which obligations under section 53 must be discharged

(1) An obligation imposed on a person by section 53(1) to notify an interest must, if he knows of the existence of the interest on the relevant day (that is to say, in a case in which he is a director or secretary at the beginning of the day on which that section comes into operation, the last previous day, and, in a case in which he thereafter becomes a director or secretary, the day on which he becomes it), be fulfilled before the expiration of the period of five days beginning with the day next following the relevant

day; otherwise it must be fulfilled before the expiration of the period of five days beginning with the day next following that on which the existence of the interest comes to his knowledge.

(2) An obligation imposed on a person by section 53(2) to notify the occurrence of an event must, if at the time at which the event occurs he knows of its occurrence, be fulfilled before the expiration of the period of five days beginning with the day next following that on which it occurs; otherwise, it must be fulfilled before the expiration of the period of five days beginning with the day next following that on which the occurrence of the event comes to his knowledge.

Cross reference

As to the contents of the disclosure notice, see CA 1990, s 57.

See CA 1990, s 4(2) in relation to how the period of five days is computed.

Definitions

'director': CA 1963, s 21.

UK legislation

See CA 1985, Sch 13, Pt II.

57 Circumstances in which obligation under section 53 is not discharged

(1) Where an event of whose occurrence a director or secretary is, by virtue of section 53(2)(a), under obligation to notify a company consists of his entering into a contract for the purchase by him of shares or debentures, the obligation shall be taken not to be discharged in the absence of inclusion in the notice of a statement of the price to be paid by him under the contract, and an obligation imposed on a director or secretary by virtue of section 53(2)(b) shall be taken not to be discharged in the absence of inclusion in the notice of the price to be received by him under the contract.

(2) An obligation imposed on a director or secretary by virtue of section 53(2)(c) to notify a company shall be taken not to be discharged in the absence of inclusion in the notice of a statement of the consideration for the assignment (or, if it be the case that there is no consideration, that fact), and where an event of whose occurrence a director is, by virtue of section 53(2)(d), under obligation to notify) a company consists in his assigning a right, the obligation shall be taken not to be discharged in the absence of inclusion in the notice of a similar statement.

(3) Where an event of whose occurrence a director or secretary is, by virtue of section 53 (2)(d), under obligation to notify a company consists in the grant to him of a right to subscribe for shares or debentures, the obligation shall not be taken to be discharged in the absence of inclusion in the notice of a statement of—

(a) the date on which the right was granted,

(b) the period during which or time at which the right is exercisable,

(c) the consideration for the grant (or, if it be the case that there is no consideration, that fact), and

(d) the price to be paid for the shares or debentures.

(4) Where an event of whose occurrence a director or secretary is, by virtue of section 53 (2)(d), under obligation to notify a company consists in the exercise of a right granted to him to subscribe for shares or debentures, the obligation shall be taken not to be discharged in the absence of inclusion in the notice of a statement of—

(a) the number of shares or amount of debentures in respect of which the right was exercised, and

(b) if it be the case that they were registered in his name, that fact, and, if not, the name or names of the person or persons in whose name or names they were registered,

together (if they were registered in the names of two persons or more) with the number or amount thereof registered in the name of each of them.

(5) For the purposes of this section any reference, however expressed, to any price paid, given or received in respect of any interest in shares or debentures shall be construed as including a reference to any consideration other than money given or received in respect of any such interest.

Definitions

'debenture': CA 1963, s 2(1); 'director': CA 1963, s 2(1); 'share': CA 1963, s 2(1).

Note

The curious way that these provisions were drafted (for which the only fault of the Irish legislators has been the faithful transcription of the original provisions of the UK 1985 Act) is exemplified by this section. Rather than there being a transparent duty imposed, eg to disclose the price under a share purchase contract, instead 'the obligation … shall be taken not to be discharged in the absence of inclusion in the notice of the price to be received … under the contract'.

UK legislation

See CA 1985, Sch 13, Pt I (amended by FSA 1986, s 212, Sch 16).

---

58 Other provisions relating to notification

(1) Where a person authorises any other person ('the agent') to acquire or dispose of, on his behalf, interests in shares in, or debentures of, a company, he shall secure that the agent notifies him immediately of acquisitions or disposals of interests in such shares or debentures effected by the agent which will or may give rise to any obligation on his part to make a notification under this Chapter with respect to his interest in those shares or debentures.

(2) An obligation to make any notification imposed on any person by this Chapter shall be treated as not being fulfilled unless the notice by means of which it purports to be fulfilled identifies him and gives his address.

(3) Where a person fails to fulfil, within the proper period, an obligation to which he is subject by virtue of section 53, no right or interest of any kind whatsoever in respect of the shares or debentures concerned shall be enforceable by him, whether directly or indirectly, by action or legal proceeding.

(4) Where any right or interest is restricted under subsection (3), any person in default under that subsection or any other person affected by such restriction may apply to the

court for relief against a disability imposed by or arising out of subsection (3) and the court on being satisfied that the default was accidental, or due to inadvertence, or some other sufficient cause, or that on other grounds it is just and equitable to grant relief, may grant such relief either generally, or as respects any particular right or interest on such terms and conditions as it sees fit.

(5) Where an applicant for relief under subsection (4) is a person referred to in subsection (3), the court may not grant such relief if it appears that the default has arisen as a result of any deliberate act or omission on the part of the applicant.

(6) Subsection (3) shall not apply to an obligation relating to a person ceasing to be interested in shares in, or debentures of, a company.

(7) A person who fails without reasonable excuse to comply with subsection (1) shall be guilty of an offence.

Cross reference

See CA 1990, s 79 for comparable provisions punishing non-compliance with the disclosure régime for major shareholders in public limited companies.

Definitions

'court': CA 1990, s 235; 'debenture': CA 1963, s 2(1); 'share': CA 1963, s 2(1).

Notes

Section 58(1) would be of relevance, for example, where the director or secretary has appointed a stockbroker to buy and sell shares on his behalf but has left the time and amount of any acquisition or disposal to the stockbroker's discretion.

Section 58(3) is superficially harsh since it prevents the director or secretary from exercising any rights in respect of the shares or debentures, not only where there has been no disclosure at all, but also where the disclosure has been marginally late and has thus fallen outside the 'proper period'. The only legal option in such circumstances would be to apply to the court for relief under sub-s (4). However, in practice, it is open to the company to recognised the directors rights, even if the director cannot enforce them.

---

59 Register of interests

(1) Every company shall keep a register for the purposes of section 53.

(2) Whenever the company receives information from a director or secretary in consequence of the fulfilment of an obligation imposed on him by that section, the company shall enter in the register, against the name of that person, that information and the date of the entry.

(3) Every company shall, whenever it grants to a director or secretary a right to subscribe for shares in, or debentures of, the company, enter in the register against his name—

- (a) the date on which the right is granted,
- (b) the period during which or time at which it is exercisable,
- (c) the consideration for the grant (or, if it be the case that there is no consideration, that fact), and

(d) the description of shares or debentures involved and the number or amount thereof, and the price to be paid therefor.

(4) Whenever such a right as is mentioned in subsection (3) is exercised by a director or secretary, the company shall enter in the said register against his name that fact (identifying the right), the number or amount of shares or debentures in respect of which it is exercised and, if it be the case that they were registered in his name, that fact, and, if not, the name or names of the person or persons in whose name or names they were registered, together (if they were registered in the names of two persons or more) with the number or amount thereof registered in the name of each of them.

(5) This section applies to shadow directors as to directors.

Definitions

'debenture': CA 1963, s 2(1); 'director': CA 1963, s 2(1): 'shadow director': CA 1990, s 3(1), s 27; 'share': CA 1963, s 2(1).

UK legislation

See CA 1985, s 325.

---

60 Provisions relating to register

(1) The register to be kept under section 59 shall be so made up that the entries therein against the several names inscribed therein appear in chronological order.

(2) An obligation imposed by section 59(2) to (4) shall be fulfilled before the expiration of the period of 3 days beginning with the day next following that on which it arises.

(3) The nature and extent of an interest recorded in the said register of a director or secretary in any shares or debentures shall, if he so requires, be recorded in the said register.

(4) The company shall not, by virtue of anything done for the purposes of this section, be affected with notice of, or put upon inquiry as to, the rights of any person in relation to any shares or debentures.

(5) The said register shall—

(a) if the company's register of members is kept at its registered office, be kept there;

(b) if the company's register of members is not so kept, be kept at the company's registered office or at the place where its register of members is kept;

and shall during business hours (subject to such reasonable restrictions as the company in general meeting may impose, so that not less than two hours in each day be allowed for inspection) be open to the inspection of any member of the company without charge and of any other person on payment of [38 cents][a] or such less sum as the company may prescribe for each inspection.

(6) The company shall send notice to the registrar of companies of the place where the said register is kept and of any change in that place, save in a case in which it has at all times been kept at its registered office.

(7) Unless the said register is in such a form as to constitute in itself an index, the company shall keep an index of the names entered therein which shall—

(a) in respect of each name, contain a sufficient indication to enable the information inscribed against it to be readily found; and

(b) be kept at the same place as the said register;

and the company shall, within 14 days after the date on which a name is entered in the said register, make any necessary alteration in the index.

(8) Any member of the company or other person may require a copy of the said register, or of any part thereof, on payment of [19 cents][b] or such less sum as the company may prescribe, for every hundred words or fractional part thereof required to be copied.

The company shall cause any copy so required by any person to be sent to that person within the period of 10 days beginning with the day next following that on which the requirement is received by the company.

(9) The said register shall also be and remain open and accessible to any person attending the company's annual general meeting at least one quarter hour before the appointed time for the commencement of the meeting and during the continuance of the meeting.

[(10) If default is made in compliance with subsection (9), the company and every officer of the company who is in default shall be guilty of an offence and liable to a fine not exceeding €1,904.61 and if default is made for 14 days in complying with subsection (6) the company and every officer of the company who is in default shall be guilty of an offence and liable to a fine not exceeding €1,904.61; and if default is made in complying with section 59 or with subsection (1), (2) or (7) of this section or if an inspection required under this section is refused or any copy required thereunder is not sent within the proper period the company and every officer of the company who is in default shall be guilty of an offence and liable to a fine not exceeding €1,904.61.][c]

(11) In the case of a refusal of an inspection required under this section of the said register, the court may by order compel an immediate inspection thereof; and in the case of a failure to send within the proper period a copy required under this section, the court may by order direct that the copy required shall be sent to the person requiring it.

Amendments

a '30p' converted to 38 cents by Council Regulations (EC) No 1103/97, No 974/98 and No 2866/98 and the European and Monetary Union Act 1998, s 6.

b '15p' converted to 19 cents by Council Regulations (EC) No 1103/97, No 974/98 and No 2866/98 and the European and Monetary Union Act 1998, s 6.

c Substituted by IFCMPA 2005, s 73(2)(a).

Cross reference

For the places at which the register of members may be kept, see CA 1963, s 116(5), (6).

Definitions

'court': CA 1990, s 235; 'debenture' CA 1963, s 2(1); 'director': CA 1963, s 2(1); 'officer': CA 1963, s 2(1); 'officer in default': CA 1963, s 383, as amended by CLEA 2001, s 100; 'member'

CA 1963, s 31; 'prescribe': CA 1990, s 3(1); 'registrar of companies': CA 1963, s 2(1); 'share': CA 1963, s 2(1).

Notes

The company cannot however disregard notice of beneficial or equitable interests in the shares or debentures of which it has actual notice.[1] See s 60(4).

Whereas a non-member's inspection of the register of members or register of directors stands to yield the sum of 7 cents or €1.27 respectively, an inspection of the register in this case yields 38 cents.

[1] *Rearden v Provincial Bank of Ireland* [1896] 1 IR 532.

UK legislation

CA 1985, Sch 13, Pt IV (amended by CA 1989, ss 143, 212).

---

61 Removal of entries from register

(1) A company may remove an entry against a person's name from the register of interests in shares and debentures kept under section 59 if more than 6 years has elapsed since the date of the entry being made, and either—

(a) that entry recorded the fact that the person in question has ceased to have an interest notifiable under this Chapter in shares in, or debentures of, the company, or

(b) it has been superseded by a later entry made under the said section 59 against the same person's name;

and in a case within paragraph (a) the company may also remove that person's name from the register.

(2) Where a name is removed from a company's register of interests in shares or debentures in pursuance of subsection (1), the company shall within 14 days of the date of that removal make any necessary alterations in any associated index.

(3) If default is made in complying with subsection (2), the company and every officer of it who is in default shall be guilty of an offence and liable to a fine.

Definitions

'debenture' CA 1963, s 2(1); 'officer': CA 1963, s 2(1); 'officer in default': CA 1963, s 383, as amended by CLEA 2001, s 100.

Notes

An entry may be superseded by a subsequent related entry eg a first entry on the grant of an option, and a second entry when it is subsequently exercised.

---

62 Entries, when not to be removed

(1) Entries in a company's register of interests in shares and debentures under this Chapter shall not be deleted except in accordance with section 61.

(2) If an entry is deleted from a company's register of interests in shares in contravention of subsection (1), the company shall restore that entry to the register as soon as is reasonable and practicable.

(3) If default is made in complying with subsection (1) or (2), the company and every officer of it who is in default shall be guilty of an offence and liable to a fine.

Definitions

'contravention': CA 1990, s 3(1); 'debenture' CA 1963, s 2(1); 'officer': CA 1963, s 2(1); 'officer in default': CA 1963, s 383, as amended by CLEA 2001, s 100; 'share': CA 1963, s 2(1).

63 Disclosure of interests in directors' report

(1) Subject to subsection (2), the directors' report or the notes to the company's accounts in respect of a financial year shall, as respects each person who, at the end of that year, was a director of the company, state—

(a) whether or not he was, at the end of that year, interested in shares in, or debentures of, the company or any other body corporate being the company's subsidiary or holding company or a subsidiary of the company's holding company;

(b) if he was so interested—

(i) the number and amount of shares in, and debentures of, each body (specifying it) in which he was then interested,

(ii) whether or not he was, at the beginning of that year (or, if he was not then a director, when he became a director), interested in shares in, or debentures of, the company or any other such body corporate, and,

(iii) if he was, the number and amount of shares in, and debentures of, each body (specifying it) in which he was interested at the beginning of that year or, as the case may be, when he became a director.

(2) The reference in subsection (1) to the directors' report and the notes to the company's accounts are references to the report and notes respectively which are required by virtue of the Companies (Amendment) Act, 1986 to be annexed to the Annual Return and where a company does not annex the report of the directors, as permitted by section 10(2) of the aforementioned Act, the information required in subsection (1) shall be contained in the notes to the company's accounts.

(3) The references in subsection (1) to the time when a person became a director shall, in the case of a person who became a director on more than one occasion, be construed as referring to the time when he first became a director.

(4) For the purposes of this section 'the directors' report' means the report by the directors of a company which, by section 158(1) of the Principal Act, is required to be attached to every balance sheet of the company.

(5) The information required by subsection (1) to be given in respect of the directors of the company shall also be given in respect of the person who was the secretary of the company at the end of the financial year concerned.

Definitions

'debenture' CA 1963, s 2(1); 'director': CA 1963, s 2(1); 'financial year': CA 1963, s 2(1); 'Principal Act': CA 1990, s 3(1); 'share': CA 1963, s 2(1).

Notes

The C(A)A 1986 does not apply to unlimited companies; instead, CA 1963, s 128 imposes comparable provisions for unlimited companies, but they are not applied to private companies.

The exemption in C(A)A 1986, s 10(2) applies to 'small companies'.

UK legislation

CA 1985, Sch 7 paras 2, 2A, 2B.

64 Extension of section 53 to spouses and children

(1) For the purposes of section 53—

(a) an interest of the spouse of a director or secretary of a company (not being himself or herself a director or secretary thereof) in shares or debentures shall be treated as being the director's or secretary's interest, and

(b) the same applies to an interest of a minor child of a director or secretary of a company (not being himself or herself a director or secretary thereof) in shares or debentures.

(2) For those purposes—

(a) a contract, assignment or right of subscription entered into, exercised or made by, or grant made to, the spouse of a director or secretary of a company (not being himself or herself a director or secretary thereof) shall be treated as having been entered into, exercised or made by, or, as the case may be, as having been made to, the director or secretary, and

(b) the same applies to a contract, assignment or right of subscription entered into, exercised or made by, or grant made to, a minor child of a director or secretary of a company (not being himself or herself a director or secretary thereof).

(3) A director or secretary of a company shall be under obligation to notify the company in writing of the occurrence, while he or she is director or secretary, of either of the following events, namely—

(a) the grant to his or her spouse or minor child by the company, of a right to subscribe for shares in, or debentures of, the company; and

(b) the exercise by the spouse or minor child of such a right as aforesaid granted by the company to the spouse or child.

(4) In a notice given to the company under subsection (3) there shall be stated—

(a) in the case of the grant of a right, the like information as is required by section 53 to be stated by the director or secretary on the grant to him by another body corporate of a right to subscribe for shares in, or debentures of, that other body corporate, and

(b) in the case of the exercise of a right, the like information as is required by that section to be stated by the director or secretary on the exercise of a right granted to him by another body corporate to subscribe for shares in, or debentures of, that other body corporate.

(5) An obligation imposed by subsection (3) on a director or secretary must be fulfilled by him before the expiration of the period of 5 days beginning with the day next following that on which the occurrence of the event that gives rise to it comes to his knowledge.

(6) A person who fails to fulfil, within the proper period, an obligation to which he is subject under subsection (3) shall be guilty of an offence.

(7) The provisions set out in sections 54 and 55, shall have effect for the interpretation of, and otherwise in relation to, subsections (1) and (2), and subsections (8) and (9) of section 53, shall, with any requisite modification, have effect for the purposes of this section as they have effect for the purposes of that section.

(8) For the purposes of section 59 an obligation imposed on a director or secretary by this section shall be treated as if imposed by section 53.

Cross reference

See CA 1990, s 66 for power of the inspector to investigate suspected breaches of ss 53, 54.

The Market Abuse (Directive 2003/6/EC) Regulations 2005 (SI 342/2005), reg 12(8) imposes a comparable responsibility on 'persons discharging managerial responsibilities' (PDMRs) to disclose the interests of persons with a connection to the PDMRs. As would be expected there is no particular harmony between this section and that regulation. The one key – and most notable – exclusion from the duty to notify under this section and under that regulation is that of a cohabiting partner, which does not require to be notified or made known under either provision.

Definitions

'child': CA 1990, s 3(1); 'debenture' CA 1963, s 2(1); 'director': CA1963, s 2(1); 'share': CA 1963, s 2(1).

UK legislation

CA 1985, s 238.

---

65 Duty of company to notify stock exchange

(1) Whenever a company in the case of whose shares or debentures dealing facilities are provided by a recognised stock exchange is notified of any matter by a director or secretary in consequence of the fulfilment of an obligation imposed on him by section 53 or 64, and that matter relates to shares or debentures for which such dealing facilities are provided, the company shall be under an obligation to notify that stock exchange of that matter; and the stock exchange may publish, in such manner as it may determine, any information received by it under this subsection.

(2) An obligation imposed by subsection (1) must be fulfilled before the end of the day next following that on which it arises.

(3) If default is made in complying with this section, the company and every officer of the company who is in default shall be guilty of an offence.

Definitions

'debenture': CA 1963, s 2(1); 'director': CA 1963, s 2(1); 'officer': CA 1963, s 2(1); 'officer in default': CA 1963, s 383, as amended by CLEA 2001, s 100; 'recognised stock exchange': CA 1990, s 3(1), (2); 'share': CA 1963, s 2(1).

UK legislation

CA 1985 (amended by FSA 1986, s 212).

66 Investigation of share dealing

(1) If it appears to the [Director][a] that there are circumstances suggesting that contraventions may have occurred, in relation to shares in, or debentures of, a company, of section 30, 53 or 64(3) to (5) he may appoint one or more competent inspectors to carry out such investigations as are requisite to establish whether or not contraventions have occurred as aforesaid and to report the result of their investigations to the [Director].[a]

(2) The appointment under this section of an inspector may limit the period to which his investigation is to extend or confine it to shares or debentures of a particular class or both.

(3) For the purposes of any investigation under this section, section 10 shall apply—

- (a) with the substitution, for references to any other body corporate whose affairs are investigated by virtue of section 9, of a reference to any other body corporate which is, or has at any relevant time been, the company's subsidiary or holding company, and
- (b) with the necessary modification of the reference, in section 10(5), to the affairs of the company or other body corporate, so, however, that it shall apply to members of a recognised stock exchange who are individuals and to officers (past as well as present) of members of such an exchange who are bodies corporate as it applies to officers of the company or of the other body corporate.

(4) The inspectors may, and, if so directed by the [Director],[a] shall, make interim reports to the [Director],[a] and, on the conclusion of the investigation, shall make a final report to the [Director][a].

(5) Any such report shall be written or printed, as the [Director][a] may direct, and the [Director][a] may cause it to be published.

(6) Sections 9, 16 to 18, 22, 23(1) and 23(3) shall, with any necessary modifications, apply for the purposes of this section.

(7) The expenses of an investigation under this section shall be defrayed by the Minister.

(8) Where a person is convicted of an offence on a prosecution instituted as a result of the investigation the High Court may, on the application of the [Director],[a] order that person to pay the said expenses to such extent as the court may direct.

Amendments

a 'Director' substituted for 'Minister' by CLEA 2001, s 14 as enacted by the Company Law Enforcement Act 2001 (Commencement) (No 3) Order 2001 (SI 523/2001) on 28 November 2001.

Definitions

'contravention': CA 1990, s 3(1); 'court': CA 1990, s 235; 'debenture': CA 1963, s 2(1); 'Minister': CA 1990, s 3(1); 'recognised stock exchange': CA 1990, s 3(1), (2); 'share': CA 1963, s 2(1).

Notes

In reaching a decision whether to appoint an inspector, the Director is not bound by the rules of natural justice.[1] Provided he acts in good faith, the Director is not required to give specific reasons for the appointment and in the warrant of appointment he need only specify the section or sections which he claims may have been contravened.[2]

If the inspector does determine facts relevant to the investigation, then he has a duty and power to include that information in his report. And if he is unable to make a positive determination as to relevant facts, but is able to form an opinion in relation thereto, he has a duty to include his findings in his report.[3]

A decision by the Director not to publish the report cannot be challenged by way of judicial review unless he mis-directed himself on questions of law or took into account irrelevant matters, or ignored relevant matters, or if his decision was wholly unreasonable in the circumstances, or if there was some other serious and substantial defect in the procedure which let to his decision.[4]

1 *Norwest Holst Ltd v Secretary of State for Trade* [1978] 3 All ER 280.

2 *Norwest Holst Ltd v Secretary of State for Trade* [1978] 3 All ER 280; *R v Secretary of State for Trade, ex p Perestrell* [1981] QB 19; *Desmond and Dedeir v Glackin* (25 February 1992, unreported) HC and (30 July 1992, unreported) SC.

3 *Lyons v Curran* [1993] ILRM 375.

4 *Lonrho plc v Secretary of State for Trade and Industry* [1989] 2 All ER 609.

UK legislation

See CA 446, as amended by FSA 1986, ss 182, 212 as amended by CA 1989, s 212).

Chapter 2
Individual and Group Acquisitions

67 Obligation of disclosure and the cases in which it may arise

(1) Where a person either—

(a) to his knowledge acquires an interest in shares comprised in a public limited company's relevant share capital, or ceases to be interested in shares so comprised (whether or not retaining an interest in other shares so comprised), or

(b) becomes aware that he has acquired an interest in shares so comprised or that he has ceased to be interested in shares so comprised in which he was previously interested, then, subject to the provisions of sections 68 to 79, he shall be under an obligation ('the obligation of disclosure') to make notification to the company of the interests which he has, or had, in its shares.

(2) In relation to a public limited company, 'relevant share capital' means the company's issued share capital of a class carrying rights to vote in all circumstances at general meetings of the company and it is hereby declared for the avoidance of doubt that—

(a) where a company's relevant share capital is divided into different classes of shares, references in this Chapter to a percentage of the nominal value of its relevant share capital are to a percentage of the nominal value of the issued shares comprised in each of the classes taken separately, and

(b) the temporary suspension of voting rights in respect of shares comprised in issued share capital of a company of any such class does not affect the application of this Chapter in relation to interests in those or any other shares comprised in that class.

(3) Where, otherwise than in circumstances within subsection (1), a person—

(a) is aware at the time when it occurs of any change of circumstances affecting facts relevant to the application of the next following section to an existing interest of his in shares comprised in a company's share capital of any description, or

(b) otherwise becomes aware of any such facts (whether or not arising from any such change of circumstances),

then, subject to the provisions of sections 68 to 79, he shall be under the obligation of disclosure.

(4) The acquisition by any person of an interest in shares or debentures of a company registered in the State shall be deemed to be a consent by that person to the disclosure by him, his agents or intermediaries of any information required to be disclosed in relation to shares or debentures by the Companies Acts.

Cross reference

The requirement to disclose an interest in shares is in addition to:

- the duty of directors and secretaries to disclose their personal, family and corporate interests in shares or debentures of a company under CA 1990, ss 53 *et seq*;
- the duty of 'persons discharging managerial responsibilities' to disclose their personal, family and corporate interests in shares of a company whose shares are admitted to trading on a regulated market, under the Market Abuse Regulations, reg 12; and
- the duty of shareholders in a company subject to the Irish Takeover Rules or the Substantial Acquisition Rules to notify dealings in shares in such a company.

The Transparency Regulations 2007, reg 81 provides that the obligation of disclosure under Chapter 2 of Part IV of CA 1990 and the related provisions of that Chapter does not apply to—

(a) an acquisition or disposal of shares which must be notified under those Regulations, or

(b) an acquisition or disposal of shares which, but for an express exemption provided by or under those Regulations (whether the word 'exempted' is used or not), would be required to be notified under those Regulations.

Definitions

'Companies Acts': CA 1990, s 3(1); 'debenture': CA 1963, s 2(1); 'share': CA 1963, s 2(1).

UK legislation

CA 1985, s 198.

---

68 Interests to be disclosed

(1) For the purposes of the obligation of disclosure, the interests to be taken into account are those in relevant share capital of the company concerned.

(2) A person has a notifiable interest at any time when he is interested in shares comprised in that share capital of an aggregate nominal value equal to or more than the percentage of the nominal value of that share capital which is for the time being the notifiable percentage.

(3) All facts relevant to determining whether a person has a notifiable interest at any time (or the percentage level of his interest) are taken to be what he knows the facts to be at that time.

(4) The obligation of disclosure arises under section 67(1) or (3) where the person has a notifiable interest immediately after the relevant time, but did not have such an interest immediately before that time.

(5) The obligation also arises under section 67(1) where—

(a) the person had a notifiable interest immediately before the relevant time, but does not have such an interest immediately after it, or

(b) he had a notifiable interest immediately before that time, and has such an interest immediately after it, but the percentage levels of his interest immediately before and immediately after that time are not the same.

(6) For the purposes of this section, 'the relevant time' means—

(a) in a case within section 67(1)(a) or (3)(a), the time of the event or change of circumstances there mentioned, and

(b) in a case within section 67(1)(b) or (3)(b), the time at which the person became aware of the facts in question.

Definitions

'share': CA 1963, s 2(1).

Notes

If the share capital is divided into different classes, disclosure is required if the person has a 'notifiable interest' in shares of the particular class or classes concerned. See CA 1990, s 67(2)(a).

The effect of sub-ss (4), (5), taken with CA 1990, ss 69, 70 is that a person must make disclosure to the company if:

(a) he was interested in less than 5% of the relevant share capital before the transaction, and as a result of the transaction is now interested in 5% or more of the relevant share capital;

(b) he was interested in 5% or more of the relevant share capital before the transaction and as a result of the transaction is not interested in less than 5% of the relevant share capital;

(c) he was interest in 5% or more of the relevant share capital before the transaction and as a result of the transaction the level of his interest has altered but is still 5% or more of the relevant share capital.

UK legislation

CA 1985, s 199, as amended by CA 1989, s 134.

---

69 'Percentage level' in relation to notifiable interests

(1) Subject to the qualification mentioned below, 'percentage level', in section 68 (5)(b), means the percentage figure found by expressing the aggregate nominal value of all the shares comprised in the share capital concerned in which the person is interested immediately before or (as the case may be) immediately after the relevant time as a percentage of the nominal value of that share capital and rounding that figure down, if it is not a whole number, to the next whole number.

(2) Where the nominal value of the share capital is greater immediately after the relevant time than it was immediately before, the percentage level of the person's interest immediately before (as well as immediately after) that time is determined by reference to the larger amount.

Definitions

'share': CA 1963, s 2(1).

Notes

If the share capital is divided into different classes, regard must be had to the percentage level of the particular class or classes concerned rather than the entire of the relevant share capital. See CA 1990, s 67(2)(a).

UK legislation

CA 1985, s 200.

---

70 The notifiable percentage

(1) The reference in section 68(2) to the notifiable percentage. is to 5 per cent, or such other percentage as may be prescribed by the Minister under this section.

(2) The Minister may prescribe the percentage to apply in determining whether a person's interest in a company's shares is notifiable under section 67; and different percentages may be prescribed in relation to companies of different classes or descriptions.

(3) Where in consequence of a reduction prescribed under this section in the percentage made by such order a person's interest in a company's shares becomes notifiable, he shall then come under the obligation of disclosure in respect of it; and the obligation must be performed within the period of 10 days next following the day on which it arises.

Definitions

'Minister': CA 1990, s 3(1); 'prescribe': CA 1990, s 3(1); 'share': CA 1963, s 2(1).

Notes

The relevant percentage level in the UK is 3%. It used be fairly common for shares in Irish quoted plcs to be twinned with shares in a UK or Northern Irish plc, so as to facilitate choice of source of dividends, in view of historically differing taxation treatments of dividends received from Irish and UK sources. Although the taxation reason for those twin share schemes has now passed, the fact of their existence means that in practice, many major shareholders are obliged to notify at the 3% level rather than the 5% level.

UK legislation

CA 1985, s 200.

---

71 Particulars to be contained in notification

(1) Subject to section 70(3) a person's obligation to make a notification under section 67 must be performed within the period of 5 days next following the day on which the obligation arises; and the notification must be in writing to the company.

(2) The notification must specify the share capital to which it relates, and must also—

(a) state the number of shares comprised in that share capital in which the person making the notification knows he was interested immediately after the time when the obligation arose, or

(b) in a case where the person no longer has a notifiable interest in shares comprised in that share capital, state that he no longer has that interest.

(3) A notification with respect to a person's interest in a company's relevant share capital (other than one stating that he no longer has a notifiable interest in shares comprised in that share capital) shall include particulars of—

(a) the identity of each registered holder of shares to which the notification relates, and

(b) the number of those shares held by each such registered holder,

so far as known to the person making the notification at the date when the notification is made.

(4) A person who has an interest in shares comprised in a company's relevant share capital, that interest being notifiable, is under obligation to notify the company in writing—

(a) of any particulars in relation to those shares which are specified in subsection (3), and

(b) of any change in those particulars,

of which in either case he becomes aware at any time after any interest notification date and before the first occasion following that date on which he comes under any further obligation of disclosure with respect to his interest in shares comprised in that share capital.

An obligation arising under this section must be performed within the period of 5 days next following the day on which it arises.

(5) The reference in subsection (4) to an interest notification date, in relation to a person's interest in shares comprised in a public limited company's relevant share capital, is to either of the following—

(a) the date of any notification made by him with respect to his interest under this Part, and

(b) where he has failed to make a notification, the date on which the period allowed for making it came to an end.

(6) A person who at any time has an interest in shares which is notifiable is to be regarded under subsection (4) as continuing to have a notifiable interest in them unless and until he comes under obligation to make a notification stating that he no longer has such an interest in those shares.

Cross reference

For the civil consequences of a failure to make disclosure within the 'proper period' see CA 1990, s 79 (3)–(8).

Definitions

'share': CA 1963, s 2(1).

UK legislation

CA 1985, s 202, as amended by CA 1989, s 134.

---

72 Notification of family and corporate interests

(1) For the purposes of sections 67 to 71 a person is taken to be interested in any shares in which his spouse or any minor child of his is interested.

(2) For those purposes, a person is taken to be interested in shares if a body corporate is interested in them and—

(a) that body or its directors are accustomed to act in accordance with his directions or instructions, or

(b) he is entitled to exercise or control the exercise of one-third or more of the voting power at general meetings of that body corporate.

(3) Where a person is entitled to exercise or control the exercise of one-third or more of the voting power at general meetings of a body corporate and that body corporate is entitled to exercise or control the exercise of any of the voting power at general meetings of another body corporate ('the effective voting power') then, for the purposes of subsection (2)(b), the effective voting power is taken as exercisable by that person.

(4) For the purposes of subsections (2) and (3) a person is entitled to exercise or control the exercise of voting power if—

(a) he has a right (whether subject to conditions or not) the exercise of which would make him so entitled, or

(b) he is under an obligation (whether or not so subject) the fulfilment of which would make him so entitled.

Cross reference

The reference to a 'body corporate' indicates that the company need not have been incorporated in the State: CA 1963, s 2(3).

Definitions

'child': CA 1990, s 3(1); 'director': CA 1963, s 2(1): 'share': CA 1963, s 2(1).

Notes

A shadow director would be regarded as having an interest in any shares held by the body corporate, under s 72(2)(a).

Under s 72(4) a person will be deemed to control the exercise of one third or more of the voting power at general meetings of the body corporate if he has entered into a legally binding contract to purchase shares enjoying such voting power, but the contract has yet to be completed.

A person could thus be regarded as having voting power at general meetings where, although not a registered shareholder of the body corporate, shares are held on his behalf by nominees or where he has entered into an agreement with shareholders of the body corporate, the terms of which entitle him to control the manner in which they exercise the votes attaching to their shares.

For example, a person will be deemed to be under an obligation the fulfilment of which would entitle him to exercise or control the exercise of voting power at general meetings of the body corporate if he has entered into a legally binding contract to purchase shares enjoying such voting power, but the contract has yet to be completed.

UK legislation

See CA 1985, s 203.

---

73 Agreement to acquire interests in a public limited company

(1) Subject to the following provisions of this section an agreement between two or more persons which includes provision for the acquisition by any one or more of the parties to the agreement of interests in shares comprised in relevant share capital of a particular public limited company ('the target company') is an agreement to which this section applies if—

(a) it also includes provisions imposing obligations or restrictions on any one or more of the parties to the agreement with respect to their use, retention or disposal of interests in that company's shares acquired in pursuance of the agreement (whether or not together with any other interests of theirs in that company's shares to which the agreement relates); and

(b) any interest in the company's shares is in fact acquired by any of the parties in pursuance of the agreement;

and in relation to such an agreement references in this section, and in sections 74 and 75, to the target company are to the company which is the target company for that agreement in accordance with this section.

(2) The reference in subsection (1)(a) to the use of interests in shares in the target company is to the exercise of any rights or of any control or influence arising from those interests (including the right to enter into any agreement for the exercise, or for control of the exercise, of any of those rights by another person).

(3) Once any interest in shares in the target company has been acquired in pursuance of such an agreement as is mentioned above, this section continues to apply to that agreement irrespective of—

(a) whether or not any further acquisitions of interests in the company's shares take place in pursuance of the agreement, and

(b) any change in the persons who are for the time being parties to it, and

(c) any variation of the agreement, so long as the agreement continues to include provisions of any description mentioned in subsection (1)(a).

References in this subsection to the agreement include any agreement having effect (whether directly or indirectly) in substitution for the original agreement.

(4) In this section, and also in references elsewhere in this Part to an agreement to which this section applies, 'agreement' includes any agreement or arrangement; and references in this section to provisions of an agreement—

(a) accordingly include undertakings, expectations or understandings operative under any arrangement, and

(b) (without prejudice to the above) also include any provisions, whether express or implied and whether absolute or not.

(5) This section does not apply to an agreement which is not legally binding unless it involves mutuality in the undertakings, expectations or understandings of the parties to it; nor does the section apply to an agreement to underwrite or sub-underwrite any offer of shares in a company, provided the agreement is confined to that purpose and any matters incidental to it.

Cross reference

The obligations of disclosure and the criteria by reference to which an obligation of disclosure arises are different from and in addition to those applicable to persons 'acting in concert' under the Takeover Rules.

Definitions

'share': CA 1963, s 2(1).

Notes

This section and CA 1990, ss 74, 75 apply where two or more persons are acting in concert for the purpose of acquiring shares in the company. In such circumstances, they are deemed to be interested in one another's shareholdings in the company, for the purpose of determining whether either or all of them have 'notifiable interests'.

For example, A and B acting in concert, each acquire 3% of the relevant share capital of the company, and agree to act in support of one another in relation to the exercise of voting rights. Together they have control of 6% of the voting shares, yet but for ss 73–75, they would not have to make disclosure pursuant to Chapter 2, unless one of them buys shares in consequence of the agreement.

UK legislation

CA 1985, s 204.

---

74 Obligation of disclosure arising under section 73

(1) In the case of an agreement to which section 73 applies, each party to the agreement shall be taken (for purposes of the obligation of disclosure) to be interested in all shares in the target company in which any other party to it is interested apart from the agreement (whether or not the interest of the other party in question was acquired, or includes any interest which was acquired, in pursuance of the agreement).

(2) For those purposes, and also for those of section 75, an interest of a party to such an agreement in shares in the target company is an interest apart from the agreement if he is interested in those shares otherwise than by virtue of the application of section 73 and this section in relation to the agreement.

(3) Accordingly, any such interest of the person (apart from the agreement) includes for those purposes any interest treated as his under section 72 or by the application of section 73 and this section in relation to any other agreement with respect to shares in the target company to which he is a party.

(4) A notification with respect to his interest in shares in the target company made to that company under this Part by a person who is for the time being a party to an agreement to which section 73 applies shall—

- (a) state that the person making the notification is a party to such an agreement,
- (b) include the names and (so far as known to him) the addresses of the other parties to the agreement, identifying them as such, and
- (c) [illegible] or not any of the shares to which the notification relates are shares in which he is interested by virtue of section 73 and this section and, if so, the number of those shares.

(5) Where a person makes a notification to a company under this Part in consequence of ceasing to be interested in any shares of that company by virtue of the fact that he or any other person has ceased to be a party to an agreement to which section 73 applies, the notification shall include a statement that he or that other person has ceased to be a party to the agreement (as the case may require) and also (in the latter case) the name and (if known to him) the address of that other.

Definitions

'share': CA 1963, s 2(1).

Notes

Section 74(1) and (2) make it clear that each party to the agreement is deemed to be interested not only in his own shares but also in all other relevant share capital held by his fellow parties, regardless of whether or not the shares were acquired in pursuance of their agreement.

The effect of s 74(3) is as follows—

- (a) Party A is deemed to be interest in shares in which a body corporate is interested where that body corporate is controlled by Party B;
- (b) Party A is deemed to be interested in shares in which the spouse and/or minor children of by Concert Party B are interested; and
- (c) Party B is also party to a similar agreement with C, then Party A is deemed to be interest in the shares in which Party C is interested.

UK legislation

CA 1985, s 205.

75 Obligation of persons acting together to keep each other informed

(1) A person who is a party to an agreement to which section 73 applies shall be subject to the requirements of this section at any other time when—

- (a) the target company is a public limited company, and he knows it to be so, and
- (b) the shares in that company to which the agreement relates consist of or include shares comprised in relevant share capital of the company, and he knows that to be the case, and
- (c) he knows the facts which make the agreement one to which section 73 applies.

(2) Such a person shall be under obligation to notify every other party to the agreement, in writing, of the relevant particulars of his interest (if any) apart from the agreement in shares comprised in relevant share capital of the target company—

- (a) on his first becoming subject to the requirements of this section, and
- (b) on each occurrence after that time while he is still subject to those requirements of any event or circumstances within section 67(1) (as it applies to his case otherwise than by reference to interests treated as his under section 74 as applying to that agreement).

(3) The relevant particulars to be notified under subsection (2) are—

- (a) the number of shares (if any) comprised in the target company's relevant share capital in which the person giving the notice would be required to state his interest if he were under the obligation of disclosure with respect to that interest (apart from the agreement) immediately after the time when the obligation to give notice under subsection (2) arose, and
- (b) the relevant particulars with respect to the registered ownership of those shares, so far as known to him at the date of the notice.

(4) A person who is for the time being subject to the requirements of this section shall be under obligation to notify every other party to the agreement, in writing—

- (a) of any relevant particulars with respect to the registered ownership of any shares comprised in relevant share capital of the target company in which he is interested apart from the agreement, and
- (b) of any change in those particulars, of which in either case he becomes aware at any time after any interest notification date and before the first occasion following that date on which he becomes subject to any further obligation to give notice under subsection (2) with respect to his interest in shares comprised in that share capital.

(5) The reference in subsection (4) to an interest notification date, in relation to a person's interest in shares comprised in the target company's relevant share capital, is to either of the following—

- (a) the date of any notice given by him with respect to his interest under subsection (2), and

(b) where he has failed to give that notice, the date on which the period allowed by this section for giving the notice came to an end.

(6) A person who is a party to an agreement to which section 73 applies shall be under an obligation to notify each other party to the agreement, in writing, of his current address—

(a) on his first becoming subject to the requirements of this section, and

(b) on any change in his address occurring after that time and while he is still subject to those requirements.

(7) A reference to the relevant particulars with respect to the registered ownership of shares is to such particulars in relation to those shares as are mentioned in section 71 (3)(a) or (b).

(8) A person's obligation to give any notice required by this section to any other person must be performed within the period of 5 days next following the day on which that obligation arose.

Definitions

'share': CA 1963, s 2(1).

Notes

The purpose of s 75 is to ensure that each party to a s 73 agreement is fully informed of the extent to which his fellow parties are interested in the relevant share capital of the company, and thus to be in a position to determine whether, because of s 73, he has a notifiable interest. See also CA 1990, s 76 and in particular s 76(5).

UK legislation

CA 1985, s 206 as amended by CA 1989, s 134.

---

76 Interest in shares by attribution

(1) Where section 67 or 68 refers to a person acquiring an interest in shares or ceasing to be interested in shares, that reference in certain cases includes his becoming or ceasing to be interested in those shares by virtue of another person's interest.

(2) This section applies where he becomes or ceases to be interested by virtue of section 72 or (as the case may be) section 74 whether—

(a) by virtue of the fact that the person who is interested in the shares becomes or ceases to be a person whose interests (if any) fall by virtue of either section to be treated as his, or

(b) in consequence of the fact that such a person has become or ceased to be interested in the shares, or

(c) in consequence of the fact that he himself becomes or ceases to be a party to an agreement to which section 73 applies to which the person interested in the shares is for the time being a party, or

(d) in consequence of the fact that an agreement to which both he and that person are parties becomes or ceases to be one to which the said section 73 applies.

(3) The person shall be treated under section 67 as knowing he has acquired an interest in the shares or (as the case may be) that he has ceased to be interested in them, if and when he knows both—

(a) the relevant facts with respect to the other person's interest in the shares, and

(b) the relevant facts by virtue of which he himself has become or ceased to be interested in them in accordance with section 72 or 74.

(4) He shall be deemed to know the relevant facts referred to in subsection (3)(a) if he knows (whether contemporaneously or not) either of the subsistence of the other person's interest at any material time or of the fact that the other has become or ceased to be interested in the shares at any such time; and 'material time' is any time at which the other's interests (if any) fall or fell to be treated as his under section 72 or 74.

(5) A person is to be regarded as knowing of the subsistence of another's interest in shares or (as the case may be) that another has become or ceased to be interested in shares if he has been notified under section 75 of facts with respect to the other's interest which indicate that he is or has become or ceased to be interested in the shares (whether on his own account or by virtue of a third party's interest in them).

Definitions

'share': CA 1963, s 2(1).

UK legislation

CA 1985, s 207.

77 Interests in shares which are to be notified

(1) This section applies, subject to section 78, in determining for purposes of sections 67 to 71 whether a person has a notifiable interest in shares.

(2) A reference to an interest in shares is to be read as including an interest of any kind whatsoever in the shares. Accordingly there are to be disregarded any restraints or restrictions to which the exercise of any right attached to the interest is or may be subject.

(3) Where property is held on trust and an interest in shares is comprised in the property, a beneficiary of the trust who apart from this subsection does not have an interest in the shares is to be taken as having such an interest; but this subsection is without prejudice to the following provisions of this section.

(4) A person is taken to have an interest in shares if—

(a) he enters into a contract for their purchase by him (whether for cash or other consideration), or

(b) not being the registered holder, he is entitled to exercise any right conferred by the holding of the shares or is entitled to control the exercise of any such right.

(5) For the purposes of subsection (4)(b), a person is entitled to exercise or control the exercise of any right conferred by the holding of shares if he—

(a) has a right (whether subject to conditions or not) the exercise of which would make him so entitled, or

(b) is under an obligation (whether so subject or not) the fulfilment of which would make him so entitled.

(6) A person is taken to have an interest in shares if, otherwise than by virtue of having an interest under a trust—

(a) he has a right to call for delivery of the shares to himself or to his order, or

(b) he has a right to acquire an interest in shares or is under an obligation to take an interest in shares,

whether in any case the right or obligation is conditional or absolute.

(7) Without prejudice to subsection (2), rights or obligations to subscribe for any shares shall not be taken for the purposes of subsection (6) to be rights to acquire, or obligations to take, any interest in shares.

(8) Where persons have a joint interest each of them shall be taken to have that interest.

(9) It is immaterial that shares in which a person has an interest are unidentifiable.

(10) Delivery to a person's order of shares in fulfilment of a contract for the purchase thereof by him or in satisfaction of a right of his to call for delivery thereof, or failure to deliver shares in accordance with the terms of such a contract or on which such a right falls to be satisfied, shall be deemed to constitute an event in consequence of the occurrence of which he ceases to be interested in them, and so shall the lapse of a person's right to call for delivery of shares.

Definitions

'share': CA 1963, s 2(1).

Notes

See, for example, CA 1990, s 72 which deems a director or secretary to be interested in shares or debentures in which his spouse or minor children have an interest or in which a body corporate controlled by him has an interest. Furthermore, subject to CA 1990, s 78(4), a mortgagee or chargee of shares would be regarded as having an interest in the shares.

In s 77(3), for example, where shares are held in the name of a nominee, the person on whose behalf the nominee acts, will be treated as having an interest in the shares.

A person could, for example, be regarded as having an interest in shares where, although not the registered shareholder, he is entitled to control the exercise of the votes attaching to the shares or is entitled to receive any dividends declared or other distributions made in respect of the shares. In this regard, see also sub-ss (5)(a) and (b).

In s 77(5)(b), a person will be deemed to be under an obligation the fulfilment of which would entitle him to exercise or control the exercise of rights conferred by the holding of shares if he has entered into a legally binding contract to purchase shares enjoying such voting power, but the contract has yet to be completed. In this regard, see sub-s (4)(a).

UK legislation

CA 1985, s 208.

---

78 Interests to be disregarded

(1) The following interests in shares shall be disregarded for the purposes of sections 67 to 71—

(a) where property is held on trust and an interest in shares is comprised in that property, an interest in reversion or remainder or of a bare trustee and any discretionary interest;

(b) an interest of a person subsisting by virtue of—

(i) his holding units in—

(I) a registered unit trust scheme within the meaning of section 3 of the Unit Trusts Act, 1972;

(II) a unit trust to which section 31 of the Capital Gains Tax Act, 1975, as amended by section 34 of the Finance Act, 1977, relates;

(III) an undertaking for collective investment in transferable securities, within the meaning of the European Communities (Undertakings for Collective Investment in Transferable Securities) Regulations, 1989 (S.I. No 78 of 1989); or

(ii) a scheme made under section 46 of the Charities Act, 1961;

(c) an interest for the life of himself or another of a person under a settlement in the case of which the property comprised in the settlement consists of or includes shares, and the conditions mentioned in subsection (3) are satisfied;

(d) an exempt security interest;

(e) an interest of the President of the High Court subsisting by virtue of section 13 of the Succession Act, 1965;

(f) an interest of the Accountant of the High Court in shares held by him in accordance with rules of court;

(g) such interests, or interests of such a class, as may be prescribed for purposes of this paragraph by regulations made by the Minister.

(2) A person shall not by virtue of section 77(4)(b) be taken to be interested in shares by reason only that he has been appointed a proxy to vote at a specified meeting of a company or of any class of its members and at any adjournment of that meeting, or has been appointed by a body corporate to act as its representative at any meeting of a company or of any class of its members.

(3) The conditions referred to in subsection (1)(c) are, in relation to a settlement—

(a) that it is irrevocable, and

(b) that the settlor (within the meaning of section 96 of the Income Tax Act, 1967) has no interest in any income arising under, or property comprised in, the settlement.

(4) An interest in shares is an exempt security interest for purposes of subsection (1)(d) if—

(a) it is held by—

(i) the holder of a licence under section 9 of the Central Bank Act, 1971, or an insurance company within the meaning of the Insurance Acts, 1909 to 1990,

(ii) a trustee savings bank (within the meaning of the Trustee Savings Banks Acts, 1863 to 1979) or a Post Office Savings Bank within the meaning of the Post Office Savings Bank Acts, 1861 to 1958,

(iii) [...][a] [...][b]

(iv) a member of a recognised stock exchange carrying on business as a stockbroker, and

(b) it is held by way of security only for the purposes of a transaction entered into by the person or body concerned in the ordinary course of business of such person or body.

Amendments

a Section 73(4)(a)(iii) repealed by ACC Bank Act 2001, s 12(1) and Pt 1 of the Schedule.

b The words 'or Industrial Credit Corporation plc' deleted by ICC Bank Act 2000, s 7(1) and Pt 1 of the Schedule.

Definitions

'court': CA 1990, s 235; 'member': CA 1963, s 31; 'Minister': CA 1990, s 3(1); 'recognised stock exchange': CA 1990, s 3(1), (2); 'share': CA 1963, s 2(1).

Notes

Interests in discretionary trust may be taken into account, where as a matter of practice, the trustees exercise their discretion in favour of the director.

Registered unit trusts, as referred to in the Unit Trusts 1972 Act are now superseded by authorised unit trusts, under the Unit Trusts Act 1990.

To date no regs have been made under s 78(1)(g).

The effect of s 78(4)(a)(i) is to require credit institutions and overseas banks which are not the holders of a Central Bank Licence.

The Irish Stock Exchange has been prescribed as a recognised stock exchange pursuant to the Companies (Stock Exchange) Regulations1995 (SI 310/1995).

UK legislation

See CA 1985, s 209.

---

79 Other provisions relating to notification

(1) Where a person authorises any other person ('the agent') to acquire or dispose of, on his behalf, interests in shares comprised in relevant share capital of a public limited company, he shall secure that the agent notifies him immediately of acquisitions or disposals of interests in shares so comprised effected by the agent which will or may give rise to any obligation on his part to make a notification under this Chapter with respect to his interest in that share capital.

(2) An obligation to make any notification imposed on any person by this Chapter shall be treated as not being fulfilled unless the notice by means of which it purports to be fulfilled identifies him and gives his address, and in a case where he is a director or secretary of the company, is expressed to be given in fulfilment of that obligation.

(3) Where a person—

(a) fails to fulfil, within the proper period, an obligation to make any notification required by this Chapter; or

(b) in purported fulfilment of any such obligation makes to a company a statement which he knows to be false or recklessly makes to a company a statement which is false; or

(c) fails to fulfil, within the proper period, an obligation to give any other person any notice required by section 75,

no right or interest of any kind whatsoever in respect of any shares in the company concerned, held by him, shall be enforceable by him, whether directly or indirectly, by action or legal proceeding.

(4) Where any right or interest is restricted under subsection (3), any person in default under that subsection or any other person affected by such restriction may apply to the court for relief against a disability imposed by or arising out of subsection (3) and the court on being satisfied that the default was accidental, or due to inadvertence, or some other sufficient cause, or that on other grounds it is just and equitable to grant relief, may grant such relief either generally, or as respects any particular right or interest on such terms and conditions as it sees fit.

(5) Where an applicant for relief under subsection (4) is a person referred to in subsection (3), the court may not grant such relief if it appears that the default has arisen as a result of any deliberate act or omission on the part of the applicant.

(6) Subsection (3) shall not apply to an obligation relating to a person ceasing to be interested in shares in any company.

(7) A person who—

(a) fails to fulfil, within the proper period, an obligation of disclosure imposed on him by this Chapter, or

(b) fails to fulfil, within the proper period, an obligation to give any other person a notice required by section 75, or

[(bb) fails to fulfil, within the period of 5 days next following the day on which he becomes aware of the matters referred to in section 91(2), the obligation to give the Exchange (within the meaning of that section) a notice required by that section, or][a]

(c) fails without reasonable excuse to comply with subsection (1),

shall be guilty of an offence.

(8) It shall be a defence for a person charged with an offence under subsection (7)(b) to prove that it was not possible for him to give the notice to that other person required by section 75 within the proper period, and either—

(a) that it has not since become possible for him to give the notice so required; or

(b) that he gave that notice as soon after the end of that period as it became possible for him to do so.

Amendments

a CLEA 2001, s 35 inserts CA 1990, s 79(7)(bb).

Definitions

'court': CA 1990, s 235; 'director': CA 1963, s 2(1); 'share': CA 1963, s 2(1).

Notes

Section 79(1) would be of relevance, for example, where the director or secretary has appointed a stockbroker to buy and sell shares on his behalf but has left the time and amount of any acquisition or disposal to the stockbroker's discretion.

The provisions of s 79(5) can be harsh since they prevent the shareholder from exercising any rights in respect of the shares or debentures, not only where there has been no disclosure or false or reckless disclosure, but also where the disclosure has been marginally late and has thus fallen outside the 'proper period'. The only option in such circumstances would be to apply to the court for relief under s 79(4).

It can catch the most likely of shareholders unawares. For example, just before the IPO of Bord Telecom Éireann plc, all the major shareholders, including two Government Ministers were concerned at the discovery that Telecom had not been informed formally of the shareholding agreements entered into with the Government when Telecom went public in 1996. Each of them brought applications under this section on 28 June 1999. Kelly J noted, generously, that the notification provisions in Chapter 2, Part 4 of the 1990 Companies Act were 'quite detailed and technical'. Noting that the court had a discretion to give relief from the consequences of the disabilities in s 79(3), he was satisfied that if there was any failure to comply with the notification provisions it was due to inadvertence and that nobody had been prejudiced or was likely to be prejudiced as a result of that failure. In the circumstances, it was just and equitable to grant the relief sought: (1999) *The Irish Times*, 29 June.

UK legislation

CA 1985, s 213.

---

80 Register of interests in shares

(1) Every public limited company shall keep a register for purposes of sections 67 to 71 and whenever the company receives information from a person in consequence of the fulfilment of an obligation imposed on him by any of those sections, it is under obligation to inscribe in the register, against that person's name, that information and the date of the inscription.

(2) Without prejudice to subsection (1), where a company receives a notification under this Part which includes a statement that the person making the notification, or any other person, has ceased to be a party to an agreement to which section 73 applies, the company shall be under obligation to record that information against the name of that person in every place where his name appears in the register as a party to that agreement (including any entry relating to him made against another person's name).

(3) An obligation imposed by subsection (1) or (2) must be fulfilled within the period of 3 days next following the day on which it arises.

(4) The nature and extent of an interest recorded in the said register of a person in any shares shall, if he so requires, be recorded in the said register.

(5) The company shall not, by virtue of anything done for the purposes of this section, be affected with notice of, or put upon enquiry as to, the rights of any person in relation to any shares.

(6) The register must be so made up that the entries against the several names entered in it appear in chronological order.

(7) Unless the register is in such form as to constitute in itself an index, the company shall keep an index of the names entered in the register which shall in respect of each name contain a sufficient indication to enable the information entered against it to be readily found; and the company shall, within 10 days after the date on which a name is entered in the register, make any necessary alteration in the index.

(8) If the company ceases to be a public limited company it shall continue to keep the register and any associated index until the end of the period of 6 years beginning with the day next following that on which it ceases to be such a company.

(9) The register and any associated index—

(a) shall be kept at the place at which the register required to be kept by the company by section 59 (register of directors' and secretaries' interests) is kept, and

(b) shall be available for inspection in accordance with section 88.

(10) If default is made in complying with any of the provisions of this section, the company and every officer of it who is in default [shall be guilty of an offence and liable to a fine][a] not exceeding [€1,904.61],[b] and for continued contravention, to a daily default fine not exceeding [€63.49].[c]

Amendments

a Words inserted by C(AA)A 2003, Sch 2.

b £1,000 increased to £1,500 by CA 1990, s 240(7) (as inserted by CLEA 2001, s 104) and converted to €1,904.61 by Council Regulations (EC) No 1103/97, No 974/98 and No 2866/98 and the Economic and Monetary Union Act 1998, s 6.

c £50 converted to €63.49 by Council Regulations (EC) No 1103/97, No 974/98 and No 2866/98 and the Economic and Monetary Union Act 1998, s 6.

Cross reference

For the places at which the register of members may be kept, see CA 1963, s 116(5), (6).

Definitions

'contravention': CA 1990, s 3(1); 'daily default fine': CA 1990, s 3(1), s 240(1); 'director': CA 1963, s 2(1); 'officer': CA 1963, s 2(1); 'officer in default': CA 1963, s 383, as amended by CLEA 2001, s 100; 'share': CA 1963, s 2(1).

Notes

The company cannot however disregard notice of beneficial or equitable interests in the shares or debentures.[1]

1 *Rearden v Provincial Bank of Ireland* [1896] 1 IR 532.

UK legislation

CA 1985, s 213.

81 Company investigations

(1) A public limited company may by notice in writing require a person whom the company knows or has reasonable cause to believe to be or, at any time during the 3 years immediately preceding the date on which the notice is issued (but excluding any

time before the commencement of this section), to have been interested in shares comprised in the company's relevant share capital—

(a) to confirm that fact or (as the case may be) to indicate whether or not it is the case, and

(b) where he holds or has during that time held an interest in shares so comprised, to give such further information as may be required in accordance with the following subsection.

(2) A notice under this section may require the person to whom it is addressed—

(a) to give particulars of his own past or present interest in shares comprised in relevant share capital of the company (held by him at any time during the 3 year period mentioned in subsection (1)),

(b) where the interest is a present interest and any other interest in shares subsists or, in any case, where another interest in the shares subsisted during that 3 year period at any time when his own interest subsisted, to give (so far as lies within his knowledge) such particulars with respect to that other interest as may be required by the notice,

(c) where his interest is a past interest, to give (so far as lies within his knowledge) particulars of the identity of the person who held that interest immediately upon his ceasing to hold it.

(3) The particulars referred to in subsection (2)(a) and (2)(b) include particulars of the identity of persons interested in the shares in question and of whether persons interested in the same shares are or were parties to any agreement to which section 73 applies or to any agreement or arrangement relating to the exercise of any rights conferred by the holding of the shares.

(4) A notice under this section shall require any information given in response to the notice to be given in writing within such reasonable time as may be specified in the notice.

(5) Sections 72 to 74 and 77 apply for the purpose of construing references in this section to persons interested in shares and to interests in shares respectively, as they apply in relation to sections 67 to 70 (but with the omission of any reference to section 78).

(6) This section applies in relation to a person who has or previously had, or is or was entitled to acquire, a right to subscribe for shares in a public limited company which would on issue be comprised in relevant share capital of that company as it applies in relation to a person who is or was interested in shares so comprised; and references in this section to an interest in shares so comprised and to shares so comprised are to be read accordingly in any such case as including respectively any such right and shares which would on issue be so comprised.

Definitions

'share': CA 1963, s 2(1).

Notes

A notice may be served on a person under s 81 even where that person is resident abroad.[1]

What is reasonable will depend on the circumstances. In the middle of a takeover offer or suspected stake-building, periods measured in hours rather than days may be reasonable.

The effect of s 81(5) appears to be that the plc may even require disclosure of interests that would otherwise be disregarded pursuant to CA 1990, s 78.

Section 81(6) clearly overrides CA 1990, s 77(7) which provides that the right to subscribe for shares is not to be regarded as an interest in shares.

1 *Re FH Lloyd Holdings plc* [1985] BCLC 293.

UK legislation

CA 1985, s 212.

---

82 Registration of interests disclosed under section 81

(1) Whenever in pursuance of a requirement imposed on a person under section 81 a company receives information to which this section applies relating to shares comprised in its relevant share capital, it is under obligation to enter against the name of the registered holder of those shares, in a separate part of its register of interests in shares—

(a) the fact that the requirement was imposed and the date on which it was imposed, and

(b) any information to which this section applies received in pursuance of the requirement.

(2) This section applies to any information received in pursuance of a requirement imposed by section 81 which relates to the present interests held by any persons in shares comprised in relevant share capital of the company in question.

(3) Subsections (3) to (10) of section 80 apply in relation to any part of the register maintained in accordance with subsection (1) of this section, reading references to subsection (1) of that section to include subsection (1) of this section.

Definitions

'share': CA 1963, s 2(1).

Notes

Apart from registering the details of the person's interests in a separate part of the register, the company should enter the information beside the person's name in the register, for ease of reference.

The requirement to enter these particulars in the register arises only for information disclosed pursuant to a notice under s 81, not a notice served under bespoke provisions in the company's articles of association, which are fairly common in the case of quoted public companies.

UK legislation

CA 1985, s 213.

---

83 Company investigations on requisition by members

(1) A company may be required to exercise its powers under section 81 on the requisition of members of the company holding at the date of the deposit of the requisition not less than one-tenth of such of the paid-up capital of the company as carries at that date the right of voting at general meetings of the company.

(2) The requisition must—

(a) state that the requisitionists are requiring the company to exercise its powers under section 81,

(b) specify the manner in which they require those powers to be exercised, and

(c) give reasonable grounds for requiring the company to exercise those powers in the manner specified,

and must be signed by the requisitionists and deposited at the company's registered office.

(3) The requisition may consist of several documents in like form each signed by one or more requisitionists.

(4) On the deposit of a requisition complying with this section the company shall exercise its powers under section 81 in the manner specified in the requisition.

(5) If default is made in complying with subsection (4), the court may, on the application of the requisitionists, or any of them, and on being satisfied that it is reasonable to do so, require the company to exercise its powers under section 81 in a manner specified in the order.

Definitions

'court': CA 1990, s 235; 'member' CA 1963, s 31.

UK legislation

CA 1985, s 214.

---

84 Company report to members

(1) On the conclusion of an investigation carried out by a company in pursuance of a requisition under section 83 it is the company's duty to cause a report of the information received in pursuance of that investigation to be prepared, and the report shall be made available at the company's registered office within a reasonable period after the conclusion of that investigation.

(2) Where—

(a) a company undertakes an investigation in pursuance of a requisition under section 83, and

(b) the investigation is not concluded before the end of 3 months beginning with the date immediately following the date of the deposit of the requisition,

the company shall cause to be prepared, in respect of that period and each successive period of 3 months ending before the conclusion of the investigation, an interim report of the information received during that period in pursuance of the investigation. Each such report shall be made available at the company's registered office within a reasonable period after the end of the period to which it relates.

(3) The period for making any report prepared under this section available as required by subsection (1) or (2) shall not exceed 15 days.

(4) The company shall, within 3 days of making any report prepared under this section available at its registered office, notify the requisitionists that the report is so available.

(5) An investigation carried out by a company in pursuance of a requisition under section 83 shall be regarded for the purposes of this section as concluded when the company has made all such inquiries as are necessary or expedient for the purposes of the requisition and in the case of each such inquiry, either a response has been received by the company or the time allowed for a response has elapsed.

(6) A report prepared under this section—

(a) shall be kept at the company's registered office from the day on which it is first available there in accordance with subsection (1) or (2) until the expiration of 6 years beginning with the day next following that day, and

(b) shall be available for inspection in accordance with section 88 so long as it is so kept.

(7) If default is made in complying with subsection (1), (2), (3), (4) or (6)(a), the company and every officer of the company who is in default shall be guilty of an offence and be liable to a fine.

Definitions

'member' CA 1963, s 31; 'officer': CA 1963, s 2(1); 'officer in default': CA 1963, s 383, CLEA 2001, s 100.

Notes

If the company does determine facts relevant to the investigation, then it has a duty and power to include that information in its report. If it is unable to make a definitive determination as to relevant facts, but is able to form an opinion thereto, it should include its findings in the report.[1]

Section 84 does not oblige the company either to inform other members of the company of the making of the report or to furnish a copy of the report to persons criticised or accused. However, disclosure to affected persons would appear to be implied as a requirement of natural justice.[2]

There is no requirement on the company under this section to make the report available after the expiry of the six-month period.

1 *Lyons v Curran* [1993] ILRM 375.

2 *Re Haughey* [1971] IR 217; *Re Pergamon Press Ltd* [1970] 3 All ER; *Maxwell v Department of Trade and Industry* [1974] QB 523.

---

85 Penalty for failure to provide information

(1) Where notice is served by a company under section 81 on a person who is or was interested in shares of the company and that person fails to give the company any information required by the notice within the time specified in it, the company may apply to the court for an order directing that the shares in question be subject to restrictions under section 16.

(2) Such an order may be made by the court notwithstanding any power contained in the applicant company's memorandum or articles enabling the company itself to impose similar restrictions on the shares in question.

(3) Subject to the following subsections, a person who fails to comply with a notice under section 81 shall be guilty of an offence.

(4) A person shall not be guilty of an offence by virtue of failing to comply with a notice under section 81 if he proves that the requirement to give the information was frivolous or vexatious.

(5) Where an order is made under this section directing that shares shall be subject to restrictions under section 16, the company or any person aggrieved by the order may apply to the court for an order directing that the shares shall cease to be subject thereto.

(6) Subsections (6) to (16) of section 16 shall apply in relation to any shares subject to the restrictions imposed by that section by virtue of an order under this section but with the omission in subsections (6) to (15) of any reference to the [Director][a].

Amendments

a 'Director' substituted for 'Minister' by CLEA 2001, s 14 as enacted by the Company Law Enforcement Act 2001 (Commencement) (No 3) Order 2001 (SI 523/2001) on 28 November 2001.

Definitions

'articles': CA 1963, s 2(1); 'court': CA 1990, s 235; 'memorandum': CA 1963, s 2(1); 'Minister': CA 1990, s 3(1): CA 1963, s 2(1).

Notes

Although the court will not exercise its discretion under sub-s (1) where the company's requirement for information was frivolous or vexatious, it is not necessary for a company to show that it had a real ground for believing that the person interested in the shares was seeking to build up a substantial holding in the company.[1]

Since a plc has an unqualified right under CA 1990, s 81 to know the identity of the real owners of its shares, where it is shown that sufficient information has not been provided under a s 81 notice, the company is entitled to a restriction order and there is no need to show that damages would not be an adequate remedy or that the company would suffer loss if the information were not provided. In addition, it is no objection to the granting of an order freezing the shares that the board of the company is seeking the information to ward off a take-over bid.[2]

The court should not impose restrictions on shares under s 85 where the information requested has been furnished after the filing and before the hearing of the application.[3]

In exercising its discretion whether or not to make an order under s 85 the court will take into consideration the interests of innocent third parties. However, once the court has determined to make a restriction order, it cannot make the order in a modified form and it cannot qualify the restrictions set out in s 85.[4]

Although the company has a right under CA 1990, s 81 to obtain information as to the persons interested in its shares, the court may decline to grant a restriction order under s 85 where the effect of such an order would be to prevent a take-over bid from proceedings, thus prejudicing other shareholders who want to accept the bit.[5]

The costs of an application under s 85 are to be borne by the parties who failed to fully comply with the notice served by the company under CA 1990, s 81.[6] See *Re FH Lloyd Holdings plc*.[7]

Orders pursuant to s 85 imposing restrictions upon shares are granted to compel the provision of information to which the company is entitled and it follows that once the information has been supplied there is no justification for their continuance.[8]

The court will refuse to lift restrictions imposed pursuant to s 85 where the information requested by the company pursuant to CA 1990, s 81 has not been furnished to it.[9]

Where an application is made to discharge an order imposing restrictions on shares under s 85 and it is shown that the omissions to provide information as a result of which the order had been made have been rectified the order should be discharged. It is not a good reason for adjourning the application or continuing the order that the company wants an opportunity to produce evidence of new and different failures to provide the requisite information where there is no prima facie evidence of such failures before the court.

1 *Re FH Lloyd Holdings plc* [1985] BCLC 293.
2 *Re TR Technology Investment Trust plc* [1988] BCLC 256.
3 *Ricardo Group plc (No 2)* [1989] BCLC 766.
4 *Re Lonrho plc (No 4)* [1990] BCLC 151.
5 *Re Ricardo Group plc (No 3)* [1989] BCLC 771.
6 *Re Bestwood plc* [1989] BCLC 606.
7 *Re FH Lloyd Holdings plc* [1988] BCLC 293.
8 *Re Ricardo Group plc* [1989] BCLC 566.
9 *Re Geers Gross plc* [1988] BCLC 140.

UK legislation

CA 1985, s 216.

86 Removal of entries from register

(1) A company may remove an entry against a person's name from its register of interests in shares if more than 6 years have elapsed since the date of the entry being made, and either—

(a) that entry recorded the fact that the person in question had ceased to have an interest notifiable under this Chapter in relevant share capital of the company, or

(b) it has been superseded by a later entry made under section 80 against the same person's name;

and in a case within paragraph (a) the company may also remove that person's name from the register.

(2) If a person in pursuance of an obligation imposed on him by any provision of this Chapter gives to a company the name and address of another person as being interested in shares in the company, the company shall, within 15 days of the date on which it was given that information, notify the other person that he has been so named and shall include in that notification—

(a) particulars of any entry relating to him made, in consequence of its being given that information, by the company in its register of interests in shares, and

(b) a statement informing him of his right to apply to have the entry removed in accordance with the following provisions of this section.

(3) A person who has been notified by a company in pursuance of subsection (2) that an entry relating to him has been made in the company's register of interests in shares may apply in writing to the company for the removal of that entry from the register; and the company shall remove the entry if satisfied that the information in pursuance of which the entry was made was incorrect.

(4) If a person who is identified in a company's register of interests in shares as being a party to an agreement to which section 73 applies (whether by an entry against his own name or by an entry relating to him made against another person's name as mentioned in subsection (2)(a)) ceases to be a party to that agreement, he may apply in writing to the

company for the inclusion of that information in the register; and if the company is satisfied that he has ceased to be a party to the agreement, it shall record that information (if not already recorded) in every place where his name appears as a party to that agreement in the register.

(5) If an application under subsection (3) or (4) is refused (in a case within subsection (4), otherwise than on the ground that the information has already been recorded) the applicant may apply to the court for an order directing the company to remove the entry in question from the register or (as the case may be) to include the information in question in the register; and the court may, if it thinks fit, make such an order.

(6) Where a name is removed from a company's register of interests in shares in pursuance of subsection (1) or (3) or an order under subsection (5), the company shall within 14 days of the date of that removal make any necessary alteration in any associated index.

(7) If default is made in complying with subsection (2) or (6), the company and every officer of it who is in default shall be guilty of an offence and liable to a fine.

Definitions

'court': CA 1990, s 235; 'officer' CA 1963, s 2(1); 'officer in default': CA 1963, s 383, as amended by CLEA 2001, s 100; 'share': CA 1963, s 2(1).

Notes

An entry may be superseded by a subsequent related entry eg a first entry on the grant of an option, and a second entry when it is subsequently exercised.

UK legislation

CA 1985, s 217.

87 Entries, when not to be removed

(1) Entries in a company's register of interests in shares under this Chapter shall not be deleted except in accordance with section 86.

(2) If an entry is deleted from a company's register of interests in shares in contravention of subsection (1), the company shall restore that entry to the register as soon as is reasonably practicable.

(3) If default is made in complying with subsection (1) or (2), the company and every officer of it who is in default shall be guilty of an offence and liable to a fine.

Definitions

'contravention': CA 1990, s 3(1); 'officer' CA 1963, s 2(1); 'officer in default': CA 1963, s 383, as amended by CLEA 2001, s 100; 'share': CA 1963, s 2(1).

Notes

An entry may be superseded by a subsequent related entry eg a first entry on the grant of an option, and a second entry when it is subsequently exercised.

UK legislation

CA 1985, s 218.

88 Inspection of register and reports

(1) Any register of interests in shares and any report which is required by section 84 (6) to be available for inspection in accordance with this section shall, during business hours (subject to such reasonable restrictions as the company may in general meeting impose, but so that not less than 2 hours in each day are allowed for inspection) be open to the inspection of any member of the company or of any other person without charge.

(2) The register referred to in subsection (1) shall also be and remain open and accessible to any person attending the company's annual general meeting at least one quarter hour before the appointed time for the commencement of the meeting and during the continuance of the meeting.

(3) Any such member or other person may require a copy of any such register or report, or any part of it, on payment of [19 cents][a] or such less sum as the company may prescribe, for every 100 words or fractional part of 100 words required to be copied; and the company shall cause any copy so required by a person to be sent to him before the expiration of the period of 10 days beginning with the day next following that on which the requirement is received by the company.

(4) If an inspection required under this section is refused or a copy so required is not sent within the proper period, the company and every officer of it who is in default shall be guilty of an offence and liable to a fine.

(5) In the case of a refusal of an inspection required under this section of any register or report, the court may by order compel an immediate inspection of it; and in the case of failure to send a copy required under this section, the court may by order direct that the copy required shall be sent to the person requiring it.

Amendments

a 'l5p' converted to 19 cents by Council Regulations (EC) No 1103/97, No 974/98 and No 2866/98 and the European and Monetary Union Act 1998, s 6.

Definitions

'court': CA 1990, s 235; 'member' CA 1963, s 312; 'officer' CA 1963, s 2(1); 'officer in default': CA 1963, s 383, as amended by CLEA 2001, s 100; 'prescribe': CA 1990, s 3(1); 'share': CA 1963, s 2(1).

Notes

Sections 89 to 96 transpose the Major Shareholdings Directive 88/627/EEC into Irish law. That Directive was consolidated into the Consolidated Admissions and Reporting Directive 2001/34/EC Articles 85 to 97 which Articles were deleted by the Transparency Directive 2004/109/EC Article 32(5). As at 1 February 2007 the Transparency Directive was about to be transposed into Irish law.

Definitions

'member': CA 1963, s 31; 'share': CA 1963, s 2(1).

Notes

Chapter 3 applies to private companies only. It is one of the Irish solo legislative adventures and is aimed at providing a judicial equivalent of Chapter 3 as applies to public limited companies so as to enable a person having dealings with a private company to ascertain who are the real owners and controllers. This might be something of relevance eg to a landlord or other counterparty to a company.

This Part of the Act is a wonderful example of a (i) a legal cure for which there was no disease in the first place, and (ii) a non-cure for where there was a disease. By and large when business people, for fair reasons or foul, choose to hide their economic interest in an enterprise, they will not choose a company from Ireland or any respectable jurisdiction. Rather they will most usually do so in one of Her Majesty's offshore colonies or dominions, or some in the United States sphere of influence where there is no law compelling such disclosure. Therefore, a non-Irish entity, Jackson Way Properties Limited, an entity not incorporated in Ireland which was the owner of valuable development land beside the M50 orbital motorway around Dublin was not subject to this section. Although it has been the subject of various court proceedings revolving around the non-disclosure of its real owners or those who stand to benefit from its assets (see *The Irish Times*, 10 October 2006) this Part of the 1990 Act, which might have been a valuable weapon in the armoury of regulators is unavailable.

98 Disclosure order

(1) For the purposes of this Chapter, 'disclosure order' means an order of the court which obliges—

(a) any person whom the court believes to have or to be able to obtain any information as to—

(i) persons interested at present, or at any time during a period specified in the order, in the shares or debentures of a company,

(ii) the names and addresses of any of those persons,

(iii) the name and address of any person who acts or has acted on behalf of any of those persons in relation to the shares or debentures,

to give such information to the court; or

(b) any person whom the court believes to be, or at any time during a period specified in the order to have been, interested in shares or debentures of a company to confirm that fact or (as the case may be) to indicate whether or not it is the case and, where he holds or has during that period held any interest in such shares or debentures, to give such further information as the court may require; or

(c) any person interested in shares or debentures of a company specified in the order to disclose to the court the information required under subparagraphs (i) and (ii) and (iii) of paragraph (a) and such further information as the court may require.

(2) Any person who has a financial interest in a company may apply to the court for a disclosure order in respect of all or any of the shares of or debentures in the company.

(3) An application under subsection (2) shall be supported by such evidence as the court may require.

(4) The court may, before hearing an application under subsection (2), require the applicant to give security for payment of the costs of hearing the application or any consequential proceedings.

(5) The court may make a disclosure order only if—

(a) it deems it just and equitable to do so; and

(b) it is of the opinion that the financial interest of the applicant is or will be prejudiced by the non-disclosure of any interest in the shares or debentures of the company.

(6) For the purposes of subsection (2) 'financial interest' includes any interest as member, contributory, creditor, employee, co-adventurer, examiner, lessor, lessee, licensor, licensee, liquidator or receiver either in relation to the company in respect of whose shares or debentures a disclosure order is sought or a related company.

(7) Where a person authorises any other person ('the agent') to acquire or dispose of, on his behalf, interests in shares comprised in relevant share capital of a company or in debentures of the company in respect of which a disclosure order is made, he shall, for the duration of that order, ensure that the agent notifies him immediately of acquisitions or disposals of interests in shares or debentures so comprised effected by the agent which will or may give rise to any obligation on his part to provide information in accordance with the terms of the order with respect to his interest in that share capital or those debentures.

Cross reference

For the scope of the information which may be obtained from a person under s 98(1), see s 100.

For the civil consequences of a contravention of disclosure order under s 98(1), see s 104.

In determining whether a person is or has been interested in shares the court will have regard to the provisions of ss 72 to 78: see CA 1990, s 100(3).

Definitions

'court': CA 1990, s 235; 'debenture': CA 1963, s 2(1); 'member': 'CA 1963, s 31; 'related company': CA 1990, ss 3(1), 140; 'share': CA 1963, s 2(1).

Notes

Another way of determining the beneficial ownership of shares in a private company is for the Minister to appoint an inspector for that purpose under s 14 or for a Ministerial enquiry as to ownership under s 15.

The disclosure order may specify a person, group or class of persons to whom it applies: CA 1990, s 101(2).

Where a court makes a disclosure order, it may impose, for a specified period of time, such conditions or restrictions on the rights or obligations attaching to the shares or debentures in respect of which the order is made, as it deems fit: CA 1990, s 101(4). These would be akin to those specified in s 16, as extended by s 85.

A person is deemed also to have an interest in shares or debentures of a company where he has or is entitled to acquire a right to subscribe for such shares or debentures: CA 1990, s 100(5).

The person in possession of information regarding interests in the shares concerned could well be a solicitor. Section 98 does not mention an entitlement to withhold information on the basis of legal professional privilege. By way of contrast, see s 23 where an express right to withhold information is acknowledged. That said, a court may only make an order where it is just and equitable to do so, and to do so in breach of legal professional privilege would appear not to be just and equitable.

99 Procedure on application for disclosure order

(1) A person intending to apply for the making of a disclosure order shall give not less than 10 days' notice of his intention to the company in respect of whose shares or debentures the order is sought and to the person to whom the order is intended to be directed.

(2) The applicant shall also serve on any person specified by the court such notice of the application as the court may direct.

(3) On the hearing of the application every person notified under subsection (1) or (2) may appear and adduce evidence.

Definitions

'court': CA 1990, s 235; 'debenture': CA 1963, s 2(1); 'share': CA 1963, s 2(1).

Notes

The application is by way of Originating Notice of Motion: RSC 1986, Ord 75B, r 3(s).

The application must be served on the registered owner of the shares, if different from the person against whom the disclosure order is sought.

100 Scope of disclosure order

(1) A disclosure order may require the person to whom it is addressed—

(a) to give particulars of his own past or present interest in shares comprised in relevant share capital of the company or in debentures of the company held by him at any time during the period mentioned in the order;

(b) where the interest is a present interest and any other interest in the shares or debentures subsists or, in any case, where another interest in the shares or debentures subsisted during that period at any time when his own interest subsisted, to give so far as lies within his knowledge such particulars with respect to that other interest as may be required by the order;

(c) where his interest is a past interest, to give so far as lies within his knowledge particulars of the identity of the person who held that interest immediately upon his ceasing to hold it.

(2) A disclosure order shall specify the information to be supplied to the court under the order in respect of any person, shares or debentures to which it refers and any such information shall be given in writing.

(3) Sections 68 to 79 shall apply as appropriate for the purposes of construing references in this Chapter to persons interested in shares and debentures and to interests in shares

and debentures respectively as they apply in relation to section 67 (disregarding section 78) and any reference in those sections to a 'percentage level' shall be disregarded.

(4) For the purposes of this section any reference in sections 67 to 79 to 'shares' shall, where appropriate and unless the contrary is stated, be deemed to include a reference to debentures.

(5) This section shall apply in relation to a person who has or previously had or is or was entitled to acquire a right to subscribe for shares in or debentures of a company which would on issue be comprised in relevant share capital of that company as it applies in relation to a person who is or was interested in shares so comprised or in debentures of the company; and references in the preceding provisions of this section to an interest in shares so comprised or an interest in debentures and to shares so comprised or debentures shall be read accordingly in any such case as including references respectively to any such right and to shares which would on issue be so comprised.

Definitions

'court': CA 1990, s 235; 'debenture': CA 1963, s 2(1); 'share': CA 1963, s 2(1).

Notes

Section 100(1) appears tautologous when read in conjunction with s 98.

101 Powers of court

(1) The court may, on cause shown, rescind or vary a disclosure order.

(2) A disclosure order may specify a person, group or class of persons to which the order applies.

(3) The court may, if it considers—

(a) that it would be just and equitable to do so, and

(b) that the financial interest of the applicant would not be prejudiced thereby,

exempt in whole or in part from the requirements of a disclosure order—

(i) any person or class of persons,

(ii) any interest or class of interest in shares or debentures,

(iii) any share, group or class of shares,

(iv) any debenture, group or class of debentures.

(4) When the court makes a disclosure order it may impose, for a specific period of time, such conditions or restrictions on the rights or obligations attaching to the shares or debentures in respect of which the order is made as it deems fit.

(5) Any person whose interests are affected by any conditions or restrictions imposed on shares or debentures under subsection (4) may apply to the court for relief from all or any of those conditions and the court may, if it considers it just and equitable to do so, grant such relief in whole or in part and on such terms and conditions as it sees fit.

Cross reference

For the consequences of contravention of a disclosure order, see CA 1990, s 104.

Definitions

'court': CA 1990, s 235; 'debenture': CA 1963, s 2(1); 'share': CA 1963, s 2(1).

Notes

An application under s 101 is by way of Originating Notice of Motion, served on the applicant for the disclosure order, the company and any other person affected by the application: RSC 1986, Ord 75B, r 3(t), (u).

It is likely that the restrictions would be akin to those specified in s 16, as extended by s 85.

---

102 Notice of disclosure order

(1) The applicant shall cause notice in the prescribed form of the making of a disclosure order together with a copy of the order to be sent by registered post within 7 days of the making of the order to—

(a) the company (at its registered office) in respect of whose shares or debentures the order has been made,

(b) the registrar of companies,

(c) the registered holder of any shares or debentures in respect of which the disclosure order has been made where it appears to the court that—

(i) such holder is not at the date of the making of the order resident in the State, and

(ii) such holder should be notified,

(d) such other person as the court sees fit.

(2) The applicant shall cause notice of the making of a disclosure order to be published, within 7 days of the making of the order, in at least 2 daily newspapers which circulate in the district in which the registered office of the company, in respect of whose shares or debentures the order has been made, is situate.

(3) For the purposes of subsection (1)(a)—

(a) the address of the registered office of the company at the date of the making of the disclosure order shall be deemed to be the address of that office which was last delivered to the registrar of companies or otherwise published, as such case may be (in accordance with and in the manner required by the law relating to the company) prior to the date of making the order; and

(b) if no address of the registered office has ever been duly delivered to the registrar of companies or if the location of the last delivered address has been destroyed, the requirements of subsection (1)(a) shall be deemed to have been complied with by sending the required notice of the order together with a copy thereof to the registrar of companies.

(4) For the purposes of subsection (1)(c)—

(a) the address of a non-resident registered holder of shares or debentures shall be deemed to be the address of that holder which was last delivered to the registrar of companies or otherwise published, as the case may be (in accordance with and in the manner required by the law relating to the company) prior to the date of making of the order; and

(b) if no address of the non-resident registered holder has ever been duly delivered to the registrar of companies the requirements of subsection (1)(c) shall be deemed to have been complied with by sending the required notice of the order together with a copy thereof to the registrar of companies.

(5) Any reference in this section to the registered office of a company shall, in the case of a company not registered under the Companies Acts, be construed as a reference to the principal office of the company.

Cross reference

See CA 1963, s 113 for procedures for notifying the change of registered office.

See CA 1963, s 379 for service of documents on a company.

See CA 1963, s 125 and Sch 5 regarding delivery of names and addresses of shareholders to the Registrar of Companies.

Definitions

'Companies Acts': CA 1990, s 3(1); 'court': CA 1990, s 235; 'debenture': CA 1963, s 2(1); 'prescribe': CA 1990, s 3(1); 'registrar of companies': CA 1963, s 2(1); 'share': CA 1963, s 2(1).

103 Information disclosed under order

(1) An obligation to provide any information imposed on any person by a disclosure order shall be treated as not being fulfilled unless the notice by means of which it purports to be fulfilled identifies him and gives his current address.

(2) Where information is given to the court in compliance with the terms of a disclosure order, a prescribed officer of the court shall, unless the court otherwise directs, cause such information to be furnished (in whole or in part as the court may direct) to the applicant and to the company in respect of whose shares or debentures the order was made.

(3) In reaching its decision under subsection (2), the court shall have regard to whether the requirements of section 102 have been complied with.

(4) Where any information is furnished to the applicant or the company in pursuance of subsection (2), the court may impose such restrictions as it sees fit as to the publication of the information by the person to whom it has been furnished.

Definitions

'court': CA 1990, s 235; 'debenture': CA 1963, s 2(1); 'prescribe': CA 1990, s 3(1); 'share': CA 1963, s 2(1).

Notes

The Examiner of the High Court (not to be confused with an examiner appointed to a company by the Court under the Companies (Amendment) Act 1999) and the Registrars of the High Court are the prescribed officers for the purposes of this section: Companies Acts 1990 (Parts IV and VII) Regulations 1991 (SI 209/1991).

104 Civil Consequences of Contravention of Disclosure Order

(1) Where a person—

(a) fails to fulfil, within the proper period, an obligation to provide information required by a disclosure order, or

(b) in purported fulfilment of any such obligation makes to the court a statement which he knows to be false or recklessly makes to the court a statement which is false,

no right or interest of any kind whatsoever in respect of any shares in or debentures of the company concerned held by him shall be enforceable by him whether directly or indirectly, by action or legal proceeding.

(2) Where any right or interest is restricted under subsection (1), any person in default under that subsection or any other person affected by such restriction may apply to the court for relief against a disability imposed by or arising out of subsection (1) and the court on being satisfied that the default was accidental, or due to inadvertence, or some other sufficient cause, or that on other grounds it is just and equitable to grant relief, may grant such relief either generally, or as respects any particular right or interest on such terms and conditions as it sees fit.

(3) Where an applicant for relief under subsection (2) is a person referred to in subsection (1), the court may not grant such relief if it appears that the default has arisen as a result of any deliberate act or omission on the part of the applicant.

(4) The acquisition by any person of an interest in shares or debentures of a company registered in the State shall be deemed to be a consent by that person to the disclosure by him, his agents or intermediaries of any information required to be disclosed in relation to shares or debentures by the Companies Acts.

Definitions

'Companies Acts': CA 1990, s 3(1); 'contravention': CA 1990, s 3(1); 'court': CA 1990, s 235; 'debenture': CA 1963, s 2(1); 'share': CA 1963, s 2(1).

Notes

Rights attaching to shares may be unenforceable by action or legal proceeding in the event of the breach of a disclosure order, but in the absence of an order to the contrary, that does not preclude the recognition of those rights by others eg the company may still pay dividends and send notices of general meetings to the holder of shares.

It would, presumably, be just and equitable to grant relief where the person subsequently complies with the disclosure order as per s 104(2).

An application for relief must be brought by way of Originating Notice of Motion and must be served upon the company and on any other person affected by the restrictions and on the applicant for the disclosure order: RSC 1986, Ord 75B, r 3(v).

One may interpret s 104(3) as potentially being applicable only for so long as the breach of the disclosure order is ongoing. Otherwise a person who deliberately disobeyed the order but later complied would be forever precluded from enforcing rights attaching to the shares.

A literal interpretation of s 104(4) means that where a person acquires shares in an Irish-incorporated company, he is deemed to waive legal professional privilege between him and his solicitor concerning the shares.

Chapter 4
General Provisions about Share Registers etc.

105 Power to alter maximum inspection etc charges

(1) The Minister may, by order, alter any of the charges referred to in—

(a) section 60(5) of this Act or section 92(1), 119(1) or 195(10) (inserted by section 51 of this Act) of the Principal Act, or

(b) section 60(8) or 88(3) of this Act, or section 92(2), 92(3), 119(2) or 146(2) of the Principal Act.

(2) The Minister may also, by order, alter the basis of any of the charges referred to in the provisions specified in subsection (1)(b) from the basis referred to in those provisions to some other basis.

(3) In making any order under this section, the Minister shall take into account the general costs incurred by a company in facilitating the inspection, or providing copies, of the registers or other documents referred to in subsection (1).

(4) Every order made under this section shall be laid before each House of the Oireachtas as soon as may be after it is made and if a resolution annulling the order is passed by either House within the next 21 days on which that House has sat after the order is laid before it, the order shall be annulled accordingly but without prejudice to the validity of anything previously done thereunder.

Definitions

'Minister': CA 1990, s 3(1); 'Principal Act': CA 1990, s 3(1).

Note

For example it costs 6c to inspect the register of members, 38c to inspect the register of directors and secretaries and €1.27 to inspect the register of directors and secretaries. No Orders have been made under this section, indicating an indifference to the costs on the part of companies and those interested.

UK legislation

CA 1985, s 723A, inserted by CA 1989, s 143.

---

106 Transitional provisions

(1) Where on the commencement of this section a person has an interest which, if it was acquired after such commencement, would be subject to a notification requirement under Chapter 1 or 2 he shall be under an obligation to make to the company the notification with respect to his interest required by the Chapter concerned.

(2) For the purposes of subsection (1), sections 56 and 71(1) shall apply as if, for the period of 5 days mentioned in each of those provisions, there were substituted a period of 14 days.

(3) Section 73 shall apply in relation to an agreement not withstanding that it was made before the commencement of this section or that any such acquisition of shares as is mentioned in subsection (1)(b) of that section took place before such commencement.

Definitions

'share': CA 1963, s 2(1).

PART V
INSIDER DEALING

Amendments

This Part has been repealed by IFCMPA 2005, s 31. However, the Investment Funds, Companies and Miscellaneous Provisions Act 2005 (Commencement) Order 2005 (SI 323/2005), art 5 provides: 'The 6th day of July 2005 is appointed as the day on which the following provisions of the Act come into operation, namely – (a) section 31 (but only for the purpose of repealing the enactments specified in that section in so far as they relate to a regulated market (within the meaning of Directive 2003/71/EC of the European Parliament and of the Council of 4 November 2003) operated by a recognised stock exchange within the meaning Part V of the Companies Act 1990 (No 33/1990)).'

Therefore, the repeal is only in so far as the securities concerned are admitted to trading on a 'regulated market', ie on the official list. Therefore this Part applies to securities admitted to trading on a 'recognised stock exchange', of which there is only one, the Irish Stock Exchange: Companies (Stock Exchange) Regulations 1995 (SI 310/1995).

Part V is anomalous in one key aspect, and that is because it was enacted in the first place in order to transpose the 1989 Insider Trading Directive (Council Directive 89/592/EEC of 13 November 1989 coordinating regulations on insider dealing OJ L 334, 18/11/1989). Now that the 1989 Directive has been repealed, it is submitted that Part V must be read on its own terms, rather than with a view to apply the principles of a now-repealed Directive.

Cross reference

See also the prohibition in CA 1990, s 30 on option dealing by directors and shadow directors.

See also the prohibition on insider dealing in financial instruments of an issuer admitted to trading on a regulated market in IFCMPA 2005 Part 4 and the Market Abuse (Directive 2003/6/EC) Regulations 2005 (SI 342/2005).

Notes

With regard to insider dealing generally, see MacCann, 'Liability for Insider Dealing' (1999) ILR (ns) 130, 151; Ashe & Murphy, 'Insider Dealing' (Round Hall Press, 1992); Suter, 'The Regulation of Insider Dealing in Britain' (Butterworths, 1989).

Quite apart from the statutory prohibition on insider dealing, a director or other fiduciary may not, except with the consent of the company in general meeting, use confidential information obtained by virtue of his position as a director in order to make a personal profit.[1] Thus he may be accountable for profits he makes from dealings in securities issued by his company or any other company where he has price sensitive information about that company which is not available to investors generally, and which information has come to him by reason of his fiduciary position.[2] In normal circumstances, such an action could only be maintained against the director or other fiduciary by the company itself and not by individual shareholders who had suffered loss as a result of the insider dealing (eg by selling their shares at an undervalue).[3] In some exceptional circumstances an individual shareholder could maintain such a claim himself as where the director had been appointed as his agent[4] or where there was a pre-existing relationship of trust and confidence between the director and the shareholder.[5]

In *Fyffes plc v DCC plc and S & L Investments Ltd and* others,[6] the plaintiff sought a declaration that sales of shares in the plaintiff constituted unlawful dealings within the meaning of Part V together with an order pursuant to s 109(1)(b) requiring the defendants to account to the plaintiff for any profit arising. In addition to the statutory claim the plaintiff sought (i) an account in equity of all profit accruing to the defendants from the share sales and (ii) damages and/or compensation for breach of fiduciary duty on behalf of one of the defendants, a former director of the plaintiff. In that case the plaintiff lost in the High Court and has brought an appeal to the Supreme Court, due to be heard in Spring 2007.

1 *Bray v Ford* (1896] AC 44; *Boardman v Phipps* [1967] Ac 46; *Regal (Hastings) Ltd v Gulliver* [1942] 1 All ER 378; *Cook v Deeks* [1916] 1 AC 554; *Canadian Aeroservice Ltd v O'Malley* [1974] 40 DLR (3d); *Industrial Developments Ltd v Cooley* [1972] 2 All ER 162.

2 *Terrapin Ltd v Builder's Supply Co (Hayes) Ltd* [1960] AC 128; *Seager v Copydex Ltd* [1967] 1 WLR 923.

3 *Percival v Wright* [1902] 2 Ch 421.

4 *Allen v Hyatt* [1941] 30 TLR 444.

5 *Coleman v Myers* [1977] 2 NZLR 225.

6 *Fyffes plc v DCC plc and S & L Investments Ltd and others* [2005] IEHC 477.

107 Interpretation

In this Part, except where the context otherwise requires

'dealing', in relation to securities, means (whether as principal or agent) acquiring, disposing of, subscribing for or underwriting the securities, or making or offering to make, or inducing or attempting to induce a person to make or to offer to make, an agreement—

(a) for or relating to acquiring, disposing of, subscribing for or underwriting the securities; or

(b) the purpose or purported purpose of which is to secure a profit or gain to a person who acquires, disposes of, subscribes for or underwrites the securities or to any of the parties to the agreement in relation to the securities;

'director' includes a shadow director within the meaning of section 27;

'officer', in relation to a company, includes—

(a) a director, secretary or employee;

(b) a liquidator;

(c) any person administering a compromise or arrangement made between the company and its creditors;

(d) an examiner;

(e) an auditor; and

(f) a receiver;

'public office' means an office or employment which is remunerated out of the Central Fund or out of moneys provided by the Oireachtas or money raised by local taxation or charges, or an appointment to or employment under any commission, committee, tribunal, board or body established by the

Government or any Minister of the Government or by or under any statutory authority;

'recognised stock exchange' includes, in particular, any exchange prescribed by the Minister which provides facilities for the buying and selling of rights or obligations to acquire stock;

'related company', in relation to a company, means any body corporate which is the company's subsidiary or holding company, or a subsidiary of the company's holding company;

'relevant authority', in relation to a recognised stock exchange, means—

(i) its board of directors, committee of management or other management body, or

(ii) its manager, however described;

'securities' means—

(a) shares, debentures or other debt securities issued or proposed to be issued, whether in the State or otherwise, and for which dealing facilities are, or are to be, provided by a recognised stock exchange;

(b) any right, option or obligation in respect of any such shares, debentures or other debt securities referred to in paragraph (a);

(c) any right, option or obligation in respect of any index relating to any such shares, debentures or other debt securities referred to in paragraph (a); or

(d) such interests as may be prescribed;

'underwrite' includes sub-underwrite.

Amendments

Section repealed in the limited manner noted in IFCMPA 2005, s 31 with effect from 6 July 2005. See IFCMPA 2005, s 31 and notes thereto.

The Companies (Stock Exchange) Regulations, 1995 (SI 310/1995), reg 3(c) obliquely amends this section, stating: 'the Irish Stock Exchange is hereby prescribed as a recognised stock exchange for the purposes of the following provisions of the Companies Acts— ... sections ... 90 to 96, 107 of the Companies Act, 1990'. It provides that 'recognised stock exchange' means 'The Irish Stock Exchange Limited'.

Definitions

'debenture': CA 1963, s 2(1); 'director': CA 1963, s 2(1); 'holding company': CA 1963, s 153; 'Minister': CA 1990, s 3(1); 'prescribe': CA 1990, s 3(1); 'recognised stock exchange': CA 1990, s 3(1), (2); 'related company': CA 1990, s 3(1), s 140; 'shadow director': CA 1990, s 3(1), s 27; 'share': CA 1963, s 2(1); 'subsidiary': CA 1963, s 155.

Notes

Note that this definition of 'related company' is different to the generally applicable definition contained in CA 1990, s 140(5).

Dealings in unlisted securities are not caught by CA 1990, Part V, and are thus subject only to the restrictions on fiduciaries outlined above. Furthermore, CA 1990 Part V does not apply to dealing outside the State in securities: CA 1990 (Insider Dealing) Regs 1992 (SI 131/1992).

UK legislation

Criminal Justice Act 1993, ss 54, 55, 60.

108 Unlawful dealings in securities by insiders

(1) It shall not be lawful for a person who is, or at any time in the preceding 6 months has been, connected with a company to deal in any securities of that company if by reason of his so being, or having been, connected with that company he is in possession of information that is not generally available, but, if it were, would be likely materially to affect the price of those securities.

(2) It shall not be lawful for a person who is, or at any time in the preceding 6 months has been, connected with a company to deal in any securities of any other company if by reason of his so being, or having been, connected with the first-mentioned company he is in possession of information that—

(a) is not generally available but, if it were, would be likely materially to affect the price of those securities, and

(b) relates to any transaction (actual or contemplated) involving both those companies or involving one of them and securities of the other, or to the fact that any such transaction is no longer contemplated.

(3) Where a person is in possession of any such information as is mentioned in subsection (1) or (2) that if generally available would be likely materially to affect the price of securities but is not precluded by either of those subsections from dealing in those securities, it shall not be lawful for him to deal in those securities if he has received the information, directly or indirectly, from another person and is aware, or ought reasonably to be aware, of facts or circumstances by virtue of which that other person is then himself precluded by subsection (1) or (2) from dealing in those securities.

(4) It shall not be lawful for a person at any time when he is precluded by subsection (1), (2) or (3) from dealing in any securities, to cause or procure any other person to deal in those securities.

(5) It shall not be lawful for a person, at any time when he is precluded by subsection (1), (2) or (3) from dealing in any securities by reason of his being in possession of any information, to communicate that information to any other person if he knows, or ought reasonably to know, that the other person will make use of the information for the purpose of dealing, or causing or procuring another person to deal, in those securities.

(6) Without prejudice to subsection (3), but subject to subsections (7) and (8), it shall not be lawful for a company to deal in any securities at a time when any officer of that company is precluded by subsection (1), (2) or (3) from dealing in those securities.

(7) Subsection (6) does not preclude a company from entering into a transaction at any time by reason only of information in the possession of an officer of that company if—

(a) the decision to enter into the transaction was taken on its behalf by a person other than the officer;

(b) it had in operation at that time written arrangements to ensure that the information was not communicated to that person and that no advice relating to the transaction was given to him by a person in possession of the information; and

(c) the information was not so communicated and such advice was not so given.

(8) Subsection (6) does not preclude a company from dealing in securities of another company at any time by reason only of information in the possession of an officer of the first-mentioned company, being information that was received by the officer in the course of the performance of his duties as an officer of the first-mentioned company and that consists only of the fact that the first-mentioned company proposes to deal in securities of that other company.

(9) This section does not preclude a person from dealing in securities, or rights or interests in securities, of a company if—

(a) he enters into the transaction concerned as agent for another person pursuant to a specified instruction of that other person to effect that transaction; and

(b) he has not given any advice to the other person in relation to dealing in securities, or rights or interests in securities, of that company that are included in the same class as the first-mentioned securities.

(10) This section does not preclude a person from dealing in securities if, while not otherwise taking advantage of his possession of information referred to in subsection (1)—

(a) he gives at least 21 days' notice to a relevant authority of the relevant stock exchange of his intention to deal, within the period referred to in paragraph (b), in the securities of the company concerned, and

(b) the dealing takes place within a period beginning 7 days after the publication of the company's interim or final results, as the case may be and ending 14 days after such publication, and

(c) the notice referred to in paragraph (a) is published by the exchange concerned immediately on its receipt.

(11) For the purposes of this section, a person is connected with a company if, being a natural person—

(a) he is an officer of that company or of a related company;

(b) he is a shareholder in that company or in a related company;or

(c) he occupies a position (including a public office) that may reasonably be expected to give him access to information of a kind to which subsections (1) and (2) apply by virtue of—

(i) any professional, business or other relationship existing between himself (or his employer or a company of which he is an officer) and that company or a related company; or

(ii) his being an officer of a substantial shareholder in that company or in a related company.

(12) For the purposes of subsection (11) 'substantial shareholder' means a person who holds shares in a company, the number of which is above the notifiable percentage for the time being in force under section 70.

(13) The prohibitions in subsections (1), (3), (4) and (5) shall extend to dealings in securities issued by the State as if the references in subsections (1), (9) and (11)(other

than paragraphs (a) and (b) of the last mentioned subsection) to a company were references to the State.

Amendments

Section repealed in the limited manner noted in IFCMPA 2005, s 31 with effect from 6 July 2005. See IFCMPA 2005, s 31 and notes thereto.

C(A)A 1999, s 2 provides: 'Section 108 of the Act of 1990, shall not be regarded as having been contravened by reason of—

(a) anything done in the State for the purpose of stabilising or maintaining the market price of securities if it is done in conformity with the Stabilisation Rules, or

(b) any action taken during the stabilising period by a person in any jurisdiction other than the State for the purpose of stabilising or maintaining the market price of securities, but only if the action taken is, in all material respects, permitted by or is otherwise in accordance with all relevant requirements applicable to such actions in the jurisdiction where such action is effected, including, if those securities are also listed on a stock exchange in that jurisdiction, the rules or other regulatory requirements governing that stock exchange.'

Cross reference

See notes to ss 109 and 111 and discussion for requirement or otherwise for *mens rea* in order to establish civil liability or criminal guilt. In *Fyffes plc v DCC plc and S & L Investments Limited and others*,[1] stated, with respect to civil liability under this section: 'The language of sub-ss (1) and (6) of s 108 is the language of strict liability. If the legislature intended that these provisions should be qualified by a requirement of knowledge, it could easily have done so. The fact that the provisions of sub-ss (3) and (5) of s 108 and s 113 expressly import the requirement of knowledge, suggests that it was not the intention of the legislature to do so in the remainder of the provisions.'

See generally IFCMPA 2005, Pt 4 and Market Abuse (Directive 2003/6/EC) Regulations 2005 (SI 342/2005) which prohibit insider dealing where the securities dealt in are admitted to trading on a regulated market.

1 *Fyffes plc v DCC plc and S & L Investments Ltd and others* [2005] IEHC 477.

Definitions

'company': CA 1963, s 2(1); 'officer': CA 1990, s 107; 'related company': CA 1990, s 3(1), s 140; 'share': CA 1963, s 2(1).

The definition of 'company' in this section is troublesome. Part V was enacted with a view to transposing Directive 89/592/EEC of 13 November 1989 on Insider Trading, repealed by the Market Abuse Directive 2003/6/EC of 28 January 2003. The 1989 Directive does not, in relation to its implementation in each member state, appear to limit its application to corporations incorporated in such member state. Therefore, for as long as Part V constituted the transposition of the 1989 Directive, it would have to be construed in accordance with that Directive.[1] In *Marleasing* the Court stated: 'The obligation of member states under a Directive is to achieve its objects, and their duty by Article 5 of the Treaty (of Rome) to take all necessary steps to ensure the fulfilment of that obligation, binds all authorities of member states, including national courts within their jurisdiction. It follows that in applying national law ... the national court asked to interpret national law is bound to do so in every way possible in light of the text and aim of the Directive to achieve the results envisaged by it ...' .

This meant that the word 'company' would have to be construed as meaning more than a company within the meaning of CA 1963, s 2(1). However, with the 1989 Directive repealed, it is submitted that the section must be construed in accordance with its own terms, and accordingly that the word 'company' has the meaning in CA 1963, s 2(1) only.

1 *Marleasing SA v La Commercial International de Alimentación SA* [1990] ECR 40 4135, (which principles were approved in *Fyffes plc v DCC plc and S & L Investments Ltd and others* [2005] IEHC 477, reversed on other grounds at [2007] IESC 36.

Notes

Inside Information: In July 2007, the Committee of European Securities Regulators (CESR) published a guidance under the Market Abuse Directive 2003/6/EC to provide illustrative examples of inside information for the purposes of that Directive. In it, CESR identifies information which, if not published, would constitute inside information. Although referable to a different enactment, the examples provide guidance as to what, if not published, would be considered by the regulators as constituting 'information which is not generally available, but if it were, would be likely materially to affect the price of those securities'. CESR divide their list of information into information which directly concerns the issuer and information relating indirectly to issuers.

Information which directly concerns the issuer:

- Operating business performance;
- Changes in control and control agreements;
- Changes in management and supervisory boards;
- Changes in auditors or any other information related to the auditors' activity;
- Operations involving the capital or the issue of debt securities or warrants to buy or subscribe securities;
- Decisions to increase or decrease the share capital;
- Mergers, splits and spin-offs;
- Purchase or disposal of equity interests or other major assets or branches of corporate activity;
- Restructurings or reorganizations that have an effect on the issuer's assets and liabilities, financial position or profits and losses;
- Decisions concerning buy-back programmes or transactions in other listed financial instruments;
- Changes in the class rights of the issuer's own listed shares;
- Filing of petitions in bankruptcy or the issuing of orders for bankruptcy proceedings;
- Significant legal disputes;
- Revocation or cancellation of credit lines by one or more banks;
- Dissolution or verification of a cause of dissolution;
- Relevant changes in the assets' value;
- Insolvency of relevant debtors;
- Reduction of real properties' values;
- Physical destruction of uninsured goods;
- New licences, patents, registered trade marks;
- Decrease or increase in value of financial instruments in portfolio;
- Decrease in value of patents or rights or intangible assets due to market innovation;
- Receiving acquisition bids for relevant assets;
- Innovative products or processes;
- Serious product liability or environmental damages cases;
- Changes in expected earnings or losses;
- Relevant orders received from customers, their cancellation or important changes;
- Withdrawal from or entering into new core business areas;
- Relevant changes in the investment policy of the issuer;

- Ex-dividend date, dividend payment date and amount of the dividend;
- changes in dividend policy payment.

Information relating indirectly to issuers:

- Data and statistics published by public institutions disseminating statistics;
- The coming publication of rating agencies' reports, research, recommendations or suggestions concerning the value of listed financial instruments;
- Central bank decisions concerning interest rate;
- Government's decisions concerning taxation, industry regulation, debt management, etc.;
- Decisions concerning changes in the governance rules of market indices, and especially as regards their composition;
- Regulated and unregulated markets' decisions concerning rules governing the markets;
- Competition and market authorities' decisions concerning listed companies;
- Relevant orders by government bodies, regional or local authorities or other public organizations;
- A change in trading mode (eg, information relating to knowledge that an issuer's financial instruments will be traded in another market segment: eg change from continuous trading to auction trading); a change of market maker or dealing conditions.

The Supreme Court has held that to be consistent with Directive 89/592/EEC on which it is based, the words 'likely materially to affect the price of those securities' must have the same meaning as 'likely to have a significant effect on the price of…' in the Directive.[1] In this regard, the test is an objective one and will typically involve a common-sense judgment as to whether a piece of information is such as would be likely to significantly affect the price of a share.[2] In undertaking this exercise in common sense, the court does not have regard to how a 'reasonable investor' would have reacted if the information had been public, but must instead try to determine how the market (both wise and unwise and reasonable and unreasonable) would in fact have reacted.[3] Thus, the function of the court is as follows:

1 to determine the generality or 'total mix' of information generally available;

2 to determine the information not generally available but available to the dealer;

3 to determine whether that information, if it were generally available, would be likely to materially affect the price of the shares having regard to the total mix of information available in the market.[4]

As to the quantification of movement in the share price necessary to be regarded as having a material effect on the price, this will depend on the particular share and in the particular circumstances of the case.[5] In this regard, the court is not precluded from looking at post-disclosure share movement in determining the question of materiality.[6]

The definition of 'inside information' has recently been considered by the ECJ in the case of *Ipourgos Ikonomikon v Georgakis*[7] where it was held that in order to constitute 'inside information' it had to fulfil a number of conditions, such as that it must not have been made public, it must have been of a precise nature related to the issuer of the transferable securities, and, if made public, that it would have been likely to have had a significant effect on the price of those securities. The ECJ further held that a mere recommendation to take certain steps, made solely on the basis of an expert analysis of the subject, could not be considered as meeting those conditions. Consequently, where shareholders undertook various sale, purchase and buy-back transactions in the company's shares to support the share price and did so on the recommendation of their financial advisers (who had in turn made that recommendation without any inside information), it was held that the recommendation itself did not constitute insider information and thus the shareholders were not guilty of insider dealing.

Persons who are or have been connected with the company within the last six months and who have price sensitive information in their possession are commonly referred to either as 'insiders' or 'primary insiders'. Persons who receive information from 'insiders'/'primary insiders' are referred to either as 'tippees' or 'secondary insiders'. Where one tippee passes price-sensitive information about a company to another tippee, the second tippee will likewise be precluded from dealing in the company's securities where he is aware or ought reasonably to be aware that the information originally emanated from an insider/primary insider.

Arguably the provision seems somewhat superfluous since s 107 already defines 'dealing' as including 'inducing or attempting to induce a person' to deal in the securities.

This prohibition is rather sweeping since it precludes the company from dealing in the securities simply where its officer has obtained price sensitive information about the securities even if he has not passed on the information to his company nor has not acquired the information in his capacity as officer of the company.

Such written arrangements are referred to as 'Chinese Walls'. For a brief explanation of their operation, see Ashe & Murphy, *Insider Dealing* (Round Hall Press, 1992), pp 67–70.

The information referred to in s 107(8) which the offer of the company has in his possession about the second company might be, for example, that the first company proposes to take over the second company. The anomaly in this subsection is that it is an exemption given only to 'companies' and not individuals or bodies corporate not being a 'company' within the meaning of the Companies Acts. This suggests that it is possible that the very fact of an imminent dealing by, for example, a company director ought in certain circumstances to be known to the market, as such dealings by directors may influence the price.

See, however, the provisions of s 113 which prohibit an agent from dealing on behalf of his principal where he has reasonable cause to believe or ought to conclude that the transaction amounts to insider dealing on the part of the principal. Section 113 applies even where the agent has not advised his principal to deal in the securities but has merely acted on his principal's instructions.

A director or other primary insider may be continuously in possession of price sensitive information concerning his company and but for the provisions of s 107(10) he could be permanently prohibited from disposing of or acquiring shares in his company. Although the primary insider is permitted to deal in securities during the 7 to 14 day period after publication of the interim or final results, as the case may be, and after such information has thus become public knowledge, he must nonetheless divorce from his mind any other price-sensitive information in his possession. Such an exercise would seem to be rather difficult to perform, however.

This subsection is sometimes, it is submitted, incorrectly, interpreted to mean that company directors may only deal in shares by complying with the procedures in s 107(10). It is however a useful procedure to follow in particular circumstances – eg where a director of a small company with a large shareholding wishes to acquire more shares or to dispose of shares. Either transaction has the possibility of moving the share price, so by announcing the intended dealing to the market it 'sanitises' it and protects it from the argument alluded to above. Note that the notice to the exchange does not require to state whether the intended dealing is a sale or purchase, which to some extent devalues the effect of a notice which does not so state.

Persons whose professional, business or other relationship might give him access to price sensitive information about the company would include the company's accountants, solicitors and financial advisers.

1 *Fyffes plc v DCC plc* [2007] IESC 36 (per Fennelly & Macken JJ).

2 *Fyffes plc v DCC plc* [2007] IESC 36 (per Fennelly, Finnegan, Denham & Macken JJ).

3 *Fyffes plc v DCC plc* [2007] IESC 36 (per Fennelly, Finnegan, Denham & Macken JJ).

4 *Fyffes plc v DCC plc* [2007] IESC 36 (per Finnegan & Macken JJ).

5 *Fyffes plc v DCC plc* [2007] IESC 36 (per Finnegan J).

6 *Fyffes plc v DCC plc* [2007] IESC 36 (per Finnegan & Macken JJ).

[7] *Ipourgos Ikonomikon v Georgakis* [2007] 2 BCLC 693.

UK legislation

Criminal Justice Act 1993, s 52.

109 Civil liability for unlawful dealing

(1) Where a person deals in or causes or procures another person to deal in securities in a manner declared unlawful by section 108 or communicates information in any such manner, that person shall, without prejudice to any other cause of action which may lie against him, be liable—

(a) to compensate any other party to the transaction who was not in possession of the relevant information for any loss sustained by that party by reason of any difference between the price at which the securities were dealt in that transaction and the price at which they would have been likely to have been dealt in such a transaction at the time when the first-mentioned transaction took place if that information had been generally available; and

(b) to account to the company that issued or made available those securities for any profit accruing to the first-mentioned person from dealing in those securities.

(2) The amount of compensation for which a person is liable under subsection (1) or the amount of the profit for which a person is liable to account under that subsection is—

(a) subject to paragraph (b), the amount of the loss sustained by the person claiming the compensation or the amount of the profit referred to in subsection (1)(b), as the case may be; or

(b) if the person so liable has been found by a court to be liable to pay an amount or amounts to any other person or persons by reason of the same act or transaction, the amount of that loss or profit less the amount or the sum of the amounts for which that person has been found to be liable.

(3) For the purposes of subsection (2), the onus of proving that the liability of a person to pay an amount to another person arose from the same act or transaction from which another liability arose lies on the person liable to pay the amount.

(4) An action under this section for recovery of a loss or profit shall not be commenced after the expiration of 2 years after the date of completion of the transaction in which the loss or profit occurred.

Amendments

Section repealed in the limited manner noted in IFCMPA 2005, s 31 with effect from 6 July 2005. See IFCMPA 2005, s 31 and notes thereto.

Definitions

'company': CA 1963, s 2(1); 'court': CA 1990, s 235.

Notes

While the affording of a remedy to a counterparty to a share transaction who has suffered loss as a result of the use of inside information has a logic, the Supreme Court has expressed the view that it is somewhat incongruous for s 109 to also afford such remedies to the company whose securities were the subject of the transaction.[1]

In *Fyffes plc v DCC plc*[2] the High Court dismissed the argument that for civil liability to apply, the *mens rea* required in order to establish guilt in a criminal case should apply in order for civil liability to apply. Laffoy J said: 'The civil liability created by s 109 in conjunction with ss 107 and 108 is wholly statutory. The jurisprudence which has developed in this jurisdiction and in other jurisdictions in relation to the common law action for damages for breach of statutory duty, in my view, is neither apposite nor helpful in the construction of the provisions of Part V governing civil liability. The ascertainment of the intention of the Oireachtas as to the factors which give rise to the civil liability are to be found within the four corners of the statute'.

Other causes of action that might lie against a primary insider would be actions for damages or an account of profits in respect of breach of fiduciary duty. In this regard see the general note to CA 1990, Pt V, supra.

The liability to account to the company for any profit made on the deal arises even where the person is not in a fiduciary relationship with the company (eg a tippee).

Thus the amount of the profits for which the person must account to the company is reduced by the amount of any compensation which he has already been ordered by the court to pay to the injured party. Similarly, if the court has already ordered the person to account to the company for profits made, then the level of damages payable to the injured party will be reduced accordingly. In the transposition of the Market Abuse Directive 2003/6/EC of 28 January 2006 in IFCMA, the comparable provision is given some teeth so that those who have a claim are not prejudiced by a prior award. IFCMPA 2005, s 33.

An action for breach of fiduciary duty may be brought beyond this period, subject to the equitable doctrine of laches.

1 *Fyffes plc v DCC plc* [2007] IESC 36.

2 *Fyffes plc v DCC plc* [2005] IEHC 477, reversed on other grounds at [2007] IESC 36.

110 Exempt transactions

(1) Nothing in section 108, shall prevent a person from—

(a) acquiring securities under a will or on the intestacy of another person; or

(b) acquiring securities in a company pursuant to an employee profit sharing scheme—

(i) approved by the Revenue Commissioners for the purposes of the Finance Acts, and

(ii) the terms of which were approved by the company in general meeting, and

(iii) under which all permanent employees of the company are offered the opportunity to participate on equal terms relative to specified objective criteria;

[(ba) acquiring a right to shares in a company pursuant to a scheme approved by the Revenue Commissioners for the purposes of the Tax Acts and the Capital Gains Tax Acts.][a]

(c) entering in good faith into a transaction to which subsection (2) applies.

(2) This subsection applies to the following kinds of transactions—

(a) the obtaining by a director of a share qualification under section 180 of the Principal Act;

(b) a transaction entered into by a person in accordance with his obligations under an underwriting agreement;

(c) a transaction entered into by a personal representative of a deceased person, a trustee, or liquidator, receiver or examiner in the performance of the functions of his office; or

(d) a transaction by way of, or arising out of, a mortgage of or charge on securities or a mortgage, charge, pledge or lien on documents of title to securities.

[(2A) A person shall be regarded as having entered in good faith into a transaction to which subsection (2)(b) relates, if such person enters in good faith into—

(a) negotiations with a view to entering an agreement to which paragraph (b) or (c) would relate, or

(b) an agreement to underwrite securities, or

(c) an agreement, in advance of dealing facilities being provided by a recognised stock exchange for securities, to acquire or subscribe for a specified number of those securities, or

(d) a transaction in accordance with such person's obligations under an agreement to which paragraph (b) or (c) relates.][b]

(3) This Part shall not apply to transactions entered into in pursuit of monetary, exchange rate, national debt management or foreign exchange reserve policies by any Minister of the Government or the Central Bank, or by any person on their behalf.

Amendments

Section repealed in the limited manner noted in IFCMPA 2005, s 31 with effect from 6 July 2005. See IFCMPA 2005, s 31 and notes thereto.

a CLEA 2001, s 103 inserts CA 1990, s 110(1)(ba).

b C(A)A 1999, s 4 inserts CA 1990, s 110(2A).

---

111 Criminal liability for unlawful dealing

A person who deals in securities in a manner declared unlawful by section 108 shall be guilty of an offence.

Amendments

Section repealed in the limited manner noted in IFCMPA 2005, s 31 with effect from 6 July 2005. See IFCMPA 2005, s 31 and notes thereto.

Notes

In the only criminal trial under Part V to date, in the Dublin Circuit Court in *DPP v Byrne*[1] Lynch J made a ruling to the effect that, as *mens rea* was an essential element to be proved in a criminal prosecution under a legal provision which outlawed an activity and provided for both civil remedies and criminal punishment, it was an essential proof that the accused knew that he had price-sensitive information at the relevant time. In the *Byrne* case this was not proven, and the accused was acquitted. In *Fyffes plc v DCC plc and S & L Investments Ltd and others*,[1] whilst acknowledging that the issue of whether mens rea is an ingredient of an offence under s 111 was not an issue in that case, Laffoy J observed that it may be reasonable to infer that the legislature intended that the common law principles applicable to offences created by statute should apply to the offence created by s 111.

1 *DPP v Byrne* [2003] IESC 54.

2 *Fyffes plc v DCC plc and S & L Investments Ltd and others* [2005] IEHC 477.

UK legislation

Criminal Justice Act 1993, s 52.

112 Restriction on dealing

(1) Subject to subsection (2), a person convicted of an offence under section 111 or this section shall not deal within the period of 12 months from the date of the conviction.

(2) Where a person convicted of an offence under subsection (1) has, before the date of his conviction, initiated a transaction under which some element of performance remains to be rendered, subsection (1) shall not prohibit him from completing the transaction where a relevant authority of a recognised stock exchange has indicated in writing, to the parties to the transaction, its satisfaction that—

(a) the transaction was initiated but not completed before the date of the conviction, and

(b) if the transaction were not concluded, the rights of an innocent third party would be prejudiced, and

(c) the transaction would not be unlawful under any other provision of this Part.

(3) A person who contravenes this section shall be guilty of an offence.

Amendments

Section repealed in the limited manner noted in IFCMPA 2005, s 31 with effect from 6 July 2005. See IFCMPA 2005, s 31 and notes thereto.

Cross reference

See s 114 for the applicable penalties.

Definitions

'recognised stock exchange': CA 1990, s 3(1), (2); 'relevant authority': CA 1990, s 107.

Notes

The Irish Stock Exchange is the only 'recognised stock exchange' for the purposes of this section: Companies (Stock Exchange) Regulations1995 (SI 310/1995).

113 Duty of agents in relation to unlawful dealing

(1) A person shall not deal on behalf of another person if he has reasonable cause to believe or ought to conclude that the deal would be unlawful, within the meaning of section 108.

(2) A person who contravenes this section shall be guilty of an offence.

Amendments

Section repealed in the limited manner noted in IFCMPA 2005, s 31 with effect from 6 July 2005. See IFCMPA 2005, s 31 and notes thereto.

Cross reference

See s 108(9) in relation to the position of agents.

See s 114 for the applicable penalties.

114 Penalties for offences under this Part

A person who commits an offence under this Part shall be liable—

(a) on summary conviction to imprisonment for a term not exceeding 12 months or to a fine not exceeding [€1,904.61][a] or to both, or

(b) on conviction on indictment, to imprisonment for a term not exceeding 10 years or to a fine not exceeding [€253,947.61][b] or to both.

Amendments

Section repealed in the limited manner noted in IFCMPA 2005, s 31 with effect from 6 July 2005. See IFCMPA 2005, s 31 and notes thereto.

a '£1,000' increased to £1,500 by CA 1990, s 240(7) as inserted by CLEA 2001, s 104(c), and converted to €1,904.61 by Council Regulations (EC) No 1103/97, No 974/98 and No 2866/98 and the Economic and Monetary Union Act 1998, s 6.

b '£200,000' converted to €253,947.61 by Council Regulations (EC) No 1103/97, No 974/98 and No 2866/98 and the Economic and Monetary Union Act 1998, s 6.

UK legislation

Criminal Justice Act 1993, s 61.

115 Duty of recognised stock exchange in relation of unlawful dealing

(1) If it appears to a relevant authority of a recognised stock exchange that any person has committed an offence under this Part, such authority shall forthwith report the matter to the [Director][a] and shall furnish to the [Director][a] such information and give to him such access to and facilities for inspecting and taking copies of any documents, being information or documents in the possession or under the control of such authority and relating to the matter in question, as the [Director][a] may require.

(2) Where it appears to a member of a recognised stock exchange that any person has committed an offence under this Part, he shall report the matter forthwith to a relevant authority of the recognised stock exchange concerned, who shall thereupon come under the duty referred to in subsection (1).

(3) If it appears to a court in any proceedings that any person has committed an offence as aforesaid, and that no report relating to the matter has been made to the [Director][a] under subsection (1), that court may, on the application of any person interested in the proceedings concerned or of its own motion, direct a relevant authority of the recognised stock exchange concerned to make such a report, and on a report being made

accordingly, this section shall have effect as though the report had been made in pursuance of subsection (1).

[(4) If, where any matter is reported or referred to the Director under this section, he has reasonable grounds for believing that an offence under this Part has been committed and—

(a) institutes proceedings in respect of the offence, or

(b) refers the matter to the Director of Public Prosecutions and the Director of Public Prosecutions institutes proceedings in respect of the offence,

it shall be the duty of a relevant authority of the recognised stock exchange concerned, and of every officer of the company whose securities are concerned, and of any other person who appears to the Director or to the Director of Public Prosecutions, as the case may be, to have relevant information (other than any defendant in the proceedings) to give all assistance in connection with the proceedings which he or they are reasonably able to give.][b]

(5) If it appears to the [Director][c], arising from a complaint to a relevant authority of a recognised stock exchange concerning an alleged offence under this Part, that there are circumstances suggesting that—

(a) the relevant authority ought to use its powers under this Part but has not done so, or

(b) that a report ought to be made to the [Director][a] under subsection (1), but that the relevant authority concerned has not so reported,

he may direct the relevant authority to use such powers or make such a report, and on a report being made accordingly, this section shall have effect as though the report had been made in pursuance of subsection (1).

[...][d].

(7) A relevant authority of a recognised stock exchange shall not be liable in damages in respect of anything done or omitted to be done by the authority in connection with the exercise by it of its functions under this Part unless the act or omission complained of was done or omitted to be done in bad faith.

Amendments

Section repealed in the limited manner noted in IFCMPA 2005, s 31 with effect from 6 July 2005. See IFCMPA 2005, s 31 and notes thereto.

a CLEA 2001, s 37(a) amends CA 1990, s 115 by the substitution for 'Director of Public Prosecutions' wherever occurring, except in subsection (4) of 'Director'.

b CLEA 2001, s 37(b) substitutes CA 1990, s 115(4).

c CLEA 2001, s 37(c) amends CA 1990, s 115(5) by the substitution for 'Minister' of 'Director'.

d CLEA 2001, s 37(d) deletes CA 1990, s 115(6).

Definitions

'court': CA 1990, s 235; 'Minister': CA 1990, s 3(1); 'officer': CA 1990, s 107; 'recognised stock exchange': CA 1990, s 3(1), 3(2); 'relevant authority': CA 1990, s 107.

Notes

The Irish Stock Exchange is the only 'recognised stock exchange' for the purposes of this section: Companies (Stock Exchange) Regulations1995 (SI 310/1995).

The power of the relevant authority include the power to appoint an 'authorised person' to investigate suspected breaches of the insider dealing provisions.

---

116 Co-operation with other authorities outside the State

(1) This section applies where a relevant authority of a recognised stock exchange receives a request for information from a similar authority in another Member State of the European Communities in relation to the exercise by the second-named authority of its functions under any enactment of the European Communities relating to unlawful dealing within the meaning of this Part, whether in the State or elsewhere.

(2) The relevant authority concerned shall, in so far as it is reasonably able to do so, and making use of its powers under this Part where appropriate, obtain the information requested and shall, subject to the following provisions of this section, provide such information accordingly.

(3) Where a relevant authority of a recognised stock exchange receives a request under subsection (1), it shall advise the [Director][a] who, on being satisfied as to any of the matters referred to in subsection (4), may direct the authority to refuse to provide all or part of the information requested.

(4) The matters referred to in subsection (3) are that—

(a) communication of the information requested might adversely affect the sovereignty, security or public policy of the State;

(b) civil or criminal proceedings in the State have already been commenced against a person in respect of any acts in relation to which a request for information has been received under subsection (1);

(c) any person has been convicted in the State of a criminal offence in respect of any such acts.

Amendments

Section repealed in the limited manner noted in IFCMPA 2005, s 31 with effect from 6 July 2005. See IFCMPA 2005, s 31 and notes thereto.

a 'Director' substituted for 'Minister' by CLEA 2001, s 14 as enacted by the Company Law Enforcement Act 2001 (Commencement) (No 3) Order 2001 (SI 523/2001) on November 2001.

Definitions

'Minister': CA 1990, s 3(1); 'the recognised stock exchange': CA 1990, s 3(1), (2); 'relevant authority': CA 1990, s 107.

Notes

The Irish Stock Exchange is the only 'recognised stock exchange' for the purposes of this section: Companies (Stock Exchange) Regulations1995 (SI 310/1995).

This provision was aimed at assisting in the enforcement throughout the EU of the now-repealed Insider Dealing Directive 89/952/EC. It is likely that the section can be used in order to assist the enforcement of the Market Abuse Directive 2003/6/EC.

The purpose of sub-s 4(b), (c) is to avoid a person being placed in double jeopardy in respect of the same act of insider dealing.

UK legislation

CA 1989 s 82, as amended by Criminal Justice Act 1993, s 79(13), Sch 5, Pt I para 16.

---

117 Authorised persons

(1) In this section and sections 118 and 121, 'authorised person' means a person approved by the [Director][a] to be an authorised person for the purposes of this Part being—

(a) the manager, however described, of a recognised stock exchange, or

(b) a person nominated by a relevant authority of a recognised stock exchange.

(2) Where an alleged offence under this Part is investigated by an authorised person, the relevant authorities of the recognised stock exchange concerned shall be under a general duty to ensure that potential conflicts of interest are avoided, as far as possible, on the part of any such authorised person.

(3) For the purpose of obtaining any information necessary for the exercise by a relevant authority of such exchange of the function referred to in section 115, an authorised person may, on production of his authorisation if so required, require any person whom he or such relevant authority has reasonable cause to believe to have dealt in securities, or to have any information about such dealings, to give the authorised person any information which he may reasonably require in regard to—

(a) the securities concerned,

(b) the company which issued the securities,

(c) his dealings in such securities, or

(d) any other information the authorised person reasonably requires in relation to such securities or such dealings,

and give him such access to and facilities for inspecting and taking copies of any documents relating to the matter as he reasonably requires.

(4) Every document purporting to be a warrant or authorisation and to be signed or authenticated by or on behalf of a relevant authority shall be received in evidence and shall be deemed to be such warrant or authorisation without further proof until the contrary is shown.

(5) An authorised person, or any person on whom he has made a requirement under this section, may apply to the court for a declaration under this section.

(6) The court, having heard such evidence as may be adduced and any representations that may be made by the authorised person and a person referred to in subsection (5), may at its discretion declare—

(a) that the exigencies of the common good do not warrant the exercise by the authorised person of the powers conferred on him by this section, or

(b) that the exigencies of the common good do so warrant.

(7) Where the court makes a declaration under subsection (6)(a), the authorised person shall, as soon as may be, withdraw the relevant requirement under this section.

(8) Where the court makes a declaration under subsection (6)(b), the person on whom the requirement was imposed shall, as soon as may be, furnish the required information to the authorised person.

(9) Where, in contravention of subsection (8), a person refuses, or fails within a reasonable time, to comply with a requirement of an authorised person, the authorised person may certify the refusal under his hand to the court, and the court may, after hearing any statement which may be offered in defence, punish the offender in like manner as if he had been guilty of contempt of court.

Amendments

Section repealed in the limited manner noted in IFCMPA 2005, s 31 with effect from 6 July 2005. See IFCMPA 2005, s 31 and notes thereto.

a 'Director' substituted for 'Minister' by CLEA 2001, 14 as enacted by the Company Law Enforcement Act 2001 (Commencement) (No 3) Order 2001 (SI 523/2001) on November 2001.

Definitions

'contravention': CA 1990, s 3(1); 'court': CA 1990, s 235; 'Minister': CA 1990, s 3(1); 'recognised stock exchange': CA 1990, s 3(1), 2(2); 'relevant authority': CA 1990, s 107.

Notes

The Irish Stock Exchange is the only 'recognised stock exchange' for the purposes of this section: Companies (Stock Exchange) Regulations1995 (SI 310/1995).

A journalist may not refuse to answer questions put to him by an authorised person on the ground that he wishes to protect the source of his information.[1]

An application under s 117(5) is by way of Originating Notice of Motion: RSC 1986, Ord 75B, r 3(y).

Section 117(9) is probably unconstitutional on the ground that it permits the Court to try summarily an offence which is not minor in character.[2]

1 *Re an Inquiry under the Company Securities (Insider Dealing) Act 1985* [1988] AC 660.

2 *Desmond and Dedeir v Glackin (No 2)* [1993] IR 67.

UK legislation

CA 1989, ss 84, 85.

---

118 Obligation of professional secrecy

(1) Information obtained by any of the following persons by virtue of the exercise by a recognised stock exchange of its functions under this Part shall not be disclosed except in accordance with law, namely—

(a) a relevant authority of the exchange,

(b) an authorised person, or

(c) any person employed or formerly employed by the exchange.

(2) Subsection (1) shall not prevent a relevant authority of a recognised stock exchange from disclosing any information to the [Director],[a] whether pursuant to a request under

section 115 (5) or otherwise, or to a similar authority in another Member State of the European Communities.

[(2A) Subsection (1) shall not prevent a member, authorised person, relevant authority or employee or former employee of a recognised stock exchange from disclosing information concerning suspected breaches of the Companies Acts to the Director and it is the duty of each such person to so report any such suspected breach to the Director.][b]

(3) Any person who contravenes subsection (1) shall be guilty of an offence.

Amendments

Section repealed in the limited manner noted in IFCMPA 2005, s 31 with effect from 6 July 2005. See IFCMPA 2005, s 31 and notes thereto.

a 'Director' substituted for 'Minister' by CLEA 2001, 14 as enacted by the Company Law Enforcement Act 2001 (Commencement) (No 3) Order 2001 (SI 523/2001) on November 2001.

b CLEA 2001, s 38 inserts CA 1990, s 118(2A).

Definitions

'authorised person': CA 1990, s 117(1); 'Minister': CA 1990, s 3(1); 'recognised stock exchange': CA 1990, s 3(1), (2); 'relevant authority': CA 1990, s 107.

Notes

The Irish Stock Exchange is the only 'recognised stock exchange' for the purposes of this section: Companies (Stock Exchange) Regulations 1995 (SI 310/1995).

UK legislation

CA 1989, ss 86, 87.

119 Extension of Council Directive 79/279/EEC

The provisions of Schedule C.5 (a) of Council Directive 79/279/EEC of 5 March 1979 co-ordinating the conditions for the admission of securities to official stock exchange listing, as given effect by the European Communities (Stock Exchange) Regulations, 1984 (S.I. No 282 of 1984), shall also apply to securities within the meaning of section 107.

Amendments

Section repealed in the limited manner noted in IFCMPA 2005, s 31 with effect from 6 July 2005. See IFCMPA 2005, s 31 and notes thereto.

Notes

This provision is now contained in art 68 of Directive 2001/34/EC of 28 May 2001 (the Consolidated Admissions and Reporting Directive or 'CARD') on the admission of securities to official stock exchange listing and on information to be published on those securities: 'Additional information: The company must inform the public as soon as possible of any major new developments in its sphere of activity which are not public knowledge and which may, by virtue of their effect on its assets and liabilities or financial position or on the general course of its business, lead to substantial movements in the prices of its shares. The competent authorities may, however, exempt the company from this requirement, if the disclosure of particular information is such as to prejudice the legitimate interests of the company.'

This CARD provision is repealed by the Transparency Directive, but if the relevant transposing enactment applies only to issuers whose securities are admitted to a regulated market, this section may continue to apply for issuers admitted to non-regulated markets of the Irish Stock Exchange.

120 Annual report of recognised stock exchange

(1) An annual report shall be presented to the Minister on behalf of every recognised stock exchange on the exercise of the functions of the relevant authorities of the exchange concerned under this Part and, in particular, the report shall include—

(a) the number of written complaints received concerning possible contraventions of this Part,

(b) the number of reports made to the Director of Public Prosecutions under this Part,

(c) the number of instances in which, following the exercise of powers by authorised persons under this Part, reports were not made to the Director of Public Prosecutions, and

(d) such other information as may be prescribed.

(2) A copy of the report referred to in subsection (1) shall, subject to subsection (3), be laid before each House of the Oireachtas.

(3) If the Minister, after consultation with a relevant authority of the recognised stock exchange concerned, is of the opinion that the disclosure of any information contained in the report referred to in subsection (1) would materially injure or unfairly prejudice the legitimate interests of any person, or that otherwise there is good reason for not divulging any part of such a report, he may lay the report under subsection (2) with that information or that part omitted.

Amendments

Section repealed in the limited manner noted in IFCMPA 2005, s 31 with effect from 6 July 2005. See IFCMPA 2005, s 31 and notes thereto.

Definitions

'contravention': CA 1990, s 3(1); 'Minister': CA 1990, s 3(1); 'recognised stock exchange': CA 1990, s 3(1), 2(2); 'relevant authority': CA 1990, s 107.

Notes

The Irish Stock Exchange is the only 'recognised stock exchange' for the purposes of this section: Companies (Stock Exchange) Regulations 1995 (SI 310/1995).

121 Power of Minister to make supplementary regulations

(1) If, in any respect, any difficulty arises in bringing any provision of this Part into operation or in relation to the operation of any such provision, the Minister may by regulations do anything which appears to him to be necessary or expedient for removing that difficulty, for bringing the provision into operation, or for securing or facilitating its

operation, and any such regulations may modify any provision of this Part so far as may be necessary or expedient for carrying such provision into effect for the purposes aforesaid.

(2) Without prejudice to the generality of subsection (1), where the Minister considers it necessary or expedient to do so for the proper and effective administration of sections 115 and 117, he may make such regulations as he thinks appropriate in relation to—

(a) the powers of authorised persons, or

(b) the matters in respect of which, or the persons from whom, authorised persons may require information under this Part.

(3) Every regulation made by the Minister under this section shall be laid before each House of the Oireachtas as soon as may be after it is made and, if a resolution annulling the regulation is passed by either House within the next 21 days on which that House has sat after the regulation is laid before it, the regulation shall be annulled accordingly, but without prejudice to the validity of anything previously done thereunder.

Amendments

Section repealed in the limited manner noted in IFCMPA 2005, s 31 with effect from 6 July 2005. See IFCMPA 2005, s 31 and notes thereto.

Definitions

'Minister': CA 1990, s 3(1).

UK legislation

Criminal Justice Act 1993, s 64.

PART VI
WINDING UP AND RELATED MATTERS

Registration of charges

122 Amendment of section 99 of the Principal Act

[...][a]

[...][b]

Amendments

a This sub-s substitutes CA 1963, s 99(2)(h).

b This sub-s inserts CA 1963, s 99(2A), (2B) & (2C).

Winding up by the court

123 Amendment of sections 214 and 345 of Principal Act

[...][a]

Amendments

a This section substitutes '£1,000' for '£50' in CA 1963, s 214(a) & s 345(a).

124 Amendment of section 231 of the Principal Act

[...][a]

Amendments

a This section inserts CA 1963, s 231(1A).

125 No lien over company's books, records etc

[...][a]

Amendments

a This section inserts CA 1963, s 244A.

126 Power of court to summon persons for examination

[...][a]

Amendments

a This section substitutes CA 1963, s 245.

127 Order for payment or delivery of property against person examined under section 245 of Principal Act

[...][a]

Amendments

a This section inserts CA 1963, s 245A.

Declaration of solvency

128 Statutory declaration of solvency in case of proposal to wind up voluntarily

[...][a]

Amendments

a This section substitutes CA 1963, s 256.

Provisions applicable to a members' voluntary winding up

129 Duty of liquidator to call creditors' meeting if he is of opinion that company is unable to pay its debts

[...][a]

Amendments

a This section substitutes CA 1963, s 261.

Provisions applicable to a Creditors' Voluntary Winding Up

130 Amendment of section 266 of the Principal Act

[...][a]

Amendments

a This section inserts ', at least ten days before the date of the meeting,' after 'advertised' in CA 1963, s 266(2).

131 Creditors' voluntary winding up

(1) This section applies where, in the case of a creditors' voluntary winding up, a liquidator has been nominated by the company.

(2) The powers conferred on the liquidator by section 276 of the Principal Act shall not be exercised, except with sanction of the court, during the period before the holding of the creditors' meeting under section 266 of that Act.

(3) Subsection (2) does not apply in relation to the power of the liquidator—

- (a) to take into his custody or under his control all the property to which the company is or appears to be entitled;
- (b) to dispose of perishable goods and other goods the value of which is likely to diminish if they are not immediately disposed of;
- (c) to do all such other things as may be necessary for the protection of the company's assets.

(4) The liquidator shall attend the creditors' meeting held under section 266 of the Principal Act and shall report to the meeting on any exercise by him of his powers (whether or not under this section or under section 276 or 280 of that Act).

(5) If default is made—

- (a) by the company in complying with subsection (1) or (2) of section 266 of the Principal Act, or
- (b) by the directors in complying with subsection (3) of the said section,

the liquidator shall, within 7 days of the relevant day, apply to the court for directions as to the manner in which that default is to be remedied.

(6) 'The relevant day' means the day on which the liquidator was nominated by the company or the day on which he first became aware of the default, whichever is the later.

(7) If a liquidator without reasonable excuse fails to comply with this section, he shall be guilty of an offence.

Definitions

CA 1963: 'company': CA 1963, s 2(1); 'the court': CA 1963, s 2(1); 'creditor': CA 1963, s 2(1); 'liquidator': CA 1963, s 2(1); 'director': CA 1963, s 2(1).

Notes

Centrebinding: In a creditors' voluntary winding up the members of the company may nominate a liquidator subject to the right of the creditors to appoint a liquidator of their own choosing pursuant to CA 1963, s 267. CA 1963, s 266(1) requires that a creditors' meeting take place on the same day or the next day following a members' general meeting that proposed the winding up of the company.

The purpose of CA 1990, s 131 was to reverse the decision in *Re Centrebind Ltd*[1] where it had been held that the person appointed as liquidator by the members had been validly appointed and had power to act in the liquidation and to realise and deal with the assets despite the fact that no creditors' meeting had ever been held under CA 1963, s 266. A practice had thus developed of only holding a members' meeting and appointing a 'friendly' liquidator who would not investigate or pursue the director and who would be in a position to transfer the company's assets on advantageous terms to a new entity established by the directors.

As a result of the enactment of CA 1990, s 131 this practice, commonly known as 'centrebinding', has been severely curtailed, with the liquidator having only limited powers to deal with the assets (otherwise than with the sanction of the court) pending the holding of the creditors' meeting. An application for the sanction of the court should be made by Originating Notice of Motion pursuant to Ord 74, r 138.

When the creditors' meeting is actually held, the liquidator is required to advise those present whether he has exercised any of his powers since his appointment.

1 *Re Centrebind Ltd* [1967] 1 WLR 377.

UK legislation

IA 1986, s 166.

Provisions applicable to every voluntary winding up

132 Amendment of section 275 of the Principal Act

[...][a]

Amendments

a This section substitutes CA 1963, s 275.

133 Consent to appointment as liquidator and notification of appointment

[...][a]

Amendments

a This section inserts CA 1963, s 276A.

Provisions applicable to every winding up

134 Preferential payments in a winding up

[...][a]

Amendments

a This section inserts CA 1963, s 285(14).

135 Fraudulent preference

[...][a]

Amendments

a This section substitutes CA 1963, s 286.

136 Circumstances in which floating charge is invalid

[...][a]

Amendments

a This section substitutes CA 1963, s 288.

137 Criminal liability of persons concerned for fraudulent trading of company

[...][a]

Amendments

a This section substitutes CA 1963, s 297.

138 Civil liability of persons concerned for fraudulent or reckless trading of company

[...][a]

Amendments

a This section insertes CA 1963, s 297A.

139 Power of the court to order the return of assets which have been improperly transferred

(1) Where, on the application of a liquidator, creditor or contributory of a company which is being wound up, it can be shown to the satisfaction of the court that—

(a) any property of the company of any kind whatsoever was disposed of either by way of conveyance, transfer, mortgage, security, loan, or in any way whatsoever whether by act or omission, direct or indirect, and

(b) the effect of such disposal was to perpetrate a fraud on the company, its creditors or members, the court may, if it deems it just and equitable to do so, order any person who appears to have the use, control or possession of such property or the proceeds of the sale or development thereof to deliver it or pay a sum in respect of it to the liquidator on such terms or conditions as the court sees fit.

(2) Subsection (1) shall not apply to any conveyance, mortgage, delivery of goods, payment, execution or other act relating to property made or done by or against a company to which section 286 (1) of the Principal Act applies.

(3) In deciding whether it is just and equitable to make an order under this section, the court shall have regard to the rights of persons who have bona fide and for value acquired an interest in the property the subject of the application.

Definitions

'company': CA 1963, s 2(1); 'the court': CA 1963, s 2(1); 'creditor': CA 1963, s 2(1); 'contributory': CA 1963, s 2(1); 'liquidator': CA 1963, s 2(1).

Cross references in other enactments

NAMA Act 2009, s 218(1) provides that an acquired bank asset within the meaning of NAMA Act 2009 is 'not invalidated or rendered void or voidable as against NAMA or a NAMA group entity or their successors in title' by operation of CA 1990, s 139.

Notes

Fraudulent dispositions: Prior to the coming into force of CA 1990, s 139 a liquidator could seek to set aside a disposition of company assets under the Conveyances (Ireland) Act 1634 where the intent had been to put the assets beyond the reach of creditors and thus to defraud them. A good example of where a liquidator successfully invoked the provisions of the 1634 Act is *Re Kill Inn Motel Ltd*.[1] In the later case of *Re Frederick Inns Ltd*[2] it was held by the Supreme Court that a disposal of assets by an insolvent company in disregard of the interests of the general body of creditors which had the effect of diminishing the fund available for them in a liquidation was not only *ultra vires* but also unlawful and thus void.

In some respects the provisions of s 139 represent a statutory embodiment of the principles enunciated in *Re Frederick Inns Ltd*. In order to set aside a disposition of assets the liquidator does not have to prove that the company intended to defraud its creditors. Rather, he has the lower evidential burden of merely establishing that the *effect* of the disposition has been to defraud the creditors. To date there has been no recorded decision where s 139 has been successfully invoked. However, in *Re Comet Food Machinery Co Ltd*[3] the Supreme Court observed, albeit obiter, that the section could be invoked if it were established that assets had been diverted with a view to frustrating a judgment against the company. This is hardly a controversial observation since, in such circumstances, the disposition would not only have had the effect of defrauding the creditors:

the administration of two investment companies. The judge described the section as a valuable remedial measure designed to facilitate the task of liquidation helping to avoid protracted liquidation on what is likely to be a futile legal exercise.[5] In relation to the extension of the provisions of s 140 to receiverships and examinerships, see CA 1990, ss 178 & 180.

1 *Power Supermarkets Ltd v Crumlin Investments Ltd* (22 June 1981, unreported) HC (Costello J). See also *Re Bray Travel Ltd and Bray Travel (Holdings) Ltd* (13 July 1981, unreported) SC; *H Albert De Bary & Co NV v TF O'Mullaney* (2 June 1992, unreported) HC (Barron J); *DHN Food Distributors Ltd v Tower Hamlets London Borough Council* [1976] 1 WLR 852.

2 *Lac Minerals Ltd v Chevron Mineral* [1995] 1 ILRM 161; *Allied Irish Coal Supplies Ltd v Powell Duffryn International Fuels Ltd* [1998] 2 IR 519; *Woolfson v Strathclyde Regional Council* (1978) SC 90; *National Dock Labour Board v Pinn & Wheeler Ltd* [1989] BCLC 647; *Adams v Cape Industries plc* [1990] Ch. 433; *Re Polly Peck International plc (No 4)* [1996] 2 All ER 433.

3 *Fyffes plc v DCC plc* (21 December 2005, unreported) HC (Laffoy J).

4 *Re Pacific Syndicates (NZ) Ltd* (1989) 4 NZCLC 64, 757

5 See generally *Rea v Barker* (1988) 4 NZCLC 64, 312; *Re Dalhoff and King Holdings Ltd* [1991] 2 NZLR 296; (1990) 5 NZCLC 66, 959.

141 Pooling of assets of related companies

(1) Where two or more related companies are being wound up and the court, on the application of the liquidator of any of the companies, is satisfied that it is just and equitable to make an order under this section, the court may order that, subject to such terms and conditions as the court may impose and to the extent that the court orders, the companies shall be wound up together as if they were one company, and, subject to the provisions of this section, the order shall have effect and all the provisions of this Part and Part VI of the Principal Act shall apply accordingly.

(2) In deciding the terms and conditions of an order under this section the court shall have particular regard to the interests of those persons who are members of some, but not all, of the companies.

(3) Where the court makes an order under subsection (1) —

- (a) the court may remove any liquidator of any of the companies, and appoint any person to act as liquidator of any one or more of the companies;
- (b) the court may give such directions as it thinks fit for the purpose of giving effect to the order;
- (c) nothing in this section or the order shall affect the rights of any secured creditor of any of the companies;
- (d) debts of a company that are to be paid in priority to all other debts of the company pursuant to section 285 of the Principal Act shall, to the extent that they are not paid out of the assets of that company, be subject to the claims of holders of debentures under any floating charge (as defined in that section) created by any of the other companies;
- (e) unless the court otherwise orders, the claims of all unsecured creditors of the companies shall rank equally among themselves.

(4) In deciding whether it is just and equitable to make an order under subsection (1) the court shall have regard to the following matters—

(a) the extent to which any of the companies took part in the management of any of the other companies;

(b) the conduct of any of the companies towards the creditors of any of the other companies;

(c) the extent to which the circumstances that gave rise to the winding up of any of the companies are attributable to the actions or omissions of any of the other companies;

(d) the extent to which the businesses of the companies have been intermingled.

(5) Notwithstanding any other provision, it shall not be just and equitable to make an order under subsection (1) if the only ground for making the order is—

(a) the fact that a company is related to another company, or

(b) that creditors of a company being wound up have relied on the fact that another company is or has been related to the first mentioned company.

(6) Notice of an application to the court for the purposes of this section shall be served on every company specified in the application, and on such other persons as the court may direct, not later than the end of the eighth day before the day the application is heard.

Definitions

'company': CA 1963, s 2(1); 'the court': CA 1963, s 2(1); 'creditor': CA 1963, s 2(1); 'debenture': CA 1963, s 2(1); 'floating charge': CA 1963, s 285; 'liquidator': CA 1963, s 2(1); 'related company': CA 1990, s 3(1) and 140(5)

Notes

Pooling orders: The provisions of s 141 echo the judgment of Costello J in *Power Supermarkets Ltd v Crumlin Investments Ltd*[1] where it was held that the court has an inherent jurisdiction, if the justice of the case so required, to pierce the corporate veil and treat two or more related companies as a single entity so that the business notionally carried on by one will be regarded as the business of the group, or another member of the group, if this conforms to the economic and commercial realities of the case. The correctness of this line of jurisprudence was questioned in later cases both in Ireland and in other jurisdictions.[2] It has, however, been reasserted in the recent decision of Laffoy J in *Fyffes plc v DCC plc*.[3]

See notes to CA 1990, s 140 and Courtney, *Law of Private Companies* (2nd edn, Tottel Publishing, 2002) paras 5.006 & 27.112–27.116 and Keane, Company Law (4th edn, Tottel Publishing, 2007), pp 139–140.

The section provides that where two or more related companies are being wound up the court, on the application of the liquidator of any of the companies, may, provided it is satisfied that it is just and equitable to do so, order that, subject to such terms and conditions as it may impose and to the extent that it orders, the companies be wound up together as if they were one company: s 141(1). In deciding the terms and conditions on any such order, the court is to have particular regard to the interests of those persons who are members of some, but not all, of the companies: s 141(2). Notice of the application is to be served on every company specified in the application, and on such persons as the court may direct, not later than the end of the eighth day before the day the application is heard: s 141(6).

In deciding whether it is just and equitable to make the order, the court is to have regard to the extent to which any of the companies took part in the management of any of the other companies, to which the circumstances of the insolvency are attributable to the acts of an of the other companies and the intermingling of the companies' businesses.

In making an order that the companies be wound up together the court may make give such directions as it thinks fit for the purpose of giving effect to the order. In particular it may remove any liquidator of any of the companies and appoint any person to act as liquidator of any of the companies and appoint any person to act as liquidator of any one or more of the companies: s 141(3)(a) & (b). Presumably, in view of the fact that the companies are to be wound up as one, it will be standard practice to have the same individual or individuals as liquidator of all of the companies to which the order relates, unless of course some conflict of interest arises.[4]

An order for the winding up together of related companies does not affect the rights of any secured creditor of any of the companies. Furthermore, creditors with preferential claims under CA 1963, s 285 as against one company may, to the extent that such claims have not been met out of the assets of that company, prove in the liquidation of the related company, after the claims of the holders of any floating charges created by that other company but before the claims of the ordinary unsecured creditors: s 141(3)(c) and (d).

The claims of all unsecured creditors of the companies rank equally among themselves, unless the court directs otherwise: s 141(3)(e). The effect of the section is that creditors of a company could find themselves ranking after not only the secured and preferential creditors of their own company, but also after the balance of any unsatisfied preferential claims of the related company. This in itself could substantially reduce the dividend available for distribution to the unsecured creditors. In addition, the very fact that the assets of the two companies are being pooled, could result in the unsecured creditors of one company receiving a lower dividend than they would have obtained if their company had been wound up on its own, whereas the unsecured creditors of the second company may obtain a higher dividend than they could otherwise have expected. This makes inroads into the property of the creditors of one company to subsidise the creditors of another company and may run a risk of being challenged on the basis of Articles 40.3.2° and 43.2.2° of the Constitution or art 1 of the ECHR.

As the affairs of related companies must be in effect co-mingled, and as this will be done by those persons appointed by the members to manage the company, ie the directors, it is arguable that the directors of a company ought to include, as a contingent liability, the debts of the company where its affairs are, according to their knowledge intermingled with a related company. Failure of a director to make himself aware of his company's relationship with related companies would seem, in light of the risk posed to the security of his company's creditors, to be a failure in his duty towards those creditors.

1 *Power Supermarkets Ltd v Crumlin Investments Ltd* (22 June 1981, unreported) HC (Costello J). See also *Re Bray Travel Ltd and Bray Travel (Holdings) Ltd* (13 July 1981, unreported) SC; *H Albert De Bary & Co NV v TF O'Mullaney* (2 June 1992, unreported) HC (Barron J); *DHN Food Distributors Ltd v Tower Hamlets London Borough Council* [1976] 3 All ER 462.

2 *Lac Minerals Ltd v Chevron Mineral* [1995] 1 ILRM 161; *Allied Irish Coal Supplies Ltd v Powell Duffryn International Fuels Ltd* [1998] 2 IR 519; *Woolfson v Strathclyde Regional Council* (1978) SC 90; *National Dock Labour Board v Pinn & Wheeler Ltd* [1989] BCLC 647; *Adams v Cape Industries plc* [1990] Ch 433; *Re Polly Peck International plc (No 4)* [1996] 2 All ER 433.

3 *Fyffes plc v DCC plc* (21 December 2005, unreported) HC (Laffoy J).

4 As to the question of conflict of interest in such a situation, see *Re P Turner (Wilsden) Ltd* [1987] BCLC 149.

142 Amendment of section 298 of the Principal Act

[...][a]

Amendments

a This section substitutes CA 1963, s 298.

143 Amendment of section 299 of the Principal Act

[...][a]

Amendments

a This section substitutes CA 1963, s 299(1).

144 Duty of liquidators and receivers to include certain information in returns etc

(1) Where a receiver or liquidator of a company is obliged by the Companies Acts to make a periodic account, abstract, statement or return in relation to his activities as receiver or liquidator he shall incorporate in such account, abstract, statement or return a report as to whether, at the date of such account, abstract, statement or return any past or present director or other officer, or any member, of the company is a person—

(a) in respect of whom a declaration has been made under any provision of the Companies Acts that he should be personally liable for all or any part of the debts of a company,

(b) who is, or is deemed to be, subject to a disqualification order under Part VII.

(2) A receiver or liquidator who contravenes subsection (1) shall be guilty of an offence and liable to a fine.

Definitions

'company': CA 1963, s 2(1); 'director': CA 1963, s 2(1); 'liquidator': CA 1963, s 2(1); 'officer': CA 1963, s 2(1); 'receiver': CA 1963, s 2(1).

Notes

This section obliges a receiver or liquidator to periodically update the relevant authority as to whether any past or present officer of the company was made personally liable under any provision of the Companies Act for the debts of the company and who is or who is deemed to be disqualified. In relation to the provisions of the Companies Acts obliging liquidators and receivers to make accounts, returns, etc, see CA 1963, ss 262, 263, 272, 273, 319 & 321 and CLEA 2001, s 56. As regards the provisions whereby personal liability may be imposed on directors, officers and members, see CA 1963, ss 256, 297A & CA 1990, ss 39, 163, 165, 204 & 251.

145 Penalty for default of receiver or liquidator in making certain accounts and returns

(1) Where a receiver or liquidator is in default in relation to the making or filing of a periodic account, abstract, statement or return in pursuance of any provision of the Companies Acts he shall be guilty of an offence and liable—

(a) on summary conviction to a fine not exceeding [€1,904.61][a] and, for continued contravention, to a daily default fine not exceeding [€63.49][b];

(b) on conviction on indictment to a fine not exceeding [€12,697.38][c] and, for continued contravention, to a daily default fine not exceeding [€317.44].[d]

(2) A person convicted of an offence under any of the following provisions, namely section 262, 272, 306, 319 (2) or 321 of the Principal Act, shall, in lieu of the penalty provided in any such section (as increased by section 15 of the Companies (Amendment) Act, 1982), be liable to the penalties specified in subsection (1).

Amendments

a '£1,000' in subsection (1)(a) increased to '£1,500' by CA 1990, s 240(7) as inserted by CLEA 2001, s 104 and converted to €1,904.61 by Council Regulations (EC) No 1103/97, No 974/98 and No 2866/98 and the Economic and Monetary Union Act 1998, s 6.

b '£50' in subsection (1)(a) converted to €63.49 by Council Regulations (EC) No 1103/97, No 974/98 and No 2866/98 and the Economic and Monetary Union Act 1998, s 6.

c '£10,000' in subsection (1)(b) converted to €12,697.38 by Council Regulations (EC) No 1103/97, No 974/98 and No 2866/98 and the Economic and Monetary Union Act 1998, s 6.

d '£250' in subsection (1)(b) converted to €317.44 by Council Regulations (EC) No 1103/97, No 974/98 and No 2866/98 and the Economic and Monetary Union Act 1998, s 6.

Supplementary provisions

146 Disqualification for appointment as liquidator

[...][a]

Amendments

a This section inserts CA 1963, s 300A.

147 Disclosure of interest by creditors etc. at creditors' meetings

[...][a]

Amendments

a This section inserts CA 1963, s 301A.

148 Extension of power of court to assess damages against directors

(1) Subsection (2) applies if in the course of winding up a company which is a subsidiary of another company, it appears that any director of the subsidiary's holding company has misapplied or retained or become liable or accountable for any money or property of the subsidiary, or has been guilty of any misfeasance or other breach of duty or trust in relation to the subsidiary.

(2) The court may, on the application of the liquidator, any creditor or contributory of the subsidiary, examine into the conduct of the director concerned and compel him—

(a) to repay or restore the money or property or any part thereof respectively with interest at such rate as the court thinks just, or

(b) to contribute such sum to the assets of the subsidiary by way of compensation in respect of the misapplication, retainer, misfeasance or other breach of duty or trust as the court thinks just.

Definitions

'company': CA 1963, s 2(1); 'the court': CA 1963, s 2(1); 'creditor': CA 1963, s 2(1); 'holding company': CA 1963, s 155(4); 'liquidator': CA 1963, s 2(1); 'subsidiary': CA 1963, s 155(1).

Notes

The effect of this section is to extend the misfeasance provisions of CA 1963, s 298 to a situation where a director of a holding company has been guilty of wrongdoing in relation to the assets or affairs of any subsidiary. See generally the notes to CA 1963, s 298.

PART VII
DISQUALIFICATIONS AND RESTRICTIONS: DIRECTORS AND OTHER OFFICERS

Chapter 1
Restriction on Directors of Insolvent Companies

149 Application of Chapter I

(1) This Chapter applies to any company if—

(a) at the date of the commencement of its winding-up it is proved to the court, or

(b) at any time during the course of its winding-up the liquidator of the company certifies, or it is otherwise proved, to the court,

that it is unable to pay its debts (within the meaning of section 214 of the Principal Act).

(2) This Chapter applies to any person who was a director of a company to which this section applies at the date of, or within 12 months prior to, the commencement of its winding-up.

(3) This Chapter shall not apply to a company which commences to be wound up before the commencement of this section.

(4) In this Chapter 'company' includes a company to which section 351 of the Principal Act applies.

(5) This Chapter applies to shadow directors as it applies to directors.

Definitions

'company': CA 1963, s 2(1); 'the court': CA 1963, s 2(1); 'creditor': CA 1963, s 2(1); 'liquidator': CA 1963, s 2(1); 'shadow director': CA 1990, s 27.

Notes

Restriction of directors: CA 1990, Pt VII, Ch 1 introduced an entirely new statutory regime for the restriction of persons who were directors or shadow directors of insolvent companies at the time of commencement of the liquidation or receivership, as the case may be, or who had been directors or shadow directors in the twelve months previously.

The primary purpose of CA 1990, s 150 is to protect the public from 'cowboy' directors who by their conduct have shown themselves to be unfit to hold the office of director and to discharge the duties imposed on directors of companies[1] The concept of limited liability offers great privileges for those who wish to trade using the corporate vehicle. The necessary corollary of this privilege is a responsibility to protect creditors and shareholders.[2] Although the function of CA 1990, Pt VII, Ch 1 is to protect the public from the danger to potential investors and traders dealing with directors who have shown themselves to be unfit, in considering whether or not to make an order under this section one must be careful not to be wise after the event and there must be no 'witch hunt' just because the business failed as businesses will.[3] The most substantial effect of a restriction order for the restricted person himself is that he cannot directly or indirectly act as a director, shadow director or secretary or be concerned in the promotion or formation of any company unless it has a minimum level of share capital paid up in cash of €317,434.51 in the case of a plc or €63,486.90 in the case of any other type of company. See s 150(3). See also ss 155 & 156 for the limitations imposed on companies that have restricted persons as directors or promoters.

The section 56 report: Under CLEA 2001, s 56 the liquidator[4] must present a report to the ODCE, dealing, *inter alia*, with the question of whether there are circumstances warranting the restriction of any persons caught by CA 1990, Pt VII, Ch 1. Unless he has been relieved of his obligation to do so by the ODCE,[5] the liquidator must commence s 150 proceedings against those persons not earlier than three months and not later than five months after the date on which he presented his s 56 Report (or within such longer period of time as may be allowed by the court). Whilst the failure to commence the s 150 proceedings in time is an offence on the part of the liquidator under CLEA 2001, s 56(3), this failure will not of invalidate the s 150 proceedings themselves.[6]

Shadow directors: Although a body corporate may be a shadow director, it has recently been held by the Supreme Court that a body corporate may not be made the subject of a restriction order under s 150.[7] CA 1990 s 27 defines a shadow director as 'a person in accordance with whose directions or instructions the directors of a company are accustomed to act … unless the directors are accustomed so to act by reason only that they do so on advice given by him in his professional capacity'. The court has on several occasions made an order pursuant to CA 1990, s 150 against shadow directors.[8]

De facto directors: The word 'director' is defined in CA 1963, s 2(1) as including a director by whatever name called. For the purposes of s 150 it includes a person who has never been formally appointed as a director but who nonetheless is a *de facto* director.[9] In *Re Lynrowan Enterprises Ltd*[10] O'Neill J distinguished between a shadow director and a de facto director, adopting the dictum of Millett J in *Hydrodam (Corby) Ltd*[11] where it was held that a *de facto* director is one who claims to act and purports to act as a director although not validly appointed,[12] whereas a shadow director does not claim to purport to act as a director. O'Neill J described a shadow director as one lurking in the shadows, sheltering behind others who he claims are the only directors of a company to the exclusion of himself. O'Neill J held that it was an invariable characteristic of a shadow director that his role was hidden behind that of a validly appointed or indeed a de facto director through whom in a concealed way a shadow director directs the affairs of the company. It would appear therefore that the positions of de facto director and shadow director are not mutually exclusive since the directions or instructions which make a person a shadow director need not extend over the whole range of the company's activities and, accordingly, a person could be a de facto director of the company for the purpose of certain activities and yet be a shadow director for the purpose of other activities.[13]

Foreign directors: Directors resident abroad are capable of being made the subject of restriction orders and in this regard s 150 proceedings may be served on them abroad even though such proceedings are nowhere mentioned in Ord 11.[14]

Foreign companies: Because of the extension of the word 'company' to include those 'companies' to which CA 1963, s 351 applies, restriction orders may be made against directors of foreign companies having a place of business in the state.

Onus of proof and potential constitutional infirmity: Whereas the onus of proof is on a director to show why he should not be restricted,[15] the onus of proof lies on the liquidator or receiver, as the case may be, to first demonstrate that the respondent is indeed a director, shadow director or de facto director.[16] Recognising the grave damage that may be done to a person's reputation as a result of being restricted, the Supreme Court has categorised the mandatory nature of s 150 as being 'draconian' and has expressed doubts as to whether the blanket reversal of the onus of proof (including the requirement for the person to show why he should not be restricted) is consistent with fundamental fairness and constitutional justice.[17]

Proof of insolvency: CA 1990, Pt VII, Ch 1 only applies if it is proved to the court at the commencement of the winding up if the liquidator subsequently certifies at any time during the course of the winding up that the company is unable to pay its debts. The certificate of a liquidator that a company is unable to pay its debts is capable of being challenged, does not give rise to any presumption of insolvency and may be challenged by the respondents.[18]

Procedure for s 150 applications: In the case of a compulsory winding up, s 150 proceedings are commenced by Notice of Motion whereas in a voluntary winding up or receivership they are commenced by Originating Notice of Motion. Evidence is on affidavit unless the court otherwise orders. See Practice Direction *HC 28 – Companies Acts – Applications under s 150(1) Companies Act 1990* and *Luby v McMahon*.[19]

1 See generally Courtney, *The Law of Private Companies* (2nd edn, Tottel Publishing, 2002), paras 12.043–12.089; see also *La Moselle Clothing Ltd v Soluahi* [1998] 2 ILRM 345; *Re Tralee Beef & Lamb Ltd, Kavanagh v Delaney* [2008] 3 IR 347; *Re Dublin Sports Cafe Ltd* (16 December 2008, unreported) SC (Finnegan J).

2 *Re Grayan Building Services Ltd* [1995] Ch D 241 as approved in *Business Communications v Baxter* (21 July 1995, unreported) HC (Murphy J).

3 *Business Communications v Baxter* (21 July 1995, unreported) HC (Murphy J); *Re Camoate Construction Ltd, Coyle v Callanan* [2006] 1 IR 447.

4 Curiously, CLEA 2001, s 56 does not appear to apply to receivers.

5 The Supreme Court has roundly criticised the ODCE for failing to gives reasons for not relieving a liquidator of the obligation to bring s 150 proceedings in circumstances where the liquidator has formed the view that the individuals in question have acted honestly and responsibly and that there is no other reason why they should be restricted: *Re Tralee Beef & Lamb Ltd, Kavanagh v Delaney* [2008] 3 IR 347. See McGrath, 'Restriction of Directors: Tralee Beef and Lamb' (2008) 2 (4) IBLQ 16. See also *Re Dublin Sports Cafe Ltd* (16 December 2008, unreported) SC (Finnegan J).

6 *Re Visual Impact and Displays Ltd* [2003] 4 IR 451; *Coyle v O'Brien* [2003] 2 IR 627.

7 *Re Worldport Ireland Ltd* [2009] 1 IR 398.

8 See for example, *Re Vehicle Imports Ltd* (23 November 2000, unreported) HC (Murphy J); *Re Gasco Ltd* [2001] IEHC 20 (McCracken J).

9 *Re Lynrowan Enterprises Ltd* (31 July 2002, unreported) HC (O'Neill J); *Re First Class Toy Traders Ltd* (9 July 2004, unreported) HC ex tempore (Finlay Geoghegan J); *Re Richborough Furniture Ltd* (1996) BCLC 507; *Secretary State for Industry v Tjolle* [1998] BCC 282; *Re Kaytech International plc* (1999) BCC 390; *Re Mitek Holdings Ltd* [2005] 4 IR 522 (Finlay Geoghegan J); *Gemma Ltd v Davies* [2008] 2 BCLC 281; *Re Lo-Line Electric Motors Ltd* [1988] BCLC 696.

10 *Re Lynrowan Enterprises Ltd* [2002] IEHC 90 (O'Neill J).

11 *Hydrodam (Corby) Ltd* [1994] 2 BCLC 180.

12 See for example, *Re Paycheck Services Ltd* [2009] 2 BCLC 309.

13 *Re Mea Corporation Ltd* [2007] 1 BCLC 618.

14 *Fennell v Frost* [2003] 3 IR 80.

15 *Business Communications v Baxter* (21 July 1995, unreported) HC (Murphy J); *La Moselle Clothing Ltd v Soluahi* [1998] 2 ILRM 345; *Re Dublin Sports Cafe Ltd* (16 December 2008, unreported) SC (Finnegan J).

16 *Re Lynrowan Enterprises Ltd* [2002] IEHC 90 (O'Neill J).

17 *Re Tralee Beef & Lamb Ltd, Kavanagh v Delaney* [2008] 3 IR 347. See McGrath, 'Restriction of Directors: Tralee Beef and Lamb' (2008) 2 (4) IBLQ 16

18 *Caraway v The Attorney General* [1996] 3 IR 300.

19 *Luby v McMahon* [2003] 4 IR 133.

150 Restriction

(1) The court shall, unless it is satisfied as to any of the matters specified in subsection (2), declare that a person to whom this Chapter applies shall not, for a period of five years, be appointed or act in any way, whether directly or indirectly, as a director or secretary or be concerned or take part in the promotion or formation of any company unless it meets the requirements set out in subsection (3); and, in subsequent provisions of this Part, the expression 'a person to whom section 150 applies' shall be construed as a reference to a person in respect of whom such a declaration has been made.

(2) The matters referred to in subsection (1) are—

(a) that the person concerned has acted honestly and responsibly in relation to the conduct of the affairs of the company and that there is no other reason why it would be just and equitable that he should be subject to the restrictions imposed by this section, or

(b) subject to paragraph (a), that the person concerned was a director of the company solely by reason of his nomination as such by a financial institution in connection with the giving of credit facilities to the company by such institution, provided that the institution in question has not obtained from any director of the company a personal or individual guarantee of repayment to it of the loans or other forms of credit advanced to the company, or

(c) subject to paragraph (a), that the person concerned was a director of the company solely by reason of his nomination as such by a venture capital company in connection with the purchase of, or subscription for, shares by it in the first-mentioned company.

(3) The requirements specified in subsection (1) are that—

(a) the nominal value of the allotted share capital of the company shall—

(i) in the case of a public limited company, be at least [€317,434.52],[a]

(ii) in the case of any other company, be at least [€63,486.90],[b]

(b) each allotted share to an aggregate amount not less than the amount referred to in subparagraph (i) or (ii) of paragraph (a), as the case may be, shall be fully paid up, including the whole of any premium thereon, and

(c) each such allotted share and the whole of any premium thereon shall be paid for in cash.

(4) Where a court makes a declaration under subsection (1), a prescribed officer of the court shall cause the registrar of companies to be furnished with prescribed particulars of the declaration in such form and manner as may be prescribed.

[(4A) An application for a declaration under subsection (1) may be made to the court by the Director, a liquidator or a receiver.][c]

[(4B) The court, on the hearing of an application for a declaration under subsection (1) by the Director, a liquidator or a receiver (in this subsection referred to as 'the applicant'), may order that the directors against whom the declaration is made shall bear—

(a) the costs of the application, and

(b) the whole (or such portion of them as the court specifies) of the costs and expenses incurred by the applicant—

(i) in investigating the matters the subject of the application, and

(ii) in so far as they do not fall within paragraph (a), in collecting evidence in respect of those matters,

including so much of the remuneration and expenses of the applicant as are attributable to such investigation and collection.][d]

(5) In this section—

'financial institution' means—

(a) a licensed bank, within the meaning of section 25, or

(b) a company the ordinary business of which includes the making of loans or the giving of guarantees in connection with loans, and

'venture capital company' means a company prescribed by the Minister the principal ordinary business of which is the making of share investments.

Amendments

a CLEA 2001, s 41(1)(a) amends CA 1990, s 150(3)(a)(i) by the substitution for '£100,000' of '£250,000'. £250,000 was converted to €317,434.52 by Council Regulations (EC) No 1103/97, No 974/98 and No 2866/98 and the Economic and Monetary Union Act 1998, s 6.

b CLEA 2001, s 41(1)(b) amends CA 1990, s 150(3)(a)(ii) by the substitution for '£20,000' of '£50,000'. £50,000 was converted to €63,486.90 by Council Regulations (EC) No 1103/97, No 974/98 and No 2866/98 and the Economic and Monetary Union Act 1998, s 6.

c CLEA 2001, s 41(1)(c) inserts CA 1990, s 150(4A).

d CLEA 2001, s 41(c) inserts sub-s (4B) which was substituted with effect from 29 January 2007 by IFCMPA 2006, s 11(1).

Definitions

'company': CA 1963, s 2(1); 'the court': CA 1963, s 2(1); 'director': CA 1963, s 2(1); the minister': 2(1); 'registrar of companies': CA 1963, s 2(1); 'licensed bank': CA 1990, s 25; 'shadow director': CA 1990, s 27.

Notes

The mandatory nature of Part VII Chapter 1: The provisions of s 150 are mandatory and the court must impose the full statutory restriction unless the directors concerned have discharged the onus of proof as set out in sub-section CA 1990: CA 1963, s 150(2).[1] Recognising the grave damage that may be done to a person's reputation as a result of being restricted, the Supreme Court has categorised the mandatory nature of s 150 as being 'draconian' and has expressed doubts as to whether the blanket reversal of the onus of proof (including the requirement for the person to show why he should not be restricted) is consistent with fundamental fairness and constitutional justice.[2]

An order pursuant to CA 1990: CA 1963, s 150 must be for a five-year period of restriction, commencing on the date that the court makes the order and not the commencement of the winding up.[3] The court may, however, put a stay on the order on such terms as it thinks fit.[4] A director may apply within one year of the making of the order, to lift the restriction order and the court may do so if it believes it is just and equitable and on whatever terms and conditions it sees fit.[5] Under CA 1990: CA 1963, s 152 the Court has discretion whether or not to lift or vary the order, whereas it is constrained in its approach when hearing an application under CA 1990: CA 1963, s 150.

1 Per Murphy J in *Business Communications v Baxter & Parsons* (21 July 1995, unreported) (Murphy J). See also *Re Cavan Crystal Group Ltd* (26 April 1996, unreported) (Murphy J); *La Moselle Clothing Ltd v Soluahi* [1998] 2 ILRM 345; *Re Dublin Sports Cafe Ltd* (16 December 2008, unreported) SC (Finnegan J); *Re MDN Rochford Construction Ltd* (18 August 2009, unreported) HC (MacMenamin J).

2 *Re Tralee Beef & Lamb Ltd, Kavanagh v Delaney* [2008] 3 IR 347. See McGrath, 'Restriction of Directors: Tralee Beef and Lamb' (2008) 2 (4) IBLQ 16. See also *Re Dublin Sports Cafe Ltd* (16 December 2008, unreported) SC (Finnegan J).

3 *Duignan v Carway* [2001] 4 IR 550.

4 Shanley J granted the directors a stay of six months in *Re Ferngara Associates Ltd, Robinson v Forrest* [1999] 1 IR 426.

5 See notes following CA 1990, s 152(1).

The La Moselle Test: Under CA 1990, s 150 the court must make a declaration of restriction in respect of persons to whom it applies unless the court is satisfied 'as to any of the matters specified in sub-section (2)'. The matters relevant to such an application are whether the director in question 'has acted honestly and responsibly in relation to the conduct of the affairs of the company'.[1] Whilst the court's scrutiny will be particularly focused on the period prior to the commencement of the liquidation or receivership, nevertheless the court must look at the entire tenure of the respondents as directors.[2]

The application to restrict a director is unusual in that the onus of establishing that he acted honestly and responsibly rests on the director.[3] A practice direction dated 24 March 2003 in relation to voluntary windings up requires a liquidator to put before the court that which he considers relevant to the court's determination of whether a director has acted honestly and responsibly. Finlay Geoghegan J has directed that the said practice direction shall apply to compulsory winding up. A director will of course be required to respond to the specific averments of the liquidator, but must also be alive to other issues of relevance because of the general evidential burden placed on him by s 150.

The matters to which the court should have regard in determining the responsibility of a director for the purposes of CA 1990: CA 1963, s 150 (2)(a), as set out by Shanley J in *La Moselle Clothing Ltd v Soualhi*[4] and as approved by the Supreme Court in *Re Squash (Ireland) Ltd*[5] are—

'(a) The extent to which the director has or has not complied with any obligation imposed on him by the Companies Acts 1963–1990.

(b) The extent to which his conduct could be regarded as so incompetent as to amount to irresponsibility.

(c) The extent of the director's responsibility for the insolvency of the company.

(d) The extent of the director's responsibility for the net deficiency in the assets of the company disclosed at the date of the winding up or thereafter.

(e) The extent to which the director, in his conduct of the affairs of the company, has displayed a lack of commercial probity or want of proper standards.'

In *Re Tralee Beef and Lamb Ltd*,[6] it was held in the High Court that the court should also have regard to the duties imposed on a director at common law. In that case, the court agreed with three general propositions derived from earlier English decisions[7] in relation to duties of directors in the following terms—

(i) 'Directors had, both collectively and individually, a continuing duty to acquire and maintain a sufficient knowledge and understanding of the company's business to enable them properly to discharge their duties as directors.

(ii) Whilst directors were entitled (subject to the articles of association of the company) to delegate particular functions to those below them in the management chain, and to trust their competence and integrity to a reasonable extent, the exercise of the power of delegation did not absolve a director from the duty to supervise the discharge of the delegated functions.

(iii) No rule of universal application can be formulated as to the duty referred to in (ii) above. The extent of the duty, and the question whether it has been discharged, depended on the facts of each particular case, including the director's role in the management of the company.'

On appeal, however, the Supreme Court left open both the question of whether the matters to be considered by the court in s 150 proceedings should indeed be amplified to include the question of an individual's compliance with his common law duties as a director and also the question of the content and wording of any such amplification.[8]

1 In the vast majority of cases that have been dealt with by the court the issue has been whether or not the directors have acted responsibly. For an example of a case where the court had to consider the issue of dishonesty, see *Re Outdoor Financial Services Ltd* [1997] IEHC 20 (Costello J) where the court found that the directors did not act honestly as they consciously and deliberately sought to benefit one of the directors personally and two outside companies owned by the directors who were not creditors of the company at the expense of the company's creditors.

2 *Re Squash Ireland Ltd* [2001] 3 I.R. 35; *Re Gasco Ltd* [2001] IEHC 20 (McCracken J); *Re Swanpool Ltd, McLaughlin v Lannen* [2006] 2 ILRM 217.

3 *Business Communications Ltd v Baxter* (21 July 1995, unreported) HC (Murphy J); *Re La Moselle Ltd* [1998] 2 ILRM 345.

4 *La Moselle Clothing Ltd v Soualhi* [1998] 2 ILRM 345. See also *Re Dublin Sports Cafe Ltd* (16 December 2008, unreported) SC (Finnegan J).

5 *Re Squash (Ireland) Ltd* [2001] 3 IR 35. See also *Re Money Markets International Ltd* [2006] IEHC 350.

6 *Re Tralee Beef and Lamb Ltd* (20 July 2004, unreported) HC (Finlay Geoghegan J).

7 Per Jonathan Parker J in *Re Barings plc. and Ors. (No 5)*; *Secretary of State for Trade and Industry v Baker and Ors* [1999] 1 BCLC 433. Approved by the Court of Appeal in *Re Barings plc (No 5)*; *Secretary of State for Trade and Industry v Baker* [2000] 1 BCLC 523 at 536.

8 *Re Tralee Beef & Lamb Ltd, Kavanagh v Delaney* [2008] 3 IR 347. See McGrath, 'Restriction of Directors: Tralee Beef and Lamb' (2008) 2 (4) IBLQ 16.

La Moselle Test No 1 – The extent to which the director has or has not complied with the Companies Acts

1.1 Books and records and financial information

Under this rubric, the courts have been concerned with the maintenance of proper books and accounts. The records may be modest, but they must exist in such a form so as to enable the directors to make reasonable commercial decisions and auditors (or liquidators) to understand and follow the transactions to which the company was engaged.[1] Maintenance of proper books and accounts and the employment of appropriate experts in relation to them goes a long way to discharge the onus of showing that the directors behaved responsibly.[2] Keeping books and records is the joint and several responsibility of each of the directors.[3] Failure to keep proper financial records[4] and failing to ensure the safety of all the books and records of the company despite the fact that the company ceased trading[5] or was 'dormant'[6] have all been held to be evidence of irresponsibility.

1 *Business Communications v Baxter & others* (21 July 1995, unreported) HC (Murphy J); *Re Hydro Klenze Ltd* (20 December 2007, unreported) HC (Smyth J); *Re Dublin Sports Cafe Ltd* (16 December 2008, unreported) SC (Finnegan J); *Re MDN Rochford Construction Ltd* (18 August 2009, unreported) HC (MacMenamin J).

2 In *Re Costello Doors Ltd* (21 July 1995, unreported) HC (Murphy J).

3 *Re Vehicle Imports Ltd* (23 November 2000, unreported) HC (Murphy J).

4 *Re Gasco Ltd* [2001] IEHC 20 (McCracken J); *Re Vehicle Imports Ltd* (23 November 2000, unreported) HC (Murphy J); *Re Ashclad Ltd* [2000] IEHC 174; *Kavanagh v Cooke* [2006] 1 ILRM 191.

5 *La Moselle Clothing Ltd v Soluahi* [1998] 2 ILRM 345; *Re Bath Glass Ltd* [1988] BCLC 329; *Re Rolus Properties Ltd* (1988) 4 BCC 446; *Re Chartmore Ltd* [1990] BCLC 673; *Re Palmstock Ltd* [1994] 1 BCLC 716; *Re Firedart Ltd, Official Receiver v Fairall* [1994] 2 BCLC 340; and *Re Richborough Furniture Ltd* [1996] 1 BCLC 507.

6 *Careca Investments Ltd (In Liquidation)* [2005] IEHC 62 (Clarke J).

1.2 Board meetings

The court will also look to see if proper board meetings were held and that the minutes were properly taken and to ensure that the company was run in accordance with the Companies Acts and the intentions of the shareholders.[1] Attending regular board meetings has also been found to be significant.[2]

1 In *Re Squash (Ireland) Ltd* [2001] 3 IR 35; *Re Hydro Klenze Ltd* (20 December 2007, unreported) HC (Smyth J); *Re MDN Rochford Construction Ltd* (18 August 2009, unreported) HC (MacMenamin J).

2 In *Re Cavan Crystal Group Ltd* (26 April 1996, unreported) Murphy J.

1.3 Technical breaches of the Companies Acts

Companies must file regulatory returns to ensure that those dealing with limited liability companies have access to certain information. Failure to make returns in accordance with the Companies Acts may constitute an offence and failure to make returns to the Companies Registration Office has been found to be a factor in favour of restriction.[1] Failure of the officers of a company to disclose their interests in the company's contracts (CA 1963, s 194) is a breach of the principle of good governance, sound commercial probity and proper standards in commercial dealings and of the parallel common law obligation to make the entire of a director's board aware of any such interest, and may justify the making of a restriction order.[2]

1 *Newcastle Timber Ltd (In liquidation)* [2001] 4 IR 586 (McCracken J); see also *Re Tansfot Ltd* [BCLC] 1991 339.

2 In *Re Xnet Information Systems Ltd; Stafford v Higgins* [2004] IEHC 82 (Finlay Geoghegan J).

La Moselle Test No 2 – The extent to which his conduct could have been regarded as so incompetent to amount to irresponsibility

Business failure does not in itself justify the making of a restriction order.[1] Insolvency tends to permit some criticism of the directors, but one has to go further than misjudgement or commercial error in order to find that there has been irresponsible behaviour on the part of the directors.[2] Conduct complained of should display a lack of commercial probity although in extreme cases of gross negligence or total incompetence, restriction may be appropriate.[3] The courts will take into consideration the professional and legal advice the directors took and the time when they took such advice and will look to see if they acted in accordance with the advice.[4] It would appear that if the directors engage in a plan which is overly optimistic but based on advice that they will be held to be acting responsibly. Directors that commenced trading with an undercapitalised company, but who were experienced businessmen and gave personal guarantees in respect of the company's borrowing were not restricted.[5]

1 *La Moselle Clothing Ltd v Soluahi* [1998] 2 ILRM 345; *Business Communications v Baxter & Others* (21 July 1995, unreported) Murphy J where Murphy J warned that one must be careful not to be wise after the event and that there must not be a witch hunt because a business failed as businesses will. See also *Re Camoate Construction Ltd* (29 July 2005, unreported) HC (O'Leary J); *Re The Computer Learning Centre Ltd* (7 February 2005, unreported) HC (Finlay Geoghegan J); *Re Money Markets International Ltd* [2006] IEHC 350; *Re Hydro Klenze Ltd* (20 December 2007, unreported) HC (Smyth J); *Re MDN Rochford Construction Ltd* (18 August 2009, unreported) HC (MacMenamin J).

2 In *Re Squash (Ireland) Ltd* [2001] 3 IR 35; *Business Communications Ltd v Baxter* (21 July 1995, unreported) HC (Murphy J); *Re USIT World plc* [2005] IEHC 285 (Peart J); *Re Money Markets International Ltd* [2006] IEHC 350; *Re MDN Rochford Construction Ltd* (18 August 2009, unreported) HC (MacMenamin J).

3 In *Re Lo Line Electric Motors Ltd* [1988] BCLC 698 where Browne-Wilkinson V-C considered the general approach to be taken in deciding whether somebody is unfit to be a director of a company in the context of an application of for a disqualification order under the English equivalent of a s 150. Shanley J approved this approach in *La Mosselle Clothing Ltd v Soluahi* [1998] 2 ILRM 345.

4 In *Re Squash (Ireland) Ltd* [2001] 3 IR 35; *Re 360Networks (Ireland) Ltd, O'Ferral v Coughlan* (21 December 2004, unreported), Finlay Geoghegan J; *Re Camoate Construction Ltd, Coyle v Callanan* [2006] 1 IR 447; *Re MDN Rochford Construction Ltd* (18 August 2009, unreported) HC (MacMenamin J).

5 In *Re First Class Toy Traders Ltd; Gray v McLoughlin* [2004] IEHC 289, ex tempore (Finlay Geoghegan J).

La Moselle Test No 3 – The extent of the directors' responsibility for the insolvency of the company

It has been emphasised by the courts in several cases that in order for a restriction order to be made, it is normally necessary to show that there is a causal link between some wrongdoing on the part of the director and the insolvency of the company.[1] Moreover, it has been pointed out that in considering whether or not to restrict a Director, the court tries to be careful not to view the actions of the Director concerned with the benefit of hindsight.[2]

1 *Business Communications Ltd v Baxter* (21 July 1995, unreported) HC (Murphy J); *Re Usit World Plc* [2005] IEHC 285 (Peart J); *Kavanagh v Cooke* [2006] 1 ILRM 191; *Re Money Markets International Ltd* [2006] IEHC 350; *Re Dublin Sports Cafe Ltd* (16 December 2008, unreported) SC (Finnegan J).

2 *La Moselle Clothing Ltd v Soluahi* [1998] 2 ILRM 345; *Business Communications v Baxter* (21 July 1995, unreported) HC (Murphy J) where Murphy J warned that one must be careful not to be wise after the event and that there must not be a witch hunt because a business failed as businesses will. See also *Re Squash (Ireland) Ltd* [2001] 3 IR 35; *Re Camoate Construction Ltd, Coyle v Callanan* [2006] 1 IR 447; *Re The Computer Learning Centre Ltd, Farrell v Gill* (7 February 2005, unreported) HC (Finlay Geoghegan J); *Re Money Markets International Ltd* [2006] IEHC 350; *Re MDN Rochford Construction Ltd* (18 August 2009, unreported) HC (MacMenamin J).

La Moselle Test No 4 – The extent of the directors' responsibility for the net deficiency of the company disclosed at the date of the winding up or thereafter

In order for a court to make a restriction order under this heading, it will be necessary for the court to find some degree of dishonesty or something very near to dishonesty.[1] Examples would include a deliberate policy of directing payments towards the company's bank overdraft and trade creditors in preference to other creditors,[2] issuing false invoices for the purposes of avoiding VAT[3] and trading using phoenix companies,[4] continuing to draw remuneration or drawing excessive remuneration when the company is insolvent,[5] and diverting corporate opportunities.[6]

Unreasonably delaying putting the company into liquidation may also be a ground for restriction under this heading[7] as can be the use of moneys due to the Revenue Commissioners to keep an otherwise hopelessly insolvent business afloat.[8]

1 *Re Squash (Ireland) Ltd* [2001] 3 IR 35.

2 *Re Structural Concrete Ltd* [2000] 26 LS Gaz R 35.

3 *Official Receiver v Doshi* [2001] 2 BCLC 235.

4 *Re Douglas Construction Services Ltd* [1988] BCLC 397; *Re Keypak Homecare Ltd* [1990] BCLC 440. *Newcastle Timber Ltd (In liquidation)* (16 October 2001, unreported) (McCracken J).

5 *Re Stanford Services Ltd* [1987] BCLC 607; *La Mosselle Clothing Ltd v Soluahi* [1998] 2 ILRM 345.

6 *Re Living Images Ltd* [1996] 1 BCLC 348.

7 *Re Shannonside Holdings Ltd* (20 May 1993, unreported) HC; *Re Halley v Nolan* (1 July 2005, unreported) HC (O'Leary J).

8 *Re Verit Hotel and Leisure (Ireland) Ltd, Duignan v Carway* (23 January 2002, unreported) HC (McCracken J); *Re Digital Channel Partners Ltd* [2004] 2 ILRM 35; *Re Pineroad Distribution Ltd* [2007] IEHC 55 (Hanna J); *Re MDN Rochford Construction Ltd* (18 August 2009, unreported) HC (MacMenamin J).

La Moselle Test No 5 –The extent to which the director, in his conduct of the affairs of the company, has displayed a lack of commercial probity or want of proper standards.

There is considerable overlap between this heading and the other four headings set out above. The courts will use an objective standard in deciding whether or not a director is in breach of proper standards or has displayed a lack of commercial probity. Not all situations of a want of responsibility will result from a breach of obligations imposed by the Companies Acts.

In *La Moselle Clothing Ltd v Soluahi*[1] Shanley J cited an inability to see ' the writing on the wall' as being sufficient to justify restriction where he meant incompetence. He also referred to *Re Continental Assurance Co of London Plc, Secretary for State for Industry v Burrows*[2] where an inability to understand the statutory accounts of a company was considered to be a ground for disqualification of a director. The court has also held that a director has acted irresponsibly in allowing credit to be extended to a company under his control at a time when the company was suffering from serious cash flow problems.[3] Likewise, repaying BES investors when the company is insolvent may amount to evidence of irresponsibility.[4] The court has made restriction orders against directors who use PAYE, PRSI and VAT moneys to keep the company alive, thus allowing huge arrears to build-up together with interest.[5] In a number of English decisions particular emphasis is placed on the special nature of the debts owned to the Crown for PAYE, VAT and National Insurance contributions. It has also been found that a director, who allowed a company to carry out business without adequate capitalisation, was found to have acted irresponsibly.[6]

However, not every instance of trading while insolvent will constitute irresponsibility. In the case of *Re Lynrowan Enterprises Ltd*[7] the company in question had continued to trade while insolvent, and the court excused this behaviour on two grounds peculiar to that particular case, namely the non-involvement of one director and the impact of a 'deeply entrenched family split'. Peart J provided some useful guidance in *Re USIT World plc*[8] in this context when he stated that:

> '… it is not incumbent on a board of directors, at the first moment at which it is becoming apparent that debts may not be capable of being paid as they fall due, to immediately call in the liquidator and cease trading ... To attempt to trade out of a difficulty is not an

irresponsible act. Care of course must be taken to ensure that effective and realistic steps are taken and that creditors' interest are kept to the fore, rather than a careless or reckless gamble is taken without proper advice and planning to an achievable end.'

Each individual case will fall to be considered on its merits, but there is some sensitivity for the commercial reality of business attempting to trade out of economic difficulties.

1 *La Moselle Clothing Ltd v Soluahi* [1998] 2 ILRM 345.

2 *Re Continental Assurance Co of London Plc, Secretary for State for Industry v Burrows* [1997] 1 BCLC 48; See also *Re Hydro Klenze Ltd* (20 December 2007, unreported) HC (Smyth J); *Re MDN Rochford Construction Ltd* (18 August 2009, unreported) HC (MacMenamin J).

3 *Re Gasco Ltd* [2001] IEHC 20 (McCracken J).

4 *Re Swanpool Ltd, McLaughlin v Lannen* [2006] 2 ILRM 217.

5 *Re Verit Hotel & Leisure Ltd* (23 January 2002, unreported) (McCracken J); *Fennell v Shanahan* (21 December 2004, unreported) HC (Finlay Geoghegan J); *Re Digital Channel Partners Ltd* [2004] 2 ILRM 35; *Re Pineroad Distribution Ltd* 2007] IEHC 55 (Hanna J); *Re MDN Rochford Construction Ltd* (18 August 2009, unreported) HC (MacMenamin J).

6 *Re Austinsuite Furniture Ltd* [1992] BCLC 1047, although see *Re First Class Toy Traders Ltd; Gray v McLoughlin* [2004] IEHC 289, ex tempore, Finlay Geoghegan J.

7 *Re Lynrowan Enterprises Ltd* [2002] IEHC 90 (O'Neill J).

8 *Re USIT WORLD plc* [2005] IEHC 285 (Peart J); see also *Re Careca Investments Ltd* [2005] IEHC 62 (Clarke J).

Otherwise just or equitable to make the restriction order

The court has considered the legal status of the actions of directors in the period after the appointment of a liquidator or receiver to see whether it was appropriate to refer to that conduct in an application for restriction pursuant to s 150 of the Companies Act 1990.[1] Clarke J confirmed that the just and equitable test permitted the court to take into account any relevant conduct of the director after the commencement of the winding up, notwithstanding the amendments to CA 1990: CA 1963, s 150.[2] In examining the actions of the directors post liquidation Clarke J pithily summed up the obligations of a director:

> 'It is axiomatic that the duties of persons who have served as directors include an obligation to be of any assistance that they can to the liquidator in the conduct of the liquidation. The rights of creditors of a company are likely to be compromised not only by the fact that a company is insolvent and unable to pay its debts as of the date of liquidation but also such rights can be further compromised where due to inappropriate action or inaction on the part of directors or former directors the liquidator is prevented from being in a position to effectually get in the assets of the company for the purposes of discharging the liabilities due to the creditors to the greatest extent possible and as soon as possible … the court is entitled to take into account any conduct on the part of directors or former directors which amounts to inappropriate retention of the companies assets subsequent to the commencement of the winding up.'

The court has also imposed a restriction order solely on the ground of the failure on the part of the director to file its statement of affairs and their failure to explain why.[3] Filing inconsistent statements of affairs with no proper explanation as to the differences was found to be an act of irresponsibility justifying a restriction order.[4]

1 In *La Moselle Clothing Ltd v Soluahi* [1998] 2 ILRM 345; Shanley J stated as follows— 'It is to be noted that acting honestly and responsibility relates to 'the conduct of the affairs of the company' and arguably as such bears no relation to any period after the commencement of the winding up or receivership of a particular company where the person may not be involved any further in the conduct of the affairs of the company. That the director must satisfy the Court that there is no other reason why it would be just and equitable to restrict a director, allows the Court to take into account, in my view, any relevant conduct of the director after the commencement of

the winding up or the receivership (for example failure to co-operate with the liquidator or receiver) in deciding whether or not to make an order under s 150 (1) of the 1990 Act.' See also *Re DCS Ltd, Fitzpatrick v Henley* [2006] IEHC 179; *Re Dublin Sports Cafe Ltd* (16 December 2008, unreported) SC (Finnegan J).

2 *Re CMC (Ireland) Ltd* (4 March 2005, unreported) HC (Clarke J).

3 *In the matter of Dunleckney Ltd* [2001] 1 IR 103.

4 *Re Lynrowan Enterprises Ltd* [2002] IEHC 90 (O'Neill J). See also *Re Tansoft Ltd* [1991] BCLC 339 where the director failed to prepare a statement of affairs. His reason for so doing was that he did not have access to the company's books and records for almost two years and that he felt that it was impossible for him to contribute in any significant way to the preparation of the statement of affairs. His view was that the official receiver should ask another director to prepare a statement of affairs on the basis that they were in a better position to submit the statement of affairs. This was not accepted by the court as a valid reason not to prepare the Statement of Affairs.

Avoiding restriction – specific issues

1 Non-executive directors

All directors, whether executive or non-executive, have duties, which they must discharge. In *Re Tralee Beef and Lamb Ltd*[1] Finlay Geoghegan J held at first instance that the standard expected of a non-executive director is different from that of an executive director, because the former will typically lack the intimate knowledge of the company's day-to-day affairs of an executive director. However, they must put themselves in the position to supervise the executive directors in their management of the company's affairs. The judge adopted the test as laid down by Jonathan Parker J in the case of *Re Barings plc (No 5)*[2] that the duty of a non-executive director was to 'inform himself about affairs and join with his co-directors in supervising and controlling them'. In this regard, delegation of day-to-day management to the executive directors does not absolve the non-executive directors from the duty to acquire information about the affairs of the company and to supervise the discharge of those delegated functions.[3] However, on appeal the Supreme Court stated that it was not prepared at this stage, and without fuller debate, to make authoritative findings as to the respective roles of executive and non-executive directors and it also expressed the view that the standards that might reasonably be expected of a director of a vast corporation are not necessarily the same as those to be expected of a small private company.[4]

Although facts coming to the attention of the non-executive director may of themselves require him to make further inquiries, nevertheless, in general, he is entitled both to rely upon information provided by his fellow directors and to rely upon the executive directors carrying out what might be normal executive or management functions.[5]

1 *Re Tralee Beef and Lamb Ltd* (20 July 2004, unreported) HC (Finlay Geoghegan J). See also *Re RMF (Ireland) Ltd: Kavanagh v Reidler* [2004] 3 IR 498.

2 *Re Barings plc (No 5)* [1999] 1 BCLC 433.

3 *Re Tralee Beef and Lamb Ltd* (20 July 2004, unreported) HC at p 10 (Finlay Geoghegan J).

4 *Re Tralee Beef & Lamb Ltd, Kavanagh v Delaney* [2008] 3 IR 347. See McGrath, 'Restriction of Directors: Tralee Beef and Lamb' (2008) 2 (4) IBLQ 16. See also *Re Dublin Sports Cafe Ltd* (16 December 2008, unreported) SC (Finnegan J).

5 *Re RMF (Ireland) Ltd; Kavanagh v Reidler* [2004] 3 IR 498.

2 Delegation

In *Re Vehicle Imports Ltd*[1] Murphy J considered a director's responsibilities in the context of delegation of functions. He accepted that a degree of delegation was a necessary part of conducting a company's business efficiently and that accordingly there was a public interest in delegation. However, he emphasised that a director retains a residual duty of supervision and control requiring him to acquire sufficient understanding of the company's business to discharge his duties. In that case he held that the delegation of responsibility for the maintenance of books and records of the company did not completely discharge the director of those duties. A matter to be considered in this regard is whether reliance on the actions of another director is itself responsible.[2]

Delegation of tasks does not in any way absolve a director of responsibilities, although it has been suggested,[3] that delegation must be examined on a case-by-case basis. A broader qualification to this is, perhaps, that certain company functions are executive functions and, as such, a non-executive director may delegate such functions and to a degree rely on the actions of the executive concerned (although it should not be assumed, without more, that this absolves a director of the need to show that he acted responsibly).[4] In this regard, the transparent nature of tax liability fixes a director with knowledge of liabilities to the Revenue Commissioners.[5]

1 *Re Vehicle Imports Ltd* (23 November 2000, unreported) HC (Murphy J)); *Re MDN Rochford Construction Ltd* (18 August 2009, unreported) HC (MacMenamin J).

2 McCracken J in *Re Gasco Ltd* (5 February 2001, unreported) (McCracken J).

3 *Re 360 Networks (Ireland) Ltd, O'Ferral v Coughlan* (21 December 2004 unreported) (Finlay Geoghegan J). In making the restriction orders sought the court commented that a decision by the directors to appoint a receiver after legal advice was indicative of taking steps to manage the company, despite criticism by the liquidator on the appropriateness of such a step.

4 As identified in *Re Colm O'Neill Engineering Services Ltd*. Also see *Re Cherby Ltd, Kavanagh v Cooke*, [2006] 1 ILRM 191.

5 *Fennell v Shanahan* (21 December 2004, unreported) HC (Finlay Geoghegan J).

3 Limited responsibility

A broader defence is that a director's limited involvement with the company in liquidation should excuse him from a potential restriction order. This argument has been rejected by the court, at least in the case of a director whose participation in the company has been somewhere between passive and non-existent.[1] Typically, such a defence has been advanced by persons who are family members of the de facto controller of the business. The court's refusal to exculpate a director merely because he was a friend, relative or spouse of the controller of a company[2] traces its roots to the dictum of Carroll J in the case of *Re Hunting Lodges*[3] in which the judge said that a director 'who continues as a director but abdicates all responsibility is not lightly to be excused'.

In practice, the court demonstrates a high degree of understanding to those who become directors in such circumstances. Murphy J declined to make a restriction order against a director who was the wife of the principal director, and who had taken no part in the management of the company or in relation to the maintenance of the company's records.[4] The court noted that the wife had opposed the increased borrowing of the company. In *Re Lynrowan Enterprises Ltd*,[5] the making of a restriction order was refused in respect of a director who took no part in the company affairs, and who did not appear to have been expected to. However, this may perhaps be explained on the basis that the director in question had 'effectively passed all control of the affairs of the company to his son … and in the context of a small family business, having effectively permitted his son to take over control of the business, he having arrived at the stage of retirement'.

What the court is prepared to do, however, is to look at the particular area of management in the company for which a particular director had delegated responsibility, and to his assess his conduct by reference to that management role.[6]

1 *Re Costello Doors Ltd*, (21 July 1995, unreported) HC (Murphy J).

2 *Re Lynrowan Enterprises Ltd* [2002] IEHC 90 (O'Neill J).

3 *Re Hunting Lodges* [1985] ILRM 75 at 85.

4 *Re Vehicle Imports Ltd* [2000] IEHC 90 (Murphy J).

5 *Re Lynrowan Enterprises Ltd* [2002] IEHC 90 (O'Neill J).

6 *Re Gasco Ltd* [2001] IEHC 20 (McCracken J); *Re USIT World plc* [2005] IEHC 285 (Peart J).

4 Size of deficit

Companies tend to accrue debts. The scale of such debts will also be considered by the courts. In a passing reference in *Kavanagh v Cummins*,[1] Finlay Geoghegan J did hold that the size of the company's deficit did not preclude her from deciding that the directors concerned had discharged the onus placed on them of establishing that they acted responsibly. The agreement of a scheme by an examiner may have influenced this decision. Peart J in *Re USIT World plc*[2] echoed this view when he stated that, 'the size of the deficit should not of itself be determinative, although obviously the greater [the] sums involved in the business the greater the care required to accompany decisions taken'.

1 *Kavanagh v Cummins* [2004] 2 ILRM 35 at 41. See also *In Re Digital Capital Partners (in Voluntary Liquidation)* (12 December 2003) ex tempore (Finlay Geoghegan J).

2 *USIT WORLD plc; Jackson v Colleary* [2005] IEHC 285 (Peart J) at p 62.

5 Nominee of a financial institution or

CA 1990, s 150 provides that if a person can satisfy the court that he was a director of a company solely by reason of a nomination by a financial institution in connection with the giving of credit facilities to the company or a person was a director of the company solely by reason of the nomination by a venture capital company in connection with the purchase of or a subscription for shares in the company then the provisions concerning the restrictions of the directors do not apply. Murphy J in *Re Cavan Crystal Group Ltd*[1] indicated in an obiter comment on CA 1990, s 150(2) that he 'would prefer to conclude that the legislature intended that where a person concerned established that he fell within the particular category of director designate in paragraphs (b) or paragraph (c) that it was not necessary for him to establish that he acted honestly and responsibly'. Murphy J indicated that there had to be some meaning given to the defences in (b) and (c).

Finlay Geoghegan J was asked to consider the defence in the High Court in *Tralee Beef and Lamb Ltd*.[2] She held that the director in question did not establish that he was appointed by either a financial institution or a venture capital group. She made an obiter comment acknowledging that there was an inconsistency in the defences offered by subsections (b) and (c) but which fell short of support for Mr Justice Murphy's opinion.

It is not possible to read sub-s (b) and (c) as providing any defence independent of sub-s (a). Giving the subsections a literal meaning, there is only one defence possible ie that contained in (a). If this is a valid interpretation, it is submitted, that the legislative intent of creating sub-ss (b) and (c) must logically be defeated, because they will have no meaning. The interpretation offered by Murphy J in *Cavan Crystal* seems, it is submitted, to do damage to the plain meaning of the words. The words do not permit a discrete defence, rather, it is submitted that subsections (b) and (c) have a meaning similar to the guidelines proffered by Finlay Geoghegan J in relation to non-executive directors, ie that they give rise to an examination of the actions of the directors in light of their duties to another agency (either the financial institution or the venture capital group). Subsections (b) and (c) have the effect, it is submitted, of varying the weighting that should be applied to the test in subsection (a) in respect of their respective factual situations.

1 *Re Cavan Crystal Group Ltd* (26 April 1996, unreported) HC.

2 *Tralee Beef and Lamb Ltd* (20 July, 2004, unreported) HC (Finlay Geoghegan J), reversed on other grounds [2008] 3 IR 347.

Costs of section 150 proceedings

For more than a decade after the coming into force of s 150 there was a practice that directors who successfully resisted the making of a restriction order against them were nevertheless expected to make a contribution to the costs of the Liquidator. However, it was noted in *Re GMT Engineering Services Ltd (in Voluntary Liquidation)*,[1] that the court's jurisdiction to award costs has been enlarged by the insertion of sub-s (4B) by the CLEA. In particular, it was held that the insertion of sub-s (4B) meant that where a director successfully defended a restriction application, there is no statutory basis for ordering him to pay costs to the liquidator. A practice then developed whereby, in the overall exercise of the Court's discretion, the court would simply make no order for costs in favour of a successful director, even when it was obvious that the case against him or her was weak. Since then, however, in *USIT (Ireland)*,[2] Peart J applied the provisions of RSC 1986, Ord 99 and directed that costs follow the event. An order for costs was thus made against the liquidator personally, as opposed to the company in liquidation, since it is the liquidator who is the applicant.

Peart J refused to hold that s 150(4A) was intended to supplant the provisions of Order 99 Rule 1 of the RSC and to remove the court's discretion as to costs even in respect of a director who successfully resisted the application. The Companies Act 1990 contained no definition of the terms 'costs' or 'costs incurred by the applicant'.

One of the changes made by the insertion of sub-s (4B) was to allow a successful liquidator his costs of investigating the matter. However, the concept of 'costs in investigating the matter' was restrictively interpreted by Finlay Geoghegan J in *Re Mitek Holdings Ltd, Grace v Kachar*,[3] as only covering moneys paid to third parties by the liquidator[4] and as therefore not covering his own fees in respect of such remuneration. This decision has since been reversed by the substitution of a new sub-s (4B) by IFCMPA 2006, s 11(1). In this regard, costs may be recovered by the successful applicant in respect of the investigation of matters which pre-dated the coming into force of sub-s (4B),[5] but only provided that the s 150 proceedings themselves post-date the coming into force of the legislative change.[6]

1 *Re GMT Engineering Services Ltd (in Voluntary Liquidation)* [2003] 4 IR 133.

2 *USIT (Ireland)* [2005] IEHC 481. See also *Kavanagh v Cummins* [2004] 2 ILRM 35; *Tre Visual Impact and Displays Ltd* [2003] 4 IR 451.

3 *Re Mitek Holdings Ltd, Grace v Kachar* [2005] 4 IR 522.

4 In *Re Moypool Ltd, Gannon v O'Hora* [2007] 3 IR 563 Finlay Geoghegan J held that recoverable costs paid by the liquidator would include pre-litigation fees charged by his solicitor in connection with the investigation of the s 150 application.

5 *Re Tipperary Fresh Foods Ltd* [2005] 2 ILRM 462.

6 *Re Sallyview Estates Ltd, Farrell v Balzarini* [2007] IEHC 424.

Discovery in restriction and disqualification applications

The court has held that RSC 1986, Ord 31, r 12 of the applies to an application under CA 1990, s 150.[1] In the context of a request to discover a s 56 report the liquidator and the Director of Corporate Enforcement had argued that a section 56 report was not relevant to the determination of the issues in a s 150 application and that its discovery would have additional effect of inhibiting a frank and candid report. However, Finlay Geoghegan J concluded that two matters were at issue in a s 150 application, namely whether the directors had acted honestly and responsibly in relation to the conduct of the affairs of the company, and whether there was any other reason why it would be just and equitable that a declaration of restriction be made. On the basis of normal discovery principles it was held two of the entries in a section 56 reports were relevant:

1. Paragraph 22(g) 'Has the person demonstrated to you that he has acted honestly and responsibly in relation to the conduct of the Company's affairs?', and
2. Paragraph 31 where a liquidator may ask the Director of Corporate Enforcement to relieve him of the requirement to seek to have the directors restricted.

It was submitted that the s 56 report was a confidential document due to CLEA 2001: CA 1963, s 17 which states: 'Information obtained by virtue of the performance by the Director of any of his functions which has not otherwise come to the notice of the public, shall not be disclosed, except in accordance with the law by any person …'. However, the court held that the phrase 'except in accordance with the law' did not prevent discovery of a s 56 report on grounds of confidentiality.

1 *Kavanagh v O'Donoghue* [2003] 4 IR 443.

Joinder of parties

An application pursuant to RSC 1986, Ord 15, r 13 to be joined as a party to the application to restrict other directors of the company has been considered by the Court. Rule 13 provides:

> 'No cause or matter shall be defeated by reason of the misjoinder or non-joinder of parties, and the Court may in every cause or matter deal with the matter in controversy so far as regards the rights and interests of the parties actually before it. The Court may at any stage of the proceedings, either upon or without the application of either party, and on such terms as may appear to the Court to be just, order that the names of any parties improperly joined, whether as plaintiffs or as defendants, be struck out and that the names of any parties, whether plaintiffs or defendants, who ought to have been joined, or whose presence before the Court may be necessary in order to enable the Court effectually and completely to adjudicate upon and settle all the questions involved in the cause or matter, be added ...'.

Finlay Geoghegan J has held[1] that however wide the discretion, the court must be satisfied that the proposed party is a person whose presence before the court may be necessary in order to enable that court effectually and completely to adjudicate upon and settle all the questions involved in the cause or matter. She distinguished the decision of Shanley J in *Re Steamline Ltd*[2] which had allowed creditors to participate in s 150 proceedings, pointing out that CA 1990, s 150(4A) now explicitly defines *locus standi* to bring such an application (ie only the Director of Corporate Enforcement, a receiver or a liquidator have such *locus standi*). The court held that the only jurisdiction that remained to join a party to a s 150 application under the 1990 Companies Act was if 'exceptional circumstances' pertained.

1 In *Re Document Imaging Systems Ltd (In Liquidation) and others* [2005] IEHC 250 (Finlay Geoghegan J).

2 *Steamline Ltd* [2001] 1 IR 103 at 106.

Delay

The Supreme Court's jurisprudence in relation to delay as set out in *Primor plc v Stokes Kennedy Crowley*[1] appears to apply in a more restrictive form to applications to restrict a director. In *Re Verit Hotel and Lesiure (Ireland) Ltd, Duignan v Carway*[2] the Supreme Court noted that section 150 applications were not 'strictly speaking *inter partes* proceedings' and held that slightly different factors ought to be taken into account:

1 The legislative intent of s 150 includes a public interest in the qualification of the rights of directors of insolvent companies and a protection for third parties;

2 The constitutional entitlements of respondent directors to have their applications determined in accordance with the constitutional guarantee of fair procedures, including a right to fair and speedy trial;

3 The special features of s 150 in imposing an onus on respondent directors to establish that they acted honestly and responsibly and the absence of any discretion of the court as to the period for restriction (five years);

4 The amount of time that has elapsed since the matters the subject matter of the application took place;

The court did not hold that there was an inherent prejudice in dealing with matters that had taken place up to 15 years previously but appeared to take judicial notice of the 'added difficulty' caused by the lapse of time. The court briefly considered the merits of the application before concluding that a period of in excess of eight years following the appointment of the liquidator would have been a last reasonable time to have commenced the s 150 proceedings and dismissed the application on the grounds of delay.

In two more recent cases, s 150 proceedings have, however, been dismissed on grounds of prejudicial delay, with the events under scrutiny dating back to eight or more years previously.[3] In addition, the question of delay is one which, in the context of disqualification proceedings, has been held to be a breach of the right to a speedy trial under the ECHR.[4]

1 *Primor plc v Stokes Kennedy Crowley* [1996] 1 IR 459.

2 *Re Verit Hotel and Lesiure (Ireland) Ltd, Duignan v Carway* [2001] 4 IR 550.

3 *Re Knocklofty House Hotel Ltd* [2005] 4 IR 497; see also *Supreme Oil Company Ltd (in liquidation)* (19 April 2005, unreported) HC (Finlay Geoghegan J).

4 *Davies v United Kingdom* (2002) 35 EHRR 29; *Eastaway v United Kingdom* [2004] ECHR 364.

Affidavit evidence

The courts have considered restriction applications on the basis of the high point of the respondent directors' cases.[1] The procedure adopted was not of importance given the very low weight attached to the issue but demonstrates the approach of the court to contradictory affidavit evidence in an application that is normally heard without any cross-examination.

The facility to cross-examine is open to all parties in a restriction application but it tends not to be availed of. For this reason the court tends to adopt the approach outlined above. Peart J has suggested an additional consideration:

> '… where matters deposed of by a director/respondent relate less to purely factual matters than to a view held by the director as to the probity of his actions, the Court may of course take into account the fact that such a director will inevitably be seeking to place as favourable an interpretation of facts and events as he can, so as to discharge the onus upon him.'[2]

1 *Re CMC (Ireland) Ltd (In Voluntary Liquidation)*, (4 March 2005, unreported) HC (Clarke J).

2 *Re USIT WORLD plc; Jackson v Colleary* [2005] IEHC 285 (Peart J).

---

151 Duty of liquidator under this Chapter

(1) Where it appears to the liquidator of a company to which under this Chapter applies that the interests of any other company or its creditors may be placed in jeopardy by the relevant matters referred to in subsection (2) the liquidator shall inform the court of his opinion forthwith and the court may, on receipt of such report, make whatever order it sees fit.

(2) The relevant matters are that a person to whom section 150 applies is appointed or is acting in any way, whether directly or indirectly, as a director or is concerned or is taking part in the promotion or formation of such other company as is referred to in subsection (1).

(3) Any liquidator who contravenes subsection (1) shall be guilty of an offence and shall be liable—

(a) on summary conviction, to a fine not exceeding [€1,904.61][a] and, for continued contravention, to a daily default fine not exceeding [€63.49][b], or

(b) on conviction on indictment, to a fine not exceeding [€12,697.38][c] and, for continued contravention, to a daily default fine not exceeding [€317.43][d].

Amendments

a '£1,000' in subsection (3)(a) increased to '£1,500' by CA 1990, s 240(7) as inserted by CLEA 2001, s 104 and converted to €1,904.61 by Council Regulations (EC) No 1103/97, No 974/98 and No 2866/98 and the Economic and Monetary Union Act 1998, s 6.

b ‘£50’ in subsection (3)(a) converted to €63.49 by Council Regulations (EC) No 1103/97, No 974/98 and No 2866/98 and the Economic and Monetary Union Act 1998, s 6.

c ‘£10,000’ in subsection (3)(b) converted to €12,697.38 by Council Regulations (EC) No 1103/97, No 974/98 and No 2866/98 and the Economic and Monetary Union Act 1998, s 6.

d ‘£250’ in subsection 3(b) converted to €317.44 by Council Regulations (EC) No 1103/97, No 974/98 and No 2866/98 and the Economic and Monetary Union Act 1998, s 6.

Definitions

CA 1963: ‘company’: CA 1963, s 2(1); ‘court’: CA 1963, s 2(1); ‘director’: CA 1963, s 2(1); ‘liquidator’: CA 1963, s 2(1).

Notes

This section requires a liquidator to form a view on the impact of conduct by a director or former director of the company in liquidation on any other company, or that other company’s creditors, where the director or former director of the insolvent company is directly or indirectly concerned with the other company. This section has the effect of placing a duty on the liquidator to have regard to the actions of the directors of the insolvent company and scrutinise their dealings. The obligation is expressed to be in order to protect the other company or its creditors and it is possible to construe this as a statutory duty toward those parties, although it could not dislodge their own duty to look after their own affairs. Non-compliance with the section may, where loss flows, give rise to liability for the liquidator. The liability would not appear to be one incurred as part of the liquidation, being a duty (if it should be properly so characterised) that arises from his position but not as an aspect of the liquidation. This may have some relevance to the terms of the indemnity or insurance protection of the liquidator in such circumstances.

---

152 Relief

(1) A person to whom section 150 applies may, within not more than one year after a declaration has been made in respect of him under that section, apply to the court for relief, either in whole or in part, from the restrictions referred to in that section or from any order made in relation to him under section 151 and the court may, if it deems it just and equitable to do so, grant such relief on whatever terms and conditions it sees fit.

(2) Where it is intended to make an application for relief under subsection (1) the applicant shall give not less than 14 days’ notice of his intention to the liquidator (if any) of the company the insolvency of which caused him to be subject to this Chapter.

(3) On receipt of a notice under subsection (2), the liquidator shall forthwith notify such creditors and contributories of the company as have been notified to him or become known to him, that he has received such notice.

(4) On the hearing of an application under this section the liquidator or any creditor or contributory of the company, the insolvency of which caused the applicant to be subject to this Chapter may appear and give evidence.

(5) Any liquidator who contravenes subsection (3) shall be guilty of an offence and liable to a fine.

Definitions

CA 1963: ‘contributory’: CA 1963, s 2(1); ‘company’: CA 1963, s 2(1); ‘court’: CA 1963, s 2(1); ‘creditor’: CA 1963, s 2(1); ‘director’: CA 1963, s 2(1); ‘liquidator’: CA 1963, s 2(1).

Notes

CA 1990, s 152 is not an appeal, but it does allow the exercise of clemency.

Application for relief: A person against whom an order pursuant to CA 1990 s 150 has been made may apply to the Court within one year after the declaration has been made for relief either in whole or in part and the Court may, if it deems just and equitable to do so, grant relief on such terms and conditions as meet the justice of the case. In exceptional circumstances, an order made under CA 1990, s 150 may even be set aside.[1]

The court has 'a very wide discretion' and the case law has revealed no limits on the factors the court can take into consideration, including the restricted person's actions as a director of another company.[2] The High Court enjoys an inherent jurisdiction to stay the enforcement of a restriction order. Such stay might permit a 'probationary' period after which an application might be made for relief this section.

1 In *Re Ferngara Associates Ltd; Robinson v Forrest* [1999] 1 IR 426 at 435–436 Laffoy J granted an order under CA 1990, s 152. It was her view that it was an exceptional case, which fell to be determined on its own peculiar facts. She stated that she was satisfied that the applicant had learned an expensive lesson from his involvement in the company and that the deterrent value of the restriction would not be undermined if the restriction was lifted. Interestingly the discretion given to the Court under CA 1990, s 152 does not apply when hearing an application under CA 1990, s 150.

2 *Re CMC Ltd* (1 November 2005, unreported) HC; *Re Ferngara Associates Ltd: F & R Robinson v Forrest* [1999] 1 IR 426 and also the judgment of Finlay Geoghegan J in *Carolan and Cosgrave v Fennell* [2005] IEHC 340.

Criteria for relief

The Court has held that the Oireachtas intended the 'relatively speedy rehabilitation of directors in respect of whom declarations of restriction were made' and gave some guidance on matters to take into account when seeking relief.[1] An applicant should demonstrate 'some need or interest' that requires clemency. The court demonstrated flexibility in its approach, suggesting a reduction of the capitalisation requirements. The applicant's conduct should be considered, including his responsible conduct separate from the events giving rise to the insolvency and restriction. The court considered the importance of the deterrent effect of restriction and granted the Director of Corporate Enforcement liberty to apply to vary the order made reducing the effect of the restriction order made. See notes after CA 1990, s 155.

The age of a restricted person has also been considered as a possible ground for relief.[2]

1 *XNet Information Systems Ltd (in voluntary liquidation)* [2006] IEHC 289 (O'Neill J).

2 *Club Tivioli Ltd (in voluntary liquidation)* [2005] IEHC 468 (MacMenamin J).

153 Register of restricted persons

(1) The registrar shall, subject to the provisions of this section, keep a register of the particulars which have been notified to him under section 150, and the following provisions of this section shall apply to the keeping of such a register.

(2) Where the court grants partial relief to a person under section 152 a prescribed officer of the court shall cause the registrar to be furnished with prescribed particulars of the relief, and the registrar shall, as soon as may be, enter the particulars on the register referred to in subsection (1).

(3) Where the court grants full relief to a person under section 152 a prescribed officer of the court shall cause the registrar to be so notified, and the registrar shall, as soon as

may be, remove the particulars of any such person from the register referred to in subsection (1).

(4) The registrar shall also remove from the register any particulars in relation to a person on the expiry of five years from the date of the declaration to which the original notification under section 150 relates.

(5) Nothing in this section shall prevent the registrar from keeping the register required by this section as part of any other system of classification, whether pursuant to section 247 or otherwise.

Definitions

CA 1963: 'company': CA 1963, s 2(1); 'registrar': CA 1963, s 2(1).

Notes

See notes following CA 1990, ss 150 and 152. The Registrar of Companies provides access to online extracts from the register of restricted persons at http://www.cro.ie.

---

154 Application of this Chapter to receivers

Where a receiver of the property of a company is appointed, the provisions of this Chapter shall, with the necessary modifications, apply as if the references therein to the liquidator and to winding up were construed as references to the receiver and to receivership.

Definitions

CA 1963: 'company': CA 1963, s 2(1); 'liquidator': CA 1963, s 2(1); 'receiver': CA 1963, s 2(1).

---

155 Restrictions on company to which section 150 (3) applies

(1) This section applies to any company in relation to which a person who is the subject of a declaration under section 150 is appointed or acts in any way, whether directly or indirectly, as a director or secretary or is concerned in or takes part in the promotion or formation of that company.

(2) Subsections (2) to (11) of section 60 of the Principal Act shall not apply to any company to which this section applies.

(3) Sections 32 to 36 of the Companies (Amendment) Act, 1983, shall, with the necessary modifications, apply to any company to which this section applies as if the company were a public limited company so, however, that for the purposes of this subsection those sections shall apply as if—

(a) in subsection (1) of section 32 the words 'during the initial period' were deleted;

(b) any other reference in any of those sections to 'initial period' were deleted; and

(c) in subsection (2) of section 32 the words 'relevant person' were defined to mean 'any subscriber to the memorandum, any director or any person involved in the promotion or formation of the company'.

(4) Without prejudice to section 39, sections 32 and 37 shall not apply to any company to which subsection (1) applies.

(5) From the date of a declaration under section 150 a person in respect of whom the declaration was made shall not accept appointment to a position or act in any manner mentioned in subsection (1) of this section in relation to a company unless he has, within the 14 days immediately preceding such appointment or so acting, sent to the registered office of the company a notification that he is a person to whom section 150 applies.

Definitions

CA 1963: 'company': CA 1963, s 2(1); 'director': CA 1963, s 2(1).

Notes

Although emphasis tends to be placed on the capitalisation requirements for a company with a director or promoter who is a restricted person, the difficulties created by s 155 are also significant and tend to be overlooked. Such a company cannot provide financial assistance for the purchase of its own shares under the whitewash provisions of CA 1963, s 60, nor can it avail of the exceptions to CA 1990, s 31 regarding the making of loans and quasi-loans to and the entering into of credit transactions with directors and persons connected with the directors. Also, any transaction involving the acquisition of non-cash assets worth at least one-tenth of the nominal value of the share capital from any subscriber, director or promoter must be independently valued and approved beforehand by ordinary resolution of the company in general meeting.

These restrictions apply irrespective of whether or not the restricted person has given the company notice of the restriction order as required by sub-s (5). However, if has failed to give the company notice and the company has thereby unwittingly breached s 155, it may apply for relief under s 157.

See also the restrictions imposed by CA 1990, s 156.

CA 1990, s 157 provides for relief for third parties in respect of any acts or omissions that are prohibited by this chapter.

---

156 Requirements as to share allotted by a company to which section 155 applies

(1) Where a company to which section 155 applies allots a share which is not fully paid up as required by section 150(3)(b) the share shall be treated as if its nominal value together with the whole of any premium had been received, but the allottee shall be liable to pay the company in cash the full amount which should have been received in respect of the share under that subsection less the value of any consideration actually applied in payment up (to any extent) of the share and any premium on it, and interest at the appropriate rate on the amount payable under this subsection.

(2) Where a company to which section 155 applies allots a share which is not fully paid for in cash as required by section 150(3)(c) the allottee of the share shall be liable to pay the company in cash an amount equal to its nominal value, together with the whole of any premium, and shall be liable to pay interest at the appropriate rate on the amount payable under this subsection.

(3) Subsection (1) shall not apply in relation to the allotment of a bonus share which is not fully paid up as required by section 150(3)(b) unless the allottee knew or ought to have known that the share was so allotted.

(4) Subsection (1) does not apply to shares allotted in pursuance of an employees' share scheme within the meaning of section 2 of the Companies (Amendment) Act, 1983.

(5) In this section, 'appropriate rate' has the meaning assigned to it by section 2 of the Companies (Amendment) Act, 1983.

(6) Section 26(4) of the Companies (Amendment) Act, 1983, shall apply for the purposes of this section as it applies for the purposes of that section.

Definitions

CA 1963: 'company': CA 1963, s 2(1); 'shares': CA 1963, s 2(1); 'the registrar of companies': CA 1963, s 2(1); 'appropriate rate': CA 1983, s 2(1).

Notes

This section contains further restrictions on a company in relation to which a person is the subject of a declaration under CA 1990, s 150 has been appointed. The effect of the section is that where a share has not been fully paid up in cash, the allottee is required to pay the full consideration in cash and this is so even though he may already have paid for the share either wholly or partly by way of a non-cash consideration. He may, however, apply to the court under C(A)A 1983, s 34 for relief. Presumably, the court will grant relief on the basis that the non-cash consideration is independently valued and the allottee is only ordered to pay whatever cash balance is found to be due and owing after deduction of the independently valued non-cash consideration from the total price.

The application of C(A)A 1983, s 26(4) means that subsequent holders of shares which are not fully paid up in cash as required by s 150(3)(b) & (c) will also be liable under CA 1990, s 156 unless they acquired the shares *bona fide* for value and without notice of the breach of s 150(3).

157 Relief for a company in respect of prohibited transactions

(1) The court may, if it deems it just and equitable to do so, grant relief to a company to which section 155 applies in respect of any act or omission which, by virtue of that section, contravened a provision of the Companies Acts or to any person adversely affected thereby, on whatever terms and conditions the court sees fit, including exemption from any such provision.

(2) Relief shall not be granted to the company where the person referred to in section 155 (1) complied with subsection (5) of that section.

Definitions

CA 1963: 'court': CA 1963, s 2(1); 'company': CA 1963, s 2(1).

Notes

This section allows any third party apply to court to obtain relief in respect of an act or omission that was prohibited by this chapter. Such relief will not be granted though if the restricted person had notified the company of his restriction under s 155(5) before the breach occurred.

158 Power to vary amounts mentioned in section 150(3)

The Minister may, by order, vary the amounts mentioned in section 150 (3)(a) and the order may—

(a) require any company to which that section applies having an allotted share capital of which the nominal value is less than the amount specified in the order to increase the value to not less than that amount;

(b) make, in connection with any such requirement provision for any of the matters for which provision is made in the Companies Acts in relation to a company's registration, Re-registration, change of name, winding-up or dissolution, payment for any share comprised in a company's capital and offers of shares in or debentures of a company to the public, including provision as to the consequences (whether in criminal law or otherwise) of a failure to comply with any requirement of the order, and

(c) contain such supplemental and transitional provisions as the Minister thinks appropriate, specify different amounts in relation to companies of different classes or descriptions and, in particular, provide for any provision of the order to come into operation on different days for different purposes.

Definitions

'court': CA 1963, s 2(1); 'company': CA 1963, s 2(1); 'debentures': CA 1963, s 2(1); 'shares': CA 1963, s 2(1); 'the Minister': CA 1990, s 3(1).

Chapter 2
Disqualification generally

159 Interpretation of Chapters 2 and 3

In this Chapter and Chapter 3, except where the context otherwise requires—

'company' includes every company and every body, whether corporate or unincorporated, which may be wound up under Part X of the Principal Act and, without prejudice to the generality of the foregoing, includes a friendly society within the meaning of the Friendly Societies Acts, 1896 to 1977;

'the court' means the High Court except in relation to a disqualification order made by a court of its own motion under section 160(2), paragraph (a), (b), (c), (d) or (f), in which case it includes any court;

'default order' means an order made against any person under section 371 of the Principal Act by virtue of any contravention of or failure to comply with any relevant requirement (whether on his own part or on the part of any company);

'disqualification order' means—

(a) an order under this Part that the person against whom the order is made shall not be appointed or act as an auditor, director or other officer, receiver, liquidator or examiner or be in any way, whether directly or indirectly, concerned or take part in the promotion, formation or management of any company, or any society registered under the Industrial and Provident Societies Acts, 1893 to 1978, or

(b) an order under section 184 of the Principal Act;

'officer' in relation to any company, includes any director, shadow director or secretary of the company;

'relevant requirement' means any provision of the Companies Acts (including a provision repealed by this Act) which requires or required any return, account or other document to be filed with, delivered or sent to, or notice of any matter to be given to, the registrar of companies.

Definitions

'court': CA 1963, s 2(1); 'company': CA 1963, s 2(1); 'director': CA 1963, s 2(1); 'examiner': CA 1963, s 2(1); 'liquidator': CA 1963, s 2(1); 'officer': CA 1963, s 2(1); 'receiver': CA 1963, s 2(1); 'the registrar of companies': CA 1963, s 2(1); 'shadow director': CA 1990, s 27.

160 Disqualification of certain persons from acting as directors or auditors of or managing companies

(1) Where a person is convicted on indictment of any indictable offence in relation to a company, or involving fraud or dishonesty, then during the period of five years from the date of conviction or such other period as the court, on the application of the prosecutor and having regard to all the circumstances of the case, may order—

(a) he shall not be appointed or act as an auditor, director or other officer, receiver, liquidator or examiner or be in any way, whether directly or indirectly, concerned or take part in the promotion, formation or management of any company or any society registered under the Industrial and Provident Societies Acts, 1893 to 1978;

(b) he shall be deemed, for the purposes of this Act, to be subject to a disqualification order for that period.

[(1A) Without prejudice to subsection (1), a person who—

(a) fails to comply with section 3A(1) of the Companies (Amendment) Act, 1982, or section 195(8) of the Principal Act, or

(b) in purported compliance with the said section 3A(1) or 195(8), permits the first-mentioned statement in the said section 3A(1) or, as the case may be, the first-mentioned notification in the said section 195(8) to be accompanied by a statement signed by him which is false or misleading in a material respect,

shall, upon the delivery to the registrar of companies of the said first-mentioned statement or notification or, as the case may be, the said statement or notification accompanied by a statement as aforesaid, be deemed, for the purposes of this Act, to be subject to a disqualification order for the period referred to in subsection (1B).

(1B) The period mentioned in subsection (1A) is—

(a) so much as remains unexpired, at the date of the delivery mentioned in that subsection, of the period for which the person concerned is disqualified under the law of the other state referred to in section 3A(1) of the Companies (Amendment) Act, 1982, or section 195(8) of the Principal Act from being appointed or acting in the manner described therein, or

(b) if the person concerned is so disqualified under the law of more than one other such state and the portions of the respective periods for which he is so disqualified that remain unexpired at the date of that delivery are not equal, whichever of those unexpired portions is the greatest.][a]

(2) Where the court is satisfied in any proceedings or as a result of an application under this section that—

(a) a person has been guilty, while a promoter, officer, auditor, receiver, liquidator or examiner of a company, of any fraud in relation to the company, its members or creditors; or

(b) a person has been guilty, while a promoter, officer, auditor, receiver, liquidator or examiner of a company, of any breach of his duty as such promoter, officer, auditor, receiver, liquidator or examiner; or

(c) a declaration has been granted under section 297A of the Principal Act (inserted by section 138 of this Act) in respect of a person; or

(d) the conduct of any person as promoter, officer, auditor, receiver, liquidator or examiner of a company, makes him unfit to be concerned in the management of a company; or

(e) in consequence of a report of inspectors appointed by the court or the [Director][b] under the Companies Acts, the conduct of any person makes him unfit to be concerned in the management of a company; or

(f) a person has been persistently in default in relation to the relevant [requirements; or][c]

[(g) a person has been guilty of 2 or more offences under section 202(10); or

(h) a person was a director of a company at the time of the sending, after the commencement of section 42 of the Company Law Enforcement Act, 2001, of a letter under subsection (1) of section 12 of the Companies (Amendment) Act, 1982, to the company and the name of which, following the taking of the other steps under that section consequent on the sending of that letter, was struck off the register under subsection (3) of that section; or

(i) a person is disqualified under the law of another state (whether pursuant to an order of a judge or a tribunal or otherwise) from being appointed or acting as a director or secretary of a body corporate or an undertaking and the court is satisfied that, if the conduct of the person or the circumstances otherwise affecting him that gave rise to the said order being made against him had occurred or arisen in the State, it would have been proper to make a disqualification order otherwise under this subsection against him;][d]

the court may, of its own motion, or as a result of the application, make a disqualification order against such a person for such period as it sees fit.

(3) (a) For the purposes of subsection (2)(f) the fact that a person has been persistently in default in relation to the relevant requirements may (without prejudice to its proof in any other manner) be conclusively proved by showing that in the five years ending with the date of the application he has been adjudged guilty (whether or not on the same occasion) of three or more defaults in relation to those requirements.

(b) A person shall be treated as being adjudged guilty of a default in relation to a relevant requirement for the purposes of this subsection if he is convicted of any offence consisting of a contravention of a relevant requirement or a default order is made against him.

[(3A) The court shall not make a disqualification order under paragraph (h) of subsection (2) against a person who shows to the court that the company referred to in that paragraph had no liabilities (whether actual, contingent or prospective) at the time its name was struck off the register or that any such liabilities that existed at that time were discharged before the date of the making of the application for the disqualification order.

(3B) A disqualification order under paragraph (i) of subsection (2) may be made against a person notwithstanding that, at the time of the making of the order, the person is deemed, by virtue of subsection (1A), to be subject to a disqualification order for the purposes of this Act, and where a disqualification order under the said paragraph (i) is made, the period of disqualification specified in it shall be expressed to begin on the expiry of the period of disqualification referred to in subsection (1B) to which the person, by virtue of subsection (1A), is subject or the said period of disqualification as varied, if such be the case, under subsection (8).][e]

(4) An application under paragraph (a), (b), (c) or (d) of subsection (2) may be made by—

(a) the Director of Public Prosecutions; or

(b) any member, contributory, officer, employee, receiver, liquidator, examiner or creditor of any company in relation to which the person who is the subject of the application—

(i) has been or is acting or is proposing to or being proposed to act as officer, auditor, receiver, liquidator or examiner, or

(ii) has been or is concerned or taking part, or is proposing to be concerned or take part, in the promotion, formation or management of any company,

and where the application is made by a member, contributory, employee or creditor of the company, the court may require security for all or some of the costs of the application.

(5) An application under [paragraph (e) or g][f] of subsection (2) may be made by the Director of Public Prosecutions.

(6) An application under paragraph (f) of subsection (2) may be made by—

(a) the Director of Public Prosecutions; or

(b) the registrar of companies.

[(6A) In addition to the persons who in pursuance of subsections (4), (5) and (6) may make such an application, an application under subsection (2)(a), (b), (c), (d), (e), (f), (g), (h) or (i) may be made by the Director.][g]

(7) Where it is intended to make an application under subsection (2) in respect of any person, the applicant shall give not less than ten days' notice of his intention to that person.

(8) Any person who is subject or deemed subject to a disqualification order by virtue of this Part may apply to the court for relief, either in whole or in part, from that disqualification and the court may, if it deems it just and equitable to do so, grant such relief on whatever terms and conditions it sees fit.

(9) A disqualification order may be made on grounds which are or include matters other than criminal convictions notwithstanding that the person in respect of whom the order is to be made may be criminally liable in respect of those matters.

[(9A) In considering the penalty to be imposed under this section, the court may as an alternative, where it adjudges that disqualification is not justified, make a declaration under section 150.][h]

[(9B) The court, on the hearing of an application for a disqualification order under subsection (2), may order that the persons disqualified or against whom a declaration under section 150 is made as a result of the application shall bear—

(a) the costs of the application, and

(b) in the case of an application by the Director, the Director of Public Prosecutions, a liquidator, a receiver or an examiner (in this paragraph referred to as 'the applicant'), in addition to the costs referred to in paragraph (a), the whole (or such portion of them as the court specifies) of the costs and expenses incurred by the applicant—

(i) in investigating the matters the subject of the application, and

(ii) in so far as they do not fall within paragraph (a), in collecting evidence in respect of those matters,

including so much of the remuneration and expenses of the applicant as are attributable to such investigation and collection.][i]

(10) A reference in any other enactment to section 184 of the Principal Act shall be construed as including a reference to this section.

Amendments

a CLEA 2001, s 42(a) inserts CA 1990, s 160(1A) and (1B).

b 'Director' substituted for 'Minister' by CLEA 2001, s 14.

c CLEA 2001, s 42(b)(i) amends CA 1990, s 160(2)(f) by the substitution for 'requirements' of 'requirements; or'.

d CLEA 2001, s 42(b)(ii) inserts CA 1990, s 160(2)(g), (h) and (i).

e CLEA 2001, s 42(c) inserts CA 1990, s 160(3A) and (3B).

f CLEA 2001, s 42(d) amends CA 1990, s 160(5) by the substitution for 'paragraph (e)' of 'paragraph (e) or (g)'.

g CLEA 2001, s 42(e) inserts CA 1990, s 160(6A).

h CLEA 2001, s 42(f) inserts CA 1990, s 160(9A).

i CLEA 2001, s 42(f) inserts CA 1990, s 160(9B) which was substituted with effect from 29 January 2007 by IFCMPA 2005, s 11(2).

Definitions

'contributory': CA 1963, s 2(1); 'creditor': CA 1963, s 2(1); 'director': CA 1963, s 2(1); 'examiner': CA 1963, s 2(1); 'liquidator': CA 1963, s 2(1); 'officer': CA 1963, s 2(1); 'receiver': CA 1963, s 2(1); 'the registrar of companies': CA 1963, s 2(1); 'company': CA 1990, s 259; 'the court: CA 1990, s 259; 'default order': CA 1990, s 259; 'disqualification order': CA 1990, s 159; 'the court': CA 1990, s 159; 'relevant requirements': CA 1990, s 259; 'the Director': CLEA 2001, s 3(1).

Notes

Nature of disqualification order: The key distinction between a restriction (under s 150) and a disqualification (under s 160) is summarised as follows by Courtney, *The Law of Private* Companies (2nd edn, Tottel Publishing, 2002) para 12.090:

> '… a person against whom a Disqualification Order is made can have no involvement, whatsoever, in the promotion, formation or management of any company for the duration of the disqualification period'.

In other words, a disqualification order constitutes a total banishment from corporate life whereas a restriction order by contrast merely places conditions on participation.

Section 160 is aimed at conduct that amounts to fraud, breach of statutory duty, gross incompetence, lack of commercial probity and persistent default in corporate obligations and is thus considered to be merited for only the most egregious behaviour.[1]

In *Business Communications Ltd v Baxter*[2] the court noted that:

> 'the comprehensive nature of a Disqualification Order… is seen as constituting an appropriately severe sentence for conduct which is manifestly more blameworthy than merely failing to exercise an appropriate degree of responsibility in relation to an insolvent company in liquidation of which the person is a Director'.

Accordingly a Disqualification Order will not be made lightly,[3] and indeed, this appears to be reflected in sub-s (9A) which empowers the court to make a restriction order instead, if it considers that an absolute disqualification would nto be appropriate. As Sir Nicholas Browne-Wilkinson VC stated, in the oft-cited case of *Re Lo-Line Ltd*:[4]

> 'The primary purpose of the section is not to punish the individual but to protect the public against future conduct of companies by persons whose past records as directors…have shown them to be a danger to creditors and others. Therefore the power is not fundamentally penal. But, if the power to disqualify is exercised, disqualification does involve a substantial interference with the freedom of the individual. It follows that the rights of the individual must be fully protected. Ordinary commercial misjudgement is in itself not sufficient to justify disqualification. In the normal case, the conduct complained of must display a lack of commercial probity, although I have no doubt that in an extreme case of gross negligence or total incompetence disqualification could be appropriate.'

This statement of the law has recently been endorsed by the Supreme Court[5] which, while emphasising the primary purpose of the section as being the protection of the public, nevertheless also acknowledged that there should be an element of deterrence in the exercise of the court's discretion.

1 *Re CB Readymix Ltd; Cahill v Grimes* [2002] 1 IR 372; *Director of Corporate Enforcement v Collery* [2006] IEHC 67; *Director of Corporate Enforcement v D'Arcy* [2006] 2 IR 163; *Director of Corporate Enforcement v Byrne* [2009] 2 ILRM 328.

2 *Business Communications Ltd v Baxter* (21 July 1995, unreported) HC (Murphy J). See also *Director of Corporate Enforcement v Byrne* [2009] 2 ILRM 328.

3 *Re Newcastle Timber Ltd* [2001] 4 IR 586.

4 *Re Lo-Line Ltd* [1988] Ch 477 at 485–6. Cited with approval in *Re CB Readymix Ltd; Cahill v Grimes* [2002] 1 IR 372; *Director of Corporate Enforcement v Collery* [2006] IEHC 67; *Director of Corporate Enforcement v D'Arcy* [2006] 2 IR 163; *Re Kentford Securities Ltd, Director of Corporate Enforcement v McCann* [2007] IEHC 1; *Director of Corporate Enforcement v Byrne* [2009] 2 ILRM 328.

5 *Director of Corporate Enforcement v McGowan* [2008] 4 IR 598; *Director of Corporate Enforcement v Byrne* [2009] 2 ILRM 328.

Automatic deemed disqualification: Any person convicted on indictment of an offence of the type described in s 160(1) is automatically deemed to be disqualified for five years unless the court imposes some other period of disqualification instead. A solicitor who allows his client account to be used to conceal the proceeds of criminal conduct by a company and who is thus convicted of money laundering, will be regarded as having been convicted of an 'offence in relation to a company' for the purpose of s 160(1).[1] It is to be noted that if the offence of which the person is convicted involves fraud or dishonesty, it matters not whether the person was involved in the affairs of any company. In addition, if a person who has been disqualified in another state fails to notify the registrar of companies of that fact upon his appointment as a director of an Irish company he will also be deemed under sub-ss (1A) and (1B) to be disqualified in the State for the unexpired of the foreign disqualification order.

1 *R v Creggy* [2008] 1 BCLC 625.

Persons who may be disqualified under s 160(2): Disqualifications under s 160(2) are not automatic. Rather, they are ordered by the court either of its own motion or on application to it by a person having appropriate *locus standi*. The provisions of sub-s (2) are directed against promoters, officers, auditors, receivers, liquidators and examiners of companies. De facto promoters, officers, auditors, receivers, liquidators and examiners are also included.[1] The word 'officer' is defined by CA 1990, s 159 as including 'any director, shadow director or secretary of the company'. This definition is clearly not exhaustive and in this regard it has been held in the English courts that a person who was not a director of a company might nevertheless be regarded as an officer of a company on the basis that he was in an elevated management position.[2] This line of case law has been described by Kelly J in *Re National Irish Bank, The Director of Corporate Enforcement v D'Arcy*[3] as being 'probably correct'. The fact that a person has previously been acquitted on criminal charges does not preclude the bringing of disqualification proceedings against him in respect of the same matters because the standard of proof in disqualification proceedings is the civil standard of proof on the balance of probabilities.[4]

1 *Re CB Readymix Ltd, Cahill v Grimes* [2002] 1 IR 372; *Re Lo-Line Ltd* [1988] Ch 477. See also *Re Tasbian Ltd (No 3)* [1991] BCLC 792; *Re Cargo Agency Ltd* [1992] BCLC 686; *Re Hydrodam (Corby) Ltd* [1994] 2 BCLC 180; *Re Moorgate Metals Ltd* [1995] 1 BCLC 503; *Re Richborough Furniture Ltd* [1996] 1 BCLC 507; *Re Sykes (Butchers) Ltd* [1998] 1 BCLC 110; *Secretary of State for Trade and Industry v Tjolle* [1998] 1 BCLC 333; *Secretary of State for Trade and Industry v Becker* [2003] 1 BCLC 555.

2 *Re a company* [1980] Ch 138; *R v Boal* [1992] QB 591; *Re Mea Corporation Ltd* [2007] 1 BCLC 618.

3 *Re National Irish Bank, The Director of Corporate Enforcement v D'Arcy* [2006] 2 IR 163. See also *Director of Corporate Enforcement v Boner* [2008] IEHC 151; *Director of Corporate Enforcement v Brennan* [2008] IEHC 132.

4 *Re Trans Tec plc (No 2)* [2007] 2 BCLC 495.

Notice of disqualification proceedings: All applications to disqualify must be preceded by not less than 10 days' notice to the proposed respondents.[1] This is a statutory time limit and not one provided for under the RSC 1986, and as such, is one to which the provisions of those rules for the abridgment of time do not apply. Nevertheless, a failure to give the prescribed period of notice will probably not invalidate the actual proceedings.[2]

1 CA 1990, s 160(7).

2 *Secretary of State for Trade and Industry v Langridge* [1991] 3 All ER 591.

***Locus standi* to seek disqualification order:** Under s 160(2) the court may, of its own motion, make a disqualification in any proceedings where it is satisfied that there are grounds for so doing. Otherwise, the ODCE may apply under paragraphs (a) to (i), the DPP may apply under (a) to (g), the registrar of companies may apply under (f) and members, contributories, officers, employees, receivers, liquidators, examiners and creditors under (a) to (d).[1]

1 See CA 1990, s 160(4) to (6A).

Onus of Proof: In contrast to applications for restriction pursuant to CA 1990, s 150, the onus of proof under CA 1990: CA 1963, s 160 is on the applicant.[1] In bringing such proceedings, the applicant is subject to the same hearsay exclusionary rule that applies to other civil proceedings.[2] In this regard, whilst proceedings under s 160 are by way of affidavit, the applicant may seek to have the respondent cross-examined on his affidavits with a view to making out a case for disqualification.[3]

1 *Re Newcastle Timber Ltd* [2001] 4 IR 586; approved by the Supreme Court in *Re Readymix Ltd Cahill v Grimes* [2002] 1 IR 372. See also *Director of Corporate Enforcement v Collery* [2006] IEHC 67; *Director of Corporate Enforcement v D'Arcy* [2006] 2 IR 163.

2 *Re Bovale Developments Ltd, Director of Corporate Enforcement v Bailey* [2008] 2 ILRM 13.

3 *Director of Corporate Enforcement v Seymour* [2006] IEHC 369.

Grounds for disqualification

Most of the grounds for disqualification are self-explanatory. Accordingly, some warrant less comment than others.

1 Fraud

Para (a) allows for the making of a disqualification order on grounds of fraud, irrespective of whether or not personal liability has also been imposed for fraudulent trading under CA 1963, s 297A. Examples of fraud that have justified the making of disqualification orders include the obtaining of local authority grants by deception,[1] the appending of false audit certificates to the annual accounts[2] and the deliberate underdeclaration of taxes and the use of those tax moneys to fund continued insolvent trading.[3]

1 *Re T & D Services (Timber Preservation & Damp Proofing Contractors) Ltd* [1990] BCC 592.

2 *Re Defence & Microwave Devices Ltd* (7 October 1992, unreported) (HC, Eng, Ch D).

3 *Re PSK Construction Ltd* (7 December 2009, unreported) HC (Finlay Geoghegan J).

2 Breach of duty

Para (b) allows for the making of a disqualification order for breach of duty. The provisions do not, however, cover breaches that are trivial or the result of mistake. In *Re Christy Kenneally Communications Ltd*,[2] in the context of proceedings under CA 1963, s 205 Costello J disqualified two directors who had refused to comply with an order of the court to prepare annual accounts and hold an AGM. In their stead, he appointed two accountants to act as the directors of the company. The failure by a director, in breach of CA 1963, s 194, to disclose to the company his interest in a transaction between the company and a third party was held to give grounds for disqualification.[3]

1 *Re Adbury Park Estates Ltd* (2003) BCC 696.

2 *Re Christy Kenneally Communications Ltd* (July 1992, unreported) HC (Costello J).

3 *Re Godwin Warren Control Systems plc* [1993] BCLC 80. The failure to disclose became active concealment and was held not only to be a breach of duty but also to amount to unfitness.

3 Fraudulent or reckless trading

Para (c) allows for a disqualification order to be made in circumstances where personal liability has already been imposed on the respondent pursuant to CA 1963, s 297A for fraudulent or reckless trading.[1]

1 For an example of a case where a person was disqualified, having been found guilty of fraudulent trading, see *Re Kellys Carpetdrome Ltd* (1 July 1983, unreported) HC (Costello J); *Re PSK Construction Ltd* (7 December 2009, unreported) HC (Finlay Geoghegan J).

4 Unfitness to be concerned in the management of a company

Paras (d) & (e) allow for the making of a disqualification order in circumstances where the person is shown to be unfit to be concerned in the management of a company. An application under para

(e) can only be made where the unfitness is disclosed in the Report of an Inspector appointed by the court or by the ODCE.

It is the question of unfitness that has given rise to most litigation both in the State and in the UK. As noted above, in order to constitute unfitness, the conduct of the respondent must be such as to display a lack of commercial probity, gross negligence or total incompetence and in this regard a director's competence or otherwise must be assessed by reference to the role in the management of the company which had in fact been assigned to him or which he had in fact assumed and by reference to his duties and responsibilities in that role.[1] This may encompass matters such as deliberate tax evasion,[2] the deliberate destruction or falsification of records to defraud creditors or to defeat their claims,[3] the sale by the directors of the assets of an insolvent company to themselves at a substantial undervalue,[4] a failure to keep proper books of account or to make annual returns,[5] the grossly negligent issuing of false and misleading financial statements,[6] the dishonest supply of false and misleading information to the directors of a company the subject of a take-over bid,[7] the misappropriation of company stock,[8] the failure to stop the misuse of company funds by another director,[9] the drawing of excessive, or even going-rate, remuneration at a time when the company is insolvent,[10] and trading whilst insolvent when the respondent knew or ought to have known that he was thereby acting to the detriment of creditors.[11] However, if the insolvent trading occurred over a limited period of time, the court may regard the conduct as insufficient to warrant a disqualification,[12] although it may justify the making of a restriction order under s 150.[13]

In relation to insolvent trading, the court will be more inclined to make a disqualification order where it is established that the directors have been deliberately causing the company not to pay its taxes and have been using those taxes as a source of revenue for the business.[14] Acting on professional advice,[15] or engaging the services of a qualified accountant to act as finance director[16] may help to exonerate the respondents, although even then, they cannot abdicate financial responsibility for the company's affairs altogether and must still take steps to satisfy themselves that the company's finances are sound.[17]

In assessing the conduct of the individual the court will take into account his entire history and not just the alleged acts of wrongdoing and will look at his behaviour and record as a whole.[18] In this regard the individual is not to be judged with the inevitable benefit of hindsight.[19]

1 *Re Lo-Line Ltd* [1988] Ch 477 at 485–6. *Re CB Readymix Ltd; Cahill v Grimes* [2002] 1 IR 372; *Director of Corporate Enforcement v Collery* [2007] 1 IR 580; *Director of Corporate Enforcement v D'Arcy* [2006] 2 IR 163; *Kappler v Secretary of State for Trade and Industry* [2008] 1 BCLC 120; *Re Grayan Building Services Ltd* [1995] Ch 241; *Re Barings plc (No 5)* [1999] 1 BCLC 433; *Official Receiver v Doshi* [2001] 2 BCLC 235; *Re Vintage Hallmark plc* [2007] 1 BCLC 788; *Director of Corporate Enforcement v Seymour* [2007] IEHC 102; *Director of Corporate Enforcement v Brennan* [2008] IEHC 132; *Director of Corporate Enforcement v Byrne* [2009] 2 ILRM 328; *Kappler v Secretary of State for Trade and Industry* [2008] 1 BCLC 120. See also *Director of Corporate Enforcement v Keane* [2008] IEHC 150; *Director of Corporate Enforcement v Curran* [2008] IEHC 181; *Re PSK Construction Ltd* (7 December 2009, unreported) HC (Finlay Geoghegan J).

2 *Director of Corporate Enforcement v Collery* [2007] 1 IR 580; *Director of Corporate Enforcement v D'Arcy* [2006] 2 IR 163.

3 *Re CB Readymix Ltd; Cahill v Grimes* [2002] 1 IR 372; *Re Nationwide Transport Ltd, Forrest v Whelan* [2006] IEHC 87; *Re Trans Tec plc (No 2)* [2007] 2 BCLC 495; *Re City Truck Group Ltd* [2007] 2 BCLC 649; *Kappler v Secretary of State for Trade and Industry* [2008] 1 BCLC 120.

4 *Re Nationwide Transport Ltd, Forrest v Whelan* [2006] IEHC 87; *Re Keypak Homecare Ltd* [1990] BCLC 440; *Re Copecrest Ltd* [1997] BCC 224; *Re Funtime Ltd* [2000] 1 BCLC 247.

5 *Re Nationwide Transport Ltd, Forrest v Whelan* [2006] IEHC 87; *Re Dev Oil and Gas Ltd, Jackson v Devlin* [2008] IEHC 252; *Re Churchill Hotel Ltd* [1988] BCLC 341; *Re J & B Lynch (Builders) Ltd* [1988] BCLC 376; *Re Cladrose Ltd* [1990] BCLC 204; *Re Sevenoaks Stationers (Retail) Ltd* [1990] BCLC 668; *Re Chartmore Ltd* [1990] BCLC 673; *Re Travel Mondial (UK)*

Ltd [1991] BCLC 120; *Re Tansoft Ltd* [1991] BCLC 339; *Re Swift 736 Ltd* [1993] BCLC 1; *Re New Generation Engineers Ltd* [1993] BCLC 435; *Re Linvale Ltd* [1993] BCLC 654; *Re Hitco 2000 Ltd* [1995] BCC 161; *Re Thorncliffe Finance Ltd* [1996] BCC 586; *Re Richborough Furniture Ltd* [1996] BCC 155; *Re Galeforce Pleating Co Ltd* [1999] 2 BCLC 704; *Re Promwalk Services Ltd* [2003] 2 BCLC 305. Failure to file annual returns may also justify disqualification under para (f).

6 *Re Nationwide Transport Ltd, Forrest v Whelan* [2006] IEHC 87; *Re Queen's Moat Houses plc (No 2)* [2005] 1 BCLC 136.

7 *Re Bunting Electric Manufacturing Co Ltd* [2006] 1 BCLC 550.

8 *Re Nationwide Transport Ltd, Forrest v Whelan* [2006] IEHC 87;*Secretary of State for Trade and Industry v Blunt* [2005] 2 BCLC 463.

9 *Re Nationwide Transport Ltd, Forrest v Whelan* [2006] IEHC 87;*Secretary of State for Trade and Industry v Goldberg* [2004] 1 BCLC 597.

10 *Re Stanford Services Ltd* (1987) 3 BCC 326; *Re Cargo Agency Ltd* [1992] BCC 388; *Re Austinsuite Furniture Ltd* [1992] BCLC 1047; *Re Synthetic Technology Ltd* [1993] BCC 549; *Re Firedart Ltd* [1994] 2 BCLC 340; *Re Moorgate Metals Ltd* [1995] BCC 143; *Re CSTC Ltd* [1995] BCC 173; *Re Ward Sherrard Ltd* [1996] BCC 418; *Re Copecrest Ltd* [1997] BCC 224; *Re Amaron Ltd* [1997] 2 BCLC 115, aff'd [1998] BCC 264; *Official Receiver v Stern (No 2)* [2002] 1 BCLC 119.

11 *Re Bath Glass Ltd* [1988] BCLC 329; *Re Sevenoaks Stationers (Retail) Ltd* [1990] BCLC 668; *Re Ward Sherrard Ltd* [1996] BCC 418; *Re City Pram and Toy Co Ltd* [1998] BCC 537; *Re Galeforce Pleating Co Ltd* [1999] 2 BCLC 704; *Official Receiver v Doshi* [2001] 2 BCLC 235.

12 *Re CU Fittings Ltd* [1989] BCLC 556; *Re Wimbledon Village Restaurant Ltd* [1994] BCC 753; *Re Moonlight Foods (UK) Ltd* [1996] BCC 678; *Secretary of State for Trade and Industry v Creegan* [2002] 1 BCLC 99.

13 See the notes to CA 1990, s 150.

14 *Re Lo-Line Ltd* [1988] Ch 477; *Re Stanford Services Ltd* [1987] BCLC 607; *Re Churchill Hotel Ltd* [1988] BCLC 341; *Re J & B Lynch (Builders) Ltd* [1988] BCLC 376; *Re Cladrose Ltd* [1990] BCLC 204; *Re Sevenoaks Stationers (Retail) Ltd* [1990] BCLC 668; *Re Melcast (Wolverhampton) Ltd* [1991] BCLC 288; *Re Swift 736 Ltd* [1993] BCLC 1; *Re GSAR Realisations Ltd* [1993] BCLC 409; *Re Linvale Ltd* [1993] BCLC 654; *Re Verby Print for Advertising Ltd* [1998] 2 BCLC 23; *Re Galeforce Pleating Co Ltd* [1999] 2 BCLC 704; *Re Hopes (Heathrow) Ltd* [2001] 1 BCLC 575; *Re Amaron Ltd, Secretary of State for Trade and Industry v Lubrani (No 2)* [2001] 1 BCLC 562; *Re City Truck Ltd* [2007] 2 BCLC 649.

15 *Re Douglas Construction Services Ltd* [1988] BCLC 397; *Re Bath Glass Ltd* [1988] BCLC 329; *Re McNulty's Interchange Ltd* [1989] BCLC 709; *Re Cladrose Ltd* [1990] BCLC 204; *Re World of Leather plc* [2004] EWHC (Ch) 2786.

16 *Re Majestic Recording Studios Ltd* [1989] BCLC 1; *Re Melcast (Wolverhampton) Ltd* [1991] BCLC 288.

17 *Re Bradcrown Ltd* [2002] BCC 428; *Re Vintage Hallmark plc* [2007] 1 BCLC 788; *Re City Truck Ltd* [2007] 2 BCLC 649; *Secretary of State for Trade and Industry v Thornbury* [2008] 1 BCLC 139; *Re AG (Manchester) Ltd, Official Receiver v Watson* [2008] 1 BCLC 321.

18 *Director of Corporate Enforcement v Byrne* [2009] 2 ILRM 328.

19 *Director of Corporate Enforcement v Byrne* [2009] 2 ILRM 328.

5 Failing to file returns

Para (f) allows for the disqualification of a person for persistent default in filing, delivering, sending or notifying the registrar of companies of any return, account, document or other matter which is meant to be so filed, etc. Persistent default is deemed to have been conclusively proved under sub-s (3) if the person has been convicted of three or more such offences in the preceding five years. Otherwise, in order to show 'persistent' default, it will be necessary to satisfy the court not only that the default has been continuous or repeated but also that there has been some other element, whether of opposition or determination.[1] The provisions of sub-s (3) are without prejudice to the entitlement of the applicant to prove persistent default in some other way.

1 *Director of Corporate Enforcement v McGowan* [2008] 4 IR 598.

6 Failure to keep proper books of account

Para (g) allows for a disqualification order to be made where the respondent has been guilty of two or more ofences of a failure to keep proper books of account. See the notes to CA 1990, s 202.

1 See CA 1990, s 160(3A).

7 Directorship of dissolved company

CLEA 2001, s 42 introduced a new para (h) which entitles the court to disqualify a person who is a director of a company which has been struck off the register for failure to file annual returns. The respondent may, however, avoid disqualification if he can demonstrate that the company had no liabilities at the time of dissolution or that any such liabilities were discharged before the making of the application under para (h). Applications for disqualification under s 160(2)(h) have become more common recently.[1] It has been held that the minimum period of disqualification on this ground should be five years.[2]

1 See, for example, *Director of Corporate Enforcement v McDonnell* [2005] 1 IR 503; *Director of Corporate Enforcement v Collins* [2008] IEHC 456.

2 See, for example, *Director of Corporate Enforcement v McDonnell* [2005] 1 IR 503; *Director of Corporate Enforcement v Collins* [2008] IEHC 456.

8 Disqualification in a foreign state

The final ground for disqualification is contained in para (i) and arises in circumstances where the person has already been disqualified in another state. If he is already subject to a deemed disqualification order under subsection (1A) for having failed to notify the fact of his foreign disqualification order to the registrar of companies, the period of his disqualification under s 160(2)(i) shall run from the expiry of his deemed disqualification under s 160(1A). See s 160(3B).

Period of disqualification: Under CA 1990, s 160 the court may make a disqualification order 'for such period as it sees fit'. In determining a period of disqualification the court must have regard to the seriousness of the sanction. The court has held that in the absence of a respondent adducing relevant evidence, it is hard to see that any period less than five years would be a more onerous sanction for the respondent than a declaration of restriction, which must be for five years.[1]

The primary purpose of an order of disqualification is not to punish the individual but to protect the public against future conduct of companies by persons whose past record had shown them to be a danger to creditors and to others.[2] The period of disqualification should reflect the gravity of the conduct concerned and should have a deterrent element to it.[3] Longer periods of disqualification should, it is submitted, be reserved for serious cases. The relevant period ought to be considered and then appropriate regard had to any mitigating factors.[4]

In one recent case,[5] factors that the court took into account included the following: the statutory purpose of protecting the public; the long period that had elapsed between the conduct giving rise to the application and the actual commencement of the application to the court; and the absence of any complaint about or, indeed, positive evidence in relation to relevant conduct in the intervening period.

The court has held that the proper way to measure the period of disqualification was to approach it in the same manner as one would when sentencing a convicted person after a criminal trial. This necessitates an examination of the gravity of the offence, consideration of the appropriate period and regard to any mitigating factors.[6]

Despite the absence of evidence from the respondent, a disqualification period of less than five years has been ordered[7] and in doing so Dunne J warned that to interpret the section as providing for a minimum period was in effect to use 'tunnel vision' that Vinelott J had referred to in *Re Pamstock Ltd*.[8]

CA 1990, s 160(9A) allows a declaration of restriction as an alternative order, where disqualification is not justified.

Because the court has a discretion under s 160, even if it finds the case against the respondent to have been proved, it may exercise its discretion not to impose a disqualification order and indeed may decide not to grant the applicant the alternative remedy of a restriction order under s 160(9A) where it considers that no useful purpose would be achieved by the making of such an order and/or where the making of such an order would adversely affect the ongoing business of the company[9] or where it considers that disqualification would be disproportionate in the circumstances.[10] Similarly, the court may exercise its discretion not to disqualify where it is satisfied that the respondent has learned the error of his way, has reformed and is no longer a danger to the public.[11]

1 See *Director of Corporate Enforcement v McDonnell* [2005] 1 IR 503; *Director of Corporate Enforcement v D'Arcy* [2006] 2 IR 163.

2 *Re Lo-Line Ltd* [1988] Ch 477; *Re Sevenoaks Stationers (Retail) Ltd* [1991] Ch 164; *Re Westmid Packing* [1998] 2 All ER 124; *Director Corporate Enforcement v D'Arcy* [2006] 2 IR 163; *Director of Corporate Enforcement v Collery* [2007] 1 IR 580; *Director of Corporate Enforcement v Byrne* [2009] 2 ILRM 328.

3 *Director of Corporate Enforcement v D'Arcy* [2006] 2 IR 163.

4 *Director of Corporate Enforcement v D'Arcy* [2006] 2 IR 163.

5 *Director of Corporate Enforcement v Collery* [2007] 1 IR 580.

6 *Re Betarose Ltd, Forrest v Harrington* (12 January 2006) HC *ex tempore* (Dunne J).

7 *Re Betarose Ltd, Forrest v Harrington* (12 January 2006) HC *ex tempore* (Dunne J).

8 *Re Pamstock Ltd* [1994] 1 BCLC 716 at 737.

9 *Director of Corporate Enforcement v McGowan* [2008] 4 IR 598.

10 *Director of Corporate Enforcement v Byrne* [2009] 2 ILRM 328.

11 *Re Kentford Securities Ltd, Director of Corporate Enforcement v McCann* [2007] IEHC 1.

Costs

Costs should normally follow the event under Ord 99. Notably, sub-s (9B) gives the Court the power to order costs of the investigation of the disqualification application. In this regard see the notes to CA 1990, s 150 regarding the corresponding provisions of s 150(4B).

Relief from disqualification: Sub-s (8) entitles a disqualified person to apply for relief, in whole or in part from the disqualification order. Relief may be granted where the court considers its just and equitable to do so. In hearing such an application, the court should be mindful both of the reasons which led to the making of the disqualification order in the first place and of the need to protect the public.[1] However, the fact that there is virtually no risk of a recurrence of the conduct in question is a factor which the court can take into account in deciding to grant relief.[2] In one case,[3] the court granted leave to the individual to act as director of one named company but only on condition that it remained a subsidiary of a particular plc and someone other than the disqualified person held the office of finance director.

1 *Re Tech Textiles Ltd* [1998] 1 BCLC 259; *Secretary of State for Trade and Industry v Barnett* [1998] 2 BCLC 64; *Re Barings plc, Secretary of State for Trade and Indusry v Baker* [1999] 1BCLC 262; *Re Britannia Homes Centres Ltd* [2001] 2 BCLC 63.

2 *Re Barings plc, Secretary of State for Trade and Industry v Baker* [1999] 1 BCLC 433.

3 *Re Tech Textiles Ltd* [1998] 1 BCLC 259.

161 Penalty for acting contrary to the provisions of Chapter 1 or 2

(1) Any person who, in relation to any company, acts in a manner or capacity which, by virtue of being a person to whom section 150 applies or being subject or deemed to be subject to a disqualification order, he is prohibited from doing shall be guilty of an offence.

(2) Where a person is convicted of an offence under subsection (1) he shall be deemed to be subject to a disqualification order from the date of such conviction if he was not, or was not deemed to be, subject to such an order on that date.

(3) Where a person convicted of an offence under subsection (1) was subject, or deemed to be subject, to a disqualification order immediately prior to the date of such conviction, the period for which he was disqualified shall be extended for a further period of ten years from such date, or such other further period as the court, on the application of the prosecutor and having regard to all the circumstances of the case, may order.

(4) Section 160 (8) shall not apply to a person convicted of an offence under subsection (1) of this section.

(5) Where—

(a) a person who is a person to whom section 150 applies is or becomes a director of a company which commences to be wound up within the period of 5 years after the date of commencement of the winding-up of the company whose insolvency caused that section to apply to him; and

(b) it appears to the liquidator of the first-mentioned company that that company is, at the date of commencement of its winding-up or at any time during the course of its winding up, unable to pay its debts;

the liquidator shall report those matters to the court and the court, on receiving the report and if it considers it proper to do so, may make a disqualification order against that person for such period as it thinks fit.

(6) If the liquidator fails to comply with subsection (5) he shall [be guilty of an offence and liable to a fine][a] not exceeding [€1,904.61][b].

Amendments

a Words inserted by C(AA)A 2003, Sch 2.

b £1,000 increased to £1,500 by CA 1990, s 240(7) as inserted by CLEA 2001, s 104 and converted to €1,904.61 by Council Regulations (EC) No 1103/97, No 974/98 and No 2866/98 and the Economic and Monetary Union Act 1998, s 6.

Definitions

'director': CA 1963, s 2(1); 'liquidator': CA 1963, s 2(1); 'company': CA 1990, s 259; 'the court: CA 1990, s 259; 'disqualification order': CA 1990, s 159.

162 Period of disqualification order to which person is deemed to be subject

Where a person is, as a consequence of his conviction of an offence under this Chapter, deemed to be subject to a disqualification order, he shall be deemed to be so subject for a period of five years from the date of such conviction or such other period as the court, on the application of the prosecutor and having regard to all the circumstances of the case, may order.

Definitions

'disqualification order': CA 1990, s 159.

163 Civil consequences of acting contrary to the provisions of Chapter 1 or 2

(1) Subsections (2) and (3) apply to any person who acts, in relation to a company, in a manner or capacity which, by virtue of being a person to whom section 150 applies or being subject or deemed to be subject to a disqualification order, he is prohibited from doing.

(2) Where any consideration is given by or on behalf of a company for an act done or service performed by a person referred to in subsection (1) while he was acting in a manner or capacity described in that subsection, the company shall be entitled to recover from him, as a simple contract debt in any court of competent jurisdiction, the consideration or an amount representing its value.

(3) Where—

- (a) a person referred to in subsection (1) acts, in relation to a company, in a manner or capacity described in that subsection, and
- (b) the company concerned commences to be wound up—
  - (i) while he is acting in such a manner or capacity, or
  - (ii) within 12 months of his so acting, and
- (c) the company is unable to pay its debts, within the meaning of section 214 of the Principal Act,

the court may, on the application of the liquidator or any creditor of the company, declare that such person shall be personally liable, without any limitation of liability, for all or any part of the debts or other liabilities of the company incurred in the period during which he was acting in such a manner or capacity.

(4) Where a company which has received a notification under section 155 (5) and which carries on business following such notification without the requirements of section 150 (3) being fulfilled within a reasonable period—

- (a) is subsequently wound up, and
- (b) is at the time of the commencement of the winding-up unable to pay its debts (taking into account the contingent and prospective liabilities),

the court may, on the application of the liquidator or any creditor or contributory of the company, declare that any person who was an officer of the company while the company so carried on business and who knew or ought to have known that the company had been so notified shall be personally responsible, without any limitation of liability, for all or any part of the debts or other liabilities of the company as the court may direct.

(5) In any proceedings brought against a person by virtue of this section the court may if, having regard to the circumstances of the case, it considers it just and equitable to do so, grant relief in whole or in part from the liability to which he would otherwise be subject thereunder and the court may attach to its order such conditions as it sees fit.

Definitions

'contributory': CA 1963, s 2(1); 'creditor': CA 1963, s 2(1); 'director': CA 1963, s 2(1); 'liquidator': CA 1963, s 2(1); 'officer: CA 1963, s 2(1); 'company': CA 1990, s 259; 'the court: CA 1990, s 259; 'disqualification order': CA 1990, s 159.

Notes

Civil consequences of acting in breach of an order under s 150 or s 160: Subsection (2) allows a company recover from a disqualified or restricted person any consideration given to that person (eg director's fees) as though it were a contractual debt. Subsection (3) permits the liquidator or any creditor of the company, in an insolvent liquidation, to apply to make the prohibited or restricted person personally liable for the debts of that company incurred during the period during which he acted in breach of the disqualification order. An application in respect of a winding up may only be made if the person was acting in breach of the disqualification order or restriction order during the 12 months prior to the commencement of the winding up.

A restricted person may only act as a director in respect of a company that has met the capitalisation requirements set out in s 150(3). If a company has been notified of the restricted status of the individual under s 155(5) and fails to meet those prescribed capitalisation requirements within a reasonable time then, if that company is wound up and unable to pay its debts, any officer of the company who knew or ought to have known of the default may be made personally liable in respect of all or any of the debts of the company. Subsection (4) contains no time limit in respect of the winding up or the scope of the debts in respect of which the officer can be made liable.

Under sub-s (5), the court has a broad discretion to grant relief from the personal liability of sub-s (4) on whatever terms it sees fit.

164 Penalty for acting under directions of disqualified person

(1) If any person while a director or other officer or a member of a committee of management or trustee of any company acts in accordance with the directions or instructions of another person knowing that such other person is disqualified or that, in giving the directions or instructions, he is acting in contravention of any provision of this Part he shall be guilty of an offence.

(2) Where a person is convicted of an offence under subsection (1) he shall be deemed to be subject to a disqualification order from the date of such conviction if he was not, or was not deemed to be, subject to such an order on that date.

Definitions

CA 1963: 'director': CA 1963, s 2(1); 'officer: CA 1963, s 2(1); CA 1990: 'company': CA 1990, s 259; 'disqualification order': CA 1990, s 159.

Notes

This section makes it an offence for directors, officers, etc to act on the instructions of a person whom they know to be acting in breach of a disqualification order or restriction order. Once convicted, the person in question is deemed to be subject to a five-year disqualification pursuant to CA 1990, s 162. See also s 165 for the civil consequences of acting on the instructions of a disqualified person.

165 Civil consequences of acting under directions of disqualified person

(1) A person who is convicted of an offence under section 164 for acting in accordance with the directions or instructions of a disqualified person shall, subject to subsection (2), be personally liable for the debts of the company concerned incurred in the period during which he was so acting.

(2) In any proceedings brought against a person for the recovery of any such debt the court may if, having regard to the circumstances of the case, it considers it just and equitable to do so, grant relief in whole or in part from the liability to which he would otherwise be subject under subsection (1) and the court may attach to its order such conditions as it sees fit.

Definitions

'company': CA 1990, s 259; 'the court: CA 1990, s 259.

Notes

Personal liability under sub-s (1) arises only where a person is convicted of acting on the instructions of a disqualified person. If he is convicted under s 164 of acting on the instructions of a restricted person (and it is to be noted that a restriction order prohibits a person from acting as a shadow director) no personal liability arises under this section.

The personal liability under s 165 is automatic upon conviction, although the convicted person may apply for relief under sub-s (2).

166 Information to be given by directors to the court

[(1) Where—

(a) a director of a company is charged with an offence or civil proceedings are instituted against such a director, and

(b) the charge or proceedings relate to the company or involve alleged fraud or dishonesty,

the court before which the proceedings consequent on that charge or those civil proceedings are pending may (either of its own motion or at the request of any of the parties to the proceedings), if satisfied that it is appropriate to do so, require the director to lodge with the office of the court a notice in writing—

(i) giving the names of all companies of which he is a director at the date of the notice,

(ii) giving the names of all companies of which he was a director within a period commencing not earlier than 12 months prior to his being charged with the offence or the commencement of the civil proceedings and ending at the date of the notice,

(iii) stating whether he is at the date of the notice or ever was subject or deemed to be subject to a disqualification order, and

(iv) giving the dates and duration of each period in respect of which he is or was disqualified.][a]

(2) This section applies to shadow directors as it applies to directors.

(3) [...][b]

Amendments

a CA 1990, s 166(1) substituted by IFCMPA 2005, s 70(a) with effect from 30 June 2005.

b Subsection (3) repealed by IFCMPA 2005, s 70(b).

Definitions

'court': CA 1963, s 2(1); 'director': CA 1963, s 2(1); 'registrar': CA 1963, s 2(1); 'company': CA 1990, s 259; 'disqualification order': CA 1990, s 159; 'shadow director': CA 1990, s 27.

Notes

The section gives the court discretion in civil and criminal proceedings against a director or shadow director to require him to give notice of his directorships and of any disqualification orders that have been made against him. The purpose of such a notice is lest a deemed disqualification order should arise under s 160(1) in the event of conviction in criminal proceedings or the court should wish to make a disqualification order of its own motion under s 160(2) in the case of civil proceedings. It also enables the court to fulfil its notification obligations under s 167 in the event that such a disqualification occurs.

167 Information to be supplied to registrar of companies

Where a court—

(a) makes a disqualification order;

(b) grants or varies relief under section 160(8); or

(c) convicts a person of an offence—

(i) which has the effect of his being deemed to be subject to a disqualification order, or

(ii) under section 161(1) or 164,

a prescribed officer of the court shall cause the registrar of companies to be furnished with prescribed particulars of the order, relief or conviction at such time and in such form and manner as may be prescribed.

Definitions

CA 1963: 'court': CA 1963, s 2(1); 'registrar': CA 1963, s 2(1); CA 1990: 'disqualification order': CA 1990, s 159.

Notes

Under the CA 1990 (Pts IV & VII)R 1991 (SI 209/1991) the following officers are prescribed for the purposes of s 167, namely—

(a) in the case of proceedings in the Supreme Court, the Registrar of the Supreme Court;

(b) in the case of proceedings in the Court of Criminal Appeal, the Registrar of the Court of Criminal Appeal;

(c) in the case of proceedings or an application in the High Court, the Examiner and Registrars of the High Court;

(d) in the case of proceedings or an application in the Central Criminal Court, the Registrar of the Central Criminal Court;

(e) in the case of proceedings in the Special Criminal Court, the Registrar of the Special Criminal Court;

(f) in the case of proceedings in the Circuit Court, the County Registrar for the county in which the proceedings are heard;

(g) in the case of proceedings in the District Court, in the Dublin Metropolitan District or in the District Court Area of Cork City, the Chief Clerk for the district or area concerned, as the case may be;

(h) in the case of proceedings elsewhere in the District Court, the principal Clerk assigned to the District Court area in which the proceedings are heard.

The particulars to be furnished are set out in the form contained in the Schedule to the CA 1990 (Pts IV & VII)R 1991 (SI 209/1991).

---

168 Register of persons subject to disqualification orders

(1) The registrar shall, subject to the provisions of this section, keep a register of the particulars which have been notified to him under section 167, and the following provisions of this section shall apply to the keeping of such a register.

(2) Where the particulars referred to in section 167(b) comprise the grant of full relief under section 160 (8), the registrar shall not enter such particulars on the register referred to in subsection (1), but shall, as soon as may be, remove any existing particulars in respect of the person concerned from the register.

(3) The registrar shall also remove from the register any particulars in relation to a person on the expiry of five years from the date of the original notification under section 167, or such other period in respect of which the person concerned is deemed to be subject to a disqualification order, unless the registrar has received a further notification in respect of that person under this section.

(4) Nothing in this section shall prevent the registrar from keeping the register required by this section as part of any other system of classification, whether pursuant to section 247 or otherwise.

Definitions

'registrar': CA 1963, s 2(1); 'disqualification order': CA 1990, s 159.

Notes

See notes following CA 1963, ss 3(6), 5(2), 8(3), 5A, 5B, 10(1), 16, 23(5) and 24.

The Registrar of Companies provides access to online extracts from the register of restricted persons at http://www.cro.ie.

---

169 Prohibition of undischarged bankrupts acting as directors or other officers of companies

[...][a]

Amendments

a This section substitutes CA 1963, s 183.

Part VIII
Receivers

170 Disqualification for appointment as receiver

[...][a]

Amendments

a This section substitutes CA 1963, s 315.

171 Amendment of section 316 of the Principal Act

[...][a]

Amendments

a This section substitutes CA 1963, s 316(1) and inserts CA 1963, s 316(1A) & (1B).

172 Duty of receiver selling property to get best price reasonably obtainable

[...][a]

Amendments

a This section inserts CA 1963, s 316A.

173 Amendment of section 320 of the Principal Act

[...][a]

Amendments

a This section substitutes CA 1963, s 320(5).

174 Consequences of contravention of section 319 or 320 of the Principal Act

[...][a]

Amendments

a This section inserts CA 1963, s 320A.

175 Removal of receiver

[...][a]

Amendments

a This section inserts CA 1963, s 322A.

176 Court may determine or limit receivership on application of liquidator

[...][a]

Amendments

a This section inserts CA 1963, s 322B.

177 Resignation of receiver

[...][a]

Amendments

a This section inserts CA 1963, s 322C.

178 Application of section 139 to receivers

The provisions of section 139, shall, with the necessary modifications, apply to a company in receivership as if the references therein to the liquidator and to winding up were construed as references to the receiver and to receivership.

Definitions

CA 1963: 'receiver: CA 1963, s 2(1); 'liquidator': CA 1963, s 2(1).

Notes

See notes following CA 1990, s 139. CA 1963, s 139, as applied, allows a receiver to apply to court to order the return of assets which have been improperly transferred.

179 Application of section 299(2), (4) and (5) of the Principal Act to receivers

Section 299 (2), (4) and (5) of the Principal Act shall apply, with the necessary modifications, to receivers as it applies to liquidators.

Definitions

CA 1963: 'receiver: CA 1963, s 2(1); 'liquidator': CA 1963, s 2(1).

Notes

See notes following CA 1963, s 299.

CA 1963, s 299(2), as applied, requires a receiver to report any appearance that a past or present officer, or any member, of the company has been guilty of any offence in relation to the company to the DPP and shall give certain assistance to the DPP in this regard.

If there is a report and it is a case in respect of which the DPP decides to prosecute, it shall be the duty of the receiver to give all reasonable assistance. The DPP may apply to court to require the receiver to comply with this section and, unless the failure to cooperate is due to an insufficiency of the assets of the company in receivership, in which case the costs may be directed to be borne personally by the receiver.

PART IX
COMPANIES COURT PROTECTION

180 Amendments to the Companies (Amendment) Act, 1990

(1) The Companies (Amendment) Act, 1990, is hereby amended as follows:

(a) […][a]

(b) […][b]

(c) […][c]

(d) […][d]

(e) […][e]

(f) […][f]

(g) […][g]

(h) […][h]

(i) […][i]

(2) Section 244A of the Principal Act (inserted by section 125 of the Companies Act, 1990) and section 139 of the Companies Act, 1990, shall apply to a company under the protection of the court as they apply to a company being wound up, and any references in those sections to a liquidator or provisional liquidator shall be construed for the purposes of this subsection as a reference to an examiner.

(3) […][j]

Amendments

a Subsection (1)(a) substitutes '3 days' for '14 days' in C(A)A 1990, s 3(6).

b Subsection (1)(b) inserts C(A)A 1990, s 5(2)(g).

c Subsection (1)(c) deletes ', or past director,' in C(A)A 1990, s 8(3).

d Subsection (1)(d) inserts 'and "director" includes any present or past director or any person connected, within the meaning of CA 1990, s 26, with such director, and any present or past shadow director' after 'Act' where it secondly occurs in C(A)A 1990, s 8(3).

e Subsection (1)(e) inserts C(A)A 1990, s 8(5A), (5B).

f Subsection (1)(f) substitutes 'Any' for 'Where an order is made under this Act for the winding-up of the company or a receiver is appointed, any' in C(A)A 1990, s 10(1).

g Subsection (1)(g) substitutes s 16(i).

h Subsection (1)(h) inserts ', a local authority' after 'Government' in s 23(5)(b).

i Subsection (1)(i) inserts C(A)A 1990, s 24(12).

j Subsection (3) repeals C(A)A 1990, ss 32 to 35.

Definitions

CA 1963: 'company': CA 1963, s 2(1); 'the court': CA 1963, s 2(1); 'liquidator': CA 1963, s 2(1); 'liquidator': CA 1963, s 2(1); C(A)A 1990: 'examiner': CA 1990, s 1.

Notes

CA 1963: CA 1963, s 244A prevents a person withholding possession of any document belonging to the company, without prejudice to that person's rights under a mortgage, charge or pledge that has been created by the deposit of those documents. It requires an examiner to make available for inspection by the receiver at all reasonable times all documents to which a receiver is entitled. CA 1963, s 139, as applied, allows an examiner apply to court to order the return of assets which have been improperly transferred.

---

181 Further amendments to the Companies (Amendment) Act, 1990

(1) The Companies (Amendment) Act, 1990, is hereby further amended as follows:

(a) [...][a]

(b) [...][b]

(c) [...][c]

(d) [...][d]

(e) [...][e]

(2) [...][f]

Amendments

a Subsection (1)(a) substitutes C(A)A 1990, s 2(1)(b).

b Subsection (1)(b) substitutes 'body corporate' for 'company' in C(A)A 1990, s 4(5)(f).

c Subsection (1)(c) inserts C(A)A 1990, s 5(2)(h).

d Subsection (1)(d) inserts 'discharging' after 'towards' in C(A)A 1990, s 11(5).

e Subsection (1)(e) inserts C(A)A 1990, s 36A.

f Subsection (2) repeals C(A)A 1990, s 30(3).

PART X
ACCOUNTS AND AUDIT

182 Interpretation of Part X

[(1)][a] In this Part—

'the Council Directive' means Council Directive No 84/253/EEC of 10 April, 1984 (OJ No L126, 12.5.1984, p 20) on the approval of persons responsible for carrying out the statutory audits of accounting documents;

'friendly society' means a society registered under the Friendly Societies Acts, 1896 to 1977;

'practising certificate' means a certificate awarded to a person by a body of accountants entitling that person to practise as auditor of a company or as a public auditor;

'public auditor' means a public auditor for the purposes of the Industrial and Provident Societies Acts, 1893 to 1978, and the Friendly Societies Acts, [1896 to 1993].[b]

['the Act of 2003' means the Companies (Auditing and Accounting) Act 2003;

'the 1993 Regulations' means the European Communities (Accounts) Regulations 1993 (S.I. No. 396 of 1993);

'the 1992 Regulations' means the European Communities (Companies: Group Accounts) Regulations 1992 (S.I. No. 201 of 1992)';][c]

[(2) For the purposes of sections 205B and 205D, each of the following is considered to be an affiliate of an auditor in a financial year:

(a) if the auditor is a firm—

(i) any other firm where, at any time during the financial year, both firms were under common ownership and control,

(ii) any body corporate in which the auditor, any firm mentioned in subparagraph (i) or (iv) or any body corporate mentioned in subparagraph (iii) or (iv) was, at any time in the financial year, entitled to exercise or control the exercise of 20 per cent or more of the voting rights at a general meeting,

(iii) any body corporate that was, at any time in the financial year, in the same group as a body corporate mentioned in subparagraph (ii),

(iv) any other firm, or body corporate, that because of the use of a common name or corporate identity or the sharing of common professional services could reasonably be considered to be associated with the auditor,

(b) if the auditor is an individual—

(i) any partnership in which the auditor was, at any time in the financial year, a partner,

(ii) any body corporate in which the auditor, any partnership mentioned in subparagraph (i) or any body corporate mentioned in subparagraph (iii) was, at any time in the financial year, entitled to exercise or control the exercise of 20 per cent or more of the voting rights at a general meeting,

(iii) any body corporate that was, at any time in the financial year, in the same group as a body corporate mentioned in subparagraph (ii).

(3) A reference in this Part to group accounts is to be construed as follows:

(a) in accordance with the 1992 Regulations, in the case of an undertaking to which those Regulations apply;

(b) in accordance with the Principal Act, in the case of any other undertaking.][a]

Amendments

a C(AA)A 2003, s 34(c) renumbers CA 1990, s 182 as CA 1990, s 182 (1) and inserts CA 1990, s 182 (2) and (3).

b C(AA)A 2003, s 34(a) amends the definition of public auditor in CA 1990, s 182 by substituting '1896 to 1993' for '1896 to 1977'.

c C(AA)A 2003, s 34(b) inserts definitions of 'the Act of 2003', 'the 1993 Regulations' and 'the 1992 Regulations' after the definition of 'public auditor' in CA 1990, s 182.

Notes

The C(AA)A 2003 was the Government's response to the Report of the Review Group on Auditing ('RGA'). The RGA was established by the Minister for Enterprise, Trade and Employment as a result of concerns regarding corporate governance practices and the auditing profession identified during the Public Accounts Committee's investigation into Deposit Interest Retention Tax and the behaviour of certain financial institutions in this regard.

The RGA reported in July 2000 and included significant recommendations aimed at improving corporate governance practices in Ireland, the regulation of statutory auditors, and audit practice in general. A copy of the report can be downloaded at http://www.entemp.ie.

The concept of an 'affiliate of an auditor' relates to additional measures introduced by the 2003 Act by the insertion of ss 205B and 205D to the CA 1990. These are aimed at promoting greater transparency regarding amounts paid by companies to auditors and their 'affiliates', and so contributing towards safeguarding auditor independence. These measures require monitoring by the audit committee and disclosure of amounts paid to auditors and their affiliates analysed under the categories of 'audit', 'audit related' and 'non-audit work'.

See ss 205(B) and 205(D) and notes thereto.

183 Appointment and removal of auditors

(a) [...][a]

(b) [...][b]

Amendments

a Subsection (a) substitutes sub-ss (5), (5A) for CA 1963, s 160(5).

b Subsection (b) substitutes CA 1963, s 160(7).

184 Resolutions relating to appointment and removal of auditors and rights of auditors who have been removed

(1) [...][a]

(2) The reference in subsection (5) of the said section 161 to a resolution to remove the first auditors by virtue of subsection (6) of section 160 of the Principal Act shall be construed as including a reference to a resolution to remove an auditor other than the first auditors before the expiration of his term of office.

Amendments

a Sub-s (1) substitutes CA 1963, s 160(1), (2).

Definitions

'Principal Act': CA 1963, s 3(1).

185 Resignation of auditors

(1) An auditor of a company may, by a notice in writing that complies with subsection (2) served on the company and stating his intention to do so, resign from the office of

auditor to the company; and the resignation shall take effect on the date on which the notice is so served or on such later date as may be specified in the notice.

(2) A notice under subsection (1) shall contain either—

- (a) a statement to the effect that there are no circumstances connected with the resignation to which it relates that the auditor concerned considers should be brought to the notice of the members or creditors of the company, or
- (b) a statement of any such circumstances as aforesaid.

(3) Where a notice under subsection (1) is served on a company—

- (a) the auditor concerned shall, within 14 days after the date of such service, send a copy of the notice to the registrar of companies, and
- (b) subject to subsection (4), the company shall, if the notice contains a statement referred to in subsection (2)(b), not later than 14 days after the date of such service send a copy of the notice to every person who is entitled under section 159 (1) of the Principal Act to be sent copies of the documents referred to in the said section 159(1).

(4) Copies of a notice served on a company under subsection (1) need not be sent to the persons specified in subsection (3)(b) if, on the application of the company concerned or any other person who claims to be aggrieved, the court is satisfied that the notice contains material which has been included to secure needless publicity for defamatory matter and the court may order the company's costs on an application under this section to be paid in whole or in part by the auditor concerned notwithstanding that he is not a party to the application.

(5) This section shall also apply to a notice given by an auditor under section 160(2)(c) of the Principal Act, indicating his unwillingness to be Re-appointed.

(6) A person who fails to comply with subsection (2) or (3)(a) shall be guilty of an offence.

(7) If default is made in complying with subsection (3)(b), the company concerned, and every officer of such company who is in default, shall be guilty of an offence.

Cross reference

In relation to the removal of auditors, see CA 1963, ss 160, 161.

Definitions

'court': CA 1990, s 235; 'member': CA 1963, s 31; 'officer': CA 1963, s 2(1); 'officer in default': CA 1963, s 383; 'Principal Act': CA 1990, s 3(1); 'registrar of companies': CA 1963, s 2(1).

Notes

Prior to the enactment of this section there was no statutory provision for the resignation of auditors before the expiry of their term of appointment.

Circumstances which should be brought to the notice of the members of creditors might include instances of fraud, misfeasance or breach of duty on the part of the officers of the company which have been discovered by the resigning auditor or the fact that the company is insolvent or threatened with insolvency.

See also CA 1990, s 186 in relation to the power of the resigning auditor to requisition an EGM at which he may explain the circumstances connected with his resignation, as well as his power to have a written statement explaining such circumstances circulated to the members either:

(a) before the requisitioned meeting, or

(b) before any general meeting at which his term of office would otherwise have expired, or

(c) before any general meeting at which it is proposed to fill the vacancy caused by his resignation.

In addition, the resigning auditor is entitled to attend and be heard at each such meeting, at least in so far as it concerns his position as former auditor: CA 1990, s 186(5).

A copy of the notice must be sent to all persons who are entitled to receive copies of the company's annual accounts, namely the members and debentureholders. There is no provision, however, for circulating the notice to the general body of creditors of the company, even if the matters specified in the notice are of more concern to the creditors than the members.

UK legislation

See CA 1985, ss 392, 394.

---

186 Requisitioning of general meeting of company by resigning auditor

(1) A notice served on a company under section 185 which contains a statement in accordance with subsection (2)(b) of that section may also requisition the convening by the directors of the company of a general meeting of the company for the purpose of receiving and considering such account and explanation of the circumstances connected with his resignation from the office of auditor to the company as he may wish to give to the meeting.

(2) Where an auditor makes a requisition under subsection (1), the directors of the company shall, within 14 days of the service on the company of the said notice, proceed duly to convene a general meeting of the company for a day not more than 28 days after such service.

(3) Subject to subsection (4), where—

(a) a notice served on a company under section 185 contains a statement in accordance with subsection (2)(b) of that section, and

(b) the auditor concerned requests the company to circulate to its members—

(i) before the general meeting at which, apart from the notice, his term of office would expire, or

(ii) before any general meeting at which it is proposed to fill the vacancy caused by his resignation or convened pursuant to a requisition under subsection (1),

a further statement in writing prepared by the auditor of circumstances connected with the resignation that the auditor considers should be brought to the notice of the members,

the company shall—

(i) in any notice of the meeting given to members of the company state the fact of the statement having been made, and

(ii) send a copy of the statement to the registrar of companies and to every person who is entitled under section 159(1) of the Principal Act to be sent copies of the documents referred to in the said section 159(1).

(4) Subsection (3) need not be complied with by the company concerned if, on the application either of the company or any other person who claims to be aggrieved, the court is satisfied that the rights conferred by this section are being abused to secure needless publicity for defamatory matter and the court may order the company's costs on an application under this section to be paid in whole or in part by the auditor concerned notwithstanding that he is not a party to the application.

(5) An auditor of a company who has resigned from the office of auditor shall be permitted by the company to attend—

(a) the annual general meeting at which, but for his resignation, his term of office would have expired, and

(b) any general meeting at which it is proposed to fill the vacancy caused by his resignation or convened pursuant to a requisition of his under subsection (1),

and the company shall send him all notices of, and other communications relating to, any such meeting that a member of the company is entitled to receive and the company shall permit him to be heard at any such meeting which he attends on any part of the business of the meeting which concerns him as a former auditor of the company.

(6) If default is made in complying with subsection (2), (3) or (5), the company concerned, and every officer of the company who is in default, shall be guilty of an offence.

Cross reference

See also CA 1963, s 132 in relation to the power of the members to requisition the convening of an EGM.

For the right of auditors who have not resigned to attend and be heard at general meetings of the company, see CA 1990, s 193.

Definitions

'court': CA 1990, s 235; 'director': CA 1963, s 2(1); 'member': CA 1963, s 31; 'officer': CA 1963, s 2(1); 'officer in default': CA 1963, s 383; 'Principal Act': CA 1963, s 3(1); 'registrar of companies': CA 1963, s 2(1).

Notes

A copy of the statement must be sent to all persons who are entitled to receive copies of the company's annual accounts, namely the members and debentureholders. There is no provision, however, for circulating the statement to the general body of creditors of the company, even if the matters specified in the statement are of more concern to the creditors than the members.

UK legislation

See CA 1985, s 392A.

---

187 Qualification for appointment as auditor

(1) Subject to section 190, a person shall not be qualified for appointment either as auditor of a company or as a public auditor unless—

(a) (i) he is a member of a body of accountants for the time being recognised by the [Supervisory Authority][a] for the purposes of this section and holds a valid practising certificate from such a body, or

(ii) he holds an accountancy qualification that is, in the opinion of the [Supervisory Authority][a], of a standard which is not less than that required for such membership as aforesaid and which would entitle him to be granted a practising certificate by that body if he were a member of it, and is for the time being authorised by the [Supervisory Authority][a] to be so appointed, or

(iii) he was, on the 31st day of December, 1990, a member of a body of accountants for the time being recognised under section 162(1)(a) of the Principal Act [and holds a valid practising certificate from such a body][b], or

[(iv) he was authorised by the Minister before the 3rd day of February, 1983, and is for the time being authorised by the Supervisory Authority to be so appointed, or][c]

(v) he is a person to whom section 188 applies, or

(vi) he is a person to whom section 189 applies, and is for the time being authorised by the [Supervisory Authority][a] to be so appointed, and

(b) the particulars required by sections 199 and 200 in respect of such a person have been forwarded to the registrar of companies.

[(1A) A firm shall be qualified for appointment as auditor of a company or as a public auditor if—

(a) at least one member of the firm is entitled to hold a practising certificate from a body referred to in subparagraph (i), (ii) or (iii) of subsection (1)(a) and is otherwise qualified under the applicable subparagraph for appointment as auditor of a company or as a public auditor, and

(b) the particulars required by sections 199 and 200 in respect of such a member have been forwarded to the registrar of companies.

(1B) A body referred to in subsection (1A) may grant a practising certificate to a firm that satisfies the conditions in that subsection, and, if a practising certificate is granted—

(a) each member of the firm who from time to time during the currency of the certificate is qualified for appointment as auditor of a company or as a public auditor is deemed to hold the certificate, and

(b) the name of such a member is deemed to be entered in the register of auditors.][d]

(2) None of the following persons shall be qualified for appointment as auditor of a company—

(a) an officer or servant of the company,

(b) a person who has been an officer or servant of the company within a period in respect of which accounts would fall to be audited by him if he were appointed auditor of the company,

(c) a parent, spouse, brother, sister or child of an officer of the company,

(d) a person who is a partner of or in the employment of an officer of the company,

(e) a person who is disqualified under this subsection for appointment as auditor of any other body corporate that is a subsidiary or holding company of the company or a subsidiary of the company's holding company, or would be so disqualified if the body corporate were a company,

(f) a person who is disqualified under subsection (3) for appointment as a public auditor of a society that is a subsidiary or holding company of the company or a subsidiary of the company's holding company,

(g) a body corporate.

[(h) a person in whose name a share in the company is registered, whether or not that person is the beneficial owner of the share.][e]

(3) None of the following persons shall be qualified for appointment as a public auditor of a society—

(a) an officer or servant of the society,

(b) a person who has been an officer or servant of the society within a period in respect of which accounts would fall to be audited by him if he were appointed auditor of the society,

(c) a parent, spouse, brother, sister or child of an officer of the society,

(d) a person who is a partner of or in the employment of an officer of the society,

(e) a person who is disqualified under this subsection for appointment as a public auditor of any other society that is a subsidiary or holding company of the society or a subsidiary of the society's holding company,

(f) a person who is disqualified under subsection (2) for appointment as auditor of a company that is a subsidiary or holding company of the society,

(g) a body corporate.

(4) None of the following persons shall be qualified for appointment as a public auditor of a friendly society—

(a) an officer or servant of the friendly society,

(b) a person who has been an officer or servant of the friendly society within a period in respect of which accounts would fall to be audited by him if he were appointed auditor of the friendly society,

(c) a parent, spouse, brother, sister or child of an officer of the friendly society,

(d) a person who is a partner of or in the employment of an officer of the friendly society,

(e) a body corporate.

(5) A person shall not, by virtue of subsection (3) or (4), be disqualified for appointment as public auditor of a society or a friendly society at any time during the period of 2 years from the commencement of this section if on such commencement he stands duly appointed as public auditor of the society or friendly society, as the case may be.

(6) Subject to subsection (5), a person shall not act as auditor of a company or as a public auditor at a time when he is disqualified under this section for appointment to that office.

(7) If, during his term of office as auditor of a company or public auditor, a person becomes disqualified under the Companies Acts for appointment to that office, he shall thereupon vacate his office and give notice in writing to the company, society or friendly society that he has vacated his office by reason of such disqualification.

(8) This section shall not apply to the Comptroller and Auditor General.

(9) A person who contravenes subsection (6) or (7) shall be guilty of an offence and liable—

(a) on summary conviction, to a fine not exceeding [€1,904.61],[f] and, for continued contravention, to a daily default fine not exceeding [€63.49],[g] or

(b) on conviction on indictment, to a fine not exceeding [€6,348.69][h] and, for continued contravention, to a daily default fine not exceeding [€126.97].[i]

(10)(a) In this section 'society' means a society registered under the Industrial and Provident Societies Acts, 1893 to 1978.

(b) References in this section to an officer or servant do not include references to an auditor or a public auditor.

(11) A recognition or authorisation by the Minister under section 162 of the Principal Act shall, notwithstanding the repeal of that section by this Act, continue in force as if given under this section—

(a) in the case of a recognition, until the time limit provided expires, or the Minister's decision is communicated to the body concerned, under section 191, whichever is the earlier, and

(b) in the case of an authorisation, until the time limit for the person to make the notification required by section 199(3) expires.

[(12)(a) The Director may demand of a person acting as an auditor of a company or as a public auditor, or purporting to be qualified to so act, the production of evidence of his qualifications under subsection (1) in respect of any time or period during which he so acted or purported to be qualified to so act, and if the person refuses or fails to produce the evidence within 30 days of the demand, or such longer period as the Director may allow, he shall be guilty of an offence.

(b) In a prosecution for an offence under this subsection, it shall be presumed, until the contrary is shown by the defendant, that the defendant did not, within 30 days, or any longer period allowed, after the day on which the production was demanded, produce evidence in accordance with paragraph (a).

(13)(a) Where a person is the subject of a prosecution under subsection (9) for a contravention of subsection (6) or (7), it shall be sufficient evidence, until the contrary is shown by the person, of non-membership of a body of accountants for the time being recognised by the Minister for the purposes of this section for any or all such bodies to certify in writing to the court such non-membership, provided that the first-mentioned person is provided by the prosecutor with a copy of the certificate or certificates, served by registered post, not later than 21 days before any such certificate is presented in evidence to the court.

(b) Where a person the subject of a prosecution proposes to contest the certification of non-membership contained in a certificate provided for by paragraph (a), he shall give written notice thereof, served by registered post, to the prosecutor within 21 days, or such longer period as the court may allow, of receipt of the certificate from the prosecutor.][j]

[(14) An authorisation granted to a person under subsection (1)(a)(iv) ceases to have effect on the expiry of 3 years after the commencement of this subsection unless, within that 3 year period, the person becomes a member of, or becomes subject to the regulations of, a body of accountants recognised for the purposes of section 187.

(15) On an authorisation ceasing to have effect under subsection (14), the person to whom it was granted ceases to be qualified for appointment as auditor of a company or as a public auditor.][k]

Amendments

a C(AA)A 2003, Sch 1, Pt 1, substitutes 'Supervisory Authority' for 'Minister'.

b CLEA 2001, s 72(a) amends CA 1990, s 187(1)(a)(iii) by the insertion after 'Principal Act' of 'and holds a valid practising certificate from such a body'.

c C(AA)A 2003, Sch 1, Pt 1, substitutes CA 1990, s 187(1)(a)(iv).

d C(AA)A 2003, s 35(a) inserts CA 1990, s 187(1A) and (1B).

e C(AA)A 2003, s 35(b) inserts CA 1990, s 187(2)(h).

f £1,000 increased to £1,500 by CA 1990, s 240(7) as inserted by CLEA 2001, s 104(c), and converted to €1,904.61 by Council Regulations (EC) No 1103/97, No 974/98 and No 2866/98 and the Economic and Monetary Union Act 1998, s 6.

g £50 converted to €63.49 by Council Regulations (EC) No 1103/97, No 974/98 and No 2866/98 and the Economic and Monetary Union Act 1998, s 6.

h £5,000 converted to €6,348.69 by Council Regulations (EC) No 1103/97, No 974/98 and No 2866/98 and the Economic and Monetary Union Act 1998, s 6.

i £100 converted to €126.97 by Council Regulations (EC) No 1103/97, No 974/98 and No 2866/98 and the Economic and Monetary Union Act 1998, s 6.

j CLEA 2001, s 72(b) inserts CA 1990, s 187(12) and (13).

k C(AA)A 2003, s 35(c) inserts CA 1990, s 187(14) and (15).

Definitions

'child': CA 1990, s 3(1); 'Companies Acts': CA 1990, s 3(1); 'contravention': CA 1990, s 3(1); 'daily default fine': CA 1990, s 3(1); 'director': CLEA 2001, s 3; 'holding company': CA 1963, s 155; 'Principal Act': CA 1990, s 3(1); 'registrar of companies'; CA 1963, s 2(1); 'subsidiary': CA 1963, s 2(1); 'Supervisory Authority': C(AA)A 2003, s 4.

Notes

A person or firm is qualified for appointment as auditor of a company or as a public auditor provided that at least one member of the firm is entitled to hold a practising certificate from a body referred to in sub-ss (1)(a)(i), (ii) or (iii). Where a firm has been granted a practising certificate, it shall be deemed to be held by all members of the firm who are themselves qualified under sub-ss (1)(a)(i), (ii) or (iii). This was effected by the Companies Act (Auditors) Regulations 1992 (SI 259/1992). The insertion of sub-ss 187(1A) and (1B) by s 35(a) of the C(AA)A 2003 means that SI 259/1992 has now been incorporated into s 187. Section 59 of C(AA)A 2003 repeals SI 259/1992. However, at the time of writing, neither s 35(a) nor s 59 of the C(AA) 2003 have been commenced.

Transfer of functions to the Supervisory Authority: The effect of C(AA)A 2003, s 32(1) is to amend CA 1990, ss 187, 189, 190, 191 and 192 by transferring certain functions thereunder from the Minister to the Supervisory Authority, namely (a) recognising accountancy bodies to act as auditors (and the attaching of conditions to such recognition), (b) continuing the authorisation of individuals who are not members of such bodies to act as auditors (and the attaching of conditions to such authorisation), (c) approving the qualifications of foreign accountants to act as auditors and (d) consulting with accountancy bodies and other persons as to the standards and qualifications of auditors.

Transitional recognition arrangements: Pursuant to C(AA)A 2003, s 32(2) every body of accountants that had been recognised by the Minister pursuant to CA 1990, s 187 prior to coming into force of this Act continues to be so recognised *pro tempore* by the Supervisory Authority. Such bodies are:

(a) the Institute of Chartered Accountants in Ireland;

(b) the Institute of Chartered Accountants in England and Wales;

(c) the Institute of Chartered Accountants of Scotland;

(d) the Institute of Certified Public Accountants in Ireland;

(e) the Association of Chartered Certified Accountants; and

(f) the Institute of Incorporated Public Accountants.

Presumably other bodies will only be recognised by IAASA if they meet the Standards of Council Directive 84/253/EEC (the Eighth Company Law Directive) relating to training, qualification, and repute of auditors. Under s 162 as amended by s 6 of C(A)A 1983, the Minister was entitled to grant authorisation to statutory auditors where:

(a) the person received his qualification from an unrecognised accounting body, but the nature of the qualification was similar to that of a recognised body; or

(b) he had obtained adequate knowledge and experience before 1 April 1964 in the course of his employment by, or under the supervision of, a member of a recognised body of accountants; or

(c) he had prior to 1 April 1964 practised in the state as an accountant.

A limited number of statutory auditors continues to hold authorisation in this manner under this sub-s 187(a)(iv), the details of whom are maintained by the Registrar of Companies. However, sub-ss 187(14) and (15), as inserted by C(AA)A 2003, will, on commencement, provide a 3-year 'sunset' period during which persons authorised under sub-s 187(1)(a)(iv) must either become members of any of the bodies authorised under s 187 or become subject to their regulations. Once such authorisations cease to have effect, such persons will no longer be qualified for appointment as auditor of a company or as a public auditor. However, as at the time of writing, the subsections have not yet been commenced.

The provisions of sub-ss (2) to (4) are aimed at ensuring the independence of auditors and, to that extent, give effect to the requirements of Section III of Council Directive 84/253/EEC. Notably, however, a recognised person is not disqualified under s 187 from acting as auditor of a company on the grounds that he is a shareholder of that company or a related company. Such a disqualification will arise under:

(a) the Ethical Standards for Auditors, issued by the Auditing Practices Board, the independent standard setter for auditors in Ireland and the UK (available from http://www.frc.org.uk/apb/publications); and

(b) the ethical codes of the professional body of which the person is a member. See also s 192(4) of CA 1990.

Interestingly, the prohibition on bodies corporate being eligible for appointment as auditor has remained in Ireland in spite of this prohibition being removed in all other EU member states.

Directive 2006/46/EC of the European Parliament and of the Council ('the Statutory Audit Directive') was published on 17 June 2006 and repeals Directive 84/253/EEC. The Statutory Audit Directive will bring about significant changes as regards the supervision of the auditors throughout the European Union and the conduct of statutory audits. The Statutory Audit Directive must be transposed into domestic legislation by mid-2008.

UK legislation

See CA 1989, ss 25, 27, 28, 31.

---

188 Persons undergoing training on 1 January, 1990

(1) Without prejudice to section 187, a person to whom this section applies shall also be qualified for appointment as auditor of a company or a public auditor.

(2) This section applies to a person—

(a) who on the 1st day of January, 1990, was a person to whom Article 18 of the Council Directive applies, and

(b) who, following his admission, before the 1st day of January, 1996, to the membership of a body of accountants recognised under section 191, was subsequently awarded a practising certificate by that body, and

(c) in respect of whom such certificate remains valid.

Notes

Article 18 of Directive 84/253/EEC applies to persons already undergoing professional or practical training when the provisions of the Directive were brought into operation but who, on the completion of their training, would otherwise not fulfil the conditions of the Directive regarding training and qualification.

---

189 Approval of qualifications obtained outside the State

(1) Without prejudice to section 187, the [Supervisory Authority][a] may declare that, subject to subsection (2), persons who hold—

(a) a qualification entitling them to audit accounts under the law of a specified country outside the State, or

(b) a specified accountancy qualification recognised under the law of a country outside the State,

shall be regarded as qualified for appointment as auditor of a company or a public auditor.

(2) Before making a declaration under subsection (1), the [Supervisory Authority][a]—

(a) must be satisfied that the qualification concerned is of a standard not less than is required by the Companies Acts to qualify a person for appointment as auditor of a company or a public auditor, and

(b) may direct that such a person shall not be treated as qualified for the purposes of subsection (1) unless he holds such additional educational qualifications as the Minister may specify for the purpose of ensuring that such persons have an adequate knowledge of the law and practice in the State relevant to the audit of accounts, and

(c) may have regard to the extent to which persons qualified under the Companies Acts for appointment as auditor of a company or a public auditor are recognised by the law of the country in question as qualified to audit accounts there.

(3) Different directions may be given under subsection (2)(b) in relation to different qualifications.

(4) The [Supervisory Authority][a] may, if he thinks fit, revoke or suspend for a specified period, in such manner and on such conditions as he may think appropriate, any declaration previously made under subsection (1).

Amendments

a C(AA)A 2003, Sch 1, Pt 1, substitutes 'Supervisory Authority' for 'Minister'.

Definitions

'Companies Acts': CA 1990, s 3(1); 'Supervisory Authority': C(AA)A 2003, s 4.

Notes

Transfer of functions to the Supervisory Authority: See corresponding notes to CA 1990, s 187.

Directive 2006/46/EC contains new provisions regarding recognition of auditors both from other EU member states and from so-called 'third countries'. When implemented this is likely to necessitate the amendment of s 189 of CA 1990.

---

190 Consultation by Minister regarding standards and qualifications

(1) Before granting, renewing, withdrawing, revoking, suspending or refusing a recognition of a body of accountants under the Companies Acts, the [Supervisory Authority][a] may consult with any person or body of persons as to the conditions imposed or standards required by the body of accountants concerned in connection with membership of that body or the awarding to persons of practising certificates.

(2) The [Supervisory Authority][a] may also consult with any person or body of persons before forming any opinion or making any declaration in relation to the qualifications held by any person or class of persons as respects qualification for appointment as auditor of a company or a public auditor.

Amendments

a C(AA)A 2003, Sch 1, Pt 1, substitutes 'Supervisory Authority' for 'Minister'.

Definitions

'Companies Acts': CA 1990, s 3(1); 'Supervisory Authority': C(AA)A 2003, s 4.

191 Recognition of bodies of accountants

[The Supervisory Authority may grant recognition to a body of accountants but only if satisfied—

(a) that the standards relating to training, qualifications and repute required by that body for the awarding of a practising certificate to a person are not less than those specified in Articles 3 to 6, 8 and 19 of the Council Directive, and

(b) as to the standards that body applies to its members in the areas of ethics, codes of conduct and practice, independence, professional integrity, auditing and accounting standards and investigation and disciplinary procedures.'][a]

Amendments

a C(AA)A 2003, Sch 1, Pt 1, substitutes CA 1990, s 191.

Definitions

'Supervisory Authority': C(AA)A 2003, s 4.

Notes

Transitional recognition arrangements: See corresponding notes after CA 1990, s 187.

Under art 3 of Council Directive 84/253/EEC the authorities of a member state shall grant approval only to persons of good repute who are not carrying on any activity which is incompatible under the law of the member state with the auditing of annual accounts.

Art 4 provides that a person may only carry out audits after having attained university entrance level, then completed a course of theoretical instruction, undergone practical training and passed an examination of professional competence of university, final examination level organised or recognised by the State. According to art 5 the examination must guarantee the necessary level of theoretical knowledge of subjects relevant to auditing and the ability to apply such knowledge in practice. In particular art 6 states the theoretical knowledge included in the examination must cover:

(i) auditing,

(ii) analysis and critical assessment of annual accounts,

(iii) general accounting,

(iv) consolidated accounts,

(v) cost and management accounting,

(vi) internal audit,

(vii) standards relating to the preparation of annual and consolidated accounts and to methods of valuing balance sheet items and of computing profits and losses,

(viii) legal and professional standards relating to the statutory auditing of accounting documents and to those carrying out such audits, and

(ix) in so far as they are relevant to auditing: company law, insolvency law, tax law, civil and commercial law, social security law, the law of employment, information and computer systems, business, general and financial economics, mathematics and statistics, and basic principles of the financial management of undertakings.

Art 8 requires trainee accountants to complete at least 3 years' practical training in *inter alia* the auditing of annual accounts, consolidated accounts or similar financial statements, of which at least two-thirds of the practical training must be spent under the supervision of a recognised person.

Finally art 19 requires that persons who are not members of recognised accounting bodies but who are nonetheless qualified under the transitional arrangements, should nonetheless be fit to carry out statutory audits.

The provisions regarding education, theoretical and practical training contained in Directive 2006/46/EC are similar to those of Directive 84/253/EEC. Directive 2006/46/EC of the European Parliament and of the Council ('the Statutory Audit Directive') was published on 17 June 2006 and repeals Directive 84/253/EEC. The Statutory Audit Directive will bring about significant changes as regards the supervision of auditors throughout the European Union and the conduct of statutory audits. The Statutory Audit Directive must be transposed into domestic legislation by mid-2008.

UK legislation

See CA 1989, Sch 12.

---

192 Provisions in relation to recognitions and authorisations by Supervisory Authority under section 187

(1) The [Supervisory Authority][a] may, at the time it is granted or at any time during the currency of a recognition or authorisation [under or for the purposes of section 187][a] by notice in writing given to the body of accountants or individual concerned, attach to the recognition or authorisation, as the case may be, such terms and conditions as he thinks necessary or expedient and specified in the notice.

(2) The [Supervisory Authority][b] may, at any time during the currency of a recognition or authorisation [under or for the purposes of section 187][a], by notice in writing given to the body of accountants or individual concerned, amend its terms or conditions or insert into it or delete from it other terms or conditions.

(3) The [Supervisory Authority][c] may, at any time during its currency, by notice in writing given to the body of accountants or individual concerned, revoke, or suspend for a specified period, a recognition or authorisation [under or for the purposes of section 187][a].

(4) (a) The [Supervisory Authority][c] may require a body of accountants recognised for the purposes of the said section 187 to prepare and, within such period as may be specified in the requirement, to submit to the [Supervisory Authority][a] for his approval a code prescribing standards of professional conduct for its members and providing for sanctions for breaches of the code, and the body of accountants shall comply with the requirement.

(b) A body of accountants may, at any time, prepare and submit to the [Supervisory Authority][c] a code amending or revoking a code prepared by it under this subsection.

(c) The [Supervisory Authority][c] may approve of a code submitted to him under this subsection.

(d) A code approved of by the [Supervisory Authority][c] under this section shall be brought into operation and enforced by the body of accountants concerned in accordance with its terms.

[...][d]

(5) References in this section to recognitions under section 187 include references to recognitions under section 162 (inserted by the Companies (Amendment) Act, 1982) of the Principal Act and references in this section to an authorisation under section 187 include references to authorisations under the said section 162.

[(6) Where a disciplinary committee or tribunal (however called) of a body of accountants recognised for the purposes of section 187 has reasonable grounds for believing that an indictable offence under the Companies Acts may have been committed by a person while the person was a member of the body, the body shall, as soon as possible, provide a report to the Director giving details of the alleged offence and shall furnish the Director with such further information in relation to the matter as the Director may require.

(7) Where a body referred to in subsection (6) fails to comply with that subsection or a requirement of the Director under that subsection, it, and every officer of the body to whom the failure is attributable, shall be guilty of an offence.][e]

Amendments

a C(AA)A 2003, Sch 1, Pt 1, Item No 5(a) substitutes 'Supervisory Authority' for 'Minister' and substitutes 'under or for the purposes of section 187' for 'under section 187'.

b C(AA)A 2003, Sch 1, Pt 1, Item No 5(b) substitutes 'Supervisory Authority' for 'Minister' and substitutes 'under or for the purposes of section 187' for 'under the said section 187'.

c C(AA)A 2003, Sch 1, Pt 1, Item No 5(c) substitutes 'Supervisory Authority' for 'Minister'.

d C(AA)A 2003, Sch 1, Pt 1, Item No 5(d) repeals CA 1990, s 192(4)(e), (f) and (g).

e CLEA 2001, s 73 inserts CA 1990, s 192(6) and (7).

Definitions

'director': CLEA 2001, s 3; 'member': C(AA)A 2003, s 4; 'Principal Act': CA 1990, s 3(1); 'Supervisory Authority': C(AA)A 2003, s 4.

Notes

Transfer of functions to the Supervisory Authority: See corresponding notes to CA 1990, s 187.

Presumably no term or condition attached to the recognition or authorisation should conflict with the provisions of Directive 84/253/EEC.

Subsections 6 and 7 were inserted by the CLEA 2001 and require that recognised accounting bodies, where a disciplinary committee or tribunal has reasonable grounds for believing that one of its members may have committed an indictable offence under the Companies Acts, shall report this matter to the Director of Corporate Enforcement and provide the Director with any further information that he may require.

See also CA 1990, s 194.

UK legislation

See CA 1989, Sch 12.

[192A Statutory backing for disciplinary procedures of prescribed accountancy bodies

(1) In this section—

'client' includes an individual, a body corporate, an unincorporated body of persons and a partnership;

'disciplinary committee' means any disciplinary committee or tribunal (however called) of a prescribed accountancy body;

'member', in relation to a prescribed accountancy body, means—

(a) a person, or

(b) a firm,

that is, or was at the relevant time, subject to the investigation and disciplinary procedures approved by the Supervisory Authority under section 9(2)(c) of the Act of 2003 for that body;

'prescribed accountancy body' has the meaning given by section 4 of the Act of 2003;

'refusal' includes failure and 'refuses' includes fails;

'relevant person', in relation to an investigation of a member of a prescribed accountancy body, means—

(a) a member of the prescribed accountancy body,

(b) a client or former client of such a member,

(c) if the client or former client is a body corporate, a person who is or was an officer, employee or agent of the client or former client, or

(d) any person whom the prescribed accountancy body reasonably believes has information or documents relating to the investigation other than information or documents the disclosure of which is prohibited or restricted by law;

'standards', in relation to a prescribed accountancy body, means the rules, regulations and standards that body applies to its members and to which, by virtue of their membership, they are obliged to adhere.

(2) For the purposes of an investigation of a possible breach of a prescribed accountancy body's standards by a member, a disciplinary committee may require a relevant person to do one or more of the following:

(a) produce to the committee all books or documents relating to the investigation that are in the relevant person's possession or control;

(b) attend before the committee;

(c) give the committee any other assistance in connection with the investigation that the relevant person is reasonably able to give.

(3) For the purposes of an investigation referred to in subsection (2), the disciplinary committee may—

(a) examine on oath, either by word of mouth or on written interrogatories, a relevant person,

(b) administer oaths for the purpose of that examination, and

(c) record, in writing, the answers of a person so examined and require that person to sign them.

(4) The disciplinary committee may certify the refusal to the High Court if a relevant person refuses to do one or more of the following:

(a) produce to the committee any book or document that it is the person's duty under this section to produce;

(b) attend before the committee when required to do so under this section;

(c) answer a question put to the person by the committee with respect to the matter under investigation.

(5) On receiving a certificate of refusal concerning a relevant person, the Court may enquire into the case and, after hearing any evidence that may be adduced, may do one or more of the following:

(a) direct that the relevant person attend or Re-attend before the disciplinary committee or produce particular books or documents or answer particular questions put to him or her by that committee;

(b) direct that the relevant person need not produce a particular book or document or answer a particular question put to him or her by that committee;

(c) make any other ancillary or consequential order or give any other direction that the Court thinks fit.

(6) The production of any books or documents under this section by a person who claims a lien on them does not prejudice the lien.

(7) Any information produced or answer given by a member of a prescribed accountancy body in compliance with a requirement under this section may be used in evidence against the member in any proceedings whatsoever, save proceedings for an offence (other than perjury in respect of such an answer).][a]

Amendments

a C(AA)A 2003, s 36 inserted CA 1990, s 192A.

Notes

Statutory backing for their disciplinary processes and, in particular, the ability of a disciplinary committee to compel witnesses who are non-members to appear before it, were measures that were sought specifically by certain of the accounting bodies during submissions at the Bill stage of C(AA) 2003.

The section has yet to be commenced so its impact is as yet untested.

---

193 Auditors' report and right of access to books and of attendance and audience at general meetings

[(1) The auditors of a company shall make a report to the members on the individual accounts examined by them, and on every balance sheet and profit and loss account or income statement, and all group accounts, laid before the company in general meeting during their tenure of office.][a]

(2) The auditors' report shall be read at the annual general meeting of the company and shall be open to inspection by any member.

(3) Every auditor of a company shall have a right of access at all reasonable times to the books, accounts and vouchers of the company and shall be entitled to require from the officers (within the meaning of section 197(5)) of the company such information and

explanations that are within their knowledge or can be procured by them as he thinks necessary for the performance of the duties of the auditors.

[(4) The auditors' report shall include—

(a) an introduction identifying the individual accounts, and where appropriate, the group accounts, that are the subject of the audit and the financial reporting framework that has been applied in their preparation, and

(b) a description of the scope of the audit identifying the auditing standards in accordance with which the audit was conducted.

(4A)(a) Except in the case of a company that has taken advantage of any of the provisions of Part III of the Sixth Schedule to the Principal Act, the auditors' report shall state clearly whether in the auditors' opinion the annual accounts have been properly prepared in accordance with the requirements of the Companies Acts (and, where applicable, Article 4 of the IAS Regulation).

(b) In the case of a company that has taken advantage of any of the provisions of Part III of the Sixth Schedule to the Principal Act, the auditors' report shall state whether, in their opinion, the annual accounts and, where it is a holding company submitting group accounts, the group accounts have been properly prepared in accordance with the Companies Acts (and, where applicable, Article 4 of the IAS Regulation) and give a true and fair view of the matters referred to in subsection (4B)(e)(i) and (ii) and, where appropriate, subsection (4B)(e)(iii) subject to the non-disclosure of any matters (to be indicated in the report) which by virtue of the said Part III are not required to be disclosed.

(4B) The auditors' report shall also state—

(a) whether they have obtained all the information and explanations which, to the best of their knowledge and belief, are necessary for the purposes of their audit,

(b) whether, in their opinion, proper books of account have been kept by the company,

(c) whether, in their opinion, proper returns adequate for their audit have been received from branches of the company not visited by them, and

(d) whether the company's balance sheet and (unless it is framed as a consolidated profit and loss account) profit and loss account are in agreement with the books of account and returns.

(4C) The auditors' report shall state, in particular—

(i) whether the annual accounts give a true and fair view in accordance with the relevant financial reporting framework–

(I) in the case of an individual balance sheet, of the state of affairs of the company as at the end of the financial year,

(II) in the case of an individual profit and loss account, of the profit or loss of the company for the financial year,

(III) in the case of group accounts, of the state of affairs as at the end of the financial year and of the profit or loss for the financial year of the undertakings included in the consolidation as a whole, so far as concerns members of the company,

and

(ii) whether, in their opinion, there existed at the balance sheet date a financial situation which under section 40(1) of the Companies (Amendment) Act 1983 would require the convening of an extraordinary general meeting of the company.

(4D) The auditors' report—

(a) shall be signed and dated by the statutory auditors,

(b) shall, in relation to each matter referred to in subsections (4A), (4B) and (4C) contain a statement or opinion, as the case may be, which shall be either—

(i) unqualified, or

(ii) qualified, and

(c) shall include a reference to any matters to which the auditors wish to draw attention by way of emphasis without qualifying the report.

(4E) For the purposes of subsection (4D)(b)(ii), a statement or opinion may be qualified, including to the extent of an adverse opinion or a disclaimer of opinion, where there is a disagreement or limitation in scope of work.

(4F) Where the individual accounts of a parent undertaking are attached to the group accounts, the auditors' report on the group accounts may be combined with the report on the individual accounts.'][b]

(5) The auditors of a company shall be entitled to attend any general meeting of the company and to receive all notices of, and other communications relating to, any general meeting which any member of the company is entitled to receive and to be heard at any general meeting which they attend on any part of the business of the meeting which concerns them as auditors.

(6) A person who is appointed as auditor of a company or as a public auditor shall be under a general duty to carry out such audit with professional integrity.

(7) Any reference in the Principal Act to section 163 of or the Seventh Schedule to that Act shall be construed as references to this section.

Amendments

a Subsection (1) substituted by EC(IFRSMA)R 2005, reg 9.

b Subsection (4) substituted and sub-ss (4A)–(4B) were added by EC(IFRSMA)R 2005, reg 8.

Notes

Duty of Care of Auditor: In so far as the Companies Acts are silent regarding the content and format of the accounts, compliance with the recognised practices and standards of the accountancy profession in preparing the accounts represents strong (but not conclusive) evidence that the accounts present a 'true and fair view' of the company's affairs.[1]

In auditing the annual accounts of the company and in preparing his report under s 193, the auditor must exercise the skill, care and caution of a reasonably competent, careful and cautious auditor.[2]

Although the duty of care imposed upon an auditor is unchanged in the last 100 years, the standard of care has become more exacting so that standards of auditing that were acceptable in the past might now be regarded as negligent.[3]

Reasonable auditing practice is to be ascertained primarily by reference to the provisions of the Companies Acts. However, in so far as the legislation is silent on a particular matter, reference should be had to the *Statements of Standard Accounting Practice and Auditing Guidelines* prepared by the accounting profession.[4]

The auditor has been referred to as 'a watchdog, not a bloodhound': per Lopes LJ in *Re Kingston Cotton Mill Co (No 2)*.[5] Nonetheless, the auditor is under a duty to make all reasonable enquiries before certifying the accounts.[6] He will, for example, be guilty of negligence where he fails to attend at, observe and verify the company's stocktaking.[7] Furthermore, if the auditor has been or ought to have been put on enquiry by irregularities discovered in the course of the audit, he is under a duty to make an exhaustive investigation of the matter. He is not entitled to simply accept the explanation given by the company's officers, but may be required to make inquiries of the customers, suppliers and other third parties who have had dealings with the company or who have knowledge of the company's affairs.[8]

An auditor who fails to exercise reasonable care and skill in the preparation of his report under s 193 will be liable in damages to the company for any loss suffered by it as a result, including the amount of any dividends paid in respect of false profits.[9]

An auditor who fails to exercise reasonable care and skill in the preparation of his report under s 193 will also be liable in damages to any third party who suffers loss as a result of reliance upon the report provided (a) the loss was reasonably foreseeable, (b) there is a sufficient degree of proximity between the auditor and the third party, and (c) it was reasonable for the third party to rely on the accounts.[10]

Thus it has been held that the auditor owes a duty of care to any third party who is considering a take-over of the company at the time of the audit provided he is aware of the identity of the potential bidder and is aware or ought to be aware that the bidder will be placing reliance on the audited accounts.[11] A contrary view was however reached in the recent English case of *James McNaughton Papers Group Ltd v Hicks Anderson & Co*[12] on the basis that there was an insufficient degree of proximity between the auditors and the bidder.

In *Scott Group Ltd v McFarlane*[13] and *JEB Fasteners Ltd v Marks, Bloom & Co*[14] it was held that the auditor owed a duty of care to potential bidders where he knew or ought to have known of the likelihood of a take-over bid, even if he was not aware of the actual identity of any such bidder. However, in the House of Lords decision in *Caparo Industries plc v Dickman*[15] it was held that the auditors do not owe a duty of care to potential investors/bidders when auditing the accounts, regardless of whether such bidders are already shareholders in the company. Likewise in *Al Saudi Banque v Clark Pixley (a firm)*[16] it was held that the auditors did not owe a duty of care to a bank which lent money to the company in reliance on the audited accounts, regardless of whether the bank was an existing creditor of the company making further advances or was only a potential creditor of the company, since in either case even if it was foreseeable that the bank might request a copy of the company's accounts and rely on them when making an advance to the company there was not a sufficiently close or direct relationship between the auditors and the bank to give rise to the degree of proximity necessary to establish a duty of care. Similarly, in *Man Nutzfahrzeuge AG v Freighliner Ltd*[17] it was held that the auditors of a subsidiary did not owe a duty of care to the parent company in circumstances where a dishonest employee of the subsidiary presented falsified accounts to a third party who was buying the subsidiary and the parent company subsequently became liable to pay damages to the third party when it was discovered that the financial position of the subsidiary as recorded in the audited accounts was inaccurate.

Subsection 4 was replaced by reg 8 of SI 116/2005. This, in turn, reflected new requirements for the format and content of reports by auditors on statutory financial statements contained in Directive 2003/51 of the European Council and of the Parliament ('the Modernisation Directive') which amended Directives 78/660/EEC, 83/349/EEC, 86/635/EEC, and 91/674/EEC relating to annual and consolidated accounts of certain types of companies, banks and other financial institutions and insurance undertakings. Article 1(18) inserted new art 51a into Directive 78/660/EEC, while art 2(11) replaces in a similar fashion art 37 of 83/349/EEC.

The amendment is essentially technical in nature reflecting current practice for audit report formats contained in International Standards of Auditing (UK and Ireland).

1 *Lloyd Cheyham Ltd v Little John & Co* [1987] BCLC 303; *Dovey v Cory* [1901] AC 477; *Dolan v AB Co Ltd* [1969] IR 247; *IRC v Duple Motor Bodies Ltd* [1961] 1 WLR 739.

2 *Re Kingston Cotton Mill Co (No 2)* [1896] 2 Ch 279; *Irish Woollen Co Ltd v Tyson* (1900) 26 The Accountant LR 13; *Leech v Stokes* [1937] IR 787 at 823.

3 *Kelly v Haughey Boland & Co* (30 July 1985, unreported) HC, Lardner J).

4 *Lloyd Cheyham & Co Ltd v Little John & Co* [1987] BCLC 303; *Dolan v AB Ltd* [1969] IR 282; *Fomento (Sterling Area) Ltd v Selsden Fountain Pen Co Ltd* [1958] 1 WLR 45.

5 *Re Kingston Cotton Mill Co (No 2)* [1896] 2 Ch 279 at p 288.

6 *Fomento (Sterling Area) Ltd v Selsden Fountain Pen Co Ltd* [1958] 1 WLR 45.

7 *Kelly v Haughey Boland & Co* (30 July 1985, unreported) HC.

8 *Re Thomas Gerrard & Son Ltd* [1967] 2 All ER 525.

9 *Re London and General Bank (No 2)* [1895] 2 Ch 673; *Re Kingston Cotton Mill Co (No 2)* [1896] 2 Ch 279; *Irish Woollen Co Ltd v Tyson* (1900) 26; *Leech v Stokes* [1937] IR 787; *Re Thomas Gerrard & Son Ltd* [1967] 2 All ER 525. In *Stone & Rolls Ltd v Moore Stephens (a firm)* [2009] 4 All ER 431 it was held that a company will not be precluded by the maxim *ex turpi causa non oritur* action from claiming damages against a firm of auditors which has failed to discover fraud committed by an officer of the company against third parties, even though a consequence of that officer's fraud is that the company may be exposed to claims against it by those third parties. However, if the fraud has been directed against the company itself so that it is the target or direct victim of the fraud, then the officer's dishonesty will not be attributed to the company and it may be entitled to proceed against the auditors for having failed to discover the wrongdoing.

10 *Kelly v Haughey Boland & Co* (30 July 1985, unreported) HC; *Candler v Crane Christmas & Co* [1951] 1 All ER 326; *Scott Group Ltd v McFarlane* [1978] 1 NZLR 553; *JEB Fasteners Ltd v Marks, Bloom & Co* [1981] 3 All ER 289; *Al Saudi Banque v Clark Pixley (a firm)* [1989] 3 All ER 361; *Caparo Industries plc v Dickman* [1990] 1 All ER 568; *James McNaughton Papers Group Ltd v Hicks Anderson & Co* [1991] 1 All ER 134; *Morgan Crucible Co plc v Hill Samuel Bank Ltd* [1991] BCLC 178; *Deloitte Haskins & Sells v National Mutual Life Nominees Ltd* [1993] 2 All ER 1015.

11 *John Sisk & Son Ltd v Flinn* (18 July 1984, unreported) HC; *Kelly v Haughey Boland & Co* (30 July 1985, unreported) HC; *Candler v Crane Christmas & Co* [1951] 1 All ER 326; *Morgan Crucible Co plc v Hill Samuel Bank Ltd* [1991] BCLC 178.

12 *James McNaughton Papers Group Ltd v Hicks Anderson & Co* [1991] 1 All ER 134.

13 *Scott Group Ltd v McFarlane* [1978] 1 NZLR 553.

14 *JEB Fasteners Ltd v Marks, Bloom & Co* [1981] 3 All ER 289.

15 *Caparo Industries plc v Dickman* [1990] 1 All ER 568. See also *Customs and Excise Commissioners v Barclays Bank plc* [2006] 4 All ER 256; *South Australia Asset Management Corpn v York Montague Ltd* [1996] 3 All ER 365.

16 *Al Saudi Banque v Clark Pixley (a firm)* [1989] 3 All ER 361.

17 *Man Nutzfahrzeuge AG v Freighliner Ltd* [2008] 2 BCLC 22.

194 Duty of auditors if proper books of account not being kept

(1) If, at any time, the auditors of a company form the opinion that the company is contravening, or has contravened, section 202 by failing to cause to be kept proper books of account (within the meaning of that section) in relation to the matters specified in subsection (1) and (2) of that section, the auditors shall—

[(a) as soon as may be, by recorded delivery, serve a notice in writing on the company stating their opinion, and][a]

(b) not later than 7 days after the service of such notice on the company, notify the registrar of companies in the prescribed form of the notice [and the registrar shall forthwith forward a copy of the notice to the Director][b].

(2) Where the auditors form the opinion that the company has contravened section 202 but that, following such contravention, the directors of the company have taken the necessary steps to ensure that proper books of account are kept as required by that section, subsection (1)(b) shall not apply.

(3) This section shall not require the auditors to make the notifications referred to in subsection (1) if they are of opinion that the contraventions concerned are minor or otherwise immaterial in nature.

[(3A) Where the auditors of a company file a notice pursuant to subsection (1)(b), they shall, if requested by the Director—

(a) furnish to the Director such information, including an explanation of the reasons for their opinion that the company had contravened section 202, and

(b) give to the Director such [access to books and documents][c], including facilities for inspecting and taking copies,

[being information, books or documents][d] in their possession or control and relating to the matter the subject of the notice, as the Director may require.

(3B) Any written information given in response to a request of the Director under subsection (3A) shall in all legal proceedings be admissible without further proof, until the contrary is shown, as evidence of the facts stated therein.][e]

(4) A person who contravenes [subsection (1), (3A), (5) or (5A)][f] shall be guilty of an offence.

[(5) Where, in the course of, and by virtue of, their carrying out an audit of the accounts of the company, information comes into the possession of the auditors of a company that leads them to form the opinion that there are reasonable grounds for believing that the company or an officer or agent of it has committed an indictable offence under the Companies Acts [...][g] [(other than an indictable offence under section 125(2) or 127(12) of the Principal Act)][h] the auditors shall, forthwith after having formed it, notify that opinion to the Director and provide the Director with details of the grounds on which they have formed that opinion.][i]

[(5A) Where the auditors of a company notify the Director of any matter pursuant to subsection (5), they shall, in addition to performing their obligations under that subsection, if requested by the Director—

(a) furnish the Director with such further information in their possession or control relating to the matter as the Director may require, including further information relating to the details of the grounds on which they formed the opinion referred to in that subsection,

(b) give the Director such access to books and documents in their possession or control relating to the matter as the Director may require, and

(c) give the Director such access to facilities for the taking of copies of or extracts from those books and documents as the Director may require.

(5B) Nothing in this section compels the disclosure by any person of any information that the person would be entitled to refuse to produce on the grounds of legal professional privilege or authorises the inspection or copying of any document containing such information that is in the person's possession.][j]

[(6) No professional or legal duty to which an auditor is subject by virtue of his appointment as an auditor of a company shall be regarded as contravened by, and no liability to the company, its shareholders, creditors or other interested parties shall attach to, an auditor, by reason of his compliance with an obligation imposed on him by or under this section.][i]

Amendments

a CLEA 2001, s 74(a) substitutes CA 1990, s 194(1)(a).

b CLEA 2001, s 74(b) amends CA 1990, s 194(1)(b) by the insertion after 'form of the notice' of 'and the registrar shall forthwith forward a copy of the notice to the Director'.

c C(AA)A 2003, s 37(a) amends CA 1990, s 194(3A)(b) by substituting 'access to books and documents' for 'access to documents'.

d C(AA)A 2003, s 37(b) amends CA 1990, s 194(3A) by substituting 'being information, books or documents' for 'being information or documents'.

e CLEA 2001, s 74(c) inserts CA 1990, s 194(3A) and (3B).

f C(AA)A 2003, s 37(c) amends CA 1990, s 194(4) by substituting 'subsection (1), (3A), (5) or (5A)' for 'subsection (1), (3A) or (5)'; which had been substituted for 'subsection (1) by CLEA 2001, s 74(d).

g C(AA)A 2003, s 37(d) amends CA 1990, s 194(5) by inserting '(other than an indictable offence under section 125(1) or 127(12) of the Principal Act)' after 'an indictable offence under the Companies Acts'; this was repealed by IFCMPA 2005, s 73(3).

h Words inserted by IFCMPA 2005, s 73(2)(d).

i CLEA 2001, s 74(e) inserts CA 1990, s 194(5) and (6).

j C(AA)A 2003, s 37(e) inserted CA 1990, s 194(5A) and (5B), which took effect from 1 March 2007.[1]

[1] Companies (Auditing and Accounting) Act 2003 (Commencement) Order 2007 (SI 61/2007).

Definitions

'contravention': CA 1990, s 3(1); 'directors': CA 1963, s 2(1); 'director': CLEA 2001, s 3; 'officer': CA 1963, s 2(1); 'registrar of companies': CA 1963, s 2(1).

Notes

Section 194 was amended substantially by CLEA 2001 and subsequently by C(AA)A 2003 and IFCMPA 2005.

Section 74 of the CLEA 2001 amended s 194 of CA 1990 by requiring auditors to report to the Director of Corporate Enforcement instances of the suspected commission of indictable offences under the Companies Acts by a company, its officers or agents. The amended section took effect from 28 November 2001.

In 2003, s 37 of the C(AA)A 2003 made further changes to s 194. These changes provide that the failure to comply with certain obligations to file annual returns would be exempted from the obligation to report to the Director. It also provided that auditors would be required to give additional assistance to the Director in his investigation of reported suspected indictable offences under the Companies Acts.

Further amendments were made by ss 73(2)(d) and (3) of the IFCMPA 2005 which provided clarification of the provision in the 2003 Act relating to the exemption of auditors from the requirement to report filing defaults.

The Auditing Practices Board ('APB') and the ODCE have together issued guidance for auditors of this reporting obligation. The APB version, Bulletin 01/2002, 'The Duty of Auditors in the Republic of Ireland to Report to the Director of Corporate Enforcement' is available to download from the APB website at http://www.frc.org.uk/apb. The ODCE version, Decision Notice D/2002/2, is available from the ODCE website at http://www.odce.ie.

A notice served by the auditors on the Registrar or the Director under subsection (1) or subsection (5), as the case may be, is not inadmissible in evidence pursuant to the hearsay exclusionary rule, at least in so far as the auditors were acting as servants or agents of the company at the time of the service of that notice.[1]

Subsections 5A, 5B and 6 have not yet been commenced. It is likely that revised guidance will be issued both by APB and ODCE once this commencement takes place.

1 *Re Bovale Developments Ltd, Director of Corporate Enforcement v Bailey* [2008] 2 ILRM 13.

---

195 Prohibition on acting in relation to audit while disqualification order in force

(1) If a person who is subject or deemed to be subject to a disqualification order—

(a) becomes, or remains after 28 days from the date of the making of the order, a partner in a firm of auditors.

(b) gives directions or instructions in relation to the conduct of any part of the audit of the accounts of a company, or

(c) works in any capacity in the conduct of an audit of the accounts of a company,

he shall be guilty of an offence.

(2) Where a person is convicted of an offence under subsection (1), the period for which he was disqualified shall be extended for a further period of ten years from such date, or such other further period as the court, on the application of the prosecutor and having regard to all the circumstances of the case, may order.

(3) In this section—

(a) 'company' has meaning assigned to it by section 159, and also includes any society registered under the Industrial and Provident Societies Acts, 1893 to 1978.

(b) 'disqualification order' has the meaning assigned to it by section 159.

Definitions

'court': CA 1990, s 235.

---

196 Powers of auditors in relation to subsidiaries

(1) Where a company (referred to in this section as 'the holding company') has a subsidiary, then—

(a) in case the subsidiary is a body corporate incorporated in the State, it shall be the duty of the subsidiary and its auditors to give to the auditors of the holding company such information and explanations as those auditors may reasonably require for the purposes of their duties as auditors of the holding company,

(b) in any other case, it shall be the duty of the holding company, if required by its auditors to do so, to take all such steps as are reasonably open to it to obtain from the subsidiary such information and explanations as aforesaid.

(2) If a company or an auditor fails to comply with subsection (1) within five days of the making of the relevant requirement under that subsection, the company and every officer thereof who is in default, or the auditor, as the case may be, shall be guilty of an offence.

(3) In a prosecution for an offence under this section, it shall be a defence for the defendant to show that it was not reasonably possible for him to comply with the requirement under subsection (1) to which the offence relates within the time specified in subsection (2) but that he complied therewith as soon as was reasonably possible after the expiration of such time.

(4) A person guilty of an offence under this section shall be liable to a fine.

Definitions

'holding company': CA 1963, s 155; 'officer': CA 1963, s 2(1); 'officer in default': CA 1963, s 383; 'subsidiary': CA 1963, s 155.

UK legislation

CA 1985, ss 389A, 390.

197 Penalty for false statements to auditors

(1) An officer of a company who knowingly or recklessly makes a statement to which this section applies that is misleading, false or deceptive in a material particular shall be guilty of an offence.

(2) This section applies to any statement made to the auditors of a company (whether orally or in writing) which conveys, or purports to convey, any information or explanation which they require under the Companies Acts, or are entitled so to require, as auditors of the company.

(3) An officer of a company who fails to provide to the auditors of the company or of the holding company of the company, within two days of the making of the relevant requirement, any information or explanations that the auditors require as auditors of the company or of the holding company of the company and that is within the knowledge of or can be procured by the officer shall be guilty of an offence.

(4) In a prosecution for an offence under this section, it shall be a defence for the defendant to show that it was not reasonably possible for him to comply with the requirement under subsection (3) to which the offence relates within the time specified in that subsection but that he complied therewith as soon as was reasonably possible after the expiration of such time.

(5) In this section 'officer', in relation to a company, includes any employee of the company.

Definitions

'Companies Acts': CA 1990, s 3(1).

UK legislation

CA 1985, s 389A.

[198 Register of auditors

(1) The registrar of companies shall maintain a register containing the names of persons or firms that have been notified to him as qualified for appointment as auditor of a company or as public auditor.

(2) A person shall not—

- (a) act as an auditor of a company or as a public auditor,
- (b) describe himself as an auditor of a company or as a public auditor, or
- (c) so hold himself out as to indicate, or be reasonably understood to indicate, that he is, or is registered as, an auditor of a company or a public auditor, unless—
  - (i) his name is entered, or is deemed under subsection (3) to be entered, in the register of auditors and he holds a valid practising certificate, or
  - (ii) he is a member of a firm that holds a valid practising certificate under section 187(1B) and he is deemed under that section to hold a practising certificate.

(3) In the following circumstances, the name of a person is deemed to be entered in the register of auditors:

- (a) if the person becomes qualified for appointment as an auditor or is granted an authorisation by the Supervisory Authority under section 187(1) and if the time allowed under section 200(1), (2) or (3) for forwarding that person's particulars to the registrar of companies has not yet expired;
- (b) if the person is entitled to have his name entered in the register of auditors and his particulars have been forwarded to the registrar of companies in accordance with section 200(1), (2) or (3) but his name has not yet been entered in that register.

(4) This section does not apply to the Comptroller and Auditor-General.

(5) A person who contravenes subsection (2) is guilty of an offence and is liable—

- (a) on summary conviction, to a fine not exceeding €2,000 and, for continued contravention, a daily default fine not exceeding €60, and
- (b) on conviction on indictment, to a fine not exceeding €12,500 and, for continued contravention, a daily default fine not exceeding €300.

(6) In this section and sections 199 and 200, 'address' in relation to a person means—

- (a) the person's usual business address, and
- (b) if the person is a partner or employee of a firm, the name of the firm and the address of its head office.][a]

Amendments

a C(AA)A 2003, s 38 substitutes CA 1990, s 198.

Notes

At the time of writing, C(AA)A 2003, s 38 has not yet been commenced. Other than the addition of subsection (2), the requirements of the original s 198 were broadly similar.

199 Transitional provisions concerning register

[(1) Subject to subsection (2), a body of accountants which has been recognised by the Supervisory Authority under section 191, shall, within one month after such recognition, deliver to the registrar of companies, the name and address of each of its members who is qualified for appointment under the Companies Acts as auditor of a company or public auditor.][a]

(2) Without prejudice to the generality of subsection (1), a body of accountants based outside the State, [whose recognition is continued under section 32(2) of the Act of 2003][b] or granted as aforesaid, shall notify details of those of its members who wish to practise in the State.

[(2A) A body of accountants referred to in subsection (1) or (2) shall, as soon as possible but not later than 6 months after the event, notify the registrar of companies of any change in the particulars previously provided to him under the applicable subsection.][c]

(3) Every person who, immediately before the commencement of this section, holds an authorisation from the Minister under the Companies Acts to act as auditor of a company or as a public auditor (otherwise than by virtue of membership of a recognised body of accountants) shall, within one month after such commencement, deliver his name and address to the registrar of companies.

[(3A) A person referred to in subsection (3) or in section 32(6) of the Act of 2003, shall notify the registrar of companies—

(a) at least once in each year during the currency of the authorisation referred to in that subsection or section, as the case may be, of the fact that the person holds the authorisation,

(b) as soon as possible but not later than one month after the event, of any change in the particulars provided by the person to the registrar, and

(c) as soon as possible but not later than one month after ceasing to hold the authorisation, of the occurrence of that event.][d]

[(4) If default is made in complying with subsection (1) or (2A), the body of accountants concerned shall be guilty of an offence.][e]

[(5) Information required to be delivered to the registrar of companies under this section shall be delivered in such form and manner as that registrar may specify.][f]

Amendments

a C(AA)A 2003, s 39(a) substitutes CA 1990, s 199(1).

b C(AA)A 2003, s 39(b) amends CA 1990, s 199(2) by substituting 'whose recognition is continued under section 32(2) of the Act of 2003' for 'whose recognition is renewed'.

c C(AA)A 2003, s 39(c) inserts CA 1990, s 199(2A).

d C(AA)A 2003, s 39(d) inserts CA 1990, s 199(3A).

e C(AA)A 2003, s 39(e) substitutes CA 1990, s 199(4).

f C(AA)A 2003, s 39(f) inserts CA 1990, s 199(5).

Definitions

'registrar of companies': CA 1963, s 2(1); 'supervisory authority': C(AA)A 2003, s 4.

Notes

Section 39 of C(AA)A 2003 has not yet been commenced. However there has been no material change from the original section.

200 Duty to keep registrar informed

(1) Subject to subsection (2), where, by virtue of his becoming a member of a body of accountants, a person (other than a person referred to in section 199 (1)) becomes qualified for appointment as auditor of a company or as a public auditor, the body concerned shall, within one month of his becoming so qualified, deliver his name and address to the registrar of companies for inclusion in the register referred to in section 198.

(2) Without prejudice to the generality of subsection (1), a recognised body of accountants based outside the State shall notify details of those of its members who wish to practise in the State.

[(2A) A body of accountants referred to in subsection (1) or a recognised body of accountants referred to in subsection (2) shall, as soon as possible but not later than 6 months after the event, notify the registrar of companies of any change in the particulars previously provided to him under the applicable subsection.][a]

(3) Every person who, after the commencement of this section, is granted an authorisation by the Minister under the Companies Acts to act as auditor of a company or as a public auditor (otherwise than by virtue of membership of a recognised body of accountants) shall, within one month after such grant, deliver his name and address to the registrar of companies.

[(3A) A person referred to in subsection (3) shall notify the registrar of companies—

(a) at least once in each year during the currency of the authorisation referred to in that subsection, of the fact that the person holds the authorisation,

(b) as soon as possible but not later than one month after the event, of any change in the particulars provided by the person to the registrar, and

(c) as soon as possible but not later than one month after ceasing to hold the authorisation, of the occurrence of that event.][b]

[(4) If default is made in complying with subsection (1) or (2A), the body of accountants concerned, or the recognised body of accountants concerned, shall be guilty of an offence.][c]

[(5) Information required to be delivered to the registrar of companies under this section shall be delivered in such form and manner as that registrar may specify.][d]

Amendments

a C(AA)A 2003, s 40(a) inserts CA 1990, s 200(2A).

b C(AA)A 2003, s 40(b) inserts CA 1990, s 200(3A).

c C(AA)A 2003, s 40(c) substitutes CA 1990, s 200(4).

d C(AA)A 2003, s 40(d) inserts CA 1990, s 200(5).

Definitions

'Companies Acts': CA 1990, s 3(1); 'Minister': CA 1990, s 3(1); 'registrar of companies': CA 1963, s 2(1).

Notes

The reference to a person's address is to be construed as a reference to his business address and to the name and address of the head office of any firm of which he is a partner or employee: Companies Act 1990 (Auditors) Regs 1992 (SI 259/1992). C(AA)A 2003, s 40 has yet to be commenced.

UK legislation

CA 1989, ss 37, 38.

201 Power to make supplementary regulations

(1) The Minister may make such supplementary regulations as he considers necessary for the proper and effective implementation of the Council Directive.

(2) Without prejudice to the generality of subsection (1), if, in any respect, any difficulty arises in regard to the implementation of the Directive, the Minister may by regulations do anything which appears to him to be necessary or expedient for removing that difficulty, and any such regulations may modify any provision of this Part so far as may be necessary or expedient to implement the Directive but no regulations shall be made under this subsection in relation to any provision of this Part after the expiration of 3 years commencing on the day on which the relevant provision of this Part came into operation.

(3) Every regulation made by the Minister under this section shall be laid before each House of the Oireachtas as soon as may be after it is made and, if a resolution annulling the regulation is passed by either House within the next 21 days on which that House has sat after the regulation is laid before it, the regulation shall be annulled accordingly, but without prejudice to the validity of anything previously done thereunder.

Notes

The only regulations made to date under this section are the Companies Act 1990 (Auditors) Regulations 1992 (SI 259/1992). These regs will be repealed on commencement of C(AA)A 2003, ss 32 and s 59.

202 Keeping of books of account

(1) Every company shall cause to be kept proper books of account, whether in the form of documents or otherwise, that—

(a) correctly record and explain the transactions of the company,

(b) will at any time enable the financial position of the company to be determined with reasonable accuracy,

[(c) will enable the directors to ensure that any annual accounts of the company comply with the requirements of the Companies Acts and, where applicable, Article 4 of the IAS Regulations, and] [a]

(d) will enable the [annual accounts][a] of the company to be readily and properly audited.

(2) The books of account of a company shall be kept on a continuous and consistent basis, that is to say, the entries therein shall be made in a timely manner and be consistent from one year to the next.

(3) Without prejudice to the generality of subsections (1) and (2), books of account kept pursuant to those subsections shall contain—

(a) entries from day to day of all sums of money received and expended by the company and the matters in respect of which the receipt and expenditure takes place,

(b) a record of the assets and liabilities of the company,

(c) if the company's business involves dealing in goods—

(i) a record of all goods purchased, and of all goods sold (except those sold for cash by way of ordinary retail trade), showing the goods and the sellers and buyers in sufficient detail to enable the goods and the sellers and buyers to be identified and a record of all the invoices relating to such purchases and sales,

(ii) statements of stock held by the company at the end of each financial year and all records of stocktakings from which any such statement of stock has been, or is to be, prepared, and

(d) if the company's business involves the provision of services, a record of the services provided and of all the invoices relating thereto.

(4) For the purposes of subsections (1), (2) and (3), proper books of account shall be deemed to be kept if they comply with those subsections and give a true and fair view of the state of affairs of the company and explain its transactions.

(5) Subject to subsection (6), the books of account shall be kept at the registered office of the company or at such other place as the directors think fit.

(6) If books of account are kept at a place outside the State, there shall be sent to and kept at a place in the State and be at all reasonable times open to inspection by the directors such accounts and returns relating to the business dealt with in the books of account so kept as will disclose with reasonable accuracy the financial position of that business at intervals not exceeding 6 months and will enable to be prepared in accordance with the Companies Acts [(and, where applicable, Article 4 of the IAS Regulation) the company's accounts and any document annexed to those accounts][b] giving information which is required by the said Acts and is thereby allowed to be so given.

(7) Books of account required by this section to be kept, and accounts and returns referred to in subsection (6), shall be kept either in written form in an official language

of the State or so as to enable the books of account and the accounts and returns to be readily accessible and readily convertible into written form in an official language of the State.

(8) A company shall make its books of account, and any accounts and returns referred to in subsection (6), available in written form in an official language of the State at all reasonable times for inspection without charge by the officers of the company and by other persons entitled pursuant to the Companies Acts to inspect the books of account of the company.

(9) A record, being a book of account required by this section to be kept or an account or return referred to in subsection (6), shall be preserved by the company concerned for a period of at least 6 years after the latest date to which it relates.

(10) A company that contravenes this section and a person who, being a director of a company, fails to take all reasonable steps to secure compliance by the company with the requirements of this section, or has by his own wilful act been the cause of any default by the company thereunder, shall be guilty of an offence:

Provided, however, that—

(a) in any proceedings against a person in respect of an offence under this section consisting of a failure to take reasonable steps to secure compliance by a company with the requirements of this section, it shall be a defence to prove that he had reasonable grounds for believing and did believe that a competent and reliable person was charged with the duty of ensuring that those requirements were complied with and was in a position to discharge that duty, and

(b) a person shall not be sentenced to imprisonment for such an offence unless, in the opinion of the court, the offence was committed wilfully.

Amendments

a Section 202(1)(c) substituted and (d) amended by EC(IFRSMA)R 2005, reg 9, Sch 1, Pt 4, Item No 6(a).

b Words substituted by EC(IFRSMA)R 2005, reg 9, Sch 1, Pt 4, Item No 6(b).

Definitions

'Companies Acts': CA 1990, s 3(1); 'court': CA 1990, s 235; 'director': CA 1963, s 2(1); 'financial year': CA 1963, s 2(1).

Notes

In relation to ss 202–204 generally see Courtney, *The Law of Private Companies* (2nd edn, Tottel Publishing, 2002), para 13.004 *et seq*; MacCann, 'Duty to keep proper Books of Account' (1991) 9 ILT (ns) 177 and Sanfey, 'Personal Liability of Directors under Section 204 of the Companies Act 1990' (1996) The Bar Review 50.

Duty to 'keep' proper books of account: The obligation under CA 1990, s 202 to 'keep' proper books of account is not an obligation to act as a mere passive custodian of books and records, but rather is a positive and continuing obligation to create books and records in a particular form and with specified contents.[1]

1 *Re Mantruck Services Ltd, Meghigan v Duignan* [1997] 1 IR 341.

Director's Right of Access to Books of Account: A director's right of access, which exists for the purpose of enabling him to enforce his duties as a director, to the books of account may be enforced by injunction if necessary[1] or by way of an application pursuant to CA 1963, s 371 for an order enforcing the statutory duty of the other directors under s 202(8) to make those books of account available for inspection by him.[2] Such an application may be brought not only against the company and its existing directors but also against any person who resigns from the board for the purpose of evading compliance with s 202.[3] In this regard, the duty to provide access to the books of account is not satisfied by providing minimal information but, instead, the information provided must be such as to render the company's transactions explicable.[4] Moreover, a director is entitled to have an accountant accompany him for the purpose of inspecting the books provided the accountant gives an undertaking to the company that information acquired by him during the course of the inspection will not be used for any purpose except giving confidential advice to the director in relation to the matter in which he has been retained.[5] The right of the director and his accountant to inspect the books of account includes a right to take copies of such books.[6] It should be noted, though, that the company will be entitled to refuse the director access to the books of account where he is seeking access for the purpose of injuring the company or for some other improper purpose.[7]

1 *Healy v Healy Homes Ltd* [1973] IR 309; *Oxford Legal Group Ltd v Sibbasbridge Services plc* [2008] 2 BCLC 381; *Burn v The London and South Wales Coal Company and the Risca Investment Company* (1890) 7 TLR 11.

2 *Brosnan v Sommerville* [2007] 4 IR 135.

3 *Brosnan v Sommerville* [2007] 4 IR 135.

4 *Brosnan v Sommerville* [2007] 4 IR 135.

5 *Healy v Healy Homes Ltd* [1973] IR 309.

6 *Healy v Healy Homes Ltd* [1973] IR 309.

7 *Oxford Legal Group Ltd v Sibbasbridge Services plc* [2008] 2 BCLC 381.

Personal Liability for failure to keep proper books of account: See the notes to CA 1990, s 204.

UK legislation

See CA 1985, s 222.

---

203 Liability of officers of company to penalty where proper books of account not kept

(1) If—

(a) a company that is being wound up and that is unable to pay all of its debts, has contravened section 202, and

(b) the court considers that such contravention has contributed to the company's inability to pay all of its debts or has resulted in substantial uncertainty as to the assets and liabilities of the company or has substantially impeded the orderly winding up thereof,

every officer of the company who is in default shall be guilty of an offence and liable—

(i) on summary conviction, to a fine not exceeding [€1,904.61][a] or to imprisonment for a term not exceeding 6 months or to both, or

(ii) on conviction on indictment, to a fine not exceeding [€12,697.38][b] or to imprisonment for a term not exceeding 5 years or to both.

(2) In a prosecution for an offence under this section it shall be a defence for the person charged with the offence to show that—

(a) he took all reasonable steps to secure compliance by the company with section 202, or

(b) he had reasonable grounds for believing and did believe that a competent and reliable person, acting under the supervision or control of a director of the company who has been formally allocated such responsibility, was charged with the duty of ensuring that that section was complied with and was in a position to discharge that duty.

Amendments

a £1,000 increased to £1,500 by CA 1990, s 240(7) as inserted by CLEA 2001, s 104(c), and converted to €1,904.61 by Council Regulations (EC) No 1103/97, No 974/98 and No 2866/98 and the Economic and Monetary Union Act 1998, s 6.

b £10,000 converted to €12,697.38 by Council Regulations (EC) No 1103/97, No 974/98 and No 2866/98 and the Economic and Monetary Union Act 1998, s 6.

Definitions

'contravention': CA 1990, s 3(1); 'court': CA 1990, s 235; 'director': CA 1963, s 2(1); 'officer': CA 1963, s 2(1); 'officer in default': CA 1963, s 383.

Notes

Such conduct could also amount to reckless trading within the meaning of s 297A of CA 1963. See in particular the comments of Knox J in *Re Produce Marketing Consortium Ltd (No 2)* [1989] BCLC 520.

UK legislation

See CA 1985, s 222.

204 Personal liability of officers of company where proper books of account not kept

(1) Subject to subsection (2), if—

(a) a company that is being wound up and that is unable to pay all of its debts has contravened section 202, and

(b) the court considers that such contravention has contributed to the company's inability to pay all of its debts or has resulted in substantial uncertainty as to the assets and liabilities of the company or has substantially impeded the orderly winding up thereof,

the court, on the application of the liquidator or any creditor or contributory of the company, may, if it thinks it proper to do so, declare that any one or more of the officers and former officers of the company who is or are in default shall be personally liable, without any limitation of liability, for all, or such part as may be specified by the court, of the debts and other liabilities of the company.

(2) On the hearing of an application under this subsection, the person bringing the application may himself give evidence or call witnesses.

(3) (a) Where the court makes a declaration under subsection (1), it may give such directions as it thinks proper for the purpose of giving effect to the declaration and in particular may make provision for making the liability of any such person under the declaration a charge on any debt or obligation due from the company to him, or on any mortgage or charge or any interest in any mortgage or charge on any assets of the company held by or vested in him or any company or other person on his behalf, or any person claiming as assignee from or through the person liable under the declaration or any company or person acting on his behalf, and may from time to time make such further order as may be necessary for the purpose of enforcing any charge imposed under this subsection.

(b) In paragraph (a) 'assignee' includes any person to whom or in whose favour, by the directions of the person liable, the debt, obligation, mortgage or charge was created, issued or transferred or the interest created, but does not include an assignee for valuable consideration (not including consideration by way of marriage) given in good faith and without notice of any of the matters on the ground of which the declaration is made.

(4) The court shall not make a declaration under subsection (1) in respect of a person if it considers that—

(a) he took all reasonable steps to secure compliance by the company with section 202, or

(b) he had reasonable grounds for believing and did believe that a competent and reliable person, acting under the supervision or control of a director of the company who has been formally allocated such responsibility, was charged with the duty of ensuring that that section was complied with and was in a position to discharge that duty.

(5) This section shall have effect notwithstanding that the person concerned may be criminally liable in respect of the matters on the ground of which the declaration is to be made.

(6) In this section 'officer', in relation to a company, includes a person who has been convicted of an offence under section 194, 197 or 242 in relation to a statement concerning the keeping of proper books of account by the company.

Definitions

'contravention': CA 1990, s 3(1); 'court': CA 1990, s 235; 'director': CA 1963, s 2(1); 'officer': CA 1963, s 2(1); 'officer in default': CA 1963, s 383.

Notes

Personal Liability for failure to keep proper books of account: The obligation under CA 1990, s 202 to 'keep' proper books of account is not an obligation to act as a mere passive custodian of books and records, but rather is a positive and continuing obligation to create books and records in a particular form and with specified contents.[1] For the court to have jurisdiction to impose personal liability under s 204, it must be satisfied that the officer or former officer of the company has committed a criminal offence under s 202(10).[2] In addition, the following statutory preconditions must be satisfied:

(a) the company must be in liquidation and unable to pay its debts;

(b) the court must consider that the breach of s 202—

(i) has contributed to the company's inability to pay all of its debts; or

(ii) has resulted in substantial uncertainty as to the company's assets and liabilities; or

(iii) has substantially impeded the orderly winding up of the company; and

(c) the officer or former officer must have knowingly and wilfully authorised the breach of s 202 or must alternatively be a person who has been convicted under CA 1990, ss 198, 197 or 242 in relation to a statement concerning the keeping of proper books of account.[2]

The standard of proof applicable to an application under s 204 is the normal civil standard on the balance of probabilities.[3] While s 204 does not require any causal relationship between the breach of s 20 and the quantum of the liability to be imposed and does not make any express allowance for different degrees of blameworthiness, nevertheless the section is to be construed by reference to the presumption of constitutionality which it enjoys and, accordingly, the court in the exercise of its discretion must have regard to (but not necessarily exclusively) the extent to which the contravention of s 202 resulted in financial loss and, if it did, whether such losses were reasonably foreseeable by the officer or former officer.[4] Nevertheless, it would appear to be permissible for the court, in appropriate circumstances, to impose personal liability in an amount which is not necessarily proportionate to the wrongdoing but which is instead punitive as to the quantum.[5]

Such conduct could also amount to reckless trading within the meaning of s 297A of CA 1963. See in particular comments of Knox J in *Re Produce Marketing Consortium Ltd (No 2)*.[6]

1 *Re Mantruck Services Ltd, Meghigan v Duignan* [1997] 1 IR 341.

2 *Re Mantruck Services Ltd, Meghigan v Duignan* [1997] 1 IR 341. See also *Re Dev Oil and Gas Ltd, Jackson v Devlin* [2008] IEHC 252.

3 *Re Mantruck Services Ltd, Meghigan v Duignan* [1997] 1 IR 341. See also *Maloc Construction Ltd v Chadwick* (1986) 3 NZCLC 99.

4 *Re Mantruck Services Ltd, Meghigan v Duignan* [1997] 1 IR 341. See also *Re Ashclad Ltd, Forrest v Harrington* [2000] IEHC 174; *Re Rayhill Property Co Ltd, Conroy v Corneill* [2003] 3 IR 588; *Re PSK Construction Ltd* (7 December 2009, unreported) HC (Finlay Geoghegan J).

5 *O'Keefe v Ferris* [1997] 3 IR 463; *Re Ashclad Ltd, Forrest v Harrington* (5 April 2000, unreported) HC (Geoghegan J); *Re Dev Oil and Gas Ltd, Jackson v Devlin* [2008] IEHC 252.

6 *Re Produce Marketing Consortium Ltd (No 2)* [1989] BCLC 520.

205 Commencement of Part X

Each of the following provisions, that is to say sections 202 to 204, shall apply as respects the accounts of a company for each financial year of the company beginning or ending after such date after the commencement of the provision as may be specified by the Minister by order.

Definitions

'Minister': CA 1990, s 3(1).

[205A Accounting standards

(1) In this section—

'accounting standards' means—

(a) statements of accounting standards, and

(b) any written interpretation of those standards,

issued by any body or bodies prescribed by regulation;

'relevant undertaking' means—

(a) a company, or

(b) an undertaking referred to in Regulation 6 of the 1993 Regulations,

but does not include a company or an undertaking of a class exempt under section 48(1)(j) of the Act of 2003 from this section.

(2) Each relevant undertaking shall ensure—

(a) that its [individual accounts][b] and, where relevant, its group accounts include a statement as to whether they have been prepared in accordance with applicable accounting standards, and

(b) that any material departure from applicable accounting standards, the effect of the departure and the reasons for it are noted in the [individual accounts][b] and, where relevant, in the group accounts.

(3) Accounting standards are applicable to a relevant undertaking's [individual accounts][b] and, where relevant, to its group accounts, if those standards are, in accordance with their terms, relevant to its circumstances and those accounts.

(4) Where a relevant undertaking fails to comply with subsection (2), each company or other entity that forms all or part of that undertaking is guilty of an offence.][a]

Amendments

a C(AA)A 2003, s 41 inserts CA 1990, s 205A.

b 'Individual accounts' substituted for 'annual account' by EC(IFRSMA)R 2005, reg 9, Sch 1, Pt 4, Item No 7.

Definitions

'individual accounts': CA 1963, s 2(1).

Notes

This section provides a definition for 'accounting standards' and also requires that companies ensure that their financial statements have been prepared in accordance with applicable accounting standards and where there is a significant departure from accounting standards which apply that the reasons for this are noted in the annual accounts. Accounting standards are those issued by a body prescribed by regulation.

The section has yet to be commenced.

Accounting standards (or Financial Reporting Standards) currently used in Ireland are those issued by the Accounting Standards Board and promulgated in the Republic of Ireland by the Institute of Chartered Accountants in Ireland. (See 149 of CA 1963).

Under SI 116/2005, companies may use IFRS when preparing annual accounts. SI 116 does recognise explicitly, therefore, IFRS. Also, IFCMPA 2005, s 28 inserts a new section, s 260A into CA 1990 permitting an investment company, in respect of its individual accounts, to prepare these in accordance with either:

(a) an alternative body of accounting standards ('ABAS') and

(b) s 149A of the Principal Act.

Section 260A(4) identifies ABAS as including standards laid down by bodies in the USA, Canada and Japan.

Thus there are already a number of bodies of accounting standards already having recognition in law. Interestingly, such legal recognition does not yet extend to those standards issued by the ASB which are the most commonly applied standards by companies. Presumably, the ASB will be prescribed as such a body on commencement of s 205A.

[205B Audit committee

(1) In this section—

'affiliate' in relation to an auditor, means a firm, body corporate or partnership considered under section 182(2) to be an affiliate of the auditor at the relevant time;

'amount of turnover' and 'balance sheet total' have the same meanings as in section 8 of the Companies (Amendment) Act 1986;

'internal audit' means an examination of the internal control system of a public limited company, a large private company or a relevant undertaking that is conducted within the public limited company, large private company or undertaking or otherwise at the request of its audit committee, directors or other officers;

'internal auditor' means a person who conducts an internal audit;

'large private company' means either of the following:

(a) a private company limited by shares that, in both the most recent financial year of the company and the immediately preceding financial year, meets the following criteria:

(i) the balance sheet total of that company exceeds for the year—

(A) €25,000,000, or

(B) if an amount is prescribed under section 48(1)(l) of the Act of 2003 for the purpose of this provision, the prescribed amount;

(ii) the amount of turnover of that company exceeds for the year—

(A) €50,000,000, or

(B) if an amount is prescribed under section 48(1)(l) of the Act of 2003 for the purpose of this provision, the prescribed amount;

(b) a private company limited by shares if the company and all its subsidiary undertakings together, in both the most recent financial year of that company and the immediately preceding financial year, meet the criteria in paragraph (a);

'parent undertaking' and 'subsidiary undertaking' have the same meaning as in the 1992 Regulations;

'relevant undertaking' means either of the following:

(a) an undertaking referred to in Regulation 6 of the 1993 Regulations that, in both the most recent financial year and the immediately preceding financial year of the undertaking, meets the following criteria:

(i) the balance sheet total of that undertaking exceeds for the year—

(A) €25,000,000, or

(B) if an amount is prescribed under section 48(1)(l) of the Act of 2003 for the purpose of this provision, the prescribed amount;

(ii) the amount of turnover of that undertaking exceeds for the year—

(A) €50,000,000, or

(B) if an amount is prescribed under section 48(1)(l) of the Act of 2003 for the purpose of this provision, the prescribed amount;

(b) an undertaking referred to in Regulation 6 of the 1993 Regulations if that undertaking and all of its subsidiary undertakings together, in both the most recent financial year and the immediately preceding financial year of the parent undertaking, meet the criteria in paragraph (a).

(2) Subject to subsection (16), the board of directors of a public limited company (whether listed or unlisted) shall establish and adequately resource a committee of directors, to be known as the audit committee, with the following responsibilities:

(a) reviewing, before they are presented to the board of directors for approval—

(i) the company's [individual accounts],[b] and

(ii) if the company is a parent undertaking, the group accounts of the group of undertakings of which the company is the parent undertaking;

(b) determining whether the [individual accounts][b] so reviewed comply with section 205A(2) and whether, in the committee's opinion, they give at the end of the financial year a true and fair view of—

(i) the state of affairs of the company, and

[(ii) the profit or loss of the company, even if, by virtue of section 7(1A) of the Companies (Amendment) Act 1986 or section 148(8) of the Act of 1963, it is not laid before the members in annual general meeting;][c]

(c) determining whether the group accounts so reviewed comply with section 205A(2) and whether, in the committee's opinion, they give at the end of the financial year a true and fair view of—

(i) the state of affairs of the group of undertakings of which the company is the parent undertaking, and

(ii) the profit or loss of that group;

(d) recommending to the board of directors whether or not to approve the [individual accounts][b] and group accounts so reviewed;

(e) determining, at least annually, whether in the committee's opinion, the company has kept proper books of account in accordance with section 202;

(f) reviewing, before its approval by the board of directors, the statement required to be made under section 205E(5) and (6);

(g) determining whether, in the committee's opinion, the statement so reviewed—

(i) complies with section 205E(5) and (6), and

(ii) is fair and reasonable and is based on due and careful enquiry;

(h) recommending to the board of directors whether or not to approve a statement reviewed under paragraph (f);

(i) advising the board of directors as to the recommendation to be made by the board to the shareholders concerning the appointment of the company's auditor;

(j) monitoring the performance and quality of the auditor's work and the auditor's independence from the company;

(k) obtaining from the auditor up to date information to enable the committee to monitor the company's relationship with the auditor, including, but not limited to, information relating to the auditor's affiliates;

(l) recommending whether or not to award contracts to the auditor or an affiliate of the auditor for non-audit work;

(m) satisfying itself that the arrangements made and the resources available for internal audits are in the committee's opinion suitable;

(n) reporting, as part of the report under section 158 of the Principal Act, on the committee's activities for the year, including, but not limited to, the discharge of its responsibilities under paragraph (j);

(o) performing any additional functions prescribed by regulation under section 48(1)(m) of the Act of 2003;

(p) performing any other functions relating to the company's audit and financial management that are delegated to it by the board of directors.

(3) Subject to subsection (16), the board of directors of each large private company and of each relevant undertaking shall either—

(a) establish an audit committee that—

(i) has all or some of the responsibilities specified in subsection (2), and

(ii) subject to subsection (8), otherwise meets the requirements of this section, or

(b) decide not to establish an audit committee.

(4) The board of directors of each large private company and of each relevant undertaking to which subsection (3) applies shall state in their report under section 158 of the Principal Act—

(a) whether the company or undertaking, as the case may be, has established an audit committee or decided not to do so,

(b) if the company or undertaking, as the case may be, has established an audit committee, whether it has only some of the responsibilities specified in subsection (2), and

(c) if the company or undertaking, as the case may be, has decided not to establish an audit committee, the reasons for that decision.

(5) For the purpose of applying subsection (2) to a large private company or relevant undertaking that decides under subsection (3)(a) to establish an audit committee with some or all of the responsibilities specified in subsection (2)—

(a) a reference in any applicable paragraph of subsection (2) to a public limited company or the company is to be construed as a reference to the large private company or relevant undertaking, as the case may be, and

(b) subsection (2) applies to the extent specified by the large private company or the relevant undertaking with any other modifications necessary for that purpose.

(6) The audit committee is to consist of such directors as the board of directors concerned thinks fit, provided, subject to subsection (8), both of the following requirements are met:

(a) the committee consists of not fewer than 2 members;

(b) all those appointed to the committee qualify under subsection (7).

(7) A director qualifies for appointment to the audit committee unless he or she—

(a) is, or was at any time during the 3 years preceding appointment to the committee—

(i) an employee of the company or undertaking concerned, or

(ii) an employee of any subsidiary of the company concerned or of a subsidiary undertaking of the undertaking concerned, or

(b) is the chairperson of the board of directors.

(8) The requirements specified in paragraphs (a) and (b) of subsection (6) do not apply if—

(a) only one director on the board of directors of the company or undertaking concerned qualifies under subsection (7),

(b) that director—

(i) is appointed as the sole member of the audit committee, or

(ii) is appointed as the chairperson of an audit committee consisting of not more than 2 members (including the chairperson) and has, in the case of an equal division of votes, a second or casting vote,

(c) any conditions prescribed under section 48(1)(m) of the Act of 2003 are met, and

(d) the directors of the company or undertaking concerned state in their report under section 158 of the Principal Act the reasons for the company's or undertaking's exemption from those requirements.

(9) Written terms of reference concerning the audit committee's role in the audit and financial management of the company or relevant undertaking concerned shall—

(a) be prepared and approved by the board of directors,

(b) be submitted for the information of the shareholders of the company or undertaking concerned at its annual general meeting, and

(c) be reviewed each year by the board of directors.

(10) Without limiting the matters that may be included under subsection (9), the terms of reference must—

(a) specify how the audit committee will discharge its responsibilities, and

(b) provide for a programme of separate and joint meetings with the management, auditor and internal auditor of the company or undertaking concerned.

(11) Subsection (9) applies also in relation to any amendments of the audit committee's terms of reference.

(12) Where the board of directors of a public limited company to which subsection (2) applies fails to establish an audit committee that is constituted in accordance with this section, each director to whom the failure is attributable is guilty of an offence.

(13) Where a director of a large private company or relevant undertaking to which subsection (3) applies fails to take all reasonable steps to comply with the requirements of subsection (4), the director is guilty of an offence.

(14) A reference in this section to the directors of a relevant undertaking is to be construed in the case of an undertaking that does not have a board of directors as a reference to the corresponding persons appropriate to that undertaking.

(15) For the purpose of applying this section to a partnership that is referred to in Regulation 6 of the 1993 Regulations and that is a relevant undertaking—

(a) the partnership is to be treated as though it were a company formed and registered under the Companies Acts,

(b) a reference in this section to a report under section 158 of the Principal Act is to be construed as a reference to a report under Regulation 14 of the 1993 Regulations, and

(c) this section applies with any other modifications necessary for that purpose.

(16) This section does not apply to—

(a) a public limited company that is a wholly owned subsidiary undertaking of another public limited company, or

(b) any company or undertaking of a class exempted under section 48(1)(j) of the Act of 2003 from the application of this section.][a]

Amendments

a C(AA)A 2003, s 42 inserts CA 1990, s 205B.

b 'Individual accounts' substituted for 'annual accounts' by EC(IFRSMA)R 2005, reg 9, Sch 1, Pt 4, Item No 8(a).

c Subsection (2)(b)(ii) substituted by EC(IFRSMA)R 2005, reg 9, Sch 1, Pt 4, Item No 8(b).

Notes

Section 205B requires the establishment of audit committees by boards of directors of companies and undertakings falling within the criteria set out in the section. The section stipulates the minimum number (2) which is to comprise the committee and other applicable criteria. The committee must have written terms of reference concerning its operation and role and details the minimum responsibilities that the committee must discharge.

Where directors of a large private company as defined in the section choose not to establish an audit committee, an explanation for this must be given in their report under s 158 of CA 1963.

This section has not yet been commenced. During 2006, the ODCE issued draft guidance on this section for consultation which was finalised and published in November 2006. It can be downloaded from the ODCE website at http://www.odce.ie.

Article 41 of Directive 2006/43/EC also contains provisions relating to the establishment of audit committee by certain classes of company. A number of differences exist between its requirements and those of s 205B which presumably will be addressed during transposition.

[205C Disclosure of accounting policies

(1) In this section 'relevant undertaking' means—

(a) a company, or

(b) an undertaking referred to in Regulation 6 of the 1993 Regulations,

but does not include a company or an undertaking of a class exempted under section 48(1)(j) of the Act of 2003 from this section;

(2) A relevant undertaking shall disclose in the notes to its annual accounts the accounting policies adopted by the undertaking in determining—

(a) the items and amounts to be included in its balance sheet, and

(b) the amounts in its profit and loss account.

(3) The accounting policies that a relevant undertaking is required to disclose under this section include, but are not limited to, those relating to the depreciation and diminution in the value of its assets.

(4) Where a relevant undertaking fails to comply with subsection (2), each company or other entity that forms all or part of that undertaking is guilty of an offence.][a]

Amendments

a C(AA)A 2003, s 43 inserts CA 1990, s 205C.

Notes

This section amends CA 1990 by defining a 'relevant undertaking' and requiring such an undertaking to disclose in the notes to its annual accounts its accounting policies in relation to the items and amounts included in its profit and loss account and balance sheet. This requirement duplicates what is already required by accounting standards.

The section has not yet been commenced.

[205D Disclosure of remuneration for audit, audit-related and non-audit work

(1) In this section—

'affiliate' in relation to an auditor, means a firm, body corporate or partnership considered under section 182(2) to be an affiliate of the auditor;

'audit committee' means the committee established under section 205B;

'audit-related work' means work required by any relevant undertaking, body or person to be done by an auditor of the relevant undertaking by virtue of his or her position as auditor of that undertaking, but does not include audit work;

'audit work' means—

(a) in relation to a relevant undertaking other than a partnership referred to in Regulation 6 of the 1993 Regulations, work required to fulfil the duties imposed under section 193 of this Act on an auditor of a company, and

(b) in relation to a partnership referred to in Regulation 6 of the 1993 Regulations, work required to fulfil the duties imposed under Regulation 22 of those Regulations on an auditor appointed by the partners;

'connected undertaking', in relation to a relevant undertaking, means an undertaking that under the 1992 Regulations, or under those Regulations as applied by Regulation 9 of the 1993 Regulations, is—

(a) a subsidiary undertaking of the relevant undertaking,

(b) a joint venture of the relevant undertaking proportionally consolidated in accordance with Regulation 32 of the 1992 Regulations, or

(c) an associated undertaking of the relevant undertaking;

'firm' means a firm that qualifies for appointment as auditor of a company or as a public auditor under section 187(1A);

'non-audit work' means work other than audit work or audit-related work;

'relevant undertaking' means—

(a) a company, or

(b) an undertaking referred to in Regulation 6 of the 1993 Regulations, but does not include a company or an undertaking of a class exempted under section 48(1)(j) of the Act of 2003 from this section;

'remuneration' includes benefits in kind and payments in cash.

(2) Subject to subsection (5), a relevant undertaking shall disclose in the notes to its annual accounts relating to each financial year beginning on or after the commencement of this section the following information:

(a) the remuneration for all work in each category specified in subsection (3) that was carried out for the relevant undertaking or a connected undertaking of the relevant undertaking, during that financial year—

(i) by an auditor of the relevant undertaking, and

(ii) by any firm or individual that, at any time during the financial year, was an affiliate of the auditor;

(b) the remuneration for all work in each category specified in subsection (3) that was carried out for the relevant undertaking or a connected undertaking of the relevant undertaking, during the preceding financial year—

(i) by an auditor of the relevant undertaking, and

(ii) by any firm or individual that, at any time during the financial year, was an affiliate of the auditor;

(c) where the remuneration referred to in paragraph (a) or (b) is for non-audit work, the nature of the work;

(d) where all or part of the remuneration referred to in paragraph (a) or (b) is in the form of a benefit in kind, the nature and estimated monetary value of the benefit.

(3) Remuneration must be disclosed under subsection (2) for each of the following categories of work carried out as described in that subsection:

(a) audit work;

(b) audit-related work;

(c) non-audit work.

(4) Where the auditor of a relevant undertaking is a firm, any work carried out by a partner in the firm is considered for the purposes of this section to have been carried out by the auditor.

(5) The disclosure requirements of this section apply in relation to a financial year of the relevant undertaking only if—

(a) the aggregate of the remuneration for all work in each specified category that was carried out as described in subsection (2)(a) in that financial year exceeds €1,000, and

(b) the aggregate of the remuneration for all work in each specified category that was carried out as described in subsection (2)(b) in the preceding financial year exceeds €1,000.

(6) Where the remuneration required to be disclosed by a relevant undertaking in respect of a financial year for non-audit work exceeds the aggregate of the remuneration required to be disclosed in respect of that year for audit work and audit-related work, the audit committee shall state in its report for that year under section 205B(2)(m)—

(a) whether it has satisfied itself that the carrying out of the non-audit work by the auditor or an affiliate of the auditor has not affected the auditor's independence from the relevant undertaking, and

(b) if it has satisfied itself to that effect, the reasons for the decision to have the non-audit work carried out by the auditor or an affiliate of the auditor.

(7) Subsection (6) applies also where the relevant undertaking has no audit committee, but in that case the required statement shall be made by the directors in their report under section 158 of the Principal Act.

(8) Where more than one firm or individual has been appointed as the auditor of a relevant undertaking in a single financial year, separate disclosure in respect of the remuneration of each of them and of their affiliates must be provided in the notes to the company's annual accounts.

(9) The auditor of a relevant undertaking shall provide the directors of that undertaking with the information necessary to enable the auditor's affiliates to be identified for the purposes of this section.

(10) Where a relevant undertaking fails to comply with subsection (2), (3) or (8), each company or other entity that forms all or part of that undertaking is guilty of an offence.

(11) Where the audit committee of a relevant undertaking fails to comply with subsection (6) or the directors of a relevant undertaking fail to comply with that subsection as applied by subsection (7), each member of the committee or each director of the undertaking, as the case may be, to whom the failure is attributable is guilty of an offence.

(12) Where an auditor fails to comply with subsection (9), the auditor is guilty of an offence.

(13) Section 205B(14) applies in relation to any reference in this section to the directors of a relevant undertaking and section 205B(15) applies for the purpose of applying this section to a partnership.][a]

Amendments

a C(AA)A 2003, s 44 inserts CA 1990, s 205D.

Notes

This section is aimed at addressing the issue of auditor independence. It requires disclosure by undertakings of all work carried out in the financial year by the auditor of the relevant undertaking in the notes to the annual accounts. The requirement also extends to the preceding financial year. 'All work' is defined as audit, audit-related, and non-audit work. The nature of non-audit work must be specified. These disclosure requirements only apply in the financial year in question where the amounts paid over the three categories amount to more than €1,000. Where remuneration for non-audit work exceeds the aggregate of amounts paid for audit and audit-related work added together, the directors or audit committee must state in their report under s 158 of CA 1963 that they have satisfied themselves that the carrying out of this non-audit work has not interfered with the auditor's independence in respect of the audit of the undertaking.

The section has not yet been commenced. Article 49 of Directive 2006/43/EC also contains requirements addressing the same issue. However, it approaches the matter by requiring fees to be disclosed under the headings of statutory audit, other assurance services, tax advisory services, and other non-audit services. Presumably s 205D will be amended to take account of this difference on transposition of this Directive.

[205E Directors' compliance statement and related statement

(1) In this section—

'amount of turnover' and 'balance sheet total' have the same meanings as in section 8 of the Companies (Amendment) Act 1986; 'relevant obligations', in relation to a company, means the company's obligations under—

(a) the Companies Acts,

(b) tax law, and

(c) any other enactments that provide a legal framework within which the company operates and that may materially affect the company's financial statements;

'tax law' means—

(a) the Customs Acts,

(b) the statutes relating to the duties of excise and to the management of those duties,

(c) the Tax Acts,

(d) the Capital Gains Tax Acts,

(e) the Value-Added Tax Act 1972 and the enactments amending or extending that Act,

(f) the Capital Acquisitions Tax Act 1976 and the enactments amending or extending that Act,

(g) the statutes relating to stamp duty and to the management of that duty, and

(h) any instruments made under an enactment referred to in any of paragraphs (a) to (g) or made under any other enactment and relating to tax.

(2) This section applies to—

(a) a public limited company (whether listed or unlisted), and

(b) a private company limited by shares, but it does not apply to a company referred to in paragraph (a) or (b) that is of a class exempted under section 48(1)(j) of the Act of 2003 from this section or to a company referred to in paragraph (b) while that company qualifies for an exemption under subsection (9).

(3) The directors of a company to which this section applies shall, as soon as possible after the commencement of this section or after this section becomes applicable to the company, prepare or cause to be prepared a directors' compliance statement containing the following information concerning the company:

(a) its policies respecting compliance with its relevant obligations;

(b) its internal financial and other procedures for securing compliance with its relevant obligations;

(c) its arrangements for implementing and reviewing the effectiveness of the policies and procedures referred to in paragraphs (a) and (b).

(4) The directors' compliance statement (including any revisions) must—

(a) be in writing,

(b) be submitted for approval by the board of directors,

(c) at least once in every 3 year period following its approval by the board, be reviewed and, if necessary, revised by the directors, and

(d) be included in the directors' report under section 158 of the Principal Act.

(5) The directors of a company to which this section applies shall also include in their report under section 158 of the Principal Act a statement—

(a) acknowledging that they are responsible for securing the company's compliance with its relevant obligations,

(b) confirming that the company has internal financial and other procedures in place that are designed to secure compliance with its relevant obligations, and, if this is not the case, specifying the reasons, and

(c) confirming that the directors have reviewed the effectiveness of the procedures referred to in paragraph (b) during the financial year to which the report relates, and, if this is not the case, specifying the reasons.

(6) In addition, the directors of a company to which this section applies shall in the statement required under subsection (5)—

(a) specify whether, based on the procedures referred to in that subsection and their review of those procedures, they are of the opinion that they used all reasonable endeavours to secure the company's compliance with its relevant obligations in the financial year to which the annual report relates, and

(b) if they are not of that opinion, specify the reasons.

(7) For the purposes of this section, a company's internal financial and other procedures are considered to be designed to secure compliance with its relevant obligations and to be effective for that purpose if they provide a reasonable assurance of compliance in all material respects with those obligations.

(8) Where the directors of a company to which this section applies fail—

- (a) to prepare, or to cause to be prepared, a directors' compliance statement as required by subsections (3) and (4)(a) to (c),
- (b) to include a directors' compliance statement in the directors' report as required by subsection (4)(d), or
- (c) to comply with subsections (5) and (6), each director to whom the failure is attributable is guilty of an offence.

(9) A private company limited by shares qualifies for an exemption from this section in respect of any financial year of the company if—

- (a) its balance sheet total for the year does not exceed—
  - (i) €7,618,428, or
  - (ii) if an amount is prescribed under section 48(1)(l) of the Act of 2003 for the purpose of this provision, the prescribed amount, and
- (b) the amount of its turnover for the year does not exceed—
  - (i) €15,236,856, or
  - (ii) if an amount is prescribed under section 48(1)(l) of the Act of 2003 for the purpose of this provision, the prescribed amount.][a]

Amendments

a C(AA)A 2003, s 45 inserts CA 1990, s 205E.

Notes

Under this new section, directors are required to prepare a compliance statement, containing certain information regarding the company, namely:

- (i) its policies in relation to compliance with its 'relevant obligations' (defined as the Companies Acts, tax law, and enactments within a legal framework in which the company operates and which could materially affect the company's financial statements);
- (ii) the procedures in place within the company to ensure compliance with these obligations; and
- (iii) the arrangements for implementing and reviewing the effectiveness of these policies and procedures.

In addition, directors must include in the report under s 158 of CA 1963 a statement acknowledging their responsibility for securing compliance by the company with its relevant obligations, confirming that the company has in place internal financial and any other necessary procedures designed to achieve compliance with relevant obligations and a confirmation that they have reviewed the effectiveness of these procedures.

If the company does not have such procedures in place or it has not conducted the review of effectiveness, the directors must give reasons for this.

This section has never been commenced and indeed provoked significant opposition from affected parties following its enactment. This opposition was based on cost, potential damage to competitiveness and the uncertainties which many believed were associated with the section. As a result, in April 2005, the Minister referred the section and the related proposed s 205F to the CLRG chaired by Dr Thomas B Courtney. The CLRG published its report on the issue late in 2005 following its deliberations and consultations on the issue. This report proposed a refined version of the requirements of s 205E which subsequently received Cabinet endorsement.

Consequently, neither s 205E or 205F will be commenced in their current form. Indeed, the revised proposal from the CLRG envisages no need for s 205F at all.

A copy of the CLRG report on this issue is available at http://www.clrg.org.

[205F Auditor's review of compliance statements and related statements

(1) The auditor of a company to which section 205E applies shall undertake an annual review of—

(a) the directors' compliance statement under subsections (3) and (4) of that section, and

(b) the directors' statement under subsections (5) and (6) of that section, to determine whether, in the auditor's opinion, each statement is fair and reasonable having regard to information obtained by the auditor, or by an affiliate of the auditor within the meaning of section 205D, in the course of and by virtue of having carried out audit work, audit-related work or non-audit work for the company.

(2) The auditor shall—

(a) include in the auditor's report appended to the company's annual accounts a report on, and the conclusions of, the review undertaken under subsection (1), and

(b) where any statement reviewed under subsection (1) is not, in the auditor's opinion, fair and reasonable—

(i) make a report to that effect to the directors, and

(ii) include that report in the auditor's report appended to the annual accounts.

(3) Where, in the auditor's opinion, the directors have failed—

(a) to prepare, or to cause to be prepared, a directors' compliance statement as required by section 205E(3) and (4)(a) to (c),

(b) to include a directors' compliance statement in the directors' report as required by section 205E(4)(d), or

(c) to comply with section 205E(5) and (6), the auditor shall report that opinion and the reasons for forming that opinion to the Director of Corporate Enforcement.

(4) Section 194(6) applies, with the necessary modifications, in relation to an auditor's compliance with an obligation imposed on him by or under this section as it applies in relation to an obligation imposed by or under section 194.

(5) A person who contravenes this section is guilty of an offence.][a]

Amendments

a C(AA)A 2003, s 45 inserts CA 1990, s 205F.

Notes

See notes to CA 1990, s 205E.

PART XI

ACQUISITION OF OWN SHARES AND SHARES IN HOLDING COMPANY

206 Interpretation

In this Part—

'the Act of 1983' means the Companies (Amendment) Act, 1983;

'company' means a company to which section 207 relates;

'distribution' has the meaning assigned to it by section 51(2) of the Act of 1983 (as amended by section 232 (d) and (e) of this Act);

'redeemable shares' includes shares which are liable at the option of the company or the shareholder to be redeemed.

Definitions

'share': CA 1963, s 2(1).

Notes

This Part updates the provisions of CA 1963 which permitted the creation, issue and redemption of redeemable preference shares only. It sets out the general prohibition on a company (or subsidiary) acquiring the company's own shares contained in C(A)A 1983, s 41(1). The principal changes made by this Part were to permit:

(i) the repurchase, as well as the redemption of shares;

(ii) the acquisition of any class of shares, not just preference shares;

(iii) the retention and reissue of repurchased shares as treasury shares;

(iv) unlike the UK, permitting the conversion of shares from non-redeemable to redeemable, and permitting acquisition of company shares by a subsidiary of the company.

The other methods whereby shares in a company may be cancelled are:

(i) by reduction of capital through the court under CA 1963, s 72;

(ii) by their being gifted to the company under C(A)A 1983, s 41(2).

The flexibility in corporate structuring created by this Part is inhibited by two factors. First, the provisions as to redeemable shares for all classes of limited company are built in enthusiastic obedience to the Second Company Law Directive 77/91/EEC of 13 December 1976 on 'the formation of public limited liability companies and the maintenance and alteration of their capital'. Provisions believed to be beneficial or appropriate of public companies are applied to all limited companies, including a confused application of a rule requiring that not more than 90% of a company's share capital ought to be redeemable.

Secondly, CA 1963, s 89, (which permits an application to the court to validate what might not be a valid allotment of shares) which is amended by this Part to apply to potentially invalid redemptions or repurchases of shares is rendered of very limited value by the strict qualifying criteria applied. In many cases where one might seek to validate a redemption or repurchase of shares, s 89 is unavailable.

Even if the shares are redeemable at the option of the member rather than at the option of the company, the enforceability of that option may be somewhat curtailed by the provisions of CA 1990, s 219 which:

(i) limits specific performance to situations where the company has sufficient distributable profits to fund the redemption; and

(ii) prevents any claim for damages in respect of the company's failure to redeem.

---

207 Power to issue redeemable shares

(1) Subject to the provisions of this Part, a company limited by shares or limited by guarantee and having a share capital may, if so authorised by its articles, issue redeemable shares and redeem them accordingly.

(2) The issue and redemption of shares by a company pursuant to subsection (1) shall be subject to the following conditions—

(a) No redeemable shares shall be issued or redeemed at any time when the nominal value of the issued share capital which is not redeemable is less than one tenth of the nominal value of the total issued share capital of the company.

(b) No such shares shall be redeemed unless they are fully paid.

(c) The terms of redemption must provide for payment on redemption.

(d) [(i) Subject to subparagraph (ii), no such shares shall be redeemed otherwise than—

(I) out of profits available for distribution, and

(II) if the company is a public limited company, in accordance with the restriction on the distribution of assets specified in section 46 of the Companies (Amendment) Act 1983.][a]

(ii) Where the company proposes to cancel shares on redemption pursuant to section 208, such shares may also be redeemed out of the proceeds of a fresh issue of shares made for the purposes of redemption.

(e) The premium, if any, payable on redemption, must, subject to paragraph (f), have been provided for out of the said profits of the company.

(f) Where the shares were issued at a premium, any premium payable on their redemption (being a redemption to which paragraph (d)(ii) applies) may be paid out of the proceeds of a fresh issue of shares made for the purposes of the redemption, up to an amount equal to—

(i) the aggregate of the premiums received by the company on the issue of the shares redeemed, or

(ii) the current amount of the company's share premium account (including any sum transferred to that account in respect of premiums on the new shares),

whichever is the less, and in any such case the amount of the company's share premium account shall, not withstanding anything in section 62(1) of the Principal Act, be reduced by a sum corresponding (or by sums in the aggregate corresponding) to the amount of any payment made by virtue of this paragraph out of the proceeds of the issue of the new shares.

(3) Subject to the provisions of this Part, the redemption of shares may be effected on such terms and in such manner as may be provided by the articles of the company.

Amendments

a CA 1990, s 207(d)(i) substituted by EC(PLC)R 2008, reg 4(a).

Cross reference

In relation to the profits available for distribution, see C(A)A 1983, Pt IV.

See CA 1963, s 62 in relation to the share premium account generally.

Definitions

'articles': CA 1963, s 2(1); 'the Principal Act': CA 1990, s 2(1); 'share': CA 1963, s 2(1).

Notes

No authorisation is contained in Table A or Table D as in s 207(i).

Section 207(a) seems to be trying to state that the amount of non-redeemable shares should not fall below 10%, but that is not what it says. It states that 'at any time when the nominal value of the issued share capital which is not redeemable is less than one tenth of the nominal value of the total issued share capital' no issues of redeemable shares may take place. It does not prohibit the issue of any amount of redeemable shares when the non-redeemable shares are in excess of 10%, even if such allotment results in the amount of the non-redeemable share capital falling below 10%. Indeed, the subsection applies only where 'the nominal value of the issued share capital which is not redeemable is less than one tenth of the nominal value of the total issued share capital', which presumes that it is legally possible to have such a situation.

The articles can provide that the terms of redemption are to be determined by the board of directors when initially issuing the shares.

It is legally permissible for a company to alter its articles of association even after going into liquidation so as to facilitate a redemption of shares.[1] Any such redemption would of course have to be in accordance with the normal rules as to priorities applicable to every winding up.

1 *Hague v Nam Tai Electronics Inc* [2007] 2 BCLC 194 at 199.

UK legislation

CA 1985, s 159A.

---

208 Cancellation of shares on redemption

Shares redeemed pursuant to this Part may be cancelled on redemption, in which case the following provisions shall apply as respects those shares:

(a) The amount of the company's issued share capital shall be reduced by the nominal value of the shares redeemed but no such cancellation shall be taken as reducing the amount of the company's authorised share capital.

(b) Where the shares are—

(i) redeemed wholly out of the profits available for distribution, or

(ii) redeemed wholly or partly out of the proceeds of a fresh issue and the aggregate amount of those proceeds (disregarding any part of those proceeds used to pay any premium on redemption) is less than the aggregate nominal value of the shares redeemed ('the aggregable difference'),

then a sum equal to, in the case of subparagraph (i), the nominal amount of the shares redeemed and, in the case of subparagraph (ii), the aggregable difference shall be transferred to a reserve fund ('the capital redemption reserve fund') and the provisions of the Principal Act relating to the reduction of the share capital of a company shall, except as provided in this section, apply as if the capital redemption reserve fund were paid-up share capital of the company.

(c) Where a company—

(i) has redeemed and cancelled shares, or

(ii) is about to redeem shares and cancel them upon redemption,

it shall have the power to issue shares up to the nominal amount of the shares redeemed or to be redeemed as if those shares had never been issued and for the purposes of [section 116 of the Stamp Duties Consolidation Act, 1999],[a] shares issued by a company in place of shares redeemed under this Part shall constitute a chargeable transaction if, but only if, the actual value of the shares so issued exceeds the actual value of the shares redeemed at the date of their redemption and, where the issue of shares does constitute a chargeable transaction for those purposes, the amount on which stamp duty on the relevant statement relating to that transaction is chargeable under [section 117 of the Stamp Duties Consolidation Act, 1999],[a] shall be the difference between—

(I) the amount on which the duty would be so chargeable if the shares had not been issued in place of shares redeemed under this section, and

(II) the value of the shares redeemed at the date of their redemption.

(d) Where new shares are issued before the redemption of the old shares, the new shares shall not, so far as relates to stamp duty, be deemed to have been issued in pursuance of paragraph (c) unless the old shares are redeemed within one month after the issue of the new shares.

(e) The capital redemption reserve fund may, notwithstanding anything in this section, be applied by the company in paying up unissued shares of the company (other than redeemable shares) to be allotted to members of the company as fully paid bonus shares.

Amendments

a Amended by SDCA 1999, s 162 which came into effect on 15 December 1999.

Cross reference

In relation to the reduction of the share capital of companies see generally CA 1963, ss 72–77.

Definitions

'member': CA 1963, s 31; 'the Principal Act': CA 1990, s 2(1); 'share': CA 1963, s 2(1).

Notes

Such reduction in the issued share capital does not require shareholder approval or court confirmation under CA 1963, s 72.

The reason for transferring to the capital redemption reserve account a sum equal to the amount of any distributable profits used for the redemption is to ensure that the amount of the capital in the company's balance sheet remains the same despite the redemption (ie the amount of the redeemed shares is replaced either in whole by an equivalent sum in the capital redemption reserve account or alternatively is replaced in part by the sum transferred to the capital redemption reserve account and in part by a fresh issue of shares).

The stamp duty referred to here is companies capital duty, the charge to which on allotments of shares made on or after 7 December 2006 was abolished by the Finance Act 2006, s 110a. Therefore, the text in paragraph (c) commencing 'and for the purposes of section 68 of the Finance Act, 1973 … together with paragraph (d) can be considered spent.

In converting the capital redemption reserve account into fully paid bonus shares, the amount of the capital in the company's balance sheet remains the same.

UK legislation

See CA 1985, s 160 (amended by CA 1989, s 133).

---

209 Treasury shares

(1) Subject to the provisions of this section, a company may instead of cancelling shares upon their redemption hold them (as 'treasury shares') and shares so held may be dealt with by the company in the manner provided for in subsection (4) but not otherwise.

(2) (a) The nominal value of treasury shares held by a company may not, at any one time, exceed ten per cent of the nominal value of the issued share capital of the company.

(b) For the purposes of paragraph (a), the following shall also be deemed to be shares held by the company—

(i) shares held in the company by any subsidiary in pursuance of section 224, and

(ii) shares held in the company by any subsidiary in pursuance of section 9 of the Insurance Act, 1990, and

(iii) shares held in the company by any person acting in his own name but on the company's behalf.

(3) For so long as the company holds shares as treasury shares—

(a) the company shall not exercise any voting rights in respect of those shares and any purported exercise of those rights shall be void; and

(b) no dividend or other payment (including any payment in a winding up of the company) shall be payable to the company in respect of those shares.

(4) Treasury shares may either be—

(a) cancelled by the company in which case the provisions of section 208 shall apply as if the shares had been cancelled on redemption, or

(b) subject to subsections (5) and (6), may be re-issued as shares of any class or classes.

(5) A re-issue of shares under this section shall be deemed for all the purposes of the Companies Acts to be an issue of shares but the issued share capital of the company shall not be regarded for any purpose (including the purposes of any enactments relating to stamp duties) as having been increased by the re-issue of the shares.

(6) (a) The maximum and minimum prices at which treasury shares may be re-issued off-market ('the re-issue price range') shall be determined in advance by the company in general meeting in accordance with paragraphs (b), (c) and (d) and such determination may fix different maximum and minimum prices for different shares.

(b) Where the treasury shares to be re-issued are derived in whole or in part from shares purchased by the company in accordance with the provisions of this Part the re-issue price range of the whole or such part (as the case may be) of those shares shall be determined by special resolution of the company passed at the meeting at which the resolution authorising the said purchase has been passed and such determination shall, for the purposes of this subsection, remain effective with respect to those shares for the requisite period.

(c) Where the treasury shares to be re-issued are derived in whole or in part from shares redeemed by the company in accordance with the provisions of this Part the re-issue price range of the whole or such part (as the case may be) of those shares shall be determined by special resolution of the company passed before any contract for the re-issue of those shares is entered into and such determination shall, for the purposes of this subsection, remain effective with respect to those shares for the requisite period.

(d) The company may from time to time by special resolution vary or renew a determination of re-issue price range under paragraph (b) or (c) with respect to particular treasury shares before any contract for re-issue of those shares is entered into and any such variation or renewal shall, for the purposes of this subsection, remain effective as a determination of the re-issue price range of those shares for the requisite period.

(e) (i) For the purposes of determining in this subsection whether treasury shares are re-issued off-market, the provisions of section 212 (off-market and market purchases) shall have effect with the substitution of the words 're-issue', 'off-market re-issue' and 'reissued' respectively for the words 'purchase', 'off market purchase' and 'purchased' in subsection (1)(a) of that section.

(ii) In this subsection, 'the requisite period' means the period of eighteen months from the date of the passing of the resolution determining the re-issue price range or varying or renewing (as the case may be) such determination or such lesser period of time as the resolution may specify.

(7) A re-issue by a company of treasury shares in contravention of any of the provisions of subsection (6) shall be unlawful.

Cross reference

In relation to the purchase of shares by the company see CA 1990, ss 212–218.

See CA 1990, s 224(2)(b)(iii) which provides similarly that votes on shares held by subsidiaries are similarly suspended.

Definitions

'Companies Acts': CA 1990, s 3(1); 'contravention': CA 1990, s 3(1); 'share' CA 1963, s 2(1).

Notes

Where the company holds the shares as treasury shares instead of cancelling them, it becomes a member of itself.

Suspending the voting rights on the treasury shares prevents the directors, inter alia, from exercising those votes to keep themselves in office.

In the case of shares which have been purchased under CA 1990, ss 212–218 it would seem therefore that they can only be re-issued off-market if the re-issue price range was determined by special resolution at the same time as the original authorisation to purchase the shares. If the re-issue price range was not so fixed then presumably the company is limited either to Re-issuing them on the stock exchange or alternatively to cancelling them under CA 1990, s 208.

UK legislation

CA 1985, ss 162A–162G, inserted by SI 2003/1116.

---

210 Power to convert shares into redeemable shares

(1) Subject to subsections (2), (3), (4) and (5) and the provisions of the Companies Acts governing the variation of rights attached to classes of shares and the alteration of a company's memorandum or articles, a company may convert any of its shares into redeemable shares.

(2) A conversion of shares under subsection (1) shall not have effect with respect to any shares, the holder of which notifies the company, before the date of conversion, of his unwillingness to have his shares converted but, subject to that and the other provisions of this section, the conversion shall have effect according to its terms.

(3) Subsection (2) shall not, where a shareholder objects to a conversion, prejudice any right he may have under the Companies Acts or otherwise to invoke the jurisdiction of the court to set aside the conversion or otherwise provide relief in respect thereof.

(4) No shares shall be converted into redeemable shares if as a result of the conversion the nominal value of the issued share capital which is not redeemable would be less than one tenth of the nominal value of the total issued share capital of the company.

(5) The provisions of sections 207, 208 and 209, shall apply to shares which have been converted into redeemable shares under this section.

Cross reference

See C(A)A 1983, s 38 for the entitlement of a dissenting shareholder to apply to the court for relief in respect of the variation of rights attaching to shares occasioned by a conversion.

Definitions

'articles': CA 1963, s 2(1); 'Companies Acts': CA 1990, s 3(1); 'court': CA 1990, s 235; 'memorandum': CA 1963, s 2(1); 'share': CA 1963, s 2(1).

Notes

Subject perhaps to provisions in a company's articles of association to the contrary, the notice of unwillingness to have one's shares converted may be given orally or in writing. The notice can therefore be given at the meeting at which the requisite resolution is passed authorising the conversion of shares.

---

211 Power of company to purchase own shares

(1) Subject to [subsection (4) and][a] the following provisions of this Part, a company may, if so authorised by its articles, purchase its own shares (including any redeemable shares).

(2) Sections 207 (2), 208 and 209 shall apply in relation to the purchase by a company under this section of any of its own shares as those sections apply in relation to the redemption of shares by a company under section 207.

(3) A company shall not purchase any of its shares under this section if as a result of such purchase the nominal value of the issued share capital which is not redeemable would be less than one tenth of the nominal value of the total issued share capital of the company.

[(4) This section has effect without prejudice to—

(a) the principle of equal treatment of all shareholders who are in the same position,

(b) the Market Abuse (Directive 2003/6/EC) Regulations 2005 (S.I. No. 342 of 2005), and

(c) Part 4 of the Investment Funds, Companies and Miscellaneous Provisions Act 2005.][b]

Amendments

a Words inserted by EC(PLC)R 2008, reg 4(b)(i).

b CA 1990, s 211(4) inserted by EC(PLC)R 2008, reg 4(b)(ii).

Definitions

'articles': CA 1963, s 2(1); 'share': CA 1963, s 2(1).

Notes

Authorisation, as per s 211(1), is not contained in Table A or Table D.

A purchase of redeemable shares might take place, for example, where the company wished to cancel the shares before the due redemption date.

UK legislation

See CA 1985, s 162 (amended by CA 1989, s 133).

---

212 Off-market and market purchases

(1) For the purposes of sections 213 and 215, a purchase by a company of its own shares is—

(a) an 'off-market purchase' if the shares are purchased either—

(i) otherwise than on a recognised stock exchange, or

(ii) on a recognised stock exchange but are not subject to a marketing arrangement on that stock exchange,

(b) a 'market purchase' if the shares are purchased on a recognised stock exchange [within the State][a] and are subject to a marketing arrangement.

[(1A) For the purposes of sections 215, 226, 226A and 229, a purchase by a company that issues shares, or by a subsidiary of that company, of the first-mentioned company's shares, is an 'overseas market purchase' if the shares are purchased on a recognised stock exchange outside the State and are subject to a marketing arrangement.][b]

(2) For the purposes of [subsections (1) and (1A)][c], a company's shares are subject to a marketing arrangement on a recognised stock exchange if either—

(a) they are listed on that stock exchange, or

(b) the company has been afforded facilities for dealings in those shares to take place on that stock exchange without prior permission for individual transactions from the authority governing that stock exchange and without limit as to the time during which those facilities are to be available.

Amendments

a Words 'within the State' inserted by C(MP)A 2009, s 3(d)(i).

b Subsection (1A) inserted by C(MP)A 2009, s 3(d)(ii).

c Words 'subsections (1) and (1A)' substituted for 'subsection (1)' by C(MP)A 2009, s 3(d)(iii).

Definitions

'recognised stock exchange': CA 1990, s 3(1), (2); 'share': CA 1963, s 2(1).

Notes

In consequence of the amendment effected to this provision by C(MP)A 2009, s 3(d)(i)–(iii), it is now recognised that a company can purchase its own shares arising from an 'off-market purchase', a 'market purchase' within the State or an 'overseas market purchase' outside of the State.

UK legislation

See CA 1985, s 163 (amended by FSA 1986, s 212, Sch 16).

---

213 Authority for off-market purchase

(1) A company shall not make an off-market purchase of its own shares otherwise than in pursuance of a contract authorised in advance in accordance with this section.

(2) The terms of the proposed contract of purchase shall be authorised by special resolution before the contract is entered into and any such authority may be varied, revoked or from time to time renewed by special resolution.

(3) A special resolution under subsection (2) shall not be effective for the purposes of this section if any member of the company holding shares to which the resolution relates exercises the voting rights carried by any of those shares in voting on the resolution and the resolution would not have been passed if he had not done so.

(4) Notwithstanding anything contained in section 137 of the Principal Act or in a company's articles, any member of the company may demand a poll on a special resolution under subsection (2).

(5) A special resolution under subsection (2) shall not be effective unless a copy of the proposed contract of purchase or, if the contract is not in writing, a written memorandum of its terms is available for inspection by members of the company both—

(a) at the registered office of the company for not less than the period of 21 days ending with the date of the meeting at which the resolution is passed, and

(b) at the meeting itself.

(6) Any memorandum of the terms of the contract of purchase made available for the purposes of this section must include the names of any members holding shares to which the contract relates, and any copy of the contract made available for those purposes must have annexed to it a written memorandum specifying any such names which do not appear in the contract itself.

(7) A company may agree to a variation of an existing contract of purchase approved under this section only if the variation is authorised by special resolution of the company before it is agreed to, and subsections (2) to (5) shall apply in relation to that authority save that a copy or memorandum (as the case may require) of the existing contract must also be available for inspection in accordance with subsection (5).

Definitions

'articles': CA 1963, s 2(1); 'member': CA 1963, s 32l; 'the Principal Act': CA 1990, s 3(1); 'share': CA 1963, s 2(1).

Notes

Subsection 213(1) is somewhat misleading since an off-market purchase could still take place pursuant to CA 1963, ss 10, 28, 72, 205 or pursuant to C(A)A 1983, s 15.

If the company wishes to be entitled to re-issue the shares off-market then the members must at the same time pass a special resolution fixing the re-issue price range: CA 1990, s 209(6)(a)(b).

The requirement for the contract of purchase to be available for inspection for 21 days means in effect that it is not possible to abridge the time for passing the resolution by consent to short notice. In practice, where all shareholders are in agreement, the way around this unhelpful provision is to convert the to-be-purchased shares to redeemable and to redeem them accordingly.

Any payment made by the company in consideration of the variation of a contract for the purchase of its own shares will be unlawful unless made out of distributable profits: CA 1990, s 218.

UK legislation

See CA 1985, s 164.

---

214 Contingent purchase contract

(1) In this section 'contingent purchase contract' means a contract entered into by a company and relating to any of its shares which does not amount to a contract to purchase those shares but under which the company may become entitled or obliged to purchase those shares.

(2) A company shall only make a purchase of its own shares in pursuance of a contingent purchase contract if the terms of the contract have been authorised by a special resolution of the company before the contract is entered into and subsections (2) to (7) of section 213 shall apply to such contract and resolution.

Cross reference

See CA 1990, s 30 in relation to the prohibition against directors and shadow directors purchasing call or put options over shares which are admitted to trading on the Irish Stock Exchange. Note however that a director may subject himself to a call option or put option on the part of the company to compel disposal or acquisition of the shares in question.

Definitions

'share': CA 1963, s 2(1).

Notes

Any payment made by the company in consideration of acquiring an option to purchase its own shares will be unlawful unless made out of distributable profits: CA 1990, s 218.

UK legislation

See CA 1985, s 165.

215 Authority for market purchase

(1) A company shall not make a market purchase [or overseas market purchase][a] of its own shares unless the purchase has first been authorised by the company in general meeting and any such authority may be varied, revoked or from time to time renewed by the company in general meeting. This subsection shall not be construed as requiring any particular contract for the market purchase [or overseas market purchase][a] of shares to be authorised by the company in general meeting and for the purposes of this Part where a market purchase [or overseas market purchase][a] of shares has been authorised in accordance with this section any contract entered into pursuant to that authority in respect of such a purchase shall be deemed also to be so authorised.

(2) Section 143 of the Principal Act shall apply to a resolution under subsection (1).

(3) In the case of a public limited company, any authority granted under subsection (1) shall—

(a) specify the maximum number of shares authorised to be acquired; and

(b) determine both the maximum and minimum prices which may be paid for the shares.

(4) A resolution to which subsection (3) applies may determine either or both the prices mentioned in paragraph (b) of that subsection by—

(a) specifying a particular sum; or

(b) providing a basis or formula for calculating the amount of the price in question without reference to any person's discretion or opinion.

Amendments

a Words 'or overseas market purchase' inserted by C(MP)A 2009, s 3(e).

Definitions

'the Principal Act': CA 1990, s 3(1); 'share': CA 1963, s 2(1).

Notes

Under the Act, an ordinary resolution will suffice in order to authorise a market purchase or overseas market purchase of shares. For the duration of such an authorisation see CA 1990, s 216. If the company wishes to be entitled to re-issue off-market then the members must at the same time pass a special resolution fixing the re-issue price range: CA 1990, s 209(6)(a),(b). However, in the case of Irish public companies admitted to trading on any of the Irish Stock Exchange's markets, regard should be had to the Guidelines of the Irish Association of Investment Managers on Acquisition of Own Shares of July 1992. These provide that the articles of association of a company to which the guidelines apply should 'provide that the authority for a company to make market purchases of its own shares under Part XI of the Companies Act 1990, should be conferred by special resolution and not an ordinary resolution as is permitted by Section 215 of the Act.'

Section 215(2) states that despite being an ordinary resolution, it must be filed with the registrar of companies.

It is difficult to envisage how s 215 could apply to any type of company other than a plc since Part XI applies only to companies limited by shares or limited by guarantee and having a share capital. Thus the only companies other than plcs to which Part XI applies are private companies. In this regard, the shares of private companies are not traded on the stock exchange so that the possibility of a market purchase or overseas market purchase of shares in a private company would not arise.

UK legislation

See CA 1985, s 166.

216 Duration of authority granted by public limited companies to purchase own shares

(1) Without prejudice to the generality of sections 213, 214 and 215, in the case of a public limited company, any authority granted under those sections shall specify the date on which the authority is to expire which shall not be later than 18 months after the date on which the special resolution or ordinary resolution, as the case may be, granting the authority is passed.

(2) A public limited company may make a purchase after the expiry of any time limit imposed by virtue of subsection (1) in any case where the contract of purchase was concluded before the authority expired and the terms of the authority permit the company to make a contract of purchase which would or might be executed wholly or partly after the authority expired.

Definitions

'share': CA 1963, s 2(1).

Notes

In the case of off-market purchases by private companies, there is no statutory time limit on the duration of the authorisation.

UK legislation

See CA 1985, s 166.

217 Assignment or release of company's right to purchase own shares

(1) Any purported assignment of the rights of a company under any contract authorised under section 213, 214 or 215 shall be void.

(2) Nothing in subsection (1) shall prevent a company from releasing its right under any contract authorised under section 213, 214 or 215 provided that, in the case of a contract authorised under section 213 or 214, the release has been authorised by special resolution of the company before the release is entered into, and any such purported release by a company which has not been authorised as aforesaid shall be void.

(3) Subsections (2) to (7) of section 213, shall apply to a resolution under subsection (2).

Definitions

'share': CA 1963, s 2(1).

Notes

Once a purchase has been authorised, only the company itself may acquire the shares. It cannot assign the right to acquire the shares to a third party as a means of simply effecting a transfer of shares from one shareholder to another.

Any payment made by the company in consideration of obtaining a release of any of its obligations with respect to the purchase of any of its shares will be unlawful unless made out of distributable profits: CA 1990, s 218.

UK legislation

See CA 1985, s 167.

218 Incidental payments with respect to purchase of own shares

(1) Any payment made by a company in consideration of—

(a) acquiring any right with respect to the purchase of its own shares in pursuance of a contract authorised under section 214, or

(b) the variation of a contract authorised under section 213 or 214, or

(c) the release of any of the company's obligations with respect to the purchase of any of its own shares under a contract authorised under section 213, 214 or 215

shall be unlawful if any such payment is made otherwise than out of distributable profits of the company.

(2) If the requirements of subsection (1) are not satisfied in relation to a contract—

(a) in a case to which paragraph (a) of that subsection applies, no purchase by the company of its own shares in pursuance of that contract shall be lawful under this Part;

(b) in a case to which paragraph (b) of that subsection applies, no such purchase following the variation shall be lawful under this Part; and

(c) in a case to which paragraph (c) of that subsection applies, the purported release shall be void.

Cross reference

In relation to the profits available for distribution see C(A)A 1983, Pt IV.

Definitions

'share': CA 1963, s 2(1).

UK legislation

See CA 1985, s 168.

---

219 Effect of company's failure to redeem or purchase

(1) This section applies to—

(a) redeemable shares issued after the coming into operation of this Part;

(b) shares which have been converted into redeemable shares pursuant to section 210; and

(c) shares which a company has agreed to purchase pursuant to section 213, 214 or 215.

(2) Without prejudice to any other right of the holder of any shares to which this section applies a company shall not be liable in damages in respect of any failure on its part to redeem or purchase any such shares.

(3) The court shall not grant an order for specific performance of the terms of redemption or purchase of the shares to which this section applies if the company shows that it is unable to meet the cost of redeeming or purchasing the shares out of profits available for distribution.

(4) Where at the commencement of the winding up of a company any shares to which this section applies have not been redeemed or purchased then, subject to subsections (5), (6) and (7), the terms of redemption or purchase may be enforced against the company and the shares when so redeemed or purchased under this subsection shall be treated as cancelled.

(5) Subsection (4) shall not apply if—

(a) the terms of redemption or purchase provided for the redemption or purchase to take place at a date later than that of the commencement of the winding-up, or

(b) during the period beginning with the date on which the redemption or purchase was to have taken place and ending with the commencement of the winding-up the company could not at any time have lawfully made a distribution equal in value to the price at which the shares were to have been redeemed or purchased.

(6) There shall be paid in priority to any amount for which the company is liable by virtue of subsection (4) to pay in respect of any shares—

(a) all other debts and liabilities of the company other than any due to members in their character as such, and

(b) if other shares carry rights, whether as to capital or to income, which are preferred to the rights as to capital attaching to the first mentioned shares, any amount due in satisfaction of those preferred rights,

but subject as aforesaid, any such amount shall be paid in priority to any amounts due to members in satisfaction of their rights (whether as to capital or income) as members.

(7) Where by virtue of the application by section 284 of the Principal Act of the rules of bankruptcy in the winding-up of insolvent companies a creditor of a company is entitled to payment of any interest only after payment of all other debts of the company, the company's debts and liabilities shall for the purposes of subsection (6) include the liability to pay that interest.

Cross reference

In relation to the profits available for distribution, see C(A)A 1983, Pt IV.

For the date of commencement of the winding up, see CA 1963, ss 220, 253.

Definitions

'court': CA 1990, s 235; 'member': CA 1963, s 2(1); 'Principal Act': CA 1990, s 3(1); 'share': CA 1963, s 2(1).

Notes

Although precluded from suing for damages, the shareholder might petition under CA 1963, s 205 for an order that the company acquire his shares, on the ground that the company's original failure to redeem or purchase his shares was oppressive or in disregard of his interests as member of the company.

The redemption or purchase of the shares would only have been lawful if the price could have been paid either out of distributable profits or (in a case where the shares were to be cancelled upon redemption or purchase) out of the proceeds of a fresh issue of shares made for that purpose: CA 1990, ss 207(2), 211(2).

Debts due to a member in his character as such would include dividends declared but not paid. See CA 1963, s 207(1)(g) and *Re Imperial Hotel (Cork)* [1950] IR 115.

With regard to the entitlement to claim interest in the liquidation of an insolvent company see Bankruptcy Act 1988, Sch 1, para 14, as applied by CA 1963, s 284 and *Re International Contract Co Ltd Hughes' Claim* [1872] LR 13 Eq 623.

UK legislation

See CA 1985, s 178.

---

220 Redemption of existing redeemable preference shares

Section 64 of the Principal Act is hereby repealed but any redeemable preference shares issued by a company limited by shares before the coming into operation of this Part which could but for the repeal of section 64 have been redeemed under that section shall be subject to redemption in accordance with the provisions of this Part save that any premium payable on redemption may, notwithstanding section 207(2)(e) and (f), be paid out of the share premium account instead of out of profits or may be paid partly out of that account and partly out of profits available for distribution.

Definitions

'Principal Act': CA 1990, s 3(1); 'share': CA 1963, s 2(1).

UK legislation

See CA 1985, s 180.

221 Construction of references to redeemable preference shares

A reference to redeemable preference shares in—

(a) section 69(1)(e) of, and the Second, Third, Fourth and Sixth Schedules to, the Principal Act, and

(b) section 55(1)(h) of the Act of 1983,

shall be construed as a reference to redeemable shares.

Cross reference

See also the Schedule to C(A)A 1986.

Definitions

'Principal Act': CA 1990, s 3(1); 'share': CA 1963, s 2(1).

222 Retention and inspection of documents

(1) Every company which enters into a contract under section 213, 214 or 215 shall, until the expiration of ten years after the contract has been fully performed, keep at its registered office a copy of that contract or, if it is not in writing, a memorandum of its terms.

(2) Every document required to be kept under subsection (1) shall during business hours (subject to such reasonable restrictions as the company in general meeting may impose, so that not less than 2 hours in each day be allowed for inspection) be open to the inspection of any member and, if the company is a public limited company, of any other person.

(3) If a company fails to comply with this section, the company and every officer of the company who is in default shall be guilty of an offence.

(4) In the case of a refusal of an inspection of a document required under subsection (2), the court may, on the application of a person who has requested an inspection and has been refused, by order require the company to allow the inspection of that document.

Definitions

'court' CA 1990, s 235; 'member': CA 1963, s 31; 'officer': CA 1963, s 2(1); 'officer in default': CA 1963, s 383.

UK legislation

See CA 1985, s 169 (as amended by CA 1989, ss 143, 212, Sch 24).

223 Application of section 108(6) to dealings by company in its own securities

Subsection (6) of section 108, in its application to dealings by a company in its own securities, shall not preclude a company from dealing in its own shares at any time by reason only of information in the possession of an officer of that company if—

(a) the decision to enter into the transaction was taken on its behalf by a person other than the officer, and

(b) the information was not communicated to that person and no advice relating to the transaction was given to him by a person in possession of the information.

Definitions

'share': CA 1963, s 2(1).

224 Holding by subsidiary of shares in its holding company

(1) Notwithstanding sections 32 and 60 of the Principal Act a company may, subject to the provisions of this section, acquire and hold shares in a company which is its holding company.

(2) The acquisition and holding by a subsidiary under subsection (1) of shares in its holding company shall be subject to the following conditions:

(a) The consideration for the acquisition of such shares shall be provided for out of the profits of the subsidiary available for distribution

(b) Upon the acquisition of such shares and for so long as the shares are held by the subsidiary—

(i) the profits of the subsidiary available for distribution shall for all purposes be restricted by a sum equal to the total cost of the shares acquired;

(ii) the shares shall, for the purposes of the consolidated accounts prepared by the holding company in accordance with sections 150 to 152 of The Principal Act, be treated in the same manner as is required in respect of shares held as treasury shares under section 43A of the Act of 1983 (inserted by section 232(c) of this Act); and.

(iii) the subsidiary shall not exercise any voting rights in respect of the shares and any purported exercise of those rights shall be void.

(3) A contract for the acquisition (whether by allotment or transfer) by a subsidiary of shares in its holding company shall not be entered into without being authorised in advance both by the subsidiary and its holding company and the provisions of sections 212 to 217 shall apply, with the necessary modifications, to the granting, variation, revocation and release of such authority.

(4) For the purposes of this section, a subsidiary's profits available for distribution shall not include the profits attributable to any shares in the subsidiary for the time being held

by the subsidiary's holding company so far as they are profits for the period before the date on or from which the shares were acquired by the holding company.

(5) This section shall not apply to shares held by a subsidiary in its holding company in the circumstances permitted by section 32 of the Principal Act.

(6) This section, except subsection (2)(b)(iii), shall not apply to shares subscribed for, purchased or held by a subsidiary in its holding company pursuant to section 9(1) of the Insurance Act, 1990.

Cross reference

In relation to profits available for distribution, see C(A)A 1983, Pt IV.

Definitions

'holding company': CA 1963, s 155; 'Principal Act': CA 1990, s 3(1); 'share': CA 1963, s 2(1); 'subsidiary': CA 1963, s 155.

Notes

Regulation 4 of SI 67/1997 widens the definition of 'company' where it first appears in subsection (1) of this section to include any body corporate.

Effectively, according to s 224(1) the shares held by the subsidiary in its holding company are treated as part of the capital of the subsidiary itself.

The shares are not to be shown in the balance sheet as an asset, but the deduction of the cost of the shares from the profits available for distribution and the nominal value of the shares must be disclosed in the notes to the accounts.

Removing the voting rights in respect of such shares prevents the directors of the holding company, inter alia, from controlling the exercise of those votes to keep themselves in office.

Subsection (4) prevents what would otherwise be a rather circular situation whereby the subsidiary returned to the holding company by way of dividend profits made by the holding company itself.

225 Civil liability for improper purchase in holding company

(1) Where the winding-up of a company which has acquired shares in its holding company in accordance with section 224 commences within six months after such acquisition and the company is at the time of the commencement of the winding-up unable to pay its debts (taking into account the contingent and prospective liabilities),the court, on the application of a liquidator, creditor, employee or contributory of the company, may subject to subsection (2), declare that the directors of the company shall be jointly and severally liable to repay to the company the total amount paid by the company for the shares.

(2) Where it appears to the court that any person in respect of whom a declaration has been sought under subsection (1) believed on reasonable grounds that the said purchase was in the best interests of the company, the court may relieve him, either wholly or in part, from personal liability on such terms as it may think fit.

Cross reference

For the date of the commencement of the winding up, see CA 1963, ss 220, 253.

For the definition of 'inability to pay debts', see CA 1963, s 214.

Definitions

'contributory': CA 1963, s 2(1), s 208; 'court': CA 1990, s 235; 'director': CA 1963, s 2(1); 'holding company': CA 1963, s 155; 'share': CA 1963, s 2(1).

226 Return to be made to registrar

(1) Every company which has purchased shares pursuant to this Part shall, within 28 days [or, in the case of an overseas market purchase, within 3 working days,][a] after delivery to the company of those shares, deliver to the registrar for registration a return in the prescribed form stating with respect to shares of each class purchased the number and nominal value of those shares and the date on which they were delivered to the company.

(2) In the case of a public limited company, the return shall also state—

(a) the aggregate amount paid by the company for the shares, and

(b) the maximum and minimum prices paid in respect of each class purchased.

(3) Particulars of shares delivered to the company on different dates and under different contracts may be included in a single return to the registrar, and in such a case the amount required to be stated under subsection (2)(a) shall be the aggregate amount paid by the company for all the shares to which the return relates.

(4) If a company fails to comply with the requirements of this section, the company and every officer who is in default shall be guilty of an offence.

(5) Summary proceedings in relation to an offence under this section may be brought and prosecuted by the registrar of companies.

Amendments

a Words 'or, in the case of an overseas market purchase, within 3 working days,' inserted by C(MP)A 2009, s 3(e).

Definitions

'officer': CA 1963, s 2(1); 'officer in default': CA 1963, s 383; 'registrar of companies' CA 1963, s 2(1); 'share': CA 1963, s 2(1).

UK legislation

See CA 1985, s 169.

[226A Duty of company to publish particulars of overseas market purchase

(1) Whenever shares for which dealing facilities are provided on a recognised stock exchange are the subject of an overseas market purchase either by the company which issued the shares or by a company which is that company's subsidiary, the company which issued the shares shall publish, on its website for a continuous period of not less than 28 days beginning on the day that next follows the overseas market purchase concerned and is a day on which the recognised stock exchange concerned is open for business, or in any other prescribed manner, the following information for total purchases on the recognised stock market concerned on each such day:

(a) the date, in the place outside the State where the recognised stock market concerned is located, of the overseas market purchase;

(b) the purchase price at which the shares were purchased, or the highest such price and lowest such price paid by that company or subsidiary;

(c) the number of shares which were purchased;

(d) the recognised stock exchange on which the shares were purchased.

(2) If default is made in complying with this section, the company and every officer of the company who is in default shall be guilty of an offence.][a]

Amendments

a CA 1990, s 226A inserted by C(MP)A 2009, s 3(g).

227 Amendment of section 89 of the Principal Act

[...][a]

Amendments

a This section substitutes CA 1963, s 89.

228 Regulations as to purchase of shares

(1) The Minister may make regulations governing the purchase by companies of their own shares or of shares in their holding company and the sale by companies of their own shares held as treasury shares and such regulations may relate to companies in general or to a particular category or class of company.

(2) Without prejudice to the generality of subsection (1), regulations under this section may provide for in particular—

(a) the class or description of shares which may (or may not) be purchased or sold,

(b) the price at which they may be purchased or sold,

(c) the timing of such purchases or sales,

(d) the method by which the shares may be purchased or sold, and

(e) the volume of trading in the shares which may be carried out by companies.

(3) If a company fails to comply with the provisions of regulations made under this section, the company and every officer who is in default shall be guilty of an offence.

Definitions

'Minister': CA 1990, s 3(1); 'officer': CA 1963, s 2(1); 'officer in default': CA 1963, s 383; 'share': CA 1963, s 2(1).

Notes

To date no regs such as s 228(1) have been made.

UK legislation

See CA 1985, s 179.

229 Duty of company to notify stock exchange

(1) Whenever shares for which dealing facilities are provided on a recognised stock exchange have been purchased either by the company which issued the shares or by a company which is that company's subsidiary[, other than when the purchase was an overseas market purchase,][a] the company whose shares have been purchased shall be under an obligation to notify that stock exchange of that matter; and the stock exchange may publish, in such manner as it may determine, any information received by it under this subsection.

(2) An obligation imposed by subsection (1) shall be fulfilled before the end of the day next following that on which it arises.

(3) If default is made in complying with this section, the company and every officer of the company who is in default shall be guilty of an offence.

Amendments

a Words ', other than when the purchase was an overseas market purchase,' inserted by C(MP)A 2009, s 3(h).

Definitions

'officer': CA 1963, s 2(1); 'officer in default': CA 1963, s 383; 'recognised stock exchange': CA 1990, s 3(1), (2); 'share': CA 1963, s 2(1); 'subsidiary': CA 1963, s 155.

Notes

The Irish Stock Exchange is prescribed as a recognised stock exchange for the purposes of CA 1990, s 229: the Companies (Stock Exchange) Regulations1995 (SI 310/1995).

230 Duty of stock exchange in relation to unlawful purchases

(1) If it appears to a relevant authority of a recognised stock exchange that a company in the case of whose shares dealing facilities have been provided on that stock exchange has committed an offence under section 228 or 229, such authority shall forthwith report the matter to the [Director][a] and shall furnish to the [Director][a] such information and give to him such access to and facilities for inspecting and taking copies of any documents, being information or documents in the possession or under the control of such authority and relating to the matter in question, as the [Director][a] may require.

(2) Where it appears to a member of a recognised stock exchange that any person has committed an offence under section 228 or 229 he shall report the matter forthwith to a relevant authority of the recognised stock exchange concerned, who shall thereupon come under the duty referred to in subsection (1).

(3) If it appears to a court in any proceedings that any person has committed an offence as aforesaid, and that no report relating to the matter has been made to the [Director][a] under subsection (1), that court may, on the application of any person interested in the proceedings concerned or of its own motion, direct the relevant authority of the

recognised stock exchange concerned to make such a report, and on a report being made accordingly, this section shall have effect as though the report had been made in pursuance of subsection (1).

[(4) If, where any matter is reported or referred to the Director under this section, he has reasonable grounds for believing that an offence under section 228 or 229 has been committed and—

(a) institutes proceedings in respect of the offence, or

(b) refers the matter to the Director of Public Prosecutions and the Director of Public Prosecutions institutes proceedings in respect of the offence,

it shall be the duty of a relevant authority of the recognised stock exchange concerned, and of every officer of the company whose shares are concerned, and of any other person who appears to the Director or to the Director of Public Prosecutions, as the case may be, to have relevant information (other than any defendant in the proceedings) to give all assistance in connection with the proceedings which he or they are reasonably able to give.][b]

(5) If it appears to the [Director],[c] arising from a complaint to a relevant authority of a recognised stock exchange concerning an alleged offence under section 228 or 229, that there are circumstances suggesting that—

(a) the relevant authority ought to use its powers under this section but has not done so, or

(b) that a report ought to be made to the [Director][a] under subsection (1), but that the relevant authority concerned has not so reported,

he may request the relevant authority to use such powers or make such a report, and on a report being made accordingly, this section shall have effect as though the report had been made in pursuance of subsection (1).

[…][d]

(7) A relevant authority of a recognised stock exchange shall not be liable in damages in respect of anything done or omitted to be done by the authority in connection with the exercise by it of its functions under this section unless the act or omission complained of was done or omitted to be done in bad faith.

(8) For the purposes of this section each of the following shall be a 'relevant authority' in relation to a recognised stock exchange—

(i) its board of directors, committee of management or other management body,

(ii) its manager, however described.

(9) A relevant authority shall have the same powers and duties for the purposes of this section as it has under sections 117 and 120.

(10) Where the Minister considers it necessary or expedient to do so for the proper and effective administration of this section, he may make such regulations 4d as he thinks appropriate in relation to—

(a) the powers of authorised persons, or

(b) the matters in respect of which, or the persons from whom, authorised persons may require information under section 117, as applied by subsection (9).

Amendments

a CLEA 2001, s 39(a) amends CA 1990, s 230 by the substitution for 'Director of Public Prosecutions' wherever occurring, except in subsection (4) of 'Director'.

b CLEA 2001, s 39(b) substitutes CA 1990, s 230(4).

c CLEA 2001, s 39(c) amends CA 1990, s 230(5) by the substitution for 'Minister' of 'Director'.

d CLEA 2001, s 39(d) deletes CA 1990, s 230(6).

Definitions

'court': CA 1990, s 235); 'director': CA 1963, s 2(1); 'recognised stock exchange': CA 1990, s 3(1); 'share' CA 1963, s 2(1).

Notes

The Irish Stock Exchange is prescribed as a recognised stock exchange for the purposes of s 229: the Companies (Stock Exchange) Regulations 1995 (SI 310/1995).

The powers of the relevant authority to which sub-ss (5)(a), (6) are the powers of investigation contained in CA 1990, s 117 as extended by s 230(9).

CA 1990, s 117 contains powers of investigation and CA 1990, s 120 imposes a duty to prepare an annual report detailing written complaints received, investigations made and reports made to the DPP during the year.

No regs such as s 230(10) have as yet been made.

231 Amendments to the Principal Act in respect of share capital

(1) The Principal Act is hereby amended—

(a) [...][a];

(b) [...][b]; and

(c) [...][c].

(2) [...][d]

Amendments

a Subsection (1)(a) amends CA 1963, s 62(1) by the insertion after 'except as provided in this section' of 'and section 207(2) of the Companies Act, 1990'.

b Subsection (1)(b) amends CA 1963, s 62(2).

c Subsection (1)(c) amends CA 1963, s 72(1) by the deletion of 'to purchase any of its shares or'.

d Subsection (2) substitutes CA 1963, Sch 6, para 12(d).

232 Amendments to the Act of 1983

The Act of 1983 is hereby amended—

(a) [...][a];

(b) [...][b];

(c) [...][c];

(d) [...][d]; and

(e) [...][e].

Amendments

a Subsection (a) substitutes C(A)A 1983, s 41(4)(a).

b Subsection (b) deletes C(A)A 1983, s 43(13).

c Subsection (c) inserts C(A)A 1983, s 43A.

d Subsection (d) substitutes C(A)A 1983, s 51(2)(b).

e Subsection (e) inserts C(A)A 1983, s 51(2)(bb).

233 Amendments to the Companies (Amendment) Act, 1986

(1) Section 14 of the Companies (Amendment) Act, 1986, is hereby amended—

(a) in paragraph (vi) by the substitution of 'acquisition or disposal' for 'disposal'; and

(b) [...][a].

(2) Part I of the Schedule to the Companies (Amendment) Act, 1986, is hereby amended—

(a) by the deletion in Format 1 of the balance sheet formats of items A.III.7, B.III.2 and H.IV.2;

(b) by the deletion in Format 2 of the balance sheet formats—

(i) under 'Assets', of items A.III.7 and B.III.2 (Assets), and

(ii) under 'liabilities', of item A.IV.2; and

(c) by the deletion of note (3) in the notes on the balance sheet formats following the aforesaid formats.

(3) Part IV of the Schedule to the Companies (Amendment) Act, 1986, is hereby amended—

(a) [...][b]; and

(b) [...][c].

Amendments

a Subsection (1)(b) inserts C(A)A 1986, s 14(vii).

b Subsection (3)(a) inserts C(A)A 1986, Sch, Pt IV para 32A.

c Subsection (3)(c) substitutes C(A)A 1986, Sch, Pt IV para 39(3).

234 Offences under this Part

(1) A company which contravenes any of the following provisions shall be guilty of an offence, namely sections 207 to 211, 218 and 222 to 224.

(2) Section 241 shall apply to an offence under this Part.

PART XII
GENERAL

235 Amendment of section 2 of the Principal Act

(1) Unless the context otherwise requires, 'the court', used in any provision of the Companies Acts in relation to a company, means—

(a) the High Court, or

(b) where another court is prescribed for the purposes of that provision, that court.

(2) The definition of 'the court' in subsection (1) is in substitution for the definition in section 2 (1) of the Principal Act.

Definitions

'Companies Acts': CA 1990, s 3(1); 'prescribe': CA 1990, s 3(1); 'the Principal Act': CA 1990, s 3(1).

Notes

To date there have been only two legislative instances where jurisdiction has been given to a court other than the High Court. Under C(A)A 1990, s 3(9) the Circuit Court is given jurisdiction in respect of companies under the protection of the court in certain circumstances. Also, under C(A)A 1982, s 12B(9) jurisdiction is conferred on the Circuit Court to hear applications for the restoration of companies to the register by creditors and/or by the Registrar of Companies.

---

236 Qualifications of secretary of public limited company

It shall be the duty of the directors of a public limited company to take all reasonable steps to secure that the secretary (or each joint secretary) of the company is a person who appears to them to have the requisite knowledge and experience to discharge the functions of secretary of the company and who—

(a) on the commencement of this section held the office of secretary of the company; or

(b) for at least three years of the five years immediately preceding his appointment as secretary held the office of secretary of a company; or

(c) is a member of a body for the time being recognised for the purposes of this section by the Minister; or

(d) is a person who, by virtue of his holding or having held any other position or his being a member of any other body, appears to the directors to be capable of discharging those functions.

Definitions

'company': CA 1963, s 2(1); 'director': CA 1963, s 2(1); 'Minister': CA 1990, s 3(1); 'public limited company': C(A)A 1983, s 2(1).

Notes

To date no regulations have been made by the Minister recognising any bodies for the purposes of para (c).

237 Qualifications of liquidators and receivers

(1) The Minister may, if he considers it necessary or expedient to do so in the interests of the orderly and proper regulation of the winding-up of companies generally, by regulations add to the list of persons in section 300A of the Principal Act (inserted by section 146) who shall not be qualified for appointment as liquidator of a company.

(2) The Minister may, if he considers it necessary or expedient to do so in the interests of the orderly and proper regulation of receiverships generally, by regulations add to the list of persons in section 315 of the Principal Act (inserted by section 170) who shall not be qualified for appointment as receiver of the property of a company.

(3) Every regulation made by the Minister under this section shall be laid before each House of the Oireachtas as soon as may be after it is made and, if a resolution annulling the regulation is passed by either House within the next 21 days on which that House has sat after the regulation is laid before it, the regulation shall be annulled accordingly, but without prejudice to the validity of anything previously done thereunder.

Definitions

'company': CA 1963, s 2(1); 'Minister': CA 1990, s 3(1); 'Principal Act': CA 1990, s 3(1).

Notes

To date no regs have been made by the Minister under sub-s(1) or sub-s(2) adding to the lists of persons who are disqualified from acting as liquidators and receivers respectively.

UK legislation

See IA 1986, ss 390, 391.

238 Amendment of section 61 of the Principal Act

[...][a]

Amendments

a This section inserts CA 1963, s 61(3).

239 Power to make regulations for transfer of securities

(1) The Minister may make provision by regulations for enabling title to securities to be evidenced and transferred without a written instrument.

[(1A) Subject to any exceptions that may be specified in the regulations, the regulations may, in respect of—

(a) securities of companies admitted to trading on a regulated market,

(b) securities of companies admitted to trading on a market other than a regulated market, or

(c) securities of public limited companies of a specified class,

provide that the means provided by the regulations for evidencing and transferring title to such securities shall constitute the sole and exclusive means for doing so (and, accordingly, that any purported transfer of such securities otherwise than by those means shall be void).][a]

(2) In this section—

(a) 'securities' means shares, stock, debentures, debenture stock, loan stock, bonds, units in undertakings for collective investments in transferable securities within the meaning of the European Communities (Undertakings for Collective Investment in Transferable Securities) Regulations, 1989 (S.I. No 78 of 1989), and other securities of any description;

(b) references to title to securities include any legal or equitable interest in securities; and

(c) references to a transfer of title include a transfer by way of security.

(3) The regulations may make provision—

(a) for procedures for recording and transferring title to securities, and

(b) for the regulation of those procedures and the persons responsible for or involved in their operation, and

(c) for dispensing with the obligations of a company under section 86 of the Principal Act to issue certificates and providing for alternative procedures.

(4) The regulations shall contain such safeguards as appear to the Minister appropriate for the protection of investors and for ensuring that competition is not restricted, distorted or prevented.

(5) (a) The regulations may for the purpose of enabling or facilitating the operation of the new procedures make provision with respect to the rights and obligations of persons in relation to securities dealt with under the procedures.

(b) The regulations shall be framed so as to secure that the rights and obligations in relation to securities dealt with under the new procedures correspond, so far as practicable, with those which would arise apart from any regulations under this section.

[(c) The regulations may—

(i) require the provision of statements by a company to holders of securities (at specified intervals or on specified occasions) of the securities held in their name;

(ii) make provision removing any requirement for the holders of securities to surrender existing share certificates to issuers; and

(iii) make provision that the requirements of the regulations supersede any existing requirements in the articles of association of a company which would be incompatible with the requirements of the regulations.][b]

[(5A) Without prejudice to the generality of subsections (4) and (5), the regulations shall not contain provisions that would result in a person who, but for the regulations, would be entitled—

(a) to have his or her name entered in the register of members of a company, or

(b) to give instructions in respect of any securities,

ceasing to be so entitled.][c]

(6) (a) The regulations may include such supplementary, incidental and transitional provisions as appear to the Minister to be necessary or expedient.

(b) In particular, provision may be made for the purpose of giving effect to—

(i) the transmission of title of securities by operation of law;

(ii) any restriction on the transfer of title to securities arising by virtue of the provisions of any enactment or instrument, court order or agreement;

(iii) any power conferred by any such provision on a person to deal with securities on behalf of the person entitled.

(7) The regulations may for the purposes mentioned in this section make provision with respect to the persons who are to be responsible for the operation of the new procedures and for those purposes may empower the Minister to delegate to any person willing and able to discharge them any functions of his under the regulations.

(8) The regulations may make different provision for different cases.

(9) Every regulation made under this section shall be laid before each House of the Oireachtas as soon as may be after it is made and if a resolution annulling the regulation is passed by either such House within the next twenty-one days on which that House has sat after the regulation is laid before it, the regulation shall be annulled accordingly, but without prejudice to the validity of anything previously done thereunder.

Amendments

a Subsection (1A) inserted by IFCMPA 2006, s 12(a).

b Subsection (5)(c) inserted by IFCMPA 2006, s 12(b).

c Subsection (5A) inserted by IFCMPA 2006, s 12(c).

Definitions

'court': CA 1963, s 2(1); 'company': CA 1963, s 2(1); 'debenture': CA 1963, s 2(1); 'Minister': CA 1990, s 3(1); 'Principal Act': CA 1990, s 3(1); 'share': CA 1963, s 2(1).

Notes

CA 1990, s 239 conferred the power on the Minister to make the regulations that empowered the transfer of uncertificated securities: SI 68/1996.

The amendments effected by IFCMPA 2006, s 12 amend CA 1990, s 239 by providing for the power to provide by regulations for *mandatory dematerialisation* (ie holding shares in electronic form *only*, where no share certificate is available) of securities of companies listed on a regulated market.

UK legislation

See CA 1989, s 207.

240 Offences

(1) A person guilty under any provision of the Companies Acts of an offence for which no punishment is specifically provided shall be liable—

(a) on summary conviction, to a fine not exceeding [€1,904.61][a] or, at the discretion of the court, to imprisonment for a term not exceeding 12 months or to both, or

(b) on conviction on indictment, to a fine not exceeding [€12,697.38][b] or, at the discretion of the court, to imprisonment for a term not exceeding [5 years][c] or to both.

(2) A person guilty under any provision of the Companies Acts of an offence made punishable by a fine of an unspecified amount shall be liable—

(a) on summary conviction to a fine not exceeding[€1,904.61],[a] or

(b) on conviction on indictment, to a fine not exceeding [€12,697.38].[b]

(3) Every offence under the Companies Acts made punishable by a fine not exceeding [€1,904.61][a] or by imprisonment for a term not exceeding 12 months, or by both, may be prosecuted summarily.

(4) Summary proceedings in relation to an offence under the Companies Acts may be brought and prosecuted by the Director of Public Prosecutions or the [Director].[d]

[(5) Notwithstanding section 10(4) of the Petty Sessions (Ireland) Act, 1851, summary proceedings in relation to an offence under the Companies Acts may be commenced—

(a) at any time within 3 years from the date on which the offence was committed, or

(b) if, at the expiry of that period, the person against whom the proceedings are to be brought is outside the State, within 6 months from the date on which he next enters the State, or

(c) at any time within 3 years from the date on which evidence that, in the opinion of the person by whom the proceedings are brought, is sufficient to justify the bringing of the proceedings comes to that person's knowledge,

whichever is the later.][e]

[(5A) For the purpose of subsection (5)(c), a certificate signed by or on behalf of the person bringing the proceedings as to the date on which the evidence referred to in that provision relating to the offence concerned came to his knowledge shall be prima facie evidence thereof and in any legal proceedings a document purporting to be a certificate issued for the purpose of this subsection and to be so signed shall be deemed to be so signed and shall be admitted as evidence without proof of the signature of the person purporting to sign the certificate.][f]

(6) Where, in relation to a contravention of any provision of the Companies Acts, it is provided that for continued contravention a person shall be liable to a daily default fine, he shall be guilty of contravening the provision on every day on which the contravention continues after conviction of the original contravention and for each such offence he shall be liable to a fine not exceeding the amount specified in the provision, instead of the penalty specified for the original contravention.

[(7) In any provision of the Companies Acts for which a fine of any amount of less than [€1,904.61][a] is provided in respect of a summary conviction, the maximum amount of that fine shall be taken to be [€1,904.61].[a]

(8) In any provision of the Companies Acts for which a term of imprisonment of less than 5 years is provided in respect of a conviction on indictment, the maximum term of imprisonment shall be taken to be 5 years.][g]

Amendments

a CLEA 2001, s 104(a) amends CA 1990, s 240 by the substitution for '£1,000' wherever occurring of '£1,500'. '£1,500' converted to '€1,904.61' by Council Regulations (EC) No 1103/97, No 974/98 and No 2866/98 and the Economic and Monetary Union Act 1998, s 6.

b '£10,000' converted to '€12,697.38' by Council Regulations (EC) No 1103/97, No 974/98 and No 2866/98 and the Economic and Monetary Union Act, 1998, s 6.

c CLEA 2001, s 104(b) amends CA 1990, s 240(1)(b) by the substitution for '3 years' of '5 years'.

d 'Director' substituted for 'Minister' by CLEA 2001, s 14(4).

e C(A)(No 2)A 1999, s 41 substitutes CA 1990, s 240(5).

f C(A)(No 2)A 1999, s 41 inserts CA 1990, s 240(5A).

g CLEA 2001, s 104(c) inserts CA 1990, s 240(7) and (8).

Definitions

'Companies Acts': CA 1990, s 3(1); 'contravention': CA 1990, s 3(1); 'court': CA 1963, s 2(1); 'daily default fine': CA 1990, s 3(1) & s 240(1); 'director': CLEA 2001, s 3(1).

Notes

Raising the maximum term of imprisonment from 3 to 5 years had the effect of applying s 4 of the Criminal Justice Act 1984 to these offences. This means that a member of An Garda Síochána has the power to arrest a suspect without warrant and detain him for up to 6 (and a further 6) hours where that is necessary for the proper investigation of the offence. See also of s 4 of the Criminal Law Act 1997 which provides that a civilian may effect an arrest in respect of an offence attracting 5 or more years' imprisonment where the arresting civilian believes with reasonable cause that the suspect would otherwise attempt to avoid, or is avoiding, arrest by a member of An Garda Síochána. See discussion in Courtney, *The Law of Private Companies* (2nd edn, Tottel Publishing, 2002) p 657.

UK legislation

See CA 1985, s 730 (amended by CA 1989, s 145), Sch 24.

[240A Court in which proceedings for certain offences may be brought

For the purposes of any provision of the Companies Acts which provides that the company and every officer of the company is guilty of an offence, summary proceedings against the company or an officer of the company may be brought, heard and determined either—

(a) in the court area in which the offence charged or, if more than one offence is stated to have been committed, any one of the offences charged, is stated to have been committed,

(b) in the court area in which the accused has been arrested,

(c) in the court area in which the accused resides,

(d) in the court area specified by order made pursuant to section 15 of the Courts Act, 1971, or

(e) in the court area in which the registered office of the company is situated.][a]

Amendments

a CLEA 2001, s 105 inserts CA 1990, s 240A.

Definitions

'Companies Acts': CA 1990, s 3(1); 'company': CA 1963, s 2(1); 'court': CA 1963, s 2(1); 'officer in default': CA 1963, s 2(1).

241 Offences by certain bodies

(1) Where an offence under section 19, 21, 79 or 242 which is committed by a body to which any such section applies is proved to have been committed with the consent or connivance of or to be attributable to any neglect on the part of any person being a director, manager, secretary or other officer of the body, or any person who was purporting to act in any such capacity, that person shall also be guilty of an offence under that section.

(2) Where the affairs of a body are managed by its members, subsection (1) shall apply in relation to the acts and defaults of a member in connection with his functions of management as if he were a director or manager of the body.

Definitions

'director': CA 1963, s 2(1); 'member': CA 1963, s 31.

Notes

The controller of a company may be convicted of aiding and abetting an offence committed by the company he controls.[1] He may also be convicted of conspiring with his company. Management of the affairs of the company may revert to the members where there is no board of directors or where the board is unable to act due to, for example, deadlock.[2]

1 *McMahon v Murtagh Properties Ltd* [1982] ILRM 342; *DPP v Roberts* [1987] IR 268.

2 *Barron v Potter* [1914] 1 Ch 895; *Foster v Foster* [1916] 1 Ch 532.

242 Furnishing false information

(1) A person who, in purported compliance with any provision of the Companies Acts, answers a question, provides an explanation, makes a statement or produces, lodges or delivers any return, report, certificate, balance sheet or other document false in a material particular, knowing it to be false, or recklessly answers a question, provides an explanation, makes a statement or [completes, signs,][a] produces, lodges or delivers any such document false in a material particular shall be guilty of an offence.

[(1A) A person who knowingly or recklessly furnishes false information to an electronic filing agent that is subsequently transmitted in a return made, on the person's behalf, to the registrar of companies shall be guilty of an offence.][b]

(2) [Where a person is convicted on indictment][c] of an offence under subsection (1) [or (1A)][d] and the court is of opinion that any act, omission or conduct which constituted that offence has—

(a) substantially contributed to a company being unable to pay its debts;

(b) prevented or seriously impeded the orderly winding-up of the company; or

(c) substantially facilitated the defrauding of the creditors of the company or creditors of any other person,

that person shall be liable [...][e] to imprisonment for a term not exceeding 7 years or to a fine not exceeding [€12,697.38][f] or to both.

Amendments

a 'completes, signs,' inserted in sub-s (1) by IFCMPA 2005, s 71.

b Sub-s (1A) inserted by IFCMPA 2005, s 71.

c CLEA 2001, s 106(a) amends CA 1990, s 242(2) by the substitution for 'Where a person is guilty' of 'Where a person is convicted on indictment'.

d 'or (1A)' inserted in sub-s (2) by by IFCMPA 2005, s 71.

e CLEA 2001, s 106(b) amends CA 1990, s 242(2) by the deletion of 'on conviction on indictment.'

f £10,000 converted to €12,697.38 by Council Regulations (EC) No 1103/97, No 974/98 and No 2866/98 and the Economic and Monetary Union Act 1998, s 6.

Definitions

'Companies Acts': CA 1990, s 3(1); 'company': CA 1963, s 2(1); 'court': CA 1990, s 235.

Notes

Under CA 1990, s 241(1) where an offence under s 242 is committed with the consent or connivance of or to be attributable to any neglect on the part of any person being a director, manager, secretary or other officer of the body, or any person who was purporting to act in any such capacity, that person is also guilty of the offence. Likewise CA 1990, s 241(2) provides that where the affairs of the company are under the management of the members, a member may be guilty of an offence if it is committed in the same circumstances.

In relation to the 'electronic filing agents' referred to in sub-s (1A) see IFCMPC 2005, s 57 and the notes thereto. See also the CRO's Information Leaflet No 15.

UK legislation

See CA 1985, s 451; IA 1986, s 211.

243 Penalisation of destruction, mutilation or falsification of documents

(1) A person, being an officer of any such body as is mentioned in paragraphs (a) to (e) of section 19(1) who destroys, mutilates or falsifies, or is privy to the destruction, mutilation or falsification of any book or document affecting or relating to the property or affairs of the body, or makes or is privy to the making of a false entry therein, shall, unless he proves that he had no intention to defeat the law, be guilty of an offence.

(2) Any such person who fraudulently either parts with, alters or makes an omission in any such book or document, or who is privy to fraudulent parting with, fraudulent

altering or fraudulent making of an omission in, any such book or document, shall be guilty of an offence.

Definitions

'officer': CA 1963, s 2(1).

UK legislation

See IA 1986, s 209.

---

244 Increase of penalties

Sections 125(2), 126(4), 127(2) and 128(3) of the Principal Act shall have effect as if for the sums mentioned therein there were substituted '[€1,269.74]'[a] in each case.

Amendments

a £1,000 converted to €1,269.74 by Council Regulations (EC) No 1103/97, No 974/98 and No 2866/98 and the Economic and Monetary Union Act 1998, s 6.

Definitions

'Principal Act': CA 1990, s 3(1).

---

245 Amendment of section 12 of Companies (Amendment) Act, 1982

[...][a]

Amendments

a This section substitutes 'two consecutive years' for 'three consecutive years' in C(A)A 1982, s 12(1).

---

246 Restoration to register of company struck off

[...][a]

Amendments

a This section inserts CA 1963, s 311A, which was in turn amended by C(A)(No 2)A 1999, s 50.

---

247 System of classification of information

(1) Where, under the Companies Acts, any information relating to any person is required to be delivered to the registrar of companies and is so received by him, the registrar may apply such system of classification as he considers appropriate to such information and may assign symbols of identification to persons or classes of persons to whom any such information relates.

(2) The Minister may make regulations requiring that the symbol assigned under subsection (1) to any person or persons of any class shall be entered on all documents which, under any provision of the Companies Acts, are required to contain the name of that person.

(3) Regulations under subsection (2) may, in particular, specify particular persons whose duty it shall be to comply or ensure compliance with the regulations.

(4) A person who makes default in complying with regulations under subsection (2) shall be guilty of an offence and liable to a fine.

Definitions

'Companies Acts': CA 1990, s 3(1); 'Minister': CA 1990, s 3(1); 'registrar of companies' CA 1963, s 2(1).

Notes

No regs have been made to date pursuant to sub-s (2).

248 Delivery to the registrar of documents in legible form

(1) This section applies to the delivery to the registrar under any provision of the Companies Acts of documents in legible form.

(2) The document must—

(a) state in a prominent position the registered number of the company to which it relates,

(b) satisfy any requirements prescribed for the purposes of this section as to the form and content of the document, and

(c) conform to such requirements as may be prescribed for the purpose of enabling the registrar to copy the document.

[...][a]

(6) Regulations made for the purposes of this section may make different provision as to the form and content of the document with respect to different descriptions of document.

(7) Every regulation made under this section shall be laid before each House of the Oireachtas as soon as may be after it is made and if a resolution annulling the regulation is passed by either such House within the next twenty-one days on which that House has sat after the regulation is laid before it, the regulation shall be annulled accordingly, but without prejudice to the validity of anything previously done thereunder.

(8) In this section, 'document' includes any periodic account, abstract, statement or return required to be delivered to the registrar.

Amendments

a CLEA 2001, s 107(2) deletes CA 1990, s 248(3), (4) and (5).

Definitions

'Companies Acts': CA 1990, s 3(1); 'company': CA 1963, s 2(1); 'contravention': CA 1990, s 3(1); 'prescribe': CA 1990, s 3(1) 'registrar': CA 1963, s 2(1).

Notes

In relation to the prescribed form and content of documents to be delivered to the Registrar, see the Companies Acts 1990 (Form and Content of Documents Delivered to Registrar) Regulations 2002 (SI 39/2002).

In relation to the delivery of documents to the Registrar in electronic form, see CA 1990, s 249.

UK legislation

See CA 1985, s 706.

---

249 Delivery to the registrar of documents otherwise than in legible form

(1) This section applies to the delivery to the registrar under any provision of the Companies Acts of documents otherwise than in legible form (whether by electronic means or otherwise).

(2) Any requirement to deliver a document to the registrar, or to deliver a document in the prescribed form, shall be satisfied by the communication to the registrar of the requisite information in any non-legible form prescribed for the purposes of this section.

(3) Where any document is required to be signed or sealed, it shall instead be authenticated in such manner as may be prescribed for the purposes of this section.

(4) The document must—

- (a) contain in a prominent position the registered number of the company to which it relates,
- (b) satisfy any requirements prescribed for the purposes of this section, and
- (c) be furnished in such manner and conform to such requirements as may be prescribed for the purposes of enabling the registrar to read and copy the document.

[...][a]

(8) The Minister may by regulations make further provision with respect to the application of this section in relation to instantaneous forms of communication.

(9) Regulations made for the purpose of this section may make different provision with respect to different descriptions of documents and different forms of communication.

(10) Every regulation made under this section shall be laid before each House of the Oireachtas as soon as may be after it is made and if a resolution annulling the regulation is passed by either such House within the next twenty-one days on which that House has sat after the regulation is laid before it, the regulation shall be annulled accordingly, but without prejudice to the validity of anything previously done thereunder.

(11) In this section, 'document' includes any periodic account, abstract, statement or return required to be delivered to the registrar.

Amendments

a CLEA 2001, s 107(2) deletes CA 1990, s 249(5), (6) and (7).

Definitions

'Companies Acts': CA 1990, s 3(1); 'company': CA 1963, s 2(1); 'contravention': CA 1990, s 3(1); 'Minister': CA 1990, s 3(1); 'precribe': CA 1990, s 3(1); 'Registrar of Companies': CA 1963, s 2(1).

UK legislation

CA 1985, s 707.

[249A Power to reject documents sent for registration and amendments consequential on that section's insertion

(1) If a document is delivered to the registrar which does not comply with—

(a) the requirements of section 248 or 249,

(b) any other requirement of the Companies Acts (and in particular the provisions of the section or sections under which a requirement to deliver the document concerned to the registrar arises), or

(c) any requirements imposed by or under any other enactment relating to the completion of a document and its delivery to the registrar,

the registrar may serve on the person by whom the document was delivered (or, if there are two or more such persons, on any of them) a notice indicating the respect in which the document does not comply.

(2) Where the registrar serves such a notice, then, unless a replacement document—

(a) is delivered to him within 14 days after the service of the notice, and

(b) complies with the requirements referred to in subsection (1) or is not rejected by him for failure to comply with those requirements,

the original document shall be deemed not to have been delivered to him.

(3) For the purposes of any provision which—

(a) imposes a penalty for failure to deliver a document, so far as it imposes a penalty for continued contravention, or

(b) provides for the payment of a fee in respect of the registration of a document being a fee of a greater amount than the amount provided under the provision in respect of the registration of such a document that has been delivered to the registrar within the period specified for its delivery to him,

no account shall be taken of the period between the delivery of the original document and the end of the period of 14 days after the service of the notice under subsection (1)(but only if, before the end of the latter period, a replacement document that complies with the requirements referred to in subsection (1) is delivered to the registrar).

(4) Nothing in this section shall have the effect of making valid any matter which a provision of the Companies Acts or of any other enactment provides is to be void or of no effect in circumstances where a document in relation to it is not delivered to the registrar within the period specified for the document's delivery to him.][a]

Amendments

a CLEA 2001, s 107(1) inserts CA 1990, s 249A.

Definitions

'Companies Acts': CA 1990, s 3(1); s 2(1); 'contravention': CA 1990, s 3(1); 'document': CA 1990, ss 248(8) and 249(11); 'prescribe': CA 1990, s 3(1); 'Registrar': CA 1963, s 2(1).

Notes

Rejection of irregular documentation: This section empowers the Registrar to serve notice on a company rejecting documents which are delivered to him otherwise than in the prescribed form as set out in CA 1990, ss 248 and 249. If within 14 days of service of the notice, the company fails to Re-deliver the document in the prescribed form, the document will be deemed never to have been delivered at all. This could have serious consequences for a company under provisions such as CA 1963, s 99 where a charge executed by the company will be void unless the prescribed particulars are delivered to the Registrar within 21 days of the date of execution.

250 Amendment of section 377 of, and Ninth Schedule to, the Principal Act

(1) [...][a]

(2) The Minister may, if he considers it necessary to do so in the interests of the orderly and proper regulation of the business of unregistered companies, make regulations adding to, or subtracting from, the list of the provisions of the Companies Acts specified in the Ninth Schedule to The Principal Act.

(3) Every regulation made by the Minister under this section shall be laid before each House of the Oireachtas as soon as may be after it is made and, if a resolution annulling the regulation is passed by either House within the next 21 days on which that House has sat after the regulation is laid before it, the regulation shall be annulled accordingly, but without prejudice to the validity of anything previously done thereunder.

Amendments

a Sub-s (1)(a) substitutes CA 1963, s 377(1) and sub-s (1)(b) substitutes CA 1963, Sch 9.

Definitions

'Companies Acts': CA 1990, s 3(1); 'Minister': CA 1990, s 3(1); 'Principal Act': CA 1990, s 3(1).

Notes

Amendments to CA 1963, Sch 9: The Minister has since amended CA 1963, Sch 9 pursuant to the Companies Act 1963 (Ninth Schedule) Regulations 1999 (SI 63/1999).

251 Application of certain provisions to companies not in liquidation

(1) This section applies in relation to a company that is not being wound up where—

(a) execution or other process issued on a judgment, decree or order of any court in favour of a creditor of the company is returned unsatisfied in whole or in part; or

(b) it is proved to the satisfaction of the court that the company is unable to pay its debts, taking into account the contingent and prospective liabilities of the company, and

it appears to the court that the reason or the principal reason for its not being wound up is the insufficiency of its assets.

(2) The following sections, with the necessary modifications, shall apply to a company to which this section applies, notwithstanding that it is not being wound up—

(a) [sections 139, 140, 148, 149 or 149A, 203 and 204, and][a]

(b) the provisions of the Principal Act mentioned in the Table to this section.

[(2A) The Director may apply to the court pursuant to this section for an order or judgement, as the case may be, under any of the sections which apply to a company to which this section applies.][b]

(3) References in the sections mentioned in subsection (2) to the commencement of the winding-up of a company, the appointment of a provisional liquidator or the making of a winding up order and to the 'relevant date' shall, for the purposes of this section, be construed as references to the date—

(a) of the judgment, decree or order mentioned in subsection (1)(a); or

(b) on which the court determines that the company is unable to pay its debts.

[(4)

(a) Where, by virtue of this section, proceedings are instituted under section 139, 140 or 204 of this Act or section 245A, 297A or 298 of the Principal Act, section 297A(7)(b) of the Principal Act shall apply in relation to any order made as a result of those proceedings except that an order made as a result of an application by the Director pursuant to subsection (2A) shall not be made in favour of the Director, otherwise than as to his costs and expenses.

(b) A person having a claim against the company may apply for an enforcement order for a share of any sums or assets recovered or available following a successful action by the Director pursuant to subsection (2A), provided that the order is sought within a period of one month from the date of judgement on behalf of the Director.][c]

(5) Where section 295 of the Principal Act is applied by virtue of this section, it shall apply as if the words 'which is subsequently ordered to be wound up or subsequently passes a resolution for voluntary winding-up' were deleted therefrom.

TABLE

SECTIONS OF PRINCIPAL ACT TO WHICH THIS SECTION APPLIES

Section	*Subject*	*Comment*
243	Inspection of books by creditors and contributories	
245	Power of court to summon persons for examination	Inserted by section 126 of this Act
245A	Order for payment or delivery of property against person examined under section 245	Inserted by section 127 of this Act

Section	Subject	Comment
247	Power to arrest absconding contributory	
295	Frauds by officers of companies which have gone into liquidation	
297	Criminal liability for fraudulent trading	Inserted by section 137 of this Act
297A	Civil liability for fraudulent trading	Inserted by section 138 of this Act
298	Power of court to assess damages against directors	Amended by section 142 of this Act

Amendments

a Sub-s (2)(a) amended by CLEA 2001, s 54 and substituted by reg 9 of and the Schedule to the EC(IFRSMA)R 2005.

b CLEA 2001, s 54(b) inserts CA 1990, s 251(2A).

c CLEA 2001, s 54(c) substitutes CA 1990, s 251(4).

Definitions

'company': CA 1963, s 2(1); 'contributory': CA 1963, s 2(1); 'court': CA 1963, s 2(1); 'director': CA 1963, s 2(1); 'the Director': CLEA 2001, s 3(1); 'inability to pay debts': CA 1963, s 214; 'Principal Act': CA 1990, s 3(1).

Notes

Invocation of liquidation remedies: The effect of this section is to allow the ODCE and individual creditors and contributories to invoke various remedies against delinquent directors and officers which would otherwise be exercisable only in a winding up. In order to be able to avail of s 251 the applicant must satisfy the court that judgment etc has been returned unsatisfied or that the company is otherwise unable to pay its debts and that the reason or main reason why the company has not been wound up is that there are insufficient assets (ie that there would not be enough assets in a winding up to even meet the costs and expenses of a liquidator).

Under s 251(4)(a) if the proceedings are successful, the court may determine which persons or classes of persons are to receive the benefit of any financial awards made by it. If the applicant was the ODCE, it will be entitled to its costs – the remainder of the award will go to such creditors and/or contributories as the court determines. Those creditors and contributories have one month from the date of judgment to apply to share in the award. Notably, the section does not lay down any procedure whereby those creditors and contributories are to learn of the award in the first place. Nor does the section confer any jurisdiction on the court to extend the time within which claimants may apply to share in the award.

With the exception of an examination under CA 1963, s 245,[1] it would appear that the various remedies referred in s 251 cannot be invoked in respect of matters which pre-dated the coming into force of that section[2].

There is an onus on a creditor of a company which is not being wound up, who is seeking an order under CA 1990, s 245 in reliance upon CA 1990, s 251 to demonstrate that the examination would probably result in a benefit accruing to him and that onus is more rigerous than the onus borne by a contributory or a creditor in a compulsory or a voluntary winding up; an examination will not be permitted for a 'fishing expedition'.[3]

1 *Alba Radio Ltd v Haltone (Cork) Ltd* [1995] 2 IR 170.

2 *Jones v Gunn* [1997] 3 IR 1.

[3] *Airscape Ltd v Powertech Logistics Ltd and others* [2008] 4 IR 438.

PART XIII
INVESTMENT COMPANIES

252 Interpretation of this Part

(1) In this Part—

[…][a]

'investment company' means a company to which this Part applies and 'company' shall be construed accordingly;

['management company' means a company designated by an investment company to undertake the management of the investment company;][b]

'property' means real or personal property of whatever kind (including securities);

['sub-fund' means a separate portfolio of assets maintained by an investment company in accordance with its articles;][c]

'the UCITS Regulations' means the European Communities (Undertakings for Collective Investment in Transferable Securities) Regulations, 1989 (S.I. No 78 of 1989).

['umbrella fund' means an investment company which has one or more sub-funds and which is authorised by the Central Bank pursuant to section 256.][d]

(2) For the purposes of the application by this Part of certain provisions of the UCITS Regulations to investment companies, the said provisions shall be construed as one with the Companies Acts.

Amendments

a Deleted by the CBFSAA 2003, Sch 1.

b Added by IFCMPA 2005, s 22.

c Added by IFCMPA 2005, s 22.

d Added by IFCMPA 2005, s 22.

Definitions

'Central Bank': CA 1990, s 3(1); 'company: CA 1963, s 2(1); 'Companies Acts': CA 1990, s 3(1).

Notes

The UCITS Regulations implement Council Directive 85/611/EEC of 20 December 1985 on the co-ordination of laws, regulations and administrative provisions relating to undertakings for collective investment in transferable securities. This Directive was amended by the Markets in Financial Instruments Directive 2004/39/EC of the European Parliament and of the Council of 21 April 2004 (OJ L145 30.4.2004, p 1).

In *Banque Bruxelles Lambert SA (BBL) v Belgian State*, Case C-8/03 [2004] STC 1643, the European Court of Justice held that open-ended investment companies which have as their sole object the collective investment in transferable securities of capital raised from the public in accordance with Council Directive 85/611/EEC of 20 December 1985 on the co-ordination of laws, regulations and administrative provisions relating to undertakings for collective investment in transferable securities (UCITS) are taxable persons within the meaning of art 4 of Sixth Council

Directive 77/388/EEC of 17 May 1977 on the harmonisation of the laws of the member states relating to turnover taxes-common system of value added tax: uniform basis of assessment, s o that, where services referred to in art 9(2)(e) of that directive are supplied to open-ended investment companies which are established in a member state other than that of the supplier of the services, the place where those services are provided is the place where the open-ended investment companies have established their business.

---

253 Share capital of investment companies

(1) Notwithstanding anything in the Companies Acts, the memorandum of a company to which this Part applies may in respect of the share capital of the company state in lieu of the matters specified in paragraph (a) of section 6 (4) of the Principal Act—

- (a) that the share capital of the company shall be equal to the value for the time being of the issued share capital of the company,[...][a]
- (b) the division of that share capital into a specified number of shares without assigning any nominal value thereto, [and][b]
- [(c) that the issued share capital of the company for the time being shall not be less than a minimum amount nor more than a maximum amount specified in the memorandum,][c]

and the form of memorandum set out in Table B of the First Schedule to the Principal Act or Part I of the Second Schedule to the Companies (Amendment) Act, 1983, as may be appropriate, s hall have effect with respect to such company with the necessary modifications.

(2) This Part applies to a company limited by shares (not being a company to which the UCITS Regulations apply)—

- (a) the sole object of which is stated in its memorandum to be the collective investment of its funds in property with the aim of spreading investment risk and giving members of the company the benefit of the results of the management of its funds; and
- (b) the articles or memorandum of which provide—
  - (i) that the actual value of the paid up share capital of the company shall be at all times equal to the value of the assets of any kind of the company after the deduction of its liabilities, and
  - (ii) that the shares of the company shall, at the request of any of the holders thereof, be purchased by the company directly or indirectly out of the company's assets.

[(2A)(a) Notwithstanding subsection (2)(b)(ii), this Part shall also apply to a company to which subsection (2) otherwise applies, the articles or memorandum of which do not provide that the shares of the company shall, at the request of any holders thereof, be purchased in the manner therein provided, to the extent as may be approved and subject to such conditions as may be applied by the [Central Bank][d].][e],

(b) [...],[f]

(3) For the purposes of subsection (2)(b)(ii), action taken by a company to ensure that the stock exchange value of its shares does not deviate from its net asset value by more

than a percentage specified in its articles (which deviation shall not be so specified as greater than 5 per cent) shall be regarded as the equivalent of purchase of its shares by the company.

(4) The memorandum or articles of a company shall be regarded as providing for the matters referred to in paragraphs (a) and (b) of subsection (2) notwithstanding the inclusion in the memorandum or articles with respect thereto of incidental or supplementary provisions.

(5) In the Companies Acts—

(a) a reference to a company limited by shares shall be construed as including an investment company within the meaning of this Part and a reference to a share in, or the share capital of, a company limited by shares shall be construed accordingly, and

(b) a reference to the nominal value of an issued or allotted share in, or of the issued or allotted share capital of, a company limited by shares shall be construed, in the case of an investment company, as a reference to the value of the consideration for which the share or share capital (as the case may be) has been issued or allotted.

Amendments

a CA 1990, s 253(1)(a) amended by C(A)(No 2)1999, s 54(1)(a)(i) by the deletion of the word 'and'.

b CA 1990, s 253(1)(b) amended by C(A)(No 2)1999, s 54(1)(a)(ii) by the insertion after 'nominal value thereto' of 'and'.

c CA 1990, s 253(1)(c) inserted by C(A)(No 2)1999, s 54(1)(a)(iii).

d CA 1990, s 253(2A)(a) amended by the CBFSA Act 2003 Part 9, s ch 3 by the insertion of the word 'Central' in before the word 'Bank'.

e CA 1990, s 253(2A) inserted by Investment Intermediaries Act 1995, s 80.

f CA 1990, s 253(2A)(b) deleted by C(A)(No 2)1999, s 54(1)(b).

Definitions

'articles': CA 1963, s 2(1); 'Central Bank': CA 1990, s 3(1); 'company: CA 1963, s 2(1); 'Companies Acts': CA 1990, s 3(1); 'investment company': CA 1990, s 252(1); 'memorandum': CA 1963, s 2(1); 'Principal Act': CA 1990, s 3(1); 'share': CA 1963, s 2(1); 'UCITS Regulations': CA 1990, s 252(1).

---

254 Power of company to purchase own shares

(1) Subject to subsection (2), the purchase by an investment company of its own shares shall be on such terms and in such manner as may be provided by its articles.

[(2) An investment company shall not purchase its own shares, for the purposes referred to in section 253(2)(*b*)(ii), unless they are fully paid, but nothing in this subsection shall prevent a purchase being made in accordance with section 255(3).][a]

(3) For the avoidance of doubt, nothing in the Companies Acts shall require an investment company to create any reserve account.

Amendments

a Section 254(2) substituted by CA 2005, s 23. The old provision read provided that 'An investment company shall not purchase its own shares unless they are fully paid.'

Definitions

'articles': CA 1963, s 2(1); 'company: CA 1963, s 2(1); 'Companies Acts': CA 1990, s 3(1); 'investment company': CA 1990, s 252(1); 'share': CA 1963, s 2(1).

Notes

This is an exception to the general rule that a company cannot purchase its own shares. See *Trevor v Whitworth* (1887) 12 App Cas 409; CA 1963, s 72(1) and C(A)A 1983, s 41(1).

The original s 254(2) baldly declared that '[a]n investment company shall not purchase its own shares unless they are fully paid'. This section replaces that absolute prohibition with a more sophisticated approach, which allows for the type of internal transfer of sub-funds envisaged in the new s 255 (3).

255 Treatment of purchased shares

(1) Shares of an investment company which have been purchased by the company shall be cancelled and the amount of the company's issued share capital shall be reduced by the amount of the consideration paid by the company for the purchase of the shares.

(2) (a) Where a company has purchased or is about to purchase any of its own shares, it shall have the power to issue an equal number of shares in place of those purchased and for the purposes of section 68 of the Finance Act, 1973, the issue of those replacement shares shall constitute a chargeable transaction if, but only if, the actual value of the shares so issued exceeds the actual value of the shares purchased at the date of their purchase and, where the issue of shares does constitute a chargeable transaction for those purposes, the amount on which stamp duty on the relevant statement relating to that transaction is chargeable under section 69 of the Finance Act, 1973, shall be the difference between—

(i) the amount on which the duty would be so chargeable if the shares had not been issued in place of shares purchased under this section, and

(ii) the value of the shares purchased at the date of their purchase.

(b) Where new shares are issued before the purchase of the old shares, the new shares shall not, s o far as relates to stamp duty, be deemed to have been issued in pursuance of paragraph (a) unless the old shares are purchased within one month after the issue of the new shares.

[(3)Notwithstanding subsection (1), an umbrella fund may, for the account of any of its sub-funds, and in accordance with conditions imposed by the Central Bank pursuant to section 257, acquire by subscription or transfer for consideration, shares of any class or classes, howsoever described, representing other sub-funds of the same umbrella fund provided that the acquisition is for a purpose otherwise than that provided for in section 253(2)(*b*)(ii).][a]

Amendments

a Subsection (3) inserted by IFCMPA 2005, s 24.

Definitions

'Central Bank': CA 1990, s 3(1); 'company: CA 1963, s 2(1); s 3(1); 'investment company': CA 1990, s 252(1); 'share': CA 1963, s 2(1); 'umbrella fund': CA 1990, s 252(1).

Notes

Sections 68 and 69 of the FA 1973 contain charging provisions in respect of stamp duty.

Subsection (3) is an entirely new sub-section, which allows an umbrella fund to acquire sub-funds from the same umbrella fund provided that the acquisition complies with conditions laid down by the Central Bank, and does not purport to satisfy the s 253(2)(b)(ii) requirement that the actual value of the company's paid up share capital remains equal to its assets less liabilities.

256 Authorisation by Bank

(1) An investment company shall not carry on business in the State unless it has been authorised to do so by the [Central Bank][a] on the basis of criteria approved by the Minister.

(2) A person shall not carry on business on behalf of an investment company, insofar as relates to the purchase or sale of the shares of the investment company, unless the investment company has been authorised in the manner referred to in subsection (1).

(3) The [Central Bank][a] shall not authorise an investment company to carry on business in the State unless the company has paid up share capital which, in the opinion of the [Central Bank][a], will be sufficient to enable it to conduct its business effectively and meet its liabilities.

(4) An application by an investment company for the authorisation referred to in subsection (1) shall be made in writing to the [Central Bank][a] and contain such information as the [Central Bank][a] may specify for the purpose of determining the application (including such additional information as the [Central Bank][a] may specify in the course of determining the application).

(5) Where the [Central Bank][a] proposes to grant an authorisation to an investment company under this section and the [Central Bank][a] is satisfied that the company will raise capital [by providing facilities for the direct or indirect participation by the public in the profits and income of the company][b], the [Central Bank][a] shall, in granting the authorisation, designate the company as an investment company which may raise capital in that manner, and 'designated company' in this section and section 257, shall be construed accordingly.

(6) In the event that a designated company does not [provide facilities for the direct or indirect participation by the public in the profits and income of the company][c] within a period, not greater than six months, which shall be specified in the authorisation under this section, the company shall, on the expiry of the period so specified, be deemed to have ceased to be a designated company.

(7) An investment company which is not a designated company shall not raise capital [by providing facilities for the direct or indirect participation by the public in the profits and income of the company].[b]

(8) A company incorporated outside the State which, if it were incorporated in the State, would be a company to which this Part applies[, other than a company to which section 256F applies,][d] shall not advertise or market its shares in any way in the State without the approval of the [Central Bank][a], which approval may be subject to such conditions as the [Central Bank][a] considers appropriate and prudent for the purposes of the orderly and proper regulation of so much of the business of companies of that type as is conducted in the State.

(9) [...][e]

Amendments

a Words inserted by CBFSAIA 2003, Sch 1.

b CA 1990, s 256(5) and (7) amended by C(A)(No 2)A 1999, s 54(2)(a) by the substitution for 'by promoting the sale of its shares to the public', in each place where it occurs, of 'by providing facilities for the direct or indirect participation by the public in the profits and income of the company'.

c CA 1990, s 256(6) amended by C(A)(No 2) A 1999, s 54(2)(b) by the substitution for 'promote the sale of its s hares to the public' of 'provide facilities for the direct or indirect participation by the public in the profits and income of the company'.

d Words ', other than a company to which section 256F applies,' inserted by C(MP)A 2009, s 3(i).

e Subsection (9) deleted by C(A)(No2)A 1999, s 54.

Definitions

'Central Bank': CA 1990, s 3(1); 'company: CA 1963, s 2(1); 'investment company': CA 1990, s 252(1); 'share': CA 1963, s 2(1).

[256A Segregated liability of investment company sub-funds

(1) Notwithstanding any statutory provision or rule of law to the contrary, but subject to subsection (2), any liability incurred on behalf of or attributable to any sub-fund of an umbrella fund shall be discharged solely out of the assets of that sub-fund, and no umbrella fund nor any director, receiver, examiner, liquidator, provisional liquidator or other person shall apply, nor be obliged to apply, the assets of any such sub-fund in satisfaction of any liability incurred on behalf of or attributable to any other sub-fund of the same umbrella fund, whether such liability was incurred before, on or after the date this section commences.

(2) Subsection (1) shall not apply to an umbrella fund which was authorised and commenced trading prior to the date this section commences unless—

(a) the members of the umbrella fund shall have resolved by special resolution that the provisions of subsection (1) should apply to that umbrella fund, and

(b) the special resolution has taken effect in accordance with subsection (4).

(3) For the purposes of subsection (2), an umbrella fund shall be deemed to have commenced to trade prior to the date this section commences if—

(a) shares, other than the subscriber shares issued for the purposes of incorporation of the umbrella fund, were issued in any sub-fund of that umbrella fund prior to that commencement date and one or more of those shares remains in issue on that commencement date, or

(b) the umbrella fund, or any person acting on its behalf, entered into an agreement with a third party prior to that commencement date, which remains in force on that commencement date and pursuant to which the assets of any sub-fund may be applied in satisfaction of any liability incurred on behalf of or attributable to any other sub-fund of the same umbrella fund.

(4) If—

(a) no application to the court is made pursuant to section 256C, a special resolution passed pursuant to subsection (2) shall take effect on the date on which such resolution is passed or the 31st day following the date of service of notice on creditors issued pursuant to subsection (5)(b), whichever is the later, or

(b) an application is or applications are made to the court pursuant to section 256C, a special resolution pursuant to subsection (2) shall not take effect until—

(i) in the event that all applications made are withdrawn, the day on which such resolution is passed or the day next following the withdrawal of the last outstanding application, whichever is the later, subject to this day being no earlier than the 31st day following the date of service of notice on creditors; and

(ii) in the event that all applications made are not withdrawn, whichever of the following is the later, that is to say, the later of the day on which such resolution is passed, and:

(I) where an order is granted by the court pursuant to section 256C or on appeal pursuant to section 256D, the date specified in that order or, if no such date is specified, the day next following the date on which the period for which the order is specified to remain in force expires or, as appropriate, following the day on which it otherwise ceases to be in force; or

(II) where no appeal against any decision of the court is lodged pursuant to section 256D, the day next following the date on which the time period for such an appeal in relation to the last such determination of the court shall have elapsed; or

(III) where an appeal is lodged against any decision of the court pursuant to section 256D, the day next following the date on which the last outstanding such appeal is disposed of or withdrawn,

unless a court has otherwise ordered under section 256C or 256D.

(5) Any notice of a meeting to consider a special resolution of the type referred to in subsection (2) shall be—

(a) accompanied by audited accounts for the umbrella fund which include a statement of the assets and liabilities of each sub-fund of the umbrella fund and which are prepared as at a date which is not more than four months before the date on which the notice convening the meeting is served (hereafter referred to in this section and section 256B as 'statement of assets and liabilities');

(b) given to all creditors of the umbrella fund accompanied by a copy of the statement of assets and liabilities, in accordance with the provisions of section 256B; and

(c) delivered to the registrar of companies, accompanied by the statement of assets and liabilities, no later than the third day after the date on which the notice is first sent to members of the umbrella fund.][a]

Amendments

a Section 256A inserted by IFCMPA 2005, s 25.

Definitions

'court': CA 1963, s 2(1); 'registrar of companies': CA 1963, s 2(1); 'umbrella fund': CA 1990, s 252(1).

Notes

The new s 256A is one of the key reforms of the new legislation, permitting, as it does, the complete segregation of liability for sub-funds of an umbrella fund. For the sake of certainty, it specifically provides that this segregation will apply to receivers, examiners, liquidators, provisional liquidators, or any other person.

This amendment is the product of extensive consultation between the funds industry and the government. The IFSC Funds Group, involving representatives of industry, key government departments and the Financial Regulator, recommended the introduction of measures along the lines of those contained in this Act.

The situation prior to the introduction of s 256A was unsatisfactory for those involved in the industry because of the way in which Irish law treated the investment company as a single legal entity. Each sub-fund was regarded as a series or class of shares within that entity with the result that individual sub-funds did not enjoy the benefits of limited liability. This had a particularly adverse impact on leveraged umbrella funds, or on those which regularly used derivatives in the course of their trading.

Although these provisions allow for segregation of liability between sub-funds, s 256E(6) specifies that a sub-fund is not to be regarded as a separate legal person.

As these reforms prevent creditors from having access to a sub-fund to offset liabilities incurred in another sub-fund, s 256E(1) introduces a measure of creditor protection by requiring an umbrella fund with segregated liability to ensure that it includes the words 'An umbrella fund with segregated liability between sub-funds' in all its letterheads and in any agreement entered into in writing with a third party, and shall be obliged to disclose that it is a segregated liability umbrella fund to any third party with which it enters into an oral contract.

Many of the details of this section are devoted to the problem posed by existing umbrella funds. The Act allows existing companies to convert to the segregated system. It also, however, attempts to provide a mechanism by which concerned creditors could oppose this development.

An existing company can only rely on s 256A(1) where it has passed a special resolution to that effect in accordance with s 256A(2).

By section 256B, notice of a meeting to pass a special resolution must be given in writing to creditors, along with a statement of the fund's assets and liabilities. A notice must also be published in a national newspaper alerting creditors to the holding of the meeting, and to their entitlement to apply to court to oppose a special resolution under s 256C.

By virtue of section 256C, a 'relevant creditor' can apply to court to prevent any resolution passed or proposed to be passed pursuant to s 256A(2) from taking effect in relation to any umbrella fund to which that section applies. The court has a discretionary power to make such an order where it feels it is just and equitable to do so. This somewhat nebulous test is to be applied by reference, *inter alia*, to the agreement between the parties, the course of dealing between them, the conduct of the umbrella fund towards the creditor and the extent to which it was reasonable for the creditor to expect to have recourse to the assets of other sub-funds.

If the court decides to prevent the passing of a resolution, it must, under s 256C(3) specify the period in respect of which the order shall remain in force. This section notes, with an obvious effort at suggestion, that the court may specify that the order shall cease to be in force on the date on which the applicant ceases to be a creditor of the umbrella fund or the date on which the applicant consents to the application of s 256A(1) to that umbrella fund.

If the court refuses the creditor's application, the decision can be appealed to the Supreme Court. Notice of appeal must be lodged within five days of the perfection of the order being appealed. If an appeal is not lodged, the resolution can take effect on the day next following the date on which the time permitted for an appeal has lapsed.

Where an application is successfully made under s 256C, a resolution under s 256(2) cannot take effect until the date specified in that order or, if no such date is specified, the day next following the date on which the order expires or ceases to otherwise have effect.

Where no application is made, a special resolution passed pursuant to s 256A(2) takes effect on the date on which the resolution is passed, or on the 31-day period following the date of service of notice on creditors, whichever is the later.

[256B Notice to creditors of special resolution under section 256A

(1) The requirement in section 256A to give all creditors of the umbrella fund notice of a meeting to consider a special resolution shall be met if—

(a) a notice in writing, accompanied by the statement of assets and liabilities, is sent to each relevant creditor of a sub-fund, and

(b) a notice is published in at least one national newspaper in accordance with the terms of the prospectus for the umbrella fund, s tating that the umbrella fund intends to avail of section 256A(1) and that an application may be made in accordance with section 256C, for an order pursuant to that section.

(2) For the purpose of this section, a relevant creditor of a sub-fund is any creditor for whom provision was made, in accordance with the articles of association, in the net asset value of the sub-fund calculated—

(a) in the case of a sub-fund in respect of which the net asset value is not calculated on a daily basis, as at the last valuation point for that sub-fund prior to the date of service of the notice pursuant to section 256A(5)(b); and

(b) in the case of a sub-fund in respect of which the net asset value is calculated on a daily basis, as at the second last valuation point for that sub-fund.][a]

Amendments

a Section 256B inserted by IFCMPA 2005, s 25.

Definitions

'umbrella fund': CA 1990, s 252(1).

[256C Application to court opposing special resolution under section 256A

(1) An application may be made to the court in accordance with this section for an order preventing any resolution passed or proposed to be passed pursuant to section 256A(2) from taking effect in relation to any umbrella fund to which that section applies.

(2) An order under this section may be granted only if the court considers that it would be just and equitable to do so.

(3) Each order granted pursuant to this section shall specify the period in respect of which the order shall remain in force and, without prejudice to the powers of the court to specify such period, may specify that the order shall cease to be in force on the date on which the applicant ceases to be a creditor of the umbrella fund or the date on which the applicant consents to the application of section 256A(1) to that umbrella fund, whichever is the later.

(4) An application under this section may only be made by a relevant creditor or relevant creditors constituting not less than 1 per cent in number of the creditors of any sub-fund, or whose debts account for not less than 1 per cent in value of the debts owed by any sub-fund, in each case as provided for in the net asset value of that sub-fund referred to in section 256B.

(5) Any application pursuant to this section must be made by a relevant creditor within 28 days after the date of service of the notice referred to in section 256A(5)(b), and may be made on behalf of the creditors entitled to make the application by one or more of their number as they may appoint in writing for such purpose.

(6) Notice of an application to the court for the purposes of this section shall be sent by the relevant creditor or relevant creditors to the umbrella fund and to the Central Bank within two days after the date on which the application is made, and the umbrella fund and the Central Bank shall each be entitled to make representations to the court before an order is made.

(7) In considering whether it is just and equitable to make an order pursuant to this section, the court shall have regard to the following matters:

(a) the terms of any agreement or arrangement between the creditor or creditors and the umbrella fund or its delegates;

(b) the course of dealings between the creditor or creditors and the umbrella fund or its delegates;

(c) the conduct of the umbrella fund or its delegates towards the creditor or creditors;

(d) the extent to which the umbrella fund or its delegates represented to the creditor or creditors that it would have recourse to the assets of any other sub-fund to discharge the liabilities owed to the creditor or creditors;

(e) the extent to which it was reasonable for the relevant creditor or relevant creditors to expect to have recourse to the assets of any other sub-fund; and

(f) any other matters which the court shall deem relevant.][a]

Amendments

a Section 256C inserted by IFCMPA 2005, s 25.

Definitions

'Central Bank': CA 1990, s 3(1); 'court': CA 1963, s 2(1); 'umbrella fund': CA 1990, s 252(1).

[256D Appeal from court order under section 256C

(1) Any creditor who has made an application pursuant to section 256C, or the umbrella fund in respect of which the application is made, may appeal to the Supreme Court against any decision of the court in respect of that application.

(2) Notice of any such appeal must be lodged within five days after the date on which the order is perfected by the court.

(3) Notice of any appeal lodged by the umbrella fund shall be sent to the Central Bank and to the relevant creditor or relevant creditors who made the application pursuant to section 256C within two days after the date on which the appeal is made.

(4) Notice of any appeal by the party which made the application pursuant to section 256C shall be sent to the Central Bank and to the umbrella fund within two days after the date on which the appeal is made.][a]

Amendments

a Section 256D inserted by IFCMPA 2005, s 25.

Definitions

'Central Bank': CA 1990, s 3(1); 'court': CA 1963, s 2(1); 'umbrella fund': CA 1990, s 252(1).

[256E Requirements to be complied with by, and other matters respecting, an umbrella fund to which section 256A applies

(1) Every umbrella fund to which section 256A applies shall be required to include the words 'An umbrella fund with segregated liability between sub-funds' in all its letterheads and in any agreement entered into in writing with a third party, and shall be obliged to disclose that it is a segregated liability umbrella fund to any third party with which it enters into an oral contract.

(2) There shall be implied in every contract, agreement, arrangement or transaction entered into by an umbrella fund to which section 256A applies the following terms, that—

(a) the party or parties contracting with the umbrella fund shall not seek, whether in any proceedings or by any other means whatsoever or wheresoever, to have recourse to any assets of any sub-fund of the umbrella fund in the discharge of all or any part of a liability which was not incurred on behalf of that sub-fund,

(b) if any party contracting with the umbrella fund shall succeed by any means whatsoever or wheresoever in having recourse to any assets of any sub-fund of the umbrella fund in the discharge of all or any part of a liability which was not incurred on behalf of that sub-fund, that party shall be liable to the umbrella fund to pay a sum equal to the value of the benefit thereby obtained by it, and

(c) if any party contracting with the umbrella fund shall succeed in seizing or attaching by any means, or otherwise levying execution against, any assets of a sub-fund of an umbrella fund in respect of a liability which was not incurred on behalf of that sub-fund, that party shall hold those assets or the direct or indirect proceeds of the sale of such assets on trust for the umbrella fund and shall keep those assets or proceeds separate and identifiable as such trust property.

(3) All sums recovered by an umbrella fund as a result of any such trust as is described in subsection (2)(c) shall be credited against any concurrent liability pursuant to the implied term set out in subsection (2)(b).

(4) Any asset or sum recovered by an umbrella fund pursuant to the implied term set out in subsection (2)(b) or (c) or by any other means whatsoever or wheresoever in the events referred to in those paragraphs shall, after the deduction or payment of any costs of recovery, be applied so as to compensate the sub-fund affected.

(5) In the event that assets attributable to a sub-fund to which section 256A applies are taken in execution of a liability not attributable to that sub-fund, and in so far as such assets or compensation in respect thereof cannot otherwise be restored to that sub-fund affected, the directors of the umbrella fund, with the consent of the custodian, s hall certify or cause to be certified, the value of the assets lost to the sub-fund affected and transfer or pay from the assets of the sub-fund or sub-funds to which the liability was attributable, in priority to all other claims against such sub-fund or sub-funds, assets or sums sufficient to restore to the sub-fund affected, the value of the assets or sums lost to it.

(6) Without prejudice to the other provisions of sections 256A to 256D and this section, a sub-fund of an umbrella fund is not a legal person separate from that umbrella fund, but an umbrella fund may sue and be sued in respect of a particular sub-fund and may exercise the same rights of set-off, if any, as between its sub-funds as apply at law in respect of companies and the property of a sub-fund is subject to orders of the court as it would have been if the sub-fund were a separate legal person.

(7) Nothing in sections 256A to 256D and this section shall prevent the application of any enactment or rule of law which would require the application of the assets of any sub-fund in discharge of some or all of the liabilities of any other sub-fund on the grounds of fraud or misrepresentation and, in particular, by reason of the application of—

(a) section 286 of the Principal Act; and

(b) section 139 of this Act.

(8) A sub-fund may be wound up in accordance with the provisions of section 213(e) and section 251(1)(c) of the Principal Act as if the sub-fund were a separate company, provided always that the appointment of the liquidator or any provisional liquidator and the powers, rights, duties and responsibilities of the liquidator or any provisional liquidator shall be confined to the sub-fund or sub-funds which is or are being wound up.

(9) For the purposes of subsection (8), all references made in sections 213(e) and 251(1)(c) of the Principal Act and all relevant provisions of the Companies Acts relating to the winding up of a company pursuant to sections 213(e) and 251(1)(c) of the Principal Act to one of the following words shall be construed as follows—

(a) 'company' shall be read as referring to the sub-fund or sub-funds which is or are being wound up;

(b) a 'member' or 'members' shall be read as referring to the holders of the shares in that sub-fund or sub-funds; and

(c) 'creditors' shall be read as referring to the creditors of that sub-fund or sub-funds.][a]

Amendments

a Section 256E inserted by IFCMPA 2005, s 25.

Definitions

'Central Bank': CA 1990, s 3(1); 'company: CA 1963, s 2(1); 'Companies Acts': CA 1990, s 3(1); 'Principal Act': CA 1990, s 3(1); 'umbrella fund': CA 1990, s 252(1).

[256F Continuation of foreign investment companies

(1) In this section—

'migrating company' means a body corporate which is established and registered under the laws of a relevant jurisdiction and which is a collective investment undertaking;

'registration documents', in relation to a migrating company, means the following documents and, when the original registration documents are not written in the Irish language or the English language, means a translation into the Irish language or the English language certified as being a correct translation thereof by a person who is competent to so certify:

(a) a copy, certified and authenticated in the prescribed manner, of the certificate of registration or equivalent certificate or document issued with respect to the migrating company under the laws of the relevant jurisdiction;

(b) a copy, certified and authenticated in the prescribed manner, of the memorandum and articles of association of the migrating company or equivalent constitutive document of the migrating company;

(c) a list setting out particulars in relation to the directors and secretary of the migrating company in accordance with the provisions of section 195 of the Principal Act;

(d) a statutory declaration of a director of the migrating company made not more than 28 days prior to the date on which the application is made to the registrar to the effect that—

(i) the migrating company is, as of the date of the declaration, established and registered in the relevant jurisdiction, no petition or other similar proceeding to wind up or liquidate the migrating company has been notified to it and remains outstanding in any place, and no order has been notified to the migrating company or resolution adopted to wind up or liquidate the migrating company in any place,

(ii) the appointment of a receiver, liquidator, examiner or other similar person has not been notified to the migrating company and, at the date of the declaration, no such person is acting in that capacity in any place with respect to the migrating company or its property or any part thereof,

(iii) the migrating company is not, at the date of the declaration, operating or carrying on business under any scheme, order, compromise or other similar arrangement entered into or made by the migrating company with creditors in any place,

(iv) at the date of the declaration the migrating company has served notice of the proposed registration on the creditors of the migrating company,

(v) any consent or approval to the proposed registration in the State required by any contract entered into or undertaking given by the migrating company has been obtained or waived, as the case may be, and

(vi) the registration is permitted by and has been approved in accordance with the memorandum and articles of association or equivalent constitutive document of the migrating company;

(e) a declaration of solvency prepared in accordance with section 256H;

(f) a schedule of the charges or security interests created or granted by the migrating company that would, if such charges created or granted by a company incorporated under the Companies Acts, have been registrable under Part IV of the Principal Act and such particulars of those security interests and charges as are specified in section 103 of the Principal Act;

(g) notification of the proposed name of the migrating company if different from its existing name; and

(h) a copy of the memorandum and articles of association of the migrating company which the migrating company has resolved to adopt, which shall be in the Irish language or the English language, which shall take effect on registration under this section and which the migrating company undertakes not to amend before registration without the prior authorisation of the registrar;

'relevant jurisdiction' means the prescribed place outside the State where the migrating company is established and registered at the time of its application under this section.

(2) A migrating company may apply to the registrar to be registered as a company in the State by way of continuation.

(3) Where an application is made under subsection (2), the registrar shall not register the migrating company as a company in the State unless he or she is satisfied that all of the requirements of the Companies Acts in respect of the registration and of matters precedent and incidental thereto have been complied with and, in particular, but without prejudice to the generality of the foregoing, he or she is satisfied that—

(a) the migrating company has delivered to the registrar an application for the purpose, in the prescribed form and signed by a director of the migrating company, together with the registration documents,

(b) the name or, if relevant, the proposed new name of the migrating company has not been determined to be undesirable pursuant to section 21 of the Principal Act,

(c) the migrating company has paid to the registrar such fee as may be specified from time to time pursuant to section 369 of the Principal Act,

(d) the migrating company has filed with the registrar notice of the address of its proposed registered office in the State,

(e) the migrating company has applied to the Central Bank to be authorised to carry on business as a company under section 256(1) and the Central Bank has notified the migrating company and the registrar that it proposes to authorise the migrating company to so carry on business.

(4) An application under this section shall be accompanied by a statutory declaration in the prescribed form made by a solicitor engaged for this purpose by the migrating company, or by a director of the migrating company, and stating that the requirements mentioned in subsection (3) have been complied with. The registrar may accept such a declaration as sufficient evidence of compliance.

(5) The registrar shall, as soon as is practicable after receipt of the application for registration, publish notice of it in the Companies Registration Office Gazette.

(6) Where the registrar receives a notification under subsection (3)(e), the registrar—

(a) may issue a certificate of registration of the migrating company by way of continuation of the migrating company as a body corporate under the laws of the State, and

(b) if he or she issues such a certificate, shall enter in the register maintained for the purpose of section 103 of the Principal Act, in relation to charges and security interests of the migrating company specified in paragraph (f) of the definition of 'registration documents' in subsection (1), the particulars prescribed by section 103 of the Principal Act which have been supplied by the migrating company.

(7) The migrating company shall, as soon as may be after being registered under subsection (6), apply to be de-registered in the relevant jurisdiction.

(8) The registrar shall enter in the register of companies the date of registration of the migrating company and shall forthwith publish notice in the Companies Registration Office Gazette of the following matters:

(a) the date of the registration of the migrating company under this section;

(b) the relevant jurisdiction; and

(c) the previous name of the migrating company if different from the name under which it is being registered.

(9) From the date of registration, the migrating company shall be deemed to be a company formed and registered under this Act and shall continue for all purposes under this Act, and the provisions of this Part shall apply to the migrating company, provided always that this section shall not operate—

(a) to create a new legal entity,

(b) to prejudice or affect the identity or continuity of the migrating company as previously established and registered under the laws of the relevant jurisdiction for the period that the migrating company was established and registered in the relevant jurisdiction,

(c) to affect any contract made, resolution passed or any other act or thing done in relation to the migrating company during the period that the migrating company was so established and registered,

(d) to affect the rights, powers, authorities, functions and liabilities or obligations of the migrating company or any other person, or

(e) to render defective any legal proceedings by or against the migrating company.

(10) Without prejudice to the generality of subsection (9)—

(a) the failure of a migrating company to send to the registrar the particulars of a charge or security interest created prior to the date of registration shall not prejudice any rights which any person in whose favour the charge was made or security interest created may have thereunder, and

(b) any legal proceedings that could have been continued or commenced by or against the migrating company before its registration under this section may, notwithstanding the registration, be continued or commenced by or against the migrating company after registration.

(11) The migrating company shall notify the registrar in the prescribed form, and notify the Central Bank, within 3 days of its de-registration in the relevant jurisdiction, of that de-registration.

(12) On registration of the migrating company under subsection (6), the Central Bank shall forthwith authorise the migrating company to carry on business under this Part.

(13) If there is any material change in any of the information contained in the statutory declaration mentioned in paragraph (d) of the definition of 'registration documents' in subsection (1) after the date of the declaration and before the date of the registration under this section, the director who made that statutory declaration, and any other director who becomes aware of that material change shall forth with deliver a new statutory declaration to the registrar relating to the change.

(14) If the migrating company fails to comply with any provision of this section, the registrar may send to the company by post a registered letter stating that, unless the migrating company rectifies the failure within 1 month of the date of the letter and confirms that it has rectified the failure, a notice may be published in the Companies Registration Office Gazette with a view to striking the name of the migrating company off the register.

(15) If the failure mentioned in subsection (14) is not rectified within 1 month after the sending of the letter referred to in that subsection, the registrar may publish in the Companies Registration Office Gazette a notice stating that, at the expiration of 1 month from the date of that notice, the name of the migrating company mentioned therein will, unless the matter is resolved, be struck off the register, and the migrating company will be dissolved.

(16) At the expiration of the time mentioned in the notice, the registrar may, unless cause to the contrary is previously shown by the migrating company, strike its name off the register, and shall publish notice thereof in the Companies Registration Office Gazette, and on that publication, the migrating company shall be dissolved.

(17) The Minister may make regulations prescribing places as relevant jurisdictions for the purposes of this section, where he or she is satisfied that the law of the place concerned makes provision for migrating companies to continue under the laws of the State or for companies to continue under the laws of that place in a substantially similar manner to continuations under this section.

(18) Every regulation made by the Minister under subsection (17) shall be laid before each House of the Oireachtas as soon as may be after it is made and, if a resolution annulling the regulation is passed by either House within the next 21 days on which that House has sat after the regulation is laid before it, the regulation shall be annulled accordingly, but without prejudice to the validity of anything previously done thereunder.][a]

Amendments

a CA 1990, s 256F inserted by C(MP)A 2009, s 3(j).

Notes

This provision, inserted by C(MP)A 2009, s 3(j), facilitates the migration to Ireland of bodies corporate which are established and registered under the laws of a relevant jurisdiction and which are collective investment undertakings (ie funds companies). It may be noted, in particular, that this provision is not generally available to companies, only those which are collective investment undertakings and also that it only applies to companies in 'relevant jurisdictions', ie jurisdictions so prescribed by the Minster for Enterprise, Trade and Employment. In order for a foreign body corporate to migrate (ie re-register) in Ireland, application must be made to the Registrar of Companies. Where that application is successful, the foreign body corporate will eschew its foreign law origins by applying to be de-registered in its jurisdiction of incorporation and become a 'company' within the meaning of CA 1963, s 2 to which the Companies Acts apply because of sub-s (9), which operates to deem the migrating company to have been 'formed and registered' in the State. It is expressly provided that the provision does not operate to create a new legal entity (ie the company registered in Ireland will be the same entity as previously existed under the laws of the relevant jurisdiction), does not affect its previous identity when a foreign body corporate or affect any contract made or resolution passed or other act or thing done in relation to the migrating company during the period that the migrating company was so established and registered.

[256G De-registration of companies when continued under the law of place outside the State

(1) In this section—

'applicant' means a company that applies to be de-registered under this section;

'relevant jurisdiction' means the prescribed place outside the State in which the company proposes to be registered;

'transfer documents', in relation to an applicant, means the following documents:

(a) a statutory declaration of a director of the applicant made not more than 28 days prior to the date on which the application is made to the registrar to the effect that—

(i) the applicant will, upon registration, continue as a body corporate under the laws of the relevant jurisdiction,

(ii) no petition or other similar proceeding to wind up or liquidate the applicant has been notified to the applicant and remains outstanding in any place, and no order has been notified to the applicant or resolution adopted to wind up or liquidate the applicant in any place,

(iii) the appointment of a receiver, liquidator, examiner or other similar person has not been notified to the applicant and, at the date of the declaration, no such person is acting in that capacity in any place with respect to the applicant or its property or any part thereof,

(iv) the applicant is not, at the date of the declaration, operating or carrying on business under any scheme, order, compromise or other similar arrangement entered into or made by the applicant with creditors in any place,

(v) the application for de-registration is not intended to defraud persons who are, at the date of the declaration, creditors of the applicant,

(vi) any consent or approval to the proposed de-registration required by any contract entered into or undertaking given by the applicant has been obtained or waived, as the case may be, and

(vii) the de-registration is permitted by the memorandum and articles of association of the applicant;

(b) a declaration of solvency prepared in accordance with the provisions of section 256H; and

(c) a copy of a special resolution of the applicant that approves the proposed de-registration and the transfer of the applicant to the relevant jurisdiction.

(2) An applicant which proposes to be registered in a relevant jurisdiction by way of continuation as a body corporate may apply to the registrar to be de-registered in the State.

(3) Where an application is made under subsection (2), the registrar shall not deregister the applicant as a company in the State unless he or she is satisfied that all of the requirements of the Companies Acts in respect of the de-registration and of matters precedent and incidental thereto have been complied with and, in particular, but without prejudice to the generality of the foregoing, he or she is satisfied that—

(a) the applicant has delivered to the registrar an application for the purpose, in the prescribed form and signed by a director of the applicant, together with the transfer documents,

(b) the applicant has paid to the registrar such fee as may be specified from time to time pursuant to section 369 of the Principal Act,

(c) the applicant has informed the Central Bank of its intention to be de-registered and the Central Bank has notified the registrar that it has no objection to the de-registration, so long as the applicant complies with any conditions that the Central Bank may impose on the applicant, and

(d) the applicant has filed with the registrar notice of any proposed change in its name and of its proposed registered office or agent for service of process in the relevant jurisdiction.

(4) An application under this section shall be accompanied by a statutory declaration in the prescribed form made by a solicitor engaged for this purpose by the applicant, or by a director of the applicant, and stating that the requirements mentioned in subsection (3) have been complied with. The registrar may accept such a declaration as sufficient evidence of compliance.

(5) The registrar shall, as soon as is practicable after receipt of the application for de-registration, publish notice of it in the Companies Registration Office Gazette.

(6) (a) Where an application is made under subsection (2), a person mentioned in paragraph (b) may apply to the High Court, on notice to the applicant, the Central Bank, the registrar and all creditors of the applicant, not later than 60 days after the publication of the notice under subsection (5), for an order preventing the proposal or passage of a resolution specified in paragraph (c) of the definition of 'transfer documents' in subsection (1) from taking effect in relation to the application.

(b) The following persons may apply for an order under this subsection:

(i) the holders of not less than 5 per cent of the issued share capital of the applicant and who have not voted in favour of the resolution, or

(ii) any creditor of the applicant.

(c) Notice of an application for an order under this subsection may be given to the creditors concerned by publication in at least one national newspaper in the State.

(d) The Central Bank and the applicant concerned shall be entitled to make representations to the High Court before an order under this subsection is made.

(7) The High Court may make an order mentioned in subsection (6) only if it is satisfied that—

(a) the proposed de-registration of the applicant would contravene the terms of an agreement or arrangement between the applicant and any shareholder or creditor of the applicant; or

(b) the proposed de-registration would be materially prejudicial to any shareholder or creditor of the applicant and the interests of shareholders and creditors or both taken as a whole would be materially prejudiced.

(8) An order made under subsection (7) shall specify the period in respect of which it shall remain in force.

(9) An order of the High Court under subsection (7) is final and conclusive.

(10) Unless the High Court orders otherwise, when one or more than one application is made under subsection (6), a resolution specified in paragraph (c) of the definition of 'transfer documents' in subsection (1) in relation to a company shall not take effect until—

(a) where the application or all the applications to the High Court are withdrawn—

(i) the day on which the resolution is passed,

(ii) the day next following the day on which the last outstanding application is withdrawn, or

(iii) the 31st day following the publication of the notice on the creditors under subsection (4),

whichever is the latest, and

(b) where all applications to the High Court are not withdrawn—

(i) the day on which the resolution is passed,

(ii) the day specified in the order or, if no date is specified in the order, the day next following the day on which the period for which the order is specified to remain in force expires or otherwise ceases to be in force, or

(iii) the day next following the decision of the High Court,

whichever is the latest.

(11) When the applicant is registered as a company under the laws of the relevant jurisdiction, it shall give notice to the registrar of that fact within 3 working days of becoming so registered, including its new name, if any, and, as soon as practicable after receiving that notice, the registrar shall issue a certificate of de-registration of the applicant.

(12) The registrar shall enter in the register of companies the date of the deregistration of the applicant and shall, within 7 days of the issuance of the certificate under subsection (11), publish in the Companies Registration Office Gazette notice of the following matters:

(a) the date of the de-registration of the applicant under this section;

(b) the relevant jurisdiction; and

(c) the new name of the applicant if different from the name under which it was registered.

(13) From the date of registration of the applicant in the relevant jurisdiction, it shall cease to be a company for all purposes of the Companies Acts and shall continue for all purposes as a body corporate under the laws of the relevant jurisdiction, provided always that this section shall not operate—

(a) to create a new legal entity,

(b) to prejudice or affect the identity or continuity of the applicant as previously constituted under the laws of the State for the period that the applicant was so constituted,

(c) to affect any contract made, resolution passed or any other act or thing done in relation to the applicant during the period that the applicant was constituted under the laws of the State,

(d) to affect the rights, powers, authorities, functions and liabilities or obligations of the applicant or any other person, or

(e) to render defective any legal proceedings by or against the applicant.

(14) Without prejudice to the generality of subsection (13), any legal proceedings that could have been continued or commenced by or against the applicant before its de-registration under this section may, notwithstanding the de-registration, be continued or commenced by or against the applicant after registration.

(15) The Minister may make regulations prescribing places as relevant jurisdictions for the purposes of this section, where he or she is satisfied that the law of the place

concerned makes provision for bodies corporate that are substantially similar to applicants under this section to continue under the laws of the State in a substantially similar manner to continuations under section 256F or for companies to continue under the laws of that place.

(16) Every regulation made by the Minister under subsection (15) shall be laid before each House of the Oireachtas as soon as may be after it is made and, if a resolution annulling the regulation is passed by either House within the next 21 days on which that House has sat after the regulation is laid before it, the regulation shall be annulled accordingly, but without prejudice to the validity of anything previously done thereunder.][a]

Amendments

a CA 1990, s 256G inserted by C(MP)A 2009, s 3(j).

Notes

This provision, inserted by C(MP)A 2009, s 3j, operates in reverse to CA 1990, s 256G, by enabling an Irish formed and registered 'applicant' company which is a collective investment undertaking, to migrate to a relevant jurisdiction and eschew its Irish registration and application of the Companies Acts.

[256H Statutory declarations

(1) Where an application is made under section 256F or 256G, a director of the migrating company or applicant, as the case may be, making the application shall make a statutory declaration stating that he or she has made a full inquiry into its affairs and has formed the opinion that it is able to pay its debts as they fall due.

(2) A declaration under subsection (1) shall have no effect for the purposes of this section unless—

(a) it is made not more than 28 days prior to the date on which the application is made to the registrar,

(b) it contains a statement of the migrating company's or applicant's assets and liabilities as at the latest practicable date before the making of the declaration, and, in any case as at a date that is not more than 3 months before the making of the declaration, and

(c) a report made by an independent person under subsection (3) is attached to the declaration, along with a statement by the independent person that he or she has given and has not withdrawn consent to the making of the declaration with the report attached to it.

(3) The report mentioned in subsection (2)(c) shall state whether, in the independent person's opinion, based on the information and explanations given to him or her, the opinion of the director mentioned in subsection (1) and the statement of the migrating company's or applicant's assets and liabilities referred to in subsection (2)(b), are reasonable.

(4) For the purposes of subsection (3), the independent person shall be a person who, at the time the report is made, is qualified to be the auditor of the company or applicant, or of bodies corporate—

(a) in the case of an application under section 256F, under the laws of the relevant jurisdiction, and

(b) in the case of an application under section 256G, under the laws of the State.

(5) A director who makes a declaration under this section without having reasonable grounds for the opinion that the migrating company or applicant is able to pay its debts as they fall due commits an offence and is liable—

(a) on summary conviction to a fine not exceeding €5,000, or imprisonment for a term not exceeding 12 months, or to both, or

(b) on conviction on indictment to a fine not exceeding €50,000, or imprisonment for a term not exceeding 5 years, or to both.

(6) Where the migrating company or applicant is wound up within 1 year of the date on which the application is made to the registrar and its debts are not paid or provided for in full within that year, it shall be presumed, unless the contrary is shown, that the director did not have reasonable grounds for his or her opinion.][a]

Amendments

a CA 1990, s 256H inserted by C(MP)A 2009, s 3(j).

257 Powers of [Central Bank][a]

(1) Notwithstanding any other powers which may be available to the [Central Bank][a] under any other enactment, order or regulation, the [Central Bank][a] may impose such conditions for the granting of an authorisation to a company under section 256 as it considers appropriate and prudent for the purposes of the orderly and proper regulation of the business of investment companies.

(2) Conditions imposed under subsection (1) may be imposed generally, or by reference to particular classes of company or business (including, but not limited to, whether or not an investment company is a designated company), or by reference to any other matter the [Central Bank][a] considers appropriate and prudent for the purposes of the orderly and proper regulation of the business of investment companies.

(3) The power to impose conditions referred to in subsection (1) shall include a power to impose such further conditions from time to time as the [Central Bank][a] considers appropriate and prudent for the purposes of the orderly and proper regulation of the business of investment companies.

(4) Without prejudice to the generality of subsections (1), (2) and (3), conditions imposed by the [Central Bank][a] on an investment company may make provision for any or all of the following matters—

(a) the prudential requirements of the investment policies of the company,

(b) prospectuses and other information disseminated by the company,

(c) the vesting of the assets or specified assets of the company in a person nominated by the [Central Bank][a] with such of the powers or duties of a trustee with regard to the company as are specified by the [Central Bank],[a]

(d) such other supervisory and reporting requirements and conditions relating to its business as the [Central Bank][a] considers appropriate and prudent to impose on the company from time to time for the purposes referred to in the aforesaid subsections [,][b]

[(e) supervisory and reporting requirements and conditions relating to the business of a management company as the Central Bank considers appropriate or prudent to impose on the management company from time to time.][c]

(5) A company shall comply with any conditions relating to its authorisation or business imposed by the [Central Bank][a].

Amendments

a 'Central Bank' substituted for 'Bank' by CBFSAIA 2003, Sch 1.

b 'subsections,' substituted for 'subsections.' by IFCMPA 2005, s 26(a).

c Para (e) of sub-s(4) inserted by IFCMPA 2005, s 26(b).

Definitions

'Central Bank': CA 1990, s 3(1); 'company: CA 1963, s 2(1); 'designated company': CA 1990, s 256(5); 'investment company': CA 1990, s 252(1); 'management company' CA 1990, s 252(1); 'prospectus': CA 1963, s 2(1).

258 Adaptation of certain provisions of UCITS Regulations

Regulations 14, 30, 63, [72(3)][a], 83(2) to (7), and 99 to 105 of the UCITS Regulations shall apply to an investment company [or, in the case of the said Regulation 72(3), such a company other than one to which section 253(2A)(a) applies][b] as they apply to the bodies to which those Regulations relate subject to the following modifications—

(a) a reference in those Regulations to a term or expression specified in the second column of the Table to this section at any reference number shall be construed, where the context admits, as a reference to the term or expression specified in the third column of the said Table at that reference number, and

(b) references to cognate terms or expressions in those Regulations shall be construed accordingly.

TABLE

Ref. No (1)	*Term or expression referred to in UCITS Regulations* (2)	*Construction of term or expression for purposes of this section* (3)
1.	'repurchase'	'purchase'
2.	'these Regulations'	'Part XIII of the Companies Act, 1990'
3.	'UCITS'	'investment company'
4.	'unit'	'share'
5.	'unit-holder'	'shareholder'

Amendments

a CLEA 2001, s 108(a) amends CA 1990, s 258 by the insertion after '63,' of '72(3),'.

b CLEA 2001, s 108(b) amends CA 1990, s 258 by the insertion after 'investment company' of 'or, in the case of the said Regulation 72(3), such a company other than one to which section 253(2A)(a) applies,'.

Definitions

'company: CA 1963, s 2(1); 'investment company': CA 1990, s 252(1); s 3(1); 'share': CA 1963, s 2(1); 'UCITS Regulations': CA 1990, s 252(1).

Notes

This section is intended to ensure clarity and ease of reference in the context of the UCITS regs.

259 Default of investment company or failure in performance of its investments

An authorisation by the [Central Bank][a] under section 256 of an investment company shall not constitute a warranty by the [Central Bank][a] as to the creditworthiness or financial standing of that company and the [Central Bank][a] shall not be liable by virtue of that authorisation or by reason of its exercise of the functions conferred on it by this Part (or any regulations made under this Part) in relation to investment companies for any default of the company unless the [Central Bank][a] acted in bad faith in exercising such functions.

Amendments

a 'Central Bank' substituted for 'Bank' by CBFSIA 2003, Sch 1.

Definitions

'Central Bank': CA 1990, s 3(1); 'company: CA 1963, s 2(1); 'investment company': CA 1990, s 252(1).

[260 Amendment and restriction of certain provisions of Companies Acts

(1) The following provisions of the Principal Act, namely sections 5(1), 36, 213(d) and 215(a)(i), are hereby amended by the insertion after 'private company', in each place where it occurs in those provisions, of 'or an investment company (within the meaning of Part XIII of the Companies Act, 1990)'.

(2) None of the following provisions of the Principal Act shall apply to an investment company, namely sections 53, 56, 58, 60, 69, 70, 72, 119 and 125.

(3) None of the following provisions of the Companies (Amendment) Act, 1983, shall apply to an investment company, namely sections 5(2), 6 and 19, subsections (3) and (4) of section 20, s ections 22, 23 to 25, 30 to 33, 40, 41, [43, 43A][b] and Part IV.

(4) Section 14 of the Companies (Amendment) Act, 1986, shall not apply to an investment company.

(5) None of the following provisions of this Act shall apply to an investment company, namely, Chapters 2 to 4 of Part IV, s ection 140 (whether as regards a case in which the investment company is being wound up or a case in which it is a related company (within the meaning of that section)) and Part XI.][a]

Amendments

a CA 1990, s 260 substituted by C(A)(No 2)A 1999, s 54(3).

b '43, 43A' inserted by IFCMPA 2005, s 27.

Definitions

'company: CA 1963, s 2(1); 'Companies Acts': CA 1990, s 3(1); 'investment company': CA 1990, s 252(1); 'Principal Act': CA 1990, s 3(1); 'private company': CA 1963, s 33.

Notes

This section clarifies those provisions of the Companies Acts that do and do not apply to investment companies.

[260A Application of section 148 of Principal Act

(1) Notwithstanding section 148(2) of the Principal Act (inserted by the European Communities (International Financial Reporting Standards and Miscellaneous Amendments) Regulations 2005 (S.I. No. 116 of 2005)) an investment company may, in respect of its individual accounts, opt to prepare those accounts in accordance with both of the following, namely—

(a) an alternative body of accounting standards, and

(b) section 149A of the Principal Act,

as if the references in that section 149A to international financial reporting standards were references to that alternative body of accounting standards.

(2) In the application of subsections (4), (5) and (6) of section 148 of the Principal Act to an investment company which has opted under subsection (1) to prepare its accounts in accordance with an alternative body of accounting standards—

(a) the reference in that subsection (4) to international financial reporting standards shall be read as a reference to that alternative body of accounting standards, and

(b) there shall be substituted for 'IFRS', in each place where it occurs in those subsections (4), (5) and (6), 'ABAS' (which shall be read as referring to that alternative body of accounting standards).

(3) For the purposes of this section, accounts shall not be regarded as having been prepared in accordance with an alternative body of accounting standards unless the accounts concerned would, were they to have been prepared by a company or undertaking registered in the relevant jurisdiction, be regarded as having been prepared in accordance with those standards.

(4) In this section—

'alternative body of accounting standards' means standards that accounts of companies or undertakings must comply with that are laid down by such body or bodies having authority to lay down standards of that kind in—

(a) United States of America,

(b) Canada,

(c) Japan, or

(d) any other prescribed state or territory,

as may be prescribed;

'relevant jurisdiction' means the state or territory in which the alternative body of accounting standards concerned have effect.

(5) Before making regulations for the purposes of subsection (4), the Minister—

(a) shall consult with the Central Bank, and

(b) may consult with any other persons whom the Minister considers should be consulted.

(6) If particular regulations for the purposes of subsection (4) are proposed to be made at a time subsequent to the commencement of Part 2 of the Companies (Auditing and Accounting) Act 2003, then, before making those regulations, the Minister shall also consult with the Irish Auditing and Accounting Supervisory Authority.][a]

Amendments

a This section was added by IFCMPA 2005, s 28.

Definitions

'Central Bank': CA 1990, s 3(1); 'company: CA 1963, s 2(1); 'investment company': CA 1990, s 252(1); 'Minister': CA 1963, s 2(1); 'Principal Act': CA 1990, s 3(1).

261 Power to make supplementary regulations

The Minister may make such regulations as he considers necessary for the purposes of giving full effect to the provisions of this Part.

Definitions

'Minister': CA 1963, s 2(1).

262 Offences

Where a company contravenes—

(a) any of the provisions of this Part, or

(b) any regulations made in relation thereto (whether under this Part or under any other enactment), or

(c) any condition in relation to its authorisation or business imposed by the [Central Bank][a] under section 257,

the company and every officer thereof who is in default shall be guilty of an offence.

Amendments

a 'Central Bank' substituted for 'Bank' by CBFSAIA 2003, Sch 1.

Definitions

'Central Bank': CA 1990, s 3(1); 'company: CA 1963, s 2(1); 'officer in default': CA 1963, s 383.

SCHEDULE

PROVISIONS SUBSTITUTED FOR NINTH SCHEDULE TO PRINCIPAL ACT

[...][a]

Amendments

a Schedule inserts new Ninth Sch of CA 1963.

COMPANIES (AMENDMENT) ACT, 1977

Subject matter	*Provisions applied*
Share certificates	Sections 2 and 3.
Company records	Section 4.

COMPANIES (AMENDMENT) ACT, 1983

Subject matter	*Provisions applied*
Maintenance of capital. Restrictions on distribution of profits and assets	Sections 40 to 42, 45, 45A (inserted by the Companies (Amendment) Act, 1986) and 49 to 51. Sections 43, 44, 46 and 47, with the modification that those sections shall apply to all bodies corporate to which section 377(1) of the Principal Act applies other than those which, if they were registered, would be private companies.

EUROPEAN COMMUNITIES (STOCK EXCHANGE) REGULATIONS, 1984
(S.I. NO 282 OF 1984)

Provisions applied

All of the Regulations.	

COMPANIES (AMENDMENT) ACT, 1986

Subject matter	Provisions applied
Power to alter form of accounts	Section 24.

EUROPEAN COMMUNITIES (MERGERS AND DIVISIONS OF COMPANIES) REGULATIONS, 1987
(S.I. NO 137 OF 1987)

Provisions applied

All of the Regulations.	

COMPANIES (AMENDMENT) ACT, 1990

Provisions applied

The whole Act.

COMPANIES ACT, 1990

Provisions applied

Parts I to III.
Part IV, with the modification that Chapter 2 of that Part shall apply to all bodies corporate to which section 377 (1) of the Principal Act applies other than those which, if they were registered, would be private companies and Chapter 3 of that Part shall apply to all such bodies corporate which, if they were registered, would be private companies.
Part V.
Part VI, except sections 122, 128 to 131 and 133.
Parts VII, IX, X and XII.

Companies (Amendment) Act 1999

Number 8 of 1999

ARRANGEMENT OF SECTIONS

An Act to amend and extend Parts IV and V of the Companies Act, 1990, to permit stabilising activity in relation to the issue or sale of securities and to provide for connected matters. [19th May, 1999]

Be It Enacted by the Oireachtas as Follows:

Notes

The purpose of Companies (Amendment) Act 1999, which came into force on 24 May 1999[1] was to introduce a mechanism known as price stabilisation for use in connection with new issues or offers for sale of securities on a stock exchange. By introducing this mechanism, Irish law was brought into line with existing international practice.[2] The immediate need for the Act had been brought about by the sale by the State of its 50.1% stake in Bord Telecom Éireann plc by way of initial public offering, in June 1999.

The primary purpose of price stabilisation is to protect investors from potential serious declines in the value of the securities following the public offering. This mechanism also protects the company itself and those selling the securities by promoting an orderly and stable market in the aftermath of the public offering.

Unless otherwise permitted by appropriate legislation, price stabilisation could amount to insider dealing. Such activity was already permitted outside the State by the Companies Act, 1990 (Insider Dealing) Regulations, 1992[3] but was potentially unlawful within the State by virtue of the provisions of CA 1990, Part V. That position has, however, been rectified by the enactment of this piece of legislation. The Companies Act, 1990 (Insider Dealing) Regulations 1992 have now been repealed[4] and price stabilisation, whether occurring within or outside the State, was governed instead by this Act.

Price stabilisation may only take place for a limited period of time after the announcement of the public offering and, even then, only in accordance with the Stabilisation Rules set out in the Schedule to the Act.

This Act, along with Part V of CA 1990 has been repealed by IFCMPA 2005 s 31. However The Investment Funds, Companies and Miscellaneous Provisions Act 2005 (Commencement) Order 2005 (SI 323/2005) art 5 provides: "The 6th day of July 2005 is appointed as the day on which the following provisions of the Act come into operation, namely – (a) section 31 (but only for the purpose of repealing the enactments specified in that section in so far as they relate to a regulated market (within the meaning of Directive 2003/71/EC of the European Parliament and of the Council of 4 November 2003) operated by a recognised stock exchange within the meaning Part V of the Companies Act 1990 (No.33 of 1990))."

Accordingly this Act applies only to Irish-incorporated companies whose shares or other securities are admitted to trading on an Irish recognised stock exchange, ie the Irish Stock Exchange.

1 Companies (Amendment) Act, 1999 (Commencement) Order, 1999 (SI 144/1999).

2 Companies (Amendment) Act, 1999 (Commencement) Order, 1999 (SI 144/1999).

3 SI 131/1992.

4 C(A)A 1999, s 6.

1 Interpretation

(1) In this Act—

'the Act of 1990' means the Companies Act, 1990;

'closing date' has the meaning assigned by the Stabilisation Rules;

'the Principal Act' means the Companies Act, 1963;

'stabilising period' has, in relation to anything done in the State pursuant to the Stabilisation Rules, the meaning assigned by the Stabilisation Rules and, in relation to anything done in a jurisdiction outside the State for the purpose of stabilising or maintaining the market price of securities, means the period beginning on—

(a) in the case of an issue or offer for sale of securities (not being an issue of debentures or other debt securities), the date on which the earliest public announcement of such issue or offer is made which states the issue price or the offer price, as the case may be, for those securities, or

(b) in the case of an issue of debentures or other debt securities, the date on which the earliest public announcement of such issue is made, whether or not that announcement states the issue price, and ending on the expiration of—

(i) the day which is 30 days after the closing date, or

(ii) the day which a manager appointed by the issuer or, as the case may be, the offeror to conduct stabilising activity shall have notified a stock exchange on which stabilising activity was being conducted as the day on which it determined that it would take no further action to stabilise or maintain the market price of the securities concerned, whichever first occurs;

'Stabilisation Rules' means the rules referred to by that name which are set out in the Schedule.

(2) In this Act—

(a) a reference to a Part, section or Schedule is a reference to a Part or section of, or a Schedule to, this Act, unless it is indicated that reference to some other enactment is intended,

(b) a reference to a subsection, paragraph, subparagraph, clause or subclause is a reference to the subsection, paragraph, subparagraph, clause or subclause of the provision in which the reference occurs unless it is indicated that reference to some other provision is intended, and

(c) a reference to any enactment is a reference to that enactment as amended, extended or adapted by or under any subsequent enactment including this Act.

Amendments

Section repealed in limited manner as per IFCMPA 2005, s 31 as enacted by SI 323/2005. See IFCMPA 2005, s 31 and notes thereto.

Definitions

'closing date': C(A)A 1990, Sch, para 1; 'debenture': CA 1963, s 2(1); 'issue': C(A)A 1990, Sch para 1; 'manager': C(A)A 1990, Sch para 1; 'public announcement': C(A) 1990, Sch para 1; 'securities': CA 1990, s 107 and C(A)A 1990, Sch, para 1; 'stabilising period': C(A)A 1990, Sch para 1.

Notes

Stabilisation period: Price stabilisation may only be conducted for a limited period of time. In the case of securities other than debentures and other debt securities, it may begin on the date of the earliest public announcement of the issue or offer which states the issue price or offer price, as the case may be.[1] In the case of debentures and other debt securities price stabilisation may begin on the date of the earliest public announcement of the issue or offer regardless of whether or not the price is stated.[2] However, regardless of the type of security involved, the price stabilisation activity must terminate at the end of the 30-day period after the closing date[3] or such earlier date on which the stabilising manager[4] (or, in the case of foreign activity, the person appointed by the issuer or offeror to carry out the equivalent role abroad) shall notify the relevant stock exchange that it has been determined that there should be no further such stabilising activity.

1 C(A)A 1990, s 1(1) and Sch, para (1).

2 C(A)A 1990, s 1(1) and Sch, para (1).

3 The 'closing date' is defined by the Stabilisation Rules as being the date on which the issuer or offeror receives the proceeds of the issue or offer or, in a case where payment is by instalments, where the issuer or offeror receives the proceeds of the first such instalment.

4 Typically an investment bank retained by the company for the purposes of the public offering.

UK legislation

Financial Services and Markets Act 2000, s 144.

2 Restriction of section 108 of Act of 1990

Section 108 of the Act of 1990 shall not be regarded as having been contravened by reason of—

(a) anything done in the State for the purpose of stabilising or maintaining the market price of securities if it is done in conformity with the Stabilisation Rules, or

(b) any action taken during the stabilising period by a person in any jurisdiction other than the State for the purpose of stabilising or maintaining the market price of securities, but only if the action taken is, in all material respects, permitted by or is otherwise in accordance with all relevant requirements applicable to such actions in the jurisdiction where such action is effected, including, if those securities are also listed on a stock exchange in that jurisdiction, the rules or other regulatory requirements governing that stock exchange.

Amendments

Section repealed in limited manner as per IFCMPA 2005, s 31 as enacted by SI 323/2005. See IFCMPA 2005, s 31 and notes thereto.

Definitions

'the Act of 1990': C(A)A 1999, s 1(1); 'stabilising period': C(A)A 1999, s 1(1); 'Stabilisation Rules': C(A)A 1999, s 1(1).

Notes

Disapplication of insider dealing rules: Participation in price stabilisation, whether as a primary or as a secondary insider, could have amounted to a breach of the insider dealing provisions of CA 1990, Part V, at least in circumstances where the participant was in possession of price-sensitive information. The effect of this section however, is to permit dealing in securities of the company if conducted in accordance with the Stabilisation Rules or (in the case of foreign dealing) if conducted in accordance with local legislative requirements. Interestingly, it would seem that if the jurisdiction has no price stabilisation provisions but also has no insider dealing provisions, the use of price-sensitive information can be availed of with impunity, regardless of the personal benefit that may be enjoyed thereby.

UK legislation

Criminal Justice Act 1993, s 53(4) and Sch 1 para 5.

Financial Services and Markets Act 2000, s 144.

---

3 Disclosure of interests in relevant share capital

(1) The acquisition or disposal of interests in relevant share capital by a person during the stabilising period concerned, which—

(a) is done for the purpose of stabilising or maintaining the market price of securities, and

(b) is so done either in conformity with the Stabilisation Rules or is an acquisition or disposal to which section 2(b) relates,

shall be disregarded during the stabilising period for the purposes of sections 67 to 79 of the Act of 1990.

(2) Any interest in relevant share capital which—

(a) was acquired by a person during the stabilising period for the purpose of stabilising or maintaining the market price of securities,

(b) was so acquired in accordance with this Act, and

(c) continues to be held by such person at the end of the stabilizing period,

shall be treated, for the purposes of sections 67 to 79 of the Act of 1990, as having been acquired by such person on the first day following the end of the stabilising period that is not a Saturday, Sunday or public holiday.

(3) Notwithstanding subsection (1), subsection (4) of section 91 of the Act of 1990 shall operate to determine the interests which are to be notified to the Irish Stock Exchange

Limited, and the manner in which they are to be so notified, under subsection (2) of that section.

(4) In this section 'relevant share capital' has the meaning assigned by section 67(2) of the Act of 1990.

Amendments

Section repealed in limited manner as per IFCMPA 2005, s 31 as enacted by SI 323/2005. See IFCMPA 2005, s 31 and notes thereto.

Definitions

'the Act of 1990': C(A)A 1999, s 1(1); 'relevant share capital': CA 1990, s 67(2); 'stabilising period': C(A)A 1999, s 1(1); 'Stabilisation Rules': C(A)A 1999, s 1(1).

Notes

Disclosure of interests in shares: In the case of a plc, normally there would be an obligation to notify any transaction which brought a person's interest in shares in the company above or below 5% or which altered the amount of a shareholding already at 5% or more. However, if the transaction in question is effected for price stabilisation purposes and in accordance with the Stabilisation Rules (or in accordance with local rules in the case of a foreign transaction) no notification obligation will arise during the stabilisation period. However, if the person holds onto the securities after the end of the stabilisation period, a notification obligation will arise, albeit that the securities in question will be deemed to have been acquired on the first business day after the end of the stabilisation period.

Despite the foregoing, if the party engaged in price stabilisation is a substantial shareholder in a listed plc, such that the price stabilisation dealing brings that party above or below any of the trigger levels of 10%, 25%, 50% or 75%, an obligation to notify the Stock Exchange will arise under CA 1990, s 91.

4 Amendment of section 110 of Act of 1990

[...][a]

Amendments

a C(A)A 1999, s 4 inserts CA 1990, s 110(2A) which in essence incorporates the provisions of the Companies Act, 1990 (Insider Dealing) Regulations, 1991[1] which have now been repealed by C(A)A 1999, s 6. See the amended Act.

[1] SI 151/1991.

5 Removal of difficulties

(1) Where, in any respect, any difficulty arises in the operation of any provision of the Stabilisation Rules, the Minister for Enterprise, Trade and Employment may by regulations amend the Stabilisation Rules to do anything which appears to him or her to be necessary or expedient for removing that difficulty, and any such regulations may modify any provision of the Stabilisation Rules or add thereto so far as may be necessary or expedient for carrying the Schedule into effect.

(2) Every regulation made under this section shall be laid before each House of the Oireachtas as soon as may be after it is made and if a resolution annulling the regulation

is passed by either such House within the next 21 days on which that House has sat after the regulation is laid before it, the regulation shall be annulled accordingly, but without prejudice to the validity of anything previously done thereunder.

Definitions

'Stabilisation Rules': C(A)A 1999, s 1(1).

Notes

Amendment of the Stabilisation Rules: C(A)A 1999, s 5 confers on the Minister a potentially wide ranging jurisdiction to make whatever changes may be considered 'necessary or expedient' with limited power for the Oireachtas to prevent such change.

UK legislation

Financial Services and Markets Act 2000, s 144.

---

6 Revocations

The Companies Act, 1990 (Insider Dealing) Regulations, 1991 (SI No 151 of 1991), and the Companies Act, 1990 (Insider Dealing) Regulations, 1992 (SI No 131 of 1992), are hereby revoked.

Amendments

Section repealed in limited manner as per IFCMPA 2005, s 31 as enacted by SI 323/2005. See IFCMPA 2005, s 31 and notes thereto.

Notes

Repeals: The repeal of the 1991 Regulations is a logical consequence of the incorporation of the provisions thereof into CA 1990, s 110(2A) as inserted by C(A)A 1990, s 4. As regards the 1992 Regulations (which had permitted foreign price stabilisation), they have been superseded by C(A)A 1990, s 2.

---

7 Short title, collective citation, construction and commencement

(1) This Act may be cited as the Companies (Amendment) Act, 1999.

(2) This Act and the Companies Acts, 1963 to 1990, may be cited together as the Companies Acts, 1963 to 1999, and shall be construed together as one.

(3) This Act shall come into operation on such day or days as may be appointed by order or orders made by the Minister for Enterprise, Trade and Employment, either generally or with reference to any particular purpose or provision, and different days may be so appointed for different purposes and different provisions of this Act.

Amendments

Section repealed in the limited manner as per IFCMPA 2005, s 31 as enacted by SI 323/2005. See IFCMPA 2005, s 31 and Notes thereto.

Notes

SI 151/1991: C(A)A 1999 came into force on 24 May 1999.[1]

[1] Companies (Amendment) Act, 1999 (Commencement) Order, 1999 (SI 144/1999).

SCHEDULE

STABILISATION RULES

Section 1(1).

1 Definitions

In these Rules—

'associated securities' means securities—

(a) which are in all respects uniform with the relevant securities, or

(b) for which the relevant securities may be exchanged or into which they may be converted, or

(c) which the holders of the relevant securities have, by virtue of their holdings of those securities, rights to acquire or to subscribe for, or

(d) which are depository receipts which represent or confer property rights in respect of relevant securities or securities to which paragraph (a), (b), (c) or (f) relates or which represent or confer a contractual right (other than an option) to acquire such securities otherwise than by subscription; or

(e) which represent or confer any right, option or obligation in respect of an index relating to relevant securities or to securities to which paragraph (a), (b), (c) or (d) relates, or

(f) which represent or confer a right to acquire a particular amount of relevant securities or of any securities to which paragraph (a), (b), (c), (d) or (e) relates at a future date at a particular price ('associated call options') or which otherwise represent or confer any right, option or obligation in respect of such securities;

'closing date' means—

(a) in the case of an issue of securities, the date on which the issuer of the securities receives the proceeds of the issue or, where the issuer receives those proceeds in instalments, the date on which it receives the first instalment; and

(b) in the case of an offer for sale of securities, the date on which the offeror or, as the case may be, the offerors receive the proceeds of the offer for sale, or where the offeror or, as the case may be, the offerors receive those proceeds in instalments, the date on which the offeror or, where there is more than one offeror, one or more of the offerors receives the first instalment;

'introductory period' means the period starting at the time of the first public announcement from which it could reasonably be deducted that the issue was intended to take place in some form and at some time, and ending with the beginning of the stabilising period;

'issue', except in the definitions of 'closing date' and 'stabilising period' and in Rule 2, includes offer for sale and 'issued' shall be construed accordingly;

'issue price' means the specified price at which the relevant securities are issued without deducting any selling concession or commission;

'issuer', except in the definition of 'closing date', includes offeror;

'manager' means the person instructed by the issuer of the securities to manage the issue;

'public announcement' means any communication made by or on behalf of the issuer or the manager, being a communication made in circumstances in which it is likely that members of the public will become aware of the communication;

'recognised stock exchange' has the meaning assigned by section 107 of the Companies Act, 1990;

'the Register' has the meaning assigned by Rule 5(1)(d);

'relevant day' means—

(a) the 30th day after the closing date or,

(b) where before the 30th day after the closing date the stabilising manager has determined that he or she would take no further action to stabilise or maintain the market price of the relevant securities and has notified the Irish Stock Exchange Limited accordingly pursuant to Rule 8; the day he or she so determined;

'relevant securities' has the meaning given by Rule 2;

'securities' has the meaning assigned by section 107 of the Companies Act, 1990;

'stabilising action' means a purchase of, or agreement to purchase or offer to purchase relevant securities or associated securities permitted to be made by Rule 3;

'stabilising manager' means the person who is manager or, if there be more than one manager, such one of the managers as shall have been agreed between them to be the one to conduct stabilising action in the State in relation to the issue of the relevant securities;

'stabilising period' means the period beginning with the date on which the earliest public announcement of the issue or offer for sale which states the issue price or offer price, as the case may be, is made and ending with the relevant day, save that, in relation to an issue of relevant securities which are debentures or other debt securities, the stabilising period means the period beginning with the date on which the earliest public announcement of the issue is made (whether or not that announcement states the issue price) and ending with the relevant day;

'takeover offer' means an offer made generally to holders of shares in a company to acquire those shares or a specified proportion of them, or to holders of a particular class of those shares to acquire the shares of that class or a specified proportion of them.

2 Application

These Rules apply to—

(a) an issue of securities for cash,

(b) an offer of securities for cash for which securities dealing facilities are not already provided by a recognised stock exchange, and

(c) an offer of securities for cash for which securities dealing facilities are already provided by a recognised stock exchange, if the total cost of the securities which are the subject of the offer is at least [€19,046,071.18][a] (or the equivalent in the currency or unit of account in which the price of the securities is stated),

and which is made other than in connection with a takeover offer and at a specified price and which securities may be dealt in on a recognised stock exchange without a formal application, or in respect of which application has been made to a recognised stock exchange for the securities to be dealt in on that exchange, and such securities are in these Rules referred to as 'relevant securities'.

Amendments

a £15,000,000 converted to €19,046,071.18 by Council Regulation (EC) No 1103/97, No 974/98 and No 2866/98 and the Economic and Monetary Union Act 1998, s 6.

---

3 Permitted stabilising action

(1) Subject to paragraph (2) and Rules 6 and 7, the stabilising manager may during the stabilising period do any or all of the following, with a view to stabilising or maintaining the market price of the relevant securities:

(a) purchase, agree to purchase or offer to purchase any of the relevant securities, and

(b) purchase, agree to purchase or offer to purchase any associated securities.

(2) A stabilising manager may effect a stabilising action pursuant to paragraph (1) only if the stabilising manager reasonably believes that the conditions specified in Rule 5 have been fulfilled.

(3) A stabilising manager who effects a stabilising action pursuant to paragraph (1) shall comply with Rule 9.

4 Permitted action ancillary to stabilising action

(1) Subject to paragraph (2) and Rule 6, the stabilising manager may—

(a) with a view to effecting stabilising actions, either or both—

(i) make allocations of a greater number of relevant securities than will be issued, and

(ii) sell, offer to sell, or agree to sell a greater number of relevant securities or associated securities than the stabilising manager has available for sale,

(b) sell, offer to sell, or agree to sell relevant securities or associated securities in order to close out or liquidate any position established by stabilising actions whether or not those actions were in accordance with Rule 3, and

(c) purchase, offer to purchase or agree to purchase relevant securities or associated securities in order to close out or liquidate any position established pursuant to clause (i) or (ii) of subparagraph (a).

(2) A stabilising manager may act pursuant to paragraph (1) only if he or she reasonably believes that the conditions specified in Rule 5 have been fulfilled.

(3) A stabilising manager who acts pursuant to paragraph (1) shall comply with Rule 9.

(4) A transaction of the type described in paragraph (1)(c) may be effected without regard to the requirements as to purchasing price limits set out in Rule 7.

5 Preliminary steps before stabilising action, etc

(1) The following are the conditions which have, in the reasonable belief of the stabilising manager, to have been fulfilled before any stabilising action or action pursuant to Rule 4(1) may be taken in accordance with these Rules:

(a) from the beginning of the introductory period—

(i) any electronic screen-based statement, including any screen facility provided by the stabilising manager through which persons are informed of the sale or purchase price of securities, or

(ii) any announcement intended for publication in any newspaper and any other announcement of a public nature, or

(iii) any invitation telex or equivalent document;

which refers to the issue concerned and is made or published by or on behalf of the issuer or the stabilising manager shall during the introductory period, include a reference to the future prospectus or to the prospectus or include the word 'Stabilisation',

(b) from the beginning of the introductory period, any preliminary offering circular, preliminary offering prospectus, final offering circular or final offering prospectus relating to the issue of the securities concerned shall include the following statement or a statement to the like effect:

'In connection with this issue [name of stabilizing manager] may over-allot or effect transactions which stabilise or maintain the market price of [description of relevant securities and of any associated securities] at a level which might not otherwise prevail. Such stabilising, if commenced, may be discontinued at any time',

and references in these Rules to a 'disclosure statement' shall be to such statement or such statement to like effect,

(c) if there are associated securities in existence the market price of which was, at the time the issue price of the relevant securities was determined, at a level higher than it otherwise would have been because of any act performed by, or any course of conduct engaged in by, any person which the stabilising manager knows or ought reasonably to know created a false or misleading impression in the market in or the price or value of that security which may induce, or may have induced, another person—

(i) to enter into, or refrain from entering into any bargain or other transaction relative to such security, or

(ii) to exercise or refrain from exercising any rights conferred by that security,

the stabilising manager is satisfied that the issue price of the relevant securities is no higher than it would have been had that act not been performed or that course of conduct not been engaged in,

and

(d) the stabilising manager has established a register (in these Rules referred to as 'the Register') to record in relation to each transaction effected in the relevant securities or associated securities the matters required to be recorded by Rule 9.

(2) (a) Any disclosure required by paragraph (1)(a) to be included in a document or communication, or any disclosure statement required by paragraph (1)(b) to be included in a circular or prospectus, shall be set out prominently and in a legible form in the document or communication concerned.

(b) The disclosure statement may be adapted or omitted to comply with the requirements of any other jurisdiction in which transactions to stabilise or maintain the market price of securities may be conducted in connection with the issue and so as not to require any person duly appointed to conduct stabilising activity in respect of a jurisdiction other than the State to commit any breach of any legal rule or requirement in respect of any communication or announcement made or advertisement or document issued in that jurisdiction.

(3) (a) Except where provided for by subparagraphs (a) and (b) of paragraph (1), this Rule shall not apply to any communication, advertisement or document.

(b) Without prejudice to the generality of subparagraph (a), a disclosure or a disclosure statement need not be set out in any—

(i) allotment telex or similar document,

(ii) pricing telex or similar document,

(iii) contract note, or

(iv) short form or image advertisement, including any newspaper, radio or television advertisement designed to generate interest in the issue of the securities concerned and any marketing brochure as long as it does not constitute a preliminary offering circular or preliminary offering prospectus.

6 Restriction on stabilising action in associated securities

No stabilising action shall be taken in any associated securities of those relevant securities which are debentures or other debt securities and which associated securities are associated securities because—

(a) the relevant securities may be exchanged for or converted into the associated securities, or

(b) the holders of the relevant securities have a right to subscribe for or to acquire the associated securities,

unless the terms on which the relevant securities may be exchanged for or converted into the associated securities, or the rights of holders of the relevant securities to subscribe for or to acquire the associated securities, have been finally settled and been made the subject of a public announcement.

7 Limits on prices

(1) No stabilising action shall be effected by the stabilising manager at a price higher than any relevant price determined in accordance with this Rule.

(2) The limits on prices at which stabilising action may be effected shall be as follows:

(a) in the case of relevant securities and associated securities which are in all respects uniform with the relevant securities (not being debentures or other debt securities)—

(i) for the initial stabilising action, the issue price,

(ii) for subsequent actions—

(I) where there has been a deal at a price above the price at which the initial stabilising action took place (the 'initial stabilising price') on the relevant exchange which has not been done by or on the instructions of the stabilising manager, the issue price, or the price at which that deal was done, whichever is the lower, or

(II) where there has been no deal of the type described in subclause (I), the issue price, or the initial stabilising price, whichever is the lower,

(b) in the case of associated securities (not being debentures or other debt securities, associated securities which are in all respects uniform with the relevant securities, or associated call options)—

(i) for the initial stabilising action, the market bid price of the associated securities at the beginning of the stabilising period,

(ii) for subsequent actions—

(I) where there has been a deal at a price above the price at which the initial stabilising action took place (the 'initial stabilising price') on the relevant exchange which has not been done by or on the instructions of the stabilising manager, the market bid price in clause (i) or the price at which that deal in the associated securities was done, whichever is the lower, or

(II) where there has been no deal of the type described in subclause (I), the market bid price as in clause (i), or the initial stabilising price for the associated securities, whichever is the lower,

and

(c) in the case of associated call options—

(i) for the initial stabilising action, the market price of the associated call option at the beginning of the stabilising period,

(ii) for subsequent actions—

(I) where there has been a deal at a price above the price at which the initial stabilising action took place (the 'initial stabilising price') on the relevant exchange which has not been done by or on the instructions of the stabilising manager, the market price in clause (i) or the price at which that deal in the associated call option was done, whichever is the lower, or

(II) where there has been no deal of the type described in subclause (I), the market price as in clause (i), or the initial stabilising price for the associated call option, whichever is the lower.

(3) (a) In this Rule 'relevant exchange' means the stock exchange which the stabilising manager reasonably believes to be the principal stock exchange on which those securities, or as the case may be, options, are dealt in at the time of the transaction.

(b) For the purposes of this Rule—

(i) where the price of any relevant securities or associated securities on the relevant exchange is in a currency other than the currency of the price of the securities to be stabilised, stabilising actions may be made at a price that reflects any movement in the relevant rate of exchange, but this shall not permit stabilising action under paragraph (2)(a) at a price above the equivalent, in the other currency, of the issue price in the currency on the relevant exchange,

(ii) any convertible bond which is both a debenture or other debt security and an associated call option shall be treated as a debenture only,

(iii) where no market bid price is quoted in respect of the associated security concerned at the beginning of the stabilising period, the relevant price shall be the closing quotation price in respect of such securities on the previous business day as published in the relevant stock exchange list.

8 Notification of termination of stabilising action

Where the stabilising manager determines, before the 30th day after the closing date that he or she will take no further action to stabilise or maintain the market price of the relevant securities, he or she shall notify the Irish Stock Exchange Limited without delay of that determination and the Irish Stock Exchange Limited shall publish that information in such form as it sees fit.

9 Recording of stabilisation transactions

(1) The stabilising manager shall record in the Register the matters specified in subparagraph (2) in relation to transactions effected pursuant to Rules 3 and 4 and that record shall be made before the opening of business on the day that is not a Saturday, Sunday or public holiday which next follows the day the transaction was effected and a copy of that record shall be communicated to the Irish Stock Exchange Limited before the end of that day.

(2) The following matters shall be recorded in the Register:

(a) the names of the persons to whom the relevant securities were allocated or issued and, in relation to each person, the amount allocated or issued to him or her;

(b) the description of the security which is the subject of the transaction;

(c) the price (excluding any commission payable) of each security which is the subject of the transaction;

(d) the number of securities which are the subject of the transaction;

(e) the date and time of the transaction; and

(f) the identity of the counterparty to the transaction.

(3) A stabilising manager who offers or effects a stabilising action at a price determined in accordance with subparagraph (a)(ii)(I), (b)(ii)(I) or (c)(ii)(I) of Rule 7(2) shall record in the Register details of the transaction which affects the maximum price of the stabilising action.

Notes

Financial threshold: In an effort to limit scope of the Stabilisation Rules, it is provided that they apply only where the total value of the securities on offer is at least £15,000,000 or the Euro equivalent thereof.[1]

1 Stabilisation Rules, r 2.

Other limitations: The offer must be in cash and at a specified price[1] and must arise otherwise than in the context of a takeover in order to be able to invoke the Stabilisation Rules.[2]

1 Stabilisation Rules, r 2.
2 Stabilisation Rules, r 2.

Permitted stabilisation: Buying or selling (and indeed overselling)[1] of the relevant securities is permitted as part of the stabilisation process.[2] However, as a prerequisite for these activities, the stabilisation manager must act in good faith to ensure that relevant electronic or 'hard copy' announcements regarding the offer or issue include a sufficient warning of potential stabilisation activity, as described in rule 5. In addition, proper records of any stabilisation transactions must be maintained in accordance with rule 9 and must be copied to the Irish Stock Exchange. Furthermore, where the company already has associated securities on the market the price of which has been artificially inflated by a person of whose conduct the stabilisation manager knows or ought reasonably to be aware, it is an essential prerequisite to any stabilisation activity that the stabilisation manager be satisfied that the issue price of the securities has not been upwardly distorted by the conduct of that third party.[3]

Where the offer or issue concerns securities other than debentures or debt securities no stabilisation activity may be undertaken in relation to any associated securities unless the terms for conversion into securities of the type currently being offered, have been publicly announced.

Rule 7 sets out limits on the permitted prices at which securities may be dealt as part of the process of stabilisation.[4] In the case of initial stabilising activity the maximum price payable is issue price. Thereafter, the price payable by the stabilisation manger (or his foreign counterpart, as the case may be) is the initial stabilisation price or the issue price, whichever is the lower.[5] Nonetheless, if there has been an independent (ie non-stabilisation) deal on the market at a price above the stabilisation price, the stabilisation manager is permitted to purchase at the issue price or the price at which the independent deal was done, whichever is the lower.

1 Stabilisation Rules, r 4(1)(a).
2 Stabilisation Rules, r 3.
3 Stabilisation Rules, r 5(1)(c).
4 An exception is, however, made for a transaction to close out a position established as part of a permitted oversell of the securities: Stabilisation Rules, r 4(4).
5 Equivalent rules apply for dealing in associated securities and associated call options: Stabilisation Rules, r 7(2)(b) and (c).

UK legislation

Financial Services and Markets Act 2000, s 144.

Companies (Amendment) (No 2) Act 1999

Number 30 of 1999

ARRANGEMENT OF SECTIONS

PART I

PRELIMINARY AND GENERAL

PART III
EXEMPTION FROM REQUIREMENT TO HAVE ACCOUNTS AUDITED

PART IV
MISCELLANEOUS

FIRST SCHEDULE

SECOND SCHEDULE

Companies (Amendment) (No 2) Act 1999

Number 30 of 1999

An Act to amend the Companies (Amendment) Act, 1990, to provide for an exemption from the requirement that the accounts of companies and certain partnerships be audited, to prohibit the formation of a company unless it appears to the registrar of companies that the company will carry on an activity in the state, to require, save in certain circumstances, one of the directors of a company to be a person resident in the state, to otherwise amend the law relating to companies and certain partnerships and to provide for related matters. [15th December, 1999]

Be it Enacted by the Oireachtas as Follows:

Notes

C(A)(No 2)A 1999 implemented, *inter alia*, many of the recommendations of the ad hoc company law review group, chaired by James Gallagher and published in February 1995.

C(A)(No 2)A 1999, Pt II introduced numerous changes to the law relating to examinerships, such as raising the standard of proof required for the appointment of an examiner and shortening the period of protection itself. Changes were also introduced regarding the treatment of certain types of liability such as those secured by a guarantee or those deriving from a lease. The entitlement of the members to vote on the examiner's proposals was also removed, thereby reflecting the fact that in most instances where an examiner has been appointed, there is a substantial net asset deficiency and thus the members have no tangible pecuniary interest in the company's fate.

C(A)(No 2)A 1999, Pt III represents an effort to relieve a range of smaller private companies from the burden of having to have their accounts audited annually. Broadly speaking, if such companies fall within the relevant financial and other thresholds and are up to date in the filing of their annual returns, they may elect to dispense with the requirement for an annual audit. However, this exemption cannot be availed of if members holding not less than 10% of voting rights insist to the contrary.

C(A)(No 2)A 1999, Pt IV introduced a range of miscellaneous amendments, the most significant of which were the introduction of the requirements that any newly-formed companies should carry on business in the State and that every Irish company should have at least one Irish resident director. As an alternative to having an Irish resident director a company could put in place a bond as security for any fines that might be imposed on the company for breaches of the Companies Acts or the Taxes Consolidation Act 1997. The number of directorships which a person could hold was also limited. A range of amendments were also made concerning the dissolution of companies and the circumstances in which application may be made to have such companies restored to the register.

[1] In April 1994, an ad hoc company law review group was established by the then Minister for Enterprise and Employment, Ruairí Quinn.

PART I

PRELIMINARY AND GENERAL

1 Short Title, collective citation, construction and commencement

(1) This Act may be cited as the Companies (Amendment) (No 2) Act, 1999.

(2) The Companies Acts, 1963 to 1986, the Companies (Amendment) Act, 1990, the Companies Act, 1990, the Companies (Amendment) Act, 1999, and this Act (other than section 40) may be cited together as the Companies Acts, 1963 to 1999.

(3) The enactments referred to in subsection (2) shall be construed together as one.

(4) This Act shall come into operation on such day or days as the Minister may appoint by order or orders either generally or with reference to any particular purpose or provision and different days may be so appointed for different purposes or different provisions.

(5) The power under subsection (4) shall be so exercised that—

(a) the one day is appointed on which every provision of Part III (other than subsections (2), (3) and (7) of section 33), the First Schedule and the Second Schedule (in so far as it relates to the said Part) shall come into operation, and

(b) the day appointed on which subsections (2), (3) and (7) of section 33 shall come into operation is the day that is 2 months earlier than the said day.

Definitions

'commencement': IA 2005, Sch, Pt 1; 'Minister': CA 1963, s 2(1).

Notes

Operative dates: C(A)(No 2)A 1999, Pt I and s 33(2), (3)[1] and (7), ss 40, 41, 52, 53 and s 54 (other than s 54(1)(a) in so far as it relates to a company the memorandum of which was delivered to the registrar of companies for registration under CA 1963, s 17 before 24 December 1999) came into force on 21 December 1999.[2] The balance of s 54(1)(a) came into force on 24 December 2000.[3]

C(A)(No 2)A 1999, Pt II and the 2nd Sch in so far as it relates to Pt II, came into force on 1 February 2000.[4]

C(A)(No 2)A 1999, Pt III (other than s 33(2), (3) and (7)), the 1st Sch and the 2nd Sch in so far as it relates to Pt III, came into force on 21 February 2000.[5]

The provisions of C(A)(No 2)A 1999, ss 46 and 49–51 came into force on 23 March 2000[6] whereas C(A)(No 2)A 1999, ss 42–45, 47 and 48 together with the Second Schedule in so far as it relates to Pt IV, came into force on 18 April 2000.[7]

1 Specific reference is made at C(A)(No 2)A 1999, s 5(b) to the power of the Minister to determine the dates on which certain sections become operative. A distinction was made between the operative dates of the various subsections of C(A)(No 2)A 1999, s 33 so as to permit the members of a company which would be entitled to avail of the audit exemption to request that the company not avail of the exemption in advance of the right to avail of the exemption being commenced.

2 Companies (Amendment) (No 2) Act 1999 (Commencement) Order 1999 (SI 406/1999), reg 3.

3 Companies (Amendment) (No 2) Act 1999 (Commencement) Order 1999 (SI 406/1999), reg 6.

4 Companies (Amendment) (No 2) Act 1999 (Commencement) Order 1999 (SI 406/1999), reg 4.

5 Companies (Amendment) (No 2) Act 1999 (Commencement) Order 1999 (SI 406/1999), reg 5.

6 Companies (Amendment) (No 2) Act 1999 (Commencement) Order 2000 (SI 61/2000), reg 2.

7 Companies (Amendment) (No 2) Act 1999 (Commencement) Order 2000 (SI 61/2000), reg 3.

Notes

Collective citation: The C(A)(No 2)A 1999 was not referred to in the collective citation prescribed in CA 1990, s 1. For this reason, C(A)(No 2)A 1999, s 1(2) specifically makes reference to the C(A)A 1999 as forming part of 'the Companies Acts 1963 to 1999'. C(A)(No 2)A

1999 amends the Limited Partnership Act 1994, however it is acknowledged in the citation of the C(A)(No 2)A 1999 that this amendment does not form part of the Companies Acts generally.

---

2 Interpretation generally

(1) In this Act—

'the Central Bank' means the Central Bank of Ireland;

'the Principal Act' means the Companies Act, 1963.

(2) In this Act—

(a) a reference to a Part, section or Schedule is a reference to a Part or section of, or a Schedule to, this Act unless it is indicated that reference to some other enactment is intended,

(b) a reference to a subsection, paragraph or subparagraph is a reference to the subsection, paragraph or subparagraph of the provision in which the reference occurs unless it is indicated that reference to some other provision is intended,

(c) a reference to any enactment is a reference to that enactment as amended, extended or adapted by or under any subsequent enactment (including this Act).

Cross reference

'Central Bank of Ireland': Central Bank Act 1942, s 2(1).

---

3 Orders

(1) The Minister may by order prescribe any matter or thing which is referred to in this Act as prescribed or to be prescribed.

(2) The Minister may by order amend or revoke an order under this Act (other than an order under section 1(4) but including an order under this subsection).

(3) Every order under this Act (other than an order under section 1(4)) shall be laid before each House of the Oireachtas as soon as may be after it is made and, if a resolution annulling the order is passed by either such House within the next 21 days on which that House has sat after the order is laid before it, the order shall be annulled accordingly but without prejudice to the validity of anything previously done thereunder.

Definitions

'Minister': CA 1963, s 2(1); 'Oireachtas': IA 2005, Sch, Pt 2; 'prescribed': CA 1963, s 2(1).

PART II
EXAMINERSHIPS

4 Definition

In this Part 'the Act of 1990' means the Companies (Amendment) Act, 1990.

5 Amendment of section 2 of Act of 1990

[...][a]

Amendments

a C(A)(No 2)A 1999, s 5(a) amended C(A)A 1990, s 2(1) by the substitution for 'Where it appears to the court that' of 'Subject to subsection (2), where it appears to the court that'. C(A)(No 2)A 1999, s 5(b) substituted C(A)A 1990, s 2(2).

6 Amendment of section 3 of Act of 1990

[...][a]

Amendments

a C(A)(No 2)A 1999, s 6 substituted C(A)A 1990, s 3(2)(b) and inserted C(A)A 1990, s 3(2)(c).

7 Pre-petition report in relation to company

[...][a]

Amendments

a C(A)(No 2)A 1999, s 7 inserted C(A)A 1990, s 3(3A) and (3B).

8 Amendment of section 3(5) of Act of 1990

[...][a]

Amendments

a C(A)(No 2)A 1999, s 8 deleted ', and until a prima facie case for protection has been established to the satisfaction of the court' in C(A)A 1990, s 3(5).

9 Interim protection pending report

[...][a]

Amendments

a C(A)(No 2)A 1999, s 9 inserted C(A)A 1990, s 3A.

10 Creditors to be heard

[...][a]

Amendments

a C(A)(No 2)A 1999, s 10 inserted C(A)A 1990, s 3B.

11 Availability of independent accountant's report

[...][a]

Amendments

a C(A)(No 2)A 1999, s 11 inserted C(A)A 1990, s 3C.

12 Amendment of section 4 of Act of 1990

[...][a]

Amendments

a C(A)(No 2)A 1999, s 12(a) substituted 'Subject to subsection (2), where the court appoints an examiner to a company' for 'Where the court appoints an examiner to a company' in C(A)A 1990, s 4(1). C(A)(No 2)A 1999, s 12(b) substituted C(A)A 1990, s 4(2).

13 Duty to act in good faith

[...][a]

Amendments

a C(A)(No 2)A 1999, s 13 inserted C(A)A 1990, s 4A.

14 Amendment of section 5 of Act of 1990

[...][a]

Amendments

a C(A)(No 2)A 1999, s 14(a) substituted C(A)A 1990, s 5(1). C(A)(No 2)A 1999, s 14(b) substituted C(A)A 1990, s 5(2)(d) and deleted C(A)A 1990, s 5(2)(h).

15 Restriction of payment of pre-petition debts

[...][a]

Amendments

a C(A)(No 2)A 1999, s 15 inserted C(A)A 1990, s 5A.

16 Amendment of section 6 of Act of 1990

[...][a]

Amendments

a C(A)(No 2)A 1999, s 16(a) amended C(A)A 1990, s 6(1) by the substitution for 'Where the court appoints an examiner to a company and' of 'Where, at the date of the presentation of a petition under section 2 in relation to a company'. C(A)(No 2)A 1999, s 16(b) amended C(A)A 1990, s 6(2) by the substitution for 'Where the court appoints an examiner to a company and' of 'Where, at the date of the presentation of a petition under section 2 in relation to a company'. C(A)(No 2)A 1999, s 16(c) substitutes C(A)A 1990, s 6(3).

17 Disapplication of section 98 of Principal Act to receivers in certain circumstances

[...][a]

Amendments

a C(A)(No 2)A 1999, s 17 inserts C(A)A 1990, s 6A.

18 Repudiation of contracts

[...][a]

Amendments

a C(A)(No 2)A 1999, s 18 inserts C(A)A 1990, s 7(5A), (5B) and (5C).

19 Amendment of section 8 of Act of 1990

[...][a]

Amendments

a C(A)(No 2)A 1999, s 19 substitutes C(A)A 1990, s 8(5) and (5A).

20 Amendment of section 12 of Act of 1990

[...][a]

Amendments

a C(A)(No 2)A 1999, s 20(1) substitutes C(A)A 1990, s 12(2)(a). C(A)(No 2)A 1999, s 20(2) substitutes C(A)A 1990, s 12(4).

21 Hearing regarding irregularities

[...][a]

Amendments

a C(A)(No 2)A 1999, s 21 inserts C(A)A 1990, s 13A.

22 Amendment of section 18 of Act of 1990

[...][a]

Amendments

a C(A)(No 2)A 1999, s 22(a) substitutes C(A)A 1990, s 18(1). C(A)(No 2)A 1999, s 22(b) amends C(A)A 1990, s 18(2) by the deletion of all the words from 'to consider such proposals' to the end of that subsection and the substitution of 'for the purpose of section 23 and shall report on those proposals to the court, within 35 days of his appointment or such longer period as the court may allow, in accordance with section 19.' C(A)(No 2)A 1999, s 22(c) amends C(A)A 1990, s 18(3) by the substitution of '70 days' for 'three months'. C(A)(No 2)A 1999, s 22(d) substitutes C(A)A 1990, s 18(5) and (6) and inserts C(A)A 1990, s 18(7), (8) and (9).

23 Amendment of section 23 of Act of 1990

[...][a]

Amendments

a C(A)(No 2)A 1999, s 23(a) amends C(A)A 1990, s 23(1) by the substitution for 'compromise or scheme of arrangement' of 'compromise or scheme of arrangement; save where expressly provided otherwise in this section, this section shall not authorise, at such a meeting, anything to be done in relation to such proposals by any member or creditor.' C(A)(No 2)A 1999, s 23(b) deletes C(A)A 1990, s 23(3). C(A)(No 2)A 1999, s 23(c) inserts C(A)A 1990, s 23(4A). C(A)(No 2)A 1999, s 23(d) amends C(A)A 1990, s 23(6) by the deletion of '(3) or'. C(A)(No 2)A 1999, s 23(e) inserts C(A)A 1990, s 23(9).

24 Amendment of section 24 of Act of 1990

[...][a]

Amendments

a C(A)(No 2)A 1999, s 24(a) inserts C(A)A 1990, s 24(2)(d). C(A)(No 2)A 1999, s 24(b) substitutes C(A)A 1990, s 24(4)(a). C(A)(No 2)A 1999, s 24(c) inserts C(A)A 1990, s 24(4A). C(A)(No 2)A 1999, s 24(d) amends C(A)A 1990, s 24(11)(b) by the deletion of 'members and'. C(A)(No 2)A 1999, s 24(e) substitutes C(A)A 1990, s 24(12).

25 Provisions with respect to guarantees

[...][a]

Amendments

a C(A)(No 2)A 1999, s 25 inserts C(A)A 1990, s 25A.

26 Provisions with respect to leases

[...][a]

Amendments

a C(A)(No 2)A 1999, s 26 inserts C(A)A 1990, s 25B.

27 Amendment of section 27 of Act of 1990

[...][a]

Amendments

a C(A)(No 2)A 1999, s 27(a) amends C(A)A 1990, s 27 by the insertion of '(1) before 'The company or any interested party'. C(A)(No 2)A 1999, s 27(b) inserts C(A)A 1990, s 27(2).

28 Priority of costs, remuneration and expenses of examiner

[...][a]

Amendments

a C(A)(No 2)A 1999, s 28 substitutes C(A)A 1990, s 29(3) and inserts C(A)A 1990, s 29(3A) and (3B).

29 Amendment of section 30 of Act of 1990

[...][a]

Amendments

a C(A)(No 2)A 1999, s 29 amends C(A)A 1990, s 30(1) by the substitution of 'section 13A, 24 or 27' for 'section 17 or 24'.

30 Repeals

[...][a]

Amendments

a C(A)(No 2)A 1999, s 30 repeals C(A)A 1990, s 3(3)(b) and (c) and ss 14, 15, 16 and 17.

PART III

EXEMPTION FROM REQUIREMENT TO HAVE ACCOUNTS AUDITED

31 Definitions

In this Part—

'the Act of 1986' means the Companies (Amendment) Act, 1986;

'the exemption' means the non-application, by virtue of section 32, of section 160 of the Principal Act and the provisions referred to in subsection (2) of section 32;

'financial year' means the financial year of the company concerned;

'private company' does not include an unlimited company other than such a company (being a private company) to which Part III of the 1993 Regulations applies;

'the 1993 Regulations' means the European Communities (Accounts) Regulations, 1993 (S.I. No. 396 of 1993).

Definitions

'company': CA 1963, s 2(1); 'private company': CA 1963, s 33; 'unlimited company': CA 1963, s 5(2).

Notes

Exemption from annual audit: Part III of C(A)(No 2)A 1999 introduces provisions enabling private limited companies which meet the criteria laid down in s 32 to be exempted from the requirement to have an auditor and to have their annual accounts audited. These changes in the law relating to the audit follow recommendations in the First Report of the CLRG. It is to be noted though that under s 33, members holding not less than 10% of the voting rights in general meeting can effectively insist on the audit being maintained or reinstated, as the case may be.

The IFCMPA 2006 increased significantly the turnover and balance sheet thresholds below which a company may avail of audit exemption (See section 32(3)(a)(ii) and (iii) below). As a result, a significant number of smaller companies are now eligible to take advantage of this relief.

---

32 Exemption from requirement to have accounts audited

(1) [Subject to sections 32A and [32B]][a], if—

(a) the directors of a private company are of opinion that the company will satisfy the conditions specified in subsection (3) in respect of a financial year and decide that the company should avail itself of the exemption in that year (and they record that decision in the minutes of the meeting concerned), and

(b) unless that financial year is the first financial year of the company, the company satisfied the said conditions in respect of the preceding financial year, then—

(i) without prejudice to section 35, section 160 of the Principal Act (which requires the appointment of an auditor to a company) shall not apply to the said company in respect of that financial year, and

(ii) [unless and until –

(I) circumstances, if any, arise in that financial year which result in one or more of the said conditions not being satisfied in respect of that year, or

(II) circumstances otherwise arise by reason of which the said company is not entitled to the exemption in respect of that financial year,

the provisions mentioned in subsection (2) shall not apply to the said company in respect of that year.][b]

(2) The provisions mentioned in subsection (1) are those provisions of the Companies Acts, 1963 to 1999, (other than this Part) the 1993 Regulations and the European Communities (Single-Member Private Limited Companies) Regulations, 1994 (S.I. No. 275 of 1994), that apply to the company, being provisions that—

(a) confer any powers on an auditor or require anything to be done by or to or as respects an auditor,

(b) make provision on the basis of a report of an auditor having been prepared in relation to the accounts of the company in a financial year, and, without prejudice to the generality of the foregoing, include the provisions specified in the First Schedule.

(3) The conditions mentioned in subsection (1) are that—

(a) in respect of the year concerned—

(i) the company is a company to which the Act of 1986 applies,

(ii) the amount of the turnover of the company does not exceed [€7.3 million][c],

(iii) the balance sheet total of the company does not exceed [€3.65 million][c],

(iv) the average number of persons employed by the company does not exceed 50,

(v) the company is not—

(I) a parent undertaking or a subsidiary undertaking (within the meaning of the European Communities (Companies: Group Accounts) Regulations, 1992 (S.I. No. 201 of 1992)),

(II) a holder of a licence under section 9 of the Central Bank Act, 1971, or a company that is exempt from the requirement under that Act to hold such a licence,

(III) a company to which the European Communities (Insurance Undertakings: Accounts) Regulations, 1996 (S.I. No. 23 of 1996) apply, [...][d]

(IV) a company referred to in the Second Schedule [(other than paragraph 18 thereof, or)][e]

[(V) a company whose securities are admitted to trading on a regulated market.][f]

[…][g]

(4) In this section 'amount of turnover' and 'balance sheet total' have the same meaning as they have in section 8 of the Act of 1986.

(5) For the purpose of subsection (3)(a)(iv), the average number of persons employed by a company shall be determined by applying the method of calculation prescribed by paragraph 42(4) of the Schedule to the Act of 1986 for determining the number required

by subparagraph (1) of that paragraph to be stated in a note to the accounts of a company.

(6) In the application of this section to any period which is a financial year of a company, but is not in fact a year, the amount specified in subsection (3)(a)(ii) shall be proportionally adjusted.

(7) Each occasion of an amendment of the kind referred to in subsection (8) being effected shall operate to enable the Minister to amend, by order, subparagraphs (ii) and (iii) of subsection (3)(a) by substituting for the amount and the total, respectively, specified in those provisions a greater amount and total (not being an amount or total that is greater than the amount or total it replaces by 25 per cent.).

(8) The amendment referred to in subsection (7) is an amendment of the total and the amount specified in paragraphs (a) and (b), respectively, of section 8(2) of the Act of 1986, being an amendment made for the purpose of giving effect to an act adopted by an institution of the European Communities.

[(9) In subsection (3), 'regulated market' has the meaning assigned to it by Article 4(1), point (14) of Directive 2004/39/EC.][h]

Amendments

a C(AA)A 2003, s 53(a) amends C(A)(No 2)A 1999, s 32(1) by substituting 'Subject to sections 32A and 33(1)' for 'Subject to section 33(1)'. The IFCMPA 2006 further amends this section by substituting '32B' for 33(1).

b The IFCMPA 2006 substitutes this wording in s 32(1)(b)(2).

c C(AA)A 2003, s 53(b) amended C(A)(No 2)A 1999, s 32(3)(a)(ii) by substituting '€1,500,000' for '£250,000'. Subsequently, the IFCMPA 2006 amended C(A)(No 2)A 1999, s 32(3)(a)(ii) by substituting €7.3 million for €1,500,000 and s 32(3)(a)(iii) by substituting €3.65 million for €1,904,607.10.

d European Communities (Directive 2006/46/EC) Regulations 2009, reg 5(a) amends C(A)(No 2)A 1999, s 32(3)(a)(v)(III) by deleting word 'or'.

e C(AA)A 2003, s 53(c) amends C(A)(No 2)A 1999, s 32(3)(a)(v)(IV) by substituting '(other than paragraph 18 thereof).' for '(other than paragraph 18 thereof),' and is further amended by European Communities (Directive 2006/46/EC) Regulations 2009, reg 5(b) by the substitution of 'paragraph 18 thereof, or for 'paragraph 18 thereof' .

f European Communities (Directive 2006/46/EC) Regulations 2009, reg 5(c) inserts C(A)(No 2)A 1999, s 32(3)(a)(v)(V).

g C(AA)A 2003, s 53(d) amends C(A)(No 2)A 1999, s 32(3) by deleting 'and' where it occurs after paragraph (a)(v)(IV) and by repealing paragraph (b).

h European Communities (Directive 2006/46/EC) Regulations 2009, reg 5(d) inserts C(A)(No 2)A 1999, s 32(9).

Definitions

'the Act of 1986': C(A)(No 2)A 1999, s 31; 'company': CA 1963, s 2(1); 'director': CA 1963, s 2(1); 'financial year': C(A)(No 2)A 1999, s 31; 'Minister': CA 1963, s 2(1); 'parent undertaking': EC(CGA)R 1992 (SI 120/1992), reg 3(1); 'the Principal Act': C(A)(No 2)A 1999, s 2(1); 'private company': C(A)(No 2)A 1999, s 31 and CA 1963, s 33; 'subsidiary undertaking': EC(CGA)R 1992 (SI 120/1992), reg 3(1).

Notes

Exemption from audit requirement: Normally, every company should have its annual accounts audited.[1] However, in the case of a private limited company[2] being one to which the provisions of C(A)A 1986 apply,[3] the requirement to appoint an auditor and to have the annual accounts audited may be disapplied provided that certain conditions are met. In essence, the directors must form the opinion that both in respect of the financial year in question and also in respect of the immediately preceding financial year,[4] the company meets the criteria set out in subsection (3), namely that—

- a its turnover does not exceed €7.3 million;
- b its balance sheet total does not exceed €3.65 million;
- c the number of its employees does not exceed 50;[5]
- d it is neither be a parent undertaking nor a subsidiary undertaking within the meaning of EC(CGA)R 1992 (SI 201/1992);[6]
- e it is not a licensed bank,[7] an insurance company[8] or a financial services company of the type referred to in Sch 2;[9]
- f the filing of its annual returns is fully up-to-date both for the year in question and, in the case of a company which is not filing its first annual return, for the preceding year as well.[10]

Once they have concluded that these criteria are being satisfied, the directors may determine to disapply the audit provisions of the Companies Acts in so far as they pertain to the company. That determination must be recorded in the board minutes.[11] Any person who records in the minutes a decision to avail of the audit exemption knowing, that the company does not in fact qualify for the exemption, is guilty of an offence.[12]

The amendments to Part III of C(A)(No 2)A 1999 took effect on enactment of the IFCMPA 2006 for financial years beginning not earlier than commencement of s 9 of that Act (24 December 2006). The revised criteria also apply to financial years ending not earlier than two months after commencement of that section. In this latter circumstance, should the minority shareholders require an audit, the formal notice must be given to the company at least one month prior to the end of the financial year.[13]

1 See in particular CA 1990, s 193.
2 See C(A)(No 2)A 1999, s 31 and s 32(1)(a).
3 See C(A)(No 2)A 1999, s 32(3)(a)(i). As to the categories of company covered by C(A)A 1986, see ss 1 and 2 thereof and the notes thereto.
4 C(A)(No 2)A 1999, s 32(1). Of course, if the company is in its first financial year, the relevant criteria need only be met in respect of that year: s 32(1)(b).
5 C(A)(No 2)A 1999, s 32(3)(a)(ii)–(iv).
6 C(A)(No 2)A 1999, s 32(3)(a)(v)(I).
7 C(A)(No 2)A 1999, s 32(3)(a)(v)(II).
8 C(A)(No 2)A 1999, s 32(3)(a)(v)(III).
9 C(A)(No 2)A 1999, s 32(3)(a)(v)(IV).
10 C(A)(No 2)A 1999, s 32A as inserted by C(AA)A 2003, s 53.
11 C(A)(No 2)A 1999, s 32(1)(a).
12 C(A)(No 2)A 1999, s 37.
13 IFCMPA 2006, s 10.

Entitlement of members to insist on an audit: Even if the directors wish to avail of the audit exemption, they may be prevented from doing so by the members. In this regard, members holding shares carrying not less than 10% of voting rights[1] may serve a notice insisting on the relevant audit provisions continuing to apply to or being reactivated in respect of the company for a given financial year.[2] Following enactment of s 9 of the IFCMPA 2006, this notice may be served at any time during the preceding financial year to which the notice relates or at least one month prior to the end of the financial year to which the notice relates.[3]

[1] In determining whether or not the 10% has been achieved regard is not had to voting rights which are only exercisable in special circumstances: C(A)(No 2)A 1999, s 33(7).

[2] C(A)(No 2)A 1999, s 33(1).

[3] C(A)(No 2)A 1999, s 33(2).

Statement in the accounts: Even if a company validly avails of the audit exemption, it must still prepare and present to its members accounts which are prepared in accordance with the Companies Acts and which present a true and fair view of the company's financial position.[1] Moreover, a statement to that effect must be contained in the balance sheet as signed by the directors.[2] The statement must also clearly state that the audit exemption is being availed of[3] and must confirm that no notice of the type referred to above, has been served on the company reactivating the audit provisions.[4] If the statement is false in any material respect, any director who participated in the making of the statement knowing it to be false, will be guilty of an offence.[5]

[1] C(A)(No 2)A 1999, s 33(4)(d).

[2] C(A)(No 2)A 1999, s 33(4)(d) and (5).

[3] C(A)(No 2)A 1999, s 33(4)(a) and (b).

[4] C(A)(No 2)A 1999, s 33(4)(c).

[5] C(A)(No 2)A 1999, s 37.

UK legislation

Companies Act 1985, ss 249A, 249B, 249C, 249D and 249E.

[32A Exemption conditional on timely filing of annual return

Notwithstanding that the conditions specified in section 32(3) are satisfied, a company is not entitled to the exemption in a financial year unless—

(a) the company's annual return to which the accounts for that financial year are annexed is delivered to the registrar of companies in compliance with section 127 of the Principal Act, and

(b) if the annual return referred to in paragraph (a) is not the company's first annual return, its annual return to which the accounts for its preceding financial year were annexed was also delivered to the registrar of companies in compliance with section 127 of the Principal Act.']a

Amendments

a C(A)(No 2)A 1999, s 32A inserted by C(AA)A 2003, s 53(e).

Definitions

'annual return': CA 1963, s 2(1); 'company': CA 1963, s 2(1); 'financial year': CA 1963, s 2(1); 'the Principal Act': C(A)(No 2)A 1999, s 2(1); 'the registrar of companies': CA 1963, s 2(1).

Notes

Exemption from audit requirement: See the notes to C(A)(No 2)A 1999, s 32.

[32B Exemption conditional on notice under section 33(1) not being served

Notwithstanding that the conditions specified in section 32(3) are satisfied, a company is not entitled to the exemption in a financial year if a notice, with respect to that year, is served, under and in accordance with section 33(1) and (2), on the company.][a]

Amendments

a Section 32B inserted by the IFCMPA 2006, s 9(1)(c).

Definitions

'company': CA 1963, s 2(1); 'financial year': CA 1963, s 2(1);

33 Section 32: supplemental provisions

[(1) Any member or members of a company holding shares in the company that confer, in aggregate, not less than one-tenth of the total voting rights in the company may serve a notice in writing on the company stating that that member or those members do not wish the exemption to be availableto the company in a financial year specified in the notice.

(2) A notice under subsection (1) may be served on the company either—

(a) during the financial year immediately preceding the financial year to which the notice relates, or

(b) during the financial year to which the notice relates (but not later than 1 month before the end of that year).][a]

(3) [...][b]

(4) If a company avails itself of the exemption in a financial year, the balance sheet prepared by the company in respect of that year shall contain a statement by the directors of the company that, in respect of that year—

(a) the company is availing itself of the exemption (and the exemption shall be expressed to be 'the exemption provided for by Part III of the Companies (Amendment) (No 2) Act, 1999)',

(b) the company is availing itself of the exemption on the grounds that it satisfies the conditions specified in section 32,

(c) [no notice under subsection (1) has, in accordance with subsection (2), been served on the company, and,][c]

(d) the directors acknowledge the obligations of the company, under the Companies Acts, 1963 to 1999, to keep proper books of account and prepare accounts which give a true and fair view of the state of affairs of the company at the end of its financial year and of its profit or loss for such a year and to otherwise comply with the provisions of those Acts relating to accounts so far as they are applicable to the company.

(5) The statement required by subsection (4) shall appear in the balance sheet in a position immediately above the signatures of the directors required by section 156 of the Principal Act or, as the case may be, the statement required by section 18(2) of the Act of 1986.

(6) If subsection (4) or (5) is not complied with, the company and every officer of the company who is in default shall be guilty of an offence and be liable to a fine.

(7) The reference in subsection (1) to a voting right in a company shall be construed as a reference to a right exercisable for the time being to cast, or to control the casting of, a vote at general meetings of members of the company, not being such a right that is exercisable only in special circumstances.

Amendments

a Section 33(1) and (2) were substituted by s 9(1)(d)(i) of the IFCMPA 2006.

b Section 33(3) was deleted by s 9(1)(d)(ii) of the IFCMPA 2006.

c Section 33(4)(c) was substituted by s 9(1)(d)(iii) of the IFCMPA 2006.

Cross reference

See IFCMPA 2006, s 10.

Definitions

'the Act of 1986': C(A)(No 2)A 1999, s 31; 'company': C(A)(No 2)A 1999, s 31 and CA 1963, s 2(1); 'director': CA 1963, s 2(1); 'financial year': C(A)(No 2)A 1999, s 31; 'member': CA 1963, s 31; 'the Principal Act': C(A)(No 2)A 1999, s 2(1); 'officer in default': CA 1963, s 383.

Notes

See C(A)(No 2)A 1999, s 32 and the notes thereto.

UK legislation

Companies Act 1985, ss 249A, 249B, 249C, 249D and 249E.

34 Removal of auditor consequent on exemption being availed of

(1) If a company—

(a) decides that the appointment of a person as auditor to the company should not be continued during the whole or part of a financial year in which the exemption is being availed of in relation to the company, and

(b) decides, accordingly, to terminate the appointment of that person as auditor to the company,

then—

(i) that person shall, within the period of 21 days beginning on the date of his or her being notified by the company of that decision, serve a notice on the company containing the statement referred to in subsection (2),

(ii) unless and until that person serves such a notice, any purported termination of his or her appointment as auditor to the company shall not have effect.

(2) The statement to be contained in a notice under subsection (1)(i) shall be whichever of the following is appropriate, namely—

(a) a statement to the effect that there are no circumstances connected with the decision of the company referred to in subsection (1) that he or she considers should be brought to the notice of the members or creditors of the company, or

(b) a statement of any such circumstances as aforesaid.

(3) Where a notice under subsection (1)(i) is served on a company—

(a) the auditor concerned shall, within 14 days after the date of such service, send a copy of the notice to the registrar of companies, and

(b) subject to subsection (4), the company shall, if the notice contains a statement referred to in subsection (2)(b), within 14 days after the date of such service, send a copy of the notice to every person who is entitled under section 159(1) of the Principal Act to be sent copies of the documents referred to in the said section 159(1).

(4) Copies of a notice served on a company under subsection (1) need not be sent to the persons specified in subsection (3)(b), if, on the application of the company concerned or any other person who claims to be aggrieved, the court is satisfied that the notice contains material which has been included to secure needless publicity for defamatory matter and the court may order the company's costs on an application under this subsection to be paid in whole or in part by the auditor concerned notwithstanding that he or she is not a party to the application.

(5) Subsection (2A) (inserted by the Companies Act, 1990) of section 161 of the Principal Act shall not apply to an auditor as respects his or her removal from office in the circumstances referred to in subsection (1).

Definitions

'company': C(A)(No 2)A 1999, s 31 and CA 1963, s 2(1); 'court': CA 1963, s 2(1); 'financial year': C(A)(No 2)A 1999, s 31; 'member': CA 1963, s 31; 'the Principal Act': C(A)(No 2)A 1999, s 2(1).

Notes

Removal of auditor: Where the directors validly resolve that the company shall avail of the audit exemption, this does not automatically result in the removal of the auditor from office, albeit that his functions and powers are suspended.[1] Rather, a separate decision must be taken to terminate the appointment of the auditor for the whole or part of the year in respect of which the exemption is be availed.[2] Normally, removal of an auditor would require a resolution of the members in general meeting[3] with all of the attendant rights on the part of the auditor to attend and be heard at the meeting and to have his written representations, if any, circulated to the members in advance of the meeting.[4] However, where the removal is consequent solely upon the company availing of the audit exemption, it would seem to be implicit that those procedures are disapplied by C(A)(No 2)A 1999, s 32(2)(a) as being provisions which 'require anything to be done … as respects an auditor.' Instead, the procedures prescribed by s 34 itself are deemed to apply. It seems, therefore, that a decision to remove the auditor before the expiration of his term of office may be taken by the board of directors.[5] However, it does not become effective[6] unless and until the auditor serves a notice on the company stating either that there are no circumstances connected with the decision to avail of the audit exemption which ought to be brought to the attention of the members or creditors, or alternatively stating what those circumstances are.[7] The auditor must serve this notice on the company within 21 days of being notified of the decision to terminate his appointment[8] and within a further 14 days thereafter he must copy same to the registrar of companies.[9] Significantly, if the notice does indeed state that there are circumstances connected with the decision to avail of the audit exemption which ought to be brought to the attention of the members or creditors, the company must within the same 14-day period send a copy of the notice to every person who would be entitled to copies of the annual accounts under CA 1963, s 159(1).[10] However, if the notice contains defamatory matter application may be made to the court by the company itself or by any other aggrieved person for an order preventing its circulation.[11] Furthermore, if the auditor's statement is false in any material particular and he made it knowing it to be false, he will be guilty of an offence.[12]

Normally, where an auditor has been removed from office, he will be entitled to attend the next AGM at which, but for his prior removal, his term of office would otherwise have expired and to attend any other general meeting (such as an EGM in advance of the next AGM) at which it is proposed to fill the vacancy occasioned by his removal.[13] However, this right of attendance is not enjoyed by an auditor removed under s 34.[14]

1 C(A)(No 2)A 1999, s 32(2) and Sch 1.

2 C(A)(No 2)A 1999, s 34(1).

3 CA 1963, s 161.

4 CA 1963, s 161.

5 Presumably, the provisions of and procedures contained in C(A)(No 2)A 1999, s 34 will also apply where the auditor is not removed from office during the course of the financial year but where his appointment lapses instead at the following AGM in accordance with CA 1963, s 160(1) as a result of no resolution being proposed and passed for his re-election.

6 C(A)(No 2)A 1999, s 34(1)(ii). Presumably, the delay in the vacation of office becoming effective also applies in the case of an auditor whose appointment lapses under s 160(1) at the following AGM in accordance with CA 1963, s 160(1) as a result of no resolution being proposed and passed for his re-election.

7 C(A)(No 2)A 1999, s 34(2).

8 C(A)(No 2)A 1999, s 34(1)(i).

9 C(A)(No 2)A 1999, s 34(3)(a).

10 C(A)(No 2)A 1999, s 34(3)(b). Under CA 1963, s 159(1) the persons entitled to receive the copies of the annual accounts are the members (whether or not entitled to receive notice of general meetings) and every holder of debentures (whether or not entitled to receive notice of general meetings) and every other person who would be entitled to receive notice of general meetings (eg where such entitlement is conferred by the articles of association).

11 C(A)(No 2)A 1999, s 34(4).

12 C(A)(No 2)A 1999, s 37.

13 CA 1963, s 161(2A).

14 C(A)(No 2)A 1999, s 34(5).

UK legislation

Companies Act 1985, ss 249A, 249B, 249C, 249D and 249E.

---

35 Appointment of auditor consequent on exemption ceasing to have effect

[(1) Whenever by reason of—

(a) circumstances referred to in section 32(1)(ii) arising in the financial year concerned the exemption ceases to have effect in relation to a company in respect of that year, or

(b) circumstances otherwise arising a company is not entitled to the exemption in respect of the financial year concerned,

it shall be the duty of the directors of the company to appoint an auditor of the company as soon as may be after those circumstances arise and such an appointment may be made by the directors notwithstanding the provisions of section 160 of the Principal Act.][a]

(2) An auditor appointed pursuant to subsection (1) shall hold office until the conclusion of the next meeting of the company held after his or her appointment at which accounts are required to be laid.

(3) If the directors of the company fail to carry out their duty under subsection (1), the company in general meeting may appoint an auditor to the company and subsection (2) shall apply to an auditor appointed by it.

Amendments

a Subsection 35(1) substituted by s 9(1)(e) of the IFCMPA 2006.

Definitions

'company': C(A)(No 2)A 1999, s 31 and CA 1963, s 2(1); 'director': CA 1963, s 2(1); 'financial year': C(A)(No 2)A 1999, s 31; 'the Principal Act': C(A)(No 2)A 1999, s 2(1).

Notes

Appointment of a new auditor:[1] Where a company ceases to be entitled to avail of the audit exemption, the directors must take steps 'as soon as may be' to appoint a new auditor,[2] assuming of course that the previous appointee has indeed ceased to hold office.[3] If the directors fail to make the appointment, the members in general meeting may do so instead.[4] In either event, the newly-appointed auditor holds office until the next general meeting at which annual accounts are to be presented.[5]

1 In relation to the appointment of auditors in normal circumstances, see CA 1963, s 160.

2 C(A)(No 2)A 1999, s 35(1).

3 The previous auditor may have been removed before the expiration of his term of office under C(A)(No 2)A 1999, s 34 or alternatively his appointment may have lapsed under CA 1963, s 160(1) in circumstances where, at the AGM following the decision to avail of the audit exemption, the members resolved not to re-elect him.

4 C(A)(No 2)A 1999, s 35(3). If neither the directors nor the members appoint an auditor, then the Minister may do so (at least where there has since been an AGM) pursuant to CA 1963, s 160(4).

5 C(A)(No 2)A 1999, s 35(2). With regard to the laying of accounts before a general meeting of the members, see CA 1963, s 148.

36 Application of Part

This Part shall apply to a company as respects a financial year that commences on or after the commencement of this Part.

Definitions

'company': C(A)(No 2)A 1999, s 31 and CA 1963, s 2(1); 'financial year': C(A)(No 2)A 1999, s 31.

Notes

Commencement date: The provisions of C(A)(No 2)A 1999, s 33(2), (3) and (7) so as to enable members to serve notice in advance insisting that the audit exemption should not be availed of.[1] The remainder of Pt III came into force on 1 February 2000[2] and accordingly it is only in respect of a financial year commencing on or after that date that the audit exemption may be availed of.

1 Companies (Amendment)(No 2) Act, 1999 (Commencement) Order 1999 (SI 406/1999).

2 Companies (Amendment)(No 2) Act, 1999 (Commencement) Order 1999 (SI 406/1999).

37 False statements in returns, balance sheets, etc

(1) If a person in any return, statement, balance sheet or other document required by or for the purposes of any provision of this Part wilfully makes a statement, false in any material particular, knowing it to be so false, he or she shall be guilty of an offence.

(2) A person guilty of an offence under this section shall be liable—

(a) on summary conviction, to a fine not exceeding [€1,904.61][a] or imprisonment for a term not exceeding 12 months or both, or

(b) on conviction on indictment, to a fine not exceeding [€12,697.38][b] or imprisonment for a term not exceeding [5 years][c] or both.

Amendments

a ‘£1,000 increased to £1,500 by CA 1990, s 240(7) as inserted by CLEA 2001, s 104(c), and converted to €1,904.61 by Council Regulations (EC) No 1103/97, No 974/98 and No 2866/98 and the Economic and Monetary Union Act 1998, s 6.

b ‘£10,000 converted to €12,697.38 by Council Regulations (EC) No 1103/97, No 974/98 and No 2866/98 and the Economic and Monetary Union Act 1998, s 6.

c 3 years increased to 5 years by CA 1990, s 240(8).

Notes

False statements: See the notes to C(A)(No 2)A 1999, ss 32, 33 and 34. For the criminal offences committed generally where false statements are contained in the annual accounts, see C(A)A 1986, s 22.

38 Application of Part to partnerships to which Part III of the 1993 Regulations applies

This Part shall apply to a partnership to which Part III of the 1993 Regulations applies as this Part applies to a private company with the following modifications—

(a) the substitution in this Part for references to section 160 of the Principal Act of references to Regulation 22 of the 1993 Regulations,

(b) the substitution in this Part for references to other provisions of the Companies Acts, 1963 to 1999, of references to so much of those provisions as are applied to partnerships by the 1993 Regulations,

(c) the substitution in this Part for references to directors of a company of references to partners of a partnership, and any other necessary modifications (including any modifications necessary to take account of the fact that such partnerships are unincorporated).

Definitions

‘the 1993 Regulations’: C(A)(No 2)A 1999, s 31; ‘company’: CA 1963, s 2(1); ‘director’: CA 1963, s 2(1); ‘the Principal Act’: C(A)(No 2)A 1999, s 2(1); ‘private company’: C(A)(No 2)A 1999, s 31 and CA 1963, s 33.

Notes

Extension of audit exemption to certain partnerships: The effect of C(A)(No 2)A 1999, s 38 is to extend the entitlement to avail of the audit exemption to partnerships covered by the 1993 Regulations, namely partnerships where all the members thereof who do not have a limit on their liability are (a) Irish or foreign limited companies or (b) unlimited companies or partnerships in respect of which all of their own members who do not have a limited on their liability are Irish or foreign limited companies or (c) any combination of (a) and (b).[1]

[1] E39C(A)R 1993, reg 6.

39 Saving

Nothing in this Part shall authorise the removal of an auditor from office which, apart from this Part, would not be lawful.

Notes

Removal of auditor: For the circumstances other than those identified in C(A)(No 2)A 1999, s 34, in which the auditor of a company may lawfully be removed, see CA 1963, ss 160 and 161 and the notes thereto.

PART IV

MISCELLANEOUS

40 Amendment of section 16 of Investment Limited Partnerships Act, 1994

Section 16 of the Investment Limited Partnerships Act, 1994, is hereby amended by the substitution of the following subsection for subsection (10):

[...][a]

Amendments

a C(A)(No 2)A 1999, s 40 substituted s 16(10) of the Investment Limited Partnerships Act 1994.

Cross reference

See Investment Limited Partnerships Act 1994, s 16(10) (as amended).

Notes

Auditors' liability: A breach of the relevant subsections of the Investment Limited Partnerships Act 1994 by an auditor will no longer result in the auditor being held liable to indemnify the person suffering a loss as a result of that breach but rather the auditor will be guilty of an offence only.

41 Amendment of section 240 of Companies Act, 1990

[...][a]

Amendments

a C(A)(No 2)A 1999, s 41 substituted CA 1990, s 240(5) and inserted CA 1990, s 240(5A).

Cross reference

See CA 1990, s 240 (as amended).

Definitions

'document': CA 1963, s 2(1); 'the Companies Acts': CA 1990, s 3(1).

Notes

Summary Proceedings under the Companies Acts[1]: Under the Petty Sessions (Ireland) Act 1851, summary proceedings[2] should be brought within six months of the date of the offence. CA 1963, s 240 already provided a derogation from this requirement. In addition this amendment permits, notwithstanding the fact that over three years may have elapsed, proceedings to be brought against any person who was outside the jurisdiction, once those proceedings are brought within six months of that person returning to Ireland. Finally, and given the fact that the prosecution of offences under the Companies Acts is frequently delayed until the appointment of a liquidator, most significantly, a mechanism[3] now exists whereby proceedings can be brought at any time within three years from the date on which the relevant evidence comes to light. The person bringing the prosecution must form the view that the evidence is sufficient to justify the bringing of the proceedings. A certificate signed by that person will be treated as prima facie evidence of the offence without need for further proof of the signature of the person bringing the prosecution[4] thus avoiding the requirement for witnesses to attend court for the purpose of proving their signature.

1 CA 1990, ss 240(5) and (5A) (as amended by C(A)(No 2)A 1999, s 41) do not apply to indictable offences. Per *B v DPP* [1997] 2 ILRM 118, there is no statutory limitation period on the prosecution of indictable offences.

2 See also generally Criminal Justice Act 2006. Since 1 August 2006, where an offence may be tried summarily and on indictment the six-month time limit imposed by the Petty Sessions (Ireland) Act 1851 (as amended by the Criminal Justice Act 1951, s 7) shall not apply; the six-month time limit now only applies to offences that may only be tried as summary offences.

3 C(A)(No 2)A 1999, s 41(5)(c).

4 C(A)(No 2)A 1999, s 41(5A).

42 Additional requirement to be complied with before company may be formed

(1) A company shall not be formed and registered under the Companies Acts, 1963 to 1999, after the commencement of this section, unless it appears to the registrar of companies that the company, when registered, will carry on an activity in the State, being an activity that is mentioned in its memorandum.

(2) The registrar of companies may accept as sufficient evidence that a company, when registered, will carry on an activity in the State a statutory declaration, in the prescribed form, that the purpose or one of the purposes for which the company is being formed is the carrying on by it of an activity in the State and which declaration includes the following particulars—

(a) if it appears to the person making the declaration that the activity belongs to a division, group and class appearing in the relevant classification system—

(i) the general nature of the activity, and

(ii) the division, group and class in that system to which the activity belongs,

(b) if it appears to the said person that the activity does not belong to any such division, group and class, a precise description of the activity,

(c) the place or places in the State where it is proposed to carry on the activity,

(d) the place, whether in the State or not, where the central administration of the company will normally be carried on.

(3) For the purposes of subsection (2), if the purpose or one of the purposes for which the company is being formed is the carrying on of 2 or more activities in the State, the particulars in respect of the matters referred to in paragraphs (a) to (c) of that subsection to be given in the statutory declaration shall be the particulars that relate to whichever of those activities the person making the declaration considers to be the principal activity for which the company is being formed to carry on in the State.

(4) The statutory declaration referred to in subsection (2) shall be made by—

(a) one of the persons named in the statement delivered under section 3 of the Companies (Amendment) Act, 1982, in relation to the company as directors of the company,

(b) the person or, as the case may be, one of the persons named in the said statement as secretary or joint secretaries of the company, or

(c) the solicitor, if any, engaged in the formation of the company.

(5) The form prescribed for the purposes of the statutory declaration referred to in subsection (2) may enable the declarant to include therein a declaration as to the matters referred to in section 5(5) of the Companies (Amendment) Act, 1983, and such a declaration that is so included shall suffice for the purposes of that section 5(5) as if it had been separately made and delivered to the registrar of companies.

(6) Without prejudice to its construction for the purposes of any other provision of that section, the expression 'the requirements mentioned in subsection (1)' in subsection (5) of section 5 of the Companies (Amendment) Act, 1983, shall not be construed as including the requirements of this section.

(7) In this section—

'activity' means any activity that a company may be lawfully formed to carry on and includes the holding, acquisition or disposal of property of whatsoever kind;

'relevant classification system' means NACE Rev 1, that is to say, the common basis for statistical classifications of economic activities within the European Community set out in the Annex to Council Regulation (EEC) No 3037/90 of 9 October 1990 (OJ No L293/1, 24 October 1990) on the statistical classification of economic activities in the European Community, as amended for the time being.

Definitions

'commencement': IA 2005, Sch, Pt 1; 'company': CA 1963, s 2(1); 'prescribed': CA 1963, s 2(1); 'registrar of companies': CA 1963, s 2(1); 'statutory declaration': IA 2005, Sch, Pt 1.

Notes

No incorporation without proof of intended activity in the State: Prior to the coming into force of this section on 18 April 2000[1] a company could lawfully be incorporated in the State even though its sole intended purpose was to operate as a non-resident company. Now, however, the company will not be registered and a certificate of incorporation will not be issued without proof that one of the activities mentioned in its objects clause will be carried on in the state.[2] However, the Registrar of Companies may accept as sufficient proof a statutory declaration in the prescribed form[3] that the purpose or one of the purposes for which the company is being formed is to carry on an activity in the state.[4] The statutory declaration, which may be made by one of the persons who is to be named in the statement to be filed with the registrar of companies under C(A)A 1982, s 3 as being the first directors of the company[5] or being the first secretary or one of the first joint secretaries of the company[6] or which may be made by a solicitor engaged in the formation of the company,[7] must give details of the activity to be carried on in the state[8] or the principal activity if two or more such activities[9] are to be carried on,[10] including details of the place or places in the State where such activity is proposed to be carried on.[11] Furthermore, details must also be given of the place (whether in the State or abroad) where the central administration of the company will normally be carried on.[12] It remains to be seen whether the requirement that every newly-formed company carry on an activity in the State amounts to an unlawful curtailment of the freedom of establishment provided for in Art 43 of the EC Treaty.

1 Companies (Amendment)(No 2) Act, 1999 (Commencement) Order 2000 (SI 61/2000).

2 C(A)(No 2)A 1999, s 42(1).

3 Companies (Forms) No 2 Order 2004 (SI 829/2004), Form A1. In this form the declarant not only confirms compliance with the provisions of C(A)(No 2)A 1999, s 42 but also confirms compliance generally with the registration requirements of the Companies Acts, as required by C(A)A 1983, s 5(5). Making this combined declaration is expressly provided by C(A)(No 2)A 1999, s 42(5).

4 C(A)(No 2)A 1999, s 42(2).

5 C(A)(No 2)A 1999, s 42(4)(a).

6 C(A)(No 2)A 1999, s 42(4)(b).

7 C(A)(No 2)A 1999, s 42(4)(c).

8 C(A)(No 2)A 1999, s 42(2)(a) and (b).

9 C(A)(No 2)A 1999, s 42(7). See also Annex to Council Regulation (EEC) No 3037/90 of 9 October 1990 (as amended) which sets out the common basis for statistical classification of economic activity in the European Union.

10 C(A)(No 2)A 1999, s 42(3).

11 C(A)(No 2)A 1999, s 42(2)(c).

12 C(A)(No 2)A 1999, s 42(2)(d). With regard to the place of a company's central administration, see the notes to CA 1963, s 113.

43 Company to have director resident in the State

(1) Subject to subsection (3) and section 44, one, at least, of the directors for the time being of a company, not being a company referred to in subsection (2), shall, on and from the commencement of this section, be a person who is resident in [a Member State of the EEA].[a]

(2) Subject to subsection (3) and section 44, one, at least, of the directors for the time being of a company, being—

(a) a company the memorandum of which was delivered to the registrar of companies for registration under section 17 of the Principal Act before the commencement of this section, or

(b) an existing company (within the meaning of the Principal Act),

shall, on and from the date that is 12 months after the commencement of this section, be a person who is resident in [a Member State of the EEA].[a]

(3) Subsection (1) or (2), as the case may be, shall not apply in relation to a company if the company for the time being holds a bond, in the prescribed form, in force to the value of [€25,394.76][b] and which provides that, in the event of a failure by the company to pay the whole or part of—

(a) a fine, if any, imposed on the company in respect of an offence under the Companies Acts, 1963 to 1999, committed by it, being an offence which is prosecutable by the registrar of companies, and

(b) (i) a fine, if any, imposed on the company in respect of an offence under section 1078 of the Taxes Consolidation Act, 1997, committed by it, being an offence that consists of a failure by the company to deliver a statement which it is required to deliver under section 882 of that Act or to comply with a notice served on it under section 884 of that Act, and

(ii) a penalty, if any, which it has been held liable to pay under section 1071 or 1073 of the Taxes Consolidation Act, 1997, there shall become payable under the bond to a person nominated for the purpose ('the nominated person') by the registrar of companies or the Revenue Commissioners, as appropriate, (or jointly by the registrar and the Commissioners in the case of both a fine referred to in paragraph (a) and a fine or penalty, or a fine and penalty, referred to in paragraph (b)), a sum of money for the purposes of that sum being applied by the nominated person in discharging the whole or part, as the case may be, of the company's liability in respect of any such fine or penalty, and any sum that becomes so payable shall be applied by the nominated person accordingly.

(4) The bond referred to in subsection (3) may be entered into and shall have effect according to its terms notwithstanding any rule of law whereby any agreement to insure or indemnify a person in respect of any punishment or liability imposed on him or her in relation to any offence or unlawful act committed by him or her is void or unenforceable.

(5) The bond referred to in subsection (3) shall also provide that, in addition to the sum referred to in that subsection, there shall become payable under the bond to the nominated person, on demand being made, with the consent of the Revenue Commissioners, by him or her in that behalf, a sum of money, not exceeding such sum as the Revenue Commissioners and the Minister may sanction, for the purpose of defraying such expenses as may have been reasonably incurred by that person in carrying out his or her duties under subsection (3).

(6) The nominated person shall keep all proper and usual accounts, including an income and expenditure account and a balance sheet, of all moneys received by him or her on foot of the bond referred to in subsection (3) and of all disbursements made by him or her from any such moneys.

(7) The Minister, after consultation with the Minister for Finance, the Revenue Commissioners and any other person whom, in the opinion of the Minister, might be concerned with or interested in the matter, may prescribe—

(a) that arrangements in relation to the bond referred to in subsection (3) shall only be entered into with persons of a prescribed class or classes,

(b) the form of that bond and the minimum period to be specified in the bond as being the period for which it shall be valid.

(8) A copy of the bond referred to in subsection (3) held by a company shall be appended—

(a) in case none of the directors of the company is resident in [a Member State of the EEA][a] the State on its incorporation, to the statement required by section 3 of the Companies (Amendment) Act, 1982, to be delivered to the registrar of companies in relation to the company,

(b) in case a notification is made under subsection (9) to the registrar of companies in relation to the company, to that notification,

(c) in case during the period to which an annual return concerning the company relates none of the directors of the company is resident in [a Member State of the EEA],[a] to that annual return (unless such a copy has been appended to a notification under subsection (9) made to the registrar of companies in that period).

(9) Without prejudice to anything in section 195 (as amended by this Act) of the Principal Act, if a person ceases to be a director of a company and, at the time of that cessation—

(a) he or she is resident in [a Member State of the EEA],[a] and

(b) to his or her knowledge, no other director of the company is resident in [a Member State of the EEA],[a] that person shall, within 14 days after that cessation, notify, in writing, the registrar of companies of that cessation and the matter referred to in paragraph (b).

(10) A notification in writing to the registrar of companies of the matter referred to in subsection (9)(b) shall not, of itself, be regarded as constituting defamatory matter.

(11) If a person fails to comply with subsection (9), he or she shall be jointly and severally liable with the company of which he or she has ceased to be a director for any fine or penalty referred to in subsection (3) imposed on the company or which it is held liable to pay after that cessation, and any such fine or penalty for which that person is so liable may be recovered by the registrar of companies or the Revenue Commissioners, as appropriate, from him or her as a simple contract debt in any court of competent jurisdiction.

[...][c]

(13) If subsection (1) or, as the case may be, subsection (2) is not complied with, the company concerned and every officer of the company who is in default shall be guilty of an offence.

(14) Summary proceedings in relation to an offence under subsection (13) may be brought and prosecuted by the registrar of companies.

(15) [...][d]

[(16) In this section—

'director' does not include an alternate director;

'Member State of the EEA' means a state that is a contracting party to the Agreement on the European Economic Area signed at Oporto on 2 May 1992, as amended for the time being.][e]

Amendments

a Words 'a Member State of the EEA' substituted for 'the State' by C(A)A 2009, s 10(1)(a).

b £20,000 converted to €25,394.76 by Council Regulation (EC)No 1103/97, No 974/98 and No 2866/98 and the Economic and Monetary Union Act 1998, s 6.

c C(A)A 2009, s 10(1)(b) repeals C(A)(No 2)A 1999, s 43(12).

d C(A)(No 2)A 1999, s 43(15) amends CA 1963, s 311.

e C(AA)A 2003, s 54 inserted C(A)(No 2)A 1999, s 43(16), which was substituted by C(A)A 2009, s 10(1)(c).

Definitions

'annual return': CA 1963, s 2(1); 'articles': CA 1963, s 2(1); 'commencement': IA 2005, Sch, Pt 1; 'company': CA 1963, s 2(1); 'director': CA 1963, s 2(1); 'existing company': CA 1963, s 2(1); 'memorandum': CA 1963, s 2(1); 'Minister for Finance': Ministers and Secretaries Act 1924, s 1(ii); 'officer in default': CA 1963, s 383; 'prescribed': CA 1963, s 2(1); 'the Principal Act': C(A)(No 2)A 1999, s 2(1); 'the registrar of companies': CA 1963, s 2(1).

Notes

Requirement of having at least one EEA resident director: Every company registered in Ireland must have at least two directors[1] which directors may not be bodies corporate.[2] However, prior to the coming into force of this and the following section on 18 April 2000,[3] there was no restriction either on the maximum number of directorships which any one person could hold or on the residence of a company's directors. Now, however, as a result of C(A)(No 2)A 1999, s 45 an upper limit is placed on the number of directorships which a person can validly hold (subject to certain exceptions). In addition, s 43 places limitations on the ability of a company registered in Ireland to operate without at least one EEA resident director[4] (excluding alternate directors).[5] Prior to the commencement of C(A)A 2009 on 12 July 2009 the requirement had been for at least one Irish resident director.

In the case of companies which had already been incorporated or in respect of which the relevant documentation had already been delivered to the Registrar for incorporation by 18 April 2000,[6] a twelve-month period of grace was afforded for compliance with the provisions of s 43.[7] Subject to these exceptions, the provisions of s 43 came into force with immediate effect.[8]

Under s 43 every company must either have at least one EEA resident director[9] or alternatively put in place a bond in the prescribed form[10] to the value of €25,394.76 which becomes payable to a person nominated by the Registrar of Companies or the Revenue Commissioners, as the case may be, for the purpose of discharging any fine imposed on the company in respect of an offence committed by it and prosecutable by the Registrar and/or for the purpose of discharging certain fines or penalties imposed on it under the Taxes Consolidation Act 1997.[11] The bond must also cover such expenses as are reasonably incurred by the nominated person in effecting the discharge of the fine or penalty out of the bond proceeds.[12] In this regard, the recoverable expenses of the nominated person (who is obliged to keep proper accounts)[13] may not exceed such sum as may be sanctioned by the Revenue Commissioners and the Minister.[14]

1 CA 1963, s 174.

2 CA 1963, s 176.

3 Companies (Amendment)(No 2) Act, 1999 (Commencement) Order 2000 (SI 61/2000).

4 With regard to the definition of Irish residence for the purposes of this section, see C(A)(No 2)A 1999, s 44(8), (9) and (10).

5 C(A)(No 2)A 1999, s 44(16) as inserted by C(AA)A 2003, s 54.

6 This is the date on which C(A)(No 2)A 1999, s 43 came into force: Companies (Amendment) (No 2) Act, 1999 (Commencement) Order 2000 (SI 61/2000).

7 C(A)(No 2)A 1999, s 43(2).

8 C(A)(No 2)A 1999, s 43(1).

9 C(A)(No 2)A 1999, s 43(1) and (2).

10 See the Companies (Amendment) (No 2) Act 1999 (Bonding) Order 2000 (SI 64/2000).

11 C(A)(No 2)A 1999, s 43(3).

12 C(A)(No 2)A 1999, s 43(5).

13 C(A)(No 2)A 1999, s 43(6).

14 C(A)(No 2)A 1999, s 43(5).

The timing of the bonding obligation: If the company is being formed without any EEA resident director, the bond must be appended to the statement which must be delivered to the Registrar of Companies under C(A)A 1982, s 3 along with the memorandum of association.[1] The timing of the bonding requirement is different, however, where the lack of an EEA resident director occurs as a result of a change in the composition of the existing board. In this regard, the section stipulates that if a person ceases to be a director and to his knowledge, this leaves the company with no EEA resident director, he must so notify the Registrar of Companies within 14 days of vacating office.[2] The bond which the company is then required to put in place as a result of the EEA resident director ceasing to hold office, must be appended to the form of notification filed by the director.[3] It appears to be implicit therefore, that there is an onus on the departing director to ensure that the company complies with the bonding obligations which are triggered by his departure. Moreover, if the departing director fails to so notify the Registrar of Companies (thereby frustrating or delaying the delivery of a bond by the company) he will become jointly and severally liable with the company for the amount of any fines and penalties which would otherwise have been covered by such a bond.[4]

1 C(A)(No 2)A 1999, s 43(8)(a).

2 C(A)(No 2)A 1999, s 43(9).

3 C(A)(No 2)A 1999, s 43(8)(b).

4 C(A)(No 2)A 1999, s 43(11). Notably, the wording of the subsection is such that personal liability arises for the departing director even if he makes the notification with the bond appended, but after the expiry of the prescribed 14-day period. Moreover, even though it is probably implicit in the subsection, there is no explicit reference to the departing director being absolved from any further personal liability in respect of fines and penalties imposed after the bond has ultimately been put in place.

Striking off non-compliant companies: If the Registrar of Companies has reasonable cause to believe that a company neither has an EEA resident director nor a bond (and does not come within the exemption in s 43) he may invoke the striking off provisions of CA 1963, s 311 against the company. He may serve a notice on the company requesting evidence of compliance with the requirements of s 43 and threatening strike off in default. If evidence of compliance is not forthcoming within one month, the Registrar may publish notice in the Companies Registration Office Gazette to the effect that one further month thereafter the name of company will be struck off the register unless cause is shown to the contrary.[1] Absent cause in fact being shown, the Registrar may proceed to strike off the company in which case he must publish a further notice to that effect in the Companies Registration Office Gazette.[2]

1 C(A)(No 2)A 1999, s 43(15).

2 CA 1963, s 311(5). In relation to the circumstances in which the company can subsequently be restored to the register and the procedure applicable to such applications for restoration, see CA 1963, s 311, s 8 and s 311A and the notes thereto.

44 Section 43: supplemental provisions

(1) Subsection (1) or, as the case may be, subsection (2) of section 43 shall not apply in relation to a company in respect of which there is in force a certificate under this section.

(2) The registrar of companies may grant to a company, on application in the prescribed form being made by it in that behalf, a certificate stating that the company has a real and continuous link with one or more economic activities that are being carried on in the State.

(3) The registrar of companies shall not grant such a certificate unless the company concerned tenders proof to him or her that it has such a link.

(4) A statement referred to in subsection (5) that is tendered by the applicant shall be deemed to be proof, for the purposes of subsection (3), that the applicant has such a link.

(5) The statement mentioned in subsection (4) is a statement in writing that has been given to the company concerned by the Revenue Commissioners within the period of 2 months ending on the date on which an application is made under subsection (2) by the company and which states that the Revenue Commissioners have reasonable grounds to believe that the company has a real and continuous link with one or more economic activities being carried on in the State.

(6) If, in consequence of information that has come into the possession of the registrar, the registrar of companies is of opinion that a company in respect of which a certificate under subsection (2) has been granted has ceased to have a real and continuous link with any economic activity being carried on in the State, he or she shall revoke that certificate.

(7) If, in consequence of information that has come into their possession, the Revenue Commissioners are of opinion that a company in respect of which a certificate under subsection (2) has been granted has ceased to have a real and continuous link with any economic activity being carried on in the State, then notwithstanding any obligations as to secrecy or other restrictions upon disclosure of information imposed by or under statute or otherwise, they may give a notice in writing to the registrar of companies stating that they are of that opinion and such a notice that is received by the registrar shall constitute information in his or her possession for the purposes of subsection (6).

(8) [So far as it is the person's residence in the State that falls to be determined for the purposes of that section, for the purposes of section 43][a], a person is resident in the State at a particular time ('the relevant time') if—

(a) he or she is present in the State at—

(i) any one time or several times in the period of 12 months preceding the relevant time ('the immediate 12 month period') for a period in the aggregate amounting to 183 days or more, or

(ii) any one time or several times—

(I) in the immediate 12 month period, and

(II) in the period of 12 months preceding the immediate 12 month period ('the previous 12 month period'), for a period (being a period comprising in the aggregate the number of days on which the person is present in the State in the immediate 12 month period and the number of days on which the person was present in the State in the previous 12 month period) in the aggregate amounting to 280 days or more, or

(b) that time is in a year of assessment (within the meaning of the Taxes Consolidation Act, 1997) in respect of which the person has made an election under section 819(3) of that Act.

(9) Notwithstanding subsection (8)(a)(ii), where in the immediate 12 month period concerned a person is present in the State at any one time or several times for a period in the aggregate amounting to not more than 30 days—

(a) the person shall not be resident in the State, for the purposes of section 43, at the relevant time concerned, and

(b) no account shall be taken of the period for the purposes of the aggregate mentioned, in subsection (8)(a)(ii).

(10) For the purposes of subsections (8) and (9)—

(a) references in this section to a person's being present in the State are references to the person's being personally present in the State, and

(b) a person shall be deemed to be present in the State for a day if the person is present in the State at the end of the day.

(11) An application under subsection (2) may be made, and a certificate under that subsection may be granted, before the commencement of subsection (1) or (2) of section 43.

[(12) For the purposes of this section a company has a real and continuous link with an economic activity that is being carried on in the State if one or more of the following conditions are satisfied by it:

(a) the affairs of the company are managed by one or more persons from a place of business established in the State and that person or those per-sons is or are authorised by the company to act on its behalf;

(b) the company carries on a trade in the State;

(c) the company is a subsidiary or a holding company of a company or another body corporate that satisfies either or both of the conditions specified in paragraphs (a) and (b);

(d) the company is a subsidiary of a company, another subsidiary of which satisfies either or both of the conditions specified in paragraphs (a) and (b).][b]

Amendments

a Words 'So far as it is the person's residence in the State that falls to be determined for the purposes of that section, for the purposes of section 43' substituted for 'For the purposes of section 43' by C(A)A 2009, s 10(2)(a).

b C(A)A 2009, s 10(2)(b) inserts C(A)(No 2)A 1999, s 44(12).

Definitions

'commencement': IA 2005, Sch, Pt 1; 'company': CA 1963, s 2(1); 'director': CA 1963, s 2(1); 'prescribed': CA 1963, s 2(1); 'the registrar of companies': CA 1963, s 2(1).

Notes

Exemption from requirements of s 43: See C(A)(No 2)A 1999, s 43 and the notes thereto.

Residence of directors: In determining whether or not a director is resident in the State for the purposes of C(A)(No 2)A 1999, s 43, specific residency rules are prescribed by s 44(8), (9) and (10). These residency rules largely mirror the residency provisions of the Taxes Consolidation Act 1997, s 819.

Exemption for companies with Irish economic activities: The requirement to either have a bond or at least one EEA resident director will be dispensed with in respect of any company which obtains from the Registrar, on application in the prescribed form,[1] a certificate stating that the company has a real and continuous link with one or more economic activities that are being carried on in the state.[2] Proof of such a link will have to be adduced before the Registrar can issue such a certificate.[3] That evidence may come in the form of a statement (not less than two months old) from the Revenue Commissioners confirming such a link.[4] However, other forms of proof would also appear to be permissible.[5]

If, having previously granted a certificate of exemption to a company, the Registrar of Companies subsequently forms the opinion that it no longer has a real and continuous link with one or more economic activities that are being carried on in the State, he must revoke the certificate.[6] Such an opinion may, *inter alia*, be formed as a result of information to that effect received from the Revenue Commissioners. In this regard, any such disclosure by the Revenue Commissioners will not be regarded as a breach of their obligations as to secrecy and confidentiality.[7]

1 Form B67: Companies (Forms) Order 2000 (SI 62/2000).

2 C(A)(No 2)A 1999, s 44(1) and (2). This discrimination between Irish economic activities and economic activities in other member states of the European Union seems hard to reconcile with the freedom of establishment enshrined in Art 43 of the EC Treaty.

3 C(A)(No 2)A 1999, s 44(3).

4 C(A)(No 2)A 1999, s 44(4) and (5).

5 C(A)(No 2)A 1999, s 44(3).

6 C(A)(No 2)A 1999, s 44(6).

7 C(A)(No 2)A 1999, s 44(7).

Residence of the Company: It is worth noting that prior to FA 1999, the residence of a company, for tax purposes, was determined by where the central management and control actually resided.[1] However, all companies incorporated in the State after 11 February 1999[2] are to be regarded as resident in the State for tax purposes and all companies incorporated prior to 11 February 1999 are to be regarded as resident in the State for tax purposes from 1 October 1999. There are certain limited exceptions to this general rule.[3] Any provision of a company's articles of association which have the effect of prohibiting a person who is resident in the State from being a director of a company, is void.[4] This provision was introduced to counteract the attempts by some promoters to demonstrate, particularly to the Revenue Commissioners, that control and management of the company was being exercised outside the state, notwithstanding the fact that the company in question was registered in Ireland. Since the changes introduced by the FA 1999, referred to above, this provision is of diminished significance.

1 *De Beers Consolidated Mines Ltd v Howe* [1906] AC 455.

2 Taxes Consolidation Act 1997, s 23A(2) as inserted by FA 1999, s 82.

3 Taxes Consolidation Act 1997, ss 23A(3) and (4) as inserted by FA 1999, s 82.

4 C(A)(No 2)A 1999, s 43(12).

Effect of certificate granted: Pursuant to C(A)(No 2)A 1999, s 44 (II) it was possible to seek a certificate under C(A)(No 2)A 1999, s 44 (2) before C(A)(No 2)A 1999, s 43 came into force, thus allowing existing companies, having a real and continuous link to avoid having to comply with the requirements of C(A)(No 2)A 1999, s 43 once brought into force.[1] It is also significant that under C(A)(No 2)A 1999, s 45(3)(a)(iii) directorships of a company in respect of which such a certificate has been granted shall not be counted towards the total permissible number of 25.[2]

1 18 April 2000: Companies (Amendment) (No 2) Act 1999 (Commencement) Order 2000 (SI 61/ 2000).

2 C(A)(No 2)A 1999, s 45(1).

45 Limitation on number of directorships

(1) A person shall not, at a particular time, be a director of more than 25 companies.

(2) In subsection (1), (but not any other subsection of this section) 'director' includes a shadow director (within the meaning of the Companies Act, 1990).

(3) In reckoning, for the purposes of subsection (1), the number of companies of which the person concerned is a director at a particular time the following provisions shall apply—

(a) without prejudice to paragraph (b) or subsection (4), there shall not be included any of the following companies of which he or she is a director at that time, namely—

(i) a public limited company,

(ii) a public company (within the meaning of the Companies (Amendment) Act, 1983),

(iii) a company in respect of which a certificate under section 44(2) is in force,

(b) there shall not be included any company of which he or she is a director at that time (not being a time that is before the date of the giving of the certificate or direction referred to hereafter in this paragraph) if—

(i) he or she, or the company, delivers to the registrar of companies a notice, in the prescribed form, stating that the company is a company falling within one or more of the categories of company specified in the Table to this section, and

(ii) either—

(I) the registrar of companies, having considered the said notice and having made such enquiries as he or she thinks fit, certifies in writing, or as the case may be the Minister under subsection (6) so certifies, that the company is a company falling within one or more of the categories aforesaid, or

(II) the Minister directs, under subsection (6), that the company is not to be included amongst the companies that shall be reckoned for the purposes aforesaid,

(c) there shall be counted as the one company of which he or she is a director at that time, 2 or more companies of which he or she is a director at that time if one of those companies is the holding company of the other or others.

(4) Without prejudice to subsection (3), in reckoning, for the purposes of subsection (1), the number of companies of which the person concerned is a director at a particular

time, being a time that is before the expiration of the period of 12 months from the commencement of this section, there shall not be included any company of which the person is a director at that time if he or she was such a director immediately before such commencement.

(5) For the purposes of subsection (3)(b)(ii), the registrar of companies may accept as sufficient evidence that the company concerned falls within a category of company specified in the Table to this section a statutory declaration, in the prescribed form, to that effect made by an officer of the company or the other person referred to in subsection (3)(b)(i).

(6) If the registrar of companies refuses to certify that the company to which a notice under subsection (3)(b) relates is a company falling within a category of company specified in the Table to this section, the company or the person referred to in that subsection may appeal to the Minister against such a refusal and the Minister may, having considered the matter and made such enquiries as he or she thinks fit, do one of the following—

- (a) confirm the decision of the registrar of companies,
- (b) certify in writing that the company is a company falling within a category aforesaid, or
- (c) notwithstanding that he or she confirms the decision of the registrar of companies, if—
  - (i) the person concerned was a director of the company before the commencement of this section, and
  - (ii) in the opinion of the Minister the inclusion of the company amongst the companies that shall be reckoned for the purposes of subsection (1), in so far as that subsection applies to the person concerned, would result in serious injustice or hardship to that person, and
  - (iii) the giving of a direction under this subsection would not operate against the common good,

direct that the company is not to be included amongst the companies that shall be reckoned for the purposes of subsection (1) in so far as that subsection applies to the person concerned.

(7) A notice referred to in subsection (3)(b)(i) may, for the purposes of that provision, be delivered to the registrar of companies before the person concerned becomes a director of the company to which the notice relates.

(8) If a person, in contravention of subsection (1), becomes or remains a director or shadow director of one or more companies he or she shall be guilty of an offence.

(9) An appointment of a person as a director of a company made after the commencement of this section shall, if it contravenes subsection (1), be void.

(10) An appointment of a person as a director of a company made before the commencement of this section, being an appointment which, but for this section, would subsist on or after the expiration of the period of 12 months from that commencement, shall, if its subsistence at any time on or after the expiration of that period contravenes subsection (1), cease to have effect upon that contravention occurring.

(11) For the avoidance of doubt—

(a) each appointment, in excess of the limit (reckoned in accordance with subsections (3) and (4)) that is provided for by subsection (1), of a person as a director of a company shall constitute a separate contravention of that subsection,

(b) an appointment, not in excess of the said limit, of a person as a director of a company shall not, by virtue of this section, become unlawful, be rendered void or cease to have effect by reason of a subsequent appointment, in excess of that limit, of the person as a director of a company,

(c) in determining whether one particular appointment referred to in subsection (10), as distinct from another such appointment, has ceased to have effect by virtue of that subsection or whether a person's remaining in office under one such appointment, as distinct from another such appointment, constitutes an offence under subsection (8), the provisions of this section (other than subsections (3)(b), (5), (6), (7) and (8)) shall be deemed to have been in operation at the time of the making of that appointment.

(12) If—

(a) the appointments of a person as a director of 2 or more companies are made at the same time, or

(b) the times at which the appointments of a person as a director of 2 or more companies were made are not capable of being distinguished from one another,

then those appointments shall, for the purposes of this section, be deemed to have been made at different times on the day concerned and in the same order as the order in which the companies to which the appointments relate were registered under the Companies Acts, 1963 to 1999.

(13) Summary proceedings in relation to an offence under subsection (8) may be brought and prosecuted by the registrar of companies.

TABLE

1. A company that is the holder of a licence under section 9 of the Central Bank Act, 1971, or is exempt from the requirement under that Act to hold such a licence.

2. A company referred to in the Second Schedule.

Definitions

'company': CA 1963, s 2(1); 'commencement': IA 2005, Sch, Pt 1; 'director': CA 1963, s 2(1); 'holding company': CA 1963, s 155; 'Minister': CA 1963, s 2(1); 'prescribed': CA 1963, s 2(1); 'private company': CA 1963, s 2(1); 'public company': C(A)A 1983, s 2(1); 'public limited company': C(A)A 1983, s 2(1); 'the registrar of companies': CA 1963, s 2(1); 'shadow director': CA 1990, s 27.

Notes

Limit on number of directorships: Prior to the coming into force of this section on 18 April 2000[1] there was no limit on the number of directorships that any one individual[2] could hold.[3] Concern had arisen at the number of Irish registered non-resident companies which had failed to file annual returns. Many of these companies had the same handful of individuals (eg company formation agents and trust company representatives) as directors.[4] The enactment of C(A)(No 2)A 1999, s 45 represented an attempt to address this problem.

The basic restriction contained in s 45 is that no individual should be a director or shadow director[5] of more than 25 Irish-registered companies.[6] Directorships of two or more companies in the same group will be counted as one directorship only.[7] Furthermore, in determining whether or not this limit has been exceeded, the following directorships (but not shadow directorships)[8] will be ignored: (a) a directorship of a plc;[9] (b) a directorship of some other public company such an a company limited by guarantee or an unlimited public company;[10] a directorship of a company which has in force a certificate from the Registrar of Companies stating that the company has a real and continuous link with one or more economic activities that are being carried on in the State;[11] a directorship of a company in respect of which there is in force a certificate from the registrar of companies or, on appeal, from the Minister,[12] to the effect that the company is a licensed bank or is a bank exempted from holding such a licence or is a financial services company of the type listed in Sch 2.[13] In order to gain such a certificate, application must be made by the company in the prescribed form[14] and indeed, may be made before the person actually becomes a director.[15]

1 Companies (Amendment) (No 2) Act, 1999 (Commencement) Order 2000 (SI 61/2000).

2 CA 1963, s 176: Prohibition on a company having a body corporate as a director. There is no prohibition contained in the Companies Acts on a company having a body corporate acting as secretary nor on an Irish registered company acting as a director of a company registered in another jurisdiction.

3 CA 1963, s 174: Every company must have at least two directors..

4 See Parliamentary Debates, Dáil Éireann, Volume 505, (27 May 1999).

5 For the definition of shadow director, see CA 1990, s 27.

6 C(A)(No 2)A 1999, s 45(1) and (2).

7 C(A)(No 2)A 1999, s 45(3)(c).

8 C(A)(No 2)A 1999, s 45(2).

9 C(A)(No 2)A 1999, s 45(3)(a)(i).

10 C(A)(No 2)A 1999, s 45(3)(a)(ii).

11 C(A)(No 2)A 1999, s 45(3)(a)(iii).

12 Even if the Minister finds, on appeal, that the company is one to which the Registrar correctly refused a certificate, he may nonetheless issue a direction that the company be ignored for the purpose of calculating the ceiling of 25 directorships if (a) the person was a director of the company before C(A)(No 2)A 1999, s 45 came into force; (b) the person would otherwise suffer serious injustice or hardship; and (c) the giving of such a direction would not be contrary to the common good.

13 C(A)(No 2)A 1999, s 45(3)(b) and s 45(6). The types of companies identified in the Table are credit institutions which are directly or indirectly supervised by the Central Bank or companies which fall into another regulated sector. Given the close scrutiny applied prior to the appointment of such persons as directors, it was thought that it was reasonable to exclude such directorships from the total of 25.

14 Form B68: Companies (Forms) Order 2000 (SI 62/2000), with effect from 18 April 2000.

15 C(A)(No 2)A 1999, s 45(7).

Consequences of limit being exceeded: An appointment which brings the number of a person's reckonable directorships above the permitted limit of 25 is automatically void.[1] In the case of multiple appointments made on the same day or made at times which cannot be distinguished from one another, the order of appointment is deemed to be the same as the order in which those appointments are registered in the Companies Registration Office.[2] Each and every[3] invalid appointment constitutes a criminal offence.[4]

1 C(A)(No 2)A 1999, s 45(9).

2 C(A)(No 2)A 1999, s 45(12). See also CA 1963, s 195 in relation to the registration of directorships.

3 C(A)(No 2)A 1999, s 45(11)(a).

4 C(A)(No 2)A 1999, s 45(8). It is the person accepting appointment rather than the company itself who commits the offence.

Transitional measure: As a transitional measure, for 12 months from 18 April 2000[1] pre-existing directorships were also ignored in determining whether the statutory ceiling had been exceeded.[2] However, after this transitional period, any of these pre-existing directorships which still subsist will have to be taken into account and to the extent that the ceiling of 25 directorships is exceeded, those directorships which result in the ceiling being exceeded, will be rendered void.[3] In this regard, the appointments which are latest in time are the first to be invalidated.[4]

1 Being the operative date of C(A)(No 2)A 1999, s 45 under Companies (Amendment) (No 2) Act, 1999 (Commencement) Order 2000 (SI 61/2000).

2 C(A)(No 2)A 1999, s 45(4).

3 C(A)(No 2)A 1999, s 45(10).

4 C(A)(No 2)A 1999, s 45(11) and (12).

---

46 Power of registrar to strike company off register for failure to make annual return

[...][a]

Amendments

a C(A)(No 2)A 1999, s 46 substitutes C(A)A 1982, s 12 and inserts C(A)A 1982, ss 12A–12D.

Cross reference

See C(A)A 1982, s 12 and ss 12A–12D (as amended).

Definitions

'annual return' CA 1963, s 2(1); 'company': CA 1963, s 2(1); 'the registrar of companies': CA 1963, s 2(1).

Notes

Operative Date: C(A)(No 2)A 1999 s 46 was brought into force on 23 March 2000 by the Companies (Amendment) (No 2) Act 1999 (Commencement) Order 2000.[1]

1 SI 61/2000.

---

47 Amendment of section 195 of Principal Act

[...][a]

[...][b]

Amendments

a C(A)(No 2)A 1999, s 47(a) deletes CA 1963, s 195(8) (as inserted by CA 1990, s 51).

b C(A)(No 2)A 1999, s 47(b) inserts CA 1963, ss 195(11A)–(11E).

Cross reference

See CA 1963, s 195 (as amended).

Definitions

'the Principal Act': C(A)(No 2)A 1999, s 2(1).

Notes

Operative Date: C(A)(No 2)A 1999 s 47 was brought into force on 18 April 2000 by the Companies (Amendment) (No 2) Act 1999 (Commencement) Order 2000.[1]

Notification to the Registrar of cessation to act as a director or secretary: The purpose of CA1963, s 195(8) was to allow any person who ceased to be a director or secretary of a company to send to the Registrar of Companies a notification of their ceasing to so act as at a particular date. However, it became apparent that such a provision would cause serious administrative difficulties as it could result in companies remaining on the register notwithstanding the fact that such companies had no registered directors or secretary. This would arise in circumstances where the company did not notify the Registrar of Companies of officers who would replace those ceasing to act. Therefore, it was decided not to commence this particular subsection of CA 1990, s 51. However, it was recognised that provision should be made for officers to be able to notify the Registrar of companies in circumstances where they had ceased to act and the company had not made the appropriate notification to the Registrar of Companies.[2] See notes in relation CA 1963, s 195(11A) in this regard.

1 SI 61/2000.

2 C(A)(No 2)A 1999, s 47(b).

---

48 Exercise of power to strike company off register where it is not carrying on business

The fact that, for the time being, in consequence of the forwarding to the registrar, under and in accordance with subsections (11A) and (11B) of section 195 of the Principal Act, of a copy of a notice of resignation or other documentary proof of a person's having ceased to be a director of the company concerned, there are no persons recorded in the office of the registrar of companies as being directors of a particular company shall, for the purposes of section 311 of the Principal Act, afford the registrar of companies good grounds for believing that the company is not carrying on business, and for so believing with the cause requisite for the exercise by him or her of the powers conferred by subsection (1) of that section 311 in relation to the company.

Definitions

'company': CA 1963, s 2(1); 'director': CA 1963, s 2(1); 'the Principal Act': C(A)(No 2)A 1999, s 2(1); 'the registrar of companies': CA 1963, s 2(1).

Notes

Operative Date: C(A)(No 2)A 1999, s 48 was brought into force on 18 April 2000 by the Companies (Amendment) (No 2) Act 1999 (Commencement) Order 2000 (SI 61/2000).

Striking defunct companies off the register: CA 1963, s 311 authorises the Registrar to strike the name of a company off the register of companies in circumstances where he has reasonable cause to believe that the company is not carrying on business. The procedure involves the sending of a letter to the company inquiring as to its status.[1] If, within one month he receives no response or alternatively receives a response to the effect that the company is no longer carrying on business, he may publish in the Companies Registration Office Gazette[2] and send to the company a notice advising that within one month thereafter the company will be dissolved unless cause is shown to the contrary.[3] The effect of C(A)(No 2)A 1999, s 48 is that if as a result of the filing of a notice of resignation under CA 1963, ss 195(11A) and (11B) or if as a result of furnishing of other documentary proof of a person's ceasing to be a director[4] there is no longer any person recorded in the Companies Registration Office as being a director of the company, the Registrar will be deemed to have good grounds for believing that the company is no longer carrying on business and he will accordingly be justified in commencing the strike-off process provided for by CA 1963, s 311. The onus will then be on the company to establish that it is indeed still carrying on business or to otherwise show cause as to why it should not be dissolved. This provision mirrors C(A)(No 2)A 1999, s 43(15), which applies in circumstances where a company fails to have an Irish resident director and does not comply with any of the exemptions provided in C(A)(No 2)A 1999 ss 43 or 44.

1 CA 1963, s 311(1).

2 CA 1963, s 311(2).

3 'the Companies Registration Office Gazette' was substituted for Iris Oifigiúil by IFCMPA 2005, s 72.

4 eg Form B 70, filed with a death certificate in respect of a deceased director.

---

49 Amendment of section 311 of Principal Act

[...][a]

[...][b]

Amendments

a C(A)(No 2)A 1999, s 49(a) amends CA 1963, s 311(8) by the substitution for 'as if the name of the company had not been struck off.' of 'as if the name of the company had not been struck off or make such other order as seems just (and such other order is referred to in subsection (8A) as an 'alternative order').'

b C(A)(No 2)A 1999, s 49(b) inserts CA 1963, s 311(8A).

Cross reference

See CA 1963, s 311 (as amended).

Definitions

'company': CA 1963, s 2(1); 'the Principal Act': C(A)(No 2)A 1999, s 2(1).

Notes

Operative Date: C(A)(No 2)A 1999 s 49 was brought into force on 23 March 2000 by the Companies (Amendment) (No 2) Act 1999 (Commencement) Order 2000.[1]

1 SI 61/2000.

Alternative Order: This amendment brings CA 1963, s 311 into line with the amendments made to C(A)A 1982, s 12 by C(A)(No 2)A 1999, s 46 whereby the court may if it considers it appropriate, make an officer of the company liable for the whole or part of the debt incurred by the company in circumstances where the company continues to trade after it has been struck off the register.[1]

1 C(A)A 1982, s 12B(4).

50 Amendment of section 311A of Principal Act

[...][a]

Amendments

a C(A)(No 2)A 1999, s 50 amends CA 1963, s 311A by the substitution for 'Without prejudice to the provisions of section 311(8) of this Act and section 12(6) of the Companies (Amendment) Act 1982' of 'Without prejudice to the provisions of section 311(8) of this Act or subsection (3) or (7) of section 12B, or subsection (1) of section 12C, of the Companies (Amendment) Act, 1982,'.

Cross reference

See CA 1963, s 311A (as amended).

Definitions

'the Principal Act': C(A)(No 2)A 1999, s 2(1).

Notes

Operative Date: C(A)(No 2)A 1999 s 50 was brought into force on 23 March 2000 by the Companies (Amendment) (No 2) Act 1999 (Commencement) Order 2000.[1] This is a consequential change to the provisions of CA 1963, s 311A, which is required so as to take into account the changes made to C(A)A 1982, s 12 by C(A)(No 2)A 1999, s 46.

1 SI 61/2000.

51 Amendment of section 8 of Companies (Amendment) Act, 1983

[...][a]

Amendments

a C(A)(No 2)A 1999, s 51 amends C(A)A 1983, s 8(3) by the substitution for '(7) and (8)' of '(7), (8) and (8A)'.

Cross reference

See CA 1983, s 8 (as amended).

Notes

Operative Date: C(A)(No 2)A 1999, s 51 was brought into force on 23 March 2000 by the Companies (Amendment) (No 2) Act 1999 (Commencement) Order 2000.[1] This is a consequential change to ensure that the provisions of CA 1963, s 311 (as amended) apply to public limited companies.

1 SI 61/2000.

52 Performance of duties of registrar of companies

(1) Any act referred to in subsection (4) of section 368 of the Principal Act which, before the commencement of this section, was done to or by—

(a) an assistant registrar appointed under subsection (2) of that section, or

(b) any other person employed in the office of the registrar of companies to perform generally duties under any enactment referred to in that subsection, shall be valid and be deemed always to have been valid as if the Minister had directed under that subsection (4) that such an act was to be done to or by such an assistant registrar or other such person (including in cases where the existing registrar of joint stock companies (or his or her successor) was not absent).

(2) On and from the commencement of this section, any act required or authorised by the Companies Acts, 1963 to 1999, the Registration of Business Names Act, 1963, or the Limited Partnerships Act, 1907, to be done to or by the registrar of companies, the registrar of joint stock companies or, as the case may be, a person referred to in the enactment concerned as 'the registrar' may be done to or by a registrar or assistant registrar appointed under section 368(2) of the Principal Act or any other person authorised in that behalf by the Minister.

(3) Subsection (4) of section 368 of the Principal Act shall cease to have effect.

Definitions

'commencement': IA 2005, Sch, Pt 1; 'the Principal Act': C(A)(No 2)A 1999, s 2(1); 'Minister': CA 1963, s 2(1); 'the registrar of companies': CA 1963, s 2(1).

Notes

Operative Date: C(A)(No 2)A 1999 s 52 was brought into force on 21 December 1999 by the Companies (Amendment) (No 2) Act 1999 (Commencement) Order 1999.[1]

[1] SI 406/1999.

Delegation to assistant registrars and other officials: CA 1963 368(2) allows for the appointment of Assistant Registrars of Companies. Under that section, however, such Assistant Registrars were not automatically authorised to exercise the functions of the actual Registrar of Companies. Delegation of authority was dependent on the making of appropriate regulations by the Minister for Enterprise, Trade and Employment. Doubt was therefore cast on the validity of acts performed on behalf of the registrar of companies by officials in the Companies Registration Office. To remove these doubts C(A)(No 2)A 1999, s 52(1) retrospectively ratifies any acts performed on behalf of the Registrar whether by an Assistant Registrar or by some other official employed in the Companies Registration Office. Furthermore, s 52(2) prospectively provides for the delegation of the Registrar's functions to assistant registrars and other officials, not only for the purposes of the Companies Acts but also for the purposes of the Registration of Business Names Act 1963 and the Limited Partnership Act 1907. CA 1963, s 368 (4) which dealt with such delegation previously, ceases to have effect, as of 21 December 1999.[1]

[1] Companies (Amendment) (No 2) Act 1999 (Commencement) Order 1999 (SI 406/1999).

---

53 Amendment of sections 20 and 21 of Companies Act, 1990

(1) [...][a]

(2) [...][b]

(3)

[...][c]

[...][d]

(4) The amendments effected by this section shall apply in relation to the publication or disclosure, after its commencement, of information, books or documents which have

been obtained under section 19 or 20 of the Companies Act, 1990, whether before or after that commencement.

Amendments

a C(A)(No 2)A 1999, s 53(1) amended CA 1990, s 20(3) by the substitution for 'any such criminal proceedings as are mentioned in section 21(1)(a) or (1)(b)' of 'any proceedings for an offence mentioned in section 21(1)(a).' CA 1990, s 20 (3) was repealed by IFCMPA 2005, s 68 with respect to material information seized under that section before 30 June 2005.

b C(A)(No 2)A 1999, s 53(2) substitutes CA 1990, s 21(1).

c C(A)(No 2)A 1999, s 53(3)(a) amends CA 1990, s 21(3)(g) by the deletion of 'and'.

d C(A)(No 2)A 1999, s 53(3)(b) substitutes CA 1990, s 21(3)(h) and inserts CA 1990, s 21(3)(i).

1 Brought into force by the Investment Funds, Companies and Miscellaneous Provisions Act 2005 (Commencement) Order 2005 (SI 323/2005), with effect from 30 June 2005.

Cross reference

See CA 1990, ss 20 and 21 (as amended).

Definitions

'books or documents': CA 1990 s 3(1); 'commencement': IA 2005, Sch, Pt 1.

Notes

Disclosure of information obtained upon enquiry: C(A)(No 2)A 1999, s 53 extended the classes of persons to whom information obtained on foot of an inquiry under CA 1990, s 19 or s 20 may be disclosed. Although this section only came into force on 21 December 1999,[1] it authorised this wider disclosure in respect of information and documentation obtained before that date as part of the enquiry process.[2]

Competent Authority: The meaning of 'competent authority' is extended to include an authority established outside the State which exercises functions of investigation or prosecution of offences similar to those specified in CA 1990, s 21(1)(a)[3].

1 Companies (Amendment) (No 2) Act 1999 (Commencement) Order 1999 (SI 406/1999).

2 C(A)(No 2)A 1999, s 53(4). See also *Chestvale Properties Ltd and Hoddle Investments Ltd v Glackin* [1992] ILRM 221.

3 C(A)(No 2)A 1999, s 53(3).

54 Amendment of Part XIII (Investment Companies) of Companies Act, 1990

(1)

(a)

[...][a]

[...][b]

[...][c]

[...][d]

(2)

[...][e]

[...][f]

[...][g]

Amendments

a C(A)(No 2)A 1999, s 54(1)(a)(i) amends CA 1990, s 253(1)(a) by the deletion of the word 'and'.

b C(A)(No 2)A 1999, s 54(1)(a)(ii) amends CA 1990, s 253(1)(b) by the insertion after 'nominal value thereto' of 'and'.

c C(A)(No 2)A 1999, s 54(1)(a)(iii) inserts CA 1990, s 253(1)(c).

d C(A)(No 2)A 1999, s 54(1)(b) deletes CA 1990, s 253(2A)(b).

e C(A)(No 2)A 1999, s 54(2)(a) amends CA 1990, s 256(5) and (7) by the substitution for 'by promoting the sale of its shares to the public', in each place where it occurs, of 'by providing facilities for the direct or indirect participation by the public in the profits and income of the company'.

f C(A)(No 2)A 1999, s 54(2)(b) amends CA 1990, s 256(6) by the substitution for 'promote the sale of its shares to the public' of 'provide facilities for the direct or indirect participation by the public in the profits and income of the company'.

g C(A)(No 2)A 1999, s 54(3) substitutes CA 1990, s 260.

Cross reference

See CA 1990, ss 253, 256 and 260 (as amended).

Definitions

'company': CA 1963, s 2(1); 'investment company': CA 1990, s 252 (1); 'share': CA 1963, s 2(1).

Notes

Operative Dates: C(A)(No 2)A 1999 s 54 (other than subs (1)(a))[1] was brought into force on 21 December 1999. C(A)(No 2)A 1999, s 54(1)(a) was brought into force on 24 February 2000.[2]

1 Companies (Amendment) (No 2) Act 1999 (Commencement) Order 1999 (SI 406/1999), r 3(d).

2 Companies (Amendment) (No 2) Act 1999 (Commencement) Order 1999 (SI 406/1999), r 6.

Investment Companies: C(A)(No 2)A 1999, s 54 was introduced by an amendment passed at Dáil Committee Stage. CA 1990, s 253 operates to disapply certain provisions of CA 1963 in relation to investment companies formed pursuant to CA 1990, Pt XIII. The Second EU Company Law Directive,1 requires that investment companies should state their minimum and maximum amount of share capital. This requirement has now been included in C(A)(No 2)A 1999, s 54(1)(a). Amendments to CA 1990, s 256 in relation to 'sales to the public' bring that section in line with the other investment company legislation, such as the Unit Trusts Act 1990 and provides for other consequential changes. See notes in relation to CA 1990, s 260, as substituted.

1 (77/91/EEC) 20 OJ, L 26, 31 January 1977, pp 1–13.

FIRST SCHEDULE

SPECIFIC PROVISIONS FROM WHICH COMPANY IS EXEMPTED UNDER PART III

Section 32

1 Sections 157 and 159 of the Principal Act in so far as they relate to an auditor's report.

2 Section 160(2) of the Principal Act.

3 Paragraphs (b), (c) and (d) of subsection (3), and subsection (4), of section 49 of the Companies (Amendment) Act, 1983.

4 Section 7 of the Companies (Amendment) Act, 1986, in so far as it relates to an auditor's report.

5 Section 15 and subsections (3), (4) and (5) of section 18 of the Companies (Amendment) Act, 1986.

6 Section 19 of the Companies (Amendment) Act, 1986, in so far as it relates to an auditor's report.

7 Sections 46 and 193 of the Companies Act, 1990.

SECOND SCHEDULE

LIST OF COMPANIES FOR PURPOSES OF SECTION 3(2)(C) OF ACT OF 1990 AND SECTIONS 32 AND 45

Sections 6, 32 and 45.

1. A company that is a member firm within the meaning of the Stock Exchange Act, 1995.
2. A company that is a stock exchange within the meaning of the Stock Exchange Act, 1995.
3. A company that is an associated undertaking or a related undertaking of a member firm or stock exchange within the meaning of the Stock Exchange Act, 1995.
4. A company that is an investment business firm within the meaning of the Investment Intermediaries Act, 1995.
5. A company that is an associated undertaking or a related undertaking of an investment business firm within the meaning of the Investment Intermediaries Act, 1995.
6. A company to which Chapter VII, VIII or IX of Part II of the Central Bank Act, 1989, applies.
7. A company that is engaged in the business of accepting deposits or other repayable funds or granting credit for its own account.
8. A company that is an associated body of a building society within the meaning of the Building Societies Act, 1989.
9. A company that is an associated enterprise of a credit institution within the meaning of the European Communities (Consolidated Supervision of Credit Institutions) Regulations, 1992 (S.I. No. 396 of 1992).
10. An investment company within the meaning of Part XIII of the Companies Act, 1990.
11. A company that is a management company or trustee within the meaning of Part XIII of the Companies Act, 1990.
12. A company that is an undertaking for collective investment in transferable securities within the meaning of the European Communities (Undertakings for

Collective Investment in Transferable Securities) Regulations, 1989 (S.I. No. 78 of 1989).

13. A company that is a management company or trustee of an undertaking for collective investment in transferable securities within the meaning of the European Communities (Undertakings for Collective Investment in Transferable Securities) Regulations, 1989 (S.I. No. 78 of 1989).
14. A company that is a management company or trustee of a unit trust scheme within the meaning of the Unit Trusts Act, 1990.
15. A company that is a general partner or custodian of an investment limited partnership within the meaning of the Investment Limited Partnerships Act, 1994.
16. A company that is an undertaking with close links with a financial undertaking within the meaning of the Supervision of Credit Institutions, Stock Exchange Member Firms and Investment Business Firms Regulations, 1996 (S.I. No. 267 of 1996).
17. Any other company the carrying on of business by which is required, by virtue of any enactment or instrument thereunder, to be authorised by the Central Bank.
18. A company that is—
    - (a) a holder of an authorisation within the meaning of—
        - (i) Regulation 2 of the European Communities (Non-Life Insurance) Regulations, 1976 (S.I. No. 115 of 1976),
        - (ii) Regulation 2 of the European Communities (Non-Life Insurance) Framework Regulations, 1994 (S.I. No. 359 of 1994),
        - (iii) Regulation 2 of the European Communities (Life Assurance) Regulations, 1984 (S.I. No. 57 of 1984),

          or
        - (iv) Regulation 2 of the European Communities (Life Assurance) Framework Regulations, 1994 (S.I. No. 360 of 1994),

      or
    - (b) a holder of an authorisation granted under the European Communities (Non-Life Insurance) (Amendment) (No 2) Regulations, 1991 (S.I. No. 142 of 1991).
19. A company that is an insurance intermediary within the meaning of the Insurance Act, 1989.
20. A company that is an excepted body within the meaning of the Trade Union Acts, 1871 to 1990.

Definitions

'company': CA 1963, s 2(1); 'Central Bank': C(A)(No 2)A 1999, s 2(1); 'undertaking': CA 1963, s 2(1).

Cross reference

'associated body': Building Societies Act 1989, s 2(1); 'associated enterprise': European Communities (Consolidated Supervision of Credit Institutions) Regulations 1992,[1] r 2(1); 'associated undertaking': Investment Intermediaries Act 1995, s 2(1); 'associated undertaking':

Stock Exchange Act 1995, s 2(1); 'authorisation': European Communities (Non-Life Insurance) Regulations 1976,[2] r 2(1); 'authorisation': European Communities (Non-Life Insurance) Framework Regulations 1994,[3] r 2(1); 'authorisation': European Communities (Life Assurance) Regulations 1984,[4] r 2(1); 'authorisation': European Communities (Life Assurance) Regulations 1994,[5] r 2(1); 'authorisation': European Communities (Non-Life Insurance) (Amendment) (No 2) Regulations 1991,[6] r 2(1); 'close links': Supervision of Credit Institutions, Stock Exchange Member Firms and Investment Business Firms Regulations 1996,[7] r 2(1); 'custodian': Investment Limited Partnerships Act 1994, s 3(1); 'excepted body': Trade Union Act 1941, s 6(3); 'financial undertaking': Supervision of Credit Institutions, Stock Exchange Member Firms and Investment Business Firms Regulations 1996,[8] r 2(1); 'general partner': Investment Limited Partnerships Act 1994, s 3(1); 'insurance intermediary': Insurance Act, 1989, s 2(1). 'investment business firm': Investment Intermediaries Act 1995, s 2(1); 'investment company': CA 1990, s 252; 'management company': CA 1990, s 252; 'management company': European Communities (Undertakings for Collective Investment in Transferable Securities) Regulations 2003,[9] r 2(1); 'management company': Unit Trusts Act 1990, s 1(2); 'member firm': Stock Exchange Act, 1995 s 2(1); 'related undertaking': Investment Intermediaries Act 1995, s (2). 'related undertaking': Stock Exchange Act 1995, s 2(1); 'stock exchange': Stock Exchange Act, 1995 s 2(1); 'trustee': Unit Trusts Act 1990,s 1(2); 'trustee' European Communities (Undertakings for Collective Investment in Transferable Securities) Regulations 2003,[10] r 2(1); 'undertaking for collective investment in transferable securities': European Communities (Undertakings for Collective Investment in Transferable Securities) Regulations 2003,[11] r 2(1).

See also notes to C(A)(No 2)A 1999, ss 6, 32 and 45.

1 SI 396/1992.

2 SI 115/1976.

3 SI 359/1994.

4 SI 57/1984.

5 SI 360/1994.

6 SI 142/1991.

7 SI 267/1996.

8 SI 267/1996.

9 SI 211/2003, which revoked and substituted European Communities (Undertakings for Collective Investment in Transferable Securities) Regulations 1989 (SI 78/1989).

10 SI 211/2003, which revoked and substituted European Communities (Undertakings for Collective Investment in Transferable Securities) Regulations 1989 (SI 78/1989).

11 SI 211/2003, which revoked and substituted European Communities (Undertakings for Collective Investment in Transferable Securities) Regulations 1989 (SI 78/1989).

Notes

Operative Dates: In so far as it relates to C(A)(No 2)A 1999, Pt II, the Second Schedule came into force on 1 February 2000.[1] Insofar as it relates to C(A)(No 2)A 1999, Pt III, the Second Schedule came into force on 21 February 2000.[2] In so far as it relates to C(A)(No 2)A 1999 Pt IV, the Second Schedule came into force on 18 April 2000.[3]

1 Companies (Amendment) (No 2) Act 1999 (Commencement) Order 1999 (SI 406/1999), r 4.

2 Companies (Amendment) (No 2) Act 1999 (Commencement) Order 1999 (SI 406/1999), r 5.

3 Companies (Amendment) (No 2) Act 1999 (Commencement) Order 2000 (SI 61/2000), r 3.

Company Law Enforcement Act 2001

Number 28 of 2001

An Act to establish a Director of Corporate Enforcement and provide for his or her appointment, terms and conditions and functions, to provide for an acting director to perform the functions of the director during exigencies, to transfer existing functions of the minister relating to the enforcement of the Companies Acts to the director, to establish a company law review group to monitor, review and advise the minister on matters relating to company law, to amend in various ways the Companies Act, 1963, the Companies Act, 1990, and various other Acts, and for related purposes. [9th July, 2001]

Be it Enacted by the Oireachtas as Follows:

Notes

CLEA 2001 gives legislative effect to many of the recommendations of the Working Group on Company Law Compliance and Enforcement which was chaired by Michael McDowell SC. Its single most important element comprises the creation of the Office of the Director of Corporate Enforcement, to whom many of the regulatory functions of the Minister have now been transferred. In addition, the Act makes substantial amendments to the provisions of CA 1990, Pt II concerning investigations and inquiries, as well as effecting changes, *inter alia*, in relation to the winding-up provisions of CA 1963. Changes have also been made concerning both the restriction and disqualification of directors and the circumstances in which a company may enter into loans, quasi-loans, credit transactions and other similar arrangements for the benefit of directors and connected persons. CLEA 2001 also established the Company Law Review Group chaired by Dr Thomas B Courtney on a statutory basis, whereas prior to this enactment the Company Law Review Group (and its predecessors the Working Group on Company Law Compliance and Enforcement chaired by Michael McDowell SC and the Company Law Review Group chaired by James Gallagher) operated on an ad hoc basis at the demand of the relevant Minister for Enterprise, Trade and Employment.

PART 1

PRELIMINARY AND GENERAL

1 Short title, collective citation and construction

(1) This Act may be cited as the Company Law Enforcement Act, 2001.

(2) This Act and the Companies Acts, 1963 to 1999, may be cited together as the Companies Acts, 1963 to 2001, and shall be construed together as one Act.

2 Commencement

This Act shall come into operation on such day or days as may be fixed by order or orders made by the Minister, either generally or with reference to any particular provision, and different days may be so fixed for different purposes and different provisions of this Act.

Definitions

'commencement': IA 2005, Sch, Pt 1; 'Minister': CLEA 2001, s 3(1).

Notes

Operative Dates: CLEA 2001 has been brought into force in stages details of which are set out below.

Part 1 and s 111 came into force on 4 August 2001.[1]

Sections 47, 62, 66–71, 75–79, 80–83, 85–87, 89, 90, 91(b), 92, 93 (except in so far as it inserts subpara (ii) of para (fa) into CA 1963, s 213), 94, 95, 98, 100, 102–106, 108 and 114, came into force on 1 October 2001.[2]

Sections 63(1)(b), 64 and 99 came into operation on 26 October 2001.[3]

Sections 7–24, 25(b), 26–39, 72–74, 96, 97, 112 and 113 and the Schedule came into operation on 28 November 2001.[4]

Sections 59, 60, 61, 63(1)(a) and (2), 65 and 84(a) came into operation on 1 March 2002,[5] as did s 88,[6] as did s 107 and s 25(a) and (c) (in so far as those paragraphs relate to investigations under CA 1990, s 8 initiated on or after that date)[7] and ss 40, 41, 42, 84(b), 91(a) and 101.[8]

Sections 43–46, 48–55, 57 and 58 came into force on 1 June 2002.[9]

Section 56 came into force on 1 June 2002 in so far as it applies to liquidators who (i) were appointed on or after June 2002 or (ii) who were appointed on or after 1 July 2001 and before 1 June 2002 where, in respect of the company to which the liquidator was appointed an order has not been made dissolving the company on the basis of the winding up having been completed.[10] Furthermore, with effect from 1 June 2003 the provisions of s 56 also apply to liquidators who were appointed on or after 1 January 2000 and before 1 July 2001, where, in respect of the company to which the liquidator was appointed, an order has not been made dissolving the company on the basis of the winding up having been completed.[11]

1 Company Law Enforcement Act, 2001 (Commencement) Order 2001 (SI 391/2001).
2 Company Law Enforcement Act, 2001 (Commencement) (No 2) Order 2001 (SI 438/2001).
3 Company Law Enforcement Act, 2001 (Commencement) (No 2) Order 2001 (SI 438/2001).
4 Company Law Enforcement Act, 2001 (Commencement) (No 3) Order 2001 (SI 523/2001).
5 Company Law Enforcement Act, 2001 (Commencement) (No 2) Order 2001 (SI 438/2001).
6 Company Law Enforcement Act, 2001 (Commencement) (No 3) Order 2001 (SI 523/2001).
7 Company Law Enforcement Act, 2001 (Commencement) (No 4) Order 2002 (SI 43/2002).
8 Company Law Enforcement Act, 2001 (Commencement) (No 5) Order 2002 (SI 53/2002).
9 Company Law Enforcement Act, 2001 (Winding Up and Insolvency Provisions) (Commencement) Order 2002 (SI 263/2002).
10 Company Law Enforcement Act 2001 (Winding Up and Insolvency Provisions) (Commencement) Order 2002 (SI 263/2002).
11 Company Law Enforcement Act 2001 (Winding Up and Insolvency Provisions) (Commencement) Order (SI 217/2003).

3 Interpretation

(1) In this Act, unless the context otherwise requires—

'Act of 1963' means the Companies Act, 1963;

'Act of 1990' means the Companies Act, 1990;

'Acting Director' means a person appointed under section 11 as the Acting Director of Corporate Enforcement;

'Companies Acts' means the Companies Act, 1963, and every enactment (including this Act) which is to be construed as one with that Act;

'Director' means the Director of Corporate Enforcement appointed under section 7(2) and includes an Acting Director while so acting and, in relation to a particular power of the Director, a delegate to whom the power is delegated under section 13;

'functions' includes powers and duties;

'Minister' means the Minister for Enterprise, Trade and Employment;

'officer of the Director' means—

(a) an officer of the Minister assigned to the Director,

(b) a member of An Garda Síochána seconded to the Director, or

(c) a person employed by the Minister or the Director under a contract for service or otherwise,

to assist the Director in carrying out functions of the Director under the Companies Acts or any other Act;

'prescribed' means prescribed by regulations made by the Minister;

'Review Group' means the Company Law Review Group established by section 67.

(2) In this Act—

(a) a reference to a Part, section or Schedule is a reference to a Part or section of, or Schedule to, this Act, unless it is indicated that reference to some other enactment is intended;

(b) a reference to a subsection, paragraph or subparagraph is to the subsection, paragraph or subparagraph of the provision in which the reference occurs, unless it is indicated that reference to some other provision is intended; and

(c) a reference to any other enactment shall, unless the context otherwise requires, be construed as a reference to that enactment as amended by or under any other enactment, including this Act.

Definitions

'Companies Acts': IA 2005, Sch, Pt 2; 'functions': IA 2005, Sch, Pt 2; 'Minister': CA 1963, s 2(1); 'prescribed': CA 1963, s 2(1).

---

4 Regulations

(1) The Minister may make regulations prescribing any matter or thing referred to in this Act as prescribed or to be prescribed, or in relation to any matter referred to in this Act as the subject of regulation.

(2) Regulations under this section may contain such incidental, supplementary and consequential provisions as appear to the Minister to be necessary or expedient for the purposes of the regulations or for giving full effect to this Act.

Definitions

'Minister': CLEA 2001, s 3(1); 'prescribed': CLEA 2001, 3(1).

---

5 Laying of regulations and orders before Houses of the Oireachtas and power to revoke or amend orders

(1) Every regulation or order (other than an order made under section 2) made under this Act shall be laid before each House of the Oireachtas as soon as may be after it is made and, if a resolution annulling the regulation or order is passed by either House within the next 21 days on which that House has sat after the regulation or order is laid before it, the regulation or order shall be annulled accordingly but without prejudice to the validity of anything previously done under it.

(2) The Minister may by order revoke or amend an order (other than an order made under section 2) made under this Act (including an order under this subsection).

Definitions

'Minister': CLEA 2001, s 3(1); 'Oireachtas': IA 2005, Sch, Pt 2.

6 Expenses of Minister

The expenses incurred by the Minister in the administration of this Act shall, to such extent as may be sanctioned by the Minister for Finance, be paid out of moneys provided by the Oireachtas.

Definitions

'Minister': CLEA 2001, s 3(1); 'Minister for Finance': Ministers and Secretaries Act 1924, s 1(ii); 'Oireachtas': IA 2005, Sch, Pt 2.

PART 2
DIRECTOR OF CORPORATE ENFORCEMENT

Director

7 Director of Corporate Enforcement

(1) There shall be a Director of Corporate Enforcement.

(2) The Minister shall, in writing, appoint a person to be the Director of Corporate Enforcement.

[(3) The Minister shall not appoint a person to be the Director unless the person has been duly selected following a competition under the Public Service Management (Recruitment and Appointments) Act 2004 for that position and the Minister has been advised accordingly].[a]

(4) The Director shall be a corporation sole and, notwithstanding any casual vacancy in the office from time to time, shall have perpetual succession and shall be capable in his or her corporate name of holding and disposing of real or personal property and of suing and being sued.

(5) The Director shall perform the functions conferred on him or her by or under this or any other Act and shall be assisted in the performance of those functions by the officers of the Director.

(6) All judges, courts or other persons or bodies acting judicially shall take judicial notice of the signature of the Director on or affixed to any document and it shall be presumed, unless the contrary is proved, that it has been duly signed or affixed.

Amendments

a Substituted by the Public Service Management (Recruitment and Appointments) Act 2004, s 61 and Sch 2.

Definitions

'Director': CLEA 2001, s 3(1); 'functions': CLEA 2001, s 3(1); 'Minister': CLEA 2001, s 3(1); 'person': IA 2005, s 18(c); 'writing': IA 2005, Sch, Pt 1.

Notes

Director of Corporate Enforcement:[1] The creation of the Office of the Director of Corporate Enforcement follows the recommendations of the Working Group on Company Law Compliance and Enforcement which was chaired by Michael McDowell SC. The Director is a corporation sole,[2] appointed by[3] and capable of being removed, for stated reasons by the Minister.[4] His functions are spelt out in CLEA 2001, s 12 as amended by C(AA)A 2003, s 51. Essentially, they involve enforcing and encouraging compliance with the Companies Acts, investigating of suspected offences under those Acts and reporting the more serious of such offences to the DPP, as well as exercising a supervisory role over liquidators and receivers.[5] Furthermore, various regulatory and other functions which had previously been exercised by the Minister, have now been transferred to the Director. These additional functions are identified in CLEA 2001, Sch and s 14. The Director is also a member of the Irish Auditing and Accounting Supervisory Authority which was established by C(AA)A 2003 and may also be appointed by the Minister to be a director of that body.[6]

The Director's staff includes a mix of lawyers, accountants, members of An Garda Síochána and others. He is expressly authorised to delegate the performance of such of his functions and the exercise of such of his powers as he sees fit to all or any of his officers.[7] He must also report on his activities annually to the Minister.[8]

Subject to the contrary being established, courts, judges and other persons acting in a judicial capacity shall accept the authenticity of the signature of the Director on documents purporting to have been so signed.[9] The purpose of this provision is to remove the need to prove the authenticity of such documentation each time it is presented in court or similar circumstances.

1 CLEA 2001, Pt 2 came into operation on 28 November 2001: Company Law Enforcement Act 2001 (Commencement) (No 3) Order 2001 (SI 523/2001).

2 CLEA 2001, s 7(4). In relation to 'corporations sole' see generally Courtney, *The Law of Private Companies* (2nd edn, Tottel Publishing, 2002) para 1.046.

3 CLEA 2001, s 7(2).

4 CLEA 2001, s 10(1).

5 CLEA 2001, s 12(1).

6 CLEA 2001, s 12(1)(h) as inserted by C(AA)A 2003, s 51(c).

7 CLEA 2001, ss 12(6) and 13. CLEA 2001, s 3(1): In order to be an 'officer of the Director' and thus a person to whom the Director's functions may lawfully be delegated, the individual must be an officer of the Minister assigned to the ODCE, a member of An Garda Síochána seconded to the ODCE or an employee of the Minister or the Director: s 3(1).

8 CLEA 2001, s 16.

9 CLEA 2001, s 7(6). See also provisions as to evidence contained in CLEA 2001, s 110A.

8 Terms and conditions of appointment of Director

(1) Subject to subsection (2), a person appointed to be the Director shall hold office for such period not exceeding 5 years beginning on the date of his or her appointment, and on such terms and conditions (which shall include a scheme of superannuation under section 9), as the Minister, with the consent of the Minister for Finance, may determine, and the Minister may, if he or she thinks fit, with the consent of the Minister for Finance, continue the appointment (including an appointment previously continued under this subsection) for such further period, not exceeding 5 years at any one time, as the Minister thinks appropriate.

(2) A person appointed as the Director is, by virtue of the appointment, a civil servant within the meaning of the Civil Service Regulation Act, 1956, as amended.

(3) The Director shall not hold any other office or employment in respect of which emoluments are payable.

Definitions

'Director': CLEA 2001, s 3(1); 'Minister': CLEA 2001, s 3(1); 'Minister for Finance': Ministers and Secretaries Act 1924, s 1 (ii); 'person': IA 2005, s 18(c); 'year': IA 2005, Sch, Pt 1.

Notes

Appointment of the Director: CLEA 2001, s 8 sets out the terms and conditions of the Director's appointment. The Director shall hold office for not more than 5 years and his/her appointment may be renewed after the first period of appointment (at the discretion of the Minister with the consent of the Minister for Finance) for an unlimited number of further periods, each being not more than 5 years.[1]

By virtue of his/her appointment, the Director is a civil servant and is therefore subject to various legislative provisions pertaining to civil servants such as the Official Secrets Act 1963. The Director is also subject to the usual conditions of employment of civil servants such as suspension and disciplinary procedures, and travel and subsistence etc.[2] In order to avoid any conflict of interest which might arise with his/her duties as Director, the Director may not take up any outside paid employment.[3]

1 CLEA 2001, s 8(1).

2 CLEA 2001, s 8(2).

3 CLEA 2001, s 8(3).

9 Superannuation

(1) The Minister shall, with the consent of the Minister for Finance, if he or she considers it appropriate to do so, make and carry out a scheme or schemes for the granting of superannuation benefits to or in respect of one or more of the following, namely, the Director, the Acting Director and any officer of the Director.

(2) Every such scheme shall fix the time and conditions of retirement for the person or persons to or in respect of whom superannuation benefits are payable under the scheme, and different times and conditions may be fixed in respect of different classes of such person.

(3) Every such scheme may be amended or revoked by a subsequent scheme made under this section with the consent of the Minister for Finance.

(4) No superannuation benefit shall be granted by the Minister to or in respect of the Director, the Acting Director or an officer of the Director otherwise than in accordance with a scheme under this section or, if the Minister, with the consent of the Minister for Finance, sanctions the granting of such a benefit, in accordance with that sanction.

(5) If any dispute arises as to the claim of any person to, or the amount of, any superannuation benefit payable in pursuance of a scheme or schemes under this section, such dispute shall be submitted to the Minister who shall refer it to the Minister for Finance, whose decision shall be final.

(6) A scheme under this section shall be laid before each House of the Oireachtas as soon as may be after it is made and, if a resolution annulling the scheme is passed by either such House within the next 21 days on which that House has sat after the scheme

is laid before it, the scheme shall be annulled accordingly, but without prejudice to the validity of anything previously done thereunder.

(7) In this section, 'superannuation benefits' means pensions, gratuities and other allowances payable on resignation, retirement or death.

Definitions

'Acting Director': CLEA 2001, s 3(1); 'Director': CLEA 2001, s 3(1); 'Oireachtas': IA 2005, Sch, Pt 1; 'officer of the Director': CLEA 2001, s 3(1);'Minister': CLEA 2001, s 3(1); 'Minister for Finance': Ministers and Secretaries Act 1924, s 1(ii); 'superannuation benefits': CLEA 2001, s 9(7).

Notes

Retirement benefits of the Director: CLEA 2001, s 9 provides that the Minister, with the consent of the Minister for Finance, may put in place a specific scheme or schemes for pension benefits (or a replacement scheme if required from time to time)[1] for the Director, an Acting Director[2] and any officers of the Director. Any disputes relating to claims relating to a scheme established under CLEA 2001, s 9 shall be decided by the Minister for Finance.[3] Any scheme made under CLEA 2001, s 9 must also be laid before both Houses of the Oireachtas for approval.[4]

1 See CLEA 2001, s 11.
2 CLEA 2001, s 9(3).
3 CLEA 2001, s 9(5).
4 CLEA 2001, s 9(6).

---

10 Removal, disqualification or cessation of Director

(1) The Minister may at any time, for stated reasons, remove the Director from office.

(2) If the Director is removed from office under this section, the Minister shall cause to be laid before each House of the Oireachtas a statement of the reasons for the removal.

(3) Where the Director is—

(a) nominated as a member of Seanad Éireann,

(b) nominated as a candidate for election to either House of the Oireachtas or to the European Parliament or becomes a member of a local authority, or

(c) regarded pursuant to Part XIII of the Second Schedule to the European Parliament Elections Act, 1997, as having been elected to the European Parliament,

he or she shall thereon cease to be the Director.

(4) A person who is for the time being—

(a) entitled under the Standing Orders of either House of the Oireachtas to sit in that House,

(b) a member of the European Parliament, or

(c) a member of a local authority,

is, while he or she is so entitled or is such a member, disqualified from being the Director.

Definitions

'Director': CLEA 2001, s 3(1); 'Minister': CLEA 2001, s 3(1).; 'Oireachtas': IA 2005, Sch, Pt 1; 'Seanad Éireann': IA 2005, Sch, Pt 1.

Notes

Removal of the Director: The Minister has the power to remove the Director from time to time, which power may only be exercised 'for stated reasons'.[1] In order to exercise this power, the Minister must cause a statement of the reasons for removal to be laid before the Houses of the Oireachtas.[2] Presumably this power would be exercised in circumstances where the Director has been found guilty of misconduct or other serious failure in respect of his/her duties. The Director shall cease to hold office on entering or being nominated for certain political positions.[3] Similarly certain holders of political positions are disqualified from being the Director.[4]

1 CLEA 2001, s 10(1).
2 CLEA 2001, s 10(2).
3 CLEA 2001, s 10(3).
4 CLEA 2001, s 10(4).

Acting Director

11 Acting Director of Corporate Enforcement

(1) Subject to subsection (2), the Minister may appoint a person to be the Acting Director of Corporate Enforcement to perform the functions of the Director during—

(a) a period, or during all periods, when the Director is absent from duty or from the State or is, for any other reason, unable to perform the functions of the Director,

(b) any suspension from office of the Director, or

(c) a vacancy in the office of Director.

(2) A person shall not be appointed to perform the functions of the Director for a continuous period of more than 6 months during a vacancy in the office of Director.

(3) The Minister may, at any time, terminate an appointment under this section.

Definitions

'Acting Director': CLEA 2001, s 3(1); 'Director': CLEA 2001, s 3(1); 'functions': CLEA 2001, s 3(1); 'Minister': CLEA 2001, s 3(1); 'month': IA 2005, Sch, Pt 1; 'person': IA 2005, s 18(c).

Notes

Appointment of an Acting Director: In the event the Director is unable to perform his/her functions, is suspended or there is a vacancy in the office of Director, the Minister may appoint an Acting Director.[1] Where the appointment is made on foot of a vacancy of the office of Director, the appointment of such an Acting Director may not be more than six months.[2] The appointment of an Acting Director may be terminated at any time by the Minister.[3]

1 CLEA 2001, s 11(1).
2 CLEA 2001, s 11(2).
3 CLEA 2001, s 11(3).

Functions of Director

12 Functions of Director

(1) The functions of the Director are—

(a) to enforce the Companies Acts, including by the prosecution of offences by way of summary proceedings,

(b) to encourage compliance with the Companies Acts,

(c) to investigate instances of suspected offences under the Companies Acts,

(d) at his or her discretion, to refer cases to the Director of Public Prosecutions where the Director of Corporate Enforcement has reasonable grounds for believing that an indictable offence under the Companies Acts has been committed,

(e) to exercise, insofar as the Director feels it necessary or appropriate, a supervisory role over the activity of liquidators and receivers in the discharge of their functions under the Companies Acts,

(f) for the purpose of ensuring the effective application and enforcement of obligations, standards and procedures to which companies and their officers are subject, to perform such other functions in respect of any matters to which the Companies Acts relate as the Minister considers appropriate and may by order confer on the Director,[...][a]

(g) to perform such other functions for a purpose referred to in paragraph (f) as may be assigned to him or her by or under the Companies Acts or [any other Act, and;][b]

[(h) to act, under the Companies (Auditing and Accounting) Act 2003, as a member of the Irish Auditing and Accounting Supervisory Authority and, if appointed under section 11 of that Act, as a director of the Authority.][c]

(2) The Director may do all such acts or things as are necessary or expedient for the purpose of the performance of his or her functions under this or any other Act.

(3) Notwithstanding that he or she has been so seconded but without prejudice to subsections (5) and (6), a member of the Garda Síochána seconded to the office of the Director shall continue to be under the general direction and control of the Commissioner of the Garda Síochána.

(4) A member of the Garda Síochána so seconded shall continue to be vested with and may exercise or perform the powers or duties of a member of the Garda Síochána for purposes other than the purposes of this Act, as well as for the purposes of this Act.

(5) The Director shall be independent in the performance of his or her functions.

(6) The Director may perform such of his or her functions as he or she thinks fit through or by an officer of the Director and in the performance of those functions the officer shall be subject to the directions of the Director only.

Amendments

a C(AA)A 2003, s 51(a) deletes the word 'and' at the end of CLEA 2001, s 12(1)(f).

b C(AA)A 2003, s 51(b) amends CLEA 2001, s 12(1)(g) by substituting 'any other Act, and' for 'any other Act'.

c C(AA)A 2003, s 51(c) inserts CLEA 2001, s 12(1)(h).

Definitions

'Companies Acts': CLEA 2001, s 3(1); 'functions': CLEA 2001, s 3(1); 'Irish Auditing and Accounting Supervisory Authority': C(AA)A 2003, s 5(1)(c); 'Director': CLEA 2001, s 3(1); 'officer': CA 1963, s 2(1); 'officer of the Director': CLEA 2001, s 3(1).

Notes

Functions of the Director:[1] CLEA 2001, s 12 details the Director's functions which include, in general:

(i) Enforcement and encouragement of compliance with the Companies Acts;[2]

(ii) Investigation of suspected offences under the Companies Acts;[3]

(iii) Prosecution of suing offences and 'on the spot fines' and referral of cases for prosecution on indictment to the Director of Public Prosecution;[4] and

(iv) Supervision of liquidators and receivers in connection with their activities under the Companies Acts.[5]

The Director is also generally empowered to do such acts or things as are necessary or expedient for the discharge of his/her functions under CLEA 2001.[6]

Gardaí seconded to the ODCE: Such Gardaí shall continue to be under the general direction and contract of the Commissioner of An Garda Síochána.[7] Gardaí seconded to the ODCE continue to be vested with their normal powers as members of An Garda Síochána and may exercise any powers gained under the CLEA 2001, in addition to their normal powers.[8]

Independence of the Director: The Director is stated to be independent in the performance of his/her functions.[9] As a further reinforcement of this statement, CLEA 2001, s 12(2) confirms that the Director may perform his/her functions 'as he or she sees fit' and that any officer of the Director acting in the performance of those functions is subject to the directions of the Director only.[10]

Acting through officers: An instrument of delegation pursuant to CLEA 2001, s 13 is not necessary where the Director obtains assistance in the carrying out of his functions through an officer pursuant to s 12(6).[11] Moreover, in appointing an officer to assist him in his functions, it is sufficient for the Director to name a firm or company as officer and he does not have to name each and every individual in that firm or company who will be providing him with such assistance.[12]

Transfer of functions of the ODCE: See CLEA 2001, s 14 and the notes thereto.

1 See generally Courtney, *The Law of Private Companies* (2nd edn, Tottel Publishing, 2002) paras 12.013–12.022.

2 CLEA 2001, s 12(1)(a) and (b).

3 CLEA 2001, s 12(1)(c); CA 1990, s 8.

4 CLEA 2001, s 12 (1)(d).

5 CLEA 2001, s 12(1)(e).

6 CLEA 2001, s 12(2).

7 CLEA 2001, s 12(3).

8 CLEA 2001, s 12(4).

9 CLEA 2001, s 12(5).

10 CLEA 2001, s 12(b). See also CLEA 2001, s 13 in relation to the delegation of powers to officers of the Director.

11 *Re Bovale Developments Ltd, Director of Corporate Enforcement v Bailey* [2008] 2 ILRM 13.

12 *Re Bovale Developments Ltd, Director of Corporate Enforcement v Bailey* [2008] 2 ILRM 13.

13 Delegation

(1) Without prejudice to the generality of section 12(6), the Director may, in writing, delegate to an officer of the Director any of the Director's powers under this or any other Act, except this power of delegation.

(2) A power delegated under subsection (1) shall not be exercised by the delegate except in accordance with the instrument of delegation.

(3) A delegate shall, on request by a person affected by the exercise of a power delegated to him or her, produce the instrument of delegation under this section, or a copy of the instrument, for inspection.

(4) A delegation under this section is revocable at will and does not prevent the exercise by the Director of a power so delegated.

Definitions

'Director': CLEA 2001, s 3(1); 'officer of the Director': CLEA 2001, s 3(1).; 'writing': IA 2005, Sch, Pt 1.

Notes

Delegation of powers: In addition to CLEA 2001, s 12(b), whereby the Director may perform his/her functions through or by his/her officers, the Director may also delegate any of his/her powers (other than the power to delegate) to his/her officers.[1] The Director may revoke that delegation of power at will and he/she may exercise the power that has been delegated simultaneously with the officer to whom the power has been delegated.[2] Such an officer may only exercise the power in accordance with the instrument delegating the power and must, on request by a relevant person, produce the instrument of delegation, or a copy thereof.[3] This power of delegation is of particular significance in the context of making applications before the courts. It should be noted, though, that a formal delegation under s 13 is not required where an officer of the Director is performing certain of the Director's functions under the supervision of the Director pursuant to CLEA 2001, s 12(6).[4]

1 CLEA 2001, s 13(1).

2 CLEA 2001, s 13(3).

3 CLEA 2001, s 13(4).

4 *Re Bovale Developments Ltd, Director of Corporate Enforcement v Bailey* [2008] 2 ILRM 13.

Transfer of Minister's Functions to Director

14 Transfer of functions

(1) Each subsection mentioned in column (3) of the sections mentioned in column (2) opposite to those subsections of the Acts mentioned in the headings to Parts 1 and 2 of the Schedule, is amended by the substitution for 'Minister', wherever occurring, of 'Director'.

(2) Where, before its relevant amendment, anything was commenced under a provision of the Companies Acts by or under the authority of the Minister, it may be carried on or completed on or after that amendment by or under the authority of the Director.

(3) A person authorised by the Minister under a relevantly amended provision shall be regarded as having been so authorised by the Director under that provision as relevantly amended.

(4) Where, before its relevant amendment, legal proceedings were pending under a provision of the Companies Acts to which the Minister is or was then the plaintiff or the prosecutor, the name of the Director shall be substituted in those proceedings for that of the Minister, or added in those proceedings as may be appropriate, and those proceedings shall not abate by reason of that substitution or addition.

(5) To avoid doubt, where, immediately before its relevant amendment, legal proceedings were pending under a provision of the Companies Acts as then in force in which the Minister was a defendant, the Director shall not be substituted for the Minister in those proceedings notwithstanding the amendment of that provision.

(6) In this section, 'relevant amendment', in relation to a provision of the Companies Acts, means an amendment by this or any other section of this Act which comprises or includes the substitution for 'Minister' of 'Director' (including the substitution of an entire provision or part of a provision which has the effect of transferring a function from the Minister to the Director), and 'relevantly amended' has a corresponding meaning.

Definitions

'Companies Acts': CLEA 2001, s 3(1); 'Director': CLEA 2001, s 3(1); 'functions': CLEA 2001, s 3(1), IA 2005, Sch, Pt 2; 'Minister': CLEA 2001, s 3(1); 'relevant amendment': CLEA 2001, s 14(6).

Notes

Transfer of functions from Minister to ODCE: The general functions of the ODCE are spelt out in CLEA 2001, s 12. In addition, under CLEA 2001, s 14, various powers, functions andresponsibilities previously exercised by or vested in the Minister and identified in the Schedule have now been transferred to the ODCE instead. These include the power to call or direct the calling of an AGM by a company which has failed to do so;[1] the power to apply to the High Court for an order for the production of books and records where it is suspected that offences have been committed;[2] the receipt of the reports of High Court appointed inspectors;[3] the presentation of a winding-up petition on foot of an inspector's report;[4] the appointment of inspectors to investigate the ownership of companies;[5] the power to direct the furnishing of information as to the ownership of shares and debentures;[6] the power to impose restrictions on shares and debentures pending investigation or enquiry as to their true ownership;[7] the investigation of share dealing;[8] the receipt of Stock Exchange reports on share ownership;[9] co-operating with the regulatory authorities of other EU states regarding suspected insider dealing;[10] approving individuals to be 'authorised persons' to investigate suspected insider dealing;[11] the receipt of reports on suspected insider dealing from the Stock Exchange;[12] the making of applications for disqualification orders;[13] and the prosecution of summary offences under the Companies Acts.[14]

1 CA 1963, s 131(3), (4), (6).

2 CA 1963, s 384(1).

3 CA 1990, s 11(3).

4 CA 1990, s 12(2).

5 CA 1990, s 14(1), (2), (5).

6 CA 1990, s 15(1).

7 CA 1990, s 16(1), (5), (6), (7), (8), (13), (16), (18).

8 CA 1990, s 66(1), (4), (5), (8).

9 CA 1990, s 94(2).

10 CA 1990, s 116(3).

11 CA 1990, s 117(1).

12 CA 1990, s 118(2).

13 CA 1990, s 160(2).

14 CA 1990, s 240(4).

Transitional provisions: In relation to activities pursuant to a statutory provision, responsibility for which has now passed to the Director, which were ongoing at the time of the coming into force of CLEA 2001, s 14 on 28 November 2001,[1] those activities may continue to be carried on by or under the authority of the Director.[2] Such activities would include ongoing inquiries under the original CA 1990, s 19 which the Minister did not elect to retain under her own control pursuant to CLEA 2001, s 34.[3] In legal proceedings initiated by the Minister (as plaintiff or prosecutor) under the Companies Acts, the Director is to be substituted for the Minister.[4] In contrast, notwithstanding the transfer to the Director of the functions to which the proceedings relate, the Director will not be substituted for the Minister as a defendant in proceedings taken against the Minister prior to the coming into force of the relevant provision of CLEA 2001.[5]

1 Company Law Enforcement Act 2001 (Commencement) (No 3) Order 2001 (SI 523/2001).

2 CLEA 2001, s 14(2) and (3).

3 *Dunnes Stores Ireland Company v Houlihan* [2003] IEHC 619 (O'Neill J).

4 CLEA 2001, s 14(4).

5 CLEA 2001, s 14(5).

General

15 Director or officer of Director indemnified against losses

Neither the Director nor any officer of the Director shall be liable in damages in respect of any thing done or omitted to be done in good faith by him or her in the performance or purported performance of a function under the Companies Acts or any other Act.

Definitions

'Companies Acts': CLEA 2001, s 3(1); 'Director': CLEA 2001, s 3(1); 'functions': CLEA 2001, s 3(1); 'officer of the Director': CLEA 2001, s 3(1).

Notes

Exclusion of liability in damages: This section expressly exempts the Director and his officers from liability in damages for anything done by them in good faith[1] in performance or purported performance of their statutory functions. Damages may, however, be recoverable against the State itself for misfeasance by these officials.[2]

1 A *male fides* or malicious abuse of power would, however, seem to expose the Director and is officials to potential personal liability.

2 *Byrne v Ireland* [1972] IR 241; *Gildea v Hipwell* [1942] IR 489; *Corliss v Ireland* [1984] IEHC 20 (Hamilton J); *Pine Valley Developments Ltd v Minister for the Environment* [1987] IR 23; *Moyne v Londonderry Port and Harbour Commissioners* [1986] IR 299; *Irish Permanent Building Society v Caldwell (No 2)* [1981] ILRM 242; *McHugh v Commissioner of the Garda Síochána* [1986] IR 228.

16 Reporting by Director

(1) The Director shall, not later than 3 months after the end of each year, present a report to the Minister about the performance of the Director's functions and other activities of the Director in that year, and the Minister shall cause a copy of the report to be laid before each House of the Oireachtas within 2 months of receipt of the report.

(2) A report under subsection (1) shall include information in such form and about such matters as the Minister may direct but nothing in that or this subsection shall be construed as requiring the Director to include in such a report information the inclusion of which therein would, in the opinion of the Director, be likely to prejudice the performance by him or her of any of his or her functions.

(3) The Director shall furnish to the Minister such information about the performance of the Director's functions as the Minister may from time to time require (other than information the provision of which under this subsection would, in the opinion of the Director, be likely to prejudice the performance by him or her of any of his or her functions).

(4) When so requested, the Director shall account to an appropriately established Committee of either House of the Oireachtas for the performance of his or her functions but in discharging his or her duties under this subsection the Director shall not be required to furnish any information or answer any questions the furnishing or answering of which would, in the opinion of the Director, be likely to prejudice the performance by him or her of any of his or her functions.

Definitions

'Director': CLEA 2001, s 3(1); 'functions': CLEA 2001, s 3(1); 'Minister': CLEA 2001, s 3(1). 'Oireachtas': IA 2005, Sch, Pt 1; 'month': IA 2005, Sch, Pt 1; 'year': IA 2005, Sch, Pt 1.

Notes

Reporting obligations and accountability: the Director must present the Minister with a formal report, detailing the activities and performance of the ODCE on an annual basis.[1] The Minister must cause a copy of each annual report to be laid before the Houses of the Oireachtas.[2] The Minister may direct the form and content of the annual report presented by the Director.[3]

The Minister may also, on an ad hoc basis, require the Director to provide information as to the performance of his/her functions.[4]

The Director must, if requested to do so, appear and answer questions before an appropriate Committee of the Oireachtas in connection with the performance of his/her duties.[5]

The Director's various obligations to provide information are subject always to the caveat that he/she will not be required to provide such information if to do so would prejudice the performance of his/her duties.[6]

1 CLEA 2001, s 16(1).
2 CLEA 2001, s 16(1).
3 CLEA 2001, s 16(2).
4 CLEA 2001, s 16(3).
5 CLEA 2001, s 16(4).
6 CLEA 2001, s 16(2), (3), (4).

---

17 Disclosure of information

(1) Information obtained by virtue of the performance by the Director of any of his or her functions which has not otherwise come to the notice of the public, shall not be disclosed, except in accordance with law, by any person, including—

(a) the Director or a former Director,

(b) a professional or other adviser (including a former adviser) to the Director, and

(c) an officer or former officer of the Director.

(2) Notwithstanding subsection (1), information referred to in that subsection which, in the opinion of the Director, may be required—

(a) for a purpose or reason specified in subsection (1) of section 21 of the Act of 1990,

(b) for the performance by a competent authority (within the meaning of that section 21) of a function or functions of the authority, or

(c) for the performance by the Director of a function or functions of the Director,

may be disclosed by or under the authority of the Director to the extent that, in the opinion of the Director, is necessary for that purpose.

(3) Notwithstanding subsection (1), information which, in the opinion of the Director or an officer of the Director, may relate to the commission of an offence which is not an offence under the Companies Acts may be disclosed to any member of An Garda Síochána.

(4) A person who contravenes this section is guilty of an offence.

Definitions

'Act of 1990': CLEA 2001, s 3(1); 'Companies Acts': CLEA 2001, s 3(1); 'competent authority': CA 1990, s 21(3); 'Director': CLEA 2001, s 3(1); 'functions': CLEA 2001, s 3(1); 'Minister': CLEA 2001, s 3(1); 'officer of the Director': CLEA 2001, s 3(1).

Notes

Confidentiality of information: This section requires the past and present members of the staff of the ODCE, including past and present professional and other advisers to keep confidential information received by them in the performance of the work of the ODCE.[1] The section does not however constitute a basis for preventing the ODCE from disclosing to a liquidator the reasons for declining to grant him relief under CLEA 2001, s 56 from the obligation to bring restriction proceedings against an individual under CA 1990, s 150.[2] Furthermore, such confidential information may, however be disclosed for the purposes specified in CA 1990, s 21(1) and may be disclosed to any of the 'competent authorities' identified in CA 1990, s 21(3) for the purpose of enabling them to perform their functions. The provisions of CLEA 2001, s 17(2)(c) would also seem to suggest that, notwithstanding the confidentiality attaching to such information, it may nonetheless be disclosed by the Director to other third parties if such disclosure is necessary for the purpose of enabling him to properly perform his functions. Such information may also be disclosed to An Garda Síochána where it relates to the commission of an offence, (other than an offence under the Companies Acts).[3]

Conversely, in relation to the receipt of information, the Competition Authority, An Garda Síochána and the Revenue Commissioners may furnish the ODCE with information regarding suspected offences under the Companies Acts, without themselves being held to have acted in breach of their own duties of confidentiality.[4]

1 CLEA 2001, s 17(1).

2 *Re Tralee Beef & Lamb Ltd, Kavanagh v Delaney* [2008] 3 IR 347.

3 CLEA 2001, s 17(3).

4 CLEA 2001, s 18.

---

18 Information relating to offences under Companies Acts may be disclosed to Director or officer of Director.

Notwithstanding any other law, information which, in the opinion of the Competition Authority or a member of An Garda Síochána or an officer of the Revenue Commissioners, may relate to the commission of an offence under the Companies Acts may be disclosed by that Authority, member or officer to the Director or an officer of the Director.

Definitions

'Companies Acts': CLEA 2001, s 3(1); 'Director': CLEA 2001, s 3(1); 'officer of the Director': CLEA 2001, s 3(1).

Notes

Disclosure of information to the ODCE: CLEA 2001, s 18 facilitates the reporting to the Director of information relating to offences under the Companies Acts, which has been gathered by the Competition Authority, members of An Garda Síochána and officers of the Revenue Commissioners. This provision confirms that such information may be disclosed to the Director, and removes any concern that the dissemination of such information to the Director might be restricted or prohibited by virtue of such information being confidential. Notably, information relayed to the Director under this section is not afforded any particular evidential status and must therefore be formally proved in civil proceedings in the same way as any other item of information.[1]

1 *Re Bovale Developments Ltd, Director of Corporate Enforcement v Bailey* [2008] 2 ILRM 13.

Disclosure of information by the ODCE: See CLEA 2001, s 17 and notes thereto.

PART 3
INVESTIGATIONS

19 Amendment of section 145 of Act of 1963

(a) [...][a]

(b) [...][b]

Amendments

a CLEA 2001, s 19(a) inserts CA 1963, s 145(3A).

b CLEA 2001, s 19(b) amends CA 1963, s 145(4) by the insertion after 'subsection (1)' of 'or (3A)'.

20 Amendment of section 7 of Act of 1990

[...][a]

Amendments

a CLEA 2001, s 20 amends CA 1990, s 7(3) by the substitution for '£500' and '£100,000' of '£5,000' and '£250,000' respectively which were converted to €6,348.69 and €317,424.51 by the Economic and Monetary Union Act 1998, s 6.

21 Amendment of section 8 of Act of 1990 — Investigation of company's affairs on application of Director

[...][a]

Amendments

a CLEA 2001, s 21 amends CA 1990, s 8(1) by the substitution for 'on the application of the Minister appoint one or more competent inspectors' of 'on the application of the Director appoint one or more competent inspectors (who may be or include an officer of officers of the Director'.

22 Amendment of section 9 of Act of 1990

[...][a]

[...][b]

Amendments

a CLEA 2001, s 22(a) amends CA 1990, s 9 by the substitution for 'If an Inspector' of '(1) If an Inspector'.

b CLEA 2001, s 22(b) inserts CA 1990, s 9(2). See the amended Act.

23 Amendment of section 10 of Act of 1990

(a) [...][a]

(b) [...][b]

(c) [...][c]

(d) [...][d]

Amendments

a CLEA 2001, s 23(a) amends CA 1990, s 10(1) by the insertion after 'reasonably able to give' of; but where any such person claims a lien on books or documents produced by the person, the production shall be without prejudice to the lien'.

b CLEA 2001, s 23(b) amends CA 1990, s 10(2) by the insertion after 'comply with the requirement' of; but where any such person claims a lien on books or documents produced by the person, the production shall be without prejudice to the lien'.

c CLEA 2001, s 23(c) substitutes CA 1990, s 10(5) and (6). See the amended Act.

d CLEA 2001, s 23(d) amends CA 1990, s 10(7) by the insertion after 'auditors' of 'accountants, book-keepers or taxation advisers,'.

24 Amendment of section 11 of Act of 1990

(a) [...][a]

(b) [...][b]

(2) [...][c]

Amendments

a CLEA 2001, s 24(1)(a) amends CA 1990, s 11(3)(b)(vi) by the deletion of 'and' from the end thereof.

b CLEA 2001, s 24(1)(b) inserts CA 1990, s 11(3)(ba).

c CLEA 2001, s 24(2) amends CA 1990, s 11(4) by the substitution for 'subsection (3)(a) or (b)' of 'subsection (3)(a), (b) or (ba)'.

25 Amendment of section 13 of Act of 1990

(a) [...][a]

(b) [...][b]

(c) [...][c]

Amendments

a CLEA 2001, s 25(a) amends CA 1990, s 13 by the substitution for 'Minister for Justice' wherever occurring of 'relevant Minister'.

b CLEA 2001, s 25(b) amends CA 1990, s 13(1) by the substitution for '£100,000' of '£250,000'.

c CLEA 2001, s 25(c) inserts CA 1990, s 13(3A). See the amended Act.

26 Amendment of section 14 of Act of 1990

[...][a]

Amendments

a CLEA 2001, s 26 inserts CA 1990, s 14(6), (7) and (8). See the amended Act.

27 Amendment of section 16 of Act of 1990

(a) [...][a]

(b) [...][b]

(c) [...][c]

(d) [...][d]

Amendments

a CLEA 2001, s 27(a) amends CA 1990, s 16(2)(d) by the deletion of 'except in a liquidation'.

b CLEA 2001, s 27(b) amends CA 1990, s 16(4) by the deletion of '(otherwise than in a liquidation)'.

c CLEA 2001, s 27(c) substitutes CA 1990, s 16(6)(a) and (b) and inserts CA 1990, s 16(6)(c).

d CLEA 2001, s 27(d) amends CA 1990, s 16(7) by the insertion after 'or the company' of 'having given notice to the Director,'.

28 Amendment of section 18 of Act of 1990

(a) [...][a]

(b) [...][b]

(c) [...][c]

Amendments

a CLEA 2001, s 28(a) amends CA 1990, s 18 by the substitution for 'An answer given by a person' of '(1) An answer given by an individual'.

b CLEA 2001, s 28(b) amends CA 1990, s 18 by the deletion of all the words from 'and a statement required' down to and including 'making it.' and the substitution of 'in any proceedings whatsoever (save proceedings for an offence (other than perjury in respect of such an answer)).'

c CLEA 2001, s 28(c) inserts CA 1990, s 18(2).

29 Repeal and substitution of section 19 of Act of 1990 — Power of Director to require production of documents

[...][a]

Amendments

a CLEA 2001, s 29 substitutes CA 1990, s 19 and inserts CA 1990, s 19A. See the amended Act.

30 Repeal and substitution of section 20 of Act of 1990

[...][a]

Amendments

a CLEA 2001, s 30 substitutes CA 1990, s 20. See the amended Act.

31 Amendment of section 21 of Act of 1990

(a) [...][a]

(b) [...][b]

(c) [...][c]

(d) [...][d]

Amendments

a CLEA 2001, s 31(a) amends CA 1990, s 21(1) by the substitution for 'Minister' where ever occurring, except in paragraph (d) of 'Director'.

b CLEA 2001, s 31(b) substitutes CA 1990, s 21(1)(a)(i)(V).

c CLEA 2001, s 31(c) inserts CA 1990, s 21(1)(fa) and (fb).

d CLEA 2001, s 31(d) substitutes CA 1990, s 21(1)(g)(ii).

32 Amendment of section 23 of Act of 1990

(a) [...][a]

(b) [...][b]

Amendments

a CLEA 2001, s 32(a) substitutes CA 1990, s 23(2).

b CLEA 2001, s 32(b) inserts CA 1990, s 23(4).

33 New section 23A of Act of 1990 — Assistance to overseas company law authorities

[...][a]

Amendments

a CLEA 2001, s 33 inserts CA 1990, s 23A. See amended Act.

34 Examination of books and documents of certain companies to be continued by Minister or authorised officer

(1) Notwithstanding subsections (2) and (3) of section 14 or any other provision of this Act, the Minister or any officer of the Minister authorised by him or her under section 19 of the Act of 1990 before the passing of this Act may, in relation to such body or bodies and to such extent as may be prescribed, continue to exercise, after such passing, the powers conferred on them respectively by sections 19 to 23 of the Act of 1990.

(2) In subsection (1), 'sections 19 to 23 of the Act of 1990' means those sections as they stand amended by this Act but with the substitution for references in them to the Director of references to the Minister or an officer of the Minister authorised by the Minister under section 19 of the Act of 1990, as appropriate.

Definitions

'Act of 1990': CLEA 2001, s 3(1); 'Director': CLEA 2001, s 3(1); 'Minister': CLEA 2001, s 3(1).

Notes

Retention of powers and functions by the Minister: Notwithstanding the transfer of various functions to the ODCE, including the power to conduct enquiries, CLEA 2001, s 34 allows the Minister, by order, to retain control of such existing enquiries, whether being conducted by her or by an authorised officer appointed by her, to such extent as she may prescribe.[1] The Minister has retained control in respect of five enquiries that were ongoing at the time of the coming into force of this Act.[2]

1 *Dunnes Stores Ireland Company v Houlihan* (9 May 2003, unreported) HC (O'Neill J).

2 Company Law Enforcement Act 2001 (Section 34) Regulations, 2001 (SI 524/2001).

35 Amendment of section 79 of Act of 1990

[...][a]

Amendments

a CLEA 2001, s 35 inserts CA 1990, s 79(7)(bb). See the amended Act.

36 Amendment of section 92 of Act of 1990 — Duty of relevant authority to report to Director

(a) [...][a]

(b) [...][b]

Amendments

a CLEA 2001, s 36(a) amends CA 1990, s 92 by the substitution for 'Director of Public Prosecutions' wherever occurring, except in subsection (4) of 'Director'.

b CLEA 2001, s 36(b) substitutes CA 1990, s 92(4).

37 Amendment of section 115 of Act of 1990

(a) [...][a]

(b) [...][b]

(c) [...][c]

(d) [...][d]

Amendments

a CLEA 2001, s 37(a) amends CA 1990, s 115 by the substitution for 'Director of Public Prosecutions' wherever occurring, except in subsection (4) of 'Director'.

b CLEA 2001, s 37(b) substitutes CA 1990, s 115(4).

c CLEA 2001, s 37(c) amends CA 1990, s 115(5) by the substitution for 'Minister' of 'Director'.

d CLEA 2001, s 37(d) deletes CA 1990, s 115(6).

38 Amendment of section 118 of Act of 1990

[...][a]

Amendments

a CLEA 2001, s 38 inserts CA 1990, s 118(2A). See the amended Act.

39 Amendment of section 230 of Act of 1990

(a) [...][a]

(b) [...][b]

(c) [...][c]

(d) [...][d]

Amendments

a CLEA 2001, s 39(a) amends CA 1990, s 230 by the substitution for 'Director of Public Prosecutions' wherever occurring, except in subsection (4) of 'Director'.

b CLEA 2001, s 39(b) substitutes CA 1990, s 230(4).

c CLEA 2001, s 39(c) amends CA 1990, s 230(5) by the substitution for 'Minister' of 'Director'.

d CLEA 2001, s 39(d) deletes CA 1990, s 230(6).

PART 4
RESTRICTIONS AND DISQUALIFICATIONS

40 New section 183A of Act of 1963 — Examination as to solvency status

[...][a]

Amendments

a CLEA 2001, s 40 inserts CA 1963, s 183A. See the amended Act.

41 Amendment of section 150 of Act of 1990

[...][a]

[...][b]

[...][c]

(2) The amendments made by paragraphs (a) and (b)of subsection (1) shall not have effect in relation to a declaration under subsection (1) of section 150 of the Act of 1990 made before the commencement of this section and, accordingly, the requirements of subsection (3) of that section 150 that shall apply in respect of a person who is the subject of such a declaration made before that commencement shall be those that applied before that commencement.

Amendments

a CLEA 2001, s 41(1)(a) amends CA 1990, s 150(3)(a)(i) by the substitution for '£100,000' of '£250,000'.

b CLEA 2001, s 41(1)(b) amends CA 1990, s 150(3)(a)(ii) by the substitution for '£20,000' of '£50,000'.

c CLEA 2001, s 41(1)(c) inserts CA 1990, s 150(4A) and (4B).

Notes

Increase of financial thresholds for restricted persons: This section increases the amount of share capital which must be paid up in cash in respect of a company which has as one of its directors a person against whom a restriction order has been made. The section came into force on 1 March 2002.[1] The increased financial thresholds only apply to restriction orders made after that date, albeit that such orders may relate to conduct of directors which occurred before the section came into operation.

1 CLEA 2001 (Commencement) (No 5) Order 2002 (SI 53/2002).

42 Amendment of section 160 of Act of 1990

[...][a]

[...][b]

[...][c]

[...][e]

[...][e]

[...][f]

Amendments

a CLEA 2001, s 42(a) inserts CA 1990, s 160(1A) and (1B).

b CLEA 2001, s 42(b)(i) amends CA 1990, s 160(2)(f) by the substitution for 'requirements' of 'requirements; or'.

c CLEA 2001, s 42(b)(ii) inserts CA 1990, s 160(2)(g), (h) and (i).

d CLEA 2001, s 42(c) inserts CA 1990, s 160(3A) and (3B). CLEA 2001, s 42(d) amends CA 1990, s 160(5) by the substitution for 'paragraph (e)' of 'paragraph (e) or (g)'.

e CLEA 2001, s 42(e) inserts CA 1990, s 160(6A).

f CLEA 2001, s 42(f) inserts CA 1990, s 160(9A) and (9B).

PART 5
WINDING-UP AND INSOLVENCY

43 Amendment of section 243 of Act of 1963 — Inspection of books by creditors, contributories and Director

[...][a]

Amendments

a CLEA 2001, s 43 inserts CA 1963, s 243(1A). See the amended Act.

44 Amendment of section 245 of Act of 1963

[...][a]

[...][b]

Amendments

a CLEA 2001, s 44(a) amends CA 1963, s 245(1) by the insertion after 'The court may' of 'of its own motion or on the application of the Director,'.

b CLEA 2001, s 44(b) substitutes CA 1963, s 245(6). See the amended Act.

45 Amendment of section 245A of Act of 1963

[...][a]

[...][b]

[...][c]

Amendments

a CLEA 2001, s 45(a) amends CA 1963, s 245A by the substitution for 'If in the course of an examination' of '(1) If in the course of an examination'.

b CLEA 2001, s 45(b) amends CA 1963, s 245A by the substitution for 'the court may order such person' of 'the court may, of its own motion or on the application of the Director, order such person'.

c CLEA 2001, s 45(c) inserts CA 1963, s 245A(2)–(6). See the amended Act.

46 Repeal and substitution of section 247 of Act of 1963 — Power to arrest absconding contributory or officer of company

[...][a]

Amendments

a CLEA 2001, s 46 substitutes CA 1963, s 247. See the amended Act.

47 Amendment of section 267 of Act of 1963

[...][a]

Amendments

a CLEA 2001, s 47 inserts CA 1963, s 267(3).

48 Amendment of section 278 of Act of 1963

[...][a]

Amendments

a CLEA 2001, s 48 amends CA 1963, s 278(1) by the insertion after 'notice of his appointment' of 'and the registrar shall forward a copy to the Director'.

49 New sections 282A to 282D of Act of 1963

[...][a]

Amendments

a CLEA 2001, s 49 inserts CA 1963, ss 282A, 282B, 282C and 282D.

50 Amendment of section 298 of Act of 1963

[...][a]

Amendments

a CLEA 2001, s 50 amends CA 1963, s 298(2) by the substitution for 'on the application of the liquidator' of 'on the application of the Director, liquidator'.

51 Amendment of section 299 of Act of 1963

[...][a]

[...][b]

[...][c]

[...][d]

[...][e]

[...][f]

Amendments

a CLEA 2001, s 51(a) inserts CA 1963, s 299(1A).

b CLEA 2001, s 51(b) amends CA 1963, s 299(2) by the substitution for 'Attorney General' wherever occurring of 'Director of Public Prosecutions'.

c CLEA 2001, s 51(c) inserts CA 1963, s 299(2A).

d CLEA 2001, s 51(d) amends CA 1963, s 299(3) by the substitution for 'the Attorney General under subsection (2)' and 'in pursuance of subsection (2)' of 'the Director of Public Prosecutions under subsection (2), or the Director under subsection (2A)' and 'in pursuance of subsection (2) or subsection (2A), as the case may be', respectively.

e CLEA 2001, s 51(e) amends CA 1963, s 299(4) by the substitution for 'Attorney General under this section, he considers' of 'Director of Public Prosecutions and the Director under this section, either the Director of Public Prosecutions or the Director considers'.

f CLEA 2001, s 51(f) amends CA 1963, s 299(5) by the substitution for 'of the Attorney General' of 'of the Director of Public Prosecutions or of the Director'.

52 Amendment of section 319 of Act of 1963

[...][a]

[...][b]

Amendments

a CLEA 2001, s 52(a) inserts CA 1963, s 319(2A).

b CLEA 2001, s 52(b) substitutes CA 1963, s 319(7) and inserts CA 1963, s 319(8).

53 New section 323A of Act of 1963 — Director may request production of receiver's books

[...][a]

Amendments

a CLEA 2001, s 53 inserts CA 1963, s 323A. See the amended Act.

54 Amendment of section 251 of Act of 1990

[...][a]

[...][b]

[...][c]

Amendments

a CLEA 2001, s 54(a) amends CA 1990, s 251(2)(a) by the insertion after '140,' of '149'.

b CLEA 2001, s 54(b) inserts CA 1990, s 251(2A).

c CLEA 2001, s 54(c) substitutes CA 1990, s 251(4).

55 Order to restrain directors and others from moving assets

The court may, on the application of a company, director, member, liquidator, receiver, creditor or the Director, order a director or other officer of a company not to remove his or her assets from the State or to reduce his or her assets within or outside the State below an amount to be specified by the court, where the court is satisfied that—

(a) the applicant has a substantive civil cause of action or right to seek a declaration of personal liability or claim for damages against the director, other officer or the company, and

(b) there are grounds for believing that the respondent may remove or dispose of his, her or the company's assets with a view to evading his, her or the company's obligations and frustrating an order of the court.

Definitions

'company': CA 1963, s 2(1); 'court': CA 1963, s 2(1); 'director': CA 1963, s 2(1); 'member': CA 1963, s 31; 'officer': CA 1963, s 2(1).

Notes

Mareva-type order against officers: CLEA 2001, s 55 confers on the High Court a statutory jurisdiction to make a Mareva-type injunction against any director or other officer of a company who, it is apprehended, proposes to place his assets beyond the reach of his creditors.[1] The applicant (who may be another director or a member, liquidator, receiver or creditor of the company, or the company itself or the Director of Corporate Enforcement) must not only show that he has a good cause of action against the individual (eg for damages or for the imposition of personal liability[2]) but must also show that there are grounds for believing that the individual is seeking to put his assets beyond the reach of his creditors (as opposed to using his assets to meet his legitimate liabilities).

Its aim is to prevent officers of the company avoiding claims. It freezes the assets of the respondent, preventing him from frustrating a possible judgment against him and prevents him removing or disposing of the company's assets. The section includes shadow directors.

1 See, eg, *Mareva Compania Naviera SA v International Bulk Carriers* [1980] 1 All ER 213; *Fleming v Ranks* [1983] ILRM 541; *Countyglen plc v Carway* [1995] 1 IR 208; *O'Mahony v Horgan* [1995] 2 IR 411.

2 eg, an action to impose personal liability for fraudulent or reckless trading under CA 1963, s 297A or for failure to keep proper books of account under CA 1990, s 204.

Grounds for obtaining a freezing order: While the statutory injunction shares the characteristics of the relief that may be obtained by a Mareva-type order it is not bound by the principles attached to injuctive relief. The section creates a statutory injunction and, accordingly, must be viewed as a self-contained code.[1] Its operation and jurisdiction are strictly limited to the provisions of the section. There is, for example, no provision in the section for giving an undertaking as to damages.

The section requires a substantive civil cause of action for either a declaration of personal liability or claim for damages against an officer of the company. "Cause of action" is understood to mean the facts that make out the necessary ingredients for a cause of action.[2] This will have the effect of ruling out a *quia timet* order – where this ingredient of the relief is not complied with. Moreover, the section may not be used in support of a criminal offence.

Assuming that a cause of action has accrued then the next requirement is that grounds exist for believing that the respondent may remove or dispose of his or the company's assets with a view to evading his or the company's obligations and frustrating an order of the court. This may be contrasted with a Mareva-type application in which it is necessary to provide evidence of the defendant's intention to evade his obligation. The other contrasts are that a Mareva-type injunction requires consideration of the strength of an applicant's case. The expression used in sub-s (b) is 'with a view to', which suggests knowledge of the effect of the actions. It clearly requires evidence of the consequence of the actions without being as neutral as an expression as 'having the effect of'. It is submitted that the combination of the court not being willing to act in vain, and the phrase 'with a view to', means that an applicant under this section will be required, at a minimum, to produce prima facie evidence of facts necessary to form a stateable case, and of facts that tend to show that a respondent is aware of the effects of his actions, or that the latter intention arises by necessary implication. It is possible that situations exist in which ostensibly innocent actions may be characterized as being 'with a view to' avoid judgment. Those facts would not arise easily and might follow the logic evinced by the court in the decision of McCracken J in *Re Genport Ltd*[3] ie an examination of the motives of the respondent in question.

In so far as the effect of an order under this section might reduce the assets available to the creditors or shareholders of the company in question, a possible difficulty with an improper but ostensibly 'innocent' reduction of the assets is that they may constitute an unjust attack on the property rights of the creditors in question. As the court is obliged to give the section a reading that accords with the Constitution, if possible, this will require clear facts to establish that an improper motive is present. This appears to be unlikely in practice.

1 See the judgment of Denham J in *Mahon v Butler* [1997] 3 IR 369.
2 *Hegarty v O'Loughran* [1990] 1 IR 161.
3 *Re Genport Ltd* [2001] IEHC 156 (McCracken J).

Procedure: The action should be brought by way of originating motion (RSC 1986, Ord 52, r 1). It may be made *ex parte* pursuant to Ord 52, r 3 and the court has jurisdiction to make the order on such terms as to costs or otherwise and subject to such undertakings as the court thinks just. However, an order for security for costs or undertaking as to damages in the context of the section might be viewed as being contrary to the legislative intent of creating a remedy that was unfettered by such considerations.

Security interest arising from an order under this section: Nothing in the section creates any security interest in the frozen asset. The assets must remain subject to any trust, equity or statutory priority as is appropriate in the circumstances.

56 Liquidator to report on conduct of directors

(1) A liquidator of an insolvent company shall, within 6 months after his or her appointment or the commencement of this section, whichever is the later, and at intervals as required by the Director thereafter, provide to the Director a report in the prescribed form.

(2) A liquidator of an insolvent company shall, not earlier than 3 months nor later than 5 months (or such later time as the court may allow and advises the Director) after the date on which he or she has provided to the Director a report under subsection (1), apply to the court for the restriction under section 150 of the Act of 1990 of each of the directors of the company, unless the Director has relieved the liquidator of the obligation to make such an application.

(3) A liquidator who fails to comply with subsection (1) or (2) is guilty of an offence.

Definitions

'Act of 1990': CLEA 2001, s 3(1); 'company': CA 1963, s 2(1); 'Director': CLEA 2001, s 3(1); 'prescribed': CLEA 2001, s 3(1).

Notes

Report by liquidator on conduct of directors: CLEA 2001, s 56 came into force on 1 June 2002 in so far as it applies to liquidators of insolvent companies who (i) were appointed on or after June 2002, or (ii) were appointed on or after 1 July 2001 and before 1 June 2002 where, in respect of the company to which the liquidator was appointed an order has not been made dissolving the company on the basis of the winding up having been completed.[1] Furthermore, with effect from 1 June 2003 the provisions of s 56 also apply to liquidators who were appointed on or after 1 January 2000 and before 1 July 2001, where, in respect of the company to which the liquidator was appointed, an order has not been made dissolving the company on the basis of the winding up having been completed.[2]

The liquidator's report to the ODCE, which must be filed within six months of the liquidator's appointment,[3] is divided into seven sections covering (1) Liquidator's Details, (2) Company Details, (3) Company Directors, (4) Statement of Affairs, Accounts and Report to Creditors, (5) Proceedings, (6) Final Report and (7) Liquidator's Statement. Detailed regulations have been published and the ODCE has prepared a guidance note for the benefit of insolvency practitioners.[4]

1 Company Law Enforcement Act 2001 (Winding Up and Insolvency Provisions) (Commencement) Order 2002 (SI 263/2002).

2 Company Law Enforcement Act 2001 (Winding Up and Insolvency Provisions) (Commencement) Order 2003 (SI 217/2003).

3 CLEA 2001, s 56(1).

4 Company Law Enforcement Act 2001 (Section 56) Regulations 2002 (SI 324/2002). See also the ODCE's *Guidance Notes for the completion of Liquidators' Reports under s 56 of the Company Law Enforcement Act 2001*. See http://www.odce.ie.

Time limit for s 150 application: Unless otherwise absolved from the obligation to do so by the ODCE, the liquidator must apply for restriction orders against the company's directors within three to five months of presenting his report.[1] The court may extend this time limit, and if does so, it must inform the ODCE of the fact that it has done do.[2] It has been held that this three- to five-month time limit is nothing more than a stipulation as to the period of time within which the liquidator can bring his application without committing an offence under CLEA 2001, s 56(3) but that it does not operate as a limitation period beyond which the liquidator is precluded from seeking restriction orders against the directors.[3]

Given the ostensible public importance of the making of a report under this section it is likely that, in the absence of particular facts giving rise to an actual prejudice, delay will not provide a defence to subsequent applications predicated on the report (such as CA 1990, s 150[4]). In effect the importance of the report is a consideration going to the balance of justice to be considered under the inherent jurisdiction of the High Court or the test as described for dismissal for want of prosecution. This was the conclusion of Finlay Geoghegan J in her *ex tempore* judgment in the case of in *Re Knocklofty Hotel Ltd (in liquidation)*[5] and her judgment in *Hughes v Duffy*.[6]

The courts have placed emphasis on the legislative intent of the time limit in the section.[7] In this regard a failure to present the s 56 report on time will not invalidate the s 150 proceedings themselves.[8]

1 CLEA 2001, s 56(2). The Supreme Court has criticised the failure on the part of the ODCE to give reasons for refusing to relieve a liquidator of the obligation to bring s 150 proceedings in circumstances where the liquidator has formed the opinion the individuals in question have acted responsibly and that there is no other reason why it would be just and equitable to have them restricted: *Re Tralee Beef & Lamb Ltd, Kavanagh v Delaney* [2008] 3 IR 347. In the opinion of the Supreme Court, in such circumstances the proceedings have 'an air of unreality' about them.

2 CLEA 2001, s 56(2). See also *Re Dublin Sports Cafe Ltd* (16 December 2008, unreported) SC (Finnegan J)

3 *Re E-Host (Europe) Ltd* (14 July 2003, unreported) HC (Finlay Geoghegan J).

4 See comments of Fennelly J in Duignan v Carway [2001] 4 IR 550.

5 *Re Knocklofty Hotel Ltd (in liquidation)* [2005] 4 IR 497.

6 *Hughes v Duffy* [2005] 1 IR 571.

7 *Duignan v Carway* [2001] 4 IR 550 and *Hughes v Duffy* [2005] 1 IR 571.

8 *Re Visual Impact and Delays Ltd* [2003] 4 IR 451; *Coyle v O'Brien* [2003] 2 IR 627.

Other reporting obligations of liquidator: In relation to the obligation of liquidators to report suspected *indictable* criminal offences to the DPP, see CA 1963, s 299. A liquidator, if a solicitor or accountant, will also be under a separate duty to consider his obligations under the requirements of the Criminal Justice Act 1994, s 57.

57 Director's power to examine liquidator's books

(1) The Director may on his or her own motion or where a complaint is made to the Director by a member, contributory or creditor of the company, request, specifying the reason why the request is being made, the liquidator of a company in liquidation to produce to the Director the liquidator's books for examination, either in relation to a particular liquidation process or to all liquidations undertaken by the liquidator, and the liquidator shall comply with the request.

(2) The liquidator shall answer any questions of the Director concerning the content of the books requested under subsection (1) to be produced and the conduct of a particular liquidation or all liquidations, and give to the Director such assistance in the matter as the liquidator is reasonably able to give.

(3) A request under subsection (1) may not be made in respect of books relating to a liquidation that has concluded more than 6 years prior to the request.

(4) A liquidator who fails to comply with a request or requirement under this section is guilty of an offence.

Definitions

'contributory': CA 1963, s 208; 'company': CA 1963, s 2(1); 'creditor': CA 1963, s 2(1); 'liquidator': CA 1963, s 2(1); 'member': CA 1963, s 31; 'officer': CA 1963, s 2(1).

'Director': CLEA 2001, s 3(1)

Notes

Examination of liquidator's books: CLEA 2001, s 57 confers a power on the ODCE either of its own motion or on foot of a complaint by a member, contributory or creditor, to examine a liquidator's books. The inspection may be confined to the books relating to a particular liquidation or may alternatively be made referable to all liquidations which have been undertaken by the liquidator[1] in the previous six years.[2] The liquidator must also answer any questions put to him by the ODCE in this regard.[3] Failure to co-operate will constitute a criminal offence.[4]

In addition, the court, on the application of the ODCE may make an order for the inspection and copying of any books and papers of a company in liquidation, in which event the liquidator and every officer of the company is under a duty to provide all necessary co-operation.[5]

The court has a separate power under CA 1963, s 243 to order inspection of books and papers of a company in liquidation. See notes following CA 1963, ss 243 and 282A.

1 CLEA 2001, s 57(1).
2 CLEA 2001, s 57(3).
3 CLEA 2001, s 57(2).
4 CLEA 2001, s 57(4).
5 CA 1963, ss 243(1A) and 282A.

58 Reporting to Director of misconduct by liquidators or receivers

Where a disciplinary committee or tribunal (however called) of a prescribed professional body finds that a member conducting a liquidation or receivership has not maintained appropriate records, or it has reasonable grounds for believing that a member has committed an indictable offence under the Companies Acts during the course of a liquidation or receivership, the body shall report the matter, giving details of the finding or, as the case may be, of the alleged offence, to the Director forthwith and if the body fails to comply with this section it, and every officer of the body to whom the failure is attributable, is guilty of an offence.

Definitions

'Companies Acts': CLEA 2001, s 3(1); 'Director': CLEA 2001, s 3(1).

Notes

Reporting misconduct of liquidators and receivers by professional bodies: Whilst liquidators and receivers must be independent of the companies to which they are appointed,[1] there is no statutory requirement for them to have any professional qualification or to be members of any professional body. However, if a liquidator or receiver is a member of a professional body and that body finds that he has failed to keep appropriate records or has reasonable grounds for believing that he has committed an offence under the Companies Acts *qua* liquidator or receiver, as the case may be, it must report the matter to the ODCE. Failure to so report is itself a criminal offence.

Plainly, there is no such obligation on liquidators that are not the members of any prescribed professional body. As for the bodies that are prescribed, see the CLEA 2001 (Section 58) Regs 2002.

1 CA 1963, ss 300A and 315.

PART 6
MEASURES TO IMPROVE COMPLIANCE WITH FILING OBLIGATIONS

59 Repeal of sections 125 and 126 of Act of 1963 and substitution of section 125 — Annual return

[...][a]

Amendments

a CLEA 2001, s 59, substitutes CA 1963, s 125 and repeals CA 1963, s 126 with effect from 1 March 2002.[1] See amended Act.

1 Company Law Enforcement Act 2001 (Commencement) (No 2) Order 2001 (SI 438/2001).

Definitions

'Act of 1963': CLEA 2001, s 3(1); 'annual return': CA 1963, s 2(1).

60 Repeal and substitution of section 127 of Act of 1963 — Annual return date[a]

[...][a]

Amendments

a CLEA 2001, s 60, substitutes CA 1963, s 127 with effect from 1 March 2002.[1] See amended Act.

1 Company Law Enforcement Act 2001 (Commencement) (No 2) Order 2001 (SI 438/2001).

Definitions

'Act of 1963': CLEA 2001, s 3(1); 'annual return': CA 1963, s 2(1).

61 Amendment of section 153 of Act of 1963 — Financial year and annual return date of holding company and subsidiary

[...][a]

Amendments

a CLEA 2001, s 61, substitutes CA 1963, s 153(2) with effect from 1 March 2002.[1] See amended Act.

[1] Company Law Enforcement Act 2001 (Commencement) (No 2) Order 2001 (SI 438/2001).

Definitions

'Act of 1963': CLEA 2001, s 3(1); 'annual return': CA 1963, s 2(1); 'financial year': CA 1963, s 2(1); 'holding company': CA 1963 s 155; 'subsidiary': CA 1963, ss 2(1) and 155.

62 Amendment of section 370 of Act of 1963

[...][a]

Amendments

a CLEA 2001, s 62 inserts CA 1963, s 370(4) with effect from 26 October 2002.[1] See amended Act.

[1] Company Law Enforcement Act 2001 (Commencement) (No 2) Order 2001 (SI 438/2001).

Definitions

'Act of 1963': CLEA 2001, s 3(1).

63 Amendment of section 395 of Act of 1963 and repeal of Fifth Schedule

(1)

(a) [...][a]

(b) [...][b]

(2) [...][c]

Amendments

a CLEA 2001, s 63(1)(a) amends CA 1963, s 395(2)(b) with effect from 1 March 2002.[1] See amended Act.

b CLEA 2001, s 63(1)(b) inserts CA 1963, s 395(3) with effect from 26 October 2002.[2] See amended Act.

c CLEA 2001, s 63(2) repeals CA 1963, Sch 5 with effect from 1 March 2002.[3] See amended Act.

[1] Company Law Enforcement Act 2001 (Commencement) (No 2) Order 2001 (SI 438/2001).

[2] Company Law Enforcement Act 2001 (Commencement) (No 2) Order 2001 (SI 438/2001).

[3] Company Law Enforcement Act 2001 (Commencement) (No 2) Order 2001 (SI 438/2001).

Definitions

'Act of 1963': CLEA 2001, s 3(1).

Notes

Form of Annual Return: CA 1963, Sch 5 outlined the format and content of the annual return to be made by companies having a share capital as required by CA 1963, 125 (as amended by CLEA 2001, s 59). Since the coming into force of CLEA 2001, ss 59 and 63[2] the format and content of the annual return may be prescribed from time to time by regulations made by the Minister for Enterprise, Trade and Employment.

1 CLEA 2001, ss 59 and 63 was brought into force by the Company Law Enforcement Act 2001 (Commencement) (No 2) Order 2001 (SI 438/2001).

2 Companies (Forms) Order 2004 (SI 133/2004).

64 Amendment of section 7 of Companies (Amendment) Act, 1986

(a) [...][a]

(b) [...][b]

Amendments

a CLEA 2001, s 64(a) with effect from 26 October 2002.[1] See amended Act.

b CLEA 2001, s 64(b) inserts C(A)A 1986, s 7(1A) with effect from 26 October 2002.[2] See amended Act.

1 Company Law Enforcement Act 2001 (Commencement) (No 2) Order 2001 (SI 438/2001).

2 Company Law Enforcement Act 2001 (Commencement) (No 2) Order 2001 (SI 438/2001).

Definitions

'conpany': CA 1963, s 2(1); 'year': IA 2005, Sch, Pt 1.

Notes

Accounts annexed to Annual Return: C(A)A 1986, s 7 sets out the various documents, including accounts, which must be annexed to an annual return.[1] Since 26 October 2006[2] it is no longer necessary that the accounts filed with an annual return have been laid before an AGM. It is sufficient to file accounts which are to be laid before the AGM. The amendment by CLEA 2001, s 60 of CA 1963, s 127 has changed the basis on which the date for filing annual returns is set. Where previously the date for filing the annual return was linked to the date of the AGM, this association no longer applies. The accounts to be filed with the annual return must be made up to a date no earlier than nine months before the date to which the annual return is made up, irrespective of when the AGM is to be held.

1 'annual return': CA 1963, s 2(1).

2 Company Law Enforcement Act 2001 (Commencement) (No 2) Order 2001 (SI 438/2001).

65 Amendment of section 17(1) of Companies (Amendment) Act, 1986

[...][a]

Amendments

a CLEA 2001, s 65 amends C(A)A 1986, s 17(1)(a) with effect from 1 March 2002.[1] See amended Act.

1 Company Law Enforcement Act 2001 (Commencement) (No 2) Order 2001 (SI 438/2001).

Definitions

'annual return date': CA 1063, s 2(1); 'company': CA 1963, s 2(1); 'financial year' CA 1963, s 2(1).

Notes

Section 17 guarantee: C(A)A 1986, s 17 sets out the terms on which wholly owned subsidiaries of holding companies established in a member state of the EU may be exempt from the obligation to annex accounts under C(A)A 1986, s 7. The amendment by CLEA 2001, s 60 of CA 1963 s 127 dispenses with the link between the date of a company's AGM and the date on which it files its annual return. Since the introduction of the concept of an annual return date it is possible that a company might hold its AGM after its annual return date or even after the date on which it has filed its annual return. If this were to happen, the company would not be able to avail of the provisions of C(A)A 1986, s 17. CLEA 2001, s 65 inserts a consequential amendment to C(A)A 1986, sub-s 17(1)(a) whereby shareholder consent, which is required to avail of the exemption, must be given on the earlier of (i) the date of the AGM held following the relevant financial year or (ii) the next annual return date of the company after the end of that financial year. See also notes to C(A)A 1986, s 17.

---

66 Special provisions applying where default in delivery of documents to registrar of companies

(1) Where the registrar of companies has reasonable grounds for believing that a person is in default in the delivery, filing or making to the registrar of a return or similar document required under the Companies Acts, the registrar may deliver to the person or, where the person believed to be in default is a company, to an officer of the company, a notice in the prescribed form stating—

(a) that the person or company has failed to deliver, file or make a specified return or similar document to the registrar under a specified section of the Companies Acts,

(b) that the person to whom the notice is delivered may, during a period of 21 days beginning on the date of the notice,

(i) remedy the default, and

(ii) make to the registrar a payment of a prescribed amount which shall be accompanied by the notice, and

(c) that a prosecution of the person to whom the notice is delivered will not be instituted during the period specified in the notice, or, if the default is remedied and the payment specified in the notice is made during that period, at all.

(2) Where a notice is delivered under subsection (1)—

(a) a person to whom it applies may, during the period specified in the notice, make to the registrar the payment specified in the notice, accompanied by the notice,

(b) the registrar may receive the payment and issue a receipt for it, and no payment so received shall in any circumstances be recoverable by the person who made it, and

(c) a prosecution in respect of the alleged default shall not be instituted in the period specified in the notice, and, if the default is remedied and the payment specified in the notice is made during that period, no prosecution in respect of the alleged default shall be instituted at all.

(3) In a prosecution for an offence to which this section applies, the onus of showing that a payment pursuant to a notice under this section has been made shall lie on the defendant or accused.

(4) All payments made to the registrar under this section shall be paid into or disposed of for the benefit of the Exchequer in such manner as the Minister for Finance may direct.

Definitions

'company': CA 1963, s 2(1); 'Companies Acts': CLEA 2001, s 3(1); 'Minister for Finance': Ministers and Secretaries Act 1924, s 1 (ii); 'officer': CA 1963, s 2(1); 'person': IA 2005, 18(c); 'prescribed': CA 1963, s 2(1); 'the registrar of companies': CA 1963, s 2(1).

Notes

Operative Date: CLEA 2001, s 66 was brought into force on 1 October 2002.

1 Company Law Enforcement Act 2001 (Commencement) (No 2) Order 2001 (SI 438/2001).

On-the-spot fines for outstanding returns: CLEA 2001, s 66 confers on the Registrar a new power, in addition to his existing powers to prosecute specific offences under the Companies Acts, namely to impose on-the-spot fines where he has reasonable grounds for believing that there has been a failure to file returns or similar documents in the Companies Registration Office. The person on whom the notice is served has 21 days to file the outstanding item or items and pay the fine to the Registrar.[1] If he does so on time that person (which in the case of a company means an officer of that company) will not be prosecuted notwithstanding the fact that his default may have constituted a criminal offence.[2] The Director of Corporate Enforcement has a similar power to impose on-the-spot fines pursuant to CLEA 2001, s 109. The responsibility for proving that a fine imposed under CLEA 2001, s 66 has been paid is placed on the defendant in any subsequent proceedings.[3] This ensures that a defendant cannot rely on the defence that the relevant amount was remitted and that it is up to the registrar to prove the contrary.

If the Registrar issues a notice under CLEA 2001, s 66 (1), during the period of 21 days beginning on the date of the notice, the alleged offence cannot be prosecuted.[4] This new power has significant advantages for the registrar of companies and the Director of Corporate Enforcement[5] in that it allows the registrar to make companies and officers aware of the likelihood of prosecutions while giving such companies and officers the opportunity to remedy their default before the Registrar has to undertake the expense and effort of prosecuting offences in court.

1 CLEA 2001, s 66(1).

2 CLEA 2001, s 66(2).

3 CLEA 2001, s 66(3).

4 CLEA 2001, s 66(2)(c).

5 CLEA 2001, s 109.

PART 7
COMPANY LAW REVIEW GROUP

67 Establishment of Company Law Review Group

There is hereby established a body to be known as the Company Law Review Group.

Notes

Company Law Review Group: In recent years there have been several non-statutory company law review groups. One group established by the Minister in May 1994 under the chairmanship of Mr James Gallagher presented its report (including various recommendations in relation to examinerships) in November 1994. Those recommendations ultimately found their way into C(A)(No 2)A 1999, Pt II. Another group established by the Minister in September 1998 under the chairmanship of Michael McDowell SC made various recommendations for improving the enforcement of company law, including the establishment of the ODCE. The contents of the McDowell Report strongly influenced the content of CLEA 2001. In anticipation of the enactment of CLEA 2001 the CLRG was set up on an ad hoc basis in February 2000. With the coming into force of s 67 it is now placed on a firm statutory footing under the chairmanship of Dr Thomas B Courtney. The CLRG presented its first report to the Minister on 31 December 2001, its second report on 31 March 2004 and reported on Directors' Compliance Statements in August 2005. Moreover, from its establishment on a statutory basis, the CLRG has published annual reports as required by s CLEA 2001, s 71.

68 Functions of Review Group

(1) The Review Group shall monitor, review and advise the Minister on matters concerning—

(a) the implementation of the Companies Acts,

(b) the amendment of the Companies Acts,

(c) the consolidation of the Companies Acts,

(d) the introduction of new legislation relating to the operation of companies and commercial practices in Ireland,

(e) the Rules of the Superior Courts and case law judgements insofar as they relate to the Companies Acts,

(f) the approach to issues arising from the State's membership of the European Union, insofar as they affect the operation of the Companies Acts,

(g) international developments in company law, insofar as they may provide lessons for improved State practice, and

(h) other related matters or issues, including issues submitted by the Minister to the Review Group for consideration.

(2) In advising the Minister the Review Group shall seek to promote enterprise, facilitate commerce, simplify the operation of the Companies Acts, enhance corporate governance and encourage commercial probity.

Definitions

'Minister': CA 1963, s 2(1).

Notes

Functions of the CLRG: The functions of the CLRG are to monitor, review and advise the Minister on all aspects of company law,[1] with particular emphasis on promoting enterprise, facilitating commerce, simplifying the operation of the Companies Acts as well as enhancing corporate governance and encouraging commercial probity.[2] The CLRG first report, wherein it unveiled its blueprint for a new Companies Consolidation Bill to replace all existing company law acts was accepted by the Government in July 2002 and since then the CLRG has been working closely with the Department of Enterprise Trade and Employment and the various users of company law (most of which are represented on the CLRG) in drafting the heads of a new Bill which is intended to go to Government in late 2006, early 2007.

1 CLEA 2001, s 68(1).

2 CLEA 2001, s 68(2).

69 Membership of Review Group

(1) The Review Group shall consist of such and so many persons as the Minister from time to time appoints to be members of the Review Group.

(2) The Minister shall from time to time appoint a member of the Review Group to be its chairperson.

(3) Members of the Review Group shall be paid such remuneration and allowances for expenses as the Minister, with the consent of the Minister for Finance, may from time to time determine.

(4) A member of the Review Group may at any time resign his or her membership of the Review Group by letter addressed to the Minister.

(5) The Minister may at any time, for stated reasons, terminate a person's membership of the Review Group.

Definitions

'Minister': CA 1963, s 2(1).

70 Meetings and business of Review Group

(1) The Minister shall, at least once in every 2 years, after consultation with the Review Group, determine the programme of work to be undertaken by the Review Group over the ensuing specified period.

(2) Notwithstanding subsection (1), the Minister may, from time to time, amend the Review Group's work programme, including the period to which it relates.

(3) The Review Group shall hold such and so many meetings as may be necessary for the performance of its functions and the achievement of its work programme and may make such arrangements for the conduct of its meetings and business (including by the establishment of sub-committees and the fixing of a quorum for a meeting) as it considers appropriate.

(4) In the absence of the chairperson from a meeting of the Review Group, the members present shall elect one of their number to be chairperson for that meeting.

(5) A member of the Review Group, other than the chairperson, who is unable to attend a meeting of the Review Group, may nominate a deputy to attend in his or her place.

Definitions

'Minister': CA 1963, s 2(1).

71 Annual Report and provision of information to Minister

(1) No later than 3 months after the end of each calendar year, the Review Group shall make a report to the Minister on its activities during that year and the Minister shall cause copies of the report to be laid before each House of the Oireachtas within a period of 2 months from the receipt of the report.

(2) A report under subsection (1) shall include information in such form and regarding such matters as the Minister may direct.

(3) The Review Group shall, if so requested by the Minister, provide a report to the Minister on any matter—

(a) concerning the functions or activities of the Review Group, or

(b) referred by the Minister to the Review Group for its advice.

Definitions

'Minister': CA 1963, s 2(1).

PART 8
AUDITORS

72 Amendment of section 187 of Act of 1990

(a) [...][a]

(b) [...][b]

Amendments

a CLEA 2001, s 72(a) amends CA 1990, s 187(1)(a)(iii) by the insertion after 'Principal Act' of 'and holds a valid practising certificate from such a body'.

b CLEA 2001, s 72(b) inserts CA 1990, s 187(12) and (13).

73 Amendment of section 192 of Act of 1990

[...][a]

Amendments

a CLEA 2001, s 73 inserts CA 1990, s 192(6) and (7).

74 Amendment of section 194 of Act of 1990 — Duty of auditors if proper books of account not being kept or other offences suspected

(a) [...][a]

(b) [...][b]

(c) [...][c]

(d) [...][d]

(e) [...][e]

Amendments

a CLEA 2001, s 74(a) substitutes CA 1990, s 194(1)(a).

b CLEA 2001, s 74(b) amends CA 1990, s 194(1)(b) by the insertion after 'form of the notice' of 'and the registrar shall forthwith forward a copy of the notice to the Director'.

c CLEA 2001, s 74(c) inserts CA 1990, s 194(3A) and (3B).

d CLEA 2001, s 74(d) amends CA 1990, s 194(4) by the substitution for 'subsection (1)' of 'subsection (1), (3A) or (5)'.

e CLEA 2001, s 74(e) inserts CA 1990, s 194(5) and (6).

PART 9
TRANSACTIONS INVOLVING DIRECTORS

75 Amendment of section 25 of Act of 1990

[…][a]

Amendments

a CLEA 2001, s 75 inserts CA 1990, s 25(3A).

76 Amendment of section 26 of Act of 1990

[…][a]

[…][b]

[…][c]

Amendments

a CLEA 2001, s 76(a) substitutes CA 1990, s 26(1).

b CLEA 2001, s 76(b) substitutes CA 1990, s 26(3).

c CLEA 2001, s 76(c) inserts CA 1990, s 26(6).

77 Amendment of section 33 of Act of 1990

[…][a]

Amendments

a CLEA 2001, s 77 inserts CA 1990, s 33(3).

78 Repeal and substitution of section 34 of Act of 1990 — Exceptions to section 31 in certain circumstances

[...][a]

Amendments

a CLEA 2001, s 78 repeals and substitutes CA 1990, s 34.

79 Amendment of section 35 of Act of 1990 — Inter-company transactions in the same group

[...][a]

Amendments

a CLEA 2001, s 79 amends CA 1990, s 35 by the substitution for 'its holding company' wherever occurring, of 'any company which is its holding company, subsidiary or a subsidiary of its holding company'.

PART 10
MISCELLANEOUS

80 Reference Memoranda and Articles of Association

(1) The registrar of companies may accept for registration a document containing standard form text from the objects clause of a memorandum of association or from articles of association and shall assign a reference number to each document so registered.

(2) Notwithstanding anything in the Companies Acts, a document filed pursuant to subsection (1) need not relate to a particular company or contain the registered number of a company.

(3) A memorandum or articles of association may contain a statement that it is to incorporate the text of a document previously registered with the registrar pursuant to subsection (1), which document shall be identified by the reference number assigned to it by the registrar.

(4) Where a memorandum or articles of association contains a statement as referred to in subsection (3), it shall be deemed for all purposes to incorporate within it the text of the relevant document filed with the registrar pursuant to subsection (1), so that it shall form and be read as one entire document, and where such a memorandum or articles of association has been registered by the registrar and is inspected by any person, the registrar shall also make available for inspection the related document filed with him or her pursuant to subsection (1).

Definitions

'articles': CA 1963, s 2(1); 'company': CA 1963, s 2(1); 'Companies Acts': CLEA 2001, s 3(1); 'memorandum': CA 1963, s 2(1); 'the registrar of companies': CA 1963, s 2(1).

Notes

Registration of standard form memoranda and articles:[1] CLEA 2001, s 80[2] allows for the filing of standard form memoranda and articles of association to which reference numbers will be assigned by the Registrar. Thereafter the promoters of a company need only file a memorandum and articles of association specifying those matters peculiar to the company itself, together with a statement identifying the reference number(s) of the standard form documents which are to be deemed also to have been incorporated therein. Reduced filing fees are payable in respect of companies incorporated in circumstances where such standard form memoranda and articles of association are used.[3]

1 See generally Companies Registration Office, 'Company Incorporation', Information Leaflet No. 1/May 2006.

2 Effective from 1 October 2001: Company Law Enforcement Act 2001 (Commencement)(No 2) Order 2001 (SI 438/2001).

3 See CA 1963, Sch 8 (as amended by Companies (Fees)(No3) Order 2005 (SI 517/2005).

81 Amendment of section 7 of Act of 1963

[...][a]

Amendments

a CLEA 2001, s 81 amends CA 1963, s 7 with effect from 1 October 2001[1] by the insertion after 'The memorandum must be printed' of 'in an entire format or in a form pursuant to section 80 of the Company Law Enforcement Act, 2001'.

1 Company Law Enforcement Act 2001 (Commencement)(No 2) Order 2001 (SI 438/2001).

Definitions

'Act of 1963': CLEA 2001, s 3(1); 'memorandum': CA 1963, s 2(1); 'printed': CA 1963, s 2(1).

Notes

Printing of memorandum: This amendment of CA 1963, s 7 ensures that by printing only that part of the memorandum of association which is specific to the company and citing a reference number identifying the document previously filed with the Registrar, the incorporators of the company will satisfy the requirements of CA 1963, s 7.

82 Amendment of section 14 of Act of 1963

[...][a]

Amendments

a CLEA 2001, s 82 amends CA 1963, s 14(a) with effect from 1 October 2001 by the insertion after 'printed' of 'in an entire format or in a form pursuant to section 80 of the Company Law Enforcement Act, 2001'

1 Company Law Enforcement Act 2001 (Commencement)(No 2) Order 2001 (SI 438/2001).

Definitions

'Act of 1963': CLEA 2001, s 3(1); 'printed': CA 1963, s 2(1).

Notes

Printing of articles: This amendment of CA 1963, s 14(a) ensures that by printing only that part of the articles of association which is specific to the company and citing a reference number identifying the document previously filed with the Registrar, the incorporators of the company will satisfy the requirements of CA 1963, s 14(a).

---

83 Amendment of section 17 of Act of 1963

[...][a]

Amendments

a CLEA 2001, s 83 amends CA 1963, s 17 with effect from 1 October 2001 by the insertion after 'shall be delivered to the registrar of companies' of 'in an entire format or in a form pursuant to section 80 of the Company Law Enforcement Act, 2001'.

1 Company Law Enforcement Act 2001 (Commencement)(No 2) Order 2001 (SI 438/2001).

Definitions

'Act of 1963': CLEA 2001, s 3(1); 'the registrar of companies': CA 1963, s 2(1).

Notes

Delivery of memorandum: CA 1963, s 17 governs the delivery of the memorandum and articles of association to the Registrar. CLEA 2001, s 83 confirms that delivery of the memorandum may be satisfied by providing that part of the memorandum of association which is specific to the company and citing a reference number identifying the document previously filed with the Registrar.

---

84 Amendment of section 2 of Act of 1963

(a) [...][a]

(b) [...][b]

Amendments

a CLEA 2001, s 84(a) amends CA 1963, s 2(1) by substituting the definition of 'annual return' and by inserting the definition of 'annual return date' with effect from 1 March 2002.[1] See amended Act.

b CLEA 2001, s 84(b) amends CA 1963, s 2(1) by substituting the definition of 'undischarged bankrupt' with effect from 1 March 2002.[2] See amended Act.

1 Company Law Enforcement Act 2001 (Commencement)(No 2) Order 2001 (SI 438/2001).

2 Company Law Enforcement Act 2001 (Commencement)(No 5) Order 2001 (SI 53/2002).

Definitions

'Act of 1963': CLEA 2001, s 3(1); 'annual return': CA 1963, s 2(1); 'undischarged bankrupt': CA 1963, s 2(1).

Cross reference

CA 1963, ss 125, 126 and 127 (as amended by CLEA 2001, ss 59 and 60).

Notes

Consequential amendments: CLEA 2001, ss 59 and 60 introduced amendments to CA 1963 relating to the content and delivery of annual returns. Changes introduced in CLEA 2001, s 84(a) are consequential to the changes introduced by CLEA 2001, ss 59 and 60. The definition of 'annual return' is substituted and the definition of 'annual return date' is introduced.

Definition of 'undischarged bankrupt': CLEA 2001, s 84 (b) introduces a broader definition of 'undischarged bankrupt' to include any jurisdiction and not just Northern Ireland, England or Scotland, being the jurisdictions referred to in the pre-amendment definition.

---

85 Amendment of section 10 of Act of 1963

[...][a]

Amendments

a CLEA 2001, s 85 amends CA 1963, s 10(8) with effect from 1 October 2001[1] by the substitution for 'Minister' (second occurring) of 'registrar of companies'.

[1] Company Law Enforcement Act 2001 (Commencement)(No 2) Order 2001 (SI 438/2001).

Definitions

'Act of 1963': CLEA 2001, s 3(1); 'Minister': CA 1963, s (1); 'the registrar of companies': CA 1963, s 2(1).

Cross reference

See CA 1963, s 21 (as amended by CLEA 2001, s 86).

See CA 1963, s 24 (as amended by CLEA 2001, s 88).

Notes

Replacement of reference to the Minister: Companies who wished to be exempt from the requirement to use the word 'limited' in their name had to apply to the Minister for Enterprise, Trade and Employment pursuant to CA 1963, s 24. CLEA 2001, s 88 amended CA 1963, s 24 so that a new system was introduced whereby companies wishing to avail of this exemption must establish eligibility by way of statutory declaration, filed with the Registrar.

[1]1 October 2001: Company Law Enforcement Act 2001 (Commencement)(No 2) Order 2001 (SI 438/2001).

---

86 Amendment of section 21 of Act of 1963

[...][a]

Amendments

a CLEA 2001, s 86 amends CA 1963, s 21 with effect from 1 October 2001[1] by the substitution for 'Minister' of 'registrar of companies'.

[1] Company Law Enforcement Act 2001 (Commencement)(No 2) Order 2001 (SI 438/2001).

Definitions

'Act of 1963': CLEA 2001, s 3(1); 'Minister': CA 1963, s 2(1); 'the registrar of companies': CA 1963, s 2(1).

Cross reference

CA 1963, s 23 (as amended by CLEA 2001, s 87).

CA 1963, s 24 (as amended by CLEA 2001, s 88).

Notes

Replacement of reference to the Minister: The discretion as to whether the proposed name of a company being incorporated is undesirable is transferred to the Registrar by virtue of CLEA 2001, s 86.

87 Amendment of section 23 of Act of 1963

(a) [...][a]

(b) [...][b]

(c) [...][c]

Amendments

a CLEA 2001, s 87(a) amends CA 1963, s 23(1) and (2) with effect from 1 October 2001[1] by the substitution for 'Minister' (wherever occurring) of 'registrar of companies'.

b CLEA 2001, s 87(b) amends CA 1963, s 23(5) with effect from 1 October 2001[2] by the substitution for 'but if the Minister is of opinion that any other Minister' and 'that other Minister' of 'but if the registrar of companies is of opinion that any Minister' and 'that Minister', respectively.

c CLEA 2001, s 87(c) inserts CA 1963, s 23(7) with effect from 1 October 2001.[3] See amended Act.

1 Company Law Enforcement Act 2001 (Commencement)(No 2) Order 2001 (SI 438/2001).

2 Company Law Enforcement Act 2001 (Commencement)(No 2) Order 2001 (SI 438/2001).

3 Company Law Enforcement Act 2001 (Commencement)(No 2) Order 2001 (SI 438/2001).

Definitions

'Act of 1963': CLEA 2001, s 3(1); 'Minister': CA 1963, 2(1); 'the registrar of companies': CA 1963, s 2(1).

Cross reference

CA 1963, s 21 (as amended by CLEA 2001, s 86).

CA 1963, s 24 (as amended by CLEA 2001, s 88).

Notes

Replacement of reference to the Minister: The discretion as to whether the proposed change of name of a company is undesirable is transferred to the Registrar by virtue of CLEA 2001, s 87(a). In the case of companies with names specified by statute, the responsibility to consult with the relevant Minister, on the change of such name transfers to the Registrar.[1] In addition to the general transfer of responsibility, the Registrar has been given additional powers to prosecute offences summarily under CA 1963, s 23.[2]

1 CA 1963, s 23(5) as amended by CLEA 2001, s 87(b).

2 CA 1963, s 23(7) as inserted by CLEA 2001, s 87(c).

88 Repeal and substitution of section 24 of Act of 1963

(1) [...][a]

(2) Notwithstanding the repeal effected by subsection (1) a licence granted by the Minister pursuant to section 24(1) or (2) of the Act of 1963 as in force immediately before the commencement of this section shall continue to have effect, and subsections (4) to (7) of section 24 of that Act as then in force shall continue in force in relation to the licence, as if the section had never been repealed, except that references in those subsections to the Minister, wherever occurring, shall be construed as references to the registrar of companies.

Amendments

a CLEA 2001, s 88(1) substitutes CA 1963, s 24 with effect from 1 March 2002.[1] See amended Act.

1 Company Law Enforcement Act 2001 (Commencement)(No 3) Order 2001 (SI 523/2001).

Definitions

'Act of 1963': CLEA 2001, s 3(1); 'Minister': CLEA 2001, s 3(1); 'the registrar of companies': CA 1963, s 2(1).

Notes

Exemption from use of 'limited' or teoranta': Under CA 1963, s 24 (as substituted), a qualifying company will automatically be entitled to exclude the word 'limited' or 'teoranta', as the case may be, from the end of its name. However, licences granted by the Minister granting similar exemption before the date of the coming into force of this section[1] will continue to be valid.

1 1 March 2002. See Company Law Enforcement Act 2001 (Commencement) (No 3) Order 2001 (SI 523/2001).

89 Amendment of section 60 of Act of 1963

(a) [...][a]

(b) [...][b]

Amendments

a CLEA 2001, s 89(a) substitutes CA 1963, s 60(2)(b) with effect from 1 October 2001.[1] See amended Act.

b CLEA 2001, s 89(b) substitutes CA 1963, s 60(6) with effect from 1 October 2001.[2] See amended Act.

1 Company Law Enforcement Act 2001 (Commencement)(No 2) Order 2001 (SI 438/2001).

2 Company Law Enforcement Act 2001 (Commencement)(No 2) Order 2001 (SI 438/2001).

Definitions

'Act of 1963': CLEA 2001, s 3(1).

90 Amendment of section 158 of Act of 1963

[...][a]

Amendments

a CLEA 2001, s 90 inserts CA 1963, s 158(6A) with effect from 1 October 2001.[1] See amended Act.

1 Company Law Enforcement Act 2001 (Commencement)(No 2) Order 2001 (SI 438/2001).

Definitions

'Act of 1963': CLEA 2001, s 3(1).

91 Amendment of section 195 of Act of 1963

(a) [...][a]

(b) [...][b]

Amendments

a CLEA 2001, s 91(a) substitutes CA 1963, s 195(8) with effect from 1 March 2002.[1] See amended Act.

b CLEA 2001, s 91(b) inserts CA 1963, s 198(10A) with effect from 1 October 2001.[2] See amended Act.

1 Company Law Enforcement Act 2001 (Commencement)(No 5) Order 2001 (SI 53/2005).

2 Company Law Enforcement Act 2001 (Commencement)(No 2) Order 2001 (SI 438/2001).

Definitions

'Act of 1963': CLEA 2001, s 3(1).

92 Amendment of section 201 of Act of 1963

[...][a]

Amendments

a CLEA 2001, s 92 inserts CA 1963, s 201(6A) and (6B) with effect from 1 October 2001.[1] See amended Act.

1 Company Law Enforcement Act 2001 (Commencement)(No 2) Order 2001 (SI 438/2001).

Definitions

'Act of 1963': CLEA 2001, s 3(1).

93 Amendment of section 213 of Act of 1963

Section 213 of the Act of 1963 is amended—

(a) [...][a]

(b) [...][b]

Amendments

a CLEA 2001, s 93(a) amends CA 1963, s 213(f) with effect from 1 October 2001[1] by the insertion after 'company' of ', other than an investment company within the meaning of Part XIII of the Companies Act, 1990, or the European Communities (Undertakings for Collective Investment in Transferable Securities) Regulations, 1989 (S.I. No. 78 of 1989),'.

b CLEA 2001, s 93(b) inserts CA 1963, s 213(fa) with effect from 1 October 2001 (except in so far as it inserts (fa)(ii) into CA 1963, s 213).[2] See amended Act.

1 Company Law Enforcement Act 2001 (Commencement)(No 2) Order 2001 (SI 438/2001).

2 Company Law Enforcement Act 2001 (Commencement)(No 2) Order 2001 (SI 438/2001).

Definitions

'Act of 1963': CLEA 2001, s 3(1); 'company': CA 1963, s 2(1); 'investment company': CA 1990, s 252(1).

94 Amendment of section 215 of Act of 1963

(a) [...][a]

(b) [...][b]

(c) [...][c]

Amendments

a CLEA 2001, s 94(a) amends CA 1963, s 215 with effect from 1 October 2001[1] by the deletion of 'and' where it occurs immediately before paragraph (f).

b CLEA 2001, s 94(b) amends CA 1963, s 215(f) with effect from 1 October 2001[2] by the substitution for 'companies.' of 'companies; and'.

c CLEA 2001, s 94(c) inserts CA 1963, s 215(g) with effect from 1 October 2001.[3] See amended Act.

1 Company Law Enforcement Act 2001 (Commencement)(No 2) Order 2001 (SI 438/2001).

2 Company Law Enforcement Act 2001 (Commencement)(No 2) Order 2001 (SI 438/2001).

3 Company Law Enforcement Act 2001 (Commencement)(No 2) Order 2001 (SI 438/2001).

Definitions

'Act of 1963': CLEA 2001, s 3(1); 'company': CA 1963, s 2(1).

95 Amendment of section 334 of Act of 1963

[...][a]

Amendments

a CLEA 2001, s 95 amends CA 1963, s 334(1) with effect from 1 October 2001[1] by the substitution for 'Minister' (twice occurring) of 'registrar of companies'.

1 Company Law Enforcement Act 2001 (Commencement)(No 2) Order 2001 (SI 438/2001).

Definitions

'Act of 1963': CLEA 2001, s 3(1); 'Minister': CA 1963, s 2(1); 'the registrar of companies': CA 1963, s 2(1).

96 Amendment of section 371 of Act of 1963

(a) [...][a]

(b) [...][b]

(c) [...][c]

Amendments

a CLEA 2001, s 96(a) amends CA 1963, s 371(1) with effect from 28 November 2001[1] by the insertion after 'by any member or creditor of the company' of ', by the Director'.

b CLEA 2001, s 96(b) amends CA 1963, s 371(3) with effect from 28 November 2001[2] by the insertion after 'penalties' of '(including restriction under section 150, or disqualification under section 160, of the Companies Act, 1990)'.

c CLEA 2001, s 96(c) inserts CA 1963, s 370(4) with effect from 28 November 2001.[3] See amended Act.

1 Company Law Enforcement Act 2001 (Commencement) (No 3) Order 2001 (SI 523/2001).

2 Company Law Enforcement Act 2001 (Commencement) (No 3) Order 2001 (SI 523/2001).

3 Company Law Enforcement Act 2001 (Commencement) (No 3) Order 2001 (SI 523/2001).

Definitions

'Act of 1963': CLEA 2001, s 3(1); 'company': CA 1963, s 2(1); 'Director': CLEA 2001, s 3(1); 'director': CA 1963, s 2(1); 'officer': CA 1963, s 2(1); 'shadow director': CA 1990, s 27.

97 New section 371A of Act of 1963 — Power to compel compliance with requirement made under section 19(3)(b) of Act of 1990

[...][a]

Amendments

a CLEA 2001, s 97 inserts CA 1963, s 371A with effect from 28 November 2001.[1] See amended Act.

1 Company Law Enforcement Act 2001 (Commencement) (No 3) Order 2001 (SI 523/2001).

Definitions

'Act of 1963': CLEA 2001, s 3(1); 'Act of 1990': CLEA 2001, s 3(1).

98 Repeal and substitution of section 381 of Act of 1963 — Improper use of 'limited' or 'teoranta'

[...][a]

Amendments

a CLEA 2001, s 98 substitutes CA 1963, s 381 with effect from 1 October 2001.[1] See amended Act.

1 Company Law Enforcement Act 2001 (Commencement) (No 2) Order 2001 (SI 438/2001).

Definitions

'Act of 1963': CLEA 2001, s 3(1); 'Act of 1990': CLEA 2001, s 3(1).

99 Amendment of section 392 of Act of 1963

[...][a]

Amendments

a CLEA 2001, s 99 amends CA 1963, s 392 with effect from 26 October 2001[1] by the insertion after 'Houses of the Oireachtas' of 'not later than 7 months after the end of the calendar year to which the report relates'.

1 Company Law Enforcement Act 2001 (Commencement) (No 2) Order 2001 (SI 438/2001).

Definitions

'Act of 1963': CLEA 2001, s 3(1); 'Oireachtas': IA 2005, Sch, Pt 1; 'year': IA 2005, Sch, Pt 1.

100 Repeal and substitution of section 383 of Act of 1963

[...][a]

Amendments

a CLEA 2001, s 100 substitutes CA 1963, s 383 with effect from 1 October 2001.[1] See amended Act.

1 Company Law Enforcement Act 2001 (Commencement) (No 2) Order 2001 (SI 438/2001).

Definitions

'Act of 1963': CLEA 2001, s 3(1).

101 New section 3A of Companies (Amendment) Act, 1982 — Additional statement to be delivered to registrar

[...][a]

Amendments

a CLEA 2001, s 101 inserts C(A)A 1982, s 3A with effect from 1 March 2002.[1] See amended Act.

1 Company Law Enforcement Act 2001 (Commencement)(No 5) Order 2002 (SI 53/2002).

Definitions

'the registrar of companies': CA 1963, s 2(1).

102 Amendment of section 30 of Act of 1990

Section 30 of the Act of 1990 is amended by the insertion of the following after subsection (3):[a]

[...][a]

Amendments

a CLEA 2001, s 102 inserts CA 1990, s 30(3A) with effect from 1 October 2001.[1] See amended Act.

1 Company Law Enforcement Act 2001 (Commencement) (No 2) Order 2001 (SI 438/2001).

Definitions

'Act of 1990': CLEA 2001, s 3(1).

103 Amendment of section 110 of Act of 1990

[...][a]

Amendments

a CLEA 2001, s 103 inserts CA 1990, s 110(1)(ba) with effect from 1 October 2001.[1] See amended Act.

1 Company Law Enforcement Act 2001 (Commencement) (No 2) Order 2001 (SI 438/2001).

Definitions

'Act of 1990': CLEA 2001, s 3(1).

104 Amendment of section 240 of Act of 1990

(a) [...][a]

(b) [...][b]

(c) [...][c]

Amendments

a CLEA 2001, s 104(a) amends CA 1990, s 240 with effect from 1 October 2001[1] by the substitution for '£1,000' (wherever occurring) of '£1,500'.

b CLEA 2001, s 104(b) amends CA 1990, s 240(1)(b) with effect from 1 October 2001[2] by the substitution for '3 years' of '5 years'

c CLEA 2001, s 104(c) inserts CA 1990, s 240(7) and (8) with effect from 1 October 2001.[3] See amended Act.

1 Company Law Enforcement Act 2001 (Commencement) (No 2) Order 2001 (SI 438/2001).

2 Company Law Enforcement Act 2001 (Commencement) (No 2) Order 2001 (SI 438/2001).

3 Company Law Enforcement Act 2001 (Commencement) (No 2) Order 2001 (SI 438/2001).

Definitions

'Act of 1990': CLEA 2001, s 3(1); 'Companies Acts': CLEA 2001, s 3(1); 'year': IA 2005, Sch, Pt 1.

105 New section 240A of Act of 1990 — Court in which proceedings for certain offences may be brought

[...][a]

Amendments

a CLEA 2001, s 105 inserts CA 1990, s 240A with effect from 1 October 2001.[1] See amended Act.

1 Company Law Enforcement Act 2001 (Commencement) (No 2) Order 2001 (SI 438/2001).

Definitions

'Act of 1990': CLEA 2001, s 3(1).

106 Amendment of section 242 of Act of 1990

Section 242(2) of the Act of 1990 is amended—

(a) [...][a]

(b) [...][b]

Amendments

a CLEA 2001, s 106(a) amends CA 1990, s 242(2) with effect from 1 October 2001[1] by the substitution for 'Where a person is guilty' of 'Where a person is convicted on indictment'.

b CLEA 2001, s 106(b) amends CA 1990, s 242(2) with effect from 1 October 2001[2] by the deletion of 'on conviction on indictment'.

1 Company Law Enforcement Act 2001 (Commencement) (No 2) Order 2001 (SI 438/2001).

2 Company Law Enforcement Act 2001 (Commencement) (No 2) Order 2001 (SI 438/2001).

Definitions

'Act of 1990': CLEA 2001, s 3(1).

107 New section 249A of Act of 1990 — Power to reject documents sent for registration and amendments consequential on that section's insertion

(1) [...][a]

(2) [...][b]

Amendments

a CLEA 2001, s 107(1) inserts CA 1990, s 249A with effect from 1 March 2002.[1] See amended Act

b CLEA 2001, s 107(2) deletes CA 1990, s 248(3), (4) and (5) and s 249(5), (6) and (7) with effect from 1 March 2002.[2] See amended Act.

1 Company Law Enforcement Act 2001 (Commencement) (No 4) Order 2002 (SI 43/2002).

2 Company Law Enforcement Act 2001 (Commencement) (No 4) Order 2002 (SI 43/2002).

Definitions

'Act of 1990': CLEA 2001, s 3(1); 'document': CA 1963, s 2(1).

108 Amendment of section 258 of Act of 1990

Section 258 of the Act of 1990 is amended—

(a) [...][a]

(b) [...][b]

Amendments

a CLEA 2001, s 108(a) amends CA 1990, s 258 with effect from 1 October 2001[1] by the insertion after '63,' of '72(3).

b CLEA 2001, s 108(b) amends CA 1990, s 258 with effect from 1 October 2001[2] by the insertion after 'investment company' of ', or, in the case of the said Regulation 72(3), such a company other than one to which section 253(2A)(a) applies.

1 Company Law Enforcement Act 2001 (Commencement) (No 2) Order 2001 (SI 438/2001).

2 Company Law Enforcement Act 2001 (Commencement) (No 2) Order 2001 (SI 438/2001).

Definitions

'Act of 1990': CLEA 2001, s 3(1); 'company': CA 1963, s 2(1); 'investment company': CA 1990, s 256(1).

109 Notice by Director of intention to prosecute

(1) Where the Director has reasonable grounds for believing that a person has committed an offence under the Companies Acts which is subject to summary prosecution, the Director may deliver to the person or, where the person believed to have committed the offence is a company, to an officer of the company, a notice in the prescribed form stating—

(a) that the person or company is alleged to have committed that offence,

(b) that the person to whom the notice is delivered may during a period of 21 days beginning on the date of the notice—

(i) remedy as far as practicable to the satisfaction of the Director any default that constitutes the offence, and

(ii) make to the Director a payment of a prescribed amount which shall be accompanied by the notice, and

(c) that a prosecution of the person to whom the notice is delivered in respect of the alleged offence will not be instituted during the period specified in the notice or, if the default is remedied to the satisfaction of the Director and the payment specified in the notice is made during that period, at all.

(2) Where a notice is given under subsection (1)—

(a) a person to whom it applies may, during the period specified in the notice, make to the Director the payment specified in the notice, accompanied by the notice,

(b) the Director may receive the payment and issue a receipt for it, and no payment so received shall in any circumstances be recoverable by the person who made it, and

(c) a prosecution in respect of the alleged offence shall not be instituted in the period specified in the notice and, if the default is remedied to the satisfaction of the Director and the payment specified in the notice is made during that period, no prosecution in respect of the alleged offence shall be instituted at all.

(3) In a prosecution for an offence to which this section applies, the onus of showing that a payment pursuant to a notice under this section has been made shall lie on the defendant.

(4) All payments made to the Director in pursuance of this section shall be paid into or disposed of for the benefit of the Exchequer in such manner as the Minister for Finance may direct.

Definitions

'Companies Acts': CLEA 2001, s 3(1); 'company': CA 1963, s 2(1); 'Director': CLEA 2001, s 3(1); 'Minister for Finance': Minister and Secretaries Act 1924, s 1(ii); 'officer': CA 1963, s 2(1); 'person': IA 2005, s 18(c); 'prescribed': CLEA 2001, s 3(1).

Cross reference

See also CLEA 2001, s 66 in relation to the enhanced enforcement powers of the Registrar.

Notes

No commencement order has been passed bringing CLEA 2001, s 109 into effect.

On-the-spot fines for outstanding returns: CLEA 2001, s 109 confers on the Director a power to impose on-the-spot fines where he has reasonable grounds for believing that a summary offence under the Companies Acts has been committed. The person on whom the notice is served has 21 days to file the outstanding item or items and pay the fine to the Director.[1] If he does so on time he will not be prosecuted notwithstanding the fact that his default may have constituted a criminal offence.[2] The Registrar has a similar power to impose on-the-spot fines in respect of failures to files returns etc pursuant to CLEA 2001, s 66.

1 CLEA 2001, s 109(1).
2 CLEA 2001, s 109(2).

---

110 Provision of information to juries

(1) In a trial on indictment of an offence under the Companies Acts, the trial judge may order that copies of any or all of the following documents be given to the jury in any form that the judge considers appropriate:

(a) any document admitted in evidence at the trial,

(b) the transcript of the opening speeches of counsel,

(c) any charts, diagrams, graphics, schedules or summaries of evidence produced at the trial,

(d) the transcript of the whole or any part of the evidence given at the trial,

(e) the transcript of the trial judge's charge to the jury,

(f) any other document that in the opinion of the trial judge would be of assistance to the jury in its deliberations including, where appropriate, an affidavit by an accountant summarising, in a form which is likely to be comprehended by the jury, any transactions by the accused or other persons relevant to the offence.

(2) If the prosecutor proposes to apply to the trial judge for an order that a document mentioned in subsection (1)(f) shall be given to the jury, the prosecutor shall give a copy of the document to the accused in advance of the trial and, on the hearing of the application, the trial judge shall take into account any representations made by or on behalf of the accused in relation to it.

(3) Where the trial judge has made an order that an affidavit mentioned in subsection (1)(f) shall be given to the jury, he or she may in an appropriate case, with a view to further assisting the jury in its deliberations, require the accountant who prepared the affidavit to explain to the jury any relevant accounting procedures or principles.

Definitions

'Companies Acts': CLEA 2001, s 3(1); 'document': CA 1963, s 2(1); 'person': IA 2005, s 18(c).

Notes

Provision of information to juries: CLEA 2001, s 110[1] provides that the court may order a variety of documents[2] be made available in a trial on indictment of an offence under the Companies Acts. In the event that the prosecution wishes to apply to have a document given to the jury it must first provide a copy to the accused who may make representations to the court as to the admissibility of that document.[3] In addition, where an affidavit of an accountant is submitted to the jury, the court may also order that the accountant providing the affidavit also attends and provides an explanation of any relevant accounting procedures or principles.[4]

1 No commencement order has been passed bringing CLEA 2001, s 110 into effect.

2 CLEA 2001, s 110(1)(a)–(f).

3 CLEA 2001, s 110(2).

4 CLEA 2001, s 110(3).

[110A Certificate evidence and other matters

(1) In this section—

'appropriate officer' means—

(a) in respect of functions that, under the Companies Acts, are to be performed by the Minister, the Minister or an officer of the Minister,

(b) in respect of functions that, under the Companies Acts, are to be performed by the Director, the Director or an officer of the Director,

(c) in respect of functions that, under the Companies Acts, are to be performed by the inspector or inspectors appointed pursuant to Part II of the Companies Act 1990, an inspector or, where more than one inspector is appointed, any inspector, [...][a]

(d) in respect of functions that, under the Companies Acts, are to be performed by the registrar of companies, a registrar, an assistant registrar or any other person authorised in that behalf by the Minister under section 52(2) of the Companies (Amendment) (No. 2) Act [1999; and][b]

[(e) in respect of functions that, under the Companies Acts, are to be performed by the Central Bank and Financial Services Authority of Ireland—

(i) the Chief Executive of the Irish Financial Services Regulatory Authority, or

(ii) a person appointed by some other person to whom the Chief Executive of the Irish Financial Services Regulatory Authority has delegated responsibility for appointing persons for the purposes of this section;][c]

'item' includes a document and any other thing;

'notice' includes—

(a) any request, notice, letter, demand, pleading or other document, and

(b) any form of obligation that an individual may have under the Companies Acts by reason of a demand or request made by an appropriate officer, whether communicated in writing, orally or by other means.

(2) In any legal proceedings (including proceedings relating to an offence) a certificate signed by an appropriate officer in the course of performing his or her functions is, in the absence of evidence to the contrary, proof of the following:

(a) if it certifies that the officer has examined the relevant records and that it appears from them that during a stated period an item was not received from a stated person, proof that the person did not during that period furnish that item and that the item was not received;

(b) if it certifies that the officer has examined the relevant records and that it appears from them that a stated notice was not issued to a stated person, proof that the person did not receive the notice;

(c) if it certifies that the officer has examined the relevant records and that it appears from them that a stated notice was duly given to a stated person on a stated date, proof that the person received the notice on that date;

(d) if it certifies that the officer has examined the relevant records and that it appears from them that a stated notice was posted to a stated person at a stated address on a stated date, proof that the notice was received by that person at that address on a date 3 days after the date on which the document was posted;

(e) if it certifies that the officer has examined the relevant records and that it appears from them that a document was filed or registered with or delivered at a stated place, on a stated date or at a stated time is, proof that the document was filed or registered with or delivered at that place, on that date or at that time.

(3) A certificate referred to in subsection (2) that purports to be signed by an appropriate officer is admissible in evidence in any legal proceedings without proof of the officer's signature or that the officer was the proper person to sign the certificate.

(4) A document prepared pursuant to any provision of the Companies Acts and purporting to be signed by any person is deemed, in the absence of evidence to the contrary, to have been signed by that person.

(5) A document submitted under the Companies Acts on behalf of a person is deemed to have been submitted by the person unless that person proves that it was submitted without that person's consent or knowledge.

(6) A document that purports to be a copy of, or extract from, any document kept by or on behalf of the Director and that purports to be certified by—

(a) the Director,

(b) an officer of the Director, or

(c) any person authorised by the Director, to be a true copy of or extract from the document so kept is, without proof of the official position of the person purporting to so certify, admissible in evidence in all legal proceedings as of equal validity with the original document.

(7) A document that purports to be a copy of, or extract from, any document kept by the Minister and that purports to be certified by—

(a) the Minister,

(b) an officer of the Minister, or

(c) any person authorised by the Minister, to be a true copy of, or extract from, the document so kept is, without proof of the official position of the person purporting to so certify, admissible in evidence in all legal proceedings as of equal validity with the original document.

(8) A document that purports to be a copy of, or extract from, any document kept by an inspector and that is certified by—

(a) the inspector, or

(b) any person authorised by the inspector,

to be a true copy of, or extract from, the document so kept is, without proof of the official position of the person purporting to so certify, admissible in evidence in all legal proceedings as of equal validity with the original document.

[(8A) A document purporting to be a copy of, or extract from, any document kept by the Central Bank and Financial Services Authority of Ireland and that is certified by—

(a) the Chief Executive of the Irish Financial Services Regulatory Authority, or

(b) any person authorised by the Chief Executive of the Irish Financial Services Regulatory Authority,

to be a true copy of, or extract from, the document so kept is, without proof of the official position of the person purporting to so certify, admissible in evidence in all legal proceedings as of equal validity with the document so kept.][d]

(9) A document that purports to have been created by a person is presumed, in the absence of evidence to the contrary, to have been created by that person, and any statement contained in the document is presumed to have been made by the person unless the document expressly attributes its making to some other person.][e]

Amendments

a IFCMPA 2005, s 74 amends CLEA 2001, s 110A(1)(c) by deleting the word 'and' with effect from 1 July 2005.[1]

b IFCMPA 2005, s 74 amends CLEA 2001, s 110A(1)(c) by substituting '1999, and' for '1999' with effect from 1 July 2005.[2]

c IFCMPA 2005, s 74 inserts CLEA 2001, s 110A(1)(e) with effect from 1 July 2005.[3]

d IFCMPA 2005, s 74 inserts CLEA 2001, s 110A(8A) with effect from 1 July 2005.[4]

e CLEA 2001, s 110A was inserted by C(AA)A 2003, s 52 with effect from 6 April 2004.[5]

1 Investment Funds, Companies and Miscellaneous Provisions Act 2005 (Commencement) Order 2005 (SI 323/2005).

2 Investment Funds, Companies and Miscellaneous Provisions Act 2005 (Commencement) Order 2005 (SI 323/2005).

3 Investment Funds, Companies and Miscellaneous Provisions Act 2005 (Commencement) Order 2005 (SI 323/2005).

4 Investment Funds, Companies and Miscellaneous Provisions Act 2005 (Commencement) Order 2005 (SI 323/2005).

5 Companies (Auditing and Accounting) Act 2003 (Commencement) Order 2004 (SI 132/2004).

Definitions

'appropriate officer' CLEA 2001, s 110A; 'Companies Acts': CLEA 2001, s 3(1); 'Director': CLEA 2001, s 3(1); 'document': CA 1963, s 2(1) 'item': CLEA 2001, s 110A; 'functions': CLEA 2001, s 3(1); 'Minister': CLEA 2001, s 3(1); 'notice': CLEA 2001, s 110A; 'officer of the Director': CLEA 2001, s 3(1); 'person': IA 2005, s 18(c);

Notes

Evidence from Companies Act officials: Following the introduction of the ODCE, it became apparent that there were a number of practical difficulties arising out of the manner in which the Director and officers of the Director were able to bring information before the courts. CLEA 2001, s 110(A) was introduced to the Company (Auditing and Accounting) Bill 2003 by way of amendment to the Bill at Select Committee Stage.[1] CLEA 2001, s 110A seeks to streamline the giving of evidence in any legal proceedings by the Minister,[2] the Director,[3] an inspector appointed under CA 1990, Pt II[4] or by the Registrar[5] in respect of the performance of their respective statutory functions. It allows for the admission in evidence of certified copies of copies of or extracts from the records of these officers or their duly authorised representatives without further proof.[6] In addition, a certificate from any of these officers (following an examination of relevant records) as to the non-receipt of an item by a person or as to the receipt or non-receipt of a notice by a person or as to the posting of a notice to a stated person on a stated date or as to the filing or registration or delivery of a document at a stated place and on a stated date or time, shall be proof of those facts in the absence of evidence to the contrary.[7] For the purpose of the legal proceedings the officer does not need to give evidence in court to prove his certificate.[8]

CLEA 2001, s 110A was further amended with effect from 1July 2005[9] to enable the evidential rules contained in that section to be adopted by the Financial Regulator or a person appointed to act on behalf of the Financial Regulator.[10]

It is to be noted that the provision for certification is limited to allowing for the introduction of copy documents rather than originals and cannot be utilised to render otherwise inadmissible documents admissible.[11]

1 The Select Committee on Enterprise and Small Business, 29SEB1 No 3 (4 December 2003).

2 CLEA 2001, s 110A(1)(a).

3 CLEA 2001, s 110A(1)(b).

4 CLEA 2001, s 110A(1)(c).

5 CLEA 2001, s 110A(1)(d).

6 CLEA 2001, s 110A(2).

7 CLEA 2001, s 110A(1) and (2).

8 CLEA 2001, s 110A(3).

9 Investment Funds, Companies and Miscellaneous Provisions Act 2005 (Commencement) Order 2005 (SI 323/2005), r 4.

10 CLEA 2001, sub-s 110A(1)(e) and (8A) as inserted by IFCMPA 2005, s 74.

11 *Re Bovale Developments Ltd, Director of Corporate Enforcement v Bailey* [2008] 2 ILRM 13.

Proof of signatures and authority of agents: If a document has been prepared in pursuance of a requirement under the Companies Acts and purports to be signed by a specified person, that person will be presumed to have in fact signed the document in the absence of evidence to the contrary.[1] Similarly, if any such document is purportedly submitted on behalf of a person (ie by an agent or representative) it will be presumed to be that person's document unless he can establish that it was submitted without his knowledge or consent.[2] A document purporting to have been created by a person is presumed to have been created by that person (unless evidence to the contrary can be adduced) and any statements contained in such a document are presumed to have been made by the same person unless the documents specifically attributes the statement to someone else.[3]

1 CLEA 2001, s 110A(4).

2 CLEA 2001, s 110A(5).

3 CLEA 2001, s 110A(9).

---

111 Non-application of certain provisions concerning acquisition by subsidiary of shares in its holding company

(1) None of the following—

(a) section 32 or 60 of the Act of 1963,

(b) Part XI of the Act of 1990, or

(c) the European Communities (Public Limited Companies Subsidiaries) Regulations, 1997 (S.I. No. 67 of 1997),

shall apply to the subscription by a subsidiary for, or the acquisition or holding by a subsidiary of, shares in its holding company if the subsidiary is a member of an approved stock exchange specified in section 17(2) of the Stock Exchange Act, 1995, acting in its capacity as a professional dealer in securities in the normal course of its business.

(2) In addition to the meaning assigned to it by section 155 of the Act of 1963, 'subsidiary' in this section means a company or other body corporate referred to in paragraph (2) of Regulation 4 of the European Communities (Public Limited Companies Subsidiaries) Regulations, 1997 (S.I. No. 67 of 1997), which, by virtue of paragraph (1) of that Regulation, is deemed to be a subsidiary of a public limited company.

Definitions

'Act of 1963': CLEA 2001, s 3(1); 'Act of 1990': CLEA 2001, s 3(1); 'company': CA 1963, s 2(1); 'holding company': CA 1963, s 155; 'share': CA 1963, s 2(1); 'subsidiary': CA 1963, s 155.

Notes

Acquisition by listed dealer of shares in holding company: In the normal circumstances a subsidiary will be restricted by CA 1963, s 32 and CA 1990, s 224 as to the circumstances in which it may acquire shares in its holding company. Moreover, since such an acquisition constitutes financial assistance of a type otherwise prohibited by CA 1963, s 60(1), the whitewash procedure contained in CLEA 2001, s 60(2)–(11) would also have to be undergone in order to validate the acquisition. However, if the subsidiary is a member of an approved stock exchange[1] acting in the ordinary course of its business as a professional dealer in securities, these restrictions and limitations on the acquisition of shares in its holding company will not apply.

1 Under the Stock Exchange Act 1995, s 17(2) authorisation for membership of an approved stock exchange may come from the Central Bank or from the competent authority of another EU member state under the Investment Services Directive 93/22/EEC or from a EC credit institution under the First Banking Co-ordination Directive 77/780/EEC, as amended.

Extended definition of subsidiary: Apart from the circumstances prescribed by CA 1963, s 155 in which one company will be regarded as being a subsidiary of another, a body corporate (including a foreign company) will, for the purposes of this section,[1] also be deemed to be a subsidiary of a plc if the plc is itself a shareholder or member of that body corporate and controls alone, pursuant to a shareholders agreement, a majority of the voting rights.[2]

1 CLEA 2001, s 111(2).

2 EC(PLC Subsidiaries)R 1997, reg 4(1).

112 Amendment of Freedom of Information Act, 1997

The Freedom of Information Act, 1997, is amended—

(a)]in section 46(1), by the insertion of the following after paragraph (b):

'(ba) a record held or created under the Companies Acts, 1963 to 2001, by the Director of Corporate Enforcement or an officer of the Director (other than a record concerning the general administration of the Director's office),][a]', and

(b) [in the First Schedule, by the insertion in paragraph 1(2) of 'the Office of the Director of Corporate Enforcement,'][b]

Amendments

a CLEA 2001, s 112(a) inserts Freedom of Information Act 1997, s 46(1)(ba) with effect from 28 November 2001.[1]

b CLEA 2001, s 112(b) amends Freedom of Information Act 1997, Sch 1, para 1(2) with effect from 28 November 2001.[2]

1 Company Law Enforcement Act 2001 (Commencement) (No 3) Order 2001 (SI 523/2001).

2 Company Law Enforcement Act 2001 (Commencement) (No 3) Order 2001 (SI 523/2001).

Notes

Freedom of Information Act 1997: The effect of this section is to exempt the records of the ODCE from the provisions of the Freedom of Information Act 1997.

113 Amendment of section 7A of Bankers' Books Evidence Act, 1879

[Section 7A (inserted by the Central Bank Act, 1989) of the Bankers' Books Evidence Act, 1879, is amended by the insertion after 'Superintendent' and 'designated by him' of 'or the Director of Corporate Enforcement' and ', or officer of the Director of Corporate Enforcement nominated by the Director, as the case may be', respectively.][a]

Amendments

a CLEA 2001, s 113 amends the Bankers' Books Evidence Act 1879, s 7A (as inserted by the Central Bank Act 1989) with effect from 28 November 2001.[1]

1 Company Law Enforcement Act 2001 (Commencement) (No 3) Order 2001 (SI 523/2001).

Notes

Bankers' Books Evidence Act 1879: CLEA 2001, s 113 extends to the Director of Corporate Enforcement and his officers the entitlement to apply to court under the Bankers' Books Evidence Act 1879 for liberty to inspect and take copies of entries in bankers' books where there are reasonable grounds for believing that an indictable offence has been committed and that there is material in the possession of a bank which is likely to be of substantial value to the investigation of the offence.

114 Amendment of section 9 of Consumer Information Act, 1978

[Section 9 of the Consumer Information Act, 1978, is amended by the substitution of the following for subsection (11):][a]

'(11)(a) Where the Director is through illness or any other cause absent from duty or the office of Director is vacant, the Minister may appoint a person to perform the functions of the Director during such absence or vacancy.

(b) The Minister shall not appoint a person under paragraph (a) of this subsection to perform the functions of the Director for a continuous period of more than 6 months during a vacancy in the office of Director.

(c) The Minister may at any time terminate an appointment under paragraph (a) of this subsection.

(d) A person appointed under paragraph (a) of this subsection has all the powers, rights and duties conferred on the Director by this Act and each reference in this Act to the Director shall be deemed to include a reference to such a person.'.

Amendments

a CLEA 2001, s 114, substitutes the Consumer Information Act 1978, s 11 with effect from 1 October 2001.[1]

1 Company Law Enforcement Act 2001 (Commencement) (No 2) Order 2001 (SI 438/2001).

SCHEDULE

TRANSFER OF FUNCTIONS FROM MINISTER TO DIRECTOR
ACTS UNDER WHICH FUNCTIONS ARE TRANSFERRED

Section 14

PART 1
COMPANIES ACT, 1963
(NO. 33 OF 1963)

Item Section *(1)*	*Subsection(s)* *(2)*	*Section Title* *(3)*	*(4)*
1	131	(3), (4), (6)	Annual general meeting
2	384	(1)	Production and inspection of books when offence suspected

Amendments

CA 1963, ss 131 (3),(4),(6) and 384(1) are amended by the substitution for 'Minister', wherever occurring, of 'Director' with effect from 28 November 2001.[1] See amended Act.

1 Company Law Enforcement Act 2001 (Commencement) (No 3) Order 2001 (SI 523/2001).

Definitions

'Director': CLEA 2001, s 3(1); 'functions': CLEA 2001, s 3(1); 'Minister': CLEA 2001, s 3(1).

Cross reference

See CLEA 2001, s 14 and notes thereto.

PART 2
COMPANIES ACT, 1990
(NO. 33 OF 1990)

Item Section (1)	*Subsection(s)* (2)	*Section Title* (3)	(4)
3	11	(3)	Inspectors' report
4	12	(2)	Proceedings on inspectors' report
5	14	(1), (2), (5)	Appointment and power of inspectors to investigate ownership of company
6	15	(1)	Power to require information as to persons interested in shares or debentures
7	16	(1), (5), (6), (7), (8), (13), (16), (18)	Power to impose restrictions on shares or debentures
8	66	(1), (4), (5), (8)	Investigation of share dealing

Item Section	*Subsection(s)*	*Section Title*	
9	85	(6)	Penalty for failure to provide information
10	94	(2)	Obligation of professional secrecy
11	116	(3)	Cooperation with other authorities outside the State
12	117	(1)	Authorised persons Section 14.
13	18	(2)	Obligation of professional secrecy
14	160	(2)	Disqualification of certain persons from acting as directors or auditors of or managing companies
15	240	(4)	Offences

Amendments

CA 1963, ss 11(3), 12(2), 14(1), (2), (5), 15(1), 16(1), (5), (6), (7), (8), (13), (16), (18), 66(1), (4), (5), (8), 85(6), 94(2), 116(3), 117(1), 118(2), 160(2), 240(4) are amended by the substitution for 'Minister', wherever occurring, of 'Director' with effect from 28 November 2001.[1] See amended Act.

1 Company Law Enforcement Act 2001 (Commencement) (No 3) Order 2001 (SI 523/2001).

Definitions

'company': CA 1963, s 2(1); 'debenture': CA 1963, s 2(1); 'director': CA 1963, s 2(1); 'share': CA 1963, s 2(1); 'Minister': CLEA 2001, s 3(1); 'person': IA 2005, s 18(c).

Cross reference

See CLEA 2001, s 14 and notes thereto.

Companies (Auditing and Accounting) Act 2003

Number 44 of 2003

ARRANGEMENT OF SECTIONS

PART 1

PRELIMINARY MATTERS

PART 3

OTHER MEASURES TO STRENGTHEN THE REGULATION OF AUDITORS

PART 4

REGULATIONS AND MISCELLANEOUS MATTERS

SCHEDULE 1

TRANSFER OF FUNCTIONS TO SUPERVISORY AUTHORITY

SCHEDULE 2

An Act to provide for the establishment of a body to be known as the Irish Auditing And Accounting Supervisory Authority or, in the Irish language, Údarás Maoirseachta Iniúchta agus Cuntasaíochta na hÉireann, to give power to it to supervise the regulatory functions of the recognised accountancy bodies and other prescribed accountancy bodies, to amend company law to transfer to the supervisory authority existing functions relating to the recognition of accountancy bodies and to otherwise amend company law in relation to auditing, accounting and other matters. [23rd December, 2003]

Be It Enacted by the Oireachtas as Follows:

PART 1

PRELIMINARY MATTERS

1 Short title, collective citation and construction

(1) This Act may be cited as the Companies (Auditing and Accounting) Act 2003.

(2) This Act and the Companies Acts 1963 to 2001 may be cited together as the Companies Acts 1963 to 2003 and are to be construed together as one.

Notes

C(AA)A 2003, as its name suggests, is primarily concerned with regulating company accounts and the auditing of those accounts. It establishes the Irish Auditing and Accounting Supervisory Authority ('the Supervisory Authority') whose principal objects are—

(a) supervising how prescribed accountancy bodies regulate and monitor their members;

(b) promoting adherence to high professional standards in the auditing and accountancy profession;

(c) monitoring whether the accounts of certain classes of companies and other undertakings comply with the Companies Acts; and

(d) acting as a specialist source of advice to the Minister on auditing and accounting matters.[1]

C(AA)A 2003 also revises the qualifications for appointment as an auditor[2] whilst at the same time increasing the financial threshold for the audit exemption which was introduced by C(A)(No 2)A 1999.[3] Other measures adopted include the setting up of audit committees for plcs and large private companies and other relevant undertakings[4] as well as requiring greater disclosure of a company's accounting policies[5] and any material departure from applicable accounting standards.[6] Also, in a move designed to identify the financial dependence or otherwise of auditors on a particular client or client, the accounts of a company must now disclose the amount (other than *de minimis* sums) paid by the company and its connected undertakings during the financial year to the auditors and affiliates of the auditor for audit work, audit-related work and non-audit work respectively.

In the case of plcs and large private companies limited by shares, one of the most significant amendments was to introduce a stipulation that the directors' report must include a compliance statement and related statement concerning the company's adherence during the financial year, not only with the requirements of the Companies Acts, but also with the requirement of the Tax Acts and any other enactments that provide a legal framework within which the company operates and that may materially affect the company's financial statements.[7] It is also provided that the reasonableness or otherwise of the directors' compliance statement and related statement should be reviewed by the auditors who must in turn report thereon as part of their auditors report.[8] The directors' compliance statement, as enacted, is now a dead letter following the CLRG's recommendations accepted by Government, that s 45 never be commenced and be replaced by a greatly mitigated, more proportionate and reasonable provision referred to in the CLRG's report as 'section x'.

1 C(AA)A 2003, s 8(1).
2 C(AA)A 2003, s 35.
3 C(AA)A 2003, s 53.
4 CA 1990, s 205B as inserted by C(AA)A 2003, s 42 (not yet commenced).
5 CA 1990, s 205C as inserted by C(AA)A 2003, s 43.
6 CA 1990, s 205A as inserted by C(AA)A 2003, s 41.
7 CA 1990, s 205E as inserted by C(AA)A 2003, s 45.
8 CA 1990, s 205F as inserted by C(AA)A 2003, s 45.

---

2 Commencement

(1) This Act comes into operation on the day that the Minister may, by order, appoint.

(2) Different days may be appointed under this section, by one or more orders, for different purposes or different provisions of this Act.

Notes

Commencement of C(AA)A 2003: The following provisions of C(AA)A 2003 have been brought into effect:

Part I:[1]

Ss 52, 53(a), (c), (d) and (e), 54, 55, 56 and 57;[1]

Schedule 2 (other than amendments at item 1 to ss 115(6) and 128(4) of the CA 1963 and the amendments at item 9 to the Companies Act 1990);[1]

S 53(b) for financial years of companies beginning on or after 1 July 2004;[1]

From 17 May 2004, s 46, and s 47 in so far as it substitutes for sub-s (6) of s 128 of CA 1963 sub-ss (6) and (6A), sub-s (6B) other than para (b) and sub-s (6C)[1].

From 1 December 2005, s 47 to the extent that it is not already in operation by virtue of SI 132/2004.[2]

From 13 December 2004:[3]

Ss 4 to 8;

Ss 11 to 14;

S 15 (other than sub-s (2));

Ss 16 to 22;

S 30, 31 and 33;

Ss 48 to 51;

S 58.

From 3 February 2006:[4]

S 9 (other than paragraph (1) of sub-s (2))

S 10;

Ss 23 to 25;

Ss 27 and 28;

S 29 (other than sub-s (5));

S 32;

Sch 1.

From 1 March 2007:[5]

S 37(a), (b), (c) and (e)

Following the Government's decision to accept the CLRG's report, section 45 will never be commenced.

1 Companies (Auditing and Accounting) Act 2003 (Commencement) Order, 2004 (SI 132/2004).
2 Companies (Auditing and Accounting) Act 2003 (Commencement) Order 2005 (SI 686/2005).
3 Companies (Auditing and Accounting) Act 2003 (Commencement) (No 2) Order 2005 (SI 791/ 2005).
4 Companies (Auditing and Accounting) Act 2003 (Commencement) Order 2006 (SI 56/2006).
5 Companies (Auditing and Accounting) Act 2003 (Commencement) Order 2006 (SI 61/2007).

3 Interpretation

(1) In this Act—

'Act of 1963' means the Companies Act 1963;

'Act of 1986' means the Companies (Amendment) Act 1986;

'Act of 1990' means the Companies Act 1990;

'Companies Acts' means the Companies Act 1963 and every enactment, including this Act, that is to be construed as one with that Act.

(2) In this Act—

(a) a reference to a section, Part or Schedule is to a section or Part of, or a Schedule to, this Act, unless it is indicated that a reference to some other enactment is intended,

(b) a reference to a subsection, paragraph or subparagraph is to the subsection, paragraph or subparagraph of the provision in which the reference occcurs, unless it is indicated that reference to some other provision is intended, and

(c) a reference to any other enactment is to that enactment as amended by or under any other enactment, including this Act, unless the context otherwise requires.

PART 2
IRISH AUDITING AND ACCOUNTING SUPERVISORY AUTHORITY

4 Interpretation of this Part

(1) In this Part, except where the context otherwise requires—

'amount of turnover' and 'balance sheet total' have the same meanings as in section 8 of the Act of 1986;

'board' means the board of directors of the Supervisory Authority;

'chief executive officer' means the Chief Executive Officer of the Supervisory Authority;

'designated body' means a body that, under section 6(2), is a designated body at the relevant time;

'disciplinary committee' means any disciplinary committee or tribunal (however called) of a prescribed accountancy body;

'enactment' means a statute or an instrument made under a power conferred by a statute;

'functions' includes duties and responsibilities;

'member', in relation to a prescribed accountancy body, means—

(a) a person, or

(b) a firm,

that is, or was at the relevant time, subject to the investigation and disciplinary procedures approved under section 9(2)(c) for that body;

'Minister' means the Minister for Enterprise, Trade and Employment;

'parent undertaking' has the same meaning as in the 1992 Regulations;

'prescribed accountancy body' means—

(a) a recognised accountancy body, or

(b) any other body of accountants that is prescribed under section 48(1)(a) for the purposes of this Act;

'recognised accountancy body' means a body of accountants recognised for the purposes of section 187 of the Act of 1990;

'reserve fund' means the fund established under section 15;

'standards', in relation to a prescribed accountancy body, means the rules, regulations and standards that body applies to its members and to which, by virtue of their membership, they are obliged to adhere;

'subsidiary undertaking' has the same meaning as in the 1992 Regulations;

'superannuation benefits' means pensions, gratuities and other allowances payable on resignation, retirement or death;

'Supervisory Authority' means the company designated by the Minister under section 5(1);

'the 1992 Regulations' means the European Communities (Companies: Group Accounts) Regulations 1992 (S.I. No. 201 of 1992);

'the 1993 Regulations' means the European Communities (Accounts) Regulations 1993 (S.I. No. 396 of 1993).

(2) In this Part 'material interest' is to be construed in accordance with section 2(3) of the Ethics in Public Office Act 1995.

Definitions

'Act of 1986': C(AA)A 2003, s 3(1); 'Act of 1990': C(AA)A 2003, s 3(1); 'prescribed': CA 1963, s 2(1).

Notes

Material Interest: The phrase 'material interest' has the same definition as in the Ethics in Public Office Act 1995, s 2(3), namely that:

'a person or a connected person has a material interest in a matter if the consequence or effect—

(a) of the performance by the person of a function of his or her office, directorship, designated position, or position as a special adviser, as the case may be, or

(b) of any decision made in relation to or in the course or as a result of the performance of such a function by the person, concerning that matter may be to confer on or withhold from the person or the connected person a significant benefit without also conferring it on or withholding it from persons in general or a class of persons which is of significant size having regard to all the circumstances and of which the person or the connected person is a member.'

Prescribed accountancy bodies

In addition to those accountancy bodies recognised for the purposes of s 187 of CA 1990, a further three bodies have been designated as 'prescribed accountancy bodies' by virtue of the Companies (Auditing and Accounting) Act 2003 (Prescribed Accountancy Bodies) Regulations 2006 (SI 57/2006). The three additional bodies are the Association of International Accountants; the Chartered Institute of Management Accountants; and the Chartered Institute of Public Finance and Accountancy. It should be noted that such prescription does not, however, confer rights to conduct statutory audits on the members of these bodies.

---

5 Establishment of Supervisory Authority

(1) The Minister may designate a public company to perform the functions and exercise the powers of the Supervisory Authority under this Act, if the following requirements are satisfied:

(a) the company is formed and registered under the Companies Acts after the commencement of this section;

(b) the company is a company limited by guarantee;

(c) the name of the company is the Irish Auditing and Accounting Supervisory Authority or in the Irish language Údarás Maoirseachta Iniúchta agus Cuntasaíochta na hÉireann;

(d) the memorandum of association and articles of association of the company are consistent with this Act.

(2) Section 6(1)(b) of the Act of 1963 does not apply to a company where the Minister informs the registrar of companies in writing that the Minister proposes to designate the company under subsection (1).

Definitions

'Act of 1963': C(AA)A 2003, s 3(1); 'articles': CA 1963, s 2(1); 'Companies Acts': C(AA)A 2003, s 3(1); 'company': CA 1963, s 2(1); 'company limited by guarantee': CA 1963, s 2(1); 'memorandum': CA 1963, s 2(1); 'the Minister': C(AA)A 2003, s 4(1); 'the registrar of companies': CA 1963, s 2(1); 'Supervisory Authority': C(AA)A 2003, s 4(1).

Notes

The Irish Auditing and Accounting Supervisory Authority: C(AA)A 2003 provides for the establishment of the Irish Auditing and Accounting Supervisory Authority ('the Supervisory Authority') as a company limited by guarantee,[1] albeit with a statutory dispensation from the requirement to have the word 'limited' at the end of its name.[2] Its membership is comprised of all prescribed accountancy bodies[3] which are incorporated[4] together with one nominee from each prescribed accountancy body which is unincorporated.[5] The various designated bodies specified (or their nominees where such parties are neither individuals nor bodies corporate) are also members.[6]

1 C(AA)A 2003, s 5(1)(b).
2 C(AA)A 2003, s 5(2).

3 See the notes to CA 1990, s 187 for the accountancy bodies that have been prescribed by the Minister.
4 C(AA)A 2003, s 6(1)(a).
5 C(AA)A 2003, s 6(1)(b).
6 C(AA)A 2003, s 6(1)(c) and (d).

The objects, powers and functions of the Supervisory Authority: The principal objects of the Supervisory Authority objects are –

(a) supervising how prescribed accountancy bodies regulate and monitor their members;
(b) promoting adherence to high professional standards in the auditing and accountancy profession;
(c) monitoring whether the accounts of certain classes of companies and other undertakings comply with the Companies Acts; and
(d) acting as a specialist source of advice to the Minister on auditing and accounting matters.[1]

To this end, the functions of the Supervisory Authority include, but are not limited to, the following—[2]

(a) granting recognition to bodies of accountants for the purposes of CA 1990, s 187;
(b) attaching conditions to the recognition of bodies of accountants, including terms and conditions—
    (i) requiring changes to and approval by the Supervisory Authority of their regulatory plans; and
    (ii) requiring their annual reports to the Supervisory Authority on their regulatory plans to be prepared in the manner and form directed by the Supervisory Authority;
(c) requiring changes to and approving the constitution and bye-laws of each prescribed accountancy body, including its investigation and disciplinary procedures and standards, as well as any amendments thereto;
(d) conducting enquiries into whether a prescribed accountancy body has complied with the investigation and disciplinary procedures approved for it under C(AA)A 2003, s 23(c);
(e) intervening in the disciplinary processes of prescribed accountancy bodies and, where appropriate, imposing sanctions on such bodies;[3]
(f) undertaking investigations into possible breaches of the standards of a prescribed accountancy body;[4]
(g) supervising how each recognised accountancy body monitors its members and undertaking reviews of those members;[5]
(h) co-operating with the recognised accountancy bodies and other interested parties in developing standards relating to the independence of auditors and monitoring the effectiveness of those standards;
(i) monitoring the effectiveness of provisions of the Companies Acts relating to the independence of auditors;
(j) supervising the investigation and disciplinary procedures of each prescribed accountancy body, *inter alia*, by requiring access to its records and by requiring explanations about the performance of its regulatory and monitoring duties;
(k) co-operating with the prescribed accountancy bodies and other interested parties in developing auditing and accounting standards and practice notes;
(l) reviewing whether the accounts of companies and undertakings of the type referred to in C(AA)A 2003, s 26 (being plcs large private companies limited by shares, and their respective parent undertakings and subsidiary undertakings) comply with the accounting

requirements of the Companies Acts and making application to the High Court to ensure compliance;[6]

(m) arranging for the regulation and supervision of individually authorised auditors by recognised accountancy bodies;[7]

(n) performing any other duties or discharging any other responsibilities imposed on it from time to time by the Companies Acts.

The Supervisory Authority may also adopt rules and issue guidelines concerning any matter that relates to its functions or powers and in the case of an actual or anticipated failure to comply with such a rule or guideline by a prescribed accountancy body or recognised accountancy body it may apply to the High Court for an order compelling compliance.[8]

1 C(AA)A 2003, s 8(1).
2 C(AA)A 2003, s 9.
3 See C(AA)A 2003, s 23 regarding the imposition of such sanctions.
4 See C(AA)A 2003, s 24 regarding the undertaking of such investigations.
5 See C(AA)A 2003, s 25 regarding the exercise of such supervision.
6 See C(AA)A 2003, s 26 regarding the extent of this power of review and regarding the categories of companies subject to such review.
7 See CA 1990, s 187 regarding the circumstances in which a person may have been individually authorised to act as an auditor.
8 C(AA)A 203, s 10(3) and (4).

The directors and chief executive of the Supervisor Authority: The board of directors of the Supervisory Authority is comprised of not more than 14 Ministerial appointments and a chief executive.[1] With regard to the Ministerial appointments, they comprise three persons nominated by the prescribed accountancy bodies, one nominee for each of the designated bodies and two Ministerial nominees (one of whom also acts as chairman of the board).[2] The Minister may remove any of these appointees for stated reason a any time, regardless of whether they were originally nominated by him or by one of the other prescribed accountancy bodies or designated bodies.[3] As for the Chief Executive, he is appointed by the other directors who, subject to Ministerial approval, may determine the terms and conditions on and subject to which he holds office (including terms and conditions relating to remuneration and allowances).[4] He has day-to-day responsibility for carrying on, managing and generally controlling the administration of the Supervisory Authority and performing such other functions as may, from time to time, be determined by the board.[5] The Chief Executive is subject to removal at any time by the other members of the board, albeit that his removal, if inconsistent with or in breach of his terms of employment, may entitle him to compensation for loss of office.[6]

In order to ensure the independence of the directors, it is expressly stipulated that the members of the Supervisory Authority cannot instruct them how to act.[7] On the other hand, whilst the Minister is not entitled to give directions to the Supervisory Authority concerning the discharge of the three-yearly work programmes which the Supervisory Authority is required to submit to him,[8] some degree of indirect control is vested in the Minister regarding the discharge of the Supervisory Authority's functions since it is he, acting with the consent of the Minister for Finance, whose approval is required for each annual programme of expenditure of the Supervisory Authority.[9]

1 C(AA)A 2003, s 11(1).
2 C(AA)A 2003, s 11(2). So as to ensure that the Supervisory Authority is not controlled by accountants, C(AA)A 2003, s 11(3) and (4) stipulate that at any one time there not more than four of the Ministerial appointments can be members of a prescribed accountancy body.
3 C(AA)A 2003, s 11(8)–(10). The Minister must fill any vacancy so arising, by appointing a director nominated by the same body that nominated the now removed director: C(AA)A 2003, s 11(11).

4 C(AA)A 2003, s 12(1) and (2).

5 C(AA)A 2003, s 12(1).

6 *Nelson v James Nelson and Sons Ltd* [1914] 2 KB 770; *Southern Foundries (1926) Ltd v Shirlaw* [1940] AC 701; *Shindler v Northern Raincoat Co Ltd* [1960] 1 WLR 1038. See, however, CA 1990, s 28 regarding the limitations on fixed term contracts of employment for directors.

7 C(AA)A 2003, s 11(7).

8 See C(AA)A 2003, s 13(1) and (10).

9 C(AA)A 2003, s 13(4).

Funding of the Supervisory Authority: In so far as the funding of the Supervisory Authority is concerned, up to 40% of each year's programme of expenditure may be funded by way of grant from the Oireachtas[1] with up to 60% being funded by way of levy on the prescribed accountancy bodies, which levy must first be approved by the Minister.[2] The Supervisory Authority is also required to establish a reserve fund into which a portion of the aforementioned moneys is to be paid.[3] This amount may be topped up by a levy on plcs and certain large private companies, undertakings and groups.[4] The amount of this levy, which requires Ministerial consent,[5] cannot exceed the amount paid into the reserve fund by the Supervisory Authority itself for that financial year out of its own current income.[6] The purpose of the reserve fund is to finance: (a) the performance of the Supervisory Authority's investigative functions under C(AA)A 2003, s 24; (b) the conduct of reviews of members of recognised accountancy bodies under C(AA)A 2003, s 25, and (c) the conduct of reviews under C(A)A 2003, s 26 as to whether the accounts of those plcs and large private limited companies, undertakings and groups comply with the accounting requirements of the Companies Acts.[7] In this regard, the Minister may specify a limit on the amount which to be held in the reserve fund at any one time.[8]

1 C(AA)A 2003, s 14(1).

2 C(AA)A 2003, s 14(2)–(9).

3 C(AA)A 2003, s 15(1)(b).

4 C(AA)A 2003, s 15(2).

5 C(AA)A 2003, s 15(3)(b).

6 C(AA)A 2003, s 15(3)(a).

7 C(AA)A 2003, s 15(1)(a).

8 C(AA)A 2003, s 15(1)(a).

6 Membership

(1) The Supervisory Authority is to consist of the following members:

(a) each prescribed accountancy body that is a body corporate;

(b) if a prescribed accountancy body is not a body corporate, an individual or body corporate nominated by that prescribed accountancy body to be a member;

(c) each designated body that is a body corporate;

(d) if a designated body is not a body corporate, an individual or body corporate nominated by that designated body to be a member.

(2) Unless a regulation under section 48(1)(b) provides otherwise, each of the following is a designated body for the purposes of this section and section 11:

(a) the Irish Business and Employers Confederation;

(b) the Irish Congress of Trade Unions;

(c) the Irish Association of Investment Managers;

(d) the Irish Stock Exchange;

(e) the Pensions Board;

(f) the Irish Financial Services Regulatory Authority;

(g) the Revenue Commissioners;

(h) the Director of Corporate Enforcement;

(i) the Law Society of Ireland;

(j) any body prescribed under section 48(1)(b) as a designated body.

Definitions

'designated body': C(AA)A 2003, s 4(1); 'the Minister': C(AA)A 2003, s 4(1); 'prescribed accountancy body': C(AA)A 2003, s 4(1); 'Supervisory Authority': C(AA)A 2003, s 4(1).

Notes

See the notes to C(AA)A 2003, s 5.

---

7 Alterations in memorandum and articles of association

Any alteration that is made in the memorandum of association or articles of association of the Supervisory Authority takes effect only if the alteration is made with the Minister's prior approval.

Definitions

'articles': CA 1963, s 2(1); 'memorandum': CA 1963, s 2(1); 'the Minister': C(AA)A 2003, s 4(1); 'Supervisory Authority': C(AA)A 2003, s 4(1).

Notes

Alteration of Memorandum and Articles of the Supervisory Authority: For the normal rules governing the alteration of the memorandum and articles of a company limited by guarantee, see CA 1963, ss 9, 10, 15, 23 and 28. In addition to complying with such of these procedures as may be applicable in any given case, the Supervisory Authority must also obtain the Minister's consent to the proposed alteration before it may become effective.[1]

1 C(AA)A 2003, s 7.

---

8 Objects

(1) The principal objects of the Supervisory Authority, which are to be included in its memorandum of association, are—

(a) to supervise how the prescribed accountancy bodies regulate and monitor their members,

(b) to promote adherence to high professional standards in the auditing and accountancy profession,

(c) to monitor whether the accounts of certain classes of companies and other undertakings comply with the Companies Acts, and, [where applicable, Article 4 of the IAS Regulation, and][a]

(d) to act as a specialist source of advice to the Minister on auditing and accounting matters.

(2) This section does not prevent or restrict the inclusion in the memorandum of association of all objects and powers, consistent with this Act, that are reasonable, necessary or proper for, or incidental or ancillary to, the due attainment of the principal objects of the Supervisory Authority.

Amendments

a Amended by Sch 1 Pt 5 of EC(IFRSMA)R 2005 (SI 116/2005).

Definitions

'Companies Acts': C(AA)A 2003, s 3(1); 'IAS Regulation': CA 1963, s 2(1); 'memorandum': CA 1963, s 2(1); 'the Minister': C(AA)A 2003, s 4(1); 'prescribed accountancy body': C(AA)A 2003, s 4(1); 'Supervisory Authority': C(AA)A 2003, s 4(1).

Notes

See the notes to C(AA)A 2003, s 5 and to CA 1963, s 148 to 151.

9 Functions

(1) The Supervisory Authority shall do all things necessary and reasonable to further its objects.

(2) Without limiting its responsibilities under subsection (1), the functions of the Supervisory Authority are as follows:

(a) to grant recognition to bodies of accountants for the purposes of section 187 of the Act of 1990;

(b) to attach under section 192 of the Act of 1990 terms and conditions to the recognition of bodies of accountants, including terms and conditions—

(i) requiring changes to and the approval by the Supervisory Authority of their regulatory plans, and

(ii) requiring their annual reports to the Supervisory Authority on their regulatory plans to be prepared in the manner and form directed by the Supervisory Authority;

(c) to require changes to and to approve—

(i) the constitution and bye-laws of each prescribed accountancy body, including its investigation and disciplinary procedures and its standards, and

(ii) any amendments to the approved constitution or bye-laws of each prescribed accountancy body, including amendments to its investigation and disciplinary procedures and to its standards;

(d) to conduct under section 23 enquiries into whether a prescribed accountancy body has complied with the investigation and disciplinary procedures approved for that body under paragraph (c);

(e) to impose under section 23 sanctions on prescribed accountancy bodies;

(f) to undertake under section 24 investigations into possible breaches of the standards of a prescribed accountancy body;

(g) to supervise how each recognised accountancy body monitors its members and to undertake under section 25 reviews of those members;

(h) to co-operate with the recognised accountancy bodies and other interested parties in developing standards relating to the independence of auditors and to monitor the effectiveness of those standards;

(i) to monitor the effectiveness of provisions of the Companies Acts relating to the independence of auditors;

(j) to supervise the investigation and disciplinary procedures of each prescribed accountancy body, including by requiring access to its records and by requiring explanations about the performance of its regulatory and monitoring duties;

(k) to co-operate with the prescribed accountancy bodies and other interested parties in developing auditing and accounting standards and practice notes;

(l) to review under section 26 whether the accounts of companies and undertakings referred to in that section comply with the Companies Acts [and, where applicable, Article 4 of the IAS Regulation][a] and to make applications to the High Court to ensure compliance;

(m) to arrange for the regulation and supervision of individually authorised auditors by recognised accountancy bodies;

[(ma) to perform the functions conferred on it by transparency (regulated markets) law (within the meaning of Part 3 of the Investment Funds, Companies and Miscellaneous Provisions Act 2006) in respect of matters referred to in Article 24(4)(h) of the Transparency (Regulated Markets) Directive (within the meaning of that Part);][b]

(n) to perform any other duties or discharge any other responsibilities imposed on it by this Act or the Companies Acts.

Amendments

a Amended by Sch 1 Pt 5 of EC(IFRSMA)R 2005.

b Section 9(2)(ma) inserted by the IFCMPA 2006, s 16.

Definitions

'Act of 1990': C(AA)A 2003, s 3(1); 'Companies Acts': C(AA)A 2003, s 3(1); 'IAS Regulation': CA 1963, s 2(1); 'the Minister': C(AA)A 2003, s 4(1); 'prescribed': CA 1963, s 2(1); 'prescribed accountancy body': C(AA)A 2003, s 4(1); 'recognised accountancy body': C(AA)A 2003, s 4(1); 'Supervisory Authority': C(AA)A 2003, s 4(1); Transparency (Regulated Markets) Directive: IFCMPA 2006, s 19(1); 'transparency (regulated markets) law': IFCMPA 2006, s 19(1).

Notes

See the notes to C(AA)A 2003, s 5 and to CA 1963, ss 148 to 151.

Article 24(4)(h)

Article 24(4)(h) of Directive 2004/109/EC ('the Transparency Directive') requires member states to establish Competent Authorities with the power that information referred to in the Transparency Directive (for example, interim or half-yearly financial information) is drawn up in accordance with the relevant reporting framework and to take appropriate measures in cases of discovered infringements. Section 9(2)(ma) confers this responsibility on the Irish Auditing and Accounting Supervisory Authority.

10 General powers

(1) The Supervisory Authority has the power to do anything that appears to it to be requisite, advantageous or incidental to, or to facilitate, the performance of its functions and that is not inconsistent with any enactment.

(2) A power conferred by subsection (1) is not to be considered to be limited merely by implication from another provision, whether of this or any other Act, that confers a power on the Supervisory Authority.

(3) The Supervisory Authority may adopt rules and issue guidelines concerning any matter that relates to its functions or powers.

(4) The Supervisory Authority may apply to the High Court for an order under section 29(7) compelling—

(a) a prescribed accountancy body to comply with a rule adopted or guideline issued under subsection (3) of this [section,][a]

(b) a recognised accountancy body to comply with a term or condition attached under section 192 of the Act of 1990 (before or after the amendment of that Act by section 32 of this Act) to the [recognition of that body, or][b]

[(c) a person on whom a relevant obligation or obligations is or are imposed to comply with that obligation or those obligations,][c]

if, in the Authority's opinion, [the body or other person concerned may fail or has failed to comply with the rule, guideline, term or condition or obligation or obligations, as the case may be.][d]

[(5) In subsection (4), the reference to a relevant obligation or obligations that is or are imposed on a person is a reference to an obligation or obligations that is or are imposed on the person by—

(a) provisions of transparency (regulated markets) law (within the meaning of Part 3 of the Investment Funds, Companies and Miscellaneous Provisions Act 2006) that implement Article 24(4)(h) of the Transparency (Regulated Markets) Directive (within the meaning of that Part), or

(b) rules adopted by the Supervisory Authority under subsection (3) concerning the matters that relate to its functions under section 9(2)(ma).][e]

Amendments

a Amended by IFCMPA 2006, s 17(a)(i).

b Amended by IFCMPA 2006, s 17(a)(ii).

c Amended by IFCMPA 2006, s 17(a)(iii).

d Amended by IFCMPA 2006, s 17(a)(iv).

e Inserted by IFCMPA 2006, s 17(b).

Definitions

'Act of 1990': C(AA)A 2003, s 3(1); 'prescribed': CA 1963, s 2(1); 'prescribed accountancy body': C(AA)A 2003, s 4(1); 'recognised accountancy body': C(AA)A 2003, s 4(1); 'Supervisory Authority': C(AA)A 2003, s 4(1); 'Transparency (Regulated Markets) Directive': IFCMPA 2006, s 19(1); 'transparency (regulated markets) law': Investment Funds, Companies and Miscellaneous Provisions Act, 2006, s 19(1).

Notes

Incidental powers: The provisions of C(AA)A 2003, s 10(1) and (2) conferring on the Supervisory Authority power to do anything appearing to be requisite, advantageous or incidental to or facilitating the performance of its statutory functions, is in essence a statutory restatement of the principles regarding implied powers which apply to every company and which are to be found in *Attorney General v Great Eastern Railway*.[1] It is important to note though, that whilst one of the implied powers normally enjoyed by a company is the power to borrow money,[2] in the case of the Supervisory Authority that power cannot be exercised except with the consent of the Minister and the Minister for Finance, and even then subject to such conditions as they may impose.[3] Similarly, the powers to engage employees and to pay them pensions, which are impliedly enjoyed by every company,[4] are circumscribed in the case of the Supervisory Authority, since the number, grades and terms and conditions of its staff and the terms of any superannuation scheme for staff members (including the chief executive) all require the consent of both the Minister and the Minister for Finance.[5]

Transparency (Regulated Markets) Directive: See Notes to s 9.

1 *Attorney General v Great Eastern Railway* (1880) 5 App Cas 473.

2 *General Auction Estate and Monetary Co v Smith* [1891] 3 Ch 432; *Re Introductions Ltd* [1970] Ch 199.

3 C(AA)A 2003, s 14(9).

4 *Ferguson v Wilson* (1866) 2 Ch App 77, 89; *Henderson v Bank of Australasia* (1888) 40 Ch D 170.

5 C(AA)A 2003, ss 17(7) and 20(3).

Making and enforcing rules and guidelines: See C(AA)A 2003, s 5 and the notes thereto.

11 Board of directors

(1) Subject to a regulation under section 48(1)(d), the board of directors of the Supervisory Authority is to consist of—

(a) not more than 14 directors (including the chairperson and the deputy chairperson) appointed by the Minister under subsection (2), and

(b) the person holding the office of chief executive officer who, by virtue of that office, is a director.

(2) Subject to a regulation under section 48(1)(d), the directors appointed by the Minister shall include—

(a) 3 persons nominated jointly by agreement among the prescribed accountancy bodies,

(b) 2 persons nominated by the Minister, one of whom—

(i) is neither an officer or employee of the Minister nor a member, officer or employee of a prescribed accountancy body, and

(ii) is appointed as chairperson by the Minister, and

(c) for each designated body, one person nominated by that body.

(3) Subject to a regulation under section 48(1)(d), the board shall not include at any one time more than 4 directors appointed under subsection (2) who are members of prescribed accountancy bodies, and of those 4 directors—

(a) 3 may be nominees of the prescribed accountancy bodies, and

(b) one may be a nominee of a designated body.

(4) If, at any time, more than one designated body proposes to nominate a member of a prescribed accountancy body for appointment to the board, the designated bodies proposing to do so shall decide among themselves which one of them is to nominate such a member.

(5) The directors may select the deputy chairperson from among those directors who are not members of a prescribed accountancy body.

(6) The term of office of a director appointed under subsection (2) shall be specified by the Minister when appointing the director and, subject to subsection (12), may not be less than 3 or more than 5 years.

(7) The members of the Supervisory Authority may not instruct the directors, at any meeting of those members or by any other means, regarding the carrying out of their duties as directors of the Supervisory Authority.

(8) Section 182 of the Act of 1963 does not apply to the Supervisory Authority.

(9) A director may resign by letter addressed to the Minister and copied to the Supervisory Authority, and the resignation takes effect on the date the Minister receives the letter.

(10) At any time, the Minister may remove for stated reasons any director appointed under subsection (2), including a director nominated under subsection (2)(b).

(11) The Minister shall fill any vacancy that arises on the board as a consequence of the resignation or removal of a director by appointing a replacement nominated in the same manner as the replaced director.

(12) A director appointed under subsection (11) to replace another holds office for the remainder of the replaced director's term of office, and the same terms and conditions apply to the new appointee.

(13) The directors may act despite one or more vacancies in their numbers.

Definitions

'Act of 1963': C(AA)A 2003, s 3(1); 'director': CA 1963, s 2(1); 'the Minister': C(AA)A 2003, s 4(1); 'prescribed': CA 1963, s 2(1); 'prescribed accountancy body': C(AA)A 2003, s 4(1); 'recognised accountancy body': C(AA)A 2003, s 4(1); 'Supervisory Authority': C(AA)A 2003, s 4(1).

Notes

See the notes to C(AA)A 2003, s 5.

---

12 Chief executive officer

(1) The directors appointed under section 11(2) shall appoint a chief executive officer to—

(a) carry on, manage and control generally the administration and business of the Supervisory Authority, and

(b) perform any other functions that may be determined by the board.

(2) The chief executive officer holds office on and subject to the terms and conditions (including terms and conditions relating to remuneration and allowances) that the directors appointed under section 11(2) may, with the approval of the Minister given with the consent of the Minister for Finance, determine.

(3) The directors appointed under section 11(2) may remove the chief executive officer from office at any time.

Definitions

'director': CA 1963, s 2(1); 'the Minister': C(AA)A 2003, s 4(1); 'Supervisory Authority': C(AA)A 2003, s 4(1).

Notes

See the notes to C(AA)A 2003, s 5.

---

13 Work programme

(1) The Supervisory Authority shall prepare and submit to the Minister a work programme for—

(a) in the case of the initial work programme, the period specified by the Minister, and

(b) in the case of each subsequent work programme, the period of 3 years beginning on the day after the last day of the period covered by the preceding work programme.

(2) In preparing the work programme, the Supervisory Authority shall have regard to the need to ensure the most beneficial, effective and efficient use of its resources and shall include the following information:

(a) the key strategies and activities the Supervisory Authority will pursue to further its objects and perform its functions;

(b) the outputs the Supervisory Authority aims to achieve and against which its performance will be assessed;

(c) the staff, resources and expenditures (including an annual programme of expenditure) necessary to pursue the strategies and activities mentioned in paragraph (a).

(3) In addition to capital and other expenditures, the annual programme of expenditure must include the amount of revenue to be received under section 14(1) and (2) that is to be paid into the reserve fund.

(4) With the consent of the Minister for Finance and after considering the views of the prescribed accountancy bodies, the Minister may approve, with or without amendment, the annual programme of expenditure.

(5) If the annual programme of expenditure is amended under subsection (4), the Supervisory Authority—

(a) may revise any other part of the work programme, and

(b) if it does so, shall submit to the Minister the revised work programme, including the annual programme of expenditure as amended under subsection (4).

(6) The Supervisory Authority may—

(a) if it considers it necessary to do so, undertake an interim review of a work programme, and

(b) submit to the Minister, within the period covered by that programme, an amended or supplementary work programme, including an amended or supplementary annual programme of expenditure.

(7) Subsections (4) and (5) apply with any necessary changes if an amended or a supplementary annual programme of expenditure is submitted to the Minister.

(8) Subject to subsection (9), the Minister shall ensure that a copy of each work programme (including each revised, amended or supplementary work programme) is laid before each House of the Oireachtas not later than 60 days after the date on which it was submitted to the Minister.

(9) If a revised work programme (including a revised amended or supplementary work programme) is submitted to the Minister before the unrevised work programme is laid before the Houses of the Oireachtas as required by subsection (8), only the revised work programme need be laid before the Houses.

(10) The Minister may not give directions to the Supervisory Authority concerning the discharge of a work programme, including an amended or a supplementary work programme.

Definitions

'the Minister': C(AA)A 2003, s 4(1); 'prescribed': CA 1963, s 2(1); 'prescribed accountancy body': C(AA)A 2003, s 4(1); 'Supervisory Authority': C(AA)A 2003, s 4(1).

Notes

See the notes to C(AA)A 2003, s 5.

---

14 Funding

(1) For the purposes specified in subsection (3), in each financial year, a grant not exceeding 40 per cent of the programme of expenditure approved for that year under section 13, shall, subject to the conditions, if any, that the Minister thinks proper, be paid to the Supervisory Authority out of money provided by the Oireachtas.

(2) For the purposes specified in subsection (3), the Supervisory Authority may impose, with the Minister's consent and subject to subsections (4) to (6), one or more levies in each financial year of the Supervisory Authority on each prescribed accountancy body.

(3) Money received by the Supervisory Authority under this section may be used only for the purposes of meeting expenses properly incurred by it in performing its functions and exercising its powers under—

(a) sections 24 and 26, in the case of money set aside for, or paid into, the reserve fund in accordance with section 15,

or

(b) any provision of this Act, other than sections 24 and 26, in the case of money not so set aside for, or paid into, that fund.

(4) The total amount levied in any financial year of the Supervisory Authority on all prescribed accountancy bodies—

(a) may not exceed 60 per cent of the programme of expenditure approved for that year under section 13, and

(b) requires the Minister's approval before consent is given to the imposition of any levy in that year.

(5) The Supervisory Authority shall—

(a) establish criteria for apportioning a levy among the classes of prescribed accountancy bodies,

(b) submit the criteria to the Minister for approval before imposing the levy, and

(c) specify the date on which the levy is due to be paid by those bodies.

(6) As a consequence of the apportionment of a levy under subsection (5), different classes of prescribed accountancy bodies may be required to pay different amounts of the levy.

(7) Before consenting to the imposition of a levy under this section, the Minister shall consult with the prescribed accountancy bodies and may consult with any other persons who, in the Minister's opinion, are interested in the matter.

(8) The Supervisory Authority may recover, as a simple contract debt in any court of competent jurisdiction, from a prescribed accountancy body from which the levy is due, a levy imposed under this section.

(9) For the purpose of providing for activities specified in its work programme, the Supervisory Authority may, from time to time, borrow money subject to the consent of the Minister and the Minister for Finance and to such conditions as they may specify.

Definitions

'financial year': CA 1963, s 2(1); 'the Minister': C(AA)A 2003, s 4(1); 'prescribed': CA 1963, s 2(1); 'prescribed accountancy body': C(AA)A 2003, s 4(1); 'Supervisory Authority': C(AA)A 2003, s 4(1).

Notes

See the notes to C(AA)A 2003, ss 5 and 10.

---

15 Reserve fund and levy

(1) The Supervisory Authority shall—

(a) subject to any limit that the Minister may specify, establish and maintain a reserve fund to be used only for the purposes of performing its functions and exercising its powers under sections 24 and 26,

(b) set aside in each financial year for the reserve fund a portion of the revenue received under section 14(1) and (2),

(c) pay into the reserve fund in each financial year—

(i) the amount set aside under paragraph (b) for the fund or, if that amount is amended under section 13(4), the amended amount,

(ii) the proceeds of any levy imposed under subsection (2) of this section, and

(iii) any amounts paid to the Supervisory Authority under section 23(5)(c) or 24(7) and any costs recovered under section 26(5) or (8),

and

(d) promptly inform the Minister if, in any financial year, the total amount in the reserve fund is likely to exceed any limit specified by the Minister for the purposes of this section.

(2) With the Minister's consent and after consulting with any persons who are interested in the matter, the Supervisory Authority may, subject to subsections (3) to (7), impose in each financial year of the Supervisory Authority one or more levies on the following:

(a) each public limited company (whether listed or unlisted);

(b) each private company limited by shares that, in both the most recent financial year and the immediately preceding financial year of the company, meets the following criteria:

(i) its balance sheet total for the year exceeds—

(A) €25,000,000, or

(B) if an amount is prescribed under section 48(1)(e) for the purpose of this provision, the prescribed amount;

(ii) the amount of its turnover for the year exceeds—

(A) €50,000,000, or

(B) if an amount is prescribed under section 48(1)(e) for the purpose of this provision, the prescribed amount;

(c) each private company limited by shares that is a parent undertaking, if the parent undertaking and all of its subsidiary undertakings together, in both the most recent financial year and the immediately preceding financial year of the parent undertaking, meet the criteria in paragraph (b);

(d) each undertaking referred to in Regulation 6 of the 1993 Regulations that, in both the most recent financial year and the immediately preceding financial year of the undertaking, meets the criteria in paragraph (b);

(e) each undertaking referred to in Regulation 6 of the 1993 Regulations that is a parent undertaking, if the parent undertaking and all of its subsidiary undertakings together, in both the most recent financial year and the immediately preceding financial year of the parent undertaking, meet the criteria in paragraph (b).

(3) The total amount levied under subsection (2) in any financial year of the Supervisory Authority on all companies and undertakings—

(a) may not exceed the total amount paid into the reserve fund for that year under subsection (1)(c)(i), and

(b) requires the Minister's approval before consent is given to the imposition of any levy in that year.

(4) In determining whether to approve the total amount referred to in subsection (3), the Minister may—

(a) have regard to the Supervisory Authority's work programme,

and

(b) give due consideration to the use to which the reserve fund was put in the previous financial year.

(5) The Supervisory Authority shall—

(a) establish criteria for apportioning a levy among the classes of companies and undertakings liable to pay the levy under subsection (2),

(b) submit the criteria to the Minister for approval before imposing the levy, and

(c) specify the date on which the levy is due to be paid by those companies and undertakings.

(6) As a consequence of the apportionment of a levy under subsection (5), different classes of companies or undertakings may be required to pay different amounts of the levy.

(7) Subsection (2) does not apply in respect of a company or an undertaking of a class exempted under section 48(1)(j) from this section.

(8) Where both a parent undertaking and one or more of its subsidiary undertakings would otherwise be liable to pay a levy imposed under this section, only the parent undertaking is required to pay the levy.

(9) Subsection (8) applies whether the parent undertaking is a public limited company, a private limited company or an undertaking referred to in Regulation 6 of the 1993 Regulations.

(10) The Supervisory Authority may recover, as a simple contract debt in any court of competent jurisdiction, from a company or undertaking from which the levy is due, a levy imposed under this section.

Definitions

'financial year': CA 1963, s 2(1); 'the Minister': C(AA)A 2003, s 4(1); 'prescribed': CA 1963, s 2(1); 'Supervisory Authority': C(AA)A 2003, s 4(1); 'the 1993 Regulations': C(AA)A 2003, s 4(1).

Notes

See the notes to C(AA)A 2003, s 5.

---

16 Excess revenue

(1) The Supervisory Authority shall apply any excess of its revenue over its expenditure in any year to meet its programme of expenditure approved for the subsequent year under section 13, and the amounts payable under section 14(1) and (2) for the subsequent year shall be appropriately reduced.

(2) Money in, or set aside for, the reserve fund is not considered to be revenue for the purposes of this section.

Definitions

'Supervisory Authority': C(AA)A 2003, s 4(1).

---

17 Staff

(1) Subject to subsection (2) and to the limits of the staffing numbers specified under section 13 in its work programme, the Supervisory Authority may, from time to time, appoint persons to be members of its staff.

(2) The numbers, grades and terms or conditions of its staff shall be determined by the Supervisory Authority with the approval of the Minister given with the consent of the Minister for Finance.

(3) The Supervisory Authority may from time to time engage the services of professional and other advisers.

Definitions

'the Minister': C(AA)A 2003, s 4(1); 'Supervisory Authority': C(AA)A 2003, s 4(1).

Notes

See the notes to C(AA)A 2003, s 10.

---

18 Disclosure of interests by directors

(1) In this section—

'meeting' means a meeting of the board of the Supervisory Authority or of a committee of its directors;

'specified matter' means—

(a) an arrangement to which the Supervisory Authority is a party or a proposed such arrangement, or

(b) a contract or other agreement with the Supervisory Authority or a proposed such contract or other agreement.

(2) Any director of the Supervisory Authority who is present at a meeting where a specified matter arises and who, otherwise than in his or her capacity as such a director, has a material interest in that matter shall—

(a) at the meeting disclose to the Authority the fact of the interest and its nature,

(b) absent himself or herself from the meeting or the part of the meeting during which the matter is discussed,

(c) take no part in any deliberations of the directors relating to the matter, and

(d) refrain from voting on any decision relating to the matter.

(3) Where a director discloses a material interest under this section—

(a) the disclosure shall be recorded in the minutes of the meeting concerned, and

(b) for as long as the matter to which the disclosure relates is being dealt with by the meeting, the director shall not be counted in the quorum for the meeting.

(4) Where at a meeting a question arises as to whether or not a course of conduct, if pursued by a director, would constitute a failure by him or her to comply with subsection (2)—

(a) the chairperson of the meeting may, subject to subsection (5), determine the question,

(b) the chairperson's determination is final, and

(c) the particulars of the determination shall be recorded in the minutes of the meeting.

(5) If the chairperson is the director in respect of whom the question arises, the other directors present at the meeting shall choose one of their number to be the chairperson of the meeting for the purposes of subsection (4).

(6) A director of the Supervisory Authority who, otherwise than in his or her capacity as such a director, has a material interest in a specified matter shall neither influence nor seek to influence any decision to be made by the Authority in relation to that matter.

(7) On being satisfied that a director of the Supervisory Authority has contravened subsection (2) or (6), the Minister may—

(a) if he or she thinks fit, remove that director from office, or

(b) if the director concerned is the chief executive officer, recommend to the board that he or she be removed from that office.

(8) A director removed from office under this section is disqualified for appointment under section 11 or 12.

(9) Section 194 of the Act of 1963 does not apply to a director of the Supervisory Authority.

(10) Nothing in this section prejudices the operation of any rule of law restricting directors of a company from having any interest in contracts with the company.

Definitions

'director': CA 1963, s 2(1); 'material interest': C(AA)A 2003, s 4(2); 'the Minister': C(AA)A 2003, s 4(1); 'Supervisory Authority': C(AA)A 2003, s 4(1).

Notes

Disclosure of material interests: The disclosure requirements of this section, regarding material interest which a director may have in a transaction with the Supervisory Authority, operate in place of the provisions of CA 1963, s 194.[1] Apart from the risk of removal which a director faces if he fails to comply with the provisions of this section,[2] he also remains exposed to the risk of having the transaction avoided and/or being sued for damages or an account of profits arising out his conflict of interest.[3]

1 C(AA)A 2003, s 18(9). See also C(AA)A 2003, s 19 for the disclosure obligations applicable to members of the staff of the Supervisory Authority who are not members of the board of directors.

2 C(AA)A 2003, s 18(7).

3 C(AA)A 2003, s 8(10). See the notes to CA 1963, s 194 regarding the circumstances in which and the extent to which such civil liability may arise.

19 Disclosure of interests by staff

(1) A member of the staff of the Supervisory Authority who, otherwise than in his or her capacity as such a member, has a material interest in a specified matter, as defined in section 18(1), shall—

(a) disclose to the Authority the fact of the interest and its nature,

(b) take no part in the negotiation of the arrangement, contract or other agreement concerned or in any deliberation by the Authority or members of its staff relating to that matter,

(c) refrain from making any recommendation relating to the matter, and

(d) neither influence nor seek to influence a decision to be made in relation to the matter.

(2) Subsection (1) does not apply to contracts or proposed contracts of employment of members of the staff of the Supervisory Authority with the Authority.

(3) Where a person contravenes this section, the Supervisory Authority may make such alterations to the person's terms and conditions of employment as it considers appropriate or terminate the person's contract of employment.

Definitions

'material interest': C(AA)A 2003, s 4(2); 'Supervisory Authority': C(AA)A 2003, s 4(1).

Notes

See the notes to C(AA)A 2003, s 18.

20 Superannuation

(1) The Supervisory Authority may, if it considers it appropriate to do so, prepare and submit to the Minister a scheme or schemes for granting superannuation benefits to or in respect of one or more of the following:

(a) the chief executive officer;

(b) any staff of the Authority.

(2) Each superannuation scheme shall fix the time and conditions of retirement for all persons to or in respect of whom superannuation benefits are payable under the scheme, and different times and conditions may be fixed in respect of different classes of persons.

(3) A superannuation scheme submitted to the Minister under this section shall, if approved by the Minister with the consent of the Minister for Finance, be carried out in accordance with its terms.

(4) A superannuation scheme may be amended or revoked by a subsequent scheme prepared, submitted and approved under this section.

(5) The Supervisory Authority may not grant, or enter any arrangement for the provision of, any superannuation benefit to or in respect of a person referred to in subsection (1) except in accordance with a superannuation scheme approved under this section or approved by the Minister with the consent of the Minister for Finance.

(6) If any dispute arises as to the claim of any person to, or the amount of, a superannuation benefit payable in pursuance of a superannuation scheme approved under this section, the dispute shall be submitted to the Minister who shall refer it to the Minister for Finance whose decision shall be final.

(7) The Minister shall ensure that a superannuation scheme approved under this section is laid before each House of the Oireachtas as soon as practicable after it is approved.

(8) Either House of the Oireachtas may, by a resolution passed within 21 sitting days after the day on which the superannuation scheme is laid before it, annul the scheme.

(9) The annulment of a superannuation scheme under subsection (8) takes effect immediately on the passing of the resolution concerned, but does not affect the validity of anything done under the scheme before the passing of the resolution.

Definitions

'the Minister': C(AA)A 2003, s 4(1); 'Supervisory Authority': C(AA)A 2003, s 4(1).

Notes

See the notes to C(AA)A 2003, s 10.

---

21 Accounts and audit

(1) The Supervisory Authority shall keep records of, and prepare all proper and usual accounts of—

(a) all income received by it, including the sources,

(b) all expenditure incurred by it, and

(c) its assets and liabilities.

(2) Not later than 3 months after the end of the financial year to which the accounts relate, the Supervisory Authority shall submit the accounts prepared under this section to the Comptroller and Auditor General for audit.

(3) After the audit, the Comptroller and Auditor General shall present to the Minister the audited accounts together with the Comptroller and Auditor General's report.

(4) The Minister shall ensure that, as soon as possible after the audited accounts and the report are presented to the Minister, copies of them are—

(a) laid before each House of the Oireachtas, and

(b) supplied to the prescribed accountancy bodies.

(5) The Supervisory Authority shall—

(a) at the Minister's request, permit any person appointed by the Minister to examine its accounts in respect of any financial year or other period,

(b) facilitate the examination of the accounts by the appointed person, and

(c) pay the fee that may be set by the Minister for the examination.

Definitions

'the Minister': C(AA)A 2003, s 4(1); 'Supervisory Authority': C(AA)A 2003, s 4(1).

Notes

Accounting records of the Supervisory Authority: Apart from the general accounting obligations imposed by this section, the Supervisory Authority as a company incorporated under the Companies Acts, has a general obligation to keep proper books and records that: (a) correctly record and explain its transactions; (b) will at any time enable its financial position to be determined with reasonable accuracy; (c) will enable the directors to ensure that its balance sheet, profit and loss account or income and expenditure account complies with the requirements of the Companies Acts; and (d) will enable its accounts to be readily and properly audited.[1]

1 CA 1990, s 202.

22 Accountability mechanisms

(1) As soon as practicable but not later than 4 months after the end of each financial year, the Supervisory Authority shall make a written report to the Minister of its activities during that year.

(2) The annual report must be prepared in such manner and form as the Minister may direct.

(3) The Minister shall ensure that a copy of the annual report is laid before each House of the Oireachtas not later than 6 months after the end of the financial year to which the report relates.

(4) Whenever required to do so by the Committee of Dáil Éireann established under the Standing Orders of Dáil Éireann to examine and report to Dáil Éireann on the appropriation accounts and reports of the Comptroller and Auditor General, the chief executive officer and the chairperson of the board shall give evidence to that Committee on the following:

(a) the regularity and propriety of the transactions recorded or to be recorded in any account subject to audit by the Comptroller and Auditor General that the Supervisory Authority is required by law to prepare;

(b) the Supervisory Authority's economy and efficiency in using its resources;

(c) systems, procedures and practices used by the Supervisory Authority for evaluating the effectiveness of its operations;

(d) any matter affecting the Supervisory Authority that is referred to in a special report under section 11(2) of the Comptroller and Auditor General (Amendment) Act 1993 or in any other report of the Comptroller and Auditor General that is laid before Dáil Éireann, in so far as the other report relates to a matter specified in any of paragraphs (a) to (c);

(5) Whenever requested by any other committee appointed by either House of the Oireachtas or appointed jointly by both Houses, the chief executive officer and the

chairperson of the board shall account to the committee for the performance of the functions and the exercise of the powers of the Supervisory Authority.

(6) The Supervisory Authority shall have regard to any recommendations relating to its functions or powers that are made by a committee in response to an account given under subsection (5).

(7) In performing duties under subsection (4) or (5), neither the chief executive officer nor the chairperson of the board shall question or express an opinion on the merits of any policy of the Government or a Minister of the Government or on the merits of the objectives of such a policy.

Definitions

'the Minister': C(AA)A 2003, s 4(1); 'Supervisory Authority': C(AA)A 2003, s 4(1).

---

23 Intervention in disciplinary process of prescribed accountancy bodies

(1) In this section, 'approved investigation and disciplinary procedures' means—

(a) in relation to a prescribed accountancy body that is a recognised accountancy body, the investigation and disciplinary procedures approved under section 9(2)(c) of this Act or approved under the Act of 1990 before or after the amendment of that Act by section 32 of this Act, and

(b) in relation to any other prescribed accountancy body, the investigation and disciplinary procedures approved under section 9(2)(c) of this Act.

(2) Following a complaint or on its own initiative, the Supervisory Authority may, for the purpose of determining whether a prescribed accountancy body has complied with the approved investigation and disciplinary procedures, enquire into—

(a) a decision by that body not to undertake an investigation into a possible breach of its standards by a member,

(b) the conduct of an investigation by that body into a possible breach of its standards by a member, or

(c) any other decision of that body relating to a possible breach of its standards by a member, unless the matter is or has been the subject of an investigation under section 24(2) relating to that member.

(3) For the purposes of an enquiry under this section, the Supervisory Authority may—

(a) inspect and make copies of all relevant documents in the possession or control of the prescribed accountancy body, and

(b) require the prescribed accountancy body to explain why it reached a decision referred to in subsection (2)(a) or (c) or to explain how it conducted its investigation.

(4) If, at any time before completing an enquiry under this section into a matter relating to a member of a prescribed accountancy body, the Supervisory Authority forms the opinion that it is appropriate or in the public interest that the matter be investigated under section 24, the Authority may apply to the High Court for permission to investigate the matter under that section.

(5) If not satisfied after completing the enquiry that the prescribed accountancy body complied with the approved investigation and disciplinary procedures, the Supervisory Authority may advise or admonish the prescribed accountancy body or may censure it by doing one or more of the following:

(a) annulling all or part of a decision of that body relating to the matter that was the subject of the enquiry;

(b) directing that body to conduct an investigation or a fresh investigation into the matter;

(c) requiring that body to pay to the Supervisory Authority an amount not exceeding the greater of the following:

(i) €125,000;

(ii) the amount prescribed under section 48(1)(f).

(6) Where the Supervisory Authority applies under this section to the High Court for permission to investigate under section 24 any matter relating to a member of a prescribed accountancy body or decides to direct a prescribed accountancy body to conduct an investigation or a fresh investigation under this section into any matter, the following rules apply:

(a) in the case of an application to the High Court for permission to investigate a matter, any decision of that body relating to the matter is suspended if and as soon as the body is notified by the Supervisory Authority that permission has been granted under section 29(3);

(b) in the case of a direction to conduct an investigation, any decision of that body relating to the matter is suspended as soon as the body is notified by the Supervisory Authority of the direction;

(c) in the case of a direction to conduct a fresh investigation, any decision of that body relating to the matter is suspended if and as soon as the body is notified by the Supervisory Authority that the direction has been confirmed under section 29(6).

(7) The Supervisory Authority may publish each decision made under subsection (5) and the reasons for the decision after giving the prescribed accountancy body and the member concerned not less than 3 months notice in writing of its intention to do so.

(8) The prescribed accountancy body or the member concerned may appeal to the High Court against a decision made by the Supervisory Authority under subsection (5).

(9) An appeal under subsection (8) must be brought before the expiry of the notice given under subsection (7) to the prescribed accountancy body and the member concerned.

(10) If not satisfied that a prescribed accountancy body has, when undertaking an investigation or a fresh investigation into the matter under subsection (5)(b), complied with the approved investigation and disciplinary procedures, the Supervisory Authority may appeal to the High Court against any decision of the prescribed accountancy body relating to the matter.

(11) An appeal under subsection (10) must be brought within 3 months after the Supervisory Authority was notified by the prescribed accountancy body of its decision.

(12) For the purposes of this section, any decision made or any investigation conducted by the disciplinary committee of a prescribed accountancy body is considered to have been made or conducted by the prescribed accountancy body.

Definitions

'Act of 1990': C(AA)A 2003, s 3(1); 'prescribed': CA 1963, s 2(1); 'prescribed accountancy body': C(AA)A 2003, s 4(1); 'recognised accountancy body': C(AA)A 2003, s 4(1); 'standards': C(AA)A 2003, s 4(1); 'Supervisory Authority': C(AA)A 2003, s 4(1).

Notes

Intervention in disciplinary processes of accountancy bodies:[1] Previously, the disciplinary processes of the various accountancy bodies had been purely internal matters in respect of which the State could not readily interfere. Now, however, by virtue of the provisions of C(AA)A 2003, s 23 the Supervisory Authority (or a committee consisting of directors of the Authority and professional and other advisers)[2] may intervene in relation to the disciplinary procedures of bodies that are prescribed accountancy bodies. The intervention may be made on the Supervisory Authority's own initiative or as a result of a complaint made to it[3] and may relate to virtually any aspect of the disciplinary process, provided that the matter is not already the subject of a court ordered investigation under C(AA)A 2003, s 24.[4] For example, it may intervene regarding: (a) a decision not to investigate a possible breach of standards; (b) the actual investigation of a suspected breach of standards; or (c) the decision of the body regarding the suspected breach of standards.

In the context of this power of intervention, the Supervisory Authority may inspect and take copies of relevant documents from the prescribed accountancy body and may require explanations regarding whatever aspect of the disciplinary process is the subject matter of the intervention.[5] It cannot, however, compel the disclosure of information or material which is protected by legal professional privilege.[6] It does, however, have a discretion to conduct an oral hearing as part of the enquiry, in which case witnesses will have the same immunities and privileges as they would enjoy before the High Court.[7]

At any stage before completing its enquiry, if it considers it to be in the public interest to do so, the Supervisory Authority may apply to the High Court for permission to conduct its own formal investigation of the member of the accountancy body pursuant to s 24.[8] If the application is acceded to by the High Court, the notification of the order to the accountancy body automatically operates to suspend any decisions of that body concerning the matter under enquiry.[9]

1 See also C(AA)A 2003, s 25 in relation to the power of the Supervisory Authority to undertake reviews of members of recognized accountancy bodies to determine whether those bodies are properly regulating their members.

2 C(AA)A 2003, s 27(1)(a).

3 C(AA)A 2003, s 23(2).

4 C(AA)A 2003, s 23(2).

5 C(AA)A 2003, s 23(3).

6 C(AA)A 2003, s 28(3).

7 C(AA)A 2003, s 28(1), (2) and (4).

8 C(AA)A 2003, s 23(4).

9 C(AA)A 2003, s 23(6)(a).

The decision of the Supervisory Authority: Once the enquiry has been concluded under C(AA)A 2003, s 23, if the Supervisory Authority is dissatisfied with the way in which the accountancy body has dealt with the matter, it may issue one or more of a range of sanctions: it may advise or admonish the body or it may censure the body—

(a) by annulling all or part of the decision of the body which was the subject of the enquiry; and/or

(b) by directing the body to conduct an investigation or fresh investigation; and/or

(c) by imposing a fine on the body of up to €125,000 or such other sum as may be prescribed by the Minister.[1]

It is to be noted, however, that none of the three orders of censure can take effect unless and until confirmed by the High Court, whether on appeal (as to which, see below) or by way of separate application made by the Supervisory Authority itself.[2]

If the decision of the Supervisory Authority is to direct the accountancy body to conduct an investigation, the notification of that direction operates to automatically suspend any other decision of the accountancy body concerning the matter in question, even before the direction has been confirmed by the High Court.[3] However, in the case of a direction to conduct a fresh investigation (as where the accountancy body's earlier investigation is found to have been flawed), the decisions of the accountancy body concerning the disciplinary process are only suspended if and when it receives notification that the direction of the Supervisory Authority has been confirmed by the High Court.[4]

1 C(AA)A 2003, s 23(5).
2 C(AA)A 2003, s 29(4).
3 C(AA)A 2003, s 23(6)(b).
4 C(AA)A 2003, s 23(6)(c).

Appeal to the High Court: Whether the decision of the Supervisory Authority is to advise, admonish or censure the prescribed accountancy body, both the body itself and the member concerned have a right of appeal to the High Court.[1] Any such appeal must be brought within three months of being notified of the Supervisory Authority's intention to publish its decision (including the reasons therefore).[2]

The right of appeal is not, however, limited to the Supervisory Authority and the member concerned. If the Supervisory Authority has given a direction to conduct an investigation or a fresh investigation, as the case may be, and it is dissatisfied with the way in which that investigation has been conducted, it too may appeal to the High Court, within three months of being notified of the prescribed accountancy body's decision on the investigation.[3]

1 C(AA)A 2003, s 23(8).
2 C(AA)A 2003, s 23(9). Under s 23(7) the Supervisory authority may be is not obliged to publish its decision. On a literal reading therefore, if the Supervisory Authority were to opt not to publish its decision, then the accountancy body and the member would have an unlimited time within which to appeal!
3 C(AA)A 2003, s 23(10) and (11).

24 Investigation of possible breaches of standards of prescribed accountancy bodies

(1) In this section—

'client' includes an individual, a body corporate, an unincorporated body of persons and a partnership;

'refusal' includes failure and 'refuses' includes fails;

'relevant person', in relation to an investigation of a member of a prescribed accountancy body, means—

(a) a member of the prescribed accountancy body,

(b) a client or former client of such member,

(c) if the client or former client is a body corporate, a person who is or was an officer, employee or agent of the client or former client,

(d) the prescribed accountancy body or a person who is or was an officer, employee or agent of that body, or

(e) any person whom the Supervisory Authority reasonably believes has information or documents relating to the investigation other than information or documents the disclosure of which is prohibited or restricted by law.

(2) If, in the Supervisory Authority's opinion, it is appropriate or in the public interest to undertake an investigation into a possible breach of a prescribed accountancy body's standards by a member, the Authority may do so—

(a) following a complaint, or

(b) on its own initiative,

but no investigation may be undertaken into a matter that is or has been the subject of an enquiry under section 23 relating to that member except with the permission of the High Court granted on application under section 23(4).

(3) For the purposes of an investigation under this section, the Supervisory Authority may require a relevant person to do one or more of the following:

(a) produce to the Supervisory Authority all books or documents relating to the investigation that are in the relevant person's possession or control;

(b) attend before the Supervisory Authority;

(c) give the Supervisory Authority any other assistance in connection with the investigation that the relevant person is reasonably able to give.

(4) For the purposes of an investigation under this section, the Supervisory Authority may—

(a) examine on oath, either by word of mouth or on written interrogatories, a relevant person,

(b) administer oaths for the purposes of the examination, and

(c) record, in writing, the answers of a person so examined and require that person to sign them.

(5) The Supervisory Authority may certify the refusal to the High Court if a relevant person refuses to do one or more of the following:

(a) produce to the Supervisory Authority any book or document that it is the person's duty under this section to produce;

(b) attend before the Supervisory Authority when required to do so under this section;

(c) answer a question put to the person by the Supervisory Authority with respect to the matter under investigation.

(6) On receiving a certificate of refusal concerning a relevant person, the Court may enquire into the case and, after hearing any evidence that may be adduced, may do one or more of the following:

(a) direct that the relevant person attend or re-attend before the Supervisory Authority or produce particular books or documents or answer particular questions put to him or her by the Supervisory Authority;

(b) direct that the relevant person need not produce particular books or documents or answer particular questions put to him or her by the Supervisory Authority;

(c) make any other ancillary or consequential order or give any other direction that the Court thinks fit.

(7) If the Supervisory Authority finds that the member committed a breach of the prescribed accountancy body's standards—

(a) the Supervisory Authority may impose on the member any sanction to which the member is liable under the approved constitution and bye-laws of the prescribed accountancy body (including a monetary sanction), and

(b) in addition, the member is liable to pay the amount specified by the Supervisory Authority towards its costs in investigating and determining the case, excluding any costs of or incidental to an enquiry by the Court under subsection (6).

(8) The member who is the subject of a decision made by the Supervisory Authority under subsection (7) may appeal to the High Court against the decision.

(9) An appeal under subsection (8) must be brought within 3 months after the member concerned was notified by the Supervisory Authority of its decision.

(10) The production of any books or documents under this section by a person who claims a lien on them does not prejudice the lien.

(11) Any information produced or answer given by a member of a prescribed accountancy body in compliance with a requirement under this section may be used in evidence against the member in any proceedings whatsoever, save proceedings for an offence (other than perjury in respect of such an answer).

(12) A finding or decision of the Supervisory Authority under this section is not a bar to any civil or criminal proceedings against the member who is the subject of the finding or decision.

Definitions

'Act of 1990': C(AA)A 2003, s 3(1); 'prescribed': CA 1963, s 2(1); 'prescribed accountancy body': C(AA)A 2003, s 4(1); 'standards': C(AA)A 2003, s 4(1); 'Supervisory Authority': C(AA)A 2003, s 4(1).

Notes

Investigation of members of prescribed accountancy bodies: Apart from being entitled under C(AA)A 2003, s 23 to intervene in the disciplinary process of a prescribed accountancy body where a member of that body is suspected of a breach of standards, the Supervisory Authority is also authorised to commence its own investigations of members of such bodies under s 24. The investigative process may be commenced on the Supervisory Authority's own initiative or as a result of a complaint made to it,[1] although the leave of the court will be required to commence the process if the matter in question already is or has been the subject of a disciplinary process into which the Supervisory Authority intervened pursuant to s 23.[2]

1 C(AA)A 2003. s 24(2).

2 C(AA)A 2003. s 24(2).

Powers of the Supervisory Authority: Where an investigation is commenced, the Supervisory Authority may require any 'relevant person', as defined in C(AA)A 2003, s 24(2), to produce books and records to it, to attend before it and to provide it with all reasonable assistance.[1] Such persons may be examined on oath as part of the investigative process.[2] It is to be noted though, that these powers of the Supervisory Authority do not entitle it to have access to books, records or information which are protected by legal professional privilege.[3] It is also to be noted that although the production of documents would appear to be required of a 'relevant person' even if he is exercising a lien over them, the yielding up of possession will not destroy his lien,[4] contrary to the position at common law.[5]

A refusal on the part of a 'relevant person' to co-operate may result in the Supervisory Authority certifying that refusal, and applying to the High Court for an order directing him to co-operate.[6] Failure to obey the order of the court would be punishable as a contempt of court.

As part of the investigative process, the Supervisory Authority has a discretion to conduct an oral hearing, in which case witnesses giving evidence will have the same immunities and privileges as they would enjoy before the High Court.[7]

1 C(AA)A 2003, s 24(3).
2 C(AA)A 2003, s 24(4).
3 C(AA)A 2003, s 28(3).
4 C(AA)A 2003, s 24(10).
5 For an analysis of the position at common law, see Bell *Modern Law of Personal property in England and Ireland* (Butterworths, 1989), Ch 6.
6 C(AA)A 2003, s 24(5) and (6).
7 C(AA)A 2003, s 28(1), (2) and (4).

The decision of the Supervisory Authority: Having concluded its investigation, if the Supervisory Authority finds that the member has committed a breach of the prescribed accountancy body's standards, it may impose the same sanctions as could have been imposed by the prescribed accountancy body itself.[1] In addition, the member will be liable to pay the costs of the investigation other than any legal costs of applications to court to compel co-operation.[2] The decision of the Supervisory Authority (which does not operate as a bar to separate civil or criminal proceedings)[3] may be appealed to the High Court within three months of the date upon which it is first notified to the member in question.[4]

1 C(AA)A 2003, s 24(7)(a).
2 C(AA)A 2003, s 24(7)(b). The legal costs will presumably have been dealt with by the court itself at the end of the application for orders directing co-operation.
3 C(AA)A 2003, s 24(12).
4 C(AA)A 2003, s 24(8) and (9).

Use of information given in the investigation: Information produced or answers given by a person under legal compulsion as part of the C(AA)A 2003, s 24 investigation may, reflecting the decision of the Supreme Court in *Re National Irish Bank Ltd (No 1)*,[1] be used against that person in separate civil proceedings but may not be used against him in criminal proceedings (other than proceedings for perjury).[2]

1 *Re National Irish Bank Ltd (No 1)* [1999] 3 IR 145.
2 C(AA)A 2003, s 24(11).

25 Review of members of recognised accountancy bodies

(1) The Supervisory Authority may, if in its opinion it is appropriate to do so, undertake a review of a member of a recognised accountancy body to determine whether that body has been or is regulating its members in the manner approved under section 9(2)(b) of

this Act or approved under the Act of 1990 before or after the amendment of that Act by section 32 of this Act.

(2) For the purposes of a review under this section—

(a) the Supervisory Authority may inspect and make copies of all relevant documents in the possession or control of the recognised accountancy body whose practices are under review,

(b) the member of the recognised accountancy body shall cooperate with the Supervisory Authority as if the recognised accountancy body were undertaking the review, and

(c) if the member fails to co-operate in accordance with paragraph (b) of this subsection, section 24(3) to (7) applies, with any necessary modifications, in relation to the member as if the review were an investigation under section 24.

Definitions

'recognised accountancy body': C(AA)A 2003, s 4(1); 'Supervisory Authority': C(AA)A 2003, s 4(1).

Notes

Review of members of recognised accountancy bodies: Allied to the power to intervene in the disciplinary processes of prescribed accountancy bodies[1] and to conduct its own investigations of suspected breaches of the standards of prescribed accountancy bodies,[2] the Supervisory Authority may also undertake reviews of members of recognised accountancy bodies under C(AA)A 2003, s 25(1) to ensure that those bodies are properly regulating their members. The member being reviewed is under an obligation to co-operate with the Supervisory Authority as if he were being reviewed by the recognised body itself,[3] albeit that he does not have to produce documents or furnish information which is protected by legal professional privilege.[4] If he fails to co-operate he may be formally investigated in the same manner as if he were subject to a formal C(AA)A 2003, s 24 investigation, with the Supervisory Authority being empowered ultimately to apply to the High Court for an order directing him to co-operate.[5]

In order to facilitate the review, the Supervisory Authority may also inspect and take copies of relevant documents from the recognised body,[6] although again, there is no entitlement to have access to documents which are protected by legal professional privilege.[7]

1 C(AA)A 2003, s 23.

2 C(AA)A 2003, s 24.

3 C(AA)A 2003, s 25(2)(b).

4 C(AA)A 2003, s 28(3).

5 C(AA)A 2003, s 25(2)(c).

6 C(AA)A 2003, s 25(2)(a).

7 C(AA)A 2003, s 28(3).

26 Review of whether accounts comply with Companies Acts

(1) In this section—

'relevant undertaking' means—

(a) a public limited company (whether unlisted or listed),

(b) a subsidiary undertaking of a public limited company referred to in paragraph (a) (whether the subsidiary undertaking is a company or is an undertaking referred to in Regulation 6 of the 1993 Regulations),

(c) a private company limited by shares that, in both the relevant financial year and the immediately preceding financial year of the company, meets the following criteria:

(i) its balance sheet total for the year exceeds—

(A) €25,000,000, or

(B) if an amount is prescribed under section 48(1)(h) for the purpose of this provision, the prescribed amount;

(ii) the amount of its turnover for the year exceeds—

(A) €50,000,000, or

(B) if an amount is prescribed under section 48(1)(h) for the purpose of this provision, the prescribed amount,

(d) a private company limited by shares that is a parent undertaking, if the parent undertaking and all of its subsidiary undertakings together, in both the relevant financial year and the immediately preceding financial year of the parent undertaking, meet the criteria in paragraph (c),

(e) each subsidiary undertaking of a parent undertaking that comes within paragraph (d),

(f) an undertaking referred to in Regulation 6 of the 1993 Regulations that, in both the relevant financial year and the immediately preceding financial year of the undertaking, meets the criteria in paragraph (c),

(g) an undertaking referred to in Regulation 6 of the 1993 Regulations that is a parent undertaking, if the parent undertaking and all of its subsidiary undertakings together, in both the relevant financial year and the immediately preceding financial year of the parent undertaking, meet the criteria in paragraph (c), or

(h) each subsidiary undertaking of a parent undertaking that comes within paragraph (g), but does not include a company or an undertaking of a class exempted under section 48(1)(j) from this section.

(2) A reference in this section to the directors of a relevant undertaking is to be construed in the case of an undertaking that does not have a board of directors as a reference to the corresponding persons appropriate to that undertaking.

(3) Subject to subsection (12), the Supervisory Authority may give notice to the directors of a relevant undertaking concerning its annual accounts where—

(a) a copy of the annual accounts has been sent out under section 159 of the Act of 1963 or laid before the undertaking at its annual general meeting or delivered to the registrar of companies, and

(b) it appears to the Supervisory Authority that there is, or may be, a question whether the annual accounts comply with the Companies Acts [and, where applicable, Article 4 of the IAS Regulation][a].

(4) The notice to the directors of the relevant undertaking must specify—

(a) the matters in respect of which it appears to the Supervisory Authority that the question of compliance with the Companies Acts [and, where applicable, Article 4 of the IAS Regulation][a] arises or may arise, and

(b) a period of not less than 30 days within which those directors are required to give the Supervisory Authority an explanation of the annual accounts or to prepare revised annual accounts that comply with the Companies Acts [and, where applicable, Article 4 of the IAS Regulation][a].

(5) If before the end of the specified period, or such longer period as the Supervisory Authority may allow, the directors of the relevant undertaking prepare revised annual accounts, the Supervisory Authority may, taking account of the circumstances of the case and the degree of co-operation by the directors with the Supervisory Authority, require that undertaking to pay some or all of the costs the Supervisory Authority incurred under this section in relation to that undertaking.

(6) If at the end of the specified period, or such longer period as the Supervisory Authority may allow, the directors of the relevant undertaking have, in the Supervisory Authority's opinion, neither given a satisfactory explanation of the annual accounts nor revised them to comply with the Companies Acts [and, where applicable, Article 4 of the IAS Regulation][a], the Supervisory Authority may apply to the High Court for a declaration of non-compliance and an order under subsection (8).

(7) If an application is made to the Court under subsection (6), the Supervisory Authority shall give to the registrar of companies for registration—

(a) notice of the application, and

(b) a general statement of the matters at issue in the proceedings.

(8) If satisfied after hearing the application that the relevant undertaking's annual accounts referred to in subsection (3) do not comply with the Companies Acts [and, where applicable, Article 4 of the IAS Regulation][a], the Court may make a declaration to that effect and may, by order, do one or more of the following:

(a) require the directors to revise the annual accounts so that they comply with those Acts [and, where applicable, Article 4 of the IAS Regulation][a];

(b) give directions respecting one or more of the following:

(i) the auditing of the revised annual accounts;

(ii) the revision of any directors' report;

(iii) the steps to be taken by the directors to bring the court order to the notice of persons likely to rely on the annual accounts that were the subject of the declaration;

(iv) such other matters as the Court thinks fit;

(c) require the directors of the relevant undertaking to pay—

(i) the costs incurred by the Supervisory Authority under subsections (3) and (4) in relation to that undertaking, and

(ii) any reasonable expenses incurred by the relevant undertaking in connection with or in consequence of the preparation of revised annual accounts.

(9) For the purpose of subsection (8)(c), every director of the relevant undertaking at the time the annual accounts were approved is considered to have been a party to their approval unless the director shows that he or she took all reasonable steps to prevent their being approved.

(10) In making an order under subsection (8)(c), the Court—

(a) shall have regard to whether any or all of the directors who approved the annual accounts that were the subject of the declaration knew, or ought to have known, that they did not comply with the Companies Acts [and, where applicable, Article 4 of the IAS Regulation][a], and

(b) may exempt one or more directors from the order or may order the payment of different amounts by different directors.

(11) On the conclusion of the proceedings, the Supervisory Authority shall give to the registrar of companies for registration—

(a) a copy of the court order, or

(b) notice that the application has failed or been withdrawn.

(12) The Supervisory Authority shall consult with the Irish Financial Services Regulatory Authority before making any decisions under this section with respect to a company regulated by the latter Authority, including a decision to give notice under subsection (3).

(13) This section applies equally to revised annual accounts, in which case references to revised annual accounts are to be construed as references to further revised annual accounts.

(14) For the purpose of applying this section to a partnership that is referred to in Regulation 6 of the 1993 Regulations and that is a relevant undertaking—

(a) the partnership is to be treated as though it were a company formed and registered under the Companies Acts, and

(b) the section applies with any modifications necessary for that purpose.

(15) Where revised annual accounts are prepared under this section, then, subject to a direction given under subsection (8)(b), any provision of the Companies Acts respecting the preparation, auditing, circulation and disclosure of annual accounts applies with the necessary changes to the revised annual accounts.

Amendments

a Amended by Sch 1 Pt 5 of EC(IFRSMA)R 2005.

Definitions

'accounts': CA 1963, s 2(1); 'Companies Acts': C(AA)A 2003, s 3(1); 'director': CA 1963, s 2(1); 'the 1993 Regulations': C(AA)A 2003, s 4(1); 'company': CA 1963, s 2(1); 'financial year': CA 1963, s 2(1); 'IAS Regulation': CA 1963 s 2(1); 'parent undertaking': C(AA)A 2003, s 4(1); 'prescribed': CA 1963, s 2(1); 'private company': CA 1963, ss 2(1) and 33; 'public limited company': C(A)A 1983, s 2(1); 'subsidiary undertaking': C(AA)A 2003, s 4(1); 'Supervisory Authority': C(AA)A 2003, s 4(1).

Notes

Review as to compliance of accounts with the Companies Acts: C(AA)A 2003, s 26 is somewhat novel in nature and empowers the Supervisory Authority to require the rectification of the accounts of larger organisations where such accounts fail in some respect to comply with the accounting requirements of the Companies Acts.

Undertakings subject to potential review: The provisions of C(AA)A 2003, s 26 apply to any 'relevant undertaking' namely—

(a) any plc;[1]

(b) any subsidiary undertaking of a plc;[2]

(c) any private company limited by shares which in the relevant financial year and in the immediately preceding financial year had a balance sheet total of not less than €25,000,000 and a turnover of not less than €50,000,000 (or such other balance sheet total and turnover as may be prescribed from time to time);[3]

(d) any private company limited by shares which is a parent undertaking and whose group had in the relevant financial year and in the immediately preceding financial year an aggregate balance sheet total of not less than €25,000,000 and an aggregate turnover of not less than €50,000,000 (or such other balance sheet total and turnover as may be prescribed from time to time);[4]

(e) every subsidiary undertaking of a private company limited by shares which is a parent undertaking and whose group had in the relevant financial year and in the immediately preceding financial year an aggregate balance sheet total of not less than €25,000,000 and an aggregate turnover of not less than €50,000,000 (or such other balance sheet total and turnover as may be prescribed from time to time);[5]

(f) any unlimited company or partnership where—

- (i) the members with unlimited liability are—
  - (I) Irish or foreign limited companies; and/or
  - (II) Irish or other EU unlimited companies or partnerships whose members with unlimited liability are in turn Irish and/or foreign limited companies; and
- (ii) in the relevant financial year and in the immediately preceding financial year it had a balance sheet total of not less than €25,000,000 and a turnover of not less than €50,000,000 (or such other balance sheet total and turnover as may be prescribed from time to time);[6]

(g) any unlimited company or partnership which is a parent undertaking where—

- (i) the members with unlimited liability are—
  - (I) Irish or foreign limited companies; and/or
  - (II) Irish or other EU unlimited companies or partnerships whose members with unlimited liability are in turn Irish and/or foreign limited companies; and
- (ii) in the relevant financial year and in the immediately preceding financial year the group had an aggregate balance sheet total of not less than €25,000,000 and an aggregate turnover of not less than €50,000,000 (or such other balance sheet total and turnover as may be prescribed from time to time);[7]

(h) every subsidiary undertaking of unlimited company or partnership which is a parent undertaking where—

- (i) the members with of that parent undertaking with unlimited liability are—
  - (I) Irish or foreign limited companies; and/or

(II) Irish or other EU unlimited companies or partnerships whose members with unlimited liability are in turn Irish and/or foreign limited companies; and

(ii) in the relevant financial year and in the immediately preceding financial year the group had an aggregate balance sheet total of not less than €25,000,000 and an aggregate turnover of not less than €50,000,000 (or such other balance sheet total and turnover as may be prescribed from time to time).[8]

It is to be noted, however, though that the Minister has power to exempt qualifying companies within the meaning of TCA 1997, s 110 and other classes of companies and undertakings from the application of s 26.[9]

1 C(AA)A 2003, s 26(1)(a).
2 C(AA)A 2003, s 26(1)(b).
3 C(AA)A 2003, s 26(1)(c).
4 C(AA)A 2003, s 26(1)(d).
5 C(AA)A 2003, s 26(1)(e).
6 C(AA)A 2003, s 26(1)(f).
7 C(AA)A 2003, s 26(1)(g).
8 C(AA)A 2003, s 26(1)(h).
9 C(AA)A 2003, s 48(1)(j).

Notice of suspected breach of accounting requirements: Where the Supervisory Authority is of the view that the annual accounts of a relevant undertaking which have been sent out to members or debenture holders or which have been laid before an AGM or which have been delivered to the Registrar of Companies are not in compliance with the accounting requirements of the Companies Acts, it may send a notice to the board[1] of that undertaking specifying the matters of concern and giving a period of not less than 30 days within which to provide a satisfactory explanation or within which to prepare correct accounts, as the case may be.[2]

1 In the case of an undertaking which is not a company, the 'directors' are those persons performing the equivalent functions: C(AA)A 2003, s 26(2).
2 C(AA)A 2003, s 26(4).

Position if explanation is given or accounts are corrected: If, within the stipulated period of time (or within such longer period as the Supervisory Authority allows), the directors provide a satisfactory explanation, that would appear to be an end to the matter. However, if it is a case that the accounts are indeed deficient but are nonetheless corrected within the allowed period of time, no further action will be taken by the Supervisory Authority, save possibly that it may look to the directors to discharge all or some of the costs incurred by it.[1]

1 C(AA)A 2003, s 26(5).

Position if no explanation given or accounts not corrected: If the directors fail either to provide a satisfactory explanation or corrected accounts within the allowed period of time, the Supervisory Authority may apply to the High Court, on notice to the Registrar of Companies for orders declaring that they have failed to comply with the relevant statutory accounting requirements and directing them to remedy the position.[1] If the court is satisfied that the Supervisory Authority has proved its case, it may not only order the directors to remedy the accounting defect but also order all or some of them to discharge the costs originally incurred by the Supervisory Authority in reviewing the accounts.[2] Moreover, insofar as the undertaking itself incurs any costs in connection with, or in consequence of, the preparation of corrected accounts the court may order all or some of the directors to reimburse those costs to the undertaking.[3] The extent to which the various directors knew or ought to have known of the non-compliance with the accounting requirements of the Companies Acts is something to which the court may have regard in determining which directors, if any, to fix with costs or to exempt from costs, and in determining the amount, if any, of the costs which each director will have to pay.[4] It would also seem that a factor relevant to the imposition of costs on a director is whether or not he was on the board at the time of the approval of the defective accounts. However, if he was a member of the board at the time, the onus will be on him to show that he had taken all reasonable steps to prevent the accounts from being approved, if he is to relieved wholly or partly from any award of costs.[5]

Apart from directing that the accounts be corrected and directing that costs be paid, the court may also give consequential directions, including a direction that any revised accounts be audited and/or that the directors' report be revised and/or that steps be taken to have the revised accounts brought to the notice of persons who would be likely to rely on them.[6] Thus, for example, the court could direct that the accounts be circulated to all or some of the undertaking's members, bankers, other major creditors and suppliers and/or that a notice be placed in one or more national newspapers drawing attention to the fact that the accounts have been so revised. It might also direct that apart from filing the revised accounts with the Registrar of Companies, the directors should also serve copies on any relevant regulatory or other authorities having an interest in the undertaking's affairs. Indeed, it is of note that in the case of undertakings regulated by the Irish Financial Services Regulatory Authority it is expressly stipulated that that body should be consulted by the Supervisory Authority from the very outset of the review process.[7]

1 C(AA)A 2003, s 26(6) and (7).
2 C(AA)A 2003, s 26(8)(a) and (8)(c)(i).
3 C(AA)A 2003, s 26(8)(c)(ii).
4 C(AA)A 2003, s 26(1).
5 C(AA)A 2003, s 26(9).
6 C(AA)A 2003, s 26(8)(b).
7 C(AA)A 2003, s 26(12).

Corrected Accounts: Where on foot of a review under C(AA)A 2003, s 26 the accounts of an undertaking are either voluntarily corrected or are corrected pursuant to a court order, all of the provisions of the Companies Acts regarding the preparation, auditing, circulation and disclosure of accounts of accounts (including filing with the Registrar of Companies) shall apply, albeit that where the correction arises pursuant to a court order the court has a discretion to dispense with some or all of these requirements or indeed to impose more onerous requirements, as the case may be.[1] Furthermore, it is to be noted that the revised accounts may themselves be the subject of a further review by the Supervisory Authority at some later stage.[2]

1 C(AA)A 2003, s 26(15).
2 C(AA)A 2003, s 26(13).

---

27 Delegation of Supervisory Authority's functions and powers

[(1) The Supervisory Authority may delegate some or all of its functions and powers under sections 23 to 26 to a committee established for that purpose and consisting of persons from one or more of the following categories of persons:

(a) persons who are, at the time the committee is established, directors of the Authority,

(b) other persons that the Authority considers appropriate.][a]

(2) Where functions or powers under a provision referred to in subsection (1) are delegated to a committee, any references in that provision to the Supervisory Authority are to be construed as references to that committee.

(3) Subject to the regulations made under section 28(4), a committee may regulate its own procedure.

(4) The Supervisory Authority may, if it reasonably considers it appropriate to do so, perform any of its other functions or exercise any of its other powers through or by any of its officers or employees or any other person duly authorised by it in that behalf[, including the determination of whether a matter should be referred to a committee established for a purpose referred to in subsection (1)].[b]

Amendments

a Subsection (1) substituted by C(MP)A 2009, s 4(1)(a).

b Words ', including the determination of whether a matter should be referred to a committee established for a purpose referred to in subsection (1)' inserted by C(MP)A 2009, s 4(1)(b).

Definitions

'functions': C(AA)A 2003, s 4(1); 'Supervisory Authority': C(AA)A 2003, s 4(1).

Notes

Delegation of certain functions of the Supervisory Authority: See the notes to C(AA)A 2003, ss 23–26.

28 Hearings, privileges and procedural rules

(1) The Supervisory Authority may for the purposes of exercising its functions under section 23 or 24 conduct an oral hearing in accordance with regulations made under subsection (4) of this section.

(2) A witness before the Supervisory Authority is entitled to the same immunities and privileges as a witness before the High Court.

(3) Nothing in section 23, 24 or 25 compels the disclosure by any person of any information that the person would be entitled to refuse to produce on the grounds of legal professional privilege or authorises the inspection or copying of any document containing such information that is in the person's possession.

(4) The Supervisory Authority shall make regulations respecting the procedures to be followed in conducting enquiries under section 23, investigations under section 24 and reviews under section 25.

Definitions

'Supervisory Authority': C(AA)A 2003, s 4(1).

Notes

Oral hearings before the Supervisory Authority: See the notes to C(AA)A 2003, ss 23 and 24.

29 Appeals to and orders of High Court, including orders confirming decisions of Supervisory Authority

(1) In an appeal under section 23(8) or (10) or 24(8), the High Court may consider any evidence adduced or argument made, whether or not adduced or made to the Supervisory Authority or other body whose decision is under appeal.

(2) On the hearing of the appeal, the Court may make any order or give any direction it thinks fit, including an order—

(a) confirming the decision under appeal, or

(b) modifying or annulling that decision.

(3) On application under section 23(4) for an order granting permission for an investigation under section 24 into a possible breach of a prescribed accountancy body's rules by a member, the Court may—

(a) grant or refuse to grant permission, and

(b) make any ancillary or consequential order it thinks fit, including, if permission is granted, an order setting aside any decision of the body relating to the member.

(4) A decision of the Supervisory Authority annulling all or part of a decision of a prescribed accountancy body under section 23(5)(a), directing a fresh investigation under section 23(5)(b) or requiring the payment of an amount under section 23(5)(c) or 24(7)(a) or (b) does not take effect until that decision is confirmed by the Court either—

(a) on appeal under section 23(8) or 24(8), or

(b) on application by the Supervisory Authority under subsection

(6) of this section.

(5) Subsection (4)(b) applies also in relation to a decision of the Supervisory Authority requiring payment of costs under section 26(5).

(6) On application by motion on notice by the Supervisory Authority for an order confirming a decision referred to in subsection (4) or (5), the Court may make an order confirming the decision or may refuse to make such an order.

[(7) On application under subsection (4) of section 10 for an order compelling compliance with—

(a) a rule adopted or guideline issued by the Supervisory Authority,

(b) a term or condition of recognition, or

(c) an obligation or obligations referred to in that subsection,

the Court may make any order or give any direction it thinks fit.][a]

Amendments

a Sub-s 7 substituted by the IFCMPA 2006, s 18.

Definitions

'the court': CA 1963, s 2(1); 'prescribed': CA 1963, s 2(1); 'prescribed accountancy body': C(AA)A 2003, s 4(1); 'Supervisory Authority': C(AA)A 2003, s 4(1).

Notes

Appeals and applications to the High Court: See the notes to C(AA)A 2003, ss 23, 24 and 26.

30 Supervisory Authority's seal and instruments

(1) Judicial notice shall be taken of the Supervisory Authority's seal.

(2) Every document that appears to be an instrument made by the Supervisory Authority and to be sealed with its seal apparently authenticated in accordance with its articles of association shall be received in evidence and be deemed to be such instrument without proof, unless the contrary is shown.

Definitions

'articles': CA 1963, s 2(1); 'Supervisory Authority': C(AA)A 2003, s 4(1).

31 Confidentiality of information

(1) No person shall disclose, except in accordance with law, information that—

(a) is obtained in performing the functions or exercising the powers of the Supervisory Authority, and

(b) has not otherwise come to the notice of members of the public.

(2) Without limiting subsection (1), the persons to whom that subsection applies include the following:

(a) a member or director or former member or director of the Supervisory Authority;

(b) an employee or former employee of the Supervisory Authority;

(c) a professional or other adviser to the Supervisory Authority, including a former adviser.

(3) Subsection (1) does not prohibit the Supervisory Authority from disclosing information referred to in that subsection—

(a) if the disclosure is, in its opinion, necessary to enable it to state the grounds on which it made a decision under section 23, 24 or 26, or

(b) if the information is, in its opinion, connected with the functions of, and if the disclosure is made to, any of the following:

(i) the Minister;

(ii) the Minister for Finance;

(iii) the Garda Síochána;

(iv) the Director of Public Prosecutions;

(v) the Director of Corporate Enforcement;

(vi) the Revenue Commissioners;

(vii) the Comptroller and Auditor General;

(viii) the Central Bank and Financial Services Authority of Ireland;

(ix) the Irish Takeover Panel;

(x) the Irish Stock Exchange;

(xi) the Pensions Board;

(xii) a prescribed accountancy body;

(xiii) a member of a recognised accountancy body who is qualified for appointment as an auditor;

(xiv) an inspector appointed under any other enactment;

(xv) any person prescribed under section 48(1)(i) for the purposes of this section.

(4) A person who contravenes subsection (1) is guilty of an offence.

Definitions

'director': CA 1963, s 2(1); 'the Minister': C(AA)A 2003, s 4(1); 'prescribed': CA 1963, s 2(1); 'prescribed accountancy body': C(AA)A 2003, s 4(1); 'recognised accountancy body': C(AA)A 2003, s 4(1); 'Supervisory Authority': C(AA)A 2003, s 4(1).

Notes

Confidentiality of information: C(AA)A 2003, s 31 imposes a duty of confidentiality on the Supervisory Authority's present and former members, directors, employees and advisers in respect of information which has been obtained in the performance of the functions or the exercise of the powers of the Supervisory Authority.[1] However, this duty of non-disclosure is not absolute. Logically, it does not arise if the information in question has already been made public.[2] Furthermore, disclosure may be made to any of the persons or authorities recited in subsection (3)(b) if the Supervisory Authority if of the opinion that such disclosure is connected with the functions of that particular person or authority. In this regard, such types of disclosure broadly mirror the types of disclosure to regulatory and other authorities that may be made by the ODCE pursuant to CA 1990, s 21 in respect of information obtained as part of enquiries made pursuant to CA 1990, ss 19 and 20.[3] In addition, reflecting the decision of the High Court in *Dunnes Stores Ireland Company v Maloney*,[4] the Supervisory Authority may disclose such information if necessary for the purpose of stating its grounds for: (a) intervening in the disciplinary process of a prescribed accountancy body under C(AA)A 2003, s 23; (b) investigation possible breaches of standards of prescribed accountancy bodies under C(AA)A 2003, s 24; or (c) conducting a review under C(AA)A 2003, s 26 as to whether a plc or larger private company limited by shares or other relevant undertaking has complied with the accounting provisions of the Companies Acts.[5]

1 C(AA)A 2003, ss 31(1)(a) and 32.

2 C(AA)A 2003, s 31(1)(b).

3 See the notes to CA 1990, s 21 for a fuller discussion of disclosure of such information to regulatory authorities.

4 *Dunnes Stores Ireland Company v Maloney* [1999] 3 IR 542.

5 C(AA)A 2003, s 31(3)(a).

---

32 Transfer of certain functions to Supervisory Authority and related transitional provisions

(1) The Acts specified in Schedule 1 are amended as indicated in that Schedule.

(2) Subject to subsections (3) to (5), each body that was a recognised body of accountants immediately before the commencement of this section is a recognised accountancy body immediately after the commencement of this section.

(3) Where, on an application made by the Institute of Incorporated Public Accountants under the Act of 1990 before 15 September 2003 as though it were not a recognised body of accountants, the Minister decides, before the commencement of this section, to grant the Institute recognition (with or without terms and conditions) for the purposes of section 187 of that Act or to refuse to grant it such recognition—

(a) the decision is not invalid or ineffectual by reason only—

(i) that the recognition granted to the Institute before 29 January 2003 had not been withdrawn before the date of application, or

(ii) that the decision to grant or refuse recognition was made before the commencement of this section,

(b) if recognition is granted, the Institute is deemed to have become a recognised body of accountants on the date of the decision, subject to such terms and conditions, if any, as may be specified by the Minister at the time of granting recognition, and

(c) if recognition is refused, the Institute is deemed to have ceased to be a recognised body of accountants on the date of the decision.

(4) If for any reason a decision in relation to the application referred to in subsection (3) has not been made before the commencement of this section, the Minister shall, on the commencement of this section, refer the application to the Supervisory Authority for a decision.

(5) If, following the referral of the application, the Supervisory Authority decides to grant the Institute of Incorporated Public Accountants recognition (with or without terms and conditions) for the purposes of section 187 of that Act or to refuse to grant it such recognition, the decision is not invalid or ineffectual by reason only that the recognition granted to the Institute before 29 January 2003 had not been withdrawn before the date of application.

(6) For the removal of doubt and subject to subsection (3), section 192 of the Act of 1990 as amended by this section applies during its currency to any recognition granted to the Institute of Incorporated Public Accountants following the application referred to in subsection (3).

(7) Each person who, on the making of an application referred to in subsection (3), was a member of and held a valid practising certificate from the Institute of Incorporated Public Accountants is considered, for the purposes of section 187 of the Act of 1990, to be a member of a recognised body of accountants until the later of—

(a) the commencement of this section, and

(b) the date on which the Minister or the Supervisory Authority, as the case may be, makes a decision in relation to the application.

(8) If the Minister or the Supervisory Authority, as the case may be, decides to refuse to grant recognition to the Institute of Incorporated Public Accountants—

(a) each person referred to in subsection (7) is, from the date on which he or she ceases under that subsection to be considered to be a member of a recognised body of accountants, considered for the time being authorised to be appointed as an auditor of a company or as a public auditor, as though he or she had been granted an authorisation by the Minister under section 187(1)(a)(iv) of the Act of 1990, and

(b) section 187(14) of the Act of 1990 applies in respect of an authorisation under this subsection, except that the 3 year period referred to in that section runs from the date referred to in paragraph (a).

(9) For the removal of doubt, section 192 of the Act of 1990 as amended by this section applies during its currency to an authorisation under subsection (8).

(10) Each person who, immediately before the commencement of this section, was for the time being authorised by the Minister under section 187 of the Act of 1990 to be appointed as an auditor of a company or as a public auditor is immediately after the commencement of this section considered for the time being authorised by the Supervisory Authority to be so appointed.

(11) Any legal proceedings against the Minister that, immediately before the commencement of this section, are pending or underway and that relate to the exercise of the Minister's powers under any provision mentioned in Schedule 1 may be continued against the Minister after the commencement of this section as if that provision had not been amended by this section.

Definitions

'the Minister': C(AA)A 2003, s 4(1); 'recognised accountancy body': C(AA)A 2003, s 4(1); 'Supervisory Authority': C(AA)A 2003, s 4(1).

Notes

Transfer of functions to the Supervisory Authority: The effect of C(AA)A 2003, s 32(1) is to amend CA 1990, ss 187, 189, 190, 191 and 192 by transferring certain functions thereunder from the Minister to the Supervisory Authority, namely: (a) recognising accountancy bodies to act as auditors (and the attaching of conditions to such recognition); (b) continuing the authorisation of individuals who are not members of such bodies to act as auditors (and the attaching of conditions to such authorisation); (c) approving the qualifications of foreign accountants to act as auditors; and (d) consulting with accountancy bodies and other persons as to the standards and qualifications of auditors.

Transitional recognition arrangements: Pursuant to C(AA)A 2003, s 32(2) every body of accountants that had been recognised by the Minister pursuant to CA 1990, s 187 prior to the coming into force of this Act continues to be so recognised *pro tempore* by the Supervisory Authority. The bodies so recognised are: the Institute of Chartered Accountants in Ireland; the Institute of Certified Public Accountants in Ireland; the Association of Chartered Certified Accountants; the Institute of Chartered Accountants in England and Wales; the Institute of Chartered Accountants of Scotland; and the Institute of Incorporated Public Accountants Ltd.[1] Provision is also made for dealing with a revised application for recognition by the Institute of Incorporated Public Accountants which was pending at the time of the passing of C(AA)A 2003.[2] Persons who had been individually authorised to act as auditors by the Minister within the meaning of CA 1990, s 187(1)(iv) also continue to be authorised *pro tempore* by virtue of C(AA)A 2003, s 32(10).

1 Companies Act 1990 (Auditors) Regs 1992 (SI 259/1992), now repealed by C(AA)A 2003, s 59.

2 C(AA)A 2003, s 32(3)–(9).

33 Liability of Supervisory Authority for acts, omissions, etc

(1) Neither the Supervisory Authority nor any person who is or was a member, director or other officer or employee of the Supervisory Authority is liable for damages for anything done, anything purported to be done or anything omitted to be done by the

Supervisory Authority or that person in performing their functions or exercising their powers under this Act, unless the act or omission is shown to have been in bad faith.

(2) The matters in respect of which subsection (1) applies include, but are not limited to, the following:

(a) any advice given, or admonition or censure administered, to a prescribed accountancy body under section 23(5);

(b) any statement published under section 23(7) concerning a prescribed accountancy body;

(c) any investigation under section 24 of a possible breach of the standards of a prescribed accountancy body by a member of that body or any sanction or penalty imposed on such a member;

(d) any certificate of refusal issued by the Supervisory Authority in connection with an investigation under section 24;

(e) any review under section 25 of a member of a recognised accountancy body;

(f) any notice given or statement made by the Supervisory Authority under section 26 respecting whether an undertaking's accounts comply with the Companies Acts.

(3) Subject to any enactment or rule of law, the Supervisory Authority may indemnify any person who is or was a member, director, officer or employee of the Supervisory Authority in respect of anything done or omitted to be done by that person in good faith in carrying out duties under this Act.

(4) The power to indemnify under subsection (3) includes, but is not limited to, the power to indemnify a person referred to in that subsection for any liability to pay damages or costs because of anything done or omitted to be done by that person in carrying out duties under this Act where the liability—

(a) has been determined in proceedings before a court or tribunal in another state or arises by virtue of an agreement entered into in settlement of such proceedings, and

(b) would not have been determined had subsections (1) and

(2) been applied in those proceedings or would not have been the subject of such an agreement but for that person's reliance in good faith on a legal opinion or advice that those subsections would not be applied by the court or tribunal in those proceedings.

Definitions

'director': CA 1963, s 2(1); 'the Minister': C(AA)A 2003, s 4(1); 'prescribed': CA 1963, s 2(1); 'prescribed accountancy body': C(AA)A 2003, s 4(1); 'recognised accountancy body': C(AA)A 2003, s 4(1); 'Supervisory Authority': C(AA)A 2003, s 4(1).

Notes

Immunity for *bona fide* acts and omissions: Provisions similar to C(AA)A 2003, s 33 are to be found in many other pieces of legislation.[1] It affords an immunity from liability in damages to the Supervisory Authority, its members, directors, officers and employees in respect of the performance of their statutory functions and the exercise of their statutory powers unless the aggrieved party can establish bad faith in respect of the act or omission in question. To this extent, the provisions of s 20(1) appear to be little more than confirmatory of the position at common law regarding the absence of any duty of care in negligence for public regulatory bodies in respect of the *bona fide* exercise by them of their discretionary powers.[2]

In order to give this immunity from suit real substance, the Supervisory Authority is empowered to indemnify its members, directors, officers and employees not in respect of any liability in damages but also in respect of any liability for costs arising out of the performance in good faith of their respective statutory duties.[3]

1 See, for example, the Stock Exchange Act 1997, s 53 and the Irish Takeover Panel Act 1997, s 20.

2 See *McMahon v Ireland* [1988] ILRM 610; *Sunderland v McGreavey* [1990] ILRM 658; *Cotter v Minister for Agriculture* (1 April 1993, unreported) SC (O'Flaherty J); *Convery v Dublin County Council* [1996] 3 IR 153; *Yuen Kun Yeu v AG of Hong Kong* [1987] 3 WLR 776; *Davis v Radcliffe* [1990] 1 WLR 821.

3 C(AA)A 2003, s 20(3) and (4). See also the provisions of CA 1963, s 200 as amended by C(AA)A 2003, s 56.

PART 3

OTHER MEASURES TO STRENGTHEN THE REGULATION OF AUDITORS

34 Amendment of section 182 of Act of 1990 (interpretation of Part X)

Section 182 of the Act of 1990 is amended as follows:

(a) in the definition of 'public auditor' by substituting '1896 to 1993;' for ['1896 to 1993.]';[a]

(b) [...][b]

(c) by renumbering that section as section 182(1) and inserting the following: [...][c]

Amendments

a C(AA)A 2003, s 34(a) amends the definition of public auditor in CA 1990, s 182 by substituting '1896 to 1993' for '1896 to 1977'.

b C(AA)A 2003, s 34(b) inserts definitions of 'the Act of 2003', 'the 1993 Regulations' and 'the 1992 Regulations' after the definition of 'public auditor' in CA 1990, s 182. See the amended Act.

c C(AA)A 2003, s 34(c) renumbers CA 1990, s 182 as CA 1990, s 182(1) and inserts CA 1990, s 182 (2) and (3). See the amended Act.

35 Amendment of section 187 of Act of 1990 (qualifications for appointment as auditor)

Section 187 of the Act of 1990 is amended as follows:

(a) […][a]

(b) […][b]

(c) […][c]

Amendments

a C(AA)A 2003, s 35(a) inserts CA 1990, s 187(1A) and (1B). See the amended Act.

b C(AA)A 2003, s 35(b) inserts CA 1990, s 187(2)(h). See the amended Act.

c C(AA)A 2003, s 35(c) inserts CA 1990, s 187(14) and (15). See the amended Act.

36 Amendment of Act of 1990 — new section 192A

[…][a]

Amendments

a C(AA)A 2003, s 36 inserts CA 1990, s 192A with effect from 27 January 2009.[1] See the amended Act.

1 Companies (Auditing and Accounting) Act 2003 (Commencement) Order 2009 (SI 13/2009).

37 Amendment of section 194 of Act of 1990 (duty of auditors)

Section 194 of the Act of 1990 is amended as follows:

(a) [...][a]

(b) i[...][b]

(c) [...][c]

(d) [...][d]

(e) […][e]

Amendments

a C(AA)A 2003, s 37(a) amends CA 1990, s 194(3A)(b) by substituting 'access to books and documents' for 'access to documents'.

b C(AA)A 2003, s 37(b) amends CA 1990, s 194(3A) by substituting 'being information, books or documents' for 'being information or documents'.

c C(AA)A 2003, s 37(c) amends CA 1990, s 194(4) by substituting 'subsection (1), (3A), (5) or (5A)' for 'subsection (1), (3A) or (5)'.

d C(AA)A 2003, s 37(d) amends CA 1990, s 194(5) by inserting '(other than an indictable offence under section 125(1) or 127(12) of the Principal Act)' after 'an indictable offence under the Companies Acts'.

e C(AA)A 2003, s 37(e) inserts CA 1990, s 194(5A) and (5B). See the amended Act.

38 Amendment of section 198 of Act of 1990 (register of auditors)

[…][a]

Amendments

a C(AA)A 2003, s 38 substitutes CA 1990, s 198. See the amended Act.

39 Amendment of section 199 of Act of 1990 (provisions concerning register of auditors)

Section 199 of the Act of 1990 is amended as follows:

(a) […][a]

(b) [...][b]

(c) […][c]

(d) […][d]

(e) […][e]

(f) […][f]

Amendments

a C(AA)A 2003, s 39(a) substitutes CA 1990, s 199(1). See the amended Act.

b C(AA)A 2003, s 39(b) amends CA 1990, s 199(2) by substituting 'whose recognition is continued under section 32(2) of the Act of 2003' for 'whose recognition is renewed'.

c C(AA)A 2003, s 39(c) inserts CA 1990, s 199(2A). See the amended Act.

d C(AA)A 2003, s 39(d) inserts CA 1990, s 199(3A). See the amended Act.

e C(AA)A 2003, s 39(e) substitutes CA 1990, s 199(4). See the amended Act.

f C(AA)A 2003, s 39(f) inserts CA 1990, s 199(5). See the amended Act.

40 Amendment of section 200 of Act of 1990 (duty to keep registrar informed)

Section 200 of the Act of 1990 is amended as follows:

(a) […][a]

(b) […][b]

(c) […][c]

(d) […][d]

Amendments

a C(AA)A 2003, s 40(a) inserts CA 1990, s 200(2A). See the amended Act.

b C(AA)A 2003, s 40(b) inserts CA 1990, s 200(3A). See the amended Act.

c C(AA)A 2003, s 40(c) substitutes CA 1990, s 200(4). See the amended Act.

d C(AA)A 2003, s 40(d) inserts CA 1990, s 200(5). See the amended Act.

41 Amendment of Act of 1990 — new section 205A

[…][a]

Amendments

a C(AA)A 2003, s 41 inserts CA 1990, s 205A. See the amended Act.

42 Amendment of Act of 1990 — new section 205B

[…][a]

Amendments

a C(AA)A 2003, s 42 inserts CA 1990, s 205B. See the amended Act.

43 Amendment of Act of 1990 — new section 205C

[…][a]

Amendments

a C(AA)A 2003, s 43 inserts CA 1990, s 205C. See the amended Act.

44 Amendment of Act of 1990 — new section 205D

[…][a]

Amendments

a C(AA)A 2003, s 44 inserts CA 1990, s 205D. See the amended Act.

45 Amendment of Act of 1990 — new sections 205E and 205F

[…][a]

Amendments

a C(AA)A 2003, s 45 inserts CA 1990, ss 205E and 205F. See the amended Act.

46 Amendment of section 127 of Act of 1963 (annual return date)

Section 127 of the Act of 1963 (inserted by section 60 of the Company Law Enforcement Act 2001) is amended as follows:

(a) [...][a]

(b) [...][b]

(c) [...][c]

Amendments

a C(AA)A 2003, s 46(a) substitutes CA 1963, s 127(1) (as inserted by CLEA 2001, s 60). See the amended Act.

b C(AA)A 2003, s 46(b) inserting ',subject to subsection (8),' after ', the annual return date is' in CA 1963, s 127 (as inserted by CLEA 2001, s 60).

c C(AA)A 2003, s 46(c) substitutes CA 1963, s 127 (8) (as inserted by CLEA 2001, s 60). See the amended Act.

47 Amendment of section 128 of Act of 1963 (documents to be annexed to annual return)

Section 128 of the Act of 1963 is amended by substituting the following for subsection (6):

[...][a]

Amendments

a C(AA)A 2003, s 47 substitutes CA 1963, s 128(6) and inserts CA 1963, s 128(6A)–(6C). See the amended Act.

PART 4
REGULATIONS AND MISCELLANEOUS MATTERS

48 Minister's power to make regulations

(1) Subject to section 49, the Minister may make regulations respecting any matter that is referred to in this Act as prescribed or that is necessary or advisable for giving effect to this Act, including regulations—

(a) prescribing bodies of accountants for the purposes of this Act,

(b) prescribing designated bodies for the purposes of sections 6 and 11,

(c) providing that, effective on a specified date, a body referred to in section 6(2) ceases to be a designated body,

(d) varying, as a consequence of a regulation under paragraph (b) or (c), the numbers specified in section 11(1), (2) and (3) as the Minister considers necessary or expedient,

(e) prescribing for the purposes of the criteria referred to in section 15(2)(b) amounts that are higher or lower than the euro amounts specified in that section and that apply instead of the euro amounts,

(f) prescribing the amount of a penalty under section 23(5)(c),

(g) prescribing for the purpose of section 23(7) the manner in which notice is to be given,

(h) prescribing, for the purposes of the criteria referred to in paragraph (c) of the definition of 'relevant undertaking' in section 26, amounts that are higher or lower than the euro amounts specified in that definition and that apply instead of the euro amounts,

(i) prescribing for the purposes of section 31(3) persons to whom the Supervisory Authority may disclose information,

(j) exempting from all or any of sections 15 and 26 of this Act and sections 205A, 205B, 205C, 205D and 205E of the Act of 1990—

(i) qualifying companies within the meaning of section 110 of the Taxes Consolidation Act 1997 (as inserted by section 48 of the Finance Act 2003), and

(ii) classes of other companies and other undertakings, if the extent to which or the manner in which they are or may be regulated under any enactment makes it, in the Minister's opinion, unnecessary or inappropriate to apply those provisions to them,

(k) prescribing for the purposes of the definition of 'accounting standards' in section 205A of the Act of 1990 one or more bodies that issue statements of accounting standards,

(l) prescribing, for the purposes of the definitions of 'large private company' and 'relevant undertaking' in section 205B of the Act of 1990 or for the purposes of section 205E(9) of that Act, amounts that are higher or lower than the euro amounts specified in those definitions or in section 205E(9), as the case may be, and that apply instead of the euro amounts,

(m) prescribing for the purposes of section 205B of the Act of 1990—

(i) additional functions to be performed by audit committees,

(ii) conditions to be met under subsection (8)(c) of that section, and

(iii) supplementary rules governing the operation of those committees, and

(n) prescribing the format in which information must be disclosed under section 205D of the Act of 1990 for audit work, audit-related work and non-audit work.

(2) On a body ceasing—

(a) to be a prescribed accountancy body because of the revocation of a regulation made under subsection (1)(a), or

(b) to be a designated body because of a regulation under subsection (1)(c),

any director who was nominated by that body under section 11 immediately ceases to hold office.

(3) Before preparing for the purposes of section 49 a draft regulation under subsection (1)(a), (e), (h) or (l) of this section, the Minister shall consider any recommendations that the Supervisory Authority may make.

(4) Subject to subsection (3), before making a regulation under this section the Minister may consult with any persons that the Minister considers should be consulted.

(5) Regulations under this section may contain any transitional and other supplementary and incidental provisions that appear to the Minister to be appropriate.

Notes

Regs made under this section must first have been laid in draft form before both Houses of the Oireachtas and must have been approved by resolutions of each House.[1]

[1] C(AA)A 2003, s 49.

---

49 Prior approval by Oireachtas required for certain regulations

A regulation may not be made under section 48(1)(a), (e), (h), (j) or (l) unless—

(a) a draft of the proposed regulation has been laid before the Houses of the Oireachtas, and

(b) a resolution approving the draft has been passed by each House.

Notes

See the notes to C(AA)A 2003, s 48.

---

50 Laying of other regulations before Oireachtas

(1) The Minister shall ensure that a regulation made under this Act, other than one to which section 49 applies, is laid before each House of the Oireachtas as soon as practicable after it is made.

(2) Either House of the Oireachtas may, by a resolution passed within 21 sitting days after the day on which the regulation is laid before it, annul the regulation.

(3) The annulment of a regulation under subsection (2) takes effect immediately on the passing of the resolution concerned, but does not affect the validity of anything done under the regulation before the passing of the resolution.

51 Amendment of Company Law Enforcement Act 2001

Section 12(1) of the Company Law Enforcement Act 2001 is amended as follows:

(a) [...][a]

(b) [...][b]

(c) by inserting the following after paragraph (g):

[...][c]

Amendments

a C(AA)A 2003, s 51(a) deletes the word 'and' at the end of CLEA 2001, s 12(1)(f).

b C(AA)A 2003, s 51(b) amends CLEA 2001, s 12(1)(g) by substituting 'any other Act, and' for 'any other Act'.

c C(AA)A 2003, s 51(c) inserts CLEA 2001, s 12(1)(h). See the amended Act.

52 Amendment of Company Law Enforcement Act 2001 (certificate evidence)

The Company Law Enforcement Act 2001 is amended by inserting the following after section 110:

[...][a]

Amendments

C(AA)A 2003, s 52 inserts CLEA 2001, s 110A. See the amended Act.

53 Amendment of Companies (Amendment) (No. 2) Act 1999 (exemption from requirement to have accounts audited)

The Companies (Amendment) (No. 2) Act 1999 is amended as follows:

(a) [...][a]

(b) [...][b]

(c) [...][c]

(d) [...][d]

(e) [...][e]

Amendments

a C(AA)A 2003, s 53(a) amends C(A)(No2)A 1999, s 32(1) by substituting 'Subject to sections 32A and 33(1)' for 'Subject to section 33(1)'.

b C(AA)A 2003, s 53(b) amends C(A)(No2)A 1999, s 32(3)(a)(ii) by substituting '€1,500,000' for '£250,000'.

c C(AA)A 2003, s 53(c) amends C(A)(No2)A 1999, s 32(3)(a)(v)(IV) by substituting '(other than paragraph 18 thereof)' for '(other than paragraph 18 thereof),'.

d C(AA)A 2003, s 53(d) amends C(A)(No2)A 1999, s 32(3) by deleting 'and' where it occurs after paragraph (a)(v)(IV) and by repealing paragraph (b).

e C(AA)A 2003, s 53(e) inserts C(A)(No2)A 1999, s 32A. See the amended Act.

54 Amendment of section 43 of Companies (Amendment) (No. 2) Act 1999 (Company to have director resident in State)

Section 43 of the Companies (Amendment) (No. 2) Act 1999 is amended by inserting the following after subsection (15):

[...][a]

Amendments

a C(AA)A 2003, s 54 inserts C(A)(No 2)A 1999, s 43(16).

55 Amendment of section 13 of Companies (Amendment) Act 1982

Section 13 of the Companies (Amendment) Act 1982 is amended by substituting the following for subsection (2):

[...][a]

Amendments

a C(AA)A 2003, s 55 substitutes C(A)A 1982, s 13(2). See the amended Act.

56 Amendment of section 200 of Act of 1963 (avoidance of provisions exempting officers and auditors from liability)

Section 200 of the Act of 1963 is amended by renumbering that section as section 200(1) and by adding the following:

[...][a]

Amendments

a C(AA)A 2003, s 56 renumbers CA 1963 as CA 1963, s 200(1) and inserts CA 1963, s 201(2)–(5). See the amended Act.

57 Amendment of Companies Acts (default provisions)

The Companies Acts specified in Schedule 2 are amended as indicated in that Schedule.

Notes

Amendment of default provisions: C(AA)A 2003, s 57 amends various provisions of the Companies Acts (as identified in Sch 2) which had heretofore provided for the imposition of fines for breaches of those measures without explicitly stating that such breaches amounted to criminal offences. Any doubt as to whether those breaches amounted to criminal offences has accordingly now been removed.

58 Amendment of Defamation Act 1961

Paragraph II of the Second Schedule to the Defamation Act 1961 (which specifies statements that carry qualified privilege subject to explanation or contradiction) is amended by inserting the following after paragraph 6:

'7. (1) A copy or fair and accurate report or summary of any decision, direction, report, investigation, statement or notice made, given, prepared, published or served by the Irish Auditing and Accounting Supervisory Authority.

(2) In this paragraph, 'statement' includes the following:

(a) any advice, admonition or censure given or administered by the Irish Auditing and Accounting Supervisory Authority under section 23 of the Companies (Auditing and Accounting) Act 2003;

(b) any certificate of refusal issued by that Authority in connection with an investigation under section 24 of the Companies (Auditing and Accounting) Act 2003;

(c) any notice given or statement made by that Authority under section 26 of the Companies (Auditing and Accounting) Act 2003 respecting whether a company's accounts comply with the Companies Acts.

(3) Nothing in this paragraph or any other provision of this Act limits section 33 of the Companies (Auditing and Accounting) Act 2003.'.

Notes

Qualified privilege for IAASA Publications: The effect of this amendment to the Defamation Act 1961 is to confer qualified privilege in respect of the publication of copies or fair and accurate reports or summaries of decisions, directions, reports, investigations, statements (including disciplinary and regulatory rulings) or notices of the Supervisory Authority. In addition to the protection afforded by this amendment, C(AA)A 2003, s 33 also affords immunity from liability in damages to the Supervisory Authority and its members, directors, officers and employees in respect of the performance of their statutory functions and the exercise of their statutory powers, provided that they have acted in good faith.

59 Revocation of regulations

The Companies Act 1990 (Auditors) Regulations 1992 (SI No 259 of 1992) are revoked.

Amendments

C(AA)A 2003, s 59 revokes the Companies Act 1990 (Auditors) Regs 1992 (SI 1259/1992).

Notes

The requirements of these Regulations are now reflected in the revised C(A)A 1990, s 187. See notes on s 187 of C(A)A 1990.

SCHEDULE 1

TRANSFER OF FUNCTIONS TO SUPERVISORY AUTHORITY

PART 1

AMENDMENT OF COMPANIES ACT 1990

Item No	*Section affected*	*Amendment*
1.	Section 187	(a) In subsection (1)(a)(i), (ii) and (vi), substitute 'Supervisory Authority' for 'Minister' wherever it appears. (b) In subsection (1)(a), substitute the following for subparagraph (iv): '(iv) he was authorised by the Minister before the 3rd day of February, 1983, and is for the time being authorised by the Supervisory Authority to be so appointed, or'.
2.	Section 189	In subsections (1), (2) and (4), substitute 'Supervisory Authority' for 'Minister' wherever it appears.
3.	Section 190	In subsections (1) and (2), substitute 'Supervisory Authority' for 'Minister' wherever it appears.
4.	Section 191	Substitute the following for section 191: 'Recognition of bodies of accountants. 191.—The Supervisory Authority may grant recognition to a body of accountants but only if satisfied— (a) that the standards relating to training, qualifications and repute required by that body for the awarding of a practising certificate to a person are not less than those specified in Articles 3 to 6, 8 and 19 of the Council Directive, and (b) as to the standards that body applies to its members in the areas of ethics, codes of conduct and practice, independence, professional integrity, auditing and accounting standards and investigation and disciplinary procedures.'.

Item No	*Section affected*	*Amendment*
5.	Section 192	(a) In subsections (1) and (2) substitute 'Supervisory Authority' for 'Minister' and substitute 'under or for the purposes of section 187' for 'under section 187'. (b) In subsection (3) substitute 'Supervisory Authority' for 'Minister' and substitute 'under or for the purposes of section 187' for 'under the said section 187'. (c) In subsection (4)(a) to (d) substitute 'Supervisory Authority' for 'Minister' wherever it appears. (d) In subsection (4), repeal paragraphs (e), (f) and (g).

PART 2
AMENDMENT OF THE INSTITUTE OF CHARTERED ACCOUNTANTS IN IRELAND (CHARTER AMENDMENT) ACT 1966

Item No	*Section affected*	*Amendment*
1.	Section 6	Substitute 'Supervisory Authority' for 'Government'.

SCHEDULE 2

Item No	*Acts and Provisions affected*	*Amendment*
	Companies Act 1963, sections 10(10), 12(3), 44(8), 46(2), 47(4), 57(3), 58(3), 59(5), 69(2), 70(3), 78(5), 84(2), 86(2), 91(5), 92(4), 100(3), 101(2), 107(3), 110(2), 113(5), 114(3), 114(4), 115(6), 116(9), 117(4), 128(4), 136(3), 136(5), 143(5), 143(6), 145(4), 156(3), 157(2), 179(4), 180(5), 188(2), 193(4), 194(5)(b), 194(6), 195(12), 197(3), 201(6),	Substitute, in each of the provisions specified in column 2, 'shall be guilty of an offence and liable to a fine' for'shall be liable to a fine'.

Item No	*Acts and Provisions affected*	*Amendment*
	202(4), 202(6), 203(3), 205(5), 224(5), 227(2), 249(3), 252(2), 256(7), 261(7), 262(2), 263(3), 263(6), 263(7), 272(2), 273(3), 273(6), 273(7), 276A(3), 278(2), 280(4), 300, 301, 301A(5), 303(2), 305(2), 306(2), 310(2), 314, 317(2), 321(2), 322C(3), 358, 377(7) and 378(2)	
2.	Companies Act 1963, section 60(5)	Substitute, in the provision specified in column 2, 'shall be guilty of an offence and liable to imprisonment for a period not exceeding 6 months or to a fine not exceeding €1,904.61 or to both' for 'shall be liable to imprisonment for a period not exceeding 6 months or to a fine not exceeding £500 or to both'.
3.	Companies Act 1963, section 102(2)	Substitute for the provision specified in column 2 the following: '(2) If a judgment creditor makes default in complying with subsection (1) he shall be guilty of an offence and liable to a fine not exceeding €1,904.61, and if a company makes default in complying with that subsection, the company and every officer who is in default shall be guilty of an offence and liable to a fine not exceeding €1,904.61.'.
4.	Companies Act 1963, sections 114(2), 131(6), 159(5), 190(9), 221(2), 234(5) and 398(3)	Substitute, in each of the provisions specified in column 2, 'shall be guilty of an offence and liable to a fine' for the words 'shall be liable to a fine' in both instances in which those words occur within that provision.

Item No	*Acts and Provisions affected*	*Amendment*
5.	Companies Act 1963, section 266(6)	Substitute for the provision specified in column 2 the following: '(6) If default is made— (a) by the company in complying with subsections (1) and (2), (b) by the directors of the company in complying with subsection (3), or
Item No	*Acts and Provisions affected*	*Amendment*
		(c) by any director of the company in complying with subsection (4), the company, directors or director, as the case may be, shall be guilty of an offence and liable to a fine not exceeding €1,904.61, and in case of default by the company, every officer of the company who is in default shall be guilty of an offence and liable to a fine not exceeding €1,904.61.'.
6.	Companies (Amendment) Act 1990 section 11(7)	Substitute, in the provision specified in column 2, 'shall be guilty of an offence and liable to a fine' for 'shall be liable to a fine'.
7.	Companies Act 1990, section 50(7)	Substitute for the provision specified in column 2 the following: '(7) If default is made in complying with subsection (1) or (5) or if an inspection required under subsection (6) is refused, the company and every officer of the company who is in default shall be guilty of an offence and liable on summary conviction to a fine not exceeding €1,904.61 and, for continued contravention, to a daily default fine not exceeding €63.49 and, if default is made for 14 days in complying with subsection (4), the company and every officer of the company who is in default shall be guilty of an offence and liable to a fine not exceeding €1,904.61 and, for continued contravention, to a daily default fine not exceeding €63.49.'.
8.	Companies Act 1990, section 60(10)	Substitute, in the provision specified in column 2, 'shall be guilty of an offence and liable to a fine' for 'shall be liable to a fine' in both instances in which those words occur within that provision.
9.	Companies Act 1990, sections 80(10) and 161(6)	Substitute, in each provision specified in column 2, 'shall be guilty of an offence and liable to a fine' for the words 'shall be liable to a fine' in both instances in which those words occur within that provision.

Investment Funds, Companies and Miscellaneous Provisions Act 2005

Number 12 of 2005

PART 1
PRELIMINARY AND GENERAL

PART 2
COMMON CONTRACTUAL FUNDS

Not reproduced here

PART 3
AMENDMENTS TO PART XIII OF ACT OF 1990

PART 4
MARKET ABUSE

PART 5
PUBLIC OFFERS OF SECURITIES

PART 6
MISCELLANEOUS COMPANY LAW AMENDMENTS

PART 7
MISCELLANEOUS AMENDMENTS

Not reproduced here

SCHEDULE

Not reproduced here

Notes

Parts 2, 7 and the Schedule are not reproduced here as they are not read as part of the Companies Acts.

An Act to make provision in relation to collective investment undertakings of the kind known as 'common contractual funds'; to amend Part XIII of the Companies Act 1990 and the European Communities (Undertakings For Collective Investment In Transferable Securities) Regulations 2003 (S.I. No. 211 of 2003); to make provision in relation to certain of the matters dealt with by Acts adopted by institutions of the European Communities in the fields of insider trading and manipulation and other abuses of financial markets and in the field of offers to the public of securities or the admittance of securities to trading; to effect certain miscellaneous amendments to the Companies Acts 1963 to 2003; to amend the Irish Takeover Panel Act 1997 and the Competition Act 2002; to increase the penalties for offences under the Prices Act 1958, the Restrictive Practices Act 1972 and certain enactments that relate to protection of the consumer; to amend the Industrial and Provident Societies Act 1893 and to provide for related matters. [29th June, 2005]

Be it Enacted by the Oireachtas as Follows:

PART 1
PRELIMINARY AND GENERAL

1 Short title, collective citation, and construction

(1) This Act may be cited as the Investment Funds, Companies and Miscellaneous Provisions Act 2005.

(2) Parts 3 to 6 and the Companies Acts 1963 to 2003 may be cited together as the Companies Acts 1963 to 2005 and shall be construed together as one.

Cross reference

'Companies Acts': IA 2005, Sch, Pt 2.

Notes

Collective Citation: It is acknowledged that IFCMPA 2005, Pts 2 and 7 do not form part of the Companies Acts so are not included for the purpose of collective citation of the Companies Acts.

2 Commencement

(1) This Act (other than sections 85 and 86) shall come into operation on such day or days as the Minister may appoint by order or orders either generally or with reference to any particular purpose or provision and different days may be so appointed for different purposes or different provisions.

(2) Without prejudice to the generality of subsection (1), an order or orders under that subsection may appoint different days for the coming into operation of section 31 so as to effect the repeal provided by that section of an enactment specified in it on different days for different purposes.

Cross reference

'commencement': IA 2005, Sch, Pt 1.

Definitions

'Minister': IFCMPA 2005, s 3(1); 'enactment': IFCMPA 2005, s 3(1).

Notes

Operative dates: IFCMPA 2005, Pts I, 2 and 3 and ss 29, 30, 38, 46, 56, 63–68, 70, 73(1), 73(2)(a)–(c), 73(4), 75–84 and 87 came into force on 30 June 2005.[1] The remaining parts of IFCMPA 2005, s 73 came into force on 1 September 2005.[2]

IFCMPA 2005, ss 39–45, 47–55 and 74 came into force on 1 July 2005.[3]

IFCMPA 2005, ss 31 (but only for the purpose of repealing the enactments specified therein as far as they relate to a regulated market[4] operated by a recognised stock exchange[5]) and 32–37 came into force on 6 July 2005.[6]

IFCMPA 2005, ss 57, 58, 61 and 71 came into force on 1 December 2005.[7]

1 Investment Funds, Companies and Miscellaneous Provisions Act (Commencement) Order 2005 (SI 323/2005), r 3.

2 Investment Funds, Companies and Miscellaneous Provisions Act (Commencement) Order 2005 (SI 323/2005), r 6.

3 Investment Funds, Companies and Miscellaneous Provisions Act (Commencement) Order 2005 (SI 323/2005), r 4.

4 Directive 2003/71/EC.

5 CA 1990, s 2(2).

6 Investment Funds, Companies and Miscellaneous Provisions Act (Commencement) Order 2005 (SI 323/2005), r 5.

7 Investment Funds, Companies and Miscellaneous Provisions Act 2005 (Commencement) (No 2) Order 2005 (SI 695/2005), r 3.

Sections 85 and 86: Reference to these sections in IFCMPA 2005, s 2(1) arises by virtue of a Government amendment to the Investment Funds, Companies and Miscellaneous Provisions Bill 2005.[1] It had been noted, in relation to the Industrial and Provident Societies Acts of 1893 and 1978, that the power of the Minister for Finance to alter certain statutory limits by means of regulations had been inadvertently removed by the Credit Union Act 1997. These amendments, therefore, had immediate effect (ie 29 June 2005).

1 Parliamentary Debates, Seanad Éireann, Vol 180, cols 269–270, 26 April 2005.

---

3 Interpretation generally

(1) In this Act—

'Act of 1963' means the Companies Act 1963;

'Act of 1990' means the Companies Act 1990;

'contravention' includes, in relation to any provision, a failure to comply with that provision and 'contravene' shall be construed accordingly;

'enactment' includes an instrument made under an enactment;

'Member State', where used without qualification, means Member State of the European Union;

'Minister' means the Minister for Enterprise, Trade and Employment.

(2) In this Act—

(a) a reference to a section or Part is a reference to a section or Part of this Act unless it is indicated that reference to some other enactment is intended,

(b) a reference to a subsection, paragraph or subparagraph is a reference to the subsection, paragraph or subparagraph of the provision in which the reference occurs, unless it is indicated that reference to some other provision is intended, and

(c) a reference to any other enactment shall, unless the context otherwise requires, be construed as a reference to that enactment as amended or adapted by or under any other enactment.

Cross reference

'contravention': CA 1990, s 3(1); 'Member State': IA 2005, Sch, Pt 2.

Definitions

'enactment': IFCMPA 2005, s 3(1). In addition to the terms and expressions defined for the purposes of Pts 4 and 5 of this Act respectively, the above terms and expression apply to those Parts also.

---

4 Orders and regulations

(1) Every order or regulation made under this Act (other than an order made under section 2 or 37) shall be laid before each House of the Oireachtas as soon as may be after it is made and, if a resolution annulling the order or regulation is passed by either such House within the next 21 days on which that House has sat after the order or regulation is laid before it, the order or regulation shall be annulled accordingly but without prejudice to the validity of anything previously done thereunder.

(2) The Minister may by order amend or revoke an order made under this Act (other than an order made under section 2 or 37 but including an order made under this subsection).

Cross reference

'Oireachtas': IA 2005, Sch, Pt 1.

Definitions

'Minister': IFCMPA 2005, s 3(1). In addition to the terms and expressions defined for the purposes of Pts 4 and 5 of this Act respectively, the above terms and expression apply to those Parts also.

Notes

Orders and regulations: It is not necessary for commencement orders made under IFCMPA 2005, s 2 to be laid before each House of the Oireachtas. While orders made to commence any section of this Act[1] may be made without further reference to the Houses of the Oireachtas, any provisional orders made by the Minister under IFCMPA 2005, s 37[2] must be confirmed by an Act of the Oireachtas[3].

1 IFCMPA 2005, s 2.

2 IFCMPA 2005, s 37 allows the Minister to prescribe, by way of provisional order, any market to which Irish Market Abuse Law (as defined in IFCMPA 2005, s 29) applies.

[3] IFCMPA 2005, s 37(3).

5 Expenses

The expenses incurred by the Minister in the administration of this Act shall, to such extent as may be sanctioned by the Minister for Finance, be paid out of moneys provided by the Oireachtas.

Cross reference

'Minister for Finance': Ministers and Secretaries Act 1924, s 1(ii); 'Oireachtas': IA 2005, Sch, Pt 1.

PART 3
AMENDMENTS TO PART XIII OF ACT OF 1990

22 Amendment of section 252 of Act of 1990

[...][a]

Amendments

a This section inserted definitions of 'management company', 'sub-fund' and 'umbrella fund' in CA 1990, s 252. See the amended Act.

23 Amendment of section 254 of Act of 1990

[...][a]

Amendments

a This section substituted CA 1990, s 254(2). See the amended Act.

24 Amendment of section 255 of Act of 1990

[...][a]

Amendments

a This section inserted CA 1990, s 255(3). See the amended Act.

25 Segregated liability of sub-funds – insertion of new sections in Part XIII of Act of 1990

[...][a]

Amendments

a This section inserted CA 1990, s 256A–256E. See the amended Act.

26 Amendment of section 257 of Act of 1990

[...][a]

Amendments

a This section inserted CA 1990, s 257(4)(e). See the amended Act.

27 Amendment of section 260 of Act of 1990

[...][a]

Amendments

a This section amended CA 1990, s 260(3) by inserting ', 43, 43A' after '41. See the amended Act.

28 Insertion of new section 260A in Act of 1990

[...][a]

Amendments

a This section inserted CA 1990, s 260A. See the amended Act.

PART 4
MARKET ABUSE

Cross references

See also the prohibition in CA 1990, s 30 on option dealing by directors and shadow directors.

See also the prohibition on insider dealing in securities of a company where the securities are not admitted to trading on a regulated market, CA 1990, Pt V.

Quite apart from the statutory prohibition on insider dealing, a director or fiduciary may not, without the consent of the company in general meeting use confidential information obtained by virtue of his position as director in order to make a personal profit. It is submitted that this may be possible by permissive provision in the articles of association of the company, *Clark-Boyce v Mouat*[1] and *Kelly v Cooper*[2] which support the position that fully-informed consent or agreement to what would otherwise be a breach of duty is possible. As the articles of association of a company are under CA 1963, s 25 a contract among the members of the company it may restrain the ability of members to require directors to disgorge profit from transactions involving directors approved by the articles of association. This is constrained by the fact that nothing in articles of association can permit what is an unlawful act. See Notes b to CA 1990, Pt V.

1 *Clark-Boyce v Mouat* [1993] 4 All ER 268.

2 *Kelly v Cooper* [1993] AC 205.

Notes

The structure of the law on market abuse is multi-faceted. All of the statute law and secondary legislation is based on EU law, itself now enacted by a four-level system often called as the 'Lamfalussy Process'.

(a) Level 1 measures set out frameworks and general principles, as the Market Abuse Directive does.

(b) Level 2 measures, which are left to the European Commission to draft and enact, implement the Level 1 measures. The three Supplemental Directives (as defined in s 29 below) and the Market Abuse Regulation (ibid) fall under this heading.

(c) Level 3 measures are informal agreements between regulators of each of the EU member states where they are considered sufficient to result in a homogeneous approach to regulation and supervision of investment business throughout the EU:

   (i) guidelines for the administrative regulations to be adopted at EU member state level;

   (ii) joint interpretative recommendations and setting common standards regarding matters not covered by EU legislation, where considered necessary by the regulators;

   (iii) comparing and reviewing regulatory practices to ensure effective enforcement throughout the EU and defining best practice.

   Examples of these relevant to the law regulating market abuse are the guidelines of the Committee of European Securities Regulators (CESR):

   – 04–505b of 11 May 2005 on: (i) accepted market practices in relation to market manipulation: (ii) what CESR members consider to constitute market manipulation: and (iii) a common reporting format for reporting suspicious transactions; and

   – 06–562b of 12 July 2007 on: (i) what constitutes 'inside information' under the Market Abuse Directive; (ii) when is it legitimate to delay the disclosure of inside information; (iii) when does information as to a client's pending orders constitute inside information; and (iv) inside lists in multiple jurisdictions.

(d) At Level 4 the European Commission is to monitor the member states' transposition and enforcement of EU-wide law and regulation of financial services, so as to inform it as to whether further measures are required.

In Ireland there is a similar but not quite parallel structure, with three levels.

At the first level is IFCMPA 2005, Pt 4, which contains the framework for the enforcement of the law, providing for criminal, civil and administrative penalties for those who breach the law, and broadening the power of the Minister to make Regulations beyond the power contained in the European Communities Acts 1972 and 1973.

At the second level is the Market Abuse (Directive 2003/6/EC) Regulations (SI 342/2003), which contain the transposition into Irish law of the Market Abuse Directive and the Supplemental Directives, as well as conveniently accommodating the text of the Market Abuse Regulation.

At the third level are the Market Abuse Rules made by the Central Bank and Financial Services Authority of Ireland, called 'the Bank' in the legislation and Rules. These Rules, most recently made in September 2008, are available at http://www.ifsra.ie.

---

29 Interpretation (*Part 4*)

(1) In this Part—

'2003 Market Abuse Directive' means Directive 2003/6/EC of the European Parliament and of the Council of 28 January 2003 on insider dealing and market manipulation (market abuse), including that Directive as it stands amended for the time being;

'Irish market abuse law' means—

(a) the measures adopted for the time being by the State to implement the 2003 Market Abuse Directive and the supplemental Directives (whether an Act of the Oireachtas, regulations under section 3 of the European Communities Act 1972, regulations under section 30 or any other enactment (other than, save where the context otherwise admits, this Part)),

(b) any measures directly applicable in the State in consequence of the 2003 Market Abuse Directive and, without prejudice to the generality of this paragraph, includes the Market Abuse Regulation, and

(c) any supplementary and consequential measures adopted for the time being by the State in respect of the Market Abuse Regulation;

'Market Abuse Regulation' means Commission Regulation 2273/2003 of 22 December 2003;

'supplemental Directives' means—

(a) Commission Directive No. 2003/124/EC of 22 December 2003,

(b) Commission Directive No. 2003/125/EC of 22 December 2003, and

(c) Commission Directive No. 2004/72/EC of 29 April 2004.

(2) A word or expression that is used in this Part and is also used in the 2003 Market Abuse Directive or the supplemental Directives shall have in this Part the same meaning as it has in the 2003 Market Abuse Directive or the supplemental Directives, unless—

(a) the contrary intention appears, or

(b) Irish market abuse law provides otherwise.

Definitions

The Market Abuse (Directive 2003/6/EC) Regulations (SI 342/2003), reg 2(1) repeats most of the terms and expressions defined by the Directives: 'inside information', 'market manipulation', financial instrument', 'regulated market', 'accepted market practices'. The Act was passed some weeks before the Market Abuse (Directive 2003/6/EC) Regulations (SI 342/2003) was enacted.

The Market Abuse Directive defines 'person' as meaning 'any natural or legal person', stating in more accessible language what the IA 2005 says on the same subject: 'Person' shall be read as importing a body corporate (whether a corporation aggregate or a corporation sole) and an unincorporated body of persons, as well as an individual, and the subsequent use of any pronoun in place of a further use of "person" shall be read accordingly'.

'Enactment' is defined in Market Abuse (Directive 2003/6/EC) Regulations (SI 342/2003), reg 2(1) as including 'an instrument made under an enactment'

1 OJ L096, 12.4.2003, p. 16.

2 OJ L336, 23.12.2003, p. 33.

3 OJ L339, 24.12.2003, p. 70.

4 OJ L339, 24.12.2003, p. 73.

5 OJ L162, 30.4.2004, p. 70.

---

30 Regulations (*Part 4*)

(1) The Minister may make regulations for the purposes of—

(a) giving effect to the 2003 Market Abuse Directive and the supplemental Directives, and

(b) supplementing and making consequential provision in respect of the Market Abuse Regulation.

(2) Regulations under this section may contain such incidental, supplementary and consequential provisions as appear to the Minister to be necessary or expedient for the purposes of those regulations, including provisions creating offences (but the regulations may only provide penalties in respect of a summary conviction for any such offence).

(3) Regulations under this section may also—

(a) make, for the purposes of those Regulations, provision analogous to that which was made by section 3 of the Companies (Amendment) Act 1999 (repealed by section 31) for the purposes of that Act,

(b) impose on a market operator a requirement similar to that which is imposed by Article 6(9) of the 2003 Market Abuse Directive on the person referred to in that Article 6(9).

(4) This section is without prejudice to section 3 of the European Communities Act 1972.

Cross reference

Section 3 of C(A)A 1999 relieves parties to stabilisation transactions from the requirement to notify the acquisition and disposal of interests in the relevant share capital of an Irish-incorporated public limited company where the interests concerned are at or above 5% of that share capital and pass through whole number percentage points of that share capital by reason of those transactions.

Section 2 of the European Communities Act 1972 provides that from 1 January 1973, the treaties governing the European Communities (now the European Union) and the existing and future acts adopted by the institutions of those Communities shall be binding on the State and shall be part of the domestic law thereof under the conditions laid down in those treaties. Section 3 provides that a Minister of State may make regulations for enabling s 2 of this Act to have full effect. Such regulations 'may contain such incidental, supplementary and consequential provisions as appear to the Minister making the regulations to be necessary for the purposes of the regulations (including provisions repealing, amending or applying, with or without modification, other law, exclusive of this Act)' but 'shall not create an indictable offence'.

Definitions

'2003 Market Abuse Directive': IFCMPA 2005, s 29(1); 'supplemental Directives': IFCMPA 2005, s 29(1); 'Market operator': Market Abuse Regs, reg 2(1); 'Minister': IFCMPA 2005, s 3(1).

Notes

The Market Abuse (Directive 2003/6/EC) Regulations 2005 (SI 342/2005) are regulations made by the Minister under this section.

---

31 Repeal of Part V of Act of 1990 and Companies (Amendment) Act 1999

The following are repealed:

(a) Part V of the Act of 1990, and

(b) the Companies (Amendment) Act 1999.

Notes

Article 6 of the Investment Funds, Companies and Miscellaneous Provisions Act 2005 (Commencement) Order 2005 (SI 323/2005), designating 6 July 2005 as the date for the commencement of s 31, does so 'only for the purpose of repealing the enactments specified in that section in so far as they relate to a regulated market (within the meaning of Directive 2003/71/EC of the European Parliament and of the Council of 4 November 2003) operated by a recognised stock exchange within the meaning Pt V of the Companies Act 1990 (No 33 of 1990).' This means that CA 1990, Pt V and C(A)A 1999 continue in force insofar as they concern securities of companies admitted to trading on one of the Irish Stock Exchange markets other than its main market for listed securities (often called the Official List).

32 Conviction on indictment of offences under Irish market abuse law: penalties

A person who is guilty of an offence created by Irish market abuse law (being an offence expressed by that law to be an offence to which this section applies) shall, without prejudice to any penalties provided by that law in respect of a summary conviction for the offence, be liable, on conviction on indictment, to a fine not exceeding €10,000,000 or imprisonment for a term not exceeding 10 years or both.

Cross Reference

The comparable provision under CA 1990, Pt V is s 114.

Definitions

'Irish market abuse law': IFCMPA 2005, s 29(1).

UK legislation

Criminal Justice Act 1993, s 61(1). FSMA 2000, s 129.

33 Civil liability for certain breaches of Irish market abuse law

(1) If a person contravenes a provision of Irish market abuse law (being a provision the purpose of which is expressed by that law to be for the implementation of Article 2, 3 or 4 of the 2003 Market Abuse Directive) the person shall be liable—

(a) to compensate any other party to the transaction concerned who was not in possession of the relevant information for any loss sustained by that party by reason of any difference between the price at which the financial instruments concerned were acquired or disposed of and the price at which they would have been likely to have been acquired or disposed of in such a transaction at the time when the first-mentioned transaction took place if that information had been generally available, and

(b) to account to the body corporate or other legal entity which issued the financial instruments concerned for any profit accruing to the first-mentioned person from acquiring or disposing of those instruments.

(2) If a person contravenes a provision of Irish market abuse law (being a provision the purpose of which is expressed by that law to be for the implementation of Article 5 of the 2003 Market Abuse Directive) the person shall be liable—

(a) to compensate any other party who acquired or disposed of financial instruments by reason of the contravention, and

(b) to account to the body corporate or other legal entity which issued the financial instruments concerned for any profit accruing to the first-mentioned person from acquiring or disposing of those instruments.

(3) Subsections (1) and (2) are without prejudice to any other cause of action which may lie against the person for contravening the provision concerned.

(4) An action under subsection (1) or (2) shall not be commenced more than 2 years after the date of the contravention concerned.

Cross reference

Article 2 deals with inside information and art 3 deals with tipping, or passing on inside information. Article 4 extends the prohibition to persons who know or ought to know that the information concerned is inside information.

The comparable provision under CA 1990, Pt V is s 109(1). However, the limit laid down by s 109(2) on recovery under the provision contained in s 109(1) is not repeated in s 33.

Article 5 is concerned with market manipulation.

Definitions

'Irish market abuse law': IFCMPA 2005, s 29(1); '2003 Market Abuse Directive': IFCMPA 2005, s 29(1); 'supplemental Directives': IFCMPA 2005, s 29(1); 'contravene': Market Abuse Regs, reg 2(1); 'contravention': Market Abuse Regs, reg 2(1); 'financial instruments: Market Abuse Regs, reg 2(1).

UK legislation

See FSMA 2000, s 150.

---

34 Supplementary rules, etc., by competent authority

(1) In this section "competent authority" means the competent authority designated under Irish market abuse law.

(2) The competent authority may make rules imposing or enabling the competent authority to impose requirements on persons on whom an obligation or obligations are imposed by Irish market abuse law, being requirements—

(a) to do or not to do specified things so as to secure that the provisions of Irish market abuse law are complied with and, in particular (without limiting the generality of this paragraph), to adopt specified procedures and use specified forms in the provision of information to the competent authority,

(b) to do or not to do specified things so as to secure the effective supervision by the competent authority of activities of the kind to which Irish market abuse law relates and, in particular (without limiting the generality of this paragraph), to make such reports or disclose such matters, at such times and in such manner, to the competent authority or other specified persons as are provided for by the rules or specified by the competent authority pursuant to the rules, being reports or a disclosure of matters that is or are required by virtue or in consequence of the operation of Irish market abuse law.

(3) Rules under this section may include rules providing for the manner in which or the matters by reference to which (or both) a determination is to be made of any issue as to whether a financial interest or interests is or are significant for the purposes of the provisions of Irish market abuse law implementing Article 5(1) of Commission Directive No 2003/125/EC of 22 December 2003.

(4) Rules under this section may contain such consequential, incidental or supplemental provisions as the competent authority considers necessary or expedient.

(5) Rules under this section shall not contain any provision that is inconsistent with Irish market abuse law or require the provision of information to any person the provision of which is not reasonably related to the purposes for which the applicable provisions of the 2003 Market Abuse Directive or the supplemental Directives have been adopted.

(6) The provisions of Irish market abuse law that are expressed by that law to be made for the purpose of enabling the imposition of administrative sanctions shall apply in relation to a contravention of rules under this section as they apply in relation to a contravention of a provision of Irish market abuse law and, accordingly, a sanction that may be imposed pursuant to the first-mentioned provisions of Irish market abuse law in respect of a contravention of a provision of that law may, in accordance with that law, be imposed in respect of a contravention of rules under this section.

(7) The competent authority may issue guidelines in writing as to the steps that may be taken to comply with Irish market abuse law.

Definitions

'Irish market abuse law': IFCMPA 2005, s 29(1); '2003 Market Abuse Directive': IFCMPA 2005, s 29(1) 'supplemental Directives': IFCMPA 2005, s 29(1); 'contravention': Market Abuse Regs, reg 2(1).

Notes

The Financial Regulator has made Market Abuse Rules, most recently in September 2008, which included the ban on short selling the shares of the four quoted Irish financial services companies.

---

35 Amendment of section 33AJ of Central Bank Act 1942

Section 33AJ (inserted by the Central Bank and Financial Services Authority of Ireland Act 2003) of the Central Bank Act 1942 is amended by substituting the following subsection for subsection (7):

> "(7) In this section, 'agent' includes a person appointed or authorised by the Bank, the Governor or the Chief Executive to perform any function or exercise a power under the Central Bank Acts or any other enactment.".

Note

The Central Bank Act 1942, s 33AK grants immunity to the Bank and connected office holders of the Bank when exercising statutory duties. This amendment substitutes the word "enactment" for the word 'Act' as the last word in this subsection, so as to ensure that the statutory immunity given to the Bank is extended to circumstances where the particular activity in respect of which immunity is relevant is conducted under secondary legislation or any instrument made under any such primary or secondary legislation, as opposed to primary legislation; 'enactment' is defined in the Market Abuse (Directive 2003/6/EC) Regulations (SI 342/2003), reg 2(1) as including 'an instrument made under an enactment'.

36 Amendment of section 33AK of Central Bank Act 1942

The definition of "Supervisory Directives" in subsection (10) of section 33AK (inserted by the Central Bank and Financial Services Authority of Ireland Act 2003) of the Central Bank Act 1942 is amended by substituting the following paragraphs for paragraph (e):

"(e) Council Directive 92/96/EEC of 10 November 1992 (OJ L360, 9.12.1992, p. 1),

(f) the 2003 Market Abuse Directive (within the meaning of Part 4 of the Investment Funds, Companies and Miscellaneous Provisions Act 2005),

(g) the supplemental Directives (within the meaning of that Part 4),

(h) the 2003 Prospectus Directive (within the meaning of Part 5 of the Investment Funds, Companies and Miscellaneous Provisions Act 2005);".

Cross reference

The Central Bank Act 1942, s 33AK imposes duties of confidentiality on the Bank and connected office holders of the Bank where disclosure of information would be in breach of certain EU measures, to which are now added the above four Directives.

Council Directive 92/96/EEC of 10 November 1992 on the coordination of laws, regulations and administrative provisions relating to direct life assurance and amending Directives 79/267/EEC and 90/619/EEC – the third life assurance Directive).

Definitions

'2003 Market Abuse Directive': IFCMPA 2005, s 29(1); 'supplemental Directives': IFCMPA 2005, s 29(1); '2003 Prospectus Directive': IFCMPA 2005, s 38(1).

37 Application of Irish market abuse law to certain markets

(1) The Minister, after consultation with the competent authority designated under Irish market abuse law, may, by provisional order, provide that one or more provisions of Irish market abuse law that apply in relation to a market to which the 2003 Market Abuse Directive applies shall, with such modifications, if any, as are specified in the order, apply to a market specified in the order.

(2) The Minister may, by provisional order, amend or revoke a provisional order under this section (including a provisional order under this subsection).

(3) A provisional order under this section shall not have effect unless or until it is confirmed by an Act of the Oireachtas.

Definitions

'Irish market abuse law': IFCMPA 2005, 29(1); '2003 Market Abuse Directive': IFCMPA 2005, s 29(1); 'Minister': IFCMPA 2005, s 3(1).

Notes

This provides the opportunity to extend IFCMPA 2005, Pt 4 and the Market Abuse Regs, reg 2(1) to unregulated markets. The usefulness of the section is undermined somewhat by the requirement that any order be confirmed by Act of the Oireachtas.

PART 5
PUBLIC OFFERS OF SECURITIES

Notes

Like the law on insider dealing and market manipulation (market abuse), the structure of the law on public offers of securities and prospectuses is multi-faceted. With few exceptions, all of the statute law and secondary legislation is based on EU law, itself now enacted by the four-level 'Lamfalussy Process' under which EU financial services law is now enacted:

(a) Level 1 measures set out frameworks and general principles, as the Prospectus Directive does.

(b) Level 2 measures, which are left to the European Commission to draft and enact, implement the Level 1 measures. The Prospectus Regulation (as defined in s 38 below) is such a measure.

(c) Level 3 measures are informal agreements between regulators of each of the EU member states where they are considered sufficient to result in a homogeneous approach to regulation and supervision of investment business throughout the EU:

  (i) guidelines for the administrative regulations to be adopted at EU member state level;

  (ii) joint interpretative recommendations and setting common standards regarding matters not covered by EU legislation, where considered necessary by the regulators;

  (iii) comparing and reviewing regulatory practices to ensure effective enforcement throughout the EU and defining best practice.

  Examples of these relevant to the law regulating prospectuses and public offers are the guidelines of the Committee of European Securities Regulators (CESR):

  – 05–054b of 10 February 2005 on the consistent implementation of the Prospectus Regulation 809/2004; and

  – 08–602 of August 2008 setting out a sixth version of frequently asked questions regarding prospectuses and common positions agreed by CESR members.

(d) At Level 4 the European Commission is to monitor the member states' transposition and enforcement of EU-wide law and regulation of financial services, so as to inform it as to whether further measures are required.

In Ireland there is a similar but not quite parallel structure, with three levels:

(i) At the first level is IFCMPA 2005, Pt 5, which contains the framework for the enforcement of the law, providing for criminal, civil and administrative penalties for those who breach the law, broadening the power of the Minister to make Regulations beyond the power contained in the European Communities Acts 1972 and 1973, and dealing with those aspects of public offers not within the score of the 2003 Prospectus Directive.

(ii) At the second level is the Prospectus Regs (SI 324/2005) which contain the transposition into Irish law of the 2003 Prospectus Directive.

(iii) At the third level are the Prospectus Rules made by the Central Bank and Financial Services Authority of Ireland, called 'the Bank' in the legislation and Rules. These Rules, most recently made in August 2008 are available at http://www.ifsra.ie.

---

38 Interpretation (*Part 5*)

(1) In this Part, unless the context otherwise requires—

"2003 Prospectus Directive" means Directive 2003/71/EC of the European Parliament and of the Council of 4 November 2003 (OJ L345, 31.12.2003, p. 64.), including that Directive as it stands amended for the time being;

"body corporate" includes a company;

"EEA Agreement" means the Agreement on the European Economic Area signed at Oporto on 2 May 1992, as amended for the time being;

"EU prospectus law" means—

(a) the measures adopted for the time being by a Member State (including the State) or a Member State of the EEA to implement the 2003 Prospectus Directive,

(b) any measures directly applicable in consequence of the 2003 Prospectus Directive and, without prejudice to the generality of this paragraph, includes the Prospectus Regulation, and

(c) any supplementary and consequential measures adopted for the time being by a Member State (including the State) or a Member State of the EEA in respect of the Prospectus Regulation;

"expert", save where a different construction in respect of that expression applies for the purposes of this Part by virtue of Irish prospectus law, includes engineer, valuer, accountant and any other individual or body (whether incorporated or unincorporated) the profession of whom, or the profession of members, officers or employees of which, gives authority to a statement made by the individual or body;

"Irish prospectus law" means—

(a) the measures adopted for the time being by the State to implement the 2003 Prospectus Directive (whether an Act of the Oireachtas, regulations under section 3 of the European Communities Act 1972, regulations under section 46 or any other enactment (other than, save where the context otherwise admits, this Part)),

(b) any measures directly applicable in the State in consequence of the 2003 Prospectus Directive and, without prejudice to the generality of this paragraph, includes the Prospectus Regulation, and

(c) any supplementary and consequential measures adopted for the time being by the State in respect of the Prospectus Regulation;

"issuer" means a body corporate or other legal entity which issues or proposes to issue securities;

"local offer" means an offer of securities to the public in the State where—

(a) the offer expressly limits the amount of the total consideration for the offer to less than €2,500,000 (and the means by which that limit shall be calculated, in particular in the case of a series of such offers of securities, shall be the same as that provided for by regulations under section 46 in relation to analogous limits specified by those regulations for any purpose),

(b) the securities are other than those referred to in any of paragraphs (a) to (g) or paragraph (i) or (j) of Article 1(2) of the 2003 Prospectus Directive, and

(c) the offer is not of a kind described in Article 3(2) of the 2003 Prospectus Directive;

"Member State of the EEA" means a state that is a contracting party to the EEA Agreement;

"offer of securities to the public" has the same meaning as it has in Irish prospectus law;

"offering document" means a document prepared for a local offer which document, if prepared in connection with an offer to which the 2003 Prospectus Directive applies, would be a prospectus;

"offeror" means a body corporate or other legal entity or an individual which or who offers securities to the public;

"promoter" means, subject to subsection (5), a promoter who was a party to the preparation of a prospectus, or of the portion thereof containing an untrue statement;

"prospectus" means a document or documents in such form and containing such information as may be required by or under this Part or EU prospectus law, howsoever the document or documents are constituted, but does not include any advertisements in newspapers or journals derived from the foregoing;

"Prospectus Regulation" means Commission Regulation (EC) No. 809/2004 of 29 April 2004 implementing Directive 2003/71/EC of the European Parliament and of the Council as regards information contained in prospectuses as well as the format, incorporation by reference and publication of such prospectuses and dissemination of advertisements[2];

"securities" has the same meaning as it has in Irish prospectus law, and includes shares and debentures of a company.

(2) A word or expression that is used in this Part and is also used in the 2003 Prospectus Directive shall have in this Part the same meaning as it has in that Directive, unless—

(a) the contrary intention appears, or

(b) Irish prospectus law provides otherwise.

(3) For the purposes of this Part—

(a) a statement included in a prospectus shall be deemed to be untrue if it is misleading in the form and context in which it is included, and

(b) a statement shall be deemed to be included in a prospectus if it is contained therein or in any report or memorandum appearing on the face thereof or by reference incorporated therein.

[(3A) Without limiting the meaning of that expression in any other context in which it is used in this Part, 'statement' in section 45(2) (other than paragraph (b) thereof) and any other section of this Part that makes provision in respect of an expert includes a report and a valuation.][a]

(4) Nothing in this Part shall limit or diminish any liability which any person may incur under the general law.

(5) For the purposes of sections 41 and 43, the following persons shall be deemed not to be a promoter or a person who has authorised the issue of the prospectus—

(a) a professional adviser to any person referred to in section 41 acting as such;

(b) an underwriter or professional adviser to an underwriter acting as such.

(6) The person referred to as the "purchaser" in the following case shall be deemed to be an underwriter for the purposes of subsection (5)(b).

(7) That case is one in which—

(a) a person (the "offeror") intends to make an offer of securities to the public, and

(b) another person (the "purchaser")—

(i) agrees to purchase those securities with the intention of their immediate resale to give effect to that intention of the offeror, at a profit or subject to payment by the offeror to the purchaser of a commission, and

(ii) binds himself or herself to purchase, or procure the purchase of, any of the securities not so resold.

Amendments

a Sub-s (3A) inserted by IFCMPA 2006, s 15(a).

Definitions

All the definitions in the 2003 Prospectus Directive are repeated in the Prospectus (Directive 2003/71/EC) Regs (SI 324/2003), reg 2(1).

The definition of 'prospectus' in CA 1963 s 2(1) has been superseded by the definition in the Prospectus Regs; 'company', for the purposes of this Part, is defined by the Prospectus Regs as including 'any body corporate', superseding the definition in CA 1963 s 2(1); 'enactment': the Prospectus Regs, reg 2(1); 'Member State': the Prospectus Regs, reg 2(1); 'publication': the Prospectus Regs, reg 2(1); 'securities': the Prospectus Regs, reg 2(1); 'offer of securities to the public': the Prospectus Regs, reg 2(1).

Notes

The definition of offer of securities to the public cross refers to the definition in the the Prospectus Regs, reg 2(1), which is drawn from the Prospectus Directive 2003/71/EC itself:

> "offer of securities to the public" or "public offer" means a communication to persons in any form and by any means, presenting sufficient information on the terms of the offer and the securities to be offered, so as to enable an investor to decide to purchase or subscribe for those securities or apply to purchase or subscribe for those securities and this definition shall be construed as—

(a) being also applicable to the placing of securities through financial intermediaries; and

(b) as not being applicable to trading on a regulated market or any other market operated by an approved stock exchange;

Reg 2(6) states: For the purpose of the definition of 'offer of securities to the public' in this Regulation "communication" shall include an invitation to treat.

In so far as the company itself offers its shares to the public, this may occur in the following ways:

A direct offer or an offer for sale: Both of these methods involve an offer of the shares to the public at large and accordingly, before they can be used, the pre-emption rights contained in C(A)A 1983, s 23 must first be waived. See notes to C(A)A, s 23:

(a) In the case of a direct offer, the shares are offered for subscription directly to the public. A direct offer will, however, have little prospect of success unless the securities have a trading facility on the Stock Exchange with or without an admission to listing.

(b) With an offer for sale, the share are not issued directly to the public. Instead, the company will agree to allot the entire issue to an issuing house, usually an investment bank or special purpose company of an investment bank, and the issuing house will in turn seek to sell the shares to members of the public. The main advantage of an offer for sale, as far as the company is concerned, is that the risk of a lack of demand for the shares lies with the issuing house rather than with the company itself. In practice therefore, most companies will opt for a direct offer rather than an offer for sale, if it is sufficiently large and well known to attract public interest and confidence, or if the issue price is so competitive that there is no real risk of under-subscription. In passing it is worth noting that in the US, an offer for sale would be an often-used method of offering securities, with the underwriting commission being replaced or substituted by a profit on the sale of the securities.

Placing: Rather than offer the shares to the general public, the company may instead agree to allot the shares to an issuing house and the issuing house will in turn seek to sell the shares with selected institutional clients. This process is known as placing, and as with an offer for sale, it removes any risk for the company of under-subscription. The risk will instead lie with the issuing house. However, before placing can take place however, the pre-emption rights of existing members under C(A)A 1983, s 23 must first be waived. These pre-emption rights are often satisfied by the making of an open offer of the shares to all existing shareholders pro rata to their holdings. The difference between this kind of pre-emptive offer and a rights issue is that the right to subscribe for the shares is not transferable and generally has no economic value unless the offeree takes up the shares where they are trading at a price higher than the open offer price.

In practice, placing will normally only occur in circumstances where application has been made to the Stock Exchange for an admission to trading on the Stock Exchange.

Rights issue: With a rights issue a company makes a provisional allotment, nil paid, of new shares to its existing shareholders and the company then invites its existing shareholders to pay up the new shares. It is usual for there to be a disapplication of pre-emption rights to take account of fractional entitlements and shareholders resident in jurisdictions where compliance with securities law is troublesome, such as Australia, Japan and the United States. Where a rights issue is made, the company will send to each member or debentureholder concerned a circular and a provisional allotment letter. By virtue of this document the securities are actually allotted to the member or debentureholder, but subject to his right to reject them or to renounce them in favour of someone else. Renunciation is effected by completing a form of renunciation which will have been included with the provisional letter of allotment. The provisional allotment letter or PAL has an economic value, as generally rights issues are made at a discount to market value.

Where a shareholder offers shares to the public, that is known in the securities market as a secondary offering of shares.

The definition of 'offer of securities to the public' does not differentiate between the various possible offerors of shares – the company itself, an investment bank or a shareholder.

Whether securities are offered to the public directly or via an issuing house, there is always a risk that public demand will not be sufficient and that the offer will not be fully taken up. If a direct offer has been used, the risk lies with the company whereas otherwise the risk lies with the issuing house. To insure against this risk, the company or the issuing house, as the case may be, will typically enter into an underwriting agreement with institutional investors and banks, pursuant to which these institutions ('underwriters') agree to subscribe for or purchase whatever securities are not taken up by the public. Underwriters receive a commission for their service, although, in the case of an allotment of shares it should be noted that it is unlawful for a company to pay a commission which exceeds 10% of the price of the shares which the underwriter agrees to take, or such lower percentage as may be fixed by the company's articles. See CA 1963, s 60(12)(m).

---

39 Construction of certain terms in Act of 1963

(1) A word or expression that is used in a provision inserted in the Act of 1963 by this Part, or in a provision of that Act amended by this Part, and which is also used in this Part shall have in that provision, as so inserted or amended, the same meaning as it has in this Part.

(2) This section does not limit the generality of section 1(2).

Note

This means that where text in the 1963 Act is inserted or amended by the 2005 Act, the 2005 Act definitions apply to the inserted or amended provisions.

---

40 Repeal of certain provisions of Act of 1963 and revocation

(1) The following are repealed:

(a) sections 43 to 47, 49 to 52, 54, 56 and 59, subsections (15B) and (15C) of section 60 and sections 61 and 361 to 367 of the Act of 1963, and

(b) the Third and Fourth Schedules to the Act of 1963.

(2) The Companies (Recognition of Countries) Order 1964 (S.I. No. 42 of 1964) is revoked to the extent that it is for the purposes of section 367 of the Act of 1963.

Note

The repeal of the 1963 Act provisions, which for 13 years had been duplicated by the European Communities (Transferable Securities) Stock Exchange Regulations 1992 (SI 202/1992), has ensure that there is no double regulation, of the type outlined in Chapter 9 of the first report of the Company Law Review Group, 31 December 2001.

---

41 Civil liability for misstatements in prospectus

[(1)][a] Subject to sections 42 and 43, the following persons shall be liable to pay compensation to all persons who acquire any securities on the faith of a prospectus for the loss or damage they may have sustained by reason of—

(a) any untrue statement included therein, or

(b) any omission of information required by EU prospectus law to be contained in the prospectus, namely—

(i) the issuer who has issued the prospectus or on whose behalf the prospectus has been issued,

(ii) the offeror of securities to which the prospectus relates,

(iii) every person who has sought the admission of the securities to which the prospectus relates to trading on a regulated market,

(iv) the guarantor of the issue of securities to which the prospectus relates,

(v) every person who is a director of the issuer at the time of the issue of the prospectus,

(vi) every person who has authorised himself or herself to be named and is named in the prospectus as a director of the issuer or as having agreed to become such a director either immediately or after an interval of time,

(vii) every person being a promoter of the issuer,

(viii) every person who has authorised the issue of the prospectus (not being the competent authority designated under Irish prospectus law).

[(2) In addition to the persons specified in subsection (1) as being liable in the circumstances there set out, an expert who has given the consent required by section 45 to the inclusion in a prospectus of a statement purporting to be made by him or her shall, subject to sections 42 and 43, be liable to pay compensation to all persons who acquire any securities on the faith of the prospectus for the loss or damage they may have sustained by reason of an untrue statement in the prospectus purporting to be made by him or her as an expert.][b]

Amendments

a Existing section re-numbered as sub-s (1) by IFCMPA 2006, s 15(b)(i).

b Sub-s (2) inserted by IFCMPA 2006, s 15(b)(ii).

Definitions

'EU prospectus law': IFCMPA 2005, s 38(1); 'Irish prospectus law': IFCMPA 2005, s 38(1); 'issuer': IFCMPA 2005, s 38(1); 'offeror': IFCMPA 2005, s 38(1); 'promoter': IFCMPA 2005, s 38(1); 'prospectus': IFCMPA 2005, s 38(1); 'offeror': the Prospectus Regs, reg 2(1); 'regulated market': the Prospectus Regs, reg 2(1); 'securities': the Prospectus Regs, reg 2(1).

Notes

Guarantees by Minister for Finance: The Financial Measures (Miscellaneous Provisions) Act 2009, reg 15(2) provides that, 'Nothing in section 41 of the Investment Funds, Companies and Miscellaneous Provisions Act 2005 renders the Minister for Finance liable to pay compensation to any person who acquires any security the issue of which has been guaranteed by that Minister.

Measure of compensation: The appropriate criteria for measuring damages are those traditionally applied in measuring damages in tort.[1]

1 *McConnell v Wright* [1903] 1 Ch 546; *Clark v Urquhart* [1930] AC 28, [1930] NI 4; *Stevens v Hoare* (1904) 20 TLR 407.

Common law and equitable remedies for untrue statements: Civil liability for misstatements or omissions in a prospectus may arise under common law under the heading of negligent or fraudulent misstatement. If a person suffers loss as a result of any untrue statement or omission, he may be able to claim damages in tort or contract or to rescind any resulting contract.

Damages against those responsible for the untrue statement: Apart from the remedy in damages under s 41, those persons who have been induced by untrue statements in the prospectus to take shares in or debentures of the company may sue the directors and other responsible agents of the company for the damages for the tort of deceit or fraudulent misrepresentation[1] or for negligent misstatement.[2] Such an action in damages is undoubtedly available to someone to whom the prospectus has been issued but does not appear to be available to other persons who incidentally obtain sight of its contents.[3]

1 *Jury v Stoker and Jackson* (1882) 9 LR Ir 385; *Derry v Peek* (1889) 14 App Cas 337; *Northern Bank Finance Corporation v Charlton* [1979] IR 149; *Potts v Miller* (1940) 64 CLR 282; *Jones v Dumbrell* [1981] VR 199; *Smith New Court Securities Ltd v Scrimgeour Vickers (Asset Management) Ltd* [1994] 4 All ER 225.

2 *Hedley Byrne and Co Ltd v Heller and Partners Ltd* [1964] AC 465; *Securities Trust Ltd v Hugh Moore and Alexander Ltd* [1964] IR 417.

3 *Securities Trust Ltd v Hugh Moore and Alexander Ltd* [1964] IR 417; *Peek v Gurney* (1873) LR 6 HL 377; *Collins v Associated Greyhound Racecourses Ltd* [1930] 1 Ch 1; *Al-Nakib Investments (Jersey) Ltd v Longcroft* [1991] BCLC 7. Cf *Possfund Custodian Trustee Ltd v Diamond* [1996] 2 All ER 774 where Lightman J questioned the correctness of the earlier case law and stated that it was arguable that persons responsible for the issue of a prospectus owed a duty of care to those investors who (as intended) rely on the contents of the prospectus to make purchases of issued shares on the market.

Rescission: Where a person has been induced by an untrue statement in the prospectus to take shares in or debentures of the company, he may also be able to rescind the contract of allotment and to recover the moneys paid with interest, provided that *restitutio in integrum* is still possible.[1] It will, therefore, be too late to rescind, once the company has gone into liquidation.[2] Rescission will also be refused where the inaccuracies in the prospectus are only minor or trivial.[3]

1 *Aaron's Reefs v Twiss* [1895] 2 IR 207, affirmed [1896] AC 273; *Components Tube Co v Naylor* [1900] 2 IR 1; *Northern Bank Finance Corporation Ltd v Charlton* [1979] IR 149; *Re Australia Slate Quarries Ltd* (1930) 31 SR (NSW) 1.

2 *Oakes v Turquand and Harding; Peek v Turquand and Harding* [1867] LR 2 HL 325; *Tennant v City of Glasgow Bank* (1880) 5 App Cas 317. See also *Challis' Case* (1871) 6 Ch App 266; *Langer's Case* (1868) 37 LJ Ch 292; *Bishop's Case* (1869) 7 Ch App 296; *Felgate's Case* (1865) 2 De GJ and Sm 456; *Woolaston's Case* (1859) 4 De G and J 437; *Barrett's Case* (1864) 4 De GJ and Sm 416; *Gower's Case* (1868) LR 6 Eq 77. Rescission may however be possible even after the allotment of the shares provided that the plaintiff has not yet been entered in the register of members: *Barnett's Case* (1874) LR 18 Eq 507.

3 *Re South of England Natural Gas and Petroleum Co Ltd* [1911] 1 Ch 573.

Damages against the company: Apart from any possible entitlement to rescission, the person who has been induced by the untrue statement in the prospectus to take the securities, may be able to sue the company itself for breach of contract on the basis that the terms of the prospectus were either incorporated by implication into the contract of allotment or alternatively constituted a collateral contract between himself and the company.[1] Similarly, he may be able to sue the company for damages for the tort of deceit or fraudulent misrepresentation or negligent misstatement. However, whether the action is in contract or in tort, it cannot be maintained by the plaintiff against the company while he remains as a member.[2] Instead, the plaintiff must first have the contract of allotment rescinded.[3]

1 *Re Addlestone Linoleum Co* (1887) 36 Ch D 191.

2 *Re Addlestone Linoleum Co* (1887) 36 Ch D 191 (action in contract); *Houldsworth v City of Glasgow Bank* (1880) 5 App Cas 317 (action in tort).

3 *Re Addlestone Linoleum Co* (1887) 37 Ch D 191 (action in contract); *Houldsworth v City of Glasgow Bank* (1880) 5 App Cas 317 (action in tort).

Reliance on prospectus: For a civil claim to be successful, it is not necessary to prove that a misstatement was the only factor inducing the plaintiff to acquire the shares; it is sufficient if the misstatement was one factor, even if not the main one.[1]

The section refers to acquisition of shares rather than subscription for shares, which was the formula under the former CA 1963, s 49, under which only the original subscriber for the shares (or where the shares were subscribed for and then sold to the public by an investment bank or other intermediary, the first public purchaser) was entitled to redress. It is submitted that subsequent purchasers of shares will not have a right of redress under this section, but, rather may have rights of action under potential breaches of market abuse law in Pt 4. The use of the expression 'acquires' reflects the fact that shares may be acquired by the public by purchase from an underwriter as well as by subscription from the issuer. Note that in so far as common law actions for misrepresentation or negligent misstatement are concerned, it has been held that the contents of the prospectus can only be relied upon by those persons to whom it was originally issued, and not by others who incidentally obtain sight of its contents,[2] where Lightman J questioned the correctness of the earlier caselaw and stated that it was arguable that persons responsible for the issue of a prospectus owed a duty of care to those investors who (as intended) rely on the contents of the prospectus to make purchases of issued shares on the market.

1 *Edington v Fitzmaurice* (1885) 29 Ch D 459.

2 *Securities Trust Ltd v Hugh Moore and Alexander Ltd* [1964] IR 417; *Peek v Gurney* (1873) LR 6 HL 377; *Collins v Associated Greyhound Racecourses Ltd* [1930] 1 Ch 1; *Al-Nakib Investments (Jersey) Ltd v Longcroft* [1991] BCLC 7. Cf *Possfund Custodian Trustee Ltd v Diamond* [1996] 2 All ER 774

Untrue statements: Any untrue statement in the prospectus that relates to a matter of substance or that is meaningful, may give rise to a liability in damages under s 41. However, matters of a merely artistic or decorative nature or which are linked to the form of presentation only, would not normally be such as to attract liability under the section.[1] The statement must be one of fact rather than of law or opinion,[2] so that a statement of belief as to future profits which ultimately turns out to be unfounded will not be actionable.[3] But, a statement that the directors hold a particular opinion, in circumstances where they do not, is misrepresentation of fact rather and is therefore actionable.[4] Similarly, a misstatement in the prospectus as to the contents of the company's memorandum is one of fact rather than law.[5] The following have also been held to be actionable misstatements of facts:

(a) a statement that the company was acquiring a solvent business whereas in reality it was insolvent and would only be rendered solvent by the injection of the moneys subscribed for the shares;[6]

(b) a representation as to the company's past and present trading results and financial position;[7]

(c) the concealment of the true identity of persons selling property to the company;[8]

(d) a statement that certain contractual commitments undertaken by the company were well within its capital whereas fulfilment of these contracts would have left the company with insufficient working capital to carry on its business;[9]

(e) a statement that a mine to be acquired by the company was 'rich' in ore, whereas in reality, the mine had already been worked unsuccessfully by three other companies;[10] and

(f) a statement that the company's assets had a particular value whereas the figure stated was the estimated cost of replacing them and not their present value.[11]

Statements contained in a prospectus are required to be made with the 'utmost candour and honesty. [12]

A statement included in the prospectus shall be deemed to be untrue if it is misleading in the form or context in which it is included.[13] Whilst concealment of facts does not per se amount to an 'untrue statement' it may nonetheless attract liability under s 41 if it results in some other statement which is actually contained in the prospectus being rendered untrue.[14] Similarly, the concept of an 'untrue statement' would include a statement which although to some degree literally true, nonetheless, conveys a false or misleading impression to those persons reading the prospectus.[15]

1 *FNCB-Waltons Corporation Ltd v CAC* [1975] 2 NSWLR 493.
2 *Bentley and Co Ltd v Black* (1893) 9 TLR 580.
3 *Bentley and Co Ltd v Black* (1893) 9 TLR 580.
4 *Aaron's Reefs Ltd v Twiss* [1896] AC 273; *Edington v Fitzmaurice* (1885) 29 Ch D 459.
5 *Oakes v Turquand and Harding* (1867) LR 2 HL 325; *Downes v Ship* (1868) LR 3 HL 343; *Re Hop and Malt Exchange and Warehouse Co,* ex parte *Briggs* (1866) LR 1 Eq 483.
6 *Peek v Gurney* (1873) LR 6 HL 377.
7 *R v Kylsant* [1932] 1 KB 442.
8 *Components Tube Co Ltd v Naylor* [1900] 2 IR 1.
9 *Central Railway Co of Venezuela v Kisch* (1867) LR 2 HL 99.
10 *Aaron's Reefs Ltd v Twiss* [1895] 2 IR 207, aff'd [1896] AC 273.
11 *Clark v Urquhart* [1930] AC 28.
12 *Components Tube Co v Naylor* [1900] 2 IR 1; *The Directors of Central Railway Co Venezuela v Kisch* (1867) LR 2 HL 99, 113; *Flavel v Giorgio* (1990) 2 ACSR 568.
13 Section 38(3)(a).
14 *Components Tube Co v Naylor* [1900] 2 IR 1, 59; *R v Kylsant* [1932] 1 KB 442*; New Brunswick and Canada Pty Ltd v Muggeridge* (1860) 1 DR and Sm 363; *Re South of England Natural Gas Co* [1911] 1 Ch 573. See also CA 1963, s 44 (5) and (6) and the notes thereto for further statutory liability where there have been omissions from the prospectus.
15 *Broome v Speak* [1903] 1 Ch 586, 602; aff'd sub nom *Shepheard v Broome* [1904] AC 342, 347; *Greenwood v Leather Shod Wheel Co* [1900] 1 Ch 421.

Omission of information: A prospectus with no misstatement of fact but which omits information required by the law will fall foul of this section. A prospectus as well as containing information specified by EU Commission Regulation 809/2004 must contain 'all information which, according to the particular nature of the issuer and of the securities offered to the public or admitted to trading, is necessary to enable investors to make an informed assessment of— (a) the assets and liabilities, financial position, profit and losses, and prospects of the issuer and of any guarantor, and (b) the rights attaching to such securities: Prospectus (Directive 2003/71/EC) Regulations 2005 (SI 325/2005), reg 19(1). Accordingly the preparation of the prospectus is not just a box-ticking exercise.

UK legislation

See FSMA 2000, s 90, amending SI 2005/1433, reg 2(1), Sch 1, para 6.

42 Section 41: exceptions and exemptions

(1) [...][a]

(2) A person shall not be liable under section 41 solely on the basis of a summary of a prospectus, including any translation thereof, unless it is misleading, inaccurate or inconsistent when read together with other parts of the prospectus.

(3) Subject to subsection (5), a person shall not be liable under section 41 if he or she proves—

(a) that, having consented to become a director of the issuer, he or she withdrew, in writing, his or her consent before the issue of the prospectus, and that it was issued without his or her authority or consent, or

(b) that the prospectus was issued without his or her knowledge or consent, and that on becoming aware of its issue he or she forthwith gave reasonable public notice that it was issued without his or her knowledge or consent, or

(c) that after the issue of the prospectus and before the acquisition of securities thereunder by the person referred to in section 41, he or she, on becoming aware of any untrue statement therein or omission of material information required by EU prospectus law to be contained therein, withdrew, in writing, his or her consent thereto and gave reasonable public notice of the withdrawal and of the reason therefor, or

(d) that—

(i) as regards—

(I) every untrue statement not purporting to be made on the authority of an expert or of a public official document or statement,

(II) the omission from the prospectus of any information required by EU prospectus law to be contained therein,

he or she had reasonable grounds to believe, and did up to the time of the issue of the securities, believe, that the statement was true or that the matter whose omission caused loss was properly omitted, and

(ii) as regards every untrue statement purporting to be a statement by an expert or contained in what purports to be a copy of or extract from a report or valuation of an expert, it fairly represented the statement, or was a correct and fair copy of or extract from the report or valuation, and he or she had reasonable grounds to believe and did up to the time of the issue of the prospectus believe that the person making the statement was competent to make it [and, where required by section 45, that that person had given his or her consent to the inclusion of the statement in the prospectus][b] and had not withdrawn, in writing, that consent before the publication of the prospectus or, to the defendant's knowledge, before issue of securities thereunder, and

(iii) as regards every untrue statement purporting to be a statement made by an official person or contained in what purports to be a copy of or extract from a public official document, it was a correct and fair representation of the statement or copy of or extract from the document.

(4) In subsections (5) and (6) "by reason of the relevant consent", in relation to an expert, means by reason of his or her having given the consent required of him or her by section 45 to [the inclusion in the prospectus of the statement concerned].[c]

(5) Subsection (3) shall not apply in the case of an expert, by reason of the relevant consent [...],[d] in respect of an untrue statement purporting to be made by him or her as an expert.

(6) An expert who, apart from this subsection, would under section 41 be liable, by reason of the relevant consent, [...][e] in respect of an untrue statement purporting to be made by him or her as an expert shall not be so liable if he or she proves—

(a) that, having given his or her consent to [the inclusion in the prospectus of the statement],[f] he or she withdrew it in writing before publication of the prospectus, or

(b) that, after publication of the prospectus and before the acquisition of securities thereunder by the person referred to in section 41 on becoming aware of the untrue statement, withdrew his or her consent in writing and gave reasonable public notice of the withdrawal, and of the reason therefor, or

(c) that he or she was competent to make the statement and that he or she had reasonable grounds to believe and did up to the time of such acquisition of the securities believe that the statement was true.

Amendments

a Sub-s (1) deleted by IFCMPA 2006, s 15(c)(i).

b Text substituted by IFCMPA 2006, s 15(c)(ii).

c Text substituted by IFCMPA 2006, s 15(c)(iii).

d Text deleted by IFCMPA 2006, s 15(c)(iv).

e Text deleted by IFCMPA 2006, s 15(c)(v)(I).

f Text substituted by IFCMPA 2006, s 15(c)(v)(II).

Definitions

'EU prospectus law': IFCMPA 2005, s 38(1); 'expert': IFCMPA 2005, s 38(1); 'issuer': IFCMPA 2005, s 38(1); 'prospectus': IFCMPA 2005, s 38(1). 'in writing': the Prospectus Regs, reg 2(1); 'publication': the Prospectus Regs, reg 2(1); 'securities': the Prospectus Regs, reg 2(1); 'summary': the Prospectus Regs, reg 2(1).

Notes

No guidance is given on what constitutes 'reasonable public notice'. Posting a comment on the Internet simpliciter would not suffice. However, issuing a statement through the regulatory news service of a regulated market or stock exchange would appear to satisfy the requirement for reasonable notice, as the information would be communicated into the milieu of those who deal or who advise those who deal in securities. No guidance is given as to the meaning of 'public official document or statement'. If a defendant pleads reasonable grounds for his belief in the truth of the statement, by way of defence to an action under s 41, he must give particulars of such grounds.[1] The uncorroborted word of a third party as to the veracity of certain statements which are easily capable of verification, will not per se afford the director reasonable grounds for believing that the statements were true.[2]

1 *Alman v Oppert* [1901] 2 KB 576.

2 *Adams v Thrift* [1915] 1 Ch 557; on appeal [1915] 2 Ch 21.

UK legislation

See FSMA 2000, s 90(2), (5), (12), Sch 10.

---

43 Restriction of liability where non-equity securities solely involved

[Where a prospectus is issued solely in respect of non-equity securities—

(a) only—

(i) the offeror or the person who has sought the admission of the securities to which the prospectus relates to trading on a regulated market, and

(ii) subject to, and to the extent provided in, paragraph (c), the guarantor (if any), and no other person referred to in section 41 shall be liable under that section in the circumstances in which that section applies unless—

(I) the prospectus expressly provides otherwise, or

(II) that other such person is convicted on indictment of an offence created by Irish prospectus law or an offence under section 48 in respect of the issue of that prospectus,

(b) section 383(3) of the Act of 1963 shall not apply to the directors or secretary of the issuer to the extent that such application would thereby impose a liability under section 41 on such directors or secretary, and

(c) no liability shall attach under section 41 to a guarantor of such securities save in respect of statements included in, or information omitted from, the prospectus that relate to the guarantor or the guarantee given by the guarantor.][a]

Amendment

a Section substituted by IFCMPA 2006, s 13.

Cross reference

CA 1963, s 383 as inserted by CLEA 2001, s 100 *inter alia* imposes a positive duty on directors and the company secretary to procure compliance by an Irish-incorporated company with the provisions of the Companies Acts. That duty is disapplied by this section.

Definitions

'Irish prospectus law': IFCMPA 2005, s 38(1); 'issuer': IFCMPA 2005, s 38(1); 'offeror': IFCMPA 2005, s 38(1); 'prospectus': IFCMPA 2005, s 38(1).

'non-equity securities': the Prospectus Regs, reg 2(1), offeror': the Prospectus Regs, reg 2(1); 'regulated market': the Prospectus Regs, reg 2(1); 'securities': the Prospectus Regs, reg 2(1).

Notes

This section makes it clear that the mere fact of a guarantee of an issue of debt securities does not of itself impose liability for misstatements in the prospectus on the guarantor.

---

44 Indemnification of certain persons

(1) This section applies where—

(a) a prospectus contains the name of a person as a director of the issuer, or as having agreed to become a director thereof, and he or she has not consented to become a director, or has withdrawn, in writing, his or her consent before the issue of the prospectus, and has not authorised or consented to the issue thereof, or

(b) the consent of an expert is required by section 45 to [the inclusion in a prospectus of a statement purporting to be made by him or her][a] and he or she either has not given that consent or has withdrawn, in writing, that consent before the issue of the prospectus.

(2) The directors of the issuer, except any without whose knowledge or consent the prospectus was issued, and any other person who authorised the issue thereof shall be liable to indemnify the person named as mentioned in subsection (1) or whose consent was required as so mentioned, as the case may be, against all damages, costs and expenses to which he or she may be made liable by reason of his or her name having been inserted in the prospectus or of the inclusion therein of a statement purporting to be made by him or her as an expert, as the case may be, or in defending himself or herself against any action or legal proceeding brought against him or her in respect thereof.

[(3)...][b]

Amendments

a Text substituted by IFCMPA 2006, s 15(d)(i).

b Subsection (3) deleted by IFCMPA 2006, s 15(d)(ii).

Definitions

'expert': IFCMPA 2005, s 38(1); 'issuer': IFCMPA 2005, s 38(1); 'prospectus': IFCMPA 2005, s 38(1); 'in writing': the Prospectus Regs, reg 2(1).

Notes

See s 41(1) subparagraphs (i) to (viii) which lists the persons liable to compensate for misstatements and omissions in prospectuses. Although separately listed under that heading, the issuer itself would obviously be a person which authorised the issue of the prospectus.

45 Expert's consent to issue of prospectus containing statement by him or her

[(1) The prohibition in subsection (2) only applies in relation to a prospectus if EU prospectus law requires the inclusion in the prospectus of a statement of the kind referred to in paragraph (b) of that subsection.

(2) A prospectus including a statement that is attributed to an expert shall not be issued unless—

(a) the expert has given and has not, before the publication of the prospectus, withdrawn, in writing, his or her consent to the inclusion in the prospectus of the statement in the form and context in which it is included, and

(b) a statement that the expert has given and not withdrawn, in writing, that consent appears in the prospectus.

(3) If any prospectus is issued in contravention of this section the issuer and every person who is knowingly a party to the issue thereof shall be guilty of an offence and liable to a fine.][a]

Amendments

a Section substituted by IFCMPA 2006, s 14.

Definitions

'EU prospectus law': IFCMPA 2005, s 38(1); 'expert': IFCMPA 2005, s 38(1); 'issuer': IFCMPA 2005, s 38(1); 'prospectus: IFCMPA 2005, s 38(1); 'contravention': the Prospectus Regs, reg 2(1); 'in writing': the Prospectus Regs, reg 2(1); 'publication': the Prospectus Regs, reg 2(1).

Notes

This section clarifies that the requirement for there to be a statement as to an expert's consent is to apply only to the extent that the law transposing the EU Prospectus Directive 2003/71/EC requires such a statement.

46 Regulations (*Part 5*)

(1) The Minister may make regulations for the purposes of

(a) giving effect to the 2003 Prospectus Directive, and

(b) supplementing and making consequential provision in respect of the Prospectus Regulation.

(2) Regulations under this section may contain such incidental, supplementary and consequential provisions as appear to the Minister to be necessary or expedient for the purposes of those regulations, including—

(a) provisions creating offences (but the regulations may only provide penalties in respect of a summary conviction for any such offence), and

(b) provisions revoking instruments made under other enactments.

(3) This section is without prejudice to section 3 of the European Communities Act 1972.

Definitions

'2003 Prospectus Directive': IFCMPA 2005, s 38(1); 'enactment' is defined in the Prospectus Regs as including 'an instrument made under an enactment'; 'Minister' IFCMPA 2005, s 3(1) and the Prospectus Regs, reg 2(1).

Notes

The Prospectus (Directive 2003/71/EC) Regulations 2005 (SI 324/2005) are regulations made by the Minister under this section.

47 Penalties on conviction on indictment and defences in respect of certain offences

(1) A person who is guilty of an offence created by Irish prospectus law (being an offence expressed by that law to be an offence to which this section applies) shall, without prejudice to any penalties provided by that law in respect of a summary conviction for the offence, be liable, on conviction on indictment, to a fine not exceeding €1,000,000 or imprisonment for a term not exceeding 5 years or both.

(2) In proceedings for an offence created by Irish prospectus law, it shall be a defence for the defendant to prove—

(a) as regards any matter not disclosed in the prospectus concerned, that he or she did not know it, or

(b) the contravention arose from an honest mistake of fact on his or her part, or

(c) the contravention was in respect of matters which, having regard to the circumstances of the case, was immaterial or as respects which, having regard to those circumstances, he or she ought otherwise reasonably to be excused.

Definitions

'Irish prospectus law', 'prospectus', IFCMPA 2005, s 38(1); 'contravention': the Prospectus Regs, reg 2(1).

---

48 Untrue statements and omissions in prospectus: criminal liability

(1) Where a prospectus is issued and—

(a) includes any untrue statement, or

(b) omits any information required by EU prospectus law to be contained in it,

any person who authorised the issue of the prospectus (not being the competent authority designated under Irish prospectus law) shall be guilty of an offence unless he or she proves—

(i) as regards an untrue statement, either that the statement was, having regard to the circumstances of the case, immaterial or that he or she honestly believed and did, up to the time of the issue of the prospectus, believe that the statement was true, or

(ii) as regards any information omitted, either that the omission was, having regard to the circumstances of the case, immaterial or that he or she did not know it, or

(iii) that the making of the statement or omission was otherwise such as, having regard to the circumstances of the case, ought reasonably to be excused.

(2) A person guilty of an offence under this section shall be liable—

(a) on summary conviction, to a fine not exceeding €5,000 or imprisonment for a term not exceeding 12 months, or

(b) on conviction on indictment, to a fine not exceeding €1,000,000 or imprisonment for a term not exceeding 5 years or both.

(3) Summary proceedings for an offence under this section may be brought and prosecuted by the competent authority designated under Irish prospectus law.

[(4)...][a]

(5) If at a trial for an offence under this section or an offence created by Irish prospectus law, the judge or jury has to consider whether the defendant honestly believed a particular thing or was honestly mistaken in relation to a particular thing, the presence or absence of reasonable grounds for such a belief or for his or her having been so mistaken

is a matter to which the judge or jury is to have regard, in conjunction with any other relevant matters, in considering whether the defendant so believed or was so mistaken.

Amendments

a Subsection (4) deleted by IFCMPA 2006, s 15(e).

Definitions

'2003 Prospectus Directive': IFCMPA 2005, s 38(1); 'expert': IFCMPA 2005, s 38(1); 'Irish prospectus law': IFCMPA 2005, s 38(1); 'prospectus': IFCMPA 2005, s 38(1).

UK legislation

FSMA 2000, s 397.

49 Local offers

(1) An offering document prepared for a local offer shall contain the following statements in print in clearly legible type:

(a) on the front page or otherwise in a prominent position:

"This document,

—has not been prepared in accordance with Directive 2003/71/EC on prospectuses or any measures made under that Directive or the laws of Ireland or of any EU Member State or EEA treaty adherent state that implement that Directive or those measures,

—has not been reviewed, prior to its being issued, by any regulatory authority in Ireland or in any other EU Member State or EEA treaty adherent state,

and therefore may not contain all the information required where a document is prepared pursuant to that Directive or those laws.",

(b) elsewhere in the offering document:

(i) where the offering document contains information on past performance:

"*Past performance may not be a reliable guide to future performance.*",

(ii) where the offering document contains information on simulated performance:

"*Simulated performance may not be a reliable guide to future performance.*",

(iii) "*Investments may fall as well as rise in value.*",

(iv) where securities are described as being likely to yield income or as being suitable for an investor particularly seeking income from his or her investment, and where the income from the securities can fluctuate:

"*Income may fluctuate in accordance with market conditions and taxation arrangements.*",

(v) where the primary market for the securities or the currency of the underlying business is in a currency other than euro:

"*Changes in exchange rates may have an adverse effect on the value, price or income of the securities.*",

(vi) where the securities do not constitute a readily realisable investment:

"It may be difficult for investors to sell or realise the securities and/or obtain reliable information about their value or the extent of the risks to which they are exposed.".

(2) Any requirement of subsection (1) as to the inclusion of a particular statement in an offering document shall be regarded as satisfied if words substantially to the effect of that statement are instead included in that document.

(3) If an offeror fails to comply with subsection (1) the offeror shall be guilty of an offence.

(4) No offering document prepared for a local offer shall be issued by or on behalf of a company or in relation to an intended company unless, on or before the date of its publication, a copy of the offering document has been delivered to the registrar of companies for registration.

(5) Summary proceedings for an offence under this section may be brought and prosecuted by the competent authority designated under Irish prospectus law or by the registrar of companies.

Definitions

'Irish prospectus law': IFCMPA 2005, s 38(1); 'local offer': IFCMPA 2005, s 38(1); 'offering document': IFCMPA 2005, s 38(1); 'offeror': IFCMPA 2005, s 38(1); 'offeror', 'publication', 'securities': the Prospectus Regs, reg 2(1).

Notes

This section regulates offers of securities outside the scope of the 2003 Prospectus Directive, such as small Business Expansion Scheme-type offers, where the amount being raised falls below €2,500,000 but the number of offerees exceeds 99. 'Company' is defined by the Prospectus Regs, reg 2(1) as including 'any body corporate', superseding the definition in CA 1963 s 2(1). 'body corporate' is defined in s 38(1).

---

50 Exclusion of Investment Intermediaries Act 1995

(1) Any document issued in connection with an offer of securities by or on behalf of an issuer, offeror or person seeking admission of securities to trading on a regulated market shall not be regarded as constituting an investment advertisement within the meaning of section 23 of the Investment Intermediaries Act 1995.

(2) "Document" in subsection (1) includes, in the case of a local offer, an offering document.

Definitions

'issuer': IFCMPA 2005, s 38(1); 'local offer': IFCMPA 2005, s 38(1); 'offer of securities to the public': IFCMPA 2005, s 38(1); 'offering document': IFCMPA 2005, s 38(1); offeror': IFCMPA 2005, s 38(1); 'offeror': the Prospectus Regs, reg 2(1); 'regulated market': the Prospectus Regs, reg 2(1); 'securities': the Prospectus Regs, reg 2(1).

Notes

The Investment Intermediaries Act 1995 is concerned with regulating intermediaries rather than primary markets activity. Due to alleged ambiguity as to the definition of 'investment business' in that Act, this provision was enacted to forestall an interpretation which would have made prospectuses subject to the content requirements of investment advertisements.

51 Power to make certain rules and issue guidelines

(1) In this section "competent authority" means the competent authority designated under Irish prospectus law.

(2) The competent authority may make rules imposing or enabling the competent authority to impose requirements on persons on whom an obligation or obligations are imposed by Irish prospectus law, being requirements—

(a) to do or not to do specified things so as to secure that the provisions of Irish prospectus law are complied with and, in particular (without limiting the generality of this paragraph), to adopt specified procedures and use specified forms in the provision of information to the competent authority,

(b) to do or not to do specified things so as to secure the effective supervision by the competent authority of activities of the kind to which Irish prospectus law relates and, in particular (without limiting the generality of this paragraph), to make such reports or disclose such matters, at such times and in such manner, to the competent authority or other specified persons as are provided for by the rules or specified by the competent authority pursuant to the rules, being reports or a disclosure of matters that is or are required by virtue or in consequence of the operation of Irish prospectus law.

(3) Rules under this section may include rules providing for the manner in which or the matters by reference to which (or both) a determination is to be made of any issue as to whether a transaction or transactions is or are of a significant size for the purposes of the provisions of Irish prospectus law implementing Article 2(2)(a) of the 2003 Prospectus Directive.

(4) The reference in subsection (2) to an obligation imposed on a person by Irish prospectus law includes a reference to an obligation imposed on a person by virtue of the person's exercising a right or option provided under Irish prospectus law.

(5) Rules under this section may contain such consequential, incidental or supplemental provisions as the competent authority considers necessary or expedient.

(6) Rules under this section shall not contain any provision that is inconsistent with Irish prospectus law or require the provision of information to any person the provision of which is not reasonably related to the purposes for which the applicable provisions of the 2003 Prospectus Directive have been adopted.

(7) The provisions of Irish prospectus law that are expressed by that law to be made for the purpose of enabling the imposition of administrative sanctions shall apply in relation to a contravention of rules under this section as they apply in relation to a contravention of a provision of Irish prospectus law and, accordingly, a sanction that may be imposed pursuant to the first-mentioned provisions of Irish prospectus law in respect of a

contravention of a provision of that law may, in accordance with that law, be imposed in respect of a contravention of rules under this section.

(8) The competent authority may issue guidelines in writing as to the steps that may be taken to comply with Irish prospectus law.

Definitions

'2003 Prospectus Directive': IFCMPA 2005, s 38(1); 'Irish prospectus law': IFCMPA 2005, s 38(1); 'contravention': the Prospectus Regs, reg 2(1); 'in writing': the Prospectus Regs, reg 2(1).

Notes

The Prospectus Rules (most recent version August 2008) are the supplementary rules made by Financial Regulator under this section.

52 Avoidance of certain agreements

A condition—

(a) requiring or binding an applicant for securities to waive compliance with any requirement of—

  (i) this Part, or

  (ii) EU prospectus law, or

(b) where EU prospectus law applies, purporting to affect him or her with notice of any contract, document or matter not specifically referred to in the prospectus concerned,

shall be void.

Definitions

'EU prospectus law': IFCMPA 2005, s 38(1); 'prospectus': IFCMPA 2005, s 38(1); 'securities': the Prospectus Regs, reg 2(1).

53 Amendment of section 53 of Act of 1963

[...][a]

Amendments

a Section 53 substitutes CA 1963, s 53(1).

54 Amendment of section 55 of Act of 1963

[...][a]

Amendments

a Section 54 substitutes CA 1963, s 55(1) and (3).

55 Amendment of section 57 of Act of 1963

[...][a]

Amendments

a Section 55 substitutes CA 1963, ss 1 and adds a new sub-s 7.

PART 6
MISCELLANEOUS COMPANY LAW AMENDMENTS

56 Amendment of section 60 of Act of 1963

(1) [...][a]

(2) Section 39 applies to the construction of a word or expression used in the provisions inserted in the Act of 1963 by subsection (1) as it applies to the construction of a word or expression used in the provisions inserted in the Act of 1963 by Part 5.

Amendments

a IFCMPA 2005, s 56 substitutes CA 1963, ss 60(12) and (13).

Cross reference

See CA 1963, ss 60(12) and (13) (as amended) and notes thereto.

Definitions

'Act of 1963': IFCMPA 2005, s 3(1).

Notes

Operative Date: IFCMPA 2005, s 56 was brought into force on 30 June 2005[1].

1 Investment Funds, Companies and Miscellaneous Provisions Act (Commencement) Order 2005 (SI 323/2005), reg 3(b).

Construction: IFCMPA 2005, s 39 provides that any words or expressions used in CA 1963 as inserted or amended by IFCMPA 2005, Pt 5, shall have the same meaning in CA 1963 as they have in IFCMPA 2005, Pt 5. Similarly IFCMPA 2005, s 56(2) operates to apply the same construction of words and expressions inserted into CA 1963 by IFCMPA 2005, s 56(1) as is applied to those expressions and words used in the provisions inserted in CA 1963 by IFCMPA 2005, Pt 5.

---

57 Electronic filing agents

(1) A company may authorise a person (who shall be known and is in this Act referred to as an 'electronic filing agent') to do the following acts on its behalf.

(2) Those acts are—

(a) the electronic signing of documents that are required or authorised, by or under the Companies Acts or any other enactment, to be delivered by the company to the registrar of companies, and

(b) the delivery to the registrar of companies, by electronic means, of those documents so signed.

(3) Subject to the following conditions being complied with, an act of the foregoing kind done by such an agent on behalf of a company pursuant to an authorisation by the company under this section that is in force shall be as valid in law as if it had been done by the company (and the requirements of the Companies Acts or the other enactment concerned with respect to the doing of the act have otherwise been complied with (such as with regard to the period within which the act is to be done)).

(4) The conditions mentioned in subsection (3) are—

(a) that prior to the first instance of the electronic filing agent's doing of an act of the kind referred to in subsection (2), pursuant to an authorisation by the company concerned under this section, the authorisation of the agent has been notified by the company to the registrar of companies in the prescribed form, and

(b) the doing of the act complies with any requirements of the registrar of companies of the kind referred to in sections 12(2)(b) and 13(2)(a) of the Electronic Commerce Act 2000.

(5) It shall be the joint responsibility of a company and the electronic filing agent authorised by it under this section to manage the control of the documents referred to in subsection (2).

(6) An electronic filing agent shall not, by virtue of his or her authorisation under this section to act as such, be regarded as an officer or servant of the company concerned for the purposes of section 187(2)(a) of the Act of 1990.

Definitions

'Act of 1990': IFCMPA 2005, s 3(1); 'agent': CA 1963, s 2(1); 'the Companies Acts': CA 1990, s 3(1); 'company': CA 1963, s 1(1); 'document': CA 1963, s 2(1); 'the registrar of companies': CA 1963, s 2(1); 'officer': CA 1963, s 2(1); 'prescribed': CA 1963, s 2(1).

Notes

Operative Dates: IFCMPA 2005, s 57 was brought into force on 1 December 2005.[1]

1 Investment Funds, Companies and Miscellaneous Provisions Act 2005 (Commencement) (No 2) Order 2005 (SI 695/2005), reg 3.

Appointment of an electronic filing agent (EFA)[1]: IFCMPA 2005, s 57 implements the recommendations of the CLRG[2] with regard to the introduction of electronic filing methods. An agent wishing to act as an EFA must apply to the registrar to act in that capacity.[3]

In order to appoint an EFA, a company must first authorise[4] the EFA to act as such and notify such authorisation to the Registrar on the prescribed form[5] and the acts of the agent must comply[6] with the relevant provisions of the Electronic Commerce Act as regards writing[7] and signatures[8]. The revocation of appointment of an EFA must also be notified to the Registrar.[9]

1 See generally http://www.cro.ie, CRO Information Leaflet No. 15/September 2005, 'Statutory Electronic Filing Agent'.

2 CLRG, First Report, Para 7.5.

3 Form J1(a); this form is not statutorily prescribed. This form serves to apply for a digital certificate for the EFA and to nominate individuals as verification signatories. See notes 'Electronic identification of EFA' below.

4 IFCMPA 2005, s 57(4)(a).

5 IFCMPA 2005, s 57(4)(b).

6 Form B77; Companies (Forms) Order 2005 (SI 694/2005).

7 Electronic Commerce Act 2000, s 12(2)(b).

8 Electronic Commerce Act 2000, s 13(2)(a).

9 IFCMPA 2005, s 58 and notes thereto.

Delegation of authority: The effect of appointment of an EFA is that the company delegates authority to the EFA to sign and deliver documents electronically to the registrar. Any electronic signature on a document or the delivery of such a document shall be as valid in law as if it had been done by the company and all relevant requirements under law have been complied with.[1] In delegating authority to execute and deliver documents to the Registrar, the CLRG recognised that it should be a matter between the EFA and the company to manage the control of such documents (and even then, where accounts are required to be annexed to the annual return, the accounts cannot be filed electronically).[2] However, IFCMPA 2005, s 57(5) specifically prescribes joint responsibility for the company and the EFA. It is not possible to appoint more than one EFA at any one time.[3] At the moment it is only possible to sign and deliver annual returns,[4] however, it is anticipated that it will be possible to file additional forms in due course. Also, where the EFA is a firm/partnership there is no statutory deeming that the EFA will be the 'new' partnership. This is to be contrasted with the position relating to a firm of auditors. CA 1963, s 169(9) provides that the appointment of a firm by its firm name shall be deemed to be an appointment of those persons who from time to time are the partners in the firm.

1 IFCMPA 2005, s 57(3).

2 CLRG, First Report, para 7.5.1.

3 CRO Information Leaflet No. 15/September 2005, 'Statutory Electronic Filing Agent', para 2.

4 Form B1; Companies Forms Order 2004 (SI 133/2004).

Electronic identification of an EFA: A person wishing to act as an EFA must apply to the registrar[1] for a personal digital certificate.[2] A personal digital certificate acts as an identity card, which the registrar uses to satisfy itself as to the identity of the sender of electronic filings made pursuant to IFCMPA 2005, s 57. An EFA may add to the list of named individuals who may verify the signing and sending of documents from time to time.[3] An individual who is a director or secretary of a company and who has been issued with an ID and PIN from the registrar does not need to make a separate application to become a verification signatory.

1 The Registrar is a 'certification service provider' for the purposes of the Electronic Commerce Act 2000 in this regard.

2 Form J1 and Form J1(a); these form are not statutorily prescribed. On form J1(a) nominated individuals within the EFA's organisation who may verify the signing of documents are listed.

3 Form J2; this form is not statutorily prescribed.

EFA being an officer or servant: It was recognised by the CLRG[1] that CA 1990, s 187(2)(a) could be interpreted to preclude the auditors of a company from becoming an EFA in respect of that company. The CLRG was of the view that the involvement of professional auditors in the process of filing documents with the registrar would be of benefit to company law compliance generally and therefore it is specifically provided[2] that an EFA, duly authorised under IFCMPA 2005, s 57, is not to be regarded as 'an officer or a servant' of the company for the purpose of CA 1990, s 187(2)(a). It would seem from IFCMPA 2005, s 57(6) that for the purposes of the Companies Acts generally[3] an EFA could be deemed an officer or servant in certain circumstances.

1 CLRG, First Report, para 7.5.2.

2 IFCMPA 2005, s 57(6).

3 ie other than under CA 1990, s 187(2)(a).

UK legislation

See generally CA 1985, s 707B (inserted by the Companies Act 1985 (Electronic Communications) Order 2000 (SI 1985/3373).

---

58 Section 57: supplemental provisions

(1) A company may revoke an authorisation by it under section 57 of an electronic filing agent.

(2) Such a revocation by a company shall be notified by it, in the prescribed form, to the registrar of companies.

(3) Unless and until the revocation is so notified to the registrar of companies, the authorisation concerned shall be deemed to subsist and, accordingly, to be still in force for the purposes of section 57(3).

(4) If a revocation, in accordance with this section, of an authorisation under section 57 constitutes a breach of contract or otherwise gives rise to a liability being incurred—

(a) the fact that it constitutes such a breach or otherwise gives rise to a liability being incurred does not affect the validity of the revocation for the purposes of section 57, and

(b) the fact of the revocation being so valid does not remove or otherwise affect any cause of action in respect of that breach or the incurring of that liability.

Definitions

'agent': CA 1963, s 2(1); 'company': CA 1963, s 2(1); 'electronic filing agent': IFCMPA 2005, s 57(1); 'prescribed': CA 1963, s 2(1); 'the registrar of companies': CA 1963, s 2(1).

Notes

Operative Date: This section was brought into force 1 December 2005.[1]

1 Investment Funds, Companies and Miscellaneous Provisions Act 2005 (Commencement)(No 2) Order 2005 (SI 695/2005), reg 3.

Revocation of authorisation of an EFA: It is possible for a company to revoke the appointment of an EFA by filing the prescribed form.[1] Unless such a form is filed with the registrar by the company, the authorisation of that EFA to act shall remain in force.[2] In the event that such a revocation constitutes a breach of contract or otherwise gives rise to a liability being incurred, the fact of that breach of contract or liability does not affect the validity of the revocation,[3] nor does the valid revocation remove or otherwise affect the fact of any breach of contract or the incurring of such a liability.[4]

1 Form B77: Companies (Forms) Order 2005 (SI 694/2005). IFCMPA 2005, s 57(2).
2 IFCMPA 2005, s 58(3).
3 IFCMPA 2005, s 58(4)(a).
4 IFCMPA 2005, s 58(4)(b).

UK legislation

See generally CA 1985, s 707B (inserted by the Companies Act 1985 (Electronic Communications) Order 2000 (SI 1985/3373).

---

59 Reservation of company name

(1) In this section—

'reserved' means reserved under subsection (4) for the purpose mentioned in subsection (3);

'specified period' means the period specified in the relevant notification made by the registrar of companies under subsection (5).

(2) During the specified period and any extension under section 60 of that period a company shall not be incorporated with a particular reserved name save on the application of the person in whose favour that name has been reserved.

(3) A person may apply to the registrar of companies to reserve a specified name for the following purpose, namely, the purpose of a company that is proposed to be formed by that person being incorporated with that name; such an application shall be accompanied by the prescribed fee.

(4) On the making of such an application, the registrar of companies may, subject to subsection (6), determine that the name specified in the application shall be reserved for the purpose mentioned in subsection (3).

(5) That determination shall be notified to the applicant by the registrar of companies and that notification shall specify the period (which shall not be greater than 28 days and which shall be expressed to begin on the making of the notification) for which the name is reserved.

(6) A name shall not be reserved that, in the opinion of the registrar of companies, is undesirable.

Cross reference

CA 1963, s 21: The Registrar of Companies shall not register a company with a name which, in his opinion is undesirable. See also IFCMPA 2005, s 60 and notes thereto.

Definitions

'company': CA 1963, s 2(1); 'prescribed': CA 1963, s 2(1); 'the registrar of companies': CA 1963, s 2(1).

Notes

Operative Date: IFCMPA 2005, s 59 came into operation on 1 September 2009.[1]

[1] Investment Funds, Companies and Miscellaneous Provisions Act 2005 (Commencement) Order 2009 (SI 303/2009).

Reservation of Company Name: IFCMPA 2005, s 59 implements the recommendations of the CLRG[1] in that it introduces the facility for company names to be reserved for a short period of time,[2] prior to incorporation. In certain circumstances it will be possible to extend this period by application in the prescribed form[3] for a further 28 days.[4] The purpose of introducing this facility is to allow swifter company incorporation.

This facility does not alter in any way the functions[5] of the Registrar with regard to assessing the suitability of a proposed company names (including having regard to similarity to names on the register). Only the person who has reserved a particular company name may apply to incorporate a company with that particular name during the period of 28 days[6] beginning on the date of making the notification of determination of the Registrar.[7] Application to the registrar shall be made with the prescribed fee.[8] If the Registrar is of the opinion that the name is undesirable, then the name may not be reserved.[9] Similarly under CA 1963, s 21 the Registrar shall refuse to incorporate a company with a name, which, in his opinion is undesirable, however there is no analogous provision under IFCMPA 2005, s 59 whereby an appeal to a decision to refuse to reserve a company name shall lie to the High Court.[10]

1 CLRG, First Report, Para 7.3.
2 28 days, subject to IFCMPA 2005, s 60.
3 The relevant form has not yet been prescribed by statutory instrument.
4 See IFCMPA 2005, s 60 and notes thereto.
5 CA 1963, s 21.
6 IFCMPA 2005, s 59(2).
7 IFCMPA 2005, s 59(5).
8 IFCMPA 2005, s 59(3).
9 IFCMPA 2005, s 59(6).
10 CA 1963, s 21.

60 Section 59: supplemental provisions

(1) A person in whose favour a name has been reserved under section 59 may, before the expiry of the specified period, apply to the registrar of companies for an extension of the specified period; such an application shall be accompanied by the prescribed fee.

(2) On the making of such an application, the registrar of companies may, if he or she considers it appropriate to do so, extend the specified period for such number of days (not exceeding 28 days) as the registrar determines and specifies in a notification of the determination to the applicant.

(3) If an application for incorporation of a company with a name that has been reserved under section 59 is received by the registrar of companies during the specified period from the person in whose favour the name has been so reserved, the fee payable to the registrar in respect of that incorporation shall be reduced by an amount equal to the amount of the fee paid under section 59(3) in respect of the reservation of that name.

(4) In this section 'specified period' has the same meaning as it has in section 59.

Cross reference

See also IFCMPA 2005, s 59 and notes thereto.

Definitions

'company': CA 1963, s 2(1); 'prescribed': CA 1963; 'the registrar of companies': CA 1963, s 2(1); 'specified period': IFCMPA 2005, s 59(1) and IFCMPA 2005, s 60(4).

Notes

Operative Date: IFCMPA 2005, s 60 came into operation on 1 September 2009.[1]

1 Investment Funds, Companies and Miscellaneous Provisions Act 2005 (Commencement) Order 2009 (SI 303/2009).

Extension of specified period: It will be possible for the person in whose favour a name has been reserved to apply to the Registrar for an extension of the specified time period (as defined in IFCMPA 2005, s 59(1)).[1] Such an extension in time shall not exceed 28 days and shall be granted at the discretion of the Registrar.[2]

1 IFCMPA 2005, s 60(1).
2 IFCMPA 2005, s 60(2).

Set off of fees: The fees payable in respect of the incorporation of a company for which a name has been reserved under IFCMPA 2005, s 59, shall be reduced by the fees paid by the applicant under IFCMPA 2005, s 59(3).[1]

1 IFCMPA 2005 s 60(3).

61 Amendment of section 128 of Act of 1963

[...][a]

Amendments

a IFCMPA 2005, s 61 inserts 'of the Act of 1990' after 'section 193' in CA 1963, s 128(6B)(b).

Cross reference

See CA 1963, s 128 (as amended) and notes thereto.

Definitions

'Act of 1963': IFCMPA 2005, s 3(1); 'Act of 1990': IFCMPA 2005, s 3(1).

Notes

Operative Date: This section came into operation on 1 December 2005.[1]

1 Investment Funds, Companies and Miscellaneous Provisions Act 2005 (Commencement)(No 2) Order 2005 (SI 695/2005), reg 3.

The purpose of this amendment is to clarify that the reference to 'section 193' is to CA 1990, s 193.

62 Amendment of section 195 of Act of 1963

Section 195 of the Act of 1963 (inserted by the Act of 1990) is amended by inserting the following subsection after subsection (6):

[...] [a]

Amendments

a IFCMPA 2005, s 62 inserts CA 1963, s 195(6A).

Cross reference

See CA 1990, s 195 (as amended) and notes thereto.

See CLRG, First Report, para 7.8.3.

Definitions

'Act of 1963': IFCMPA 2005, s 3(1); 'Act of 1990': IFCMPA 2005, s 3(1).

Notes

Operative Date: IFCMPA 2005, s 62 has not yet been commenced.

63 Amendment of section 302(1) of Act of 1963

[...] [a]

Amendments

a IFCMPA 2005, s 63 inserts 'or such greater period as may be required in the notice' after 'notice requiring him to do so' in CA 1963, s 302(1).

Cross reference

See CA 1963, s 302 (as amended) and notes thereto.

Definitions

'Act of 1963': IFCMPA 2005, s 3(1).

Notes

Operative Date: This section came into force on 30 June 2005.[1]

1 Investment Funds, Companies and Miscellaneous Provisions Act 2005 (Commencement) Order 2005 (SI 323/2005), reg 3(b).

Enforcement of liquidators' compliance: The Registrar and any contributory or creditor may seek a court order to enforce compliance, where there has been default in complying with any filing requirement, and following a notice requiring the default to be rectified, the liquidator remains in default. The purpose of this amendment is to encourage more widespread use of CA 1963, s 302 generally. By extending the time within which the liquidator may make good any default, it is hoped that unnecessary and expensive High Court applications could be avoided[1]. This is similar to the amendment of CA 1963, s 371(1) by IFCMPA 2005, s 64 with regard to compliance of companies and directors.

1 Dáil Debates, Seanad Éireann, Vol 179, col 1894, 14 April 2005.

UK legislation

See generally Insolvency Act 1986, s 170.

64 Amendment of section 371(1) of Act of 1963

[...][a]

Amendments

a IFCMPA 2005, s 64 inserts 'or such greater period as may be required in the notice' after 'notice on the company or officer requiring it or him to do so' in CA 1963, s 371(1).

Cross reference

See CA 1963, s 371(1) (as amended) and notes thereto.

Definitions

'Act of 1963': IFCMPA 2005, s 3(1); 'company': CA 1963, s 2(1); 'officer': CA 1963, s 2(1).

Notes

Operative Date: This section was brought into force on 30 June 2005.[1]

1 Investment Funds, Companies and Miscellaneous Provisions Act 2005 (Commencement) Order 2005, (SI 2005/323), r 3(b).

Enforcement of companies' and officers' compliance: The Registrar, the Director of Corporate Enforcement (the Director) and any member or creditor of a company may seek a court order to enforce compliance where there has been default in complying with any filing requirement by a company or an officer, and following a notice requiring the default to be rectified, that company or officer remains in default. The purpose of this amendment is to encourage more widespread use of CA 1963, s 371 generally. By extending the time within which any company or officer may make good any default it is hoped that unnecessary and expensive High Court applications could be avoided.[1] This is similar to the amendment of CA 1963, s 302 by IFCMPA 2005 s 63, with regard to compliance of liquidators.

1 Dáil Debates, Seanad Éireann, Vol 179, col 1894, 14 April 2005.

UK legislation

See generally CA 1985 s 713 (as amended by the CA 1989, s 127(4)).

65 Amendment of section 12B of Companies (Amendment) Act 1982

Section 12B of the Companies (Amendment) Act 1982 (inserted by the Companies (Amendment) (No. 2) Act 1999) is amended by inserting the following subsection after subsection (8):

[...] [a]

Amendments

a IFCMPA 2005, s 65 inserts C(A)A 1982, s 12B(8A).

Cross reference

See C(A)A 1982, s 12B(8A) (as amended) and notes thereto.

Notes

Operative Date: This section came in to force 30 June 2005.[1]

1 Investment Funds, Companies and Miscellaneous Provisions Act 2005 (Commencement) Order 2005 (SI 323/2005), reg 3(b).

66 Amendment of section 22 of Companies (Amendment) Act 1986

Section 22 of the Companies (Amendment) Act 1986 is amended—

(a) in subsection (1)—

(i) [...] [a]

(ii) [...] [b]

(b) [...] [c]

Amendments

a IFCMPA 2005, s 66(a) substitutes 'shall be guilty of an offence' for 'shall be liable on summary conviction to a fine not exceeding €1,269.74' in C(A)A 1986, s 22(1), para (a).

b IFCMPA 2005, s 67(b) substitutes 'Summary proceedings' for 'Proceedings' in C(A)A 1986, s 22(1), para (b).

c IFCMPA 2005, s 67(c) substitutes 'in respect of each such failure be guilty of an offence, but—' for 'in respect of each offence be liable on summary conviction to imprisonment for a term not exceeding 6 months, or, at the discretion of the court to a fine not exceeding €1,269.74 or to both so, however, that—' in C(A)A 1986, s 22(2).

Cross reference

See C(A)A 1986, s 22 (as amended) and notes thereto.

Definitions

'the court': CA 1963, s 2(1).

Notes

Operative Date: This section was brought into force on 30 June 2005.[1]

1 Investment Funds, Companies and Miscellaneous Provisions Act 2005 (Commencement) Order 2005 (SI 323/2005), reg 3(b).

Offences prosecuted on indictment: This section was introduced by way of Government amendment to the Investment Funds, Companies and Miscellaneous Provisions Bill 2005[1] in order to provide for more serious offences under C(A)A 1986 to be prosecuted on indictment.

1 Dáil Debates, Seanad Éireann, Vol 180, col 291, 26 April 2005.

UK legislation

See generally CA 1985, s 730 (as amended by the CA 1989, s 145, Sch 9, para 17 and Sch 24).

---

67 Amendment of section 19 of Act of 1990

Section 19(2) of the Act of 1990 is amended—

(a) by inserting the following after paragraph (d):

[...][a]

(b) [...][b]

(c) [...][c]

Amendments

a IFCMPA 2005, s 67(a) inserts CA 1990, para 19(2)(da).

b IFCMPA 2005, s 67(b) substitutes 'have been, are or would be' for 'are or would be' in CA 1990, para 19(2)(e).

c IFCMPA 2005, s 67(c) substitutes 'have been, are or are likely' for 'are or are likely' in CA 1990, para 19(2)(e).

Cross reference

See CA 1990, s 19[1] (as amended) and notes thereto.

1 CA 1990, s 19 was substituted by CLEA 2001, s 29 with effect from 28 November 2001, following which amendment the Director rather than the Minister for Enterprise, Trade and Employment was vested with powers under CA 1990, s 19.

Definitions

'the Act of 1990': IFCPMA 2005, s 3(1).

Notes

Operative Date: This section came into operation on 30 June 2005.[1]

1 Investment Funds, Companies and Miscellaneous Provisions Act 2005 (Commencement) Order 2005 (SI 2005/323), reg 3(b).

Extension of powers: The Director may now require a body to produce specified books or documents in circumstances suggesting that the affairs of the body are being or have been conducted in a manner which is unfairly prejudicial to some or all of the creditors of that body. Similarly the Director may now exercise this power where certain acts or omissions of the body have been (rather than are or will be) unlawful or unfairly prejudicial to any of the creditors of that body.

UK legislation

See CA 1985, s 447 (as amended by CA 1989, ss 63(1)–(7) and 212, and Sch 24).

---

68 Amendment of section 20 of Act of 1990

(1) Subsection (3) of section 20 of the Act of 1990 is repealed.

(2) Notwithstanding the repeal by this section of subsection (3) of that section 20, that subsection (3) shall continue to apply to material information (within the meaning of that section 20) seized under that section before the commencement of this section.

Amendments

IFCMPA 2005, s 68(1) repeals CA1990, s 20(3).

Cross reference

'commencement': IA 2005, Sch, Pt 1; 'the Act of 1990': IFCMPA 2005, s 3(1).

Notes

Operative Date: IFCMPA 2005, s 68 came into force on 30 June 2005.[1]

1 Investment Funds, Companies and Miscellaneous Provisions Act (Commencement) Order 2005 (SI 323/2005), r 3(b).

Retention of material information: CA 1990, s 20(3) limited the length of time the Director (or his officers) could retain material information which had been seized pursuant to CA 1990 s 20(2).[1] This caused significant practical difficulties for the Director in terms of having to apply to the District Court on a regular basis to have warrants renewed.[2] Since 30 June 2005, such limitations no longer apply,[3] save to the extent that the information in question had been seized prior to 30 June 2005.[4]

1 ie under a search warrant issued by a judge of the District Court.

2 Dáil Debates, Seanad Éireann, Vol 180, col 292, 26 April 2005.

3 IFCMPA 2005, s 68(1).

4 IFCMPA 2005, s 68(2).

UK legislation

See CA 1985, s 448 (as substituted by CA 1989, s 64(1)).

---

69 Amendment of section 21 of Act of 1990

Section 21(3) of the Act of 1990 is amended by inserting the following after paragraph (e):

[...] [a]

Amendments

IFCMPA 2005, s 69 inserts CA 1990, s 21(ea) with effect from 23 August 2009.[1]

1 Investment Funds, Companies and Miscellaneous Provisions Act 2005 (Commencement) Order 2009 (SI 335/2009).

Cross reference

'Irish Auditing and Accounting Supervisory Authority': C(A)A 2003, s 5. See CA 1990, s 21(3) (as amended) and notes thereto.

Definitions

'the Act of 1990': IFCMPA 2005, s 3(1).

Notes

Sharing of information: The inclusion of the Irish Accounting and Auditing Supervisory Authority (IAASA) as a 'competent authority'[1] will permit the Director to share information obtained by virtue of CA 1990, ss 19[2] and 20[3] with IAASA for the purposes relevant to IAASA's statutory functions.

1 CA 1990, s 21(3).
2 CA 1990, s 19: Power of Director to require production of documents.
3 CA 1990, s 20: Entry and search of premises.

70 Amendment of section 166 of Act of 1990

Section 166 of the Act of 1990 is amended—

(a) by substituting the following subsection for subsection (1):

[...][a]

(b) by repealing subsection (3).

[...][b]

Amendments

a IFCMPA 2005, s 70(a) substitutes CA 1990, s 166(1).
b IFCMPA 2005, s 70(b) repeals CA 1990, s 166(3).

Cross reference

See CA 1990, s 166 (as amended) and notes thereto.

Definitions

'the Act of 1990': IFCMPA 2005, s 3(1).

Notes

Operative Date: This section came into effect on 30 June 2005.[1]

1 Investment Funds, Companies and Miscellaneous Provisions Act 2005 (Commencement) Order 2005 (SI 323/2005), reg 3(b).

71 Amendment of section 242 of Act of 1990

Section 242 of the Act of 1990 is amended—

(a) [...][a]

(b) by inserting the following subsection after subsection (1):

[...][b]

and

(c) in subsection (2), by inserting after 'subsection (1)' 'or (1A)'.

[...][c]

Amendments

a CA 1990, s 242(1) is amended by inserting 'completes, signs' before 'produces, lodges or delivers' in each places where those words occur.

b CA 1990, s 242 is amended by inserting CA 1990, s 242(1A).

c CA 1990, s 242(2) is amended by inserting in CA 1990, s 242(2). 'or (1A)' after 'subsection (1)'.

Cross reference

CA 1990, s 242 (as amended) and notes thereto.

'electronic filing agent': IFCMPA 2005, s 57.

Definitions

'the Act of 1990': IFCMPA 2005, s 3(1).

Notes

Operative Date: This section was brought into force on 1 December 2005.[1]

1 Investment Funds, Companies and Miscellaneous Provisions Act 2005 (Commencement)(No 2) Act 2005 (SI 695/2005), reg 3.

Additional offences: IFCMPA 2005, s 71 implements the recommendations of the CLRG[1] with regard to expanding the offence described in CA 1990, s 242(1). The CLRG was concerned that it would be possible for a person who 'produced lodged or delivered' a document but who had no knowledge of the contents of the document, to fall outside the ambit of CA 1990, s 242(1). Similarly, a person who falsely completed or signed a form would not have 'produced, lodged or delivered' the form to the registrar. The amendment extends the offence committed under CA 1990, s 242(1) to a person who completes or signs such a document.[2] The offences outlined in CA 1990, s 242(1) are also extended[3] to deal with the situation where documents are filed by an electronic filing agent appointed pursuant to IFCMPA 2001, s 57.

1 CLRG, First Report, Para 7.6.

2 IFCMPA 2005, s 71(a).

3 IFCMPA 2005, s 71(b).

UK legislation

See generally CA 1985, s 451 (substituted by the Companies (Audit, Investigations and Community Enterprise) Act 2004, s 25(1), Sch 2, Pt 3, paras 16, 19); and CA 1985, Sch 24 (as amended by the Companies Act 1985 (Electronic Communications) Order 2000 (SI 2000/3373).

---

72 Replacement of references to Companies Registration Office Gazette for references to *Iris Oifigiúil.*

Each enactment mentioned in column (2) of the Table to this section at a particular reference number is amended, in each provision of that enactment mentioned in column (3) of that Table at that reference number, by substituting for '*Iris Oifigiúil*' 'the Companies Registration Office Gazette'.

TABLE

Reference Number	*Enactment*	*Provision*
(1)	(2)	(3)
1.	Companies Act 1963	Sections 65(1)(*e*), 107(1), 227(1), 252(1) and 261(1); Subsections (1), (2), (3), (5) and (8) of section 311 (including those subsections as they have effect by virtue of section 43(15) of the Companies (Amendment) (No 2) Act 1999) and section 311A(1).
2.	Companies (Amendment) Act 1982	Subsections (1), (2) and (3) of section 12; Subsections (1), (2) and (3) of section 12A; Subsections (3) and (7) of section 12B and section 12C(1).
3.	Companies (Amendment) Act 1983	Sections 8(1), 23(7) and 55(1).
4.	Companies (Amendment) Act 1990	Subsection (2)(*a*) and (*b*) of section 12 and section 30(1).
5.	Companies Act 1990	Section 16(18).

Cross reference

See also CA 1963, ss 65, 107, 227, 252, 261, 311 and 311(A); C(A)A 1982, ss 12, 12A, 12B and 12C; C(A)A 1983, ss 8, 23 and 55; C(A)A 1990, ss 12 and 30; and CA 1990, s 16 (as amended).

Definitions

'enactment': IFCMPA 2005, s 3(1).

Notes

Operative Date: IFCMPA 2005, s 72 has not yet been commenced.

Establishment of Companies Registration Office Gazette (CRO Gazette): IFCMPA 2005, s 72 makes amendments throughout the Companies Acts, which amendments are required to give effect to the replacement of reference to *Iris Oifigiúil* with reference to the CRO Gazette. The First EU Directive on Company Law,[1] as implemented in Ireland,[2] provided for the official notification by companies of certain documents and particulars by means of publication in *Iris Oifigiúil*. The establishment of the CRO Gazette was first provided for in 2004[3] in order to further facilitate Ireland's implementation of the First EU Directive on Company Law.[4] Under the

European Communities (Companies) Regulations 2004 the CRO Gazette is to be kept solely in electronic form.[5] The CRO Gazette is to be maintained on the CRO's website.[6]

1 (68/151/EEC) OJ, Special Edition 1968(1), pp 41–45, as amended by (2003/58/EC) OJ L 221.

2 European Communities (Companies) Regulations 1973 (SI 163/1973).

3 European Communities (Companies) Regulations 2004 (SI 839/2004), implementing (2003/58/EC) OJ L 221.

4 (68/151/EEC) OJ Special Edition 1968(1), as amended by (2003/58/EC) OJ L 221.

5 European Communities (Companies) Regulations 2004 (SI 839/2004), reg 3.

6 http://www.cro.ie; European Communities (Companies) Regulations 2004 (SI 839/2004), reg 4.

---

73 Miscellaneous amendments of Companies Acts related to penalties

(1) The Act of 1963 is amended—

(a) in section 115, by substituting the following subsection for subsection (6):

[...] [a]

and

(b) [...][b]

(2) The Act of 1990 is amended—

(a) in section 60, by substituting the following subsection for subsection (10):

[...][c]

(b) [...][d]

(c) [...][e]

(d) [...][f]

(3) [...][g]

(4) Schedule 2 to the Companies (Auditing and Accounting) Act 2003 is amended—

(a) [...][h]

(b) [...][i]

Amendments

a IFCMPA 2005, s 73(1)(a) substitutes CA 1963, s 115(6).

b IFCMPA 2005, s 73(1)(b) substitutes 'shall be guilty of an offence and liable for a fine' for 'shall be liable to a fine' in CA 1963, s 128(3).

c IFCMPA 2005, s 73(2)(a) substitutes CA 1990, s 60(10).

d IFCMPA 2005, s 73(2)(b) substitutes 'shall be guilty of an offence and liable for a fine' for 'shall be liable for a fine' in CA 1990, s 80(10).

e IFCMPA 2005, s 73(2)(c) substitutes 'shall be guilty of an offence and liable to a fine' for 'shall be liable for a fine' in CA 1990, s 161(6).

f IFCMPA 2005 s 73(2)(d) inserts '(other than an indictable offence under section 125(2) or 127(12) of the Principal Act)' after 'an indictable offence under the Companies Acts' in CA 1990, s 194(5).

g IFCMPA 2005, s 73(3) repeals C(AA)A 2003, s 37, para (d).

h IFCMPA 2005, s 73(4)(a) deletes '116(6)' and '128(4)' in C(AA)A 2003, Sch 2, Item No 1, col 2.

i IFCMPA 2005, s 73(4)(b) deletes C(AA)A 2003, Sch 2, Items No 8 and 9.

Cross reference

See CA 1963, ss 115(6) and 128(3) (as amended) and notes thereto.

See CA 1990, ss 60(10), 80(10), 161(6) and 194(5) (as amended) and notes thereto.

See C(AA)A 2003, s 37 and Sch 2 (as amended) and notes thereto.

Definitions

'Act of 1963': IFCMPA 2005, s 3(1); 'Act of 1990': IFCMPA 2005, s 3(1).

Notes

Operative Date: IFCMPA 2005, ss 73(1), 73(2)(a)–(c) and 73(4) came into force on 30 June 2005[1]. IFCMPA 2005, s 73(2)(d) and 73(3) came into force on 1 September 2005.[2]

1 Investment Funds, Companies and Miscellaneous Provisions Act 2005 (Commencement) Order 2005 (SI 323/2005), reg 3(b).

2 Investment Funds, Companies and Miscellaneous Provisions Act 2005 (Commencement) Order 2005 (SI 323/2005), reg 6.

74 Amendment of section 110A of Company Law Enforcement Act 2001

Section 110A of the Company Law Enforcement Act 2001 (inserted by the Companies (Auditing and Accounting) Act 2003) is amended—

(a) in subsection (1)—

(i) [...][a]

(ii) [...][b]

(iii) by inserting the following after paragraph (d):

[...][c]

(b) by inserting the following after subsection 8:

[...][d]

Amendments

a IFCMPA 2005, s 74(a)(i) deletes 'and' in CLEA 2001, s 110A(1), para (c).

b IFCMPA 2005, s 74(a)(ii) substitutes '1999, and' for '1999,' in CLEA 2001, s 110A(1), para (d).

c IFCMPA 2005, s 74(a)(iii) inserts CLEA 2001, s 110A(1), para (e).

d IFCMPA 2005, s 74(b) inserts CLEA 2001, s 110A(8A).

Cross reference

See CLEA 2001, s 110A (as amended) and notes thereto.

Notes

Operative Date: This section came into force 1 July 2005.[1]

1 Investment Funds, Companies and Miscellaneous Provisions Act 2005 (Commencement) Act 2005 (SI 323/2005), reg 4.

Investment Funds, Companies and Miscellaneous Provisions Act 2006

Number 41 of 2006

ARRANGEMENT OF SECTIONS

PART 1
PRELIMINARY AND GENERAL

PART 2
AMENDMENTS OF COMPANIES ACTS

PART 3
TRANSPARENCY REQUIREMENTS REGARDING ISSUERS OF SECURITIES ADMITTED TO TRADING ON CERTAIN MARKETS

PART 4
MISCELLANEOUS

Not reproduced here.

Notes

Part 4 is not reproduced here as it is not read as part of the Companies Acts.

An Act to amend and extend the Companies Acts, the Irish Takeover Panel Act 1997, The Central Bank Act 1942, the Consumer Information Act 1978 And The Netting Of Financial Contracts Act 1995, to Provide for the Implementation of Directive 2004/109/ EC of the European Parliament and of the Council of 15 December 2004 and to Provide for Related Matters.

Be It Enacted By The Oireachtas As Follows:

PART 1

PRELIMINARY AND GENERAL

1 Short title, collective citation and construction

(1) This Act may be cited as the Investment Funds, Companies and Miscellaneous Provisions Act 2006.

(2) The Companies Acts and Parts 2 and 3 shall be read together as one.

Notes

It will be noted that the citation and construction provisions in IFCMPA 2006 departs from that used in IFCMPA 2005 and previous Companies Acts. Specifically, IFCMPA 2006 s 1 *does not* provide that the Companies Acts 1963 to 2005[1] and Parts 2 and 3 of that Act may be cited together as the Companies Acts 1963 to 2006. Rather, s 1(2) merely provides 'The Companies Acts and Parts 2 and 3 shall be read together as one'.

IFCMPA 2006 is the first company law statute to be passed since the citation of the Companies Acts was amended by the Interpretation Act 2005 (IA 2005). IA 2005, s 21(2) and Part 2 of the Schedule provide that in an enactment which comes into operation after the commencement of the IA 2005, 'Companies Acts' means the Companies Acts 1963 to 2001 and every other enactment which is to be read together with any of those Acts". This definition is not without difficulty since when IA 2005 was enacted, the then correct collective citation of the Companies Acts was to the Companies Acts 1963 to 2003, not to the Companies Acts 1963 to 2001.[2] There has to be some concern that the term 'Companies Acts' as used in IFCMPA 2006 s 1(2) does not include the C(AA)A 2003 since it has never been provided in statute that it is to be 'read together' with the 'Companies Acts.'[3]

It should also be noted that the words Companies Acts in a private document, such as a contract, will not be deemed to have the foregoing meaning since such meaning is confined to where Companies Acts is used in an enactment and that is defined as being 'an Act or a statutory instrument or any portion of an Act or statutory instrument': IA 2005 s 2(1).

Moreover, there is, therefore, no statutory meaning assigned to the collective term, 'Companies Acts 1963 to 2006' and where that term is used in a contract or other private document, it may need to be defined there. It may be noted that the Companies Registration Office has not dropped the requirement to use the year of the latest statutory provision to be read as one with the Companies Acts and has specified that persons forming companies must use the citation 'Companies Acts 1963 to 2006' in all memoranda and articles of association filed with them, despite that formulation of words having no prescribed statutory meaning.[4]

1 The use of a comma after the word Acts in the phrase the Companies Acts 1963 to 2005 was rendered optional by IA 2005 s 14(3) which provides that in citing an Act by its short title or any

other enactment by its citation a comma immediately before a reference to a year and a comma immediately after such a reference that is not required for the purpose of punctuation may be omitted.

2 The reference in IA 2005 to the Companies Acts 1963 to 2001, when the then most recent authorised reference was to the Companies Acts 1963 to 2003 (as authorised by C(AA)A 2003 s 1(2)) may be explained as an updating oversight resulting from the fact that the IA 2005 started out as a Bill several years before it was enacted.

3 It should also not be forgotten that a significant number of statutory instruments were also passed between 2001 and 2005 which did not strictly provide that they were to be read together with the Companies Acts but that they were 'to be read as one with' (eg EC(FVA)R 2004, SI 765/2004, Reg 1(3) and EC (IFRSMA)R 2005, SI 116 of 2005), Reg 1(2)) the Companies Act 1963 to 2003.

4 See the Companies Registration Office CRO E-zine (Issue 44 – 5 February 2007).

2 Commencement

(1) Subject to subsections (2) and (3), this Act shall come into operation on such day or days as the Minister may appoint by order or orders either generally or with reference to any particular purpose or provision and different days may be so appointed for different purposes or different provisions.

(2) Section 1, this section and sections 3 to 6 and 9, 10, 13, 14, 15 and 35 shall come into operation on the passing of this Act.

(3) Sections 7 and 8 shall be deemed to have come into operation on 1 July 2005.

Notes

IFCMPA 2006 was signed into law by the President on 24 December 2006. Somewhat unusually, a significant number of its company law provisions were commenced from that date.

Sections 7 and 8 provide for a new definition of private company are deemed to have come into operation on 1 July 2005.

Sections 11, 12, 16 to 22 and 24 to 34 were commenced on 22 January 2007: Investment Funds, Companies and Miscellaneous Provisions Act 2006 (Commencement) Order 2007 (SI 23/2007). It will be noted that IFCMPA 2006, s 23 has not been commenced.

3 Definitions

In this Act—

'Act of 1990' means the Companies Act 1990;

'Act of 1997' means the Irish Takeover Panel Act 1997;

'Act of 2005' means the Investment Funds, Companies and Miscellaneous Provisions Act 2005;

'Minister' means the Minister for Enterprise, Trade and Employment;

'Regulations of 2006' means the European Communities (Takeover Bids (Directive 2004/25/EC)) Regulations 2006 (S.I. No. 255 of 2006).

4 Orders and regulations

Every order or regulation made under this Act (other than an order made under section 2 or 24) shall be laid before each House of the Oireachtas as soon as may be after it is made and, if a resolution annulling the order or regulation is passed by either such

House within the next 21 days on which that House has sat after the order or regulation is laid before it, the order or regulation shall be annulled accordingly but without prejudice to the validity of anything previously done thereunder.

5 Expenses

The expenses incurred by the Minister in the administration of this Act shall, to such extent as may be sanctioned by the Minister for Finance, be paid out of moneys provided by the Oireachtas.

Definitions

'Minister': IFCMPA 2006, s 3.

PART 2
AMENDMENTS OF COMPANIES ACTS

6 Statutory declarations for purposes of Companies Acts

(1) A statutory declaration made in a place outside the State (in pursuance of or for the purposes of the Companies Acts) shall be regarded as having been validly made (in pursuance of those Acts or for the purposes of them) if it is made in such a place before—

(a) a person entitled under the Solicitors Act 1954 to practise as a solicitor in the State, or

(b) a person authorised, under the law of that place, to administer oaths in that place and subsection (3), (4) or (5), as the case may be, is complied with.

(2) Subsection (1) is—

(a) without prejudice to the circumstances set out in the Statutory Declarations Act 1938 in which a statutory declaration may be made, and

(b) in addition to, and not in substitution for, the circumstances provided under the Diplomatic and Consular Officers (Provision of Services) Act 1993 or any other enactment in which a statutory declaration made by a person in a place outside the State is regarded as a statutory declaration validly made (whether for purposes generally or any specific purpose).

(3) In cases falling within subsection (1) (b) and unless subsection (4) or (5) applies, the signature of the person making the declaration (the 'declarer') and, to the extent that that law requires either or both of the following to be authenticated:

(a) the capacity in which the declarer has acted in making that declaration,

(b) the seal or stamp of the person who has administered the oath to the declarer,

shall be authenticated in accordance with the law of the place referred to in subsection (1)(b).

(4) If the place referred to in subsection (1) (b) is situate in a state that is a contracting party to the EC Convention, then (unless that Convention does not extend to that particular place) the provisions of that Convention with regard to authentication shall apply in relation to the statutory declaration concerned, including the procedures for

verification of any matter in circumstances where serious doubts, with good reason, arise in respect of that matter.

(5) If the place referred to in subsection (1)(b) is situate in a state that is a contracting party to the Hague Convention but is not a contracting party to the EC Convention, then (unless the Hague Convention does not extend to that particular place) the provisions of the Hague Convention with regard to authentication shall apply in relation to the statutory declaration concerned, including the procedures for verification of any matter in circumstances where serious doubts, with good reason, arise in respect of that matter.

(6) The registrar of companies may, before receiving any statutory declaration purporting to be made in pursuance of, or for the purposes of, the Companies Acts, being a declaration—

(a) falling within subsection (1)(b), and

(b) to which neither the provisions of the EC Convention nor the Hague Convention apply as regards the authentication of it,

require such proof, as he or she considers appropriate, of any paricular requirements of the law referred to in subsection (3).

(7) A statutory declaration made before the passing of this Act—

(a) in a place outside the State,

(b) before—

(i) if the place is not a place in England and Wales, Northern Ireland or Scotland, a person authorised, under the law of that place, to administer oaths or a person entitled under the Solicitors Act 1954 to practise as a solicitor in the State, or

(ii) if the place is a place in England and Wales, Northern Ireland or Scotland—

(I) a person entitled under the law of England and Wales, Northern Ireland or Scotland, as the case may be, to practise as a solicitor in England and Wales, Northern Ireland or Scotland, as the case may be, or to administer oaths there, or

(II) a person entitled under the Solicitors Act 1954 to practise as a solicitor in the State,

and

(c) purporting to be made in pursuance of, or for the purposes of, the Companies Acts,

shall, if the declaration was delivered to the registrar of companies before that passing, be valid and deemed always to have been valid notwithstanding anything in the Diplomatic and Consular Officers (Provision of Services) Act 1993 or any other enactment and any-thing done on foot of that declaration's delivery to the registrar, including any subsequent registration of that declaration by the registrar, shall be valid and be deemed always to have been valid notwithstanding anything in that Act or any other enactment.

(8) Nothing in subsection (7) affects any proceedings commenced before the passing of this Act.

(9) In this section—

"EC Convention" means the Convention Abolishing the Legalisation of Documents in the Member States of the European Communities of 25 May 1987;

"Hague Convention" means the Convention Abolishing the Requirement of Legalisation for Foreign Public Documents done at the Hague on 5 October 1961;

"statutory declaration", in addition to the meaning assigned to it by the IA 2005, means a declaration that conforms with the requirements of the Statutory Declarations Act 1938, save for any requirements contained in section 1 of that Act, or any other provision of it, expressly or impliedly limiting the class of persons who may take and receive a declaration or the places in which a declaration may be received or taken.

Notes

Statutory declarations made in a place outside of the state: Section 1(1) of the Statutory Declarations Act 1938 provides:

> 'It shall be lawful for any of the following persons, that is to say:— (a) a notary public, (b) a commissioner for oaths, (c) a peace commissioner, (d) a person authorised by law to take and receive statutory declarations, to take and receive the declaration in writing of any person making the same before him in the form set out in the Schedule to this Act.'

The Solicitors (Amendment) Act 1994, s 72 provides *inter alia* that 'every solicitor who holds a practising certificate which is in force shall ... have all the powers conferred by any enactment ... and any reference to such a commissioner in any such enactment ... whether passed or made before or after the commencement of this section, shall include a reference to such a solicitor'.

Neither the 1938 nor 1994 Acts are specific as to where such statutory declarations may be made: the key point is the individual before whom – not the location where – the declaration is made. However, a number of other enactments are also relevant.

First, the Diplomatic and Consular Officers (Provision of Services) Act 1993 applies to (a) a civil servant employed as a head of mission, a member of the diplomatic staff of a mission or a career consular officer; and (b) an honorary consular officer appointed by the Minister for Foreign Affairs. This Act has a section on "Powers as to oaths and notarial acts abroad", providing that:

> '(1) Every person to whom this section applies may, in any country or place outside the State in which he is for the time being exercising the functions of his office, administer any oath and take any affidavit, and may also do any notarial act which a notary public can do in the State, and every oath, affidavit and notarial act administered, sworn or done by or before such person in such country or place shall be as effectual as if duly administered, sworn or done by or before any lawful authority in the State.
>
> (2) Any document purporting to have affixed thereon or thereto, or to have impressed thereon, the seal of any person or of a mission and to have subscribed thereto the signature of such person, being a person to whom this section applies, in testimony of any oath, affidavit or act being administered, taken or done by or before him, shall be admitted in evidence (saving all just exceptions) without proof of the seal or signature being the seal of such person or mission or signature of such person, or of the status and official character of such person.'

The implication of this section, which is concentrated on notarial acts, is that acts by Irish notaries overseas may not have validity. Although not alluding to any other persons before whom declarations may be made, the implication of this Act is that statutory declarations outside the State would have validity only if made before a diplomatic or consular official.

Secondly, Ord 40, r 7 of the Rules of the Superior Court 1986 provides:

> 'All examinations, affidavits, declarations, affirmations and attestations of honour in causes or matters pending in the High Court or the Supreme Court, and also acknowledgements required for the purpose of enrolling any deed in the said Courts, may be taken in any foreign country or place before any Irish diplomatic or consular representative or agent exercising his functions in that country or place or, when there is no such representative or agent or no such representative or agent conveniently near to the deponent in such country or place, before any notary public lawfully authorised to administer oaths in that country or place, or where such country or place is a part of the British Commonwealth of Nations or a British possession, before any judge, court, notary public or person authorised to administer oaths in such part or possession; and the Judges and officers of the High Court and of the Supreme Court shall take judicial notice of the seal or signature, as the case may be, of any such diplomatic or consular representative or agent, judge, court, notary public or other person attached, appended or subscribed to any such examination, affidavit, declaration, affirmation, attestation of honour, or acknowledgement, or to any other deed or document.'

This Rule is aimed at affidavits, but it includes the word 'declarations' on the first line. For the purposes of such documents in proceedings before the Irish courts, it broadens the class of persons authorized to take oaths etc to diplomatic and consular representatives, overseas notaries public, and in the case of British possessions to those authorized to take oaths etc in such possessions. This carries an implication that declarations made for other purposes might not be similarly capable of being made overseas as provided in the RSC.

This section therefore clarifies that statutory declarations for the purposes of the Companies Acts made overseas before Irish solicitors or local notaries or other persons authorised to take declarations are valid.

Statutory declarations required under the Companies Acts – Statutory declarations currently required by the Companies Acts arise as follows:

CA 1963, s 24(1)(c)	statutory declaration as to compliance with requirements for dispensing with the word 'limited' from the end of a limited company's name (inserted by CLEA 2001, s 88);
CA 1963, s 60(3)	statutory declaration of solvency for the purposes of proposed financial assistance;
CA 1963, s 115(1)(d)	statutory declaration of compliance by a public limited company for the purpose of obtaining a trading certificate;
CA 1963, s 179(1)(b)(iv)	as to compliance with share qualification requirements as to appointment of a director named in a prospectus;
CA 1963, s 195(11A)	statutory declaration as to due resignation of a director (inserted by C(A)(No 2)A 1999, s 47(b));
CA 1963, s 256	statutory declaration of solvency in case of proposal to wind up voluntarily;
CA 1963, s 320(2)	statutory declaration of directors verifying statement of affairs to receiver appointed by instrument;
CA 1963, s 332	verification of lists of members and directors of company for purposes of re-registration of a joint stock company;
C(A)A 1983, s 5(5)	statutory declaration of compliance with requirements of Companies Acts on incorporation;

C(A)A 1983, s 6(3)	statutory declaration of compliance by a public limited company on incorporation for the purpose of obtaining a trading certificate;
C(A)A 1983, s 9(3)(e)	statutory declaration of compliance with requirements for re-registration of private company as public limited company;
C(A)A 1983, s 18(4)(e)	statutory declaration of compliance with requirements for re-registration of joint stock company as public limited company;
C(A)A 1983, s 52(3)(b)	statutory declaration of compliance with requirements for re-registration of limited company as unlimited;
CA 1990, s 34(3)	statutory declaration for the purposes of validating a guarantee or provision of security in connection with a loanm quasi-loan or a credit transaction in favour of a director or person connected therewith (inserted by CLEA 2001, s 78);
C(A)(No 2)A 1999, s 42(2)	statutory declaration as to a proposed new company's carrying on a business in the State.

In addition, the CRO requires the complete or partial discharge of a charge to be verified by statutory declaration on Forms C5 and C6.

7 Amendment of section 33 of Companies Act 1963

[...][a]

Amendments

a Substitutes the text of CA 1963, s 33.

8 Amendment of section 21 of Companies (Amendment) Act 1983

[...][a]

Amendments

a Substitutes the text of C(A)A 1983, s 21.

9 Exemption from audit requirement

(1) [...][a]

(2) Nothing in subsection (1)(b) prejudices the future exercise of the power under subsection (7) of section 32 of the Companies (Amendment) (No. 2) Act 1999 in relation to subsection (3) (as it stands amended by subsection (1)(b)) of that section 32.

Amendments

a Subsection (1) amends C(A)(No2)A 1999, ss 32(1), 32(3), 33 and 35 and inserts a new s 32B.

10 Application of section 9 and transitional provisions

(1) The amendments effected by section 9 shall apply as respects—

(a) a financial year of a company that commences not earlier than the commencement of that section, and

(b) subject to subsection (2), a financial year of a company that ends not earlier than 2 months after the commencement of that section (not being a financial year to which paragraph (a) applies).

(2) In cases falling within subsection (1)(b), section 9 shall have effect as if, instead of the subsection (2) inserted by that section in section 33 of the Companies (Amendment) (No. 2) Act 1999, there were inserted the following subsection in that section 33:

> "(2) In cases falling within section 10(1) (b) of the Investment Funds, Companies and Miscellaneous Provisions Act 2006, a notice under subsection (1) may be served on the company not later than 1 month before the end of the financial year to which the notice relates.".

11 Restrictions on, and disqualifications of, persons from acting as directors, etc

[...][a]

Amendments

a Amends CA 1990, ss 150 and 160.

12 Dematerialisation

[...][a]

Amendments

a Amends CA 1990, s 239.

13 Amendment of section 43 of Act of 2005

[...][a]

Amendments

a Substitutes IFCMPA 2005, s 43.

14 Amendment of section 45 of Act of 2005

[...][a]

Amendments

a Substitutes IFCMPA 2005, s 43.

15 Amendments of Act of 2005 consequential on amendment made by section 14

[...][a]

Amendments

a Amends IFCMPA 2005, ss 38, 41 42, 44 and 48.

16 Amendment of section 9 of Companies (Auditing and Accounting) Act 2003

[...][a]

Amendments

a Amends C(AA)A 2003, s 9(2).

17 Amendment of section 10 of Companies (Auditing and Accounting) Act 2003

[...][a]

Amendments

a Amends C(AA) 2003, s 10.

18 Amendment of section 29 of Companies (Auditing and Accounting) Act 2003

[...][a]

Amendments

a Substitutes sub-s (7) of C(AA)A 2003, s 29.

PART 3

TRANSPARENCY REQUIREMENTS REGARDING ISSUERS OF SECURITIES ADMITTED TO TRADING ON CERTAIN MARKETS

Notes

The structure of this Part is modelled on IFCMPA 2005, Parts 4 and 5 respectively, and provides the statutory basis for civil liability and enforcement of the statutory instrument transposing the Transparency Obligations Directive 2004/109/EC of 15 December 2004 [1 OJ L390, 31.12.2004, p.38]. This law applies to issuers, either Irish or non-Irish with Ireland as home member state, whose 'securities' (as defined in the Directive) are admitted to trading on a 'regulated market' (as defined in the Directive). The law is concerned with the disclosure by issuers to the market of interim accounting and management information as well as particulars of major shareholdings held in the issuer.

The Directive is a 'Level 1' directive in the Lamfalussy scheme of things. See the Notes to Parts 4 and 5 of the IFCMPA 2005 above.

At present there are two Level 2 measures:

(1) a Level 2 Commission Decision 2006/891/EC of 4 December 2006 (OJ 8.12.2006 L343, p 96); and

(2) a Level 2 Commission Directive 2007/14/EC of 8 March 2007 (OJ 9.3.2007 L69, p 27).

The three-level Irish legislation is made up of:

– this Part;

– SI 277/2007, which transposes the Directive and level 2 measures (see below); and

– the Financial Regulator's Interim Transparency Rules of June 2007.

Section 24 permits the Minister to apply this law to issuers whose securities are traded on other markets, such as the Irish Enterprise Exchange. Pending such a Ministerial order, the provisions of CA 1990, ss 67 et seq relating to disclosure by major shareholders of interests in the relevant share capital of Irish-incorporated and registered public limited companies continue to apply.

---

19 Interpretation (Part 3)

(1) In this Part—

"Transparency (Regulated Markets) Directive" means Directive 2004/109/EC[1] of the European Parliament and of the Council of 15 December 2004 on the harmonisation of transparency requirements in relation to information about issuers whose securities are admitted to trading on a regulated market and amending Directive 2001/34/EC, including the first-mentioned Directive as it stands amended for the time being;

"transparency (regulated markets) law" means—

(a) the measures adopted for the time being by the State to implement the Transparency (Regulated Markets) Directive and any supplemental Directive (whether an Act of the Oireachtas, regulations under section 3 of the European Communities Act 1972, regulations under section 20 or any other enactment (other than, save where the context otherwise admits, this Part)),

(b) any measures directly applicable in the State in con-sequence of the Transparency (Regulated Markets) Directive and, without prejudice to the generality of this paragraph, includes any Regulation or Decision made by the Commission pursuant to the procedure referred to in Article 27(2) of that Directive, and

(c) any supplementary and consequential measures adopted for the time being by the State in respect of any Regulation or Decision made by the Commission in consequence of the Transparency (Regulated Markets) Directive pursuant to the foregoing procedure;

"supplemental Directive" means any Directive made by the Commission in consequence of the Transparency (Regulated Markets) Directive pursuant to the procedure referred to in Article 27(2) of that Directive.

(2) A word or expression that is used in this Part and is also used in the Transparency (Regulated Markets) Directive shall have in this Part the same meaning as it has in that Directive.

Definitions

"securities": Transparency Directive, art 2.1(a) applied by IFCMPA 2006, s 19(2); Issuer: Transparency Directive, art 2.1(d) applied by IFCMPA 2006, s 19(2).

20 Power to make certain regulations

(1) The Minister may make regulations for the purposes of—

(a) giving effect to the Transparency (Regulated Markets) Directive or any supplemental Directive, and

(b) supplementing and making consequential provision in respect of any Regulation or Decision made by the Commission in consequence of the first-mentioned Directive in paragraph (a) pursuant to the procedure referred to in Article 27(2) of that Directive.

(2) Regulations under this section may contain such incidental, supplementary and consequential provisions as appear to the Minister to be necessary or expedient for the purposes of those regulations, including—

(a) provisions creating offences (but the regulations may only provide penalties in respect of a summary conviction for any such offence), and

(b) provisions creating civil liability in respect of contraventions of the regulations so as to enable any person suffering loss thereby to recover compensation for that loss.

(3) Civil liability shall not be created by regulations under subsection (2) in respect of a contravention of regulations under this section save in respect of such a contravention that involves either—

(a) an untrue or misleading statement, or

(b) the omission from a statement of any matter required to be included in it,

being, in either case, a statement—

(i) that is contained in a publication made in purported compliance with a provision of transparency (regulated markets) law specified in the regulations, and

(ii) in respect of which a person suffers a loss by reason of the person's acquiring or contracting to acquire securities (or an interest in them) in reliance on that publication at a time when, and in circumstances in which, it was reason-able for the person to rely on that publication,

and the following condition is fulfilled in respect of that publication.

(4) That condition is that a person discharging responsibilities within the issuer of the securities referred to in subsection (3) in relation to that publication (being responsibilities of a kind specified in regulations under this section)—

(a) knew the statement concerned to be untrue or misleading or was reckless as to whether it was untrue or misleading, or

(b) knew the omission concerned to be dishonest concealment of a material fact.

(5) Regulations under this section may also make, for the purposes of those regulations, provision analogous to that which is made by Part IV of the Act of 1990.

(6) This section is without prejudice to section 3 of the European Communities Act 1972.

Definitions

'Act of 1990': IFCMPA 2006, s 3; 'Minister': IFCMPA 2006, s 3; 'Transparency (Regulated Markets) Directive': IFCMPA 2006, s 19(1); 'transparency (regulated markets) law': IFCMPA 2006, s 19(1); 'supplemental Directive': IFCMPA 2006, s 19(1); 'securities': Transparency Directive Art 2.1(a) applied by IFCMPA 2006, s 19(2); 'issuer': Transparency Directive Art 2.1(d) applied by IFCMPA 2006, s 19(2).

21 Conviction on indictment of offences under transparency (regulated markets) law

A person who is guilty of an offence created by transparency (regulated markets) law (being an offence expressed by that law to be an offence to which this section applies) shall, without prejudice to any penalties provided by that law in respect of a summary conviction for the offence, be liable, on conviction on indictment, to a fine not exceeding €1,000,000 or imprisonment for a term not exceeding 5 years or both.

Definitions

'transparency (regulated markets) law': IFCMPA 2006, s 19(1).

Notes

The Transparency (Directive 2004/109/EC) Regulations 2007 (SI 277/2007) are the regulations made by the Minister under this section. See below.

22 Supplementary rules, etc., by competent authority

(1) In this section "competent authority" means the competent authority designated under transparency (regulated markets) law for the purposes of the provisions of the Transparency (Regulated Markets) Directive (other than Article 24(4)(h) of that Directive).

(2) The competent authority may make rules imposing or enabling the competent authority to impose requirements on persons on whom an obligation or obligations are imposed by transparency (regulated markets) law, being requirements—

(a) to do or not to do specified things so as to secure that the provisions of transparency (regulated markets) law are complied with and, in particular (without limiting the generality of this paragraph), to adopt specified procedures and use specified forms in the provision of information to the competent authority,

(b) to do or not to do specified things so as to secure the effective supervision by the competent authority of activities of the kind to which transparency (regulated markets) law relates and, in particular (without limiting the generality of this paragraph), to make such reports or disclose such matters, at such times and in such manner, to the competent authority or other specified persons as are provided for by the rules or specified by the competent authority pursuant to the rules, being reports or a disclosure of matters that is or are required by virtue or in consequence of the operation of transparency (regulated markets) law.

(3) Rules under this section may, in particular, include rules necessary for the performance by the competent authority of the functions under Article 24 of the Transparency (Regulated Markets) Directive, other than paragraph (4)(h) of that Article.

(4) Rules under this section may contain such consequential, incidental or supplemental provisions as the competent authority considers necessary or expedient.

(5) Rules under this section shall not contain any provision that is inconsistent with transparency (regulated markets) law or require the provision of information to any person the provision of which is not reasonably related to the purposes for which the applicable provisions of the Transparency (Regulated Markets) Directive have been adopted.

(6) The provisions of transparency (regulated markets) law that are expressed by that law to be made for the purpose of enabling the imposition of administrative sanctions shall apply in relation to a contravention of—

(a) rules under this section, and

(b) rules adopted by the Irish Auditing and Accounting Supervisory Authority under section 10(3) of the Companies (Auditing and Accounting) Act 2003 concerning the matters that relate to its functions under section 9(2)(ma) of that Act,

as they apply in relation to a contravention of a provision of transparency (regulated markets) law and, accordingly, a sanction that may be imposed pursuant to the first-mentioned provisions of transparency (regulated markets) law in respect of a contravention of a provision of that law may, in accordance with that law, be imposed in respect of a contravention of rules referred to in either of the foregoing paragraphs.

(7) The competent authority may issue guidelines in writing as to the steps that may be taken to comply with transparency (regulated markets) law.

Definitions

'Transparency (Regulated Markets) Directive': IFCMPA 2006, s 19(1); transparency (regulated markets) law: IFCMPA 2006, s 19(1).

Notes

The Interim Transparency Rules of June 2007 are the supplementary rules made by Financial Regulator under this section.

23 Amendment of section 33AK of Central Bank Act 1942

The definition of "Supervisory Directives" in subsection (10) of section 33AK (inserted by the Central Bank and Financial Services Authority of Ireland Act 2003) of the Central Bank Act 1942 is amended by substituting the following paragraphs for paragraph (h) (inserted by the Act of 2005):

"(h) the 2003 Prospectus Directive (within the meaning of Part 5 of the Investment Funds, Companies and Miscellaneous Provisions Act 2005),

(i) the Transparency (Regulated Markets) Directive (within the meaning of Part 3 of the Investment Funds, Companies and Miscellaneous Provisions Act 2006);".

Cross reference

The Central Bank Act 1942, s 33AK imposes duties of confidentiality on the Bank and connected offfice holders of the Bank where disclosure of information would be in breach of certain EU measures, to which is now added the Transparency Directive.

Definitions

'Act of 2005': IFCMPA 2006, s 3.

---

24 Application of transparency (regulated markets) law to certain markets

(1) The Minister, after consultation with the competent authority referred to in section 22(1), may, by provisional order, provide that one or more provisions of transparency (regulated markets) law that apply in relation to a market to which the Transparency (Regulated Markets) Directive applies shall, with such modifications, if any, as are specified in the order, apply to a market specified in the order.

(2) A provisional order under this section shall not have effect unless or until it is confirmed by an Act of the Oireachtas.

Definitions

'Minister': IFCMPA 2006, s 3; Transparency (Regulated Markets) Directive: s 19(1); transparency (regulated markets) law: IFCMPA 2006, s 19(1).

Companies (Amendment) Act 2009

(Number 20 of 2009)

ARRANGEMENT OF SECTIONS

Section

Companies (Amendment) Act 2009

Number 20 of 2009

An Act to remove certain exceptions contained in the companies acts that apply in the cases of companies holding licences under section 9 of the Central Bank Act 1971 (or holding companies of such companies) regarding disclosure of loans to directors and transactions of an analogous nature, to otherwise amend the companies acts in respect of loans by companies (of whatever type) to directors or certain related par-ties and transactions of an analogous nature and, in particular, to amend section 40 of the Companies Act 1990 concerning criminal liability in that regard, to confer additional powers on the director of corporate enforcement with respect to access to information in the possession of companies, including information kept by them in certain registers or books, or in the possession of third parties, to amend sections 20 and 23 of the Companies Act 1990 in relation to search warrants and procedures to be followed in cases of claims of legal professional privilege, to amend sections 43 and 44 of the Companies (Amendment) (No 2) Act 1999 and to provide for related matters. [12th July, 2009]

Be it enacted by the Oireachtas as follows:

Notes

The C(A)A was commenced immediately upon being signed by the President of Ireland on 12 July 2009 and was not the subject of any commencement orders. The purpose of the Act is essentially compliance and enforcement related and it would seem that its enactment was prompted largely by concerns raised when it became known that certain large loans had been made to the Chairman and former CEO of Anglo Irish Bank Corporation plc (as it was then known before it was nationalised by the Anglo Irish Bank Corporation Act 2009; No 1 of 2009) which had not been disclosed in that company's financial statements because of the existence of certain exemptions from disclosing loans in the accounts of companies which hold a banking license. In amending the law to remove this exemption the opportunity was taken to tighten up the law and confer additional powers on the ODCE in a number of other areas too. These other changes are summarised in the following extract from the Tanaiste's speech in the Seanad upon the introduction of the Bill when she said that:

> 'the Bill will improve overall enforcement of compliance with company law by, *inter alia*, providing for the ODCE's right of access to certain company and third party records and allowing for extensions to search warrants granted to the office. It will introduce a mechanism, together with appropriate safeguards, for an extended power of seizure so that large volumes of paper or electronic information that may contain relevant material can be removed for later examination. It will lighten the evidential burden on the Director of Corporate Enforcement when taking action against companies in default of existing provisions regarding loans to their directors and will amend existing requirements relating to the disclosure of loans to directors in the annual accounts of licensed banks.'[1]

[1] Seanad Debates, Vol 195, No 5.

---

1 Definitions

In this Act—

'Act of 1990' means the Companies Act 1990;

'Act of 2001' means the Company Law Enforcement Act 2001;

'Act of 2003' means the Companies (Auditing and Accounting) Act 2003;

'Principal Act' means the Companies Act 1963.

2 Amendment of section 194 of Principal Act

Section 194 (as amended by the Act of 2003) of the Principal Act is amended—

(a) in subsection (5)(b), by substituting 'fails to comply with this subsection or subsection (5A)' for 'fails to comply with this subsection'; and

(b) […][a]

Amendments

a C(A)A 2009, s 2 inserts CA 1963, s 194(5A).

---

3 Amendment of section 371A of Principal Act

Section 371A (inserted by the Act of 2001) of the Principal Act is amended, in subsection (1), by substituting 'section 19(3)(c)' for 'section 19(3)(b)'.

4 Amendment of section 19 of Act of 1990

(1) Section 19 (inserted by the Act of 2001) of the Act of 1990 is amended—

(a) […][a]

(b) in subsection (4), by substituting 'subsection (3)(c)' for 'subsection (3)(b)' in each place where it occurs; and

(c) in subsection (9), by substituting 'a direction under subsection (1) or (3A)' for 'a direction under subsection (1)'.

(2) Nothing in subsection (1) shall be construed to mean that, but for the amendment effected by it, a direction given by the Director of Corporate Enforcement, before the passing of this Act, under section 19(3) of the Act of 1990 was limited in any way as to its effect or extent of operation or that any books or documents produced on foot of it to the Director of Corporate Enforcement were not lawfully produced to him.

Amendments

a C(A)A 2009, s 4(1)(a) substitutes CA 1990, s 19(3).

5 Amendment of section 20 of Act of 1990

Section 20 of the Act of 1990 is amended—

(a) in subsection (2), by substituting 'at any time or times within the period of validity of the warrant' for 'at any time or times within 1 month from the date of issue of the warrant';

(b) […][a];

and

(c) […][b].

Amendments

a C(A)A 2009, s 5(b) inserts CA 1990, s 20(2A)–(2J).

b C(A)A 2009, s 5(c) inserts CA 1990, s 20(8)–(11).

6 Amendment of section 23 of Act of 1990

[…][a].

Amendments

a C(A)A 2009, s 6 substitutes CA 1990, s 23(1) and inserts CA 1990, s 23(1A)–(1F).

7 Amendment of section 40 of Act of 1990

[…][a].

Amendments

a C(A)A 2009, s 7 substitutes CA 1990, s 40.

8 Disclosure of loans, etc., — amendment of exceptions applicable to directors of licensed banks and provisions as to offences and other matters

(1) Section 41 of the Act of 1990 is amended—

(a) […][a];

and

(b) […][b].

(2) […][c].

(3) Section 43 of the Act of 1990 is further amended—

(a) in subsection (7), by substituting 'subsection (2) or (5)' for 'subsection (2), (5) or (6)';

(b) in subsection (8), by substituting 'subsections (2) and (5)' for 'subsections (2), (5) and (6)';

(c) by deleting subsection (9); and

(d) […][d].

Amendments

a C(A)A 2009, s 8(1)(a) substitutes CA 1990, s 41(6).

b C(A)A 2009, s 8(1)(b) inserts CA 1990, s 41(10)–(12).

c C(A)A 2009, s 8(2) substitutes CA 1990, s 43(5) and (6) and inserts s 43(6A).

d C(A)A 2009, s 8(3)(d) inserts CA 1990, s 43(11) and (12).

9 Amendments of other provisions of Act of 1990 concerning licensed banks and disclosure of loans, etc.

Section 44 of the Act of 1990 is amended—

(a) in subsection (1), by substituting 'are required by subsection (1) or (2) of section 41 or would, but for section 41(6), be required by subsection (1) or (2) of that section' for 'would, but for section 41(6), be required by subsection (1) or (2) of that section';

(b) […][a];

(c) in subsection (8), by substituting 'subsection (1), (3) or (4C)' for 'subsection (1) or (3)'; and

(d) […][b].

Amendments

a C(A)A 2009, s 9(b) inserts CA 1990, s 44(4A)–(4C).

b C(A)A 2009, s 9(d) substitutes CA 1990, s 44(9).

10 Amendment of sections 43 and 44 of Companies (Amendment) (No 2) Act 1999

(1) Section 43 of the Companies (Amendment) (No. 2) Act 1999 is amended—

(a) in subsections (1), (2), (8) and (9), by substituting 'a Member State of the EEA' for 'the State';

(b) by repealing subsection (12); and

(c) […][a].

(2) Section 44 of the Companies (Amendment) (No. 2) Act 1999 is amended—

(a) in subsection (8), by substituting 'So far as it is the person's residence in the State that falls to be determined for the purposes of that section, for the purposes of section 43,' for 'For the purposes of section 43,'; and

(b) [...][b].

Amendments

a C(A)A 2009, s 10(1)(c) substitutes C(A)(No 2)A 1999, s 43(16).

b C(A)A 2009, s 10(2)(b) inserts C(A)(No 2)A 1999, s 44(12).

11 Short title and construction

(1) This Act may be cited as the Companies (Amendment) Act 2009.

(2) The Companies Acts and this Act shall be read as one.

Companies (Miscellaneous Provisions) Act 2009

(Number 45 of 2009)

ARRANGEMENT OF SECTIONS

An Act to provide, in limited circumstances, for the transitional use by certain parent undertakings of internationally recognised accounting standards other than those generally accepted accounting principles and policies used in the state, to amend the Companies Act 1990, the Companies (Auditing And Accounting) Act 2003 and the European Communities (Undertakings for Collective Investment in Transferable Securities) Regulations 2003, and to provide for related matters.

Be it enacted by the Oireachtas as follows:

1 Transitional accounting standards

(1) In this section—

"accounts" means Companies Act individual accounts and Companies Act group accounts;

"relevant parent undertaking" means a parent undertaking—

(a) which does not have securities admitted to trading on a regulated market,

(b) whose securities (or whose receipts in respect of those securities) are registered with the Securities and Exchange Commission of the United States of America, or which is otherwise subject to reporting to that Commission, under the laws of the United States of America, and

(c) which, prior to the commencement of this section, has not made and was not required to make an annual return to the registrar of companies to which accounts were required to have been annexed;

"US generally accepted accounting principles" means the standards and interpretations, in relation to accounting and financial statements, issued by any of the following bodies constituted under the laws of the United States of America or of a territorial unit of the United States of America:

(a) the Financial Accounting Standards Board;

(b) the American Institute of Certified Public Accountants;

(c) the Securities and Exchange Commission.

(2) This section applies to the accounts of a relevant parent undertaking that are prepared for such of its first 4 financial years after it is incorporated in the State as end or ends not later than 31 December 2015.

(3) To the extent that the use of US generally accepted accounting principles does not contravene any provision of the Companies Acts or of any regulations made thereunder—

(a) a true and fair view of the state of affairs and profit or loss of a relevant parent undertaking may be given by the use by that undertaking of those principles in the preparation of its Companies Act individual accounts, and

(b) a true and fair view of the state of affairs and profit or loss of a relevant parent undertaking and its subsidiary undertakings as a whole may be given by the use by that relevant parent undertaking of those principles in the preparation of its Companies Act group accounts.

(4) Where accounts are prepared in accordance with this section, the notes to those accounts shall contain a statement to that effect.

Notes

The background to this change in Irish company law is the migration to Ireland of a number of US listed companies. Prior to moving to Ireland, these companies had their headquarters in jurisdictions like Bermuda and the Caymen Islands. Many of these migrations involved a scheme of arrangement under the law of the jurisdictions where they were incorporated whereby their shareholders would in a share-for-share sway receive shares or interests in shares in a newly incorporated Irish company. Most of these companies have their shares listed with the US Securities and Exchange Commission ('US SEC') and whilst held internationally, many of their shareholders hold *American depository receipts* ('ADRs') and are based in the USA.

Prior to migrating to Ireland, these companies prepared their financial statements in accordance with US generally accepted accounting principles ('US GAAP') and whilst ultimately US companies will switch to IFRS, it will be a number of years before this changeover happens. Accordingly, it was recognised that it would have been needlessly costly, time-consuming and wasteful for these companies to be forced, prematurely, to switch to IFRS or Irish GAAP and a transition exemption has been introduced by C(MP)A 2009, s 1.

For a transition period, companies which meet certain strict criteria will be permitted to use US GAAP in the preparation of their Companies Act individual accounts and Companies Act group accounts. The first criterion is that only '*relevant parent undertakings*' (a) which do not have their securities admitted to trading on a regulated market (ie in the EU or EEA), (b) whose securities (or ADRs) are registered with the US SEC or which are otherwise subject to reporting to that commission under the laws of the USA, and (c) which, prior to the commencement of s 1, have not made and were not required to make an annual return to the Registrar of Companies to which accounts were required to have been annexed can avail of the transitional regime.

If any of the foregoing conditions are not met, a company cannot avail of the transitional regime. So, for example, if a company has already filed an annual return to which its financial statements were annexed, it is disqualified or if a company was obliged to file its annual return to which financial statements ought to have been annexed but failed to meet that obligation, it is disqualified. On the other hand, a company which has filed its first annual return six months after its incorporation to which no financials were appended is not disqualified because companies are not required to file financial statements with their first annual return; and neither is a company disqualified which filed financial statements in order to pay an interim dividend.

A qualifying 'relevant parent undertaking' can avail of the transitional regime in relation to its accounts prepared for such of its first four financial years after it is incorporated in the State as end or ends not later than 31 December 2015: s 1(2).

The extent of the provision should also be borne in mind and s 1(3) provides that it is only 'to the extent that the use of US GAAP does not contravene any provision of the Companies Acts or of any regulations made thereunder' that (a) a true and fair view of the state of affairs and profit or loss of a relevant parent undertaking may be given by the use by that undertaking of those principles in the preparation of its Companies Act individual accounts, and (b) a true and fair view of the state of affairs and profit or loss of a relevant parent undertaking and its subsidiary undertakings as a whole may be given by the use by that relevant parent undertaking of those principles in the preparation of its Companies Act group accounts. It is also provided what where accounts are prepared in accordance with this provision, the notes to those accounts must contain a statement to that effect: s 1(4).

---

2 Regulations

(1) In this section "accounts" means Companies Act individual accounts and Companies Act group accounts.

(2) The Minister may make regulations providing for specified categories of parent undertakings which do not have securities admitted to trading on a regulated market and providing that—

- (a) a true and fair view of the state of affairs and profit or loss of a parent undertaking in such a category may be given by the preparation by it of its Companies Act individual accounts for a specified number, not to exceed 4, of its first financial years in accordance with specified accounting standards, and
- (b) a true and fair view of the state of affairs and profit or loss of a parent undertaking in such a category and its subsidiary undertakings as a whole may be given by the preparation by that parent undertaking of its Companies Act group accounts for a specified number, not to exceed 4, of its first financial years in accordance with specified accounting standards.

(3) Regulations made under subsection (2) shall—

- (a) specify the accounting standards, which shall be—
  - (i) internationally recognised, and
  - (ii) generally accepted accounting principles or practice of a jurisdiction—
    - (I) to which a majority of the subsidiaries of the parent undertaking have a substantial connection, or
    - (II) in which the market on which the shares of the parent undertaking are primarily admitted to trading is situated,
- (b) specify the number of financial years in respect of which the regulations apply, and the date on which the latest of such financial years shall end, which shall be not later than 31 December 2015, and
- (c) provide that the preparation of such accounts shall not contravene any provision of the Companies Acts or of any regulations made thereunder.

(4) Every regulation under this section shall be laid before each House of the Oireachtas as soon as may be after it is made and, if a resolution annulling the regulation is passed by either such House within the next 21 days on which that House has sat after the regulation is laid before it, the regulation shall be annulled accordingly but without prejudice to the validity of anything previously done thereunder.

(5) Where accounts are prepared in accordance with regulations made under this section, the notes to those accounts shall contain a statement to that effect.

Notes

C(MP)A 2009, s 2 empowers the Minister to make regulations that may prescribe other specified internationally recognised accounting standards subject to specified criteria.

3 Amendment of Companies Act 1990

The Companies Act 1990 is amended—

(a) in section 3(2), by substituting the following for paragraph (a):

[...][a]

(b) in section 7(3), by deleting ", to an amount not less than £5,000 and not exceeding £250,000,",

(c) in section 13(1), by substituting "relevant Minister." for 35 "relevant Minister, provided that no such liability on the part of the applicant or applicants shall exceed in the aggregate £250,000.",

(d) in section 212—

(i) in subsection (1)(b), by inserting "within the State" after "exchange",

(ii) by inserting the following subsection after subsection (1):

[...][b] and

(iii) in subsection (2), by deleting "subsection (1)" and substituting "subsections (1) and (1A)",

(e) in section 215(1), by inserting "or overseas market purchase" after "market purchase" in each place where it occurs,

(f) in section 226(1), by inserting "or, in the case of an overseas market purchase, within 3 working days," after "28 days",

(g) by inserting the following section after section 226:

[...][c]

(h) in section 229(1), by inserting ", other than when the purchase was an overseas market purchase," after "subsidiary",

(i) in section 256(8), by inserting ", other than a company to which section 256F applies," after "this Part applies", and

(j) by inserting the following after section 256E:

[...][d]

Amendments

a C(MP)A 2009, s 3(a) substitutes CA 1990, s 3(2)(a).

b C(MP)A 2009, s 3(d)(ii) inserts CA 1990, s 212(1A).

c C(MP)A 2009, s 3(g) inserts CA 1990, s 226A.

d C(MP)A 2009, s 3(j) inserts CA 1990, ss 256F, 256G, 256H.

4 Amendment of Companies (Auditing and Accounting) Act 2003

(1) Section 27 of the Companies (Auditing and Accounting) Act 2003 is amended—

(a) by substituting the following for subsection (1):

[...][a]

and

(b) by inserting in subsection (4) ", including the determination of whether a matter should be referred to a committee established for a purpose referred to in subsection (1)" after "behalf".

(2) For the avoidance of doubt, a committee that was established under subsection (1) of section 27 of the Companies (Auditing and Accounting) Act 2003 prior to the commencement of section 4 of the Companies (Miscellaneous Provisions) Act 2009 shall be deemed to have been properly constituted, and shall be deemed to have and to have had all the powers necessary to perform its functions notwithstanding that any of its members was a director when he or she was appointed to the committee but ceased to be such a director before the completion.

Amendments

a C(MP)A 2009, s 4(1)(a) substitutes C(AA)A 2003, s 27(1).

---

5 Amendment of UCITS Regulations

(1) The UCITS Regulations are amended by inserting the following after Regulation 36F (inserted by section 77 of and the Schedule to the Investment Funds, Companies and Miscellaneous Provisions Act 2005):

> "Application of jurisdiction transfer provisions to investment companies established as UCITS
>
> 36G.—The provisions of sections 256F to 256H of the Companies Act 1990 (inserted by section 3 of the Companies (Miscellaneous Provisions) Act 2009) shall apply to any investment company authorised pursuant to these Regulations and for this purpose the references to authorisation shall be read as referring to authorisation pursuant to these Regulations.".

(2) In this section "UCITS Regulations" means the European Communities (Undertakings for Collective Investment in Transferable Securities) Regulations 2003 (S.I. No. 211 of 2003) as amended.

6 Short title, commencement and construction

(1) This Act may be cited as the Companies (Miscellaneous Provisions) Act 2009.

(2) This Act (other than sections 1 and 2, paragraphs (a) to (h) of section 3, and section 4) shall come into operation on such day or days as may be appointed by order or orders of the Minister for Enterprise, Trade and Employment, either generally or with reference to a particular purpose or provision, and different days may be so appointed for different purposes and different provisions.

(3) The Companies Acts and this Act are to be read together as one.

Division B: Secondary Legislation

European Communities (Companies) Regulations 1973

SI 163/1973

The Minister for Industry and Commerce, in exercise of the powers conferred on a Minister of State by section 3 of the European Communities Act, 1972 (No. 27 of 1972), and to give effect to the Council Directive of the European Communities of 9 March, 1968 (68/151/EEC), hereby makes the following regulations:

1 Citation and commencement

These regulations may be cited as the European Communities (Companies) Regulations, 1973, and shall come into operation on the 1st day of July, 1973.

Notes

Implementation of First Company Law Directive: The First Company Law Directive[1] had as its objective the co-ordination of safeguards for the protection of the interests of members and creditors of companies. Section I provides for the registration and publication of various important company documents and particulars including:

(a) the memorandum and articles of association and any amendments thereto;

(b) annual returns as to the capital of the company;

(c) the annual accounts;

(d) notice of transfer of the 'seat', ie the registered office, of the company;

(e) notice of the appointment of a liquidator; and

(f) notice of any annulment/dissolution of the company.

Section II provided for the enforcement by outsiders of transactions which were either *ultra vires* the company itself or which were perhaps within the company's capacity, but were beyond the actual authority of the director or other agent of the company.

Finally, Section III of the Directive provided, *inter alia*, for the protection of persons dealing with companies which were in fact annulled or dissolved.

To a large extent the provisions of the Directive were already part of Irish company law when Ireland joined the European Community.[2] Legal effect was given to the remainder of the Directive by EC(C) Regs 1973.

The EC(C)(A)R 2007 (SI 49/2007) give effect to Directive 2003/58/EC, which amended the First Company Law Directive, and amend (EC(C)R 1973, by inserting reg 2A, amending reg 4 and substituting regs 9 and 12. The most significant change is the extension of the media required to comply with the disclosure requirements in reg 9 to websites and, through the amendment of the definition of 'letters and forms' to extend from paper to any other medium, to emails.

1 68/151/EEC.

2 The relevant provisions of CA 1963 were as follows: s 8 (enforcement of *ultra vires* transactions; s 17 (registration of memorandum and articles of association); s 19 (conclusiveness of certificate of incorporation. This section has since been replaced by C(A)A 1983, s 5); s 113 (registration of particulars of registered office; ss 125–129 (filing of annual returns); s 143 (registration of special resolutions, winding up resolutions etc); s 195 (registration of particulars of directors); s 221 (registration of winding up order); s 249 (registration of order for the solution of a company); ss 263 and 273 (registration of voluntary liquidators' final returns.

---

2 Construction

These regulations shall be construed as one with the Companies Act, 1963 (No. 33 of 1963), in these regulations referred to as 'the Act'.

[**2A**(1) In these Regulations—

'certified translation' means certified to be a true and correct translation in accordance with rules drawn up by the registrar of companies and published in the Companies Registration Office Gazette;

'Directive' means First Council Directive 68/151/EEC of the Council of the European Communities of 9 March 1968 (OJ No L 65, 14.3.1963, p 8), as amended by Directive 2003/58/EC of the European Parliament and of the Council of 15 July 2003 (OJ No L 221, 4.9.2003, p 13);

'letters and order forms' means letters and order forms in paper form or in any other medium.

(2) A word or expression that is used in these Regulations and is also used in the Directive has the same meaning in these Regulations as it has in the Directive.][a]

Amendments

a Section 2A inserted by EC(C)(A)R 2007 (SI 49/2007), reg 3(a) with effect from 1 April 2007.

3 Application

These regulations apply to every company, being a company registered under the Act with limited liability or an unregistered company with limited liability to which certain provisions are applied by section 377(1) of the Act, and the terms 'company' and 'unregistered company' shall be construed accordingly.

Definitions

'company': CA 1963, s 2(1).

Notes

Application of regulations: Since the Directive itself is directed only to limited companies, these regulations have been similarly restricted in their application.[1] They apply to limited companies registered under CA and to unregistered companies of the type to which CA 1963, s 377(1) applies (ie companies trading for gain which have been formed by private Act of Parliament or by charter or by letters patent eg The Governor and Company of the Bank of Ireland). It follows that the regulations do not apply to unlimited companies.[2]

1 EC(C)R 1973, art 1.

2 For an example of a case where the regulations could not be availed of to protect a person dealing with an unlimited company, see *Northern Bank Finance Corporation Ltd v Quinn* [1979] ILRM 221.

4 Publication of notices

(1) A company shall [cause to be published in the Companies Registration Office Gazette][a] notice of the delivery to or the issue by the registrar of companies after the commencement of these regulations of the following documents and particulars—

(a) any certificate of incorporation of the company;

(b) the memorandum and articles of association, or the charter, statutes or other instrument constituting or defining the constitution of the company (in these regulations included in the term 'memorandum and articles of association');

(c) any document making or evidencing an alteration in its memorandum or articles of association;

(d) every amended text of its memorandum and articles of association;

(e) any return relating to its register of directors or notification of a change among its directors;

(f) any return relating to the persons, other than the board of directors, authorised to enter into transactions binding the company, or notification of a change among such persons;

(g) [its annual return and the accounting documents that are required to be published in accordance with—

(i) Fourth Council Directive 78/660/EEC of 25 July 1978 (OJ No. L222, 14.8.1978, p. 11),

(ii) Seventh Council Directive 83/349/EEC of 13 June 1983 (OJ No. L193, 18.7.1983, p. 1),

(iii) Council Directive 86/635/EEC of 8 December 1986 (OJ No. L372, 31.12.1986, p.1), and

(iv) Council Directive 91/674/EEC of 19 December 1991 (OJ No. L374, 31.12.1999, p. 7)][b];

(h) any notice of the situation of its registered office, or of any change therein;

(i) any copy of a winding up order in respect of the company;

(j) any order for the dissolution of the company on a winding up;

(k) any return by a liquidator of the final meeting of the company on a winding up.

(2) A notice shall be published within six weeks of the relevant delivery or issue.

(3) In a voluntary winding up, the liquidator shall within 14 days after his appointment [cause to be published in the Companies Registration Office Gazette][a] a notice of his appointment in addition to delivering notice to the registrar of companies as required by section 278 of the Act.

[(4) For the purposes of the provisions of Article 3(3) of the Directive the registrar of companies shall ensure that certification of electronic copies of documents or particulars guarantees both the authenticity of their origin and the integrity of their contents, by means at least of an advanced electronic signature within the meaning of Article 2(2) of Directive 1999/93/EC of the European Parliament and of the Council of 13 December 1999 (OJ No. L13, 19.1.2000, p.12).

(5) Any document or particular specified in these Regulations that is required to be delivered to the registrar of companies shall be drawn up in the Irish or English

language, and may be accompanied by a certified translation of that document or particular into any other official language of the European Communities.

(6) Where a certified translation pursuant to paragraph (5) has been voluntarily disclosed and there is a discrepancy between—

(a) a document or particular required to be delivered or disclosed to the registrar of companies under paragraph (5), and

(b) the certified translation accompanying it,

the certified translation—

(i) may not be relied upon by the company as against any person dealing with the company, and

(ii) may be relied upon by a person dealing with the company as against that company, unless the company proves that the person dealing with the company had knowledge of the document or particular in the Irish or English version.][c]

Amendments

a Reg 5 of the EC(C)R 2004 (SI 839/2004) substituted the words 'cause to be published in the Companies Registration Office Gazette' for 'publish in *Iris Oifigiúil*'.

b Subparagraph (g) of reg 4(1) substituted by EC(C)(A)R 2007 (SI 49/2007), reg 3(b)(i) with effect from 1 April 2007.

c Paragraphs (4), (5) and (6) inserted by EC(C)(A)R 2007 (SI 49/2007), reg 3(b)(ii) with effect from 1 April 2007.

Definitions

'annual return': CA 1963, s 2(1); 'articles': CA 1963, s 2(1): 'company': CA 1963, s 2(1); 'directors': CA 1963, s 2(1); 'documents': CA 1963, s 2(1); 'memorandum': CA 1963, s 2(1); Registrar of Companies': CA 1963, s 2(1).

Notes

Publication in the Companies Registration Office Gazette: Under CA various documents and particulars must be delivered to or issued by the Registrar of Companies.[1] If they are documents or particulars of the type referred to in:

- regs 4 and 7 of EC(C) Regs 1973;
- regs 11, 21, 30 & 40 of EC (MDC) Regs 1987;
- reg 9 of EC (EEIG) Regs 1989;
- reg 10 of EC (BDC) Regs 1993; or
- CA 1963, s 227B

then companies must cause them to be published in the Companies Registration Office Gazette. Delivery of the requisite particulars to the Registrar of Companies will discharge this duty since the Registrar of Companies effects the actual publication of the particulars delivered, without companies having to do anything further.

Publication in *Iris Oifigiúil*: Other company law items which must be published in *Iris Oifigiúil* as opposed to the Companies Registration Office Gazette include the following:

(a) an order appointing a liquidator;[2]

(b) a resolution for the voluntary winding up of the company;[3]

(c) the appointment of an examiner;[4]

(d) notice of the dissolution of a company by the Registrar because it is defunct or has failed to file its annual returns;[5]

(e) notice of the dissolution of a plc by the Registrar for failure to obtain a certificate authorising it to do business;[6]

(f) the imposition of restrictions on shares or debentures by the Minister in connection with an investigation or enquiry into their ownership;[7]

(g) in the case of a plc, the various classes of documents prescribed by C(A)A 1983, s 55.

1 The main provisions of relevance in CA 1963 are as follows: s 17 (registration of memorandum and articles of association); s 113 (registration of particulars of registered office); ss 125–129 (filing of annual returns); s 143 (registration of special resolutions, winding up resolutions etc); s 195 (registration of particulars of directors); s 221 (registration of winding up order); s 249 (registration of order for the solution of a company); ss 263 and 273 (registration of voluntary liquidators' final returns).

2 CA 1963, s 227.

3 CA 1963, s 252.

4 C(A)A 1990, s 12(1).

5 CA 1963, s 311(3) and C(A)A 1982, s 12(3).

6 C(A)A 1983, s 8.

7 CA 1990, s 16(18).

Consequences of non-publication: Publication of the items listed in regs 4(1) & 7(2) must take place within a period of six weeks of delivery to or issue by the Registrar.[1] If publication has not yet taken place, the documents and particulars may not be relied upon by the company against a third party unless the company proves that the third party had actual knowledge of them.[2] Moreover, even if the documents or particulars have been published in the Companies Registration Office Gazette they may not be relied upon by the company against a third party in connection with transactions taking place before the sixteenth day after publication if the third party proves that it would have been impossible for him to have had knowledge of them.[3] For a discussion of the doctrine of constructive notice and its application in company law, see reg 6 and the notes thereto.

1 EC(C)R 1973, reg 4(2).

2 EC(C)R 1973, reg 10.

3 EC(C)R 1973, reg 10.

5 Text of altered memorandum and articles

Where any alteration is made in a company's memorandum or articles of association, notice of which the company is required to publish under Regulation 4, the company shall deliver to the registrar of companies, in addition to the alteration, a copy of the text of the memorandum and articles as so altered.

Definitions

'company': CA 1963, s 2(1); 'memorandum': CA 1963, s 2(1); 'Registrar of Companies': CA 1963, s 2(1).

Notes

Registration of altered memorandum and articles: Prior to the coming into force of these Regulations, the company was only required to deliver to the Registrar copies of any special resolutions amending the memorandum or articles.[1] Now, however, a copy of the text of the document as so amended must also be delivered for registration.

1 CA 1963, s 143.

6 Organs authorised to bind company

(1) In favour of a person dealing with a company in good faith, any transaction entered into by any organ of the company, being its board of directors or any person registered under these regulations as a person authorised to bind the company, shall be deemed to be within the capacity of the company and any limitation of the powers of that board or person, whether imposed by the memorandum or articles of association or otherwise, may not be relied upon as against any person so dealing with the company.

(2) Any such person shall be presumed to have acted in good faith unless the contrary is proved.

(3) For the purpose of this Regulation, the registration of a person authorised to bind the company shall be effected by delivering to the registrar of companies a notice giving the name and description of the person concerned.

Definitions

'articles': CA 1963, s 2(1); 'company': CA 1963, s 2(1); 'directors': CA 1963, s 2(1); 'memorandum': CA 1963, s 2(1); 'Registrar of Companies': CA 1963, s 2(1).

Notes

Scope of regulation: This regulation gives effect to art 9 of the First Companies Directive. It applies to transactions which are *ultra vires* the company as well as to transactions which, although within the capacity of the company, are nonetheless beyond the authority of the directors or other agent of the company. The enforcement of *ultra vires* transactions was already largely provided for by CA 1963, s 8. Accordingly, the real importance of the regulation is in relation to the enforcement of unauthorised acts of the company's agents.

Acts beyond the authority of the company's agent

1. Actual, apparent and usual authority

Since a company is an artificial legal entity it must, of necessity, operate through agents. The authority of an agent to act on his behalf may be divided into two or possibly three broad categories, namely actual, apparent and usual.[1]

(a) Actual authority, as its name suggests, is the authority which an agent in fact possesses from his principal, and may be express or implied. An express or implied grant of actual authority will normally be subject to an implied condition that the agent should act honestly for the benefit of his principal, the company, and thus if he acts for his own benefit rather than that of the company he will be acting without actual authority.[2] Where the authority of an agent is conferred in such ambiguous terms, or the instructions given to him are so uncertain as to be fairly capable of more than one construction, an act reasonably done by him in good faith which is justified by any one of those constructions, will be deemed to be within his actual authority, and the company will be bound accordingly.[3]

(b) Apparent or ostensible authority, on the other hand, derives not from any consensual arrangement between the principal and the agent, but is founded on a representation by the principal to the third party which is intended to convey, and does convey, to the third party that the arrangement entered into by the agent will be binding on the principal.[4] Apparent authority may therefore be greater than the agent's actual authority. The representation as to the possession of authority, if it is to be binding, must be *intra vires* the company,[5] and must come from the principal rather than the agent since an agent cannot clothe himself with authority.[6] Within a company it is a matter of looking at the internal structure to determine which organ is the 'principal' capable of making the representation as to the authority of the agent. If the case involves the acts of the board of directors or purported directors, the representation must come from the company in general meeting since it is the company in general meeting which appoints the board in the first place.[7] However, if the agent is a managing director or other officer or servant of the company, the representation will need to come from the board, since his appointment will come from the board.[8]

The representation as to authority may take the form of a positive statement by the principal or it may be passive, as where the principal knowingly allows the agent to engage in unauthorised transactions and does nothing to stop him.[9]

The representation by the principal may be that the 'agent' holds a particular post such as that of director or managing director in circumstances where no such appointment has been made[10] or it may be that the agent (who has in fact been so appointed) possesses a greater authority than is in fact the case.[11]

Under normal agency rules, the principal will be bound by an act which is beyond the agent's actual authority but which is within his apparent authority, unless the third party knows or has actual notice of the fact the agent was indeed exceeding his actual authority.[12] If there are suspicious circumstances or abnormalities in the transaction to which the agent is purportedly binding the company, the third party has a duty to make all reasonable enquiries to satisfy himself that the agent is indeed acting with actual authority.[13]

(c) Some commentators[14] suggest the addition of another class of authority namely 'usual authority', ie the authority which an agent of the type in question normally possesses. Depending on the facts of the particular case, usual authority may be less than, the same as or greater than the agent's actual authority. In reality, therefore, it is probably fair to say that usual authority is no more than another way of describing implied actual authority or apparent authority, as the case may be.

The usual authority of a company's agents is to be derived from the provisions of the standard form articles of association in Table A.

Board of directors: By virtue of reg 80, the board, acting collectively, has usual authority to engage in all acts of management on behalf of the company.[15]

Managing Director: A managing director's usual authority is commensurate with that of the board of directors because, under reg 112, the board is entitled upon appointing such an officer to delegate some or all of their functions to him.[16]

Individual director: As a matter of general company law, the directors must make their decisions collectively.[17] Accordingly, an ordinary director has very little usual authority when acting individually rather than as part of the board and an outsider acts at his own risk in contracting with him.[18] Apart from attesting the affixing of the company's seal under reg 115, model form articles do not confer any particular authority on him. Even then his actual authority may be less than his usual authority, since he is only entitled to witness the affixing of the seal if so authorised by resolution of the board.

Chairman of the board: The functions of a chairman vary from company to company. In some cases he will be little more than a figurehead whilst in others he may have the functions of a managing director.[19] His usual authority is, however, somewhat limited, extending only to the signing of the minutes which then become *prima facie* evidence of what transpired at the meeting.[20]

Company secretary: The company secretary has usual authority to enter into contracts on the company's behalf of an administrative nature which relate to the day to day running of its business.[21] He does not, however, have usual authority to contract generally on behalf of the company.[22]

Auditors: The company's auditors do not have any usual authority to enter into contracts or to make binding representations on its behalf.[23]

Individual shareholder: Traditionally, individual shareholders have not had any usual authority to act on behalf of the company. However, in one exceptional case[24] a shareholder who held 49,000 of 50,000 shares and who was also the chairman was found to have actual and ostensible authority to bind the company. It is unclear from the judgment as to how such authority was found to exist. It may perhaps be regarded as an example of the court implicitly lifting the veil of incorporation so as to attribute to the company the acts of its beneficial owner and controller.

Since the coming into force of EC (SMPLC) Regs 1994 the sole member of a company is now empowered to exercise all the powers of the company without necessarily having to do so through the medium of a formal general meeting.[25] Arguably, therefore, the usual authority of the sole member of a single-member company should be regarded as entailing the power to bind the company to any transaction which is neither *ultra vires* nor illegal.

1 For a more detailed discussion of the authority of corporate agents, see Courtney, *The Law of Private Companies* (2nd edn, Tottel Publishing, 2002) paras 7.096–7.131 and, on the authority of agents generally, *Bowstead on Agency* (15th edn, Sweet and Maxwell, 1985), ch 3).

2 *Hopkins v TL Dallas Group Ltd* [2005] 1 BCLC 543.

3 *SMC Electronics Ltd v Akhter Computers Ltd* [2001] 1 BCLC 433.

4 *Kett v Shannon & English* [1987] ILRM 364; *Criterion Properties plc v Stratford UK Properties LLC* [2006] 1 BCLC 729; *Ford v Polymer Vision Ltd* [2009] 2 BCLC 160.

5 *Thomas Williamson Ltd v Bailieborough Co-Operative Agricultural Society Ltd* (31 July 1986, unreported) HC (Costello J).

6 *Freeman & Lockyer v Buckhurst Park Properties (Mangal) Ltd* [1964] 2 QB 480; *Kett v Shannon & English* [1987] ILRM 364; *ESS-Food Eksportlagtiernes Sallgsforening v Crown Shipping (Ireland) Ltd* [1991] ILRM 97; *Armagas Ltd v Mundogas SA, The Ocean Frost* [1986] AC 717; *First Energy (UK) Ltd v Hungarian International Bank Ltd* [1993] BCLC 1409; *MCI WorldCom International Inc v Primus Telecommunications Inc* [2004] 1 BCLC 42.

7 *Mahony v East Holyford Mining Co Ltd* (1875) LR 7 HL 869.

8 *Freeman & Lockyer v Buckhurst Park Properties (Mangal) Ltd* [1964] 2 QB 480; *Unicorn Investments Ltd v Ewart plc* (29 June 1995, unreported) HC (Costello P) at pp 8 and 9 of the transcript; *Ulster Factors Ltd v Entonglen Ltd* (21 February 1997, unreported) HC (Laffoy J).

9 *Mahony v East Holyford Mining Co Ltd* (1875) LR 7 HL 869; *Freeman & Lockyer v Buckhurst Park Properties (Mangal) Ltd* [1964] 2 QB 480; *Ulster Factors Ltd v Entonglen Ltd* [1997] IEHC 34 (Laffoy J).

10 *Mahony v East Holyford Mining Co Ltd* (1875) LR 7 HL 869; *Freeman & Lockyer v Buckhurst Park Properties (Mangal) Ltd* [1964] 2 QB 480; *Hely-Hutchinson v Brayhead Ltd* [1968] 1 QB 549.

11 *Watteau v Fenwick* [1893] 1 QB 346; *Waugh v HB Clifford & Sons* [1982] 1 All ER 1095.

12 *Freeman & Lockyer v Buckhurst Park Properties (Mangal) Ltd* [1964] 2 QB 480.

13 *Hopkins v TL Dallas Group Ltd* [2005] 1 BCLC 543.

14 Powell, *The Law of Agency* (2nd edn), ch 2; Treitel, *The Law of Contract* (6th edn, Sweet and Maxwell), pp 533–535,

15 *Mahony v East Holyford Mining Co Ltd* (1875) LR 7 HL 869; *Re Shannonside Holdings Ltd* (20 May 1993, unreported) HC (Costello J).

16 *Freeman & Lockyer v Buckhurst Park Properties (Mangal) Ltd* [1964] 2 QB 480; *Hely-Hutchinson v Brayhead Ltd* [1968] 1 QB 549; *Thomas Williamson Ltd v Bailieborough Co-Operative Agricultural Society Ltd* (31 July 1986, unreported) HC (Costello J); *Dey v Pullinger Engineering Co* [1921] 1 KB 77; *Bank of New South Wales v Goulburn Valley Butter Co Pty Ltd* [1902] AC 543; *Biggerstaff v Rowatt's Wharf Ltd* [1896] 2 Ch 93; *Clay Hill Brick and Tile Co Ltd v Rawlings* [1938] 4 All ER 100; *Hely-Hutchinson v Brayhead Ltd* [1968] 1 QB 549; *British Thomson-Houston Co Ltd v Federated European Bank Ltd* [1932] 2 KB 176.

17 *Re Athenaeum Life Insurance Society, ex parte Eagle Insurance Co* (1858) 4 K & J 549 at 558; *D'Arcy v Tamar, Kit Hill and Callington Rly Co* (1867) LR 2 Exch 158; *Re Haycraft Gold Reduction and Mining Co* [1900] 2 Ch 230.

18 *Houghton & Co Nothard, Lowe and Wills Ltd* [1927] 1 KB 246, aff'd [1928] AC 1; *Rama Corp'n Ltd v Proved Tin and General Investments Ltd* [1952] 2 QB 147.

19 For a case where the actual authority of the chairman equated with that of a managing director, see *Nash v Lancegaye Safety Glass (Ireland) Ltd* (1958) 92 ILTR 11. In *Kilgobbin Mink and Stud Farms Ltd v National Credit Company Ltd* [1980] IR 175 the chairman, who held 49,999 of 50,000 shares in the company was found to have both ostensible and implied actual authority to enter into a contract on its behalf with a third party). Whilst the rationale behind this decision is hard to discern, it may be explicable as an example of the court at least implicitly lifting the veil of incorporation so as to identify the company with its beneficial owner.

20 CA 1963, s 145.

21 *Panorama Developments (Guildford) Ltd v Fidelis Furnishing Fabrics Ltd* [1971] 3 All ER 16.

22 *Barnett, Hoares & Co v South London Tramways Co* [1887] 18 QBD 815; *Re Cleadon Trust Ltd* [1939] Ch 286.

23 *Re Transplanters (Holding Co) Ltd* [1958] 2 All ER 711.

24 *Kilgobbin Mink and stud Farms Ltd v National Credit Company Ltd* [1980] IR 175.

25 EC(SMPLC)R 1994, reg 9.

2. Doctrine of constructive notice

The normal agency rules regarding apparent/usual authority are modified in the company law context by the doctrine of constructive notice which provides that third parties dealing with the company are deemed to have constructive notice of the contents of any documents which are required to be registered in the Companies Registration Office.[1] These would include the memorandum and articles,[2] particulars as to the identity of the directors and secretary,[3] as well as details of any special resolutions passed in general meeting.[4]

The doctrine of constructive notice does not apply in circumstances where the outsider is in a position to avail of the protection afforded by reg 6. In the absence of this protection, however, the outsider will be deemed to be on notice of restrictions contained in the registered documents and will be bound thereby even though the transaction in question would otherwise have been within the agent's usual or apparent authority. So, for example, where the articles of a company prohibited the board from borrowing money except on foot of a special resolution of the members, the outsider was deemed to be aware of the board's lack of authority, both because the restriction itself was contained in a registerable document, ie the articles, and also because the special resolution, if passed, would likewise have been registerable. It followed therefore that the transaction could not be enforced against the company.[5] Some limits are placed on the operation of the doctrine of constructive notice by reg 10 of EC(C) Regs 1973 which provides that if publication of the registerable documents has not yet taken place in the Companies Registration Office Gazette, they may not be relied upon by the company against a third party unless the company proves that the third party had actual knowledge of them. Moreover, even if the documents or particulars have been published in the Companies Registration Office Gazette they may not be relied upon by the company against a third party in connection with transactions taking place before the sixteenth day after publication if the third party proves that it would have been impossible for him to have had knowledge of them.

1 *Ernest v Nicholls* (1857) 6 HL Cas 401 at 419; *Mahony v East Holyford Mining Co Ltd* (1875) LR 7 HL 869 at 893; *Re Jon Beauforte (London) Ltd* [1953] 1 All ER 634.

2 CA 1963, s 17.

3 CA 1963, s 195 and C(A)A 1982, s 3.

4 CA 1963, s 143.

5 *Irvine v Union Bank of Australia* (1887) 2 App Cas 366. In *Mahony v East Holyford Mining Co* (1875) LR 7 HL 869 because of representations to that effect by the shareholders, a third party was entitled to assume that certain individuals constituted the duly appointed board of directors of the company. It is debateable whether this case would still represent good law on the particular facts since particulars of the names and addresses of the directors and secretary are now registerable under CA 1963, s 195 and C(A)A 1982, s 3 and accordingly outsiders would be deemed to have constructive notice of this information.

3. Indoor Management Rule

The harshness of the doctrine of constructive notice is also curtailed somewhat by the mitigating influence of a common law rule known as the Indoor Management Rule or the Rule in *Royal British Bank v Turquand*.[1] This rule entitles an outsider acting in good faith to assume that any acts of internal management which are necessary to perfect the agent's authority, other than acts requiring registration in the Companies Registration Office, have in fact been taken.[2] The following are examples of the successful invocation of the rule:

(a) The articles provided that the directors could not borrow beyond a specific sum without the authorisation of an ordinary resolution of the members. The outsider was deemed to be aware of that limitation because it was contained in a registerable document, namely the articles, but was entitled to assume that the ordinary resolution, not being registerable, had in fact been passed.[3]

(b) A mortgage was executed by two directors at an inquorate board meeting. The outsider, not having notice of the absence of the quorum, was entitled to assume that the meeting had been validly held and was therefore entitled to enforce the mortgage.[4]

(c) Company borrowings were authorised at a board meeting which was technically invalid because of the failure to give notice to one of the directors. The bank, being unaware of the irregularity in the meeting and in the resolution passed thereat, was entitled to enforce the loan against the company.[5]

(d) A charge was executed over several properties belonging to the company. The bank was also furnished with a copy of the board resolution authorising the execution of charge. The resolution extended to fewer properties than the charge itself. In response to a request for a copy of the resolution authorising the charging of the additional properties, the bank received assurances from the managing director that such a resolution had been passed and would be forthcoming. The resolution had not in fact been passed and was therefore never furnished to the bank. The court held, however, that the bank was still entitled to assume that all necessary internal steps had been taken to perfect the security, including the passing of the resolution charging the additional properties and accordingly it was entitled to enforce the security against these properties as well.[6]

(e) A debenture had been executed in circumstances where, contrary to the requirements of the articles of association, one of the countersignatories to the affixing of the seal was not in fact a director or secretary. The bank in whose favour the debenture had been created was entitled to assume that all necessary acts of internal management had been complied with by the company and was accordingly entitled to enforce the debenture.[7]

The Indoor Management Rule is of no protection to the outsider if he actually knows of the failure to comply with the necessary internal procedures[8] or if he knows facts which would lead a reasonable person to enquire further and to discover the non-compliance.[9] Nor is the rule of any avail in the case of a forgery.[10] Insiders, such as directors, dealing with the company will not normally be allowed to rely on the Indoor Management Rule, at least insofar as they know what internal procedures have been followed and ought therefore to be able to recognise that the requirements of the memorandum or articles of association have not been complied with.[11] However, if the director is dealing with the company in his capacity as an outsider and is not on notice of the facts giving rise to the non-compliance, he may be entitled to invoke the rule and to enforce the irregular transaction against the company.[12] Similarly, an individual shareholder seeking the consent of the board to transfer their shares, is entitled to assume that the consent as communicated to him, has been given on foot a properly made of passed board resolution.[13]

Finally, it should be noted that the Indoor Management Rule affects only the usual authority of an agent and cannot be relied upon to perfect an authority which although perhaps capable of being conferred under the articles, is nonetheless wider than would be normal for an agent of that type.[14]

1 *Royal British Bank v Turquand* (1856) 6 E & B 327.

2 *Re Motor Racing Circuits Ltd* (31 January 1997, unreported) SC, per Blayney J, nem diss.

3 *Royal British Bank v Turquand* (1856) 6 E & B 327; *Re Hampshire Land Co* [1896] 2 Ch 743).

4 *Gloucester County Bank v Rudry Merthyr Steam and House Colliery Co* [1895] 1 Ch 629; *Re Bank of Syria, Owen and Ashworth's Claim* [1901] 1 Ch 115; *Montreal and St Lawrence Light and Power Co v Robert* [1906] AC 196; *Re Fireproof Doors Ltd* [1916] 2 Ch 142; *Cox v Dublin City Distillery Co (No 2)* [1915] IR 345; *Ulster Investment Bank Ltd v Euro Estates Ltd* [1982] ILRM 57).

5 *Allied Irish Banks Ltd v Ardmore Studios International (1972) Ltd* (1963–1993) Irish Company Law Reports 276.

6 *Ulster Investment Bank Ltd v Euro Estates Ltd* [1982] ILRM 57). See also *Re Irish Grain (Trading Board) Ltd* [1984] IEHC 52 (McWilliam J) and *Davies v R Bolton & Co* [1894] 3 Ch 678.

7 *Re Motor Racing Circuits Ltd* (31 January 1997, unreported) SC, per Blayney J, nem diss.

8 *Howard v Patent Ivory Manufacturing Co* (1888) 38 Ch D 156.

9 *AL Underwood Ltd v Bank of Liverpool* [1924] 1 KB 775; *Houghton & Co v Northard Lowe & Wills Ltd* [1927] 1 KB 246; *B Liggett (Liverpool) Ltd v Barclays Bank Ltd* [1928] 1 KB 48; *Lloyds Bank Ltd v Chartered Bank of India, Australia and China* [1929] 1 KB 40; *EBM Co Ltd v Dominion Bank* [1937] 3 All ER 555; *Kanssen v Rialto (West End) Ltd* [1944] Ch 346, aff'd sub nom *Morris v Kanssen* [1946] AC 459.

10 *Ruben v Great Fingall Consolidated* [1906] AC 439. A document signed by a director without the authority of a proper board meeting is not a forgery: *Re Land Credit Co of Ireland* (1869) 4 Ch App 460.

11 *Cox v Dublin City Distillery Co (No 2)* [1915] IR 345; *Howard v Patent Ivory Manufacturing Co* (1888) 38 Ch D 156; *Morris v Kanssen* [1946] AC 459.

12 *Hely-Hutchinson v Brayhead Ltd* [1968] 1 QB 549.

13 *Bargate v Shortridge* (1855) 5 HL Cas 297; *Re British Provident Life and Fire Assurance Society, Grady's Case* (1863) 1 De GJ & Sm 488.

14 *Houghton & Co v Northard Lowe and Wills Ltd* [1928] AC 1; *Kreditbank Cassel GmbH v Schenkers Ltd* [1927] 1 KB 826; *Rama Corp'n Ltd v Proved Tin and General Investments Ltd* [1952] 2 QB 147.

4. Effect of Regulation 6

The main effect of reg 6, which implements art 9 of the First Companies Directive, is to abolish the doctrine of constructive notice in respect of transactions falling within its ambit.[1]

(a) Good faith

The first requirement of reg 6 is that the person should be dealing with the company 'in good faith'. Whilst there is a legal presumption of good faith,[2] there is no statutory definition of the phrase. Nor does the phrase appear anywhere in art 9. However, in an effort to construe the Regulation and its UK equivalent in a manner which is consistent with art 9, the courts have held that a person is to be deemed to be acting in good faith unless he was aware or could not have been unaware of the lack of authority on the part of the agent or the lack of capacity on the part of the company.[3] Furthermore, although the person dealing in good faith with the company will normally be an outsider (ie a person having no connection with the company) the phrase 'a person dealing with a company in good faith' is wide enough to extend to a shareholder receiving an allotment of additional shares[4] and possibly even a director having dealings with the company.[5] However, the provisions of reg 6 will not be of avail to a chairman of the board of directors dealing with the company in circumstances where it was he whose duty it was to ensure that the limitations in the company's constitution were duly observed.[6]

(b) Dealing

The second requirement of reg 6 is that the person should have been 'dealing' with the company. It has been held that the phrase 'dealing' refers only to transactions in which consideration has been or is to be provided by the outsider and does not extend to transactions which are gratuitous from the company's perspective.[7]

(c) Transactions with Directors or Registered Agent

The third requirement in order to be able to avail of the protection of reg 6 is that the 'dealing' should be with the board of directors or with a person who has been registered in the Companies Registration Office as having authority to bind the company. In practice Irish companies tend not to register agents under reg 6 so that the Regulation is really only of relevance insofar as the dealing can be described as being with the board of directors.[8] In this regard, a transaction may be regarded as an act of the board of directors, if, although not formally approved at a board meeting, it has been approved by each director individually.[9] However, an act of an inquorate board does not constitute a transaction entered into by the company's board of directors and accordingly an outsider dealing with the company in such circumstances cannot enjoy the protection of reg 6.[10] So, for example, if the board is rendered incapable of acting under its constitution, because of conflicts of interest, acts purportedly effected by it will not be regarded as transactions of the board for the purposes of reg 6.[11] On the other hand, a transaction may be regarded as an act of the board of directors, if it has been carried out by some person to whom a quorate board of directors has delegated authority to act.[12]

1 *International Sales and Agencies Ltd v Marcus* [1982] 3 All ER 551; *International Factors (NI) Ltd v Streeve Construction Ltd* [1984] NI 245; *TCB Ltd v Gray* [1986] 1 All ER 587.

2 EC(C)R 1973, reg 6(2).

3 *International Sales and Agencies Ltd v Marcus* [1982] 3 All ER 551; *International Factors (NI) Ltd v Streeve Construction Ltd* [1984] NI 245; *TCB Ltd v Gray* [1986] 1 All ER 587.

4 *EIC Services Ltd v Phipps* [2003] 3 All ER 804.

5 *Smith v Henniker-Major & Co* [2002] 2 BCLC 655.

6 *Smith v Henniker-Major & Co* [2002] 2 BCLC 655.

7 *International Sales and Agencies Ltd v Marcus* [1982] 3 All ER 551.

8 *Re Frederick Inns Ltd* [1994] 1 ILRM 387 at 394, per Blayney J.

9 *TCB Ltd v Gray* [1986] 1 All ER 587.

10 *Smith v Henniker-Major & Co* [2002] 2 BCLC 655.

11 *Cooperatieve Rabobank Vecht en Plassengebied BA v Minderhoud* [1998] 2 BCLC 507.

12 *International Sales and Agencies Ltd v Marcus* [1982] 3 All ER 551; *International Factors (NI) Ltd v Streeve Construction Ltd* [1984] NI 245. See also *Unicorn Investments Ltd v Ewart plc* (29 June 1995, unreported) HC (Costello P) at pp 8 and 9.

5. Ultra vires *transactions*

It is unclear as to whether, in respect of *ultra vires* transactions, reg 6 in fact adds anything to the protection already afforded to outsiders by CA 1963, s 8.[1] Section 8 already protected outsiders unless they were 'actually aware' of the lack of capacity on the part of the company. Moreover, to some extent the protection afforded by s 8 is wider than that contained in reg 6, since—

(a) it applies to both limited and unlimited companies;

(b) it is not confined to dealings in which the company is to receive consideration, but also includes gratuitous transactions; and

(c) it applies to transactions effected by any of the company's representatives and not just to the transactions with the board of directors or registered agents.

It has, however, been argued by Keane[2] that although for the purposes of s 8 an outsider will be deemed to be 'actually aware' of the company's lack of capacity where he reads but misconstrues the objects clause,[3] he might nonetheless be regarded as having acted in 'good faith' so as to be entitled to the protection of reg 6. Furthermore, although it may be difficult for an insider such as a director or shareholder to bring himself within the protection of s 8, the phrase 'a person dealing with a company in good faith' in reg 6 is potentially wide enough to extend to a shareholder receiving an allotment of additional shares[4] and possibly even a director having dealings with the company.[5] That said, however, the provisions of reg 6 will not be of avail to a chairman of the board of directors dealing with the company in circumstances where it was he whose duty it was to ensure that the limitations in the company's constitution were duly observed.[6]

1 For a more detailed discussion of the protection afforded by s 8 see the notes thereto.

2 Keane, *Company Law* (4th edn, Tottel Publishing, 2007) at para 12.17.

3 See *Northern Bank Finance Corporation Ltd v Quinn* [1979] ILRM 221.

4 *EIC Services Ltd v Phipps* [2003] 3 All ER 804.

5 *Smith v Henniker-Major & Co* [2002] 2 BCLC 655.

6 *Smith v Henniker-Major & Co* [2002] 2 BCLC 655.

7 Registration of unregistered companies

(1) Every unregistered company shall, within one month after the commencement of these regulations or, if it is incorporated after such commencement, within one month of its incorporation, deliver to the registrar of companies for registration a certified copy of the memorandum and articles of association of the company as amended to date.

(2) The company shall [cause to be published in the Companies Registration Office Gazette][a] notice of the delivery of all documents required to be delivered under paragraph (1), stating in the notice the name of the company, the description of the documents and the date of delivery.

Amendments

a Reg 5 of the EC(C)R 2004 (SI 839/2004) substituted the words 'cause to be published in the Companies Registration Office Gazette' for 'publish in *Iris Oifigiúil*'.

Definitions

'articles': CA 1963, s 2(1); 'company': CA 1963, s 2(1); 'documents': CA 1963, s 2(1); 'memorandum': CA 1963, s 2(1); 'registrar of companies': CA 1963, s 2(1).

Notes

Registration of unregistered companies: This regulation imposed an obligation on unregistered companies to deliver copies of their constitutional documents to the Registrar for registration. As to the classes of companies which constitute 'unregistered companies' see CA 1963, s 377 and the notes thereto.

8 Application of Act to unregistered companies

[...][a]

Amendments

a Repealed by CA 1990, s 6, effective 1 August 1991.

9 [Letters, order forms and websites

(1) Every company shall include the following particulars on its letters and order forms:

(a) the name and legal form of the company;

(b) the place of registration of the company and the number with which it is registered;

(c) the address of the registered office of the company;

(d) in the case of a company exempt from the obligation to use the word 'limited' or 'teoranta' as part of its name, the fact that it is a limited company;

(e) in the case of a company that is being wound up, the fact that it is being wound up;

(f) if reference is made in the letter or order form to the share capital of the company, the reference shall be to the capital that is sub-scribed and paid up.

(2) Where a company has a website, it shall display in a prominent and easily accessible place on that website the particulars referred to in subparagraphs (a) to (f) of paragraph (1), except that the reference in subparagraph (f) to 'in the letter or order forms' shall be construed as a reference to 'on the website'.][a]

Amendments

a Reg 9 substituted by EC(C)(A)R 2007 (SI 49/2007), reg 3(c) with effect from 1 April 2007.

Definitions

'company': CA 1963, s 2(1); 'share': CA 1963, s 2(1).

Notes

Display of information on letter heads and order forms: The company's name must be stated in legible characters on all of its business letters, notices and other official publications, bills of exchange, promissory notes, endorsements, cheques, orders for money or goods, invoices, receipts and letters of credit.[1] All business letters must also give particulars of the names of the company's directors and their nationalities, if not Irish.[2] Moreover, if the company is one to which these Regulations apply[3] all business letters and order forms must state the place of registration of the company, its registered number, its registered address[4] and, if applicable, the fact that it is exempted under CA 1963, s 24 from the obligation to use the word 'limited' or 'teoranta' at the end of its name[5]. If the company elects to refer to its share capital on the letter or order form, the reference must be to the paid-up share capital.[6]

Where a company is being wound up, or is in receivership or is under the protection of the court, that fact must be stated on all business letters, invoices and orders for goods issued by it or on its behalf.[7]

1 CA 1963, s 114(1)(c).

2 CA 1963, s 196(1).

3 ie limited companies EC(C)R 1973, reg 3.

4 EC(C)R 1973, reg 9(1)(a) and (b). Similar disclosure obligations are imposed on foreign companies which establish a branch in the State: EC(BD)R 1993, regs 5 and 8.

5 EC(C)R 1973, reg 9(1)(c).

6 EC(C)R 1973, reg 9(2).

7 CA 1963, ss 303 and 317 and C(A)A 1990, s 12(4). In view of the fact that CA 1963, s 303 already required disclosure of the fact that the company was being wound to be made on letters, etc, EC(C)R 1973, reg 9(1)(e) seems to have been somewhat superfluous.

Websites: By reason of reg 9(2) companies to which the regs apply, now obliged to display in a prominent and easily accessible place the particulars referred to therein.

Emails: Since the introduction of the definition of letters and order forms' in reg 2A(i) to mean 'letters and order forms in paper format or in any other medium' certain emails (eg those with a business letter as an attachment) sent by companies to which the regulations apply, will have to comply with the requirements in reg 9(1).

---

10 Failure to notify documents

The documents and particulars, notice of which is required by these regulations to be [published in the Companies Registration Office Gazette],[a] may not be relied upon by the company as against any other person until after such publication unless the company proves that such person had knowledge of them. However, with regard to transactions taking place before the sixteenth day after the date of publication, they shall not be relied upon against a person who proves that it was impossible for him to have had knowledge of them.

Amendments

a Reg 5 of the EC (C) R 2004 (SI 839/2004) substituted the words 'published in the Companies Registration Office Gazette' for 'published in *Iris Oifigiúil*'.

Definitions

'company': CA 1963, s 2(1); 'documents': CA 1963, s 2(1).

Notes

See the notes to EC(C)R 1973, regs 4 and 6.

---

11 Extension of time for delivery of documents

The court may by order at any time extend the time for delivery of documents under these regulations for such period as the court may think proper.

Definitions

'court': CA 1963, s 2(1).

---

12 [Offences and penalties

(1) If a company fails to comply with Regulation 4, 5, 7 or 9, the company and—

(a) every officer of the company who is in default, and

(b) any person in accordance with whose directions or instructions the directors of the company are accustomed to act and to whose directions or omissions the default is attributable,

shall be guilty of an offence.

(2) A person who is convicted of an offence under these Regulations shall be liable, on summary conviction, to a fine not exceeding €2,000.

(3) Where a person has been convicted of an offence under these Regulations and there is a continuation of the offence by the person after his or her conviction, the person shall be guilty of a further offence on every day on which the contravention continues and for each such offence shall be liable, on summary conviction, to a fine not exceeding €100 for each day on which the offence is so continued.][a]

Amendments

a Reg 12 substituted by EC(C)(A)R 2007 (SI 49/2007), reg 3(d) with effect from 1 April 2007.

Definitions

'company': CA 1963, s 2(1); 'directors': CA 1963, s 2(1); 'memorandum': CA 1963, s 2(1); 'Registrar of Companies': CA 1963, s 2(1).

Given under my Official Seal, this 20th day of June, 1973.

EXPLANATORY NOTE

These Regulations give effect to Council Directive of the European Communities of 9th March, 1968 (68/151/EEC). The Regulations, which apply to companies including unregistered companies with limited liability, provide for the official notification by companies of certain registered documents and particulars by means of publication in Iris Oifigiúil [now, the Companies Registration Office Gazette] and for the publication of additional information on a company's business letters and order forms. They also modify the ultra vires rule in regard to the board of directors or any person authorised to bind a company. The Regulations extend to unregistered companies certain provisions of the Companies Act, 1963.

European Communities (Mergers and Division of Companies) Regulations 1987

SI 137/1987

ARRANGEMENT OF REGULATIONS

PART 1
PRELIMINARY

PART II
MERGERS

PART III
DIVISIONS

1, ALBERT REYNOLDS, Minister of Industry and Commerce, in exercise of the powers conferred on me by section 3 of the European Communities Act, 1972 (No. 27 of 1972) and for the purpose of giving effect to Council Directive No. 78/855/EEC of 9 October, 1978 (OJ No L295/36, 20.10.78) and No. 82/891/EEC of 17 December, 1982 (OJ L378/ 47, 31.12.82) hereby make the following Regulations;

PART 1
PRELIMINARY

1 Citation and commencement

(1) These Regulations may be cited as the European Communities (Mergers and Divisions of Companies) Regulations, 1987.

(2) These Regulations shall be construed as one with the Companies Acts.

(3) These Regulations shall come into operation on the 1st day of June, 1987.

Notes

These regulations apply only to Irish-incorporated and registered public limited companies and transpose the Third and Sixth Company Law Directives on mergers and divisions respectively of public limited liability companies. Part II applies to mergers whereby the assets and liabilities of one or more plcs are being acquired by another plc. Part III, on the other hand, applies to divisions whereby the assets and liabilities of a plc are being acquired by other plcs. It should be noted, however, that these Regulations do not apply to conventional take-overs or a transaction whereby one plc simply acquires a controlling interest in the share capital of another plc.

The Third Directive is the basis of the Tenth Company Law Directive 2005/56/EC of 26 October 2005 on cross-border mergers of limited liability companies, which was transposed into Irish law by European Communities (Cross-Border Mergers) Regulations 2008 (SI 157/2008).

---

2 Interpretation

(1) In these Regulations, unless the context otherwise requires—

"the Act of 1963" means the Companies Act, 1963;

"the Companies Acts" means the Act of 1963 and every enactment (including these and other Regulations made under the European Communities Act, 1972) which is to be construed as one with that Act;

"company" means a pubic limited company, within the meaning of the Companies (Amendment) Act, 1983, or a body corporate to which certain provisions of the Act of 1963 are applied by section 377(1) of that Act;

"director", in relation to a company which is being wound up, means liquidator;

"division" has the meaning assigned to it by Regulation 24;

"merger" has the meaning assigned to it by Regulation 4;

"Minister" means the Minister for Industry and Commerce.

(2) In these Regulations a reference to any enactment shall, unless the context otherwise requires, be construed as a reference to that enactment as amended by any other enactment including these Regulations.

Cross reference

For companies other than public limited companies, it may be possible to effect a merger or division pursuant to CA 1963, ss 201–204, 260, 271.

For the definition of 'director' in respect of a company which is not being wound up, see CA 1963, s 2(1).

---

3 Penalties

A person convicted of an offence under these Regulations shall be liable, on summary conviction, to a fine not exceeding [€1,904.61][a] or, at the discretion of the court, to imprisonment for a term not exceeding 12 months or both.

Amendments

a £1,000 increased to £1,500 by CA 1990, s 240(7) as inserted by CLEA 2001, s 104. £1,500 converted to €1,904.61 by Council Regulations (EC) No 1103/97, No 974/98 and No 2866/98 and the Economic and Monetary Union Act 1988, s 6.

Definitions

'court'; CA 1963, s 2(1).

PART II
MERGERS

Notes

The basic requirements of Part II are that draft terms of the merger and an explanatory report are prepared by the directors of each company which is a party to the proposed merger. In addition, each merging company must commission an independent person to examine and prepare a written report on the draft terms of the merger.

Each merging company must deliver a copy of the draft terms of the merger to the Registrar of Companies and publish notice of such delivery in the Companies Registration Office Gazette. They must then make the draft terms of the merger, the explanatory report and the independent person's report, together with the last three years' accounts and any accounting statement required by reg 9 to update the company's financial position, available for inspection at their respective registered offices for at least one month prior to the date of the general meeting at which the proposed merger is to be considered.

If the merger is to be effected by the formation of a new company, it must be approved by special resolution of the shareholders of each merging company. However, if the merger simply involves the acquisition of one or more companies by another existing company, then it need only be approved by special resolution of the company or companies being acquired. Dissenting shareholders are entitled to demand that their shares be acquired for cash.

Finally, for the merger to take effect, it must be confirmed by order of the court upon the application of all merging companies.

4 Interpretation of Part II

In this Part, unless the context otherwise requires—

"acquiring company", has the meaning assigned to it by Regulation 5;

"merger" means "merger by acquisition" or "merger by formation of a new company" within the meaning of Regulation 5(1);

"merging company" means a company which is a party to a proposed merger.

Definitions

'company': EC(MDC)R 1987, reg 2; 'merger': EC(MDC)R 1987, reg 2.

Notes

The 'merging companies' would appear to include both the acquiring company and the company or companies whose assets and liabilities are being acquired.

5 Mergers to which Part II applies

(1) In this Part—

(a) "merger by acquisition" means an operation whereby an existing company ("the acquiring company") acquires all the assets and liabilities of another company or companies in exchange for the issue to the shareholders of the company or companies being acquired of shares in the acquiring company, with or without any cash payment, and with a view to the dissolution of the company or companies being acquired; and

(b) "merger by formation of a new company" means a similar operation where the acquiring company has been formed for the purpose of such acquisition.

(2) Where a company is being wound up it may—

(a) become a party to a merger by acquisition or by formation of a new company, provided that the distribution of its assets to its shareholders has not begun at the date, under Regulation 6 (4), of the draft terms of merger, or

(b) opt to avail of the provisions of sections 201 to 204, 260 and 271 of the Act of 1963.

(3) Subject to paragraph (2), the said provisions shall not apply to merger by acquisition or by formation of a new company.

Definitions

'Act of 1963': EC(MDC)R 1987, reg 2: 'company'; EC(MDC)R 1987, reg 2: 'merger': EC(MDC)R 1987, regs 2, 4.

6 Draft terms of merger

(1) Where a merger is proposed to be entered into, the directors of the merging companies shall draw up draft terms of the merger in writing.

(2) The draft terms of merger shall state, at least—

- (a) the name and registered office of each of the merging companies;
- (b) as to each of such companies, whether it is a public company limited by shares, a public company limited by guarantee and having a share capital or a body corporate to which section 377(1) of the Act of 1963 relates;
- (c) the proposed share exchange ratio and the amount of any cash payment;
- (d) the proposed terms relating to allotment of shares in the acquiring company;
- (e) the date from which holders of such shares will become entitled to participate in the profits of the acquiring company;
- (f) the date from which the transactions of the company or companies being acquired shall be treated for accounting purposes as being those of the acquiring company;
- (g) any special conditions, including special rights or restrictions, whether in regard to voting, participation in profits, share capital or otherwise, which will apply to shares or other securities issued by the acquiring company in exchange for shares or other securities in the company or companies being acquired;
- (h) any payment or benefit in cash or otherwise, paid or given or intended to be paid or given to any independent person referred to in Regulation 8 and to any director of any of the merging companies insofar as it differs from the payment or benefit paid or given to other persons in respect of the merger and the consideration, if any, for any such payment or benefit.

(3) Where the merger is a merger by formation of a new company the draft terms of merger shall include or be accompanied by the memorandum or draft memorandum and the articles or draft articles of association of the new company.

(4) The draft terms of merger shall be signed and dated on behalf of each of the merging companies by two directors of each such company and that date shall, for the purposes of this Part, be the date of the draft terms of merger.

Definitions

'Act of 1963': EC(MDC)R 1987, reg 2: 'company': EC(MDC)R 1987, reg 2; 'director': EC(MDC)R 1987, reg 2, CA 1963, s 2(1); 'merger': EC(MDC)R 1987, reg 2, reg 4.

7 Directors' explanatory report

(1) A separate written report ("the explanatory report") shall be drawn up in respect of each of the merging companies by the directors of each such company.

(2) The explanatory report shall at least detail and explain—

(a) the draft terms of merger;

(b) the legal and economic grounds for and implications of the draft terms of merger with particular reference to the proposed share exchange ratio, organisation and management structures, recent and future commercial activities and the financial interests of the holders of the shares and other securities in the company;

(c) the methods used to arrive at the proposed share exchange ratio and the reasons for the use of these methods;

(d) any special valuation difficulties which have arisen.

(3) The explanatory report shall be signed and dated on behalf of each of the merging companies by two directors of each such company.

Definitions

'company': EC(MDC)R 1987, reg 2; 'director': EC(MDC)R 1987, reg 2, CA 1963, s 2(1); 'merger': EC(MDC)R 1987, reg 2, reg 4.

8 Independent person's report

(1) [Subject to paragraph (11), each][a] of the merging companies shall appoint an independent person to examine the draft terms of merger and to prepare a written report on them to the shareholders of the company concerned.

(2) No person shall act as an independent person for the purposes of paragraph (1) unless he is authorised by the Minster on application by the company concerned to be such a person for the purposes of the proposed merger.

(3) One or more independent persons may be authorised by the Minister on joint application by the merging companies for all the said companies.

(4) None of the following persons shall be qualified to act as an independent person in respect of a proposed merger—

(a) a person who is or, within 12 months of the date of the draft terms of merger, has been, an officer or servant of the company;

(b) except with the leave of the Minister, a parent, spouse, brother, sister or child of an officer of the company;

(c) a person who is a partner or in the employment of an officer or servant of the company.

(5) If an independent person becomes disqualified by virtue of this regulation he shall thereupon cease to hold office and shall give notice in writing of his disqualification to the Minister within 14 days thereof, but without prejudice to the validity of any acts done by him in his capacity as independent person.

(6) Any person who acts as an independent person when disqualified from doing so under this regulation or who makes default in complying with paragraph (5) shall be guilty of an offence.

(7) The report referred to in paragraph (1) shall—

(a) state the method or methods used to arrive at the proposed share exchange ratio;

(b) give the opinion of the person making the report as to whether the proposed share exchange ratio is fair and reasonable;

(c) give the opinion of the person making the report as to whether the method or methods used are adequate in the case in question;

(d) indicate the values arrived at using each such method;

(e) give the opinion of the person making the report as to the relative importance attributed to such methods in arriving at the values decided on;

(f) any special valuation difficulties which have arisen.

(8) A person making a report under this regulation shall be entitled to require from the merging companies and their officers such information and explanation (whether orally or in writing) and to carry out such investigations as he thinks necessary to enable him to make the report.

(9) Any of the merging companies and any officer thereof who—

(a) fails to supply to an independent person any information or explanation in his power, possession or procurement which that person thinks necessary for the purposes of this report, or

(b) knowingly or recklessly makes a statement or provides a document which—

(i) is misleading, false or deceptive in a material particular, and

(ii) is a statement or document to which this paragraph applies,

shall be guilty of an offence.

(10) Paragraph (9) applies to any statement made, whether orally or in writing, or any document provided to any person making a report under this regulation being a statement or document which conveys or purports to convey any information or explanation which that person requires, or is entitled to require, under paragraph (8).

[(11) Paragraph (1) does not apply if all of the holders of shares and other securities conferring the right to vote in general meetings of each of the merging companies have so agreed.][b]

Amendments

a Words 'Subject to paragraph (11), each' substituted for 'Each' by EC(MDC)(A)R 2008, reg 2(a)(i).

b EC(MDC)R 1987, reg 8(11) inserted by EC(MDC)(A)R 2008, reg 2(a)(ii).

Definitions

'company': EC(MDC)R 1987, reg 2; 'merger': EC(MDC)R 1987, reg 2, reg 4; 'Minister': EC(MDC)R 1987, reg 2; 'officer': CA 1963, s 2(1).

9 Accounting statement

(1) Where the latest annual accounts of any of the merging companies relate to a financial year ended more than six months before the date of the draft terms of merger, that company shall prepare an accounting statement in accordance with the provisions of this regulation.

(2) The accounting statement shall, where required under paragraph (1), be drawn up—

- (i) in the format of the last annual balance sheet and in accordance with the provisions of the Companies Acts; and
- (ii) as at a date not earlier than the first day of the third month preceding the date of the draft terms of merger.

(3) Valuations shown in the last annual balance sheet shall, subject to the exceptions outlined in paragraph (4), only be altered to reflect entries in the books of account.

(4) Notwithstanding the provisions of paragraph (3), the following shall be taken into account in preparing the accounting statement—

- (a) interim depreciation and provisions, and
- (b) material changes in actual value not shown in the books of account.

(5) The provisions of the Companies Acts relating to the Auditor's report on the last annual accounts shall apply, with any necessary modifications, to the accounting statement required by paragraph (1).

Cross reference

With regard to the relevant accounting provisions of the Companies Acts generally, see CA 1963, ss 148–164, C(A)A 1986 and EC(CGA)R 1992.

For the balance sheet format see C(A)A 1986, Sch, Part I, and the EC(CGA)R 1992.

In relation to the books of account, see CA 1990, s 202.

For the provisions dealing with the auditor's report, see CA 1963, ss 157, 191, 192; C(A)A 1986, ss 15, 18; EC(CGA)R 1992, regs 38, 40 and CA 1990, ss 193, 194.

Definitions

'company': EC(MDC)R 1987, reg 2: 'Companies Acts'; EC(MDC)R 1987, reg 2; 'financial year': CA 1963, s 291); 'merger': EC(MDC)R 1987, reg 2, reg 4.

---

10 Companies (Amendment) Act 1983: sections 30 and 31 restricted

The provisions of sections 30 and 31 of the Companies (Amendment) Act, 1983, shall not apply to the issue of shares by any company formed for the purposes of a merger by formation of a new company.

Definitions

'company': EC(MDC)R 1987, reg 2; 'merger': EC(MDC)R 1987, reg 2, reg 4; 'share': CA 1963, s 2(1).

Notes

It would seem that ss 30, 31 would probably not apply in any case by virtue of the provisions of s 30(2)(b).

11 Registration and publication of documents

(1) Each of the merging companies shall—

(a) deliver for registration to the registrar of companies a copy of the draft terms of merger, signed and dated as required by Regulation 6; and

(b) [cause to be published in the Companies Registration Office Gazette][a] and once at least in 2 daily newspapers circulating in the district where the registered office or principal place of business of the company is situate notice of delivery to the registrar of companies of the draft terms of merger.

(2) The requirements of paragraph (1) shall be fulfilled by each of the merging companies at least one month before the date of the general meeting of each such company which by virtue of Regulation 13 is to consider the draft terms of merger.

Amendments

a The Companies Registration Office Gazette was substituted for *Iris Oifigiúil* by EC(C)R 2004, (SI 839/2004), reg 6(a) with effect from 15 December 2004.

Definitions

'company': EC(MDC)R 1987, reg 2; 'documents': CA 1963, s 2(1); 'merger': EC(MDC)R 1987, reg 2, reg 4; 'registrar of companies': CA 1963, s 2(1).

12 Inspection of documents

(1) Each of the merging companies shall, subject to paragraph (2), make available for inspection free of charge by any member of the company at its registered office during business hours (subject to such reasonable restrictions as the company in general meeting may impose so that not less than 2 hours in each day be allowed for inspection)—

(a) the draft terms of merger;

(b) the audited annual accounts for the preceding three financial years of each company or, where a company has traded for less than 3 financial years before the date of the draft terms of merger, the audited annual accounts for those financial years for which the company has traded;

(c) the explanatory reports relating to each of the merging companies referred to in Regulation 7;

(d) [where applicable][a] the independent person's report relating to each of the merging companies referred to in Regulation 8;

(e) any accounting statement in relation to any of the merging companies which is required to be prepared pursuant to Regulation 9.

(2) The provisions of paragraph (1) shall apply in the case of each of the merging companies for a period of one month before the general meeting which is to consider the draft of merger.

Amendments

a Words 'where applicable' inserted by EC(MDC)(A)R 2008, reg 2(b).

Definitions

'company': EC(MDC)R 1987, reg 2; 'financial year'; CA 1963, s 2(1); 'member'; CA 1963, s 31; 'merger': EC(MDC)R 1987, reg 2, reg 4.

13 General meetings of merging companies

(1) Subject to paragraph (4) of this regulation and to Regulation 14, the draft terms of merger shall be approved by a special resolution passed at a general meeting of each of the merging companies.

(2) Where the merger is a merger by formation of a new company, the memorandum or draft memorandum and articles or draft articles of association of the new company shall be approved by a special resolution of each of the companies being acquired.

(3) The notice convening the general meeting referred to in paragraph (1) shall contain a statement of every shareholder's entitlement to obtain on request, free of charge, full or, if so desired, partial copies of the documents listed in Regulation 12.

(4) In the case of—

(a) a merger by acquisition, or

(b) an operation whereby one or more companies are acquired by another company which holds ninety per cent or more, but not all, of their shares and other securities conferring the right to vote at general meetings (**"a voting right"**) (whether such shares and other securities are held either by the acquiring company together with or solely by other persons in their own names but on behalf of that company), or

(c) an operation to which paragraph (8) of this regulation applies,

approval of the draft terms of merger by means of a special resolution shall not be required in the case of the acquiring company provided that the following conditions are fulfilled—

(i) the provisions of Regulations 11 and 12 are complied with at least one month before the date of the general meeting of each of the companies being acquired, and

(ii) one or more members of the company holding paid up share capital amounting in total value to not less that 5% of such of the paid up share capital as confers voting right, whether or not the shares held confer a voting right, shall be entitled, under the articles of association of the company, to require the convening of a general meeting of the company to consider the draft terms of merger.

(5) The directors of each of the companies being acquired shall inform—

(a) the general meeting of that company, and

(b) the directors of the acquiring company

of any material change in the assets and liabilities of the company or companies being acquired between the date of the draft terms of merger and the date of such general meeting.

(6) The directors of the acquiring company shall inform the general meeting of that company of the matters referred to in paragraph (5).

(7) Regulations 7, 8 and 12 shall not apply in the case of an operation under paragraph (4) (b) of this regulation provided that the conditions under Regulation 15 are fulfilled.

(8) Notwithstanding anything contained in Regulation 5, but subject to paragraph (9) of this regulation, these Regulations shall apply to an operation whereby a company ("the acquiring company") acquires all the assets and liabilities of another company or companies and the acquiring company is the holder of all of the shares and other securities conferring the right to vote at general meetings of the company or companies being acquired, whether such shares and other securities are held either by the acquiring company together with or solely by other persons in their own name but on behalf of that company.

(9) The following provisions of these Regulations shall not apply to an operation under paragraph (8), namely, Regulations 6(2)(c), 6(2)(d), 6(2)(e), 7, 8, 12(1)(c), 12 1)(d), 19(1)(b) and 21.

Definitions

'articles'; CA 1963, s 2(1): 'company': EC(MDC)R 1987, reg 2; 'memorandum'; CA 1963, s 2(1); 'merger': EC(MDC)R 1987, reg 2, reg 4.

Notes

The exemption from the requirement in such a case to prepare an explanatory report and independent person's report and to have the documentation referred to in reg 12 available for inspection is presumably because the acquiring company already has such a large degree of control over the company being acquired so that the passing of the special resolution approving the merger is a foregone conclusion.

---

14 Meetings of classes of shareholders

Where the share capital of any of the merging companies is divided into shares of different classes, section 38 of the Companies (Amendment) Act, 1983, shall apply.

Definitions

'company': EC(MDC)R 1987, reg 2; 'share': CA 1963, s 2(1).

---

15 Purchase of minority shares

(1) Any person being—

(a) a shareholder in any of the merging companies who voted against the special resolution of the company concerned relating to the draft terms of merger, or

(b) in a case to which Regulation 13(4)(b) relates, any shareholder other than the acquiring company,

may, not later than 15 days after the relevant date, request the acquiring company in writing to acquire his shares for cash.

(2) In this regulation "the relevant date" in relation to a company means the date on which the latest general meeting of that company to consider the draft terms of merger, or of any class of the holders of shares or other securities of such company, as required by these Regulations, is held.

(3) Nothing in this regulation shall prejudice the power of the court to make any order necessary for the protection of the interests of a dissenting minority in a merging company.

Definitions

'company': EC(MDC)R 1987, reg 2; 'court': CA 1963, s 2(1); 'merger': EC(MDC)R 1987, reg 2, reg 4; 'share': CA 1963, s 2(1).

Notes

It would seem that in the case of a merger of the type to which reg 13(4)(b) refers, any shareholder other than the acquiring company is entitled to demand that his shares be acquired for cash, even if he has voted for the merger.

The court order would presumably be made as a condition of the confirmation of the merger under EC(MDC)R 1987, reg 16.

16 Application for confirmation of merger by court

(1) An application to the court for an order confirming a merger shall be made jointly by all the merging companies.

(2) The application shall be accompanied by a statement of the size of the shareholding of any shareholder who has requested the purchase of his shares under Regulation 15 and of the measures which the acquiring company proposes to take to comply with such shareholder's request.

Definitions

'company': EC(MDC)R 1987, reg 2; 'court': CA 1963, s 2(1); 'merger': EC(MDC)R 1987, reg 2, reg 4; 'share': CA 1963, s 2(1).

Notes

The application (including the settling of a list of creditors under EC(MDC)R 1987, reg 17) is somewhat similar to that involved in the confirmation of a reduction of capital pursuant to CA 1963, s 72. Since a s 72 application is by way of petition, it would seem that the same procedure should be used for EC(MDC)R 1987, reg 16.

17 Protection of creditors

(1) A creditor of any of the merging companies who, at the date of publication of the notice under Regulation 11(1)(b), is entitled to any debt or claim against the company, shall be entitled to object to the confirmation by the court of the merger.

(2) If the court deems if necessary in order to secure the adequate protection of creditors of any of the merging companies it may—

(a) determine a list of creditors entitled to object and the nature and amount of their debts or claims, and may publish notices fixing a period within which creditors not entered on the list may have a claim for inclusion on that list considered;

(b) where an undischarged creditor on the list referred to in subparagraph (a) does not consent to the merger, the court may dispense with the consent of that creditor, on the company securing payment of the debt or claim by apportioning to that creditor such following amount as the court may direct—

(i) if the company concerned admits the full amount of the debt or claim, that amount;

(ii) if the company concerned does not admit the debt or claim, or if the amount is contingent or not ascertained, an amount fixed by the court after the like inquiry and adjudication as if the company were being wound up by the court.

(3) If, having regard to any special circumstances of the case it thinks proper so to do, the court may direct that paragraph (2) shall not apply as regards as regards any class of creditors.

Definitions

'company': EC(MDC)R 1987, reg 2; 'court': CA 1963, s 2(1); 'merger': EC(MDC)R 1987, reg 2, reg 4.

---

18 Preservation of rights of holders of securities

(1) Subject to paragraph (2), holders of securities, other than shares, in any of the companies being acquired to which special rights are attached shall be given rights in the acquiring company at least equivalent to those they possessed in the company being acquired.

(2) Paragraph (1) shall not apply—

(a) where the alteration of the rights in the acquiring company has been approved—

(i) by a majority of the holders of such securities at a meeting held for that purpose, or

(ii) by the holders of those securities individually, or

(b) where the holders of those securities are entitled under the terms of those securities to have their securities purchased by the acquiring company.

Definitions

'company': EC(MDC)R 1987, reg 2; 'share': CA 1963, s 2(1).

Notes

The phrase 'securities other than shares' would extend to debentures in the company.

19 Confirmation order

(1) The court, on being satisfied that—

(a) the requirements of these Regulations have been complied with,

(b) proper provision has been made for—

(i) any dissenting shareholder of any of the merging companies who has made a request under Regulation 15, and

(ii) any creditor of any of the merging companies who objects to the merger in accordance with Regulation 17, and

(c) the rights of holders of securities other than shares in any of the companies being acquired are safeguarded in accordance with Regulation 18,

may, subject to Regulation 20, make an order confirming the merger with effect from such date as the court appoints ("the appointed date").

(2) The order of the court confirming the merger shall, with effect from the appointed date, have the following effects—

(a) all the assets and liabilities of the company or companies being acquired shall stand transferred to the acquiring company in accordance with the draft terms of merger as approved by the court;

(b) the shareholders of the company or companies being acquired shall become shareholders in the acquiring company in accordance with the draft terms of the merger as approved by the court;

(c) the company or companies being acquired shall, subject to paragraph (4), be dissolved;

(d) all legal proceedings pending by or against any of the dissolved companies shall be continued with the substitution, for the dissolved company, of the acquiring company.

(3) The court may, either by the order confirming the merger or by a separate order, make provision for such matters as the court considers necessary to secure that the merger shall be fully and effectively carried out.

(4) The court may, in particular, by order—

(a) direct that the acquiring company shall, on a date specified by the court, purchase the shares of a dissenting shareholder who has made a request under Regulation 15 and pay therefor the sum determined by the court, being not less than the market sale price of the shares on the appointed date, and

(b) provide for the reduction accordingly of the company's capital.

(5) Section 41 (1) of the Companies (Amendment) Act, 1983 (which restricts the right of a company to purchase its own shares) shall not apply to the purchase of any shares in pursuance of an order of the court under this regulation.

(6) If it is necessary for any of the companies being acquired to take any steps to ensure that its assets and liabilities are fully transferred, the court may specify a date which, save in exceptional cases, shall not be later than 6 months after the appointed date by which such steps must be taken and for that purpose may order that the dissolution of such company shall take effect on that date.

Definitions

'company': EC(MDC)R 1987, reg 2; 'court': CA 1963, s 2(1); 'merger': EC(MDC)R 1987, reg 2, reg 4; 'share': CA 1963, s 2(1).

20 Limitation on power of court to make orders

An order of the court shall not be made under these Regulations in respect of a proposed merger to which the Mergers, Take-overs and Monopolies (Control) Act, 1978 applies until either—

(a) the Minister has stated in writing that he has decided not to make an order under section 9 of that Act, in relation to the proposed merger, or

(b) the Minister has stated in writing that he has made a conditional order under that section in relation to the proposed merger, or

(c) the relevant period within the meaning of section 6 of that Act (which relates to a limitation on the commencement of a merger) has elapsed without the Minister's having made an order under the said section 9 in relation to the proposed merger.

whichever first occurs.

Definitions

'court': CA 1963, s 2(1); 'merger': EC(MDC)R 1987, reg 2, reg 4; 'minister': EC(MDC)R 1987, reg 2.

Notes

The Mergers, Take-Overs and Monopolies (Control) Act 1978 has since been repealed by the Competition Act 2002, s 48(b). Part 3 of the Competition Act 2002 now regulates mergers to which the EU Merger Regulation (Council Regulation (EC) No 139/2004 of 20 January 2004 on the control of concentrations between undertakings (OJ L 24, 29.01.2004, pages 1–22) does not apply.

21 Registration and publication of confirmation of merger

(1) Where the court has made an order confirming a merger an office copy thereof shall forthwith be sent to the registrar of companies for registration by such officer of the court as the court may direct.

(2) The acquiring company shall [cause to be published in the Company Registration Office Gazette][a] notice of delivery to the registrar of companies of the order of the court confirming the merger within fourteen days of such delivery and if default is made in complying with this paragraph the company and every officer of the company who is in default shall be guilty of an offence.

(3) It shall be a defence for a person charged with an offence under paragraph (2) to show that non-compliance was not due to any delay or negligence on the part of the company or person concerned.

(4) Proceedings in relation to an offence under this regulation may be brought and prosecuted by the registrar of companies.

Amendments

a The Companies Registration Office Gazette was substituted for *Iris Oifigiúil* by EC(C)R 2004, (SI 839/2004), reg 6(b) with effect from 15 December 2004.

Definitions

'company': EC(MDC)R 1987, reg 2; 'court': CA 1963, s 2(1); 'merger': EC(MDC)R 1987, reg 2, reg 4; 'registrar of companies': CA 1963, s 2(1).

22 Civil liability of directors and independent persons

(1) Any shareholder of any of the merging companies who has suffered loss or damage by reason of misconduct in the preparation or implementation of the merger by a director of any such company or by the independent person who has made a report under Regulation 8 shall be entitled to have such loss or damage made good to him by—

(a) in the case of misconduct by a person who was a director of that company at the date of the draft terms of merger – that person,

(b) in the case of misconduct by any independent person who prepared a report under Regulation 8 in respect of any of the merging companies – that person.

(2) Without prejudice to the generality of paragraph (1), any shareholder of any of the merging companies who has suffered loss or damage arising from the inclusion of any untrue statement in the draft terms of merger, the explanatory report, the independent person's report or the accounting statement provided for under Regulation 9 shall, subject to paragraphs (3) and (4), be entitled to have such loss or damage made good to him by every person who was a director of that company at the date of the draft terms of merger or, in the case of the independent person's report, by the person who made that report in relation to that company.

(3) A director of a company shall not be liable under paragraph (2) if he proves—

(a) that any of the documents referred to in paragraph (2) was issued without his knowledge or consent and that on becoming aware of their issue he forthwith informed the shareholders of that company that they were issued without his knowledge or consent, or

(b) that as regards every untrue statement he had reasonable grounds, having exercised all reasonable care and skill, for believing and did, up to the time the merger took effect, believe that the statement was true.

(4) A person who makes a report required by Regulation 8 in relation to a company shall not be liable in the case of untrue statements in his own report if he proves—

(i) that on becoming aware of the statement he forthwith informed the company concerned and its shareholders of the untruth, or

(ii) that he was competent to make the statement and that he had reasonable grounds for believing and did up to the time the merger took effect believe that the statement was true.

Definitions

'company': EC(MDC)R 1987, reg 2; 'documents': CA 1963, s 2(1); 'director': EC(MDC)R 1987, reg 2; 'merger': EC(MDC)R 1987, reg 2, reg 4.

Notes

This regulation is analogous to, but admittedly not exactly the same as IFCMPA 2005, s 41 which imposes civil liability for 'untrue statements' in a prospectus.

With regard to the meaning of the phrase 'untrue statement', see Notes to IFCMPA 2005, s 41.

23 Criminal liability for untrue statements to merger documents

(1) Where any untrue statement has been included in the draft terms of merger, the explanatory report or the accounting statement, each of the directors and any person who authorised the issue of those documents shall be guilty of an offence.

(2) Where any untrue statement has been included in the independent person's report the independent person and any person who authorised the issue of the report shall be guilty of an offence.

(3) It shall be a defence for a person charged with an offence under paragraph (1) or (2) to show that, having exercised all reasonable care and skill, he had reasonable grounds for believing and did, up to the time of the issue of the documents, believe that the statement was true.

Definitions

'director': EC(MDC)R 1987, reg 2, CA 1963, s 2(1); 'merger': EC(MDC)R 1987, reg 2, reg 4.

Notes

This regulation is analogous to, but admittedly not exactly the same as IFCMPA 2005 s 48 which imposes criminal liability for 'untrue statements' in a prospectus. With regard to the meaning of the phrase 'untrue statement', see Notes to IFCMPA, s 41.

PART III
DIVISIONS

Notes

The basic requirements of Part III are that draft terms of the division and an explanatory report are prepared by the directors of each company which is a party to the proposed division. In addition, each company must commission an independent person to examine and prepare a written report on the draft terms of the division.

Each company involved in the division must deliver a copy of the draft terms of division to the registrar of companies and publish notice of such delivery in the Companies Registration Office Gazette. They must then make the draft terms of division, the explanatory report and the independent person's report, together with the last three years' accounts and any accounting statement required by reg 29 to up date the company's financial position, available for inspection at their respective registered offices for at least one month prior to the date of the general meeting at which the proposed division is to be considered.

The next step is for the division to be approved by special resolution of the company whose assets and liabilities are being acquired. Dissenting shareholders are entitled to demand that their shares be acquired for cash.

Finally, for the division to take effect, it must be confirmed by order of the court upon the application of all companies involved in the division.

---

24 Interpretation of Part III

In this Part, unless the context otherwise requires—

"**acquiring companies**" has the meaning assigned to it by Regulation 25;

"**division**" means "division by acquisition" or "division by formation of new companies", within the meaning of Regulation 25(1).

Definitions

'company': EC(MDC)R 1987, reg 2.

---

25 Division to which Part II applies

(1) In this Part—

(a) "division by acquisition" means an operation whereby two or more companies ("the acquiring companies") of which one or more but not all may be a new company acquire between them all the assets and liabilities of another company in exchange for the issue to the shareholders of that company of shares in one or more of the acquiring companies with or without any cash payment and with a view to the dissolution of the company being acquired, and

(b) "division by formation of new companies" means a similar operation whereby the acquiring companies have been formed for the purposes of such acquisition.

(2) Where a company is being wound up it may—

(a) become a party to a division by acquisition or by formation of new companies, provided that the distribution of its assets to its shareholders has not begun at the date, under Regulation 26 (4), of the draft terms of a division, or

(b) opt to avail of the provisions of sections 201 to 204, 260 and 271 of the Act of 1963.

(3) Subject to paragraph (2), the said provisions shall not apply to a division by acquisition or by formation of new companies.

Definitions

'Act of 1963': EC(MDC)R 1987, reg 2; 'company': EC(MDC)R 1987, reg 2; 'division'; EC(MDC)R 1987, reg 2, reg 24; 'share': CA 1963, s 2(1).

26 Draft terms of division

(1) Where a division is proposed to be entered into, the directors of the companies involved in the division shall draw up draft terms of the division in writing.

(2) The draft terms of division shall state, at least—

- (a) the name and registered office of each of the companies involved in the division;
- (b) as to each of such companies, whether it is a public company limited by shares, a public company limited by guarantee and having a share capital or a body corporate to which section 377(1) of the Act of 1963 relates;
- (c) the proposed share exchange ratio and the amount of any cash payment;
- (d) the proposed terms relating to allotment of shares in the acquiring companies.;
- (e) the date from which holders of such shares will become entitled to participate in the profits of one or more of the acquiring companies;
- (f) the date from which the transactions of the company being acquired shall be treated for accounting purposes as being those of any of the acquiring companies;
- (g) any special conditions, including special rights or restrictions, whether in regard to voting, participation in profits, share capital or otherwise, which will apply to shares or other securities issued by the acquiring companies in exchange for shares or other securities in the company being acquired;
- (h) any payment or benefit in cash or otherwise paid or given or intended to be paid or given to any independent person referred to in Regulation 28 and to any director of any of the companies involved in the division insofar as it differs from the payment or benefit paid or given or intended to be paid or given to other persons in respect of the division and the consideration, if any, for any such payment or benefit;
- (i) the precise description and allocation of the assets and liabilities of the company being acquired to be transferred to each of the acquiring companies;
- (j) the allocation of shares in the acquiring companies to the shareholders of the company being acquired and the criteria on which such allocation is based.

(3) Where the division involves the formation of one or more new companies the draft terms of division shall include or be accompanied by the memorandum or draft memorandum and the articles or draft articles of association of each of the new companies.

(4) The draft terms of division shall be signed and dated on behalf of each of the companies involved in the division by two directors of each such company and that date shall for the purposes of this Part, be the date of the draft terms of division.

(5) Where an asset of the company being acquired is not allocated by the draft terms of division and where the interpretation of those terms does not make a decision on its allocation possible, the asset or the consideration therefor shall be allocated to the acquiring companies in proportion to the share of the net assets allocated to each of those companies under the draft terms of division.

Definitions

'Act of 1963': EC(MDC)R 1987, reg 2; 'company': EC(MDC)R 1987, reg 2; 'director': EC(MDC)R 1987, reg 2, CA 1963, s 2(1); 'division'; EC(MDC)R 1987, reg 2, reg 24.

Notes

The 'companies involved in the division' include both the acquiring companies and the company whose assets and liabilities are being acquired.

27 Directors' explanatory report

(1) A separate written report ("the explanatory report") shall be drawn up in respect of each of the companies involved in the division by the directors of each such company.

(2) The explanatory report shall at least detail and explain—

(a) the draft terms of division;

(b) The legal and economic grounds for and implications of the draft terms of division with particular reference to the proposed share exchange ratio, organisation and management structures, recent and future commercial activities and the financial interests of holders of the shares and other securities in the company;

(c) the methods used to arrive at the proposed share exchange ratio and the reasons for the use of these methods;

(d) any special valuation difficulties which have arisen.

(3) Where it is proposed that any of the acquiring companies will allot shares for a consideration other than in cash, the explanatory report shall state that the report required by section 30 of the Companies (Amendment) Act, 1983, is being or has been prepared and that it will be delivered to the registrar of companies for registration in accordance with section 31 of that Act.

(4) The explanatory report shall be signed and dated on behalf of each of the companies involved in the division by two directors of each such company.

Cross reference

In the case of a merger, however, a valuation under ss 30, 31 will not be required. See EC(MDC)R 1987, reg 10.

Definitions

'company': EC(MDC)R 1987, reg 2; 'director': EC(MDC)R 1987, reg 2, CA 1963, s 2(1); 'division'; EC(MDC)R 1987, reg 2, reg 24; 'registrar of companies: CA 196,3, s 2(1); 'share': CA 1963, s 2(1).

28 Independent person's report

(1) [Subject to paragraph (12), each][a] of the companies involved in the division shall appoint an independent person to examine the draft terms of division and to prepare a written report on them to the shareholders of the company concerned.

(2) No person shall act as an independent person for the purposes of paragraph (1) unless he is authorised by the Minister on application by the company concerned to be such a person for the purposes of the proposed division.

(3) One or more independent persons may be authorised by the Minister on joint application by the companies involved in the division for all the said companies.

(4) None of the following persons shall be qualified to act as an independent person in respect of a proposed division—

(a) a person who is or, within 12 months of the date of the draft terms of division, has been an officer or servant of the company;

(b) except with the leave of the Minister, a parent, spouse, brother, sister or child or an officer of the company;

(c) a person who is a partner or in the employment of an officer or servant of the company.

(5) If an independent person becomes disqualified by virtue of this regulation he shall thereupon cease to hold office and shall give notice in writing of his disqualification to the Minister within 14 days thereof, but without prejudice to the validity of any acts done by him in his capacity as independent person.

(6) Any person who acts as an independent person when disqualified from doing so under this regulation or who makes default in complying with paragraph (5) shall be guilty of an offence.

(7) The report referred to in paragraph (1) shall—

(a) state the method or methods used to arrive at the proposed share exchange ratio;

(b) give the opinion of the person making the report as to whether the proposed share exchange ratio is fair and reasonable;

(c) give the opinion of the person making the report as to whether such method or methods are adequate in the case in question;

(d) indicate the values arrived at using each such method;

(e) give the opinion of the person making the report as to the relative importance attributed to such methods in arriving at the values decided on;

(f) any special valuation difficulties which have arisen.

(8) The report required by section 30 of the Companies (Amendment) Act, 1983, may be prepared by the person preparing the report required by this regulation.

(9) A person making a report under this regulation shall be entitled to require from the companies involved in the division and their officers such information and explanation (whether orally or in writing) and to carry out such investigations as the independent person thinks necessary to enable him to make the report.

(10) Any of the companies involved in the division and any officer thereof who—

(a) fails to supply to an independent person any information or explanation in his power, possession or procurement, and which that person thinks necessary for the purpose of his report, or

(b) knowingly or recklessly makes a statement or provides a document which—

(i) is misleading, false or deceptive in a material particular, and

(ii) is a statement or document to which this paragraph applies,

shall be guilty of an offence.

(11) Paragraph (10) applies to any statement made, whether orally or in writing, or any document provided to any person making a report under this regulation being a statement or document which conveys or purports to convey any information or explanation which that person requires, or is entitled to require, under paragraph (9).

[(12) Paragraph (1) does not apply if all of the holders of shares and other securities conferring the right to vote in general meetings of each of the companies involved in the division have so agreed.][b]

Amendments

a Words 'Subject to paragraph (12), each' substituted for 'Each' by EC(MDC)(A)R 2008, reg 2(c)(i).

b EC(MDC)R 1987, reg 28(12) inserted by EC(MDC)(A)R 2008, reg 2(c)(ii).

Definitions

'company': EC(MDC)R 1987, reg 2; 'division'; EC(MDC)R 1987, reg 2, reg 24; 'minister': EC(MDC)R 1987, reg 2; 'officer'; CA 1963, s 2(1).

29 Accounting statement

(1) Where the latest annual accounts of any of the companies involved in the division relate to a financial year ended more than six months before the date of the draft terms of division, that company shall prepare an accounting statement in accordance with the provisions of this regulation.

(2) The accounting statement shall, where required under paragraph (1), be drawn up—

(i) in the format of the last annual balance sheet and in accordance with the provisions Companies Acts; and

(ii) as a date not earlier than the first day of the third month preceding the date of the draft terms of division.

(3) Valuations shown in the last annual balance sheet shall, subject to the exceptions outlined in paragraph (4), only be altered to reflect entries in the books of account.

(4) Notwithstanding the provisions of paragraph (3), the following shall be taken into account in preparing the accounting statement—

(a) interim depreciation and provisions; and

(b) material changes in actual value not shown in the books of account.

(5) The provisions of the Companies Acts relating to the auditor's report on the last annual accounts shall apply, with any necessary modifications, also to the accounting statement required by paragraph (1).

Cross reference

With regard to the relevant accounting provisions of the Companies Acts generally, see CA 1963, ss 148–164, C(A)A 1986 and EC(CGA)R 1992.

For the balance sheet format see C(A)A 1986, Sch, Pt I, and EC(CGA)R 1992.

In relation to the books of account, see CA 1990, s 202.

For the provisions dealing with the auditors' report, see CA 1963, ss 157, 191, 192, C(A)A 1986, ss 15, 18, EC(CGA)R 1992, regs 38, 40 and CA 1990, ss 193, 194.

Definitions

'company': EC(MDC)R 1987, reg 2; 'Companies Acts': EC(MDC)R 1987, reg 2; 'division'; EC(MDC)R 1987, reg 2, reg 24; 'financial year'; CA 1963, s 2(1).

30 Registration and publication of documents

(1) Each of the companies involved in the division shall—

(a) deliver for registration to the registrar of companies a copy of the draft terms of division, signed and dated as required by Regulation 26; and

(b) [cause to be published in the Companies Registration Office Gazette][a] and once at least in 2 daily newspapers circulating in the district where the registered office or principal place of business of the company is situate notice of delivery to the registrar of the draft terms of division.

(2) The requirements of paragraph (1) shall be fulfilled by each of the companies at lease one month before the date of the general meeting of each such company which by virtue of Regulation 32 is to consider the draft terms of division.

Amendments

a "'cause to be published in the Companies Registration Office Gazette' was substituted for 'publish in *Iris Oifigiúil*' by EC(C)R 2004, (SI 839/2004), reg 6(a) with effect from 15 December 2004.

Definitions

'company': EC(MDC)R 1987, reg 2; 'division'; EC(MDC)R 1987, reg 2, reg 24; 'registrar of companies'; CA 1963, s 2(1).

31 Inspection of documents

(1) Each of the companies involved in the division shall, subject to paragraph (2), make available for inspection free of charge by any member of the company at its registered office during business hours (subject to such reasonable restrictions as the company in general meeting may impose so that not less than 2 hours in each day be allowed for inspection)—

(a) the draft terms of division;

(b) the audited annual accounts for the preceding three financial years of each company, or where a company has traded for less than 3 financial years before the date of the draft terms of division, the audited annual accounts for those financial years for which the company has traded;

(c) the explanatory reports relating to each of the companies referred to in Regulation 27;

(d) [where applicable][a] the independent person's report relating to each of the companies referred to in Regulation 28;

(e) accounting statement in relation to any of the companies which is required to be prepared pursuant to Regulation 29.

(2) The provisions of paragraph (1) shall apply in the case of each of the companies for a period of one month before the general meeting which is to consider the draft terms of division.

Amendments

a Words 'where applicable' inserted by EC(MDC)(A)R 2008, reg 2(d).

Definitions

'company': EC(MDC)R 1987, reg 2; 'division': EC(MDC)R 1987, reg 2, reg 24; 'financial year': CA 1963, s 2(1); 'member' CA 1963, s 31.

32 General meetings of the companies involved in a division

(1) Subject to paragraph (4) of this regulation and to Regulation 33, the draft terms of division shall be approved by a special resolution passed at a general meeting of each of the companies involved in the division.

(2) Where the division involves the formation of one or more new companies, the memorandum or draft memorandum and articles or draft articles of association of each of the new companies shall also be approved by a special resolution of the company being acquired.

(3) The notice convening the general meeting referred to in paragraph (1) shall contain a statement of every shareholder's entitlement to obtain on request, free of charge, full or, if so desired, partial copies of the documents listed in Regulation 31.

(4) This regulation shall not apply in the case of an acquiring company provided that the following conditions are fulfilled—

(i) the provisions of Regulations 30 and 31 are complied with at least one month before the date of the general meeting of the company being acquired, and

(ii) one or more members of the company holding paid up share capital amounting in total value to not less than 5% of such of the paid up share capital as confers the right to vote at general meetings, whether or not the shares held confer such voting right, shall be entitled, under the articles of association of the company, to require the convening of a general meeting of the company to consider the draft terms of division.

(5) The directors of the company being acquired shall inform—

(a) the general meeting of that company, and

(b) the directors of the acquiring companies,

of any material change in the assets and liabilities of the company being acquired between the date of the draft terms of division and the date of the general meeting.

(6) The directors of each acquiring company shall inform the general meeting of that company of the matters referred to in paragraph (5).

(7) This regulation shall not apply in the case of the company being acquired where the acquiring companies together hold all the shares and other securities conferring the right to vote at general meetings of that company and where the information delivered under paragraph (4) covers any material change in the assets and liabilities after the date of the draft terms of division.

Definitions

'articles': CA 1963, s 2(1); 'company': EC(MDC)R 1987, reg 2; 'director': EC(MDC)R 1987, reg 2, CA 1963, s 2(1); 'division'; EC(MDC)R 1987, reg 2, reg 24; 'documents': CA 1963, s 2(1); 'member' CA 1963, s 31; 'memorandum' CA 1963, s 2(1).

33 Meetings of classes of shareholder

Where the share capital of any of the companies involved in a division is divided into shares of different classes, section 38 of the Companies (Amendment) Act 1983, shall apply.

Definitions

'company': EC(MDC)R 1987, reg 2; 'division'; EC(MDC)R 1987, reg 2, reg 24; 'share': CA 1963, s 2(1).

34 Purchase of minority shares

(1) Any of the shareholders in any of the companies involved in a division who voted against the special resolution of the company concerned relating to the draft terms of division may, not later than 15 days after the relevant date request the acquiring company in writing to acquire his shares for cash.

(2) In this regulation "the relevant date" in relation to a company means the date on which the latest general meeting of that company to consider the draft terms of division, or of any class of the holders of shares or other securities of such company, as required by these Regulations, is held.

(3) Nothing in this regulation shall prejudice the power of the court to make any order necessary for the protection of the interests of a dissenting minority in a company involved in a division.

Definitions

'company': EC(MDC)R 1987, reg 2; 'court': CA 1963, s 2(1); 'division': EC(MDC)R 1987, reg 2, reg 24; 'share': CA 1963, s 2(1).

Notes

The court order would presumably be made as a condition of the confirmation of the merger under EC(MDC)R 1987, reg 16.

35 Application for confirmation of division by court

(1) An application to the court for an order confirming a division shall be made by all the companies involved in a division.

(2) The application shall be accompanied by a statement of the size of the shareholding of any shareholder who has requested the purchase of his shares under Regulation 34 and of the measures which the acquiring companies propose to take to comply with such shareholder's request.

Definitions

'company': EC(MDC)R 1987, reg 2; 'court': CA 1963, s 2(1); 'division'; EC(MDC)R 1987, reg 2, reg 24; 'share': CA 1963, s 2(1).

Notes

The application (including the settling of a list of creditors in reg 36) is somewhat similar to that involved in the confirmation of a reduction of capital pursuant to CA 1963, s 72. Since a s 72 application is by way of petition, it would seem that the same procedure should be used for EC(MDC)R 1987, reg 35.

36 Protection of creditors

(1) A creditor of any of the companies involved in a division who, at the date of publication of the notice under Regulation 30(1)(b), is entitled to any debt or claim against the company, shall be entitled to object to the confirmation by the court of the division.

(2) If the court deems it necessary in order to secure the adequate protection of creditors of any of the companies involved in a division it may—

- (a) determine a list of creditors entitled to object and the nature and amount of their debts or claims, and may publish notices fixing a period within which creditors not entered on the list may have a claim for inclusion on that list considered;
- (b) where an undischarged creditor on the list referred to in subparagraph (a) does not consent to the division, the court may dispense with the consent of that creditor, on the company securing payment of the debt or claim by appropriating to that creditor such following amount as the court may direct—
  - (i) if the company concerned admits the full amount of the debt or claim, that amount;
  - (ii) if the company concerned does not admit the debt or claim, or if the amount is contingent or not ascertained, an amount fixed by the court after the like inquiry and adjudication as if the company were being wound up by the court.

(3) If, having regard to any special circumstances of the case, it thinks proper so to do, the court may direct that paragraph (2) shall not apply as regards any class of creditors.

(4) Each of the acquiring companies shall be jointly and severally liable for all the liabilities of the company being acquired.

Definitions

'company': EC(MDC)R 1987, reg 2; 'court': CA 1963, s 2(1); 'division'; EC(MDC)R 1987, reg 2, reg 24.

37 Preservation of rights of holders of securities

(1) Subject to paragraph (2), holders of securities, other than shares, in any of the companies being acquired, to which special rights are attached shall be given rights in the acquiring companies at least equivalent to those they possessed in the company being acquired.

(2) Paragraph (1) shall not apply—

- (a) where the alteration of the rights in an acquiring company has been approved
  - (i) by a majority of the holders of such securities at a meeting held for that purpose, or
  - (ii) by the holders of those securities individually, or
- (b) where the holders of those securities are entitled under the terms of those securities to have their securities purchased by an acquiring company.

Definitions

'company': EC(MDC)R 1987, reg 2; 'share': CA 1963, s 2(1).

Notes

The phrase 'securities other than shares' would extend to debentures in the company.

38 Confirmation order

(1) The court, on being satisfied that—

- (a) the requirements of these Regulations have been complied with,
- (b) proper provision has been made for—
  - (i) any dissenting shareholder of any of the companies involved in the division who has made a request under Regulation 34, and
  - (ii) any creditor of any of the companies who objects to the division in accordance with Regulation 36, and
- (c) the rights of holders of securities other than shares in any of the companies being acquired are safeguarded in accordance with Regulation 37,

may make an order confirming the division with effect from such date as the court appoints ("the appointed date").

(2) The order of the court confirming the division shall, with effect from the appointed date, have the following effects—

(a) all the assets and liabilities of the company or companies being acquired shall stand transferred to the acquiring companies in accordance with the draft terms of division as approved by the court;

(b) the shareholders of the company being acquired shall become shareholders in the acquiring companies or any of them in accordance with the draft terms of division as approved by the court;

(c) the company or companies being acquired shall, subject to paragraph (4), be dissolved;

(d) all legal proceedings pending by or against any of the dissolved companies shall be continued with the substitution, for the dissolved company, of the acquiring companies or such of them as the court having seisin of the proceedings may order.

(3) The court may, either by the order confirming the division or by a separate order, make provision for such matters as the court considers necessary to secure that the division shall be fully and effectively carried out.

(4) The court may, in particular, by order—

(a) direct that an acquiring company shall, on a date specified by the court, purchase the shares of a dissenting shareholder who has made a request under Regulation 34 and pay therefor the sum determined by the court, being not less than the market sale price of the shares on the appointed date, and

(b) provide for the reduction accordingly of the company's capital.

(5) If it is necessary for the company being acquired to take any steps to ensure that its assets and liabilities are fully transferred, the court may specify a date which, save in exceptional cases, shall not be later than 6 months after the appointed date, by which such steps must be taken and for that purpose may order that the dissolution of such company shall take effect on that date.

(6) Section 41(1) of the Companies (Amendment) Act, 1983 (which restricts the right of a company to purchase its own shares) shall not apply to the purchase of any shares in pursuance of an order of the court under this regulation.

Definitions

'company': EC(MDC)R 1987, reg 2; 'court': CA 1963, s 2(1); 'division'; EC(MDC)R 1987, reg 2, reg 24; 'share': CA 1963, s 2(1).

---

39 Limitation on power to make orders

An order of the court shall not be made in respect of a proposed division which involves a take-over to which the Mergers, Take-Overs and Monopolies (Control) Act, 1978 applies until either—

(a) the Minister has stated in writing that he has decided not to make an order under section 9 of that Act, in relation to the proposed take-over, or

(b) the Minister has stated in writing that he has made a conditional order under that section in relation to the proposed take-over, or

(c) the relevant period within the meaning of section 6 of that Act (which refers to a limitation on the commencement of a take-over) has elapsed without the Minister's having made an order under the said section 9 in relation to the proposed take-over,

whichever first occurs.

Definitions

'court': CA 1963, s 2(1); 'division'; EC(MDC)R 1987, reg 2, reg 24; 'Minister'; EC(MDC)R 1987, reg 2.

Notes

The Mergers, Take-Overs and Monopolies (Control) Act 1978 has since been repealed by the Competition Act 2002, s 48(b). Part 3 of the Competition Act 2002 now regulates mergers to which the EU Merger Regulation (Council Regulation (EC) No 139/2004 of 20 January 2004 on the control of concentrations between undertakings OJ L 24, 29.01.2004, pages 1–22) does not apply.

---

40 Registration and publication of confirmation of division

(1) Where the court has made an order confirming a division an office copy thereof shall forthwith be sent to the registrar of companies for registration by such officer of the court as the court may direct.

(2) Each of the acquiring companies shall [cause to be published in the Companies Registration Office Gazette][a] notice of delivery to the registrar of companies of the order of the court confirming the division within fourteen days of such delivery and if default is made in complying with this paragraph each company and every officer of the company who is in default shall be guilty of an offence.

(3) It shall be a defence for a person charged with an offence under paragraph (2) to show that non-compliance was not due to any delay or negligence on the part of the company or person concerned.

(4) Proceedings in relation to an offence under this regulation may be brought and prosecuted by the registrar of companies.

Amendments

a 'cause to be published in the Companies Registration Office Gazette' was substituted for 'publish in *Iris Oifigiúil*' by EC(C)R 2004, (SI 839/2004), reg 6(a) with effect from 15 December 2004.

Definitions

'company': EC(MDC)R 1987, reg 2; 'court': CA 1963, s 2(1); 'division'; EC(MDC)R 1987, reg 2, reg 24; 'registrar of companies' CA 1963, s 2(10).

---

41 Civil liability of directors and independent persons

(1) Any shareholder of any of the companies involved in a division who has suffered loss or damage by reason of misconduct in the preparation or implementation of the

division by a director of any such company or by the independent person who has made a report under Regulation 28 shall be entitled to have such loss or damage made good to him by—

(a) in the case of misconduct by a person who was a director of that company at the date of the draft terms of division – that person.

(b) in the case of misconduct by any independent person who prepared a report under Regulation 28 in respect of any of the companies – that person.

(2) Without prejudice to the generality of paragraph (1), any shareholder of any of the companies who has suffered loss or damage arising from the inclusion of any untrue statement in the draft terms of division, the explanatory report, the independent person's report or the accounting statement shall, subject to paragraphs (3) and (4), be entitled to have such loss or damage made good to him by every person who was a director of that company at the date of the draft terms of division or, in the case of the independent person's report, by the person who made that report, in relation to that company.

(3) A director of a company shall not be liable under paragraph (2) if he proves—

(a) that any of the documents referred to in paragraph (2) was issued without his knowledge or consent, and that on becoming aware of their issue he forthwith informed the shareholders of that company that they were issued without his knowledge or consent, or

(b) that as regards every untrue statement he had reasonable grounds, having exercised all reasonable care and skill, for believing and did, up to the time the division took effect, believe that the statement was true.

(4) A person who made a report required by Regulation 28 in relation to a company shall not be liable in the case of untrue statements in his own report if he proves—

(i) that on becoming aware of the statement, he forthwith informed the company concerned and its shareholders of the untruth, or

(ii) that he was competent to make the statement and that he had reasonable grounds for believing and did up to the time the division took effect believe that the statement was true.

Definitions

'company': EC(MDC)R 1987, reg 2; 'director': reg 2, CA 1963, s 2(1); 'division'; EC(MDC)R 1987, reg 2, reg 24; 'share': CA 1963, s 2(1).

Notes

This regulation is analogous to, but admittedly not exactly the same as IFCMPA 2005, s 41 which imposes civil liability for 'untrue statements' in a prospectus. With regard to the meaning of the phrase 'untrue statement' see Notes to IFCMPA 2005, s 41.

---

42 Criminal liability for untrue statements in division documents

(1) Where any untrue statement has been included in the draft terms of division, the explanatory report or the accounting statement, each of the directors and any person who authorised the issue of those documents shall be guilty of an offence.

(2) Where any untrue statement has been included in the independent person's report, the independent person and any person who authorised the issue of the report shall be guilty of an offence.

(3) It shall be a defence for a person charged with an offence under paragraph (1) or (2) to show that, having exercised all reasonable care and skill, he had reasonable grounds for believing and did, up to the time of the issue of the documents, believe that the statement was true.

Definitions

'director': EC(MDC)R 1987, reg 2, CA 1963, s 2(1); 'division'; EC(MDC)R 1987, reg 2, reg 24.

Notes

This regulation is analogous to, but admittedly not exactly the same as IFCMPA 2005, s 48 which imposes criminal liability for 'untrue statements' in a prospectus. With regard to the meaning of the phrase 'untrue statement' see Notes to IFCMPA 2005 s 41.

EXPLANATORY NOTE

(*This note is not part of the Instrument and does not purport to be a legal interpretation.*)

These Regulations implement the EEC Third and Sixth Company Law Directives concerning the mergers and divisions of public limited companies. The Regulations apply only to public limited companies, and certain unregistered companies defined in the Regulations.

MERGERS

In the case of a merger, the Regulations apply to an operation whereby all the assets and liabilities of one or more companies are transferred to another company (the acquiring company), the shareholders of the company or companies being acquired become shareholders in the acquiring company and the company or companies being acquired are dissolved.

DIVISIONS

In the case of a division, the Regulations apply to an operation whereby all the assets and liabilities of a company are transferred to more than on other company, the shareholders of the company being acquired become shareholders in the acquiring company or companies and the company being acquired is dissolved.

The provisions of the Companies Acts in relation to arrangements and reconstructions (Sections 201 to 204) are expressly disapplied in the case of the specific mergers and divisions covered in the Regulations.

The Regulations are divided into three Parts. Part 1 contains the usual preliminary provisions relating to interpretation and penalties. Part II sets out the new procedure and requirements in respect of mergers and Part III sets out the new procedure and requirements in respect of divisions.

The provisions of Parts II and III broadly cover;

(a) reporting requirements by directors of a company and by an independent person to the members of the company;

(b) approval of the merger or division by general meeting of the companies involved;

(c) inspection of relevant documents by members of the companies involved;

(d) confirmation of the merger or division by the High Court and registration and publication of the Court's decision;

(e) protection of the interests of creditors, dissenting minorities and holders of securities other than shares.

The Regulations also provide for civil liability of directors and independent person to shareholders for misconduct in relation to the merger or division and for criminal liability for false statements in any document published in connection with the merger or division.

European Communities (European Economic Interest Groupings) Regulations 1989

SI 191/1989

ARRANGEMENT OF REGULATIONS

PRELIMINARY

PART 1

FORMATION AND REGISTRATION OF GROUPINGS

PART II

MEMBERSHIP OF GROUPINGS

ADMINISTRATION, ACTIVITIES ETC

FIRST SCHEDULE
COUNCIL REGULATION (EEC) NO. 2137/85 OF 25 JULY 1985 ON THE EUROPEAN ECONOMIC INTEREST GROUPING

SECOND SCHEDULE
FORMS RELATING TO EEIGs

I, DESMOND O'MALLEY, Minister for Industry and Commerce, in exercise of the powers conferred on me by section 3 of the European Communities Act, 1972 (No. 27 of 1972) and for the purpose of giving full effect to the provisions of Council Regulation (EEC) No. 2137/85 of the 25th day of July, 1985on the European Economic Interest Grouping (EEIG), hereby make the following Regulations.

Notes

OJ No L 199, 31/7/1985, pp 1–9.

Notice of the making of this Statutory Instrument was published in '*Iris Oifigiúil*' of 4th August 1989.

PRELIMINARY

1 Citation and commencement

(1) These Regulations may be cited as the European Communities (European Economic Interest Groupings) Regulations, 1989.

(2) These Regulations shall come into operation on the 1st day of August, 1989.

Notes

These Regulations implement Council Regulation (EEC) No 2137/85 and provide for the creation of a special type of corporate body known as the 'European Economic Interest Grouping' (EEIG). The purpose of the EEIG is to facilitate certain types of joint venture between natural persons, firms and companies from different member states of the EU. In particular, its purpose is to 'facilitate or develop the economic activities of its members and to improve or increase the results of those activities; its purpose is not to make profits for itself.' (Council Regulation (EEC) No 2137/85, art 3). Thus, the profits resulting from the EEIG's activities 'shall be deemed to be the profits of the members and shall be apportioned among them.' (Council Regulation (EEC) No 2137/85, art 21).

The process for establishing an EEIG involves the members first drafting a contract of formation. This is the constitutional document of the EEIG and is thus the equivalent of the memorandum and articles of association of a company. The EEIG is then registered in a member state and upon registration it becomes a body corporate with a separate legal personality from those of its members. However, despite the fact that the EEIG has legal personality, its members are jointly and severally liable for its debts and liabilities, in much the same way as if the EEIG were an unlimited company incorporated under CA 1963–1990.

The EEIG must have not more than 20 members, at least two of which must be from different member states. The EEIG is prohibited from employing more than 500 persons and is also prohibited from inviting investment from the public.[1]

The EC(EEIG)R 1989 are not to be read as one or construed as one with company law legislation so these regulations stand alone.

[1] For a general discussion of EEIG's see Corporate Law – The European Dimension, (London, 1991) ch 2, Ronald Mackay QC 'The European Economic Interest Grouping'. See also Linnane 'The European Economic Interest Grouping' (1989) 9 ILT (ns) 213; 'Forming an EEIG in Ireland' (1991) 11 ILT (ns) 36; 'Managing an EEIG' (1992) 12 ILT (ns) 163; Power 'The European Economic Interest Grouping' (1990) 10 ILT (ns) 19.

2 Interpretation

(1) In these Regulations, unless the context otherwise requires:

'the Companies Acts' means the Companies Act, 1963, and every enactment which is to be constructed as one with that Act;

'the Council Regulation' means Council Regulation (EEC) No. 2137/85 of 25th July, 1985 on the European Economic Interest Grouping, being the Regulation set out in the First Schedule to these Regulations;

'the court' means the High Court;

'director' includes any person occupying the position of director by whichever name called;

'grouping' means a European Economic Interest Grouping, whether formed and registered in the State or elsewhere;

'the Minister' means the Minister for Industry and Commerce;

'officer' in relation to a body corporate includes a director or company secretary;

'registry' has the meaning assigned to it under Regulation 5(1) of these Regulations;

'registrar' means the registrar of groupings, within the meaning of Regulation 5(2) of these Regulations.

(2) A word or expression that is used in these Regulations and is also used in the Council Regulation shall, unless the contrary intention appears, have the same meaning in these Regulations as it has in the Council Regulation.

PART 1

FORMATION AND REGISTRATION OF GROUPINGS

3 Formation of a grouping

A grouping shall be formed upon the terms, in the matter and with the effects laid down in the Council Regulation and these Regulations.

Definitions

'Council Regulation': EC(EEIG)R 1989, reg 2(1).

Notes

The Council reg is set out in EC(EEIG)R 1989, Sch 1.

4 Name of grouping

(1) The name of a grouping registered in the State shall include:

(a) the words 'European Economic Interest Groupings' or the initials 'EEIG', or

(b) the words 'Grupáil Eorpach um Leas Eacnamaíoch' or the initials 'GELE' unless those words or initials already form part of the name.

(2) Every invoice, order for goods or business letter issued by or on behalf of a grouping shall include the name of the grouping referred to in paragraph (1) of this Regulation.

(3) No grouping shall be registered under these Regulations by a name which, in the opinion of the Minister, is undesirable but an appeal shall lie to the court against a refusal to register on such a ground.

(4) A grouping registered under these Regulations may, subject to the approval of the Minister signified in writing, change its name.

Definitions

'court': EC(EEIG)R 1989, reg 2(1); 'Minister': EC(EEIG)R 1989, reg 2(1).

Notes

This paragraph echoes the provisions of CA 1963 s 6(1)(a), (b).

A similar provision applies to companies registered under the Irish Companies Acts. See CA 1963, s 114(1)(c).

In addition, however, the invoices, order forms and letters must also include the other information prescribed by Council Regulation (EEC) No 2137/85, art 25.

The registrar of companies has issued a leaflet indicating names which may be refused registration. In particular, a name will not be registered if—

(a) it is identical to a name already appearing on the register of companies;

(b) in the opinion of the Minister, it is offensive;

(c) it would suggest State sponsorship;

(d) the name includes 'bank' or cognate words, unless an appropriate licence or exemption has been granted by the Central Bank;

(e) the name includes the word 'insurance' or cognate words unless an appropriate licence has been granted by the Minister;

(f) the name includes the words 'society', 'co-op' or 'co-operative'.

Presumably, the provisions of this leaflet will apply equally to EEIG's. Associated EEIG's may, however, be registered with similar names.[1]

The court may grant an injunction restraining an EEIG from registering a name which is calculated to mislead or deceive the public into thinking that the business of the EEIG is that of another company or EEIG.[2]

In deciding whether a name is likely to deceive the court should consider (1) the respective businesses of the old company/EEIG and the new EEIG; and (2) the name of the old company/EEIG. Moreover, the court will not restrain the use of a word which is in ordinary use in the English or Irish language and which is descriptive only.[3]

With regard to the requisite majority for a resolution altering the name of the EEIG, see Council Regulation (EEC) No 2137/85, art 17.

1 *Irish Permanent Building Society v Cauldwell* [1981] ILRM 240.

2 *Ewing v Buttercup Margarine Co* [1917] Ch 1; Waring & Gillow Ltd v Gillow & Gillow Ltd (1916) 32 TLR 389.

3 *Aerators Ltd v Tolitt* [1902] 2 Ch 319.

---

5 Designation of registrar and registry

(1) The Companies Registration Office, being the office maintained for the purpose of the registration of companies under the Companies Acts, is hereby designated as the registry of the purpose of Articles 6, 7, 10 and 39 of the Council Regulation.

(2) For the purposes specified in paragraph (1) of this Regulation, the person for the time being holding the office of registrar of companies under the Companies Acts shall also have the function of registrar of groupings under the Council Regulation and these Regulations and is referred to in these Regulations as 'the registrar'.

Definitions

'Companies Acts': EC(EEIG)R 1989, reg 2(1); 'Council Regulation': EC(EEIG)R 1989, reg 2(1); 'registrar': EC(EEIG)R 1989, reg 2(1), reg 5(2), CA 1963 s 2(1).

Notes

For the documents which must be delivered to the registrar of companies see in particular Council Regulation (EEC) No 2137/85, arts 7, 10, EC(EEIG)R 1989, reg 6.

6 Registration of a grouping

(1) Where the official address of a grouping is in the State, the contract for the formation of the grouping shall be delivered to the registrar.

(2) The registrar shall retain and register in a register maintained by him for that purpose any contracts for the formation of groupings delivered to him.

Definitions

'registrar': EC(EEIG)R 1989, reg 2(1), EC(EEIG)R 1989, reg 5(2), CA 1963 s 2(1).

Notes

See also Council Regulation (EEC) No 2137/85, art 7.

7 Effect of registration

(1) On the registration of a contract forming a grouping the registrar shall certify under his hand that the grouping is incorporated as a European Economic Interest Grouping.

(2) A grouping, from the date of its registration under these Regulations, shall:

(a) be a body corporate,

(b) have perpetual succession and a common seal, and

(c) have legal personality.

Definitions

'grouping': EC(EEIG)R 1989, reg 2(1); 'registrar': EC(EEIG)R 1989, reg 2(1), reg 5(2), CA 1963 s 2(1).

Notes

Unlike the certificate of incorporation issued by the registrar for companies under C(A)A 1983 s 5, the certificate of incorporation for EEIG's does not amount to conclusive evidence that the registration requirements of these Regulations have been complied with.

---

8 Time for filing documents and other particulars

Where a document or particular is to be filed at the registry pursuant to Article 7 of the Council Regulation, it shall be so filed within 14 days of the amendment, decision or other event giving rise to the requirement under that Article.

Definitions

'Council Regulation': EC(EEIG)R 1989, reg 2(1); 'registry': EC(EEIG)R 1989, reg 2(1).

---

9 Publication of information by grouping

(1) A grouping registered in the State shall, within 21 days of its registration, cause to be published in the *Iris Oifigiúil*:

(a) the particulars referred to in Article 5 of the Council Regulation, and

(b) notice of the number, date and place of its registration.

(2) A grouping registered in the State shall, within 21 days of delivery to the registrar of the documents referred to in Article 7 (b) to (j) and 14.1 of the Council Regulation, cause to be published in the *Iris Oifigiúil* notice of such delivery.

(3) A grouping registered in the State shall, within 21 days of the termination of its registration, cause to be published in the *Iris Oifigiúil*, notice of such termination.

Definitions

'Council Regulation': EC(EEIG)R 1989, reg 2(1); 'grouping': EC(EEIG)R 1989, reg 2(1); 'registrar': EC(EEIG)R 1989, reg 2(1), reg 5(2), CA 1963 s 2(1).

Notes

The particulars referred to in Council Regulation (EEC) No 2137/85, art 5 are:

(a) the name of the EEIG;

(b) the official address of the EEIG;

(c) the objects for which the EEIG is formed;

(d) the name, business name, legal form, permanent address or registered office, and the number and place of registration, if any, of each member of the EEIG;

(e) the duration of the EEIG, except where this is indefinite.

---

10 Groupings registered outside the State

(1) Any document delivered to the registrar, pursuant to Article 10 of the Council Regulation, by a grouping registered outside the State shall be certified, in the country in which the grouping is registered, as follows:

(a) certified as a true copy by an official of the registry to whose custody the original is committed, or

(b) certified as a true copy in accordance with the provisions of the Companies (Forms) Order, 1964.

(2) Any such document shall, if it is not expressed in the Irish or English language, be accompanied by a certified translation thereof.

(3) In this Regulation 'certified translation' means a translation certified to be a correct translation by:

(a) if made outside the State, an Irish diplomatic or consular officer, or any person whom any such officer certifies to be known to him as competent to translate it into the Irish or English language;

(b) if made within the State, a notary public, solicitor or barrister.

Definitions

'Council Regulation': EC(EEIG)R 1989, reg 2(1); 'grouping': EC(EEIG)R 1989, reg 2(1); 'registry': EC(EEIG)R 1989, reg 2(1); 'registrar': EC(EEIG)R 1989, reg 2(1), reg 5(2), CA 1963 s 2(1).

Notes

Council Regulation (EEC) No 2137/85, art 10 applies to any EEIG which is situate within the State but has its official address in another member state. Such an EEIG must deliver to the registrar of companies the documents referred to in art 7.

---

11 Notification of information by registrar

The duty of forwarding the information mentioned in Article 39.2 of the Council Regulation to the Office for Official Publications of the European Communities shall lie with the registrar.

Definitions

'Council Regulation': EC(EEIG)R 1989, reg 2(1); 'registrar': EC(EEIG)R 1989, reg 2(1), reg 5(2), CA 1963 s 2(1).

Notes

The information referred to in Council Regulation (EEC) No 2137/85, art 39(2) is that the EEIG has been formed or gone into liquidation, as the case may be. The notice must also state the number, date and place of registration of the EEIG together with details of the date, place and title of publication of such information. In Ireland, publication must be effected in Iris Oifigiúil: EC(EEIG)R 1989, reg 9.

---

12 Transfer of official address outside the State

(1) Where a grouping registered in the State proposes to transfer its official address to a place outside the State, the registrar may, after consultation with any Minister of the Government, the Revenue Commissioners, the Attorney General or the Director of

Public Prosecutions, refuse to terminate the registration of the grouping in the State if any such person indicates that it would be in the public interest to do so.

(2) (a) Where the registrar refuses to terminate the registration of a grouping under paragraph (1) of this Regulation, the grouping may apply to the court in a summary manner to have such refusal reviewed.

(b) Where an application to review a decision by the registrar is brought pursuant to subparagraph (a) of this paragraph, the court shall confirm the decision of the registrar unless it is satisfied that the procedures laid down by, or the requirements of, these Regulations or the Council Regulation have not been compiled with in any material respect.

(c) Where the court is satisfied that the procedures laid down by, or the requirements of, these Regulations or the Council Regulation have not been compiled with in any material respect, the court may set aside the decision of the registrar and in such case shall remit the matter to the registrar who shall thereupon reconsider the matter and make a further decision in accordance with such procedures and requirements.

Definitions

'Council Regulation': EC(EEIG)R 1989, reg 2(1); 'court': EC(EEIG)R 1989, reg 2(1); 'grouping': EC(EEIG)R 1989, reg 2(1); 'registrar': EC(EEIG)R 1989, reg 2(1), reg 5(2), CA 1963 s 2(1).

Notes

In relation to the transfer of the official address of the EEIG outside the State see also Council Regulation (EEC) No 2137/85, art 14.

The procedures and requirements which must be complied with are:

(a) that the refusal be made on grounds of public interest (EC(EEIG)R 1989, reg 12(1) and Council Regulation (EEC) No 2137/85, art 14(4));

(b) that the refusal be made within 2 months of the publication of the notice of intention to change the official address of the EEIG (Council Regulation (EEC) No 2137/85, art 14(4)).

PART II
MEMBERSHIP OF GROUPINGS

13 Permissible number of members

(1) No grouping consisting of more than 20 members shall be registered in the State.

(2) In this Regulation, 'member' includes a partner in a partnership, but does not include a partner in a partnership exempted under section 13 of the Companies (Amendment) Act, 1982.

Definitions

'grouping': EC(EEIG)R 1989, reg 2(1).

Notes

Under Council Regulation (EEC) No 2137/85, art 4(3) member states were given an option whether or not to place an upper limit of 20 on membership of an EEIG. The effect of EC(EEIG)R 1989, reg 13(1) is that even if other member states permit unlimited membership of EEIGs, a foreign EEIG validly incorporated abroad with more than 20 members will not be to locate in Ireland since the size of its membership will prevent registration pursuant to EC(EEIG)R 1989, reg 10, Council Regulation (EEC) No 2137/85, art 10.

It would appear from EC(EEIG)R 1989, reg 16(b), Council Regulation (EEC) No 2137/85, art 4 that the partnership itself is also deemed to be a member of the EEIG.

14 Disqualification from membership

(1) The following persons shall be disqualified from membership of a grouping, namely:

(a) an undischarged bankrupt,

(b) a person convicted on indictment of any offence involving fraud or dishonesty,

(c) a person convicted on indictment of any offence in relation to a company formed and registered under the Companies Acts,

(d) a person to whom section 297 of the Companies Act, 1963, applies,

(e) a body corporate in respect of which winding-up or analogous proceedings have commenced.

(2) A person who becomes disqualified under this Regulation shall, within five days of becoming disqualified, resign from membership of a grouping and shall not act as a member of a grouping when disqualified from doing so.

Definitions

'Companies Acts': EC(EEIG)R 1989, reg 2(1); 'grouping': EC(EEIG)R 1989, reg 2(1).

Notes

CA 1963 s 297, in its original form, imposed both civil and criminal liability for fraudulent trading. As a result of CA 1990 ss 137, 138, only criminal liability for fraudulent trading is now dealt with by CA 1963 s 297A. Civil liability for fraudulent trading as well as civil liability for reckless trading are now dealt with by an entirely separate section, namely CA 1963 s 297A. It would appear that someone guilty only of reckless trading is not therefore disqualified under EC(EEIG)R 1989, reg 14(1)(d).

See also EC(EEIG)R 1989, reg 17 in relation to the cessation of membership upon liquidation, bankruptcy or (in the case of an individual) the making of any arrangement or composition with his creditors.

15 Expulsion of member of grouping

The jurisdiction to hear and decide on applications under Article 27.2 of the Council Regulation shall lie with the court.

Definitions

'Council Regulation': EC(EEIG)R 1989, reg 2(1); 'court': EC(EEIG)R 1989, reg 2(1); 'grouping': EC(EEIG)R 1989, reg 2(1).

Notes

Council Regulation (EEC) No 2137/85, art 27(2) deals with the expulsion of members from an EEIG.

16 Reduction of number of members below two

If at any time the number of members of a grouping is reduced below two, and it carries on any trade, activity or business for more than one month while the number is so reduced, the following persons shall, if they know that the grouping is carrying on business with less than two members, be severally liable for the payment of the whole debts of the grouping contracted during that time, and may be severally sued thereof, namely:

(a) if the remaining member is a natural person, that person,

(b) if the remaining member is a partnership, every member of that partnership,

(c) if the remaining member is a body corporate, every person who was a director or other officer of the body corporate during the period mentioned in this Regulation.

Definitions

'body corporate': CA 1963 s 2(3); 'director': EC(EEIG)R 1989, reg 2(1), CA 1963 s 2(1); 'grouping': EC(EEIG)R 1989, reg 2(1); 'officer': EC(EEIG)R 1989, reg 2(1).

Notes

This provision appears to be broadly based on CA 1963 s 36.

Although it is not specified in EC(EEIG)R 1989, reg 16, the minimum membership of two for the EEIG must come from different member states.

The difference between personal liability under EC(EEIG)R 1989, reg 16 and the general unlimited liability of members under Council Regulation (EEC) No 2137/85, art 24 is that in art 24 liability will only arise if the EEIG is in liquidation or if the EEIG has failed to comply with a demand for payment within a reasonable period of time, whereas liability under reg 16 may arise and be enforced whilst the EEIG is still in operation and without having to first demand payment from the EEIG itself. Furthermore the liability under reg 16 only relates to debts of the EEIG, whereas art 24 relates not only to such debts but also to other corporate liabilities such as claims for damages for breach of contract, breach of statutory duty or tortious acts and omissions. If a person incurs personal liability under reg 16 he is entitled to an indemnity from the EEIG since the EEIG is still primarily liable to discharge the debt.[1]

If the partnership is not one exempted under C(A)A 1982 s 13, then each partner will also be deemed a member of the EEIG and thus the EEIG will be regarded as having at least two members. In this regard, see EC(EEIG)R 1989, reg 13(2). However, Council Regulation (EEC) No 2137/85, art 4 requires that the minimum membership of two should come from different member states and thus, unless the partners themselves are from different member states it would appear that reg 16 ought to apply.

EC(EEIG)R 1989, reg 16(c) differs from CA 1963 s 36 in that the directors of a sole surviving corporate shareholder have no personal liability for debts incurred whilst the membership is below the statutory minimum. Instead, liability attaches only to the corporate shareholder itself.

[1] *Brook's Wharf Ltd v Goodman Bros* [1937] 1 KB 534.

17 Cessation of membership of a grouping

(1) Membership of grouping by a person shall cease in the event of his being adjudged bankrupt, or if he makes any arrangement or composition with his creditors generally.

(2) Membership of a grouping by a body (whether or not incorporated) shall cease on the commencement of the winding up of that body.

Definitions

'grouping': EC(EEIG)R 1989, reg 2(1).

Notes

It would seem from EC(EEIG)R 1989, reg 17(1) that in the case of an individual member, his membership will cease even in the case of an informal composition or arrangement with his creditors outside the provisions of the Bankruptcy Act 1988.

In the case of a company, membership of the EEIG will not however cease simply because it is placed either in receivership or under the protection of the court.

Administration, Activities Etc

18 Manager of a grouping

(1) The manager of a grouping may be a natural person or a body corporate.

(2) Where the manager is a body corporate:

(a) the grouping shall designate one or more natural persons as the representative of the manager,

(b) such representative shall have the same liability as if he were himself the manager, and

(c) the grouping shall deliver to the registrar particulars in relation to such representative as if he were the manager.

Definitions

'grouping': EC(EEIG)R 1989, reg 2(1); 'registrar': EC(EEIG)R 1989, reg 2(1), reg 5(2), CA 1963 s 2(1).

Notes

Compare the position for companies where bodies corporate are prohibited from acting as directors: CA 1963 s 176. In relation to the manager of an EEIG see also Council Regulation (EEC) No 2137/85, arts 19 and 20 and Linnane 'Managing an EEIG' (1992) 12 ILT (ns) 163.

---

19 Annual Return

(1) A grouping whose official address is in the State shall, not later than 1st July in every year, make a return to the registrar in the form set out in the Second Schedule to these Regulations.

(2) Paragraph (1) shall also apply to a grouping which has a grouping establishment in the State.

(3) Nothing in this Regulation shall require a grouping to make a return before 1st July in a particular year if the date of registration in the State of such grouping or grouping establishment, as the case may be, under these Regulations was less than fifteen months before that date.

Definitions

'grouping': EC(EEIG)R 1989, reg 2(1); 'registrar': EC(EEIG)R 1989, reg 2(1), reg 5(2), CA 1963 s 2(1).

Notes

The appropriate form is IG8.

---

20 Prohibition on invitation of investment from the public

(1) A grouping shall not invite investment from the public.

(2) Where a grouping is convicted of an offence under this Regulation and the grouping is in the course of being wound up on the date of the conviction or commences to be wound up within 12 months after that date, the court may, on the application of the liquidator or any creditor of the grouping, declare that any of the following persons shall be personally liable, without any limitation of liability, for all or any of the debts or other liabilities of the grouping incurred in the period during which such person was acting in the capacity mentioned, namely:

(a) any member of the grouping who is a natural person,

(b) a director or member of the committee of management of any member of the grouping which is a body corporate,

(c) the manager of the grouping or, where the manager is a body corporate, the natural person who is the representative of the manager, within the meaning of Regulation 18(2).

Definitions

'court': EC(EEIG)R 1989, reg 2(1); 'director': EC(EEIG)R 1989, reg 2(1), CA 1963 s 2(1); 'grouping': EC(EEIG)R 1989, reg 2(1).

Notes

The prohibition on the invitation of investment from the public is similar to the prohibition contained in CA 1963, s 33; C(A)A 1983, s 21 against private companies offering to or inviting the public to subscribe for their shares, debentures or other securities.

No definition of the phrase 'the public' is contained in the regs.

A member who is a natural person has unlimited liability in any event under Council Regulation (EEC) No 2137/85, art 24.

---

21 Winding-up of grouping

(1) For the purposes of Articles 35 and 36 of the Council Regulation, a grouping shall be deemed to be an unregistered company, within the meaning of Part X of the Companies Act, 1963.

(2) For the purposes of that Part, the manager of a grouping shall be treated as if he were a director of a company.

(3) The Minister shall be the competent authority for the purposes of Article 32.1 of the Council Regulation.

Definitions

'Council Regulation': EC(EEIG)R 1989, reg 2(1); 'director': EC(EEIG)R 1989, reg 2(1), CA 1963 s 2(1); 'grouping': EC(EEIG)R 1989, reg 2(1); 'Minister': EC(EEIG)R 1989, reg 2(1).

Notes

CA 1963, Pt X provides for the application of the winding up provisions of the Companies Acts to unregistered companies.

Under Council Regulation (EEC) No 2137/85, art 32(1) the Minister must petition for the winding up of the EEIG if infringes art 3 (permitted purposes of EEIG), art 4(2) (minimum number of members) or art 12 (official address of EEIG to be within EEC).

22 Provisions of Companies Acts applied to groupings

(1) The provisions of the Companies Act set out in the Table to this Regulation shall, with any necessary modifications, apply to groupings as they apply to companies formed and registered under those Acts.

(2) A person convicted of an offence under a provision of the Companies Acts, as applied by this Regulation, shall, in lieu of the penalties therefor set out in those Acts, be liable to the penalties set out in Regulation 28.

TABLE

Act	*Provisions applied*
Companies Act, 1963	
	Sections 99 to 112.
	Section 165 to 173.
	Section 184.
	Section 205.
	Sections 293, 295 and 297.
	Section 311.
	Sections 344 to 350.
	Sections 368, 370, 379, 389, 390, and 394.
Companies (Amendment) Act, 1982	Section 12.

Definitions

'Companies Acts': EC(EEIG)R 1989, reg 2(1); 'grouping': EC(EEIG)R 1989, reg 2(1).

Notes

CA 1963, ss 99–112 deal with the registration of charges.

CA 1963, ss 165–173 which dealt with the investigation of companies have been repealed and replaced by CA 1990, Pt II.

CA 1963, s 184 which dealt with the disqualification of directors has been repealed and replaced by CA 1990, Pt VII.

CA 1963, s 205 entitles members to petition for relief where the affairs of the company are being conducted or the powers of the directors are being exercised in an oppressive manner or in disregard of the interests of members.

CA 1963, ss 293, 295 create various offences where officers of the company are guilty of default in a winding up. CA 1963, s 297, in its original form, imposed both civil and criminal liability for fraudulent trading. As a result of CA 1990, ss 137, 138, only criminal liability for fraudulent trading is now dealt with by CA 1963, s 297. Civil liability for fraudulent trading as well as civil liability for reckless trading are now dealt with by an entirely separate section, namely CA 1963, s 297A.

CA 1963, s 311 empowers the registrar of companies to strike defunct companies off the register.

CA 1963, ss 344–350 1963 provide for the winding up of unregistered companies. In this regard see also EC(EEIG)R 1989, reg 21(1).

CA 1963, ss 368, 370 provide for the maintenance by the registrar and the inspection by the public of the register at the Companies Registration Office. CA 1963, s 379 provides for the service of documents on the registered office. CA 1963, s 389 deals with the evidentiary status of the certificate of incorporation. CA 1963, s 390 sets out the circumstances in which security for costs may be obtained against a plaintiff company. CA 1963, s 394 deals with the authentication of documents issued by the Minister.

C(A)A 1982, s 12 empowers the Minister to strike companies off the register for failing to file the requisite returns.

---

23 Activity contrary to public interest

(1) The Minister shall be the competent authority for the purposes of Article 38 of the Council Regulation.

(2) For the said purposes, the Minister may direct a grouping to cease or refrain from any activity which, in his opinion, is or is likely to be against the public interest, and the grouping shall comply with any such direction.

Definitions

'Council Regulation': EC(EEIG)R 1989, reg 2(1); 'grouping': EC(EEIG)R 1989, reg 2(1); 'Minister': EC(EEIG)R 1989, reg 2(1).

Notes

Under Council Regulation (EEC) No 2137/85, art 38 where an EEIG carries on any activity in the State in contravention of the public interest of the State, the Minister may prohibit that activity. the Minister's decision is expressed to be amenable to judicial review.

---

24 Furnishing false information

A person shall not, in purported compliance with any provision of the Council Regulation or these Regulations, make a statement or produce, lodge or deliver any return, report, account or other document, knowing it to be false, or recklessly make a statement or produce, lodge or deliver any such document false in a material particular.

Definitions

'Council Regulation': EC(EEIG)R 1989, reg 2(1).

25 Destruction, mutilation or falsification of documents

(1) A person shall not destroy, mutilate or falsify, or be privy to the destruction, mutilation or falsification of any book or document affecting or relating to the property or affairs of a grouping, or make or be privy to the making of a false entry therein.

(2) A person shall not fraudulently part with, alter or make an omission in, any such book or document.

(3) A person shall not be convicted of an offence under this Regulation if he proves that he had no intention to defeat the law.

Definitions

'**grouping**': EC(EEIG)R 1989, reg 2(1).

26 Fees

In respect of the several matters mentioned in the first column of the Table to this Regulation, there shall be paid to the registrar the several fees specified in the second column of that Table.

TABLE

Matter in respect of which fee is payable.	*Amount of fee* £ (€)
For registration of a grouping to be registered in the State	[€1,904.61][a]
For registration of a grouping establishment in the State, where a grouping is registered in another Member State of the European Communities	[€1,904.61][a]
For registration of change of a grouping name.	[€1,904.61][a]
For registration of transfer of official address of a grouping.	[€1,904.61][a]
For termination of registration of a grouping.	[€31.74][b]
For registering any other document by these Regulations required to be delivered, forwarded or sent to the registrar or filed in the registry.	[€31.74][b]

Amendments

a £150 increased to £1,500 by CA 1990, s 240(7) as inserted by CLEA 2001, s 104(c) and converted to €1,904.61 by Council Regulation (EC)No 1103/97, No 974/98 and No 2866/98 and the Economic and Monetary Union Act 1998, s 6.

b £25 converted to €31.74 by Council Regulation (EC)No 1103/97, No 974/98 and No 2866/98 and the Economic and Monetary Union Act 1998, s 6.

Definitions

'grouping': EC(EEIG)R 1989, reg 2(1); 'registry': EC(EEIG)R 1989, reg 2(1); 'registrar': EC(EEIG)R 1989, reg 2(1), reg 5(2), CA 1963 s 2(1).

27 Forms

(1) The forms referred to in the Table to this Regulation and set out in the Second Schedule to these Regulations are, subject to paragraph (2), hereby prescribed as the forms to be used by groupings for the various purposes required under the Council Regulation and these Regulations.

(2) For the purpose of giving full and better effect to the Council Regulation and these Regulations, the registrar may require groupings generally to furnish him with such further information, and in such form, as he may from time to time determine, or may make such adjustments and alterations in the forms set out in the Second Schedule to these Regulations as he deems appropriate.

TABLE

Purpose	*Form*
Registration of grouping whose official address is in the State.	IG1
Registration of grouping establishment in Ireland for grouping whose official address is outside the State.	IG2
Notice of setting up of grouping establishment of grouping whose official address is in the State.	IG3
Notice of closure of grouping establishment of grouping.	IG4
Notice of manager's particulars and of termination of appointment	IG5
Notice of documents and particulars required to be filed.	IG6
Notice of proposal to transfer official address of grouping.	IG7

Definitions

'Council Regulation': EC(EEIG)R 1989, reg 2(1); 'grouping': EC(EEIG)R 1989, reg 2(1); 'registrar': EC(EEIG)R 1989, reg 2(1), reg 5(2), CA 1963 s 2(1).

28 Offences and penalties

(1) A person or grouping who contravenes Article 3(2), 4(1), 7, 10, 18, 19, 25, 29, 31 or 35(4) of the Council Regulation or Regulations 4, 8, 9,14,18,19, 20(1), 24 or 25 of these Regulations, or a direction of the Minister under Regulation 23 of these Regulations shall be guilty of an offence and shall be liable on summary conviction to a fine not exceeding [€1,269.74][a] or to imprisonment for a term not exceeding 12 months or to both.

(2) Where an offence which is committed by a grouping under the Council Regulation or these Regulations is proved to have been committed with the consent or connivance of or to be attributable to any neglect on the part of any member of that grouping or any person or body who was purporting to act in such capacity, that person or body shall also be guilty of an offence and shall be liable to be proceeded against accordingly as if he were guilty of the first-mentioned offence.

(3) Summary proceedings in relation to an offence under the Council Regulation or these Regulations may be brought and prosecuted by the Minister or the registrar.

(4) Notwithstanding section 10(4) of the Petty Sessions (Ireland) Act, 1851, summary proceedings under the Council Regulation or these Regulations may be instituted within three years from the date of the offence.

Amendments

a £1,000 converted to €1,269.74 by Council Regulation (EC)No 1103/97, No 974/98 and No 2866/98 and the Economic and Monetary Union Act 1998, s 6.

Definitions

'Council Regulation': EC(EEIG)R 1989, reg 2(1); 'grouping': EC(EEIG)R 1989, reg 2(1); 'Minister': EC(EEIG)R 1989, reg 2(1); 'registrar': EC(EEIG)R 1989, reg 2(1), reg 5(2), CA 1963 s 2(1).

SCHEDULES

Regulation 2

FIRST SCHEDULE

COUNCIL REGULATION (EEC) NO 2137/85 OF 25 JULY 1985 ON THE EUROPEAN ECONOMIC INTEREST GROUPING (EEIG)

THE COUNCIL OF THE EUROPEAN COMMUNITIES

Having regard to the Treaty establishing the European Economic Community, and in particular Article 235 thereof.

Having regard to the proposal from the Commission

Having regard to the opinion of the European Parliament,

Having regard to the opinion of the Economic and Social Committee,

Where a harmonious development of economic activities and a continuous and balanced expansion throughout the Community depends on the establishment and smooth functioning of a common market offering conditions analogous to those of a national market; whereas to bring about this single market and to increase its unity a legal framework which facilities the adaptation of their activities to the economic conditions of the Community should be created for natural persons, companies, firms and other legal bodies in particular; whereas to that end it is necessary that those natural persons, companies, firms and other legal bodies should be able to co-operate effectively across frontiers;

Whereas co-operation of this nature can encounter legal, fiscal or psychological difficulties; whereas the creation of an appropriate Community legal instrument in the form of a European Economic Interest Grouping would contribute to the achievement of the above mentioned objectives and therefore proves necessary;

Whereas the Treaty does not provide the necessary powers for the creation of such a legal instrument;

Whereas a grouping's ability to adapt to economic conditions must be guaranteed by the considerable freedom for its members in their contractual relations and the internal organisation of the grouping;

Whereas a grouping differs from a firm or company principally in its purpose, which is only to facilitate or develop the economic activities of its members to enable them to improve their own results; whereas, by reason of that ancillary nature, a grouping's activities must be related to the economic activities of its members but not replace them so that, to that extent, for example, a grouping may not itself, with regard to third parties, practise a profession, the concept of economic activities being interpreted in the widest sense;

Whereas access to grouping form must be made as widely available as possible to natural persons, companies, firms and other legal bodies, in keeping with the aims of this Regulation; whereas this Regulation shall not, however, prejudice the application at national level of legal rules and/or ethical codes concerning the conditions for the pursuit of business and professional activities;

Whereas this Regulation does not itself confer on any person the right to participate in a grouping, even where the conditions it lays down are fulfilled;

Whereas the power provided by this Regulation to prohibit or restrict participation in grouping on grounds of public interest is without prejudice to the laws of member states which govern the pursuit of activities and which may provide further prohibitions or restrictions or otherwise control or supervise participation in a grouping by any natural person, company, firm or other legal body or any class of them;

Whereas, to enable a grouping to achieve its purpose, it should be endowed with legal capacity and provision should be made for it to be represented vis-a-vis third parties by an organ legally separate from its membership;

Whereas the protection of third parties requires widespread publicity; whereas the members of a grouping have unlimited joint and several liability for the grouping's debts and other liabilities, including those relating to tax or social security, without, however, that principle's affecting the freedom to exclude or restrict the liability of one or more of its members in respect of a particular debt or other liability by means of a specific contract between the grouping and a third party;

Whereas matters relating to the status or capacity of natural persons and to the capacity of legal persons are governed by national law:

Whereas the grounds for winding up which are peculiar to the grouping should be specific while referring to national law for its liquidation and the conclusion thereof;

Whereas groupings are subject to national laws relating to insolvency and cessation of payments; whereas such laws may provide other grounds for the winding up of groupings;

Whereas this Regulation provides that the profits or losses resulting from the activities of a grouping shall be taxable only in the hands of its members; whereas it is understood that otherwise national tax laws apply, particularly as regards the apportionment of profits, tax procedures and any obligations imposed by national tax law;

Whereas in matters not covered by this Regulation the laws of the member states and Community law are applicable, for example with regard to: social and labour laws, competition law, intellectual property law;

Whereas the activities of groupings are subject to the provisions of member states' laws on the pursuit and supervision of activities; whereas in the event of abuse or circumvention of the laws of a Member State by a grouping or its members that Members State may impose appropriate sanctions;

Whereas the Member States are free to apply or to adopt any laws, regulations or administrative measures which do not conflict with the scope or objective of this Regulation;

Whereas this Regulation must enter into force immediately in its entirety; whereas the implementation of some provisions must nevertheless be deferred in order to allow the Member States first to set up the necessary machinery for the registration of groupings in their territories and the disclosure of certain matters relating to groupings; whereas, with effect from the date of implementation of this Regulation, groupings set up may operate without territorial restrictions.

HAS ADOPTED THIS REGULATION:

Definitions

'grouping': EC(EEIG)R 1989, reg 2(1).

Notes

OJ No C 14,15, 2.1974, p 30 and OJ No C 103, 28, 4.1978, p 4.
OJ No C 163,11, 7,1977, p 17.
OJ No C 108,15, 5,1975, p 46.

Article 1

1. European Economic Interest Groupings shall be formed upon the terms, in the manner and with the effects laid down in this Regulation. Accordingly, parties intending to form a grouping must conclude a contract and have the registration provided for in Article 6 carried out.

2. A grouping so formed shall, from the date of its registration as provided for in Article 6, have the capacity, in its own name, to have rights and obligations of all kinds, to make contracts or accomplish other legal acts, and to sue and be sued.

3. The Member States shall determine whether or not groupings registered at their registries, pursuant to Article 6, have legal personality.

Definitions

'grouping': EC(EEIG)R 1989, reg 2(1); 'registry': EC(EEIG)R 1989, reg 2(1).

Notes

See also EC(EEIG)R 1989, reg 7.

Under reg 7 the EEIG is given legal personality once registration has been effected.

Article 2

1. Subject to the provisions of this Regulation, the law applicable, on the one hand, to the contract for the formation of a grouping, except as regards matters relating to the status or capacity of natural persons and to the capacity of legal persons and, on the other hand, to the internal organisation of a grouping shall be the internal law of the State in which the official address is situated, as laid down in the contract for the formation of the grouping.

2. Where a State comprises several territorial units, each of which has its own rules of law applicable to the matters referred to in paragraph 1, each territorial unit shall be considered as a State for the purposes of identifying the law applicable under this Article.3

Definitions

'grouping': EC(EEIG)R 1989, reg 2(1).

Article 3

1. The purpose of a grouping shall be to facilitate or develop the economic activities of its members and to improve or increase the results of those activities; its purpose is not to make profits for itself.Its activity shall be related to the economic activities of its members and must not be more than ancillary to those activities.

2. Consequently, a grouping may not:

(a) exercise, directly or indirectly, a power of management or supervision over its members' own activities or over the activities of another undertaking, in particular in the fields of personnel, finance and investment;

(b) directly or indirectly, on any basis whatsoever, hold shares of any kind in a member undertaking; the holding of shares in another undertaking shall be possible only in so far as it is necessary for the achievement of the grouping's objects and if it is done on its members' behalf;

(c) employ more than 500 persons;

(d) be used by a company to make a loan to a director of a company, or any person connected with him, when the making of such loans is restricted or controlled under the Member States' laws governing companies. Nor must a grouping be used for the transfer of any property between a company and a director, or any person connected with him, except to the extent allowed by the Member States' laws governing companies. For the purposes of this provision the making of a loan includes entering into any transaction or arrangement of similar effect, and property includes moveable and immovable property;

(e) be a member of another European Economic Interest Grouping.

Definitions

'director': EC(EEIG)R 1989, reg 2(1), CA 1963 s 2(1); 'grouping': EC(EEIG)R 1989, reg 2(1).

Notes

Under Council Regulation (EEC) No 2137/85, art 21 profits made from the activities of the EEIG are to be treated as the profits of the members and thus under Council Regulation (EEC) No 2137/85, art 40 such profits are taxable only in the hands of the members.

The following are examples quoted by Linnane[1] of activities which although not having as their object the making of profit for the EEIG, would nonetheless involve facilitating or developing the economic activities of its members or which would involve improving or increasing the results of those activities:

- joint buying office,
- joint sales/marketing office,
- co-ordination of particular technical activities, such as research and development activities of members,
- representation of members in particular transactions, such as a combined tender for a contract whose scope exceeds the capacity of any one member to fulfil,
- administration of specialist services essential to all members, such as joint salaries office or a computerised accounting system.

This provision is somewhat similar to the rule in *AG v Great Eastern Rly Co*[2] which empowers a company to do anything that is 'reasonably incidental' to its objects. It is a matter for objective assessment as to whether the activities of the EEIG can be described as reasonably incidental or ancillary to the economic activities of its members.

For the prohibition on loans by a company to its directors and shadow directors, the directors and shadow directors of its holding company and any person connected with such directors and shadow directors, see CA 1990, ss 31–40.

For the statutory restrictions on transactions between a company and directors, shadow directors and persons connected with such directors and shadow directors, see CA 1963, s 194; C(A)A 1983, s 32, s 29; CA 1990, s 29.

1 See also Linnane 'The European Economic Interest Grouping' (1989) 9 ILT (ns) 213; 'Forming an EEIG in Ireland' (1991) 11 ILT (ns) 36; 'Managing an EEIG' (1992) 12 ILT (ns) 163; Power 'The European Economic Interest Grouping' (1990) 10 ILT (ns) 19.

2 *AG v Great Eastern Rly Co* (1880) 5 AC 473.

Article 4

1. Only the following may be members of a grouping:

(a) companies or firms within the meaning of the second paragraph of Article 58 of the Treaty and other legal bodies governed by public or private law, which have been formed in accordance with the law of a Member State and which have their registered or statutory office and central administration in the Community; where, under the law of a Member State, a company, firm or other legal body is not obliged to have a registered or statutory office, it shall be sufficient for such a company, firm or other legal body to have its central administration in the Community;

(b) natural persons who carry on any industrial, commercial, craft or agricultural activity or who provide professional or other services in the Community.

2. A grouping must comprise at least:

(a) two companies, firms or other legal bodies, within the meaning of paragraph 1, which have their central administrations in different Member States, or

(b) two natural person, within the meaning of paragraph 1, who carry on their principal activities in different Members States, or

(c) a company, firm or other legal body within the meaning of paragraph 1 and a natural person, of which the first has its central administration in one Member State and the second carries on his principal activity in another Member State.

3. A Member State may provide that groupings registered at its registries in accordance with Article 6 may have no more than 20 members. For this purpose, that Member State may provide that, in accordance with its laws, each member of a legal body formed under its laws, other than a registered company, shall be treated as a separate member of a grouping.

4. Any Member State may, on grounds of that State's public interest, prohibit or restrict participation in groupings by certain classes of natural persons, companies, firms, or other legal bodies.

Definitions

'grouping': EC(EEIG)R 1989, reg 2(1).

Notes

In relation to membership of an EEIG see EC(EEIG)R 1989, regs 13–17.

With regard to the minimum membership of an EEIG and the consequences where the membership falls below the legal minimum, see EC(EEIG)R 1989, reg 16.

Article 5

A contract for the formation of a grouping shall include at least:

(a) the name of the grouping preceded or followed either by the words 'European Economic Interest Grouping' or by the initials 'EEIG', unless those words or initials already form part of the name;

(b) the official address of the grouping;

(c) the objects for which the grouping is formed;

(d) the name, business name, legal form, permanent address or registered office, and the number and place of registration, if any, of each member of the grouping;

(e) the duration of the grouping, except where this is indefinite.

Definitions

'grouping': EC(EEIG)R 1989, reg 2(1).

Notes

The contract of formation is the constitutional document of the EEIG and thus equates with the memorandum and articles of association of a company.

The EEIG may not be registered with an undesirable name: EC(EEIG)R 1989, reg 4(3).

In relation to the objects of the EEIG see also Council Regulation (EEC) No 2137/85, art 3.

Article 6

A grouping shall be registered in the State in which it has its official address, at the registry designated pursuant to Article 39(1).

Definitions

'grouping': EC(EEIG)R 1989, reg 2(1); 'registry': EC(EEIG)R 1989, reg 2(1).

Notes

The designated registry is the Companies Registration Office: EC(EEIG)R 1989, reg 5(1).

Article 7

A contract for the formation of a grouping shall be filed at the registry referred to in Article 6. The following documents and particulars must also be filed at that registry:

(a) any amendment to the contract for the formation of a grouping, including any change in the composition of a grouping;

(b) notice of a setting up or closure of any establishment of the grouping;

(c) any judicial decision establishing or declaring the nullity of a grouping, in accordance with Article 15;

(d) notice of the appointment of the manager or managers of a grouping, their names and any other identification particulars required by the law of the Member State in which the register is kept, notification that they may act alone or must act jointly, and the termination of any manager's appointment;

(e) notice of a member's assignment of his participation in a grouping or a proportion thereof, in accordance with Article 22 (1);

(f) any decision by members ordering or establishing the winding up of a grouping, in accordance with Articles 31 or 32;

(g) notice of the appointment of the liquidator or liquidators of a grouping, as referred to in Article 35, their names and any other identification particulars required by the law of the Member State in which the register is kept, and the termination of any liquidator's appointment;

(h) notice of the conclusion of a grouping's liquidation, as referred to in Article 35 (2);

(i) any proposal to transfer the official address, as referred to in Article 14 (1);

(j) any clause exempting a new member from the payment of debts and other liabilities which originated prior to his admission in accordance with Article 26 (2).

Definitions

'grouping': EC(EEIG)R 1989, reg 2(1); 'registry': EC(EEIG)R 1989, reg 2(1).

In relation to the managers of an EEIG see also Council Regulation (EEC) No 2137/85, arts 19, 20, EC(EEIG)R 1989, reg 18.

Article 8

The following must be published, as laid down in Article 39, in the gazette referred to in paragraph 1 of that Article:

(a) the particulars which must be included in the contract for the formation of a grouping, pursuant to Article 5, and any amendments thereto;

(b) the number, date and place of registration as well as notice of the termination of that registration;

(c) the documents and particulars referred to in Article 7(b) to (j).

The particulars referred to in (a) and (b) must be published in full. The documents and particulars referred to in (c) may be published either in full or in extract form or by means of a reference to their filing at the registry, in accordance with the national legislation applicable.

Definitions

'grouping': EC(EEIG)R 1989, reg 2(1); 'registry': EC(EEIG)R 1989, reg 2(1).

Article 9

1. The documents and particulars which must be published pursuant to this Regulation may be relied on by a grouping as against third parties under the conditions laid down by the national law applicable pursuant to Article 3(5) and (7) of the Council Directive 68/151/EEC of 9 March 1968 on co-ordination of safeguards which, for the protection of the interests of members and others, are required by Member States of companies within the meaning of the second paragraph of Article 58 of the Treaty, with a view to making such safeguards equivalent throughout the Community.

2. If activities have been carried on on behalf of a grouping before its registration in accordance with Article 6 and if the grouping does not, after its registration, assume the obligations arising out of such activities, the natural persons, companies, firms or other legal bodies which carried on those activities shall bear unlimited joint and several liability for them.

Definitions

'grouping': EC(EEIG)R 1989, reg 2(1).

Notes

OJ No L 65,14.3.1968 p 8.

The effect of this sub-article is to impose the doctrine of constructive notice on third parties dealing with an EEIG, at least with regard to documents which have been duly published in Iris Oifigiúil. However, see Council Regulation (EEC) No 2137/85, art 20 for the entitlement of innocent third parties to enforce ultra vires transactions against an EEIG which have been entered into on its behalf by its manager.

For a similar provision in relation to pre-incorporation contracts for companies, see CA 1963 s 37. A pre-incorporation contract may be informally or impliedly ratified by an EEIG.[1] Furthermore, the liquidator may ratify the pre-incorporation contract on behalf of the EEIG after

Notes

See EC(EEIG)R 1989, reg 9(2) in relation to the obligation on an EEIG to publish notice of its intention to transfer its official address abroad.

See EC(EEIG)R 1989, reg 12 for the power of the registrar to refuse to terminate the registration of the EEIG in the State. Such refusal may be made on grounds of public interest.

Article 15

1. Where the law applicable to a grouping by virtue of Article 2 provides for the nullity of that grouping, such nullity must be established or declared by judicial decision. However, the court to which the matter is referred must, where it is possible for the affairs of the grouping to be put in order, allow time to permit that to be done.

2. The nullity of a grouping shall entail its liquidation in accordance with the conditions laid down in Article 35.

3. A decision establishing or declaring the nullity of a grouping may be relied on as against third parties in accordance with the conditions laid down in Article 9(1). Such a decision shall not of itself affect the validity of liabilities, owed by or to a grouping, which originated before it could be relied on as against third parties in accordance with the conditions laid down in the previous subparagraph.

Definitions

'court': EC(EEIG)R 1989, reg 2(1); 'grouping': EC(EEIG)R 1989, reg 2(1).

Notes

In breach of the provisions of Council Regulation (EEC) No 2137/85, art 15, the regs allow for the registrar to strike the name of the EEIG off the register (and thereby to annul the EEIG) without a liquidation, pursuant to CA 1963, s 311 and C(A)A 1982, s 12. See EC(EEIG)R 1989, reg 22.

Article 16

1. The organs of a grouping shall be the members acting collectively and the manager or managers. A contract for the formation of a grouping may provide for other organs; if it does it shall determine their powers.

2. The members of a grouping, acting as a body, may take any decision for the purpose of achieving the objects of the grouping.

Definitions

'grouping': EC(EEIG)R 1989, reg 2(1).

Notes

The power of the members of an EEIG broadly equate to the power of the members of a company in general meeting. Likewise, the position of the manager of the EEIG equates with that of the board of directors of a company.

The contract for the formation of the EEIG is the constitutional document of the EEIG and is thus equivalent to the memorandum and articles of association of a company.

With regard to the taking of decisions by the members, see Council Regulation (EEC) No 2137/85, art 17.

Article 17

1. Each member shall have one vote. The contract for the formation of a grouping may, however, give more than one vote to certain members, provided that no one member holds a majority of the votes.

2. A unanimous decision by the members shall be required to:

(a) alter the objects of a grouping;

(b) alter the number of votes allotted to each member;

(c) alter the conditions for the taking of decision;

(d) extend the duration of a grouping beyond any period fixed in the contract for the formation of the grouping;

(e) alter the contribution by every member or by some members of the grouping's financing;

(f) alter any other obligation of a member, unless otherwise provided by the contract for the formation of the grouping;

(g) make any alteration to the contract for the formation of the grouping not covered by this paragraph, unless otherwise provided by that contract.

3. Except where this Regulation provides that decisions must be taken unanimously, the contract for the formation of a grouping may prescribe the conditions for the quorum and for a majority, in accordance with which the decisions, or some of them, shall be taken. Unless otherwise provided for by the contract, decisions shall be taken unanimously.

4. On the initiative of a manager or at the request of a member, the manager or managers must arrange for the members to be consulted so that the latter can take a decision.

Definitions

'grouping': EC(EEIG)R 1989, reg 2(1).

Notes

In relation to the objects of the EEIG see generally Council Regulation (EEC) No 2137/85, art 3.

Clearly, Council Regulation (EEC) No 2137/85, art 17 leaves much of the procedural aspects of decision taking to be governed by the contract of formation and thus it will be necessary to ensure that the contract is properly and adequately drafted since the EEIG does not have the equivalent of a Table A to fall back on, in the event of the contract of formation failing to deal with a particular matter of management and organisation. Similarly many other matters such as admission to and termination of membership of the EEIG are largely left to be dealt with by the contract of formation. See in particular Council Regulation (EEC) No 2137/85, arts 26, 27.

Article 18

Each member shall be entitled to obtain information from the manager or managers concerning the grouping's business and to inspect the grouping's books and business records.

Definitions

'grouping': EC(EEIG)R 1989, reg 2(1).

Notes

The members' right of access to the books and records in greater than that afforded to the members of a company. The members of a company are only entitled to the annual accounts (CA 1963 s 159) and have no right to inspect the company's basic records (CA 1990, s 202).

Article 19

1. A grouping shall be managed by one or more natural persons appointed in the contract for the formation of the grouping or by decision of the members. No person may be a manager of a grouping if: by virtue of the law applicable to him, or by virtue of the internal law of the State in which the grouping has its official address, or following a judicial or administrative decision made or recognised in a Member State he may not belong to the administrative or management body of a company, may not manage an undertaking or may not act as manager of a European Economic Interest Grouping.

2. A Member State may, in the case of groupings registered at their registries pursuant to Article 6, provide that legal persons may be managers on condition that such legal persons designate one or more natural persons, whose particulars shall be the subject of the filing provisions of Article 7(d) to represent them. If a Member State exercises this option, it must provide that the representative or representatives shall be liable as if they were themselves managers of the groupings concerned. The restrictions imposed in paragraph 1 shall also apply to those representatives.

3. The contract for the formation of a grouping or, failing that, a unanimous decision by the members shall determine the conditions for the appointment and removal of the manager or managers and shall lay down their powers.

Definitions

'grouping': EC(EEIG)R 1989, reg 2(1); 'registry': EC(EEIG)R 1989, reg 2(1).

Notes

In relation to the manager of the EEIG see also Council Regulation (EEC) No 2137/85, art 20, EC(EEIG)R 1989, reg 18. The appointment of the manager must be registered pursuant to Council Regulation (EEC) No 2137/85, art 7.

The manager is the equivalent of the board of directors of a company. See in particular, Council Regulation (EEC) No 2137/85, art 20(1).

For the restriction and disqualification of directors, see CA 1990, Pt VII.

EC(EEIG)R 1989, reg 18 permits bodies corporate to be managers of EEIG's.

Reg 18 contains such a provision.

For the power of the manager to bind the company, even in respect of acts which are either intra vires the EEIG but beyond his actual authority or alternatively which are ultra vires the EEIG itself, see Council Regulation (EEC) No 2137/85, art 20.

Article 20

1. Only the manager or, where there are two or more, each of the managers shall represent a grouping in respect of dealings with third parties. Each of the managers shall bind the grouping as regards third parties when he acts on behalf of the grouping, even where his acts do not fall within the objects of the groupings, unless the grouping proves that the third party knew or could not, under the circumstances, have been unaware that the act fell outside the objects of the grouping; publication of the particulars referred to in Article 5(c) shall not of itself be proof thereof. No limitation on the powers of the manager or managers, whether deriving from the contract for the formation of the grouping or from a decision by the members, may be relied on as against third parties even if it is published.

2. The contract for the formation of the grouping may provide that the grouping shall be validly bound only by two or more managers acting jointly. Such a clause may be relied on as against third parties in accordance with the conditions referred to in Article 9(1) only if it is published in accordance with Article 8.

Definitions

'grouping': EC(EEIG)R 1989, reg 2(1).

Notes

The protection afforded to outsiders where the manager acts beyond his actual authority or acts beyond the capacity of the EEIG itself, is similar to that afforded to innocent outsiders pursuant to CA 1963 s 8 and of the EC(C)R 1973 reg 6 in respect of their dealings with companies. The protection afforded by EC(EEIG)R 1989, reg 20(1) is however subject to one important exception contained in r 20(2), the effect of which is that the outsider will be deemed to have constructive notice of a limitation in the contract of formation which provides that the EEIG may only be bound by two or more managers acting jointly, provided that the clause containing the limitation has been duly published in Iris Oifigiúil pursuant to Council Regulation (EEC) No 2137/85, art 8.

The requirement that the managers act jointly should be stated on the EEIG's letters, invoices and order forms. See Council Regulation (EEC) No 2137/85, art 25(d).

Article 21

1. The profits resulting from a grouping's activities shall be deemed to be the profits of the members and shall be apportioned among them in the proportions laid down in the contract for the formation of the grouping or, in the absence of any such provision, in equal shares.

2. The members of a grouping shall contribute to the payment of the amount by which expenditure exceeds income in the proportions laid down in the contract for the formation of the grouping or, in the absence of any such provision, in equal shares.

Definitions

'grouping': EC(EEIG)R 1989, reg 2(1).

Notes

See also Council Regulation (EEC) No 2137/85, art 3 which prohibits an EEIG from making a profit for itself. Under art 40 profits or losses resulting from the activities of the EEIG are taxable only in the hands of its members.

See also Council Regulation (EEC) No 2137/85, art 24 in relation to the unlimited liability of the members of an EEIG.

Article 22

1. Any member of a grouping may assign his participation in the grouping, or a proportion thereof, either to another member or to a third party; the assignment shall not take effect without the unanimous authorisation of the other members.

2. A member of a grouping may use his participation in the grouping as security only after the other members have given their unanimous authorisation, unless otherwise laid down in the contract for the formation of the grouping. The holder of the security may not at any time become a member of the grouping by virtue of that security.

Definitions

'grouping': EC(EEIG)R 1989, reg 2(1).

Notes

For the consequences if an assignment from one member to another brings the membership of the EEIG below the prescribed minimum, see EC(EEIG)R 1989, reg 16. The assignment of the member's interest in the EEIG must be registered pursuant to Council Regulation (EEC) No 2137/85, art 7 and published pursuant to art 8.

Article 23

No grouping may invite investment by the public.

Definitions

'grouping': EC(EEIG)R 1989, reg 2(1).

Notes

See also EC(EEIG)R 1989, reg 20(1).

Article 24

1. The members of a grouping shall have unlimited joint and several liability for its debts and other liabilities of whatever nature. National law shall determine the consequences of such liability.

2. Creditors may not proceed against a member for payment in respect of debts and other liabilities, in accordance with the conditions laid down in paragraph 1, before the liquidation of a grouping is concluded, unless they have first requested the grouping to pay and payment has not been made within an appropriate period.

Definitions

'grouping': EC(EEIG)R 1989, reg 2(1).

Notes

The unlimited liability of the members is similar but not identical to that of members of an unlimited company. In the case of an unlimited company however, CA 1963, s 207 provides that the unlimited liability only arises once the company goes into liquidation and can only be enforced by the liquidator of the company. For the liability of past members see Council Regulation (EEC) No 2137/85, arts 26(2), 34, 37.

Article 25

Letters, order forms and similar documents must indicate legibly:

(a) the name of the grouping preceded or followed either by the words 'European Economic Interest Grouping' or by the initials 'EEIG', unless those words or initials already occur in the name;

(b) the location of the registry referred to in Article 6, in which the grouping is registered, together with the number of the grouping's entry at the registry;

(c) the grouping's official address;

(d) where applicable, that the managers must act jointly;

(e) where applicable, that the grouping is in liquidation, pursuant to Articles 15, 31, 32 or 36.

Every establishment of a grouping, when registered in accordance with Article 10, must give the above particulars, together with those relating to its own registration, on the documents referred to in the first paragraph of this Article uttered by it.

Definitions

'grouping': EC(EEIG)R 1989, reg 2(1); 'registry': EC(EEIG)R 1989, reg 2(1).

Notes

See also EC(EEIG)R 1989, reg 4(2).

With regard to the significance of the requirement that managers should act jointly, see Council Regulation (EEC) No 2137/85, art 20(2).

Article 26

1. A decision to admit new members shall be taken unanimously by the members of the grouping.

2. Every new member shall be liable, in accordance with the conditions laid down in Article 24, for the grouping's debts and other liabilities, including those arising out of the grouping's activities before his admission. He may, however, be exempted by a clause in the contract for the formation of the grouping or in the instrument of admission from the payment of debts and other liabilities which originated before his admission. Such a clause may be relied on as against third parties, under the conditions referred to in Article 9(1), only if it is published in accordance with Article 8.

Definitions

'grouping': EC(EEIG)R 1989, reg 2(1).

Notes

The clause must also be registered pursuant to Council Regulation (EEC) No 2137/85, art 7.

Article 27

1. A member of a grouping may withdraw in accordance with the conditions laid down in the contract for the formation of a grouping or, in the absence of such conditions, with the unanimous agreement of the other members. Any member of a grouping may, in addition, withdraw on just and proper grounds.

2. Any member of a grouping may be expelled for the reasons listed in the contract for the formation of the grouping and, in any case, if he seriously fails in his obligations or if he causes or threatens to cause serious disruption in the operation of the grouping. Such expulsion may occur only by the decision of a court to which joint application has been made by a majority of the other members, unless otherwise provided by the contract for the formation of a grouping.

Definitions

'court': EC(EEIG)R 1989, reg 2(1); 'grouping': EC(EEIG)R 1989, reg 2(1).

Article 28

1. A member of a grouping shall cease to belong to it on death or when he no longer complies with the conditions laid down in Article 4(1). In addition, a Member State may provide, for the purposes of its liquidation, winding up, insolvency or cessation of payments laws, that a member shall cease to be a member of any grouping at the moment determined by those laws.

2. In the event of the death of a natural person who is a member of a grouping, no person may become a member in his place except under the conditions laid down in the contract for the formation of the grouping or, failing that, with the unanimous agreement of the remaining members.

Definitions

'grouping': EC(EEIG)R 1989, reg 2(1).

Notes

The conditions in Council Regulation (EEC) No 2137/85, art 4(1) will be infringed in the case of a company, if it ceases to have its central administration in a member state of the EEC, and in the case of a natural person, if he ceases to carry on a business or profession within the European Community.

EC(EEIG)R 1989, reg 17 provides that membership of the EEIG ceases upon the liquidation or bankruptcy of the member.

Article 29

As soon as a member ceases to belong to a grouping, the manager or managers must inform the other members of that fact; they must also take the steps required as listed in Articles 7 and 8. In addition, any person concerned may take those steps.

Definitions

'grouping': EC(EEIG)R 1989, reg 2(1).

Article 30

Except where the contract for the formation of a grouping provides otherwise and without prejudice to the rights acquired by a person under Articles 22(1) or 28(2), grouping shall continue to exist for the remaining members after a member has ceased to belong to it, in accordance with the conditions laid down in the contract for the formation of the grouping or determined by unanimous decision of the members in question.

Definitions

'grouping': EC(EEIG)R 1989, reg 2(1).

Notes

For the consequences where a member ceases to belong to the EEIG and the membership thus falls below the legal minimum, see EC(EEIG)R 1989, reg 16.

Article 31

1. A grouping may be wound up by a decision of its members ordering its winding up. Such a decision shall be taken unanimously, unless otherwise laid down in the contract for the formation of the grouping.

2. A grouping must be wound up by a decision of its members:

(a) noting the expiry of the period fixed in the contract for the formation of the grouping or the existence of any other cause for winding up provided for in the contract, or

(b) noting the accomplishment of the grouping's purpose or the impossibility of pursuing it further.

Where, three months after one of the situations referred to in the first subparagraph has occurred, a members' decision establishing the winding up of the grouping has not been taken, any member may petition the court to order winding up.

3. A grouping must also be wound up by a decision of its members of the remaining member when the conditions laid down in Article (2) are no longer fulfilled.

4. After a grouping has been wound up by decision of its members, the manager or managers must take the steps required as listed in Articles 7 and 8. In addition, any person concerned may take those steps.

Definitions

'court': EC(EEIG)R 1989, reg 2(1); 'grouping': EC(EEIG)R 1989, reg 2(1).

Notes

The EEIG is treated as an unregistered company for the purpose of winding up: EC(EEIG)R 1989, reg 21. Thus, under CA 1963, s 345(3) the EEIG may only be wound up by the court and cannot be wound up voluntarily.

Even where the decision of the members has been taken, it will still be necessary to petition for a winding up order: CA 1963, s 345(3).

Article 32

1. On application by any person concerned or by a competent authority, in the event of the infringement of Articles 3, 12 or 31(3), the court must order a grouping to be wound up, unless its affairs can be and are put in order before the court has delivered a substantive ruling.

2. On applications by a member, the court may order a grouping to be wound up on just and proper grounds.

3. A Member State may provide that the court may, on application by a competent authority, order the winding up of a grouping which has its official address in the State to which that authority belongs, wherever the grouping acts in contravention of that State's public interest, if the law of that State provides for such a possibility in respect of registered companies or other legal bodies subject to it.

Definitions

'court': EC(EEIG)R 1989, reg 2(1); 'grouping': EC(EEIG)R 1989, reg 2(1).

Notes

The competent authority for the purposes of Council Regulation (EEC) No 2137/85, art 32 is the Minister: EC(EEIG)R 1989, reg 21(3).

No such provision has been made in the regs.

Article 33

When a member ceases to belong to a grouping for any reason other than the assignment of his rights in accordance with the conditions laid down in Article 22 (1), the value of his rights and obligations shall be determined taking into account the assets and liabilities of the grouping as they stand when he ceases to belong to it. The value of the rights and obligations of a departing member may not be fixed in advance.

Definitions

'grouping': EC(EEIG)R 1989, reg 2(1).

Article 34

Without prejudice to Article 37(1), any member who ceases to belong to a grouping shall remain answerable, in accordance with the conditions laid down in Article 24, for the debts and other liabilities arising out of the grouping's activities before he ceased to be a member.

Definitions

'grouping': EC(EEIG)R 1989, reg 2(1).

Notes

Council Regulation (EEC) No 2137/85, art 37(1) places a 5 year limitation period after publication of the notice of termination of membership, within which actions may be brought against a past member for payment of debts and liabilities of the EEIG incurred before he ceased to be a member.

Article 35

1. The winding up of a grouping shall entail its liquidation.

2. The liquidation of a grouping and the conclusion of its liquidation shall be governed by national law.

3. A grouping shall retain its capacity, within the meaning of Article 1(2), until its liquidation is concluded.

4. The liquidator or liquidators shall take the steps required as listed in Articles 7 and 8.

Definitions

'grouping': EC(EEIG)R 1989, reg 2(1).

Notes

The EEIG is treated as an unregistered company for the purpose of winding up: EC(EEIG)R 1989, reg 21. Thus, under CA 1963, s 345(3) the EEIG may only be wound up by the court and cannot be wound up voluntarily. This means the liquidator must register and publish notice of his appointment and notice of the conclusion of the liquidation.

Article 36

Groupings shall be subject to national laws governing insolvency and cessation of payments. The commencement of proceedings against a grouping on grounds of its solvency or cessation of payments shall not by itself cause the commencement of such proceedings against its members.

Definitions

'grouping': EC(EEIG)R 1989, reg 2(1).

Article 37

1. A period of limitation of five years after the publication, pursuant to Article 8, of notice of a member's ceasing to belong to a grouping shall be substituted for any longer period which may be laid down by the relevant national law for actions against that member in connection with debts and other liabilities arising out of the grouping's activities before he ceased to be a member.

2. A period of limitation of five years after the publication, pursuant to Article 8, of notice of the conclusion of the liquidation of a grouping shall be substituted for any longer period which may be laid down by the relevant national law for actions against a member of the grouping in connection with debts and other liabilities arising out of the grouping's activities.

Definitions

'grouping': EC(EEIG)R 1989, reg 2(1).

Article 38

Where a grouping carries on any activity in a Member State in contravention of that State's public interest, a competent authority of that State may prohibit that activity. Review of that competent authority's decision by a judicial authority shall be possible.

Definitions

'grouping': EC(EEIG)R 1989, reg 2(1).

Notes

See also EC(EEIG)R 1989, reg 23.

Article 39

1. The Member States shall designate the registry or registries responsible for effecting the registration referred to in Articles 6 and 10 and shall lay down the rules governing registration. They shall prescribe the conditions under which the documents referred to in Articles 7 and 10 shall be filed. They shall ensure that the documents and particulars referred to in Article 8 are published in the appropriate official gazette of the Member

State in which the grouping has its official address and may prescribe the manner of publication of the documents and particulars referred to in Article 8(c). The Member States shall also ensure that anyone may, at the appropriate registry pursuant to Article 6 or, where appropriate, Article 10, inspect the documents referred to in Article 7 and obtain, even by post, full or partial copies thereof. The Member States may provide for the payment of fees in connection with the operations referred to in the preceding subparagraphs; those fees may not, however, exceed the administrative cost thereof.

2. The Member States shall ensure that the information to be published in the Official Journal of the European Communities pursuant to Article 11 is forwarded to the Office for Official Publications of the European Communities within one month of its publication in the official gazette referred to in paragraph 1.

3. The Member States shall provide for appropriate penalties in the event of failure to comply with the provisions of Articles 7, 8 and 10 on disclosure and in the event of failure to comply with Article 25.

Definitions

'registry': EC(EEIG)R 1989, reg 2(1).

Notes

The designated registry is the Companies Registration Office: EC(EEIG)R 1989, reg 5(1).

The right to inspect and take copies of documents on the register is conferred by CA 1963, s 370 as applied by EC(EEIG)R 1989, reg 22.

Article 40

The profits or losses resulting from the activities of a grouping shall be taxable only in the hands of its members.

Definitions

'grouping': EC(EEIG)R 1989, reg 2(1).

Notes

See also Council Regulation (EEC) No 2137/85, art 21 which provides that any profits resulting from the activities of the EEIG are to be treated as the profits of its members.

Article 41

1. The Member States shall take the measures required by virtue of Article 39 before 1 July 1989. They shall immediately communicate them to the Commission.

2. For information purposes, the Member States shall inform the Commission of the classes of natural persons, companies, firms and other legal bodies which they prohibit from participating in groupings pursuant to Article 4(4). The Commission shall inform the other Member States.

Article 42

1. Upon the adoption of this Regulation, a Contact Committee shall be set up under the auspices of the Commission. Its function shall be:

(a) to facilitate, without prejudice to Articles 169 and 170 of the Treaty, application of this Regulation through regular consultation dealing in particular with particular problems arising in connection with its application;

(b) to advise the Commission, if necessary, on additions or amendments to this Regulation.

2. The Contact Committee shall be composed of representatives of the Member States and representatives of the Commission. The chairman shall be a representative of the Commission. The Commission shall provide the secretariat.

3. The Contact Committee shall be convened by its chairman either on his own initiative or at the request of one of its members.

Article 43

This Regulation shall enter into force on the third day following its publication in the Official Journal of the European Communities. It shall apply from 1 July 1989, with the exception of Articles 39, 41 and 42 which shall apply as from the entry force of the Regulation. This Regulation shall be binding in its entirety and directly applicable in all Member States.

Second Schedule

EUROPEAN ECONOMIC INTEREST GROUPING

Regulation of EEIG whose official address is in Ireland Registration 27 of the 1989 Regulations	Council Regulation (EEC) No 213/85 and European Communities (European Economic Interest Groupings) Regulations 1989 Grouping registration number in Ireland	Registration for stamp to be affixed above
	IR ☐☐☐☐☐☐☐	**IGI**

Name of grouping *in full*

____

____

Official address of grouping

____

Membership *Note one*

Names (including business name if different) and particulars of the members of the grouping

Name

____

____

Registered number and place of registration (if any)__________________

Legal form *Note two*______________________________

Address *Note three*______________________________

____

Name____________________________________

Registered number and place of registration (if any)__________________

Legal form *Note two*______________________________

Address *Note three*______________________________

____

Name____________________________________

Registered number and place of registration (if any)__________________

Legal form *Note two*______________________________

Address *Note three*______________________________

Presenter's Name Address

____

____

____

Telephone Number Reference

Number of continuation sheets attached ☐

Names (including business name if different) and particulars of the members of the grouping

Name

____

____

Registered number and place of registration (if any)______________________________

Legal form *Note two*______________________________

Address *Note three*______________________________

____

Name

____

____

Registered number and place of registration (if any)______________________________

Legal form *Note two*______________________________

Address *Note three*______________________________

____

Objects of the grouping______________________________

____

____

Duration of grouping *Note four*______________________________

____

Attachments

The contract establishing the above named grouping is herewith for registration

☐ that contract not being written in english or Irish a certified translation is herewith for registration______________________________

Declaration of Compliance

I,______________________________

☐ A member of the above grouping

☐ A person authorised on behalf of a member of the above grouping

declare that the particulars on this form are correct and that all the requirements of the above Regulations in respect of the registration of the above grouping and of matters precedent and incidental to it have been complied with.

And I make this solemn declaration conscientiously believing the same to be true and by virtue of the provisions of the Statutory Declarations Act 1938.

Signature of Declarant______________________________

Declared before me by______________________________

who is personally known to me or who is identified to me by:

who is personally known to me

at ______________________________

this______________________day of__________________19__________

Signed____________________

☐ Commissioner for Oaths

☐ Notary Public

☐ Peace Commissioner

Please complete using black block capitals or typewriting

Note one

Particulars of further members should be given on the prescribed continuation sheet prescribed continuation sheet

Note two

Insert 'natural person' if an individual, 'legal person' if a body corporate or 'partnership' as appropriate

Note three

Business address or registered office address as appropriate

Note four

If the duration is indefinite this should be stated

EUROPEAN ECONOMIC INTEREST GROUPING

Regulation of EEIG whose official address is in Ireland Registration 27 of the 1989 Regulations	Council Regulation (EEC) No 213/85 and European Communities (European Economic Interest Groupings) Regulations 1989 Grouping registration number in Ireland	Registration for stamp to be affixed above

IR 815

IG2

Name of grouping *in full*

Official address of grouping

County

Establishment in Ireland

Membership *Note one*

Names (including business name if different) and particulars of the members of the grouping

Name

Registered number and place of registration (if any)

Legal form *Note two*

Address *Note three*

Name

Registered number and place of registration (if any)

Legal form *Note two*

Address *Note three*

Presenter's Name

Address

Telephone Number

Reference

Number of continuation sheets attached ☐

Names (including business name if different) and particulars of the members of the grouping

Name

____

____

Registered number and place of registration (if any)____________________

Legal form *Note two*____________________

Address *Note three*____________________

____

Name

____

____

Registered number and place of registration (if any)____________________

Legal form *Note two*____________________

Address *Note three*____________________

____

Attachments

A certified copy of the contract establishing the above named grouping is herewith for registration

☐ that contract not being written in English or Irish a certified translation is herewith for registration.

Declaration of Compliance

I,____________________

☐ A member of the above grouping

☐ A person authorised on behalf of a member of the above grouping

declare that the particulars on this form are correct and that all the requirements of the above Regulations in respect of the registration of the above grouping and of matters precedent and incidental to it have been complied with.

And I make this solemn declaration conscientiously believing the same to be true and by virtue of the provisions of the Statutory Declarations Act 1938.

Signature of Declarant____________________

Declared before me by____________________

who is personally known to me or who is identified to me by:

who is personally known to me

at ____________________

this__________day of__________19__________

Signed____________________

☐ Commissioner for Oaths

☐ Notary Public

☐ Peace Commissioner

Please complete using black block capitals or typewriting

Note one

Particulars of further members should be given on the prescribed continuation sheet

Note two

Insert 'natural person' if an individual, 'legal person' if a body corporate or 'partnership' as appropriate

Note three

Business address or registered office address as appropriate.

EUROPEAN ECONOMIC INTEREST GROUPING

Regulation of EEIG whose official address is in Ireland

Registration 27 of the 1989 Regulations

Council Regulation (EEC) No 213/85 and European Communities (European Economic Interest Groupings) Regulations 1989

Grouping registration number in Ireland

IR ☐☐☐☐☐☐

Registration for stamp to be affixed above

IG3

Name of grouping *in full*____

____

Official address of grouping______________________________________

____

____

Address of grouping establishment being set up__________________________

____

____

____

Declaration

I,____

☐ a member of the above grouping

☐ a person authorised on behalf of a member of the above group

☐ a manager of the above grouping

declare that the particulars on this form are correct

Signature of Declarant______________________Date__________________

Presenter's Name

Telephone Number

Address

Reference

Number of continuation sheets attached ☐

Please complete using block capitals or typewriting.

EUROPEAN ECONOMIC INTEREST GROUPING

Regulation of EEIG whose official address is in Ireland Registration 27 of the 1989 Regulations	Council Regulation (EEC) No 213/85 and European Communities (European Economic Interest Groupings) Regulations 1989 Grouping registration number in Ireland IR ☐☐☐☐☐☐☐	Registration for stamp to be affixed above **IG4**

Name of grouping *in full*________________________

____

Official address of grouping________________________

____

____

Address of grouping establishment being set up________________________

____

____

____

Declaration

I,________________________

☐ a member of the above grouping

☐ a person authorised on behalf of a member of the above group

☐ a manager of the above grouping

declare that the particulars on this form are correct

Signature of Declarant____________ Date____________

Presenter's Name | Address
Telephone Number | Reference

Number of continuation sheets attached ☐

Please complete using black block capitals or typewriting

EUROPEAN ECONOMIC INTEREST GROUPING

Regulation of EEIG whose official address is in Ireland Registration 27 of the 1989 Regulations	Council Regulation (EEC) No 213/85 and European Communities (European Economic Interest Groupings) Regulations 1989 Grouping registration number in Ireland IR ☐☐☐☐☐☐☐	Registration for stamp to be affixed above **IG5**

Section A

Name of grouping *in full*__________

Official address of grouping__________

Section B

Name of Manager__________ Date of Appointment__________

Address__________

Section C (i)

Attachments

A certified copy of the manager's particulars

☐ those particulars not being written in Irish or English a certified translation thereof (other than the manager's name and address is attached.

Signature of Declarant__________ Date__________

Presenter's Name

Address

Telephone Number

Reference

Number of continuation sheets attached ☐

Section D

I consent to act singly/jointly* as manager of the grouping named above

Signature__________ Date__________

Section E

If the grouping has more than one manager does the manager have the power to bind the grouping acting singly?

YES/NO*

If NO please specify the conditions under which managers can bind the grouping__________

Section F

The appointment of the person named above as manager of the above grouping was terminated on

______________________________19________________________

____

Declaration

I,____

☐ a member of the above grouping

☐ a person authorised on behalf of a member of the above group

☐ a manager of the above grouping

declare that the particulars on this form are correct

Signature of Declarant________________________Date__________________

Notes on the completion of this form

1. If this form relates to the appointment of a manager(s), omit Section F.
2. If this form relates to the termination of the appointment of a manager(s), omit Section C, D and E.

Please complete using black block capitals or typewriting

To be completed only if official address of EEIG is in Ireland

To be completed only if official address of EEIG is outside Ireland

*Delete as approrprate

EUROPEAN ECONOMIC INTEREST GROUPING

Regulation of EEIG whose official address is in Ireland

Registration 27 of the 1989 Regulations

Council Regulation (EEC) No 213/85 and European Communities (European Economic Interest Groupings) Regulations 1989

Grouping registration number in Ireland

IR ☐☐☐☐☐☐

Registration for stamp to be affixed above

IG6

Name of grouping *in full*____________________

____

Official address of grouping____________________

____

____

Certified copy(ies) of the following document(s) is/are* attached:
Please tick appropriate box(es)

☐ an amendment to the grouping's formation contract

☐ a document evidencing a judicial decision regarding nullity

☐ an assignment of all/part* of a member's participation

☐ a document evidencing a judicial decision/members' order or decision* to wind up the grouping

☐ Liquidator's appointment/termination of appointment*

☐ a document evidencing the conclusion of liquidation

☐ an exemption clause relieving a new member from payment of debts and other liabilities which originated before his admission to membership of a grouping

Signature of Declarant____________________Date____________

Presenter's Name

Telephone Number

Address

Reference

Number of continuation sheets attached ☐

Declaration

I,____________________

☐ a member of the above grouping

☐ a person authorised on behalf of a member of the above group

☐ a manager of the above grouping

declare that the particulars on this form are correct

Signature of Declarant____________________Date____________

Please complete using black block capitals or typewriting
*Delete as appropriate

EUROPEAN ECONOMIC INTEREST GROUPING

Regulation of EEIG whose official address is in Ireland Registration 27 of the 1989 Regulations	Council Regulation (EEC) No 213/85 and European Communities (European Economic Interest Groupings) Regulations 1989 Grouping registration number in Ireland IR ☐☐☐☐☐☐	Registration for stamp to be affixed above **IG7**

Section A

Name of grouping *in full*____________________

____

Official address of grouping____________________

____

____

Prosposed new official address____________________

____

Section B

Proposal to transfer the official address from Ireland

A copy of the Iris Oifigiúil is attached as evidence of the publication of the transfer proposal

Signed____________________Date__________

☐ a member of the above grouping

☐ a person authorised on behalf of a member of the above group

Presenter's Name Address

Telephone Number Reference

Number of continuation sheets attached ☐

Section C

Proposal to transfer the official address into Ireland

The following documents (or certified copies thereof) are attached, together with certified translations of such of the documents as are not written in Irish or English:

☐ the contract for the formation of the grouping, together with any amendments thereto

☐ any documents filed, pursuant to the Council Regulation, at the registry in the country from which it is proposed to transfer the official address,

☐ A copy of____________________as evidence of the publication of the transfer proposal

I declare that no competent authority has opposed the transfer under Article 14(4) of the Council Regulation.

Signature of Declarant____________________Date__________

☐ a member of the above grouping

☐ a person authorised on behalf of a member of the above group

Please complete using black block capitals or typewriting

EUROPEAN ECONOMIC INTEREST GROUPING

Regulation of EEIG whose official address is in Ireland Registration 27 of the 1989 Regulations	Council Regulation (EEC) No 213/85 and European Communities (European Economic Interest Groupings) Regulations 1989 Grouping registration number in Ireland IR8 [8]	Registration for stamp to be affixed above **IG8**

Name of grouping *in full*____________________

Official address of grouping

Addresses of grouping establishments in Ireland

Membership *Note one*

Names including business name if different) and particulars of the members of the grouping

Name____________________

Registered number and place of registration (if any)____________________

Legal form *Note two*____________________

Address *Note three*____________________

Name____________________

Registered number and place of registration (if any)____________________

Legal form *Note two*____________________

Address *Note three*____________________

Name____________________

Registered number and place of registration (if any)____________________

Legal form NLegal form *Note two*____________________

Address *Note three*____________________

Presenter's Name Address

Telephone Number Reference

Number of continuation sheets attached ☐

Membership continued

Name____________________

Registered number and place of registration (if any)____________________

Legal form *Note two*____________________

Address *Note three*____________________

Changes in year ending 30 June 19___

Please tick appropriate box(es)

- ☐ amendment to the grouping's formation contract
- ☐ notifiable event concerning a manager
- ☐ judicial decision regarding nullity
- ☐ assignment of all/part* of a member's participation
- ☐ judicial decision/members' order or decision* to wind up the grouping
- ☐ Liquidator's appointment/termination of appointment*
- ☐ conclusion of liquidation
- ☐ proposal to transfer the official address of the grouping
- ☐ exemption clause relieving a new member from payment of debts and other liabilities which originated before his admission to membership of a grouping

Declaration

I,____

- ☐ a member of the above grouping
- ☐ a person authorised on behalf of a member of the above group

declare that the particulars on this form are correct

Signature of Declarant____________________ Date______________

Please complete using black block capitals or typewriting

Note one

Particulars of further members should be given on the prescribed continuation sheet

Note two

Insert 'natural person' if an individual, 'legal person' if a body corporate or 'partnership' as appropriate

Note three

Business address or registered office address as appropriate

* Delete as appropriate

EUROPEAN ECONOMIC INTEREST GROUPING

Continuation Sheet for Forms IG to IG8	Council Regulation (EEC) No 213/85 and European Communities (European Economic Interest Groupings) Regulations 1989	Continuation of Form
Registration 27 of the 1989 Regulations	Grouping registration number in Ireland IR8 8	**IG....**

Name of grouping *in full*________________________

____

____

____

____

____

Please complete using black block capitals or typewriting

EXPLANATORY NOTE

(THIS NOTE IS NOT PART OF THE INSTRUMENT AND DOES NOT PURPORT TO BE A LEGAL INTERPRETATION.)

These Regulations give full effect to Council Regulations (EEC) No. 2137/85 on the European Economic Interest Grouping (EEIG). They provide a legal framework for groupings of natural persons, companies and other legal entities to enable them to co-operate effectively in economic activities across national frontiers within the European Community. Such groupings, if their official address is in Ireland, will be bodies corporate and have legal personality.

The Council Regulation is directly applicable in Irish Law but certain provisions within the Council Regulations need supplementary legislation. These include the designation of the registry and registrar for groupings (the Companies Registration Office and the Registrar of Companies respectively), management of groupings, qualifications and limits on membership, and winding-up. These Regulations also designate the forms to be used in relation to the registration, setting-up, closure or transfer of a grouping or in any other prescribed event.

The Regulations come into operation on 1st August, 1989.

Companies Act 1990 (Parts IV And VII) Regulations 1991

SI 209/1991

The Minister for Industry and Commerce, in exercise of the powers conferred on him by sections 3 of the Companies Act, 1990 (No. 33 of 1990), hereby makes the following Regulations:

1. (1) These Regulations may be cited as the Companies Act, 1990 (Parts IV and VII) Regulations, 1990.

(2) These Regulations shall come into operation on the 1st day of August, 1991.

2. In these Regulations, "the Act" means the Companies Act, 1990 (No. 33 of 1990).

3. (1) The Examiner and the Registrars of the High Court are hereby prescribed for the purposes of sections 103, 150 and 153 of the Act.

(2) The following officers are hereby prescribed for the purposes of section 167 of the Act, namely—

(a) in the case of proceedings in the Supreme Court, the Registrar of the Supreme Court,

(b) in the case of proceedings in the Court of Criminal Appeal, the Registrar of the Court of Criminal Appeal,

(c) in the case of proceedings or an application in the High Court, the Examiner and Registrars of the High Court,

(d) in the case of proceedings or an application in the Central Criminal Court, the Registrar of the Central Criminal Court,

(e) in the case of proceedings in the Special Criminal Court, the Registrar of the Special Criminal Court,

(f) in the case of proceedings in the Circuit Court, the County Registrar for the county in which the proceedings are heard,

(g) in the case of proceedings in the District Court, in the Dublin Metropolitan District or in the District Court Area of Cork City, the Chief Clerk for the district or area concerned, as the case may be,

(h) in the case of proceedings elsewhere in the District Court, the principal Clerk assigned to the District Court area in which the proceedings are heard.

Definitions

'examiner': Courts and Courts Officers Act 1926, Pt 1; 'Registrar': CA 1963, s 2(1).

Notes

CA 1990, s 105 requires that where information is furnished to the relevant court on foot of a disclosure order under CA 1990, s 98 by a prescribed officer of the court then that information shall, unless the relevant court orders otherwise, be furnished to the applicant and the company in respect of whose shares or debentures the order was made.[1] A disclosure order overrides the protections of the Data Protection Acts 1988 to 2003 and, in doing so, would be compatible with the Data Protection Directives.[2]

CA 1990, s 150(4)[3] requires the court to request a prescribed officer to furnish the particulars of the declaration of restriction that the court intends to make in respect of a person under CA 1990, s 150(1). CA 1990, s 153 imposes an identical obligation on the court in respect of orders made to vary a declaration under CA 1990, s 150(1).

CA 1990, s 167 requires a prescribed officer to inform the Registrar of Companies of the particulars of the order, relief or conviction made by the relevant court in certain stated circumstances. The obligation arises when the court in question makes an order of disqualification,[4] varies a disqualification order,[5] convicts a person of an offence that has the effect of deeming him to be disqualified, or an offence of breaching a disqualification order[6] or convicts a person of having connived in the breach of a disqualification order.[7]

Proceedings within the High Court include actions adopted into the Commercial List in accordance with Order 63A of the Rules of the Superior Courts.

1 CA 1990, s 105(2).

2 EU Directive 95/46/EC and Directive 2002/58/EC of the European Parliament and of the Council.

3 CA 1990, s 150(3)(a)(i) and (ii) as amended: amount substituted and 150(4A) and (B) inserted by CLEA 2001, s 41 with effect from 1 March 2002.

4 CA 1990, s 160.

5 CA 1990, s 160(8).

6 CA 1990, s 161(1).

7 CA 1990, s 164.

---

4. (1) The particulars specified in a form set out in the Schedule to these Regulations in relation to section 150, 153 or 167 of the Act are hereby prescribed for the purposes of the relevant section.

(2) The period of 21 days is hereby prescribed for the purposes of section 167 of the Act.

Notes

The prescribed persons have 21 days to furnish the particulars required under CA 1990, s 167. See the notes following SI 209/1990, reg 3.

Schedule

Particulars of a court declaration of a restriction under section 150, Companies Act, 1990

Companies Acts 1963 to 1990

NO FEE

H6

Please complete using black block capitals or typewriting

TO REGISTRAR OF COMPANIES

I hereby notify you that the following person

Surname________________ Forename________________

Note one
Insert usual residential address

of *note one* ________________________________

____

____

Date of Birth________________________________

is the subject of a court declaration pursuant to section 150 (1) of the Companies Act, 1990

Note two
Insert date

made on *note two*________________________________

The declaration arises from an action in respect of the following company

Company Name Company Number________________

____

____________________________________Limited

Note three This form is to be completed by an officer of the court, prescribed for the purpose pursuant to section 150(4).

Signature *note three* Date____________

Name Block letters please

OFFICIAL STAMP

Particulars of partial relief granted by a court pursuant to section 152, Companies Act, 1990

Companies Acts 1963 to 1990

NO FEE

H7

Please complete using black block capitals or typewriting

TO REGISTRAR OF COMPANIES

I hereby notify you that the following person

Note one
Insert usual residential address

of *note one* ________________________

the court granted partial relief under section 152 of the Companies Act, 1990 to the following person

Surname_______________ Forename_______________

Note two
Insert usual residential address

of *note two*________________________

____

____

Date of Birth________________________

who is the subject of a declaration pursuant to section 150 of the Companies Act, 1990

Note three
Insert the date of the original declaration by the court

made on *note three*________________________

The following are the details of the partial relief granted note four

Note four Include in particular the date of the expiration of the restrictions if varied by the court

____

____

____

____

____

____

The original declaration arose in respect of the following company

Company Name Company Number____________

____

____________________________Limited

Note five
This form is to be completed by an officer of the court, prescribed for the purpose pursuant to section 153 (2).

Signature *note five* Date____________

Name Block letters please

OFFICIAL STAMP

Particulars of a disqualification order pursuant to section 160 of the Companies Act, 1990 ; a conviction which has the effect of a person being deemed to be subject to a disqualification order under section 160, 161, or 164, or section 183 of the Companies Act,1963 (inserted by section 169 of the Companies Act, 1990); or a conviction under section 161(1) or 164

Companies Acts 1963 to 1990

NO FEE

H8

Please complete using black block capitals or typewriting

TO REGISTRAR OF COMPANIES

I hereby notify you that the following person

Surname________________ Forename________________

of *note two* ________________________________

____

____

Note one
Notification must be made within 21 days of the court decision

Note two
Insert usual residential address

Date of Birth________________________________

note three

☐ is the subject of a disqualification order

☐ was convicted of an offence which has the effect of his being deemed to be subject to a disqualification order

☐ was convicted of an offence under section 161(1) of the Companies Act, 1990

☐ was convicted of an offence under section 164 of the Companies Act, 1990

Note three Tick appropriate box

From ______________________________________

To ____

Date of court decision__________________________

Signature *note four* Date__________

Name Block letters please

OFFICIAL STAMP

Note four
This form is to be completed by an officer of the court, prescribed for the purpose pursuant to section 167.

Particulars of relief granted or varied by a court pursuant to section 160 (8), Company Act , 1990

Companies Acts 1963 to 1990

NO FEE

H9

Please complete using black block capitals or typewriting

Note one
Notification must be made within 21 days of the court decision

Note two
Insert date on which the relief was granted or varied

Note three
Insert usual residential address

Note four
Insert the date of the original disqualification

Note five
Tick appropriate box

Note six
Include in particular the date of expiration of the disqualification if varied by the court

Note seven
This form is to be completed by an officer of the court, prescribed for the purpose pursuant to section 167

TO REGISTRAR OF COMPANIES

I hereby notify you that the following person

of *note two* ____________________

the court granted or varied relief under section 160 (8) of the Companies Act, 1990 in respect of the following person

Surname____________________ Forename____________________

of *note three* ____________________

____

____

Date of Birth____________________

who was the subject of a disqualification order

dated *note four* ____________________

The following are the details of the court decision note five

☐ Full relief granted

☐ Partial relief granted note six

☐ Relief varied note six____________________

____

____

____

____

Company Name Company Number____________________

____

____________________Limited

Signature *note seven* Date____________

Name Block letters please

OFFICIAL STAMP

Explanatory Note

The purpose of these Regulations is to prescribe officers of the court, and the particulars, form and time within which information is to be furnished by them to the registrar of companies, for the purposes of certain sections of the Companies Act, 1990.

European Communities (Companies: Group Accounts) Regulations, 1992

SI 201/1992

I, Desmond O'Malley, Minister for Industry and Commerce, in exercise of the powers conferred on me by section 3 of the European Communities Act, 1972 (No. 27 of 1972), and for the purpose of giving effect to the provisions of Council Directive No. 83/349/EEC of 13 June, 1983 (OJ L493, 18.7.1983, pp 1–17) hereby make the following Regulations:

PRELIMINARY AND GENERAL

Citation, commencement and construction

1.(1) These Regulations may be cited as the European Communities (Companies: Group Accounts) Regulations, 1992.

(2) These Regulations shall be construed as one with the Companies Acts, 1963 to 1990.

Notes

These regulations give legal effect to the provisions of the Seventh Companies Directive (83/349/EEC) which governs the format and content of group accounts for certain types of limited companies. For a further discussion of the scope of the regulations see the notes to EC(CGA)R 1992, reg 2.

The provisions of the Directive should have been implemented in this jurisdiction before 1 January 1988 and should have applied to group accounts for financial years beginning not later than 1990.[1] However, these Regs were made only on 17 July 1992 and apply only to group accounts and directors' reports for financial years on or after 1 September 1992.[2]

1 Directive 83/349/EEC, art 49.

2 EC(CGA)R 1992, reg 2.

Application

2. These Regulations shall apply to [Companies Act group accounts][a] and directors' reports for financial years beginning on or after the 1st day of September, 1992.

Amendments

a Amended by EC(IFRSMA)R 2005 (SI 116/2005), reg 6(a).

Definitions

'companies act group accounts': CA 1963, s 2(1).

Notes

Obligation to prepare group accounts: The requirement to prepare group accounts and the form and content of those accounts were originally all governed by CA 1963, ss 150, 151, 152 & 154. Over the last three decades, however, the relevance and applicability of these provisions has been largely eroded by the following enactments:

EC(CGA)R 1992[1]: These Regulations implement Council Directive 83/349/EEC and deal with the format and content of group accounts of public and private limited holding companies[2] which are engaged for gain in the production, supply or distribution of goods, the provision of a service or the making or holding of investments[3]. The Regulations do not apply, however, to the following:-

(a) licensed banks[4];

(b) certified trustee savings banks[5];

(c) other companies engaged in the business of accepting deposits or other repayable funds or granting credit for its own account[6];

(d) companies engaged solely in the making of hire-purchase agreements and credit-sale agreements[7];

(e) authorised life and non-life insurance companies[8];

(f) companies which meet at least two of the three following criteria—

(i) the group balance sheet does not exceed €7,618,428,

(ii) the group turnover does not exceed €15,236,858 per annum,

(iii) the group workforce does not exceed 250,[9]

and in respect of which neither the parent company not any of its subsidiaries is listed on a stock exchange established in a member state;[10]

(k) certain parent companies which are themselves subsidiaries of other EC companies.[11]

EC(CI:A)R 1992: These regs, which give effect to Council Directive 86/635/EEC, govern the form and content of annual accounts and group accounts for banks and other financial institutions. *EC(A)R 1993*: These regs give legal effect, *inter alia*, to Council Directive 90/605/EEC and govern the format and content of the annual accounts for unlimited companies in circumstances where, broadly speaking, the members of the company are themselves either Irish or foreign limited companies.[12] The group accounts of such companies are, with some modifications, to be drawn up in accordance with the provisions of EC(CGAC)R 1992.[13]

EC(IUA)R 1996: These regs implement Council Directive 91/674/EEC and govern the form and content of annual accounts and group accounts for insurance companies to which the European Communities (Non-Life Insurance) Regs 1976 or the European Communities (Life Assurance) Regs 1984 apply, as well as reinsurance companies.

However, more recently the European Communities (International Financial Reporting Standards and Miscellaneous Amendments) Regulations 2005, (SI 116/2005) ('EC(IFRSMA)R 2005') have made fundamental changes to the Companies Acts provisions as regards the preparation of accounts.

EC(IFRSMA)R 2005 was a direct consequence of Council Regulation (EC) No 1606/2002 of the European Parliament and of the Council. This Regulation applied directly to the group accounts of listed entities throughout the European Union by requiring these to be prepared in accordance with International Financial Reporting Standards ('IFRS').

The main purpose of the EC(IFRSMA)R 2005 was to avail of a number of EU member state options contained in Council Regulation (EC) 1606/2002 of the European Parliament of the Council ('the EU IAS Regulation'). The EU IAS Regulation requires all listed entities required to prepare consolidated (or group) accounts to do so in accordance with IFRS as adopted for use in the EU. IFRS (previously known as International Accounting Standards or 'IAS') are issued by the International Accounting Standards Board ('IASB'). Each IFRS requires formal adoption by the European Union, after which, when published in the Official Journal, has full legal recognition.

The EU IAS regulation also allows member states to 'permit or require' the use of IFRS for the preparation of individual company accounts, regardless of whether such companies are listed or not. In implementing the IFRS Regulations, Ireland has opted for a permissive regime and the following choices have been reflected in CA 1963:

(i) debt-only listed parent companies may avail of an option not to prepare group accounts in accordance with IFRS until accounting periods beginning on or after 1 January 2007; and

(ii) all other companies have the option to use IFRS in preparing their group or individual accounts.

Therefore as a result of the IFRS Regulations, all companies and groups (that are not directly impacted by the EU IAS Regulation) have a choice as to the financial reporting framework they apply in preparing their individual and group accounts.

The choice is not available to the following types of company:

(i) a company not trading for the acquisition of gain by members;

(ii) a company not having a share capital formed for charitable purposes (see section 128(4)(c) of CA 1963); and

(iii) a company in respect of which an order under CA 1963, s 128(5) is in force.

Such companies must continue to prepare Companies Act accounts. Companies Act accounts are prepared in accordance with the formats accounting requirements of the Companies Acts, including EC(CI:A)R 1992 (SI 294/1992), EC(A)R 1993 (SI 396/1993), and EC(IUA)R 1996 (SI 23/1996), and accounting standards. The applicable standards are the Financial Reporting Standards ('FRS') issued by the Accounting Standards Board ('ASB') and promulgated in the Republic of Ireland by the Institute of Chartered Accountants in Ireland.

Generally, if a company opts to move from preparing Companies Act accounts to IFRS accounts, it is a one-way street. Such a company may not subsequently revert to preparing Companies Act accounts except where there has been a 'relevant change of circumstances'. Subsection (5) sets out the situations when such a change may arise.

The IFRS Regulations apply to accounting periods beginning on or after 1 January 2005.

As a result of EC(IFRSMA)R 2005, CA 1963, ss 148–151 were repealed and replaced by new ss 148, 149, 149A, 150, 150A, 150B, 150C and 151. A principal consequence of this, is that the primary obligation to prepare financial statements previously contained in C(A)A 1986, s 3 and EC(G:AR) 1992, reg 5, EC(CI:A)R 1992, EC(IUA)R 1996 is now contained in CA 1963, s 148 (individual accounts) and CA 1963, s 150 (group accounts), irrespective of what type of company is involved – eg general companies, credit institutions, or insurance undertakings.

See also notes to CA 1063, ss 148–151.

1 For a general review of the regs, see Rue, *Guide to the 1992 Group Accounts Regulations* (1992).
2 EC(CGA)R 1992, reg 5.
3 EC(CGA)R 1992, reg 3(1).
4 EC(CGA)R 1992, reg 6(2)(a).
5 EC(CGA)R 1992, reg 6(2)(b).
6 EC(CGA)R 1992, reg 6(2)(d).
7 EC(CGA)R 1992, reg 6(2)(c).
8 EC(CGA)R 1992, reg 6(2)(g).
9 EC(CGA)R 1992, reg 7(1).
10 EC(CGA)R 1992, reg 7(8).
11 EC(CGA)R 1992, regs 8 and 9.
12 EC(A)R 1993, reg 6. The regs also apply to partnerships.
13 EC(A)R 1993, reg 9.

Interpretation

3.(1) In these Regulations, unless the context otherwise requires—

'associated undertaking' has the meaning assigned to it by Regulation 34;

'the Directive' means EEC Council Directive 83/349/EEC;

'directors' report' is the report referred to in Regulation 37;

['Companies Act group accounts' shall be read in accordance with Regulation 13][a];

'Member State' means a State which is a member of the European Communities;

'the Minister' means the Minister for Industry and Commerce;

'parent undertaking' means an undertaking that has one or more subsidiary undertakings;

'participating interest' has the meaning assigned to it by Regulation 35;

'the Principal Act' means the Companies Act, 1963;

'an undertaking' means a body corporate, a partnership, or an unincorporated body of persons engaged for gain in the production, supply or distribution of goods, the provision of a service or the making or holding of investments;

'undertakings dealt with in the group accounts' shall be construed as a reference to the parent undertaking drawing up the group accounts together with any subsidiary undertakings of that parent dealt with in the group accounts (excluding any undertakings dealt with in the group accounts in accordance with Regulation 32);

'the 1986 Act' means the Companies (Amendment) Act, 1986;

'the 1990 Act' means the Companies Act, 1990.

(2) In these Regulations, a reference to the directors of a company shall be construed, in the case of an undertaking which does not have a board of directors, as references to the corresponding persons appropriate to such an undertaking.

(3) In these Regulations, unless the context otherwise requires, a reference to a Regulation is to a Regulation of these Regulations, a reference to a paragraph is to the paragraph of the Regulation and a reference to a subparagraph is to the subparagraph of the paragraph, in which the reference occurs.

(4) In these Regulations, a reference to voting rights in an undertaking means the rights conferred on shareholders in respect of their shares or, in the case of an undertaking not having a share capital, on members, to vote at general meetings of the undertaking on all, or substantially all, matters.

(5) In these Regulations, in relation to an undertaking which does not have general meetings at which matters are decided by the exercise of voting rights, the references to holding a majority of the voting rights in an undertaking shall be construed as references to having the right under the constitution of the undertaking to direct the overall policy of the undertaking or to alter the terms of its constitution.

Amendments

a Amended by EC(IFRSMA)R 2005 (SI 116/2005), reg 6(b).

Definitions

'body corporate': CA 1963, s 2(3); 'subsidiary undertaking': EC(CGA)R 1992, reg 4.

Notes

Undertaking: Although the obligation to prepare group accounts under these regs applies only to parent undertakings which are companies limited either by shares or by guarantee[1], the definition of 'undertaking' makes it clear that the accounts must deal with the affairs of any subsidiaries, whether incorporated or not and whether Irish or foreign, which carry on business for gain.

[1] EC(CGA)R 1992, reg 5(1) and (3).

Board of directors: Because the subsidiary undertakings dealt with in the group accounts might not all be incorporated companies, it has been necessary to widen somewhat the definition of 'board of directors' for the purpose of these regs to include any equivalent body of persons having responsibility for the management of the undertaking. In the case of a partnership, it would include the partners themselves, whereas in other unincorporated companies, it might be a committee of management or some similarly styled body.

Voting rights: Since an undertaking might not be a company having a share capital, the term 'voting rights' is deemed to include not only a right to vote in respect of shares, but also any right to vote at general meetings 'on all or substantially all matters'[1] as well as a right under the constitution of an undertaking which does not have general meetings at which matters are decided on a vote, to direct overall policy or to alter the terms of its constitution.[2]

[1] EC(CGA)R 1992, reg 3(4).
[2] EC(CGA)R 1992, reg 3(5).

Subsidiary undertaking

4.(1) For the purposes of these Regulations, an undertaking shall be deemed to be a subsidiary of another, if but only if—

(a) that other—

(i) holds a majority of the shareholders' or members' voting rights in the undertaking, or

(ii) is a shareholder or member of it and controls the composition of its board of directors, or

(iii) is a shareholder or member of it and controls alone, pursuant to an agreement with other shareholders or members, a majority of the shareholders' or members' voting rights; or

(b) that other has the right to exercise a dominant influence over it—

(i) by virtue of provisions contained in its memorandum or articles, or

(ii) by virtue of a control contract; or

[(c) that other has the power to exercise, or actually exercises, dominant influence or control over it, or

(ca) that other and the subsidiary undertaking are managed on a unified basis, or][a]

(d) the undertaking is a subsidiary of any undertaking which is that other's subsidiary undertaking.

(2) In determining whether one undertaking controls the composition of the board of directors of another for the purposes of paragraph 1(a)(ii), subsection (2) of section 155 of the Principal Act shall apply to undertakings subject to these Regulations as it applies to companies subject to that section.

(3) For the purposes of paragraph (l)(a)—

(a) subject to paragraphs (c) and (d), any shares held or power exercisable—

(i) by any person as a nominee for that other; or

(ii) by, or by a nominee for, a subsidiary undertaking of that other, not being the subsidiary undertaking whose shares or board of directors are involved;

shall be treated as held or exercisable by that other,

(b) any shares held or power exercisable by that other or a subsidiary undertaking of that other, on behalf of a person or undertaking that is neither that other nor a subsidiary undertaking of that other shall be treated as not held or exercisable by that other,

(c) any shares held or power exercisable by that other or a nominee for that other or its subsidiary undertaking shall be treated as not held or exercisable by that other if they are held as aforesaid by way of security provided that such power or the rights attaching to such shares are exercised in accordance with instructions received from the person providing the security,

(d) any shares held or power exercisable by that other or a nominee for that other or its subsidiary undertaking shall be treated as not held or exercisable by that other if the ordinary business of that other or its subsidiary undertaking, as the case may be, includes the lending of money and the shares are held as aforesaid by way of security provided that such power or the rights attaching to such shares are exercised in the interests of the person providing the security.

(4) For the purposes of paragraphs (l)(a)(i) and (iii), the total of the voting rights of the shareholders or members in the subsidiary undertaking shall be reduced by the following:

(a) the voting rights attached to shares held by the subsidiary undertaking in itself, and

(b) the voting rights attached to shares held in the subsidiary undertaking by any of its subsidiary undertakings, and

(c) the voting rights attached to shares held by a person acting in his own name but on behalf of the subsidiary undertaking or one of its subsidiary undertakings.

(5) For the purposes of paragraph l(b) an undertaking shall not be regarded as having the right to exercise a dominant influence over another undertaking unless it has a right to give directions with respect to the operating and financial policies of that other undertaking which its directors are obliged to comply with.

(6) A 'control contract' as specified in paragraph l(b) means a contract in writing conferring such a right which-

(a) is of a kind authorised by the memorandum or articles of the undertaking in relation to which the right is exercisable, and

(b) is permitted by the law under which that undertaking is established.

(7) Paragraph (5) shall not be read as affecting the construction of the expression 'actually exercises a dominant influence' in paragraph 1(c).

Amendments

a Amended by EC(IFRSMA)R 2005 (SI 116/2005), reg 6(c).

Definitions

'control contract': EC(CGA)R 1992, reg 4(6); 'director': EC(CGA)R 1992, reg 3(2), CA 1963, s 2(1); 'dominant influence': EC(CGA)R 1992, reg 4(5); 'member': CA 1963, s 31; 'participating interest': EC(CGA)R 1992, reg 35; 'Principal Act': EC(CGA)R 1992, reg 3(1); 'board of directors': EC(CGA)R 1992, reg 3(2); 'voting rights': EC(CGA)R 1992, reg 3(4) and (5).

Notes

Exhaustive definition: The wording of EC(CGA)R 1992, reg 4(1) makes it quite clear that the definition of 'subsidiary undertaking' contained therein is exhaustive. However, EC(IFRSMA)R 2005 has amended this definition. Previously, where a company actually exercised dominant influence over another or was managed on a unified basis with that other company, it was necessary for the company to have a participating interest in the other before it met the definition of a subsidiary. This requirement has now been removed. A company will now be a subsidiary of another where that other company has the power to exercise, or actually exercises, dominant influence or control over it, or where they are both managed on a unified basis. The several ways in which the relationship of parent undertaking and subsidiary undertaking can arise are as follows:

1. *Holding a majority of voting rights*:[1] Since the subsidiary undertaking might not be a company having a share capital, the term 'voting rights' is deemed to include not only a right to vote in respect of shares, but also any right to vote at general meetings 'on all or substantially all matters'[2] as well as the right (in respect of undertakings which do not have general meetings at which matters are decided on a vote) under the constitution of that undertaking to direct overall policy or to alter the terms of its constitution.[3] Voting rights held through a nominee on behalf of the parent undertaking or on behalf of one of its other subsidiaries, are also to be taken into account in determining whether or not it holds a majority of voting rights.[4] Excluded from consideration, however, are the following:
   (a) any shares held or power exercisable by the parent undertaking or one of its subsidiaries on behalf of a third party in circumstances where that third party is not itself part of the same group of companies;[5]
   (b) any shares held or power exercisable by or on behalf of the parent undertaking or one of its subsidiaries by way of security, provided that the power or the rights attaching to the shares are exercised in accordance with instructions received from the person providing the security;[6]
   (c) any shares held or power exercisable by or on behalf of the parent undertaking or one of its subsidiaries, if the ordinary business of the parent or that subsidiary, as the case may be, includes the lending of money, and the shares are held as security, and provided that the power or the rights attaching to the shares are exercised in the interests of the person providing the security.[7]

   In determining whether or not the parent undertaking holds a majority of voting rights in the subsidiary undertaking, the total voting rights of shareholders or members in that subsidiary must be reduced by the amount of any voting rights attaching to shares held by or on behalf of the subsidiary itself or held by or on behalf of any of its own subsidiaries[8]. Thus, although Undertaking A might not, at first sight, appear to have a majority of voting rights in Undertaking B, such a majority may in fact be deemed to arise after one has excluded such voting rights as are exercisable by or behalf of Undertaking B itself or by on behalf of any subsidiaries of Undertaking B.

1 See, generally, Courtney *The Law of Private Companies* (2nd edn, Tottel Publishing, 2002), Ch 17; EC(CGA)R 1992, reg 4(1)(a)(i).

2 EC(CGA)R 1992, reg 3(4).

3 EC(CGA)R 1992, reg 3(5).

4 EC(CGA)R 1992, reg 4(3)(a).

5 EC(CGA)R 1992, reg 4(3)(b).

6 EC(CGA)R 1992, reg 4(3)(c).

7 EC(CGA)R 1992, reg 4(3)(d).

8 EC(CGA)R 1992, reg 4(4). The only circumstance in which a company may acquire shares in itself and exercise voting rights attaching to such shares is where the company has acquired any of its own fully paid shares otherwise than for valuable consideration: C(A)A 1983, s 41(2). If the shares have been acquired by way of purchase or redemption pursuant to CA 1990, Part XI and are not cancelled, they must instead be held as 'treasury shares' and thus voting rights cannot be exercised in relation to them: CA 1990, s 209(3)). With regard to the entitlement of a subsidiary to acquire shares in its holding company, see CA 1963, s 32 and CA 1990, s 224 as well as EC(Plcs)R 1997, reg 5(2).

2. *Controlling a majority of voting rights*:[1] The difference between holding and controlling a majority of voting rights is a subtle one. A member 'holds' a majority of voting rights in circumstances where such rights are conferred on him pursuant to the undertaking's constitution or attach to the shares which are held by him. 'Control' of a majority of voting rights, is slightly different. It refers to a situation where the member although not automatically having a majority of votes under the constitution, or by virtue of his shareholding, nonetheless has control of a majority of votes pursuant to the terms of a shareholder's agreement between himself and other members of the undertaking. For example, Undertaking A might only hold shares carrying 25% of voting rights in general meeting of Undertaking B, but under the terms of an agreement with other shareholders, Undertaking A is in fact contractually entitled to direct not only how its own votes are cast but also how the votes of the other members are cast as well. Such a contractual entitlement amounts to 'control' for the purposes of reg 4.

The various rules referred to above under the heading '*holding a majority of voting rights*' which deal with the taking into account of votes held through nominees, etc,[2] and dealing with how to calculate the total voting rights in the subsidiary, apply equally in determining whether one undertaking 'controls' a majority of votes in the other.[3]

1 EC(CGA)R 1992, reg 4(1)(a)(iii).

2 EC(CGA)R 1992, reg 4(3).

3 EC(CGA)R 1992, reg 4(4).

3. *Control of composition of board*:[1] This involves an entitlement on the part of Undertaking A without the consent or concurrence of any other person to appoint or remove a majority of the board of Undertaking B or to exercise a right of veto in respect of the appointment of a majority of the board.[2] A person may be able to control the composition of the board of directors by reason, *inter alia*, of (i) having a majority of the votes in general meeting; (ii) a shareholders' agreement giving such control; (iii) a provision in the memorandum or articles of association conferring a power to appoint and dismiss the board or a majority of the board.

Powers exercisable by a nominee on behalf of the parent undertaking or on behalf of one of its other subsidiaries are also to be taken into account in determining whether or not it controls the composition of the board.[3] Excluded from consideration, however, are the following:

(a) any shares held or power exercisable by the parent undertaking or one of its subsidiaries on behalf of a third party in circumstances where that third party is not itself part of the same group of companies;[4]

(b) any shares held or power exercisable by or on behalf of the parent undertaking or one of its subsidiaries by way of security, provided that the power or the rights attaching to the

(b) where the undertakings to be dealt with in group accounts comprise principally undertakings to which this Regulation applies.

(2) This Regulation applies to the following undertakings:

(a) an undertaking that is the holder of a licence under the Central Bank Act, 1971,

(b) an undertaking that is a trustee savings bank certified under the Trustee Savings Banks Acts, 1863 to 1965,

(c) an undertaking engaged solely in the making of hire-purchase agreements (within the meaning of the Hire-Purchase Act, 1946) and credit-sale agreements (within the meaning of that Act), in respect of goods owned by the undertaking,

(d) an undertaking engaged in the business of accepting deposits or other repayable funds or granting credit for its own account,

[....][a],

[...][b],

(g) an undertaking that is the holder of an authorisation under the European Communities (Non-Life Insurance) Regulations, 1976 (S.I. No. 115 of 1976), or an authorisation under the European Communities (Life Assurance) Regulations, 1984 (S.I No 57 of 1984).

Amendments

a Reg 6(2)(e) was repealed by ACC Bank Act 2001, s 12(2).

b Reg 6(2)(f) was repealed by ICC Bank Act 2000, s 7(2) and Sch, Pt 2.

Definitions

'group accounts': EC(CGA)R 1992, reg 3(1), reg 13; 'undertaking': EC(CGA)R 1992, reg 3(1).

Notes

Departure from Regulations in respect of financial institutions and insurance companies: This reg permits departure from the provisions of EC(CGA)R 1992 concerning the layout of group accounts, the valuation methods to be used and the information to be contained in the notes to the accounts—

(a) with regard to banks and other financial institutions, hire-purchase companies and other finance companies, trustee savings banks and insurance companies; and

(b) where the majority of undertakings to be dealt with in the group accounts are undertakings of the type described above.[1]

Instead, banks and other financial institutions, as well as hire-purchase companies and other finance companies are governed by EC(CI:A)R 1992, with insurance companies being governed by EC(IUA)R 1996.

1 EC(CI:A)R 1992, reg 2(1)). Notably, trustee savings banks are excluded from the operation of these regs.

2 EC(IUA)R 1996, reg 3.

Exemptions related to size of group

7.(1) Subject to paragraphs (2) to (8), Regulation 5 shall not apply to a parent undertaking that is a private company in any financial year if, at the balance sheet date of the parent undertaking in that financial year and in the financial year of that undertaking immediately preceding that year, the parent undertaking and all of its subsidiary undertakings together, on the basis of their latest annual accounts satisfy two of the following three qualifying conditions:

(a) the balance sheet total of the parent undertaking and its subsidiary undertakings together does not exceed [€7,618,428],[a]

(b) the amount of the turnover of the parent undertaking and its subsidiary undertakings together does not exceed [€15,236,858],[b] and

(c) the average number of persons employed by the parent undertaking and its subsidiary undertakings together does not exceed 250.

(2) In this Regulation, 'balance sheet total' in relation to any financial year, means—

(a) where Format 1 of the balance sheet Formats set out in the Schedule to the 1986 Act is adopted in the group accounts, the aggregate of the amounts shown in the consolidated balance sheet for that year under the headings corresponding to items A and B in that Format, and

(b) where Format 2 of those formats is adopted by the company, the aggregate amounts so shown under 'Assets'.

(3) In this Regulation, 'amount of the turnover', in relation to any financial year, means the amounts of the turnover shown in the consolidated profit and loss account under headings corresponding to the relevant items in any of the Formats of profit and loss accounts set out in the Schedule to the 1986 Act.

(4) In the application of this Regulation to any period which is a financial year for the purpose of the group accounts but is not in fact a year, the amounts specified in paragraph (1)(b) shall be proportionally adjusted.

(5) An undertaking which before the commencement of these Regulations is not a parent undertaking but which becomes a parent undertaking on or after the commencement of these Regulations may avail of the exemption in paragraph (l) in respect of the financial year in which it becomes a parent if the requirements of paragraph (1) are met in that financial year.

(6) An undertaking which was a parent undertaking before such commencement may avail of the exemption in paragraph (1) in the first financial year in which accounts of the group are to be prepared in accordance with these Regulations if the requirements of paragraph (1) are met in that financial year or in the financial year immediately preceding that year.

(7) Where a parent undertaking qualifies to avail of the exemption provided for in paragraph (1) it shall continue to be so qualified, unless in the latest financial year of the undertaking and the financial year of the undertaking immediately preceding that year the requirements of paragraph (1) are not met.

(8) This Regulation shall not apply where—

[(a) any shares, debentures or other debt securities of the parent undertaking or of one of its subsidiary undertakings have been admitted to trading on a regulated market of any EEA State.][c]

(b) the parent undertaking or any of its subsidiary undertakings is an undertaking to which Regulation 6 applies.

(9) For the purposes of this Regulation, the average number of persons employed shall be that required to be disclosed in accordance with paragraph 15 of the Schedule to these Regulations.

(10) In determining for the purposes of paragraph (6) whether two of the three qualifying conditions therein mentioned have been met in respect of a financial year in a case where consolidated accounts in respect of that year are not prepared in accordance with these Regulations, paragraph (2) shall be construed as referring to the aggregate of any amounts included in the balance sheets of the parent and its subsidiary undertakings which correspond to the amounts mentioned in subparagraph (a) or (b), as may be appropriate, of that paragraph.

Amendments

a £6,000,000 converted to €7,618,428 by Council Regulations (EC) No 1103/97, No 974/98 and No 2866/98 and the Economic and Monetary Union Act 1998, s 6.

b £12,000,000 converted to €15,236,858 by Council Regulations (EC) No 1103/97, No 974/98 and No 2866/98 and the Economic and Monetary Union Act 1998, s 6.

c Paragraph 8(a) substituted by EC(IFRSMA)R 2005 (SI 116/2005), reg 6(e).

Definitions

'EEA State': CA 1963, s 2(1)'group accounts': EC(CGA)R 1992, reg 3(1), reg 13; 'Member State': EC(CGA)R 1992, reg 3(1); 'private company': CA 1963, s 33; '1986 Act': EC(CGA)R 1992, reg 3(1); 'financial year': CA 1963, s 2(1); 'parent undertaking': EC(CGA)R 1992, reg 3(1); 'accounts': CA 1963, s 2(1); 'undertaking': EC(CGA)R 1992, reg 3(1); 'subsidiary undertaking': EC(CGA)R 1992, reg 4.

Notes

Exemptions for smaller unlisted groups: If a group of undertakings meets at least two of the three conditions as to size set out in EC(CGA)R 1992, reg 7(1), and none of the members of that group is listed on a stock exchange established in any EEA State, the parent undertaking will not be required to prepare group accounts in accordance with EC(CGA)R 1992. Instead, it will be obliged to prepare group accounts which comply with the provisions of CA 1963, ss 150–153, as amended by C(A)A 1986, s 3(1) and s 16.

Loss of exemption: If a parent undertaking qualifies for exemption under EC(CGA)R 1992, reg 7, it will cease to be so qualified if the group fails to meet at least two of the three conditions as to size for two successive financial years.[1]

1 EC(CGA)R 1992, reg 7(7).

Exemptions for parent undertakings that are fully or 90 per cent owned subsidiary undertakings of EC undertakings

8.(1) Subject to paragraphs (3) and (4), Regulation 5 shall not apply to a parent undertaking if that parent undertaking ('the exempted parent') is itself a subsidiary undertaking of another undertaking established under the laws of [an EEA State][a] ('that other parent undertaking'), and

(a) that other parent undertaking holds all the shares in the exempted parent undertaking; or

(b) that other parent undertaking holds 90 per cent or more of the shares of the exempted parent undertaking and the remaining shareholders in or members of the exempted parent have approved the exemption.

(2) In determining whether paragraph (1)(a) applies shares held by directors of the exempted parent pursuant to an obligation in law or in its articles of association shall be disregarded.

(3) Paragraph (1) shall only apply if the following conditions are met:

(a) the exempted parent and, without prejudice to [Regulations 10 and 11],[b] all of its subsidiary undertakings must be dealt with in group accounts prepared by a parent undertaking which is established under the law of [a EEA State],[c] and of which the exempted parent is a subsidiary undertaking;

(b) the group accounts referred to in subparagraph (a) and the report of the directors of the parent undertaking drawing up those group accounts must be prepared and audited according to the law of the [EEA State][d] in which that parent undertaking is established and in accordance with the Directive [or in accordance with international financial reporting standards;][e]

(c) the following must be annexed to the annual return of the exempted parent next after the group accounts have been prepared in accordance with subparagraph (a):

(i) the group accounts referred to in subparagraph (a),

(ii) the directors' report referred to in subparagraph (b), and

(iii) the report of the person responsible for auditing the accounts referred to in subparagraph (a);

(d) the notes on the annual accounts of the exempted parent must disclose:

(i) the name and registered office of the parent undertaking that draws up the group accounts referred to in subparagraph (a), and

(ii) the exemption from the obligation to draw up group accounts and a directors' report;

(e) If the group accounts, directors' report or auditor's report referred to in subparagraph (c) are in a language other than the English language or the Irish language, there shall be annexed to each such document a translation in the English language or the Irish language certified in the prescribed manner to be a correct translation.

[(4) Paragraph (1) shall not apply to a parent undertaking any of whose shares, debentures or other debt securities have been admitted to trading on a regulated market of any EEA State.][f]

Amendments

a Amended by EC(IFRSMA)R 2005 (SI 116/2005), reg 6(f)(i).

b Amended by EC(IFRSMA)R 2005 (SI 116/2005), reg 6(f)(ii)(I).

c Amended by EC(IFRSMA)R 2005 (SI 116/2005), reg 6(f)(ii)(II).

d Amended by EC(IFRSMA)R 2005 (SI 116/2005), reg 6(f)(iii)(I).

e Amended by EC(IFRSMA)R 2005 (SI 116/2005), reg 6(f)(iii)(II).

f Substituted by EC(IFRSMA)R 2005 (SI 116/2005), reg 6(f)(iv).

Definitions

'Directive': EC(CGA)R 1992, reg 3(1); 'EEA State': CA 1963, s 2(1); 'group accounts': EC(CGA)R 1992, reg 3(1), reg 13; 'international financial reporting standards': CA 1963, s 2(1); 'member': CA 1963, s 31; 'parent undertaking': EC(CGA)R 1992, reg 3(1); 'undertaking': EC(CGA)R 1992, reg 3(1); 'subsidiary undertaking': EC(CGA)R 1992, reg 4.

Notes

Exemption for parent undertakings which are themselves wholly-owned or 90% owned subsidiaries: This Regulation exempts an unlisted[1] parent undertaking ('the exempted parent') from the obligation to prepare group accounts in accordance with EC(CGA)R 1992 if:

(a) it is in turn a wholly-owned subsidiary of another parent undertaking incorporated under the laws of a EEA State ('the other parent undertaking') or the other parent undertaking holds at least 90% of its issued share capital, and the holders of remaining 10% approve of the exemption;[2]

(b) the exempted parent and its subsidiary undertakings are dealt with in group accounts of the other parent undertaking which (along with the directors' report) are drawn up in accordance with the provisions of the Seventh companies Directive;[3]

(c) the other parent undertaking's group accounts, directors' report and auditors' report together with any necessary translations thereof into English or Irish, are annexed to the exempted parent's annual return;[4] and

(d) the notes to the exempted parent's annual accounts disclose the name and registered office of the other parent undertaking as well as the fact that the exemption has been availed of.[5]

Extension of exemptions to EEA States

EC(IFRSMA)R 2005 (SI 116/2005) extends the exemptions available to undertakings incorporated in a EEA State, as permitted under Directive 83/349/EEC but heretofore not taken up in Irish company law

1 EC(CGA)R 1992, reg 8(4).

2 EC(CGA)R 1992, reg 8(1)). In ascertaining the extent of the second parents' shareholding in the exempted parent, reg 8(2) states that any shares held by directors of the exempted parent in pursuance of a share qualification imposed either by statute or by the articles of association will be disregarded). Under CA 1963, s 180 there is no automatic share qualification imposed on directors, although the section permits same to be imposed by the articles). Moreover, Table A, art 77 provides that no such share qualification shall be required only unless so resolved upon by the company in general meeting.

3 EC(CGA)R 1992, reg 8(3)(a) & (b).

4 EC(CGA)R 1992, reg 8(3)(c) & (e).

5 EC(CGA)R 1992, reg 8(3)(d).

Exemption for other parent undertakings which are themselves subsidiaries: See reg 9 and the notes thereto.

Exemptions for other parent undertakings that are subsidiary undertakings of EC undertakings

9.(1) In cases not falling within Regulation 8(1), and subject to paragraphs (2) and (3), Regulation 5 shall not apply to a parent undertaking if that parent undertaking ('the exempted parent') is itself a subsidiary undertaking of another undertaking established under the law of [an EEA State],[a] and shareholders or members holding an aggregate of 10 per cent or more in nominal value of the total share capital of the exempted parent undertaking have not, at least six months before the end of the financial year of that undertaking, requested the preparation of group accounts in accordance with Regulation 5.

(2) Paragraph (l) shall only apply if the conditions set out in paragraph (3) of Regulation 8 are met.

[(3) Paragraph (1) shall not apply to a parent undertaking any of whose shares, debentures or other debt securities have been admitted to trading on a regulated market of any EEA State.][b]

Amendments

a Amended by EC(IFRSMA)R 2005 (SI 116/2005), reg 6(g)(i).

b Paragraph 3 substituted by EC(IFRSMA)R 2005 (SI 116/2005), reg 6(g)(ii).

Definitions

'EEA State': CA 1963, s 2(1); 'group accounts': EC(CGA)R 1992, reg 3(1), reg 13; 'Member State': EC(CGA)R 1992, reg 3(1); 'member': CA 1963, s 31; 'parent undertaking': EC(CGA)R 1992, reg 3(1); 'undertaking': EC(CGA)R 1992, reg 3(1); 'subsidiary undertaking': EC(CGA)R 1992, reg 4.

Notes

Exemption for parent undertakings which are themselves wholly-owned or 90% owned subsidiaries: See EC(CGA)R 1992, reg 8 and the notes thereto. EC(IFRSMA)R 2005 (SI 116/2005) extends these exemptions to undertakings incorporated under the laws of a EEA State.

Exemption for other parent undertakings which are themselves subsidiaries: If an unlisted[1] parent undertaking ('the exempted parent') is itself a subsidiary of another undertaking incorporated under the laws of a EEA State ('the second parent') but is held as to less than 90% of its share capital by the second parent, it will be exempted from the obligation to prepare group accounts in accordance with EC(CGA)R 1992 if—

(a) the holders of not less than 10% of its issued share capital have not made a request for such accounts at least six months before the end of the relevant financial year;[2]

(b) the exempted parent and its subsidiary undertakings are dealt with in group accounts of the second parent which (along with the directors' report) are drawn up in accordance with the provisions of the Seventh Companies Directive;[3]

(c) the second parent's group accounts, directors' report and auditors' report together with any necessary translations thereof into English or Irish, are annexed to the exempted parent's annual return;[4] and

(d) the notes to the exempted parent's annual accounts disclose the name and registered office of the second parent as well as the fact that the exemption has been availed of.[5]

1 EC(CGA)R 1992, reg 9(3).

2 EC(CGA)R 1992, reg 9(1).

3 EC(CGA)R 1992, reg 9(2) and reg 8(3)(a) and (b).

4 EC(CGA)R 1992, reg 9(2) and reg 8(3)(c) and (e).

5 EC(CGA)R 1992, reg 9(2) and reg 8(3)(d).

[Exemption for parent undertakings included in non-EEA group accounts.

9A.(1) A parent undertaking (the 'exempted parent') is exempt from the requirement in Regulation 5 to prepare group accounts where that undertaking is itself a subsidiary undertaking and its parent undertaking ('that other parent undertaking') is not established under the law of an EEA State where—

(a) the exempted parent is a wholly-owned subsidiary of that other parent undertaking;

(b) that other parent undertaking holds more than 50 per cent of the shares in the exempted parent and notice requesting the preparation of group accounts has not been served in accordance with paragraph (2) on the exempted parent by shareholders holding in aggregate—

(i) more than half of the remaining shares in the company, or

(ii) 5 per cent of the total shares in the company.

(2) The notice referred to in paragraph (1)(b) must be served not later than 6 months after the end of the financial year before that to which it relates.

(3) Exemption under this Regulation is conditional upon compliance with all of the following conditions—

(a) that the exempted parent and all of its subsidiary undertakings are included in consolidated accounts for a larger group drawn up to the same date, or to an earlier date in the same financial year by that other parent undertaking,

(b) that those accounts and, where appropriate, the group's annual report, are drawn up in accordance with the provisions of the Seventh Council Directive 83/349/EEC of 13 June 1983 (where applicable, as modified by Council Directive 86/635/EEC of 8 December 1986 or Council Directive 91/674/EEC of 23 December 1991), or in a manner equivalent to consolidated accounts and consolidated annual reports so drawn up,

(c) that the consolidated accounts are audited by one or more persons authorised to audit accounts under the law under which that other parent undertaking which draws them up is established,

(d) that the exempted parent discloses in its individual accounts that it is exempt from the obligation to prepare and deliver group accounts,

(e) that the exempted parent states in its individual accounts the name of that other parent undertaking which draws up the group accounts referred to in subparagraph (d) and—

(i) where that other parent undertaking is incorporated outside the State, the country in which it is incorporated, or

(ii) where that other parent undertaking is unincorporated, the address of its principal place of business,

(f) that the exempted parent delivers to the registrar, within the period allowed for delivering its individual accounts, copies of that other parent's group accounts and, where appropriate, of the consolidated annual report, together with the auditors' report on them, and

(g) where any document comprised in accounts and reports delivered in accordance with paragraph (f) is in a language other than the English language or the Irish language, there is annexed to the copy of that document delivered a translation of it into the English language or the Irish language, certified in the prescribed manner to be a correct translation.

(4) The exemption under this Regulation does not apply to a parent undertaking any of whose securities are admitted to trading on a regulated market of any EEA State.

(5) Shares held by directors of a company for the purpose of complying with any share qualification requirement shall be disregarded in determining for the purposes of paragraph (1)(a) whether the company is a wholly-owned subsidiary.

(6) For the purpose of paragraph (1)(b), shares held by a wholly-owned subsidiary of that other parent undertaking, or held on behalf of that other parent undertaking or a wholly-owned subsidiary, shall be attributed to that other parent undertaking.

(7) In paragraph (4) 'securities' includes—

(a) shares and stock,

(b) debentures, including debenture stock, loan stock, bonds, certificates of deposit and other instruments creating or acknowledging indebtedness,

(c) warrants or other instruments entitling the holder to subscribe for securities falling within subparagraph (a) or (b), and

(d) certificates or other instruments which confer—

(i) property rights in respect of a security falling within subparagraph (a), (b) or (c),

(ii) any right to acquire, dispose of, underwrite or convert a security, being a right to which the holder would be entitled if the holder held any such security to which the certificate or other instrument relates, or

(iii) a contractual right (other than an option) to acquire any such security otherwise than by subscription.][a]

Amendments

a Paragraph 9A inserted by EC(IFRSMA)R 2005 (SI 116/2005), reg 6(h).

Notes

Exemptions for parent undertakings included in non-EEA group accounts: Reg 9A sets out the conditions under which a parent company which itself is a subsidiary of a non-EEA parent company is exempt from the requirement to prepare group accounts. That non-EEA parent company must itself produce group accounts which incorporate the Irish entity and all of its subsidiaries. In particular, to avail of this exemption the group accounts of the non-EEA parent are drawn up in accordance with the provisions of the Seventh Company Law Directive (83/349/EEC) or in a manner equivalent. Use of this exemption therefore requires an analysis of the particular set of consolidated accounts to determine whether they are drawn up in a manner that is consistent with the Seventh Directive.

Guidance on conducting such an assessment is contained in a pronouncement by the Urgent Issues Task Force of the Accounting Standards Board (UITF), UITF abstract 43. UITF 43 also concludes that consolidated accounts of the higher parent prepared in accordance with the Generally Accepted Accounting Principles (GAAP) of certain other jurisdictions, namely US GAAP. Canadian GAAP, and Japanese GAAP will normally meet the test of equivalence with the

Seventh Directive subject to certain considerations. The text of UITF 43 is available on the website of the Accounting Standards Board at http://www.frc.org.uk/asb.

Exclusions from consolidation

10.(1) A subsidiary undertaking need not be included in group accounts where its inclusion is not material for the purposes of Regulation 14(1).

(2) Where two or more undertakings satisfy the requirements of paragraph (1) they shall, notwithstanding that paragraph, be included in group accounts if taken together they are material for the purpose of Regulation 14(1).

Definitions

'group accounts': EC(CGA)R 1992, reg 3(1), reg 13; 'subsidiary undertaking': EC(CGA)R 1992, reg 4.

Notes

Exclusion of immaterial subsidiaries: Subsidiary undertakings may be excluded from the group accounts if, whether looked at in isolation or taken together, their inclusion would not be material for the purpose of ensuring that the accounts give a true and fair view of the state of affairs of the group as a whole.

Exclusion of subsidiaries in respect of which the parent's rights of management are severely restricted: A parent undertaking may exclude a subsidiary undertaking from the group accounts in circumstances where severe long-term restrictions exist which substantially hinder its rights over the assets or management of that subsidiary[1]. According to para 78(c) of Financial Reporting Standard (FRS) No 2,[2] entitled 'Accounting for Subsidiary Undertakings'—

> 'The rights affected must be those by reason of which the undertaking holding them is the parent undertaking and without which it would not be the parent undertaking. Severe long-term restrictions justify excluding a subsidiary undertaking from consolidation only where the effect of those restrictions is that the parent undertaking does not control its subsidiary undertaking. Severe long-term restrictions are identified by their effect in practice rather than by the way in which the restrictions are imposed. For example, a subsidiary undertaking should not be excluded because restrictions are threatened or because another party has the power to impose them unless such threats or the existence of such a power has a severe and restricting effect in practice in the long-term on the rights of the parent undertaking. Generally, restrictions are dealt with better by disclosure than non-consolidation. However, the loss of the parent undertaking's control over its subsidiary undertaking resulting from severe long-term restrictions would make it misleading to include that subsidiary undertaking in the consolidation.'

Examples of long-term restrictions which would justify exclusion from the group accounts include situations where the subsidiary undertaking is in liquidation or receivership.[3]

1 EC(CGA)R 1992, reg 11(a).

2 Issued by the Accounting Standards Board and the Institute of Chartered Accountants in Ireland.

3 FRS No 2, para 78(c)). As to the manner in which such subsidiaries should be treated in the accounts, see FRS No 2, para 79(a).

Exclusion of subsidiary because of disproportionate expense or delay: A subsidiary undertaking may also be excluded from the group accounts if the information concerning its affairs, which would otherwise have to be included in the accounts, cannot be obtained without disproportionate expense or delay[1]. However, it would still appear that the entitlement to make such an exclusion is still subject to the overriding requirement that the information should not be omitted if it is material for the purpose of ensuring that the accounts give a true and fair view of the group as a whole[2].

1 EC(CGA)R 1992, reg 11(b)). This section replicates CA 1963, s 150(2)(b)(i).

2 See EC(CGA)R 1992, reg 14(1) and FRS No 2, para 24.

Exclusion of a subsidiary which is to be resold: If the shares of a subsidiary undertaking are held exclusively with a view to their subsequent resale, that subsidiary may be excluded from the group accounts. According to FRS No 2,[1] para 11, an interest is held 'exclusively with a view to ... subsequent resale' if it is—

'(a) an interest for which a purchaser has been identified or is being sought, and which is reasonably expected to be disposed of within approximately one year of its date of acquisition; or

(b) an interest that was acquired as a result of the enforcement of a security, unless the interest has become part of the continuing activities of the group or the holder acts as if it intends the interest to become so.'

Furthermore, FRS, para 78(d) states that an interest may also be regarded as being held exclusively for resale where the sale has not been completed within one year of the date of acquisition provided that on the date the accounts are signed, the terms of the sale have been agreed and the process of disposing of the interest in the shares is substantially complete.[2]

1 Issued by the Accounting Standards Board and the Institute of Chartered Accountants in Ireland.

2 As to the manner in which such subsidiaries should be treated in the accounts, see FRS No 2, para 79(b).

---

11. A subsidiary undertaking need not be included in group accounts where:

(a) severe long-term restrictions substantially hinder the parent undertaking in the exercise of its right over the assets or management of that subsidiary undertaking, or

(b) the information necessary for the preparation of group accounts in accordance with these Regulations cannot be obtained without disproportionate expense or undue delay, or

(c) the shares of the subsidiary undertaking are held by the parent undertaking exclusively with a view to their subsequent resale.

Definitions

'group accounts': EC(CGA)R 1992, reg 3(1), reg 13; 'parent undertaking': EC(CGA)R 1992, reg 3(1); 'subsidiary undertaking': EC(CGA)R 1992, reg 4.

Notes

Exclusion of subsidiaries from group accounts: See EC(CGA)R 1992, reg 10 and the notes thereto.

---

12. [...][a]

Amendments

a Regulation 12 deleted by EC(IFRSMA)R 2005 (SI 116/2005), reg 6(i).

General provisions in relation to group accounts

13. For the purpose of these Regulations group accounts shall comprise—

(a) a consolidated balance sheet dealing, as provided for in these Regulations, with the state of affairs of the parent undertaking and its subsidiary undertakings as a whole,

(b) a consolidated profit and loss account dealing, as provided for in these Regulations, with the profit or loss of the parent undertaking and its subsidiary undertakings as a whole, and

(c) notes on the accounts giving additional information as provided for in these Regulations.

Definitions

'group accounts': EC(CGA)R 1992, reg 3(1), reg 13; 'parent undertaking': EC(CGA)R 1992, reg 3(1); 'subsidiary undertaking': EC(CGA)R 1992, reg 4.

Notes

Obligation to lay group accounts before AGM of parent undertaking: In addition to laying its own annual accounts before the members at the AGM, the parent undertaking must also lay before them a copy of the group accounts as prepared in accordance with the provisions of these regs.[1]

1 EC(CGA)R 1992, reg 5(1).

14.(1) Group accounts shall give a true and fair view of the state of affairs as at the end of the financial year and the profit or loss for the financial year of the parent undertaking and subsidiary undertakings as a whole.

(2) Where group accounts drawn up in accordance with these Regulations would not provide sufficient information to comply with paragraph (1), any necessary additional information shall be provided in those accounts.

(3) Where, owing to special circumstances, the preparation of group accounts in accordance with Regulations 15 to 36 and the Schedule would prevent those accounts from complying with paragraph (1) (even if additional information were provided under paragraph (2) of this Regulation), the directors of the parent undertaking shall depart from the requirements of those Regulations in preparing those group accounts so far as is necessary in order to comply with that paragraph.

(4) Where, pursuant to paragraph (3), the directors of a parent undertaking depart from the requirements of these Regulations, they shall attach a note to the group accounts giving details of the particular departures made, the reasons therefor and the effect of those departures on the group accounts.

Definitions

'group accounts': EC(CGA)R 1992, reg 3(1), reg 13; 'parent undertaking': EC(CGA)R 1992, reg 3(1); 'subsidiary undertaking': EC(CGA)R 1992, reg 4.

Notes

True and fair view: EC(CGA)R 1992, reg 14 imposes an overriding obligation that the group accounts should give a true and fair view of the state of affairs of the parent undertaking and subsidiary undertakings as a whole.[1] To a large extent, the provisions of EC(CGA)R 1992 are themselves determinative as to what constitutes a properly prepared set of group accounts. However, to the extent that the legislation is silent on any particular matter, compliance with the relevant financial reporting framework, including accounting standards, in preparing group accounts will be strong, but not conclusive evidence that the accounts give a 'true and fair view' of the group's financial position.[2]

Indeed, even where the legislation specifically deals with an aspect of the accounts, a departure will be permitted if strict adherence would result in the 'true and fair view' not being achieved.[3] Details of the departure must, however, be given in the notes to the accounts together with the reasons therefor.[4]

See also section 205A of CA 1990, s 205A and notes thereon.

1 EC(CGA)R 1992, reg 14(1).

2 *Dolan v AB Ltd* [1969] IR 282; *Lloyd Cheyham & Co Ltd v Littlejohn & Co* [1987] BCLC 303; *IRC v Duple Motor Bodies Ltd* [1961] 1 WLR 739. The recognised practices of the accountancy profession may be found in its Statements of Standard Accounting Practice (SSAPs) and in its Auditing Guidelines.

3 EC(CGA)R 1992, reg 14(3).

4 EC(CGA)R 1992, reg 14(4).

Format of accounts

15.(1) Section 4 and the Schedule to the 1986 Act shall apply to group accounts prepared in compliance with these Regulations as they apply to annual accounts prepared under that Act, with any necessary modifications to take account of differences between group accounts and annual accounts or the provisions of these Regulations.

(2) In particular, for the purposes of paragraph 45 of the Schedule to the 1986 Act, as substituted by Paragraph 4(2) of the Schedule to these Regulations, (dealings with or interests in group undertakings) as it applies to group accounts—

(a) any subsidiary undertakings of the parent undertaking not dealt with in the group accounts shall be treated as a subsidiary undertaking of the group, and

(b) if the parent undertaking is itself a subsidiary undertaking, the group shall be treated as a subsidiary undertaking of any parent undertaking of the parent undertaking, and the reference to fellow subsidiary undertakings shall be construed accordingly.

(3) Where, in the opinion of the directors, undue expense would be incurred in showing separately items B.I1 to B.I4 in Balance Sheet Formats 1 and 2, those items may be combined in the group balance sheet and shown as a single item under the heading 'Stocks'.

Definitions

'group accounts': EC(CGA)R 1992, reg 3(1), reg 13; '1986 Act': EC(CGA)R 1992, reg 3(1); 'parent undertaking': EC(CGA)R 1992, reg 3(1); 'subsidiary undertaking': EC(CGA)R 1992, reg 4.

Notes

Dealings with or interests in group undertakings: The effect of EC(CGA)R 1992, reg 15(2) is that even though certain subsidiary undertakings may have been excluded from the group accounts,[1] details must be given, either in the balance sheet or in the notes to the accounts, of any other members of the group's dealings with or interests in those excluded subsidiary undertakings during the relevant financial year.

[1] For the circumstances in which such exclusion is permissible, see EC(CGA)R 1992, regs 10–11.

Group balance sheet and group profit and loss account

16. The group balance sheet and group profit and loss account shall combine in full the information contained in the separate balance sheets and profit and loss accounts of the parent undertaking and of the subsidiary undertakings included in the group accounts but with adjustments required or permitted under these Regulations.

Definitions

'group accounts': EC(CGA)R 1992, reg 3(1), reg 13; 'parent undertaking': EC(CGA)R 1992, reg 3(1); 'subsidiary undertaking': EC(CGA)R 1992, reg 4.

Notes

Format and content of annual accounts of parent undertaking and individual subsidiary undertakings: The form and content of a company's annual accounts were originally governed by CA 1963, s 149. Over the last three decades, however, the relevance and applicability of these provisions have been largely eroded by the following enactments:

C(A)A 1986: This Act gives legal effect to Council Directive 78/660/EEC. It governs the format and contents of the annual accounts of all private and public limited companies[1] other than—

- (a) companies not trading for the acquisition of gain by its members;[2]
- (b) religious charitable companies limited by guarantee;[3]
- (c) any charitable company limited by guarantee in respect of which the Commissioners of Charitable Donations and Bequests for Ireland have made an order exempting it from the obligation to annex its accounts to the annual return;[4]
- (d) licensed banks;[5]
- (e) certified trustee savings banks;[6]
- (f) other companies engaged in the business of accepting deposits or other repayable funds or granting credit for its own account;[7]
- (g) companies engaged solely in the making of hire-purchase agreements and credit-sale agreements;[8] and
- (h) authorised life and non-life insurance companies.[9]

EC(CI:A)R 1992: These regs which give effect to Council Directive 86/635/EEC, govern the form and content of annual accounts for banks and other financial institutions.

EC(A)R 1993: These regs give legal effect, *inter alia*, to Council Directive 90/605/EEC and govern the format and content of the annual accounts for unlimited companies in circumstances where, broadly speaking, the members of the company are themselves either Irish or foreign limited companies.[10]

EC(IUA)R 1996: These regs implement Council Directive 91/674/EEC and govern the form and content of annual accounts for insurance companies to which the European Communities (Non-Life Insurance) Regs 1976 or the European Communities (Life Assurance) Regs 1984 apply, as well as reinsurance companies.

However, more recently the EC(IFRSMA)R 2005 (SI 116/2005) have made fundamental changes to the companies acts provisions as regards the preparation of accounts.

EC(IFRSMA)R 2005 was a direct consequence of Council Regulation (EC) No 1606/2002 of the European Parliament and of the Council. This reg applied directly to the group accounts of listed entities throughout the European Union by requiring these to be prepared in accordance with International Financial Reporting Standards ('IFRS').

The main purpose of the IFRS regs was to avail of a number of EU member state options contained in Council Regulation (EC) 1606/2002 of the European Parliament of the Council ('the EU IAS reg). The EU IAS reg requires all listed entities required to prepare consolidated (or group) accounts to do so in accordance with International Financial Reporting Standards ('IFRS') as adopted for use in the European Union. IFRS (previously known as International Accounting Standards or 'IAS') are issued by the International Accounting Standards Board ('IASB'). Each IFRS requires formal adoption by the European Union, after which, when published in the Official Journal, has full legal recognition.

The EU IAS reg also allows member states to 'permit or require' the use of IFRS for the preparation of individual company accounts, regardless of whether such companies are listed or not. In implementing the IFRS regs, Ireland has opted for a permissive regime and the following choices have been reflected in CA 1963:

(i) debt-only listed parent companies may avail of an option not to prepare group accounts in accordance with IFRS until accounting periods beginning on or after 1 January 2007; and

(ii) all other companies have the option to use IFRS in preparing their group or individual accounts.

Therefore, as a result of the IFRS regs, all companies and groups (that are not directly impacted by the EU IAS reg) have a choice as to the financial reporting framework they apply in preparing their individual and group accounts.

The choice is not available to the following types of company:

(i) a company not trading for the acquisition of gain by members;

(ii) a company not having a share capital formed for charitable purposes (see CA 1963, s 128(4)(c);

(iii) a company in respect of which an order under CA 1963, s 128(5) is in force.

Such companies must continue to prepare Companies Act accounts. Companies Act accounts are prepared in accordance with the formats accounting requirements of the Companies Acts, including EC(CI:A) R 1992 (SI 294/1992), EC(A)R 1993 (SI 396/1993), and EC(IUA)R 1996 (SI 23/1996), and accounting standards. The applicable standards are the Financial Reporting Standards ('FRS') issued by the Accounting Standards Board ('ASB') and promulgated in the Republic of Ireland by the Institute of Chartered Accountants in Ireland.

Generally, if a company opts to move from preparing Companies Act accounts to IFRS accounts is a one-way street. Such a company may not subsequently revert to preparing Companies Act accounts except where there has been a 'relevant change of circumstances'. Subsection 5 sets out the situations when such a change may arise.

The IFRS regs apply to accounting periods beginning on or after 1 January 2005.

As a result of EC(IFRSMA)R 2005, CA 1963, ss 148–151 were repealed and replaced by new ss 148, 149, 149A, 150, 150A, 150B, 150C and 151. A principal consequence of this, the primary obligation to prepare financial statements previously contained in C(A)A 1986, s 3 and EC(G:AR) 1992, reg 5, EC(CI:A) R, 1992, EC(IUA)R, 1996 is now contained in CA 1963, s 148 (individual accounts) and CA 1963, s 150 (group accounts), irrespective of what type of company is involved – eg general companies, credit institutions, or insurance undertakings.

See also notes to CA 1963, ss 148–151.

1 C(A)A 1986, s 1(1).
2 C(A)A 1986, s 2(1)(a).
3 C(A)A 1986, s 2(1)(b).
4 C(A)A 1986, s 2(1)(c).
5 C(A)A 1986, s 2(2)(a).
6 C(A)A 1986, s 2(2)(b).
7 C(A)A 1986, s 2(2)(d).
8 C(A)A 1986, s 2(2)(g).
9 C(A)A 1986, s 2(3).
10 EC(A)R 1993, reg 6. The regs also apply to partnerships.

Acquisition and merger accounting

17.(1) The provisions set out in Regulations 18 to 22 shall apply where an undertaking becomes a subsidiary undertaking of the parent undertaking.

(2) The event described in paragraph (1) is referred to in those provisions as an 'acquisition', and references to the 'undertaking acquired' shall be construed accordingly.

Definitions

'parent undertaking': EC(CGA)R 1992, reg 3(1); 'subsidiary undertaking': EC(CGA)R 1992, reg 4.

Notes

Acquisition and merger accounting: This refers to the accounting methods to be adopted when one undertaking becomes a subsidiary of another. Prior to the making of these regs, such accounting methods were on a non-statutory footing only and were governed by SSAP 22 and SSAP 23.

18. An acquisition shall be accounted for by the acquisition method of accounting unless the conditions for accounting for it as a merger are met and the merger method of accounting is adopted.

Definitions

'acquisition': EC(CGA)R 1992, reg 17(2).

19.(1) The acquisition method of accounting is as follows.

(2) The identifiable assets and liabilities of the undertaking acquired shall be included in the consolidated balance sheet at their fair values as at the date of acquisition. In this

paragraph the 'identifiable assets or liabilities' means the assets or liabilities which are capable of being disposed of or discharged separately, without disposing of a business of the undertaking.

(3) The income and expenditure of the undertaking acquired shall be brought into the group accounts only as from the date of acquisition.

(4) There shall be set off against the acquisition cost of the interest in the shares of the undertaking held by the undertakings dealt with in the group accounts, the interest of the undertakings dealt with in the group accounts in the adjusted capital and reserves of the undertaking acquired.

For this purpose—

'the acquisition cost' means the amount of any cash consideration and the fair value of any other consideration, together with such amounts (if any) in respect of fees and other expenses of the acquisition as the parent undertaking may determine, and

'the adjusted capital and reserves' of the undertaking acquired means its capital and reserves at the date of the acquisition after adjusting the identifiable assets and liabilities of the undertaking to fair values as at that date.

(5) The resulting amount if positive shall be treated as goodwill and the provisions of the Schedule to the 1986 Act in relation to goodwill shall apply.

(6) The resulting amount if negative shall be treated as a negative consolidation difference.

Definitions

'group accounts': EC(CGA)R 1992, reg 3(1), reg 13; 'undertakings dealt with in the group accounts': EC(CGA)R 1992, reg 3(1), reg 32; '1986 Act': EC(CGA)R 1992, reg 3(1); 'parent undertaking': EC(CGA)R 1992, reg 3(1); 'undertaking' EC(CGA)R 1992, reg 3(1); 'undertaking acquired': EC(CGA)R 1992, reg 17(2).

20.(1) Paragraph (2) shall apply where a parent undertaking acquired a subsidiary undertaking before the introduction of these Regulations but has not previously included that subsidiary undertaking in its group accounts.

(2) For the purposes of applying the acquisition method of accounting in accordance with Regulation 19, where:

- (a) there is no record of—
  - (i) the fair values as at the date of acquisition of the identifiable assets and liabilities of the undertaking acquired, or
  - (ii) the acquisition cost of the interest in the shares of the acquired undertaking held by the undertakings dealt with in the group accounts, or
- (b) where any such records cannot be obtained without unreasonable expense or delay,

the values of the identifiable assets and liabilities and the acquisition cost shall be taken to be the values and cost ascribed to them in the earliest available record made after the acquisition of that subsidiary undertaking.

Definitions

'group accounts': EC(CGA)R 1992, reg 3(1), reg 13; 'undertakings dealt with in the group accounts': EC(CGA)R 1992, reg 3(1), reg 32; 'parent undertaking': EC(CGA)R 1992, reg 3(1); 'subsidiary undertaking': EC(CGA)R 1992, reg 4.

21.(1) The conditions for accounting for an acquisition as a merger are—

(a) that at least 90 per cent of the nominal value of the relevant shares in the undertaking acquired is held by or on behalf of the undertakings dealt with in the group accounts,

(b) that the proportion referred to in paragraph (a) was attained pursuant to the arrangement providing for the issue of equity shares by the undertakings dealt with in the group accounts,

(c) that the fair value of any consideration other than the issue of equity shares given pursuant to the arrangement by the undertakings dealt with in the group accounts did not exceed 10 per cent of the nominal value of the equity shares issued.

(2) The reference in paragraph (l)(a) to the 'relevant shares' in an undertaking acquired is to those carrying unrestricted rights to participate both in distributions and in the assets of the undertaking upon liquidation.

Definitions

'group accounts': EC(CGA)R 1992, reg 3(1), reg 13; 'undertakings dealt with in the group accounts': EC(CGA)R 1992, reg 3(1), reg 32; 'acquisition': EC(CGA)R 1992, reg 17(2); 'undertaking acquired': EC(CGA)R 1992, reg 17(2); 'undertaking' EC(CGA)R 1992, reg 3(1); 'equity share capital': CA 1963, s 155(5).

Notes

Merger: For the purposes of these regs, a merger occurs where Undertaking A, directly and/or through nominees, acquires not less than 90% of the 'relevant shares' of Undertaking B in consideration for the allotment to the members of Undertaking B of equity shares in Undertaking B.

22.(1) The merger method of accounting is as follows.

(2) The assets and liabilities of the undertaking acquired shall be brought into the group accounts at the figures at which they stand in the undertaking's accounts, subject to any adjustment authorised or required by these Regulations.

(3) The income and expenditure of the undertaking acquired shall be included in the group accounts for the entire financial year, including the period before the acquisition.

(4) The group accounts shall show corresponding amounts relating to the previous financial year as if the undertaking had been included in the consolidation throughout that year.

(5) There shall be set off against the aggregate of—

(a) the appropriate amount in respect of shares issued by the undertakings dealt with in the group accounts as part of the arrangement referred to in Regulation 20(1)(b) in consideration for the acquisition of shares in the undertaking acquired, and

(b) the fair value of any other consideration for the acquisition of shares in the undertaking acquired, determined as at the date when those shares were acquired,

the nominal value of the issued share capital of the undertaking acquired held by the undertakings dealt with in the group accounts.

(6) The resulting amount shall be shown as an adjustment to the consolidated reserves.

Definitions

'group accounts': EC(CGA)R 1992, reg 3(1), reg 13; 'undertakings dealt with in the group accounts': EC(CGA)R 1992, reg 3(1), reg 32; 'undertaking acquired': EC(CGA)R 1992, reg 17(2); 'undertaking': EC(CGA)R 1992, reg 3(1); 'financial year': CA 1963, s 2(1).

23.(1) Where a group is acquired, Regulations 18 to 22 apply with the following adaptations.

(2) References to shares of the undertaking acquired shall be construed as references to shares of the parent undertaking of the group.

(3) Other references to the undertaking acquired shall be construed as references to the group; and references to the assets and liabilities, income and expenditure and capital and reserves of the undertaking acquired shall be construed as references to the assets and liabilities, income and expenditure and capital and reserves of the group after making the set offs and other adjustments required by these Regulations in the case of group accounts.

Definitions

'group accounts': EC(CGA)R 1992, reg 3(1), reg 13; 'undertaking acquired': EC(CGA)R 1992, reg 17(2); 'undertaking' EC(CGA)R 1992, reg 3(1); 'parent undertaking': EC(CGA)R 1992, reg 3(1).

Methods of consolidation

24.(1) The methods of consolidation shall be applied consistently from one financial year to the next.

(2) If it appears to the directors of a parent undertaking that there are special reasons for departing from the principle specified in paragraph (1), they may so depart, but particulars of the departure, the reasons for it and its effect on the balance sheet and profit or loss of the parent undertaking and subsidiaries as a whole must be disclosed in the notes to the accounts.

Definitions

'group accounts': EC(CGA)R 1992, reg 3(1), reg 13; 'undertakings dealt with in the group accounts': EC(CGA)R 1992, reg 3(1), reg 32; 'director': CA 1963, s 2(1); 'financial year': CA 1963, s 2(1); 'parent undertaking': EC(CGA)R 1992, reg 3(1).

Notes

Departure from previous method of consolidation: The primary requirement of reg 24 is that the methods of consolidation should be applied consistently from one financial year to the next.[1] However, if the directors consider that there are special reasons for so doing, they may depart from this principle provided they give particulars of the nature of the departure, the reasons therefor and the effect thereof, in a note to the accounts.[2] Moreover, they must also ensure that the accounts still meet the overriding requirement of giving a true and fair view of the state of affairs of the group as a whole.[3]

1 EC(CGA)R 1992, reg 24(1).
2 EC(CGA)R 1992, reg 24(2).
3 EC(CGA)R 1992, reg 14.

25. Group accounts shall show the assets, liabilities, state of affairs as at the end of the financial year and profit or loss of the parent undertaking and its subsidiary undertakings dealt with in the group accounts as if they were a single undertaking. In particular:

(i) debts and claims between the undertakings dealt with in the group accounts shall be eliminated from those accounts,

(ii) income and expenditure relating to transactions between the undertakings dealt with in the group accounts shall be eliminated from those accounts,

(iii) where profits and losses resulting from transactions between the undertakings dealt with in the group accounts are included in the book values of assets, they shall be eliminated from those accounts,

(iv) paragraphs (i) to (iii) need not be complied with where the amounts involved are not material for the purpose of giving a true and fair view as required by Regulation 14.

Definitions

'group accounts': EC(CGA)R 1992, reg 3(1), reg 13; 'financial year': CA 1963, s 2(1); 'undertaking' EC(CGA)R 1992, reg 3(1); 'parent undertaking': EC(CGA)R 1992, reg 3(1); 'subsidiary undertaking': EC(CGA)R 1992, reg 4.

Notes

True and fair view: To a large extent, the provisions of EC(CGA)R 1992 are themselves determinative as to what constitutes a properly prepared set of group accounts. However, to the extent that the legislation is silent on any particular matter, compliance with the relevant financial reporting framework, including accounting standards, used in preparing the company's accounts will be strong but not conclusive evidence that the accounts give a 'true and fair view' of the company's financial position.[1]

Indeed, even where the legislation specifically deals with an aspect of the accounts, a departure will be permitted if strict adherence would result in the 'true and fair view' not being achieved.[2] Details of the departure must, however, be given in the notes to the accounts together with the reasons therefor.[3]

See also CA 1990, s 205A and notes thereon.

1 *Dolan v AB Ltd* [1969] IR 282; *Lloyd Cheyham & Co Ltd v Littlejohn & Co* [1987] BCLC 303; *IRC v Duple Motor Bodies Ltd* [1961] 1 WLR 739). The recognised practices of the accountancy profession may be found in its Statements of Standard Accounting Practice (SSAPs) and in its Auditing Guidelines.

2 EC(CGA)R 1992, reg 14(3).

3 EC(CGA)R 1992, reg 14(4).

26.(1) Group accounts must be drawn up as at the same date as the annual accounts of the parent undertaking.

(2) If the financial year of a subsidiary undertaking dealt with in the group accounts differs from that of the parent undertaking, the group accounts shall be drawn up—

(a) from the accounts of the subsidiary undertaking for its financial year last ending before the end of the parent undertaking's financial year provided that year ended no more than three months before that of the parent undertaking, or

(b) from interim accounts drawn up by the subsidiary undertaking as at the end of the parent undertaking's financial year.

Definitions

'group accounts': EC(CGA)R 1992, reg 3(1), reg 13; 'undertakings dealt with in the group accounts': EC(CGA)R 1992, reg 3(1), reg 32; 'financial year': CA 1963, s 2(1); 'parent undertaking': EC(CGA)R 1992, reg 3(1); 'subsidiary undertaking': EC(CGA)R 1992, reg 4.

Notes

Coincidence of financial year for group accounts and parent undertaking's accounts: The group accounts and the parent undertaking's own annual accounts must be drawn up as at the same date.[1] If any subsidiary undertaking has a different financial year, the group accounts must be drawn up from that subsidiary's last annual accounts provided same are made up to a date not less than three months before the end of the parent undertaking's financial year, and otherwise from specifically prepared interim accounts.[2]

1 EC(CGA)R 1992, reg 26(1).

2 EC(CGA)R 1992, reg 26(2).

Coincidence of financial year for parent and subsidiary undertakings: Adjustments to group accounts because of a subsidiary undertaking with a different financial year, may be largely overcome if that undertaking is also a 'subsidiary' within the meaning of CA 1963, s 155. This is because the directors of a holding company are under a duty to secure that except where there are good reasons against it, the financial year of each of its subsidiaries shall coincide with the parent company's own financial year.[1] Furthermore, where it appears desirable to the Minister for a holding company or a subsidiary to extend its financial year, so that the subsidiary's financial year coincides with that of the holding company, and for that purpose to postpone the submission of the annual accounts to an AGM from one calendar year to the next, he may, on the application or with the consent of the directors of the company whose financial year is to be extended, direct that in the case of that company, the submission of annual accounts to an AGM, the holding of an

AGM or the making of an annual return shall not be required in the earlier of the two calendar years.[2]

[1] CA 1963, s 153(1).

[2] CA 1963, s 153(2).

Changes in composition of group

27. If the composition of the undertakings dealt with in the group accounts has changed significantly in the course of a financial year, the group accounts must include information which makes the comparison of successive sets of group accounts meaningful.

Definitions

'group accounts': EC(CGA)R 1992, reg 3(1), reg 13; 'undertakings dealt with in the group accounts': EC(CGA)R 1992, reg 3(1), reg 32; 'financial year': CA 1963, s 2(1); 'undertaking' EC(CGA)R 1992, reg 3(1).

Notes

Changes in composition of group: Where an undertaking has joined or left the group during the course of a financial year, the following information may be appropriate to include in the accounts for the purpose of allowing for a meaningful comparison between one set of group accounts and another:

(a) the name of the undertaking in question;[1]

(b) the extent to which the profit or loss of the group is attributable to that undertaking;[2] and

(c) details of the amount paid by the group for the undertaking, in the event of an acquisition, and details of the amount received, in the case of a disposal, together with details of the effect of the sale or disposal on group cash flow.[3]

[1] Such information is required to be contained in the notes to the accounts in the UK by CA 1985, Sch 4A, para 15.

[2] Such information is required to be contained in the notes to the accounts in the UK by CA 1985, Sch 4A, para 15.

[3] FRS No 1 requires that such information be contained in a note to the cash flow statements.

Valuation

28. In determining the amounts to be included in the group accounts, sections 5 and 6 of, and the valuation methods contained in the Schedule to, the 1986 Act shall apply and shall be applied consistently within those accounts.

Definitions

'group accounts': EC(CGA)R 1992, reg 3(1), reg 13; '1986 Act': EC(CGA)R 1992, reg 3(1).

29.(1) Subject to paragraph (2), a parent undertaking shall apply the same methods of valuation in drawing up group accounts as it applies in drawing up its [individual accounts].[a]

[(2) Subject to Regulation 28, paragraph (1) shall not apply where, in the opinion of the directors, a departure from the provisions of that paragraph is necessary for the purposes of Regulation 14(1) or, where in accordance with section 1 50(2)(a) or (3)(b) of the Principal Act, the parent company prepares IFRS group accounts.][b]

(3) Any application of paragraph (2) and the reasons therefor shall be disclosed in the notes to the group accounts.

Amendments

a Amended by EC(IFRSMA) 2005 (SI 116/2005), reg 6(j)(i).

b Paragraph 2 substituted by EC(IFRSMA) 2005 (SI 116/2005), reg 6(j)(i).

Definitions

'IFRS group accounts': CA 1963, s 2(1); 'individual accounts': CA 1963, s 2(1); 'parent undertaking' EC(CGA)R 1992, reg 3(1).

Notes

Departure from valuation methods used for accounts of parent undertaking: The group accounts may adopt different valuation methods from those used in drawing up the parent undertaking's annual accounts, where the directors deem it necessary to do so to ensure that the group accounts give a true and fair view of the affairs of the group as a whole.[1] Any such departure must be noted in the accounts,[2] and furthermore, the valuation methods actually adopted must still be of a type specified in C(A)A 1986.[3]

1 EC(CGA)R 1992, reg 29(1) and (2). As to what constitutes a 'true and fair view' see EC(CGA)R 1992, reg 14 and the notes thereto.
2 EC(CGA)R 1992, reg 29(3).
3 EC(CGA)R 1992, reg 29(2).

Revaluation of undertakings' assets and liabilities: If the valuation method which is used for the group accounts differs from that used in the annual accounts of any of the members of the group, that member's assets and liabilities will first have to be revalued in accordance with the group valuation method before being included in the group accounts.[1] Such a valuation will not, however, be required, if, without same, the accounts will still give a true and fair view of the affairs of the group as a whole.[2]

1 EC(CGA)R 1992, reg 30(1).
2 EC(CGA)R 1992, reg 30(2)). For the meaning of 'true and fair view' see EC(CGA)R 1992, reg 14 and the notes thereto.

30.(1) Where the assets and liabilities of an undertaking to be dealt with in the group accounts have been valued by a different method to that being used in the group accounts they shall be revalued in accordance with the method used in the group accounts and subject to paragraphs (2) and (3), shall be included in the group accounts on the basis of such revaluation.

(2) The revaluation in paragraph (l) need not be made where it is not material for the purposes of Regulation 14(1).

(3) If in the opinion of the directors of the parent undertaking there are special reasons for departing from the provisions of paragraph (l) they may do so and any such departure and the reasons therefor shall be stated in the notes to the group accounts.

Definitions

'group accounts': EC(CGA)R 1992, reg 3(1), reg 13; 'undertaking' EC(CGA)R 1992, reg 3(1); 'parent undertaking': EC(CGA)R 1992, reg 3(1).

Notes

See the notes to EC(CGA)R 1992, reg 29.

31. Account shall be taken in the group accounts of any difference arising on consolidation between the tax chargeable for the financial year and for preceding financial years and the amount of tax paid or payable in respect of those years, provided that it is probable that an actual charge to tax will arise within the foreseeable future for one of the undertakings dealt with in the group accounts.

Definitions

'group accounts': EC(CGA)R 1992, reg 3(1), reg 13; 'undertakings dealt with in the group accounts': EC(CGA)R 1992, reg 3(1), reg 32; 'financial year: CA 1963, s 2(1); 'undertaking': EC(CGA)R 1992, reg 3(1).

Joint ventures

32.(1) Where a parent undertaking or one of its subsidiary undertakings dealt with in the group accounts manages another undertaking jointly with one or more undertakings not dealt with in the group accounts, that other undertaking ('the joint venture') may, if it is not—

(a) a body corporate, or

(b) a subsidiary undertaking of the parent undertaking,

be proportionally consolidated in the group accounts in proportion to the rights in its capital held by the parent undertaking or the subsidiary undertakings dealt with in the group accounts as the case may be.

(2) The provisions of these Regulations relating to the preparation of group accounts shall apply, with any necessary modifications, to the inclusion of joint ventures in the consolidated accounts by proportional consolidation in accordance with paragraph (1).

Definitions

'group accounts': EC(CGA)R 1992, reg 3(1), reg 13; 'undertakings dealt with in the group accounts': EC(CGA)R 1992, reg 3(1), reg 32; 'undertaking': EC(CGA)R 1992, reg 3(1); 'parent undertaking': EC(CGA)R 1992, reg 3(1); 'subsidiary undertaking': EC(CGA)R 1992, reg 4.

Notes

Joint venture: For the purposes of EC(CGA)R 1992, reg 32 an entity must satisfy the following criteria to constitute a 'joint venture'—

(a) it must be an unincorporated body;

(b) it must not be a subsidiary undertaking of the parent undertaking; and

(c) it must be jointly managed with one or more other undertakings not dealt with in the group accounts.

If the entity satisfies (b) and (c) but is a body corporate, it will fall to be dealt with, if at all, as an 'associated undertaking' under EC(CGA)R 1992, reg 33.

Associated undertakings

33.(1) The interest of an undertaking dealt with in the group accounts in an associated undertaking, and the amount of profit or loss attributable to such an interest, shall be shown in the group accounts by way of the equity method of accounting including dealing with any goodwill arising in accordance with paragraphs 5 to 7 and 9 of the Schedule to the 1986 Act.

(2) Where the associated undertaking is itself a parent undertaking, the net assets and profits or losses to be taken into account are those of the parent and its subsidiary undertakings (after making any consolidation adjustments).

(3) The equity method of accounting need not be applied if the amounts in question are not material for the purpose of giving a true and fair view.

Definitions

'associated undertaking': EC(CGA)R 1992, reg 3(1), reg 34; 'group accounts': EC(CGA)R 1992, reg 3(1), reg 13; 'undertakings dealt with in the group accounts': EC(CGA)R 1992, reg 3(1), reg 32; '1986 Act': EC(CGA)R 1992, reg 3(1); 'undertaking': EC(CGA)R 1992, reg 3(1); 'parent undertaking': EC(CGA)R 1992, reg 3(1).

Notes

Meaning of 'associated undertaking': An 'associated undertaking' is defined as one in which an undertaking dealt with in the group accounts has a 'participating interest'[1] and over whose operating and financial policy it exercises a significant influence and which is neither a subsidiary undertaking of the parent undertaking nor a 'joint venture' which has proportionally consolidated into the accounts under reg 32.[2] It will be presumed, unless the contrary is shown, that one undertaking exercises a significant influence over the operating and financial policy of another, in circumstances where it holds 20% or more of the voting rights in that other undertaking.[3] In SSAP 1 it is stated at para 13 that 'significant influence' is not to be necessarily equated with 'control.' It suggests that having representation at board level is indicative but by no means conclusive of a 'significant influence'.

Inclusion of associated undertakings: Unlike subsidiary undertakings, the affairs of 'associated undertakings' are not fully consolidated into the group accounts. Instead, the accounts must simply include details of the parent undertaking's interest in the associated undertaking together with details of the amount of profit or loss attributable to that interest.[4] If the associated undertaking is itself a parent undertaking, the net assets and profits or losses of its own subsidiary undertakings will have to be taken into account in ascertaining amount of the profit or loss attributable to the interest in the associated undertaking.[5]

1 For the meaning of 'participating interest' see EC(CGA)R 1992, reg 34.

2 EC(CGA)R 1992, reg 34(1).

3 EC(CGA)R 1992, reg 34(2)). The same rules apply in determining whether or not at least 20% of such voting rights are held as apply in determining whether one undertaking holds a majority of voting rights in another undertaking so as to make one undertaking a subsidiary of the other: EC(CGA)R 1992, reg 34(3).

[4] EC(CGA)R 1992, reg 33(1).
[5] EC(CGA)R 1992, reg 33(2).

34.(1) For the purpose of these Regulations an 'associated undertaking' means an undertaking in which an undertaking dealt with in the group accounts has a participating interest and over whose operating and financial policy it exercises a significant influence and which is not—

(a) a subsidiary undertaking of the parent undertaking, or

(b) a joint venture proportionally consolidated in accordance with Regulation 32.

(2) Where an undertaking holds 20 per cent or more of the voting rights in another undertaking, it shall be presumed to exercise such an influence over it unless the contrary is shown.

(3) Paragraphs (3) and (4) of Regulation 4 shall apply in determining for the purposes of this Regulation whether an undertaking holds 20 per cent or more of the voting rights in another undertaking.

Definitions

'associated undertaking': EC(CGA)R 1992, reg 3(1), reg 34; 'group accounts': EC(CGA)R 1992, reg 3(1), reg 13; 'participating interest': EC(CGA)R 1992, reg 35; 'undertaking': EC(CGA)R 1992, reg 3(1); 'parent undertaking': EC(CGA)R 1992, reg 3(1); 'voting rights': EC(CGA)R 1992, reg 3(4) and (5); 'subsidiary undertaking': EC(CGA)R 1992, reg 4.

Notes

See the notes to EC(CGA)R 1992, reg 33.

Participating interest

35.(1) A 'participating interest' means a qualifying capital interest held by one undertaking in another on a long-term basis for the purpose of securing a contribution to that undertaking's own activities by the exercise of control or influence arising from or related to that interest.

(2) In this Regulation 'qualifying capital interest'

(a) in relation to an undertaking with share capital means an interest in shares comprised in the allotted share capital of that undertaking,

(b) in relation to an undertaking with capital but no share capital means an interest conferring rights to share in the capital of the undertaking,

(c) in relation to an undertaking without capital means interests—

(i) conferring any right to share in the profits or liability to contribute to the losses of the undertaking, or

(ii) giving rise to an obligation to contribute to the debts or expenses of the undertaking in the event of a winding up; and

(d) includes an interest which is convertible into a qualifying capital interest as well as an option to acquire any such qualifying capital interest.

(3) Where an undertaking holds a qualifying capital interest in another undertaking and such an interest represents 20 per cent or more of all such interests in the other

undertaking it shall be presumed to hold that interest on the basis and for the purpose mentioned in paragraph (1) of this Regulation unless the contrary is shown.

(4) The percentage of qualifying capital interests held in an undertaking with share capital shall be the percentage that the nominal value of the shares held represents of the nominal value of the allotted share capital of that undertaking.

(5) For the purpose of this Regulation an interest held on behalf of an undertaking shall be treated as held by it.

(6) [...][a]

(7) In the balance sheet and profit and loss formats set out in the Schedule to the 1986 Act, as amended by the Schedule to these Regulations, 'participating interest' does not include an interest in a group undertaking.

Amendments

a Paragraph 6 deleted by EC(IFRSMA) 2005 (SI 116/2005), reg 6(k).

Definitions

'1986 Act': EC(CGA)R 1992, reg 3(1); 'undertaking': EC(CGA)R 1992, reg 3(1); 'subsidiary undertaking': EC(CGA)R 1992, reg 4.

Notes

Interest held on a long-term basis: EC(CGA)R 1992, reg 35 gives very little guidance as to when an interest in an undertaking is to be regarded as being held 'on a long-term basis for the purpose of securing a contribution to another undertaking's own activities by the exercise of control or influence arising from or related to that interest.' Where the interest represents not less than 20% of all such interests in the undertaking, it shall be presumed to be held on that basis and for that purpose.[1] Ultimately, however, it is a question of fact in each case, and quite conceivably an interest of less than 20% could qualify as well.

Some guidance on the matter is to be found in FRS No 2[2] at para 10 where it is stated that an interest should be deemed to be held 'on a long-term basis' where it is held other than exclusively with a view to subsequent resale.

1 EC(CGA)R 1992, reg 35(3).

2 Issued by the Accounting Standards Board and the Institute of Chartered Accountants in Ireland.

Options and convertible debentures: An interest in debentures which are convertible into shares would constitute a 'qualifying capital interest' as would an option to acquire shares in the company.[3]

1 EC(CGA)R 1992, reg 35(2)(d).

Publication of information

36.(1) Subject to paragraph (2) the information specified in paragraphs 18 to 22 of the Schedule to these Regulations may, in lieu of being stated in the notes to the group accounts for any particular financial year, be given in a statement in writing signed by a director and the secretary of the parent undertaking and annexed to the first annual return made by the parent undertaking next after the group accounts for that year are laid before the annual general meeting of the parent undertaking if, in the opinion of the directors of the parent undertaking, compliance with paragraphs 18 to 22 would require a note to the group accounts of excessive length.

(2) Paragraph (1) of this Regulation shall not apply in relation to information concerning any particular undertaking if the financial state of that undertaking, as disclosed by its accounts, has in the opinion of the directors of the parent undertaking, a substantial effect on the profit or loss, or the amount of the assets of the parent undertaking and its subsidiaries taken as a whole.

(3) A copy of a statement annexed, pursuant to paragraph (1) of this Regulation, to the annual return referred to in that paragraph made by a parent undertaking shall be certified both by a director and the secretary of the parent undertaking to be a true copy of such statement.

Definitions

'group accounts': EC(CGA)R 1992, reg 3(1), reg 13; 'director': CA 1963, s 2(1); 'financial year': CA 1963, s 2(1); 'parent undertaking': EC(CGA)R 1992, reg 3(1); 'subsidiary undertaking': EC(CGA)R 1992, reg 4.

Notes

Information in paragraphs 18 to 22: Paragraphs 18–22 of the Schedule require that details be given of the aggregate amount of 'qualifying capital interests'[1] held by group members in each undertaking, associated undertaking,[2] 'undertaking of substantial interest'[3] and joint venture[4] which is dealt with in the accounts.

1 For the meaning of 'qualifying capital interest' see EC(CGA)R 1992, reg 35(2).

2 For the meaning of 'associated undertaking' see EC(CGA)R 1992, reg 33.

3 For the meaning of 'undertaking of substantial interest' see EC(CGA)R 1992, Sch, para 22(1).

4 For the meaning of 'joint venture' see EC(CGA)R 1992, reg 32.

Information in separate statement rather than in the notes: By including this information in a statement annexed to the annual return, rather than in the notes to the accounts, the directors would seem to be able to avoid presenting such information to the members at the annual general meeting.

Annual return of group accounts: See reg 39 and the notes thereto.

37.(1) In the case of a parent undertaking preparing group accounts in accordance with these Regulations, the report of the directors of that undertaking under section 158 of the Principal Act, shall contain, in addition to the information specified in that section, the following information:

[(a) a fair review of the development and performance of the parent undertaking and of the development and performance of its subsidiary undertakings and of the position of the group as a whole, together with a description of the principal risks and uncertainties that they face, which review—

(i) shall be a balanced and comprehensive analysis of the development and performance of the business and of the position of the undertakings included in the group taken as a whole, consistent with the size and complexity of the business, and

(ii) to the extent necessary for an understanding of such development, performance or position, shall include an analysis of financial, and, where appropriate, non-financial key performance indicators relevant to the particular business, including information relevant to environmental and employee matters,

and, where appropriate, the report shall include additional explanations of amounts included in the group accounts;][a]

(b) particulars of any important events affecting the parent undertaking or any of its subsidiary undertakings which have occurred since the end of that year;

(c) an indication of likely future developments in the business of the parent undertaking and its subsidiary undertakings, taken as a group;

[(d) an indication of the activities, if any, of the parent undertaking and its subsidiary undertakings, taken as a group, in the field of research and development;

(e) the number and nominal value of shares in the parent undertaking held by that undertaking itself, by its subsidiary undertakings or by a person acting in the person's own name but on behalf of those undertakings, and

(f) in relation to the use of financial instruments by the parent undertaking and its subsidiary undertakings, taken as a group, and where material for the assessment of the assets, liabilities, financial position and profit or loss of the parent undertaking and its subsidiary undertakings, taken as a group—

(i) the financial risk management objectives and policies of the parent undertaking and its subsidiary undertakings, taken as a group, including its policies for hedging each major type of forecasted transaction for which hedge accounting is used, and

(ii) the exposure of the parent undertaking and its subsidiary undertakings, taken as a group to price risk, credit risk, liquidity risk and cash flow risk.][b]

(2) The information required by subparagraph (l)(e) may be given in the notes to the group accounts.

(3) Subsections (4) and (5) of section 158 of the Principal Act shall not apply to an undertaking to which this Regulation applies.

Amendments

a Paragraph (a) substituted by EC(IFRSMA) 2005 (SI 116/2005), reg 6(l).

b Paragraphs (d) and (e) substituted and (f) inserted by EC(FVA)R 2004 (SI 765/2004), reg 4.

Definitions

'group accounts': EC(CGA)R 1992, reg 3(1), reg 13; 'Principal Act': EC(CGA)R 1992, reg 3(1); 'director': CA 1963, s 2(1); 'financial year': CA 1963, s 2(1); 'parent undertaking': EC(CGA)R 1992, reg 3(1); 'subsidiary undertaking': EC(CGA)R 1992, reg 4.

Notes

Contents of directors' report: See CA 1963, s 158 and the notes thereto. This reg is the group equivalent of C(A)A 1986, s 13. See also notes to C(A)A 1986, s 13.

Shares held by subsidiary undertaking: With regard to the entitlement of a subsidiary to hold shares in a parent company, see CA 1963, s 32 and CA 1990, s 224 and EC(PLCS)R 1997, reg 5.

---

38. It shall be the duty of the auditors of a parent undertaking, in preparing the report on group accounts required by section 193 of the Companies Act, 1990, to consider whether the information given in the report of the directors on the state of affairs of the parent undertaking and its subsidiary undertakings, as a group, relating to the financial year concerned is consistent with the group accounts for that year and they shall state in the report whether, in their opinion, such information is consistent with those accounts.

Definitions

'group accounts': EC(CGA)R 1992, reg 3(1), reg 13; 'director': CA 1963, s 2(1); 'financial year': CA 1963, s 2(1); 'parent undertaking': EC(CGA)R 1992, reg 3(1); 'subsidiary undertaking': EC(CGA)R 1992, reg 4.

Notes

Contents of auditors' report: See CA 1990, s 193 and CA 1963, s 191(8). This particular reg echoes the provisions of C(A)A 1986, s 15.

39.(1) Subject to the provisions of these Regulations, copies of the following documents shall be documents to be annexed to the annual return of the parent undertaking:

(a) group accounts drawn up by the parent undertaking in accordance with these Regulations;

(b) the report of the directors required by Regulation 37;

(c) the auditor's report referred to in Regulation 38;

and each such copy document shall be certified both by a director, and the secretary, of the parent undertaking to be a true copy of such accounts or reports, as the case may be.

(2) Where any such document is in a language other than the English language or the Irish language, there shall be annexed to each such document a translation in the English language or the Irish language certified in the prescribed manner to be a correct translation.

Definitions

'group accounts': EC(CGA)R 1992, reg 3(1), reg 13; 'director': CA 1963, s 2(1); 'financial year': CA 1963, s 2(1); 'parent undertaking': EC(CGA)R 1992, reg 3(1); 'subsidiary undertaking': EC(CGA)R 1992, reg 4.

Notes

Duty to make annual return and contents thereof: See CA 1963, ss 125–129 and the notes thereto.

40.(1) Where a parent undertaking publishes its full group accounts, it shall also publish with those accounts the auditor's report in relation to those accounts referred to in Regulation 38.

(2) Where a parent undertaking publishes abbreviated group accounts relating to any financial year, it shall also publish a statement indicating—

(a) that the group accounts are not the group accounts, copies of which are required by these Regulations to be annexed to the annual return,

(b) whether the copies of the group accounts so required to be annexed have in fact been so annexed,

(c) whether the auditors of the parent undertaking have made a report under section 193 of the 1990 Act in respect of the group accounts of the parent undertaking which relate to any financial year with which the abbreviated group accounts purport to deal,

[(d) whether any matters referred to in the auditors' report were qualified or unqualified, or whether the auditors' report included a reference to any matters to which the auditors drew attention by way of emphasis without qualifying the report.][a]

(3) Where a parent undertaking publishes abbreviated group accounts, it shall not publish with those accounts the report of the auditors mentioned in subparagraph (2)(c) of this Regulation.

(4) In this Regulation—

'abbreviated group accounts', in relation to a parent undertaking, means any group balance sheet or group profit and loss account, or summary or abstract of a group balance sheet or group profit and loss account, relating to a financial year of the parent undertaking which is published by the parent undertaking otherwise than as part of the full group accounts of the parent undertaking and its subsidiary undertakings for that financial year;

'full group accounts', in relation to a parent undertaking, means group accounts and the report of the directors of the parent undertaking referred to in Regulation 37.

'publish', in relation to a document, includes issue, circulate or otherwise make it available for public inspection in a manner calculated to invite the public generally, or any class of members of the public, to read the document, and cognate words shall be construed accordingly.

Amendments

a Paragraph (d) substituted by EC(IFRSMA) 2005 (SI 116/2005), reg 6(m).

Definitions

'group accounts': EC(CGA)R 1992, reg 3(1), reg 13; '1990 Act': EC(CGA)R 1992, reg 3(1); 'director': CA 1963, s 2(1); 'financial year': CA 1963, s 2(1); 'parent undertaking': EC(CGA)R 1992, reg 3(1); 'subsidiary undertaking': EC(CGA)R 1992, reg 4.

Notes

Publication of group accounts: The reference to publication in EC(CGA)R 1992, reg 40 is to situations such as the publishing of the full or abbreviated accounts of the company in a national newspaper, rather than to the filing of accounts with the annual return.

Publication of annual accounts: With regard to the obligations arising upon the publication of full or abbreviated annual accounts for individual members of the group, see C(A)A 1986, s 19.

Offences

41.(1) If a parent undertaking fails to comply with a provision of Regulation 39 or 40, the parent undertaking and every officer of the undertaking who is in default shall be liable on summary conviction to a fine not exceeding [€1,904.61].[a]

(2) If any person, being a director of a company to which these Regulations apply, fails to take all reasonable steps to secure compliance with a requirement of Regulation 39 or 40, he shall, in respect of each offence, be liable on summary conviction to imprisonment for a term not exceeding 12 months or, at the discretion of the court, to a fine not exceeding [€1,904.61],[a] or to both.

(3) In any proceedings against a person for an offence under paragraph (2) of this regulation, it shall be a defence for a director to prove that he had reasonable grounds to believe and did believe that a competent and reliable person was charged with the duty of ensuring that the provisions of these regulations were complied with and that the latter person was in a position to discharge that duty, and a person shall not be liable to be sentenced to imprisonment for an offence under the said paragraph (2) unless, in the opinion of the court, the offence was committed wilfully.

Amendments

a £1,000 increased to £1,500 by CA 1990, s 240(7) as inserted by CLEA 2001, s 104(c), and converted to €1,904.61 by Council Regulations (EC) No 1103/97, No 974/98 and No 2866/98 and the Economic and Monetary Union Act 1998, s 6.

Definitions

'officer in default': CA 1963, s 383; 'director': CA 1963, s 2(1); 'undertaking': EC(CGA)R 1992, reg 3(1); 'parent undertaking': EC(CGA)R 1992, reg 3(1); 'subsidiary undertaking': EC(CGA)R 1992, reg 4.

Amendments to the 1986 Act

42. [...][a]

Amendments

a This reg inserted CA 1986, s 1(3).

43. [...][a]

Amendments

a This reg amended C(A)A 1986, s 3(2), (3).

44. [...][a]

Amendments

a This reg amended C(A)A 1986, s 16.

45. [...][a]

Amendments

a This reg amended C(A)A 1986, s 17.

46. [...][a]

Amendments

a This reg amended C(A)A 1986, s 19(3).

Schedule

PART 1

AMENDMENTS TO THE SCHEDULE TO THE 1986 ACT

1 [...][a]

Amendments

a This para substituted 'group undertakings' for 'group companies' in C(A)A 1986, Sch.

2 [...][a]

Amendments

a This para substituted 'participating interests' for 'shares in related companies' in C(A)A 1986, Sch.

3 [...][a]

Amendments

a This paragraph substituted 'undertakings in which a participating interest is held' for 'related companies' in C(A)A 1986, Sch.

4 [...][a]

Amendments

a This para substituted C(A)A 1986, Sch, Pt V.

5 [...][a]

Amendments

a This para substituted C(A)A 1986, Sch, para 63.

6 [...][a]

Amendments

a This paragraph substituted C(A)A 1986, Sch, para 64.

7 [...][a]

Amendments

a This paragraph substituted C(A)A 1986, Sch, para 73.

Application of Formats of Schedule to 1986 Act to Group Accounts

Minority Interest

8.(1) In applying Balance Sheet Formats 1 and 2 of the 1986 Act to group accounts a separate item under the heading 'Minority Interest' shall be shown—

(a) in Format 1 after item H, and

(b) in Format 2 under the general heading 'Liabilities', between items A and B.

(2) The amount to be shown under the heading 'Minority Interest' referred to in paragraph (l) shall be the amount of capital and reserves attributable to shares in subsidiary undertakings dealt with in the group accounts held by or on behalf of persons other than the parent undertaking and its subsidiary undertakings.

Definitions

'undertakings dealt with in the group accounts': EC(CGA)R 1992, reg 3(1), reg 32; '1986 Act': EC(CGA)R 1992, reg 3(1); 'group accounts': EC(CGA)R 1992, reg 3(1); 'parent undertaking': EC(CGA)R 1992, reg 3(1); 'subsidiary undertaking': EC(CGA)R 1992, reg 4.

9.(1) In applying Profit and Loss Formats 1, 2, 3 and 4 of the 1986 Act to group accounts a separate item under the heading 'Minority Interest' shall be shown—

(a) in Format 1, between items 14 and 15,

(b) in Format 2, between items 16 and 17,

(c) in Format 3, between items 7 and 8 in both Section A and Section B, and

(d) in Format 4, between items 9 and 10 in both Section A and in Section B.

(2) The amount to be shown under the heading minority interest in accordance with paragraph (l) shall be the amount of any profit or loss on ordinary activities attributable to shares in subsidiaries dealt with in the group accounts held by or on behalf of persons other than the parent undertaking and its subsidiary undertakings.

(3) In applying Profit and Loss Formats 1, 2, 3 and 4 of the 1986 Act to group accounts a separate item under the heading 'Minority Interest' shall be shown—

(a) in Format 1, between items 18 and 19,

(b) in Format 2, between items 20 and 21,

(c) in Format 3, between items 9 and 10 in Section A and between items 8 and 9 in Section B, and

(d) in Format 4, between items 11 and 12 in Section A and between items 10 and 11 in Section B.

(4) The amount to be shown under the heading minority interest in accordance with paragraph (3) shall be the amount of any profit or loss on extraordinary activities attributable to shares in subsidiaries dealt with in the group accounts held by or on behalf of persons other than the parent undertaking and its subsidiary undertakings.

Definitions

'1986 Act': EC(CGA)R 1992, reg 3(1); 'group accounts': EC(CGA)R 1992, reg 3(1); 'subsidiary': CA 1963, s 155; 'parent undertaking': EC(CGA)R 1992, reg 3(1); 'subsidiary undertaking': EC(CGA)R 1992, reg 4.

10.(1) The formats set out in the Schedule to the 1986 Act, as amended by this Schedule, shall have effect in relation to group accounts with the following modifications.

(2) In the Balance Sheet Formats the items headed 'Participating interests', that is—

(a) in Format 1, item A.III.3, and

(b) in Format 2, item A.III.3 under the heading 'ASSETS',

shall be replaced by two items, 'Interests in associated undertakings' and 'Other participating interests'.

(3) In the Profit and Loss Account Formats, the items headed 'Income from participating interests', that is—

(a) in Format 1, item 8,

(b) in Format 2, item 10,

(c) in Format 3, item B.4, and

(d) in Format 4, item B.6,

shall be replaced by two items, 'Income from interests in associated undertakings' and 'Income from other participating interests'.

Definitions

'associated undertaking': EC(CGA)R 1992, reg 3(1), reg 34; '1986 Act': EC(CGA)R 1992, reg 3(1); 'group accounts': EC(CGA)R 1992, reg 3(1).

Part 2
Information required by way of notes to the group accounts

11. Without prejudice to Regulation 15, the notes to the group accounts shall also state the information required by the following provisions of this Part.

Definitions

'group accounts': EC(CGA)R 1992, reg 3(1).

12.(1) In relation to the resulting amounts referred to in Regulation 19(5) and 19(6), there shall be stated in the notes to the group accounts the methods used in calculating those amounts and the reasons for any significant difference between such amounts for the financial year to which the group accounts refer and those for the preceding financial year.

(2) In relation to acquisitions taking place in the financial year, there shall be stated in the notes to the group accounts—

(a) the name and registered office of the undertaking acquired, or where a group was acquired, the name and registered office of the parent undertaking of that group, and

(b) whether the acquisition has been accounted for by the acquisition or the merger method of accounting.

Definitions

'group accounts': EC(CGA)R 1992, reg 3(1); 'financial year': CA 1963, s 2(1); 'parent undertaking': EC(CGA)R 1992, reg 3(1); 'undertaking': EC(CGA)R 1992, reg 3(1); 'undertaking acquired': EC(CGA)R 1992, reg 17(2); 'acquisition': EC(CGA)R 1992, reg 17(2).

13. Where sums originally denominated in currencies, other than the currency in which the group accounts are drawn up, have been brought into account under any items shown in the balance sheet or profit and loss account, the basis on which those sums have been translated into the currency in which the group accounts are drawn up shall be stated.

Definitions

'group accounts': EC(CGA)R 1992, reg 3(1).

14. In respect of the aggregate of the amounts shown in the group balance sheet under the heading 'Creditors' there shall be stated—

(a) the aggregate amount of any debts included under that heading which are payable or repayable otherwise than by instalments and fall due for payment or repayment after the end of the period of five years beginning with the day next following the end of the financial year,

(b) the aggregate amount of any debts so included which are payable or repayable by instalments any of which fall due for payment after the end of that period,

(c) the aggregate amount of any debts included under that heading in respect of which any security has been given, and

(d) an indication of the nature of the securities so given.

Definitions

'financial year': CA 1963, s 2(1).

15.(1) The following information shall be given with respect to the employees of the undertakings dealt with in the group accounts—

(a) the average number of persons employed in the financial year, by the undertakings dealt with in the group accounts, and

(b) the average number of persons employed within each category of persons employed of those undertakings.

(2) In respect of all persons employed by the undertakings dealt with in the group accounts during the financial year who are taken into account in determining the relevant annual number for the purposes of subparagraph (1)(a) of this paragraph, there shall also be stated the aggregate amount of staff costs, save insofar as this amount is stated in the group profit and loss account.

(3) The categories of persons employed by the undertakings included in the group accounts by reference to which the number required to be disclosed by subparagraph (1)(b) is to be determined shall be such as the directors of the parent undertaking may select, having regard to the manner in which the activities of the undertakings dealt with in the group accounts are organised.

(4) For the purposes of clauses (a) and (b) of subparagraph (1) of this paragraph, the average number of persons employed by the undertakings dealt with in the group accounts shall be determined by adding together the averages, for each such undertaking, calculated by the method set out in subparagraph (4) of paragraph 42 of the Schedule to the 1986 Act.

(5) The average number of persons employed during the financial year by an undertaking proportionally consolidated pursuant to Regulation 32, calculated by the manner specified in subparagraph (4), shall also be stated.

Definitions

'undertakings dealt with in the group accounts': EC(CGA)R 1992, reg 3(1), reg 32; '1986 Act': EC(CGA)R 1992, reg 3(1); 'group accounts': EC(CGA)R 1992, reg 3(1); 'financial year': CA 1963, s 2(1); 'director': CA 1963, s 2(1); 'undertaking': EC(CGA)R 1992, reg 3(1); 'parent undertaking': EC(CGA)R 1992, reg 3(1); 'subsidiary undertaking': EC(CGA)R 1992, reg 4.

16.(1) In the case of group accounts, the pension commitments referred to in paragraph 36(4) and the emoluments and compensation referred to in paragraph 39(6) of the Schedule to the 1986 Act shall be to such commitments, emoluments and compensation relating to directors or past directors of the parent undertaking in respect of duties relating to the parent undertaking, to any of its subsidiary undertakings, to any undertakings proportionally consolidated in accordance with Regulation 32, or to associated undertakings.

(2) Section 191 of the Principal Act shall not apply to group accounts prepared in accordance with these Regulations.

Definitions

'associated undertaking': EC(CGA)R 1992, reg 3(1), reg 34; 'Principal Act': EC(CGA)R 1992, reg 3(1); '1986 Act': EC(CGA)R 1992, reg 3(1); 'group accounts': EC(CGA)R 1992, reg 3(1); 'director': CA 1963, s 2(1); 'undertaking': EC(CGA)R 1992, reg 3(1); 'parent undertaking': EC(CGA)R 1992, reg 3(1); 'subsidiary undertaking': EC(CGA)R 1992, reg 4.

[16A. (1) This paragraph applies where financial instruments have been included at fair value pursuant to Part IIIA of the Schedule to the 1986 Act.

(2) There shall be stated—

(a) the significant assumptions underlying the valuation models and techniques where fair values have been determined in accordance with paragraph 22B(4) (inserted by the European Communities (Fair Value Accounting) Regulations 2004) of the Schedule to the 1986 Act,

(b) for each category of financial instrument the fair value of the financial instruments in that category and the amounts—

(i) included in the profit and loss account, and

(ii) credited to or debited from the fair value reserve,

in respect of instruments in that category,

(c) for each class of derivative financial instrument, the extent and nature of the instruments including significant terms and conditions that may affect the amount, timing and certainty of future cash flows, and

(d) a table showing movements in the fair value reserve during the financial year.

16B. Where valuation of financial instruments at fair value has not been applied, for each class of derivative financial instrument there shall be stated—

(a) the fair value of the instruments in that class, if such a value can be determined in accordance with paragraph 22B(1) to (5) (inserted by the European Communities (Fair Value Accounting) Regulations 2004) of the Schedule to the1986 Act, and

(b) the extent and nature of the instruments.][a]

[16C. (1) Sub-paragraph (2) applies where—

(a) a parent undertaking and its subsidiary undertakings taken as a group has financial fixed assets that could be included at fair value by virtue of paragraph 22A (inserted by the European Communities (Fair Value Accounting) Regulations 2004) [or 22AA][b] of the Schedule to the Act of 1986,

(b) the amount at which those assets are included under any item in the accounts of the parent undertaking and the subsidiary undertakings taken as a group is in excess of their fair value, and

(c) the parent undertaking and its subsidiary undertakings taken as a group has not made provision for the diminution in value of those assets in accordance with paragraph 7(1) of the Schedule to the Act of 1986.

(2) There shall be stated—

(a) the amount at which either the individual assets or appropriate groupings of those assets is stated in the company's group accounts,

(b) the fair value of those assets or groupings, and

(c) the reasons for not making a provision for diminution in value of those assets, including the nature of the evidence that provides the basis for the belief that the book value will be recovered.][c]

[16D. (1) This paragraph applies where the amounts to be included in a company's group accounts in respect of investment property or living animals and plants have been determined in accordance with paragraph 22CA (inserted by the European Communities (International Financial Reporting Standards and Miscellaneous Amendments) Regulations 2005) of the Schedule to the Act of 1986.

(2) The balance sheet items affected and the basis of valuation adopted in determining the amounts of net assets concerned in the case of each such item shall be disclosed in a note to the group accounts.

(3) In the case of investment property, for each balance sheet item affected there shall be shown, either separately in the consolidated balance sheet or in a note to the group accounts—

(a) the comparable amounts determined according to the historical cost accounting rules, or

(b) the differences between those amounts and the corresponding amounts actually shown in the consolidated balance sheet in respect of that item.

(4) In subparagraph (3), references in relation to any item to the comparable amounts determined in accordance with that subparagraph are references to—

(a) the aggregate amount which would be required to be shown in respect of that item if the amounts to be included in respect of all the assets covered by that item were determined according to the historical cost accounting rules, and

(b) the aggregate amount of the cumulative provisions for depreciation or diminution in value which would be permitted or required in determining those amounts according to those rules.][d]

Amendments

a Paragraphs 16A and 16B inserted by EC(FVA)R 2004 (SI 765/2004), reg 4.

b Words inserted by European Communities (Directive 2006/46/EC) Regulations 2009, reg 10.

c Paragraph 16C, inserted by EC(FVA)R 2004 (SI 765/2004), reg 4, was substituted by EC(IFRSMA)R 2005 (SI 116/2005), reg 6(r).

d Paragraph 16D inserted by EC(IFRSMA)R 2005 (SI 116/2005), reg 6(o).

17.(1) Subject to subparagraph (2), sections 41 to 43 of the Companies Act, 1990 shall apply to group accounts prepared under these Regulations.

(2) The particulars of any transaction, arrangement or agreement referred to in those sections, entered into with a director of the parent undertaking by an undertaking proportionally consolidated in accordance with Regulation 32, or an associated undertaking, shall be similarly stated.

Definitions

'associated undertaking': EC(CGA)R 1992, reg 3(1), reg 34; 'group accounts': EC(CGA)R 1992, reg 3(1); 'parent undertaking': EC(CGA)R 1992, reg 3(1); 'undertaking': EC(CGA)R 1992, reg 3(1); 'director': CA 1963, s 2(1).

18.(1)(a) The information detailed in subparagraph (2) shall be stated in relation to each undertaking dealt with in the group accounts.

(b) For the purposes of subparagraph (a), the information required by subparagraph (2)(b)(i) does not include such interests in the parent undertaking.

(2) (a) The name and registered office of the undertaking;

(b) (i) the aggregate of the qualifying capital interests held in that undertaking by the undertakings dealt with in the group accounts as a proportion of the total of such interests,

(ii) in this paragraph 'qualifying capital interest' shall have the meanings assigned to it in Regulation 35, and

(iii) for the purposes of this subparagraph, paragraph (4) of Regulation 35 shall apply in determining the percentage of qualifying capital interests held in the undertaking with share capital;

(c) by virtue of which of the provisions of Regulation 4 has the undertaking been dealt with in the group accounts;

(d) the information required by subparagraph (c) may be omitted where the undertaking has been dealt with in the group accounts by virtue of Regulation 4(1)(a), and where the proportion of capital and the proportion of voting rights held are the same.

Definitions

'undertakings dealt with in the group accounts': EC(CGA)R 1992, reg 3(1), reg 32; 'group accounts': EC(CGA)R 1992, reg 3(1); 'undertaking': EC(CGA)R 1992, reg 3(1); 'qualifying capital interest': EC(CGA)R 1992, reg 35(2).

---

19. The information detailed in paragraph 18(2) of this Schedule shall also be given in respect of each undertaking which has been excluded from the group accounts by virtue of the application of Regulations 10 to 12.

Definitions

'group accounts': EC(CGA)R 1992, reg 3(1); 'undertaking': EC(CGA)R 1992, reg 3(1).

20.(1) The information detailed in paragraph 18(2)(a) and (b) shall be stated in relation to each associated undertaking.

(2) The information required by paragraph (1) shall also be stated in relation to associated undertakings, the interest in which has been dealt with in accordance with Regulation 33(3).

Definitions

'associated undertaking': EC(CGA)R 1992, reg 3(1), reg 34.

21.(1) The information detailed in paragraph 18(2)(a) and (b) shall be stated in relation to each undertaking that has been proportionally consolidated in accordance with Regulation 32.

(2) The nature of the joint management of each joint venture proportionally consolidated shall also be stated.

Definitions

'undertaking': EC(CGA)R 1992, reg 3(1); 'joint venture': EC(CGA)R 1992, reg 32.

22.(1) The information set out in paragraph 18(2)(a) and (b) shall be stated in relation to each undertaking ('undertaking of substantial interest'), other than those referred to in paragraphs 18 to 21 in which undertakings dealt with in the group accounts and undertakings not dealt with by virtue of the application of Regulation 12, or persons acting in their own name but on behalf of such undertakings, between them hold a qualifying capital interest representing 20 per cent or more of such interests.

(2) There shall also be stated in relation to each undertaking of substantial interest, the amount of its capital and reserves and its profit or loss for its latest financial year for which accounts have been adopted.

(3) The information required by subparagraphs (1) and (2) may be omitted, where for the purposes of Regulation 14, it is of negligible importance.

(4) The information concerning capital and reserves and the profit or loss required by subparagraph (2) may also be omitted where the undertaking concerned is not required to attach its balance sheet to its annual return and where the qualifying capital interest held as described in subparagraph (1) is less than 50 per cent.

(5) For the purposes of this paragraph, paragraph (4) of Regulation 35 shall apply in determining the percentage of qualifying capital interests held in an undertaking with share capital.

Definitions

'undertakings dealt with in the group accounts': EC(CGA)R 1992, reg 3(1), reg 32; 'group accounts': EC(CGA)R 1992, reg 3(1); 'undertaking': EC(CGA)R 1992, reg 3(1); 'qualifying capital interest': EC(CGA)R 1992, reg 35(2).

23. For the avoidance of doubt, paragraphs 34, 36(5) and 42 (except subparagraph (4) as applied by paragraph 15(4) of this Schedule), of the Schedule to the 1986 Act shall not apply to group accounts prepared in accordance with these Regulations.

Definitions

'1986 Act': EC(CGA)R 1992, reg 3(1); 'group accounts': EC(CGA)R 1992, reg 3(1).

EXPLANATORY NOTE

(*This note is not part of the Instrument and does not purport to be a legal interpretation*).

The purpose of these Regulations is to give legal effect to a Council Directive (No. 83/349/EEC) on the co-ordination of national legislation on consolidated accounts.

The Regulations require Irish limited companies which have subsidiary undertakings to draw up group accounts comprising a consolidated balance sheet, a consolidated profit and loss account and notes to the accounts. The Regulations define when one undertaking is a subsidiary of another for the purposes of the preparation of the group accounts. They provide for exemptions from the requirement to prepare group accounts in particular circumstances and under specified conditions. They also allow the exclusion of some subsidiaries from the group accounts in certain specified circumstances.

The Regulations contain provisions governing the preparation of group accounts, the content of those accounts, their format and the valuation of items to be included therein. They also specify information to be included in the notes to the group accounts.

The Regulations stipulate what is to be included in the report of the directors of a parent undertaking and provide for the examination of such reports by the auditors to assess their consistency with the group accounts.

The Regulations also provide for the making available to the public of group accounts prepared in accordance with their provisions.

The Regulations contain some provisions relating to annual accounts which are consequential to the provisions of Council Directive 83/349.EEC.

Companies Act 1990 (Auditors) Regulations 1992

SI 259/1992

WHEREAS certain difficulties have arisen in regard to the implementation in Part X of the Companies Act, 1990 (No. 33 of 1990), of Council Directive No. 84/253/EEC of 10 April, 1984,[1] on the approval of persons responsible for carrying out the statutory audits of accounting documents;

AND WHEREAS it appears to me to be necessary for the purpose of implementing the said Directive to modify certain provisions of the said Part X;

NOW I, DESMOND O'MALLEY, Minister for Industry and Commerce, in exercise of the powers conferred on me by section 201 of the Companies Act, 1990, hereby make the following Regulations:

1 (1) These Regulations may be cited as the Companies Act, 1990 (Auditors) Regulations, 1992.

(2) These Regulations shall come into operation on the 21st day of September, 1992.

Notes

These regs were introduced because of difficulties in implementing certain provisions of CA 1990, Pt X. Primarily these related to uncertainty as to whether 'firms' as well as natural persons were eligible for appointment as statutory auditors. SI 259/1992 clarified that a firm was eligible for appointment as auditor provided it met the specified criteria.

These regs were incorporated into CA 1990, Pt X by C(AA)A 2003 (see CA 1990. Pt X) and the Regulations themselves were repealed by s 59 of that Act.

However, at the time of writing, these amendments have not yet been commenced.

---

2 In these Regulations, "the Act" means the Companies Act, 1990 (No. 33 of 1990).

3 Subparagraph (iii) of section 187(1)(a) of the Act shall not be regarded as having been complied with by a person appointed to be the auditor of a company or a public auditor unless, both on the 31st day of December, 1990, and on the date of such appointment, he was a member of a body referred to in that subparagraph and on the later date he held a valid practising certificate from that body.

4 (1) Notwithstanding section 187 of the Act, a firm shall be qualified for appointment as auditor of a company or as a public auditor:

Provided that at least one member of the firm is entitled to hold a practising certificate from a body referred to in subparagraph (i), (ii) or (iii) of subsection (1)(a) of that section and is otherwise qualified under the said subparagraph (i), (ii) or (iii), as may be appropriate, and paragraph (b) of subsection (1) of that section for appointment as auditor of a company or as a public auditor.

(2) A practising certificate may be granted by a body referred to in paragraph (1) of this Regulation to a firm that complies with the proviso to that paragraph and, where such a certificate is so granted, it shall be deemed to be held by the member or members of the firm from time to time during the currency of the appointment who so complies or comply.

5 The references in sections 198, 199 and 200 of the Act to the address of a person shall be construed as references to his business address and to the name and address of the head office of any firm of which he is a partner or employee.

6 Information furnished to the registrar of companies pursuant to section 199 or 200 of the Act shall be so furnished in such form and manner as he may specify.

7 (1) Sections 199 and 200 of the Act shall be construed as—

(a) requiring a body of accountants referred to therein, to notify the registrar of companies of any change in the particulars previously furnished to him pursuant to those sections, as soon as may be, but not later than 6 months after its occurrence, and

(b) requiring a person referred to in subsection (3) of either of those sections to notify the registrar of companies—

(i) at least once in each year, if it be the case, that he holds an authorisation referred to in those subsections, and

(ii) as soon as may be, but not later than one month after its occurrence, of his ceasing to hold such an authorisation or of any change in the particulars delivered by him to the registrar of companies under either of those sections.

Explanatory Note

These Regulations modify certain provisions in Part X of the Companies Act, 1990 and are designed to facilitate the proper and effective implementation of EC Council Directive No. 84/253/EEC (OJ No L126 12.5.1984 pp 20–26), provision for the implementation of which is already provided for in that Part of the Act.

European Communities (Credit Institutions: Accounts) Regulations 1992

SI 294/1992

TABLE OF CONTENTS

Regulations

I, BERTIE AHERN, Minister for Finance, in exercise of the powers conferred on me by section 3 of the European Communities Act, 1972 (No. 27 of 1972), and for the purpose of giving effect to Council Directives 86/635/EEC of 8 December 1986[1] and 89/117/EEC of 13 February 1989[2] hereby make the following regulations:

[1] OJ No L372 of 31/12/1986.
[2] OJ No L44 of 16/2/1989.

1 Citation and Construction

(1) These Regulations may be cited as the European Communities (Credit Institutions: Accounts) Regulations, 1992.

(2) These Regulations shall be construed as one with the Companies Acts, 1963 to 1990.

Notes

Scope of Regulations: These Regulations, which give legal effect to Council Directive 86/635/EEC, deal with the following—

(a) the obligation of various types of credit institutions to prepare annual accounts and group accounts; and

(b) the form and content of such accounts.

The need for separate legislation in respect of these institutions arises by virtue of the fact that the accounting provisions of both C(A)A 1986 and EC (GAC) 1992 were expressly stated not to apply to them[1]. The institutions caught by the regs are 'section 2(2) companies'[2] and (in the case of group accounts) 'section 2(2) parent companies'[3].

A 'section 2(2) company' is one incorporated in the State and referred to in C(A)A 1986, s 2(2)(a) or (c)–(g),[4] and comprises the following:

(a) licensed banks;[5]

(b) other companies engaged in the business of accepting deposits or other repayable funds or granting credit for its own account;[6] and

(c) companies engaged solely in the making of hire-purchase agreements and credit-sale agreements;[7] and

A 'section 2(2) parent company' is simply one of the above companies which is also a parent company.[8]

1 See C(A)A 1986, s 2(2) and EC(CGA)R 1992, reg 6.
2 EC(CI:A)R 1992, reg 5.
3 EC(CI:A)R 1992, reg 7.
4 EC(CI:A)R 1992, reg 2(1).
5 C(A)A 1986, s 2(2)(a).
6 C(A)A 1986, s 2(2)(d).
7 C(A)A 1986, s 2(2)(c).
8 EC(CI:A)R 1992, reg 7.

Insurance companies: Authorised life and non-life insurance companies[1] were also excluded from the operation of C(A)A 1986[2] and European Communities (Companies: Group Accounts) Regulations 1992[3], and are now governed instead by European Communities (Insurance Undertakings Accounts) Regulations 1996.

1 C(A)A 1986, s 2(3).
2 C(A)A 1986, s 2(3).
3 EC(CGA)R 1992, reg 2(g).

2 Interpretation

(1) In these Regulations, unless the context otherwise requires—

"accounts" means the balance sheet, profit and loss account and any notes on the accounts or statements forming part of the accounts whether or not required by law;

"annual return" means the annual return made to the registrar of companies under the Principal Act;

"associated undertaking" has the same meaning as in the European Communities (Companies: Group Accounts) Regulations 1992, (S.I. No. 201 of 1992);

["Bank" means the Central Bank and Financial Services Authority of Ireland][a];

"the Directive" means Council Directive 86/635/EEC of 8 December 1986;

"the Principal Act" means the Companies Act, 1963;

"the Act of 1986" means the Companies (Amendment) Act, 1986 (No. 25 of 1986);

"group accounts" means the accounts prepared in accordance with Regulation 7;

"individual accounts" means the accounts prepared in accordance with Regulation 5;

['investment property' means land or buildings (or both) held to earn rentals or for capital appreciation (or both);][b]

"parent company" means a company that has subsidiaries;

"section 2(2) company" means any company incorporated in the State and referred to in subsection (2) (other than paragraph (b)) of section 2 of the Act of 1986;

"section 2(2) parent company" has the meaning assigned to it by Regulation 7(1);

"undertaking" and "subsidiary undertaking" have the same meanings as in the European Communities (Companies: Group Accounts) Regulations, 1992.

[(1A) References in these Regulations to annual accounts giving a 'true and fair view' are references—

(a) in the case of Companies Act individual accounts, to the requirement under Regulation 5 that those accounts give a true and fair view,

(b) in the case of Companies Act group accounts, to the requirement under Regulation 7 that those accounts give a true and fair view, and

(c) in the case of IFRS accounts, to the equivalent requirement under international financial reporting standards.][c]

(2) A word or expression in these Regulations shall have the same meaning as in the Council Directive 86/635/EEC of 8 December 1986 unless the contrary is indicated.

(3) In these Regulations, unless the context otherwise requires, a reference to a regulation is to a regulation of these Regulations, a reference to a paragraph is to the paragraph of the regulation, and a reference to a subparagraph is to the subparagraph of the paragraph, in which the reference occurs.

(4) In these Regulations, unless the context otherwise requires, a reference to a balance sheet or profit and loss account shall include a reference to any notes to or documents annexed to the accounts in question giving information which is required by any provision of the Companies Acts, 1963 to 1990, [these Regulations, or international financial reporting standards][d] and required or allowed by any such provision to be given in a note to or a document annexed to a company's accounts.

(5) In these Regulations:

(i) a reference to directors shall be construed, in the case of an undertaking which does not have a board of directors, as a reference to the corresponding persons appropriate to such undertaking;

(ii) a reference to voting rights in an undertaking means the rights conferred on shareholders in respect of their shares or, in the case of an undertaking not having a share capital, on members, to vote at general meetings of the undertaking on all, or substantially all, matters;

(iii) in relation to an undertaking which does not have general meetings at which matters are decided by the exercise of voting rights, the references to holding a majority of the voting rights in an undertaking shall be construed as references to having the right under the constitution of the undertaking to direct the overall policy of the undertaking to alter the terms of its constitution.

Amendments

a "Bank" definition substituted by CBFSIA 2003, s 35 and Sch 2.

b Inserted by reg 10 and Sch 2, Item No 1(a) of EC(IFRSMA)R 2005 .

c Inserted by reg 10 and Sch 2, Item No 1(b) of EC(IFRSMA)R 2005.

d Inserted by reg 10 and Sch 2, Item No 1(c) of EC(IFRSMA)R 2005.

Definitions

'associated undertaking' EC(CGA)R 1992, reg 34; 'Companies Act group accounts': CA 1963, s 2(1); 'Companies Act individual accounts': CA 1963, s 2(1); 'IFRS accounts': CA 1963, s 2(1); 'international financial reporting standards': CA 1963, s 2(1); subsidiary' CA 1963, s 155; 'undertaking': EC(CGA)R 1992, reg 3(1); 'subsidiary undertaking': EC(CGA)R, reg 4.

Notes

Board of directors: Throughout these regs there are various references to 'undertakings' which are in turn defined by EC (CGA) Regs 1992[1] as including certain types of unincorporated bodies and associations. Because of this fact, it has been necessary to widen somewhat the definition of 'board of directors' to include any equivalent body of persons having responsibility for the management of the undertaking.[2] In the case of a partnership, it would include the partners themselves, whereas in other unincorporated companies, it might be a committee of management or some similarly styled body.

1 EC(CGA)R 1992, reg 3(1).

2 EC(CI:A)R 1992, reg 2(5)(i).

Voting rights: Since an undertaking might not be a company having a share capital, the term 'voting rights' is deemed to include not only a right to vote in respect of shares, but also any right to vote at general meetings 'on all or substantially all matters',[1] as well as a right under the constitution of an undertaking which does not have general meetings at which matters are decided on a vote, to direct overall policy or to alter the terms of its constitution[2].

1 EC(CI:A)R 1992, reg 2(5)(ii).

2 EC(CI:A)R 1992, reg 2(5)(iii).

3 Amendment of Act of 1986

[...][a]

Amendment

a This section inserted CA(A) 1986, s 7(1)(a)(ii). See the amended Act.

Notes

Annual return: The effect of this reg has been to amend C(A)A 1986, s 7, so as to extend the provisions of that Act which deal with the annexing of documents to the annual return, to companies governed by these regs.

4 Date of Application

These Regulations shall apply to the individual and group accounts of a section 2(2) company drawn up in respect of every financial year beginning on or after the 1st day of January 1993 and the requirements of section 7(1)(a)(ii) of the Act of 1986 shall come into operation on that date.

Definitions

'group accounts': European Communities (Credit Institutions: Accounts) Regulations 1992, reg 2(1), reg 7; 'individual accounts': EC(CI:A)R 1992, reg 2(1), reg 5; 'section 2(2) company': EC(CI:A)R 1992, reg 2(1), C(A)A 1986 s 2.

Notes

Amendment to C(A)A 1986: See notes to EC(CI:A)R 1992, reg 3.

5 Drawing up of Accounts

[(1) Subject to paragraph (2), every balance sheet and profit and loss account of a section 2 (2) company laid before the annual general meeting of the company, pursuant to section 148 of the Principal Act shall be prepared in accordance with:

(a) section 149 of the Principal Act as modified by these Regulations, or

(b) international financial reporting standards (in these Regulations referred to as "IFRS individual accounts") and section 149A of the Principal Act as modified by these Regulations,

and in either case shall comply with section 150C of the Principal Act.

(1A) Companies Act individual accounts of a section 2 (2) company prepared in accordance with section 149 of the Principal Act shall comply with the following requirements and section 149 (other than subsection (5) and, insofar as it relates to (5), subsection (7)) of that Act shall not apply to any such balance sheet or profit and loss account:

(a) every such balance sheet and profit and loss account shall comply with the Schedule to these Regulations;

(b) every such balance sheet of a company shall give a true and fair view of the state of affairs of the company as at the end of its financial year and every such profit and loss account of a company shall give a true and fair view of the profit and loss of the company for the financial year;

(c) where a balance sheet or profit and loss account drawn up in accordance with subparagraph (a) would not provide sufficient information to comply with subparagraph (b), any necessary additional information shall be provided in that balance sheet or profit and loss account or in a note to the accounts;

(d) where owing to special circumstances, the preparation of individual accounts of a company in compliance with subparagraph (a) would prevent those accounts from complying with subparagraph (b) (even if additional information were provided under subparagraph (c)) the directors of a company shall depart from the requirements of the Schedule to these Regulations in preparing those accounts insofar as is necessary in order to comply with that subparagraph;

(e) where the directors of a company depart from the requirements of this Regulation, they shall attach a note to the individual accounts of the company giving details of the particular departures made, the reasons therefor and the effect of those departures on the accounts,

and, accordingly, in the Companies Acts 1963 to 2003, in relation to a company to which these Regulations apply—

(i) references to the said section 149 shall be read as references to that section as modified by the provisions of these Regulations, and

(ii) references to the Sixth Schedule of the Principal Act shall be read as references to the corresponding provisions of these Regulations.

(1B) Where the directors of a section 2 (2) company prepare IFRS individual accounts in accordance with international financial reporting standards and section 149A of the Principal Act they shall ensure that instead of making the disclosures specified in section 149A(2) the notes to the accounts include the information required by—

(a) paragraph 74 (4) of Part I of the Schedule to these Regulations (details of directors' remuneration),

(b) sections 41 to 45 of the Companies Act 1990 to be disclosed in individual accounts (transactions with directors),

(c) section 63 of the Companies Act 1990 unless it is disclosed in the directors' report (interests in shares and debentures),

(d) Regulation 10 of these Regulations (details of group undertakings),

(e) paragraph 77 of Part I of the Schedule to these Regulations (details of staff numbers and remuneration),

(f) paragraphs 51 to 54 of Part I of the Schedule to these Regulations (details of share capital and debentures),

(g) paragraph 73(4) of Part I of the Schedule to these Regulations (restriction on distributability of profits),

(h) paragraph 66 of Part I of the Schedule to these Regulations (guarantees and other financial commitments),

(i) paragraph 73(2) of Part I of the Schedule to these Regulations (financial assistance for the purchase of own shares),

(j) paragraph 6 of Part III of the Schedule to these Regulations (shares and debentures held by subsidiary undertakings), and

(k) paragraph 74(3) of Part I of the Schedule to these Regulations and section 205D (inserted by section 44 of the Companies (Auditing and Accounting) Act 2003) of the Companies Act 1990 (auditors' [remuneration), and][a]

[(l) where appropriate, paragraph 66A of Part I of the Schedule.][b]

(2) The references in paragraph (1) to the profit and loss account of a company being laid before the annual general meeting of a company shall not apply to the profit and loss account of a company if the company prepares Companies Acts individual accounts and—

(a) the company is a parent undertaking, and

(b) the company is required to prepare and does prepare Companies Acts group accounts in accordance with these Regulations, and

(c) the notes to the company's individual balance sheet show the company's profit and loss for the financial year determined in accordance with these Regulations.][c]

(3) Where, in the case of a company, advantage is taken of paragraph (2), that fact shall be disclosed in a note to the individual and group accounts of the company.

(4) Subparagraph (b) of paragraph (1) overrides the requirements of the Schedule to these Regulations and all other requirements of the Companies Acts, 1963 to 1990, as to the matters to be included in the accounts of a company or in notes to those accounts and, accordingly, where a balance sheet or profit and loss account of a company drawn up in accordance with those requirements would not provide sufficient information to comply with the said subparagraph, any necessary additional information shall be provided in that balance sheet or profit and loss account or in a note to the accounts.

Amendments

a Words substituted by European Communities (Directive 2006/46/EC) Regulations 2009, reg 14(a)(i).

b Subparagraph (l) inserted by European Communities (Directive 2006/46/EC) Regulations 2009, reg 14(a)(ii).

c Paragraphs (1) and (2) of reg 5 were substituted by reg 10 and Schedule 2, Item No 2 of Sch II Item No 2 of EC(IFRSMA)R 2005.

Definitions

'accounts': EC(CI:A)R 1992, reg 2(1); 'company': CA 1963, s 2(1); 'companies act individual accounts': CA 1963, s 2(1); 'director': CA 1963, s 2(1) and EC(CI:A)R 1992, reg 2(5)(i); 'group accounts': EC(CI:A)R 1992, reg 2(1), reg 7; 'IFRS individual accounts': CA 1963, s 2(1); 'international financial reporting standards': CA 1963 s 2(1)'the Principal Act': EC(CI:A)R 1992, reg 2(1); 'section 2(2) company': EC(CI:A)R 1992, reg 2(1), C(A)A 1986 s 2.

Notes

The European Communities (International Financial Reporting Standards and Miscellaneous Amendments) Regulations 2005, (SI 116/2005) ('EC(IFRSMA)R 2005' have made fundamental changes to the companies acts provisions as regards the preparation of accounts.

It was a direct consequence of Regulation (EC) No. 1606/2002 of the European Parliament and of the Council. This reg applied directly to the group accounts of listed entities throughout the European Union by requiring these to be prepared in accordance with International Financial Reporting Standards ('IFRS').

The main purpose of the EC(IFRSMA)R 2005 was to avail of a number of EU member state options contained in Regulation EC 1606/2002 of the European Parliament of the the Council ('the EU IAS Regulation'). The EU IAS Regulation requires all listed entities required to prepare consolidated (or group) accounts to do so in accordance with International Financial Reporting

Standards ('IFRS') as adopted for use in the European Union. IFRS (previously known as International Accounting Standards or 'IAS') are issued by the International Accounting Standards Board ('IASB'). Each IFRS requires formal adoption by the European Union, after which, when published in the Official Journal, has full legal recognition.

The EU IAS Regulation also allows member states to 'permit or require' the use of IFRS for the preparation of individual company accounts, regardless of whether such companies are listed or not. In implementing the EU IAS Regulation, Ireland has opted for a permissive regime and the following choices have been reflected in CA 1963:

(i) debt-only listed parent companies may avail of an option not to prepare group accounts in accordance with IFRS until accounting periods beginning on or after 1 January 2007; and

(ii) all other companies have the option to use IFRS in preparing their group or individual accounts.

Therefore as a result of the EC(IFRSMA)R 2005, all companies and groups (that are not directly impacted by the EU IAS Regulation) have a choice as to the financial reporting framework they apply in preparing their individual and group accounts.

The choice is not available to the following types of company:

(i) a company not trading for the acquisition of gain by members;

(ii) a company not having a share capital formed for charitable purposes (see section 128(4)(c) of CA 1963); or

(iii) a company in respect of which an order under s 128(5) is in force.

Such companies must continue to prepare Companies Act accounts. Companies Act accounts are prepared in accordance with the formats, accounting requirements of the Companies Acts, including EC(CI:A) R 1992, European Communities (Accounts) Regulations 1993 (SI 396/1993), and EC(IUA)R 1996, and accounting standards. The applicable standards are the Financial Reporting Standards ('FRS') issued by the Accounting Standards Board ('ASB') and promulgated in Ireland by the Institute of Chartered Accountants in Ireland.

Generally, if a company opts to move from preparing Companies Act accounts to IFRS accounts, it is a one-way street. Such a company may not subsequently revert to preparing Companies Act accounts except where there has been a 'relevant change of circumstances'.

The EC(IFRSMA)R 2005 apply to accounting periods beginning on or after 1 January 2005.

As a result of EC(IFRSMA)R 2005, ss 148 to 151 of CA 1963 were repealed and replaced by new sections 148, 149, 149A, 150, 150A, 150B, 150C and 151. A principal consequence of this, the primary obligation to prepare financial statements previously contained in s 3, C(A)A 1986 and Regulation 5 of EC(G:AR) 1992, EC(CI:A) R, 1992, EC(IUA)R, 1996 is now contained in section 148 CA 1963 (individual accounts) and SI 150 CA 1963 (group accounts), irrespective of what type of company is involved eg general companies, credit institutions, or insurance undertakings.

See also notes to ss 148 to 151 of CA 1963.

True and fair view: The basic and overriding requirement for a company's annual accounts is that they should give a 'true and fair view' of the financial state of affairs of the company for the year in question.[1] To a large extent, the provisions of EC(CI:A)R 1992 are themselves determinative as to what constitutes a properly prepared set of annual accounts. However, insofar as the legislation is silent on any particular matter, compliance with the recognised practices and standards of the accountancy profession in preparing the company's accounts will be strong but not conclusive evidence that the accounts give a 'true and fair view' of the company's financial position.[2] Indeed, even where the legislation specifically deals with an aspect of the accounts, a departure will be permitted if strict adherence would result in the 'true and fair view' not being achieved.[3] Details of the departure must, however, be given in the notes to the accounts together with the reasons therefor.[4] With the introduction of International Financial Reporting Standards through EC(IFRSMA)R 2005, a new term, 'presents fairly' entered into financial reporting language. The United Kingdom's Financial Reporting Council, of which the Accounting Standards Board is a constituent body, published a paper in August 2005 entitled 'The implications of new accounting and auditing standards for the 'true and fair view' and auditors' responsibilities'. In this paper, the FRC concludes that the concept of 'true and fair' remains a cornerstone of financial reporting and that the intent and substance of the two expressions 'presents fairly' and 'true and fair' are similar. The paper is available from the FRC website at http://www.frc.org.uk/publications.

1 EC(CI:A)R 1992, reg 5(1)(b)–(d) and reg 5(4).

2 *Dolan v AB Ltd* [1969] IR 282; *Lloyd Cheyham & Co Ltd v Littlejohn & Co* [1987] BCLC 303; *IRC v Duple Motor Bodies Ltd* [1961] 1 WLR 739). The recognised practices of the accountancy profession may be found in its Statements of Standard Accounting Practice (SSAPs) and in its Auditing Guidelines.

3 EC(CI:A)R 1992, reg 5(1)(d).

4 EC(CI:A)R 1992, reg 5(1)(e).

Parent companies: Rather than prepare a separate profit and loss account, a parent company which is required by these Regulations to prepare group accounts[1] may instead disclose the details of its profit and loss for the particular financial year by way of notes to its individual balance sheet.[2] The fact that the parent company has availed of this exemption must also be disclosed in a note to both its individual accounts and its group accounts.[3]

1 The requirement to prepare group accounts is to be found in EC(CI:A)R 1992, reg 7.

2 EC(CI:A)R 1992, reg 5(2).

3 EC(CI:A)R 1992, reg 5(3).

---

6 Publication of Accounts in Full or Abbreviated Form

(1) Where a company publishes its full accounts, it shall also publish with those accounts any report in relation to those accounts by the auditors of the company under section 193 of the Companies Act, 1990.

(2) Where a company publishes abbreviated accounts relating to any financial year, it shall also publish a statement indicating—

(a) that the accounts are not the accounts copies of which are required to be annexed to the annual return,

(b) whether the copies of the accounts so required to be so annexed have in fact been so annexed,

(c) whether the auditors of the company have made a report under section 193 of the Companies Act, 1990, in respect of the accounts of the company which relate to any financial year with which the abbreviated accounts purport to deal,

[(d) whether any matters referred to in the auditors' report were qualified or unqualified, or whether the auditors' report included a reference to any matters to which the auditors drew attention by way of emphasis without qualifying the report.][a]

(3) Where a company publishes abbreviated accounts, it shall not publish with those accounts any such report of the auditors as is mentioned in paragraph (2)(c).

(4) Where a company publishes its full individual accounts for a financial year it shall indicate if group accounts have been prepared and if so where those group accounts can be obtained.

(5) In this regulation—

"abbreviated accounts", in relation to a company, means any balance sheet or profit and loss account, or summary or abstract of a balance sheet or profit and loss account, relating to a financial year of the company which is published by the company otherwise than as part of the full accounts of the company for that financial year and, in relation to a parent company, includes an account in any form purporting to be a balance sheet or profit and loss account, or a summary or abstract of a balance sheet or profit and loss account, of the group consisting of the parent company and its subsidiaries;

"company" means a section 2(2) company;

"full accounts" means the individual or group accounts required to be annexed to the annual return;

"publish", in relation to a document, includes issue, circulate or otherwise make it available for public inspection in a manner calculated to invite the public generally, or any class of members of the public, to read the document, and cognate words shall be construed accordingly.

Amendments

a Paragraph (2)(d) of reg 6 was substituted by reg 10 and Sch 2, Item No 3 of EC(IFRSMA)R 2005.

Definitions

'accounts': EC(CI:A)R 1992, reg 2(1); 'annual return': EC(CI:A)R 1992, reg 2(1), CA 1963, s 2(1); 'financial year': CA 1963, s 2(1); 'group accounts': EC(CI:A)R 1992, reg 2(1), reg 7; 'parent company': EC(CI:A)R 1992, reg 2(1); 'section 2(2) company': EC(CI:A)R 1992, reg 2(1), C(A)A 1986 s 2.

Notes

Publication of accounts: The reference to publication in reg 6 is to situations such as the publishing of the full or abbreviated annual or group accounts of the company in a national newspaper, rather than to the filing of such accounts with the annual return.

Annual return of credit institution: See CA 1963, ss 125–129, C(A)A 1986, s 7 and EC(CI:A)R 1992, reg 3, as well as the Notes thereto.

---

7 Group Accounts

[(1) This Regulation applies to a parent company which is a section 2(2) company (in these Regulations referred to as a 'section 2(2) parent company') whether or not it is itself a subsidiary of another undertaking.

(2) A parent company to which this Regulation applies shall not be entitled to take advantage of section 154 of the Principal Act in relation to the preparation of group accounts or of section 151(1A), (2) and (3) of the Principal Act in relation to the form of group accounts.

(3) Every parent company to which this Regulation applies shall, in accordance with section 150 of the Principal Act, prepare group accounts at the end of its financial year dealing with the state of affairs and profit or loss of the company and its subsidiaries (including those in liquidation and those with registered offices outside the State) and those group accounts shall be laid before the next annual general meeting of the company at the same time as the individual accounts of the company are so laid and shall be annexed to the annual return of the company.

(4) The report of the auditors on the group accounts laid before the annual general meeting shall be annexed to the annual return referred to in paragraph (3).

(5) Where, in accordance with section 150 (2) or (3)(b) of the Principal Act, the directors of a section 2 (2) parent company prepare IFRS group accounts, they shall ensure that instead of making the disclosures specified in section 1 50B (2) (inserted by the European Communities (International Financial Reporting Standards and Miscellaneous Amendments) Regulations 2005) the notes to those group accounts include the information required by—

- (a) paragraph 4 of Part IV of the Schedule to these Regulations (details of directors' remuneration,
- (b) sections 41 to 45 of the Companies Act 1990 to be disclosed in group accounts (transactions with directors),
- (c) section 63 of the Companies Act 1990 unless it is disclosed in the directors' report (interests in shares and debentures),
- (d) Regulation 10 of these Regulations (details of group undertakings),
- (e) paragraph 77 of Part I of the Schedule to these Regulations (details of staff numbers and remuneration),
- (f) paragraphs 51 to 54 of Part I of the Schedule to these Regulations (details of share capital and debentures),
- (g) paragraph 73(4) of Part I of the Schedule to these Regulations (restriction on distributability of profits),
- (h) paragraph 66 of Part I of the Schedule to these Regulations (guarantees and other financial commitments),
- (i) paragraph 73(2) of Part I of the Schedule to these Regulations (financial assistance for the purchase of own shares),
- (j) paragraph 6 of Part III of the Schedule to these Regulations (shares and debentures held by subsidiary undertakings),
- (k) paragraph 74(3) of Part I of the Schedule to these Regulations and section 205D (inserted by section 44 of the Companies (Auditing and Accounting) Act 2003) of the Companies Act 1990 (auditors' [remuneration), and][b]
- [(l) where appropriate, paragraph 7A(a) of Part II of the Schedule.][c]

(6) Where in accordance with section 150(3)(a) of the Principal Act, the directors of a section 2(2) parent company prepare Companies Acts group accounts they shall, subject to paragraph (7), be prepared in accordance with Part 1 of the Schedule to these Regulations, as modified by Part II of the Schedule.

(7) (a) The Companies Act group accounts laid before the annual general meeting of a company shall give a true and fair view of the state of affairs and profit or loss

of the company and subsidiaries dealt with thereby as a whole, so far as concerns members of the company.

(b) The Companies Act group accounts shall comprise the consolidated balance sheet dealing with the state of affairs of the parent and its subsidiaries as a whole, the consolidated profit and loss account dealing with the profit and loss of the parent and its subsidiaries as a whole and the notes on the accounts giving the information required by these Regulations or otherwise provided by the company.

(c) Where Companies Act group accounts drawn up in accordance with paragraph (6) would not provide sufficient information to comply with subparagraph (a), any necessary additional information shall be given in the group accounts or in a note to the accounts.

(d) Where, owing to special circumstances, the preparation of Companies Act group accounts in compliance with paragraph (6) would prevent those accounts from complying with subparagraph (a) (even if additional information were given under subparagraph (c)), the directors of the parent company shall depart from the requirements of Parts I and II (other than paragraph 2 of Part II) of the Schedule to these Regulations in preparing those accounts insofar as it is necessary to comply with that paragraph.

(e) Where the directors of a parent company depart from the requirements of these Regulations in compliance with subparagraph (d), they shall attach a note to the Companies Act group accounts of the company giving details of the particular departures made, the reasons therefor and the effect of those departures on the accounts.

(8) Where a document annexed to the annual return under this Regulation or Regulation 8, 8A, 9, 10 or 11 is in a language other than English or Irish, there shall be annexed to any such document a translation in the English or Irish language certified in the prescribed manner to be a correct translation.

(9) The individual and group accounts, if any, of a subsidiary undertaking excluded from group accounts by virtue of the application of paragraph 2 of Part II of the Schedule to these Regulations shall be attached to the group accounts, or annexed to the annual return, of the parent company.

(10) Paragraph (9) shall not apply where the subsidiary undertaking has otherwise annexed the relevant accounts referred to in that paragraph to its annual return.][a]

Amendments

a Regulation 7 was substituted by reg 10 and Schedule 2, Item No 4 of EC(IFRSMA)R 2005 (SI 116/2005).

b Words substituted by European Communities (Directive 2006/46/EC) Regulations 2009, reg 14(b)(i).

c Subparagraph (l) inserted by European Communities (Directive 2006/46/EC) Regulations 2009, reg 14(b)(ii).

Definitions

'accounts': EC(CI:A)R 1992, reg 2(1); 'annual return': EC(CI:A)R 1992, reg 2(1), CA 1963, s 2(1); 'companies act group accounts': CA 1963, s 2(1); 'group accounts': EC(CI:A)R 1992, reg 2(1), reg 7; 'IFRS group accounts': CA 1963, s 2(1); 'parent company': EC(CI:A)R 1992, reg 2(1); 'the Principal Act': EC(CI:A)R 1992, reg 2(1); 'section 2(2) company': EC(CI:A)R 1992, reg 2(1), C(A)A 1986, s 2; 'section 2(2) parent company': EC(CI:A)R 1992, reg 2(1), reg 7(1); 'subsidiary undertaking': EC(CI:A)R 1992, reg 2(1); 'subsidiary': CA 1963, s 155; 'undertaking': EC(CGA)R 1992, reg 3(1).

Notes

True and fair view: The basic and overriding requirement for group accounts is that they should give a 'true and fair view' of the financial state of affairs of the group as a whole for the year in question.[1] To a large extent, the provisions of EC(CI:A)R 1992 are themselves determinative as to what constitutes a properly prepared set of group accounts. However, in so far as the legislation is silent on any particular matter, compliance with the recognised practices and standards of the accountancy profession in preparing the group's accounts will be strong but not conclusive evidence that the accounts give a 'true and fair view' of the group's financial position.[2] Indeed, even where the legislation specifically deals with an aspect of the accounts, a departure will be permitted if strict adherence would result in the 'true and fair view' not being achieved.[3] Details of the departure must, however, be given in the notes to the accounts together with the reasons therefor.[4] With the introduction of International Financial Reporting Standards through EC(IFRSMA)R 2005, a new term, 'presents fairly' entered into financial reporting language. The United Kingdom's Financial Reporting Council, of which the Accounting Standards Board is a constituent body, published a paper in August 2005 entitled 'The implications of new accounting and auditing standards for the 'true and fair view' and auditors' responsibilities'. In this paper, the FRC concludes that the concept of 'true and fair' remains a cornerstone of financial reporting and that the intent and substance of the two expressions 'presents fairly' and 'true and fair' are similar. The paper is available from the FRC website at http://www.frc.org.uk/publications.

See also notes to reg 5.

1 EC(CI:A)R 1992, reg 7(5).

2 *Dolan v AB Ltd* [1969] IR 282; *Lloyd Cheyham & Co Ltd v Littlejohn & Co* [1987] BCLC 303; *IRC v Duple Motor Bodies Ltd* [1961] 1 WLR 739). The recognised practices of the accountancy profession may be found in its Statements of Standard Accounting Practice (SSAPs) and in its Auditing Guidelines.

3 EC(CI:A)R 1992, reg 7(5)(iv).

4 EC(CI:A)R 1992, reg 7(5)(v).

Bank holding companies: The obligation to prepare group accounts in accordance with reg 7 applies not only to credit institutions, but also to companies which do not carry on any material business other than the acquisition, management and disposal of interests in subsidiaries, and whose principal subsidiaries are wholly or mainly credit institutions[1]. In this regard, the 'principal subsidiaries' are those whose results or financial position would principally affect the figures shown in the group accounts[2].

1 EC(CI:A)R 1992, reg 9(1)). For the purposes of the Regulations, the management of interests in subsidiaries includes the provision of services to such subsidiaries: EC(CI:A)R 1992, reg 9(2).

2 EC(CI:A)R 1992, reg 9(2).

Exemption for parent companies which are themselves wholly-owned or 90% owned subsidiaries: This Regulation exempts an unlisted[1] parent company from the obligation to prepare group accounts in accordance with EC(CI:A)R 1992 if:

(a) it is in turn a wholly-owned subsidiary of another parent undertaking incorporated under the laws of a EEA State ("parent undertaking") or the parent undertaking holds at least 90% of its issued share capital, and the holders of the remaining 10% approve of the exemption;[2]

(b) the parent company and its subsidiaries are dealt with in group accounts of the parent undertaking which (along with the 'group report'[3]) are drawn up in accordance with the provisions of either Council Directive 86/635/EEC or the Seventh Companies Directive;[4]

(c) the parent undertaking's group accounts, group report and auditors' report are annexed to the parent company's annual return;[5] and

(d) the notes to the parent company's annual accounts disclose the name and registered office of the parent undertaking as well as the fact that the exemption has been availed of.[6]

1 EC(CI:A)R 1992, reg 8(4).

2 EC(CI:A)R 1992, reg 8(2).

3 The phrase 'group report' is not defined). Presumably it means the directors' report which is attached to the group accounts). See EC(CGA)R 1992, reg 8(3)(b).

4 EC(CI:A)R 1992, reg 8(3)(a) and (b).

5 EC(CI:A)R 1992, reg 8(3)(c).

6 EC(CI:A)R 1992, reg 8(3)(d).

Exemption for other parent companies which are themselves subsidiaries: The above exemptions also apply to an unlisted[1] parent company which is itself a subsidiary of a another parent undertaking incorporated under the laws of a EEA State but which is held as to less than 90% of its share capital by the parent undertaking, provided that the holders of not less than 10% of its issued share capital have not made a request for the preparation of such accounts at least six months before the end of the relevant financial year.[2]

1 EC(CI:A)R 1992, reg 8(4).

2 EC(CI:A)R 1992, reg 8(6).

Annual return of credit institution: See CA 1963, ss 125–129, C(A)A 1986, s 7 and EC(CI:A)R 1992, reg 3, as well as the notes thereto.

---

8 Wholly-owned Subsidiaries

(1) Paragraph (3) of regulation 7 shall not apply to a section 2(2) parent company which is itself a wholly-owned subsidiary of another undertaking [established in an EEA State][a] ("the parent undertaking") if paragraph (3) of this regulation is complied with; provided that the fact that the advantage of this regulation is being availed of shall be disclosed in a note to the accounts of the section 2(2) parent company annexed to its annual return under the Principal Act.

(2) In this regulation, a company shall be deemed to be a wholly-owned subsidiary of another if:

(a) it would be so deemed for the purposes of section 150 of the Principal Act, or

(b) that other holds 90% or more of the shares in the company and the remaining shareholders in the company have approved the treatment of the company as a wholly-owned subsidiary under this regulation.

(3) The requirements referred to in paragraph (1) are as follows:

(a) The company and its subsidiaries must be dealt with in group accounts prepared by the parent undertaking;

(b) the group accounts and the group report of the parent undertaking must be prepared and audited in accordance with the Directive or Directive 83/349/EEC of 13 June 1983 (OJ No L193 of 18/7/1983), [or prepared in accordance with international financial reporting standards and audited in accordance with either such Directive, as applicable,][b] as the case may be;

(c) the following must be annexed to the annual return of the company next after the group accounts have been prepared in accordance with subparagraph (a):

(i) the group accounts referred to in subparagraph (b),

(ii) the group annual report referred to in subparagraph (b), and

(iii) the report of the person responsible for auditing the accounts referred to in subparagraph (b);

(d) the notes on the annual accounts of the company must disclose:

(i) the name and registered office of the parent undertaking that draws up the group accounts referred to in subparagraph (b), and

(ii) the exemption from the obligation to draw up group accounts and a group annual report.

[(4) The exemption does not apply to a company any of whose securities are admitted to trading on a regulated market of any EEA State.][c]

(5) The Minister may, after consultation with the Bank, require that additional information shall be provided in the consolidated accounts of the parent undertaking or the individual accounts of the section 2(2) parent company referred to in paragraph (1) of this regulation in accordance with Article 9 of Directive 83/349 EEC.

(6) This regulation shall also apply to a section 2(2) parent company not falling under the provisions of paragraph (2) of this regulation which is itself a subsidiary of a parent undertaking [established in an EEA State][d] if the shareholders or members holding in total 10% or more of the nominal value of the shares of the parent company concerned have not at any time that is not later than six months before the end of the financial year in question requested the preparation of group accounts by that parent company in respect of that financial year.

Amendments

a Words substituted by reg 10 and Sch 2, Item No 5(a) of EC(IFRSMA)R 2005.

b Words inserted by reg 10 and Sch 2, Item No 5(b) of EC(IFRSMA)R 2005.

c Paragraph (4) substituted by reg 10 and Sch 2, Item No 5(c) of EC(IFRSMA)R 2005.

d Words substituted by reg 10 and Sch 2, Item No 5(d) of EC(IFRSMA)R 2005.

Definitions

'accounts': EC(CI:A)R 1992, reg 2(1); 'annual return': EC(CI:A)R 1992, reg 2(1), CA 1963 s 2(1); 'the bank': EC(CI:A)R 1992, reg 2(1); 'the Directive': EC(CI:A)R 1992, reg (1); 'EEA State': CA 1963, s 2(1); 'group accounts': EC(CI:A)R 1992, reg 2(1), reg 7; 'international financial reporting standards': CA 1963, s 2(1); 'parent company': EC(CI:A)R 1992, reg 2(1); 'the Principal Act': EC(CI:A)R 1992, reg 2(1); 'section 2(2) parent company': EC(CI:A)R 1992, reg 2(1), reg 7(1); 'subsidiaries': CA 1963 s 155; 'company': CA 1963, s 2(1); 'financial year': CA 1963, s 2(1); 'member': CA 1963, s 31 'undertaking': EC(CGA)R 1992, reg 3(1).

Notes

See the notes to EC(CI:A)R 1992, reg 7.

Extension of exemptions to EEA States

EC(IFRSMA)R 2005 extends the exemptions available to undertakings incorporated in a EEA State, as permitted under Directive 86/635/EEC but heretofore not taken up in Irish company law.

[8A Exemption for parent undertakings included in non-EEA group accounts

(1) A section 2 (2) parent undertaking (the 'exempted parent') is exempt from the requirement in Regulation 7(3) to prepare group accounts where that undertaking is itself a subsidiary undertaking and its parent undertaking ('that other parent undertaking') is not established under the law of an EEA State where:

(a) the exempted parent is a wholly-owned subsidiary of that other parent undertaking;

(b) that other parent undertaking holds more than 50 per cent of the shares in the exempted parent and notice requesting the preparation of group accounts has not been served in accordance with paragraph (2) on the exempted parent by shareholders holding in aggregate –

(i) more than half of the remaining shares in the company, or

(ii) 5 per cent of the total shares in the company.

(2) The notice referred to in paragraph (1)(b) must be served not later than 6 months after the end of the financial year before that to which it relates.

(3) Exemption under this Regulation is conditional upon compliance with all of the following conditions—

(a) that the exempted parent and all of its subsidiary undertakings are included in consolidated accounts for a larger group drawn up to the same date, or to an earlier date in the same financial year by that other parent undertaking,

(b) that those accounts and, where appropriate, the group's annual report, are drawn up in accordance with the provisions of the Seventh Council Directive 83/349/EEC of 13 June 1983 (where applicable as modified by the Directive or Council Directive No.91/674/EEC of 23 December 1991), or in a manner equivalent to consolidated accounts and consolidated annual reports so drawn up,

(c) that the consolidated accounts are audited by one or more persons authorised to audit accounts under the law under which that other parent undertaking which draws them up is established,

(d) that the exempted parent discloses in its individual accounts that it is exempt from the obligation to prepare and deliver group accounts;

(e) that the exempted parent states in its individual accounts the name of that other parent undertaking which draws up the group accounts referred to in subparagraph (d) and—

(i) where that other parent undertaking is incorporated outside the State, the country in which it is incorporated, or

(ii) where that other parent undertaking is unincorporated, the address of its principal place of business,

(f) that the exempted parent delivers to the registrar, within the period allowed for delivering its individual accounts, copies of that other parent's group accounts and, where appropriate, of the consolidated annual report, together with the auditors' report on them, and

(g) where any document comprised in accounts and reports delivered in accordance with paragraph (f) is in a language other than the English language or the Irish language, there is annexed to the copy of that document delivered a translation of it into the English language or the Irish language, certified in the prescribed manner to be a correct translation.

(4) The exemption under this Regulation does not apply to a parent undertaking any of whose securities are admitted to trading on a regulated market of any EEA State.

(5) The Minister may, after consultation with the Bank, require that additional information shall be provided in the consolidated accounts of that other parent undertaking or of the individual accounts of the section 2(2) parent referred to in paragraph (1).

(6) Shares held by directors of a company for the purpose of complying with any share qualification requirement shall be disregarded in determining for the purposes of paragraph 1(a) whether the company is a wholly-owned subsidiary.

(7) For the purpose of paragraph (1)(b), shares held by a wholly-owned subsidiary of that other parent undertaking, or held on behalf of that other parent undertaking or a wholly-owned subsidiary, are attributed to that other parent undertaking.

(8) In paragraph (3) 'securities' includes:

(a) shares and stock,

(b) debentures, including debenture stock, loan stock, bonds, certificates of deposit and other instruments creating or acknowledging indebtedness,

(c) warrants or other instruments entitling the holder to subscribe for securities falling within subparagraph (a) or (b), and

(d) certificates or other instruments which confer—

(i) property rights in respect of a security falling within subparagraph (a), (b) or (c),

(ii) any right to acquire, dispose of, underwrite or convert a security, being a right to which the holder would be entitled if the holder held any such security to which the certificate or other instrument relates, or

(iii) a contractual right (other than an option) to acquire any such security otherwise than by subscription.][a]

Amendments

a Inserted by reg 10 and Sch 2, Item No 6 of EC(IFRSMA)R 2005.

Definitions

'accounts': EC(CI:A)R 1992, reg 2(1); 'annual return': EC(CI:A)R 1992, reg 2(1), CA 1963 s 2(1); 'the bank': EC(CI:A)R 1992, reg 2(1); 'the Directive': EC(CI:A)R 1992, reg (1); 'EEA State': CA 1963, s 2(1); 'group accounts': EC(CI:A)R 1992, reg 2(1), reg 7; 'international financial reporting standards': CA 1963, s 2(1); 'parent company': EC(CI:A)R 1992, reg 2(1); 'the Principal Act': EC(CI:A)R 1992, reg 2(1); 'section 2(2) parent company': EC(CI:A)R 1992, reg 2(1), reg 7(1); 'subsidiaries': CA 1963 s 155; 'company': CA 1963, s 2(1); 'financial year': CA 1963, s 2(1); 'member': CA 1963, s 31 'undertaking': EC(CGA)R 1992, reg 3(1).

Notes

Exemptions for parent undertakings included in non-EEA group accounts: Reg 8A sets out the conditions under which a parent company which itself is a subsidiary of a non EEA parent company is exempt from the requirement to prepare group accounts. That non-EEA parent company must itself produce group accounts which incorporate the Irish entity and all of its subsidiaries. In particular, to avail of this exemption the group accounts of the non-EEA parent should be drawn up in accordance with the provisions of the Seventh Company Law Directive (83/349/EEC) (where applicable as modified by Directive 91/674/EEC) or in a manner equivalent. Use of this exemption therefore requires an analysis of the particular set of consolidated accounts to determine whether they are drawn up in a manner that is consistent with the Seventh Directive.

Guidance on conducting such an assessment is contained in a pronouncement by the Urgent Issues Task Force of the Accounting Standards Board (UITF), UITF abstract 43. UITF 43 also concludes that consolidated accounts of the higher parent prepared in accordance with Generally Accepted Accounting Principles (GAAP) of certain other jurisdictions, namely US GAAP. Canadian GAAP, and Japanese GAAP will normally meet the test of equivalence with the Seventh Directive subject to certain considerations. The text of UITF 43 is available on the website of the Accounting Standards Board at www.frc.org.uk/asb.

9 Bank holding Companies

(1) The obligation to prepare group accounts in accordance with regulation 7 also applies to a parent company:

(i) which does not itself carry on any material business apart from the acquisition, management and disposal of interests in subsidiaries; and

(ii) whose principal subsidiaries are wholly or mainly credit institutions.

(2) In paragraph (1), the management of interests in subsidiaries includes the provision of services to such subsidiaries and a parent company's principal subsidiaries are those subsidiaries of the company whose results or financial position would principally affect the figures shown in the group accounts.

Definitions

'group accounts': EC(CI:A)R 1992, reg 2(1), reg 7; 'parent company': EC(CI:A)R 1992, reg 2(1); 'subsidiary': CA 1963, s 155.

Notes

See the notes to EC(CI:A)R 1992, reg 7.

10 Information on Related Undertakings

(1) A company to which these Regulations apply shall give the information required by Part III of the Schedule to these Regulations by way of a note to [its individual accounts][a] or group accounts as the case may be.

(2) (a) Subject to subparagraph (b), the information specified in paragraph (1) may, in lieu of being stated in a note to the accounts of the company concerned for any particular financial year of the company, be given in a statement in writing signed by a director and the secretary, of the company and annexed to the first annual return made by the company next after its accounts for that year are laid before the annual general meeting of the company if, in the opinion of the directors of the company, compliance with paragraph (1) would require a note to the accounts of the company of excessive length.

(b) Subparagraph (a) shall not apply—

(i) in relation to information concerning a subsidiary of or an undertaking of substantial interest to a company (referred to subsequently in this subparagraph as the "second-mentioned company") if the financial state of that subsidiary or undertaking, as disclosed by its accounts, has, in the opinion of the directors of the second-mentioned company, a substantial effect on the profit or loss, or the amount of the assets, of the second-mentioned company and its subsidiaries; or

(ii) in relation to any subsidiary excluded from consolidated accounts by virtue of paragraph 2 of Part II of the Schedule to these Regulations.

(c) A copy of a statement annexed, pursuant to subparagraph (a), to the annual return referred to in that subparagraph made by a company shall be certified both by a director and the secretary of the company to be a true copy of such statement.

(3) Section 16 of the Companies (Amendment) Act, 1986, and subsections (4) and (5) of section 158 of the Principal Act shall not apply to a company to which this regulation applies.

(4) If advantage is taken of paragraph 2(a), the company shall indicate that the information required by Part III of the Schedule to these Regulations to be given in the notes to the accounts refers only to the undertakings referred to in paragraph 2(b) and that the full information required has been annexed to the annual return referred to in paragraph 2(a).

(5) In this regulation, the expression "undertaking of substantial interest" means an undertaking falling within any of paragraphs 7, 18 or 19 of Part III of the Schedule to these Regulations.

Amendments

a Words substituted by reg 10 and Sch 2, Item No 7 of EC(IFRSMA)R 2005.

Definitions

'accounts': EC(CI:A)R 1992, reg 2(1); 'annual return': EC(CI:A)R 1992, reg 2(1), CA 1963, s 2(1); 'group accounts': EC(CI:A)R 1992, reg 2(1), reg 7; 'the Principal Act': EC(CI:A)R 1992, reg 2(1); 'company': CA 1963, s 2(1); 'director': CA 1963, s 2(1) and EC(CI:A)R 1992, reg 2(5)(i); 'subsidiary': CA 1963, s 155.

Notes

Part III of the Schedule: The information required by Part III of the Schedule is in relation to the company's subsidiary undertakings, associated undertakings and other related companies and joint ventures. The extent of the disclosure depends on whether or not the company is required by these Regulations to prepare group accounts.

Information in separate statement rather than in notes: If the directors are of the opinion that to include such information in the notes to the accounts would result in the notes being of excessive length, then unless—

(a) the financial state of the subsidiary or undertaking of substantial interest has a substantial effect on the financial position of the company itself; or

(b) the subsidiary is one excluded from consolidated accounts by virtue of the Sch, Pt II, para (2),

the directors may instead set out the information in a separate statement which must be signed by one director and the secretary and which must be annexed to the annual return[1]. The fact that the information has been put into the statement rather than into the notes to the accounts, must itself be disclosed in the accounts[2].

1 EC(CI:A)R 1992, reg 10(2)). By including the information about subsidiaries or undertakings of substantial interest in a statement annexed to the annual return, rather than in the notes to the accounts, the directors would seem to be able to avoid presenting such information to the members at the annual general meeting.

2 EC(CI:A)R 1992, reg 10(4).

11 Directors' Report

In the case of a section 2(2) parent company preparing group accounts in accordance with these Regulations, the report of the directors of that company under section 158 of the Principal Act, shall contain, in addition to the information specified in that section, the following information:

[(a) a fair review of the development and performance of the company's business and of its position and, in relation to its subsidiary undertakings, if any, of the development and performance of their business and of their position, during the financial year ending with the relevant balance sheet date together with a description of the principal risks and uncertainties that they face, which review—

(i) shall be a balanced and comprehensive analysis of the development and performance of the company's business and of its position and, in relation to its subsidiary undertakings, if any, of the development and performance of their business and of their position, consistent with the size and complexity of the business, and

(ii) to the extent necessary for an understanding of the company's development, performance or position, and that of its subsidiary undertakings, if any, shall include an analysis of financial, and, where appropriate, non-financial key performance indicators relevant to the particular business, including information relevant to environmental and employee matters,

and, where appropriate, the report shall include additional explanations of amounts included in the annual accounts;][a]

(b) particulars of any important events affecting the parent company or any of its subsidiary undertakings which have occurred since the end of that year;

(c) an indication of likely future developments in the business of the parent company and its subsidiary undertakings, taken as a group;

(d) an indication of the activities, if any, of the parent company and its subsidiary undertakings, taken as a group, in the field of research and development, [...][b]

(e) the number and nominal value of shares in the parent company held by the company itself, by its subsidiary undertakings or by a person acting in his own name but on behalf of the company or [subsidiary and,][c]

[(f) in relation to the company's use of financial instruments and where material for the assessment of its assets, liabilities, financial position and profit or loss—

(i) the company's financial risk management objectives and policies, including its policy for hedging each major type of forecasted transaction for which hedge accounting is used, and

(ii) the company's exposure to price risk, credit risk, liquidity risk and cash flow risk.][d]

(2) The information required by subparagraph (1)(e) may be given in the notes to the group accounts.

Amendments

a Paragraph (a) substituted by reg 10 and Sch 2, Item No 8 of EC(IFRSMA)R 2005.

b Amended by reg 3 of EC(CI) (FVA)R 2004.

c Amended by reg 3 of EC(CI) (FVA)R 2004.

d Amended by reg 3 of EC(CI) (FVA)R 2004.

Definitions

'group accounts': EC(CI:A)R 1992, reg 2(1), reg 7; 'parent company': EC(CI:A)R 1992, reg 2(1); 'the Principal Act': EC(CI:A)R 1992, reg 2(1); 'section 2(2) parent company': EC(CI:A)R 1992, reg 2(1), reg 7(1); 'subsidiary undertaking': EC(CI:A)R 1992, reg 2(1); 'director': CA 1963, s 2(1) and EC(CI:A)R 1992, reg 2(5)(i); 'financial year': CA 1963, s 2(1).

Notes

Directors' report: EC(CI:A)R 1992, reg 11 only applies in relation to the contents of the directors' report which accompanies the group accounts. The contents of the directors' report which accompanies the annual accounts are as prescribed by CA 1963, s 158 (as modified by EC(CI:A)R 1992, reg 12) and C(A)A 1986, ss 13 and 14. See notes thereon.

Shares in the parent held by the parent itself or by subsidiaries: In the directors' report which accompanies the group accounts details must be given of shares in the parent which are held by the parent itself or by any of its subsidiaries, whether directly or through nominees[1]. For the circumstances in which a company may acquire and hold shares in itself, see C(A)A 1983, ss 41–

43 and the notes thereto. For the circumstances in which a subsidiary may hold shares in its holding company, see CA 1963, s 32, CA 1990, s 224 and EC(PLCS)R 1997, reg 5.

1 EC(CI:A)R 1992, reg 11(e).

[11A Corporate Governance Statement

(1) Where a section 2(2) parent company has its securities admitted to trading on a regulated market, is preparing group accounts in accordance with these Regulations, the corporate governance statement included in the report by the directors of that company under section 158 of the Principal Act, shall contain, in addition to the information specified in that section, a description of the main features of the internal control and risk management systems of that section 2(2) parent company and its subsidiaries in relation to the process for preparing such group accounts.

(2)Where the consolidated annual report and the annual report are presented as a single report the description referred to in paragraph (1) shall be included in the section of the report by the directors referred to in paragraph (1) containing the corporate governance statement.

(3)Where a section 2(2) parent company referred to in paragraph (1), produces a corporate governance statement in the form of a separate report published in conjunction with the annual report in accordance with section 158 of the Principal Act, the description required by paragraph (1) shall form part of that separate report.

(4)In this Regulation, 'regulated market' has the meaning assigned to it by Article 4(1), point (14) of Directive 2004/39/EC.][a]

Amendments

a Regulation 11A inserted by European Communities (Directive 2006/46/EC) Regulations 2009, reg 15.

12 Non-Application of Principal Act

[Sections 151, 152, 158(4), (5) and (6) and 191 of the Principal Act shall not apply to a company to which Regulation 7 applies.][a]

Amendments

a Regulation 12 substituted by reg 10 and Sch 2, Item No 5(b) of EC(IFRSMA)R 2005.

Definitions

'the Principal Act': EC(CI:A)R 1992, reg 2(1); 'company': CA 1963, s 2(1).

13 Auditors' Reports

(1) The auditors of a section 2(2) company shall make a report to the members in accordance with section 193 of the Companies Act, 1990, and the company shall not be entitled to rely on the exemption referred to in [section 193(4A)(b)(inserted by the European Communities (International Financial Reporting Standards and Miscellaneous Amendments) Regulations 2005)][a] in relation to the preparation of its accounts.

(2) The report of the auditors shall also contain the information required by section 15 of the Companies (Amendment) Act, 1986, in relation to both the individual and group accounts prepared by the company to which these Regulations apply.

[(3) Where a section 2(2) parent company referred to in Regulation 11A(1) produces a corporate governance statement under section 158 of the Principal Act, the auditors of that parent company, when preparing a report required by section 193 of the Companies Act 1990 (No. 33 of 1990) shall—

(a) provide an opinion as to whether the description of the main features of the internal control and risk management systems of that section 2(2) parent company and its subsidiaries, in relation to the process for preparing consolidated accounts, is consistent with their evaluation and testing of the relevant systems for the purposes of preparing such report on such group accounts, and

(b) consider whether, in their opinion, the description referred to in subparagraph (a) is consistent with their evaluation and testing of the systems referred to in paragraph (a).][b]

Amendments

a Words substituted by reg 10 and Schedule 2, Item No 5(b) of EC(IFRSMA)R 2005 (SI 116/2005).

b Subsection (3) inserted by European Communities (Directive 2006/46/EC) Regulations 2009, reg 16.

Definitions

'accounts': EC(CI:A)R 1992, reg 2(1); 'group accounts': EC(CI:A)R 1992, reg 2(1), reg 7; 'section 2(2) company': EC(CI:A)R 1992, reg 2(1), C(A)A 1986, s 2; 'member': CA 1963, s 31.

Notes

Contents of auditors' report: In addition, to CA 1990, s 193 and C(A)A 1986, s 15, as modified by this Regulation, see also CA 1963 s 192(3). The provisions of CA 1963, s 191(8) do not apply by virtue of EC(CI:A)R 1992, reg 12.

See notes to s 193 of CA 1990.

14 Publication of Accounts of Credit Institutions incorporated outside the State

(1) Every credit institution incorporated outside the State which has a place of business in the State shall publish its individual accounts and its group accounts, together with the report of the directors and auditors, in such manner as may be prescribed by the Bank in accordance with Article 44 of the Directive.

(2) In implementing the provisions of this regulation, the bank shall apply the provisions of Directive 89/117/EEC of 13 February 1989 (OJ No L44 of 16/2/1989) and, in particular, Articles 2, 3 and 4 thereof.

(3) This regulation shall also apply to any financial institution incorporated outside the State with a place of business in the State which would, if it were incorporated in the State, be subject to licensing or supervision by the Bank.

(4) In paragraph (3), "financial institution" does not include an insurance company or undertaking.

Definitions

'the bank': EC(CI:A)R 1992, reg 2(1); 'the Directive': EC(CI:A)R 1992, reg 2(1); 'group accounts': EC(CI:A)R 1992, reg 2(1), reg 7; 'undertaking': EC(CI:A)R 1992, reg 2(1).

Notes

Licensing of financial institutions: In relation to the licensing of financial institutions by the Central Bank, see the Central Bank Acts 1942–1989 and the European Communities (Licensing and Supervision of Banks) Regulations 1979.

15 Offences

(1) (a) If a company to which these Regulations apply fails to comply with a provision of these Regulations, the company and every officer of the company who is in default shall be liable on summary conviction to a fine not exceeding [€3,000].[a]

(b) Proceedings for an offence under this regulation may be brought and prosecuted by the Bank or, in the case of a failure by a company to annex or attach any document required by these Regulations to be annexed or attached to the annual return of that company, by the registrar of companies.

(2) If any person, being a director of a company to which these Regulations apply, fails to take all reasonable steps to secure compliance with a requirement of these Regulations, he shall, in respect of each offence, be liable on summary conviction to imprisonment for a term not exceeding [3 months][b] or, at the discretion of the court, to a fine not exceeding [€3,000],[c] or to both.

(3).In any proceedings against a person for an offence under paragraph (2), it shall be a defence for a director to prove that he had reasonable grounds to believe and did believe that a competent and reliable person was charged with the duty of ensuring that the provisions of these Regulations were complied with and that the latter person was in a position to discharge that duty, and a person shall not be liable to be sentenced to imprisonment for an offence under the said paragraph (2) unless, in the opinion of the court, the offence was committed wilfully.

(4) If any person in any balance sheet, profit and loss account, report, note or other document required by or for the purposes of any provision of these Regulations wilfully makes a statement false in any material particular, knowing it to be false, he shall be liable on summary conviction, to imprisonment for a term not exceeding [3 months][d] of to a fine not exceeding [€3,000][e] or to both.

(5) In this section "director" and "officer" includes any person in accordance with whose instruction or directions the directors of the company are accustomed to act.

Amendments

a '€3,000' substituted for '£1,000' by EC(CI)(FVA)R 2004, reg 4(a).

b '3 months' substituted for '12 months' by EC(CI)(FVA)R 2004, reg 4(b)(i).

c '€3,000' substituted for '£1,000' by EC(CI)(FVA)R 2004, reg 4(b)(ii).

d ‘3 months’ substituted for ‘12 months’ by EC(CI)(FVA)R 2004, reg 4(c)(i).

e ‘€3,000’ substituted for ‘£1,000’ by EC(CI)(FVA)R 2004, reg 4(c)(ii).

Definitions

‘annual return’: EC(CI:A)R 1992, reg 2(1), CA 1963, s 2(1); ‘the bank’: EC(CI:A)R 1992, reg 2(1); ‘company’: CA 1963, s 2(1).

Notes

Meaning of ‘officer’ and ‘director’: The definition of ‘officer’ and ‘director’ for the purposes of EC(CI:A)R 1992, reg 15 is deemed to include any person in accordance with whose directions or instructions the directors of the company are accustomed to act[1]. This definition is similar to that of ‘shadow director’ contained in CA 1990, s 27. Notably, however, unlike in CA 1990, s 27, there is no saving provision for circumstances where the directors are accustomed to so act by reason only that they do so on advice given by the person in a professional capacity. It is at least arguable therefore that if the directors are accustomed to acting on the professional advice of an accountant regarding, for example, the filing of the annual return and the annexing of documents thereto, that accountant could be regarded as being a ‘director’ or ‘officer’ for the purposes of reg 15.

1 EC(CI:A)R 1992, reg 15(5).

SCHEDULE

FORM AND CONTENT OF ACCOUNTS OF CREDIT INSTITUTIONS AND GROUPS

Regulation 5

PART I

INDIVIDUAL ACCOUNTS

Chapter 1

General Rules And Formats

SECTION A

GENERAL RULES

1. (1) [Where the directors of a company prepare Companies Act individual accounts and subject to the following provisions of this Part:][a]

(a) every balance sheet of a company shall show the items listed in the balance sheet format set out below in section B of this Chapter of this Schedule; and

(b) every profit and loss account of a company shall show the items listed in either of the profit and loss account formats so set out;

in either case in the order and under the headings and sub-headings given in the format adopted.

(2) Subparagraph (1) above is not to be read as requiring the heading or sub-heading for any item to be distinguished by any number or letter assigned to that item in the format adopted.

Amendments

a Words substituted by reg 10 and Schedule 2, Item No 11(a) of EC(IFRSMA)R 2005 (SI 116/2005).

Definitions

'company': CA 1963, s 2(1); 'companies act individual accounts': CA 1963, s 2(1); 'director': CA 1963, s 2(1); 'financial year': CA 1963, s 2(1); 'member': CA 1963, s 2(1).

2. (1) Where in accordance with paragraph 1 a company's profit and loss account for any financial year has been prepared by reference to one of the formats set out in section B below, the directors of the company shall adopt the same format in preparing the profit and loss account for subsequent financial years of the company unless in their opinion there are special reasons for a change.

(2) Particulars of any change in the format adopted in preparing a company's profit and loss account in accordance with paragraph 1 shall be disclosed, and the reasons for the change shall be explained, in a note to the accounts in which the new format is first adopted.

Definitions

'accounts': EC(CI:A)R 1992, reg 2(1); 'company': CA 1963, s 2(1); 'director': CA 1963, s 2(1); 'financial year': CA 1963, s 2(1); 'member': CA 1963, s 2(1).

3. (1) Any item required in accordance with paragraph 1 to be shown in a company's balance sheet or profit and loss account may be shown in greater detail than so required.

(2) A company's balance sheet or profit and loss account may include an item representing or covering the amount of any asset or liability, income or expenditure not specifically covered by any of the items listed in the balance sheet format provided or the profit and loss account format adopted, but the following shall not be treated as assets in any company's balance sheet:

(i) preliminary expenses;

(ii) expenses of and commission on any issue of shares or debentures; and

(iii) costs of research.

(3) Items to which lower case letters are assigned in any of the formats set out in section B below may be combined in a company's accounts for any financial year if either:

(a) their individual amounts are not material for the purpose of giving a true and fair view; or

(b) the combination facilitates the assessment of the state of affairs or profit or loss of the company for that year;

but in a case within paragraph (b) the individual amounts of any items so combined shall be disclosed in a note to the accounts and any notes required by this Schedule to the items so combined shall, notwithstanding the combination, be given.

(4) Subject to paragraph 4(3) below, a heading or sub-heading corresponding to an item listed in the balance sheet format or the profit and loss account format adopted in preparing a company's balance sheet or profit and loss account shall not be included if there is no amount to be shown for that item in respect of the financial year to which the balance sheet or profit and loss account relates.

Definitions

'accounts': EC(CI:A)R 1992, reg 2(1); 'company': CA 1963, s 2(1); 'director': CA 1963, s 2(1); 'financial year': CA 1963, s 2(1); 'member': CA 1963, s 2(1).

4. (1) In respect of every item shown in the balance sheet or profit and loss account, there shall be shown or stated the corresponding amount for the financial year immediately preceding that to which the accounts relate.

[(2) Where the corresponding amount is not comparable with the amount to be shown for the item in question in respect of the financial year to which the balance sheet or profit and loss account relates, the former amount may be adjusted, and, if the former amount is adjusted, particulars as regards the respect or respects in which the foregoing amounts are not comparable and of the adjustment shall be given in a note to the accounts.][a]

(3) Paragraph 3(4) does not apply in any case where an amount can be shown for the item in question in respect of the financial year immediately preceding that to which the balance sheet or profit and loss account relates, and that amount shall be shown under the heading or sub-heading required by paragraph 1 for that item.

Amendments

a Subparagraph (2) substituted by SI 840/2005, reg 6.

Definitions

'accounts': EC(CI:A)R 1992, reg 2(1); 'company': CA 1963, s 2(1); 'director': CA 1963, s 2(1); 'financial year': CA 1963, s 2(1); 'member': CA 1963, s 2(1).

5. (1) Subject to the following provisions of this paragraph and without prejudice to note (6) to the balance sheet format, amounts in respect of items representing assets or income may not be set off against amounts in respect of items representing liabilities or expenditure (as the case may be), or vice versa.

(2) Charges required to be included in profit and loss account format 1, items 11(a) and 11(b) or format 2, items A7(a) and A7(b) may however be set off against income required to be included in format 1, items 12(a) and 12(b) or format 2, items B5(a) and B5(b) and the resulting figure shown as a single item (in format 2 at position A7 if negative and at position B5 if positive).

(3) Charges required to be included in profit and loss account format 1, item 13 or format 2, item A8 may also be set off against income required to be included in format 1, item 14 or format 2, item B6 and the resulting figure shown as a single item (in format 2 at position A8 if negative and at position B6 (if positive).

Definitions

'company': CA 1963, s 2(1); 'director': CA 1963, s 2(1); 'financial year': CA 1963, s 2(1); 'member': CA 1963, s 2(1).

6. (1) Assets shall be shown under the relevant balance sheet headings even where the company has pledged them as security for its own liabilities or for those of third parties or has otherwise assigned them as security to third parties.

(2) A company shall not include in its balance sheet assets pledged or otherwise assigned to it as security unless such assets are in the form of cash in the hands of the company.

Definitions

'company': CA 1963, s 2(1); 'director': CA 1963, s 2(1); 'financial year': CA 1963, s 2(1); 'member': CA 1963, s 2(1).

7. Assets acquired in the name of and on behalf of third parties shall not be shown in the balance sheet.

Definitions

'company': CA 1963, s 2(1); 'director': CA 1963, s 2(1); 'financial year': CA 1963, s 2(1); 'member': CA 1963, s 2(1).

[8. (1) The notes to the profit and loss account shall show—

(a) dividends paid (other than dividends for which a liability existed at the immediately preceding balance sheet date) or which the company is liable to pay,

(b) separately, any transfers between the profit and loss account and other reserves,

(c) any increase or reduction in the balance on the profit and loss account since the immediately preceding financial year,

(d) the profit or loss brought forward at the beginning of the financial year, and

(e) the profit or loss carried forward at the end of the financial year.

(2) There shall be shown in the notes to the accounts the aggregate amount of any dividends proposed before the date of approval of the accounts which have not been shown in the notes to the profit and loss account in accordance with subparagraph (1).][a]

Amendments

a Paragraph (8) substituted by reg 10 and Sch 2, Item No 11(b) of EC(IFRSMA)R 2005.

Section B
The Required Formats for Accounts

Preliminary

9. (1) References in this Part of this Schedule to the balance sheet format or to profit and loss account formats are to the balance sheet format or profit and loss account formats set out below and references to the items listed in any of the formats are to those items read together with any of the notes following the formats for alternative positions for any particular item.

(2) The requirement imposed by paragraph 1 of this Part of this Schedule to show the items listed in any such format in the order adopted in the format is subject to any provision in the notes following the formats for alternative positions for any particular items.

Definitions

'company': CA 1963, s 2(1); 'director': CA 1963, s 2(1); 'financial year': CA 1963, s 2(1); 'member': CA 1963, s 2(1).

---

10. A number in brackets following any item in any of the formats set out below is a reference to the note of that number in the notes following the formats.

BALANCE SHEET FORMAT
ASSETS

1. Cash and balances at central and post office banks (1)
2. Central Government bills and other bills eligible for refinancing with a central bank (20)
   (a) Exchequer bills and similar securities (2)
   (b) Other eligible bills (3)
3. Loans and advances to banks (4), (20)
   (a) Repayable on demand
   (b) Other loans and advances
4. Loans and advances to customers (5), (20)
5. Debt securities and other fixed income securities (6), (20)
   (a) Issued by public bodies
   (b) Issued by other issuers
6. Equity shares and other variable-yield securities
7. Participating interests
8. Shares in group undertakings
9. Intangible fixed assets (7)
10. Tangible fixed assets (8)
11. Called up capital not paid (9)
12. Own shares (10)
13. Other assets
14. Called up capital not paid (9)
15. Prepayments and accrued income

Total assets

LIABILITIES

1. Deposits by banks (11), (20)
   (a) Repayable on demand
   (b) With agreed maturity dates or periods of notice
2. Customer accounts (12), (20)
   (a) Repayable on demand
   (b) With agreed maturity dates or periods of notice
3. Debt securities in issue (13), (20)
   (a) Bonds and medium term notes
   (b) Others
4. Other liabilities
5. Accruals and deferred income
6. [Provisions for liabilities][a]
   (a) Provisions for pensions and similar obligations
   (b) Provisions for tax
   (c) Other provisions
7. Subordinated liabilities (14), (20)
8. Called up share capital (15)
9. Share premium account
10. Reserves
   (a) Capital redemption reserve
   (b) Reserve for own shares
   (c) Reserves provided for by the articles of association
   (d) Other reserves
11. Revaluation reserve
12. Profit and loss account

Total Liabilities

OFF-BALANCE SHEET ITEMS

1. Contingent liabilities (16)
   (1) Acceptances and endorsements
   (2) Guarantees and assets pledged as collateral security (17)
   (3) Other contingent liabilities
2. Commitments (18)
   (1) Commitments arising out of sale and option to resell transactions (19)
   (2) Other commitments

Amendments

a Words substituted by reg 10 and Sch 2, Item No 11(c) of EC(IFRSMA)R 2005.

Notes on the Balance Sheet Format and Off-Balance Sheet Items

(1) Cash and balances at central and post office banks

(ASSETS ITEM 1)

Cash shall comprise all currency including foreign notes and coins.

Only those balances which may be withdrawn without notice and which are deposited with central or post office banks of the country or countries in which the company is established shall be included in this item. All other claims on central banks must be shown under Assets items 3 or 4.

(2) Central Government bills and other eligible bills: Exchequer bills and similar securities

(ASSETS ITEM 2(a)

Central Government bills and similar securities shall comprise Exchequer bills and similar debt instruments issued by public bodies which are eligible for refinancing with central banks of the country or countries in which the company is established. Any bills or similar debt instruments not so eligible shall be included under Assets item 5, sub-item (a).

(3) Exchequer bills and other eligible bills: other eligible bills

(ASSETS ITEM 2(b)

Other eligible bills shall comprise all bills purchased to the extent that they are eligible, under national law, for refinancing with the central banks of the country or countries in which the company is established.

(4) Loans and advances to banks

(ASSETS ITEM 3)

Loans and advances to banks shall comprise all loans and advances to domestic or foreign credit institutions made by the company arising out of banking transactions. However loans and advances to credit institutions represented by debt securities or other fixed income securities shall be included under Asset item 5 and not this item.

(5) Loans and advances to customers

(ASSETS ITEM 4)

Loans and advances to customers shall comprise all types of assets in the form of claims on domestic and foreign customers other than credit institutions. However loans and advances represented by debt securities or other fixed income securities shall be included under Assets item 5 and not this item.

(6) Debt securities and other fixed income securities

(ASSETS ITEM 5)

This item shall comprise transferable debt securities and any other transferable fixed income securities issued by credit institutions, other undertakings or public bodies. Debt securities and other fixed income securities issued by public bodies shall however only be included in this item if they may not be shown under Assets item 2.

Where a company holds its own debt securities these shall not be included under this item but shall be deducted from Liabilities item 3 (a) or (b), as appropriate.

Securities bearing interest rates that vary in accordance with specific factors, for example the interest rate on the inter-bank market or on the Euromarket, shall also be regarded as fixed income securities to be included under this item.

(7) Intangible fixed assets

(ASSETS ITEM 9)

This item shall comprise:

(a) development costs;

(b) concessions, patents, licenses, trade marks and similar rights and assets;

(c) goodwill; and

(d) payments on account.

Amounts shall, however,be included in respect of (b) only if the assets were acquired for valuable consideration or the assets in question were created by the company itself.

Amounts representing goodwill shall only be included to the extent that the goodwill was acquired for valuable consideration.

There shall be disclosed, in a note to the accounts, the amount of any goodwill included in this item.

(8) Tangible fixed assets

(ASSETS ITEM 10)

This item shall comprise:

- land and buildings;
- plant and machinery;
- fixtures and fittings, tools and equipment; and
- payments on account and assets in the course of construction.

There shall be disclosed in a note to the accounts the amount included in this item with respect to land and buildings occupied by the company for its own activities.

(9) Called up capital not paid

(ASSETS ITEM 11 AND 14)

The two positions shown for this item are alternatives.

(10) Own Shares

(ASSETS ITEM 12)

The nominal value of the shares held shall be shown separately under this item.

(11) Deposits by banks

(LIABILITIES ITEM 1)

Deposits by banks shall comprise all amounts arising out of banking transactions owed to other domestic or foreign credit institutions by the company. However liabilities in the form of debt securities and any liabilities for which transferable certificates have been issued shall be included under Liabilities item 3 and not this item.

(12) Customer accounts

(LIABILITIES ITEM 2)

This item shall comprise all amounts owed to creditors that are not credit institutions. However liabilities in the form of debt securities and any liabilities for which transferable certificates have been issued shall be shown under Liabilities item 3 and not this item.

(13) Debt securities in issue

(LIABILITIES ITEM 3)

This item shall include both debt securities and debts for which transferable certificates have been issued, including liabilities arising out of own acceptances and promissory notes. (Only acceptances which a company has issued for its own refinancing and in respect of which it is the first party liable shall be treated as own acceptances).

(14) Subordinated liabilities

(LIABILITIES ITEM 7)

This item shall comprise all liabilities in respect of which there is a contractual obligation that, in the event of winding up or bankruptcy, they are to be repaid only after the claims of other creditors have been met.

This item shall include all subordinated liabilities, whether or not a ranking has been agreed between the subordinated creditors concerned.

(15) Called up share capital

(LIABILITIES ITEM 8)

The amount of allotted share capital and the amount of called up share capital which has been paid up shall be shown separately.

(16) Contingent liabilities

(OFF-BALANCE SHEET ITEM 1)

This item shall include all transactions whereby the company has underwritten the obligations of a third party.

Liabilities arising out of the endorsement of rediscontinued bills shall be included in this item. Acceptances other than own acceptance shall also be included.

(17) Contingent liabilities: Guarantees and assets pledged as collateral security

(OFF-BALANCE SHEET ITEM 1 (2)

This item shall include all guarantee obligations incurred and assets pledged as collateral security on behalf of third parties, particularly in respect of sureties and irrevocable letters of credit.

(18) Commitments

(OFF-BALANCE SHEET ITEM 2)

This item shall include every irrevocable commitment which could give rise to a credit risk.

(19) Commitments: Commitments arising out of sale and option to resell transactions

(OFF-BALANCE SHEET ITEM 2(1))

This sub-item shall comprise commitments entered into by the company in the context of sale and option to resell transactions.

(20) Claims on, and liabilities to, undertakings in which a participating interest is held or group undertakings

(ASSETS ITEMS 2 TO 5, LIABILITIES ITEMS 1 TO 3 AND 7)

The following information must be given either by way of subdivision of the relevant items or by way of notes to the accounts.

The amount of the following must be shown for each of Assets items 2 to 5:

(a) claims on group undertakings included therein; and

(b) claims on undertakings in which the company has a participating interest included therein.

The amount of the following must be shown for each of Liabilities items, 1, 2, 3 and 7:

(i) liabilities to group undertakings included therein; and

(ii) liabilities to undertakings in which the company has a participating interest included therein.

Definitions

'accounts': EC(CI:A)R 1992, reg 2(1); 'company': CA 1963, s 2(1); 'director': CA 1963, s 2(1); 'financial year': CA 1963, s 2(1); 'member': CA 1963, s 2(1); 'undertaking': EC(CI:A)R 1992, reg 2(1); 'banking transactions': EC(CI:A)R 1992, Sch, Pt IV; 'group undertakings: EC(CI:A)R 1992, Sch, Pt IV; 'participating interest: EC(CI:A)R 1992, Sch, Pt IV; 'sale and option to resell transaction': EC(CI:A)R 1992, Sch, Pt IV.

Special Rules

Subordinated assets

11. (1) The amount of any assets that are subordinated must be shown either as a subdivision of any relevant asset item or in the notes to the accounts; in the latter case disclosure shall be by reference to the relevant asset item or items in which the assets are included.

(2) In the case of Assets items 2 to 5 in the balance sheet format, the amounts required to be shown by note (20) to the format as sub-items of those items shall be further subdivided so as to show the amount of any claims included therein that are subordinated.

(3) For this purpose, assets are subordinated if there is a contractual obligation to the effect that, in the event of winding up or bankruptcy, they are to be repaid only after the claims of other creditors have been met, whether or not a ranking has been agreed between the subordinated creditors concerned.

Definitions

'accounts': EC(CI:A)R 1992, reg 2(1); 'company': CA 1963, s 2(1); 'director': CA 1963, s 2(1); 'financial year': CA 1963, s 2(1); 'member': CA 1963, s 2(1).

Syndicated loans

12. (1) Where a company is a party to a syndicated loan transaction the company shall include only that part of the total loan which it itself has funded.

(2) Where a company is a party to a syndicated loan transaction and has agreed to reimburse (in whole or in part) any other party to the syndicate any funds advanced by that party or any interest thereon upon the occurrence of any event, including the default of the borrower, any additional liability by reason of such a guarantee shall be included as a contingent liability in off-balance sheet item 1, sub-item (2).

Definitions

'company': CA 1963, s 2(1); 'director': CA 1963, s 2(1); 'financial year': CA 1963, s 2(1); 'member': CA 1963, s 2(1).

Sale and repurchase transactions

13. (1) The following rules apply where a company is a party to a sale and repurchase transaction.

(2) Where the company is the transferor of the assets under the transaction:

(a) the assets transferred shall, notwithstanding the transfer, be included in its balance sheet;

(b) the purchase price received by it shall be included in its balance sheet as an amount owed to the transferee; and

(c) the value of the assets transferred shall be disclosed in a note to its accounts.

(3) Where the company is the transferee of the assets under the transaction it shall not include the assets transferred in its balance sheet but the purchase price paid by it to the transferor shall be so included as an amount owed by the transferor.

Definitions

'accounts': EC(CI:A)R 1992, reg 2(1); 'company': CA 1963, s 2(1); 'director': CA 1963, s 2(1); 'financial year': CA 1963, s 2(1); 'member': CA 1963, s 2(1); 'sale and repurchase transaction': EC(CI:A)R 1992, Sch, Pt IV.

Sale and option to resell transactions

14. (1) The following rules apply where a company is a party to a sale and option to resell transaction.

(2) Where the company is the transferor of the assets under the transaction it shall not include in its balance sheet the assets transferred but it shall enter under off-balance sheet item 2 an amount equal to the price agreed in the event of repurchase.

(3) Where the company is the transferee of the assets under the transaction it shall include those assets in its balance sheet.

Definitions

'accounts': EC(CI:A)R 1992, reg 2(1); 'company': CA 1963, s 2(1); 'director': CA 1963, s 2(1); 'financial year': CA 1963, s 2(1); 'member': CA 1963, s 2(1); 'sale and option to resell transaction': EC(CI:A)R 1992, Sch, Pt IV.

Managed funds

15. (1) For the purpose of this paragraph "managed funds" are funds which the company administers in its own name but on behalf of others and to which it has legal title.

(2) The company shall, in any case where claims and obligations arising in respect of managed funds fall to be treated as claims and obligations of the company, adopt the following accounting treatment: claims and obligations representing managed funds are to be included in the company's balance sheet, with the notes to the accounts disclosing the total amount included with respect to such assets and liabilities in the balance sheet and showing the amount included under each relevant balance sheet item in respect of such assets or (as the case may be) liabilities.

Definitions

'accounts': EC(CI:A)R 1992, reg 2(1); 'company': CA 1963, s 2(1); 'director': CA 1963, s 2(1); 'financial year': CA 1963, s 2(1); 'member': CA 1963, s 2(1).

PROFIT AND LOSS ACCOUNT FORMATS

FORMAT 1

Vertical Layout

1. Interest receivable and similar income (1)
   (1) Interest receivable and similar income arising from debt securities and other fixed income securities
   (2) Other interest receivable and similar income
2. Interest payable and similar charges (2)
3. Dividend income
   (a) Income from equity shares and other variable-yield securities
   (b) Income from participating interests
   (c) Income from shares in group undertakings

4. Fees and commissions receivable (3)
5. Fees and commissions payable (4)
6. Dealing profits or losses (5)
7. Other operating income
8. Administrative expenses
   (a) Staff costs
      (i) Wages and salaries
      (ii) Social security costs
      (iii) Other pension costs
   (b) Other administrative expenses
9. Depreciation and amortisation (6)
10. Other operating charges
11. Provisions
   (a) Provisions for bad and doubtful debts (7)
   (b) Provisions for contingent liabilities and commitments (8)
12. Adjustments to provisions
   (a) Adjustments to provisions for bad and doubtful debts (9)
   (b) Adjustments to provisions for contingent liabilities and commitments (10)
13. Amounts written off fixed asset investments (11)
14. Adjustments to amounts written off fixed asset investments (12)
15. Profit or loss on ordinary activities before tax
16. Tax on profit or loss on ordinary activities.
17. Profit or loss on ordinary activities after tax
18. Extraordinary income
19. Extraordinary charges
20. Extraordinary profit or loss
21. Tax on extraordinary profit or loss
22. Extraordinary profit or loss after tax
23. Other taxes not shown under the preceding items
24. Profit or loss for the financial year

FORMAT 2

Horizontal layout

A. Charges

1. Interest payable and similar charges (2)
2. Fees and commission payable (4)
3. Dealing losses (5)
4. Administrative expenses
   (a) Staff costs
      (i) Wages and salaries
      (ii) Social security costs
      (iii) Other pension costs
   (b) Other administrative expenses

5. Depreciation and amortisation (6)
6. Other operating charges
7. Provisions
   (a) Provisions for bad and doubtful debts (7)
   (b) Provisions for contingent liabilities and commitments (8)
8. Amounts written off fixed asset investments (11)
9. Profit on ordinary activities before tax
10. Tax on profit or loss on ordinary activities
11. Profit on ordinary activities after tax
12. Extraordinary charges
13. Tax on extraordinary profit or loss
14. Extraordinary loss after tax
15. Other taxes not shown under the preceding items
16. Profit for the financial year.

B. Income

1. Interest receivable and similar income (1)
   (1) Interest receivable and similar income arising from debt securities and other fixed income securities
   (2) Other interest receivable and similar income
2. Dividend income
   (a) Income from equity shares and other variable-yield securities
   (b) Income from participating interests
   (c) Income from shares in group undertakings
3. Fees and commissions receivable (3)
4. Dealing profits (5)
5. Adjustments to provisions
   (a) Adjustments to provisions for bad and doubtful debts (9)
   (b) Adjustments to provisions for contingent liabilities and commitments (10)
6. Adjustments to amounts written off fixed asset investments (12)
7. Other operating income
8. Loss on ordinary activities before tax
9. Loss on ordinary activities after tax
10. Extraordinary income
11. Extraordinary profit after tax
12. Loss for the financial year

Notes on the Profit and Loss Account Formats

(1) Interest receivable and similar income

(FORMAT 1, ITEM 1; FORMAT 2, ITEM B1)

This item shall include all income arising out of banking activities, including:

(a) income from assets included in Assets items 1 to 5 in the balance sheet format, however calculated;

(b) income resulting from covered forward contracts, spread over the actual duration of the contract and similar in nature to interest; and

(c) fees and commissions receivable similar in nature to interest and calculated on a time basis or by reference to the amount of the claim (but not other fees and commissions receivable).

(2) Interest payable and similar charges

(FORMAT 1, ITEM 2; FORMAT 2, ITEM A1)

This item shall include all expenditure arising out of banking activities, including:

(a) charges arising out of liabilities included in Liabilities items 1, 2, 3 and 7 in the balance sheet format, however calculated;

(b) charges resulting from covered forward contracts, spread over the actual duration of the contract and similar in nature to interest; and

(c) fees and commissions payable similar in nature to interest and calculated on a time basis or by reference to the amount of the liability (but not other fees and commissions payable).

(3) Fees and commissions receivable

(FORMAT 1, ITEM 4; FORMAT 2, ITEM B3)

Fees and commissions receivable shall comprise income in respect of all services supplied by the company to third parties, but not fees or commissions required to be included under interest receivable.

(FORMAT 1, ITEM 1; FORMAT 2, ITEM B1)

In particular the following fees and commissions receivable must be included (unless required to be included under interest receivable):

– fees and commissions for guarantees, loan administration on behalf of other lenders and securities transactions;

– fees, commissions and other income in respect of payment transactions, account administration charges and commissions for the safe custody and administration of securities;

– fees and commissions for foreign currency transactions and for the sale and purchase of coin and precious metals; and

– fees and commissions charged for brokerage services in connection with savings and insurance contracts and loans.

(4) Fees and commissions payable

(FORMAT 1, ITEM 5; FORMAT 2, ITEM A2)

Fees and commissions payable shall comprise charges for all services rendered to the company by third parties but not fees or commissions required to be included under interest payable (Format 1, item 2; Format 2, item A1).

In particular the following fees and commissions payable must be included (unless required to be included under interest payable):

- fees and commissions for guarantees, loan administration and securities transactions;
- fees, commissions and other charges in respect of payment transactions, account administration charges and commission for the safe custody and administration of securities;
- fees and commissions for foreign currency transactions and for the sale and purchase of coin and precious metals; and
- fees and commissions for brokerage service in connection with savings and insurance contracts and loans.

(5) Dealing profits or losses

(FORMAT 1, ITEM 6, FORMAT 2, ITEMS B4 AND A3)

This item shall comprise:

(a) the net profit or net loss on transactions in securities which are not held as financial fixed assets together with amounts written off or written back with respect to such securities, including amounts written off or written back as a result of the application of paragraph 34(1) below;

(b) the net profit or loss on exchange activities, save in so far as the profit or loss is included in interest receivable or interest payable (format 1, items 1 or 2; format 2, items B1 or A1); and

(c) the net profits and losses on other dealing operations involving financial instruments, including precious metals.

(6) Depreciation and amortisation

(FORMAT 1, ITEM 9; FORMAT 2, ITEM A5)

This item shall comprise depreciation and other amounts written off in respect of balance sheet Assets items 9 and 10.

(7) Provisions: Provisions for bad and doubtful debts

(FORMAT 1, ITEM 11(a); FORMAT 2, ITEM 7(a))

Provisions for bad or doubtful debts shall comprise charges for amount written off and for provisions made in respect of loans and advances shown under balance sheet Assets items 3 and 4.

(8) Provisions: Provisions for contingent liabilities and commitments

(FORMAT 1, ITEM 11(b); FORMAT 2, ITEM A7(b))

This item shall comprise charges for provisions for contingent liabilities and commitments of a type which would, if not provided for, be shown under off-balance sheet items 1 and 2.

(9) Adjustments to provisions: Adjustments to provisions for bad and doubtful debts

(FORMAT 1, ITEM 12 (a); FORMAT 2, ITEM B5(a))

This item shall include credits from the recovery of loans that have been written off, from other advances written back following earlier write offs and from the reduction of provisions previously made with respect to loans and advances.

(10) Adjustments to provisions: Adjustments to provisions for contingent liabilities and commitments

(FORMAT 1, ITEM 12(b); FORMAT 2, ITEM B5(b))

This item comprises credits from the reduction of provisions previously made with respect to contingent liabilities and commitments.

(11) Amounts written off fixed assets investments

(FORMAT 12, ITEM 13; FORMAT 2, ITEM A8)

Amounts written off fixed assets investments shall comprise amounts written off in respect of assets which are transferable securities held as financial fixed assets, participating interests and shares in group undertakings and which are included in Assets items 5 to 8 in the balance sheet format.

(12) Adjustments to amounts written off fixed asset investments

(FORMAT 1, ITEM 14; FORMAT 2, ITEM B6)

Adjustments to amounts written off fixed assets investments shall include amounts written back following earlier write offs and provisions in respect of assets which are transferable securities held as financial fixed assets, participating interests and group undertakings and which are included in Assets items 5 to 8 in the balance sheet format.

Definitions

'company': CA 1963, s 2(1); 'director': CA 1963, s 2(1); 'financial year': CA 1963, s 2(1); 'member': CA 1963, s 2(1); 'banking activities': Sch, Pt IV; 'financial fixed assets': Sch, Pt IV; 'group undertakings: Sch, Pt IV; 'participating interest: Sch, Pt IV.

Chapter II
Accounting Principles and Rules

Section A
Accounting Principles

16. Subject to paragraph 22 below, the amounts to be included in respect of all items shown in [Companies Act individual accounts][a] shall be determined in accordance with the principles set out in paragraphs 17 to 21.

Amendments

a Words substituted by reg 10 and Schedule 2, Item No 11(d) of EC(IFRSMA)R 2005 (SI 116/2005).

Definitions

'accounts': reg 2(1); 'company': CA 1963, s 2(1); 'Companies act individual accounts': CA 1963, s 2(1); 'director': CA 1963, s 2(1); 'financial year': CA 1963, s 2(1); 'member': CA 1963, s 2(1).

Accounting principles

17. The company shall be presumed to be carrying on business as a going concern.

Definitions

'company': CA 1963, s 2(1); 'director': CA 1963, s 2(1); 'financial year': CA 1963, s 2(1); 'member': CA 1963, s 2(1).

18. Accounting policies shall be applied consistently within the same accounts and from one financial year to the next.

Definitions

'accounts': EC(CI:A)R 1992, reg 2(1); 'company': CA 1963, s 2(1); 'director': CA 1963, s 2(1); 'financial year': CA 1963, s 2(1); 'member': CA 1963, s 2(1).

19. The amount of any item shall be determined on a prudent basis and, in particular:

(a) only profits realised at the balance sheet date shall be included in the profit and loss account; and

(b) [all liabilities which have arisen][a] in respect of the financial year to which the accounts relate or a previous financial year shall be taken into account, including those which only become apparent between the balance sheet date and the date on which it is signed on behalf of the board of directors in pursuance of section 156 of the Principal Act.

Amendments

a Words substituted by reg 10 and Schedule 2, Item No 11(e) of EC(IFRSMA)R 2005 (SI 116/2005).

Definitions

'accounts': EC(CI:A)R 1992, reg 2(1); 'company': CA 1963, s 2(1); 'director': CA 1963, s 2(1); 'financial year': CA 1963, s 2(1); 'member': CA 1963, s 2(1); 'the Principal Act': EC(CI:A)R 1992, reg 2(1).

20. All income and charges relating to the financial year to which the accounts relate shall be taken into account, without regard to the date of receipt or payment.

Definitions

'accounts': EC(CI:A)R 1992, reg 2(1); 'company': CA 1963, s 2(1); 'director': CA 1963, s 2(1); 'financial year': CA 1963, s 2(1); 'member': CA 1963, s 2(1).

[20A. The directors of a company shall, in determining how amounts are presented within items in the profit and loss account and balance sheet, have regard to the substance of the reported transaction or arrangement, in accordance with generally accepted accounting principles or practice.][a]

Amendments

a Words substituted by reg 10 and Schedule 2, Item No 11(f) of EC(IFRSMA)R 2005 (SI 116/2005).

21. In determining the aggregate amount of any item the amount of each individual asset or liability that falls to be taken into account shall be determined separately.

Departure from the Accounting Principles

22. If it appears to the directors of a company that there are special reasons for departing from any of the principles stated above in preparing the company's accounts in respect of any financial year they may do so, but particulars of the departure, the reasons for it and its effect on the accounts shall be given in a note to the accounts.

Definitions

'accounts': EC(CI:A)R 1992, reg 2(1); 'company': CA 1963, s 2(1); 'director': CA 1963, s 2(1); 'financial year': CA 1963, s 2(1); 'member': CA 1963, s 2(1).

Section B
Valuation Rules

HISTORICAL COST ACCOUNTING RULES

Preliminary

23. Subject to paragraphs 39 to 44 of this part of this Schedule, the amounts to be included in respect of all items shown in [Companies Act individual accounts][a] shall be determined in accordance with the rules set out in paragraph 24 to 38 of this part of the Schedule.

Amendments

a Words substituted by reg 10 and Schedule 2, Item No 11(g) of EC(IFRSMA)R 2005 (SI 116/2005).

Definitions

'accounts': EC(CI:A)R 1992, reg 2(1); 'company': CA 1963, s 2(1); 'Companies Act individual accounts'; CA 1963, s 2(1);'director': CA 1963, s 2(1); 'financial year': CA 1963, s 2(1); 'member': CA 1963, s 2(1).

Fixed Assets

General Rules

24. Subject to any provision for depreciation or diminution in value made in accordance with paragraph 25 or 26 the amount to be included in respect of any fixed asset shall be its cost.

Definitions

'accounts': EC(CI:A)R 1992, reg 2(1); 'company': CA 1963, s 2(1); 'director': CA 1963, s 2(1); 'financial year': CA 1963, s 2(1); 'member': CA 1963, s 2(1).

---

25. In the case of any fixed asset which has a limited useful economic life, the amount of:

(a) its cost, or

(b) where it is estimated that any such asset will have a residual value at the end of the period of its useful economic life, its cost less that estimated residual value,

shall be reduced by provisions for depreciation calculated to write off that amount systematically over the period of the asset's useful economic life.

Definitions

'accounts': EC(CI:A)R 1992, reg 2(1); 'company': CA 1963, s 2(1); 'director': CA 1963, s 2(1); 'financial year': CA 1963, s 2(1); 'member': CA 1963, s 2(1).

---

26. (1) Where a fixed asset investment of a description falling to be included under Assets items 7 (participating interests) or 8 (shares in group undertakings) in the balance sheet format, or any other holding of securities held as a financial fixed asset, has diminished in value, provisions for diminution in value may be made in respect of it and the amount to be included in respect of it may be reduced accordingly; and any such provisions which are not shown separately in the profit and loss account shall be disclosed (either separately or in aggregate) in a note to the accounts.

(2) Provisions for diminution in value shall be made in respect of any fixed asset which has diminished in value if the reduction of its value is expected to be permanent (whether its useful economic life is limited or not), and the amount to be included in respect of it shall be reduced accordingly; and any such provisions which are not shown separately in the profit and loss account shall be disclosed (either separately or in aggregate) in a note to the accounts.

(3) Where the reasons for which any provision was made in accordance with subparagraph (1) or (2) have ceased to apply to any extent, that provision shall be written back to the extent that it is no longer necessary; and any amounts written back in accordance with this subparagraph which are not shown separately in the profit and loss account shall be disclosed (either separately or in aggregate) in a note to the accounts.

Definitions

'accounts': EC(CI:A)R 1992, reg 2(1); 'company': CA 1963, s 2(1); 'director': CA 1963, s 2(1); 'financial year': CA 1963, s 2(1); 'member': CA 1963, s 2(1); 'group undertakings: EC(CI:A)R 1992, Sch, Pt IV; 'participating interest: EC(CI:A)R 1992, Sch, Pt IV.

Development Costs

27. (1) Notwithstanding that amounts representing "development costs" may be included under Assets item 9 in the balance sheet format, an amount may only be included in a company's balance sheet in respect of development costs in special circumstances.

(2) If any amount is included in a company's balance sheet in respect of development costs the following information shall be given in a note to the accounts—

(a) the period over which the amount of those costs originally capitalised is being or is to be written off; and

(b) the reasons for capitalising the development costs in question.

Definitions

'accounts': EC(CI:A)R 1992, reg 2(1); 'company': CA 1963, s 2(1); 'director': CA 1963, s 2(1); 'financial year': CA 1963, s 2(1); 'member': CA 1963, s 2(1).

Goodwill

28. (1) The application of paragraphs 24 to 26 in relation to goodwill (in any case where goodwill is treated as an asset) is subject to the following provisions of this paragraph.

(2) Subject to subparagraph (3) below the amount of the consideration for any goodwill acquired by a company shall be reduced by provisions for depreciation calculated to write off that amount systematically over a period chosen by the directors of the company.

(3) The period chosen shall not exceed the useful economic life of the goodwill in question.

(4) In any case where any goodwill acquired by a company is included as an asset in the company's balance sheet the period chosen for writing off the consideration for that goodwill and the reasons for choosing that period shall be disclosed in a note to the accounts.

Definitions

'accounts': EC(CI:A)R 1992, reg 2(1); 'company': CA 1963, s 2(1); 'director': CA 1963, s 2(1); 'financial year': CA 1963, s 2(1); 'member': CA 1963, s 2(1).

Intangible and tangible fixed assets

29. Assets included in Assets items 9 (Intangible fixed assets) and 10 (Tangible fixed assets) in the balance sheet format shall be valued as fixed assets.

Definitions

'accounts': EC(CI:A)R 1992, reg 2(1); 'company': CA 1963, s 2(1); 'director': CA 1963, s 2(1); 'financial year': CA 1963, s 2(1); 'member': CA 1963, s 2(1).

Other fixed assets

30. Other assets falling to be included in the balance sheet shall be valued as fixed assets where they are intended for use on a continuing basis in the company's activities.

Financial fixed assets

31. (1) Debts securities, including fixed income securities, held as financial fixed assets shall be included in the balance sheet at an amount equal to their maturity value plus any premium, or less any discount, on their purchase, subject to the following provisions of this paragraph.

(2) The amount included in the balance sheet with respect to such securities purchased at a premium shall be reduced each financial year on a systematic basis, in accordance with best accounting practices, so as to write the premium off over the period to the maturity date of the security and the amounts so written off shall be charged to the profit and loss account for the relevant financial years.

(3) The amount included in the balance sheet with respect to such securities purchased at a discount shall be increased each financial year on a systematic basis, in accordance with best accounting practices, so as to extinguish the discount over the period to the maturity date of the security and the amounts by which the amount is increased shall be credited to the profit and loss account for the relevant years.

(4) The notes to the accounts shall disclose the amount of any unamortised premium or discount not extinguished which is included in the balance sheet by virtue of subparagraph (1).

(5) For the purposes of this paragraph "premium" means any excess of the amount paid for a security over its maturity value and "discount" means any deficit of the amount paid for a security over its maturity value.

Cross reference

EC(CI)(FVA)R 2004 provides para (1) of this regulation shall not apply in respect of current assets and liabilities valued in accordance with paras 46A, 46B, 46C and 46D.

Definitions

'accounts': EC(CI:A)R 1992, reg 2(1); 'company': CA 1963, s 2(1); 'director': CA 1963, s 2(1); 'financial year': CA 1963, s 2(1); 'member': CA 1963, s 2(1); 'financial fixed assets': EC(CI:A)R 1992, Sch, Pt IV.

Current Assets

32. The amount to be included in respect of loans and advances, debt or other fixed income securities and equity shares or other variable yield securities not held as financial fixed assets shall be their cost, subject to paragraphs 33 and 34 below.

Cross reference

EC(CI)(FVA)R 2004 provides this paragraph of this regulation shall not apply in respect of current assets and liabilities valued in accordance with paras 46A, 46B, 46C and 46D.

Definitions

'company': CA 1963, s 2(1); 'director': CA 1963, s 2(1); 'financial year': CA 1963, s 2(1); 'member': CA 1963, s 2(1); 'financial fixed assets': EC(CI:A)R 1992, Sch, Pt IV.

---

33. (1) If the net realisable value of any asset referred to in paragraph 32 is lower than its cost the amount to be included in respect of that asset shall be the net realisable value.

(2) Where the reasons for which any provision for diminution in value was made in accordance with subparagraph (1) have ceased to apply to an extent that provision shall be written back to the extent that it is no longer necessary.

Cross reference

EC(CI)(FVA)R 2004 provides this paragraph of this regulation shall not apply in respect of current assets and liabilities valued in accordance with paras 46A, 46B, 46C and 46D.

Definitions

'company': CA 1963, s 2(1); 'director': CA 1963, s 2(1); 'financial year': CA 1963, s 2(1); 'member': CA 1963, s 2(1).

---

34. (1) Subject to paragraph 33 above, the amount to be included in the balance sheet in respect of transferable securities not held as financial fixed assets may be the higher of their cost or their market value at the balance sheet date.

(2) The difference between the cost of any securities included in the balance sheet at a valuation under subparagraph (1) and their market value shall be shown (in aggregate) in the notes to the accounts.

Cross reference

EC(CI)(FVA)R 2004 provides this paragraph of this regulation shall not apply in respect of current assets and liabilities valued in accordance with paras 46A, 46B, 46C and 46D.

Definitions

'accounts': EC(CI:A)R 1992, reg 2(1); 'company': CA 1963, s 2(1); 'director': CA 1963, s 2(1); 'financial year': CA 1963, s 2(1); 'member': CA 1963, s 2(1); 'financial fixed assets': EC(CI:A)R 1992, Sch, Pt IV.

Miscellaneous and Supplementary Provisions

Excess of money owed over value received as an asset item

35. (1) Where the amount repayable on any debt owed by a company is greater than the value of the consideration received in the transaction giving rise to the debt, the amount of the difference may be treated as an asset.

(2) Where any such amount is so treated:

(a) it shall be written off by reasonable amounts each year and must be completely written off before repayment of the debt; and

(b) if the current amount is not shown as a separate item in the company's balance sheet it must be disclosed in a note to the accounts.

Definitions

'accounts': EC(CI:A)R 1992, reg 2(1); 'company': CA 1963, s 2(1); 'director': CA 1963, s 2(1); 'financial year': CA 1963, s 2(1); 'member': CA 1963, s 2(1).

Determination of cost

36. (1) The cost of an asset that has been acquired by the company shall be determined by adding to the actual price paid any expenses incidental to its acquisition.

(2) The cost of an asset constructed by the company shall be determined by adding to the purchase price of the raw materials and consumables used the amount of the costs incurred by the company which are directly attributable to the construction of that asset.

(3) In addition, there may be included in the cost of an asset constructed by the company:

(a) a reasonable proportion of the costs incurred by the company which are only indirectly attributable to the construction of that asset, but only to the extent that they relate to the period of construction; and

(b) interest on capital borrowed to finance the construction of that asset, to the extent that it accrues in respect of the period of construction;

provided, however, in a case within subparagraph (b) above, that the inclusion of the interest in determining the cost of that asset and the amount of the interest so included is disclosed in a note to the accounts.

Definitions

'accounts': EC(CI:A)R 1992, reg 2(1); 'company': CA 1963, s 2(1); 'director': CA 1963, s 2(1); 'financial year': CA 1963, s 2(1); 'member': CA 1963, s 2(1).

37. (1) Subject to the qualification mentioned below, the cost of any assets which are fungible assets (including investments) may be determined by the application of any of the methods mentioned in subparagraph (2) below in relation to any such assets of the same class.

The method chosen must be one which appears to the directors to be appropriate in the circumstances of the company.

(2) Those methods are:

(a) the method known as "first in, first out" (FIFO);

(b) a weighted average price; and

(c) any other method similar to any of the methods mentioned above.

(3) Where in the case of any company:

(a) the cost of assets falling to be included under any item shown in the company's balance sheet has been determined by the application of any method permitted by this paragraph; and

(b) the amount shown in respect of that item differs materially from the relevant alternative amount given below in this paragraph;

the amount of that difference shall be disclosed in a note to the accounts.

(4) Subject to subparagraph (5) below, for the purposes of subparagraph (3)(b) above, the relevant alternative amount, in relation to any item shown in company's balance sheet, is the amount which would have been shown in respect of that item if assets of any class included under that item at an amount determined by any method permitted by this paragraph had instead been included at their replacement cost as at the balance sheet date.

(5) The relevant alternative amount may be determined by reference to the most recent actual purchase price before the balance sheet date of assets of any class included under the item in question instead of by reference to their replacement cost as at that date, but only if the former appears to the directors of the company to constitute the more appropriate standard of comparison in the case of assets of that class.

Definitions

'accounts': EC(CI:A)R 1992, reg 2(1); 'company': CA 1963, s 2(1); 'director': CA 1963, s 2(1); 'financial year': CA 1963, s 2(1); 'member': CA 1963, s 2(1); 'fungible assets': EC(CI:A)R 1992, Sch, Pt IV.

Substitution of original amount where price or cost unknown

38. Where there is no record of the purchase price of any asset acquired by a company or of any price, expenses or costs relevant for determining its cost in accordance with paragraph 36, or any such record cannot be obtained without unreasonable expense or delay, its cost shall be taken for the purposes of paragraphs 24 to 34 to be the value ascribed to it in the earliest available record on its value made on or after its acquisition by the company.

Alternative Accounting Rules

Preliminary

39. (1) The rules set out in paragraphs 24 to 38 are referred to below in this Schedule as the historical cost accounting rules.

(2) Paragraphs 24 to 27 and 31 to 35 are referred to below in this section of this Part of this Schedule as the depreciation rules; and references below in this Schedule to the historical cost accounting rules do not include the depreciation rules as they apply by virtue of paragraph 42.

Definitions

'company': CA 1963, s 2(1); 'director': CA 1963, s 2(1); 'financial year': CA 1963, s 2(1); 'member': CA 1963, s 2(1).

40. Subject to paragraphs 42 to 44, the amounts to be included in respect of assets of any description mentioned in paragraph 41 may be determined on any basis so mentioned.

Definitions

'company': CA 1963, s 2(1); 'director': CA 1963, s 2(1); 'financial year': CA 1963, s 2(1); 'member': CA 1963, s 2(1).

Alternative Accounting Rules

41. (1) Intangible fixed assets, other than goodwill, may be included at their current cost.

(2) Tangible fixed assets may be included at a market value determined as at the date of their last valuation or at their current cost.

[(3)Investments of any description falling to be included under Assets items 7 (Participating interests) or 8 (Shares in group undertakings) of the balance sheet format and any other securities held as financial fixed assets may be included:

(a) at a market value determined as at the date of their last valuation,

(b) at a value determined on any basis which appears to the directors to be appropriate in the circumstances of the company, or

(c) at fair value determined in accordance with paragraphs 46A to 46D,

but in the case of (b) or (c) particulars of the method of valuation determined and the reasons for its determination shall be disclosed in a note to the accounts.][a]

(4) Securities of any description not held as financial fixed assets (if not valued in accordance with paragraph 34 above) may be included at their current cost.

Amendments

a Substituted by reg 5 of EC(CI) (FVA)R 2004.

Definitions

'accounts': EC(CI:A)R 1992, reg 2(1); 'company': CA 1963, s 2(1); 'director': CA 1963, s 2(1); 'financial year': CA 1963, s 2(1); 'member': CA 1963, s 2(1); 'financial fixed assets': EC(CI:A)R 1992, Sch, Pt IV; 'group undertakings': Sch, Pt IV; 'participating interest: EC(CI:A)R 1992, Sch, Pt IV.

Application of the depreciation rules

42. (1) Where the value of any asset of a company is determined in accordance with paragraph 41, that value shall be, or (as the case may require) be the starting point for determining, the amount to be included in respect of that asset in the company's accounts, instead of its cost or any value previously so determined for that asset; and the depreciation rules shall apply accordingly in relation to any such asset with the substitution for any reference to its cost of a reference to the value most recently determined for that asset in accordance with paragraph 41.

(2) The amount of any provision for depreciation required in the case of any fixed asset by paragraph 25 or 26 as it applies by virtue of subparagraph (1) is referred to below in this paragraph as the "adjusted amount", and the amount of any provision which would be required by that paragraph in the case of that asset according to the historical cost accounting rules is referred to as the "historical cost amount".

(3) Where subparagraph (1) applies in the case of any fixed asset the amount of any provision for depreciation in respect of that asset included in any item shown in the profit and loss account in respect of amounts written off assets of the description in question may be the historical cost amount instead of the adjusted amount, provided that the amount of any difference between the two is shown separately in the profit and loss account or in a note to the accounts.

Definitions

'accounts': EC(CI:A)R 1992, reg 2(1); 'company': CA 1963, s 2(1); 'director': CA 1963, s 2(1); 'financial year': CA 1963, s 2(1); 'member': CA 1963, s 2(1).

Additional Information to be Provided in Case of Departure from Historical Cost Accounting Rules

43. (1) This paragraph applies where amounts to be included in respect of assets covered by any items shown in a company's accounts have been determined in accordance with paragraph 41.

(2) The items affected and the basis of valuation adopted in determining the amounts of the assets in question in the case of each such item shall be disclosed in a note to the accounts.

(3) In the case of each balance sheet item affected either:

(a) the comparable amounts determined according to the historical cost accounting rules; or

(b) the difference between those amounts and the corresponding amounts actually shown in the balance sheet in respect of that item;

shall be shown separately in the balance sheet or in a note to the accounts.

(4) In subparagraph (3) above, references in relation to any item to the comparable amounts determined as there mentioned are references to:

(a) the aggregate amount which would be required to be shown in respect of that item if the amounts to be included in respect of all the assets covered by that item were determined according to the historical cost accounting rules; and

(b) the aggregate amount of the cumulative provisions for depreciation or diminution in value which would be permitted or required in determining those amounts according to those rules.

Definitions

'accounts': EC(CI:A)R 1992, reg 2(1); 'company': CA 1963, s 2(1); 'director': CA 1963, s 2(1); 'financial year': CA 1963, s 2(1); 'member': CA 1963, s 2(1).

Revaluation Reserve

44. (1) With respect to any determination of the value of an asset of a company in accordance with paragraph 41, the amount of any profit or loss arising from that determination (after allowing, where appropriate, for any provisions for depreciation or diminution in value made otherwise than by reference to the value so determined and any adjustments of any such provisions made in the light of that determination) shall be credited or (as the case may be) debited to a separate reserve ("the revaluation reserve").

(2) The amount of the revaluation reserve shall be shown in the company's balance sheet under Liabilities item 11 in the balance sheet format, but need not be shown under that name.

(3) An amount may be transferred from the revaluation reserve:

(a) to the profit and loss account, if the amount was previously charged to that account or represents realised profit, or

(b) on capitalisation;

and the revaluation reserve shall be reduced to the extent that the amounts transferred to it are no longer necessary for the purposes of the valuation method used.

(4) In subparagraph (3)(b) "capitalisation", in relation to an amount standing to the credit of the revaluation reserve, means applying it in wholly or partly paying up unissued shares in the company to be allotted to members of the company as fully or partly paid shares.

(5) The revaluation reserve shall not be reduced except as mentioned in this paragraph.

(6) The treatment for taxation purposes of amounts credited or debited to the revaluation reserve shall be disclosed in a note to the accounts.

Definitions

'accounts': EC(CI:A)R 1992, reg 2(1); 'company': CA 1963, s 2(1); 'director': CA 1963, s 2(1); 'financial year': CA 1963, s 2(1); 'member': CA 1963, s 2(1).

Assets and Liabilities Denominated in Foreign Currencies

45. (1) Subject to the following subparagraphs, amounts to be included in respect of assets and liabilities denominated in foreign currencies shall be in Irish pounds (or the currency in which the accounts are drawn up) after translation at an appropriate spot rate of exchange prevailing at the balance sheet date.

(2) An appropriate rate of exchange prevailing on the date of purchase may however be used for assets held as financial fixed assets and assets to be included under Assets item 9 (Intangible fixed assets) and 10 (Tangible fixed assets) in the balance sheet format, if they are not covered or not specifically covered in either the spot or forward currency markets.

(3) An appropriate spot rate of exchange prevailing at the balance sheet date shall be used for translating uncompleted spot exchange transactions.

(4) An appropriate forward rate of exchange prevailing at the balance sheet date shall be used for translating uncompleted forward exchange transactions.

(5) This paragraph does not apply to any assets or liabilities held, or any transactions entered into, for hedging purposes or to any assets or liabilities which are themselves hedged.

Definitions

'accounts': EC(CI:A)R 1992, reg 2(1); 'company': CA 1963, s 2(1); 'director': CA 1963, s 2(1); 'financial year': CA 1963, s 2(1); 'member': CA 1963, s 2(1); 'financial fixed assets': EC(CI:A)R 1992, Sch, Pt IV.

46. (1) Subject to subparagraph (2), any difference between the amount to be included in respect of an asset or liability under paragraph 45 and the book value, after translation into Irish pounds (or the currency in which the accounts are drawn up) at an appropriate rate, of that asset or liability shall be credited or, as the case may be, debited to the profit and loss account.

(2) In the case, however, of assets held as financial fixed assets, of assets to be included under Assets items 9 (Intangible fixed assets) and 10 (Tangible fixed assets) in the balance sheet format and of transactions undertaken to cover such assets, any such difference may be deducted from or credited to any non-distributable reserve available for the purpose.

Definitions

'accounts': EC(CI:A)R 1992, reg 2(1); 'company': CA 1963, s 2(1); 'director': CA 1963, s 2(1); 'financial year': CA 1963, s 2(1); 'member': CA 1963, s 2(1); 'financial fixed assets': EC(CI:A)R 1992, Sch, Pt IV.

[Valuation at fair value

46A.(1) A company is permitted to make a valuation at fair value of financial instruments (including derivatives) at fair value.

(2) For the purposes of this Schedule commodity-based contracts that give either contracting party the right to settle in cash or some other financial instrument are considered to be derivative financial instruments, except when—

(a) they were entered into and continue to meet the company's expected purchase, sale or usage requirements,

(b) they were designated for such purpose at their inception, and

(c) they are expected to be settled by delivery of the commodity.

(3) Subparagraph (1) applies only to liabilities that are—

(a) held as part of a trading portfolio, or

(b) derivative financial instruments.

(4) Valuation according to subparagraph (1) does not apply to—

(a) non-derivative financial instruments held to maturity,

(b) loans and receivables originated by the company and not held for trading purposes, and

(c) interests in subsidiaries, associated undertakings and joint ventures, equity instruments issued by the company, contracts for contingent consideration in a business combination as well as other financial instruments with such special characteristics that the instruments, according to what is generally accepted, should be accounted for differently from other financial instruments.

[(4A) Valuation at fair value may be made by a company in respect of financial instruments which constitute liabilities other than the liabilities referred to in subparagraphs (3)(a) and (3)(b) if—

(a) the valuation is in accordance with international accounting standards as adopted by the Commission Regulation on or before 5 September 2006, and

(b) the associated disclosure requirements, provided for in international financial reporting standards adopted in accordance with the IAS Regulation, are made.

(4B) Valuation at fair value may be made by a company in respect of financial instruments referred to in subparagraph (4) if—

(a) the valuation is in accordance with international accounting standards as adopted by the Commission Regulation on or before 5 September 2006, and

(b) the associated disclosure requirements, provided for in international financial reporting standards adopted in accordance with the IAS Regulation, are made.

(4C) In subparagraphs (4A) and (4B)—

'Commission Regulation' means the Commission Regulation (EC) No. 1725/20035 of 29 September 2003;

'international financial reporting standards' has the meaning assigned to it by the Principal Act;

'IAS Regulation' has the meaning assigned to it by the Principal Act.][b]

(5) Assets and liabilities which qualify as hedged items under a fair value hedge accounting system, or identified portions of such assets or liabilities, may be valued at the specific amount required under that system.

46B. (1) The fair value referred to in paragraph 46A shall be determined by reference to—

(a) a market value, for those financial instruments for which a reliable market can readily be identified. Where a market value is not readily identifiable for an instrument but can be identified for its components or for a similar instrument, the market value may be derived from that of its components or of the similar instrument, or

(b) a value resulting from generally accepted valuation models and techniques, for those instruments for which a reliable market cannot be readily identified. Such valuation models and techniques shall ensure a reasonable approximation of the market value.

(2) Those financial instruments that cannot be measured reliably by any of the methods described in subparagraph (1), shall be measured in accordance with paragraphs 24 to 38.][a]

Amendments

a Amended by reg 6 of EC(CI)(FVA)R 2004.

b Subparagraphs (4A)–(4C) inserted by European Communities (Directive 2006/46/EC) Regulations 2009, reg 17.

[Other assets that may be included at fair value

46BA. (1) This paragraph applies to—

(a) investment property, and

(b) living animals and plants,

that, under relevant international financial reporting standards, may be included in accounts at fair value.

(2) Investment property and living animals and plants referred to in subparagraph (1), may be included at fair value, provided that all such investment property or, living animals and plants, as the case may be, are so included where their fair value can reliably be determined.

(3) In this paragraph, 'fair value' means fair value determined in accordance with relevant international financial reporting standards.][a]

Amendments

a Inserted by reg 10 and Sch 2, Item No 11(i) of EC(IFRSMA)R 2005.

[46C. (1) Notwithstanding paragraph 19(a), where a financial instrument is valued in accordance with paragraph 46B or an asset is valued in accordance with paragraph 46BA, a change in the value shall be included in the profit and loss account. However, such a change shall be included directly in equity, in a fair value reserve, where—

(a) the financial instrument accounted for is a hedging instrument under a system of hedge accounting that allows some or all of the change in value not to be shown in the profit and loss account, or

(b) the change in value relates to an exchange difference arising on a monetary item that form part of a company's net investment in a foreign entity.][a]

Amendments

a Substituted by reg 10 and Sch 2, Item No 11(j) of EC(IFRSMA)R 2005.

[46D. Where valuation at fair value of financial instruments has been applied, the notes on the accounts shall disclose—

(a) the significant assumptions underlying the valuation models and techniques where fair values have been determined in accordance with paragraph 46B(1)(a),

(b) per category of financial instruments, for fair value, the changes in value included directly in the profit and loss account as well as changes included in the fair value reserve,

(c) for each class of derivative financial instruments, information about the extent and the nature of the instruments, including significant terms and conditions that may affect the amount, timing and certainty of future cash flows, and

(d) a table showing movements in the fair value reserve during the financial year.][d]

Amendments

a Amended by reg 6 of EC(CI)(FVA)R 2004.

Information where investment property and living animals and plants are included at fair value

[46E. (1) This paragraph applies where the amounts to be included in a company's accounts in respect of investment property or living animals and plants have been determined in accordance with paragraph 46BA of this Schedule.

(2) The balance sheet items affected and the basis of valuation adopted in determining the amounts of the net assets concerned in the case of each such item shall be disclosed in a note to the accounts.

(3) In the case of investment property, for each balance sheet item affected there shall be shown, either separately in the balance sheet or in a note to the accounts—

(a) the comparable amounts determined according to the historical cost accounting rules, or

(b) the differences between those amounts and the corresponding amounts actually shown in the balance sheet in respect of that item.

(4) In subparagraph (3), references in relation to any item to the comparable amounts determined in accordance with that subparagraph are references to—

(a) the aggregate amount which would be required to be shown in respect of that item if the amounts to be included in respect of all the assets covered by that item were determined according to the historical cost accounting rules, and

(b) the aggregate amount of the cumulative provisions for depreciation or diminution in value which would be permitted or required in determining those amounts according to those rules.][a]

Amendments

a Inserted by reg 10 and Sch 2, Item No 11(k) of EC(IFRSMA)R 2005.

Notes

EC(CI)(FVA)R 2004 implements Directive 2001/65/EC ('the Fair Value Directive') as regards banks and other financial institutions. The Fair Value Directive amended the EU Accounting Directives to permit certain financial instruments to be recorded at fair value in accordance with the IAS 32 (Financial Instruments: Disclosure and Presentation) and IAS 39 (Financial Instruments: Recognition and Measurement)[1] The Fair Value Directive also amended Directives 86/635/EEC and 91/674/EEC dealing with the accounts of banks and other financial institutions and insurance undertakings. The Fair Value regs have been implemented in a manner that permits all companies to use fair value accounting for certain financial instruments in both their annual and consolidated accounts. As such the Regulations amend primarily the Schedule to the Companies (Amendment) Act 1986 and the Group Accounts Regulations 1992.

1 See CA 1963 section 148 to 149.

Chapter III
Notes to the Accounts

Preliminary

47. Any information required in the case of a company by the following provisions of this Part of this Schedule shall be given by way of a note to the accounts, unless otherwise provided.

Definitions

'accounts': EC(CI:A)R 1992, reg 2(1); 'company': CA 1963, s 2(1); 'director': CA 1963, s 2(1); 'financial year': CA 1963, s 2(1); 'member': CA 1963, s 2(1).

General

Disclosure of accounting policies

48. The accounting policies adopted by the company in determining the amounts to be included in respect of items shown in the balance sheet and in determining the profit or loss of the company shall be stated (including such policies with respect to the depreciation and diminution in value of assets).

49. If there are changes to the accounting policies adopted by the company from one year to the next, these changes shall be stated together with the reasons for the changes and their effect on the accounts of the company.

Definitions

'accounts': EC(CI:A)R 1992, reg 2(1); 'company': CA 1963, s 2(1); 'director': CA 1963, s 2(1); 'financial year': CA 1963, s 2(1); 'member': CA 1963, s 2(1).

Sums denominated in foreign currencies

50. Where any sums originally denominated in foreign currencies have been brought into accounts under any items shown in the balance sheet format or the profit and loss account formats, the basis on which those sums have been translated into Irish pounds (or the currency in which the accounts are drawn) shall be stated.

Definitions

'accounts': EC(CI:A)R 1992, reg 2(1); 'company': CA 1963, s 2(1); 'director': CA 1963, s 2(1); 'financial year': CA 1963, s 2(1); 'member': CA 1963, s 2(1).

(a) on the basis of cost (determined in accordance with paragraphs 36 and 37), or

(b) on any basis permitted by paragraph 41;

(leaving out of account in either case any provisions for depreciation or diminution in value).

(3) In addition, in respect of any fixed assets of the company included in any assets item in the company's balance sheet, there shall be stated (by reference to each such item):

(a) the cumulative amount of provisions for depreciation or diminution in value of those assets included under the item as at each date mentioned in sub-paragraph (1)(a),

(b) the amount of any such provisions made in respect of the financial year,

(c) the amount of any adjustment made in respect of any such provisions during that year in consequence of the disposal of any of those assets, and

(d) the amount of any other adjustments made in respect of any such provisions during that year.

(4) The requirements of this paragraph need not be complied with to the extent that a company takes advantage of the option of setting off charges and income afforded by paragraph 5(3) of this Part of this Schedule.

Definitions

'company': CA 1963, s 2(1); 'director': CA 1963, s 2(1); 'financial year': CA 1963, s 2(1); 'member': CA 1963, s 2(1).

56. Where any fixed assets of the company (other than listed investments) are included under any item shown in the company's balance sheet at an amount determined in accordance with paragraph 41, the following information shall be given:

(a) the years (so far as they are known to the directors) in which the assets were severally valued and the several values; and

(b) in the case of assets that have been valued during the financial year, the names of the persons who valued them or particulars of their qualifications for doing so and (in either case) the bases of valuation used by them.

Definitions

'company': CA 1963, s 2(1); 'director': CA 1963, s 2(1); 'financial year': CA 1963, s 2(1); 'member': CA 1963, s 2(1).

57. In relation to any amount which is included under Assets item 10 in the balance sheet format (Tangible fixed assets) with respect to land and buildings there shall be stated:

(a) how much of that amount is ascribable to land of freehold tenure and how much to land of leasehold tenure; and

(b) how much of the amount ascribable to land of leasehold tenure is ascribable to land held on long lease and how much to land held on short lease.

Definitions

'company': CA 1963, s 2(1); 'director': CA 1963, s 2(1); 'financial year': CA 1963, s 2(1); 'member': CA 1963, s 2(1); 'long lease': EC(CI:A)R 1992, Sch, Pt IV.

58. There shall be disclosed separately the amount of:

(a) any participating interests; and

(b) any shares in group undertakings

that are held in credit institutions.

Definitions

'company': CA 1963, s 2(1); 'director': CA 1963, s 2(1); 'financial year': CA 1963, s 2(1); 'member': CA 1963, s 2(1); 'group undertakings': EC(CI:A)R 1992, Sch, Pt IV; 'participating interest': EC(CI:A)R 1992, Sch, Pt IV.

Reserves and provisions

59. (1) Where any amount is transferred—

(a) to or from any reserves,

(b) to any provisions for liabilities [...][a],

(c) from any provision for liabilities [...][a] otherwise than for the purpose for which the provision was established,

and the reserves or provisions are or would but for paragraph 3(3) of this Part of this Schedule be shown as separate items in the company's balance sheet, the information mentioned in the following sub-paragraph shall be given in respect of the aggregate of reserves or provisions included in the same item.

(2) That information is:

(a) the amount of the reserves or provisions as at the date of the beginning of the financial year and as at the balance sheet date respectively,

(b) any amounts transferred to or from the reserve or provisions during that year, and

(c) the source and application respectively of any amounts so transferred.

(3) Particulars shall be given of each provision included in Liabilities item 6(c) (Other provisions) in the company's balance sheet in any case where the amount of that provision is material.

Amendments

a Words deleted by reg 10 and Sch 2, Item No 11(h) of EC(IFRSMA)R 2005.

Definitions

'company': CA 1963, s 2(1); 'director': CA 1963, s 2(1); 'financial year': CA 1963, s 2(1); 'member': CA 1963, s 2(1).

Provision for taxation

60. The amount of any provision for deferred taxation shall be stated separately from the amount of any provision for other taxation.

Definitions

'company': CA 1963, s 2(1); 'director': CA 1963, s 2(1); 'financial year': CA 1963, s 2(1); 'member': CA 1963, s 2(1).

Maturity analysis

61. (1) A company shall disclose separately for each of Assets items 3(b) and 4 and Liabilities items 1(b), 2(b) and 3(b) the aggregate amount of the loans and advances and liabilities included in those items broken down into the following categories:

(a) those repayable in not more than three months;

(b) those repayable in more than three months but not more than one year;

(c) those repayable in more than one year but not more than five years;

(d) those repayable in more than five years

from the balance sheet date.

(2) A company shall also disclose the aggregate amounts of all loans and advances falling within Assets item 4 (Loans and advances to customers) which are:

(a) repayable on demand; or

(b) are for an indeterminate period, being repayable upon short notice.

(3) For the purposes of sub-paragraph (1), where a loan or advance or liability is repayable by instalments, each such instalment is to be treated as a separate loan or advance or liability.

Definitions

'company': CA 1963, s 2(1); 'director': CA 1963, s 2(1); 'financial year': CA 1963, s 2(1); 'member': CA 1963, s 2(1); 'repayable on demand': EC(CI:A)R 1992, Sch, Pt IV.

Debt and other fixed income securities

62. A company shall disclose the amount of debt and fixed income securities included in Assets item 5 (Debt securities and other fixed income securities) and the amount of such securities included in Liabilities item 3(a) (Bonds and medium term notes) that in each case will become due within one year of the balance sheet date.

Definitions

'company': CA 1963, s 2(1); 'director': CA 1963, s 2(1); 'financial year': CA 1963, s 2(1); 'member': CA 1963, s 2(1).

Subordinated liabilities

63. (1) The following information must be disclosed in relation to any borrowing included in Liabilities item 7 (subordinated liabilities) that exceeds 10 per cent of the total for that item:

(a) its amount;

(b) the currency in which it is denominated;

(c) the rate of interest and the maturity date (or the fact that it is perpetual);

(d) the circumstances in which early repayment may be demanded;

(e) the terms of the subordination; and

(f) the existence of any provisions whereby it may be converted into capital or some other form of liability and the terms of any such provisions.

(2) The general terms of any other borrowings included in Liabilities item 7 shall also be stated.

Definitions

'company': CA 1963, s 2(1); 'director': CA 1963, s 2(1); 'financial year': CA 1963, s 2(1); 'member': CA 1963, s 2(1).

Fixed cumulative dividends

64. If any fixed cumulative dividends on the company's shares are in arrear, there shall be stated:

(a) the amount of the arrears; and

(b) the period for which the dividends or, if there is more than one class, each class of them are in arrear.

Definitions

'company': CA 1963, s 2(1); 'director': CA 1963, s 2(1); 'financial year': CA 1963, s 2(1); 'member': CA 1963, s 2(1).

Details of assets charged

65. (1) There shall be disclosed, in relation to each liabilities and off-balance sheet item of the balance sheet format, the aggregate amount of any assets of the company which have been charged to secure any liability or potential liability included thereunder, the aggregate amount of the liabilities or potential liabilities so secured and an indication of the nature of the security given.

(2) Particulars shall also be given of any other charge on the assets of the company to secure the liabilities of any other person, including, where practicable, the amount secured.

Definitions

'company': CA 1963, s 2(1); 'director': CA 1963, s 2(1); 'financial year': CA 1963, s 2(1); 'member': CA 1963, s 2(1).

Guarantees and other financial commitments

66. (1) There shall be stated, where practicable:

(a) the aggregate amount or estimated amount of contracts for capital expenditure, so far as not provided for; and

(b) the aggregate amount or estimated amount of capital expenditure authorised by the directors which has not been contracted for.

(2) Particulars shall be given of:

(a) any pension commitments included under any provision shown in the company's balance sheet; and

(b) any such commitments for which no provision has been made;

and where any such commitment relates wholly or partly to pensions payable to past directors of the company separate particulars shall be given of that commitment so far as it relates to such pensions.

(3) The following information shall also be given:

(a) the nature of every pension scheme operated by or on behalf of the company including information as to whether or not each scheme is a defined benefit scheme or a defined contribution scheme,

(b) whether each such scheme is externally funded or internally financed,

(c) whether any pension costs and liabilities are assessed in accordance with the advice of a professionally qualified actuary and, if so, the date of the most recent relevant actuarial valuation,

(d) whether and, if so, where any such actuarial valuation is available for public inspection.

(4) Particulars shall also be given of any other financial commitments, including any contingent liabilities, which:

(a) have not been provided for;

(b) have not been included in the off-balance sheet items in the balance sheet format; and

(c) are relevant to assessing the company's state of affairs.

(5) Commitments within any of the preceding subparagraphs taken on behalf of or for the benefit of:

(a) any parent company or fellow subsidiary undertaking of the company; or

(b) any subsidiary undertaking of the company;

shall be stated separately from the other commitments within that sub-paragraph (and commitments within paragraph (a) shall be stated separately from those within paragraph (b)).

(6) There shall be disclosed the nature and amount of any contingent liabilities and commitments included in off-balance sheet items 1 and 2 which are material in relation to the company's activities.

Definitions

'company': CA 1963, s 2(1); 'director': CA 1963, s 2(1); 'financial year': CA 1963, s 2(1); 'member': CA 1963, s 2(1); 'parent company': EC(CI:A)R 1992, reg 2(1); 'subsidiary undertaking': EC(CI:A)R 1992, reg 2(1); 'fellow subsidiary': EC(CI:A)R 1992, Sch, Pt IV.

[Information concerning off-balance sheet arrangements not included in balance sheet

66A. (1) The nature and business purpose of the arrangements of the company that are not included in its balance sheet and the financial impact on the company of those arrangements shall be provided in the notes to the accounts of the company if the risks or benefits arising from such arrangements are material and in so far as the disclosure of such risks or benefits is necessary for assessing the financial position of the company.

Related party transactions

66B. (1) Particulars shall be given in the notes to the accounts of the section 2(2) company of transactions which have been entered into with related parties by the company if such transactions are material and have not been concluded under normal market conditions and the particulars shall include the amount of such transactions, the nature of the related party relationship and other information about the transactions which is necessary for an understanding of the financial position of that company.

(2) Subject to subparagraph (4), the provision of particulars and other information about individual transactions may be aggregated according to their nature, except where separate information is necessary for an understanding of the effects of related party transactions on the financial position of the section 2(2) company.

(3) Subparagraph (1) shall not apply to transactions which are entered into between 2 or more members of a group if any subsidiary undertaking which is a party to the transaction is wholly owned by such a member.

(4) Subparagraph (2) shall not apply to a company whose securities are admitted to trading on a regulated market within the meaning of Article 4(1), point (14) of Directive 2004/39/EC6.

(5) A word or expression used in this paragraph has the same meaning as it has in Directive 2006/46/EC][a].

Amendments

a Paragraphs 66A–66C inserted by European Communities (Directive 2006/46/EC) Regulations 2009, reg 18.

Off-balance sheet items: group undertakings

67. (1) With respect to contingent liabilities required to be included under off-balance sheet item 1 in the balance sheet format, there shall be stated in a note to the accounts the amount of such contingent liabilities incurred on behalf of or for the benefit of:

(a) any parent undertaking or fellow subsidiary undertaking, or

(b) any subsidiary undertaking,

of the company; in addition the amount incurred in respect of the undertakings referred to in paragraph (a) shall be stated separately from the amount incurred in respect of the undertakings referred to in paragraph (b).

(2) With respect to commitments required to be included under off-balance sheet item 2 in the balance sheet format, there shall be stated in a note to the accounts the amount of such commitments undertaken on behalf of or for the benefit of:

(a) any parent undertaking or fellow subsidiary undertaking, or

(b) any subsidiary undertaking,

of the company; in addition the amount incurred in respect of the undertakings referred to in paragraph (a) shall be stated separately from the amount incurred in respect of the undertakings referred to in paragraph (b).

Definitions

'accounts': EC(CI:A)R 1992, reg 2(1); 'company': CA 1963, s 2(1); 'director': CA 1963, s 2(1); 'financial year': CA 1963, s 2(1); 'member': CA 1963, s 2(1); 'undertaking': EC(CI:A)R 1992, reg 2(1); 'subsidiary undertaking': reg 2(1); 'fellow subsidiary': Sch, Pt IV; 'group undertakings: EC(CI:A)R 1992, Sch, Pt IV.

Transferable securities

68. (1) There shall be disclosed for each of Assets items 5 to 8 in the balance sheet format the amount of transferable securities that are listed on a recognised stock exchange and the amount of those that are unlisted.

(2) In the case of each amount shown in respect of listed securities under subparagraph (1) above, there shall also be disclosed the aggregate market value of those securities, if different from the amount shown.

(3) There shall be disclosed for each of assets items 5 and 6 the amount of transferable securities included under those items that are held as financial fixed assets and the amount of those that are not so held, together with the criterion used by the directors to distinguish those held as financial fixed assets.

Definitions

'company': CA 1963, s 2(1); 'director': CA 1963, s 2(1); 'financial year': CA 1963, s 2(1); 'member': CA 1963, s 2(1); 'financial fixed assets': EC(CI:A)R 1992, Sch, Pt IV.

Leasing transactions

69. The aggregate amount of all property (other than land) leased by the company to other persons shall be disclosed, broken down so as to show the aggregate amount included in each relevant balance sheet item.

Definitions

'company': CA 1963, s 2(1); 'director': CA 1963, s 2(1); 'financial year': CA 1963, s 2(1); 'member': CA 1963, s 2(1).

Assets and liabilities denominated in a currency other than Irish pounds (or the currency in which the accounts are drawn up)

70. (1) The aggregate amount in Irish pounds (or the currency in which the accounts are drawn up) of all assets denominated in a currency other than Irish pounds (or the currency used), together with the aggregate amount in Irish pounds (or the currency used) of all liabilities so denominated, shall be disclosed.

(2) For the purposes of this paragraph an appropriate rate of exchange prevailing at the balance sheet date shall be used to determine the amounts concerned.

Definitions

'accounts': EC(CI:A)R 1992, reg 2(1); 'company': CA 1963, s 2(1); 'director': CA 1963, s 2(1); 'financial year': CA 1963, s 2(1); 'member': CA 1963, s 2(1).

Sundry assets and liabilities

71. Where any amount shown under either of the following items is material, particulars shall be given of each type of asset or liability included therein, including an explanation of the nature of the asset or liability and the amount included with respect to assets or liabilities of that type;

(a) Assets item 13 (Other assets),

(b) Liabilities item 4 (Other liabilities).

Unmatured forward transactions

72. (1) The following shall be disclosed with respect to unmatured forward transactions outstanding at the balance sheet date:

(a) the categories of such transactions, by reference to an appropriate system of classification;

(b) whether, in the case of each such category, they have been made, to any material extent, for the purpose of hedging the effects of fluctuations in interest rates, exchange rates and market prices or whether they have been made, to any material extent, for dealing purposes.

(2) Transactions falling within subparagraph (1) shall include all those in relation to which income or expenditure is to be included in:

(a) format 1, item 6 or format 2, items B4 or A3 (Dealing profits or losses),

(b) format 1, item 1 or format 2, item B1, by virtue of note (1)(b) to the profit and loss account formats (forward contracts, spread over the actual duration of the contract and similar in nature to interest).

[Where fair valuation has not been applied

72A. Where fair valuation has not been applied in accordance with paragraphs [46A to 46E][a]—

(a) for each class of derivative financial instruments—

(i) the fair value of the instruments, if such a value can be determined by any of the methods mentioned in paragraph 46B(1),

(ii) information about the extent and the nature of the instruments, and

(b) for financial fixed assets covered by paragraph 46A, carried at an amount in excess of their fair value and without use being made of the option to make a value adjustment in accordance with paragraph 31(2)—

(i) the book value and the fair value of either the individual assets or appropriate groupings of those individual assets,

(ii) the reasons for not reducing the book value, including the nature of the evidence that provides the basis for the belief that the book value will be recovered.][b]

Amendments

a Words substituted by reg 10 and Sch 2, Item No 11(L) of EC(IFRSMA)R 2005.

b Inserted by reg 7 of EC(CI)(FVA)R 2004.

Miscellaneous matters

73. (1) Particulars shall be given of any case where the cost of any asset is for the first time determined under paragraph 38 of this Part of this Schedule.

(2) Where any outstanding loans made under the authority of section 60 of the Principal Act, other than subsection (13)(a) of that section (various cases of financial assistance by a company for purchase of its own shares) are included under any item shown in the company's balance sheet, the aggregate amount of those loans shall be disclosed for each item in question.

(3) The aggregate amount which is recommended for distribution by way of dividend shall be stated.

Particulars of any restriction on profits available for distribution by virtue of section 224(2)(b)(1) of the Companies Act, 1990, must be stated.

Definitions

'company': CA 1963, s 2(1); 'director': CA 1963, s 2(1); 'financial year': CA 1963, s 2(1); 'member': CA 1963, s 2(1); 'the Principal Act': EC(CI:A)R 1992, reg 2(1).

Information Supplementing the Profit and Loss Account

Separate statement of certain items of income and expenditure

74. (1) The amount respectively provided for the purchase of the company's share capital, for redemption of share capital and for redemption of loans shall be stated.

(2) The amount of income from listed and unlisted investments shall be stated.

(3) The amount of the remuneration of the auditors and the expenses of the auditors shall be stated.

(4) The aggregate amount of the emoluments of, and compensation in respect of loss of office to, directors and compensation paid to past directors shall be stated.

Particulars of tax

75. (1) The basis on which the charge for corporation tax, income tax and other taxation on profits (whether payable inside or outside the State) is computed shall be stated.

(2) Particulars shall be given of any special circumstances which affect liability in respect of taxation of profits, income or capital gains for the financial year concerned or liability in respect of taxation of profits, income or capital gains for succeeding financial years. [This includes the extent to which the calculation of the profit or loss is affected by the fair valuation of financial instruments and separately the extent to which it is affected by the fair valuation of other assets in accordance with paragraph 46BA.][a]

(3) The following amounts shall be stated:

(a) the amount of the charge for corporation tax;

(b) if that amount would have been greater but for relief from double taxation, the amount which it would have been but for such relief;

(c) the amount of the charge for income tax; and

(d) the amount of the charge for taxation payable outside the State of profits, income and (so far as charged to revenue) capital gains.

These amounts shall be stated separately in respect of each of the amounts which is shown under the following items in the profit and loss account, that is to say format 1 item 16, format 2 item A10 (Tax on profit or loss on ordinary activities) and format 1 item 21, format 2 item A13 (Tax on extraordinary profit or loss).

Amendments

a The sentence inserted by reg 7 of EC(CI)(FVA)R 2004 was substituted by reg 10 and Sch 2, Item No 11(m) of EC(IFRSMA)R 2005.

Particulars of income

76. (1) A company shall disclose, with respect to income included in the following items in the profit and loss account formats, the amount of that income attributable to each of the geographical markets in which the company has operated during the financial year:

(a) format 1 item 1, format 2 item B1 (Interest receivable);

(b) format 1 item 3, format 2 item B2 (Dividend income);

(c) format 1 item 4, format 2 item B3 (Fees and commissions receivable);

(d) format 1 item 6, format 2 item B4 (Dealing profits); and

(e) format 1 item 7, format 2 item B7 (Other operating income).

(2) In analysing for the purposes of this paragraph the source of any income, the directors shall have regard to the manner in which the company's activities are organised.

(3) For the purposes of this paragraph, markets which do not differ substantially from each other shall be treated as one market.

(4) Where in the opinion of the directors the disclosure of any information required by this paragraph would be seriously prejudicial to the interests of the company, that information need not be disclosed, but the fact that any such information has not been disclosed must be stated.

Particulars of staff

77. (1) The following information shall be given with respect to the employees of the company:

(a) the average number of persons employed by the company in the financial year; and

(b) the average number of persons so employed within each category of persons employed by the company.

(2) The average number required by subparagraph (1)(a) or (b) shall be determined by dividing the relevant annual number by the number of weeks in the financial year.

(3) The relevant annual number shall be determined by ascertaining for each week in the financial year:

(a) for the purposes of subparagraph (1)(a), the number of persons employed under contracts of service by the company in that week (whether throughout the week or not); and

(b) for the purposes of subparagraph (1)(b), the number of persons in the category in question of persons so employed;

and, in either case, adding together all the weekly numbers.

(4) In respect of all persons employed by the company during the financial year who are taken into account in determining the relevant annual number for the purposes of subparagraph (1)(a) there shall also be stated the aggregate amounts respectively of:

(a) wages and salaries paid or payable in respect of that year to those persons;

(b) social security costs incurred by the company on their behalf; and

(c) other pension costs so incurred.

save insofar as those amounts or any of them are stated in the profit and loss account.

(5) The categories of persons employed by the company by reference to which the number required to be disclosed by subparagraph (1)(b) is to be determined shall be such as the directors may select, having regard to the manner in which the company's activities are organised.

Management and agency services

78. A company providing any management and agency services to customers shall disclose that fact if the scale of such services provided is material in the context of its business as a whole.

Subordinated liabilities

79. Any amounts charged to the profit and loss account representing charges incurred during the year with respect to subordinated liabilities shall be disclosed.

Sundry income and charges

80. Where any amount to be included in any of the following items is material, particulars shall be given of each individual component of the figure, including an explanation of their nature and amount:

(a) in format 1:

(i) items 7 and 10 (Other operating income and charges);

(ii) items 18 and 19 (Extraordinary income and charges);

(b) in format 2:

(i) items A6 and B7 (Other operating charges and income);

(ii) items A12 and B10 (Extraordinary charges and income).

Miscellaneous matters

81. (1) Where any amount relating to any preceding financial year is included in any item in the profit and loss account, the effect shall be stated.

(2) The effect shall be stated on any transactions that are exceptional by virtue of size or incidence though they fall within the ordinary activities of the company.

(3) Particulars shall be given of any extraordinary income or charges arising in the financial year.

PART II
FORM AND CONTENT OF GROUP ACCOUNTS

Regulation 7

General rules

1. (1)[Where the directors of a company prepare Companies Act group accounts, those group accounts][a] shall comply so far as practicable with the provisions of Part I of this Schedule as if the undertakings included in the consolidation ("the group") were a single company.

(2) In particular, for the purposes of note (20) to the balance sheet format set out in Section B of Chapter 1 of Part 1 of this Schedule and paragraphs 66 (5) and 67 of Part 1 of this Schedule as it applies to group accounts—

(a) any subsidiary undertakings of the parent company not included in the consolidation shall be treated as subsidiary undertakings of the group, and

(b) if the parent company is itself a subsidiary undertaking, the group shall be treated as a subsidiary undertaking of any parent undertaking of that company, and the reference to fellow-subsidiary undertakings shall be construed accordingly.

Amendments

a Words substituted by reg 10 and Schedule 2, Item No 12(a) (what was meant to be No 12 but mistakenly called "(1)") of EC(IFRSMA)R 2005 (SI 116/2005).

Definitions

'accounts': EC(CI:A)R 1992, reg 2(1); 'company': CA 1963, s 2(1); 'director': CA 1963, s 2(1); 'financial year': CA 1963, s 2(1); 'group accounts': EC(CI:A)R 1992, reg 2(1), reg 7; 'member': CA 1963, s 2(1); 'parent company': EC(CI:A)R 1992, reg 2(1); 'undertaking': EC(CI:A)R 1992, reg 2(1); 'subsidiary undertaking': EC(CI:A)R 1992, reg 2(1); 'included in the consolidation': EC(CI:A)R 1992, Sch, Pt IV.

2. (1) Subject to the exceptions authorised or required by this paragraph, all the subsidiary undertakings of the parent company shall be included in the consolidation.

(2) A subsidiary undertaking may be excluded from consolidation if its inclusion is not material for the purpose of giving a true and fair view; but two or more undertakings may be excluded only if they are not material taken together.

(3) In addition, a subsidiary undertaking may be excluded from consolidation where—

(a) severe long-term restrictions substantially hinder the exercise of the rights of the parent company over the assets or management of that undertaking, or

(b) the information necessary for the preparation of group accounts cannot be obtained without disproportionate expense or undue delay, or

(c) the interest of the parent company is held exclusively with a view to subsequent resale and the undertaking has not previously been included in consolidated group accounts prepared by the parent company.

The reference in paragraph (a) to the right of the parent company and the reference in paragraph (c) to the interest of the parent company are, respectively, references to rights and interests held by or attributed to the company in the absence of which it would not be the parent company.

[...][a]

(8) Where all the subsidiary undertakings of a parent company fall within the above exclusions, no group accounts shall be required.

Amendments

a Sub-paragraphs (4), (5), (6) and (7) deleted by reg 10 and Schedule 2, Item No 12(b) (what was meant to be No 12 but mistakenly called "(1)") of EC(IFRSMA)R 2005.

Definitions

'company': CA 1963, s 2(1); 'director': CA 1963, s 2(1); 'financial year': CA 1963, s 2(1); 'group accounts': EC(CI:A)R 1992, reg 2(1), reg 7; 'member': CA 1963, s 2(1); 'parent company':

reg 2(1); 'undertaking': EC(CI:A)R 1992, reg 2(1); 'subsidiary undertaking': EC(CI:A)R 1992, reg 2(1); 'included in the consolidation': EC(CI:A)R 1992, Sch, Pt IV; 'included in consolidated group accounts': EC(CI:A)R 1992, Sch, Pt IV.

3. (1) The consolidated balance sheet and profit and loss account shall incorporate in full the information contained in the individual accounts of the undertakings included in the consolidation, subject to the adjustments authorised or required by the following provisions to this Schedule and to such other adjustments (if any) as may be appropriate in accordance with generally accepted accounting principles or practice.

(2) Group accounts shall be drawn up as at the same date as the individual accounts of the parent company.

(3) If the financial year of a subsidiary undertaking included in the consolidation differs from that of the parent company, the group accounts shall be made up—

(a) from the accounts of the subsidiary undertaking for its financial year last ending before the end of the parent company's financial year, provided that year ended no more than three months before that of the parent company, or

(b) from interim accounts prepared by the subsidiary undertaking as at the end of the parent company's financial year.

Definitions

'company': CA 1963, s 2(1); 'director': CA 1963, s 2(1); 'financial year': CA 1963, s 2(1); 'member': CA 1963, s 2(1); 'accounts': EC(CI:A)R 1992, reg 2(1); 'group accounts': EC(CI:A)R 1992, reg 2(1), reg 7; 'individual accounts': EC(CI:A)R 1992, reg 2(1), reg 5; 'parent company': EC(CI:A)R 1992, reg 2(1); 'undertaking': EC(CI:A)R 1992, reg 2(1); 'subsidiary undertaking': EC(CI:A)R 1992, reg 2(1); 'included in the consolidation': EC(CI:A)R 1992, Sch, Pt IV.

4. (1) Where assets and liabilities to be included in the group accounts have been valued or otherwise determined by undertakings according to accounting rules differing from those used for the group accounts, the values or amounts shall be adjusted so as to accord with the rules used for the group accounts.

(2) If it appears to the directors of the parent company that there are special reasons for departing from subparagraph (1) they may do so, but particulars of any such departure, the reasons for it and its effect shall be given in a note to the accounts.

(3) The adjustments referred to in this paragraph need not be made if they are not material for the purpose of giving a true and fair view.

Definitions

'company': CA 1963, s 2(1); 'director': CA 1963, s 2(1); 'financial year': CA 1963, s 2(1); 'member': CA 1963, s 2(1); 'accounts': EC(CI:A)R 1992, reg 2(1); 'group accounts': EC(CI:A)R 1992, reg 2(1), reg 7; 'parent company': EC(CI:A)R 1992, reg 2(1); 'undertaking': EC(CI:A)R 1992, reg 2(1).

5. Any differences of accounting rules as between a parent company's individual accounts for a financial year and its group accounts shall be disclosed in a note to the latter accounts and the reasons for the difference given.

Definitions

'company': CA 1963, s 2(1); 'director': CA 1963, s 2(1); 'financial year': CA 1963, s 2(1); 'member': CA 1963, s 2(1); 'group accounts': EC(CI:A)R 1992, reg 2(1), reg 7; 'individual accounts': EC(CI:A)R 1992, reg 2(1), reg 5; 'parent company': EC(CI:A)R 1992, reg 2(1).

6. Amounts which in the particular context of any provision of this Part of the Schedule are not material may be disregarded for the purposes of that provision.

7. (1) Debts and claims between undertakings included in the consolidation, and income and expenditure relating to transactions between such undertakings, shall be eliminated in preparing the group accounts.

(2) Where profits and losses resulting from transactions between undertakings included in the consolidation are included in the book value of assets, they shall be eliminated in preparing the group accounts.

(3) Subparagraphs (1) and (2) need not be complied with if the amounts concerned are not material for the purpose of giving a true and fair view.

Definitions

'company': CA 1963, s 2(1); 'director': CA 1963, s 2(1); 'financial year': CA 1963, s 2(1); 'member': CA 1963, s 2(1); 'group accounts': EC(CI:A)R 1992, reg 2(1), reg 7; 'undertaking': EC(CI:A)R 1992, reg 2(1); 'included in the consolidation': EC(CI:A)R 1992, Sch, Pt IV.

[7A. The notes on the accounts shall set out information relating to—

(a) the nature and business purpose of any arrangement that is not included in the consolidated balance sheet, and the financial impact of such arrangement if the risks or benefits arising from the arrangement are material, and in so far as the disclosure of such risks or benefits is necessary for assessing the financial position, taken as a whole, of the section 2(2) parent undertaking and its subsidiaries included in the consolidated balance sheet, and

(b) subject to paragraph 7B, transactions entered into by—

(i) the section 2(2) parent company, or

(ii) by a subsidiary of the section 2(2) parent company included in the group accounts,

with related parties, if the transactions are material and have not been concluded under normal market conditions and the information shall include the amounts of such transactions, the nature of the related party relationship and other information about the transactions which is necessary for an understanding of the financial position, taken as a whole, of the section 2(2) parent company and its subsidiaries included in the group accounts.

7B.A transaction referred to in paragraph 7A(b) does not include an intra-group transaction.

7C. Information provided pursuant to paragraph 7A(b) concerning individual transactions may be aggregated according to their nature except where separate information is necessary for an understanding of the effects of the related party transactions on the financial position, taken as a whole, of the section 2(2) parent company and its subsidiaries included in the group accounts.

7D. In paragraph 7A, 'consolidated balance sheet' means the balance sheet for the section 2(2) parent company and its subsidiaries.

7E. A word or expression used in paragraphs 7A to 7C has the same meaning as it has in Directive 2006/46/EC.][a]

Amendments

a Paragraphs 7A–7E inserted by European Communities (Directive 2006/46/EC) Regulations 2009, reg 19.

Acquisition and Merger Accounting

8. (1) The following provisions apply where an undertaking becomes a subsidiary undertaking of the parent company.

(2) That event is referred to in those provisions as an "acquisition", and references to the "undertaking acquired" shall be construed accordingly.

Definitions

'company': CA 1963, s 2(1); 'director': CA 1963, s 2(1); 'financial year': CA 1963, s 2(1); 'member': CA 1963, s 2(1); 'parent company': EC(CI:A)R 1992, reg 2(1); 'undertaking': EC(CI:A)R 1992, reg 2(1); 'subsidiary undertaking': EC(CI:A)R 1992, reg 2(1).

9. An acquisition shall be accounted for by the acquisition method of accounting unless the conditions for accounting for it as a merger are met and the merger method of accounting is adopted.

10. (1) The acquisition method of accounting is as follows.

(2) The identifiable assets and liabilities of the undertaking acquired shall be included in the consolidated balance sheet at their fair values as at the date of acquisition.

In this paragraph the "identifiable" assets or liabilities of the undertaking acquired means the assets or liabilities which are capable of being disposed of or discharged separately, without disposing of a business of the undertaking.

(3) The income and expenditure of the undertaking acquired shall be brought into the group accounts only as from the date of the acquisition.

(4) There shall be set off against the acquisition cost of the interest in the shares of the undertaking held by the parent company and its subsidiary undertakings the interest of the parent company and its subsidiary undertakings in the adjusted capital and reserves of the undertaking acquired.

For this purpose—

"the acquisition cost" means the amount of any cash consideration and the fair value of any other consideration, together with such amount (if any) in respect of fees and other expenses of the acquisition as the company may determine, and

"the adjusted capital and reserves" of the undertaking acquired means its capital and reserves at the date of the acquisition after adjusting the identifiable assets and liabilities of the undertaking to fair values as at that date.

(5) The resulting amount if positive shall be treated as goodwill, and if negative as a negative consolidation difference.

(6) Where in applying the acquisition method of accounting—

(a) there is no record of—

(i) the fair values as at the date of acquisition of the identifiable assets and liabilities of the undertaking acquired, or

(ii) the acquisition cost of the interest in the shares of the acquired undertaking by the undertakings dealt with in the group accounts, or

(b) such records cannot be obtained without unreasonable expense or delay,

the values of the identifiable assets and liabilities and the acquisition cost shall be taken to be the values and cost ascribed to them in the earliest available record made after the acquisition of that subsidiary undertaking.

Definitions

'company': CA 1963, s 2(1); 'director': CA 1963, s 2(1); 'financial year': CA 1963, s 2(1); 'member': CA 1963, s 2(1); 'group accounts': EC(CI:A)R 1992, reg 2(1), reg 7; 'parent company': EC(CI:A)R 1992, reg 2(1); 'undertaking': EC(CI:A)R 1992, reg 2(1); 'subsidiary undertaking': EC(CI:A)R 1992, reg 2(1).

---

11. (1) The conditions for accounting for an acquisition as a merger are—

(a) that at least 90 per cent of the nominal value of the relevant shares in the undertaking acquired is held by or on behalf of the parent company and its subsidiary undertakings,

(b) that the proportion referred to in paragraph (a) was attained pursuant to an arrangement providing for the issue of equity shares by the parent company or one or more of its subsidiary undertakings, and

(c) that the fair value of any consideration other than the issue of equity shares given pursuant to the arrangement by the parent company and its subsidiary undertakings did not exceed 10 per cent of the nominal value of the equity shares issued.

(2) The reference in subparagraph (1)(a) to the "relevant shares" in an undertaking acquired is to those carrying unrestricted rights to participate both in distributions and in the assets of the undertaking upon liquidation.

Definitions

'company': CA 1963, s 2(1); 'director': CA 1963, s 2(1); 'financial year': CA 1963, s 2(1); 'member': CA 1963, s 2(1); 'parent company': EC(CI:A)R 1992, reg 2(1); 'undertaking': EC(CI:A)R 1992, reg 2(1); 'subsidiary undertaking': EC(CI:A)R 1992, reg 2(1).

12. (1) The merger method of accounting is as follows:

(2) The assets and liabilities of the undertaking acquired shall be brought into the group accounts at the figures at which they stand in the undertaking's accounts, subject to any adjustment authorised or required by this Part of the Schedule.

(3) The income and expenditure of the undertaking acquired shall be included in the group accounts for the entire financial year, including the period before the acquisition.

(4) The group accounts shall show corresponding amounts relating to the previous financial year as if the undertaking acquired had been included in the consolidation throughout that year.

(5) There shall be set off against the aggregate of—

(a) the appropriate amount in respect of shares issued by the parent company or its subsidiary undertakings in consideration for the acquisition of shares in the undertaking acquired, and

(b) the fair value of any other consideration for the acquisition of shares in the undertaking acquired, determined as at the date when those shares were acquired,

the nominal value of the issued share capital of the undertaking acquired held by the parent company and its subsidiary undertakings.

(6) The resulting amount shall be shown as an adjustment to the consolidated reserves.

Definitions

'company': CA 1963, s 2(1); 'director': CA 1963, s 2(1); 'financial year': CA 1963, s 2(1); 'member': CA 1963, s 2(1); 'group accounts': EC(CI:A)R 1992, reg 2(1), reg 7; 'parent company': EC(CI:A)R 1992, reg 2(1); 'undertaking': EC(CI:A)R 1992, reg 2(1); 'subsidiary undertaking': EC(CI:A)R 1992, reg 2(1); 'included in the consolidation': EC(CI:A)R 1992, Sch, Pt IV.

13. (1) Where a group of undertakings is acquired, paragraphs 10 to 12 apply with the following adaptations.

(2) References to shares of the undertaking acquired shall be construed as references to shares of the parent undertaking of the group.

(3) Other references to the undertaking acquired shall be construed as references to the group; and references to the assets and liabilities, income and expenditure and capital and reserves of the undertaking acquired shall be construed as references to the assets and liabilities, income and expenditure and capital and reserves of the group after making the set-offs and other adjustments required by this Part of the Schedule in the case of group accounts.

Definitions

'company': CA 1963, s 2(1); 'director': CA 1963, s 2(1); 'financial year': CA 1963, s 2(1); 'member': CA 1963, s 2(1); 'group accounts': EC(CI:A)R 1992, reg 2(1), reg 7; 'undertaking': EC(CI:A)R 1992, reg 2(1).

14. (1) The following information with respect to acquisitions taking place in the financial year shall be given in a note to the accounts.

(2) There shall be stated—

(a) the name of the undertaking acquired or, where a group was acquired, the name of the parent undertaking of that group, and

(b) whether the acquisition has been accounted for by the acquisition or the merger method of accounting.

Definitions

'company': CA 1963, s 2(1); 'director': CA 1963, s 2(1); 'financial year': CA 1963, s 2(1); 'member': CA 1963, s 2(1); 'accounts': EC(CI:A)R 1992, reg 2(1); 'undertaking': EC(CI:A)R 1992, reg 2(1).

15. In relation to the resulting amounts referred to in paragraphs 10(5) and 12(6) of this Part of the Schedule, there shall be stated in a note to the group accounts the methods used in calculating those amounts and the reasons for any significant difference between those amounts for the financial year to which the group accounts refer and the preceding financial year.

Definitions

'company': CA 1963, s 2(1); 'director': CA 1963, s 2(1); 'financial year': CA 1963, s 2(1); 'member': CA 1963, s 2(1); 'group accounts': EC(CI:A)R 1992, reg 2(1), reg 7.

Changes in Composition of the Group

16. If the composition of the undertakings dealt with in the group accounts has changed significantly in the course of a financial year, the group accounts must include information which makes the comparison of successive sets of group accounts meaningful.

Definitions

'company': CA 1963, s 2(1); 'director': CA 1963, s 2(1); 'financial year': CA 1963, s 2(1); 'member': CA 1963, s 2(1); 'group accounts': EC(CI:A)R 1992, reg 2(1), reg 7; 'undertaking': EC(CI:A)R 1992, reg 2(1).

Differences in Tax Treatment

17. Account shall be taken in the group accounts of any difference arising on consolidation between the tax chargeable for the financial year and for preceding

financial years and the amount of tax paid or payable in respect of those years, provided that it is probable that an actual charge to tax will arise within the foreseeable future for one of the undertakings dealt with in the group accounts.

Definitions

'company': CA 1963, s 2(1); 'director': CA 1963, s 2(1); 'financial year': CA 1963, s 2(1); 'member': CA 1963, s 2(1); 'group accounts': EC(CI:A)R 1992, reg 2(1), reg 7; 'undertaking': EC(CI:A)R 1992, reg 2(1).

Minority Interests

18. (1) The formats set out in Part I of this Schedule have effect in relation to group accounts with the following additions.

(2) In the Balance Sheet Format a further item headed "Minority interests" shall be added—

(a) either between "liabilities" items 7 and 8, or

(b) after "liabilities" item 12;

and under that item shall be shown the amount of capital and reserves attributable to shares in subsidiary undertakings included in the consolidation held by or on behalf of persons other than the parent company and its subsidiary undertakings.

(3) In the Profit and Loss Account Formats a further item headed "Minority interests" shall be added—

(a) in Format 1, between items 17 and 18; and

(b) in Format 2, between items A11 and A12 or between items B9 and B10;

and under that item shall be shown the amount of any profit or loss on ordinary activities attributable to shares in subsidiary undertakings included in the consolidation held by or on behalf of persons other than the parent company and its subsidiary undertakings.

(4) In the Profit and Loss Account Formats a further item headed "Minority interests" shall be added—

(a) in Format 1, between items 22 and 23, and

(b) in Format 2, between items A14 and A15 or between items B11 and B12;

and under that item shall be shown the amount of any profit or loss on extraordinary activities attributable to shares in subsidiary undertakings included in the consolidation held by or on behalf of persons other than the parent company and its subsidiary undertakings.

(5) For the purposes of paragraph 3(3) of Part I of this Schedule (power to combine items) the additional items required by the foregoing provisions of this paragraph shall be treated as items to which a letter is assigned.

Definitions

'company': CA 1963, s 2(1); 'director': CA 1963, s 2(1); 'financial year': CA 1963, s 2(1); 'member': CA 1963, s 2(1); 'group accounts': EC(CI:A)R 1992, reg 2(1), reg 7; 'parent company': EC(CI:A)R 1992, reg 2(1); 'subsidiary undertaking': EC(CI:A)R 1992, reg 2(1); 'included in the consolidation': EC(CI:A)R 1992, Sch, Pt IV.

Interests in Subsidiary Undertakings Excluded from Consolidation

19. (1) The interest of the group in subsidiary undertakings excluded from consolidation under paragraph 2(4) of this Part of the Schedule (undertakings with activities different from those of undertakings included in the consolidation), and the amount of profit or loss attributable to such an interest, shall be shown in the consolidated balance sheet or, as the case may be, in the consolidated profit and loss account by the equity method of accounting (including dealing with any goodwill arising in accordance with paragraphs 24, 26 and 28 of Part 1 of this Schedule).

Definitions

'company': CA 1963, s 2(1); 'director': CA 1963, s 2(1); 'financial year': CA 1963, s 2(1); 'member': CA 1963, s 2(1); 'undertaking': EC(CI:A)R 1992, reg 2(1); 'subsidiary undertaking': EC(CI:A)R 1992, reg 2(1); 'included in the consolidation': EC(CI:A)R 1992, Sch, Pt IV.

Joint Ventures

20. (1) Where an undertaking included in the consolidation manages another undertaking jointly with one or more undertakings not included in the consolidation, that other undertaking ("the joint venture") may, if it is not—

(a) a body corporate, or

(b) a subsidiary undertaking of the parent company,

be dealt with in the group accounts by the method of proportional consolidation.

(2) The provisions of this Part relating to the preparation of consolidated accounts apply, with any necessary modifications, to proportional consolidation under this paragraph.

Definitions

'company': CA 1963, s 2(1); 'director': CA 1963, s 2(1); 'financial year': CA 1963, s 2(1); 'member': CA 1963, s 2(1); 'group accounts': EC(CI:A)R 1992, reg 2(1), reg 7; 'parent company': EC(CI:A)R 1992, reg 2(1); 'undertaking': EC(CI:A)R 1992, reg 2(1); 'subsidiary undertaking': EC(CI:A)R 1992, reg 2(1); 'included in the consolidation': EC(CI:A)R 1992, Sch, Pt IV.

Associated Undertakings

21. (1) An "associated undertaking" means an undertaking in which an undertaking included in the consolidation has a participating interest and over whose operating and financial policy it exercises a significant influence, and which is not—

(a) a subsidiary undertaking of the parent company, or

(b) a joint venture dealt with in accordance with paragraph 20.

(2) Where an undertaking holds 20 per cent or more of the qualifying capital interest in another undertaking, it shall be presumed to exercise such an influence over it unless the contrary is shown.

(3) Paragraphs (3) and (4) of Regulation 4 of the European Communities (Companies: Group Accounts) Regulations, 1992, shall apply for determining whether subparagraph (2) above applies.

Definitions

'company': CA 1963, s 2(1); 'director': CA 1963, s 2(1); 'financial year': CA 1963, s 2(1); 'member': CA 1963, s 2(1); associated undertaking': EC(CI:A)R 1992, reg 2(1); 'parent company': reg 2(1); 'undertaking': EC(CI:A)R 1992, reg 2(1); 'subsidiary undertaking': EC(CI:A)R 1992, reg 2(1); 'included in the consolidation': EC(CI:A)R 1992, Sch, Pt IV; 'participating interests: EC(CI:A)R 1992, Sch, Pt IV; 'qualifying capital interest': EC(CI:A)R 1992, Sch, Pt IV.

22. (1) The formats in Part 1 of this Schedule shall have effect in relation to group accounts with the following modifications.

(2) In the Balance Sheet format assets item 7 (Participating Interests) shall be replaced by two items headed

"Interests in associated undertakings" and

"Other participating interests".

(3) In the Profit and Loss Account formats the following items, namely:

(a) format 1, item 3(b), (Income from participating interests), and

(b) format 2, item B2(b) (Income from participating interests),

shall be replaced by the following two replacement items:

(i) "Income from participating interests other than associated undertakings", which shall be shown at position 3(b) in format 1 and position B2(b) in format 2; and

(ii) "Income from associated undertakings", which shall be shown at an appropriate position.

Definitions

'company': CA 1963, s 2(1); 'director': CA 1963, s 2(1); 'financial year': CA 1963, s 2(1); 'member': CA 1963, s 2(1); 'associated undertaking': EC(CI:A)R 1992, reg 2(1); 'group accounts': EC(CI:A)R 1992, reg 2(1), reg 7; 'participating interests: EC(CI:A)R 1992, Sch, Pt IV.

23. (1) The interest of an undertaking in an associated undertaking, and the amount of profit or loss attributable to such an interest, shall be shown by the equity method of accounting (including dealing with any goodwill arising in accordance with paragraphs 24, 26 and 28 of Part 1 of this Schedule).

(2) Where the associated undertaking is itself a parent undertaking, the net assets and profits or losses to be taken into account are those of the parent and its subsidiary undertaking (after making any consolidation adjustments).

(3) The equity method of accounting need not be applied if the amounts in question are not material for the purpose of giving a true and fair view.

Definitions

'company': CA 1963, s 2(1); 'director': CA 1963, s 2(1); 'financial year': CA 1963, s 2(1); 'member': CA 1963, s 2(1); 'associated undertaking': EC(CI:A)R 1992, reg 2(1); 'undertaking': EC(CI:A)R 1992, reg 2(1); 'subsidiary undertaking': EC(CI:A)R 1992, reg 2(1).

Foreign Currency Translation

24. Any difference between:

(a) the amount included in the consolidated account for the previous financial year with respect to any undertaking included in the consolidation or the group's interest in any associated undertaking, together with the amount of any transactions undertaken to cover any such interest; and

(b) the opening amount for the financial year in respect of those undertakings and in respect of any such transactions arising as a result of the application of paragraph 45 of Part I of this Schedule may be credited to (where (a) is less than (b)), or deducted from (where (a) is greater than (b)), (as the case may be) consolidated reserves.

Definitions

'company': CA 1963, s 2(1); 'director': CA 1963, s 2(1); 'financial year': CA 1963, s 2(1); 'member': CA 1963, s 2(1); 'associated undertaking': EC(CI:A)R 1992, reg 2(1); 'undertaking': EC(CI:A)R 1992, reg 2(1); 'included in the consolidation': EC(CI:A)R 1992, Sch, Pt IV.

25. Any income and expenditure of undertakings included in the consolidation and associated undertakings in a foreign currency may be translated for the purposes of the consolidated accounts at the average rates of exchange prevailing during the financial year.

Definitions

'company': CA 1963, s 2(1); 'director': CA 1963, s 2(1); 'financial year': CA 1963, s 2(1); 'member': CA 1963, s 2(1); 'associated undertaking': EC(CI:A)R 1992, reg 2(1); 'undertaking': EC(CI:A)R 1992, reg 2(1); 'included in the consolidation': EC(CI:A)R 1992, Sch, Pt IV.

Information as to Undertaking in which Shares are Held as a Result of a Financial Assistance Operation

26. (1) The following provisions apply where the parent company of a banking group has a subsidiary undertaking which:

(a) is a credit institution of which shares are held as a result of a financial assistance operation with a view to its reorganisation or rescue; and

(b) is excluded from consolidation under paragraph 2(3)(c) (interest held with a view to resale).

(2) Information as to the nature and terms of the operations shall be given in a note to the group accounts and there shall be appended to the copy of the group accounts annexed to the annual return of the parent company a copy of the undertaking's latest individual accounts and, if it is a parent undertaking, its latest group accounts.

If the accounts appended are required by law to be audited, a copy of the auditors' report shall also be appended.

(3) If any document required to be appended is in a language other than Irish or English, the directors shall annex a translation of it into Irish or English, certified to be a correct translation.

(4) The above requirements are subject to the following qualifications:

(a) an undertaking is not required to prepare for the purposes of this paragraph accounts which would not otherwise be required to be prepared, and if no accounts satisfying the above requirements are prepared none need be appended;

(b) the accounts of an undertaking need not be appended if they would not otherwise be required to be published, or made available for public inspection, anywhere in the world, but in that case the reason for not appending the accounts shall be stated in a note to the consolidated accounts.

(5) Where a copy of an undertaking's accounts is required to be appended to the copy of the group accounts annexed to the annual return, that fact shall be stated in a note to the group accounts.

Definitions

'company': CA 1963, s 2(1); 'director': CA 1963, s 2(1); 'financial year': CA 1963, s 2(1); 'member': CA 1963, s 2(1); 'accounts': reg 2(1); 'annual return': EC(CI:A)R 1992, reg 2(1), CA 1963 s 2(1); 'group accounts': EC(CI:A)R 1992, reg 2(1), reg 7; 'individual accounts': EC(CI:A)R 1992, reg 2(1), reg 5; 'parent company': EC(CI:A)R 1992, reg 2(1); 'undertaking': EC(CI:A)R 1992, reg 2(1); 'subsidiary undertaking': EC(CI:A)R 1992, reg 2(1).

PART III

DISCLOSURE OF INFORMATION: RELATED UNDERTAKINGS

A. Companies not Required to Prepare Group Accounts

Regulation 10

Subsidiary Undertakings

1. (1) The following information shall be given where at the end of the financial year the company has subsidiary undertakings.

(2) The name of each subsidiary undertaking shall be stated.

(3) There shall be stated with respect to each subsidiary undertaking—

(a) if it is incorporated, the country in which it is incorporated;

(b) if it is unincorporated, the address of its principal place of business.

(4) The reason why the company is not required to prepare group accounts shall be stated.

(5) If the reason is that all the subsidiary undertakings of the company fall within the exclusions provided for in paragraph (2) of Part II of this Schedule, it shall be stated with respect to each subsidiary undertaking which of those exclusions applies.

Definitions

'company': CA 1963, s 2(1); 'director': CA 1963, s 2(1); 'financial year': CA 1963, s 2(1); 'member': CA 1963, s 2(1); 'group accounts': EC(CI:A)R 1992, reg 2(1), reg 7; 'subsidiary undertaking': EC(CI:A)R 1992, reg 2(1).

Holdings in Subsidiary Undertakings

2. There shall be stated in relation to shares of each class held by the company in a subsidiary undertaking—

(a) the identity of the class, and

(b) the proportion of the nominal value of the shares of that class represented by those shares.

Definitions

'company': CA 1963, s 2(1); 'director': CA 1963, s 2(1); 'financial year': CA 1963, s 2(1); 'member': CA 1963, s 2(1); 'subsidiary undertaking': EC(CI:A)R 1992, reg 2(1).

Financial Information about Subsidiary Undertakings

3. (1) There shall be disclosed with respect to each subsidiary undertaking—

(a) the aggregate amount of its capital and reserves as at the end of its relevant financial year, and

(b) its profit or loss for that year.

(2) That information need not be given if the company is exempt by virtue of regulation 8 [or 8A][a] of these Regulations from the requirement to prepare group accounts (parent company included in accounts of larger group).

(3) That information need not be given if—

(a) the subsidiary undertaking is not otherwise required to publish its accounts, and

(b) the company's holding is less than 50 per cent of the nominal value of the shares in the undertaking.

(4) Information otherwise required by this paragraph need not be given if it is not material.

(5) For the purposes of this part of the Schedule the "relevant financial year" of a subsidiary undertaking is—

(a) if its financial year ends with that of the company, that year, and

(b) if not, its financial year ending last before the end of the company's financial year.

Amendments

a Words inserted by reg 10 and Schedule 2, Item No 13 of EC(IFRSMA)R 2005 (SI 116/2005).

Definitions

'company': CA 1963, s 2(1); 'director': CA 1963, s 2(1); 'financial year': CA 1963, s 2(1); 'member': CA 1963, s 2(1); 'accounts': EC(CI:A)R 1992, reg 2(1); 'group accounts': EC(CI:A)R 1992, reg 2(1), reg 7; 'parent company': EC(CI:A)R 1992, reg 2(1); 'undertaking': EC(CI:A)R 1992, reg 2(1); 'subsidiary undertaking': EC(CI:A)R 1992, reg 2(1).

Financial Years of Subsidiary Undertakings

4. Where the financial year of one or more subsidiary undertakings did not end with that of the company, there shall be stated in relation to each such undertaking—

(a) the reasons why the company's directors consider that its financial year should not end with that of the company, and

(b) the date on which its last financial year ended (last before the end of the company's financial year).

Instead of the date required by paragraph (b) being given for each subsidiary undertaking the earliest and latest of those dates may be given.

Definitions

'company': CA 1963, s 2(1); 'director': CA 1963, s 2(1); 'financial year': CA 1963, s 2(1); 'member': CA 1963, s 2(1); 'undertaking': EC(CI:A)R 1992, reg 2(1); 'subsidiary undertaking': EC(CI:A)R 1992, reg 2(1).

Further Information about Subsidiary Undertakings

5. (1) There shall be disclosed—

(a) any qualifications contained in the auditors' reports on the accounts of subsidiary undertakings for financial years ending with or during the financial year of the company, and

(b) any note or saving contained in such accounts to call attention to a matter which, apart from the note or saving, would properly have been referred to in such a qualification,

insofar as the matter which is the subject of the qualification or note is not covered by the company's own accounts and its material from the point of view of its members.

(2) The aggregated amount of the total investment of the company in the shares of subsidiary undertakings shall be stated by way of the equity method of valuation, unless—

(a) the company is exempt from the requirement to prepare group accounts by virtue of regulation 8 [or 8A][a] of these Regulations (parent company included in accounts of larger group), and

(b) the directors state their opinion that the aggregate value of the assets of the company consisting of shares in, or amounts owing (whether on account of a loan or otherwise) from, the company's subsidiary undertakings is not less than the aggregate of the amounts at which those assets are stated or included in the company's balance sheet.

(3) Insofar as information required by this paragraph is not obtainable, a statement to that effect shall be given instead.

Amendments

a Words inserted by reg 10 and Sch 2, Item No 13 of EC(IFRSMA)R 2005.

Definitions

'company': CA 1963, s 2(1); 'director': CA 1963, s 2(1); 'financial year': CA 1963, s 2(1); 'member': CA 1963, s 2(1); 'accounts': EC(CI:A)R 1992, reg 2(1); 'group accounts': EC(CI:A)R 1992, reg 2(1), reg 7; 'parent company': EC(CI:A)R 1992, reg 2(1); 'subsidiary undertaking': EC(CI:A)R 1992, reg 2(1).

Shares and Debentures of Company Held by Subsidiary Undertakings

6. (1) The number, description and amount of the shares in and debentures of the company held by or on behalf of its subsidiary undertakings shall be disclosed.

(2) Sub-paragraph (1) does not apply in relation to shares or debentures in the case of which the subsidiary undertaking is concerned as personal representative or, subject as follows, as trustee.

(3) The exception for shares or debentures in relation to which the subsidiary undertaking is concerned as trustee does not apply if the company, or any subsidiary undertaking of the company, is beneficially interested under the trust, otherwise than by way of security only for the purposes of a transaction entered into by it in the ordinary course of a business which includes the lending of money.

Definitions

'company': CA 1963, s 2(1); 'director': CA 1963, s 2(1); 'financial year': CA 1963, s 2(1); 'member': CA 1963, s 2(1); 'subsidiary undertaking': EC(CI:A)R 1992, reg 2(1).

Significant Holdings in Undertakings Other than Subsidiary Undertakings

7. (1) The information required by paragraphs 8 and 9 shall be given where at the end of the financial year the company has a significant holding in an undertaking which is not a subsidiary undertaking of the company.

(2) A holding is significant for this purpose if it amounts to 20 per cent or more of all interests held by the company in an undertaking.

Definitions

'company': CA 1963, s 2(1); 'director': CA 1963, s 2(1); 'financial year': CA 1963, s 2(1); 'member': CA 1963, s 2(1); 'undertaking': EC(CI:A)R 1992, reg 2(1); 'subsidiary undertaking': EC(CI:A)R 1992, reg 2(1).

8. (1) The name of the undertaking shall be stated.

(2) There shall be stated—

(a) if the undertaking is incorporated, the country in which it is incorporated;

(b) if it is unincorporated, the address of its principal place of business.

(3) There shall also be stated—

(a) the identity of each class of shares in the undertaking held by the company, and

(b) the proportion of the nominal value of the shares of that class represented by those shares.

Definitions

'company': CA 1963, s 2(1); 'director': CA 1963, s 2(1); 'financial year': CA 1963, s 2(1); 'member': CA 1963, s 2(1); 'undertaking': EC(CI:A)R 1992, reg 2(1).

9. (1)There shall also be stated—

(a) the aggregate amount of the capital and reserves of the undertaking as at the end of its relevant financial year, and

(b) its profit or loss for that year.

(2) That information need not be given if—

(a) the company is exempt by virtue of regulation 8 [or 8A][a] of these Regulations from the requirement to prepare group accounts (parent company included in accounts of larger group), and

(b) the investment of the company in all undertakings in which it has such holding as is mentioned in subparagraph (1) is shown, in aggregate, in the notes to the accounts by way of the equity method of valuation.

(3) That information need not be given in respect of an undertaking if—

(a) the undertaking is not otherwise required to publish its accounts, and

(b) the company's holding is less than 50 per cent. of the nominal value of the shares in the undertaking.

Amendments

a Words inserted by reg 10 and Sch, Item No 13 of EC(IFRSMA)R 2005.

Definitions

'company': CA 1963, s 2(1); 'director': CA 1963, s 2(1); 'financial year': CA 1963, s 2(1); 'member': CA 1963, s 2(1); 'accounts': EC(CI:A)R 1992, reg 2(1); 'group accounts': EC(CI:A)R

1992, reg 2(1), reg 7; 'parent company': EC(CI:A)R 1992, reg 2(1); 'undertaking': EC(CI:A)R 1992, reg 2(1).

Parent undertaking drawing up accounts for larger group

10. (1) Where the company is a subsidiary undertaking, the following information shall be given with respect to the parent undertaking of—

(a) the largest group of undertakings for which group accounts are drawn up and of which the company is a member, and

(b) the smallest such group of undertakings.

(2) The name of the parent undertaking shall be stated.

(3) There shall be stated—

(a) if the undertaking is incorporated, the country in which it is incorporated;

(b) if it is unincorporated, the address of its principal place of business.

(4) If copies of the group accounts referred to in subparagraph (1) are available to the public, there shall also be stated the addresses from which copies of the accounts can be obtained.

Definitions

'company': CA 1963, s 2(1); 'director': CA 1963, s 2(1); 'financial year': CA 1963, s 2(1); 'member': CA 1963, s 2(1); 'accounts': EC(CI:A)R 1992, reg 2(1); 'group accounts': EC(CI:A)R 1992, reg 2(1), reg 7; 'undertaking': EC(CI:A)R 1992, reg 2(1); 'subsidiary undertaking': EC(CI:A)R 1992, reg 2(1).

B. Companies Required to Prepare Group Accounts

Subsidiary undertakings

11. (1) The following information shall be given with respect to the undertakings which are subsidiary undertakings of the parent company at the end of the financial year.

(2) The name of each undertaking shall be stated.

(3) There shall be stated—

(a) if the undertaking is incorporated, the country in which it is incorporated;

(b) if it is unincorporated, the address of its principal place of business.

(4) It shall also be stated whether the subsidiary undertaking is included in the consolidation and, if it is not, the reasons for excluding it from consolidation shall be given.

(5) The relevant provisions of regulation 4, other than subparagraph 1 (a), of the European Communities (Companies: Group Accounts) Regulations 1992 which apply to each subsidiary shall be stated.

Definitions

'company': CA 1963, s 2(1); 'director': CA 1963, s 2(1); 'financial year': CA 1963, s 2(1); 'member': CA 1963, s 2(1); 'parent company': EC(CI:A)R 1992, reg 2(1); 'undertaking': EC(CI:A)R 1992, reg 2(1); 'subsidiary undertaking': EC(CI:A)R 1992, reg 2(1); 'included in the consolidation': EC(CI:A)R 1992, Sch, Pt IV.

Holdings in Subsidiary Undertakings

12. (1) The following information shall be given with respect to the shares of a subsidiary undertaking held—

(a) by the parent company, and

(b) by the group;

and the information under paragraphs (a) and (b) shall (if different) be shown separately.

(2) There shall be stated—

(a) the identity of each class of shares held, and

(b) the proportion of the nominal value of the shares of that class represented by those shares.

Definitions

'company': CA 1963, s 2(1); 'director': CA 1963, s 2(1); 'financial year': CA 1963, s 2(1); 'member': CA 1963, s 2(1); 'parent company': EC(CI:A)R 1992, reg 2(1); 'subsidiary undertaking': EC(CI:A)R 1992, reg 2(1).

Financial Information about Subsidiary Undertakings not Included in the Consolidation

13. (1) There shall be shown with respect to each subsidiary undertaking not included in the consolidation—

(a) the aggregate amount of its capital and reserves as at the end of its relevant financial year, and

(b) its profit or loss for that year.

(2) That information need not be given if the group's investment in the undertaking is included in the accounts by way of the equity method of valuation or if—

(a) the undertaking is not otherwise required to publish its accounts, and

(b) the holding of the group is less than 50 per cent of the nominal value of the shares in the undertaking.

(3) Information otherwise required by this paragraph need not be given if it is not material.

Definitions

'company': CA 1963, s 2(1); 'director': CA 1963, s 2(1); 'financial year': CA 1963, s 2(1); 'member': CA 1963, s 2(1); 'accounts': EC(CI:A)R 1992, reg 2(1); 'undertaking': EC(CI:A)R 1992, reg 2(1); 'subsidiary undertaking': EC(CI:A)R 1992, reg 2(1); 'included in the consolidation': EC(CI:A)R 1992, Sch, Pt IV.

Further Information about Subsidiary Undertakings Excluded from Consolidation

14. (1) The following information shall be given with respect to subsidiary undertakings excluded from consolidation.

(2) There shall be disclosed—

(a) any qualifications contained in the auditors' reports on the accounts of the undertaking for financial years ending with or during the financial year of the company, and

(b) any note or saving contained in such accounts to call attention to a matter which, apart from the note or saving, would properly have been referred to in such a qualification,

in so far as the matter which is the subject of the qualification or note is not covered by the consolidated accounts and is material from the point of view of the members of the parent company.

(3) In so far as information required by this paragraph is not obtainable, a statement to the effect shall be given instead.

Definitions

'company': CA 1963, s 2(1); 'director': CA 1963, s 2(1); 'financial year': CA 1963, s 2(1); 'member': CA 1963, s 2(1); 'accounts': EC(CI:A)R 1992, reg 2(1); 'parent company': EC(CI:A)R 1992, reg 2(1); 'undertaking': EC(CI:A)R 1992, reg 2(1); 'subsidiary undertaking': EC(CI:A)R 1992, reg 2(1).

Financial Years of Subsidiary Undertakings

15. Where the financial year of one or more subsidiary undertakings did not end with that of the company, there shall be stated in relation to each such undertaking—

(a) the reasons why the company's directors consider that its financial year should not end with that of the company, and

(b) the date on which its last financial year ended (last before the end of the company's financial year).

Instead of the dates required by paragraph (b) being given for each subsidiary undertaking the earliest and latest of those dates may be given.

Definitions

'company': CA 1963, s 2(1); 'director': CA 1963, s 2(1); 'financial year': CA 1963, s 2(1); 'member': CA 1963, s 2(1); 'undertaking': EC(CI:A)R 1992, reg 2(1); 'subsidiary undertaking': EC(CI:A)R 1992, reg 2(1).

Shares and Debentures of Company Held by Subsidiary Undertakings

16. (1) The number, description and amount of the shares in and debentures of the company held by or on behalf of its subsidiary undertakings shall be disclosed.

(2) Subparagraph (1) does not apply in relation to shares or debentures in the case of which the subsidiary undertaking is concerned as personal representative or, subject as follows, as trustee.

(3) The exception for shares or debentures in relation to which the subsidiary undertaking is concerned as trustee does not apply if the company, or any of its subsidiary undertakings, is beneficially interested under the trust, otherwise than by way of security only for the purposes of a transaction entered into by it in the ordinary course of a business which includes the lending of money.

Definitions

'company': CA 1963, s 2(1); 'director': CA 1963, s 2(1); 'financial year': CA 1963, s 2(1); 'member': CA 1963, s 2(1); 'subsidiary undertaking': EC(CI:A)R 1992, reg 2(1).

Joint Ventures

17. (1) The following information shall be given where an undertaking is dealt with in the consolidated accounts by the method of proportional consolidation in the case of joint ventures—

(a) the name of the undertaking;

(b) the address of the principal place of business of the undertaking;

(c) the factors on which joint management of the undertaking is based; and

(d) the proportion of the capital of the undertaking held by undertakings included in the consolidation.

(2) Where the financial year of the undertaking did not end with that of the company, there shall be stated the date on which a financial year of the undertaking last ended before that date.

Definitions

'company': CA 1963, s 2(1); 'director': CA 1963, s 2(1); 'financial year': CA 1963, s 2(1); 'member': CA 1963, s 2(1); 'undertaking': EC(CI:A)R 1992, reg 2(1); 'included in the consolidation': EC(CI:A)R 1992, Sch, Pt IV.

Associated Undertakings

18. (1) The following information shall be given where an undertaking included in the consolidation has an interest in an associated undertaking.

(2) The name of the associated undertaking shall be stated.

(3) There shall be stated—

(a) if the undertaking is incorporated, the country in which it is incorporated;

(b) if it is unincorporated, the address of its principal place of business.

(4) The following information shall be given with respect to the shares of the undertaking held—

(a) by the parent company, and

(b) by the group;

and the information under paragraphs (a) and (b) shall be shown separately.

(5) There shall be stated—

(a) the identity of each class of shares held, and

(b) the proportion of the nominal value of the shares of that class represented by those shares.

(6) In this paragraph "associated undertakings" has the meaning given by paragraph 21 of Part II of this Schedule and the information required by this paragraph shall be given notwithstanding that paragraph 6 of that Schedule (materiality) applies in relation to the accounts themselves.

Definitions

'company': CA 1963, s 2(1); 'director': CA 1963, s 2(1); 'financial year': CA 1963, s 2(1); 'member': CA 1963, s 2(1); 'accounts': EC(CI:A)R 1992, reg 2(1); associated undertaking': EC(CI:A)R 1992, reg 2(1); 'parent company': EC(CI:A)R 1992, reg 2(1); 'undertaking': EC(CI:A)R 1992, reg 2(1); 'included in the consolidation': EC(CI:A)R 1992, Sch, Pt IV.

Other Significant Holdings of Parent Company

19. (1) The information required by paragraphs 20 and 21 shall be given where at the end of the financial year the parent company has a significant holding in an undertaking which is not one of its subsidiary undertakings and does not fall within paragraph 17 (joint ventures) or paragraph 18 (associated undertakings).

(2) A holding is significant for this purpose if it amounts to 20 per cent or more of all interests in an undertaking.

Definitions

'company': CA 1963, s 2(1); 'director': CA 1963, s 2(1); 'financial year': CA 1963, s 2(1); 'member': CA 1963, s 2(1); 'associated undertaking': EC(CI:A)R 1992, reg 2(1); 'parent company': EC(CI:A)R 1992, reg 2(1); 'undertaking': EC(CI:A)R 1992, reg 2(1); 'subsidiary undertaking': EC(CI:A)R 1992, reg 2(1).

20.(1) The name of the undertaking shall be stated.

(2) There shall be stated—

(a) if the undertaking is incorporated, the country in which it is incorporated;

(b) if it is unincorporated, the address of its principal place of business.

(3) The following information shall be given with respect to the shares of the undertaking held by the parent company.

(4) There shall be stated—

(a) the identity of each class of shares held, and

(b) the proportion of the nominal value of the shares of that class represented by those shares.

Definitions

'company': CA 1963, s 2(1); 'director': CA 1963, s 2(1); 'financial year': CA 1963, s 2(1); 'member': CA 1963, s 2(1); 'parent company': EC(CI:A)R 1992, reg 2(1); 'undertaking': EC(CI:A)R 1992, reg 2(1).

21.(1) There shall also be stated—

(a) the aggregate amount of the capital and reserves of the undertakings as at the end of its relevant financial year, and

(b) its profit or loss for that year.

(2) That information need not be given in respect of an undertaking if—

(a) the undertaking is not otherwise required to publish its accounts, and

(b) the company's holding is less than 50 per cent of the nominal value of the shares in the undertaking.

(3) Information otherwise required by this paragraph need not be given if it is not material.

Definitions

'company': CA 1963, s 2(1); 'director': CA 1963, s 2(1); 'financial year': CA 1963, s 2(1); 'member': CA 1963, s 2(1); 'accounts': EC(CI:A)R 1992, reg 2(1); 'undertaking': EC(CI:A)R 1992, reg 2(1).

Parent Undertaking Drawing up Accounts for Larger Group

22. (1) Where the parent company is itself a subsidiary undertaking, the following information shall be given with respect to that parent undertaking of the company which heads—

(a) the largest group of undertakings for which group accounts are drawn up and of which that company is a member, and

(b) the smallest such group of undertakings.

(2) The name of the parent undertaking shall be stated.

(3) There shall be stated—

(a) if the undertaking is incorporated, the country in which it is incorporated;

(b) if it is unincorporated, the address of its principal place of business.

(4) If copies of the group accounts referred to in subparagraph (1) are available to the public, there shall also be stated the addresses from which copy of the accounts can be obtained.

Definitions

'company': CA 1963, s 2(1); 'director': CA 1963, s 2(1); 'financial year': CA 1963, s 2(1); 'member': CA 1963, s 2(1); 'accounts': EC(CI:A)R 1992, reg 2(1); 'group accounts': EC(CI:A)R 1992, reg 2(1), reg 7; 'parent company': EC(CI:A)R 1992, reg 2(1); 'undertaking': EC(CI:A)R 1992, reg 2(1); 'subsidiary undertaking': EC(CI:A)R 1992, reg 2(1).

23. References in this part to shares held by a company shall be construed as being held or not being held by that company in accordance with the rules set out in regulation 4(3) of the European Communities (Companies: Group Accounts) Regulations, 1992.

PART IV
INTERPRETATION

General

1. The following definitions apply for the purposes of this Schedule and its interpretation:

"Banking activities" means activities normally undertaken by a bank or building society;

"Banking Transactions" means transactions entered into in the normal course of a deposit-taking business within the meaning of the Central Bank Act 1989;

"Fellow subsidiary": an undertaking shall be treated as a fellow subsidiary of another undertaking if both are subsidiaries of the same undertaking but neither is the other's;

"Financial fixed assets" means loans and advances and securities held as fixed assets; participating interests and shareholdings in group undertakings shall be regarded as financial fixed assets;

"Fungible assets" means assets of any description which are substantially indistinguishable one from another;

"Group" means a parent undertaking and its subsidiary undertakings;

"Group Undertakings" has the meaning assigned to it by paragraph 64 of the Schedule to the Act of 1986 as amended by the Schedule to the European Communities (Companies: Group Accounts) Regulations, 1992;

"Included in the consolidation" in relation to group accounts, or "included in consolidated group accounts", means that the undertaking is included in the accounts by the method of full (and not proportional) consolidation, and references to an undertaking excluded from consolidation shall be construed accordingly;

"Lease" includes an agreement for a lease;

"Listed security" means a security listed on a recognised stock exchange, and the expression "unlisted security" shall be construed accordingly;

"Long lease" means a lease in the case of which the portion of the term for which it was granted remaining unexpired at the end of the financial year is not less than 50 years;

"Parent" means a holding company;

"Participating interest" and "qualifying capital interest" have the meanings assigned to them by regulation 35 of the European Communities (Companies: Group Accounts) Regulations, 1992;

"Repayable on demand", in connection with deposits, loans or advances, means those amounts which can at any time be withdrawn or demanded without notice or for which a maturity or period of notice of not more than 24 hours or one working day has been agreed;

"Sale and repurchase transaction" means a transaction which involves the transfer by a credit institution or customer ("the transferor") to another credit institution or customer ("the transferee") of assets subject to an agreement that the same assets, or (in the case of fungible assets) equivalent assets, will subsequently be transferred back to the transferor at a specified price on a date specified or to be specified by the transferor; but the following shall not be regarded as sale and repurchase transactions: forward exchange transactions, options, transactions involving the issue of debt securities with a commitment to repurchase all or part of the issue before maturity or any similar transactions;

"Sale and option to resell transaction" means a transaction which involves the transfer by a credit institution or customer ("the transferor") to another credit institution or customer ("the transferee") of assets subject to an agreement that the transferee is entitled to require the subsequent transfer of the same assets, or (in the case of fungible assets) equivalent assets, back to the transferor at the purchase price or another price agreed in advance on a date specified or to be specified; and

"Short lease" means a lease which is not a long lease.

Definitions

'company': CA 1963, s 2(1); 'director': CA 1963, s 2(1); 'financial year': CA 1963, s 2(1); 'member': CA 1963, s 2(1); 'undertaking': EC(CI:A)R 1992, reg 2(1); 'subsidiary undertaking': EC(CI:A)R 1992, reg 2(1); 'fungible assets': EC(CI:A)R 1992, Sch, Pt IV; 'sale and repurchase transaction': EC(CI:A)R 1992, Sch, Pt IV.

Loans

2. For the purposes of this Schedule a loan or advance (including a liability comprising a loan or advance) is treated as falling due for repayment, and an instalment of a loan or advance is treated as falling due for payment, on the earliest date on which the lender could require repayment or (as the case may be) payment, if he exercised all options and rights available to him.

Definitions

'company': CA 1963, s 2(1); 'director': CA 1963, s 2(1); 'financial year': CA 1963, s 2(1); 'member': CA 1963, s 2(1).

Materiality

3. For the purposes of this Schedule amounts which in the particular context of any provision of this Schedule are not material may be disregarded for the purposes of that provision.

Pensions and Emoluments

4. In the case of group accounts, the pension commitments referred to in paragraph 66(2) and the emoluments and compensation referred to in paragraph 74(5) of Part I of this Schedule shall be a reference to commitments, emoluments and compensation relating to directors or past directors of the parent company in respect of duties relating to that parent or any of its subsidiary undertakings or undertakings proportionally consolidated in accordance with paragraph 20 of Part II of this Schedule.

Definitions

'company': CA 1963, s 2(1); 'director': CA 1963, s 2(1); 'financial year': CA 1963, s 2(1); 'member': CA 1963, s 2(1); 'group accounts': EC(CI:A)R 1992, reg 2(1), reg 7; 'parent company': EC(CI:A)R 1992, reg 2(1); 'undertaking': EC(CI:A)R 1992, reg 2(1); 'subsidiary undertaking': EC(CI:A)R 1992, reg 2(1).

Provisions

5. For the purposes of this Schedule and its interpretation:

(a) references to provisions for depreciation or diminution in value of assets are to any amount written off by way of providing for depreciation or diminution in value of assets;

(b) any reference in the profit and loss account formats or the notes thereto set out in Section B of Part I to the depreciation of, or amounts written off, assets of any description is to any provision for depreciation or diminution in value of assets of that description; and

(c) references to provisions for liabilities [...][a] are to any amount retained as reasonably necessary for the purpose of providing for any liability [the nature of which is clearly defined and][b] which is either likely to be incurred, or certain to be incurred but certain as to amount or as to the date on which it will arise.

Amendments

a Words deleted by reg 10 and Sch, Item No 14(a) of EC(IFRSMA)R 2005.

b Words substituted by reg 10 and Sch 2, Item No 14(b) of EC(IFRSMA)R 2005.

Staff Costs

6. In this Schedule –

(a) "Social security costs" means any contributions by the company to any state social security or pension scheme, fund or arrangement;

(b) "Pension costs" includes any other contributions by the company for the purposes of any pension scheme established for the purpose of providing pensions for persons employed by the company, any sums set aside for that purpose and any amounts paid by the company in respect of pensions without first being so set aside; and

(c) any amount stated in respect of either of the above items or in respect of the item "wages and salaries" in the company's profit and loss account shall be determined by reference to payments made or costs incurred in respect of all persons employed by the company during the financial year who are taken into account in determining the relevant annual number for the purposes of paragraph 77(1)(a).

Given under my Official Seal, this 12th day of October 1992.

Bertie Ahern,

Minister of Finance

Definitions

'company': CA 1963, s 2(1); 'director': CA 1963, s 2(1); 'financial year': CA 1963, s 2(1); 'member': CA 1963, s 2(1).

EXPLANATORY NOTE

(*This note is not part of the Instrument and does not purport to be a legal interpretation*).

The purpose of these Regulations is to give legal effect to Council Directive 86/635/EC on the annual accounts and consolidated accounts of banks and other financial institutions, and to Council Directive 89/117/EC on the obligations of branches established in a Member State of credit institutions and financial institutions having their head offices outside the Member State regarding the publication of annual accounting documents.

The Regulations apply to licensed banks in the State and to the ACC Bank and ICC Bank. They require the banks in question to draw up and publish individual and group accounts in accordance with the Regulations and the Schedule to the Regulations. They contain provisions relating to the accounting treatment and disclosure requirements of subsidiaries, associated undertakings and joint ventures and the material to be contained in the report of the directors and the auditors. The Regulations also provide for penalties for non-compliance of up to £1,000 and 12 months' imprisonment.

The Schedule to the Regulations contains provisions governing the form and content of accounts, the format of the balance sheet and profit and loss account, the valuation of items in the accounts and the information to be given in the notes to the accounts. The Schedule also deals with the rules regarding the preparation of group accounts and sets out the nature and content of the information to be given in relation to subsidiary and other related undertakings.

The Regulations require branches of foreign banks in the State to publish the accounts of the undertaking to which they belong. The Central Bank may also require branches to publish certain information about the activities of the branches themselves in accordance with the EC Directives referred to above.

The Regulations apply in respect of all financial years of the relevant institutions beginning on or after 1 January 1993.

European Communities (Branch Disclosures) Regulations 1993

SI 395/1993

I, RUAIRÍ QUINN, Minister for Enterprise and Employment, in exercise of the powers conferred on me by section 3 of the European Communities Act, 1972 (No. 27 of 1972), and for the purpose of giving effect to Council Directive No. 89/666/EEC of 21 December 1989 [OJ No 395, 30.12.89, pp 36–39], hereby make the following regulations:

PART I

PRELIMINARY

1 Citation, commencement and construction

(1) These Regulations may be cited as the European Communities (Branch Disclosures) Regulations, 1993.

(2) These Regulations shall come into operation on the 1st day of February, 1994.

(3) These Regulations shall be construed as one with the Companies Acts, 1963 to 1990.

Notes

Scope of regulations: Under CA 1963, Pt XI, a foreign company which establishes a place of business in the State is required to deliver to the Registrar of Companies copies of various classes of documents such as its memorandum and articles of association or other constitutional documents,[1] a list of its directors and secretary,[2] the address of its principal place of business in the State,[3] the names and addresses of one or more persons resident in the State who were authorised to accept service of notices, processes etc on behalf of the company[4] and, except in the case of private companies, copies of its annual accounts[5]. Any alterations in the above details also had to be delivered for registration.[6]

The purpose of the regulations is to give legal effect to Council Directive 89/666/EEC which imposes disclosure requirements on foreign limited companies whether incorporated in another member state or elsewhere, that establish a branch in the state.[7] Such companies are no longer governed by the provisions of CA 1963, Pt XI unless the place of business established in the State does not constitute a branch.[8] Whether the place of business is or is not a 'branch', Part XI continues to apply where the company has unlimited liability.

1 CA 1963, s 352(1)(a).

2 CA 1963, s 352(1)(b).

3 CA 1963, s 352(1)(c).

4 CA 1963, s 352(1)(c))

5 CA 1963, s 354.

6 CA 1963, s 353.

7 EC(BD)R 1993, Pt II of the Regulation applies to companies incorporated in another member state, whereas Pt III applies to non-EU companies.

8 EC(BD)R 1993, reg 14(1).

Establishes a branch: For an explanation of what constitutes the establishment of a branch in the State, see EC(BD)R 1993, reg 3 and the notes thereto.

---

2 Interpretation

(1) In these Regulations, unless the context otherwise requires—

"accounting documents" means the documents referred to in Regulation 12;

"certified" means certified in the prescribed manner to be a true copy or a correct translation;

"company" in Part II of Part III, means a company to which that Part applies;

"financial year" in relation to a company, means the period for which the company draws up its accounts in accordance with the law of the country in which it is incorporated;

"memorandum of articles of association" means the documents referred to in Regulations 4(1) and 7(1);

"the Principal Act" means the Companies Act, 1963 (No. 33 of 1963);

"the 1968 Directive" means Council Directive No. 68/151/EEC of 9 March 1968 [OJ No 6, 14.3.68, pp 8–12];

"the 1989 Directive" means Council Directive No. 89/666/EEC of 21 December, 1989.

(2) A word or expression that is used in these Regulations and is also used in the 1989 Directive shall, unless the contrary intention appears, have the same meaning in these Regulations as it has in the Directive concerned.

PART II
BRANCHES OF COMPANIES FROM OTHER MEMBER STATES OF THE EUROPEAN COMMUNITIES

3 Application of this Part

This Part applies to a company—

(a) to which article 1 of the 1968 Directive applies,

(b) which is incorporated in another Member State of the European Communities, and

(c) which establishes a branch in the State,

and references in this Part to a company shall be construed accordingly.

Definitions

'company': EC(BD)R 1993, reg 2(1); 'the 1968 Directive': EC(BD)R 1993, reg 2(1).

Notes

Company: For the purposes of EC(BD)R 1993, Pt II a 'company' is one to which art 1 of Directive 68/151/EEC applies,[1] (ie a limited company) which is incorporated under the laws of another member state and which establishes a branch in the State. Limited companies incorporated outside the European Union that establish branches in the State are governed by Pt III of the regulations, whereas foreign unlimited companies, wherever incorporated, continue to be governed by CA 1963, Pt XI.

[1] EC(BD)R 1993, reg 3(a).

Establishes a branch: In order for these regulations to apply, the place of business established in the State must constitute a 'branch' of the foreign company. If it is not a branch, then CA 1963,

Part XI will apply instead.[1] The word 'branch' is not defined but does appear to involve a greater than is required by CA 1963, Pt XI.[2] Thus, although every 'branch' will be regarded as an 'established place of business', not every 'established place of business' will be regarded a 'branch'.[3]

There are certain features common to an 'established place of business' or 'branch'. They both involve more than simply showing that the foreign company carries on business in the State.[4] There should be some visible sign or physical indication that the company has an ongoing or permanent connection with a particular premises from which habitually, or with some degree of regularity, business is conducted,[5] and whilst, for the purposes of CA 1963, Pt XI it might not be necessary to show that the premises are owned or even leased by the company,[6] some degree of interest in the property, whether by lease, licence or otherwise, would probably be required to satisfy the requirements for a branch. Furthermore, if the place of business is to rank as a branch, there should be a locally based management team which is materially equipped to negotiate business and contracts directly with third parties.[7]

1 EC(BD)R 1993, reg 14.

2 See EC(BD)R 1993, reg 14(2) and (3).

3 For the meaning of 'established place of business' see CA 1963, ss 111 and 351 as well as the notes thereto.

4 *Re Oriel Ltd* [1985] BCLC 343.

5 *Re Oriel Ltd* [1985] BCLC 343; *South India Shipping Corp Ltd v The Export-Import Bank of Korea* [1985] BCLC 163; *Rome v Punjab National Bank (No 2)* [1989] BCLC 328; *Cleveland Museum of Art v Capricorn Art International SA* [1990] BCLC 546; *Derverall v Grant Advertising Inc* [1954] 3 All ER 389; *Lord Advocate v Huron & Erie Loan and Savings Co* 1911 SC 612; *Établissements Somafer SA v Saar-Ferngas AG* [1978] ECR 2183; *Schotte GmbH v Parfums Rothschild Sarl* [1987] ECR 4905; *Établissements A de Bloos Sprl v Société en Commandite par Actions Bouyer* [1976] ECR 1497.

6 *Re Oriel Ltd* [1985] BCLC 343.

7 *Établissements Somafer SA v Saar-Ferngas AG* [1978] ECR 2183; *Schotte GmbH v Parfums Rothschild Sarl* [1987] ECR 4905; *Établissements A de Bloos Sprl v Société en Commandite par Actions Bouyer* [1976] ECR 1497.

4 Documents to be delivered to the Registrar

(1) A company shall, within one month of the date of the establishment of a branch in the State, deliver to the registrar for registration a certified copy of the memorandum and articles of association or the charter, statutes or other instrument constituting or defining the constitution of the company.

(2) A company shall notify the registrar in the prescribed form of the following matters at the same time as the delivery of the matter referred to in paragraph (1), namely—

(a) the name and legal form of the company and the name of the branch if that is different from the name of the company;

(b) a certificate of incorporation of the company;

(c) the address of the branch;

(d) the activities of the branch;

(e) the place of registration of the company and the number with which it is registered;

(f) a list of the persons who are authorised to represent the company in accordance with Article 2.1(e) of the 1989 Directive together with the following details relating to each such person:

(i) present forename and surname and any former forename and surname;

(ii) date of birth;

(iii) usual residential address;

(iv) nationality;

(v) business occupation, if any;

(vi) particulars of any other directorships of bodies corporate, whether incorporated in the State or elsewhere, held by that person, and

(vii) the extent of that person's powers in relation to the activities of the branch;

(g) without prejudice to the generality of subparagraph (f), the name and addresses of some one or more persons resident in the State authorised to accept on behalf of the company service of process and any notices required to be served on the company;

(h) without prejudice to the generality of subparagraph (f), the name and address of every person resident in the State authorised by the company to ensure compliance with the provisions of these Regulations together with a consent signed by each such person to act in this capacity;

(i) copies of the latest accounting documents prepared in relation to a financial year of the company to have been publicly disclosed in accordance with the law of the State in which it is incorporated before the end of the period allowed for compliance with a paragraph (1) in respect of the branch, or if earlier, the date on which the company complies with paragraph (1) in respect of the branch.

(3) A company shall also deliver to the registrar for registration, under cover of the prescribed form, the following documents and notices within 14 days of the occurrence of the event concerned, namely—

(a) any document making or evidencing an alteration in its memorandum or articles of association;

(b) every amended text of its memorandum or articles of association;

(c) notice of a change among the persons referred to in paragraphs (2)(f), (g), or (h) or in any of the particulars relating to such persons specifying the date of the change;

(d) notice of a change in the address referred to in paragraph (2)(c) together with the new address of the branch;

(e) notice of the winding-up of the company, the appointment of liquidators, particulars concerning them and their powers and the termination of the liquidation in accordance with disclosure by the company as provided for in Article 2 (1)(h), (i) and (j) of the 1968 Directive and particulars concerning insolvency proceedings, arrangements, compositions or any analogous proceedings to which the company is subject;

(f) the closure of the branch.

(4) Subsection (15) of section 195 of the Principal Act, as inserted by section 51 of the Companies Act, 1990, shall apply for the purposes of paragraph (2)(f).

Definitions

'accounting documents': EC(BD)R 1993, reg 2(1); 'certified': EC(BD)R 1993, reg 2(1); 'company': EC(BD)R 1993, reg 2(1); 'financial year': EC(BD)R 1993, reg 2(1); 'the Principal Act': EC(BD)R 1993, reg 2(1); 'the 1968 Directive': EC(BD)R 1993, reg 2(1); 'the 1989 Directive': EC(BD)R 1993, reg 2(1); 'the registrar': CA 1963, s 2(1).

Notes

Delivery of documents to Registrar: Within one month of the establishment of a branch in the State, the foreign company must deliver to the Registrar the documentation and information referred to in paras (1) and (2) thereof. If there are any changes in the information referred to in paras (2), details of the change must be delivered to the registrar within 14 days of the occurrence of the event in question.[1] These registration requirements are in place of those previously stipulated by CA 1963, ss 352–354 and are akin to those imposed on Irish companies by CA 1963, ss 17, 143 & 195 and by C(A)A 1982, s 3.

1 EC(BD)R 1993, reg 4(3).

Accounts: Under CA 1963, Part XI, only public companies with branches in the State were required to deliver copies of their accounts to the Registrar.[1] Under EC(BD)R, however, all limited companies, whether public or private are required to make such disclosure.[2] In this regard the 'accounting documents' which must be delivered to the Registrar include not only the annual accounts themselves but also any group accounts, the directors' report and the auditors' report.[3] For the ongoing obligation to file accounts after the branch has been established, see reg 11 and the notes thereto.

1 CA 1963, s 354(4).

2 EC(BD)R 1993, reg 4(2)(i).

3 EC(BD)R 1993, reg 12.

Establishes a branch: For an explanation of what constitutes the establishment of a branch in the state, see reg 3 and the notes thereto.

Prescribed forms: For the prescribed forms to be used in delivering the information referred to in EC(BD)R 1993, reg 4(2) and (3), see Companies (Forms) Order 1994.

5 Letterheads

(1) Every letter and order form used by a branch of a company shall bear the following particulars—

(a) the place of registration of the company and the number with which it is registered;

(b) the legal form of the company and the address of its registered office;

(c) in the case of a company which is being wound up, the fact that that is so;

(d) the place of registration of the branch and the number with which it is registered.

(2) If on any letters or order forms there is reference to the share capital of the company, the reference shall be to the paid-up share capital.

Definitions

'company': EC(BD)R 1993, reg 2(1); 'share': CA 1963, s 2(1).

Notes

Letterheads and order forms: The particulars to be set out on the branches, letters and order forms were equivalent to the information required of Irish companies by EC(C)R 1973, reg 9 prior to its amendment by EC(C)(A)R 2007 (SI 49/2007).

PART III

BRANCHES OF COMPANIES FROM STATES OTHER THAN THOSE UNDER PART II

6 Application of this Part

This Part applies to a company—

(a) which is incorporated outside the State, other than a company to which Part II applies,

(b) which is of a legal form comparable to a company to which Article 1 of the 1968 Directive applies, and

(c) which establishes a branch in the State,

and references in this Part to a company shall be construed accordingly.

Definitions

'company': EC(BD)R 1993, reg 2(1); 'the 1968 Directive': EC(BD)R 1993, reg 2(1).

Notes

Company: For the purposes of EC(BD)R 1993, Pt III, a 'company' is one which is incorporated with limited liability[1] outside the EU and which establishes a place of business in the State. Limited companies incorporated within the EU are governed by Pt II of the regulations whereas foreign unlimited companies, wherever incorporated, continue to be governed by CA 1963, Pt XI.

1 Council Directive 68/151/EEC, art 1 applies only to limited companies).

Establishes a branch: For an explanation of what constitutes the establishment of a branch in the state, see EC(BD)R 1993, reg 3 and the notes thereto.

7 Documents to be delivered to the registrar

(1) A company shall, within one month of the date of establishment of a branch in the State, deliver to the registrar for registration a certified copy of the memorandum and articles of association, or the charter, statutes or other instrument constituting or defining the constitution of the company.

(2) A company shall notify the registrar in the prescribed form of the following matters at the same time as the delivery of the matter referred to in paragraph (1), namely—

(a) the name and legal form of the company, its principal place of business and its objects, where this information is not in the documents referred to in paragraph (1);

(b) a certificate of incorporation of the company;

(c) the address of the branch;

(d) the activities of the branch;

(e) the name of the branch if that is different from the name of the company;

(f) the State in which the company is incorporated and, where the law of that State so provides, the place of registration of the company and the number with which it is registered;

(g) a list of the persons who are authorised to represent the company in accordance with Article 8(h) of the 1989 Directive together with the following details relating to each such person:

(i) present forename and surname and any former forename and surname;

(ii) date of birth;

(iii) usual residential address;

(iv) nationality;

(v) business occupation, if any;

(vi) particulars of any other directorships of bodies corporate, whether incorporated in the State or elsewhere, held by that person, and

(vii) the extent of that person's powers in relation to the activities of the branch together with a statement whether that person may represent the company alone or jointly with any other person or persons;

(h) without prejudice to the generality of subparagraph (g), the names and addresses of some one or more persons resident in the State authorised to accept on behalf of the company service of process and any notices required to be served on the company;

(i) without prejudice to the generality of subparagraph (g), the name and address of each person resident in the State authorised by the company to ensure compliance with the provisions of these Regulations together with a consent signed by each such person to act in this capacity;

(j) copies of the latest accounting documents prepared in relation to a financial year of the company to have been publicly disclosed in accordance with the law of the State in which it is incorporated before the end of the period allowed for compliance with paragraph (1) in respect of the branch, or if earlier, the date on which the company complies with paragraph (1) in respect of the branch.

(3) A company shall also deliver to the registrar for registration, under cover of the prescribed form, the following documents and notices within 14 days of the occurrence of the event concerned, namely—

(a) any document making or evidencing an alteration in its memorandum or articles of association;

(b) every amended text of its memorandum or articles of association:

(c) notice of a change among the persons referred to in paragraphs (2)(g), (h) or (i), or in any of the particulars relating to such persons specifying the date of the change;

(d) notice of a change in the address referred to in paragraph (2)(c) together with the new address of the branch;

(e) the winding-up of the company, the appointment of liquidators, particulars concerning them and their powers and the termination of the liquidation, insolvency proceedings, arrangements, compositions or any analogous proceedings to which the company is subject;

(f) the closure of the branch.

(4) Subsection (15) of section 195 of the Principal Act, as inserted by section 51 of the Companies Act, 1990, shall apply for the purposes of paragraph (2)(g).

Definitions

'accounting documents': EC(BD)R 1993, reg 2(1); 'certified': EC(BD)R 1993, reg 2(1); 'company': EC(BD)R 1993, reg 2(1); 'financial year': EC(BD)R 1993, reg 2(1); 'the Principal Act': EC(BD)R 1993, reg 2(1); 'the 1989 Directive': EC(BD)R 1993, reg 2(1); `registrar': CA 1963, s 2(1).

Notes

Delivery of documents to Registrar: Within one month of the establishment of a branch in the State, the foreign company must deliver to the Registrar the documentation and information referred to in paras (1) and (2) thereof. If there are any changes in the information referred to in para (2), details of the change must be delivered to the Registrar within 14 days of the occurrence of the event in question.[1] These registration requirements are in place of those previously stipulated by CA 1963, ss 352–354 and are akin to those imposed on Irish companies by CA 1963, ss 17, 143 & 195 and by C(A)A 1982, s 3.

1 EC(BD)R 1993, reg 7(3).

Accounts: Under CA 1963, Pt XI, only public companies with branches in the State were required to deliver copies of their accounts to the Registrar.[1] Under EC(BD)R 1993, however, all limited companies, whether public or private, are required to make such disclosure.[2] In this regard the 'accounting documents' which must be delivered to the Registrar includes not only the annual accounts themselves but also any group accounts, the directors' report and the auditors' report.[3] For the ongoing obligation to file accounts after the branch has been established, see EC(BD)R 1993, reg 11 and the notes thereto.

1 CA 1963, s 354(4).

2 EC(BD)R 1993, reg 7(2)(j).

3 EC(BD)R 1993, reg 12.

Establishes a branch: For an explanation of what constitutes the establishment of a branch in the state, see EC(BD)R 1993, reg 3 and the notes thereto.

Prescribed forms: For the prescribed forms to be used in delivering the information referred to in EC(BD)R 1993, reg 7(2) and (3), see Companies (Forms) Order 1994.

---

8 Letterheads

(1) Every letter and order form used by a branch of a company shall bear the following particulars—

(a) the place of registration of the branch and the number with which it is registered;

(b) if the law of the State in which the company is incorporated requires entry in a register, the place of registration of the company and the number with which it is registered.

(2) If on any letters or order forms there is reference to the share capital of the company, the reference shall be to the paid-up share capital.

Definitions

'company': EC(BD)R 1993, reg 2(1); 'share': CA 1963, s 2(1).

Notes

Letterheads and order forms: The particulars to be set out on the branches, letters and order forms were broadly equivalent to the information required of Irish companies by EC(C)R 1973, reg 9 prior to its amendment by EC(C)(A)R 2007. Notably, however, there is no requirement to state the legal form of the company or to state that it has been incorporated with limited liability, notwithstanding the fact that under the laws of the country of incorporation there might be no obligation whatsoever to include the word 'limited' or some equivalent thereof in the company's name.

---

9 Capital

(1) Subject to paragraph (2), every company shall, at the same time as it returns to the registrar the accounts referred to in Regulation 11, return a statement, in the prescribed form, indicating the amount of the called up share capital of the company.

(2) Paragraph (1) shall not apply where the information which would be contained in the statement is contained in the documentation referred to in Regulation 7(1).

Definitions

'company': EC(BD)R 1993, reg 2(1); 'registrar': CA 1963, s 2(1).

Notes

Return as to capital: If the company's constitution does not itself include details of the amount of the called up share capital, a separate statement must be filed along with the annual accounts, detailing this information.

Prescribed form: For the prescribed form of return, see Companies (Forms) Order 1994 (SI 100/1994).

PART IV

PROVISIONS APPLICABLE TO ALL COMPANIES TO WHICH THESE REGULATIONS APPLY

10 Publication of notices

A company within the meaning of Part II or Part III of these Regulations shall [cause to be published in the Companies Registration Office Gazette] [a] notice of the delivery to the registrar of the documents and particulars referred to in Regulations 4 and 7, as appropriate, within 21 days of such delivery.

Amendments

a Reg 5 of the EC (C) R 2004 (SI 839/2004) substituted the words “cause to be published in the Companies Registration Office Gazette” for “publish in *Iris Oifigiuil*”.

Definitions

‘company’: EC(BD)R 1993, reg 2(1); ‘registrar’: CA 1963, s 2(1).

Notes

Publication of notices: The publication requirements imposed on foreign companies with branches in the State are equivalent to those imposed on Irish companies by EC(C)R 1973, reg 4.

11 Accounting Documents to be delivered to the registrar

(1) Subject to paragraphs (2) to (6) every company within the meaning of Part II or Part III of these Regulations shall, once in every year, deliver to the registrar the accounting documents of the company as drawn up, audited and, where so required, disclosed in accordance with the law of the State in which it is incorporated and in the case of a company to which Part II applies in accordance with Council Directives 78/660/EEC (OJ No 222, 14.08.78, pp 11–31), 83/349/EEC [OJ No 193, 18.07.83, pp 1–17] and 84/253/EEC (OJ No 126, 12.05.84, pp 20–26).

(2) A company to which Part III applies, shall, where there is no requirement in the law of the State in which it is incorporated to have accounting documents drawn up, deliver to the registrar accounting documents drawn up and audited in accordance with Council Directives 78/660/EEC and 83/349/EEC.

(3) A company to which Part III applies may, in lieu of returning accounting documents of the company drawn up and where so required disclosed, in accordance with the law of the State in which it is incorporated, return accounting documents for the company drawn up and audited in accordance with Council Directives 78/660/EEC and 83/349/EEC.

(4) The accounting documents referred to in paragraphs (1) and (3) shall be delivered under cover of the prescribed form within eleven months from the end of the company’s financial year or at the same time as the accounting documents of the company are published pursuant to the law of the State in which the company is incorporated or are due to be so published, whichever is the earlier.

(5) The accounting documents referred to in paragraph (2) shall be delivered under cover of the prescribed form within eleven months of the end of the company’s financial year.

(6) This Regulation shall not apply to companies that are credit institutions and financial institutions within the meaning of Council Directive 89/117/EEC (OJ No 44, 16.02.89, pp 40-42).

Definitions

‘accounting documents’: EC(BD)R 1993, reg 2(1); ‘company’: EC(BD)R 1993, reg 2(1); ‘financial year’: EC(BD)R 1993, reg 2(1); `registrar’: CA 1963, s 2(1).

Notes

Filing of annual accounts: Within 14 days of the establishment of the branch, the foreign company must deliver to the Registrar of Companies copies of its latest accounting documents[1], including any group accounts and the directors' report and auditors' report.[2] Thereafter, audited accounts must be delivered to the Registrar on an annual basis.[3]

If the company is incorporated in another member state, its accounts must comply with the provisions of the Fourth and Seventh Companies Directives, and must have been audited by persons qualified in accordance with the provisions of the Eighth Companies Directive.[4]

If the company is incorporated outside the EU it has the option either of filing accounts drawn up in accordance with its own domestic law[5] or alternatively of filing accounts drawn up and audited in accordance with the provisions of the Fourth and Eighth Directives.[6] However, if the law of incorporation does not require the preparation of annual accounts, then the accounts to be filed under EC(BD)R 1993, reg 11 must be drawn up in accordance with the provisions of these two directives.[7]

1 EC(BD)R 1993, regs 4(2)(i) and 7(2)(j).

2 EC(BD)R 1993, reg 12.

3 EC(BD)R 1993, reg 11(1).

4 EC(BD)R 1993, reg 11(1). The Fourth and Seventh Companies Directives deal with annual accounts and group accounts respectively and were implemented in this jurisdiction by C(A)A 1986 and EC(CGA)R 1992). The Eighth Companies Directive was implemented by CA 1990, Pt X.

5 EC(BD)R 1993, reg 11(1).

6 EC(BD)R 1993, reg 11(3).

7 EC(BD)R 1993, reg 11(2).

Prescribed form: For the prescribed form to be used in filing the annual accounts, see Companies (Forms) Order 1994.

Financial institutions: The provisions of reg 11 do not apply to financial institutions or credit institutions[1]. Such companies are instead governed by EC(CI:A)R 1992 and, in particular, reg 14 thereof.

1 EC(BD)R 1993, reg 11(6).

12 Reference to accounting documents

References in Regulations 4(2)(i), 7(2)(j) and 11 to accounting documents, in relation to a financial year of a company, are to—

(a) the accounts of the company for the period, including, if it has one or more subsidiaries, any consolidated accounts of the group,

(b) any annual report of the directors for the period,

(c) the report of the auditors on the accounts mentioned in subparagraph (a), and

(d) any report of the auditors on the report mentioned in sub-paragraph (b).

Definitions

'accounting documents': EC(BD)R 1993, reg 2(1); 'accounts': CA 1963, s 2(1); 'company': EC(BD)R 1993, reg 2(1); 'director': CA 1963, s 2(1); 'financial year': EC(BD)R 1993, reg 2(1); `subsidiary'; CA 1963, ss 2(1) and 155.

Notes

Accounts: See the notes to EC(BD)R 1993, regs 4, 7 and 11.

13 Translations

Every document required to be delivered or notified to the registrar under Regulations 4(1), 4(2)(i), 4(3)(a) or (b), 7(1), 7(2)(j), 7(3)(a) or (b) or 11 shall, if they are not written in the Irish or the English language, have annexed to them a certified translation thereof.

Definitions

'registrar': CA 1963, s 2(1).

14 Miscellaneous Provisions

(1) Subject to paragraph (3), Part XI of the Principal Act shall not apply to a company as a result of that company having established a branch, where, by virtue of having established that branch, these Regulations apply.

(2) For the avoidance of doubt and subject to paragraph (4), references in these Regulations to the establishment of a branch shall include the changing of a place of business that is not a branch within the meaning of the 1989 Directive into such a branch and the date of establishment of the branch shall be construed as the date on which such change occurs.

(3) For the further avoidance of doubt, references in Part XI of the Principal Act to the establishment of a place of business shall include the changing of a branch within the meaning of the 1989 Directive into a place of business that is not a branch within the meaning of the 1989 Directive and the date of establishment of that place of business shall, for the purposes of the said Part XI, be construed as the date on which such change occurs and from that date the exemption in paragraph (1) shall not apply.

(4) (a) Subject to subparagraph (b), where a company to which these Regulations apply established a branch in the State before the commencement of the Regulations and where that branch has not closed a reference in these Regulations to the date of establishment of a branch shall in the case of that branch be construed as a reference to the date of the commencement of these Regulations.

(b) Where a company to which subparagraph (a) applies has, in respect of a branch established in the State, complied with all the requirements of Part XI of the Principal Act applicable following the establishment of that branch, the date of establishment of that branch for the purposes of applying these Regulations shall be construed as the date which is three months after the date of commencement of these Regulations.

Definitions

'company': EC(BD)R 1993, reg 2(1); 'the Principal Act': EC(BD)R 1993, reg 2(1); 'the 1989 Directive': EC(BD)R 1993, reg 2(1).

Notes

Distinction between branch and place of business: See the notes to EC(BD)R 1993, reg 3. If the company has a place of business in the State which is not a branch, CA 1963, Pt XI will apply. However, if the place of business subsequently becomes a branch, these regs will be triggered instead[1]. Conversely, if the company has a branch in the State so that it is governed by these regs, but it subsequently downscales operations so that the place of business no longer constitutes a branch, then CA 1963, Pt XI will be triggered.[2]

1 EC(BD)R 1993, reg 14(2).

2 EC(BD)R 1993, reg 14(3).

15 Statement in prescribed form in lieu of return under regulation 4

(1) Where prior to the date referred to in Regulation 4(1) or Regulation 7(1), as appropriate, a company which has established a branch in the State, in complying with either Part XI of the Principal Act or in complying with these Regulations in respect of another branch established in the State, had returned to the registrar documents which are the same in all respects as the documents required by Regulation 4(1) or 7(1), as appropriate, and it has no outstanding obligation to make a return to the registrar so far as concerns any alterations to those documents, then the company may return, in lieu of the documents required by regulation 4(1) or 7(1), a statement in the prescribed form that this information has already been returned to the registrar.

(2) Where prior to the date referred to in Regulation 4(1) or Regulation 7(1), as appropriate, a company which has established a branch in the State, in complying with either Part XI of the Principal Act or in complying with these Regulations in respect of another branch established in the State, had returned to the registrar particulars which are the same in all respects as the corresponding particulars required by Regulation 4(2)(f), (g) or (h) or Regulation 7(2)(g), (h) or (i), as appropriate, and it has no outstanding obligation to make a return to the registrar so far as concerns any alterations to those particulars, then the company may return, in lieu of the corresponding particulars required by Regulation 4(2)(f), (g), or (h), or Regulation 7(2)(g), (h) or (i), as appropriate, a statement in the prescribed form that this information has already been returned to the registrar.

(3) Where paragraph (1) applies, a reference to the delivery of the matter referred to in Regulation 4(1) or Regulation 7(1) shall be construed as a reference to the return of the statement referred to in paragraph (1).

Definitions

'company': EC(BD)R 1993, reg 2(1); 'the Principal Act': EC(BD)R 1993, reg 2(1); 'registrar': CA 1963, s 2(1).

Notes

Duplication of information: If the company, by virtue of having established a place of business in the State, has already delivered to the Registrar copies of its constitutional documents as well as particulars of its place of incorporation, registered number, authorised agents and persons authorised to accept service of notices etc, it need not duplicate these disclosure requirements when the place of business is upgraded to a branch. Instead, it can file a statement in the prescribed form advising that the documents and information have already been furnished.

Prescribed form: For the prescribed form to be used in making a return under EC(BD)R 1993, reg 15, see Companies (Forms) Order 1994 (SI 100/1994).

16 Statement in prescribed form in lieu of return under section 352

(1) Where Part XI of the Principal Act applies to a company by virtue of its having established a place of business and where prior to the establishment of that place of business, the company has, in complying with these Regulations, returned to the registrar documents which are the same in all respects as the documents required by section 352(1)(a), and it has no outstanding obligation to make a return to the registrar under the said Regulations, so far as concerns any alterations to those documents, then the company may return, in lieu of the documents required by section 352(1)(a), a statement in the prescribed form, that this information has already been returned pursuant to the said Regulations.

(2) Where Part XI of the Principal Act applies to a company by virtue of its having established a place of business and where prior to the establishment of that place of business, the company has, in complying with these Regulations, returned to the registrar particulars which are the same in all respects as the particulars required by section 352 (1)(b) and (2), and it has no outstanding obligation to make a return to the registrar under the said Regulations, so far as concerns any alterations to those particulars, then the company may return, in lieu of the documents required by section 352 (1)(b) and (2), a statement in the prescribed form, that this information has already been returned pursuant to the said Regulations.

Definitions

'company': EC(BD)R 1993, reg 2(1); 'the Principal Act': EC(BD)R 1993, reg 2(1); 'registrar': CA 1963, s 2(1).

Notes

Duplication of information: If the company, by virtue of having established a branch in the State, has already delivered to the Registrar copies of its constitutional documents as well as particulars of its directors, secretary, corporate name and registered number, it need not duplicate these disclosure requirements if the place of business is downgraded to a place of business which is not a branch. Instead, it can file a statement in the prescribed form advising that the documents and information have already been furnished.

Prescribed form: For the prescribed form to be used in making a return under EC(BD)R 1993, reg 16, see Companies (Forms) Order 1994 (SI 100/1994).

17 Service of process or notice

(1) Subject to paragraph (2), any process or notice required to be served on a company to which these Regulations apply shall be sufficiently served if addressed to any person whose name has been delivered to the registrar under Regulation 4(2)(g) or 7(2)(h) (or any changes notified thereto) and left at or sent by post to the address which has been so delivered.

(2) A document may be served on any such company by leaving it at or sending it by post to any branch established by the company in the State—

(a) where the company makes default it in delivering to the registrar the name and address of a person resident in the State who is authorised to accept on behalf of the company service of process; or

(b) if at any time all the persons whose names and addresses have been so delivered are dead or have ceased to so reside, or refuse to accept service on behalf of the company, or for any reason it cannot be served.

Definitions

'company': EC(BD)R 1993, reg 2(1).

Notes

Service of documents: For companies governed by the regs, the provisions of EC(BD)R 1993, reg 17 replace CA 1963, s 356.[1]

1 For service of documents on Irish companies, see CA 1963, s 379 and the notes thereto.

---

18 Duty of compliance

The duty of securing compliance by a company with the provisions of these Regulations shall, without prejudice to the duty of the company concerned, also lie upon the persons appointed by a company to ensure compliance with these Regulations.

Definitions

'company': EC(BD)R 1993, reg 2(1).

Notes

Compliance officer: Every company establishing a place of business in the State must deliver to the Registrar details of the name and address of a person or persons resident in the country authorised to ensure compliance with these regulations.[1] A signed consent to so act must also be delivered to the Registrar in respect of each and every such person.[2] Having been so appointed, the relevant officer may be made criminally liable if the company defaults in its filing obligations[3]. The penalising of the officer is, however, without prejudice to the imposition of liability on any other officer of the company who is in default.[4]

1 EC(BD)R 1993, regs 4(2)(h) and 7(2)(h).
2 EC(BD)R 1993, regs 4(2)(h) and 7(2)(h).
3 EC(BD)R 1993, reg 18.
4 EC(BD)R 1993, reg 18.

---

19 Offences

(1) A person who contravenes any provision of these Regulations shall be guilty of an offence.

(2) A person guilty of an offence under paragraph (1) shall be liable on summary conviction to a fine not exceeding [€1,904.61] [a] or, at the discretion of the court in the case of an individual, to imprisonment for a term not exceeding 12 months or to both.

(3) A person shall not be liable to be sentenced to imprisonment for such an offence unless, in the opinion of the court, the offence was committed wilfully.

(4) Where an offence referred to in paragraph (1) committed by a body or by a person purporting to act on behalf of a body is proved to have been so committed with the consent or connivance of or to be attributable to, or to have been facilitated by, any neglect on the part of any officer or employee of that body, that person shall also be guilty of an offence.

(5) In this Regulation, a reference to a contravention includes a reference to a failure to comply.

Amendments

a £1,000 increased to £1,500 by CA 1990, s 240(7) as inserted by CLEA 2001, s 104 and £1,500 converted to €1,904.61 by Council Regulations (EC) No 1103/97, No 974/98 and No 2866/98 and the Economic and Monetary Union Act, 1988, s 6.

Explanatory Note

(This note is not part of the Instrument and does not purport to be a legal interpretation).

The purpose of these Regulations is to give legal effect to Council Directive (No. 89/666/EEC) concerning disclosure requirements in respect of branches opened in a Member State by certain types of company governed by the law of another State (Council Directive 89/666/EEC).

Part XI of the Companies Act, 1963 contains disclosure requirements where companies incorporated outside the State establish a place of business in the State. Where, as a result of having opened a branch, the Regulations now made apply, the requirements of Part XI will not apply in respect of that branch. The Regulations also facilitate movement between the regime now imposed and that imposed by Part XI of the 1963.

Part I of the Regulations provides for commencement, citation and interpretation of the Regulations.

Part II (Regulations 2 to 5) provides for disclosures by European Communities First Directive companies (limited companies) that establish a branch in the State.

Part III (Regulations 6 to 9) provides for disclosures by non-European Communities companies of a legal form comparable to Part II companies that establish a branch in the State.

Part IV (Regulations 10 to 19) introduce a variety of provisions applicable to both Part II and Part III companies.

European Communities (Accounts) Regulations 1993

SI 396/1993

I, RUAIRÍ QUINN, Minister for Enterprise and Employment, in exercise of the powers conferred on me by section 3 of the European Communities Act 1972 (No 27 of 1972), and for the purpose of giving effect to the provisions of Council Directives 90/604/EEC (OJ No L 317, 16.11.1990, pp 57–59) and 90/605/EEC (OJ No L 317, 16.11.1990, pp 60–62) of 8 November 1990 and Article 11 of Council Directive 89/666/EEC (OJ No L 395, 21.12.1989, pp 36–39) of 21 December 1989 hereby make the following Regulations:

PART I

PRELIMINARY AND GENERAL

Citation and construction

1.(1) These Regulations may be cited as European Communities (Accounts) Regulations, 1993.

(2) These Regulations shall be construed as one with the Companies Acts.

Definitions

'the Companies Acts': EC(A)R 1993, reg 3(1).

Application

2.(1) Parts I and II of these Regulations shall come into operation on the 1st day of January 1994.

(2) Part III of these Regulations shall apply to accounts prepared for financial years commencing on or after 1 January 1994.

(3) Part IV of these Regulations shall apply to directors' reports attached to balance sheets for financial years commencing on or after 30 June 1993.

Definitions

'accounts': CA 1963, s 2(1); 'financial year': CA 1963, s 2(1); 'the Companies Acts: EC(A)R 1993, reg 3(1).

Notes

Application of regs: The primary function of these regs is to implement Council Directive 90/605/EEC which in turn widens the categories of company to which the Fourth Companies Directive[1] and the Seventh Companies Directive[2] apply.

The Fourth and Seventh Companies Directives respectively deal with the form and content of a company's annual accounts and a parent company's group accounts, as well as with the requirement to annex the annual accounts or group accounts, as the case may be, to the company's annual return. The two Directives were implemented in this jurisdiction by C(A)A 1986 and by EC(CGA)R 1992 and originally applied only to limited companies trading for gain.[3] However, because of these regs they now apply to unlimited companies and partnerships of the type described in EC(A)R 1993, reg 6.

The imposition of accounting and disclosure requirements on partnerships is a new development in Irish law. However, unlimited companies were already obliged to prepare accounts which complied with the provisions of CA 1963,[4] and in the case of public unlimited companies, there was an additional requirement to annex those accounts to the annual return.[5]

1 78/660/EEC.

2 83/349/EEC.

3 C(A)A 1986, s 2 and EC(CGA)R 1992, regs 5–9 and 39. Financial institutions and insurance companies are excluded from the scope of this legislation by C(A)A 1986 s 2(2) and (3) and EC(CGA)R 1992, reg 6, being dealt with instead by EC(CI:A)R 1992 and EC (IUA)R 1996, respectively.

4 See CA 1963, s 149A and the notes thereto.

5 CA 1963, s 128. See also the notes to CA 1963, s 125.

Interpretation

3.(1) In these Regulations, unless the context otherwise requires—

"the Companies Acts" means the Companies Act, 1963, and any enactment to be construed as one with that Act;

"Member State" means a State which is a member of the European Communities;

"partnership" has the same meaning as in the Partnerships Act, 1890;

"limited partnership" means a partnership to which the Limited Partnerships Act 1907, applies;

"the 1992 Group Accounts Regulations" means the European Communities (Companies: Group Accounts), Regulations, 1992;

"the 1986 Act" means the Companies (Amendment) Act, 1986;

"undertaking" has the same meaning as in the 1992 Group Accounts Regulations.

(2) In these Regulations, unless the context otherwise requires, a reference to a Part is to a Part of these Regulations, a reference to a Regulation is to a Regulation of these Regulations, a reference to a paragraph is to the paragraph of the Regulation and a reference to a subparagraph is to the subparagraph of the paragraph in which the reference occurs.

Definitions

'undertaking': EC(CGA)R 1992, reg 3(1).

PART II

IMPLEMENTATION OF COUNCIL DIRECTIVE 90/604/EEC

4. [...][a]

Amendments

a EC(A)R 1993, reg 4 amends C(A)A 1986, s 8(2). See amended Act.

Definitions

'the 1986 Act': EC(A)R 1993, reg 3(1).

Notes

EC(A)R 1993, reg 4 amended C(A)A 1986, s 8 by increasing the balance sheet and turnover thresholds for the purpose of availing of the small and medium-sized companies' accounting and disclosure exemptions[1].

1 For the nature and extent of the accounting and disclosure exemptions for such companies, see C(A)A 1986, ss 10–12 and s 18 as well as the notes thereto.

5.(1) The documents to be delivered to the registrar of companies under section 7 or 18 of the 1986 Act or Regulation 39 of the 1992 Group Accounts Regulations or Regulation 20 of these Regulations, as the case may be, may have the money amounts referred to therein expressed in European currency units, in addition to their expression in the currency in which the documents concerned were drawn up.

(2) Where a company avails itself of the option in paragraph (1), the exchange rate used shall be that prevailing on the date of the balance sheet, and that rate shall be disclosed in a note to the accounts.

(3) In this Regulation, "European currency unit" has the meaning assigned to it by Regulation (EEC) No. 3180/78 (OJ No L379, 30.12.1978, p 1), as amended by Regulation (EEC) No. 2626/84 (OJ No L247, 16.9.1984, p 1, and by Regulation (EEC) No. 1971/89. (OJ No L189, 4.7.1989, p 1).

Definitions

'company': CA 1963, s 2(1); 'the 1992 Group Accounts Regulations': EC(A)R 1993, reg 3(1); 'the 1986 Act': EC(A)R 1993, reg 3(1).

Notes

Figures in annexed accounts expressed in ECUs: If a company is required by these Regulations or by C(A)A 1986 or by EC(CGA)R 1992 to annex copy accounts to its annual returns, it may, if it so wishes, have the monetary amounts in those accounts expressed in ECUs as well as in the currency in which the accounts were originally drawn up[1]. This may be of particular assistance where there is an international dimension to the company's business. The applicable exchange rate (which must be disclosed in a note to the accounts) is that prevailing on the date of the balance sheet[2].

1 EC(A)R 1993, reg 5(1).

2 EC(A)R 1993, reg 5(2).

PART III

IMPLEMENTATION OF COUNCIL DIRECTIVE 90/605/EEC

6. This Part shall apply to the following undertakings:

(1) Unlimited companies and partnerships where all the members thereof who do not have a limit on their liability are

(a) companies limited by shares or by guarantee, or

(b) bodies not governed by the law of the State but equivalent to those in paragraph (a), or

(c) any combination of the types of bodies referred to in subparagraphs (a) and (b), and

(2) Unlimited companies and partnerships where all the members thereof who do not have a limit on their liability are

(a) (i) unlimited companies or partnerships of the type referred to in paragraph (1) that are governed by the laws of a Member State, or

(ii) bodies governed by the laws of a Member State that are of a legal form comparable to those referred to in paragraph (i), or

(b) any combination of the types of bodies referred to in subparagraph (a) and subparagraphs (a) and (b) of paragraph (1).

Definitions

'undertaking': EC(CGA)R 1992, reg 3(1); 'company': CA 1963, s 2(1); 'Member State': EC(A)R 1993, reg 3(1); 'partnership': EC(A)R 1993, reg 3(1).

Notes

Member or partner with unlimited liability: The apparent intent of this Regulation is to apply the accounting and disclosure provisions of the Fourth and Seventh Companies Directives to any unlimited company or partnership in which there is not a person who ultimately has unlimited liability for the debts of the business. Previously, it had been possible to circumvent the disclosure obligations of C(A)A 1986 by trading through an Irish unlimited company whose shares were in turn held by an off-shore limited company. The effectiveness of such schemes would now, however, appear to be somewhat curtailed.

Unlimited companies: An unlimited company will be caught by the provisions of these Regulations if all its members are—

(a) Irish and/or foreign limited companies; or

(b) unlimited companies incorporated in the state or in another member state, whose members are in turn all Irish and/or foreign limited companies, or

(c) a combination of (a) and (b).

The regs will not apply, however, if there is at least one member who is an individual, since he will have unlimited liability in the true sense of the phrase. Nor would the regs seem to apply to an Irish unlimited company all of whose shares are held by an unlimited company incorporated in a country other than a member state of the European Union, and whose shares are in turn held by a limited company which is likewise incorporated outside the European Union[1]. So, for example, an Irish unlimited company which is a wholly-owned subsidiary of an unlimited company incorporated under the laws of the Cayman Islands which is in turn owned by a limited company incorporated under the laws of the British Virgin Islands, would appear to be exempt from having to annex a copy of its accounts to the annual return.

1 This conclusion is founded on the fact that, for whatever reason, reg 6(2) only applies to unlimited companies incorporated in the EU, whereas reg 6(1) applies to companies wherever incorporated.

Partnerships: Not all partnerships are caught by these regs. For the reasons expounded above in relation to unlimited companies, the regs will not apply if there is at least one human being who is a general partner. For the same reasons, Irish partnerships owned by non-EU partnerships and/or by non-EU unlimited companies, which are in turn owned by other non-EU limited companies, would appear to be exempt.

In the case of a limited partnership, however, where the only human partner is a limited partner, and all the general partners are limited companies, the regs will apply.

7.(1) Subject to these Regulations, the 1986 Act shall apply to an undertaking to which this Part applies as it applies to companies to which that Act applies.

(2) Notwithstanding section 1(1) of the 1986 Act, the term "company" in that Act shall include an unlimited company to which this Part applies and the term "private company" shall include such unlimited companies that are not public companies.

(3) Subject to these Regulations, the 1986 Act shall be applied to partnerships to which this Part applies as though those partnerships were companies formed and registered under the Companies Acts with any modifications necessary to take account of the fact that such partnerships are unincorporated.

[(4) Notwithstanding paragraphs (1), (2) and (3), an undertaking to which this Part applies shall prepare its annual individual accounts in accordance with—

(a) section 149 of the Companies Act 1963 (in these Regulations referred to as 'Companies Act individual accounts'), or

(b) international financial reporting standards (in these Regulations referred to as 'IFRS individual accounts') and section 149A of the Companies Act 1963,][a]

Amendments

a Inserted by EC(IFRS)R 2005, reg 7.

Definitions

'undertaking': EC(CGA)R 1992, reg 3(1); 'company': CA 1963, s 2(1); 'companies act individual accounts': CA 1963, s 2(1); 'IFRS individual accounts:' CA 1963, s 2(1); 'individual accounts': CA 1963 s 2(1);'international financial reporting standards': CA 1963, s 2(1); 'private company': CA 1963, s 2(1) and s 33; 'the Companies Acts': EC(A)R 1993, reg 3(1); 'partnership': EC(A)R 1993, reg 3(1); 'the 1986 Act': EC(A)R 1993, reg 3(1); 'undertaking': EC(A)R 1993, reg 3(1); 'unlimited company': CA 1963, s 2(1) and s 5(2).

Notes

Application of C(A)A 1986 to unlimited companies and partnerships: The original effect of EC(A)R 1993, reg 7 is to apply the accounting and disclosure provisions of C(A)A 1986, with modifications, to unlimited companies and partnerships of the type described in reg 7. Heretofore, C(A)A 1986 had applied only to limited companies trading for gain[1].

However, as a result of EC(IFRS)R 2005, ss 148 to 151 of CA 1963 were repealed and replaced by new ss 148, 149, 149A, 150, 150A, 150B, 150C and 151. A principal consequence of this, the primary obligation to prepare financial statements previously contained in s 3, C(A)A 1986 and reg 5 of EC(G:AR) 1992, EC(CI:A) R, 1992, EC(IUA)R, 1996 and reg 7 of EC(A)R, 1993 is now contained in s 148 CA 1963 (individual accounts) and CA 1963, s 150 (group accounts), irrespective of what type of company is involved – eg general companies, credit institutions or insurance undertakings.

See also Notes to CA 1963, ss 148–151.

1 See C(A)A 1986, ss 1(1) and 2, as well as the notes thereto.

8.(1) Save as otherwise provided, in these Regulations the term "partner" shall not include a limited partner.

(2) The compliance by a limited partner with Regulations 16(2)(b) and 22 (1) shall not constitute taking part in the management of the partnership business for the purposes of section 6(1) of the Limited Partnerships Act, 1907.

Definitions

'limited partnership': EC(A)R 1993, reg 3(1); 'partnership': EC(A)R 1993, reg 3(1).

Notes

Types of partner: Irish law recognises two types of partner: the general partner and the limited partner. The general partner has unlimited liability, but is entitled subject to anything to the contrary in any partnership agreement, to participate in the business of the partnership and to bind his fellow partners.[1] By contrast, a limited partner has his liability limited to the amount of the capital which he has contributed to the partnership, but is not entitled to participate in the management of the business of the firm, nor is he entitled to bind his fellow partners.[2] For the purpose of these regs, unless the contrary is stated, a reference to a 'partner' is to be construed as a reference to a general partner.[3]

1 Partnership Act 1890, ss 4(1) and 5. For a general overview of the law of partnership, see Ivamy, Underhill's *Principles of the Law of Partnership* (2nd edn, 1986) and Twomey *Partnership Law* (Tottel Publishing, 2000).

2 Limited Partnership Act 1907, ss 4(2) and 6(1).

3 EC(A)R 1993, reg 8(1).

Participation by limited partner in the affairs of the partnership: In normal circumstances, if a limited partner takes part in the management of the business of the firm, he loses his limited liability and becomes a general partner[1]. Nonetheless, neither of the following acts is to be construed as participation in the management of the business such as would expose the partner to the possibility of unlimited liability:-

(i) the giving of consent under EC(A)R 1993, reg 16(2)(b) for a firm which is a subsidiary undertaking to avail of the exemption from having to annex a copy of its accounts to the annual return; and

(ii) the appointment of an auditor under EC(A)R 1993, reg 22(1).[2]

1 Limited Partnership Act 1907, s 6(1).

2 EC(A)R 1993, reg 8(2).

9.(1) Subject to these Regulations, the 1992 Group Accounts Regulations shall apply to an undertaking to which this Part applies that is a parent undertaking as they apply to the parent undertakings referred to in Regulation 5 (3) of those Regulations.

(2) In the case of a partnership to which this Part applies the partners shall prepare the group accounts referred to in Regulation 5(1) of the 1992 Group Accounts Regulations and in the case of such partnerships any reference to group accounts prepared by the company shall be construed as a reference to group accounts prepared by the partners.

(3) Subject to these Regulations, the 1992 Group Accounts Regulations shall be applied to partnerships to which this Part applies as though those partnerships were companies

formed and registered under the Companies Act with any modifications necessary to take account of the fact that such partnerships are unincorporated.

[(4) Notwithstanding paragraphs (1), (2) and (3), an undertaking to which this Part applies shall prepare its annual group accounts in accordance with—

(a) section 150A of the Companies Act 1963 (in these Regulations referred to as 'Companies Act group accounts'), or

(b) international financial reporting standards (in these Regulations referred to as 'IFRS group accounts') and section 150B of the Companies Act 1963,

and in either case shall comply with section 150C of the Companies Act 1963.][a]

Amendments

a Inserted by EC(IFRS)R 2005, reg 7(b).

Definitions

'undertaking': EC(CGA)R 1992, reg 3(1); 'parent undertaking': EC(CGA)R, reg 3(1); 'Companies act group accounts': CA 1963, s 2(1); 'international financial reporting standards': CA 1963, s 2(1); 'IFRS group accounts': CA 1963 s 2(1);'partnership': EC(A)R 1993, reg 3(1); 'the 1992 Group Accounts Regulations': EC(A)R 1993, reg 3(1); 'undertaking': EC(A)R 1993, reg 3(1).

Notes

Group accounts: The effect of EC(A)R 1993, reg 9 as amended by EC(IFRS)R 2005 is to apply the group accounting and disclosure provisions of CA 1963, s 150 to unlimited companies and partnerships of the type described in reg 9. Heretofore, the requirement to prepare group accounts under EC(CGA)R 1992 arose only if the parent undertaking was a limited company[1], albeit that the subsidiaries, undertakings which had to be included in the group accounts, might themselves have been unlimited companies, partnerships or other unincorporated associations[2].

1 EC(CGA)R 1992, reg 5(3).

2 See the definitions of 'undertaking' and 'subsidiary undertaking' in EC(CGA)R 1992, reg 3(1) and reg 4 which clearly envisage such bodies being included in the group accounts.

10.(1) Every balance sheet and profit and loss account of a partnership to which this Part applies shall be approved by the partners and shall be signed on behalf of the partners by two of the partners authorised by the partners to do so.

(2) In the case of a partnership to which this Part applies any reference in the 1986 Act to Section 156 of the Principal Act shall be construed as a reference to paragraph (1).

Definitions

'partnership': EC(A)R 1993, reg 3(1); '1986 Act': EC(A)R 1993, reg 3(1).

Notes

Signing of partnership accounts: This regulation which requires the annual accounts of the partnership to be signed by two duly authorised officers is the equivalent of CA 1963, s 156 which requires the accounts of a company to be signed by two directors.

Balance sheet as an acknowledgement of debt: Once signed, the balance sheet is capable of operating as an acknowledgement of debt for the purposes of the Statute of Limitations 1957, s 56[1].

1 *Re Atlantic and Pacific Fibre Importing and Manufacturing Co* [1928] Ch 836; *Jones v Bellgrove Properties Ltd* [1949] 2 KB 700; *Re Gee & Co (Woolwich) Ltd* [1975] Ch 152; *Re Compania de Electricidad de la Provincia de Buenos Aires Ltd* [1978] 3 All ER 668; *Re The Stage Club Ltd v Millers Hotel Pty Ltd* (1982) 56 ALJR 113; *Re Overmark Smith Warden Ltd* [1982] 1 WLR 1195) provided that the creditor is not also a member of the firm (*Re Coliseum (Barrow) Ltd* [1930] 2 Ch 44; *Re Transplanters (Holding Co)* Ltd [1958] 1 WLR 822.

11. Without prejudice to the generality of Regulation 3 (2) of the 1992 Group Accounts Regulations and save as otherwise provided in these Regulations, any reference in the 1986 Act or in the 1992 Group Accounts Regulations to directors shall, in the case of a partnership to which this Part applies, be construed as a reference to the partners of such partnerships and any duties, obligations or discretion imposed on or granted to such directors shall be deemed to be imposed on or granted to such partners.

Definitions

'partnership': EC(A)R 1993, reg 3(1); 'the 1992 Group Accounts Regulations' EC(A)R 1993, reg 3(1); 'the 1986 Act' EC(A)R 1993, reg 3(1).

Annual Accounts of Partnerships

12.(1) In the case of a partnership to which this Part applies, the partners shall, at some date not later than 18 months after the appropriate date and subsequently once at least in every calendar year, so however that not more than 15 months shall elapse between the preparation of the account, draw up a profit and loss account for the period, in the case of the first account, since the formation of the partnership, and in any other case, since the preceding account.

(2) The partners shall cause to be made out in every calendar year a balance sheet as at the date to which the profit and loss account is made up.

[(3) In the case of such partnerships the reference in section 3 of the 1986 Act to Companies Act individual accounts shall be read as a reference to balance sheets and profit and loss accounts drawn up pursuant to this Regulation, which, in accordance with Regulation 7(4), may be Companies Act individual accounts or IFRS individual accounts.][a]

(4) For the purposes of this Regulation the "appropriate date" shall be;

(i) in the case of the partnership formed before the commencement of these Regulations, the date referred to in Regulation 2(2), and

(ii) in the case of a partnership formed after the commencement of these Regulations, the date of the formation of the partnership.

Amendments

a Substituted by EC(IFRS)R 2005, reg 7(c).

Definitions

'partnership': EC(A)R 1993, reg 3(1).

13.(1) Subject to paragraphs (3) to (6), the provisions of sections 10, 12(1) and 18 of the 1986 Act applicable to a company qualified to be treated as a small company shall apply mutatis mutandis to a partnership to which this Part applies in respect of any financial year of the partnership if, in respect of that year and the financial year of the partnership immediately preceding that year, the partnership satisfies at least two of the conditions specified in subsection (2) of section 8 of the 1986 Act, as amended by Regulation 4.

(2) Subject to paragraphs (3) to (6), the provisions of sections 11, 12 (2) and 18 of the 1986 Act applicable to a company qualified to be treated as a medium-sized company shall apply mutatis mutandis to any partnership to which this Part applies in respect of any financial year of the partnership if, in respect of that year and the financial year of the partnership immediately preceding that year, the partnership satisfies at least two of the conditions specified in subsection (3) of section 8 of the 1986 Act, as amended by Regulation 4.

(3) Subject to paragraph (4), in determining whether a partnership to which this Part applies is qualified to be treated in the same manner as a small company or a medium-sized company subsections (4) to (12) of section 8 and section 9 of the 1986 Act shall apply.

(4) In the case of partnerships to which this Part applies the references in subsections (7) and (8) of section 8 of the 1986 Act to incorporation shall be construed as references to the formation of such partnerships and a reference in those subsections to the commencement of the said section 7 shall be construed as a reference to the date referred to in Regulation 2 (2).

(5) In the case of partnerships to which this Part applies the statement required by section 18 (2) of the 1986 Act shall be in a position on the balance sheet immediately above the signatures required by Regulation 10.

(6) In the case of partnerships to which this Part applies the copy of the report of the auditors referred to in subsection (5) of section 18 shall be certified by two of the partners to be a true copy of such report.

Definitions

'financial year': CA 1963, s 2(1); 'small company': C(A)A 1986, s 8(1)(a); 'medium-sized company': C(A)A 1986, s 8(1)(b); 'partnership': EC(A)R 1993, reg 3(1); 'the 1986 Act': EC(A)R 1993, reg 3(1).

Notes

Small and medium-sized partnerships: The effect of this reg is to afford to small and medium-sized partnerships of the type described in EC(A)R 1993, reg 6 the same accounting and disclosure exemptions as are afforded to small and medium-sized companies under C(A)A 1986.

14.(1) In the case of a partnership to which this Part applies, there shall be attached to every balance sheet drawn up pursuant to Regulation 12, a report of the partners containing the following information:

[(a) a fair review of the development and performance of the business of the partnership and of the development and performance of its subsidiary undertakings, if any, together with a description of the principal risks and uncertainties that they face, which review—

(i) shall be a balanced and comprehensive analysis of the development and performance of the business of the partnership and of its subsidiary undertakings, if any, consistent with the size and complexity of the business, and

(ii) to the extent necessary for an understanding of the partnership's development, performance or position, and that of its subsidiary undertakings, if any, shall include an analysis of financial, and, where appropriate, non-financial key performance indicators relevant to the particular business, including information relevant to environmental and employee matters,

and, where appropriate, the report shall include additional explanations of amounts included in the annual accounts;][a]

(b) particulars of any important events affecting the partnership or any of its subsidiary undertakings, if any, which have occurred since the end of that year;

(c) an indication of likely future developments in the business of the partnership and any of its subsidiary undertakings, if any;

(d) an indication of the activities, if any, of the partnership and any of its subsidiary undertakings, if any, in the field of research and development, and

(e) an indication of the existence of branches (within the meaning of Council Directive 89/666/EEC (OJ No L395, 21.12.1989, pp 36–39)) of the partnership outside the State and the country in which each such branch is located.

(2) The said report shall be signed on behalf of the partners by two of the partners authorised by the partners to so do.

(3) Section 13 of the 1986 Act shall not apply in the case of a partnership referred to in paragraph (1) and a reference in the 1986 Act to the report of the directors of a company shall in the case of such partnerships be construed as a reference to the report of the partners prepared pursuant to this Regulation.

Amendments

a Substituted by EC(IFRS)R 2005, reg 7(d).

Definitions

'financial year': CA 1963, s 2(1); 'partnership': has the same meaning as in the Partnerships Act, 1890; 'subsidiary undertaking': EC(CGA)R 1992, reg 4; 'the 1986 Act': EC(A)R 1993, reg 3(1); 'undertaking': EC(A)R 1993, reg 3(1).

Notes

Partners' report: The partners' report which is required to be drawn up and attached to the balance sheet of the partnership's accounts is the equivalent for a firm of the type described in reg 6, to a directors' report for an incorporated company[1].

[1] In relation to the directors' report generally, see CA 1963 s 158, C(A)A 1986, ss 13 and 14 and EC(CGA)R 1992, reg 37 as well as the notes thereto.

---

15. Where, in the case of a partnership to which this Part applies, the partners decide to give the information specified in subsection (1) of section 16 of the 1986 Act, as amended by Regulation 44 of the 1992 Group Accounts Regulations, by way of a separate statement in accordance with subsection (3) of that section, the said statement shall be signed on behalf of the partners by two of the partners and a copy of that statement, certified by two of the partners to be a true copy of such a statement shall be returned to the registrar with the accounts for that particular financial year.

Definitions

'partnership': EC(A)R 1993, reg 3(1); 'the 1992 Group Accounts Regulations' EC(A)R 1993, reg 3(1); 'the 1986 Act': EC(A)R 1993, reg 3(1).

Notes

Statement concerning subsidiary undertakings and undertakings of substantial interest: See the notes to C(A)A 1986, s 16.

16.(1) Subject to paragraph (2), section 17 of the 1986 Act, as substituted by Regulation 45 of the 1992 Group Accounts Regulations, shall apply to a partnership to which this Part applies as it applies to a private company.

(2) In the case of a partnership to which this Part applies;

(a) the reference in section 17 to the provisions of section 7 shall be construed in accordance with Regulation 20(4), and

(b) paragraph (a) of subsection 1 of the said section 17 shall not apply but all the partners including, in the case of a limited partnership, a limited partner must declare, in writing, their consent to the exemption in respect of a financial year before the partnership can stand exempted from the requirement in respect of that year, and

(c) the notification procedure referred to in subsection (1)(b) of the said section 17 shall not apply, but a certified copy of the guarantee referred to in that subsection in respect of a financial year must be forwarded to all the partners including, in the case of a limited partnership, a limited partner before the partnership can stand exempted from the requirement in respect of that year, and

(d) paragraphs (d) and (f) of subsection (1) of the said section 17 shall not apply but the partners shall, in respect of each financial year for which it avails of the exemption, return to the registrar, in lieu of the accounts referred to in Regulation 20:

(i) a notice stating that the partnership has availed of the exemption under the said section 17,

(ii) the declarations referred to in paragraph (h) in respect of that financial year,

(iii) a certified copy of the guarantee referred to in paragraph (c) for that financial year,

[(iv) the group accounts of the parent undertaking prepared in accordance with the Seventh Council Directive or international financial reporting standards and audited in accordance with Article 37 of the Seventh Council Directive.][a]

Amendments

a Substituted by EC(IFRS)R 2005, reg 7(e).

Definitions

'limited partnership': EC(A)R 1993, reg 3(1); 'private company': CA 1963, s 2(1) and s 33; 'financial year': CA 1963, s 2(1); 'the 1992 Group Accounts Regulations': EC(A)R 1993, reg 3(1); 'the 1986 Act': EC(A)R 1993, reg 3(1).

Notes

Subsidiary partnership: The effect of this reg to a partnership of the type described in EC(A)R 1993, reg 6, is an exemption from the obligation to annex copy accounts to the annual return, which is similar to the exemption afforded by C(A)A 1986, s 17 to a private company which is a subsidiary undertaking of a parent company which files its own group accounts in accordance with the provisions of EC(CGA)R 1992.

Consent to availing of exemption: The giving of consent under EC(A)R 1993, reg 16(2)(b) for a firm which is a subsidiary undertaking to avail of the exemption from having to annex a copy of its accounts to the annual return will not be construed as participation in the management of the business such as would expose a limited partner to the possibility of unlimited liability (EC(A)R 1993, reg 8(2)).

Group Accounts of Partnerships to which this Part applies

17. Regulation 7 of the 1992 Group Accounts Regulations shall apply to a parent undertaking that is a partnership to which this Part applies as it applies to private companies under that Regulation.

Definitions

'director': CA 1963, s 2(1); 'private company': CA 1963, s 2(1) and s 33; 'financial year': CA 1963, s 2(1); 'parent undertaking': EC(CGA)R 1992, reg 3(1). Also add in any applicable definitions from reg 3; 'partnership': EC(A)R 1993, reg 3(1); 'the 1992 Group Accounts Regulations': EC(A)R 1993, reg 3(1); 'undertaking': EC(A)R 1993, reg 3(1).

Notes

Exemptions related to size of group: If the parent undertaking of a group of undertakings is a partnership of the type described in reg 6, it will be afforded the same exemptions from having to file group accounts as are afforded to parent companies under EC(CGA)R 1992, reg 7.

18.(1) In the case of a parent undertaking that is a partnership to which this Part applies, the requirement in paragraphs (1) and (3) of Regulation 36 of the 1992 Group Accounts Regulations to have statements signed and certified by a director and the secretary shall be construed as a requirement to have such statements signed and certified by two of the partners authorised by the partners to do so.

(2) In the case of a parent undertaking that is a partnership to which this Part applies, the statements referred to in paragraph (1) shall be returned to the Registrar with the accounts for that particular financial year.

Definitions

'director': CA 1963, s 2(1); 'parent undertaking': EC(CGA)R 1992, reg 3(1); 'partnership': EC(A)R 1993, reg 3(1); 'the 1992 Group Accounts Regulations': EC(A)R 1993, reg 3(1); 'undertaking': EC(A)R 1993, reg 3(1).

Notes

Publication of information: See the notes to EC(CGA)R 1992, reg 36.

19. In the case of a parent undertaking that is a partnership to which this Part applies, the reference in Regulation 37 of the 1992 Group Accounts Regulations to the report of the directors under section 158 of the Principal Act shall be construed as a reference to the report of the partners under Regulations 14 of these Regulations.

Definitions

'director': CA 1963, s 2(1); 'parent undertaking': EC (GAC) Regs 1992, reg 3(1); 'partnership': EC(A)R 1993, reg 3(1); 'the 1992 Group Accounts Regulations': EC(A)R 1993, reg 3(1); 'undertaking': EC(A)R 1993, reg 3(1).

Notes

Partners' report: See EC(A)R 1993, reg 14 and the notes to EC(CGA)R 1992, reg 37.

Return by Partnership of Documents to the Register of Companies

20.(1) Subject to Regulation 13, in the case of a partnership to which this Part applies the partners shall, under cover of the prescribed form, forward to the register of companies, within six months from the end of the financial year of the partnership, a copy of the balance sheet and profit and loss account for that financial year drawn up in accordance with Regulation 12 and each such copy shall be certified, by two of the partners authorised by the partners to do so, to be a true copy of such balance sheet or profit and loss account, as the case may be.

(2) Where a partnership to which this Part applies is a parent undertaking whose partners are required to prepare group accounts in accordance with the 1992 Group Accounts Regulations, the partners shall forward a copy of the group accounts to the registrar at the same time as the documentation referred to in paragraph (1) and each such copy shall be certified, by two of the partners authorised by the partners to do so, to be a true copy.

(3) There shall be attached to the balance sheet, profit and loss accounts and group accounts referred to in paragraphs (1) and (2) a copy of the report of the auditors on and report of the partners accompanying each such balance sheet, profit and loss account or

group accounts and each such copy shall be certified, by two of the partners authorised by the partners to do so, to be a true copy of each such report.

(4) Section 7 of the 1986 Act shall not apply to a partnership to which this Part applies and a reference in that Act to a provision of the said section 7 shall be construed in the case of such a partnership as a reference to the corresponding provision in this Regulation.

(5) Regulation 39 of the 1992 Group Accounts Regulations shall not apply to a partnership to which paragraph (2) applies.

(6) In the case of a partnership to which this Part applies, a reference, in the 1986 Act or in the 1992 Group Accounts Regulations to the annual return shall be construed as a reference to the return made to the registrar pursuant to this Regulation and a reference to any documents to be annexed to the annual return shall be construed as a reference to the corresponding documents to be returned pursuant to these Regulations.

Definitions

'financial year': CA 1963, s 2(1); 'parent undertaking': EC(CGA)R 1992, reg 3(1); 'partnership': EC(A)R 1993, reg 3(1); 'the 1992 Group Accounts Regulations': EC(A)R 1993, reg 3(1); 'the 1986 Act': EC(A)R 1993, reg 3(1); 'undertaking': EC(A)R 1993, reg 3(1).

Notes

Annual return for partnerships: This Regulation imposes on partnerships of the type described in EC(A)R 1993, reg 6, an obligation to make annual returns and to annex thereto copies of the annual accounts and group accounts, if any. For the prescribed form of the annual return, see EC(A)(F)R 1995.

---

21. Where a document, being a balance sheet, profit and loss account, report or statement, returned to the registrar pursuant to these Regulations, is in a language other than the English language or the Irish language, there shall be annexed to each such document a translation in the English language or the Irish language certified in the prescribed manner to be a correct translation.

Audit Provisions

22.(1) In the case of a partnership to which this Part applies, the partners, including a limited partner, if any, shall appoint auditors who shall make a report on the accounts examined by them and on every balance sheet and profit and loss account, and all group accounts drawn up pursuant to these Regulations by the partners during their tenure of office as auditors.

(2) A person shall not be qualified for appointment as an auditor under paragraph (1) unless he is qualified under the Companies Acts for appointment as auditor of a company.

(3) In the case of a partnership to which this Part applies the reference in section 15, section 18 (3)(b) and section 19 (2)(c) and (d) of the 1986 Act to an auditor's report under section 163 of the Principal Act and the reference in Regulation 38 of the 1992 Group Accounts Regulations to an auditor's report under section 193 of the 1990 Act shall be construed as references to the auditor's report referred to in paragraph (1).

Definitions

'the Companies Acts': EC(A)R 1993, reg 3(1); 'partnership': EC(A)R 1993, reg 3(1); 'the 1992 Group Accounts Regulations' EC(A)R 1993, reg 3(1); 'the 1986 Act': EC(A)R 1993, reg 3(1).

Notes

Holding of audit and preparation of auditor's report: For partnerships of the type described in reg 6, this Regulation imposes an audit requirement similar to that for incorporated companies and also requires the preparation of an auditor's report in respect of the annual or group accounts, as the case may be. An auditor of such a partnership must have the same qualifications as an auditor of an incorporated company[1]. Curiously, however, the regs are silent as to whether or not the other provisions of the Companies Acts relating to auditors, such as the provisions governing the procedure tenure of office[2], removal from office[3] and resignation[4] apply also to auditors of partnerships.

1 See CA 1990, ss 187–192 and s 195 for the qualifications of auditors.
2 CA 1963, ss 160 and 161.
3 CA 1963, ss 160 and 161.
4 CA 1990, ss 185 and 186.

Unlimited Liability

23. [...][a]

Amendments

a EC(A)R 1993, reg 23 amends C(A)A 1986, by the insertion of s 16A. See the amended Act.

Definitions

'the 1986 Act': EC(A)R 1993, reg 3(1); 'undertaking': EC(A)R 1993, reg 3(1).

Offences

24.(1) If any person, being a partner of a partnership to which this Part applies, fails to take all reasonable steps to secure compliance with a requirement of Regulations 10(1), 12(1) and (2), 13(5) and (6), 14(1) and (2), 15, 16, 20, 21 and 22, that partner and any officer of that partner who is in default, shall in respect of each offence, be liable on summary conviction to imprisonment for a term not exceeding 12 months or, at the discretion of the court, to a fine not exceeding [€1,904.61],[a] or to both.

(2) In any proceedings against a person for an offence under paragraph (1) of this Regulation, it shall be a defence for a partner to prove that he had reasonable grounds to believe and did believe that a competent and reliable person was charged with the duty of ensuring that the provisions of these Regulations were complied with and that the latter person was in a position to discharge that duty, and a person shall not be liable to be sentenced to imprisonment for an offence under the said paragraph (1) unless, in the opinion of the court, the offence was committed wilfully.

(3) If any person in any return, report, certificate, balance sheet or other documents required by or for the purpose of any of the provisions of these Regulations wilfully makes a statement false in any material particular, knowing it to be false, he shall be

liable on summary conviction to imprisonment for a term not exceeding 12 months or, at the discretion of the court, to a fine not exceeding [€1,904.61],[a] or to both.

(4) A partner shall be deemed to be an officer of the partnership for the purposes of section 22 of the 1986 Act and Regulation 41 of the 1992 Group Accounts Regulations.

(5) Proceedings for an offence under this Regulation, in relation to regulations 13 (5) and (6), 15, 20, and 21 may be brought and prosecuted by the registrar of companies.

Amendments

a £1,000 increased to £1,500 by CA 1990, s 240(7) as inserted by CLEA 2001, s 104(c), and converted to €1,904.61 by Council Regulations (EC) No 1103/97, No 974/98 and No 2866/98 and the Economic and Monetary Union Act 1998, s 6.

Definitions

'officer in default': CA 1963, s 383; 'partnership': EC(A)R 1993, reg 3(1); 'the 1992 Group Accounts Regulations': EC(A)R 1993, reg 3(1); 'the 1986 Act': EC(A)R 1993, reg 3(1).

PART IV

IMPLEMENTATION OF ARTICLE 11 OF COUNCIL DIRECTIVE 89/666/EEC

25. Section 13 of the Companies (Amendment) Act 1986, is hereby amended by the insertion of the following new subsection:

[...][a]

GIVEN under my Official Seal, this 20th day of December, 1993.

RUAIRÍ QUINN, Minister for Enterprise and Employment.

Amendments

a EC(A)R 1993, reg 25 amends C(A)A 1986, s 13 by the insertion of sub-s (e). See the amended Act.

EXPLANATORY NOTE

(This note is not part of the Instrument and does not purport to be a legal interpretation).

The purpose of these Regulations is to give legal effect to Council Directive 90/604/EEC on accounting exemptions for small and medium sized undertakings, Council Directive 90/605/EEC extending the Scope of the 4th (annual accounts) and 7th (group accounts) Company Law Directives and Article 11 of Council Directive 89/666/EEC (branch disclosures).

Part I of the Regulations contains preliminary and general provisions eg Interpretation Provisions.

Part II of the Regulations implements Council Directive 90/604/EEC. It increases the balance sheet and turnover thresholds set out in the Companies (Amendment) Act 1986 for the purpose of availing of exemptions for small and medium-sized companies. It also clarifies that a company can file accounts in ECUs as well as the currency in which they are drawn up.

Part III of the Regulations implements Council Directive 90/605/EEC. It extends the scope of the 1986 Act implementing the 4th Directive and the 1992 Group Accounts Regulations to certain types of unlimited companies and partnerships.

Part IV implements Article 11 of Council Directive 89/666/EEC (the Eleventh Directive) on disclosures by branches. Regulation 25 contains the relevant provision which requires disclosure in accounts of the existence of branches.

European Communities (Single-Member Private Limited Companies) Regulations 1994

SI 275/1994

I, RUAIRÍ QUINN, Minister for Enterprise and Employment, in exercise of the powers conferred on me by section 3 of the European Communities Act, 1972 (No. 27 of 1972), and for the purpose of giving effect to Council Directive No. 89/667/EEC of 21 December 1989 (OJ No L395, 30–12–1989, pp 40-42), hereby make the following Regulations:

1 Citation, Commencement and Construction

(1) These Regulations may be cited as the European Communities (Single-Member Private Limited Companies) Regulations, 1994.

(2) These Regulations shall come into operation on the 1st day of October, 1994.

(3) These Regulations shall be construed as one with the Companies Acts, 1963 to 1990.

Definitions

'commencement': IA, 2005, Sch, Pt 1.

Notes

Single-member companies: EC(SMPLC) Regs 1994 implement the Twelfth EU Directive[1] on company law[2] the purpose of which was to introduce in member states a common legal framework whereby small enterprises could enjoy the benefits of incorporation, including limited liability, notwithstanding the fact that such a company was formed with only one member. The CLRG has recommended the repeal of EC(SMPLC) Regs 1994 and their replacement with a provision that any private company can be formed with one member.[3]

1 For an analysis of the Twelfth EU Directive on Company Law, see MacCann, 'Company Law Reform: One Man Companies' (1990) 8 ILT 166, Courtney and Hutchinson, 'The Single-Member Private Company Regulations: Perpetuating an anomaly?' (1994) 1 CLP 307 and Courtney, *The Law of Private Companies* (2nd edn, Tottel Publishing, 2002) paras 1.119–1.125.

2 Council Directive No 89/667/EEC (OJ No L395, 30 December 1989, pp 40–42).

3 The Company Law Review Group, First Report (2001), para 4.9.2.

UK legislation

See generally CA 1985, s 24 and Companies (Single Member Private Limited Companies) Regulations 1992 (SI 1992/1699).

2 Interpretation

(1) In these Regulations, unless the context otherwise requires—

"accounts" means the balance sheet and profit and loss account of a company referred to in section 148 of the Principal Act, together with any notes to or other documents annexed to the accounts in question giving information which is required by any provision of the Companies Acts, and required or allowed by any such provision to be given in a note to or a document annexed to a company's accounts;

"the Act of 1990" means the Companies Act, 1990 (No. 33 of 1990);

"the Companies Acts" means the Principal Act, and every enactment which is to be construed as one with that Act;

"the Directive" means Council Directive No. 89/667/EEC of 21 December 1989;

"enactment" includes an instrument made under an enactment;

"the Principal Act" means the Companies Act, 1963 (No. 33 of 1963);

"single-member company" shall be construed in accordance with Regulation 3(1);

(2) A word or expression that is used in these Regulations and is also used in the Directive has, unless the contrary intention appears, the meaning in these Regulations that it has in the Directive.

(3) In these Regulations—

(a) a reference to a regulation is a reference to a regulation of these Regulations unless it is indicated that reference to some other Regulation is intended,

(b) a reference to a paragraph or subparagraph is a reference to the paragraph or subparagraph of the provision in which the reference occurs unless it is indicated that reference to some other provision is intended.

Definitions

'Companies Act': EC(SMPLC)R 1994, reg 2(1); 'Directive': EC(SMPLC)R 1994, reg 2(1); 'enactment': IA 2005, Sch, Pt 1; 'Principal Act': EC(SMPLC)R 1994, reg 2(1).

---

3 Single-member private companies, limited by shares or by guarantee

(1) Notwithstanding any enactment or rule of law to the contrary, a private company limited by shares or by guarantee may be formed by one person, and may have one member (in these Regulations referred to as a single-member company), to the extent permitted by the Companies Acts and these Regulations.

(2) Any enactment or rule of law which applies in relation to a private company limited by shares or guarantee incorporated under the Companies Acts shall, in the absence of any express provision to the contrary, apply with any necessary modifications in relation to a single-member company as it applies in relation to such a company which is formed by two or more persons or which has two or more persons as members.

(3) Without prejudice to the generality of paragraphs (1) and (2), the Companies Acts shall have effect with the modifications specified in these Regulations.

Definitions

'Companies Acts': EC(SMPLC)R 1994, reg 2 (1); 'company limited by guarantee': CA 1963, s 5(2)(b); 'company limited by shares': CA 1963, s 5(2)(a); 'enactment': EC(SMPLC)R 1994, reg 2(1); 'private company': CA 1963, ss 2(1) and 33(1); 'member': CA 1963, s 31; 'person': IA 2005, s 18(c); 'single-member company': EC(SMPLC)R 1994, reg 2(1).

Notes

Private limited companies: Rather curiously, EC(SMPLC)R 1994, reg 3(1) would appear to suggest that it is possible to have a private company which is limited either by shares or by guarantee. However, according to CA 1963, s 33 a 'private company' must have, inter alia, a share capital. If a company is limited purely by guarantee then, by definition, it must be a public company. It is unclear from the text of the legislation as to whether EC(SMPLC)R 1994 are intended to apply to such companies or whether they are only intended to apply to companies limited by shares and to companies limited by guarantee and having a share capital.[1] If EC(SMPLC)R 1994 were to apply to companies limited purely by guarantee, then it would no longer be necessary for such a company (being a public company) to have at least seven subscribers to its memorandum of association.[2] A company limited by guarantee and having a share capital is something of a hybrid and although permitted by statute, since 13 October 1983 it has only been possible to form such companies as private companies.[3]

Even though it is now possible to form single-member companies, such companies must still have at least two directors.[4] It has been said that this requirement is somewhat anomalous and ought to be dispensed with.[5] In this regard, it is now possible in the UK to have single-member private companies with one director only.[6]

1 Although companies limited by guarantee and having a share capital are not expressly mentioned in CA 1963, s 5, they are nonetheless provided for by CA 1963, s 26(2).

2 See CA 1963, s 5 and notes thereto. See also views of Courtney, *The Law of Private Companies* (2nd edn, Tottel Publishing, 2002) para 2.017.

3 See C(A)A 1983, s 7.

4 CA 1963, s 174.

5 See the recommendations of The Company Law Review Group, First Report (2001), para 11.8.11.

6 CA 1985, s 282(3).

UK legislation

Companies (Single Member Private Limited Companies) Regulations 1992 (SI 1992/1699), reg 2.

4 Formation of a single-member company

Notwithstanding section 5(1) of the Principal Act, one person may, for any lawful purpose, by subscribing his or her name to a memorandum of association and otherwise complying with the requirements of the Companies Acts and these Regulations relating to registration, form an incorporated company being a private company limited by shares or by guarantee.

Definitions

'company': CA 1963, s 2(1); 'Companies Acts': EC(SMPLC)R 1994, reg 2(1); 'company limited by guarantee': CA 1963, s 5(2)(b); 'company limited by shares': CA 1963, s 5(2)(a); 'member': CA 1963, s 31; 'memorandum': CA 1963, s 2(1); 'person': IA 2005, s 18(c); 'Principal Act': EC(SMPLC)R 1994, reg 2(1); 'private company': CA 1963, ss 2(1) and 33(1); 'single-member company': EC(SMPLC)R 1994, reg 2(1).

Cross reference

See CA 1963, s 5 and notes thereto.

Notes

Single subscriber required: Notwithstanding the general requirement contained in CA 1963, s 5 that at least two persons sign the memorandum of association of a private company, EC(SMPLC) Regs 1994, reg 4 authorises the formation of a single-member private company (limited by shares or by guarantee) by having one person subscribe his/her name to the memorandum of association.

UK legislation

See CA 1985, s 1(3A) (as inserted by Companies (Single Member Private Limited Companies) Regulations 1992 (SI 1992/1699), reg 2(1)(b), Sch para 1).

---

5 Company becoming a single-member company

(1) A private company limited by shares or by guarantee registered with two or more subscribers to its memorandum of association, in accordance with the Companies Acts, shall become a single-member company, on such date as the number of members is reduced to one and all the shares in the company are registered in the name of a sole person.

(2) Where a company becomes a single-member company pursuant to paragraph (1) it shall cause that fact and the date on which it became a single-member company and the identity of the sole member to be notified in writing in the prescribed form to the registrar of companies within 28 days after the date on which the number of members is reduced to one.

(3) If a company fails to comply with the requirements of paragraph (2), the company and every officer of the company who is in default shall be guilty of an offence.

Definitions

'company': CA 1963, s 2(1); 'Companies Acts': EC(SMPLC)R 1994, reg 2(1); 'company limited by guarantee': CA 1963, s 5(2)(b); 'company limited by shares': CA 1963, s 5(2)(a); 'member': CA 1963, s 31; 'memorandum': CA 1963, s 2(1); 'officer': CA 1963, s 2(1); 'officer in default': CA 1963, s 383; 'person': IA 2005, s 18(c); 'prescribed': CA 1963, s 2(1); 'Principal Act': EC(SMPLC)R 1994, reg 2(1); 'private company': CA 1963, ss 2(1) and 33(1); 'the registrar of companies': CA 1963, s 2(1); 'single-member company': EC(SMPLC)R 1994, reg 2(1).

Notes

Conversion to a single-member company: A private company limited by shares or by guarantee becomes a single member company on the date on which its members are reduced to one and the single-member is registered in the register of members as such.[1] Within 28 days of that event, the company is obliged to notify the Registrar of Companies in the prescribed form.[2] Failure to notify the Registrar, as required, is an offence punishable on summary conviction, by a fine of up to €1,904.61.[3]

1 EC(SMPLC)R 1994, reg 5(1).

2 EC(SMPLC)R 1994, reg 5(2). European Communities (Single-Member Private Limited Companies)(Forms) Regulations 1994, Sch, Pt 1: Form M1. See also Companies Registration Office, Information Leaflet No 12, Single-Member Company, December 2005.

3 EC(SMPLC)R 1994, regs 5(3) and 14.

UK legislation

See generally CA 1985, s 352A(1): There is no analogous requirement to notify the Registrar of Companies; rather a statement as to the occurrence of the event must be entered in the company's register of members.

6 Change in status of a single-member company

(1) A company which is incorporated as, or becomes, a single-member company, in accordance with the Companies Acts and these Regulations, shall cease to be a single-member company on such date as the number of members increases to more than one but shall continue to be a private company limited by shares or guarantee, as the case may be, while the number of members does not exceed 50.

(2) Where a single-member company ceases to be such pursuant to paragraph (1), it shall cause that fact and the date on which it ceased to be a single-member company to be notified in writing in the prescribed form to the registrar of companies within 28 days after the date when the number of members increased to more than one.

(3) If a company fails to comply with the requirements of paragraph (2), the company and every officer of the company who is in default shall be guilty of an offence.

Definitions

'company': CA 1963, s 2(1); 'Companies Acts': EC(SMPLC)R 1994, reg 2(1); 'company limited by guarantee': CA 1963, s 5(2)(b); 'company limited by shares': CA 1963, s 5(2)(a); 'member': CA 1963, s 31; 'officer': CA 1963, s 2(1); 'officer in default': CA 1963, s 383; 'prescribed': CA 1963, s 2(1); 'private company': CA 1963, s 2(1); 'single-member company': EC(SMPLC)R 1994, s 2(1); 'the registrar of companies': CA 1963, s 2(1).

Cross reference

See CA 1963, s 33 (as amended by IFCMPA 2006) and notes thereto: the maximum number of members of a private company is now 99 rather than 50.

Notes

Conversion from a single-member company: A private company limited by shares or by guarantee ceases to be a single-member company on the date on which its members exceed one.[1] Within 28 days of that event, the company is obliged to notify the Registrar of Companies in the prescribed form.[2] Failure to notify the Registrar, as required, is an offence punishable on summary conviction, by a fine of up to €1,904.61.[3]

1 EC(SMPLC)R 1994, reg 6(1).

2 EC(SMPLC)R 1994, reg 6(2). European Communities (Single-Member Private Limited Companies)(Forms) Regulations 1994, Sch, Pt 2: Form M2. See also Companies Registration Office, Information Leaflet No 12, Single-Member Company, December 2005.

3 EC(SMPLC)R 1994, regs 6(3) and 14.

UK legislation

See generally CA 1985, s 352A(2). There is no analogous requirement to notify the Registrar of Companies; rather a statement as to the occurrence of the event must be entered in the company's register of members.

7 Non-application of section 36 of Principal Act

(1) Section 36 of the Principal Act shall not apply to a private company limited by shares or by guarantee.

(2) Without prejudice to paragraph (1), a person who, before the coming into force of these Regulations, is liable by virtue of section 36 of the Principal Act (members severally liable for debts where business carried on with fewer than, in the case of private company, two members) for the payment of the debts of a private company limited by shares or by guarantee, shall not be so liable for the payment of the company's debts contracted on or after the date on which these Regulations come into force.

Definitions

'company': CA 1963, s 2(1); 'company limited by guarantee': CA 1963, s 5(2)(b); 'company limited by shares': CA 1963, s 5(2)(a); 'member': CA 1963, s 31; 'person': IA 2005, s 18(c); 'Principal Act': EC (SMPLC) 1994, reg 2(1); 'private company': CA 1963 ss 2(1) and 33.

Cross reference

See CA 1963, s 36 and notes thereto.

Notes

Private limited companies: The provisions of CA 1963, s 36 no longer apply to private companies limited by shares or limited by guarantee and having a share capital, since such companies are now permitted by EC(SMPLC)R 1994 to become single-member companies.[1] In the circumstances, therefore, CA 1963, s 36 only remains of relevance for the following:

(a) public companies; and

(b) unlimited private companies.

The main significance of CA 1963, s 36 for the members of an unlimited private company is that they may be sued directly by the creditor concerned without the company first having to be wound up, whereas in the normal course of events their liability would have been indirect, in that they would only have been liable to contribute to the debts of the company, and even then their liability would only have arisen upon the liquidation of the company.[2] The CLRG has recommended the repeal of CA 1963, s 36.[3] EC (SMPLC) 1994, reg 6(1) does not have retrospective effect for personal liability incurred prior to 1 October 1994.[4]

1 EC(SMPLC)R 1994, regs 3, 5 and 7 and notes thereto. See also CA 1963, s 5 and notes thereto.

2 CA 1963, s 207.

3 The Company Law Review Group, First Report (2001), para 4.9.3.

4 EC (SMPLC) 1994, reg 6(2).

UK legislation

See CA 1985, s 24 (as amended by Companies (Single Member Private Limited Companies) Regulation 1992 (SI 1992/1699), reg 2, Sch para 2).

8 Annual General Meeting

(1) The sole member of a single-member company may decide, in the manner provided for in Regulation 9, to dispense with the holding of annual general meetings and, if he or she does so, section 131 of the Principal Act shall not apply to the company.

(2) A decision pursuant to paragraph (1) shall have effect for the year in which it is made and subsequent years, but shall not affect any liability already incurred by reason of default in holding an annual general meeting.

(3) In any year in which an annual general meeting would, but for a decision pursuant to paragraph (1) be required to be held, and in which no such meeting has been held, the sole member or the auditor of a single-member company may, by notice to the company not later than three months before the end of the year, require the holding of an annual general meeting in that year.

(4) If such a notice is given, the provisions of section 131 of the Principal Act, other than subsection (2) thereof, shall apply with respect to the calling of the meeting and the consequence of default.

(5) Where a decision to dispense with the holding of annual general meetings for a single-member company pursuant to paragraph (1) is in force, the requirements in—

- (a) section 148 of the Principal Act that the directors lay accounts before the annual general meeting,
- (b) section 158 of the Principal Act that a directors' report shall be attached to the balance sheet,
- (c) section 193 of the Act of 1990 that the auditors shall make a report on the accounts of the company at the annual general meeting, and
- (d) Regulation 5 of the European Communities (Companies: Group Accounts) Regulations, 1992 (S.I. No. 201 of 1992) that a parent undertaking lay group accounts before the annual general meeting,

shall be deemed to be satisfied where the said accounts and reports are sent to the sole member of the single-member company in accordance with section 159 of the Principal Act, with the modification that they shall be sent not less than 21 days before the appropriate date.

(6) A reference in any other provision of the Companies Acts to the accounts of a company laid before the annual general meeting of a company or the report of the auditors on or the report of the directors accompanying such accounts shall, in the case of a single-member company where a decision to dispense with the holding of annual general meetings pursuant to paragraph (1) is in force, be construed as a reference to the accounts and reports sent to the sole member in accordance with paragraph (5).

(7) If a decision to dispense with the holding of annual general meetings under paragraph (1) ceases to have effect, sections 148 and 158 of the Principal Act, section 193 of the Act of 1990, and Regulation 5 of the European Communities (Companies: Group Accounts) Regulations, 1992 shall, with any necessary modifications, apply in relation to the accounts and reports in respect of the financial year in which the decision ceases to have effect and subsequent financial years.

(8) For the purposes of the Principal Act, the requirements—

- (a) in section 127 that the annual return must be completed within 60 days after the annual general meeting,
- (b) in section 148 that the accounts must be made up to a date not earlier than the date of the annual general meeting by more than 9 months, and

(c) in paragraph 5 of Part I of the Fifth Schedule that the list containing specified particulars of persons who are members on the 14th day after the company's annual general meeting

shall in the case of a single-member company where a decision to dispense with the holding of annual general meetings pursuant to paragraph (1) is in force, be read as relating to a similar period relative to the appropriate date.

(9) For the purposes of this Regulation, each year the "appropriate date" shall be—

(a) in the case of a single-member company formed as such and where a decision to dispense with the holding of annual general meetings is taken before the first such meeting is due, the last day of the month in which the anniversary of its formation falls;

(b) in the case of a private company limited by share or by guarantee formed after the commencement of these Regulations which becomes a single-member company pursuant to Regulation 5 before holding its first annual general meeting and where a decision to dispense with the holding of annual general meetings is taken before the first such meeting is due, the last day of the month in which the anniversary of its formation falls; and

(c) in the case of all other single-member companies, the last day of the month in which the anniversary of the last annual general meeting of the company was held falls.

Definitions

'accounts': CA 1963, s 2(1); 'annual return': CA 1963, s 2(1); 'appropriate date': EC (SMPLC) 1994, reg 9(a); 'company' CA 1963, s 2(1); 'a company limited by guarantee': CA 1963, s 5(2)(b); 'a company limited by shares': CA 1963, s 5(2)(a); 'Companies Acts': EC(SMPLC)R 1994, reg 2(1); 'director': CA 1963, s 2(1); 'financial year'; CA 1963, s 2(1); 'member': CA 1963, s 31; 'Principal Act': EC(SMPLC) R 1994, reg 2(1); 'private company': CA 1963, ss 2(1) and 33; 'single-member company': EC(SMPLC)R 1994, reg 2(1).

Cross reference

See generally CA 1963, s 131.

Notes

Dispensing with AGM for single-member companies: The sole member of a single-member private limited company may, at any time, dispense with the holding of AGMs.[1] He is meant to do so by drawing up a decision to that effect in writing and by forwarding a copy of the decision to the company,[2] whereupon the company is meant to record that decision, and any other decisions made by him, in a separate book or by some other suitable means maintained for that purpose.[3] Notwithstanding these procedural requirements, there is considerable authority to support the proposition that an unwritten decision of the sole member to dispense with the holding of AGMs should be just as valid as a written decision to that effect.[4] Indeed, it is notable that under the EC(SMPLC)R 1994 it is expressly stated that neither a failure to give written notice of the decision to the company, nor a failure by the company to record the decision, will affect the validity of the decision itself.[5]

A decision to dispense with the holding of AGMs shall have effect for the year in which it is made and subsequent years, but will not affect any liability already incurred for failing to comply with CA 1963, s 131 in the past.[6] Moreover, even if the sole member decides to dispense with

AGMs, either he or the company's auditor can, in any given year, still require such a meeting be held, by serving notice to that effect on the company itself at least three months before the end of the year in question.[7]

If the AGM is dispensed with, annual accounts must still be prepared. However, rather than presenting a balance sheet, profit and loss account, auditor's report and directors' report and, if appropriate, group accounts, to the company in an AGM, copies of these documents will simply be sent directly to the sole member within 21 days.[8]

The time limits for sending copies of the accounts to the member vary depending on the particular circumstances of the case. If the company was formed as or converted into a single-member company, and the decision to dispense with AGMs was made before the due date for the first such meeting, the accounts will have to be sent to the member within 21 days of the end of the month in which the anniversary of incorporation falls.[9] In all other cases, the accounts must be sent to the member within 21 days of the end of the month in which the anniversary of the last AGM falls.[10] The accounts themselves must be made up to a date not more than 9 months prior to the date upon which they have to be furnished to the member.[11]

Finally, in relation to the filing of annual returns, this obligation continues to apply regardless of the fact that the company now has single-member status and has dispensed with the holding of AGMs.[12]

1 EC(SMPLC)R 1994, reg 8(1).
2 EC(SMPLC)R 1994, reg 9(3) and (4).
3 EC(SMPLC)R 1994, reg 9(4).
4 *Re Express Engineering Works Ltd* [1920] 1 Ch 466; *Re Oxted Motor Co* [1921] 3 KB 32; *Re Duomatic Ltd* [1969] 2 Ch 365; *Cane v Jones* [1981] 1 All ER 533; *Re SM Barker Ltd* [1950] IR 123; *Peter Buchanan Ltd v McVey* [1954] IR 89; *Re PMPA Garage (Longmile) Ltd (No 1)* [1992] 1 ILRM 337; *Re Shannonside Holdings Ltd* (20 May 1993, unreported) HC (Costello J).
5 EC(SMPLC)R 1994, reg 9(8).
6 EC(SMPLC)R 1994, reg 8(2).
7 EC(SMPLC)R 1994, reg 8(3).
8 EC(SMPLC)R 1994, reg 8(5) and (6).
9 EC(SMPLC)R 1994, reg 8(9)(a) and (b).
10 EC(SMPLC)R 1994, reg 8(9)(c).
11 CA 1963, s 148, as amended by EC(SMPLC)R 1994, reg 8(8)(b).
12 CA 1963, s 127 as amended by EC(SMPLC)R 1994, reg 8(8)(a) and reg 8(9). Reference to CA 1963, Sch 5 in EC(SMPLC)R 1994, reg 8(8)(c) is obsolete as CA 1963, Sch 5 was repealed by CLEA 2001, s 63(2).

UK legislation

See generally CA 1989, s 366A which allows private companies (not just single-member private limited companies) to dispense with holding an AGM.

---

9 General Meetings — powers exercisable by sole member

(1) Subject to paragraph (2), all the powers exercisable by a company in general meeting under the Companies Acts or otherwise shall be exercisable, in the case of a single-member company, by the sole member without the need to hold a general meeting for that purpose.

(2) Paragraph (1) shall not empower the sole member of a single-member company to exercise the powers in sections 160(2)(b), 160(5), and 160(6) of the Principal Act to remove an auditor from office without holding the requisite meeting provided for in the said provisions.

(3) Subject to paragraph (2), any provision of the Companies Acts which—

(a) enables or requires any matter to be done or to be decided by a company in general meeting, or

(b) requires any matter to be decided by a resolution of the company,

shall be deemed to be satisfied, in the case of a single-member company, by a decision of the member which is drawn up in writing and notified to the company in accordance with this Regulation.

(4) Where the sole member of a single-member company takes any decision which may be taken by the company in general meeting and which has effect, pursuant to paragraphs (1) and (3), as if agreed by the company in general meeting, he shall, unless the decision is taken by way of written resolution which he has already forwarded to the company, provide the company with a written record of that decision.

(5) Where the sole member notifies a decision taken by way of written resolution, or a written record of a decision taken pursuant to paragraph (4), to a single-member company of which he is the sole member, the notification shall be recorded and retained by the company in a book or by some other suitable means maintained for the purpose.

(6) The exercise by the sole member of a single-member company of any power, right or obligation under this Regulation, to which section 143 of the Principal Act, as amended, applies, shall, within 15 days, be notified by the company in writing to the registrar of companies and be recorded by him.

(7) If the sole member fails to comply with paragraph (4), or if a company fails to comply with paragraphs (5) or (6) the sole member, the company and every officer of the company who is in default shall be guilty of an offence.

(8) Failure by the sole member to comply with paragraph (4) shall not affect the validity of any decision referred to in that paragraph.

Definitions

'articles': CA 1963, s 2(1); 'company' CA 1963, s 2(1); 'single-member company': EC(SMPLC)R 1994, reg 2(1); 'member': CA 1963, s 31; 'person': IA 2005, s 18(c); 'the registrar of companies': CA 1963, s 2(1).

Cross reference

See generally CA 1963, s 134 and notes thereto.

Notes

Informal acts in single-member companies: In the case of a single-member company, all the powers capable of being exercised by a company in general meeting, other than those relating to the removal of an auditor from office, are exercisable by the sole member without the need to hold a general meeting for that purpose.[1] The member is required to draw up his decision in writing and forward a copy to the company which is in turn to record that decision in a book or by some other suitable means maintained for that purpose.[2] Although a failure to comply with these procedures may constitute an offence,[3] the inherent validity of the decision itself would not appear to be affected.[4]

1 EC(SMPLC)R 1994, reg 9(1) and (2).

2 EC(SMPLC)R 1994, reg 9(3)–(5).

3 EC(SMPLC)R 1994, reg 9(7).

4 EC(SMPLC)R 1994, reg 9(8). See also the notes below on the validity at common law of informal acts of the members which are not necessarily recorded in writing.

Informal acts of the members: Notwithstanding the notice requirements of the Companies Acts, an informal decision made by all of the members who have voting rights, will be as valid and effective as if it had been passed as a formal resolution at a properly convened general meeting of the company.[1] Although CA 1963, s 141(8) provides that a resolution in writing signed by all the members is as valid as if passed at a properly convened general meeting, it would appear from *Re PMPA Garage (Longmile) Ltd* and *Re Shannonside Holdings Ltd* that an oral resolution or decision of all the members will still suffice. On the same basis, although EC(SMPLC)R 1994, reg 9(3) requires the decision of a single-member to be recorded in writing, it seems that an oral decision or resolution which is not so recorded will still be valid. In relation to the Duomatic Principle generally, see CA 1963, s 141 and notes thereto.

1 *Re Oxted Motor Co* [1921] 3 KB 32; *Re Duomatic Ltd* [1969] 2 Ch 365; *Cane v Jones* [1981] 1 All ER 533; *Re SM Barker Ltd* [1950] IR 123; *Peter Buchanan Ltd v McVey* [1954] IR 89; *Re PMPA Garage (Longmile) Ltd (No 1)* [1992] 1 ILRM 337; *Re Shannonside Holdings Ltd* (20 May 1993, unreported) HC (Costello J); *Euro Brokers Holdings Ltd v Monecor (London) Ltd* [2003] 1 BCLC 506.

Documents required to be registered: Under CA 1963, s 143(4) all special resolutions must be registered[1] as well as any informal resolutions which, if passed at formal meetings, would have been passed as special resolutions.[2] Resolutions affecting class rights must also be registered.[3] Although ordinary resolutions do not generally require registration, there are some exceptions, namely resolutions increasing the share capital[4] or authorising market purchases of the company's own shares[5] as well as certain resolutions to wind up a company voluntarily[6] and resolutions which by giving, varying, revoking or renewing the authority of a board of directors to allot shares, thereby amend the Articles.[7] Similarly, most board resolutions will not have to be registered, although a notable exception is in relation to any resolution of the directors of a plc to cancel shares which have been forfeited or surrendered or which have been acquired by the company otherwise than for valuable consideration.[8] Resolutions of the type described in s 143(4) which are passed informally by the sole member of a single-member company must also be registered.[9]

1 CA 1963, s 413(4)(a). See CA 1963, s 141(1) for the definition of a special resolution.

2 CA 1963, s 143(4)(b). See CA 1963, s 141(8) and the notes thereto in relation to the effectiveness of informal resolutions.

3 CA 1963, s 143(4)(c),(f),(g) and (i). In relation to the variation of class rights generally, see CA 1963, s 78 and C(A)A 1983, s 38.

4 CA 1963, s 143(4)(d). The authority for such resolutions is to be found in CA 1963, s 68.

5 CA 1990, s 215(2).

6 CA 1963, s 143(4)(e).

7 C(A)A 1983, s 20(6).

8 CA 1963, s 143(4)(j). See also C(A)A 1983, ss 41 and 43.

9 EC(SMPLC)R 1994, reg 9(6).

UK legislation

Companies Act 1985, s 370A (inserted by Companies (Single Member Private Limited Companies) Regulation 1992 (SI 1992/1699), reg 2, Sch para 5).

---

10 Quorum

Notwithstanding any provision to the contrary in the articles of a single-member company, one member present in person or by proxy shall be a quorum.

Definitions

'articles': CA 1963, s 2(1); 'company' CA 1963, s 2(1); 'single-member company': EC(SMPLC)R 1994, reg 2(1); 'member': CA 1963, s 31; 'person': IA 2005, s 18(c).

Cross reference

See generally CA 1963, s 134 and notes thereto.

Notes

Quorum for general meetings: In the case of single-member companies, the provisions of CA 1963, s 134(c) are superseded by EC(SMPLC)R 1994 which state that a quorum is deemed to be the sole member present either in person or by proxy.[1]

1 EC(SMPLC)R 1994, reg 10.

UK legislation

Companies Act 1985, s 370A (inserted by Companies (Single Member Private Limited Companies) Regulation 1992 (SI 1992/1699), reg 2, Sch para 5).

11 Non-application of other provisions of Principal Act

Sections 213(d) and 215(a)(i) of the Principal Act shall not apply to a private company limited by shares or by guarantee.

Definitions

'company' CA 1963, s 2(1); 'company limited by guarantee': CA 1963, s 5(2)(b); 'company limited by shares': CA 1963, s 5(2)(a); 'Principal Act': EC(SMPLC)R 1994, reg 2(1); 'private company': CA 1963, ss 2(1) and 33; 'share': CA 1963, s 2(1).

Notes

Grounds for petition to wind up a company: Where the number of members is reduced, in the case of a private unlimited company, below two and in the case of any public company, below seven, there exists grounds for a petition to the court to wind up the company. However, where that company is a private company limited by shares or by guarantee these grounds for such a petition no longer apply.[1]

1 EC(SMPLC)R 1994, reg 11.

UK legislation

Companies (Single Member Private Limited Companies) Regulations 1992 (SI 1992/1699), reg 2, Sch para 8.

12 Connected person

[...][a]

Amendments

a Deleted by European Communities (Single Member Private Limited Companies) Regulations 1994 (Amendment) Regulations 2001 (SI 437/2001), reg 3 with effect from 1 October 2001.

Definitions

'connected person': CA 1990, ss 3(1) and 26.

Notes

Connected person: Prior to its deletion, EC(SMPLC)R 1994, reg 12 deemed the sole member of a single-member company to be a 'connected person' for the purposes of CA 1990, s 26. However, CA 1990, s 26(6) (as inserted by CLEA 2001, s 76(c)) now provides that it is merely presumed that such a member is a connected person. The onus is placed on the sole member to rebut the presumption that he/she is a person connected to the single-member company.

---

13 Contracts with sole members

(1) Subject to paragraph (2), where a single-member company enters into a contract with the sole member of the company and the sole member also represents the company in the transaction, whether as a director or otherwise, the company shall, unless the contract is in writing, ensure that the terms of the contract are forthwith set out in a written memorandum or are recorded in the minutes of the first meeting of the directors of the company following the making of the contract.

(2) Paragraph (1) shall not apply to contracts entered into in the ordinary course of the company's business.

(3) If a company fails to comply with paragraph (1), the company and every officer of the company who is in default shall be guilty of an offence.

(4) Subject to paragraph (5), nothing in this Regulation shall be taken to prejudice the operation of any other enactment or rule of law applying to contracts between a company and a director of that company.

(5) Failure to comply with paragraph (1) with respect to a contract shall not affect the validity of that contract.

Definitions

'company' CA 1963, s 2(1); 'director': CA 1963, s 2(1); 'enactment': EC(SMPLC)R 1994, reg 2(1); 'member': CA 1963, s 31; 'officer': CA 1963, s 2(1); 'officer in default': CA 1963, s 383.

Notes

Contracts with sole members: Contracts which may be validly made by parol by an individual, may also be validly made by parol on behalf of a company by its duly authorised agent.[1] However, if a single-member private limited company enters into an oral contract with its sole member otherwise than in the ordinary course of business and the sole member also represents the company in the transaction, the terms of the contract must forthwith be set out in a written memorandum or alternatively must be recorded in the minutes of the next board meeting.[2] Failure to do so will not affect the validity of the contract[3] but may expose the company and every officer in default to criminal liability.[4]

1 CA 1963, s 38(c).

2 EC(SMPLC)R 1994, reg 13(1).

3 EC(SMPLC)R 1994, reg 13(5).

4 EC(SMPLC)R 1994, reg 13(3).

UK legislation

See generally CA 1985, s 322B (as inserted by Companies (Single Member Private Limited Companies) Regulations 1992 (SI 1992/1699), reg 2, Sch para 3(1)) in relation to 'Contracts with sole members who are directors'.

14 Offences

A person guilty of an offence under any provision of these Regulations shall be liable, on summary conviction, to a fine not exceeding [€1,904.61].[a]

Amendments

a £1,000 increased to £1500 by CA 1990, s 240(7), as inserted by CLEA 2001, s 104(c), and converted to €1904,61 by Council Regulations (EC) No 1103/97, No 974/98 and No 2866/98 and the Economic and Monetary Union Act 1998, s 6.

Definitions

'person': IA 2005, s 18(c).

UK legislation

See CA 1985, s 729 and Sch 24.

Explanatory Note

These Regulations implement Council Directive No. 89/667/EEC on single-member private limited liability companies. The Directive requires Member States to provide for the formation of a company having one member and to permit a company to be a single member company, subject to certain safeguards. In relation to Ireland, it applies to private companies limited by shares or guarantee.

The Regulations provide that a sole person, whether natural or legal, will now be able to form or become a single-member limited liability company. The Regulations further provide that, subject to certain modifications, all the provisions of the Companies Acts which apply to private companies limited by shares or by guarantee will apply to single-member companies. For instance, the sole member, if he so decides, can dispense with the holding of General Meetings, including Annual General Meetings (AGM). However, certain notifications will have to be made. Also the accounts and reports that would normally be laid before the AGM of a company will still need to be prepared and forwarded to the member.

European Communities (Insurance Undertakings: Accounts) Regulations 1996

SI 23/1996

ARRANGEMENT OF REGULATIONS

Chapter 2 Accounting/Valuation

Chapter 3 Information required by way of Notes to the Group Accounts

I, RICHARD BRUTON, Minister for Enterprise and Employment, in exercise of the powers conferred on me by section 3 of the European Communities Act, 1972 (No. 27 of 1972), and for the purpose of giving effect to Council Directive No. 91/674/EEC of 23 December, 1991, hereby make the following Regulations:

1 Citation and Construction

(1) These Regulations may be cited as the European Communities (Insurance Undertakings: Accounts) Regulations, 1996.

(2) These Regulations shall be construed as one with the Companies Acts, 1963 to 1990.

Notes

Accounts of insurance companies: The provisions of C(A)A 1986 and EC(CGA)R 1992 concerning the form and content of annual accounts and group accounts were expressed not to apply to insurance companies.[1] Instead, the accounts of such companies and of reinsurance companies fall to be dealt with under the provisions of these regs. The purpose of the regs is to give legal effect to the provisions of Council Directive 91/674/EEC.

1 C(A)A 1986, s 2(3) and EC(CGA)R 1992, reg 6(2)(g).

---

2 Interpretation

(1) In these Regulations, unless the context otherwise requires—

"accounts" means the balance sheet, profit and loss account and any notes on the accounts or statements forming part of the accounts, whether or not required by law;

"the Act of 1986" means the Companies (Amendment) Act, 1986 (No. 25 of 1986);

"the Act of 1990" means the Companies Act, 1990 (No. 33 of 1990);

"annual return" means the annual return made to the registrar of undertakings under the Principal Act;

"associated undertaking" has the meaning assigned by paragraph 21 of Chapter 2 of Part IV of the Schedule;

["Bank" means the Central Bank and Financial Services Authority of Ireland];[a]

"company" means an undertaking as defined in Regulation 3;

"the Directive" means Council Directive 91/674/EEC of 23 December, 1991;

"group accounts" means the accounts prepared in accordance with Regulations 10 to 18;

"holding company", in relation to one or more undertakings that are subsidiaries of another undertaking, means that other undertaking;

"individual accounts" means the accounts prepared in accordance with Regulations 5 to 9;

['investment property' means land or buildings (or both) held to earn rentals or for capital appreciation (or both);][b]

[...][c];

"parent undertaking" means an undertaking that has one or more subsidiary undertakings;

"participating interest" shall be construed in accordance with paragraph 23 of Part IV of the Schedule;

"the Principal Act" means the Companies Act, 1963;

"subsidiary" shall be construed in accordance with Regulation 11;

"undertaking" means an undertaking to which these Regulations apply by virtue of Regulation 3.

[(1A) References in these Regulations to annual accounts giving a 'true and fair view' are references—

(a) in the case of Companies Act individual accounts, to the requirement under Regulation 5 that those accounts give a true and fair view,

(b) in the case of Companies Act group accounts, to the requirement under Regulation 10 that those accounts give a true and fair view, and

(c) in the case of IFRS accounts, to the equivalent requirement under international financial reporting standards.][d]

(2) In these Regulations, unless the context otherwise requires, a reference to a balance sheet or profit and loss account shall include a reference to any notes or documents annexed to the accounts in question giving information which is required by any provision of the Companies Acts, 1963 to 1990, [these Regulations or international financial reporting standards][e] and required or allowed by any such provision to be given in a note or document annexed to an undertaking's accounts.

(3) In these Regulations—

(a) a reference to directors shall be construed, in the case of an undertaking which does not have a board of directors, as a reference to the corresponding persons appropriate to such undertaking;

(b) a reference to voting rights in an undertaking means the rights conferred on shareholders in respect of their shares or, in case of an undertaking not having a share capital, on members, to vote at general meetings of the undertaking on all, or substantially all, matters;

(c) in relation to an undertaking which does not have general meetings at which matters are decided by the exercise of voting rights, the references to holding a majority of the voting rights in an undertaking shall be construed as references to having the right under the constitution of the undertaking to direct the overall policy of the undertaking to alter the terms of its constitution.

(4) A word or expression that is used in these Regulations and is also used in the Council Directive has, unless the context otherwise requires, the same meaning in these Regulations as it has in the Council Directive.

(5) In these Regulations, unless the context otherwise requires—

(a) a reference to a Regulation or a Schedule is to a Regulation of or a Schedule to these Regulations unless it is indicated that a reference to some other enactment is intended.

(b) a reference to a paragraph or a subparagraph is to a paragraph or subparagraph of the provision in which the reference occurs, unless it is indicated that reference to some other provision is intended.

Amendments

a Definition inserted by CBFSAIA 2003, s 35 and Sch 2, Item 1(a).

b Inserted by reg 11 and Sch 3, Item No 1(a) of EC(IFRSMA)R 2005.

c Definition of "Minister" deleted by CBFSAIA 2003, s 35 and Sch 2, Item 1(b).

d Inserted by reg 11 and Sch 3, Item No 1(a) of EC(IFRSMA)R 2005.

e Words substituted by reg 11 and Sch 3, Item No 1(a) of EC(IFRSMA)R 2005.

Definitions

'undertaking': EC(IUA)R 1996, reg 2(1) & EC(CGA)R 1992, reg 3(1).

Notes

Undertaking: The obligation to prepare accounts under these Regulations applies only to 'undertakings' to which the European Communities (Non-Life Insurance) Regs 1976 or the European Communities (Life Assurance) Regs 1984 apply or which carry on reinsurance business[1]. In this regard, the definition of 'undertaking' includes any body, whether incorporated or not and whether Irish or foreign, which carries on such a business for gain.[2]

Board of directors: Because the undertaking dealt with in the accounts might not be an incorporated company, it has been necessary to widen somewhat the definition of 'board of directors' for the purpose of these regs to include any equivalent body of persons having responsibility for the management of the undertaking. In the case of a partnership, it would include the partners themselves, whereas in other unincorporated companies, it might be a committee of management or some similarly styled body.

Voting rights: Since an undertaking might not be a company having a share capital, the term 'voting rights' is deemed to include not only a right to vote in respect of shares, but also any right to vote at general meetings 'on all or substantially all matters'[3] as well as a right under the constitution of an undertaking which does not have general meetings at which matters are decided on a vote, to direct overall policy or to alter the terms of its constitution[4].

1 EC(IUA)R 1996, reg 3.

2 EC(CGA)R 1992, reg 3(1).

3 EC(IUA)R 1996, reg 2(3)(b))

4 EC(IUA)R 1996, reg 2(3)(c).

3 Application

These Regulations shall, except where otherwise provided for, only apply—

(a) to undertakings to which the European Communities (Non-Life Insurance) Regulations, 1976 (S.I. No. 115 of 1976), the European Communities (Non-Life Insurance) Framework Regulations, 1994 (S.I. No. 359 of 1994) or the European Communities (Life Assurance) Regulations, 1984 (S.I. No. 57 of 1984), the European Communities (Life Assurance) Framework Regulations, 1994 (S.I. No. 360 of 1994) apply and shall also apply to undertakings carrying on reinsurance business, and

(b) in respect of individual and group accounts of undertakings drawn up in respect of every financial year beginning on or after 1 January, 1995.

Definitions

'group accounts': EC(IUA)R 1996, reg 2(1); 'undertaking': EC(IUA)R 1996, reg 2(1) & EC(CGA)R 1992, reg 3(1).

Notes

Application of regulations: See the notes to EC(IUA)R 1996, reg 1.

4 Modification

(1) For the purposes of enabling the Directive to have full effect, the [Bank][a] may, with the consent or on the application of any undertaking, issue a direction in writing that specified provisions of these Regulations shall apply to that undertaking with such modifications as may be specified in the direction.

(2) A direction under paragraph (1) may be subject to such conditions as the [Bank][a] considers appropriate to impose.

(3) A direction under paragraph (1) may be revoked at any time by the Minister and the Minister may at any time vary the direction on the application or with the consent of the undertaking to which it relates.

(4) A direction under paragraph (1) shall, subject to paragraph (3), apply for such period as shall be stated in the direction.

Amendments

a 'Bank' substituted for 'Minister' by CBFSAIA 2003, s 35 and Sch 2, Pt 16, Item 2.

Definitions

'the Directive': EC(IUA)R 1996, reg 2(1); 'the Minister': EC(IUA)R 1996, reg 2(1); 'undertaking': EC(IUA)R 1996, reg 2(1) & EC(CGA)R 1992, reg 3(1).

5 Drawing up of accounts

[(1) Subject to paragraph (2), every balance sheet and profit and loss account of an undertaking laid before the annual general meeting of the undertaking, pursuant to section 148 of the Principal Act shall be prepared in accordance with—

(a) section 149 of the Principal Act as modified by these Regulations, or

(b) international financial reporting standards (in these Regulations referred to as 'IFRS individual accounts') and section 149A (inserted by the European Communities (International Financial Reporting Standards and Miscellaneous Amendments) Regulations 2005)) of the Principal Act as modified by these Regulations,

and in either case shall comply with section 150C (inserted by the European Communities (International Financial Reporting Standards and Miscellaneous Amendments) Regulations 2005) of the Principal Act.

(1A) Companies Act individual accounts of an undertaking prepared in accordance with section 149 of the Principal Act shall comply with the following requirements and section 149 (other than subsection (5) and, insofar as it relates to the said subsection (5), subsection (7)) of that Act shall not apply to any such balance sheet or profit and loss account:

(a) every such balance sheet and profit and loss account shall comply with the Schedule,

(b) every such balance sheet of an undertaking shall give a true and fair view of the state of affairs of the undertaking as at the end of its financial year and every such profit and loss account of an undertaking shall give a true and fair view of the profit and loss of the undertaking for the financial year,

(c) where a balance sheet or profit and loss account drawn up in accordance with subparagraph (a) would not provide sufficient information to comply with subparagraph (b), any necessary additional information shall be provided in that balance sheet or profit and loss account or in a note to the accounts,

(d) where owing to special circumstances, the preparation of individual accounts of an undertaking in compliance with subparagraph (a) would prevent those accounts from complying with subparagraph (b) (even if additional information were provided under subparagraph (c)) the directors of an undertaking shall depart from the requirements of the Schedule in preparing those accounts insofar as is necessary in order to comply with that subparagraph,

(e) where the directors of a company depart from the requirements of this Regulation, they shall attach a note to the individual accounts of the undertaking giving details of the particular departures made, the reasons therefor and the effect of those departures on the accounts,

and, accordingly, in the Companies Acts 1963 to 2003, in relation to a undertaking—

(i) references to the said section 149 shall be read as references to that section as modified by the provisions of these Regulations, and

(ii) references to the Sixth Schedule of the Principal Act shall be read as references to the corresponding provisions of these Regulations.

(1B) Where the directors of an undertaking prepare IFRS individual accounts in accordance with international financial reporting standards and section 149A of the Principal Act they shall ensure that instead of making the disclosures specified in section 149A (2) the notes to the accounts include the information required by—

(a) paragraph 21 (e) of Part III of the Schedule (details of directors' remuneration),

(b) sections 41 to 45 of the Act of 1990 to be disclosed in individual accounts and paragraph 31 (2) of Part IV of the (transactions with directors),

(c) section 63 of the Act of 1990 unless it is disclosed in the directors' report (interests in shares and debentures),

(d) paragraphs 32 to 36 of Part IV of the Schedule (details of group undertakings),

(e) paragraph 27 of Part III of the Schedule (details of staff numbers and remuneration),

Companies Act accounts except where there has been a 'relevant change of circumstances'. Subsection 5 sets out the situations when such a change may arise.

The IFRS regs apply to accounting periods beginning on or after 1 January 2005.

As a result of EC(IFRSMA)R 2005 (SI 116/2005), CA 1963, ss 148–151 of were repealed and replaced by new ss 148, 149, 149A, 150, 150A, 150B, 150C and 151. A principal consequence of this, the primary obligation to prepare financial statements previously contained in C(A)A 1986, s 3 and EC(G:AR) 1992, reg 5, EC(CI:A) R, 1992, EC(IUA)R, 1996 is now contained in CA 1963, s 148 (individual accounts) and CA 1963, s 150 (group accounts), irrespective of what type of company is involved – eg general companies, credit institutions, or insurance undertakings.

See also notes to CA 1963, ss 148–151.

True and fair view: EC(IUA)R 1996, reg 5 imposes an overriding obligation that the annual accounts should give a true and fair view of the state of affairs of the undertaking concerned.[1] To a large extent, the provisions of EC(IUA)R 1996 are themselves determinative as to what constitutes a properly prepared set of annual accounts. However, to the extent that the legislation is silent on any particular matter, compliance with the recognised practices and standards of the accountancy profession in preparing group accounts will be strong but not conclusive evidence that the accounts give a 'true and fair view' of the group's financial position.[2]

Indeed, even where the legislation specifically deals with an aspect of the accounts, a departure will be permitted if strict adherence would result in the 'true and fair view' not being achieved[3]. Details of the departure must, however, be given in the notes to the accounts together with the reasons therefor.[4] With the introduction of International Financial Reporting Standards through EC(IFRSMA)R 2005, a new term, 'presents fairly' entered into financial reporting language. The United Kingdom's Financial Reporting Council, of which the Accounting Standards Board is a constituent body, published a paper in August 2005 entitled 'The implications of new accounting and auditing standards for the 'true and fair view' and auditors' responsibilities'. In this paper, the FRC concludes that the concept of 'true and fair' remains a cornerstone of financial reporting and that the intent and substance of the two expressions 'presents fairly' and 'true and fair' are similar. The paper is available from the FRC website at http://www.frc.org.uk/publications.

Parent undertaking: A parent undertaking of the type described in reg 3 will not be required to draw up its annual accounts in the manner described in reg 5(1) but may instead draw up those accounts in some other manner provided that—

(a) it also prepares group accounts in accordance with the provisions of reg 10;[5]

(b) the notes to its individual balance sheet show its profit and loss for the financial year determined in accordance with the provisions of these regs;[6] and

(c) the departure from reg 5(1) is disclosed by way of a note to both the individual and group accounts.[7]

1 EC(IUA)R 1996, reg 5(1)(b) & Reg 5(4).

2 *Dolan v AB Ltd* [1969] IR 282; *Lloyd Cheyham & Co Ltd v Littlejohn & Co* [1987] BCLC 303; *IRC v Duple Motor Bodies Ltd* [1961] 1 WLR 739. The recognised practices of the accountancy profession may be found in its Statements of Standard Accounting Practice (SSAPs) and Financial Reporting Standards ('FRSs) or their international equivalents (International Financial Reporting Standards ('IFRS).

3 EC(IUA)R 1996, reg 5(1)(d).

4 EC(IUA)R 1996, reg 5(1)(e).

5 EC(IUA)R 1996, reg 5(2)(b).

6 EC(IUA)R 1996, reg 5(2)(c).

7 EC(IUA)R 1996, reg 5(3).

6 Format of accounts

(1) [Where the directors of an undertaking prepare Companies Act individual accounts and subject to these Regulations –][a]

(a) every balance sheet of an undertaking shall show the items listed in the balance sheet format set out in Chapter 2 of Part I of the Schedule, and

(b) every profit and loss account of an undertaking shall show the items listed in the profit and loss account format so set out,

in the order and under the headings and sub-headings given in the format concerned.

(2) Paragraph (1) shall not be construed as requiring the heading or sub-heading for any item in the balance sheet, or profit and loss account, of an undertaking to be distinguished by any letter or number assigned to that item in the formats set out in the Schedule.

(3) Where the balance sheet or profit and loss account of an undertaking has been prepared by reference to the options set out in the Schedule, the directors of the undertaking shall adopt the same options in preparing the accounts for subsequent financial years unless, in their opinion, there are special reasons for a change.

(4) Where any change is made in the format adopted in preparing a balance sheet, or profit and loss account, of an undertaking, the reasons for the change, together with full particulars of the change, shall be given in a note to the accounts in which the new format is first adopted.

(5) Any item required in accordance with the Schedule to be shown in the balance sheet or profit and loss account, of an undertaking, may be shown in greater detail than that required by the format adopted.

[(6) In respect of every item shown in the balance sheet, or profit and loss account, of an undertaking, the corresponding amount for the financial year immediately preceding that to which the balance sheet or profit and loss account refers shall also be shown and, if that corresponding amount is not comparable with the amount to be shown for the item in question in respect of the financial year to which the balance sheet or profit and loss account relates, the former amount shall be adjusted, and particulars of the adjustment and the reasons therefor shall be given in a note to the accounts.][b]

(7) Subject to paragraph (8), a heading or sub-heading corresponding to an item listed in the balance sheet format or the profit and loss account format of an undertaking, shall not be included in the balance sheet or profit and loss account, as the case may be, if there is no amount to be shown for that item in respect of the financial year to which the balance sheet or profit and loss account relates.

(8) Paragraph (7) shall not apply in any case where an amount can be shown for the item in question in respect of the financial year immediately preceding that to which the balance sheet or profit and loss account relates, and that amount shall be shown under the heading or sub-heading required by paragraph (1).

(9) Subject to the provisions of these Regulations and the provisions of the Schedule, amounts in respect of items representing assets or income may not be set off in the accounts of an undertaking against amounts in respect of items representing liabilities or expenditure, as the case may be, or vice versa.

(10) The balance sheet, or profit and loss account, of an undertaking may include an item representing or covering the amount of any asset or liability or income or expenditure not otherwise covered by any of the items listed in the format adopted but the following shall not be treated as assets in the balance sheet of an undertaking:

(a) preliminary expenses,

(b) expenses of, and commission on, any issue of shares or debentures, and

(c) costs of research.

(11) Every profit and loss account of an undertaking shall show the amount of the profit or loss of the undertaking on ordinary activities before taxation.

Amendments

a Words substituted by reg 11 and Sch 3, Item No 3 of EC(IFRSMA)R 2005.

b Subparagraph (6) substituted by SI 840/2005, reg 7.

Definitions

'accounts': EC(IUA)R 1996, reg 2(1); 'undertaking': EC(IUA)R 1996, reg 2(1) & EC(CGA)R 1992, reg 3(1).

Notes

True and fair view: See the notes to reg 5.

7 Accounting Principles

Subject to Regulation 8, the amounts to be included in the [Companies Act accounts][a] of an undertaking in respect of the items shown shall be determined in accordance with the following principles:

(a) the undertaking shall be presumed to be carrying on business as a going concern,

(b) accounting policies shall be applied consistently from one financial year to the next,

(c) subject to the provisions of the Schedule, the amount of any item in the accounts shall be determined on a prudent basis and in particular—

(i) only profits which have arisen by the balance sheet date shall be included in the profit and loss account, and

(ii) [all liabilities which have arisen][b] in respect of the financial year to which the accounts relate, or a previous financial year, shall be taken into account, including those liabilities and losses which only become apparent between the balance sheet date and the date on which the accounts are signed in pursuance of section 156 of the Principal Act,

(d) all income charges relating to the financial year to which the accounts relate shall be taken into account without regard to the date of receipt or payment, [...][c]

(e) in determining the aggregate amount of any item the amount of each individual asset or liability that falls to be taken into account shall be determined [separately, and][d] [(f) The directors of a company shall, in determining how amounts are presented within items in the profit and loss account and balance sheet, have regard to the substance of the reported transaction or arrangement, in accordance with generally accepted accounting principles or practice.][e]

Amendments

a Words substituted by reg 11 and Sch 3, Item No 4(a) of EC(IFRSMA)R 2005 .

b Words substituted by reg 11 and Sch 3, Item No 4(b) of EC(IFRSMA)R 2005.

c Word "and" deleted by reg 11 and Sch 3, Item No 4(c) of EC(IFRSMA)R 2005.

d Words substituted by reg 11 and Sch 3, Item No 4(d) of EC(IFRSMA)R 2005.

e Paragraph (f) inserted by reg 11 and Sch 3, Item No 4(e) of EC(IFRSMA)R 2005.

Definitions

'accounts': EC(IUA)R 1996, reg 2(1); 'companies act accounts' CA 1963, s 2(1) 'the Principal Act': EC(IUA)R 1996, reg 2(1); 'undertaking': EC(IUA)R 1996, reg 2(1) & EC(CGA)R 1992, reg 3(1).

Notes

True and fair view: See the notes to reg 5.

8 Departure from Accounting Principles

If it appears to the directors of an undertaking that there are special reasons for departing from any of the principles specified in Regulation 7 [when preparing Companies Act accounts][a], they may so depart, but particulars of the departure, the reasons for it and its effect on the balance sheet and profit and loss account of the undertaking shall be stated in a note to the accounts. for the financial year concerned, of the undertaking.

Amendments

a Words substituted by reg 11 and Sch 3, Item No 5 of EC(IFRSMA)R 2005 (SI 116/2005).

Definitions

'accounts': EC(IUA)R 1996, reg 2(1); 'undertaking': EC(IUA)R 1996, reg 2(1) & EC(CGA)R 1992, reg 3(1).

Notes

Departure from accounting principles: Although under reg 8 the directors may in special circumstances depart from the accounting principles set out in reg 7, they remain under an overriding obligation to ensure that the accounts present a true and fair view of the company's financial position.[1]

[1] See reg 5 and the notes thereto.

9 Publication of accounts in full or abbreviated form

(1) Where an undertaking publishes its full accounts, it shall also publish with those accounts any report in relation to those accounts by the auditors of the undertaking under section 193 of the Act of 1990.

(2) Where an undertaking publishes abbreviated accounts relating to any financial year, it shall also publish a statement indicating—

(a) that the accounts are not the accounts copies of which are required to be annexed to the annual return,

(b) whether the copies of the accounts so required to be so annexed have in fact been so annexed,

(c) whether the auditors of the undertaking have made a report under section 193 of the Act of 1990, in respect of the accounts of the undertaking which relate to any financial year with which the abbreviated accounts purport to deal,

[(d) whether any matters referred to in the auditors' report were qualified or unqualified, or whether the auditors' report included a reference to any matters to which the auditors drew attention by way of emphasis without qualifying the report.][a]

(3) Where an undertaking publishes abbreviated accounts, it shall not publish with those accounts any such report of the auditors as is mentioned in paragraph (2)(c).

(4) Where an undertaking publishes its full individual accounts for a financial year it shall indicate if group accounts have been prepared and if so where those group accounts can be obtained.

(5) Every undertaking to which these Regulations apply shall—

(a) make available its full or abbreviated accounts in accordance with paragraphs (1) to (5) for public inspection at its head office, and

(b) make available to the public copies of its accounts on request at a price which does not exceed the cost of making the copy.

(6) In this Regulation—

"abbreviated accounts", in relation to an undertaking, means any balance sheet or profit and loss account. or summary or abstract of a balance sheet or profit and loss account, relating to a financial year of the undertaking which is published by the undertaking otherwise than as part of the full accounts of the undertaking for that financial year and. in relation to a parent undertaking, includes an account in any form purporting to be a balance sheet or profit and loss account, or a summary or abstract of a balance sheet or profit and loss account of the group consisting of the parent undertaking and its subsidiaries;

"full accounts" means the individual or group accounts required to be annexed to the annual return;

"publish", in relation to a document includes issue, circulate or otherwise make it available for public inspection in a manner calculated to invite the public generally, or any class of members of the public, to read the document, and cognate words shall be constructed accordingly.

Amendments

a Paragraph 2(d) substituted by reg 11 and Sch 3, Item No 6 of EC(IFRSMA)R 2005.

Definitions

'accounts': EC(IUA)R 1996, reg 2(1); 'the Act of 1990': EC(IUA)R 1996, reg 2(1); 'annual return': EC(IUA)R 1996, reg 2(1); 'group accounts': EC(IUA)R 1996, reg 2(1); 'individual accounts': EC(IUA)R 1996, reg 2(1); 'parent undertaking': EC(IUA)R 1996, reg 2(1); 'undertaking': EC(IUA)R 1996, reg 2(1) & EC(CGA)R 1992, reg 3(1).

Notes

Publication of accounts: The reference to publication in reg 9, is to situations such as the publishing of the full or abbreviated accounts of the company in a national newspaper, rather than to the filing of accounts with the annual return.

Similar obligations are imposed with regard to the publication of group accounts (reg 18).

10 Group accounts

[(1) This Regulation applies to a parent undertaking whether or not it is itself a subsidiary of another undertaking.

(2) A parent undertaking to which this Regulation applies shall not be entitled to take advantage of section 154 of the Principal Act in relation to the preparation of group accounts or of section 151 (2) and (3) of the Principal Act in relation to the form of group accounts.

(3) Every parent undertaking to which this Regulation applies shall, in accordance with section 150 of the Principal Act, prepare group accounts at the end of its financial year dealing with the state of affairs and profit or loss of the company and its subsidiaries (including those in liquidation and those with registered offices outside the State) and those group accounts shall be laid before the next annual general meeting of the company at the same time as the individual accounts of the company are so laid and shall be annexed to the annual return of the company.

(4) The report of the auditors on the group accounts laid before the annual general meeting shall be annexed to the annual return referred to in paragraph (3).

(5) Where, in accordance with section 150 (2) or (3)(b) of the Principal Act, the directors of an undertaking prepare IFRS group accounts, they shall ensure that instead of making the disclosures specified in section 1 50B (2) (inserted by the European Communities (International Financial Reporting Standards and Miscellaneous Amendments) Regulations 2005) the notes to those group accounts include the information required by—

(a) paragraph 30 (1) of Part IV of the Schedule (details of directors' remuneration),

(b) sections 41 to 45 of the Act of 1990 to be disclosed in individual accounts and the information required by paragraph 31 (2) of Part IV of the Schedule (transactions with directors),

(c) section 63 of the Act of 1990 unless it is disclosed in the directors' report (interests in shares and debentures),

(d) paragraphs 32 to 36 of Part IV of the Schedule (details of group undertakings),

(e) paragraph 29 of Part IV of the Schedule (details of staff numbers and remuneration),

(f) paragraphs 6 to 9 of Part III of the Schedule (details of share capital and debentures),

(g) paragraph 20 (4) of Part III of the Schedule (restriction on distributibility of profits),

(h) paragraph 18 of Part III of the Schedule (guarantees and other financial commitments),

(i) paragraph 20 (2) of Part III of the Schedule (financial assistance for purchase of own shares),

(j) paragraph 21 (d) of Part III of the Schedule and by section 205D of the Act of 1990 (auditors' remuneration),

[(k) where appropriate, paragraph 37(a) of Part IV of the Schedule.][b]

(6) Where in accordance with section 1 50(3)(a) of the Principal Act, the directors of an undertaking to which this regulation applies prepare Companies Acts group accounts they shall, subject to paragraph (7), be prepared in accordance with the provisions of Part I to Part III of the Schedule, as modified by Part IV of the Schedule.

(7) (a) The Companies Act group accounts laid before the annual general meeting of an undertaking shall give a true and fair view of the state of affairs and profit or loss of the undertaking and subsidiaries dealt with thereby as a whole, so far as concerns members of the undertaking.

(b) The Companies Act group accounts shall comprise the consolidated balance sheet dealing with the sate of affairs of the parent and its subsidiaries as a whole, the consolidated profit and loss account dealing with the profit and loss of the parent and its subsidiaries as a whole and the notes on the accounts giving the information required by these Regulations or otherwise provided by the undertaking.

(c) Where Companies Act group accounts drawn up in accordance with paragraph (6) would not provide sufficient information to comply with subparagraph (a), any necessary additional information shall be given in the group accounts or in a note to the accounts.

(d) Where, owing to special circumstances, the preparation of Companies Act group accounts in compliance with paragraph (5) would prevent those accounts from complying with subparagraph (a) (even if additional information were given under subparagraph (c)), the directors of the parent undertaking shall depart from the requirements of Parts I, II, III and IV (other than paragraph 2 of Part IV) of the Schedule in preparing those accounts insofar as it is necessary to comply with that paragraph.

(e) Where the directors of a parent undertaking depart from the requirements of these Regulations in compliance with subparagraph (d), they shall attach a note to the Companies Act group accounts of the undertaking giving details of the particular departures made, the reasons therefor and the effect of those departures on the accounts.

(8) Where a document annexed to the annual return under this Regulation or Regulation 11, 12, 12A or 13 is in a language other than English or Irish, there shall be annexed to any such document a translation in the English or Irish language certified in the prescribed manner to be a correct translation.

(9) The individual and group accounts, if any, of a subsidiary undertaking excluded from group accounts by virtue of the application of paragraph 2 of Part IV of the Schedule shall be attached to the group accounts, or annexed to the annual return, of the parent undertaking.

(10) Paragraph (9) shall not apply where the subsidiary undertaking has otherwise annexed the relevant accounts referred to in that paragraph to its annual return.][a]

Amendments

a Regulation 10 substituted by reg 11 and Sch 3, Item No 7 of EC(IFRSMA)R 2005.

b Regulation 10(5)(k) inserted by European Communities (Directive 2006/46/EC) Regulations 2009, reg 21.

Definitions

'financial year': CA 1963, s 2(1); 'annual return': EC(IUA)R 1996, reg 2(1); 'Companies Act group accounts': CA 1963, s 2(1); 'group accounts': EC(IUA)R 1996, reg 2(1); 'IFRS group accounts': CA 1963, s 2(1); 'individual accounts': EC(IUA)R 1996, reg 2(1); 'parent undertaking': EC(IUA)R 1996, reg 2(1); 'the Principal Act': EC(IUA)R 1996, reg 2(1); 'subsidiary': EC(IUA)R 1996, reg 2(1); 'undertaking': EC(IUA)R 1996, reg 2(1) & EC(CGA)R 1992, reg 3(1).

Notes

Parent and subsidiary undertakings: For the circumstances in which one undertaking is deemed to the subsidiary of another, see reg 11 and the notes thereto.

Financial holding undertakings: The obligation to prepare group accounts in accordance with the provisions of reg 10 applies not only to insurance and reinsurance undertakings, but also to any other parent undertaking where—

(a) it does not itself carry on any material business apart from the acquisition, management and disposal of interests in subsidiaries, and

(b) its principal subsidiaries are wholly or mainly insurance and/or reinsurance undertakings of the type described in reg 3.[1]

In this regard the parent's principal subsidiaries are those whose results or financial position would principally affect the figures in the group accounts.[2]

True and fair view: EC(IUA)R 1996, reg 10 imposes an overriding obligation that the annual accounts should give a true and fair view of the state of affairs of the group as a whole.[3] To a large extent, the provisions of EC(IUA)R 1996 are themselves determinative as to what constitutes a properly prepared set of group accounts. However, to the extent that the legislation is silent on any particular matter, compliance with the recognised practices and standards of the accountancy profession in preparing group accounts will be strong but not conclusive evidence that the accounts give a 'true and fair view' of the group's financial position.[4]

Indeed, even where the legislation specifically deals with an aspect of the accounts, a departure will be permitted if strict adherence would result in the 'true and fair view' not being achieved.[5] Details of the departure must, however, be given in the notes to the accounts together with the reasons therefor.[6] With the introduction of International Financial Reporting Standards through EC(IFRSMA)R 2005, a new term, 'presents fairly' entered into financial reporting language. The United Kingdom's Financial Reporting Council, of which the Accounting Standards Board is a constituent body, published a paper in August 2005 entitled 'The implications of new accounting and auditing standards for the 'true and fair view' and auditors' responsibilities'. In this paper, the FRC concludes that the concept of 'true and fair' remains a cornerstone of financial reporting and that the intent and substance of the two expressions 'presents fairly' and 'true and fair' are similar. The paper is available from the FRC website at http://www.frc.org.uk/publications.

Excluded subsidiary undertaking: If the affairs of a subsidiary undertaking are legitimately excluded from the group accounts, copies of that subsidiary's individual accounts must be either attached to the group accounts or annexed to the parent company's annual return,[7] unless the subsidiary has already filed an annual return of its own with the accounts annexed thereto.[8]

1 EC(IUA)R 1996, reg 13(1). For the purposes of this reg, 'management of interest in subsidiaries' includes the provisions of services to such subsidiaries by the parent undertaking.

2 EC(IUA)R 1996, reg 13(2).

3 EC(IUA)R 1996, reg 10(5)(a) & (c).

4 *Dolan v AB Ltd* [1969] IR 282; *Lloyd Cheyham & Co Ltd v Littlejohn & Co* [1987] BCLC 303; *IRC v Duple Motor Bodies Ltd* [1961] 1 WLR 739. The recognised practices of the accountancy profession may be found in its Statements of Standard Accounting Practice (SSAPs) and Financial Reporting Standards (FRSs) or their international equivalents, international financial reporting standards (IFRSs).

5 EC(IUA)R 1996, reg 10(5)(d).

6 EC(IUA)R 1996, reg 10(5)(e).

7 EC(IUA)R 1996, reg 10(9).

8 EC(IUA)R 1996, reg 10(10)).

---

11 Subsidiary undertaking

(1) For the purpose of Regulations 10 to 19 and Part IV of the Schedule, an undertaking shall be deemed to be a subsidiary of another, if, but only if—

(a) that other—

(i) holds a majority of the shareholders' or members' voting rights in the undertaking, or

(ii) is a shareholder or member of it and controls the composition of its board of directors, or

(iii) is a shareholder or member of it and controls alone, pursuant to an agreement with other shareholders or members, a majority of the shareholders' or members' voting rights;

or

(b) that other has the right to exercise a dominant influence over it—

(i) by virtue of provisions contained in its memorandum or articles, or

(ii) by virtue of a control contract:

or

[(c) that other has the power to exercise, or actually exercises, dominant influence or control over it, or

(ca) that other and the subsidiary undertaking are managed on a unified basis; or][a]

(d) the undertaking is a subsidiary of any undertaking which is that other's subsidiary undertaking.

(2) In determining whether one undertaking controls the composition of the board of directors of another for the purposes of paragraph (1)(a)(ii), subsection (2) of section 155 of the Principal Act shall apply to undertakings subject to these Regulations as it applies to undertakings subject to that section.

(3) For the purpose of paragraph (1)(a)—

(a) subject to paragraphs (c) and (d), any shares held or power exercisable—

(i) by any person as a nominee for that other, or

(ii) by, or by a nominee for, a subsidiary undertaking of that other, not being the subsidiary undertaking whose shares or board of directors are involved,

shall be treated as held or exercisable by that other,

(b) any shares held or power exercisable by that other or a subsidiary undertaking of that other. on behalf of a person or undertaking that is neither that other nor a subsidiary undertaking of that other shall be treated as not held or exercisable by that other,

(c) any shares held or power exercisable by that other, or a nominee for that other or its subsidiary undertaking shall be treated as not held or exercisable by that other if they are held as aforesaid by way of security provided that such power or the rights attaching to such shares are exercised in accordance with instructions received from the person providing the security,

(d) any shares held or power exercisable by that other or a nominee for that other or its subsidiary undertaking shall be treated as not held or exercisable by that other if the ordinary business of that other or its subsidiary undertaking, as the case may be, includes the lending of money and the shares are held as aforesaid by way of security provided that such power or the rights attaching to such shares are exercised in the interests of the person providing the security.

(4) For the purposes of clauses (i) and (ii) of paragraph (1)(a), the total of the voting rights of the shareholders or members in the subsidiary undertaking shall be reduced by the following—

(a) the voting rights attached to shares held by the subsidiary undertaking in itself, and

(b) the voting rights attached to shares held by the subsidiary undertaking by any of its subsidiary undertakings, and

(c) the voting rights attached to shares held by a person acting in his own name but on behalf of the subsidiary undertaking or one of its subsidiary undertakings.

(5) For the purposes of paragraph (1)(b) an undertaking shall not be regarded as having the right to exercise a dominant influence over another undertaking unless it has a right to give directions with respect to the operating and financial policies of that other undertaking which its directors are obliged to comply with.

(6) In paragraph (1)(b) "control contract" means a contract in writing conferring such a right which—

(a) is of a kind authorised by the memorandum or articles of the undertaking in relation to which the right is exercisable, and

(b) is permitted by the law under which that undertaking is established.

(7) Paragraph (5) shall not be read as affecting the construction of the expression "actually exercises a dominant influence" in paragraph (1)(c).

Amendments

a Paragraph substituted by reg 11 and Sch 3, Item No 8 of EC(IFRSMA)R 2005.

Definitions

'participating interest': EC(IUA)R 1996, reg 2(1); 'the Principal Act': EC(IUA)R 1996, reg 2(1); 'subsidiary': EC(IUA)R 1996, reg 2(1); 'undertaking': EC(IUA)R 1996, reg 2(1) & EC(CGA)R 1992, reg 3(1).

Notes

Exhaustive definition: The wording of reg 11(1) makes it quite clear that the definition of 'subsidiary undertaking' contained therein is exhaustive. However, EC(IFRSMA)R 2005 has amended this definition. Previously, where a company actually exercised dominant influence over another or was managed on a unified basis with that other company, it was necessary for the company to have a participating interest in the other before it met the definition of a subsidiary. This requirement has now been removed. A company will now be a subsidiary of another where that other company has the power to exercise, or actually exercises, dominant influence or control over it, or where they are both managed on a unified basis. The several ways in which the relationship of parent undertaking and subsidiary undertaking can arise are as follows—

1. *Holding a majority of voting rights*[1]: Since the subsidiary undertaking might not be a company having a share capital, the term "voting rights" is deemed to include not only a right to vote in respect of shares, but also any right to vote at general meetings "on all or substantially all matters"[2] as well as the right (in respect of undertakings which do not have general meetings at which matters are decided on a vote) under the constitution of that undertaking to direct overall policy or to alter the terms of its constitution.[3] Voting rights held through a nominee on behalf of the parent undertaking or on behalf of one of its other subsidiaries, are also to be taken into account in determining whether or not it holds a majority of voting rights.[4] Excluded from consideration, however, are the following—

   (a) any shares held or power exercisable by the parent undertaking or one of its subsidiaries on behalf of a third party in circumstances where that third party is not itself part of the same group of companies;[5]

   (b) any shares held or power exercisable by or on behalf of the parent undertaking or one of its subsidiaries by way of security, provided that the power or the rights attaching to the shares are exercised in accordance with instructions received from the person providing the security;[6]

   (c) any shares held or power exercisable by or on behalf of the parent undertaking or one of its subsidiaries, if the ordinary business of the parent or that subsidiary, as the case may be, includes the lending of money, and the shares are held as security, and provided that the power or the rights attaching to the shares are exercised in the interests of the person providing the security.[7]

   In determining whether or not the parent undertaking holds a majority of voting rights in the subsidiary undertaking, the total voting rights of shareholders or members in that subsidiary must be reduced by the amount of any voting rights attaching to shares held by or on behalf of the subsidiary itself or held by or on behalf of any of its own subsidiaries. Thus, although Undertaking A might not, at first sight, appear to have a majority of voting rights in Undertaking B, such a majority may in fact be deemed to arise after one has excluded such voting rights as are exercisable by or on behalf of Undertaking B itself or by on behalf of any subsidiaries of Undertaking B.[8]

1 EC(IUA)R 1996, reg 11(1)(a)(i).

2 EC(IUA)R 1996, reg 2(3)(b).

3 EC(IUA)R 1996, reg 2(3)(c).

4 EC(IUA)R 1996, reg 11(3)(a).

5 EC(IUA)R 1996, reg 11(3)(b).

6 EC(IUA)R 1996, reg 11(3)(c).

7 EC(IUA)R 1996, reg 11(3)(d).

8 EC(IUA)R 1996, reg 11(4). The only circumstance in which a company may acquire shares in itself and exercise voting rights attaching to such shares is where the company has acquired any of its own fully paid shares otherwise than for valuable consideration: C(A)A 1983, s 41(2). If the shares have been acquired by way of purchase or redemption pursuant to CA 1990, Part XI and are not cancelled, they must instead be held as `treasury shares' and thus voting rights cannot be exercised in relation to them: CA 1990, s 209(3). With regard to the entitlement of a subsidiary to acquire shares in its holding company, see CA 1963, s 32, CA 1990, s 224 and EC(PLCS)R 1997 (SI 67/1997), reg 5(2).

2. *Controlling a majority of voting rights*[1]: The difference between holding and controlling a majority of voting rights is a subtle one. A member 'holds' a majority of voting rights in circumstances where such rights are conferred on him pursuant to the undertaking's constitution or attach to the shares which are held by him. 'Control' of a majority of voting rights is slightly different. It refers to a situation where the member although not automatically having a majority of votes under the constitution or by virtue of his shareholding, nonetheless has control of a majority of votes pursuant to the terms of a shareholders' agreement between himself and other members of the undertaking. For example, Undertaking A might hold only shares carrying 25% of voting rights in a general meeting of Undertaking B, but under the terms of an agreement with other shareholders, Undertaking A is in fact contractually entitled to direct not only how its own votes are cast but how the votes of the other members are cast as well. Such a contractual entitlement amounts to 'control' for the purposes of reg 11.

   The various rules referred to above under the heading '*holding a majority of voting rights*' which deal with the taking into account of votes held through nominees, etc,[2] and dealing with how to calculate the total voting rights in the subsidiary, apply equally in determining whether one undertaking 'controls' a majority of votes in the other.[3]

1 EC(IUA)R 1996, reg 11(1)(a)(iii).

2 EC(IUA)R 1996, reg 11(3).

3 EC(IUA)R 1996, reg 11(4).

3. *Control of composition of board*[1]: This involves an entitlement on the part of Undertaking A without the consent or concurrence of any other person to appoint or remove a majority of the board of Undertaking B or to exercise a right of veto in respect of the appointment of a majority of the board.[2] A person may be able to control the composition of the board of directors by reason, inter alia, of (i) having a majority of the votes in general meeting; (ii) a shareholders' agreement giving such control; (iii) a provision in the memorandum or articles of association conferring a power to appoint and dismiss the board or a majority of the board.

   Powers exercisable by a nominee on behalf of the parent undertaking or on behalf of one of its other subsidiaries, are also to be taken into account in determining whether or not it controls the composition of the board.[3] Excluded from consideration, however, are the following—

(a) any shares held or power exercisable by the parent undertaking or one of its subsidiaries on behalf of a third party in circumstances where that third party is not itself part of the same group of companies;[4]

(b) any shares held or power exercisable by or on behalf of the parent undertaking or one of its subsidiaries by way of security, provided that the power or the rights attaching to the shares are exercised in accordance with instructions received from the person providing the security;[5]

(c) any shares held or power exercisable by or on behalf of the parent undertaking or one of its subsidiaries, if the ordinary business of the parent or that subsidiary, as the case may be, includes the lending of money, and the shares are held as security, and provided that the power or the rights attaching to the shares are exercised in the interests of the person providing the security.[6]

1 EC(IUA)R 1996, reg 11(1)(a)(ii).
2 CA 1963, s 155(2) as applied by EC(IUA)R 1996, reg 11(2).
3 EC(IUA)R 1996, reg 11(3)(a)).
4 EC(IUA)R 1996, reg 11(3)(b).
5 EC(IUA)R 1996, reg 11(3)(c).
6 EC(IUA)R 1996, reg 11(3)(d).

4. *Right to exercise a dominant influence*[1]: Where Undertaking A has a right to exercise a 'dominant influence'[2] over Undertaking B by virtue of a provision in the memorandum or articles of association of Undertaking B, or by virtue of a 'control contract', then the latter undertaking will be deemed to be a subsidiary of the former.

For the purposes of this Regulation a 'control contract' is one which is in writing and is of a kind authorised by the memorandum or articles of Undertaking B, and is permitted by the law of the State pursuant to which Undertaking B is established.[3] Such a contract, if valid, could therefore result in Undertaking B being deemed to be a subsidiary of Undertaking A, even though the latter undertaking is not a member of the former.

1 EC(IUA)R 1996, reg 11(1)(b).
2 A right to exercise a dominant influence is deemed to exist in circumstances where Undertaking A has a legal entitlement to give directions with respect to the operating and financial policies of Undertaking B, which the latter's directors are required to obey: EC(IUA)R 1996, reg 11(5).
3 EC(IUA)R 1996, reg 11(6).

5. *Actual exercise of dominant interest*[1]: This involves a situation where Undertaking A has the power to exercise or actually exercises dominant influence or control over Undertaking B, even though not having a strict legal entitlement to do so.

1 EC(IUA)R 1996, reg 11(1)(c).

6. *Management on a unified basis*[1]: Where Undertaking A and Undertaking B are managed on a 'unified basis' the relationship of parent and subsidiary will also be deemed to arise. No indication is given as to what amounts to management of undertakings on a 'unified basis.' Does it mean simply that the undertakings have the same board of directors, or does it perhaps mean that the separate legal personalities of the respective undertakings have been ignored and that they are effectively being run as a single economic entity?[2] Of some influence in this regard is the Financial Reporting Standard No 2 "Accounting for Subsidiary Undertakings" issued by the Accounting Standards Board and the Institute of Chartered Accountants in Ireland, which states at para 12 that management on a unified basis occurs if the whole of the operations of the undertakings are integrated and they are managed as a single unit, but that unified management does not arise simply because one undertaking manages another.

1 EC(IUA)R 1996, reg 11(1)(c).
2 As to the circumstances in which the veil of incorporation may be lifted on a group of companies, see the notes to CA 1963, s 18.

7. *Subsidiary of a subsidiary*[1] If Undertaking B is a subsidiary of Undertaking A, but in turn has its own subsidiary, Undertaking C, then Undertaking C will also be deemed to be a subsidiary of Undertaking A.

1 EC(IUA)R 1996, reg 11(1)(d).

12 Wholly-owned subsidiaries

(1) Paragraph (3) of Regulation 10 shall not apply to a parent undertaking (in this Regulation referred to as "the exempted parent undertaking") which is itself a wholly-owned subsidiary of another undertaking [established in an EEA State][a] (in this Regulation referred to as "the parent undertaking") if the requirements set out in paragraph (3) of this Regulation are complied with provided that the fact that the advantage of this Regulation is being availed of shall be disclosed in a note to the accounts of the insurance parent undertaking annexed to its annual return under the Principal Act.

(2) In this Regulation, an undertaking shall be deemed to be a wholly-owned subsidiary of another if—

(a) that other parent undertaking holds all the shares in the exempted parent undertaking, or

(b) that other holds 90 per cent or more of the shares in the undertaking and the remaining shareholders in or members of the undertaking have approved the exemption.

(3) The requirements referred to in paragraph (1) are as follows:

(a) the undertaking and its subsidiaries shall be dealt with in group accounts prepared by the parent undertaking;

(b) the group accounts and the group annual report of the parent undertaking shall be prepared and audited in accordance with the Directive or Council Directive No. 3/349/EEC of 13 June 1983, [or prepared in accordance with international financial reporting standards and audited in accordance with either such Directive, as applicable,][b] as the case may be;

(c) there shall be annexed to the annual return of the exempted parent next after the group accounts have been prepared in accordance with subparagraph (a)—

(i) the group accounts referred to in subparagraph (b);

(ii) the group annual report referred to in subparagraph (b); and

(iii) the report of the person responsible for auditing the accounts referred to in subparagraph (b).

(d) The notes on the annual accounts of the undertaking shall disclose—

(i) the name and registered office of the parent undertaking that draws up the group accounts referred to in subparagraph (b), and

(ii) the exemption from the obligation to draw up group accounts and a group annual report.

[(4) The exemption does not apply to a company any of whose securities are admitted to trading on a regulated market of any EEA State.][c]

(5) The [Bank][d] may require that additional information shall be provided in the consolidated accounts of the parent undertaking or the individual accounts of the undertaking referred to in paragraph (1) in accordance with Article 9 of Council Directive No. 83/349/EEC.

(6) This Regulation shall also apply to a parent undertaking which is not for the purposes of paragraph (2) a wholly-owned subsidiary of another undertaking where—

(a) the parent undertaking is itself a subsidiary of a parent undertaking [established in an EEA State,][e] and

(b) the shareholders or members holding in total 10 per cent or more of the nominal value of the shares of the parent undertaking concerned have not at any time that is not later than six months before the end of the financial year in question requested the preparation of group accounts by that parent undertaking in respect of that financial year.

Amendments

a Words substituted by reg 11 and Sch 3, Item No 9(a) of EC(IFRSMA)R 2005.

b Words inserted by reg 11 and Sch 3, Item No 9(b) of EC(IFRSMA)R 2005.

c Paragraph substituted by reg 11 and Sch 3, Item No 9(c) of EC(IFRSMA)R 2005.

d "Bank" substituted for "Minister" by CBFSAIA 2003, s 35 and Sch 2, Pt 16, Item 3.

e Words substituted by reg 11 and Sch 3, Item No 9(e) of EC(IFRSMA)R 2005.

Definitions

'accounts': EC(IUA)R 1996, reg 2(1); 'annual return': EC(IUA)R 1996, reg 2(1); 'the Directive': EC(IUA)R 1996, reg 2(1); 'EEA State'; CA 1963, s 2(1); 'group accounts': EC(IUA)R 1996, reg 2(1); 'individual accounts': EC(IUA)R 1996, reg 2(1); 'international financial reporting standards': CA 1963, s 2(1); 'the Minister': EC(IUA)R 1996, reg 2(1); 'parent undertaking': EC(IUA)R 1996, reg 2(1); 'the Principal Act': EC(IUA)R 1996, reg 2(1); 'subsidiary': EC(IUA)R 1996, reg 2(1); 'undertaking': EC(IUA)R 1996, reg 2(1) & EC(CGA)R 1992, reg 3(1).

Notes

Exemption for parent undertakings which are themselves wholly-owned or 90% owned subsidiaries: This Regulation exempts an unlisted[1] parent undertaking ('the exempted parent') from the obligation to prepare group accounts in accordance with EC(IUA)R 1996 if—

(a) it is in turn a wholly-owned subsidiary of another parent undertaking incorporated under the laws of a EEA State ("the other parent undertaking") or the other parent undertaking holds at least 90% of its issued share capital, and the holders of the remaining 10% approve of the exemption;[2]

(b) the exempted parent and its subsidiary undertakings are dealt with in group accounts of the other parent undertaking which (along with the directors' report) are drawn up in accordance with the provisions of Council Directive 91/674/EEC or the Seventh Companies Directive;[3]

(c) the other parent undertaking's group accounts, directors' report and auditors' report are annexed to the exempted parent's annual return;[4] and

(d) the notes to the exempted parent's annual accounts disclose the name and registered office of the other parent undertaking as well as the fact that the exemption has been availed of.[5]

1 EC(IUA)R 1996, reg 11(4).
2 EC(IUA)R 1996, reg 12(1) & (2).
3 EC(IUA)R 1996, reg 11(3)(a) & (b).
4 EC(IUA)R 1996, reg 11(3)(c).
5 EC(IUA)R 1996, reg 11(3)(d).

Extension of exemptions to EEA States: EC(IFRSMA)R 2005 extends the exemptions available to undertakings incorporated in a EEA State, as permitted under Directive 86/635/EEC but heretofore not taken up in Irish company law.

Exemption for other parent undertakings which are themselves subsidiaries: If an unlisted[1] parent undertaking ('the exempted parent') is itself a subsidiary of another undertaking incorporated under the laws of a member state ('the second parent') but is held as to less than 90% of its share capital by the second parent, it will be exempted from the obligation to prepare group accounts in accordance with EC(CIA)R 1992 if—

(a) the holders of not less than 10% of its issued share capital have not made a request for such accounts at least six months before the end of the relevant financial year;[2]

(b) the exempted parent and its subsidiary undertakings are dealt with in group accounts of the second parent which (along with the directors' report) are drawn up in accordance with the provisions of Council Directive 91/674/EEC or the Seventh Companies Directive;[3]

(c) the second parent's group accounts, directors' report and auditors' report are annexed to the exempted parent's annual return;[4] and

(d) the notes to the exempted parent's annual accounts disclose the name and registered office of the second parent as well as the fact that the exemption has been availed of.[5]

1 EC(IUA)R 1996, reg 11(4) & (6).
2 EC(IUA)R 1996, reg 11(6).
3 EC(IUA)R 1996, reg 11(3)(a) & (b) & reg 11(6).
4 EC(IUA)R 1996, reg 11(3)(c) & reg 11(6).
5 EC(IUA)R 1996, reg 11(3)(d) & reg 11(6).

[12A Exemption for parent undertakings included in non-EEA group accounts

(1) A parent undertaking (the 'exempted parent') is exempt from the requirement in Regulation 10(3) to prepare group accounts where that undertaking is itself a subsidiary undertaking and its parent undertaking ('that other parent undertaking') is not established under the law of an EEA State where—

(a) the exempted parent is a wholly-owned subsidiary of that other parent undertaking;

(b) that other parent undertaking holds more than 50 per cent of the shares in the exempted parent and notice requesting the preparation of group accounts has not been served in accordance with paragraph (2) on the exempted parent by shareholders holding in aggregate—

(i) more than half of the remaining shares in the company, or

(ii) 5 per cent of the total shares in the company.

(2) The notice referred to in paragraph (1)(b) must be served not later than 6 months after the end of the financial year before that to which it relates.

(3) Exemption under this Regulation is conditional upon compliance with all of the following conditions—

(a) that the exempted parent and all of its subsidiary undertakings are included in consolidated accounts for a larger group drawn up to the same date, or to an earlier date in the same financial year by that other parent undertaking,

(b) that those accounts and, where appropriate, the group's annual report, are drawn up in accordance with the provisions of the Seventh Council Directive 83/349/EEC of 13 June 1983 (where applicable as modified by Council Directive 86/635/EEC of 8 December 1986 or the Directive), or in a manner equivalent to consolidated accounts and consolidated annual reports so drawn up,

(c) that the consolidated accounts are audited by one or more persons authorised to audit accounts under the law under which that other parent undertaking which draws them up is established,

(d) that the exempted parent discloses in its individual accounts that it is exempt from the obligation to prepare and deliver group accounts,

(e) that the exempted parent states in its individual accounts the name of that other parent undertaking which draws up the group accounts referred to in subparagraph (d) and—

(i) where that other undertaking is incorporated outside the State, the country in which it is incorporated, or

(ii) where that other undertaking is unincorporated, the address of its principal place of business;

(f) that the exempted parent delivers to the registrar, within the period allowed for delivering its individual accounts, copies of that other parent's group accounts and, where appropriate, of the consolidated annual report, together with the auditors' report on them, and

(g) where any document comprised in accounts and reports delivered in accordance with paragraph (f) is in a language other than the English language or the Irish language, there is annexed to the copy of that document delivered a translation of it into the English language or the Irish language, certified in the prescribed manner to be a correct translation.

(3) The exemption under this Regulation does not apply to a parent undertaking any of whose securities are admitted to trading on a regulated market of any EEA State.

(4) The Minister may require that additional information shall be provided in the consolidated accounts of that other parent undertaking or of the individual accounts of the section 2 (3) parent referred to in paragraph (1).

(5) Shares held by directors of a company for the purpose of complying with any share qualification requirement are disregarded in determining for the purposes of paragraph 1(a) whether the company is a wholly-owned subsidiary.

(6) For the purpose of paragraph (1)(b), shares held by a wholly-owned subsidiary of that other parent undertaking, or held on behalf of that other parent undertaking or a wholly-owned subsidiary, are attributed to that other parent undertaking.

(7) In paragraph (3) 'securities' includes—

(a) shares and stock,

(b) debentures, including debenture stock, loan stock, bonds, certificates of deposit and other instruments creating or acknowledging indebtedness,

(c) warrants or other instruments entitling the holder to subscribe for securities falling within subparagraph (a) or (b), and

(d) certificates or other instruments which confer –

(i) property rights in respect of a security falling within subparagraph (a), (b) or (c),

(ii) any right to acquire, dispose of, underwrite or convert a security, being a right to which the holder would be entitled if the holder held any such security to which the certificate or other instrument relates, or

(iii) a contractual right (other than an option) to acquire any such security otherwise than by subscription.][a]

Amendments

a Reg 12A inserted by reg 11 and Sch 3, Item No 9 of EC(IFRSMA)R 2005.

Definitions

'accounts': EC(IUA)R 1996, reg 2(1); 'annual return': EC(IUA)R 1996, reg 2(1); 'the Directive': EC(IUA)R 1996, reg 2(1); 'EEA State'; CA 1963, s 2(1); 'group accounts': EC(IUA)R 1996, reg 2(1); 'individual accounts': EC(IUA)R 1996, reg 2(1); 'international financial reporting standards': CA 1963, s 2(1); 'the Minister': EC(IUA)R 1996, reg 2(1); 'parent undertaking': EC(IUA)R 1996, reg 2(1); 'the Principal Act': EC(IUA)R 1996, reg 2(1); 'subsidiary': EC(IUA)R 1996, reg 2(1); 'undertaking': EC(IUA)R 1996, reg 2(1) & EC(CGA)R 1992, reg 3(1).

Notes

Exemptions for parent undertakings included in non-EEA group accounts: EC(IUA)R 1996, reg 12A sets out the conditions under which a parent company which itself is a subsidiary of a non EEA parent company is exempt from the requirement to prepare group accounts. That non-EEA parent company must itself produce group accounts which incorporate the Irish entity and all of its subsidiaries. In particular, to avail of this exemption the group accounts of the non-EEA parent must be drawn up in accordance with the provisions of the Seventh Company Law Directive (83/349/EEC) (where applicable as modified by Directive 91/674/EEC) or in a manner equivalent. Use of this exemption therefore requires an analysis of the particular set of consolidated accounts to determine whether they are drawn up in a manner that is consistent with the Seventh Directive.

Guidance on conducting such an assessment is contained in a pronouncement by the Urgent Issues Task Force of the Accounting Standards Board (UITF), UITF abstract 43. UITF 43 also concludes that consolidated accounts of the higher parent prepared in accordance with Generally Accepted Accounting Principles (GAAP) of certain other jurisdictions, namely US GAAP. Canadian GAAP, and Japanese GAAP will normally meet the test of equivalence with the Seventh Directive subject to certain considerations. The text of UITF 43 is available on the website of the Accounting Standards Board at http://www.frc.org.uk/asb.

---

13 Financial holding undertakings

(1) The obligation to prepare group accounts in accordance with Regulation 10 shall also apply to a parent undertaking, including a parent undertaking to whom Regulation 3 does not apply—

(a) which does not itself carry on any material business apart from the acquisition, management and disposal of interests in subsidiaries, and

(b) whose principal subsidiaries are wholly or mainly undertakings to which these Regulations apply.

(2) In paragraph (I), the management of interests in subsidiaries includes the provision of service to such subsidiaries and a parent undertaking's principal subsidiaries are those subsidiaries of the undertaking whose results or financial position would principally affect the figures shown in the group accounts.

Definitions

'group accounts': EC(IUA)R 1996, reg 2(1); 'parent undertaking': EC(IUA)R 1996, reg 2(1); 'undertaking': EC(IUA)R 1996, reg 2(1) & EC(CGA)R 1992, reg 3(1).

Notes

Financial holding undertakings: See the notes to reg 10.

---

14 Directors' Report

(1) In the case of a parent undertaking preparing group accounts in accordance with these Regulations, the report of the directors of that undertaking under section 158 of the Principal Act, shall contain, in addition to the information specified in that section, the following information:

[(a) a fair review of the development and performance of the undertaking's business and of its position and, in relation to its subsidiaries, if any, of the development and performance of their business and of their position, during the financial year ending with the relevant balance sheet date together with a description of the principal risks and uncertainties that they face, which review—

(i) shall be a balanced and comprehensive analysis of the development and performance of the undertaking's business and of its position and, in relation to its subsidiaries, if any, of the development and performance of their business and of their position, consistent with the size and complexity of the business;

(ii) to the extent necessary for an understanding of the undertaking's development, performance or position, and that of its subsidiaries, if any, shall include an analysis of financial, and, where appropriate, non-financial key performance indicators relevant to the particular business, including information relevant to environmental and employee matters, and, where appropriate, the report shall include additional explanations of amounts included in the annual accounts;][a]

(b) particulars of any important events affecting the parent undertaking or any of its subsidiary undertakings which have occurred since the end of that year;

(c) an indication of likely future developments in the business of the parent undertaking and its subsidiary undertakings, taken as a group;

(d) an indication of the activities, if any, of the parent undertaking and its subsidiary undertakings, taken as a group, in the field of research and development, and

(e) the number and nominal value of shares in the parent undertaking held by the undertaking itself, by its subsidiary undertakings or by a person acting in his or her own name but on behalf of the undertaking or subsidiary.

(2) The information required by subparagraph (1)(e) may be given in the notes to the group accounts.

(3) This report shall be annexed to the group's annual report.

Amendments

a Paragraph (a) of reg 14(1) substituted by reg 11 and Sch 3, Item No 10 of EC(IFRSMA)R 2005.

Definitions

'group accounts': EC(IUA)R 1996, reg 2(1); 'parent undertaking': EC(IUA)R 1996, reg 2(1); 'the Principal Act': EC(IUA)R 1996, reg 2(1); 'subsidiary': EC(IUA)R 1996, reg 2(1); 'undertaking': EC(IUA)R 1996, reg 2(1) & EC(CGA)R 1992, reg 3(1).

Notes

Directors' report: This reg applies only to the directors' report of a parent undertaking which is preparing group accounts. In all other cases the contents of the directors' report are as set out in CA 1963, s 158 & C(A)A 1986, ss 13 & 14. See also notes thereon.

[14A Corporate Governance Statement

(1) Where a parent undertaking which has its securities admitted to trading on a regulated market is preparing group accounts the corporate governance statement included in the report by the directors of that undertaking under section 158 of the Principal Act, shall contain, in addition to the information specified in that section, a description of the main features of the internal control and risk management systems of that parent undertaking and its subsidiaries, taken as a whole, in relation to the process for preparing such group accounts for the parent undertaking and its subsidiaries taken as a whole.

(2) Where the consolidated annual report and the annual report are presented as a single report the description referred to in paragraph (1) shall be included in the section of the report by the directors referred to in paragraph (1) containing the corporate governance statement.

(3)Where a parent undertaking referred to in paragraph (1) produces a corporate governance statement in the form of a separate report published in conjunction with the annual report in accordance with section 158 of the Principal Act, the description required by paragraph (1) shall form part of that separate report.

(4) In paragraph (1), 'regulated market' has the meaning assigned to it by Directive 2004/39/EC.][a]

Amendments

a Regulation 14A inserted by European Communities (Directive 2006/46/EC) Regulations 2009, reg 22.

15 Non-application of Principal Act

[Sections 151, 152, 158 (4) and (5) and 191 of the Principal Act shall not apply to a company to which Regulation 10 applies.][a]

Amendments

a Words substituted by reg 11 and Sch 3, Item No 11 of EC(IFRSMA)R 2005.

Definitions

'the Principal Act': EC(IUA)R 1996, reg 2(1); 'undertaking': EC(IUA)R 1996, reg 2(1) & EC(CGA)R 1992, reg 3(1).

16 Auditors' Report

[(1)][a] It shall be the duty of the auditors of a parent undertaking, in preparing the report on group accounts required by section 193 of the Act of 1990, to consider whether the information given in the report of the directors on the state of affairs of the parent undertaking and its subsidiary undertakings, as a group, relating to the financial year concerned is consistent with the group accounts for that year and the auditors shall state in their report whether, in their opinion, such information is consistent with those accounts.

[(2) Where a parent undertaking referred to in Regulation 14A produces a corporate governance statement under section 158 of the Principal Act, the auditors of that parent undertaking, when preparing a report required by section 193 of the Act of 1990 shall—

(a) provide an opinion as to whether the description of the main features of the internal control and risk management systems of the parent undertaking and its subsidiaries, as a group, in relation to the process for preparing consolidated accounts, is consistent with their evaluation and testing of the relevant systems for the purposes of preparing the report or such group accounts, and

(b) consider whether, in their opinion, the description referred to in paragraph (a) is consistent with their evaluation and testing of the systems referred to in paragraph (a).][b]

Amendments

a Regulation 16 renumbered by European Communities (Directive 2006/46/EC) Regulations 2009, reg 23.

b Regulation 16(2) inserted by European Communities (Directive 2006/46/EC) Regulations 2009, reg 23.

Definitions

'the Act of 1990': EC(IUA)R 1996, reg 2(1); 'group accounts': EC(IUA)R 1996, reg 2(1); 'parent undertaking': EC(IUA)R 1996, reg 2(1); 'subsidiary': EC(IUA)R 1996, reg 2(1); 'undertaking': EC(IUA)R 1996, reg 2(1) & EC(CGA)R 1992, reg 3(1).

Notes

Contents of auditors' report: See CA 1990, s 193 and the notes thereto.

---

17 Documents to be annexed to annual return of parent undertaking

(1) Subject to the provisions of these Regulations, copies of the following documents shall be documents to be annexed to the annual return of a parent undertaking:

(a) the group accounts, in respect of the period to which the return relates, drawn up by the parent undertaking in accordance with these Regulations;

(b) the report of the directors, in respect of the period to which the return relates, required by Regulation 14;

(c) the auditors' report, in respect of the period to which the return relates, referred to in Regulation 16;

and each such copy document shall be certified both by a director and the secretary of the parent undertaking to be a true copy of such accounts or reports, as the case may be.

(2) Where any document annexed to the annual return under this Regulation is in a language other than the English language or the Irish language, there shall be annexed to each such document a translation in the English language or the Irish language certified in the prescribed manner to be a correct translation.

Definitions

'annual return': EC(IUA)R 1996, reg 2(1); 'group accounts': EC(IUA)R 1996, reg 2(1); 'parent undertaking': EC(IUA)R 1996, reg 2(1).

Notes

Duty to make annual return and contents thereof: See CA 1963, ss 125–129 and the notes thereto.

---

18 Publication of accounts in full or abbreviated form

(1) Where a parent undertaking publishes its full group accounts, the auditors' report under Regulation 16 in respect of those accounts shall also be published by the parent undertaking.

(2) Where a parent undertaking publishes abbreviated group accounts relating to any financial year, it shall also publish a statement indicating—

(a) that the group accounts are not the group accounts, copies of which are required by these Regulations to be annexed to the annual return,

(b) whether the copies of the group accounts so required to be annexed have in fact been so annexed,

(c) whether the auditors of the parent undertaking have made a report under section 193 of the Act of 1990 in respect of the group accounts of the parent undertaking which relate to any financial year with which the abbreviated group accounts purport to deal,

[(d) whether any matters referred to in the auditors' report were qualified or unqualified, or whether the auditors' report included a reference to any matters to which the auditors drew attention by way of emphasis without qualifying the report.][a]

(3) Where a parent undertaking publishes abbreviated group accounts, it shall not publish with those accounts the report of the auditors mentioned in subparagraph (2)(c) of this Regulation.

(4) In this Regulation—

"abbreviated group accounts", in relation to a parent undertaking, means any group balance sheet or group profit and loss account, or summary or abstract of a group balance sheet or group profit and loss account, relating to a financial year of the parent undertaking which is published by the parent undertaking otherwise than as part of the full group accounts of the parent undertaking and its subsidiary undertakings for that financial year;

"full group accounts". in relation to a parent undertaking, means group accounts and the report of the directors of the parent undertaking referred to in Regulation 14:

"publish", in relation to a document, includes issue, circulate or otherwise make it available for public inspection in a manner calculated to invite the public generally, or any class of members of the public, to read the document, and cognate words shall be construed accordingly.

Amendments

a Paragraph 2(d) substituted by reg 11 and Sch 3, Item No 12 of EC(IFRSMA)R 2005.

Definitions

'accounts': EC(IUA)R 1996, reg 2(1); 'the Act of 1990': EC(IUA)R 1996, reg 2(1); 'annual return': EC(IUA)R 1996, reg 2(1); 'group accounts': EC(IUA)R 1996, reg 2(1); 'parent undertaking': EC(IUA)R 1996, reg 2(1); 'subsidiary': EC(IUA)R 1996, reg 2(1); 'undertaking': EC(IUA)R 1996, reg 2(1) & EC(CGA)R 1992, reg 3(1).

Notes

Publication of accounts: The reference to publication in reg 18 is to situations such as the publishing of the full or abbreviated accounts of the company in a national newspaper, rather than to the filing of accounts with the annual return.

Similar obligations are imposed with regard to the publication of annual accounts.[1]

1 EC(IUA)R 1996, reg 9.

---

19 Offences

(1) If an undertaking to which these Regulations apply fails after the making of these Regulations, to comply with a provision of these Regulations, the undertaking and every

officer of the undertaking who is in default shall be guilty of an offence and shall be liable on summary conviction to a fine not exceeding [€1,904.61].[a]

(2) (a) If any person, being a director of an undertaking to which these Regulations apply, fails. after the making of these Regulations, to take all reasonable steps to secure compliance with a requirement of these Regulations. that person shall be guilty of an offence and shall be liable on summary conviction to imprisonment for a term not exceeding 12 months, or, at the discretion of the court, to a fine not exceeding [€1,904.61],[a] or to both.

(b) In any proceedings against a person for an offence under this paragraph, it shall be a defence for a director to prove that he or she had reasonable grounds to believe and did believe that a competent and reliable person was charged with the duty of ensuring that the provisions of these Regulations were complied with and that the latter person was in a position to discharge that duty, and a person shall not be liable to be sentenced to imprisonment for an offence under the said paragraph (2) unless, in the opinion of the court, the offence was committed wilfully.

(3) If after the making of these Regulations, any person in any balance sheet, profit and loss account, report, note or other document required by or for the purposes of any provision of these Regulations wilfully makes a statement false in any material particular, knowing it to be false, that person shall be guilty of an offence and shall be liable on summary conviction, to imprisonment for a term not exceeding 12 months or to a fine not exceeding [€1,904.61][a] or to both.

(4) In this section "director" and "officer" includes any person in accordance with whose instructions or directions the directors of the undertaking are accustomed to act.

Amendments

a £1,000 increased to £1,500 by CA 1990, s 240(7) as inserted by CLEA 2001, s 104(c), and converted to €1,904.61 by Council Regulations (EC) No 1103/97, No 974/98 and No 2866/98 and the Economic and Monetary Union Act 1998, s 6.

Definitions

'officer in default': CA 1963, s 383; 'undertaking': EC(IUA)R 1996, reg 2(1) & EC(CGA)R 1992, reg 3(1).

Notes

Meaning of 'officer' and 'director': The definition of 'officer' and 'director' for the purposes of reg 19 is deemed to include any person in accordance with whose directions or instructions the directors of the company are accustomed to act. This definition is similar to that of 'shadow director' contained in CA 1990, s 27. Notably, however, unlike CA 1990, s 27, there is no saving provision for circumstances where the directors are accustomed to so act by reason only that they do so on advice given by the person in a professional capacity. It is at least arguable therefore that if the directors are accustomed to act on the professional advice of an accountant regarding, for example, the filing of the annual return and the annexing of documents thereto, that accountant could be regarded as being a 'director' or 'officer' for the purposes of reg 19.

1 EC(IUA)R 1996, reg 19(4).

20 Repeals and Amendments

(1) Section 7(4) of the Assurance Companies Act, 1909, (c. 49) and section 128(4)(b) of the Principal Act are hereby repealed.

(2) The Act of 1986 is hereby amended—

(a) in section (2) by the substitution of the following subsection for subsection (3):

"(3) Sections 3 to 6, 8, 12, 17, 18 and 24 of this Act do not apply in relation to undertakings to which the European Communities (Insurance Undertakings: Accounts) Regulations 1996 (No. 23 of 1996) apply by virtue of regulation 3 of those Regulations."

(b) In subsection (I) of section 7 by the insertion of the following subparagraph after subparagraph (ii) (inserted by the European Communities (Credit Institutions: Accounts) Regulations, 1992 (S.I. No. 294 of 1992)) of paragraph (a):

"(iii) in the case of an undertaking to which subsection (3) of section 2 of this Act applies, a copy of the balance sheet and profit and loss account of the undertaking drawn up in accordance with the European Communities (Insurance Undertakings: Accounts) Regulations, 1996."

Definitions

'the Act of 1986': EC(IUA)R 1996, reg 2(1); 'the Principal Act': EC(IUA)R 1996, reg 2(1); 'undertaking': EC(IUA)R 1996, reg 2(1) & EC(CGA)R 1992, reg 3(1).

SCHEDULE

FORM AND CONTENTS OF ACCOUNTS OF INSURANCE UNDERTAKINGS

PART I

THE REQUIRED FORMATS FOR ACCOUNTS

Chapters 1

General Rules

1. References in this Part of the Schedule to the items listed in the formats set out in this Part are references to those items read together with any notes following the formats which apply to any of those items.

2. (a) A number in brackets following any item in, or any heading to, the formats set out in this Part is a reference to the note of that number in the notes following the formats.

(b) In the notes following the formats the heading of each note gives the required heading or subheading for the item to which it applies and a reference to any letters and numbers assigned to that item in the formats set out in this Part.

3. (1) Items to which arabic numbers are assigned in the balance sheet format set out in Chapter 2 of this Part (except for items concerning technical provisions and the reinsurers' share of technical provisions), and items to which lower case letters are assigned in the profit and loss account format so set out (except for items I.1, I.4, II.1, II.5 and II.6) may be combined in an undertaking's accounts for any financial year in any case where—

(a) the individual amounts of such items are not material to assessing the state of affairs or profit and loss of the undertaking for the financial year concerned, or

(b) in any case where the combination of such items facilitates that assessment.

(2) Where items are combined in an undertaking's accounts pursuant to subparagraph (1), the individual amounts of any items so combined shall be disclosed in a note to the accounts.

Definitions

'accounts': EC(IUA)R 1996, reg 2(1); 'undertaking': EC(IUA)R 1996, reg 2(1) & EC(CGA)R 1992, reg 3(1).

4.(1) Funds of a group pension fund within the meaning of subparagraphs (c) and (d) of paragraph (2) of Article 1 of Council Directive 791267/EEC of March 1979[C] which an insurance undertaking administers in its own name but on behalf of third parties shall be shown in the balance sheet if the undertaking acquires legal title to the assets concerned and the total amount of such assets and liabilities shall be shown separately or in the notes to the accounts, broken down according to the various assets and liabilities items.

(2) Assets acquired in the name of and on behalf of third parties shall not be shown in the balance sheet.

Definitions

'accounts': EC(IUA)R 1996, reg 2(1); 'undertaking': EC(IUA)R 1996, reg 2(1) & EC(CGA)R 1992, reg 3(1).

5. The provisions of this Schedule which relate to life assurance shall apply to health insurance written by undertakings which write only health insurance and which is transacted exclusively or principally according to the technical principles of life assurance.

Definitions

'undertaking': EC(IUA)R 1996, reg 2(1) & EC(CGA)R 1992, reg 3(1).

6.[(1) The notes to the profit and loss account shall show—

(a) dividends paid (other than dividends for which a liability existed at the immediately preceding balance sheet date) or which the company is liable to pay,

(b) separately, any transfers between the profit and loss account and other reserves,

(c) any increase or reduction in the balance on the profit and loss account since the immediately preceding financial year,

(d) the profit or loss brought forward at the beginning of the financial year, and

(e) the profit or loss carried forward at the end of the financial year.

(1A) There shall be shown in the notes to the accounts the aggregate amount of any dividends proposed before the date of approval of the accounts which have not been shown in the notes to the profit and loss account in accordance with subparagraph (1).][a]

(2) In the profit and loss account format set out below in Section B of Chapter 2 of this Part—

(a) the heading "Technical account – non-life business" is for those classes of direct insurance which are within the scope of the European Communities (Non-Life Insurance) Regulations, 1976 (S.I. No. 115 of 1976), the European Communities (Non-Life Insurance) Framework Regulations, 1994 (S.I. No. 359 of 1994) and for the corresponding classes of reinsurance business. and

(b) the heading Technical account— life assurance business is for those classes of direct insurance which are within the scope of the European Communities (Life Assurance) Regulations, 1984 (S.I. No. 57 of 1984), the European Communities (Life Assurance) Framework Regulations, 1994 (S.I. No. 360 of 1994) and for the corresponding classes of reinsurance business.

(3) Undertakings whose activities consist wholly of reinsurance or whose activities consist of direct non-life insurance and reinsurance may use the format "Technical account non life business" for all of their business.

Amendments

a Paragraph 6(1) substituted by reg 11 and Sch 3, Item No 13 of EC(IFRSMA)R 2005.

Definitions

'undertaking': EC(IUA)R 1996, reg 2(1) & EC(CGA)R 1992, reg 3(1).

Chapter 2

Section A—The Balance Sheet

FORMAT

ASSETS

A. Called up share capital not paid (1)

B. Intangible assets (2)

- I. Goodwill (3)

C. Investments

- I. Land and buildings (4)
- II. Investments in group undertakings and participating interests:
  1. Shares in group undertakings
  2. Debt securities issued by, and loans to group undertakings
  3. Participating interests
  4. Debt securities issued by, and loans to. undertakings in which the undertaking has a participating interest
- III. Other financial investments:
  1. Shares and other variable-yield securities and units in unit trusts
  2. Debt securities and other fixed income securities (5)

3. Participation in investment pools (6)
4. Loans secured by mortgages (7)
5. Other loans (7)
6. Deposits with credit institutions (8)
7. Other (9)

IV. Deposits with ceding undertakings (10)

D. Investments for the benefit of life assurance policyholders who bear the investment risk (11)

Da. Reinsurers' share of technical provisions (12)

1. Provision for unearned premiums
2. Life assurance provision
3. Claims outstanding
4. Provision for bonuses and rebates (unless shown under (2).
5. Other technical provisions
6. Technical provisions for life-assurance policies where the investment risk is borne by the policyholders

E. Debtors (13)

I. Debtors arising out of direct insurance operations
   1. Policyholders
   2. Intermediaries

II. Debtors arising out of reinsurance operations

III. Other debtors

IV. Called up share capital not paid (1)

F. Other assets

I. Tangible assets and stocks
   1. Plant and machinery
   2. Fixtures, fittings, tools and equipment
   3. Payments on account (other than deposits paid on land and buildings) and assets (other than buildings) in course of construction.
   4. Raw materials and consumables
   5. Work in progress
   6. Finished goods and goods for resale

II. Cash at bank and in hand

III. Own shares (14)

IV. Other (15)

G. Prepayments and accrued income

I. Accrued interest and rent (16)

II. Deferred acquisition costs (17)

III. Other prepayments and accrued income

LIABILITIES

A. Capital and reserves

I. Called up share capital or equivalent funds (18)

II. Share premium account

III. Revaluation reserve

IV. Reserves (19)

1. The capital redemption reserve fund
2. Reserves for own shares
3. Reserves provided for by the articles of association
4. Other reserves

V. Profit or loss brought forward

VI. Profit or loss for the financial year

B. Subordinated liabilities (20)

Ba. Fund for future appropriations (21)

C. Technical provisions (22)

1. Provisions for unearned premiums: (23)
   (a) gross amount
   (b) reinsurance amount(-)(12)

2. Life assurance provision: (23) (25) (29)
   (a) gross amount
   (b) reinsurance amount(-)(12)

3. Claims outstanding: (26)
   (a) gross amount
   (b) reinsurance amount(-)(12)

4. Provision for bonuses and rebates: (27)
   (a) gross amount
   (b) reinsurance amount(-)(12)

5. Equalisation provision (28)

6. Other technical provisions: (24)
   (a) gross amount
   (b) reinsurance amount(-)(12)

D. Technical provisions for life assurance policies where the investment risk is borne by the policyholders (29)
   (a) gross amount
   (b) reinsurance amount(-)(12)

E.[Provisions for other risks][a]

1. Provisions for pensions and similar obligations
2. Provisions for taxation
3. Other provisions

F.Deposits received from reinsurers (30)

G.Creditors

I. Creditors arising out of direct insurance operations
II. Creditors arising out of reinsurance operations
III. Debenture loans
IV. Amounts owed to credit institutions
V. Other creditors including tax and social welfare

H.Accruals and deferred income

NOTES ON THE BALANCE SHEET FORMAT

(1) Called-up share capital not paid
(Assets items A and E.IV)

This item may be shown in either of the positions given in the format.

(2) Intangible assets
(Assets item B)

Amounts in respect of assets shall only be included in an undertaking's balance sheet under this item if either—

(a) the assets were acquired for valuable consideration and are not required to be shown under goodwill, or
(b) the assets in question were created by the undertaking itself.

Amendments

a Words substituted by reg 11 and Sch 3, Item No 12(b) of EC(IFRSMA)R 2005.

Definitions

'undertaking': EC(IUA)R 1996, reg 2(1) & EC(CGA)R 1992, reg 3(1).

(3) Goodwill
(Assets item B.I)

Amounts representing goodwill shall only be included to the extent that the goodwill was acquired for valuable consideration.

(4) Land and buildings
(Assets item C.l)

The amount of any land and buildings occupied by the undertaking for its own activities shall be shown separately.

Definitions

'undertaking': EC(IUA)R 1996, reg 2(1) & EC(CGA)R 1992, reg 3(1).

(5) Debt securities and other fixed income securities
(Assets item C.III.2)

This item shall comprise negotiable debt securities and other fixed income securities issued by credit institutions. other undertakings or public bodies, insofar as they are not covered by Assets item C.II.2 or C.II.4.

Securities bearing interest rates that vary in accordance with specific factors, for example the interest rate on the inter-bank market or on the Euro market, shall also be regarded as debt securities and other fixed income securities and so be included under this item.

Definitions

'undertaking': EC(IUA)R 1996, reg 2(1) & EC(CGA)R 1992, reg 3(1).

(6) Participation in investment pools
(Assets item C.III.3)

This item shall comprise shares held by the undertaking in joint investments constituted by several undertakings or pension funds, the management of which has been entrusted to one of those undertakings or to one of those pension funds.

Definitions

'undertaking': EC(IUA)R 1996, reg 2(1) & EC(CGA)R 1992, reg 3(1).

(7) Loans secured by mortgages and other loans
(Assets items C.III.4 and C.III.5)

Loans to policy holders for which the policy is the main security shall be included under "Other loans" and their amount shall be disclosed in the notes to the accounts. Loans guaranteed by mortgages shall be shown as such even where they are also secured by insurance policies. Where the amount of "Other loans" not secured by policies is material, an appropriate breakdown shall be given in the notes to the accounts.

Definitions

'accounts': EC(IUA)R 1996, reg 2(1).

(8) Deposits with credit institutions

(Assets item C.111.6)

This item shall comprise sums the withdrawal of which is subject to a time restriction. Sums deposited with no such restriction shall be shown under Assets item F.II even if they bear interest.

(9) Other
(Assets item C.III.7)

This item shall comprise those investments which are not covered by Assets items C.III.1 to 6. Where the amount of such investments is significant, they shall be disclosed in the notes to the accounts.

Definitions
'accounts': EC(IUA)R 1996, reg 2(1).

(10) Deposits with ceding undertakings
(Assets item C.IV)

Where the undertaking accepts reinsurance this item shall comprise amounts, owed by the ceding undertakings and corresponding to guarantees, which are deposited with those ceding undertakings or with third parties or which are retained by those undertakings.

These amounts may not be combined with other amounts owed by the ceding insurer to the reinsurer or set off against amounts owed by the reinsurer to the ceding insurer.

Securities deposited with ceding undertakings or third parties which remain the property of the undertaking accepting reinsurance shall be entered in the undertaking's accounts as an investment, under the appropriate item.

Definitions

'accounts': EC(IUA)R 1996, reg 2(1); 'undertaking': EC(IUA)R 1996, reg 2(1) & EC(CGA)R 1992, reg 3(1).

(11) Investments for the benefit of life assurance policyholders who bear the investment risk
(Assets item D)

In respect of life assurance this item shall comprise, on the one hand, investments the value of which is used to determine the value of or the return on policies relating to an investment fund, and on the other hand, investments serving as cover for liabilities which are determined by reference to an index. This item shall also comprise investments which are held on behalf of the members of a tontine and are intended for distribution among them.

(12) Reinsurance amounts

(Assets item Da)

(Liabilities items C.1(b), 2(b), 3(b), 4(b) and 6(b) and D(b)).

The reinsurance amounts may be shown either under Assets item D(a) or under Liabilities items C.l(b), 2(b), 3(b), 4(b) and 6(b) and D(b).

The reinsurance amounts shall comprise the actual or estimated amounts which, under contractual reinsurance arrangements, are deducted from the gross amounts of technical provisions. Where reinsurance amounts are shown as assets under item Da, they shall be sub-divided as shown. Notwithstanding paragraph 3 of this Part, these items shall not be combined. The disclosure of reinsurance amounts shall be in the same form from one accounting year to the next. If the directors decide that a change is necessary, the reason for that change should be disclosed in the notes together with a statement of what the position would have been had the original treatment been retained.

As regards the provision for unearned premiums, the reinsurance amounts shall be calculated according to the methods referred to in paragraph 24 of Part II of this Schedule or in accordance with the terms of the reinsurance policy.

(13) Debtors

(Assets item E)

Amounts owed by group undertaking and undertakings in which the undertaking has a participating interest shall be shown separately as sub-items of Assets items E.I, E.II and E.III.

Definitions

'participating interest': EC(IUA)R 1996, reg 2(1); 'undertaking': EC(IUA)R 1996, reg 2(1) & EC(CGA)R 1992, reg 3(1).

---

(14) Own Shares

(Assets item F.111)

The nominal value of the shares shall be shown separately under this item.

(15) Other

(Assets item F.IV)

This item shall comprise those assets which are not covered by Assets items F.I, II and III. Where such assets are material they shall be disclosed in the notes to the accounts.

Definitions

'accounts': EC(IUA)R 1996, reg 2(1).

---

(16) Accrued interest and rent

(Assets item G.I)

This item shall comprise those items that represent interest and rent that have been earned up to the balance-sheet date but have not yet become receivable.

(17) Deferred acquisition costs

(Assets item G.II)

The costs of acquiring insurance policies which are incurred during the financial year but which relate to a subsequent financial year (referred to as "deferred acquisition costs") shall be treated as follows:

(a) Costs incurred in respect of non-life shall be disclosed under this item and shall be calculated on a basis compatible with that used for unearned premiums:

(b) (i) Costs incurred in respect of life assurance business shall be deferred. Such deferral should be over such a period as is recognised to be prudent.

(ii) Costs incurred in respect of life assurance may be either disclosed under this item on the balance sheet or may be deducted by a recognised actuarial method from the mathematical reserves; where the latter method is used, the amounts deducted from the provisions shall be disclosed in the notes to the accounts.

(iii) The method of treatment of deferred acquisition costs in the accounts of a life assurance undertaking, should be the same from one financial year to the next. If, in the opinion of the directors of the undertaking, a change is necessary, the reasons for that change should be disclosed in the notes together with a statement of what the position would have been had the original method been retained.

Definitions

'accounts': EC(IUA)R 1996, reg 2(1); 'undertaking': EC(IUA)R 1996, reg 2(1) & EC(CGA)R 1992, reg 3(1).

---

(18) Called up capital or equivalent funds

(Liabilities item A.I)

This item shall comprise all amounts which are regarded, in accordance with the Companies Acts, 1963 to 1990, as equity capital subscribed and fully paid up or subscribed and partly paid up, to the extent paid up.

(19) Reserves

(Liabilities item A. IV)

Reserves shall be shown separately, as sub items of liabilities item A.IV in the balance sheet except for the revaluation reserve, which shall be shown as a liability under A.III.

Should it be considered necessary, the [Bank][a] may, in the future under this item, require other types of reserves for insurance undertakings not covered by Council Directive No. 78/660/EEC.

Amendments

a 'Bank' substituted for 'Minister' by CBFSAIA 2003, s 35 and Sch 2, Pt 16. Item 4.

Definitions

'the Minister': EC(IUA)R 1996, reg 2(1); 'undertaking': EC(IUA)R 1996, reg 2(1) & EC(CGA)R 1992, reg 3(1).

(20) Subordinated liabilities
(Liabilities item B)

This item shall comprise all liabilities, whether or not represented by certificates, in respect of which there is a contractual obligation that, in the event of winding up or of bankruptcy, they are to be repaid only after the claims of all other creditors have been met.

(21) Fund for future appropriations
(Liabilities item Ba)

This item shall comprise all funds the allocation of which either to policy holders or to shareholders has not been determined by the end of the financial year.

Transfers to and from this item shall be shown in item II.12a (Transfers to or from the fund for future appropriation) in the profit and loss account.

(22) Technical provisions
(Liabilities item C)

Regulation 7(c)(ii) shall apply to the technical provisions, subject to Note (12) and Notes (23) to (28).

(23) Provision for unearned premiums
(Liabilities items C.1 and C.2)

In the case of life assurance the provision for unearned premiums may be included in Liabilities item C.2 rather than in this item.

The provision for unearned premiums shall comprise the amount representing that part of gross premiums written which is estimated to be earned in the following financial year or in subsequent financial years.

Where, in accordance with Note (24) this item also includes the amount of the provision for unexpired risks, the description of the item shall be "Provision for unearned premiums and unexpired risks".

(24) Other technical provisions
(Liabilities item C.6)

This item shall include the provision for unexpired risks. being the amount set aside in addition to unearned premiums in respect of risks to be borne by the insurance undertaking after the end of the financial year, in order to provide for all claims and expenses in connection with insurance contracts in force in excess of the related unearned premiums and any premiums receivable on those contracts. However, the provision for unexpired risks may be added to the provision for unearned premiums under item C.l. Where the amount of unexpired risks is material, it shall be disclosed separately in the notes to the accounts.

Ageing reserves should be disclosed under this item.

Definitions

'accounts': EC(IUA)R 1996, reg 2(1); 'undertaking': EC(IUA)R 1996, reg 2(1) & EC(CGA)R 1992, reg 3(1).

---

(25) Life assurance provision

(Liabilities item C.2)

This item shall comprise the actuarially estimated value of the undertaking's liabilities including bonuses already declared and after deducting the actuarial value of future premiums, excluding amounts covered by Note 29.

Definitions

'undertaking': EC(IUA)R 1996, reg 2(1) & EC(CGA)R 1992, reg 3(1).

---

(26) Claims outstanding

(Liabilities item C.3)

This item shall comprise the total estimated ultimate cost to the undertaking of settling all claims arising from events which have occurred up to the end of the financial year, whether reported or not, less amounts already paid in respect of such claims.

Definitions

'undertaking': EC(IUA)R 1996, reg 2(1) & EC(CGA)R 1992, reg 3(1).

---

(27) Provision for bonuses and rebates

(Liabilities item C.4)

This item shall comprise amounts intended for policy holders or contract beneficiaries by way of bonuses and rebates as defined in Note (5) on the profit and loss account format to the extent that such amounts have not been credited to policy holders or contract beneficiaries or included in Liabilities item Ba or in Liabilities item C.2.

(28) Equalisation provision

(Liabilities item C.5)

This item shall comprise any amounts required by law to be set aside by an undertaking to equalise fluctuations in loss ratios in future years or to provide for special risks.

An undertaking which otherwise constitutes reserves, falling to be included under liabilities item A.IV to equalise fluctuations in loss ratios in future years or to provide for special risks shall disclose that fact in the notes to the accounts.

Definitions

'accounts': EC(IUA)R 1996, reg 2(1); 'undertaking': EC(IUA)R 1996, reg 2(1) & EC(CGA)R 1992, reg 3(1).

(29) Technical provisions for life assurance policies where the investment risk is borne by the policyholders

(Liabilities items D and C.2)

This item shall comprise technical provisions constituted to cover liabilities relating to investment in the context of the assurance policies for which the policy holder bears the risk, the value of or the return on which is determined by reference to investments or by reference to an index.

Any additional technical provisions constituted to cover death risks, operating expenses or other risks (such as benefits payable at the maturity date or guaranteed surrender values) shall be included under Liabilities item C.2.

This item shall also comprise technical provisions representing the obligations of a tontine's organiser in relation to its members.

(30) Deposits received from reinsurers

(Liabilities item F)

Where the undertaking cedes reinsurance this item shall comprise amounts deposited by or withheld from other insurance undertakings under re insurance contracts. These amounts may not be merged with other amounts owed to or by those other undertakings.

Where the undertaking cedes reinsurance and has received as a deposit securities which have been transferred to its ownership, this item shall comprise the amount owed by the undertaking by virtue of the deposit.

Definitions

'undertaking': EC(IUA)R 1996, reg 2(1) & EC(CGA)R 1992, reg 3(1).

Section B—The Profit and Loss Account

FORMAT

I. TECHNICAL ACCOUNT— NON-LIFE INSURANCE

1. Earned premiums, net of reinsurance:

(a) gross premiums written (1) ——

(b) outward reinsurance premiums (-)(2) —— ——

(c) change in the gross provision for unearned premiums and in the gross provision for unexpired risks (+/-)(3) ——

(d) change in the provision for unearned premiums, reinsurers' share (+/-)(3)

2. Allocated investment return transferred from the non-technical account (Item III.6)(8)(9)

(a) allocated by class of business

accident and health

motor

marine, aviation and transport

fire and other damage to property

liability business

miscellaneous pecuniary loss

(b) total:

3. Other technical income, net of reinsurance

4. Claims incurred, net of reinsurance: (4)

(a) claims paid

(aa) gross amount

(bb) reinsurers' share(-)

(b) change in the provision for claims

(aa) gross amount

(bb) reinsurers' share(-)

5. Changes in other technical provisions, net of reinsurance, not shown under other headings (+/-).

6. Bonuses and rebates, net of reinsurance (5)

7. Net operating expenses:

(a) acquisition costs (6)

(b) change in deferred acquisition costs (+/-)

(c) administrative expenses (7)

(d) reinsurance commissions and profit participation (+/-)

7a Investment charges (8)

(a) By class of business:

accident and health

motor

marine, aviation and transport

fire and other damage to property

liability business

miscellaneous pecuniary loss

(aa) investment management expenses, including interest

(bb) value adjustments in investments

(cc) Losses on the realisation of investments

(b) total:

8. Other technical charges, net of reinsurance

9. Change in the equalisation provisions (+/-)

10. Sub-total (balance on the technical account for non-life insurance business (item III.1)

II. TECHNICAL ACCOUNT – LIFE ASSURANCE BUSINESS

1. Earned premiums, net of reinsurance:

(a) gross premiums written (1)

(b) outward reinsurance premiums (-)(2)

(c) change in the provision for unearned premiums, net of reinsurance (+/-)(3)

2. Investment income: (8) (9)

(a) income from participating interests, with a separate indication of that derived from group undertakings

(b) income from other investments, with a separate indication of that derived from group undertakings

(aa) income from land and buildings

(bb) income from other investments

(c) value readjustments on investments

(d) gains on the realisation of investments

3. Unrealised gains on investments (10)

4. Other technical income, net of reinsurance

5. Claims incurred, net of reinsurance: (4)

(a) claims paid

(aa) gross amount

(bb) reinsurers' share (-)

(b) change in the provision for claims

(aa) gross amount

(bb) reinsurers' share (-)

6. Changes in other technical provisions, net of reinsurance, not shown under other headings (+/-):

(a) Life assurance provision, net of reinsurance (3)

(aa) gross amount

(bb) reinsurers' share (-)

(b) Other technical provisions, net of reinsurance

7. Bonuses and rebates, net of reinsurance (5)

8. Net operating expenses:

(a) acquisition costs (6)

(b) change in deferred acquisition costs

(c) administrative expenses (7)

(d) reinsurance commissions and profit participation

9. Investment expenses and charges: (8)

(a) investment management expenses, including interest

(b) value adjustments on investments ______

(c) losses on the realisation of investments ______

10. Unrealised losses on investments (10)

11. Other technical charges, net of reinsurance

11a. Tax attributable to the life assurance business

12. Allocated investment return transferred to the non-technical account (-) (item III.4) (9)

12a. Transfers to or from the fund for future appropriations

13. Sub-total (balance on the technical account—life assurance business) (item III.2)

III. NON-TECHNICAL ACCOUNT

1. Balance on the technical account – non-life insurance business (item I.10)

2. Balance on the technical account – life assurance business (item II.13)

3. Investment income (8)

(a) income from participating interests with a separate indication of that derived from group undertakings ______

(b) income from other investments, with a separate indication of that derived from group undertakings ______

(aa) income from land and buildings ______

(bb) income from other investments ______

(c) value readjustments on investments

(d) gains on the realisation of investments

3a. Unrealised gains on investments (10)

4. Allocated investment return transferred from the life assurance technical account (item II.12) (9)

5. Investment charges: (8)

(a) investment management expenses, including interest

(b) value adjustments on investments

(c) losses on the realisation of investments

5a. Unrealised losses on investments (10)

6. Allocated investment return transferred to the non-life insurance technical account (item I.2) (9).

7. Other income

8. Other charges, including value adjustments

9. Tax on profit or loss on ordinary activities

10. Profit or loss on ordinary activities after tax

11. Extraordinary income

12. Extraordinary charges

13. Extraordinary profit or loss

14. Tax on extraordinary profit or loss

15. Other taxes not shown under the preceding items

16. Profit or loss for the financial year

NOTES ON THE PROFIT AND LOSS ACCOUNT FORMAT

(1) Gross premiums written

(Non-life insurance technical account: item I.l.(a)).

(Life assurance technical account: item II.l.(a)).

This item shall comprise all amounts due during the financial year in respect of insurance contracts entered into regardless of the fact that such amounts may relate in whole or in part to a later financial year, and shall include *inter alia*:

(a) premiums yet to be written, where the premium calculation can be done only at the end of the year;

(b) single premiums including annuity premiums and, in life assurance business, single premiums resulting from bonus and rebate provisions insofar as they shall be considered as premium under the terms of the contract;

(c) additional premiums in the case of half-yearly, quarterly or monthly payments and additional payments from policyholders for expenses borne by the undertaking;

(d) in the case of co-insurance, the undertaking's portion of total premiums;

(e) reinsurance premiums due from ceding and retroceding insurance undertakings, including portfolio entries, after deduction of—

  (i) portfolio withdrawals credited to ceding and retroceding insurance undertakings, and

  (ii) cancellations.

The amounts to which this note relates shall not include the amounts of taxes or duties levied with premiums.

(2) Outward reinsurance premiums

(Non-life insurance technical account: item I.1.(b))

(Life assurance technical account: item II.1.(b))

This item shall comprise all premiums paid or payable in respect of outward reinsurance contracts entered into by the undertaking. Portfolio entries payable on the conclusion or amendment of outward reinsurance contracts shall be added; portfolio withdrawals receivable shall be deducted.

Definitions

'undertaking': EC(IUA)R 1996, reg 2(1) & EC(CGA)R 1992, reg 3(1).

---

(3) Change in the provision for unearned premiums, net of reinsurance

(Non-life insurance technical account: items I.1.(c) and I.1.(d))

(Life assurance technical account: items II.l.(c) and II.6.(a))

In the case of life assurance, the change in unearned premiums may be included either in item II.l(c) or in item II.6.(a) of the life assurance technical account.

(4) Claims incurred, net of reinsurance

(Non-life insurance technical account: item I.4)

(Life assurance technical account: item II.5)

This item shall comprise all payments made in respect of the financial year including the provision for claims but excluding the provision for claims for the preceding financial year.

These amounts shall include annuities, surrenders, entries and withdrawals of loss provisions to and from ceding insurance undertakings and reinsurers, external and internal claims management costs and charges for claims incurred but not reported such as are referred to in paragraphs 27(3) and 29 of Part II (Valuation Rules) of this Schedule.

Sums recoverable on the basis of subrogation and salvage within the meaning of subparagraph (7) of the said paragraph 27 shall be deducted.

Where the difference between:

(a) the loss provision made at the beginning of the year for outstanding claims incurred in previous years, and

(b) the payments made during the year on account of claims incurred in previous years and the loss provision shown at the end of the year for such outstanding claims,

is material it shall be shown in the notes to the accounts, broken down by category and amount.

Definitions

'accounts': EC(IUA)R 1996, reg 2(1); 'undertaking': EC(IUA)R 1996, reg 2(1) & EC(CGA)R 1992, reg 3(1).

---

(5) Bonuses and rebates, net of reinsurance

(Non-life insurance technical account: item I.6)

(Life assurance technical account: item II.7)

Bonuses shall comprise all amounts chargeable for the financial year which are paid or payable to policyholders and other insured parties or provided for their benefit, including amounts used to increase technical provisions or applied to the reduction of future premiums, to the extent that such amounts represent an allocation of surplus or profit arising on business as a whole or a section of business, after deduction of amounts provided in previous years which are no longer required.

Rebates shall comprise such amounts to the extent that they represent a partial refund of premiums resulting from the experience of individual contracts.

Where material, the amount charged for bonuses and that charged for rebates shall be disclosed separately in the notes to the accounts.

Definitions

'accounts': EC(IUA)R 1996, reg 2(1).

(6) Acquisition costs

(Non-life insurance technical account: item I.7.(a))

(Life assurance technical account: item II.8.(a))

This item shall comprise the costs arising from the conclusion of insurance contracts. They shall cover both direct costs, such as acquisition commissions or the cost of drawing up the insurance document or including the insurance contract in the portfolio, and indirect costs, such as advertising costs or the administrative expenses connected with the processing of proposals and the issuing of policies.

In the case of life assurance. policy renewal commissions shall be included under item II.8.(c) in the life assurance technical account.

(7) Administrative expenses

(Non-life insurance technical account: item 1.7.(c))

(Life assurance technical account: item 11.8.(c))

This item shall include the costs arising from premium collection, portfolio administration, handling of bonuses and rebates, and inward and outward reinsurance.

They shall, in particular. include staff costs and depreciation provisions in respect of office furniture and equipment insofar as these need not be shown under acquisition costs, claims incurred or investment charges.

Item 11.8.(c) shall also include policy renewal commissions in respect of life assurance.

(8) Investment income and charges

(Non-life insurance technical account: items 1.2 and 7a)

(Life assurance technical account: items II.2 and II.9)

(Non-technical account: items III.3 and III.5)

(a) Investment income and charges relating to non-life insurance shall be disclosed in the non-technical account. Investment income and those charges attributable to the non-life technical account shall be allocated to that account by class of business, grouped as in the Revenue Account of the annual returns submitted in accordance with the European Communities (Non-life Insurance Accounts) Regulations, 1977 (S.I. No. 401 of 1977). The proportion of this and the basis on which they have been allocated as between the various classes shall be disclosed in the notes to the accounts.

(b) Investment income and charges relating to life assurance shall be disclosed in the life assurance technical account.

(c) In the case of an undertaking carrying on both life assurance and non-life insurance business, investment income and charges shall, to the extent that they are directly connected with the carrying on of the life assurance business be disclosed in the life assurance technical account.

Definitions

'annual return': EC(IUA)R 1996, reg 2(1), 'undertaking': EC(IUA)R 1996, reg 2(1) & EC(CGA)R 1992, reg 3(1).

(9) Allocated investment return

(Non-life insurance technical account: item I.2)

(Life assurance technical account: item II.2)

(Non-technical account: items III.4 and III.6)

Where part of the investment return is transferred to the non-life insurance technical account, the transfer from the non-technical account shall be deducted from item III.6 and added to item I.2.

Part of the investment return disclosed in the life assurance technical account may (to the extent that it is not attributable in the life assurance fund) be transferred to the non-technical account. The amount transferred shall be deducted from item II.12 and added to item III.4.

In the case of non-life insurance, allocated return may be transferred from one part of the profit and loss account to another in accordance with best accounting practices. The amount and reasons for such transfers and the bases on which they are made shall be disclosed in the notes to the accounts.

Definitions

'accounts': EC(IUA)R 1996, reg 2(1).

(10) Unrealised gains and losses on investments

(Life assurance technical account: items II.3 and II.10)

(Non-technical account: items III.3a and III.5a)

Variations between the valuation of investments at their current value or by means of one of the methods referred to in paragraph 19 of the Schedule to the Act of 1986 and their valuation at purchase price shall be treated as follows:

(a) where they relate to investments shown as assets under D of the balance sheet format they shall be fully disclosed in items II.3 and II.10 in the profit and loss account.

(b) in life assurance business those which do not fall under paragraph *(a)* of this note may be disclosed in full or in part in items II.3 and II.10 in the profit and loss account.

(c) in non-life insurance business they may be disclosed in full or in part in items III.3a and III.5a in the profit and loss account.

In the case of both paragraphs (b) and (c) of this note, where a partial disclosure is made, that shall be disclosed in the notes to the accounts, together with the full amount of the unrealised gains or losses, as the case may be, and the reasons for which the partial disclosure was made.

Definitions

'accounts': EC(IUA)R 1996, reg 2(1); 'the Act of 1986': EC(IUA)R 1996, reg 2(1).

PART II
VALUATION RULES

Chapter 1
Historical Cost Accounting Rules

PRELIMINARY

1. Subject to paragraphs 12 to 21 of this Part, the amounts to be included in respect of all items shown in an undertaking's [Companies Act individual accounts][a] shall be determined in accordance with the rules set out in paragraphs 2 to 11 of this Part of the Schedule.

Amendments

a Words substituted by reg 11 and Sch 3, Item No 13 of EC(IFRSMA)R 2005.

Definitions

'accounts': EC(IUA)R 1996, reg 2(1); 'undertaking': EC(IUA)R 1996, reg 2(1) & EC(CGA)R 1992, reg 3(1).

General rules

2.(1) Subject to any provision for depreciation or diminution in value made in accordance with paragraph 3 the amount to be included in respect of any asset shall be its purchase price or production cost.

(2) Where investments are shown as provided in subparagraph (1), their current value shall be disclosed on the balance sheet or in the notes to the accounts.

Definitions

'accounts': EC(IUA)R 1996, reg 2(1).

3.(1) In the case of any asset included under Assets item B, (intangible assets), C.l (investments: land and buildings) or Fl (tangible assets and stocks) in the balance sheet format (set out in Chapter 2 of Part I of this Schedule) which has a limited useful economic life, the amount of—

(a) its purchase price or production cost, or

(b) where it is estimated that any such asset will have a residual value at the end of the period of its useful economic life, its cost less that estimated residual value,

shall be reduced by provisions for depreciation calculated to write off that amount systematically over the period of the asset's useful economic life.

(2) Where an asset falling to be included under Assets item C.II, C.III, C.IV or F.III in the balance sheet format (set out in Chapter 2 of Part I of this Schedule) has diminished in value, provisions for diminution in value may be made in respect of it and the amount to be included in respect of it may be reduced accordingly, and any such provisions which are not shown separately in the profit and loss account shall be disclosed (either separately or in aggregate) in a note to the accounts.

(3) Provisions for diminution in value shall be made in respect of any asset to which this paragraph applies which has diminished in value if the reduction of its value is expected to be permanent (whether its useful economic life is limited or not), and the amount to be included in respect of it shall be reduced accordingly; and any such provisions which are not shown separately in the profit and loss account shall be disclosed (either separately or in aggregate) in a note to the accounts.

(4) Where the reasons for which any provision was made in accordance with subparagraph (2) or (3) have ceased to apply to any extent, that provision shall be written back to the extent that it is no longer necessary, and any amounts written back in accordance with this subparagraph which are not shown separately in the profit and loss account shall be disclosed (either separately or in aggregate) in a note to the accounts.

Definitions

'accounts': EC(IUA)R 1996, reg 2(1).

Goodwill

4. (1) The application of paragraphs 1 to 3 in relation to goodwill (in any case where goodwill is treated as an asset) is subject to the following provisions of this paragraph.

(2) Subject to subparagraph (3), the amount of the consideration for any goodwill acquired by an undertaking shall be reduced by provisions for depreciation calculated to write off that amount systematically over a period chosen by the directors of the undertaking.

(3) The period chosen shall not exceed the useful economic life of the goodwill in question.

(4) In any case where any goodwill acquired by an undertaking is included as an asset in the undertaking's balance sheet the period chosen for writing off the consideration for that goodwill and the reasons for choosing that period shall be disclosed in a note to the accounts.

Definitions

'accounts': EC(IUA)R 1996, reg 2(1); 'undertaking': EC(IUA)R 1996, reg 2(1) & EC(CGA)R 1992, reg 3(1).

5.(1) This paragraph applies to assets included under Assets items E.I, E.II and E.III (debtors) and F.II (cash at bank and in hand) in the balance sheet.

(2) If the net realisable value of any asset referred to in subparagraph (1) is lower than its cost the amount to be included in respect of that asset shall be the net realisable value.

(3) Where the reasons for which any provision for diminution in value was made in accordance with subparagraph (2) have ceased to apply to any extent, that provision shall be written back to the extent that it is no longer necessary.

MISCELLANEOUS AND SUPPLEMENTARY PROVISIONS

Excess of money owed over value received as an asset item

6. (1) Where the amount repayable on any debt owed by an undertaking is greater than the value of the consideration received in the transaction giving rise to the debt, the amount of the difference may be treated as an asset.

(2) Where any such amount is treated as an asset, then—

(a) it shall be written off by reasonable amounts each year and shall be completely written off before repayment of the debt, and

(b) if the current amount is not shown as a separate item in the undertaking's balance sheet it shall be disclosed in a note to the accounts.

Definitions

'accounts': EC(IUA)R 1996, reg 2(1); 'undertaking': EC(IUA)R 1996, reg 2(1) & EC(CGA)R 1992, reg 3(1).

Determination of cost

7. The cost of an asset that has been acquired by the undertaking shall be determined by adding to the actual price paid any expenses incidental to its acquisition.

Definitions

'undertaking': EC(IUA)R 1996, reg 2(1) & EC(CGA)R 1992, reg 3(1).

8. (1) The cost of an asset constructed by the undertaking shall be determined by adding to the purchase price of the raw materials and consumables used the amount of the costs incurred by the undertaking which are directly attributable to the construction of that asset.

(2) In addition, there may be included in the cost of an asset constructed by the undertaking—

(a) a reasonable proportion of the costs incurred by the undertaking which are only indirectly attributable to the construction of that asset, but only to the extent that they relate to the period of construction; and

(b) interest on capital borrowed to finance the construction of that asset, to the extent that it accrues in respect of the period of construction;

provided that, in a case to which subparagraph (h) relates, the inclusion of the interest in determining the cost of that asset and the amount of the interest so included is disclosed in a note to the accounts.

Definitions

'accounts': EC(IUA)R 1996, reg 2(1); 'undertaking': EC(IUA)R 1996, reg 2(1) & EC(CGA)R 1992, reg 3(1).

9.(1) Subject to the qualification mentioned in this subparagraph, the cost of any assets which are fungible assets as defined in paragraph 15(6) of the Schedule to the Act of 1986 may be determined by the application of any of the methods mentioned in subparagraph (2) in relation to any such assets of the same class and the method chosen shall be one which appears to the directors to be appropriate in the circumstances of the undertaking.

(2) The methods to which subparagraph (1) relates are the following:

(a) the method known as "first in, first out" (FIFO);

(b) a weighted average price;

(c) any other method similar to either of the other methods mentioned in this subparagraph.

(3) Where in the case of any undertaking:

(a) the cost of assets falling to be included under any item shown in the undertaking's balance sheet has been determined by the application of any method permitted by this paragraph, and

(b) the amount shown in respect of that item differs materially from the relevant alternative amount given below in this paragraph,

the amount of that difference shall be disclosed in a note to the accounts.

(4) Subject to subparagraph (5), for the purposes of subparagraph (3)(b), the relevant alternative amount, in relation to any item shown in an undertaking's balance sheet, is the amount which would have been shown in respect of that item if assets of any class included under that item at an amount determined by any method permitted by this paragraph had instead been included at their replacement cost as at the balance sheet date.

(5) The relevant alternative amount may be determined by reference to the most recent actual purchase price before the balance sheet date of assets of any class included under the item in question instead of by reference to their replacement cost as at that date, but only if the former appears to the directors of the undertaking to constitute the more appropriate standard of comparison in the case of assets of that class.

Definitions

'accounts': EC(IUA)R 1996, reg 2(1); 'the Act of 1986': EC(IUA)R 1996, reg 2(1); 'undertaking': EC(IUA)R 1996, reg 2(1) & EC(CGA)R 1992, reg 3(1).

Substitution of original amount where price or cost unknown

10. Where there is no record of the purchase price of any asset acquired by an undertaking or of any price, expenses or costs relevant for determining its cost in accordance with paragraph 9, or any such record cannot be obtained without unreasonable expenses or delay, its cost shall be taken for the purposes of paragraphs 2 to 7 to be the value ascribed to it in the earliest available record of its value made on or after its acquisition by the undertaking.

Definitions

'undertaking': EC(IUA)R 1996, reg 2(1) & EC(CGA)R 1992, reg 3(1).

11.(1) Subject to subparagraph (2), assets which fall to be included under Assets item FI (tangible assets and stocks) in the balance sheet format (set out in Chapter 2 of Part I of this Schedule) may be included at a fixed quantity and value.

(2) Subparagraph (1) applies to assets of a kind which are constantly being replaced, where—

(a) their overall value is not material to assessing the undertaking's state of affairs; and

(b) their quantity, value and composition are not subject to material variation.

Definitions

'undertaking': EC(IUA)R 1996, reg 2(1) & EC(CGA)R 1992, reg 3(1).

Chapter 2
Current Value Accounting Rules

PRELIMINARY

12. (1) The rules set out in paragraphs 2 to 11 are referred to subsequently in this Schedule as "the historical cost accounting rules".

(2) Paragraphs 2, 3, 4 and 5 are referred to in this Chapter as "the depreciation rules" and references subsequently in this Schedule to the historical cost accounting rules do not include the depreciation rules as they apply by virtue of paragraph 19.

13. Subject to paragraphs 19 to 21, the amounts to be included in respect of assets of any description mentioned in paragraph 14 may be determined on any basis so mentioned.

Current value accounting rates

14. (1) Investments falling to be included under Assets item C (investments) may be included at their current value calculated in accordance with paragraphs 17 and 18.

(2) Investments falling to be included under Assets item D (unit-linked investments) shall be shown at their current value.

15. (1) Intangible assets, other than goodwill, and assets falling to be included under Assets item F.II (cash at bank and in hand), F.III (own shares) and F.IV (other) may be included at their current cost.

(2) Assets falling to be included under Assets item F.I (tangible assets and stocks) in the balance sheet format (set out in Chapter 2 of Part I of this Schedule) may be included at a market value determined as at the date of their last valuation or at their current cost.

16. The same valuation method shall be applied to all investments included in any item denoted by an arabic number or shown as assets under Assets item C.I.

Valuation of investments

17. (1) Subject to subparagraph (5) in the case of investments other than land and buildings, current value shall mean market value determined in accordance with this paragraph.

(2) Where investments are officially listed on an official stock exchange, market value shall mean the value on the balance sheet date or, when the balance sheet date is not a stock exchange trading day, on the last stock exchange trading day before that date.

(3) Where a market exists for unlisted investments, market value shall mean the average price at which such investments were traded on the balance sheet date or, when the balance sheet date is not a trading day, on the last trading day before that date.

(4) Where on the date on which the accounts are drawn up listed or unlisted investments have been sold or are to be sold within the short term, the market value shall be reduced by the actual or estimated realisation costs.

(5) Except where the equity method is applied all investments other than those referred to in subparagraphs (2) and (3) shall be valued on a basis which has prudent regard to the likely realisable value.

(6) In all cases the method of valuation shall be precisely described and the reason for adopting it disclosed in the notes to the accounts.

Definitions

'accounts': EC(IUA)R 1996, reg 2(1).

18.(1) In the case of land and buildings, current value shall mean the market value on the date of valuation, where relevant, reduced as provided in subparagraphs (4) and (5).

(2) Market value shall mean the price at which land and buildings could be sold under private contract between a willing seller and an arm's length buyer on the date of valuation, it being assumed that the property is publicly exposed to the market, that market conditions permit orderly disposal and that a normal period, having regard to the nature of the property, is available for the negotiation of the sale.

(3) The market value shall be determined through the separate valuation of each land and buildings item. carried out at least every five years in accordance with generally accepted methods of valuation.

(4) Where the value of any land and buildings item has diminished since the preceding valuation under subparagraph (3), an appropriate value adjustment shall be made and the lower value arrived at shall not be increased in subsequent balance sheets unless such increase results from a new determination of market value arrived at in accordance with subparagraphs (2) and (3).

(5) Where on the date on which the accounts are drawn up and buildings have been sold or are to be sold within the short term, the value arrived at in accordance with subparagraphs (2) and (4) shall be reduced by the actual or estimated realisation costs.

(6) Where it is impossible to determine the market value of a land and buildings item, the value arrived at on the basis of the principle of purchase price or production cost shall be deemed to be its current value.

(7) The method by which the current value of land and buildings has been arrived at and their breakdown by financial year of valuation shall be disclosed in the notes to the accounts.

Definitions

'accounts': EC(IUA)R 1996, reg 2(1).

Application of the depreciation rules

19.(1) Where the value of any asset of an undertaking is determined in accordance with paragraph 14 (in the case of assets falling to be included under assets item C.I) or paragraph 15, that value shall be, or (as the case may require) be the starting point for determining, the amount to be included in respect of that asset in the undertaking's accounts, instead of its cost or any value previously so determined for that asset; and the depreciation rules shall apply accordingly in relation to any such asset with the substitution for any reference to its cost of a reference to the value most recently determined for that asset in accordance with paragraph 14 or 15 (as the case may be).

(2) The amount of any provision for depreciation required in the case of any asset by paragraph 3 as it applies by virtue of subparagraph (1) is referred to below in this paragraph as the "adjusted amount", and the amount of any provision which would be required by that paragraph in the case of that asset according to the historical cost accounting rules is referred to as the "historical cost amount".

(3) Where subparagraph (1) applies in the case of any asset the amount of any provision for depreciation in respect of that asset included in any item shown in the profit and loss account in respect of amounts written off assets of the description in question may be the historical cost amount instead of the adjusted amount, provided that the amount of any difference between the two is shown separately in the profit and loss account or in a note to the accounts.

Definitions

'accounts': EC(IUA)R 1996, reg 2(1); 'undertaking': EC(IUA)R 1996, reg 2(1) & EC(CGA)R 1992, reg 3(1).

Additional Information to be provided

20.(1) This paragraph applies where the amounts to be included in respect of assets covered by any items shown in an undertaking's accounts have been determined in accordance with paragraph 14 or 15.

(2) The items affected and the basis of valuation adopted in determining the amounts of the assets in question in the case of each such item shall be disclosed in a note to the accounts.

(3) The purchase price of investments valued in accordance with paragraph 14 shall be disclosed in the notes to the accounts.

(4) In the case of each balance sheet item valued in accordance with paragraph 15 either—

(a) the comparable amounts determined according to the historical cost accounting rules, or

(b) the differences between those amounts and the corresponding amounts actually shown in the balance sheet in respect of that item,

shall be shown separately in the balance sheet or in a note to the accounts.

(5) In subparagraph (4) references. in relation to any item to the comparable amounts determined as there mentioned are references to—

(a) the aggregate amount which would be required to be shown in respect of that item if the amounts to be included in respect of all the assets covered by that item were determined according to the historical cost accounting rules, and

(b) the aggregate amount of the cumulative provisions for depreciation or diminution in value which would be permitted or required in determining those amounts according to those rules.

Definitions

'accounts': EC(IUA)R 1996, reg 2(1); 'undertaking': EC(IUA)R 1996, reg 2(1) & EC(CGA)R 1992, reg 3(1).

21.(1) With respect to any determination of the value of an asset of an undertaking in accordance with paragraph 14, the amount of any profit or loss arising from that determination (after allowing, where appropriate, for any provisions for depreciation or diminution in value made otherwise than by reference to the value so determined and any adjustments of any such provisions made in the light of that determination) shall be credited or (as the case may be) debited to a separate reserve (referred to in this paragraph as "the revaluation reserve"), except insofar as it has already been recognised in the life assurance technical account or the non-technical account in accordance with note 10 to the profit and loss account.

(2) The amount of the revaluation reserve shall be shown in the undertaking's balance sheet under Liabilities item A.III in the balance sheet format (set out in Chapter 2 of Part I of this Schedule).

(3) An amount may be transferred from the revaluation reserve to the profit and loss account—

(a) if the amount was previously charged to that account or represents realised profit, or

(b) on capitalisation,

and the revaluation reserve shall be reduced to the extent that the amounts transferred to it are no longer necessary for the purpose of the valuation method used.

(4) The revaluation reserve shall not be reduced except as mentioned in this paragraph.

(5) The treatment for taxation purposes of amounts credited or debited to the revaluation reserve shall be disclosed in a note to the accounts.

(6) In subparagraph (3)(b), capitalisation, in relation to an amount standing to the credit of the revaluation reserve, means applying it in wholly or partly paying up unissued shares in the undertaking to be allotted to members of the undertaking as fully or partly paid shares.

Definitions

'accounts': EC(IUA)R 1996, reg 2(1); 'undertaking': EC(IUA)R 1996, reg 2(1) & EC(CGA)R 1992, reg 3(1).

Chapter 3
General Rules

22.(1) This paragraph applies to debt securities and other fixed income securities shown as assets under C.II and C.III of the balance sheet format (set out in Chapter 2 of Part I of this Schedule) which have not been valued at market value.

(2) The amount included in the balance sheet in respect of these assets shall be their purchase price.

(3) Where the purchase price of these assets exceeds the amount repayable at maturity, the amount of the difference shall be charged to the profit and loss account or reduced each financial year on a systematic basis, in accordance with best accounting practice, so that it is completely written off when the securities are repaid. That difference shall be shown separately in the balance sheet or in the notes to the accounts.

(4) Where the purchase price of those assets is less than the amount repayable at maturity, the amount of the difference may be released to income in instalments over the period remaining until repayment. That difference shall be shown separately in the balance sheet or in the notes to the accounts.

Definitions

'accounts': EC(IUA)R 1996, reg 2(1).

Technical Provisions

23. The amount of technical provisions shall at all times be sufficient to cover any liabilities arising out of insurance contracts as far as can reasonably be foreseen.

Provision for unearned premiums

24.(1) Subject to subparagraph (2), the provision for unearned premiums shall be computed separately for each insurance contract.

(2) Notwithstanding subparagraph (1) statistical methods, in particular proportional and flat rate methods, may be used where they may be expected to give approximately the same results as would be obtained if individual calculations were made under subparagraph (1).

(3) In classes of insurance where the pattern of risk varies over the life of a contract, this shall be taken into account in the calculation methods.

Provision for unexpired risks

25. (1) The provision for unexpired risks shall be computed on the basis of claims and administrative expenses likely to arise after the end of the financial year from contracts concluded before that date, insofar as their estimated value exceeds the provision for unearned premiums and any premiums receivable under those contracts.

(2) In this paragraph, "unexpired risks" has the same meaning as it has in note 24 on the balance sheet format which is set out in Chapter 2 of Part I of this Schedule.

Life assurance

26.(1) Subject to subparagraph (2), the life assurance provision shall be computed separately for each life assurance contract.

(2) Notwithstanding subparagraph (1), statistical or mathematical methods may be used where they may be expected to give approximately the same results as would be obtained if individual calculations were made under subparagraph (1).

(3) A summary of the principal assumptions in making the provision under subparagraph (1) or (2) shall be given in the notes to the accounts.

(4) The computation shall be made on the basis of recognised actuarial methods annually by a Fellow Member of the Society of Actuaries in Ireland, with due regard to the actuarial principles laid down in Council Directive 92/96/EEC.

Definitions

'accounts': EC(IUA)R 1996, reg 2(1).

PROVISIONS FOR CLAIMS OUTSTANDING

Non-life insurance

27. (1) Subject to subparagraph (2). a provision for claims outstanding shall be computed separately for each case on the basis of the costs still expected to arise.

(2) Notwithstanding subparagraph (1), statistical methods may be used if they result in an adequate provision for claims outstanding having regard to the nature of the risks.

(3) A provision for claims outstanding shall also allow for claims incurred but not reported by the balance sheet date, the amount of the allowance being determined having regard to past experience as to the number and magnitude of claims reported after previous balance sheet dates.

(4) All claims settlement costs shall be included in the calculation of the provision for claims outstanding, irrespective of their origin.

(5) Recoverable amounts arising out of subrogation or salvage shall be estimated on a prudent basis and either deducted from the provision for claims outstanding (in which case if the amounts are material they shall be shown in the notes to the accounts) or shown as assets.

(6) Where benefits resulting from a claim are required to be paid in the form of annuity, the amounts to be set aside for that purpose shall be calculated by recognised actuarial methods.

(7) In subparagraph (5)—

"salvage" means the acquisition of the legal ownership of insured property:

"subrogation" means the acquisition of the rights of policy holders with respect to third parties.

Definitions

'accounts': EC(IUA)R 1996, reg 2(1).

28.(1) There shall be no implicit discounting or deductions (including by way of financial reinsurance), whether resulting from the placing of a present value on a provision for an outstanding claim which is expected to be settled later at a higher figure or otherwise effected.

(2) The [Bank][a] may, on application by the undertaking concerned. permit explicit discounting or deductions (including by way of financial reinsurance) to take account of investment income subject to compliance with the following conditions and any other conditions which the Minister may from time to time consider necessary:

(a) the expected date for the settlement of claims shall be on average at least four years after the accounting date;

(b) the discounting or deduction shall be effected on a recognised prudential basis; any change in that basis shall be notified, in advance, to the Minister;

(c) when calculating the total cost of settling claims, an undertaking shall take account of all factors that could cause increases in that cost;

(d) an undertaking shall have adequate data at its disposal to construct a reliable model of the rate of claims settlements;

(e) the rate of interest used for the calculation of present value shall not exceed a prudent estimate of the investment income from assets invested as a provision for claims during the period necessary for the payment of such claims and that rate shall not exceed either of the following:

    (i) a rate derived from the investment income from such assets over the preceding five years;

    (ii) a rate derived from the investment income from such assets during the year preceding the balance sheet date.

(3) When discounting or effecting deductions, an undertaking shall, in the notes on its accounts, disclose the total amount of provisions before discounting or deduction, the

categories of claims which are discounted or from which deductions have been made and, for each category of claims, the methods used, in particular the rates used for the estimates referred to in the clauses (c) and (e) of subparagraph (2), and the criteria adopted for estimating the period that will elapse before the claims are settled.

Amendments

a 'Bank' substituted for 'Minister' by CBFSAIA 2003, s 35.

Definitions

'accounts': EC(IUA)R 1996, reg 2(1); 'the Minister': EC(IUA)R 1996, reg 2(1); 'undertaking': EC(IUA)R 1996, reg 2(1) & EC(CGA)R 1992, reg 3(1).

Life assurance business

29. The amount of the provision for claims shall—

(a) be equal to the sums due to beneficiaries, plus the costs of settling claims,

(b) include the provision for claims incurred but not reported and

(c) be disclosed in Liabilities item C(2).

30. Any equalisation provision established under the European Communities (Non-Life Insurance) (Amendment) Regulations, 1991 (S.I. No. 5 of 1991), shall be valued in accordance with the provisions of those Regulations.

Accounting on a non-annual basis

31. (1) Where, because of the nature of the class or type of insurance in question, information relating to premiums receivable or claims payable or to both in respect of the underwriting year is, when the annual accounts are drawn up, insufficient for accurate estimates to be made, then either of the methods set out in the Table to this paragraph may be adopted and applied.

(2) The method adopted shall be disclosed in the notes together with the reasons for adopting it.

(3) The method adopted shall be applied systematically in successive years unless circumstances justify a change and where there is a change in the method applied, the effect on the assets, liabilities, financial position and profit or loss shall be disclosed in the notes to the accounts.

(4) In this paragraph and the Table hereto "underwriting year" means the financial year in which the insurance contracts in the class or type of insurance in question commenced.

Definitions

'accounts': EC(IUA)R 1996, reg 2(1).

TABLE

METHOD 1

(a) The excess of the premiums written over the claims and expenses paid in respect of contracts commencing in the underwriting year shall form a technical provision included in the technical provision for claims outstanding shown in the balance sheet under Liabilities item C.3.

(b) The provision may also be computed on the basis of a given percentage of the premiums written where such a method is appropriate for the type of risk insured.

(c) If necessary, the amount of this technical provision shall be increased to make it sufficient to meet present and future obligations.

(d) The technical provision constituted under this method shall be replaced by a provision for claims outstanding estimated in accordance with paragraphs 27 to 29 as soon as sufficient information has been gathered and not later than the end of the third year following the underwriting year.

(e) The length of time that elapses before a provision for claims outstanding is constituted in accordance with paragraph (d) of this method shall be disclosed in the notes to the accounts.

Definitions

'accounts': EC(IUA)R 1996, reg 2(1).

METHOD 2

(a) The figures shown in the technical account or in certain items within it shall relate to a year which wholly or partly precedes the financial year but by no more than 12 months.

(b) The amounts of the technical provisions shown in the accounts shall, if necessary, be increased to make them sufficient to meet present and future obligations.

(c) The length of time by which the earlier year to which the figures relate precedes the financial year and the magnitude of the transactions concerned shall be disclosed in the notes to the accounts.

Definitions

'accounts': EC(IUA)R 1996, reg 2(1).

PART III
NOTES TO THE ACCOUNTS

Preliminary

1. Any information required in the case of an undertaking by the following provisions of this Part of this Schedule shall be given by way of a note to the [Companies Act accounts][a], unless otherwise provided.

Amendments

a Words substituted by reg 11 and Sch 3, Item No 14(a) of EC(IFRSMA)R 2005.

Definitions

'accounts': EC(IUA)R 1996, reg 2(1); 'undertaking': EC(IUA)R 1996, reg 2(1) & EC(CGA)R 1992, reg 3(1).

General

Disclosure of accounting policies

2. The accounting policies adopted by the undertaking in determining the amounts to be included in respect of items shown in the balance sheet and in determining the profit or loss of the undertaking shall be stated, including such policies with respect to the depreciation and diminution in value of assets.

Definitions

'undertaking': EC(IUA)R 1996, reg 2(1) & EC(CGA)R 1992, reg 3(1).

3. If there are changes to the accounting policies adopted by the undertaking from one year to the next, these changes shall be stated together with the reasons for the changes and their effect on the accounts of the undertaking.

Definitions

'accounts': EC(IUA)R 1996, reg 2(1); 'undertaking': EC(IUA)R 1996, reg 2(1) & EC(CGA)R 1992, reg 3(1).

Sums denominated in foreign currencies

4. Where any sums originally denominated in a currency other than the currency of the State have been brought into accounts under any items shown in the balance sheet format (which is set out in Chapter 2 of Part I of this Schedule) or the profit and loss account format (which is so set out), the basis on which those sums have been translated into Irish Pounds, or the currency in which the accounts are drawn, shall be stated.

5. It shall be stated whether the accounts have been prepared in accordance with applicable accounting standards and particulars of any material departure from those standards and the reason for it shall be given.

Definitions

'accounts': EC(IUA)R 1996, reg 2(1).

INFORMATION SUPPLEMENTING THE BALANCE SHEET

Share capital and debentures

6.(1) The following information shall be given with respect to the undertaking's share capital:

(a) the authorised share capital, and

(b) where shares of more than one class have been allotted, the number and aggregate nominal value of shares of each class allotted.

(2) In the case of any part of the allotted share capital that consists of redeemable shares, the following information shall be given:

(a) the earliest and latest dates on which the undertaking has power to redeem those shares,

(b) whether those shares have to be redeemed in any event or are liable to be redeemed at the option of the undertaking or of the shareholder, and

(c) whether any premium is payable on redemption and, if so payable, the amount of that premium.

Definitions

'undertaking': EC(IUA)R 1996, reg 2(1) & EC(CGA)R 1992, reg 3(1).

---

7. If the undertaking has allotted any shares during the financial year, the following information shall be given:

(a) the reason for making the allotment,

(b) the classes of shares allotted, and

(c) as respects each class of shares, the number allotted, their aggregate nominal value and the consideration received by the undertaking for the allotment.

Definitions

'undertaking': EC(IUA)R 1996, reg 2(1) & EC(CGA)R 1992, reg 3(1).

---

8. (1) With respect to any contingent right to the allotment of shares in the undertaking the following particulars shall be given:

(a) the number, description and amount of the shares in relation to which the right is exercisable,

(b) the period during which it is exercisable, and

(c) the price to be paid for the shares allotted.

(2) In subparagraph (1) "contingent right to the allotment of shares" means any option to subscribe for shares and any other right to require the allotment of shares to any person whether arising on the conversion into shares of securities of any other description or otherwise.

Definitions

'undertaking': EC(IUA)R 1996, reg 2(1) & EC(CGA)R 1992, reg 3(1).

9.(1) If the undertaking has issued any debentures during the financial year to which the accounts relate, the following information shall be given:

(a) the reason for making the issue.

(b) the classes of debentures issued, and

(c) as respects each class of debentures, the amount issued and the consideration received by the undertaking for the issue.

(2) Particulars of any redeemed debentures which the undertaking has power to reissue shall also be given.

(3) Where any of the undertaking's debentures are held by a nominee of or trustee for the undertaking, the nominal amount of the debentures and the amount at which they are stated in the accounting records kept by the undertaking in accordance with section 202 of the Act of 1990, shall be stated.

Definitions

'accounts': EC(IUA)R 1996, reg 2(1); 'the Act of 1990': EC(IUA)R 1996, reg 2(1); 'undertaking': EC(IUA)R 1996, reg 2(1) & EC(CGA)R 1992, reg 3(1).

Assets

10.(1) In respect of any assets of the undertaking included in Assets item B (intangible assets), C.I (land and buildings) and C.II (investments in group undertakings and participating interests) in the undertaking's balance sheet the following information shall be given by reference to each such item:

(a) the appropriate amounts in respect of those assets included in the item as at the date of the beginning of the financial year and as at the balance sheet date respectively;

(b) the effect on any amount included in Assets item B in respect of those assets of—

(i) any determination during that year of the value to be ascribed to any of those assets in accordance with paragraph 15;

(ii) acquisitions during that year of any assets;

(iii) disposal during that year of any assets; and

(iv) any transfers of assets of the undertaking to and from the item during that year.

(2) The reference in subparagraph (I)(a) to the appropriate amounts in respect of any assets (included in an assets item) as at any date there mentioned is a reference to amounts representing the aggregate amounts determined, as at that date, in respect of assets falling to be included under the item on either of the following bases, that is to say:

(a) on the basis of cost, determined in accordance with paragraphs 7, 8 and 9; or

(b) on any basis permitted by paragraph 14 or 15;

leaving out of account in either case any provision for depreciation or diminution in value.

(3) In addition, in respect of any assets of the undertaking included in any assets item in the undertaking's balance sheet, there shall be stated (by reference to each such item)—

(a) the cumulative amount of provisions for depreciation or diminution in value of those assets included under the item as at each date mentioned in subparagraph (1)(a);

(b) the amount of any such provision made in respect of the financial year;

(c) the amount of any adjustments made in respect of any such provisions during that year in consequence of the disposal of any of those assets; and

(d) the amount of any other adjustments made in respect of any such provisions during that year.

Definitions

'participating interest': EC(IUA)R 1996, reg 2(1); 'undertaking': EC(IUA)R 1996, reg 2(1) & EC(CGA)R 1992, reg 3(1).

11. Where any assets, other than listed investments, of the undertaking are included under any item shown in the undertaking's balance sheet at an amount determined on any basis mentioned in paragraph 14 or 15 of Part II of this Schedule, the following information shall be given:

(a) the years, insofar as they are known to the directors in which the assets were severally valued and the several values; and

(b) in the case of assets that have been valued during the financial year, the names of the persons who valued them or particulars of their qualifications for doing so and, in either case, the bases of valuation used by them.

Definitions

'undertaking': EC(IUA)R 1996, reg 2(1) & EC(CGA)R 1992, reg 3(1).

12. In relation to any amount which is included under Assets item C.I. (land and buildings) the following shall be stated:

(a) how much of that amount is ascribable to land of freehold tenure and how much to land of leasehold tenure; and

(b) how much of the amount ascribable to land of leasehold tenure is ascribable to land held on long lease and how much to land held on short lease.

Investments

13. In respect of the amount of each item which is shown in the undertaking's balance sheet under Assets item C (investments) the following shall be stated:

(a) how much of that amount is ascribable to listed investments; and

(b) how much of any amount so ascribable is ascribable to investments in respect of which there has been granted a listing on a recognised stock exchange and how much to other listed investments.

Definitions

'undertaking': EC(IUA)R 1996, reg 2(1) & EC(CGA)R 1992, reg 3(1).

Reserves and provisions

14.(1) Where any amount is transferred—

(a) to or from any reserves, or

(b) to any [provision for other risks][a], or

(c) from any provision for [provision for other risks][a] otherwise than for the purpose for which the provision was established,

and the reserves or provisions are or would be but for paragraph 3 of Part I of this Schedule shown as separate items in the undertaking's balance sheet, the information mentioned in subparagraph (2) shall be given in respect of the aggregate of reserves or provisions included in the same item.

(2) The information to which subparagraph (1) relates is as follows:

(a) the amount of the reserves or provisions as at the date of the beginning of the financial year and as at the balance sheet date respectively.

(b) any amounts transferred to or from the reserves or provisions during that year, and

(c) the source and application respectively of any amounts so transferred.

(3) Particulars shall be given of each provision included in Liabilities item E.III (other provisions) in the undertaking's balance sheet in any case where the amount of that provision is material.

Amendments

a Words substituted by reg 11 and Sch 3, Item No 14(b) of EC(IFRSMA)R 2005.

Definitions

'undertaking': EC(IUA)R 1996, reg 2(1) & EC(CGA)R 1992, reg 3(1).

Provision for taxation

15. The amount of any provision for deferred taxation shall be stated separately from the amount of any provision for other taxation.

Details of indebtedness

16.(1). In respect of each item shown under "creditors" in the undertaking's balance sheet there shall be stated—

(a) the aggregate amount of any debts included under that item which are payable or repayable otherwise than by instalments and fall due for payment or repayment after the end of the period of five years beginning with the day next following the end of the financial year, and

(b) the aggregate amount of any debts so included which are repayable or repayable by instalments any of which fall due for payment after the end of that period;

and in the case of debts to which subparagraph *(b)* relates the aggregate amount of instalments falling due after the end of that period shall also be disclosed for each such item.

(2) Subject to subparagraph *(3),* in relation to each debt falling to be taken into account under subparagraph (1), the terms of payment or repayment and the rate of any interest payable on the debt shall be stated.

(3) If the number of debts is such that, in the opinion of the directors, compliance with subparagraph (2) would result in a statement of excessive length, it shall be sufficient to give a general indication of the terms of payment or repayment and the rates of any interest payable on the debts.

(4) In respect of each item shown under "creditors" in the undertaking's balance sheet there shall be stated—

(a) the aggregate amount of any debts included under that item in respect of which any security has been given by the undertaking; and

(b) an indication of the nature of the securities so given.

(5) References in this paragraph to an item shown under "creditors" in the undertaking's balance sheet include references, where amounts falling due to creditors within one year and after more than one year are distinguished in the balance sheet—

(a) in a case within subparagraph (1), to an item shown under the latter of those categories, and

(b) in a case within subparagraph (4), to an item shown under either of those categories,

and references to items shown under "creditors" include references to items which would but for paragraph 3(1)(b) of Part I of this Schedule be shown under that heading.

Definitions

'undertaking': EC(IUA)R 1996, reg 2(1) & EC(CGA)R 1992, reg 3(1).

17. If any fixed cumulative dividends on the undertaking's shares are in arrears, there shall be stated—

(a) the amount of the arrears, and

(b) the period for which the dividends or, if there is more than one class, each class of them are in arrears.

Definitions

'undertaking': EC(IUA)R 1996, reg 2(1) & EC(CGA)R 1992, reg 3(1).

Guarantees and other financial commitments

18.(1) Particulars shall be given of any charge on the assets of the undertaking to secure the liabilities of any other person, including, where practicable, the amount secured.

(2) The following information shall be given with respect to any other contingent liability not provided for (other than a contingent liability arising out of an insurance contract):

(a) the amount or estimated amount of that liability;

(b) its legal nature; and

(c) whether or not any valuable security has been provided by the undertaking in connection with that liability and, if such security has been so provided, what that security is.

(3) Where practicable, there shall be stated—

(a) the aggregate amount or estimated amount of contracts for capital expenditure, so far as not provided for, and

(b) the aggregate amount or estimated amount of capital expenditure authorised by the directors which has not been contracted for.

(4) Particulars shall be given of—

(a) any pension commitments included under any provision shown in the undertaking's balance sheet, and

(b) any such commitments for which no provision has been made,

and where any such commitment relates wholly or partly to pensions payable to past directors of the undertaking separate particulars shall be given of that commitment so far as it relates to such pensions.

(5) Particulars shall also be given of any other financial commitments, other than commitments arising out of insurance contracts, which—

(a) have not been provided for, and

(b) are relevant to assessing the undertaking's state of affairs.

(6) Commitments, being commitments to which any subparagraph of this paragraph relates, which are undertaken on behalf of or for the benefit of—

(a) any parent undertaking or fellow subsidiary undertaking of the undertaking, or

(b) any subsidiary undertaking of the undertaking,

shall be stated separately from the other commitments within that subparagraph, and commitments within clause (a) of this subparagraph shall also be stated separately from those within clause (b) of this subparagraph.

Definitions

'parent undertaking': EC(IUA)R 1996, reg 2(1); 'subsidiary': EC(IUA)R 1996, reg 2(1); 'undertaking': EC(IUA)R 1996, reg 2(1) & EC(CGA)R 1992, reg 3(1).

Dealings with or interests in group undertakings

19. Where an undertaking is a parent undertaking or a subsidiary undertaking and any item required by Part I of this Schedule to be shown in the undertaking's balance sheet in relation to group undertakings includes—

(a) amounts attributable to dealings with or interests in any parent undertaking or fellow subsidiary undertaking, or

(b) amounts attributable to dealings with or interests in any subsidiary undertaking of the undertaking,

the aggregate amounts within subparagraphs (a) and (b) respectively. shall be shown as separate items, in the balance sheet.

Definitions

'parent undertaking': EC(IUA)R 1996, reg 2(1); 'subsidiary': EC(IUA)R 1996, reg 2(1); 'undertaking': EC(IUA)R 1996, reg 2(1) & EC(CGA)R 1992, reg 3(1).

[Information on arrangements not included in balance sheet

19A. (1) The following information shall be provided in the notes to the accounts for an undertaking:

(a) the nature and business purpose of the arrangements of the undertaking that are not included in its balance sheet;

(b) the financial impact on the undertaking of the arrangements referred to in clause (a) if the risks or benefits arising from such arrangements are material and in so far as the disclosure of such risks or benefits is necessary for assessing the financial position of the undertaking.

Related party transactions

19B.(1) Particulars shall be given in the notes to the accounts of an undertaking of transactions which have been entered into with related parties by the undertaking, and if such transactions are material and have not been concluded under normal market conditions and the particulars of transactions shall include the amount of such transactions, the nature of the related party relationship, and other information concerning the transactions which is necessary for an understanding of the financial position of the undertaking.

(2) Subject to subparagraph (4), the provision of particulars and other information concerning individual transactions may be aggregated according to their nature, except where separate information is necessary for an understanding of the effects of related party transactions on the financial position of the undertaking.

(3) Subparagraph (1) shall not apply to transactions which are entered into between 2 or more members of a group if any subsidiary undertaking which is a party to the transaction is wholly owned by such a member.

(4) Subparagraph (2) shall not apply to a company whose securities are admitted to trading on a regulated market within the meaning of Article 4(1), point (14) of Directive 2004/39/EC.

(5) A word or expression used in subparagraphs (1) to (4) has the same meaning as it has in Directive 2006/46/EC.][a]

Amendments

a Paragraphs 19A and 19B inserted by European Communities (Directive 2006/46/EC) Regulations 2009, reg 24.

Miscellaneous Matters

20.(1) Particulars shall be given of any case where the cost of any asset is for the first time determined under paragraph 11 of Part I of this Schedule.

(2) Where any outstanding loans made under the authority of section 60) of the Principal Act, other than subsection (13)(a) of that section (which relates to various cases of financial assistance by an undertaking for purchase of its own shares) are included under any item shown in the undertaking's balance sheet, the aggregate amount of those loans shall be disclosed for each item in question.

(3) The aggregate amount which is recommended for distribution by way of dividend shall be stated.

(4) Particulars of any restriction on profits available for distribution by virtue of section 224(2)(b)(i) of the Act of 1990 shall be stated.

Definitions

'the Act of 1990': EC(IUA)R 1996, reg 2(1); 'the Principal Act': EC(IUA)R 1996, reg 2(1); 'undertaking': EC(IUA)R 1996, reg 2(1) & EC(CGA)R 1992, reg 3(1).

INFORMATION SUPPLEMENTING THE PROFIT AND LOSS ACCOUNT

Separate statement of certain items of income and expenditure

21. Subject to the following provisions of this paragraph, each of the following amounts shall be stated:

(a) the amount of the interest on or any similar charges in respect of—

(i) bank loans and overdrafts, and loans made to the undertaking (other than bank loans and overdrafts) which—

(I) are repayable otherwise than by instalments and fall due for repayment before the end of the period of five years beginning with the day next following the end of the financial year, or

(II) are repayable by instalments the last of which falls due for payment before the end of that period,

and

(ii) loans of any other kind made to the undertaking:

Provided that this subparagraph shall not apply to interest or charges on loans to the undertaking from group undertakings, but shall apply to interest or charges on all loans, whether made on the security of debentures or not;

(b) the amounts respectively set aside for redemption of share capital and for redemption of loans;

(c) the amount of income from listed and unlisted investments;

(d) the amount of the remuneration of the auditors and the expenses of the auditors;

(e) the aggregate amounts of the emoluments of, and compensation in respect of loss of office to, directors and compensation paid to past directors.

Definitions

'undertaking': EC(IUA)R 1996, reg 2(1) & EC(CGA)R 1992, reg 3(1).

Particulars of tax

22.(1) The basis on which the charge for corporation tax, income tax and other taxation on profits, whether payable in the State or outside the State, is computed shall be stated.

(2) Particulars shall be given of any special circumstances which affect liability in respect of taxation of profits, income or capital gains for the financial year concerned or liability in respect of taxation of profits, income or capital gains for succeeding financial years.

(3) The following amounts shall be stated:

(a) the amount of the charge for corporation tax;

(b) if the amount of the charge to corporation tax would have been greater but for relief from double taxation, the amount which it would have been but for such relief;

(c) the amount of the charge for income tax; and

(d) the amount of the charge for taxation payable outside the State of profits, income and (so far as charged to revenue) capital gains.

These amounts shall be stated separately in respect of each of the amounts which is shown under the following items in the profit and loss account, that is to say item III.9 (tax on profit or loss on ordinary activities) and item III.14 (tax on extraordinary profit or loss).

Particulars of business

23. (1) As regards non-life insurance, the notes to the accounts shall disclose—

(a) gross premiums written,

(b) gross premiums earned,

(c) gross claims incurred,

(d) gross operating expenses, and

(e) the reinsurance balance.

(2) The amounts required to be disclosed by subparagraph (1) shall be broken down between direct insurance and reinsurance acceptances, if reinsurance acceptances amount to 10 per cent or more of gross premiums written.

(3) Subject to subparagraph (4), the amounts required to be disclosed by subparagraphs (1) and (2) with respect to direct insurance shall be further broken down into the following groups of classes—

(a) accident and health,

(b) motor third party liability,

(c) motor other classes,

(d) marine, aviation and transport,

(e) fire and other damage to property,

(f) third-party liability,

(g) credit and suretyship,

(h) legal expenses,

(i) assistance, and

(j) miscellaneous,

where the amount of the gross premiums written in direct insurance for each such group exceeds ten million ECUs.

(4) The amounts relating to the three largest groups of classes in an undertaking's business shall in any event be disclosed.

Definitions

'undertaking': EC(IUA)R 1996, reg 2(1) & EC(CGA)R 1992, reg 3(1).

24.(1) As regards life assurance, the notes to the accounts shall disclose—

(a) gross premiums written, and

(b) the reinsurance balance.

(2) The notes relating to gross premiums written shall be broken down between direct insurance and reinsurance acceptances, where reinsurance acceptances amount to 10 per cent or more of gross premiums written, and within direct insurance shall be broken down to indicate—

(a) (i) individual premiums,

(ii) premiums under group contracts,

(b) (i) periodic premiums,

(ii) single premiums,

(c) (i) premiums from non-participating contracts,

(ii) premiums from participating contracts,

(iii) premiums from contracts where the investment risk is borne by policy holders.

(3) Disclosures of any amount required by clause (a), (b) or (c) of subparagraph (2) shall not be required where that amount does not exceed 10 per cent of the gross premiums written in direct insurance.

Definitions

'accounts': EC(IUA)R 1996, reg 2(1).

25.(1) Subject to subparagraph (2), there shall be disclosed as regards both non-life insurance and life assurance the total gross direct insurance premiums resulting from contracts concluded by the undertaking—

(a) in the member state of the European Union where there is situated its head office,

(b) in the other member states of the European Union, and

(c) in other countries.

(2) Disclosure of any figure referred to in subparagraph (1) above shall not be required if it does not exceed 5 per cent of total gross premiums.

Definitions

'undertaking': EC(IUA)R 1996, reg 2(1) & EC(CGA)R 1992, reg 3(1).

Commissions

26. There shall be disclosed the total amount of commissions of any kind for direct insurance business accounted for in the financial year, including acquisition, renewal, collection and portfolio management commission.

Particulars of staff

27.(1) The following information shall be given with respect to the employees of the undertaking:

(a) the average number of persons employed by the undertaking in the financial year, and

(b) the average number of persons employed within each category of persons employed by the undertaking.

(2) The average number required by clause (a) or (b) of subparagraph (1) shall be determined by dividing the relevant annual number by the number of weeks in the financial year.

(3) For the purposes of this paragraph, the relevant annual number shall be determined by ascertaining for each week in the financial year—

(a) for the purpose of subparagraph (1)(a), the number of persons employed under contracts of service by the undertaking in that week, whether throughout the week or not, and

(b) for the purpose of subparagraph (1)(b), the number of persons in the category in question of persons so employed.

and, in either case, adding together all the weekly numbers.

(4) In respect of all persons employed by the undertaking during the financial year who are taken into account in determining the relevant annual number for the purpose of subparagraph (1)(a) there shall also be stated the aggregate amounts respectively of—

(a) wages and salaries paid or payable in respect of that year to those persons,

(b) social welfare costs incurred by the undertaking on their behalf, and

(c) other pension costs so incurred.

save in so far as those amounts or any of them are stated in the profit and loss account.

(5) The categories of person employed by the undertaking by reference to which the number required to be disclosed by subparagraph (I)(b) is to be determined shall be such as the directors may select, having regard to the manner in which the undertaking's activities are organised.

Definitions

'undertaking': EC(IUA)R 1996, reg 2(1) & EC(CGA)R 1992, reg 3(1).

Miscellaneous matters

28.(1) Where any amount relating to any preceding financial year is included in any item in the profit and loss account, the effect shall be stated.

(2) Particulars shall be given of any extraordinary income or charges arising in the financial year.

(3) The effect shall be stated of any transactions that are exceptional by virtue of size or incidence though they fall within the ordinary activities of the undertaking.

Definitions

'undertaking': EC(IUA)R 1996, reg 2(1) & EC(CGA)R 1992, reg 3(1).

PART IV

FORM AND CONTENT OF GROUP ACCOUNTS

Chapter 1

General Rules

1.(1) [Where the directors of an undertaking prepare Companies Act group accounts, those group accounts][a] shall comply so far as practicable with the provisions of Parts I and 111 of this Schedule as if the undertakings included in the consolidation (in this Part referred to as "the group") were a single undertaking.

(2) In particular, for the purpose of note 13 to the balance sheet format (which is set out in Chapter 2 of Part I of this Schedule) and paragraphs 18(6) and 19 of Part 111 of this Schedule as it applies to group accounts—

(a) any subsidiary undertakings of the parent undertaking not included in the consolidation shall be treated as subsidiary undertakings of the group, and

(b) if the parent undertaking is itself a subsidiary undertaking, the group shall be treated as a subsidiary undertaking of any parent undertaking of that undertaking, and the reference to fellow subsidiary undertakings shall be construed accordingly.

Amendments

a Words substituted by reg 11 and Sch 3, Item No 14(a) of EC(IFRSMA)R 2005 (SI 116/2005).

Definitions

'accounts': EC(IUA)R 1996, reg 2(1); 'group accounts': EC(IUA)R 1996, reg 2(1); 'parent undertaking': EC(IUA)R 1996, reg 2(1); 'subsidiary': EC(IUA)R 1996, reg 2(1); 'undertaking': EC(IUA)R 1996, reg 2(1) & EC(CGA)R 1992, reg 3(1).

Notes

True and fair view: EC(IUA)R 1996, reg 10 imposes an overriding obligation that the annual accounts should give a true and fair view of the state of affairs of the group as a whole.[1] To a large extent, the provisions of EC(IUA)R 1996 are themselves determinative as to what constitutes a properly prepared set of group accounts. However, to the extent that the legislation is silent on any particular matter, compliance with the recognised practices and standards of the accountancy profession in preparing group accounts will be strong but not conclusive evidence that the accounts give a 'true and fair view' of the group's financial position.[2]

Indeed, even where the legislation specifically deals with an aspect of the accounts, a departure will be permitted if strict adherence would result in the 'true and fair view' not being achieved.[3] Details of the departure must, however, be given in the notes to the accounts together with the reasons therefor.[4] With the introduction of International Financial Reporting Standards through SI 116/2005, a new term, 'presents fairly' entered into financial reporting language. The United Kingdom's Financial Reporting Council, of which the Accounting Standards Board is a constituent body, published a paper in August 2005 entitled 'The implications of new accounting and auditing standards for the 'true and fair view' and auditors' responsibilities'. In this paper, the FRC concludes that the concept of 'true and fair' remains a cornerstone of financial reporting and that the intent and substance of the two expressions 'presents fairly' and 'true and fair' are similar. The paper is available from the FRC website at http://www.frc.org.uk/publications.

1 EC(IUA)R 1996, reg 10(5)(a) & (c).

2 *Dolan v AB Ltd* [1969] IR 282; *Lloyd Cheyham & Co Ltd v Littlejohn & Co* [1987] BCLC 303; *IRC v Duple Motor Bodies Ltd* [1961] 1 WLR 739. The recognised practices of the accountancy profession may be found in its Statements of Standard Accounting Practice (SSAPs) and Financial Reporting Standards (FRSs) or their international equivalents, international financial reporting standards ('IFRSs').

3 EC(IUA)R 1996, reg 10(5)(d).

4 EC(IUA)R 1996, reg 10(5)(e).

2.(1) Subject to the exceptions authorised or required by this paragraph, all the subsidiary undertakings of the parent undertaking shall be included in the consolidation.

(2) A subsidiary undertaking may be excluded from consolidation if its inclusion is not material for the purpose of giving a true and fair view, but two or more undertakings may be excluded only if they are not material taken together.

(3) In addition, a subsidiary undertaking may be excluded from consolidation where—

(a) severe long-term restrictions substantially hinder the exercise of the rights of the parent undertaking over the assets or management of that undertaking, or

(b) the information necessary for the preparation of group accounts cannot be obtained without disproportionate expense or undue delay, or

(c) the interest of the parent undertaking is held exclusively with a view to subsequent resale and the undertaking has not previously been included in consolidated group accounts prepared by the parent undertaking.

[...][a]

Amendments

a Sub-paras (4), (5) and (6) of para 2 deleted by reg 11 and Sch 3, Item No 14(b) of EC(IFRSMA)R 2005 (SI 116/2005).

Definitions

'group accounts': EC(IUA)R 1996, reg 2(1); 'parent undertaking': EC(IUA)R 1996, reg 2(1); 'subsidiary': EC(IUA)R 1996, reg 2(1); 'undertaking': EC(IUA)R 1996, reg 2(1) & EC(CGA)R 1992, reg 3(1).

Notes

Exclusion of immaterial subsidiaries: Subsidiary undertakings may be excluded from the group accounts if, whether looked at in isolation or taken together, their inclusion would not be material for the purpose of ensuring that the accounts give a true and fair view of the state of affairs of the group as a whole.[1]

Exclusion of subsidiaries in respect of which the parent's rights of management are severely restricted: A parent undertaking may exclude a subsidiary undertaking from the group accounts in circumstances where severe long-term restrictions exist which substantially hinder its rights over the assets or management of that subsidiary[2]. According to para 78(c) of Financial Reporting Standard (FRS) No 2,[3] entitled 'Accounting for Subsidiary Undertakings'—

> "The rights affected must be those by reason of which the undertaking holding them is the parent undertaking and without which it would not be the parent undertaking. Severe long-term restrictions justify excluding a subsidiary undertaking from consolidation only where the effect of those restrictions is that the parent undertaking does not control its subsidiary undertaking. Severe long-term restrictions are identified by their effect in practice rather than by the way in which the restrictions are imposed. For example, a subsidiary undertaking should not be excluded because restrictions are threatened or because another party has the power to impose them unless such threats or the existence of such a power has a severe and restricting effect in practice in the long-term on the rights of the parent undertaking. Generally, restrictions are dealt with better by disclosure than non-consolidation. However, the loss of the parent undertaking's control over its subsidiary undertaking resulting from severe long-term restrictions would make it misleading to include that subsidiary undertaking in the consolidation."

Examples of long-term restrictions which would justify exclusion from the group accounts include situations where the subsidiary undertaking is in liquidation or receivership.[4]

Exclusion of subsidiary because of disproportionate expense or delay: A subsidiary undertaking may also be excluded from the group accounts if the information concerning its affairs which would otherwise have to be included in the accounts, cannot be obtained without disproportionate expense or delay.[5] However, it would still appear that the entitlement to make such an exclusion is still subject to the overriding requirement that the information should not be omitted if it is material for the purpose of ensuring that the accounts give a true and fair view of the group as a whole.[6]

Exclusion of a subsidiary which is to be resold: If the shares of a subsidiary undertaking are held exclusively with a view to their subsequent resale, that subsidiary may be excluded from the group accounts.[7] According to FRS No 2,[8] para 11 an interest is held 'exclusively with a view to ... subsequent resale' if it is—

"(a) an interest for which a purchaser has been identified or is being sought, and which is reasonably expected to be disposed of within approximately one year of its date of acquisition; or

(b) an interest that was acquired as a result of the enforcement of a security, unless the interest has become part of the continuing activities of the group or the holder acts as if it intends the interest to become so."

Furthermore, FRS, para 78(d) states that an interest may also be regarded as being held exclusively for resale where the sale has not been completed within one year of the date of acquisition provided that on the date the accounts are signed, the terms of the sale have been agreed and the process of disposing of the interest in the shares is substantially complete.[9]

1 Sch, Pt IV, para 2(2).

2 Sch, Pt IV, para 2(3)(a).

3 Issued by the Accounting Standards Board and the Institute of Chartered Accountants in Ireland.

4 FRS No 2, para 78(c)). As to the manner in which such subsidiaries should be treated in the accounts, see FRS No 2, para 79(a).

5 Sch, Pt IV, para 2(3)(b)). This section replicates CA 1963, s 150(2)(b)(i).

6 See reg 10(5) and FRS No 2, para 24.

7 Sch, Pt IV, para 2(3)(c).

8 Issued by the Accounting Standards Board and the Institute of Chartered Accountants in Ireland.

9 As to the manner in which such subsidiaries should be treated in the accounts, see FRS No 2, para 79(b).

10 This overriding obligation is to be found in reg 10(5).

3.(1) The group balance sheet and group profit and loss account shall incorporate in full the information contained in the individual accounts of the parent undertaking and subsidiary undertakings included in the group accounts, subject to the adjustments authorised or required by the following provisions of this Schedule.

(2) Group accounts shall be drawn up as at the same date as the annual accounts of the parent undertaking.

(3) If the financial year of a subsidiary undertaking included in the group accounts differs from that of the parent undertaking, the group accounts shall be made up—

(a) from the accounts of the subsidiary undertaking for its financial year last ending before the end of the parent undertaking's financial year, provided that year ended no more than three months before that of the parent undertaking,

(b) where an undertaking's balance sheet date precedes the group balance sheet by more than three months, but not more than six months, that undertaking shall be included in the group accounts on the basis of interim accounts drawn up as at the group balance sheet date.

Definitions

'group accounts': EC(IUA)R 1996, reg 2(1); 'individual accounts': EC(IUA)R 1996, reg 2(1); 'parent undertaking': EC(IUA)R 1996, reg 2(1); 'subsidiary': EC(IUA)R 1996, reg 2(1).

Notes

Coincidence of financial year for group accounts and parent undertaking's accounts: The group accounts and the parent undertaking's own annual accounts must be drawn up as at the same date.[1] If any subsidiary undertaking has a different financial year, the group accounts must be drawn up from that subsidiary's last annual accounts provided same are made up to a date not less than three months before the end of the parent undertaking's financial year, and otherwise from specifically prepared interim accounts.[2]

Coincidence of financial year for parent and subsidiary undertakings: Adjustments to group accounts because of a subsidiary undertaking with a different financial year may be largely overcome if that undertaking is also a 'subsidiary' within the meaning of CA 1963, s 155. This is because the directors of a holding company are under a duty to secure that except where there are good reasons against it, the financial year of each of its subsidiaries shall coincide with the parent company's own financial year.[3] Furthermore, where it appears desirable to the Minister for a holding company or a subsidiary to extend its financial year, so that the subsidiary's financial year coincides with that of the holding company, and for that purpose to postpone the submission of the annual accounts to an AGM from one calendar year to the next, he may, on the application or with the consent of the directors of the company whose financial year is to be extended, direct that in the case of that company, the submission of annual accounts to an AGM, the holding of an AGM or the making of an annual return shall not be required in the earlier of the two calendar years.[4]

1 Sch, Pt IV, para 3(2).
2 Sch, Pt IV, para 3(3).
3 CA 1963, s 153(1).
4 CA 1963, s 153(2).

4.(1) The methods of consolidation shall be applied consistently from one financial year to the next.

(2) If it appears to the directors of a parent undertaking that there are special reasons for departing from the principle specified in subparagraph (1) they may so depart, but particulars of the departure, the reasons for it and its effect on the balance sheet and profit or loss of the parent undertaking and subsidiaries as a whole shall be disclosed in the notes to the accounts.

Definitions

'accounts': EC(IUA)R 1996, reg 2(1); 'parent undertaking': EC(IUA)R 1996, reg 2(1).

Notes

Departure from previous method of consolidation: The primary requirement of para 4 is that the methods of consolidation should be applied consistently from one financial year to the next.[1] However, if the directors consider that there are special reasons for so doing, they may depart from this principle provided they give particulars of the nature of the departure, the reasons therefor and the effect thereof, in a note to the accounts.[2] Moreover, they must also ensure that the accounts still meet the overriding requirement of giving a true and fair view of the state of affairs of the group as a whole.[3]

1 Sch, Pt IV, para 4(1).
2 Sch, Pt IV, para 4(2).
3 See EC(IUA)R 1996, reg 10(5).

---

5. (a) Group accounts shall show the assets, liabilities, state of affairs as at the end of the financial year and profit or loss of the parent undertaking and its subsidiary undertakings dealt with in the group accounts as if they were a single undertaking and, in particular, shall show—
   (i) debts and claims between the undertakings dealt with in the group accounts shall be eliminated from those accounts,
   (ii) income and expenditure relating to transactions between the undertakings dealt with in the group accounts shall be eliminated from those accounts,
   (iii) where profits and losses resulting from transactions between the undertakings dealt with in the group accounts are included in the book value of assets, they shall be eliminated from those accounts,

   (b) clauses (i) to (iii) of subparagraph (a) need not be complied with where the amounts involved are not material for the purpose of giving a true and fair view as required by Regulation 10.

Definitions

'group accounts': EC(IUA)R 1996, reg 2(1); 'parent undertaking': EC(IUA)R 1996, reg 2(1); 'subsidiary': EC(IUA)R 1996, reg 2(1); 'undertaking': EC(IUA)R 1996, reg 2(1) & EC(CGA)R 1992, reg 3(1).

Notes

True and fair view: EC(IUA)R 1996, reg 10 imposes an overriding obligation that the annual accounts should give a true and fair view of the state of affairs of the group as a whole.[1] To a large extent, the provisions of EC(IUA)R 1996 are themselves determinative as to what constitutes a properly prepared set of group accounts. However, to the extent that the legislation is silent on any particular matter, compliance with the recognised practices and standards of the accountancy profession in preparing group accounts will be strong but not conclusive evidence that the accounts give a 'true and fair view' of the group's financial position.[2]

Indeed, even where the legislation specifically deals with an aspect of the accounts, a departure will be permitted if strict adherence would result in the 'true and fair view' not being achieved.[3] Details of the departure must, however, be given in the notes to the accounts together with the reasons therefor.[4] With the introduction of International Financial Reporting Standards through EC(IFRSMA)R 2005, a new term, 'presents fairly' entered into financial reporting language. The United Kingdom's Financial Reporting Council, of which the Accounting Standards Board is a constituent body, published a paper in August 2005 entitled 'The implications of new accounting and auditing standards for the 'true and fair view' and auditors' responsibilities'. In this paper, the FRC concludes that the concept of 'true and fair' remains a cornerstone of financial reporting and that the intent and substance of the two expressions 'presents fairly' and 'true and fair' are similar. The paper is available from the FRC website at http://www.frc.org.uk/publications.

1 EC(IUA)R 1996, reg 10(5)(a) & (c).

2 *Dolan v AB Ltd* [1969] IR 282; *Lloyd Cheyham & Co Ltd v Littlejohn & Co* [1987] BCLC 303; *IRC v Duple Motor Bodies Ltd* [1961] 1 WLR 739). The recognised practices of the accountancy profession may be found in its Statements of Standard Accounting Practice (SSAPs) and Financial Reporting Standards (FRSs) or their international equivalents, international financial reporting standards (IFRSs).

3 EC(IUA)R 1996, reg 10(5)(d).

4 EC(IUA)R 1996, reg 10(5)(e).

6. If the composition of the undertakings dealt with in the group accounts has changed significantly in the course of a financial year, the group accounts shall include information which makes the comparison of successive sets of group accounts meaningful.

Definitions

'group accounts': EC(IUA)R 1996, reg 2(1); 'undertaking': EC(IUA)R 1996, reg 2(1) & EC(CGA)R 1992, reg 3(1).

Notes

Changes in composition of group: Where an undertaking has joined or left the group during the course of a financial year, the following information may be appropriate to include in the accounts for the purpose of allowing for a meaningful comparison between one set of group accounts and another:-

(a) the name of the undertaking in question;[1]

(b) the extent to which the profit or loss of the group is attributable to that undertaking;[2]

(c) details of the amount paid by the group for the undertaking, in the event of an acquisition, and details of the amount received, in the case of a disposal, together with details of the effect of the sale or disposal on group cash flow.[3]

1 Such information is required to be contained in the notes to group accounts generally in the UK by CA 1985, Sch 4A, para 15.

2 Such information is required to be contained in the notes to the group accounts generally in the UK by CA 1985, Sch 4A, para 15.

3 FRS No 1 requires that such information be contained in a note to the cash flow statements.

Chapter 2
Accounting/Valuation

ACQUISITION AND MERGER ACCOUNTING

7. The following provisions of this Chapter shall apply where an undertaking becomes a subsidiary undertaking of the parent undertaking and that event is referred to in those provisions as an "acquisition", and references to the "undertaking acquired" shall be construed accordingly.

Definitions

'parent undertaking': EC(IUA)R 1996, reg 2(1); 'subsidiary': EC(IUA)R 1996, reg 2(1); 'undertaking': EC(IUA)R 1996, reg 2(1) & EC(CGA)R 1992, reg 3(1).

Notes

Acquisition and merger accounting: This refers to the accounting methods to be adopted when one undertaking becomes a subsidiary of another. Prior to the making of these Regulations, such accounting methods were on a non-statutory footing only and were governed by SSAP 22 and SSAP 23.

---

8. An acquisition shall be accounted for by the acquisition method of accounting unless the conditions for accounting for it as a merger are met and the merger method of accounting is adopted.

Notes

See the notes to Sch, Pt IV, para 7. For the definition of a 'merger' see Sch, Pt IV, para 10.

9.(1) The acquisition method of accounting is as set out in this paragraph.

(2) The identifiable assets and liabilities of the undertaking acquired shall be included in the consolidated balance sheet at their fair values as at the date of acquisition.

(3) The income and expenditure of the undertaking acquired shall be brought into the group accounts only as from the date of the acquisition.

(4) (a) There shall be set off against the acquisition cost of the interest in the shares of the undertaking held by the undertakings dealt with in the group accounts the interest of undertakings dealt with in the group accounts in the adjusted capital and reserves of the undertaking acquired.

(b) In clause (a) of this subparagraph "the adjusted capital and reserves of the undertaking acquired" means its capital and reserves at the date of the acquisition after adjusting the identifiable assets and liabilities of the undertaking to fair values as at that date.

(5) The resulting amount if positive shall be treated as goodwill, and if negative as a negative consolidation difference.

(6) Where in applying the acquisition method of accounting—

(a) there is no record of—

(i) the fair values as at the date of acquisition of the identifiable assets and liabilities of the undertaking acquired, or

(ii) the acquisition cost of the interest in the shares of the acquired undertaking by the undertakings dealt with in the group accounts,

or

(b) such records cannot be obtained without unreasonable expense or delay,

then the values of the identifiable assets and liabilities and the acquisition cost shall be taken to be the values and cost ascribed to them in the earliest available record made after the acquisition of that subsidiary undertaking.

(7) In this paragraph

"the acquisition cost" means the amount of any cash consideration and the fair value of any other consideration, together with such amount (if any) in respect of fees and other expenses of the acquisition as the parent undertaking may determine;

the "identifiable assets and liabilities" in relation to the undertaking acquired means the assets and liabilities which are capable of being disposed of or discharged separately, without disposing of a business of the undertaking.

Definitions

'group accounts': EC(IUA)R 1996, reg 2(1); 'parent undertaking': EC(IUA)R 1996, reg 2(1); 'subsidiary': EC(IUA)R 1996, reg 2(1); 'undertaking': EC(IUA)R 1996, reg 2(1) & EC(CGA)R 1992, reg 3(1).

Notes

Merger: For the purposes of these regs, a merger occurs where Undertaking A, directly and/or through nominees, acquires not less than 90% of the 'relevant shares' of Undertaking B in consideration for the allotment to the members of Undertaking B of equity shares in Undertaking B.

10.(1) The conditions for accounting for an acquisition as a merger are as follows:

(a) that at least 90 per cent of the nominal value of the relevant shares in the undertaking acquired is held by or on behalf of the undertakings dealt with in the group accounts,

(b) that the proportion referred to in clause (a) of this subparagraph was attained pursuant to an arrangement providing for the issue of equity shares by the undertakings dealt with in the group accounts, and

(c) that the fair value of any consideration other than the issue of equity shares given pursuant to the arrangement by the undertakings dealt with in the group accounts did not exceed 10 per cent of the nominal value of the equity shares issued.

(2) In subparagraph (1)(a) "relevant shares in an undertaking acquired" means those shares carrying unrestricted rights to participate both in distributions and in the assets of the undertaking upon liquidation.

Definitions

'group accounts': EC(IUA)R 1996, reg 2(1); 'undertaking': EC(IUA)R 1996, reg 2(1) & EC(CGA)R 1992, reg 3(1).

11.(1) The merger method of accounting is set out in this paragraph.

(2) The assets and liabilities of the undertaking acquired shall be brought into the group accounts at the figures at which they stand in the undertaking's accounts, subject to any adjustment authorised or required by this Part of the Schedule.

(3) The income and expenditure of the undertaking acquired shall be included in the group accounts for the entire financial year, including the period before the acquisition.

(4) The group accounts shall show corresponding amounts relating to the previous financial year as if the undertaking acquired had been included in the consolidation throughout that year.

(5) There shall be set off against the aggregate of—

(a) the appropriate amount in respect of shares issued by the undertakings dealt with in the group accounts in consideration for the acquisition of shares in the undertaking acquired, and

(b) the fair value of any other consideration for the acquisition of shares in the undertaking acquired, determined as at the date when those shares were acquired,

the nominal value of the issued share capital of the undertaking acquired held by the undertakings dealt with in the group accounts.

(6) The resulting amount by virtue of this paragraph shall be shown as an adjustment to the consolidated reserves.

12.(1) Where a group of undertakings is acquired, paragraphs 8 to 11 apply with the following adaptations.

(2) Reference to shares of the undertaking acquired shall be construed as references to shares of the parent undertaking of the group.

(3) Other references to the undertaking acquired shall be construed as references to the group, and references to the assets and liabilities, income and expenditure and capital and reserves of the undertaking acquired shall be construed as references to the assets and liabilities, income and expenditure and capital and reserves of the group after making the set-offs and other adjustments required by this Part of the Schedule in the case of group accounts.

Definitions

'group accounts': EC(IUA)R 1996, reg 2(1); 'parent undertaking': EC(IUA)R 1996, reg 2(1); 'undertaking': EC(IUA)R 1996, reg 2(1) & EC(CGA)R 1992, reg 3(1).

VALUATION

13.(1) In determining the amounts to be included in the group accounts, Regulations 7 and 8 and the valuation rules contained in Part II of this Schedule shall apply and shall be applied consistently within those accounts.

(2) Subparagraph (1) shall not apply to those liabilities items the valuation of which by the insurance undertakings included in group accounts is based on the application of provisions specific to insurance undertakings nor to those assets items changes in the values of which also affect or establish policyholders' rights.

(3) Where subparagraph (2) applies, that fact shall be disclosed in the notes to the group accounts.

Definitions

'group accounts': EC(IUA)R 1996, reg 2(1); 'undertaking': EC(IUA)R 1996, reg 2(1) & EC(CGA)R 1992, reg 3(1).

---

14. (1) Subject to subparagraph (2) a parent undertaking shall apply the same methods of valuation in drawing up group accounts as it applies in drawing up its annual accounts.

(2) Subject to paragraph 13, subparagraph (1) shall not apply where, in the opinion of the directors, a departure from the provisions of that paragraph is necessary for the purpose of Regulation 10(5)(i).

(3) Any application of subparagraph (2) and the reasons therefor shall be disclosed in the notes to the group accounts.

Definitions

'group accounts': EC(IUA)R 1996, reg 2(1); 'parent undertaking': EC(IUA)R 1996, reg 2(1).

Notes

Departure from valuation methods used for accounts of parent undertaking: The group accounts may adopt different valuation methods from those used in drawing up the parent undertaking's annual accounts, where the directors deem it necessary to do so to ensure that the group accounts give a true and fair view of the affairs of the group as a whole.[1] Any such departure must be noted in the accounts,[2] and furthermore, the valuation methods actually adopted must still be of a type specified in Pt II of the Schedule.

1 Sch, Pt IV, para 14(2). As to what constitutes a 'true and fair view' see Reg 10(5) and the notes thereto.

2 Sch, Pt IV, para 14(3).

15.(1) Where assets and liabilities to be included in the group accounts have been valued or otherwise determined by undertakings according to accounting rules differing from those used for the group accounts, the values or amounts shall be adjusted so as to accord with the rules used for the group accounts.

(2) If it appears to the directors of the parent undertaking that there are special reasons for departing from subparagraph (1) they may do so, but particulars of any such departure, the reasons for it and its effect shall be given in a note to the accounts.

(3) The adjustments referred to in this paragraph need not be made if they are not material for the purpose of giving a true and fair view.

Definitions

'group accounts': EC(IUA)R 1996, reg 2(1); 'parent undertaking': EC(IUA)R 1996, reg 2(1); 'undertaking': EC(IUA)R 1996, reg 2(1) & EC(CGA)R 1992, reg 3(1).

Notes

Revaluation of undertakings' assets and liabilities: If the valuation method which is used for the group accounts, differs from that used in the annual accounts of any of the members of the group, then unless there are special reasons for not doing so, that member's assets and liabilities will first have to be re-valued in accordance with the group's valuation method before being included in the group accounts.[1] Such a valuation will not, however, be required, if, without same, the accounts will still give a true and fair view of the affairs of the group as a whole.[2]

1 Sch, Pt IV, para 15(1) & (2). If, for special reasons, a revaluation does not take place, this fact and the reasons therefor, as well as the effect thereof, must be disclosed in a note to the accounts: para 15(2).

2 Sch, Pt IV, para 15(3). For the meaning of 'true and fair view' see reg 10(5) and the notes thereto.

---

16. Any differences of accounting rules as between a parent undertaking's individual accounts for a financial year and its group accounts shall be disclosed in a note to the latter accounts and the reasons for the difference given.

Definitions

'group accounts': EC(IUA)R 1996, reg 2(1); 'individual accounts': EC(IUA)R 1996, reg 2(1); 'parent undertaking': EC(IUA)R 1996, reg 2(1).

17. Amounts which in the particular context of any provision of this Part of the Schedule are not material may be disregarded for the purposes of that provision.

DIFFERENCES IN TAX TREATMENT

18. Account shall be taken in the group accounts of any difference arising on consolidation between the tax chargeable for the financial year and for preceding financial years and the amount of tax paid or payable in respect of those years, provided that it is probable that an actual charge to tax will arise within the foreseeable future for one of the undertakings dealt with in the group accounts.

Definitions

'group accounts': EC(IUA)R 1996, reg 2(1); 'undertaking': EC(IUA)R 1996, reg 2(1) & EC(CGA)R 1992, reg 3(1).

MINORITY INTERESTS

19.(1) The formats set out in Part I of this Schedule shall have effect in relation to group accounts with the modifications set out in this paragraph.

(2) In the Balance Sheet Format (which is set out in Chapter 2 of Part I of this Schedule) a further item headed "Minority interests" shall be added as Liabilities item Aa and under that item shall be shown the amount of capital and reserves attributable to shares in subsidiary undertakings included in the consolidation held by or on behalf of persons other than the parent undertaking and its subsidiary undertakings.

(3) In the profit and loss account format (which is set out in Chapter 2 of Part I of this Schedule) a further item headed "Minority interests" shall be added as item l0(a) in the non-technical account and under the said item l0(a) there shall be shown the amount of any profit or loss on ordinary activities attributable to shares in subsidiary undertakings included in the consolidation held by or on behalf of persons other than the parent undertaking and its subsidiary undertakings.

(4) In the profit and loss account format (which is set out in Chapter 2 of Part I of this Schedule) a further item headed "Minority interests" shall be added in as item 13(a) in the non-technical account and under the said item 13(a) there shall be shown the amount of any profit or loss on extraordinary activities attributable to shares in subsidiary undertakings included in the consolidation held by or on behalf of persons other than the parent undertaking and its subsidiary undertakings.

(5) For the purposes of paragraph 3 of Part I of this Schedule (power to combine items) the additional items required by the foregoing provisions of this paragraph shall be treated as items to which a letter is assigned.

(6) Investment income and charges attributable to life assurance shall be shown in the technical account. Investment income and charges attributable to non-life business may be disclosed in the non-technical account.

Definitions

'group accounts': EC(IUA)R 1996, reg 2(1); 'parent undertaking': EC(IUA)R 1996, reg 2(1); 'subsidiary': EC(IUA)R 1996, reg 2(1); 'undertaking': EC(IUA)R 1996, reg 2(1) & EC(CGA)R 1992, reg 3(1).

JOINT VENTURES

20.(1) Where a parent undertaking or one of its subsidiaries dealt with in the group accounts manages another undertaking jointly with one or more undertakings not dealt with in the group accounts, that other undertaking (in this paragraph referred to as the "joint venture") may be dealt with in the group accounts by the method of proportional consolidation if it is neither a body corporate nor a subsidiary undertaking of the parent undertaking.

(2) The provisions of this Part relating to the preparation of group accounts shall, with any necessary modifications, apply to proportional consolidation under this paragraph.

Definitions

'group accounts': EC(IUA)R 1996, reg 2(1); 'parent undertaking': EC(IUA)R 1996, reg 2(1); 'subsidiary': EC(IUA)R 1996, reg 2(1); 'undertaking': EC(IUA)R 1996, reg 2(1) & EC(CGA)R 1992, reg 3(1).

Notes

Joint venture: For the purposes of para 20 an entity must satisfy the following criteria to constitute a 'joint venture':

(a) it must be an unincorporated body;

(b) it must not be a subsidiary undertaking of the parent undertaking; and

(c) it must be jointly managed with one or more other undertakings not dealt with in the group accounts.

If the entity satisfies (b) and (c) but is a body corporate, it will fall to be dealt with, if at all, as an 'associated undertaking' under Sch, Pt IV, para 21.

ASSOCIATED UNDERTAKINGS

21.(1) In this Part of the Schedule "associated undertaking" means an undertaking in which an undertaking dealt with in the group accounts has a participating interest and over whose operating and financial policy it exercises a significant influence, and which is not—

(a) a subsidiary undertaking of the parent undertaking, or

(b) a joint venture dealt with in accordance with paragraph 20.

(2) Where an undertaking holds 20 per cent or more of the voting rights in another undertaking, it shall be presumed to exercise such an influence over it unless the contrary is shown.

(3) Paragraphs (3) and (4) of Regulation 11 shall apply for determining whether subparagraph (2) applies.

Definitions

'associated undertaking': EC(IUA)R 1996, reg 2(1); 'group accounts': EC(IUA)R 1996, reg 2(1); 'parent undertaking': EC(IUA)R 1996, reg 2(1); 'participating interest': EC(IUA)R 1996, reg 2(1); 'subsidiary': EC(IUA)R 1996, reg 2(1); 'undertaking': EC(IUA)R 1996, reg 2(1) & EC(CGA)R 1992, reg 3(1).

Notes

Meaning of 'associated undertaking': An 'associated undertaking' is defined as one in which an undertaking dealt with in the group accounts has a 'participating interest'[1] and over whose operating and financial policy it exercises a significant influence and which is neither a subsidiary undertaking of the parent undertaking nor a 'joint venture' which has proportionally consolidated into the accounts under Sch, Pt IV, para 20.[2] It will be presumed, unless the contrary is shown, that one undertaking exercises a significant influence over the operating and financial policy of another, in circumstances where it holds 20% or more of the voting rights in that other undertaking.[3] In SSAP 1 it is stated at para 13 that 'significant influence' is not necessarily to be equated with 'control.' It suggests that having representation at board level is indicative but by no means conclusive of a 'significant influence.'

Inclusion of associated undertakings: Unlike subsidiary undertakings, the affairs of 'associated undertakings' are not fully consolidated into the group accounts. Instead, the accounts must simply include details of the parent undertaking's interest in the associated undertaking together with details of the amount of profit or loss attributable to that interest.[4] If the associated undertaking is itself a parent undertaking, the net assets and profits or losses of its own subsidiary undertakings will have to be taken into account in ascertaining the amount of the profit or loss attributable to the interest in the associated undertaking.[5]

1 For the meaning of 'participating interest' see Sch, Pt IV, para 23.

2 Sch, Pt IV, para 21(1).

3 Sch, Pt IV, para 21(2)). The same rules apply in determining whether or not at least 20% of such voting rights are held, as apply in determining whether one undertaking holds a majority of voting rights in another undertaking so as to make one undertaking a subsidiary of the other: para 21(3).

4 Sch, Part IV, para 22(1).

5 Sch, Part IV, para 22(2).

22.(1) The interest of an undertaking dealt with in the group accounts in an associated undertaking, and the amount of profit or loss attributable to such an interest, shall be shown in the group accounts by way of the equity method of accounting including dealing with any goodwill arising in accordance with paragraphs 2 to 4 of Part 11 of this Schedule.

(2) Where the associated undertaking is itself a parent undertaking, the net assets and profits or losses to be taken into account are those of the parent and its subsidiary undertakings, after making any consolidation adjustments.

(3) The equity method of accounting need not be applied if the amounts in question are not material for the purpose of giving a true and fair view.

Definitions

'associated undertaking': EC(IUA)R 1996, reg 2(1); 'group accounts': EC(IUA)R 1996, reg 2(1); 'parent undertaking': EC(IUA)R 1996, reg 2(1); 'subsidiary': EC(IUA)R 1996, reg 2(1); 'undertaking': EC(IUA)R 1996, reg 2(1) & EC(CGA)R 1992, reg 3(1).

Notes

See the notes to Sch, Pt IV, para 21.

PARTICIPATING INTEREST

23.(1) In this paragraph—

"participating interest" means a qualifying capital interest held by one undertaking in another on a long-term basis for the purpose of securing a contribution to that undertaking's own activities by the exercise of control or influence arising from or related to that interest;

"qualifying capital interest", means—

- (a) in relation to an undertaking with share capital, an interest in shares comprised in the allotted share capital of that undertaking,
- (b) in relation to an undertaking with capital but no share capital, an interest conferring rights to share in the capital of the undertaking,
- (c) in relation to an undertaking without capital, interests—
  - (i) conferring any right to share in the profits or liability to contribute to the losses of the undertaking, or
  - (ii) giving rise to an obligation to contribute to the debts or expenses of the undertaking in the event of a winding up,

and includes an interest which is convertible into a qualifying capital interest as well as an option to acquire any such qualifying capital interest.

(2) Where an undertaking holds a qualifying capital interest in another undertaking and such an interest represents 20 per cent or more of all such interests in the other undertaking it shall be presumed to hold that interest on the basis and for the purpose mentioned in subparagraph (1) unless the contrary is shown.

(3) The percentage of qualifying capital interests held in an undertaking with share capital shall be the percentage that the nominal value of the shares held represents of the nominal value of the allotted share capital of that undertaking.

(4) For the purpose of this paragraph an interest held on behalf of an undertaking shall be treated as held by it.

(5) For the purpose of this paragraph as it applies in relation to "participating interest" in Regulation 11(1)(c) (subsidiary undertaking)—

(a) there shall be attributed to an undertaking any interests held by any of its subsidiary undertakings, and

(b) the references in subparagraph (1) of this paragraph to the purpose and activities of an undertaking include the purpose and activities of any of its subsidiary undertakings and of the group as a whole.

(6) In the balance sheet and profit and loss formats set out in Part I of this Schedule as applied to group accounts by this Part of the Schedule "participating interest" does not include an interest in a group undertaking.

Definitions

'group accounts': EC(IUA)R 1996, reg 2(1); 'participating interest': EC(IUA)R 1996, reg 2(1); 'subsidiary': EC(IUA)R 1996, reg 2(1); 'undertaking': EC(IUA)R 1996, reg 2(1) & EC(CGA)R 1992, reg 3(1).

Notes

Interest held on a long-term basis: Para 23 gives very little guidance as to when an interest in an undertaking is to be regarded as being held 'on a long-term basis for the purpose of securing a contribution to [another] undertaking's own activities by the exercise of control or influence arising from or related to that interest'. Where the interest represents not less than 20% of all such interests in the undertaking, it shall be presumed to be held on that basis and for that purpose.[1] Ultimately, however, it is a question of fact in each case, and quite conceivably an interest of less than 20% could qualify as well.

Some guidance on the matter is to be found in FRS No 2[2] at para 10 where it is stated that an interest should be deemed to be held 'on a long-term basis' where it is held other than exclusively with a view to subsequent resale.

Options and convertible debentures: An interest in debentures which are convertible into shares would constitute a 'qualifying capital interest' as would an option to acquire shares in the company.[3]

1 Sch, Pt IV, para 23(2).

2 Issued by the Accounting Standards Board and the Institute of Chartered Accountants in Ireland.

3 Sch, Pt IV, para 23(1).

24.(1) The formats in Part I of this Schedule shall have effect in relation to group accounts with the following modifications.

(2) In the balance sheet format (which is set out in Chapter 2 of Part I of this Schedule) assets item C.II.3 (Participating Interests) shall be replaced by two items headed "Interests in associated undertakings" and "Other participating interests".

(3) In the profit and loss account format (which is set out in Chapter 2 of Part I of this Schedule) the following items, namely:

(a) item I.2(a) of the technical account – non-life insurance;

(b) item II.2(a) of the technical account – life assurance business, and

(c) item III.3(a) of the non-technical account

shall be replaced by two items, "income from interests in associated undertakings" and "income from other participating interests".

Definitions

'associated undertaking': EC(IUA)R 1996, reg 2(1); 'group accounts': EC(IUA)R 1996, reg 2(1); 'participating interest': EC(IUA)R 1996, reg 2(1).

Chapter 3
Information Required
BY WAY OF NOTES TO THE GROUP ACCOUNTS

25. Without prejudice to Regulation 10, the notes to the group accounts shall also set out the information required by the following provisions of this Chapter.

Definitions

'group accounts': EC(IUA)R 1996, reg 2(1).

26.(1) In relation to the resulting amounts referred to in paragraph 9(5) and 11(6), there shall be stated in the notes to the group accounts the methods used in calculating those amounts and the reasons for any significant difference between such amounts for the financial year to which the group accounts refer and those for the preceding financial year.

(2) In relation to acquisitions taking place in the financial year, there shall be stated in the notes to the group accounts the following:

(a) the name and registered office of the undertaking acquired, or where a group was acquired, the name and registered office of the parent undertaking of that group, and

(b) whether the acquisition has been accounted for by the acquisition or the merger method of accounting.

Definitions

'group accounts': EC(IUA)R 1996, reg 2(1); 'parent undertaking': EC(IUA)R 1996, reg 2(1); 'undertaking': EC(IUA)R 1996, reg 2(1) & EC(CGA)R 1992, reg 3(1).

27. Where sums originally denominated in currencies, other than the currency in which the group accounts are drawn up, have been brought into account under any items shown in the balance sheet or profit and loss account, the basis on which those sums have, for the purposes of the accounts, been converted into the currency in which the group accounts are drawn up shall be stated.

Definitions

'group accounts': EC(IUA)R 1996, reg 2(1).

28. In respect of the aggregate of the amounts shown in the group balance sheet under the heading "Creditors" there shall be stated the following:

(a) the aggregate amount of any debts included under that heading which are payable or repayable otherwise than by instalments and fall due for payment or repayment after the end of the period of five years beginning with the day next following the end of the financial year,

(b) the aggregate amount of any debts so included which are payable or repayable by instalments any of which fall due for payment after the end of that period,

(c) the aggregate amount of any debts included under that heading in respect of which any security has been given, and

(d) an indication of the nature of the securities so given.

29.(1) The following information shall be given with respect to the employees of the undertakings dealt with in the group accounts:

(a) the average number of persons employed in the financial year, by the undertakings dealt with in the group accounts, and

(b) the average number of persons employed within each category of persons employed by those undertakings.

(2) In respect of all persons employed by the undertakings dealt with in the group accounts during the financial year who are taken into account in determining the relevant annual number for the purposes of subparagraph (1)(a), there shall also be stated the aggregate amount of staff costs, save insofar as this amount is stated in the group profit and loss account.

(3) The categories of persons employed by the undertakings included in the group accounts by reference to which the number required to be disclosed by subparagraph (1)(b) is to be determined shall be such as the directors of the parent undertaking may select, having regard to the manner in which the activities of the undertakings dealt with in the group accounts are organised.

(4) For the purposes of clauses (a) and (b) of subparagraph (1) the average number of persons employed by the undertakings dealt with in the group accounts shall be determined by adding together the averages, for each such undertaking, calculated by the method set out in paragraph 27(3) of Part III of this Schedule.

(5) The average number of persons employed during the financial year by an undertaking proportionally consolidated pursuant to paragraph 21 of this Part, calculated by the manner specified in subparagraph (4), shall also be stated.

Definitions

'group accounts': EC(IUA)R 1996, reg 2(1); 'parent undertaking': EC(IUA)R 1996, reg 2(1); 'undertaking': EC(IUA)R 1996, reg 2(1) & EC(CGA)R 1992, reg 3(1).

30.(1) In the case of group accounts, the pension commitments referred to in paragraph 18(4) of Part III of this Schedule and the emoluments and compensation referred to in paragraph 58(6) of the Schedule to the 1986 Act shall be to such commitments, emoluments and compensation relating to directors or past directors of the parent undertaking in respect of duties relating to the parent undertaking, to any of its subsidiary undertakings, to any undertakings proportionally consolidated in accordance with paragraph 21 of this Part or to associated undertakings.

(2) Section 191 of the Principal Act shall not apply to group accounts prepared in accordance with these Regulations.

Definitions

'group accounts': EC(IUA)R 1996, reg 2(1); 'parent undertaking': EC(IUA)R 1996, reg 2(1); 'the Principal Act': EC(IUA)R 1996, reg 2(1); 'subsidiary': EC(IUA)R 1996, reg 2(1); 'undertaking': EC(IUA)R 1996, reg 2(1) & EC(CGA)R 1992, reg 3(1).

31.(1) Subject to subparagraph (2), sections 41 to 43 of the Act of 1990 shall apply to group accounts prepared under these Regulations.

(2) The particulars of any transaction, arrangement or agreement referred to in those sections, entered into with a director of the parent undertaking by an undertaking proportionally consolidated in accordance with paragraph 21 of this Part of this Schedule, or an associated undertaking, shall be similarly stated.

Definitions

'the Act of 1990': EC(IUA)R 1996, reg 2(1); 'associated undertaking': EC(IUA)R 1996, reg 2(1); 'group accounts': EC(IUA)R 1996, reg 2(1); 'parent undertaking': EC(IUA)R 1996, reg 2(1); 'undertaking': EC(IUA)R 1996, reg 2(1) & EC(CGA)R 1992, reg 3(1).

32.(1)(a) The information set out in subparagraphs (2), (3) and (4) shall be stated in relation to each undertaking dealt with in the group accounts.

(b) For the purpose of clause (a), the information required by subparagraph (3)(a) does not include such interests in the parent undertaking.

(2) The names and registered offices of the undertakings included in the group accounts shall be set out therein.

(3) (a) The aggregate of the qualifying capital interests held in that undertaking by the undertakings dealt with in the group accounts as a proportion of the total of such interests shall be stated for the purposes of paragraph 25.

(b) In this subparagraph "qualifying capital interest" has the meanings assigned to it in paragraph 23.

(c) For the purpose of this subparagraph, paragraph 23(3) shall apply in determining the percentage of qualifying capital interests held in an undertaking with share capital.

(4) (a) There shall be set out for the purposes of paragraph 25 a note indicating by virtue of which of the provisions of Regulation 11 has the undertaking been dealt with in the group accounts.

(b) The information required by clause (c) of this subparagraph may be omitted where the undertaking has been dealt with in the group accounts by virtue of Regulation 11(1)(a), and where the proportion of capital and the proportion of voting rights held are the same.

Definitions

'group accounts': EC(IUA)R 1996, reg 2(1); 'parent undertaking': EC(IUA)R 1996, reg 2(1); 'undertaking': EC(IUA)R 1996, reg 2(1) & EC(CGA)R 1992, reg 3(1).

33. The information set out in subparagraphs (2), (3) and (4) of paragraph 32 shall also be given in respect of each undertaking which has been excluded from the group accounts by virtue of the application of paragraph 2.

Definitions

'group accounts': EC(IUA)R 1996, reg 2(1); 'undertaking': EC(IUA)R 1996, reg 2(1) & EC(CGA)R 1992, reg 3(1).

34.(1) The information set out in subparagraphs (2) and (3) of paragraph 32 shall be stated in relation to each associated undertaking.

(2) The information required by subparagraph (1) shall also be stated in relation to associated undertakings, the interest in which has been dealt with in accordance with paragraph 22(3).

Definitions

'associated undertaking': EC(IUA)R 1996, reg 2(1).

35.(1) The information set out in subparagraphs (2) and (3) of paragraph 32 shall be stated in relation to each undertaking that has been proportionally consolidated in accordance with paragraph 20.

(2) The nature of the joint management of each joint venture, to which paragraph 20 applies, proportionally consolidated shall also be stated.

36.(1) The information set out in subparagraphs (2) and (3) of paragraph 32 shall be stated in relation to each undertaking (in this paragraph referred to as an "undertaking of substantial interest"), other than those referred to in paragraphs 32 to 35 in which undertakings dealt with in the group accounts and undertakings not dealt with by virtue of the application of subparagraphs (4) to (6) of paragraph 2, or persons acting in their own name but on behalf of such undertakings, between them hold a qualifying capital interest representing 20 per cent or more of such interests.

(2) There shall also be stated in relation to each undertaking of substantial interest, the amount of its capital and reserves and its profit or loss for its latest financial year for which accounts have been adopted.

(3) The information required by subparagraphs (1) and (2) may be omitted, where for the purposes of Regulation 10(5), it is of negligible importance.

(4) The information concerning capital and reserves and the profit or loss required by subparagraph (2) may also be omitted where the undertaking concerned is not required to attach its balance sheet to its annual return and where the qualifying capital interest held as described in subparagraph (1) is less than 50 per cent.

(5) For the purpose of this paragraph, paragraph 23(3) shall apply in determining the percentage of qualifying capital interest held in an undertaking with share capital.

Definitions

'accounts': EC(IUA)R 1996, reg 2(1); 'annual return': EC(IUA)R 1996, reg 2(1); 'group accounts': EC(IUA)R 1996, reg 2(1); 'undertaking': EC(IUA)R 1996, reg 2(1) & EC(CGA)R 1992, reg 3(1).

[37. The notes on the group accounts shall set out information relating to—

(a) the nature and business purpose of any arrangement which is not included in the consolidated balance sheet, and the financial impact of such arrangement if the risks or benefits arising from the arrangement are material, and in so far as the disclosure of such risks or benefits is necessary for assessing the financial position, taken as a whole, of the parent undertaking and its subsidiaries included in the consolidated balance sheet, and

(b) subject to paragraph 38, transactions entered into by—

(i) the parent undertaking, or

(ii) a subsidiary of that parent undertaking included in the group accounts,

with related parties if the transactions are material and have not been concluded under normal market conditions and the information shall include the amounts of such transactions, the nature of the related party relationship and other information concerning the transactions which is necessary for an understanding of the financial position, taken as a whole, of the parent undertaking and its subsidiaries included in the group accounts.

38. A transaction referred to in paragraph 37(b) does not include an intragroup transaction.

39 Information provided pursuant to paragraph 37(b) concerning individual transactions may be aggregated according to their nature except where separate information is necessary for an understanding of the effects of the related party transactions on the financial position, taken as a whole, of the parent undertaking and its subsidiaries included in the group accounts.

40. In paragraph 37 'consolidated balance sheet' means the balance sheet prepared in respect of the group accounts.

41. A word or expression that is used in paragraphs 37 to 39 has the same meaning as it has in Directive 2006/46/EC][a].

Amendments

a Paragraphs 37–41 inserted by European Communities (Directive 2006/46/EC) Regulations 2009, reg 25.

Explanatory Note

(*This note is not part of the Instrument and does not purport to be a legal interpretation*).

These Regulations give effect to the Council Directive on the annual accounts and consolidated accounts of insurance undertakings (91/674/EEC, O.J. No. L374/7). This Directive provides for the application of the fourth and seventh company law directives to insurance companies, taking account of specific features of the accounts of insurance companies.

The fourth directive (78/60/EEC, O.J. No. L222/11) provides for co-ordinated national legislation concerning presentation of accounts and uniform valuation of assets and liabilities brought to account by all undertakings within the European Union, aimed at providing comparable sets of accounts within a range of options. It was implemented by the Companies (Amendment) Act, 1986 (No. 25 of 1986). The seventh directive (83/349/EEC, O.J. L193/1) provided for co-ordinated national legislation concerning consolidated accounts. It was implemented by the European Communities (Companies: Group Accounts) Regulations, 1992 (No. 201 of 1992).

These Regulations require insurance undertakings to prepare and to publish annually accounts (balance sheet, profit and loss account and notes), in accordance with the provisions of these Regulations. They also require (with provision for exceptions) insurance undertakings which have subsidiary undertakings or non-insurance holding companies, the most important of whose subsidiaries are insurance undertakings, to prepare and to publish group accounts in accordance with the provisions of these Regulations.

The Regulations contain provisions governing the preparation of accounts, including group accounts, the content of those accounts, their format and the valuation of items to be included. They specify information to be included in the notes to the accounts.

Companies Act, 1990 (Uncertificated Securities) Regulations 1996

SI 68/1996

ARRANGEMENT OF REGULATIONS

CHAPTER I
CITATION, COMMENCEMENT & INTERPRETATION

CHAPTER II
TRANSFERRING & RECORDING SHARES & SECURITIES

CHAPTER III
APPROVAL AND COMPLIANCE OF OPERATOR

Notes

These regs, made under s 239 of the Companies Act 1990, facilitate the transfer and evidencing of title to shares and other securities without stock transfer forms or certificates.

Following the collapse in 1993 of the London Stock Exhange's 'Taurus' scheme, a new attempt was made to computerise the transfer of quoted securities, with the Bank of England co-ordinating key City of London players in the setting up of the Securities Settlement Task Force, which decided on a different system called 'CREST'. During 1995 this team developed the present CREST system, beginning testing in January 1996 and starting operations in July 1996. CREST replaced share certificates and stock transfer forms with authentic electronic instructions, for those companies who wished to use it.

Under the Companies Act 1963 companies are obliged to issue share certificates to shareholders. In the absence of these regs, they could only register the transfer of shares on receipt of a stock transfer form. To facilitate the CREST system, it was necessary to change the law to allow an electronic transfer system to work. This need had been foreseen in CA 1990, s 239, which enabled the making of these regs, taking cognisance of advances in technology. CRESTCo is at present the sole operator of a 'relevant system' as defined by the Regulations although it is possible for a competitor to establish itself.

These regs are, with minor changes and adjustments, identical to the UK Uncertificated Securities Regulations 1995. The relevant UK Minister, when moving the UK 1995 Regulations made the point that no computerised system would ever be perfect, and continued: 'I do not believe that this system will stand still. This is the start of a system which will greatly assist matters. ... with computers one has to keep going. One cannot just stop at any point and say, 'This is fine.' One has to keep going. The process will be continued.' Hansard 14 Dec 1995, columns 1390 et seq. And in both the UK and Ireland this has proven to be the case. The UK regs were repealed and re-enacted with amendments in 2001. The enabling Irish section, s 239 of the 1990 Act, was extensively amended by the Investment Funds, Companies and Miscellaneous Provisions Act 2006, s 12.

I, PAT RABBITTE, Minister of State at the Department of Enterprise and Employment, in exercise of the powers conferred on me by section 4 of the Companies (Amendment) Act, 1977 (No. 31 of 1977) and section 239 of the Companies Act, 1990 (No. 33 of 1990) and the Enterprise and Employment (Delegation of Ministerial Functions) Order, 1995

(S.I. No. 42 of 1995), to enable title to securities to be evidenced otherwise than by a certificate and transferred without a written instrument, and make provision for certain supplemental and incidental matters, hereby make the following regulations:

CHAPTER I

CITATION, COMMENCEMENT AND INTERPRETATION

1 Citation and Construction

(1) These regulations may be cited as the Companies Act, 1990 (Uncertificated Securities) Regulations, 1996.

(2) These regulations shall be construed as one with the Companies Acts.

Definitions

'the Companies Acts': CA 1990(US)R 1996, reg 3(1).

UK legislation

Uncertificated Securities Regulations 2001, reg 1.

---

2 Commencement

These regulations shall come into force on the 1st April, 1996.

UK legislation

Uncertificated Securities Regulations 2001, reg 1.

---

3 Interpretation

(1) In these regulations except where the context otherwise requires—

'the 1963 Act' means the Companies Act, 1963;

'the 1977 Act' means the Companies (Amendment) Act, 1977;

'the 1990 Act' means the Companies Act, 1990;

'the 1995 Act' means the Stock Exchange Act, 1995;

'articles of association', in the case of a company which is not a company within the meaning of section 2 (1) of the 1963 Act, shall include its charter, bye-laws or other constituent documents;

'certificate', means any certificate, instrument or other document of, or evidencing, title to, a unit or units of security;

'certificated unit of a security' means a unit of a security other than an uncertificated unit of a security as defined in this regulation;

'the Companies Acts' means the 1963 Act and any enactment which is to be construed therewith;

'company' means a company within the meaning of section 2(1) of the 1963 Act and any body corporate within the meaning of section 377(1) of the 1963 Act;

'competent authority' means any person authorised under the laws of a Member State to approve persons to operate a relevant system;

'computer' means any device or combination or succession of devices for storing and processing information, and any reference to information being derived from other information is a reference to its being derived therefrom by calculation, comparison or any other process;

'court' means a court of competent jurisdiction;

'dematerialised instruction' means an instruction sent or received by means of a relevant system;

'director', in the case of a company which is not a company within the meaning of section 2(1) of the 1963 Act, includes a member of the governing body of the company;

'enactment' includes an enactment comprised in any subordinate legislation within the meaning of the Interpretation Act, 1937;

'generate', in relation to an operator-instruction, means to initiate the procedures by which an operator-instruction comes to be sent;

'guidance', in relation to an operator, means guidance issued by the operator which is intended to have continuing effect and is issued in writing or other legible form, which if it were a rule, would come within the definition of a rule;

'instruction' includes any instruction, election, acceptance or any other message of any kind;

'interest in a security' means any legal or equitable interest or right in relation to a security, including—

(a) an absolute or contingent right to acquire a security created, allotted or issued or to be created, allotted or issued; and

(b) the interests or rights of a person for whom a security is held by a custodian or depository;

'issue', in relation to a new unit of a security, means to confer title to that unit on a person;

'issuer-instruction' means a properly authenticated dematerialised instruction attributable to a participating issuer;

'officer', in relation to a participating issuer, includes—

(a) where the participating issuer is a company, such persons as are mentioned in section 2 (1) of the 1963 Act;

(b) where the participating issuer is a partnership, a partner; or in the event that no partner is situated in the State, a person in the State who is acting on behalf of the partner; and

(c) where the participating issuer is neither a company nor a partnership, any member of its governing body; or in the event that no member of its governing body is situated in the State, a person in the State who is acting on behalf of its governing body;

'operator' means any person specified in regulation 28 or approved by the Minister under these regulations as operator of a relevant system;

'operator-instruction' means a properly authenticated dematerialised instruction attributable to an operator;

'operator-system' means those facilities and procedures which are part of the relevant system, which are maintained and operated by or for an operator, by which the operator generates operator-instructions and receives dematerialised instructions from system-participants and by which persons change the form in which units of a participating security are held;

'participating issuer' means a person who has issued a security which is a participating security;

'participating security' means a security, title to units of which is permitted by an operator to be transferred by means of a relevant system;

'practices' in relation to an operator means non-binding guidance issued by the operator;

'register of members' means a register of members maintained by a company under section 116 (1) of the 1963 Act;

'register of securities'—

(a) in relation to shares, means a register of members, and

(b) in relation to units of a security other than shares, means a register maintained by the issuer, whether by virtue of these regulations or otherwise, of persons holding the units;

'relevant system' means a computer based system and procedures which enable title to units of a security to be evidenced and transferred without a written instrument, and which facilitate supplementary and incidental matters and 'relevant system' includes an operator-system;

'rules' in relation to an operator, means rules made or conditions imposed by the operator with respect to the provision of the relevant system;

'securities' means shares, stock, debentures, debenture stock, loan stock, bonds, units in undertakings for collective investments in transferable securities within the meaning of the European Communities (Undertakings for Collective Investment in Transferable Securities) Regulations, 1989 (S.I. No. 78 of 1989), and other securities of any description;

['settlement', in relation to a transfer of uncertificated units of a security between 2 system-members by means of a relevant system, means the delivery of those units to the transferee and, where appropriate, the creation of any associated obligation to make payments, in accordance with the rules and practices of the operator, and 'settle' shall be construed accordingly;][a]

'settlement-bank' in relation to a relevant system, means a person who has contracted to make payments in connection with transfers of title to uncertificated units of a security by means of that system;

'share' means share or stock in the share capital of a company;

'system entry' means any entry or record made, supplied or stored in legible or non-legible form by any operator or any system-participant in any register of securities or in connection with the operation of a relevant system and any dematerialised instruction issued by any such persons;

'system-member', in relation to a relevant system, means a person permitted by an operator to transfer title to uncertificated units of a security by means of that system and includes, where relevant, two or more persons who are jointly so permitted;

'system-member instruction' means a properly authenticated dematerialised instruction attributable to a system-member;

'system-participant' in relation to a relevant system, means a person who is permitted by an operator to send and receive properly authenticated dematerialised instructions and 'sponsoring system-participant' means a system-participant who is permitted by an operator to send properly authenticated dematerialised instructions attributable to another person and to receive properly authenticated dematerialised instructions on another person's behalf;

'system-user', in relation to a relevant system, means a person who as regards that system is a participating issuer, system-member, system-participant or settlement-bank;

'uncertificated unit of a security' means a unit of a security title to which is recorded on the relevant register of securities as being held in uncertificated form, and title to which, by virtue of these regulations, may be transferred by means of a relevant system and corresponding expressions shall be construed accordingly;

'unit of a security' means the smallest possible transferable unit of the security (for example a single share);

and any other expression bears the meaning given to it in the 1963 Act or the 1990 Act.

(2) For the purposes of these Regulations—

(a) a dematerialised instruction is properly authenticated if it complies with the specifications in that regard contained in the rules made and practices instituted by an operator corresponding to those in paragraph 5 (b) of the Schedule to these regulations; and

(b) a dematerialised instruction is attributable to a person if it is expressed to have been sent by that person, or if it is expressed to have been sent on behalf of that person, in each case in accordance with the specifications in that regard contained in the rules made and practices instituted by an operator corresponding to those in paragraph 5 (c) of the Schedule to these regulations; and a dematerialised instruction may be attributable to more than one person.

(3) In these regulations, except where otherwise indicated—

(a) a reference to a numbered regulation is a reference to the regulation of these regulations so numbered;

(b) a reference in a regulation to a numbered paragraph is a reference to the paragraph of that regulation so numbered;

(c) a reference in the Schedule to a numbered paragraph is a reference to the paragraph of that Schedule so numbered;

(d) a reference in a paragraph to a numbered sub-paragraph is a reference to the sub-paragraph of that paragraph so numbered.

(4) References to title to securities include any legal or equitable interest in securities and references to a transfer of title include a transfer by way of security.

(5) Where, in these regulations, anything is required or allowed to be done within a number of days not exceeding six a day that is Saturday, Sunday or public holiday shall not be reckoned in computing that number.

Amendment

a Definition of 'settlement' inserted by the CA1990 (US)(A)R 2005, reg 2(a), with effect from 10 November 2005.

UK legislation

Uncertificated Securities Regulations 2001, reg 3.

CHAPTER II

TRANSFERRING AND RECORDING SHARES AND SECURITIES

4 Formalities of Transfer of securities

(1) Notwithstanding section 79 or section 81 of the 1963 Act or section 2 (1) of the Stock Transfer Act, 1963, title to securities may be evidenced and transferred without a written instrument provided that such title is evidenced and transferred in accordance with these regulations.

(2) References in any enactment or rule of law to a proper instrument of transfer or to a transfer with respect to securities, or any expression having like meaning, shall be taken to include a reference to an operator-instruction to a participating issuer to register a transfer of title on the relevant register of securities in accordance with the operator-instruction.

(3) Paragraphs (1) and (2) of this regulation shall not have effect in relation to an operator instruction—

(a) unless the operator giving the instruction has entered into an agreement with the Revenue Commissioners in relation to the payment of any stamp duty chargeable on transfers of title to securities through the relevant system,

(b) in the event of such an agreement having been terminated prior to the performance of the instruction, unless the instruction has been performed within seven days of the termination, and for the purpose of this paragraph an agreement shall be deemed to have been terminated on the date notice of the termination is published by the Revenue Commissioners in Iris Oifigiúil and in two national newspapers, and

(c) an agreement for the purpose of this regulation shall not impose an obligation on the operator giving the instruction to pay over to the Revenue Commissioners an amount of stamp duty greater than that collected on foot of transfers of title to securities through the relevant system.

Definitions

'the 1963 Act': CA 1990(US)R 1996, reg 3(1); 'enactment': CA 1990(US)R 1996, reg 3(1); 'instruction': CA 1990(US)R 1996, reg 3(1); 'operator': CA 1990(US)R 1996, reg 3(1); 'operator-instruction': CA 1990(US)R 1996, reg 3(1); 'participating issuer': CA 1990(US)R 1996, reg 3(1); 'register of securities': CA 1990(US)R 1996, reg 3(1); 'relevant system': CA 1990(US)R 1996, reg 3(1); 'securities': CA 1990(US)R 1996, reg 3(1).

UK legislation

Uncertificated Securities Regulations 2001, reg 37, Sch 7, Pt 1, para 7.

5 Transfer in writing

Section 6 of the Statute of Frauds Act (Ireland), 1695 and section 28(6) of the Supreme Court of Judicature (Ireland) Act, 1877 and any other rule of law requiring the execution under hand or seal of a document in writing for the transfer of property, shall not apply (if they would otherwise do so) to any transfer of title to uncertificated units of a security through a relevant system.

Definitions

'certificated unit of a security': CA 1990(US)R 1996, reg 3(1); 'court': CA 1990(US)R 1996, reg 3(1); 'relevant system': CA 1990(US)R 1996, reg 3(1); 'uncertificated unit of a security': CA 1990(US)R 1996, reg 3(1); 'document' CA 1963, s 2(1).

UK legislation

Uncertificated Securities Regulations 2001, reg 38(5), (7).

6 Participation in respect of shares

(1) Where an operator permits a class of shares in relation to which regulation 7 applies, or in relation to which a directors' resolution passed in accordance with regulation 8 is effective, to be a participating security, title to shares of that class which are recorded in a register of members as being held in uncertificated form may be transferred by means of the relevant system to which the permission relates.

(2) For the purposes of regulations 7 and 8 any shares with respect to which share warrants to bearer are issued under section 88 of the 1963 Act shall be regarded as forming a separate class of share.

Definitions

'the 1963 Act': CA 1990(US)R 1996, reg 3(1); 'director': CA 1990(US)R 1996, reg 3(1); 'operator': CA 1990(US)R 1996, reg 3(1); 'participating security': CA 1990(US)R 1996, reg 3(1); 'register of members': CA 1990(US)R 1996, reg 3(1); 'relevant system': CA 1990(US)R 1996, reg 3(1); 'share': CA 1990(US)R 1996, reg 3(1); 'directors' resolution': CA 1990(US)R 1996, reg 8(2).

UK legislation

Uncertificated Securities Regulations 2001, reg 14.

7

(1) This regulation applies to a class of shares if a company's articles of association are consistent with—

(a) the holding of shares in that class in uncertificated form,

(b) the transfer of title to shares in that class by means of a relevant system, and

(c) these regulations.

(2) A company may provide for the holding of shares in such a class to which this regulation applies in uncertificated form, and the transfer of title to any such shares by means of a relevant system.

Definitions

'articles of association': CA 1990(US)R 1996, reg 3(1); 'company': CA 1990(US)R 1996, reg 3(1); 'relevant system': CA 1990(US)R 1996, reg 3(1); 'share': CA 1990(US)R 1996, reg 3(1).

UK legislation

Uncertificated Securities Regulations 2001, reg 15.

8

(1) This regulation applies to a class of shares if a company's articles of association are inconsistent with—

(a) the holding of shares in that class in uncertificated form,

(b) the transfer of title to shares in that class by means of a relevant system, or

(c) any provision of these regulations.

(2) A company may resolve, subject to paragraph 6 (a), by resolution of its directors (in this Chapter referred to as a 'directors' resolution') that title to shares of a class issued or to be issued by it may be transferred by means of a relevant system.

(3) Upon a directors' resolution becoming effective in accordance with its terms, and for as long as it is in force, the articles of association in relation to the class of shares which were the subject of the directors' resolution, shall not apply to any uncertificated shares of that class to the extent that they are inconsistent with—

(a) the holding of shares of that class in uncertificated form;

(b) the transfer of title to shares of that class by means of a relevant system; and

(c) any provision of these regulations.

(4) Unless a company has given notice to every member of the company in accordance with its articles of association of its intention to pass a directors' resolution before the passing of such a resolution, it shall give such notice within 60 days of the passing of the resolution and a printed copy of such a directors' resolution shall be forwarded to and recorded by the registrar of companies.

(5) Notice given by the company before the coming into force of these regulations of its intention to pass a directors' resolution which, if it had been given after the coming into force of these regulations, would have satisfied the requirements of paragraph (4) shall be taken to satisfy the requirements of that paragraph.

(6) In respect of a class of shares the members of a company may by ordinary resolution—

(a) if a directors' resolution has not been passed, resolve that the directors of the company shall not pass a directors' resolution, or

(b) if a directors' resolution has been passed but not yet come into effect in accordance with its terms, resolve that it shall not come into effect; or

(c) if a directors' resolution has been passed and is effective in accordance with its terms but the class of shares has not yet been permitted by the operator to be a participating security, resolve that the directors' resolution shall cease to have effect; or

(d) if a directors' resolution has been passed and is effective in accordance with its terms and the class of shares has been permitted by the operator to be a participating security, resolve that the directors shall take the necessary steps to ensure that title to shares of the class that was the subject of the directors' resolution shall cease to be transferable by means of a relevant system and that the directors' resolution shall cease to have effect;

and the directors shall be bound by the terms of any such ordinary resolution. A printed copy of any such resolution shall be forwarded to and recorded by the registrar of companies.

(7) If default is made in complying with paragraphs (4) and (6), the participating issuer and every officer of the participating issuer who is in default shall be liable to a fine not exceeding [€1,904.61].[a]

(8) A company shall not permit the holding of shares in such a class as is referred to in paragraph (1) in un-certificated form, or the transfer of title to shares in such a class by means of a relevant system, unless in relation to that class of shares a directors' resolution is effective.

(9) This regulation shall not be taken to exclude the right of the members of a company to amend the articles of association of the company, in accordance with the articles, to allow the holding of any class of its shares in uncertificated form and the transfer of title to shares in such class by means of a relevant system.

Amendments

a £250 increased to £1,500 by CA 1990, s 240(7) and converted to €1,904.61 by Council Regulations (EC) No 1103/97, No 974/98 and No 2866/98 and the Economic and Monetary Union Act 1988, s 6.

Definitions

'articles of association': CA 1990(US)R 1996, reg 3(1); 'company':CA 1990(US)R 1996, reg 3(1); 'director': CA 1990(US)R 1996, reg 3(1); 'officer': CA 1990(US)R 1996, reg 3(1); 'operator': CA 1990(US)R 1996, reg 3(1); 'participating issuer': CA 1990(US)R 1996, reg 3(1);

'participating security': CA 1990(US)R 1996, reg 3(1); 'relevant system': CA 1990(US)R 1996, reg 3(1); 'share': CA 1990(US)R 1996, reg 3(1); 'printed': CA 1963, s 2(1).

UK legislation

Uncertificated Securities Regulations 2001, reg 16.

9 Participation in respect of securities other than shares

(1) Subject to paragraph (2), where the operator permits a security other than a share to be a participating security, title to units of that security which are recorded in a register of securities as being held in uncertificated form shall be transferred by means of a relevant system.

(2) If, in relation to any security (other than a share), the law under which it was constituted, or a current term of its issue, is consistent with—

(a) the holding of title to units of that security in uncertificated form,

(b) the transfer of title to units of that security by means of a relevant system, or

(c) these regulations,

the issuer shall not permit the holding of units of that security in uncertificated form, or the transfer of title to units of that security, by means of a relevant system.

(3) In this regulation the terms of issue of a security shall be taken to include the terms prescribed by the issuer on which units of the security are held and title to them is transferred.

Definitions

'issue': CA 1990(US)R 1996, reg 3(1); 'operator': CA 1990(US)R 1996, reg 3(1); 'participating security': CA 1990(US)R 1996, reg 3(1); 'register of securities': CA 1990(US)R 1996, reg 3(1); 'relevant system': CA 1990(US)R 1996, reg 3(1); 'securities': CA 1990(US)R 1996, reg 3(1); 'share': CA 1990(US)R 1996, reg 3(1).

UK legislation

Uncertificated Securities Regulations 2001, reg 19.

10 Entries on registers

(1) A participating issuer which is a company shall enter on its register of members, in respect of any class of shares which is a participating security, the number of shares each member holds in uncertificated form and certificated form respectively.

(2) In addition to the requirements of sections 91 and 92 of the 1963 Act, a participating issuer, who, apart from this regulation, is required by or under an enactment or instrument to maintain in the State a register of persons holding securities (other than shares) issued by it, shall enter on that register in respect of any class of security which is a participating security—

(a) the names and addresses of the persons holding units of that security, and

(b) the number of units of that security each person holds in uncertificated form and certificated form respectively.

(3) A participating issuer who, apart from this regulation, is not required by or under an enactment or instrument to maintain in the State in respect of a participating security issued by it a register of persons holding units of that participating security, shall maintain in the State a register recording—

(a) the names and addresses of the persons holding units of that security in uncertificated form; and

(b) the number of such units of that security each person holds in that form.

(4) If default is made in complying with paragraphs (1), (2) or (3), the participation issuer and every officer of the participating issuer who is in default shall be liable to a fine not exceeding [€1,904.61][a].

(5) For the purpose of paragraph (1) any shares with respect to which share warrants to bearer are issued under section 88 of the 1963 Act shall be regarded as a separate class of shares.

(6) No notice of any trust, expressed, implied or constructive, shall be entered on a register of securities which is maintained by virtue of paragraph (3) in relation to uncertificated units of a security, or be receivable by the registrar of such a register.

Amendments

a £500 increased to £1,500 by CA 1990, s 240(7) and converted to €1,904.61 by Council Regulations (EC) No 1103/97, No 974/98 and No 2866/98 and the Economic and Monetary Union Act 1988, s 6.

Definitions

'the 1963 Act': CA 1990(US)R 1996, reg 3(1); 'certificated unit of a security': CA 1990(US)R 1996, reg 3(1); 'company': CA 1990(US)R 1996, reg 3(1); 'enactment': CA 1990(US)R 1996, reg 3(1); 'officer': CA 1990(US)R 1996, reg 3(1); 'participating issuer': CA 1990(US)R 1996, reg 3(1); 'participating security': CA 1990(US)R 1996, reg 3(1); 'register of members': CA 1990(US)R 1996, reg 3(1); 'register of securities': CA 1990(US)R 1996, reg 3(1); 'securities': CA 1990(US)R 1996, reg 3(1); 'share': CA 1990(US)R 1996, reg 3(1); 'uncertificated unit of a security', CA 1990(US)R 1996, reg 3(1).

UK legislation

Uncertificated Securities Regulations 2001, reg 20.

11 Effect of entries on registers

(1) Subject to regulation 16 (7), an entry on a register mentioned in paragraph (1) or (2) of regulation 10 which records a person as holding units of a security in uncertificated form shall be evidence of such title to the units as would be evidenced if the entry on the register related to units of that security held in certificated form.

(2) Subject to regulation 16 (7), an entry on a register maintained by virtue of paragraph (3) of regulation 10 shall be prima facie evidence that the person to whom the entry relates has such title to the units of the security which that person is recorded as holding in uncertificated form as if the units were held in certificated form.

Definitions

'unit of a security': CA 1990(US)R 1996, reg 3(1).

UK legislation

Uncertificated Securities Regulations 2001, reg 24.

12 Rectification of and changes to registers of securities

(1) A participating issuer shall not rectify a register of securities in relation to uncertificated units of a security held by a system-member except—

(a) with the consent of the operator, or

(b) by order of the High Court.

(2) A participating issuer who rectifies or otherwise changes an entry on a register of securities in relation to uncertificated units of a security (except in response to an operator-instruction) shall immediately—

(a) notify the operator, and

(b) inform the system-members concerned,

of the change to the entry.

Definitions

'certificated unit of a security': CA 1990(US)R 1996, reg 3(1); 'operator': CA 1990(US)R 1996, reg 3(1); 'operator-instruction': CA 1990(US)R 1996, reg 3(1); 'participating issuer': CA 1990(US)R 1996, reg 3(1); 'register of securities': CA 1990(US)R 1996, reg 3(1); 'system-member': CA 1990(US)R 1996, reg 3(1); 'uncertificated unit of a security': CA 1990(US)R 1996, reg 3(1).

UK legislation

Uncertificated Securities Regulations 2001, reg 25.

13 Closing of registers

Notwithstanding section 121 of the 1963 Act, a participating issuer shall not close a register of securities relating to a participating security without the consent of the operator.

Definitions

'the 1963 Act': CA 1990(US)R 1996, reg 3(1); 'operator': CA 1990(US)R 1996, reg 3(1); 'participating issuer': CA 1990(US)R 1996, reg 3(1); 'participating security': CA 1990(US)R 1996, reg 3(1); 'register of securities': CA 1990(US)R 1996, reg 3(1).

UK legislation

Uncertificated Securities Regulations 2001, reg 26.

14 Attendance and Voting at meetings

(1) For the purposes of determining which persons are entitled to attend or vote at a meeting, and how many votes such persons may cast, the participating issuer may specify in the notice of the meeting a time, not more than 48 hours before the time fixed for the meeting, by which a person must be entered on the relevant register of securities in order to have the right to attend or vote at the meeting.

(2) Changes to entries on the relevant register of securities after the time specified by virtue of paragraph (1) shall be disregarded in determining the rights of any person to attend or vote at the meeting, notwithstanding any provisions in any enactment, articles of association or other instrument to the contrary.

Definitions

'articles of association': CA 1990(US)R 1996, reg 3(1); 'enactment': CA 1990(US)R 1996, reg 3(1); 'participating issuer': CA 1990(US)R 1996, reg 3(1); 'register of securities': CA 1990(US)R 1996, reg 3(1).

Note

This ability to close the register obviates the need to close the register under CA 1963, s 131 in order to crystallise those entitled to attend at a meeting.

UK legislation

Uncertificated Securities Regulations 2001, reg 41.

---

15 Notice of meetings

(1) For the purposes of serving notices of meetings, whether under section 134(a) of the 1963 Act, any other enactment, a provision in the Articles of Association or any other instrument, a participating issuer may determine that persons entitled to receive such notices are those persons entered on the relevant register of securities at the close of business on a day determined by the participating issuer.

(2) The day determined by a participating issuer under paragraph (1) may not be more than 7 days before the day that the notices of the meeting are sent.

Definitions

'the 1963 Act': CA 1990(US)R 1996, reg 3(1); 'articles of association': CA 1990(US)R 1996, reg 3(1); 'enactment': CA 1990(US)R 1996, reg 3(1); 'participating issuer': CA 1990(US)R 1996, reg 3(1); 'register of securities': CA 1990(US)R 1996, reg 3(1).

UK legislation

Uncertificated Securities Regulations 2001, reg 41.

---

16 Registration of transfers of securities

(1) A participating issuer shall register a transfer of title to uncertificated units of a security on a register of securities in accordance with an operator-instruction unless—

(a) the transfer is prohibited—

(i) by order of the High Court, provided both the participating issuer and the relevant operator shall both have had actual notice of the order before the operator-instruction is sent and the fact of such actual notice on the part of both such persons shall have been established to the satisfaction of the court by the person seeking to rely on the order, or

(ii) by or under an enactment, or

(b) the participating issuer it has actual notice that the transfer is—

(i) avoided by or under an enactment, or

(ii) a transfer to a deceased person, or

(c) the circumstances described in paragraph (2) apply, or

(d) the participating issuer is entitled by virtue of paragraph (3) to refuse to register the transfer.

(2) The circumstances referred to in paragraph (1)(c) are that the transfer is one of two or more transfers in respect of which the operator has notified the participating issuer in accordance with regulation 17(1), and that to those transfers regulation 17 (2) does not apply by virtue of regulation 17(3).

(3) A participating issuer may refuse to register a transfer of title to uncertificated units of a security in accordance with an operator-instruction if the instruction requires a transfer of units—

(a) to an entity which is not a natural or legal person,

(b) to a minor,

(c) to be held jointly in the names of more persons than is permitted under the terms of issue of the security, or

(d) where in relation to the operator-instruction the participating issuer has actual notice from the operator of any of the matters specified in regulation 35 (5) (a).

(4) A participating issuer shall notify the operator by issuer-instruction that the transfer has been registered in response to an operator-instruction to do so.

(5) A participating issuer shall not register a transfer of title to uncertificated units of a security on a register of securities unless required to do so—

(a) by an operator-instruction,

(b) by order of the High Court,

(c) by or under an enactment, or

(d) by regulation 36(2).

(6) Paragraph (5) shall not be taken to prevent a participating issuer from entering a person on a register of securities to whom the title to uncertificated units of a security has been transmitted by operation of law.

(7) Any purported registration of a transfer of title to an uncertificated unit of a security other than in accordance with this regulation shall be of no effect.

(8) If a participating issuer refuses to register a transfer of any shares or debentures, the participating issuer shall, within 2 months after the date on which the transfer was lodged with the participating issuer, send to the transferee notice of the refusal.

(9) If default is made in complying with paragraph (8), the participating issuer and every officer of the participating issuer who is in default shall be liable to a fine not exceeding [€1,904.61].[a]

Amendments

a £250 increased to £1,500 by CA 1990, s 240(7) and converted to €1,904.61 by Council Regulations (EC) No 1103/97, No 974/98 and No 2866/98 and the Economic and Monetary Union Act, 1988, s 6.

Definitions

'court': CA 1990(US)R 1996, reg 3(1); 'enactment': CA 1990(US)R 1996, reg 3(1); 'instruction': CA 1990(US)R 1996, reg 3(1); 'issue': CA 1990(US)R 1996, reg 3(1); 'issuer-instruction': CA 1990(US)R 1996, reg 3(1); 'officer': CA 1990(US)R 1996, reg 3(1); 'operator': CA 1990(US)R 1996, reg 3(1); 'operator-instruction': CA 1990(US)R 1996, reg 3(1); 'participating issuer': CA 1990(US)R 1996, reg 3(1); 'register of securities': CA 1990(US)R 1996, reg 3(1); 'share': CA 1990(US)R 1996, reg 3(1); 'uncertificated unit of a security': CA 1990(US)R 1996, reg 3(1); 'debentures': CA 1963, s 2(1).

UK legislation

Uncertificated Securities Regulations 2001, reg 27.

17 Registration of linked transfers

(1) Where an operator sends two or more operator-instructions requiring a participating issuer to register two or more transfers of title to uncertificated units of a security, and it appears to the operator—

(a) either—

(i) that there are fewer units of the security registered in the name of a person identified in any one of the operator-instructions as a transferor than the number of units to be transferred from that person, or

(ii) that any one of the transfers taken alone is one in relation to which it has not been established in accordance with the procedures of the relevant system that a settlement-bank has agreed to make a payment, and

(b) that registration of all of the transfers would result in each of the persons identified in the operator-instructions as a transferor having title to a number of units of a security equal to or greater than nil, and

(c) that the combined effect of all the transfers taken together would result in payment being made by the settlement-bank,

the operator may notify the participating issuer that the transfers are linked transfers.

(2) Except in the circumstances described in paragraph (3), notwithstanding that there may be fewer uncertificated units of the security registered in the name of a person identified in any one of the operator-instructions as a transferor than the number of uncertificated units to be transferred from that person, where an operator notifies a participating issuer that transfers are linked transfers, the participating issuer may either—

(a) register the combined effect of all the transfers taken together, or

(b) register all the transfers simultaneously.

(3) Paragraph (2) does not apply in a case in which—

(a) registration of the combined effect of the linked transfers, or simultaneous registration of all the transfers (as the case may be), would not result in each of the persons identified in the operator-instructions as a transferor having title to a number of uncertificated units of the security equal to or greater than nil, or

(b) one or more of the transfers constituting the linked transfers may not be registered by virtue of the circumstances specified in regulation 16(1)(a) or (b), or is to be refused registration by virtue of regulation 16(3).

Definitions

'operator': CA 1990(US)R 1996, reg 3(1); 'operator-instruction': CA 1990(US)R 1996, reg 3(1); 'participating issuer': CA 1990(US)R 1996, reg 3(1); 'relevant system': CA 1990(US)R 1996, reg 3(1); 'settlement-bank': CA 1990(US)R 1996, reg 3(1); 'uncertificated unit of a security', CA 1990(US)R 1996, reg 3(1).

UK legislation

Uncertificated Securities Regulations 2001, reg 30.

18 Position of a transferee prior to entry on register

(1) At the time an operator-instruction is sent requiring a participating issuer to register on a register of securities a transfer of title to any uncertificated units of a security—

(a) the transferee shall acquire an equitable interest in the requisite number of uncertificated units of the security of the kind specified in the operator-instruction in which the transferor has an equitable interest by virtue of this regulation, or in relation to which the transferor is recorded on the relevant register of securities as having title, and

(b) the equitable interest shall subsist until the time specified in paragraph (3).

(2) For the purposes of paragraph (1)(a) it shall not be denied that the transferee has obtained the equitable interest referred to in paragraph (1)(a), solely by reason of the fact that the transferor acquired the equitable interest by virtue of paragraph (1)(a) at the same time as the transferee's equitable interest arises in that interest.

(3) Subject to any enactment or rule of law, an interest acquired under paragraph (1)—

(a) in a case other than one in which under regulation 17(2)(a) a participating issuer registers the combined effect of linked transfers, shall subsist until the time that the transferee is entered on the register of securities in respect of the transfer of the units, and

(b) in a case in which under regulation 17(2)(a) a participating issuer registers the combined effect of linked transfers, shall subsist until the time that the combined effect of all the linked transfers is registered.

(4) The requisite number for the purposes of this regulation is whichever of the following is the lower at the time that the operator-instruction is sent, namely—

(a) the number of units which are specified in the operator-instruction, and

(b) the total of the number of uncertificated units in relation to which the transferor is recorded on the register of securities as having title and the number in which the transferor has an interest by virtue of paragraph (1), less that number of units in which such interests subsist in favour of a third party by virtue of an earlier operator-instruction requiring a participating issuer to register on a register of securities a transfer of title to those units.

(5) This regulation has effect notwithstanding that the units to which the operator-instruction relates, or in which an interest arises by virtue of paragraph 1, of any of them, may be unascertained.

(6) Subject to paragraph (5), this regulation shall not be construed as conferring a proprietary interest (whether of the kind referred to in paragraph (1) or any other kind) in units of a security if the conferring of such an interest at the time specified in these regulations would otherwise be void by or under an enactment or rule of law.

(7) In this regulation—

(a) 'the transferee' means the person identified in the operator-instruction as the transferee, and

(b) 'the transferor' means the person identified in the operator-instruction as the transferor.

Definitions

'enactment': CA 1990(US)R 1996, reg 3(1); 'interest in a security': CA 1990(US)R 1996, reg 3(1); 'operator-instruction': CA 1990(US)R 1996, reg 3(1); 'participating issuer': CA 1990(US)R 1996, reg 3(1); 'register of securities': CA 1990(US)R 1996, reg 3(1); 'uncertificated unit of a security': CA 1990(US)R 1996, reg 3(1).

UK legislation

Uncertificated Securities Regulations 2001, reg 31.

---

19 Prohibition on issue of certificates

(1) Notwithstanding any enactment, or rule of law, and in particular section 86 of the 1963 Act, but subject to regulation 20, a participating issuer shall not issue a certificate in relation to any uncertificated units of a participating security.

(2) A document issued by or on behalf of a participating issuer purportedly evidencing title to an uncertificated unit of a participating security shall not be evidence of title to the unit of the security; and in particular section 87(1) of the 1963 Act shall not apply to any document issued with respect to uncertificated shares.

Definitions

'the 1963 Act': CA 1990(US)R 1996, reg 3(1); 'certificate': CA 1990(US)R 1996, reg 3(1); 'enactment': CA 1990(US)R 1996, reg 3(1); 'issue': CA 1990(US)R 1996, reg 3(1); 'participating issuer': CA 1990(US)R 1996, reg 3(1); 'participating security': CA 1990(US)R 1996, reg 3(1); 'share': CA 1990(US)R 1996, reg 3(1); 'uncertificated unit of a security': CA 1990(US)R 1996, reg 3(1); 'document': CA 1963, s 2(1).

UK legislation

Uncertificated Securities Regulations 2001, reg 38(2), (3)(a).

20 Conversion of securities into certificated form

(1) A participating issuer shall not change a unit of a participating security from uncertificated to certificated form except—

(a) where permitted by the rules made and practices instituted by an operator, or

(b) following receipt of an operator-instruction requiring the conversion into certificated form of uncertificated units of a participating security registered in the name of a system-member, or

(c) subject to regulation 16, following receipt of an operator-instruction requiring the registration of a transfer of title to uncertificated units of a security to a person who is not a system-member, or

(d) on the registration, in accordance with regulation 36(2), of an offeror who is not a system-member as holder of the units of the security referred to in that regulation.

(2) In the circumstances specified in paragraph (1) (b), (c) and (d) a participating issuer shall—

(a) record on the register of securities that the units of the security are held in certificated form;

(b) where a certificate can be issued for the security, issue a certificate in respect of the units of the security to the relevant person; and

(c) notify the operator that the units are no longer held in uncertificated form.

(3) Every participating issuer shall, within 2 months after the date on which the issuer receives a relevant operator-instruction which can be complied with in accordance with paragraph (2), complete and have ready for delivery the certificates of all securities transferred pursuant to the operator-instruction.

(4) If default is made in complying with paragraph (3), the participating issuer and every officer of the participating issuer who is in default shall be liable to a fine not exceeding [€1,904.61].[a]

(5) If any participating issuer served with a notice requiring the participating issuer to make good any default in complying with the provisions of paragraph (3) fails to make good the default within 10 days after the service of the notice, the court may on the application of the person entitled to have the certificates delivered, make an order directing the participating issuer and any officers of the participating issuer to make good the default within such time as may be specified in the order, and any such order may provide that all costs of and incidental to the application shall be borne by the participating issuer or by any officer of the participating issuer responsible for the default.

Amendments

a £250 increased to £1,500 by CA 1990, s 240(7) and converted to €1,904.61 by Council Regulations (EC) No 1103/97, No 974/98 and No 2866/98 and the Economic and Monetary Union Act, 1988, s 6.

Definitions

'certificate': CA 1990(US)R 1996, reg 3(1); 'court': CA 1990(US)R 1996, reg 3(1); 'issue': CA 1990(US)R 1996, reg 3(1); 'officer': CA 1990(US)R 1996, reg 3(1); 'operator': CA 1990(US)R 1996, reg 3(1); 'operator-instruction': CA 1990(US)R 1996, reg 3(1); 'participating issuer': CA 1990(US)R 1996, reg 3(1); 'participating security': CA 1990(US)R 1996, reg 3(1); 'practices': CA 1990(US)R 1996, reg 3(1); 'register of securities': CA 1990(US)R 1996, reg 3(1); 'rules': CA 1990(US)R 1996, reg 3(1); 'securities': CA 1990(US)R 1996, reg 3(1); 'system-member': CA 1990(US)R 1996, reg 3(1); 'uncertificated unit of a security': CA 1990(US)R 1996, reg 3(1).

UK legislation

Uncertificated Securities Regulations 2001, reg 32.

21 Endorsements on certificates

Any requirement in or under any enactment to endorse any statement or information on a certificate evidencing title to a unit of security (including any such requirement in section 104 of the 1963 Act)—

(a) shall not prohibit the conversion into, or issue of, units of the security in uncertificated form, and

(b) in relation to uncertificated units of the security, shall be taken to be a requirement to provide the holder of the units of security on request with the statement or information.

Definitions

'the 1963 Act': CA 1990(US)R 1996, reg 3(1); 'certificate': CA 1990(US)R 1996, reg 3(1); 'enactment': CA 1990(US)R 1996, reg 3(1); 'issue': CA 1990(US)R 1996, reg 3(1); 'uncertificated unit of a security': CA 1990(US)R 1996, reg 3(1).

UK legislation

Uncertificated Securities Regulations 2001, reg 38(4).

22 Interests in uncertificated units

The operator shall not be bound by or compelled to recognise any express, implied or constructive trust or other interest in respect of uncertificated units of a security, even if the operator has actual or constructive notice of the said trust or interest.

Definitions

'operator': CA 1990(US)R 1996, reg 3(1); 'uncertificated unit of a security': CA 1990(US)R 1996, reg 3(1).

UK legislation

Uncertificated Securities Regulations 2001, reg 40(3).

23 Liabilities of trustees

(1) Unless expressly prohibited from transferring units of a security by means of any computer based system, a person being a trustee or personal representative shall not be chargeable with a breach of trust or, as the case may be, with default in administering the estate by reason only of the fact that—

(a) for the purpose of acquiring units of a security which that person has the power to acquire in connection with the trust or estate, the units are paid for under arrangements which provide for them to be transferred from a system-member but not to be so transferred until after the payment of the price;

(b) for the purpose of disposing of units of security which that person has power to dispose of in connection with the trust or estate, the units are transferred to a system-member under arrangements which provide that the price is not to be paid until after the transfer is made; or

(c) for the purposes of holding units of a security belonging to the trust or estate in uncertificated form and for transferring title to them by means of a relevant system, that person has become a system-member.

(2) A trustee of a trust deed for securing an issue of debentures shall not be chargeable with a breach of trust by reason only of having consented to an amendment of the trust deed only for the purposes of—

(a) allowing the holding of the debentures in uncertificated form;

(b) allowing the exercise of rights attaching to the debentures by means of a relevant system; or

(c) allowing the transfer of title to the debentures by means of a relevant system;

provided that notice of the amendment has been given to all persons having title to the debentures at least 30 days prior to such consent becoming effective.

Definitions

'computer': CA 1990(US)R 1996, reg 3(1); 'issue': CA 1990(US)R 1996, reg 3(1); 'relevant system': CA 1990(US)R 1996, reg 3(1); 'system-member': CA 1990(US)R 1996, reg 3(1); 'debentures' CA 1963, s 2(1).

UK legislation

Uncertificated Securities Regulations 2001, reg 40.

24 Conversion of securities into uncertificated form

(1) A participating issuer shall not change a unit of a participating security from certificated form to uncertificated form except in the circumstances specified in paragraph (2).

(2) The circumstances referred to in paragraph (1) are—

(a) where the unit of the participating-security is held by a system-member, that the participating issuer has received—

(i) a request in writing in the form required by the rules made and practices instituted by an operator to register the system-member as holding the unit in uncertificated form; and

(ii) subject to paragraph (4), the certificate relating to the certificated unit which is to be converted into uncertificated form;

(b) where the unit of the participating security is to be registered on a register of securities in the name of a system-member following a transfer of the unit to that person from a person other than a stock exchange nominee, that the participating issuer—

(i) subject to paragraph (3), has received by means of the operator-system a proper instrument of transfer in favour of the system-member relating to the unit to be transferred;

(ii) subject to paragraph (4), has received by means of the operator-system the certificate relating to the certificated unit which is to be transferred and converted into uncertificated form; and

(iii) may accept by virtue of the rules made and practices instituted by an operator that the system-member to whom the unit is to be transferred wishes to hold it in uncertificated form; and

(c) where the unit of the participating security is to be registered on a register of securities in the name of a system-member following a transfer of the unit to him from a stock exchange nominee, that the participating issuer—

(i) has received a proper instrument of transfer in favour of the system-member from the nominee relating to the unit to be transferred; and

(ii) may accept by virtue of the rules made and practices instituted by an operator that the system-member to whom the unit is to be transferred wishes to hold it in uncertificated form.

(3) The requirement in paragraph (2)(b)(i) that the participating issuer shall have received an instrument of transfer relating to the unit of the participating security shall not apply in a case where for a transfer of a unit of that security no instrument of transfer is required.

(4) The requirements in paragraph (2)(a)(ii) and (2)(b)(ii) that the participating issuer shall have received a certificate relating to the unit of the participating security shall not apply in a case where the system-member or transferor (as the case may be) does not have a certificate in respect of the unit to be converted into uncertificated form because no certificate has yet been issued to him.

(5) In the circumstances specified in paragraph (2 (a), on receipt of the request referred to in paragraph (2)(a)(i) and (except where paragraph (4) applies) the certificate referred to in paragraph (2)(a)(ii), the participating issuer shall, within two months—

(a) enter on the register of securities that the system-member holds the unit in uncertificated form; and

(b) send the operator an issuer-instruction of the entry on the relevant register of securities.

(6) In the circumstances specified in paragraph (2)(b), on receipt of the instrument of transfer referred to in paragraph (2)(b)(i) (except where paragraph (3) applies) and the certificate referred to in paragraph (2)(b)(ii) (except where paragraph (4) applies), the participating issuer shall—

(a) upon recording that the system-member holds the unit, enter on the register of securities that the unit is held in uncertificated form; and

(b) within 2 months thereafter, send the operator an issuer-instruction of the entry on the register of securities.

(7) In the circumstances specified in paragraph (2)(c), on receipt of the instrument of transfer referred to in paragraph (2)(c)(i), the participating issuer shall—

(a) upon recording that the system-member holds the unit, enter on the register of securities that the unit is held in uncertificated form; and

(b) within 2 months thereafter, send the operator an issuer-instruction of the entry on the register of securities.

(8) If default is made in complying with paragraphs (5), (6) or (7) the participating issuer and every officer of the participating issuer who is in default shall be liable to a fine not exceeding [€1,904.61].[a]

(9) In this regulation, 'stock exchange nominee' has the same meaning as in the 1977 Act.

Amendments

a £250 increased to £1,500 by CA 1990, s 240(7) and converted to €1,904.61 by Council Regulations (EC) No 1103/97, No 974/98 and No 2866/98 and the Economic and Monetary Union Act, 1988, s 6.

Definitions

'the 1977 Act': CA 1990(US)R 1996, reg 3(1); 'certificate': CA 1990(US)R 1996, reg 3(1); 'certificated unit of a security': CA 1990(US)R 1996, reg 3(1); 'issuer-instruction': CA 1990(US)R 1996, reg 3(1); 'officer': CA 1990(US)R 1996, reg 3(1); 'operator': CA 1990(US)R 1996, reg 3(1); 'operator-system': CA 1990(US)R 1996, reg 3(1); 'participating issuer': CA 1990(US)R 1996, reg 3(1); 'participating security': CA 1990(US)R 1996, reg 3(1); 'practices': CA 1990(US)R 1996, reg 3(1); 'register of securities': CA 1990(US)R 1996, reg 3(1); 'rules': CA 1990(US)R 1996, reg 3(1); 'system-member': CA 1990(US)R 1996, reg 3(1).

UK legislation

Uncertificated Securities Regulations 2001, reg 33.

25 New issues in uncertificated form

(1) A participating issuer may issue new units of a participating security in uncertificated form to a person if, and only if, that person is a system-member.

(2) For the purposes of calculating the number of new units to which a system-member is entitled, a participating issuer may treat a system-member's holdings of certificated and uncertificated units of a security as if they were separate holdings.

(3) On the issue in uncertificated form of new units of a participating security, the participating issuer shall by issuer-instruction notify the operator of the persons to whom the uncertificated units of a security have been issued and of the number of such units issued to each of those persons.

Definitions

'issue': CA 1990(US)R 1996, reg 3(1); 'issuer-instruction': CA 1990(US)R 1996, reg 3(1); 'operator': CA 1990(US)R 1996, reg 3(1); 'participating issuer': CA 1990(US)R 1996, reg 3(1); 'participating security': CA 1990(US)R 1996, reg 3(1); 'system-member': CA 1990(US)R 1996, reg 3(1); 'uncertificated unit of a security': CA 1990(US)R 1996, reg 3(1).

UK legislation

Uncertificated Securities Regulations 2001, reg 34.

CHAPTER III
APPROVAL AND COMPLIANCE OF OPERATOR

26 Application for Approval

(1) A person may apply to the Minister to be approved operator of a relevant system.

(2) Any such application—

(a) shall be made in such a manner as the Minister may direct, and

(b) shall be accompanied by such information as the Minister may reasonably require for the purpose of determining the application.

(3) At any time after receiving an application and before determining it, the Minister may require the applicant to furnish additional information.

(4) The directions and requirements given or imposed under paragraphs (2) and (3) may differ as between different applications.

(5) Any information to be furnished to the Minister under this regulation shall, if the Minister so requires, be in such form or verified in such manner as the Minister may specify.

(6) Every application shall be accompanied by a copy of any rules and guidance to be issued by the applicant.

Definitions

'guidance': CA 1990(US)R 1996, reg 3(1); 'operator': CA 1990(US)R 1996, reg 3(1); 'relevant system': CA 1990(US)R 1996, reg 3(1); 'rules': CA 1990(US)R 1996, reg 3(1); 'Minister', CA 1990 s 3(1).

UK legislation

Uncertificated Securities Regulations 2001, reg 4.

27 Grant of Approval

(1) If, on an application made under regulation 26, it appears that the requirements of the Schedule are satisfied with respect to the application, the Minister may, subject to

the following paragraphs of this regulation, approve a person (in these regulations referred to as an approved operator) to operate a relevant system.

(2) Approval of an operator under this regulation shall be by written instrument and may be subject to the fulfilment of conditions specified by the Minister to ensure compliance with these regulations and shall state the date on which it takes effect and may state the date on which it terminates.

(3) Approval under this regulation shall be without prejudice to the requirements of the Competition Act, 1991.

(4) Where the Minister refuses to approve an operator on the basis of an application made under regulation 26 the Minister shall so inform the applicant in writing stating the reasons for the refusal.

Cross reference

The Competition Act 1991 referred to in reg 27(3) has been repealed and replaced by the Competition Act 2002.

Definitions

'operator': CA 1990(US)R 1996, reg 3(1); 'relevant system': CA 1990(US)R 1996, reg 3(1); 'Minister', CA 1990, s 3(1).

UK legislation

Uncertificated Securities Regulations 2001, reg 5.

28 Recognition of operator approved by competent authority

(1) A person approved by a competent authority to operate a relevant system may be granted recognition by the Minister to act as an operator for the purposes of these regulations, subject, in particular, to regulation 32.

(2) The Minister may make the recognition subject to certain conditions, either when granted or during its currency.

Definitions

'competent authority': CA 1990(US)R 1996, reg 3(1); 'operator': CA 1990(US)R 1996, reg 3(1); 'relevant system': CA 1990(US)R 1996, reg 3(1); 'Minister', CA 1990, s 3(1).

29 Delegation of Minister's Functions

(1) The Minister may delegate any approval and other supervisory functions under this Chapter to a designated body.

(2) The Minister may by written instrument revoke a designation under paragraph (1)—

(a) at the request of, or with the consent of, the designated body, or

(b) if at any time it appears to the Minister that the designated body is unable or unwilling to discharge all or any of the functions delegated to it.

Definitions

'Minister': CA 1990, s 3(1).

UK legislation

Uncertificated Securities Regulations 2001, reg 11.

30 Appeal to Minister

(1) Where a body designated under regulation 29(1) refuses to approve a proposed operator, it shall serve notice on the proposed operator, and on the Minister, of its refusal to grant approval and state the reason therefor.

(2) A proposed operator on whom a notice has been served under paragraph (1) of this regulation, may within 21 days of receipt of the notice, appeal to the Minister and the Minister shall consider any such appeal and may uphold or reject it.

(3) When considering an appeal under this section, the Minister shall consult with the designated body and the proposed operator concerned and any other party the Minister thinks proper, provided that the period taken for consideration does not exceed three months.

(4) If the Minister upholds an appeal made under this section, the designated body shall grant approval of the proposed operator.

(5) An appeal under this section shall be accompanied by such fee as the Minister may by regulation prescribe.

(6) The Public Offices Fees Act, 1879, shall not apply to any fees charged under this section.

Definitions

'operator': CA 1990(US)R 1996, reg 3(1); 'Minister': CA 1990, s 3(1).

UK legislation

Uncertificated Securities Regulations 2001, Sch 3.

31 Withdrawal of Approval

(1) The Minister may revoke approval of an operator in all or any of the following circumstances, namely, where—

- (a) a request has been made in that behalf by the operator, or
- (b) the operator—
  - (i) has failed to operate a relevant system within 12 months of the date on which the approval to be an operator was granted, or
  - (ii) has failed to operate as a relevant system for a period of more than 6 months, or
  - (iii) is being wound up.

(2) Without prejudice to the power of the Minister to revoke an approval under paragraph (1), the Minister may apply to the High Court, in a summary manner, for an order revoking the approval in any or all of the following circumstances, namely, if—

(a) at any time it appears to the Minister that any requirement of the Schedule is not satisfied by an approved operator, or

(b) it is expedient to do so in the interest of the proper and orderly regulation of operators, or their system users, or in order to protect investors,

(c) the operator has, on indictment, been convicted of any offence under the Companies Acts or any offence involving fraud, dishonesty or breach of trust;

(d) the approval was obtained by the operator knowingly or recklessly making false or misleading statements, or by knowingly or recklessly using false or misleading information;

(e) the operator has failed to comply to a material degree with a requirement of these regulations having been first called upon to do so;

(f) the operator no longer fulfils a condition or requirement imposed when approval was granted;

(g) the operator becomes unable or, in the opinion of the Minister, is likely to become unable to meet its obligations to its creditors or suspends payments lawfully due.

(3) When the Minister proposes to revoke the approval of an operator or proposes to apply to the court for an order to revoke approval of an operator, the Minister shall serve notice on the operator concerned of the proposal and the reasons therefor.

(4) Where an application is made to the court under this regulation the court may make such order or orders as the circumstances may require.

(5) Where approval of an operator is revoked and where the operator concerned is not a company which is being wound up.

(a) the former operator and its system-users shall continue to be subject to the duties and obligations imposed by these regulations until all the liabilities, duties and obligations of the said operator have been discharged to the satisfaction of the Minister, and

(b) the former operator shall, as soon as possible, after the revocation, notify the Minister, its system users and such other persons, if any, as the Minister indicates are to be notified of the measures being taken to discharge without undue delay the liabilities, duties and obligations of the said operator.

(6) The Minister shall publish notice of any revocation of an approval of an operator in Iris Oifigiúil within 28 days of revocation.

(7) An operator whose approval has been revoked under these regulations shall cease to operate a relevant system.

(8) An application under this regulation may be heard otherwise than in public.

Definitions

'the Companies Acts': CA 1990(US)R 1996, reg 3(1); 'company': CA 1990(US)R 1996, reg 3(1); 'court': CA 1990(US)R 1996, reg 3(1); 'operator': CA 1990(US)R 1996, reg 3(1); 'relevant system': CA 1990(US)R 1996, reg 3(1); 'system-user': CA 1990(US)R 1996, reg 3(1); 'Minister': CA 1990, s 3(1).

UK legislation

Uncertificated Securities Regulations 2001, reg 7, Sch 2.

32 Withdrawal of Recognition

(1) The Minister may withdraw a grant of recognition in all or any of the following circumstances, namely, where—

(a) a request has been made in that behalf by the operator;

(b) if the competent authority which approved the operator has withdrawn its approval;

(c) if the operator—

(i) has failed to operate a relevant system within 12 months of the date on which recognition was granted, or

(ii) has failed to operate as a relevant system for a period of more than 6 months, or

(iii) is being wound up, or

(d) on any other grounds which seem reasonable to the Minister.

(2) The Minister shall serve on the operator notice of a proposal to withdraw a grant and shall state the reasons therefor.

(3) An operator whose grant of recognition is withdrawn pursuant to paragraph 1 (d) may appeal the Minister's decision to the Court.

(4) On hearing an application under paragraph (3), the Court may confirm or rescind the Minister's decision or make such other ancillary order as it deems fit.

(5) The operator may apply to the Court and the Court may grant an order providing for such interim or interlocutory relief as it considers appropriate.

Definitions

'competent authority': CA 1990(US)R 1996, reg 3(1); 'court': CA 1990(US)R 1996, reg 3(1); 'operator': CA 1990(US)R 1996, reg 3(1); 'relevant system': CA 1990(US)R 1996, reg 3(1); 'Minister': CA 1990, s 3(1).

33 Compliance order and directions

(1) If at any time it appears to the Minister that any requirement of the Schedule to these regulations is not satisfied by an approved operator, or that an approved operator has failed to comply with any obligation under these regulations, the Minister may—

(a) apply to the High Court for relief, or

(b) subject to paragraph (3), give to the operator such directions as the Minister thinks fit for securing that the relevant requirement is satisfied or obligation complied with.

(2) If on any application by the Minister under paragraph (1) (a) the court is satisfied that the requirement is not satisfied or, as the case may be, that the operator has failed to comply with the obligation in question, it may order the operator to take such steps as the court directs for securing that the requirement is satisfied or that the obligation is complied with.

(3) Before giving a direction under paragraph (1) (b) the Minister shall—

(a) if circumstances permit, consult with and afford the operator an opportunity to make representations; and

(b) so far as it is practicable to estimate it, have regard to the cost to the operator of complying with any term of any direction and to the costs to other persons resulting from the operator's compliance.

Definitions

'court': CA 1990(US)R 1996, reg 3(1); 'operator': CA 1990(US)R 1996, reg 3(1); 'Minister': CA 1990, s 3(1).

UK legislation

Uncertificated Securities Regulations 2001, reg 8.

34 Requests for information from the Operator

(1) The Minister may in writing, require an approved operator to provide the Minister with specified information.

(2) The Minister, may, in writing, require an approved operator to furnish the Minister, at specified times or in respect of specified periods, with specified information, verified in a specified manner, relating to that operator for the exercise of the Minister's functions under these regulations.

(3) An approved operator who amends, revokes or adds to any rules or guidance shall within seven days given written notice to the Minister of the amendment, revocation or addition.

Definitions

'guidance': CA 1990(US)R 1996, reg 3(1); 'operator': CA 1990(US)R 1996, reg 3(1); 'rules': CA 1990(US)R 1996, reg 3(1); 'Minister': CA 1990, s 3(1).

UK legislation

Uncertificated Securities Regulations 2001, reg 10.

CHAPTER IV
OPERATION OF AUTOMATED TRANSFER AND REGISTRATION

35 Properly authenticated dematerialised instructions

(1) This regulation has effect for the purpose of determining the rights and obligations of persons to whom properly authenticated dematerialised instructions are attributable and of persons to whom properly authenticated dematerialised instructions are

addressed when such instructions relate to an uncertificated unit of a security, or relate to a right, benefit or privilege attaching to or arising from such a unit, or relating to the details of a holder of such a unit.

(2) Where a properly authenticated dematerialised instruction is expressed to have been sent on behalf of a person by a sponsoring system-participant or the operator—

(a) the person on whose behalf the instruction is expressed to have been sent shall not be able to deny to the addressee—

(i) that the properly authenticated dematerialised instruction was sent with that person's authority, or

(ii) that the information contained in the properly authenticated dematerialised instruction is correct; and

(b) the sponsoring system-participant or the operator (as the case may be) shall not be able to deny to the addressee—

(i) that he has authority to send the properly authenticated dematerialised instruction, or

(ii) that he has sent the properly authenticated dematerialised instruction.

(3) Where a properly authenticated dematerialised instruction is expressed to have been sent by a person and is not expressed to have been sent on behalf of another person, the person shall not be able to deny to the addressee—

(a) that the information contained in the properly authenticated dematerialised instruction is correct, or

(b) that the properly authenticated dematerialised instruction was sent.

(4) An addressee who receives (whether directly, or by means of the facilities of a sponsoring system-participant acting on the addressee's behalf) a properly authenticated dematerialised instruction may, subject to paragraph (5), accept that at the time at which the properly authenticated dematerialised instruction was sent—

(a) the information contained in the instruction was correct;

(b) the system-participant or the operator (as the case may be) identified in the instruction as having sent the instruction sent the instruction; and

(c) the instruction, where relevant, has been sent with the authority of the person on whose behalf it is expressed to have been sent.

(5) Subject to paragraph (6), an addressee may not accept any of the matters specified in paragraph (4) if at the time of receipt of the properly authenticated dematerialised instruction—

(a) the addressee was a person other than a participating issuer or a sponsoring system-participant receiving properly authenticated dematerialised instructions on behalf of a participating issuer, and had actual notice—

(i) that any information contained in it was incorrect;

(ii) that the system participant or the operator (as the case may be) expressed to have sent the instruction did not send the instruction; or

(iii) where relevant, that the person on whose behalf it was expressed to have been sent had not given to the operator or the sponsoring system-participant (as the case may be), identified in the properly authenticated dematerialised instruction as having sent it, authority to send the instruction on that persons behalf; or

(b) the addressee was a participating issuer or a sponsoring system-participant receiving the instruction on behalf of a participating issuer, and

(i) had actual notice from the operator of any of the matters specified in sub-paragraph (a); or

(ii) the instruction was an operator- instruction requiring the registration of title in the circumstances specified in regulation 16(1)(a), (b) or (c); or

(c) the addressee was an operator and the instruction related to a transfer of units of a security which was in excess of any limit imposed on a sponsoring system participant, by a system-member, in accordance with the rules and procedures of an operator.

(6) Notwithstanding that an addressee has received in respect of a properly authenticated dematerialised instruction actual notice of the kind referred to in paragraph (5), the addressee may accept the matters specified in paragraph (4) if at the time that the actual notice was received it was not practical for the addressee to halt processing of the instruction.

(7) A person who is permitted by this regulation to accept any matter shall not be liable in damages or otherwise to any person by reason of having relied on that matter.

(8) Subject to paragraph (7) this regulation has effect without prejudice to the liability of any person for causing or permitting a dematerialised instruction—

(a) to be sent without authority; or

(b) to contain information which is incorrect; or

(c) to be expressed to have been sent by a person who did not send it.

(9) For the purposes of this regulation—

(a) a properly authenticated dematerialised instruction is expressed to have been sent by a person or on behalf of a person if it is attributable to that person; and

(b) an addressee is the person to whom the instruction indicates it is addressed in accordance with the specifications of the operator.

Definitions

'dematerialised instruction': CA 1990(US)R 1996, reg 3(1); 'operator': CA 1990(US)R 1996, reg 3(1); 'participating issuer': CA 1990(US)R 1996, reg 3(1); 'rules': CA 1990(US)R 1996, reg 3(1); 'system-member': CA 1990(US)R 1996, reg 3(1); 'system-participant': CA 1990(US)R 1996, reg 3(1); 'uncertificated unit of a security': CA 1990(US)R 1996, reg 3(1).

UK legislation

Uncertificated Securities Regulations 2001, reg 35.

CHAPTER V
MINORITY SHAREHOLDERS

36 Notices under section 204 of the 1963 Act

(1) This regulation shall apply in relation to any uncertificated units of a security to which a notice given pursuant to section 204(1) of the 1963 Act relates.

(2) On receipt of a notice transmitted pursuant to section 204(5) of the 1963 Act, a company which is a participating issuer shall on the expiration of one month from the date on which this notification was made enter the transferee company in its register of securities as the holder of the uncertificated units of the security to which the notice relates in place of the system-member who was immediately prior to such entry registered as the holder of such units as if it had received an operator-instruction requiring it to amend its register of securities in such manner.

(3) A company which amends its register of securities in accordance with paragraph (2) shall forthwith notify the operator by issuer-instruction of the amendment.

(4) In this regulation, 'the transferee company' has the same meaning as in section 204 (1) of the 1963 Act.

Definitions

'the 1963 Act': CA 1990(US)R 1996, reg 3(1); 'company': CA 1990(US)R 1996, reg 3(1); 'issuer-instruction': CA 1990(US)R 1996, reg 3(1); 'operator': CA 1990(US)R 1996, reg 3(1); 'operator-instruction': CA 1990(US)R 1996, reg 3(1); 'participating issuer': CA 1990(US)R 1996, reg 3(1); 'register of securities': CA 1990(US)R 1996, reg 3(1); 'system-member': CA 1990(US)R 1996, reg 3(1); 'uncertificated unit of a security': CA 1990(US)R 1996, reg 3(1).

UK legislation

Uncertificated Securities Regulations 2001, reg 42.

CHAPTER VI
SUPPLEMENTARY AND INCIDENTAL

37 Evidence of system-entries.

(1) Subject to the provisions of this regulation, a copy or reproduction of a system-entry or the relevant part of it in a legible form shall in all legal proceedings be received as prima facie evidence of such entry or record and of the matters and transactions therein entered or recorded.

(2) A copy or reproduction of a system-entry shall not be received in evidence under this regulation unless it be first proved that the system-entry was at the time of the making of the entry or record one of the ordinary entries or records of the operator or system-participant, as applicable, and that the entry or record was made, supplied or stored in the usual and ordinary course of business, and that the system-entry is in the custody or control of such person. Such proof may be given by a director, secretary or officer of such person, and may be given orally or by an affidavit sworn before any commissioner or person authorised to take affidavits.

(3) A copy or reproduction of a system-entry which was originally made in legible form shall not be received in evidence under this regulation unless it be further proved that the

copy or reproduction has been examined with the original system-entry and is correct. Such proof shall be given by some person who has examined the copy or reproduction with the original entry, and may be given either orally or by an affidavit sworn before any commissioner or person authorised to take affidavit.

(4) A copy or reproduction of a system-entry which was originally made in non-legible form shall not be received in evidence under this regulation unless it be further proved that where the copy or reproduction was produced by computer, any such computer was operating properly throughout the relevant period, or if not, the circumstances were not such as to affect the reproduction of the system-entry or its contents in legible form and that the information contained in the copy or reproduction reproduces or is derived from information supplied to the computer or computers. Such proof may be given by any person occupying a responsible position in relation to the relevant device or the management of the relevant activities (whichever is appropriate) and may be given orally or by affidavit sworn before any commissioner or person authorised to take affidavits.

(5) An operator or system-participant or any officer of such person shall not, in any legal proceedings to which such person is not a party, be compellable to produce any system-entry the contents of which can be proved under this regulation, or to appear as a witness to prove the entries, records, matters or transactions therein entered or recorded, unless by an order of a court made for special cause.

(6) On the application of any party to a legal proceeding a court may order that such party be at liberty to inspect and take copies or reproductions of any entries in a system-entry for any of the purposes of such proceeding. An order under this paragraph may be made either with or without summoning the person who has custody or control of the system-entry or any other party, and shall be served on the person who has custody or control of the system-entry three clear days before the same is to be obeyed, unless the court otherwise directs.

(7) The costs of any application to a court under or for the purposes of this regulation, and the costs of anything done or to be done under an order of a court made under or for the purposes of this regulation shall be in the discretion of the court, who may order the same or any part thereof to be paid to any party by the person who has custody or control of the system-entry, where the same have been occasioned by any default or delay on the part of such person. Any such order against such person may be enforced as if such person was a party to the proceedings.

(8) In this regulation—

> 'legal proceeding' means any civil or criminal proceeding or enquiry in which evidence is or may be given, and includes an arbitration;
>
> 'the court' means the court, judge, arbitrator, person or persons before whom a legal proceeding is held or taken;

information shall be taken to be supplied to a computer if it is supplied thereto in any appropriate form and whether it is so supplied directly or (with or without human intervention) by means of any appropriate equipment;

where in the ordinary course of business carried on by any individual or body, information is supplied with a view to its being stored or processed for the purposes of that business by a computer operated otherwise than in the ordinary course of that business, that information, if duly supplied to that computer, shall be taken to be supplied to it in the ordinary course of that business;

a document shall be taken to have been produced by a computer whether it was produced by it directly or (with or without human intervention) by means of any appropriate equipment.

Definitions

'computer': CA 1990(US)R 1996, reg 3(1); 'court': CA 1990(US)R 1996, reg 3(1); 'director': CA 1990(US)R 1996, reg 3(1); 'officer': CA 1990(US)R 1996, reg 3(1); 'operator': CA 1990(US)R 1996, reg 3(1); 'system entry': CA 1990(US)R 1996, reg 3(1); 'system-participant': CA 1990(US)R 1996, reg 3(1); 'document': CA 1963, s 2(1).

UK legislation

Uncertificated Securities Regulations 2001, reg 24(7), (8), Sch 4, para 13(5).

Schedule

REQUIREMENTS FOR APPROVAL OF AN OPERATOR

Arrangements and Resources

1. (a) An approved operator must have adequate arrangements and resources for the effective monitoring and enforcement of compliance with the rules of the operator or, as respects monitoring, arrangements providing for that function to be performed on the operator's behalf (and without affecting the operator's responsibility) by another body or person who is able and willing to perform it.

(b) The operator's business and corporate structure must be so organised to be capable of being supervised under the regulations to the satisfaction of the Minister.

Financial Resources

2. An approved operator must have financial resources sufficient for the proper performance of the functions of an operator.

Promotion and Maintenance of Standards

3. An approved operator must be able and willing to promote and maintain high standards of integrity and fair dealing in the operation of the relevant system and to co-operate, by the sharing of information or otherwise, with the Minister and any other authority, body or person having responsibility for the supervision or regulation of investment business or other financial services.

Operation of the Relevant System

4. Where an operator causes or permits a part of the relevant system which is not the operator-system to be operated by another person (other than as his agent) the operator—

(a) shall monitor compliance by the person and that part with the requirements of this Schedule; and

(b) shall have arrangements to ensure that the person provides such information and such assistance as the operator may require in order to meet obligations under these regulations.

System Security

5. A relevant system must be constructed and operate in such a way—

(a) so as to minimise the possibility of unauthorised access to or modification of any program or data held in any computer forming part of the operator's system; and

[(b) that each dematerialised instruction is properly authenticated—

(i) in accordance with the specifications of the operator, which shall provide that each dematerialised instruction—

(I) is identifiable as being from the computers of a particular system-participant, and

(II) is designed to minimise fraud and forgery, or

(ii) if it is sent to the operator by, or by the operator to, a depository, a clearing house or a stock exchange, in accordance with specifications of that depository, clearing house or exchange to which the operator has agreed and which shall provide that each dematerialised instruction –

(I) is identifiable as being from the computers of the operator or of the depositary, clearing house or exchange which sent it, and

(II) is designed to minimise fraud and forgery;][a]

(c) that each dematerialised instruction, in accordance with the specifications of the operator, expresses by whom it has been sent and, where relevant, on whose behalf it has been sent;

(d) that each dematerialised instruction, in accordance with the specifications of the operator, indicates—

(i) where it is sent to a system-participant or the operator, that it is addressed to that system-participant or the operator; and

(ii) where it is sent to a person who is using the facilities of a sponsoring system-participant to receive dematerialised instructions, that it is addressed to that person and the sponsoring system-participant; and

(iii) where it is sent to the operator in order to send an operator-instruction to a system-participant, that it is addressed to the operator, to the system-participant and, if the system-participant is acting as a sponsoring system-participant, to the relevant person on whose behalf the sponsoring system-participant receives dematerialised instructions; and

(e) that the possibility for a system-participant to send a dematerialised instruction on behalf of a person from whom the participant has no authority is minimised.

[5A. For the purposes of paragraph 5—

'clearing house' means a body or association which provides services related to the clearing and settlement of transactions and payments and the management of risks associated with the resulting contracts and which is regulated or supervised in the provision of those services by a regulatory body, or an agency of government, of a Member State;

'depositary' means a body or association carrying on business outside the State with whom an operator has made arrangements—

(i) to enable system-members to hold (whether directly or indirectly) and transfer title to securities (other than participating securities) by means of facilities provided by that body or association; or

(ii) to enable that body or association to permit persons to whom it provides services in the course of its business to hold (whether directly or indirectly) and transfer title to participating securities by means of the operator's relevant system;

'stock exchange' means—

(i) a person who has been approved as such under section 9 of the Stock Exchange Act 1995, or

(ii) a body or association which provides services outside the State which are similar in nature to those provided by a person referred to in paragraph (i) and which is regulated or supervised in the provision of those services by a regulatory body, or an agency of government, of a Member State.][b]

Amendments

a Subparagraph 5(b) substituted by CA1990(US)(A)R 2005, reg 2(b)(i), with effect from 10 November 2005.

b Paragraph 5A inserted by CA1990(US)(A)R 2005, reg 2(b)(ii), with effect from 10 November 2005.

System Capabilities

6. A relevant system must ensure that the operator-system can send and respond to properly authenticated dematerialised instructions in sufficient volume and speed.

7. Before an operator-instruction to a participating issuer to register a transfer of uncertificated units of a security is generated, a relevant system must—

(a) be able to establish that the transferor is likely to have title to or, by virtue of regulation 18(1), an interest in, such number of units of the security as is in aggregate at least equal to the number to be transferred; or

(b) be able to notify the participating issuer, in accordance with regulation 17(1), that the transfer is one of two or more transfers which may be registered in accordance with regulation 17(2).

8. A relevant system must maintain adequate records of all dematerialised instructions.

9. A relevant system must be able—

(a) to permit each system-member to obtain a copy of any records relating to the member as are maintained by the relevant system in order to comply with paragraph 7 (a) or 8; and

(b) to make correcting entries in such records as are maintained in order to comply with paragraph 7(a) which are inaccurate.

10. A relevant system must be able to establish, where there is a transfer of uncertificated units of a security to a system-member for value, that a settlement-bank

has agreed to make payment in respect of the transfer, whether alone or taken together with another transfer for value.

11. A relevant system must ensure that the operator-system is able to generate operator-instructions—

(a) requiring participating issuers to amend the appropriate registers of securities kept by them; and

(b) informing settlement-banks of their payment obligations.

12. A relevant system must—

(a) enable a system-member—

(i) to grant authority to a sponsoring system-participant to send properly authenticated dematerialised instructions on the member's behalf; and

(ii) to limit such authority by reference to the net value of the units of securities to be transferred in any one day; and

(b) prevent the transfer of units in excess of that limit.

13. A relevant system must enable system-members—

(a) to change the form in which they hold or are to hold units of a participating security; and

(b) where appropriate, to require participating issuers to issue certificates relating to units of a participating security held or to be held by them.

Operating Procedures

14. A relevant system must comprise procedures which provide that it responds only to properly authenticated dematerialised instructions which are attributable to a system-user or an operator.

15. (1) Subject to sub-paragraph (2), a relevant system must comprise procedures which provide that an operator- instruction requiring a participating issuer to register a transfer of uncertificated units of a security, or informing a settlement-bank of its payment obligations in respect of such a transfer is generated only if—

(a) it has—

(i) received a system-member instruction from the transferor; or

(ii) been required to do so by a court or by or under an enactment;

(b) it has—

(i) established that the transferor is likely to have title to, or is likely to have by virtue of regulation 18(1) an interest in, such number of units as is in aggregate at least equal to the number to be transferred; or

(ii) established that the transfer is one of two or more transfers which may be notified to the participating issuer in accordance with regulation 17(1);

(c) in the case of a transfer to a system-member for value, it has established that a settlement-bank has agreed to make payment in respect of the transfer, whether alone or taken together with another transfer for value; and

(d) the transfer is not in excess of any limit which by virtue of paragraph 12 (a) (ii) the transferor has set on an authority given to a sponsoring system-participant.

(2) A relevant system must comprise procedures which provide that an operator-instruction requiring a participating- issuer to register a transfer of uncertificated units of a security, or informing a settlement-bank of its payment obligations in respect of such a transfer may be generated if necessary to correct an error and if in accordance with the rules and practices of an operator instituted in order to comply with this Schedule.

16. (1) Subject to sub-paragraph (2), a relevant system must comprise procedures which provide that an operator- instruction to a participating issuer relating to a right, privilege or benefit attaching to or arising from an uncertificated unit of a security is generated only if it has—

(a) received a properly authenticated dematerialised instruction attributable to the system-member having the right, privilege or benefit requiring the operator to generate an operator-instruction to the participating issuer; or

(b) been required to do so by a court or by or under an enactment.

(2) A relevant-system must comprise procedures which provide that an operator-instruction to a participating issuer relating to a right, privilege or benefit attaching to or arising from an uncertificated unit of a security may be generated if necessary to correct an error and if in accordance with the rules and practices of an operator instituted in order to comply with this Schedule.

17. A relevant system must comprise procedures which ensure that, where the relevant system maintains records in order to comply with paragraph 15(b)(i), the records are regularly reconciled with the registers of securities maintained by participating issuers.

18. A relevant system must comprise procedures which—

(a) enable system-users to notify the operator of an error in or relating to a dematerialised instruction; and

(b) ensure that, where the operator becomes aware of an error in or relating to a dematerialised instruction, appropriate corrective action is taken.

Rules and Practices

19. An operator's rules and practices—

(a) must bind system-members and participating issuers—

(i) so as to ensure the efficient processing of transfers of title to uncertificated units of a security in response to operator-instructions; and

(ii) as to the action to be taken where transfer of title in response to an operator-instruction cannot be effected;

(b) must make provision for a participating issuer to cease to participate in respect of a participating security so as—

(i) to minimise so far as practicable any disruption to system-members in respect of their ability to transfer the relevant security; and

(ii) to provide the participating issuer with any relevant information held by the operator relating to uncertificated units of the relevant security held by system-members;

(c) must make provision for the orderly termination of participation by system-members and system-participation whose participating is disruptive to other system-members or system-participants or to participating issuers; and

(d) if they make provision for the designation of a subsidiary undertaking as a relevant nominee, must require that the relevant nominee maintain adequate records of—

(i) the names of the persons who have an interest in the securities it holds; and

(ii) the nature and extent of their interests,

20. An operator's rules and practices must require—

(a) that each system-participant is able to send and receive properly authenticated dematerialised instructions:

(b) that each system-member has arrangements—

(i) for properly authenticated dematerialised instructions attributable to the member to be sent;

(ii) for properly authenticated dematerialised instructions to be received by or for the member; and

(iii) with a settlement-bank for payments to be made, where appropriate, for the units of a security transferred by means of the relevant system;

(c) that each participating issuer is able to respond with sufficient speed to operator- instructions.

21. An operator must have rules which require system-users and former system-users to provide the operator with such information in their possession as the operator may require in order to meet obligations under these regulations.

Definitions

'certificate': CA 1990(US)R 1996, reg 3(1); 'computer': CA 1990(US)R 1996, reg 3(1); 'court': CA 1990(US)R 1996, reg 3(1); 'dematerialised instruction': CA 1990(US)R 1996, reg 3(1); 'enactment': CA 1990(US)R 1996, reg 3(1); 'generate': CA 1990(US)R 1996, reg 3(1); 'interest in a security': CA 1990(US)R 1996, reg 3(1); 'issue': CA 1990(US)R 1996, reg 3(1); 'operator': CA 1990(US)R 1996, reg 3(1); 'operator-instruction': CA 1990(US)R 1996, reg 3(1); 'operator-system': CA 1990(US)R 1996, reg 3(1); 'participating issuer': CA 1990(US)R 1996, reg 3(1); 'participating security': CA 1990(US)R 1996, reg 3(1); 'practices': CA 1990(US)R 1996, reg 3(1); 'relevant system': CA 1990(US)R 1996, reg 3(1); 'rules': CA 1990(US)R 1996, reg 3(1); 'securities': CA 1990(US)R 1996, reg 3(1); 'settlement-bank': CA 1990(US)R 1996, reg 3(1); 'system-member': CA 1990(US)R 1996, reg 3(1); 'system-member instruction': CA 1990(US)R 1996, reg 3(1); 'system-participant': CA 1990(US)R 1996, reg 3(1); 'system-user': CA 1990(US)R 1996, reg 3(1); 'uncertificated unit of a security', reg 3(1).

UK legislation

Uncertificated Securities Regulations 2001, Sch 1.

EXPLANATORY NOTE

These Regulations make provision for the transfer without a written instrument, and the evidencing otherwise than by a certificate, of title to a unit of a security, in accordance with a computer-based system and procedures known as the 'relevant system'. The relevant system centres on a person known as the 'operator'. The legal framework underlying the operation of the relevant system, together with the criteria which the operator and the relevant system must meet, are enshrined in these Regulations.

Chapter I, inter alia, sets out the purpose and definitions in the Regulations. A unit of a security which may be transferred by means of the relevant system is referred to as an 'uncertificated unit'. A security, the units of which may become uncertificated, is referred to as a 'participating security'. An issuer which issues a participating security is, in relation to that security, referred to as a 'participating issuer'. Instructions sent by means of the relevant system are referred to as 'dematerialised instructions'.

Chapter II mainly provides for a range of matters relating to transfers of title to securities (including transfer of uncertificated holdings, transfer from uncertificated to certificated holdings and vice-versa) through a dematerialised system, the recording and registration of such transfers and the obligations imposed on participating issuers in regard to this and certain other matters.

Chapter III provides for the approval of an operator or recognition of an operator already approved by a competent authority of a Member State of the EU, by the Minister and associated matters. Provision is also made for the Minister to delegate his approval and supervisory functions under Chapter III to a designated body, if he so wishes.

Chapter IV makes provision to prevent persons sending dematerialised instructions, and persons on whose behalf they are sent, denying particular matters relating to them. It also makes provision for persons receiving such instructions to accept with certain exceptions, that the information contained in them and matters relating to them are correct.

Chapter V makes provision for certain notices to be issued in respect of minority shareholdings resulting from a take-over situation.

Chapter VI contains certain supplementary and incidental provisions designed to overcome evidential problems which may arise in relation to system entries.

The Schedule to the Regulations sets out the requirements for approval and continuing operation of a person as an operator.

European Communities (Public Limited Companies Subsidiaries) Regulations 1997

SI 67/1997

Notes

These Regulations transpose Council Directive 92/101/EEC of 23 November 1992 amending Directive 77/91/EEC on formation of public limited-liability companies and the maintenance and alteration of their capital (the Second Company Law Directive). This amending Directive aimed to prevent the use by subsidiaries of public limited-liability companies in order to circumvent the capital maintenance rules applicable to public limited liability companies under the Second Company Law Directive.

I, RICHARD BRUTON, Minister for Enterprise and Employment, in exercise of the powers conferred on me by section 3 of the European Communities Act, 1972 (No. 27 of 1972), and for the purpose of giving effect to the provisions of Council Directive No. 92/101/EEC of 23 November, 1992 hereby make the following Regulations:

PRELIMINARY AND GENERAL

1 Citation and construction

(1) These Regulations may be cited as the European Communities (Public Limited Companies Subsidiaries) Regulations, 1997.

(2) These Regulations shall be construed as one with the Companies Acts.

Definitions

'the Companies Acts': EC(PLCS)R 1997, reg 3(1).

---

2 Commencement

These Regulations shall come into operation on the 1st day of March 1997.

3 Interpretation

(1) In these Regulations, unless the context otherwise requires—

"the Companies Acts" means the Principal Act, and every enactment (including these Regulations) which is to be construed as one with that Act;

"the Principal Act" means the Companies Act, 1963 (No. 33 of 1963);

"the Act of 1986" means the Companies (Amendment) Act, 1986 (No. 25 of 1986);

"the Act of 1990" means the Companies Act, 1990 (No. 33 of 1990);

"the Directive of 1968" means Council Directive No. 68/151/EEC of 9 March 1968.

(2) In these Regulations, unless the context otherwise requires, a reference to a Regulation is to a Regulation of these Regulations, a reference to a paragraph is to a paragraph of the Regulation, and a reference to a subparagraph is to the subparagraph of the paragraph, in which the reference occurs.

Definitions

'the Directive of 1968': EC(PLCS)R 1997, reg 3(1).

4 Extension of meaning of 'subsidary'

(1) For the purposes of Part XI of the Act of 1990, in addition to the circumstances where a company (including a body corporate) is deemed to be a subsidiary of a public limited company by virtue of section 155 of the Principal Act, a limited company (including a body corporate) within the meaning of paragraph (2) shall also be deemed to be a subsidiary of a public limited company if, but only if, the public limited company is itself a shareholder or member of the said limited company and controls alone, pursuant to an agreement with other shareholders or members, a majority of the shareholders' or members' voting rights in the company in question.

(2) For the purposes of this Regulation, a limited company (including a body corporate) is a company—

(a) to which Article 1 of the Directive of 1968 applies, or

(b) which is incorporated other than in a Member State of the European Union and is of a legal form comparable to the type of company referred to in paragraph (a).

(3) For the purposes of Part XI of the Act of 1990, a public limited company exercises its control indirectly where the control of a subsidiary is exercised through another subsidiary, pursuant to section 155(1)(b) of the Principal Act.

(4) The first reference to a company in section 224(1) of the Act of 1990 includes a body corporate.

Definitions

'the Act of 1990': EC(PLCS)R 1997, reg 3(1); 'the Directive of 1968': EC(PLCS)R 1997, reg 3(1); 'the Principal Act': EC(PLCS)R 1997, reg 3(1).

Notes

The expression "public limited company" is not defined, but it appears to refer only to a public limited company formed and registered under the Irish Companies Acts. This can be deduced from, first, the expression "including a body corporate" being used in relation to subsidiaries but not holding companies and secondly para (2) of this Regulation expressly broadening the meaning of "limited company" to include a company within the meaning of the First Company Law Directive of 1968, but without a similar provision for "public limited company" to include comparable companies as listed in the Second Company Law Directive 77/91/EEC of 13 December 1976. Directive 92/101/EEC of 23 November 1992, which these Regulations purport to transpose, amends the Second Company Law Directive, which applies only to the various public company forms in each of the member states.

Therefore, to the extent that an Irish-incorporated company were to acquire shares in a public limited liability company incorporated in another member state, this Irish law does not appear to apply. It is arguable that these regs have not correctly implemented the Directive.

In the case of *Marleasing SA v La Commercial International de Alimentación SA*[1] the European Court stated:

'The obligations of member states under a Directive is to achieve its objects, and their duty by Article 5 of the Treaty (of Rome) to take all necessary steps to ensure the fulfilment of that obligation, binds all authorities of member states, including national courts within their jurisdiction. It follows that in applying national law … the national court asked to interpret national law is bound to do so in every way possible in light of the text and aim of the Directive to achieve the results envisaged by it …".

It is therefore possible that these regs may be construed by a court as preventing an Irish company from acquiring shares in a non-Irish public limited liability company or providing financial assistance in connection with such an acquisition, as though the public limited liability company concerned were incorporated as an Irish public limited company.

[1] *Marleasing SA v La Commercial International de Alimentación SA* Case C–106/89 [1990] ECR 4135.

---

5 Extension to section 224 of 1990 on holding of shares by subsidiaries

(1) In addition to section 224 of the Act of 1990, this Regulation shall apply where any holding company is a public limited company (in this Regulation referred to as a 'parent public company') and where its subsidiary (not being a subsidiary solely by virtue of paragraph (a)(ii) or (b) of subsection (1) of section 155 of the Principal Act) is a limited company (including a body corporate) of the type referred to in Regulation 4(2) (in this Regulation referred to as a 'public company subsidiary').

(2) A public company subsidiary shall not—

(a) subscribe for the shares of its parent public company, or

(b) purchase shares in its parent public company which are not fully paid, or

(c) provide financial assistance in accordance with subsections (2) to (11) of section 60 of the Principal Act for the purchase of or subscription for shares in its parent public company.

(3) If a public company subsidiary purports to act in contravention of paragraph (2)(a), it shall be guilty of an offence and the purported subscription shall be void.

(4) Where shares in a parent public company are subscribed for by a nominee of a public company subsidiary in contravention of paragraph (2), then for all purposes the shares shall be treated as held by the nominee on his own account and the public company subsidiary shall be regarded as having no beneficial interest in them, and the provisions of subsections (2) to (6) of section 42 of the Companies (Amendment) Act, 1983, shall, with any necessary modifications, apply.

(5) Without prejudice to any other requirements contained in or penalties imposed by the Companies Acts, where a public company subsidiary purchases, subscribes for or holds shares in its parent public company, and—

(a) the shares were not fully paid when they were purchased, or

(b) the authorisation required by section 224(3) of the Act of 1990 has not been obtained, or

(c) the shares are held as treasury shares in excess of the limit referred to in section 209(2) of that Act, or

(d) the purchase or subscription was in contravention of paragraph (2)(c), then, unless the shares or any interest of the public company subsidiary in them are previously disposed of, the provisions of section 43(3) of the Companies (Amendment) Act, 1983, shall, with the modification that the 'relevant period' in relation to any shares shall be 12 months and with any other necessary modifications, apply to the public company subsidiary in respect of such shares.

(6) This Regulation shall not affect or prohibit—

(a) the subscription for, acquisition or holding of, shares in its parent public company by a public company subsidiary where the public company subsidiary is concerned as personal representative or where it is concerned as trustee unless the parent public company or a subsidiary thereof is beneficially interested under the trust and is not so interested only by way of security for the purposes of a transaction entered into by it in the ordinary course of a business which includes the lending of money;

(b) the allotment to, or holding by, a public company subsidiary of shares in its parent public company in the circumstances set out in section 32(5) of the Principal Act, but where the shares so allotted are held as treasury shares and the nominal value of treasury shares held by the public company subsidiary exceeds the limit referred to in section 209(2) of the Act of 1990 then, unless the shares or any interest of the public company subsidiary in them are previously disposed of, the provisions of section 43(3) of the Companies (Amendment) Act, 1983, shall with the modification that the relevant period in relation to any shares shall be 3 years and with any other necessary modifications, apply to the public company subsidiary in respect of such shares;

(c) the subscription, acquisition or holding of shares in its parent public company by a public company subsidiary where the subscription, acquisition or holding is effected on behalf of a person other than the person subscribing, acquiring or holding the shares, who is neither the parent public company itself nor a subsidiary within the meaning of Part XI of the Act of 1990 of the said parent public company;

(d) the subscription, acquisition or holding of shares in its parent public company by a public company subsidiary which is a member of an approved stock exchange specified in section 17(2) of the Stock Exchange Act, 1995 (No. 9 of 1995), acting in its capacity as a professional dealer in securities in the normal course of its business.

(7) A person guilty of an offence under this Regulation shall be liable on summary conviction to a fine not exceeding [€1,904.61][a] or to imprisonment for a term not exceeding 6 months, or to both such fine and such imprisonment.

(8) (a) Where an offence under this Regulation has been committed by a public company subsidiary and is proved to have been committed with the consent or connivance of or to be attributable to any neglect on the part of a person being a director, manager, secretary or other similar officer of the public company subsidiary, or a person who was purporting to act in any such capacity, that person as well as the body corporate shall be guilty of an offence and shall be

liable to be proceeded against and punished as if he or she were guilty of the first-mentioned offence.

(b) Where the affairs of a public company subsidiary are managed by its members, paragraph (a) shall apply in relation to the acts and defaults of a member in connection with his or her functions of management as if he or she were a director of the public company subsidiary.

Amendments

a £500 increased to £1,500 by CA 1990, s 240(7) (as inserted by CLEA 2001, s 104(c)), and converted to €1,904.61 by Council Regulations (EC) No 1103/97, No 974/98 and No 2866/98 and the Economic and Monetary Union Act 1998, s 6.

Definitions

'the Act of 1990': EC(PLCS)R 1997, reg 3(1); 'the Principal Act': EC(PLCS)R 1997, reg 3(1); 'the Companies Acts': EC(PLCS)R 1997, reg 3(1).

---

6 Information in directors' report regarding acquisitions by company of own shares

Section 14 of the Act of 1986 shall also apply where, in any financial year of a company, shares in the company are acquired in a public limited company by a subsidiary pursuant to section 224 of the Act of 1990, and references in paragraphs (i), (ii) and (iii) of that section to 'another person' shall be read as including a subsidiary company of a public limited company, pursuant to Part XI of that Act.

Definitions

'the Act of 1986': EC(PLCS)R 1997, reg 3(1); 'the Act of 1990': EC(PLCS)R 1997, reg 3(1).

Given under my Official Seal, this 5th day of February 1997

Richard Bruton

Minister for Enterprise and Employment

EXPLANATORY NOTE

The purpose of these Regulations is to give legal effect to Council Directive 92/101/EEC which amends the Second Directive (Formation and Capital of Public Limited Companies) to apply conditions on the purchase of shares in a PLC by subsidiaries of that PLC.

Part XI of the Companies Act, 1990 already substantially implements Directive 92/101/EEC. It is proposed to complete the implementation process by extending the definition of subsidiary for the purposes of Part XI of the 1990 Act, and applying the additional requirements of the Directive to directly controlled subsidiaries.

Regulations 1–3 provide for citation, commencement and interpretation of the Regulations.

Regulation 4 extends the definition of subsidiary of a public limited company for the purposes of Part XI of the Companies Act, 1990.

Regulation 5 applies the conditions relating to the subscription, acquisition or holding of shares by a public company itself to the subscription, acquisition or holding of shares by any subsidiary of the type referred to in the Directive in its parent public limited company. It also sets out the penalty for those found guilty of an offence.

Regulation 6 extends the requirements on directors to disclose information about acquisition by a PLC of its own shares, to acquisition by a subsidiary (as defined) company of shares in its parent PLC.

Companies Act 1963 (Section 377(1)) Order 1999

SI 64/1999

I, NOEL TREACY, Minister of State at the Department of Enterprise, Trade and Employment, in exercise of the powers conferred on me by section 377(1) of the Companies Act, 1963 (No. 33 of 1963), (inserted by section 250 of the Companies Act, 1990 (No. 33 of 1990)), as adapted by the Enterprise and Employment (Alteration of Name of Department and Title of Minister) Order, 1997 (S.I. No. 305 of 1997), and the Enterprise, Trade and Employment (Delegation of Ministerial Functions) Order, 1998 (S.I. No. 265 of 1998), hereby order as follows:

1. This Order may be cited as the Companies Act, 1963 (section 377(1)) Order, 1999.

Cross references

See 1963, s 377 and notes thereto.

See also IA 2005, s 19: 'A word or expression used in a statutory instrument has the same meaning in the statutory instrument as it has in the enactment under which the instrument is made'.

Notes

The most important 'unregistered company' is The Governor and Company of the Bank of Ireland. The provisions of the Companies Acts listed in CA 1963, Sch 9 apply to all bodies corporate[1] incorporated in and having a place of business in the State by virtue of CA 1963, s 377 ie, unregistered companies. CA 1963(s 377(1))O 1999 modifies and adapts certain provisions of the Companies Act for application to such unregistered companies. CA 1963(s 377(1))O 1999 does not stipulate the date on which the order comes into effect; however, it was made on 5 March 1999.

1 All bodies corporate other than those specifically excepted by CA 1963, s 377(2).

---

2. In this Order—

"the Act of 1990" means the Companies Act, 1990 (No. 33 of 1990);

"the Companies Acts" means the Companies Act, 1963 (No. 33 of 1963), and every enactment which is to be construed as one with that Act;

"the provisions of the Companies Acts as applied" means the provisions of the Companies Acts which, by virtue of section 377(1) of, and the Ninth Schedule to, the Companies Act, 1963 (as altered by the Companies Act, 1963 (Ninth Schedule) Regulations, 1999), apply to the bodies corporate specified in the said section 377(1);

"the provisions of the Act of 1990 as applied" means the provisions of Part XI of the Act of 1990 which, by virtue of section 377(1) of, and the Ninth Schedule to, the Companies Act, 1963 (as altered by the Companies Act, 1963 (Ninth Schedule) Regulations, 1999), apply to the bodies corporate specified in the said section 377(1).

Definitions

'body corporate': CA 1963, s 2(3).

3. There is hereby prescribed the following adaptation of the provisions of the Companies Acts as applied, namely, each of the references to articles in those provisions shall be constructed as including references to the bye-laws of the body corporate concerned.

Definitions

'articles': CA 1963, s 2(1); 'body corporate': CA 1963, s 2(3); 'Companies Acts': CA 1963 (s 377(1)) O 1999, r 2; 'prescribed': CA 1963, s 2(1) and CA 1990, s 3(1).

Notes

The Companies Acts are adapted by CA 1963 (s 377(1)) O 1999 such that reference to articles of association shall be read as reference to 'bye-laws' of the relevant body corporate.

4. There are hereby prescribed the following modifications of the provisions of the Act of 1990 as applied, namely—

(a) subsection (1) of section 210 of the Act of 1990 shall have effect as if there were inserted the following sentence at the end of that subsection—

> "For the purposes of this section the provisions of the Companies Acts governing the variation of rights attached to classes of shares shall apply to the body corporate concerned.",

(b) sections 215, 216, 222 and 226 of the Act of 1990, in so far as they apply to a public limited company, shall apply to all bodies corporate to which section 377(1) of the Companies Act, 1963, applies, other than those which, if they were registered under the Companies Acts, would be private companies.

Definitions

'Act of 1990': CA 1963 (s 377(1)) O 1999, r 2; 'body corporate': CA 1963, s 2(3); 'Companies Acts': CA 1963 (s 377(1)) O 1999, r 2; 'private company': CA 1963, s 2(1); 'prescribed': CA 1963, s 2(1) and CA 1990, s 3(1); 'public limited company': C(A)A 1983, s 2(1).

Notes

Application of CA 1990, Pt IX: CA 1963 (s 377(1)) O 1999 facilitates the application of CA 1990, Pt IX to unregistered companies. In particular provisions as to the acquisition of own shares and shares in a holding company are applied to unregistered companies. EC (PLCS) R 1997 applies to such unregistered companies by virtue of CA 1963(9th Sch)R 1999 which came into force on 1 April 1999.

EXPLANATORY NOTE

(*This note is not part of the Instrument and does not purport to be a legal interpretation.*)

The purpose of this Order is to facilitate the application of Part IX of the Companies Act, 1990, as altered by the Companies Act 1963 (Ninth Schedule) Regulations, 1999 to unregistered companies, by making some necessary modifications in the application of that Part to such unregistered companies.

Companies Act 1990 (Form and Content of Documents Delivered to Registrar) Regulations 2002

SI 39/2002

I, Noel Treacy, Minister of State at the Department of Enterprise, Trade and Employment, in exercise of the powers conferred on me by sections 3(3) and 248 of the Companies Act 1990 (No. 33 of 1990) as adapted by the Enterprise and Employment (Alteration of Name of Department and Title of Minister) Order 1997 (S.I. No. 305 of 1997) and the Enterprise, Trade and Employment (Delegation of Ministerial Functions) Order 1998 (S.I. No. 265 of 1998), hereby order as follows:

1. These Regulations may be cited as the Companies Act 1990 (Form and Content of Documents Delivered to Registrar) Regulations 2002.

Definitions

'document': CA 1963, s 2(1) and CA 1990, s 248(8); 'the registrar of companies': CA 1963, s 2(1).

UK legislation

See generally Companies Act 2006, s 1068 (so far as is brought into force by the Companies Act 2006 (Commencement No. 1, Transitional Provisions and Savings) Order 2006 (SI 2006/3428)) and Companies Act 1985 ss 706 (as substituted by Companies Act 1989, s 125) and 707B (as inserted by the Companies Act 1985 (Electronic Communications) Order 2000 (SI 2000/3373).

---

2. These Regulations shall come into operation on 1st March 2002.

Cross-references

See CA 1990, s 248 'Delivery to the registrar of documents in legible form' which came into force on 28 February 2002.[1]

See CA 1990, s 249A 'Power to reject documents for registration and amendments consequential on that section's insertion' which came into force on 1 March 2002.[2]

1 Companies Act 1990 (Commencement) Order 2002 (SI 57/2002).

2 Company Law Enforcement Act 2001 (Commencement) (No 4) Order 2002 (SI 2002/43). See also Leaflet No 21, 'Grounds for Returning Documents to Presenters', Companies Registration Office, September 2002 in relation to the commencement of operation of CA 1990, s 249A and CA1990(FCDDR)R 2002.

---

3. (1) In these Regulations—

"Acts" means the Companies Acts 1963 to 2001;

"delivered" means delivered to the registrar;

"documents" has the same meaning as in section 248 of the Companies Act 1990 (No. 33 of 1990);

"registrar" means the registrar of companies.

(2) A word or expression used in these Regulations that is also used in the Acts shall, unless the context otherwise requires, have in these Regulations the meaning that it has in those Acts.

(3) In these Regulations, unless the contrary intention appears—

(a) a reference to a paragraph is a reference to the paragraph of the provision in which the reference occurs, and

(b) a reference to a section is to a section of the Companies Act 1963 (No. 33 of 1963).

Definitions

'the registrar of companies': CA 1963, s 2 (1).

4. Documents shall be easily legible and suitable for electronic scanning and electronic copying.

Definitions

'documents': CA1990(FCDDR)R 2002, reg 3(1).

Notes

Documents suitable for scanning and copying: The First EU Directive on Company Law[1] provides that member states are obliged, as from 1 January 2007, to ensure that filings done pursuant to that directive are kept in a file or entered in the register in electronic form. CA1990(FCDDR)R 2002, reg 4 facilitates the satisfaction of this requirement by providing that documents that are required to be delivered to the Registrar of Companies (the Registrar) and which are delivered in legible form are delivered in such a format that they are easily scanned and therefore may be converted into electronic form. This was implemented in Ireland by EC(C)(A)R 2007 (SI 49/2007).

1 (68/151/EEC) OJ Special Edition 1968, r 3 (as amended by Directive 2003/58/EC of the European Parliament and of the Council, OJ NL 221, 4.9.2003, p 13).

5. A page of a document shall be—

(a) 297 millimetres in length and 210 millimetres in width, that is to say, A4 size, and

(b) made of white paper with a matt finish weighing not less than 80 grams per square millimetre.

Definitions

'documents': CA 1990(FCDDR)R 2002, reg 3(1).

6. The print in a document shall be—

(a) black in colour,

(b) not less than 1.8 millimetres in height, and

(c) suitable and adequate for electronic scanning.

Definitions

'documents': CA1990(FCDDR)R 2002, reg 3(1); 'printed': CA 1963, s 2(1).

7. The layout of the printed matter on a page of a document shall be such as to provide a margin of not less than one centimetre all around the printed matter, that is to say, on the top and bottom and on each side, of it.

Definitions

'documents': CA1990(FCDDR)R 2002, reg 3(1); 'printed': CA 1963, s 2(1).

8. A document shall not contain any colour other than the white of the paper and the black of the printed matter.

Definitions

'documents': CA1990(FCDDR)R 2002, reg 3(1); 'printed': CA 1963, s 2(1).

9. If an original document contains coloured print or any of its pages consist of glossy paper, a copy of the document, or a printer's proof of the document, complying with these Regulations shall be delivered.

Definitions

'documents': CA1990(FCDDR)R 2002, reg 3(1); 'printed': CA 1963, s 2(1).

10. Pages of a document shall be kept together by means of a clip or staple at the top left-hand corner and shall not be stitched together or otherwise bound and shall not bear any adhesive tape.

Definitions

'documents': CA1990(FCDDR)R 2002, reg 3(1).

11. A document shall not consist of or contain a carbon copy or photocopy or printed matter from a dot matrix computer printer.

Definitions

'documents': CA1990(FCDDR)R 2002, reg 3(1); 'printed': CA 1963, s 2(1).

12. A space in a document for the insertion of information shall not be left blank but, as appropriate, "not applicable", "nil" or "none" or another similar word shall be inserted in the space.

Definitions

'documents': CA1990(FCDDR)R 2002, reg 3(1).

13.(1) An amendment inserted in the contents of a document shall be initialled and dated by at least one of the signatories to the document or, if there are no signatories, by at least one of the persons who authorised its production.

(2) Subject to paragraph (3), if a document delivered by a person is returned by the registrar to the person for amendment, either, as the registrar may determine, a new document shall be prepared or the contents of the document shall be amended and initialled and dated in accordance with paragraph (1), and thereafter the document shall be delivered.

(3) If the document referred to in paragraph (2) is a statutory declaration, the person who made the declaration shall make another statutory declaration and deliver it as soon as practicable.

Definitions

'delivered': CA1990(FCDDR)R 2002, reg 3(1); 'documents': CA1990(FCDDR)R 2002, reg 3(1); 'registrar': CA1990(FCDDR)R 2002, reg 3(1); 'statutory declaration': IA 2005, Sch, Pt 1 and IFCMPA 2006, s 6(9).

Cross reference

See IFCMPA 2006, s 6 and notes thereto in relation to statutory declarations under the Companies Acts.

Notes

Amendment of documents: CA 1990, s 249A provides that the Registrar can serve on a person who delivers a document which does not comply with CA 1990 (FCDDR) 2002 or CA 1990, ss 248 or 249 a notice indicating the deficiency in the document. If within 14 days the Registrar does not receive a replacement document, satisfying the relevant requirements, then the original document is deemed not to have been delivered to the Registrar.[1] Where the Registrar returns a document he/she may stipulate whether an amendment or a new document is required.[2] Where an amendment only is required, it is sufficient that the amendment is initialled by at least one of the original signatories or if there are no signatories, by one of the persons who authorised the production of that document.[3]

1 CA 1990, s 249A.

2 CA1990(FCDDR)R 2002, reg 13(2).

3 CA1990(FCDDR)R 2002, reg 13(1).

14.(1) Subject to paragraphs (2) and (3), the name of a company (as stated in its memorandum of association) and the address of its registered office shall be entered on the first page of a document in a prominent position.

(2) The name and address referred to in paragraph (1) shall correspond with the information previously delivered to the registrar in accordance with the Acts.

(3) If the name of the company includes one of the words or expressions "limited", "teoranta", "public limited company" or "cuideachta phoiblí theoranta", an abbreviated

form of the word or expression may be used in the entry made under paragraph (1) in a document other than a document relating to the incorporation of a company, a change of name or the re-registration of a company or the memorandum or articles of association of a company.

(4) The address of the registered office of a company on a document may not be given as a post office box number.

Definitions

'Acts': CA1990(FCDDR)R 2002, reg 3(1); 'articles': CA 1963, s 2(1); 'company': CA 1963, s 2(1); 'documents': CA1990(FCDDR)R 2002, reg 3(1); 'memorandum': CA 1963, s 2(1); 'registrar': CA1990(FCDDR)R 2002, reg 3(1).

15.(1) An individual shall be referred to in a document by his or her surname and all of his or her first names.

(2) Where the address of an individual is required to be stated in a document, his or her residential address shall be stated, unless some other address is required by law to be stated.

(3) If a document is required to be signed—

(a) the signature shall be the original, handwritten signature of the person, and

(b) the date of the signature shall be stated on the document.

Definition

'documents: CA1990(FCDDR)R 2002, reg 3(1).

UK legislation

See generally in relation to the provision of residential addresses CA 1985, s 723B '*Confidentiality Orders*'.

---

16. The form and content of a document delivered under a scheme of the registrar for giving priority to the examination and registration by the registrar of the document or documents of a specified class shall be in compliance with the rules and requirements of the scheme.

Definitions

'documents': CA1990(FCDDR)R 2002, reg 3(1); 'registrar': CA1990(FCDDR)R 2002, reg 3(1).

Notes

Currently, documents filed using the CRO's 'Companies Online Registration Environment (CORE) are processed more quickly than documents filed by other means.[1]

[1] See generally http://www.cro.ie.

---

17. Where any matter is included in a document under a provision of the Acts, or of an instrument made under the Acts, or such a provision is otherwise relevant to the matter, the provision shall be identified in the document.

Definitions

'Acts': CA1990(FCDDR)R 2002, reg 3(1); 'documents': CA1990(FCDDR)R 2002, reg 3(1).

18.(1) An application to the registrar in the form prescribed for the purposes of the Acts in relation to the registration of a company—

(a) shall correspond and be in compliance with the articles of association where the articles of association—

(i) provide for a minimum number of directors, or

(ii) contain the names of the first-appointed directors and the first-appointed secretary,

and

(b) subject to paragraph (2), may be signed by an individual acting as agent for all or any of the subscribers to the memorandum of association, but may not be completed on behalf of a company acting as such an agent.

(2) Where a subscriber referred to in paragraph (1)(b) is a company, the application to the registrar shall be signed by an officer of the company authorised in that behalf.

(3) A statutory declaration referred to in section 5(5) of the companies (Amendment) Act 1983 (No. 13 of 1983) and section 42(2) of the Companies (Amendment) (No.2) Act 1999 (No. 30 of 1999) shall be made on or after—

(a) the date of the form prescribed for the purposes of the Acts in relation to the registration of a company, or

(b) the date of the memorandum and articles of association of the company concerned,

whichever is the later.

Definitions

'Acts': CA1990(FCDDR)R 2002, reg 3(1); 'agent': CA 1963, s 2(1); 'articles': CA 1963, s 2(1); 'company': CA 1963, s 2(1); 'director': CA 1963, s 2(1); 'memorandum': CA 1963, s 2(1); 'Officer': CA 1963, s 2(1); 'prescribed': CA 1963, s 2(1); 'registrar': CA1990(FCDDR)R 2002, reg 3(1); 'statutory declaration': IA 2005, Sch, Pt 1 and IFCMPA 2006, s 6(9).

Cross reference

See Companies (Forms) No 2 Order 2004 (SI 829/2004), Form A1.[1] In this form, the declarant not only confirms compliance with the provisions of C(A)(No 2)A 1999, s 42 but also confirms compliance generally with the registration requirements of the Companies Acts, as required by C(A)A 1983, s 5(5). Making this combined declaration is expressly provided by C(A)(No 2)A 1999, s 42(5).

See IFCMPA 2006, s 6 and notes thereto in relation to statutory declarations under the Companies Acts.

[1] See also CRO Information Leaflet No. 1" Company Incorporation" May 2006.

19. If a statutory declaration of solvency for the purposes of section 256(1) (inserted by the Companies Act 1990) is made on the date of the passing of the resolution for winding up the company concerned—

(a) the time of the making of the statutory declaration shall be stated in the declaration, and

(b) the time of the passing of the resolution shall be stated in the resolution.

Definitions

'company': CA 1963, s 2(1); 'statutory declaration'; IA 2005, s 2(1) and IFCMPA 2006, s 6(9).

Cross reference

See CA 1963, s 256(1) (as amended) and notes thereto.

See IFCMPA 2006, s 6 and notes thereto in relation to statutory declarations under the Companies Acts.

20. A copy of a resolution passed by a company for the purpose of a creditors' voluntary winding up of the company and delivered must bear a certificate signed by the liquidator of the company to the effect that the copy is a true copy of the resolution.

Definitions

'company': CA 1963, s 2(1); 'creditors' voluntary winding up': CA 1963, s 2(1); 'delivered': CA1990(FCDDR)R 2004, reg 3(1).

21. A document shall not refer to a person who is an officer, liquidator, receiver, or examiner, of a company or a person referred to in section 352(1)(c) unless the registrar has been notified, as required under the Acts, of the name and appointment of the person.

Definitions

'Acts': CA1990(FCDDR)R 2002, reg 3(1); 'company': CA 1963, s 2(1); 'documents': CA1990(FCDDR)R 2002, reg 3(1); 'officer': CA 1963, s 2(1); 'person': IA 2005, Sch, Pt 1; 'registrar': CA 1990 (FCDDR) R 2004, r 3(1).

Cross reference

See CA 1963, ss 107, 195(6), 227(1), 278 and 352(1)(c) and notes thereto.

See also C(A)A 190 s 12(2)(b) and notes thereto.

22.(1) Documents delivered by the liquidator of a company shall not relate to a period, or to accounts for a period, beginning at any time after its incorporation and after a period for which accounts of the company, or any other documents of the company for that period required by or under the Acts to be delivered, have not been delivered.

(2) The return in relation to a company of a liquidator—

(a) under section 263, in the case of a members' voluntary winding up,

(b) under section 273, in the case of a creditors' voluntary winding up, or

(c) under section 306 or Order 74 Rule 130 of the Rules of the Superior Courts (S.I. No. 15 of 1986) or any rules of court for the time being amending or replacing that Order, in the case of a court winding up,

shall not relate to a period that is after another period during the liquidation for which no return in relation to the company has been delivered.

Definitions

'accounts': CA 1963, s 2(1); 'Acts': CA1990(FCDDR)R 2002, reg 3(1); 'company': CA 1963, s 2(1); 'creditors' voluntary winding up': CA 1963, s 2(1); 'delivered': CA1990(FCDDR)R 2002, reg 3(1); 'documents': CA1990(FCDDR)R 2002, reg 3(1); 'members' voluntary winding up': CA 1963, s 2(1).

Cross reference

See CA 1963, ss 262, 272, 263, 273 and 306 and notes thereto.

Notes

Returns by a liquidator: Filings under CA 1963, ss 262, 272, 263, 273 and 306 and any other relevant provision of the Companies Act may not be filed by the liquidator of the company in respect of a particular period, if there has been a failure to make a return in respect of a prior period.

23.(1) A copy of the text of a resolution passed by a company that is delivered shall be signed either by a director of the company whose appointment as a director has been notified to the registrar or, if the appointment of the secretary of the company as secretary has been so notified, by the secretary.

(2) A document shall not consist of or include a copy of the text of a resolution of a company in a voluntary winding up of the company if a statutory declaration of solvency under section 256 has not been delivered.

Definitions

'company': CA 1963, s 2(1); 'delivered': CA 1990 R 2002, r 3(1); 'director': CA 1963, s 2(1); 'documents': CA1990(FCDDR)R 2003, reg 3(1); 'registrar': CA1990(FCDDR)R 2002, reg 3(1); 'statutory declaration': IA 2005, Sch, Pt 1 and IFCMPA 2006, s 6(9).

Cross reference

See IFCMPA 2006, s 6 and notes thereto in relation to statutory declarations under the Companies Acts.

Notes

Notification of appointment: Notwithstanding the fact that an individual may have been appointed as a director or secretary, if the Registrar has not been notified of such appointment then the Registrar will not recognise such individual as a director or secretary (as appropriate), and entitled to sign such a resolution. See also obligations under CA 1990 (FCDDR) R 2004, r 21.

Statutory declaration as to solvency: It is not possible to file a resolution of the members approving the winding up of the Company[1] if a statutory declaration as to the solvency of the Company has not yet been filed.

1 CA 1963, s 256.

---

24. The registrar shall not accept any documents relating to the winding up of a company unless the registrar has received—

(a) a copy of the resolution for the winding up of the company, in the case of a voluntary liquidation, or

(b) an office copy of the order of the court directing the winding up of the company, in any other case.

Definitions

'company': CA 1963, s 2(1); 'the court': CA 1963, s 2(1); 'documents': CA1990(FCDDR)R 2002, reg 3(1); 'registrar': CA1990(FCDDR)R 2002, reg 3(1).

Cross reference

See CA 1963, s 143: obligation on the Company to deliver a copy of the resolution to the Registrar within 15 days of its being passed.

See CA 1963, s 221(1): obligation on the Company (or such other person as the Court may direct) to deliver an office copy of the order forthwith to the Registrar.

Explanatory Note

(This note is not part of the Instrument and does not purport to be a legal interpretation)

The purpose of these regulations is to deal with the manner of completion of documents deposited with the Companies Registration Office. They will support the Registrar on enforcement of proper quality control on documents deposited with him. The Regulations cover both the manner of delivery and return of documents. From the effective date any document sent back to the presenters if not corrected and returned within 14 days will be deemed not to have been filed.

Company Law Enforcement Act 2001 (Section 56) Regulations 2002

SI 324/2002

I, Mary Harney, Minister for Enterprise, Trade and Employment, in exercise of the powers conferred on me by section 4 of the Company Law Enforcement Act 2001 (No. 28 of 2001), hereby make the following regulations:

Notes

See CA 1990, s 150 and notes thereto.

---

1. These Regulations may be cited as the Company Law Enforcement Act 2001 (Section 56) Regulations 2002.

2. The form set out in the Schedule to these regulations is hereby prescribed for the purposes of section 56(1) of the Company Law Enforcement Act 2001 (No. 28 of 2001).

Schedule

Liquidator's Report under Section 56 of the Company Law Enforcement Act 2001

Please refer to the Guidance Notes when completing this Report. These are available from the ODCE website at www.odce.ie/publications/decision.asp

Name of Company: ______________________________

Registration Number of Company: ______________________

Please indicate if this is the first, second, etc. or final Report filed for the above company:______

Section 1: Liquidator Details

(Question 1 to be completed in every Report. Questions 2 to 9 to be completed as part of the first Report and in every subsequent Report where a change in details arises.)

1. Name of Liquidator: ______________________________

2. Name of Liquidator's firm *(if applicable)*: ______________________

3. Address of Liquidator: ______________________________

4. If you are a member of a professional body, please state which one: __________

5. Liquidation Type *(please tick one)*:

    Creditors' Voluntary Liquidation:

    Official Liquidation:

6. If a Creditors' Voluntary Liquidation, were you the members' nominee?

Yes: No:

7. Date of your appointment as Liquidator:______________________

8. Name of Liquidator's staff member with day-to-day responsibility for the Liquidation (*where applicable*)

____

9. Contact Details for *(please tick one)*:

    the Liquidator:

    Staff Member:

Telephone Number(s): ____________ Fax Number: ____________

E-mail Address: ____________

Section 2: Company Details

(To be completed as part of the first Report and every subsequent Report where a change in details arises)

10. Business/Trading Name(s) (please include all those used in the 12 months prior to the date of commencement of the winding up):

____

____

11. Address of Current Registered Office:

____

____

____

12. Address of any other Registered Office used in the 12 months prior to the date of commencement of the winding up:

____

____

____

13. Principal Trading Address(es) (*please include all those used in the 12 months prior to the date of commencement of the winding up, if different from the Registered Office(s) above*):

____

____

____

14. Nature of the Company's Business:

a Please state the most relevant NACE Classification at the date of commencement of the liquidation *(see Guidance Notes)*:

____

b. Please give a precise description of the Company's activities at the date of commencement of the liquidation:

____

____

____

15. Number of Company employees at the date of commencement of the liquidation:

____

16. Turnover for each of the last three financial years preceding the date of commencement of the liquidation:

Financial Year Ended (date): ____________ Turnover: ____________(€ amount)

Financial Year Ended (date): ____________ Turnover: ____________(€ amount)

Financial Year Ended (date): ____________ Turnover: ____________(€ amount)

17. Trading Details *(please state as a minimum month and year)*:

a. Date of Commencement of Trading: ____________________

b. Date of Cessation of Trading *(if applicable)*: ____________________

18. Please state, in your opinion, the reasons for the liquidation of the Company, and cite the evidence to support this opinion on a separate sheet.

19. Has there been any Scheme of Arrangement/Receivership/Examinership/ Liquidation in the Company in the 36 months prior to the date of this report?

Yes: No:

If yes, please provide relevant information, including type, name and address of any office-holder(s), date(s) of appointment/termination of appointment, copies of all notices of appointment and reports of receivers/examiners/liquidators or other office holders of the Company during that period:

____

____

____

____

____

____

20. Is there a deficiency in any tax return or payment of taxes?

Yes: No:

If so, please specify the periods, if any, for which returns are overdue and/or the amounts due:

____

____

____

____

____

____

21. Have you any information which may lead you to believe that there was a person acting as a shadow director of the Company?
(Please note that the expression 'shadow director' may include an individual or a body corporate):

Yes: No:

If yes, please provide the following details for the individual/body corporate in question:

a. Full Name:

____

b. Current or last known address:

____

____

____

____

c. What was the Person's role in the Company?

____

____

____

____

d. Has the Person demonstrated to you that s/he has acted honestly and responsibly in relation to the conduct of the Company's affairs?

Yes: No:

Please provide on a separate sheet details of the factors which support this answer and any other relevant information.

Section 3: Company Directors

(To be completed as part of the first Report and every subsequent Report where a change in details arises)

22. In this Section, you are required to include every person who appears to you to be, or have been, a director of the Company at the date of commencement of the winding up or at any time in the 12 months prior to the date of commencement of the winding up.

A separate copy of this Section should be used for each Person.

____

a. Full name *(including other known names)*: ________________

b. Current or last known address: ________________

____

c. Date of birth: ________________

d. PPS number: ________________

e. Period as director: ________________

From *(date)*: ________________ To *(date)*: ________________

f. What was the Person's role in the Company? ________________

____

____

g. Has the Person demonstrated to you that s/he has acted honestly and responsibly in relation to the conduct of the Company's affairs?

Yes: No:

Please provide on a separate sheet details of the factors which support this answer.

h. Other Directorships

(please provide full details of present/past companies of which this Person is/was a Director in the period from 12 months prior to the date of commencement of the winding up of the Company to date and include the company registration number, the date(s) of appointment/termination of the period as Director in each case and please indicate if any of these companies operated in a sector similar to the Company in liquidation):

____

____

____

Section 4: Statement of Affairs, Accounts and Report to Creditors

(To be completed as part of the first Report and every subsequent Report where a change in details arises)

23. Directors' Statement of Affairs or similar document (please attach a copy to this Report. If a copy is not attached, please state why not and attach details of the known assets and liabilities of the Company):

24. Is there a material difference between the Statement of Affairs or similar document and the expected final position?

Yes: No:

If so, please provide details of the amount and the reason for this material difference on a separate sheet.

25. Audited/Other Accounts

(please attach to this Report a copy of the last two sets of the audited accounts of the Company and the most recent draft or management accounts prepared after the last set of audited accounts. If the Company is exempted from audit, please provide a copy of the accounts laid before the AGM for the same period and the most recent draft or management accounts. If none are attached, please state why not.):

26. Report to Creditors and any other relevant material, e.g., minutes of creditors' meeting and Chairperson's statement to meeting

(please attach these documents and if they are not available, state why not):

27. Has a Committee of Inspection been appointed?

Yes: No:

If so, please provide the names and addresses of the members:

28. Will the winding up be completed within 18 months from the date of this report?

Yes: No:

29. Was there any material transfer of assets of the Company *(see Guidance Notes)* to any person during the period commencing 12 months prior to the date of commencement of its winding up and ending on the date of this report?

Yes: No:

If yes, please provide details, e.g., date(s) of transfer, nature of asset(s), beneficiary(ies), on a separate sheet.

30. On what date was the Company unable to trade out of its financial difficulties?

____

Section 5: Proceedings

(To be completed as part of the first Report and every subsequent Report where a change in details arises)

31. Are you asking the Director of Corporate Enforcement at this time to relieve you from the requirement to apply, pursuant to section 150 of the Companies Act 1990, for the restriction of one or more of the directors of the Company?

Yes: No:

If yes, is relief being sought for?, (please tick one)

All directors:

Certain named directors:

In either case, please name each director for which relief is sought and state the grounds upon which you consider that an application for restriction should not now be taken against each individual.

____

____

____

____

In respect of any remaining directors, please name them and indicate the grounds upon which the application for restriction will be made in each case:

____

____

____

____

32. In respect of this Company will you be applying to the High Court to disqualify any person, pursuant to section 160 of the Companies Act 1990?

Yes: No:

If yes, please name the person(s) in question and indicate the grounds upon which the application to disqualify will be taken:

____

____

33. Are any other proceedings being undertaken, or contemplated, by you against officers of the Company?

Yes: No:

If yes, please specify the nature of the proceedings, the person(s) against whom the proceedings are being or may be taken and the date/expected date of commencement of the proceedings. If proceedings have commenced please state whether they are in the High Court or Circuit Court and cite the Court record number of the case:

34. Are any other civil or criminal proceedings being undertaken, or contemplated, by any other person against the Company or any of its officers?

Yes: No:

If yes, please specify the nature of the proceedings, the person(s) against whom the proceedings are being or may be taken, the date/expected date of commencement of the proceedings and the name, address and telephone number of the person taking or contemplating the proceedings. If proceedings have commenced, please state whether they are in the High Court or Circuit Court and cite the Court record number of the case:

35. Have you made, or are you contemplating making, a report to the Director of Public Prosecutions and the Director of Corporate Enforcement under section 299 of the Companies Act 1963 (as amended by section 51 of the Company Law Enforcement Act 2001)?

Yes: No:

If yes, please specify the nature of any suspected offence(s), the person(s) to whom the report relates, the relationship of each such person to the Company and the date/expected date of submission of the report:

Section 6: Final Report

36. Outcome of restriction application(s) to the High Court (if applicable) *(please provide details for each person)*:

____

____

____

____

37. Outcome of any other court proceedings taken under the circumstances set out in questions 32, 33 and 34:

____

____

____

38. If the liquidation has been completed, please attach a copy of Form 14 as required to be submitted to the Companies Registration Office.

Section 7: Liquidator's Statement

(To be completed on every occasion a report is made)

I, ____________________, being the liquidator of the above company, state that the details and particulars contained in this Report and all associated documentation prepared by me are true, correct and complete, to the best of my knowledge and belief.

Signed:____________________________________

Date:____________________________________

Please ensure that copies of the following are attached to this Report:

- Separate sheets (if applicable) [items 18, 22(g), 24, 29];
- Copies of notices of appointment and reports of receivers/examiners/ liquidators/other office-holders (if applicable) 19;
- Statement of Affairs (or details of assets and liabilities) 23;
- Last two sets of audited accounts and draft or management accounts subsequently prepared, if any 25;
- Report to Creditors and other relevant material, including minutes of creditors' meeting, Chairperson's statement to meeting 26;
- Additional copies of Section 3: Details of Company Directors;
- Copy of CRO Form 14 (if applicable) 38;
- Any further information or documentation that you deem to be required.

EXPLANATORY NOTE

(*This note is not part of the Instrument and does not purport to be a legal interpretation*)

The purpose of these Regulations is to prescribe the form of the liquidators report for the purposes of section 56(1) of the Company Law Enforcement Act 2001.

European Communities (Corporate Insolvency) Regulations 2002

SI 333/2002

I, Mary Harney, Minister for Enterprise, Trade and Employment, in exercise of the powers conferred on me by section 3 of the European Communities Act 1972 (No. 27 of 1972) and, together with the European Communities (Personal Insolvency) Regulations 2002 (S.I. No. 334 of 2002), for the purpose of giving full effect to Council Regulation (EC) No. 1346/2000 (OJ L160 of 30.6.2000) of 29 May 2000 on insolvency proceedings, make the following regulations:

PART 1

PRELIMINARY AND GENERAL

1 Citation and construction

1. These Regulations—

(a) may be cited as the European Communities (Corporate Insolvency) Regulations 2002, and

(b) shall be construed as one with the Companies Acts, 1963 to 2001.

Definitions

'Companies Acts': IA 2005, s 21(2).

Notes

Until 31 May 2002 the procedures for administering the affairs of insolvent companies and for realising their assets were left to be determined by the domestic laws of the respective Member States of the European Union. 'Exporting' a winding-up order depended on the relevant rules of private international law of all jurisdictions concerned.[1]

The Brussels Convention 1968, the Lugano Convention 1988 and, more recently, the Brussels Regulation[2] all expressly excluded from their application: 'Bankruptcy, proceedings relating to the winding up of insolvent companies or other legal persons, judicial arrangements, compositions and analogous proceedings'.[3]

Thus, an Irish court could legitimately wind up a company and hope (and perhaps expect) that both a winding-up order and the appointment of a liquidator would be recognised extraterritorially, notwithstanding the fact that the company might have no link with Ireland other than being the place of incorporation.[4]

Whether the courts of a foreign jurisdiction would in fact recognise and enforce the orders of the Irish court winding up a company and appointing a liquidator, depended on the laws of that foreign jurisdiction and, inevitably therefore, the ability to give extraterritorial effect to Irish insolvency orders varied from one country to another.

Case law established that in order to wind up a foreign company in this jurisdiction as an unregistered company, the following had to be shown:

(i) that there was a sufficient connection between the company and Ireland;

(ii) that there was a reasonable possibility of persons benefiting from the making of the winding-up order; and

(iii) that there were one or more persons interested in the distribution of assets of the company over whom the Irish courts could exercise jurisdiction.[5]

In order to establish a sufficient connection between the company and Ireland it was not necessary to show that the foreign company carried on business in the jurisdiction,[6] although clearly if there was neither a business nor assets in the jurisdiction, it was always going to be somewhat difficult to convince the courts of the existence of a sufficient connection with Ireland such as to warrant the making of a winding-up order in the first place.[7]

Factors that were held by the court to give rise to a sufficient connection with Ireland such as to warrant the making of a winding-up order included the drawing down of loans in the jurisdiction[8] or the possibility of a liquidator being in a position to bring proceedings against directors for the imposition of personal liability in respect of fraudulent and/or reckless trading.[9]

Since 31 May 2002 the private international law dimensions of insolvency proceedings (other than proceedings involving Denmark)[10] have been governed by Council Regulation (EC) No 1346/2000[11] ('the Insolvency Regulation'). In order to give better effect to the provisions of the Insolvency Regulation various consequential amendments were made to the provisions of the Companies Acts pursuant to the EC(CI)R 2002.[12]

1 See Fletcher, *The Law of Insolvency*, (3rd edn, Sweet and Maxwell, 2002) 30–030; Courtney, *The Law of Private Companies* (2nd edn, Tottel Publishing, 2002) para. 26.064.

2 Council Regulation (EC) No. 44/2001 of 22 December 2000 on Jurisdiction and the Recognition and Enforcement of Judgments in Civil and Commercial Matters.

3 See Article 1 of the Brussels Convention, Article 1 of the Lugano Convention and Article 1 of the Brussels I Regulation.

4 See Binchy, *Irish Conflicts of Law* (Butterworths, 1988) at p 485.

5 *Re Real Estate Development Company* [1991] BCLC 210; *Re Paramount Airways Ltd* [1993] Ch 223; *Banco Nacional De Cuba v Cosmos Trading Corporation* [2000] 1 BCLC 116; *Stocznia Gdanska SA v Latreefers Inc (No 2)* [2001] BCLC 116.

6 *Banque des Marchandes de Moscou v Kindersley* [1951] Ch 112; *Re Azoff-Don Commercial Bank* [1954] Ch 315; *Re Compania Merabello San Nicholas SA* [1973] Ch 75; *International Westminster Bank v Okeanos* [1987] BCLC 450.

7 See, for example, *Re Real Estate Development Company* [1991] BCLC 210; *Re Titan International Inc* [1998] 1 BCLC 102.

8 *Re A Company (No 00359 of 1987)* [1988] Ch 210; *Re A Company (No 003102 of 1991) Ex Parte Nyckelyn Finance Co Ltd* [1991] BCLC 539.

9 *Re A Company (No 00359 of 1987)* [1988] Ch 210.

10 Denmark has opted out of the Regulation pursuant to Articles 1 and 2 of the Protocol on the position of Denmark annexed to the EU Treaty and based on Articles 61(c) and 67(1) of the EC Treaty, as amended by the Treaty of Amsterdam.

11 Insolvency proceedings commenced before 31 May 2002 do not fall to be governed by the Insolvency Regulation, even if they were still ongoing as of that date: Art 43. See also *Oakley v Vehicle Design Ltd* [2005] EWHC 872 (Ch); *Re Ultra Motorhomes International Ltd* [2006] BCC 57.

12 (SI 333/2002). These regulations came into effect on 1 July 2002. In relation to the Insolvency Regulation see, generally, Fletcher, *The Law of Insolvency* (3rd edn, Sweet and Maxwell, 2002) ch 31; Moss, Fletcher and Isaacs, *EC Regulation on Insolvency Proceedings* (OUP, 2002).

UK legislation

See Insolvency (Amendment) Rules 2002.

---

2 Interpretation

(1) In these Regulations—

'enforcement order' means an order under Regulation 6(5);

'insolvency proceedings' means insolvency proceedings opened in a member state of the European Communities other than the State and Denmark under Article 3 where the proceedings relate to a body corporate;

'Insolvency Regulation' means Council Regulation (EC) No 1346/2000 of 29 May 2000 on insolvency proceedings, the text of which, in the English language, is set out in the Schedule to these Regulations for convenience of reference.

(2) Unless provided otherwise, a word or expression used in these Regulations and also in the Insolvency Regulation has the same meaning in these Regulations as it has in that Regulation.

(3) References in these Regulations (other than Regulation 6) to numbered Articles without qualification are references to the Articles so numbered of the Insolvency Regulation.

Notes

See Article 1(2) and the exclusion of 'insolvency proceedings concerning insurance undertakings, credit institutions, investment undertakings which provide services involving the holding of funds or securities for third parties, or to collective investment undertakings'. See instead Directive 2001/17 of 19 March 2001 on the reorganisation and winding up of insurance undertakings, and Directive 2001/24 of 4 April 2001 on the reorganisation and winding up of credit institutions. See generally, *EU Banking and Insurance Insolvency*, edited by Gabriel Moss QC and Bob Wessels (OUP, 2006).

IA 2005 does not make reference to official EC documents when it prescribes documents in respect of which the courts must take judicial notice, although all Acts shall be so noted as public documents. Accordingly, it is necessary to open EC law materials to the court in the appropriate official format, according to European law. Although the text of the Insolvency Regulation is set out in the Schedule to this statutory instrument, it is stated to have been done for convenience only and, in the unlikely event of any difference occurring, reliance may only be had on the official copy, according to European law.

3 Amendment of Companies Act 1963

The Companies Act 1963 (No. 33 of 1963) is amended—

(a) […][a]

(b) […][b]

(c) […][c]

(d) […][d]

(e) […][e]

(f) […][f]

and

(g) […][g]

Amendments

a Reg 3(a) amends CA 1963, s 2(1) by the insertion of definitions of 'insolvency proceedings', 'Insolvency Regulation' and 'property'.

b Reg 3(b) inserts CA 1963, s 205A.

c Reg 3(c) inserts CA 1963, ss 227A and 227B.

d Reg 3(d) inserts CA 1963, s 250(4).

e Reg 3(e) inserts CA 1963, s 267A.

f Reg 3(f) inserts CA 1963, s 313A.

g Reg 3(g) inserts Ca 1963, s 343A.

Cross reference

See notes following CA 1963, ss 2, 205A, 227A, 227B, 250, 267A, 313A and 343A.

4 Amendment of Companies (Amendment) Act 1990

[...][a]

Amendments

a Reg 4 inserts C(A)A 1990, s 1A.

Notes

Not all forms of Irish insolvency proceedings are caught by the provisions of the Insolvency Regulation. Rather, the Regulation applies only to those types of personal and corporate insolvency proceedings listed in Annex A. On the corporate side, these comprise the following:

(i) compulsory winding up by the court;

(ii) creditors' voluntary winding up (with confirmation of the court); and

(iii) examinership.

In relation to a creditors' voluntary winding up with the confirmation of the court, this involves the voluntary liquidator, following his appointment, applying to the Master of the High Court pursuant to CA 1963, s 267A as amended for an order of confirmation which, once made, enables the winding-up resolution and the appointment of the liquidator to be recognised and enforced in the courts of the other member states.[1]

Certain classes of proceedings relating to insolvent companies are not, however, covered by the Insolvency Regulation. These include receiverships and schemes of arrangement pursuant to the provisions of CA 1963, ss 201–203. Also falling outside of the scope of the Regulation is the members' voluntary winding-up procedure, since this applies to solvent companies only.

In relation to personal debt, the Insolvency Regulation covers:

(i) bankruptcy;

(ii) the administration in bankruptcy of the estate of persons dying insolvent; and

(iii) arrangements under the control of the court which involve the vesting of all or part of the property of the debtor in the Official Assignee for realisation and distribution.

The European Communities (Personal Insolvency) Regulations (SI 334/2002) assist in the operation of the Insolvency Regulation as it applies to personal insolvency.

[1] For an English example of a creditors' voluntary winding up confirmed by the court and governed by the Regulation, see *Re TXU Europe German Finance BV* [2005] BPIR 209.

5 Registration of insolvency judgments

(1) A request by a liquidator under Article 22 that the judgment opening the insolvency proceedings be registered in a public register shall be made to the person or authority responsible for keeping the register concerned.

Notes

The Companies Registration Office and the Registrar of Friendly Societies.

6 Enforcement in State of insolvency judgments

(1) In this Regulation—

'Brussels 1 Regulation' means Council Regulation (EC) No 44/2001 of 22 December 2000 (OJ L12 of 16.1.2001) on jurisdiction and the recognition and enforcement of judgments in civil and commercial matters;

'insolvency judgment' means a judgment referred to in Article 25 of the Insolvency Regulation;

and, except where the context otherwise requires, references to numbered Articles are references to Articles so numbered of the Brussels 1 Regulation.

(2) Having regard to Article 68 of the Brussels 1 Regulation, references in Article 25 of the Insolvency Regulation to enforcement of insolvency judgments in accordance with certain Articles of the Brussels Convention are to be read as references to enforcement of those judgments in accordance with Articles 38 to 58 of the Brussels 1 Regulation.

(3) An application under the Brussels 1 Regulation for the enforcement in the State of an insolvency judgment shall be made to the Master of the High Court.

(4) The Master shall determine the application by order in accordance with the Brussels 1 Regulation.

(5) The Master shall declare the insolvency judgment enforceable immediately on completion of the formalities provided for in Article 53 without any review under Articles 34 and 35 and shall make an enforcement order in relation to the judgment.

(6) An order under paragraph (5) of this Regulation may provide for the enforcement of only part of the insolvency judgment concerned.

(7) An application to the Master under Article 39 for an enforcement order in respect of an insolvency judgment may include an application for any preservation measures the High Court has power to grant in proceedings that, apart from these Regulations, are within its jurisdiction.

(8) Where an enforcement order is made, the Master shall grant any such preservation measures so applied for.

(9) For the purposes of these Regulations references in Articles 42, 43, 45, 47, 48, 52, 53 and 57 to a declaration of enforceability are to be treated as references to an enforcement order under this Regulation.

(10) Subject to the restrictions on enforcement contained in Article 47(3), if an enforcement order has been made respecting an insolvency judgment, the judgment—

(a) shall, to the extent to which its enforcement is authorised by the enforcement order, be of the same force and effect as a judgment of the High Court, and

(b) may be enforced by the High Court, and proceedings taken on it, as if it were a judgment of that Court.

Notes

Enforcement of insolvency judgments: An insolvency judgment, within the meaning of Article 25 of the Insolvency Regulation, may be declared enforceable by the Master of the High Court immediately on completion of the various formalities in Article 53 of the Brussels 1 Regulation. The Master may grant any preservation measures that are contained in the judgment where the High Court has jurisdiction to grant such relief. Requests pursuant to Article 38 of the Brussels 1 Regulation to preserve and secure assets located in the State require application to the High Court per EC(CI)R 2002, reg 9(1).

Subpara (7) permits any application for any protective measure and, presumably, the requirement of an undertaking for damages and any counterapplication for security for costs, subject to the normal rules governing those procedures. This is an expansion of the Master's power for the purposes of the application, although, as seen subpara (8), his discretion is dramatically curtailed.

Subpara (8) cauterises the Master's discretion to refuse an application once the orders sought are 'preservation measures'. The effect of this subpara is to prevent the Master from examining the evidence further than satisfying himself that the relief sought is within the jurisdiction of the High Court and that the orders sought are preservation measures associated with the enforcement of an insolvency order.

7 Interest on insolvency judgments and payment of costs

(1) Where, on application for an enforcement order respecting an insolvency judgment, it is shown—

(a) that the judgment provides for the payment of a sum of money, and

(b) that, in accordance with the law of the member state in which the judgment was given, interest on the sum is recoverable under the judgment at a particular rate or rates and from a particular date or time, the enforcement order, if made, shall provide that the person liable to pay the sum shall also be liable to pay the interest, apart from any interest on costs recoverable under paragraph (2), in accordance with the particulars noted in the order, and the interest shall be recoverable by the applicant as though it were part of the sum.

(2) An enforcement order may provide for the payment to the applicant by the respondent of the reasonable costs of or incidental to the application for the enforcement order.

(3) A person required by an enforcement order to pay costs shall be liable to pay interest on the costs as if they were the subject of an order for the payment of costs made by the High Court on the date on which the enforcement order was made.

(4) Interest shall be payable on a sum referred to in paragraph (1)(a) only as provided for in this Regulation.

Notes

Regulation 7 does not prevent the application of the Statute of Limitations 1957 (as amended). A money judgment may apply interest according to the law of a foreign state but it does not exclude the operation of the Statute of Limitations. It might have done so, had subpara (1)(b) included the phrase 'for or until a particular date or time' instead of 'from a particular date or time'. Similarly, an enforcement order for costs shall be treated as though it were an order for the payment of costs ordered by the High Court. The Statute of Limitations applies to the enforcement of the judgment and to the interest arising therefrom, including interest on costs. The Courts Act 1981 interest applies by virtue of subpara (3), even if the order enforced does not provide for interest on costs.

---

8 Currency of payments under enforceable insolvency judgments

(1) An amount payable in the State under an insolvency judgment by virtue of an enforcement order shall be payable in the currency of the State.

(2) If the amount is stated in the insolvency judgment in any currency except the euro, payment shall be made on the basis of the exchange rate prevailing, on the date the enforcement order is made, between the currency of the State and any such currency.

(3) For the purposes of this Regulation a certificate purporting to be signed by an officer of an authorised institution and to state the exchange rate prevailing on a specified date between a specified currency and the currency of the State shall be admissible as evidence of the facts stated in the certificate.

(4) In this Regulation, 'authorised institution' means any of the following:

(a) a body licensed to carry on banking business under the Central Bank Acts, 1942 to 1998, or authorised to carry on such business under the ACC Bank Acts, 1978 to 2001, or regulations under the European Communities Acts, 1972 to 1998,

(b) a building society within the meaning of the Building Societies Act 1989 (No. 17 of 1989);

(c) a trustee savings bank within the meaning of the Trustee Savings Banks Acts, 1989 and 2001,

(d) An Post.

Notes

The date the enforcement order is made: The term used in reg 8(2) is 'made', not 'perfected', so the perfected order, unless done on the same day as the order, will refer to some prior day for determination of the exchange rate.

Reg 8(3): Although not relevant unless related to substantial sums of money or large changes in exchange rate, the term 'the exchange rate prevailing' means the rate that is predominant on a given day rather than a rate that was quoted at any one time that day. This is merely an evidentiary facility rather than a presumption, evidentiary or otherwise.

9 Preservation measures

(1) A request under Article 38 for measures to secure and preserve any of the debtor's assets in the State shall be made to the High Court.

(2) On such a request the High Court—

(a) may grant any such measures that the Court has power to grant in proceedings that, apart from these Regulations, are within its jurisdiction, and

(b) may refuse to grant the measures sought if, in its opinion, the fact that, apart from this Regulation, the Court does not have jurisdiction in relation to the subject matter of the proceedings makes it inexpedient for it to grant the measures.

Notes

According to reg 9(2), the High Court has discretion to grant these measures.

10 Venue

The jurisdiction of the Circuit Court or District Court in proceedings that may be instituted in the State by a liquidator in exercise of his or her powers under Article 18 may be exercised by the judge for the time being assigned—

(a) in the case of the Circuit Court, to the circuit, and

(b) in the case of the District Court, to the district court district,

in which the defendant ordinarily resides or carries on any profession, business or occupation.

11 Language of claims

A claim lodged with a liquidator (within the meaning of the Companies Acts, 1963 to 2001) by a creditor referred to in Article 42(2) may, if not in Irish or English, be required by the liquidator to be translated, in whole or in part, into either of these languages.

Definitions

'Companies Acts': IA 2005, s 21(2).

12 Non-recognition or non-enforcement of judgments

It shall be for the High Court to determine whether judgments referred to in Article 25(1), or insolvency proceedings or judgments referred to in Article 26, should not be recognised or enforced on grounds mentioned in those provisions.

13 Revocation

Paragraph 2 of the Companies (Recognition of Countries) Order 1964 (S.I. No. 42 of 1964) is amended by the substitution of 'section 367' for 'sections 250 and 367'.

Schedule
Text of Insolvency Regulation

Regulation 2(1)

COUNCIL REGULATION (EC) No 1346/2000 of 29 May 2000 on insolvency proceedings

THE COUNCIL OF THE EUROPEAN UNION,

Having regard to the Treaty establishing the European Community, and in particular Articles 61 (c) and 67 (1) thereof,

Having regard to the initiative of the Federal Republic of Germany and the Republic of Finland,

Having regard to the opinion of the European Parliament[1],

Having regard to the opinion of the Economic and Social Committee [2],

[1] Opinion delivered on 2 March 2000 (not yet published in the Official Journal).

[2] Opinion delivered on 26 January 2000 (not yet published in the Official Journal).

Notes

Article 61(c) deals with measures in the field of judicial cooperation in civil matters having cross-border implications in so far as necessary for the proper functioning of the internal market.

Whereas:

(1) The European Union has set out the aim of establishing an area of freedom, security and justice.

(2) The proper functioning of the internal market requires that cross-border insolvency proceedings should operate efficiently and effectively and this Regulation needs to be adopted in order to achieve this objective which comes within the scope of judicial cooperation in civil matters within the meaning of Article 65 of the Treaty.

Notes

Article 65 deals with measures in the field of judicial cooperation in civil matters having cross-border implications, and in so far as is necessary for the proper functioning of the internal market, shall include: (a) improving and simplifying the system for cross-border service of judicial and extrajudicial documents, cooperation in the taking of evidence, the recognition and enforcement of decisions in civil and commercial cases, including decisions in extrajudicial cases; (b) promoting the compatibility of the rules applicable in the member states concerning the conflict of laws and of jurisdiction; and (c) eliminating obstacles to the effective functioning of civil proceedings, if necessary by promoting the compatibility of the rules on civil procedure applicable in the member states.

---

(3) The activities of undertakings have more and more cross-border effects and are therefore increasingly being regulated by Community law. While the insolvency of such undertakings also affects the proper functioning of the internal market, there is a need for a Community act requiring coordination of the measures to be taken regarding an insolvent debtor's assets.

(4) It is necessary for the proper functioning of the internal market to avoid incentives for the parties to transfer assets or judicial proceedings from one Member State to another, seeking to obtain a more favourable legal position (forum shopping).

(5) These objectives cannot be achieved to a sufficient degree at national level and action at Community level is therefore justified.

(6) In accordance with the principle of proportionality this Regulation should be confined to provisions governing jurisdiction for opening insolvency proceedings and judgments which are delivered directly on the basis of the insolvency proceedings and are closely connected with such proceedings. In addition, this Regulation should contain provisions regarding the recognition of those judgments and the applicable law which also satisfy that principle.

(7) Insolvency proceedings relating to the winding-up of insolvent companies or other legal persons, judicial arrangements, compositions and analogous proceedings are excluded from the scope of the 1968 Brussels Convention on Jurisdiction and the Enforcement of Judgments in Civil and Commercial Matters (OJ L 299, 31.12.1972, p. 32.), as amended by the Conventions on Accession to this Convention (OJ L 204, 2.8.1975, p. 28; OJ L 304, 30.10.1978; p. 1; OJ L 388, 31.12.1982, p. 1; OJ L 285, 3.10.1989, p. 1; OJ C 15, 15.1.1997, p.1).

(8) In order to achieve the aim of improving the efficiency and effectiveness of insolvency proceedings having cross-border effects, it is necessary, and appropriate, that the provisions on jurisdiction, recognition and applicable law in this area should be contained in a Community law measure which is binding and directly applicable in Member States.

(9) This Regulation should apply to insolvency proceedings, whether the debtor is a natural person or a legal person, a trader or an individual. The insolvency proceedings to which this Regulation applies are listed in the Annexes. Insolvency proceedings concerning insurance undertakings, credit institutions, investment undertakings holding funds or securities for third parties and collective investment undertakings should be excluded from the scope of this Regulation. Such undertakings should not be covered by this Regulation since they are subject to special arrangements and, to some extent, the national supervisory authorities have extremely wide-ranging powers of intervention.

(10) Insolvency proceedings do not necessarily involve the intervention of a judicial authority; the expression 'court' in this Regulation should be given a broad meaning and include a person or body empowered by national law to open insolvency proceedings. In order for this Regulation to apply, proceedings (comprising acts and formalities set down in law) should not only have to comply with the provisions of this Regulation, but they should also be officially recognised and legally effective in the Member State in which the insolvency proceedings are opened and should be collective insolvency proceedings which entail the partial or total divestment of the debtor and the appointment of a liquidator.

(11) This Regulation acknowledges the fact that as a result of widely differing substantive laws it is not practical to introduce insolvency proceedings with universal scope in the entire Community. The application without exception of the law of the State of opening of proceedings would, against this background, frequently lead to difficulties. This applies, for example, to the widely differing laws on security interests

to be found in the Community. Furthermore, the preferential rights enjoyed by some creditors in the insolvency proceedings are, in some cases, completely different. This Regulation should take account of this in two different ways. On the one hand, provision should be made for special rules on applicable law in the case of particularly significant rights and legal relationships (e.g. rights in rem and contracts of employment). On the other hand, national proceedings covering only assets situated in the State of opening should also be allowed alongside main insolvency proceedings with universal scope.

(12) This Regulation enables the main insolvency proceedings to be opened in the Member State where the debtor has the centre of his main interests. These proceedings have universal scope and aim at encompassing all the debtor's assets. To protect the diversity of interests, this Regulation permits secondary proceedings to be opened to run in parallel with the main proceedings. Secondary proceedings may be opened in the Member State where the debtor has an establishment. The effects of secondary proceedings are limited to the assets located in that State. Mandatory rules of coordination with the main proceedings satisfy the need for unity in the Community.

(13) The 'centre of main interests' should correspond to the place where the debtor conducts the administration of his interests on a regular basis and is therefore ascertainable by third parties.

(14) This Regulation applies only to proceedings where the centre of the debtor's main interests is located in the Community.

(15) The rules of jurisdiction set out in this Regulation establish only international jurisdiction, that is to say, they designate the Member State the courts of which may open insolvency proceedings. Territorial jurisdiction within that Member State must be established by the national law of the Member State concerned.

(16) The court having jurisdiction to open the main insolvency proceedings should be enabled to order provisional and protective measures from the time of the request to open proceedings. Preservation measures both prior to and after the commencement of the insolvency proceedings are very important to guarantee the effectiveness of the insolvency proceedings. In that connection this Regulation should afford different possibilities. On the one hand, the court competent for the main insolvency proceedings should be able also to order provisional protective measures covering assets situated in the territory of other Member States. On the other hand, a liquidator temporarily appointed prior to the opening of the main insolvency proceedings should be able, in the Member States in which an establishment belonging to the debtor is to be found, to apply for the preservation measures which are possible under the law of those States.

(17) Prior to the opening of the main insolvency proceedings, the right to request the opening of insolvency proceedings in the Member State where the debtor has an establishment should be limited to local creditors and creditors of the local establishment or to cases where main proceedings cannot be opened under the law of the Member State where the debtor has the centre of his main interest. The reason for this restriction is that cases where territorial insolvency proceedings are requested before the main insolvency proceedings are intended to be limited to what is absolutely necessary. If the main insolvency proceedings are opened, the territorial proceedings become secondary.

(18) Following the opening of the main insolvency proceedings, the right to request the opening of insolvency proceedings in a Member State where the debtor has an establishment is not restricted by this Regulation. The liquidator in the main proceedings or any other person empowered under the national law of that Member State may request the opening of secondary insolvency proceedings.

(19) Secondary insolvency proceedings may serve different purposes, besides the protection of local interests. Cases may arise where the estate of the debtor is too complex to administer as a unit or where differences in the legal systems concerned are so great that difficulties may arise from the extension of effects deriving from the law of the State of the opening to the other States where the assets are located. For this reason the liquidator in the main proceedings may request the opening of secondary proceedings when the efficient administration of the estate so requires.

(20) Main insolvency proceedings and secondary proceedings can, however, contribute to the effective realisation of the total assets only if all the concurrent proceedings pending are coordinated. The main condition here is that the various liquidators must cooperate closely, in particular by exchanging a sufficient amount of information. In order to ensure the dominant role of the main insolvency proceedings, the liquidator in such proceedings should be given several possibilities for intervening in secondary insolvency proceedings which are pending at the same time. For example, he should be able to propose a restructuring plan or composition or apply for realisation of the assets in the secondary insolvency proceedings to be suspended.

(21) Every creditor, who has his habitual residence, domicile or registered office in the Community, should have the right to lodge his claims in each of the insolvency proceedings pending in the Community relating to the debtor's assets. This should also apply to tax authorities and social insurance institutions. However, in order to ensure equal treatment of creditors, the distribution of proceeds must be coordinated. Every creditor should be able to keep what he has received in the course of insolvency proceedings but should be entitled only to participate in the distribution of total assets in other proceedings if creditors with the same standing have obtained the same proportion of their claims.

(22) This Regulation should provide for immediate recognition of judgments concerning the opening, conduct and closure of insolvency proceedings which come within its scope and of judgments handed down in direct connection with such insolvency proceedings. Automatic recognition should therefore mean that the effects attributed to the proceedings by the law of the State in which the proceedings were opened extend to all other Member States. Recognition of judgments delivered by the courts of the Member States should be based on the principle of mutual trust. To that end, grounds for non-recognition should be reduced to the minimum necessary. This is also the basis on which any dispute should be resolved where the courts of two Member States both claim competence to open the main insolvency proceedings. The decision of the first court to open proceedings should be recognised in the other Member States without those Member States having the power to scrutinise the court's decision.

(23) This Regulation should set out, for the matters covered by it, uniform rules on conflict of laws which replace, within their scope of application, national rules of private international law, Unless otherwise stated, the law of the Member State of the opening of the proceedings should be applicable (*lex concursus*). This rule on conflict of laws

should be valid both for the main proceedings and for local proceedings; the *lex concursus* determines all the effects of the insolvency proceedings, both procedural and substantive, on the persons and legal relations concerned. It governs all the conditions for the opening, conduct and closure of the insolvency proceedings.

(24) Automatic recognition of insolvency proceedings to which the law of the opening State normally applies may interfere with the rules under which transactions are carried out in other Member States. To protect legitimate expectations and the certainty of transactions in Member States other than that in which proceedings are opened, provisions should be made for a number of exceptions to the general rule.

(25) There is a particular need for a special reference diverging from the law of the opening State in the case of rights in rem, since these are of considerable importance for the granting of credit. The basis, validity and extent of such a right in rem should therefore normally be determined according to the *lex situs* and not be affected by the opening of insolvency proceedings. The proprietor of the right in rem should therefore be able to continue to assert his right to segregation or separate settlement of the collateral security. Where assets are subject to rights in rem under the *lex situs* in one Member State but the main proceedings are being carried out in another Member State, the liquidator in the main proceedings should be able to request the opening of secondary proceedings in the jurisdiction where the rights in rem arise if the debtor has an establishment there. If a secondary proceeding is not opened, the surplus on sale of the asset covered by rights in rem must be paid to the liquidator in the main proceedings.

(26) If a set-off is not permitted under the law of the opening State, a creditor should nevertheless be entitled to the set-off if it is possible under the law applicable to the claim of the insolvent debtor. In this way, set-off will acquire a kind of guarantee function based on legal provisions on which the creditor concerned can rely at the time when the claim arises.

(27) There is also a need for special protection in the case of payment systems and financial markets. This applies for example to the position-closing agreements and netting agreements to be found in such systems as well as to the sale of securities and to the guarantees provided for such transactions as governed in particular by Directive 98/26/EC. of the European Parliament and of the Council of 19 May 1998 on settlement finality in payment and securities settlement systems (OJ L 166, 11.6.1998, p. 45). For such transactions, the only law which is material should thus be that applicable to the system or market concerned. This provision is intended to prevent the possibility of mechanisms for the payment and settlement of transactions provided for in the payment and set-off systems or on the regulated financial markets of the Member States being altered in the case of insolvency of a business partner. Directive 98/26/EC contains special provisions which should take precedence over the general rules in this Regulation.

(28) In order to protect employees and jobs, the effects of insolvency proceedings on the continuation or termination of employment and on the rights and obligations of all parties to such employment must be determined by the law applicable to the agreement in accordance with the general rules on conflict of law. Any other insolvency-law questions, such as whether the employees' claims are protected by preferential rights and what status such preferential rights may have, should be determined by the law of the opening State.

(29) For business considerations, the main content of the decision opening the proceedings should be published in the other Member States at the request of the liquidator. If there is an establishment in the Member State concerned, there may be a requirement that publication is compulsory. In neither case, however, should publication be a prior condition for recognition of the foreign proceedings.

(30) It may be the case that some of the persons concerned are not in fact aware that proceedings have been opened and act in good faith in a way that conflicts with the new situation. In order to protect such persons who make a payment to the debtor because they are unaware that foreign proceedings have been opened when they should in fact have made the payment to the foreign liquidator, it should be provided that such a payment is to have a debt-discharging effect.

(31) This Regulation should include Annexes relating to the organisation of insolvency proceedings. As these Annexes relate exclusively to the legislation of Member States, there are specific and substantiated reasons for the Council to reserve the right to amend these Annexes in order to take account of any amendments to the domestic law of the Member States.

(32) The United Kingdom and Ireland, in accordance with Article 3 of the Protocol on the position of the United Kingdom and Ireland annexed to the Treaty on European Union and the Treaty establishing the European Community, have given notice of their wish to take part in the adoption and application of this Regulation.

(33) Denmark, in accordance with Articles 1 and 2 of the Protocol on the position of Denmark annexed to the Treaty on European Union and the Treaty establishing the European Community, is not participating in the adoption of this Regulation, and is therefore not bound by it nor subject to its application,

HAS ADOPTED THIS REGULATION:

CHAPTER I
GENERAL PROVISIONS

Article 1

Scope

1. This Regulation shall apply to collective insolvency proceedings which entail the partial or total divestment of a debtor and the appointment of a liquidator.

2. This Regulation shall not apply to insolvency proceedings concerning insurance undertakings, credit institutions, investment undertakings which provide services involving the holding of funds or securities for third parties, or to collective investment undertakings.

Article 2

Definitions

For the purposes of this Regulation:

(a) 'insolvency proceedings' shall mean the collective proceedings referred to in Article 1(1). These proceedings are listed in Annex A;

(b) 'liquidator' shall mean any person or body whose function is to administer or liquidate assets of which the debtor has been divested or to supervise the administration of his affairs. Those persons and bodies are listed in Annex C;

(c) 'winding-up proceedings' shall mean insolvency proceedings within the meaning of point (a) involving realising the assets of the debtor, including where the proceedings have been closed by a composition or other measure terminating the insolvency, or closed by reason of the insufficiency of the assets. Those proceedings are listed in Annex B;

(d) 'court' shall mean the judicial body or any other competent body of a Member State empowered to open insolvency proceedings or to take decisions in the course of such proceedings;

(e) 'judgment' in relation to the opening of insolvency proceedings or the appointment of a liquidator shall include the decision of any court empowered to open such proceedings or to appoint a liquidator;

(f) 'the time of the opening of proceedings' shall mean the time at which the judgment opening proceedings becomes effective, whether it is a final judgment or not;

(g) 'the Member State in which assets are situated' shall mean, in the case of:

- tangible property, the Member State within the territory of which the property is situated,
- property and rights ownership of or entitlement to which must be entered in a public register, the Member State under the authority of which the register is kept,
- claims, the Member State within the territory of which the third party required to meet them has the centre of his main interests, as determined in Article 3(1);

(h) 'establishment' shall mean any place of operations where the debtor carries out a non-transitory economic activity with human means and goods.

Notes

Insolvency proceedings: All of the corporate insolvency procedures described require the participation of the court. A creditors' voluntary winding up does not require an order of the High Court, but for the purposes of the Insolvency Regulation, it is necessary to obtain an 'order of confirmation of a creditors' voluntary winding-up'. CA 1963, s 267A provides that the Master may make such an order on application.

Winding-up proceedings: 'Winding-Up' proceedings do not include examinership, as per Annex B of the Insolvency Regulation. It is not possible to obtain any extraterritorial effect for an examinership through the insolvency Regulation and a litigant would have to rely on the pre-existing procedures (see notes following reg 1).

Goods: It is probably inappropriate to interpret the word 'goods' too literally. The phrase is frequently used in EC documents in the more general sense of 'assets' and that is probably what is meant here, as well as the 'restricted assets' referred to in Art 3(2).

Establishment: The definition of 'establishment' is important to an application to open secondary insolvency proceedings, as described at Art 3(2) below.

Article 3

International jurisdiction

1. The courts of the Member State within the territory of which the centre of a debtor's main interests is situated shall have jurisdiction to open insolvency proceedings. In the case of a company or legal person, the place of the registered office shall be presumed to be the centre of its main interests in the absence of proof to the contrary.

2. Where the centre of a debtor's main interests is situated within the territory of a Member State, the courts of another Member State shall have jurisdiction to open insolvency proceedings against that debtor only if he possesses an establishment within the territory of that other Member State. The effects of those proceedings shall be restricted to the assets of the debtor situated in the territory of the latter Member State.

3. Where insolvency proceedings have been opened under paragraph 1, any proceedings opened subsequently under paragraph 2 shall be secondary proceedings. These latter proceedings must be winding-up proceedings.

4. Territorial insolvency proceedings referred to in paragraph 2 may be opened prior to the opening of main insolvency proceedings in accordance with paragraph 1 only:

(a) where insolvency proceedings under paragraph 1 cannot be opened because of the conditions laid down by the law of the Member State within the territory of which the centre of the debtor's main interests is situated; or

(b) where the opening of territorial insolvency proceedings is requested by a creditor who has his domicile, habitual residence or registered office in the Member State within the territory of which the establishment is situated, or whose claim arises from the operation of that establishment.

Notes

The Regulation divides insolvency proceedings into two broad categories, namely main proceedings and secondary proceedings. Under Art 3(1) main insolvency proceedings may only be opened in the member state in which the company has its 'centre of main interests'. Subject to some limitations, main insolvency proceedings essentially apply to the entire of a company's assets and affairs irrespective of where they are actually situate.

In contrast, pursuant to Art 3(2), secondary insolvency proceedings are restricted to the assets of a company situated in the territory of the member state of which such proceedings are opened. In other words, they are territorial in nature.

Secondary insolvency proceedings can only be opened in a member state in which the company possesses an 'establishment'. Art 3 envisages that, normally, main insolvency proceedings will be opened in the member state in which the country has its 'centre of main interest', before the opening of any secondary (ie territorial) proceedings. Nevertheless, Art 3(4) does allow for the secondary, or territorial, proceedings to be opened first in time in the following circumstances:

(a) where main insolvency proceedings cannot be opened because of conditions laid down by the law of the member state within the territory for which the company has its centre of main interest; or

(b) where the opening of territorial insolvency proceedings is requested by a creditor who has its domicile, habitual residence or registered office in the member state within the territory of which the company's establishment is situated, or whose claim arises from the operation of that establishment.

So, for example, in the case of a Polish company which has its centre of main interest in Poland but also has a place of business, and thus an establishment, in Ireland, it would be open to an Irish creditor to petition to have the Irish establishment wound up in Ireland by way of secondary insolvency proceedings at a point in time before main insolvency proceedings had been opened in Poland.

It should be noted though that under Art 3(3) it is expressly stipulated that the only type of insolvency proceedings that may be opened as secondary proceedings are proceedings for the winding up of the company. In other words, one cannot have secondary examinership proceedings. Thus, an examinership can only be commenced in the country in which the company has its centre of main interests.

Centre of main interests: There is no definition of the 'centre of main interests' within the body of the Regulation itself. However, in Recital (13) of the Preamble to the Regulation it is stated that the centre of main interests '... should correspond to the place where the debtor conducts the administration of his interest on a regular basis and is therefore ascertainable by third parties.'

In the case of a company or other legal person, Art 3(1) specifically states that the place of the registered office shall be presumed to be the centre of main interest in the absence of proof to the contrary.[1] Since the coming into force of the Regulation there has been a reasonable amount of judicial consideration of what is meant by the 'centre of main interest'. The leading case in point is the decision of the ECJ in *Re Eurofood IFSC Ltd*,[2] a reference to the ECJ from the Supreme Court.

Eurofood was a member of the Parmalat Group and was a wholly-owned subsidiary of an Italian company, Parmalat Spa. It was incorporated in Ireland and had its registered office in the IFSC. It operated in the IFSC pursuant to a certificate issued by the Minister for Finance under FA 1980, s 39(b)(2). Its day-to-day administration was conducted on its behalf in Ireland by Bank of America pursuant to an administration agreement which was governed by Irish law and contained an Irish jurisdiction clause. It prepared annual accounts, which it filed in the CRO and it paid Irish taxes. It maintained books of account in Dublin and its auditors and solicitors were Irish. It had four directors, two of whom were Irish and two of whom were Italian. With one exception, all board meetings were held in Dublin. The only meeting not physically held in Dublin was one held by telephone with the two Irish directors being present on the call from Dublin with the two Italian directors being present on the call from Italy.

An Extraordinary Administrator was appointed to Parmalat SpA in Italy following the collapse of the Parmalat Group. A creditor of Eurofood then presented a petition in the High Court in Dublin for the winding up of the company. A Provisional Liquidator was appointed by order of Mr Justice Lavan on 27 January 2004. Shortly thereafter, in February 2004, a court in Parma, Italy purported to appoint an extraordinary administrator to Eurofood, being the same individual who had also been appointed as Extraordinary Administrator of Parmalat SpA and of other companies in the Parmalat Group.

In purporting to appoint the Extraordinary Administrator to Eurofood, the court in Parma determined that Eurofood's centre of main interest was in Italy rather than in Ireland. Thus, the Italian court was purporting to open main insolvency proceedings in respect of Eurofood in Italy.

When the winding-up petition came on for hearing in the Irish High Court,[3] the Extraordinary Administrator objected to the making of any winding-up order on the basis that main insolvency proceedings had already been opened in Italy. In rejecting the Extraordinary Administrator's arguments, Kelly J held that the appointment of the Provisional Liquidator (which occurred before any insolvency proceedings in Italy) constituted a judgment of the court opening insolvency proceedings in Ireland. He held that since the Irish insolvency proceedings were first in time, the

Italian courts ought to have recognised the Irish order and ought therefore to have declined to make any order of its own purporting to appoint an Extraordinary Administrator.

In addition, Kelly J found, as a matter of fact, that the centre of main interests of Eurofood was in Ireland. Having referred to Recital (13) of the Regulation which describes what is meant by 'centre of main interests', Kelly J cited with approval the following extract from Moss, Fletcher and Isaacs, *EC Regulation on Insolvency Proceedings* wherein the authors said of the said recital that it:

> 'It intended to provide a test in which the attributes of transparency and objective ascertainability are dominant factors. This should enable parties who having dealings with the debtor to find their expectations on the reasonable conclusions to be drawn from systematic conduct and arrangements for which the debtor is responsible. In principle therefore it ought not be possible for a debtor to gain advantages, at creditors' expense, from having resorted to evasive or confusing techniques of organising its business or personal affairs, in a way calculated to conceal the true location from which interests are systematically administered.'

The Judge also cited from the Virgos-Schmit Report[4] and the Draft Bankruptcy Convention wherein the following was stated:

> 'The concept of 'centre of main interest' must be interpreted as the place where the debtor conducts the administration of his interest on a regular basis and is therefore ascertainable by third parties. The rationale of this rule is not difficult to explain. Insolvency is a foreseeable risk. It is therefore important that international jurisdiction (which, as we will see, entails the application of the insolvency laws of that Contracting State), be based on a place known to the debtors' potential creditors. This enables the legal risks which would have to be assumed in the case of insolvency to be calculated. By using the term 'interests', the intention was to encompass not only commercial, industrial or professional activities, but also general economic activities, so as to include the activities of private individuals (eg consumers). The expression 'main' serves as a criterion for the cases where these interests include activities of different types which are run from different centres. In principle, the centre of main interest will, in the case of professionals, be the place of their professional domicile and for natural persons in general, the place of their habitual residence. Where companies and legal persons are concerned, the Convention presumes, unless proved to the contrary, that the debtor's centre of main interest is the place of its registered office. This place normally corresponds to the debtor's head office.'

In determining that the centre of main interests of Eurofood was in Ireland, Kelly J was influenced not only by the company (a) being incorporated in Ireland, (b) having its registered office in the IFSC, (c) having a certificate from the Minister pursuant to the Finance Act, (d) filing accounts in Ireland, (e) maintaining day-to-day records in Ireland, (f) being managed from Ireland and (g) paying tax in Ireland, etc, but also by the fact that the evidence from certain creditors, namely bond holders, was that they were dealing with investments issued by a company that was located in Ireland and was subject to Irish fiscal and regulatory provisions.

The matter was appealed to the Supreme Court,[5] which in turn referred the matter to the European Court of Justice. The Extraordinary Administrator argued, *inter alia*, that the centre of main interests ought to be determined as being in Italy in circumstances where Eurofood was a wholly-owned subsidiary of an Italian company and thus the Italian company, through its shareholding in Eurofood was in a position to control decision making, at least in general meeting. That argument was rejected by the ECJ which noted that the concept of the centre of main interest is peculiar to the Regulation and thus has an autonomous meaning which must be interpreted in a uniform way, independently of national legislation.

Having referred to the definition of 'centre of main interests' in Recital 13 of the Preamble to the Regulation, the Court went on to conclude as follows:

The Court of Justice held that the German courts had not lost their jurisdiction as a result of the actions of Miss Staubitz-Schreiber to move to Spain. The ECJ placed considerable emphasis on the need to avoid the transfer of jurisdiction and to increase the commercial certainty of creditors. See Dammann, 'L'application du règlement CE No. 1346-2000 après les arrêts Staubitz-Schreiber et Eurofood de la CJCE', Dalloz 2006, 2329.

Article 4

Law applicable

1. Save as otherwise provided in this Regulation, the law applicable to insolvency proceedings and their effects shall be that of the Member State within the territory of which such proceedings are opened, hereafter referred to as the 'State of the opening of proceedings'.

2. The law of the State of the opening of proceedings shall determine the conditions for the opening of those proceedings, their conduct and their closure. It shall determine in particular:

(a) against which debtors insolvency proceedings may be brought on account of their capacity;

(b) the assets which form part of the estate and the treatment of assets acquired by or devolving on the debtor after the opening of the insolvency proceedings;

(c) the respective powers of the debtor and the liquidator;

(d) the conditions under which set-offs may be invoked;

(e) the effects of insolvency proceedings on current contracts to which the debtor is party;

(f) the effects of the insolvency proceedings on proceedings brought by individual creditors, with the exception of lawsuits pending;

(g) the claims which are to be lodged against the debtor's estate and the treatment of claims arising after the opening of insolvency proceedings;

(h) the rules governing the lodging, verification and admission of claims;

(i) the rules governing the distribution of proceeds from the realisation of assets, the ranking of claims and the rights of creditors who have obtained partial satisfaction after the opening of insolvency proceedings by virtue of a right in rem or through a set-off;

(j) the conditions for and the effects of closure of insolvency proceedings, in particular by composition;

(k) creditors' rights after the closure of insolvency proceedings;

(l) who is to bear the costs and expenses incurred in the insolvency proceedings;

(m) the rules relating to the voidness, voidability or unenforceability of legal acts detrimental to all the creditors.

Cross reference

Articles 5 to 15 provide for variation to the general rules established by this Article.

Notes

Article 4(1) provides that the applicable law for insolvency proceedings is the *lex forum concursus*, subject, per Article 4(2)(f), to 'lawsuits' pending. There are exceptions to this general rule ('save where otherwise provided' in the Insolvency Regulation). Article 5 protects the rights *in rem* of creditors or third parties in respect of assets that were situate in the territory of another Member State at the commencement of proceedings. Article 15 stipulates that the effect of insolvency proceedings on a lawsuit pending in concerning an asset or right of which the debtor has been divested shall be governed by the law of the member state in which that lawsuit is pending.

In *Re Flightlease Ireland Limited (in voluntary liquidation)*[1] examined the operation of Article 4(1). The parent company of Flightlease Ireland Limited ('the Company') was sued in November of 2001 for approximately €290m by a French company ('the Frenchco'). Frenchco went into liquidation in France in 2003, and its claim was rejected by the liquidator of the Company in January 2005. Frenchco requested a stay on the Irish liquidation of the Company until its suit for €290m was determined and preliminary issues relating to the application of the Insolvency Regulation were set down.

Frenchco argued that it would be prejudicial to refuse to allow it pursue its claim in France for €290m and referred to the English decision in *Mazur Media Ltd v Mazur Media GmbH*.[2] In *Mazur* both claimants were in receivership and had claimed in English proceedings that the defendant had failed to deliver up copyright in certain sound recordings. After the commencement of those proceedings one of the defendants was placed into provisional insolvency in Germany and an application was made to the English court to stay the copyright proceedings until the determination of the German insolvency. In his decision, Lawrence Collins J acknowledged that the effect of Articles 4(1)(h) and 15 only permitted the English Chancery Division to rule upon the claim for the return of assets of which the claimants had been divested.

Murphy J summed up the provisions relating to claims thus:

> 'Accordingly, we are left with a distinction between a third party's rights in rem (Article 5), an asset or right of which the debtor has been divested (Article 4(2)(f) and 15) and proceedings brought by individual creditors. It is only the latter that are subject to the law of the Memebr State within the territory of which such proceedings are opened.'

Murphy J held that in relation to the lodging, verification and admission of claims in insolvency, the liquidation of the Company was governed by Irish law. The court held that the effect of Article 15 was to apply French law to the claim for €290m. The court also referred to the decision in *Mazur* where Laurence Collins J held that the English Insolvency Act applied to the winding-up of a foreign company in England but not to foreign insolvency proceedings.[3] The English court held that it had an inherent jurisdiction to stay English litigation 'whenever it was necessary to prevent injustice' but not in a manner that would be 'inconsistent with the Brussels or Lugano Conventions', and that it would take exceptional circumstances to justify the operation of that power[4] The rationale for the need for 'exceptional circumstances' is that to require otherwise (in this case the German company had included arguments that it could be categorised as forum conveniens arguments) would permit the Brussels 1 Regulation to be avoided. As to the conflict of law issues raised, see the subsequent judgment in *Re Flightlease Ireland Ltd*.[5]

The rule for the avoidance of legal acts that are detrimental to all the creditors shall be determined according to that of the State opening the proceedings. The rule in sub-art (2)(m) is also included at Articles 5(4), 6(2) and 7(3). See the notes following Art 13.

1 *Re Flightlease Ireland Ltd* (in voluntary liquidation) (27 July 2005, unreported) HC (Murphy J).

2 *Mazur Media Ltd v Mazur Media GmbH* [2004] 1 WLR 2966.

3 *Stocznia Gdanska v Latreefers (No. 2)* [2001] BCLC 116.

4 Laurence Collins J held that this inherent jurisdiction was 'reinforced' by the Supreme Court Act 1981, s. 49(3).

5 *Re Flightlease Ireland Ltd* [2006] IEHC 193 (Clarke J).

Article 5

Third parties' rights in rem

1. The opening of insolvency proceedings shall not affect the rights in rem of creditors or third parties in respect of tangible or intangible, moveable or immoveable assets — both specific assets and collections of indefinite assets as a whole which change from time to time — belonging to the debtor which are situated within the territory of another Member State at the time of the opening of proceedings.

2. The rights referred to in paragraph 1 shall in particular mean:

(a) the right to dispose of assets or have them disposed of and to obtain satisfaction from the proceeds of or income from those assets, in particular by virtue of a lien or a mortgage;

(b) the exclusive right to have a claim met, in particular a right guaranteed by a lien in respect of the claim or by assignment of the claim by way of a guarantee;

(c) the right to demand the assets from, and/or to require restitution by, anyone having possession or use of them contrary to the wishes of the party so entitled;

(d) a right in rem to the beneficial use of assets.

3. The right, recorded in a public register and enforceable against third parties, under which a right in rem within the meaning of paragraph 1 may be obtained, shall be considered a right in rem.

4. Paragraph 1 shall not preclude actions for voidness, voidability or unenforceability as referred to in Article 4(2)(m).

Notes

The rights *in rem* of creditors and third parties in respect of assets of the debtor located within another member state at the time of opening of proceedings are determined according to the law of that State (*lex situs*), subject to the rule in Art 4(2)(m). There is considerable divergence between the Civil and Common Law jurisdictions with the EU on this issue, especially concerning non-possessory security (floating charges or fixed charges over book debts).

Article 6

Set-off

1. The opening of insolvency proceedings shall not affect the right of creditors to demand the set-off of their claims against the claims of the debtor, where such a set-off is permitted by the law applicable to the insolvent debtor's claim.

2. Paragraph 1 shall not preclude actions for voidness, voidability or unenforceability as referred to in Article 4(2)(m).

Notes

This Article supplements Art 4(2)(d) and reflects the divisions between common law and civil law member states on the operation of set-off. Set-off in civil law States is usually limited to debits and credits occurring between the same parties to a single transaction. Common law States usually require a set-off where the same parties have been dealing with each other across a broader front. Article 4(2)(d) provides that the law of the State opening proceedings (*lex forum concursus*) shall govern set-off, but this is without prejudice to the right of a creditor to claim set-off under the law of applicable to the insolvent debtor's claim. The effect of this Article does not require a creditor to subject his claim to the law applicable to the insolvent debtor's claim, it merely offers him an opportunity to avail of an alterative jurisdiction if he elects.

Article 7

Reservation of title

1. The opening of insolvency proceedings against the purchaser of an asset shall not affect the seller's rights based on a reservation of title where at the time of the opening of proceedings the asset is situated within the territory of a Member State other than the State of opening of proceedings.

2. The opening of insolvency proceedings against the seller of an asset, after delivery of the asset, shall not constitute grounds for rescinding or terminating the sale and shall not prevent the purchaser from acquiring title where at the time of the opening of proceedings the asset sold is situated within the territory of a Member State other than the State of the opening of proceedings.

3. Paragraphs 1 and 2 shall not preclude actions for voidness; voidability or unenforceability as referred to in Article 4(2)(m).

Notes

Insolvency proceedings against the purchaser of an asset do not affect retention of title clauses where the asset in question is located in a state other than that in which proceedings are opened. Where the proceedings are against the seller of an asset, then the opening of insolvency proceedings is not a ground to terminate the sale or prevent the buyer from obtaining title where the asset in question is located in a state other than that in which proceedings are opened.

The rule may prevent a liquidator taking possession of a potentially valuable asset, or oblige a buyer to prove as an unsecured creditor to the value of the asset lost to the insolvency.

Article 8

Contracts relating to immoveable property

The effects of insolvency proceedings on a contract conferring the right to acquire or make use of immoveable property shall be governed solely by the law of the Member State within the territory of which the immoveable property is situated.

Notes

This Article can have no application to immovable property outside of the Member States of the EU at the date of the transaction in question.

Article 9

Payment systems and financial markets

1. Without prejudice to Article 5, the effects of insolvency proceedings on the rights and obligations of the parties to a payment or settlement system or to a financial market shall be governed solely by the law of the Member State applicable to that system or market.
2. Paragraph 1 shall not preclude any action for voidness, voidability or unenforceability which may be taken to set aside payments or transactions under the law applicable to the relevant payment system or financial market.

Notes

This exception to Article 5 does not apply to the rights and obligations of the parties to a payment or settlement system or to a financial market that is governed by the law a third country.

Article 10

Contracts of employment

The effects of insolvency proceedings on employment contracts and relationships shall be governed solely by the law of the Member State applicable to the contract of employment.

Notes

This Article can have no application to contracts of employment governed by the law of a third country. All Member States are parties to the Rome Convention of 20 June 1980 on the Law Applicable to Contractual Obligations, which contains relevant rules to determine the governing law of a contract. Article 6 of the Rome Convention deals with employment contracts. If the choice of law clause in the contract of employment or if the place of performance of the contractual obligation is outside of the EU, then the Insolvency Regulation plainly has no application. If, however, the choice of law clause applies the law of another member state then this Article will supplant the law of the State in which proceedings were opened. As stated above at Art 4(2)(h), the Insolvency Regulation will govern the priority of employee claims, regardless of the law applicable to the contract of employment.

Article 11

Effects on rights subject to registration

The effects of insolvency proceedings on the rights of the debtor in immoveable property, a ship or an aircraft subject to registration in a public register shall be determined by the law of the Member State under the authority of which the register is kept.

Notes

This Article refers to registerable property but fails to accord an exclusive or sole jurisdiction to any one state. The Article is open to the theoretical possibility of an interaction between more than one jurisdiction.

Article 12

Community patents and trade marks

For the purposes of this Regulation, a Community patent, a Community trade mark or any other similar right established by Community law may be included only in the proceedings referred to in Article 3(1).

Notes

This prevents a Community patent or trade mark or similar right (presumably intellectual property such as industrial design or plant rights) from becoming the subject matter of secondary insolvency proceedings.

Article 13

Detrimental acts

Article 4(2) (m) shall not apply where the person who benefited from an act detrimental to all the creditors provides proof that:

— the said act is subject to the law of a Member State other than that of the State of the opening of proceedings, and

— that law does not allow any means of challenging that act in the relevant case.

Notes

The operation of Art 4(2)(m) is excluded by Art 13 when the person benefiting from the act detrimental to all the creditors proves that the act in question is subject to the law of a member state other than that of the State of the opening of proceedings, and that that law does not allow any means of challenging that act in the relevant case. This enigmatically benefits a party that relies upon the validity of an act in another member state if that act is unassailable under the general law (including insolvency law) of that State. For example, in the insolvency of a company with its centre of main interests in Germany and book debts subject to a floating charge here in Ireland, the effect of the application of the fixed charge would be detrimental to the creditors of the company. Assuming that the German state law did not permit a floating charge the charge-holder could benefit from the exception to Art 4(2)(m) contained in Art 13. As the fixed charge is subject to Irish law and, subject to the formalities being in order, unimpeachable as a charge that took the assets outside of the insolvency. The plain meaning of the second indent is stark. It describes circumstances where the law cannot challenge the act in question. The addition of the sub-clause 'in the relevant case' must be given some meaning, so that in order to rely on the exception contained in the Article one must establish a dreadnought-like quality of the act in

The importance of the automatic recognition of the judgment of a court of a member state opening insolvency proceedings was emphasised by the Irish courts and by the ECJ in *Re Eurofood IFSC Ltd*. In the High Court[2] Kelly J emphasised that where main insolvency proceedings have been commenced by a judgment of the courts of a Member State, the courts of the other Member States are obliged to recognise that judgment and are precluded from seeking to scrutinise it themselves. In so concluding, Kelly J placed some emphasise on Recital (22) in the Preamble to the Insolvency Regulation wherein it is stated that:

> 'This Regulation shall provide for immediate recognition of judgments concerning the opening, conduct enclosure of insolvency proceedings which come within its scope and of judgments handed down in direct connection with such insolvency proceedings. Automatic recognition should therefore mean that the effects attributed to the proceedings by the law of the State in which the proceedings were opened extend to all other Member States. Recognition of judgments delivered by the Courts of the Member States should be based on the principle of mutual trust. To that end, grounds for non-recognition should be reduced to the minimum necessary. This is also the basis on which any dispute should be resolved where the Courts of two Member States both claim competence to open the main insolvency proceedings. The decision of the first Court to open proceedings should be recognised in the other Member States without those Member States having the power to scrutinize the Court's decision.'

These sentiments were echoed by the ECJ in its ruling[3] where it held as follows:

> 'In return, as the 22nd Recital of the Preamble to the Regulation makes it clear, the principle of mutual trust requires that the Courts of the other Member States recognise the decision opening main insolvency proceedings, without being able to review the assessment made by the first Court as to its jurisdiction.
>
> If an interested party, taking the view that the centre of the debtor's main interest is situated in a member state other than that in which the main insolvency proceedings were opened, wishes to challenge the jurisdiction assumed by the court which opened those proceedings, it may use, before the courts of the member state in which they were opened, the remedies prescribed by the national law of that member state against the opening decision.'

So, for example, if a creditor of a company is unhappy about the purported opening of main insolvency proceedings in the United Kingdom and believe that the centre of main interest is in fact in Ireland and that main insolvency proceedings ought to have been opened in Ireland instead, his remedy is not to petition the Irish High Court for the making of a winding up order, at least in the first instance. Rather, he must first go before the English courts and challenge the order purporting to open main insolvency proceedings in that jurisdiction. If, and only if, he is successful in challenging the UK order, can he then take steps to open the main insolvency proceedings in Ireland.

1 Art 33.

2 *Re Eurofood IFSC Ltd* [2004] 4 IR 370.

3 [2006] 3 WLR 309.

Judgment opening insolvency proceedings: As noted above, Article 17 provides for the automatic recognition of 'judgments' opening insolvency proceedings. In *Re Eurofood IFSC Ltd*[1] the Supreme Court held that the mere presentation of a petition for the winding up of a company did not amount to a 'judgment' opening insolvency proceedings. However it held, upholding the decision of Kelly J that the appointment of a Provisional Liquidator did amount to such a 'judgment'. This view was subsequently endorsed by the ECJ.[2]

Of course, in most liquidations there will be no appointment of a Provisional Liquidator. In such circumstances, it is the winding-up order itself, pursuant to which the Official Liquidator is appointed, which constitutes the 'judgment' opening the insolvency proceedings.[3]

In the case of an examinership it would be the order appointing the Examiner, whether on an interim basis or otherwise, that would constitute the 'judgment' opening the insolvency proceedings.

Of course, in the case of a creditors' voluntary winding up, there would not normally be a 'judgment' opening the proceedings since the winding up commences by way of a resolution of the members, followed by a meeting of the creditors in which the creditors have an opportunity either to accept the members' nominee or alternatively to appoint someone else of their own choosing as the Voluntary Liquidator.

However, as a result of amendments effected by the EC(CI)R 2002, where the company's centre of main interest is situated in Ireland, the Voluntary Liquidator may apply to the Master of the High Court pursuant to CA 1963, s 267A o, as amended, for an order confirming the creditors voluntary winding up for the purposes of the Insolvency Regulation. That order of confirmation constitutes the 'judgment' opening the winding up proceedings for Regulation purposes. That application for confirmation should be made by the Voluntary Liquidator by way of an originating notice of motion pursuant to Ord 74, r 138.

1 *Re Eurofood IFSC Ltd* [2004] 4 IR 370.

2 [2006] 3 WLR 309.

3 *Re Collins & Aikman Corp Group* [2005] EWHC 1754.

Article 18

Powers of the liquidator

1. The liquidator appointed by a court which has jurisdiction pursuant to Article 3(1) may exercise all the powers conferred on him by the law of the State of the opening of proceedings in another Member State, as long as no other insolvency proceedings have been opened there nor any preservation measure to the contrary has been taken there further to a request for the opening of insolvency proceedings in that State. He may in particular remove the debtor's assets from the territory of the Member State in which they are situated, subject to Articles 5 and 7.

2. The liquidator appointed by a court which has jurisdiction pursuant to Article 3(2) may in any other Member State claim through the courts or out of court that moveable property was removed from the territory of the State of the opening of proceedings to the territory of that other Member State after the opening of the insolvency proceedings. He may also bring any action to set aside which is in the interests of the creditors.

3. In exercising his powers, the liquidator shall comply with the law of the Member State within the territory of which he intends to take action, in particular with regard to procedures for the realisation of assets. Those powers may not include coercive measures or the right to rule on legal proceedings or disputes.

Notes

A liquidator appointed in the *forum concursus* may exercise his powers as a liquidator in another member state, as long as no secondary proceedings have been opened in that state, subject to reservation of title and rights in *rem* as permitted in Articles 5 and 7. See Courtney, *The Law of Private Companies* (2nd edn, Tottel Publishing, 2002) para 26.059.

A liquidator appointed in secondary proceedings in a member state, in which a debtor has an establishment, may seek to recover moveable property that was removed from the member state in which the debtors COMI is located. That recovery action may take place in any other member state and may include any action to set aside that is interests of the creditors. All the creditors of the debtor, wheresoever located, must be included in the phrase 'all the creditors'.

Article 19

Proof of the liquidator's appointment

The liquidator's appointment shall be evidenced by a certified copy of the original decision appointing him or by any other certificate issued by the court which has jurisdiction.

A translation into the official language or one of the official languages of the Member State within the territory of which he intends to act may be required. No legalisation or other similar formality shall be required.

Cross references

See CA 1963, s 227B, which requires publication in the Companies Registration Office Gazette and at least two national morning newspapers.

Notes

There is no requirement to obtain an *exequatur* or 'executive judgment' authorising the execution of a foreign judgment whose validity has been authorised after a thorough examination of the issues and law of a case.

Article 20

Return and imputation

1. A creditor who, after the opening of the proceedings referred to in Article 3(1) obtains by any means, in particular through enforcement, total or partial satisfaction of his claim on the assets belonging to the debtor situated within the territory of another Member State, shall return what he has obtained to the liquidator, subject to Articles 5 and 7.

2. In order to ensure equal treatment of creditors a creditor who has, in the course of insolvency proceedings, obtained a dividend on his claim shall share in distributions made in other proceedings only where creditors of the same ranking or category have, in those other proceedings, obtained an equivalent dividend.

Article 21

Publication

1. The liquidator may request that notice of the judgment opening insolvency proceedings and, where appropriate, the decision appointing him, be published in any other Member State in accordance with the publication procedures provided for in that State. Such publication shall also specify the liquidator appointed and whether the jurisdiction rule applied is that pursuant to Article 3(1) or Article 3(2).

2. However, any Member State within the territory of which the debtor has an establishment may require mandatory publication. In such cases, the liquidator or any authority empowered to that effect in the Member State where the proceedings referred to in Article 3(1) are opened shall take all necessary measures to ensure such publication.

Cross reference

See CA 1963, s 227A(1).

Article 22

Registration in a public register

1. The liquidator may request that the judgment opening the proceedings referred to in Article 3(1) be registered in the land register, the trade register and any other public register kept in the other Member States.

2. However, any Member State may require mandatory registration. In such cases, the liquidator or any authority empowered to that effect in the Member State where the proceedings referred to in Article 3(1) have been opened shall take all necessary measures to ensure such registration.

Article 23

Costs

The costs of the publication and registration provided for in Articles 21 and 22 shall be regarded as costs and expenses incurred in the proceedings.

Article 24

Honouring of an obligation to a debtor

1. Where an obligation has been honoured in a Member State for the benefit of a debtor who is subject to insolvency proceedings opened in another Member State, when it should have been honoured for the benefit of the liquidator in those proceedings, the person honouring the obligation shall be deemed to have discharged it if he was unaware of the opening of proceedings.

2. Where such an obligation is honoured before the publication provided for in Article 21 has been effected, the person honouring the obligation shall be presumed, in the absence of proof to the contrary, to have been unaware of the opening of insolvency proceedings; where the obligation is honoured after such publication has been effected, the person honouring the obligation shall be presumed, in the absence of proof to the contrary, to have been aware of the opening of proceedings.

Article 25

Recognition and enforceability of other judgments

1. Judgments handed down by a court whose judgment concerning the opening of proceedings is recognised in accordance with Article 16 and which concern the course and closure of insolvency proceedings, and compositions approved by that court shall also be recognised with no further formalities. Such judgments shall be enforced in

accordance with Articles 31 to 51, with the exception of Article 34(2), of the Brussels Convention on Jurisdiction and the Enforcement of Judgments in Civil and Commercial Matters, as amended by the Conventions of Accession to this Convention.

The first subparagraph shall also apply to judgments deriving directly from the insolvency proceedings and which are closely linked with them, even if they were handed down by another court.

The first subparagraph shall also apply to judgments relating to preservation measures taken after the request for the opening of insolvency proceedings.

2. The recognition and enforcement of judgments other than those referred to in paragraph 1 shall be governed by the Convention referred to in paragraph 1, provided that that Convention is applicable.

3. The Member States shall not be obliged to recognise or enforce a judgment referred to in paragraph 1 which might result in a limitation of personal freedom or postal secrecy.

Article 26[1]

Public policy

Any Member State may refuse to recognise insolvency proceedings opened in another Member State or to enforce a judgment handed down in the context of such proceedings where the effects of such recognition or enforcement would be manifestly contrary to that State's public policy, in particular its fundamental principles or the constitutional rights and liberties of the individual.

1 Note the Declaration by Portugal concerning the application of Articles 26 and 37 (OJ C 183, 30.6.2000, p. 1).

Notes

Although the judgment of a court of a Member State opening insolvency proceedings ought normally to be automatically recognised, there is a public policy exception contained in Art 26 of the Regulation. It states that:

> 'Any Member State may refuse to recognise insolvency proceedings opened in another Member State or to enforce a judgment handed down in the context of such proceedings where the effects of such recognition or enforcement would be manifestly contrary to that State's public policy, in particular its fundamental principles or the constitutional rights and liberties of the individual.'

This public policy exception also came up for consideration in the case of *Re Eurofood IFSC Limited*. In this regard, the evidence before the court was that the creditors of Eurofood had not been heard on the petition of the appointment of the Extraordinary Administrator and no opportunity had been given to them to be heard by the Parma court. Moreover, the Provisional Liquidator was only notified after close of business on 13 February 2004 that the hearing would take place at midday on the following Tuesday in Parma. Moreover, he was not furnished with the petition or other papers grounding the application until after the hearing before the Parma court had actually concluded.

In the circumstances Kelly J concluded[1] there had been a breach of fair procedures so that even if the judgment of the Parma court had been the first in time, so as to purportedly open main insolvency proceedings in respect of *Eurofood* (which was not the case) the Irish court would in any event have been entitled not to recognise that order on public policy grounds.

The judgment of Kelly J was resoundingly endorsed by the Supreme Court.[2] In delivering the judgment of the court, Fennelly J concluded that it would be 'manifestly contrary to public policy, as a matter of Irish law' to give recognition to the decision of the Parma court in circumstances where the Provisional Liquidator had not been given the protection of fundamental aspects of fair procedures.

A similar approach was adopted by the ECJ in its ruling.[3] Having referred to Art 26 and various of its own decisions recognising the general principle of community law that everyone is entitled to a fair legal process, the Court observed as follows:

> 'Concerning more particularly the right to be notified of procedural documents and, more generally, the right to be heard … those rights occupy an eminent position in the organisation and conduct of a fair legal process. In the context of insolvency proceedings, the right of creditors or their representatives to participate in accordance with the equality of arms principle is of particular importance. Though this specific detailed rule concerning the right to be heard may vary according to the urgency for a ruling to be given, any restriction on the exercise of that right must be duly justified and surrounded by procedural guarantees ensuring that persons concerned by such proceedings actually have the opportunity to challenge the measures adopted in urgency.'

The decision in *Re Eurofood IFSC Ltd* is to be contrasted with *Re SAS Rover France*[4] where the Commercial Court of Nanterre was concerned with a French subsidiary of the MG Rover Group, which had been put into administration in England. The French Public Prosecutor claimed that the English decision should not be recognised on public policy grounds, arguing that safeguards imposed by French employment and social security legislation might be jeopardised. The Nanterre Commercial Court held that the English court order should be recognised under Article 16 and accepted undertakings offered by the Administrators that these safeguards would be respected. The Court of Appeal in Versailles has since upheld this ruling.[5]

1. *Re Eurofood IFSC Ltd* [2004] 4 IR 370.
2. [2004] 2 IR 370.
3. *Re Eurofood IFSC Ltd* [2006] 3 WLR 309.
4. *Re SAS Rover France* [2005] 18 Insolv. Int 118.
5. [2006] 19 Insolv. Int 31.

CHAPTER III

SECONDARY INSOLVENCY PROCEEDINGS

Article 27

Opening of proceedings

The opening of the proceedings referred to in Article 3(1) by a court of a Member State and which is recognised in another Member State (main proceedings) shall permit the opening in that other Member State, a court of which has jurisdiction pursuant to Article 3(2), of secondary insolvency proceedings without the debtor's insolvency being examined in that other State. These latter proceedings must be among the proceedings listed in Annex B. Their effects shall be restricted to the assets of the debtor situated within the territory of that other Member State.

Article 28

Applicable law

Save as otherwise provided in this Regulation, the law applicable to secondary proceedings shall be that of the Member State within the territory of which the secondary proceedings are opened.

Article 29

Right to request the opening of proceedings

The opening of secondary proceedings may be requested by:

(a) the liquidator in the main proceedings;

(b) any other person or authority empowered to request the opening of insolvency proceedings under the law of the Member State within the territory of which the opening of secondary proceedings is requested.

Article 30

Advance payment of costs and expenses

Where the law of the Member State in which the opening of secondary proceedings is requested requires that the debtor's assets be sufficient to cover in whole or in part the costs and expenses of the proceedings, the court may, when it receives such a request, require the applicant to make an advance payment of costs or to provide appropriate security.

Article 31

Duty to cooperate and communicate information

1. Subject to the rules restricting the communication of information, the liquidator in the main proceedings and the liquidators in the secondary proceedings shall be duty bound to communicate information to each other. They shall immediately communicate any information which may be relevant to the other proceedings, in particular the progress made in lodging and verifying claims and all measures aimed at terminating the proceedings.

2. Subject to the rules applicable to each of the proceedings, the liquidator in the main proceedings and the liquidators in the secondary proceedings shall be duty bound to cooperate with each other.

3. The liquidator in the secondary proceedings shall give the liquidator in the main proceedings an early opportunity of submitting proposals on the liquidation or use of the assets in the secondary proceedings.

Article 32

Exercise of creditors' rights

1. Any creditor may lodge his claim in the main proceedings and in any secondary proceedings.

2. The liquidators in the main and any secondary proceedings shall lodge in other proceedings claims which have already been lodged in the proceedings for which they were appointed, provided that the interests of creditors in the latter proceedings are

served thereby, subject to the right of creditors to oppose that or to withdraw the lodgement of their claims where the law applicable so provides.

3. The liquidator in the main or secondary proceedings shall be empowered to participate in other proceedings on the same basis as a creditor, in particular by attending creditors' meetings.

Article 33

Stay of liquidation

1. The court, which opened the secondary proceedings, shall stay the process of liquidation in whole or in part on receipt of a request from the liquidator in the main proceedings, provided that in that event it may require the liquidator in the main proceedings to take any suitable measure to guarantee the interests of the creditors in the secondary proceedings and of individual classes of creditors. Such a request from the liquidator may be rejected only if it is manifestly of no interest to the creditors in the main proceedings. Such a stay of the process of liquidation may be ordered for up to three months. It may be continued or renewed for similar periods.

2. The court referred to in paragraph 1 shall terminate the stay of the process of liquidation:

— at the request of the liquidator in the main proceedings,

— of its own motion, at the request of a creditor or at the request of the liquidator in the secondary proceedings if that measure no longer appears justified, in particular, by the interests of creditors in the main proceedings or in the secondary proceedings.

Article 34

Measures ending secondary insolvency proceedings

1. Where the law applicable to secondary proceedings allows for such proceedings to be closed without liquidation by a rescue plan, a composition or a comparable measure, the liquidator in the main proceedings shall be empowered to propose such a measure himself.

Closure of the secondary proceedings by a measure referred to in the first subparagraph shall not become final without the consent of the liquidator in the main proceedings; failing his agreement, however, it may become final if the financial interests of the creditors in the main proceedings are not affected by the measure proposed.

2. Any restriction of creditors' rights arising from a measure referred to in paragraph 1 which is proposed in secondary proceedings, such as a stay of payment or discharge of debt; may not have effect in respect of the debtor's assets not covered by those proceedings without the consent of all the creditors having an interest.

3. During a stay of the process of liquidation ordered pursuant to Article 33, only the liquidator in the main proceedings or the debtor, with the former's consent, may propose measures laid down in paragraph 1 of this Article in the secondary proceedings; no other proposal for such a measure shall be put to the vote or approved.

Article 35

Assets remaining in the secondary proceedings

If by the liquidation of assets in the secondary proceedings it is possible to meet all claims allowed under those proceedings, the liquidator appointed in those proceedings shall immediately transfer any assets remaining to the liquidator in the main proceedings.

Article 36

Subsequent opening of the main proceedings

Where the proceedings referred to in Article 3(1) are opened following the opening of the proceedings referred to in Article 3(2) in another Member State, Articles 31 to 35 shall apply to those opened first, in so far as the progress of those proceedings so permits.

Article 37[1]

Conversion of earlier proceedings

The liquidator in the main proceedings may request that proceedings listed in Annex A previously opened in another Member State be converted into winding-up proceedings if this proves to be in the interests of the creditors in the main proceedings.

The court with jurisdiction under Article 3(2) shall order conversion into one of the proceedings listed in Annex B.

1 Note the Declaration by Portugal concerning the application of Articles 26 and 37 (O) C. 183, 30.6.2000, p. 1).

Article 38

Preservation measures

Where the court of a Member State which has jurisdiction pursuant to Article 3(1) appoints a temporary administrator in order to ensure the preservation of the debtor's assets, that temporary administrator shall be empowered to request any measures to secure and preserve any of the debtor's assets situated in another Member State, provided for under the law of that State, for the period between the request for the opening of insolvency proceedings and the judgment opening the proceedings.

CHAPTER IV

PROVISION OF INFORMATION FOR CREDITORS AND LODGEMENT OF THEIR CLAIMS

Article 39

Right to lodge claims

Any creditor who has his habitual residence, domicile or registered office in a Member State other than the State of the opening of proceedings, including the tax authorities and social security authorities of Member States, shall have the right to lodge claims in the insolvency proceedings in writing.

Notes

This Article provides for an exception to the established principle of international law that one state will not enforce the revenue law of a foreign country[1]. The exception applies only to the tax authorities of other member states. The exception was heralded after the completion of the Insolvency Regulation[2] and confirmed by Laffoy J in *Re Cedarlease Ltd* [2005] 1 IR 470 when she overruled the common law rule and permitted a claim for Stg£839,404.25 for VAT owed by to a foreign Revenue:

1 See *Buchanan Ltd v McVey* [1954] IR 89; *Governor and Company of* the Bank of *Ireland v Meeneghan* [1994] 3 IR 111; *Government of India v Taylor* [1955] AC 491.

2 Smart, 'The rule against foreign revenue laws' LQR 2000, 116 (July) 360; Fletcher, 'A new age of international insolvency' Insolvency Intelligence 2000, 13(8), 57.

3 *Re Cedarlease Ltd* [2005] 1 IR 470.

Article 40

Duty to inform creditors

1. As soon as insolvency proceedings are opened in a Member State, the court of that State having jurisdiction or the liquidator appointed by it shall immediately inform known creditors who have their habitual residences, domiciles or registered offices in the other Member States.

2. That information, provided by an individual notice, shall in particular include time limits, the penalties laid down in regard to those time limits, the body or authority empowered to accept the lodgement of claims and the other measures laid down. Such notice shall also indicate whether creditors whose claims are preferential or secured in rem need lodge their claims.

Article 41

Content of the lodgement of a claim

A creditor shall send copies of supporting documents, if any, and shall indicate the nature of the claim, the date on which it arose and its amount, as well as whether he alleges preference, security in rem or a reservation of title in respect of the claim and what assets are covered by the guarantee he is invoking.

Article 42

Languages

1. The information provided for in Article 40 shall be provided in the official language or one of the official languages of the State of the opening of proceedings. For that purpose a form shall be used bearing the heading 'Invitation to lodge a claim. Time limits to be observed' in all the official languages of the institutions of the European Union.

2. Any creditor who has his habitual residence, domicile or registered office in a Member State other than the State of the opening of proceedings may lodge his claim in the official language or one of the official languages of that other State. In that event, however, the lodgement of his claim shall bear the heading 'Lodgement of claim' in the official language or one of the official languages of the State of the opening of proceedings. In addition, he may be required to provide a translation into the official language or one of the official languages of the State of the opening of proceedings.

Notes

The heading of the notification must be in all of the official languages of the institutions but the notice itself need only by in an official language of the member state in question. Creditors, on the other hand, may lodge their claim in the official language of their habitual residence, domicile or registered office, but the liquidator may require them to translate this into an official language of the state opening the proceedings.

CHAPTER V

TRANSITIONAL AND FINAL PROVISIONS

Article 43

Applicability in time

The provisions of this Regulation shall apply only to insolvency proceedings opened after its entry into force. Acts done by a debtor before the entry into force of this Regulation shall continue to be governed by the law which was applicable to them at the time they were done.

Notes

This Article prevents retrospective effect of the Insolvency Regulation and limits its operation to acts of a debtor done after the entry into force of the Insolvency Regulation. A debtor's actions are governed by the law in effect at the time of those actions. The Virgos-Schmidt Report contained a similar recommendation (EU Council Document 6500/96, DRS 8 (CFC), Brussels, 3 May 1996, at para 306).

The Article has been interpreted as requiring courts to treat jurisdiction as having been confirmed once the request to open insolvency proceedings is received. See Case C-1/04 *Susanne Staubitz-Scheiber*, Judgment, 17 January 2006. Read in light of preamble recitals 2, 4 and 8, the need to avoid a transfer of jurisdiction from a court originally seised, the need for judicial certainty for creditors who have assumed certain risks in relation to their creditors based on their centre of main interests and the existence of effective and adequate protection for creditors in secondary proceedings. Miss Staubitz-Scheiber moved from Germany to Spain after a request had been made to open insolvency proceedings in Germany. The German Bundesgerichtshof referred the question to the court, which ruled that the German courts retained jurisdiction.

Article 44

Relationship to Conventions

1. After its entry into force, this Regulation replaces, in respect of the matters referred to therein, in the relations between Member States, the Conventions concluded between two or more Member States, in particular:

(a) the Convention between Belgium and France on Jurisdiction and the Validity and Enforcement of Judgments, Arbitration Awards and Authentic Instruments, signed at Paris on 8 July 1899;

(b) the Convention between Belgium and Austria on Bankruptcy, Winding-up, Arrangements, Compositions and Suspension of Payments (with Additional Protocol of 13 June 1973), signed at Brussels on 16 July 1969;

(c) the Convention between Belgium and the Netherlands on Territorial Jurisdiction, Bankruptcy and the Validity and Enforcement of Judgments, Arbitration Awards and Authentic Instruments, signed at Brussels on 28 March 1925;

(d) the Treaty between Germany and Austria on Bankruptcy, Winding-up, Arrangements and Compositions, signed at Vienna on 25 May 1979;

(e) the Convention between France and Austria on Jurisdiction, Recognition and Enforcement of Judgments on Bankruptcy, signed at Vienna on 27 February 1979;

(f) the Convention between France and Italy on the Enforcement of Judgments in Civil and Commercial Matters, signed at Rome on 3 June 1930;

(g) the Convention between Italy and Austria on Bankruptcy, Winding-up, Arrangements and Compositions, signed at Rome on 12 July 1977;

(h) the Convention between the Kingdom of the Netherlands and the Federal Republic of Germany on the Mutual Recognition and Enforcement of Judgments and other Enforceable Instruments in Civil and Commercial Matters, signed at The Hague on 30 August 1962;

(i) the Convention between the United Kingdom and the Kingdom of Belgium providing for the Reciprocal Enforcement of Judgments in Civil and Commercial Matters, with Protocol, signed at Brussels on 2 May 1934;

(j) the Convention between Denmark, Finland, Norway, Sweden and Iceland on Bankruptcy, signed at Copenhagen on 7 November 1933;

(k) the European Convention on Certain International Aspects of Bankruptcy, signed at Istanbul on 5 June 1990.

2. The Conventions referred to in paragraph 1 shall continue to have effect with regard to proceedings opened before the entry into force of this Regulation.

3. This Regulation shall not apply:

(a) in any Member State, to the extent that it is irreconcilable with the obligations arising in relation to bankruptcy from a convention concluded by that State with one or more third countries before the entry into force of this Regulation;

(b) in the United Kingdom of Great Britain and Northern Ireland, to the extent that is irreconcilable with the obligations arising in relation to bankruptcy and the winding-up of insolvent companies from any arrangements with the Commonwealth existing at the time this Regulation enters into force.

Article 45

Amendment of the Annexes

The Council, acting by qualified majority on the initiative of one of its members or on a proposal from the Commission, may amend the Annexes.

Article 46

Reports

No later than 1 June 2012, and every five years thereafter, the Commission shall present to the European Parliament, the Council and the Economic and Social Committee a report on the application of this Regulation. The report shall be accompanied if need be by a proposal for adaptation of this Regulation.

Article 47

Entry into force

This Regulation shall enter into force on 31 May 2002.

This Regulation shall be binding in its entirety and directly applicable in the Member States in accordance with the Treaty establishing the European Community.

ANNEX A

INSOLVENCY PROCEEDINGS REFERRED TO IN ARTICLE 2(A)

BELGIË—BELGIQUE

— Het faillissement/La faillite

— Het gerechtelijk akkoord/Le concordat judiciaire

— De collectieve schuldenregeling/Le règlement collectif de dettes

DEUTSCHLAND

— Das Konkursverfahren

— Das gerichtliche Vergleichsverfahren

— Das Gesamtvollstreckungsverfahren

— Das Insolvenzverfahren

ΕΛΛΑΣ

— Πτώχευση

Η ειδική εκκαθάριση

— Η ειδική εκκαθάριση

— Η προσωρινή διαχείριση εταιρίας. Η διοίκηση και η διαχείριση των πιστωτών

— Η υπαγωγή επιχείρησης υπό επίτροπο με σκοπό τη σύναψη συμβιβασμού με τους πιστωτές

ESPAÑA

— Concurso de acreedores

— Quiebra

— Suspensión de pagos

FRANCE

— Liquidation judiciaire

— Redressement judiciaire avec nomination d'un administrateur

IRELAND

— Compulsory winding up by the court

— Bankruptcy

— The administration in bankruptcy of the estate of persons dying insolvent

— Winding-up in bankruptcy of partnerships

— Creditors' voluntary winding up (with confirmation of a Court)

— Arrangements under the control of the court which involve the vesting of all or part of the property of the debtor in the Official Assignce for realisation and distribution

— Company examinership

ITALIA

— Fallimento

— Concordato preventivo

— Liquidazione coatta amministrativa

— Amministrazione straordinaria

— Amministrazione controllata

LUXEMBOURG

— Faillite

— Gestion contrôlée

— Concordat préventif de faillite (par abandon d'acrif)

— Régime spécial de liquidation du notariat

NEDERLAND

— Het faillissement

— De surséance van betaling

— De schuldsaneringsregeling natuurlijke personen

ÖSTERREICH

— Das Konkursverfahren

— Das Ausgleichsverfahren

PORTUGAL

— O processo de falência

— Os processos especiais de recuperação de empresa, ou seja:

— A concordata

— A reconstituição empresarial

— A reestruturação financeira

— A gest ào controlada

SUOMI-FINLAND

— Konkurssi/konkurs

— Yrityssaneeraus/företagssanering

SVERIGE

— Konkurs

— Företagsrekonstruktion

UNITED KINGDOM

— Winding up by or subject to the supervision of the court

— Creditors' voluntary winding up (with confirmation by the court)

— Administration

— Voluntary arrangements under insolvency legislation

— Bankruptcy or sequestration

ANNEX B

WINDING UP PROCEEDINGS REFERRED TO IN ARTICLE 2(C)

BELGIË—BELGIQUE

— Het faillissement/La faillite

DEUTSCHLAND

— Das Konkursverfahren

— Das Gesamtvollstreckungsverfahren

— Das Insolvenzverfahren

ΕΛΛΑΣ

— Πτώχευση

— Η ειδική εκκαθάρισηε

ESPAÑA

— Concurso de acreedores

— Quiebra

— Suspensión de pagos basada en la insolvencia definitiva

FRANCE

— Liquidation judiciaire

IRELAND

— Compulsory winding up

— Bankruptcy

— The administration in bankruptcy of the estate of persons dying insolvent

— Winding-up in bankruptcy of partnerships

— Creditors' voluntary winding up (with confirmation of a court)

— Arrangements under the control of the court which involve the vesting of all or part of the property of the debtor in the Official Assignee for realisation and distribution

ITALIA

— Fallimento

— Liquidazione coatta amministrativa

LUXEMBOURG

— Faillite

— Régime spécial de liquidation du notariat

NEDERLAND

— Het faillissement

— De schuldsaneringsregeling natuurlijke personen

ÖSTERREICH

— Das Konkursverfahren

PORTUGAL

— O processo de falência

SUOMI-FINLAND

— Konkurssi/konkurs

SVERIGE

— Konkurs

UNITED KINGDOM

— Winding up by or subject to the supervision of the court

— Creditors' voluntary winding up (with confirmation by the court)

— Bankruptcy or sequestration

ANNEX C

LIQUIDATORS REFERRED TO IN ARTICLE 2(B)

BELGIË—BELGIQUE

— De curator/Le curateur

— De commissaris inzake opschorting/Le commissaire au sursis

— De schuldbemiddelaar/Le médiateur de dettes

DEUTSCHLAND

— Konkursverwalter

— Vergleichsverwalter

— Sachwalter (nach der Vergleichsordnung)

— Verwalter

— Insolvenzverwalter

— Sachwalter (nach der Insolvenzordnung)

— Treuhänder

— Vorläufiger Insolvenzverwalter

ΕΛΛΑΣ

— Ο σύνδικο

— Ο προσωρινός διαχειριστής. Η διοικούσα επιτροπή των πιστωτών

— Ο ειδικός εκκαθαριστής

— Ο επίτροπος

ESPAÑA

— Depositario-administrador

— Interventor o Interventores

— Síndicos

— Comisario

FRANCE

— Représentant des créanciers

— Mandataire liquidateur

— Administrateur judiciaire

— Commissaire à l'exécution de plan

IRELAND

— Liquidator

— Official Assignee

— Trustee in bankruptcy

— Provisional Liquidator

— Examiner

ITALIA

— Curatore

— Commissario

LUXEMBOURG

— Le curateur

— Le commissaire

— Le liquidateur

— Le conseil de gérance de la section d'assainissement du notariat

NEDERLAND

— De curator in het faillissement

— De bewindvoerder in de surséance van betaling

— De bewindvoerder in de schuldsaneringsregeling natuurlijke personen

ÖSTERREICH

— Masseverwalter

— Ausgleichsverwalter

— Sachwalter

— Treuhänder

— Besondere Verwalter

— Vorläufiger Verwalter

— Konkursgericht

PORTUGAL

— Gestor judicial

— Liquidatário judicial

— Comissão de credores

SUOMI—FINLAND

— Pesänhoitaja/boförvaltare

— Selvittäjä/utredare

SVERIGE

— Förvaltare

— God man

— Rekonstruktör

UNITED KINGDOM

— Liquidator

— Supervisor of a voluntary arrangement

— Administrator
— Official Receiver
— Trustee
— Judicial factor

EXPLANATORY NOTE

(*This note is not a part of the Instrument and does not purport to be a legal interpretation*)

These Regulations are intended to facilitate the operation of Council Regulation (EC) No. 1346/2000 of 29 May 2000 on Insolvency Proceedings, insofar as they concern corporate insolvency. The Regulations set out the necessary amendments to domestic legislation (the Companies Acts 1963 to 2001) and make necessary provisions for the good administration of the Council Regulation, which came into effect on 31 May, 2002.

The facilitation of the operation of the Council Regulation with regard to personal insolvency is set out in Statutory Instrument No. 334 of 2002.

European Communities (Credit Institutions) (Fair Value Accounting) Regulations 2004

SI 720/2004

I, Brian Cowen, Minister for Finance, in exercise of the powers conferred on me by section 3 of the European Communities Act 1972 (No. 27 of 1972), for the purpose of giving effect to Directive 2001/65/EC of the European Parliament and of the Council of 27 September 2001[1]*, hereby make the following regulations:*

1.(1) These Regulations may be cited as the European Communities (Credit Institutions) (Fair Value Accounting) Regulations 2004.

(2) These Regulations come into operation on 1 January 2005.

Notes

These Regs implement Directive 2001/65/EC ('the Fair Value Directive') as regards banks and other financial institutions. The Fair Value Directive amended the EU Accounting Directives to permit certain financial instruments to be recorded at fair value in accordance with the *IAS 32 (Financial Instruments: Disclosure and Presentation)* and *IAS 39 (Financial Instruments: Recognition and Measurement).*[1] The Fair Value Directive also amended Directives 86/635/EEC and 91/674/EEC dealing with the accounts of banks and other financial institutions and insurance undertakings. The Fair Value Regulations have been implemented in a manner that permits all companies to use fair value accounting for certain financial instruments in both their annual and consolidated accounts. As such, the Regulations amend primarily the Schedule to the C(A)A 1986 and the EC(CGA)R, 1992.

1 See CA 1963 section 148 to 149.

2.(1) In these Regulations "Principal Regulations" means the European Communities (Credit Institutions: Accounts) Regulations 1992 (S.I. No. 294 of 1992).

(2) A word or expression that is used in these Regulations (including provisions inserted into the Principal Regulations by these Regulations) and is also used in Directive 2001/65/EC of the European Parliament and of the Council of 27 September 2001 (O.J. No. L283, 27.10.01, p.28) has, unless the contrary is indicted, the same meaning in these Regulations as it has in that Directive.

3. Regulation 11 of the Principal Regulations is amended—

(a) in paragraph (d), by deleting "and" at the end of that paragraph,

(b) in paragraph (e), by substituting "subsidiary, and" for "subsidiary.", and

(c) by inserting after paragraph (e) the following:

[.....][a]

Amendments

a Reg 11(f) of EC(CI:A)R 1992 inserted. See the amended Regs.

Notes

See Reg 11 of European Communities (Credit Institutions: Accounts) Regulations 1992.

---

4. Regulation 15 of the Principal Regulations is amended by substituting—

(a) in paragraph (1)(a), "€3,000" for "£1,000",

(b) in paragraph (2)—

(i) "3 months" for "12 months", and

(ii) "€3,000" for "£1,000", and

(c) in paragraph (4)—

(i) "3 months" for "12 months", and

(ii) "€3,000" for "£1,000".

5. Paragraph 41 of Chapter II of Part I of the Schedule to the Principal Regulations is amended, by substituting for subparagraph (3) the following:

[...][a]

Amendments

a Reg 5 substitutes EC(CI:A)R 1992, Sch, Pt 1, ch II para 41(3).

6. Part I of the Schedule to the Principal Regulations is amended by inserting after paragraph 46 the following:

[...][a].

Amendments

a Reg 6 inserts EC(CI:A)R 1992, Sch, Pt 1, ch II para 46A–46D.

7. Chapter III of Part I of the Schedule to the Principal Act is amended—

(a) in paragraph 75(2), by inserting the following sentence:

'This includes the extent to which the calculation of the profit or loss is affected by the fair valuation of financial instruments', and

(b) after paragraph 72, by inserting the following:

[...][a]

Amendments

a Reg 7(b) inserts EC(CI:A)R 1992, Sch, Pt 1, ch III para 72A.

8. Paragraphs 31(1), 32, 33, 34, 45 and 46 of Part I of the Schedule to the Principal Regulations do not apply with respect to assets and liabilities that are valued in accordance with paragraphs 46A to 46D (inserted by Regulation 6 of these Regulations) of Part I of the Schedule to the Principal Regulations.

EXPLANATORY NOTE

(*This note is not part of the instrument and does not purport to be a legal interpretation*).

The purpose of these Regulations is to give effect to Directive 2001/65/EC of 27 September 2001 which deals with the valuation rules for the annual and consolidated accounts of banks and other financial institutions.

These Regulations allow banks and other financial institutions in the EU to prepare their consolidated financial statements in accordance with generally accepted accounting principles. The impetus for this is the harmonisation of the capital markets in the EU and the desire to have a consistent set of accounting principles used in the consolidated financial statements ("group accounts") of all EU banks and financial institutions.

European Communities (Fair Value Accounting) Regulations 2004

SI 765/2004

I, Michéal Martin, Minister for Enterprise, Trade and Employment, in exercise of the powers conferred on me by section 3 of the European Communities Act 1972 (No. 27 of 1972), for the purpose of giving effect to Directive 2001/65/EC of the European Parliament and of the Council of 27 September 2001 (OJ No. L283, 27.10.01, p 28), hereby make the following regulations:

1.(1) These Regulations may be cited as the European Communities (Fair Value Accounting) Regulations 2004.

(2) These Regulations come into operation on 1 January 2005.

(3) These Regulations shall be read as one with the Companies Acts 1963 to 2003.

2. A word or expression that is used in these Regulations (including provisions inserted by these Regulations into the Companies (Amendment) Act 1986 (No. 25 of 1986) and the European Communities (Companies: Group Accounts) Regulations 1992 (S.I. No. 201 of 1992)) and is also used in Directive 2001/65/EC of the European Parliament and of the Council of 27 September 2001 has, unless the contrary is indicated, the same meaning in these Regulations as it has in that Directive.

Notes

These regs implement Directive 2001/65/EC ('the Fair Value Directive'). The Fair Value Directive amended the EU Accounting Directives to permit certain financial instruments to be recorded at fair value in accordance with the IAS 32 (Financial Instruments: Disclosure and Presentation) and IAS 39 (Financial Instruments: Recognition and Measurement)[1]. The Fair Value Regulations have been implemented in a manner that permits all companies to use fair value accounting for certain financial instruments in both their annual and consolidated accounts. As such, the regs amend primarily the Schedule to C(A)A 1986 and the Group (Accounts) Regulations 1992. The Fair Value Directive also amended Directives 86/635/EEC and 91/674/EEC dealing with the accounts of banks and other financial institutions and insurance undertakings. EC(CI)(FVA)R 2004 implement the requirements of the Fair Value Directive as regards banks and other financial institutions.

[1] See CA 1963, ss 148–149.

---

3. The Companies (Amendment) Act 1986 is amended—

(a) in section 12(1), by inserting "31B, 31C," after "27,",

(b) in section 13 (as amended by the European Communities (Accounts) Regulations 1993 (S.I. No. 396 of 1993)), by substituting the following for paragraphs (c), (d) and (e)—

[…][a]

and

(c) in the Schedule—

(i) in Part II (HISTORICAL COST RULES IN RELATION TO THE DRAWING UP OF ACCOUNTS), in paragraph 4 (Preliminary), by substituting "Parts III and IIIA" for "Part III",

(ii) by inserting the following after paragraph 22—

[…][b]

(iii) in Part IV (INFORMATION REQUIRED BY WAY OF NOTES TO ACCOUNTS), by inserting the following after paragraph 31—

[…][c]

and

in Part VII (INTERPRETATION OF SCHEDULE), by inserting the following after paragraph 76—

[…][d]

Amendments

a Reg 3(b) substitutes C(A)A 1986, s 13(c), (d) and (e).

b Reg 3(c)(ii) inserts C(A)A 1986, ss 22A–22E.

c Reg 3(c)(iii) inserts C(A)A 1986, ss 31A–31C.

d Reg 3(c)(iv) inserts C(A)A 1986, ss 77–78.

4. The European Communities (Companies: Group Accounts) Regulations 1992 are amended—

(a) in Regulation 37(1), by substituting the following for paragraphs (d) and (e)—

[…][a]

and

(b) In Part 2 (Information required by way of notes to the group accounts) of the Schedule, by inserting the following after paragraph 16—

[…][b]

Amendments

a Reg 4(a) substitutes EC(CGA)R 1992, reg 37(1)(d) and (e).

b Reg 4(b) inserts EC(CGA)R 1992, Sch, Pt 2, paras 16A and 16B.

EXPLANATORY NOTE

(*This note is not part of the instrument and does not purport to be a legal interpretation*).

These Regulations give effect to Directive 2001/65/EC of the European Parliament and of the Council of 27 September, 2001 to allow for the fair valuation of financial instruments in accounts.

European Communities (International Financial Reporting Standards and Miscellaneous Amendments) Regulations 2005

SI 116/2005

I, Micheál Martin, Minister for Enterprise, Trade and Employment, in exercise of the powers conferred on me by section 3 of the European Communities Act 1972 (No. 27 of 1972) and for the purpose of giving full effect to Regulation (EC) No. 1606/2002 of the European Parliament and of the Council of 19 July 2002[1], for the purpose of giving further effect to the Fourth Council Directive 78/660/EEC of 25 July 1978[2], the Seventh Council Directive 83/349/EEC of 13 June 1983[3], Council Directive 86/635/EEC of 8 December 1986[4] and Council Directive 91/674/EEC[5] of 19 December 1991 and for the purpose of giving effect to Directive 2003/51 /EC of the European Parliament and of the Council of 18 June 2003[6], hereby make the following regulations:

1 OJ No. L243, 11.9.2002, p.1
2 OJ No. L222, 14.8.1978, p.11
3 OJ No. L193, 18.7.1983, p.1
4 OJ No. L372, 31.12.1986, p.1
5 OJ No. L374, 31.12.1991, p.7
6 OJ No. L178, 17.7.2003, p.16

PART I
PRELIMINARY AND GENERAL

Citation and construction

1.(1) These Regulations may be cited as the European Communities (International Financial Reporting Standards and Miscellaneous Amendments) Regulations 2005.

(2) These Regulations are to be read as one with the Companies Acts 1963 to 2003.

Notes

Three pieces of legislation passed by the EU in recent years have made a number of significant changes to the EU accounting requirements for companies. These are:

- Regulation (EC) No 1606/2002 of the European Parliament and of the Council on the application of International Accounting Standards ('the IAS Regulation');
- Directive 2003/51/EC of the European Parliament and of the Council amending Council Directives 78/660/EEC, 83/349/EEC, 86/635/EEC and 91/674/EEC on the annual and consolidated accounts of certain types of companies, banks and other financial institutions and insurance undertakings ('the Modernisation Directive'); and
- Directive 2001/65/EC of the European Parliament and of the Council amending Council Directives 78/660/EEC, 83/349/EEC, 86/635/EEC as regards the valuation rules for the annual and consolidated accounts of certain types of companies as well as banks and other financial institutions ('the Fair Value Directive').

These regs, EC(IFRSMA)R 2005, give effect in Irish company law to the first two of these European instruments. The Fair Value Directive has been implemented by SI 720/2004 and SI 765/2004.

Application

2.(1) These Regulations apply to the preparation of annual accounts in the case of a company or undertaking the financial year of which commences on or after 1 January 2005.

(2) In the case of a company or undertaking that prepares its first annual accounts for a period ending after 1 January 2005, it may prepare IFRS accounts (within the meaning of section 2 of the Principal Act) even though its date of incorporation or formation, as the case may be, is before 1 January 2005.

Interpretation

3.(1) In these Regulations—

'Credit Institutions Regulations' means the European Communities (Credit Institutions: Accounts) Regulations 1992 (S.I. No. 294 of 1992);

'Fair Value Regulations' means the European Communities (Fair Value Accounting) Regulations 2004 (S.I. No. 765 of 2004);

'Insurance Undertakings Regulations' means the European Communities (Insurance Undertakings: Accounts) Regulations 1996 (S.I. No. 23 of 1996);

'Principal Act' means the Companies Act 1963 (No. 33 of 1963).

(2) A word or expression that is used in these Regulations (including provisions inserted by these Regulations into the Principal Act, the Companies (Amendment) Act 1983 (No. 13 of 1983), the Companies (Amendment) Act 1986 (No. 25 of 1986), the Companies Act 1990 (No. 27 of 1990), the Companies (Auditing and Accounting) Act 2003 (No. 44 of 2003), the European Communities (Companies: Group Accounts) Regulations 1992 (S.I. No. 201 of 1992), the Credit Institutions Regulations, the European Communities (Accounts) Regulations 1993 (S.I. No. 396 of 1993) or the Insurance Undertakings Regulations) and is also used in Regulation (EC) No. 1606/2002 of the European Parliament and of the Council of 19 July 2002, the Fourth Council Directive 78/660/EEC of 25 July 1978, the Seventh Council Directive 83/349/EEC of 13 June 1983, Council Directive 86/635/EEC of 8 December 1986, Council Directive 91/674/EEC of 19 December 1991 and Directive 2003/51/EC of the European Parliament and of the Council of 18 June 2003 has, unless the contrary is indicated, the same meaning in these Regulations as it has in that Regulation and those Directives.

PART 2
PREPARATION OF INDIVIDUAL AND GROUP ACCOUNTS

Preparation of individual and group accounts

4.The Principal Act is amended by substituting the following for sections 148 to 151—

[...][a]

Amendments

a EC(IFRSMA)R 2005, reg 4 substituted ss 148–151 of CA 1963.

PART 3
MISCELLANEOUS AMENDMENTS TO PROVISIONS RELATING TO ACCOUNTS

Chapter 1
Amendments to Companies (Amendment) Act 1986

5. The Companies (Amendment) Act 1986 is amended as follows-

(a) in section 3—

[…][a]

(b) in section 4—

[…][b]

(c) in section 5—

(i) in paragraph (c)(ii), by substituting 'all liabilities which have arisen' for 'all liabilities and losses which have arisen or are likely to arise',

(ii) in paragraph (d), by substituting 'payment,' for 'payment, and',

(iii) in paragraph (e), by substituting 'separately,' for 'separately.', and

(iv) by inserting the following after paragraph (e):

[...][c]

(d) in section 7—

(i) in subsection (1)(a), by substituting the following for subparagraphs (i), (ii) and (iii) and all the words from 'and a copy of the report' down to and including 'for that year, and':

[….][d]

and

(ii) by inserting the following after subsection (1) and by renumbering subsection (1A) (inserted by section 64 of the Company Law Enforcement Act 2001) as subsection (1C)—

[…][e]

(e) in section 8(4)—

(i) in paragraph (a), by deleting 'and',

(ii) in paragraph (b), by substituting 'under 'Assets', and' for 'under 'Assets'.', and

(iii) by inserting the following after paragraph (b):

[...][f]

(f) by substituting the following for sections 10, 11 and 12—

[…][g]

(g) in section 13—

(i) by substituting the following for paragraph (a):

[…][h]

and

(ii) by renumbering the existing provision as subsection (1) of that section and inserting the following:

[…][i]

(h) in section 15, by substituting 'section 193 of the Companies Act 1990' for 'section 163 of the Principal Act',

(i) in section 16(2), by substituting the following for paragraph (a):

[…][j]

(j) in section 17(1)—

(i) by substituting the following for paragraph (b):

[…][k]

and

(ii) by substituting the following for paragraph (e):

[…][l]

(k) in section 18—

(i) by substituting the following for subsection (1):

[…][m]

(ii in subsection (2), by substituting 'An abridged balance sheet' for 'A copy of a balance sheet',

(iii) by substituting the following for subsection (3):

[…][n]

and

(iv) in subsection (4), by substituting 'abridged accounts' for 'accounts' wherever it occurs,

(l) in section 19—

(i) by substituting the following for subsection (1):

[…][o]

(ii) in subsection (2), by substituting the following for paragraph (d):

[…][p]

and

(iii) in subsection (4)–

(I) by inserting the following after the definition of 'abbreviated accounts:

[…][q]

and

(II) by substituting the following for the definition of 'full accounts':

[…][r]

and

(m) in the Schedule—

(i) in Part 1, in the Balance Sheet Formats—

(I) in Format 1, Item G, by substituting 'Provisions for liabilities' for 'provisions for liabilities and charges', and

(II) in Format 2, Item B under the heading 'LIABILITIES', by substituting 'Provisions for liabilities' for 'Provisions for liabilities and charges',

(ii) by inserting the following after paragraph 22C (inserted by Regulation 3 of the Fair Value Regulations):

[…][s],

(iii) in paragraph 22D (inserted by Regulation 3 of the Fair Value Regulations)—

(I) in subparagraph (1), by inserting 'or where the fair value at which an asset is included in accordance with paragraph 22CA of this Schedule' after 'Schedule' and

(II) in subparagraph (2), by inserting 'of the financial instrument or of the investment property or living animals or plants' after 'difference in value',

(iv) by substituting the following for paragraph 31C (inserted by the Fair Value Regulations):

[…][t],

(v) by inserting the following after paragraph 31C:

[…][u],

(vi) in paragraph 32—

(I) in subparagraph (1)(b), by substituting 'provisions for liabilities' for 'provisions for liabilities and charges', and

(II) in subparagraph (1)(c), by substituting 'provision for liabilities' for 'provision for liabilities and charges',

(vii) in paragraph 57 by renumbering the existing provision as subparagraph (1) and inserting the following:

[…][v],

(viii) by inserting the following after paragraph 65:

[…][w],

and

(ix) in paragraph 70—

(I) by deleting 'or charges', and

(II) by substituting 'the nature of which is clearly defined and' for 'or loss'.

Amendments

a Reg 5(a) amends C(A)A 1986, s 3.

b Reg 5(b) amends C(A)A 1986, s 4.

c Reg 5(c)(iv) inserts C(A)A 1986, s 5(f).

d Reg 5(d) amends C(A)A 1986, s 7(1)(a).

e Reg 5(e)(ii) inserts C(A)A 1986, ss 1A and 1B and renumbers s 1C.

f Reg 5(e)(iii) inserts C(A)A 1986, s 8(4)(c).

g Reg 5(f) substitutes C(A)A 1986, ss 10, 11 and 12.

h Reg 5(g)(i) substitutes C(A)A 1986, s 13(a).

i Reg 5(g)(ii) inserts C(A)A 1986, s 13(2).

j Reg 5(i) substitutes C(A)A 1986, s 16(2)(a).

k Reg 5(j)(i) substitutes C(A)A 1986, s 17(1)(b).

l Reg 5(j)(ii) substitutes C(A)A 1986, s 17(1)(e).

m Reg 5(k)(i) substitutes C(A)A 1986, s 18(1).

n Reg 5(k)(ii) substitutes C(A)A 1986, s 18(3).

o Reg 5(l)(i) substitutes C(A)A 1986, s 19(1).

p Reg 5(l)(ii) substitutes C(A)A 1986, s 19(2)(d).

q Reg 5(l)(iii)(I) inserts a definition of 'abridged accounts' in C(A)A 1986, s 19(4).

r Reg 5(l)(iii)(II) substitutes the definition of 'full individual accounts' in C(A)A 1986, s 19(4).

s Reg 5(m)(ii) inserts C(A)A 1986, Sch, para 22(CA).

t Reg 5(m)(iv) substitutes C(A)A 1986, Sch, para 31(C).

u Reg 5(m)(v) inserts C(A)A 1986, Sch, para 31(D).

v Reg 5(m)(vii) inserts C(A)A 1986, Sch, para 57(2).

w Reg 5(m)(viii) inserts C(A)A 1986, Sch, para 65A.

Chapter 2

Amendments to European Communities (Companies: Group Accounts) Regulations 1992

6. The European Communities (Companies: Group Accounts) Regulations 1992 are amended—

(a) in Regulation 2, by substituting 'Companies Act group accounts' for 'group accounts',

(b) in Regulation 3, by substituting the following for the definition of 'group accounts':

[…][a],

(c) in Regulation 4(1), by substituting the following for paragraph (c):

[…][b],

(d) in Regulation 5—

(i) by substituting the following for paragraph (1):

[…][c]

(ii) in paragraph (2), by substituting 'Regulations 10 and 11' for 'Regulations 10, 11 and 12', and

(iii) in paragraph (4), by substituting 'Companies Act group accounts' for 'group accounts' wherever those words occur,

(e) in Regulation 7(8), by substituting the following for paragraph (a):

[...][d]

(f) in Regulation 8—

(i) in paragraph (1), by substituting 'an EEA State' for 'a Member State,

(ii) in paragraph (3)(a)—

(I) by substituting 'Regulations 10 and 11' for 'Regulations 10, 11 and 12', and

(II) by substituting 'EEA State' for 'Member State',

(iii) in paragraph (3)(b)—

(I) by substituting 'EEA State' for 'Member State', and

(II) by inserting 'or in accordance with international financial reporting standards' after 'with the Directive',

and

(iv) by substituting the following for paragraph (4):

[…][e]

(g) in Regulation 9—

(i) in paragraph (1), by substituting 'an EEA State' for 'a Member State', and

(ii) by substituting the following for paragraph (3):

[…][f],

(h) by inserting the following after Regulation 9:

[…][g]

(i) by deleting Regulation 12,

(j) in Regulation 29—

(i) in paragraph (1), by substituting 'individual accounts' for 'annual accounts', and

(ii) by substituting the following for paragraph (2):

[…][h]

(k) in Regulation 35, by deleting paragraph (6),

(l) in Regulation 37, by substituting the following for paragraph (a):

[…][i]

(m) in Regulation 40(2), by substituting the following for paragraph (d):

[…][j]

(n) in Part 2 of the Schedule, by substituting the following for paragraph 16C (inserted by Regulation 4 of the Fair Value Regulations):

[…][k]

(o) by inserting the following after paragraph 16C:

[…][l]

Amendments

a Reg 6(b) substitutes the definition of 'group accounts' in EC(CGA)R 1992, reg 3.

b Reg 6(c) substitutes EC(CGA)R 1992, reg 4(1)(c) and inserts reg 4(1)(ca).

c Reg 6(d)(i) substitutes EC(CGA)R 1992, reg 5(1).

d Reg 6(e) substitutes EC(CGA)R 1992, reg 7(8)(a).

e Reg 6(f)(iv) substitutes EC(CGA)R 1992, reg 8(4).

f Reg 6(g) substitutes EC(CGA)R 1992, reg 9(3).

g Reg 6(h) inserts EC(CGA)R 1992, reg 9A.

h Reg 6(j) substitutes EC(CGA)R 1992, reg 29(2).

i Reg 6(l) substitutes EC(CGA)R 1992, reg 37(a).

j Reg 6(m) substitutes EC(CGA)R 1992, reg 40(2)(d).
k Reg 6(n) substitutues EC(CGA)R 1992, Sch, Pt 2, para 16C.
l Reg 6(o) inserts EC(CGA)R 1992, Sch, Pt 2, para 16D.

Chapter 3
Amendments to European Communities (Accounts) Regulations 1993

7. The European Communities (Accounts) Regulations 1993 are amended—

(a) by inserting the following after paragraph 7(3):

[…][a],

(b) by inserting the following after paragraph 9(3):

[…][b],

(c) in Regulation 12, by substituting the following for paragraph (3):

[…][c]

(d) in Regulation 14(1), by substituting the following for paragraph (a):

[…][d]

and

(e) in Regulation 16(2), by substituting the following for paragraph (d)(iv):

[…][e].

Amendments

a Reg 7(a) inserts EC(A)R 1993, para 7(4).
b Reg 7(b) inserts EC(A)R 1993, para 9(4).
c Reg 7(c) substitutes EC(A)R 1993, reg 12, para (3).
d Reg 7(d) substitutes EC(A)R 1993, reg 14(1), para (a).
e Reg 7(e) substitutes EC(A)R 1993, reg 16(2), para (d)(iv).

Chapter 4
Amendment to the Companies Act 1990

8. The Companies Act 1990 is amended in section 193 by substituting the following for subsection (4):

[…][a]

Amendments

a Reg 8 substitutes CA 1990, s 193(4).

PART 4
CONSEQUENTIAL AND MINOR AMENDMENTS

Amendments to Companies Acts 1963 to 2003

9. The Acts specified in Schedule 1 are amended as indicated in that Schedule.

Amendments to Credit Institutions Regulations

10. The Credit Institutions Regulations are amended as indicated in Schedule 2.

Amendments to Insurance Undertakings Regulations

11. The Insurance Undertakings Regulations are amended as indicated in Schedule 3.

Schedule 1

Amendments to Companies Acts 1963 To 2003

PART 1

AMENDMENTS TO PRINCIPAL ACT

Item No	*Section affected*	*Amendment*
1.	Section 2	(a) In subsection (1)— (i) substitute the following for the definition of 'accounts': […][a], (ii) insert the following after the definition of 'books and paper': […][b], (iii) insert the following after the definition of 'the Court' (inserted by section 235 of the Act of 1990): […][c], (iv) insert the following after the definition of 'document': […][d], (v) insert the following after the definition of 'group accounts': […][e], (vi) insert the following after the definition of 'Insolvency Regulation' (inserted by Regulation 3(a) of the European Communities (Corporate Insolvency) Regulations 2002 (S.I. No. 333 of 2002): […][f], (vii) insert the following after the definition of 'private company': […][g], (viii) in the definition of 'financial year' insert 'subject to subsection (1A),' after 'means,', (ix) [...][h]

Item No	*Section affected*	*Amendment*
		(x) insert the following after the definition of the 'registrar of companies': [...][i];', and (xi) insert the following after the definition of 'the time of the opening of the subscription lists': […][j]. (b) Insert the following after subsection (1): […][k].
2.	Section 60	Substitute the following for subsection (15C) (inserted by the Companies (Amendment) Act 1983): […][l].
3.	Section 152	(a) In subsection (1), substitute 'Companies Act group accounts prepared in accordane with sections 151 to 155 of this Act' for 'The group accounts'. (b) In subsections (2) and (3), substitute 'the group accounts referred to in subsection (1)' for 'group accounts' in each place where it occurs.
4.	Section 156	Substitute the following for subsections (1) and (2): […][m].

Amendments

a Sch 1, Pt 1, item 1(a)(i) inserts definitions of 'accounts', 'Act of 1986', 'Act of 1990' and 'Act of 2003' in CA 1963, s 2(1).

b Sch 1, Pt 1, item 1(a)(ii) inserts definitions of 'Companies Act accounts', 'Companies Act group accounts' and 'Companies Act individual accounts' in CA 1963, s 2(1).

c Sch 1, Pt 1, item 1(a)(iii) inserts definitions of '1993 Regulations' and 'Credit Institutions Regulations' in CA 1963, s 2(1).

d Sch 1, Pt 1, item 1(a)(iv) inserts definitions of 'EEA state' and 'EEA Agreement' in CA 1963, s 2(1).

e Sch 1, Pt 1, item 1(a)(v) inserts definitions of 'Group Accounts Regulations', 'IAS Regulation', 'income statement', 'individual accounts', 'IFRS accounts', 'IFRS group accounts' and 'IFRS individual accounts' in CA 1963, s 2(1).

f Sch 1, Pt 1, item 1(a)(vi) inserts definitions of 'Insurance Undertakings Regulations' and 'international financial reporting standards' in CA 1963, s 2(1).

g Sch 1, Pt 1, item 1(a)(vii) inserts a definition of 'profit and loss account' in CA 1963, s 2(1).

h Sch 1, Pt 1, item 1(a)(ix) inserts definitions of 'parent company' and 'parent undertaking' in CA 1963, s 2(1).

i Sch 1, Pt 1, item 1(a)(x) inserts a definition of 'regulated market' in CA 1963, s 2(1).

j Sch 1, Pt 1, item 1(a)(xi) inserts a definition of 'undertaking' in CA 1963, s 2(1).

k Sch 1, Pt 1, item 1(b) inserts CA 1963, s 2(1A) and (1B).

l Sch 1, Pt 1, item 2 substitutes CA 1963, s 60(15C).

m Sch 1, Pt 1, item 4 substitutes CA 1963, s 156(1) and (2).

PART 2
AMENDMENTS TO COMPANIES (AMENDMENT) ACT 1983

Item No	*Section affected*	*Amendment*
1.	Section 2	In subsection (4)— (a) in paragraph (a), insert 'or by international financial reporting standards' after 'Companies Acts', and (b) substitute the following for subsection (c) and for all the words from 'and in paragraph (c)' down to and including 'of the company': […][a].
2.	Section 9	In subsection (13), in the definition of 'unqualified report', substitute the following for paragraph (a): […][b].
3.	Section 45	Substitute the following for subsection (4)— […][c].
4.	Section 45A (inserted by section 20 of the Companies (Amendment) Act 1986)	In subsection (3), substitute the following for paragraph (b): […][d].
5.	Section 47	Substitute the following for subsection (2): […][e].
6.	Section 49	(a) In subsection (2)(a), insert '(and, where applicable, in accordance with the requirements of Article 4 of the IAS Regulation)' after 'Principal Act'. (b) In subsection (9)— (i) […][f], and (ii) […][g], (c) In subsection (10), substitute 'section 148 and either section 149 or 149A of the Principal Act, where applicable, of' for 'section 149 of'.

Amendments

a Sch 1, Pt 2, item 1(b) substitutes C(A)A 1983, s 2(c).

b Sch 1, Pt 2, item 2 substitutes C(A)A 1983, s 9(13)(a).

c Sch 1, Pt 2, item 3 substitutes C(A)A 1983, s 45(4).

d Sch 1, Pt 2, item 4 substitutes C(A)A 1983, s 45A(3)(b).

e Sch 1, Pt 2, item 5 substitutes C(A)A 1983, s 47(2).

f Sch 1, Pt 2. item 6(b)(i) substitutes C(A)A 1983, s 49(9), paras (a) and (b) in the definition of 'properly prepared'.

g Sch 1, Pt 2, item 6(b)(ii) substitutes the definition of 'relevant item' in C(A)A 1983, s 49(9).

PART 3
AMENDMENT TO THE COMPANIES (AMENDMENT) ACT 1986

Item No	*Section affected*	*Amendment*
1.	Section 1	In subsection (1), before the definition of 'company' insert the following: 'abridged accounts' has the meaning given to it by section 19 of the Principal Act;'.

PART 4
AMENDMENT TO COMPANIES ACT 1990

Item No	*Section affected*	*Amendment*
1.	Section 29	In subsection (9), substitute the following for paragraph (c): […][a].
2.	Section 41	In subsection (4), substitute 'sections 151 (2) and 154' for 'sections 150 (2) and 154'.
3.	Section 43	In subsection (8), substitute 'sections 151 (2) and 154' for 'sections 150(2) and 154'.
4.	Section 63	In subsection (2), substitute 'section 10 (1)' for 'section 10(2)'.
5.	Section 193	Substitute the following for subsection (1): […][b]
6.	Section 202	(a) In subsection (1)— (i) substitute the following for paragraph (c): […][c], and (ii) in paragraph (d), substitute 'annual accounts' for 'accounts'. (b) In subsection (6), substitute the following for 'the company's balance sheet, its profit and loss account or income and expenditure account and document annexed to any of those documents': '(and, where applicable, Article 4 of the IAS Regulation) the company's accounts and any document annexed to those accounts'.
7.	Section 205A (inserted by section 41 of the Companies (Auditing and Accounting) Act 2003)	Substitute 'individual accounts' for 'annual accounts' wherever occurring in that section.

Item No	Section affected	Amendment
8.	Section 205B (inserted by section 42 the Companies (Auditing and Accounting) Act 2003)	In subsection (2)— (a) in paragraphs (a), (b) and (d), substitute 'individual accounts' for 'annual accounts' wherever occurring, and (b) substitute the following for paragraph (b)(ii): […][d].
9.	Section 251	In subsection (2), substitute the following for paragraph (a): '(a) sections 139, 140, 148, 149 or 149A, 203 and 204, and'.

Amendments

a Sch 1, Pt 4, item 1 substitutes CA 1990, s 29(9)(c).

b Sch 1, Pt 4, item 5 substitutes CA 1990, s 193(1).

c Sch 1, Pt 4, item 6(a)(i) substitutes CA 1990, s 202(1)(c).

d Sch 1, Pt 4, item 8(b) substitutes CA 1990, s 205B(2)(b)(ii).

PART 5

AMENDMENTS TO COMPANIES (AUDITING AND ACCOUNTING) ACT 2003

Item No	Section affected	Amendment
1.	Sections 8(1)(c), 9(2)(l), and 26(3)(b), (4)(a) and (b), (6), (8) and (10)(a).	Insert 'and, where applicable, Article 4 of the IAS Regulation' after 'Companies Acts' wherever occurring in those provisions.
2.	Section 26	In subsection (8)(a), insert 'and, where applicable, Article 4 of the IAS Regulation' after 'those Acts'.

Schedule 2

Amendments to Credit Institutions Regulations

Item No	*Provision affected*	*Amendment*
1.	Regulation 2	(a) In paragraph (1), insert the following after the definition of 'individual accounts': 'investment property' means land or buildings (or both) held to earn rentals or for capital appreciation (or both);'. (b) Insert the following after paragraph (1): […][a]. (c) In paragraph (4), substitute 'these Regulations, or international financial reporting standards' for 'or these Regulations'.
2.	Regulation 5	Substitute the following for paragraphs (1) and (2): […][b].
3.	Regulation 6	Substitute the following for paragraph (2)(d): […][c].
4.	Regulation 7	Substitute the following for Regulation 7: […][d].
5.	Regulation 8	(a) In paragraph (1), substitute 'established in an EEA State' for 'established in a Member State of the Community'. (b) In paragraph (3)(b), insert 'or prepared in accordance with international financial reporting standards and audited in accordance with either such Directive, as applicable,' after '1983,'. (c) Substitute the following for paragraph (4): […][e]. (d) In paragraph (6), substitute 'established in an EEA State' for 'established in a Member State of the Community'.
6.	Regulation 8A	Insert the following after Regulation 8: […][f]
7.	Regulation 10	In paragraph (1), substitute 'its individual accounts' for 'its accounts'.
8.	Regulation 11	Substitute the following for paragraph (a): […][g].
9.	Regulation 12	Substitute the following for Regulation 12: '12. Sections 151, 152, 158 (4), (5) and (6) and 191 of the Principal Act shall not apply to a company to which Regulation 7 applies.'.

Item No	*Provision affected*	*Amendment*
10.	Regulation 13	In paragraph (1), substitute 'section 193(4A)(b)(inserted by the European Communities (International Financial Reporting Standards and Miscellaneous Amendments) Regulations 2005)' for 'subsection (4)(f) of section 193'.
11.	Part I of Schedule	(a) In paragraph 1(1), substitute 'Where the directors of a company prepare Companies Act individual accounts and subject to the following provisions of this Part:'. See paragraph 1(1) of Part I of the Schedule to the European Communities (Credit Institutions: Accounts) Regulations 1992. (b) Substitute the following for paragraph 8: […][h]. (c) In Section B at item number 6 under the heading 'LIABILITIES', substitute 'provisions for liabilities' for 'provisions for liabilities and charges'. (d) In paragraph 16, substitute 'Companies Act individual accounts' for 'a company's accounts'. (e) In paragraph 19(b), substitute 'all liabilities which have arisen' for 'all liabilities and losses which have arisen or are likely to arise'. (f) Insert the following after paragraph 20: […][i]. (g) In paragraph 23, substitute 'Companies Act individual accounts' for 'a company's accounts'. (h) In paragraph 59(1)(b) and (c), delete 'and charges' wherever occurring. (i) Insert the following after paragraph 46B (inserted by the European Communities (Credit Institutions) (Fair Value Accounting) Regulations 2004 (S.I. No. 720 of 2004)): […][j]. (j) Substitute the following for paragraph 46C(1) (inserted by the European Communities (Credit Institution) (Fair Value Accounting) Regulations 2004). […][k]. (k) Insert the following after paragraph 46D (inserted by the European Communities (Credit Institution) (Fair Value Accounting) Regulations 2004). […][l]. (l) In paragraph 72A, (inserted by the European Communities (Credit Institution) (Fair Value Accounting) Regulations 2004 (S.I. No. 720 of 2004)) substitute '46A to 46E' for '46A to 46D'.

Item No	*Provision affected*	*Amendment*
		(m) In paragraph 75(2) (as amended by the European Communities (Credit Institution) (Fair Value Accounting) Regulations 2004) substitute— 'This includes the extent to which the calculation of the profit or loss is affected by the fair valuation of financial instruments and separately the extent to which it is affected by the fair valuation of other assets in accordance with paragraph 46BA.' for 'This includes the extent to which the calculation of the profit or loss is affected by the fair valuation of financial instruments.'.
12.	Part II of Schedule	(a) In paragraph 1 (1), substitute 'Where the directors of a company prepare Companies Act group accounts, those group accounts' for 'Accounts'. (b) In paragraph 2, delete subparagraphs (4), (5), (6) and (7).
13.	Part III of Schedule	In paragraphs 3(2), 5(2)(a) and 9(2)(a), insert 'or 8A' after 'Regulation 8', where it occurs in each of those provisions.
14.	Part IV of Schedule	In paragraph 5(c)— (a) delete 'or charges', and (b) substitute 'the nature of which is clearly defined and' for 'or loss'.

Amendments

a Sch 2, item 1(b) inserts EC(CIA)R 1992, reg 2, para (1A).

b Sch 2, item 2, substitutes EC(CIA)R 1992, reg 5, paras (1) and (2).

c Sch 2, item 3 substitutes EC(CIA)R 1992, reg 6, para (2)(d).

d Sch 2, item 4 substitutes EC(CIA)R 1992, reg 7.

e Sch 2, item 5(c) substitutes EC(CIA)R 1992, reg 8(4).

f Sch 2, item 6 inserts EC(CIA)R 1992, reg 8A.

g Sch 2, item 8 substitutes EC(CIA)R 1992, reg 11(a).

h Sch 2, item 11(b) substitutes EC(CIA)R 1992, Sch, Pt 1, para 8.

i Sch 2, item 11(f) inserts EC(CIA)R 1992, Sch, Pt 1, para 20A.

j Sch 2, item 11(i) inserts EC(CIA)R 1992, Sch, Pt 1, para 46BA.

k Sch 2, item 11(j) substitutes EC(CIA)R 1992, Sch, Pt 1, para 46C(1).

l Sch 2, item 11(k) inserts EC(CIA)R 1992, Sch, Pt 1, para 46E.

Schedule 3

Amendments to Insurance Undertakings Regulations

Item No	Provision affected	Amendment
1.	Regulation 2	(a) In paragraph (1), insert the following after the definition of 'individual accounts': ''investment property' means land or buildings (or both) held to earn rentals or for capital appreciation (or both);'. (b) Insert the following after paragraph (1): […][a]. (c) In paragraph (2), substitute 'these Regulations or international financial reporting standards' for 'or these Regulations'.
2.	Regulation 5	Substitute the following for paragraphs (1) and (2): […][b].
3.	Regulation 6	In paragraph (1), substitute 'Where the directors of an undertaking prepare Companies Act individual accounts and subject to these Regulations –' for 'Subject to the provisions of this Regulation –'.
4.	Regulation 7	(a) Substitute 'Companies Act accounts' for 'accounts' where it first occurs in that Regulation. (b) In paragraph (c)(ii), substitute 'all liabilities which have arisen' for 'all liabilities and losses which have arisen or are likely to arise'. (c) In paragraph (d), delete 'and'. (d) In paragraph (e), substitute 'separately, and' for 'separately.'. (e) Insert the following after paragraph (e): […][c].
5.	Regulation 8	Insert 'when preparing Companies Act accounts' after 'Regulation 7'.
6.	Regulation 9	Substitute the following for paragraph (2)(d): […][d].
7.	Regulation 10	Substitute the following for Regulation 10: […][e].
8.	Regulation 11	Substitute the following for paragraph (1)(c): […][f].
9.	Regulation 12	(a) In paragraph (1), substitute 'established in an EEA State' for 'established in a Member State of the European Union'.

Item No	*Provision affected*	*Amendment*
		(b) In paragraph (3)(b), insert 'or prepared in accordance with international financial reporting standards and audited in accordance with either such Directive, as applicable,' after '1983,'.
		(c) Substitute the following for paragraph (4): […][g].
		(d) In paragraph (6)(a), substitute 'established in an EEA State' for 'established in a Member State of the European Union'.
9	Regulation 12A	Insert the following after Regulation 12: […][h].
10.	Regulation 14	Substitute the following for paragraph (a): […][i].
11.	Regulation 15	Substitute the following for Regulation 15: […][j].
12.	Regulation 18	Substitute the following for paragraph 2(d): […][k].
13.	Part I of Schedule	(a) Substitute the following for paragraph 6 (1): […][l].
		(b) In Section A of Chapter 2 at item E under the heading 'LIABILITIES', substitute 'provisions for other risks' for 'provisions for other risks and charges'.
13.	Part II of Schedule	In paragraph 1, substitute 'Companies Act individual accounts' for 'accounts'.
14.	Part III of Schedule	(a) In paragraph 1, substitute 'Companies Act accounts' for 'accounts'.
		(b) In paragraph 14(1)(b) and (c), substitute 'provision for other risks' for 'provisions for liabilities and charges' in each place where it occurs.
14.	Part IV of Schedule	(a) In paragraph 1(1), substitute 'Where the directors of an undertaking prepare Companies Act group accounts, those group accounts' for 'Accounts'.
		(b) In paragraph 2, delete subparagraphs (4), (5) and (6).

Amendments

a Sch 3, item 1(b) inserts EC(IUA)R 1996, reg 2(1A).

b Sch 3, item 2 substitutes EC(IUA)R 1996, reg 5, paras (1) and (2).

c Sch 3, item 4 (e) inserts EC(IUA)R 1996, reg 7, para (f).

d Sch 3, item 6 substitutes EC(IUA)R 1996, reg 9, para 2(d).

e Sch 3, item 7 substitutes EC(IUA)R 1996, reg 10.

f Sch 3, item 8 substitutes EC(IUA)R 1996, reg 11, para (1)(c).

Prospectus (Directive 2003/71/EC) Regulations 2005

SI 324/2005

PART 1

PRELIMINARY AND GENERAL

PART 2

SECURITIES OUTSIDE THE AMBIT OF THESE REGULATIONS

PART 3

EXEMPTIONS FROM THE OBLIGATION TO PUBLISH A PROSPECTUS

PART 4

OBLIGATION TO PUBLISH A PROSPECTUS

PART 5

DRAWING UP OF THE PROSPECTUS – CONTENT, FORMAT AND VALIDITY

PART 6

RESPONSIBILITY ATTACHING TO THE PROSPECTUS

PART 7

APPROVAL OF PROSPECTUS

PART 8

PUBLICATION OF PROSPECTUS

PART 9

CROSS-BORDER OFFERS AND ADMISSIONS TO TRADING

PART 10

USE OF LANGUAGES

PART 11

ANNUAL INFORMATION DOCUMENT

PART 12

ADVERTISEMENTS

PART 13

COMPETENT AUTHORITY

PART 14

POWERS OF COMPETENT AUTHORITY

PART 15

ADMINISTRATIVE SANCTIONS

PART 16

PENALTIES, GENERAL AND OTHER MISCELLANEOUS PROVISIONS

SCHEDULE 1

SCHEDULE 2

SCHEDULE 3

Notes

On 11 May 1999 the European Commission adopted an Action Plan outlining a series of policy objectives and specific measures to improve the European single market for financial services during the five years following. The FSAP suggested indicative priorities and time-scales for legislative and other measures to tackle three strategic objectives:

(i) a single market for wholesale financial services;

(ii) open and secure retail markets for retail financial services; and

(iii) financial market stability with state-of-the-art prudential rules and supervision.

Although the fulfilment of these objectives, or at least the adoption of measures relied upon to achieve these objectives, took an extra couple of years, the years since 1999 have seen a complete renewal and expansion of EU measures in financial services law.

The centrepiece of the measures to fulfil the second of these three objectives is the Prospectus Directive (2003/71/EC), which was adopted on 4 November 2003, and was to be transposed into Member States' law no later than 1 July 2005. The Prospectus (Directive 2003/71/EC) Regulations transpose this Directive.

The Directive, as transposed by the Regulation, introduced a number of key reforms:

(i) Instead of the previous distinction between a prospectus (for public offers of securities) or a listing particulars (for admission of securities to listing), now there is one document only, a prospectus. It is the disclosure document, containing key financial and non-financial information, that a company makes available to potential investors when it is offering securities to the public (shares, bonds, derivative securities, etc.) to raise capital and/or when it wants its securities admitted to trading on a regulated market.

(ii) Instead of the previous requirement for convoluted rules for mutual recognition of prospectuses as listing particulars and vice versa, and mutual recognition of prospectuses in different member states, there is now a requirement for a once-off single approval process for any public issue of shares or admission to trading: once a prospectus has been approved in one member state, then that prospectus can be used for public offers or admissions to trading on a regulated market in any EU member state (and any EEA member state). As issuer has a home member state which is its regulator to the exclusion of other member states' regulators. Non-EEA issuers ("third country" issuers) are regulated by one member state only also, and the Regulations transpose the Directive's rules as to how an issuer ends up with a particular home member state.

(iii) A prospectus must contain 'all information which, according to the particular nature of the issuer and of the securities offered to the public or admitted to trading on a regulated market, is necessary to enable investors to make an informed assessment of the assets and liabilities, financial position, profit and losses, and prospects of the issuer and of any guarantor, and of the rights attaching to such securities. The information must be presented in an easily analysable and comprehensible form.' That has generally always been the case under the previous law. However it was open to the member states to require the inclusion of other information eg in Ireland with the infamous requirements of the now repealed Third Schedule of CA 1963.

Instead of these previous national variations as to the information to be included in a prospectus, there is now a standard set of requirements for the contents of a prospectus, which requirements are set out in EU Commission Regulation (EC) 809/2005 of 29 April 2004. (OJ: 30 April 2004, L 149 p 1; Corrigendum : 16 June 2004, L 215 p 3.].

Under the Lamfalussy process,[1] the Prospectus Directive is a Level 1 measure, providing frameworks and general principles. The principal Level 2 measure (which measures are left to the

European Commission to draft and enact in order to implement the Level 1 measures), in Regulation (EC) 809/2004 is referred to above. The Level 3 measures under this Directive are the Guidelines of the Committee of European Securities Regulators (CESR) whose guidance is available at http://www.cesr-eu.int. CESR has published guidance on financial information to be provided in a prospectus, as well as a series of frequently asked questions regarding prospectuses with common positions agreed by CESR members. The most recent of these Q&As issued in August 2008.

These Regulations must be read in conjunction with IFCMPA 2005, Pt 5, which provides the regime for statutory liability, both civil and criminal, for breaches of prospectus law. In addition, the Central Bank and Financial Services Authority of Ireland, more commonly referred to (at present) as 'the Financial Regulator' and in the Regulations as 'the Bank' has made "Prospectus Rules" which further clarify the law. The Commission Level 2 regs and CESR Level 3 guidance must be noted also.

1 See the introductory note to Pt 4 of IFCMPA 2005.

I, Micheál Martin, Minister for Enterprise, Trade and Employment, in exercise of the powers conferred on me by section 46 of the Investment Funds, Companies and Miscellaneous Provisions Act 2005 (No. 12 of 2005) and for the purpose of giving effect to Directive 2003/71/EC of the European Parliament and the Council of 4 November 2003 and for the other purposes mentioned in that section, hereby make the following regulations:

PART I
PRELIMINARY AND GENERAL

Citation

1.(1) These Regulations may be cited as the Prospectus (Directive 2003/71/EC) Regulations 2005.

These Regulations shall come into operation on 1 July 2005.

These Regulations shall be construed as one with the Companies Acts 1963 to 2005.

Interpretation

2.(1) In these Regulations, except where the context otherwise requires:

'Act of 2005' means the Investment Funds, Companies and Miscellaneous Provisions Act 2005;

'admission to trading' means admission of securities to trading on a regulated market and 'admission to trading in the State' means admission of securities to trading on a regulated market situated or operating in the State;

'approval' means the positive act at the outcome of the scrutiny of the completeness of the prospectus by the competent authority of the Home Member State including the consistency of the information given and its comprehensibility and 'approved' shall be construed accordingly;

'approved stock exchange' has the same meaning as it has in the Stock Exchange Act 1995 (No. 9 of 1995);

'Bank' means the Central Bank and Financial Services Authority of Ireland;

'base prospectus' means a prospectus containing all relevant information as specified in Regulations 19 and 20, and in case there is a supplement, Regulation 51, concerning the issuer and the securities to be offered to the public or admitted to trading, and, at the choice of the issuer, the final terms of the offering;

'collective investment undertaking other than the closed-end type' means unit trusts and investment companies:

(a) the object of which is the collective investment of capital provided by the public and which operate on the principle of risk-spreading;

(b) the units of which are, at the holder's request, repurchased or redeemed, directly or indirectly, out of the assets of the undertaking;

'Community act' means an act adopted by an institution of the European Communities;

'company' includes any body corporate;

'competent authority of a Home Member State' means—

(a) where the State is the Home Member State, the Bank, or

(b) where the State is a Host Member State, the central competent administrative authority designated as such under the national law of the Home Member State for the purposes of the Directive;

'contravention' includes, in relation to any provision, a failure to comply with that provision and 'contravene' shall be construed accordingly;

'Court' means the High Court;

'credit institution' means an undertaking as defined by Article 1(1)(a) of Directive 2000/1 2/EC of the European Parliament and of the Council of 20 March 2000 relating to the taking up and pursuit of the business of credit institutions;

'Directive' means Directive 2003/71/EC of the European Parliament and of the Council of 4 November 2003;

'EEA Agreement' means the Agreement on the European Economic Area signed at Oporto on 2 May 1992, as adjusted by the Protocol signed at Brussels on 17 March 1993;

'EEA State' means a state which is a contracting party to the EEA Agreement;

'enactment' includes an instrument made under an enactment;

'equity securities' means shares and other transferable securities equivalent to shares in companies, as well as any other type of transferable securities giving the right to acquire any of the aforementioned securities as a consequence of their being converted or the rights conferred by them being exercised, provided that securities of the latter type are issued by the issuer of the underlying shares or by an entity belonging to the group of the said issuer;

'EU prospectus law' has the same meaning as it has in the Act of 2005;

'functions' includes powers and duties and references to the performance of functions include, as respects the powers and duties, references to the exercise of the powers and the carrying out of the duties;

'Home Member State' means:

(a) for all issuers incorporated or formed in a Member State save in respect of securities mentioned in paragraph (c) of this definition, the Member State where the issuer has its registered office,

(b) for all issuers incorporated or formed in a state or territory which is not a Member State, save in respect of securities mentioned in paragraph (c)of this definition, the Member State where the securities are or were the subject of a public offer for the first time after 31 December 2003 or where the first application for admission to trading is or was made, at the choice of the issuer, the offeror or the person asking for admission, as the case may be, subject to a subsequent election by such an issuer if the Home Member State was not determined by its choice (but by the choice of an offeror or a person seeking admission to trading) pursuant to this paragraph,

(c) for:

(i) any issues of non-equity securities whose denomination per unit amounts to at least €1,000,

(ii) any issues of non-equity securities in a currency other than euro, whose denomination per unit amounts to at least €1,000 or the nearest practical equivalent thereto, and

(iii) any issues of non-equity securities giving the right to acquire any transferable securities or to receive a cash amount, as a consequence of their being converted or the rights conferred by them being exercised, provided that the issuer of the non-equity securities is not the issuer of the underlying securities or an entity belonging to the group of the latter issuer,

the Member State where the issuer has its registered office, or where the securities were or are to be admitted to trading or where the securities are the subject of a public offer, at the choice of the relevant person;

'Host Member State' means the state where an offer to the public is made or admission to trading is sought, when different from the Home Member State;

'implementing measures' means any measures directly applicable in consequence of the Directive and, without prejudice to the generality of the foregoing, includes the Prospectus Regulation;

'in writing' includes by facsimile;

'Irish prospectus law' has the same meaning as it has in the Act of 2005;

'issuer' means a body corporate or other legal entity which issues or proposes to issue securities;

'market operator' means one or more persons who manage or operate the business of a regulated market (or who do both those things), and may be the regulated market itself;

'Member State' means a Member State of the European Union or an EEA State;

'Minister' means the Minister for Enterprise, Trade and Employment;

'non-equity securities' means all securities that are not equity securities;

'offering programme' means a plan which would permit the issuance of non-equity securities, including warrants in any form, of a similar type or class (or both), in a continuous or repeated manner during a specified issuing period;

(5) In any case other than that referred to in paragraph (4), the Home Member State shall be determined (by reference to the issuer whose securities are being offered to the public or admitted to trading) in accordance with paragraph (a) or (b), as the case may be, of the definition of 'Home Member State' in paragraph (1).

(6) For the purpose of the definition of 'offer of securities to the public' in this Regulation 'communication' shall include an invitation to treat.

(7) Where the total balance sheet amount of an undertaking falls to be determined for the purposes of the definition of 'small and medium enterprises' in this Regulation and the accounts of the undertaking are denominated in a currency other than the Euro, the currency in which those accounts are stated shall be converted into the Euro at the rate prevailing at the end of the financial year to which they relate.

Notes

Definition of 'company' is broader than in the Companies Act 1963, s 2(1).

The European Commission issued an interpretative statement in September 2005 to clarify what offers to the public would trigger a home member state election. In brief, in order for an offer of security to the public between 31 December 2003 and 30 June 2005 to trigger a choice of home member state under this paragraph, that offer must have been: (i) an 'offer of securities to the public' within the meaning of the Prospectus Directive (2003/71/EC); and (ii) an offer considered to be a public offer under then national law. If it was an offer to the public under one but not the other, then it would not trigger the choice of home member state. What is not clear from that statement is whether an offer benefiting from a prospectus publication exemption is or is not to be considered a public offer and likewise, an offer with a value of securities offered of less than €2,500,000.

The interpretative statement also clarified that the date upon which an existing admission of securities to trading on a regulated market was to be considered was 1 July 2005. Therefore a listing which lapsed before that date would not trigger a home member state election.

The Recommendations of the Committee of European Securities Regulators (CESR) must be consulted also with respect to the interpretation of the Prospectus Regulation. The current CESR guidance is found in:

> CESR Recommendations (Ref.CESR/05-054b) of 10 February 2005 regarding the provision to disclose financial information on a range of areas and to promote greater transparency in the way in which supervisors will apply the Regulation, without imposing further obligations on issuers.
>
> CESR frequently asked questions regarding prospectuses and common positions agreed by CESR members, 6th version of August 2008 (Ref: CESR 08/602), consisting of everyday questions which are commonly posed to the CESR secretariat or CESR members, with corresponding answers. These are available at http://www.cesr-eu.org.

Interim Prospectus Rules were made in July 2005, and Final Rules were made in March 2006. These are available at http://www.financialregulator.ie.

The definition of 'transferable securities' from Directive 93/22/EC (the original Investment Services Directive, about to be superseded by the Directive on Markets in Financial Instruments (MiFID)) is as follows:

'transferable securities' shall mean:

(a) shares in companies and other securities equivalent to shares in companies,

(b) bonds and other forms of securitized debt which are negotiable on the capital market and

(c) any other securities normally dealt in giving the right to acquire any such transferable securities by subscription or exchange or giving rise to a cash settlement excluding instruments of payment.'

The MiFID definition is:

'Transferable securities' means those classes of securities which are negotiable on the capital market, with the exception of instruments of payment, such as:

(a) shares in companies and other securities equivalent to shares in companies, partnerships or other entities, and depositary receipts in respect of shares;

(b) bonds or other forms of securitised debt, including depositary receipts in respect of such securities;

(c) any other securities giving the right to acquire or sell any such transferable securities or giving rise to a cash settlement determined by reference to transferable securities, currencies, interest rates or yields, commodities or other indices or measures.'

In CESR's common positions, a common view has been expressed, now with diminishing dissent, that non-transferable employee share options do not constitute securities, and therefore are out of the scope of the Prospectus Directive, and, by extension, Member States' laws transposing the Directive.

The definition of 'money market instruments from Directive 93/22/EC is ''those classes of instruments which are normally dealt in on the money market'. The MiFID definition expands on this to read as follows:

'Money-market instruments' means those classes of instruments which are normally dealt in on the money market, such as treasury bills, certificates of deposit and commercial papers and excluding instruments of payment.'

UK legislation

FSMA 2000, ss 1, 417.

Register of Natural Persons and Small and Medium-Sized Enterprises as Qualified Investors

3. In Regulations 4 to 7—

'registrant' means a natural person or small or medium-sized enterprise whose name is for the time being entered in the register;

'register' means the register referred to in Regulation 4(1).

Definitions

'small and medium-sized enterprises': Prospectus Regs, reg 2(1).

UK legislation

FSMA 2000, s 87R, inserted by SI 2005/1433.

4.(1) The Bank shall establish and maintain a register in which there shall be entered the name of every natural person and every small and medium-sized enterprise who or which—

(a) applies in writing for inclusion on the register in accordance with the prospectus rules, and

(b) satisfies the conditions for inclusion on the register specified in paragraph (2) or (3), as appropriate.

(2) The conditions for inclusion on the register in respect of a natural person are as follows:

(a) he or she is resident in the State,

(b) he or she meets at least two of the following requirements—

(i) he or she has carried out transactions of a significant size on securities markets at an average frequency of, at least, 10 per quarter over the 4 quarters immediately prior to the application being made,

(ii) the value of his or her securities portfolio exceeds €0.5 million,

(iii) he or she works or has worked for at least one year in the financial sector in a professional position which requires knowledge of securities investment.

(3) The condition for inclusion on the register in respect of a small and medium-sized enterprise is that it has its registered office in the State.

(4) For the purposes of paragraph (2)(a) the question as to whether a natural person is resident in the State shall be determined in accordance with subsections (8) (other than paragraph (b) thereof), (9) and (10) of section 48 of the Companies (Amendment)(No.2) Act 1999.

(5) For the purposes of paragraph (2)(b)(i) the question as to whether a transaction is of significant size shall be determined in accordance with the prospectus rules.

(6) For the purposes of paragraph (2)(b)(iii) 'financial sector' includes the entities referred to in paragraph (a) of the definition of 'qualified investors' in Regulation 2.

Definitions

'Bank': Prospectus Regs, reg 2(1); 'in writing': Prospectus Regs, reg 2(1); 'qualified investors': Prospectus Regs, reg 2(1); 'prospectus rules': Prospectus Regs, reg 2(1); 'securities': Prospectus Regs, reg 2(1); 'small and medium-sized enterprises': Prospectus Regs, reg 2(1).

UK legislation

FSMA 2000, s 87R inserted by SI 2005/1433.

5.(1) The Bank may require a natural person or a small and medium-sized enterprise who or which applies for inclusion on the register to furnish such information or documents to the Bank as the Bank may reasonably specify in order to demonstrate that he or she or it satisfies the appropriate conditions referred to in Regulation 4.

(2) The Bank may require each registrant to demonstrate that he or she or it continues to satisfy the appropriate conditions referred to in Regulation 4, including, in the case of an enterprise, that it continues to fall within the definition of 'small and medium-sized enterprises' in Regulation 2.

(3) For the purpose of the registrant's demonstrating the matters referred to in paragraph (2), pursuant to a requirement made of the registrant thereunder, Regulation 4(2)(b)(i)

shall apply as if for 'the 4 quarters immediately prior to the application being made' in that provision there were substituted 'the 4 quarters immediately prior to the requirement being made under Regulation 5(2)'.

(4) The Bank shall delete from the register any registrant that fails to demonstrate to the Bank's reasonable satisfaction, pursuant to paragraph (2), that the registrant continues to satisfy the appropriate conditions referred to in Regulation 4, including, in the case of an enterprise, that it continues to fall within the definition of 'small and medium-sized enterprises' in Regulation 2.

Definitions

'Bank': Prospectus Regs, reg 2(1); 'small and medium-sized enterprises': Prospectus Regs, reg 2(1).

UK legislation

FSMA 2000, s 87R inserted by SI 2005/1433.

6. Without prejudice to the Bank's obligations under the Data Protection Acts 1988 to 2003, the Bank shall—

(a) take due care in respect of the security of the information and data provided to it by a natural person or small and medium-sized enterprise applying for inclusion on the register,

(b) take appropriate measures to establish the bona fides of an issuer or offeror seeking to have made available to him, her or it information included on the register pursuant to Regulation 7,

(c) update promptly the information and data relating to a registrant on the register when instructed by a registrant to do so,

(d) upon notification in writing at any time from a registrant that the registrant no longer wishes to have his, her or its name included on the register the Bank shall, as soon as practicable after the notification, delete the name from the register.

Definitions

'Bank': Prospectus Regs, reg 2(1); 'in writing': Prospectus Regs, reg 2(1); 'issuer: Prospectus Regs, reg 2(1); 'offeror': Prospectus Regs, reg 2(1); 'small and medium-sized enterprises': Prospectus Regs, reg 2(1).

UK legislation

FSMA 2000, s 348.

7.(1) Subject to Regulation 6 (b), the Bank shall make the register available to issuers and offerors on such conditions as it may reasonably specify provided such conditions are not inconsistent with these Regulations or the Directive.

(2) Issuers and offerors shall only use the information made available to them under paragraph (1) for the purposes of making or contemplating the making of an offer of securities to be addressed to qualified investors in the State.

(3) An issuer or offeror who or which fails to comply with paragraph (2) shall be guilty of an offence.

Definitions

'Bank': Prospectus Regs, reg 2(1); 'Directive': Prospectus Regs, reg 2(1); 'issuer': Prospectus Regs, reg 2(1); 'offeror': Prospectus Regs, reg 2(1); 'qualified investors': Prospectus Regs, reg 2(1); 'securities': Prospectus Regs, reg 2(1).

UK legislation

FSMA 2000, s 347.

PART 2
SECURITIES OUTSIDE THE AMBIT OF THESE REGULATIONS

8.(1) These Regulations shall not apply to—

(a) units issued by collective investment undertakings other than the closed-end type,

(b) non-equity securities issued by a Member State or by one of a Member State's regional or local authorities, by public international bodies of which one or more Member States are members, by the European Central Bank or by the central banks of the Member States,

(c) shares in the capital of a central bank of a Member State,

(d) securities unconditionally and irrevocably guaranteed by a Member State or by one of a Member State's regional or local authorities,

(e) securities issued by associations with legal status or non-profit-making bodies, recognised by a Member State, with a view to their obtaining the means necessary to achieve their non-profit-making objectives,

(f) non-equity securities issued in a continuous or repeated manner by credit institutions provided that these securities—

(i) are not subordinated, convertible or exchangeable,

(ii) do not give a right to subscribe to or acquire other types of securities and that they are not linked to a derivative instrument,

(iii) materialise reception of repayable deposits,

(iv) are covered by a deposit guarantee scheme under Directive 94/19/EC of the European Parliament and of the Council on deposit-guarantee schemes,

(g) non-fungible shares of capital whose main purpose is to provide the holder with a right to occupy an apartment, or other form of immovable property or a part thereof and where the shares cannot be sold on without this right being given up;

(h) securities included in an offer where the offer expressly limits the amount of the total consideration for the offer to less than €2,500,000,

(i) 'bostadsobligationer' issued repeatedly by credit institutions in Sweden whose main purpose is to grant mortgage loans, provided that—

(i) the 'bostadsobligationer' issued are of the same series,

(ii) the 'bostadsobligationer' are issued on tap during a specified issuing period,

(iii) the terms and conditions of the 'bostadsobligationer' are not changed during the issuing period,

(iv) the sums deriving from the issue of the said 'bostadsobligationer', in accordance with the articles of association of the issuer, are placed in assets which provide sufficient coverage for the liability deriving from securities,

(j) non-equity securities issued in a continuous or repeated manner by credit institutions where the total consideration of the offer is less than €50,000,000, which limit shall be calculated over a period of 12 months, provided that these securities—

(i) are not subordinated, convertible or exchangeable,

(ii) do not give a right to subscribe to or acquire other types of securities and that they are not linked to a derivative instrument.

(2) For the purposes of paragraph (1)(e) an association or body is recognised by a Member State if it has been established by, under or pursuant to the national legislation of the Member State.

(3) No offer of securities by an offeror or issuer shall be deemed to fall within paragraph (1)(h) unless the amount of the total consideration for the offer when aggregated with the consideration for all previous offers of securities of the same type in the issuer concerned made by the same offeror or issuer within the period of 12 months expiring on the date the offer is made is less than €2,500,000 (but excluding for the purposes of such aggregation any offer of securities made prior to the commencement of these Regulations).

(4) For the purposes of any other enactment, it is declared that paragraph (3) provides the means by which the limit specified by paragraph (1)(h) is calculated.

(5) Notwithstanding subparagraph (b), (d), (h), (i) or (j) of paragraph (1), where the State is the Home Member State a relevant person may draw up a prospectus in respect of the securities mentioned in that subparagraph and submit it to the Bank for approval in accordance with these Regulations and the other provisions of Irish prospectus law.

Definitions

'approval': Prospectus Regs, reg 2(1); 'Bank': Prospectus Regs, reg 2(1); 'collective investment undertaking other than the closed-end type': Prospectus Regs, reg 2(1); 'credit institution': Prospectus Regs, reg 2(1); 'enactment': Prospectus Regs, reg 2(1); 'Home Member State': Prospectus Regs, reg 2(1); 'Irish prospectus law': Prospectus Regs, reg 2(1); 'issuer': Prospectus Regs, reg 2(1); 'Member State': Prospectus Regs, reg 2(1); 'non-equity securities': Prospectus Regs, reg 2(1); 'offeror': Prospectus Regs, reg 2(1); 'prospectus': Prospectus Regs, reg 2(1);

'relevant person': Prospectus Regs, reg 2(1); 'securities': Prospectus Regs, reg 2(1); 'securities issued in a continuous or repeated manner': Prospectus Regs, reg 2(1); 'units of a collective investment undertaking': Prospectus Regs, reg 2(1).

UK legislation

FSMA 2000, Sch 11A Part 1 inserted by SI 2005/1433.

PART 3

EXEMPTIONS FROM THE OBLIGATION TO PUBLISH A PROSPECTUS

Excluded Offers

9.(1) The obligation to publish a prospectus under Regulation 12 shall not apply to an offer of securities in the State falling within one or more than one of the following subparagraphs—

(a) an offer of securities addressed solely to qualified investors,

(b) an offer of securities addressed to fewer than 100 persons, other than qualified investors,

(c) an offer of securities addressed to investors where the minimum consideration payable pursuant to the offer is at least €50,000 per investor, for each separate offer,

(d) an offer of securities whose denomination per unit amounts to at least €50,000,

(e) an offer of securities where the offer expressly limits the amount of the total consideration for the offer to less than €100,000.

(2) Any subsequent resale of securities which were previously the subject of an offer described in paragraph (1) shall be regarded as a separate offer for the purposes of determining whether it is an offer of securities to the public within the meaning of these Regulations.

(3) The obligation to publish a prospectus pursuant to Regulation 12 shall apply to the placement of securities through financial intermediaries, if none of subparagraphs (a) to (e) of paragraph (1) apply at the final placement.

(4) No offer of securities shall be deemed to come within paragraph (1)(e) unless the amount of the total consideration for the offer when aggregated with the consideration for all previous offers of securities of the same type in the issuer concerned made by the same offeror or issuer within the period of 12 months expiring on the date the offer is made is less than €100,000 (but excluding for the purpose of such aggregation any offer of securities made prior to the commencement of these Regulations).

Definitions

'issuer': Prospectus Regs, reg 2(1); 'offer of securities to the public': Prospectus Regs, reg 2(1); 'offeror': Prospectus Regs, reg 2(1); 'prospectus': Prospectus Regs, reg 2(1); 'publication': Prospectus Regs, reg 2(1); 'qualified investors': Prospectus Regs, reg 2(1); 'securities': Prospectus Regs, reg 2(1).

Note

This reg (when contrasted against art 3 of the Prospectus Directive 2003/71/EC on which it is based) is focused on an offer of securities in the State, ie made to persons located in Ireland, rather than across the European Economic Area (which is, naturally, how the Prospectus Directive is focused). Rather than seeking to invigilate what offers are made in other jurisdictions, the Irish law is concerned only with offers in Ireland and in that context (and by reference to such offers only) exempts offers in the State from the prospectus requirements made, inter alia, to fewer than 100 persons.

It is technically possible to interpret the words 'offer of securities addressed to fewer than 100 persons' by reference to the entire EEA – however, if that were the intention of the transposition, it would clearly be an incorrect transposition of Art 3.2, which refers to fewer than 100 persons per member state, meaning potentially up to 2,772 persons in the entire EEA.

The more correct interpretation is to construe 'offer of securities addressed to fewer than 100 persons' by reference to the 'offer of securities in the State' in the first phrase of the reg; ie when considering whether a prospectus is required for an offer in Ireland, one does not need to consider the contemporaneous offer or offers made in other jurisdictions, where such jurisdictions' laws will regulate matters.

It is important to remember that the Prospectus Directive is not directly applicable EU federal law. Rather, even in a maximum harmonization measure, it provides the framework within which the individual member states transpose the law; subject to that transposition being consistent with the Directive, it is the transposition, not the Directive, which constitutes Irish law.

UK legislation

FSMA 2000, s 86 inserted by SI 2005/1433.

10.(1) The obligation to publish a prospectus pursuant to Regulation 12 shall not apply to offers of securities to the public in the State of the following types of securities—

(a) shares issued in substitution for shares of the same class already issued, if the issuing of such new shares does not involve any increase in the issued capital,

(b) securities offered in connection with a takeover by means of an exchange offer, provided that a document is available containing information which is regarded by the Bank as being equivalent to that of a prospectus, taking into account the requirements of any Community act,

(c) securities offered, allotted or to be allotted in connection with a merger, provided that a document is available containing information which is regarded by the Bank as being equivalent to that of a prospectus, taking into account the requirements of any Community act,

(d) shares offered, allotted or to be allotted free of charge to existing shareholders, and dividends paid out in the form of shares of the same class as the shares in respect of which such dividends are paid, provided that a document is made available containing information on the number and nature of the shares and the reasons for and details of the offer,

(e) securities offered, allotted or to be allotted to existing or former directors or employees by their employer or by an affiliated undertaking which in either case has securities already admitted to trading on a regulated market and provided that a document is made available containing information on the number and nature of the securities and the reasons for and details of the offer; for the purposes of this subparagraph 'affiliated undertaking' includes any parent undertaking or subsidiary undertaking of the employer or another subsidiary undertaking of that parent undertaking.

(2) The reference in paragraph (1)(e) to the offering or allotment of securities by an employer or an affiliated undertaking shall, in the case of such an offer or allotment that takes place for the purpose of an employees' share scheme or an employee share ownership trust, be construed as a reference to such offering or allotment, whether effected directly or indirectly by the employer or the affiliated undertaking.

(3) In paragraph (2)—

'employees' share scheme' means a scheme which is approved for the purposes of Chapter 1 of Part 17 of the Taxes Consolidation Act 1997 and Schedule 11 to that Act;

'employee share ownership trust' means a trust which is approved for the purposes of Chapter 2 of Part 17 of the Taxes Consolidation Act 1997 and Schedule 12 to that Act.

Definitions

'admission to trading': Prospectus Regs, reg 2(1); 'Bank': Prospectus Regs, reg 2(1); 'Community act': Prospectus Regs, reg 2(1); 'prospectus': Prospectus Regs, reg 2(1); 'publication': Prospectus Regs, reg 2(1); 'regulated market': Prospectus Regs, reg 2(1); 'securities': Prospectus Regs, reg 2(1).

Notes

Reg 10(1)(b) is in fact not an exemption, as it provides that one is exempt from the requirement to produce a prospectus provided one prepares a document which is effectively the same as a prospectus.

Reg 10(1)(e), from the requirement to prepare a prospectus for a public offer should be contrasted with that for admission of securities to a regulated market in reg 11(1)(f). In this reg 10, the exemption arises if the issuer has *any* securities admitted to trading whereas in reg 11(1)(f) it is necessary for those securities admitted to trading to be of the same class. This exemption under this reg has been transposed faithfully from the Directive, as has its UK counterpart. The European Commission Internal Market Directorate has expressed the view that the broad nature of the exemption for public offers is an anomaly, and ought to be construed as though it were drafted along the lines of that underpinning the reg 11(1)(f) exemption. This means that in a number of EU jurisdictions this exemption is framed differently, along the lines of the Commission's preferred interpretation.

In the Guidance of the Committee of European Securities Regulators (CESR) of 18 July 2006 (Ref. CESR/06-296d) CESR outlines the information which the respective Regulators would expect to find in a document containing 'information on the number and nature of the securities and the reasons for and details of the offer'.

UK legislation

FSMA 2000, s 85(5)(b); Prospectus Rules, Rule 1.2.2.

11.(1) The obligation to publish a prospectus under Regulation 13 shall not apply to the admission to trading in the State of the following types of securities—

(a) shares representing, over a period of 12 months, less than 10 per cent of the number of shares of the same class already admitted to trading on the same regulated market,

(b) shares issued in substitution for shares of the same class already admitted to trading on the same regulated market, if the issuing of such shares does not involve any increase in the issued capital,

(c) securities offered in connection with a takeover by means of an exchange offer, provided that a document is available containing information which is regarded by the Bank as being equivalent to that of a prospectus, taking into account the requirements of any Community act,

(d) securities offered, allotted or to be allotted in connection with a merger, provided that a document is available containing information which is regarded by the Bank as being equivalent to that of a prospectus, taking into account the requirements of any Community act,

(e) shares offered, allotted or to be allotted free of charge to existing shareholders, and dividends paid out in the form of shares of the same class as the shares in respect of which such dividends are paid, provided that the first-mentioned shares are of the same class as the shares already admitted to trading on the same regulated market and that a document is made available containing information on the number and nature of the shares and the reasons for and details of the offer,

(f) securities offered, allotted or to be allotted to existing or former directors or employees by their employer or an affiliated undertaking, which in either case has securities already admitted to trading on the same regulated market, provided that the first-mentioned securities are of the same class as the securities already admitted to trading on that market and that a document is made available containing information on the number and nature of the securities and the reasons for and detail of the offer; for the purposes of this subparagraph 'affiliated undertaking' includes any parent undertaking or subsidiary undertaking of the employer or another subsidiary undertaking of that parent undertaking,

(g) shares resulting from the conversion or exchange of other securities or from the exercise of the rights conferred by other securities, provided that the said shares are of the same class as the shares already admitted to trading on the same regulated market,

(h) securities already admitted to trading on another regulated market, if the following conditions are satisfied—

(i) that these securities, or securities of the same class, have been admitted to trading on that other regulated market for more than 18 months,

(ii) that, for securities first admitted to trading on a regulated market after 31 December 2003, the admission to trading on that other regulated market was associated with an approved prospectus made available to the public in conformity with EU prospectus law,

(iii) that, unless subparagraph (ii) applies, for securities first admitted to listing after 30 June 1983, listing particulars were approved in accordance with the requirements of Directive 80/390/EEC or Directive 2001/34/EC,

(iv) that the ongoing obligations for trading on that other regulated market have been fulfilled,

Definitions

'admission to trading': Prospectus Regs, reg 2(1); 'contravention': Prospectus Regs, reg 2(1); 'issuer': Prospectus Regs, reg 2(1); 'offeror: Prospectus Regs, reg 2(1); 'securities': Prospectus Regs, reg 2(1).

UK legislation

FSMA 2000, s 85(3).

16.(1) A market operator that admits securities to trading in circumstances where it knows that that admission involves a contravention of Regulation 13 shall be guilty of an offence.

(2) A market operator in the State shall be entitled to rely on a copy of a notice of the decision of the Bank to approve a prospectus under Regulation 35, or, as the case may be, a copy of the certificate of approval from the competent authority of the Home Member State as evidence of compliance of the prospectus with EU prospectus law.

Definitions

'admission to trading': Prospectus Regs, reg 2(1); 'approval': Prospectus Regs, reg 2(1); 'Bank': Prospectus Regs, reg 2(1); 'competent authority of a Home Member State': Prospectus Regs, reg 2(1); 'contravention': Prospectus Regs, reg 2(1); 'EU prospectus law': Prospectus Regs, reg 2(1); 'market operator': Prospectus Regs, reg 2(1); 'prospectus': Prospectus Regs, reg 2(1); 'securities': Prospectus Regs, reg 2(1).

17. Without prejudice to its right to stipulate conditions for admission to trading and the production of evidence (whether in documentary form or otherwise) of compliance with those conditions following the commencement of these Regulations, a market operator in the State shall not require any person applying for admission of securities to trading on a regulated market to produce a prospectus, listing particulars or any other document equivalent thereto as a condition of admission of the securities to trading other than a prospectus drawn up and approved in compliance with the applicable provisions of EU prospectus law.

Definitions

'admission to trading': Prospectus Regs, reg 2(1); 'approval': Prospectus Regs, reg 2(1); 'EU prospectus law': Prospectus Regs, reg 2(1); 'market operator': Prospectus Regs, reg 2(1); 'prospectus': Prospectus Regs, reg 2(1); 'regulated market': Prospectus Regs, reg 2(1); 'securities': Prospectus Regs, reg 2(1).

PART 5
DRAWING UP OF THE PROSPECTUS – CONTENT, FORMAT AND VALIDITY

18. The provisions of this Part shall apply to prospectuses relating to issuers or securities, as the case may be, in respect of which the State is the Home Member State.

Definitions

'Home Member State': Prospectus Regs, reg 2(1); 'issuer': Prospectus Regs, reg 2(1); 'prospectus': Prospectus Regs, reg 2(1); 'securities': Prospectus Regs, reg 2(1).

Contents of Prospectus

19.(1) Without prejudice to Regulations 24 and 25, a prospectus shall contain all information which, according to the particular nature of the issuer and of the securities offered to the public or admitted to trading, is necessary to enable investors to make an informed assessment of—

(a) the assets and liabilities, financial position, profit and losses, and prospects of the issuer and of any guarantor, and

(b) the rights attaching to such securities.

(2) The information contained in the prospectus shall be consistent and presented in an easily analysable and comprehensible form.

(3) The prospectus shall contain information concerning the issuer and the securities to be offered to the public or to be admitted to trading.

(4) In the circumstances in which paragraph 4(b) of Schedule 2 to these Regulations applies, the prospectus shall also contain the information referred to in that paragraph.

Definitions

'admission to trading': Prospectus Regs, reg 2(1); 'issuer': Prospectus Regs, reg 2(1); 'prospectus': Prospectus Regs, reg 2(1); 'securities': Prospectus Regs, reg 2(1).

UK legislation

FSMA 2000, s 87A(2) inserted by SI 2005/1433.

Minimum Information

20. Without prejudice to the generality of Regulation 19 and subject to Regulation 26, the prospectus shall contain the minimum information required under the Prospectus Regulation.

Definitions

'prospectus': Prospectus Regs, reg 2(1); 'Prospectus Regulation': Prospectus Regs, reg 2(1).

Note

The information specified in the Prospectus Regulation is identical for all member states, in view of the fact that the Regulation is directly applicable, rather than being a Directive requiring transposition.

UK legislation

FSA Prospectus Rules, Rule 2.3.1.

Summary

21.(1) Subject to paragraph (4), a prospectus shall include a summary.

(2) The summary shall, in a brief manner and in non-technical language, convey the essential characteristics and risks associated with the issuer, any guarantor and the securities, in the language in which the prospectus was originally drawn up.

(3) The summary shall also contain a warning that—

(a) it should be read as an introduction to the prospectus,

(b) any decision to invest in the securities should be based on consideration of the prospectus as a whole by the investor,

(c) where a claim relating to the information contained in a prospectus is brought before a court, the plaintiff investor might, under the national legislation of the Member States, have to bear the costs of translating the prospectus before the legal proceedings are initiated, and

(d) civil liability attaches to those persons responsible under law for the contents of the prospectus but only if the summary is misleading, inaccurate or inconsistent when read together with the other parts of the prospectus.

(4) Where the prospectus relates to the admission to trading of non-equity securities having a denomination of at least €50,000, this Regulation shall not apply.

Definitions

'admission to trading': Prospectus Regs, reg 2(1); 'issuer: Prospectus Regs, reg 2(1); 'Member State': Prospectus Regs, reg 2(1); 'non-equity securities': Prospectus Regs, reg 2(1); 'prospectus': Prospectus Regs, reg 2(1); 'securities': Prospectus Regs, reg 2(1).

UK legislation

FSMA 2000, s 87A(5), (6) inserted by SI 2005/1433.

Single or Separate Documents

22.(1) Subject to Regulation 23, a prospectus may be drawn up as a single document or separate documents.

(2) A prospectus composed of separate documents shall divide the required information into—

(a) a registration document containing the required information relating to the issuer,

(b) a securities note containing the required information concerning the securities offered to the public or to be admitted to trading, and

(c) a summary.

Definitions

'admission to trading': Prospectus Regs, reg 2(1); 'issuer': Prospectus Regs, reg 2(1); 'prospectus': Prospectus Regs, reg 2(1); 'securities': Prospectus Regs, reg 2(1).

UK legislation

FSA Prospectus Rules, Rule 2.2.1.

Base Prospectus

23.(1) In the following cases, at the election of a relevant person, a prospectus may consist of a base prospectus—

(a) in a case where the securities are non-equity securities, including warrants in any form, issued under an offering programme,

(b) in a case where the securities are non-equity securities issued in a continuous or repeated manner by credit institutions—

(i) if the sums deriving from the issue of those securities, under national legislation, are placed in assets which provide sufficient coverage for the liability deriving from securities until their maturity date, and

(ii) if, in the event of the insolvency of the related credit institution, the said sums are intended, as a priority, to repay the capital and interest falling due, without prejudice to the provisions of Directive 2001/24/EC of the European Parliament and of the Council of 4 April 2001 on the reorganisation and winding up of credit institutions.

(2) The information given in the base prospectus shall be supplemented, if necessary, in accordance with Regulation 51, with updated information on the issuer and on the securities to be offered to the public or to be admitted to trading.

(3) If the final terms of the offer are not included in either the base prospectus or a supplement, the final terms shall be filed with the Bank in accordance with the prospectus rules and published in accordance with Part 8 when each public offer is made as soon as practicable and, if possible, in advance of the beginning of the offer.

(4) The provisions of Regulation 24(1)(a) shall be applicable in any case coming within paragraph (3).

Definitions

'admission to trading': Prospectus Regs, reg 2(1); 'Bank': Prospectus Regs, reg 2(1); 'base prospectus': Prospectus Regs, reg 2(1); 'credit institution': Prospectus Regs, reg 2(1); 'issuer': Prospectus Regs, reg 2(1); 'non-equity securities': Prospectus Regs, reg 2(1); 'offering programme': Prospectus Regs, reg 2(1); 'public offer': Prospectus Regs, reg 2(1); 'prospectus': Prospectus Regs, reg 2(1); 'prospectus rules': Prospectus Regs, reg 2(1); 'publication': Prospectus Regs, reg 2(1); 'relevant person': Prospectus Regs, reg 2(1); 'securities': Prospectus Regs, reg 2(1); 'securities issued in a continuous or repeated manner': Prospectus Regs, reg 2(1).

UK legislation

FSA Prospectus Rules, Rule 2.2.7.

Omission of Information

24.(1) Where pursuant to Regulation 23 the final offer price or amount of securities (or both) to be subject to a public offer cannot be included in the prospectus—

(a) the criteria or the conditions (or both) in accordance with which the above elements will be determined or, in the case of price, the maximum price, shall be disclosed in the prospectus, or

(b) it shall be a term of the offer that acceptances of or applications for the purchase or subscription of securities (whether accepted by the issuer or not) may be withdrawn or revoked during a period expiring not less

than 2 working days after a statement of the final offer price and amount of securities which will be offered to the public has been filed and published in accordance with Regulation 23(3).

Definitions

'issuer': Prospectus Regs, reg 2(1); 'public offer': Prospectus Regs, reg 2(1); 'prospectus': Prospectus Regs, reg 2(1); 'publication': Prospectus Regs, reg 2(1); 'securities': Prospectus Regs, reg 2(1); 'working day': Prospectus Regs, reg 2(1).

UK legislation

FSA Prospectus Rules, Rule 2.3.2.

25. The Bank may authorise the omission from a prospectus of information required under these Regulations or any other provision of Irish prospectus law, if it considers that—

(a) disclosure of such information would be contrary to the public interest, or

(b) disclosure of such information would be seriously detrimental to the issuer, provided that the omission would not be likely to mislead the public with regard to facts and circumstances essential for an informed assessment of the issuer, offeror or guarantor, if any, and of the rights attached to the securities to which the prospectus relates, or

(c) such information is of minor importance only for a specific offer or admission to trading and is not such as will influence the assessment of the financial position and prospects of the issuer, offeror or guarantor, if any.

Definitions

'admission to trading': Prospectus Regs, reg 2(1); 'Bank': Prospectus Regs, reg 2(1); 'Irish prospectus law': Prospectus Regs, reg 2(1); 'issuer': Prospectus Regs, reg 2(1); 'offeror': Prospectus Regs, reg 2(1); 'prospectus': Prospectus Regs, reg 2(1); 'securities': Prospectus Regs, reg 2(1).

UK legislation

FSMA 2000, s 87B(1) inserted by SI 2005/1433.

26. Without prejudice to the requirement to give adequate information to investors, where, in exceptional cases, certain information required by any implementing measures to be included in a prospectus would be inappropriate to the issuer's sphere of activity or to the legal form of the issuer or to the securities to which the prospectus relates, the prospectus may omit that required information but, unless there is no such equivalent information, shall contain information equivalent to that required information.

Definitions

'implementing measures': Prospectus Regs, reg 2(1); 'issuer': Prospectus Regs, reg 2(1); 'prospectus': Prospectus Regs, reg 2(1); 'securities': Prospectus Regs, reg 2(1).

UK legislation

FSA Prospectus Rules, Rule 2.5.1.

Incorporation by Reference

27.(1) Subject to paragraph (3) information may be incorporated in a prospectus by reference to one or more previously or simultaneously published documents that have been approved by the Bank or filed with it in accordance with the EU prospectus law, in particular pursuant to Part 11, or filed with the competent authority for the time being for the purposes of Titles IV and V of Directive 2001/34/EC and in accordance with those Titles.

(2) The information incorporated by reference in accordance with paragraph (1) shall be the latest available to the issuer.

(3) The summary shall not incorporate information by reference.

Definitions

'approval': Prospectus Regs, reg 2(1); 'Bank': Prospectus Regs, reg 2(1); 'EU prospectus law': Prospectus Regs, reg 2(1); 'issuer': Prospectus Regs, reg 2(1); 'prospectus': Prospectus Regs, reg 2(1); 'publication': Prospectus Regs, reg 2(1).

UK legislation

FSA Prospectus Rules, Rule 2.4.

---

28. When information is incorporated by reference pursuant to Regulation 27, a cross-reference list must be provided in order to enable investors to identify easily specific items of information.

UK legislation

FSA Prospectus Rules, Rule 2.4.5.

Prospectuses Consisting of Separate Documents

29.(1) A relevant person may apply to the Bank for approval of the registration document referred to in Regulation 22.

(2) A relevant person who has a registration document approved by the Bank under paragraph (1) shall only be required to draw up a securities note and a summary when its securities are offered to the public or to be admitted to trading.

(3) In the circumstances referred to in paragraph (2), the securities note shall provide information that would normally be provided in the registration document if there has been a material change or recent development which could affect investors' assessments since the latest updated registration document or any supplement was approved.

(4) In the circumstances referred to in paragraph (2), the securities note and summary shall be subject to separate approval under these Regulations and any other provisions of Irish prospectus law.

(5) Where a registration document has been filed but not approved in accordance with these Regulations and any other provisions of Irish prospectus law, the entire documentation, including updated information, shall be subject to approval in accordance with these Regulations and any other provisions of such law.

Definitions

'admission to trading': Prospectus Regs, reg 2(1); 'approval': Prospectus Regs, reg 2(1); 'Bank': Prospectus Regs, reg 2(1); 'Irish prospectus law': Prospectus Regs, reg 2(1); 'relevant person': Prospectus Regs, reg 2(1); 'securities': Prospectus Regs, reg 2(1).

UK legislation

FSA Prospectus Rules, Rules 2.2.4, 2.2.5, 2.2.6.

Validity of a Prospectus, Base Prospectus and Registration Document

30.(1) Provided it is updated by the issue of a supplement where required, the period of validity of a prospectus or a related document for the purposes of an offer of securities to the public or admission to trading shall be as follows—

(a) subject to subparagraphs (b) to (d), an approved prospectus shall be valid for 12 months after its publication,

(b) in the case of securities referred to in Regulation 23(1)(a), the base prospectus, previously filed and published, shall be valid for 12 months after its filing,

(c) in the case of non-equity securities referred to in Regulation 23(1)(b), the base prospectus as previously filed and published shall be valid until no more of the securities concerned are issued in a continuous or repeated manner,

(d) a registration document, as referred to in Regulation 22(2)(a), previously filed, shall be valid for the purposes of Regulation 29(2) for 12 months after its filing.

(2) The registration document accompanied by the securities note, updated if applicable in accordance with Regulation 29(3), and the summary shall, together, be considered to constitute a valid prospectus.

Definitions

'admission to trading': Prospectus Regs, reg 2(1); 'approval': Prospectus Regs, reg 2(1); 'base prospectus': Prospectus Regs, reg 2(1); 'non-equity securities': Prospectus Regs, reg 2(1); 'offer of securities to the public': Prospectus Regs, reg 2(1); 'prospectus': Prospectus Regs, reg 2(1); 'publication': Prospectus Regs, reg 2(1); 'publication': Prospectus Regs, reg 2(1); 'securities': Prospectus Regs, reg 2(1); 'securities issued in a continuous or repeated manner': Prospectus Regs, reg 2(1).

UK legislation

FSA Prospectus, Rule 2.2.3.

PART 6

RESPONSIBILITY ATTACHING TO THE PROSPECTUS

31.(1) The provisions of this Part shall govern responsibility in respect of the contents of a prospectus relating to issuers or securities, as the case may be, in respect of which the State is the Home Member State.

(2) For the purposes of these Regulations, responsibility for the information given in a prospectus attaches, subject to the provisions of that Schedule, in each of the cases specified in Schedule 1 to these Regulations to the persons specified in the relevant case, and references in these Regulations to responsible persons shall be construed accordingly.

Definitions

'Home Member State': Prospectus Regs, reg 2(1); 'issuer': Prospectus Regs, reg 2(1); 'prospectus': Prospectus Regs, reg 2(1); 'securities': Prospectus Regs, reg 2(1).

UK legislation

FSMA 2000, s 84(1)(d).

32.(1) The responsible persons shall be clearly identified in a prospectus by their names and functions or, in the case of legal persons, their names and registered offices.

(2) A prospectus shall contain declarations by the responsible persons that, to the best of their knowledge:

(a) the information contained in the prospectus is in accordance with the facts, and

(b) that the prospectus makes no omission likely to affect its import save information if any omitted in accordance with Regulation 25 (a).

but shall be deemed to have been made on publication of the prospectus.

(3) Neither this Regulation nor Regulation 31 prejudices section 41 of the Act of 2005.

Definitions

'functions': Prospectus Regs, reg 2(1); 'prospectus': Prospectus Regs, reg 2(1); 'publication': Prospectus Regs, reg 2(1).

UK legislation

FSA Prospectus Rules, Appendix 3.

PART 7

APPROVAL OF PROSPECTUS

Approval of the Prospectus

33. For the purposes of this Part—

'applicant' means a relevant person who applies to the Bank for approval;

'time limits' means the time limits provided for under Regulations 35 and 36.

34. The provisions of Regulations 35 to 39 shall apply in circumstances where the State is the Home Member State or where the function of approving of a prospectus has been transferred to the Bank in accordance with Regulation 41.

Definitions

'approval': Prospectus Regs, reg 2(1); 'Bank': Prospectus Regs, reg 2(1); 'functions': Prospectus Regs, reg 2(1); 'Home Member State': Prospectus Regs, reg 2(1); 'prospectus': Prospectus Regs, reg 2(1); 'relevant person': Prospectus Regs, reg 2(1).

UK legislation

FSMA 2000, ss 87A(1)(a), 87F, inserted by SI 2005/1433.

35.(1) An applicant shall submit a draft of the prospectus to the Bank and any other information and documents the Bank may require in accordance with the prospectus rules.

(2) Subject to paragraph (3), the Bank shall notify the applicant of its decision regarding the approval of the prospectus in writing within 10 working days after the submission of the draft prospectus in accordance with paragraph (1).

(3) The reference in paragraph (2) to 10 working days shall be construed as a reference to 20 working days if the public offer involves securities issued by an issuer which does not have any securities admitted to trading and which has not previously offered securities to the public.

(4) If the Bank fails to give a decision as to whether to approve a prospectus within the time limits, such failure shall not be deemed to constitute approval by it of the application.

Definitions

'admission to trading': Prospectus Regs, reg 2(1); 'applicant': Prospectus Regs, reg 33; 'approval': Prospectus Regs, reg 2(1); 'Bank': Prospectus Regs, reg 2(1); 'in writing': Prospectus Regs, reg 2(1); 'issuer': Prospectus Regs, reg 2(1); 'public offer': Prospectus Regs, reg 2(1); 'prospectus': Prospectus Regs, reg 2(1); 'prospectus rules': Prospectus Regs, reg 2(1); 'securities': Prospectus Regs, reg 2(1); 'working day': Prospectus Regs, reg 2(1) 'time limits': Prospectus Regs, reg 33.

Note

The Bank has, pursuant to its entitlement to do so under reg 79, delegated certain tasks under the regs to the Irish Stock Exchange, including the task of reviewing prospectuses. The Prospectus Rules issued by the Bank stipulate that the prospectus be filed with the Irish Stock Exchange as its delegate authority.

UK legislation

FSMA 2000, ss 87B, 87C inserted by SI 2005/1433.

36.(1) If the Bank finds, on reasonable grounds, that the documents submitted to it are incomplete or that supplementary information is needed, the time limits referred to in Regulation 35 shall apply only from the date on which such supplementary information is provided by the applicant.

(2) If the documents submitted to it are incomplete or supplementary information is needed the Bank shall, within 10 working days of the submission of the application, notify the applicant of that fact.

Definitions

'applicant': Prospectus Regs, reg 33; 'Bank': Prospectus Regs, reg 2(1); 'time limts': Prospectus Regs, reg 33; 'working day': Prospectus Regs, reg 2(1).

UK legislation

FSMA 2000, s 87C(4)–(6) inserted by SI 2005/1433.

37. The Bank shall not approve a prospectus unless it is satisfied that the applicable requirements imposed by or under these Regulations and any other provisions of Irish prospectus law have been complied with.

Definitions

'approval': Prospectus Regs, reg 2(1); 'Bank': Prospectus Regs, reg 2(1); 'Irish prospectus law': Prospectus Regs, reg 2(1); 'prospectus': Prospectus Regs, reg 2(1).

UK legislation

FSMA 2000, s 87A(1)(b), (c), inserted by SI 2005/1433.

38.(1) Upon the prospectus being approved, the applicant shall file the prospectus—

- (a) with the Bank forthwith, and
- (b) if the issuer is a company registered under the Companies Acts 1963 to 2005, with the registrar of companies within 14 days after its publication in accordance with Part 8.

(2) An applicant who fails to comply with paragraph (1) shall be guilty of an offence.

Definitions

'applicant': Prospectus Regs, reg 33; 'approval': Prospectus Regs, reg 2(1); 'Bank': Prospectus Regs, reg 2(1); 'company': Prospectus Regs, reg 2(1); 'issuer': Prospectus Regs, reg 2(1); 'prospectus': Prospectus Regs, reg 2(1); 'publication': Prospectus Regs, reg 2(1).

Application to Court

39.(1) If the Bank refuses to approve a prospectus the applicant may apply to the Court in a summary manner to have such refusal reviewed.

(2) An application under paragraph (1) shall be made within 28 days after the date of notification of the Bank's decision under Regulation 35.

(3) On the hearing of an application under this Regulation, the Court shall confirm the decision of the Bank unless the applicant establishes to the Court's satisfaction that the applicant has complied with the procedures specified by these Regulations and any other provisions of Irish prospectus law in all material respects and that the prospectus

meets the requirements of these Regulations and any other such provisions in all material respects.

(4) If the Court is satisfied that those procedures and requirements have been complied with in all material respects the Court may set aside the decision of the Bank and in such a case shall remit the matter to the Bank which shall thereupon reconsider the matter and make a further decision in accordance with those procedures and requirements.

Definitions

'applicant': Prospectus Regs, reg 33; 'approval': Prospectus Regs, reg 2(1); 'Bank': Prospectus Regs, reg 2(1); 'Court': Prospectus Regs, reg 2(1); 'Irish prospectus law': Prospectus Regs, reg 2(1); 'prospectus': Prospectus Regs, reg 2(1).

UK legislation

FSMA 2000, s 87N, inserted by SI 2005/1433.

Transfer to Another Competent Authority

40.(1) The Bank may, with the consent of the competent authority, transfer the function of approving a prospectus to the competent authority of another Member State.

(2) Any transfer under paragraph (1) shall be notified to the applicant within 3 working days after the date on which the decision by the Bank to make the transfer is made.

Definitions

'applicant': Prospectus Regs, reg 33; 'Bank': Prospectus Regs, reg 2(1); 'competent authority of a Home Member State': Prospectus Regs, reg 2(1); 'functions': Prospectus Regs, reg 2(1); 'prospectus': Prospectus Regs, reg 2(1); 'working day': Prospectus Regs, reg 2(1).

UK legislation

FSMA 2000, s 87E, inserted by SI 2005/1433.

Transfer from Another Competent Authority

41.(1) In circumstances where the State is not the Home Member State, subject to the consent of the Bank, the competent authority of the Home Member State may transfer the function of approving a prospectus to the Bank in accordance with EU prospectus law.

(2) In the case of a transfer such as is referred to in paragraph (1) the relevant time limits shall apply from the date on which the decision by the competent authority of the Home Member State to transfer the function is made.

Definitions

'approval': Prospectus Regs, reg 2(1); 'Bank': Prospectus Regs, reg 2(1); 'competent authority of a Home Member State': Prospectus Regs, reg 2(1); 'EU prospectus law': Prospectus Regs, reg 2(1); 'functions': Prospectus Regs, reg 2(1); 'Home Member State': Prospectus Regs, reg 2(1); 'prospectus': Prospectus Regs, reg 2(1); 'time limits': Prospectus Regs, reg 33.

UK legislation

FSMA 2000, s 87F, inserted by SI 2005/1433.

42. Where—

(a) the Bank has transferred the function of approving a prospectus to the competent authority of another Member State under Regulation 40, or

(b) in circumstances where the State is not the Home Member State, the competent authority of the Home Member State has transferred the function of approving a prospectus to the competent authority of another Member State under EU prospectus law,

then if the prospectus is approved by such competent authority under EU prospectus law the prospectus shall be deemed to have been approved for the purposes of these Regulations.

Definitions

'approval': Prospectus Regs, reg 2(1); 'Bank': Prospectus Regs, reg 2(1); 'competent authority of a Home Member State': Prospectus Regs, reg 2(1); 'EU prospectus law': Prospectus Regs, reg 2(1); 'functions': Prospectus Regs, reg 2(1); 'Home Member State': Prospectus Regs, reg 2(1); 'Member State': Prospectus Regs, reg 2(1); 'prospectus': Prospectus Regs, reg 2(1).

UK legislation

FSMA 2000, s 85(1), (7).

Liability of Bank and Other Bodies

43. Without prejudice to the generality of section 33AJ of the Central Bank Act 1942, approval of a prospectus by the Bank shall not be deemed to be or construed as a representation or warranty as to the solvency or credit – worthiness of the issuer or the truth or accuracy of the contents of the prospectus.

Definitions

'approval': Prospectus Regs, reg 2(1); 'Bank': Prospectus Regs, reg 2(1); 'issuer': Prospectus Regs, reg 2(1); 'prospectus': Prospectus Regs, reg 2(1).

PART 8
PUBLICATION OF PROSPECTUS

44.(1) This Part shall apply to offers of securities to the public or admissions to trading in respect of which the State is the Home Member State.

(2) Upon a prospectus having been approved and filed in accordance with these Regulations, the relevant person shall:

(a) make the prospectus available to the public as soon as practicable and in any case, at a reasonable time in advance of, and at the latest at the beginning of, the offer to the public or the admission to trading of the securities involved,

(b) in the case of an initial public offer of a class of shares not already admitted to trading that is to be admitted to trading for the first time, make the prospectus available to the public at the earlier of the time referred to in paragraph (a) or 6 working days before the end of the offer.

(3) A relevant person who fails to comply with paragraph (2) shall be guilty of an offence.

Definitions

'admission to trading': Prospectus Regs, reg 2(1); 'approval': Prospectus Regs, reg 2(1); 'Home Member State': Prospectus Regs, reg 2(1); 'offers of securities to the public': Prospectus Regs, reg 2(1); 'public offer': Prospectus Regs, reg 2(1); 'prospectus': Prospectus Regs, reg 2(1); 'relevant person': Prospectus Regs, reg 2(1); 'working day': Prospectus Regs, reg 2(1).

UK legislation

FSMA 2000, s 85(3), FSA Prospectus Rules, Rules 1.2.1, 3.2.2, 3.2.3.

45.(1) Subject to paragraph (2), a prospectus shall be deemed available to the public in accordance with Regulation 44 when published in one of the following ways—

(a) by insertion in one or more newspapers circulated throughout, or widely circulated in, the Member State or Member States in which the public offer is to be made or admission to trading is to be sought,

(b) in a printed form to be made available, free of charge, to the public at the offices of the market on which the securities are being admitted to trading, or at the registered office of the issuer and at the offices of the financial intermediaries placing or selling the securities, including paying agents,

(c) in an electronic form on the issuer's website and, if applicable, on the website of the financial intermediaries placing or selling the securities, including paying agents,

(d) in an electronic form on the website of the regulated market or markets where the admission to trading is sought, or

(e) in electronic form on the website of the Bank (if the Bank decides to provide a service of publishing prospectuses on its website).

(2) The issuer of equity securities (other than equity securities issued by a collective investment undertaking subject to these Regulations) which publishes a prospectus in respect of such securities in accordance with subparagraph (a) or (b) of paragraph (1) shall also publish the prospectus in an electronic form in accordance with subparagraph (c) of paragraph (1).

Definitions

'admission to trading': Prospectus Regs, reg 2(1); 'Bank': Prospectus Regs, reg 2(1); 'equity securities': Prospectus Regs, reg 2(1); 'issuer': Prospectus Regs, reg 2(1); 'Member State': Prospectus Regs, reg 2(1); 'public offer': Prospectus Regs, reg 2(1); 'prospectus': Prospectus Regs, reg 2(1); 'publication': Prospectus Regs, reg 2(1); 'regulated market': Prospectus Regs, reg 2(1); 'securities': Prospectus Regs, reg 2(1).

Note

Under the Bank's Prospectus Rules it is provided that the Bank will keep and publish a copy of the prospectus on its website http://www.financialregulator.ie.

UK legislation

FSMA 2000, s 85(3), FSA Prospectus Rules, Rule 3.2.4.

46.(1) In respect of a prospectus relating to equity securities (other than equity securities issued by a collective investment undertaking subject to these Regulations), the relevant person shall publish a notice stating how the prospectus has been made available pursuant to Regulation 45 and where it can be obtained by the public.

(2) A relevant person who fails to comply with paragraph (1) shall be guilty of an offence.

Definitions

'equity securities': Prospectus Regs, reg 2(1); 'prospectus': Prospectus Regs, reg 2(1); 'publication': Prospectus Regs, reg 2(1).

UK legislation

FSMA 2000, s 85(3); FSA Prospectus Rules, Rule 3.1.1(10).

47.(1) In the case of a prospectus comprising several documents or incorporating information by reference (or both), the documents and information making up the prospectus may be published and circulated separately provided that the documents are made available to the public in accordance with the arrangements referred to in Regulation 45.

(2) Each such document shall indicate where the other documents constituting the full prospectus may be obtained.

Definitions

'prospectus': Prospectus Regs, reg 2(1); 'publication': Prospectus Regs, reg 2(1); 'relevant person': Prospectus Regs, reg 2(1).

UK legislation

FSMA 2000, s 85(3), FSA Prospectus Rules, Rule 3.2.8.

---

48. The text and the format of the prospectus, and of any of the supplements published, shall at all times be identical to the original version approved by the Bank.

Definitions

'approval': Prospectus Regs, reg 2(1); 'Bank': Prospectus Regs, reg 2(1); 'prospectus': Prospectus Regs, reg 2(1); 'publication': Prospectus Regs, reg 2(1).

UK legislation

FSMA 2000, s 85(3), FSA Prospectus Rules, Rule 3.2.5.

49.(1) Where the prospectus is made available by publication in electronic form pursuant to Regulation 45, a paper copy of it must nevertheless be delivered to each investor who purchases or subscribes for the securities involved (or intends to purchase or subscribes for such securities or bona fide contemplates such purchase or subscription) upon the investor's request and free of charge by the relevant person or the financial intermediaries placing or selling the securities.

(2) A relevant person of financial intermediary who fails to comply with a request under paragraph (1) shall be guilty of an offence (unless a prior request by the investor concerned in respect of the particular prospectus has already been complied with by another person referred to in that paragraph).

Definitions

'prospectus': Prospectus Regs, reg 2(1); 'publication': Prospectus Regs, reg 2(1); 'relevant person': Prospectus Regs, reg 2(1); 'securities': Prospectus Regs, reg 2(1).

UK legislation

FSMA 2000, s 85(3), FSA Prospectus Rules, Rule 3.2.6.

50. The Bank shall publish on its website over a period of 12 months all the prospectuses approved(or, alternatively, at its discretion, the list of prospectuses) approved by it in accordance with Part 7, including, if applicable, a hyperlink to the prospectus published on the website of the issuer, or on the website of the regulated market.

Definitions

'approval': Prospectus Regs, reg 2(1); 'Bank': Prospectus Regs, reg 2(1); 'issuer': Prospectus Regs, reg 2(1); 'prospectus': Prospectus Regs, reg 2(1); 'publication': Prospectus Regs, reg 2(1); 'regulated market': Prospectus Regs, reg 2(1).

UK legislation

FSMA 2000, s 85(3), FSA Prospectus Rules, Rule 3.2.7.

Supplements to the Prospectus

51.(1) A relevant person shall include in a supplement to the prospectus every significant new factor, material mistake or inaccuracy relating to the information included in a prospectus which is capable of affecting the assessment of the securities and which arises or is noted between the time when the prospectus is approved and the final closing of the offer to the public or, as the case may be, the time when trading on a regulated market begins.

(2) Such a supplement shall be the subject of the procedures under Part 7 in relation to approval of prospectuses in the same way as the original prospectus but those procedures shall, in general, be completed in a maximum of 7 working days and the

supplement shall be published at least in the manner in which the original prospectus was published.

(3) The summary, and any translations thereof, shall also be supplemented, if necessary, to take account of the new information included in the supplement.

(4) Where there are significant new factors, material mistakes or inaccuracies as referred to in paragraph (1) of which the Bank becomes aware the Bank shall require the approval and publication of a supplement.

(5) In exercising its powers under paragraph (4) the Bank shall have regard to any significant new factors, material mistakes or inaccuracies brought to its attention by the competent authority of a Host Member State.

Definitions

'approval': Prospectus Regs, reg 2(1); 'Bank': Prospectus Regs, reg 2(1); 'Host Member State': Prospectus Regs, reg 2(1); 'in writing': Prospectus Regs, reg 2(1); 'prospectus': Prospectus Regs, reg 2(1); 'public offer': Prospectus Regs, reg 2(1); 'publication': Prospectus Regs, reg 2(1); 'regulated market': Prospectus Regs, reg 2(1); 'relevant person': Prospectus Regs, reg 2(1); 'securities': Prospectus Regs, reg 2(1); 'working day': Prospectus Regs, reg 2(1).

UK legislation

FSMA 2000, s 87G(1), inserted by SI 2005/1433.

52. It shall be an implied term of all public offers to which this Part applies that persons who agree to purchase or subscribe for, or apply to purchase or subscribe for, the securities concerned before a supplement is published shall have the right, exercisable within a period not to be less than 2 working days after the publication of the supplement, to withdraw their applications or acceptances by notice in writing to the issuer or offeror, as the case may be.

Definitions

'issuer': Prospectus Regs, reg 2(1); 'offeror': Prospectus Regs, reg 2(1); 'securities': Prospectus Regs, reg 2(1); 'working day': Prospectus Regs, reg 2(1).

UK legislation

FSMA 2000, s 87Q(4), inserted by SI 2005/1433.

PART 9

CROSS-BORDER OFFERS AND ADMISSIONS TO TRADING

53. In this Part 'third country issuer' means an issuer incorporated or having its registered office in a state or territory which is not a Member State.

Definitions

'issuer': Prospectus Regs, reg 2(1); 'Member State': Prospectus Regs, reg 2(1).

UK legislation

FSMA 2000, s 87H, inserted by SI 2005/1433.

Community Scope of Approvals of Prospectuses

54.(1) Where the State is a Host Member State and without prejudice to Regulations 89 and 90, a prospectus approved by the competent authority of the Home Member State (including any prospectus drawn up under Article 1(3) of the Directive or the national legislation of the Home Member State implementing the said Article 1(3)) shall be valid for a public offer or an admission to trading in the State, provided that the Bank is notified in accordance with Regulation 55.

(2) The Bank shall not undertake any approval or administrative procedures relating to prospectuses falling within paragraph (1).

(3) If there are significant new factors, material mistakes or inaccuracies, as referred to in Regulation 51, arising since the approval of a prospectus falling within paragraph (1), the Bank may draw the attention of the competent authority of the Home Member State to the need for any new information to be included in a supplement to the prospectus.

Definitions

'admission to trading': Prospectus Regs, reg 2(1); 'approval': Prospectus Regs, reg 2(1); 'Bank': Prospectus Regs, reg 2(1); 'competent authority of a Home Member State': Prospectus Regs, reg 2(1); 'Directive': Prospectus Regs, reg 2(1); 'Home Member State': Prospectus Regs, reg 2(1); 'Host Member State': Prospectus Regs, reg 2(1); 'prospectus': Prospectus Regs, reg 2(1); 'public offer': Prospectus Regs, reg 2(1).

UK legislation

FSMA 2000, s 87H, inserted by SI 2005/1433.

---

55. The notification referred to in Regulation 54(1) shall consist of—

(a) the certificate referred to in Regulation 57,

(b) a copy of the prospectus, and

(c) if required by the Bank, a translation of the summary of the prospectus into English or Irish (at the election of the relevant person).

Definitions

'Bank': Prospectus Regs, reg 2(1); 'prospectus': Prospectus Regs, reg 2(1); 'relevant person': Prospectus Regs, reg 2(1).

Note

The Bank's Prospectus Rules set out the procedure for 'passporting' prospectuses from other member states. It is noteworthy that the Rules stipulate that the home Member State's competent authority notifies the Bank directly, as opposed to accepting a letter tendered by the applicant for administrative sign-off by the Bank.

UK legislation

FSMA 2000, s 87H(1)(a)-(c), inserted by SI 2005/1433.

56.(1) In circumstances where the State is the Home Member State and the Bank has approved a prospectus (including a prospectus submitted under Regulation 8(5)), the Bank shall, at the request of the relevant person or the person responsible for drawing up the prospectus, provide the competent authority of each Host Member State specified in the request with the certificate referred to in Regulation 57, together with a copy of the prospectus.

(2) A request of the Bank made under paragraph (1) shall be complied with by it within 3 working days after the making of the request or, if the request is submitted together with the draft prospectus, within 1 working day after the approval of the prospectus.

(3) If required by the competent authority of the Host Member State under EU prospectus law, the notification under paragraph (1) shall be accompanied by a translation of the summary produced under the responsibility of the relevant person or person responsible for drawing up the prospectus.

Definitions

'approval': Prospectus Regs, reg 2(1); 'Bank': Prospectus Regs, reg 2(1); 'EU prospectus law': Prospectus Regs, reg 2(1); 'Home Member State': Prospectus Regs, reg 2(1); 'Host Member State': Prospectus Regs, reg 2(1); 'prospectus': Prospectus Regs, reg 2(1); 'relevant person': Prospectus Regs, reg 2(1); 'working day': Prospectus Regs, reg 2(1).

UK legislation

FSMA 2000, s 87E, inserted by SI 2005/1433.

57. The certificate referred to in Regulations 55 and 56 is a certificate of approval attesting that the prospectus has been drawn up in accordance with the Directive and recording whether any information has been omitted from the prospectus in accordance with Article 8(2) and (3) of the Directive or the relevant provision of EU prospectus law implementing the said Article and, if so, the justification for such omission.

Definitions

'approval': Prospectus Regs, reg 2(1); 'Directive': Prospectus Regs, reg 2(1); 'EU prospectus law': Prospectus Regs, reg 2(1); 'prospectus': Prospectus Regs, reg 2(1).

UK legislation

FSMA 2000, s 87H(2),(3), inserted by SI 2005/1433.

58. Regulations 54 to 57 shall apply to any supplement.

Issuers Incorporated in Third Countries

59.(1) This Regulation shall apply to third country issuers in respect of which the State is the Home Member State.

(2) The Bank may approve a prospectus pursuant to Part 7 for an offer of securities to the public or for admission to trading, drawn up in accordance with the legislation of the third country governing an issuer referred to in paragraph (1), provided that:

(a) the prospectus has been drawn up in accordance with international standards set by international securities commission organisations, including the IOSCO disclosure standards, and

(b) the information requirements, including information of a financial nature, are equivalent to the requirements under the Directive.

Definitions

'admission to trading': Prospectus Regs, reg 2(1); 'approval': Prospectus Regs, reg 2(1); 'Bank': Prospectus Regs, reg 2(1); 'Directive': Prospectus Regs, reg 2(1); 'Home Member State': Prospectus Regs, reg 2(1); 'offer of securities to the public': Prospectus Regs, reg 2(1); 'prospectus': Prospectus Regs, reg 2(1).

Note

The transitional provisions as to accounting principles to be applied in Art 35 of the Prospectus Regs are now extended by a further period of two years to accommodate the discussion between the US and the EU on equivalence of financial information: Commission Regulation (EC) 1787/2006 (OJ L 337 5.12.2006, p 17).

UK legislation

FSA Prospectus Rules, Rule 4.2.1.

60. In the case of an offer of securities to the public or admission to trading of securities, issued by a third country issuer, in circumstances where the State is a Host Member State, the requirements of Regulations 54 and 55 and Part 10 shall apply.

Definitions

'admission to trading': Prospectus Regs, reg 2(1); 'Host Member State': Prospectus Regs, reg 2(1); 'offer of securities to the public': Prospectus Regs, reg 2(1); 'securities': Prospectus Regs, reg 2(1).

UK legislation

FSA Prospectus Rules, Rule 4.2.2.

Co-operation between Authorities

61.(1) The Bank shall—

(a) co-operate with the competent authorities of other Member States designated under EU prospectus law whenever necessary for the purpose of performing its functions, and

(b) render assistance to competent authorities of other Member States in the performance of their functions under EU prospectus law.

(2) In particular and without prejudice to the generality of paragraph (1), the Bank shall—

(a) exchange information and cooperate with competent authorities in other Member States when an issuer has more than one home competent authority because of its various classes of securities, or where the function of approving a prospectus has been transferred to the competent authority of another Member State pursuant to Regulation 40,

(b) closely cooperate with competent authorities in other Member State when requiring suspension or prohibition of trading for securities traded in various Member States in order to ensure (in so far as practicable) equivalent treatment between trading venues and protection of investors.

(3) Where appropriate, the competent authority of the Host Member State may request the assistance of the competent authority of the Home Member State from the stage at which a particular case is scrutinised for the purposes of approval in accordance with EU prospectus law, in particular as regards a new type or rare forms of securities.

(4) The competent authority of the Home Member State may request the competent authority of the Host Member State to furnish to it information in relation to any items specific to the relevant market.

Definitions

'approval': Prospectus Regs, reg 2(1); 'Bank': Prospectus Regs, reg 2(1); 'competent authority of a Home Member State': Prospectus Regs, reg 2(1); 'EU prospectus law': Prospectus Regs, reg 2(1); 'functions': Prospectus Regs, reg 2(1); 'Host Member State': Prospectus Regs, reg 2(1); 'issuer': Prospectus Regs, reg 2(1); 'Member State': Prospectus Regs, reg 2(1); 'prospectus': Prospectus Regs, reg 2(1); 'securities': Prospectus Regs, reg 2(1).

UK legislation

FSMA 2000, s 87I inserted by SI 2005/1433.

---

62. Without prejudice to its powers under Regulations 87 and 88 and 95, the Bank may consult with market operators if, in the Bank's opinion, it is necessary to do so and, in particular, when deciding to suspend, or to request a regulated market to suspend or prohibit trading.

Definitions

'Bank': Prospectus Regs, reg 2(1); 'market operator': Prospectus Regs, reg 2(1); 'regulated market': Prospectus Regs, reg 2(1).

PART 10

USE OF LANGUAGES

Use of Languages

63. Where the State is the Home Member State the following provisions shall apply in respect of the language or languages in which the prospectus is to be drawn up and published:

(a) where an offer of securities to the public is made or admission to trading is sought only in the State, the prospectus shall be drawn up and published in a language accepted by the Bank,

(b) where an offer of securities to the public is made or admission to trading is sought in one or more Member States other than the State—

(i) the prospectus shall be drawn up and published in each Host Member State either in a language accepted by the competent authority of the Host Member State or in a language customary in the sphere of international finance, at the election of the relevant person,

(ii) the competent authority of each Host Member State may only require that the summary be translated into the official language of the Host Member State,

(iii) for the purposes of the scrutiny of the prospectus by the Bank pursuant to Part 7, the prospectus shall be drawn up either in a language accepted by the Bank or in a language customary in the sphere of international finance, at the election of the relevant person,

(c) where an offer of securities to the public is made or admission to trading is sought in more than one Member State including the State—

(i) the prospectus shall be drawn up and published in a language accepted by the Bank,

(ii) the prospectus shall also be drawn up and published in each Host Member State in a language accepted by the competent authority of the Host Member State or in a language customary in the sphere of international finance, at the election of the relevant person, and

(iii) the competent authority of each Host Member State may only require that the summary be translated into the official language of the Host Member State.

Definitions

'admission to trading': Prospectus Regs, reg 2(1); 'Bank': Prospectus Regs, reg 2(1); 'Home Member State': Prospectus Regs, reg 2(1); 'Host Member State': Prospectus Regs, reg 2(1); 'Member State': Prospectus Regs, reg 2(1); 'offer of securities to the public': Prospectus Regs, reg 2(1); 'prospectus': Prospectus Regs, reg 2(1); 'publication': Prospectus Regs, reg 2(1); 'relevant person': Prospectus Regs, reg 2(1); 'a language customary in the sphere of international finance': Prospectus Regs, reg 67.

Note

The Bank in its Prospectus Rules states that English and Irish are acceptable languages.

UK legislation

FSA Prospectus Rules, Rules 4.1.1, 4.1.2, 4.1.3(1).

---

64. In circumstances where the State is the Host Member State the following provisions shall apply in relation to the language in which a prospectus is to be drawn up and published in the State—

(a) where a public offer is made or admission to trading is sought in one or more Member States other than the Home Member State then—

(i) the prospectus shall be drawn up in a language accepted by the Bank or in a language customary in the sphere of international finance, at the election of the relevant person,

(ii) the Bank may only require that the summary be translated into Irish or English, at the election of the relevant person,

(b) where the public offer is made or admission to trading is sought in more than one Member State including the Home Member State then—

(i) the prospectus shall be drawn up in a language accepted by the competent authority of the Home Member State,

(ii) the prospectus shall also be drawn up in a language accepted by the Bank or in a language customary in the sphere of international finance, at the election of the relevant person,

(iii) the Bank may only require that the summary be translated into Irish or English, at the election of the relevant person.

Definitions

'admission to trading': Prospectus Regs, reg 2(1); 'Bank': Prospectus Regs, reg 2(1); 'competent authority of a Home Member State': Prospectus Regs, reg 2(1); 'Home Member State': Prospectus Regs, reg 2(1); 'Host Member State': Prospectus Regs, reg 2(1); 'Member State': Prospectus Regs, reg 2(1); 'prospectus': Prospectus Regs, reg 2(1); 'public offer': Prospectus Regs, reg 2(1); 'publication': Prospectus Regs, reg 2(1); 'relevant person': Prospectus Regs, reg 2(1).

Note

The Bank, in its Prospectus Rules, states that English and Irish are acceptable languages.

UK legislation

FSA Prospectus Rules, Rule 4.1.3(2).

---

65. Whether the State is the Home Member State or a Host Member State where admission to trading on a regulated market of non-equity securities whose denomination per unit amounts to at least €50,000 is sought in one or more Member States the prospectus shall be drawn up either in a language accepted by the competent authority of the Home Member State and competent authorities of the Host Member States or in a language customary in the sphere of international finance, at the election of the relevant person.

Definitions

'admission to trading': Prospectus Regs, reg 2(1); 'competent authority of a Home Member State': Prospectus Regs, reg 2(1); 'Home Member State': Prospectus Regs, reg 2(1); 'Host Member State': Prospectus Regs, reg 2(1); 'Member State': Prospectus Regs, reg 2(1); 'non-equity securities': Prospectus Regs, reg 2(1); 'prospectus': Prospectus Regs, reg 2(1); 'regulated market': Prospectus Regs, reg 2(1); 'relevant person': Prospectus Regs, reg 2(1); 'a language customary in the sphere of international finance': Prospectus Regs, reg 67.

Note

The Bank, in its Prospectus Rules, states that English and Irish are acceptable languages.

UK legislation

FSA Prospectus Rules, Rule 4.1.4.

---

66. The Bank shall, from time to time, publish in such manner as it thinks fit a notice specifying—

(a) the languages accepted by it, for the time being, for the purpose of these Regulations, and

(b) any other requirements, for the time being, of it for the purposes of this Part.

Definitions

'Bank': Prospectus Regs, reg 2(1); 'publication': Prospectus Regs, reg 2(1).

Note

The Bank, in its Prospectus Rules, states that English and Irish are acceptable languages.

UK legislation

FSMA 2000, s 84(1)(c).

---

67. For the purposes of this Part 'a language customary in the sphere of international finance' includes the English language.

UK legislation

FSA Prospectus Rules, Rules 4.1.5.

PART 11

ANNUAL INFORMATION DOCUMENT

68. This Part shall apply to—

(a) issuers in respect of which the State is the Home Member State, and

(b) issuers, not falling within paragraph (a), of securities in respect of which the State is the Home Member State.

Definitions

'Home Member State': Prospectus Regs, reg 2(1); 'issuer': Prospectus Regs, reg 2(1); 'securities': Prospectus Regs, reg 2(1).

69.(1) Issuers which have securities admitted to trading shall at least annually draw up a document that contains or refers to all information that they have published or made available to the public over the preceding 12 months in one or more Member States and in third countries in compliance with their obligations under Community acts dealing with the regulation of securities, issuers of securities and securities markets.

(2) Without prejudice to the generality of paragraph (1), the document referred to in that paragraph shall refer to the information required pursuant to Community acts relating to companies, Directive 2001/34/EC and Regulation (EC) No 1606/2002 of the European Parliament and of the Council of 19 July 2002 on the application of international accounting standards.

(3) An issuer which fails to comply with paragraph (1) shall be guilty of an offence.

Definitions

'admission to trading': Prospectus Regs, reg 2(1); 'Community act': Prospectus Regs, reg 2(1); 'company': Prospectus Regs, reg 2(1); 'issuer': Prospectus Regs, reg 2(1); 'Member State': Prospectus Regs, reg 2(1); 'publication': Prospectus Regs, reg 2(1); 'securities': Prospectus Regs, reg 2(1).

UK legislation

FSA Prospectus Rules, Rule 5.2.1.

70.(1) The document referred to in Regulation 69 shall be filed with the Bank in accordance with the prospectus rules and published in accordance with Article 27 of the Prospectus Regulation.

(2) Where that document refers to information, it shall state where the information can be obtained.

(3) An issuer which fails to comply with paragraph (1) shall be guilty of an offence.

Definitions

'Prospectus Regulation': Prospectus Regs, reg 2(1); 'prospectus rules': Prospectus Regs, reg 2(1); 'publication': Prospectus Regs, reg 2(1).

UK legislation

FSA Prospectus Rules, Rule 5.2.9.

71. Regulations 69 and 70 shall not apply to issuers whose only securities admitted to trading are non-equity securities the denomination per unit of which amounts to at least €50,000.

Definitions

'admission to trading': Prospectus Regs, reg 2(1); 'Bank': Prospectus Regs, reg 2(1); 'issuer': Prospectus Regs, reg 2(1); 'non-equity securities': Prospectus Regs, reg 2(1); 'securities': Prospectus Regs, reg 2(1).

UK legislation

FSA Prospectus Rules, Rule 5.2.2.

72. Issuers admitted to trading in the State in circumstances where the State is not the Home Member State shall file annual information documents within the meaning of Article 10 of the Directive with the competent authority of the Home Member State.

Definitions

'admission to trading': Prospectus Regs, reg 2(1); 'competent authority of a Home Member State': Prospectus Regs, reg 2(1); 'Directive': Prospectus Regs, reg 2(1); 'Home Member State': Prospectus Regs, reg 2(1); 'issuer': Prospectus Regs, reg 2(1).

PART 12
ADVERTISEMENTS

73. This Part shall apply to advertisements relating to a public offer or an admission to trading in one or more Member States—

(a) made in or from the State by or on behalf of any relevant person, or

(b) made in or from any other Member State by or on behalf of any relevant person,

in connection with a public offer or an admission to trading in respect of which the State is the Home Member State.

Definitions

'admission to trading': Prospectus Regs, reg 2(1); 'Home Member State': Prospectus Regs, reg 2(1); 'Member State': Prospectus Regs, reg 2(1); 'public offer': Prospectus Regs, reg 2(1); 'relevant person': Prospectus Regs, reg 2(1).

UK legislation

FSA Prospectus Rules, Rule 3.3.

74.(1) Subject to paragraph (2), an advertisement to which this Part applies shall comply with the principles set out in Schedule 2 to these Regulations.

(2) Paragraph 4 of Schedule 2 to these Regulations shall not apply to cases where a relevant person is obliged to draw up a prospectus pursuant to EU prospectus law (or not being so obliged nevertheless draws up a prospectus pursuant to Regulation 8 (5) or the corresponding provisions of the national legislation of the other Member State concerned implementing the Directive).

(3) An advertisement that complies with paragraph (1) shall not be considered as a prospectus for the purpose of these Regulations.

(4) A relevant person shall be guilty of an offence if an advertisement that fails to comply with paragraph (1) is made or issued in or from the State by or on behalf of the relevant person.

Definitions

'Directive': Prospectus Regs, reg 2(1); 'EU prospectus law': Prospectus Regs, reg 2(1); 'Member State': Prospectus Regs, reg 2(1); 'prospectus': Prospectus Regs, reg 2(1); 'relevant person': Prospectus Regs, reg 2(1).

UK legislation

FSA Prospectus Rules, Rule 3.3.2.

75. Without prejudice to any power exercisable by the Bank under any other enactment, the Bank may monitor and supervise compliance by relevant persons with the principles set out in Schedule 2 to these Regulations.

Definitions

'Bank': Prospectus Regs, reg 2(1); 'enactment': Prospectus Regs, reg 2(1); 'relevant person': Prospectus Regs, reg 2(1).

UK legislation

FSMA 2000, s 87K inserted by SI 2005/1433.

76. For the purpose of its function under Regulation 75, the Bank may give a direction to a relevant person to do or not to do such things as are necessary to ensure compliance with the principles set out in Schedule 2 to these Regulations.

Definitions

'Bank': Prospectus Regs, reg 2(1); 'functions': Prospectus Regs, reg 2(1); 'relevant person': Prospectus Regs, reg 2(1).

UK legislation

FSMA 2000, s 87K inserted by SI 2005/1433.

77.(1) Without prejudice to the generality of Regulation 76, a direction under that Regulation may do all or any of the following:

(a) prohibit the issue of a specified advertisement,

(b) require the relevant person to modify a specified advertisement or an advertisement of a specified description in a specified manner,

(c) prohibit the issue by the person of any advertisements which are substantial repetitions of a specified advertisement,

(d) require the relevant person to withdraw any specified advertisement or any advertisement of a specified description,

(e) require the relevant person to include specified information in any advertisement to be published by the person or on person's behalf,

(f) require the relevant person to arrange the publication of a correction of an advertisement which contravenes Regulation 74,

(g) require the relevant person to arrange the publication, in a manner specified by the Bank, of the fact that an offence under Regulation 74 has been committed by the relevant person and that a fine or term of imprisonment, if any, has been imposed on the relevant person in respect of a conviction therefor.

(2) In this Regulation 'specified' means specified in a direction under this Regulation.

(3) Where a direction has been given by the Bank under this Regulation the provisions of Regulation 88(4) to (13) shall, with any necessary modifications, apply to the direction.

(4) A direction under this Regulation may be given to any relevant person referred to in Regulation 73.

Definitions

'Bank': Prospectus Regs, reg 2(1); 'contravene': Prospectus Regs, reg 2(1); 'publication': Prospectus Regs, reg 2(1); 'relevant person': Prospectus Regs, reg 2(1).

UK legislation

FSMA ss 77(1), 87L(2)(b), 87L(3)(b), inserted by SI 2005/1433.

PART 13
COMPETENT AUTHORITY

Designation of Competent Authority

78.(1) The Bank is designated as the central competent administrative authority for the purposes of Article 21(1) of the Directive and shall be responsible for carrying out the obligations provided for in the Directive and for ensuring that the provisions adopted pursuant to the Directive are applied.

(2) The Bank shall be independent in the performance of its functions under these Regulations.

Definitions

'Bank': Prospectus Regs, reg 2(1); 'Directive': Prospectus Regs, reg 2(1); 'functions': Prospectus Regs, reg 2(1).

UK legislation

FSMA ss 72(1), 72(2), Sch 7, inserted by SI 2005/1433.

Delegation of functions

79.(1) The Bank may delegate to an approved stock exchange, subject to such conditions as the Bank specifies, any of the functions that it is obliged or authorised to perform under Irish prospectus law or under the Directive other than the following functions—

(a) the approval of prospectuses and supplements pursuant to Part 7 (but not any act involving the scrutiny of prospectuses or supplements),

(b) the issuing of a certificate referred to in Regulation 57,

(c) functions under Regulations 40, 41, 5 1(2), 56(1), 59(2), 79, 85, 88, 89 and 90 or this Regulation,

(d) Parts 15 and 16.

(2) Any person to whom functions are delegated under paragraph (1) shall have, by virtue of the delegation, all such powers as are necessary to perform those functions.

(3) Any delegation of functions shall be in writing and specify the functions to be performed and the conditions subject to which they are to be performed.

(4) The conditions referred to in paragraph (3) shall include a provision obliging the stock exchange to whom a function or functions concerned are delegated to act and be organised in such a manner as to avoid conflicts of interest and so that information obtained from performing the function is not used unfairly or to prevent competition.

(5) A delegation under this Regulation shall not prevent the performance by the Bank of the function delegated.

(6) Notwithstanding any delegation under this Regulation, the final responsibility for supervising compliance with the Directive and the applicable provisions of EU prospectus law and for approving prospectuses under these Regulations shall be with the Bank.

(7) The Bank shall notify the Minister of any such delegation of a function promptly and of the conditions subject to which it has been delegated.

(8) Following such notification, the Minister shall inform the Commission and the competent authorities of other Member States designated pursuant to the Directive of any arrangements entered into with regard to the functions under this Regulation, including the conditions subject to which such functions are delegated.

(9) Where a function is delegated pursuant to this Regulation, then nothing in the Stock Exchange Act 1995 shall prevent there being specified as a condition subject to which the function is to be performed a condition requiring the rules of the stock exchange concerned or an amendment thereof to be approved by the Bank in so far as they are relevant to the function delegated.

Definitions

'approval': Prospectus Regs, reg 2(1); 'approved stock exchange': Prospectus Regs, reg 2(1); 'Bank': Prospectus Regs, reg 2(1); 'Directive': Prospectus Regs, reg 2(1); 'EU prospectus law': Prospectus Regs, reg 2(1); 'functions': Prospectus Regs, reg 2(1); 'Irish prospectus law': Prospectus Regs, reg 2(1); 'in writing': Prospectus Regs, reg 2(1); 'Member State': Prospectus Regs, reg 2(1); 'Minister': Prospectus Regs, reg 2(1); 'prospectus': Prospectus Regs, reg 2(1).

UK legislation

FSMA 2000, s 72(3), Sch 8, inserted by SI 2005/1433.

PART 14

POWERS OF COMPETENT AUTHORITY

Definitions

80. In this Part—

'authorised officer' means an authorised officer appointed under Regulation 85;

'person to whom these Regulations apply' means any relevant person or a market operator;

'records' means any book, document or any other written or printed material in any form including any information (including phone and data traffic records) stored, maintained or preserved by means of any mechanical or electronic device, whether or not stored, maintained or preserved in a legible form;

'relevant records' means records relating to the activities of persons to whom these Regulations apply;

'responsible authority' means:—

(a) the Chief Executive of the Irish Financial Services Regulatory Authority, or

(b) any person to whom the Chief Executive of that Authority has delegated responsibility for appointing authorised persons.

Definitions

'market operator': Prospectus Regs, reg 2(1); 'relevant person': Prospectus Regs, reg 2(1).

81.(1) The Bank shall have all the powers necessary for the performance of its functions under Irish prospectus law or the Directive.

(2) The powers provided for in this Part shall not be exercised in a manner or for a purpose inconsistent with the Directive or these Regulations.

Definitions

'Bank': Prospectus Regs, reg 2(1); 'Directive': Prospectus Regs, reg 2(1); 'functions': Prospectus Regs, reg 2(1); 'Irish prospectus law': Prospectus Regs, reg 2(1).

UK legislation

FSMA 2000, s 72.

82.(1) Following receipt of an application for approval of a prospectus the Bank (or any person to whom the Bank has delegated the function of scrutinising prospectuses under Regulation 79) shall have the power to:

(a) require the relevant person to include in the prospectus supplementary information, if necessary for investor protection,

(b) require the relevant person and the persons that control the relevant person to provide information and documents to the Bank or delegate,

(c) require auditors and managers of the relevant person as well as financial intermediaries commissioned to carry out the offer to the public or ask for admission to trading, to provide information to the Bank or delegate.

(2) The Bank shall have the following powers (by means of giving a direction under Regulation 88 in that behalf) for the purpose of regulating public offers or admissions to trading in respect of which it is the Home Member State or for the purposes specified in Regulation 90(1).

(a) to suspend a public offer or admission to trading, for a maximum of 10 consecutive working days on any single occasion, if it has reasonable grounds for suspecting that the provisions of the Directive or of EU prospectus law have not been complied with as respects the offer or admission to trading;

(b) to prohibit or suspend advertisements for a maximum of 10 consecutive working days on any single occasion if it has reasonable grounds for believing that the provisions of the Directive or of EU prospectus law have not been complied with as respects the advertisement;

(c) to prohibit a public offer if it finds that the provisions of the Directive or of EU prospectus law have not been complied with as respects the offer to trading of the securities concerned, or if it has reasonable grounds for suspecting that they will not be complied with as respects the offer;

(d) to suspend or ask the relevant regulated markets to suspend trading on a regulated market, for a maximum of 10 consecutive working days on any single occasion, if it has reasonable grounds for believing that the provisions of the Directive or of EU prospectus law have not been complied with as respects the admission to trading of the securities concerned;

(e) to prohibit trading on a regulated market if it finds that the provisions of the Directive or of EU prospectus law have not been complied with as respects the admission to trading of the securities concerned;

(f) to disclose to public the fact a relevant person is failing to comply with its obligations under EU prospectus law.

Definitions

'admission to trading': Prospectus Regs, reg 2(1); 'approval': Prospectus Regs, reg 2(1); 'Bank': Prospectus Regs, reg 2(1); 'Directive': Prospectus Regs, reg 2(1); 'EU prospectus law': Prospectus Regs, reg 2(1); 'functions': Prospectus Regs, reg 2(1); 'Home Member State': Prospectus Regs, reg 2(1); 'prospectus': Prospectus Regs, reg 2(1); 'public offer': Prospectus Regs, reg 2(1); 'regulated market': Prospectus Regs, reg 2(1); 'relevant person': Prospectus Regs, reg 2(1); 'securities': Prospectus Regs, reg 2(1); 'working day': Prospectus Regs, reg 2(1).

UK legislation

FSMA ss 87J, 87K, 87L inserted by SI 2005/1433.

83. Once the securities have been admitted to trading the Bank may (by means of giving a direction under Regulation 88 in that behalf):

(a) require the issuer to disclose all material information which may have an effect on the assessment of the securities admitted to trading in order to ensure investor protection or the smooth operation of the market,

(b) suspend or require the relevant regulated market to suspend the securities from trading if, in its opinion, the issuer's situation is such that trading would be detrimental to investors' interests,

(c) ensure that issuers whose securities are traded on regulated markets comply with the obligations provided for in Articles 102 and 103 of Directive 2001/34/EC and that equivalent information is provided to investors and equivalent treatment is granted by the issuer to all securities holders who are in the same position, in all Member States where the offer to the public is made or the securities are admitted to trading.

Definitions

'admission to trading': Prospectus Regs, reg 2(1); 'Bank': Prospectus Regs, reg 2(1); 'issuer': Prospectus Regs, reg 2(1); 'Member State': Prospectus Regs, reg 2(1); 'regulated market': Prospectus Regs, reg 2(1); 'securities': Prospectus Regs, reg 2(1).

UK legislation

FSMA 2000, ss 87J, 87K, 87L,inserted by SI 2005/1433.

84. The powers of the Bank under this Part are without prejudice to the powers of the Bank under any other Part of these Regulations or any other enactment.

Definitions

'Bank': Prospectus Regs, reg 2(1); 'enactment': Prospectus Regs, reg 2(1).

Power to appoint authorised officers

85.(1) A responsible authority may, in writing—

(a) authorise such and so many persons as the authority considers necessary to be authorised officers for the purposes of these Regulations, and

(b) revoke any such authorisation.

(2) An appointment under paragraph (1)(a) may be for a specified or unspecified period.

(3) Every authorised officer shall—

(a) be furnished with a certificate of his or her appointment as an authorised officer, and

(b) when exercising a power under these Regulations of an authorised officer, produce the certificate, together with some form of personal identification, if requested to do so by a person affected by the exercise of that power.

(4) An appointment under paragraph (1) of a person as an authorised officer ceases—

(a) when the responsible authority concerned revokes the appointment,

(b) the person dies or resigns from the appointment,

(c) if the appointment is for a specified period, when the period ends,

(d) if the person appointed is an officer of the Irish Financial Services Regulatory Authority, when the person ceases to be such an officer, or

(e) if the person appointed is an officer of an approved stock exchange to which the Bank has delegated functions under Regulation 79, when the person ceases to be such an officer.

Definitions

'approved stock exchange': Prospectus Regs, reg 2(1); 'authorised officer': Prospectus Regs, reg 80; 'Bank': Prospectus Regs, reg 2(1); 'functions': Prospectus Regs, reg 2(1); 'in writing': Prospectus Regs, reg 2(1); 'responsible authority': Prospectus Regs, reg 80.

UK legislation

FSMA 2000, ss 165, 167.

Powers of authorised officers

86.(1) An authorised officer may, for the purpose of carrying out an investigation under these Regulations, do all or any of the following—

- (a) at all reasonable times enter any premises at which there are reasonable grounds to believe that there are any relevant records,
- (b) search and inspect the premises referred to in subparagraph (a) and any relevant records on the premises,
- (c) secure for later inspection the premises or any part of the premises in which relevant records are kept or in which the officer has reasonable grounds for believing the relevant records are kept,
- (d) require any person to whom these Regulations apply to produce to the officer relevant records, and if the information is in a non-legible form, to reproduce it in a legible form or to give to the officer such information as the officer reasonably requires in relation to entries in the relevant records,
- (e) inspect and take copies of relevant records inspected or produced under this Regulation (including, in the case of information in a non-legible form, a copy of all or part of the information in a permanent legible form),
- (f) remove and retain any of the relevant records inspected or produced under this Regulation for such period as may be reasonable to facilitate further examination,
- (g) require a person to give to the officer information (including give information by way of a written report) that the officer reasonably requires in relation to activities covered by these Regulations and to produce to the officer any relevant records that the person has or has access to,
- (h) require a person by or on whose behalf data equipment is or has been used, or any person who has charge of, or is otherwise concerned with the operation of, the data equipment or any associated apparatus or material, to give the officer all reasonable assistance in relation thereto, and
- (i) require a person to explain entries in any relevant records.

(2) An authorised officer shall not, except with the consent of the occupier, enter a private dwelling (other than a part of the dwelling used as a place of work) unless the officer has obtained a warrant from a judge of the District Court.

(3) Where any person from whom production of a relevant record is required claims a lien thereon, the production of it shall be without prejudice to the lien.

(4) The requirement to produce any relevant record or report or to provide information or assistance under this Regulation extends to—

(a) a liquidator or receiver of, or any person who is or has been an officer or employee or agent of, a person to whom these Regulations apply, or

(b) any other person who appears to the Bank or the authorised officer to have the relevant record or report in his or her possession or under his or her control or the ability to provide information or assistance, as the case may be.

(5) An authorised officer may, if the officer considers it necessary, be accompanied by a member of the Garda Síochána or by another authorised officer when exercising a power under this Part.

(6) A person who obstructs or impedes an authorised officer in the exercise of his or her powers under this Regulation shall be guilty of an offence.

Definitions

'authorised officer': Prospectus Regs, reg 80; 'Bank': Prospectus Regs, reg 2(1); 'person to whom these regulations apply': Prospectus Regs, reg 80; 'records': Prospectus Regs, reg 80; 'relevant records': Prospectus Regs, reg 80.

UK legislation

FSMA 2000, ss 171, 172, 175.

Warrants

87.(1) When an authorised officer in the exercise of the authorised officer's powers under Regulation 86(1)—

(a) is prevented from entering any premises, or

(b) believes that there are relevant records in a private dwelling,

the authorised officer or the responsible authority by whom the authorised officer was appointed may apply to a judge of the District Court for a warrant under this Regulation authorising the entry by the authorised officer into the premises or the private dwelling, as the case may be.

(2) If on an application under paragraph (1) a judge of the District Court is satisfied, on the information of the applicant, that the authorised officer concerned—

(a) has been prevented from entering any premises, or

(b) has reasonable grounds for believing that there are relevant records in a private dwelling,

then the judge may issue a warrant under the judge's hand authorising the authorised officer, accompanied, if the judge considers it appropriate to so provide, by such number of members of the Garda Síochána as may be specified in the warrant, at any time within 4 weeks from the date of issue of the warrant, to enter, if need be by force, the premises or private dwelling and exercise any of the powers referred to in Regulation 86(1).

(2) The provisions of this Part are made for the purposes of enabling the imposition of administrative sanctions.

Definitions

'Bank': Prospectus Regs, reg 2(1); 'contravention': Prospectus Regs, reg 2(1); 'EU prospectus law': Prospectus Regs, reg 2(1).

Bank may appoint assessor

93.(1) Where the Bank has reason to suspect that a prescribed contravention is being committed or has been committed, the Bank may appoint an assessor (or, if the Bank thinks fit to do so, more than one assessor) to conduct an assessment as to—

(a) whether or not the assessee is committing or has committed the contravention, and

(b) if the assessor finds that the assessee is committing or has committed the contravention, the sanction or sanctions, if any, which the assessor considers are appropriate to be imposed on the assessee in respect of the contravention.

(2) The Bank may appoint an assessor who is not an officer, employee or official of the Bank and any such assessor so appointed is an agent of the Bank for the purpose of performing the functions of an assessor under this Part.

(3) The Bank shall provide the assessor with such administrative services (including technical and legal advice) as the Bank considers necessary to enable the assessor to perform the assessor's functions.

(4) The assessor shall, as soon as is practicable after the assessor's appointment as an assessor, give notice of the appointment to the assessee.

(5) The notice under paragraph (4) given to the assessee by the assessor shall contain—

(a) a statement that the assessor is appointed by the Bank under this Regulation,

(b) a statement in summary form of the grounds for conducting the assessment,

(c) the notice, the assessee may—

(i) make submissions in writing to the assessor, and

(ii) request the assessor to be permitted to make oral submissions about the matters to which the notice relates, and

(d) a statement that the assessor shall conduct the assessment even if no submissions referred to in subparagraph (c) are made.

(6) The assessor shall—

(a) consider any submissions made by the assessee, and

(b) conduct such investigations relating to the assessment as the assessor considers appropriate before issuing the assessment.

(7) The assessor shall issue the assessment to the Bank when the assessment is made.

(8) Where the assessor decides that a prescribed contravention is being committed or has been committed, the assessor shall ensure that the assessment includes—

(a) a statement of the grounds upon which the assessor made the assessment that the assessee is committing or has committed the contravention,

(b) a statement in summary form of the evidence upon which the assessment is based, and

(c) a statement of the sanction or sanctions, if any, which the assessor considers are appropriate to be imposed on the assessee in respect of the contravention.

(9) The appointment of an assessor may be for a specified or unspecified period.

(10) Subject to Regulation 100(2), the assessment shall constitute the decision of the Bank, and references in this Part to an adverse assessment shall be construed accordingly.

Definitions

'adverse assessment': Prospectus Regs, reg 92; 'assessee': Prospectus Regs, reg 92; 'assessment': Prospectus Regs, reg 92; 'adverse assessor': Prospectus Regs, reg 92; 'Bank': Prospectus Regs, reg 2(1); 'functions': Prospectus Regs, reg 2(1); 'in writing': Prospectus Regs, reg 2(1); 'prescribed contravention': Prospectus Regs, reg 92.

UK legislation

FSMA 2000, ss 167, 168, 170.

Revocation of appointment of assessor

94.(1) Where the Bank is satisfied that the assessor has contravened paragraph (2) or is incapacitated, the Bank may revoke the appointment of the assessor at any time.

(2) The assessor (including a person proposed to be appointed as an assessor) shall—

(a) disclose to the Bank any material interest that the assessor may have in any matter that may arise during the assessment,

(b) disclose to the Bank any actual or potential conflict of interest that the assessor may have in conducting an assessment,

(c) not use any inside information (within the meaning of the Market Abuse (Directive 2003/6/EC) Regulations 2005) obtained during an assessment for any purpose other than the performance of the assessor's functions under this Part,

(d) not engage in misconduct during the assessment,

(e) perform the assessor's functions in accordance with the provisions of this Part, and

(f) issue an assessment that is not contrary to law.

Definitions

'assessment': Prospectus Regs, reg 92; 'assessor': Prospectus Regs, reg 92; 'Bank': Prospectus Regs, reg 2(1); 'functions': Prospectus Regs, reg 2(1).

UK legislation

FSMA 2000, s 170(8)(c).

Power to require witnesses to appear and give evidence

95.(1) The assessor may by notice given in or outside the State to a person require the person to do one or more of the following—

(a) appear before the assessor to give evidence (including give evidence on oath), custody or control,

(b) for the purposes of subparagraph (a) or (b), attend before the assessor from day to day unless excused from attendance or released from further attendance by the assessor.

(2) The assessor may administer oaths for the purposes of the evidence referred to in paragraph (1) (a).

(3) A witness at a hearing before the assessor has the same liabilities, privileges and immunities as a witness before the Court.

(4) Where a person ('person concerned')—

(a) fails to comply with a notice under paragraph (1),

(b) threatens or insults the assessor or any witness or person required to attend before the assessor,

(c) interrupts the proceedings of, or does not behave in an appropriate manner before, the assessor,

(d) obstructs or attempts to obstruct the assessor, 92

(e) discloses, or authorises the disclosure of, evidence given before the assessor or any of the contents of a document produced to the assessor that the assessor has instructed not to be published, or

(f) does anything else that, if the assessor were a court of law having power to commit for contempt, would be contempt for that court,then—

(i) the assessor may apply to the Court for an order requiring the person concerned to do one or both of the following—

(I) to comply with the notice under paragraph (1),

(II) to discontinue or not repeat the behaviour falling within any of the provisions of subparagraphs (b) to (f), or behaviour of any similar kind, and

(ii) the Court, if satisfied that there is no reasonable excuse for the failure to comply with the notice under paragraph (1) or for the behaviour concerned, as the case may be, grant the order and such other orders as it considers appropriate to ensure that the person concerned cooperates with the assessor.

Definitions

'assessor': Prospectus Regs, reg 92; 'Court': Prospectus Regs, reg 2(1).

UK legislation

FSMA 2000, ss 171, 174, 177.

Referral to Court on question of law

96.(1) The Bank or the assessor may (including at the request of the assessee) refer a question of law arising in the assessment to the Court for determination by the Court.

(2) Where a question of law is referred under paragraph (1)—

(a) the assessor shall send to the Court all documents before him or her that are relevant to the matter in question, and

(b) at the end of the proceedings in the Court in relation to the reference, the Court shall cause the documents to be returned to the assessor.

Definitions

'assessee': Prospectus Regs, reg 92; 'assessment': Prospectus Regs, reg 92; 'assessor': Prospectus Regs, reg 92; 'Bank': Prospectus Regs, reg 2(1); 'Court': Prospectus Regs, reg 2(1).

UK legislation

FSMA 2000, s 137.

Assessee to be issued copy of any adverse assessment, etc.

97.(1) Where the assessment of the assessor is that the assessee is committing or has committed a prescribed contravention, the Bank shall—

(a) issue the assessee with a copy of the adverse assessment (or, as the Bank thinks fit, so much of the adverse assessment as constitutes the statements referred to in Regulation 93(8)), and

(b) advise the assessee that—

(i) the assessee may appeal against the adverse assessment to the Court under Regulation 98, and

(ii) the Bank may apply to the Court under Regulation 102 for an order confirming the adverse assessment (including the specified sanctions).

(2) Where the assessment of the assessor is that the assessee is neither committing nor has committed a prescribed contravention, the Bank shall issue the assessee with a statement to that effect.

Definitions

'adverse assessment': Prospectus Regs, reg 92; 'assessee': Prospectus Regs, reg 92; 'adverse assessor': Prospectus Regs, reg 92; 'Bank': Prospectus Regs, reg 2(1); 'Court': Prospectus Regs, reg 2(1); 'prescribed contravention': Prospectus Regs, reg 92; 'specified sanctions': Prospectus Regs, reg 92.

UK legislation

FSMA 2000, s 87M(2), inserted by SI 2005/1433.

Right of appeal against adverse assessment (including specified sanctions)

98.(1) The assessee may appeal to the Court against the adverse assessment (including the specified sanctions) not later than 28 days after the Bank has complied with

Regulation 97(1) in relation to the assessee or within such further period as the Court allows.

(2) An appeal under paragraph (1) may be heard otherwise than in public.

(3) The Court may, pending the hearing and determination of an appeal under paragraph (1), make such interim or interlocutory orders as the Court considers necessary in the circumstances.

(4) The Court shall determine an appeal under paragraph (1) by making—

(a) an order confirming, varying or setting aside the adverse assessment (including the specified sanctions), whether in whole or in part, or

(b) an order remitting the case to be decided again by the Bank in accordance with the directions of the Court.

(5) The determination of the Court on the hearing of an appeal under paragraph (1) shall be final, except that a party to the appeal may apply to the Supreme Court to review the determination on a question of law.

(6) For the avoidance of doubt, it is declared that no variation of an adverse assessment under paragraph (4)(a) may provide for the imposition of a sanction on the assessee which is not a sanction referred to in paragraphs (a) to (f) of Regulation 99.

Definitions

'adverse assessment': Prospectus Regs, reg 92; 'assessee': Prospectus Regs, reg 92; 'Bank': Prospectus Regs, reg 2(1); 'Court': Prospectus Regs, reg 2(1); 'sanctions': Prospectus Regs, reg 92; 'specified sanctions': Prospectus Regs, reg 92.

UK legislation

FSMA 2000, ss 87N inserted by SI 2005/1433.

Sanctions that may be imposed by Bank

99. In the case of an adverse assessment, the Bank may impose on the assessee such of the following sanctions as are the specified sanctions—

(a) a private caution or reprimand,

(b) a public caution or reprimand,

(c) subject to Regulation 104(2), a direction to pay to the Bank a monetary penalty (but not exceeding €2,500,000 in any case),

(d) a direction disqualifying the assessee from being concerned in the management of, or having a qualifying holding in, any regulated financial service provider for such time as is specified in the order,

(e) if the assessee is continuing to commit a prescribed contravention, a direction ordering the assessee to cease committing the prescribed contravention,

(f) a direction to pay to the Bank all or a specified part of the costs incurred by the Bank in investigating the matter to which the assessment relates and in holding the assessment (including any costs incurred by authorised officers).

Definitions

'adverse assessment': Prospectus Regs, reg 92; 'assessee': Prospectus Regs, reg 92; 'Bank': Prospectus Regs, reg 2(1); 'prescribed contravention': Prospectus Regs, reg 92; 'regulated financial service provider': Prospectus Regs, reg 92; 'specified sanctions': Prospectus Regs, reg 92; 'qualifying holding': Prospectus Regs, reg 92.

Notes

'Authorised officer' is defined in reg 80 for the purposes of Pt 14 only. It would appear logical that such definition should apply for the purposes of this reg also.

UK legislation

FSMA 2000, ss 87M, 87L, 89, 91, inserted by SI 2005/1433.

Power to correct assessments

100.(1) Where the assessor or the Bank is satisfied that there is an obvious error in the text of an assessment, the assessor or the Bank, as the case may be, may alter the text of the assessment to remove the error.

(2) Where the text of an assessment is altered under paragraph (1), the text as so altered shall be taken to be the decision of the Bank under Regulation 93(10).

(3) In paragraph (1), 'obvious error', in relation to the text of an assessment, includes—

(a) a clerical or typographical error,

(b) an error arising from an accidental slip or omission, or

(c) a defect of form.

Definitions

'assessment': Prospectus Regs, reg 92; 'assessor': Prospectus Regs, reg 92; 'Bank': Prospectus Regs, reg 2(1).

When specified sanctions take effect

101.(1) Where—

(a) no appeal under Regulation 98 against the adverse assessment is lodged with the Court within the period for lodging the appeal, or

(b) an appeal under Regulation 98 against the adverse assessment which has been lodged with the Court within the period for lodging the appeal is withdrawn or abandoned,

then the specified sanctions, as confirmed or varied in the order, if any, obtained under Regulation 102(2)(a), shall take effect on the date of that order or such other date as the Court may specify in that order.

(2) Where an appeal under Regulation 98 against the adverse assessment is lodged with the Court within the period for lodging the appeal, then the specified sanctions, as

confirmed or varied in the order, if any, obtained under Regulation 98(4)(a), shall take effect on the date of that order or such other date as the Court may specify in that order.

Definitions

'adverse assessment': Prospectus Regs, reg 92; 'Court': Prospectus Regs, reg 2(1); 'specified sanctions': Prospectus Regs, reg 92.

Enforcement of adverse assessment (including specified sanctions)

102.(1) Where—

(a) no appeal under Regulation 98 against the adverse assessment is lodged with the Court within the period for lodging the appeal, or

(b) an appeal under Regulation 98 against the adverse assessment which has been lodged with the Court within the period for lodging the appeal is withdrawn or abandoned,

then the Bank may apply to the Court for an order confirming the adverse assessment (including the specified sanctions).

(2) The Court shall determine an application under para graph (1) by making—

(a) an order confirming, varying or setting aside the adverse assessment (including the specified sanctions), whether in whole or in part, or

(b) an order remitting the case to be decided again by the Bank in accordance with the directions of the Court.

(3) The Court shall not hear an application under para graph (1) unless—

(a) the assessee appears at the hearing as respondent to the application, or

(b) if the assessee does not so appear, the Court is satisfied that a copy of the application has been served on the assessee.

(4) An application under paragraph (1) may be heard otherwise than in public.

(5) The Court may, on an application under paragraph (1), make such interim or interlocutory orders as the Court considers necessary in the circumstances.

(6) The determination of the Court on the hearing of an application under paragraph (1) shall be final, except that the Bank or the respondent, if any, may apply to the Supreme Court to review the determination on a question of law.

(7) For the avoidance of doubt, it is hereby declared that no variation of an adverse assessment under paragraph (2)(a) may provide for the imposition of a sanction on the assessee which is not a sanction referred to in paragraphs (a) to (f) of Regulation 99.

Definitions

'adverse assessment': Prospectus Regs, reg 92; 'assessee': Prospectus Regs, reg 92; 'Bank': Prospectus Regs, reg 2(1); 'Court': Prospectus Regs, reg 2(1); 'sanction': Prospectus Regs, reg 92; 'specified sanctions': Prospectus Regs, reg 92.

UK legislation

FSMA 2000, s 133(11).

Publication of certain specified sanctions

103. The Bank shall publicly disclose the specified sanctions referred to in paragraphs (c) to (f) of Regulation 99, as confirmed or varied in the order concerned obtained under Regulation 98(4)(a) or 102(2)(a), that are imposed on the assessee unless the Bank considers that the disclosure would—

(a) seriously jeopardise the financial markets, or

(b) cause disproportionate damage to the parties involved.

Definitions

'assessee': Prospectus Regs, reg 92; 'Bank': Prospectus Regs, reg 2(1); 'specified sanctions': Prospectus Regs, reg 92.

Person not liable to be penalised twice for same contravention

104.(1) Where—

(a) a sanction referred to in Regulation 99(c) is to be imposed on the assessee by virtue of an order obtained under Regulation 98(4)(a) or 102(2)(a), and

(b) the acts which constitute the prescribed contravention to which the sanction relates also constitute an offence under a law of the State,

then the asses see is not, in respect of those acts, liable to be prosecuted or punished for that offence under that law.

(2) A sanction referred to in Regulation 99(c) in respect of a prescribed contravention shall not be imposed on the assessee where—

(a) the assessee has been found guilty or not guilty of having committed an offence under a provision of—

(i) these Regulations, or

(ii) Part 5 of the Investment Funds, Companies and Miscellaneous Pensions 2005 Act, and

(b) all or some of the acts constituting that offence also constitute the prescribed contravention.

Definitions

'assessee': Prospectus Regs, reg 92; 'prescribed contravention': Prospectus Regs, reg 92; 'sanction': Prospectus Regs, reg 92

Person not to be concerned in management of regulated financial service provider while disqualified

105.(1) A regulated financial service provider shall ensure that a person shall not be concerned in the management of, or have a qualifying holding in, the financial service provider while the person is subject to a sanction referred to in Regulation 99(d) that is in force.

(2) A regulated financial service provider who contravenes paragraph (1) shall be guilty of an offence.

Definitions

'qualifying holding': Prospectus Regs, reg 92; 'regulated financial service provider': Prospectus Regs, reg 92.

UK legislation

FSMA 2000, s 56(6).

Power of the Bank to resolve suspected contraventions, etc.

106.(1) Where the Bank has reason to suspect that a person ('relevant party') is committing or has committed a prescribed contravention, it may enter into an agreement in writing with the relevant party to resolve the matter (including at any time before an assessment, if any, has been issued in respect of the relevant party).

(2) An agreement entered into under paragraph (1)—

(a) is binding on the Bank and the relevant party, and

(b) may include terms under which the relevant party accepts the imposition of sanctions.

(3) An agreement entered into under paragraph (1) may be enforced by the Bank or the relevant party in a court of competent jurisdiction.

Definitions

'assessment': Prospectus Regs, reg 92; 'Bank': Prospectus Regs, reg 2(1); 'in writing': Prospectus Regs, reg 2(1); 'prescribed contravention': Prospectus Regs, reg 92; 'sanction': Prospectus Regs, reg 92.

PART 16

PENALTIES, GENERAL AND OTHER MISCELLANEOUS PROVISIONS

Certain Offences and Penalties generally

107.(1) If the contravention in respect of which a person is convicted of an offence under these Regulations is continued after the conviction, the person shall be guilty of a further offence on every day on which the contravention continues.

(2) Where any offence is committed under these Regulations by a body corporate and is proved to have been committed with the consent, connivance or approval of or to have been attributable to the wilful neglect on the part of any person, being a director, manager, secretary or other officer of the body corporate or a person who was purporting to act in any such capacity, that person as well as the body corporate shall be guilty of an offence and is liable to be proceeded against and punished as if he or she was guilty of the first mentioned offence.

(3) A person who is guilty of—

(a) an offence under these Regulations other than an offence referred to in subparagraph (b), or

(b) one or more further offences under paragraph (1), for each such offence,

shall be liable on summary conviction to a fine not exceeding €5,000 or imprisonment for a term not exceeding 12 months or both.

(4) Each of the following is an offence to which section 47 (penalties on indictment) of the Investment Funds, Companies and Miscellaneous Provisions Act 2005 applies—

(a) an offence under Regulation 14,

(b) an offence under Regulation 15,

(c) an offence under paragraph (1) or (2) that relates to an offence referred to in subparagraph (a) or (b).

Definitions

'contravention': Prospectus Regs, reg 2(1).

UK legislation

FSMA 2000, s 400.

Annual Report of Bank

108. The Bank shall provide the Minister with a copy of the extract relating to the performance of its functions under these Regulations from its annual report to the Minster for Finance under section 300 of the Central Bank Act 1942.

Definitions

'Bank': Prospectus Regs, reg 2(1); 'functions': Prospectus Regs, reg 2(1); 'Minister': Prospectus Regs, reg 2(1).

UK legislation

FSMA 2000, Sch 1, para 10.

Fees

109. Fees shall be payable pursuant to section 33K of the Central Bank Act 1942 in respect of the performance by the Bank of its functions under these Regulations.

Definitions

'Bank': Prospectus Regs, reg 2(1); 'functions': Prospectus Regs, reg 2(1).

UK legislation

FSMA 2000, Sch 1, para 17.

Revocations and Amendments

110.(1) The following are revoked—

(a) the European Communities (Stock Exchange) (Amendment) Regulations 1991 (S.I. No. 18 of 1991),

(b) the European Communities (Transferable Securities and Stock Exchange) Regulations 1992 (S.I. No. 202 of 1992),

(c) the European Communities (Stock Exchange) (Amendment) Regulations 1994 (S.I. No. 234 of 1994).

(2) The European Communities (Stock Exchange) Regulations 1984 (S.I. No. 282 of 1984) are amended as specified in Schedule 3 to these Regulations.

Transitional Provisions

111. Issuers which are incorporated in a third country and whose securities have already been admitted to trading on a regulated market prior to 31 December 2003 and who choose the State as their competent authority in accordance with these Regulations shall notify their decision in writing to the Bank by 31 December 2005.

Definitions

'admission to trading': Prospectus Regs, reg 2(1); 'Bank': Prospectus Regs, reg 2(1); 'in writing': Prospectus Regs, reg 2(1); 'issuer': Prospectus Regs, reg 2(1); 'regulated market': Prospectus Regs, reg 2(1); 'securities': Prospectus Regs, reg 2(1).

---

112. Notwithstanding Regulation 12, credit institutions or other financial institutions equivalent to credit institutions within the meaning of Article 5 of Directive 89/29 8/EEC may continue to make public offers of debt securities or other transferable securities equivalent to debt securities issued in a continuous or repeated manner within the State up to 31 December 2008 without the need to publish a prospectus under these Regulations in circumstances where but for this Regulation they would have been obliged to publish a prospectus under these Regulations.

Definitions

'credit institution': Prospectus Regs, reg 2(1); 'prospectus': Prospectus Regs, reg 2(1); 'public offer': Prospectus Regs, reg 2(1); 'publication': Prospectus Regs, reg 2(1); 'securities': Prospectus Regs, reg 2(1); 'securities issued in a continuous or repeated manner': Prospectus Regs, reg 2(1).

---

113. Regulations 111 and 112 are in addition to the provisions of Article 35 of the Prospectus Regulation (which also contains transitional provisions).

Definitions

'Prospectus Regulation': Prospectus Regs, reg 2(1).

Schedule 1

Regulation 31

1. Responsible Persons

Subject to the provisions of this Schedule, responsibility for the information given in a prospectus attaches in the following cases.

Definitions

'prospectus': Prospectus Regs, reg 2(1).

2. Equity securities

(1) This paragraph applies to a case in which the prospectus relates to equity securities (other than securities convertible into shares issued by the issuer of the underlying shares or by an entity belonging to the issuer's group).

(2) In a case to which this paragraph applies, each of the following persons is, subject to the other provisions of this Schedule, responsible for the prospectus:

- (a) the issuer of the securities;
- (b) if the issuer is a body corporate:
  - (i) each person who is a director of that body corporate when the prospectus is published; and
  - (ii) each person who has authorised himself or herself to be named, and is named, in the prospectus as a director or as having agreed

  to become a director of that body corporate either immediately or at a future time;
- (c) each person who accepts, and is stated in the prospectus as accepting, responsibility for the prospectus;
- (d) if the case involves an offer of securities to the public:
  - (i) the offeror of the securities, if this is not the issuer; and
  - (ii) if the offeror is a body corporate and is not the issuer, each person who is a director of that body corporate when the prospectus is published;
- (e) if the case involves the admission to trading of securities:
  - (i) the person seeking admission, if this is not the issuer; and
  - (ii) if the person seeking admission is a body corporate and is not the issuer, each person who is a director of that body corporate when the prospectus is published; and
- (f) each person not falling within any of the preceding provisions of this subparagraph who has authorised the contents of the prospectus.

Definitions

'admission to trading': Prospectus Regs, reg 2(1); 'equity securities': Prospectus Regs, reg 2(1); 'issuer': Prospectus Regs, reg 2(1); 'offer of securities to the public': Prospectus Regs, reg 2(1); 'offeror': Prospectus Regs, reg 2(1); 'prospectus': Prospectus Regs, reg 2(1); 'publication': Prospectus Regs, reg 2(1); 'securities': Prospectus Regs, reg 2(1).

UK legislation

FSA Prospectus Rules, Rule 5.5.3.

3. All other securities

(1) This paragraph applies to a case in which the prospectus relates to securities that are not securities to which paragraph 2 applies.

(2) In a case to which this paragraph applies, each of the following persons is, subject to the other provisions of this Schedule, responsible for the prospectus:

(a) the issuer of the securities;

(b) each person who accepts, and is stated in the prospectus as accepting, responsibility for the prospectus;

(c) if the case involves an offer of securities to the public, the offeror of the securities, if this is not the issuer;

(d) if the case involves the admission to trading of securities, the person seeking admission, if this is not the issuer;

(e) if there is a guarantor for the issue, the guarantor in relation to information in the prospectus that relates to the guarantor and the guarantee; and

(f) each person not falling within any of the preceding provisions of this subparagraph who has authorised the contents of the prospectus.

Definitions

'admission to trading': Prospectus Regs, reg 2(1); 'issuer': Prospectus Regs, reg 2(1); 'offer of securities to the public': Prospectus Regs, reg 2(1); 'offeror': Prospectus Regs, reg 2(1); 'prospectus': Prospectus Regs, reg 2(1); 'securities': Prospectus Regs, reg 2(1).

UK legislation

FSA Prospectus Rules, Rule 5.5.4.

4. Issuer not responsible if it has not authorised offer or admission to trading

An issuer is not responsible for a prospectus under paragraph 2(2)(a) or (b) or paragraph 3(2)(a) unless the issuer has made or authorised the offer of securities to the public or the application for admission to trading in relation to which the prospectus was published.

Definitions

'admission to trading': Prospectus Regs, reg 2(1); 'issuer': Prospectus Regs, reg 2(1); 'offer of securities to the public': Prospectus Regs, reg 2(1); 'prospectus': Prospectus Regs, reg 2(1); 'publication': Prospectus Regs, reg 2(1).

UK legislation

FSA Prospectus Rules, Rule 5.5.5.

5. Publication without directors consent

A person is not responsible for a prospectus under paragraph 2(2)(b)(i) if it is published without his or her knowledge or consent and on becoming aware of its publication he or she, as soon as practicable, gives reasonable public notice that it was published without his or her knowledge or consent.

Definitions

'prospectus': Prospectus Regs, reg 2(1); 'publication': Prospectus Regs, reg 2(1); 'publication': Prospectus Regs, reg 2(1).

UK legislation

FSA Prospectus Rules, Rule 5.5.6.

---

6. Offeror not responsible in certain circumstances

A person is not responsible for a prospectus under paragraph 2(2)(d) or paragraph 3(2)(c) if:

(a) the issuer is responsible for the prospectus in accordance with this Schedule;

(b) the prospectus was drawn up primarily by the issuer, or by one or more persons acting on behalf of the issuer; and

(c) the offeror is making the offer in association with the issuer.

Definitions

'issuer': Prospectus Regs, reg 2(1); 'offeror': Prospectus Regs, reg 2(1); 'prospectus': Prospectus Regs, reg 2(1).

UK legislation

FSA Prospectus Rules, Rule 5.5.7.

---

7. Person may accept responsibility for, or authorise, part of contents

When accepting responsibility for a prospectus under—

(a) paragraph 2(2)(c) or paragraph 3(2)(b), or

(b) authorising the contents of a prospectus under paragraph 2(2)(f),

a person may state that her or she does so only in relation to specified parts of the prospectus, or only in specified respects, and in that case the person is responsible under those paragraphs:

(i) only to the extent specified; and

(ii) only if the material in question is included in (or substantially in) the form and context to which the person has agreed.

Definitions

'prospectus': Prospectus Regs, reg 2(1).

Market Abuse (Directive 2003/6/EC) Regulations 2005

SI 342/2005

ARRANGEMENT OF REGULATIONS

PART 4
POWERS OF THE BANK

PART 5
ENFORCEMENT PROVISIONS

PART 6
OFFENCES AND REPORTS

SCHEDULE 1
PROVISIONS APPLICABLE TO THE DEFINITION OF "ACCEPTED MARKET PRACTICES"

SCHEDULE 2
PROVISIONS APPLICABLE TO PARAGRAPH (A) OF THE DEFINITION OF "MARKET MANIPULATION"

SCHEDULE 3

PROVISIONS APPLICABLE TO PARAGRAPH (B) OF THE DEFINITION OF "MARKET MANIPULATION"

SCHEDULE 4

PROVISIONS APPLICABLE TO LISTS DRAWN UP UNDER REGULATION 11

SCHEDULE 5

TEXT OF THE MARKET ABUSE REGULATION

Notes

These Regulations transpose the Market Abuse Directive 2003/6/EC of 28 January 2003 (OJ 12.4.2003 L96 p 16) a Lamfalussy procedure Level 1 measure,[1] and three Level 2 Commission Directives – 2003/124/EC (OJ 24.12.2003 L339 p 70) and 2003/125/EC of 22 December 2003 (OJ 24.12.2003 L339 p 70) and 2004/72/EC of 29 April 2004 (OJ 30.4.2004 L162 p 70). They also accommodate the directly applicable Commission Regulation (EC) 2273/2003 of 22 December 2003 (OJ 24.12.2003 L336 p 33).

The Market Abuse Directive and its associated measures are concerned with the integrity of European financial markets, and seek to establish and implement common standards against market abuse throughout the EU, with a view to enhancing investor confidence in these markets. The Directive repeals and re-enacts provisions against insider dealing originally contained in Directive 89/592/EEC of 13 November 1989 (OJ 18.11.89 L334 p 30) with a view to ensuring that persons cannot use information which is not publicly available to their own advantage or the advantage of others. In addition, the Directive contains, for the first time, measures aimed against those seeking to manipulate the market, eg by distorting the price-setting mechanism of securities or by disseminating false or misleading information.

The law in these Regulations applies only to companies, Irish or non-Irish, whose securities are admitted to trading on a regulated market in the European Economic Area. The only Irish regulated market at present is the Official List of the Irish Stock Exchange. IFCMPA 2005, s 37 enables the Minister for Enterprise Trade and Employment, after consulting with the Central Bank and Financial Services Authority of Ireland, apply the Regulations to markets other than the regulated markets.

The law which at present applies to companies whose securities are traded on other markets is limited to the insider dealing provisions of CA 1990 Part V, and as appears from the introductory note to CA 1990, Pt V, that law appears to apply only to Irish companies whose securities are traded on a non-regulated markets of the Irish Stock Exchange, such as the Irish Enterprise

Exchange (IEX). Accordingly insider dealing *(i)* in Irish companies on overseas markets such as the London Stock Exchange's Alternative Investment Market (AIM) or *(ii)* in non-Irish companies IEX would not appear to be regulated by this law. Of course the victims of such trading may seek redress under the law of tort eg misrepresentation. And where the trading is subject to overseas enforcement – eg an Irish company whose shares are traded on AIM, the relevant UK law would apply to prohibit and punish such trading.

The Regulations contain the Directive's general definition of what constitutes market abuse. This definition was chosen at EU level in order to be flexible enough to ensure that new abusive practices which might emerge are adequately covered. At the same time it is sufficiently clear to provide adequate guidance for behaviour to market participants.

Trading in securities when in possession of 'inside information' is prohibited. This includes not only straightforward dealing with inside information, but also tipping for the purpose of dealing, dealing when acting on a tip and aiding or procuring a dealing.

But issuers are obliged, subject to a narrow exemption, to disclose in a timely manner what would otherwise be inside information so as to be able to limit the possibilities of insider dealing.

The Regulations prohibit persons engaging in manipulative behaviour which would have the effect of misleading or distorting the market.

The Regulations contain administrative procedures requiring persons discharging managerial responsibilities in a listed company to disclose their dealings in the securities of that listed company. In addition lists of insiders must be kept by listed issuers so that the individuals both inside the company and in, for example, external advisory firms who would come into possession of inside information on an episodic or continuous basis can be identified. These procedures are aimed at providing further disincentives both to insider dealing and to market manipulation.

The Regulations go beyond regulating issuers and persons dealing in their securities to regulate the originators of research on companies and their securities. They must take reasonable care to ensure that such information is fairly presented and disclose their interests or declare conflicts of interest. Public institutions disseminating statistics must do so in a fair and transparent way.

The Regulations conveniently set out the Commission Regulation (EC) 2273/2003 dealing with stabilisation procedures – ie over allotment and repurchase of securities in connection with a public issue in order to smooth out the peaks and troughs in market prices which might otherwise obtain, to the detriment of investors in the market. The ethic of the Regulation is that trading in own shares and stabilisation must be carried out transparently in order to avoid insider dealing or giving misleading signals to the markets.

The Regulations should be read in conjunction with IFCMPA 2005, Pt 4 which provides the regime for statutory liability, both civil and criminal, for breaches of market abuse law. In addition, the Central Bank and Financial Services Authority of Ireland, more commonly referred to (at present) as 'the Financial Regulator' and in the Regulations as 'the Bank' has made Market Abuse Rules which further clarify the law. And the Commission Level 2 Regulations[2] and CESR Level 3 guidance must be noted also.

1 For a commentary on the Lamfalussy process and the four-level structure of enactment of EU securities legislation, see the introductory note to IFCMPA 2005, Pt 4 and the introductory note to the Prospectus (Directive 2003/71/EC) Regulations 2005.

2 In addition to the Level 2 Directives and Regulation the Commission has published a communication of 12 December 2006 Ref: COM 2006/789, as at 1 February 2007 not yet published in the Official Journal, to provide practical guidance on the provisions of recent European legislation relating to investment research and financial analysts, principally the Market Abuse Directive and also the Transparency Directive.

I, Micheál Martin, Minister for Enterprise, Trade and Employment, in exercise of the powers conferred on me by section 30 of the Investment Funds, Companies and Miscellaneous Provisions Act 2005 (No. 12 of 2005) and for the purpose of giving effect to the 2003 Market Abuse Directive (being Directive 2003/6/EC of the European Parliament and of the Council of 28 January 2003 (OJ L096, 12.04.2003, p.16) on insider dealing and market manipulation (market abuse)) and for the other purposes mentioned in that section, hereby make the following regulations:

Definitions

'2003 Market Abuse Directive': IFCMPA 2005, s 29(1).

PART 1
PRELIMINARY

1 Citation, construction and commencement

(1) These Regulations may be cited as the Market Abuse (Directive 2003/6/EC) Regulations 2005.

(2) These Regulations and the Companies Acts 1963 to 2005 shall be construed together as one.

(3) Subject to paragraph (4), these Regulations shall come into operation on 6 July 2005.

(4) Regulations 11 and 12 and Part 3 shall come into operation on 1 October 2005.

2 Interpretation generally

(1) In these Regulations, unless the context otherwise requires—

'accepted market practices' means practices that are—

(a) reasonably expected in one or more financial markets, and

(b) accepted by the Bank in accordance with Schedule 1;

'act' includes an omission (and, accordingly, any reference to an act done includes an omission made);

'approved stock exchange' has the same meaning as it has in the Stock Exchange Act 1995 (No. 9 of 1995);

'Bank' means the Central Bank and Financial Services Authority of Ireland;

'contravention' includes, in relation to any provision, a failure to comply with that provision and 'contravene' shall be construed accordingly;

'Court' means the High Court;

'credit institution' means any person as defined in Article 1(1) of Directive 2000/1 2/EC of the European Parliament and of the Council of 20 March 2000 (OJ L126, 26.05.2000, p. 1) relating to the taking up and pursuit of the business of credit institutions;

'EEA Agreement' means the Agreement on the European Economic Area signed at Oporto on 2 May 1992, as amended for the time being;

'EEA State' means a state which is a contracting party to the EEA Agreement;

'enactment' includes an instrument made under an enactment;

'financial instrument' means—

(a) transferable securities as defined in Article 4 of Council Directive 93/22/EEC of 10 May 1993 (OJ L141, 11.06.1993, p. 27) on investment services in the securities field,

(b) units in collective investment undertakings,

(c) money-market instruments,

(d) financial futures contracts, including equivalent cash-settled instruments,

(e) forward interest rate agreements,

(f) interest-rate, currency and equity swaps,

(g) derivatives on commodities,

(h) any other instrument admitted to trading on a regulated market in a Member State or for which a request for admission to trading on such a market has been made, and

(i) options to acquire or dispose of any instrument falling into any of paragraphs (a) to (h) of this definition, including equivalent cash-settled instruments in particular options on currency and on interest rates;

'functions' includes powers and duties, and references to the performance of functions include, as respects powers and duties, references to the exercise of powers and the carrying out of duties;

'information of a precise nature' means information that—

(a) indicates—

(i) a set of circumstances which exists or may reasonably be expected to come into existence, or

(ii) an event which has occurred or may reasonably be expected to occur, and

(b) is specific enough to enable a conclusion to be drawn as to the possible effect of that set of circumstances or event, as the case may be, on the prices of financial instruments or related derivative financial instruments;

'information which, if it were made public, would be likely to have a significant effect on the prices of financial instruments or related derivative financial instruments' means information that a reasonable investor would be likely to use as part of the basis of the investor's investment decisions, and includes cognate expressions;

'inside information' means—

(a) information of a precise nature relating directly or indirectly to one or more issuers of financial instruments or to one or more financial instruments which has not been made public and which, if it were made public, would be likely to have a significant effect on the price of those financial instruments or on the price of related derivative financial instruments,

(b) in relation to derivatives on commodities and subject to paragraph (2), information of a precise nature which has not been made public, and relating, directly or indirectly, to one or more such derivatives and which users of markets on which such derivatives are traded would expect to receive in accordance with accepted market practices on those markets, or

(c) for persons charged with the execution of orders concerning financial instruments, information conveyed by a client and relating to the client's pending orders, which is of a precise nature, which relates directly or indirectly to one or more issuers of financial instruments or to one or more financial instruments, and which, if it were made public, would be likely to have a significant effect on the prices of those financial instruments or on the price of related derivative financial instruments;

'insider dealing' means any act which contravenes Regulation 5(1) or (2);

'investment firm' means investment firm as defined in Article 1(2) of Council Directive 93/22/EEC;

'issuer' means an issuer of any financial instrument to which these Regulations apply pursuant to Regulation 4;

'market abuse' means—

(a) insider dealing, or

(b) market manipulation;

'market manipulation' means—

(a) transactions or orders to trade—

(i) which give, or are likely to give, false or misleading signals as to the supply of, demand for or price of financial instruments, or

(ii) which secure, by a person, or persons acting in collaboration, the price of one or several financial instruments at an abnormal or artificial level,

unless the person who entered into the transactions or issued the orders to trade establishes that the person's reasons for so doing are legitimate and the transactions or orders to trade, as the case may be, conform to accepted market practices on the regulated market concerned,

(b) transactions or orders to trade which employ fictitious devices or any other form of deception or contrivance, or

(c) dissemination of information through the media, including the Internet, or by any other means, which gives, or is likely to give, false or misleading signals as to financial instruments, including the dissemination of rumours and false or misleading news, where the person who made the dissemination knew, or ought to have known, that the information was false or misleading;

'market operator'—

(a) means a person who—

(i) manages the business of a regulated market,

(ii) operates the business of a regulated market, or

(iii) manages and operates the business of a regulated market,

(b) includes a regulated market which—

(i) manages its own business as a regulated market,

(ii) operates its own business as a regulated market, or

(iii) manages and operates its own business as a regulated market;

'Member State' means a Member State of the European Communities and an EEA State;

'notify' means notify in writing;

'regulated market' means regulated market as defined in Article 1(13) of Council Directive 93/22/EEC;

'relevant community acts' means—

(a) the 2003 Market Abuse Directive,

(b) the supplemental Directives, and

(c) the Market Abuse Regulation.

(2) For the purposes of paragraph (b) of the definition of 'inside information', users of markets on which derivatives on commodities are traded shall be deemed to expect to receive information—

(a) relating, directly or indirectly, to one or more such derivatives, and

(b) which is—

(i) routinely made available to the users of those markets, or

(ii) required to be disclosed in accordance with legal or regulatory provisions, market rules, contracts or customs on the relevant underlying commodity market or commodity derivatives market.

(3) For the purposes of demonstrating the operation of the definition of 'market manipulation', the following examples are derived from that definition—

(a) conduct by a person, or persons acting in collaboration, to secure a dominant position over the supply of or demand for a financial instrument which has the effect of fixing, directly or indirectly, purchase or sale prices or creating other unfair trading conditions,

(b) the buying or selling of financial instruments at the close of the market with the effect of misleading investors acting on the basis of closing prices,

(c) taking advantage of occasional or regular access to the traditional or electronic media by voicing an opinion about a financial instrument (or indirectly about its issuer) while having previously taken positions on that instrument and profiting subsequently from the impact of opinions voiced on the price of that instrument, without having simultaneously disclosed that conflict of interest to the public in a proper and effective way.

(4) Without prejudice to the examples set out in paragraph (3) and for the purposes of applying paragraph (a) of the definition of 'market manipulation', the non-exhaustive signals set out in Schedule 2, which should not necessarily be deemed in themselves to constitute market manipulation, shall be taken into account when transactions or orders to trade are examined by market participants and competent authorities.

(5) Without prejudice to the examples set out in paragraph (3) and for the purposes of applying paragraph (b) of the definition of 'market manipulation', the non-exhaustive signals set out in Schedule 3, which should not necessarily be deemed in themselves to constitute market manipulation, shall be taken into account when transactions or orders to trade are examined by market participants and competent authorities.

(6) A word or expression that is used in these Regulations and is also used in the relevant community acts shall have in these Regulations the same meaning as it has in the relevant community acts unless the contrary intention appears.

(7) A reference in these Regulations—

(a) to any other enactment or to a Directive or Regulation of the Council or Commission of the European Communities shall, unless the context otherwise requires, be construed as a reference to that enactment, Directive or Regulation as amended or extended by any other enactment or, as the case may be, Directive or Regulation of the Council or Commission of the European Communities European Communities (including, in the case of an enactment, by a Regulation of these Regulations),

(b) a reference to a Regulation or Part is a reference to a Regulation or Part of these Regulations unless it is indicated that a reference to some other provision is intended,

(c) a reference to a Schedule is a reference to a Schedule to these Regulations unless it is indicated that a reference to some other provision is intended,

(d) a reference to a paragraph, subparagraph or clause is a reference to a paragraph, subparagraph or clause of the provision in which the reference occurs unless it is indicated that a reference to some other provision is intended.

Cross reference

Directive 93/22/EC has been superseded by Directive 2004/39/EC (MiFID), which provides that a 'regulated market' means a 'multilateral system operated and/or managed by a market operator, which brings together or facilitates the bringing together of multiple third-party buying and selling interests in financial instruments – in the system and in accordance with its non-discretionary rules – in a way that results in a contract, in respect of the financial instruments admitted to trading under its rules and/or systems, and which is authorised and functions regularly and in accordance with the provisions of Title III [of MiFID].'

Definitions

'2003 Market Abuse Directive': IFCMPA 2005, s 29(1); 'Market Abuse Regulation': IFCMPA 2005, s 29(1); 'supplemental Directives': IFCMPA 2005, s 29(1).

Notes

CESR has published guidance to assist the interpretation of the Market Abuse Directive (06–562b) of 12 July 2007, exploring, *inter alia*, the four constituent parts of the definition of insider dealing:

(a) information of a precise nature;

(b) which has not been made public;

(c) relating, directly or indirectly, to one or more issuers of financial instruments or to one or more financial instruments;

(d) which, if it were made public, would be likely to have a significant effect on the prices of those financial instruments or on the price of related derivative financial instruments.

In the guidance it identifies the following illustrative examples of such insider information:

Information which directly concerns the issuer:

- Operating business performance;
- Changes in control and control agreements;
- Changes in management and supervisory boards;
- Changes in auditors or any other information related to the auditors' activity;
- Operations involving the capital or the issue of debt securities or warrants to buy or subscribe securities;
- Decisions to increase or decrease the share capital;
- Mergers, splits and spin-offs;
- Purchase or disposal of equity interests or other major assets or branches of corporate activity;
- Restructurings or reorganizations that have an effect on the issuer's assets and liabilities, financial position or profits and losses;
- Decisions concerning buy-back programmes or transactions in other listed financial instruments;
- Changes in the class rights of the issuer's own listed shares;
- Filing of petitions in bankruptcy or the issuing of orders for bankruptcy proceedings;
- Significant legal disputes;
- Revocation or cancellation of credit lines by one or more banks;
- Dissolution or verification of a cause of dissolution;
- Relevant changes in the assets' value;
- Insolvency of relevant debtors;
- Reduction of real properties' values;
- Physical destruction of uninsured goods;
- New licences, patents, registered trade marks;
- Decrease or increase in value of financial instruments in portfolio;
- Decrease in value of patents or rights or intangible assets due to market innovation;
- Receiving acquisition bids for relevant assets;
- Innovative products or processes;
- Serious product liability or environmental damages cases;
- Changes in expected earnings or losses;
- Relevant orders received from customers, their cancellation or important changes;
- Withdrawal from or entering into new core business areas;
- Relevant changes in the investment policy of the issuer;
- Ex-dividend date, dividend payment date and amount of the dividend;
- Changes in dividend policy payment.

The draft guidance also discusses information which relates indirectly to issuers or financial instruments. The following is a list of examples:

- Data and statistics published by public institutions disseminating statistics;
- The coming publication of rating agencies' reports, research, recommendations or suggestions concerning the value of listed financial instruments;
- Central bank decisions concerning interest rate;
- Government's decisions concerning taxation, industry regulation, debt management, etc.
- Decisions concerning changes in the governance rules of market indices, and especially as regards their composition;

- Regulated and unregulated markets' decisions concerning rules governing the markets;
- Competition and market authorities' decisions concerning listed companies;
- Relevant orders by government bodies, regional or local authorities or other public organizations;
- A change in trading mode (eg, information relating to knowledge that an issuer's financial instruments will be traded in another market segment: eg change from continuous trading to auction trading); a change of market maker or dealing conditions.

The draft guidance also discusses the price sensitivity of an order to trade and the precise nature of such an order.

'The price sensitivity of an order is likely to be influenced by:

a. its dimension/size, compared, for example, with the average size of the orders in that market or the daily trading volume. The greater the size of the order as compared with the average size of orders in that market, the more likely it is to have an influence on the price of the financial instrument;

b. the liquidity of the market during the period of the order execution;

c. the bid-ask spread: the wider the spread, the more likely that an order may have an impact on the price;

d. the price limit for the order and the relationship of that price limit to the current bid-ask spread;

e. the execution timeframe as instructed by the client (e.g. the quicker the client wants the order executed, the more likely there is to be a price impact);

f. the execution timing in relation to determining relevant or reference prices such as opening, closing minimum or maximum prices or exercise prices of related financial instruments such as derivatives, covered warrants, structured bonds, etc;

g. the identity of the client;

h. whether the order is likely to influence the behaviour of other market participants.

The test for the precise nature of an order is more likely to be satisfied:

a. the more defined are the order's size, price limit and execution period;

b. the more predictable the pattern of the trading behaviour of a client,

the more precise will be the nature of a particular order from that client.'

Part IV of CESR Guidance Ref: 04-505b available at http://www.cesr-eu.org which out the types of practice which CESR members (including the Irish Financial Regulator) would consider to constitute market manipulation. These are described in non-technical terms under the headings of: (i) false and misleading transactions (para 4.11); (ii) price positioning (para 4.12); (iii) transactions involving fictitious devices or deception (para 4.13); and (iv) dissemination of false and misleading information.

'**False/Misleading Transactions**

(a) Wash trades. This is the practice of entering into arrangements for the sale or purchase of a financial instrument where there is no change in beneficial interests or market risk or where the transfer of beneficial interest or market risk is only between parties who are acting in concert or collusion. (Repo transactions and stock lending/borrowing or other transactions involving transfer of securities as collateral do not constitute wash trades.)

(b) Painting the tape. This practice involves engaging in a transaction or series of transactions which are shown on a public display facility to give the impression of activity or price movement in a financial instrument.

(c) Improper matched orders. These are transactions where both buy and sell orders are entered at or nearly at the same time, with the same price and quantity by different but colluding parties, unless the transactions are legitimate trades carried out in conformity with the rules of the relevant trading platform (e.g. crossing trades).

(d) Placing orders with no intention of executing them. This involves the entering of orders, especially into electronic trading systems, which are higher/lower than the previous bid/offer. The intention is not to execute the order but to give a misleading impression that there is demand for or supply of the financial instrument at that price. The orders are then withdrawn from the market before they are executed. (A variant on this type of market manipulation is to place a small order to move the bid/offer price of the financial instrument and being prepared for that order to be executed if it cannot be withdrawn in time.)

Price Positioning

(a) Marking the close. This practice involves deliberately buying or selling securities or derivatives contracts at the close of the market in an effort to alter the closing price of the security or derivatives contract. This practice may take place on any individual trading day but is particularly associated with dates such as future/option expiry dates or quarterly/annual portfolio or index reference/valuation points.

(b) Colluding in the after market of an Initial Public Offer. This practice is particularly associated with Initial Public Offers of securities immediately after trading in the security begins. Parties which have been allocated stock in the primary offering collude to purchase further tranches of stock when trading begins in order to force the price of the security to an artificial level and generate interest from other investors – at which point they sell their holdings.

(c) Abusive squeeze. This involves a party or parties with a significant influence over the supply of, or demand for, or delivery mechanisms for a financial instrument and/or the underlying product of a derivative contract exploiting a dominant position in order materially to distort the price at which others have to deliver, take delivery or defer delivery of the instrument/product in order to satisfy their obligations. (It should be noted that the proper interaction of supply and demand can and often does lead to market tightness but that this is not of itself market manipulation. Nor does having a significant influence over the supply of, demand for, or delivery mechanisms for an investment/product by itself constitute market manipulation.)

(d) Creation of a floor in the price pattern. This practice is usually carried out by issuers or other entities which control them, and involves transactions or orders to trade employed in such a way that obstacles are created to the share prices falling below a certain level, mainly in order to avoid negative consequences for their share or credit ratings. This needs to be distinguished from legitimate trading in shares as part of 'buy-back' programmes or the stabilisation of financial instruments.

(e) Excessive bid-ask spreads. This conduct is carried out by intermediaries which have market power – such as specialists or market makers acting in cooperation – in such a way intentionally to move the bid-ask spread to and/or to maintain it at artificial levels and far from fair values, by abusing of their market power, i.e. the absence of other competitors.

(f) Trading on one market to improperly position the price of a financial instrument on a related market. This practice involves undertaking trading in one market with a view to improperly influencing the price of the same or a related financial instrument in another market. Examples might be conducting trades in an equity to position the price of its derivative traded on another market at a distorted level or trading in the underlying product of a commodity derivative to distort the price of the derivative contract. (Transactions to take legitimate advantage of differences in the prices of financial instruments or underlying products as traded in different locations would not constitute manipulation.)

Transactions involving fictitious devices/deception

(a) Concealing ownership. This is a transaction or series of transactions which is designed to conceal the ownership of a financial instrument via the breach of disclosure requirements through the holding of the instrument in the name of a colluding party (or parties). The disclosures are misleading in respect of the true underlying holding of the instrument. (This practice does not cover cases where there are legitimate reasons for financial instruments to be held in the name of a party other than the beneficial owner – e.g. nominee holdings. Nor do all failures to make a required disclosure necessarily constitute market manipulation.)

(b) Dissemination of false or misleading market information through media, including the internet, or by any other means (in some jurisdictions this is known as 'scalping'). This is done with the intention of moving the price of a security, a derivative contract or the underlying asset in a direction that is favourable to the position held or a transaction planned by the person disseminating the information.

(c) Pump and dump. This practice involves taking a long position in a security and then undertaking further buying activity and/or disseminating misleading positive information about the security with a view to increasing the price of the security. Other market participants are misled by the resulting effect on price and are attracted into purchasing the security. The manipulator then sells out at the inflated price

(d) 'Trash and cash'. This is the opposite of pump and dump. A party will take a short position in a security; undertake further selling activity and/or spread misleading negative information about the security with the purpose of driving down its price. The manipulator then closes their position after the price has fallen.

(e) Opening a position and closing it immediately after its public disclosure. This practice is typically carried out by portfolio managers and other large investors whose investment decisions are usually valued by market participants as relevant signals of future price dynamics. The canonical unfair conduct consists in closing the position previously acquired immediately after having publicly disclosed it putting emphasis on the long holding period of the investment. However, making a report or disclosure will not, in itself, give rise to a false or misleading impression if it was made in the way specified by any applicable legal or regulatory requirement and was expressly required or permitted by such a requirement.

Dissemination of false and misleading information

This type of market manipulation involves dissemination of false and misleading information without necessarily undertaking any accompanying transaction. This could include creating a misleading impression by failure properly to disclose a price sensitive piece of information which should be disclosed. For example, an issuer with information which would meet the Directive definition of 'inside information' fails properly to disclose that information and the result that the public is likely to be misled.

(a) Spreading false/misleading information through the media. This involves behaviour such as posting information on an internet bulletin board or issuing a press release which contains false or misleading statements about a company whose shares are admitted to trading on a regulated market. The person spreading the information knows that it is false or misleading and is disseminating the information in order to create a false or misleading impression. Spreading false/misleading information through an officially recognised channel for disseminating information to users of a regulated market is particularly serious as it is important that market participants are able to rely on information dissemination via such official channels.

(b) Other behaviour designed to spread false/misleading information. This type of market manipulation would cover a course of conduct designed to give false and misleading impression through means other than the media. An example might be the movement of physical commodity stocks to create a misleading impression as to the supply or demand for a commodity or the deliverable into a commodity futures contract.'

UK legislation

Criminal Justice Act 1993, s 56, FSMA 2000, ss 102A, 103, inserted by SI 2005/1433; FSMA 2000, s 118, 118C, 130A, inserted by SI 2005/381.

3 Single administrative competent authority

The Bank is designated as the single administrative competent authority for the purposes of the Directive.

Definitions

'Bank': Market Abuse Regs, reg 2(1).

UK legislation

FSMA 2000, ss 1(1), 2(1), Pt VIII generally.

4 Application

(1) Subject to Regulations 5(4), 10(12) and 11(6), these Regulations shall apply to any financial instrument—

(a) admitted to trading on a regulated market in at least one Member State, or

(b) for which a request for admission to trading on a regulated market in at least one Member State has been made,

whether or not any transaction in or relating to the financial instrument takes place on that market.

(2) These Regulations shall apply to—

(a) actions carried out in the State or abroad concerning financial instruments that—

(i) are admitted to trading on a regulated market situated in or operating in the State, or

(ii) for which a request for admission to trading on a regulated market situated in or operating in the State has been made, and

(b) actions carried out in the State concerning financial instruments that—

(i) are admitted to trading on a regulated market in a Member State, or

(ii) for which a request for admission to trading on a regulated market in a Member State has been made.

(3) These Regulations do not apply to transactions carried out in pursuit of monetary, exchange rate or public debt management policy by—

(a) a Member State,

(b) the European System of Central Banks,

(c) the Bank,

(d) the Minister for Finance, or

(e) the National Treasury Management Agency.

a particular security – especially if the client is insistent that the order is carried out very urgently or must be conducted before a particular time specified by the client;

(b) The client's requested transaction or investment behaviour is significantly out of character with the client's previous investment behaviour. (e.g. type of security; amount invested; size of order; duration of holding). (One case reported by a CESR member involved a client wanting to sell his whole portfolio and immediately invest the proceeds in the securities of a specific company. Others have involved a client who had previously invested only in mutual funds suddenly requesting the purchase of the securities of a single company or a client who had previously only invested in 'blue chip' stocks who made a sudden switch into illiquid securities. In a further case a 'buy and hold' client suddenly conducted a purchase of a particular security just before the announcement of inside information and then a sale directly after the announcement.)

(c) The client specifically requests immediate execution of an order regardless of the price at which the order would be executed (this indicator pre-supposes more than the simple placing of a 'market order' by the client);

(d) Significant trading by major shareholders or other insiders before the announcement of important corporate events.

(e) Unusual trading in the shares of a company before the announcement of price sensitive information relating to the company; transactions resulting in sudden and unusual changes in the volume of orders and shares prices before public announcements regarding the security in question;

(f) Employees' own account transactions and related orders timed just before clients' transactions and related orders in the same financial instrument.'

UK legislation

FSMA 2000, ss 118, 118A, 119, inserted by SI 2005/381, FSA Code of Market Conduct generally.

---

6 Market manipulation

(1) A person shall not engage in market manipulation.

(2) Having regard to section 33(2) of the Investment Funds, Companies and Miscellaneous Provisions Act 2005, it is declared that the purpose of paragraph (1) is to implement Article 5 of the 2003 Market Abuse Directive.

Definitions

'market manipulation': Market Abuse Regs, reg 2(1); '2003 Market Abuse Directive': IFCMPA 2005, s 29(1).

Notes

Whereas there is a parallel law of insider dealing for the securities of companies not admitted to trading on a regulated market, there is no equivalent statutory provision regulating market manipulation on a non-regulated market.

UK legislation

FSMA ss 118, 118A, 119, inserted by SI 2005/381, FSA Code of Market Conduct.

---

7 Preventing and detecting market manipulation practices

(1) The Bank shall require that market operators—

(a) so structure their operations such that market manipulation practices are prevented and detected, and

(b) report to it on a regular basis in accordance with arrangements drawn up by the Bank.

(2) Without prejudice to the generality of paragraph (1), the Bank may impose requirements under that paragraph concerning transparency of transactions concluded, total disclosure of price- regularisation agreements, a fair system of order pairing, introduction of an effective atypical order detection scheme, sufficiently robust financial instrument reference price-fixing schemes and clarity of rules on the suspension of transactions.

Definitions

'Bank': Market Abuse Regs, reg 2(1); 'financial instrument': Market Abuse Regs, reg 2(1); 'market manipulation': Market Abuse Regs, reg 2(1); 'market operator': Market Abuse Regs, reg 2(1).

UK legislation

FSMA 2000, s 2, 6(2).

8 Exemption for actions taken in conformity with takeover rules

(1) A word or expression that is used in this Regulation and is also used in the Irish Takeover Panel Act 1997 (No. 5 of 1997) shall have the same meaning in this Regulation as it has in that Act.

(2) Having access to inside information relating to another company and using it in the context of a public takeover offer for the purpose of gaining control of that company or proposing a merger with that company in conformity with rules made under section 8 of the Irish Takeover Panel Act 1997 does not of itself constitute market abuse and is not a contravention of Regulation 5 or 6.

(3) Regulation 5(3)(c) does not preclude a company ('first-mentioned company') from dealing in the financial instruments of another company ('second-mentioned company') at any time by reason only of information in the possession of an officer of the first-mentioned company that—

(a) was received by the officer in the course of the carrying out of the officer's duties, and

(b) consists only of the fact that the first-mentioned company proposes to acquire or attempt to acquire financial instruments of the second-mentioned company.

(4) Actions taken in compliance with rules made under section 8 of the Irish Takeover Panel Act 1997 (in particular rules relating to the timing, dissemination or availability, content and standard of care applicable to a disclosure, announcement, communication or release of information during the course of a public takeover offer) does not of itself constitute market abuse and is not a contravention of Regulation 5 or 6 provided that the relevant general principles set out in the Irish Takeover Panel Act 1997 are also complied with.

(5) Nothing in these Regulations affects the jurisdiction and role of the Irish Takeover Panel under the Irish Takeover Panel Act 1997.

(6) Without prejudice to the generality of paragraph (5), the Irish Takeover Panel, in performing its functions under the Irish Takeover Panel Act 1997, and the Bank, in performing its functions under these Regulations, shall have due regard to the other's performance of functions under that Act or these Regulations, as the case may be.

Definitions

'Bank': Market Abuse Regs, reg 2(1); 'financial instrument': Market Abuse Regs, reg 2(1); 'functions': Market Abuse Regs, reg 2(1); 'inside information': Market Abuse Regs, reg 2(1); 'market abuse': Market Abuse Regs, reg 2(1); 'contravention': Market Abuse Regs, reg 2(1).

UK legislation

FSMA 2000, s 120.

9 Buy-back programmes or stabilisation measures

(1) Regulations 5 and 6 do not apply—

(a) to trading in own shares in buy-back programmes, or to trading to secure the stabilisation of a financial instrument, provided that such trading is carried out in accordance with the Market Abuse Regulation (the text of which is set out, for convenience of reference, in Schedule 5), or

(b) to the purchase of own shares carried out in accordance with Part XI of the Companies Act 1990 (No. 33 of 1990).

(2) Subject to paragraph (4), the acquisition or disposal of interests in relevant share capital by a person during the stabilising period concerned, which—

(a) is done for the purpose of stabilising or maintaining the market price of securities, and

(b) is done in conformity with the Market Abuse Regulation,

shall be disregarded during the stabilising period for the purposes of sections 67 to 79 of the Companies Act 1990.

(3) Any interest in relevant share capital which—

(a) was acquired by a person during the stabilising period for the purpose of stabilising or maintaining the market price of securities,

(b) was so acquired in accordance with the Market Abuse Regulation, and

(c) continues to be held by such person at the end of the stabilising period as provided in the Market Abuse Regulation,

shall be treated, for the purposes of sections 67 to 79 of the Companies Act 1990, as having been acquired by the person on the first day following the end of the stabilising period that is not a Saturday, Sunday or public holiday.

(4) Section 91(4) of the Companies Act 1990 shall operate to determine the interests which are to be notified to the Irish Stock Exchange Limited, and the manner in which they are to be so notified, under section 91(2) of that Act.

(5) For the purposes of this Regulation—

'buy-back programme' means a programme as described in, and operated in accordance with, the Market Abuse Regulation;

'relevant share capital' has the same meaning as it has in section 67(2) of the Companies Act 1990;

'stabilising period' means the limited time period provided in Article 8(2) of the Market Abuse Regulation.

Definitions

'financial instrument': Market Abuse Regs, reg 2(1); 'notify': Market Abuse Regs, reg 2(1); 'Market Abuse Regulation', IFCMPA 2005, s 29(1); 'buy-back programmes': Market Abuse Regs, art 2.3; 'stabilisation': Market Abuse Regs, art 2.7.

UK legislation

FSMA 2000, s 118A(5), inserted by SI 2005/381.

---

10 Disclosure of inside information

(1) Subject to paragraph (7), the issuer of a financial instrument shall publicly disclose without delay inside information—

(a) which directly concerns the issuer, and

(b) in a manner that enables fast access and complete, correct and timely assessment of the information by the public.

(2) Without prejudice to any measures taken under paragraph (1), the issuer shall, for a period of not less than 6 months, post on the issuer's Internet site or sites any inside information that the issuer is required to publicly disclose.

(3) Subject to paragraph (7), the issuer shall not combine, in a manner likely to be misleading, the provision of inside information to the public with the marketing of the issuer's activities.

(4) The issuer shall be deemed to have complied with paragraph (1) where, upon the coming into existence of a set of circumstances or the occurrence of an event, albeit not yet formalised, the issuer has without delay informed the public of those circumstances or that event, as the case may be.

(5) Where there is any significant change concerning already publicly disclosed inside information, the issuer shall publicly and without delay disclose the change—

(a) immediately after the change occurs, and

(b) through the same channel as the one used for public disclosure of the original information.

(6) The issuer shall take reasonable care to ensure that the disclosure of inside information to the public is synchronised as closely as possible between all categories of investors in regulated markets in all Member States on which—

(a) the issuer's financial instruments concerned are admitted to trading, or

(b) the issuer has requested admission to trading of the financial instruments concerned.

(7) The issuer may delay the public disclosure of inside information to avoid prejudicing the issuer's legitimate interests provided that—

(a) the failure to disclose the information would not be likely to mislead the public, and

(b) the issuer is able to ensure the confidentiality of the information.

(8) For the purposes of paragraph (7), 'legitimate interests' may include any of the following circumstances—

(a) negotiations in course, or related elements, where the outcome or normal pattern of those negotiations would be likely to be affected by public disclosure (in particular, in the event that the financial viability of the issuer is in grave and imminent danger, although not within the scope of the applicable insolvency law, public disclosure of information may be delayed for a limited period where such a public disclosure would seriously jeopardise the interest of existing and potential shareholders by undermining the conclusion of specific negotiations designed to ensure the long-term financial recovery of the issuer),

(b) decisions taken or contracts made by the management body of the issuer which need the approval of another body of the issuer in order to become effective, provided that—

(i) the organisation of the issuer requires separation between those bodies, and

(ii) a public disclosure of the information before such approval together with the simultaneous announcement that this approval is still pending would jeopardise the correct assessment of the information by the public.[c]

(9) In order to ensure the confidentiality of inside information that is not disclosed to the public under paragraph (7), the issuer shall control access to the information and, in particular—

(a) take effective measures to deny access to the information to persons other than those who require it for the exercise of their functions within the issuer,

(b) take the measures necessary to ensure that a person with access to the information acknowledges the legal and regulatory duties entailed and is aware of the sanctions attaching to the misuse or improper circulation of the information, and

(c) without prejudice to paragraph (11), have in place measures which allow immediate public disclosure in case the issuer was not able to ensure the confidentiality of the information.

(10) Subject to paragraph (11), where the issuer, or a person acting on the issuer's behalf or for the issuer's account, discloses any inside information to any third party in the normal exercise of the issuer's or person's employment, profession or duties, the issuer or person, as the case may be, shall make complete and effective public disclosure of that information, simultaneously in the case of an intentional disclosure and without delay in the case of a non-intentional disclosure.

(11) Paragraph (10) does not apply where the third party receiving the inside information is a person under an obligation of confidentiality.

(12) This Regulation does not apply to the issuer of the financial instrument concerned where the issuer neither—

(a) made a request for the financial instrument to be admitted to trading on a regulated market, nor

(b) approved the admission of the financial instrument to trading on a regulated market.

Cross references

CA 1990, s 119 imposes a comparable requirement on companies to whose securities Pt V of that Act applies to inform the public as son as possible of any major new developments in its sphere of activity which might affect the price of those securities.

Definitions

'financial instrument': Market Abuse Regs, reg 2(1); 'functions': Market Abuse Regs, reg 2(1); 'inside information': Market Abuse Regs, reg 2(1); 'issuer': Market Abuse Regs, reg 2(1); 'regulated market': Market Abuse Regs, reg 2(1); 'Member State': Market Abuse Regs, reg 2(1).

Notes

It is worth emphasising that this provision entitles, but does not oblige, an issuer to withhold inside information. It is also worth emphasising that there are three conditions which must be satisfied before the information may be withheld:

(a) the withholding of information must be so as 'to avoid prejudicing the issuer's legitimate interests;'

(b) the non-disclosure must not be likely to mislead the public; and

(c) the issuer must be able to ensure the confidentiality of the undisclosed information.

If any one of these three conditions cannot be satisfied, then the disclosure of the inside information is mandatory.

The Financial Regulator, in Rule 5 of the Market Abuse Rules made under IFCMPA 2005, s 34 provides guidance on the disclosure of information mandated by this Regulation.

CESR's second guidance on the Market Abuse Directive (06–562b of 12 July 2007) provides illustrative examples of circumstances contemplated by the exemption:

'– Confidentiality constraints relating to a competitive situation (e.g. where a contract was being negotiated but had not been finalized and the disclosure that negotiations were taking place would jeopardise the conclusion of the contract or threaten its loss to another party). This is subject to the provision that any confidentiality arrangement entered into by an issuer with a third party does not prevent it from meeting its disclosure obligations;

– Product development, patents, inventions etc where the issuer needs to protect its rights provided that significant events that impact on major product developments (for example the results of clinical trials in the case of new pharmaceutical products) should be disclosed as soon as possible;

– When an issuer decides to sell a major holding in another issuer and the deal will fail with premature disclosure;

– Impending developments that could be jeopardised by premature disclosure.'

UK legislation

FSA Disclosure Rules, Rules 2.2–2.7

(7) The Bank shall ensure that public access to information concerning the transactions notified to it under this Regulation is readily available, at least on an individual basis, without delay.

(8) For the purposes of this Regulation—

'person closely associated', in relation to a person discharging managerial responsibilities within an issuer of financial instruments, means—

(a) the spouse of the person discharging managerial responsibilities,

(b) dependent children of the person discharging managerial responsibilities,

(c) other relatives of the person discharging managerial responsibilities, who have shared the same household as that person for at least one year on the date of the transaction concerned,

(d) any person—

(i) the managerial responsibilities of which are discharged by a person—

(I) discharging managerial responsibilities within the issuer, or

(II) referred to in paragraph (a), (b) or (c) of this definition,

(ii) that is directly or indirectly controlled by a person referred to in subparagraph (i) of paragraph (d) of this definition,

(iii) that is set up for the benefit of a person referred to in subparagraph (i) of paragraph (d) of this definition, or

(iv) the economic interests of which are substantially equivalent to those of a person referred to in subparagraph (i) of paragraph (d) of this definition;

'person discharging managerial responsibilities', in relation to an issuer of financial instruments, means a person who is—

(a) a member of the administrative, management or supervisory bodies of the issuer, or

(b) a senior executive—

(i) who is not a member of the bodies referred to in paragraph (a) of this definition,

(ii) having regular access to inside information relating, directly or indirectly, to the issuer, and

(iii) having the power to make managerial decisions affecting the future developments and business prospects of the issuer.

Cross references

See CA 1990, ss 53 et seq which impose a duty of directors to inform their companies of any acquisition or disposal of interests in shares or debentures of the company or of its holding or subsidiary companies.

Definitions

'Bank': Market Abuse Regs, reg 2(1); 'financial instrument': Market Abuse Regs, reg 2(1); 'inside information': Market Abuse Regs, reg 2(1); 'notify': Market Abuse Regs, reg 2(1); 'Member State': Market Abuse Regs, reg 2(1).

Notes

The Financial Regulator, in Rule 7 of the Market Abuse Rules made under IFCMPA 2005, s 34 provides guidance on the requirements imposed on persons discharging managerial responsibilities.

There is no definition of 'relative'. A second cousin twice removed is a relative, but a partner in the sense of partner for life is not. A person discharging managerial responsibilities must therefore be attentive to the share dealings of his or her estranged spouse, but can, in the absence of suspicious transactions, stay mute in the full knowledge of share dealings of a partner with whom he or she is cohabiting.

UK legislation

FSA Disclosure Rules, Rule 3.1.

---

13 Suspicious transactions to be notified

(1) Any prescribed person who reasonably suspects that a transaction might constitute market abuse shall notify the Bank without delay (which notification may be a telephone call to a telephone number specified by the Bank provided that a notification in writing to the same effect is made as soon as is practicable after that call).

(2) Any prescribed person shall decide on a case-by-case basis whether there are reasonable grounds for suspecting that a transaction involves market abuse after taking into account the elements constituting market abuse.

(3) The Bank shall, on receipt of a notification under paragraph (1), transmit the notification immediately to the relevant competent authority of each regulated market on which the financial instrument concerned—

(a) is admitted to trading, or

(b) is the subject of a request to be admitted to trading of which the Bank is aware.

(4) A prescribed person required under paragraph (1) to notify the Bank shall transmit to the Bank the following information—

(a) a description of the transactions concerned, including the type of order (such as limit order, market order or other characteristics of the order) and the type of trading market (such as block trade),

(b) the reason or reasons for suspecting that the transactions might constitute market abuse,

(c) the names, or means of identification, of the persons on behalf of whom the transactions have been carried out, and of other persons involved in the transactions,

(d) the capacity in which the prescribed person operates (such as for own account or on behalf of third parties), and

(e) any other information which may be significant in reviewing the transactions.

(5) Where the information specified in paragraph (4) is not available at the time of notification—

(a) the notification shall include at least the reason or reasons why the prescribed person suspects that the transactions might constitute market abuse as specified in paragraph (4)(b), and

(b) the other information required by paragraph (4) shall be provided to the Bank as soon as it becomes available.

(6) A prescribed person shall not be liable for any act done, or purporting to be done, in good faith by the person pursuant to paragraph (1).

(7) An act referred to in paragraph (6) does not contravene any restriction on the disclosure of information.

(8) For the purposes of this Regulation, 'prescribed person' means any person (including any investment firm, credit institution or market operator) professionally arranging transactions in financial instruments who—

(a) is registered in the State, or

(b) consists of a branch operating in the State of any person (including any investment firm, credit institution or market operator)—

(i) professionally arranging transactions in financial instruments, and

(ii) registered in another Member State.

Definitions

'act': Market Abuse Regs, reg 2(1); 'Bank': Market Abuse Regs, reg 2(1); 'credit institution': Market Abuse Regs, reg 2(1); 'financial instrument': Market Abuse Regs, reg 2(1); 'investment firm': Market Abuse Regs, reg 2(1); 'market abuse': Market Abuse Regs, reg 2(1); 'market operator': Market Abuse Regs, reg 2(1); 'regulated market': Market Abuse Regs, reg 2(1); 'contravene': Market Abuse Regs, reg 2(1); 'Member State': Market Abuse Regs, reg 2(1).

Note

The Financial Regulator, in Rule 8 of the Market Abuse Rules Rules made under IFCMPA 2005, s 34 provides guidance on the requirements to notify suspicious transactions imposed by this Regulation.

UK legislation

FSA Supervision Rules, Rule 15.10.

14 Restrictions on disclosure of notification under Regulation 13 and of identity of notifier

(1) A person notifying the Bank under Regulation 13 shall not inform any other person, in particular the persons on behalf of whom the transactions concerned have been carried out or parties related to those persons, of the notification, unless under an obligation to do so under an enactment or rule of law.

(2) Without prejudice to the provisions of Part 5 or the rules on the transfer of personal data laid down in Directive 95/46/EC of the European Parliament and of the Council of 24 October 1995 (OJ L281, 23.11.1995, p 31) on the protection of individuals with regard to the processing of personal data and on the free movement of such data, the Bank shall not disclose to any person the identity of the person ('notifier') having notified it under Regulation 13 of the transactions concerned if the disclosure would, or would be likely to, harm the notifier.

Definitions

'Bank': Market Abuse Regs, reg 2(1); 'notify': Market Abuse Regs, reg 2(1); 'enactment': Market Abuse Regs, reg 2(1); 'enactment': Market Abuse Regs, reg 2(1), IFCMPA 2005, s 3(1).

UK legislation

FSA Supervision Rules, Rule 15.10.9.

15 Cooperation with other competent authorities

(1) The Bank shall cooperate with and render assistance to competent authorities in other Member States whenever necessary for the purpose of performing the functions of competent authorities under the relevant community acts (in particular, the exchange of information and cooperation in investigation activities).

(2) Subject to paragraph (3), the Bank shall, on receipt of a request for information from a competent authority for the purpose referred to in paragraph (1)—

(a) immediately supply the information to that competent authority,

(b) if necessary, immediately take the measures necessary to collect the required information, or

(c) if unable to supply the requested information immediately, notify that competent authority of the reasons.

(3) The Bank may refuse to supply information requested by a competent authority for the purpose referred to in paragraph (1) where—

(a) communication may adversely affect the sovereignty, security or public policy of the State,

(b) judicial proceedings have already been initiated in the State in respect of the same actions and against the same person before the authorities of the State, or

(c) a final judgment of a court of competent jurisdiction has already been delivered in relation to such persons for the same actions in the State.

(4) The Bank shall—

(a) notify the competent authority of a refusal under paragraph (3), and

(b) if the reason for the refusal falls within paragraph (3) (b) or (c), provide as detailed information as is possible on the relevant judicial proceedings or final judgment, as the case may be.

(5) Without prejudice to the obligations of the Bank with respect to criminal proceedings in the State, the Bank shall use information received from competent authorities of other Member States pursuant to Article 16(1) of the 2003 Market Abuse Directive only—

(a) for the exercise of its function under the relevant community acts, and

(b) in the context of administrative or judicial proceedings specifically related to the exercise of those functions,

unless the Bank seeks and receives the consent of the competent authority that sent the information to use such information for other purposes or to forward the information received to competent authorities of other Member States.

(6) Without prejudice to the obligations of the competent authorities in other Member States with respect to criminal proceedings in such Member States, the Bank shall not give information to competent authorities of other Member States pursuant to Article 16(1) of the 2003 Market Abuse Directive unless such other competent authority of such other Member State agrees to use such information only—

(a) for the exercise of its functions under the relevant community acts, and

(b) in the context of administrative or judicial proceedings specifically related to the exercise of those functions,

unless the competent authority receiving information from the Bank seeks and receives the consent of the Bank to use such information for other purposes or to forward the information received to competent authorities of other Member States.

(7) The Bank shall give notice to the competent authority of another Member State, in as specific manner as possible, if it believes that—

(a) acts contrary to the relevant community acts are being, or have been, carried out within the territory of the Member State, or

(b) acts are affecting financial instruments traded on a regulated market situated in the Member State.

(8) Upon receipt by the Bank of any notice from a competent authority of another Member State that—

(a) acts contrary to the relevant community acts are being, or have been, carried out within the territory of the State, or

(b) acts are affecting financial instruments traded on a regulated market situated in the State,

then, without prejudice to the competence of that notifying competent authority, the Bank shall take appropriate action and inform the notifying competent authority of the outcome and, so far as possible, of significant interim developments.

(9) The Bank shall consult with the appropriate competent authorities on any proposed follow-up with respect to any matter which is or was the subject of any notice given or received by the Bank under paragraph (7) or (8).

(10) The Bank—

(a) may request that an investigation be carried out by a competent authority of another Member State in the territory of the Member State, and

(b) may further request that agents or employees of the Bank may accompany the personnel of the competent authority of the Member State during the course of the investigation.

(11) Subject to paragraph (13), upon receipt of a request from a competent authority of another Member State, the Bank shall conduct an investigation in the State with respect to the subject matter of the request.

(12) Subject to paragraph (13), if requested by a competent authority of another Member State, the Bank may permit personnel of the competent authority to accompany personnel of the Bank during the course of an investigation conducted under paragraph (11).

(13) The Bank may refuse to initiate an investigation upon receipt of a notice under paragraph (11), or refuse to permit the personnel of another competent authority to accompany its personnel pursuant to a request under paragraph (12), where—

(a) the investigation might adversely affect the sovereignty, security or public policy of the State,

(b) judicial proceedings have already been initiated in respect of the same actions and against the same persons before the authorities of the State, or

(c) a final judgment of a court of competent jurisdiction has already been delivered in relation to such persons for the same actions in the State.

(14) The Bank shall—

(a) notify the competent authority concerned of a refusal under paragraph (13), and

(b) if the reason for the refusal falls with paragraph (13)(b) or (c), provide as detailed information as is possible on the relevant judicial proceedings or final judgment, as the case may be.

Definitions

'Bank': Market Abuse Regs, reg 2(1); 'financial instrument': Market Abuse Regs, reg 2(1); 'functions': Market Abuse Regs, reg 2(1); 'notify': Market Abuse Regs, reg 2(1); 'regulated market': Market Abuse Regs, reg 2(1); 'relevant community acts': Market Abuse Regs, reg 2(1); '2003 Market Abuse Directive', IFCMPA 2005, s 29(1); 'Member State': IFCMPA 2005, s 2(1).

UK legislation

FSMA 2000, ss 47, 354.

PART 3
FAIR PRESENTATION OF RECOMMENDATIONS

16 Interpretation (Part 3)

In this Part, unless the context otherwise requires—

'distribution channels' means a channel through which information is, or is likely to become, publicly available;

'issuer' means an issuer of a financial instrument to which—

(a) these Regulations apply pursuant to Regulation 4, and

(b) a recommendation relates, directly or indirectly,

'likely to become publicly available information' means information to which a large number of persons have access;

'recommendation' means research or other information recommending or suggesting an investment strategy, explicitly or implicitly, concerning one or several financial instruments or the issuers of financial instruments, including any opinion as to the present or future value or price of such instruments, intended for distribution channels or for the public;

'related company' means a related company within the meaning of section 140 of the Companies Act 1990;

'relevant person' means a person producing or disseminating recommendations in the exercise of the person's profession or the conduct of the person's business;

'research or other information recommending or suggesting investment strategy' means—

(a) information—

(i) produced by an independent analyst, an investment firm, a credit institution, any other person whose main business is to produce recommendations or a person working for any of them under a contract of employment or otherwise, and

(ii) that, directly or indirectly, expresses a particular investment recommendation in respect of a financial instrument or an issuer of financial instruments, or

(b) information produced by persons other than the persons referred to in paragraph (a)(i) of this definition which directly recommends a particular investment decision in respect of a financial instrument.

Definitions

'credit institution': Market Abuse Regs, reg 2(1); 'financial instrument': Market Abuse Regs, reg 2(1); 'investment firm': Market Abuse Regs, reg 2(1).

17 Production and dissemination of recommendations

A person who produces or disseminates recommendations shall—

(a) take reasonable care to ensure that the recommendations are fairly presented, and

(b) disclose any interests in or conflicts of interest concerning the financial instruments and issuer to which the recommendation relates.

Definitions

'financial instrument': Market Abuse Regs, reg 2(1); 'issuer': Market Abuse Regs, reg 16(1); 'recommendation': Market Abuse Regs, reg 16(1).

UK legislation

FSA Code of Market Conduct Rules, Rule 1.8; FSA Conduct of Business Rules, Rules 7.16, 7.17.

18 Identity of producer of recommendation

(1) Without prejudice to the generality of Regulation 17 but subject to Regulation 26, any person who produces a recommendation shall ensure that the recommendation discloses clearly and prominently—

(a) the name and job title of the individual who prepared the recommendation, and

(b) the name of the person responsible for its production.

(2) Subject to Regulation 26, where the relevant person responsible for the preparation or production of a recommendation is an investment firm or a credit institution, the

investment firm or credit institution shall ensure that the recommendation indicates clearly and prominently the identity of the relevant competent authority of the investment firm or credit institution, as the case may be.

(3) Subject to Regulation 26, where the relevant person responsible for the preparation or production of a recommendation is neither a credit institution nor an investment firm but is subject to self-regulatory standards or codes of conduct, the relevant person shall ensure that a reference to those standards or codes, as the case may be, is disclosed clearly and prominently in the recommendation.

Definitions

'credit institution': Market Abuse Regs, reg 2(1); 'investment firm': Market Abuse Regs, reg 2(1); 'recommendation': Market Abuse Regs, reg 16(1); 'relevant person': Market Abuse Regs, reg 16(1).

UK legislation

FSA Conduct of Business Rules, Rule 7.16.

19 General standard for fair presentation of recommendations

(1) Subject to Regulation 26, a relevant person responsible for the preparation or production of recommendations shall take reasonable care to ensure that—

(a) facts are clearly distinguished from interpretations, estimates, opinions and other types of non-factual information,

(b) all sources are reliable or, where there is any doubt as to whether a source is reliable, this is clearly indicated, and

(c) all projections, forecasts and price targets are clearly labelled as such and that the material assumptions made in producing or using them are indicated.

(2) Subject to Regulation 26, a relevant person shall take reasonable care to ensure that any recommendation can be justified to the Bank if the Bank requests justification of the recommendation.

Definitions

'Bank': Market Abuse Regs, reg 2(1); 'recommendation': Market Abuse Regs, reg 16(1); 'relevant person': Market Abuse Regs, reg 16(1).

UK legislation

FSA Conduct of Business Rules, Rule 17.17.

20 Additional obligations in relation to fair presentation of recommendations

(1) Without prejudice to the generality of Regulation 19, where a relevant person is an independent analyst, an investment firm, a credit institution, any related company, any other relevant person whose main business is to produce recommendations, or a person working for any of them under a contract of employment or otherwise, the relevant person shall take reasonable care to ensure that—

(a) subject to paragraph (2), all substantially material sources are indicated, including—
   (i) a description of the relevant issuer,
   (ii) whether or not the recommendation has been disclosed to that issuer, and
   (iii) whether or not following such a disclosure the recommendation has been amended before its dissemination,

(b) subject to paragraph (2), any basis of valuation or other methodology used to evaluate a financial instrument or an issuer of a financial instrument, or to set a price target for a financial instrument, is adequately summarised,

(c) subject to paragraph (2), the meaning of any recommendation made, such as buy, sell or hold, which may include the time horizon of the investment to which the recommendation relates, is adequately explained and any appropriate risk warning, including a sensitivity analysis of the relevant assumptions, indicated,

(d) reference is made to the planned frequency, if any, of updates of the recommendation and to any major changes in the coverage policy previously announced,

(e) the date on which the recommendation was first released for distribution is indicated clearly and prominently, as well as the relevant date and time for any financial instrument price mentioned, and

(f) where a recommendation differs from a recommendation concerning the same financial instrument or issuer, issued during the 12 months immediately preceding its release, this change and the date of the earlier recommendation are indicated clearly and prominently.

(2) Where the requirements of paragraph (1)(a), (b) or (c) would be disproportionate in relation to the length of the recommendation distributed, it is sufficient to make clear and prominent reference in the recommendation to a place where the required information can be directly and easily accessed by the public, such as a direct Internet link to that information on an appropriate Internet site of the relevant person, provided that there has been no change in the methodology or basis of valuation used.

Definitions

'credit institution': Market Abuse Regs, reg 2(1); 'financial instrument': Market Abuse Regs, reg 2(1); 'investment firm': Market Abuse Regs, reg 2(1); 'issuer': Market Abuse Regs, reg 16(1); 'recommendation': Market Abuse Regs, reg 16(1); 'related company': Market Abuse Regs, reg 16(1); 'relevant person': Market Abuse Regs, reg 16(1).

UK legislation

FSA Conduct of Business Rules, Rule 17.17.

---

21 General standard for disclosure of interests and conflicts of interest

(1) Subject to paragraphs (2), (3) and (4) and Regulation 26, a relevant person shall disclose in any recommendation all relationships and circumstances that may reasonably be expected to impair the objectivity of the recommendation, in particular where the relevant person has—

(a) a significant financial interest in one or more of the financial instruments which are the subject of the recommendation, or

(b) a significant conflict of interest with respect to an issuer to which the recommendation relates.

(2) Where a relevant person is a legal person, paragraph (1) also applies to any person working for, or providing a service to, the relevant person under a contract of employment or otherwise, who was involved in preparing the recommendation.

(3) Where the relevant person is a legal person, the information to be disclosed in accordance with paragraph (1) shall include the following—

(a) any interests or conflicts of interest of the relevant person or of related companies that are accessible or reasonably expected to be accessible to the persons involved in the preparation of the recommendation, and

(b) any interests or conflicts of interest of the relevant person or of related companies known to persons who, although not involved in the preparation of the recommendation, had or could reasonably be expected to have access to the recommendation prior to its dissemination to customers or the public.

(4) Where a disclosure under this Regulation would be disproportionate in relation to the length of the recommendation distributed, it is sufficient to make clear and prominent reference in the recommendation to a place where the disclosure can be directly and easily accessed by the public, such as a direct Internet link to the disclosure on an appropriate Internet site of the relevant person.

Definitions

'financial instrument': Market Abuse Regs, reg 2(1); 'issuer': Market Abuse Regs, reg 16(1); 'recommendation': Market Abuse Regs, reg 16(1).

UK legislation

FSA Conduct of Business Rules, Rule 17.17.

---

22 Additional obligations in relation to disclosure of interests or conflicts of interest

(1) Without prejudice to the generality of Regulation 21 but subject to paragraph (4), where a relevant person is an independent analyst, an investment firm, a credit institution, any related company, or any other relevant person whose main business is to produce recommendations, the relevant person shall, in any recommendation produced by the relevant person, disclose clearly and prominently the following information on their interests and conflicts of interest—

(a) any major shareholdings that exist between the relevant person or any related company on the one hand and the issuer on the other hand,

(b) any other significant interests held by the relevant persons or any related company in relation to the issuer,

(c) where applicable, a statement that the relevant person or any related company is a market maker or liquidity provider in the financial instruments of the issuer,

(d) where applicable, a statement that the relevant person or any related company has been lead manager or co-lead manager during the previous 12 months of any publicly disclosed offer of financial instruments of the issuer,

(e) where applicable, a statement that the relevant person or any related company is party to any other agreement with the issuer relating to the provision of investment banking services, provided that this would not entail the disclosure of any confidential commercial information and that the agreement—

(i) has been in effect during the previous 12 months, or

(ii) has given rise during the same period to a payment of compensation or to a promise to pay compensation, and

(f) where applicable, a statement that the relevant person or any related company is party to an agreement with the issuer relating to the production of the recommendation.

(2) For the purposes of paragraph (1)(a), 'major shareholdings' include—

(a) a shareholding held by the relevant person or any related company that exceeds 5% of the total issued share capital in the issuer, and

(b) a shareholding held by the issuer exceeding 5% of the total issued share capital in the relevant person or any related company.

(3) Without prejudice to the generality of Regulation 21 and of paragraph (1), a relevant person which is an investment firm or a credit institution shall disclose clearly and prominently—

(a) in general terms, the organisational and administrative arrangements set up within the investment firm or the credit institution, as the case may be, for the prevention and avoidance of conflicts of interest with respect to recommendations, including information barriers,

(b) with respect to persons working for the investment firm or the credit institution, as the case may be, under a contract of employment or otherwise who are involved in preparing a recommendation, whether or not the remuneration of such persons is tied to investment banking transactions performed by the investment firm or credit institution, as the case may be, or any related company,

(c) where persons referred to in subparagraph (b) receive or purchase the shares of the issuers prior to a public offering of the shares, the price at which the shares were acquired and the date of acquisition, and

(d) on a quarterly basis, the proportion of all recommendations that fall within the categories buy, hold, sell or equivalent terms, as well as the proportion of issuers corresponding to each of those categories to which the investment firm or the credit institution, as the case may be, has supplied material investment banking services over the previous 12 months.

(4) Where a disclosure under this Regulation would be disproportionate in relation to the length of the recommendation distributed, it is sufficient to make clear and prominent reference in the recommendation to a place where the disclosure can be directly and easily accessed by the public, such as a direct Internet link to the disclosure on an appropriate Internet site of the relevant person.

Definitions

'credit institution': Market Abuse Regs, reg 2(1); 'financial instrument': Market Abuse Regs, reg 2(1); 'investment firm': Market Abuse Regs, reg 2(1); 'issuer': Market Abuse Regs, reg 16(1); 'recommendation': Market Abuse Regs, reg 16(1); 'related company': Market Abuse Regs, reg 16(1); 'relevant person': Market Abuse Regs, reg 16(1).

UK legislation

FSA Conduct of Business Rules, Rule 17.17.

23 Dissemination of recommendations produced by third parties

(1) Subject to paragraph (5), a relevant person who disseminates a recommendation produced by a third party shall ensure that the recommendation indicates clearly and prominently the identity of the relevant person.

(2) Subject to paragraph (5), where a recommendation produced by a third party is substantially altered within the disseminated information, the person disseminating the information shall clearly indicate the substantial alteration in detail.

(3) Subject to paragraph (5), where a substantial alteration referred to in paragraph (2) consists of a change of the direction of the recommendation (such as changing a buy recommendation into a hold or sell recommendation or vice versa), the person disseminating the substantial alteration shall comply with the requirements of Regulations 18 to 21 as respects the substantial alteration.

(4) Subject to paragraph (5), a relevant person who disseminates a substantially altered recommendation shall have a formal written policy so that the persons receiving the information may be directed to where they can have access to such of the following that are publicly available—

(a) the identity of the producer of the recommendation,

(b) the recommendation, and

(c) the disclosure of the producer's interests or conflicts of interest.

(5) Paragraphs (1) to (4) do not apply to news reporting on recommendations produced by a third party where the substance of the recommendation is not altered.

(6) Where there is dissemination of a summary of a recommendation produced by a third party, the relevant persons disseminating the summary shall ensure that the summary—

(a) is clear and not misleading, and

(b) mentions such of the following that are publicly available—

(i) the source document, and

(ii) where disclosures relating to the source document can be directly and easily accessed by the public.

Definitions

'recommendation': Market Abuse Regs, reg 16(1); 'relevant person': Market Abuse Regs, reg 16(1).

UK legislation

FSA Conduct of Business Rules, Rule 17.17.

24 Additional obligations for investment firms and credit institutions

(1) Without prejudice to the generality of Regulation 23, where the relevant person—

(a) is an investment firm or credit institution or a person working for the investment firm or credit institution, as the case may be, under a contract of employment or otherwise, and

(b) disseminates recommendations produced by a third party,

then the relevant person shall ensure that the recommendation includes a clear and prominent disclosure of the name of the competent authority of the investment firm or credit institution, as the case may be.

(2) Where the producer of a recommendation referred to in paragraph (1) has not already disseminated the recommendation through a distribution channel, the requirements of Regulation 22 shall be met by the disseminator of the recommendation.

(3) Where an investment firm or credit institution referred to in paragraph (1) has substantially altered a recommendation, Regulations 18 to 22 shall apply with all necessary modifications.

Definitions

'credit institution': Market Abuse Regs, reg 2(1); 'investment firm': Market Abuse Regs, reg 2(1); 'distribution channels': Market Abuse Regs, reg 16(1); 'recommendation': Market Abuse Regs, reg 16(1), 'relevant person': Market Abuse Regs, reg 16(1).

UK legislation

FSA Conduct of Business Rules, Rule 7.17.

25 Non-written recommendations

The requirements of Regulations 18, 19, 20, 21(1) and 22 may be satisfied, in the case of a recommendation which is not in writing, by reference to a place where the information concerned may be directly and easily accessed by the public, such as a direct Internet link to an appropriate Internet site of the relevant person.

Definitions

'recommendation': Market Abuse Regs, reg 16(1); 'relevant person': Market Abuse Regs, reg 16(1).

UK legislation

FSA Conduct of Business Rules, Rule 7.17.

26 Exemption for journalists

(1) Regulations 18, 19 and 21 do not apply to recommendations produced or disseminated by journalists in the State subject to equivalent appropriate regulation.

(2) Without prejudice to paragraph (1), where a journalist acts in a journalist's professional capacity, the dissemination of information will be assessed, for the purposes of the definition of 'market manipulation', taking into account the code of conduct governing the journalist's profession, unless the journalist derives, directly or indirectly, an advantage or profit from the dissemination of the information concerned.

(3) For the purposes of this Regulation, 'equivalent appropriate regulation' means such regulation (including self-regulation) as the Bank considers equivalent to the requirements of Regulations 18, 19 and 21.

Definitions

'Bank': Market Abuse Regs, reg 2(1); 'market manipulation': Market Abuse Regs, reg 2(1); 'recommendation': Market Abuse Regs, reg 16(1).

UK legislation

FSMA 2000, s 118A(4), inserted by SI 2005/381.

PART 4
POWERS OF THE BANK

27 Definitions (Part 4)

In this Part, unless the context otherwise requires—

'authorised officer' means an authorised officer appointed under Regulation 28(1);

'records' means any book, document or any other written or printed material in any form including any information (including phone and data traffic records) stored, maintained or preserved by means of any mechanical or electronic device, whether or not stored, maintained or preserved in a legible form;

'relevant records' means records relating to the activities of persons to whom these Regulations apply;

'responsible authority' means—

(a) the Chief Executive of the Irish Financial Services Regulatory Authority, or

(b) any person to whom the Chief Executive of that Authority has delegated responsibility for appointing authorised officers.

Definitions

'Bank': Market Abuse Regs, reg 2(1).

---

28 Power to appoint authorised officers

(1) A responsible authority may, in writing—

(a) authorise such and so many persons as the authority considers necessary to be authorised officers for the purposes of these Regulations, and

(b) revoke any such authorisation.

(2) An appointment under paragraph (1)(a) may be for a specified or unspecified period.

(3) Every authorised officer shall—

(a) be furnished with a certificate of his or her appointment as an authorised officer, and

(b) when exercising a power under these Regulations of an authorised officer, produce the certificate, together with some form of personal identification, if requested to do so by a person affected by the exercise of that power.

(4) An appointment under paragraph (1) of a person as an authorised officer ceases—

(a) when the responsible authority concerned revokes the appointment,

(b) the person dies or resigns from the appointment,

(c) if the appointment is for a specified period, when the period ends,

(d) if the person appointed is an officer of the Irish Financial Services Regulatory Authority, when the person ceases to be such an officer, or

(e) if the person appointed is an officer of an authority or market undertaking to which the Bank has delegated powers and functions under Regulation 33(1)(c), when the person ceases to be such an officer.

Definitions

'authorised officer': Market Abuse Regs, reg 27; 'Bank': Market Abuse Regs, reg 2(1); 'functions': Market Abuse Regs, reg 2(1); 'responsible authority': Market Abuse Regs, reg 27.

UK legislation

FSMA 2000, ss 165, 167.

29 Powers of authorised officers

(1) An authorised officer may, for the purposes of enforcing compliance with these Regulations (including carrying out investigations in relation thereto), do all or any of the following—

(a) at all reasonable times enter any premises at which there are reasonable grounds to believe that there are any relevant records,

(b) search and inspect the premises referred to in subparagraph (a) and any relevant records on the premises,

(c) secure for later inspection the premises or any part of the premises in which relevant records are kept or in which the officer has reasonable grounds for believing the relevant records are kept,

(d) require any person to whom these Regulations apply to produce to the officer relevant records, and if the information is in a non-legible form, to reproduce it in a legible form or to give to the officer such information as the officer reasonably requires in relation to entries in the relevant records,

(e) inspect and take copies of relevant records inspected or produced under this Regulation (including, in the case of information in a non-legible form, a copy of all or part of the information in a permanent legible form),

(f) remove and retain any of the relevant records inspected or produced under this Regulation for such period as may be reasonable to facilitate further examination,

(g) require a person to give to the officer information (including give information by way of a written report) that the officer reasonably requires in relation to activities covered by these Regulations and to produce to the officer any relevant records that the person has or has access to,

(h) require a person by or on whose behalf data equipment is or has been used, or any person who has charge of, or is otherwise concerned with the operation of, the data equipment or any associated apparatus or material, to give the officer all reasonable assistance in relation thereto, and

(i) require a person to explain entries in any relevant records.

(2) An authorised officer shall not, except with the consent of the occupier, enter a private dwelling (other than a part of the dwelling used as a place of work) unless the officer has obtained a warrant from a judge of the District Court.

(3) Where any person from whom production of a relevant record is required claims a lien thereon, the production of it shall be without prejudice to the lien.

(4) The requirement to produce any relevant record or report or to provide information or assistance under this Regulation extends to—

(a) a liquidator or receiver of, or any person who is or has been an officer or employee or agent of, a person to whom these Regulations apply, or

(b) any other person who appears to the Bank or the authorised officer to have the relevant record or report in his or her possession or under his

(c) or her control or the ability to provide information or assistance, as the case may be.

(5) An authorised officer may, if the officer considers it necessary, be accompanied by a member of the Garda Síochána or by another authorised officer when exercising a power under this Part.

Definitions

'authorised officer': Market Abuse Regs, reg 27; 'Bank': Market Abuse Regs, reg 2(1); 'relevant records': Market Abuse Regs, reg 27.

UK legislation

FSMA 2000, ss 171, 172, 175.

---

30 Warrants

(1) When an authorised officer in the exercise of the authorised officer's powers under Regulation 29(1)—

(a) is prevented from entering any premises, or

(b) believes that there are relevant records in a private dwelling,

(c) the authorised officer or the responsible authority by whom the authorised officer was appointed may apply to a judge of the District Court for a warrant under this Regulation authorising the entry by the authorised officer into the premises or the private dwelling, as the case may be.

(2) If on an application under paragraph (1) a judge of the District Court is satisfied, on the information of the applicant, that the authorised officer concerned—

(a) has been prevented from entering any premises, or

(b) has reasonable gounds for beleiving that there relevant records in a private dwelling,

then the judge may issue a warrant under the judge's hand authorising the authorised officer, accompanied, if the judge considers it appropriate to so provide, by such number of members of the Garda Síochána as may be specified in the warrant, at any time within 4 weeks from the date of issue of the warrant, to enter, if need be by force, the premises or private dwelling and exercise any of the powers referred to in Regulation 29(1).

Definitions

'authorised officer': Market Abuse Regs, reg 27; 'relevant records': Market Abuse Regs, reg 27; 'responsible authority': Market Abuse Regs, reg 27.

UK legislation

FSMA 2000, s 176.

---

31 Directions by Bank

(1) Without prejudice to the power of the Bank to impose directions, conditions or other requirements under any enactment, where the Bank considers it necessary to do so in order to—

(a) ensure the integrity of financial markets in Member States,

(b) enhance investor confidence in those markets, or

(c) prevent any person from contravening or continuing to contravene a provision of these Regulations or any other provision of Irish market abuse law,

the Bank may, subject to paragraphs (2) and (3), issue a direction in writing to any person.

(2) A direction under paragraph (1) shall—

(a) subject to subparagraph (b), take effect on and after such date, or the occurrence of such event, as is specified in the direction for the purpose, and

(b) shall cease to have effect—

(i) on such date, or the occurrence of such event, as is specified in the direction for the purpose, or

(ii) on the expiration of the period of 12 months immediately following the day on which the direction takes effect,

whichever is the earlier.

(3) A direction under paragraph (1) shall be a direction to do one or more of the following—

(a) suspend the trading of any financial instrument,

(b) not to dispose of or otherwise dissipate any assets or specified assets of any person or not to do any of those things save where specified conditions are complied with,

(c) not to dispose of or otherwise dissipate any assets or specified assets the beneficial interest in which is vested in another person or persons or not to do any of those things save where specified conditions are complied with,

(d) being a credit institution, not to make any payments from an account held with the institution by a specified person or persons save with the prior consent of the Bank,

(e) not to accept, process or execute any further subscription or orders on behalf of a specified person,

(f) not to carry on a business (whether on the person's behalf or another's behalf) in a specified manner or otherwise than in a specified manner,

(g) not to engage in any practice that contravenes a provision of these Regulations or any other provision of Irish market abuse law,

(h) not to enter into of transactions of a specified kind or not to enter into such transactions except to a specified extent or except where specified conditions are complied with,

(i) not to publish a specified recommendation,

(j) to publish or disseminate in a specified manner information relating to a recommendation or an issuer or a financial instrument.

(4) A person may apply to the Court for, and the Court may, if it considers it appropriate to do so, grant an order setting aside or varying a direction under paragraph (1).

(5) The Bank may, as respects a direction under this Regulation which, in its opinion has not been complied with or is unlikely to be complied with, (or, in the case of a direction referred to in paragraph (2)(b) or (c), irrespective of whether it is of that opinion) apply to the Court in a summary manner for such order as may be appropriate by way of enforcement of the direction and the Court may, as it thinks fit, on the hearing of the application, make or refuse to make an order providing for such relief.

(6) An application for an order under paragraph (5) shall be by motion, and the Court when considering the motion may make such interim or interlocutory order as it considers appropriate.

(7) An application under paragraph (4) may not be made if the direction concerned has been the subject of an order granted under paragraph (5) (but without prejudice to the right of a person, the subject of an order granted under paragraph (5), to apply subsequently to the Court to have the order varied or discharged).

(8) The Court may direct the hearing together of applications made under paragraphs (4) and (5) that relate to the same direction.

(9) The Court may, if it thinks fit, vary or discharge an order made under paragraph (5).

(10) An application under paragraph (4) or (5) may be heard otherwise than in public.

(11) The Bank may give a direction amending or revoking a direction given by it under paragraph (1) but this power may not be exercised—

Definitions

'Bank': Market Abuse Regs, reg 2(1); 'Court': Market Abuse Regs, reg 2(1); 'contravention': Market Abuse Regs, reg 2(1), IFCMPA 2005, s 3(1); 'adverse assessment': Market Abuse Regs, reg 34(1); 'assessee': Market Abuse Regs, reg 34(1); 'assessment': Market Abuse Regs, reg 34(1); 'assessor': Market Abuse Regs, reg 34(1); 'prescribed contravention': Market Abuse Regs, reg 34(1); 'specified sanctions': Market Abuse Regs, reg 34(1).

UK legislation

FSMA 2000, s 87M(2), inserted by SI 2005/1433.

40 Right of appeal against adverse assessment (including specified sanctions)

(1) The assessee may appeal against the adverse assessment (including the specified sanctions) not later than 28 days after the Bank has complied with Regulation 39(1) in relation to the assessee or within such further period as the Court allows.

(2) An appeal under paragraph (1) may be heard otherwise than in public.

(3) The Court may, pending the hearing and determination of an appeal under paragraph (1), make such interim or interlocutory orders as the Court considers necessary in the circumstances.

(4) The Court shall determine an appeal under paragraph (1) by making—

(a) an order confirming, varying or setting aside the adverse assessment (including the specified sanctions), whether in whole or in part, or

(b) an order remitting the case to be decided again by the Bank in accordance with the directions of the Court.

(5) The determination of the Court on the hearing of an appeal under paragraph (1) shall be final, except that a party to the appeal may apply to the Supreme Court to review the determination on a question of law.

(6) For the avoidance of doubt, it is declared that no variation of an adverse assessment under paragraph (4) (a) may provide for the imposition of a sanction on the assessee which is not a sanction referred to in paragraphs (a) to (f) of Regulation 41.

Definitions

'Bank': Market Abuse Regs, reg 2(1); 'Court': Market Abuse Regs, reg 2(1); 'adverse assessment': Market Abuse Regs, reg 34(1); 'assessee': Market Abuse Regs, reg 34(1); 'assessment': Market Abuse Regs, reg 34(1); 'sanction': Market Abuse Regs, reg 34(1); 'specified sanctions': Market Abuse Regs, reg 34(1).

UK legislation

FSMA 2000, ss 87N(1), inserted by SI 2005/1433, 133.

41 Sanctions that may be imposed by Bank

In the case of an adverse assessment, the Bank may impose on the assessee such of the following sanctions as are the specified sanctions—

(a) a private caution or reprimand,

(b) a public caution or reprimand,

(c) subject to Regulation 46(2), a direction to pay to the Bank a monetary penalty (but not exceeding €2,500,000 in any case),

(d) a direction disqualifying the assessee from being concerned in the management of, or having a qualifying holding in, any regulated financial service provider for such time as is specified in the order,

(e) if the assessee is continuing to commit a prescribed contravention, a direction ordering the assessee to cease committing the prescribed contravention,

(f) a direction to pay to the Bank all or a specified part of the costs incurred by the Bank in investigating the matter to which the assessment relates and in holding the assessment (including any costs incurred by authorised officers).

Definitions

'Bank': Market Abuse Regs, reg 2(1); 'contravention': IFCMPA 2005, s 3(1); 'adverse assessment': Market Abuse Regs, reg 34(1); 'assessee': Market Abuse Regs, reg 34(1); 'assessment': Market Abuse Regs, reg 34(1); 'prescribed contravention': Market Abuse Regs, reg 34(1); 'qualifying holding': Market Abuse Regs, reg 34(1); 'regulated financial service provider': Market Abuse Regs, reg 34(1); 'sanction': Market Abuse Regs, reg 34(1); 'specified sanctions': Market Abuse Regs, reg 34(1).

UK legislation

FSMA 2000, s 89, s 91, s 87M, s 87L inserted by SI 2005/1433.

---

42 Power to correct assessments

(1) Where the assessor or the Bank is satisfied that there is an obvious error in the text of an assessment, the assessor or the Bank, as the case may be, may alter the text of the assessment to remove the error.

(2) Where the text of an assessment is altered under paragraph (1), the text as so altered shall be taken to be the decision of the Bank under Regulation 35(10).

(3) In paragraph (1), 'obvious error', in relation to the text of an assessment, includes—

(a) a clerical or typographical error,

(b) an error arising from an accidental slip or omission, or

(c) a defect of form.

Definitions

'Bank': Market Abuse Regs, reg 2(1); 'assessment': Market Abuse Regs, reg 34(1); 'assessor': Market Abuse Regs, reg 34(1).

---

43 When specified sanctions take effect

(1) Where—

(a) no appeal under Regulation 40 against the adverse assessment is lodged with the Court within the period for lodging the appeal, or

Definitions

'contravention': IFCMPA 2005, s 3(1); 'assessee': Market Abuse Regs, reg 34(1); 'prescribed contravention': Market Abuse Regs, reg 34(1); 'sanction': Market Abuse Regs, reg 34(1).

47 Person not to be concerned in management of regulated financial service provider while disqualified

A regulated financial service provider shall ensure that a person shall not be concerned in the management of, or have a qualifying holding in, the financial service provider while the person is subject to a sanction referred to in Regulation 41(d) that is in force.

Definitions

'qualifying holding': Market Abuse Regs, reg 34(1); 'regulated financial service provider': Market Abuse Regs, reg 34(1); 'sanction': Market Abuse Regs, reg 34(1).

UK legislation

FSMA 2000, s 56(6).

48 Power of Bank to resolve suspected contraventions, etc

(1) Where the Bank has reason to suspect that a person ('relevant party') is committing or has committed a prescribed contravention, it may enter into an agreement in writing with the relevant party to resolve the matter (including at any time before an assessment, if any, has been issued in respect of the relevant party).

(2) An agreement entered into under paragraph (1)—

- (a) is binding on the Bank and the relevant party, and
- (b) may include terms under which the relevant party accepts the imposition of sanctions.

(3) An agreement entered into under paragraph (1) may be enforced by the Bank or the relevant party in a court of competent jurisdiction.

Definitions

'Bank': Market Abuse Regs, reg 2(1); 'contravention': IFCMPA 2005, s 3(1); 'assessment': Market Abuse Regs, reg 34(1); 'prescribed contravention': Market Abuse Regs, reg 34(1); 'sanction': Market Abuse Regs, reg 34(1).

PART 6

OFFENCES AND REPORTS

49 Offences generally and application of section 32 of Investment Funds, Companies and Miscellaneous Provisions Act 2005

(1) A person who contravenes—

- (a) any provision of Regulation 5 or 6,

(b) any provision of Regulation 10, 11, 12 (except Regulation 12(7)), 13 (except Regulation 13(3)), 14 (except Regulation 14(2)), 17, 18, 19, 20, 21, 22, 23, 24 or 47, or

(c) a requirement under any provision of Regulation 7,

is guilty of an offence and liable on summary conviction to a fine not exceeding €5,000 or imprisonment for a term not exceeding 12 months or both.

(2) Each offence under paragraph (1) consisting of a contravention of any provision of Regulation 5 or 6 is an offence to which section 32 of the Investment Funds, Companies and Miscellaneous Provisions Act 2005 applies.

(3) Where the contravention in respect of which a person is convicted of an offence under these Regulations is continued after the conviction, the person shall be guilty of a further offence on every day on which the contravention continues and liable on summary conviction to a fine not exceeding €5,000 or imprisonment for a term not exceeding 12 months or both for each such further offence.

Definitions

'contravene': Market Abuse Regs, reg 2(1), IFCMPA 2005, s 3(1); 'contravention': Market Abuse Regs, reg 2(1), IFCMPA 2005, s 3(1).

UK legislation

Criminal Justice Act 1993, ss 52, 61.

---

50 Obstruction, etc. of authorised officer

A person who—

(a) obstructs an authorised officer (within the meaning of Regulation 27) in the exercise of the powers of an authorised officer under Part 4,

(b) without reasonable excuse, fails to comply with a request or requirement made by such an officer under Part 4, or

(c) gives such an officer information that the person knows or ought reasonably to know is false or misleading in a material particular,

is guilty of an offence and liable upon summary conviction to a fine not exceeding €5,000 or imprisonment for a term not exceeding 12 months or both.

UK legislation

FSMA 2000, s 177.

---

51 False, etc. information

A person who—

(a) gives the Bank a notification under Regulation 13, or

(b) gives the assessor (within the meaning of Regulation 34) information pursuant to a requirement under Part 5, that the person knows is false or misleading in a material particular or that the person does not believe to be true is guilty of an offence and liable upon summary conviction to a fine not exceeding €5,000 or imprisonment for a term not exceeding 12 months or both.

Definitions

'Bank': Market Abuse Regs, reg 2(1); 'notify': Market Abuse Regs, reg 2(1); 'assessor': Market Abuse Regs, reg 34(1).

UK legislation

FSMA 2000, s 398.

52 Offences by bodies corporate, etc

(1) Where an offence is committed under these Regulations by a body corporate and is proved to have been committed with the consent, connivance or approval of or to have been attributable to the wilful neglect on the part of any person, being a director, manager, secretary or other officer of the body corporate or a person who was purporting to act in any such capacity, that person as well as the body corporate is guilty of an offence and is liable to be proceeded against and punished as if that person were guilty of the first-mentioned offence.

(2) A person may be charged with having committed an offence under these Regulations even if the body corporate concerned is not charged with having committed an offence under these Regulations in relation to the same matter.

UK legislation

FSMA 2000, s 400.

53 Summary proceedings may be brought by Bank

Summary proceedings for an offence under these Regulations may be brought and prosecuted by the Bank.

Definitions

'Bank': Market Abuse Regs, reg 2(1).

UK legislation

FSMA 2000, s 402.

54 Annual report of Bank

The Bank shall provide the Minister with a copy extract relating to the performance of its functions under these Regulations of its annual report to the Minister for Finance pursuant to section 330 of the Central Bank Act 1942 (No. 22 of 1942) as inserted by section 26 of the Central Bank and Financial Services Authority of Ireland Act 2003 (No. 12 of 2003).

Definitions

'Bank': Market Abuse Regs, reg 2(1); 'functions': Market Abuse Regs, reg 2(1); 'Minister': IFCMPA 2005, s 3.

UK legislation

FSMA 2000, Sch 1, Pt 1, para 10.

Schedule 1

Provisions Applicable to the Definition of 'accepted Market Practices'

Regulation 2(1)

Factors to be taken into account when considering market practices

1.1 For the purposes of applying the definitions of 'inside information' and 'market manipulation' in Regulation 2(1), the following non-exhaustive factors shall be taken into account by the Bank, without prejudice to collaboration with other authorities, when assessing whether they can accept a particular market practice—

(a) the level of transparency of the relevant market practice to the whole market,

(b) the need to safeguard the operation of market forces and the proper interplay of the forces of supply and demand,

(c) the degree to which the relevant market practice has an impact on market liquidity and efficiency,

(d) the degree to which the relevant practice takes into account the trading mechanism of the relevant market and enables market participants to react properly and in a timely manner to the new market situation created by that practice,

(e) the risk inherent in the relevant practice for the integrity of, directly or indirectly, related markets, whether regulated or not, in the relevant financial instrument within the whole Community,

(f) the outcome of any investigation of the relevant market practice by any competent authority or other authority mentioned in Article 12(1) of the 2003 Market Abuse Directive, in particular whether the relevant market practice breached rules or regulations designed to prevent market abuse, or codes of conduct, be it on the market in question or on directly or indirectly related markets within the Community, and

(g) the structural characteristics of the relevant market including whether it is regulated or not, the types of financial instruments traded and the type of market participants, including the extent of retail investors participation in the relevant market.

The Bank shall, when considering the need to safeguard the operation of market forces and the proper interplay of the forces of supply and demand referred to in subparagraph (b), in particular, analyse the impact of the relevant market practice against the main market parameters, such as the specific market conditions, before carrying out the relevant market practice, the weighted average price of a single session or the daily closing price.

1.2. The Bank shall not assume that practices, in particular new or emerging market practices, are unacceptable simply because they have not been previously accepted by the Bank.

1.3. The Bank shall regularly review the market practices it has accepted, in particular, taking into account significant changes to the relevant market environment, such as changes to trading rules or to market infrastructure.

Definitions

'accepted market practices': Market Abuse Regs, reg 2(1); 'Bank': Market Abuse Regs, reg 2(1); 'financial instrument': Market Abuse Regs, reg 2(1); 'inside information': Market Abuse Regs, reg 2(1); 'market abuse': Market Abuse Regs, reg 2(1); 'market manipulation': Market Abuse Regs, reg 2(1); '2003 Market Abuse Directive': IFCMPA 2005, s 29(1).

UK legislation

FSMA 2000, s 119(2)(c), FSA Code of Market Conduct, Annex 2.

Consultation procedures and disclosure of decisions

2.1. For the purposes of applying the definitions of 'inside information' and 'market manipulation' in Regulation 2, the procedures set out in subparagraphs 2.2, 2.3 and 2.4 shall be observed by the Bank when considering whether to accept or continue to accept a particular market practice.

2.2. The Bank shall, before issuing a decision as to whether to accept or continue to accept the market practice concerned, consult as appropriate relevant bodies such as representatives of issuers, financial services providers, consumers, other authorities and market operators. The consultation procedure shall include consultation with other competent authorities, in particular where there exist comparable markets (that is, in structures, volume, type of transactions).

2.3. The Bank shall publicly disclose any decision regarding the acceptability of the market practice concerned, including an appropriate description of such practice. The disclosure shall include a description of the factors taken into account in determining whether the relevant practice is regarded as acceptable, in particular where different conclusions have been reached regarding the acceptability of the same practice on different Member States' markets.

2.4. The Bank shall transmit its decision as soon as possible to the Committee of European Securities Regulators.

2.5. When investigatory actions on specific cases have already started, the consultation procedures set out in subparagraphs 2.2 and 2.3 may be delayed until the end of such investigation and possible related sanctions.

2.6. A market practice which was accepted following the consultation procedures set out in subparagraphs 2.2 and 2.3 shall not be changed without using the same consultation procedures.

Definitions

'Member State': IFCMPA 2005, s 2(1); 'accepted market practices': Market Abuse Regs, reg 2(1); 'Bank': Market Abuse Regs, reg 2(1); 'inside information': Market Abuse Regs, reg 2(1); 'market manipulation': Market Abuse Regs, reg 2(1); 'market operator': Market Abuse Regs, reg 2(1); 'sanctions' defined in: Market Abuse Regs, reg 34(1) for the purposes of Part 5 of the Regulations only, but may assist the interpretation of para 2.5; 'issuer', is defined in: Market Abuse Regs, reg 16(1) for the purposes of Part 3 only.

UK legislation

FSMA 2000, s 396.

Schedule 2

Provisions Applicable to Paragraph (A) of the Definition of 'Market Manipulation'

Regulation 2(4)

Manipulative behaviour related to false or misleading signals and to price securing

Without prejudice to the examples of market manipulation set out in Regulation 2, and for the purposes of applying paragraph (a) of the definition of 'market manipulation' in that Regulation, the non-exhaustive signals set out below, which should not necessarily be deemed in themselves to constitute market manipulation, shall be taken into account when transactions or orders to trade are examined by market participants and the Bank:

(a) the extent to which orders to trade given or transactions undertaken represent a significant proportion of the daily volume of transactions in the relevant financial instrument on the regulated market concerned, in particular when these activities lead to a significant change in the price of the financial instrument,

(b) the extent to which orders to trade given or transactions undertaken by persons with a significant buying or selling position in a financial instrument lead to significant changes in the price of the financial instrument or related derivative or underlying asset admitted to trading on a regulated market,

(c) whether transactions undertaken lead to no change in beneficial ownership of a financial instrument admitted to trading on a regulated market,

(d) the extent to which orders to trade given or transactions undertaken include position reversals in a short period and represent a significant proportion of the daily volume of transactions in the relevant financial instrument on the regulated market concerned, and might be associated with significant changes in the price of a financial instrument admitted to trading on a regulated market,

(e) the extent to which orders to trade given or transactions undertaken are concentrated within a short time span in the trading session and lead to a price change which is subsequently reversed,

(f) the extent to which orders to trade given change the representation of the best bid or offer prices in a financial instrument admitted to trading on a regulated market, or more generally the representation of the order book available to market participants, and are removed before they are executed, and

(g) the extent to which orders to trade are given or transactions are undertaken at or around a specific time when reference prices, settlement prices and valuations are calculated and lead to price changes which have an effect on such prices and valuations.

Definitions

'financial instrument': Market Abuse Regs, reg 2(1); 'market manipulation': Market Abuse Regs, reg 2(1); 'regulated market': Market Abuse Regs, reg 2(1).

Note

See Part IV of CESR Guidance Ref: 04-505b available at http://www.cesr-eu.org which sets out the types of practice which CESR members (including the Irish Financial Regulator) would consider to constitute illustrative examples of market manipulation.

'Possible Signals of Insider Dealing or Market Manipulation

(a) An unusual concentration of transactions in a particular security (for example, with one or more institutional investors known to be affiliated with the issuer or a party with a particular interest in the issuer such as a bidder/potential bidder);

(b) An unusual repetition of a transaction among a small number of clients over a certain period of time

(c) Unusual concentration of transactions and/or orders with only one client; or with the different securities accounts of one client; or with a limited number of clients (especially if the clients are related to one another) ...

Possible signals of Market Manipulation

(a) Transactions with no other apparent justification than to increase/decrease the price of or to increase the volume of trading in a financial instrument. Particular attention might be given to orders of this kind which result in the execution of transactions near to a reference point during the trading day – e.g. near the close;

(b) The client submits orders which, because of their size in relation to the market in that security, will clearly have a significant impact on the supply of or demand for or the price or value of the security. Again, particular attention might be given to orders of this kind which result in the execution of transactions near to a reference point during the trading day – e.g. near the close;

(c) Transactions which appear to have the purpose of increasing the price of a financial instrument during the days preceding the issue of a related derivative/convertible;

(d) Transactions which appear to have the purpose of maintaining the price of a financial instrument during the days preceding the issue of a related derivative/convertible when the market trend is downward;

(e) Transactions which appear to be seeking to modify the valuation of a position while not decreasing/increasing the size of that position;

(f) Transactions which appear to be seeking to increase/decrease the weighted average price of the day or of a period during the session;

(g) Transactions which appear to be seeking to set a market price when the liquidity of the financial instrument is not sufficient to fix a price within the session (unless the rules or regulation of the regulated market explicitly allow such operations);

(h) Transactions which appear to be seeking to bypass the trading safeguards of the market (e.g. as regards volume limits; bid/offer spread parameters; etc);

(i) When a transaction is to be concluded/executed, changing the bid-ask prices (as computed by the trading system) when this spread is a factor in the determination of the price of that transaction;

(j) Entering significant orders in the central order book of the trading system a few minutes before the price determination phase of the auction and cancelling these orders a few seconds before the order book is frozen for computing the auction price so that the theoretical opening price might look higher or lower than it otherwise would do;

(k) Transactions which appear to be seeking to maintain the price of the underlying financial instrument below the strike price of a related derivative at expiration date;

(l) Transactions which appear to be aimed at modifying the price of the underlying financial instrument so that it crosses over the strike price of a related derivative at expiration date;

(m) Transactions which appear to be seeking to modify the settlement price of a financial instrument when this price is used as a reference/determinant in the calculation of margins requirements.'

UK legislation

FSMA 2000, s 119(2)(a), (b), s 122(2), FSA Code of Market Conduct, Rule 1.6.9.

Schedule 3

Provisions Applicable to Paragraph (B) of the Definition of 'Market Manipulation'

Regulation 2(5)

Manipulative behaviours related to the employment of fictitious devices or any other form of deception or contrivance

Without prejudice to the examples of market manipulation set out in Regulation 2 and for the purposes of applying paragraph (b) of the definition of 'market manipulation' in that Regulation, the non-exhaustive signals set out below, which should not necessarily be deemed in themselves to constitute market manipulation, are taken into account when transactions or orders to trade are examined by market participants and the Bank:

(a) whether orders to trade given or transactions undertaken by persons are preceded or followed by dissemination of false or misleading information by the same persons or persons linked to them, and

(b) whether orders to trade are given or transactions are undertaken by persons before or after the same persons or persons linked to them produce or disseminate research or investment recommendations which are erroneous or biased or demonstrably influenced by material interest.

Definitions

'market manipulation': Market Abuse Regs, reg 2(1).

Note

See Pt IV of CESR Guidance Ref: 04-505b available at http://www.cesr-eu.org which sets out the types of practice which CESR members (including the Irish Financial Regulator) would consider to constitute market manipulation. These are described in non-technical terms under the headings of (i) False and Misleading Transactions (para 4.11) (ii) Price Positioning (para 4.12), (iii) Transactions involving fictitious devices or deception (Para 4.13) and (iv) Dissemination of false and misleading information.

UK legislation

FSA Code of Market Conduct, Rule 1.7.3.

Schedule 4

Provisions Applicable to Lists Drawn up under Regulation 11

Regulation 11(1)

Content and form of list of persons privy to inside information

1. For the purposes of Regulation 11, lists of insiders include all persons covered by that Regulation who have access to inside information relating, directly or indirectly, to the issuer, whether on a regular or occasional basis.

2. Lists of insiders shall state—

(a) the identity of any person having access to inside information,

(b) the reason why any such person is on the list, and

(c) the date at which the list of insiders was created and updated.

3. Lists of insiders shall be promptly updated—

(a) whenever there is a change in the reason why any person is already on the list,

(b) whenever any new person has to be added to the list, and

(c) by mentioning whether and when any person already on the list has no longer access to inside information.

4. Lists of insiders shall be kept for at least 5 years after being drawn up or updated.

5. Persons required to draw up lists of insiders shall take the necessary measures to ensure that any person on such a list that has access to inside information acknowledges the legal and regulatory duties entailed and is aware of the sanctions attaching to the misuse or improper circulation of such information.

Definitions

'inside information': Market Abuse Regs, reg 2(1); 'sanctions' defined in Market Abuse Regs, reg 34(1) for the purposes of Pt 5 of the regs only, but may assist the interpretation of para 5.

Notes

'issuer', is defined in Market Abuse Regs, reg 16(1) for the purposes of Pt 3 only.

UK legislation

FSA Disclosure, Rule 2.8.

Schedule 5

Text of the Market Abuse Regulation

Regulation 9(1)(a)

THE COMMISSION OF THE EUROPEAN COMMUNITIES, Having regard to the Treaty establishing the European Community,

Having regard to Directive 2003/6/EC of the European Parliament and the Council of 28 January 2003 on insider dealing and market manipulation (market abuse)[1], and in particular Article 8 thereof,

After consulting the Committee of European Securities Regulators (CESR)[2] for technical advice,

Whereas:

(1) Article 8 of Directive 2003/6/EC provides that the prohibitions provided therein shall not apply to trading in own shares in 'buy back' programmes or to the stabilisation of a financial instrument, provided such trading is carried out in accordance with implementing measures adopted to that effect.

(2) Activities of trading in own shares in 'buy-back' programmes and of stabilisation of a financial instrument which would not benefit from the exemption of the prohibitions of Directive 2003/6/EC as provided for by Article 8 thereof, should not in themselves be deemed to constitute market abuse.

(3) On the other hand, the exemptions created by this Regulation only cover behaviour directly related to the purpose of the buy-back and stabilisation activities. Behaviour which is not directly related to the purpose of the buy-back and stabilisation activities shall therefore be considered as any other action covered by Directive 2003/6/EC and may be the object of administrative measures or sanctions, if the competent authority establishes that the action in question constitutes market abuse.

(4) As regards trading in own shares in 'buy-back' programmes, the rules provided for by this Regulation are without prejudice to the application of Council Directive 77/91/EEC on coordination of safeguards which, for the protection of the interests of members and others, are required by Member States of companies within the meaning of the second paragraph of Article 58 of the Treaty, in respect of the formation of public limited liability companies and the maintenance and alteration of their capital, with a view to making such safeguards equivalent[3].

(5) Allowable 'buy back' activities in order to benefit from the exemption of the prohibitions of Directive 2003/6/EC include issuers needing the possibility to reduce their capital, to meet obligations arising from debt financial instruments exchangeable into equity instruments, and to meet obligations arising from allocations of shares to employees.

(6) Transparency is a prerequisite for prevention of market abuse. To this end Member States may officially appoint mechanisms to be used for public disclosure of information required to be publicly disclosed under this Regulation.

(7) Issuers having adopted 'buy-back' programmes shall inform their competent authority and, wherever required, the public.

(8) Trading in own shares in 'buy-back' programmes may be carried out through derivative financial instruments.

(9) In order to prevent market abuse, the daily volume of trading in own shares in 'buy-back' programmes shall be limited. However, some flexibility is necessary in order to respond to given market conditions such as a low level of transactions.

(10) Particular attention has to be paid to the selling of own shares during the life of a 'buy-back' programme, to the possible existence of closed periods within issuers during which transactions are prohibited and to the fact that an issuer may have legitimate reasons to delay public disclosure of inside information.

(11) Stabilisation transactions mainly have the effect of providing support for the price of an offering of relevant securities during a limited time period if they come under selling pressure, thus alleviating sales pressure generated by short term investors and maintaining an orderly market in the relevant securities. This is in the interest of those investors having subscribed or purchased those relevant securities in the context of a significant distribution, and of issuers. In this way, stabilisation can contribute to greater confidence of investors and issuers in the financial markets.

(12) Stabilisation activity may be carried out either on or off a regulated market and may be carried out by use of financial instruments other than those admitted or to be admitted to the regulated market which may influence the price of the instrument admitted or to be admitted to trading on a regulated market.

(13) Relevant securities shall include financial instruments that become fungible after an initial period because they are substantially the same, although they have different initial dividend or interest payment rights.

(14) In relation to stabilisation, block trades shall not be considered as a significant distribution of relevant securities as they are strictly private transactions.

(15) When Member States permit, in the context of an initial public offer, trading prior to the beginning of the official trading on a regulated market, the permission covers 'when issued trading'.

(16) Market integrity requires the adequate public disclosure of stabilisation activity by issuers or by entities undertaking stabilisation, acting or not on behalf of these issuers. Methods used for adequate public disclosure of such information should be efficient and can take into account market practices accepted by competent authorities.

(17) There should be adequate coordination in place between all investment firms and credit institutions undertaking stabilisation. During stabilisation, one investment firm or credit institution shall act as a central point of inquiry for any regulatory intervention by the competent authority in each Member State concerned.

(18) In order to avoid confusion of market participants, stabilisation activity should be carried out by taking into account the market conditions and the offering price of the relevant security and transactions to liquidate positions established as a result of stabilisation activity should be undertaken to minimise market impact having due regard to prevailing market conditions.

(19) Overallotment facilities and 'greenshoe options' are closely related to stabilisation, by providing resources and hedging for stabilisation activity.

(20) Particular attention should be paid to the exercise of an overallotment facility by an investment firm or a credit institution for the purpose of stabilisation when it results in a position uncovered by the 'greenshoe option'.

(21) The measures provided for in this Regulation are in accordance with the opinion of the European Securities Committee,

HAS ADOPTED THIS REGULATION

1 OJ L 96, 12.4.2003, p. 16.

2 CESR was established by Commission Directive 2001/521/EC (OJ L191, 13.7.2001, p. 43).

3 OJ L 26, 31.1.1977, p. 1.

Chapter I
Definitions

Article 1

Subject matter

This Regulation lays down the conditions to be met by buy-back programmes and the stabilisation of financial instruments in order to benefit from the exemption provided for in Article 8 of Directive 2003/6/EC.

Definitions

'financial instrument': Market Abuse Directive 2003/6/EC, art 1.3; 'buy-back programmes': art 2.3 of this Market Abuse Regulation; 'stabilisation': art 2.7 of this Market Abuse Regulation.

Notes

As the Regulation is directly applicable it is the Directive's definitions rather than those in the transposing regulations which apply. This is reinforced by the reference in art 2 of this Regulation that the definitions in that article apply 'in addition to those laid down in Directive 2003/6/EC'.

UK legislation

Same as Ireland, as this reg is directly applicable to all EU Member States.

Definitions

For the purposes of this Regulation, the following definitions shall apply in addition to those laid down in Directive 2003/6/EC:

1 'investment firm' means any legal person as defined in point (2) of Article 1 of Council Directive 93/22/EEC (OJ L 141, 11.6.1993, p. 27);

2 'credit institution' means a legal person as defined in Article 1(1) of Directive 2000/12/EC of the European Parliament and the Council (OJ L 126, 26.5.2005, p. 1);

3 'buy-back programmes' means trading in own shares in accordance with Articles 19 to 24 of Council Directive 77/91/EEC;

4 'time-scheduled 'buy-back' programme' means a 'buy-back' programme where the dates and quantities of securities to be traded during the time period of the programme are set out at the time of the public disclosure of the 'buy-back' programme;

5 'adequate public disclosure' means disclosure made in accordance with the procedure laid down in Articles 102(1) and 103 of Directive 2001/34/EC of the European Parliament and of the Council (OJ L 184, 6.7.2001, p. 1);

6 'relevant securities' means transferable securities as defined in Directive 93/22/EEC, which are admitted to trading on a regulated market or for which a request for admission to trading on such a market has been made, and which are the subject of a significant distribution;

7 'stabilisation' means any purchase or offer to purchase relevant securities, or any transaction in associated instruments equivalent thereto, by investment firms or credit institutions, which is undertaken in the context of a significant distribution of such relevant securities exclusively for supporting the market price of these relevant securities for a predetermined period of time, due to a selling pressure in such securities;

8 'associated instruments' means the following financial instruments (including those which are not admitted to trading on a regulated market, or for which a request for admission to trading on such a market has not been made, provided that the relevant competent authorities have agreed to standards of transparency for transactions in such financial instruments):

(a) contracts or rights to subscribe for, acquire or dispose of relevant securities;

(b) financial derivatives on relevant securities;

(c) where the relevant securities are convertible or exchangeable debt instruments, the securities into which such convertible or exchangeable debt instruments may be converted or exchanged;

(d) instruments which are issued or guaranteed by the issuer or guarantor of the relevant securities and whose market price is likely to materially influence the price of the relevant securities, or vice versa;

(e) where the relevant securities are securities equivalent to shares, the shares represented by those securities (and any other securities equivalent to those shares).

9 'significant distribution' means an initial or secondary offer of relevant securities, publicly announced and distinct from ordinary trading both in terms of the amount in value of the securities offered and the selling methods employed;

10 'offer or' means the prior holders of, or the entity issuing, the relevant securities;

11 'allotment' means the process or processes by which the number of relevant securities to be received by investors who have previously subscribed or applied for them is determined;

12 'ancillary stabilisation' means the exercise of an overallotment facility or of a greenshoe option by investment firms or credit institutions, in the context of a significant distribution of relevant securities, exclusively for facilitating stabilisation activity;

13 'overallotment facility' means a clause in the underwriting agreement or lead management agreement which permits acceptance of subscriptions or offers to purchase a greater number of relevant securities than originally offered;

14 'greenshoe option' means an option granted by the offeror in favour of the investment firm(s) or credit institution(s) involved in the offer for the purpose of covering overallotments, under the terms of which such firm(s) or institution(s) may purchase up to a certain amount of relevant securities at the offer price for a certain period of time after the offer of the relevant securities.

Definitions

'financial instrument': Market Abuse Directive 2003/6/EC, arts 1.3 and 1.4; 'regulated market': Market Abuse Directive 2003/6/EC, arts 1.3 and 1.4.

Notes

As the Regulation is directly applicable it is the Directive's definitions rather than those in the transposing regulations which apply. This is reinforced by the statement in this art 2 that the definitions in this article apply 'in addition to those laid down in Directive 2003/6/EC'.

'1.3. 'Financial instrument' shall mean:

- transferable securities as defined in Council Directive 93/22/EEC of 10 May 1993 on investment services in the securities field (1),
- units in collective investment undertakings,
- money-market instruments,
- financial-futures contracts, including equivalent cash settled instruments,
- forward interest-rate agreements,
- interest-rate, currency and equity swaps,
- options to acquire or dispose of any instrument falling into these categories, including equivalent cash-settled instruments. This category includes in particular options on currency and on interest rates,
- derivatives on commodities,
- any other instrument admitted to trading on a regulated market in a Member State or for which a request for admission to trading on such a market has been made.

1.4 'Regulated market' shall mean a market as defined by Article 1(13) of Directive 93/22/EEC.'

UK legislation

Same as Ireland, as this reg is directly applicable to all EU member states.

Chapter II
'Buy-back' Programmes

Article 3

Objectives of buy-back programmes

In order to benefit from the exemption provided for in Article 8 of Directive 2003/6/EC, a buy-back programme must comply with Articles 4, 5 and 6 of this Regulation and the sole purpose of that buy-back programme must be to reduce the capital of an issuer (in value or in number of shares) or to meet obligations arising from any of the following:

(a) debt financial instruments exchangeable into equity instruments;

(b) employee share option programmes or other allocations of shares to employees of the issuer or of an associate company.

Definitions

'buy-back programmes': art 2.3 of this Market Abuse Regulation; 'financial instrument': Market Abuse Directive (2003/6/EC), art 1.3.

Notes

As the Regulation is directly applicable it is the Directive's definitions rather than those in the transposing regulations which apply. This is reinforced by the reference in art 2 of this Regulation that the definitions in that article apply 'in addition to those laid down in Directive 2003/6/EC'. See Definitions note under art 2.3 of this Market Abuse Regulation.

UK legislation

Same as Ireland, as this reg is directly applicable to all EU Member States.

Article 4

Conditions for 'buy-back' programmes and disclosure

1. The 'buy-back' programme must comply with the conditions laid down by Article 19(1) of Directive 77/91/EEC.

2. Prior to the start of trading, full details of the programme approved in accordance with Article 19(1) of Directive 77/91/EEC must be adequately disclosed to the public in Member States in which an issuer has requested admission of its shares to trading on a regulated market.

Those details must include the objective of the programme as referred to in Article 3, the maximum consideration, the maximum number of shares to be acquired and the duration of the period for which authorisation for the programme has been given. Subsequent changes to the programme must be subject to adequate public disclosure in Member States.

3. The issuer must have in place the mechanisms ensuring that it fulfils trade reporting obligations to the competent authority of the regulated market on which the shares have been admitted to trading. These mechanisms must record each transaction related to 'buy-back' programmes, including the information specified in Article 20(1) of Directive 93/22/EEC.

4. The issuer must publicly disclose details of all transactions as referred to in paragraph 3 no later than the end of the seventh daily market session following the date of execution of such transactions.

Definitions

'regulated market': Market Abuse Directive 2003/6/EC, art 1.4; 'adequate public disclosure' art 2.5 of this Market Abuse Regulation.

Notes

As the Regulation is directly applicable it is the Directive's definitions rather than those in the transposing regulations which apply. This is reinforced by the reference in Article 2 of this Regulation that the definitions in that Article apply 'in addition to those laid down in Directive 2003/6/EC'. See Definitions note under art 2 of this Market Abuse Regulation. In Ireland the expression 'competent authority' will be interpreted as the Central Bank and Financial Services Authority of Ireland.

UK legislation

Same as Ireland, as this reg is directly applicable to all EU Member States.

Article 5

Conditions for trading

1. In so far as prices are concerned, the issuer must not, when executing trades under a 'buy-back' programme, purchase shares at a price higher than the higher of the price of the last independent trade and the highest current independent bid on the trading venues where the purchase is carried out.

If the trading venue is not a regulated market, the price of the last independent trade or the highest current independent bid taken in reference shall be the one of the regulated market of the Member State in which the purchase is carried out.

Where the issuer carries out the purchase of own shares through derivative financial instruments, the exercise price of those derivative financial instruments shall not be above the higher of the price of the last independent trade and the highest current independent bid.

2. In so far as volume is concerned, the issuer must not purchase more than 25% of the average daily volume of the shares in any one day on the regulated market on which the purchase is carried out.

The average daily volume figure must be based on the average daily volume traded in the month preceding the month of public disclosure of that programme and fixed on that basis for the authorised period of the programme.

Where the programme makes no reference to that volume, the average daily volume figure must be based on the average daily volume traded in the 20 trading days preceding the date of purchase.

3. For the purposes of paragraph 2, in cases of extreme low liquidity on the relevant market, the issuer may exceed the 25% limit, provided that the following conditions are met:

(a) the issuer informs the competent authority of the relevant market, in advance, of its intention to deviate from the 25% limit;

(b) the issuer discloses adequately to the public the fact that it may deviate from the 25% limit;

(c) the issuer does not exceed 50 % of the average daily volume.

Definitions

'financial instrument': Market Abuse Directive 2003/6/EC, art 1.3 and 1.4; 'regulated market': Market Abuse Directive 2003/6/EC, art 1.3 and 1.4.

Notes

As the Regulation is directly applicable it is the Directive's definitions rather than those in the transposing regulations which apply. This is reinforced by the reference in art 2 of this Regulation that the definitions in that Article apply 'in addition to those laid down in Directive 2003/6/EC'.

See Definitions note under art 2 of this Market Abuse Regulation. In Ireland the expression 'competent authority' will be interpreted as the Central Bank and Financial Services Authority of Ireland.

UK legislation

Same as Ireland, as this reg is directly applicable to all EU Member States.

Article 6

Restrictions

1. In order to benefit from the exemption provided by Article 8 of Directive 2003/6/EC, the issuer shall not, during its participation in a buy-back programme, engage in the following trading:

(a) selling of own shares during the life of the programme;

(b) trading during a period which, under the law of the Member State in which trading takes place, is a closed period;

(c) trading where the issuer has decided to delay the public disclosure of inside information in accordance with Article 6(2) of Directive 2003/6/EC.

2. Paragraph 1(a) shall not apply if the issuer is an investment firm or credit institution and has established effective information barriers (Chinese Walls) subject to supervision by the competent authority, between those responsible for the handling of inside information related directly or indirectly to the issuer and those responsible for any decision relating to the trading of own shares (including the trading of own shares on behalf of clients), when trading in own shares on the basis of such any decision. Paragraphs 1(b) and (c) shall not apply if the issuer is an investment firm or credit institution and has established effective information barriers (Chinese Walls) subject to supervision by the competent authority, between those responsible for the handling of inside information related directly or indirectly to the issuer (including trading decisions under the 'buy-back' programme) and those responsible for the trading of own shares on behalf of clients, when trading in own shares on behalf of those clients.

3. Paragraph 1 shall not apply if:

(a) the issuer has in place a time-scheduled 'buy-back' programme; or

(b) the 'buy-back' programme is lead-managed by an investment firm or a credit institution which makes its trading decisions in relation to the issuer's shares independently of, and without influence by, the issuer with regard to the timing of the purchases.

Definitions

'inside information', Market Abuse Directive 2003/6/EC, art 1.1. 'investment firm': art 2.1 of this Market Abuse Regulation; 'credit institution': art 2.2 of this Market Abuse Regulation; art 2.3 of this Market Abuse Regulation; 'time-scheduled 'buy-back' programme': art 2.4 of this Market Abuse Regulation.

Notes

As the Regulation is directly applicable it is the Directive's definitions rather than those in the transposing regulations which apply. This is reinforced by the reference in art 2 of this Regulation that the definitions in that article apply 'in addition to those laid down in Directive 2003/6/EC'.

> ' 1.1. 'Inside information' shall mean information of a precise nature which has not been made public, relating, directly or indirectly, to one or more issuers of financial instruments or to one or more financial instruments and which, if it were made public, would be likely to have a significant effect on the prices of those financial instruments or on the price of related derivative financial instruments.
>
> In relation to derivatives on commodities, 'inside information' shall mean information of a precise nature which has not been made public, relating, directly or indirectly, to one or more such derivatives and which users of markets on which such derivatives are traded would expect to receive in accordance with accepted market practices on those markets.
>
> For persons charged with the execution of orders concerning financial instruments, 'inside information' shall also mean information conveyed by a client and related to the client's pending orders, which is of a precise nature, which relates directly or indirectly to one or more issuers of financial instruments or to one or more financial instruments, and which, if it were made public, would be likely to have a significant effect on the prices of those financial instruments or on the price of related derivative financial instruments.'

In Ireland this expression 'competent authority' will be interpreted as the Central Bank and Financial Services Authority of Ireland.

UK legislation

Same as Ireland, as this reg is directly applicable to all EU Member States.

Chapter III
Stabilisation of a Financial Instrument

Article 7

Conditions for stabilisation

In order to benefit from the exemption provided for in Article 8 of Directive 2003/6/EC, stabilisation of a financial instrument must be carried out in accordance with Articles 8, 9 and 10 of this Regulation.

Definitions

'financial instrument': Market Abuse Directive 2003/6/EC, art 1.3; 'stabilisation': art 2.7 of this Market Abuse Regulation.

Notes

As the Regulation is directly applicable it is the Directive's definitions rather than those in the transposing regulations which apply. This is reinforced by the reference in art 2 of this Regulation that the definitions in that article apply 'in addition to those laid down in Directive 2003/6/EC'. See Definitions note under the art 2 of this Market Abuse Regulation.

UK legislation

Same as Ireland, as this reg is directly applicable to all EU Member States.

Article 8

Time-related conditions for stabilisation

1. Stabilisation shall be carried out only for a limited time period.

2. In respect of shares and other securities equivalent to shares, the time period referred to in paragraph 1 shall, in the case of an initial offer publicly announced, start on the date of commencement of trading of the relevant securities on the regulated market and end no later than 30 calendar days thereafter.

Where the initial offer publicly announced takes place in a Member State that permits trading prior to the commencement of trading on a regulated market, the time period referred to in paragraph 1 shall start on the date of adequate public disclosure of the final price of the relevant securities and end no later than 30 calendar days thereafter, provided that any such trading is carried out in compliance with the rules, if any, of the regulated market on which the relevant securities are to be admitted to trading, including any rules concerning public disclosure and trade reporting.

3. In respect of shares and other securities equivalent to shares, the time period referred to in paragraph 1 shall, in the case of a secondary offer, start on the date of adequate public disclosure of the final price of the relevant securities and end no later than 30 calendar days after the date of allotment.

4. In respect of bonds and other forms of securitised debt (which are not convertible or exchangeable into shares or into other securities equivalent to shares), the time period referred to in paragraph 1 shall start on the date of adequate public disclosure of the terms of the offer of the relevant securities (i.e. including the spread to the benchmark, if any, once it has been fixed) and end, whatever is earlier, either no later than 30 calendar days after the date on which the issuer of the instruments received the proceeds of the issue, or no later than 60 calendar days after the date of allotment of the relevant securities.

5. In respect of securitised debt convertible or exchangeable into shares or into other securities equivalent to shares, the time period referred to in paragraph 1 shall start on the date of adequate public disclosure of the final terms of the offer of the relevant securities and end, whatever is earlier, either no later than 30 calendar days after the date on which the issuer of the instruments received the proceeds of the issue, or no later than 60 calendar days after the date of allotment of the relevant securities.

Definitions

'regulated market': Market Abuse Directive 2003/6/EC, art 1.3. 'adequate public disclosure': art 2.5 of this Market Abuse Regulation; 'relevant securities': art 2.6 of this Market Abuse Regulation; 'stabilisation': art 2.7 of this Market Abuse Regulation; 'allotment': art 2.11 of this Market Abuse Regulation.

Notes

As the Regulation is directly applicable it is the Directive's definitions rather than those in the transposing regulations which apply. This is reinforced by the reference in art 2 of this Regulation that the definitions in that article apply 'in addition to those laid down in Directive 2003/6/EC'. See Definitions note under art 2 of this Market Abuse Regulation.

UK legislation

Same as Ireland, as this reg is directly applicable to all EU Member States.

Article 9

Disclosure and reporting conditions for stabilisation

1. The following information shall be adequately publicly disclosed by issuers, offerors, or entities undertaking the stabilisation acting, or not, on behalf of such persons, before the opening of the offer period of the relevant securities:

(a) the fact that stabilisation may be undertaken, that there is no assurance that it will be undertaken and that it may be stopped at any time;

(b) the fact that stabilisation transactions are aimed to support the market price of the relevant securities;

(c) the beginning and end of the period during which stabilisation may occur;

(d) the identity of the stabilisation manager, unless this is not known at the time of publication in which case it must be publicly disclosed before any stabilisation activity begins;

(e) the existence and maximum size of any overallotment facility or greenshoe option, the exercise period of the greenshoe option and any conditions for the use of the overallotment facility or exercise of the greenshoe option.

The application of the provisions of this paragraph shall be suspended for offers under the scope of application of the measures implementing Directive 2004/.. ../EC (Prospectus Directive), from the date of application of these measures.

2. Without prejudice to Article 12(1)(c) of Directive 2003/6/EC, the details of all stabilisation transactions must be notified by issuers, offerors, or entities undertaking the stabilisation acting, or not, on behalf of such persons, to the competent authority of the relevant market no later than the end of the seventh daily market session following the date of execution of such transactions.

3. Within one week of the end of the stabilisation period, the following information must be adequately disclosed to the public by issuers, offerors, or entities undertaking the stabilisation acting, or not, on behalf of such persons:

(a) whether or not stabilisation was undertaken;

(b) the date at which stabilisation started;

(c) the date at which stabilisation last occurred;

(d) the price range within which stabilisation was carried out, for each of the dates during which stabilisation transactions were carried out.

4. Issuers, offerors, or entities undertaking the stabilisation, acting or not, on behalf of such persons, must record each stabilisation order or transaction with, as a minimum, the information specified in Article 20(1) of Directive 93/22/EEC extended to financial instruments other than those admitted or going to be admitted to the regulated market.

5. Where several investment firms or credit institutions undertake the stabilisation acting, or not, on behalf of the issuer or offeror, one of those persons shall act as central point of inquiry for any request from the competent authority of the regulated market on which the relevant securities have been admitted to trading.

Definitions

'financial instrument': Market Abuse Directive 2003/6/EC, arts 1.3 and 1.4; 'regulated market': Market Abuse Directive 2003/6/EC, arts 1.3 and 1.4; 'investment firm': art 2.1 of this Market Abuse Regulation; 'credit institution': art 2.2 of this Market Abuse Regulation; 'relevant securities': art 2.6 of this Market Abuse Regulation; 'stabilisation': art 2.7 of this Market Abuse Regulation; 'offeror': art 2.10 of this Market Abuse Regulation; 'overallotment facility': art 2.13 of this Market Abuse Regulation; 'greenshoe option': art 2.14 of this Market Abuse Regulation.

Notes

As the Regulation is directly applicable it is the Directive's definitions rather than those in the transposing regulations which apply. This is reinforced by the reference in art 2 of this Regulation that the definitions in that article apply 'in addition to those laid down in Directive 2003/6/EC'. See Definitions note under art 2 of this Market Abuse Regulation.

UK legislation

Same as Ireland, as this reg is directly applicable to all EU Member States.

Article 10

Specific price conditions

1. In the case of an offer of shares or other securities equivalent to shares, stabilisation of the relevant securities shall not in any circumstances be executed above the offering price.

2. In the case of an offer of securitised debt convertible or exchangeable into instruments as referred to in paragraph 1, stabilisation of those instruments shall not in any circumstances be executed above the market price of those instruments at the time of the public disclosure of the final terms of the new offer.

Definitions

'relevant securities': art 2.6 of this Market Abuse Regulation; 'stabilisation': art 2.7 of this Market Abuse Regulation.

UK legislation

Same as Ireland, as this reg is directly applicable to all EU Member States.

Article 11

Conditions for ancillary stabilisation

In order to benefit from the exemption provided for in Article 8 of Directive 2003/6/EC, ancillary stabilisation must be undertaken in accordance with Article 9 of this Regulation and with the following:

(a) relevant securities may be overallotted only during the subscription period and at the offer price;

(b) a position resulting from the exercise of an overallotment facility by an investment firm or credit institution which is not covered by the greenshoe option may not exceed 5 % of the original offer;

(c) the greenshoe option may be exercised by the beneficiaries of such an option only where relevant securities have been overallotted;

(d) the greenshoe option may not amount to more than 15 % of the original offer;

(e) the exercise period of the greenshoe option must be the same as the stabilisation period required under Article 8;

(f) the exercise of the greenshoe option must be disclosed to the public promptly, together with all appropriate details, including in particular the date of exercise and the number and nature of relevant securities involved.

Definitions

'investment firm': art 2.1 of this Market Abuse Regulation; 'credit institution': art 2.2 of this Market Abuse Regulation; 'relevant securities': art 2.6 of this Market Abuse Regulation; 'stabilisation': art 2.7 of this Market Abuse Regulation; 'ancillary stabilisation': art 2.12 of this Market Abuse Regulation; 'overallotment facility': art 2.13 of this Market Abuse Regulation; 'greenshoe option': art 2.14 of this Market Abuse Regulation.

UK legislation

Same as Ireland, as this reg is directly applicable to all EU Member States.

Chapter IV
Final Provision

Article 12

Entry into force

This Regulation shall enter into force in Member States on the day of its publication in the Official Journal of the European Union.

This Regulation shall be binding in its entirety and directly applicable in all Member States. Done at Brussels, 22 December 2003.

UK legislation

Same as Ireland, as this reg is directly applicable to all EU Member States.

Explanatory Note

(*This note is not part of the instrument and does not purport to be a legal interpretation*).

These Regulations along with Part 4 of The Investment Funds, Companies and Miscellaneous Provisions Act 2005 give effect to Directive 2003/6/EC and the implementing Directives 2003/124/EC, 2003/125/EC and 2004/72/EC on insider dealing and market manipulation (market abuse).

European Communities (Adjustment of Non-Comparable Amounts in Accounts and Distributions by Certain Investment Companies) Regulations 2005

SI 840/2005

I, Micheál Martin, Minister for Enterprise, Trade and Employment, in exercise of the powers conferred on me by section 3 of the European Communities Act 1972 (No. 27 of 1972) and for the purpose of giving further effect to the Second Council Directive 77/91/EEC (OJ No.L026, 31.1.1977, p.1) of 13 December 1976, the Fourth Council Directive 78/660/EEC of 25 July 1978 (OJ No.L222, 14.8.1978, p 11), the Seventh Council Directive 83/349/EEC of 13 June 1983 (OJ No.L193, 18.7.1983, p 1), Council Directive 86/635/EEC of 8 December 1986 (OJ No.L372, 31.12.1986, p 1), Council Directive 90/605 of 8 November 1990 (OJ No.317, 16.11.1990, p.60) and Council Directive 91/674/EEC of 19 December 1991 (OJ No.374, 31.12.1991, p 7), hereby make the following regulations:

PART I

PRELIMINARY AND GENERAL

Citation

1. These Regulations may be cited as the European Communities (Adjustment of Non-comparable Amounts in Accounts and Distributions by Certain Investment Companies) Regulations 2005.

Notes

SI 840/2005: Companies that opt to prepare accounts in accordance with International Accounting Standards ('IAS'), now known as International Financial Reporting Standards ('IFRS') no longer have to comply with the detailed accounting requirements of the Companies Acts, save for certain disclosures as detailed in section 149A(1)(b) of CA 1963. Companies continuing to prepare 'companies act accounts' continue to comply with the companies act requirements.

IFRS 1 'First-time adoption of International Financial Reporting Standards' provides exemption from the requirement to restate comparative information relating primarily to financial instruments, now required to be accounted for at 'fair value'. SI 840/2005 (along with FRS 28 'Corresponding Amounts') provides a similar exemption for companies preparing 'companies act accounts'. It removes from law the requirement to restate corresponding amounts where they are not comparable – although it remains a legal requirement to provide corresponding amounts in respect of the balance sheet and the profit and loss account, and the law permits them to be restated where these are not comparable. The amendments also remove from the law the requirement to provide corresponding amounts for items disclosed in the notes to the financial statements. Henceforth, it will fall to accounting standards to specify when corresponding amounts should be restated.

Application

2. These Regulations apply to the preparation of annual accounts in the case of a company or undertaking the financial year of which commences on or after 1 January 2005.

Definitions

3. In these Regulations—

'Credit Institutions Regulations' means the European Communities (Credit Institutions: Accounts) Regulations 1992 (S.I. No. 294 of 1992);

'Insurance Undertakings Regulations' means the European Communities (Insurance Undertakings: Accounts) Regulations 1996 (S.I. No. 23 of 1996).

PART 2

ADJUSTMENT OF NON-COMPARABLE AMOUNTS IN ACCOUNTS

4. Section 4 of the Companies (Amendment) Act 1986 is amended by substituting the following for subsection (8):

[...][a]

Amendments

a Substitutes C(A)A 1986, s 4(8).

5. Paragraph 44 of the Schedule to the Companies (Amendment) Act 1986 is amended by substituting the following for subparagraph (2):

[...][a]

Amendments

a Amends C(A)A 1986, Sch, para 44(2).

6. Paragraph 4 of the Schedule to the Credit Institutions Regulations is amended by substituting the following for subparagraph (2):

[...][a]

Amendments

a Amends EC(CI)R 1992, Sch para 4(2).

7. Regulation 6 of the Insurance Undertakings Regulations is amended by substituting the following for paragraph (6):

[...][a]

Amendments

a Substitutes EC(IU)R 1996, reg 6(6).

PART 3

DISTRIBUTIONS BY CERTAIN INVESTMENT COMPANIES

8. Section 47 of the Companies (Amendment) Act 1983, as amended by the European Communities (International Financial Reporting Standards and Miscellaneous Amendments) Regulations 2005 (S.I. No. 116 of 2005), is amended—

(a) in subsection (1)(a), by inserting, after "liabilities", "to creditors",

(b) in subsection (2)—

  (i) by substituting 'liabilities to creditors' for 'liabilities',

  (ii) by inserting after "any provision" , in each place where that expression occurs, "for liabilities to creditors".

EXPLANATORY NOTE

(*This note is not part of the instrument and does not purport to be a legal interpretation*).

These regulations make amendments to the Companies Acts 1963–2005 consequential on changes in accounting practice for financial years beginning on or after 1 January 2005. Similar changes are also made for Credit Institutions and Insurance Companies.

(7) The requirements of this Regulation apply in relation to reports of directors for financial years beginning on or after 20 May 2006.

Definitions

'bid': EC(TB)R 2006, reg 2(1); 'company': EC(TB)R 2006, reg 2(1); 'regulated market': EC(TB)R 2006, reg 2(1); 'securities': EC(TB)R 2006, reg 2(1).

PART 5

RIGHTS TO BUY OUT OR BE BOUGHT OUT IN CERTAIN CIRCUMSTANCES

22 Application of Part

(1) This Part applies in relation to a bid for a body corporate, being either—

(a) a company within the meaning of the Companies Acts 1963, or

(b) a body corporate established in the State by charter,

and which is a company a bid in respect of which the Panel has (by virtue of Regulation 6) jurisdiction to supervise.

(2) Section 204 of the Companies Act 1963 shall not apply to a bid for a company or other body corporate falling within paragraph (1) in so far as it relates to securities.

Definitions

'bid': EC(TB)R 2006, reg 2(1); 'Panel': EC(TB)R 2006, reg 2(1); 'securities': EC(TB)R 2006, reg 2(1).

Notes

Regulation 6 states the bids which the Panel has the competence to supervise:

(1) (a) if the offeree company has its registered office in the State – in a case where its securities are admitted to trading on a regulated market in the state (whether or not they are also admitted to trading on relevant markets in one or more other member states);

(b) if the offeree company has its registered office in a member state other than the state – in a case where its securities are admitted solely to trading on a regulated market in the state;

(c) in each of the cases specified in para (2) if the following conditions are satisfied:

(i) the offeree company does not have its registered office in the state, and

(ii) none of the member states referred to in the cases so specified is the state in which the offeree company has its registered office.

(2) The cases in para (1)(c) are:

(a) the securities of the offeree company are admitted to trading on regulated markets in more than one member state (including the state) but the regulated market on which they were first admitted to trading is a regulated market in the state;

(b) the securities of the offeree company have been admitted to trading on regulated markets in more than one member state (including the state) simultaneously and the offeree company determines, in accordance with art 4(2)(c) of the Directive, that the Panel shall be the competent authority to supervise the bid;

(2) On an application under paragraph (1), the Court may, as it considers appropriate, annul the decision to transfer, require the SE to acquire for cash the securities of the shareholders opposed to the transfer or grant such other remedy as it considers just.

(3) Where a company proposes to form an SE through a merger pursuant to Article 2(1), then, notwithstanding any other provision in the Companies Acts, any member or members holding, in the aggregate, not less than 10 per cent in nominal value of the issued share capital of the company, being persons who did not consent to or vote in favour of the resolution for the merger, may apply to the Court—

(a) to have the decision to merge annulled,

(b) to require the SE to acquire for cash the securities of the shareholders opposed to the merger, or

(c) for such other remedy as the Court considers just.

(4) On an application under paragraph (3), the Court may, as it considers appropriate, annul the decision to merge, require the SE to acquire for cash the securities of the shareholders opposed to the merger or grant such other remedy as it considers just.

(a) An application under paragraph (1) shall be made not later than 28 days following the day on which the resolution for the transfer is passed.

(b) An application under paragraph (3) shall be made no later than 28 days following the day on which the resolution for the merger is passed.

Definitions

'Member State': EC(EPLLC)R 2007, reg 2(1).

Notes

A proposal to transfer an SE's registered office from one member state to another would 'appear' to require the approval of the shareholders in general meeting; whereas art 8(4) of the Council Directive confers a positive right on shareholders to examine the transfer proposal and the directors are required to draw up 'one month before the general meeting called upon to decide on the transfer', this is the only reference to a general meeting! Nevertheless, it would seem that a general meeting is required. In the absence of a requirement for a qualified majority to vote in favour of the matter, it would appear that an ordinary resolution will suffice although one would have thought such a significant decision should have the support of a special resolution. Reg 12 provides additional protection for dissentient shareholders, by giving any member or members holding in the aggregate not less than 10% in nominal value of the issued share capital who did not vote in favour of the resolution, the right to apply to court to have the decision annulled, or to have the opposing shareholders bought out or for such other remedy as the court thinks just.

Moreover, reg (3) extends this right of objection, *mutatis mutandis*, to any proposal to form an SE through merger pursuant to art 2(1).

---

13 Extension of protection given by Article 8(7) to liabilities incurred prior to transfer

The first sub-paragraph of Article 8(7) shall apply to liabilities that arise (or may arise) prior to the transfer.

Notes

Reg 13 is also an exercise of a member state's right to avail of an option; in this case it is the option in the second paragraph of art 8(7) to extend the application of the first paragraph of art 8(7) to liabilities that arise (or may arise) prior to the transfer of registered office.

14 Power of competent authority in the State to oppose a transfer on public interest grounds

The Director as competent authority may exercise the power given by Article 8(14) to oppose the transfer of a registered office.

Definitions

'Director': EC(EPLLC)R 2007, reg 2(1).

Notes

Reg 14 prescribes the ODCE as the competent authority with the power to oppose a proposed transfer of a registered office.

15 Management or administrative organ of SE may amend statutes where in conflict with employee involvement arrangements

Where there is a conflict between the arrangements for employee involvement made pursuant to the European Communities (European Public Limited-Liability Company) (Employee Involvement) Regulations 2006 (S.I. No. 623 of 2006) and the existing statutes of an SE, the management or administrative organ of the SE may amend those statutes in accordance with Article 12(4) without any further decision of a general meeting of shareholders.

Notes

Reg 15 asserts the primacy of the employee involvement provisions in EC(EPLLC)(EI)R 2006 (SI 623/2006) so that where they conflict with the statutes of an SE, the directors of an SE may amend them in accordance with art 12(4) of the Council Directive without ever reverting to the SE's shareholders.

16 Power of competent authority in the State to oppose the participation of a merging company

The Director as competent authority may exercise the power given by Article 19 to oppose the taking part, by a public company, in the formation of an SE by merger.

Definitions

'Director': EC(EPLLC)R 2007, reg 2(1).

Definitions

'CRO Gazette': EC(EPLLC)R 2007, reg 2(1); 'Registrar': EC(EPLLC)R 2007, reg 2(1).

Notes

This provision is also designed to ensure publicity of the formation of a holding SE.

---

24 Publication of other documents or information

(1) Where, in respect of Article 59(3) or 65 of the EC Regulation, the occurrence of an event is required to be publicised, the Registrar shall cause to be published in the CRO Gazette notice of the receipt by him or her of the particulars of the event mentioned in that Article.

(2) Where, in respect of Article 8(12) or 15(2) of the EC Regulation, the registration of an SE, whether on formation under Title II, or on the transfer of the registered office of an SE under Article 8 or the deletion of a registration under that Article is required to be publicised, the Registrar shall cause to be published in the CRO Gazette notice of that registration or the deletion of that registration and of the receipt of the documents and particulars related to that registration or deletion required to be delivered to the registrar by the EC Regulation or these Regulations.

Definitions

'CRO Gazette': EC(EPLLC)R 2007, reg 2(1); 'EC Regulation': EC(EPLLC)R 2007, reg 2(1); 'Registrar': EC(EPLLC)R 2007, reg 2(1).

Notes

This reg also makes provision for publicity of events by means of publication in the CRO Gazette.

---

25 Power to require SE to take steps to comply with requirements of Article 7

(1) If it appears to the Director that an SE no longer complies with the requirements specified in Article 7, he or she may give a direction in writing to the SE to take steps, in accordance with Article 64(1)(a) or (b), to ensure that it complies with those requirements.

(2) Such a direction shall—

(a) include a statement of the reasons upon which the direction is being given, and

(b) specify the period within which steps concerned are to be taken.

(3) Where an SE has failed to comply with a direction under paragraph (1), the Director may apply to the High Court for an order directing the SE to comply with the direction and, on the hearing of the application, the Court may make such order as it sees fit and may provide that all costs of and incidental to the application shall be borne by the SE.

(4) Section 213 of the Act of 1963 is amended by inserting the following after paragraph (e):

[...][a]

Definitions

'CRO Gazette': EC(EPLLC)R 2007, reg 2(1); prescribed': EC(EPLLC)R 2007, reg 2(1); 'Registrar': EC(EPLLC)R 2007, reg 2(1).

33 Annual return date

(1) On the registration of an SE, the Registrar shall assign to the SE an annual return date for the purposes of section 127 of the Act of 1963 (inserted by the Company Law Enforcement Act 2001 (No.28 of 2001) and amended by the Companies (Auditing and Accounting) Act 2003 (No.44 of 2003)) and that date shall, subject to paragraphs (3) and (5), be the annual return date of the SE for those purposes accordingly.

(2) The secretary of the SE may serve on the Registrar, not later than 6 weeks from its date of registration, a notice in the prescribed form—

- (a) requesting the Registrar to assign, as an annual return date in respect of the SE, a date specified in the notice and which is different from that assigned under paragraph (1),

  and

- (b) stating the reason or reasons why, in the secretary's opinion, the date so specified is more suitable than that assigned under paragraph (1).

(3) The Registrar shall consider such a notice and, if the Registrar is of the opinion that the reason or reasons (or any of them) referred to in paragraph (2)(b) and stated in the notice disclose good and substantial grounds for the secretary's opinion that the date specified in the notice is more suitable than that assigned under paragraph (1), the Registrar shall assign that date as the annual return date of the SE in place of that assigned under paragraph (1). Upon service of the notice referred to in paragraph (4) on the secretary of the SE the date so assigned shall have effect in place of the date assigned under paragraph (1) and, accordingly, shall, subject to paragraph (5), be the annual return date of the SE for the purposes of section 127 of the Act of 1963.

(4) The Registrar shall, by notice in writing served on the secretary of the SE, inform him or her whether the request made by the secretary in the notice served under paragraph (2) has been acceded to.

(5) The annual return date assigned by the Registrar under paragraph (1) or, as the case may be, paragraph (3) may be altered by the SE in accordance with the provisions of section 127 of the Act of 1963 as to the establishment of a new annual return date.

Definitions

'Act of 1963': EC(EPLLC)R 2007, reg 2(1); prescribed': EC(EPLLC)R 2007, reg 2(1); 'Registrar': EC(EPLLC)R 2007, reg 2(1).

34 Offences

(1) If an SE or any of its officers fails to comply with Regulation 7, 11, 23 or 32 or Article 11 or 13, the SE and every officer who is in default shall be guilty of an offence and shall be liable on summary conviction to a fine not exceeding €3,000.

(2) Proceedings for an offence under paragraph (1) may be brought and prosecuted by the Director or the Registrar, save in the case of proceedings in respect of an offence under that paragraph consisting of a failure to comply with Article 11 or 13 which may only be brought and prosecuted by the Director.

Definitions

'Director': EC(EPLLC)R 2007, reg 2(1); 'Registrar': EC(EPLLC)R 2007, reg 2(1).

35 Relationship of certain Regulations to Council Regulation

Regulations 10, 17(2) and 27 are made in consequence of, and are to be construed as being supplemental to, Article 9 and, accordingly, do not affect the direct application in the State of Article 9 or any other provision of the EC Regulation.

Definitions

'EC Regulation': EC(EPLLC)R 2007, reg 2(1).

Notes

This reg seeks to assert the primacy of the direct effect of Council Regulation No 2157/2001 by making clear that regs 10, 17(2) and 27, all of which provide for the application of the Irish law that applies to Irish public limited companies to apply also to SE's in particular situations, are to be construed as being supplemental to art 9 of the Council Regulation.

Schedule

COUNCIL REGULATION (EC) NO 2157/2001 OF 8 OCTOBER 2001 ON THE STATUTE FOR A EUROPEAN COMPANY (SE)

THE COUNCIL OF THE EUROPEAN UNION,

Having regard to the Treaty establishing the European Community, and in particular Article 308 thereof,

Having regard to the proposal from the Commission(1),

Having regard to the opinion of the European Parliament(2),

Having regard to the opinion of the Economic and Social Committee(3),

Whereas:

(1) The completion of the internal market and the improvement it brings about in the economic and social situation throughout the Community mean not only that barriers to trade must be removed, but also that the structures of production must be adapted to the Community dimension. For that purpose it is essential that companies the business of which is not limited to satisfying purely local needs should be able to plan and carry out the reorganisation of their business on a Community scale.

(2) Such reorganisation presupposes that existing companies from different Member States are given the option of combining their potential by means of mergers. Such operations can be carried out only with due regard to the rules of competition laid down in the Treaty.

(3) Restructuring and cooperation operations involving companies from different Member States give rise to legal and psychological difficulties and tax problems. The approximation of Member States' company law by means of Directives based on Article 44 of the Treaty can overcome some of those difficulties. Such approximation does not, however, release companies governed by different legal systems from the obligation to choose a form of company governed by a particular national law.

(4) The legal framework within which business must be carried on in the Community is still based largely on national laws and therefore no longer corresponds to the economic framework within which it must develop if the objectives set out in Article 18 of the Treaty are to be achieved. That situation forms a considerable obstacle to the creation of groups of companies from different Member States.

(5) Member States are obliged to ensure that the provisions applicable to European companies under this Regulation do not result either in discrimination arising out of unjustified different treatment of European companies compared with public limited-liability companies or in disproportionate restrictions on the formation of a European company or on the transfer of its registered office.

(6) It is essential to ensure as far as possible that the economic unit and the legal unit of business in the Community coincide. For that purpose, provision should be made for the creation, side by side with companies governed by a particular national law, of companies formed and carrying on business under the law created by a Community Regulation directly applicable in all Member States.

(7) The provisions of such a Regulation will permit the creation and management of companies with a European dimension, free from the obstacles arising from the disparity and the limited territorial application of national company law.

(8) The Statute for a European public limited-liability company (hereafter referred to as 'SE') is among the measures to be adopted by the Council before 1992 listed in the Commission's White Paper on completing the internal market, approved by the European Council that met in Milan in June 1985. The European Council that met in Brussels in 1987 expressed the wish to see such a Statute created swiftly.

(9) Since the Commission's submission in 1970 of a proposal for a Regulation on the Statute for a European public limited-liability company, amended in 1975, work on the approximation of national company law has made substantial progress, so that on those points where the functioning of an SE does not need uniform Community rules reference may be made to the law governing public limited-liability companies in the Member State where it has its registered office.

(10) Without prejudice to any economic needs that may arise in the future, if the essential objective of legal rules governing SEs is to be attained, it must be possible at least to create such a company as a means both of enabling companies from different Member States to merge or to create a holding company and of enabling companies and other legal persons carrying on economic activities and governed by the laws of different Member States to form joint subsidiaries.

(11) In the same context it should be possible for a public limited-liability company with a registered office and head office within the Community to transform itself into an SE without going into liquidation, provided it has a subsidiary in a Member State other than that of its registered office.

(12) National provisions applying to public limited-liability companies that offer their securities to the public and to securities transactions should also apply where an SE is formed by means of an offer of securities to the public and to SEs wishing to utilise such financial instruments.

(13) The SE itself must take the form of a company with share capital, that being the form most suited, in terms of both financing and management, to the needs of a company carrying on business on a European scale. In order to ensure that such companies are of reasonable size, a minimum amount of capital should be set so that they have sufficient assets without making it difficult for small and medium-sized undertakings to form SEs.

(14) An SE must be efficiently managed and properly supervised. It must be borne in mind that there are at present in the Community two different systems for the administration of public limited-liability companies. Although an SE should be allowed to choose between the two systems, the respective responsibilities of those responsible for management and those responsible for supervision should be clearly defined.

(15) Under the rules and general principles of private international law, where one undertaking controls another governed by a different legal system, its ensuing rights and obligations as regards the protection of minority shareholders and third parties are governed by the law governing the controlled undertaking, without prejudice to the obligations imposed on the controlling undertaking by its own law, for example the requirement to prepare consolidated accounts.

(16) Without prejudice to the consequences of any subsequent coordination of the laws of the Member States, specific rules for SEs are not at present required in this field. The rules and general principles of private international law should therefore be applied both where an SE exercises control and where it is the controlled company.

(17) The rule thus applicable where an SE is controlled by another undertaking should be specified, and for this purpose reference should be made to the law governing public limited-liability companies in the Member State in which the SE has its registered office.

(18) Each Member State must be required to apply the sanctions applicable to public limited-liability companies governed by its law in respect of infringements of this Regulation.

(19) The rules on the involvement of employees in the European company are laid down in Directive 2001/86/EC(4), and those provisions thus form an indissociable complement to this Regulation and must be applied concomitantly.

(20) This Regulation does not cover other areas of law such as taxation, competition, intellectual property or insolvency. The provisions of the Member States' law and of Community law are therefore applicable in the above areas and in other areas not covered by this Regulation.

(21) Directive 2001/86/EC is designed to ensure that employees have a right of involvement in issues and decisions affecting the life of their SE. Other social and labour legislation questions, in particular the right of employees to information and consultation as regulated in the Member States, are governed by the national provisions applicable, under the same conditions, to public limited-liability companies.

(22) The entry into force of this Regulation must be deferred so that each Member State may incorporate into its national law the provisions of Directive 2001/86/EC and set up in advance the necessary machinery for the formation and operation of SEs with registered offices within its territory, so that the Regulation and the Directive may be applied concomitantly.

(23) A company the head office of which is not in the Community should be allowed to participate in the formation of an SE provided that company is formed under the law of a Member State, has its registered office in that Member State and has a real and continuous link with a Member State's economy according to the principles established in the 1962 General Programme for the abolition of restrictions on freedom of establishment. Such a link exists in particular if a company has an establishment in that Member State and conducts operations therefrom.

(24) The SE should be enabled to transfer its registered office to another Member State. Adequate protection of the interests of minority shareholders who oppose the transfer, of creditors and of holders of other rights should be proportionate. Such transfer should not affect the rights originating before the transfer.

(25) This Regulation is without prejudice to any provision which may be inserted in the 1968 Brussels Convention or in any text adopted by Member States or by the Council to replace such Convention, relating to the rules of jurisdiction applicable in the case of transfer of the registered offices of a public limited-liability company from one Member State to another.

(26) Activities by financial institutions are regulated by specific directives and the national law implementing those directives and additional national rules regulating those activities apply in full to an SE.

(27) In view of the specific Community character of an SE, the 'real seat' arrangement adopted by this Regulation in respect of SEs is without prejudice to Member States' laws and does not pre-empt any choices to be made for other Community texts on company law.

(28) The Treaty does not provide, for the adoption of this Regulation, powers of action other than those of Article 308 thereof.

(29) Since the objectives of the intended action, as outlined above, cannot be adequately attained by the Member States in as much as a European public limited-liability company is being established at European level and can there-fore, because of the scale and impact of such company, be better attained at Community level, the Community may take measures in accordance with the principle of subsidiarity enshrined in Article 5 of the Treaty. In accordance with the principle of proportionality as set out in the said Article, this Regulation does not go beyond what is necessary to attain these objectives,

HAS ADOPTED THIS REGULATION:

Notes

The preamble to this Council Regulation clearly sets out its purpose: to complete the internal market so that companies with a business in more than one member states should be able to reorganise their business on a community scale. The Council recognises the legal, tax and indeed 'psychological' difficulties in restructuring groups with members from different member states and acknowledges that the approximation of company laws through harmonising directives has only gone so far and has not released companies governed by different legal systems from the obligation to choose a form of company governed by one particular national member state law. This is of course at the heart of the necessity for a Council Regulation: there is no federal structure available which can be utilised.

This Council Directive is, therefore, an attempt, albeit one likely to be of very limited success, to provide a harmonised statute for a European Company that is directly applicable in all Member States. The intention is that the reg will permit the creation and management of companies with a European dimension, 'free from the obstacles arising from the disparity and the limited territorial application of national company law'. The reason why it is thought that the Statute for a European public limited-liability company (called an SE) will be of limited success is that the Council Regulation does not go (and may not be capable of going) far enough. So in para (9) of the preamble, it is acknowledged that on matters where the functioning of an SE does not need uniform Community rules, reference may be made to the law governing public limited-liability companies in the member states where it has its registered office. This, of course, means that the law applicable to many aspects of the SE's administration and ownership will depend upon where the SE has its registered office.

The preamble to the Council Regulation is intended, particularly, to facilitate the formation of an SE through merger, or to create a holding company and to create subsidiaries. It is also considered important to allow an existing public limited-liability company to convert into an SE without having to liquidate, provided that it has a subsidiary in a member state other than the member state where it has its registered office.

Now we turn to the specifics of company law applicable to the SE that are contained in the Regulation. First, it is considered appropriate to provided that the SE is to be a company having a share capital and to provide for a minimum amount that is not too high to dissuade SMEs from forming an SE. Second, an SE is permitted to have either a one-tier or two-tier management structure. Although an Irish formed and registered company could before the Regulation have a two-tier management structure by appropriately drafting the articles of association, such was very rarely utilised and the formal recognition of the two-tier structure in an Irish formed and registered SE is one of the more significant changes to the law. Third, the preamble proposes to make no change to the current position in private international law that where a holding company controls a subsidiary that is registered under the law of a different member state, then the holding company's rights and obligations regarding the protection of minority shareholders and third parties are governed by the law of the subsidiary company. Fourth, it is not proposed that the Regulation would cover other areas of law such as taxation, competition, intellectual property or insolvency. The preamble also alludes to Directive 2001/86/EC which is designed to ensure that employees have a right of involvement in issues and decisions affecting the life of the SE that employs them and because this was considered central to the operation of the Regulation for the SE, the Regulation's commencement was deferred so that each member state might incorporate the Directive's provisions in their national laws. Among the other matters mentioned in the preamble are that an SE should be able to transfer its registered office to another member state.

Title I
General Provisions

Article 1

1. A company may be set up within the territory of the Community in the form of a European public limited-liability company (Societas Europaea or SE) on the conditions and in the manner laid down in this Regulation.

2. The capital of an SE shall be divided into shares. No shareholder shall be liable for more than the amount he has subscribed.

3. An SE shall have legal personality.

4. Employee involvement in an SE shall be governed by the provisions of Directive 2001/86/EC.

Article 2

1. Public limited-liability companies such as referred to in Annex I, formed under the law of a Member State, with registered offices and head offices within the Community may form an SE by means of a merger provided that at least two of them are governed by the law of different Member States.

2. Public and private limited-liability companies such as referred to in Annex II, formed under the law of a Member State, with registered offices and head offices within the Community may promote the formation of a holding SE provided that each of at least two of them:

(a) is governed by the law of a different Member State, or

(b) has for at least two years had a subsidiary company governed by the law of another Member State or a branch situated in another Member State.

3. Companies and firms within the meaning of the second paragraph of Article 48 of the Treaty and other legal bodies governed by public or private law, formed under the law of a Member State, with registered offices and head offices within the Community may form a subsidiary SE by subscribing for its shares, provided that each of at least two of them:

(a) is governed by the law of a different Member State, or

(b) has for at least two years had a subsidiary company governed by the law of another Member State or a branch situated in another Member State.

4. A public limited-liability company, formed under the law of a Member State, which has its registered office and head office within the Community may be transformed into an SE if for at least two years it has had a subsidiary company governed by the law of another Member State.

5. A Member State may provide that a company the head office of which is not in the Community may participate in the formation of an SE provided that company is formed under the law of a Member State, has its registered office in that Member State and has a real and continuous link with a Member State's economy.

Article 3

1. For the purposes of Article 2(1), (2) and (3), an SE shall be regarded as a public limited-liability company governed by the law of the Member State in which it has its registered office.

2. An SE may itself set up one or more subsidiaries in the form of SEs. The provisions of the law of the Member State in which a subsidiary SE has its registered office that require a public limited-liability company to have more than one shareholder shall not apply in the case of the subsidiary SE. The pro-visions of national law implementing the twelfth Council Company Law Directive (89/667/EEC) of 21 December 1989 on single-member private limited-liability companies(5) shall apply to SEs mutatis mutandis.

Article 4

1. The capital of an SE shall be expressed in euro.

2. The subscribed capital shall not be less than EUR 120000.

3. The laws of a Member State requiring a greater subscribed capital for companies carrying on certain types of activity shall apply to SEs with registered offices in that Member State.

Article 5

Subject to Article 4(1) and (2), the capital of an SE, its maintenance and changes thereto, together with its shares, bonds and other similar securities shall be governed by the provisions which would apply to a public limited-liability company with a registered office in the Member State in which the SE is registered.

Article 6

For the purposes of this Regulation, 'the statutes of the SE' shall mean both the instrument of incorporation and, where they are the subject of a separate document, the statutes of the SE.

Article 7

The registered office of an SE shall be located within the Community, in the same Member State as its head office. A Member State may in addition impose on SEs registered in its territory the obligation of locating their head office and their registered office in the same place.

Article 8

1. The registered office of an SE may be transferred to another Member State in accordance with paragraphs 2 to 13. Such a transfer shall not result in the winding up of the SE or in the creation of a new legal person.

2. The management or administrative organ shall draw up a transfer proposal and publicise it in accordance with Article 13, without prejudice to any additional forms of publication provided for by the Member State of the registered office. That proposal shall state the current name, registered office and number of the SE and shall cover:

(a) the proposed registered office of the SE;

(b) the proposed statutes of the SE including, where appropriate, its new name;

(c) any implication the transfer may have on employees' involvement;

(d) the proposed transfer timetable;

(e) any rights provided for the protection of shareholders and/or creditors.

3. The management or administrative organ shall draw up a report explaining and justifying the legal and economic aspects of the transfer and explaining the implications of the transfer for shareholders, creditors and employees.

4. An SE's shareholders and creditors shall be entitled, at least one month before the general meeting called upon to decide on the transfer, to examine at the SE's registered office the transfer proposal and the report drawn up pursuant to paragraph 3 and, on request, to obtain copies of those documents free of charge.

5. A Member State may, in the case of SEs registered within its territory, adopt provisions designed to ensure appropriate protection for minority share-holders who oppose a transfer.

6. No decision to transfer may be taken for two months after publication of the proposal. Such a decision shall be taken as laid down in Article 59.

7. Before the competent authority issues the certificate mentioned in paragraph 8, the SE shall satisfy it that, in respect of any liabilities arising prior to the publication of the transfer proposal, the interests of creditors and holders of other rights in respect of the SE (including those of public bodies) have been adequately protected in accordance with requirements laid down by the Member State where the SE has its registered office prior to the transfer.

A Member State may extend the application of the first subparagraph to liabilities that arise (or may arise) prior to the transfer.

The first and second subparagraphs shall be without prejudice to the application to SEs of the national legislation of Member States concerning the satisfaction or securing of payments to public bodies.

8. In the Member State in which an SE has its registered office the court, notary or other competent authority shall issue a certificate attesting to the completion of the acts and formalities to be accomplished before the transfer.

9. The new registration may not be effected until the certificate referred to in paragraph 8 has been submitted, and evidence produced that the formalities required for registration in the country of the new registered office have been completed.

10. The transfer of an SE's registered office and the consequent amendment of its statutes shall take effect on the date on which the SE is registered, in accordance with Article 12, in the register for its new registered office.

11. When the SE's new registration has been effected, the registry for its new registration shall notify the registry for its old registration. Deletion of the old registration shall be effected on receipt of that notification, but not before.

12. The new registration and the deletion of the old registration shall be publicised in the Member States concerned in accordance with Article 13.

13. On publication of an SE's new registration, the new registered office may be relied on as against third parties. However, as long as the deletion of the SE's registration from the register for its previous registered office has not been publicised, third parties may continue to rely on the previous registered office unless the SE proves that such third parties were aware of the new registered office.

14. The laws of a Member State may provide that, as regards SEs registered in that Member State, the transfer of a registered office which would result in a change of the law applicable shall not take effect if any of that Member State's competent authorities opposes it within the two-month period referred to in paragraph 6. Such opposition may be based only on grounds of public interest.

Where an SE is supervised by a national financial supervisory authority according to Community directives the right to oppose the change of registered office applies to this authority as well.

Review by a judicial authority shall be possible.

15. An SE may not transfer its registered office if proceedings for winding up, liquidation, insolvency or suspension of payments or other similar proceedings have been brought against it.

16 An SE which has transferred its registered office to another Member State shall be considered, in respect of any cause of action arising prior to the transfer as determined in paragraph 10, as having its registered office in the Member States where the SE was registered prior to the transfer, even if the SE is sued after the transfer.

Article 9

1. An SE shall be governed:

(a) by this Regulation,

(b) where expressly authorised by this Regulation, by the provisions of its statutes or

(c) in the case of matters not regulated by this Regulation or, where matters are partly regulated by it, of those aspects not covered by it, by:

(i) the provisions of laws adopted by Member States in implementation of Community measures relating specifically to SEs;

(ii) the provisions of Member States' laws which would apply to a public limited-liability company formed in accordance with the law of the Member State in which the SE has its registered office;

(iii) the provisions of its statutes, in the same way as for a public limited-liability company formed in accordance with the law of the Member State in which the SE has its registered office.

2. The provisions of laws adopted by Member States specifically for the SE must be in accordance with Directives applicable to public limited-liability companies referred to in Annex I.

3. If the nature of the business carried out by an SE is regulated by specific provisions of national laws, those laws shall apply in full to the SE.

Article 10

Subject to this Regulation, an SE shall be treated in every Member State as if it were a public limited-liability company formed in accordance with the law of the Member State in which it has its registered office.

Article 11

1. The name of an SE shall be preceded or followed by the abbreviation SE.

2. Only SEs may include the abbreviation SE in their name.

3. Nevertheless, companies, firms and other legal entities registered in a Member State before the date of entry into force of this Regulation in the names of which the abbreviation SE appears shall not be required to alter their names.

Article 12

1. Every SE shall be registered in the Member State in which it has its registered office in a register designated by the law of that Member State in accordance with Article 3 of the first Council Directive (68/151/EEC) of 9 March 1968 on coordination of safeguards which, for the protection of the interests of members and others, are required by Member States of companies within the meaning of the second paragraph of Article 58 of the Treaty, with a view to making such safeguards equivalent throughout the Community(6).

2. An SE may not be registered unless an agreement on arrangements for employee involvement pursuant to Article 4 of Directive 2001/86/EC has been concluded, or a decision pursuant to Article 3(6) of the Directive has been taken, or the period for negotiations pursuant to Article 5 of the Directive has expired without an agreement having been concluded.

3. In order for an SE to be registered in a Member State which has made use of the option referred to in Article 7(3) of Directive 2001/86/EC, either an agreement pursuant to Article 4 of the Directive must have been concluded on the arrangements for employee involvement, including participation, or none of the participating companies must have been governed by participation rules prior to the registration of the SE.

3. The statutes of the SE must not conflict at any time with the arrangements for employee involvement which have been so determined. Where new such arrangements determined pursuant to the Directive conflict with the existing statutes, the statutes shall to the extent necessary be amended.

In this case, a Member State may provide that the management organ or the administrative organ of the SE shall be entitled to proceed to amend the statutes without any further decision from the general shareholders meeting.

Article 13

Publication of the documents and particulars concerning an SE which must be publicised under this Regulation shall be effected in the manner laid down in the laws of the Member State in which the SE has its registered office in accordance with Directive 68/151/EEC.

Article 14

1. Notice of an SE's registration and of the deletion of such a registration shall be published for information purposes in the Official Journal of the European Communities after publication in accordance with Article 13. That notice shall state the name, number, date and place of registration of the SE, the date and place of publication and the title of publication, the registered office of the SE and its sector of activity.

2. Where the registered office of an SE is transferred in accordance with Article 8, notice shall be published giving the information provided for in paragraph 1, together with that relating to the new registration.

3. The particulars referred to in paragraph 1 shall be forwarded to the Office for Official Publications of the European Communities within one month of the publication referred to in Article 13.

Title II

Formation

Section 1

General

Article 15

1. Subject to this Regulation, the formation of an SE shall be governed by the law applicable to public limited-liability companies in the Member State in which the SE establishes its registered office.

2. The registration of an SE shall be publicised in accordance with Article 13.

Article 16

1. An SE shall acquire legal personality on the date on which it is registered in the register referred to in Article 12.

2. If acts have been performed in an SE's name before its registration in accordance with Article 12 and the SE does not assume the obligations arising out of such acts after its registration, the natural persons, companies, firms or other legal entities which performed those acts shall be jointly and severally liable therefor, without limit, in the absence of agreement to the contrary.

Section 2
Formation by merger

Article 17

1. An SE may be formed by means of a merger in accordance with Article 2(1).
2. Such a merger may be carried out in accordance with:
   (a) the procedure for merger by acquisition laid down in Article 3(1) of the third Council Directive (78/855/EEC) of 9 October 1978 based on Article 54(3)(g) of the Treaty concerning mergers of public limited-liability companies(7) or
   (b) the procedure for merger by the formation of a new company laid down in Article 4(1) of the said Directive.

In the case of a merger by acquisition, the acquiring company shall take the form of an SE when the merger takes place. In the case of a merger by the formation of a new company, the SE shall be the newly formed company.

Article 18

For matters not covered by this section or, where a matter is partly covered by it, for aspects not covered by it, each company involved in the formation of an SE by merger shall be governed by the provisions of the law of the Member State to which it is subject that apply to mergers of public limited-liability companies in accordance with Directive 78/855/EEC.

Article 19

The laws of a Member State may provide that a company governed by the law of that Member State may not take part in the formation of an SE by merger if any of that Member State's competent authorities opposes it before the issue of the certificate referred to in Article 25(2).

Such opposition may be based only on grounds of public interest. Review by a judicial authority shall be possible.

Article 20

1. The management or administrative organs of merging companies shall draw up draft terms of merger. The draft terms of merger shall include the following particulars:

(a) the name and registered office of each of the merging companies together with those proposed for the SE;

(b) the share-exchange ratio and the amount of any compensation;

(c) the terms for the allotment of shares in the SE;

(d) the date from which the holding of shares in the SE will entitle the holders to share in profits and any special conditions affecting that entitlement;

(e) the date from which the transactions of the merging companies will be treated for accounting purposes as being those of the SE;

(f) the rights conferred by the SE on the holders of shares to which special rights are attached and on the holders of securities other than shares, or the measures proposed concerning them;

(g) any special advantage granted to the experts who examine the draft terms of merger or to members of the administrative, management, supervisory or controlling organs of the merging companies;

(h) the statutes of the SE;

(i) information on the procedures by which arrangements for employee involvement are determined pursuant to Directive 2001/86/EC.

2. The merging companies may include further items in the draft terms of merger.

Article 21

For each of the merging companies and subject to the additional requirements imposed by the Member State to which the company concerned is subject, the following particulars shall be published in the national gazette of that Member State:

(a) the type, name and registered office of every merging company;

(b) the register in which the documents referred to in Article 3(2) of Directive 68/151/EEC are filed in respect of each merging company, and the number of the entry in that register;

(c) an indication of the arrangements made in accordance with Article 24 for the exercise of the rights of the creditors of the company in question and the address at which complete information on those arrangements may be obtained free of charge;

(d) an indication of the arrangements made in accordance with Article 24 for the exercise of the rights of minority shareholders of the company in question and the address at which complete information on those arrangements may be obtained free of charge;

(e) the name and registered office proposed for the SE.

Article 22

As an alternative to experts operating on behalf of each of the merging companies, one or more independent experts as defined in Article 10 of Directive 78/855/EEC, appointed for those purposes at the joint request of the companies by a judicial or administrative authority in the Member State of one of the merging companies or of the proposed SE, may examine the draft terms of merger and draw up a single report to all the shareholders.

The experts shall have the right to request from each of the merging companies any information they consider necessary to enable them to complete their function.

Article 23

1. The general meeting of each of the merging companies shall approve the draft terms of merger.

2. Employee involvement in the SE shall be decided pursuant to Directive 2001/86/EC. The general meetings of each of the merging companies may reserve the right to make registration of the SE conditional upon its express ratification of the arrangements so decided.

Article 24

1. The law of the Member State governing each merging company shall apply as in the case of a merger of public limited-liability companies, taking into account the cross-border nature of the merger, with regard to the protection of the interests of:

(a) creditors of the merging companies;

(b) holders of bonds of the merging companies;

(c) holders of securities, other than shares, which carry special rights in the merging companies.

2. A Member State may, in the case of the merging companies governed by its law, adopt provisions designed to ensure appropriate protection for minority shareholders who have opposed the merger.

Article 25

1. The legality of a merger shall be scrutinised, as regards the part of the procedure concerning each merging company, in accordance with the law on mergers of public limited-liability companies of the Member State to which the merging company is subject.

2. In each Member State concerned the court, notary or other competent authority shall issue a certificate conclusively attesting to the completion of the pre-merger acts and formalities.

3. If the law of a Member State to which a merging company is subject provides for a procedure to scrutinise and amend the share-exchange ratio, or a procedure to compensate minority shareholders, without preventing the registration of the merger, such procedures shall only apply if the other merging companies situated in Member States which do not provide for such procedure explicitly accept, when approving the draft terms of the merger in accordance with Article 23(1), the possibility for the shareholders of that merging company to have recourse to such procedure. In such cases, the court, notary or other competent authorities may issue the certificate referred to in paragraph 2 even if such a procedure has been commenced. The certificate must, however, indicate that the procedure is pending. The decision in the procedure shall be binding on the acquiring company and all its shareholders.

Article 26

1. The legality of a merger shall be scrutinised, as regards the part of the procedure concerning the completion of the merger and the formation of the SE, by the court, notary or other authority competent in the Member State of the proposed registered office of the SE to scrutinise that aspect of the legality of mergers of public limited-liability companies.

2. To that end each merging company shall submit to the competent authority the certificate referred to in Article 25(2) within six months of its issue together with a copy of the draft terms of merger approved by that company.

3. The authority referred to in paragraph 1 shall in particular ensure that the merging companies have approved draft terms of merger in the same terms and that arrangements for employee involvement have been determined pursuant to Directive 2001/86/EC.

4. That authority shall also satisfy itself that the SE has been formed in accordance with the requirements of the law of the Member State in which it has its registered office in accordance with Article 15.

Article 27

1. A merger and the simultaneous formation of an SE shall take effect on the date on which the SE is registered in accordance with Article 12.

2. The SE may not be registered until the formalities provided for in Articles 25 and 26 have been completed.

Article 28

For each of the merging companies the completion of the merger shall be publicised as laid down by the law of each Member State in accordance with Article 3 of Directive 68/151/EEC.

Article 29

1. A merger carried out as laid down in Article 17(2)(a) shall have the following consequences ipso jure and simultaneously:

(a) all the assets and liabilities of each company being acquired are transferred to the acquiring company;

(b) the shareholders of the company being acquired become shareholders of the acquiring company;

(c) the company being acquired ceases to exist;

(d) the acquiring company adopts the form of an SE.

2. A merger carried out as laid down in Article 17(2)(b) shall have the following consequences ipso jure and simultaneously:

(a) all the assets and liabilities of the merging companies are transferred to the SE;

(b) the shareholders of the merging companies become shareholders of the SE;

(c) the merging companies cease to exist.

3. Where, in the case of a merger of public limited-liability companies, the law of a Member State requires the completion of any special formalities before the transfer of certain assets, rights and obligations by the merging companies becomes effective against third parties, those formalities shall apply and shall be carried out either by the merging companies or by the SE following its registration.

4. The rights and obligations of the participating companies on terms and conditions of employment arising from national law, practice and individual employment contracts or employment relationships and existing at the date of the registration shall, by reason of such registration be transferred to the SE upon its registration.

Article 30

A merger as provided for in Article 2(1) may not be declared null and void once the SE has been registered.

The absence of scrutiny of the legality of the merger pursuant to Articles 25 and 26 may be included among the grounds for the winding-up of the SE.

Article 31

1. Where a merger within the meaning of Article 17(2)(a) is carried out by a company which holds all the shares and other securities conferring the right to vote at general meetings of another company, neither Article 20(1)(b), (c) and (d), Article 29(1)(b) nor Article 22 shall apply. National law governing each merging company and mergers of public limited-liability companies in accordance with Article 24 of Directive 78/855/EEC shall nevertheless apply.

2. Where a merger by acquisition is carried out by a company which holds 90 % or more but not all of the shares and other securities conferring the right to vote at general meetings of another company, reports by the management or administrative body, reports by an independent expert or experts and the documents necessary for scrutiny shall be required only to the extent that the national law governing either the acquiring company or the company being acquired so requires.

Member States may, however, provide that this paragraph may apply where a company holds shares conferring 90 % or more but not all of the voting rights.

Section 3
Formation of a holding SE

Article 32

1. A holding SE may be formed in accordance with Article 2(2).

A company promoting the formation of a holding SE in accordance with Article 2(2) shall continue to exist.

2. The management or administrative organs of the companies which promote such an operation shall draw up, in the same terms, draft terms for the formation of the holding SE. The draft terms shall include a report explaining and justifying the legal and economic aspects of the formation and indicating the implications for the shareholders and for the employees of the adoption of the form of a holding SE. The draft terms shall also set out the particulars provided for in Article 20(1)(a), (b), (c), (f), (g), (h) and (i) and shall fix the minimum pro-portion of the shares in each of the companies promoting the operation which the shareholders must contribute to the formation of the holding SE. That pro-portion shall be shares conferring more than 50 % of the permanent voting rights.

3. For each of the companies promoting the operation, the draft terms for the formation of the holding SE shall be publicised in the manner laid down in each Member State's national law in accordance with Article 3 of Directive 68/151/EEC at least one month before the date of the general meeting called to decide thereon.

4. One or more experts independent of the companies promoting the operation, appointed or approved by a judicial or administrative authority in the Member State to which each company is subject in accordance with national provisions adopted in implementation of Directive 78/855/EEC, shall examine the draft terms of formation drawn up in accordance with paragraph 2 and draw up a written report for the shareholders of each company. By agreement between the companies promoting the operation, a single written report may be drawn up for the shareholders of all the companies by one or more independent experts, appointed or approved by a judicial or administrative authority in the Member State to which one of the companies promoting

the operation or the proposed SE is subject in accordance with national provisions adopted in implementation of Directive 78/855/EEC.

5. The report shall indicate any particular difficulties of valuation and state whether the proposed share-exchange ratio is fair and reasonable, indicating the methods used to arrive at it and whether such methods are adequate in the case in question.

6. The general meeting of each company promoting the operation shall approve the draft terms of formation of the holding SE.

Employee involvement in the holding SE shall be decided pursuant to Directive 2001/86/EC. The general meetings of each company promoting the operation may reserve the right to make registration of the holding SE conditional upon its express ratification of the arrangements so decided.

7. These provisions shall apply mutatis mutandis to private limited-liability companies.

Article 33

1. The shareholders of the companies promoting such an operation shall have a period of three months in which to inform the promoting companies whether they intend to contribute their shares to the formation of the holding SE. That period shall begin on the date upon which the terms for the formation of the holding SE have been finally determined in accordance with Article 32.

2. The holding SE shall be formed only if, within the period referred to in paragraph 1, the shareholders of the companies promoting the operation have assigned the minimum proportion of shares in each company in accordance with the draft terms of formation and if all the other conditions are fulfilled.

3. If the conditions for the formation of the holding SE are all fulfilled in accordance with paragraph 2, that fact shall, in respect of each of the promoting companies, be publicised in the manner laid down in the national law governing each of those companies adopted in implementation of Article 3 of Directive 68/151/EEC.

Shareholders of the companies promoting the operation who have not indicated whether they intend to make their shares available to the promoting companies for the purpose of forming the holding SE within the period referred to in paragraph 1 shall have a further month in which to do so.

4. Shareholders who have contributed their securities to the formation of the SE shall receive shares in the holding SE.

5. The holding SE may not be registered until it is shown that the formalities referred to in Article 32 have been completed and that the conditions referred to in paragraph 2 have been fulfilled.

Article 34

A Member State may, in the case of companies promoting such an operation, adopt provisions designed to ensure protection for minority shareholders who oppose the operation, creditors and employees.

Section 4
Formation of a subsidiary SE

Article 35

An SE may be formed in accordance with Article 2(3).

Article 36

Companies, firms and other legal entities participating in such an operation shall be subject to the provisions governing their participation in the formation of a subsidiary in the form of a public limited-liability company under national law.

Section 5
Conversion of an existing public limited-liability company into an SE

Article 37

1. An SE may be formed in accordance with Article 2(4).

2. Without prejudice to Article 12 the conversion of a public limited-liability company into an SE shall not result in the winding up of the company or in the creation of a new legal person.

3. The registered office may not be transferred from one Member State to another pursuant to Article 8 at the same time as the conversion is effected.

4. The management or administrative organ of the company in question shall draw up draft terms of conversion and a report explaining and justifying the legal and economic aspects of the conversion and indicating the implications for the shareholders and for the employees of the adoption of the form of an SE.

5. The draft terms of conversion shall be publicised in the manner laid down in each Member State's law in accordance with Article 3 of Directive 68/151/EEC at least one month before the general meeting called upon to decide thereon.

6. Before the general meeting referred to in paragraph 7 one or more independent experts appointed or approved, in accordance with the national pro-visions adopted in implementation of Article 10 of Directive 78/855/EEC, by a judicial or administrative authority in the Member State to which the company being converted into an SE is subject shall certify in compliance with Directive 77/91/EEC(8) mutatis mutandis that the company has net assets at least equivalent to its capital plus those reserves which must not be distributed under the law or the Statutes.

7. The general meeting of the company in question shall approve the draft terms of conversion together with the statutes of the SE. The decision of the general meeting shall be passed as laid down in the provisions of national law adopted in implementation of Article 7 of Directive 78/855/EEC.

8. Member States may condition a conversion to a favourable vote of a qualified majority or unanimity in the organ of the company to be converted within which employee participation is organised.

9. The rights and obligations of the company to be converted on terms and conditions of employment arising from national law, practice and individual employment contracts or employment relationships and existing at the date of the registration shall, by reason of such registration be transferred to the SE.

Title III
Structure of the SE

Article 38

Under the conditions laid down by this Regulation an SE shall comprise:

(a) a general meeting of shareholders and

(b) either a supervisory organ and a management organ (two-tier system) or an administrative organ (one-tier system) depending on the form adopted in the statutes.

Section 1
Two-tier system

Article 39

1. The management organ shall be responsible for managing the SE. A Member State may provide that a managing director or managing directors shall be responsible for the current management under the same conditions as for public limited-liability companies that have registered offices within that Member State's territory.

2. The member or members of the management organ shall be appointed and removed by the supervisory organ.

A Member State may, however, require or permit the statutes to provide that the member or members of the management organ shall be appointed and removed by the general meeting under the same conditions as for public limited-liability companies that have registered offices within its territory.

3. No person may at the same time be a member of both the management organ and the supervisory organ of the same SE. The supervisory organ may, however, nominate one of its members to act as a member of the management organ in the event of a vacancy. During such a period the functions of the person concerned as a member of the supervisory organ shall be suspended. A Member State may impose a time limit on such a period.

4. The number of members of the management organ or the rules for determining it shall be laid down in the SE's statutes. A Member State may, however, fix a minimum and/or a maximum number.

5. Where no provision is made for a two-tier system in relation to public limited-liability companies with registered offices within its territory, a Member State may adopt the appropriate measures in relation to SEs.

Article 40

1. The supervisory organ shall supervise the work of the management organ. It may not itself exercise the power to manage the SE.

2. The members of the supervisory organ shall be appointed by the general meeting. The members of the first supervisory organ may, however, be appointed by the statutes. This shall apply without prejudice to Article 47(4) or to any employee participation arrangements determined pursuant to Directive 2001/86/EC.

3. The number of members of the supervisory organ or the rules for determining it shall be laid down in the statutes. A Member State may, however, stipulate the number of

members of the supervisory organ for SEs registered within its territory or a minimum and/or a maximum number.

Article 41

1. The management organ shall report to the supervisory organ at least once every three months on the progress and foreseeable development of the SE's business.

2. In addition to the regular information referred to in paragraph 1, the management organ shall promptly pass the supervisory organ any information on events likely to have an appreciable effect on the SE.

3. The supervisory organ may require the management organ to provide information of any kind which it needs to exercise supervision in accordance with Article 40(1). A Member State may provide that each member of the supervisory organ also be entitled to this facility.

4. The supervisory organ may undertake or arrange for any investigations necessary for the performance of its duties.

5. Each member of the supervisory organ shall be entitled to examine all information submitted to it.

Article 42

The supervisory organ shall elect a chairman from among its members. If half of the members are appointed by employees, only a member appointed by the general meeting of shareholders may be elected chairman.

Section 2

The one-tier system

Article 43

1. The administrative organ shall manage the SE. A Member State may provide that a managing director or managing directors shall be responsible for the day-to-day management under the same conditions as for public limited-liability companies that have registered offices within that Member State's territory.

2. The number of members of the administrative organ or the rules for determining it shall be laid down in the SE's statutes. A Member State may, however, set a minimum and, where necessary, a maximum number of members.

The administrative organ shall, however, consist of at least three members where employee participation is regulated in accordance with Directive 2001/86/EC.

3. The member or members of the administrative organ shall be appointed by the general meeting. The members of the first administrative organ may, however, be appointed by the statutes. This shall apply without prejudice to Article 47(4) or to any employee participation arrangements determined pursuant to Directive 2001/86/EC.

4. Where no provision is made for a one-tier system in relation to public limited-liability companies with registered offices within its territory, a Member State may adopt the appropriate measures in relation to SEs.

Article 44

1. The administrative organ shall meet at least once every three months at intervals laid down by the statutes to discuss the progress and foreseeable development of the SE's business.

2. Each member of the administrative organ shall be entitled to examine all information submitted to it.

Article 45

The administrative organ shall elect a chairman from among its members. If half of the members are appointed by employees, only a member appointed by the general meeting of shareholders may be elected chairman.

Section 3

Rules common to the one-tier and two-tier systems

Article 46

1. Members of company organs shall be appointed for a period laid down in the statutes not exceeding six years.

2. Subject to any restrictions laid down in the statutes, members may be reappointed once or more than once for the period determined in accordance with paragraph 1.

Article 47

1. An SE's statutes may permit a company or other legal entity to be a member of one of its organs, provided that the law applicable to public limited-liability companies in the Member State in which the SE's registered office is situated does not provide otherwise.

That company or other legal entity shall designate a natural person to exercise its functions on the organ in question.

2. No person may be a member of any SE organ or a representative of a member within the meaning of paragraph 1 who:

(a) is disqualified, under the law of the Member State in which the SE's registered office is situated, from serving on the corresponding organ of a public limited-liability company governed by the law of that Member State, or

(b) is disqualified from serving on the corresponding organ of a public limited-liability company governed by the law of a Member State owing to a judicial or administrative decision delivered in a Member State.

3. An SE's statutes may, in accordance with the law applicable to public limited-liability companies in the Member State in which the SE's registered office is situated, lay down special conditions of eligibility for members representing the shareholders.

4. This Regulation shall not affect national law permitting a minority of share-holders or other persons or authorities to appoint some of the members of a company organ.

Article 48

1. An SE's statutes shall list the categories of transactions which require authorisation of the management organ by the supervisory organ in the two-tier system or an express decision by the administrative organ in the one-tier system.

A Member State may, however, provide that in the two-tier system the supervisory organ may itself make certain categories of transactions subject to authorisation.

2. A Member State may determine the categories of transactions which must at least be indicated in the statutes of SEs registered within its territory.

Article 49

The members of an SE's organs shall be under a duty, even after they have ceased to hold office, not to divulge any information which they have concerning the SE the disclosure of which might be prejudicial to the company's interests, except where such disclosure is required or permitted under national law pro-visions applicable to public limited-liability companies or is in the public interest.

Article 50

1. Unless otherwise provided by this Regulation or the statutes, the internal rules relating to quorums and decision-taking in SE organs shall be as follows:

(a) quorum: at least half of the members must be present or represented;

(b) decision-taking: a majority of the members present or represented.

2. Where there is no relevant provision in the statutes, the chairman of each organ shall have a casting vote in the event of a tie. There shall be no provision to the contrary in the statutes, however, where half of the supervisory organ consists of employees' representatives.

3. Where employee participation is provided for in accordance with Directive 2001/86/EC, a Member State may provide that the supervisory organ's quorum and decision-making shall, by way of derogation from the provisions referred to in paragraphs 1 and 2, be subject to the rules applicable, under the same conditions, to public limited-liability companies governed by the law of the Member State concerned.

Article 51

Members of an SE's management, supervisory and administrative organs shall be liable, in accordance with the provisions applicable to public limited-liability companies in the Member State in which the SE's registered office is situated, for loss or damage sustained by the SE following any breach on their part of the legal, statutory or other obligations inherent in their duties.

Section 4

General meeting

Article 52

The general meeting shall decide on matters for which it is given sole responsibility by:

(a) this Regulation or

(b) the legislation of the Member State in which the SE's registered office is situated adopted in implementation of Directive 2001/86/EC.

Furthermore, the general meeting shall decide on matters for which responsibility is given to the general meeting of a public limited-liability company governed by the law of the Member State in which the SE's registered office is situated, either by the law of that Member State or by the SE's statutes in accordance with that law.

Article 53

Without prejudice to the rules laid down in this section, the organisation and conduct of general meetings together with voting procedures shall be governed by the law applicable to public limited-liability companies in the Member State in which the SE's registered office is situated.

Article 54

1. An SE shall hold a general meeting at least once each calendar year, within six months of the end of its financial year, unless the law of the Member State in which the SE's registered office is situated applicable to public limited-liability companies carrying on the same type of activity as the SE provides for more frequent meetings. A Member State may, however, provide that the first general meeting may be held at any time in the 18 months following an SE's incorporation.

2. General meetings may be convened at any time by the management organ, the administrative organ, the supervisory organ or any other organ or competent authority in accordance with the national law applicable to public limited-liability companies in the Member State in which the SE's registered office is situated.

Article 55

1. One or more shareholders who together hold at least 10 % of an SE's subscribed capital may request the SE to convene a general meeting and draw up the agenda therefor; the SE's statutes or national legislation may provide for a smaller proportion under the same conditions as those applicable to public limited-liability companies.

2. The request that a general meeting be convened shall state the items to be put on the agenda.

3. If, following a request made under paragraph 1, a general meeting is not held in due time and, in any event, within two months, the competent judicial or administrative authority within the jurisdiction of which the SE's registered office is situated may order that a general meeting be convened within a given period or authorise either the shareholders who have requested it or their representatives to convene a general meeting. This shall be without prejudice to any national provisions which allow the shareholders themselves to convene general meetings.

Article 56

One or more shareholders who together hold at least 10 % of an SE's subscribed capital may request that one or more additional items be put on the agenda of any general meeting. The procedures and time limits applicable to such requests shall be laid down by the national law of the Member State in which the SE's registered office is situated or, failing that, by the SE's statutes. The above pro-portion may be reduced by the statutes or by the law of the Member State in which the SE's registered office is situated under the same conditions as are applicable to public limited-liability companies.

Article 57

Save where this Regulation or, failing that, the law applicable to public limited-liability companies in the Member State in which an SE's registered office is situated requires a larger majority, the general meeting's decisions shall be taken by a majority of the votes validly cast.

Article 58

The votes cast shall not include votes attaching to shares in respect of which the shareholder has not taken part in the vote or has abstained or has returned a blank or spoilt ballot paper.

Article 59

1. Amendment of an SE's statutes shall require a decision by the general meeting taken by a majority which may not be less than two thirds of the votes cast, unless the law applicable to public limited-liability companies in the Member State in which an SE's registered office is situated requires or permits a larger majority.

2. A Member State may, however, provide that where at least half of an SE's subscribed capital is represented, a simple majority of the votes referred to in paragraph 1 shall suffice.

3. Amendments to an SE's statutes shall be publicised in accordance with Article 13.

Article 60

1. Where an SE has two or more classes of shares, every decision by the general meeting shall be subject to a separate vote by each class of shareholders whose class rights are affected thereby.

2. Where a decision by the general meeting requires the majority of votes specified in Article 59(1) or (2), that majority shall also be required for the separate vote by each class of shareholders whose class rights are affected by the decision.

Title IV
Annual Accounts and Consolidated Accounts

Article 61

Subject to Article 62 an SE shall be governed by the rules applicable to public limited-liability companies under the law of the Member State in which its registered office is situated as regards the preparation of its annual and, where appropriate, consolidated accounts including the accompanying annual report and the auditing and publication of those accounts.

Article 62

1. An SE which is a credit or financial institution shall be governed by the rules laid down in the national law of the Member State in which its registered office is situated in implementation of Directive 2000/12/EC of the European Parliament and of the Council of 20 March 2000 relating to the taking up and pursuit of the business of credit institutions(9) as regards the preparation of its annual and, where appropriate, consolidated accounts, including the accompanying annual report and the auditing and publication of those accounts.

2. An SE which is an insurance undertaking shall be governed by the rules laid down in the national law of the Member State in which its registered office is situated in implementation of Council Directive 91/674/EEC of 19 December 1991 on the annual

accounts and consolidated accounts of insurance undertakings(10) as regards the preparation of its annual and, where appropriate, consolidated accounts including the accompanying annual report and the auditing and publication of those accounts.

Title V

Winding Up, Liquidation, Insolvency and Cessation Of Payments

Article 63

As regards winding up, liquidation, insolvency, cessation of payments and similar procedures, an SE shall be governed by the legal provisions which would apply to a public limited-liability company formed in accordance with the law of the Member State in which its registered office is situated, including pro-visions relating to decision-making by the general meeting.

Article 64

1. When an SE no longer complies with the requirement laid down in Article 7, the Member State in which the SE's registered office is situated shall take appropriate measures to oblige the SE to regularise its position within a specified period either:

(a) by re-establishing its head office in the Member State in which its registered office is situated or

(b) by transferring the registered office by means of the procedure laid down in Article 8.

2.The Member State in which the SE's registered office is situated shall put in place the measures necessary to ensure that an SE which fails to regularise its position in accordance with paragraph 1 is liquidated.

3.The Member State in which the SE's registered office is situated shall set up a judicial remedy with regard to any established infringement of Article 7. That remedy shall have a suspensory effect on the procedures laid down in paragraphs 1 and 2.

4. Where it is established on the initiative of either the authorities or any interested party that an SE has its head office within the territory of a Member State in breach of Article 7, the authorities of that Member State shall immediately inform the Member State in which the SE's registered office is situated.

Article 65

Without prejudice to provisions of national law requiring additional publication, the initiation and termination of winding up, liquidation, insolvency or cessation of payment procedures and any decision to continue operating shall be publicised in accordance with Article 13.

Article 66

1. An SE may be converted into a public limited-liability company governed by the law of the Member State in which its registered office is situated. No decision on conversion may be taken before two years have elapsed since its registration or before the first two sets of annual accounts have been approved.

2. The conversion of an SE into a public limited-liability company shall not result in the winding up of the company or in the creation of a new legal person.

3. The management or administrative organ of the SE shall draw up draft terms of conversion and a report explaining and justifying the legal and economic aspects of the conversion and indicating the implications of the adoption of the public limited-liability company for the shareholders and for the employees.

4. The draft terms of conversion shall be publicised in the manner laid down in each Member State's law in accordance with Article 3 of Directive 68/151/EEC at least one month before the general meeting called to decide thereon.

5. Before the general meeting referred to in paragraph 6, one or more independent experts appointed or approved, in accordance with the national pro-visions adopted in implementation of Article 10 of Directive 78/855/EEC, by a judicial or administrative authority in the Member State to which the SE being converted into a public limited-liability company is subject shall certify that the company has assets at least equivalent to its capital.

6. The general meeting of the SE shall approve the draft terms of conversion together with the statutes of the public limited-liability company. The decision of the general meeting shall be passed as laid down in the provisions of national law adopted in implementation of Article 7 of Directive 78/855/EEC.

Title VI
Additional and Transitional Provisions

Article 67

1. If and so long as the third phase of economic and monetary union (EMU) does not apply to it each Member State may make SEs with registered offices within its territory subject to the same provisions as apply to public limited-liability companies covered by its legislation as regards the expression of their capital. An SE may, in any case, express its capital in euro as well. In that event the national currency/euro conversion rate shall be that for the last day of the month preceding that of the formation of the SE.

2. If and so long as the third phase of EMU does not apply to the Member State in which an SE has its registered office, the SE may, however, prepare and publish its annual and, where appropriate, consolidated accounts in euro. The Member State may require that the SE's annual and, where appropriate, consolidated accounts be prepared and published in the national currency under the same conditions as those laid down for public limited-liability companies governed by the law of that Member State. This shall not prejudge the additional possibility for an SE of publishing its annual and, where appropriate, consolidated accounts in euro in accordance with Council Directive 90/604/EEC of 8 November 1990 amending Directive 78/60/EEC on annual accounts and Directive 83/349/EEC on consolidated accounts as concerns the exemptions for small and medium-sized companies and the publication of accounts in ecu(11).

Title VII
Final Provisions

Article 68

1. The Member States shall make such provision as is appropriate to ensure the effective application of this Regulation.

2. Each Member State shall designate the competent authorities within the meaning of Articles 8, 25, 26, 54, 55 and 64. It shall inform the Commission and the other Member States accordingly.

Article 69

Five years at the latest after the entry into force of this Regulation, the Commission shall forward to the Council and the European Parliament a report on the application of the Regulation and proposals for amendments, where appropriate. The report shall, in particular, analyse the appropriateness of:

(a) allowing the location of an SE's head office and registered office in different Member States;

(b) broadening the concept of merger in Article 17(2) in order to admit also other types of merger than those defined in Articles 3(1) and 4(1) of Directive 78/855/EEC;

(c) revising the jurisdiction clause in Article 8(16) in the light of any pro-vision which may have been inserted in the 1968 Brussels Convention or in any text adopted by Member States or by the Council to replace such Convention;

(d) allowing provisions in the statutes of an SE adopted by a Member State in execution of authorisations given to the Member States by this Regulation or laws adopted to ensure the effective application of this Regulation in respect to the SE which deviate from or are complementary to these laws, even when such provisions would not be authorised in the statutes of a public limited-liability company having its registered office in the Member State.

Article 70

This Regulation shall enter into force on 8 October 2004.

This Regulation shall be binding in its entirety and directly applicable in all Member States.

(1) OJ C 263, 16.10.1989, p. 41 and OJ C 176, 8.7.1991, p. 1.

(2) Opinion of 4 September 2001 (not yet published in the Official Journal).

(3) OJ C124, 21.5.1990, p. 34.

(4) See p 22 of this Official Journal.

(5) OJ L395, 30.12.1989, p. 40. Directive as last amended by the 1994 Act of Accession.

(6) OJ L65, 14.3.1968, p. 8. Directive as last amended by the 1994 Act of Accession.

(7) OJ L295, 20.10.1978, p. 36. Directive as last amended by the 1994 Act of Accession.

(8) Second Council Directive 77/91/EEC of 13 December 1976 on coordination of safeguards which, for the protection of the interests of members and others, are required by Member States of companies within the meaning of the second paragraph of Article 58 of the Treaty, in respect of the formation of public limited liability companies and the maintenance and alteration

of their capital, with a view to making such safeguards equivalent (OJ L 26, 31.1.1977, p. 1). Directive as last amended by the 1994 Act of Accession.

(9) OJ L126, 26.5.2000, p. 1.

(10) OJ L374, 31.12.1991, p. 7.

(11) OJ L317, 16.11.1990, p. 57.

ANNEX I

PUBLIC LIMITED-LIABILITY COMPANIES REFERRED TO IN ARTICLE 2(1)

BELGIUM:

la société anonyme/de naamloze vennootschap

DENMARK:

aktieselskaber

GERMANY:

die Aktiengesellschaft

GREECE:

ανωνυμη εταιρία

SPAIN:

la sociedad anónima

FRANCE:

la société anonyme

IRELAND:

public companies limited by shares

public companies limited by guarantee having a share capital

ITALY:

società per azioni

LUXEMBOURG:

la société anonyme

NETHERLANDS:

de naamloze vennootschap

AUSTRIA:

die Aktiengesellschaft

PORTUGAL:

a sociedade anónima de responsabilidade limitada

FINLAND:

julkinen osakeyhtiö/publikt aktiebolag

SWEDEN:

publikt aktiebolag

UNITED KINGDOM:

public companies limited by shares

public companies limited by guarantee having a share capital

ANNEX II
PUBLIC AND PRIVATE LIMITED-LIABILITY COMPANIES REFERRED TO IN ARTICLE 2(2)

BELGIUM:

la société anonyme/de naamloze vennootschap,

la société privée à responsabilité limitée/besloten vennootschap met beperkte aansprakelijkheid

DENMARK:

aktieselskaber,

anpartselskaber

GERMANY:

die Aktiengesellschaft,

die Gesellschaft mit beschränkter Haftung

GREECE:

ανωνυμη εταιρία
εταιρία περιοριομένης ευνύης

SPAIN:

la sociedad anónima,

la sociedad de responsabilidad limitada

FRANCE:

la société anonyme,

la société responsabilit limite

IRELAND:

public companies limited by shares,

public companies limited by guarantee having a share capital,

private companies limited by shares,

private companies limited by guarantee having a share capital

ITALY:

società per azioni,

società a responsabilità limitata

LUXEMBOURG:

la société anonyme,

la société à responsabilité limitée

NETHERLANDS:

de naamloze vennootschap,

de besloten vennootschap met beperkte aansprakelijkheid

AUSTRIA:

die Aktiengesellschaft,

die Gesellschaft mit beschränkter Haftung

PORTUGAL:

a sociedade anónima de responsabilidade limitada,

a sociedade por quotas de responsabilidade limitada

FINLAND:

osakeyhtiö

aktiebolag

SWEDEN:

aktiebolag

UNITED KINGDOM:

public companies limited by shares,

public companies limited by guarantee having a share capital,

private companies limited by shares,

private companies limited by guarantee having a share capital

EXPLANATORY NOTE

(This note is not part of the instrument and does not purport to be a legal interpretation).

These Regulations along with the European Communities (European Public Limited-Liability Company) Forms Regulations 2006 give full effect to Council Regulation (EC) No. 2157/2001 of 8 October 2001 on the Statute for a European company (SE).

It is a new legal instrument based on European Community law that gives companies with commercial interests in more than one Member State the option of forming a European Company known formally by its Latin name of 'Societas Europaea' (SE). The European Company Statute makes it easier for companies to expand and to manage cross-border operations without the red tape of having to set up a network of subsidiaries.

European Communities (European Public Limited-Liability Company) (Forms) Regulations 2007

SI 22/2007

I, MICHEAL MARTIN, Minister for Enterprise, Trade and Employment, in exercise of the powers conferred on me by section 3 of the European Communities Act 1972 (No. 27 of 1972), as amended, for the purpose of giving full effect to Council Regulation (EC) No. 2157/2001 of 8 October 2001 (OJ L294, 10/11/2001, p 1) on the Statute for a European company (SE) and the European Communities (European Public Limited-Liability Company) Regulations 2007 hereby make the following regulations:

1. (1) These Regulations may be cited as the European Communities (European Public Limited-Liability Company) (Forms) Regulations 2007.

(2) The Companies Acts and these Regulations shall be construed together as one.

2. These Regulations shall come into effect on 22nd of January 2007.

3. In these Regulations—

'Act of 1963' means the Companies Act 1963 (No. 33 of 1963);

'Act of 1982' means the Companies (Amendment) Act 1982 (No. 10 of 1982); 'Act of 1983' means the Companies (Amendment) Act 1983 (No. 13 of 1983); 'Act of 1990' means the Companies Act 1990 (No.33 of 1990);

'Act of 1999' means the Stamp Duties Consolidation Act 1999(No. 31 of 1999); 'Act of 2001' means the Company Law Enforcement Act 2001(No. 28 of 2001);

'Council Regulation' means Council Regulation 2157/2001/EC of 8 October 2001[1] on the Statute for a European Company;

'European Regulations' mean the European Communities (European Public Limited-Liability Company) Regulations 2007;

'No. 2 Act of 1999' means the Companies (Amendment) (No 2) Act 1999 (No. 30 of 1999);

'Regulations of 2002' means the Companies Act 1990 (Form and Content of Documents delivered to Registrar) Regulations 2002 (SI 39 of 2002).

4. A reference in these Regulations to a numbered Article is a reference to the Article so numbered in the Council Regulation.

Definitions

'Council Regulation': EC(EPLLC)(F)R 2007, reg 3.

---

5. A word or expression used in these Regulations, which is also used in the European Regulations, has the same meaning as it has in those Regulations.

Definitions

'European Regulations': EC(EPLLC)(F)R 2007, reg 3.

---

6. The form set out in Part 1 of the Schedule to these Regulations (SE 1), or a form to like effect, is prescribed as the form to be used for the purposes of Articles 2(1) and 25(2) of the Council Regulation, Regulations 4(1)(a) and 28 of the European Regulations, section 3 and 3A (inserted by section 101 of the Act of 2001) of the Act of 1982, section 5 of the Act of 1983, sections 42 and 43, section 44 (other than subsection (2)) and section 45 (other than subsections (3)(b) and (5)) of the No. 2 Act of 1999, section 117 of the Act of 1999 and the Regulations of 2002.

Definitions

'Act of 1982': EC(EPLLC)(F)R 2007, reg 3; 'Act of 1999': EC(EPLLC)(F)R 2007, reg 3; 'Council Regulation': EC(EPLLC)(F)R 2007, reg 3; 'European Regulations': EC(EPLLC)(F)R 2007, reg 3; 'No. 2 Act of 1999: EC(EPLLC)(F)R 2007, reg 3; 'Regulations of 2002': EC(EPLLC)(F)R 2007, reg 3.

7. The form set out in Part II of the Schedule to these Regulations (SE 2), or a form to like effect, is prescribed as the form to be used for the purposes of Article 2(2) of the Council Regulation, Regulations 4(1)(b) and 28 of the European Regulations, section 3 and 3A (inserted by section 101 of the Act of 2001) of the Act of 1982, section 5 of the Act of 1983, sections 42 and 43, section 44 (other than subsection (2)) and section 45 (other than subsections (3)(b) and (5)) of the No. 2 Act of 1999, section 117 of the Act of 1999 and the Regulations of 2002.

Definitions

'Act of 1982': EC(EPLLC)(F)R 2007, reg 3; 'Act of 1999': EC(EPLLC)(F)R 2007, reg 3; 'Council Regulation': EC(EPLLC)(F)R 2007, reg 3; 'European Regulations': EC(EPLLC)(F)R 2007, reg 3; 'No. 2 Act of 1999: EC(EPLLC)(F)R 2007, reg 3; 'Regulations of 2002': EC(EPLLC)(F)R 2007, reg 3.

8. The form set out in Part III of the Schedule to these Regulations (SE 3), or a form to like effect, is prescribed as the form to be used for the purposes of Article 2(3) of the Council Regulation, Regulations 4(1)(c) and 28 of the European Regulations, section 3 and 3A (inserted by section 101 of the Act of 2001) of the Act of 1982, section 5 of the Act of 1983, sections 42 and 43, section 44 (other than subsection (2)) and section 45 (other than subsections (3)(b) and (5)) of the No. 2 Act of 1999, section 117 of the Act of 1999 and the Regulations of 2002.

Definitions

'Act of 1982': EC(EPLLC)(F)R 2007, reg 3; 'Act of 1999': EC(EPLLC)(F)R 2007, reg 3; 'Council Regulation': EC(EPLLC)(F)R 2007, reg 3; 'European Regulations': EC(EPLLC)(F)R 2007, reg 3; 'No. 2 Act of 1999: EC(EPLLC)(F)R 2007, reg 3; 'Regulations of 2002': EC(EPLLC)(F)R 2007, reg 3.

9. The form set out in part IV of the Schedule to these Regulations (SE 4), or a form to like effect, is prescribed as the form to be used for the purposes of Article 2(4) of the

Council Regulation, Regulations 4(1)(d) and 28 of the European Regulations, section 3 and 3A (inserted by section 101 of the Act of 2001) of the Act of 1982, section 5 of the Act of 1983, sections 42 and 43, section 44 (other than subsection (2)) and section 45 (other than subsections (3)(b) and (5)) of the No. 2 Act of 1999, section 117 of the Act of 1999 and the Regulations of 2002.

Definitions

'Act of 1982': EC(EPLLC)(F)R 2007, reg 3; 'Act of 1999': EC(EPLLC)(F)R 2007, reg 3; 'Council Regulation': EC(EPLLC)(F)R 2007, reg 3; 'European Regulations': EC(EPLLC)(F)R 2007, reg 3; 'No. 2 Act of 1999: EC(EPLLC)(F)R 2007, reg 3; 'Regulations of 2002': EC(EPLLC)(F)R 2007, reg 3.

10. The form set out in Part V of the Schedule to these Regulations (SE 5), or a form to like effect, is prescribed as the form to be used for the purposes of Article 3(2) of the Council Regulation, Regulations 4(1)(e) and 28 of the European Regulations, section 3 and 3A (inserted by section 101 of the Act of 2001) of the Act of 1982, section 5 of the Act of 1983, sections 42 and 43, section 44 (other than subsection (2)) and section 45 (other than subsections (3)(b) and (5)) of the No. 2 Act of 1999, section 117 of the Act of 1999 and the Regulations of 2002.

Definitions

'Act of 1982': EC(EPLLC)(F)R 2007, reg 3; 'Act of 1999': EC(EPLLC)(F)R 2007, reg 3; 'Council Regulation': EC(EPLLC)(F)R 2007, reg 3; 'European Regulations': EC(EPLLC)(F)R 2007, reg 3; 'No. 2 Act of 1999: EC(EPLLC)(F)R 2007, reg 3; 'Regulations of 2002': EC(EPLLC)(F)R 2007, reg 3.

11. The form set out in Part VI of the Schedule to these Regulations (SE 6), or a form to like effect, is prescribed as the form to be used for the purposes of Article 8 of the Council Regulation, Regulations 5 and 28 of the European Regulations, Section 195 (8) (inserted by section 91 of the Act of 2001) of the Act of 1963, section 117 of the Act of 1999, section 43, section 44 (other than subsection (2)) and section 45 (other than subsections (3)(b) and (5)) of the No. 2 Act of 1999 and the Regulations of 2002.

Definitions

'Act of 1982': EC(EPLLC)(F)R 2007, reg 3; 'Act of 1999': EC(EPLLC)(F)R 2007, reg 3; 'Council Regulation': EC(EPLLC)(F)R 2007, reg 3; 'European Regulations': EC(EPLLC)(F)R 2007, reg 3; 'No. 2 Act of 1999: EC(EPLLC)(F)R 2007, reg 3; 'Regulations of 2002': EC(EPLLC)(F)R 2007, reg 3.

12. The form set out in Part VII of the Schedule to these Regulations (SE 7), or a form to like effect, is prescribed as the form to be used for the purposes of Article 8 of the Council Regulation, Regulation 7 and 11 of the European Regulations, section 249A (inserted by section 107 of the Act of 2001) of the Act of 1990 and the Regulations of 2002.

Definitions

'Council Regulation': EC(EPLLC)(F)R 2007, reg 3; 'European Regulations': EC(EPLLC)(F)R 2007, reg 3; 'Regulations of 2002': EC(EPLLC)(F)R 2007, reg 3.

13. The form set out in Part VIII of the Schedule to these Regulations (SE 8), or a form to like effect, is prescribed as the form to be used for the purposes of Article 8(7) of the Council Regulation, Regulation 7 of the European Regulations, section 249A (inserted by section 107 of the Act of 2001) of the Act of 1990 and the Regulations of 2002.

Definitions

'Council Regulation': EC(EPLLC)(F)R 2007, reg 3; 'European Regulations': EC(EPLLC)(F)R 2007, reg 3; 'Regulations of 2002': EC(EPLLC)(F)R 2007, reg 3.

14. The form set out in Part IX of the Schedule to these Regulations (SE 9), or a form to like effect, is prescribed as the form to be used for the purposes of Regulation 33(2) of the European Regulations, section 249A (inserted by section 107 of the Act of 2001) of the Act of 1990 and the Regulations of 2002.

Definitions

'European Regulations': EC(EPLLC)(F)R 2007, reg 3; 'Regulations of 2002': EC(EPLLC)(F)R 2007, reg 3.

15. The form set out in Part X of the Schedule to these Regulations (SE 10), or a form to like effect, is prescribed as the form to be used for the purposes of Articles 8(2) and 13 of the Council Regulation, Regulations 7 and 21 (1) of the European Regulations, section 249A (inserted by section 107 of the Act of 2001) of the Act of 1990 and the Regulations of 2002.

Definitions

'Council Regulation': EC(EPLLC)(F)R 2007, reg 3; 'European Regulations': EC(EPLLC)(F)R 2007, reg 3; 'Regulations of 2002': EC(EPLLC)(F)R 2007, reg 3.

16. The form set out in Part XI of the Schedule to these Regulations (SE 11), or a form to like effect, is prescribed as the form to be used for the purposes of Articles 13 and 32(3) of the Council Regulation, Regulation 21(1) of the European Regulations, section 249A (inserted by section 107 of the Act of 2001) of the Act of 1990 and the Regulations of 2002.

Definitions

'Council Regulation': EC(EPLLC)(F)R 2007, reg 3; 'European Regulations': EC(EPLLC)(F)R 2007, reg 3; 'Regulations of 2002': EC(EPLLC)(F)R 2007, reg 3.

17. The form set out in Part XII of the Schedule to these Regulations (SE 12), or a form to like effect, is prescribed as the form to be used for the purposes of Articles 13 and 37(5) of the Council Regulation, Regulation 21(1) of the European Regulations, section 249A (inserted by section 107 of the Act of 2001) of the Act of 1990 and the Regulations of 2002.

Definitions

'Council Regulation': EC(EPLLC)(F)R 2007, reg 3; 'European Regulations': EC(EPLLC)(F)R 2007, reg 3; 'Regulations of 2002': EC(EPLLC)(F)R 2007, reg 3.

18. The form set out in Part X III of the Schedule to these Regulations (SE 13), or a form to like effect, is prescribed as the form to be used for the purposes of Articles 13 and 33(3) of the Council Regulation, Regulation 23 of the European Regulations, section 249A (inserted by section 107 of the Act of 2001) of the Act of 1990 and the Regulations of 2002.

Definitions

'Council Regulation': EC(EPLLC)(F)R 2007, reg 3; 'European Regulations': EC(EPLLC)(F)R 2007, reg 3; 'Regulations of 2002': EC(EPLLC)(F)R 2007, reg 3.

19. The form set out in Part XIV of the Schedule to these Regulations (SE 14), or a form to like effect, is prescribed as the form to be used for the purposes of Articles 13 and 59(3) of the Council Regulation, Regulations 24(1) and 32(a) of the European Regulations, section 249A (inserted by section 107 of the Act of 2001) of the Act of 1990 and the Regulations of 2002.

Definitions

'Council Regulation': EC(EPLLC)(F)R 2007, reg 3; 'European Regulations': EC(EPLLC)(F)R 2007, reg 3; 'Regulations of 2002': EC(EPLLC)(F)R 2007, reg 3.

20. The form set out in Part XV of the Schedule to these Regulations (SE 15), or a form to like effect, is prescribed as the form to be used for the purposes of Articles 13 and 65 of the Council Regulation, Regulations 24(1) and 32(b) of the European Regulations, section 249A (inserted by section 107 of the Act of 2001) of the Act of 1990 and the Regulations of 2002.

Definitions

'Council Regulation': EC(EPLLC)(F)R 2007, reg 3; 'European Regulations': EC(EPLLC)(F)R 2007, reg 3; 'Regulations of 2002': EC(EPLLC)(F)R 2007, reg 3.

Note: The forms set out in the Schedule to this Instrument are not replicated here.

Explanatory Note

(*This note is not part of the instrument and does not purport to be a legal interpretation*).

This Regulation along with the European Communities (European Public Limited-Liability Company) Regulations 2007 give full effect to Council Regulation (EC) No. 2157/2001 of 8 October 2001 on the Statute for a European company (SE).

European Communities (Companies) (Amendment) Regulations 2007

SI 49/2007

I, MICHEÁL MARTIN, Minister for Enterprise, Trade and Employment, in exercise of the powers conferred on me by section 3 of the European Communities Act 1972 (No. 27 of 1972) and for the purpose of giving effect to Directive 2003/58/EC of the European Parliament and of the Council of 15 July 2003(OJ L221, 4.9.2–3. p 13) hereby make the following regulations:

1. (1) These Regulations may be cited as the European Communities (Companies) (Amendment) Regulations 2007.

(2) The Companies Acts and these Regulations shall be construed together as one.

(3) These Regulations shall come into operation on 1 April 2007.

2. In these Regulations 'Principal Regulations' means the European Communities (Companies) Regulations 1973 (S.I. No. 163 of 1973), as amended by the European Communities (Companies) Regulations 2004 (S.I. No. 839 of 2004).

3. The Principal Regulations are amended—

(a) [...][a]

(b) [...][b]

(c) [...][c]

(d) [...][d]

Amendments

a EC(C)R 1973 is amended by the insertion of reg 2A.

b EC(C)R 1973, reg 4 is amended by the substitution of para (1)(g) and the insertion of paras (4), (5) and (6).

c EC(C)R 1973 is amended by the substitution of reg 9.

d EC(C)R 1973 is amended by the substitution of reg 12.

Definitions

'Principal Regulations': EC(C)(A)R 2007, reg 2.

EXPLANATORY NOTE

(*This note is not part of the Instrument and does not purport to be a legal interpretation*).

These Regulations give further effect to Directive 2003/58/EC amending Directive 68/151/EEC ('First Company Law Directive'). They provide for the certification of electronic copies of company documents and particulars obtainable from the Companies Registration Office. The Regulations also make provision for the voluntary filing of certified translations of company documents and particulars filed obligatorily in Irish or English. They also extend existing information disclosure requirements concerning letter and order forms to such communication in electronic form and to company websites.

Publication of company documents and particulars by electronic means in the Companies Registration Office Gazette was provided for by S.I. No. 839 of 2004.

Transparency (Directive 2004/109/EC) Regulations 2007

SI 277/2007

ARRANGEMENT OF REGULATIONS

Regulations

PART 1

PRELIMINARY AND GENERAL

PART 2

PERIODIC FINANCIAL REPORTING

PART 3

EXEMPTIONS/THIRDCOUNTRY EQUIVALENCE IN RESPECT OF PART 2

PART 4

LIABILITY FOR FALSE OR MISLEADING STATEMENTS IN CERTAIN PUBLICATIONS

PART 5

ONGOING INFORMATION ABOUT MAJOR SHAREHOLDINGS

PART 6

CONTINUING OBLIGATIONS AND ACCESS TO INFORMATION

PART 7

DISSEMINATION OF INFORMATION

PART 8

COMPETENT AUTHORITIES

PART 9

POWERS OF COMPETENT AUTHORITIES

PART 10

ADMINISTRATIVE SANCTIONS

PART 11

CO-OPERATION BETWEEN COMPETENT AUTHORITIES

PART 12

PENALTIES, GENERAL AND OTHER MISCELLANEOUS PROVISIONS

Notes

These regulations transpose into Irish law:

- the Transparency Directive 2004/109/EC of 15 December 2004 (OJ 31.12.2004 L390, p 38), a Lamfalussy procedure Level 1 measure;

- a Level 2 Commission Decision 2006/891/EC of 4 December 2006 (OJ 8.12.2006 L343, p 96); and
- a Level 2 Commission Directive 2007/14/EC of 8 March 2007 (OJ 9.3.2007 L69, p 27).

The Transparency Directive, along with the associated measures relating to the drawing up of prospectuses in connection with offers of securities and admissions to trading, market manipulation and insider dealing, and admission requirements, are all concerned with the integrity of the European financial markets.

The Transparency Directive has repealed and replaced those parts of the Consolidated Admissions and Reporting Directive 2001/34/EC (CARD) as related to interim financial reporting and the notification and disclosure of major shareholdings.

I, MICHAEL AHERN TD, Minister of State at the Department of Enterprise, Trade and Employment, in exercise of the powers conferred on me by section 20 of the Investment Funds, Companies and Miscellaneous Provisions Act 2006 (No. 41 of 2006) and the Enterprise, Trade and Employment (Delegation of Ministerial Functions) Order 2007 (S.I. No. 51 of 2007), and for the purpose of giving effect to Directive 2004/109/EC of the European Parliament and of the Council of 15 December 2004 and for the other purposes mentioned in that section, hereby make the following regulations:

PART 1
PRELIMINARY AND GENERAL

1. Citation, commencement and construction

(1) These Regulations may be cited as the Transparency (Directive 2004/109/EC) Regulations 2007.

(2) These Regulations shall come into operation on 13th June 2007.

(3) These Regulations shall be read as one with the Companies Acts.

2. Interpretation and application

(1) In these Regulations:

'Act of 2006' means the Investment Funds, Companies and Miscellaneous Pro-visions Act 2006 (No.41 of 2006);

'admitted to trading on a regulated market' means admitted to trading on a regulated market situated or operating within a Member State;

'approved stock exchange' has the same meaning as it has in the Stock Exchange Act 1995 (No. 9 of 1995);

'Bank' means the Central Bank and Financial Services Authority of Ireland;

'collective investment undertaking other than the closed-end type' means unit trusts and investment companies:

(a) the object of which is the collective investment of capital provided by the public and which operate on the principle of risk spreading; and

(b) the units of which are, at the holder's request, repurchased or redeemed, directly or indirectly, out of the assets of the undertaking;

'company' includes any body corporate;

'central competent authority of a home Member State' means—

(a) where the State is the home Member State, the Bank, or

(b) where the State is a host Member State, the central competent administrative authority designated as such under the national law of the home Member State for the purposes of the Directive;

'contravention' includes, in relation to any provision, a failure to comply with that provision;

'controlled undertaking' means any undertaking—

(a) in which a person has a majority of the voting rights, or

(b) of which a person has the right to appoint or remove a majority of the members of the administrative, management or supervisory body and is at the same time a shareholder in, or member of, the under-taking in question, or

(c) of which a person is a shareholder or member and alone controls a majority of the shareholders' or members' voting rights, respectively, pursuant to an agreement entered into with other shareholders or members of the undertaking in question, or

(d) over which a person has the power to exercise, or actually exercises, dominant influence or control;

'Court' means the High Court;

'credit institution' means an undertaking as defined by Article 4(1)(a) of Directive 2006/48/EC of the European Parliament and of the Council of 14 June 2006 relating to the taking up and pursuit of the business of credit institutions;

'debt securities' means bonds or other forms of transferable securitised debts, with the exception of securities which are equivalent to shares in companies or which, if converted or if the rights conferred by them are exercised, give rise to a right to acquire shares or securities equivalent to shares;

'Directive' means Directive 2004/109/EC of the European Parliament and of the Council of 15 December 2004;

'EEA Agreement' means the Agreement on the European Economic Area signed at Oporto on 2 May 1992, as adjusted by the Protocol signed at Brussels on 17 March 1993;

'EEA State' means a state that is a contracting party to the EEA Agreement;

'electronic means' are means of electronic equipment for the processing (including digital compression), storage and transmission of data, employing wires, radio, optical technologies, or any other electromagnetic means;

'enactment' includes an instrument made under an enactment; 'home Member State' means—

(a) in the case of an issuer of debt securities the denomination per unit of which is less than €1,000 or an issuer of shares:

(i) if the issuer is incorporated or formed in a Member State, the Member State in which it has its registered office,

(ii) if the issuer is incorporated or formed in a state or territory which is not a Member State, the Member State in which it is required to file the annual information with the competent authority in accordance with Article 10 of Directive 2003/71/EC of the European Parliament and of the Council of 4 November 2003, and

(b) in the case of an issuer of debt securities not falling within paragraph (a), the Member State chosen by the issuer from among the Member State in which the issuer has its registered office and those Member States which have admitted its securities to trading on a regulated market on their territory,

and paragraph (2) has effect for the purposes of this definition;

'host Member State' means a Member State in which securities are admitted to trading on a regulated market, if different from the home Member State;

'IAASA' means the Irish Auditing and Accounting Supervisory Authority;

'IFRS' means International Financial Reporting Standards within the meaning of Regulation (EC) No. 1606/2002;

'implementing measures' means any measures directly applicable in con-sequence of the Directive and, without prejudice to the generality of the foregoing, includes Commission Decision 2006/891/EC of 4 December 2006;

'in writing' includes by facsimile;

'issuer' means a legal entity governed by private or public law, including a State, whose securities are admitted to trading on a regulated market, the issuer being, in the case of depository receipts representing securities, the issuer of the securities represented;

'management company' means a company as defined in Article 1a(2) of Council Directive 85/611/EEC of 20 December 1985 on the coordination of laws, regulations and administrative provisions relating to undertakings for collective investment in transferable securities (UCITS);

'market maker' means a person who holds himself or herself out on the financial markets on a continuous basis as being willing to deal on own account by buying and selling financial instruments against his or her proprietary capital at prices defined by him or her;

'market operator' means one or more persons who manage or operate the business of a regulated market (or who do both those things), and may be the regulated market itself;

'Member State' means a Member State of the European Union or an EEA State;

'Minister' means the Minister for Enterprise, Trade and Employment;

'regulated information' means all information which the issuer, or any other person who has applied for the admission of securities to trading on a regulated market without the issuer's consent, is required to disclose—

(a) under the Directive,

(b) under Article 6 of Directive 2003/6/EC of the European Parliament and of the Council of 28 January 2003, or

(c) by virtue of more stringent requirements made by the Bank in exercise of the powers under Regulation 40(3) or under other laws, regulations or administrative provisions of the State adopted under Article 3(1) of the Directive;

'regulated market' means a market as defined by Article 4(1), point 14, of Directive 2004/39/EC of the European Parliament and of the Council of 21 April 2004;

'RIS' means a service of the kind commonly known as a regulatory information service;

'securities' means transferable securities as defined in Article 4(1), point 18, of Directive 2004/39/EC of the European Parliament and of the Council of 21 April 2004 with the exception of money-market instruments, as defined in Article 4(1), point 19, of that Directive having a maturity of less than 12 months;

'securities issued in a continuous or repeated manner' means debt securities of the same issuer on tap or at least two separate issues of securities of a similar type or class (or both);

'shareholder' means any person governed by private or public law, who holds, directly or indirectly:

(a) shares of the issuer in the person's own name and on the person's own account,

(b) shares of the issuer in the person's own name, but on behalf of another person,

(c) depository receipts, in which case the holder of the depository receipt shall be considered as the shareholder of the underlying shares rep-resented by the depository receipts;

'supplemental Directive' has the same meaning as it has in the Act of 2006;

'transparency (regulated markets) law' has the same meaning as it has in the Act of 2006;

'treasury shares' has the same meaning as it has in the Companies Acts;

'units of a collective investment undertaking' means securities issued by a collective investment undertaking and representing the rights of the participants in such an undertaking over its assets.

(2) (a) The definition of 'home Member State' in paragraph (1) shall be applicable to debt securities in a currency other than euro, provided that the value of such denomination per unit is, at the date of the issue, less than €1,000, unless it is nearly equivalent to €1,000.

(b) For the purposes of paragraph (b) of the definition of 'home Member State' in paragraph (1), the issuer may choose only one Member State as its home Member State. Its choice shall remain valid for at least three years unless its securities are no longer admitted to trading on any regulated market in the Community.

(3) For the purposes of the definition of 'controlled undertaking' in paragraph (1), the references to the holder's rights in relation to voting, appointment and removal include references to the rights of any other undertaking controlled by the shareholder and those of any person acting, albeit in the person's own name, on behalf of the shareholder or of any other undertaking controlled by the shareholder.

(4) A word or expression that is used in these Regulations and is also used in the Directive or a supplemental Directive, as the case may be, shall have in these Regulations the same meaning as it has in the Directive or the supplemental Directive, as the case may be.[a]

(5) A reference in these Regulations to a Directive or Regulation of the Council or Commission of the European Communities shall be construed as a reference to the Directive or Regulation as amended or extended by any other Directive or Regulation of the Council or Commission of the European Communities.

(6) These Regulations shall not apply to units issued by collective investment undertakings other than the closed-end type or units acquired or disposed of in such collective investment undertakings.

Definitions

'undertaking controlled': see 'controlled undertaking' in Transparency Regs, reg 2(1).

a Note: All terms defined in the Directive have been set out in reg 2(1).

UK

FSA Handbook Glossary; FSA Disclosure and Transparency Rule 1A.1.2

3. Application of Parts 2, 3, 5, 6 and 7 subject to Regulation 40(3)

(1) Any requirement specified in Part 2, 3, 5, 6 or 7 shall be read as being, and shall operate, subject to the Bank's not having exercised the power under Regulation 40(3) (in the circumstances where such power is exercisable) to make the person concerned subject to a more stringent requirement.

(2) Where that power is so exercised, the relevant requirement specified in any of the Parts mentioned in paragraph (1) shall, accordingly, be read and operate subject to such modifications as are necessary in consequence of the exercise of that power.

Definitions

'Bank': Transparency Regs, reg 2(1).

PART 2
PERIODIC FINANCIAL REPORTING

4. Annual financial report

(1) Subject to Part 3, this Regulation applies to an issuer:

(a) whose securities are admitted to trading on a regulated market, and

(b) whose home Member State is the State.

(2) An issuer shall make public its annual financial report at the latest 4 months after the end of each financial year and ensure that it remains publicly available for at least 5 years.

(3) The annual financial report shall include:

(a) the audited financial statements,

(b) a management report, and

(c) responsibility statements.

(4) (a) If an issuer is required to prepare consolidated accounts according to the Seventh Council Directive 83/349/EEC of 13 June 1983, the audited financial statements shall comprise:

(i) consolidated accounts prepared in accordance with Regulation (EC) No 1606/2002 of the European Parliament and of the Council of 19 July 2002, and

(ii) accounts of the parent company prepared in accordance with the national law of the Member State in which the parent company is incorporated.

(b) If an issuer is not required to prepare consolidated accounts, the audited financial statements shall comprise accounts prepared in accordance with the national law of the Member State in which the issuer is incorporated.

Definitions

'admitted to trading on a regulated market': Transparency Regs, reg 2(1); 'company': Transparency Regs, reg 2(1); 'home Member State': Transparency Regs, reg 2(1); 'issuer': Transparency Regs, reg 2(1); 'Member State': Transparency Regs, reg 2(1); 'regulated market': Transparency Regs, reg 2(1); 'securities': Transparency Regs, reg 2(1).

UK

FSA Disclosure and Transparency Rules 4.1.1, 4.1.3, 4.1.5, 4.1.6.

5. Supplemental provisions in relation to Regulation 4

(1) References in this Regulation to consolidated accounts, financial statements, a management report or a responsibility statement are references to consolidated accounts, financial statements, a management report or a responsibility statement referred to in Regulation 4.

(2) (a) If an issuer is required to prepare consolidated accounts, the financial statements shall be audited in accordance with Article 37 of the Seventh Council Directive 83/349/EEC of 13 June 1983 (the most recent measure adopted by the State for its implementation being the European Communities (Financial Reporting Standards and Miscellaneous Amendments) Regulations 2005 (S.I. No. 116 of 2005)).

(b) If an issuer is not required to prepare consolidated accounts, the financial statements shall be audited in accordance with Articles 51 and 51a of the Fourth Council Directive 78/660/EEC of 25 July 1978 (the most recent measure adopted by the State for their implementation being the regulations referred to in subparagraph (a)).

(c) The audit report, signed by the person or persons responsible for auditing the financial statements, shall be disclosed in full to the public together with the annual financial report.

(3) (a) If an issuer is required to prepare consolidated accounts, the management report shall be drawn up in accordance with Article 36 of the Seventh Council Directive 83/349/EEC of 13 June 1983 (the most recent measure adopted by the State for its implementation being the regulations referred to in paragraph (2)(a)).

(b) If the issuer is not required to prepare consolidated accounts, the management report shall be drawn up in accordance with Article 46 of the Fourth Council Directive 78/660/EEC of 25 July 1978 (the most recent measure adopted by the State for its implementation being the regulations referred to in paragraph (2)(a)).

(4) (a) Responsibility statements shall be made by the persons responsible within the issuer.

(b) The name and function of any person who makes a responsibility statement shall be clearly indicated in the responsibility statement.

(c) For each person making a responsibility statement, the statement shall set out that to the best of his or her knowledge:

(i) the financial statements, prepared in accordance with the applicable set of accounting standards, give a true and fair view of the assets, liabilities, financial position and profit or loss of the issuer and the undertakings included in the consolidation taken as a whole; and

(ii) the management report includes a fair review of the development and performance of the business and the position of the issuer and the undertakings included in the consolidation taken as a whole, together with a description of the principal risks and uncertainties that they face.

(5) The issuer is responsible for all information drawn up and made public in accordance with Regulation 4 and this Regulation.

Definitions

'issuer': Transparency Regs, reg 2(1).

UK

FSA Disclosure and Transparency Rules 4.1.7, 4.1.12, 4.1.13.

---

6. Half-yearly financial reports

(1) Subject to Part 3, this Regulation applies to an issuer:

(a) whose shares or debt securities are admitted to trading on a regulated market, and

(b) whose home Member State is the State.

(2) (a) An issuer shall make public a half-yearly financial report covering the first 6 months of the financial year.

(b) The half-yearly financial report shall be made public as soon as possible, but no later than 2 months, after the end of the period to which the report relates.

(c) An issuer shall ensure that the half-yearly financial report remains available to the public for at least 5 years.

(3) The half-yearly financial report shall include:

(a) a condensed set of financial statements,

(b) an interim management report, and

(c) responsibility statements.

Definitions

'admitted to trading on a regulated market': Transparency Regs, reg 2(1); 'debt securities': Transparency Regs, reg 2(1); 'home Member State': Transparency Regs, reg 2(1); 'issuer': Transparency Regs, reg 2(1); 'regulated market': Transparency Regs, reg 2(1).

UK

FSA Disclosure and Transparency Rules 4.2.1–3.

7. Supplemental provisions in relation to Regulation 6

(1) In this Regulation, 'condensed set of financial statements' means the financial statements referred to in Regulation 6(3)(a).

(2) (a) If an issuer is required to prepare consolidated accounts, the condensed set of financial statements shall be prepared in accordance with the international accounting standard applicable to the interim financial reporting adopted pursuant to the procedure provided for under Article 6 of Regulation (EC) No. 1606/2002 of the European Parliament and of the Council of 19 July 2002.

(b) If an issuer is not required to prepare consolidated accounts, the condensed set of financial statements shall contain, as a minimum, the following:

(i) a condensed balance sheet,

(ii) a condensed profit and loss account, and

(iii) explanatory notes on these accounts.

(3) (a) This paragraph applies to an issuer that is not required to prepare consolidated accounts.

(b) In preparing the condensed balance sheet and the condensed profit and loss account an issuer shall follow the same principles for recognising and measuring as when preparing annual financial reports.

(c) The condensed balance sheet and condensed profit and loss account shall show each of the headings and subtotals included in the most recent annual financial statements of the issuer. Additional line items shall be included if, as a result of their omission, the half-yearly financial statements would give a misleading view of the assets, liabilities, financial position and profit or loss of the issuer.

(d) The half-yearly financial information shall include comparative information presented as follows:

(i) balance sheet as at the end of the first 6 months of the current financial year and comparative balance sheet as at the end of the immediate preceding financial year; and

(ii) profit and loss account for the first 6 months of the current financial year with, from 2 years after 29 March 2007, comparative information for the comparable period for the preceding financial year.

(e) The explanatory notes shall include the following:

(i) sufficient information to ensure the comparability of the condensed half-yearly financial statements with the annual financial statements; and

(ii) sufficient information and explanations to ensure a user's proper understanding of any material changes in amounts and of any developments in the half-year period concerned, which are reflected in the balance sheet and the profit and loss account.

Definitions

'issuer': Transparency Regs, reg 2(1).

UK

FSA Disclosure and Transparency Rules 4.2.4, 4.2.5.

8. Further supplemental provisions in relation to Regulation 6.

(1) In this Regulation—

'condensed set of financial statements' means the financial statements referred to in Regulation 6(3)(a);

'interim management report' means the report referred to in Regulation 6(3)(b);

(2) The interim management report shall include at least:

(a) an indication of important events that have occurred during the first 6 months of the financial year, and their impact on the condensed set of financial statements, and

(b) a description of the principal risks and uncertainties for the remaining 6 months of the financial year.

(3) (a) In addition to the requirement contained in the preceding paragraph, an issuer of shares shall disclose in the interim management report the following information, as a minimum:

(i) related parties' transactions that have taken place in the first 6 months of the current financial year and that have materially affected the financial position or the performance of the enterprise during that period; and

(ii) any changes in the related parties' transactions described in the last annual report that could have a material effect on the financial position or performance of the enterprise in the first 6 months of the current financial year.

(b) If an issuer of shares is not required to prepare consolidated accounts, it shall disclose, as a minimum, any transactions which have been entered into with related parties by the issuer, including the amount of such transactions, the nature of the related party relationship and other information about the transactions necessary for an understanding of the financial position of the issuer, if such transactions are material and have not been concluded under normal market conditions.

(c) In relation to transactions referred to in subparagraph (b), information about such transactions may be aggregated according to their nature except where separate information is necessary for an understanding of the effects of related party transactions on the financial position of the issuer.

(4) (a) If the half-yearly financial report has been audited or reviewed by auditors pursuant to the Auditing Practices Board guidance on Review of Interim Financial Information, the audit report or review report shall be reproduced in full.

(b) If the half-yearly financial report has not been audited or reviewed by auditors pursuant to the Auditing Practices Board guidance on Review of Interim Financial Information, an issuer shall make a statement to this effect in its report.

(5) (a) Responsibility statements shall be made by the persons responsible within the issuer.

(b) The name and function of any person who makes a responsibility statement shall be clearly indicated in the responsibility statement.

(c) For each person making a responsibility statement, the statement shall confirm that to the best of his or her knowledge:

(i) the condensed set of financial statements, which has been pre-pared in accordance with the applicable set of accounting standards, gives a true and fair view of the assets, liabilities, financial position and profit or loss of the issuer, or the undertakings included in the consolidation as a whole as required by Regulation 7(2);

(ii) the interim management report includes a fair review of the information required by paragraph (2), and

(iii) the interim management report includes a fair review of the information required by paragraph (3), in the case of an issuer of shares.

(d) A person making a responsibility statement shall be regarded as satisfying the requirement contained in subparagraph (c) (i) by including a statement that the condensed set of financial statements have been prepared in accordance with:

(i) the international accounting standard applicable to the interim financial reporting adopted pursuant to the procedure provided for under Article 6 of Regulation (EC) No. 1606/2002 of the European Parliament and of the Council of 19 July 2002; or

(ii) for Irish issuers not using IFRS, pronouncements on half-yearly reports issued by the Accounting Standards Board; or

(iii) for all other issuers not using IFRS, a national accounting standard relating to interim reporting,

provided always that a person making such a statement has reason-able grounds to be satisfied that the condensed set of financial statements prepared in accordance with such a standard is not misleading.

(e) This application of true and fair view has no effect on the interpretation of the true and fair view for annual accounts in accordance with the Fourth Council Directive 78/660/EEC of 25 July 1978 and the Seventh Council Directive 83/349/EEC of 13 June 1983, and Regulation (EC) No 1606/2002 of the European Parliament and of the Council of 19 July 2002.

(f) In subparagraph (d)(ii) 'Irish issuers' means issuers incorporated in the State as public limited companies (within the meaning of the Companies (Amendment) Act 1983 (No. 13 of 1983)).

(6) The issuer shall be responsible for all information drawn up and made public in accordance with Regulations 6 and 7 and this Regulation.

Definitions

'issuer': Transparency Regs, reg 2(1).

UK

FSA Disclosure and Transparency Rules 4.2.7–11.

9. Interim management statements

(1) Subject to Part 3, this Regulation applies to an issuer:

(a) whose shares are admitted to trading on a regulated market; and

(b) whose home Member State is the State.

(2) (a) An issuer, other than an issuer specified in paragraph (5), shall make public a statement by its management during the first 6 month period of the financial year and another statement by its management during the second 6 month period of the financial year, each of which is referred to in this Regulation as an 'interim management statement'.

(b) The statement required by this paragraph shall be made in a period between 10 weeks after the beginning, and 6 weeks before, the end of the relevant 6 month period.

(3) The interim management statement shall contain information that covers the period between the beginning of the relevant 6 month period and the date of publication of the statement.

(4) The interim management statement shall provide:

(a) an explanation of material events and transactions that have taken place during the relevant period and their impact on the financial position of the issuer and its controlled undertakings, and

(b) a general description of the financial position and performance of the issuer and its controlled undertakings during the relevant period.

(5) The issuer referred to in paragraph (2) (a) is an issuer that publishes quarterly financial reports:

(a) in accordance with the legislation of a Member State; or

(b) in accordance with the rules of a regulated market; or

(c) of its own initiative.

Definitions

'admitted to trading on a regulated market': Transparency Regs, reg 2(1); 'controlled undertaking': Transparency Regs, reg 2(1); 'home Member State': Transparency Regs, reg 2(1); 'issuer': Transparency Regs, reg 2(1); 'Member State': Transparency Regs, reg 2(1); 'regulated market': Transparency Regs, reg 2(1).

UK

FSA Disclosure and Transparency Rules 4.3.1–6.

PART 3
EXEMPTIONS/THIRD COUNTRY EQUIVALENCE IN RESPECT OF PART 2

10. Exemptions not dependent on a decision of Bank

(1) Regulations 4 to 9 shall not apply to the following issuers, namely a state, a regional or local authority of a state, a public international body of which at least one Member State is a member, the European Central Bank and

Member States' national central banks, whether or not they issue shares or other securities.

(2) (a) Regulations 4 to 9 shall not apply to an issuer that issues exclusively debt securities admitted to trading on a regulated market the denomination per unit of which is at least €50,000 (or an equivalent amount).

(b) Regulations 6 to 8 shall not apply to a credit institution whose shares are not admitted to trading on a regulated market and which has, in a continuous or repeated manner, only issued debt securities provided that:

(i) the total nominal amount of all such debt securities remains below €100,000,000; and

(ii) the credit institution has not published a prospectus in accordance with Directive 2003/71/EC of the European Parliament and of the Council of 4 November 2003.

(c) Regulations 6 to 8 shall not apply to issuers already existing at the date of the entry into force of Directive 2003/71/EC of the European Parliament and of the Council of 4 November 2003 which exclusively issue debt securities unconditionally and irrevocably guaranteed by the State or by one of its regional or local authorities, on a regulated market.

Definitions

'admitted to trading on a regulated market': Transparency Regs, reg 2(1); 'Bank': Transparency Regs, reg 2(1); 'credit institution' Transparency Regs, reg 2(1); 'debt securities': Transparency Regs, reg 2(1); 'issuer': Transparency Regs, reg 2(1); 'Member State': Transparency Regs, reg 2(1); 'regulated market': Transparency Regs, reg 2(1); 'securities': Transparency Regs, reg 2(1); 'securities issued in a continuous or repeated manner': Transparency Regs, reg 2(1).

UK

FSA Disclosure and Transparency Rules 4.4.1–4.

11. Exemptions in respect of issuers whose registered office is in third country

(1) Where—

(a) the registered office of an issuer is in a third country, and

(b) that issuer is an issuer in respect of which the State is the home Member State,

the Bank, subject to paragraphs (2) to (9), may exempt that issuer from requirements under Regulations 4 to 9 provided that the law of the third country in question lays down equivalent requirements or such an issuer complies with requirements of the law of a third country that the Bank considers as equivalent.

(2) A third country shall be deemed to lay down requirements equivalent to those of Regulation 4(3)(b) where, under the law of that country, the annual management report is required to include at least the following information:

(a) a fair review of the development and performance of the issuer's business and of its position, together with a description of the principal risks and uncertainties that it faces, such that the review presents a balanced and comprehensive analysis of the development and performance of the issuer's business and of its position, consistent with the size and complexity of the business;

(b) an indication of any important events that have occurred since the end of the financial year;

(c) indications of the issuer's likely future development.

(3) The analysis referred to in paragraph (2) (a) shall, to the extent necessary for an understanding of the issuer's development, performance or position, include both financial and, where appropriate, non-financial key performance indicators relevant to the particular business.

(4) A third country shall be deemed to lay down requirements equivalent to those of Regulation 8(2) and (3) where, under the law of that country, a condensed set of financial statements is required in addition to the interim management report, and the interim management report is required to include at least the following information:

(a) review of the period covered;

(b) indications of the issuer's likely future development for the remaining six months of the financial year;

(c) for issuers of shares and if already not disclosed on an ongoing basis, major related parties transactions.

(5) A third country shall be deemed to lay down requirements equivalent to those of Regulations 5(3) and 8(5) where, under the law of that country, a person or persons within the issuer are responsible for the annual and half-yearly financial information, and in particular for the following:

(a) the compliance of the financial statements with the applicable reporting framework or set of accounting standards;

(b) the fairness of the management review included in the management report.

(6) A third country shall be deemed to lay down requirements equivalent to those of Regulation 9 where, under the law of that country, an issuer is required to publish quarterly financial reports.

(7) A third country shall be deemed to lay down requirements equivalent to those of Regulation 4(4)(a) where, under the law of that country, the provision of individual accounts by the parent company is not required but the issuer whose registered office is in that third country is required, in preparing consolidated accounts, to include the following information:

(a) for issuers of shares, dividends computation and ability to pay dividends;

(b) for all issuers, where applicable, minimum capital and equity requirements and liquidity issues.

(8) For the purposes of equivalence, the issuer must also be able to provide the Bank with additional audited disclosures giving information on the individual accounts of the issuer as a standalone, relevant to the elements of information referred to in subparagraphs (a) and (b) of paragraph (7). Those disclosures may be prepared under the accounting standards of the third country.

(9) (a) A third country shall be deemed to lay down requirements equivalent to those of Regulation 4(4)(b) in relation to individual accounts where, under the law of a third country, an issuer whose registered office is in that third country is not required to prepare consolidated accounts but is required to prepare its individual accounts in accordance with international accounting standards recognised pursuant to Article 3 of Regulation (EC) No 1606/2002 of the European Parliament and of the Council of 19 July 2002 as applicable within the Community or with third country national accounting standards equivalent to those standards.

(b) For the purposes of equivalence, if such financial information is not in line with those standards, it must be presented in the form of restated financial statements.

(c) In addition, the individual accounts must be audited independently.

(10) Notwithstanding that the Bank has, under this Regulation, exempted an issuer from requirements referred to in paragraph (1), the issuer shall comply with the requirements of Articles 19, 20 and 21 of the Directive (as implemented in the State by Parts 6 and 7) in respect of the information covered by the requirements laid down in the third country in question.

Definitions

'Bank': Transparency Regs, reg 2(1); 'company': Transparency Regs, reg 2(1); 'Directive': Transparency Regs, reg 2(1); 'home Member State': Transparency Regs, reg 2(1); 'issuer': Transparency Regs, reg 2(1).

UK

FSA Disclosure and Transparency Rules 4.4.8.

PART 4

LIABILITY FOR FALSE OR MISLEADING STATEMENTS IN CERTAIN PUBLICATIONS

12.

(1) The publications to which this Regulation applies are any reports and statements published in compliance with any of Regulations 4 to 9 and 26.

(2) The securities to which this Regulation applies are—

(a) securities that are traded on a regulated market situated or operating in the State, and

(b) securities that—

(i) are traded on a regulated market situated or operating outside the State, and

(ii) are issued by an issuer for which the State is the home Member State.

(3) The issuer of securities to which this Regulation applies is liable to pay compensation to a person who has—

(a) acquired such securities issued by it, and

(b) suffered loss in respect of them as a result of—

(i) any untrue or misleading statement in a publication to which this section applies, or

(ii) the omission from any such publication of any matter required to be included in it.

(4) The issuer is so liable only if a person discharging managerial responsibilities within the issuer in relation to the publication—

(a) knew the statement to be untrue or misleading or was reckless as to whether it was untrue or misleading, or

(b) knew the omission to be dishonest concealment of a material fact.

(5) A loss is not regarded as suffered as a result of the statement or omission in the publication unless the person suffering it acquired the relevant securities—

(a) in reliance on the information in the publication, and

(b) at a time when, and in circumstances in which, it was reasonable for him to rely on that information.

(6) Except as mentioned in paragraph (8)—

(a) the issuer is not subject to any other liability than that provided for by this Regulation in respect of loss suffered as a result of reliance by any person on—

(i) an untrue or misleading statement in a publication to which this Regulation applies, or

(ii) the omission from any such publication of any matter required to be included in it, and

(b) a person other than the issuer is not subject to any liability, other than to the issuer, in respect of any such loss.

(7) Any reference in paragraph (6) to a person being subject to a liability includes a reference to another person being entitled as against him or her to be granted any civil remedy or to rescind or repudiate an agreement.

(8) This Regulation does not affect—

(a) liability to be the subject of an administrative sanction; or

(b) liability for a criminal offence.

(9) For the purposes of this Regulation—

(a) the following persons shall be regarded as persons discharging managerial responsibilities in relation to a publication—

(i) any director of the issuer (or person occupying the position of director, by whatever name called),

(ii) in the case of an issuer whose affairs are managed by its members, any member of the issuer,

(iii) in the case of an issuer that has no persons falling within clause (i) or (ii), any senior executive of the issuer having responsibilities in relation to the publication;

(b) references to the acquisition by a person of securities include references to his or her contracting to acquire them or any interest in them.

Definitions

'home Member State': Transparency Regs, reg 2(1); 'issuer': Transparency Regs, reg 2(1); 'regulated market': Transparency Regs, reg 2(1); 'securities': Transparency Regs, reg 2(1).

UK

FSMA 90A (1)–(9).

PART 5
ON-GOING INFORMATION ABOUT MAJOR SHAREHOLDINGS

Note:

The duty on the part of a major holder to disclose the level of voting rights under this Part is in addition to:

- the duty of directors and secretaries to disclose their personal, family and corporate interests in shares or debentures of a company under CA 1990, ss 53 *et seq*;
- the duty of 'persons discharging managerial responsibilities' to disclose their personal, family and corporate interests in shares of a company whose shares are admitted to trading on a regulated market, under the Market Abuse Regs, reg 12;
- the duty of shareholders in a company subject to the Irish Takeover Rules or the Substantial Acquisition Rules to notify certain dealings in shares in such a company.

Regulation 81 provides that the obligation of disclosure under Chapter 2 of Part IV of the CA 1990 and the related provisions of that Chapter does not apply to:

- an acquisition or disposal of shares which must be notified under these Regulations, or
- an acquisition or disposal of shares which, but for an express exemption provided by or under these Regulations (whether the word 'exempted' is used or not), would be required to be notified under these Regulations.

---

13. Application of Part 5

This Part applies to an issuer:

(a) whose shares are admitted to trading on a regulated market; and

(b) whose home Member State is the State.

Definitions

'admitted to trading on a regulated market': Transparency Regs, reg 2(1); 'home Member State': Transparency Regs, reg 2(1); 'issuer': Transparency Regs, reg 2(1); 'regulated market': Transparency Regs, reg 2(1).

---

14. Notification of acquisition or disposal of major shareholdings

(1) A person shall notify the issuer of the percentage of voting rights he or she holds if, as a result of either or both of the events specified in paragraph (2), the percentage of voting rights which he or she holds reaches, exceeds or falls below one or more of the percentages specified in paragraph (4).

(2) The events referred to in paragraph (1) are:

- (a) the acquisition or disposal by the person referred to in that paragraph of shares in the issuer, being shares to which voting rights attach;
- (b) events changing the breakdown of voting rights and on the basis of information disclosed by the issuer in accordance with Regulation 20.

(3) In the case of an issuer that is not incorporated in a Member State, subparagraph (b) of paragraph (2) also applies in circumstances where events equivalent to the events specified in that subparagraph occur and on the basis of equivalent disclosed information to that mentioned in that subparagraph.

(4) The percentages referred to in paragraph (1) are: 5%, 10%, 15%, 20%, 30%, 50% and 75%, each being a percentage of the total voting rights in the issuer; each such percentage is subsequently referred to in this Part as a 'threshold'.

(5) The following shall be disregarded for the purposes of determining whether a person has an obligation to make a notification under paragraph (1), namely, voting rights attaching to:

- (a) shares acquired for the sole purpose of clearing and settlement within a settlement cycle not exceeding the period beginning with the trans-action and ending at the close of the third trading day following the day of the execution of the transaction (irrespective of whether the transaction is conducted on-exchange);
- (b) shares held by a custodian (or nominee) in its custodian (or nominee) capacity provided such a person can only exercise the voting rights attached to such shares under instructions given in writing or by electronic means;
- (c) shares held by a market maker acting in that capacity subject to the percentage of such shares not being equal to or in excess of 10% and subject to the market maker satisfying the criteria and complying with the conditions and operating requirements specified in paragraph (4);
- (d) shares held by a credit institution or investment firm provided that:
  - (i) the shares are held within the trading book, as defined in Article 2(6) of Council Directive 93/6/EEC of 15 March 1993, of the credit institution or investment firm;
  - (ii) the voting rights attached to such shares do not exceed 5%; and
  - (iii) the credit institution, or as the case may be investment firm, ensures that the voting rights attached to shares in the trading book are not exercised or otherwise used to intervene in the management of the issuer,
- (e) shares held by a collateral taker under a collateral transaction which involves the outright transfer of securities provided the collateral taker does not declare any intention of exercising (and does not exercise) the voting rights attaching to such shares,

(f) shares acquired by a borrower under a stock lending agreement as determined by rules of the Bank from time to time.

(4) (a) References in paragraph (3) to a market maker are references to a market maker which—

(i) is authorised by its home Member State under Directive 2004/39/EC of the European Parliament and of the Council of 21 April 2004, and

(ii) does not intervene in the management of the issuer concerned, and does not exert any influence on the issuer to buy such shares or back the share price.

(b) A market maker relying upon the exemption for shares held by it in that capacity must notify the competent authority which regulates it in respect of such activities, at the latest within the time limit provided for by Regulation 21(3), that it conducts or intends to conduct market making activities on a particular issuer and shall equally make such a notification to the relevant competent authority if it ceases to conduct market making activities on the issuer concerned.

Definitions

'Bank': Transparency Regs, reg 2(1); 'competent authority': not defined, but see 'central competent authority of a home Member State' in Reg 2(1); 'credit institution': Transparency Regs, reg 2(1); 'electronic means' Transparency Regs, reg 2(1); 'home Member State': Transparency Regs, reg 2(1); 'market maker': Transparency Regs, reg 2(1); 'in writing': Transparency Regs, reg 2(1); 'issuer': Transparency Regs, reg 2(1); 'Member State': Transparency Regs, reg 2(1); 'securities': Transparency Regs, reg 2(1).

Notes

The Financial Regulator's Transparency Rules extend the duty to notify voting interests substantially to parallel those for unquoted public limited companies under CA 1990, ss 67 *et seq*, where notifications of 5% + and interests that pass through a whole percentage point above that must be notified. Rule 7.1 states:

> 'Subject to the exemptions in Regulation 14(5) a person shall notify the issuer (other than where the issuer is a collective investment undertaking of the closed-end type) of the percentage of its voting rights if the percentage of voting rights which he holds as shareholder or through his direct or indirect holding of financial instruments or a combination of such holdings:
>
> (1) reaches, exceeds or falls below 3%, 4%, 5%, 6%, 7%, 8%, 9%, 10% and each 1% threshold thereafter up to 100% or in the case of a non-Irish issuer on the basis of thresholds at 5%, 10%, 15%, 20%, 25%, 30%, 50% and 75% as a result of an acquisition or disposal of shares or financial instruments; or
>
> (2) reaches, exceeds or falls below an applicable threshold in (1) as a result of events changing the breakdown of voting rights and on the basis of information disclosed by the issuer in accordance with Regulation 20;
>
> and in the case of an issuer which is not incorporated in an EEA state a notification under (2) shall be made on the basis of equivalent events and disclosed information.'

UK

FSA Disclosure and Transparency Rules 5.1.2–4.

15. Acquisition or disposal of major proportions of voting rights

(1) The notification requirements under Regulation 14(1) shall also apply to a person to the extent the person is entitled to acquire, to dispose of, or to exercise voting rights in any of the following cases or a combination of them:

(a) voting rights held by a third party with whom that person has concluded an agreement, which obliges them to adopt, by concerted exercise of the voting rights they hold, a long-term common policy towards the management of the issuer in question;

(b) voting rights held by a third party under an agreement concluded with that person providing for the temporary transfer for consideration of the voting rights in question;

(c) voting rights attaching to shares that are lodged as collateral with that person provided the person controls the voting rights and declares an intention to exercise them;

(d) voting rights attaching to shares in which that person has a life interest;

(e) voting rights that are held, or may be exercised within the meaning of subparagraphs (a) to (d), by an undertaking controlled by that person;

(f) voting rights attaching to shares deposited with that person which the person has a discretion to exercise in the absence of specific instructions from the shareholders;

(g) voting rights held by a third party in the third party's own name on behalf of that person;

(h) voting rights which that person may exercise as a proxy where the person has a discretion to exercise the voting rights in the absence of specific instructions from the shareholders.

Definitions

'undertaking controlled': see 'controlled undertaking' in Transparency Regs, reg 2(1); 'issuer': Transparency Regs, reg 2(1); 'shareholder': Transparency Regs, reg 2(1).

UK

FSA Disclosure and Transparency Rule 5.2.1.

16. Non-application of Regulations 14(1) and 15(1)(c) in certain cases

Regulations 14(1) and 15(1)(c) shall not apply in respect of voting rights attaching to shares provided to or by members of the European System of Central Banks in carrying out their functions as monetary authorities, including shares provided to or by such members under pledge or repurchase or similar agreement for liquidity granted for monetary policy purposes or within a payment system provided:

(a) the exemption under this Regulation shall apply only for a short period following the provision of the shares; and

(b) the voting rights attached to the shares during this period are not exercised.

Definitions

'Bank': Transparency Regs, reg 2(1).

UK

FSA Disclosure and Transparency Rule 5.2.4.

17. Notification of voting rights arising from holding of certain financial instruments

(1) The notification requirements under Regulation 14(1) shall also apply to a person who holds, directly or indirectly, financial instruments which result in an entitlement to acquire, on such holder's own initiative alone, under a formal agreement, shares to which voting rights are attached, already issued, of an issuer.

(2) (a) Transferable securities and options, futures, swaps, forward rate agreements and any other derivative contracts, as referred to in Section C of Annex 1 of Directive 2004/39/EC of the European Parliament and of the Council of 21 April 2004, shall be considered to be financial instruments falling within paragraph (1) provided that the condition specified in subparagraph (b) is complied with and they result in an entitlement to acquire, on the holder's own initiative alone, under a formal agreement, shares to which voting rights are attached, already issued, of an issuer.

(b) The condition referred to in subparagraph (a) is that the instrument holder must enjoy, on maturity, either the unconditional right to acquire the underlying shares or the discretion as to his or her right to acquire such shares or not.

(3) In this Regulation "formal agreement" means an agreement that is binding under applicable law.

(4) For the purpose of paragraph (1) the holder of financial instruments falling within that paragraph is required to aggregate and, if necessary, notify all such instruments as relate to the same underlying issuer.

Definitions

'issuer': Transparency Regs, reg 2(1); 'securities': Transparency Regs, reg 2(1).

UK

FSA Disclosure and Transparency Rules 5.3.1–4.

18. Aggregation of managed holdings

(1) (a) The parent undertaking of a management company shall not be required to aggregate its holdings with the holdings managed by the management company under the conditions laid down in Council Directive 85/611/EC of 20

December 1985, provided such management company exercises its voting rights independently from the parent undertaking.

(b) But the requirement for the aggregation of holdings under Regulation 17(4) applies if the parent undertaking, or another controlled under-taking of the parent undertaking, has invested in holdings managed by such management company and the management company has no discretion to exercise the voting rights attached to such holdings and may only exercise such voting rights under direct or indirect instructions from the parent or another controlled undertaking of the parent undertaking.

(2) (a) The parent undertaking of an investment firm authorised under Directive 2004/39/EC of the European Parliament and of the Council of 21 April 2004 shall not be required to aggregate its holdings under Regulations 14 and 15 with the holdings which such investment firm manages on a client-by-client basis within the meaning of Article 4(1), point 9, of that Directive, provided that:

(i) the investment firm is authorised to provide such portfolio management under point 4 of Section A of Annex 1 to that Directive;

(ii) it may only exercise the voting rights attached to such shares under instructions given in writing or by electronic means or it ensures that individual portfolio management services are con-ducted independently of any other services under conditions equivalent to those provided for under Council Directive 85/611/EEC of 20 December 1985 by putting into place appropriate mechanisms; and

(iii) the investment firm exercises its voting rights independently from the parent undertaking.

(b) But the requirement for the aggregation of holdings shall apply if the parent undertaking, or another controlled undertaking of the parent undertaking, has invested in holdings managed by such investment firm and the investment firm has no discretion to exercise the voting rights attached to such holdings and may only exercise such voting rights under direct or indirect instructions from the parent or another controlled undertaking of the parent undertaking.

(3) For the purposes of the exemption in relation to the aggregation of holdings provided by paragraph (1) or (2), a parent undertaking of a management company or of an investment firm shall comply with the following conditions:

(a) it shall not interfere by giving direct or indirect instructions or in any other way in the exercise of the voting rights held by the management company or investment firm;

(b) that management company or investment firm must be free to exercise, independently of the parent undertaking, the voting rights attached to the assets it manages.

(4) A parent undertaking which wishes to make use of either of the foregoing exemptions shall (in relation to shares which are admitted to trading on a regulated market) without delay, notify the following to the competent authority of the home Member State of issuers whose voting rights are attached to holdings managed by the management companies or investment firms:

(a) a list of the names of those management companies and investment firms, indicating the competent authorities that supervise them or that no competent authority supervises them, but with no reference to the issuers concerned;

(b) a statement that, in the case of each such management company or investment firm, the parent undertaking complies with the conditions specified in paragraph (3).

(5) The parent undertaking shall update the list referred to in paragraph (4) on an ongoing basis.

(6) Where the parent undertaking intends to benefit from either of the fore-going exemptions only in relation to the financial instruments referred to in Regulation 17, it shall (in relation to financial instruments giving an entitlement to acquire shares which are admitted to trading on a regulated market) notify to the competent authority of the home Member State of the issuer only the list referred to in paragraph (4).

(7) Without prejudice to Part 9, a parent undertaking of a management company or of an investment firm shall (in relation to shares which are admitted to trading on a regulated market) be able to demonstrate to the competent authority of the home Member State of the issuer on request that:

(a) the organisational structures of the parent undertaking and the management company or investment firm are such that the voting rights are exercised independently of the parent undertaking;

(b) the persons who decide how the voting rights are exercised are not the same for the parent undertaking and the management company or investment firm and act independently;

(c) if the parent undertaking is a client of its management company or investment firm or has a holding in the assets managed by the management company or investment firm, there is a clear written mandate for an arms-length customer relationship between the parent under-taking and the management company or investment firm.

(8) Paragraph (7) (a) shall be construed as requiring, as a minimum, that the parent undertaking and the management company or investment firm shall have established written policies and procedures reasonably designed to prevent the distribution of information between the parent undertaking and the management company or investment firm in relation to the exercise of voting rights.

(9) For the purposes of paragraph (3)—

"direct instruction" means any instruction given by the parent undertaking, or another controlled undertaking of the parent undertaking, specifying how the voting rights are to be exercised by the management company or investment firm in particular cases;

"indirect instruction" means any general or particular instruction, regardless of the form, given by the parent undertaking, or another controlled undertaking of the parent undertaking, that limits the discretion of the management company or investment firm in relation to the exercise of voting rights in order to serve specific business interests of the parent undertaking or another controlled undertaking of the parent undertaking.

(10) An undertaking whose registered office is in a third country which would have required authorisation in accordance with Article 5 (1) of Council Directive 85/611/

EEC of 20 December 1985 or with regard to portfolio management under point 4 of section A of Annex 1 to Directive 2004/39/EC of the European Parliament and of the Council of 21 April 2004 if it had its registered office or, only in the case of an investment firm, its head office within the Community, shall be exempted from aggregating holdings with the holdings of its parent undertaking under paragraphs (1) and (2) provided that it complies with equivalent conditions of independence as management companies or investment firms.

(11) A third country shall be deemed to set conditions of independence equivalent to those specified in paragraphs (1) and (2) where, under the law of that country, a management company or investment firm as referred to in paragraph (10) is required to meet the following conditions:

(a) the management company or investment firm shall be free in all situations to exercise, independently of its parent undertaking, the voting rights attached to the assets it manages;

(b) the management company or investment firm shall disregard the interests of the parent undertaking or of any other controlled under-taking of the parent undertaking whenever conflicts of interest arise.

(12) A parent undertaking of a third country undertaking shall comply with the notification requirements under paragraphs (4)(a) and (6) and in addition:

(a) shall make a statement that in respect of each management company or investment firm concerned, the parent undertaking complies with the conditions of independence specified in paragraph (1);and

(b) without prejudice to Article 24 of the Directive, shall be able to demonstrate to the competent authority of the home Member State of the issuer on request that the requirements of paragraph (7) are complied with.

Definitions

'admitted to trading on a regulated market': Transparency Regs, reg 2(1); 'management company': Transparency Regs, reg 2(1); 'competent authority' not defined, but see 'central competent authority of a home Member State' in Reg 2(1); 'controlled undertaking': Transparency Regs, reg 2(1); 'Directive': Transparency Regs, reg 2(1); 'electronic means' Transparency Regs, reg 2(1); 'home Member State': Transparency Regs, reg 2(1); 'in writing': Transparency Regs, reg 2(1); 'issuer': Transparency Regs, reg 2(1); 'regulated market': Transparency Regs, reg 2(1).

UK

FSA Disclosure and Transparency Rules 5.4.1–11.

19. Acquisition or disposal by issuer of shares

(1) An issuer of shares shall, if it acquires or disposes of its own shares, either itself or through a person acting in his or her own name but on the issuer's behalf, make public the percentage of voting rights attributable to those shares as soon as possible, but not later than 4 trading days following such acquisition or disposal, where that percentage reaches, exceeds or falls below either or both of the following thresholds, namely, the thresholds of 5% or 10% of the voting rights.

(2) The percentage shall be calculated on the basis of the total number of shares to which voting rights are attached.

Definitions

'issuer': Transparency Regs, reg 2(1).

UK

FSA Disclosure and Transparency Rules 5.5.1–2.

20. Disclosure by issuer

(1) An issuer shall, at the end of each calendar month during which an increase or decrease of such total number has occurred, disclose to the public—

(a) the total number of voting rights and capital in respect of each class of share that it issues,

(b) the total number of voting rights attaching to shares of the issuer that are held as treasury shares.

(2) Responsibility for all information drawn up and made public in accordance with paragraph (1) shall lie with the issuer.

Definitions

'issuer': Transparency Regs, reg 2(1); "treasury shares": CA 1990, s 209(1).

UK

FSA Disclosure and Transparency Rules 5.6.1, 5.6.3.

21. Procedures for notification and disclosure of major holdings

(1) A notification required under Regulations 14(1) and 15 shall include the following information:

(a) the resulting situation in terms of voting rights;

(b) the chain of controlled undertakings through which voting rights are effectively held, if applicable;

(c) the date on which the threshold was reached or crossed; and

(d) the identity of the shareholder even if that shareholder is not entitled to exercise voting rights under the conditions specified in Regulation 15 and of the person entitled to exercise voting rights on behalf of that shareholder.

(2) (a) A notification required under Regulation 17(1) arising from the holding of financial instruments shall include the following information:

(i) the resulting situation in terms of voting rights;

(ii) if applicable, the chain of controlled undertakings through which financial instruments are effectively held;

(iii) the date on which the threshold was reached or crossed;

(iv) for instruments with an exercise period, an indication of the date or time period where shares will or can be acquired, if applicable;

(v) date of maturity or expiration of the instrument;

(vi) identity of the holder; and

(vii) name of the underlying issuer.

(b) The notification shall be made to the issuer of each of the underlying shares to which the financial instrument relates and, in the case of shares admitted to trading on a regulated market, to each competent authority of the home Member States of such issuers.

(c) If a financial instrument relates to more than one underlying share, a separate notification shall be made to each issuer of the underlying shares.

(3) (a) The notification to the issuer shall be effected as soon as possible, but not later than 4 trading days, the first of which shall be the day after the date on which the shareholder or the person referred to in Regulation 15—

(i) learns of the acquisition or disposal or of the possibility of exercising voting rights, or on which, having regard to the circumstances, should have learned of it, regardless of the date on which the acquisition, disposal or possibility of exercising voting rights takes effect; or

(ii) is informed about the event specified in Regulation 14(2)(b).

(b) For the purposes of subparagraph (a), the shareholder, or the person referred to in Regulation 15, shall be deemed to have knowledge of the acquisition, disposal or possibility to exercise voting rights no later than 2 trading days following the transaction.

(4) (a) For the purposes of paragraph (3), the notification obligation which arises as soon as the proportion of voting rights held reaches, exceeds or falls below the applicable thresholds following transactions of the type referred to in Regulation 15 shall be an individual obligation incumbent upon each shareholder, or each person as referred to in Regulation 15, or both in case the proportion of voting rights held by each party reaches, exceeds or falls below the applicable threshold.

(b) In the circumstances referred to in Regulation 15(1)(a), the notification obligation shall be a collective obligation shared by all parties to the agreement.

(c) In the circumstances referred to in Regulation 15(1)(h) if a share-holder gives the proxy in relation to one shareholder meeting, notification may be made by means of a single notification when the proxy is given provided it is made clear in the notification what the resulting situation in terms of voting rights will be when the proxy may no longer exercise the voting rights discretion.

(d) If in the circumstances referred to in Regulation 15(1)(h) the proxy holder receives one or several proxies in relation to one shareholder meeting, notification may be made by means of a single notification on or after the deadline for receiving proxies provided that it is made clear in the notification what the resulting situation in terms of voting rights will be when the proxy may no longer exercise the voting rights at its discretion.

(e) When the duty to make notification lies with more than one person, notification may be made by means of a single common notification but this subparagraph does not release any of those persons from their responsibilities in relation to the notification.

(5) An undertaking is not required to make a notification in accordance with paragraph (1) if, instead, it is made by its parent undertaking or, where the parent undertaking is itself a controlled undertaking, by its own parent undertaking.

(6) Voting rights shall be calculated on the basis of all the shares to which voting rights are attached even if the exercise of such rights is suspended and shall be given in respect of all shares which are in the same class to which voting rights are attached.

(7) The number of voting rights to be considered when calculating whether a threshold is reached, exceeded or fallen below shall be the number of voting rights in existence according to the issuer's most recent disclosure made in accordance with Regulation 20(1)(a) but disregarding voting rights attached to any treasury shares held by the issuer (in accordance with the issuer's most recent disclosure of such holdings).

(8) (a) For the purposes of paragraphs (3) and (9) and Regulation 19, the calendar of trading days of the home Member State of the issuer shall apply.

(b) The Bank shall publish in its Internet site the calendar of trading days applicable in the State for purposes of subparagraph (a).

(9) On receipt of the notification under paragraph (1), but no later than 3 trading days thereafter, the issuer shall make public all the information contained in the notification.

Definitions

'admitted to trading on a regulated market': Transparency Regs, reg 2(1); 'Bank': Transparency Regs, reg 2(1); 'competent authority': not defined, but see 'central competent authority of a home Member State' in Reg 2(1); 'controlled undertaking': Transparency Regs, reg 2(1); 'home Member State': Transparency Regs, reg 2(1); 'issuer': Transparency Regs, reg 2(1); 'regulated market': Transparency Regs, reg 2(1); 'shareholder': Transparency Regs, reg 2(1); 'treasury shares': CA 1990, s 209(1).

Notes

Transparency Rule 7.4 requires the notification to the issuer to be effected:

> "as soon as possible, but not later than four trading days in the case of a non-Irish issuer and a collective investment undertaking of the closed-end type, and two trading days in all other cases, the first of which shall be the day after the date on which the relevant person:
>
> (a) learns of the acquisition or disposal or of the possibility of exercising voting rights, or on which, having regard to the circumstances, should have learned of it, regardless of the date on which the acquisition, disposal or possibility of exercising voting rights takes effect; or
>
> (b) is informed about the event in Regulation 14(1).
>
> For the purpose of a) above a person shall, in relation to a transaction to which he is a party or which he has instructed, be deemed to have knowledge of the acquisition, disposal or possibility to exercise voting rights no later than two trading days following the transaction in question. Where a transaction is conditional upon the approval by public authorities of the transaction or on a future uncertain event the occurrence of which is outside the control of the parties to the agreement, the parties are deemed to have knowledge of the acquisition, disposal or possibility of exercising voting rights only when the relevant approvals are obtained or when the event happens."

Transparency Rule 7.8 requires disclosure by the issuer to the market by the day following notification by the holder of the voting rights.

UK

FSA Disclosure and Transparency Rules 5.8.1–4, 5.8.6–9, 5.8.12.

22. Filing of information with competent authority

A person making a notification to an issuer in accordance with Regulation 14, 15, 17(1) or 21(1) shall, if the notification relates to shares admitted to trading on a regulated market, at the same time file a copy of such notification with the competent authority of the home Member State of the issuer.

Definitions

'admitted to trading on a regulated market': Transparency Regs, reg 2(1); 'competent authority': not defined, but see 'central competent authority of a home Member State' in Reg 2(1); 'home Member State': Transparency Regs, reg 2(1); 'issuer': Transparency Regs, reg 2(1); 'regulated market': Transparency Regs, reg 2(1).

UK

FSA Disclosure and Transparency Rule 5.9.1.

23. Use of electronic means for notifications and filing

Information filed with the Bank for the purposes of this Part shall be filed using electronic means.

Definitions

'Bank': Transparency Regs, reg 2(1); 'electronic means': Transparency Regs, reg 2(1).

UK

FSA Disclosure and Transparency Rule 5.10.1.

24. Third country issuers — equivalence

(1) Where the registered office of an issuer is in a third country, the Bank, subject to paragraphs (2) to (4), may exempt that issuer, in respect of which the State is the home Member State, from requirements under Regulations 19, 20 and 21(9) provided that the law of the third country in question lays down equivalent requirements or such an issuer complies with requirements of the law of a third country that the Bank considers as equivalent.

(2) A third country shall be deemed to set requirements equivalent to those specified in Regulation 21(9) where, under the law of that country, the period of time within which an issuer whose registered office is in that third country must be notified of major holdings and within which it must disclose to the public those major holdings is in total equal to or shorter than 7 trading days.

(3) (a) A third country shall be deemed to set requirements equivalent to those specified in Regulation 19 where, under the law of that country, an issuer whose registered office is in that third country is required to comply with the following conditions:

(i) in the case of an issuer only allowed to hold up to a maximum of 5% of its own shares to which voting rights are attached, it must make a notification whenever that threshold is reached or crossed;

(ii) in the case of an issuer allowed to hold up to a maximum of between 5% and 10% of its own shares to which voting rights are attached, it must make a notification whenever a 5% threshold or that maximum threshold is reached or crossed;

(iii) in the case of an issuer allowed to hold more than 10% of its own shares to which voting rights are attached, it must make a notification whenever that 5% threshold or that 10% threshold is reached or crossed.

(b) Notification above the 10% threshold is not required for the foregoing purpose.

(4) An issuer whose registered office is in a third country shall be deemed to meet requirements equivalent to those specified in Regulation 20 provided that the issuer is required under the law of the third country to disclose to the public the total number of voting rights and capital within 30 calendar days after an increase or decrease of such total number has occurred.

(5) Notwithstanding that the Bank has, under this Regulation, exempted an issuer from requirements referred to in paragraph (1), the issuer shall comply with the requirements of Articles 19, 20 and 21 of the Directive (as implemented in the State by Parts 6 and 7) in respect of the information covered by the requirements laid down in the third country in question.

Definitions

'Bank': Transparency Regs, reg 2(1); 'Directive': Transparency Regs, reg 2(1); 'home Member State': Transparency Regs, reg 2(1); 'issuer': Transparency Regs, reg 2(1).

UK

FSA Disclosure and Transparency Rules 5.11.1–4.

PART 6

CONTINUING OBLIGATIONS AND ACCESS TO INFORMATION

25. Information requirements for issuers of shares and debt securities

(1) (a) Subject to Regulations 29 and 30, this Regulation applies in relation to an issuer whose home Member State is the State.

(b) References in this Regulation to securities, shares and debt securities are references to such instruments as are admitted to trading on a regulated market.

(2) (a) If an issuer of securities proposes to amend its instruments of incorporation, it must communicate the draft amendment to:

(i) the Bank, and

(ii) the regulated market on which its securities have been admitted to trading.

(b) The communication referred to in subparagraph (a) shall be effected without delay but at the latest on the date of calling the general meeting which is to vote on, or be informed of, the amendment.

(3) (a) An issuer of shares shall ensure equal treatment for all holders of shares who are in the same position.

(b) An issuer of debt securities shall ensure that all holders of debt securities ranking pari passu are given equal treatment in respect of all the rights attaching to those debt securities.

(4) An issuer of shares or debt securities shall ensure that all the facilities and information necessary to enable holders of shares or debt securities to exercise their rights are available in the home Member State and that the integrity of data is preserved.

(5) (a) Shareholders and debt securities holders shall not be prevented from exercising their rights by proxy, subject to the law of the country in which the issuer is incorporated.

(b) An issuer of shares or debt securities shall make available a proxy form, on paper or, where applicable, by electronic means to each per-son entitled to vote at a meeting of shareholders or a meeting of debt securities holders.

(c) The proxy form shall be made available either:

(i) together with the notice concerning the meeting; or

(ii) on request, after the announcement of the meeting.

(6) An issuer of shares or debt securities shall designate, as its agent, a financial institution through which shareholders or debt securities holders may exercise their financial rights.

(7) An issuer of shares or debt securities may use electronic means to convey information to shareholders or debt securities holders.

(8) To use electronic means to convey information to holders, an issuer shall comply with the following:

(a) a decision to use electronic means to convey information to share-holders or debt securities holders shall be taken in a general meeting;

(b) the use of electronic means shall not depend upon the location of the seat or residence of:

(i) the shareholder; or

(ii) persons referred to in subparagraphs (a) to (h) of Regulation 15(1); or

(iii) the debt security holder; or

(iv) a proxy representing a debt security holder;

(c) identification arrangements shall be put in place so that the share-holders, debt security holders or other persons entitled to exercise or to direct the exercise of voting rights are effectively informed;

(d) shareholders, debt security holders or persons referred to in subparagraphs (a) to (h) of Regulation 15(1) who are entitled to acquire, dispose of or exercise voting rights shall be:

(i) contacted in writing to request their consent for the use of electronic means for conveying information and, if they do not object within a reasonable period of time, their consent can be considered to have been given; and

(ii) able to request at any time in the future that information be conveyed in writing; and

(e) any apportionment of the costs entailed in the conveyance of information by electronic means shall be determined by the issuer in compliance with the principle of equal treatment referred to in paragraph (3).

Definitions

'admitted to trading on a regulated market': Transparency Regs, reg 2(1); 'Bank': Transparency Regs, reg 2(1); 'debt securities': Transparency Regs, reg 2(1); 'electronic means': Transparency Regs, reg 2(1); 'home Member State': Transparency Regs, reg 2(1); 'in writing': Transparency Regs, reg 2(1); 'issuer': Transparency Regs, reg 2(1); 'regulated market': Transparency Regs, reg 2(1); 'securities': Transparency Regs, reg 2(1); 'shareholder': Transparency Regs, reg 2(1).

UK

FSA Disclosure and Transparency Rules 6.1.1–8.

26. Information about changes in rights attaching to securities

(1) An issuer of shares shall without delay disclose to the public any change in the rights attaching to its various classes of shares, including changes in the rights attaching to derivative securities issued by the issuer giving access to the shares of that issuer.

(2) An issuer of securities, other than shares admitted to trading on a regulated market, shall disclose to the public without delay any changes in the rights of holders of securities other than shares, including changes in the terms and conditions of such securities which could indirectly affect those rights, resulting in particular from a change in loan terms or in interest rates.

(3) An issuer of securities admitted to trading on a regulated market (other than an issuer which is a public international body of which at least one Member State is a member) shall disclose to the public without delay any new loan issues and in particular any guarantee or security in respect of such issues.

Definitions

'admitted to trading on a regulated market': Transparency Regs, reg 2(1); 'issuer': Transparency Regs, reg 2(1); 'Member State': Transparency Regs, reg 2(1); 'regulated market': Transparency Regs, reg 2(1); 'securities': Transparency Regs, reg 2(1).

UK

FSA Disclosure and Transparency Rules 6.1.9–11.

27. Information about meetings, issue of new shares and payment of dividends — share issuers

(1) An issuer of shares shall provide information to holders on:

(a) the place, time and agenda of meetings;

(b) the total number of shares and voting rights; and

(c) the rights of holders to participate in meetings.

(2) An issuer of shares shall publish notices or distribute circulars concerning the allocation and payment of dividends and the issue of new shares, including information on any arrangements for allotment, subscription, cancellation or conversion.

Definitions

'issuer': Transparency Regs, reg 2(1).

UK

FSA Disclosure and Transparency Rules 6.1.12–13.

28. Information about meetings, and payment of interest — debt security issuers

(1) An issuer of debt securities shall publish notices or distribute circulars concerning:

(a) the place, time and agenda of meetings of debt securities holders;

(b) the payment of interest;

(c) the exercise of any conversion, exchange, subscription or cancellation rights and repayment; and

(d) the rights of holders to exercise their rights in relation to the matters mentioned in subparagraphs (a) to (c).

(2) If only holders of debt securities whose denomination per unit amounts to at least €50,000 (or an equivalent amount) are to be invited to a meeting, the issuer may choose as a venue any Member State, provided that all the facilities and information necessary to enable such holders to exercise their rights are made available in that Member State.

Definitions

'debt securities': Transparency Regs, reg 2(1); 'issuer': Transparency Regs, reg 2(1); 'Member State': Transparency Regs, reg 2(1).

UK

FSA Disclosure and Transparency Rules 6.1.14–15.

29. State, regional and local authority exemption

A State, regional or local authority with securities admitted to trading on a regulated market is not required to comply with the following:

(a) Regulations 25(4) to (7) and 26(3) in so far as those provisions relate to debt securities, and

(b) Regulation 28(1) and (2).

Definitions

'admitted to trading on a regulated market': Transparency Regs, reg 2(1); 'debt securities': Transparency Regs, reg 2(1); 'regulated market': Transparency Regs, reg 2(1); 'securities': Transparency Regs, reg 2(1).

UK

FSA Disclosure and Transparency Rule 6.1.18.

30. Third country equivalence

(1) Where—

(a) the registered office of an issuer is in a third country, and

(b) that issuer is an issuer in respect of which the State is the home Member State,

the Bank, subject to paragraph (2), may exempt that issuer from requirements under Regulations 25(3) to 28(2), provided that the law of the third country in question lays down equivalent requirements or such an issuer complies with requirements of the law of a third country that the Bank considers as equivalent.

(2) A third country shall be deemed to set requirements equivalent to those set out in Articles 17(2) (a) and 18(2) (a) of the Directive, as far as the content of the information about meetings is concerned, where, under the law of that country, an issuer whose registered office is in that third country is required to provide at least information on the place, time and agenda of meetings.

(3) Notwithstanding that the Bank has, under this Regulation, exempted an issuer from requirements referred to in paragraph (1), the issuer shall comply with the requirements of Articles 19, 20 and 21 of the Directive (as implemented in the State by this Part and Part 7) in respect of the information covered by the requirements laid down in the third country in question.

Definitions

'Bank': Transparency Regs, reg 2(1); 'Directive': Transparency Regs, reg 2(1); 'home Member State': Transparency Regs, reg 2(1); 'issuer': Transparency Regs, reg 2(1).

UK

FSA Disclosure and Transparency Rules 6.1.16, 6.1.12.

31. Filing of information with Bank

(1) This Regulation applies to:

(a) an issuer:

(i) whose securities are admitted to trading on a regulated market; and

(ii) whose home Member State is the State; and

(b) a person who has requested, without the issuer's consent, the admission of its securities to trading on a regulated market.

(2) An issuer or person referred to in paragraph (1) that discloses regulated information shall, at the same time, file that information with the Bank.

Definitions

'admitted to trading on a regulated market': Transparency Regs, reg 2(1); 'Bank': Transparency Regs, reg 2(1); 'home Member State': Transparency Regs, reg 2(1); 'issuer': Transparency Regs, reg 2(1); 'regulated information': Transparency Regs, reg 2(1); 'regulated market': Transparency Regs, reg 2(1); 'securities': Transparency Regs, reg 2(1).

UK

FSA Disclosure and Transparency Rules 6.2.1–2.

32. Use of languages

(1) Subject to paragraph (6), if securities are admitted to trading only on a regulated market in the State and the State is the home Member State, regulated information shall be disclosed in a language accepted by the Bank.

(2) Subject to paragraph (6), if securities are admitted to trading in more than one Member State including the State and the State is the home Member State regulated information shall be disclosed:

(a) in a language accepted by the Bank; and

(b) either in a language accepted by the competent authorities of each host Member State or in a language customary in the sphere of inter-national finance, at the election of the issuer.

(3) (a) Subject to paragraph (6), if securities are admitted to trading in one or more Member States excluding the State and the State is the home Member State, regulated information shall be disclosed either:

(i) in a language accepted by the competent authorities of those host Member States; or

(ii) in a language customary in the sphere of international finance, at the election of the issuer.

(b) In addition, where the State is the home Member State, regulated information shall be disclosed in a language accepted by the Bank or in another language customary in the sphere of international finance, at the election of the issuer.

(4) Subject to paragraph (6), if securities are admitted to trading on a regulated market without the issuer's consent:

(a) paragraphs (1) to (3) shall not apply to the issuer; and

(b) paragraphs (1) to (3) shall apply to the person who has requested such admission without the issuer's consent.

(5) Shareholders and a person referred to in Regulations 14, 15 and 17 shall be permitted to notify information to an issuer under these Regulations and transparency (regulated markets) law only in a language customary in the sphere of international finance. If an issuer receives such a notification, the Bank may not require the issuer to provide a translation into a language accepted by it.

(6) If securities whose denomination per unit amounts to at least €50,000 (or an equivalent amount) are admitted to trading on a regulated market in the State or in one or more Member States, regulated information shall be disclosed to the public in either a language accepted by the competent authorities of the home Member State and host Member States or in a language customary in the sphere of international finance, at the election of the issuer or of the person who, without the issuer's consent, has requested such admission.

(7) If an action concerning the content of regulated information is brought before a court or tribunal in the State, responsibility for the payment of costs incurred in the translation of that information for the purposes of the proceedings shall be in accordance with the law of the State.

(8) For the purposes of this Regulation "a language customary in the sphere of international finance" includes the English language.

Definitions

'admitted to trading on a regulated market': Transparency Regs, reg 2(1); 'Bank': Transparency Regs, reg 2(1); 'competent authority': not defined, but see 'central competent authority of a home Member State' in Reg 2(1); 'home Member State': Transparency Regs, reg 2(1); 'host Member State' Transparency Regs, reg 2(1); 'issuer': Transparency Regs, reg 2(1); 'Member State': Transparency Regs, reg 2(1); 'regulated information': Transparency Regs, reg 2(1); 'regulated market': Transparency Regs, reg 2(1) 'securities': Transparency Regs, reg 2(1); 'shareholder': Transparency Regs, reg 2(1);'transparency (regulated markets) law': IFCMPA 2006, s 19(1).

UK

FSA Disclosure and Transparency Rules 6.2.4–8.

PART 7

DISSEMINATION OF INFORMATION

33.

(1) This Regulation applies to:

(a) an issuer:

(i) whose securities are admitted to trading on a regulated market; and

(ii) whose home Member State is the State;

(b) a person who has applied, without the issuer's consent, for the admission of its securities to trading on a regulated market; and

(c) securities that are admitted to trading only on a regulated market in the State which is the host Member State and not in the home Member State.

(2) An issuer referred to in paragraph (1)(a), a person referred to in paragraph (1)(b) ("other person") or an issuer of securities referred to in paragraph (1)(c) shall disclose regulated information in the manner specified in paragraphs (3) to (8).

(3) When disseminating regulated information an issuer or other person shall ensure that the minimum standards specified in paragraphs (4) to (8) are complied with.

(4) Regulated information shall be disseminated in a manner ensuring that it is capable of being disseminated to as wide a public as possible, and as close to simultaneously as possible in the home Member State, and in other Member States.

(5) (a) Regulated information, other than regulated information referred to in subparagraph (b), shall be communicated to the media in unedited full text.

(b) (i) An annual financial report that is required by Regulation 4 to be made public is not required to be communicated to the media in unedited full text except for the information referred to in clause (ii).

(ii) If information is of a type that would be required to be disseminated in a half-yearly financial report then information of such a type that is contained in an annual financial report shall be communicated to the media in unedited full text.

(c) The announcement relating to the publication of the following regulated information shall include an indication of the website on which the relevant documents are available:

(i) an annual financial report that is required by Regulation 4 to be made public;

(ii) a half-yearly financial report that is required by Regulation 6 to be made public; and

(iii) an interim management statement that is required by Regulation 9 to be made public or an equivalent quarterly financial report.

(6) Regulated information shall be communicated to the media in a manner which ensures the security of the communication, minimises the risk of data corruption and unauthorised access, and provides certainty as to the source of the regulated information. Security of receipt shall be ensured by remedying as soon as possible any failure or disruption in the communication of regulated information. An issuer or other person shall not be responsible for systemic errors or shortcomings in the media to which the regulated information has been communicated.

(7) Regulated information shall be communicated to a RIS in a way which:

(a) makes clear that the information is regulated information;

(b) identifies clearly:

(i) the issuer concerned;

(ii) the subject matter of the regulated information; and

(iii) the time and date of the communication of the regulated information by the issuer or other person.

(8) Upon request, an issuer or other person shall be able to communicate to the Bank, in relation to any disclosure of regulated information:

(a) the name of the person who communicated the regulated information to the RIS;

(b) the security validation details;

(c) the time and date on which the regulated information was communicated; and

(d) the medium in which the regulated information was communicated; and

(e) details of any embargo placed by the issuer on the regulated information, if applicable.

(9) An issuer or other person shall not charge investors any specific cost for providing regulated information.

Definitions

'admitted to trading on a regulated market': Transparency Regs, reg 2(1); 'Bank': Transparency Regs, reg 2(1); 'home Member State': Transparency Regs, reg 2(1); Transparency Regs, reg 2(1); 'host Member State': Transparency Regs, reg 2(1); 'issuer': Transparency Regs, reg 2(1);

'Member State': Transparency Regs, reg 2(1); 'regulated information': Transparency Regs, reg 2(1); 'regulated market': Transparency Regs, reg 2(1); 'RIS': Transparency Regs, reg 2(1); 'securities': Transparency Regs, reg 2(1).

UK

FSA Disclosure and Transparency Rules 6.3.1–9.

---

34. Disclosure of information in third country

(1) Information that is disclosed in a third country which may be of importance to the public in the Member States shall be disclosed in accordance with the provisions of Regulations 32 and 33.

(2) In addition, paragraph (1) applies to information that is not regulated information.

Definitions

'Member State': Transparency Regs, reg 2(1); 'regulated information': Transparency Regs, reg 2(1).

UK

FSA Disclosure and Transparency Rules 6.3.10.

---

35. Choice of home Member State and notifications by third country issuers

An issuer that chooses the State as its home Member State, by virtue of paragraph (b) of the definition of "home Member State" in Regulation 2(1), shall disclose that choice in accordance with this Part.

Definitions

'home Member State': Transparency Regs, reg 2(1); 'issuer': Transparency Regs, reg 2(1).

UK

FSA Disclosure and Transparency Rule 6.4.1.

PART 8
COMPETENT AUTHORITIES

36. Designation of Competent Authorities

(1) Subject to paragraph (2), the Bank is designated as the central competent administrative authority for purposes of the Directive and shall be responsible for carrying out the obligations provided for in the Directive and for ensuring that the provisions adopted pursuant to the Directive are applied.

(2) IAASA is designated as the competent authority for purposes of subparagraph (h) of Article 24(4) of the Directive and shall be responsible for carrying out the obligations provided for in that subparagraph and for ensuring that the provisions adopted pursuant to the Directive in respect thereof are applied.

(3) The Bank and IAASA shall each be independent in the performance of its functions under these Regulations.

Definitions

'Bank': Transparency Regs, reg 2(1); 'competent authority' and 'central competent administrative authority' not defined, but see 'central competent authority of a home Member State' in Reg 2(1); 'Directive': Transparency Regs, reg 2(1); 'IAASA': Transparency Regs, reg 2(1).

UK

See FSMA, Sch 7.

37. Delegation of functions

(1) The Bank may delegate to an approved stock exchange, subject to such conditions as the Bank specifies, any of the functions that it is obliged or authorised to perform under transparency (regulated markets) law or under the Directive other than the functions under Regulations 37, 39, 40, 53, 56, 57 and 58 and Parts 10 and 12.

(2) Any person to whom functions are delegated under paragraph (1) shall have, by virtue of the delegation, all such powers as are necessary to perform those functions.

(3) Any delegation of functions shall be in writing and specify the functions to be performed and the conditions subject to which they are to be performed.

(4) The conditions referred to in paragraph (3) shall include a provision obliging the stock exchange to whom a function or functions concerned are delegated to act and be organised in such a manner as to avoid conflicts of interest and so that information obtained from performing the function is not used unfairly or to prevent competition.

(5) A delegation under this Regulation shall not prevent the performance by the Bank of the function delegated.

(6) Notwithstanding any delegation under this Regulation, the final responsibility for supervising compliance with the applicable provisions of the Directive and of transparency (regulated markets) law shall be with the Bank.

(7) The Bank shall notify the Minister of any such delegation of a function promptly and of the conditions subject to which it has been delegated.

(8) Following such notification, the Minister shall inform the Commission and the competent authorities of other Member States designated pursuant to the Directive of any arrangements entered into with regard to the functions under this Regulation, including the conditions subject to which such functions are delegated.

(9) Where a function is delegated pursuant to this Regulation, then nothing in the Stock Exchange Act 1995 (No. 9 of 1995) shall prevent there being specified as a condition subject to which the function is to be performed a condition requiring the rules of the stock exchange concerned or an amendment thereof to be approved by the Bank in so far as they are relevant to the function delegated.

Definitions

'approved stock exchange': Transparency Regs, reg 2(1); 'Bank': Transparency Regs, reg 2(1); 'competent authorities' not defined, but see 'central competent authority of a home Member State' in Reg 2(1); 'Directive': Transparency Regs, reg 2(1); 'in writing': Transparency Regs, reg 2(1); 'Member State': Transparency Regs, reg 2(1); 'Minister': Transparency Regs, reg 2(1);

'regulated market': Transparency Regs, reg 2(1); 'transparency (regulated markets) law': IFCMPA 2006, s 19(1).

UK

See FSMA, Sch 8.

PART 9
POWERS OF COMPETENT AUTHORITIES

38. Definitions

In this Part—

"authorised officer" means an authorised officer appointed under Regulation 53;

"person to whom these Regulations apply" means any relevant person or a market operator;

"records" means any book, document or any other written or printed material in any form including any information (including phone and data traffic records) stored, maintained or preserved by means of any mechanical or electronic device, whether or not stored, maintained or preserved in a legible form;

"relevant person" means an issuer or any other person (other than a market operator) on whom an obligation is imposed by these Regulations;

"relevant records" means records relating to the activities of persons to whom these Regulations apply;

"responsible authority" means:—

(a) the Chief Executive of—

(i) the Irish Financial Services Regulatory Authority or

(ii) IAASA, or

(b) any person to whom the Chief Executive of either of those Authorities has delegated responsibility for appointing authorised persons.

Definitions

'IAASA': Transparency Regs, reg 2(1); 'issuer': Transparency Regs, reg 2(1); 'market operator': Transparency Regs, reg 2(1).

39. Powers of Bank

(1) The Bank shall have all the powers necessary for the performance of its functions under transparency (regulated markets) law or the Directive.

(2) The powers provided for in this Part in respect of the Bank shall not be exercised in a manner or for a purpose inconsistent with the Directive or these Regulations.

Definitions

'Bank': Transparency Regs, reg 2(1); 'Directive': Transparency Regs, reg 2(1); 'transparency (regulated markets) law': IFCMPA 2006, s 19(1).

40. Particular powers of Bank

(1) Without prejudice to—

(a) the generality of Regulation 39, and

(b) the subsequent provisions of this Regulation, the Bank shall, in particular, have the power to:

(i) require auditors, issuers, holders of shares or other financial instruments, or persons referred to in Regulation 14 or 17, and the persons that control them or are controlled by them, to provide information and documents to the Bank or delegate;

(ii) require the issuer to disclose the information required under sub-paragraph (i) to the public by the means and within the time limits the Bank considers necessary;

(iii) require managers of the issuers and of the holders of shares or other financial instruments, or of persons referred to in Regulation 14 or 17, to notify the information required under the Directive, or under transparency (regulated markets) law, and, if necessary, to provide further information and documents to the Bank or delegate;

(iv) monitor that the issuer discloses timely information with the objective of ensuring effective and equal access to the public in all Member States where the securities are traded and take appropriate action if that is not the case;

(v) make public the fact that an issuer, or a holder of shares or other financial instruments, or a person referred to in Regulation 14 or 17, is failing to comply with its or his or her obligations.

(2) The Bank may publish the information referred to in paragraph (1)(ii) of its own initiative in the event that the issuer or the persons that control it or are controlled by it, fail to do so and after having heard the issuer.

(3) (a) This paragraph applies where the State is the home Member State in respect of an issuer admitted to trading on a regulated market.

(b) Where this paragraph applies, the Bank may (by means of rules under section 22 of the Act of 2006) make—

(i) the issuer,

(ii) the holder of shares, or

(iii) a person referred to in Regulation 15 or 17(1),

subject to a requirement or requirements that is or are more stringent than a requirement or requirements specified in Part 2, 3, 5, 6 or 7.

(c) In exercising the power under subparagraph (b), the Bank shall have regard to the interests of investors and to the public interest.

(d) As soon as may be after it has exercised that power, the Bank shall notify, in writing, the Minister of the fact of its exercise and provide to the Minister such particulars in relation to that exercise as the Minister may request.

(4) The Bank shall arrange for the putting in place of at least one official mechanism for the central storage of regulated information in accordance with Article 21 of the Directive.

(5) The Bank shall have the following powers (by means of giving a direction under Regulation 56 in that behalf) for the purpose of regulating the disclosure of periodic and ongoing information about issuers whose securities are already admitted to trading on a regulated market and in respect of which the State is the home Member State:

(a) suspend, or request the relevant regulated market to suspend, trading in securities for a maximum of 10 days at a time if it has reasonable grounds for suspecting that the provisions of the Directive or of transparency (regulated markets) law, have been infringed by the issuer;

(b) prohibit trading on the relevant regulated market if it finds that the provisions of the Directive or of transparency(regulated markets) law have been infringed, or if it has reasonable grounds for suspecting that they would be infringed.

(6) The disclosure to the Bank by an auditor of any information, document, fact or decision on foot of a requirement made by the Bank under paragraph (1)(i) shall not be regarded as constituting a breach of any restriction on disclosure of information imposed by contract or by any law, regulation or administrative provision and shall not involve the auditor in liability of any kind.

Definitions

'Act of 2006': Transparency Regs, reg 2(1); 'admitted to trading on a regulated market': Transparency Regs, reg 2(1); 'Bank': Transparency Regs, reg 2(1); 'Directive': Transparency Regs, reg 2(1); 'home Member State': Transparency Regs, reg 2(1); 'in writing': Transparency Regs, reg 2(1); 'issuer': Transparency Regs, reg 2(1); 'Member State': Transparency Regs, reg 2(1); 'Minister': Transparency Regs, reg 2(1); 'regulated information': Transparency Regs, reg 2(1); 'regulated market': Transparency Regs, reg 2(1); 'securities': Transparency Regs, reg 2(1); 'transparency (regulated markets) law': IFCMPA 2006, s 19(1).

UK

FSMA, ss 89H–89J, 165.

---

41. Other powers of Bank not prejudiced

The powers of the Bank under this Part are without prejudice to the powers of the Bank under any other Part of these Regulations or any other enactment.

Definitions

'Bank': Transparency Regs, reg 2(1); 'enactment': Transparency Regs, reg 2(1).

---

42. Functions of IAASA

(1) IAASA shall have all the powers necessary for the performance of its functions under Regulation 36(2).

(2) IAASA shall examine information drawn up pursuant to Regulations 4 to 8 by issuers whose home Member State is the State for the purpose of considering whether such information is in accordance with the relevant reporting framework.

(3) The powers provided for in this Part in respect of IAASA shall not be exercised in a manner or for a purpose inconsistent with the Directive or transparency (regulated markets) law.

Definitions

'Directive': Transparency Regs, reg 2(1); 'home Member State': Transparency Regs, reg 2(1); 'IAASA': Transparency Regs, reg 2(1); 'issuer': Transparency Regs, reg 2(1); 'transparency (regulated markets) law': IFCMPA 2006, s 19(1).

43. Particular powers of IAASA — supply of information

(1) Without prejudice to the generality of Regulation 42, IAASA shall, in particular, have the power to:

- (a) require any of the following persons to produce any document in his or her possession or control and to make copies of such documents, or to provide any information or explanations that it may reasonably require, for the purpose of examining and reviewing information published pursuant to Regulations 4 to 8:
  - (i) an issuer;
  - (ii) any director, manager, officer or employee of an issuer;
  - (iii) any persons who control or are controlled by a person referred to in clause (i) or (ii);
  - (iv) any person discharging managerial responsibilities of the issuer;
  - (v) an auditor of an issuer;
  - (vi) any person who fell within any of clauses (i) to (v) at a time when the document or information required by IAASA was prepared or came into existence; and
- (b) certify to the Court the refusal or failure of any person referred to in any of clauses (i) to (v) of subparagraph (a) to comply with a requirement made by IAASA pursuant to that subparagraph.

(2) The disclosure to IAASA by an auditor of any information, document, fact or decision on foot of a requirement made by IAASA under paragraph (1)(a) shall not be regarded as constituting a breach of any restriction on disclosure of information imposed by contract or by any law, regulation or administrative provision and shall not involve the auditor in liability of any kind.

Definitions

'IAASA': Transparency Regs, reg 2(1); 'issuer': Transparency Regs, reg 2(1).

UK

FSMA, ss 89H–89J.

44. Further particular powers of IAASA — directions to issuers, etc

Where it appears to IAASA that there is, or may be, a failure by an issuer whose home Member State is the State to ensure that an annual financial report published pursuant to Regulation 4 or a half-yearly financial report published pursuant to Regulation 5 complies with the relevant reporting framework, IAASA may give notice to the issuer and to the directors of such issuer specifying:

(a) the matters in respect of which it appears to IAASA that the information fails to comply with the relevant reporting framework; and

(b) a period of not less than 30 days within which the issuer shall either:

  (i) provide IAASA with a written explanation of the information; or

  (ii) prepare revised information;

(c) that, in the absence of a written explanation under paragraph (b)(i) or the issuance of revised information under paragraph (b)(ii), IAASA may:

  (i) give a direction requiring the issuer to revise the information in accordance with instructions of IAASA specified in the direction;

  (ii) seek an order of confirmation from the Court of that direction issued by IAASA; and

  (iii) recover its costs from the issuer;

(d) that, in the event that IAASA seeks an order of the Court to enforce its direction, IAASA may publish notice of such application in such manner as it thinks fit.

Definitions

'Court': Transparency Regs, reg 2(1); 'home Member State': Transparency Regs, reg 2(1); 'IAASA': Transparency Regs, reg 2(1); 'issuer': Transparency Regs, reg 2(1).

UK

FSMA, s 165.

45. Provisions consequent on issuer's response to notice under Regulation 44

(1) If, at or before the end of the period specified in the notice under Regulation 44 in accordance with paragraph (b) thereof, or such longer period as IAASA may permit, the issuer prepares revised information as directed by IAASA in that notice, IAASA may, taking into account the circumstances of the matter, require the issuer to pay some or all of the costs IAASA incurred in examining the information published by such issuer and in performing its functions under these Regulations.

(2) If, at the end of the period specified in the notice under Regulation 44 in accordance with paragraph (b) thereof, or such longer period as IAASA may permit—

(a) the issuer has not issued revised information; and

(b) IAASA, having considered any explanations provided by the issuer or its directors or both and considered any information or documents or both provided by the issuer in response to requests from it, IAASA remains of the opinion that the information does not comply with the relevant reporting framework,

IAASA may give a direction to the issuer requiring the issuer or its directors or both to do one or more of the following:

(i) revise the annual financial report or half-yearly financial report, as applicable, in accordance with instructions of IAASA specified in the direction;

(ii) publish the revised information in the same manner as required by Regulations 4 to 8 and to make any consequential amendments to the annual or interim financial reports published in accordance with instructions of IAASA specified in the direction;

(iii) publish notice of the direction given by IAASA under this paragraph in a format and containing such information as is specified by IAASA in the direction;

(iv) pay costs specified in the direction, being costs incurred by IAASA in examining and reviewing the financial reports.

(3) A direction under paragraph (2) shall—

(a) be in writing,

and

(b) specify the date from which it shall have effect and the period for which it shall have effect (which shall not exceed 12 months).

Definitions

'IAASA': Transparency Regs, reg 2(1); 'in writing': Transparency Regs, reg 2(1); 'issuer': Transparency Regs, reg 2(1).

---

46. Application to Court to set aside or vary direction under Regulation 45

An issuer or its directors or both may apply to the Court for, and the Court may, if it considers it appropriate to do so, grant, an order setting aside or varying a direction under Regulation 45. An application under this Regulation shall be made within 30 days after the notification of the direction or within such extended period as the Court allows.

Definitions

'Court': Transparency Regs, reg 2(1); 'issuer': Transparency Regs, reg 2(1).

---

47. Enforcement of direction under Regulation 45

(1) IAASA may, as respects a direction under Regulation 45 which, in its opinion, has not been complied with, apply to the Court in a summary manner for such order as may be appropriate by way of enforcement of the direction and the Court may, as it thinks fit, on the hearing of the application, make or refuse to make an order providing for such relief.

(2) An application for an order under this Regulation shall be by motion, and the Court when considering the motion may make such interim or interlocutory order as it considers appropriate.

Definitions

'Court': Transparency Regs, reg 2(1); 'IAASA': Transparency Regs, reg 2(1).

48. Applications under Regulations 46 and 47: supplemental provisions

(1) An application under Regulation 46 may not be made if the direction concerned has been the subject of an order granted under Regulation 47 (but without prejudice to the right of a person to apply subsequently to the Court to have the order varied or discharged).

(2) The Court may direct the hearing together of applications made under Regulations 46 and 47 that relate to the same direction.

(3) The Court may, if it thinks fit, vary or discharge an order made under Regulation 47.

(4) An application under Regulation 46 or 47 may be heard otherwise than in public.

Definitions

'Court': Transparency Regs, reg 2(1); 'IAASA': Transparency Regs, reg 2(1).

49. Particular powers of Court on application to it under Regulation 47

(1) If satisfied, after hearing an application of IAASA pursuant to Regulation 47, that an issuer's annual or half-yearly financial report does not comply with the relevant reporting framework in whole or in part, the Court may make a declaration to that effect and may, by order, do one or more of the following:

(a) require the issuer or its directors or both to revise the financial report at issue so that it complies with the relevant reporting framework;

(b) give directions respecting one or more of the following:

(i) the auditing of the revised annual accounts;

(ii) the revision of any matter contained in any annual financial report or half-yearly financial report as appropriate;

(iii) the steps to be taken by the issuer or directors or both to bring the order of the Court to the notice of persons likely to rely on the information that was the subject of the declaration;

(iv) such other matters as the Court sees fit;

(c) require the issuer or directors or both to pay the costs incurred by IAASA in performing its functions under Regulations 44 to 46 in relation to such issuer.

(2) For the purposes of making an order under paragraph (1), the Court may:

(a) have regard to the extent to which any or all of the directors who approved the annual or half-yearly financial report that was the subject of the direction knew, or ought to have known, that it did not comply with the relevant reporting framework; and

(b) exempt one or more directors from any order made under paragraph (1) or may order the payment of different amounts by different directors.

Definitions

'Court': Transparency Regs, reg 2(1); 'IAASA': Transparency Regs, reg 2(1); 'issuer': Transparency Regs, reg 2(1).

50. Dissemination of court order

At the conclusion of proceedings before the Court, IAASA shall disseminate in such manner as it thinks fit:

(a) a copy of the court order, or

(b) notice that the application has failed or been withdrawn.

Definitions

'Court': Transparency Regs, reg 2(1); 'IAASA': Transparency Regs, reg 2(1).

51. Provisions in relation to revised annual and half-yearly financial reports

(1) Regulations 44, 45, 47, 48, 49 and 50 apply equally to revised annual financial reports and half-yearly financial reports, as applicable, in which case references to revised annual reports and half-yearly financial reports are to be construed as references to further revised annual financial reports and half-yearly financial reports.

(2) Where revised annual financial reports or half-yearly financial reports are prepared under any of the Regulations referred to in paragraph (1), then, subject to a direction given under Regulation 45 or any order of the Court made on foot of an application to it under Regulation 47, any provision of these Regulations or the Companies Acts respecting the preparation, auditing, circulation and disclosure of annual accounts applies with the necessary changes to the revised annual financial report or half-yearly financial report, as applicable.

Definitions

'Court': Transparency Regs, reg 2(1).

52. Supplemental provisions in relation to directions of IAASA

(1) IAASA may give a direction amending or revoking a direction given by it under Regulation 45(2) but this power may not be exercised—

(a) if an order of the Court made on foot of an application to it under Regulation 47 is for the time being in force in relation to the direction, or

(b) to extend the period specified in the direction for which it is to have effect.

(2) On the expiry of the period specified in a direction for which it is to have effect, IAASA may give another direction under these Regulations if it considers it necessary to do so, in like or different terms to the person concerned.

(6) An application for an order under paragraph (5) shall be by motion, and the Court when considering the motion may make such interim or interlocutory order as it considers appropriate.

(7) An application under paragraph (4) may not be made if the direction concerned has been the subject of an order granted under paragraph (5) (but without prejudice to the right of a person, the subject of an order granted under paragraph (5), to apply subsequently to the Court to have the order varied or discharged).

(8) The Court may direct the hearing together of applications made under paragraphs (4) and (5) that relate to the same direction.

(9) The Court may, if it thinks fit, vary or discharge an order made under paragraph (5).

(10) An application under paragraph (4) or (5) may be heard otherwise than in public.

(11) The Bank may give a direction amending or revoking a direction given by it under this Regulation but this power may not be exercised—

(a) if an order under paragraph (5) is for the time being in force in relation to the direction,

or

(b) to extend the period specified in the direction for which it is to have effect.

(12) On the expiry of the period specified in a direction for which it is to have effect, the Bank may give another direction under this Regulation (if it considers it necessary to do so on the grounds specified in paragraph (1)), in like or different terms, to the person concerned.

(13) The powers of the Bank under this Regulation are in addition to those conferred on it by any other enactment to give directions or impose conditions or requirements.

Definitions

'Bank': Transparency Regs, reg 2(1); 'contravene': see 'contravention' in Transparency Regs, reg 2(1); 'Court': Transparency Regs, reg 2(1); 'credit institution' Transparency Regs, reg 2(1); 'Directive': Transparency Regs, reg 2(1); 'enactment': Transparency Regs, reg 2(1); 'in writing': Transparency Regs, reg 2(1); 'transparency (regulated markets) law': IFCMPA 2006, s 19(1).

57. Precautionary measures

In circumstances where the State is a host Member State and where the Bank or IAASA, as appropriate, finds or has grounds for suspecting that an issuer or the holder of shares or other financial instruments or the person referred to in Regulation 14 has contravened a provision of these Regulations or another provision of transparency (regulated markets) law, it shall refer those findings or the fact of those grounds' existence to the competent authority of the home Member State.

Definitions

'Bank': Transparency Regs, reg 2(1); 'competent authority of the home Member State' not defined, but see 'central competent authority of a home Member State' in Reg 2(1); 'contravene', see 'contravention' in Transparency Regs, reg 2(1); 'home Member State': Transparency Regs, reg 2(1); Transparency Regs, reg 2(1); 'host Member State': Transparency Regs, reg 2(1);

'IAASA': Transparency Regs, reg 2(1); 'issuer': Transparency Regs, reg 2(1); 'transparency (regulated markets) law': IFCMPA 2006, s 19(1).

58. Supplemental provision in relation to Regulation 57

(1) If, despite the measures taken by the competent authority of the home Member State in response to a referral of matters under Regulation 57 by the Bank or IAASA to it (whether because those measures are inadequate or otherwise) the contravention referred to in that Regulation still persists, the Bank or IAASA, as the case may be, after informing the competent authority of the home Member State, shall take all the appropriate measures within its power under these Regulations in order to protect investors.

(2) The Bank or IAASA, as the case may be, shall inform the Commission of any measures taken by it under paragraph (1) at the earliest opportunity.

Definitions

'Bank': Transparency Regs, reg 2(1); 'competent authority of the home Member State "not defined, but see "central competent authority of a home Member State' in Reg 2(1); 'contravention': Transparency Regs, reg 2(1); 'home Member State': Transparency Regs, reg 2(1); "IAASA": Transparency Regs, reg 2(1).

59. Privilege

Nothing in these Regulations shall compel the disclosure by any person of any information which he or she would, in the opinion of the Court, be entitled to refuse to produce on the grounds of legal professional privilege or authorise the taking possession of any document containing such information which is in his or her possession.

Definitions

'Court': Transparency Regs, reg 2(1).

PART 10
ADMINISTRATIVE SANCTIONS

60. Interpretation (Part 10)

(1) In this Part—

"adverse assessment" means an assessment in which the assessor has decided that the assessee is committing or has committed a prescribed contravention;

"assessee" means the person the subject of an assessment; "assessment" means an assessment referred to in Regulation 61; "assessor" means an assessor appointed under Regulation 61; "prescribed contravention" means a contravention of—

(a) these Regulations,

(b) any obligation imposed by the Bank pursuant to a power exercised under these Regulations, or

(c) any other provision of transparency (regulated markets) law;

"qualifying holding" means—

(a) a direct or indirect holding of shares or other interest in a regulated financial service provider which represents 10% or more of the capital or the voting rights, or

(b) a direct or indirect holding of shares or other interest in a regulated financial service provider which represents less than 10% of the capital or voting rights but which, in the opinion of the Bank, makes it possible to control or exercise a significant influence over the management of the regulated financial service provider;

"regulated financial service provider" has the same meaning as it has in section 2(1) of the Central Bank Act 1942 (No. 22 of 1942) as amended by section 2(g) of the Central Bank and Financial Services Authority of Ireland Act 2004 (No. 21 of 2004);

"sanction" means any sanction referred to in any of subparagraphs (a) to (f) of Regulation 67(1);

"specified sanctions", in relation to an adverse assessment, means the sanction or sanctions referred to in Regulation 61(8) which may be imposed on the assessee.

(2) The provisions of this Part are made for the purposes of enabling the imposition of administrative sanctions.

Definitions

'Bank': Transparency Regs, reg 2(1); 'contravention': Transparency Regs, reg 2(1); 'transparency (regulated markets) law': IFCMPA 2006, s 19(1).

---

61. Bank may appoint assessor

(1) Where—

(a) the Bank, in the performance of the functions assigned to it as central competent administrative authority under Regulation 36(1), has reason to suspect that a prescribed contravention is being committed or has been committed, the Bank may appoint, or

(b) IAASA, in the performance of the functions assigned to it as competent authority under Regulation 36(2), has reason to suspect that a prescribed contravention is being committed or has been committed and requests the Bank to do so, the Bank shall appoint,

an assessor (or, if the Bank thinks fit to do so, more than one assessor) to conduct an assessment as to—

(i) whether or not the assessee is committing or has committed the contravention, and

(ii) if the assessor finds that the assessee is committing or has committed the contravention, the sanction or sanctions, if any, which the assessor considers are appropriate to be imposed on the assessee in respect of the contravention.

(2) The Bank may appoint an assessor who is not an officer, employee or official of the Bank and any such assessor so appointed is an agent of the Bank for the purpose of performing the functions of an assessor under this Part.

(3) The Bank shall provide the assessor with such administrative services (including technical and legal advice) as the Bank considers necessary to enable the assessor to perform the assessor's functions.

(4) The assessor shall, as soon as is practicable after the assessor's appointment as an assessor, give notice of the appointment to the assessee.

(5) The notice under paragraph (4) given to the assessee by the assessor shall contain—

(a) a statement that the assessor is appointed by the Bank under this Regulation and, if the appointment has been made at the request of IAASA, shall specify that to be the case,

(b) a statement in summary form of the grounds for conducting the assessment,

(c) a statement that, within a reasonable time specified by the assessor in the notice, the assessee may—

(i) make submissions in writing to the assessor, and

(ii) request the assessor to be permitted to make oral submissions about the matters to which the notice relates, and

(d) a statement that the assessor shall conduct the assessment even if no submissions referred to in subparagraph (c) are made.

(6) The assessor shall—

(a) consider any submissions made by the assessee, and

(b) conduct such investigations relating to the assessment as the assessor considers appropriate before issuing the assessment.

(7) The assessor shall issue the assessment to the Bank when the assessment is made and, if the appointment of the assessor has been made at the request of IAASA, the Bank shall, on receipt of the assessment, immediately transmit it to IAASA.

(8) Where the assessor decides that a prescribed contravention is being committed or has been committed, the assessor shall ensure that the assessment includes—

(a) a statement of the grounds upon which the assessor made the assessment that the assessee is committing or has committed the contravention,

(b) a statement in summary form of the evidence upon which the assessment is based, and

(c) a statement of the sanction or sanctions, if any, which the assessor considers are appropriate to be imposed on the assessee in respect of the contravention.

(9) The appointment of an assessor may be for a specified or unspecified period.

(10) Subject to Regulation 68(2), the assessment shall constitute the decision of the Bank, and references in this Part to an adverse assessment shall be construed accordingly.

Definitions

'adverse assessment': Transparency Regs, reg 60(1); 'assessee': Transparency Regs, reg 60(1); 'assessment': Transparency Regs, reg 60(1); 'assessor': Transparency Regs, reg 60(1); 'Bank': Transparency Regs, reg 2(1); 'competent authority': not defined, but see 'central competent authority of a home Member State' in reg 2(1); 'contravention': Transparency Regs, reg 2(1);

'IAASA': Transparency Regs, reg 2(1); 'in writing': Transparency Regs, reg 2(1); 'sanction': Transparency Regs, reg 60(1).

UK

FSMA, ss 167, 168(3), 168(5).

---

62. Revocation of appointment of assessor

(1) (a) Where the Bank is satisfied that the assessor has contravened paragraph (2) or is incapacitated, the Bank may revoke the appointment of the assessor at any time.

(b) Where IAASA is satisfied that the assessor has contravened paragraph (2) or is incapacitated, it may request the Bank to revoke the appointment of the assessor and the Bank, on the making of such a request, if it considers it appropriate to do so, shall revoke that appointment.

(2) The assessor (including a person proposed to be appointed as an assessor) shall—

(a) disclose to the Bank, and, where appropriate, to IAASA for its information, any material interest that the assessor may have in any matter that may arise during the assessment,

(b) disclose to the Bank, and where appropriate, to IAASA for its information, any actual or potential conflict of interest that the assessor may have in conducting an assessment,

(c) not use any inside information (within the meaning of the Market Abuse (Directive 2003/6/EC) Regulations 2005 (S.I. No. 342 of 2005)) obtained during an assessment for any purpose other than the performance of the assessor's functions under this Part,

(d) not engage in misconduct during the assessment,

(e) perform the assessor's functions in accordance with the provisions of this Part, and

(f) issue an assessment that is not contrary to law.

Definitions

'assessment': Transparency Regs, reg 60(1); 'assessor': Transparency Regs, reg 60(1); 'Bank': Transparency Regs, reg 2(1); 'contravene', see 'contravention' in Transparency Regs, reg 2(1); 'IAASA': Transparency Regs, reg 2(1).

---

63. Power to require witnesses to appear and give evidence

(1) The assessor may by notice given in or outside the State to a person require the person to do one or more of the following—

(a) appear before the assessor to give evidence (including give evidence on oath),

(b) produce documents specified in the notice which are in the person's custody or control,

(c) for the purposes of subparagraph (a) or (b), attend before the assessor from day to day unless excused from attendance or released from further attendance by the assessor.

(2) The assessor may administer oaths for the purposes of the evidence referred to in paragraph (1)(a).

(3) A witness at a hearing before the assessor has the same liabilities, privileges and immunities as a witness before the Court.

(4) Where a person ("person concerned")—

(a) fails to comply with a notice under paragraph (1),

(b) threatens or insults the assessor or any witness or person required to attend before the assessor,

(c) interrupts the proceedings of, or does not behave in an appropriate manner before, the assessor,

(d) obstructs or attempts to obstruct the assessor,

(e) discloses, or authorises the disclosure of, evidence given before the assessor or any of the contents of a document produced to the assessor that the assessor has instructed not to be published, or

(f) does anything else that, if the assessor were a court of law having power to commit for contempt, would be contempt for that court, then

(i) the assessor may apply to the Court for an order requiring the person concerned to do one or both of the following—

(I) to comply with the notice under paragraph (1),

(II) to discontinue or not repeat the behaviour falling within any of the provisions of subparagraphs (b) to (f), or behaviour of any similar kind, and

(ii) the Court, if satisfied that there is no reasonable excuse for the failure to comply with the notice under paragraph (1) or for the behaviour concerned, as the case may be, grant the order and such other orders as it considers appropriate to ensure that the person concerned cooperates with the assessor.

Definitions

'assessor': Transparency Regs, reg 60(1); 'Court': Transparency Regs, reg 2(1).

UK

FSMA, ss 171–173, 175.

64. Referral to Court on question of law

(1) (a) The Bank or the assessor may (including at the request of the assessee) refer a question of law arising in the assessment to the Court for determination by the Court.

(b) Without prejudice to paragraph (a), where the assessor has been appointed at the request of IAASA, the Bank may, at the request of IAASA, refer a question of law arising in the assessment to the Court for determination by the Court.

(2) Where a question of law is referred under paragraph (1)—

(a) the assessor shall send to the Court all documents before him or her that are relevant to the matter in question, and

(b) at the end of the proceedings in the Court in relation to the reference, the Court shall cause the documents to be returned to the assessor.

Definitions

'assessee': Transparency Regs, reg 60(1); 'assessment': Transparency Regs, reg 60(1); 'assessor': Transparency Regs, reg 60(1); 'Bank': Transparency Regs, reg 2(1); 'Court': Transparency Regs, reg 2(1); 'IAASA': Transparency Regs, reg 2(1).

65. Assessee to be issued copy of any adverse assessment, etc

(1) Where the assessment of the assessor is that the assessee is committing or has committed a prescribed contravention, the Bank shall—

(a) issue the assessee with a copy of the adverse assessment (or, as the Bank thinks fit, so much of the adverse assessment as constitutes the statements referred to in Regulation 61(8)) and provide a copy of the assessment to IAASA where the assessor has been appointed by the Bank at the request of IAASA, and

(b) advise the assessee that—

(i) the assessee may appeal against the adverse assessment to the Court under Regulation 66, and

(ii) the Bank may apply to the Court under Regulation 70 for an order confirming the adverse assessment (including the specified sanctions).

(2) Where the assessment of the assessor is that the assessee is neither committing nor has committed a prescribed contravention, the Bank shall issue the assessee with a statement to that effect and, where the assessor has been appointed by the Bank at the request of IAASA, shall inform IAASA accordingly.

Definitions

'adverse assessment': Transparency Regs, reg 60(1); 'assessee': Transparency Regs, reg 60(1); 'assessment': Transparency Regs, reg 60(1); 'assessor': Transparency Regs, reg 60(1); 'Bank': Transparency Regs, reg 2(1); 'contravention': Transparency Regs, reg 2(1); 'Court': Transparency Regs, reg 2(1); 'IAASA': Transparency Regs, reg 2(1); 'specified sanctions': Transparency Regs, reg 60(1).

UK

FSMA, s 207.

66. Right of appeal against adverse assessment (including specified sanctions)

(1) The assessee may appeal to the Court against the adverse assessment (including the specified sanctions) not later than 28 days after the Bank has complied with Regulation 65(1) in relation to the assessee or within such further period as the Court allows.

(2) An appeal under paragraph (1) may be heard otherwise than in public.

(3) The Court may, pending the hearing and determination of an appeal under paragraph (1), make such interim or interlocutory orders as the Court considers necessary in the circumstances.

(4) The Court shall determine an appeal under paragraph (1) by making—

(a) an order confirming, varying or setting aside the adverse assessment (including the specified sanctions), whether in whole or in part, or

(b) an order remitting the case to be decided again by the Bank in accordance with the directions of the Court.

(5) The determination of the Court on the hearing of an appeal under paragraph (1) shall be final, except that a party to the appeal may apply to the Supreme Court to review the determination on a question of law.

(6) For the avoidance of doubt, it is declared that no variation of an adverse assessment under paragraph (4) (a) may provide for the imposition of a sanction on the assessee which is not a sanction referred to in subparagraphs (a) to (f) of Regulation 67(1).

Definitions

'adverse assessment': Transparency Regs, reg 60(1); 'assessee': Transparency Regs, reg 60(1); 'assessment': Transparency Regs, reg 60(1); 'Bank': Transparency Regs, reg 2(1); 'Court': Transparency Regs, reg 2(1); 'sanction': Transparency Regs, reg 60(1); 'specified sanctions': Transparency Regs, reg 60(1).

UK

FSMA, ss 57, 58, 208.

67. Sanctions that may be imposed by Bank

(1) In the case of an adverse assessment, the Bank may impose on the assessee such of the following sanctions as are the specified sanctions—

(a) a private caution or reprimand,

(b) a public caution or reprimand,

(c) subject to Regulation 72(2), a direction to pay to the Bank, or, if the assessor has been appointed by the Bank at the request of IAASA, to IAASA, a monetary penalty (but not exceeding €2,500,000 in any case),

(d) a direction disqualifying the assessee from being concerned in the management of, or having a qualifying holding in, any regulated financial service provider for such time as is specified in the order,

(e) if the assessee is continuing to commit a prescribed contravention, a direction ordering the assessee to cease committing the prescribed contravention,

(f) a direction to pay to the Bank all or a specified part of the costs incurred by the Bank in investigating the matter to which the assessment relates and in holding the assessment (including any costs incurred by authorised officers).

(2) Where the assessor had been appointed by the Bank at the request of IAASA, the Bank shall consult with IAASA before exercising the powers under paragraph (1).

Definitions

'adverse assessment': Transparency Regs, reg 60(1); 'assessee': Transparency Regs, reg 60(1); 'assessment': Transparency Regs, reg 60(1); 'assessor': Transparency Regs, reg 60(1); 'authorised officer': Transparency Regs, reg 38; 'Bank': Transparency Regs, reg 2(1); 'contravention': Transparency Regs, reg 2(1); 'IAASA': Transparency Regs, reg 2(1); 'qualifying holding': Transparency Regs, reg 60(1); 'regulated financial service provider': Transparency Regs, reg 60(1); 'sanction': Transparency Regs, reg 60(1); 'specified sanctions': Transparency Regs, reg 60(1).

UK

FSMA, ss 56, 205, 206.

68. Power to correct assessments

(1) Where the assessor or the Bank is satisfied that there is an obvious error in the text of an assessment, the assessor or the Bank, as the case may be, may alter the text of the assessment to remove the error.

(2) Where the text of an assessment is altered under paragraph (1), the text as so altered shall be taken to be the decision of the Bank under Regulation 61(10).

(3) In paragraph (1), "obvious error", in relation to the text of an assessment, includes—

- (a) a clerical or typographical error,
- (b) an error arising from an accidental slip or omission, or
- (c) a defect of form.

Definitions

'assessor': Transparency Regs, reg 60(1); 'assessment': Transparency Regs, reg 60(1); 'Bank': Transparency Regs, reg 2(1).

69. When specified sanctions take effect

(1) Where—

- (a) no appeal under Regulation 66 against the adverse assessment is lodged with the Court within the period for lodging the appeal, or
- (b) an appeal under Regulation 66 against the adverse assessment which has been lodged with the Court within the period for lodging the appeal is withdrawn or abandoned,

then the specified sanctions, as confirmed or varied in the order, if any, obtained under Regulation 70(3)(a), shall take effect on the date of that order or such other date as the Court may specify in that order.

(2) Where an appeal under Regulation 66 against the adverse assessment is lodged with the Court within the period for lodging the appeal, then the specified sanctions, as confirmed or varied in the order, if any, obtained under Regulation 66(4)(a), shall take effect on the date of that order or such other date as the Court may specify in that order.

Definitions

'adverse assessment': Transparency Regs, reg 60(1); 'Court': Transparency Regs, reg 2(1); 'specified sanctions': Transparency Regs, reg 60(1).

70. Enforcement of adverse assessment (including specified sanctions)

(1) Where—

(a) no appeal under Regulation 66 against the adverse assessment is lodged with the Court within the period for lodging the appeal, or

(b) an appeal under Regulation 66 against the adverse assessment which has been lodged with the Court within the period for lodging the appeal is withdrawn or abandoned,

then, subject to paragraph (2), the Bank may apply to the Court for an order confirming the adverse assessment (including the specified sanctions).

(2) Where the assessor was appointed by the Bank at the request of IAASA, such an application shall not be made otherwise than at the request of IAASA but, if IAASA does make a request of the Bank to make such an application, it shall be the duty of the Bank to comply with that request.

(3) The Court shall determine an application under paragraph (1) by making—

(a) an order confirming, varying or setting aside the adverse assessment (including the specified sanctions), whether in whole or in part, or

(b) an order remitting the case to be decided again by the Bank in accordance with the directions of the Court.

(4) The Court shall not hear an application under paragraph (1) unless—

(a) the assessee appears at the hearing as respondent to the application, or

(b) if the assessee does not so appear, the Court is satisfied that a copy of the application has been served on the assessee.

(5) An application under paragraph (1) may be heard otherwise than in public.

(6) The Court may, on an application under paragraph (1), make such interim or interlocutory orders as the Court considers necessary in the circumstances.

(7) The determination of the Court on the hearing of an application under paragraph (1) shall be final, except that the Bank or the respondent, if any, may apply to the Supreme Court to review the determination on a question of law.

(8) For the avoidance of doubt, it is declared that no variation of an adverse assessment under paragraph (3)(a) may provide for the imposition of a sanction on the assessee which is not a sanction referred to in subparagraphs (a) to (f) of Regulation 67(1).

Definitions

'adverse assessment': Transparency Regs, reg 60(1); 'assessee': Transparency Regs, reg 60(1); 'assessor': Transparency Regs, reg 60(1); 'Bank': Transparency Regs, reg 2(1); 'Court':

Transparency Regs, reg 2(1); 'IAASA': Transparency Regs, reg 2(1); 'sanction': Transparency Regs, reg 60(1); 'specified sanctions': Transparency Regs, reg 60(1).

71. Publication of certain specified sanctions

The Bank shall publicly disclose the specified sanctions referred to in sub-paragraphs (c) to (f) of Regulation 67(1), as confirmed or varied in the order concerned obtained under Regulation 66(4)(a) or 70(3)(a), that are imposed on the assessee unless the Bank considers that the disclosure would—

(a) seriously jeopardise the financial markets, or

(b) cause disproportionate damage to the parties involved.

Definitions

'assessee': Transparency Regs, reg 60(1); 'Bank': Transparency Regs, reg 2(1); 'specified sanctions': Transparency Regs, reg 60(1).

72. Person not liable to be penalised twice for same contravention

(1) Where—

(a) a sanction referred to in Regulation 67(1)(c) is to be imposed on the assessee by virtue of an order obtained under Regulation 66(4)(a) or 70(3)(a), and

(b) the acts which constitute the prescribed contravention to which the sanction relates also constitute an offence under a law of the State,

then the assessee is not, in respect of those acts, liable to be prosecuted or punished for that offence under that law.

(2) A sanction referred to in Regulation 67(1)(c) in respect of a prescribed contravention shall not be imposed on the assessee where—

(a) the assessee has been found guilty or not guilty of having committed an offence under a provision of these Regulations, and

(b) all or some of the acts constituting that offence also constitute the prescribed contravention.

Definitions

'assessee': Transparency Regs, reg 60(1); 'contravention': Transparency Regs, reg 2(1); 'sanction': Transparency Regs, reg 60(1).

73. Person not to be concerned in management of regulated financial service provider while disqualified

A regulated financial service provider shall ensure that a person shall not be concerned in the management of, or have a qualifying holding in, the financial service provider while the person is subject to a sanction referred to in Regulation 67(1)(d) that is in force.

Definitions

'qualifying holding': Transparency Regs, reg 60(1); 'regulated financial service provider': Transparency Regs, reg 60(1); 'sanction': Transparency Regs, reg 60(1).

UK

FSMA, ss 56(6).

74. Power of Bank or IAASA to resolve suspected contraventions, etc

(1) Where—

(a) the Bank, in the performance of the functions assigned to it as central competent administrative authority under Regulation 36(1), has reason to suspect, or

(b) IAASA, in the performance of the functions assigned to it as competent authority under Regulation 36(2), has reason to suspect,

that a person ("relevant party") is committing or has committed a prescribed contravention, it may enter into an agreement in writing with the relevant party to resolve the matter (including at any time before an assessment, if any, has been issued in respect of the relevant party).

(2) An agreement entered into under paragraph (1)—

(a) is binding on the Bank or IAASA, as the case may be, and the relevant party, and

(b) may include terms under which the relevant party accepts the imposition of sanctions.

(3) An agreement entered into under paragraph (1) may be enforced by the Bank or IAASA, as the case may be, or the relevant party in a court of competent jurisdiction.

Definitions

'assessment': Transparency Regs, reg 60(1); 'Bank': Transparency Regs, reg 2(1); 'competent authority': not defined, but see 'central competent authority of a home Member State' in reg 2(1); 'contravention': Transparency Regs, reg 2(1); 'IAASA': Transparency Regs, reg 2(1); 'in writing': Transparency Regs, reg 2(1); 'sanction': Transparency Regs, reg 60(1).

PART 11
CO-OPERATION BETWEEN COMPETENT AUTHORITIES

75. Co-operation between Competent Authorities

(1) The Bank and IAASA shall each—

(a) co-operate with the competent authorities of other Member States, designated under the Directive, whenever necessary, for the purpose of the performance by each of the competent authorities of the Member States (including the Bank or IAASA, as appropriate) of their functions and the making use of their powers (whether set out in the Directive, transparency (regulated markets) law or the measures for the time being adopted by another Member State to implement the Directive), and

(b) render assistance to competent authorities of other Member States in the performance of their functions (whether set out in the Directive or the measures for the time being adopted by another Member State to implement the Directive).

(2) In particular and without prejudice to its obligations under section 33AK(10) of the Central Bank Act 1942, as amended, or section 31 of the Companies (Auditing and Accounting) Act 2003, as the case may be, nothing in any law shall prevent the Bank or IAASA from exchanging confidential information. Information thus exchanged shall be covered by the obligation of professional secrecy to which the persons employed or formerly employed by the competent authorities receiving the information are subject.

(3) The Bank or IAASA may conclude, for their respective purposes, cooperation agreements with the competent authorities or bodies of third countries enabled by their respective legislation providing for the exchange of information so as to allow the carrying out of any of the tasks assigned by the Directive to the competent authorities in accordance with Article 24 of the Directive.

(4) Such an exchange of information—

(a) is subject to the authority with whom the information is exchanged guaranteeing that a level of professional secrecy at least equivalent to that referred to in Article 25 of the Directive shall apply to the information, and

(b) shall be intended for the performance of the supervisory task of the authorities or bodies mentioned in paragraph (3).

(5) Without prejudice to paragraph (4), where the information proposed to be exchanged originates in another Member State—

(a) it shall not be exchanged without the express consent of the competent authority which disclosed it in the first place, and

(b) if the purpose for which it was so disclosed was limited to any extent specified in that consent, shall be exchanged only for the purpose so specified.

Definitions

'Bank': Transparency Regs, reg 2(1); 'competent authorities': not defined, but see 'central competent authority of a home Member State' in reg 2(1); 'Directive': Transparency Regs, reg 2(1); 'IAASA': Transparency Regs, reg 2(1); 'measures for the time being adopted by another Member State to implement": not defined but see "implementing measures" in Transparency Regs, reg 2(1); 'Member State': Transparency Regs, reg 2(1); 'transparency (regulated markets) law': IFCMPA 2006, s 19(1).

PART 12
PENALTIES, GENERAL AND OTHER MISCELLANEOUS PROVISIONS

76. Offences and penalties generally

(1) If the contravention in respect of which a person is convicted of an offence under another provision of this Regulation is continued after the conviction, the person shall be guilty of a further offence on every day on which the contravention continues.

(2) Where any offence is committed under another provision of this Regulation by a body corporate and is proved to have been committed with the consent, connivance or approval of or to have been attributable to the wilful neglect on the part of any person, being a director, manager, secretary or other officer of the body corporate or a person who was purporting to act in any such capacity, that person as well as the body corporate shall be guilty of an offence and is liable to be proceeded against and punished as if he or she was guilty of the first mentioned offence.

(3) A person who contravenes Regulation 54(6) or 73 shall be guilty of an offence.

(4) A person who, knowing the information to be so false or misleading, or being reckless as to whether or not it is so false or misleading, discloses information in purported compliance with a requirement imposed on the person by or pursuant to these Regulations which is false or misleading in a material respect shall be guilty of an offence.

(5) A person who is guilty of—

(a) an offence under this Regulation other than an offence referred to in subparagraph (b),

or

(b) one or more further offences under paragraph (1), for each such offence,

shall be liable on summary conviction to a fine not exceeding €5,000 or imprisonment for a term not exceeding 12 months or both.

(6) Every offence under this Regulation is an offence to which section 21 (penalties on indictment) of the Investment Funds, Companies and Miscellaneous Provisions Act 2006 applies.

Definitions

'contravention': Transparency Regs, reg 2(1).

---

77. Annual report of Bank and IAASA

(1) The Bank shall provide the Minister with a copy of the extract relating to the performance of its functions under these Regulations from its annual report to the Minister for Finance under section 300 of the Central Bank Act 1942.

(2) IAASA shall give an account of the performance of its functions under these Regulations in its annual report under section 22 of the Companies (Auditing and Accounting) Act 2003.

Definitions

'Bank': Transparency Regs, reg 2(1); 'IAASA': Transparency Regs, reg 2(1); 'Minister': Transparency Regs, reg 2(1).

78. Fees and charges

(1) Fees shall be payable pursuant to section 33K of the Central Bank Act 1942 in respect of the performance by the Bank of its functions under these Regulations.

(2) IAASA may, for the purpose of defraying the expenses incurred by it in performing its functions under these Regulations, impose charges on issuers admitted to trading on a regulated market at such rates as are from time to time determined by it with the consent of the Minister.

(3) The Minister shall, where he or she considers it appropriate to do so, consult with any persons who are, in the Minister's opinion, interested in the matter before he or she consents to any determination by IAASA of rates of charges under paragraph (2).

(4) Charges imposed by IAASA under paragraph (2) shall be recoverable by IAASA from the person on whom they have been imposed as a simple contract debt in any court of competent jurisdiction.

Definitions

'admitted to trading on a regulated market': Transparency Regs, reg 2(1); 'Bank': Transparency Regs, reg 2(1); 'IAASA': Transparency Regs, reg 2(1); 'issuer': Transparency Regs, reg 2(1); 'Minister': Transparency Regs, reg 2(1); 'regulated market': Transparency Regs, reg 2(1).

79. Transitional — provisions of a substantive nature

(1) (a) An issuer whose financial year begins on or after 20 January 2007 shall comply with Regulations 4 to 9 on and from 13th June 2007.

(b) An issuer whose financial year begins before 20 January 2007 shall comply with Regulations 4 to 9 on and from the beginning of its next financial year.

(2) (a) This paragraph applies to an issuer of debt securities which were admitted to trading on a regulated market in a Member State before 1 January 2005 if the home Member State had decided to allow such an issuer to benefit from the provisions of Article 27 of Directive 2001/34/EC of the European Parliament and of the Council of 28 May 2001 at the point of admission of those securities.

(b) For the financial years falling within the period for which this paragraph applies, such an issuer need not disclose its half-yearly financial report in accordance with Regulations 6 to 8.

(c) This paragraph applies for the period of 10 years following 1 January 2005.

(3) An issuer need not prepare its financial statements in accordance with Regulation 4(4) or 7(2) for any financial year beginning before 1 January 2007 if:

(a) the issuer's registered office is in a third country; and

(b) the issuer prepares its financial statements in accordance with inter-nationally accepted standards.

(4) (a) This paragraph applies to an issuer:

(i) whose debt securities only are admitted to trading; and

(ii) whose home Member State is the State.

(b) Such an issuer is not required to disclose financial statements in accordance with Regulation 7(2)(a) for the financial year (and that financial year only) beginning on or after 1 January 2006.

(5) (a) This paragraph applies to an issuer of debt securities:

(i) that is incorporated in a third country ("the third country");

(ii) whose home Member State is the State; and

(iii) whose debt securities were admitted to trading in a Member State prior to 1 January 2005.

(b) Such an issuer need not draw up its annual financial statements in accordance with Regulation 4(4) or its management report in accordance with Regulation 5 (3) if:

(i) the annual financial statements prepared by issuers from the third country give a true and fair view of the issuer's assets and liabilities, financial position and results;

(ii) the third country has not made mandatory the application of accounting standards referred to in Article 2 of Regulation (EC) No.1606/2002 of the European Parliament and of the Council of 19 July 2002; and

(iii) the Commission has not taken any decision, in accordance with Article 23(4)(ii) of the Directive, as to whether there is an equivalence between IAS and IFRS and:

(I) the accounting standards laid down in the law, regulations or administrative provisions of the third country; or

(II) the accounting standards of a third country (not being that referred to in subparagraph (a)(i)) with which such an issuer has elected to comply.

(6) Prior to financial years starting on or after 1 January 2009, an issuer whose registered office is in a third country may prepare its annual consolidated financial statements and half-yearly consolidated financial statements in accordance with the accounting standards of a third country provided the Bank is satisfied that one of the conditions set out in Article 1 of Commission Decision 2006/891/EC of 4 December 2006 is complied with.

(7) Notwithstanding paragraph (3) of Regulation 21, a person who holds a percentage of voting rights in respect of which there is a notification requirement under these Regulations shall notify the issuer referred to in that paragraph (3), not later than 2 months after 13th June 2007, of the percentage of voting rights he or she holds at 13th June 2007, unless he or she has already made a notification of that percentage of those voting rights in accordance with Regulation 14(1) before that date.

(8) Notwithstanding Regulation 21(9), an issuer shall disclose, in accordance with these Regulations, information the subject of a notification referred to in paragraph (7) not later than 3 months after 13th June 2007.

Definitions

'admitted to trading on a regulated market': Transparency Regs, reg 2(1); 'Bank': Transparency Regs, reg 2(1); 'debt securities': Transparency Regs, reg 2(1); 'Directive': Transparency Regs, reg 2(1); 'home Member State': Transparency Regs, reg 2(1); 'IFRS': Transparency Regs, reg 2(1); 'issuer': Transparency Regs, reg 2(1); 'Member State': Transparency Regs, reg 2(1); 'regulated market': Transparency Regs, reg 2(1).

80. Transitional — construction of certain references

(1) References in these Regulations to a person authorised under Directive 2004/39/EC of the European Parliament and of the Council of 21 April 2004 shall be read as including references to a person authorised under Council Directive 93/22/EEC of 10 May 1993.

(2) The reference in Regulation 18 to portfolio management under point 4 of Section A of Annex 1 to Directive 2004/39/EC of the European Parliament and of the Council of 21 April 2004 shall be read as including a reference to the service of portfolio management under point 3 of Annex A of Council Directive 93/22/EEC of 10 May 1993.

(3) References in these Regulations to a regulated market shall be read as including references to a market as defined by point 13 of Article 1 of Council Directive 93/22/EEC of 10 May 1993.

Definitions

'regulated market': Transparency Regs, reg 2(1).

81. Relationship with Chapter 2 of Part IV of Companies Act 1990

The obligation of disclosure under Chapter 2 of Part IV of the Companies Act 1990 and the related provisions of that Chapter shall not apply to—

(a) an acquisition or disposal of shares which is required to be notified under these Regulations, or

(b) an acquisition or disposal of shares which, but for an express exemption provided by or under these Regulations (whether the word "exempted" is used or not), would be required to be notified under these Regulations.

EXPLANATORY NOTE

(*This note is not part of the instrument and does not purport to be a legal interpretation*)

These regulations along with Part 3 of the Investment Funds, Companies and Miscellaneous Provisions Act 2006 and certain rules which may be made by the competent authority (The Central Bank and Financial Services Authority of Ireland) under regulation 40(3) of the Regulations give effect to Directive 2004/109EC of the European Parliament and of the Council of 15 December 2004 on the harmonisation of transparency requirements in relation to information about issuers whose securities are admitted to trading on a regulated market and Commission Directive 2007/14/EC laying down detailed rules for the implementation of certain provisions of Directive 2004/109/EC.

European Communities (Admissions to Listing and Miscellaneous Provisions) Regulations 2007

SI 286/2007

I, MICHEÁL MARTIN, Minister for Enterprise, Trade and Employment, in exercise of the powers conferred on me by section 3 of the European Communities Act 1972 (No. 27 of 1972), and for the purpose of giving effect to Directive 2001/34/EC of the European Parliament and of the Council of 28 May 2001 (O.J. No. L 184, 6.7.2001, pp.1-66), as amended by Directive 2003/71/EC of the European Parliament and of the Council of 4 November 2003 (O.J. No. L 345, 31.12.2003, pp 64-89), and Directive 2004/109/EC of the European Parliament and of the Council of 15 December 2004 (O.J. No. L 390, 31.12.2004, pp 38-57) and giving further effect to Article 32(5) of the last-mentioned Directive, hereby make the following regulations:

1. Citation, commencement and construction

(1) These Regulations may be cited as the European Communities (Admissions to Listing and Miscellaneous Provisions) Regulations 2007.

(2) These Regulations shall come into operation on 13 June 2007.

(3) These Regulations shall be read as one with the Companies Acts.

Notes

These regulations transpose Directive 2001/34/EC – the Consolidated Admissions and Reporting Directive or 'CARD' – into Irish law. CARD was, when first adopted, a consolidation of four Directives – the Admissions Directive 79/279/EEC, the Listing Particulars Directive 80/390/EEC, as amended, the Interim Reports Directive 82/121/EEC and the Major Holdings Directive 88/627/EEC.

Since then:

- those parts of CARD relating to Listing Particulars were repealed and replaced by the Prospectus Directive 2003/71/EC, which has been transposed into Irish law by SI 324/2005; and
- those parts of CARD relating to interim reports and the disclosure of major holdings were repealed and replaced by Transparency Directive 2003/109/EC, which has been transposed into Irish law by SI 277/2007.

Accordingly, CARD has gone from being a consolidation directive to being, in effect, a re-enactment of the Admissions Directive 79/279/EEC. CARD is now exclusively concerned with the conditions for the admission of securities to 'official listing' on a stock exchange situated or operating within an EU member state. 'Official listing' is generally, but not always, associated with the admission of securities to a 'regulated market'.

Uniquely in the suite of legislation regulating securities markets activity which is to be construed with 'the Companies Acts' (the other such legislation being that transposing the Prospectus Directive 2003/71/EC, the Market Abuse Directive 2003/6/EC and the Transparency Directive 2004/109/EC):

- it is the Irish Stock Exchange which is the competent authority and publishes the admissions and listing rules; and
- there is no primary legislation regulating admissions to listing comparable to those parts of the IFCMPA 2005 and 2006 which underpin the implementation of the

transposition of the Prospectus Directive 2003/71/EC, the Market Abuse Directive 2003/6/EC and the Transparency Directive 2004/109/EC.

These regulations repeal and replace SI 282/1984, which transposed the Admissions Directive 79/279/EEC, the Listing Particulars Directive 80/390/EEC and the Interim Reports Directive 82/121/EEC. SI 282/1984 set out the full text of those directives, whereas these Regulations do not.

2. Interpretation

(1) In these Regulations—

'admission to official listing' means the admission of securities to the Official List of the Irish Stock Exchange and 'official listing' shall be construed accordingly;

'Bank' means the Central Bank and Financial Services Authority of Ireland; 'Council' means the Board of the Irish Stock Exchange;

'Directive' means Directive 2001/34/EC of the European Parliament and of the Council of 28 May 2001 on the admission of securities to official stock exchange listing and on information to be published on those securities, as amended by Directive 2003/71/EC of the European Parliament and of the Council of 4 November 2003 on the prospectus to be published when securities are offered to the public or admitted to trading and amending Directive 2001/34/EC, and further amended by the Transparency (Regulated Markets) Directive;

'Irish Stock Exchange' has the meaning given to it by section 3(1) of the Stock Exchange Act 1995 (No. 9 of 1995);

'listing rules' means the rules of the Irish Stock Exchange relating to the admission to the Official List of the Irish Stock Exchange;

'Minister' means the Minister for Enterprise, Trade and Employment;

'Transparency (Regulated Markets) Directive' means Directive 2004/109/EC of the European Parliament and of the Council of 15 December 2004 on the harmonisation of transparency requirements in relation to information about issuers whose securities are admitted to trading on a regulated market and amending Directive 2001/34/EC;

'transparency (regulated markets) law' has the same meaning as it has in the Investment Funds, Companies and Miscellaneous Provisions Act 2006 (No. 41 of 2006).

(2) A reference in these Regulations to an Article or other provision of the Directive shall be construed as a reference to that Article or that provision as amended.

(3) A word or expression that is used in these Regulations and is also used in the Directive shall have in these Regulations the same meaning as it has in the Directive.

Definitions

'issuer': CARD, art 1(a).

3. Application of Directive

(1) Subject to the provisions of these Regulations, the requirements of the Directive relating to the admission of securities to official listing shall have effect and be applied accordingly.

(2) The Irish Stock Exchange may make the admission of securities to official listing subject to more stringent conditions than those set out in Articles 42 to 63 of the Directive or to additional conditions:

Provided that those more stringent or additional conditions—

(i) apply generally for all such issuers or for individual classes of such issuers,

(ii) are published before application for admission of such securities is made, and

(iii) are not otherwise inconsistent with, or imposed in a manner inconsistent with, any provision of the Directive taking account of the prohibitions provided for in Article 7 and Articles 42 to 63 of the Directive. [Note]

(3) The Irish Stock Exchange may also make the issuers of securities admitted to official listing subject to additional obligations:

Provided that those additional obligations—

(i) apply generally for all such issuers or for individual classes of such issuers,

(ii) do not—

(I) relieve a person of obligations arising under, or

(II) make provision for specific matters dealt with by,

transparency (regulated markets) law (including any more stringent requirements applied on foot of the Transparency (Directive 2004/109/EC) Regulations 2007 by the Bank (being the central competent administrative authority designated for the purposes of the Transparency (Regulated Markets) Directive)),and

(iii) are not inconsistent with, or imposed in a manner inconsistent with, any provision of the Directive.

(4) For the purpose of achieving the result specified in paragraph (5), the Irish Stock Exchange shall consult with the Bank before it makes issuers generally or any individual class of issuer subject to additional obligations under paragraph (3).

(5) The result mentioned in paragraph (4) is ensuring that the requirements of—

(a) these Regulations (including any more stringent or additional conditions under paragraph (2) and any additional obligations under paragraph (3)), and

(b) transparency (regulated markets) law (including any more stringent requirements referred to paragraph (ii) of the proviso to paragraph (3)),

operate in a manner that is consistent with one another.

(6) Nothing in these Regulations shall affect or derogate from any power of the Minister for Finance under the Stock Exchange Act 1995.

Definitions

'admission to official listing': Admissions Regs, reg 2(1); 'Bank': Admissions Regs, reg 2(1); 'Directive': Admissions Regs, reg 2(1); 'Irish Stock Exchange': Admissions Regs, reg 2(1); 'issuer': CARD, art 1(a); 'Minister' Admissions Regs, reg 2(1); 'Transparency (Regulated Markets) Directive': Admissions Regs, reg 2(1); 'transparency (regulated markets) law': Admissions Regs, reg 2(1).

Notes

The power of the Irish Stock Exchange to impose more onerous obligations emanates from art 8 of CARD. With regard to the requirements of the Irish Stock Exchange in relation to the admission of securities to listing and with regard to the obligations on listed issuers, see the Irish Stock Exchange's Listing Rules and Admission to Trading Rules.

The Irish Listing Rules largely track the comparable UKLA Listing Rules.

The Listing Rules provide for extra requirements, such as the requirement for shareholder consent to major transactions, independent shareholders' approval of related-party transactions and disclosure of information required by the Combined Code on corporate governance issued by the Financial Reporting Council.

4. Limited discretions conferred on Member States by Directive

The provisions of the Schedule have effect in consequence of the exercise by the State of the discretions conferred on each Member State by the Directive as to its implementation.

Definitions

'Directive': Admissions Regs, reg 2(1).

5. Offence

(1) The restrictions referred to in Article 107(1) of the Directive shall apply to all persons employed or formerly employed by the Irish Stock Exchange in the performance of its functions as competent authority.

(2) Any person who fails to comply with paragraph (1) or who publishes any information required to be published by the Directive which is false or misleading in a material respect knowing the information to be so false or misleading or being reckless as to whether it is so false or misleading shall be guilty of an offence.

(3) A person guilty of an offence under paragraph (2) shall be liable on summary conviction to a fine not exceeding €5,000.

(4) Where an offence under paragraph (2) is committed by a body corporate and is proved to have been committed with the consent, connivance or approval of or to have been attributable to the wilful neglect on the part of any person, being a director, manager, secretary or other officer of the body corporate or a person who was purporting to act in any such capacity, that person as well as the body corporate shall be guilty of an offence and is liable to be proceeded against and punished as if he or she was guilty of the first-mentioned offence

(5) Proceedings in relation to an offence under paragraph (2) may be brought and prosecuted by the Director of Public Prosecutions or the Director of Corporate Enforcement.

Definitions

'Directive': Admissions Regs, reg 2(1); 'Irish Stock Exchange': Admissions Regs, reg 2(1).

Notes

Article 107 of CARD requires member states to provide that all existing or former employees of the competent authority (in Ireland, the Irish Stock Exchange) are bound by professional secrecy. Any confidential information received by them in the course of their duties must not be divulged except by virtue of provisions laid down by law.

6. Competent authority for purposes of Directive

(1) The Irish Stock Exchange shall be the competent authority for the purposes of the Directive and shall have all the powers required to be conferred on, or which the State is permitted to confer on, the competent authority by the Directive.

(2) The Irish Stock Exchange may arrange for the discharge of its functions as competent authority by any committee, sub-committee, officer or employee of the Irish Stock Exchange and nothing in this Regulation shall prevent the Irish Stock Exchange from being assisted in, or advised on, the discharge of these functions by any committee, sub-committee, officer or employee of the Council.

Definitions

'Council': Admissions Regs, reg 2(1); 'Directive': Admissions Regs, reg 2(1); 'Irish Stock Exchange': Admissions Regs, reg 2(1).

Notes

Whereas the Irish Stock Exchange is a delegate authority under the transposition of the Prospectus Directive 2003/71/EC, it is the actual competent authority under these Regulations.

7. Liability of competent authority

(1) Subject to paragraph (2), neither the Irish Stock Exchange nor any person referred to in Regulation 6(2) shall be liable in damages by reason only of non-compliance with or contravention of any obligation imposed by or by virtue of these Regulations, nor shall the Exchange or that person be so liable in respect of anything done or omitted to be done by it or him or her in connection with the performance by the Exchange of its functions as competent authority.

(2) Paragraph (1) does not apply if the act or omission complained of was done or made in bad faith.

(3) No transaction shall be void or voidable by reason only of the fact that it was entered into in contravention of, or otherwise than in conformity with, these Regulations.

Definitions

'Irish Stock Exchange': Admissions Regs, reg 2(1).

8. Office of competent authority

(1) For the purposes of the performance of its functions as competent authority pursuant to these Regulations, the Irish Stock Exchange shall maintain and administer an office in the State.

(2) The Irish Stock Exchange shall notify the Minister of the address and of any change in the address of such office.

(3) Any document may be served on the competent authority in connection with the discharge by it of its functions under these Regulations by leaving it at, or by sending it by post to, the office maintained by the Irish Stock Exchange pursuant to paragraph (1).

Definitions

'Irish Stock Exchange': Admissions Regs, reg 2(1); 'Minister' Admissions Regs, reg 2(1).

9. Application to High Court

(1) Where, in the performance of its functions under these Regulations, the competent authority refuses an application for admission to official listing, or where it discontinues such a listing, the issuer of the securities may apply to the High Court in a summary manner to have such refusal or discontinuation reviewed.

(2) On the hearing of an application under this Regulation, the High Court shall confirm the decision of the competent authority unless it is satisfied that the procedures specified by, or the requirements of, these Regulations or the Directive have not been complied with in any material respect.

(3) In any case where the High Court is satisfied that the procedures specified by, or the requirements of, these Regulations or the Directive have not been complied with in any material respect, the High Court may set aside the decision of the competent authority and in such a case shall remit the matter to the competent authority which shall thereupon reconsider the matter and make a further decision in accordance with such procedures and requirements.

Definitions

'admission to official listing': Admissions Regs, reg 2(1); 'Directive': Admissions Regs, reg 2(1); 'issuer': CARD, art 1(a).

10. Annual report of competent authority

The Irish Stock Exchange shall report annually to the Minister on the performance of its functions as competent authority in the State under the Directive and under these Regulations and, in particular, by means of such a report, shall inform the Minister of—

(a) any amendment of the listing rules or revision of its procedures pursuant to the Directive or otherwise, including—

  (i) any conditions imposed for the admission of securities to official listing which are more stringent than, or additional to, the requirements for admission to official listing, and

  (ii) any additional obligations imposed on the issuers of securities admitted to official listing,

(b) the nature of all securities which are admitted to official listing,

(c) the refusal of any application for admission to official listing,

(d) the suspension or discontinuation of any official listing, and

(e) any special arrangements which have been made with other Member States pursuant to Article 13 of the Directive.

Definitions

'admission to official listing': Admissions Regs, reg 2(1); 'Directive': Admissions Regs, reg 2(1); 'Irish Stock Exchange': Admissions Regs, reg 2(1); 'issuer': CARD, art 1(a); 'listing rules': Admissions Regs, reg 2(1); 'Minister' Admissions Regs, reg 2(1).

---

11. Saving of other duties of issuers

For the avoidance of doubt, it is declared that nothing in these Regulations shall affect any obligation on issuers of securities admitted to official listing imposed by or under any other enactment.

Definitions

'admission to official listing': Admissions Regs, reg 2(1); 'issuer': CARD, art 1(a).

---

12. Revocations

The following Regulations are revoked:

(a) the European Communities (Stock Exchange) Regulations 1984 (S.I. No. 282 of 1984); and

(b) the European Communities (Stock Exchange) (Amendment) Regulations 1995 (S.I. No. 311 of 1995).

13. Repeals

Sections 89 to 96 of the Companies Act 1990 (No. 33 of 1990) are repealed.

Notes

The sections repealed relate to the duty of holders of shares in Irish-incorporated companies, whose shares are admitted to official listing, to notify the Irish Stock Exchange when the holder's percentage holding passes up or down through particular thresholds. Comparable law is now found in Part 5 of SI 277/2007.

Schedule

Provisions consequent on exercise of certain limited discretions by State in relation to Directive's implementation

1. These Regulations shall not apply to—

(a) units issued by collective investment undertakings other than of the closed-end type, or

(b) securities issued by a Member State or by its regional or local authorities.

2. The conditions and obligations referred to in Article 10 of the Directive shall not apply to the securities issued by persons referred to in that Article.

3. Shares may be admitted to official listing where the condition referred to in Article 43 (1) of the Directive is not fulfilled, provided that the requirements of Article 43(2) of the Directive are satisfied.

4. Debt securities may be admitted to official listing where the condition referred to in Article 58 (1) of the Directive is not fulfilled, provided that the requirements of Article 58(2) of the Directive are satisfied.

5. Convertible or exchangeable debentures and debentures with warrants may be admitted to official listing if the requirement in Article 59(2) of the Directive is satisfied.

Definitions

'admission to official listing': Admissions Regs, reg 2(1); 'Directive': Admissions Regs, reg 2(1); 'collective investment undertakings other than the closed-end type': CARD, art 1(b); 'units of a collective investment undertaking': CARD, art 1(e).

EXPANATORY NOTE

(This note is not part of the instrument and does not purport to be a legal interpretation).

These regulations replace the European Communities (Stock Exchange) Regulations 1984 (S.I. No. 282 of 1984), as amended over the years, and include amendments arising on foot of the implementation into Irish law of Directive 2004/109/EC on the harmonisation of transparency requirements in relation to information about issuers whose securities are admitted to trading on a regulated market. These Regulations also repeal Sections 89 to 96 of the Companies Act 1990 as a consequence of Article 32(5) of Directive 2004/109/EC.

European Communities (Public Limited Companies — Directive 2006/68/EC) Regulations 2008

SI 89/2008

I, MICHEÁL MARTIN, Minister for Enterprise, Trade and Employment, in exercise of the powers conferred on me by section 3 (amended by section 2 of the European Communities Act 2007 (No. 18 of 2007)) of the European Communities Act 1972 (No. 27 of 1972) and for the purpose of giving effect to Directive 2006/68/EC (OJ L264, 25.9.2006, p 64) of the European Parliament and of the Council of 6 September 2006 amending Council Directive 77/91/EEC, as regards the formation of public limited liability companies and the maintenance and alteration of their capital, hereby make the following regulations:

1. Citation, commencement and construction.

(1) These Regulations may be cited as the European Communities (Public Limited Companies — Directive 2006/68/EC) Regulations 2008.

(2) These Regulations shall come into operation on 15 April 2008.

2. Interpretation

(1) In these Regulations—

"Act of 1963" means the Companies Act 1963 (No. 33 of 1963);

"Act of 1990" means the Companies Act 1990 (No. 33 of 1990);

(2) A word or expression that is used in the amendments to the Act of 1963 or the Act of 1990, effected by these Regulations, and that is also used in the Directive has, in those amendments, the same meaning as it has in the Directive.

3. Amendment of Act of 1963

The Act of 1963 is amended—

(a) in section 73(2), by—

[...][a]

(b) in section 77 by [...][b]

Amendments

a EC(PLC)R 2008, reg 3(a) substitutes CA 1963, s 73(2).

b EC(PLC)R 2008, reg 3(b) amends CA 1963, s 77.

---

4. Amendment of Act of 1990

The Act of 1990 is amended—

(a) in section 207(2)(d), by substituting the following subparagraph for subparagraph (i):

[...][a]

(b) in section 211—

(i) [...][b]

(ii) [...][c]

Amendments

a EC(PLC)R 2008, reg 4(a) substitutes CA 1990, s 207(2)(d)(i).

b EC(PLC)R 2008, reg 4(b)(i) amends CA 1990, s 211(1).

c EC(PLC)R 2008, reg 4(b)(ii) inserts CA 1990, s 211(4).

EXPLANATORY NOTE

(*This note is not part of the Instrument and does not purport to be a legal interpretation*).

These Regulations give effect to certain provisions of Directive 2006/68/EC of the European Parliament and the Council of 6 September 2006 which amended Council Directive 77/91/EEC as regards the formation of public limited liability companies and the maintenance and alteration of their capital. The areas covered by the Regulations are matters relating to creditor protection in cases of capital reduction and purchase by a company of its own shares.

European Communities (Cross-Border Mergers) Regulations 2008

SI 157/2008

I, MARY COUGHLAN, Minister for Enterprise, Trade and Employment, in exercise of the powers conferred on me by section 3 (as amended by section 2 of the European Communities Act 2007 (No. 18 of 2007)) of the European Communities Act 1972 (No. 27 of 1972) and for the purpose of giving effect to Council Directive No. 2005/56/EC of 26 October 2005 (OJ L 310, 25.11.2005, p 1) hereby make the following regulations:

PART 1
PRELIMINARY AND GENERAL

1. Citation and construction

(1) These Regulations may be cited as the European Communities (Cross-Border Mergers) Regulations 2008.

(2) Parts 1 and 2 of these Regulations shall be construed as one with the Companies Acts 1963 to 2006.

Notes

Background: As a matter of domestic law it had always been possible to effect mergers between Irish companies pursuant to the provisions of CA 1963, ss 210–203. The EC(MDC)Regs 1987, which implemented Council Directive 78/855/EEC and Council Directive 82/891/EEC, provided an additional set of procedures whereby Irish plcs could merge or divide, as the case might be. However, what the EC(CBM)R 2008 do is implement Council Directive No 2005/56/EC of 26 October 2005 ('the CBM Directive') which provides for a set of procedures for the merger of companies from different states within the European Economic Area ('the EEA'). Broadly speaking, the procedures for cross-border mergers under the 2008 Regs mirror those for domestic mergers in the 1987 Regs.[1]

[1] Under Reg 2(1) the only Irish companies which may avail of these cross-border merger provisions are companies limited by shares or companies limited by guarantee and having a share capital, as well as bodies corporate with limited liability to which CA 1963, s 377(1) applies.

Types of Cross-Border Mergers: The 2008 Regs deal with two types of merger scenario. The first is where an Irish company is the 'transferor company', with its assets and liabilities being transferred to another EEA company by way of cross-border merger. The second is where an Irish company is the 'successor company' to which the assets and liabilities of other EEA companies are transferred by way of cross-border merger.

Both the CBM Directive and the 2008 Regs provide for three types of merger process, namely 'merger by absorption', 'merger by acquisition' and 'merger by formation of a new company'.[1]

A 'merger by absorption' is a process whereby, on being dissolved and without going into liquidation, a wholly owned subsidiary transferred all of its assets and liabilities to its holding company.[2]

A 'merger by acquisition' is a process pursuant to which an existing company acquires all the assets and liabilities of one or more transferor companies in exchange for the allotment by it of shares to the members of those transferor companies and pursuant to which those transferor companies are dissolved without going into liquidation.[3]

A 'merger by formation of a new company' is, as its name suggests, a process whereby a new company is formed and it acquires all of the assets and liabilities of one or more transferor companies in exchange for the allotment by it of shares to the members of those transferor companies and pursuant to which those transferor companies are dissolved without going into liquidation.[4]

1 Reg 2(1).
2 Reg 2(1).
3 Reg 2(1).
4 Reg 2(1).

The documents to be prepared: The first step in the cross-border merger process is for the participant companies to draw up written common draft terms of merger setting out the information prescribed by reg 5(2). At least one month before the general meeting at which the common draft terms of merger are to be voted on:

- the board of directors of each Irish company involved in the process must prepare and make available to its members and to its employee representatives (or to its employees if there are no such representatives) an explanatory report explaining the implications of the merger for members, creditors and employees of the company and stating the legal and economic grounds for the draft terms;[1] and
- subject to some exceptions set out in reg 7(1), there must also be drawn up for the members of each Irish company involved in the proposed merger an expert's report dealing with the matters specified in reg 7.

1 Reg 6.

Registration, publication and inspection of documents: Each Irish company involved in the proposed merger must deliver a copy of the common draft terms of merger and a notice in the form set out in Schedule 3 of the 2008 Regs to the Registrar of Companies.[1] Notice of the registration of these documents must then be published by the Registrar in the CRO Gazette and by the company in two national daily newspapers at least one month before the general meeting at which the proposed merger is to be voted on.[2] This notice must state that the common draft terms, the directors' explanatory report and (where relevant) the expert's report are available for inspection by the members and employee representatives (or by the employees if there are no such representatives) at the Irish company's registered office and must further state that a copy of the common draft terms may be obtained from the Registrar.[3] The notice convening the general meeting at which the merger is to be voted on must also advise members of their right to obtain copies of these documents, free of charge, on request.[4]

1 Reg 8(1).
2 Reg 8(2).
3 Reg 8(3). This right of inspection may be exercised free of charge for at least two hours per day during the month prior to the general meeting at which the merger is to be voted on: reg 9(1).
4 Reg 9(2).

General Meeting to Approve the Merger: In order for the proposed merger to proceed further, the common draft terms must be approved by special resolution at a general meeting of each Irish merging company.[1] This approval may be made subject to conditions such as the obtaining of relevant regulatory approvals and/or the ratification of arrangements for employee participation in the successor company in accordance with Part 3 of the 2008 Regs and/or an order of a competent authority of another EEA state amending the exchange ratio or compensating minority members pursuant to Art 10.3 of the CBM Directive.[2] Notably, shareholder approval of the common draft terms is not required in the case of a merger by absorption or in the case of an Irish successor company in a merger by acquisition, where certain specified conditions have been satisfied.[3] However, even if the Irish company proposes to avail of this exemption, nevertheless members holding not less than 5 per cent of the paid up voting share capital may requisition a general meeting to consider the common draft terms.[4] Furthermore, there is provision for dissenting shareholders of a transferor company who do not want to become members of the successor company to require the successor company to buy them out at a price determined in accordance with the share exchange ratio set out in the common draft terms.[5]

1 Reg 10(1).
2 Reg 10(2).
3 Reg 11(1). The conditions that must be satisfied for exemption in the case of an Irish successor company in a merger by acquisition are specified in reg 11(2).
4 Reg 11(4).
5 Reg 12.

Application for Certificate of Compliance: Assuming that the necessary shareholder approval has been obtained, the next step in the process is for each Irish merging company to apply to the Irish High Court for a certificate confirming that they have properly completed all of the above-mentioned pre-merger requirements of the 2008 Regs.[1]

1 Reg 13.

Approval of the Cross-Border Merger: Assuming that the Irish High Court issues a Certificate of Compliance, all of the companies involved in the merger apply to the competent authority in the state in which the successor company is situated, for approval of the merger itself.[1] If the successor company is incorporated in Ireland, the application for approval is made to the Irish High Court.[2] The application for approval must be made within six months of the date of issue of the Certificate of Compliance[3] and must not only give details of dissenting shareholders of transferor companies who have demanded that they be bought out[4] but must also demonstrate both that the requirements of the Regs have been complied with[5] and that all other relevant regulatory approvals have been obtained.[6] The creditors of all Irish merging companies are entitled to be heard by the court.[7] If the merger is approved, the court sends a copy of its order to the Registrar of Companies who must register it and publish notice thereof within 14 days in the CRO.[8] If the merger is approved, it operates from the effective date specified by the court, so as to, *inter alia*, automatically:

- vest the assets and liabilities (including contracts of employment) of the transferor companies in the successor company;
- render the shareholders of the transferor companies (other than dissentients who have asked to be bought out) members of the successor company; and
- dissolve the transferor companies.[9]

1 CBM Directive, Art 11.
2 Reg 14(1).
3 Reg 14(3)(d).
4 Reg 14(2).
5 Reg 14(3).
6 Reg 16.
7 Reg 15.
8 Reg 17(1) and (2). There is similar provision under reg 17(3) for the registration and publication of a foreign court order where the successor company is incorporated in another EEA state and where, as a result, the approval of that foreign court, rather than the Irish court, has been necessary in order for the merger to become effective.
9 Reg 19.

2. Interpretation

(1) In these Regulations— 'Act of 1963' means the Companies Act 1963 (No. 33 of 1963);

'common draft terms' means the proposed terms of a cross-border merger drawn up and adopted in accordance with Regulation 5;

'company' means an Irish company or an EEA Company;

'Companies Acts' means the Companies Acts 1963 to 2006;

'Companies Register' means the register of companies maintained by the Registrar in accordance with the Companies Acts;

'cross-border merger' means a merger involving at least one Irish company and at least one EEA company, being—

(a) a merger by acquisition,

(b) a merger by formation of a new company, or

(c) a merger by absorption;

'CRO Gazette' means the Companies Registration Office Gazette maintained by the Registrar pursuant to Regulation 4 of the European Communities (Companies) Regulations 2004 (S.I. No. 839 of 2004);

'Directive' means Directive 2005/56/EC on cross-border mergers of limited liability companies (OJ L 310, 25.11.2005, p 1);

'directors' explanatory report' means a report prepared and adopted in accordance with Regulation 6;

'EEA' means the European Economic Area constituted by the EEA Agreement;

'EEA Agreement' means the Agreement on the European Economic Area signed at Oporto on 2 May 1992, as adjusted by the Protocol signed at Brussels on 17 March 1993 and any subsequent amendments;

'EEA company' means a limited liability company, within the meaning of Article 2 of the Directive, that is governed by the law of an EEA State other than the State;

'EEA State' means a State that is a contracting party to the EEA Agreement;

'effective date' means—

(a) in relation to a cross-border merger in which the successor company is an Irish company, the date specified under Regulation 14(4), or

(b) in relation to a cross-border merger in which the successor company is an EEA company, the date fixed in accordance with the law of the EEA State concerned for the purposes of Article 12 of the Directive;

'expert's report' means a report prepared in accordance with Regulation 7;

'First Company Law Directive' means First Council Directive No. 68/151/EEC of 9 March 1968 (OJ L 065, 14.03.1968, p. 8) as amended by Directive 2003/58/EC of 15 July 2003 (OJ L 221, 04.09.2003, p 13);

'holding company' has the meaning assigned by section 155 of the Act of 1963;

'Irish company' means—

(a) a company within the meaning of the Act of 1963 with limited liability (other than a company limited by guarantee), or

(b) a body corporate with limited liability to which section 377(1) of the Act of 1963 applies;

'Irish merging company' means a merging company which is an Irish company;

'Irish successor company' means a successor company which is an Irish company;

'Irish transferor company' means a transferor company which is an Irish company;

'merger' includes a proposed merger;

'merger by absorption' means an operation in which, on being dissolved and without going into liquidation, a company transfers all of its assets and liabilities to a company that is the holder of all the shares or other securities representing the capital of the first-mentioned company;

'merger by acquisition' means an operation in which a company (other than a company formed for the purpose of the operation) acquires all the assets and liabilities of another company that is, or other companies that are, dissolved without going into liquidation in exchange for the issue to the members of that company, or the members of those companies, of securities or shares in the first-mentioned company, with or without any cash payment;

'merger by formation of a new company' means an operation in which 2 or more companies, on being dissolved without going into liquidation, transfer all their assets and liabilities to a company that they form, the new company, in exchange for the issue to their members of securities or shares representing the capital of that new company, with or without any cash payment;

'merging company' means—

(a) in relation to a merger by acquisition or a merger by absorption, a company that is, in relation to that merger, a transferor company or the successor company; and

(b) in relation to a merger by formation of a new company, a company that is, in relation to that merger, a transferor company;

'Merger Control Regulation' means Council Regulation (EC) No 139/2004 of 20 January 2004 on the control of concentrations between undertakings (OJ L 24, 29.01.2004, p 1.).

'Minister' means the Minister for Enterprise, Trade and Employment;

'pre-merger requirements' means the requirements of Regulations 5 to 13;

'Registrar' means the Registrar of Companies;

'Registry' in relation to an EEA State means the register maintained by that State in accordance with Article 3 of the First Company Law Directive;

'successor company', in relation to a cross-border merger, means the Irish company or EEA company to which assets and liabilities are to be, or have been, transferred from the transferor companies by way of that cross-border merger;

'transferor company', in relation to a cross-border merger, means a company, whether an Irish company or an EEA company, the assets and liabilities of which are to be, or have been, transferred by way of that cross-border merger;

'wholly-owned subsidiary', in relation to a company, means a subsidiary (within the meaning assigned to it by section 155 of the Act of 1963) the entire issued share capital of which is directly or indirectly beneficially owned by the first-mentioned company.

(2) A word or expression used but not defined in these Regulations that is also used in the Directive has the same meaning in these Regulations as it has in the Directive.

Definitions

'director': CA 1963, s 2(1); 'member': CA 1963, s 31; 'share': CA 1963, s 2(1).

3. Penalties

A person convicted of an offence under these Regulations is liable, on summary conviction, to a fine not exceeding €5,000 or imprisonment for a term not exceeding 6 months, or to both.

PART 2
COMPANY LAW PROVISIONS

Chapter 1
Preliminary

4. Definition

In this Part 'Court' means the High Court.

Chapter 2
Pre-merger Requirements

5. Common draft terms

(1) Where a cross-border merger is proposed to be entered into, common draft terms shall be drawn up in writing by all of the merging companies and adopted by the board of directors of each Irish merging company.

(2) The common draft terms of the merging companies shall state, at least—

(a) in relation to each of the transferor companies—

(i) its name,

(ii) its registered office,

(iii) its legal form and the law by which it is governed,

(iv) the register in which it is entered (including details of the relevant State), and

(v) its registration number in that register,

(b) in relation to the successor company—

(i) where the successor company is an existing company, the particulars specified in clauses (i) to (v) of subparagraph (a), or

(ii) where the successor company is a new company yet to be formed, what is proposed as the particulars specified in clauses (i) to (iv) of that subparagraph,

(c) except in the case of a merger by absorption—

(i) the proposed exchange ratio and amount of any cash payment,

(ii) the proposed terms relating to allotment of shares or other securities in the successor company, and

(iii) the date from which the holding of shares or other securities in the successor company will entitle the holders to participate in profits and any special conditions affecting that entitlement,

(d) the likely repercussions of the cross-border merger on employment,

(e) the date from which the transactions of the transferor companies are to be treated for accounting purposes as being those of the successor company,

(f) the rights to be conferred by the successor company on members of the transferor companies enjoying special rights or on holders of securities other than shares representing a transferor company's capital, and the measures (if any) proposed concerning them,

(g) any special advantages granted to—

(i) any director of a merging company, or

(ii) any person appointed under Regulation 7(2), or under a corresponding provision of a law of an EEA State, in relation to the merger,

(h) the successor company's articles of association or, if it does not have articles, the instrument constituting the company or defining its constitution,

(i) where appropriate, information on the procedures by which arrangements for the involvement of employees in the definition of their rights to participation in the company resulting from the cross-border merger are determined under Part 3,

(j) information on the evaluation of the assets and liabilities to be transferred to the successor company, and

(k) the dates of the accounts of every merging company which were used for the purpose of preparing the common draft terms.

(3) The common draft terms may include such additional terms as are not inconsistent with these Regulations.

(4) The common draft terms shall not provide for any shares in the successor company to be exchanged for shares in a transferor company held either—

(a) by the successor company itself or its nominee on its behalf; or

(b) by the transferor company itself or its nominee on its behalf.

Definitions

'articles of association': CA 1963, s 2(1); 'common draft terms': EC(CBM)R 2008, reg 2(1); 'company': EC(CBM)R 2008, reg 2(1); 'cross-border merger': EC(CBM)R 2008, reg 2(1); 'director': CA 1963, s 2(1); 'EEA State': EC(CBM)R 2008, reg 2(1); 'Irish merging company': EC(CBM)R 2008, reg 2(1); 'merger': EC(CBM)R 2008, reg 2(1); 'merger by absorption': EC(CBM)R 2008, reg 2(1); 'merging company': EC(CBM)R 2008, reg 2(1); 'share': CA 1963, s 2(1); 'successor company': EC(CBM)R 2008, reg 2(1); 'transferor company': EC(CBM)R 2008, reg 2(1).

Notes

Common draft terms of merger: See the notes to reg 1 above entitled 'The documents to be prepared'.

---

6. Directors' explanatory report

(1) The board of directors of an Irish merging company shall—

(a) draw up a directors' explanatory report for the members of the company, to be made available pursuant to these Regulations, and

(b) make that report available, not less than 1 month before the date of the general meeting referred to in Regulation 10, to—

(i) the members, and

(ii) the representatives of employees or, where there are no representatives, to the employees, in accordance with these Regulations.

(2) The report shall—

(a) explain the implications of the cross-border merger for members, creditors and employees of the company,

(b) state the legal and economic grounds for the draft terms of merger.

Definitions

'company': EC(CBM)R 2008, reg 2(1); 'cross-border merger': EC(CBM)R 2008, reg 2(1); 'director': CA 1963, s 2(1); 'Irish merging company': EC(CBM)R 2008, reg 2(1); 'merger': EC(CBM)R 2008, reg 2(1).

Notes

Directors' explanatory report: See the note to reg 1 above entitled 'The documents to be prepared'.

---

7. Expert's report

(1) In relation to each Irish merging company, a report to the members of the company on the common draft terms shall be drawn up in accordance with this Regulation, unless—

(a) the cross-border merger is a merger by absorption,

(b) the cross-border merger is a merger in which the successor company (not being a company formed for the purpose of the merger) holds 90% or more (but not all) of the shares or other securities carrying the right to vote at general meetings of each transferor company, or

(c) every member of every merging company agrees that such report is not necessary.

(2) The report shall be prepared by a person or persons (in this Regulation referred to as the 'expert'), being—

(a) a qualified person appointed for the Irish merging company by its directors,

(b) a qualified person, or qualified persons, appointed by the Court, on the application of all of the merging companies, for all of them, or

(c) a person appointed for all the merging companies for the purposes of Article 8 of the Directive by a competent authority of another EEA State.

(3) A person is a qualified person for the purposes of subparagraphs (a) and (b) of paragraph (2), and of paragraphs (7) and (8), if that person—

(a) is eligible for appointment as an auditor in accordance with section 187 of the Companies Act 1990, and

(b) is not—

(i) a person who is or, within 12 months of the date of the common draft terms, has been an officer or employee of that company;

(ii) except with the leave of the Court, a parent, spouse, brother, sister or child of an officer of that company; or

(iii) a person who is a partner, or in the employment, of an officer or employee of that company.

(4) The report shall be made available not less than 1 month before the date of the general meeting referred to in Regulation 10 and shall be in writing and shall—

(a) state the method or methods used to arrive at the proposed exchange ratio,

(b) give the opinion of the expert whether the proposed exchange ratio is fair and reasonable,

(c) give the opinion of the expert as to the adequacy of the method or methods used in the case in question,

(d) indicate the values arrived at using each such method,

(e) give the opinion of the expert as to the relative importance attributed to such methods in arriving at the values decided on, and

(f) specify any special valuation difficulties which have arisen.

(5) The expert is entitled to require from each of the merging companies and their officers such information and explanation (whether oral or in writing), and to carry out such investigations, as the expert thinks necessary for the purposes of preparing the report.

(6) Where a company, being an Irish merging company—

(a) fails, on request, to supply to the expert any information or explanation in the power, possession or procurement of that person that the expert thinks necessary for the purposes of the report that company, being an Irish merging company and every officer in default shall be guilty of an offence, or

(b) knowingly or recklessly, makes a statement (whether orally or in writing), or provides a document, to the expert, being a statement or document which—

(i) conveys or purports to convey any information or explanation that the expert requires, or is entitled to require, under paragraph (5), and

(ii) is misleading, false or deceptive in a material particular,

that company, being an Irish merging company and every officer in default shall be guilty of an offence.

(7) If a person appointed under paragraph (a) or (b) of paragraph (2) ceases to be a qualified person, that person—

(a) shall immediately cease to hold office, and

(b) shall give notice in writing of the disqualification to the Company or to the Court (as the case requires) within 14 days of ceasing to be a qualified person,

but without prejudice to the validity of any acts done by the person under this Regulation before ceasing to be a qualified person.

(8) A person who purports to carry out the functions of an expert under this Regulation after ceasing to be a qualified person shall be guilty of an offence.

Definitions

'common draft terms': EC(CBM)R 2008, reg 2(1); 'company': EC(CBM)R 2008, reg 2(1); 'cross-border merger': EC(CBM)R 2008, reg 2(1); 'Court': EC(CBM)R 2008, reg 4; 'director': CA 1963, s 2(1); 'EEA State': EC(CBM)R 2008, reg 2(1); 'expert's report': EC(CBM)R 2008, reg 2(1); 'Irish merging company': EC(CBM)R 2008, reg 2(1); 'merger': EC(CBM)R 2008, reg 2(1); 'merger by absorption': EC(CBM)R 2008, reg 2(1); 'merging company': EC(CBM)R 2008, reg 2(1); 'officer': CA 1963, s 2(1); 'officer in default': CA 1963, s 383; 'share': CA 1963, s 2(1); 'successor company': EC(CBM)R 2008, reg 2(1); 'transferor company': EC(CBM)R 2008, reg 2(1).

Notes

Expert's Report: See the note to reg 1 above entitled 'The documents to be prepared'. An expert's report must be prepared for the members of each Irish merging company unless the cross-border merger is a merger by absorption or the successor company holds 90 per cent or more but not all of the voting shares of each transferor company or every member of every merging company agrees to dispense with the report.[1] The person preparing the report must be appointed either by the directors of the Irish merging company or, on the application of all merging companies, by the Irish High Court or other foreign competent authority, as the case may be.[2] The person must be qualified to act as an auditor and must be independent of the company.[3] His report must be in writing and must be available at least one month before the general meeting of the company at which the proposed merger is to be voted on.[4] It must deal with the matters set out in reg 7(4). In order to enable the expert to prepare his report he may carry out such investigations and require the merging companies and their officers to provide him with whatever information and explanations he considers necessary.[5] Failure to co-operate with him and the making of false statements to him attract potential criminal liability.[6]

1 Reg 7(1).

2 Reg 7(2).

3 Reg 7(3).

4 Reg 7(4).

5 Reg 7(5).

6 Reg 7(6).

8. Registration and publication of documents

(1) Each Irish merging company shall deliver to the Registrar for registration—

(a) a copy of the common draft terms, and

(b) a notice, in the form set out in Schedule 3, specifying in relation to each merging company—

(i) its name,

(ii) its registered office,

(iii) its legal form and the law by which it is governed,

(iv) in the case of an Irish Company, its registered number,

Definitions

'common draft terms': EC(CBM)R 2008, reg 2(1); 'company': EC(CBM)R 2008, reg 2(1); 'cross-border merger': EC(CBM)R 2008, reg 2(1); 'Court': EC(CBM)R 2008, reg 4; 'Directive': EC(CBM)R 2008, reg 2(1); 'director': CA 1963, s 2(1); 'EEA State': EC(CBM)R 2008, reg 2(1); 'Irish merging company': EC(CBM)R 2008, reg 2(1); 'merger': EC(CBM)R 2008, reg 2(1); 'merger by absorption': EC(CBM)R 2008, reg 2(1); 'merging company': EC(CBM)R 2008, reg 2(1); 'officer': CA 1963, s 2(1); 'officer in default': CA 1963, s 383; 'special resolution': CA 1963, s 141(1); 'successor company': EC(CBM)R 2008, reg 2(1); 'transferor company': EC(CBM)R 2008, reg 2(1).

Notes

Approval of cross-border merger: See the note to Reg 1 above entitled 'General Meeting to approve the Merger'.

11. Exemption from requirement to hold general meeting

(1) Shareholder approval of the common draft terms is not required—

(a) in the case of any transferor company in a merger by absorption, or

(b) in the case of the successor company in a merger by acquisition, if the conditions specified in paragraph (2) have been satisfied.

(2) The conditions referred to in paragraph (1)(b) are the following:

(a) the notice required to be published under Regulation 8(2) was published in accordance with Regulation 8(2) in respect of the successor company before the commencement of the period (in this paragraph referred to as the 'notice period') of 1 month before the date of the general meeting of the transferor company (or, where there is more than one transferor company, of the first of them to hold such a general meeting);

(b) the members of the successor company were entitled, during the notice period—

(i) to inspect, at the registered office of the successor company, during ordinary hours of business, copies of—

(I) the documents referred to in Regulation 9,

(II) the audited annual accounts for the preceding 3 financial years of each merging company (or, where a merging company has traded for less than 3 financial years before the date of the common draft terms, the audited annual accounts for the financial years for which the company has traded), and

(III) the accounting statement, if any, in relation to each merging company which is required to be prepared pursuant to paragraph (3),

and

(ii) to obtain copies of those documents or any part of them on request;

(c) the right, conferred by paragraph (4), to requisition a general meeting has not been exercised during the notice period.

(3) Where the latest annual accounts of any merging company relate to a financial year that ended more than 6 months before the date of the common draft terms, that company shall prepare an accounting statement in accordance with the following requirements:

(a) the accounting statement shall be drawn up, as at a date not earlier than the first day of the third month preceding the date of the common draft terms—

(i) in the format of the last annual balance sheet, and

(ii) in accordance with—

(I) the Companies Acts in the case of an Irish merging company, or

(II) the law of the relevant EEA State in the case of an EEA merging company,

(b) subject to subparagraph (c), valuations shown in the last annual balance sheet shall only be altered to reflect entries in the books of account,

(c) the following shall be taken into account in preparing the accounting statement—

(i) interim depreciation and provisions, and

(ii) material changes in actual value not shown in books of account, and

(d) the provisions of the Companies Acts relating to the auditor's report on the last annual accounts apply, with any necessary modifications, to the accounting statement.

(4) One or more members of the successor company who together hold not less than 5% of the paid-up capital of the company which carries the right to vote at general meetings of the company (excluding any shares held as treasury shares) may require the convening of a general meeting of the company to consider the common draft terms, and section 132 of the Act of 1963 applies, with any necessary modifications, in relation to the requisition.

Definitions

'Act of 1963': EC(CBM)R 2008, reg 2(1); 'common draft terms': EC(CBM)R 2008, reg 2(1); 'Companies Acts': EC(CBM)R 2008, reg 2(1); 'company': EC(CBM)R 2008, reg 2(1); 'cross-border merger': EC(CBM)R 2008, reg 2(1); 'Court': EC(CBM)R 2008, reg 4; 'Directive': EC(CBM)R 2008, reg 2(1); 'director': CA 1963, s 2(1); 'EEA State': EC(CBM)R 2008, reg 2(1); 'Irish merging company': EC(CBM)R 2008, reg 2(1); 'merger': EC(CBM)R 2008, reg 2(1); 'merger by absorption': EC(CBM)R 2008, reg 2(1); 'merger by acquisition': EC(CBM)R 2008, reg 2(1); 'merging company': EC(CBM)R 2008, reg 2(1); 'share': CA 1963, s 2(1); 'successor company': EC(CBM)R 2008, reg 2(1); 'transferor company': EC(CBM)R 2008, reg 2(1).

Notes

Exemption from holding of general meeting: See the note to Reg 1 above entitled 'General Meeting to approve the Merger'.

---

12. Purchase of minority shares

(1) Where a majority of votes cast at the general meeting of a transferor company was in favour of the special resolution proposed pursuant to Regulation 10, a minority shareholder in that company may, not later than 15 days after the relevant date, request

the successor company in writing to acquire his or her shares in the transferor company for cash.

(2) Where a request is made by a minority shareholder in accordance with paragraph (1), the successor company shall purchase the shares of the minority shareholder at a price determined in accordance with the share exchange ratio set out in the common draft terms.

(3) Nothing in this Regulation limits the power of the Court to make any order necessary for the protection of the interests of a dissenting minority in a merging company.

(4) In this Regulation—

'minority shareholder', in relation to a transferor company, means—

(a) in a case where the successor company (not being a company formed for the purpose of the merger) holds 90% or more (but not all) of the shares or other securities carrying the right to vote at general meetings of the transferor company, any other shareholder in the company, or

(b) in any other case, a shareholder in the company who voted against the special resolution;

'relevant date' means—

(a) in relation to a minority shareholder referred to in paragraph (a) of the definition of 'minority shareholder', the date of publication of the notice of delivery of the common draft terms under Regulation 8(2), or

(b) in relation to a minority shareholder referred to in paragraph (b) of the definition of 'minority shareholder', the date on which the general meeting of the transferor company was held.

Definitions

'common draft terms': EC(CBM)R 2008, reg 2(1); 'company': EC(CBM)R 2008, reg 2(1); 'Court': EC(CBM)R 2008, reg 4; 'merging company': EC(CBM)R 2008, reg 2(1); 'share': CA 1963, s 2(1); 'successor company': EC(CBM)R 2008, reg 2(1); 'transferor company': EC(CBM)R 2008, reg 2(1).

Notes

Exemption from holding of general meeting: See the note to Reg 1 above entitled 'General meeting to approve the merger'.

13. Certificate of compliance with pre-merger requirements

On application by an Irish merging company, the Court shall, if it is satisfied that the company has completed properly the pre-merger requirements, issue a certificate to that effect, and such a certificate is conclusive evidence that the company has properly completed the pre-merger requirements.

Definitions

'Act of 1963': EC(CBM)R 2008, reg 2(1); 'common draft terms': EC(CBM)R 2008, reg 2(1); 'Companies Acts': EC(CBM)R 2008, reg 2(1); 'company': EC(CBM)R 2008, reg 2(1); 'cross-border merger': EC(CBM)R 2008, reg 2(1); 'Court': EC(CBM)R 2008, reg 4; 'Directive': EC(CBM)R 2008, reg 2(1); 'director': CA 1963, s 2(1); 'EEA State': EC(CBM)R 2008, reg 2(1); 'Irish merging company': EC(CBM)R 2008, reg 2(1); 'merger': EC(CBM)R 2008, reg 2(1); 'merger by absorption': EC(CBM)R 2008, reg 2(1); 'merger by acquisition': EC(CBM)R 2008, reg 2(1); 'merging company': EC(CBM)R 2008, reg 2(1); 'share': CA 1963, s 2(1); 'successor company': EC(CBM)R 2008, reg 2(1); 'transferor company': EC(CBM)R 2008, reg 2(1).

Notes

Application for Certificate of Compliance: See the note to Reg 1 above entitled 'Application for Certificate of Compliance'. There are as yet no Rules of Court specifically governing the procedure whereby a company can apply for a Certificate of Compliance. However, in a recent *ex tempore* decision, Kelly J directed that the application should be made by way of advertised petition on notice to the company's members, employees and creditors.[1] In a further application in the same case, Dunne J confirmed that it was not necessary for a transferor company to also have the proposed cross-border merger confirmed pursuant to CA 1963, s 72 notwithstanding the fact that the net value of the assets being transferred to the successor company was greater than the value of the transferor company's distributable profits.[2]

1 *Re Sachsen LB Europe plc* (31 July 2008, unreported) HC (Kelly J).

2 *Re Sachsen LB Europe plc* (19 August 2008, unreported) HC (Dunne J).

Chapter 2
Approval in State of Cross-Border Mergers

14. Court scrutiny of cross-border merger

(1) Where the successor company in a cross-border merger is an Irish company, the Court may, on application made jointly by all the merging companies, make an order confirming scrutiny of the legality of the cross-border merger as regards that part of the procedure which concerns the completion of the cross-border merger and, where appropriate, the formation of an Irish successor company.

(2) The application shall be accompanied by a statement detailing the number and class of shares of each shareholder, if any, who has requested the purchase of his or her shares under Regulation 12 and of the measures which the successor company proposes to take to comply with each such request.

(3) Subject to Regulations 15 and 16, the Court may make an order referred to in paragraph (1) if—

(a) the successor company is an Irish company,

(b) a certificate has been issued under Regulation 13 in relation to each Irish merging company,

(c) in relation to each merging company which is an EEA company, a certificate to the same effect as a certificate issued under Regulation 13 has been issued by the competent authority of the EEA State under the law of which that company is governed,

(d) the application is made not more than 6 months after the issuing of a certificate referred to in subparagraph (b) and (c),

(e) the common draft terms to which each certificate, referred to in subparagraphs (b) and (c), relates are the same terms,

(f) any arrangements for employee participation in the successor company as are required by Part 3 have been determined,

(g) provision has been made for each creditor of any of the merging companies who establishes to the satisfaction of the Court that that creditor would otherwise be unfairly prejudiced by an order under Regulation 14, and

(h) where a request for the purchase of shares, referred to in paragraph (2), has been made, that measures have been proposed to comply with each such request.

(4) The Court shall specify, in an order, referred to in paragraph (1), the date on which the merger is to have effect.

(5) After the cross-border merger has taken effect, an order made under this Regulation is conclusive evidence that—

(a) the conditions set out in paragraph (3) have been satisfied, and

(b) the pre-merger requirements have been complied with.

Definitions

'Act of 1963': EC(CBM)R 2008, reg 2(1); 'common draft terms': EC(CBM)R 2008, reg 2(1); 'company': EC(CBM)R 2008, reg 2(1); 'cross-border merger': EC(CBM)R 2008, reg 2(1); 'Court': EC(CBM)R 2008, reg 4; 'EEA company': EC(CBM)R 2008, reg 2(1); 'EEA State': EC(CBM)R 2008, reg 2(1); 'Irish Company': EC(CBM)R 2008, reg 2(1); 'Irish merging company': EC(CBM)R 2008, reg 2(1); 'merger': EC(CBM)R 2008, reg 2(1); 'merging company': EC(CBM)R 2008, reg 2(1); 'share': CA 1963, s 2(1); 'successor company': EC(CBM)R 2008, reg 2(1); 'transferor company': EC(CBM)R 2008, reg 2(1).

Notes

Approval of Cross-Border Merger: See the note to Reg 1 above entitled 'Approval of the Cross-Border Merger'.

---

15. Protection of creditors

A creditor of an Irish merging company who, at the date of publication of the notice under Regulation 8, is entitled to any debt or claim against the company, is entitled to be heard in relation to the confirmation by the Court of the cross-border merger under Regulation 14.

Definitions

'company': EC(CBM)R 2008, reg 2(1); 'Court': EC(CBM)R 2008, reg 4; 'cross-border merger': EC(CBM)R 2008, reg 2(1); 'Irish merging company': EC(CBM)R 2008, reg 2(1).

Notes

Protection of creditors: See the note to Reg 1 above entitled 'Approval of the Cross-Border Merger'.

---

16. Compliance with other laws relating to mergers and take-overs

(1) The Court shall not make an order under Regulation 14 in respect of a cross-border merger that is a merger or acquisition which is referred to in section 16 of the Competition Act 2002 (No. 14 of 2002) and to which paragraph (a) or (b) of section 18(1) of that Act applies or which is referred to in section 18(3) of that Act and which has been notified to the Competition Authority in accordance with that subsection, unless—

- (a) the Competition Authority has determined under section 21 or 22 of that Act that the merger may be put into effect,
- (b) the Competition Authority has made a conditional determination (within the meaning of that Act) in relation to the merger,
- (c) the period specified in subsection (2) of section 21 of that Act has elapsed without the Competition Authority having informed the undertakings which made the notification concerned of the determination (if any) it has made under paragraph (a) or (b) of that subsection in relation to the merger, or
- (d) a period of 4 months has elapsed since the appropriate date (within the meaning of that Act) without the Competition Authority having made a determination under section 22 of that Act in relation to the merger.

(2) The Court shall not make an order under Regulation 14 in respect of a cross-border merger that is a concentration with a Community dimension (within the meaning of the Merger Control Regulation) unless—

- (a) the European Commission has issued a decision under Article 8 of that Regulation declaring the concentration compatible with the common market,
- (b) the concentration is deemed to have been declared compatible with the common market pursuant to Article 10(6) of that Regulation, or
- (c) after a referral by the European Commission to the Competition Authority under Article 9 of that Regulation, of one of the events specified in subparagraphs (a) to (d) of paragraph (1), has occurred.

(3) The Court shall not make an order under Regulation 14 in respect of a cross-border merger while any requirement under an enactment for any other authorisation, approval, consent, waiver, licence, permission or agreement that affects the merger remains unsatisfied.

(4) Nothing in these Regulations shall be taken to imply that the satisfaction of a requirement mentioned in paragraph (3) in relation to a merging company is effective in relation to the successor company.

(5) Nothing in this Regulation shall affect any conditions to which a determination by the Competition Authority, a decision of the European Commission or an authorisation of a Regulator is subject.

(6) Nothing in these Regulations limits the jurisdiction of the Irish Takeover Panel under the Irish Takeover Panel Act 1997 (No. 5 of 1997) with respect to a cross-border merger that—

- (a) involves a relevant company (within the meaning of that Act), and
- (b) constitutes a takeover (within the meaning of that Act),

and, accordingly—

(i) the Irish Takeover Panel has power to make rules under section 8 of that Act in relation to cross-border mergers of that kind, to the same extent and subject to the same conditions, as it has power to make rules under that section in relation to any other kind of takeover, and

(ii) the Court, in exercising its powers under these Regulations, shall have due regard to the exercise of powers under that Act.

(7) In this Regulation 'Regulator' means any body or authority constituted by, or pursuant to, the provisions of any enactment and includes the Central Bank and Financial Services Authority of Ireland and any Minister of the Government or Minister of State.

Definitions

'company': EC(CBM)R 2008, reg 2(1); 'cross-border merger': EC(CBM)R 2008, reg 2(1); 'Court': EC(CBM)R 2008, reg 4; 'merger': EC(CBM)R 2008, reg 2(1); 'merging company': EC(CBM)R 2008, reg 2(1); 'successor company': EC(CBM)R 2008, reg 2(1).

Notes

Obtaining regulatory clearance: The effect of reg 16 is to preclude the Irish High Court from approving a cross-border merger until relevant regulatory clearance (or clearance by default) has been obtained from the Irish Competition Authority and, if applicable, from the European Commission as well. Regulation 16(4) also requires the court to be satisfied that all other relevant statutory clearances, permissions etc have been obtained.

Chapter 3
Consequences of Approval of Cross-Border Mergers

17. Copies of orders to be delivered to the Registrar

(1) The Registrar of the Court shall cause an office copy of an order under Regulation 14 to be sent to the Registrar for registration in the Companies Register.

(2) The Registrar shall cause to be published in the CRO Gazette notice of delivery to the Registrar of the order of the Court within 14 days of the delivery referred to in paragraph (1).

(3) Where an order is made by a competent authority of another EEA State in respect of a cross-border merger for the purposes of Article 11 of the Directive, every transferor company which is an Irish company shall—

(a) deliver a copy of that order to the Registrar for registration not more than 14 days after the date on which it was made, and

(b) specify in writing to the Registrar, the date on which the competent authority of that EEA State determined, pursuant to Article 12 of the Directive, the date on which the cross border merger takes effect.

(4) Where a company fails to comply with paragraph (3) the company and every officer in default shall be guilty of an offence.

Definitions

'company': EC(CBM)R 2008, reg 2(1); 'cross-border merger': EC(CBM)R 2008, reg 2(1); 'Court': EC(CBM)R 2008, reg 4; 'CRO Gazette': EC(CBM)R 2008, reg 2(1); 'Directive': EC(CBM)R 2008, reg 2(1); 'EEA State': EC(CBM)R 2008, reg 2(1); 'Irish Company': EC(CBM)R 2008, reg 2(1); 'merger': EC(CBM)R 2008, reg 2(1); 'officer in default': CA 1963, s 383; 'Registrar': EC(CBM)R 2008, reg 2(1).

Notes

Registration of court order: Where the successor company is Irish, the Irish High Court send a copy of its order approving the cross-border merger to the Registrar of Companies for registration and publication in the CRO Gazette.[1] The Registrar in turn must notify the order to his counterparts in any EEA states where transferor companies were incorporated.[2] If the successor company is from another EEA state and the approval of the cross-border merger has therefore been obtained from a foreign competent authority under Art 11 of the CBM Directive instead, the Irish transferor company is required to deliver a copy of the order of that foreign competent authority to the Registrar of Companies for registration and must inform him in writing of the date that has been specified by the foreign competent authority for the cross-border merger to take effect.[3]

1 Regs 17(1) and (2).

2 Reg 18(1).

3 Reg 17(3).

18. Action to be taken by Registrar on receipt of orders

(1) Where the Registrar receives a copy of an order made under Regulation 14 the Registrar shall—

(a) in relation to each transferor company which is an EEA company, give notice of that order as soon as practicable to the authority responsible for maintaining the register in which the company file for that EEA company is kept pursuant to Article 3 of the First Company Law Directive in the EEA State concerned, and

(b) in relation to an Irish transferor company, register the copy order in respect of that company on, or as soon as practicable after, the effective date in the Companies Register.

(2) Where the Registrar receives from the authority responsible for maintaining the register of another EEA State notice, under Article 13 of the Directive, that the cross-border merger has taken effect the Registrar shall register—

(a) that notice, and

(b) the date of the receipt of that notice.

(3) The deletion of the registration of the company which is the subject of the notice referred to in paragraph (2) shall not be effected until the Registrar has received that notice.

Definitions

'company': EC(CBM)R 2008, reg 2(1); 'cross-border merger': EC(CBM)R 2008, reg 2(1); 'Companies Register': EC(CBM)R 2008, reg 2(1); 'EEA Company': EC(CBM)R 2008, reg 2(1); 'EEA State': EC(CBM)R 2008, reg 2(1); 'First Company Law Directive': EC(CBM)R 2008, reg 2(1); 'Registrar': EC(CBM)R 2008, reg 2(1); 'transferor company': EC(CBM)R 2008, reg 2(1).

Notes

See the notes to reg 17.

19. Consequences of a cross-border merger

(1) Subject to paragraph (2), the consequences of a cross-border merger are that, on the effective date—

(a) all the assets and liabilities of the transferor companies are transferred to the successor company,

(b) in the case of a merger by acquisition or a merger by formation of a new company, where no application has been made by minority shareholders under Regulation 12, all remaining members of the transferor companies except the successor company (if it is a member of a transferor company) become members of the successor company,

(c) the transferor companies are dissolved,

(d) all legal proceedings pending by or against any transferor company shall be continued with the substitution, for the transferor companies, of the successor company as a party,

(e) the successor company is obliged to make to the members of the transferor companies any cash payment required by the terms of the common draft terms,

(f) the rights and obligations arising from the contracts of employment of the transferor companies are transferred to the successor company,

(g) every contract, agreement or instrument to which a transferor company is a party shall, notwithstanding anything to the contrary contained in that contract, agreement or instrument, be construed and have effect as if—

(i) the successor company had been a party thereto instead of the transferor company,

(ii) for any reference (however worded and whether express or implied) to the transferor company there were substituted a reference to the successor company, and

(iii) any reference (however worded and whether express or implied) to the directors, officers, representatives or employees of the transferor company, or any of them, were, respectively, a reference to the directors, officers, representatives or employees of the successor company or to such director, officer, representative or employee of the successor company as the successor company nominates for that purpose or, in default of nomination, to the director, officer, representative or employee of the successor company who corresponds as nearly as may be to the first-mentioned director, officer, representative or employee,

(h) every contract, agreement or instrument to which a transferor company is a party becomes a contract, agreement or instrument between the successor company and the counterparty with the same rights, and subject to the same obligations, liabilities and incidents (including rights of set-off), as would have been applicable thereto if that contract, agreement or instrument had continued in force between the transferor company and the counterparty, and any money due and owing (or payable) by or to the transferor company under or by virtue of any such contract, agreement or instrument shall become due and owing (or payable) by or to the successor company instead of the transferor company, and

(i) an offer or invitation to treat made to or by a transferor company before the effective date shall be construed and have effect, respectively, as an offer or invitation to treat made to or by the successor company.

(2) The successor company shall comply with filing requirements and any other special formalities required by law (including the law of another EEA State) for the transfer of the assets and liabilities of the transferor companies to be effective in relation to other persons.

Definitions

'company': EC(CBM)R 2008, reg 2(1); 'cross-border merger': EC(CBM)R 2008, reg 2(1); 'EEA State': EC(CBM)R 2008, reg 2(1): 'effective date': EC(CBM)R 2008, reg 2(1); 'merger': EC(CBM)R 2008, reg 2(1); 'merger by acquisition': EC(CBM)R 2008, reg 2(1); 'merger by formation of a new company': EC(CBM)R 2008, reg 2(1); 'successor company': EC(CBM)R 2008, reg 2(1); 'transferor company': EC(CBM)R 2008, reg 2(1).

Notes

Consequences of cross-border merger: Regulation 19 spells out the consequences of the cross-border merger becoming effective. It operates to automatically dissolve the transferor companies and to vest all of their assets and liabilities (including contracts of employment) in the successor company. The remaining members of the transferor companies (ie excluding those dissentients who have already been bought out under reg 12 or its foreign equivalent) also automatically become members of the successor company at the exchange ratio specified in the common draft terms. Moreover, if the common draft terms provide for cash payments to be made to them, the successor becomes immediately liable to make those payments. In addition, reg 19 provides for other automatic consequences such as the continuation against the successor company of any legal proceedings that were pending against the now dissolved transferor companies.

---

20. Validity

A cross-border merger which has taken effect as provided for in Regulation 14(4) may not be declared null and void and the order made under Regulation 14, specifying the date on which the cross-border merger is to have effect, shall constitute conclusive evidence of the effectiveness of the cross-border merger.

Definitions

'cross-border merger': EC(CBM)R 2008, reg 2(1).

21. Certain provisions of the Companies Acts not to apply

(1) Sections 30 and 31 of the Companies (Amendment) Act 1983 (No. 13 of 1983) do not apply to the issue of shares by any company as a consequence of a cross-border merger.

(2) A cross-border merger does not create a subsidiary relationship to which subsection (5) of section 149 of the Act of 1963 applies, and accordingly the restrictions in that subsection have no application to the profits, losses or accounts of an Irish successor company.

(3) Section 41(1) of the Companies (Amendment) Act 1983 (which restricts the right of a Company to purchase its own shares) does not apply to the purchase of any shares in pursuance of an order of the Court under this Regulation.

Definitions

'company': EC(CBM)R 2008, reg 2(1); 'Companies Acts': EC(CBM)R 2008, reg 2(1); 'cross-border merger': EC(CBM)R 2008, reg 2(1); 'Court': EC(CBM)R 2008, reg 2(1); 'merger': EC(CBM)R 2008, reg 2(1); 'subsidiary': CA 1963, s 155; 'successor company': EC(CBM)R 2008, reg 2(1).

Notes

Disapplication of provisions of the Companies Acts: Apart from the specific statutory provisions which are expressly disapplied by reg 20, it has been held that the provisions of CA 1963, s 72 do not apply to a proposed cross-border merger even though the net value of the assets being transferred to the successor company is greater than the value of the transferor company's distributable profits.[1]

1 *Re Sachsen LB Europe plc* (19 August 2008, unreported) HC (Dunne J).

PART 3
EMPLOYEE PARTICIPATION

Chapter 1
Preliminary and General

22. Interpretation

In this Part—

'appointed' means, in the absence of an election, appointed by the employees and the basis on which that appointment is made may, if the employees so determine, be such as is agreed by them with the merging companies, or the successor company, as the case may be;

'consultation' means the establishment of dialogue and exchange of views between the representative body or the employees' representatives (or both) and the competent organ of the successor company at a time, in a manner and with a content which allows the employees' representatives, on the basis of the information provided, to express an opinion on measures envisaged by the competent organ which may be taken into account in the decision making process within the successor company;

'Commission' means the Labour Relations Commission;

'Court' means the Labour Court;

'employee' means a person who has entered into or works under a contract of employment and references, in relation to a merging company or a successor company, to an employee shall be read as references to an employee employed by any of them;

'employee participation' means the influence of the representative body or the employees' representatives (or both) in the affairs of a company by the way of—

(a) the right to elect or appoint some of the members of the company's supervisory or administrative organ, or

(b) the right to recommend or oppose, or both to recommend and oppose, the appointment of some or all of the members of the company's supervisory or administrative organ;

'employees' representative' means a representative elected or appointed for the purposes of these Regulations;

'establishment' means in relation to a company, a division (however described) of the undertaking physically separated from other parts of the company;

'excepted body' has the meaning assigned to it by section 6(3) of the Trade Union Act 1941 (No.22 of 1941, as amended);

'expert' means an individual, and may be the holder from time to time of a named office or position in a body corporate or other body or organisation;

'information' means the informing of the representative body or the employees' representatives (or both), by the competent organ of the successor company on questions which concern the company itself and any of its subsidiaries or establishments situated in another EEA State or which exceed the powers of the decision-making organs in a single EEA State at a time, in a manner and with a content which allows the employees' representatives to undertake an in-depth assessment of the possible impact and, where appropriate, prepare consultations with the competent organ of the company;

'involvement of employees' means any mechanism including information, consultation and employee participation, through which employees' representatives may exercise an influence on decisions to be taken within the company;

'representative body' means the body representative of the employees referred to in Schedule 1 set up for the purpose of informing and consulting the employees of a successor company situated in the EEA and, where applicable, of exercising employee participation rights in relation to the successor company;

'special negotiating body' means the body established in accordance with Regulation 25 to negotiate with the competent body of the merging companies regarding the establishment of arrangements for the involvement of employees within the successor company;

'Standard Rules' means the rules set out in Schedule 1;

'trade union' means a trade union which holds a negotiation licence under Part II of the Trade Union Act 1941 (No. 22 of 1941, as amended);

'wages' has the meaning assigned to it by the Payment of Wages Act 1991 (No. 25 of 1991, as amended).

Definitions

'company': EC(CBM)R 2008, reg 2(1); 'EEA State': EC(CBM)R 2008, reg 2(1); 'merging company': EC(CBM)R 2008, reg 2(1); 'successor company': EC(CBM)R 2008, reg 2(1).

Notes

Employee participation: The purpose and effect of Part 3 of the 2008 Regs is to provide for employee participation in an Irish successor company following a cross-border merger. The employee participation may involve board representation or the right to recommend or oppose the appointment of some or all of the members of the board. Under reg 24, negotiations for employee participation must begin as soon as possible after the draft terms of the cross-border merger have been published. In this regard, Chapter 2 of Part 3 provides for the establishment of an elected special negotiating body to represent the employees of the merging companies in that process. This special negotiating body is empowered by reg 30 to engage experts, including trade union officials, to assist it with its work and under reg 31 its reasonable expenses must be funded by the merging companies. Regulation 34 provides for the negotiations to continue for up to six months from the establishment of the special negotiating body, although there is also provision to extend the negotiations for up to a period of one year. Under reg 35 there is provision for a set of Standard Rules on employee participation (as set out in Schedule 1) to apply, subject to certain caveats, in the event that the parties cannot otherwise negotiate an agreed form of participation.

23. Requirement for employee participation

(1) Arrangements for the participation of employees in every Irish successor company shall be established in accordance with these Regulations.

(2) Without prejudice to paragraph (3), the successor company shall be subject to the rules in force in the State concerning employee participation, if any.

(3) Notwithstanding paragraph (2), the rules in force concerning employee participation in the State, if any, shall not apply, where—

(a) at least one of the merging companies has, in the 6 months before the publication of the common draft terms, an average number of employees that exceeds 500 and is operating under an employee participation system within the meaning of Regulation 2(1) of the European Communities (European Public Limited-Liability Company) (Employee Involvement) Regulations 2006 (S.I. No. 623 of 2006), or

(b) there is no provision in any enactment—

(i) for at least the same level of employee participation as operated in the relevant merging companies, measured by reference to the proportion of employee representatives amongst the members of the administrative or supervisory organ or their committees or of the management group which covers the profit units of the company, subject to employee representation, or

(ii) for employees of establishments of the successor company that are situated in other EEA States of the same entitlement to exercise employee participation rights as is enjoyed by those employees employed in the State.

(4) In the cases referred to in paragraph (3), the participation of employees in the successor company and their involvement in the definition of such rights shall be regulated in accordance with Regulations 24 to 44 and in accordance with Article 12(2), (3) and (4) of Regulation (EC) No 2157/2001 (OJ L 294, 10.11.2001, p.1.) as given full effect by the European Communities (European Public Limited Liability Company) Regulations 2007 (S.I. No. 21 of 2007).

Definitions

'company': EC(CBM)R 2008, reg 2(1); 'EEA State': EC(CBM)R 2008, reg 2(1); 'employee': EC(CBM)R 2008, reg 22; 'employee participation': EC(CBM)R 2008, reg 22; 'successor company': EC(CBM)R 2008, reg 2(1).

24. Requirement to begin negotiations with employees

(1) As soon as possible after the publication of the draft terms of a cross-border merger, the management or administrative organ of each merging company shall take the necessary steps to start negotiations with the representatives of the employees of that company on arrangements for the involvement of those employees in the successor company.

(2) The steps to start negotiations shall include the provision of information about the identity of the merging companies, the number of employees in each (identified according to the EEA State in which they are located), and the number of such employees covered by an employee participation system.

(3) The information referred to in paragraph (2) shall be supplied to the employees' representative for that merging company or, where there is no such representative, to the employees themselves.

Definitions

'company': EC(CBM)R 2008, reg 2(1); 'cross border merger': EC(CBM)R 2008, reg 2(1); 'EEA State': EC(CBM)R 2008, reg 2(1); 'employee': EC(CBM)R 2008, reg 22; 'employee participation': EC(CBM)R 2008, reg 22; 'employees' representative': EC(CBM)R 2008, reg 22; 'information': EC(CBM)R 2008, reg 22; 'merging company': EC(CBM)R 2008, reg 2(1); 'successor company': EC(CBM)R 2008, reg 2(1).

Chapter 2
Special Negotiating Body

25. Creation of special negotiating body

(1) For the purposes of the negotiations mentioned in Regulation 24, the management or administrative organs of the merging companies shall make arrangements, in accordance with this Regulation, for the establishment of a special negotiating body that is representative of the employees of the merging companies.

(2) The membership of the special negotiating body shall be determined in accordance with paragraphs (3) to (5) and the members shall be elected or appointed—

(a) in the case of members to be elected or appointed to represent employees in the State, in accordance with the procedure specified in Regulations 26 and 27, and

(b) in the case of members to be elected or appointed to represent employees in any other EEA State, in accordance with such procedures specified in laws or measures adopted by that EEA State.

(3) Subject to paragraphs (4) and (5), seats on the special negotiating body shall be distributed in proportion to the number of workers employed in each EEA State by the merging companies by allocating in respect of a relevant EEA State one seat for each portion of employees employed in that EEA State which equals 10%, or a fraction thereof, of the total number of employees employed by the merging companies in all relevant EEA States taken together.

(4) There shall be such further additional members from each EEA State as are necessary to ensure that the special negotiating body includes at least one member representing each transferor company which is registered and has employees in that EEA State, but so that—

(a) the number of additional members does not exceed 20% of the number of members provided for by paragraph (3), and

(b) the addition of members under this paragraph does not result in double representation of the employees concerned.

(5) In the application of paragraph (4), if the number of those transferor companies is greater than the number of additional seats available, those additional seats shall be allocated in relation to those companies in decreasing order of the number of employees they employ.

Definitions

'company': EC(CBM)R 2008, reg 2(1); 'EEA State': EC(CBM)R 2008, reg 2(1); 'employee': EC(CBM)R 2008, reg 22; 'merging company': EC(CBM)R 2008, reg 2(1); 'special negotiating body': EC(CBM)R 2008, reg 22; 'transferor company': EC(CBM)R 2008, reg 2(1).

26. Representation of Irish employees on special negotiating body

(1) The representation on a special negotiating body of the employees in the State of the merging companies is allocated as specified in this Regulation.

(2) Where the number of seats on the special negotiating body allocated to the State is equal to the number of merging companies which have employees in the State, there shall be at least one seat for each of the merging companies, and each member elected or appointed to fill such a seat shall be considered as representing the employees of the merging company that elected or appointed them.

(3) Where the number of seats on the special negotiating body allocated to the State is greater than the number of merging companies which have employees in the State, there shall be one seat for each of the merging companies, and additional seats shall be allocated to merging companies in decreasing order of the number of employees they employ, and each member elected or appointed to fill a seat in accordance with this

paragraph shall be taken to represent those employees of the companies that elected or appointed them.

(4) Where the number of seats on the special negotiating body allocated to the State is less than the number of merging companies which have employees in the State, the number of members equal to the number of available seats shall be elected or appointed according to the greatest number of votes won, and the representatives so elected or appointed shall between them represent the employees of the merging companies in the State that elected or appointed them.

(5) The references in paragraphs (2), (3) and (4) to merging companies include the concerned subsidiaries or establishments of a merging company and, where the presence of a merging company in the State is only by virtue of the presence of its concerned subsidiaries or establishments, those entities are to be taken, for the purposes of those paragraphs, to constitute that merging company.

(6) Employees of a merging company in which there are no employees' representatives shall not, by virtue of that fact alone, be prevented from exercising their right to elect or appoint members of the special negotiating body.

(7) An employee who is employed in the State by a merging company on the day the date or dates for the election of members of the special negotiating body conducted in accordance with Regulation 27 is fixed and who is, on the election day or days, an employee of such a company shall be entitled to vote in the election.

(8) Each of the following is eligible to stand as a candidate in the election of members of the special negotiating body conducted in accordance with Regulation 27, namely:

(a) an employee who has been employed in the State by one or more of the merging companies for a continuous period of not less than one year on the nomination day,

(b) a trade union official, whether or not he or she is an employee, and

(c) an official of an excepted body, whether or not he or she is an employee,

provided that, in each case, he or she is nominated as such a candidate by—

(i) a trade union or an excepted body which is already recognised by the relevant merging companies located in the State for collective bargaining or information and consultation purposes, or

(ii) at least 2 employees.

Definitions

'company': EC(CBM)R 2008, reg 2(1); 'consultation': EC(CBM)R 2008, reg 22; 'employee': EC(CBM)R 2008, reg 22; 'employees' representative': EC(CBM)R 2008, reg 22; 'excepted body': EC(CBM)R 2008, reg 22; 'information': EC(CBM)R 2008, reg 22; 'merging company': EC(CBM)R 2008, reg 2(1); 'special negotiating body': EC(CBM)R 2008, reg 22; 'trade union': EC(CBM)R 2008, reg 22.

---

27. Conduct of election

(1) Where elections of members of a special negotiating body fall to be conducted, being elections by employees in the State of merging companies, the management or

administrative organs of the merging companies shall arrange for the conducting of those elections in accordance with this Regulation.

(2) The management or administrative organs of the merging companies shall, in consultation with employees or their representatives (or both), appoint one or more persons as returning officers (referred to collectively in this Regulation as the 'returning officer'), whose duties include the organisation and conduct of nominations and the election, and any person so appointed may authorise other persons to assist in the performance of those duties.

(3) Where the number of candidates on the nomination day exceeds the number of members to be elected, a poll or polls shall be taken by the returning officer and voting in the poll shall take place by a secret ballot on a day or days to be decided by the returning officer.

(4) The returning officer shall perform the duties of that office in a fair and reasonable manner and in the interests of an orderly and proper conduct of nomination and election procedures.

(5) As soon as is reasonably practicable after the result of the election is known, the returning officer shall make such arrangements as are necessary to ensure that the result is sent to the candidates, employees and employees' representatives and to the management or administrative organs of the merging companies.

(6) Once the result of the election is sent by the returning officer in accordance with paragraph (5), the candidates concerned shall be regarded as having been duly elected.

(7) All reasonable costs of the nomination and election procedure in the election shall be borne by the management or administrative organs of the merging companies.

(8) Where, for any reason, a vacancy arises amongst those of the members of the special negotiating body who have been elected in accordance with this Regulation, arrangements shall be made by the competent organs of the merging companies and the special negotiating body for that vacancy to be filled.

(9) Where a member of the special negotiating body whose nomination for election was on the basis of his or her satisfying the requirement contained in Regulation 26(8)(a) ceases to be employed by any of the merging companies, that person shall cease to be a member of the special negotiating body.

(10) Where a member of the special negotiating body whose nomination for election was on the basis of his or her satisfying the requirement contained in Regulation 26(8)(b) or (c) ceases to be an official of the trade union or excepted body concerned, that person shall cease to be a member of the special negotiation body.

Definitions

'company': EC(CBM)R 2008, reg 2(1); 'employee': EC(CBM)R 2008, reg 22; 'employees' representative': EC(CBM)R 2008, reg 22; 'excepted body': EC(CBM)R 2008, reg 22; 'merging company': EC(CBM)R 2008, reg 2(1); 'special negotiating body': EC(CBM)R 2008, reg 22; 'trade union': EC(CBM)R 2008, reg 22.

---

28. Remit of special negotiating body

(1) The special negotiating body and the management or administrative organs of the merging companies shall negotiate and determine, by written agreement, arrangements for the involvement of employees within the successor company in accordance with the principles set out in Regulation 32.

(2) With a view to concluding that agreement, the management or administrative organs of the merging companies shall—

(a) convene a meeting with the special negotiating body and shall inform local managements accordingly, and

(b) inform the special negotiating body of the plan, the expected timetable, and the actual process of carrying out the cross-border merger, up to its registration.

(3) The management or administrative organs of the merging companies shall convene regular meetings as necessary with the special negotiating body in order to facilitate the negotiation of a written agreement referred to in paragraph (1).

(4) The agreement referred to in paragraph (1) shall be binding on the entire group of companies within the company resulting from the cross-border merger, irrespective of the EEA State in which it was signed and the location of those companies.

Definitions

'company': EC(CBM)R 2008, reg 2(1); 'employee': EC(CBM)R 2008, reg 22; 'cross-border merger': EC(CBM)R 2008, reg 2(1); 'EEA State': EC(CBM)R 2008, reg 2(1); 'merging company': EC(CBM)R 2008, reg 2(1); 'special negotiating body': EC(CBM)R 2008, reg 22; 'successor company': EC(CBM)R 2008, reg 2(1).

---

29. Voting procedure in the special negotiating body

(1) Subject to paragraph (2), the special negotiating body shall take its decisions (including the final decision whether to approve the entering into of an agreement under Regulation 28) by both—

(a) an absolute majority of its members, with each member having one vote, and

(b) an absolute majority of the employees represented by those members.

(2) If—

(a) at least 25% of the overall number of employees of the merging companies are covered by employee participation, and

(b) the result of negotiations would lead to a reduction of employee participation rights,

the majority required for a decision to approve the entering into of an agreement under Regulation 28 is the votes of two thirds of the members of the special negotiating body representing at least two thirds of the total number of employees, including the votes of members representing employees employed in at least two EEA States.

(3) For the purposes of paragraph (2), a reduction of employee participation rights occurs when the proportion of members of the organs of the successor company having employee participation rights is lower than the highest proportion existing within the merging companies.

(4) Any decision made in accordance with paragraph (2) shall be brought to the attention of the employees by the special negotiation body as soon as reasonably practicable and, in any event, no later than 14 days after the making of the decision.

Definitions

'EEA State': EC(CBM)R 2008, reg 2(1); 'employee': EC(CBM)R 2008, reg 22; 'employee participation': EC(CBM)R 2008, reg 22; 'merging company': EC(CBM)R 2008, reg 2(1); 'special negotiating body': EC(CBM)R 2008, reg 22.

30. Engagement of experts by special negotiating body

(1) For the purpose of the negotiations, the special negotiating body may engage experts of its choice to assist with its work.

(2) The experts may be representatives of appropriate EEA-level trade union organisations.

(3) The experts may be present at negotiation meetings in an advisory capacity at the request of the special negotiating body, where appropriate to promote coherence and consistency at EEA level.

(4) The special negotiating body may decide to inform the representatives of appropriate external organisations, including trade unions and excepted bodies, of the start of the negotiations.

Definitions

'excepted body': EC(CBM)R 2008, reg 22; 'expert': EC(CBM)R 2008, reg 22; 'special negotiating body': EC(CBM)R 2008, reg 22; 'trade union': EC(CBM)R 2008, reg 22.

31. Expenses

The reasonable expenses relating to the functioning of the special negotiating body and, in general, to negotiations under these Regulations shall be borne by the merging companies so as to enable the special negotiating body to carry out its functions in an appropriate manner.

Definitions

'company' EC(CBM)R 2008, reg 2(1); 'merging company': EC(CBM)R 2008, reg 2(1); 'special negotiating body': EC(CBM)R 2008, reg 22.

Chapter 3

Negotiations and Agreement

32. Spirit of cooperation

(1) The parties shall negotiate or work together, as the case may be, in a spirit of cooperation with due regard for their reciprocal rights and obligations, and taking into account the interests both of the successor company and of the employees.

(2) In paragraph (1), 'parties' means—

(a) the competent organs of the merging companies and the special negotiating body, in relation to reaching an agreement in accordance with Regulation 28 on arrangements for the involvement of the employees within the successor company;

(b) the competent organ of the successor company and the representative body as set out in Schedule 1; and

(c) the supervisory or administrative organ of the successor company and the employees or their representatives (or both), with regard to a procedure for the information and consultation of employees.

Definitions

'company': EC(CBM)R 2008, reg 2(1); 'consultation': EC(CBM)R 2008, reg 22; 'employee': EC(CBM)R 2008, reg 22; 'information': EC(CBM)R 2008, reg 22; 'merging company': EC(CBM)R 2008, reg 2(1); 'representative body': EC(CBM)R 2008, reg 22; 'successor company': EC(CBM)R 2008, reg 2(1).

33. Content of agreement

(1) Without prejudice to the autonomy of the parties, the agreement referred to in Regulation 28 shall specify—

(a) the scope of the agreement;

(b) the substance of any arrangements for employee participation that, in the course of the negotiations, the parties decide to establish, including, where applicable—

(i) the number of members of the administrative or supervisory body of the successor company whom the employees will be entitled to elect, appoint, recommend or oppose,

(ii) the procedures as to how the members referred to in clause (i) may be elected, appointed, recommended or opposed by employees, and their rights; and

(c) the date of entry into force of the agreement, its duration, the circumstances requiring renegotiation of the agreement and the procedure for its renegotiation.

(2) Unless it otherwise provides, the agreement is not subject to the Standard Rules.

Definitions

'employee': EC(CBM)R 2008, reg 22; 'employee participation' EC(CBM)R 2008, reg 22; 'Standard Rules': EC(CBM)R 2008, reg 22; 'successor company': EC(CBM)R 2008, reg 2(1).

34. Duration of negotiations

(1) The management or administrative organs of the merging companies and the special negotiating body shall commence negotiations as soon as the special negotiating body is

established and those negotiations may continue for up to 6 months from the establishment of that body.

(2) The parties may decide, by joint agreement, to extend negotiations beyond the period referred to in paragraph (1) up to a total of one year from the establishment of the special negotiating body.

(3) The special negotiating body may decide, by a majority of two thirds of its members representing at least two thirds of the employees, including the votes of members representing employees in at least two different EEA States, not to open negotiations or to terminate negotiations already opened and to rely on the rules on employee participation in force in each of the EEA States (including the State) where the successor company has its employees.

(4) A decision under paragraph (3) shall terminate the procedure referred to in Regulation 28 for the conclusion of an agreement, and the provisions of Schedule 1 shall not apply.

Definitions

'company': EC(CBM)R 2008, reg 2(1); 'EEA State': EC(CBM)R 2008, reg 2(1); 'employee': EC(CBM)R 2008, reg 22; 'employee participation': EC(CBM)R 2008, reg 22; 'merging company': EC(CBM)R 2008, reg 2(1); 'special negotiating body': EC(CBM)R 2008, reg 22; 'successor company': EC(CBM)R 2008, reg 2(1).

35. Standard Rules

(1) In order to ensure the establishment of arrangements for the involvement of employees in the successor company, the Standard Rules apply, from the date of its registration, to the successor company if its registered office is located in the State and—

(a) the parties so agree, or

(b) no agreement has been concluded within the time limit specified in Regulation 34 and—

(i) the management or administrative organs of the merging companies decide to accept the application of the Standard Rules in relation to the successor company and, on that basis, to continue with the merger, and

(ii) the special negotiating body has not made a decision under Regulation 29(2).

(2) Part 3 of Schedule 1 applies to the successor company only if, before registration of the successor company—

(a) one or more forms of employee participation applied to one or more of the merging companies employing at least $33^{1}/_{3}$ of the total number of employees in all merging companies in each of the EEA States concerned, or

(b) one or more forms of employee participation applied in one or more of the merging companies employing less than $33^{1}/_{3}$ of the total number of employees in all the merging companies in the EEA States and the special negotiating body decides that the rules set out in that Part are to apply.

(3) Where there was more than one form of employee participation within the various merging companies, the special negotiating body shall choose which of those forms shall be established in the company resulting from the cross-border merger.

(4) The special negotiating body shall inform the management or administrative organs of the merging companies of any decisions taken pursuant to paragraph (3).

(5) The relevant organs of the merging companies may choose without any prior negotiation to be directly subject to the Standard Rules and to abide by them from the date of registration of the successor company.

(6) Where, following prior negotiations, the Standard Rules apply, the parties may, notwithstanding those Rules, agree to limit the proportion of employee representatives in the administrative organ of the successor company, but if in one of the merging companies employee representatives constituted at least one third of the administrative or supervisory board, the limitation may not result in a lower proportion of employee representatives in the administrative organ of the successor company than one third.

(7) Where, in accordance with paragraph (6), the parties agree to limit the proportion of employee representatives in the administrative organ, the majority required for such a decision shall be the votes of—

- (a) two-thirds of the employees including the votes of employees employed in at least two Member States, or
- (b) two-thirds of the members of the representative body representing at least two thirds of the total number of employees, including the votes of members representing employees employed in at least two Member States.

Definitions

'company': EC(CBM)R 2008, reg 2(1); 'EEA State': EC(CBM)R 2008, reg 22; 'employee': EC(CBM)R 2008, reg 22; 'employee participation': EC(CBM)R 2008, reg 22; 'merger': EC(CBM)R 2008, reg 2(1); 'merging company': EC(CBM)R 2008, reg 2(1); 'special negotiating body': EC(CBM)R 2008, reg 22; 'Standard Rules': EC(CBM)R 2008, reg 22; 'successor company': EC(CBM)R 2008, reg 2(1);

Chapter 4
Supplementary

36. Definition

In this Chapter 'relevant company' means—

- (a) a merging company, and
- (b) in relation to a merger by formation of a new company, the successor company.

Definitions

'merger': EC(CBM)R 2008, reg 2(1); 'merger by formation of a new company': EC(CBM)R 2008, reg 2(1); 'merging company': EC(CBM)R 2008, reg 2(1); 'successor company': EC(CBM)R 2008, reg 2(1).

---

37. Protection of employee participation rights

When the successor company is operating under an employee participation system, that company shall ensure that employees' participation rights are protected in the event of subsequent domestic mergers for a period of three years after the cross-border merger has taken effect, by applying, mutatis mutandis, the rules laid down in these Regulations.

Definitions

'company': EC(CBM)R 2008, reg 2(1); 'cross-border merger': EC(CBM)R 2008, reg 2(1); 'employee' EC(CBM)R 2008, reg 22; 'employee participation': EC(CBM)R 2008, reg 22; 'merger': EC(CBM)R 2008, reg 2(1); 'successor company': EC(CBM)R 2008, reg 2(1).

38. Confidential information

(1) An individual who is or at any time was—

(a) an employee of a relevant company,

(b) a member of—

(i) the special negotiating body, or

(ii) the representative body,

(c) an employees' representative for the purposes of these Regulations, or

(d) an expert providing assistance,

shall not reveal any information which, in the legitimate interest of any relevant company, has been expressly provided in confidence to him or her or to the body by a relevant company.

(2) The duty of confidentiality imposed by paragraph (1) continues to apply after the cessation of the employment of the individual concerned or the expiry of his or her term of office.

(3) A relevant company may refuse to communicate information to a special negotiating body where the nature of that information is such that, by reference to objective criteria, it would—

(a) seriously harm the functioning of any relevant company, or

(b) be prejudicial to any relevant company.

(4) The Court or any member of the Court or the registrar or any officer or servant of the Court, including any person or persons appointed by the Court as an expert or mediator, shall not disclose any information obtained in confidence in the course of any proceedings before the Court under these Regulations.

Definitions

'company': EC(CBM)R 2008, reg 2(1); 'Court': EC(CBM)R 2008, reg 22; 'employee': EC(CBM)R 2008, reg 22; 'employees' representative': EC(CBM)R 2008, reg 22; 'expert': EC(CBM)R 2008, reg 22; 'information': EC(CBM)R 2008, reg 22; 'relevant company':

EC(CBM)R 2008, reg 36; 'representative body': EC(CBM)R 2008, reg 22; 'special negotiating body': EC(CBM)R 2008, reg 22.

39. Protection of employees' representatives

(1) A relevant company shall not penalise—

(a) a member of the special negotiating body,

(b) a member of the representative body,

(c) an employees' representative performing functions under these Regulations, or

(d) an employees' representative in the supervisory or administrative organ of a successor company who is an employee of that company or of a merging company,

for the performance of his or her functions in accordance with these Regulations.

(2) For the purposes of this Regulation, a person referred to in paragraph (1) is penalised if that person—

(a) is dismissed or suffers any unfavourable change to his or her conditions of employment or any unfair treatment (including selection for redundancy), or

(b) is the subject of any other action prejudicial to his or her employment.

(3) Schedule 2 has effect in relation to an alleged contravention of paragraph (1).

(4) Subject to paragraph (6), a person referred to in paragraph (1) shall be afforded any reasonable facilities, including time off, that will enable him or her to perform promptly and efficiently his or her functions as a member of the special negotiating body or representative body or as an employees' representative, as the case may be.

(5) A person referred to in paragraph (1) shall be paid his or her wages for any period of absence afforded to him or her in accordance with paragraph (4).

(6) The granting of facilities under paragraph (4) shall have regard to the needs, size and capabilities of the relevant company and shall not impair the efficient operation of that company.

(7) This Regulation applies in particular to attendance by representatives at meetings of the special negotiating body or representative body or any other meetings within the framework of an agreement referred to in Regulation 33 or Schedule 1 or any meeting of the administrative or supervisory organ.

(8) Subject to paragraph (9), this Regulation is in addition to, and not in substitution for, any rights enjoyed by an employees' representative, whether under any enactment or otherwise.

(9) If a penalisation of a person referred to in paragraph (1), in contravention of that paragraph, constitutes a dismissal of that person within the meaning of the Unfair Dismissals Acts 1977 to 2007, relief may not be granted to that person in respect of that penalisation both under Schedule 2 and under those Acts.

Definitions

'company': EC(CBM)R 2008, reg 2(1); 'employee': EC(CBM)R 2008, reg 22; 'employees' representative': EC(CBM)R 2008, reg 22; 'merging company': EC(CBM)R 2008, reg 2(1);

'relevant company': EC(CBM)R 2008, reg 36; 'representative body': EC(CBM)R 2008, reg 22; 'special negotiating body': EC(CBM)R 2008, reg 22; 'successor company': EC(CBM)R 2008, reg 2(1).

40. Dispute Resolution

(1) Subject to paragraph (2), a dispute between any relevant company and employees or their representatives (or both) concerning—

(a) matters provided for in Regulations 25 to 31 relating to the special negotiating body,

(b) the negotiation, interpretation or operation of an agreement in relation to Regulation 24, 33 or 34,

(c) the interpretation or operation of the Standard Rules as provided for in Regulation 35 and Schedule 1, and

(d) a matter provided for in paragraph (4), (5), (6) or (7) of Regulation 39, or

(e) a complaint by an employee or his or her representative (or both) that, in relation to Regulation 37, the company resulting from any subsequent domestic merger is being or will be misused for the purpose of depriving employees of their rights to employee involvement or of withholding those rights,

may be referred by one or more relevant company, employees employed in the State or their representatives (or both) to the Court for investigation.

(2) Such a dispute may be referred to the Court only after—

(a) recourse to the internal dispute resolution procedure (if any) in place in the relevant company concerned has failed to resolve the dispute, and

(b) the dispute has been referred to the Commission, and, having made available such of its services as are appropriate for the purpose of resolving the dispute, the Commission provides a certificate to the Court stating that the Commission is satisfied that no further efforts on its part will advance the resolution of the dispute.

(3) Having investigated a dispute under paragraph (1), the Court may make a recommendation in writing, giving its opinion in the matter.

(4) Where, in the opinion of the Court, a dispute that is the subject of a recommendation under paragraph (3) has not been resolved, the Court may, at the request of—

(a) one or more relevant company, or

(b) one or more employees or their representatives (or both),

and, following a review of all relevant matters make a determination in writing.

(5) Disputes between any relevant company and employees or their representatives (or both) concerning matters of confidential information provided for in Regulation 38 may be referred by—

(a) one or more relevant company, or

(b) any employee of the company or his or her representatives (or both),

to the Court for determination.

(6) In relation to a dispute referred to it under this Regulation, the Court shall—

(a) give the parties an opportunity to be heard by it and to present any evidence relevant to the dispute,

(b) make a recommendation or determination, as the case requires, in writing in relation to the dispute, and

(c) communicate the recommendation or determination to the parties.

(7) The following matters, or procedures to be followed in relation to them, shall be determined by the Court, namely:

(a) the procedure in relation to all matters concerning the initiation and hearing by the Court of a dispute under this Regulation;

(b) the times and places of hearings of such disputes;

(c) the publication and notification of recommendations and determinations of the Court;

(d) any matters consequential on, or incidental to, the matters referred to in subparagraphs (a) to (c).

(8) In deciding what constitutes confidential information, the Court may be assisted by a panel of experts.

(9) A party to a dispute under this Regulation may appeal from a determination of the Court to the High Court on a point of law and the decision of the High Court shall be final and conclusive.

(10) The Court may refer a question of law arising in proceedings before it under this Regulation to the High Court for determination and the decision of the High Court shall be final and conclusive.

Definitions

'company': EC(CBM)R 2008, reg 2(1); 'Court': EC(CBM)R 2008, reg 22; 'employee': EC(CBM)R 2008, reg 22; 'employees' representative': EC(CBM)R 2008, reg 22; 'information': EC(CBM)R 2008, reg 22; 'merger': EC(CBM)R 2008, reg 2(1); 'relevant company': EC(CBM)R 2008, reg 22; 'special negotiating body': EC(CBM)R 2008, reg 22; 'Standard Rules': EC(CBM)R 2008, reg 22.

---

41. Power of Court to administer oaths and compel witnesses

(1) The Court shall, on the hearing of a dispute referred to it for recommendation or determination under Regulation 40 or on the hearing of an appeal under Schedule 2, have power to take evidence on oath and for that purpose may cause to be administered oaths to persons attending as witnesses at that hearing.

(2) Any person who, upon examination on oath authorised by this Regulation, wilfully makes any statement which is material for that purpose and which he or she knows to be false or does not believe to be true commits an offence.

(3) The Court may, by giving notice in that behalf in writing to any person, require that person to attend at such time and place as is specified in the notice to give evidence in relation to a dispute referred to the Court for recommendation or determination under Regulation 40 or an appeal under Schedule 2, or to produce any documents in the person's possession, custody or control which relate to any such matter.

(4) A notice under paragraph (3) may be given either by delivering it to the person to whom it relates or by sending it by post in a prepaid registered letter addressed to that person at the address at which he or she ordinarily resides or, in the case of a relevant company, at the address at which the relevant company ordinarily carries on any profession, business or occupation.

(5) If a person to whom a notice under paragraph (3) has been given refuses or wilfully neglects to attend in accordance with the notice or, having so attended, refuses to give evidence or refuses or wilfully fails to produce any document to which the notice relates, that person commits an offence.

(6) A witness in a hearing of a dispute or appeal before the Court has the same privileges and immunities as a witness before the High Court.

Definitions

'company': EC(CBM)R 2008, reg 2(1); 'Court': EC(CBM)R 2008, reg 22; 'relevant company': EC(CBM)R 2008, reg 36.

42. Enforcement

(1) If—

(a) a party to a Court determination fails to carry out in accordance with its terms a determination of the Court in relation to a dispute under Regulation 40, or

(b) a party to a complaint under Schedule 2 fails to carry out in accordance with its terms a decision of a rights commissioner or a determination of the Court under that Schedule in relation to the complaint,

within the period specified in the determination or decision or if no such period is so specified within 6 weeks from the date on which the determination or decision is communicated to the parties, the Circuit Court shall, on application to it in that behalf by one or more of the parties to the dispute or complaint, without hearing any evidence (other than in relation to the matters aforesaid) make an order directing the party concerned to carry out the determination or decision in accordance with its terms.

(2) The reference in paragraph (1) to a determination of the Court or a decision of a rights commissioner is a reference to such a determination or decision in relation to which, at the end of the time for bringing an appeal against it, no such appeal has been brought or, if such an appeal has been brought it has been abandoned, and the references to the date on which the determination or decision is communicated to the parties shall, in a case where such an appeal is abandoned, be read as references to the date of that abandonment.

(3) In an order under this Regulation providing for the payment of compensation of the kind referred to in paragraph 2(3)(c) of Schedule 2, the Circuit Court may, if in all the circumstances it considers it appropriate to do so, direct a relevant company to pay to the employee concerned interest on the compensation at the rate referred to in section 22 of the Courts Act 1981 (No.11 of 1981), in respect of the whole or any part of the period beginning 6 weeks after the date on which the determination of the Court or the decision of the rights commissioner is communicated to the parties and ending on the date of the order.

(4) An application under this Regulation to the Circuit Court shall be made to the judge of the Circuit Court for the circuit in which the relevant company concerned has its principal place of business.

Definitions

'company': EC(CBM)R 2008, reg 2(1); 'Court': EC(CBM)R 2008, reg 22; 'relevant company': EC(CBM)R 2008, reg 36.

---

43. Workforce thresholds in other legislation

The extension of employee participation rights to employees of establishments of the successor company employed in other EEA States, referred to in Regulation 23(3)(b)(ii), shall not entail any obligation to take those employees into account when calculating the size of workforce thresholds giving rise to participation rights under national law.

Definitions

'company': EC(CBM)R 2008, reg 2(1).'EEA State': EC(CBM)R 2008, reg 2(1); 'employee': EC(CBM)R 2008, reg 22; 'employee participation': EC(CBM)R 2008, reg 22; 'successor company': EC(CBM)R 2008, reg 2(1).

---

44. Legal form of company

When at least one of the merging companies is operating under an employee participation system and the successor company is to be governed by such a system in accordance with the rules referred to in Regulation 23, that company shall take a legal form allowing for the exercise of employee participation rights.

Definitions

'company': EC(CBM)R 2008, reg 2(1); 'employee participation': EC(CBM)R 2008, reg 22; 'merging company': EC(CBM)R 2008, reg 2(1).

SCHEDULE 1
Standard Rules

Regulation 22

PART 1
COMPOSITION OF BODY REPRESENTATIVE OF EMPLOYEES

1. In cases falling within Regulation 35, a representative body shall be set up in accordance with the provisions of this Part.

2. The representative body shall be composed of employees of the successor company and its subsidiaries and establishments elected or appointed from their number by the employees' representatives or, in the absence thereof, by the entire body of employees.

3. The members of the representative body shall be elected or appointed in proportion to the number of employees employed in each EEA State by the merging companies, by

allocating in respect of an EEA State one seat per portion of employees employed in that EEA State which equals 10% or a fraction thereof, of the number of employees employed by the merging companies in all the EEA States taken together.

4. The election or appointment of members of the representative body shall be carried out in accordance with a procedure agreed by the special negotiating body.

5. The number of members of, and allocation of seats on, the representative body shall be adapted to take account of changes occurring within the successor company, and the representative body shall take any steps it deems necessary to ensure this.

6. Where its size so warrants, the representative body shall elect a select committee from among its members, comprising at most three members.

7. The representative body shall adopt its own rules of procedure.

8. The competent organ of the successor company shall be informed of the composition of the representative body as soon as is reasonably practicable.

9. (1) Four years after the representative body is established, it shall examine whether to open negotiations for the conclusion of an agreement referred to in Regulation 28 or to continue to apply the Standard Rules as provided for in this Schedule.

(2) If such a decision has been taken to negotiate an agreement, Regulations 29 to 31 and 33 and 34 apply with the necessary modifications and, for that purpose, references in those Regulations to 'special negotiating body' shall be construed as references to 'representative body'.

(3) Where, on the expiry of the time limit specified in Regulation 34 (as applied by this paragraph), no such agreement has been concluded, the arrangements initially adopted in accordance with the provisions of this Schedule continue to apply.

PART 2

STANDARD RULES FOR INFORMATION AND CONSULTATION

10. The competence and powers of the representative body set up in the successor company are governed by the provisions of this Part.

11. (1) The competence of the representative body shall be limited to questions which concern the successor company situated in another EEA State or which exceed the powers of the decision-making organs in a single EEA State.

(2) Without prejudice to meetings held pursuant to paragraph 13(1), the representative body has the right to be informed and consulted and, for that purpose, to meet with the competent organ of the successor company at least once a year, on the basis of regular reports drawn up by the competent organ, on the progress of the business of the successor company and its prospects, and the local management shall be informed accordingly.

(3) The competent organ of the successor company shall provide the representative body with the agenda for meetings of the administrative, or, where appropriate, the management and supervisory organ, and with copies of all documents submitted to the general meeting of its shareholders.

(4) The meeting shall relate in particular to the structure, economic and financial situation, the probable development of the business and of production and sales, the situation and probable trend of employment, investments, and substantial changes

concerning organisation, introduction of new working methods or production processes, transfers of production, mergers, cut-backs or closures of undertakings, establishments or important parts thereof, and collective redundancies.

12. (1) Where there are exceptional circumstances affecting the employees' interests to a considerable extent, particularly in the event of relocations, transfers, the closure of establishments or undertakings or collective redundancies, the representative body has the right to be informed.

(2) The representative body, or where it so decides, in particular for reasons of urgency, the select committee, has the right to meet at its request the competent organ of the successor company, or any more appropriate level of management within the successor company having its own powers of decision, so as to be informed and consulted on measures significantly affecting employees' interests.

(3) Where the competent organ decides not to act in accordance with the opinion expressed by the representative body, the representative body has the right to a further meeting with the competent organ of the successor company with a view to seeking agreement.

(4) In the case of a meeting organised with a select committee, those members of the representative body who represent employees who are directly concerned by the measures in question also have the right to participate.

(5) The meetings referred to in this paragraph do not affect the prerogatives of the competent organ.

13.(1) Before any meeting with the competent organ of the successor company, the representative body or the select committee, where necessary enlarged in accordance with paragraph 12(4), is entitled to meet without the representatives of the competent organ being present.

(2) Without prejudice to Regulation 38, the members of the representative body shall inform the employees of the successor company or their representatives (or both), of the content and outcome of the information and consultation procedures.

14.(1) The representative body or the select committee may be assisted by experts of its choice.

(2) The reasonable costs of the representative body shall be borne by the successor company, which shall provide the body's members with the financial and material resources needed to enable them to perform their duties in an appropriate manner.

(3) In so far as is necessary for the fulfilment of their duties, the members of the representative body shall be entitled to time off for training without loss of wages.

PART 3
STANDARD RULES FOR EMPLOYEE PARTICIPATION

15.(1) Subject to paragraphs (6) and (7) of Regulation 35, the employees of the successor company and their representative body (or both) have the right to elect, appoint, recommend or oppose the appointment of a number of members of the administrative or supervisory body of that company equal to the highest proportion in force in the merging companies concerned before registration of the successor company.

(2) If none of the participating companies was governed by employee participation rules before registration of the successor company, the company is not required to establish provisions for employee participation.

(3) The representative body shall decide on the allocation of seats within the administrative or supervisory body among the members representing the employees from the various EEA States or on the way in which the employees of the successor company may recommend or oppose the appointment of the members of these bodies according to the proportion of the company's employees in each EEA State.

(4) If, as a consequence of a decision under subparagraph (3), the employees of one or more EEA States are not covered by the proportional criterion, the representative body shall, where possible, appoint a member from one of those EEA States, in particular the EEA State where the successor company has its registered office where that is appropriate.

(5) For the purposes of subparagraph (4) and the determination of the allocation of the seats given within the administrative or supervisory body to employees in the State, those members of the representative body representing employees in the State shall select, from amongst their number, a number of representatives equal to the number of seats available.

16. Every member of the administrative body or, where appropriate, the supervisory body of the successor company who has been elected, appointed or recommended by the representative body or, depending on the circumstances, by the employees shall be a full member with the same rights and obligations as the members representing the shareholders, including the right to vote.

Definitions

'EEA State': EC(CBM)R 2008, reg 2(1); 'employee': EC(CBM)R 2008, reg 22; 'employees' representative': EC(CBM)R 2008, reg 22; 'representative body': EC(CBM)R 2008, reg 22; 'subsidiary': CA 1963, s 155; 'successor company': EC(CBM)R 2008, reg 2(1).

SCHEDULE 2
Redress for Contravention of Regulation 39

Regulation 39

COMPLAINTS TO RIGHTS COMMISSIONER

1. In this Schedule 'relevant companies' has the same meaning as in Regulation 36.

2. (1) A person referred to in Regulation 39(1) may present a complaint to a rights commissioner that a relevant company has contravened Regulation 39(1) in relation to him or her.

(2) Where a complaint under subparagraph (1) is made, the rights commissioner shall—

(a) give the parties an opportunity to be heard by the commissioner and to present to the commissioner any evidence relevant to the complaint,

(b) give a decision in writing in relation to it, and

(c) communicate the decision to the parties.

(3) A decision of a rights commissioner under subparagraph (2) shall do one or more of the following:

(a) declare that the complaint was or, as the case may be, was not well founded;

(b) require the relevant company to take a specified course of action;

(c) require the relevant company to pay to the person referred to in subparagraph (1) compensation of such amount (if any) as is just and equitable having regard to all the circumstances but not exceeding 2 years' remuneration in respect of the person's employment.

(4) A rights commissioner shall not entertain a complaint under this Schedule if it is presented to him or her after the expiration of the period of 6 months beginning on the date of the contravention to which the complaint relates.

(5) Notwithstanding subparagraph (4), a rights commissioner may entertain a complaint under this Schedule presented to him or her not later than 6 months after the expiration of the period referred to in subparagraph (4) if he or she is satisfied that the failure to present the complaint within that period was due to reasonable cause.

(6) A complaint shall be presented by giving notice of it in writing to a rights commissioner.

(7) A copy of a notice under subparagraph (6) shall be given to the other party concerned by the rights commissioner concerned.

(8) Proceedings under this paragraph before a rights commissioner shall be conducted otherwise than in public.

APPEALS FROM DECISIONS OF RIGHTS COMMISSIONER

3.(1) A party concerned may appeal to the Court from a decision of a rights commissioner under paragraph 2, and, if the party does so, the Court shall give the parties an opportunity to be heard by it and to present to it any evidence relevant to the appeal, shall make a determination in writing in relation to the appeal affirming, varying or setting aside the decision and shall communicate the determination to the parties.

(2) An appeal under this paragraph shall be initiated by the party concerned giving, within 6 weeks (or such greater period as the Court determines in the particular circumstances) from the date on which the decision to which it relates was communicated to the party, a notice in writing to the Court containing such particulars as are determined by the Court under subparagraph (4) and stating the intention of the party concerned to appeal against the decision.

(3) A copy of a notice under subparagraph (2) shall be given by the Court to any other party concerned as soon as practicable after the receipt of the notice by the Court.

(4) The following matters, or the procedures to be followed in relation to them, shall be determined by the Court, namely:

(a) the procedure in relation to all matters concerning the initiation and the hearing by the Court of appeals under this paragraph,

(b) the times and places of hearings of such appeals,

(c) the representation of the parties to such appeals,

(d) the publication and notification of determinations of the Court,

Particulars of the company's arrangements for exercise of the rights of creditors and members

Arrangements made for the exercise of the rights of the creditors and any minority members of the merging companies:

Full information on the arrangements made for the exercise of the rights of the creditors and any minority members of the merging companies, may be obtained free of charge, from the following address:

Particulars of other merging companies

Name of Company:

The registered office of the company:

Legal form of the company and the law by which it is governed:

Arrangements made for the exercise of the rights of the creditors and any minority members of the merging companies: *note five*

Full information on the arrangements made for the exercise of the rights of the creditors and any minority members of the merging companies, may be obtained free of charge, from the following address:

☐ If the Company is an Irish Company, Information relating to the Company is kept by the Registrar under registered number:

note one

☐ If the Company is an EEA Company, particulars of the national register in which the Company's file is kept and its registration number in that register, are as follows:

Particulars of other merging companies

Name of Company:

The registered office of the company:

Legal form of the company and the law by which it is governed:

Arrangements made for the exercise of the rights of the creditors and any minority members of the merging companies: *note five*

Full information on the arrangements made for the exercise of the rights of the creditors and any minority members of the merging companies, may be obtained free of charge, from the following address:

☐ If the Company is an Irish Company, Information relating to the Company is kept by the Registrar under registered number:

note one

☐ If the Company is an EEA Company, particulars of the national register in which the Company's file is kept and its registration number in that register, are as follows:

NOTES ON COMPLETION OF FORM CBM1
These notes should be read in conjunction with the relevant legislation.

General This form must be completed correctly, in full and in accordance with the following notes. Every section of the form must be completed.

Where "not applicable", "nil" or "none" is appropriate, please state.
Where the space provided on Form CBM1 is considered inadequate, the information should be presented on a continuation sheet in the same format as the relevant section in the form. The use of a continuation sheet must be so indicated in the relevant section.

For the purposes of this form, "EEA Company" means a company governed by the law of an EEA State other than Ireland. An EEA State is a State that is a contracting party to the Agreement on the European Economic Area, signed at Oporto on 2nd May 1992, as adjusted by the Protocol signed at Brussels on the 17th March 1993, and any subsequent amendments.

"Irish registered company" refers to a company incorporated in Ireland under the Companies Acts and does not include a company registered in Northern Ireland.

note one Please tick the relevant box.

note two Any change of registered office must be notified to the CRO.

note three This form **must** be certified by a director of the company on behalf of the Board.

note four This section must be completed by the person who is presenting Form CBM1 to the CRO. This may be either the applicant or a person on his/her behalf.

note five Where space is considered inadequate, a continuation sheet should be completed, in the same format as the relevant section.

EXPLANATORY NOTE

(*This note is not part of the Instrument and does not purport to be a legal interpretation.*)

These Regulations give effect to Directive 2005/56/EC of the European Parliament and of the Council of 26 October 2005 on cross-border mergers of limited liability companies.

European Communities (Mergers and Divisions of Companies) (Amendment) Regulations 2008

SI 572/2008

I, MARY COUGHLAN, Minister for Enterprise, Trade and Employment, in exercise of the powers conferred on me by section 3 of the European Communities Act 1972 (No. 27 of 1972) and for the purpose of giving effect to Directive No. 2007/63/EC of the European Parliament and of the Council of 13 November 2007 (OJ L 300 of 17.11.2007, p 47), hereby make the following regulations:

1. (1) These Regulations may be cited as the European Communities (Mergers and Divisions of Companies) (Amendment) Regulations 2008.

(2) These Regulations come into operation on 31 December 2008.

2. The European Communities (Mergers and Divisions of Companies) Regulations 1987 (S.I. No. 137 of 1987) are amended—

- (a) in Regulation 8—
  - (i) by substituting "Subject to paragraph (11), each" for "Each" in paragraph (1), and
  - (ii) [...][a],
- (b) in Regulation 12(1)(d) by inserting "where applicable," before "the independent person's report",
- (c) in Regulation 28—
  - (i) by substituting "Subject to paragraph (12), each" for "Each" in paragraph (1), and
  - (ii) [...][b], and
- (d) in Regulation 31(1)(d) by inserting "where applicable," before "the independent person's report".

Amendments

a EC(MDC)(A)R 2008, reg 2(a)(ii) inserts EC(MDC)R 1987, reg 8(11).

b EC(MDC)(A)R 2008, reg 2(c)(ii) inserts EC(MDC)R 1987, reg 28(12).

Explanatory Note

(*This note is not part of the Instrument and does not purport to be a legal interpretation.*)

These Regulations give effect to Directive 2007/63/EC of the European Parliament and of the Council of 13 November 2007 amending Directives 78/855/EEC and 82/891/EEC concerning the requirement of an independent expert's report on the occasion of merger or division of public limited liability companies.

The change being effected to these Directives through the present Regulations is to give holders of shares and other securities with voting rights at general meetings of each of the merging companies (in the case of a merger) and each of the companies involved in a division (in the case of a division), the option, if they all so agree, to dispense with the requirement to have an examination of the draft terms of merger/written expert's report on the draft terms of a merger or division.

Companies Act 1963 (Alteration of Eighth Schedule) Order 2009

SI 302/2009

I, MARY COUGHLAN, Minister for Enterprise, Trade and Employment, in exercise of the powers conferred on me by section 395 (amended by section 63(1) of the Company Law Enforcement Act 2001 (No. 28 of 2001)) of the Companies Act 1963 (No. 33 of 1963) (as adapted by the Enterprise and Employment (Alteration of Name of Department and Title of Minister) Order 1997 (S.I. No. 305 of 1997)), hereby order as follows:

1. (1) This Order may be cited as the Companies Act 1963 (Alteration of Eighth Schedule) Order 2009.

(2) This Order shall come into operation on 1st September, 2009.

2. The Eighth Schedule (inserted by the Companies (Fees) (No. 3) Order 2005 (S.I. No. 517 of 2005)) to the Companies Act 1963 (No. 33 of 1963) is altered by substituting the Part set out in the Schedule to this Order for Part 1.

3. The Companies (Fees) (No. 4) Order 2005 (S.I. No. 737 of 2005) and Companies (Fees) Order 2006 (S.I. No. 502 of 2006) are revoked.

SCHEDULE

[...][a]

Amendments

a CA 1963 (A8S) O 2009, Sch substitutes CA 1963, Sch 8, Pt 1.

EXPLANATORY NOTE

(This Note is not part of the instrument and does not purport to be a legal interpretation)

This Order alters the Eight Schedule to the Companies Act 1963 by substituting Part 1 of the Schedule.

The Order revokes the Companies (Fees) (No 4) Order 2005 (S.I. No. 737 of 2005 and the Companies (Fees) Order 2006 (S.I. No. 502 of 2006)

Shareholders' Rights (Directive 2007/36/EC) Regulations 2009

SI 316/2009

I, MARY COUGHLAN, Minister for Enterprise, Trade and Employment, in exercise of the powers conferred on me by section 3 (amended by section 2 of the European Communities Act 2007 (No. 18 of 2007)) of the European Communities Act 1972 (No. 27 of 1972) and for the purpose of giving effect to Directive 2007/36/EC of the European Parliament and of the Council of 11 July 2007 (OJ L 184, 14.7.2007, p 17), hereby make the following regulations:

1 Citation, commencement and construction

(1) These Regulations may be cited as the Shareholders' Rights (Directive 2007/36/EC) Regulations 2009.

(2) These Regulations shall come into operation on the date on which they are made and shall apply in relation to meetings of which notice is given, or first given, on or after that date.

(3) These Regulations shall be read as one with the Companies Acts.

2 Definition

In these Regulations, "Act of 1963" means the Companies Act 1963 (No. 33 of 1963).

3 Amendment of section 2 (General provisions as to interpretation) of Act of 1963

Section 2 of the Act of 1963 is amended—

(a) […][a]; and

(b) […][b].

Amendments

a Shareholders' Rights Regulations 2009, reg 3(a) inserts definitions of 'company traded on a regulated market', 'Directive 2004/25/EC' and 'electronic means' into CA 1963, s 2.

b Shareholders' Rights Regulations 2009, reg 3(b) substitutes the definition of 'regulated market' in CA 1963, s 2.

---

4 Amendment of section 132 (Convening of extraordinary general meeting on requisition) of Act of 1963

Section 132 of the Act of 1963 is amended by inserting the following subsection after subsection (1):

[…][a].

Amendments

a Shareholders' Rights Regulations 2009, reg 4 inserts CA 1963, s 132(1A).

---

5 New section 132A in Act of 1963

The Act of 1963 is amended by inserting the following section after section 132:

[…][a].

Amendments

a Shareholders' Rights Regulations 2009, reg 5 inserts CA 1963, s 132A.

6 Amendment of section 133 (Length of notice for calling meetings) of Act of 1963

Section 133 of the Act of 1963 is amended—

(a) in subsection (1)(b), by substituting "or an unlimited company, and" for "or an unlimited company.",

(b) […][a],

(c) in subsection (2)(b), by substituting "or an unlimited company, and" for "or an unlimited company.",

(d) […][b],

and

(e) in subsection (3) by inserting ", other than a company traded on a regulated market," after "A meeting of a company".

Amendments

a Shareholders' Rights Regulations 2009, reg 6(b) inserts CA 1963, s 133(1)(c).

b Shareholders' Rights Regulations 2009, reg 6(d) inserts CA 1963, s 133(2)(c).

7 New sections 133A and 133B in Act of 1963

The Act of 1963 is amended by inserting the following sections after section 133:

[…][a].

Amendments

a Shareholders' Rights Regulations 2009, reg 7 inserts CA 1963, ss 133A and 133B.

8 New sections 134A, 134B and 134C in Act of 1963

The Act of 1963 is amended by inserting the following sections after section 134:

[…][a].

Amendments

a Shareholders' Rights Regulations 2009, reg 8 inserts CA 1963, ss 134A–C.

9 Amendment of section 136 (Proxies) of Act of 1963

Section 136 of the Act of 1963 is amended by—

(a) […][a], and

(b) […][b], and

(c) […][c].

Amendments

a Shareholders' Rights Regulations 2009, reg 9(a) inserts CA 1963, s 136(1A) and (1B).

b Shareholders' Rights Regulations 2009, reg 9(b) inserts CA 1963, s 136(2A).

c Shareholders' Rights Regulations 2009, reg 9(c) inserts CA 1963, s 136(4A).

10 Substitution of section 138 of Act of 1963

The Act of 1963 is amended by substituting the following section for section 138:

[…][a].

Amendments

a Shareholders' Rights Regulations 2009, reg 10 substitutes CA 1963, s 138.

11 Amendment of section 139 of Act of 1963

Section 139(1) of the Act of 1963 is amended—

(a) in paragraph (a) by deleting "and",

(b) in paragraph (b) by substituting "may be, and" for "may be.", and

(c) […][a].

Amendments

a Shareholders' Rights Regulations 2009, reg 11(c) inserts CA 1963, s 139(1)(c).

12 New section 145A of Act of 1963

The Act of 1963 is amended by inserting the following section after section 145:

[…][a].

Amendments

a Shareholders' Rights Regulations 2009, reg 12 inserts CA 1963, s 145A.

L.S. GIVEN under my Official Seal,

6 August 2009.

MARY COUGHLAN,

Minister for Enterprise, Trade and Employment.

Companies (Auditing and Accounting) Act 2003 (Procedures Governing the Conduct of Section 24 Investigations) Regulations 2009

SI 355/2009

The IRISH AUDITING AND ACCOUNTING SUPERVISORY AUTHORITY, in exercise of its powers conferred on it by section 28(4) of the Companies (Auditing and Accounting) Act 2003 (No. 44 of 2003), hereby makes the following regulations:

PART 1
PRELIMINARY AND GENERAL

1 Citation and application

(1) These Regulations may be cited as the Companies (Auditing and Accounting) Act 2003 (Procedures Governing the Conduct of Section 24 Investigations) Regulations, 2009.

(2) Section 24 of the Companies (Auditing and Accounting) Act, 2003 provides that, following a complaint or on its own initiative, the Authority may, if in its opinion it is appropriate or in the public interest to do so, undertake an investigation into a possible breach of a prescribed accountancy body's standards by a member or member firm of that body.

(3) Section 28(4) of the Act provides, inter alia, that the Authority shall make Regulations respecting the procedures to be followed in conducting investigations under section 24 of the Companies (Auditing and Accounting) Act, 2003.

(4) These Regulations apply to any matter that appears to the Authority may constitute grounds for the initiation of an investigation under section 24 of the Companies (Auditing and Accounting) Act, 2003.

(5) These Regulations shall be construed in accordance with the Companies Acts 1963 to 2009.

(6) Headings and sub-headings are for convenience only and shall not affect the interpretation of these Regulations.

2 Interpretation

(1) Except where otherwise stated, words and expressions used in these Regulations that are used in the Companies (Auditing and Accounting) Act, 2003 have the same meaning.

(2) In these Regulations, unless the context otherwise requires—

"the Act" means the Companies (Auditing and Accounting) Act 2003, as amended (No. 44 of 2003);

"the Authority" means the Irish Auditing and Accounting Supervisory Authority, and includes any committee established to assist the Authority under section 27(1) of the Act;

"client" includes an individual, a body corporate, an unincorporated body of persons and a partnership;

"complainant" means a person (other than an officer or employee of the Authority) who has lodged a complaint with the Authority regarding a possible breach of a prescribed accountancy body's standards by a member or member firm of that prescribed accountancy body;

"Court" means the High Court;

"documents" include any books, documents, records, telephone recordings or computer held information of whatsoever kind;

"investigation" means an investigation initiated under section 24(2) of the Act and includes a preliminary investigation initiated under these Regulations;

"Investigation Committee" means a committee established by the Authority to conduct a full investigation in accordance with these Regulations;

"member" has the same meaning as provided for in section 4 of the Act and includes a member firm unless otherwise indicated in these Regulations;

"Preliminary Investigation Committee" means a committee established by the Authority to conduct a preliminary investigation in accordance with these Regulations;

"relevant person" means—

(a) a member of a prescribed accountancy body,

(b) a client or former client of such member,

(c) if the client or former client is a body corporate, a person who is or was an officer, employee or agent of the client or former client,

(d) the prescribed accountancy body or any person who is or was an officer, employee or agent of that body, or

(e) any person whom the Authority reasonably believes has information or documents relating to the investigation other than information or documents the disclosure of which is prohibited or restricted by law.

"standards" means the rules, regulations and standards that a prescribed accountancy body applies to its members and to which, by virtue of their membership, they are obliged to adhere.

PART 2
SECTION 24 COMMITTEES

3 Section 24 Committees

(1) Subject to paragraph (2) and in accordance with section 27(1) of the Act, a Section 24 Committee shall consist of directors of the Authority and such professional and other advisers as the Authority considers necessary or appropriate.

(2) Neither the Chief Executive of the Authority nor any member of the staff of the Authority shall be a member of a Section 24 Committee.

(3) Each Section 24 Committee shall number at least 3 persons, with no more than one half of the members of the committee being directors of the Authority. The members who are not directors shall be chosen from a panel of suitable independent persons which shall be prepared and maintained by the Authority. The Chairperson of each Section 24 Committee shall be chosen by the Chairperson of the Authority.

(4) The quorum necessary for the transaction of the business by a Section 24 Committee may be fixed by the Authority and, unless so fixed, shall be three, provided that three persons are personally present, that the majority of members present are not members of a prescribed accountancy body and that at least one person present is a director of the Authority.

(5) Any decision of a Section 24 Committee shall be decided by a majority of votes. In case of an equality of votes, the Chairperson of the Committee shall have a second or casting vote.

(6) No serving member of the governing body of any prescribed accountancy body, or any officer or employee of any of the prescribed accountancy bodies, may be appointed to a Section 24 Committee.

(7) No person who, in the view of the Authority may have (or may appear to have) any interest in the outcome of the investigation or any relationship with any party to the matters which are the subject of the investigation which may create, or appear to create, a conflict of interest may be appointed to a Section 24 Committee.

(8) Any person who served as a member of a Preliminary Investigation Committee may not be appointed as a member of an Investigation Committee with respect to the same investigation.

(9) No person who is a member of the same prescribed accountancy body as the member or member firm under investigation may take part in the deliberations of a Section 24 Committee involved in such matter.

(10) The Secretary to the Authority or another person selected and appointed by the Authority may act as Secretary to a Section 24 Committee.

4 Preliminary Investigation Committee

(1) If, in the Authority's opinion, it is appropriate or in the public interest to undertake a preliminary investigation into a possible breach of a prescribed accountancy body's standards, then the Authority may appoint a Preliminary Investigation Committee ("Preliminary Investigation Committee"), to determine whether the Authority should initiate a full investigation.

(2) In appointing a Preliminary Investigation Committee, the Authority shall be deemed to have delegated to that Preliminary Investigation Committee such of its functions and powers under section 24 of the Act as are required to conduct the functions of the Preliminary Investigation Committee for which these Regulations provide.

(3) No preliminary investigation may be undertaken into a matter that is, or has been, the subject of an enquiry under section 23 of the Act relating to such member except with the permission of the High Court.

(4) Save in exceptional cases, the Authority should not refer the matter to a Preliminary Investigation Committee on the basis of an anonymous complaint.

(5) The Preliminary Investigation Committee shall notify the member affected and the prescribed accountancy body of which the member is a member of its appointment and of the initiation of the Preliminary Investigation.

(6) A full investigation will be initiated if the Preliminary Investigation Committee determines that:

(a) there is a prima facie case that a member has breached a prescribed accountancy body's standards; and

(b) in its opinion, it is appropriate or in the public interest that there should be a full investigation by the Authority into such possible breach.

(7) In determining whether it is appropriate or in the public interest that there should be such a full investigation, the Preliminary Investigation Committee shall take into account such matters as it considers appropriate, including but not limited to the question (a) of whether the possible breach has already been investigated or is in the course of investigation by a prescribed accountancy body or another supervisory body, and (b) of whether a possible breach ought to be referred to a prescribed accountancy body or another supervisory body for investigation.

(8) Where the Preliminary Investigation Committee forms the view that a matter before it ought to be referred to a prescribed accountancy body or another supervisory body for investigation, it will refer the matter to such prescribed accountancy body or other supervisory body, provided however that the Authority shall subsequently be entitled to refer the same matter once again to the Preliminary Investigation Committee for its consideration.

(9) Where the Preliminary Investigation Committee forms the view that the matter before it is better dealt with by way of the exercise by the Authority of any of its other powers, or by way of recommendations and observations by the Authority, rather than through the initiation of a full investigation, it will report its view and the facts and circumstances of the matter to the Authority and the Authority may, if it considers it appropriate to do so, direct that the Preliminary Investigation Committee report such facts and circumstances to the Chief Executive and the Head of Regulatory and Monitoring Supervision of the Authority.

(10) If, in the course of considering whether there is a prima facie case that a member has breached the standards of the prescribed accountancy body and whether a full investigation should be initiated, the Preliminary Investigation Committee discovers facts or circumstances which appear to warrant examination but which are outside the scope of its remit, the Preliminary Investigation Committee will report such facts and circumstances to the Authority and the Authority may, provided such matters fall within the scope of section 24 of the Act, direct in writing that the scope of the preliminary investigation shall include such facts or circumstances and shall inform the member and relevant prescribed accountancy body accordingly.

(11) For the avoidance of doubt and for the purpose of these Regulations, a preliminary investigation shall only be initiated where the alleged breach of the standards of a prescribed accountancy body occurred after 3 February, 2006.

(12) The Preliminary Investigation Committee may, if considered appropriate and in accordance with law, inform the complainant, if any, of the appointment of the Preliminary Investigation Committee, of the initiation of the preliminary investigation and of any extension of the scope of the preliminary investigation made under paragraph (10), if such extension is relevant to such complainant.

(13) The Preliminary Investigation Committee shall, prior to making a determination under paragraph (6), provide the member that is the subject of the preliminary

investigation and the prescribed accountancy body of which the member is a member with:

(a) a statement of the grounds upon which the preliminary investigation has been initiated;

(b) any relevant information and copies of all relevant documentation relating to such grounds; and

(c) an opportunity to comment in writing on such grounds, documentation and information, if any.

(14) The Preliminary Investigation Committee shall reach its determination on the basis of written material alone. To assist the Preliminary Investigation Committee in determining whether there is a prima facie case that a member has breached the standards of a prescribed accountancy body and whether a full investigation should be initiated, the Committee may require any relevant person to do one or more of the following:

(a) provide to the Preliminary Investigation Committee all books or documents relating to the preliminary investigation that are in the relevant person's possession or control; and

(b) give the Preliminary Investigation Committee any other assistance in connection with the investigation that the relevant person is reasonably able to give.

(15) The Preliminary Investigation Committee may also consider any submissions made to it during its preliminary investigation by any person (including a complainant, a prescribed accountancy body or any member) if it determines that such submissions are relevant to the matters at issue. It is not possible, however, to guarantee the anonymity or the confidentiality of a submission received from any person, including a complainant who participates in a preliminary investigation.

(16) The Preliminary Investigation Committee shall complete its determination as expeditiously as is reasonably practicable and shall notify the Authority, the relevant prescribed accountancy body, and the member who is the subject of the investigation of the decision made by it. If considered appropriate and in accordance with law, the Preliminary Investigation Committee at its sole discretion may notify the complainant, if any, of such decision.

(17) Confidential information provided in confidence by a Preliminary Investigation Committee to any person, including a member or a prescribed accountancy body under these Regulations, and any confidential information submitted by any person to the Preliminary Investigation Committee under these Regulations, shall be treated as information the disclosure of which to any other party, save as herein provided, is governed by the provisions of section 31 of the Act.

5 Investigation Committee

(1) Where the Preliminary Investigation Committee notifies the Authority of its determination that:

(a) there is a prima facie case that a member has breached the standards of the prescribed accountancy body of which he or she is a member; and

(b) in its opinion, it is appropriate or in the public interest that there should be a full investigation by the Authority into such possible breach,

the Authority shall appoint an Investigation Committee to conduct a full investigation on behalf of the Authority.

(2) Where an application to the High Court under section 23(4) of the Act has occurred and where the relevant permission under section 23(4) has been given by the High Court,

(3) In appointing an Investigation Committee, the Authority shall be deemed to have delegated to that Investigation Committee such of its functions and powers under section 24 of the Act as are required by the Investigation Committee to conduct the full investigation for which these Regulations provide.

(4) The Investigation Committee shall issue a Notice to the member who was the subject of the determination of the Preliminary Investigation Committee under paragraph (1), or the decision of the High Court under section 23(4) as appropriate, setting out:

(a) a statement of the allegations against the member;

(b) formal notification of the Authority's decision to establish an Investigation Committee, or the decision of the High Court under section 23(4) of the Act as appropriate, and the composition of the Committee;

(c) all documents and any other material that will be presented to the Investigation Committee, provided that the Investigation Committee will be entitled subsequently to give notice of further documents to the member;

(d) the Investigation Committee's powers of investigation to:

(i) require production to the Investigation Committee of all books or documents relating to the investigation that are in the relevant person's possession or control;

(ii) require a relevant person to attend before the Investigation Committee;

(iii) require a relevant person to give the Investigation Committee any other assistance in connection with the investigation that the relevant person is reasonably able to give; and conduct oral hearings;

(e) a statement to the effect that, within a reasonable period of time, as specified in the Notice, the member may make submissions in writing to the Investigation Committee, requesting an oral hearing; and

(f) a statement that the Investigation Committee shall conduct the investigation, and may conduct an oral hearing, irrespective of whether submissions referred to in subparagraph (e) above are made.

(5) The Investigation Committee shall notify the prescribed accountancy body (whose member is the member the subject of the full investigation) of the appointment of the Investigation Committee and of the initiation of the full investigation, and may forward such material to the prescribed accountancy body as the Investigation Committee considers necessary to enable it to make observations upon the investigation.

(6) An Investigation Committee may, if considered appropriate and in accordance with law, notify or direct the notification of any other relevant person, including a complainant, if any, of the appointment of the Investigation Committee and of the

initiation of the full investigation, and may forward such material to the complainant as is necessary to enable him or her to make observations upon the investigation.

(7) It is not possible to guarantee the anonymity of, or the confidentiality of observations received from, any person, including a complainant.

(8) An Investigation Committee shall conduct a full investigation into whether the member has breached the standards of the relevant prescribed accountancy body and, if the Investigation Committee makes a finding that the allegation is proved under Regulation 10(1), shall determine what sanctions, if any, to impose under these Regulations.

(9) Information provided in confidence by an Investigation Committee to any person, including a prescribed accountancy body or a member under these Regulations, and any confidential information submitted by any person to the Investigation Committee under these Regulations shall remain confidential and shall be treated as information the disclosure of which to any other party save as herein provided is governed by the provisions of section 31 of the Act.

6 Appointment of Legal Advisers

The Authority may appoint legal advisers to provide assistance to a Section 24 Committee, to bring evidence against the member the subject of the preliminary or full investigation before a Section 24 Committee and to act otherwise as considered appropriate. A legal adviser may also examine witnesses, participate in any oral hearing and perform any other functions necessary or as required for the conduct of the investigation.

7 Conduct of the full Investigation

(1) An Investigation Committee established under these Regulations shall consider any submissions made by the member concerned and may conduct such investigations as the Investigation Committee considers appropriate before issuing its decision. Such investigations shall be conducted in accordance with rules of fair procedure and natural and constitutional justice.

(2) An Investigation Committee may also consider any submissions made to it during the full investigation by any other person (including a complainant and a prescribed accountancy body) if it determines that such submissions are relevant to the matters at issue. It is not possible, however, to guarantee the anonymity of, or the confidentiality of a submission received from, any person, including a complainant who participates in a full investigation.

(3) A member may submit any statement or information in answer to the allegation(s) within the time provided by the Investigation Committee, which shall be reasonable under the circumstances.

(4) An Investigation Committee may require any relevant person to do one or more of the following:—

(a) produce to the Investigation Committee all books or documents relating to the investigation that are in the relevant person's possession or control;

(b) attend before the Investigation Committee; and

(c) give the Investigation Committee any other assistance in connection with the investigation that the relevant person is reasonably able to give.

(5) An Investigation Committee may for the purposes of exercising its functions under these Regulations conduct an oral hearing.

(6) The Investigation Committee may, for the purposes of an investigation, and whether in the context of an oral hearing or otherwise:

(a) examine on oath, either by word of mouth or on written interrogatories, a relevant person;

(b) administer oaths for the purposes of the examination; and

(c) record in writing, the answers of a person so examined and require that person to sign them.

(7) An Investigation Committee may take into account any relevant information, whether or not such evidence would be admissible in a court. The strict rules of evidence do not apply to the full investigation, although the Investigation Committee will employ fair procedures.

(8) Any information produced or answer given by a member of a prescribed accountancy body in compliance with a requirement under these Regulations may be used in evidence against the member in any proceedings whatsoever, save proceedings for an offence (other than perjury in respect of such an answer).

(9) Nothing in these Regulations:

(a) compels the disclosure by any person of any information that the person would be entitled to refuse to produce on the grounds of legal professional privilege, or

(b) authorises the inspection or copying of any document containing such information that is in the person's possession.

(10) The production of any books or documents under these Regulations by a person who claims a lien on the books or documents does not prejudice the lien.

8 Oral Hearings

(1) As provided for by section 28(1) of the Act, the Investigation Committee may conduct an oral hearing at its own behest or upon the reasonable request of the member that is the subject of the investigation if it considers that an oral hearing is necessary and appropriate in order to conduct the investigation.

(2) Members of the public shall be admitted to oral hearings, provided however that—

(a) an Investigation Committee may, at its sole discretion, exclude the public from all or part of a hearing to the extent it considers it necessary, for example, where, in the opinion of the Investigation Committee, the circumstances are such that holding an oral hearing, or part thereof, in public would prejudice the interests of justice or adversely affect to an undue extent the rights of a third party, and

(b) an Investigation Committee shall in any event exclude the public from all or part of a hearing where, in the opinion of the Investigation Committee, the admission of the public would lead to the disclosure to the public of information falling within the scope of section 31(1) of the Act.

(3) Any member of an Investigation Committee who is absent during an oral hearing shall not take part in the deliberations on, and the making of, the decision of the Investigation Committee.

(4) Oral hearings shall be conducted in accordance with rules of fair procedure and natural and constitutional justice. Without prejudice to the generality of that provision, where an oral hearing is taking place, the Investigation Committee will, save as may be appropriate, permit the member concerned:

(a) to be legally represented;

(b) to call and to give evidence;

(c) to present information and submissions in his or her behalf; and

(d) to cross-examine witnesses

during the oral hearing.

(5) Subject to Section 31 of the Act, an Investigation Committee may, at its sole discretion, permit any other person with an interest in the proceedings (including a complainant and a prescribed accountancy body) to participate in an oral hearing and to present relevant information and submissions on his or her behalf.

9 Standard of Proof

The standard of proof on which an Investigation Committee shall make its findings is on the balance of probabilities.

10 Decision of the Authority

(1) An Investigation Committee shall, in respect of each alleged breach of a standard of a prescribed accountancy body, make a finding either that the allegation is proved or that the allegation is not proved.

(2) Where the Investigation Committee makes a finding that an allegation is proved it will make a decision as to:

(a) which, if any, of the sanctions set out in Regulation 11(1) shall apply; and

(b) the amount (if any) that the member is liable to pay to the Authority towards its costs in investigating and determining the case.

(3) An Investigation Committee shall issue its decision to the Authority when its decision is made, which shall occur as soon as is reasonably practicable from the date of the initiation of the full investigation, taking into account the circumstances of the case.

(4) An Investigation Committee's decision must provide the reasons underlying its decision, including any decision that there has not been a breach.

(5) An Investigation Committee's decision shall set out the sanctions to be imposed and the reasons underlying the imposition of such sanctions and the amount (if any) that the member is liable to pay to the Authority towards its costs in investigating and determining the case.

(6) The decision of the Investigation Committee issued to the Authority under paragraph (3) shall be the decision of the Authority.

(7) Where an Investigation Committee notifies the Authority of a finding that an allegation has been proved, the Authority shall—

(a) issue the member and the prescribed accountancy body of which the member is a member and any other relevant person as may be determined by the Authority with a copy of the findings of the Investigation Committee, including the decision of the Investigation Committee as to the imposition of sanctions, if any, and the amount that the member is liable to pay to the Authority under section 24(7)(a) or (b) of the Act, if any;

(b) advise the member of the Authority's obligation to seek and obtain High Court approval for decisions to require the payment of an amount under section 24(7)(a) or (b) of the Act;

(c) advise the affected member of the right of appeal to the High Court under section 24(8) of the Act and the time limits for making such an appeal; and

(d) advise the affected member that the Authority may, in accordance with the provisions of section 31(3)(a) of the Act, publish details of the decision.

(8) Where the Investigation Committee notifies the Authority of a finding that an allegation has not been proved, the Authority shall issue the relevant prescribed accountancy body and the member concerned with a statement to that effect.

11 Sanctions

(1) In the case of a finding that an allegation has been proved, the Investigation Committee may impose on the member any sanction to which the member is liable under the approved constitution and bye-laws of the prescribed accountancy body (including a monetary sanction). The Investigation Committee shall not impose a sanction on a member unless the relevant prescribed accountancy body could, if finding the member guilty of the breach in question, have imposed that sanction upon him. In addition, the member is liable to pay the amount specified by the Authority towards its costs in investigating and determining the case.

(2) In determining the level of sanctions to apply, the Investigation Committee will have regard to all of the circumstances of the matter, which may include, among other things, the following factors:

(a) whether the failure to comply with the standard(s) was deliberate, dishonest, reckless or negligent;

(b) the duration and frequency of the breach of standard; and

(c) the gravity and nature of the breach of standard.

(3) The Investigation Committee shall set out in its decision issued to the Authority under Regulation 10(3) the reasons underlying the imposition or non-imposition of sanctions and the level and type of any sanctions imposed.

12 When Decision takes effect

A decision of the Authority requiring the payment of an amount under Regulation 11(1) takes effect when such decision is confirmed by the Court either on appeal by the member under section 24(8) of the Act or on application by the Authority under section 29(6) of the Act.

13 Appeal

A member may appeal a decision of the Investigation Committee to the High Court within three months after the member has been notified by the Authority of the Investigation Committee's decision pursuant to Regulation 10(7).

14 Publication of decision

Subject to the provisions of section 31(3)(a) of the Act, the Authority may publish a decision made under these Regulations and the grounds on which the decision was made in any manner in which it sees fit after giving written notice of no less than 3 months to the member concerned of its intention to do so and in such manner as it thinks fit, provided that, in the event of the member exercising his or her right of appeal to the High Court, there shall be no such publication until after the conclusion of the appeal.

15 Settlement

(1) At any time prior to the conclusion of an investigation, the matter may be resolved by entering into a binding settlement agreement between the Authority and the member that is the subject of the investigation, whereby the Authority can make on consent a decision under section 24(7) of the Act.

(2) Any proposed settlement between the Authority and a member must be approved by parties who are duly authorised to sign on behalf of each party.

(3) Any proposed settlement must be approved by a majority of the members of the Authority. Directors of the Authority who served as members of any Section 24 Committee that conducted proceedings in the matter shall not take part in the decision of the Authority as to whether to approve a proposed settlement.

(4) The Authority may, in its absolute discretion but subject to section 31 of the Act, publish notice of any decision reached on foot of a settlement agreement and the terms thereof in summary form or in its entirety after giving written notice of no less than 3 months to the member or members concerned unless it determines that such publication would be contrary to the public interest or otherwise inappropriate.

16 Notices

(1) Where any document is required or authorised by or under these Regulations to be furnished to any person, unless otherwise expressly provided under a Regulation, such document shall be furnished by delivering it to that person or by sending it by registered post in an envelope addressed to that person at his or her last known place of business or residence in the State or, if the person is a member, at the last address last notified by him or her to the prescribed accountancy body to which he or she belongs.

(2) In the case of a member firm, subject to paragraphs (3) and (4) below, all notices and other communications required by these Regulations to be given or made to a member firm shall be delivered to the senior member/partner or equivalent in the case of a partnership, or to the managing director or equivalent in the case of a body corporate, at its present or last known principal place of business. If a member firm so requests in writing, all notices and communications directed to that member firm may thereafter be addressed to a partner designated by such member firm to receive them on behalf of the member firm.

(3) If a member firm ceases to be a member firm, discontinues its business or otherwise ceases to exist, the Preliminary Investigation Committee or the Investigation Committee may designate a partner or equivalent in the case of a partnership, or the managing director or equivalent in the case of a body corporate, to receive all notices or documents to be given to such member firm by the Authority (subject to prior notice to

all members who were partners at the material time in such member firm as far as is practical).

(4) If a member so requests in writing, all notices and communications directed to that member or member firm may thereafter be addressed to his or her legal adviser.

(5) Where a person to whom a document is required or authorised by these Regulations to be furnished is absent from the State, or his or her whereabouts are unknown and cannot be ascertained by reasonable enquiries, or where the document, having been sent by registered post in the manner specified in paragraphs (1) to (2) has been returned undelivered, the Authority or other applicant may make application to the Court for an order for substituted service of notice of the content of the document, by advertisement or otherwise, as may seem just.

17 Designation of an "authorised person" by a relevant person

(1) Where a relevant person is a member firm, body corporate or prescribed accountancy body and the relevant person has an obligation to:

(a) produce books or documents relating to the investigation that are in the relevant person's possession or control;

(b) attend before the Preliminary Investigation or Investigation Committee;

(c) give the Authority any other assistance in connection with the investigation that the relevant person is reasonably able to give;

(d) attend any oral hearing; or

(e) be examined under oath under Regulation 7(6);

that obligation shall be performed by an "authorised person", being either:

(i) a partner designated by such member firm,

(ii) a competent person designated by the body corporate, or

(iii) a competent person designated by the prescribed accountancy body.

(2) A designation of an "authorised person" does not limit the Authority's power to require any relevant person (including any person who is, or was, an officer, employee or agent of any member firm, body corporate or prescribed accountancy body) to comply with any of the obligations listed above pursuant to any other provision of the Act.

(3) If a member firm, body corporate or prescribed accountancy body fails to designate a partner or competent person as an "authorised person", the Section 24 Committee, as appropriate, may do so.

(4) Where a member firm, body corporate or prescribed accountancy body has a right to submit any statement or information or to make oral and written submissions and any other right as provided in the Regulations, that right may be exercised by an "authorised person".

(5) The partner or competent person designated as an "authorised person" under paragraph (1) shall be authorised and competent to exercise the functions of the designated partner or competent person and to have the power to bind the member firm, body corporate or prescribed accountancy body with respect to the rights exercised and obligations performed on behalf of the member firm, body corporate or prescribed accountancy body, as relevant.

(6) For the avoidance of doubt, anything said, done or omitted by:

(a) an employee of a member firm within the scope of his or her employment, actual or ostensible; or

(b) an agent of the member firm within the scope of his or her employment, actual or ostensible,

shall be taken as having been said, done or omitted by that member firm.

18 Deferral of Investigation

The investigation of the matter may, if the Preliminary Investigation or Investigation Committee so decides, be deferred, or where a Section 24 Committee's investigations have been commenced, suspended, if the relevant Committee decides that it is appropriate to do so, such as where, for example, criminal or civil proceedings concerning the matters under investigation are subsequently initiated or pending.

19 Transcripts and copies of evidence

(1) If so requested by any witness who has given oral evidence to it, the Investigation Committee may in its discretion provide that witness, at a charge, if any, to be determined by the Investigation Committee, with a transcript of his or her evidence.

(2) The Investigation Committee shall, at a charge, if any, to be determined by the Investigation Committee, provide a transcript of the proceedings and copies of any documentary evidence given before it, if so requested, to a member who is a party to the proceedings under these Regulations or their legal adviser.

20 Confidentiality of Information

(1) All information that has not otherwise come to the notice of members of the public and which was obtained in performing the functions or exercising the powers of the Authority is subject to the confidentiality provisions imposed by section 31(1) of the Act.

(2) All persons who are involved in the investigatory process under the provisions of these Regulations are persons to whom section 31(1) of the Act applies, a breach of which may constitute a criminal offence and/or result in possible civil liability.

(3) Confidential information provided to the member under these Regulations shall be treated as information the disclosure to any other party of which may be prohibited under section 31 of the Act.

(4) Notwithstanding paragraphs (1) to (3), nothing in these Regulations prohibits the disclosure of information by any person during the course of the investigation under these Regulations:

(a) at a public hearing;

(b) to his or her legal advisers for the purposes of obtaining advice in relation to the Investigation;

(c) if he is partner in or director of, or employed by, a member firm, to the partners in or directors of that firm;

(d) to any person to whom disclosure is necessary for the purpose of ensuring fair procedures, or for the purpose of obtaining evidence, information or assistance in connection with the investigation; or

(e) as otherwise required by these Regulations or by the law generally.

21 Payments

(1) Any decision that a sum be paid must be complied with within 30 days from the date the decision becomes effective (unless the Authority otherwise agrees).

(2) Where the Investigation Committee makes a decision imposing a financial penalty and/or costs against a member, such moneys shall be due from and paid by the member even if he or she ceased to be a member on or after the date of the issuance of notice of the Committee under these Regulations.

(3) Where the subject of the decision to pay a sum is a member firm, such moneys—

(a) shall be due from the member firm concerned; and/or

(b) shall be jointly and severally due from, and shall be paid by, those members who were partners in, members of, directors of or the proprietor of such member firm during any part of the time relevant to the adverse finding or thereafter, whether or not they were members or it was a member firm during any part of that time; and/or

(c) shall be so due from, and shall be paid by, the member firm and the persons referred to in Regulation 21(3)(b) even if it ceased to be a member firm or they ceased to be members on or after the date of the report of the Committee.

EXPLANATORY NOTE

(This note is not part of the Instrument and does not purport to be a legal interpretation).

These Regulations set out the procedures governing the conduct of investigations by the Irish Auditing and Accounting Supervisory Authority pursuant to section 24 of the Companies (Auditing and Accounting) Act 2003.

European Communities (Directive 2006/46/EC) Regulations 2009

SI 450/2009

I, MARY COUGHLAN, Minister for Enterprise, Trade and Employment, in exercise of the powers conferred on me by section 3 of the European Communities Act 1972 (No. 27 of 1972) and for the purpose of giving effect to Directive 2006/46/EC of the European Parliament and of the Council of 14 June 20061, hereby make the following regulations:

1. (1) These Regulations may be cited as the European Communities (Directive 2006/46/EC) Regulations 2009.

(2) The Companies Acts and these Regulations shall be read together as one.

2. (1) In these Regulations—

"Act of 1986" means the Companies (Amendment) Act 1986 (No. 25 of 1986);

"Act of 1990" means the Companies Act 1990 (No. 33 of 1990);

"annual accounts" has the meaning assigned to it by the Principal Act;

"company" has the meaning assigned to it by the Principal Act;

"consolidated balance sheet" means the balance sheet dealing with the state of the affairs of a parent undertaking and its subsidiary undertakings as a whole;

"Credit Institutions Regulations" means the European Communities (Credit Institutions: Accounts) Regulations 1992 (S.I. No. 294 of 1992);

"Directive" means Directive 2006/46/EC of the European Parliament and of the Council of 14 June 2006 (OJ No L 224, 16.8.2006, p.1)1;

"Fair Value Regulations" means the European Communities (Fair Value Accounting) Regulations 2004 (SI No 765 of 2004);

"IFRS group accounts" has the meaning assigned to it by the Principal Act;

"Insurance Undertakings Regulations" means the European Communities (Insurance Undertakings: Accounts) Regulations 1996 (S.I. No. 23 of 1996);

"parent undertaking" means a body corporate, a partnership or an unincorporated body of persons engaged for gain in the production, supply or distribution of goods, the provision of a service or the making or holding of investments which has one or more subsidiary undertakings;

"Principal Act" means the Companies Act 1963 (No. 33 of 1963);

"Regulations of 1992" means the European Communities (Companies: Group Accounts) Regulations 1992 (S.I. No. 201 of 1992);

"Regulations of 2005" means the European Communities (International Financial Reporting Standards and Miscellaneous Amendments) Regulations 2005 (S.I. No. 116 of 2005);

"subsidiary undertaking" is a subsidiary of a parent undertaking;

"undertaking" has the meaning assigned to it by the Principal Act.

(2) A word or expression that is used in these Regulations (including provisions inserted by these Regulations into the Principal Act, the Act of 1986, the Regulations of 1992, the Credit Institutions Regulations or the Insurance Undertakings Regulations) and is

also used in the Directive, Regulation (EC) No. 1606/2002 of the European Parliament and of the Council of 19 July 2002 (OJ No. L 243, 11.9.2002, p.1)2, the Fourth Council Directive 78/660/EEC of 25 July 1978 (OJ L 222, 14.8.1978, p.11)3 and the Seventh Council Directive 83/349/EEC of 13 June 1983 (OJ L 193, 18.7.1983, p.1)4 has, unless the contrary is indicated, the same meaning in these Regulations and those provisions as it has in the Directive, that Regulation and those Directives.

3. Part IIIA (inserted by the Fair Value Regulations) of the Schedule to the Act of 1986 is amended—

(a) in paragraph 22A(1) by inserting "and paragraph 22AA" after "of this paragraph",

(b) by inserting the following paragraph after paragraph 22A of that Part:

[...][a]

Amendments

a European Communities (Directive 2006/46/EC) Regulations 2009, reg 3(b) inserts new para 22AA into CA 1986, Sch, Pt IIIA.

4. Section 8 of the Act of 1986 is amended—

(a) in subsection (1)(a), by inserting ", subject to subsection (1A)," after "a private company",

(b) in subsection (1)(b), by inserting ", subject to subsection (1B)," after "a private company",

(c) by inserting the following subsections after subsection (1):

[...][a]

(d) by inserting the following subsection after subsection (12):

[...][b]

Amendments

a European Communities (Directive 2006/46/EC) Regulations 2009, reg 4(c) inserts new sub-s (1A) into CA 1986, s 8.

b European Communities (Directive 2006/46/EC) Regulations 2009, reg 4(d) inserts new sub-s (13) into CA 1986, s 8.

5. (1) Section 32 of the Companies (Amendment) (No. 2) Act 1999 (No. 30 of 1999) is amended—

(a) in subsection (3)(a)(v)(III) by deleting "or",

(b) in subsection (3)(a)(v)(IV) by substituting "paragraph 18 thereof, or" for "paragraph 18 thereof.",

(c) section (3)(a)(v), by inserting the following clause after clause (IV):

[...][a]

(d) by inserting the following subsection after subsection (8):

[...][b]

Amendments

a European Communities (Directive 2006/46/EC) Regulations 2009, reg 5(c) inserts new sub-s (V) into CA 1986, s 32(a)(v).

b European Communities (Directive 2006/46/EC) Regulations 2009, reg 5(d) inserts new sub-s (9) into CA 1986, s 32.

6. Part IV of the Schedule to the Act of 1986 is amended by inserting the following paragraphs after paragraph 36:

[...][a]

Amendments

a European Communities (Directive 2006/46/EC) Regulations 2009, reg 6 inserts new paras 36A and 36 in CA 1986, Sch, Pt IV.

7. (1) The notes on the consolidated accounts prepared in respect of a parent undertaking and its subsidiary undertakings shall set out information relating to—

(a) the nature and business purpose of any arrangement that is not included in the consolidated balance sheet, and the financial impact of such arrangement if the risks or benefits arising from the arrangement are material, and in so far as the disclosure of such risks or benefits is necessary for assessing the financial position, taken as a whole, of the parent undertaking and its subsidiary undertakings included in the consolidated balance sheet, and

(b) subject to paragraph (2), transactions entered into by—

(i) the parent undertaking, or

(ii) a subsidiary undertaking of that parent undertaking included in the consolidation,

with related parties, if the transactions are material and have not been concluded under normal market conditions and the information shall include the amounts of such transactions, the nature of the related party relationship and other information about the transactions which is necessary for an understanding of the financial position, taken as a whole, of the parent undertaking and its subsidiary undertakings included in the consolidation.

(2) A transaction referred to in paragraph (1)(b) does not include an intragroup transaction.

(3) Information provided pursuant to paragraph (1)(b) concerning individual transactions may be aggregated according to their nature except where separate information is necessary for an understanding of the effects of the related party transactions on the financial position, taken as a whole, of the parent undertaking and its subsidiary undertakings included in the consolidation.

8.(1) Where a parent undertaking which has its securities admitted to trading on a regulated market is preparing consolidated accounts the corporate governance statement included in the report by the directors of that undertaking under section 158 of the Principal Act shall contain, in addition to the information specified in that section, a description of the main features of the internal control and risk management systems of that parent undertaking and its subsidiary undertakings in relation to the process for preparing such consolidated accounts for the parent undertaking and its subsidiary undertakings.

(2) Where the consolidated annual report and the annual report are presented as a single report the description referred to in paragraph (1) shall be included in the section of the report by the directors referred to in paragraph (1) containing the corporate governance statement.

(3) Where a parent undertaking referred to in paragraph (1) produces a corporate governance statement in the form of a separate report published in conjunction with the annual report, in accordance with section 158 of the Principal Act, the description required by paragraph (1) shall form part of that separate report.

(4) In paragraph (4), "regulated market" has the meaning assigned to it by Directive 2004/39/EC.

9. Where a parent undertaking referred to in Regulation 9 produces a corporate governance statement under section 158 of the Principal Act, the auditors of the parent undertaking, when preparing a report required by section 193 of the Act of 1990 shall—

(a) provide an opinion as to whether the description of the main features of the internal control and risk management systems of the parent undertaking and its subsidiary undertakings, in relation to the process for preparing consolidated accounts, is consistent with their evaluation and testing of the relevant systems for the purposes of preparing such report on such group accounts, and

(b) consider whether, in their opinion, the description referred to in paragraph (a) is consistent with their evaluation and testing of the systems referred to in paragraph (a).

10. Part 2 of the Schedule to the Regulations of 1992 is amended in paragraph 16C(a) by inserting "or 22AA" after "(inserted by the European Communities (Fair Value Accounting) Regulations 2004)".

11. Section 149A (inserted by the Regulations of 2005) of the Principal Act is amended—

(a) in subsection (1)(b)(x), by substituting "subsidiary undertakings)," for "subsidiary undertakings), and",

(b) in subsection (1)(b)(xi) by substituting "(remuneration of auditors), and" for "(remuneration of auditors).", and

(c) in subsection (1)(b), by inserting the following subparagraph after subparagraph (xi):

[...][a]

Amendments

a European Communities (Directive 2006/46/EC) Regulations 2009, reg 11(c) inserts CA 1963, s 149A(1)(b)(xii).

12. Section 150B(2) (inserted by the Regulations of 2005) of the Principal Act is amended—

(a) in paragraph (j), by substituting "subsidiary undertakings)," for "subsidiary undertakings), and",

(b) in paragraph (k) by substituting "(remuneration of auditors), and" for "(remuneration of auditors).", and

(c) by inserting the following paragraph after paragraph (k):

[...][a]

Amendments

a European Communities (Directive 2006/46/EC) Regulations 2009, reg 12(c) inserts CA 1963, s 150B(2)(l).

13. Section 158 of the Principal Act is amended by inserting the following subsections after subsection (6B) (inserted by the Central Bank and Financial Services Authority of Ireland Act 2003):

[....][a]

Amendments

a European Communities (Directive 2006/46/EC) Regulations 2009, reg 13 inserts CA 1963, s 158(6C)–(6J).

14. The Credit Institutions Regulations are amended—

(a) in Regulation 5(1B)—

(i) in subparagraph (k), by substituting "remuneration), and" for "remuneration).", and

(ii) by inserting the following subparagraph after subparagraph (k):

[...][a]

(b) in Regulation 7(5)—

(i) in subparagraph (k), by substituting "remuneration), and" for "remuneration)." and

(ii) by inserting the following subparagraph after subparagraph (k):

[...][b]

Amendments

a European Communities (Directive 2006/46/EC) Regulations 2009, reg 14(a)(ii) inserts EC(CIA)R 1992, reg 5(1B)(l).

b European Communities (Directive 2006/46/EC) Regulations 2009, reg 14(b)(ii) inserts EC(CIA)R 1992, reg 7(5)(l).

15. The Credit Institutions Regulations are amended by inserting the following Regulation after Regulation 11:

[...][a]

Amendments

a European Communities (Directive 2006/46/EC) Regulations 2009, reg 15 inserts EC(CIA)R 1992, reg 11A.

16. Regulation 13 of the Credit Institutions Regulations is amended by inserting the following paragraph after paragraph (2):

[...][a]

Amendments

a European Communities (Directive 2006/46/EC) Regulations 2009, reg 16 inserts EC(CIA)R 1992, reg 13(3).

17. Paragraph 46A (inserted by the Fair Value Regulations) of Part I of the Schedule to the Credit Institutions Regulations is amended by inserting the following subparagraphs after subparagraph (4):

[...][a]

Amendments

a European Communities (Directive 2006/46/EC) Regulations 2009, reg 17 inserts EC(CIA)R 1992, Sch, Pt I, paras 46A(4A)–(4C).

18. Part I of the Schedule to the Credit Institutions Regulations is amended by inserting the following paragraphs after paragraph 66:

[...][a]

Amendments

a European Communities (Directive 2006/46/EC) Regulations 2009, reg 18 inserts EC(CIA)R 1992, Sch, Pt I, paras 66A–66C.

19. Part II of the Schedule to the Credit Institutions Regulations is amended by inserting the following paragraphs after paragraph 7:

[...][a]

Amendments

a European Communities (Directive 2006/46/EC) Regulations 2009, reg 19 inserts EC(CIA)R 1992, Sch, Pt II, paras 7A–7E.

20. Regulation 5(1B) of the Insurance Undertakings Regulations is amended—

(a) in subparagraph (i), by substituting "own shares)," for "own shares), and",

(b) in subparagraph (j), by substituting "auditor's remuneration), and" for "auditors' remuneration).", and

(c) by inserting the following subparagraph after subparagraph (j):

[...][a]

Amendments

a European Communities (Directive 2006/46/EC) Regulations 2009, reg 20(c) inserts EC(IUA)R 1996, reg 5(1B)(k)).

21. Regulation 10(5) of the Insurance Undertakings Regulations is amended by inserting the following subparagraph after subparagraph (j):

[...][a]

Amendments

a European Communities (Directive 2006/46/EC) Regulations 2009, reg 21 amends EC(IUA)R 1996, reg 10(5).

22. The Insurance Undertakings Regulations are amended by inserting the following Regulation after Regulation 14:

[...][a]

Amendments

a European Communities (Directive 2006/46/EC) Regulations 2009, reg 22 inserts EC(IUA)R 1996, reg 14A.

23. Regulation 16 of the Insurance Undertakings Regulations is amended by renumbering the existing provision as paragraph (1) and inserting the following paragraph after paragraph (1):

[...][a]

Amendments

a European Communities (Directive 2006/46/EC) Regulations 2009, reg 23 inserts EC(IUA)R 1996, reg 16(2).

24. Part III of the Schedule to the Insurance Undertakings Regulations is amended by inserting the following paragraphs after paragraph 19:

[...][a]

Amendments

a European Communities (Directive 2006/46/EC) Regulations 2009, reg 24 inserts EC(IUA)R 1996, Sch, Pt III, paras 19A and 19B.

25. Chapter 3 of Part IV of the Schedule to the Insurance Undertakings Regulations is amended by inserting the following paragraphs after paragraph 36:

[...][a]

Amendments

a European Communities (Directive 2006/46/EC) Regulations 2009, reg 24 inserts EC(IUA)R 1996, Sch, Pt IV, paras 37–41.

26. (1) A person who contravenes Regulation 7, 8 or 9 is guilty of an offence and liable—

(a) on summary conviction to a fine of \5,000 or 3 months imprisonment or both, or

(b) on conviction on indictment, to a fine of \50,000 or imprisonment for a term not exceeding 3 years or both.

(2) Where an offence under these Regulations is committed by a body corporate and is proved to have been so committed with the consent or connivance of, or to be attributable to any neglect on the part of, any person, being a director, manager, secretary or other officer of the body corporate, or a person who was purporting to act in any such capacity, that person shall be guilty of an offence and shall be liable to be proceeded against and punished as if he or she were guilty of the first-mentioned offence.

(3) If the affairs of a body corporate are managed by its members, paragraph (2) shall apply in relation to the acts and defaults of a member in connection with the functions of management as if the member is a director or manager of the body corporate.

GIVEN under my Official Seal, 18 November 2009.

MARY COUGHLAN,

Minister for Enterprise, Trade and Employment.

EXPLANATORY NOTE

(*This note is not part of the Instrument and does not purport to be a legal interpretation*)

These Regulations give effect to Directive 2006/46/EC of the European Parliament and of the Council, of 14 June 2006 amending Council Directives 78/660/EEC on the annual accounts of certain types of companies, 83/349/EEC on consolidated accounts, 86/635/EEC on the annual accounts and consolidated accounts of banks and other financial institutions and 91/674/EEC on the annual accounts and consolidated accounts of insurance undertakings.

Division C: European Legislation

Commission Regulation (EC) No 809/2004

of 29 April 2004

implementing Directive 2003/71/EC of the European Parliament and of the Council as regards information contained in prospectuses as well as the format, incorporation by reference and publication of such prospectuses and dissemination of advertisements

(Text with EEA relevance)

Notes

This Regulation is directly applicable in all EU member states. It specifies the specific 'tick-the-box' information which is required to be included in a prospectus. These 'tick-the-box' requirements vary, depending on whether the securities offered are equity or debt securities. These requirements should, however, be read in the light of the overarching requirement of the Prospectus Directive, Art 5.1, which states:

> '... the prospectus shall contain all information which, according to the particular nature of the issuer and of the securities offered to the public or admitted to trading on a regulated market, is necessary to enable investors to make an informed assessment of the assets and liabilities, financial position, profit and losses, and prospects of the issuer and of any guarantor, and of the rights attaching to such securities. This information shall be presented in an easily analysable and comprehensible form.'

Article 5 is transposed into Irish law by reg 19 of SI 324/2005.

THE COMMISSION OF THE EUROPEAN COMMUNITIES,

Having regard to the Treaty establishing the European Community,

Having regard to Directive 2003/71/EC of the European Parliament and the Council of 4 November 2003 on the prospectus to be published when securities are offered to the public or admitted to trading and amending Directive 2001/34/EC (OJ L 345, 31.12.2003, p. 64), and in particular Article 5(5), Article 7, Article 10(4), Article 11(3), Article 14(8) and Article 15(7) thereof,

After consulting the Committee of European Securities Regulators (CESR) (CESR was established by Commission Decision 2001/527/EC (OJ L 191, 13.7.2001, p. 43) for technical advice,

Whereas:

(1) Directive 2003/71/EC lays down principles to be observed when drawing up prospectuses. These principles need to be supplemented as far as the information to be given therein, the format and aspects of publication, the information to be incorporated by reference in a prospectus and dissemination of advertisements are concerned.

(2) Depending on the type of issuer and securities involved, a typology of minimum information requirements should be established corresponding to those schedules that are in practice most frequently applied. The schedules should be based on the information items required in the IOSCO 'Disclosure Standards for cross-border offering and initial listings' (part I) and on the

existing schedules of Directive 2001/34/EC of the European Parliament and of the Council of 28 May on the admission of securities to official stock exchange listing and on information to be published on those securities (OJ L 184, 6.7.2001, p. 1. Directive as last amended by Directive 2003/71/EC).

(3) Information given by the issuer, the offeror or the person asking for admission to trading on a regulated market, according to this Regulation, should be subject to European Union provisions relating to data protection.

(4) Care should be taken that, in those cases where a prospectus is composed of separate documents, duplication of information is avoided; to this end separate detailed schedules for the registration document and for the securities note, adapted to the particular type of issuer and the securities concerned, should be laid down in order to cover each type of security.

(5) The issuer, the offeror or the person asking for admission to trading on a regulated market are entitled to include in a prospectus or base prospectus additional information going beyond the information items provided for in the schedules and building blocks. Any additional information provided should be appropriate to the type of securities or the nature of the issuer involved.

(6) In most cases, given the variety of issuers, the types of securities, the involvement or not of a third party as a guarantor, whether or not there is a listing etc, one single schedule will not give the appropriate information for an investor to make his investment decision. Therefore the combination of various schedules should be possible. A non exhaustive table of combinations, providing for different possible combinations of schedules and 'building blocks' for most of the different type of securities, should be set up in order to assist issuers when drafting their prospectus.

(7) The share registration document schedule should be applicable to shares and other transferable securities equivalent to shares but also to other securities giving access to the capital of the issuer by way of conversion or exchange. In the latter case this schedule should not be used where the underlying shares to be delivered have already been issued before the issuance of the securities giving access to the capital of the issuer; however this schedule should be used where the underlying shares to be delivered have already been issued but are not yet admitted to trading on a regulated market.

(8) Voluntary disclosure of profit forecasts in a share registration document should be presented in a consistent and comparable manner and accompanied by a statement prepared by independent accountants or auditors. This information should not be confused with the disclosure of known trends or other factual data with material impact on the issuers' prospects. Moreover, they should provide an explanation of any changes in disclosure policy relating to profit forecasts when supplementing a prospectus or drafting a new prospectus.

(9) Pro forma financial information is needed in case of significant gross change, i. e. a variation of more than 25 % relative to one or more indicators of the size of the issuer's business, in the situation of an issuer due to a particular transaction, with the exception of those situations where merger accounting is required.

(10) The schedule for the share securities note should be applicable to any class of share since it considers information regarding a description of the rights attached to the securities and the procedure for the exercise of any rights attached to the securities.

(11) Some debt securities such as structured bonds incorporate certain elements of a derivative security, therefore additional disclosure requirements related to the derivative component in the interest payment should be included in the securities note schedule for debt securities.

(12) The additional 'building block' related to guarantee should apply to any obligation in relation to any kind of security.

(13) The asset backed securities registration document should not apply to mortgage bonds as provided for in Article 5(4)(b) of Directive 2003/71/EC and other covered bonds. The same should apply for the asset backed securities additional 'building block' that has to be combined with the securities note for debt securities.

(14) Wholesale investors should be able to make their investment decision on other elements than those taken into consideration by retail investors. Therefore a differentiated content of prospectus is necessary for debt and derivative securities aimed at those investors who purchase debt or derivative securities with a denomination per unit of at least EUR 50,000 or a denomination in another currency provided that the value of such minimum denomination when converted to EURO amounts to at least EURO 50,000.

(15) In the context of depository receipts, emphasis should be put on the issuer of the underlying shares and not on the issuer of the depository receipt. Where there is legal recourse to the depository over and above a breach of its fiduciary or agency duties, the risk factors section in the prospectus should contain full information on this fact and on the circumstances of such recourse. Where a prospectus is drafted as a tripartite document (i.e. registration document, securities note and summary), the registration document should be limited to the information on the depository.

(16) The banks registration document schedule should be applicable to banks from third countries which do not fall under the definition of credit institution provided for in Article 1(1)(a) of Directive 2000/12/EC of the European Parliament and of the Council of 20 March 2000 relating to the taking up and pursuit of the business of credit institutions (OJ L 126, 26.5.2000, p. 1. Directive as last amended by the 2003 Act of Accession) but have their registered office in a state which is a member of the OECD.

(17) If a special purpose vehicle issues debt and derivative securities guaranteed by a bank, it should not use the banks registration document schedule.

(18) The schedule 'securities note for derivative securities' should be applicable to securities which are not covered by the other schedules and building blocks. The scope of this schedule is determined by reference to the other two generic categories of shares and debt securities. In order to provide a clear and comprehensive explanation to help investors understand how the value of their investment is affected by the value of the underlying, issuers should be able to use appropriate examples on a voluntary basis. For instance, for

some complex derivatives securities, examples might be the most effective way to explain the nature of those securities.

(19) The additional information 'building block' on the underlying share for certain equity securities should be added to the securities note for debt securities or substitute the item referring to 'information required in respect of the underlying' of the schedule securities note for derivative securities, depending on the characteristics of the securities being issued.

(20) Member States and their regional or local authorities are outside the scope of Directive 2003/71/EC. However, they may choose to produce a prospectus in accordance with this Directive. Third country sovereign issuers and their regional or local authorities are not outside the scope of Directive 2003/71/EC and are obliged to produce a prospectus if they wish to make a public offer of securities in the Community or wish their securities to be admitted to trading on a regulated market. For those cases, particular schedules should be used for the securities issued by States, their regional and local authorities and by public international bodies.

(21) A base prospectus and its final terms should contain the same information as a prospectus. All the general principles applicable to a prospectus are applicable also to the final terms. Nevertheless, where the final terms are not included in the base prospectus they do not have to be approved by the competent authority.

(22) For some categories of issuers the competent authority should be entitled to require adapted information going beyond the information items included in the schedules and building blocks because of the particular nature of the activities carried out by those issuers. A precise and restrictive list of issuers for which adapted information may be required is necessary. The adapted information requirements for each category of issuers included in this list should be appropriate and proportionate to the type of business involved. The Committee of European Securities Regulators could actively try to reach convergence on these information requirements within the Community. Inclusion of new categories in the list should be restricted to those cases where this can be duly justified.

(23) In the case of completely new types of securities which cannot be covered by the existing schedules or any of their combinations, the issuer should still have the possibility to apply for approval for a prospectus. In those cases he should be able to discuss the content of the information to be provided with the competent authority. The prospectus approved by the competent authority under those circumstances should benefit from the single passport established in Directive 2003/71/EC. The competent authority should always try to find similarities and make use as much as possible of existing schedules. Any additional information requirements should be proportionate and appropriate to the type of securities involved.

(24) Certain information items required in the schedules and building blocks or equivalent information items are not relevant to a particular security and thus may be inapplicable in some specific cases; in those cases the issuer should have the possibility to omit this information.

(25) The enhanced flexibility in the articulation of the base prospectus with its final terms compared to a single issue prospectus should not hamper the easy access to material information for investors.

(26) With respect to base prospectuses, it should be set out in an easily identifiable manner which kind of information will have to be included as final terms. This requirement should be able to be satisfied in a number of different ways, for example, if the base prospectus contains blanks for any information to be inserted in the final terms or if the base prospectus contains a list of the missing information.

(27) Where a single document includes more than one base prospectus and each base prospectus would require approval by a different home competent authority, the respective competent authorities should act in cooperation and, where appropriate, transfer the approval of the prospectus in accordance with Article 13(5) of Directive 2003/71/EC, so that the approval by only one competent authority is sufficient for the entire document.

(28) Historical financial information as required in the schedules should principally be presented in accordance with Regulation (EC) No 1606/2002 of the European Parliament and of the Council of 19 July 2002 on the application of international accounting standard (OJ L 243, 11.9.2002, p. 1.) or Member States' accounting standards. Specific requirements should, however, be laid down for third country issuers.

(29) For the purposes of publication of the document referred to in Article 10 of Directive 2003/71/EC, issuers should be allowed to choose the method of publication they consider adequate among those referred to in Article 14 of that Directive. In selecting the method of publication they should consider the objective of the document and that it should permit investors a fast and cost-efficient access to that information.

(30) The aim of incorporation by reference, as provided for in Article 11 of Directive 2003/71/EC, is to simplify and reduce the costs of drafting a prospectus; however this aim should not be achieved to the detriment of other interests the prospectus is meant to protect. For instance, the fact that the natural location of the information required is the prospectus, and that the information should be presented in an easily and comprehensible form, should also be considered. Particular attention should be granted to the language used for information incorporated by reference and its consistency with the prospectus itself. Information incorporated by reference may refer to historical data, however if this information is no more relevant due to material change, this should be clearly stated in the prospectus and the updated information should also be provided.

(31) Where a prospectus is published in electronic form, additional safety measures compared to traditional means of publication, using best practices available, are necessary in order to maintain the integrity of the information, to avoid manipulation or modification from unauthorised persons, to avoid altering its comprehensibility and to escape from possible adverse consequences from different approaches on offer of securities to the public in third countries.

(32) The newspaper chosen for the publication of a prospectus should have a wide area of distribution and a high circulation.

(33) A home Member State should be able to require publication of a notice stating how the prospectus has been made available and where it can be obtained by the public. Where a home Member State requires publication of notices in its legislation, the content of such a notice should be kept to the necessary items information to avoid duplication with the summary. These home Member States may also require that an additional notice in relation to the final terms of a base prospectus is to be published.

(34) In order to facilitate centralising useful information for investors a mention should be included in the list of approved prospectuses posted in the web-site of the competent authority of the home Member State, indicating how a prospectus has been published and where it can be obtained.

(35) Member States should ensure effective compliance of advertising rules concerning public offers and admission to trading on a regulated market. Proper co-ordination between competent authorities should be achieved in cross-border offerings or cross-border admission to trading.

(36) In view of the interval between the entry into force of Regulation (EC) No 1606/2002 and the production of certain of its effects, a number of transitional arrangements for historical financial information to be included in a prospectus should be provided for, in order to prevent excessive burden on issuers and enable them to adapt the way they prepare and present historical financial information within a reasonable period of time after the entry into force of Directive 2003/71/EC.

(37) The obligation to restate in a prospectus historical financial information according to Regulation (EC) N0 1606/2002 does not cover securities with a denomination per unit of at least EUR 50,000; consequently such transitional arrangements are not necessary for such securities.

(38) For reasons of coherence it is appropriate that this Regulation applies from the date of transposition of Directive 2003/71/EC.

(39) Whereas the measures provided for in this Regulation are in accordance with the opinion of the European Securities Committee,

HAS ADOPTED THIS REGULATION:

CHAPTER I
SUBJECT MATTER AND DEFINITIONS

Article 1
Subject matter

This Regulation lays down:

1. the format of prospectus referred to in Article 5 of Directive 2003/71/EC;
2. the minimum information requirements to be included in a prospectus provided for in Article 7 of Directive 2003/71/EC;
3. the method of publication referred to in Article 10 of Directive 2003/71/EC;

4. the modalities according to which information can be incorporated by reference in a prospectus provided for in Article 11 of Directive 2003/71/EC;
5. the publication methods of a prospectus in order to ensure that a prospectus is publicly available according to Article 14 of Directive 2003/71/EC;
6. the methods of dissemination of advertisements referred to in Article 15 of Directive 2003/71/EC.

Article 2
Definitions

For the purposes of this Regulation, the following definitions shall apply in addition to those laid down in Directive 2003/71/EC:

1. 'schedule' means a list of minimum information requirements adapted to the particular nature of the different types of issuers and/or the different securities involved;
2. 'building block' means a list of additional information requirements, not included in one of the schedules, to be added to one or more schedules, as the case may be, depending on the type of instrument and/or transaction for which a prospectus or base prospectus is drawn up;
3. 'risk factors' means a list of risks which are specific to the situation of the issuer and/or the securities and which are material for taking investment decisions;
4. 'special purpose vehicle' means an issuer whose objects and purposes are primarily the issue of securities;
5. 'asset backed securities' means securities which:
   (a) represent an interest in assets, including any rights intended to assure servicing, or the receipt or timeliness of receipts by holders of assets of amounts payable there under;
   or
   (b) are secured by assets and the terms of which provide for payments which relate to payments or reasonable projections of payments calculated by reference to identified or identifiable assets;
6. 'umbrella collective investment undertaking' means a collective investment undertaking invested in one or more collective investment undertakings, the asset of which is composed of separate class(es) or designation(s) of securities;
7. 'property collective investment undertaking' means a collective investment undertaking whose investment objective is the participation in the holding of property in the long term;
8. 'public international body' means a legal entity of public nature established by an international treaty between sovereign States and of which one or more Member States are members;
9. 'advertisement' means announcements:
   (a) relating to an specific offer to the public of securities or to an admission to trading on a regulated market;

and

(b) aiming to specifically promote the potential subscription or acquisition of securities.

10. 'profit forecast' means a form of words which expressly states or by implication indicates a figure or a minimum or maximum figure for the likely level of profits or losses for the current financial period and/or financial periods subsequent to that period, or contains data from which a calculation of such a figure for future profits or losses may be made, even if no particular figure is mentioned and the word 'profit' is not used.

11. 'profit estimate' means a profit forecast for a financial period which has expired and for which results have not yet been published.

12. 'regulated information' means all information which the issuer, or any person who has applied for the admission of securities to trading on a regulated market without the issuer's consent, is required to disclose under Directive 2001/34/EC or under Article 6 of Directive 2003/6/EC of the European Parliament and of the Council (OJ L 96, 12.4.2003, p. 16).

CHAPTER II
MINIMUM INFORMATION

Article 3
Minimum information to be included in a prospectus

A prospectus shall be drawn up by using one or a combination of the following schedules and building blocks set out in Articles 4 to 20, according to the combinations for various types of securities provided for in Article 21.

A prospectus shall contain the information items required in Annexes I to XVII depending on the type of issuer and securities involved, provided for in the schedules and building blocks set out in Articles 4 to 20. [Subject to Article 4a(1), a competent authority shall not request that a prospectus contain information items which are not included in Annexes I to XVII.][a]

In order to ensure conformity with the obligation referred to in Article 5 (1) of Directive 2003/71/EC, the competent authority of the home Member State, when approving a prospectus in accordance with Article 13 of that Directive, may require that the information provided by the issuer, the offeror or the person asking for admission to trading on a regulated market be completed, for each of the information items, on a case by case basis.

Amendments

a Inserted by Commission Regulation (EC) No 211/2007 of 27 February 2007 OJ L337 5.12.2006, p 17.

Article 4
Share registration document schedule

1 For the share registration document information shall be given in accordance with the schedule set out in Annex I.

2 The schedule set out in paragraph 1 shall apply to the following:

1. shares and other transferable securities equivalent to shares;
2. other securities which comply with the following conditions:
   (a) they can be converted or exchanged into shares or other transferable securities equivalent to shares, at the issuer's or at the investor's discretion, or on the basis of the conditions established a the moment of the issue, or give, in any other way, the possibility to acquire shares or other transferable securities equivalent to shares;
   and
   (b) provided that these shares or other transferable securities equivalent to shares are or will be issued by the issuer of the security and are not yet traded on a regulated market or an equivalent market outside the Community at the time of the approval of the prospectus covering the securities, and that the underlying shares or other transferable securities equivalent to shares can be delivered with physical settlement.

[Article 4a
Share registration document schedule in cases of complex financial history or significant financial commitment

1. Where the issuer of a security covered by Article 4(2) has a complex financial history, or has made a significant financial commitment, and in consequence the inclusion in the registration document of certain items of financial information relating to an entity other than the issuer is necessary in order to satisfy the obligation laid down in Article 5(1) of Directive 2003/71/EC, those items of financial information shall be deemed to relate to the issuer. The competent authority of the home Member State shall in such cases request that the issuer, the offeror or the person asking for admission to trading include those items of information in the registration document.

Those items of financial information may include pro forma information prepared in accordance with Annex II. In this context, where the issuer has made a significant financial commitment any such pro forma information shall illustrate the anticipated effects of the transaction that the issuer has agreed to undertake, and references in Annex II to 'the transaction' shall be read accordingly.

2. The competent authority shall base any request pursuant to paragraph 1 on the requirements set out in item 20.1 of Annex I as regards the content of financial information and the applicable accounting and auditing principles, subject to any modification which is appropriate in view of any of the following factors:

(a) the nature of the securities;

(b) the nature and range of information already included in the prospectus, and the existence of financial information relating to an entity other than the issuer in a form that might be included in a prospectus without modification;

(c) the facts of the case, including the economic substance of the transactions by which the issuer has acquired or disposed of its business undertaking or any part of it, and the specific nature of that undertaking;

(d) the ability of the issuer to obtain financial information relating to another entity with reasonable effort.

Where, in the individual case, the obligation laid down in Article 5(1) of Directive 2003/71/EC may be satisfied in more than one way, preference shall be given to the way that is the least costly or onerous.

3. Paragraph 1 is without prejudice to the responsibility under national law of any other person, including the persons referred to in Article 6(1) of Directive 2003/71/EC, for the information contained in the prospectus. In particular, those persons shall be responsible for the inclusion in the registration document of any items of information requested by the competent authority pursuant to paragraph 1.

4. For the purposes of paragraph 1, an issuer shall be treated as having a complex financial history if all of the following conditions apply:

(a) its entire business undertaking at the time that the prospectus is drawn up is not accurately represented in the historical financial information which it is required to provide under item 20.1 of Annex I;

(b) that inaccuracy will affect the ability of an investor to make an informed assessment as mentioned in Article 5(1) of Directive 2003/71/EC; and

(c) information relating to its business undertaking that is necessary for an investor to make such an assessment is included in financial information relating to another entity.

5. For the purposes of paragraph 1, an issuer shall be treated as having made a significant financial commitment if it has entered into a binding agreement to undertake a transaction which, on completion, is likely to give rise to a significant gross change.

In this context, the fact that an agreement makes completion of the transaction subject to conditions, including approval by a regulatory authority, shall not prevent that agreement from being treated as binding if it is reasonably certain that those conditions will be fulfilled.

In particular, an agreement shall be treated as binding where it makes the completion of the transaction conditional on the outcome of the offer of the securities that are the subject matter of the prospectus or, in the case of a proposed takeover, if the offer of securities that are the subject matter of the prospectus has the objective of funding that takeover.

6. For the purposes of paragraph 5 of this Article, and of item 20.2 of Annex I, a significant gross change means a variation of more than 25 %, relative to one or more indicators of the size of the issuer's business, in the situation of an issuer.][a]

Amendments

a Inserted by Commission Regulation (EC) No 211/2007 of 27 February 2007 OJ L337 5.12.2006, p 17.

Article 5

Pro forma financial information building block

For pro forma financial information, information shall be given in accordance with the building block set out in Annex II.

Pro forma financial information should be preceded by an introductory explanatory paragraph that states in clear terms the purpose of including this information in the prospectus.

Article 6

Share securities note schedule

1 For the share securities note information is necessary to be given in accordance with the schedule set out in Annex III.

2 The schedule shall apply to shares and other transferable securities equivalent to shares.

Article 7

Debt and derivative securities registration document schedule for securities with a denomination per unit of less than EUR 50,000

For the debt and derivative securities registration document concerning securities which are not covered in Article 4 with a denomination per unit of less than EUR 50,000 or, where there is no individual denomination, securities that can only be acquired on issue for less than EUR 50,000 per security, information shall be given in accordance with the schedule set out in Annex IV.

Article 8

Securities note schedule for debt securities with a denomination per unit of less than EUR 50,000

1 For the securities note for debt securities with a denomination per unit of less than EUR 50,000 information shall be given in accordance with the schedule set out in Annex V.

2 The schedule shall apply to debt where the issuer has an obligation arising on issue to pay the investor 100 % of the nominal value in addition to which there may be also an interest payment.

Article 9

Guarantees building block

For guarantees information shall be given in accordance with the building block set out in Annex VI.

Article 10
Asset backed securities registration document schedule

For the asset backed securities registration document information shall be given in accordance with the schedule set out in Annex VII.

Article 11
Asset backed securities building block

For the additional information building block to the securities note for asset backed securities information shall be given in accordance with the building block set out in Annex VIII.

Article 12
Debt and derivative securities registration document schedule for securities with a denomination per unit of at least EUR 50,000

For the debt and derivative securities registration document concerning securities which are not covered in Article 4 with a denomination per unit of at least EUR 50,000 or, where there is no individual denomination, securities that can only be acquired on issue for at least EUR 50,000 per security, information shall be given in accordance with the schedule set out in Annex IX.

Article 13
Depository receipts schedule

For depository receipts issued over shares information shall be given in accordance with the schedule set out in Annex X.

Article 14
Banks registration document schedule

1 For the banks registration document for debt and derivative securities and those securities which are not covered by Article 4 information shall be given in accordance with the schedule set out in Annex XI.

2 The schedule set out in paragraph 1 shall apply to credit institutions as defined in point (a) of Article 1(1) of Directive 2000/12/EC as well as to third country credit institutions which do not fall under that definition but have their registered office in a state which is a member of the OECD.
These entities may also use alternatively the registration document schedules provided for under in Articles 7 and 12.

Article 15
Securities note schedule for derivative securities

1 For the securities note for derivative securities information shall be given in accordance with the schedule set out in Annex XII.

2 The schedule shall apply to securities which are not in the scope of application of the other securities note schedules referred to in Articles 6, 8 and 16, including certain securities where the payment and/or delivery obligations are linked to an underlying.

Article 16

Securities note schedule for debt securities with a denomination per unit of at least EUR 50,000

1 For the securities note for debt securities with a denomination per unit of at least EUR 50,000 information shall be given in accordance with the schedule set out in Annex XIII.

2 The schedule shall apply to debt where the issuer has an obligation arising on issue to pay the investor 100 % of the nominal value in addition to which there may be also an interest payment.

Article 17

Additional information building block on the underlying share

1 For the additional information on the underlying share, the description of the underlying share shall be given in accordance with the building block set out in Annex XIV.

In addition, if the issuer of the underlying share is an entity belonging to the same group, the information required by the schedule referred to in Article 4 shall be given in respect of that issuer.

2 The additional information referred to in the first subparagraph of paragraph 1 shall only apply to those securities which comply with both of the following conditions:

1. they can be converted or exchanged into shares or other transferable securities equivalent to shares, at the issuer's or at the investor's discretion, or on the basis of the conditions established a the moment of the issue or give, in any other way, the possibility to acquire shares or other transferable securities equivalent to shares;

   and

2. provided that these shares or other transferable securities equivalent to shares are or will be issued by the issuer of the security or by an entity belonging to the group of that issuer and are not yet traded on a regulated market or an equivalent market outside the Community at the time of the approval of the prospectus covering the securities, and that the underlying shares or other transferable securities equivalent to shares can be delivered with physical settlement.

Article 18

Registration document schedule for collective investment undertakings of the closed-end type

1 In addition to the information required pursuant to items 1, 2, 3, 4, 5.1, 7, 9.1, 9.2.1, 9.2.3, 10.4, 13, 14, 15, 16, 17.2, 18, 19, 20, 21, 22, 23, 24, 25 of Annex I, for the registration document for securities issued by collective investment undertakings of the closed-end type information shall be given in accordance with the schedule set out in Annex XV.

2 The schedule shall apply to collective investment undertakings of the closed-end type holding a portfolio of assets on behalf of investors that:

1. are recognised by national law in the Member State in which it is incorporated as a collective investment undertaking of the closed end type;

   or

2. do not take or seek to take legal or management control of any of the issuers of its underlying investments. In such a case, legal control and/or participation in the administrative, management or supervisory bodies of the underlying issuer(s) may be taken where such action is incidental to the primary investment objective, necessary for the protection of shareholders and only in circumstances where the collective investment undertaking will not exercise significant management control over the operations of that underlying issuer(s).

Article 19

Registration document schedule for Member States, third countries and their regional and local authorities

1 For the registration document for securities issued by Member States, third countries and their regional and local authorities information shall be given in accordance with the schedule set out in Annex XVI.

2 The schedule shall apply to all types of securities issued by Member States, third countries and their regional and local authorities.

Article 20

Registration document schedule for public international bodies and for issuers of debt securities guaranteed by a member state of the OECD

1 For the registration document for securities issued by public inter-national bodies and for securities unconditionally and irrevocably guaranteed, on the basis of national legislation, by a state which is member of the OECD information shall be given in accordance with the schedule set out in Annex XVII.

2 The schedule shall apply to:

- all types of securities issued by public international bodies,
- to debt securities unconditionally and irrevocably guaranteed, on the basis of national legislation, by a state which is member of the OECD.

Article 21

Combination of schedules and building blocks

1 The use of the combinations provided for in the table set out in Annex XVIII shall be mandatory when drawing up prospectuses for the types of securities to which those combinations correspond according to this table.

However, for securities not covered by those combinations further combinations may be used.

2 The most comprehensive and stringent registration document schedule, i.e. the most demanding schedule in term of number of information items and the extent of the information included in them, may always be used to issue securities for which a less

comprehensive and stringent registration document schedule is provided for, according to the following ranking of schedules:

1. share registration document schedule;
2. debt and derivative securities registration document schedule for securities with a denomination per unit of less than EUR 50,000;
3. debt and derivative securities registration document schedule for securities with a denomination per unit at least EUR 50,000.

Article 22

Minimum information to be included in a base prospectus and its related final terms

1 A base prospectus shall be drawn up by using one or a combination of schedules and building blocks provided for in Articles 4 to 20

according to the combinations for various types of securities set out in Annex XVIII.

A base prospectus shall contain the information items required in Annexes I to XVII depending on the type of issuer and securities involved, provided for in the schedules and building blocks set out in Articles 4 to 20. A competent authority shall not request that a base prospectus contains information items which are not included in Annexes I to XVII.

In order to ensure conformity with the obligation referred to in Article 5 (1) of Directive 2003/71/EC, the competent authority of the home Member State, when approving a base prospectus in accordance with Article 13 of that Directive, may require that the information provided by the issuer, the offeror or the person asking for admission to trading on a regulated market be completed, for each of the information items, on a case by case basis.

2 The issuer, the offeror or the person asking for admission to trading on a regulated market may omit information items which are not known when the base prospectus is approved and which can only be determined at the time of the individual issue.

3 The use of the combinations provided for in the table in Annex XVIII shall be mandatory when drawing up base prospectuses for the types of securities to which those combinations correspond according to this table.

However, for securities not covered by those combinations further combinations may be used.

4 The final terms attached to a base prospectus shall only contain the information items from the various securities note schedules according to which the base prospectus is drawn up.

5 In addition to the information items set out in the schedules and building blocks referred to in Articles 4 to 20 the following information shall be included in a base prospectus:

1. indication on the information that will be included in the final terms;
2. the method of publication of the final terms; if the issuer is not in a position to determine, at the time of the approval of the prospectus, the method of publication of the final terms, an indication of how the

public will be informed about which method will be used for the publication of the final terms;

3. in the case of issues of non equity securities according to point (a) of Article 5(4) of Directive 2003/71/EC, a general description of the programme.

6 Only the following categories of securities may be contained in a base prospectus and its related final terms covering issues of various types of securities:

1. asset backed securities;
2. warrants falling under Article 17;
3. non-equity securities provided for under point (b) of Article 5(4) of Directive 2003/71/EC;
4. all other non-equity securities including warrants with the exception of those mentioned in (2).

In drawing up a base prospectus the issuer, the offeror or the person asking for admission to trading on a regulated market shall clearly segregate the specific information on each of the different securities included in these categories.

7 Where an event envisaged under Article 16(1) of Directive 2003/71/EC occurs between the time that the base prospectus has been approved and the final closing of the offer of each issue of securities under the base prospectus or, as the case may be, the time that trading on a regulated market of those securities begins, the issuer, the offeror or the person asking for admission to trading on a regulated market shall publish a supplement prior to the final closing of the offer or the admission of those securities to trading.

Article 23

Adaptations to the minimum information given in prospectuses and base prospectuses

1 Notwithstanding Articles 3 second paragraph and 22(1) second subparagraph, where the issuer's activities fall under one of the categories included in Annex XIX, the competent authority of the home Member State, taking into consideration the specific nature of the activities involved, may ask for adapted information, in addition to the information items included in the schedules and building blocks set out in Articles 4 to 20, including, where appropriate, a valuation or other expert's report on the assets of the issuer, in order to comply with the obligation referred to in Article 5(1) of Directive 2003/71/EC. The competent authority shall forthwith inform the Commission thereof.

In order to obtain the inclusion of a new category in Annex XIX a Member State shall notify its request to the Commission. The Commission shall update this list following the Committee procedure provided for in Article 24 of Directive 2003/71/EC.

2 By way of derogation of Articles 3 to 22, where an issuer, an offeror or a person asking for admission to trading on a regulated market applies for approval of a prospectus or a base prospectus for a security which is not the same but comparable to the various types of securities mentioned in the table of combinations set out in Annex XVIII, the issuer, the offeror or the person asking for admission to trading on a regulated market shall add the relevant information items from another securities note schedule provided for in Articles 4 to 20 to the main securities note schedule chosen. This addition shall be done

in accordance with the main characteristics of the securities being offered to the public or admitted to trading on a regulated market.

3 By way of derogation of Articles 3 to 22, where an issuer, an offeror or a person asking for admission to trading on a regulated market applies for approval of a prospectus or a base prospectus for a new type of security, the issuer, the offeror or the person asking for admission to trading on a regulated market shall notify a draft prospectus or base prospectus to the competent authority of the home Member State.

The competent authority shall decide, in consultation with the issuer, the offeror or the person asking for admission to trading on a regulated market, what information shall be included in the prospectus or base prospectus in order to comply with the obligation referred to in Article 5(1) of Directive 2003/71/EC. The competent authority shall forthwith inform the Commission thereof.

The derogation referred to in the first subparagraph shall only apply in case of a new type of security which has features completely different from the various types of securities mentioned in Annex XVIII, if the characteristics of this new security are such that a combination of the different information items referred to in the schedules and building blocks provided for in Articles 4 to 20 is not pertinent.

4 By way of derogation of Articles 3 to 22, in the cases where one of the information items required in one of the schedules or building blocks referred to in 4 to 20 or equivalent information is not pertinent to the issuer, to the offer or to the securities to which the prospectus relates, that information may be omitted.

Article 24
Content of the summary of prospectus and base prospectus

The issuer, the offeror or the person asking for admission to trading on a regulated market shall determine on its own the detailed content of the summary to the prospectus or base prospectus referred to in Article 5(2) of Directive 2003/71/EC.

CHAPTER III
FORMAT OF THE PROSPECTUS, BASE PROSPECTUS AND SUPPLEMENTS

Article 25
Format of the prospectus

1 Where an issuer, an offeror or a person asking for the admission to trading on a regulated market chooses, according to Article 5(3) of Directive 2003/71/EC to draw up a prospectus as a single document, the prospectus shall be composed of the following parts in the following order:

1. a clear and detailed table of contents;
2. the summary provided for in Article 5 (2) of Directive 2003/71/EC;
3. the risk factors linked to the issuer and the type of security covered by the issue;
4. the other information items included in the schedules and building blocks according to which the prospectus is drawn up.

2 Where an issuer, an offeror or a person asking for the admission to trading on a regulated market chooses, according to in Article 5(3) of Directive 2003/71/EC, to draw

up a prospectus composed of separate documents, the securities note and the registration document shall be each composed of the following parts in the following order:

1. a clear and detailed table of content;
2. as the case may be, the risk factors linked to the issuer and the type of security covered by the issue;
3. the other information items included in the schedules and building blocks according to which the prospectus is drawn up.

3 In the cases mentioned in paragraphs 1 and 2, the issuer, the offeror or the person asking for admission to trading on a regulated market shall be free in defining the order in the presentation of the required information items included in the schedules and building blocks according to which the prospectus is drawn up.

4 Where the order of the items does not coincide with the order of the information provided for in the schedules and building blocks according to which the prospectus is drawn up, the competent authority of the home Member State may ask the issuer, the offeror or the person asking for the admission to trading on a regulated market to provide a cross reference list for the purpose of checking the prospectus before its approval. Such list shall identify the pages where each item can be found in the prospectus.

5 Where the summary of a prospectus must be supplemented according to Article 16(1) of Directive 2003/71/EC, the issuer, the offeror or the person asking for admission to trading on a regulated market shall decide on a case-by-case basis whether to integrate the new information in the original summary by producing a new summary, or to produce a supplement to the summary.

If the new information is integrated in the original summary, the issuer, the offeror or the person asking for admission to trading on a regulated market shall ensure that investors can easily identify the changes, in particular by way of footnotes.

Article 26

Format of the base prospectus and its related final terms

1 Where an issuer, an offeror or a person asking for the admission to trading on a regulated market chooses, according to Article 5 (4) of Directive 2003/71/EC to draw up a base prospectus, the base prospectus shall be composed of the following parts in the following order:

1. a clear and detailed table of contents;
2. the summary provided for in Article 5 (2) of Directive 2003/71/EC;
3. the risk factors linked to the issuer and the type of security or securities covered by the issue(s);
4. the other information items included in the schedules and building blocks according to which the prospectus is drawn up.

2 Notwithstanding paragraph 1, the issuer, the offeror or the person asking for admission to trading on a regulated market shall be free in defining the order in the presentation of the required information items included in the schedules and building blocks according to which the prospectus is drawn up. The information on the different securities contained in the base prospectus shall be clearly segregated.

3 Where the order of the items does not coincide with the order of the information provided for by the schedules and building blocks according to which the prospectus is drawn up, the home competent authority may ask the issuer, the offeror or the person asking for admission to trading on a regulated market to provide a cross reference list for the purpose of checking the prospectus before its approval. Such list should identify the pages where each item can be found in the prospectus.

4 In case the issuer, the offeror or the person asking for admission to trading on a regulated market has previously filed a registration document for a particular type of security and, at a later stage, chooses to draw up base prospectus in conformity with the conditions provided for in points (a) and (b) of Article 5(4) of Directive 2003/71/ EC, the base prospectus shall contain:

1. the information contained in the previously or simultaneously filed and approved registration document which shall be incorporated by reference, following the conditions provided for in Article 28 of this Regulation;
2. the information which would otherwise be contained in the relevant securities note less the final terms where the final terms are not included in the base prospectus.

5 The final terms attached to a base prospectus shall be presented in the form of a separate document containing only the final terms or by inclusion of the final terms into the base prospectus.

In the case that the final terms are included in a separate document containing only the final terms, they may replicate some information which has been included in the approved base prospectus according to the relevant securities note schedule that has been used for drawing up the base prospectus. In this case the final terms have to be presented in such a way that they can be easily identified as such.

A clear and prominent statement shall be inserted in the final terms indicating that the full information on the issuer and on the offer is only available on the basis of the combination of base prospectus and final terms and where the base prospectus is available.

6 Where a base prospectus relates to different securities, the issuer, the offeror or the person asking for admission to trading on a regulated market shall include a single summary in the base prospectus for all securities. The information on the different securities contained in the summary, however, shall be clearly segregated.

7 Where the summary of a base prospectus must be supplemented according to Article 16(1) of Directive 2003/71/EC, the issuer, the offeror or the person asking for admission to trading on a regulated market shall decide on a case-by-case basis whether to integrate the new information in the original summary by producing a new summary, or by producing a supplement to the summary.

If the new information is integrated in the original summary of the base prospectus by producing a new summary, the issuer, the offeror or the person asking for admission to trading on a regulated market shall ensure that investors can easily identify the changes, in particular by way of footnotes.

8 Issuers, offerors or persons asking for admission to trading on a regulated market may compile in one single document two or more different base prospectuses.

CHAPTER IV
INFORMATION AND INCORPORATION BY REFERENCE

Article 27
Publication of the document referred to in Article 10(1) of Directive 2003/71/EC

1 The document referred to in Article 10(1) of Directive 2003/71/EC shall be made available to the public, at the choice of the issuer, the offeror or the person asking for admission to trading on a regulated market, through one of the means permitted under Article 14 of that Directive in the home Member State of the issuer.

2 The document shall be filed with the competent authority of the home Member State and made available to the public at the latest 20 working days after the publication of the annual financial statements in the home Member State.

3 The document shall include a statement indicating that some information may be out-of-date, if such is the case.

Article 28
Arrangements for incorporation by reference

1 Information may be incorporated by reference in a prospectus or base prospectus, notably if it is contained in one the following documents:

1. annual and interim financial information;
2. documents prepared on the occasion of a specific transaction such as a merger or de-merger;
3. audit reports and financial statements;
4. memorandum and articles of association;
5. earlier approved and published prospectuses and/or base prospectuses;
6. regulated information;
7. circulars to security holders.

2 The documents containing information that may be incorporated by reference in a prospectus or base prospectus or in the documents composing it shall be drawn up following the provisions of Article 19 of Directive 2003/71/EC.

3 If a document which may be incorporated by reference contains information which has undergone material changes, the prospectus or base prospectus shall clearly state such a circumstance and shall give the updated information.

4 The issuer, the offeror or the person asking for admission to trading on a regulated market may incorporate information in a prospectus or base prospectus by making reference only to certain parts of a document, provided that it states that the non-incorporated parts are either not relevant for the investor or covered elsewhere in the prospectus.

5 When incorporating information by reference, issuers, offerors or persons asking for admission to trading on a regulated market shall endeavour not to endanger investor protection in terms of comprehensibility and accessibility of the information.

CHAPTER V
PUBLICATION AND DISSEMINATION OF ADVERTISEMENTS

Article 29
Publication in electronic form

1 The publication of the prospectus or base prospectus in electronic form, either pursuant to points (c) (d) and (e) of Article 14(2) of Directive 2003/71/EC, or as an additional means of availability, shall be subject to the following requirements:

1. the prospectus or base prospectus shall be easily accessible when entering the web-site;
2. the file format shall be such that the prospectus or base prospectus cannot be modified;
3. the prospectus or base prospectus shall not contain hyper-links, with exception of links to the electronic addresses where information incorporated by reference is available;
4. the investors shall have the possibility of downloading and printing the prospectus or base prospectus.

The exception referred to in point 3 of the first subparagraph shall only be valid for documents incorporated by reference; those documents shall be available with easy and immediate technical arrangements.

2 If a prospectus or base prospectus for offer of securities to the public is made available on the web-sites of issuers and financial intermediaries or of regulated markets, these shall take measures, to avoid targeting residents in Members States or third countries where the offer of securities to the public does not take place, such as the insertion of a disclaimer as to who are the addressees of the offer.

Article 30
Publication in newspapers

1 In order to comply with point (a) of Article 14(2) of Directive 2003/71/EC the publication of a prospectus or a base prospectus shall be made in a general or financial information newspaper having national or supra-regional scope;

2 If the competent authority is of the opinion that the newspaper chosen for publication does not comply with the requirements set out in paragraph 1, it shall determine a newspaper whose circulation is deemed appropriate for this purpose taking into account, in particular, the geographic area, number of inhabitants and reading habits in each Member State.

Article 31
Publication of the notice

1 If a Member State makes use of the option, referred to in Article 14(3) of Directive 2003/71/EC, to require the publication of a notice stating how the prospectus or base prospectus has been made available and where it can be obtained by the public, that notice shall be published in a newspaper that fulfils the requirements for publication of prospectuses according to Article 30 of this Regulation.

If the notice relates to a prospectus or base prospectus published for the only purpose of admission of securities to trading on a regulated market where securities of the same class are already admitted, it may alternatively be inserted in the gazette of that regulated market, irrespective of whether that gazette is in paper copy or electronic form.

2 The notice shall be published no later than the next working day following the date of publication of the prospectus or base prospectus pursuant to Article 14(1) of Directive 2003/71/EC.

3 The notice shall contain the following information:

1. the identification of the issuer;
2. the type, class and amount of the securities to be offered and/or in respect of which admission to trading is sought, provided that these elements are known at the time of the publication of the notice;
3. the intended time schedule of the offer/admission to trading;
4. a statement that a prospectus or base prospectus has been published and where it can be obtained;
5. if the prospectus or base prospectus has been published in a printed form, the addresses where and the period of time during which such printed forms are available to the public;
6. if the prospectus or base prospectus has been published in electronic form, the addresses to which investors shall refer to ask for a paper copy;
7. the date of the notice.

Article 32

List of approved prospectuses

The list of the approved prospectuses and base prospectuses published on the web-site of the competent authority, in accordance with Article 14(4) of Directive 2003/71/EC, shall mention how such prospectuses have been made available and where they can be obtained.

Article 33

Publication of the final terms of base prospectuses

The publication method for final terms related to a base prospectus does not have to be the same as the one used for the base prospectus as long as the publication method used is one of the publication methods indicated in Article 14 of the Directive 2003/71/EC.

Article 34

Dissemination of advertisements

Advertisements related to an offer to the public of securities or to an admission to trading on a regulated market may be disseminated to the public by interested parties, such as issuer, offeror or person asking for admission, the financial intermediaries that participate in the placing and/or underwriting of securities, notably by one of the following means of communication:

1. addressed or unaddressed printed matter;
2. electronic message or advertisement received via a mobile telephone or pager;
3. standard letter;
4. Press advertising with or without order form;
5. catalogue;
6. telephone with or without human intervention;
7. seminars and presentations;
8. radio;
9. videophone;
10. videotext;
11. electronic mail;
12. facsimile machine (fax);
13. television;
14. notice;
15. bill;
16. poster;
17. brochure;
18. web posting including internet banners.

CHAPTER VI
TRANSITIONAL AND FINAL PROVISIONS

Article 35
Historical financial information

1 The obligation for Community issuers to restate in a prospectus historical financial information according to Regulation (EC) No 1606/2002, set out in Annex I item 20.1, Annex IV item 13.1, Annex VII items 8.2, Annex X items 20.1 and Annex XI item 11.1 shall not apply to any period earlier than 1 January 2004 or, where an issuer has securities admitted to trading on a regulated market on 1 July 2005, until the issuer has published its first consolidated annual accounts with accordance with Regulation (EC) No 1606/2002.

2 Where a Community issuer is subject to transitional national provisions adopted pursuant Article 9 of Regulation (EC) No 1606/2002, the obligation to restate in a prospectus historical financial information does not apply to any period earlier than 1 January 2006 or, where an issuer has securities admitted to trading on a regulated market on 1 July 2005, until the issuer has published its first consolidated annual accounts with accordance with Regulation (EC) No 1606/2002.

3 Until 1 January 2007 the obligation to restate in a prospectus historical financial information according to Regulation (EC) No 1606/2002, set out in Annex I item 20.1, Annex IV item 13.1, Annex VII items 8.2, Annex X items 20.1 and Annex XI item 11.1 shall not apply to issuers from third countries:

1. who have their securities admitted to trading on a regulated market on 1 January 2007;

and

2. who have presented and prepared historical financial information according to the national accounting standards of a third country.

In this case, historical financial information shall be accompanied with more detailed and/or additional information if the financial statements included in the prospectus do not give a true and fair view of the issuer's assets and liabilities, financial position and profit and loss.

4 Third country issuers having prepared historical financial information according to internationally accepted standards as referred to in Article 9 of Regulation (EC) No 1606/2002 may use that information in any prospectus filed before 1 January 2007, without being subject to restatement obligations.

[5. Subject to paragraph 5A, from 1 January 2007, third country issuers referred to in paragraphs 3 and 4 shall present their historical financial information in accordance with international accounting standards adopted under Regulation (EC) No 1606/2002 or a third country's national accounting standards equivalent to those standards. If such historical financial information is not in accordance with any such standards, it must be presented in the form of restated financial statements.

5A. Third country issuers are not subject to a requirement, under Annex I, item 20.1; Annex IV, item 13.1; Annex VII, item 8.2; Annex X, item 20.1 or Annex XI, item 11.1, to restate historical financial information or to a requirement under Annex VII, item 8.2. bis; Annex IX, item 11.1; or Annex X, item 20.1.bis, to provide a narrative description of the differences between international accounting standards adopted under Regulation (EC) No 1606/2002 and the accounting principles in accordance with which such information is drawn up, included in a prospectus filed with a competent authority before 1 January 2009, where one of the following conditions is met:

(a) the notes to the financial statements that form part of the historical financial information contain an explicit and unreserved statement that they comply with International Financial Reporting Standards in accordance with IAS 1 Presentation of Financial Statements;

(b) the historical financial information is prepared in accordance with the Generally Accepted Accounting Principles of either Canada, Japan or the United States of America;

(c) the historical financial information is prepared in accordance with the Generally Accepted Accounting Principles of a third country other than Canada, Japan or the United States of America, and the following conditions are satisfied:

(i) the third country authority responsible for the national accounting standards in question has made a public commitment, before the start of the financial year in which the prospectus is filed, to converge those standards with Inter-national Financial Reporting Standards;

(ii) that authority has established a work programme which demonstrates the intention to progress towards convergence before 31 December 2008; and

(iii) the issuer provides evidence that satisfies the competent authority that the conditions in (i) and (ii) are met.

5B. By 1 April 2007, the Commission shall present to the European Securities Committee and the European Parliament a first report on the work timetable of the authorities responsible for national accounting standards in the US, Japan and Canada for the convergence between IFRS and the Generally Accepted Accounting Principles of those countries.

The Commission shall closely monitor, and regularly inform the European Securities Committee and the European Parliament about the amount of progress in the convergence between International Financial Reporting Standards and the Generally Accepted Accounting Principles of Canada, Japan and the United States of America and of progress on the elimination of reconciliation requirements that apply to Community issuers in those countries. In particular, it shall inform the European Securities Committee and the European Parliament immediately if the process is not proceeding satisfactorily.

5C. The Commission shall also regularly inform the European Securities Committee and the European Parliament about the development of regulatory discussions and the amount of progress in the convergence between International Financial Reporting Standards and the Generally Accepted Accounting Principles of third countries mentioned in paragraph 5A(c) and progress towards the elimination of any reconciliation requirements. In particular, the Commission shall inform the European Securities Committee and the European Parliament immediately if the process is not proceeding satisfactorily.

5D. In addition to the obligations under paragraphs 5B and 5C, the Commission shall engage in and maintain a regular dialogue with third country authorities and, before 1 April 2008 at the latest, the Commission shall present a report to the European Securities Committee and to the European Parliament on the progress in convergence and progress towards the elimination of any reconciliation requirements that apply to Community issuers under the rules of a third country covered by paragraph 5A (b) or (c). The Commission may request or require another person to prepare the report.

5E. At least six months before 1 January 2009, the Commission shall ensure a determination of the equivalence of the Generally Accepted Accounting Principles of third countries, pursuant to a definition of equivalence and an equivalence mechanism that it will have established before 1 January 2008 in accordance with the procedure referred to in Article 24 of Directive 2003/71/EC. When complying with this paragraph, the Commission shall first consult the Committee of European Securities Regulators on the appropriateness of the definition of equivalence, the equivalence mechanism and the determination of the equivalence that is made.][a]

6. The provisions of this Article shall also apply to AnnexVI, item 3.

Amendments

a Inserted by Commission Regulation (EC) No 1787/2006 of 4 December 2006 OJ L337 5.12.2006, p 17.

Article 36
Entry into force

This Regulation shall enter into force in Member States on the twentieth day after its publication in the *Official Journal of the European Union*.

It shall apply from 1 July 2005.

This Regulation shall be binding in its entirety and directly applicable in all Member States.

ANNEXES

ANNEXES I TO XVII: SCHEDULES AND BUILDING BLOCKS

ANNEX XVIII: TABLE OF COMBINATIONS OF SCHEDULES AND BUILDING BLOCKS

ANNEX XIX: LIST OF SPECIALIST ISSUERS

ANNEX I

MINIMUM DISCLOSURE REQUIREMENTS FOR THE SHARE REGISTRATION DOCUMENT

(SCHEDULE)

1. Persons Responsible

1.1. All persons responsible for the information given in the Registration Document and, as the case may be, for certain parts of it, with, in the latter case, an indication of such parts. In the case of natural persons including members of the issuer's administrative, management or supervisory bodies indicate the name and function of the person; in case of legal persons indicate the name and registered office.

1.2. A declaration by those responsible for the registration document that, having taken all reasonable care to ensure that such is the case, the information contained in the registration document is, to the best of their knowledge, in accordance with the facts and contains no omission likely to affect its import. As the case may be, a declaration by those responsible for certain parts of the registration document that, having taken all reasonable care to ensure that such is the case, the information contained in the part of the registration document for which they are responsible is, to the best of their knowledge, in accordance with the facts and contains no omission likely to affect its import.

2. Statutory Auditors

2.1. Names and addresses of the issuer's auditors for the period covered by the historical financial information (together with their membership in a professional body).

2.2. If auditors have resigned, been removed or not been re-appointed during the period covered by the historical financial information, indicate details if material.

3. Selected Financial Information

3.1. Selected historical financial information regarding the issuer, presented for each financial year for the period covered by the historical financial information, and any subsequent interim financial period, in the same currency as the financial information.

The selected historical financial information must provide the key figures that summarise the financial condition of the issuer.

3.2. If selected financial information for interim periods is provided, comparative data from the same period in the prior financial year must also be provided, except that the requirement for comparative balance sheet information is satisfied by presenting the year end balance sheet information.

4. **Risk Factors**

Prominent disclosure of risk factors that are specific to the issuer or its industry in a section headed 'Risk Factors'.

5. **Information about the Issuer**

5.1 *History and development of the issuer*

5.1.1. The legal and commercial name of the issuer

5.1.2. The place of registration of the issuer and its registration number

5.1.3. The date of incorporation and the length of life of the issuer, except where indefinite

5.1.4. The domicile and legal form of the issuer, the legislation under which the issuer operates, its country of incorporation, and the address and telephone number of its registered office (or principal place of business if different from its registered office)

5.1.5. The important events in the development of the issuer's business.

5.2. *Investments*

5.2.1. A description, (including the amount) of the issuer's principal investments for each financial year for the period covered by the historical financial information up to the date of the registration document

5.2.2. A description of the issuer's principal investments that are in progress, including the geographic distribution of these investments (home and abroad) and the method of financing (internal or external)

5.2.3. Information concerning the issuer's principal future investments on which its management bodies have already made firm commitments.

6. **Business Overview**

6.1. *Principal Activities*

6.1.1. A description of, and key factors relating to, the nature of the issuer's operations and its principal activities, stating the main categories of products sold and/or services performed for each financial year for the period covered by the historical financial information; and

6.1.2. An indication of any significant new products and/or services that have been introduced and, to the extent the development of new products or services has been publicly disclosed, give the status of development.

6.2. *Principal Markets*

A description of the principal markets in which the issuer competes, including a breakdown of total revenues by category of activity and geographic market for each financial year for the period covered by the historical financial information.

6.3. Where the information given pursuant to items 6.1 and 6.2 has been influenced by exceptional factors, mention that fact.

6.4. If material to the issuer's business or profitability, a summary information regarding the extent to which the issuer is dependent, on patents or licences, industrial, commercial or financial contracts or new manufacturing processes.

6.5. The basis for any statements made by the issuer regarding its competitive position.

7. Organisational Structure

7.1. If the issuer is part of a group, a brief description of the group and the issuer's position within the group.

7.2. A list of the issuer's significant subsidiaries, including name, country of incorporation or residence, proportion of ownership interest and, if different, proportion of voting power held.

8. Property, Plants and Equipment

8.1. Information regarding any existing or planned material tangible fixed assets, including leased properties, and any major encumbrances thereon.

8.2. A description of any environmental issues that may affect the issuer's utilisation of the tangible fixed assets.

9. Operating and Financial Review

9.1. *Financial Condition*

To the extent not covered elsewhere in the registration document, provide a description of the issuer's financial condition, changes in financial condition and results of operations for each year and interim period, for which historical financial information is required, including the causes of material changes from year to year in the financial information to the extent necessary for an understanding of the issuer's business as a whole.

9.2. *Operating Results*

9.2.1. Information regarding significant factors, including unusual or infrequent events or new developments, materially affecting the issuer's income from operations, indicating the extent to which income was so affected.

9.2.2. Where the financial statements disclose material changes in net sales or revenues, provide a narrative discussion of the reasons for such changes.

9.2.3. Information regarding any governmental, economic, fiscal, monetary or political policies or factors that have materially affected, or could materially affect, directly or indirectly, the issuer's operations.

10. Capital Resources

10.1. Information concerning the issuer's capital resources (both short and long term);

10.2. An explanation of the sources and amounts of and a narrative description of the issuer's cash flows;

10.3. Information on the borrowing requirements and funding structure of the issuer;

10.4. Information regarding any restrictions on the use of capital resources that have materially affected, or could materially affect, directly or indirectly, the issuer's operations.

10.5. Information regarding the anticipated sources of funds needed to fulfil commitments referred to in items 5.2.3 and 8.1.

11. Research and Development, Patents And Licences

Where material, provide a description of the issuer's research and development policies for each financial year for the period covered by the historical financial information, including the amount spent on issuer-sponsored research and development activities.

12. Trend Information

12.1. The most significant recent trends in production, sales and inventory, and costs and selling prices since the end of the last financial year to the date of the registration document.

12.2. Information on any known trends, uncertainties, demands, commitments or events that are reasonably likely to have a material effect on the issuer's prospects for at least the current financial year.

13. Profit Forecasts or Estimates

If an issuer chooses to include a profit forecast or a profit estimate the registration document must contain the information set out in items 13.1 and 13.2:

13.1. A statement setting out the principal assumptions upon which the issuer has based its forecast, or estimate.

There must be a clear distinction between assumptions about factors which the members of the administrative, management or supervisory bodies can influence and assumptions about factors which are exclusively outside the influence of the members of the administrative, management or supervisory bodies; the assumptions must be readily understandable by investors, be specific and precise and not relate to the general accuracy of the estimates underlying the forecast.

13.2. A report prepared by independent accountants or auditors stating that in the opinion of the independent accountants or auditors the forecast or estimate has been properly compiled on the basis stated and that the basis of accounting used for the profit forecast or estimate is consistent with the accounting policies of the issuer.

13.3. The profit forecast or estimate must be prepared on a basis comparable with the historical financial information.

13.4. If a profit forecast in a prospectus has been published which is still outstanding, then provide a statement setting out whether or not that forecast is still correct as at the time of the registration document, and an explanation of why such forecast is no longer valid if that is the case.

14. Administrative, Management, and Supervisory Bodies and Senior Management

14.1. Names, business addresses and functions in the issuer of the following persons and an indication of the principal activities performed by them outside that issuer where these are significant with respect to that issuer:

(a) members of the administrative, management or supervisory bodies;

(b) partners with unlimited liability, in the case of a limited partnership with a share capital;

(c) founders, if the issuer has been established for fewer than five years; and

(d) any senior manager who is relevant to establishing that the issuer has the appropriate expertise and experience for the management of the issuer's business.

The nature of any family relationship between any of those persons.

In the case of each member of the administrative, management or supervisory bodies of the issuer and of each person mentioned in points (b) and (d) of the first subparagraph, details of that person's relevant management expertise and experience and the following information:

(a) the names of all companies and partnerships of which such person has been a member of the administrative, management or supervisory bodies or partner at any time in the previous five years, indicating whether or not the individual is still a member of the administrative, management or supervisory bodies or partner. It is not necessary to list all the subsidiaries of an issuer of which the person is also a member of the administrative, management or supervisory bodies;

(b) any convictions in relation to fraudulent offences for at least the previous five years;

(c) details of any bankruptcies, receiverships or liquidations with which a person described in (a) and (d) of the first subparagraph who was acting in the capacity of any of the positions set out in (a) and (d) of the first subparagraph was associated for at least the previous five years;

(d) details of any official public incrimination and/or sanctions of such person by statutory or regulatory authorities (including designated professional bodies) and whether such person has ever been disqualified by a court from acting as a member of the administrative, management or supervisory bodies of an issuer or from acting in the management or conduct of the affairs of any issuer for at least the previous five years.

If there is no such information to be disclosed, a statement to that effect is to be made.

14.2. Administrative, Management, and Supervisory bodies' and Senior Management conflicts of interests

Potential conflicts of interests between any duties to the issuer, of the persons referred to in item 14.1 and their private interests and or other duties must be clearly stated. In the event that there are no such conflicts, a statement to that effect must be made.

Any arrangement or understanding with major shareholders, customers, suppliers or others, pursuant to which any person referred to in item 14.1 was selected as a member of the administrative, management or supervisory bodies or member of senior management.

Details of any restrictions agreed by the persons referred to in item 14.1 on the disposal within a certain period of time of their holdings in the issuer's securities.

15. **Remuneration and Benefits**

In relation to the last full financial year for those persons referred to in points (a) and (d) of the first subparagraph of item 14.1:

15.1. The amount of remuneration paid (including any contingent or deferred compensation), and benefits in kind granted to such persons by the issuer and its subsidiaries for services in all capacities to the issuer and its subsidiaries by any person.

That information must be provided on an individual basis unless individual disclosure is not required in the issuer's home country and is not otherwise publicly disclosed by the issuer.

15.2. The total amounts set aside or accrued by the issuer or its subsidiaries to provide pension, retirement or similar benefits.

16. **Board Practices**

In relation to the issuer's last completed financial year, and unless otherwise specified, with respect to those persons referred to in point (a) of the first subparagraph of 14.1:

16.1. Date of expiration of the current term of office, if applicable, and the period during which the person has served in that office.

16.2. Information about members of the administrative, management or supervisory bodies' service contracts with the issuer or any of its subsidiaries providing for benefits upon termination of employment, or an appropriate negative statement.

16.3. Information about the issuer's audit committee and remuneration committee, including the names of committee members and a summary of the terms of reference under which the committee operates.

16.4. A statement as to whether or not the issuer complies with its country's of incorporation corporate governance regime(s). In the event that the issuer does not comply with such a regime, a statement to that effect must be included together with an explanation regarding why the issuer does not comply with such regime.

17. **Employees**

17.1. Either the number of employees at the end of the period or the average for each financial year for the period covered by the historical financial information up to the date of the registration document (and changes in such numbers, if material) and, if possible and material, a breakdown of persons employed by main category of activity and geographic location. If the issuer employs a significant number of temporary employees, include disclosure of the number of temporary employees on average during the most recent financial year.

17.2. Shareholdings and stock options

With respect to each person referred to in points (a) and (d) of the first subparagraph of item 14.1. provide information as to their share ownership and any options over such shares in the issuer as of the most recent practicable date.

17.3. Description of any arrangements for involving the employees in the capital of the issuer.

18. Major Shareholders

18.1. In so far as is known to the issuer, the name of any person other than a member of the administrative, management or supervisory bodies who, directly or indirectly, has an interest in the issuer's capital or voting rights which is notifiable under the issuer's national law, together with the amount of each such person's interest or, if there are no such persons, an appropriate negative statement.

18.2. Whether the issuer's major shareholders have different voting rights, or an appropriate negative statement.

18.3. To the extent known to the issuer, state whether the issuer is directly or indirectly owned or controlled and by whom and describe the nature of such control and describe the measures in place to ensure that such control is not abused.

18.4. A description of any arrangements, known to the issuer, the operation of which may at a subsequent date result in a change in control of the issuer.

19. Related Party Transactions

Details of related party transactions (which for these purposes are those set out in the Standards adopted according to the Regulation (EC) No 1606/2002), that the issuer has entered into during the period covered by the historical financial information and up to the date of the registration document, must be disclosed in accordance with the respective standard adopted according to Regulation (EC) No 1606/2002 if applicable.

If such standards do not apply to the issuer the following information must be disclosed:

(a) the nature and extent of any transactions which are - as a single transaction or in their entirety - material to the issuer. Where such related party transactions are not concluded at arm's length provide an explanation of why these transactions were not concluded at arms length. In the case of outstanding loans including guarantees of any kind indicate the amount outstanding;

(b) the amount or the percentage to which related party transactions form part of the turnover of the issuer.

20. Financial Information Concerning the Issuer's Assets and Liabilities, Financial Position and Profits and Losses

20.1. *Historical Financial Information*

Audited historical financial information covering the latest 3 financial years (or such shorter period that the issuer has been in operation), and the audit report in respect of each year. [If the issuer has changed its accounting reference date during the period for which historical financial information is required, the audited historical information shall cover at least 36 months, or the entire period for which the issuer has been in operation, whichever is the shorter.][a] Such financial information must be prepared according to

Regulation (EC) No 1606/2002, or if not applicable to a Member State national accounting standards for issuers from the Community. For third country issuers, such financial information must be prepared according to the international accounting standards adopted pursuant to the procedure of Article 3 of Regulation (EC) No 1606/2002 or to a third country's national accounting standards equivalent to these standards. If such financial information is not equivalent to these standards, it must be presented in the form of restated financial statements.

The last two years audited historical financial information must be presented and prepared in a form consistent with that which will be adopted in the issuer's next published annual financial statements having regard to accounting standards and policies and legislation applicable to such annual financial statements.

If the issuer has been operating in its current sphere of economic activity for less than one year, the audited historical financial information covering that period must be prepared in accordance with the standards applicable to annual financial statements under the Regulation (EC) No 1606/2002, or if not applicable to a Member State national accounting standards where the issuer is an issuer from the Community. For third country issuers, the historical financial information must be prepared according to the international accounting standards adopted pursuant to the procedure of Article 3 of Regulation (EC) No 1606/2002 or to a third country's national accounting standards equivalent to these standards. This historical financial information must be audited.

If the audited financial information is prepared according to national accounting standards, the financial information required under this heading must include at least:

(a) balance sheet;

(b) income statement;

(c) a statement showing either all changes in equity or changes in equity other than those arising from capital transactions with owners and distributions to owners;

(d) cash flow statement;

(e) accounting policies and explanatory notes.

The historical annual financial information must be independently audited or reported on as to whether or not, for the purposes of the registration document, it gives a true and fair view, in accordance with auditing standards applicable in a Member State or an equivalent standard.

20.2. *Pro forma financial information*

In the case of a significant gross change, a description of how the transaction might have affected the assets and liabilities and earnings of the issuer, had the transaction been undertaken at the commencement of the period being reported on or at the date reported.

This requirement will normally be satisfied by the inclusion of pro forma financial information.

This pro forma financial information is to be presented as set out in Annex II and must include the information indicated therein.

Pro forma financial information must be accompanied by a report prepared by independent accountants or auditors.

20.3. *Financial statements*

If the issuer prepares both own and consolidated annual financial statements, include at least the consolidated annual financial statements in the registration document.

20.4. *Auditing of historical annual financial information*

20.4.1. A statement that the historical financial information has been audited. If audit reports on the historical financial information have been refused by the statutory auditors or if they contain qualifications or disclaimers, such refusal or such qualifications or disclaimers must be reproduced in full and the reasons given.

20.4.2. Indication of other information in the registration document which has been audited by the auditors.

20.4.3. Where financial data in the registration document is not extracted from the issuer's audited financial statements state the source of the data and state that the data is unaudited.

20.5. *Age of latest financial information*

20.5.1. The last year of audited financial information may not be older than one of the following:

(a) 18 months from the date of the registration document if the issuer includes audited interim financial statements in the registration document;

(b) 15 months from the date of the registration document if the issuer includes unaudited interim financial statements in the registration document.

20.6. *Interim and other financial information*

20.6.1. If the issuer has published quarterly or half yearly financial information since the date of its last audited financial statements, these must be included in the registration document. If the quarterly or half yearly financial information has been reviewed or audited, the audit or review report must also be included. If the quarterly or half yearly financial information is unaudited or has not been reviewed state that fact.

20.6.2. If the registration document is dated more than nine months after the end of the last audited financial year, it must contain interim financial information, which may be unaudited (in which case that fact must be stated) covering at least the first six months of the financial year.

The interim financial information must include comparative statements for the same period in the prior financial year, except that the requirement for comparative balance sheet information may be satisfied by presenting the years end balance sheet.

20.7. *Dividend policy*

A description of the issuer's policy on dividend distributions and any restrictions thereon.

20.7.1. The amount of the dividend per share for each financial year for the period covered by the historical financial information adjusted, where the number of shares in the issuer has changed, to make it comparable.

20.8. *Legal and arbitration proceedings*

Information on any governmental, legal or arbitration proceedings (including any such proceedings which are pending or threatened of which the issuer is aware), during a period covering at least the previous 12 months which may have, or have had in the recent past significant effects on the issuer and/or group's financial position or profitability, or provide an appropriate negative statement.

20.9. Significant change in the issuer's financial or trading position

A description of any significant change in the financial or trading position of the group which has occurred since the end of the last financial period for which either audited financial information or interim financial information have been published, or provide an appropriate negative statement.

Amendments

a Inserted by Commission Regulation (EC) No 211/2007 of 27 February 2007 OJ L337 5.12.2006, p 17.

---

21. Additional Information

21.1. *Share Capital*

The following information as of the date of the most recent balance sheet included in the historical financial information:

21.1.1. The amount of issued capital, and for each class of share capital:

(a) the number of shares authorised;

(b) the number of shares issued and fully paid and issued but not fully paid;

(c) the par value per share, or that the shares have no par value; and

(d) a reconciliation of the number of shares outstanding at the beginning and end of the year. If more than 10 % of capital has been paid for with assets other than cash within the period covered by the historical financial information, state that fact.

21.1.2. If there are shares not representing capital, state the number and main characteristics of such shares.

21.1.3. The number, book value and face value of shares in the issuer held by or on behalf of the issuer itself or by subsidiaries of the issuer.

21.1.4. The amount of any convertible securities, exchangeable securities or securities with warrants, with an indication of the conditions governing and the procedures for conversion, exchange or subscription.

21.1.5. Information about and terms of any acquisition rights and or obligations over authorised but unissued capital or an undertaking to increase the capital.

21.1.6. Information about any capital of any member of the group which is under option or agreed conditionally or unconditionally to be put under option and details of such options including those persons to whom such options relate.

21.1.7. A history of share capital, highlighting information about any changes, for the period covered by the historical financial information.

21.2. *Memorandum and Articles of Association*

21.2.1. A description of the issuer's objects and purposes and where they can be found in the memorandum and articles of association.

21.2.2. A summary of any provisions of the issuer's articles of association, statutes, charter or bylaws with respect to the members of the administrative, management and supervisory bodies.

21.2.3. A description of the rights, preferences and restrictions attaching to each class of the existing shares.

21.2.4. A description of what action is necessary to change the rights of holders of the shares, indicating where the conditions are more significant than is required by law.

21.2.5. A description of the conditions governing the manner in which annual general meetings and extraordinary general meetings of shareholders are called including the conditions of admission.

21.2.6. A brief description of any provision of the issuer's articles of association, statutes, charter or bylaws that would have an effect of delaying, deferring or preventing a change in control of the issuer.

21.2.7. An indication of the articles of association, statutes, charter or bylaw provisions, if any, governing the ownership threshold above which shareholder ownership must be disclosed.

21.2.8. A description of the conditions imposed by the memorandum and articles of association statutes, charter or bylaw governing changes in the capital, where such conditions are more stringent than is required by law.

22. Material Contracts

A summary of each material contract, other than contracts entered into in the ordinary course of business, to which the issuer or any member of the group is a party, for the two years immediately preceding publication of the registration document.

A summary of any other contract (not being a contract entered into in the ordinary course of business) entered into by any member of the group which contains any provision under which any member of the group has any obligation or entitlement which is material to the group as at the date of the registration document.

23. Third Party Information and Statement by Experts and Declarations of Any Interest

23.1. Where a statement or report attributed to a person as an expert is included in the registration document, provide such person's name, business address, qualifications and material interest if any in the issuer. If the report has been produced at the issuer's request a statement to the effect that such statement or report is included, in the form and context in which it is included, with the consent of the person who has authorised the contents of that part of the registration document.

23.2. Where information has been sourced from a third party, provide a confirmation that this information has been accurately reproduced and that as far as the issuer is aware and is able to ascertain from information published by that third party, no facts have been omitted which would render the reproduced information inaccurate or misleading. In addition, identify the source(s) of the information.

24. Documents on Display

A statement that for the life of the registration document the following documents (or copies thereof), where applicable, may be inspected:

(a) the memorandum and articles of association of the issuer;

(b) all reports, letters, and other documents, historical financial information, valuations and statements prepared by any expert at the issuer's request any part of which is included or referred to in the registration document;

(c) the historical financial information of the issuer or, in the case of a group, the historical financial information for the issuer and its subsidiary undertakings for each of the two financial years preceding the publication of the registration document.

An indication of where the documents on display may be inspected, by physical or electronic means.

25. Information on Holdings

Information relating to the undertakings in which the issuer holds a proportion of the capital likely to have a significant effect on the assessment of its own assets and liabilities, financial position or profits and losses.

Annex II
Pro forma financial information building block

1. The pro forma information must include a description of the trans-action, the businesses or entities involved and the period to which it refers, and must clearly state the following:
   (a) the purpose to which it has been prepared;
   (b) the fact that it has been prepared for illustrative purposes only;
   (c) the fact that because of its nature, the pro forma financial information addresses a hypothetical situation and, therefore, does not represent the company's actual financial position or results.
2. In order to present pro forma financial information, a balance sheet and profit and loss account, and accompanying explanatory notes, depending on the circumstances may be included.
3. Pro forma financial information must normally be presented in columnar format, composed of:
   (a) the historical unadjusted information;
   (b) the pro forma adjustments;
   and
   (c) the resulting pro forma financial information in the final column.

   The sources of the pro forma financial information have to be stated and, if applicable, the financial statements of the acquired businesses or entities must be included in the prospectus
4. The pro forma information must be prepared in a manner consistent with the accounting policies adopted by the issuer in its last or next financial statements and shall identify the following:
   (a) the basis upon which it is prepared;
   (b) the source of each item of information and adjustment.
5. Pro forma information may only be published in respect of:
   (a) the current financial period;
   (b) the most recently completed financial period;
   and/or
   (c) the most recent interim period for which relevant unadjusted information has been or will be published or is being published in the same document.
6. Pro forma adjustments related to the pro forma financial information must be:
   (a) clearly shown and explained;
   (b) directly attributable to the transaction;
   (c) factually supportable.

   In addition, in respect of a pro forma profit and loss or cash flow statement, they must be clearly identified as to those expected to have a continuing impact on the issuer and those which are not.

7. The report prepared by the independent accountants or auditors must state that in their opinion:

   (a) the pro forma financial information has been properly compiled on the basis stated;

   (b) that basis is consistent with the accounting policies of the issuer.

Annex III
Minimum disclosure requirements for the share securities note (schedule)

1. Persons Responsible

1.1. All persons responsible for the information given in the prospectus and, as the case may be, for certain parts of it, with, in the latter case, an indication of such parts. In the case of natural persons including members of the issuer's administrative, management or supervisory bodies indicate the name and function of the person; in case of legal persons indicate the name and registered office.

1.2. A declaration by those responsible for the prospectus that, having taken all reasonable care to ensure that such is the case the information contained in the prospectus is, to the best of their knowledge, in accordance with the facts and contains no omission likely to affect its import. As the case may be, declaration by those responsible for certain parts of the prospectus that, having taken all reasonable care to ensure that such is the case the information contained in the part of the prospectus for which they are responsible is, to the best of their knowledge, in accordance with the facts and contains no omission likely to affect its import.

2. Risk Factors

Prominent disclosure of risk factors that are material to the securities being offered and/or admitted to trading in order to assess the market risk associated with these securities in a section headed 'Risk Factors'.

3. Key Information

3.1. *Working capital Statement*

Statement by the issuer that, in its opinion, the working capital is sufficient for the issuer's present requirements or, if not, how it proposes to provide the additional working capital needed.

3.2. *Capitalisation and indebtedness*

A statement of capitalisation and indebtedness (distinguishing between guaranteed and unguaranteed, secured and unsecured indebtedness) as of a date no earlier than 90 days prior to the date of the document. Indebtedness also includes indirect and contingent indebtedness.

3.3. *Interest of natural and legal persons involved in the issue/offer*

A description of any interest, including conflicting ones that is material to the issue/offer, detailing the persons involved and the nature of the interest.

3.4. *Reasons for the offer and use of proceeds*

Reasons for the offer and, where applicable, the estimated net amount of the proceeds broken into each principal intended use and presented by order of priority of such uses. If the issuer is aware that the anticipated proceeds will not be sufficient to fund all the proposed uses, state the amount and sources of other funds needed. Details must be given with regard to the use of the proceeds, in particular when they are being used to acquire assets, other than in the ordinary course of business, to finance announced acquisitions of other business, or to *discharge*, reduce or retire indebtedness.

4. Information Concerning the Securities to be Offered/admitted to Trading

4.1. A description of the type and the class of the securities being offered and/or admitted to trading, including the ISIN (international security identification number) or other such security identification code.

4.2. Legislation under which the securities have been created.

4.3. An indication whether the securities are in registered form or bearer form and whether the securities are in certificated form or book-entry form. In the latter case, name and address of the entity in charge of keeping the records.

4.4. Currency of the securities issue.

4.5. A description of the rights attached to the securities, including any limitations of those rights, and procedure for the exercise of those rights.

- Dividend rights:
  - fixed date(s) on which the entitlement arises,
  - time limit after which entitlement to dividend lapses and an indication of the person in whose favour the lapse operates,
  - dividend restrictions and procedures for non-resident holders,
  - rate of dividend or method of its calculation, periodicity and cumulative or non-cumulative nature of payments.
- Voting rights.
- Pre-emption rights in offers for subscription of securities of the same class.
- Right to share in the issuer's profits.
- Rights to share in any surplus in the event of liquidation.
- Redemption provisions.
- Conversion provisions.

4.6 In the case of new issues, a statement of the resolutions, authorisations and approvals by virtue of which the securities have been or will be created and/or issued.

4.7 In the case of new issues, the expected issue date of the securities.

4.8 A description of any restrictions on the free transferability of the securities.

4.9 An indication of the existence of any mandatory takeover bids and/or squeeze-out and sell-out rules in relation to the securities.

4.10 An indication of public takeover bids by third parties in respect of the issuer's equity, which have occurred during the last financial year and the current financial year. The price or exchange terms attaching to such offers and the outcome thereof must be stated.

4.11. In respect of the country of registered office of the issuer and the country(ies) where the offer is being made or admission to trading is being sought:

- information on taxes on the income from the securities withheld at source,

— indication as to whether the issuer assumes responsibility for the withholding of taxes at the source.

5. Terms and Conditions of the Offer

5.1. *Conditions, offer statistics, expected timetable and action required to apply for the offer*

5.1.1. Conditions to which the offer is subject.

5.1.2. Total amount of the issue/offer, distinguishing the securities offered for sale and those offered for subscription; if the amount is not fixed, description of the arrangements and time for announcing to the public the definitive amount of the offer.

5.1.3. The time period, including any possible amendments, during which the offer will be open and description of the application process.

5.1.4. An indication of when, and under which circumstances, the offer may be revoked or suspended and whether revocation can occur after dealing has begun.

5.1.5. A description of the possibility to reduce subscriptions and the manner for refunding excess amount paid by applicants.

5.1.6. Details of the minimum and/or maximum amount of application (whether in number of securities or aggregate amount to invest).

5.1.7 An indication of the period during which an application may be withdrawn, provided that investors are allowed to withdraw their subscription.

5.1.8 Method and time limits for paying up the securities and for delivery of the securities.

5.1.9 A full description of the manner and date in which results of the offer are to be made public.

5.1.10 The procedure for the exercise of any right of pre-emption, the negotiability of subscription rights and the treatment of subscription rights not exercised.

5.2. Plan of distribution and allotment

5.2.1. The various categories of potential investors to which the securities are offered. If the offer is being made simultaneously in the markets of two or more countries and if a tranche has been or is being reserved for certain of these, indicate any such tranche.

5.2.2. To the extent known to the issuer, an indication of whether major shareholders or members of the issuer's management, supervisory or administrative bodies intended to subscribe in the offer, or whether any person intends to subscribe for more than five per cent of the offer.

5.2.3. Pre-allotment disclosure:

(a) the division into tranches of the offer including the institutional, retail and issuer's employee tranches and any other tranches;

(b) the conditions under which the clawback may be used, the maximum size of such claw back and any applicable minimum percentages for individual tranches;

(c) the allotment method or methods to be used for the retail and issuer's employee tranche in the event of an over-subscription of these tranches;

(d) a description of any pre-determined preferential treatment to be accorded to certain classes of investors or certain affinity groups (including friends and family programmes) in the allotment, the percentage of the offer reserved for such preferential treatment and the criteria for inclusion in such classes or groups;

(e) whether the treatment of subscriptions or bids to subscribe in the allotment may be determined on the basis of which firm they are made through or by;

(f) a target minimum individual allotment if any within the retail tranche;

(g) the conditions for the closing of the offer as well as the date on which the offer may be closed at the earliest;

(h) whether or not multiple subscriptions are admitted, and where they are not, how any multiple subscriptions will be handled.

5.2.4. Process for notification to applicants of the amount allotted and indication whether dealing may begin before notification is made.

5.2.5. Over-allotment and 'green shoe':

(a) the existence and size of any over-allotment facility and/or 'green shoe'.

(b) the existence period of the over-allotment facility and/or 'green shoe'.

(c) any conditions for the use of the over-allotment facility or exercise of the 'green shoe'.

5.3. *Pricing*

5.3.1. An indication of the price at which the securities will be offered. If the price is not known or if there is no established and/or liquid market for the securities, indicate the method for determining the offer price, including a statement as to who has set the criteria or is formally responsible for the determination. Indication of the amount of any expenses and taxes specifically charged to the subscriber or purchaser.

5.3.2. Process for the disclosure of the offer price.

5.3.3. If the issuer's equity holders have pre-emptive purchase rights and this right is restricted or withdrawn, indication of the basis for the issue price if the issue is for cash, together with the reasons for and beneficiaries of such restriction or withdrawal.

5.3.4 Where there is or could be a material disparity between the public offer price and the effective cash cost to members of the administrative, management or supervisory bodies or senior management, or affiliated persons, of securities acquired by them in transactions during the past year, or which they have the right to acquire, include a comparison of the public contribution in the proposed public offer and the effective cash contributions of such persons.

5.4. *Placing and Underwriting*

5.4.1 Name and address of the coordinator(s) of the global offer and of single parts of the offer and, to the extend known to the issuer or to the offeror, of the placers in the various countries where the offer takes place.

5.4.2 Name and address of any paying agents and depository agents in each country.

5.4.3. Name and address of the entities agreeing to underwrite the issue on a firm commitment basis, and name and address of the entities agreeing to place the issue without a firm commitment or under 'best efforts' arrangements. Indication of the material features of the agreements, including the quotas. Where not all of the issue is underwritten, a statement of the portion not covered. Indication of the overall amount of the underwriting commission and of the placing commission.

5.4.4. When the underwriting agreement has been or will be reached.

6. Admission to Trading and Dealing Arrangements

6.1. An indication as to whether the securities offered are or will be the object of an application for admission to trading, with a view to their distribution in a regulated market or other equivalent markets with indication of the markets in question. This circumstance must be mentioned, without creating the impression that the admission to trading will necessarily be approved. If known, the earliest dates on which the securities will be admitted to trading.

6.2. All the regulated markets or equivalent markets on which, to the knowledge of the issuer, securities of the same class of the securities to be offered or admitted to trading are already admitted to trading.

6.3. If simultaneously or almost simultaneously with the creation of the securities for which admission to a regulated market is being sought securities of the same class are subscribed for or placed privately or if securities of other classes are created for public or private placing, give details of the nature of such operations and of the number and characteristics of the securities to which they relate.

6.4. Details of the entities which have a firm commitment to act as intermediaries in secondary trading, providing liquidity through bid and offer rates and description of the main terms of their commitment.

6.5. *Stabilisation: where an issuer or a selling shareholder has granted an over-allotment option or it is otherwise proposed that price stabilising activities may be entered into in connection with an offer:*

6.5.1. The fact that stabilisation may be undertaken, that there is no assurance that it will be undertaken and that it may be stopped at any time,

6.5.2. The beginning and the end of the period during which stabilisation may occur,

6.5.3. The identity of the stabilisation manager for each relevant jurisdiction unless this is not known at the time of publication,

6.5.4. The fact that stabilisation transactions may result in a market price that is higher than would otherwise prevail.

7. Selling Securities Holders

7.1. Name and business address of the person or entity offering to sell the securities, the nature of any position office or other material relationship that the selling persons has had within the past three years with the issuer or any of its predecessors or affiliates.

7.2. The number and class of securities being offered by each of the selling security holders.

7.3. Lock-up agreements

The parties involved.

Content and exceptions of the agreement. Indication of the period of the lock up.

8. Expense of the Issue/offer

8.1. The total net proceeds and an estimate of the total expenses of the issue/offer.

9. Dilution

9.1. The amount and percentage of immediate dilution resulting from the offer.

9.2. In the case of a subscription offer to existing equity holders, the amount and percentage of immediate dilution if they do not subscribe to the new offer.

10. Additional Information

10.1. If advisors connected with an issue are mentioned in the Securities Note, a statement of the capacity in which the advisors have acted.

10.2. An indication of other information in the Securities Note which has been audited or reviewed by statutory auditors and where auditors have produced a report. Reproduction of the report or, with permission of the competent authority, a summary of the report.

10.3. Where a statement or report attributed to a person as an expert is included in the Securities Note, provide such persons' name, business address, qualifications and material interest if any in the issuer. If the report has been produced at the issuer's request a statement to the effect that such statement or report is included, in the form and context in which it is included, with the consent of the person who has authorised the contents of that part of the Securities Note.

10.4. Where information has been sourced from a third party, provide a confirmation that this information has been accurately reproduced and that as far as the issuer is aware and is able to ascertain from information published by that third party, no facts have been omitted which would render the reproduced information inaccurate or misleading. In addition, identify the source(s) of the information.

Annex IV
Minimum disclosure requirements for the debt and derivative securities registration document (schedule)

(Debt and derivative securities with a denomination per unit of less than EUR 50,000)

1. Persons Responsible

1.1. All persons responsible for the information given in the registration document and, as the case may be, for certain parts of it, with, in the latter case, an indication of such parts. In the case of natural persons including members of the issuer's administrative, management or supervisory bodies indicate the name and function of the person; in case of legal persons indicate the name and registered office.

1.2. A declaration by those responsible for the registration document that, having taken all reasonable care to ensure that such is the case the information contained in the registration document is, to the best of their knowledge, in accordance with the facts and contains no omission likely to affect its import. As the case may be, declaration by those responsible for certain parts of the registration document that, having taken all reasonable care to ensure that such is the case, the information contained in the part of the registration document for which they are responsible is, to the best of their knowledge, in accordance with the facts and contains no omission likely to affect its import.

2. Statutory Auditors

2.1. Names and addresses of the issuer's auditors for the period covered by the historical financial information (together with their membership in a professional body).

2.2. If auditors have resigned, been removed or not been re-appointed during the period covered by the historical financial information, details if material.

3. Selected Financial Information

3.1. Selected historical financial information regarding the issuer, presented, for each financial year for the period covered by the historical financial information, and any subsequent interim financial period, in the same currency as the financial information.

The selected historical financial information must provide key figures that summarise the financial condition of the issuer.

3.2. If selected financial information for interim periods is provided, comparative data from the same period in the prior financial year must also be provided, except that the requirement for comparative balance sheet data is satisfied by presenting the year end balance sheet information.

4. Risk Factors

Prominent disclosure of risk factors that may affect the issuer's ability to fulfil its obligations under the securities to investors in a section headed 'Risk Factors'.

5. **Information about the Issuer**

5.1. *History and development of the Issuer*

5.1.1. the legal and commercial name of the issuer;

5.1.2. the place of registration of the issuer and its registration number;

5.1.3. the date of incorporation and the length of life of the issuer, except where indefinite;

5.1.4. the domicile and legal form of the issuer, the legislation under which the issuer operates, its country of incorporation, and the address and telephone number of its registered office (or principal place of business if different from its registered office);

5.1.5. any recent events particular to the issuer which are to a material extent relevant to the evaluation of the issuer's solvency.

5.2. *Investments*

5.2.1. A description of the principal investments made since the date of the last published financial statements.

5.2.2. Information concerning the issuer's principal future investments, on which its management bodies have already made firm commitments.

5.2.3. Information regarding the anticipated sources of funds needed to fulfil commitments referred to in item 5.2.2.

6. **Business Overview**

6.1. *Principal activities*

6.1.1. A description of the issuer's principal activities stating the main categories of products sold and/or services performed;

and

6.1.2. an indication of any significant new products and/or activities.

6.2. Principal markets

A brief description of the principal markets in which the issuer competes.

6.3. The basis for any statements made by the issuer regarding its competitive position.

7. **Organisational Structure**

7.1. If the issuer is part of a group, a brief description of the group and of the issuer's position within it.

7.2. If the issuer is dependent upon other entities within the group, this must be clearly stated together with an explanation of this dependence.

8. **Trend Information**

8.1. Include a statement that there has been no material adverse change in the prospects of the issuer since the date of its last published audited financial statements.

In the event that the issuer is unable to make such a statement, provide details of this material adverse change.

8.2. Information on any known trends, uncertainties, demands, commitments or events that are reasonably likely to have a material effect on the issuer's prospects for at least the current financial year.

9. Profit Forecasts or Estimates

If an issuer chooses to include a profit forecast or a profit estimate, the registration document must contain the information items 9.1 and 9.2:

9.1. A statement setting out the principal assumptions upon which the issuer has based its forecast, or estimate.

There must be a clear distinction between assumptions about factors which the members of the administrative, management or supervisory bodies can influence and assumptions about factors which are exclusively outside the influence of the members of the administrative, management or supervisory bodies; the assumptions must be readily understandable by investors, be specific and precise and not relate to the general accuracy of the estimates underlying the forecast.

9.2. A report prepared by independent accountants or auditors must be included stating that in the opinion of the independent accountants or auditors the forecast or estimate has been properly compiled on the basis stated and that the basis of accounting used for the profit forecast or estimate is consistent with the accounting policies of the issuer.

9.3. The profit forecast or estimate must be prepared on a basis comparable with the historical financial information.

10. Administrative, Management, and Supervisory Bodies

10.1. Names, business addresses and functions in the issuer of the following persons, and an indication of the principal activities performed by them outside the issuer where these are significant with respect to that issuer:

(a) members of the administrative, management or supervisory bodies;

(b) partners with unlimited liability, in the case of a limited partnership with a share capital.

10.2. *Administrative, Management, and Supervisory bodies' conflicts of interests*

Potential conflicts of interests between any duties to the issuing entity of the persons referred to in item 10.1 and their private interests and or other duties must be clearly stated. In the event that there are no such conflicts, make a statement to that effect.

11. Board Practices

11.1. Details relating to the issuer's audit committee, including the names of committee members and a summary of the terms of reference under which the committee operates.

11.2. A statement as to whether or not the issuer complies with its country's of incorporation corporate governance regime(s). In the event that the issuer does not comply with such a regime a statement to that effect must be included together with an explanation regarding why the issuer does not comply with such regime.

12. **Major Shareholders**

12.1. To the extent known to the issuer, state whether the issuer is directly or indirectly owned or controlled and by whom and describe the nature of such control, and describe the measures in place to ensure that such control is not abused.

12.2. A description of any arrangements, known to the issuer, the operation of which may at a subsequent date result in a change in control of the issuer.

13. **Financial Information Concerning the Issuer's Assets and Liabilities, Financial Position and Profits and Losses**

13.1. *Historical Financial Information*

Audited historical financial information covering the latest 2 financial years (or such shorter period that the issuer has been in operation), and the audit report in respect of each year. [If the issuer has changed its accounting reference date during the period for which historical financial information is required, the audited historical information shall cover at least 24 months, or the entire period for which the issuer has been in operation, whichever is the shorter.][a] Such financial information must be prepared according to Regulation (EC) No 1606/2002, or if not applicable to a Member States national accounting standards for issuers from the Community. For third country issuers, such financial information must be prepared according to the international accounting standards adopted pursuant to the procedure of Article 3 of Regulation (EC) No 1606/2002 or to a third country's national accounting standards equivalent to these standards. If such financial information is not equivalent to these standards, it must be presented in the form of restated financial statements.

The most recent year's historical financial information must be presented and prepared in a form consistent with that which will be adopted in the issuer's next published annual financial statements having regard to accounting standards and policies and legislation applicable to such annual financial statements.

If the issuer has been operating in its current sphere of economic activity for less than one year, the audited historical financial information covering that period must be prepared in accordance with the standards applicable to annual financial statements under the Regulation (EC) No 1606/2002, or if not applicable to a Member States national accounting standards where the issuer is an issuer from the Community. For third country issuers, the historical financial information must be prepared according to the international accounting standards adopted pursuant to the procedure of Article 3 of Regulation (EC) No 1606/2002 or to a third country's national accounting standards equivalent to these standards. This historical financial information must be audited.

If the audited financial information is prepared according to national accounting standards, the financial information required under this heading must include at least:

(a) balance sheet;

(b) income statement;

(c) cash flow statement;

and

(d) accounting policies and explanatory notes

The historical annual financial information must have been independently audited or reported on as to whether or not, for the purposes of the registration document, it gives a true and fair view, in accordance with auditing standards applicable in a Member State or an equivalent standard.

13.2. *Financial statements*

If the issuer prepares both own and consolidated financial statements, include at least the consolidated financial statements in the registration document.

13.3. Auditing of historical annual financial information

13.3.1. A statement that the historical financial information has been audited. If audit reports on the historical financial information have been refused by the statutory auditors or if they contain qualifications or disclaimers, such refusal or such qualifications or disclaimers must be reproduced in full and the reasons given.

13.3.2. An indication of other information in the registration document which has been audited by the auditors.

13.3.3. Where financial data in the registration document is not extracted from the issuer's audited financial statements state the source of the data and state that the data is unaudited.

13.4. Age of latest financial information

13.4.1. The last year of audited financial information may not be older than 18 months from the date of the registration document.

13.5. *Interim and other financial information*

13.5.1. If the issuer has published quarterly or half yearly financial information since the date of its last audited financial statements, these must be included in the registration document. If the quarterly or half yearly financial information has been reviewed or audited the audit or review report must also be included. If the quarterly or half yearly financial information is unaudited or has not been reviewed state that fact.

13.5.2. If the registration document is dated more than nine months after the end of the last audited financial year, it must contain interim financial information, covering at least the first six months of the financial year. If the interim financial information is un-audited state that fact.

The interim financial information must include comparative statements for the same period in the prior financial year, except that the requirement for comparative balance sheet information may be satisfied by presenting the years end balance sheet.

13.6. *Legal and arbitration proceedings*

Information on any governmental, legal or arbitration proceedings (including any such proceedings which are pending or threatened of which the issuer is aware), during a period covering at least the previous 12 months which may have, or have had in the recent past, significant effects on the issuer and/or group's financial position or profitability, or provide an appropriate negative statement.

13.7. *Significant change in the issuer's financial or trading position*

A description of any significant change in the financial or trading position of the group which has occurred since the end of the last financial period for which either audited financial information or interim financial information have been published, or an appropriate negative statement.

Amendments

a Inserted by Commission Regulation (EC) No 211/2007 of 27 February 2007 OJ L337 5.12.2006, p 17.

---

14. Additional Information

14.1. *Share Capital*

14.1.1. The amount of the issued capital, the number and classes of the shares of which it is composed with details of their principal characteristics, the part of the issued capital still to be paid up, with an indication of the number, or total nominal value, and the type of the shares not yet fully paid up, broken down where applicable according to the extent to which they have been paid up.

14.2. *Memorandum and Articles of Association*

14.2.1. The register and the entry number therein, if applicable, and a description of the issuer's objects and purposes and where they can be found in the memorandum and articles of association.

15. Material Contracts

A brief summary of all material contracts that are not entered into in the ordinary course of the issuer's business, which could result in any group member being under an obligation or entitlement that is material to the issuer's ability to meet its obligation to security holders in respect of the securities being issued.

16. Third Party Information and Statement by Experts and Declarations of Any Interest

16.1. Where a statement or report attributed to a person as an expert is included in the registration document, provide such person's name, business address, qualifications and material interest if any in the issuer. If the report has been produced at the issuer's request a statement to that effect that such statement or report is included, in the form and context in which it is included, with the consent of that person who has authorised the contents of that part of the registration document.

16.2. Where information has been sourced from a third party, provide a confirmation that this information has been accurately reproduced and that as far as the issuer is aware and is able to ascertain from information published by that third party, no facts have been omitted which would render the reproduced information inaccurate or misleading. In addition, the issuer shall identify the source(s) of the information.

17. Documents on Display

A statement that for the life of the registration document the following documents (or copies thereof), where applicable, may be inspected:

(a) the memorandum and articles of association of the issuer;

(b) all reports, letters, and other documents, historical financial information, valuations and statements prepared by any expert at the issuer's request any part of which is included or referred to in the registration document;

(c) the historical financial information of the issuer or, in the case of a group, the historical financial information of the issuer and its subsidiary undertakings for each of the two financial years preceding the publication of the registration document.

An indication of where the documents on display may be inspected, by physical or electronic means.

Annex V

Minimum disclosure requirements for the securities note related to debt securities (schedule)

(Debt securities with a denomination per unit of less than EUR 50,000)

1. **Persons Responsible**

1.1. All persons responsible for the information given in the prospectus and, as the case may be, for certain parts of it, with, in the latter case, an indication of such parts. In the case of natural persons including members of the issuer's administrative, management or supervisory bodies indicate the name and function of the person; in case of legal persons indicate the name and registered office.

1.2. A declaration by those responsible for the prospectus that, having taken all reasonable care to ensure that such is the case, the information contained in the prospectus is, to the best of their knowledge, in accordance with the facts and contains no omission likely to affect its import. As the case may be, declaration by those responsible for certain parts of the prospectus that the information contained in the part of the prospectus for which they are responsible is, to the best of their knowledge, in accordance with the facts and contains no omission likely to affect its import.

2. **Risk Factors**

2.1. Prominent disclosure of risk factors that are material to the securities being offered and/or admitted to trading in order to assess the market risk associated with these securities in a section headed 'Risk Factors'.

3. **Key Information**

3.1. *Interest of natural and legal persons involved in the issue/offer*

A description of any interest, including conflicting ones, that is material to the issue/offer, detailing the persons involved and the nature of the interest.

3.2. *Reasons for the offer and use of proceeds*

Reasons for the offer if different from making profit and/or hedging certain risks. Where applicable, disclosure of the estimated total expenses of the issue/offer and the estimated net amount of the proceeds. These expenses and proceeds shall be broken into each principal intended use and presented by order of priority of such uses. If the issuer is aware that the anticipated proceeds will not be sufficient to fund all the proposed uses, state the amount and sources of other funds needed.

4. **Information Concerning the Securities to be Offered/admitted to Trading**

4.1. A description of the type and the class of the securities being offered and/or admitted to trading, including the ISIN (International Security Identification Number) or other such security identification code.

4.2. Legislation under which the securities have been created.

4.3. An indication of whether the securities are in registered form or bearer form and whether the securities are in certificated form or book-entry form. In the latter case, name and address of the entity in charge of keeping the records.

4.4. Currency of the securities issue.

4.5. Ranking of the securities being offered and/or admitted to trading, including summaries of any clauses that are intended to affect ranking or subordinate the security to any present or future liabilities of the issuer.

4.6. A description of the rights attached to the securities, including any limitations of those rights, and procedure for the exercise of those rights.

4.7. The nominal interest rate and provisions relating to interest payable.

— The date from which interest becomes payable and the due dates for interest

— The time limit on the validity of claims to interest and repayment of principal.

Where the rate is not fixed, description of the underlying on which it is based and of the method used to relate the two and an indication where information about the past and the further performance of the underlying and its volatility can be obtained.

— A description of any market disruption or settlement disruption events that affect the underlying

— Adjustment rules with relation to events concerning the underlying

— Name of the calculation agent.

If the security has a derivative component in the interest payment, provide a clear and comprehensive explanation to help investors understand how the value of their investment is affected by the value of the underlying instrument(s), especially under the circumstances when the risks are most evident.

4.8. Maturity date and arrangements for the amortisation of the loan, including the repayment procedures. Where advance amortisation is contemplated, on the initiative of the issuer or of the holder, it shall be described, stipulating amortisation terms and conditions.

4.9. An indication of yield. Describe the method whereby that yield is calculated in summary form.

4.10. Representation of debt security holders including an identification of the organisation representing the investors and provisions applying to such representation. Indication of where the public may have access to the contracts relating to these forms of representation.

4.11. In the case of new issues, a statement of the resolutions, authorisations and approvals by virtue of which the securities have been or will be created and/or issued.

4.12. In the case of new issues, the expected issue date of the securities.

4.13. A description of any restrictions on the free transferability of the securities.

4.14. In respect of the country of registered office of the issuer and the country(ies) where the offer being made or admission to trading is being sought:

— information on taxes on the income from the securities withheld at source;

— indication as to whether the issuer assumes responsibility for the withholding of taxes at the source.

5. **Terms and Conditions of the Offer**

5.1. *Conditions, offer statistics, expected timetable and action required to apply for the offer*

5.1.1. Conditions to which the offer is subject.

5.1.2. Total amount of the issue/offer; if the amount is not fixed, description of the arrangements and time for announcing to the public the definitive amount of the offer.

5.1.3. The time period, including any possible amendments, during which the offer will be open and description of the application process.

5.1.4. A description of the possibility to reduce subscriptions and the manner for refunding excess amount paid by applicants.

5.1.5. Details of the minimum and/or maximum amount of application, (whether in number of securities or aggregate amount to invest).

5.1.6. Method and time limits for paying up the securities and for delivery of the securities.

5.1.7. A full description of the manner and date in which results of the offer are to be made public.

5.1.8. The procedure for the exercise of any right of pre-emption, the negotiability of subscription rights and the treatment of subscription rights not exercised.

5.2. *Plan of distribution and allotment*

5.2.1. The various categories of potential investors to which the securities are offered. If the offer is being made simultaneously in the markets of two or more countries and if a tranche has been or is being reserved for certain of these, indicate any such tranche.

5.2.2. Process for notification to applicants of the amount allotted and indication whether dealing may begin before notification is made.

5.3. *Pricing*

5.3.1. An indication of the expected price at which the securities will be offered or the method of determining the price and the process for its disclosure. Indicate the amount of any expenses and taxes specifically charged to the subscriber or purchaser.

5.4. *Placing and Underwriting*

5.4.1. Name and address of the co-ordinator(s) of the global offer and of single parts of the offer and, to the extend known to the issuer or to the offeror, of the placers in the various countries where the offer takes place.

5.4.2. Name and address of any paying agents and depository agents in each country.

5.4.3. Name and address of the entities agreeing to underwrite the issue on a firm commitment basis, and name and address of the entities agreeing to place the issue without a firm commitment or under 'best efforts' arrangements. Indication of the material features of the agreements, including the quotas. Where not all of the issue is underwritten, a statement of the portion not covered. Indication of the overall amount of the underwriting commission and of the placing commission.

5.4.4. When the underwriting agreement has been or will be reached.

6. Admission to Trading and Dealing Arrangements

6.1. An indication as to whether the securities offered are or will be the object of an application for admission to trading, with a view to their distribution in a regulated market or other equivalent markets with indication of the markets in question. This circumstance must be mentioned, without creating the impression that the admission to trading will necessarily be approved. If known, give the earliest dates on which the securities will be admitted to trading.

6.2. All the regulated markets or equivalent markets on which, to the knowledge of the issuer, securities of the same class of the securities to be offered or admitted to trading are already admitted to trading.

6.3. Name and address of the entities which have a firm commitment to act as intermediaries in secondary trading, providing liquidity through bid and offer rates and description of the main terms of their commitment.

7. Additional Information

7.1. If advisors connected with an issue are mentioned in the Securities Note, a statement of the capacity in which the advisors have acted.

7.2. An indication of other information in the Securities Note which has been audited or reviewed by statutory auditors and where auditors have produced a report. Reproduction of the report or, with permission of the competent authority, a summary of the report.

7.3. Where a statement or report attributed to a person as an expert is included in the Securities Note, provide such persons' name, business address, qualifications and material interest if any in the issuer. If the report has been produced at the issuer's request a statement to that effect that such statement or report is included, in the form and context in which it is included, with the consent of that person who has authorised the contents of that part of the Securities Note.

7.4. Where information has been sourced from a third party, provide a confirmation that this information has been accurately reproduced and that as far as the issuer is aware and is able to ascertain from information published by that third party, no facts have been omitted which would render the reproduced information inaccurate or misleading. In addition, identify the source(s) of the information.

7.5. Credit ratings assigned to an issuer or its debt securities at the request or with the co-operation of the issuer in the rating process. A brief explanation of the meaning of the ratings if this has previously been published by the rating provider.

Annex VI
Minimum disclosure requirements for guarantees
(Additional building block)

1. Nature of the Guarantee

A description of any arrangement intended to ensure that any obligation material to the issue will be duly serviced, whether in the form of guarantee, surety, Keep well Agreement, Mono-line Insurance policy or other equivalent commitment (hereafter referred to generically as 'guarantees' and their provider as 'guarantor' for convenience).

Without prejudice to the generality of the foregoing, such arrangements encompass commitments to ensure obligations to repay debt securities and/or the payment of interest and the description shall set out how the arrangement is intended to ensure that the guaranteed payments will be duly serviced.

2. Scope of the Guarantee

Details shall be disclosed about the terms and conditions and scope of the guarantee. Without prejudice to the generality of the foregoing, these details should cover any conditionality on the application of the guarantee in the event of any default under the terms of the security and the material terms of any mono-line insurance or keep well agreement between the issuer and the guarantor. Details must also be disclosed of any guarantor's power of veto in relation to changes to the security holder's rights, such as is often found in Mono-line Insurance.

3. Information to be disclosed about the guarantor

The guarantor must disclose information about itself as if it were the issuer of that same type of security that is the subject of the guarantee.

4. Documents on display

Indication of the places where the public may have access to the material contracts and other documents relating to the guarantee.

Annex VII

Minimum disclosure requirements for asset-backed securities registration document (schedule)

1. Persons Responsible

1.1. All persons responsible for the information given in the registration document and, as the case may be, for certain parts of it, with, in the latter case, an indication of such parts. In the case of natural persons including members of the issuer's administrative, management or supervisory bodies indicate the name and function of the person; in case of legal persons indicate the name and registered office.

1.2. A declaration by those responsible for the registration document that, having taken all reasonable care to ensure that such is the case, the information given in the registration document is, to the best of their knowledge, in accordance with the facts and does not omit anything likely to affect its import. As the case may be, declaration by those responsible for certain parts of the registration document that having taken all reasonable care to ensure that such is the case, the information contained in that part of the registration document for which they are responsible is, to the best of their knowledge, in accordance with the facts and contains no omission likely to affect its import.

2. Statutory Auditors

2.1. Names and addresses of the issuer's auditors for the period covered by the historical financial information (together with any membership of any relevant professional body).

3. Risk Factors

3.1. The document must prominently disclose risk factors in a section headed 'Risk Factors' that are specific to the issuer and its industry.

4. Information about the Issuer:

4.1. A statement whether the issuer has been established as a special purpose vehicle or entity for the purpose of issuing asset backed securities;

4.2. The legal and commercial name of the issuer;

4.3. The place of registration of the issuer and its registration number;

4.4. The date of incorporation and the length of life of the issuer, except where indefinite;

4.5. The domicile and legal form of the issuer, the legislation under which the issuer operates its country of incorporation and the address and telephone number of its registered office (or principal place of business if different from its registered office).

4.6. Description of the amount of the issuer's authorised and issued capital and the amount of any capital agreed to be issued, the number and classes of the securities of which it is composed.

5. Business Overview

5.1. A brief description of the issuer's principal activities.

5.2. A global overview of the parties to the securitisation program including information on the direct or indirect ownership or control between those parties.

6. Administrative, Management and Supervisory Bodies

6.1. Names, business addresses and functions in the issuer of the following persons, and an indication of the principal activities performed by them outside the issuer where these are significant with respect to that issuer:

(a) members of the administrative, management or supervisory bodies;

(b) partners with unlimited liability, in the case of a limited partnership with a share capital.

7. Major Shareholders

7.1. To the extent known to the issuer, state whether the issuer is directly or indirectly owned or controlled and by whom, and describe the nature of such control and describe the measures in place to ensure that such control is not abused.

8. Financial Information Concerning the Issuer's Assets and Liabilities, Financial Position, and Profits And Losses

8.1. Where, since the date of incorporation or establishment, an issuer has not commenced operations and no financial statements have been made up as at the date of the registration document, a statement to that effect shall be provided in the registration document.

8.2. *Historical Financial Information*

Where, since the date of incorporation or establishment, an issuer has commenced operations and financial statements have been made up, the registration document must contain audited historical financial information covering the latest 2 financial years (or shorter period that the issuer has been in operation) and the audit report in respect of each year. [If the issuer has changed its accounting reference date during the period for which historical financial information is required, the audited historical information shall cover at least 24 months, or the entire period for which the issuer has been in operation, whichever is the shorter.][a] Such financial information must be prepared according to Regulation (EC) No 1606/2002, or if not applicable to a Member's State national accounting standards for issuers from the Community. For third country issuers, such financial information must be prepared according to the international accounting standards adopted pursuant to the procedure of Article 3 of Regulation (EC) No 1606/2002 or to a third country's national accounting standards equivalent to these standards. If such financial information is not equivalent to these standards, it must be presented in the form of restated financial statements.

The most recent year's historical financial information must be presented and prepared in a form consistent with that which will be adopted in the issuer's next annual published financial statements having regard to accounting standards and policies and legislation applicable to such annual financial statements.

If the issuer has been operating in its current sphere of economic activity for less than one year, the audited historical financial information covering that period must be prepared in accordance with the standards applicable to annual financial statements under Regulation (EC) No 1606/2002, or if not applicable to a Member States national accounting standards where the issuer is from the Community. For third country issuers, the historical financial information must be prepared according to the international accounting standards adopted pursuant to the procedure of Article 3 of Regulation (EC) No 1606/2002 or to a third country's national accounting standards equivalent to these standards. This historical financial information must be audited.

If the audited financial information is prepared according to national accounting standards, the financial information required under this heading must include at least the following:

(a) the balance sheet;

(b) the income statement;

(c) the accounting policies and explanatory notes.

The historical annual financial information must be independently audited or reported on as to whether or not, for the purposes of the registration document, it gives a true and fair view, in accordance with auditing standards applicable in a Member State or an equivalent standard.

Amendment

a Inserted by Commission Regulation (EC) No 211/2007 of 27 February 2007 OJ L337 5.12.2006, p 17.

8.2a This paragraph may be used only for issues of asset backed securities having a denomination per unit of at least EUR 50,000.

Where, since the date of incorporation or establishment, an issuer has commenced operations and financial statements have been made up, the registration document must contain audited historical financial information covering the latest 2 financial years (or shorter period that the issuer has been in operation) and the audit report in respect of each year. [If the issuer has changed its accounting reference date during the period for which historical financial information is required, the audited historical information shall cover at least 24 months, or the entire period for which the issuer has been in operation, whichever is the shorter.][a] Such financial information must be prepared according to Regulation (EC) No 1606/2002 or, if not applicable, to a Member's State national accounting standards for issuers from the Community. For third country issuers, such financial information must be prepared according to the international accounting standards adopted pursuant to the procedure of Article 3 of Regulation (EC) No 1606/2002 or to a third country's national accounting standards equivalent to these standards. Otherwise, the following information must be included in the registration document:

(a) a prominent statement that the financial information included in the registration document has not been prepared in accordance with the international accounting standards adopted pursuant to the procedure of Article 3 of Regulation (EC) No 1606/2002 and that there may be material differences in the financial information had Regulation (EC) No 1606/2002 been applied to the historical financial information;

(b) immediately following the historical financial information a narrative description of the differences between the international accounting standards adopted pursuant to the procedure of Article 3 of Regulation (EC) No 1606/2002 and the accounting principles adopted by the issuer in preparing its annual financial statements.

The most recent year's historical financial information must be presented and prepared in a form consistent with that which will be adopted in the issuer's next annual financial statements having regard to accounting standards and policies and legislation applicable to such annual financial statements.

If the audited financial information is prepared according to national accounting standards, the financial information required under this heading must include at least the following:

(a) the balance sheet;

(b) the income statement;

(c) the accounting policies and explanatory notes.

The historical annual financial information must be independently audited or reported on as to whether or not, for the purposes of the registration document, it gives a true and fair view, in accordance with auditing standards applicable in a Member State or an equivalent standard. Otherwise, the following information must be included in the registration document:

(a) a prominent statement disclosing which auditing standards have been applied;

(b) an explanation of any significant departures from International Standards on Auditing.

Amendment

a Inserted by Commission Regulation (EC) No 211/2007 of 27 February 2007 OJ L337 5.12.2006, p 17.

8.3. *Legal and arbitration proceedings*

Information on any governmental, legal or arbitration proceedings (including any such proceedings which are pending or threatened of which the company is aware), during a period covering at least the previous 12 months, which may have, or have had in the recent past, significant effects on the issuer and/or group's financial position or profitability, or provide an appropriate negative statement.

8.4. *Material adverse change in the issuer's financial position*

Where an issuer has prepared financial statements, include a statement that there has been no material adverse change in the financial position or prospects of the issuer since the date of its last published audited financial statements. Where a material adverse change has occurred, this must be disclosed in the registration document.

9. Third Party Information and Statement by Experts and Declarations of Any Interest

9.1. Where a statement or report attributed to a person as an expert is included in the registration document, provide such person's name, business address, qualifications and material interest if any in the issuer. If the report has been produced at the issuer's request a statement to that effect that such statement or report is included, in the form and context in which it is included, with the consent of that person who has authorised the contents of that part of the registration document.

9.2. Where information has been sourced from a third party, provide a confirmation that this information has been accurately reproduced and that as far as the issuer is aware and is able to ascertain from information published by that third party, no facts have been omitted which would render the reproduced information inaccurate or misleading In addition, the issuer shall identify the source(s) of the information.

10. Documents on Display

10.1. A statement that for the life of the registration document the following documents (or copies thereof), where applicable, may be inspected:

(a) the memorandum and articles of association of the issuer;

(b) all reports, letters, and other documents, historical financial information, valuations and statements prepared by any expert at the issuer's request any part of which is included or referred to in the registration document;

(c) the historical financial information of the issuer or, in the case of a group, the historical financial information of the issuer and its subsidiary undertakings for each of the two financial years preceding the publication of the registration document.

An indication of where the documents on display may be inspected, by physical or electronic means.

Annex VIII

Minimum disclosure requirements for the asset-backed securities additional building block

1. The Securities

1.1. The minimum denomination of an issue.

1.2. Where information is disclosed about an undertaking/obligor which is not involved in the issue, provide a confirmation that the information relating to the undertaking/obligor has been accurately reproduced from information published by the undertaking/obligor. So far as the issuer is aware and is able to ascertain from information published by the undertaking/obligor no facts have been omitted which would render the reproduced information misleading.

In addition, identify the source(s) of information in the Securities Note that has been reproduced from information published by an undertaking/obligor.

2. The Underlying Assets

2.1. Confirmation that the securitised assets backing the issue have characteristics that demonstrate capacity to produce funds to service any payments due and payable on the securities.

2.2. *In respect of a pool of discrete assets backing the issue:*

2.2.1. The legal jurisdiction by which the pool of assets is governed

2.2.2.

(a) In the case of a small number of easily identifiable obligors, a general description of each obligor.

(b) In all other cases, a description of: the general characteristics of the obligors; and the economic environment, as well as global statistical data referred to the securitised assets.

2.2.3 the legal nature of the assets;

2.2.4 the expiry or maturity date(s) of the assets;

2.2.5 the amount of the assets;

2.2.6 loan to value ratio or level of collateralisation;

2.2.7 the method of origination or creation of the assets, and for loans and credit agreements, the principal lending criteria and an indication of any loans which do not meet these criteria and any rights or obligations to make further advances;

2.2.8 an indication of significant representations and collaterals given to the issuer relating to the assets;

2.2.9 any rights to substitute the assets and a description of the manner in which and the type of assets which may be so substituted; if there is any capacity to substitute assets with a different class or quality of assets a statement to that effect together with a description of the impact of such substitution;

2.2.10 a description of any relevant insurance policies relating to the assets. Any concentration with one insurer must be disclosed if it is material to the transaction.

2.2.11 Where the assets comprise obligations of 5 or fewer obligors which are legal persons or where an obligor accounts for 20 % or more of the assets, or where an obligor accounts for a material portion of the assets, so far as the issuer is aware and/or is able to ascertain from information published by the obligor(s) indicate either of the following:

(a) information relating to each obligor as if it were an issuer drafting a registration document for debt and derivative securities with an individual denomination of at least EUR 50,000;

(b) if an obligor or guarantor has securities already admitted to trading on a regulated or equivalent market or the obligations are guaranteed by an entity admitted to trading on a regulated or equivalent market, the name, address, country of incorporation, nature of business and name of the market in which its securities are admitted.

2.2.12. If a relationship exists that is material to the issue, between the issuer, guarantor and obligor, details of the principal terms of that relationship.

2.2.13. Where the assets comprise obligations that are not traded on a regulated or equivalent market, a description of the principal terms and conditions of the obligations.

2.2.14. Where the assets comprise equity securities that are admitted to trading on a regulated or equivalent market indicate the following:

(a) a description of the securities;

(b) a description of the market on which they are traded including its date of establishment, how price information is published, an indication of daily trading volumes, information as to the standing of the market in the country and the name of the market's regulatory authority;

(c) the frequency with which prices of the relevant securities, are published.

2.2.15. Where more than ten (10) per cent of the assets comprise equity securities that are not traded on a regulated or equivalent market, a description of those equity securities and equivalent information to that contained in the schedule for share registration document in respect of each issuer of those securities.

2.2.16. Where a material portion of the assets are secured on or backed by real property, a valuation report relating to the property setting out both the valuation of the property and cash flow/income streams.

Compliance with this disclosure is not required if the issue is of securities backed by mortgage loans with property as security, where there has been no revaluation of the properties for the purpose of the issue, and it is clearly stated that the valuations quoted are as at the date of the original initial mortgage loan origination.

2.3. *In respect of an actively managed pool of assets backing the issue:*

2.3.1. equivalent information to that contained in items 2.1 and 2.2 to allow an assessment of the type, quality, sufficiency and liquidity of the asset types in the portfolio which will secure the issue;

2.3.2. the parameters within which investments can be made, the name and description of the entity responsible for such management including a description of that entity's expertise and experience, a summary of the provisions relating to the termination of the appointment of such entity and the appointment of an alternative management entity, and a description of that entity's relationship with any other parties to the issue.

2.4. Where an issuer proposes to issue further securities backed by the same assets, a prominent statement to that effect and unless those further securities are fungible with or are subordinated to those classes of existing debt, a description of how the holders of that class will be informed.

3. **Structure and Cash Flow**

3.1. Description of the structure of the transaction, including, if necessary, a structure diagram.

3.2. Description of the entities participating in the issue and description of the functions to be performed by them.

3.3. Description of the method and date of the sale, transfer, novation or assignment of the assets or of any rights and/or obligations in the assets to the issuer or, where applicable, the manner and time period in which the proceeds from the issue will be fully invested by the issuer.

3.4. *An explanation of the flow of funds including:*

3.4.1. how the cash flow from the assets will meet the issuer's obligations to holders of the securities, including, if necessary, a financial service table and a description of the assumptions used in developing the table;

3.4.2. information on any credit enhancements, an indication of where material potential liquidity shortfalls may occur and the availability of any liquidity supports and indication of provisions designed to cover interest/principal shortfall risks;

3.4.3. without prejudice to item 3.4.2, details of any subordinated debt finance;

3.4.4. an indication of any investment parameters for the investment of temporary liquidity surpluses and description of the parties responsible for such investment;

3.4.5. how payments are collected in respect of the assets;

3.4.6. the order of priority of payments made by the issuer to the holders of the class of securities in question;

3.4.7. details of any other arrangements upon which payments of interest and principal to investors are dependent;

3.5. the name, address and significant business activities of the originators of the securitised assets.

3.6. Where the return on, and/or repayment of the security is linked to the performance or credit of other assets which are not assets of the issuer, items 2.2 and 2.3 are necessary;

3.7. the name, address and significant business activities of the administrator, calculation agent or equivalent, together with a summary of the administrator's/calculation agents responsibilities, their relationship with the originator or the creator of the assets and a summary of the provisions relating to the termination of the appointment of the administrator/calculation agent and the appointment of an alternative administrator/calculation agent;

3.8. the names and addresses and brief description of:

(a) any swap counterparties and any providers of other material forms of credit/liquidity enhancement;

(b) the banks with which the main accounts relating to the transaction are held.

4. Post Issuance Reporting

4.1. Indication in the prospectus whether or not it intends to provide post-issuance transaction information regarding securities to be admitted to trading and the performance of the underlying collateral. Where the issuer has indicated that it intends to report such information, specify in the prospectus what information will be reported, where such information can be obtained, and the frequency with which such information will be reported.

Annex IX

Minimum disclosure requirements for the debt and derivative securities registration document (schedule)

(Debt and derivative securities with a denomination per unit of at least EUR 50,000)

1. **Persons Responsible**

1.1. All persons responsible for the information given in the registration document and, as the case may be, for certain parts of it, with, in the latter case, an indication of such parts. In the case of natural persons including members of the issuer's administrative, management or supervisory bodies indicate the name and function of the person; in case of legal persons indicate the name and registered office.

1.2. A declaration by those responsible for the registration document that, having taken all reasonable care to ensure that such is the case, the information contained in the registration document is, to the best of their knowledge, in accordance with the facts and contains no omission likely to affect its import. As the case may be, declaration by those responsible for certain parts of the registration document that, having taken all reasonable care to ensure that such is the case, the information contained in the part of the registration document for which they are responsible is, to the best of their knowledge, in accordance with the facts and contains no omission likely to affect its import.

2. **Statutory Auditors**

2.1. Names and addresses of the issuer's auditors for the period covered by the historical financial information (together with their membership in a professional body).

2.2. If auditors have resigned, been removed or not been re-appointed during the period covered by the historical financial information, details if material.

3. **Risk Factors**

3.1. Prominent disclosure of risk factors that may affect the issuer's ability to fulfil its obligations under the securities to investors in a section headed 'Risk Factors'.

4. **Information about the Issuer**

4.1 *History and development of the Issuer*

4.1.1 the legal and commercial name of the issuer;

4.1.2 the place of registration of the issuer and its registration number;

4.1.3 the date of incorporation and the length of life of the issuer, except where indefinite;

4.1.4. the domicile and legal form of the issuer, the legislation under which the issuer operates, its country of incorporation, and the address and telephone number of its registered office (or principal place of business if different from its registered office;

4.1.5. any recent events particular to the issuer and which are to a material extent relevant to the evaluation of the issuer's solvency.

5. Business Overview

5.1. *Principal activities:*

5.1.1. A brief description of the issuer's principal activities stating the main categories of products sold and/or services performed;

5.1.2. The basis for any statements in the registration document made by the issuer regarding its competitive position.

6. Organisational Structure

6.1. If the issuer is part of a group, a brief description of the group and of the issuer's position within it.

6.2. If the issuer is dependent upon other entities within the group, this must be clearly stated together with an explanation of this dependence.

7. Trend Information

7.1. Include a statement that there has been no material adverse change in the prospects of the issuer since the date of its last published audited financial statements.

In the event that the issuer is unable to make such a statement, provide details of this material adverse change.

8. Profit Forecasts or Estimates

If an issuer chooses to include a profit forecast or a profit estimate, the registration document must contain the information items 8.1 and 8.2 the following:

8.1. A statement setting out the principal assumptions upon which the issuer has based its forecast, or estimate.

There must be a clear distinction between assumptions about factors which the members of the administrative, management or supervisory bodies can influence and assumptions about factors which are exclusively outside the influence of the members of the administrative, management or supervisory bodies; be readily understandable by investors; be specific and precise; and not relate to the general accuracy of the estimates underlying the forecast.

8.2. Any profit forecast set out in the registration document must be accompanied by a statement confirming that the said forecast has been properly prepared on the basis stated and that the basis of accounting is consistent with the accounting policies of the issuer.

8.3. The profit forecast or estimate must be prepared on a basis comparable with the historical financial information.

9. Administrative, Management, and Supervisory Bodies

9.1. Names, business addresses and functions in the issuer of the following persons, and an indication of the principal activities performed by them outside the issuer where these are significant with respect to that issuer:

(a) members of the administrative, management or supervisory bodies;

(b) partners with unlimited liability, in the case of a limited partnership with a share capital.

9.2. *Administrative, Management, and Supervisory bodies' conflicts of interests*

Potential conflicts of interests between any duties to the issuing entity of the persons referred to in item 9.1 and their private interests and or other duties must be clearly stated. In the event that there are no such conflicts, a statement to that effect.

10. Major Shareholders

10.1. To the extent known to the issuer, state whether the issuer is directly or indirectly owned or controlled and by whom, and describe the nature of such control, and describe the measures in place to ensure that such control is not abused.

10.2. A description of any arrangements, known to the issuer, the operation of which may at a subsequent date result in a change in control of the issuer.

11. Financial Information Concerning the Issuer's Assets and Liabilities, Financial Position and Profits And Losses

11.1. *Historical Financial Information*

Audited historical financial information covering the latest two financial years (or such shorter period that the issuer has been in operation), and the audit report in respect of each year. [If the issuer has changed its accounting reference date during the period for which historical financial information is required, the audited historical information shall cover at least 24 months, or the entire period for which the issuer has been in operation, whichever is the shorter.][a] Such financial information must be prepared according to Regulation (EC) No 1606/2002, or if not applicable to a Member's State national accounting standards for issuers from the Community. For third country issuers, such financial information must be prepared according to the international accounting standards adopted pursuant to the procedure of Article 3 of Regulation (EC) No 1606/2002 or to a third country's national accounting standards equivalent to these standards. Otherwise, the following information must be included in the registration document:

(a) a prominent statement that the financial information included in the registration document has not been prepared in accordance with the international accounting standards adopted pursuant to the procedure of Article 3 of Regulation (EC) No 1606/2002 and that there may be material differences in the financial information had Regulation (EC) No 1606/2002 been applied to the historical financial information.

(b) immediately following the historical financial information a narrative description of the differences between the international accounting standards adopted pursuant to the procedure of Article 3 of Regulation (EC) No 1606/2002 and the accounting principles adopted by the issuer in preparing its annual financial statements.

The most recent year's historical financial information must be presented and prepared in a form consistent with that which will be adopted in the issuer's next published annual financial statements having regard to accounting standards and policies and legislation applicable to such annual financial statements.

If the audited financial information is prepared according to national accounting standards, the financial information required under this heading must include at least the following:

(a) the balance sheet;

(b) the income statement;

(c) the accounting policies and explanatory notes.

The historical annual financial information must be independently audited or reported on as to whether or not, for the purposes of the registration document, it gives a true and fair view, in accordance with auditing standards applicable in a Member State or an equivalent standard. Otherwise, the following information must be included in the registration document:

(a) a prominent statement disclosing which auditing standards have been applied;

(b) an explanation of any significant departures from international standards on auditing.

Amendments

a Inserted by Commission Regulation (EC) No 211/2007 of 27 February 2007 OJ L337 5.12.2006, p 17.

11.2. *Financial statements*

If the issuer prepares both own and consolidated financial statements, include at least the consolidated financial statements in the registration document.

11.3. *Auditing of historical annual financial information*

11.3.1 A statement that the historical financial information has been audited. If audit reports on the historical financial information have been refused by the statutory auditors or if they contain qualifications or disclaimers, such refusal or such qualifications or disclaimers must be reproduced in full and the reasons given.

11.3.2. An indication of other information in the registration document which has been audited by the auditors.

11.3.3. Where financial data in the registration document is not extracted from the issuer's audited financial statements, state the source of the data and state that the data is unaudited.

11.4. *Age of latest financial information*

11.4.1. The last year of audited financial information may not be older than 18 months from the date of the registration document.

11.5. *Legal and arbitration proceedings*

Information on any governmental, legal or arbitration proceedings (including any such proceedings which are pending or threatened of which the issuer is aware), during a period covering at least the previous 12 months which may have, or have had in the recent past, significant effects on the issuer and/or group's financial position or profitability, or provide an appropriate negative statement.

11.6. *Significant change in the issuer's financial or trading position*

A description of any significant change in the financial or trading position of the group which has occurred since the end of the last financial period for which either audited financial information or interim financial information have been published, or an appropriate negative statement.

12. Material Contracts

A brief summary of all material contracts that are not entered into in the ordinary course of the issuer's business, which could result in any group member being under an obligation or entitlement that is material to the issuer's ability to meet its obligation to security holders in respect of the securities being issued.

13. Third Party Information and Statement by Experts and Declarations of Any Interest

13.1. Where a statement or report attributed to a person as an expert is included in the registration document, provide such person's name, business address, qualifications and material interest if any in the issuer. If the report has been produced at the issuer's request a statement to that effect that such statement or report is included, in the form and context in which it is included, with the consent of that person who has authorised the contents of that part of the registration document.

13.2. *Third party information*

Where information has been sourced from a third party, provide a confirmation that this information has been accurately reproduced and that as far as the issuer is aware and is able to ascertain from information published by that third party, no facts have been omitted which would render the reproduced information inaccurate or misleading; in addition, identify the source(s) of the information.

14. Documents on Display

A statement that for the life of the registration document the following documents (or copies thereof), where applicable, may be inspected:

(a) the memorandum and articles of association of the issuer;

(b) all reports, letters, and other documents, historical financial information, valuations and statements prepared by any expert at the issuer's request any part of which is included or referred to in the registration document;

(c) the historical financial information of the issuer or, in the case of a group, the historical financial information of the issuer and its subsidiary undertakings for each of the two financial years preceding the publication of the registration document.

An indication of where the documents on display may be inspected, by physical or electronic means.

Annex X
Minimum disclosure requirements for the depository receipts issued over shares (schedule)

Information about the Issuer of the Underlying Shares

1. Persons Responsible

1.1. All persons responsible for the information given in the prospectus and, as the case may be, for certain parts of it, with, in the latter case, an indication of such parts. In the case of natural persons including members of the issuer's administrative, management or supervisory bodies indicate the name and function of the person; in case of legal persons indicate the name and registered office.

1.2. A declaration by those responsible for the prospectus that, having taken all reasonable care to ensure that such is the case, the information contained in the prospectus is, to the best of their knowledge, in accordance with the facts and contains no omission likely to affect its import. As the case may be, declaration by those responsible for certain parts of the prospectus that, having taken all reasonable care to ensure that such is the case, the information contained in the part of the prospectus for which they are responsible is, to the best of their knowledge, in accordance with the facts and contains no omission likely to affect its import.

2. Statutory Auditors

2.1. Names and addresses of the issuer's auditors for the period covered by the historical financial information (together with their membership in a professional body).

2.2. If auditors have resigned, been removed or not been re-appointed during the period covered by the historical financial information, indicate details if material.

3. Selected Financial Information

3.1. Selected historical financial information regarding the issuer, presented for each financial year for the period covered by the historical financial information, and any subsequent interim financial period, in the same currency as the financial information.

The selected historical financial information must provide the key figures that summarise the financial condition of the issuer.

3.2. If selected financial information for interim periods is provided, comparative data from the same period in the prior financial year shall also be provided, except that the requirement for comparative balance sheet information is satisfied by presenting the year end balance sheet information.

4. Risk Factors

Prominent disclosure of risk factors that are specific to the issuer or its industry in a section headed 'Risk Factors'.

5. Information about the Issuer

5.1 *History and development of the issuer*

5.1.1 the legal and commercial name of the issuer;

5.1.2 the place of registration of the issuer and its registration number;

5.1.3 the date of incorporation and the length of life of the issuer, except where indefinite;

5.1.4. the domicile and legal form of the issuer, the legislation under which the issuer operates, its country of incorporation, and the address and telephone number of its registered office (or principal place of business if different from its registered office);

5.1.5. the important events in the development of the issuer's business.

5.2. *Investments*

5.2.1. A description, (including the amount) of the issuer's principal investments for each financial year for the period covered by the historical financial information up to the date of the prospectus;

5.2.2.A description of the issuer's principal investments that are currently in progress, including the distribution of these investments geographically (home and abroad) and the method of financing (internal or external);

5.2.3.Information concerning the issuer's principal future investments on which its management bodies have already made firm commitments.

6. Business Overview

6.1. *Principal Activities*

6.1.1. A description of, and key factors relating to, the nature of the issuer's operations and its principal activities, stating the main categories of products sold and/or services performed for each financial year for the period covered by the historical financial information.

6.1.2. An indication of any significant new products and/or services that have been introduced and, to the extent the development of new products or services has been publicly disclosed, give the status of development.

6.2. *Principal Markets*

A description of the principal markets in which the issuer competes, including a breakdown of total revenues by category of activity and geographic market for each financial year for the period covered by the historical financial information.

6.3. Where the information given pursuant to items 6.1 and 6.2 has been influenced by exceptional factors, mention that fact.

6.4. If material to the issuer's business or profitability, disclose summary information regarding the extent to which the issuer is dependent, on patents or licences, industrial, commercial or financial contracts or new manufacturing processes.

6.5. The basis for any statements made by the issuer regarding its competitive position.

7. Organisational Structure

7.1. If the issuer is part of a group, a brief description of the group and the issuer's position within the group.

7.2. A list of the issuer's significant subsidiaries, including name, country of incorporation or residence, proportion of ownership interest and, if different, proportion of voting power held.

8. Property, Plants and Equipment

8.1. Information regarding any existing or planned material tangible fixed assets, including leased properties, and any major encumbrances thereon.

8.2. A description of any environmental issues that may affect the issuer's utilisation of the tangible fixed assets.

9. Operating and Financial Review

9.1. *Financial condition*

To the extent not covered elsewhere in the prospectus, provide a description of the issuer's financial condition, changes in financial condition and results of operations for each year and interim period, for which historical financial information is required, including the causes of material changes from year to year in the financial information to the extent necessary for an understanding of the issuer's business as a whole.

9.2. *Operating results*

9.2.1. Information regarding significant factors, including unusual or infrequent events or new developments, materially affecting the issuer's income from operations, indicating the extent to which income was so affected.

9.2.2. Where the financial statements disclose material changes in net sales or revenues, provide a narrative discussion of the reasons for such changes.

9.2.3. Information regarding any governmental, economic, fiscal, monetary or political policies or factors that have materially affected, or could materially affect, directly or indirectly, the issuer's operations.

10. Capital Resources

10.1. Information concerning the issuer's capital resources (both short and long term).

10.2. An explanation of the sources and amounts of and a narrative description of the issuer's cash flows.

10.3. Information on the borrowing requirements and funding structure of the issuer.

10.4. Information regarding any restrictions on the use of capital resources that have materially affected, or could materially affect, directly or indirectly, the issuer's operations.

10.5. Information regarding the anticipated sources of funds needed to fulfil commitments referred to in items 5.2.3 and 8.1.

11. Research and Development, Patents And Licences

Where material, provide a description of the issuer's research and development policies for each financial year for the period covered by the historical financial information, including the amount spent on issuer-sponsored research and development activities.

12. Trend Information

12.1. The most significant recent trends in production, sales and inventory, and costs and selling prices since the end of the last financial year to the date of the prospectus.

12.2. Information on any known trends, uncertainties, demands, commitments or events that are reasonably likely to have a material effect on the issuer's prospects for at least the current financial year.

13. Profit Forecasts or Estimates

If an issuer chooses to include a profit forecast or a profit estimate the prospectus must contain the information items 13.1 and 13.2.

13.1. A statement setting out the principal assumptions upon which the issuer has based its forecast, or estimate.

There must be a clear distinction between assumptions about factors which the members of the administrative, management or supervisory bodies can influence and assumptions about factors which are exclusively outside the influence of the members of the administrative, management or supervisory bodies; the assumptions must be readily understandable by investors, be specific and precise and not relate to the general accuracy of the estimates underlying the forecast.

13.2. A report prepared by independent accountants or auditors stating that in the opinion of the independent accountants or auditors the forecast or estimate has been properly compiled on the basis stated and that the basis of accounting used for the profit forecast or estimate is consistent with the accounting policies of the issuer.

13.3. The profit forecast or estimate prepared on a basis comparable with the historical financial information.

13.4. If the issuer has published a profit forecast in a prospectus which is still outstanding, provide a statement setting out whether or not that forecast is still correct as at the time of the prospectus, and an explanation of why such forecast is no longer valid if that is the case.

14. Administrative, Management, and Supervisory Bodies and Senior Management

14.1. Names, business addresses and functions in the issuer of the following persons and an indication of the principal activities performed by them outside that issuer where these are significant with respect to that issuer:

(a) members of the administrative, management or supervisory bodies;

(b) partners with unlimited liability, in the case of a limited partnership with a share capital;

(c) founders, if the issuer has been established for fewer than five years;

(d) any senior manager who is relevant to establishing that the issuer has the appropriate expertise and experience for the management of the issuer's business.

The nature of any family relationship between any of those persons.

In the case of each member of the administrative, management or supervisory bodies of the issuer and person described in points (b) and (d) of the first subparagraph, details of that person's relevant management expertise and experience and the following information:

(a) the names of all companies and partnerships of which such person has been a member of the administrative, management or supervisory bodies or partner at any time in the previous five years, indicating whether or not the individual is still a member of the administrative, management or supervisory bodies or partner. It is not necessary to list all the subsidiaries of an issuer of which the person is also a member of the administrative, management or supervisory bodies;

(b) any convictions in relation to fraudulent offences for at least the previous five years;

(c) details of any bankruptcies, receiverships or liquidations with which a person described in points (a) and (d) of the first subparagraph who was acting in the capacity of any of the positions set out in points (a) and (d) of the first subparagraph member of the administrative, management or supervisory bodies was associated for at least the previous five years;

(d) details of any official public incrimination and/or sanctions of such person by statutory or regulatory authorities (including designated professional bodies) and whether such person has ever been disqualified by a court from acting as a member of the administrative, management or supervisory bodies of an issuer or from acting in the management or conduct of the affairs of any issuer for at least the previous five years.

If there is no such information to be disclosed, a statement to that effect must be made.

14.2. *Administrative, Management, and Supervisory bodies' and Senior Management conflicts of interests*

Potential conflicts of interests between any duties to the issuer of the persons referred to in the first subparagraph of item 14.1 and their private interests and or other duties must be clearly stated. In the event that there are no such conflicts, make a statement to that effect.

Any arrangement or understanding with major shareholders, customers, suppliers or others, pursuant to which any person referred to in the first subparagraph of item 14.1 was selected as a member of the administrative, management or supervisory bodies or member of senior management.

15. Remuneration and Benefits

In relation to the last full financial year for those persons referred to in points (a) and (d) of the first subparagraph of item 14.1:

15.1. The amount of remuneration paid (including any contingent or deferred compensation), and benefits in kind granted, to such persons by the issuer and its subsidiaries for services in all capacities to the issuer and its subsidiaries by any person.

This information must be provided on an individual basis unless individual disclosure is not required in the issuer's home country and is not otherwise publicly disclosed by the issuer.

15.2. The total amounts set aside or accrued by the issuer or its subsidiaries to provide pension, retirement or similar benefits.

16. Board Practices

In relation to the issuer's last completed financial year, and unless otherwise specified, with respect to those persons referred to in point (a) of the first subparagraph of item 14.1:

16.1. Date of expiration of the current term of office, if applicable, and the period during which the person has served in that office.

16.2. Information about members of the administrative, management or supervisory bodies' service contracts with the issuer or any of its subsidiaries providing for benefits upon termination of employment, or an appropriate negative statement.

16.3. Information about the issuer's audit committee and remuneration committee, including the names of committee members and a summary of the terms of reference under which the committee operates.

16.4. A statement as to whether or not the issuer complies with its country's of incorporation corporate governance regime(s). In the event that the issuer does not comply with such a regime, a statement to that effect together with an explanation regarding why the issuer does not comply with such regime.

17. Employees

17.1. Either the number of employees at the end of the period or the average for each financial year for the period covered by the historical financial information up to the date of the prospectus (and changes in such numbers, if material) and, if possible and material, a breakdown of persons employed by main category of activity and geographic location. If the issuer employs a significant number of temporary employees, include disclosure of the number of temporary employees on average during the most recent financial year.

17.2. Shareholdings and stock options

With respect to each person referred to in points (a) and (b) of the first subparagraph of item 14.1, provide information as to their share ownership and any options over such shares in the issuer as of the most recent practicable date.

17.3. Description of any arrangements for involving the employees in the capital of the issuer.

18. Major Shareholders

18.1. In so far as is known to the issuer, the name of any person other than a member of the administrative, management or supervisory bodies who, directly or indirectly, has an interest notifiable under the issuer's national law in the issuer's capital or voting rights, together with the amount of each such person's interest or, if there are no such persons, an appropriate negative statement.

18.2. Whether the issuer's major shareholders have different voting rights, or an appropriate negative statement.

18.3. To the extent known to the issuer, state whether the issuer is directly or indirectly owned or controlled and by whom and describe the nature of such control and describe the measures in place to ensure that such control is not abused.

18.4. A description of any arrangements, known to the issuer, the operation of which may at a subsequent date result in a change in control of the issuer.

19. Related Party Transactions

Details of related party transactions (which for these purposes are those set out in the Standards adopted according to Regulation (EC) No 1606/2002), that the issuer has entered into during the period covered by the historical financial information and up to the date of the prospectus must be disclosed in accordance with the respective standard adopted according to Regulation (EC) No 1606/2002 if applicable.

If such standards do not apply to the issuer the following information must be disclosed:

(a) the nature and extent of any transactions which are - as a single transaction or in their entirety - material to the issuer. Where such related party transactions are not concluded at arm's length provide an explanation of why these transactions were not concluded at arms length. In the case of outstanding loans including guarantees of any kind indicate the amount outstanding;

(b) the amount or the percentage to which related party transactions form part of the turnover of the issuer.

20. Financial Information Concerning the Issuer's Assets and Liabilities, Financial Position and Profits and Losses

20.1. *Historical financial information*

Audited historical financial information covering the latest 3 financial years (or such shorter period that the issuer has been in operation), and the audit report in respect of each year. [If the issuer has changed its accounting reference date during the period for which historical financial information is required, the audited historical information shall cover at least 36 months, or the entire period for which the issuer has been in operation, whichever is the shorter.][a] Such financial information must be prepared according to Regulation (EC) No 1606/2002, or if not applicable to a Member States national accounting standards for issuers from the Community. For third country issuers, such financial information must be prepared according to the international accounting standards adopted pursuant to the procedure of Article 3 of Regulation (EC) No 1606/2002 or to a third country's national accounting standards equivalent to these standards. If such financial information is not equivalent to these standards, it must be presented in the form of restated financial statements.

The last two years audited historical financial information must be presented and prepared in a form consistent with that which will be adopted in the issuer's next published annual financial statements having regard to accounting standards and policies and legislation applicable to such annual financial statements.

If the issuer has been operating in its current sphere of economic activity for less than one year, the audited historical financial information covering that period must be prepared in accordance with the standards applicable to annual financial statements under Regulation (EC) No 1606/2002, or if not applicable to a Member States national accounting standards where the issuer is an issuer from the Community. For third country issuers, the historical financial information must be prepared according to the international accounting standards adopted pursuant to the procedure of Article 3 of Regulation (EC) No 1606/2002 or to a third country's national accounting standards equivalent to these standards. This historical financial information must be audited.

If the audited financial information is prepared according to national accounting standards, the financial information required under this heading must include at least the following:

(a) the balance sheet;

(b) the income statement;

(c) a statement showing either all changes in equity or changes in equity other than those arising from capital transactions with owners and distributions to owners;

(d) the cash flow statement;

(e) the accounting policies and explanatory notes.

The historical annual financial information must be independently audited or reported on as to whether or not, for the purposes of the prospectus, it gives a true and fair view, in accordance with auditing standards applicable in a Member State or an equivalent standard.

Amendments

a Inserted by Commission Regulation (EC) No 211/2007 of 27 February 2007 OJ L337 5.12.2006, p 17.

20.1a *This paragraph may be used only for issues of depository receipts having a denomination per unit of at least EUR 50,000.*

Audited historical financial information covering the latest three financial years (or such shorter period that the issuer has been in operation), and the audit report in respect of each year. [If the issuer has changed its accounting reference date during the period for which historical financial information is required, the audited historical information shall cover at least 36 months, or the entire period for which the issuer has been in operation, whichever is the shorter.][a] Such financial information must be prepared according to Regulation (EC) No 1606/2002, or if not applicable to a Member State's national accounting standards for issuers from the Community. For third country issuers, such financial information must be prepared according to the international accounting standards adopted pursuant to the procedure of Article 3 of Regulation (EC) No 1606/2002 or to a third country's national accounting standards equivalent to these standards. Otherwise, the following information must be included in the prospectus:

(a) a prominent statement that the financial information included in the registration document has not been prepared in accordance with the international accounting standards adopted pursuant to the procedure of Article 3 of Regulation (EC) No 1606/2002 and that there may be material differences in the financial information had Regulation (EC) No 1606/2002 been applied to the historical financial information;

(b) immediately following the historical financial information a narrative description of the differences between the international accounting standards adopted pursuant to the procedure of Article 3 of Regulation (EC) No 1606/2002 and the accounting principles adopted by the issuer in preparing its annual financial statements.

The last two years audited historical financial information must be presented and prepared in a form consistent with that which will be adopted in the issuer's next published annual financial statements having regard to accounting standards and policies and legislation applicable to such annual financial statements.

If the audited financial information is prepared according to national accounting standards, the financial information required under this heading must include at least the following:

(a) the balance sheet;

(b) the income statement;

(c) a statement showing either all changes in equity or changes in equity other than those arising from capital transactions with owners and distributions to owners;

(d) the cash flow statement;

(e) the accounting policies and explanatory notes.

The historical annual financial information must be independently audited or reported on as to whether or not, for the purposes of the prospectus, it gives a true and fair view, in accordance with auditing standards applicable in a Member State or an equivalent standard. Otherwise, the following information must be included in the prospectus:

(a) a prominent statement disclosing which auditing standards have been applied;

(b) an explanation of any significant departures from international standards on auditing.

Amendment

a Inserted by Commission Regulation (EC) No 211/2007 of 27 February 2007 OJ L337 5.12.2006, p 17.

20.2. *Financial statements*

If the issuer prepares both own and consolidated annual financial statements, include at least the consolidated annual financial statements in the prospectus.

20.3. *Auditing of historical annual financial information*

20.3.1. A statement that the historical financial information has been audited. If audit reports on the historical financial information have been refused by the statutory auditors or if they contain qualifications or disclaimers, such refusal or such qualifications or disclaimers must be reproduced in full and the reasons given.

20.3.2. Indication of other information in the prospectus which has been audited by the auditors.

20.3.3. Where financial data in the prospectus is not extracted from the issuer's audited financial statements state the source of the data and state that the data is unaudited.

20.4. *Age of latest financial information*

20.4.1 The last year of audited financial information may not be older than:

(a) 18 months from the date of the prospectus if the issuer includes audited interim financial statements in the prospectus;

(b) 15 months from the date of the prospectus if the issuer includes unaudited interim financial statements in the prospectus.

20.5. *Interim and other financial information*

20.5.1. If the issuer has published quarterly or half yearly financial information since the date of its last audited financial statements, these must be included in the prospectus. If the quarterly or half yearly financial information has been reviewed or audited the audit or review report must also be included. If the quarterly or half yearly financial information is unaudited or has not been reviewed, state that fact.

20.5.2. If the prospectus is dated more than nine months after the end of the last audited financial year, it must contain interim financial information, which may be unaudited (in which case that fact shall be stated) covering at least the first six months of the financial year.

The interim financial information must include comparative statements for the same period in the prior financial year, except that the requirement for comparative balance sheet information may be satisfied by presenting the years end balance sheet.

20.6. *Dividend policy*

A description of the issuer's policy on dividend distributions and any restrictions thereon.

20.6.1. The amount of the dividend per share for each financial year for the period covered by the historical financial information adjusted, where the number of shares in the issuer has changed, to make it comparable.

20.7. *Legal and arbitration proceedings*

Information on any governmental, legal or arbitration proceedings (including any such proceedings which are pending or threatened of which the issuer is aware), during a period covering at least the previous 12 months which may have, or have had in the recent past significant effects on the issuer and/or group's financial position or profitability, or provide an appropriate negative statement.

20.8. *Significant change in the issuer's financial or trading position*

A description of any significant change in the financial or trading position of the group which has occurred since the end of the last financial period for which either audited financial information or interim financial information have been published, or provide an appropriate negative statement.

21. Additional Information

21.1. *Share capital*

The following information as of the date of the most recent balance sheet included in the historical financial information:

21.1.1. The amount of issued capital, and for each class of share capital:

(a) the number of shares authorised;

(b) the number of shares issued and fully paid and issued but not fully paid;

(c) the par value per share, or that the shares have no par value;

(d) a reconciliation of the number of shares outstanding at the beginning and end of the year. If more than 10 % of capital has been paid for with assets other than cash within the period covered by the historical financial information, state that fact.

21.1.2. If there are shares not representing capital, state the number and main characteristics of such shares.

21.1.3. The number, book value and face value of shares in the issuer held by or on behalf of the issuer itself or by subsidiaries of the issuer.

21.1.4. The amount of any convertible securities, exchangeable securities or securities with warrants, with an indication of the conditions governing and the procedures for conversion, exchange or subscription.

21.1.5. Information about and terms of any acquisition rights and or obligations over authorised but unissued capital or an undertaking to increase the capital.

21.1.6. Information about any capital of any member of the group which is under option or agreed conditionally or unconditionally to be put under option and details of such options including those persons to whom such options relate.

21.1.7. A history of share capital, highlighting information about any changes, for the period covered by the historical financial information.

21.2. *Memorandum and Articles of Association*

21.2.1. A description of the issuer's objects and purposes and where they can be found in the memorandum and articles of association.

21.2.2. A summary of any provisions of the issuer's articles of association, statutes or charter and bylaws with respect to the members of the administrative, management and supervisory bodies.

21.2.3. A description of the rights, preferences and restrictions attaching to each class of the existing shares.

21.2.4. A description of what action is necessary to change the rights of holders of the shares, indicating where the conditions are more significant than is required by law.

21.2.5. A description of the conditions governing the manner in which annual general meetings and extraordinary general meetings of shareholders are called including the conditions of admission.

21.2.6. A brief description of any provision of the issuer's articles of association, statutes, charter or bylaws that would have an effect of delaying, deferring or preventing a change in control of the issuer.

21.2.7. An indication of the articles of association, statutes, charter or bylaws provisions, if any, governing the ownership threshold above which shareholder ownership must be disclosed.

21.2.8. A description of the conditions imposed by the memorandum and articles of association statutes, charter or bylaws governing changes in the capital, where such conditions are more stringent than is required by law.

22. Material Contracts

A summary of each material contract, other than contracts entered into in the ordinary course of business, to which the issuer or any member of the group is a party, for the two years immediately preceding publication of the prospectus.

A summary of any other contract (not being a contract entered into in the ordinary course of business) entered into by any member of the group which contains any provision under which any member of the group has any obligation or entitlement which is material to the group as at the date of the prospectus.

23. Third Party Information, Statement by Experts and Declarations of any Interest

23.1. Where a statement or report attributed to a person as an expert is included in the prospectus provide such person's name, business address, qualifications and material interest if any in the issuer. If the report has been produced at the issuer's request a statement to that effect that such statement or report is included, in the form and context in which it is included, with the consent of that person who has authorised the contents of that part of the prospectus.

23.2. Where information has been sourced from a third party, provide a confirmation that this information has been accurately reproduced and that as far as the issuer is aware and is able to ascertain from information published by that third party, no facts have been omitted which would render the reproduced information inaccurate or misleading. In addition, the issuer shall identify the source(s) of the information.

24. Documents on Display

A statement that for the life of the prospectus the following documents (or copies thereof), where applicable, may be inspected:

(a) the memorandum and articles of association of the issuer;

(b) all reports, letters, and other documents, historical financial information, valuations and statements prepared by any expert at the issuer's request any part of which is included or referred to in the prospectus;

(c) the historical financial information of the issuer or, in the case of a group, the historical financial information for the issuer and its subsidiary undertakings for each of the two financial years preceding the publication of the prospectus.

An indication of where the documents on display may be inspected, by physical or electronic means.

25. Information on Holdings

25.1. Information relating to the undertakings in which the issuer holds a proportion of the capital likely to have a significant effect on the assessment of its own assets and liabilities, financial position or profits and losses.

26. Information about the Issuer of the Depository Receipts

26.1. Name, registered office and principal administrative establishment if different from the registered office.

26.2. Date of incorporation and length of life of the issuer, except where indefinite.

26.3. Legislation under which the issuer operates and legal form which it has adopted under that legislation.

27. Information about the Underlying Shares

27.1. A description of the type and the class of the underlying shares, including the ISIN (International Security Identification Number) or other such security identification code.

27.2. Legislation under which the underlying shares have been created.

27.3. An indication whether the underlying shares are in registered form or bearer form and whether the underlying shares are in certificated form or book-entry form. In the latter case, name and address of the entity in *charge* of keeping the records.

27.4. Currency of the underlying shares.

27.5. A description of the rights, including any limitations of these, attached to the underlying shares and procedure for the exercise of said rights.

27.6. Dividend rights:

(a) fixed date(s) on which the entitlement arises;

(b) time limit after which entitlement to dividend lapses and an indication of the person in whose favour the lapse operates;

(c) dividend restrictions and procedures for non-resident holders;

(d) rate of dividend or method of its calculation, periodicity and cumulative or non-cumulative nature of payments.

27.7. Voting rights

Pre-emption rights in offers for subscription of securities of the same class

Right to share in the issuer's profits

Rights to share in any surplus in the event of liquidation

Redemption provisions

Conversion provisions

27.8 The issue date of the underlying shares if new underlying shares are being created for the issue of the depository receipts and they are not in existence at the time of issue of the depository receipts.

27.9 If new underlying shares are being created for the issue of the depository receipts, state the resolutions, authorisations and approvals by virtue of which the new underlying shares have been or will be created and/or issued.

27.10 A description of any restrictions on the free transferability of the underlying shares.

27.11 In respect of the country of registered office of the issuer and the country(ies) where the offer is being made or admission to trading is being sought:

(a) information on taxes on the income from the underlying shares withheld at source;

(b) indication as to whether the issuer assumes responsibility for the withholding of taxes at the source.

27.12. An indication of the existence of any mandatory takeover bids and/or squeeze-out and sell-out rules in relation to the underlying shares.

27.13. An indication of public takeover bids by third parties in respect of the issuer's equity, which have occurred during the last financial year and the current financial year. The price or exchange terms attaching to such offers and the outcome thereof must be stated.

27.14. Lock up agreements:

— the parties involved,

— content and exceptions of the agreement,

— indication of the period of the lock up.

27.15. *Information about selling share holders if any*

27.15.1. Name and business address of the person or entity offering to sell the underlying shares, the nature of any position office or other material relationship that the selling persons has had within the past three years with the issuer of the underlying shares or any of its predecessors or affiliates.

27.16. *Dilution*

27.16.1. Amount and percentage of immediate dilution resulting from the offer of the depository receipts.

27.16.2. In the case of a subscription offer of the depository receipts to existing shareholders, disclose the amount and percentage of immediate dilutions if they do not subscribe to the offer of depository receipts.

27.17. *Additional information where there is a simultaneous or almost simultaneous offer or admission to trading of the same class of underlying shares as those underlying shares over which the depository receipts are being issued.*

27.17.1. If simultaneously or almost simultaneously with the creation of the depository receipts for which admission to a regulated market is being sought underlying shares of the same class as those over which the depository receipts are being issued are subscribed for or placed privately, details are to be given of the nature of such operations and of the number and characteristics of the underlying shares to which they relate.

27.17.2. Disclose all regulated markets or equivalent markets on which, to the knowledge of the issuer of the depository receipts, underlying shares of the same class of those over which the depository receipts are being issued are offered or admitted to trading.

27.17.3. To the extent known to the issuer of the depository receipts, indicate whether major shareholders, members of the administrative, management or supervisory bodies intended to subscribe in the offer, or whether any person intends to subscribe for more than five per cent of the offer.

28. Information Regarding the Depository Receipts

28.1. A description of the type and class of depository receipts being offered and/or admitted to trading.

28.2. Legislation under which the depository receipts have been created.

28.3. An indication whether the depository receipts are in registered or bearer form and whether the depository receipts are in certificated or book-entry form. In the latter case, include the name and address of the entity in charge of keeping the records.

28.4. Currency of the depository receipts.

28.5. Describe the rights attaching to the depository receipts, including any limitations of these attached to the depository receipts and the procedure if any for the exercise of these rights.

28.6. If the dividend rights attaching to depository receipts are different from the dividend rights disclosed in relation to the underlying disclose the following about the dividend rights:

(a) fixed date(s) on which the entitlement arises;

(b) time limit after which entitlement to dividend lapses and an indication of the person in whose favour the lapse operates;

(c) dividend restrictions and procedures for non-resident holders;

(d) rate of dividend or method of its calculation, periodicity and cumulative or non-cumulative nature of payments.

28.7. If the voting rights attaching to the depository receipts are different from the voting rights disclosed in relation to the underlying shares disclose the following about those rights:

— Voting rights.

— Pre-emption rights in offers for subscription of securities of the same class.

— Right to share in the issuer's profits.

— Rights to share in any surplus in the event of liquidation.

— Redemption provisions.

— Conversion provisions.

28.8. Describe the exercise of and benefit from the rights attaching to the underlying shares, in particular voting rights, the conditions on which the issuer of the depository receipts may exercise such rights, and measures envisaged to obtain the instructions of the depository receipt holders - and the right to share in profits and any liquidation surplus which are not passed on to the holder of the depository receipt.

28.9. The expected issue date of the depository receipts.

28.10. A description of any restrictions on the free transferability of the depository receipts.

28.11. In respect of the country of registered office of the issuer and the country(ies) where the offer is being made or admission to trading is being sought:

(a) information on taxes on the income from the depository receipts withheld at source;

(b) indication as to whether the issuer assumes responsibility for the withholding of taxes at the source.

28.12. Bank or other guarantees attached to the depository receipts and intended to underwrite the issuer's obligations.

28.13. Possibility of obtaining the delivery of the depository receipts into original shares and procedure for such delivery.

29. Information about the Terms and Conditions of the Offer of the Depository Receipts

29.1. *Conditions, offer statistics, expected timetable and action required to apply for the offer*

29.1.1. Total amount of the issue/offer, distinguishing the securities offered for sale and those offered for subscription; if the amount is not fixed, description of the arrangements and time for announcing to the public the definitive amount of the offer.

29.1.2. The time period, including any possible amendments, during which the offer will be open and description of the application process.

29.1.3. An indication of when, and under what circumstances, the offer may be revoked or suspended and whether revocation can occur after dealing has begun.

29.1.4. A description of the possibility to reduce subscriptions and the manner for refunding excess amount paid by applicants.

29.1.5. Details of the minimum and/or maximum amount of application (whether in number of securities or aggregate amount to invest).

29.1.6. An indication of the period during which an application may be withdrawn, provided that investors are allowed to withdraw their subscription.

29.1.7. Method and time limits for paying up the securities and for delivery of the securities.

29.1.8. A full description of the manner and date in which results of the offer are to be made public.

29.1.9. The procedure for the exercise of any right of pre-emption, the negotiability of subscription rights and the treatment of subscription rights not exercised.

29.2. *Plan of distribution and allotment*

29.2.1. The various categories of potential investors to which the securities are offered. If the offer is being made simultaneously in the markets of two or more countries and if a tranche has been or is being reserved for certain of these, indicate any such tranche.

29.2.2. To the extent known to the issuer, indicate whether major shareholders or members of the issuer's management, supervisory or administrative bodies intended to subscribe in the offer, or whether any person intends to subscribe for more than five per cent of the offer.

29.2.3. Pre-allotment Disclosure:

29.2.3.1. The division into tranches of the offer including the institutional, retail and issuer's employee tranches and any other tranches.

29.2.3.2. The conditions under which the claw-back may be used, the maximum size of such claw back and any applicable minimum percentages for individual tranches.

29.2.3.3. The allotment method or methods to be used for the retail and issuer's employee tranche in the event of an over-subscription of these tranches.

29.2.3.4. A description of any pre-determined preferential treatment to be accorded to certain classes of investors or certain affinity groups (including friends and family programmes) in the allotment, the percentage of the offer reserved for such preferential treatment and the criteria for inclusion in such classes or groups.

29.2.3.5. Whether the treatment of subscriptions or bids to subscribe in the allotment may be determined on the basis of which firm they are made through or by.

29.2.3.6. A target minimum individual allotment if any within the retail tranche.

29.2.3.7. The conditions for the closing of the offer as well as the date on which the offer may be closed at the earliest;

29.2.3.8. Whether or not multiple subscriptions are admitted, and where they are not, how any multiple subscriptions will be handled.

29.2.3.9. Process for notification to applicants of the amount allotted and indication whether dealing may begin before notification is made.

29.2.4. Over-allotment and 'green shoe':

29.2.4.1. The existence and size of any over-allotment facility and/or 'green shoe'.

29.2.4.2. The existence period of the over-allotment facility and/or 'green shoe'.

29.2.4.3. Any conditions for the use of the over-allotment facility or exercise of the 'green shoe'.

29.3. *Pricing*

29.3.1. An indication of the price at which the securities will be offered. When the price is not known or when there is not an established and/or liquid market for the securities, indicate the method for determination of the offer price, including who has set the criteria or is formally responsible for its determination. Indication of the amount of any expenses and taxes specifically *charged* to the subscriber or purchaser.

29.3.2. Process for the disclosure of the offer price.

29.3.3. Where there is or could be a material disparity between the public offer price and the effective cash cost to members of the administrative, management or supervisory bodies or senior management, or affiliated persons, of securities acquired by them in transactions during the past year, or which they have the right to acquire, include a comparison of the public contribution in the proposed public offer and the effective cash contributions of such persons.

29.4. *Placing and underwriting*

29.4.1. Name and address of the co-coordinator(s) of the global offer and of single parts of the offer and, to the extend known to the issuer, of the placers in the various countries where the offer takes place.

29.4.2. Name and address of any paying agents and depository agents in each country.

29.4.3. Name and address of the entities agreeing to underwrite the issue on a firm commitment basis, and name and address of the entities agreeing to place the issue without a firm commitment or under 'best efforts' arrangements. Indication of the material features of the agreements, including the quotas. Where not all of the issue is underwritten, a statement of the portion not covered. Indication of the overall amount of the underwriting commission and of the placing commission.

29.4.4. When the underwriting agreement has been or will be reached.

30. Admission to Trading and Dealing Arrangements in the Depository Receipts

30.1. An indication as to whether the securities offered are or will be the object of an application for admission to trading, with a view to their distribution in a regulated market or other equivalent markets with indication of the markets in question. This circumstance must be mentioned, without creating the impression that the admission to trading necessarily will be approved. If known, the earliest dates on which the securities will be admitted to trading must be given.

30.2. All the regulated markets or equivalent markets on which, to the knowledge of the issuer, securities of the same class of the securities to be offered or admitted to trading are already admitted to trading.

30.3. If simultaneously or almost simultaneously with the creation of the securities for which admission to a regulated market is being sought securities of the same class are subscribed for or placed privately or if securities of other classes are created for public or private placing, details must be given of the nature of such operations and of the number and characteristics of the securities to which they relate.

30.4. Name and address of the entities which have a firm commitment to act as intermediaries in secondary trading, providing liquidity through bid and offer rates and description of the main terms of their commitment.

30.5. Stabilisation: where an issuer or a selling shareholder has granted an over-allotment option or it is otherwise proposed that price stabilising activities may be entered into in connection with an offer:

30.6. The fact that stabilisation may be undertaken, that there is no assurance that it will be undertaken and that it may be stopped at any time.

30.7. The beginning and the end of the period during which stabilisation may occur.

30.8. The identity of the stabilisation manager for each relevant jurisdiction unless this is not known at the time of publication.

30.9. The fact that stabilisation transactions may result in a market price that is higher than would otherwise prevail.

31. Key Information about the Issue of the Depository Receipts

31.1. *Reasons for the offer and use of proceeds*

31.1.1. Reasons for the offer and, where applicable, the estimated net amount of the proceeds broken into each principal intended use and presented by order of priority of such uses. If the issuer is aware that the anticipated proceeds will not be sufficient to fund all the proposed uses, state the amount and sources of other funds needed. Details must be given with regard to the use of the proceeds, in particular when they are being used to acquire assets, other than in the ordinary course of business, to finance announced acquisitions of other business, or to *discharge*, reduce or retire indebtedness.

31.2. *Interest of natural and legal persons involved in the issue/offer*

31.2.1. A description of any interest, including conflicting ones, that is material to the issue/offer, detailing the persons involved and the nature of the interest.

31.3. *Risk factors*

31.3.1.Prominent disclosure of risk factors that are material to the securities being offered and/or admitted to trading in order to assess the market risk associated with these securities in a section headed 'Risk factors'.

32. Expense of the Issue/offer of the Depository Receipts

32.1. The total net proceeds and an estimate of the total expenses of the issue/offer.

Annex XI
Minimum Disclosure Requirements for the Banks Registration Document (schedule)

1. Persons Responsible

1.1. All persons responsible for the information given in the registration document and, as the case may be, for certain parts of it, with, in the latter case, an indication of such parts. In the case of natural persons including members of the issuer's administrative, management or supervisory bodies indicate the name and function of the person; in case of legal persons indicate the name and registered office.

1.2. A declaration by those responsible for the registration document that, having taken all reasonable care to ensure that such is the case, the information contained in the registration document is, to the best of their knowledge, in accordance with the facts and contains no omission likely to affect its import. As the case may be, declaration by those responsible for certain parts of the registration document that, having taken all reasonable care to ensure that such is the case, the information contained in the part of the registration document for which they are responsible is, to the best of their knowledge, in accordance with the facts and contains no omission likely to affect its import.

2. Statutory Auditors

2.1. Names and addresses of the issuer's auditors for the period covered by the historical financial information (together with their membership in a professional body).

2.2. If auditors have resigned, been removed or not been reappointed during the period covered by the historical financial information, details if material.

3. Risk Factors

3.1. Prominent disclosure of risk factors that may affect the issuer's ability to fulfil its obligations under the securities to investors in a section headed 'Risk factors'.

4 Information about the Issuer

4.1 *History and development of the Issuer*

4.1.1 the legal and commercial name of the issuer;

4.1.2 the place of registration of the issuer and its registration number;

4.1.3 the date of incorporation and the length of life of the issuer, except where indefinite;

4.1.4. the domicile and legal form of the issuer, the legislation under which the issuer operates, its country of incorporation, and the address and telephone number of its registered office (or principal place of business if different from its registered office);

4.1.5. any recent events particular to the issuer which are to a material extent relevant to the evaluation of the issuer's solvency.

5. Business Overview

5.1. *Principal activities:*

5.1.1. A brief description of the issuer's principal activities stating the main categories of products sold and/or services performed;

5.1.2. An indication of any significant new products and/or activities.

5.1.3. Principal markets

A brief description of the principal markets in which the issuer competes.

5.1.4. The basis for any statements in the registration document made by the issuer regarding its competitive position.

6. Organisational Structure

6.1. If the issuer is part of a group, a brief description of the group and of the issuer's position within it.

6.2. If the issuer is dependent upon other entities within the group, this must be clearly stated together with an explanation of this dependence.

7. Trend Information

7.1. Include a statement that there has been no material adverse change in the prospects of the issuer since the date of its last published audited financial statements.

In the event that the issuer is unable to make such a statement, provide details of this material adverse change.

7.2. Information on any known trends, uncertainties, demands, commitments or events that are reasonably likely to have a material effect on the issuer's prospects for at least the current financial year.

8. Profit Forecasts or Estimates

If an issuer chooses to include a profit forecast or a profit estimate the registration document must contain the information items 8.1 and 8.2.

8.1. A statement setting out the principal assumptions upon which the issuer has based its forecast, or estimate.

There must be a clear distinction between assumptions about factors which the members of the administrative, management or supervisory bodies can influence and assumptions about factors which are exclusively outside the influence of the members of the administrative, management or supervisory bodies; be readily understandable by investors; be specific and precise; and not relate to the general accuracy of the estimates underlying the forecast.

8.2. A report prepared by independent accountants or auditors stating that in the opinion of the independent accountants or auditors the forecast or estimate has been properly compiled on the basis stated and that the basis of accounting used for the profit forecast or estimate is consistent with the accounting policies of the issuer.

8.3. The profit forecast or estimate must be prepared on a basis comparable with the historical financial information.

9. Administrative, Management, And Supervisory Bodies

9.1. Names, business addresses and functions in the issuer of the following persons, and an indication of the principal activities performed by them outside the issuer where these are significant with respect to that issuer:

(a) members of the administrative, management or supervisory bodies;

(b) partners with unlimited liability, in the case of a limited partnership with a share capital.

9.2. *Administrative, Management, and Sup ervisory bodies conflicts of interests*

Potential conflicts of interests between any duties to the issuing entity of the persons referred to in item 9.1 and their private interests and or other duties must be clearly stated. In the event that there are no such conflicts, make a statement to that effect.

10. Major Shareholders

10.1. To the extent known to the issuer, state whether the issuer is directly or indirectly owned or controlled and by whom, and describe the nature of such control, and describe the measures in place to ensure that such control is not abused.

10.2. A description of any arrangements, known to the issuer, the operation of which may at a subsequent date result in a change in control of the issuer.

11. Financial Information concerning the Issuer's Assets and Liabilities, Financial Position and Profits and Losses

11.1. *Historical Financial Information*

Audited historical financial information covering the latest two financial years (or such shorter period that the issuer has been in operation), and the audit report in respect of each year. [If the issuer has changed its accounting reference date during the period for which historical financial information is required, the audited historical information shall cover at least 24 months, or the entire period for which the issuer has been in operation, whichever is the shorter.][a] Such financial information must be prepared according to Regulation (EC) No 1606/2002, or if not applicable to a Member State national accounting standards for issuers from the Community. For third country issuers, such financial information must be prepared according to the international accounting standards adopted pursuant to the procedure of Article 3 of Regulation (EC) No 1606/2002 or to a third country's national accounting standards equivalent to these standards. If such financial information is not equivalent to these standards, it must be presented in the form of restated financial statements.

The most recent year's audited historical financial information must be presented and prepared in a form consistent with that which will be adopted in the issuer's next published annual financial statements having regard to accounting standards and policies and legislation applicable to such annual financial statements.

If the issuer has been operating in its current sphere of economic activity for less than one year, the audited historical financial information covering that period must be prepared in accordance with the standards applicable to annual financial statements under Regulation (EC) No 1606/2002, or if not applicable to a Member State national accounting standards where the issuer is an issuer from the Community. For third country issuers, the historical financial information must be prepared according to the international accounting standards adopted pursuant to the procedure of Article 3 of Regulation (EC) No 1606/2002 or to a third country's national accounting standards equivalent to these standards. This historical financial information must be audited.

If the audited financial information is prepared according to national accounting standards, the financial information required under this heading must include at least the following:

(a) the balance sheet;

(b) the income statement;

(c) in the case of an admission of securities to trading on a regulated market only, a cash flow statement;

(d) the accounting policies and explanatory notes.

The historical annual financial information must be independently audited or reported on as to whether or not, for the purposes of the registration document, it gives a true and fair view, in accordance with auditing standards applicable in a Member State or an equivalent standard.

Amendments

a Inserted by Commission Regulation (EC) No 211/2007 of 27 February 2007 OJ L337 5.12.2006, p 17.

11.2. *Financial statements*

If the issuer prepares both own and consolidated financial statements, include at least the consolidated financial statements in the registration document.

11.3. *Auditing of historical annual financial information*

11.3.1. A statement that the historical financial information has been audited. If audit reports on the historical financial information have been refused by the statutory auditors or if they contain qualifications or disclaimers, such refusal or such qualifications or disclaimers must be reproduced in full and the reasons given.

11.3.2. An indication of other information in the registration document which has been audited by the auditors.

11.3.3. Where financial data in the registration document is not extracted from the issuer's audited financial statements state the source of the data and state that the data is un-audited.

11.4. *Age of latest financial information*

11.4.1. The last year of audited financial information may not be older than 18 months from the date of the registration document.

11.5. *Interim and other financial information*

11.5.1 If the issuer has published quarterly or half yearly financial information since the date of its last audited financial statements, these must be included in the registration document. If the quarterly or half yearly financial information has been reviewed or audited the audit or review report must also be included. If the quarterly or half yearly financial information is unaudited or has not been reviewed state that fact.

11.5.2. If the registration document is dated more than nine months after the end of the last audited financial year, it must contain interim financial information, covering at least the first six months of the financial year. If the interim financial information is un-audited state that fact.

The interim financial information must include comparative statements for the same period in the prior financial year, except that the requirement for comparative balance sheet information may be satisfied by presenting the years end balance sheet.

11.6. *Legal and arbitration proceedings*

Information on any governmental, legal or arbitration proceedings (including any such proceedings which are pending or threatened of which the issuer is aware), during a period covering at least the previous 12 months which may have, or have had in the recent past, significant effects on the issuer and/or group's financial position or profitability, or provide an appropriate negative statement.

11.7. *Significant change in the issuer's financial position*

A description of any significant change in the financial position of the group which has occurred since the end of the last financial period for which either audited financial information or interim financial information have been published, or an appropriate negative statement.

12. Material Contracts

A brief summary of all material contracts that are not entered into in the ordinary course of the issuer's business, which could result in any group member being under an obligation or entitlement that is material to the issuer's ability to meet its obligation to security holders in respect of the securities being issued.

13. Third Party Information and Statement by Experts And Declarations of Any Interest

13.1. Where a statement or report attributed to a person as an expert is included in the registration document, provide such person's name, business address, qualifications and material interest if any in the issuer. If the report has been produced at the issuer's request a statement to that effect that such statement or report is included, in the form and context in which it is included, with the consent of that person who has authorised the contents of that part of the registration document.

13.2. Where information has been sourced from a third party, provide a confirmation that this information has been accurately reproduced and that as far as the issuer is aware and is able to ascertain from information published by that third party, no facts have been omitted which would render the reproduced information inaccurate or misleading In addition, the issuer shall identify the source(s) of the information.

14. Documents On Display

A statement that for the life of the registration document the following documents (or copies thereof), where applicable, may be inspected:

(a) the memorandum and articles of association of the issuer;

(b) all reports, letters, and other documents, historical financial information, valuations and statements prepared by any expert at the issuer's request any part of which is included or referred to in the registration document;

(c) the historical financial information of the issuer or, in the case of a group, the historical financial information of the issuer and its subsidiary undertakings for each of the two financial years preceding the publication of the registration document.

An indication of where the documents on display may be inspected, by physical or electronic means.

Annex XII

Minimum Disclosure Requirements for the Securities Note for derivative securities (schedule)

1. Persons Responsible

1.1. All persons responsible for the information given in the prospectus and, as the case may be, for certain parts of it, with, in the latter case, an indication of such parts. In the case of natural persons including members of the issuer's administrative, management or supervisory bodies indicate the name and function of the person; in case of legal persons indicate the name and registered office.

1.2. A declaration by those responsible for the prospectus that, having taken all reasonable care to ensure that such is the case, the information contained in the prospectus is, to the best of their knowledge, in accordance with the facts and contains no omission likely to affect its import. As the case may be, declaration by those responsible for certain parts of the prospectus that, having taken all reasonable care to ensure that such is the case, the information contained in the part of the prospectus for which they are responsible is, to the best of their knowledge, in accordance with the facts and contains no omission likely to affect its import.

2. Risk Factors

Prominent disclosure of risk factors that are material to the securities being offered and/or admitted to trading in order to assess the market risk associated with these securities in a section headed 'risk factors'. This must include a risk warning to the effect that investors may lose the value of their entire investment or part of it, as the case may be, and/or, if the investor's liability is not limited to the value of his investment, a statement of that fact, together with a description of the circumstances in which such additional liability arises and the likely financial effect.

3. Key Information

3.1. *Interest of natural and legal persons involved in the issue/offer*

A description of any interest, including conflicting ones that is material to the issue/offer, detailing the persons involved and the nature of the interest.

3.2. *Reasons for the offer and use of proceeds when different from making profit and/or hedging certain risks*

If reasons for the offer and use of proceeds are disclosed provide the total net proceeds and an estimate of the total expenses of the issue/ offer.

4. Information Concerning the Securities to be Offered/admitted to Trading

4.1. *Information concerning the securities*

4.1.1. A description of the type and the class of the securities being offered and/or admitted to trading, including the ISIN (International Security Identification Number) or other such security identification code.

4.1.2. A clear and comprehensive explanation to help investors understand how the value of their investment is affected by the value of the underlying instrument (s), especially under the circumstances when the risks are most evident unless the securities have a denomination per unit of at least EUR 50,000 or can only be acquired for at least EUR 50,000 per security.

4.1.3. Legislation under which the securities have been created.

4.1.4. An indication whether the securities are in registered form or bearer form and whether the securities are in certificated form or book-entry form. In the latter case, name and address of the entity in charge of keeping the records.

4.1.5. Currency of the securities issue.

4.1.6. Ranking of the securities being offered and/or admitted to trading, including summaries of any clauses that are intended to affect ranking or subordinate the security to any present or future liabilities of the issuer.

4.1.7. A description of the rights, including any limitations of these, attached to the securities and procedure for the exercise of said rights.

4.1.8. In the case of new issues, a statement of the resolutions, authorisations and approvals by virtue of which the securities have been or will be created and/or issued.

4.1.9. The issue date of the securities.

4.1.10. A description of any restrictions on the free transferability of the securities.

4.1.11.

— The expiration or maturity date of the derivative securities.

— The exercise date or final reference date.

4.1.12. A description of the settlement procedure of the derivative securities.

4.1.13. A description of how any return on derivative securities takes place, the payment or delivery date, and the way it is calculated.

4.1.14. In respect of the country of registered office of the issuer and the country(ies) where the offer is being made or admission to trading is being sought:

(a) information on taxes on the income from the securities withheld at source;

(b) indication as to whether the issuer assumes responsibility for the withholding of taxes at the source.

4.2. *Information concerning the underlying*

4.2.1. The exercise price or the final reference price of the underlying.

4.2.2. A statement setting out the type of the underlying and details of where information on the underlying can be obtained:

— an indication where information about the past and the further performance of the underlying and its volatility can be obtained,

— where the underlying is a security,

— the name of the issuer of the security,

— the ISIN (international security identification number) or other such security identification code,

— where the underlying is an index,

— the name of the index and a description of the index if it is composed by the issuer. If the index is not composed by the issuer, where information about the index can be obtained,

— where the underlying is an interest rate,

— a description of the interest rate,

— others:

— Where the underlying does not fall within the categories specified above the securities note shall contain equivalent information.

— where the underlying is a basket of underlyings,

— disclosure of the relevant weightings of each underlying in the basket.

4.2.3. A description of any market disruption or settlement disruption events that affect the underlying.

5. Terms and Conditions Of The Offer

5.1. *Conditions, offer statistics, expected timetable and action required to apply for the offer*

5.1.1. Conditions to which the offer is subject.

5.1.2. Total amount of the issue/offer; if the amount is not fixed, description of the arrangements and time for announcing to the public the amount of the offer.

5.1.3. The time period, including any possible amendments, during which the offer will be open and description of the application process.

5.1.4. Details of the minimum and/or maximum amount of application, (whether in number of securities or aggregate amount to invest).

5.1.5. Method and time limits for paying up the securities and for delivery of the securities.

5.1.6. A full description of the manner and date in which results of the offer are to be made public.

5.2. *Plan of distribution and allotment*

5.2.1. The various categories of potential investors to which the securities are offered. If the offer is being made simultaneously in the markets of two or more countries and if a tranche has been or is being reserved for certain of these, indicate any such tranche.

5.2.2. Process for notification to applicants of the amount allotted and indication whether dealing may begin before notification is made.

5.3. *Pricing*

Indication of the expected price at which the securities will be offered or the method of determining the price and the process for its disclosure. Indicate the amount of any expenses and taxes specifically *charged* to the subscriber or purchaser.

5.4. *Placing and underwriting*

5.4.1. Name and address of the coordinator(s) of the global offer and of single parts of the offer and, to the extend known to the issuer or to the offeror, of the placers in the various countries where the offer takes place.

5.4.2. Name and address of any paying agents and depository agents in each country.

5.4.3. Entities agreeing to underwrite the issue on a firm commitment basis, and entities agreeing to place the issue without a firm commitment or under 'best efforts' arrangements. Where not all of the issue is under-written, a statement of the portion not covered.

5.4.4. When the underwriting agreement has been or will be reached.

5.4.5. Name and address of a calculation agent.

6. Admission to Trading and Dealing Arrangements

6.1. An indication as to whether the securities offered are or will be the object of an application for admission to trading, with a view to their distribution in a regulated market or other equivalent markets with indication of the markets in question. This circumstance shall be mentioned, without creating the impression that the admission to trading necessarily will be approved. If known, the earliest dates on which the securities will be admitted to trading shall be given.

6.2. All the regulated markets or equivalent markets on which, to the knowledge of the issuer, securities of the same class of the securities to be offered or admitted to trading are already admitted to trading.

6.3. Name and address of the entities which have a firm commitment to act as intermediaries in secondary trading, providing liquidity through bid and offer rates and description of the main terms of their commitment.

7. Additional Information

7.1. If advisors connected with an issue are mentioned in the Securities Note, a statement of the capacity in which the advisors have acted.

7.2. An indication of other information in the Securities Note which has been audited or reviewed by statutory auditors and where auditors have produced a report. Reproduction of the report or, with permission of the competent authority, a summary of the report.

7.3. Where a statement or report attributed to a person as an expert is included in the Securities Note, provide such person's name, business address, qualifications and material interest, if any, in the issuer. If the report has been produced at the issuer's request a statement to that effect that such statement or report is included, in the form and context in which it is included, with the consent of that person who has authorised the contents of that part of the Securities Note.

7.4. Where information has been sourced from a third party, provide a confirmation that this information has been accurately reproduced and that as far as the issuer is aware and is able to ascertain from information published by that third party, no facts have been omitted which would render the reproduced information inaccurate or misleading. In addition, the issuer shall identify the source(s) of the information.

7.5. An indication in the prospectus whether or not the issuer intends to provide post-issuance information. Where the issuer has indicated that it intends to report such information, the issuer shall specify in the prospectus what information will be reported and where such information can be obtained.

Annex XIII
Minimum Disclosure Requirements for the Securities Note for debt securities with a denomination per unit of at least EUR 50,000 (Schedule)

1. Persons Responsible

1.1. All persons responsible for the information given in the prospectus and, as the case may be, for certain parts of it, with, in the latter case, an indication of such parts. In case of natural persons including members of the issuer's administrative, management or supervisory bodies indicate the name and function of the person; in case of legal persons indicate the name and registered office.

1.2. A declaration by those responsible for the prospectus that, having taken all reasonable care to ensure that such is the case, the information contained in the prospectus is, to the best of their knowledge, in accordance with the facts and contains no omission likely to affect its import. As the case may be, declaration by those responsible for certain parts of the prospectus that the information contained in the part of the prospectus for which they are responsible is, to the best of their knowledge, in accordance with the facts and contains no omission likely to affect its import.

2. Risk Factors

Prominent disclosure of risk factors that are material to the securities admitted to trading in order to assess the market risk associated with these securities in a section headed 'Risk factors'.

3. Key Information

Interest of natural and legal persons involved in the issue

A description of any interest, including conflicting ones, that is material to the issue, detailing the persons involved and the nature of the interest.

4. Information Concerning the Securities to be Admitted to Trading

4.1. Total amount of securities being admitted to trading.

4.2. A description of the type and the class of the securities being admitted to trading, including the ISIN (international security identification number) or other such security identification code.

4.3. Legislation under which the securities have been created.

4.4. An indication of whether the securities are in registered or bearer form and whether the securities are in certificated or book-entry form. In the latter case, name and address of the entity in charge of keeping the records.

4.5. Currency of the securities issue.

4.6. Ranking of the securities being admitted to trading, including summaries of any clauses that are intended to affect ranking or subordinate the security to any present or future liabilities of the issuer.

4.7. A description of the rights, including any limitations of these, attached to the securities and procedure for the exercise of said rights.

4.8. The nominal interest rate and provisions relating to interest payable:

— The date from which interest becomes payable and the due dates for interest.

— The time limit on the validity of claims to interest and repayment of principal.

Where the rate is not fixed, description of the underlying on which it is based and of the method used to relate the two:

— A description of any market disruption or settlement disruption events that affect the underlying.

— Adjustment rules with relation to events concerning the underlying.

— Name of the calculation agent.

4.9. Maturity date and arrangements for the amortisation of the loan, including the repayment procedures. Where advance amortisation is contemplated, on the initiative of the issuer or of the holder, it must be described, stipulating amortisation terms and conditions.

4.10. An indication of yield.

4.11. Representation of debt security holders including an identification of the organisation representing the investors and provisions applying to such representation. Indication of where investors may have access to the contracts relating to these forms of representation.

4.12. A statement of the resolutions, authorisations and approvals by virtue of which the securities have been created and/or issued.

4.13. The issue date of the securities.

4.14. A description of any restrictions on the free transferability of the securities.

5. Admission to Trading and Dealing Arrangements

5.1. Indication of the market where the securities will be traded and for which prospectus has been published. If known, give the earliest dates on which the securities will be admitted to trading.

5.2. Name and address of any paying agents and depository agents in each country.

6. Expense of the Admission to Trading

An estimate of the total expenses related to the admission to trading.

7. Additional Information

7.1. If advisors are mentioned in the Securities Note, a statement of the capacity in which the advisors have acted.

7.2. An indication of other information in the Securities Note which has been audited or reviewed by auditors and where auditors have produced a report. Reproduction of the report or, with permission of the competent authority, a summary of the report.

7.3. Where a statement or report attributed to a person as an expert is included in the Securities Note, provide such person's name, business address, qualifications and material interest if any in the issuer. If the report has been produced at the issuer's request a statement to that effect that such statement or report is included, in the form and context in which it is included, with the consent of that person who has authorised the contents of that part of the Securities Note.

7.4. Where information has been sourced from a third party, provide a confirmation that this information has been accurately reproduced and that as far as the issuer is aware and is able to ascertain from information published by that third party, no facts have been omitted which would render the reproduced information inaccurate or misleading. In addition, identify the source(s) of the information.

7.5. Credit ratings assigned to an issuer or its debt securities at the request or with the co-operation of the issuer in the rating process.

Annex XIV

Additional information building block on underlying share for some equity securities

1. Description of the underlying share

1.1. Describe the type and the class of the shares

1.2. Legislation under which the shares have been or will be created

1.3. Indication whether the securities are in registered form or bearer form and whether the securities are in certificated form or book-entry form. In the latter case, name and address of the entity in charge of keeping the records

1.4. Indication of the currency of the shares issue

1.5. A description of the rights, including any limitations of these, attached to the securities and procedure for the exercise of those rights:

- Dividend rights:
  - fixed date(s) on which the entitlement arises,
  - time limit after which entitlement to dividend lapses and an indication of the person in whose favour the lapse operates,
  - dividend restrictions and procedures for non resident holders,
  - rate of dividend or method of its calculation, periodicity and cumulative or non-cumulative nature of payments.
- Voting rights.
- Pre-emption rights in offers for subscription of securities of the same class.
- Right to share in the issuer's profits.
- Rights to share in any surplus in the event of liquidation.
- Redemption provisions.
- Conversion provisions.

1.6. In the case of new issues, a statement of the resolutions, authorisations and approvals by virtue of which the shares have been or will be created and/or issued and indication of the issue date.

1.7. Where and when the shares will be or have been admitted to trading.

1.8. Description of any restrictions on the free transferability of the shares.

1.9. Indication of the existence of any mandatory takeover bids/or squeeze-out and sell-out rules in relation to the shares.

1.10. Indication of public takeover bids by third parties in respect of the issuer's equity, which have occurred during the last financial year and the current financial year. The price or exchange terms attaching to such offers and the outcome thereof must be stated.

1.11. Impact on the issuer of the underlying share of the exercise of the right and potential dilution effect for the shareholders.

2. When the issuer of the underlying is an entity belonging to the same group, the information to provide on this issuer is the one required by the share registration document schedule.

Annex XV
Minimum disclosure requirements for the registration document for securities issued by collective investment undertakings of the closed-end type (schedule)

In addition to the information required in this schedule, the collective investment undertaking must provide the following information as required under paragraphs and items 1, 2, 3, 4, 5.1, 7, 9.1, 9.2.1, 9.2.3, 10.4, 13, 14, 15, 16, 17.2, 18, 19, 20, 21, 22, 23, 24, 25 in Annex I (minimum disclosure requirements for the share registration document schedule).

1. Investment objective and policy

1.1. A detailed description of the investment objective and policy which the collective investment undertaking will pursue and a description of how that investment objectives and policy may be varied including any circumstances in which such variation requires the approval of investors. A description of any techniques and instruments that may be used in the management of the collective investment undertaking.

1.2. The borrowing and/or leverage limits of the collective investment undertaking. If there are no such limits, include a statement to that effect.

1.3. The regulatory status of the collective investment undertaking together with the name of any regulator in its country of incorporation.

1.4. The profile of a typical investor for whom the collective investment undertaking is designed.

2. Investment Restrictions

2.1. A statement of the investment restrictions which apply to the collective investment undertaking, if any, and an indication of how the holders of securities will be informed of the actions that the investment manager will take in the event of a breach.

2.2. Where more than 20 % of the gross assets of any collective investment undertaking (except where items 2.3 or 2.5 apply) may be:

(a) invested in, either directly or indirectly, or lent to any single underlying issuer (including the underlying issuer's subsidiaries or affiliates);

or

(b) invested in one or more collective investment undertakings which may invest in excess of 20 % of its gross assets in other collective investment undertakings (open-end and/or closed-end type);

or

(c) exposed to the creditworthiness or solvency of any one counterparty (including its subsidiaries or affiliates);

the following information must be disclosed:

(i) information relating to each underlying issuer/collective investment undertaking/counterparty as if it were an issuer for the purposes of the minimum disclosure requirements for the share registration document schedule (in the case of (a)) or minimum disclosure requirements for the registration document schedule for securities issued by collective investment undertaking of the closed-end type (in the case of (b)) or the minimum disclosure requirements for the debt and derivative securities with an individual denomination per unit of at least EUR 50,000 registration document schedule (in the case of (c));

or

(ii) if the securities issued by the underlying issuer/collective investment undertaking/counterparty have already been admitted to trading on a regulated or equivalent market or the obligations are guaranteed by an entity admitted to trading on a regulated or equivalent market, the name, address, country of incorporation, nature of business and name of the market in which its securities are admitted.

This requirement shall not apply where the 20 % is exceeded due to appreciations or depreciations, changes in exchange rates, or by reason of the receipt of rights, bonuses, benefits in the nature of capital or by reason of any other action affecting every holder of that investment, provided the investment manager has regard to the threshold when considering changes in the investment portfolio.

2.3. Where a collective investment undertaking may invest in excess of 20 % of its gross assets in other collective investment undertakings (open ended and/or closed ended), a description of if and how risk is spread in relation to those investments. In addition, item 2.2 shall apply, in aggregate, to its underlying investments as if those investments had been made directly.

2.4. With reference to point (c) of item 2.2, if collateral is advanced to cover that portion of the exposure to any one counterparty in excess of 20 % of the gross assets of the collective investment undertaking, details of such collateral arrangements.

2.5. Where a collective investment undertaking may invest in excess of 40 % of its gross assets in another collective investment undertaking either of the following must be disclosed:

(a) information relating to each underlying collective investment undertaking as if it were an issuer under minimum disclosure requirements for the registration document schedule for securities issued by collective investment undertaking of the closed-end type;

(b) if securities issued by an underlying collective investment under-taking have already been admitted to trading on a regulated or equivalent market or the obligations are guaranteed by an entity admitted to trading on a regulated or equivalent market, the name, address, country of incorporation, nature of business and name of the market in which its securities are admitted.

2.6. *Physical Commodities*

Where a collective investment undertaking invests directly in physical commodities a disclosure of that fact and the percentage that will be so invested.

2.7. *Property Collective investment undertakings*

Where a collective investment undertaking is a property collective investment undertaking, disclosure of that fact, the percentage of the portfolio that is to be invested in the property, as well as a description of the property and any material costs relating to the acquisition and holding of such property. In addition, a valuation report relating to the properties must be included.

Disclosure of item 4.1. applies to:

(a) the valuation entity;

(b) any other entity responsible for the administration of the property.

2.8. *Derivatives Financial instruments/Money Market Instruments/ Currencies*

Where a collective investment undertaking invests in derivatives financial instruments, money market instruments or currencies other than for the purposes of efficient portfolio management (i.e. solely for the purpose of reducing, transferring or eliminating investment risk in the underlying investments of a collective investment under-taking, including any technique or instrument used to provide protection against exchange and credit risks), a statement whether those investments are used for hedging or for investment purposes, and a description of if and how risk is spread in relation to those investments.

2.9 Item 2.2 does not apply to investment in securities issued or guaranteed by a government, government agency or instrumentality of any Member State, its regional or local authorities, or OECD Member State.

2.10 Point (a) of item 2.2 does not apply to a collective investment under-taking whose investment objective is to track, without material modification, that of a broadly based and recognised published index. A description of the composition of the index must be provided.

3. The applicant's service providers

3.1. The actual or estimated maximum amount of all material fees payable directly or indirectly by the collective investment undertaking for any services under arrangements entered into on or prior to the date of the registration document and a description of how these fees are calculated.

A description of any fee payable directly or indirectly by the collective investment undertaking which cannot be quantified under item 3.1 and which is or may be material.

If any service provider to the collective investment undertaking is in receipt of any benefits from third parties (other than the collective investment undertaking) by virtue of providing any services to the collective investment undertaking, and those benefits may not accrue to the collective investment undertaking, a statement of that fact, the name of that third party, if available, and a description of the nature of the benefits.

The name of the service provider which is responsible for the determination and calculation of the net asset value of the collective investment undertaking.

A description of any material potential conflicts of interest which any of the service providers to the collective investment undertaking may have as between their duty to the collective investment undertaking and duties owed by them to third parties and their other interests. A description of any arrangements which are in place to address such potential conflicts.

4. Investment Manager/Advisers

4.1. In respect of any Investment Manager such information as is required to be disclosed under items 5.1.1 to 5.1.4 and, if material, under item 5.1.5 of Annex I together with a description of its regulatory status and experience.

4.2. In respect of any entity providing investment advice in relation to the assets of the collective investment undertaking, the name and a brief description of such entity.

5. Custody

5.1. A full description of how the assets of the collective investment under-taking will be held and by whom and any fiduciary or similar relationship between the collective investment undertaking and any third party in relation to custody:

Where a custodian, trustee, or other fiduciary is appointed:

(a) such information as is required to be disclosed under items 5.1.1 to 5.1.4 and, if material, under item 5.1.5 of Annex I;

(b) a description of the obligations of such party under the custody or similar agreement;

(c) any delegated custody arrangements;

(d) the regulatory status of such party and delegates.

5.2. Where any entity other than those entities mentioned in item 5.1, holds any assets of the collective investment undertaking, a description of how these assets are held together with a description of any additional risks.

6. Valuation

6.1. A description of how often, and the valuation principles and the method by which, the net asset value of the collective investment undertaking will be determined, distinguishing between categories of investments and a statement of how such net asset value will be communicated to investors.

6.2. Details of all circumstances in which valuations may be suspended and a statement of how such suspension will be communicated or made available to investors.

7. Cross Liabilities

7.1. In the case of an umbrella collective investment undertaking, a statement of any cross liability that may occur between classes or investments in other collective investment undertakings and any action taken to limit such liability.

8. Financial Information

8.1. Where, since the date of incorporation or establishment, a collective investment undertaking has not commenced operations and no financial statements have been made up as at the date of the registration document, a statement to that effect.

Where a collective investment undertaking has commenced operations, the provisions of item 20 of Annex I on the Minimum Disclosure Requirements for the share registration document apply.

8.2. A comprehensive and meaningful analysis of the collective investment undertaking's portfolio (if un-audited, clearly marked as such).

8.3. An indication of the most recent net asset value per security must be included in the securities note schedule (and, if un-audited, clearly marked as such).

Annex XVI

Minimum disclosure requirements for the registration document for securities issued by Member States, third countries and their regional and local authorities (schedule)

1. Persons Responsible

1.1. All persons responsible for the information given in the registration document and, as the case may be, for certain parts of it, with, in the latter case, an indication of such parts. In the case of natural persons including members of the issuer's administrative, management or supervisory bodies indicate the name and function of the person; in case of legal persons indicate the name and registered office.

1.2. A declaration by those responsible for the registration document that, having taken all reasonable care to ensure that such is the case, the information contained in the registration document is, to the best of their knowledge in accordance with the facts and contains no omission likely to affect its import. As the case may be, declaration by those responsible for certain parts of the registration document that, having taken all reasonable care to ensure that such is the case the information contained in the part of the registration document for which they are responsible is, to the best of their knowledge, in accordance with the facts and contains no omission likely to affect its import.

2. Risk Factors

Prominent disclosure of risk factors that may affect the issuer's ability to fulfil its obligations under the securities to investors in a section headed 'Risk factors'.

3. Information about the Issuer

3.1. The legal name of the issuer and a brief description of the issuer's position within the national governmental framework.

3.2. The domicile or geographical location and legal form of the issuer and its contact address and telephone number.

3.3. Any recent events relevant to the evaluation of the issuer's solvency.

3.4. A description of the issuer's economy including:

(a) the structure of the economy with details of the main sectors of the economy;

(b) gross domestic product with a breakdown by the issuer's economic sectors over for the previous two fiscal years.

3.5. A general description of the issuer's political system and government including details of the governing body of the issuer.

4. Public Finance and Trade

Information on the following for the two fiscal years prior to the date of the registration document:

(a) the tax and budgetary systems;

(b) gross public debt including a summary of the debt, the maturity structure of outstanding debt (particularly noting debt with a residual maturity of less than one year) and debt payment record, and of the parts of debt denominated in the domestic currency of the issuer and in foreign currencies;

(c) foreign trade and balance of payment figures;

(d) foreign exchange reserves including any potential encumbrances to such foreign exchange reserves as forward contracts or derivatives;

(e) financial position and resources including liquid deposits available in domestic currency;

(f) income and expenditure figures.

Description of any auditing or independent review procedures on the accounts of the issuer.

5. Significant Change

5.1. Details of any significant changes to the information provided pursuant to item 4 which have occurred since the end of the last fiscal year, or an appropriate negative statement.

6. Legal and Arbitration Proceedings

6.1. Information on any governmental, legal or arbitration proceedings (including any such proceedings which are pending or threatened of which the issuer is aware), during a period covering at least the previous 12 months which may have, or have had in the recent past, significant effects on the issuer financial position, or provide an appropriate negative statement.

6.2. Information on any immunity the issuer may have from legal proceedings.

7. Statement by Experts and Declarations of Any Interest

Where a statement or report attributed to a person as an expert is included in the registration document, provide such person's name, business address and qualifications. If the report has been produced at the issuer's request a statement to that effect, that such statement or report is included, in the form and context in which it is included, with the consent of that person, who has authorised the contents of that part of the registration document.

To the extent known to the issuer, provide information in respect of any interest relating to such expert which may have an effect on the independence of the expert in the preparation of the report.

8. Documents on Display

A statement that for the life of the registration document the following documents (or copies thereof), where applicable, may be inspected:

(a) financial and audit reports for the issuer covering the last two fiscal years and the budget for the current fiscal year;

(b) all reports, letters, and other documents, valuations and statements prepared by any expert at the issuer's request any part of which is included or referred to in the registration document.

An indication of where the documents on display may be inspected, by physical or electronic means.

Annex XVII

Minimum disclosure requirements for the registration document for securities issued by public international bodies and for debt securities guaranteed by a Member State of the OECD (schedule)

1. Persons Responsible

1.1. All persons responsible for the information given in the registration document and, as the case may be, for certain parts of it, with, in the latter case, an indication of such parts. In the case of natural persons including members of the issuer's administrative, management or supervisory bodies indicate the name and function of the person; in case of legal persons indicate the name and registered office.

1.2. A declaration by those responsible for the registration document, that, having taken all reasonable care to ensure that such is the case, the information contained in the registration document is, to the best of their knowledge, in accordance with the facts and contains no omission likely to materially affect its import. As the case may be, declaration by those responsible for certain parts of the registration document that, having taken all reasonable care to ensure that such is the case the information contained in the part of the registration document for which they are responsible is, to the best of their knowledge, in accordance with the facts and contains no omission likely to affect its import.

2. Risk Factors

Prominent disclosure of risk factors that may affect the issuer's ability to fulfil its obligations under the securities to investors in a section headed 'Risk factors'.

3. Information about the Issuer

3.1. The legal name of the issuer and a brief description of the issuer's legal status.

3.2. The location of the principal office and the legal form of the issuer and its contact address and telephone number.

3.3. Details of the governing body of the issuer and a description of its governance arrangements, if any.

3.4. A brief description of the issuer's purpose and functions.

3.5. The sources of funding, guarantees and other obligations owed to the issuer by its members.

3.6. Any recent events relevant to the evaluation of the issuer's solvency.

3.7. A list of the issuer's members.

4. Financial Information

The two most recently published audited annual financial statements prepared in accordance with the accounting and auditing principles adopted by the issuer, and a brief description of those accounting and auditing principles.

Details of any significant changes to the issuer's financial position which has occurred since the end of the latest published audited annual financial statement, or an appropriate negative statement.

5. **Legal and Arbitration Proceedings**

5.1. Information on any governmental, legal or arbitration proceedings (including any such proceedings which are pending or threatened of which the issuer is aware), during a period covering at least the previous 12 months which are likely to have, or have had in the recent past, significant effects on the issuer's financial position, or provide an appropriate negative statement.

5.2. Information on any immunity the issuer may have from legal proceedings pursuant to its constituent document.

6. **Statement by Experts and Declaration of Any Interests**

Where a statement or report attributed to a person as an expert is included in the registration document, provide such person's name, business address and qualifications. If the report has been produced at the issuer's request a statement to that effect, that such statement or report is included, in the form and context in which it is included, with the consent of that person.

To the extent known to the issuer, provide information in respect of any conflict of interests relating to such expert which may have an effect on the independence of the expert in the preparation of the report.

7. **Document on Display**

A statement that for the life of the registration document the following documents (or copies thereof), where applicable, will be made available on request:

(a) annual and audit reports of the issuer for each of the last two financial years prepared in accordance with the accounting and auditing principles adopted by the issuer;

(b) all reports, letters, and other documents, valuations and statements prepared by any expert at the issuer's request any part of which is included or referred to in the registration document;

(c) the issuer's constituent document.

An indication of where the documents on display may be inspected, by physical or electronic means.

ANNEX XVIII

TABLE OF COMBINATIONS

TYPES OF SECURITIES	REGISTRATION DOCUMENT					
	SCHEDULES					BUILDING BLOCK
	Share	Debt and derivative (< EUR 50 000)	Debt and derivative (> or = EUR 50 000)	Asset -backed securities	Banks debt and derivative	Pro forma information
Shares (preference shares, redeemable shares, shares with preferential subscription rights; etc.)						
Bonds (vanilla bonds, income bonds, structured bonds, etc.) with a denomination of less than EUR 50 000		or			or	
Bonds (vanilla bonds, income bonds, structured bonds, etc.) with a denomination of at least EUR 50 000			or		or	
Debt securities guaranteed by a third party		or	or		or	
Derivative securities guaranteed by a third party		or	or		or	
Asset-backed securities						
Bonds exchangeable or convertible into third-party shares or issuers' or group shares which are admitted on a regulated market		or	or		or	
Bonds exchangeable or convertible into the issuer's shares not admitted on a regulated market						

TYPES OF SECURITI ES	REGISTRATION DOCUMENT					
	SCHEDULES					BUILDING BLOCK
	Share	Debt and derivative (< EUR 50 000)	Debt and derivative (> or = EUR 50 000)	Asset -backed securities	Banks debt and derivative	Pro forma information
Bonds exchangeableor convertible into group's shares not admittedon a regulatedmarket		or	or		or	
Bonds with warrants to acquire the issuer's shares not admittedto trading on a regulatedmarket						
Shares with warrants to acquire the issuer's shares not admittedto trading on a regulatedmarket						
Derivatives securities giving the right to subscribe or to acquire the issuer's shares not admittedon a regulatedmarket						
Derivatives securities giving the right to acquire group's shares not admittedon a regulatedmarket		or	or		or	
Derivatives securities giving the right to subscribe or to acquire issuer's or group shares which are admitted on a regulated market and derivatives sec. linked to any other underlying than issuer's or group shares which are not admitted on a regulated market (including any derivatives sec. entitling to cash settlement)		or	or		or	

	REGISTRATION DOCUMENT		
	SCHEDULES		
TYPES OF SECURITIES	Collective investment undertaking of the closed-end type	States and their regional and local authorities	Public international bodies/Debt Securities guaranteed by a Member State of the OECD
Shares (preference shares, redeemable shares, shares with preferential subscription rights; etc.)			
Bonds (vanilla bonds, income bonds, structured bonds, etc with a denomination of less than EUR 50 000			
Bonds (vanilla bonds, income bonds, structured bonds, etc.) with a denomination of at least EUR 50 000			
Debt securities guaranteed by a third party			
Derivative securities guaranteed by a third party			
Asset-backed securities			
Bonds exchangeable or convertible into third party shares or issuers' or group shares which are admitted on a regulated market			
Bonds exchangeable or convertible into the issuer's shares not admitted on a regulated market			
Bonds exchangeable or convertible into group's shares not admitted on a regulated market			

	REGISTRATION DOCUMENT		
	SCHEDULES		
TYPES OF SECURITIES	Collective investmentundertakingof the closed-endtype	States and their regional and local authorities	Public internationalbodies/DebtSecurities guaranteedby a Member State of the OECD
Bonds with warrants to acquire the issuer's shares not admitted to trading on a regulatedmarket			
Shares with warrants to acquire the issuer's shares not admitted to trading on a regulatedmarket			
Derivatives securities giving the right to subscribe or to acquire the issuer's shares not admittedon a regulatedmarket			
Derivatives securities giving the right to acquire group's shares not admittedon a regulatedmarket			
Derivatives securities giving the right to subscribe or to acquire issuer's or group shares which are admitted on a regulated market and derivatives sec. linked to any other underlying than issuer's or group shares which are not admittedon a regulated market (including any derivatives securities entitling to cash settlement)			

TYPES OF SECURITI ES	SECURITIES NOTE						
	SCHEDULES				ADDITIONAL BUILDING BLOCKS		
	Share	Debt (<EUR 50 000)	Debt (> or = EUR 50 000)	Derivatives securities	Guarantees	Asset-backed securities	Underlying share
Shares (preference shares, redeemable shares, shares with preferential subscription rights; etc.)							
Bonds (vanilla bonds, income bonds, structured bonds, etc with a denomination of less than EUR 50 000							
Bonds (vanilla bonds, income bonds, structured bonds, etc) with a denomination of at least EUR 50 000							
Debt securities guaranteed by a third party		or	or				
Derivative securities guaranteed by a third party							
Asset-backed securities		or	or				
Bonds exchangeable or convertible into third party shares or issuers' or group shares which are admitted on a regulated market		or	or	Only point 4.2.2			
Bonds exchangeable or convertible into the issuer's shares not admitted on a regulated market		or	or				
Bonds exchangeable or convertible into group's shares not admitted on a regulated market		or	or				

	SECURITIES NOTE						
	SCHEDULES				ADDITIONAL BUILDING BLOCKS		
TYPES OF SECURITI ES	Share	Debt (<EUR 50 000)	Debt (> or = EUR 50 000)	Derivatives securities	Guarantees	Asset-backed securities	Underlying share
Bonds with warrants to acquire the issuer's shares not admittedto trading on a regulatedmarket		or	or	and except point 4.2.2			
Shares with warrants to acquire the issuer's shares not admittedto trading on a regulatedmarket				and except point 4.2.2			
Derivatives securities giving the right to subscribe or to acquire the issuer's shares not admittedon a regulatedmarket				except point 4.2.2			
Derivatives securities giving the right to acquire group's shares not admittedon a regulatedmarket				except point 4.2.2			
Derivatives securities giving the right to subscribe or to acquire issuer's or group shares which are admitted on a regulated market and derivatives securities linked to any other underlying than issuer's or group shares which are not admitted on a regulated market (including any derivatives securities entitling to cash settlement)							

Annex XIX
List of specialist issuers

- Property companies
- Mineral companies
- Investment companies
- Scientific research based companies
- Companies with less than three years of existence (start-up companies)
- Shipping companies.

Commission Regulation (EC) No 1569/2007

of 21 December 2007

establishing a mechanism for the determination of equivalence of accounting standards applied by third country issuers of securities pursuant to Directives 200 3/71/EC and 2004/109/EC of the European Parliament and of the Council

THE COMMISSION OF THE EUROPEAN COMMUNITIES,

Having regard to the Treaty establishing the European Community,

Having regard to Directive 2003/71/EC of the European Parliament and of the Council of 4 November 2003 on the prospectus to be published when securities are offered to the public or admitted to trading and amending Directive 2001/34/EC (OJ L 345, 31.12.2003, p. 64), and in particular Article 7(1) thereof,

Having regard to Directive 2004/109/EC of the European Parliament and of the Council of 15 December 2004 on the harmonisation of transparency requirements in relation to information about issuers whose securities are admitted to trading on a regulated market and amending Directive 2001/34/EC (OJ L 390, 31.12.2004, p. 38), and in particular Article 23(4)(i) thereof,

Whereas:

(1) Article 23(4) of Directive 2004/109/EC requires the Commission to set up a mechanism for the determination of the equivalence of the information required under this Directive, including financial statements and the corresponding requirements under the law, regulations or administrative provisions of third countries. This Article also requires the Commission to take decisions in relation to the equivalence of accounting standards used by third country issuers, and enables the Commission to allow the use of third country accounting standards during an appropriate transitional period. Given the close interconnection of the information required under Directive 2004/109/EC with the information required under Directive 2003/71/EC, it is appropriate that the same criteria for determination of equivalence apply in the framework of both Directives.

(2) Given the objectives of Directive 2003/71/EC to ensure that investors are able to make an informed assessment of the assets and liabilities, financial position, profit and losses and prospects of an issuer, and the objectives of Directive 2004/109/EC to enable investors to make an informed assessment of the financial situation of issuers with securities admitted to trading on a regulated market, it is appropriate that equivalence should be defined by reference to the ability of investors to make a similar assessment of the issuer's financial position and prospects, irrespective of whether financial statements are drawn up in accordance with the accounting standards of a third country or with International Financial Reporting Standards (hereinafter IFRS).

(3) In order to ensure that a determination of the equivalence of third country accounting standards is made in all cases that are relevant to Community markets, the Commission should assess the equivalence of third country accounting standards either upon a request from the competent authority of a Member State or an authority responsible for accounting standards or market supervision of a third country, or on its own initiative. The Commission will first consult the Committee of the European Securities Regulators (CESR) with regard to the assessment of equivalence of the accounting standards in question. In addition, the Commission will actively monitor ongoing progress in the work by the relevant third country authorities to eliminate any requirement for Community issuers accessing the financial markets of a third country to reconcile financial statements prepared using IFRS adopted pursuant to Regulation (EC) No 1606/2002 of the European Parliament and of the Council of 19 July 2002 on the application of international accounting standards (OJ L 243, 11.9.2002, p. 1). The decision of the Commission will have to be such that Community issuers are permitted to use IFRS adopted pursuant to Regulation (EC) No 1606/2002 in the third country concerned.

(4) The President of the European Council, the President of the Commission and the President of the United States have agreed in April 2007 to promote and secure conditions for US Generally Accepted Accounting Principles (GAAP) and IFRS to be recognised in both jurisdictions without the need for reconciliation by 2009 or sooner. The Commission and the US Securities and Exchange Commission (SEC) have pursued their dialogue towards the acceptance of IFRS adopted pursuant to Regulation (EC) No 1606/2002 in the United States, which would relieve issuers using IFRS from costly reconciliation requirements. Steps should be taken to achieve similar arrangements with other countries on whose exchanges EU companies list their securities before the end of 2008. The Accounting Standards Board of Japan (ASBJ) is pursuing the implementation of its joint work programme with the International Accounting Standards Board (IASB) towards the convergence of Japanese GAAP with IFRS. The Accounting Standards Board of Canada (ACSB) published an Implementation Plan for incorporating IFRS into Canadian GAAP as from 1 January 2011.

(5) In order to promote the objectives of Regulation (EC) No 1606/2002 and to encourage the use of IFRS throughout the global financial markets, and to minimise disruption to markets in the Community, it is appropriate to take account of any convergence programme with IFRS or commitment on the part of the relevant authority of the third country to adopt IFRS. Therefore it is necessary to further specify under which conditions convergence programmes can be considered as providing a sufficient basis for allowing third country issuers to apply their national accounting standards for a transitional period. The Commission will first consult CESR on the convergence programme or the progress towards adoption of IFRS, as the case may be.

(6) The measures provided for in this Regulation are in accordance with the opinion of the European Securities Committee,

HAS ADOPTED THIS REGULATION:

Article 1
Subject matter

This Regulation lays down the conditions under which the Generally Accepted Accounting Principles of a third country may be considered equivalent to International Financial Reporting Standards (hereinafter IFRS) and introduces a mechanism for the determination of such equivalence.

Article 2
Equivalence

The Generally Accepted Accounting Principles of a third country may be considered equivalent to IFRS adopted pursuant to Regulation (EC) No 1606/2002 if the financial statements drawn up in accordance with Generally Accepted Accounting Principles of the third country concerned enable investors to make a similar assessment of the assets and liabilities, financial position, profit and losses and prospects of the issuer as financial statements drawn up in accordance with IFRS, with the result that investors are likely to make the same decisions about the acquisition, retention or disposal of securities of an issuer.

Article 3
Equivalence mechanism

The decision on the determination of the equivalence of the Generally Accepted Accounting Principles of a third country may be taken on the initiative of the Commission, upon application submitted by the competent authority of a Member State or upon application of an authority responsible for accounting standards or market supervision of a third country.

Where the Commission decides to make a determination of equivalence, whether on an application or on its own initiative, it shall make that decision public.

Article 4
Conditions for the acceptance of third country accounting standards for a limited period

1. Third country issuers may be permitted to use financial statements drawn up in accordance with the accounting standards of a third country in order to comply with obligations under Directive2004/109/EC and, by derogation from Article35(5) of Regulation(EC)No809/2004, to provide historical financial information under that Regulation for a period commencing any time after 31 December 2008 and expiring no later than 31 December 2011 in the following cases:

1. the third country authority responsible for the national accounting standards concerned has made a public commitment before 30 June 2008 to converge these standards with International Financial Reporting Standards before 31 December 2011 and both the following conditions are met:

   (a) the third country authority responsible for the national accounting standards concerned has established a convergence programme before 31 December 2008 that is comprehensive and capable of being completed before 31 December 2011;

(b) the convergence programme is effectively implemented, without delay, and the resources necessary for its completion are allocated to its implementation;

2. the third country authority responsible for the national accounting standards concerned has made a public commitment before 30 June 2008 to adopt International Financial Reporting Standards before 31 December 2011 and effective measures are taken in the third country to secure the timely and complete transition to International Financial Reporting Standards by that date, or has reached a mutual recognition agreement with the EU before 31 December 2008.

2. Any decision under paragraph 1 to permit the continued acceptance of financial statements drawn up in accordance with the accounting standards of a third country shall be made in accordance with the procedure referred to in Article 24 of Directive 2003/71/EC and Article 27(2) of Directive 2004/109/EC.

3. Where the Commission permits the continued acceptance of financial statements drawn up in accordance with the accounting standards of a third country in accordance with paragraph 1, it shall review regularly whether the conditions specified in point (a) or (b) (as the case may be) continue to be met, and shall report accordingly to the European Securities Committee and to the European Parliament.

4. If the conditions in point (a) or (b) of paragraph 1 are no longer met, the Commission shall take a decision in accordance with the procedure referred to in Article 24 of Directive 2003/71/EC and Article 27(2) of Directive 2004/109/EC amending its decision under paragraph 1 in respect of these accounting standards.

5. When complying with this Article, the Commission shall first consult CESR on the convergence programme or the progress towards adoption of IFRS, as the case may be.

Article 5

This Regulation shall enter into force on the third day following its publication in the *Official Journal of the European Union*.

This Regulation shall be binding in its entirety and directly applicable in all Member States.

Done at Brussels, 21 December 2007.

Division D: Rules

Interim Transparency Rules

June 2007

Notes

These Rules are made by the Financial Regulator, as competent authority under the Irish transposition of the Transparency Directive 2003/109/EC, effected by ICMPA 2006, Pt 3 and SI 277/2007. They consist of actual Rules, which are binding, and guidelines as to compliance, which are intended to be persuasive, but do not have the same character as the actual Rules. The power to make these rules is conferred by ICMPA 2006, s 22. Interim Rules only have been published to date, published in June 2007.

Contents

1. Introduction

1.1 Title

These Rules are issued by the Irish Financial Services Regulatory Authority ("the Financial Regulator") under Section 22 of the Investment Funds, Companies and Miscellaneous Provisions Act, 2006 and shall be known as the "Transparency Rules".

1.2 Transparency (regulated markets) Law

Persons falling within the scope of the Transparency Rules shall have regard to:

(a) Part 3 of the Investment Funds, Companies and Miscellaneous Provisions Act, 2006 ("the Act of 2006");

(b) the Transparency (Directive 2004/109/EC) Regulations 2007 ("the Regulations");

(c) Commission Directive 2007/14/EC of 8 March 2007 "(the Implementing Directive"); and

(d) these Transparency Rules.

1.3 Rules and Guidance

In accordance with the provisions of Section 22(7) of the Act of 2006, where appropriate the Financial Regulator has also included guidance in these Transparency Rules on the steps that may be taken to comply with Transparency (regulated markets) law.

In the interests of clarity, Transparency Rules are set out in boxed bold typeface in order to distinguish them from guidance provided in these Transparency Rules.

It is not the policy of the Financial Regulator to provide legal advice on matters arising pursuant to the Regulations, the Implementing Directive or the Directive. Any guidance provided in these Transparency Rules should not be construed as legal advice or a legal interpretation of the Regulations, the Implementing Directive or the Directive. It is a matter for any person who may fall within the scope of the Regulations, the Implementing Directive or the Directive to seek legal advice regarding the application or otherwise of the Regulations, the Implementing Directive or the Directive to their particular set of circumstances.

1.4 Administrative Sanctions

In accordance with the provisions of Section 22(6) of the Act of 2006, the imposition of administrative sanctions shall apply in relation to a contravention of the Transparency Rules.

1.5 Interpretation

In these Transparency Rules, except where otherwise stated, words and expressions used that are also used in the Act of 2006, the Regulations or the Implementing Directive have the same meaning as in the Act of 2006, the Regulations or the Implementing Directive.

2. Competent Authority and Delegate Authority

2.1 Central Competent Authority

In relation to these Transparency Rules, the Financial Regulator is exercising its functions as Central Competent Authority pursuant to Regulation 36(1) of the Regulations.

2.2 Delegation of Certain Powers

In accordance with the provisions of Regulation 37 of the Regulations, the Financial Regulator has chosen to exercise certain of its functions as Central Competent Authority under the Regulations by delegating such functions to the Irish Stock Exchange Limited, which will be known as the Delegate Authority for the purposes of these Transparency Rules.

2.3 Enforcement of the Transparency Rules

Persons falling within the scope of these Transparency Rules will at all times be subject to the powers granted to the Financial Regulator under Part 9 of the Regulations and the enforcement provisions set out in Parts 10 and 12 of the Regulations and Part 3 of the Act of 2006.

3. Definitions

3.1 In these Transparency Rules, except where otherwise stated, words and expressions used that are also used in the Act of 2006, the Regulations or the

Implementing Directive have the same meaning as in the Act of 2006, the Regulations or the Implementing Directive.

The following definitions must be used for the purposes of the Transparency Rules or the Regulations as applicable:

"CAO" shall mean the Company Announcements Office of the Irish Stock Exchange Limited (the Delegate Authority).

"RIS" shall mean a Regulatory Information Service provided by or approved for use by the regulated market on which the relevant financial instruments are admitted to trading or in respect of which a request for admission to trading on such a regulated market has been made.

"debt security" shall mean bonds or other forms of transferable securitised debts, with the exception of securities which are equivalent to shares in companies or which, if converted or if the rights conferred by them are exercised, give rise to a right to acquire shares or securities equivalent to shares.

"financial instrument" shall mean the instruments specified in Section C of Annex 1 of Directive on Markets in Financial Instruments 2004/39/EC (MiFID).

"shareholder" shall mean any natural person or legal entity governed by private or public law, who holds directly or indirectly:

(a) shares of the issuer in its own name and on its own account;

(b) shares of the issuer in its own name, but on behalf of another natural person or legal entity;

(c) depository receipts or other bearer instruments howsoever called, in which case the holder of the depository receipt or other bearer instrument shall be considered as the shareholder of the underlying shares represented by the depository receipts or other bearer instruments.

"third country investment firm" shall mean an investment firm within the meaning of Directive 2004/39/EC which has its head office outside of the EEA.

"trading day" shall mean a day included in the calendar of trading days published by the Financial Regulator on its website: www.financialregulator.ie

4. GENERAL PROVISIONS

4.1 Obligations under the Transparency Rules

A person on whom obligations are imposed under these Transparency Rules is required:

(a) to provide to the Financial Regulator or the Delegate Authority, as appropriate, in a timely manner following a request, any information or explanation that the Financial Regulator or the Delegate Authority may reasonably require;

(b) to be open and co-operative in their dealings with the Financial Regulator or the Delegate Authority in respect of any request made in accordance with paragraph (a); and

(c) to participate in such meetings as the Financial Regulator or the Delegate Authority consider necessary in respect of any request made in accordance with paragraph (a) and any information or explanations received in respect of any such request.

5. Disclosure of Regulated Information

5.0 General Guidance

Part 2 of the Regulations provides for the publication of Periodic Financial Information by issuers. This section of the Transparency Rules applies to issuers whose securities are admitted to trading on a regulated market and whose Home Member State is the State. An issuer must take all reasonable care to ensure that any information it notifies to a RIS is not misleading, false or deceptive and does not omit anything likely to affect the import of the information.

5.0.1 Guidance in relation to the Publication of Regulated Information

An issuer referred to at Guidance 5.0 which is disseminating regulated information in accordance with Rule 5.1, must disclose that regulated information either:

(a) directly to a RIS; or

(b) indirectly to a RIS through the CAO.

Please note that announcements of regulated information to the CAO must be in MS Word format and any tables included in the announcement must be created in Word (rather than imported from another program).

5.1 Publication of Regulated Information

An issuer or person shall disseminate regulated information using a RIS and shall ensure that the RIS complies with the minimum standards contained in Sections 33(4) to 33(8) of the Regulations.

5.2 Simultaneous Notification to the CAO

Where an issuer or person discloses regulated information in accordance with the Guidance 5.0.1(a), they shall simultaneously notify the CAO.

5.0.3 Guidance in relation to Notification when a RIS is not Available

The fact that a RIS is not open for business is not, in itself, sufficient grounds for delaying the disclosure or distribution of regulated information.

5.3 Notification when a RIS is not Available

An issuer who is required to disseminate regulated information via a RIS at a time outside business hours, when the RIS is not open for business shall distribute the information without delay to:

(a) not less than two national newspapers in the Member State where the financial instruments are admitted to trading;

(b) two news wire services operating in the Member State where the financial instruments have been admitted to trading; and

(c) a RIS for release as soon as it re-opens.

6. Publication of Periodic Financial Information

6.0 Guidance regarding Compliance with the Listing Rules

An issuer that is admitted to the official list of the Irish Stock Exchange should consider its obligations under the Listing Rules in addition to the requirements in these rules.

Annual Financial Report

6.0.1 Guidance regarding Content of Annual Management Report

The financial key performance indicators referred to in paragraph 2(i) of Rule 6.1 are factors by reference to which the development, performance or position of the issuer's business can be measured effectively.

6.1 Content of Annual Management Report

The annual management report referred to in Regulation 4(3)(b) must contain:

(a) a fair review of the issuer's business; and

(b) a description of the principal risks and uncertainties facing the issuer.

The review required by (a) above must:

(1) be a balanced and comprehensive analysis of:

(i) the development and performance of the issuer's business during the financial year; and

(ii) the position of the issuer's business at the end of that year, consistent with the size and complexity of the business;

(2) include, to the extent necessary for an understanding of the development, performance or position of the issuer's business:

(i) analysis using financial key performance indicators (see Guidance 6.0.1 above); and

(ii) where appropriate, analysis using other key performance indicators including information relating to environmental matters and employee matters; and

(3) include references to, and additional explanations of, amounts included in the issuer's annual financial statements, where appropriate.

The management report shall also give an indication of:

(1) any important events that have occurred since the end of the financial year;

(2) the issuer's likely future development;

(3) activities in the field of research and development;

(4) the information concerning acquisitions of own shares prescribed by Article 22 (2) of Directive 77/91/EEC;

(5) the existence of branches of the issuer; and

(6) in relation to the issuer's use of financial instruments and where material for the assessment of its assets, liabilities, financial position and profit or loss:

(a) the issuer's financial risk management objectives and policies, including its policy for hedging each major type of forecasted transaction for which hedge accounting is used, and

(b) the issuer's exposure to price risk, credit risk, liquidity risk and cash flow risk.

Half-Yearly Financial Reports

6.2 Accounting Policies and Presentation applied to Half-Yearly Figures

The accounting policies and presentation applied to half-yearly figures shall be consistent with those applied in the latest published annual accounts except where:

(1) the accounting policies and presentation are to be changed in the subsequent annual financial statements, in which case the new accounting policies and presentation should be followed and the changes and the reasons for the changes shall be disclosed in the half-yearly report; or

(2) the Financial Regulator otherwise agrees.

6.3 Change in Accounting Date

(1) An issuer shall notify a RIS as soon as possible of:

(a) any change in its accounting reference date; and

(b) the new accounting reference date.

(2) An issuer shall prepare and publish a second interim report in accordance with Regulation 6 if the effect of the change in the accounting reference date is to extend the accounting period to more than 14 months.

(3) The second interim report shall be prepared and published in respect of either:

(a) the period up to the old accounting reference date; or

(b) the period up to a date not more than six months prior to the new accounting reference date.

7. Publication of Ongoing Information Regarding Major Shareholdings

7.0 General Guidance

Part 5 of the Regulations provides for the publication of ongoing information about major shareholdings. This section of the Transparency Rules applies to issuers whose securities are admitted to trading on a regulated market and whose Home Member State is the State and to issuers whose shares are admitted to trading in a market prescribed by the Minister in accordance with Section 24 of the Act of 2006.

7.0.1 Guidance regarding the Notification of the Acquisition or Disposal of Major Shareholdings

In Part 5 of the Regulations:

(i) an acquisition or disposal of shares is to be regarded as effective when the relevant transaction is executed unless the transaction provides for settlement to be subject to conditions which are beyond the control of the parties in which case the acquisition or disposal is to be regarded as effective on the settlement of the transaction;

(ii) a stock-lending agreement which provides for the outright transfer of securities and which provides the lender with a right to call for redelivery of the lent stock (or its equivalent) is not (as respects the lender) to be taken as involving a disposal of any shares which may be the subject of the stock loan; and

(iii) for the purposes of calculating whether any percentage threshold is reached, exceeded or fallen below and in any resulting notification, the proportion of voting rights held shall if necessary be rounded down to the next whole number.

Rule 7.1 does not apply to voting rights held in collective investment undertakings of the closed end type. For the avoidance of doubt, for collective investment undertakings of the closed end type that issue shares or units or securities equivalent to these, the requirements in Regulation 14(1) to 14(4) apply.

7.1 Notification of the Acquisition or Disposal of Major Shareholdings and Voting Rights

Subject to the exemptions in Regulation 14(5) a person shall notify the issuer (other than where the issuer is a collective investment undertaking of the closed-end type) of the percentage of its voting rights if the percentage of voting rights which he holds as shareholder or through his direct or indirect holding of financial instruments or a combination of such holdings:

(1) reaches, exceeds or falls below 3%, 4%, 5%, 6%, 7%, 8%, 9%, 10% and each 1% threshold thereafter up to 100% or in the case of a non-Irish issuer on the basis of thresholds at 5%, 10%, 15%, 20%, 25%, 30%, 50% and 75% as a result of an acquisition or disposal of shares or financial instruments; or

(2) reaches, exceeds or falls below an applicable threshold in (1) as a result of events changing the breakdown of voting rights and on the basis of information disclosed by the issuer in accordance with Regulation 20;

and in the case of an issuer which is not incorporated in an EEA state a notification under (2) shall be made on the basis of equivalent events and disclosed information.

7.2 Voting Rights Disregarded on Shares Acquired by a Borrower under a Stock Lending Agreement

Voting rights on shares acquired by a borrower under a stock lending agreement can be disregarded provided:

(a) such shares (or equivalent stock) are on-lent or otherwise disposed of by the borrower by not later than close of business on the next trading day; and

(b) the borrower does not declare any intention of exercising (and does not exercise) the voting rights attaching to the shares.

7.0.2 Guidance regarding to Third Country Investment Firms acting as a Market Maker

References to a market maker in Regulation 14(6) also include a third country investment firm and a credit institution when acting as a market maker and which, in relation to that activity, is subject to regulatory supervision under the laws of a Member State. (See Rule 7.7 below regarding notification of information to the Financial Regulator in accordance with Regulation 14(6)(b)).

7.0.3 Guidance regarding the Acquisition or Disposal of Major Proportions of Voting Rights

Cases (a) to (h) in Regulation 15 identify situations where a person may be able to control the manner in which voting rights are exercised and where, (taking account of any aggregation with other holdings) a notification to the issuer may need to be made.

In the Financial Regulator's view:

(1) Case (e) produces the result that it is always necessary for the parent undertaking of a controlled undertaking to aggregate its holding with any holding of the controlled undertaking (subject to the exemptions implicit in Case (e) and others in Regulation 18);

(2) Case (f) includes a person carrying on investment management and which is also the custodian of shares to which voting rights are attached;

(3) Case (g) does not result in a unit holder in a collective investment scheme or other investment entity being treated as the holder of voting rights in the scheme property (provided always such persons do not have any entitlement to exercise, or control the exercise of, such voting rights); neither are such persons to be regarded as holding shares "indirectly";

(4) Case (h), although referring to proxies, also describes and applies to a person undertaking investment management, and to a management company, and which is able effectively to determine the manner in which voting rights attached to shares under its control are exercised (for example through instructions given directly or indirectly to a nominee or independent custodian). Case (e) provides for the voting rights which are under the control of such a person to be aggregated with those of its parent undertaking.

A person falling within Cases (a) to (h) is an indirect holder of shares for the purpose of the definition of shareholder. These indirect holdings have to be aggregated, but also separately identified in a notification to the issuer. Apart from those identified in the Cases (a) to (h), the Financial Regulator does not expect any other significant category "indirect shareholder" to be identified. Cases (a) to (h) are also relevant in determining whether a person is an indirect holder of qualifying financial instruments which result in an entitlement to acquire shares.

7.0.4 Guidance regarding the Notification of Voting Rights arising from the holding of certain Financial Instruments

For the purposes of the Directive, financial instruments should be taken into account in the context of notifying major holdings, to the extent that such instruments give the holder an unconditional right to acquire the underlying shares or cash on maturity. Consequently, financial instruments should not be considered to include instruments entitling the holder to receive shares depending on the price of the underlying share reaching a certain level at a certain moment in time. Nor should they be considered to cover those instruments that allow the instrument issuer or a third party to give shares or cash to the instrument holder on maturity.

7.0.5 Guidance regarding the Notification of Combined Holdings

A person may have to make a notification if the overall percentage level of his voting rights remains the same but there is a notifiable change in the percentage level of one or more of the categories of voting rights held.

7.3 Notification of Combined Holdings

A person making a notification in accordance with Regulation 14(1) to 14(4) shall do so by reference to each of the following:

(1) the aggregate of all voting rights which the person holds as shareholder and as the direct or indirect holder of financial instruments;

(2) the aggregate of all voting rights held as direct or indirect shareholder (disregarding for this purpose holdings of financial instruments); and

(3) the aggregate of all direct and indirect holdings of financial instruments.

7.0.6 Guidance regarding Notification and Disclosure of Major Holdings

When a shareholder acquires or disposes of a major holding of shares of an issuer to which voting rights are attached the shareholder shall notify the issuer.

7.4 Notification to the Issuer

The notification to the issuer shall be effected as soon as possible, but not later than four trading days in the case of a non-Irish issuer and a collective investment undertaking of the closed-end type, and two trading days in all other cases, the first of which shall be the day after the date on which the relevant person:

(a) learns of the acquisition or disposal or of the possibility of exercising voting rights, or on which, having regard to the circumstances, should have learned of it, regardless of the date on which the acquisition, disposal or possibility of exercising voting rights takes effect; or

(b) is informed about the event in Regulation 14(1).

For the purpose of a) above a person shall, in relation to a transaction to which he is a party or which he has instructed, be deemed to have knowledge of the acquisition, disposal or possibility to exercise voting rights no later than two trading days following the transaction in question. Where a transaction is conditional upon the approval by public authorities of the transaction or on a future uncertain event the occurrence of which is outside the control of the parties to the agreement, the parties are deemed to have knowledge of the acquisition, disposal or possibility of exercising voting rights only when the relevant approvals are obtained or when the event happens.

7.0.7 Guidance regarding Notification Obligation for the Relevant Shareholder and Proxy Holder

It may be necessary for both the relevant shareholder and proxy holder to make a notification. For example, if a direct holder of shares has a notifiable holding of voting rights and gives a proxy in respect of those rights (such that the recipient has discretion as to how the votes are cast) then for the purposes of Regulation 14(1) to 14(4) this is a disposal of such rights giving rise to a notification obligation. The proxy holder may also have such an obligation by virtue of his holding under Regulation 15.

Separate notifications will not however be necessary provided a single notification (whether made by the direct holder of the shares or by the proxy holder) makes clear what the situation will be when the proxy has expired. Where a proxy holder receives several proxies then one notification may be made in respect of the aggregated voting rights held by the proxy holder on or as soon as is reasonably practicable following the proxy deadline. Unless it discloses what the position will be in respect of each proxy after the proxies have expired, such a notification will not relieve any direct holder of the shares of its notification obligation (if there is a notifiable disposal). A proxy which confers only minor and residual discretions (such as to vote on an adjournment) will not result in the proxy holder (or shareholder) having a notification obligation.

7.5 Notification Obligations for Transactions referred to in Regulation 10

The notification obligation following transactions of a kind mentioned in Regulation 15 are individual obligations incumbent upon each direct shareholder or indirect shareholder mentioned in Regulation 15 or both if the proportion of voting rights held by each party reaches, exceeds or falls below an applicable threshold.

7.0.8 Guidance regarding Calendar of Trading Days

The Financial Regulator maintains and publishes on its website at www.financialregulator.ie a calendar of trading days which applies in Ireland for the purposes of Part 5 of the Regulations.

7.0.9 Guidance regarding the Standard Form TR-1 (Voting Rights Attached to Shares)

The information to be filed with the Financial Regulator in accordance with Regulation 22 and Rule 7.1 must:

(1) include the details required in the Annex to the Standard Form TR-1 (details contained in the separate Annex should not be sent to the issuer);

(2) clearly state in a prominent place on the first page that the notification is "for filing purposes only in accordance with Regulation 22 of the Transparency (Directive 2004/109/EC) Regulations 2007"; and

(3) be sent by email to the Irish Stock Exchange at TR1filing@ise.ie, for the period of the delegation to the ISE (the Delegate Authority).

7.6 Standard Form TR-1 (Voting Rights Attached to Shares)

A notification in relation to shares admitted to trading on a regulated market or in a market prescribed by the Minister in accordance with Section 24 of the Investment Funds, Companies and Miscellaneous Provisions Act 2006, shall be made using the Standard Form (TR-1) available in electronic format at the Financial regulator's website at www.financialregulator.ie.

7.0.10 Guidance regarding the Standard Form TR-2 (Notification by Market Makers)

The information to be filed with the Financial Regulator in accordance with Regulation 14(6)(b) must:

(1) clearly state in a prominent place on the first page that the notification is "for filing purposes only in accordance with Regulation 14(6)(b) of the Transparency (Directive 2004/109/EC) Regulations 2007"; and

(2) be sent by email to the Financial Regulator.

7.7 Standard Form TR-2 (Notification by Market Makers)

A notification by market makers in accordance with Regulation 14(6)(b) shall be made using the Standard Form (TR-2) available in electronic format at the Financial regulator's website at www.financialregulator.ie.

7.0.11 Guidance determining whether a notification is required

In determining whether a notification is required a person's net (direct or indirect) holding in a share (and of relevant financial instruments) may be assessed by reference to that person's holdings at a point in time up to midnight of the day for which the determination is made (taking account of acquisitions and disposals executed during that day).

7.8 Issuer obligation to publish information contained in the notification

(1) An issuer not falling within (2) shall, in relation to shares admitted to trading on a regulated market, on receipt of a notification as soon as possible and in any event by not

later than the end of the trading day following receipt of the notification make public all of the information contained in the notification.

(2) A non-Irish issuer, a collective investment undertaking of the closed-end type and any other issuers whose shares are admitted to trading on a market prescribed by the Minister in accordance with Section 24 of the Act of 2006 (but not a regulated market) shall, on receipt of a notification, as soon as possible and in any event by not later than the end of the third trading day following receipt of the notification, make public all of the information contained in the notification.

8. Filing of Regulated and other Information with the Competent Authority

8.0 General Guidance regarding Filing of Information with the Competent Authority

An issuer or person that discloses regulated information may comply with Regulation 31 by notifying the Company Announcements Office of the Irish Stock Exchange (the Delegate Authority).

An issuer that disseminates its annual financial report in accordance with Regulation 33(5)(a) must also file a copy of the unedited full text report with the relevant listing department or the CAO of the Irish Stock Exchange, as appropriate, by email (see email addresses on page 37).

The email notification must clearly state that the unedited full text report has been submitted for filing purposes.

8.1 Filing of Information with the Financial Regulator (Regulation 31)

An issuer or person is deemed to have filed regulated information with the Financial Regulator in accordance with Regulation 31 by disseminating the information in accordance with Rules 5.1 and 5.2.

8.0.1 General Guidance regarding Communication of Amendments to Instruments of Incorporation to the Bank

An issuer may communicate draft amendments to its instruments of incorporation in accordance with Regulation 25(2)(a) by submitting these by electronic means to the relevant listing department of the Irish Stock Exchange (the Delegate Authority).

The communication must state in a prominent place on the first page that it is "for filing purposes only in accordance with Regulation 25(2) of the Transparency (Directive 2004/109/EC) Regulations 2007".

9. Continuing Obligations and Access to Information

9.0 General Guidance

The requirements Rules 9.1 to 9.4 below apply to an issuer of shares (other than a collective investment undertaking of the closed end type) whose Home State is the State.

9.1 Statement of Dividends

In addition to Regulation 27(2), an issuer of shares (other than a collective investment undertaking of the closed-end type) shall notify a RIS as soon as possible after the board has approved any decision to pay or make any dividend or other distribution on listed equity or to withhold any dividend or interest payment on listed securities giving details of:

(1) the exact net amount payable per share;

(2) the payment date;

(3) the record date (where applicable); and

(4) any foreign income dividend election, together with any income tax treated as paid at the lower rate and not repayable.

9.2 Proxy Forms

In addition to Regulation 25(5)(b), an issuer of shares (other than a collective investment undertaking of the closed-end type) shall ensure that a proxy form:

(1) is sent with the notice convening a meeting of holders of shares to each person entitled to vote at the meeting;

(2) provides for two-way voting on all resolutions intended to be proposed (except that it is not necessary to provide proxy forms with two-way voting on procedural resolutions);

(3) states that a shareholder is entitled to appoint a proxy of his own choice and that it provides a space for insertion of the name of the proxy; and

(4) states that if it is returned without an indication as to how the proxy shall vote on any particular matter, the proxy will exercise his discretion as to whether, and if so how, he votes.

9.3 Proxy Forms for Re-Election of Retiring Directors

In addition to Regulation 25(5)(b), an issuer of shares (other than a collective investment undertaking of the closed-end type) shall ensure that, if the resolutions to be proposed include the re-election of retiring directors and the number of retiring directors standing for re-election exceeds five, the proxy form may give shareholders the opportunity to vote for or against the re-election of the retiring directors as a whole but shall also allow votes to be cast for or against the re-election of the retiring directors individually.

9.4 Notification Relating to Capital

In addition to Regulation 27(2), an issuer of shares (other than a collective investment undertaking of the closed-end type) shall notify a RIS as soon as possible of the results of any new issue of equity securities or preference shares or of a public offering of existing shares or other equity securities.

9.0.1 General Guidance regarding Notification Relating to Capital Issued Subject to an Underwriting Agreement

Where the securities are subject to an underwriting agreement an issuer of shares (other than a collective investment undertaking of the closed end type) may, at its discretion and subject to Regulation 10 of the Market Abuse (Directive 2003/6/EC) Regulations 2005 of Ireland and the related Market Abuse Rules (disclosure of inside information), delay notifying a RIS as required by Rule 9.4 for up to 2 business days until the obligation by the underwriter to take or procure others to take securities is finally determined or lapses. In the case of an issue or offer of securities, which is not underwritten, notification of the result must be made in accordance with Rule 9.4.

10. EXEMPTIONS

10.1 Exemptions

Issuers of convertible securities

The rules on half-yearly financial reports (Regulation 6) and Interim management statements (Regulation 9) do not apply to an issuer of transferable securities convertible into shares.

Issuers of preference shares

The rules on interim management statements (Regulation 9) do not apply to an issuer of preference shares.

Issuers of depository receipts

The rules on half-yearly financial reports (Regulation 6) and interim management statements (Regulation 9) do not apply to an issuer of depository receipts.

10.2 Exemptions

Regulations 25(3) to 25(8) and Regulations 27 and 28 do not apply to:

(1) an issuer of securities convertible into shares in respect of those securities convertible into shares;

(2) an issuer of preference shares in respect of those preference shares; and

(3) an issuer of depository receipts in respect of those depository receipts.

11. Third Country Equivalence

11.0.1 Guidance regarding Equivalence – Third Country States

The Financial Regulator will maintain a published list of Third Country States which, for the purpose of Article 23.1 of the Directive, are judged to have laws which lay down requirements equivalent to those imposed upon issuers under Part 2 of Regulations (Periodic Financial Reporting), Part 5 of the Regulations (On-Going Information about Major Shareholdings) and Part 6 of the Regulations (Continuing Obligations and Access to Information).

Such issuers remain subject to the following requirements of Part 6 of Regulations (Continuing Obligations and Access to Information):

(1) the filing of information with the Financial Regulator;

(2) the language provisions; and

(3) the dissemination of information provisions.

11.1 Third Country States – Equivalence

An issuer whose registered office is in a Third Country States whose relevant laws are considered equivalent by the Financial Regulator is exempted from the requirements in the Regulations and rules relating to annual financial reports (Regulation 4), half-yearly financial reports (Regulation 6) and interim management statements (Regulation 9).

11.2 Third Country States – Equivalence

An issuer whose registered office is in a Third Country States whose relevant laws are considered equivalent by the Financial Regulator is exempted from Regulations 25(3) to 28 and related Transparency Rules.

11.3 Third Country States – Equivalence

An issuer whose registered office is in a Third Country States whose relevant laws are considered equivalent by the Financial Regulator is exempted from Regulations 21(9) and related Transparency Rules.

11.4 Third Country States – Equivalence

An issuer whose registered office is in a Third Country State whose relevant laws are considered equivalent by the Financial Regulator is exempted from Regulations 19 and 20 of Part 5 of the Regulations (On-Going Information about Major Shareholdings).

11.5 Third Country States – Equivalence

The notification requirements in Regulation 14(2)(b) and Rule 7.1(2) of Chapter 7 apply to a person in respect of the shares of an issuer which has its registered office in a Third Country State on the basis of events equivalent to those in Regulation 14(2)(b) and information disclosed by that issuer in accordance with Regulation 24(4).

11.6 Third Country States – Equivalence

An issuer whose registered office is in a Third Country State, whose relevant laws are considered equivalent by the Financial Regulator, and who is exempt from Regulations 4-9, 19, 20, 21(9) and 25(3) - 28(2) is subject to Regulations 22, 25(2), 31, 32 and 33.

12. Storage of Regulated Information

12.0 General Guidance regarding the Storage of Regulated Information

Under the Directive regulated information, in addition to being disseminated and filed, must also be stored in the Officially Appointed Mechanism ("OAM") for a five year period. The Directive requires that there is at least one OAM for the central storage of regulated information in each Member State. The European Commission is due to set detailed standards for OAMs but this will not happen until sometime after the deadline for Directive implementation. For the interim period the Irish Stock Exchange (the Delegate Authority) will operate a storage mechanism in Ireland. Regulated information will be available on the Irish Stock Exchange website: www.ise.ie.

13. Transitional Provisions

13.0 General Guidance regarding Transitional Provisions

The transitional provisions arise in relation to periodic financial reporting and disclosure of major shareholding matters

13.1 Confirmation of Number of Voting Rights

Each issuer is required, within 21 calendar days of the Regulations 2007 taking effect, to make an announcement via a RIS (in accordance with Rules 5.1 and 5.2) of:

(1) the total number of voting rights in respect of each class of share which it issues and which is admitted to trading on a regulated market or admitted to trading in a market prescribed by the Minister in accordance with Section 24 of the Act of 2006; and

(2) distinguishing the number of voting rights attaching to any shares held by the issuer in treasury.

APPENDIX 1
TRANSPARENCY RULES, INFORMATION & CONTACT DETAILS

For further information on the Transparency Directive and these Transparency Rules please contact:

Markets Supervision Department

Financial Regulator

PO Box 9138

College Green

Dublin 2

Telephone: 01 410 4761

Fax: 01 410 4070

E-mail: markets@financialregulator.ie

Website: www.financialregulator.ie

For further information and details on notifications, dissemination of regulated information using the CAO, please contact:

Company Announcements Office

Irish Stock Exchange

28 Anglesea Street

Dublin 2

Telephone: 01 617 4200

Fax: 01 677 6045

E-mail: announcements@ise.ie

Website: www.ise.ie

For further information on monitoring compliance with Transparency Regulation and Transparency Rules, please contact the relevant section of the Listing Department of the Irish Stock Exchange (the Delegate Authority) at:

Listing Department

Irish Stock Exchange

28 Anglesea Street

Dublin 2

Telephone: 01 617 4200 (general)

01 617 4229 (Company Listings)

01 617 4270 (Debt Listings)

01 617 4255 (Investment Fund Listings)

Fax: 01 677 6045 (general)

01 617 4290 (Company Listings)

01 617 4244 (Debt Listings)

01 670 7394 (Investment Fund Listings)

E-mail: companylistings@ise.ie (Company Listings)

funds@ise.ie (Investment Fund Listings)

abs@ise.ie (Debt Listings)

Website: www.ise.ie

For further information on trading and regulation on the Irish Stock Exchange (the Delegate Authority), please contact:

Trading and Regulation Department

Irish Stock Exchange

28 Anglesea Street

Dublin 2

Telephone: 01 617 4200

Fax: 01 679 5432

E-mail: iseregulation@ise.ie

Website: www.ise.ie

APPENDIX 2
STANDARD FORMS

STANDARD FORM TR-1

VOTING RIGHTS ATTACHED TO SHARES– ARTICLE 12(1) OF DIRECTIVE 2004/109/EC

FINANCIAL INSTRUMENTS – ARTICLE 11(3) OF THE COMMISSION DIRECTIVE 2007/14/EC[i]

1. Identity of the issuer or the underlying issuer of existing shares to which voting rights are attached [ii]:
2. Reason for the notification (please tick the appropriate box or boxes):

   [ ] an acquisition or disposal of voting rights

   [ ] an acquisition or disposal of financial instruments which may result in the acquisition of shares already issued to which voting rights are attached

   [ ] an event changing the breakdown of voting rights
3. Full name of person(s) subject to the notification obligation[iii]:
4. Full name of shareholder(s) (if different from 3.)[iv]:
5. Date of the transaction and date on which the threshold is crossed or reached[v]:
6. Date on which issuer notified:
7. Threshold(s) that is/are crossed or reached:
8. Notified details:

A) Voting rights attached to shares							
Class/type of shares (if possible using the ISIN CODE)	Situation previous to the Triggering transaction [vi]		Resulting situation after the triggering transaction[vii]				
	Number of Shares[viii]	Number of Voting rights[ix]	Number of shares[x]	Number of voting rights[xi]		% of voting rights	
			Direct	Direct[xii]	Indirect [xiii]	Direct	Indirect
SUBTOTAL A (based on aggregate voting rights)							

B) Financial Instruments				
Resulting situation after the triggering transaction[xiv]				
Type of financial instrument	Expiration Date[xv]	Exercise/ Conversion Period/ Date[xvi]	Number of voting rights that may be acquired if the instrument is exercised/ converted	% of voting rights
		SUBTOTAL B (in relation to all expiration dates)		

Total (A+B)	**number of voting rights**	**% of voting rights**

9. Chain of controlled undertakings through which the voting rights and/or the financial instruments are effectively held, if applicable[xvii]:
10. In case of proxy voting: [*name of the proxy holder*] will cease to hold [*number*] voting rights as of [*date*].
11. Additional information:

Done at [*place*] on [*date*].

ANNEX TO THE STANDARD FORM TR-1 [xviii]

a) Identity of the person or legal entity subject to the notification obligation:

Full name (including legal form for legal entities) ....

Contact address (registered office for legal entities) ....

....

Phone number ....

Other useful information (at least legal representative for legal persons) ....

b) Identity of the notifier, if applicable[xix]:

Full name ....

Contact address ....

....

Phone number ....

Other useful information (e.g. functional relationship with the person or legal entity subject to the notification obligation)

c) Additional information

STANDARD FORM TR-2

NOTIFICATION BY MARKET MAKERS – ARTICLE 6(1) OF THE COMMISSION DIRECTIVE 2007/14/EC

(THIS FORM IS TO BE FILED WITH THE COMPETENT AUTHORITY OF THE HOME MEMBER STATE OF THE ISSUER)

1. Identity of the Market Maker

Full name (including legal form for legal entities) ....

Contact address (registered office for legal entities) ....
....

Phone number, fax and e-mail address ....

Other useful information (at least legal representative for legal persons) ....

2. Identity of the notifier, if applicable [if another person makes the notification on behalf of the market maker identified in (1)]

Full name ....

Contact address ....
....

Phone number, fax and e-mail address ....

Other useful information (e.g. functional relationship with the person or legal entity subject to the notification obligation)

3. Reason for notification

[ ] The Market maker identified in (1) intends to conduct market making activities in relation to the following issuer:

[ ] The Market maker identified in (1) ceases to conduct market making activities in relation to the following issuer:

Issuer	

4. In case the Market Maker identified in (1) intends to conduct market making activities,

   - Please indicate the Competent Authority that authorised the Market Maker under Directive 2004/39/EC ....

   - Please indicate when this authorisation was obtained: ....

5. The Market Maker identified under (1) declares that it does not intervene in the management of the issuer identified in (2) nor exerts any influence on that issuer to buy such shares or back the shares price.

Done at [*place*] on [*date*].

Notes to Form TR-1

I This form is to be sent to the issuer or underlying issuer and to be filed with the competent authority.

ii Either the full name of the legal entity or another method for identifying the issuer or underlying issuer, provided it is reliable and accurate.

iii This should be the full name of (a) the shareholder; (b) the natural person or legal entity acquiring, disposing of or exercising voting rights in the cases provided for in Article 10 (b) to (h) of Directive 2004/109/EC; (c) all the parties to the agreement referred to in Article 10 (a) of that Directive, or (d) the holder of financial instruments entitled to acquire shares already issued to which voting rights are attached, as appropriate.

In relation to the transactions referred to in points (b) to (h) of Article 10 of that Directive, the following list is provided as indication of the persons who should be mentioned:

– in the circumstances foreseen in letter (b) of Article 10 of that Directive, the natural person or legal entity that acquires the voting rights and is entitled to exercise them under the agreement and the natural person or legal entity who is transferring temporarily for consideration the voting rights;

– in the circumstances foreseen in letter (c) of Article 10 of that Directive, the natural person or legal entity holding the collateral, provided the person or entity controls the voting rights and declares its intention of exercising them, and natural person or legal entity lodging the collateral under these conditions;

– in the circumstances foreseen in letter (d) of Article 10 of that Directive, the natural person or legal entity who has a life interest in shares if that person or entity is entitled to exercise the voting rights attached to the shares and the natural person or legal entity who is disposing of the voting rights when the life interest is created;

– in the circumstances foreseen in letter (e) of Article 10 of that Directive, the controlling natural person or legal entity and, provided it has a notification duty at an individual level under Article 9, under letters (a) to (d) of Article 10 of that Directive or under a combination of any of those situations, the controlled undertaking;

– in the circumstances foreseen in letter (f) of Article 10 of that Directive, the deposit taker of the shares, if he can exercise the voting rights attached to the shares deposited with him at his discretion, and the depositor of the shares allowing the deposit taker to exercise the voting rights at his discretion;

- in the circumstances foreseen in letter (g) of Article 10 of that Directive, the natural person or legal entity that controls the voting rights;
- in the circumstances foreseen in letter (h) of Article 10 of that Directive, the proxy holder, if he can exercise the voting rights at his discretion, and the shareholder who has given his proxy to the proxy holder allowing the latter to exercise the voting rights at his discretion.

iv Applicable in the cases provided for in Article 10 (b) to (h) of Directive 2004/109/EC. This should be the full name of the shareholder who is the counterparty to the natural person or legal entity referred to in Article 10 of that Directive unless the holdings of the shareholder would be lower than 3% of the total number of voting rights.

v The date of the transaction should normally be, in the case of an on exchange transaction, the date on which the matching of orders occurs; in the case of an off exchange transaction, date of the entering into an agreement.

The date on which threshold is crossed should normally be the date on which the acquisition, disposal or possibility to exercise voting rights takes effect. For passive crossings, the date when the corporate event took effect.

vi Please refer to the situation disclosed in the previous notification. In case the situation previous to the triggering transaction was below 3%, please state "below 3%".

vii If the holding has fallen below the minimum threshold, the notifying party should not be obliged to disclose the extent of the holding, only that the new holding is below 3%.

For the case provided for in Article 10(a) of Directive 2004/109/EC, there should be no disclosure of individual holdings per party to the agreement unless a party individually crosses or reaches an Article 9 threshold. This applies upon entering into, introducing changes to or terminating an agreement.

viii To be used in Member States where applicable.

ix Direct and indirect.

x To be used in Member States where applicable.

xi In case of combined holdings of shares with voting rights attached "direct holding" and voting rights "indirect holding", please split the voting rights number and percentage into the direct and indirect columns – if there is no combined holdings, please leave the relevant box blank.

xii Voting rights attached to shares held by the notifying party (Article 9 of Directive 2004/109/EC).

xiii Voting rights held by the notifying party independently of any holding of shares (Article 10 of Directive 2004/109/EC).

xiv If the holding has fallen below the minimum threshold, the notifying party should not be obliged to disclose the extent of the holding, only that the new holding is below 3%.

xv Date of maturity/expiration of the financial instrument i.e. the date when right to acquire shares ends.

xvi If the financial instrument has such a period – please specify this period – for example once every 3 months starting from [date].

xvii The notification should include the name(s) of the controlled undertakings through which the voting rights are held. The notification should also include the amount of voting rights and the percentage held by each controlled undertaking, insofar as individually the controlled undertaking holds 3% or more, and insofar as the notification by the parent undertaking is intended to cover the notification obligations of the controlled undertaking.

xviii This annex is only to be filed with the competent authority.

xix Whenever another person makes the notification on behalf of the shareholder or the natural person/legal entity referred to in Articles 10 and 13 of Directive 2004/109/EC.

T +353 1 410 4000

Consumer help-line

lo call 1890 77 77 77

Register of Financial Service Providers help-line

lo call 1890 20 04 69

F +353 1 410 4900

www.financialregulator.ie

www.itsyourmoney.ie

Information Centre: 6-8 College Green, Dublin 2

PO Box No 9138

College Green,

Dublin 2, Ireland

Prospectus Rules

August 2008

Notes

These Rules are made by the Financial Regulator, as competent authority under the Irish transposition of the Prospectus Directive 2003/71/EC, effected by ICMPA 2005, Pt 5 and SI 324/2005. They consist of actual Rules, which are binding, and guidelines as to compliance, which are intended to be persuasive, but do not have the same character as the actual Rules. The power to make these rules is conferred by ICMPA 2005, s 51. Interim Rules were first published in 2005, updated in March 2006 and the current set are dated August 2008.

Contents

1. Introduction

Title

1.1 These Prospectus Rules are issued by the Irish Financial Services Regulatory Authority (the Financial Regulator) under Section 51 of the Investment Funds, Companies and Miscellaneous Provisions Act, 2005 and shall be known as the "Prospectus Rules". While further changes to these Prospectus Rules are likely in the future, these Prospectus Rules have been produced at this time to facilitate the efficiency of the market.

Irish and EU Prospectus Law and Guidance

1.2 An issuer, offeror or person seeking admission to trading (a relevant person) falling within the scope of the Prospectus (Directive 2003/71/EC) Regulations 2005 (the Regulation) must have regard to:

(a) Part 5 of the Investment Funds, Companies and Miscellaneous Provisions Act, 2005 (the Act of 2005);

(b) the Regulation;

(c) Commission Regulation (EC) No 809/2004 (the Prospectus Regulation), as amended from time to time;

(d) CESR's[1] Recommendations for the consistent implementation of the Prospectus Regulation (CESR Ref: 05-054b) (the CESR Recommendations);[2]

(e) these Prospectus Rules;

(f) CESR document entitled "Frequently asked questions regarding Prospectuses: Common Positions agreed by CESR Members" (CESR Common Positions);[3] and

(g) Guidance Notes issued by the Financial Regulator in respect of any of the documents referred to at (a) to (f) above (the Guidance Notes).[4]

Application

1.3 These Prospectus Rules apply to:

(a) an offer of securities to the public, or an admission to trading of securities, in Ireland, which under Regulation 12 or 13 of the Regulation requires the publication of a prospectus approved by the Financial Regulator;

(b) an offer of securities to the public, or admission to trading of securities, referred to in Regulation 8(5) of the Regulation, where the relevant person concerned elects to draw up a prospectus; and

(c) an offer of securities to the public, or an admission to trading of securities, where another competent authority has transferred, with the agreement of the Financial Regulator, the function of approving the prospectus to the Financial Regulator under Regulation 41 of the Regulation.

Rules and Guidance

1.4 In accordance with the provisions of Section 51(8) of the Act of 2005, where appropriate, the Financial Regulator has also included guidance with these Prospectus Rules on appropriate approaches which can be taken by a relevant person endeavouring to comply with Irish and EU prospectus law.

1.5 In the interests of clarity, Prospectus Rules are set out in boxed bold typeface to distinguish them from guidance provided with these Prospectus Rules.

It is not the policy of the Financial Regulator to provide legal advice on matters arising pursuant to the Regulation or the Prospectus Regulation or the Prospectus Directive

---

1. The Financial Regulator is a member of CESR. CESR is an independent Committee of European Securities Regulators. The role of CESR is to (i) improve co-ordination among securities regulators (ii) act as an advisory group to the EU Commission and (iii) work to ensure more consistent and timely day-to-day implementation of community legislation in Member States. Further information about CESR can be found on its website: www.cesr-eu.org.

2. The CESR Recommendations are available on CESR's website: http://www.cesr-eu.org/popup2.php?id=2999.

3. The CESR Common Positions are available on CESR's website and are updated regularly: http://www.cesr.eu/index.php?page=groups&mac=0&id=40.

4. The Guidance Notes are available on the Financial Regulator's website: www.financialregulator.ie.

2003/71/EC (the Directive) and any guidance provided with these Prospectus Rules should not be construed as legal advice or a legal interpretation of the Regulation or the Prospectus Regulation or the Directive. It is a matter for any relevant person who may fall within the scope of the Regulation or the Prospectus Regulation or the Directive to seek legal advice regarding the application or otherwise of the Regulation or the Prospectus Regulation or the Directive to their particular set of circumstances.

Compliance with CESR Recommendations

1.6 In considering whether the Prospectus Regulation has been complied with, the Financial Regulator will take into account whether a relevant person has complied with Paragraphs 1–127 and 146-172 of the CESR Recommendations referred to at 1.2(d).

CESR Common Positions

1.7 In considering whether the Regulation, the Prospectus Regulation and the Directive have been complied with, the Financial Regulator will take into account whether a relevant person has complied with the CESR Common Positions referred to at 1.2(f).

Compliance with the Guidance Notes

1.8 In considering whether the Regulation, the Prospectus Regulation and the Directive have been complied with, the Financial Regulator will take into account whether a relevant person has complied with the Guidance Notes referred to at 1.2(g).

Administrative Sanctions

1.9 In accordance with the provisions of Section 51(7) of the Act of 2005 and Part 15 of the Regulation, the Financial Regulator may impose a sanction for the contravention of Irish and EU prospectus law.

Interpretation

1.10 In these Prospectus Rules, except where otherwise stated, words and expressions used that are also used in the Act of 2005 or the Regulation or the Prospectus Regulation or the Directive shall have the same meaning as in the Act of 2005 or the Regulation or the Prospectus Regulation or the Directive.

For the purposes of these Prospectus Rules, the phrase "Irish and EU prospectus law" means the following:

(i) Irish prospectus law;

(ii) EU prospectus law; and

(iii) these Prospectus Rules.

1.11 Unless the context otherwise requires, a reference in these Prospectus Rules to a prospectus includes a base prospectus, registration document, securities note, summary and supplement.

Financial Regulator's Stakeholder Protocol

1.12 The Stakeholder Protocol is a statement describing the timelines the Financial Regulator aims to deliver on certain interactions with key stakeholders. These timelines include those relating to the approval and publication of prospectusess. [5]

Application

1.13 These Prospectus Rules shall apply to prospectus documents submitted to the Financial Regulator for approval on or after 15 September 2008. Until further notice and from 15 September 2008, these Prospectus Rules replace the Prospectus Rules issued in March 2006.

2 Competent Authority and Delegate

Competent Authority

2.1 In relation to these Prospectus Rules, the Financial Regulator is exercising its functions as Competent Authority under Regulation 78 of the Regulation.

Delegation of Certain Tasks

2.2 In accordance with the provisions of Regulation 79 of the Regulation, the Financial Regulator has chosen to administer the exercise of its functions as Competent Authority under the Regulation by delegating certain tasks to the Irish Stock Exchange Limited, which will be known as the Delegate for the purposes of these Prospectus Rules. In accordance with the provisions of Regulation 79 of the Regulation, this delegation of tasks does not include the final approval of a prospectus, which is granted by the Financial Regulator and communicated directly to the relevant person or their nominated agent.

Enforcement of the Prospectus Rules

2.3 A relevant person falling within the scope of these Prospectus Rules will at all times be subject to the powers granted to the Financial Regulator under Part 14 of the Regulation and the enforcement provisions set out in Parts 15 and 16 of the Regulation and Part 5 of the Act of 2005, albeit that certain tasks have been delegated by the Financial Regulator to the Delegate.

3. General Provisions

3.1 Obligations under Irish and EU prospectus law

A relevant person on whom obligations are imposed under Irish and EU prospectus law is required to:

(a) exercise due care and attention in the preparation of a prospectus and when participating in the prospectus review process;

(b) provide the Financial Regulator or the Delegate, as appropriate, in a timely manner following a request, any information or explanation that the Financial Regulator or the Delegate may reasonably require to verify whether Irish and EU prospectus law has been adhered to and complied with;

(c) be open and co-operative in their dealings with the Financial Regulator or the Delegate in respect of any request made in accordance with paragraph (b);

(d) participate in such meetings as the Financial Regulator or the Delegate considers appropriate in respect of any request made in accordance with paragraph (b) and any information or explanations received in respect of any such request; and

5. The Stakeholder Protocol is available on the Financial Regulator's website: www.financialregulator.ie.

(e) maintain such records as will secure the effective supervision by the Financial Regulator of the activities to which Irish and EU prospectus law relates.

Guidance in relation to Rule 3.1

3.1(a) Where a relevant person appoints an agent to discharge its obligations arising under Irish and EU prospectus law, it is expected that the agent will also satisfy the provisions of Rule 3.1. In this regard, a relevant person should ensure that it has appropriate contractual arrangements in place with each appointed agent to ensure adherence to and compliance with the provisions of Rule 3.1.

3.1(b) While a relevant person may appoint an agent to discharge its obligation arising under Irish and EU prospectus law, responsibility for ensuring adherence to and compliance with Irish and EU prospectus law rests with the relevant person. Therefore, any breach of Irish and EU prospectus law by an agent, appointed by a relevant person to act on its behalf, will be considered a breach of Irish and EU prospectus law by the relevant person.

3.1(c) Without prejudice to the generality of Rule 3.1(e), to comply with this Rule, records which evidence due care and attention in complying with Irish and EU prospectus law should be maintained.

4. Application for Approval of a Prospectus

4.1 Designation of Home Member State

A relevant person seeking approval of a prospectus is required to conduct a review to satisfy itself, prior to first submitting a draft prospectus to the Delegate in accordance with Rule 4.3, that Ireland has been validly and correctly designated as the relevant Home Member State, pursuant to the provisions of Regulation 2 of the Regulation.

Guidance in relation to Rule 4.1

4.1(a) It is recommended that appropriate documentary evidence be maintained by a relevant person to demonstrate adherence to and compliance with Rule 4.1. Appropriate documentary evidence generally means a dated and signed memorandum setting out the basis on which the relevant person is satisfied that Ireland has been validly and correctly designated as Home Member State. The content of the memorandum should evidence the exercise of a considered judgement. The memorandum should be available for disclosure to the Financial Regulator upon it making a request pursuant to Rule 3.1.

4.2 Activities falling within the scope of Annex XIX of the Prospectus Regulation

Where an issuer's activities fall into one of the categories listed in Annex XIX of the Prospectus Regulation, any person preparing a prospectus in relation to a public offer of that issuer's securities or seeking admission to trading of that issuer's securities is required to comply with the disclosure requirements set out in Paragraphs 128–145 of the CESR Recommendations referred to at 1.2(d), as applicable.

4.3 Submission of Prospectus for Approval

A relevant person seeking approval of a prospectus is required to submit the prospectus to the Delegate for scrutiny.

Guidance in relation to Rule 4.3

4.3(a) If the prospectus is not a single document but is comprised of separate documents:

(i) an application for approval of a prospectus submitted to the Delegate in accordance with Rule 4.3 may relate to one or more of those separate documents; and

(ii) a reference in this section to a prospectus is, unless the context otherwise requires, to be taken as a reference to the document or documents to which the application for approval relates.

4.3(b) The Delegate will scrutinise a prospectus submitted to it in accordance with Rule 4.3 to assess whether or not it has been drawn up in accordance with the Regulation, the Prospectus Regulation and these Prospectus Rules. Following the completion of this process, the Financial Regulator will decide whether to approve a prospectus and will communicate its decision in writing to the registered office of the relevant person or their nominated agent.

4.3(c) Where agreement between the relevant person and the Delegate cannot be reached in relation to whether or not a prospectus submitted to the Delegate in accordance with Rule 4.3 is drawn up in accordance with the Regulation, the Prospectus Regulation and these Prospectus Rules, the relevant person may refer the matter directly, in writing, to the Financial Regulator.

4.3(d) The application and operation of these Prospectus Rules is triggered by the first submission of the first draft of a prospectus to the Delegate in accordance with Rule 4.3. The application and operation of these Prospectus Rules is not triggered by preliminary correspondence with the Delegate and/or the Financial Regulator prior to the submission of the first draft of a prospectus to the Delegate in accordance with Rule 4.3. Hereafter, this submission is referred to in these Prospectus Rules as the "initial submission". Irrespective of whether these Prospectus Rules are complied with, the submission of the first draft of a prospectus to the Delegate in accordance with Rule 4.3 constitutes an initial submission.

4.4 Approval Statement

A relevant person is required to ensure that a statement contained in a prospectus submitted to the Financial Regulator for approval in accordance with Rule 4.3 relating to the approval by the Financial Regulator includes the following wording regarding the approval:

"The [prospectus – amend as appropriate to the type of document] has been approved by the Irish Financial Services Regulatory Authority, as competent authority under the Prospectus Directive 2003/71/EC.

The Irish Financial Services Regulatory Authority only approves this [prospectus – amend as appropriate to type of document] as meeting the requirements imposed under Irish and EU law pursuant to the Prospectus Directive 2003/71/EC."

A relevant person is required to ensure that the above wording is displayed in a *prominent* position within the prospectus.

Guidance in relation to Rule 4.4

4.4(a) "Prominent" position should normally mean displayed on the cover page of a prospectus. If a relevant person wishes to place the statement elsewhere in a prospectus, the relevant person should seek the Financial Regulator's view, via the Delegate, as to whether such positioning is considered to be prominent.

4.4(b) Where reference is made in a prospectus to the Irish Financial Services Regulatory Authority, it is recommended that the only abbreviation used thereafter is the "Financial Regulator".

4.4(c) It is not appropriate to refer in a prospectus to it having been approved by the Delegate.

4.5 Application Statement

A relevant person is required to ensure that a statement contained in a prospectus submitted to the Financial Regulator for approval in accordance with Rule 4.3 relating to securities for which admission to trading to the Irish Stock Exchange is sought includes the following wording regarding the application:

"Application has been made to the Irish Stock Exchange for the securities [insert relevant details] to be admitted to the Official List and trading on its regulated market."

A relevant person is required to ensure that the above wording is displayed in a *prominent* position within the prospectus.

Guidance in relation to Rule 4.5

4.5(a) "Prominent" position should normally mean displayed on the cover page of the prospectus. If a relevant person wishes to place the statement elsewhere in the prospectus, the relevant person should seek the Financial Regulator's view, via the Delegate, as to whether such positioning is considered to be prominent.

4.6 Scope of Approval by Financial Regulator

A relevant person is required to ensure that a prospectus submitted to the Financial Regulator for approval in accordance with Rule 4.3, which contains wording that suggests that it may be used other than for the purpose of an admission to trading on a regulated market or for a public offer in the European Economic Area (EEA), includes the following wording in respect of that approval:

> "Such approval relates only to the securities [insert relevant details] which are to be admitted to trading on the regulated market of the Irish Stock Exchange or other regulated markets for the purposes of Directive 2004/39/EC or which are to be offered to the public in any Member State of the European Economic Area."

A relevant person is required to ensure that the above wording is displayed in a *prominent* position within the prospectus.

Guidance in relation to Rule 4.6

4.6(a) "Prominent" position should normally mean displayed on the cover page of the prospectus. If a relevant person wishes to place the statement elsewhere in the prospectus, the relevant person should seek the Financial Regulator's view, via the Delegate, as to whether such positioning is considered to be prominent.

4.7 Documents for Submission with an Application for Approval

A relevant person is required to submit the following documents to the Delegate in respect of an application for approval by the Financial Regulator of a prospectus submitted to the Delegate in accordance with Rule 4.3:

(a) in draft form at the time of initial submission of the prospectus or, where appropriate, during the prospectus review process; and

(b) in final form on the day on which approval of a prospectus by the Financial Regulator is sought:

(i) the prospectus;

(ii) if requested, where the order of items in the prospectus does not coincide with the order in the Annexes and building blocks in the Prospectus Regulation, a cross-reference list identifying the pages where each item can be found in the prospectus;

(iii) a letter identifying any items from the Annexes and building blocks in the Prospectus Regulation that have not been included in the prospectus because they are not applicable;

(iv) if the relevant person is requesting the Financial Regulator to authorise the omission of information from the prospectus, the information required by Rule 4.11;

(v) if applicable, the formal notice in final draft form required by Regulation 46 of the Regulation;

(vi) if the relevant person wishes the Financial Regulator to provide a competent authority of a relevant Host Member State with a certificate of approval in accordance with Regulation 56 of the Regulation where the prospectus is approved, a letter requesting the Financial Regulator to provide this notification in accordance with Rule 8.1; and

(vii) any other information that the Financial Regulator and/or Delegate may require.

Guidance in relation to Rule 4.7

4.7(a) For the purposes of Rule 4.7(b)(v), the content of the formal notice required by Regulation 46 of the Regulation must comply with Article 31(3) of the Prospectus Regulation. The details set out in the formal notice should be consistent with the prospectus.

4.7(b) In accordance with Article 31(1) of the Prospectus Regulation, the formal notice must be published in a newspaper that fulfils the requirements for publication of prospectuses according to Article 30 of the Prospectus Regulation.

4.8 Drafts of Documents for Submission with an Application for Approval

A relevant person is required to ensure that draft documents submitted to the Delegate in accordance with Rule 4.7 are:

(a) in a substantially complete form;

(b) in duplicate in hard copy or in an agreed electronic format; and

(c) annotated in the margin to indicate compliance with all applicable requirements of the Regulation, the Prospectus Regulation and these Prospectus Rules.

Guidance in relation to Rule 4.8

4.8(a) For the purposes of Rule 4.8, an agreed electronic format means PDF format. To the extent possible, the prospectus should be electronically searchable.

4.9 Rule 4.9 – Further Drafts of Documents for Submission with an Application for Approval

A relevant person is required to ensure that further drafts of any documents submitted to the Delegate in accordance with Rules 4.7 and 4.8 are:

(a) marked to show all changes made since the last draft was scrutinised by the Delegate;

(b) in duplicate in hard copy or in an agreed electronic format; and

(c) annotated in the margin to indicate compliance with all applicable requirements of the Regulation, Prospectus Regulation and these Prospectus Rules.

Guidance in relation to Rule 4.9

4.9(a) For the purposes of Rule 4.9, an agreed electronic format means PDF format. To the extent possible, the prospectus should be electronically searchable.

4.10 Final Form of a Prospectus Submitted for Approval

A relevant person is required to submit the prospectus in final form and in an agreed electronic format to the Delegate on the day on which approval of a prospectus by the Financial Regulator is sought.

Guidance in relation to Rule 4.10

4.10(a) For the purposes of Rule 4.10, an agreed electronic format means PDF format. To the extent possible, the prospectus should be electronically searchable.

4.10(b) To ensure compliance with Rule 4.10, those preparing a prospectus are advised to have appropriate safeguards and an audit trail in place to ensure that the final version of a prospectus submitted for approval reflects fully and accurately working documents finalised with the Delegate. The Financial Regulator relies on relevant persons and their advisors in this regard and would consider any failure or errors in the process a serious matter. It is a breach of Rule 4.10 to submit a prospectus purportedly in final form, which is missing any text previously included in the final draft of a prospectus agreed with the Delegate irrespective of the reason, or which includes text not previously submitted in the final draft of a prospectus.

4.10(c) Where the Financial Regulator has approved a prospectus and the offer has not closed or, as the case may be, trading on a regulated market has not begun, amendments to that prospectus can be made via a supplement pursuant to the provisions of Regulation 51 of the Regulation.

4.10(d) A prospectus cannot be amended by way of a supplement after the offer has closed or, as the case may be, trading on a regulated market has begun.

4.10(e) Where an announcement is made by a relevant person, which amends a previously approved prospectus after the offer has closed and/or trading on a regulated market has begun, the relevant person must be satisfied that it has the appropriate legal power to prepare such an announcement.

4.10(f) During the period of validity of the base prospectus (i.e., 12 months), a supplement can be used to amend information included in the base prospectus.

4.10(g) For the avoidance of doubt, announcements cannot be used where a prospectus or supplement would otherwise be required.

4.11 Rule 4.11 – Request for Authorisation of Omission of Information

A relevant person who wishes to request the Financial Regulator to authorise the omission of certain information required by the Regulation or the Prospectus Regulation is required to submit that request in writing to the Delegate, for consideration by the Financial Regulator, and to ensure that any such request:

(a) identifies the specific information concerned and the specific reasons for its omission;

(b) states the reasons the relevant person is of the opinion that one or more of the grounds set out in Regulation 25 of the Regulation apply; and

(c) warrants that the information could not be deemed material to an investor's decision to invest in the relevant securities (where appropriate).

Guidance in relation to Rule 4.11

4.11(a) The request will be submitted to the Financial Regulator once it has been finalised with the Delegate. In the normal course, unless exceptional issues arise, the Financial Regulator will adjudicate on a request to authorise the omission of information within five business days. Therefore, for the purposes of Rule 4.11, the Financial Regulator should receive the omission of information request at least five business days before the approval of a prospectus is required.

4.12 Rule 4.12 – Filing of Certain Documents

A relevant person is required to submit the following documents to the Delegate:

(a) the final terms of the base prospectus or supplement of the type referred to in Regulation 23 of the Regulation in an agreed electronic format;

(b) the final offer price and amount of securities notification referred to in Regulation 24 of the Regulation in an agreed electronic format; and

(c) the documents referred to in Regulation 27 of the Regulation to be incorporated in a prospectus by reference in an agreed electronic format.

Guidance in relation to Rule 4.12

4.12(a) Rule 4.12 is applicable in all cases when Ireland has been designated as Home Member State for a relevant prospectus.

4.12(b) The Delegate will forward documents received in accordance with Rule 4.12 to the Financial Regulator for filing.

4.12(c) For the purposes of Rule 4.12, an agreed electronic format means PDF format.

4.12(d) For the purposes of Part 8 of the Regulation, the Financial Regulator reserves the right to publish final terms submitted to the Delegate in accordance with Rule 4.12, and filed with the Financial Regulator in accordance with the guidance provided at 4.12(b), in electronic form on its website (www.financialregulator.ie) as provided for in Regulation 23 of the Regulation.

4.12(e) For the purposes of Part 8 of the Regulation, the Financial Regulator reserves the right to publish final offer price and amount of securities notifications submitted to the Delegate in accordance with Rule 4.12, and filed with the Financial Regulator in accordance with the guidance provided at 4.12(b), in electronic form on its website (www.financialregulator.ie) as provided for by Regulation 24 of the Regulation.

4.12(f) A relevant person is required to ensure that where documents are incorporated by reference in a prospectus, the requirements of Article 28 of the Prospectus Regulation are complied with.

4.13 References in Final Terms

Where a relevant person chooses to include a reference in final terms submitted to the Delegate in accordance with Rule 4.12, for filing with the Financial Regulator in accordance with the guidance provided at 4.12(b), to either the approval by the Financial Regulator of the relevant base prospectus or the provision by the Financial Regulator of a certificate of approval attesting that the relevant base prospectus has been drawn up in accordance with the provisions of the Directive and the Prospectus Regulation, the relevant person is required to ensure that the reference states, as appropriate:

> "The Irish Financial Services Regulatory Authority has approved the [base prospectus - insert details of relevant base prospectus] under Part 7 of the Prospectus Directive (2003/71/EC) Regulations 2005 (the Regulation) as having been drawn up in accordance with the Regulation and Commission Regulation (EC) No 809/2004."; and/or

> "The Irish Financial Services Regulatory Authority has provided the competent authority(ies) of [insert details of relevant Host Member State(s)] with a certificate of approval attesting that the [base prospectus - insert details of relevant base prospectus] has been drawn up in accordance with the provisions of the Prospectus Directive 2003/71/EC and Commission Regulation (EC) No 809/2004."

Guidance in relation to Rule 4.13

4.13(a) Where references are made in final terms to a previously approved base prospectus and supplement(s) (where appropriate), the details in respect of the previously approved base prospectus and supplement(s) must be correct.

4.13(b) In addition to the requirements of these Prospectus Rules, the final terms must comply with all relevant requirements set out in the Prospectus Regulation.

4.14 Assessment of Equivalence of Information

A relevant person who wishes to request the Financial Regulator to assess the equivalence of information contained in a document to which Regulations 10(b), 10(c), 11(c) or 11(d) of the Regulation applies is required to submit that request in writing to the Delegate for consideration by the Financial Regulator and to ensure that any such request includes:

(a) a cross reference list identifying any items from the most appropriate Annex(es) to the Prospectus Regulation in respect of the relevant securities that have been included in the document, on the basis that the relevant person is of the view that such items are equivalent to the disclosure items required for a prospectus, and any items that have been excluded from the document on the basis that the relevant person is of the view that they are not applicable; and

(b) a warranty of equivalence and sets out in detail the basis for its view.

Guidance in relation to Rule 4.14

4.14(a) The Financial Regulator will consider each request received in accordance with Rule 4.14 on a case-by-case basis to determine whether or not the information contained in the document to which Regulations 10(b), 10(c), 11(c) or 11(d) of the Regulation applies is equivalent to that of a prospectus. On each occasion a relevant person is preparing a request under Rule 4.14, the relevant person should have regard to the most appropriate Annex(es) to the Prospectus Regulation in respect of the relevant securities when preparing a document to which the aforementioned Regulations apply.

4.14(b) Documents deemed "equivalent" by the Financial Regulator in accordance with the provisions of Regulations 10(b), 10(c), 11(c) or 11(d) of the Regulation cannot avail of the passporting provisions of the Regulation and Directive. If such a document is to be used in another Member State for the purposes of an offer of securities to the public or an admission to trading on a regulated market, it will require the approval of the competent authority of that Member State.

4.14(c) For the purposes of Rule 4.14(b), a "warranty of equivalence" means a declaration by the relevant person that, in their considered opinion, the disclosure items in a document are equivalent to the disclosure items required in a prospectus and any items that have been excluded from the document are on the basis that the relevant person is of the view that they are not applicable.

4.14(d) The request will be submitted to the Financial Regulator once it has been finalised with the Delegate. In the normal course, unless exceptional issues arise, the Financial Regulator will adjudicate on a request to assess the equivalence of information within 10 business days. Therefore, for the purposes of Rule 4.14, the Financial Regulator must receive the request at least ten business days before the decision of the Financial Regulator is required.

5. Publication of a Prospectus

5.1 Guidance in relation to Part 8 & Regulation 48 of the Regulation

5.1(a) For the purposes of Part 8 of the Regulation, the Financial Regulator will publish a prospectus it has approved in accordance with Part 7 of the Regulation in electronic form on its website (www.financialregulator.ie) as provided for in Regulation 45 of the Regulation.

5.1(b) For the purposes of Regulation 48 of the Regulation, the prospectus that the Financial Regulator publishes on its website in accordance with the guidance provided at 5.1(a) shall be considered to be the original version approved by the Financial Regulator.

5.2 Non-Publication of a Prospectus by the Financial Regulator

A relevant person is required to notify the Financial Regulator in writing where it does not wish the Financial Regulator to publish a prospectus it has approved in accordance with Part 7 of the Regulation in electronic form on its website (www.financialregulator.ie) as provided for in Regulation 45 of the Regulation.

A relevant person must ensure that any such notification is submitted to the Financial Regulator, via the Delegate, by 11am on the day on which approval of the prospectus is required and that any such notification specifies the method of publication to be adopted by the relevant person in accordance with Regulation 45 of the Regulation.

Guidance in relation to Rule 5.2

5.2(a) For the purposes of Rule 5.2, the Financial Regulator will publish a notification on its website specifying the method of publication to be adopted by the relevant person pursuant to Regulation 45 of the Regulation in respect of a prospectus approved by the Financial Regulator in accordance with Part 7 of the Regulation.

5.2(b) A non-publication request pursuant to Rule 5.2, received by the Financial Regulator after a prospectus has been approved and published on the website of the Financial Regulator will not be accepted.

5.3 Non-publication of final terms and/or final offer price and amount of securities notifications (together "the announcements") by the Financial Regulator

A relevant person is required to notify the Financial Regulator in writing where it does not wish the Financial Regulator to publish the announcements submitted to the Delegate in accordance with Rule 4.12, and filed with the Financial Regulator in accordance with the guidance provided at 4.12(b), in electronic form on its website (www.financialregulator.ie) as provided for in Article 33 of the Prospectus Regulation.

A relevant person must ensure that any such notification is submitted to the Financial Regulator, via the Delegate, in advance of publication of the announcements by the Financial Regulator and to ensure that any such notification specifies the method of publication to be adopted by the relevant person in accordance with Article 33 of the Prospectus Regulation.

Guidance in relation to Rule 5.3

5.3(a) Unless notified otherwise by a relevant person, the Financial Regulator will treat a non-publication request received relating to a base prospectus, pursuant to Rule 5.2, as covering all final terms of that base prospectus filed with the Financial Regulator in accordance with the guidance provided at 4.12(b).

5.3(b) Unless notified otherwise by a relevant person, the Financial Regulator will treat a non-publication request received relating to a prospectus, pursuant to Rule 5.2, as covering all final offer price and amount of securities notifications of that prospectus filed with the Financial Regulator in accordance with the guidance provided at 4.12(b).

5.3(c) While Article 33 of the Prospectus Regulation refers only to final terms, the Financial Regulator is of the view that these provisions apply equally to final offer price and amount of securities notifications.

6. USE OF LANGUAGES

6.1 Guidance in relation to Part 10 of the Regulation

For the purposes of Part 10 of the Regulation a language accepted by the Financial Regulator means Irish or English. For this reason, a prospectus submitted to the Financial Regulator for approval must be drawn up in the Irish or English languages (an "approved language").

A relevant person may choose to include non-approved language text ("foreign language text"), which is considered to be any language other than Irish or English, with the prospectus.

6.2 Foreign Language Text

A relevant person is required to ensure that where foreign language text is added one of the following forms of wording must be included in the prospectus:

(a) Where there are instances of continuous foreign language text within a document, the following wording must be used:

"The language of the prospectus is [Insert Irish or English]. Any foreign language text that is included with or within this document has been included for convenience purposes only and does not form part of the prospectus."; or

(b) Where foreign language text is used to give correct technical meaning, the following wording must be used:

"The language of the prospectus is [Insert Irish or English]. Certain legislative references and technical terms have been cited in their original language in order that the correct technical meaning may be ascribed to them under applicable law."; or

(c) Where foreign language text is included in whole parts of the document (other than the summary), for example the terms and conditions, the following wording must be used:

"This prospectus is drawn up in the [Insert Irish or English] language. In case there is any discrepancy between the [Insert Irish or English] text and the [Insert name of the foreign language] text, the [Insert Irish or English] text stands approved for the purposes of approval under the Prospectus (Directive 2003/71/EC) Regulations 2005."

7. ANNUAL INFORMATION DOCUMENT

7.1 Submission of an Annual Information Document

An issuer who is required to draw up an annual information document in accordance with Part 11 of the Regulation is required to submit the annual information document to the Delegate within 20 working days of the publication of the issuer's annual financial statements in an agreed electronic format.

Guidance in relation to Rule 7.1

7.1(a) For the purposes of Rule 7.1, an agreed electronic format is PDF format.

7.1(b) The Delegate will forward each annual information document received in accordance with Rule 7.1 to the Financial Regulator for filing.

7.1(c) For the purposes of Part 11 of the Regulation, but subject to Rule 7.3, the Financial Regulator will publish an annual information document that has been submitted to the Delegate in accordance with Rule 7.1 and forwarded to the Financial Regulator for filing in accordance with the guidance provided at 7.1(b) in electronic form on its website (www.financialregulator.ie) as provided for in Article 27 of the Prospectus Regulation.

7.1(d) Where errors are identified in references to Irish and European legislation in any annual information document submitted to the Delegate in accordance with Rule 7.1 for filing with the Financial Regulator in accordance with the guidance provided at 7.1(b), the annual information document will be returned to the relevant person for amendment.

For the avoidance of doubt, the legislation implementing the Prospectus Directive in Ireland is the Prospectus (Directive 2003/71/EC) Regulations 2005. This is the legislation that should be referenced in relation to the drawing up of an annual information document in respect of which Ireland is the Home Member State under the Directive.

7.2 Legislative Reference

A relevant person is required to ensure that an annual information document submitted to the Delegate in accordance with Rule 7.1 for filing with the Financial Regulator in accordance with the guidance provided at 7.1(b) which contains wording that refers to the legislation under which the annual information document is drawn up includes the following wording:

> "This annual information document has been prepared by [insert name of issuer] in accordance with the provisions of Part 11 of the Prospectus Directive (2003/71/EC) Regulations 2005 and has been submitted to the Irish Stock Exchange for filing with the Irish Financial Services Regulatory Authority (the Financial Regulator) in accordance with the provisions of the Prospectus Rules issued by the Financial Regulator."

7.3 Rule 7.3 – Non-Publication of an Annual Information Document by the Financial Regulator

An issuer is required to notify the Financial Regulator in writing where it does not wish the Financial Regulator to publish an annual information document submitted to the Delegate in accordance with Rule 7.1, and filed with the Financial Regulator in accordance with the guidance provided at 7.1(b), in electronic form on its website (www.financialregulator.ie) as provided for in Article 27 of the Prospectus Regulation.

An issuer is required to ensure that any such notification is submitted to the Financial Regulator, via the Delegate, in advance of the publication of the annual information document by the Financial Regulator and to ensure that any such notification specifies the method of publication to be adopted by the relevant person in accordance with Article 27 of the Prospectus Regulation.

Guidance in relation to Rule 7.3

7.3(a) A non-publication request pursuant to Rule 7.3 received by the Financial Regulator after the annual information document has been published on the website of the Financial Regulator will not be accepted.

7.4 Rule 7.4 – Format of Annual Information Document

An issuer submitting an annual information document to the Delegate in accordance with Rule 7.1 for filing with the Financial Regulator in accordance with the guidance provided at 7.1(b), is required to ensure that the annual information document contains an introductory paragraph setting out:

(a) the financial year-end of the issuer;

(b) the date of publication of the issuer's annual financial statements;

(c) whether the issuer intends to rely solely on the Financial Regulator publishing the annual information document in accordance with the guidance provided at 7.1(c) to fulfil its obligation to publish the annual information document in accordance with the provisions of Part 11 of the Regulation; and

(d) the date and methods of publication of the annual information document where the issuer does not intend to rely solely on the Financial Regulator publishing the annual information document in accordance with the guidance provided at 7.1(c).

7.5 Accuracy of Information

An issuer is required to ensure that the information provided in accordance with Rule 7.4 (a), (b), (c) and (d) is correct.

8. Passport Notification to Other Member States

8.1 Outward Passport Notification Requests

A relevant person who requests the Financial Regulator to provide a competent authority of a relevant Host Member State with a certificate of approval attesting that a prospectus has been drawn up in accordance with the Directive is required to make such a request in writing and is required to ensure that any such request includes the following information:

(a) the name of the relevant Host Member State(s) to whom the request relates;

(b) the summary of the prospectus translated into a language accepted by the relevant Host Member State(s) (where applicable);

(c) the number(s) of the Annex(es) to the Prospectus Regulation in accordance with which the prospectus was drawn up;

(d) confirmation as to whether a public offer or admission to trading on a regulated market or both is being made in the relevant Host Member State(s);

(e) the name of the guarantor(s) in respect of the prospectus (where applicable);

(f) confirmation as to whether any information has been omitted from the prospectus and details of the relevant information (such omission having been authorised by the Financial Regulator in accordance with Regulation 25 of the Regulation); and

(g) confirmation that all of the relevant disclosures required by the Annex(es) to the Prospectus Regulation in accordance with which the prospectus was drawn up relating to the Host Member State(s) have been included in the prospectus.

Guidance in relation to Rule 8.1

8.1(a) The Financial Regulator considers that it is the duty of the relevant person to provide the Financial Regulator with all the necessary information and translations of the summary (where applicable) to allow the Financial Regulator to fulfil its obligation of notification according to Regulation 56 of the Regulation.

8.1(b) A request made to the Financial Regulator in accordance with Rule 8.1 prior to the approval of the prospectus by the Financial Regulator shall be made to the Delegate. Where the request is made after the approval of the prospectus by the Financial Regulator, it shall be made directly to the Financial Regulator.

8.1(c) The Financial Regulator will communicate a confirmation in writing to the registered office of the relevant person or their nominated agent that it has notified the competent authority(ies) of the Host Member State(s) identified in its request received in accordance with Rule 8.1 of the intention of the relevant person to passport the prospectus into its(their) jurisdiction(s).

8.1(d) Where a prospectus has been provided by the Financial Regulator to a relevant Host Member State(s) pursuant to a passport notification request, the Financial Regulator will automatically passport all subsequent supplements to that prospectus, approved by the Financial Regulator, to the same Host Member State(s). A relevant person is not required to submit a passport notification request pursuant to Rule 8.1 in respect of any such supplements.

8.1(e) For the purposes of Rule 8.1(g), these disclosures would include, inter alia, those required by Item 4.11 of Annex III or Item 4.14 of Annex V of the Prospectus Regulation.

9. Passport Notification from Other Member States

9.1 Guidance in relation to Inward Passport Notifications

9.1(a) Where a relevant person wishes to passport a prospectus into Ireland, they must request the competent authority of their Home Member State to provide the Financial Regulator with a certificate of approval attesting that the prospectus has been drawn up in accordance with the Directive. The competent authority of the Home Member State will forward the documentation referred to in Regulation 55 of the Regulation directly to the Financial Regulator.

9.1(b) The Financial Regulator will maintain a list of the passport notifications it has received from the competent authorities of other Home Member States on its website (www.financialregulator.ie).

9.1(c) A relevant person who has requested the competent authority of their Home Member State to provide the Financial Regulator with a certificate of approval attesting that a base prospectus has been drawn up in accordance with the Directive, is not required to file any relevant final terms relating to the base prospectus with the Financial Regulator. The relevant person should file any such final terms with the competent authority of their Home Member State.

9.1(d) The Financial Regulator will, at the request of a relevant person, communicate a confirmation in writing to the registered office of the relevant person or their nominated agent that it has received a notification from its Home Member State of its intention to passport its prospectus into Ireland.

9.1(e) A relevant person who has requested the competent authority of their Home Member State to provide the Financial Regulator with a certificate of approval attesting that a prospectus has been drawn up in accordance with the Directive is not required to publish a notice in Ireland setting out the manner in which the relevant prospectus has been made available to the public pursuant to the provisions of Article 14 of the Directive. Notwithstanding this position, the relevant person is subject to the publication requirements set out in Article 14 of the Directive.

10. Qualified Investors Register

10.1 Guidance in relation to Qualified Investors Register

For the purpose of the requirements set out in this section, an "accountant" is a person who is a member of a body that is representative of the profession of accountants and which has functions in regard to the regulation of its members and a "solicitor" is a person who holds a practising certificate within the meaning of the Solicitors Acts, 1954 to 1994.

10.2 Application for Inclusion on the Register of Qualified Investors

A small or medium sized enterprise or a natural person that applies to the Financial Regulator to be registered as a qualified investor and included on the register established and maintained by the Financial Regulator in accordance with Regulation 4 of the Regulation is required to submit the application in writing and to include with that application:

(a) a letter from an accountant or a solicitor certifying:

(i) in respect of a small or medium sized enterprise, that the enterprise has its registered office in the State and satisfies at least two of the criteria set out in Regulation 2 of the Regulation and specifying which criteria are satisfied; or

(ii) in respect of a natural person, that the person satisfies the criteria set out in Regulation 4(2) of the Regulation and specifying which criteria set out in Regulation 4(2)(b) of the Regulation are satisfied; and

(b) relevant contact details and confirmation that the small or medium sized enterprise or natural person, as appropriate, acknowledges that the Financial Regulator may disclose the information on the register in accordance with Regulation 7 of the Regulation.

Guidance in relation to Rule 10.2

10.2(a) Where a small or medium sized enterprise or a natural person has received confirmation from the Financial Regulator that an application made in accordance with Rule 10.2 is in order and the small or medium sized enterprise or natural person has been included on the register maintained by the Financial Regulator in accordance with Regulation 4 of the Regulation, the registration will be valid from 1 July (or such later date as registration occurs) until 30 June each year.

10.3 Renewal of Registration on Register of Qualified Investors

A small or medium sized enterprise or natural person wishing to remain on the register maintained by the Financial Regulator in accordance with Regulation 4 of the Regulation is required to apply to the Financial Regulator in accordance with the provisions of Rule 10.2 to renew their registration each year.

10.4 Request for Removal from Register of Qualified Investors

A small or medium sized enterprise or natural person wishing to be removed from the register maintained by the Financial Regulator in accordance with Regulation 4 of the Regulation is required to submit a written request to the Financial Regulator.

Guidance in relation to Rule 10.4

10.4(a) The Financial Regulator will remove a small or medium sized enterprise or natural person from the register maintained by the Financial Regulator in accordance with Regulation 4 of the Regulation within 10 working days of the receipt of the request.

10.5 Requests for a Copy of the Register of Qualified Investors

An offeror wishing to obtain a copy of the register maintained by the Financial Regulator in accordance with Regulation 4 of the Regulation is required to apply in writing to the Financial Regulator at least two days before the copy of the register is sought and to include with that application:

(a) confirmation that it intends to use the information solely in connection with that offer; and

(b) a letter from an accountant or solicitor confirming that the offeror intends to offer securities to the public in Ireland.

10.6 Guidance in relation to Regulation 4(5) of the Regulation

For the purposes of Regulation 4(5) of the Regulation "a transaction of a significant size" will be considered by the Financial Regulator as one whose value is greater than €7,500.[6]

11. Collective Investment Undertakings of the Closed End Type

11.1 Definition of "Collective Investment Undertaking of the Closed End Type"

For the purposes of the Regulation and the Prospectus Regulation a "Collective Investment Undertaking of the Closed End Type" shall mean a collective investment scheme which does not permit the redemption of its units at the holder's request. Action taken by a collective investment undertaking to ensure that the stock exchange value of its units does not significantly vary from its net asset value shall be regarded as equivalent to such redemption.

---

6. CESR has defined an order customarily undertaken by a retail investor as an order whose value is less than €7,500.

Guidance in relation to Rule 11.1

11.1(a) For the purposes of the definition set out in Rule 11.1 "action taken by a collective investment undertaking" does not include the appointment of a market maker or other intermediary to assist in the provision of liquidity to investors in the collective investment undertaking on the secondary market. The reference to "action taken by the collective investment undertaking" relates to collective investment undertakings which are obliged, under their fund rules, to ensure that, while investors cannot request redemption, they are assured that their holding can be sold at a price which does not significantly vary from the net asset value of the collective investment undertaking.

11.1(b) For the purposes of the definition set out in Rule 11.1, a collective investment undertaking which provides for the redemption of its units at the holder's request, albeit that such redemption is subject to the discretion of its directors shall not be regarded as a collective investment undertaking of the closed end type.

11.1(c) For the purposes of the definition set out in Rule 11.1, a collective investment undertaking which provides for the compulsory repurchase of its units at the sole discretion of its directors shall be regarded as a collective investment undertaking of the closed end type where:

(i) the collective investment undertaking is not obliged, under its fund rules, to ensure that, while investors cannot request redemption, they are assured that their holding can be sold at a price which does not significantly vary from the net asset value of the collective investment undertaking.

Appendix 1
PROSPECTUS CONTACT DETAILS

For further information on the Prospectus Rules, please contact:

Markets Supervision Department
Financial Regulator
PO Box 9138
College Green
Dublin 2

Telephone: 01 410 4711
Fax: 01 410 4030
E-mail: markets@financialregulator.ie
Website: www.financialregulator.ie

For further information relating to the review of prospectuses by the Irish Stock Exchange Limited (the Delegate), please contact:

Irish Stock Exchange
28 Anglesea Street
Dublin 2

Telephone: 01 617 4200 (general)
01 617 4229 (Company Listings)
01 617 4270 (Debt Listings)
01 617 4255 (Investment Fund Listings)

Fax: 01 677 6045 (general)
01 617 4289 (Company Listings)
01 617 4244 (Debt Listings)
01 670 7394 (Investment Fund Listings)

E-mail: info@ise.ie
companylistings@ise.ie (Company Listings)
abs@ise.ie (Debt Listings)
funds@ise.ie (Investment Fund Listings)

Website: www.ise.ie

T +353 1 410 4000

Consumer help-line

lo call 1890 77 77 77

Register of Financial Service Providers help-line

lo call 1890 20 04 69

F +353 1 410 4900

www.financialregulator.ie

www.itsyourmoney.ie

Information Centre: 6-8 College Green, Dublin 2

PO Box No 9138

College Green,

Dublin 2, Ireland

Market Abuse Rules

September 2008

Notes

These Rules are made by the Financial Regulator, as competent authority under the Irish transposition of the Market Abuse Directive 2003/6/EC, effected by ICMPA 2005, Pt 4 and SI 342/2005. They consist of actual Rules, which are binding, and guidelines as to compliance, which are intended to be persuasive, but do not have the same character as the actual Rules. The power to make these rules is conferred by ICMPA 2005, s 34. Interim Rules were first published in 2005, updated in February 2006 and the current set are dated September 2008.

Contents

1. Introduction

1.1 Title

These Rules are issued by the Irish Financial Services Regulatory Authority (the Financial Regulator) under Section 34 of the Investment Funds, Companies and Miscellaneous Provisions Act, 2005 and shall be known as the "Market Abuse Rules".

1.2 Irish Market Abuse Law

Persons falling within the scope of the Market Abuse Rules must have regard to:

(a) Part 4 of the Investment Funds, Companies and Miscellaneous Provisions Act, 2005 (the Act of 2005);

(b) Market Abuse (Directive 2003/6/EC) Regulations 2005 (the Regulation);

(c) Commission Regulation (EC) 2273/2003 of 22 December 2003 (the Market Abuse Regulation);

(d) CESR[1]1 Guidance and Information on the Common Operation of the Market Abuse Directive (CESR/04-505b and CESR/06-562b) (the CESR Guidance); and

(e) these Market Abuse Rules.

1.3 Rules and Guidance

In accordance with Section 34(7) of the Act of 2005, where appropriate the Financial Regulator has also included guidance on the steps that may be taken to comply with Irish Market Abuse law.

In the interests of clarity, Market Abuse Rules are boxed in bold typeface to distinguish them from guidance provided in these Market Abuse Rules.

It is not the policy of the Financial Regulator to provide legal advice on matters arising pursuant to the Regulation or the Directive and any guidance provided in these Market Abuse Rules should not be construed as legal advice or a legal interpretation of the Regulation or the Directive. It is a matter for any relevant person who may fall within the scope of the Regulation or the Directive to seek legal advice regarding the application or otherwise of the Regulation or the Directive to their particular set of circumstances.

1.4 Compliance with CESR Guidance

In considering whether the Regulation has been complied with the Financial Regulator will take into account any relevant CESR Guidance as set out in the CESR documents entitled Market Abuse CESR Guidance 04-505b and Market Abuse CESR Guidance 06-562b.

1.5 Administrative Sanctions

In accordance with Section 34(6) of the Act of 2005, the imposition of administrative sanctions shall apply in relation to a contravention of the Market Abuse Rules.

1.6 Interpretation

In these Market Abuse Rules, except where otherwise stated, words and expressions used that are also used in the Act of 2005 or the Regulation or the Market Abuse Regulation have the same meaning as in the Act of 2005 or the Regulation or the Market Abuse Regulation.

2. COMPETENT AUTHORITY AND DELEGATE AUTHORITY

2.1 Competent Authority

In relation to these Market Abuse Rules, the Financial Regulator is exercising its functions as Competent Authority under Regulation 3 of the Regulation.

---

1. The Financial Regulator is a member of CESR.

CESR is an independent Committee of European Securities Regulators. The role of CESR is to:

(i) Improve co-ordination among securities regulators;

(ii) Act as an advisory group to assist the EU Commission; and

(iii) Work to ensure more consistent and timely day-to-day implementation of community legislation in Member States.

Further information about CESR can be found on its web-site: www.cesr-eu.org

2.2 Delegation of Certain Powers

In accordance with the provisions of Regulation 33 of the Regulation, the Financial Regulator has chosen to exercise certain of its functions as Competent Authority under the Regulation by delegation of such functions to the Irish Stock Exchange Limited, which will be known as the Delegate Authority for the purposes of these Market Abuse Rules.

2.3 Enforcement of the Market Abuse Rules

Persons falling within the scope of these Market Abuse Rules will at all times be subject to the powers granted to the Financial Regulator under Part 4 of the Regulation and the enforcement provisions set out in Parts 5 and 6 of the Regulation and Part 4 of the Act of 2005, albeit that certain functions have been delegated by the Financial Regulator to the Delegate Authority.

3. DEFINITIONS

3.1 In these Market Abuse Rules, except where otherwise stated, words and expressions used that are also used in the Act of 2005 or the Regulation or the Market Abuse Regulation have the same meaning as in the Act of 2005 or the Regulation or the Market Abuse Regulation.

The following definitions must be used for the purposes of the Market Abuse Rules or the Regulation as applicable:

"CAO" shall mean the Company Announcements Office of the Irish Stock Exchange Limited (the Delegate Authority).

"RIS" shall mean a Regulatory Information Service provided by or approved for use by the regulated market on which the relevant financial instruments are admitted to trading or in respect of which a request for admission to trading on such a regulated market has been made.

"significant financial interest" for the purposes of Part 3 of the Regulation "a significant financial interest" will be considered by the Financial Regulator as one whose value is greater that €7,500.

4. GENERAL PROVISIONS

4.0 Guidance in relation to the Regulation

For the purposes of the Regulation, the Financial Regulator or the Delegate Authority may exercise, as applicable, any or all of the powers prescribed in Part 4 of the Regulation.

4.1 Obligations under the Market Abuse Rules

A person on whom obligations are imposed under these Market Abuse Rules is required:

(a) to provide to the Financial Regulator or the Delegate Authority, as appropriate, in a timely manner following a request, any information or explanation that the Financial Regulator or the Delegate Authority may reasonably require to verify whether the Market Abuse Rules have been adhered to and complied with;

(b) to be open and co-operative in their dealings with the Financial Regulator or the Delegate Authority in respect of any request made in accordance with paragraph (a); and

(c) to participate in such meetings as the Financial Regulator or the Delegate Authority consider necessary in respect of any request made in accordance with paragraph (a) and any information or explanations received in respect of any such request.

5. Disclosure of Inside Information

5.0 General Guidance

Regulation 10 of the Regulation provides for the disclosure of inside information. This section of the Market Abuse Rules applies to the following issuers whose obligations arise under Regulation 10 of the Regulation:

(a) issuers of financial instruments that are admitted to trading on a regulated market in the State or for which a request for admission to trading on such a regulated market has been made; and

(b) Irish registered companies whose financial instruments are admitted to trading on a regulated market in a Member State other than the State or for which a request for admission to trading on such a regulated market has been made.

5.0.1 Guidance in relation to the Assessment of Inside Information

It is a matter for each issuer to make an initial assessment of whether a particular piece of information amounts to inside information. The decision as to whether a piece of information is inside information may be finely balanced and the issuer (with the aide of its advisors) will need to exercise its judgement.

5.0.2 Guidance in relation to the Making of an Announcement

An issuer referred to at Guidance 5.0 (a) may make any announcement required in Section 5 of these Market Abuse Rules either:

(a) directly to a RIS; or

(b) indirectly to a RIS through the CAO.

5.0.3 Guidance regarding Selective Disclosure

Where an issuer under its own responsibility avails of the provisions of Regulation 10(7) of the Regulation to delay the public disclosure of inside information to avoid prejudicing its legitimate interests, the issuer may selectively disclose the information to persons owing it a duty of confidentiality.

Such selective disclosure may be made to another person if it is in the normal course of the exercise of his employment, profession or duties but must not be made to any person simply because they owe the issuer a duty of confidentiality.

5.0.4 Example of Selective Disclosure

An issuer contemplating a major transaction which requires shareholder support or which could significantly impact its lending arrangements or credit-rating may selectively disclose details of the proposed transaction to major shareholders, its lenders and/or credit-rating agency provided that the recipients are bound by a duty of confidentiality. An issuer may, depending on the circumstances, be justified in disclosing inside information to certain categories of recipient in addition to those employees of the issuer who require the information to perform their functions. The relevant categories of recipient include:

(a) the issuer's advisers and advisers of any other persons involved or who may be involved in the matter in question;

(b) persons with whom the issuer is negotiating, or intends to negotiate, any commercial, financial or investment transaction (including prospective underwriters or placees of the financial instruments of the issuer);

(c) representatives of its employees or trade unions acting on their behalf;

(d) any government department or any other statutory or regulatory body or authority;

(e) major shareholders of the issuer;

(f) the issuer's lenders; and

(g) credit-rating agencies.

Selective disclosure to any or all of the persons referred to at (a) to (g) above may not be justified in every circumstance where an issuer delays disclosure of inside information in accordance with the provisions of Regulation 10(7) of the Regulation.

5.0.5 Guidance in relation to the Assessment of "Legitimate Interest"

Whether or not an issuer has a legitimate interest that would be prejudiced by the public disclosure of certain inside information is an assessment that must be made by the issuer in the first instance. Other than impending developments that could be jeopardised by premature public disclosure, requests or restrictions placed by statutory authorities for the purposes of a legal obligation or matters described in Regulation 10(8) of the Regulation, there are unlikely to be other circumstances where delay would be justified.

5.0.6 Guidance regarding Regulation 10(8)(b): Dual Board Structure

The provisions of Regulation 10(8)(b) of the Regulation refer to an issuer with a dual board structure (e.g., a management board and supervisory board if and to the extent that decisions of the management board require ratification by the supervisory board). An issuer with a unitary board structure would be unable to avail of the provisions of Regulation 10(8)(b).

5.1 Disclosure of Inside Information

Subject to Regulation 10(7) of the Regulation, an issuer is required to make an announcement via a RIS without delay of any inside information which directly or indirectly concerns the issuer or the financial instruments of the issuer.

5.2 Simultaneous Notification to the CAO

Where an issuer falling within the scope of Guidance 5.0 (a) makes any announcement required in Section 5 of these Market Abuse Rules in accordance with the Guidance 5.0.2 (a), it is required to simultaneously notify the CAO.

5.3 Identifying Inside Information: Reasonable Investor Test

In determining the likely price significance of information the issuer is required to assess whether the information in question would be likely to be used by a reasonable investor as part of the basis of his investment decision and would therefore be likely to have a significant impact on the price of the issuer's financial instruments or related derivative financial instruments ("the reasonable investor test").

In conducting the reasonable investor test, the issuer is required:

(a) to take into account that the significance of the information in question will vary widely from issuer to issuer depending on a number of factors such as the issuer's size, recent developments and the market sentiment about the issuer and the sector in which it operates; and

(b) to assume that a reasonable investor will make investment decisions relating to the relevant financial instruments or related derivative financial instruments to maximise his economic self interest.

In undertaking such an assessment, the issuer is required to take into consideration the anticipated impact of the information in light of the totality of the issuer's activities, the reliability of the source of information and any other market variables likely to affect the related financial instrument or derivative financial instrument in the given circumstances.

5.3.1 Guidance relating to information relevant to a reasonable investor's decision

It is not possible to prescribe how the reasonable investor test will apply in all possible circumstances. However, information that is likely to be considered relevant to a reasonable investor's investment decision includes information that affects:

(a) the assets and liabilities of the issuer;

(b) the performance or the expectation of the performance of the issuer's business;

(c) the financial condition of the issuer;

(d) events that may significantly affect the issuer's ability to meet its commitments;

(e) the course of the issuer's business;

(f) major new developments in the business of the issuer; or

(g) information already previously disclosed to the market.

5.4 Disclosure of Significant Changes

An issuer is required to announce via a RIS any significant changes concerning already publicly disclosed inside information without delay after these changes occur.

5.5 Directors' Obligations to Monitor Changes

The directors of the issuer are required to carefully and continuously monitor whether changes in the circumstances of the issuer are such that an announcement obligation under Rule 5.1 arises.

5.6 Reasonable Care in Relation to Any Announcement

An issuer is required to exercise all reasonable care to ensure that any statement, forecast or any other information it announces via a RIS is not misleading, false or deceptive and does not omit anything likely to effect the import of such statement, forecast or other information.

5.7 Publication of Information on Internet Site

Where an issuer has an internet site(s), it is required to ensure that inside information announced via a RIS is available on its internet site(s) by the close of the business day following the day of the RIS announcement. This Rule is in addition to the disclosure Rule outlined at Rule 5.1.

5.8 Prohibition and Sequence of Disclosure via Internet

An issuer is prohibited from disclosing inside information on its internet site(s) as an alternative to or in advance of its disclosure via a RIS. An issuer is required to ensure that inside information is announced via a RIS before, or simultaneously with, publication of such inside information on its internet site(s).

5.9 Announcements at Meetings

Where an issuer proposes to announce, at any meeting of holders of its financial instruments, information that might lead to a significant effect on the price of those financial instruments or on the price of related derivative instruments, the issuer is required to arrange an announcement of that information in accordance with Rule 5.1 in order that the announcement at the meeting is made no earlier than the time at which the information is publicly disclosed.

5.10 Dealing with Press Speculation or Market Rumour

Where there is press speculation or market rumour regarding an issuer, the issuer is required to assess whether a disclosure obligation arises under Rule 5.1.

5.11 Interim Disclosure in the Event of the Leak of Information

An issuer is required to make an announcement in accordance with Rule 5.1 where the implications of the facts are not yet in a position to be confirmed but where the issuer believes that the information has or is likely to leak. In these circumstances, the issuer is required to ensure that the interim announcement should:

(a) detail as much of the subject matter as possible;

(b) set out the reasons why a more comprehensive announcement cannot be made; and

(c) provide an undertaking to announce further details without delay.

5.12 Notification to Delegate Authority of Inability to make an Announcement under Rule 5.11

Where an issuer, falling within the scope of Guidance 5.0 (a), is unable to make an announcement in accordance with Rule 5.11 the issuer is required to notify the Delegate Authority without delay in the form of electronic mail to the Company Listings Department of the Irish Stock Exchange at the address stated in Appendix 1 of these Market Abuse Rules, with the necessary documentation attached in PDF or Word format.

The e-mail shall include:

(a) the name and contact details of the person sending the email,

(b) the corporate entity (if any) on whose behalf the person is sending the e-mail.

5.13 Notification to Financial Regulator of Inability to make an Announcement under Rule 5.11

Where an issuer falling within the scope of Guidance 5.0 (b) is unable to make an announcement in accordance with Rule 5.11 the issuer is required to notify the Financial Regulator without delay in the form of electronic mail to the Markets Section of the Financial Regulator at the address stated in Appendix 1 of these Market Abuse Rules, with the necessary documentation attached in PDF or Word format.

The e-mail shall include:

(a) the name and contact details of the person sending the email,

(b) the corporate entity (if any) on whose behalf the person is sending the e-mail.

5.14 Obligations regarding Selective Disclosure

An issuer is required to ensure that the recipients of the information referred to at Guidance 5.0.4 (a) to (g) are aware that they must not deal in the financial instruments of the issuer before the relevant information has been publicly disclosed.

5.15 Delaying Disclosure of Inside Information

Where an issuer under its own responsibility avails of the provisions of Regulation 10(7) of the Regulation to delay the public disclosure of inside information to avoid prejudicing its legitimate interests, the issuer is required to have appropriate measures in place which enable public disclosure of inside information via a RIS without delay in cases where failure to disclose the inside information would mislead the public or where the issuer is unable to ensure the confidentiality of the inside information.

5.16 Records of Delayed Disclosure

Where an issuer under its own responsibility avails of the provisions of Regulation 10(7) of the Regulation to delay the public disclosure of inside information to avoid prejudicing its legitimate interests, it is required to document and maintain sufficient records to reasonably demonstrate the existence of such legitimate interest.

5.17 Continuing Obligations relating to Delayed Disclosure

Where an issuer under its own responsibility avails of the provisions of Regulation 10(7) of the Regulation to delay the public disclosure of inside information to avoid prejudicing its legitimate interests, the issuer is required to monitor a developing situation in order that if circumstances change it can make an immediate announcement in accordance with Rule 5.1.

5.18 Notification when a RIS is not Available

An issuer who is required to announce inside information via a RIS at a time outside business hours, when the RIS is not open for business must distribute the information without delay to:

(a) not less than two national newspapers in the Member State where the financial instruments are admitted to trading or in respect of which a request for admission to trading has been made;

(b) two news wire services operating in the Member State where the financial instruments have been admitted to trading or in respect of which a request for admission to trading has been made; and

(c) a RIS for release as soon as it re-opens.

5.18.1 Guidance in relation to Notification when a RIS is not Available

The fact that a RIS is not open for business is not, in itself, sufficient grounds for delaying the disclosure or distribution of inside information.

6. Insider Lists

6.0 General Guidance

Regulation 11 of the Regulation provides for the obligation to draw up and maintain a list of insiders. This section of the Market Abuse Rules applies to the following issuers whose obligations arise under Regulation 11 of the Regulation:

(a) issuers of financial instruments who are admitted to trading on a regulated market in the State or for which a request for admission to trading on such a regulated market has been made; and

(b) Irish registered companies whose financial instruments are admitted to trading on a regulated market in a Member State other than the State or for which a request for admission to trading on such a regulated market has been made.

6.1 Maintenance of an Insider List

Subject to Regulation 11(6) of the Regulation, an issuer is required to maintain a list of:

(a) its own employees that have access to inside information; and

(b) the principal contacts at any other relevant person who also have access to inside information regarding either the issuer or the financial instruments of the issuer.

6.1.1 Guidance relating to Maintenance of Insider Lists

It is not necessary for an issuer to maintain a list of all the persons working for another relevant person where it has:

(a) recorded the name of principal contact(s) at that relevant person;

(b) made effective arrangements, for that relevant person to maintain a list drawn up in accordance with the provisions of Rule 6.1 and paragraphs 2, 3, 4 and 5 of Schedule 4 of the Regulation, of persons both acting on behalf of the issuer and with access to inside information on either the issuer or the financial instruments of the issuer; and

(c) made effective arrangements for that relevant person to provide a copy of its list to the issuer as soon as possible upon request.

All relevant persons are responsible for the maintenance of their respective lists drawn up in accordance with Regulation 11 of the Regulation. It is a matter for each relevant person to implement the appropriate organisational arrangements for the preparation and maintenance of its own insider list or lists.

7. Managers' Transactions

7.0 General Guidance

Regulation 12 of the Regulation provides the managers' transaction notification obligations. This section of the Market Abuse Rules, with the exception of Guidance 7.6, applies to persons discharging managerial responsibilities within an issuer, and where applicable persons closely associated with such persons, where the issuer is:

(a) registered in the State and whose financial instruments are admitted to trading on a regulated market in the State, or in respect of which a request for admission to trading on such a regulated market has been made; or

(b) registered in the State and whose financial instruments are admitted to trading on a regulated market in a Member State other than in the State, or in respect of which a request for admission to trading on such a regulated market has been made; or

(c) not registered in the State or in another Member State but required to file the annual information in relation to shares in accordance with Article 10 of Directive 2003/71/EC of the European Parliament and of the Council of 4 November 2003 on the prospectus to be published when securities are offered to the public or admitted to trading and amending Directive 2001/34/EC (Prospectuses Directive) in the State and whose financial instruments are admitted to trading on a regulated market in the State; or

(d) not registered in the State or in another Member State but required to file the annual information in relation to shares in accordance with Article 10 of the Prospectuses Directive in the State and whose financial instruments are admitted to trading on a regulated market other than in the State.

7.0.1 Guidance in relation to the Scope of the Obligation to notify Managerial Transactions

The obligation to notify transactions as provided by Regulation 12 of the Regulation extends only to shares admitted to trading on a regulated market or to derivatives or other financial instruments linked to such shares.

7.0.2 Guidance regarding Compliance with Regulation 12 of the Regulation

Persons referred to in Guidance 7.0 are deemed to have complied with the notification obligations of Regulation 12 (1), (2)(b) and (3) of the Regulation as applicable by compliance with Rule 7.1 of these Market Abuse Rules. Issuers who have not been notified by persons referred to in Guidance 7.0 in accordance with Rule 7.1 are not liable for breaches of this Section of the Market Abuse Rules.

7.0.3 Guidance regarding the possible exemption provided in Regulation 12(4)

In reference to Regulation 12 (4) of the Market Abuse Regulations, notifications of transactions required by Regulation 12 of the Regulation shall not be exempted nor delayed by reason that the total amount of the transaction in any calendar year is less than €5,000.

7.1 Notification to the Relevant Issuer

Persons discharging responsibilities within an issuer falling within the scope of Guidance 7.0 (a) to (d), and where applicable persons closely associated with such persons, are required to notify the relevant issuer, in writing, of the occurrence of all transactions conducted on their own account relating to shares of the said issuer or to derivatives or other financial instruments linked to them within 4 business days of the date on which the transaction occurred. The notification to the relevant issuer must contain the information set out in Regulation 12(6) of the Regulation.

7.2 Announcement of Notification by the Issuer

Where the relevant issuer falls within the scope of Guidance 7.0 (a) to (d), it is required to announce via a RIS all transactions notified to it in accordance with Rule 7.1 without delay and in any event not later than the end of the business day following receipt of the information by the issuer.

7.2.1 Guidance regarding Disclosure by Issuer

Where the relevant issuer falls within the scope of Guidance 7.0 (a) or (c), it may make the announcement required in Rule 7.2 either:

(a) directly to a RIS; or

(b) indirectly to a RIS through the CAO.

7.3 Format of the Announcement by the Issuer

Where the relevant issuer falls within the scope of Guidance 7.0 (a) or (c), it is required to make the announcement required by Rule 7.2 in the standard reporting format specified in Appendix 3 attached.

7.4 Notification to CAO

Where a relevant issuer falls within the scope of Guidance 7.0 (a) or (c) and makes an announcement required in Rule 7.2 directly to a RIS, it is required to simultaneously notify the CAO.

7.5 Notification to Financial Regulator

Where the relevant issuer falls within the scope of Guidance 7.0 (b) or (d), it is required to notify the Financial Regulator of all transactions notified to it in accordance with Rule 7.1 without delay and in any event not later than the end of the business day following the receipt of the information by the issuer. The relevant issuer is also required to confirm to the Financial Regulator:

(a) the date that it received the notification required under Rule 7.1 and

(b) that all such notifications have been announced via a RIS.

The notification shall be in the form of electronic mail to the Markets Section of the Financial Regulator at the address stated in Appendix 1 of these Market Abuse Rules, with the necessary documentation attached in PDF or Word format. The e-mail shall state:

(a) the name and contact details of the person sending the email, and

(b) the corporate entity (if any) on whose behalf the person is sending the e-mail.

7.6 Guidance in relation to Regulation 12(2) of the Regulation

The obligation to notify transactions required under Regulation 12(2) of the Regulation, by persons not falling within the scope of Guidance 7.0 (a) to (d), who are conducting transactions on their own account relating to shares issued by collective investment undertakings other than the closed-ended type who elect to notify these transactions to the Financial Regulator should do so in accordance with Rules 7.1 to 7.4 of these Market Abuse Rules inclusive.

8. SUSPICIOUS TRANSACTIONS

8.0 General Guidance

Regulation 13 of the Regulation imposes the obligation to report suspicious transactions. This section of the Market Abuse Rules applies to the following:

(a) persons professionally arranging transactions in financial instruments that are admitted to trading on a regulated market in a Member State, or in respect of which a request for admission to trading on such a market has been made, who are registered in the State or who have their head office in the State or who have a branch situated in the State; and

(b) market operators who operate and/or manage the business of a regulated market in a Member State and regulated markets that operate and/or manage their own business as a regulated market, where financial instruments are admitted to trading, or in respect of which a request for admission to trading on such a market has been made, who are registered in the State or who have their head office in the State or who have a branch situated in the State.

8.0.1 Guidance on Notification by Telephone

For the purposes of Regulation 13 of the Regulation, the telephone number that notifications may initially be made to the Financial Regulator is specified in Appendix 1.

8.1 Notification to Financial Regulator

Persons professionally arranging transactions, market operators and regulated markets falling within the scope of Guidance 8.0 (a) and (b) are required to notify the Financial Regulator without delay of transactions in such financial instruments they reasonably suspect might constitute insider dealing or market manipulation.

8.2 Notification to Financial Regulator

Notifications required in Rule 8.1 must be submitted in writing to the Financial Regulator using the standard reporting format set out in Appendix 2 as soon as practicable after any initial telephone call.

8.3 Records of Notifications

Records supporting the notifications made to the Financial Regulator in accordance with Rule 8.1 are required to be maintained by the persons professionally arranging transactions, market operators and regulated markets for at least six years after the date of the last transaction was entered into, or order to trade was received, by such persons professionally arranging transactions, market operators or regulated markets, as appropriate.

9. Stabilisation Notifications

9.0 Guidance regarding Adequate Public Disclosure

The Financial Regulator accepts the use of a RIS to satisfy the requirements of adequate public disclosure as defined in Article 2 of the Market Abuse Regulation and Article 102 of the Consolidated Admissions and Reporting Directive 2001/34/EC.

10. Short Selling

10.1 A person, other than a market maker, may not enter into any transaction, transactions or arrangements which have the effect of generating a net economic benefit which would arise from a fall in the price of the shares of either the Governor and Company of the Bank of Ireland, Allied Irish Banks Plc, Irish Life and Permanent Plc or Anglo Irish Bank Corporation Plc.

10.2 On 23rd September 2008, and each business day thereafter, by 3.30pm each person who has on that day an economic interest involving 0.25% or more of the issued share capital to which Rule 10.1 would have applied if entered into after the issuance of this Rule, shall make disclosure on an RIS system setting out the name of the person who has the position, the company in which the position is held and the amount of that position.

10.3 Guidance in relation to 'Short Selling'

The prohibition in Rule 10.1 applies to any new short positions, including increases in existing short positions. Where a person has an existing short position on 18th September, 2008, the rule does not prevent that short position being continued, nor does it prevent trading to reduce or close out the short position. Where a net short position arises, but does not arise because the person entered into transactions after 18th September to create that short position, Rule 10.1 does not apply, but Rule 10.2 may apply depending solely on whether 0.25% of the shares of the company are involved or not.

10.4 For the purposes of Rules 10.1 and 10.2, regard should be had to the following points in interpreting the application of the exemption for market makers:-

(a) a person is a market maker only to the extent that they are or have been operating as a market maker ordinarily as part of their business;

(b) market maker includes but is not confined to persons recognised as a market maker by a Market Operator (as defined in the Markets in Financial Instruments Directive) when operating as such;

(c) a person who operates as a market maker may also undertake other activities and those are not covered by the market maker exemption;

(d) operating as a market maker means trading in good faith as principal to fulfil orders or instructions received from clients;

(e) operating as a market maker may include trading in good faith to hedge positions arising from client orders or instructions;

(f) no discretionary management activity or proprietary trading for the purpose of achieving trading gains falls, other than in compliance with (b) above, within the scope of market making activity.

10.5 These rules apply to spread betting and Contracts for Difference as it does to all other ways in which an economic interest, whether direct or indirect, can be created.

10.6 These rules apply throughout each day. It is not complied with if short positions are taken on an intra-day basis and closed out before the end of the day.

10.7 These rules apply to any person who benefits from creating a short position, including the contracting party and an intermediary who assists in putting the transactions or arrangements in place, while understanding its purpose or consequence.

10.8 While shorting the ISEQ Index is covered by the rule, as drafted, the Financial Regulator does not propose to take action in relation to shorting of the ISEQ Index at this time. We will keep this matter under review. If shorting of the index becomes, in effect, a proxy for shorting financial stock, such that market abuse concerns are raised, we will review this guidance.

10.9 A disclosure obligation arising under these Rules applies to the holder of the net short position. A disclosure under Rule 10.2 is required even if the size of the net short position has not changed since the previous disclosure.

10.10 A disclosure under Rule 10.2 may be made either:-

(a) directly to an RIS; or

(b) indirectly to an RIS through the CAO

Where a person makes a disclosure in accordance with (a) above, the person is required simultaneously to notify the CAO.

10.11 Market making positions are exempt from Rule 10.2 disclosures.

10.12 A person may establish a short position, post 19 September 2008, provided that the short position offsets or partially offsets a long position in relation to the same company.

10.13 Rule 10.2 requires that the aggregate net short position of 0.25% or above be disclosed. There is no requirement to disclose any individual short and long positions underlying the net position. A person who has previously made disclosures under Rule 10.2 and whose net short position then falls below 0.25% should advise the Financial Regulator that this is the case.

10.14 When disclosing the amount of the aggregate net short position the percentage of the issued share capital of the company should be stated.

Appendix 1
Market Abuse Notification Information & Contact Details

For further information on Market Abuse, these Market Abuse Rules or to submit a suspicious transaction notification, please contact:

Markets Supervision Department

Financial Regulator,

PO Box 9138,

College Green,

Dublin 2

Telephone: 01 410 4794

Fax: 01 410 4070

E-mail: marketmonitoring@financialregulator.ie

Website: www.financialregulator.ie

For further information and details on notifications regarding inside information or managers' transactions, please contact:

Company Announcements Office

Irish Stock Exchange

28 Anglesea Street

Dublin 2

Telephone: 01 617 4200

Fax: 01 677 6045

E-mail: announcements@ise.ie

Website: www.ise.ie

For notifications under Rule 5.12 of these Market Abuse Rules, please contact the Company Listings Department of the Irish Stock Exchange (the Delegate Authority) at:

Email: companylistings@ise.ie

For further information on trading and regulation on the Irish Stock Exchange (the Delegate Authority), please contact:

Regulation Department

Irish Stock Exchange

28 Anglesea Street

Dublin 2

Telephone: 01 617 4200

Fax: 01 679 5432

E-mail: iseregulation@ise.ie

Website: www.ise.ie

Appendix 2
Suspicious Transaction Report

Description of the transaction(s) **Please include details of the financial instrument(s), including the ISIN code of the instrument; the market(s) concerned; the original order's entry date/time, price and size; the times and sizes of the transaction(s); the type and characteristics of the order, etc**
Reasons for suspecting that the transaction(s) might constitute insider dealing/ market manipulation
Identities of persons carrying out transaction(s) **Names, address, telephone number, date of birth, account number, client identification code used by the firm, etc**
Identities of any other persons known to be involved in the transaction(s) **Names, address, telephone number, location, date of birth, relation to person carrying out transaction; position held, role played, etc**
Capacity in which the person performing the transaction(s) acts *e.g. broker, underwriter, agent*
Further information which may be of significance (please list any accompanying material you are supplying)

Details of the person making notification. *Name of person, name of firm, position held within firm, contact details etc*
Signed ………………………………………….. (person making notification) Dated ……………………………………… ……... (date of notification)

Appendix 3
Notification of Transactions of Directors/Persons Discharging Managerial Responsibility and Connected Persons Reporting Format

This form is intended for use by an issuer to make a RIS notification required by the Market Abuse Rules and section 53 (as extended by section 64 of the Companies Act 1990) or entered into the issuer's register in accordance with section 59 of the Companies Act 1990.

(1) An issuer making a notification in respect of a transaction relating to the shares or debentures of the issuer should complete boxes 1 to 16, 23 and 24.

(2) An issuer making a notification in respect of a derivative relating to the shares of the issuer should complete boxes 1 to 4, 6, 8, 13, 14, 16, 23 and 24.

(3) An issuer making a notification in respect of options granted to a director/person discharging managerial responsibilities should complete boxes 1 to 3 and 17 to 24

(4) An issuer making a notification in respect of a financial instrument relating to the shares of the issuer (other than a debenture) should complete the boxes 1 to 4, 6, 8, 9, 11, 13, 14, 16, 23 and 24.

All relevant boxes should be completed in block capital letters

1	Name of the Issuer	2	Name of the Issuer (i) a transaction notified in accordance with Market Abuse Rules; (ii) a disclosure made in accordance with section 53 (as extended by section 64 of the Companies Act 1990) or entered into the issuer's register in accordance with section 59 of the Companies Act 1990; or (iii) both (i) and (ii).
3	Name of person discharging managerial responsibilities/director	4	State whether notification relates to a person connected with a person discharging managerial responsibilities/director named in 3 and identify the connected person
5	Indicate whether the notification is in respect of a holding of the person referred to in 3 or 4 above or in respect of a non-beneficial interest	6	Description of shares (including class) debentures or derivatives or financial instruments relating to shares
7	Name of registered shareholder(s) and, if more than one, number of shares held by each of them	8	State the nature of the transaction

9	Number of shares, debentures or financial instruments relating to shares acquired	10	Percentage of issued class acquired (treasury shares of that class should not be taken into account when calculating percentage)
11	11 Number of shares, debentures or financial instruments relating to shares disposed	12	Percentage of issued class disposed (treasury shares of that class should not be taken into account when calculating percentage)
13	Price per share or value of transaction	14	Date and place of transaction
15	Total holding following notification and total percentage holding following notification (any treasury shares should not be taken into account when calculating percentage)	16	Date issuer informed of transaction

If a person discharging managerial responsibilities has been granted options by the issuer, complete the following boxes:

17	Date of grant	18	Period during which or date on which it can be exercised
19	Total amount paid (if any) for grant of the option	20	Description of shares or debentures involved (class and number)
21	Exercise price (if fixed at time of grant) or indication that the price is to be fixed at the time of exercise	22	Total number of shares or debentures over which options are held following notification
23	Any additional information	24	Name of contact and telephone number for queries
Name and signature of duly designated officer of issuer responsible for making notification ______________________________ **Date of notification**________________________			

T +353 1 410 4000

Consumer help-line

lo call 1890 77 77 77

Register of Financial Service Providers help-line

lo call 1890 20 04 69

F +353 1 410 4900

www.financialregulator.ie

www.itsyourmoney.ie
Information Centre: 6-8 College Green, Dublin 2

PO Box No 9138
College Green,
Dublin 2, Ireland

Index

[*all references are to the provisions of the relevant legislation*]